THIS
HOLY BIBLE
IS PRESENTED TO

_____

BY

_____

_____

ON

_____

_____

**YOUR WORD IS A LAMP TO MY FEET
AND A LIGHT TO MY PATH.**

PSALM 119:105

THE
HOLY BIBLE

THE
HOLY BIBLE

Containing the Old and New Testaments

THOMAS NELSON
Since 1798

www.ThomasNelson.com

NKJV Single-Column Wide-Margin Reference Bible
Copyright © 2021 by Thomas Nelson.

Holy Bible, New King James Version®, copyright © 1982 by Thomas Nelson

Published in Nashville, TN, by Thomas Nelson. Thomas Nelson is a registered trademark of HarperCollins Christian Publishing, Inc.

Library of Congress Catalog Card Number 2021935168

This Bible was set in the Thomas Nelson NKJV Typeface, created at the 2K/DENMARK type foundry.

Printed in China

21 22 23 24 25 26 27 28 /AMC/ 15 14 13 12 11 10 9 8 7 6 5 4 3 2 1

TABLE OF CONTENTS

OLD TESTAMENT

NEW TESTAMENT

ALPHABETICAL ORDER OF THE BOOKS OF THE BIBLE

The books of the New Testament are indicated by *italics*.

PREFACE TO THE
NEW KING JAMES VERSION®

PURPOSE

In the preface to the 1611 edition, the translators of the Authorized Version, known popularly as the King James Bible, state that it was not their purpose "to make a new translation ... but to make a good one better." Indebted to the earlier work of William Tyndale and others, they saw their best contribution to consist in revising and enhancing the excellence of the English versions which had sprung from the Reformation of the sixteenth century. In harmony with the purpose of the King James scholars, the translators and editors of the present work have not pursued a goal of innovation. They have perceived the Holy Bible, New King James Version, as a continuation of the labors of the earlier translators, thus unlocking for today's readers the spiritual treasures found especially in the Authorized Version of the Holy Scriptures.

A LIVING LEGACY

For more than four hundred years, and throughout several revisions of its English form, the King James Bible has been deeply revered among the English-speaking peoples of the world. The precision of translation for which it is historically renowned, and its majesty of style, have enabled that monumental version of the Word of God to become the mainspring of the religion, language, and legal foundations of our civilization.

Although the Elizabethan period and our own era share in zeal for technical advance, the former period was more aggressively devoted to classical learning. Along with this awakened concern for the classics came a flourishing companion interest in the Scriptures, an interest that was enlivened by the conviction that the manuscripts were providentially handed down and were a trustworthy record of the inspired Word of God. The King James translators were committed to producing an English Bible that would be a precise translation, and by no means a paraphrase or a broadly approximate rendering. On the one hand, the scholars were almost as familiar with the original languages of the Bible as with their native English. On the other hand, their reverence for the divine Author and His Word assured a translation of the Scriptures in which only a principle of utmost accuracy could be accepted.

In 1786 Catholic scholar Alexander Geddes said of the King James Bible, "If accuracy and strictest attention to the letter of the text be supposed to constitute an excellent version, this is of all versions the most excellent." George Bernard Shaw became a literary legend in the twentieth century because of his severe and often humorous criticisms of our most cherished values. Surprisingly, however, Shaw paid the following tribute to the scholars commissioned by King James: "The translation was extraordinarily well done because to the translators what they were translating was not merely a curious collection of ancient books written by different authors in different stages of culture, but the Word of God divinely revealed through His chosen and expressly inspired scribes. In this conviction they carried out their work with boundless reverence and care and achieved a beautifully artistic result." History agrees with these estimates. Therefore, while seeking to unveil the excellent *form* of the traditional English Bible, special care has also been taken in the present edition to preserve the work of *precision* which is the legacy of the 1611 translators.

COMPLETE EQUIVALENCE IN TRANSLATION

Where new translation has been necessary in the New King James Version, the most complete representation of the original has been rendered by considering the history of usage and etymology of words in their contexts. This principle of complete equivalence seeks to preserve *all* of the information in the text, while presenting it in good literary form. Dynamic equivalence, a recent procedure in Bible translation, commonly results in paraphrasing where a more literal rendering is needed to reflect a specific and vital sense. For example, complete equivalence truly renders the original text in expressions such as "lifted her voice and wept" (Gen. 21:16); "I gave you cleanness of teeth" (Amos 4:6); "Jesus met them, saying, 'Rejoice!'" (Matt. 28:9); and "Woman, what does your concern have to do with Me?" (John 2:4). Complete equivalence translates fully, in order to provide an English text that is both accurate and readable.

In keeping with the principle of complete equivalence, it is the policy to translate interjections which are commonly omitted in modern language renderings of the Bible. As an example, the interjection *behold*, in the older King James editions, continues to have a place in English usage, especially in dramatically calling attention to a spectacular scene or an event of profound importance such as the Immanuel prophecy of Isaiah 7:14. Consequently, *behold* is retained for these occasions in the present edition. However, the Hebrew and Greek originals for this word can be translated variously, depending on the circumstances in the passage. Therefore, in addition to *behold*, words such as *indeed*, *look*, *see*, and *surely* are also rendered to convey the appropriate sense suggested by the context in each case.

In faithfulness to God and to our readers, it was deemed appropriate that all participating scholars sign a statement affirming their belief in the verbal and plenary inspiration of Scripture, and in the inerrancy of the original autographs.

DEVOTIONAL QUALITY

The King James scholars readily appreciated the intrinsic beauty of divine revelation. They accordingly disciplined their talents to render well-chosen English words of their time, as well as a graceful, often musical arrangement of language, which has stirred the hearts of Bible readers through the years. The translators, the committees, and the editors of the present edition, while sensitive to the late-twentieth-century English idiom, and while adhering faithfully to the Hebrew, Aramaic, and Greek texts, have sought to maintain those lyrical and devotional qualities that are so highly regarded in the Authorized Version. This devotional quality is especially apparent in the poetic and prophetic books, although even the relatively plain style of the Gospels and Epistles cannot strictly be likened, as sometimes suggested, to modern newspaper style. The Koine Greek of the New Testament is influenced by the Hebrew background of the writers, for whom even the gospel narratives were not merely flat utterance, but often song in various degrees of rhythm.

THE STYLE

Students of the Bible applaud the timeless devotional character of our historic Bible. Yet it is also universally understood that our language, like all living languages, has undergone profound change since 1611. Subsequent revisions of the King James Bible have sought to keep abreast of changes in English speech. The present work is a further step toward this objective. Where obsolescence and other reading difficulties exist, present-day vocabulary, punctuation, and grammar have been carefully integrated. Words representing ancient objects, such as *chariot* and *phylactery*, have no modern substitutes and are therefore retained.

A special feature of the New King James Version is its conformity to the thought flow of the 1611 Bible. The reader discovers that the sequence and selection of words, phrases, and clauses of the new edition, while much clearer, are so close to the traditional that there is remarkable ease in listening to the reading of either edition while following with the other.

In the discipline of translating biblical and other ancient languages, a standard method of transliteration, that is, the English spelling of untranslated words, such as names of persons and places, has never been commonly adopted. In keeping with the design of the present work, the King James spelling of untranslated words is retained, although made uniform throughout. For example, instead of the spellings *Isaiah* and *Elijah* in the Old Testament, and *Esaias* and *Elias* in the New Testament, *Isaiah* and *Elijah* now appear in both Testaments.

King James doctrinal and theological terms, for example, *propitiation*, *justification*, and *sanctification*, are generally familiar to English-speaking peoples. Such terms have been retained except where the original language indicates need for a more precise translation.

Readers of the Authorized Version will immediately be struck by the absence of several pronouns: *thee*, *thou*, and *ye* are replaced by the simple *you*, while *your* and *yours* are substituted for *thy* and *thine* as applicable. *Thee*, *thou*, *thy*, and *thine* were once forms of address to express a special relationship to human as well as divine persons. These pronouns are no longer part of our language. However, reverence for God in the present work is preserved by capitalizing pronouns, including *You*, *Your*, and *Yours*, which refer to Him. Additionally, capitalization of these pronouns benefits the reader by clearly distinguishing divine and human persons referred to in a passage. Without such capitalization the distinction is often obscure, because the antecedent of a pronoun is not always clear in the English translation.

In addition to the pronoun usages of the seventeenth century, the *-eth* and *-est* verb endings, so familiar in the earlier King James editions, are now obsolete. Unless a speaker is schooled in these verb endings, there is common difficulty in selecting the correct form to be used with a given subject of the verb in vocal prayer. That is, should we use *love*, *loveth*, or *lovest*? *do*, *doeth*, *doest*, or *dost*? *have*, *hath*, or *hast*? Because these forms are obsolete, contemporary English usage has been substituted for the previous verb endings.

In older editions of the King James Version, the frequency of the connective *and* far exceeded the limits of present English usage. Also, biblical linguists agree that the Hebrew and Greek original words for this conjunction

may commonly be translated otherwise, depending on the immediate context. Therefore, instead of *and*, alternatives such as *also, but, however, now, so, then*, and *thus* are accordingly rendered in the present edition, when the original language permits.

The real character of the Authorized Version does not reside in its archaic pronouns or verbs or other grammatical forms of the seventeenth century, but rather in the care taken by its scholars to impart the letter and spirit of the original text in a majestic and reverent style.

THE FORMAT

The format of the New King James Version is designed to enhance the vividness and devotional quality of the Holy Scriptures:

- Subject headings assist the reader to identify topics and transitions in the biblical content.
- Words or phrases in *italics* indicate expressions in the original language which require clarification by additional English words, as also done throughout the history of the King James Bible.
- Prose is divided into paragraphs to indicate the structure of thought.
- Poetry is structured as contemporary verse to reflect the poetic form and beauty of the passage in the original language.
- The covenant name of God was usually translated from the Hebrew as LORD or GOD (using capital letters as shown) in the King James Old Testament. This tradition is maintained. In the present edition the name is so capitalized whenever the covenant name is quoted in the New Testament from a passage in the Old Testament.

THE OLD TESTAMENT TEXT

The Hebrew Bible has come down to us through the scrupulous care of ancient scribes who copied the original text in successive generations. By the sixth century A.D. the scribes were succeeded by a group known as the Masoretes, who continued to preserve the sacred Scriptures for another five hundred years in a form known as the Masoretic Text. Babylonia, Palestine, and Tiberias were the main centers of Masoretic activity; but by the tenth century A.D. the Masoretes of Tiberias, led by the family of ben Asher, gained the ascendancy. Through subsequent editions, the ben Asher text became in the twelfth century the only recognized form of the Hebrew Scriptures.

Daniel Bomberg printed the first Rabbinic Bible in 1516 – 17; that work was followed in 1524 – 25 by a second edition prepared by Jacob ben Chayyim and also published by Bomberg. The text of ben Chayyim was adopted in most subsequent Hebrew Bibles, including those used by the King James translators. The ben Chayyim text was also used for the first two editions of Rudolph Kittel's *Biblia Hebraica* of 1906 and 1912. In 1937 Paul Kahle published a third edition of *Biblia Hebraica*. This edition was based on the oldest dated manuscript of the ben Asher text, the Leningrad Manuscript B19a (A.D. 1008), which Kahle regarded as superior to that used by ben Chayyim.

For the New King James Version the text used was the 1967/1977 Stuttgart edition of the *Biblia Hebraica*, with frequent comparisons being made with the Bomberg edition of 1524 – 25. The Septuagint (Greek) Version of the Old Testament and the Latin Vulgate also were consulted. In addition to referring to a variety of ancient versions of the Hebrew Scriptures, the New King James Version draws on the resources of relevant manuscripts from the Dead Sea caves. In the few places where the Hebrew was so obscure that the 1611 King James was compelled to follow one of the versions, but where information is now available to resolve the problems, the New King James Version follows the Hebrew text. Significant variations are recorded in the New King James translators' notes.

THE NEW TESTAMENT TEXT

There is more manuscript support for the New Testament than for any other body of ancient literature. Over five thousand Greek, eight thousand Latin, and many more manuscripts in other languages attest the integrity of the New Testament. There is only one basic New Testament used by Protestants, Roman Catholics, and Orthodox, by conservatives and liberals. Minor variations in hand copying have appeared through the centuries, before mechanical printing began about A.D. 1450.

Some variations exist in the spelling of Greek words, in word order, and in similar details. These ordinarily do not show up in translation and do not affect the sense of the text in any way.

Other manuscript differences such as omission or inclusion of a word or a clause, and two paragraphs in the Gospels, should not overshadow the overwhelming degree of *agreement* which exists among the ancient records. Bible readers may be assured that the most important differences in English New Testaments of today are due, not to manuscript divergence, but to the way in which translators view the task of translation: How literally should the text be rendered? How does the translator view the matter of biblical inspiration? Does the translator adopt a paraphrase when a literal rendering would be quite clear and more to the point? The New King James Version follows the historic precedent of the Authorized Version in maintaining a literal approach to translation, except where the idiom of the original language cannot be translated directly into our tongue.

The King James New Testament was based on the traditional text of the Greek-speaking churches, first published in 1516, and later called the Textus Receptus or Received Text. Although based on the relatively few available manuscripts, these were representative of many more which existed at the time but only became known later. In the late nineteenth century, B. Westcott and F. Hort taught that this text had been officially edited by the fourth-century church, but a total lack of historical evidence for this event has forced a revision of the theory. It is now widely held that the Byzantine Text that largely supports the Textus Receptus has as much right as the Alexandrian or any other tradition to be weighed in determining the text of the New Testament.

Since the 1880s most contemporary translations of the New Testament have relied upon a relatively few manuscripts discovered chiefly in the late nineteenth and early twentieth centuries. Such translations depend primarily on two manuscripts, Codex Vaticanus and Codex Sinaiticus, because of their greater age. The Greek text obtained by using these sources and the related papyri (our most ancient manuscripts) is known as the Alexandrian Text. However, some scholars have grounds for doubting the faithfulness of Vaticanus and Sinaiticus, since they often disagree with one another, and Sinaiticus exhibits excessive omission.

A third viewpoint of New Testament scholarship holds that the best text is based on the consensus of the majority of existing Greek manuscripts. This text is called the Majority Text. Most of these manuscripts are in substantial agreement. Even though many are late, and none is earlier than the fifth century, usually their readings are verified by papyri, ancient versions, quotations from the early church fathers, or a combination of these. The Majority Text is similar to the Textus Receptus, but it corrects those readings which have little or no support in the Greek manuscript tradition.

Today scholars agree that the science of New Testament textual criticism is in a state of flux. Very few scholars still favor the Textus Receptus as such, and then often for its historical prestige as the text of Luther, Calvin, Tyndale, and the King James Version. For about a century most have followed a Critical Text (so called because it is edited according to specific principles of textual criticism) which depends heavily upon the Alexandrian type of text. More recently many have abandoned this Critical Text (which is quite similar to the one edited by Westcott and Hort) for one that is more eclectic. Finally, a small but growing number of scholars prefer the Majority Text, which is close to the traditional text except in the Revelation.

In light of these facts, and also because the New King James Version is the fifth revision of a historic document translated from specific Greek texts, the editors decided to retain the traditional text in the body of the New Testament and to indicate major Critical and Majority Text variant readings in the translators' notes. Although these variations are duly indicated in the translators' notes of the present edition, it is most important to emphasize that fully eighty-five percent of the New Testament text is the same in the Textus Receptus, the Alexandrian Text, and the Majority Text.

NEW KING JAMES TRANSLATORS' NOTES

Significant textual explanations, alternate translations, and New Testament citations of Old Testament passages are supplied in the New King James translators' notes.

Important textual variants in the Old Testament are identified in a standard form.

The textual notes in the present edition of the New Testament make no evaluation of readings, but do clearly indicate the manuscript sources of readings. They objectively present the facts without such tendentious remarks as "the best manuscripts omit" or "the most reliable manuscripts read." Such notes are value judgments that differ according to varying viewpoints on the text. By giving a clearly defined set of variants the New King James Version benefits readers of all textual persuasions.

Where significant variations occur in the New Testament Greek manuscripts, textual notes are classified as follows:

NU-Text

These variations from the traditional text generally represent the Alexandrian or Egyptian type of text described previously in "The New Testament Text." They are found in the Critical Text published in the twenty-seventh edition of the Nestle-Aland Greek New Testament (N) and in the United Bible Societies' fourth edition (U), hence the acronym, "NU-Text."

M-Text

This symbol indicates points of variation in the Majority Text from the traditional text, as also previously discussed in "The New Testament Text." It should be noted that M stands for whatever reading is printed in the published *Greek New Testament According to the Majority Text*, whether supported by overwhelming, strong, or only a divided majority textual tradition.

The textual notes reflect the scholarship of the past two centuries and will assist the reader to observe the variations between the different manuscript traditions of the New Testament. Such information is generally not available in English translations of the New Testament.

OLD TESTAMENT

THE FIRST BOOK OF MOSES CALLED
GENESIS

THE HISTORY OF CREATION

(Gen. 2:4–9; Job 38:4–11; John 1:1–5)

1 In the ᵃbeginning ᵇGod created the heavens and the earth. ²The earth was ᵃwithout form, and void; and darkness ¹*was* on the face of the deep. ᵇAnd the Spirit of God was hovering over the face of the waters.

³ᵃThen God said, ᵇ"Let there be ᶜlight"; and there was light. ⁴And God saw the light, that *it was* good; and God divided the light from the darkness. ⁵God called the light Day, and the ᵃdarkness He called Night. ¹So the evening and the morning were the first day.

⁶Then God said, ᵃ"Let there be a ¹firmament in the midst of the waters, and let it divide the waters from the waters." ⁷Thus God made the firmament, ᵃand divided the waters which *were* under the firmament from the waters which *were* ᵇabove the firmament; and it was so. ⁸And God called the firmament Heaven. So the evening and the morning were the second day.

⁹Then God said, ᵃ"Let the waters under the heavens be gathered together into one place, and ᵇlet the dry *land* appear"; and it was so. ¹⁰And God called the dry *land* Earth, and the gathering together of the waters He called Seas. And God saw that *it was* good.

¹¹Then God said, "Let the earth ᵃbring forth grass, the herb *that* yields seed, *and* the ᵇfruit tree *that* yields fruit according to its kind, whose seed *is* in itself, on the earth"; and it was so. ¹²And the earth brought forth grass, the herb *that* yields seed according to its kind, and the tree *that* yields fruit, whose seed *is* in itself according to its kind. And God saw that *it was* good. ¹³So the evening and the morning were the third day.

¹⁴Then God said, "Let there be ᵃlights in the firmament of the heavens to divide the day from the night; and let them be for signs and ᵇseasons, and for days and years; ¹⁵and let them be for lights in the firmament of the heavens to give light on the earth"; and it was so. ¹⁶Then God made two great ¹lights: the ᵃgreater light to rule the day, and the ᵇlesser light to rule the night. *He made* ᶜthe stars also. ¹⁷God set them in the firmament of the ᵃheavens to give light on the earth, ¹⁸and to ᵃrule over the day and over the night, and to divide the light from the darkness. And God saw that *it was* good. ¹⁹So the evening and the morning were the fourth day.

²⁰Then God said, "Let the waters abound with an abundance of living ¹creatures, and let birds fly above the earth across the face of the ²firmament of the heavens." ²¹So ᵃGod created great sea creatures and every living thing that moves,

1:1 ᵃPs. 102:25;
Is. 40:21;
[John 1:1–3;
Heb. 1:10]
ᵇGen. 2:4;
[Ps. 8:3; 89:11;
90:2]; Is. 44:24;
Acts 17:24;
Rom. 1:20;
[Heb. 1:2; 11:3];
Rev. 4:11

1:2 ᵃJer. 4:23
ᵇ[Gen. 6:3];
Job 26:13;
Ps. 33:6; 104:30;
Is. 40:13, 14

1:3 ᵃPs. 33:6, 9
ᵇ2 Cor. 4:6
ᶜ[Heb. 11:3]

1:5 ᵃJob 37:18;
Ps. 19:2; 33:6;
74:16; 104:20;
136:5; Jer. 10:12

1:6 ᵃJob 37:18;
Jer. 10:12;
2 Pet. 3:5

1:7 ᵃJob 38:8–11;
Prov. 8:27–29
ᵇPs. 148:4

1:9 ᵃJob 26:10;
Ps. 104:6–9;
Prov. 8:29;
Jer. 5:22;
2 Pet. 3:5
ᵇPs. 24:1, 2;
33:7; 95:5

1:11 ᵃPs. 65:9–13;
104:14; Heb. 6:7
ᵇ2 Sam. 16:1;
Luke 6:44

1:14 ᵃDeut. 4:19;
Ps. 74:16;
136:5–9
ᵇPs. 104:19

1:16 ᵃPs. 136:8
ᵇDeut. 17:3;
Ps. 8:3
ᶜDeut. 4:19;
Job 38:7;
Is. 40:26

1:17 ᵃGen. 15:5;
Jer. 33:20, 25

1:18 ᵃJer. 31:35

1:21
ᵃPs. 104:25–28

1:2 ¹Words in italic type have been added for clarity. They are not found in the original Hebrew or Aramaic.   1:5 ¹Lit. *And evening was, and morning was, a day, one.*   1:6 ¹*expanse*   1:16 ¹*luminaries*   1:20 ¹*souls*   ²*expanse*

with which the waters abounded, according to their kind, and every winged bird according to its kind. And God saw that *it was* good. ²²And God blessed them, saying, ᵃ"Be fruitful and multiply, and fill the waters in the seas, and let birds multiply on the earth." ²³So the evening and the morning were the fifth day.

²⁴Then God said, "Let the earth bring forth the living creature according to its kind: cattle and creeping thing and beast of the earth, *each* according to its kind"; and it was so. ²⁵And God made the beast of the earth according to its kind, cattle according to its kind, and everything that creeps on the earth according to its kind. And God saw that *it was* good.

²⁶Then God said, ᵃ"Let Us make man in Our image, according to Our likeness; ᵇlet them have dominion over the fish of the sea, over the birds of the air, and over the cattle, over ¹all the earth and over every creeping thing that creeps on the earth." ²⁷So God created man ᵃin His *own* image; in the image of God He created him; ᵇmale and female He created them. ²⁸Then God blessed them, and God said to them, ᵃ"Be fruitful and multiply; fill the earth and ᵇsubdue it; have dominion over the fish of the sea, over the birds of the air, and over every living thing that ¹moves on the earth."

²⁹And God said, "See, I have given you every herb *that* yields seed which *is* on the face of all the earth, and every tree whose fruit yields seed; ᵃto you it shall be for food. ³⁰Also, to ᵃevery beast of the earth, to every ᵇbird of the air, and to everything that creeps on the earth, in which *there is* ¹life, *I have given* every green herb for food"; and it was so. ³¹Then ᵃGod saw everything that He had made, and indeed *it was* very good. So the evening and the morning were the sixth day.

2 Thus the heavens and the earth, and ᵃall the host of them, were finished. ²ᵃAnd on the seventh day God ended His work which He had done, and He rested on the seventh day from all His work which He had done. ³Then God ᵃblessed the seventh day and sanctified it, because in it He rested from all His work which God had created and made.

⁴ᵃThis *is* the ¹history of the heavens and the earth when they were created, in the day that the LORD God made the earth and the heavens, ⁵before any ᵃplant of the field was in the earth and before any herb of the field had grown. For the LORD God had not ᵇcaused it to rain on the earth, and *there was* no man ᶜto till the ground; ⁶but a mist went up from the earth and watered the whole face of the ground.

⁷And the LORD God formed man *of* the ᵃdust of the ground, and ᵇbreathed into his ᶜnostrils the breath of life; and ᵈman became a living being.

LIFE IN GOD'S GARDEN

⁸The LORD God planted ᵃa garden ᵇeastward in ᶜEden, and there He put the man whom He had formed. ⁹And out of the ground the LORD God made ᵃevery tree grow that is pleasant to the sight and good for food. ᵇThe tree of life *was* also in the midst of the garden, and the tree of the knowledge of good and ᶜevil.

1:22 ᵃGen. 8:17

1:26 ᵃGen. 9:6; Ps. 100:3; Eccl. 7:29; [Eph. 4:24]; James 3:9 ᵇGen. 9:2; Ps. 8:6–8

1:27 ᵃGen. 5:2; 1 Cor. 11:7 ᵇMatt. 19:4; [Mark 10:6–8]

1:28 ᵃGen. 9:1, 7; Lev. 26:9 ᵇ1 Cor. 9:27

1:29 ᵃGen. 9:3; Ps. 104:14, 15

1:30 ᵃPs. 145:15 ᵇJob 38:41

1:31 ᵃ[Ps. 104:24; 1 Tim. 4:4]

2:1 ᵃPs. 33:6

2:2 ᵃEx. 20:9–11; 31:17; Heb. 4:4, 10

2:3 ᵃ[Is. 58:13]

2:4 ᵃGen. 1:1; Ps. 90:1, 2

2:5 ᵃGen. 1:11, 12 ᵇGen. 7:4; Job 5:10; 38:26–28 ᶜGen. 3:23

2:7 ᵃGen. 3:19, 23; Ps. 103:14 ᵇJob 33:4 ᶜGen. 7:22 ᵈ1 Cor. 15:45

2:8 ᵃIs. 51:3 ᵇGen. 3:23, 24 ᶜGen. 4:16

2:9 ᵃEzek. 31:8 ᵇ[Gen. 3:22; Rev. 2:7; 22:2, 14] ᶜ[Deut. 1:39]

1:26 ¹Syr. *all the wild animals of*   1:28 ¹*moves about on*   1:30 ¹*a living soul*
2:4 ¹Heb. *toledoth*, lit. *generations*

¹⁰Now a river went out of Eden to water the garden, and from there it parted and became four riverheads. ¹¹The name of the first *is* Pishon; it *is* the one which skirts ^athe whole land of Havilah, where *there is* gold. ¹²And the gold of that land *is* good. ^aBdellium and the onyx stone *are* there. ¹³The name of the second river *is* Gihon; it *is* the one which goes around the whole land of Cush. ¹⁴The name of the third river *is* ^aHiddekel;¹ it *is* the one which goes toward the east of ²Assyria. The fourth river *is* the Euphrates.

¹⁵Then the Lord God took ¹the man and put him in the garden of Eden to ²tend and keep it. ¹⁶And the Lord God commanded the man, saying, "Of every tree of the garden you may freely eat; ¹⁷but of the tree of the knowledge of good and evil ^ayou shall not eat, for in the day that you eat of it ^byou¹ shall surely ^cdie."

¹⁸And the Lord God said, "*It is* not good that man should be alone; ^aI will make him a helper comparable to him." ^{19a}Out of the ground the Lord God formed every beast of the field and every bird of the air, and ^bbrought *them* to ¹Adam to see what he would call them. And whatever Adam called each living creature, that *was* its name. ²⁰So Adam gave names to all cattle, to the birds of the air, and to every beast of the field. But for Adam there was not found a helper comparable to him.

²¹And the Lord God caused a ^adeep sleep to fall on Adam, and he slept; and He took one of his ribs, and closed up the flesh in its place. ²²Then the rib which the Lord God had taken from man He ¹made into a woman, ^aand He ^bbrought her to the man.

²³And Adam said:

> "This *is* now ^abone of my bones
> And flesh of my flesh;
> She shall be called ¹Woman,
> Because she was ^btaken out of ²Man."

^{24a}Therefore a man shall leave his father and mother and ^bbe¹ joined to his wife, and they shall become one flesh.

^{25a}And they were both naked, the man and his wife, and were not ^bashamed.

THE TEMPTATION AND FALL OF MAN
(Rom. 5:12–21)

3 Now ^athe serpent was ^bmore cunning than any beast of the field which the Lord God had made. And he said to the woman, "Has God indeed said, 'You shall not eat of every tree of the garden'?"

²And the woman said to the serpent, "We may eat the ^afruit of the trees of the garden; ³but of the fruit of the tree which *is* in the midst of the garden, God has said, 'You shall not eat it, nor shall you ^atouch it, lest you die.'"

^{4a}Then the serpent said to the woman, "You will not surely die. ⁵For God knows that in the day you eat of it your eyes will be opened, and you will be like God, knowing good and evil."

⁶So when the woman ^asaw that the tree *was* good for food, that it *was* ¹pleasant to the eyes, and a tree desirable to make

---

2:11 ^aGen. 25:18

2:12 ^aNum. 11:7

2:14 ^aDan. 10:4

2:17 ^aGen. 3:1, 3, 11, 17 ^bGen. 3:3, 19; [Rom. 6:23] ^cRom. 5:12; 1 Cor. 15:21, 22

2:18 ^a1 Cor. 11:8, 9; 1 Tim. 2:13

2:19 ^aGen. 1:20, 24 ^bPs. 8:6

2:21 ^aGen. 15:12; 1 Sam. 26:12

2:22 ^aGen. 3:20; 1 Tim. 2:13 ^bHeb. 13:4

2:23 ^aGen. 29:14; Eph. 5:28–30 ^b1 Cor. 11:8, 9

2:24 ^aMatt. 19:5; Eph. 5:31 ^bMark 10:6–8; 1 Cor. 6:16

2:25 ^aGen. 3:7, 10 ^bIs. 47:3

3:1 ^a1 Chr. 21:1; [Rev. 12:9; 20:2, 10] ^b2 Cor. 11:3

3:2 ^aGen. 2:16, 17

3:3 ^aEx. 19:12, 13; Rev. 22:14

3:4 ^aJohn 8:44; [2 Cor. 11:3]; 1 Tim. 2:14]

3:6 ^a1 John 2:16

2:14 ¹Or *Tigris* ²Heb. *Ashshur* **2:15** ¹Or *Adam* ²*cultivate* **2:17** ¹Lit. *dying you shall die* **2:19** ¹Or *the man* **2:22** ¹Lit. *built* **2:23** ¹Heb. *Ishshah* ²Heb. *Ish* **2:24** ¹Lit. *cling* **3:6** ¹Lit. *a desirable thing*

one wise, she took of its fruit ^band ate. She also gave to her husband with her, and he ate. ⁷Then the eyes of both of them were opened, ^aand they knew that they *were* naked; and they sewed fig leaves together and made themselves ¹coverings.

⁸And they heard ^athe ¹sound of the LORD God walking in the garden in the ²cool of the day, and Adam and his wife ^bhid themselves from the presence of the LORD God among the trees of the garden.

⁹Then the LORD God called to Adam and said to him, "Where *are* you?"

¹⁰So he said, "I heard Your voice in the garden, ^aand I was afraid because I was naked; and I hid myself."

¹¹And He said, "Who told you that you *were* naked? Have you eaten from the tree of which I commanded you that you should not eat?"

¹²Then the man said, ^a"The woman whom You gave *to be* with me, she gave me of the tree, and I ate."

¹³And the LORD God said to the woman, "What *is* this you have done?"

The woman said, ^a"The serpent deceived me, and I ate."

¹⁴So the LORD God said to the serpent:

"Because you have done this,
You *are* cursed more than all cattle,
And more than every beast of the field;
On your belly you shall go,
And ^ayou shall eat dust
All the days of your life.
¹⁵ And I will put enmity
Between you and the woman,
And between ^ayour seed and ^bher Seed;
^cHe shall bruise your head,
And you shall bruise His heel."

¹⁶To the woman He said:

"I will greatly multiply your sorrow and your conception;
^aIn pain you shall bring forth children;
^bYour desire *shall be* ¹for your husband,
And he shall ^crule over you."

¹⁷Then to Adam He said, ^a"Because you have heeded the voice of your wife, and have eaten from the tree ^bof which I commanded you, saying, 'You shall not eat of it':

^c"Cursed *is* the ground for your sake;
^dIn toil you shall eat *of* it
All the days of your life.
¹⁸ Both thorns and thistles it shall ¹bring forth for you,
And ^ayou shall eat the herb of the field.
¹⁹ ^aIn the sweat of your face you shall eat bread
Till you return to the ground,
For out of it you were taken;
^bFor dust you *are,*
And ^cto dust you shall return."

²⁰And Adam called his wife's name ^aEve,¹ because she was the mother of all living.

3:6 ^b1 Tim. 2:14
3:7 ^aGen. 2:25
3:8 ^aJob 38:1
^bJob 31:33;
Jer. 23:24
3:10 ^aGen. 2:25;
Ex. 3:6;
Deut. 9:19;
1 John 3:20
3:12
^a[Prov. 28:13]
3:13 ^aGen. 3:4;
2 Cor. 11:3;
1 Tim. 2:14
3:14
^aDeut. 28:15–20;
Is. 65:25;
Mic. 7:17
3:15 ^aJohn 8:44;
Acts 13:10;
1 John 3:8
^bIs. 7:14;
Luke 1:31, 34, 35;
Gal. 4:4
^cRom. 16:20;
[Rev. 12:7, 17]
3:16 ^aIs. 13:8;
John 16:21
^bGen. 4:7
^c1 Cor. 11:3;
Eph. 5:22;
1 Tim. 2:12, 15
3:17
^a1 Sam. 15:23
^bGen. 2:17
^cGen. 5:29;
Rom. 8:20–22;
Heb. 6:8
^dJob 5:7; 14:1;
Eccl. 2:23
3:18 ^aPs. 104:14
3:19
^a2 Thess. 3:10
^bGen. 2:7; 5:5
^cJob 21:26;
Eccl. 3:20
3:20 ^a2 Cor. 11:3;
1 Tim. 2:13

3:7 ¹*girding coverings*   **3:8** ¹Or *voice*   ²Or *wind, breeze*   **3:16** ¹Lit. *toward*   **3:18** ¹*cause to grow*   **3:20** ¹Lit. *Life* or *Living*

21Also for Adam and his wife the LORD God made tunics of skin, and clothed them.

22Then the LORD God said, "Behold, the man has become like one of Us, to know good and evil. And now, lest he put out his hand and take also of the tree of life, and eat, and live forever"— 23therefore the LORD God sent him out of the garden of Eden ato till the ground from which he was taken. 24So aHe drove out the man; and He placed bcherubim cat the east of the garden of Eden, and a flaming sword which turned every way, to guard the way to the tree of dlife.

CAIN MURDERS ABEL
(Luke 11:51; Heb. 11:4; 12:24)

4 Now Adam knew Eve his wife, and she conceived and bore 1Cain, and said, "I have acquired a man from the LORD." 2Then she bore again, this time his brother 1Abel. Now aAbel was a keeper of sheep, but Cain was a tiller of the ground. 3And 1in the process of time it came to pass that Cain brought an offering of the fruit aof the ground to the LORD. 4Abel also brought of athe firstborn of his flock and of btheir fat. And the LORD crespected Abel and his offering, 5but He did not respect Cain and his offering. And Cain was very angry, and his countenance fell.

6So the LORD said to Cain, "Why are you angry? And why has your countenance fallen? 7If you do well, will you not be accepted? And if you do not do well, sin lies at the door. And its desire is 1for you, but you should rule over it."

8Now Cain 1talked with Abel his 2brother; and it came to pass, when they were in the field, that Cain rose up against Abel his brother and akilled him.

9Then the LORD said to Cain, "Where is Abel your brother?"

He said, a"I do not know. Am I bmy brother's keeper?"

10And He said, "What have you done? The voice of your brother's blood acries out to Me from the ground. 11So now ayou are cursed from the earth, which has opened its mouth to receive your brother's blood from your hand. 12When you till the ground, it shall no longer yield its strength to you. A fugitive and a vagabond you shall be on the earth."

13And Cain said to the LORD, "My 1punishment is greater than I can bear! 14Surely You have driven me out this day from the face of the ground; aI shall be bhidden from Your face; I shall be a fugitive and a vagabond on the earth, and it will happen that canyone who finds me will kill me."

15And the LORD said to him, 1"Therefore, whoever kills Cain, vengeance shall be taken on him asevenfold." And the LORD set a bmark on Cain, lest anyone finding him should kill him.

THE FAMILY OF CAIN

16Then Cain awent out from the bpresence of the LORD and dwelt in the land of 1Nod on the east of Eden. 17And Cain knew his wife, and she conceived and bore Enoch. And he built a city, aand called the name of the city after the name of his

---

3:23
aGen. 4:2; 9:20

3:24
aEzek. 31:3, 11
bEx. 25:18–22;
Ps. 104:4;
Ezek. 10:1–20;
Heb. 1:7
cGen. 2:8
dGen. 2:9;
[Rev. 22:2]

4:2
aLuke 11:50, 51

4:3 aNum. 18:12

4:4 aNum. 18:17
bLev. 3:16
cHeb. 11:4

4:8
aMatt. 23:35;
Luke 11:51;
[1 John 3:12–15];
Jude 11

4:9 aJohn 8:44
b1 Cor. 8:11–13

4:10
aNum. 35:33;
Deut. 21:1–9;
Heb. 12:24;
Rev. 6:9, 10

4:11 aGen. 3:14;
Deut. 11:28;
28:15–20;
Gal. 3:10

4:14 aPs. 51:11
bDeut. 31:18;
Is. 1:15
cGen. 9:6;
Num. 35:19,
21, 27

4:15 aGen. 4:24;
Ps. 79:12
bGen. 9:6;
Ezek. 9:4, 6

4:16
a2 Kin. 13:23;
24:20;
Jer. 23:39; 52:3
bJon. 1:3

4:17 aPs. 49:11

4:1 1Lit. Acquire 4:2 1Lit. Breath or Nothing 4:3 1Lit. at the end of days 4:7 1Lit. toward 4:8 1Lit. said to 2Sam., LXX, Syr., Vg. add "Let us go out to the field." 4:13 1iniquity 4:15 1So with MT, Tg.; LXX, Syr., Vg. Not so; 4:16 1Lit. Wandering

son—Enoch. ¹⁸To Enoch was born Irad; and Irad begot Mehujael, and Mehujael begot Methushael, and Methushael begot Lamech.

¹⁹Then Lamech took for himself ^atwo wives: the name of one *was* Adah, and the name of the second *was* Zillah. ²⁰And Adah bore Jabal. He was the father of those who dwell in tents and have livestock. ²¹His brother's name *was* Jubal. He was the father of all those who play the harp and ¹flute. ²²And as for Zillah, she also bore Tubal-Cain, an instructor of every craftsman in bronze and iron. And the sister of Tubal-Cain *was* Naamah.

²³Then Lamech said to his wives:

"Adah and Zillah, hear my voice;
Wives of Lamech, listen to my speech!
For I have ¹killed a man for wounding me,
Even a young man ²for hurting me.
²⁴ ^aIf Cain shall be avenged sevenfold,
Then Lamech seventy-sevenfold."

A NEW SON

²⁵And Adam knew his wife again, and she bore a son and ^anamed him ¹Seth, "For God has appointed another seed for me instead of Abel, whom Cain killed." ²⁶And as for Seth, ^ato him also a son was born; and he named him ¹Enosh. Then *men* began ^bto call on the name of the LORD.

THE FAMILY OF ADAM

(1 Chr. 1:1–4; Luke 3:36–38)

5 This is the book of the ^agenealogy of Adam. In the day that God created man, He made him in ^bthe likeness of God. ²He created them ^amale and female, and ^bblessed them and called them Mankind in the day they were created. ³And Adam lived one hundred and thirty years, and begot *a son* ^ain his own likeness, after his image, and ^bnamed him Seth. ⁴After he begot Seth, ^athe days of Adam were eight hundred years; ^band he had sons and daughters. ⁵So all the days that Adam lived were nine hundred and thirty years; ^aand he died.

⁶Seth lived one hundred and five years, and begot ^aEnosh. ⁷After he begot Enosh, Seth lived eight hundred and seven years, and had sons and daughters. ⁸So all the days of Seth were nine hundred and twelve years; and he died.

⁹Enosh lived ninety years, and begot ¹Cainan. ¹⁰After he begot Cainan, Enosh lived eight hundred and fifteen years, and had sons and daughters. ¹¹So all the days of Enosh were nine hundred and five years; and he died.

¹²Cainan lived seventy years, and begot Mahalalel. ¹³After he begot Mahalalel, Cainan lived eight hundred and forty years, and had sons and daughters. ¹⁴So all the days of Cainan were nine hundred and ten years; and he died.

¹⁵Mahalalel lived sixty-five years, and begot Jared. ¹⁶After he begot Jared, Mahalalel lived eight hundred and thirty years, and had sons and daughters. ¹⁷So all the days of Mahalalel were eight hundred and ninety-five years; and he died.

¹⁸Jared lived one hundred and sixty-two years, and begot

4:19 ^aGen. 2:24; 16:3; 1 Tim. 3:2
4:24 ^aGen. 4:15
4:25 ^aGen. 5:3
4:26 ^aGen. 5:6
^bGen. 12:8; 26:25; 1 Kin. 18:24; Ps. 116:17; Joel 2:32; Zeph. 3:9; 1 Cor. 1:2

5:1 ^aGen. 2:4; 6:9; 1 Chr. 1:1; Matt. 1:1
^bGen. 1:26; 9:6; [Eph. 4:24; Col. 3:10]
5:2 ^aGen. 1:27; Deut. 4:32; Matt. 19:4; Mark 10:6
^bGen. 1:28; 9:1
5:3 ^a1 Cor. 15:48, 49 ^bGen. 4:25
5:4 ^a1 Chr. 1:1–4; Luke 3:36–38
^bGen. 1:28; 4:25
5:5 ^aGen. 2:17; 3:19; 6:17; [Heb. 9:27]
5:6 ^aGen. 4:26

4:21 ¹pipe 4:23 ¹slain a man for my wound ²for my hurt 4:25 ¹Lit. Appointed 4:26 ¹Gr. Enos, Luke 3:38 5:9 ¹Heb. Qenan

5:18
ªJude 14, 15

5:22
ªGen. 6:9; 17:1;
24:40; 48:15;
2 Kin. 20:3;
Ps. 16:8;
[Mic. 6:8];
Mal. 2:6;
1 Thess. 2:12;
[Heb. 11:39]

5:24 ª2 Kin. 2:11;
Jude 14
ᵇ2 Kin. 2:10;
Ps. 49:15; 73:24;
Heb. 11:5

5:29
ªLuke 3:36;
Heb. 11:7;
1 Pet. 3:20
ᵇGen. 3:17–19;
4:11

5:32 ªGen. 6:10;
7:13 ᵇGen. 10:21

6:1 ªGen. 1:28

6:2 ªDeut. 7:3, 4

6:3 ªGen. 41:38;
[Gal. 5:16, 17];
1 Pet. 3:19, 20
ᵇ2 Thess. 2:7
ᶜPs. 78:39

6:4
ªNum. 13:32, 33;
Luke 17:27

6:5 ªGen. 8:21;
Ps. 14:1–3;
Prov. 6:18;
Matt. 15:19;
Rom. 1:28–32

6:6 ªGen. 6:7;
1 Sam. 15:11, 29;
2 Sam. 24:16;
Jer. 18:7–10;
Zech. 8:14
ᵇPs. 78:40;
Is. 63:10;
Eph. 4:30
ᶜMark 3:5

6:7 ªGen. 7:4,
23; Deut. 28:63;
29:20; Ps. 7:11

6:8 ªGen. 19:19;
Ex. 33:12, 17;
Luke 1:30;
Acts 7:46

6:9 ªGen. 7:1;
Ezek. 14:14,
20; Heb. 11:7;
2 Pet. 2:5
ᵇGen. 5:22, 24;
2 Kin. 23:3

6:10
ªGen. 5:32; 7:13

6:11
ªDeut. 31:29;
Judg. 2:19;
Rom. 2:13
ᵇEzek. 8:17

ªEnoch. ¹⁹After he begot Enoch, Jared lived eight hundred years, and had sons and daughters. ²⁰So all the days of Jared were nine hundred and sixty-two years; and he died.

²¹Enoch lived sixty-five years, and begot Methuselah. ²²After he begot Methuselah, Enoch ªwalked with God three hundred years, and had sons and daughters. ²³So all the days of Enoch were three hundred and sixty-five years. ²⁴And ªEnoch walked with God; and he *was* not, for God ᵇtook him.

²⁵Methuselah lived one hundred and eighty-seven years, and begot Lamech. ²⁶After he begot Lamech, Methuselah lived seven hundred and eighty-two years, and had sons and daughters. ²⁷So all the days of Methuselah were nine hundred and sixty-nine years; and he died.

²⁸Lamech lived one hundred and eighty-two years, and had a son. ²⁹And he called his name ªNoah,¹ saying, "This *one* will comfort us concerning our work and the toil of our hands, because of the ground ᵇwhich the LORD has cursed." ³⁰After he begot Noah, Lamech lived five hundred and ninety-five years, and had sons and daughters. ³¹So all the days of Lamech were seven hundred and seventy-seven years; and he died.

³²And Noah was five hundred years old, and Noah begot ªShem, Ham, ᵇand Japheth.

THE WICKEDNESS AND JUDGMENT OF MAN

6 Now it came to pass, ªwhen men began to multiply on the face of the earth, and daughters were born to them, ²that the sons of God saw the daughters of men, that they *were* beautiful; and they ªtook wives for themselves of all whom they chose.

³And the LORD said, ª"My Spirit shall not ᵇstrive¹ with man forever, ᶜfor he *is* indeed flesh; yet his days shall be one hundred and twenty years." ⁴There were ¹giants on the earth in those ªdays, and also afterward, when the sons of God came in to the daughters of men and they bore *children* to them. Those *were* the mighty men who *were* of old, men of renown.

⁵Then ¹the LORD saw that the wickedness of man *was* great in the earth, and *that* every ªintent² of the thoughts of his heart *was* only evil ³continually. ⁶And ªthe LORD was sorry that He had made man on the earth, and ᵇHe was grieved in His ᶜheart. ⁷So the LORD said, "I will ªdestroy man whom I have created from the face of the earth, both man and beast, creeping thing and birds of the air, for I am sorry that I have made them." ⁸But Noah ªfound grace in the eyes of the LORD.

NOAH PLEASES GOD

⁹This is the genealogy of Noah. ªNoah was a just man, ¹perfect in his generations. Noah ᵇwalked with God. ¹⁰And Noah begot three sons: ªShem, Ham, and Japheth.

¹¹The earth also was corrupt ªbefore God, and the earth was ᵇfilled with violence. ¹²So God ªlooked upon the earth, and indeed it was corrupt; for ᵇall flesh had corrupted their way on the earth.

6:12 ªPs. 14:2; 53:2, 3 ᵇPs. 14:1–3; Is. 28:8

5:29 ¹Lit. *Rest*   6:3 ¹LXX, Syr., Tg., Vg. *abide*   6:4 ¹Heb. *nephilim, fallen* or *mighty ones*   6:5 ¹So with MT, Tg.; Vg. *God;* LXX LORD *God*   ²*thought*   ³*all the day*   6:9 ¹*blameless* or *having integrity*

THE ARK PREPARED
(Heb. 11:7; 1 Pet. 3:20)

13And God said to Noah, a"The end of all flesh has come before Me, for the earth is filled with violence through them; band behold, cI will destroy them with the earth. 14Make yourself an ark of gopherwood; make 1rooms in the ark, and cover it inside and outside with pitch. 15And this is how you shall make it: The length of the ark *shall be* three hundred 1cubits, its width fifty cubits, and its height thirty cubits. 16You shall make a window for the ark, and you shall finish it to a cubit from above; and set the door of the ark in its side. You shall make it *with* lower, second, and third *decks*. 17aAnd behold, I Myself am bringing bfloodwaters on the earth, to destroy from under heaven all flesh in which *is* the breath of life; everything that *is* on the earth shall cdie. 18But I will establish My acovenant with you; and byou shall go into the ark—you, your sons, your wife, and your sons' wives with you. 19And of every living thing of all flesh you shall bring atwo of every *sort* into the ark, to keep *them* alive with you; they shall be male and female. 20Of the birds after their kind, of animals after their kind, and of every creeping thing of the earth after its kind, two of every *kind* awill come to you to keep *them* alive. 21And you shall take for yourself of all food that is eaten, and you shall gather *it* to yourself; and it shall be food for you and for them."

22aThus Noah did; baccording to all that cGod commanded him, so he did.

THE GREAT FLOOD
(Luke 17:26, 27)

7 Then the aLORD said to Noah, b"Come into the ark, you and all your household, because I have seen *that* cyou *are* righteous before Me in this generation. 2You shall take with you seven each of every aclean animal, a male and his female; btwo each of animals that *are* unclean, a male and his female; 3also seven each of birds of the air, male and female, to keep 1the species alive on the face of all the earth. 4For after aseven more days I will cause it to rain on the earth bforty days and forty nights, and I will 1destroy from the face of the earth all living things that I have made." 5aAnd Noah did according to all that the LORD commanded him. 6Noah *was* asix hundred years old when the floodwaters were on the earth.

7aSo Noah, with his sons, his wife, and his sons' wives, went into the ark because of the waters of the flood. 8Of clean animals, of animals that *are* unclean, of birds, and of everything that creeps on the earth, 9two by two they went into the ark to Noah, male and female, as God had commanded Noah. 10And it came to pass after seven days that the waters of the flood were on the earth. 11In the six hundredth year of Noah's life, in the second month, the seventeenth day of the month, on athat day all bthe fountains of the great deep were broken up, and the cwindows of heaven were opened. 12aAnd the rain was on the earth forty days and forty nights.

13On the very same day Noah and Noah's sons, Shem,

6:13 aIs. 34:1–4;
Jer. 51:13;
Ezek. 7:2, 3;
Amos 8:2;
1 Pet. 4:7
bGen. 6:17
c2 Pet. 2:4–10

6:17 aGen. 7:4,
21–23; 2 Pet. 2:5
b2 Pet. 3:6
cLuke 16:22

6:18
aGen. 8:20—
9:17; 17:7
bGen. 7:1, 7,
13; 1 Pet. 3:20;
2 Pet. 2:5

6:19 aGen. 7:2,
8, 9, 14–16

6:20
aGen. 7:9, 15

6:22 aGen. 7:5;
12:4, 5; Heb. 11:7
bGen. 7:5, 9, 16
c[1 John 5:3]

7:1 aMatt. 11:28
bMatt. 24:38;
Luke 17:26;
Heb. 11:7;
1 Pet. 3:20;
2 Pet. 2:5
cGen. 6:9;
Ps. 33:18;
Prov. 10:9;
2 Pet. 2:9

7:2 aLev. 11;
Deut. 14:3–20
bLev. 10:10;
Ezek. 44:23

7:4 aGen. 7:10;
Ex. 7:25
bGen. 7:12, 17

7:5 aGen. 6:22

7:6 aGen. 5:4, 32

7:7 aGen. 6:18;
7:1, 13;
Matt. 24:38;
Luke 17:27

7:11
aMatt. 24:39;
Luke 17:27;
2 Pet. 2:5; 3:6
bGen. 8:2;
Prov. 8:28;
Is. 51:10;
Ezek. 26:19
cGen. 8:2;
Ps. 78:23

7:12
aGen. 7:4, 17;
1 Sam. 12:18

6:14 1Lit. *compartments* or *nests*   6:15 1A cubit is about 18 inches.   7:3 1Lit. *seed*   7:4 1Lit. *blot out*

Ham, and Japheth, and Noah's wife and the three wives of his sons with them, entered the ark— [14a]they and every beast after its kind, all cattle after their kind, every creeping thing that creeps on the earth after its kind, and every bird after its kind, every bird of every [b]sort. [15]And they [a]went into the ark to Noah, two by two, of all flesh in which *is* the breath of life. [16]So those that entered, male and female of all flesh, went in [a]as God had commanded him; and the LORD shut him in.

[17a]Now the flood was on the earth forty days. The waters increased and lifted up the ark, and it rose high above the earth. [18]The waters prevailed and greatly increased on the earth, [a]and the ark moved about on the surface of the waters. [19]And the waters prevailed exceedingly on the earth, and all the high hills under the whole heaven were covered. [20]The waters prevailed fifteen cubits upward, and the mountains were covered. [21a]And all flesh died that moved on [1]the earth: birds and cattle and beasts and every creeping thing that creeps on the earth, and every man. [22]All in [a]whose nostrils *was* the breath [1]of the spirit of life, all that *was* on the dry *land,* died. [23]So He destroyed all living things which were on the face of the ground: both man and cattle, creeping thing and bird of the air. They were destroyed from the earth. Only [a]Noah and those who *were* with him in the ark remained *alive.* [24a]And the waters prevailed on the earth one hundred and fifty days.

NOAH'S DELIVERANCE

8 Then God [a]remembered Noah, and every living thing, and all the animals that *were* with him in the ark. [b]And God made a wind to pass over the earth, and the waters subsided. [2a]The fountains of the deep and the windows of heaven were also [b]stopped, and [c]the rain from heaven was restrained. [3]And the waters receded continually from the earth. At the end [a]of the hundred and fifty days the waters decreased. [4]Then the ark rested in the seventh month, the seventeenth day of the month, on the mountains of Ararat. [5]And the waters decreased continually until the tenth month. In the tenth *month,* on the first *day* of the month, the tops of the mountains were seen.

[6]So it came to pass, at the end of forty days, that Noah opened [a]the window of the ark which he had made. [7]Then he sent out a raven, which kept going to and fro until the waters had dried up from the earth. [8]He also sent out from himself a dove, to see if the waters had receded from the face of the ground. [9]But the dove found no resting place for the sole of her foot, and she returned into the ark to him, for the waters *were* on the face of the whole earth. So he put out his hand and took her, and drew her into the ark to himself. [10]And he waited yet another seven days, and again he sent the dove out from the ark. [11]Then the dove came to him in the evening, and behold, a freshly plucked olive leaf *was* in her mouth; and Noah knew that the waters had receded from the earth. [12]So he waited yet another seven days and sent out the dove, which did not return again to him anymore.

[13]And it came to pass in the six hundred and first year, in the first *month,* the first *day* of the month, that the waters were dried up from the earth; and Noah removed the covering

7:14 [a]Gen. 6:19
[b]Gen. 1:21

7:15 [a]Gen. 6:19, 20; 7:9

7:16 [a]Gen. 7:2, 3

7:17 [a]Gen. 7:4, 12; 8:6

7:18 [a]Ps. 104:26

7:21 [a]Gen. 6:7, 13, 17; 7:4

7:22 [a]Gen. 2:7

7:23 [a]Matt. 24:38, 39; Luke 17:26, 27; Heb. 11:7; 1 Pet. 3:20; 2 Pet. 2:5

7:24 [a]Gen. 8:3, 4

8:1 [a]Gen. 19:29; Ex. 2:24; 1 Sam. 1:19; Ps. 105:42; 106:4 [b]Ex. 14:21; 15:10; Job 12:15; Ps. 29:10; Is. 44:27; Nah. 1:4

8:2 [a]Gen. 7:11 [b]Deut. 11:17 [c]Gen. 7:4, 12; Job 38:37

8:3 [a]Gen. 7:24

8:6 [a]Gen. 6:16

of the ark and looked, and indeed the surface of the ground was dry. [14]And in the second month, on the twenty-seventh day of the month, the earth was dried.

[15]Then God spoke to Noah, saying, [16]"Go out of the ark, [a]you and your wife, and your sons and your sons' wives with you. [17]Bring out with you every living thing of all flesh that *is* with you: birds and cattle and every creeping thing that creeps on the earth, so that they may abound on the earth, and [a]be fruitful and multiply on the earth." [18]So Noah went out, and his sons and his wife and his sons' wives with him. [19]Every animal, every creeping thing, every bird, *and* whatever creeps on the earth, according to their families, went out of the ark.

GOD'S COVENANT WITH CREATION

[20]Then Noah built an [a]altar to the LORD, and took of [b]every clean animal and of every clean bird, and offered [c]burnt offerings on the altar. [21]And the LORD smelled [a]a soothing aroma. Then the LORD said in His heart, "I will never again [b]curse the ground for man's sake, although the [c]imagination[1] of man's heart *is* evil from his youth; [d]nor will I again destroy every living thing as I have done.

22 "While the earth [a]remains,
Seedtime and harvest,
Cold and heat,
Winter and summer,
And [b]day and night
Shall not cease."

9 So God blessed Noah and his sons, and said to them: [a]"Be fruitful and multiply, and fill the earth. [2a]And the fear of you and the dread of you shall be on every beast of the earth, on every bird of the air, on all that move *on* the earth, and on all the fish of the sea. They are given into your hand. [3a]Every moving thing that lives shall be food for you. I have given you [b]all things, even as the [c]green herbs. [4a]But you shall not eat flesh with its life, *that is,* its blood. [5]Surely for your lifeblood I will demand *a reckoning;* [a]from the hand of every beast I will require it, and [b]from the hand of man. From the hand of every [c]man's brother I will require the life of man.

6 "Whoever [a]sheds man's blood,
By man his blood shall be shed;
[b]For in the image of God
He made man.
7 And as for you, [a]be fruitful and multiply;
Bring forth abundantly in the earth
And multiply in it."

[8]Then God spoke to Noah and to his sons with him, saying: [9]"And as for Me, [a]behold, I establish [b]My covenant with you and with your [1]descendants after you, [10a]and with every living creature that *is* with you: the birds, the cattle, and every beast of the earth with you, of all that go out of the ark, every beast of the earth with you. [11]Thus [a]I establish My covenant with you: Never again shall all flesh be cut off by the waters of the flood; never again shall there be a flood to destroy the earth."

8:16 [a]Gen. 7:13

8:17 [a]Gen. 1:22, 28; 9:1, 7

8:20 [a]Gen. 12:7; Ex. 29:18, 25
[b]Gen. 7:2; Lev. 11
[c]Gen. 22:2; Ex. 10:25

8:21 [a]Ex. 29:18, 25; Lev. 1:9; Ezek. 20:41; 2 Cor. 2:15; Eph. 5:2
[b]Gen. 3:17; 6:7, 13, 17; Is. 54:9
[c]Gen. 6:5; 11:6; Job 14:4; Ps. 51:5; Jer. 17:9; Rom. 1:21; 3:23; Eph. 2:1–3
[d]Gen. 9:11, 15

8:22 [a]Is. 54:9
[b]Ps. 74:16; Jer. 33:20, 25

9:1 [a]Gen. 1:28, 29; 8:17; 9:7, 19; 10:32

9:2 [a]Gen. 1:26, 28; Ps. 8:6

9:3 [a]Deut. 12:15; 14:3, 9, 11; Acts 10:12, 13
[b]Rom. 14:14, 20; 1 Cor. 10:23, 26; Col. 2:16; [1 Tim. 4:3, 4]
[c]Gen. 1:29

9:4 [a]Lev. 7:26; 17:10–16; 19:26; Deut. 12:16, 23; 15:23; 1 Sam. 14:33, 34; Acts 15:20, 29

9:5 [a]Ex. 21:28
[b]Gen. 4:9, 10; Ps. 9:12
[c]Acts 17:26

9:6 [a]Ex. 21:12–14; Lev. 24:17; Num. 35:33; Matt. 26:52
[b]Gen. 1:26, 27

9:7 [a]Gen. 9:1, 19

9:9 [a]Gen. 6:18
[b]Is. 54:9

9:10 [a]Ps. 145:9

9:11 [a]Gen. 8:21; Is. 54:9

8:21 [1]*intent* or *thought*   **9:9** [1]Lit. *seed*

¹²And God said: ᵃ"This *is* the sign of the covenant which I make between Me and you, and every living creature that *is* with you, for perpetual generations: ¹³I set ᵃMy rainbow in the cloud, and it shall be for the sign of the covenant between Me and the earth. ¹⁴It shall be, when I bring a cloud over the earth, that the rainbow shall be seen in the cloud; ¹⁵and ᵃI will remember My covenant which *is* between Me and you and every living creature of all flesh; the waters shall never again become a flood to destroy all flesh. ¹⁶The rainbow shall be in the cloud, and I will look on it to remember ᵃthe everlasting covenant between God and every living creature of all flesh that *is* on the earth." ¹⁷And God said to Noah, "This *is* the sign of the covenant which I have established between Me and all flesh that *is* on the earth."

NOAH AND HIS SONS

¹⁸Now the sons of Noah who went out of the ark were Shem, Ham, and Japheth. ᵃAnd Ham *was* the father of Canaan. ¹⁹ᵃThese three *were* the sons of Noah, ᵇand from these the whole earth was populated.

²⁰And Noah began *to be* ᵃa farmer, and he planted a vineyard. ²¹Then he drank of the wine ᵃand was drunk, and became uncovered in his tent. ²²And Ham, the father of Canaan, saw the nakedness of his father, and told his two brothers outside. ²³ᵃBut Shem and Japheth took a garment, laid *it* on both their shoulders, and went backward and covered the nakedness of their father. Their faces *were* ¹turned away, and they did not see their father's nakedness.

²⁴So Noah awoke from his wine, and knew what his younger son had done to him. ²⁵Then he said:

ᵃ"Cursed *be* Canaan;
A ᵇservant of servants
He shall be to his brethren."

²⁶And he said:

ᵃ"Blessed *be* the LORD,
The God of Shem,
And may Canaan be his servant.
²⁷ May God ᵃenlarge Japheth,
ᵇAnd may he dwell in the tents of Shem;
And may Canaan be his servant."

²⁸And Noah lived after the flood three hundred and fifty years. ²⁹So all the days of Noah were nine hundred and fifty years; and he died.

NATIONS DESCENDED FROM NOAH

(1 Chr. 1:5–27)

10 Now this *is* the genealogy of the sons of Noah: Shem, Ham, and Japheth. ᵃAnd sons were born to them after the flood.

²ᵃThe sons of Japheth *were* Gomer, Magog, Madai, Javan, Tubal, Meshech, and Tiras. ³The sons of Gomer *were* Ashkenaz, ¹Riphath, and Togarmah. ⁴The sons of Javan *were* Elishah, Tarshish, Kittim, and ¹Dodanim. ⁵From these ᵃthe

---

9:12 ᵃGen. 9:13, 17; 17:11
9:13 ᵃEzek. 1:28; Rev. 4:3
9:15 ᵃLev. 26:42, 45; Deut. 7:9; Ezek. 16:60
9:16 ᵃGen. 17:13, 19; 2 Sam. 23:5; Is. 55:3; Jer. 32:40; Heb. 13:20
9:18 ᵃGen. 9:25–27; 10:6
9:19 ᵃGen. 5:32 ᵇGen. 9:1, 7; 10:32; 1 Chr. 1:4
9:20 ᵃGen. 3:19, 23; 4:2; Prov. 12:11; Jer. 31:24
9:21 ᵃProv. 20:1; Eph. 5:18
9:23 ᵃEx. 20:12; Gal. 6:1
9:25 ᵃDeut. 27:16; Josh. 9:23, 27 ᵇJosh. 9:23; 1 Kin. 9:20, 21
9:26 ᵃGen. 14:20; 24:27; Ps. 144:15; Heb. 11:16
9:27 ᵃGen. 10:2–5; 39:3; Is. 66:19 ᵇLuke 3:36; John 1:14; Eph. 2:13, 14; 3:6
10:1 ᵃGen. 9:1, 7, 19
10:2 ᵃ1 Chr. 1:5–7
10:5 ᵃGen. 11:8; Ps. 72:10; Jer. 2:10; 25:22

9:23 ¹Lit. *backwards* 10:3 ¹*Diphath,* 1 Chr. 1:6 10:4 ¹Sam. *Rodanim* and 1 Chr. 1:7

coastland *peoples* of the Gentiles were separated into their lands, everyone according to his language, according to their families, into their nations.

6ªThe sons of Ham *were* Cush, Mizraim, ¹Put, and Canaan. ⁷The sons of Cush *were* Seba, Havilah, Sabtah, Raamah, and Sabtechah; and the sons of Raamah *were* Sheba and Dedan.

⁸Cush begot ªNimrod; he began to be a mighty one on the earth. ⁹He was a mighty ªhunter ᵇbefore the LORD; therefore it is said, "Like Nimrod the mighty hunter before the LORD." ¹⁰ªAnd the beginning of his kingdom was ᵇBabel, Erech, Accad, and Calneh, in the land of Shinar. ¹¹From that land he went ªto Assyria and built Nineveh, Rehoboth Ir, Calah, ¹²and Resen between Nineveh and Calah (that *is* the principal city).

¹³Mizraim begot Ludim, Anamim, Lehabim, Naphtuhim, ¹⁴Pathrusim, and Casluhim ª(from whom came the Philistines and Caphtorim).

¹⁵Canaan begot Sidon his firstborn, and ªHeth; ¹⁶ªthe Jebusite, the Amorite, and the Girgashite; ¹⁷the Hivite, the Arkite, and the Sinite; ¹⁸the Arvadite, the Zemarite, and the Hamathite. Afterward the families of the Canaanites were dispersed. ¹⁹ªAnd the border of the Canaanites was from Sidon as you go toward Gerar, as far as Gaza; then as you go toward Sodom, Gomorrah, Admah, and Zeboiim, as far as Lasha. ²⁰These *were* the sons of Ham, according to their families, according to their languages, in their lands *and* in their nations.

²¹And *children* were born also to Shem, the father of all the children of Eber, ¹the brother of Japheth the elder. ²²The ªsons of Shem *were* Elam, Asshur, ᵇArphaxad, Lud, and Aram. ²³The sons of Aram *were* Uz, Hul, Gether, and ¹Mash. ²⁴¹Arphaxad begot ªSalah, and Salah begot Eber. ²⁵ªTo Eber were born two sons: the name of one *was* ¹Peleg, for in his days the earth was divided; and his brother's name *was* Joktan. ²⁶Joktan begot Almodad, Sheleph, Hazarmaveth, Jerah, ²⁷Hadoram, Uzal, Diklah, ²⁸¹Obal, Abimael, Sheba, ²⁹Ophir, Havilah, and Jobab. All these *were* the sons of Joktan. ³⁰And their dwelling place was from Mesha as you go toward Sephar, the mountain of the east. ³¹These *were* the sons of Shem, according to their families, according to their languages, in their lands, according to their nations.

³²ªThese *were* the families of the sons of Noah, according to their generations, in their nations; ᵇand from these the nations were divided on the earth after the flood.

THE TOWER OF BABEL

11 Now the whole earth had one language and one ¹speech. ²And it came to pass, as they journeyed from the east, that they found a plain in the land ªof Shinar, and they dwelt there. ³Then they said to one another, "Come, let us make bricks and ¹bake *them* thoroughly." They had brick for stone, and they had asphalt for mortar. ⁴And they said, "Come, let us build ourselves a city, and a tower ªwhose top *is* in the heavens; let us make a ᵇname for ourselves, lest we ᶜbe scattered abroad over the face of the whole earth."

10:6
ª1 Chr. 1:8–16

10:8 ªMic. 5:6

10:9 ªJer. 16:16;
Mic. 7:2
ᵇGen. 21:20

10:10 ªMic. 5:6
ᵇGen. 11:9

10:11
ªGen. 25:18;
2 Kin. 19:36;
Mic. 5:6

10:14 ª1 Chr. 1:12

10:15 ªGen. 23:3

10:16 ªGen. 14:7;
15:19–21;
Deut. 7:1;
Neh. 9:8

10:19
ªGen. 13:12, 14,
15, 17; 15:18–21;
Num. 34:2–12

10:22
ªGen. 11:10–26;
1 Chr. 1:17–28
ᵇGen. 10:24;
11:10; Luke 3:36

10:24
ªGen. 11:12;
Luke 3:35

10:25 ª1 Chr. 1:19

10:32 ªGen. 10:1
ᵇGen. 9:19; 11:8

11:2 ªGen. 10:10;
14:1; Dan. 1:2

11:4 ªDeut. 1:28;
9:1; Ps. 107:26
ᵇGen. 6:4;
2 Sam. 8:13
ᶜDeut. 4:27

10:6 ¹Or *Phut*   10:21 ¹Or *the older brother of Japheth*   10:23 ¹LXX *Meshech* and 1 Chr. 1:17   10:24 ¹So with MT, Vg., Tg.; LXX *Arphaxad begot Cainan, and Cainan begot Salah* (cf. Luke 3:35, 36)   10:25 ¹Lit. *Division*   10:28 ¹*Ebal*, 1 Chr. 1:22   11:1 ¹Lit. *lip*   11:3 ¹Lit. *burn*

11:5 ᵃGen. 18:21;
Ex. 3:8; 19:11,
18, 20

11:6 ᵃGen. 9:19;
Acts 17:26
ᵇGen. 11:1
ᶜDeut. 31:21;
Ps. 2:1

11:7 ᵃGen. 1:26
ᵇGen. 42:23;
Ex. 4:11;
Deut. 28:49;
Is. 33:19;
Jer. 5:15

11:8 ᵃGen. 11:4;
Deut. 32:8;
Ps. 92:9;
[Luke 1:51]
ᵇGen. 10:25, 32

11:9 ᵃ1 Cor. 14:23

11:10
ᵃGen. 10:22–25;
1 Chr. 1:17

11:12 ᵃLuke 3:35

11:16 ᵃ1 Chr. 1:19
ᵇLuke 3:35

11:20 ᵃLuke 3:35

11:24 ᵃGen. 11:31;
Josh. 24:2;
Luke 3:34

11:26
ᵃJosh. 24:2;
1 Chr. 1:26

11:27 ᵃGen. 11:31;
17:5

11:29
ᵃGen. 17:15;
20:12
ᵇGen. 22:20, 23;
24:15

11:30
ᵃGen. 16:1, 2;
Luke 1:36

11:31 ᵃGen. 12:1
ᵇGen. 15:7;
Neh. 9:7;
Acts 7:4

⁵ᵃBut the Lᴏʀᴅ came down to see the city and the tower which the sons of men had built. ⁶And the Lᴏʀᴅ said, "Indeed ᵃthe people *are* one and they all have ᵇone language, and this is what they begin to do; now nothing that they ᶜpropose to do will be withheld from them. ⁷Come, ᵃlet Us go down and there ᵇconfuse their language, that they may not understand one another's speech." ⁸So ᵃthe Lᴏʀᴅ scattered them abroad from there ᵇover the face of all the earth, and they ceased building the city. ⁹Therefore its name is called ¹Babel, ᵃbecause there the Lᴏʀᴅ confused the language of all the earth; and from there the Lᴏʀᴅ scattered them abroad over the face of all the earth.

SHEM'S DESCENDANTS
(1 Chr. 1:17–27; Luke 3:34–36)

¹⁰ᵃThis *is* the genealogy of Shem: Shem *was* one hundred years old, and begot Arphaxad two years after the flood. ¹¹After he begot Arphaxad, Shem lived five hundred years, and begot sons and daughters.

¹²Arphaxad lived thirty-five years, ᵃand begot Salah. ¹³After he begot Salah, Arphaxad lived four hundred and three years, and begot sons and daughters.

¹⁴Salah lived thirty years, and begot Eber. ¹⁵After he begot Eber, Salah lived four hundred and three years, and begot sons and daughters.

¹⁶ᵃEber lived thirty-four years, and begot ᵇPeleg. ¹⁷After he begot Peleg, Eber lived four hundred and thirty years, and begot sons and daughters.

¹⁸Peleg lived thirty years, and begot Reu. ¹⁹After he begot Reu, Peleg lived two hundred and nine years, and begot sons and daughters.

²⁰Reu lived thirty-two years, and begot ᵃSerug. ²¹After he begot Serug, Reu lived two hundred and seven years, and begot sons and daughters.

²²Serug lived thirty years, and begot Nahor. ²³After he begot Nahor, Serug lived two hundred years, and begot sons and daughters.

²⁴Nahor lived twenty-nine years, and begot ᵃTerah. ²⁵After he begot Terah, Nahor lived one hundred and nineteen years, and begot sons and daughters.

²⁶Now Terah lived seventy years, and ᵃbegot ¹Abram, Nahor, and Haran.

TERAH'S DESCENDANTS

²⁷This *is* the genealogy of Terah: Terah begot ᵃAbram, Nahor, and Haran. Haran begot Lot. ²⁸And Haran died before his father Terah in his native land, in Ur of the Chaldeans. ²⁹Then Abram and Nahor took wives: the name of Abram's wife *was* ᵃSarai,¹ and the name of Nahor's wife, ᵇMilcah, the daughter of Haran the father of Milcah and the father of Iscah. ³⁰But ᵃSarai was barren; she had no child.

³¹And Terah ᵃtook his son Abram and his grandson Lot, the son of Haran, and his daughter-in-law Sarai, his son Abram's wife, and they went out with them from ᵇUr of the

---

11:9 ¹Lit. *Confusion*, Babylon   11:26 ¹*Abraham*, Gen. 17:5   11:29 ¹*Sarah*, Gen. 17:15

Chaldeans to go to ^cthe land of Canaan; and they came to Haran and dwelt there. ³²So the days of Terah were two hundred and five years, and Terah died in Haran.

PROMISES TO ABRAM

(Acts 7:2–5)

12 Now the ^aLORD had said to Abram:

"Get ^bout of your country,
From your family
And from your father's house,
To a land that I will show you.
2 ^aI will make you a great nation;
^bI will bless you
And make your name great;
^cAnd you shall be a blessing.
3 ^aI will bless those who bless you,
And I will curse him who curses you;
And in ^byou all the families of the earth shall be ^cblessed."

⁴So Abram departed as the LORD had spoken to him, and Lot went with him. And Abram *was* seventy-five years old when he departed from Haran. ⁵Then Abram took Sarai his wife and Lot his brother's son, and all their possessions that they had gathered, and ^athe ¹people whom they had acquired ^bin Haran, and they ^cdeparted to go to the land of Canaan. So they came to the land of Canaan. ⁶Abram ^apassed through the land to the place of Shechem, ^bas far as ¹the terebinth tree of Moreh. ^cAnd the Canaanites *were* then in the land.

^{7a}Then the LORD appeared to Abram and said, ^b"To your ¹descendants I will give this land." And there he built an ^caltar to the LORD, who had appeared to him. ⁸And he moved from there to the mountain east of Bethel, and he pitched his tent *with* Bethel on the west and Ai on the east; there he built an altar to the LORD and ^acalled on the name of the LORD. ⁹So Abram journeyed, ^agoing on still toward the ¹South.

ABRAM IN EGYPT

¹⁰Now there was ^aa famine in the land, and Abram ^bwent down to Egypt to dwell there, for the famine *was* ^csevere in the land. ¹¹And it came to pass, when he was close to entering Egypt, that he said to Sarai his wife, "Indeed I know that you *are* ^aa woman of beautiful countenance. ¹²Therefore it will happen, when the Egyptians see you, that they will say, 'This *is* his wife'; and they ^awill kill me, but they will let you live. ^{13a}Please say you *are* my ^bsister, that it may be well with me for your sake, and that ¹I may live because of you."

¹⁴So it was, when Abram came into Egypt, that the Egyptians saw the woman, that she *was* very beautiful. ¹⁵The princes of Pharaoh also saw her and commended her to Pharaoh. And the woman was taken to Pharaoh's house. ¹⁶He ^atreated Abram well for her sake. He ^bhad sheep, oxen, male donkeys, male and female servants, female donkeys, and camels.

¹⁷But the LORD ^aplagued Pharaoh and his house with great plagues because of Sarai, Abram's wife. ¹⁸And Pharaoh called

11:31 ^cGen. 10:19

12:1 ^aGen. 15:7; Acts 7:2, 3; [Heb. 11:8] ^bGen. 13:9

12:2 ^a[Gen. 17:4–6]; 18:18; 46:3; Deut. 26:5; 1 Kin. 3:8 ^bGen. 22:17; 24:35 ^cGen. 28:4; Zech. 8:13; Gal. 3:14

12:3 ^aGen. 24:35; 27:29; Ex. 23:22; Num. 24:9 ^bGen. 18:18; 22:18; 26:4; 28:14; Ps. 72:17; Matt. 1:1; Luke 3:34; Acts 3:25; [Gal. 3:8] ^cIs. 41:27

12:5 ^aGen. 14:14 ^bGen. 11:31 ^cGen. 13:18

12:6 ^aHeb. 11:9 ^bDeut. 11:30; Judg. 7:1 ^cGen. 10:18, 19

12:7 ^aGen. 17:1; 18:1 ^bGen. 13:15; 15:18; 17:8; Deut. 34:4; Ps. 105:9–12; Acts 7:5; Gal. 3:16 ^cGen. 13:4, 18; 22:9

12:8 ^aGen. 4:26; 13:4; 21:33

12:9 ^aGen. 13:1, 3; 20:1; 24:62

12:10 ^aGen. 26:1 ^bPs. 105:13 ^cGen. 43:1

12:11 ^aGen. 12:14; 26:7; 29:17

12:12 ^aGen. 20:11; 26:7

12:13 ^aGen. 20:1–18; 26:6–11 ^bGen. 20:12

12:16 ^aGen. 20:14 ^bGen. 13:2

12:17 ^aGen. 20:18; 1 Chr. 16:21; [Ps. 105:14]

12:5 ¹Lit. *souls* **12:6** ¹Heb. *Alon Moreh* **12:7** ¹Lit. *seed* **12:9** ¹Heb. *Negev* **12:13** ¹Lit. *my soul*

12:18
[a]Gen. 20:9, 10;
26:10

12:20
[a][Prov. 21:1]

13:1 [a]Gen. 12:4;
14:12, 16
[b]Gen. 12:9

13:2
[a]Gen. 24:35;
26:14; Ps. 112:3;
Prov. 10:22

13:3
[a]Gen. 12:8, 9

13:4 [a]Gen. 12:7,
8; 21:33
[b]Ps. 116:17

13:6 [a]Gen. 36:7

13:7 [a]Gen. 26:20
[b]Gen. 12:6;
15:20, 21

13:8 [a]1 Cor. 6:7;
[Phil. 2:14, 15]

13:9
[a]Gen. 20:15;
34:10 [b]Gen. 13:11,
14 [c][Rom. 12:18]

13:10
[a]Gen. 19:17–29;
Deut. 34:3
[b]Gen. 19:24
[c]Gen. 2:8,
10; Is. 51:3
[d]Gen. 14:2, 8;
19:22; Deut. 34:3

13:12
[a]Gen. 19:24, 25,
29 [b]Gen. 14:12;
19:1

13:13
[a]Gen. 18:20, 21;
Ezek. 16:49;
2 Pet. 2:7, 8
[b]Gen. 6:11; 39:9;
Num. 32:23

13:14 [a]Gen. 13:11
[b]Gen. 28:14

13:15 [a]Gen. 12:7;
13:17; 15:7, 18;
17:8; Deut. 34:4;
Acts 7:5
[b]2 Chr. 20:7;
Ps. 37:22

13:16
[a]Gen. 22:17;
Ex. 32:13;
Num. 23:10

13:18
[a]Gen. 26:17
[b]Gen. 14:13
[c]Gen. 23:2;
35:27
[d]Gen. 8:20;
22:8, 9

14:1 [a]Gen. 10:10;
11:2 [b]Is. 11:11;
21:2; Dan. 8:2

Abram and said, [a]"What *is* this you have done to me? Why did you not tell me that she *was* your wife? [19]Why did you say, 'She *is* my sister'? I might have taken her as my wife. Now therefore, here is your wife; take *her* and go your way." [20][a]So Pharaoh commanded *his* men concerning him; and they sent him away, with his wife and all that he had.

ABRAM INHERITS CANAAN

13 Then Abram went up from Egypt, he and his wife and all that he had, and [a]Lot with him, [b]to the [1]South. [2][a]Abram *was* very rich in livestock, in silver, and in gold. [3]And he went on his journey [a]from the South as far as Bethel, to the place where his tent had been at the beginning, between Bethel and Ai, [4]to the [a]place of the altar which he had made there at first. And there Abram [b]called on the name of the LORD.

[5]Lot also, who went with Abram, had flocks and herds and tents. [6]Now [a]the land was not able to [1]support them, that they might dwell together, for their possessions were so great that they could not dwell together. [7]And there was [a]strife between the herdsmen of Abram's livestock and the herdsmen of Lot's livestock. [b]The Canaanites and the Perizzites then dwelt in the land.

[8]So Abram said to Lot, [a]"Please let there be no strife between you and me, and between my herdsmen and your herdsmen; for we *are* brethren. [9][a]Is not the whole land before you? Please [b]separate from me. [c]If *you take* the left, then I will go to the right; or, if *you go* to the right, then I will go to the left."

[10]And Lot lifted his eyes and saw all [a]the plain of Jordan, that it *was* well watered everywhere (before the LORD [b]destroyed Sodom and Gomorrah) [c]like the garden of the LORD, like the land of Egypt as you go toward [d]Zoar. [11]Then Lot chose for himself all the plain of Jordan, and Lot journeyed east. And they separated from each other. [12]Abram dwelt in the land of Canaan, and Lot [a]dwelt in the cities of the plain and [b]pitched *his* tent even as far as Sodom. [13]But the men of Sodom [a]*were* exceedingly wicked and [b]sinful against the LORD.

[14]And the LORD said to Abram, after Lot [a]had separated from him: "Lift your eyes now and look from the place where you are—[b]northward, southward, eastward, and westward; [15]for all the land which you see [a]I give to you and [b]your [1]descendants forever. [16]And [a]I will make your descendants as the dust of the earth; so that if a man could number the dust of the earth, *then* your descendants also could be numbered. [17]Arise, walk in the land through its length and its width, for I give it to you."

[18][a]Then Abram moved *his* tent, and went and [b]dwelt by [1]the terebinth trees of Mamre, [c]which *are* in Hebron, and built an [d]altar there to the LORD.

LOT'S CAPTIVITY AND RESCUE

14 And it came to pass in the days of Amraphel king [a]of Shinar, Arioch king of Ellasar, Chedorlaomer king of [b]Elam, and Tidal king of [1]nations, [2]*that* they made war with Bera king of Sodom, Birsha king of Gomorrah, Shinab king of

---

13:1 [1]Heb. *Negev*   13:6 [1]Lit. *bear*   13:15 [1]Lit. *seed*   13:18 [1]Heb. *Alon Mamre*
14:1 [1]Heb. *goyim*

ᵃAdmah, Shemeber king of Zeboiim, and the king of Bela (that is, ᵇZoar). ³All these joined together in the Valley of Siddim ᵃ(that is, the Salt Sea). ⁴Twelve years ᵃthey served Chedorlaomer, and in the thirteenth year they rebelled.

⁵In the fourteenth year Chedorlaomer and the kings that *were* with him came and attacked ᵃthe Rephaim in Ashteroth Karnaim, ᵇthe Zuzim in Ham, ᶜthe Emim in Shaveh Kiriathaim, ⁶ᵃand the Horites in their mountain of Seir, as far as El Paran, which *is* by the wilderness. ⁷Then they turned back and came to En Mishpat (that *is,* Kadesh), and attacked all the country of the Amalekites, and also the Amorites who dwelt ᵃin Hazezon Tamar.

⁸And the king of Sodom, the king of Gomorrah, the king of Admah, the king of Zeboiim, and the king of Bela (that *is,* Zoar) went out and joined together in battle in the Valley of Siddim ⁹against Chedorlaomer king of Elam, Tidal king of ¹nations, Amraphel king of Shinar, and Arioch king of Ellasar—four kings against five. ¹⁰Now the Valley of Siddim *was full of* ᵃasphalt pits; and the kings of Sodom and Gomorrah fled; *some* fell there, and the remainder fled ᵇto the mountains. ¹¹Then they took ᵃall the goods of Sodom and Gomorrah, and all their provisions, and went their way. ¹²They also took Lot, Abram's ᵃbrother's son ᵇwho dwelt in Sodom, and his goods, and departed.

¹³Then one who had escaped came and told Abram the ᵃHebrew, for ᵇhe dwelt by ¹the terebinth trees of Mamre the Amorite, brother of Eshcol and brother of Aner; ᶜand they *were* allies with Abram. ¹⁴Now ᵃwhen Abram heard that ᵇhis brother was taken captive, he armed his three hundred and eighteen trained *servants* who were ᶜborn in his own house, and went in pursuit ᵈas far as Dan. ¹⁵He divided his forces against them by night, and he and his servants ᵃattacked them and pursued them as far as Hobah, which *is* ¹north of Damascus. ¹⁶So he ᵃbrought back all the goods, and also brought back his brother Lot and his goods, as well as the women and the people.

¹⁷And the king of Sodom ᵃwent out to meet him at the Valley of Shaveh (that *is,* the ᵇKing's Valley), ᶜafter his return from the ¹defeat of Chedorlaomer and the kings who *were* with him.

ABRAM AND MELCHIZEDEK
(*Heb.* 7:1, 2)

¹⁸Then ᵃMelchizedek king of Salem brought out ᵇbread and wine; he *was* ᶜthe priest of ᵈGod Most High. ¹⁹And he blessed him and said:

ᵃ"Blessed be Abram of God Most High,
ᵇPossessor of heaven and earth;
20 And ᵃblessed be God Most High,
Who has delivered your enemies into your hand."

And he ᵇgave him ¹a tithe of all.

²¹Now the king of Sodom said to Abram, "Give me the ¹persons, and take the goods for yourself."

²²But Abram ᵃsaid to the king of Sodom, "I ᵇhave raised my hand to the LORD, God Most High, ᶜthe Possessor of heaven

14:2 ᵃGen. 10:19; Deut. 29:23
ᵇGen. 13:10; 19:22

14:3
ᵃNum. 34:12; Deut. 3:17; Josh. 3:16

14:4 ᵃGen. 9:26

14:5 ᵃGen. 15:20
ᵇDeut. 2:20
ᶜNum. 32:37; Deut. 2:10

14:6
ᵃGen. 36:20; Deut. 2:12, 22

14:7 ᵃ2 Chr. 20:2

14:10 ᵃGen. 11:3
ᵇGen. 19:17, 30

14:11 ᵃGen. 14:16, 21

14:12
ᵃGen. 11:27; 12:5
ᵇGen. 13:12

14:13
ᵃGen. 39:14; 40:15 ᵇGen. 13:18
ᶜGen. 14:24; 21:27, 32

14:14
ᵃGen. 19:29
ᵇGen. 13:8; 14:12
ᶜGen. 12:5; 15:3; 17:27; Eccl. 2:7
ᵈDeut. 34:1; Judg. 18:29; 1 Kin. 15:20

14:15 ᵃIs. 41:2, 3

14:16
ᵃGen. 31:18; 1 Sam. 30:8, 18, 19

14:17
ᵃ1 Sam. 18:6
ᵇ2 Sam. 18:18
ᶜHeb. 7:1

14:18 ᵃPs. 110:4; Heb. 7:1–10
ᵇGen. 18:5; Ex. 29:40; Ps. 104:15
ᶜPs. 110:4; Heb. 5:6
ᵈActs 16:17

14:19 ᵃRuth 3:10
ᵇGen. 14:22; Matt. 11:25

14:20
ᵃGen. 24:27
ᵇGen. 28:22; Heb. 7:4

14:22
ᵃGen. 14:2, 8, 10
ᵇDan. 12:7
ᶜGen. 14:19

14:9 ¹Heb. *goyim*   14:13 ¹Heb. *Alon Mamre*   14:15 ¹Lit. *on the left hand of*
14:17 ¹Lit. *striking*   14:20 ¹*one-tenth*   14:21 ¹Lit. *souls*

14:23
[a]2 Kin. 5:16;
Esth. 9:15, 16

15:1 [a]Gen. 15:4;
46:2;
1 Sam. 15:10;
Dan. 10:1
[b]Gen. 21:17;
26:24; Is. 41:10;
Dan. 10:12
[c]Deut. 33:29;
Ps. 3:3;
84:11; 91:4
[d]Num. 18:20;
Ps. 58:11;
Prov. 11:18

15:2 [a]Gen. 17:18
[b]Acts 7:5

15:3 [a]Gen. 14:14

15:4
[a]2 Sam. 7:12;
Gal. 4:28

15:5 [a]Gen. 22:17;
26:4; Deut. 1:10;
Ps. 147:4
[b]Jer. 33:22
[c]Ex. 32:13;
Rom. 4:18;
Heb. 11:12
[d]Gen. 17:19

15:6 [a]Gen. 21:1;
Rom. 4:3, 9,
22; Gal. 3:6;
James 2:23
[b]Ps. 32:2; 106:31

15:7 [a]Gen. 12:1
[b]Gen. 11:28, 31
[c]Gen. 13:15, 17;
Ps. 105:42, 44

15:8
[a]Gen. 24:13, 14;
Judg. 6:36–40;
1 Sam. 14:9, 10;
Luke 1:18

15:10
[a]Gen. 15:17;
Jer. 34:18
[b]Lev. 1:17

15:12 [a]Gen. 2:21;
28:11; Job 33:15

15:13 [a]Ex. 1:11;
Acts 7:6
[b]Ex. 12:40

15:14 [a]Ex. 6:6
[b]Ex. 12:36

15:15 [a]Job 5:26
[b]Gen. 25:8;
47:30 [c]Gen. 25:8

15:16
[a]Gen. 15:13;
Ex. 12:41
[b]Gen. 48:22;
Lev. 18:24–28;
1 Kin. 21:26
[c]1 Kin. 11:12;
Matt. 23:32

15:17
[a]Jer. 34:18, 19

and earth, [23]that [a]I *will take* nothing, from a thread to a sandal strap, and that I will not take anything that *is* yours, lest you should say, 'I have made Abram rich'— [24]except only what the young men have eaten, and the portion of the men who went with me: Aner, Eshcol, and Mamre; let them take their portion."

GOD'S COVENANT WITH ABRAM

(Heb. 11:8–10)

15 After these things the word of the LORD came to Abram [a]in a vision, saying, [b]"Do not be afraid, Abram. I *am* your [c]shield, [1]your exceedingly [d]great reward."

[2a]But Abram said, "Lord GOD, what will You give me, [b]seeing I [1]go childless, and the heir of my house *is* Eliezer of Damascus?" [3]Then Abram said, "Look, You have given me no offspring; indeed [a]one[1] born in my house is my heir!"

[4]And behold, the word of the LORD *came* to him, saying, "This one shall not be your heir, but one who [a]will come from your own body shall be your heir." [5]Then He brought him outside and said, "Look now toward heaven, and [a]count the [b]stars if you are able to number them." And He said to him, [c]"So shall your [d]descendants be."

[6]And he [a]believed in the LORD, and He [b]accounted it to him for righteousness.

[7]Then He said to him, "I *am* the LORD, who [a]brought you out of [b]Ur of the Chaldeans, [c]to give you this land to inherit it."

[8]And he said, "Lord GOD, [a]how shall I know that I will inherit it?"

[9]So He said to him, "Bring Me a three-year-old heifer, a three-year-old female goat, a three-year-old ram, a turtledove, and a young pigeon." [10]Then he brought all these to Him and [a]cut them in two, down the middle, and placed each piece opposite the other; but he did not cut [b]the birds in two. [11]And when the vultures came down on the carcasses, Abram drove them away.

[12]Now when the sun was going down, [a]a deep sleep fell upon Abram; and behold, horror *and* great darkness fell upon him. [13]Then He said to Abram: "Know certainly [a]that your descendants will be strangers in a land *that is* not theirs, and will serve them, and [b]they will afflict them four hundred years. [14]And also the nation whom they serve [a]I will judge; afterward [b]they shall come out with great possessions. [15]Now as for you, [a]you shall [1]go [b]to your fathers in peace; [c]you shall be buried at a good old age. [16]But [a]in the fourth generation they shall return here, for the iniquity [b]of the Amorites [c]*is* not yet complete."

[17]And it came to pass, when the sun went down and it was dark, that behold, there appeared a smoking oven and a burning torch that [a]passed between those pieces. [18]On the same day the LORD [a]made a covenant with Abram, saying:

[b]"To your descendants I have given this land, from the river of Egypt to the great river, the River Euphrates— [19]the Kenites, the Kenezzites, the Kadmonites, [20]the Hittites, the Perizzites, the Rephaim, [21]the Amorites, the Canaanites, the Girgashites, and the Jebusites."

15:18 [a]Gen. 24:7 [b]Gen. 12:7; 17:8; Ex. 23:31; Num. 34:3; Deut. 11:24; Josh. 1:4; 21:43; Acts 7:5

15:1 [1]Or *your reward shall be very great* 15:2 [1]*am childless* 15:3 [1]*a servant* 15:15 [1]Die and join your ancestors

HAGAR AND ISHMAEL

16 Now Sarai, Abram's wife, [a]had borne him no *children.* And she had [b]an Egyptian maidservant whose name was [c]Hagar. [2][a]So Sarai said to Abram, "See now, the LORD [b]has restrained me from bearing *children.* Please, [c]go in to my maid; perhaps I shall [1]obtain children by her." And Abram [d]heeded the voice of Sarai. [3]Then Sarai, Abram's wife, took Hagar her maid, the Egyptian, and gave her to her husband Abram to be his wife, after Abram [a]had dwelt ten years in the land of Canaan. [4]So he went in to Hagar, and she conceived. And when she saw that she had conceived, her mistress became [a]despised in her [1]eyes.

[5]Then Sarai said to Abram, [1]"My wrong *be* upon you! I gave my maid into your embrace; and when she saw that she had conceived, I became despised in her eyes. [a]The LORD judge between you and me."

[6a]So Abram said to Sarai, "Indeed your maid *is* in your hand; do to her as you please." And when Sarai dealt harshly with her, [b]she fled from her presence.

[7]Now the [a]Angel of the LORD found her by a spring of water in the wilderness, [b]by the spring on the way to [c]Shur. [8]And He said, "Hagar, Sarai's maid, where have you come from, and where are you going?"

She said, "I am fleeing from the presence of my mistress Sarai."

[9]The Angel of the LORD said to her, "Return to your mistress, and [a]submit yourself under her hand." [10]Then the Angel of the LORD said to her, [a]"I will multiply your descendants exceedingly, so that they shall not be counted for multitude." [11]And the Angel of the LORD said to her:

"Behold, you *are* with child,
[a]And you shall bear a son.
You shall call his name [1]Ishmael,
Because the LORD has heard your affliction.
[12] [a]He shall be a wild man;
His hand *shall be* against every man,
And every man's hand against him.
[b]And he shall dwell in the presence of all his brethren."

[13]Then she called the name of the LORD who spoke to her, You-Are-[1]the-God-Who-Sees; for she said, "Have I also here [2]seen Him [a]who sees me?" [14]Therefore the well was called [a]Beer Lahai Roi;[1] observe, *it is* [b]between Kadesh and Bered.

[15]So [a]Hagar bore Abram a son; and Abram named his son, whom Hagar bore, Ishmael. [16]Abram *was* eighty-six years old when Hagar bore Ishmael to Abram.

THE SIGN OF THE COVENANT
(Ex. 12:43—13:2)

17 When Abram was ninety-nine years old, the LORD [a]appeared to Abram and said to him, [b]"I *am* [1]Almighty God; [c]walk before Me and be [d]blameless. [2]And I will make My [a]covenant between Me and you, and [b]will multiply you

16:1 [a]Gen. 11:30; 15:2, 3
[b]Gen. 12:16; 21:9
[c]Gal. 4:24

16:2 [a]Gen. 30:3
[b]Gen. 20:18
[c]Gen. 30:3, 9
[d]Gen. 3:17

16:3
[a]Gen. 12:4, 5

16:4 [a]1 Sam. 1:6, 7; [Prov. 30:21, 23]

16:5 [a]Gen. 31:53; Ex. 5:21

16:6 [a]1 Pet. 3:7
[b]Gen. 16:9; Ex. 2:15

16:7 [a]Gen. 21:17, 18; 22:11, 15; 31:11
[b]Gen. 20:1; 25:18
[c]Ex. 15:22

16:9 [a][Titus 2:9]

16:10
[a]Gen. 17:20

16:11
[a]Luke 1:13, 31

16:12
[a]Gen. 21:20; Job 24:5; 39:5–8
[b]Gen. 25:18

16:13
[a]Gen. 31:42

16:14
[a]Gen. 24:62
[b]Gen. 14:7; Num. 13:26

16:15 [a]Gal. 4:22

17:1 [a]Gen. 12:7;
18:1 [b]Gen. 28:3; 35:11; Ex. 6:3; Job 42:2
[c]2 Kin. 20:3
[d]Gen. 6:9; Deut. 18:13

17:2 [a]Gen. 15:18; Ex. 6:4; [Gal. 3:19]
[b]Gen. 12:2; 13:16; 15:5; 18:18

16:2 [1]Lit. *be built up from*   16:4 [1]*sight*   16:5 [1]*The wrong done to me be*
16:11 [1]Lit. *God Hears*   16:13 [1]Heb. *El Roi*   [2]Seen the back of   16:14 [1]Lit.
Well of the One Who Lives and Sees Me   17:1 [1]Heb. *El Shaddai*

exceedingly." ³Then Abram fell on his face, and God talked with him, saying: ⁴"As for Me, behold, My covenant is with you, and you shall be ᵃa father of ¹many nations. ⁵No longer shall ᵃyour name be called ¹Abram, but your name shall be ²Abraham; ᵇfor I have made you a father of ³many nations. ⁶I will make you exceedingly fruitful; and I will make ᵃnations of you, and ᵇkings shall come from you. ⁷And I will ᵃestablish My covenant between Me and you and your descendants after you in their generations, for an everlasting covenant, ᵇto be God to you and ᶜyour descendants after you. ⁸Also ᵃI give to you and your descendants after you the land ᵇin¹ which you are a stranger, all the land of Canaan, as an everlasting possession; and ᶜI will be their God."

⁹And God said to Abraham: "As for you, ᵃyou shall keep My covenant, you and your descendants after you throughout their generations. ¹⁰This *is* My covenant which you shall keep, between Me and you and your descendants after you: ᵃEvery male child among you shall be circumcised; ¹¹and you shall be circumcised in the flesh of your foreskins, and it shall be ᵃa sign of the covenant between Me and you. ¹²He who is eight days old among you ᵃshall be circumcised, every male child in your generations, he who is born in your house or bought with money from any foreigner who is not your descendant. ¹³He who is born in your house and he who is bought with your money must be circumcised, and My covenant shall be in your flesh for an everlasting covenant. ¹⁴And the uncircumcised male child, who is not circumcised in the flesh of his foreskin, that person ᵃshall be cut off from his people; he has broken My covenant."

¹⁵Then God said to Abraham, "As for Sarai your wife, you shall not call her name Sarai, but ¹Sarah *shall be* her name. ¹⁶And I will bless her ᵃand also give you a son by her; then I will bless her, and she shall be *a mother* ᵇof nations; ᶜkings of peoples shall be from her."

¹⁷Then Abraham fell on his face ᵃand laughed, and said in his heart, "Shall *a child* be born to a man who is one hundred years old? And shall Sarah, who is ninety years old, bear *a child?*" ¹⁸And Abraham ᵃsaid to God, "Oh, that Ishmael might live before You!"

¹⁹Then God said: "No, ᵃSarah your wife shall bear you a son, and you shall call his name Isaac; I will establish My ᵇcovenant with him for an everlasting covenant, *and* with his descendants after him. ²⁰And as for Ishmael, I have heard you. Behold, I have blessed him, and will make him fruitful, and ᵃwill multiply him exceedingly. He shall beget ᵇtwelve princes, ᶜand I will make him a great nation. ²¹But My ᵃcovenant I will establish with Isaac, ᵇwhom Sarah shall bear to you at this ᶜset time next year." ²²Then He finished talking with him, and God went up from Abraham.

²³So Abraham took Ishmael his son, all who were born in his house and all who were bought with his money, every male among the men of Abraham's house, and circumcised the flesh of their foreskins that very same day, as God had said to him. ²⁴Abraham *was* ninety-nine years old when he

17:4 ᵃ[Rom. 4:11, 12, 16]

17:5 ᵃNeh. 9:7
ᵇRom. 4:17

17:6 ᵃGen. 17:16; 35:11 ᵇMatt. 1:6

17:7 ᵃ[Gal. 3:17]
ᵇGen. 26:24; 28:13; Lev. 11:45; 26:12, 45; Heb. 11:16
ᶜRom. 9:8; Gal. 3:16

17:8 ᵃGen. 12:7; 13:15, 17; Acts 7:5
ᵇGen. 23:4; 28:4
ᶜEx. 6:7; 29:45; Lev. 26:12; Deut. 29:13; Rev. 21:7

17:9 ᵃEx. 19:5

17:10
ᵃJohn 7:22; Acts 7:8

17:11 ᵃEx. 12:13, 48; [Rom. 4:11]

17:12 ᵃLev. 12:3

17:14
ᵃEx. 4:24–26

17:16 ᵃGen. 18:10
ᵇGen. 35:11; Gal. 4:31; 1 Pet. 3:6
ᶜGen. 17:6; 36:31; 1 Sam. 8:22

17:17 ᵃGen. 17:3; 18:12; 21:6

17:18
ᵃGen. 18:23

17:19
ᵃGen. 18:10; 21:2; [Gal. 4:28]
ᵇGen. 22:16; Matt. 1:2; Luke 3:34

17:20
ᵃGen. 16:10
ᵇGen. 25:12–16
ᶜGen. 21:13, 18

17:21
ᵃGen. 26:2–5
ᵇGen. 21:2
ᶜGen. 18:14

17:4 ¹Lit. *a multitude of nations*   17:5 ¹Lit. *Exalted Father*   ²Lit. *Father of a Multitude*   ³*a multitude of*   17:8 ¹Lit. *of your sojournings*   17:15 ¹Lit. *Princess*

was circumcised in the flesh of his foreskin. ²⁵And Ishmael his son *was* thirteen years old when he was circumcised in the flesh of his foreskin. ²⁶That very same day Abraham was circumcised, and his son Ishmael; ²⁷and ᵃall the men of his house, born in the house or bought with money from a foreigner, were circumcised with him.

THE SON OF PROMISE

(Heb. 13:2)

18 Then the LORD appeared to him by ¹the ᵃterebinth trees of Mamre, as he was sitting in the tent door in the heat of the day. ²ᵃSo he lifted his eyes and looked, and behold, three men were standing by him; ᵇand when he saw *them,* he ran from the tent door to meet them, and bowed himself to the ground, ³and said, "My Lord, if I have now found favor in Your sight, do not pass on by Your servant. ⁴Please let ᵃa little water be brought, and wash your feet, and rest yourselves under the tree. ⁵And ᵃI will bring a morsel of bread, that ᵇyou may refresh your hearts. After that you may pass by, ᶜinasmuch as you have come to your servant."

They said, "Do as you have said."

⁶So Abraham hurried into the tent to Sarah and said, "Quickly, make ready three measures of fine meal; knead *it* and make cakes." ⁷And Abraham ran to the herd, took a tender and good calf, gave *it* to a young man, and he hastened to prepare it. ⁸So ᵃhe took butter and milk and the calf which he had prepared, and set *it* before them; and he stood by them under the tree as they ate.

⁹Then they said to him, "Where *is* Sarah your wife?"

So he said, "Here, ᵃin the tent."

¹⁰And He said, "I will certainly return to you ᵃaccording to the time of life, and behold, ᵇSarah your wife shall have a son."

(Sarah was listening in the tent door which *was* behind him.) ¹¹Now ᵃAbraham and Sarah were old, well advanced in age; *and* ¹Sarah ᵇhad passed the age of childbearing. ¹²Therefore Sarah ᵃlaughed within herself, saying, ᵇ"After I have grown old, shall I have pleasure, my ᶜlord being old also?"

¹³And the LORD said to Abraham, "Why did Sarah laugh, saying, 'Shall I surely bear *a child,* since I am old?' ¹⁴ᵃIs anything too hard for the LORD? ᵇAt the appointed time I will return to you, according to the time of life, and Sarah shall have a son."

¹⁵But Sarah denied *it,* saying, "I did not laugh," for she was afraid.

And He said, "No, but you did laugh!"

ABRAHAM INTERCEDES FOR SODOM

¹⁶Then the men rose from there and looked toward Sodom, and Abraham went with them ᵃto send them on the way. ¹⁷And the LORD said, ᵃ"Shall I hide from Abraham what I am doing, ¹⁸since Abraham shall surely become a great and mighty nation, and all the nations of the earth shall be ᵃblessed in him? ¹⁹For I have known him, in order ᵃthat he may command his children and his household after him, that

---

18:1 ¹Heb. *Alon Mamre*   18:11 ¹Lit. *the manner of women had ceased to be with Sarah*

17:27 ᵃGen. 18:19

18:1 ᵃGen. 13:18; 14:13

18:2 ᵃGen. 18:16, 22; 32:24; Josh. 5:13; Judg. 13:6–11; Heb. 13:2
ᵇGen. 19:1; 1 Pet. 4:9

18:4 ᵃGen. 19:2; 24:32; 43:24

18:5 ᵃJudg. 6:18, 19; 13:15, 16
ᵇJudg. 19:5; Ps. 104:15
ᶜGen. 19:8; 33:10

18:8 ᵃGen. 19:3

18:9 ᵃGen. 24:67

18:10
ᵃ2 Kin. 4:16
ᵇGen. 17:19, 21; 21:2; Rom. 9:9

18:11 ᵃGen. 17:17; Luke 1:18; Rom. 4:19; Heb. 11:11, 12, 19
ᵇGen. 31:35

18:12 ᵃGen. 17:17
ᵇLuke 1:18
ᶜ1 Pet. 3:6

18:14
ᵃNum. 11:23; Jer. 32:17; Zech. 8:6; Matt. 3:9; 19:26; Luke 1:37; Rom. 4:21
ᵇGen. 17:21; 18:10; 2 Kin. 4:16

18:16 ᵃActs 15:3; Rom. 15:24

18:17
ᵃGen. 18:22, 26, 33; Ps. 25:14; Amos 3:7; [John 15:15]

18:18
ᵃ[Gen. 12:3; 22:18]; Matt. 1:1; Luke 3:34; [Acts 3:25, 26; Gal. 3:8]

18:19
ᵃ[Deut. 4:9, 10; 6:6, 7]

they keep the way of the LORD, to do righteousness and justice, that the LORD may bring to Abraham what He has spoken to him." 20And the LORD said, "Because ªthe outcry against Sodom and Gomorrah is great, and because their ᵇsin is very grave, 21ªI will go down now and see whether they have done altogether according to the outcry against it that has come to Me; and if not, ᵇI will know."

22Then the men turned away from there ªand went toward Sodom, but Abraham still stood before the LORD. 23And Abraham ªcame near and said, ᵇ"Would You also ᶜdestroy the ᵈrighteous with the wicked? 24Suppose there were fifty righteous within the city; would You also destroy the place and not spare *it* for the fifty righteous that were in it? 25Far be it from You to do such a thing as this, to slay the righteous with the wicked, so ªthat the righteous should be as the wicked; far be it from You! ᵇShall not the Judge of all the earth do right?"

26So the LORD said, ª"If I find in Sodom fifty righteous within the city, then I will spare all the place for their sakes."

27Then Abraham answered and said, "Indeed now, I who *am* ª*but* dust and ashes have taken it upon myself to speak to the Lord: 28Suppose there were five less than the fifty righteous; would You destroy all of the city for *lack of* five?"

So He said, "If I find there forty-five, I will not destroy *it*."

29And he spoke to Him yet again and said, "Suppose there should be forty found there?"

So He said, "I will not do *it* for the sake of forty."

30Then he said, "Let not the Lord be angry, and I will speak: Suppose thirty should be found there?"

So He said, "I will not do *it* if I find thirty there."

31And he said, "Indeed now, I have taken it upon myself to speak to the Lord: Suppose twenty should be found there?"

So He said, "I will not destroy *it* for the sake of twenty."

32Then he said, ª"Let not the Lord be angry, and I will speak but once more: Suppose ten should be found there?"

ᵇAnd He said, "I will not destroy *it* for the sake of ten." 33So the LORD went His way as soon as He had finished speaking with Abraham; and Abraham returned to his place.

SODOM'S DEPRAVITY

19 Now ªthe two angels came to Sodom in the evening, and ᵇLot was sitting in the gate of Sodom. When Lot saw *them,* he rose to meet them, and he bowed himself with his face toward the ground. 2And he said, "Here now, my lords, please ªturn in to your servant's house and spend the night, and ᵇwash your feet; then you may rise early and go on your way."

And they said, ᶜ"No, but we will spend the night in the open square."

3But he insisted strongly; so they turned in to him and entered his house. ªThen he made them a feast, and baked ᵇunleavened bread, and they ate.

4Now before they lay down, the men of the city, the men of Sodom, both old and young, all the people from every quarter, surrounded the house. 5ªAnd they called to Lot and said to him, "Where are the men who came to you tonight? ᵇBring them out to us that we ᶜmay know them *carnally.*"

18:20
ªGen. 4:10;
19:13;
Ezek. 16:49, 50
ᵇGen. 13:13

18:21 ªGen. 11:5;
Ex. 3:8; Ps. 14:2
ᵇDeut. 8:2; 13:3;
Josh. 22:22;
Luke 16:15;
2 Cor. 11:11

18:22
ªGen. 18:16; 19:1

18:23
ª[Heb. 10:22]
ᵇEx. 23:7;
Num. 16:22;
2 Sam. 24:17;
Ps. 11:4–7
ᶜJob 9:22
ᵈGen. 20:4

18:25 ªJob 8:20;
Is. 3:10, 11
ᵇDeut. 1:16, 17;
32:4; Job 8:3,
20; 34:17;
Ps. 58:11; 94:2;
Is. 3:10, 11;
Rom. 3:5, 6

18:26 ªJer. 5:1;
Ezek. 22:30

18:27
ª[Gen. 3:19];
Job 4:19;
30:19; 42:6;
[1 Cor. 15:47, 48]

18:32
ªJudg. 6:39
ᵇJames 5:16

19:1 ªGen. 18:2,
16, 22
ᵇGen. 18:1–5

19:2 ªGen. 24:31;
[Heb. 13:2]
ᵇGen. 18:4;
24:32
ᶜLuke 24:28

19:3
ªGen. 18:6–8;
Ex. 23:15;
Num. 9:11; 28:17
ᵇEx. 12:8

19:5 ªIs. 3:9
ᵇJudg. 19:22
ᶜGen. 4:1;
Rom. 1:24, 27;
Jude 7

⁶So ᵃLot went out to them through the doorway, shut the door behind him, ⁷and said, "Please, my brethren, do not do so wickedly! ⁸ᵃSee now, I have two daughters who have not known a man; please, let me bring them out to you, and you may do to them as you wish; only do nothing to these men, ᵇsince this is the reason they have come under the shadow of my roof."

⁹And they said, "Stand back!" Then they said, "This one ᵃcame in to ¹stay here, ᵇand he keeps acting as a judge; now we will deal worse with you than with them." So they pressed hard against the man Lot, and came near to break down the door. ¹⁰But the men reached out their hands and pulled Lot into the house with them, and shut the door. ¹¹And they ᵃstruck the men who were at the doorway of the house with blindness, both small and great, so that they became weary trying to find the door.

SODOM AND GOMORRAH DESTROYED
(Matt. 11:23, 24; Luke 17:28–32)

¹²Then the men said to Lot, "Have you anyone else here? Son-in-law, your sons, your daughters, and whomever you have in the city—ᵃtake them out of this place! ¹³For we will destroy this place, because the ᵃoutcry against them has grown great before the face of the LORD, and ᵇthe LORD has sent us to destroy it."

¹⁴So Lot went out and spoke to his sons-in-law, ᵃwho had married his daughters, and said, ᵇ"Get up, get out of this place; for the LORD will destroy this city!" ᶜBut to his sons-in-law he seemed to be joking.

¹⁵When the morning dawned, the angels urged Lot to hurry, saying, ᵃ"Arise, take your wife and your two daughters who are here, lest you be consumed in the punishment of the city." ¹⁶And while he lingered, the men ᵃtook hold of his hand, his wife's hand, and the hands of his two daughters, the ᵇLORD being merciful to him, ᶜand they brought him out and set him outside the city. ¹⁷So it came to pass, when they had brought them outside, that ¹he said, ᵃ"Escape for your life! ᵇDo not look behind you nor stay anywhere in the plain. Escape ᶜto the mountains, lest you be ²destroyed."

¹⁸Then Lot said to them, "Please, ᵃno, my lords! ¹⁹Indeed now, your servant has found favor in your sight, and you have increased your mercy which you have shown me by saving my life; but I cannot escape to the mountains, lest some evil overtake me and I die. ²⁰See now, this city is near enough to flee to, and it is a little one; please let me escape there (is it not a little one?) and my soul shall live."

²¹And he said to him, "See, ᵃI have favored you concerning this thing also, in that I will not overthrow this city for which you have spoken. ²²Hurry, escape there. For ᵃI cannot do anything until you arrive there."

Therefore ᵇthe name of the city was called ¹Zoar.

²³The sun had risen upon the earth when Lot entered Zoar. ²⁴Then the LORD rained ᵃbrimstone and ᵇfire on Sodom and Gomorrah, from the LORD out of the heavens. ²⁵So He ¹overthrew those cities, all the plain, all the inhabitants of the cities, and ᵃwhat grew on the ground.

19:9 ¹As a resident alien 19:17 ¹LXX, Syr., Vg. they ²Lit. swept away
19:22 ¹Lit. Little or Insignificant 19:25 ¹devastated

19:6
ᵃJudg. 19:23

19:8
ᵃJudg. 19:24
ᵇGen. 18:5

19:9
ᵃ2 Pet. 2:7, 8
ᵇEx. 2:14

19:11
ᵃGen. 20:17, 18

19:12 ᵃGen. 7:1;
2 Pet. 2:7, 9

19:13
ᵃGen. 18:20
ᵇLev. 26:30–33;
Deut. 4:26;
28:45;
1 Chr. 21:15

19:14 ᵃMatt. 1:18
ᵇNum. 16:21, 24,
26, 45; Rev. 18:4
ᶜEx. 9:21;
Jer. 43:1, 2;
Luke 17:28; 24:11

19:15 ᵃPs. 37:2;
Rev. 18:4

19:16
ᵃDeut. 5:15; 6:21;
7:8; 2 Pet. 2:7
ᵇEx. 34:7;
Ps. 32:10; 33:18,
19; Luke 18:13
ᶜPs. 34:22

19:17
ᵃ1 Kin. 19:3;
Jer. 48:6
ᵇGen. 19:26;
Matt. 24:16–18;
Luke 9:62;
Phil. 3:13, 14
ᶜGen. 14:10

19:18 ᵃActs 10:14

19:21
ᵃJob 42:8, 9;
Ps. 145:19

19:22 ᵃEx. 32:10;
Deut. 9:14
ᵇGen. 13:10; 14:2

19:24
ᵃDeut. 29:23;
Ps. 11:6; Is. 13:19;
Jer. 20:16; 23:14;
49:18; 50:40;
Ezek. 16:49,
50; Hos. 11:8;
Amos 4:11;
Zeph. 2:9;
Matt. 10:15;
Mark 6:11;
Luke 17:29;
Rom. 9:29;
2 Pet. 2:6;
Jude 7; Rev. 11:8
ᵇLev. 10:2

19:25
ᵃPs. 107:34

²⁶But his wife looked back behind him, and she became ᵃa pillar of salt.

²⁷And Abraham went early in the morning to the place where ᵃhe had stood before the LORD. ²⁸Then he looked toward Sodom and Gomorrah, and toward all the land of the plain; and he saw, and behold, ᵃthe smoke of the land which went up like the smoke of a furnace. ²⁹And it came to pass, when God destroyed the cities of the plain, that God ᵃremembered Abraham, and sent Lot out of the midst of the overthrow, when He overthrew the cities in which Lot had dwelt.

THE DESCENDANTS OF LOT

³⁰Then Lot went up out of Zoar and ᵃdwelt in the mountains, and his two daughters were with him; for he was afraid to dwell in Zoar. And he and his two daughters dwelt in a cave. ³¹Now the firstborn said to the younger, "Our father *is* old, and *there is* no man on the earth ᵃto come in to us as is the custom of all the earth. ³²Come, let us make our father drink wine, and we will lie with him, that we ᵃmay preserve the ¹lineage of our father." ³³So they made their father drink wine that night. And the firstborn went in and lay with her father, and he did not know when she lay down or when she arose.

³⁴It happened on the next day that the firstborn said to the younger, "Indeed I lay with my father last night; let us make him drink wine tonight also, and you go in *and* lie with him, that we may preserve the ¹lineage of our father." ³⁵Then they made their father drink wine that night also. And the younger arose and lay with him, and he did not know when she lay down or when she arose.

³⁶Thus both the daughters of Lot were with child by their father. ³⁷The firstborn bore a son and called his name Moab; ᵃhe *is* the father of the Moabites to this day. ³⁸And the younger, she also bore a son and called his name Ben-Ammi; ᵃhe *is* the father of the people of Ammon to this day.

ABRAHAM AND ABIMELECH

20 And Abraham journeyed from ᵃthere to the South, and dwelt between ᵇKadesh and Shur, and ᶜstayed in Gerar. ²Now Abraham said of Sarah his wife, ᵃ"She *is* my sister." And Abimelech king of Gerar sent and ᵇtook Sarah.

³But ᵃGod came to Abimelech ᵇin a dream by night, and said to him, ᶜ"Indeed you *are* a dead man because of the woman whom you have taken, for she *is* ¹a man's wife."

⁴But Abimelech had not come near her; and he said, "Lord, ᵃwill You slay a righteous nation also? ⁵Did he not say to me, 'She *is* my sister'? And she, even she herself said, 'He *is* my brother.' ᵃIn the ¹integrity of my heart and innocence of my hands I have done this."

⁶And God said to him in a dream, "Yes, I know that you did this in the integrity of your heart. For ᵃI also withheld you from sinning ᵇagainst Me; therefore I did not let you touch her. ⁷Now therefore, restore the man's wife; ᵃfor he *is* a prophet, and he will pray for you and you shall live. But if you do not restore *her*, ᵇknow that you shall surely die, you ᶜand all who *are* yours."

Cross references (margin):

19:26 ᵃGen. 19:17; Luke 17:32

19:27 ᵃGen. 18:22

19:28 ᵃRev. 9:2; 18:9

19:29 ᵃGen. 8:1; 18:23; Deut. 7:8; 9:5, 27

19:30 ᵃGen. 19:17, 19

19:31 ᵃGen. 16:2, 4; 38:8, 9; Deut. 25:5

19:32 ᵃ[Mark 12:19]

19:37 ᵃNum. 25:1; Deut. 2:9

19:38 ᵃNum. 21:24; Deut. 2:19

20:1 ᵃGen. 18:1 ᵇGen. 12:9; 16:7, 14 ᶜGen. 26:1, 6

20:2 ᵃGen. 12:11–13; 26:7 ᵇGen. 12:15

20:3 ᵃPs. 105:14 ᵇJob 33:15 ᶜGen. 20:7

20:4 ᵃGen. 18:23–25; Num. 16:22

20:5 ᵃ1 Kin. 9:4; 2 Kin. 20:3; Ps. 7:8; 26:6

20:6 ᵃGen. 31:7; 35:5; Ex. 34:24; 1 Sam. 25:26, 34 ᵇGen. 39:9; 2 Sam. 12:13

20:7 ᵃ1 Sam. 7:5; 2 Kin. 5:11; Job 42:8; James 5:14, 15 ᵇGen. 2:17 ᶜNum. 16:32, 33

19:32 ¹Lit. *seed*   19:34 ¹Lit. *seed*   20:3 ¹Lit. *married to a husband*
20:5 ¹*innocence*

⁸So Abimelech rose early in the morning, called all his servants, and told all these things in their hearing; and the men were very much afraid. ⁹And Abimelech called Abraham and said to him, "What have you done to us? How have I ¹offended you, ᵃthat you have brought on me and on my kingdom a great sin? You have done deeds to me ᵇthat ought not to be done." ¹⁰Then Abimelech said to Abraham, "What did you have in view, that you have done this thing?"

¹¹And Abraham said, "Because I thought, surely ᵃthe fear of God *is* not in this place; and ᵇthey will kill me on account of my wife. ¹²But indeed ᵃ*she is* truly my sister. She *is* the daughter of my father, but not the daughter of my mother; and she became my wife. ¹³And it came to pass, when ᵃGod caused me to wander from my father's house, that I said to her, 'This *is* your kindness that you should do for me: in every place, wherever we go, ᵇsay of me, "He *is* my brother."'"

¹⁴Then Abimelech ᵃtook sheep, oxen, and male and female servants, and gave *them* to Abraham; and he restored Sarah his wife to him. ¹⁵And Abimelech said, "See, ᵃmy land *is* before you; dwell where it pleases you." ¹⁶Then to Sarah he said, "Behold, I have given your brother a thousand *pieces* of silver; ᵃindeed this ¹vindicates you ᵇbefore all who *are* with you and before everybody." Thus she was ²rebuked.

¹⁷So Abraham ᵃprayed to God; and God ᵇhealed Abimelech, his wife, and his female servants. Then they bore *children;* ¹⁸for the LORD ᵃhad closed up all the wombs of the house of Abimelech because of Sarah, Abraham's wife.

ISAAC IS BORN
(Heb. 11:11)

21 And the LORD ᵃvisited Sarah as He had said, and the LORD did for Sarah ᵇas He had spoken. ²For Sarah ᵃconceived and bore Abraham a son in his old age, ᵇat the set time of which God had spoken to him. ³And Abraham called the name of his son who was born to him—whom Sarah bore to him—ᵃIsaac.¹ ⁴Then Abraham ᵃcircumcised his son Isaac when he was eight days old, ᵇas God had commanded him. ⁵Now ᵃAbraham was one hundred years old when his son Isaac was born to him. ⁶And Sarah said, ᵃ"God has ¹made me laugh, *and* all who hear ᵇwill laugh with me." ⁷She also said, "Who would have said to Abraham that Sarah would nurse children? ᵃFor I have borne *him* a son in his old age."

HAGAR AND ISHMAEL DEPART
(Gal. 4:21–30)

⁸So the child grew and was weaned. And Abraham made a great feast on the same day that Isaac was weaned.

⁹And Sarah saw the son of Hagar ᵃthe Egyptian, whom she had borne to Abraham, ᵇscoffing.¹ ¹⁰Therefore she said to Abraham, ᵃ"Cast out this bondwoman and her son; for the son of this bondwoman shall not be heir with my son, *namely* with Isaac." ¹¹And the matter was very ¹displeasing in Abraham's sight ᵃbecause of his son.

20:9
ᵃGen. 26:10; 39:9; Ex. 32:21; Josh. 7:25
ᵇGen. 34:7

20:11
ᵃGen. 42:18; Neh. 5:15; Ps. 36:1; Prov. 16:6
ᵇGen. 12:12; 26:7

20:12
ᵃGen. 11:29

20:13
ᵃGen. 12:1–9, 11; [Heb. 11:8]
ᵇGen. 12:13; 20:5

20:14
ᵃGen. 12:16

20:15
ᵃGen. 13:9; 34:10; 47:6

20:16
ᵃGen. 26:11
ᵇMal. 2:9

20:17
ᵃNum. 12:13; 21:7; Job 42:9; [James 5:16]
ᵇGen. 21:2

20:18
ᵃGen. 12:17

21:1 ᵃ1 Sam. 2:21
ᵇGen. 17:16, 19, 21; 18:10, 14; [Gal. 4:23, 28]

21:2 ᵃActs 7:8; Gal. 4:22; Heb. 11:11, 12
ᵇGen. 17:21; 18:10, 14; Gal. 4:4

21:3
ᵃGen. 17:19, 21

21:4 ᵃActs 7:8
ᵇGen. 17:10, 12; Lev. 12:3

21:5
ᵃGen. 17:1, 17

21:6 ᵃGen. 18:13; Ps. 126:2; Is. 54:1
ᵇLuke 1:58

21:7
ᵃGen. 18:11, 12

21:9 ᵃGen. 16:1, 4, 15 ᵇ[Gal. 4:29]

21:10
ᵃGen. 25:6; 36:6, 7; Gal. 3:18; 4:30

21:11 ᵃGen. 17:18

20:9 ¹*sinned against*   20:16 ¹Lit. *is a covering of the eyes for you to all* ²Or *justified*   21:3 ¹Lit. *Laughter*   21:6 ¹Lit. *made laughter for me* 21:9 ¹Lit. *laughing*   21:11 ¹*distressing*

12But God said to Abraham, "Do not let it be displeasing in your sight because of the lad or because of your bondwoman. Whatever Sarah has said to you, listen to her voice; for ªin Isaac your seed shall be called. 13Yet I will also make ªa nation of the son of the bondwoman, because he *is* your ¹seed."

14So Abraham rose early in the morning, and took bread and ¹a skin of water; and putting *it* on her shoulder, he gave *it* and the boy to Hagar, and ªsent her away. Then she departed and wandered in the Wilderness of Beersheba. 15And the water in the skin was used up, and she placed the boy under one of the shrubs. 16Then she went and sat down across from *him* at a distance of about a bowshot; for she said to herself, "Let me not see the death of the boy." So she sat opposite *him*, and lifted her voice and wept.

17And ªGod heard the voice of the lad. Then the ᵇangel of God called to Hagar out of heaven, and said to her, "What ails you, Hagar? Fear not, for God has heard the voice of the lad where he *is*. 18Arise, lift up the lad and hold him with your hand, for ªI will make him a great nation."

19Then ªGod opened her eyes, and she saw a well of water. And she went and filled the skin with water, and gave the lad a drink. 20So God ªwas with the lad; and he grew and dwelt in the wilderness, ᵇand became an archer. 21He dwelt in the Wilderness of Paran; and his mother ªtook a wife for him from the land of Egypt.

A COVENANT WITH ABIMELECH

22And it came to pass at that time that ªAbimelech and Phichol, the commander of his army, spoke to Abraham, saying, ᵇ"God *is* with you in all that you do. 23Now therefore, ªswear¹ to me by God that you will not deal falsely with me, with my offspring, or with my posterity; but that according to the kindness that I have done to you, you will do to me and to the land in which you have dwelt."

24And Abraham said, "I will swear."

25Then Abraham rebuked Abimelech because of a well of water which Abimelech's servants ªhad seized. 26And Abimelech said, "I do not know who has done this thing; you did not tell me, nor had I heard *of it* until today." 27So Abraham took sheep and oxen and gave them to Abimelech, and the two of them ªmade a ¹covenant. 28And Abraham set seven ewe lambs of the flock by themselves.

29Then Abimelech asked Abraham, ª"What *is the meaning of* these seven ewe lambs which you have set by themselves?"

30And he said, "You will take *these* seven ewe lambs from my hand, that ªthey may be my witness that I have dug this well." 31Therefore he ªcalled that place ¹Beersheba, because the two of them swore an oath there.

32Thus they made a covenant at Beersheba. So Abimelech rose with Phichol, the commander of his army, and they returned to the land of the Philistines. 33Then *Abraham* planted a tamarisk tree in Beersheba, and ªthere called on the name of the LORD, ᵇthe Everlasting God. 34And Abraham stayed in the land of the Philistines many days.

21:12 ªMatt. 1:2; Luke 3:34; [Rom. 9:7, 8]; Heb. 11:18
21:13 ªGen. 16:10; 17:20; 21:18; 25:12–18
21:14 ªJohn 8:35
21:17 ªEx. 3:7; Deut. 26:7; Ps. 6:8 ᵇGen. 22:11
21:18 ªGen. 16:10; 21:13; 25:12–16
21:19 ªGen. 3:7; Num. 22:31; 2 Kin. 6:17; Luke 24:31
21:20 ªGen. 28:15; 39:2, 3, 21 ᵇGen. 16:12
21:21 ªGen. 24:4
21:22 ªGen. 20:2, 14; 26:26 ᵇGen. 26:28; Is. 8:10
21:23 ªJosh. 2:12; 1 Sam. 24:21
21:25 ªGen. 26:15, 18, 20–22
21:27 ªGen. 26:31; 31:44; 1 Sam. 18:3
21:29 ªGen. 33:8
21:30 ªGen. 31:48, 52
21:31 ªGen. 21:14; 26:33
21:33 ªGen. 4:26; 12:8; 13:4; 26:25 ᵇGen. 35:11; Ex. 15:18; Deut. 32:40; 33:27; Ps. 90:2; 93:2; Is. 40:28; Jer. 10:10; Hab. 1:12; Heb. 13:8

21:13 ¹*descendant*   21:14 ¹A water bottle made of skins   21:23 ¹*take an oath*   21:27 ¹*treaty*   21:31 ¹Lit. *Well of the Oath* or *Well of the Seven*

ABRAHAM'S FAITH CONFIRMED
(Heb. 11:17–19)

22 Now it came to pass after these things that [a]God tested Abraham, and said to him, "Abraham!"

And he said, "Here I am."

[2]Then He said, "Take now your son, [a]your only *son* Isaac, whom you [b]love, and go [c]to the land of Moriah, and offer him there as a [d]burnt offering on one of the mountains of which I shall tell you."

[3]So Abraham rose early in the morning and saddled his donkey, and took two of his young men with him, and Isaac his son; and he split the wood for the burnt offering, and arose and went to the place of which God had told him. [4]Then on the third day Abraham lifted his eyes and saw the place afar off. [5]And Abraham said to his young men, "Stay here with the donkey; the [1]lad and I will go yonder and worship, and we will [a]come back to you."

[6]So Abraham took the wood of the burnt offering and [a]laid *it* on Isaac his son; and he took the fire in his hand, and a knife, and the two of them went together. [7]But Isaac spoke to Abraham his father and said, "My father!"

And he said, "Here I am, my son."

Then he said, "Look, the fire and the wood, but where *is* the [1]lamb for a burnt offering?"

[8]And Abraham said, "My son, God will provide for Himself the [a]lamb for a [b]burnt offering." So the two of them went together.

[9]Then they came to the place of which God had told him. And Abraham built an altar there and placed the wood in order; and he bound Isaac his son and [a]laid him on the altar, upon the wood. [10]And Abraham stretched out his hand and took the knife to slay his son.

[11]But the [a]Angel of the LORD called to him from heaven and said, "Abraham, Abraham!"

So he said, "Here I am."

[12]And He said, [a]"Do not lay your hand on the lad, or do anything to him; for [b]now I know that you fear God, since you have not [c]withheld your son, your only *son*, from Me."

[13]Then Abraham lifted his eyes and looked, and there behind *him was* a ram caught in a thicket by its horns. So Abraham went and took the ram, and offered it up for a burnt offering instead of his son. [14]And Abraham called the name of the place, [1]The-LORD-Will-Provide; as it is said *to* this day, "In the Mount of the LORD it shall be provided."

[15]Then the Angel of the LORD called to Abraham a second time out of heaven, [16]and said: [a]"By Myself I have sworn, says the LORD, because you have done this thing, and have not withheld your son, your only *son*— [17]blessing I will [a]bless you, and multiplying I will multiply your descendants [b]as the stars of the heaven [c]and as the sand which *is* on the seashore; and [d]your descendants shall possess the gate of their enemies. [18][a]In your seed all the nations of the earth shall be blessed, [b]because you have obeyed My voice." [19]So Abraham returned to his young men, and they rose and went together to [a]Beersheba; and Abraham dwelt at Beersheba.

22:1 [a]Deut. 8:2, 16; 1 Cor. 10:13; Heb. 11:17; [James 1:12–14; 1 Pet. 1:7]

22:2 [a]Gen. 22:12, 16; John 3:16; Heb. 11:17; 1 John 4:9 [b]John 5:20 [c]2 Chr. 3:1 [d]Gen. 8:20; 31:54

22:5 [a][Heb. 11:19]

22:6 [a]John 19:17

22:8 [a]John 1:29, 36 [b]Ex. 12:3–6

22:9 [a][Heb. 11:17–19; James 2:21]

22:11 [a]Gen. 16:7–11; 21:17, 18; 31:11

22:12 [a]1 Sam. 15:22 [b]Gen. 26:5; James 2:21, 22 [c]Gen. 22:2, 16; John 3:16

22:16 [a]Ps. 105:9; Luke 1:73; [Heb. 6:13, 14]

22:17 [a]Gen. 17:16; 26:3, 24 [b]Gen. 15:5; 26:4; Deut. 1:10; Jer. 33:22; Heb. 11:12 [c]Gen. 13:16; 32:12; 1 Kin. 4:20 [d]Gen. 24:60

22:18 [a]Gen. 12:3; 18:18; 26:4; Matt. 1:1; Luke 3:34; [Acts 3:25, 26]; Gal. 3:8, 9, 16, 18 [b]Gen. 18:19; 22:3, 10; 26:5

22:19 [a]Gen. 21:31

22:5 [1]Or *young man*   22:7 [1]Or *goat*   22:14 [1]Heb. YHWH Yireh

THE FAMILY OF NAHOR

20Now it came to pass after these things that it was told Abraham, saying, "Indeed aMilcah also has borne children to your brother Nahor: 21aHuz his firstborn, Buz his brother, Kemuel the father bof Aram, 22Chesed, Hazo, Pildash, Jidlaph, and Bethuel." 23And aBethuel begot 1Rebekah. These eight Milcah bore to Nahor, Abraham's brother. 24His concubine, whose name was Reumah, also bore Tebah, Gaham, Thahash, and Maachah.

SARAH'S DEATH AND BURIAL

23 Sarah lived one hundred and twenty-seven years; *these were* the years of the life of Sarah. 2So Sarah died in aKirjath Arba (that *is*, bHebron) in the land of Canaan, and Abraham came to mourn for Sarah and to weep for her.

3Then Abraham stood up from before his dead, and spoke to the sons of aHeth, saying, 4a"I *am* a foreigner and a visitor among you. bGive me property for a burial place among you, that I may bury my dead out of my sight."

5And the sons of Heth answered Abraham, saying to him, 6"Hear us, my lord: You *are* aa 1mighty prince among us; bury your dead in the choicest of our burial places. None of us will withhold from you his burial place, that you may bury your dead."

7Then Abraham stood up and bowed himself to the people of the land, the sons of Heth. 8And he spoke with them, saying, "If it is your wish that I bury my dead out of my sight, hear me, and 1meet with Ephron the son of Zohar for me, 9that he may give me the cave of aMachpelah which he has, which *is* at the end of his field. Let him give it to me at the full price, as property for a burial place among you."

10Now Ephron dwelt among the sons of Heth; and Ephron the Hittite answered Abraham in the presence of the sons of Heth, all who aentered at the gate of his city, saying, 11a"No, my lord, hear me: I give you the field and the cave that *is* in it; I give it to you in the presence of the sons of my people. I give it to you. Bury your dead!"

12Then Abraham bowed himself down before the people of the land; 13and he spoke to Ephron in the hearing of the people of the land, saying, "If you *will give it,* please hear me. I will give you money for the field; take *it* from me and I will bury my dead there."

14And Ephron answered Abraham, saying to him, 15"My lord, listen to me; the land *is worth* four hundred ashekels of silver. What *is* that between you and me? So bury your dead." 16And Abraham listened to Ephron; and Abraham aweighed out the silver for Ephron which he had named in the hearing of the sons of Heth, four hundred shekels of silver, currency of the merchants.

17So athe field of Ephron which *was* in Machpelah, which *was* before Mamre, the field and the cave which *was* in it, and all the trees that *were* in the field, which *were* within all the surrounding borders, were deeded 18to Abraham as a possession in the presence of the sons of Heth, before all who went in at the gate of his city.

22:20
aGen. 11:29;
24:15
22:21 aJob 1:1
bJob 32:2
22:23
aGen. 24:15
23:2
aGen. 35:27;
Josh. 14:15; 15:13;
21:11 bGen. 13:18;
23:19
23:3
aGen. 10:15;
15:20; 2 Kin. 7:6
23:4
a[Gen. 17:8];
Lev. 25:23;
1 Chr. 29:15;
Ps. 39:12;
105:12; 119:19;
[Heb. 11:9, 13]
bActs 7:5, 16
23:6 aGen. 13:2;
14:14; 24:35
23:9 aGen. 25:9
23:10
aGen. 23:18;
34:20, 24;
Ruth 4:1, 4, 11
23:11
a2 Sam. 24:21–24
23:15 aEx. 30:13;
Ezek. 45:12
23:16
a2 Sam. 14:26;
Jer. 32:9, 10;
Zech. 11:12
23:17
aGen. 25:9;
49:29–32; 50:13;
Acts 7:16

22:23 1*Rebecca,* Rom. 9:10 23:6 1Lit. *prince of God* 23:8 1*entreat*

¹⁹And after this, Abraham buried Sarah his wife in the cave of the field of Machpelah, before Mamre (that *is,* Hebron) in the land of Canaan. ²⁰So the field and the cave that *is* in it ᵃwere deeded to Abraham by the sons of Heth as property for a burial place.

A BRIDE FOR ISAAC

24 Now Abraham ᵃwas old, well advanced in age; and the LORD ᵇhad blessed Abraham in all things. ²So Abraham said ᵃto the oldest servant of his house, who ᵇruled over all that he had, "Please, ᶜput your hand under my thigh, ³and I will make you ᵃswear¹ by the LORD, the God of heaven and the God of the earth, that ᵇyou will not take a wife for my son from the daughters of the Canaanites, among whom I dwell; ⁴ᵃbut you shall go ᵇto my country and to my family, and take a wife for my son Isaac."

⁵And the servant said to him, "Perhaps the woman will not be willing to follow me to this land. Must I take your son back to the land from which you came?"

⁶But Abraham said to him, "Beware that you do not take my son back there. ⁷The LORD God of heaven, who ᵃtook me from my father's house and from the land of my family, and who spoke to me and swore to me, saying, ᵇ'To your ¹descendants I give this land,' ᶜHe will send His angel before you, and you shall take a wife for my son from there. ⁸And if the woman is not willing to follow you, then ᵃyou will be released from this oath; only do not take my son back there." ⁹So the servant put his hand under the thigh of Abraham his master, and swore to him concerning this matter.

¹⁰Then the servant took ten of his master's camels and departed, ᵃfor all his master's goods *were in* his hand. And he arose and went to Mesopotamia, to ᵇthe city of Nahor. ¹¹And he made his camels kneel down outside the city by a well of water at evening time, the time ᵃwhen women go out to draw *water.* ¹²Then he ᵃsaid, "O LORD God of my master Abraham, please ᵇgive me success this day, and show kindness to my master Abraham. ¹³Behold, *here* ᵃI stand by the well of water, and ᵇthe daughters of the men of the city are coming out to draw water. ¹⁴Now let it be that the young woman to whom I say, 'Please let down your pitcher that I may drink,' and she says, 'Drink, and I will also give your camels a drink'—*let her be the one* You have appointed for Your servant Isaac. And ᵃby this I will know that You have shown kindness to my master."

¹⁵And it happened, ᵃbefore he had finished speaking, that behold, ᵇRebekah,¹ who was born to Bethuel, son of ᶜMilcah, the wife of Nahor, Abraham's brother, came out with her pitcher on her shoulder. ¹⁶Now the young woman ᵃ*was* very beautiful to behold, a virgin; no man had known her. And she went down to the well, filled her pitcher, and came up. ¹⁷And the servant ran to meet her and said, "Please let me drink a little water from your pitcher."

¹⁸ᵃSo she said, "Drink, my lord." Then she quickly let her pitcher down to her hand, and gave him a drink. ¹⁹And when she had finished giving him a drink, she said, "I will draw *water*

23:20
ᵃ Jer. 32:10, 11

24:1 ᵃGen. 18:11;
21:5 ᵇGen. 12:2;
13:2; 24:35;
Ps. 112:3;
Prov. 10:22;
[Gal. 3:9]

24:2 ᵃGen. 15:2
ᵇGen. 24:10;
39:4–6
ᶜGen. 47:29;
1 Chr. 29:24

24:3
ᵃGen. 14:19, 22
ᵇGen. 26:35;
28:2; Ex. 34:16;
Deut. 7:3;
2 Cor. 6:14–17

24:4 ᵃGen. 28:2
ᵇGen. 12:1;
Heb. 11:15

24:7 ᵃGen. 12:1;
24:3 ᵇGen. 12:7;
13:15; 15:18;
17:8; Ex. 32:13;
Deut. 1:8;
34:4; Acts 7:5
ᶜGen. 16:7; 21:17;
22:11; Ex. 23:20,
23; 33:2;
Heb. 1:4, 14

24:8
ᵃJosh. 2:17–20

24:10
ᵃGen. 24:2, 22
ᵇGen. 11:31, 32;
22:20; 27:43;
29:5

24:11 ᵃEx. 2:16;
1 Sam. 9:11

24:12
ᵃGen. 24:27,
42, 48; 26:24;
32:9; Ex. 3:6,
15 ᵇGen. 27:20;
Neh. 1:11;
Ps. 37:5

24:13
ᵃGen. 24:43
ᵇEx. 2:16

24:14
ᵃJudg. 6:17, 37;
1 Sam. 14:10;
16:7; 20:7;
2 Kin. 20:9;
Prov. 16:33;
Acts 1:26

24:15 ᵃIs. 65:24
ᵇGen. 24:45;
25:20
ᶜGen. 22:20, 23

24:16
ᵃGen. 12:11; 26:7;
29:17

24:18
ᵃGen. 24:14, 46;
[1 Pet. 3:8, 9]

24:3 ¹*take an oath*　24:7 ¹Lit. *seed*　24:15 ¹*Rebecca,* Rom. 9:10

for your camels also, until they have finished drinking." 20Then she quickly emptied her pitcher into the trough, ran back to the well to draw *water,* and drew for all his camels. 21And the man, wondering at her, remained silent so as to know whether athe LORD had made his journey prosperous or not.

22So it was, when the camels had finished drinking, that the man took a golden anose ring weighing half a shekel, and two bracelets for her wrists weighing ten *shekels* of gold, 23and said, "Whose daughter *are* you? Tell me, please, is there room *in* your father's house for us ¹to lodge?"

24So she said to him, a"I *am* the daughter of Bethuel, Milcah's son, whom she bore to Nahor." 25Moreover she said to him, "We have both straw and feed enough, and room to lodge."

26Then the man abowed down his head and worshiped the LORD. 27And he said, a"Blessed *be* the LORD God of my master Abraham, who has not forsaken bHis mercy and His truth toward my master. As for me, being on the way, the LORD cled me to the house of my master's brethren." 28So the young woman ran and told her mother's household these things.

29Now Rebekah had a brother whose name *was* aLaban, and Laban ran out to the man by the well. 30So it came to pass, when he saw the nose ring, and the bracelets on his sister's wrists, and when he heard the words of his sister Rebekah, saying, "Thus the man spoke to me," that he went to the man. And there he stood by the camels at the well. 31And he said, "Come in, aO blessed of the LORD! Why do you stand outside? For I have prepared the house, and a place for the camels."

32Then the man came to the house. And he unloaded the camels, and aprovided straw and feed for the camels, and water to bwash his feet and the feet of the men who *were* with him. 33*Food* was set before him to eat, but he said, a"I will not eat until I have told about my errand."

And he said, "Speak on."

34So he said, "I *am* Abraham's servant. 35The LORD ahas blessed my master greatly, and he has become great; and He has given him flocks and herds, silver and gold, male and female servants, and camels and donkeys. 36And Sarah my master's wife abore a son to my master when she was old; and bto him he has given all that he has. 37Now my master amade me swear, saying, 'You shall not take a wife for my son from the daughters of the Canaanites, in whose land I dwell; 38abut you shall go to my father's house and to my family, and take a wife for my son.' 39aAnd I said to my master, 'Perhaps the woman will not follow me.' 40aBut he said to me, 'The LORD, bbefore whom I walk, will send His angel with you and ¹prosper your way; and you shall take a wife for my son from my family and from my father's house. 41aYou will be clear from this oath when you arrive among my family; for if they will not give *her* to you, then you will be released from my oath.'

42"And this day I came to the well and said, a'O LORD God of my master Abraham, if You will now prosper the way in which I go, 43abehold, I stand by the well of water; and it shall come to pass that when the virgin comes out to draw *water,*

24:21
aGen. 24:12–14, 27, 52

24:22
aGen. 24:47; Ex. 32:2, 3; Is. 3:19–21

24:24
aGen. 22:23; 24:15

24:26
aGen. 24:48, 52; Ex. 4:31

24:27
aGen. 24:12, 42, 48; Ex. 18:10; Ruth 4:14; 1 Sam. 25:32, 39; 2 Sam. 18:28; Luke 1:68
bGen. 32:10; Ps. 98:3
cGen. 24:21, 48

24:29
aGen. 29:5, 13

24:31
aGen. 26:29; Judg. 17:2; Ruth 3:10; Ps. 115:15

24:32
aGen. 43:24; Judg. 19:21
bGen. 19:2; John 13:5, 13–15

24:33
aJob 23:12; John 4:34; Eph. 6:5–7

24:35
aGen. 13:2; 24:1

24:36
aGen. 21:1–7
bGen. 21:10; 25:5

24:37
aGen. 24:2–4

24:38
aGen. 24:4

24:39
aGen. 24:5

24:40
aGen. 24:7
bGen. 5:22, 24; 17:1; 1 Kin. 8:23

24:41 aGen. 24:8

24:42
aGen. 24:12

24:43
aGen. 24:13

24:23 ¹to spend the night   24:40 ¹make your way successful

and I say to her, "Please give me a little water from your pitcher to drink," 44and she says to me, "Drink, and I will draw for your camels also,"—let her be the woman whom the LORD has appointed for my master's son.'

45a"But before I had finished bspeaking in my heart, there was Rebekah, coming out with her pitcher on her shoulder; and she went down to the well and drew water. And I said to her, 'Please let me drink.' 46And she made haste and let her pitcher down from her shoulder, and said, 'Drink, and I will give your camels a drink also.' So I drank, and she gave the camels a drink also. 47Then I asked her, and said, 'Whose daughter are you?' And she said, 'The daughter of Bethuel, Nahor's son, whom Milcah bore to him.' So I put the nose ring on her nose and the bracelets on her wrists. 48aAnd I bowed my head and worshiped the LORD, and blessed the LORD God of my master Abraham, who had led me in the way of truth to btake the daughter of my master's brother for his son. 49Now if you will adeal kindly and truly with my master, tell me. And if not, tell me, that I may turn to the right hand or to the left."

50Then Laban and Bethuel answered and said, a"The thing comes from the LORD; we cannot bspeak to you either bad or good. 51aHere is Rebekah before you; take her and go, and let her be your master's son's wife, as the LORD has spoken."

52And it came to pass, when Abraham's servant heard their words, that ahe worshiped the LORD, bowing himself to the earth. 53Then the servant brought out ajewelry of silver, jewelry of gold, and clothing, and gave them to Rebekah. He also gave bprecious things to her brother and to her mother.

54And he and the men who were with him ate and drank and stayed all night. Then they arose in the morning, and he said, a"Send me away to my master."

55But her brother and her mother said, "Let the young woman stay with us a few days, at least ten; after that she may go."

56And he said to them, "Do not ¹hinder me, since the LORD has prospered my way; send me away so that I may go to my master."

57So they said, "We will call the young woman and ask her personally." 58Then they called Rebekah and said to her, "Will you go with this man?"

And she said, "I will go."

59So they sent away Rebekah their sister aand her nurse, and Abraham's servant and his men. 60And they blessed Rebekah and said to her:

"Our sister, may you become
aThe mother of thousands of ten thousands;
bAnd may your descendants possess
The gates of those who hate them."

61Then Rebekah and her maids arose, and they rode on the camels and followed the man. So the servant took Rebekah and departed.

62Now Isaac came from the way of aBeer Lahai Roi, for he dwelt in the South. 63And Isaac went out ato meditate in the field in the evening; and he lifted his eyes and looked, and

24:45
aGen. 24:15
b1 Sam. 1:13

24:48
aGen. 24:26, 52
bGen. 22:23;
24:27; Ps. 32:8;
48:14; Is. 48:17

24:49
aGen. 47:29;
Josh. 2:14

24:50
aPs. 118:23;
Matt. 21:42;
Mark 12:11
bGen. 31:24, 29

24:51
aGen. 20:15

24:52
aGen. 24:26, 48

24:53
aGen. 24:10,
22; Ex. 3:22;
11:2; 12:35
b2 Chr. 21:3;
Ezra 1:6

24:54
aGen. 24:56, 59;
30:25

24:59
aGen. 35:8

24:60
aGen. 17:16
bGen. 22:17;
28:14

24:62
aGen. 16:14;
25:11

24:63
aJosh. 1:8;
Ps. 1:2; 77:12;
119:15, 27, 48;
143:5; 145:5

24:56 ¹delay

there, the camels *were* coming. 64Then Rebekah lifted her eyes, and when she saw Isaac ªshe dismounted from her camel; 65for she had said to the servant, "Who *is* this man walking in the field to meet us?"

The servant said, "It *is* my master." So she took a veil and covered herself.

66And the servant told Isaac all the things that he had done. 67Then Isaac brought her into his mother Sarah's tent; and he ªtook Rebekah and she became his wife, and he loved her. So Isaac ᵇwas comforted after his mother's *death.*

ABRAHAM AND KETURAH
(1 Chr. 1:32, 33)

25 Abraham again took a wife, and her name *was* ªKeturah. 2And ªshe bore him Zimran, Jokshan, Medan, Midian, Ishbak, and Shuah. 3Jokshan begot Sheba and Dedan. And the sons of Dedan were Asshurim, Letushim, and Leummim. 4And the sons of Midian *were* Ephah, Epher, Hanoch, Abidah, and Eldaah. All these *were* the children of Keturah.

5And ªAbraham gave all that he had to Isaac. 6But Abraham gave gifts to the sons of the concubines which Abraham had; and while he was still living he ªsent them eastward, away from Isaac his son, to ᵇthe country of the east.

ABRAHAM'S DEATH AND BURIAL

7This *is* the sum of the years of Abraham's life which he lived: one hundred and seventy-five years. 8Then Abraham breathed his last and ªdied in a good old age, an old man and full *of years,* and ᵇwas gathered to his people. 9And ªhis sons Isaac and Ishmael buried him in the cave of ᵇMachpelah, which *is* before Mamre, in the field of Ephron the son of Zohar the Hittite, 10ªthe field which Abraham purchased from the sons of Heth. ᵇThere Abraham was buried, and Sarah his wife. 11And it came to pass, after the death of Abraham, that God blessed his son Isaac. And Isaac dwelt at ªBeer Lahai Roi.

THE FAMILIES OF ISHMAEL AND ISAAC
(1 Chr. 1:29–31)

12Now this *is* the ªgenealogy of Ishmael, Abraham's son, whom Hagar the Egyptian, Sarah's maidservant, bore to Abraham. 13And ªthese *were* the names of the sons of Ishmael, by their names, according to their generations: The firstborn of Ishmael, Nebajoth; then Kedar, Adbeel, Mibsam, 14Mishma, Dumah, Massa, 15¹Hadar, Tema, Jetur, Naphish, and Kedemah. 16These *were* the sons of Ishmael and these *were* their names, by their towns and their ¹settlements, ªtwelve princes according to their nations. 17These *were* the years of the life of Ishmael: one hundred and thirty-seven years; and ªhe breathed his last and died, and was gathered to his people. 18ª(They dwelt from Havilah as far as Shur, which *is* east of Egypt as you go toward Assyria.) He ¹died ᵇin the presence of all his brethren.

19This *is* the ªgenealogy of Isaac, Abraham's son. ᵇAbraham begot Isaac. 20Isaac was forty years old when he took Rebekah as wife, ªthe daughter of Bethuel the Syrian of Padan

Cross-references (margin)

24:64
ª Josh. 15:18
24:67
ª Gen. 25:20;
29:20;
Prov. 18:22
ᵇ Gen. 23:1, 2;
38:12
25:1
ª 1 Chr. 1:32, 33
25:2
ª 1 Chr. 1:32, 33
25:5
ª Gen. 24:35, 36
25:6 ª Gen. 21:14
ᵇ Judg. 6:3
25:8 ª Gen. 15:15;
47:8, 9
ᵇ Gen. 25:17;
35:29; 49:29, 33
25:9
ª Gen. 35:29;
50:13
ᵇ Gen. 23:9, 17;
49:30
25:10
ª Gen. 23:3–16
ᵇ Gen. 49:31
25:11 ª Gen. 16:14
25:12
ª Gen. 11:10, 27;
16:15
25:13
ª 1 Chr. 1:29–31
25:16
ª Gen. 17:20
25:17
ª Gen. 25:8;
49:33
25:18
ª Gen. 20:1;
1 Sam. 15:7
ᵇ Gen. 16:12
25:19
ª Gen. 36:1, 9
ᵇ Matt. 1:2
25:20
ª Gen. 22:23;
24:15, 29, 67

25:15 ¹MT *Hadad*   25:16 ¹*camps*   25:18 ¹*fell*

Aram, ᵇthe sister of Laban the Syrian. ²¹Now Isaac pleaded with the LORD for his wife, because she *was* barren; ᵃand the LORD granted his plea, ᵇand Rebekah his wife conceived. ²²But the children struggled together within her; and she said, "If *all is* well, why *am I like* this?" ᵃSo she went to inquire of the LORD.

²³And the LORD said to her:

ᵃ"Two nations *are* in your womb,
Two peoples shall be separated from your body;
One people shall be stronger than ᵇthe other,
ᶜAnd the older shall serve the younger."

²⁴So when her days were fulfilled *for her* to give birth, indeed *there were* twins in her womb. ²⁵And the first came out red. *He was* ᵃlike a hairy garment all over; so they called his name ¹Esau. ²⁶Afterward his brother came out, and ᵃhis hand took hold of Esau's heel; so ᵇhis name was called ¹Jacob. Isaac *was* sixty years old when she bore them.

²⁷So the boys grew. And Esau was ᵃa skillful hunter, a man of the field; but Jacob was ᵇa ¹mild man, ᶜdwelling in tents. ²⁸And Isaac loved Esau because he ᵃate *of his* game, ᵇbut Rebekah loved Jacob.

ESAU SELLS HIS BIRTHRIGHT
(Heb. 12:16)

²⁹Now Jacob cooked a stew; and Esau came in from the field, and he *was* weary. ³⁰And Esau said to Jacob, "Please feed me with that same red *stew,* for I *am* weary." Therefore his name was called ¹Edom.

³¹But Jacob said, "Sell me your birthright as of this day."

³²And Esau said, "Look, I *am* about to die; so ᵃwhat *is* this birthright to me?"

³³Then Jacob said, ¹"Swear to me as of this day."

So he swore to him, and ᵃsold his birthright to Jacob. ³⁴And Jacob gave Esau bread and stew of lentils; then ᵃhe ate and drank, arose, and went his way. Thus Esau ᵇdespised *his* birthright.

ISAAC AND ABIMELECH

26 There was a famine in the land, besides ᵃthe first famine that was in the days of Abraham. And Isaac went to ᵇAbimelech king of the Philistines, in Gerar.

²Then the LORD appeared to him and said: ᵃ"Do not go down to Egypt; live in ᵇthe land of which I shall tell you. ³ᵃDwell in this land, and ᵇI will be with you and ᶜbless you; for to you and your descendants ᵈI give all these lands, and I will perform ᵉthe oath which I swore to Abraham your father. ⁴And ᵃI will make your descendants multiply as the stars of heaven; I will give to your descendants all these lands; ᵇand in your seed all the nations of the earth shall be blessed; ⁵ᵃbecause Abraham obeyed My voice and kept My charge, My commandments, My statutes, and My laws."

⁶So Isaac dwelt in Gerar. ⁷And the men of the place asked about his wife. And ᵃhe said, "She *is* my sister"; for ᵇhe was afraid to say, "*She is* my wife," *because he thought,* "lest the

---

25:20
ᵇGen. 24:29

25:21
ᵃ1 Sam. 1:17;
1 Chr. 5:20;
2 Chr. 33:13;
Ezra 8:23;
Ps. 127:3
ᵇRom. 9:10–13

25:22
ᵃ1 Sam. 1:15; 9:9;
10:22

25:23
ᵃGen. 17:4–6,
16; 24:60;
Num. 20:14;
Deut. 2:4–8
ᵇ2 Sam. 8:14
ᶜGen. 27:29, 40;
Mal. 1:2, 3;
Rom. 9:12

25:25
ᵃGen. 27:11,
16, 23

25:26 ᵃHos. 12:3
ᵇGen. 27:36

25:27
ᵃGen. 27:3, 5
ᵇJob 1:1, 8
ᶜHeb. 11:9

25:28
ᵃGen. 27:4,
19, 25, 31
ᵇGen. 27:6–10

25:32
ᵃMatt. 16:26;
Mark 8:36, 37

25:33
ᵃHeb. 12:16

25:34
ᵃEccl. 8:15;
Is. 22:13;
1 Cor. 15:32
ᵇHeb. 12:16, 17

26:1 ᵃGen. 12:10
ᵇGen. 20:1, 2

26:2 ᵃGen. 12:7;
17:1; 18:1; 35:9
ᵇGen. 12:1

26:3 ᵃGen. 20:1;
Ps. 39:12;
Heb. 11:9
ᵇGen. 28:13,
15 ᶜGen. 12:2
ᵈGen. 12:7;
13:15; 15:18
ᵉGen. 22:16;
Ps. 105:9

26:4 ᵃGen. 15:5;
22:17; Ex. 32:13
ᵇGen. 12:3;
22:18; Gal. 3:8

26:5
ᵃGen. 22:16, 18

26:7 ᵃGen. 12:13;
20:2, 12, 13
ᵇProv. 29:25

25:25 ¹Lit. *Hairy*   25:26 ¹*Supplanter* or *Deceitful,* lit. *One Who Takes the Heel*
25:27 ¹Lit. *complete*   25:30 ¹Lit. *Red*   25:33 ¹*Take an oath*

men of the place kill me for Rebekah, because she *is* ^cbeautiful to behold." ⁸Now it came to pass, when he had been there a long time, that Abimelech king of the Philistines looked through a window, and saw, and there was Isaac, ¹showing endearment to Rebekah his wife. ⁹Then Abimelech called Isaac and said, "Quite obviously she *is* your wife; so how could you say, 'She *is* my sister'?"

Isaac said to him, "Because I said, 'Lest I die on account of her.'"

¹⁰And Abimelech said, "What *is* this you have done to us? One of the people might soon have lain with your wife, and ^ayou would have brought guilt on us." ¹¹So Abimelech charged all *his* people, saying, "He who ^atouches this man or his wife shall surely be put to death."

¹²Then Isaac sowed in that land, and reaped in the same year ^aa hundredfold; and the Lord ^bblessed him. ¹³The man ^abegan to prosper, and continued prospering until he became very prosperous; ¹⁴for he had possessions of flocks and possessions of herds and a great number of servants. So the Philistines ^aenvied him. ¹⁵Now the Philistines had stopped up all the wells ^awhich his father's servants had dug in the days of Abraham his father, and they had filled them with earth. ¹⁶And Abimelech said to Isaac, "Go away from us, for ^ayou are much mightier than we."

¹⁷Then Isaac departed from there and ¹pitched his tent in the Valley of Gerar, and dwelt there. ¹⁸And Isaac dug again the wells of water which they had dug in the days of Abraham his father, for the Philistines had stopped them up after the death of Abraham. ^aHe called them by the names which his father had called them.

¹⁹Also Isaac's servants dug in the valley, and found a well of running water there. ²⁰But the herdsmen of Gerar ^aquarreled with Isaac's herdsmen, saying, "The water *is* ours." So he called the name of the well ¹Esek, because they quarreled with him. ²¹Then they dug another well, and they quarreled over that *one* also. So he called its name ¹Sitnah. ²²And he moved from there and dug another well, and they did not quarrel over it. So he called its name ¹Rehoboth, because he said, "For now the Lord has made room for us, and we shall ^abe fruitful in the land."

²³Then he went up from there to Beersheba. ²⁴And the Lord ^aappeared to him the same night and said, ^b"I *am* the God of your father Abraham; ^cdo not fear, for ^dI *am* with you. I will bless you and multiply your descendants for My servant Abraham's sake." ²⁵So he ^abuilt an altar there and ^bcalled on the name of the Lord, and he pitched his tent there; and there Isaac's servants dug a well.

²⁶Then Abimelech came to him from Gerar with Ahuzzath, one of his friends, ^aand Phichol the commander of his army. ²⁷And Isaac said to them, "Why have you come to me, ^asince you hate me and have ^bsent me away from you?"

²⁸But they said, "We have certainly seen that the Lord ^ais with you. So we said, 'Let there now be an oath between us, between you and us; and let us make a ¹covenant with you, ²⁹that you will do us no harm, since we have not touched

26:7 ^cGen. 12:11; 24:16; 29:17

26:10 ^aGen. 20:9

26:11 ^aPs. 105:15

26:12 ^aMatt. 13:8, 23; Mark 4:8 ^bGen. 24:1; 25:8, 11; 26:3; Job 42:12; Prov. 10:22

26:13 ^aGen. 24:35; [Prov. 10:22]

26:14 ^aGen. 37:11; Eccl. 4:4

26:15 ^aGen. 21:25, 30

26:16 ^aEx. 1:9

26:18 ^aGen. 21:31

26:20 ^aGen. 21:25

26:22 ^aGen. 17:6; 28:3; 41:52; Ex. 1:7

26:24 ^aGen. 26:2 ^bGen. 17:7, 8; 24:12; Ex. 3:6; Acts 7:32 ^cGen. 15:1 ^dGen. 26:3, 4

26:25 ^aGen. 12:7, 8; 13:4, 18; 22:9; 33:20 ^bGen. 21:33; Ps. 116:17

26:26 ^aGen. 21:22

26:27 ^aJudg. 11:7 ^bGen. 26:16

26:28 ^aGen. 21:22, 23

26:8 ¹*caressing*　26:17 ¹*camped*　26:20 ¹Lit. *Quarrel*　26:21 ¹Lit. *Enmity*
26:22 ¹Lit. *Spaciousness*　26:28 ¹*treaty*

you, and since we have done nothing to you but good and have sent you away in peace. ªYou *are* now the blessed of the LORD.'"

30ªSo he made them a feast, and they ate and drank. 31Then they arose early in the morning and ªswore an oath with one another; and Isaac sent them away, and they departed from him in peace.

32It came to pass the same day that Isaac's servants came and told him about the well which they had dug, and said to him, "We have found water." 33So he called it 1Shebah. ªTherefore the name of the city *is* 2Beersheba to this day.

34ªWhen Esau was forty years old, he took as wives Judith the daughter of Beeri the Hittite, and Basemath the daughter of Elon the Hittite. 35And ªthey were a grief of mind to Isaac and Rebekah.

ISAAC BLESSES JACOB

27 Now it came to pass, when Isaac was ªold and bhis eyes were so dim that he could not see, that he called Esau his older son and said to him, "My son."

And he answered him, "Here I am."

2Then he said, "Behold now, I am old. I ªdo not know the day of my death. 3ªNow therefore, please take your weapons, your quiver and your bow, and go out to the field and hunt game for me. 4And make me 1savory food, such as I love, and bring *it* to me that I may eat, that my soul ªmay bless you before I die."

5Now Rebekah was listening when Isaac spoke to Esau his son. And Esau went to the field to hunt game and to bring *it.* 6So Rebekah spoke to Jacob her son, saying, "Indeed I heard your father speak to Esau your brother, saying, 7'Bring me game and make 1savory food for me, that I may eat it and bless you in the presence of the LORD before my death.' 8Now therefore, my son, ªobey my voice according to what I command you. 9Go now to the flock and bring me from there two choice kids of the goats, and I will make ªsavory food from them for your father, such as he loves. 10Then you shall take *it* to your father, that he may eat *it,* and that he ªmay bless you before his death."

11And Jacob said to Rebekah his mother, "Look, ªEsau my brother *is* a hairy man, and I *am* a smooth-*skinned* man. 12Perhaps my father will ªfeel me, and I shall seem to be a deceiver to him; and I shall bring ba curse on myself and not a blessing."

13But his mother said to him, ª"*Let* your curse *be* on me, my son; only obey my voice, and go, get *them* for me." 14And he went and got *them* and brought *them* to his mother, and his mother ªmade 1savory food, such as his father loved. 15Then Rebekah took ªthe choice clothes of her elder son Esau, which *were* with her in the house, and put them on Jacob her younger son. 16And she put the skins of the kids of the goats on his hands and on the smooth part of his neck. 17Then she gave the savory food and the bread, which she had prepared, into the hand of her son Jacob.

18So he went to his father and said, "My father."

26:29
ªGen. 24:31;
Ps. 115:15

26:30
ªGen. 19:3

26:31
ªGen. 21:31

26:33
ªGen. 21:31;
28:10

26:34
ªGen. 28:8;
36:2

26:35
ªGen. 27:46;
28:1, 8

27:1 ªGen. 35:28
bGen. 48:10;
1 Sam. 3:2

27:2
ª[Prov. 27:1;
James 4:14]

27:3
ªGen. 25:27, 28

27:4
ªGen. 27:19,
25, 27, 31; 48:9,
15, 16; 49:28;
Deut. 33:1;
Heb. 11:20

27:8
ªGen. 27:13, 43

27:9 ªGen. 27:4

27:10
ªGen. 27:4;
48:16

27:11
ªGen. 25:25

27:12
ªGen. 27:21,
22 bGen. 9:25;
Deut. 27:18

27:13
ªGen. 43:9;
1 Sam. 25:24;
2 Sam. 14:9;
Matt. 27:25

27:14
ªProv. 23:3;
Luke 21:34

27:15
ªGen. 27:27

26:33 1Lit. *Oath* or *Seven*   2Lit. *Well of the Oath* or *Well of the Seven*
27:4 1*tasty*   27:7 1*tasty*   27:14 1*tasty*

And he said, "Here I am. Who *are* you, my son?"

19Jacob said to his father, "I *am* Esau your firstborn; I have done just as you told me; please arise, sit and eat of my game, ᵃthat your soul may bless me."

20But Isaac said to his son, "How *is it* that you have found *it* so quickly, my son?"

And he said, "Because the LORD your God brought *it* to me."

21Isaac said to Jacob, "Please come near, that I ᵃmay feel you, my son, whether you *are* really my son Esau or not." 22So Jacob went near to Isaac his father, and he felt him and said, "The voice *is* Jacob's voice, but the hands *are* the hands of Esau." 23And he did not recognize him, because ᵃhis hands were hairy like his brother Esau's hands; so he blessed him.

24Then he said, "*Are* you really my son Esau?"

He said, "I *am.*"

25He said, "Bring *it* near to me, and I will eat of my son's game, ᵃso that my soul may bless you." So he brought *it* near to him, and he ate; and he brought him wine, and he drank. 26Then his father Isaac said to him, "Come near now and kiss me, my son." 27And he came near and ᵃkissed him; and he smelled the smell of his clothing, and blessed him and said:

"Surely, ᵇthe smell of my son
  Is like the smell of a field
  Which the LORD has blessed.
28 Therefore may ᵃGod give you
  Of ᵇthe dew of heaven,
  Of ᶜthe fatness of the earth,
  And ᵈplenty of grain and wine.
29 ᵃLet peoples serve you,
  And nations bow down to you.
  Be master over your brethren,
  And ᵇlet your mother's sons bow down to you.
  ᶜCursed *be* everyone who curses you,
  And blessed *be* those who bless you!"

ESAU'S LOST HOPE
(Heb. 12:17)

30Now it happened, as soon as Isaac had finished blessing Jacob, and Jacob had scarcely gone out from the presence of Isaac his father, that Esau his brother came in from his hunting. 31He also had made ¹savory food, and brought it to his father, and said to his father, "Let my father arise and ᵃeat of his son's game, that your soul may bless me."

32And his father Isaac said to him, "Who *are* you?"

So he said, "I *am* your son, your firstborn, Esau."

33Then Isaac trembled exceedingly, and said, "Who? Where *is* the one who hunted game and brought *it* to me? I ate all *of it* before you came, and I have blessed him—ᵃand indeed he shall be blessed."

34When Esau heard the words of his father, ᵃhe cried with an exceedingly great and bitter cry, and said to his father, "Bless me—me also, O my father!"

35But he said, "Your brother came with deceit and has taken away your blessing."

27:19 ᵃGen. 27:4

27:21
ᵃGen. 27:12

27:23
ᵃGen. 27:16

27:25
ᵃGen. 27:4, 10, 19, 31

27:27
ᵃGen. 29:13
ᵇSong 4:11;
Hos. 14:6

27:28
ᵃHeb. 11:20
ᵇGen. 27:39;
Deut. 33:13, 28;
2 Sam. 1:21;
Ps. 133:3;
Prov. 3:20;
Mic. 5:7;
Zech. 8:12
ᶜGen. 45:18;
Num. 18:12
ᵈDeut. 7:13;
33:28

27:29
ᵃGen. 9:25;
25:23; Is. 45:14;
49:7; 60:12, 14
ᵇGen. 37:7, 10;
49:8 ᶜGen. 12:2,
3; Zeph. 2:8, 9

27:31 ᵃGen. 27:4

27:33
ᵃGen. 25:23;
28:3, 4;
Num. 23:20;
Rom. 11:29

27:34
ᵃ[Heb. 12:17]

27:31 ¹tasty

36And *Esau* said, a"Is he not rightly named 1Jacob? For he has supplanted me these two times. He took away my birthright, and now look, he has taken away my blessing!" And he said, "Have you not reserved a blessing for me?"

37Then Isaac answered and said to Esau, a"Indeed I have made him your master, and all his brethren I have given to him as servants; with bgrain and wine I have 1sustained him. What shall I do now for you, my son?"

38And Esau said to his father, "Have you only one blessing, my father? Bless me—me also, O my father!" And Esau lifted up his voice aand wept.

39Then Isaac his father answered and said to him:

"Behold, ayour dwelling shall be of the 1fatness of the
  earth,
And of the dew of heaven from above.
40 By your sword you shall live,
And ayou shall serve your brother;
And bit shall come to pass, when you become restless,
That you shall break his yoke from your neck."

JACOB ESCAPES FROM ESAU

41So Esau ahated Jacob because of the blessing with which his father blessed him, and Esau said in his heart, b"The days of mourning for my father 1are at hand; cthen I will kill my brother Jacob."

42And the words of Esau her older son were told to Rebekah. So she sent and called Jacob her younger son, and said to him, "Surely your brother Esau acomforts himself concerning you *by intending* to kill you. 43Now therefore, my son, obey my voice: arise, flee to my brother Laban ain Haran. 44And stay with him a afew days, until your brother's fury turns away, 45until your brother's anger turns away from you, and he forgets what you have done to him; then I will send and bring you from there. Why should I be bereaved also of you both in one day?"

46And Rebekah said to Isaac, a"I am weary of my life because of the daughters of Heth; bif Jacob takes a wife of the daughters of Heth, like these *who are* the daughters of the land, what good will my life be to me?"

28 Then Isaac called Jacob and ablessed him, and 1charged him, and said to him: b"You shall not take a wife from the daughters of Canaan. 2aArise, go to bPadan Aram, to the house of cBethuel your mother's father; and take yourself a wife from there of the daughters of dLaban your mother's brother.

3 "May aGod Almighty bless you,
And make you bfruitful and multiply you,
That you may be an assembly of peoples;
4 And give you athe blessing of Abraham,
To you and your descendants with you,
That you may inherit the land
bIn1 which you are a stranger,
Which God gave to Abraham."

27:36
aGen. 25:26,
32–34

27:37
a2 Sam. 8:14
bGen. 27:28, 29

27:38
aHeb. 12:17

27:39
aGen. 27:28;
Heb. 11:20

27:40
aGen. 25:23;
27:29;
2 Sam. 8:14;
[Obad. 18–20]
b2 Kin. 8:20–22

27:41
aGen. 26:27;
32:3–11; 37:4, 5, 8
bGen. 50:2–4,
10 cObad. 10

27:42 aPs. 64:5

27:43
aGen. 11:31;
25:20; 28:2, 5

27:44
aGen. 31:41

27:46
aGen. 26:34, 35;
28:8 bGen. 24:3

28:1 aGen. 27:33
bGen. 24:3

28:2 aHos. 12:12
bGen. 25:20
cGen. 22:23
dGen. 24:29;
27:43; 29:5

28:3 aGen. 17:16;
35:11; 48:3
bGen. 26:4, 24

28:4
aGen. 12:2, 3;
22:17; Gal. 3:8
bGen. 17:8;
23:4; 36:7;
1 Chr. 29:15;
Ps. 39:12

27:36 1*Supplanter* or *Deceitful*, lit. *One Who Takes the Heel*   27:37 1*provided support for*   27:39 1*fertility*   27:41 1*are soon here*   28:1 1*commanded*
28:4 1Lit. *Of your sojournings*

28:8
ªGen. 24:3;
26:34, 35; 27:46

28:9
ªGen. 26:34, 35
ᵇGen. 36:2, 3
ᶜGen. 25:13

28:10
ªGen. 26:23;
46:1; Hos. 12:12
ᵇGen. 12:4, 5;
27:43; 29:4;
2 Kin. 19:12;
Acts 7:2

28:12
ªGen. 31:10;
41:1; Num. 12:6
ᵇJohn 1:51;
Heb. 1:4, 14

28:13
ªGen. 35:1;
48:3; Amos 7:7
ᵇGen. 26:24
ᶜGen. 13:15, 17;
26:3; 35:12

28:14
ªGen. 13:16;
22:17
ᵇGen. 13:14, 15;
Deut. 12:20
ᶜGen. 12:3;
18:18; 22:18;
26:4; Matt. 1:2;
Luke 3:34;
Gal. 3:8

28:15
ªGen. 26:3,
24; 31:3
ᵇGen. 48:16;
Num. 6:24;
Ps. 121:5, 7, 8
ᶜGen. 35:6;
48:21;
Deut. 30:3
ᵈLev. 26:44;
Deut. 7:9;
31:6, 8;
Josh. 1:5;
1 Kin. 8:57;
Heb. 13:5
ᵉNum. 23:19

28:16 ªEx. 3:5;
Josh. 5:15;
Ps. 139:7–12

28:18
ªGen. 31:13, 45
ᵇLev. 8:10–12

28:19
ªJudg. 1:23, 26

28:20
ªGen. 31:13;
Judg. 11:30;
2 Sam. 15:8
ᵇGen. 28:15
ᶜ1 Tim. 6:8

28:21
ªJudg. 11:31;
2 Sam. 19:24, 30
ᵇDeut. 26:17;
2 Sam. 15:8

⁵So Isaac sent Jacob away, and he went to Padan Aram, to Laban the son of Bethuel the Syrian, the brother of Rebekah, the mother of Jacob and Esau.

ESAU MARRIES MAHALATH

⁶Esau saw that Isaac had blessed Jacob and sent him away to Padan Aram to take himself a wife from there, *and that* as he blessed him he gave him a charge, saying, "You shall not take a wife from the daughters of Canaan," ⁷and that Jacob had obeyed his father and his mother and had gone to Padan Aram. ⁸Also Esau saw ªthat the daughters of Canaan did not please his father Isaac. ⁹So Esau went to Ishmael and ªtook ᵇMahalath the daughter of Ishmael, Abraham's son, ᶜthe sister of Nebajoth, to be his wife in addition to the wives he had.

JACOB'S VOW AT BETHEL

¹⁰Now Jacob ªwent out from Beersheba and went toward ᵇHaran. ¹¹So he came to a certain place and stayed there all night, because the sun had set. And he took one of the stones of that place and put it at his head, and he lay down in that place to sleep. ¹²Then he ªdreamed, and behold, a ladder *was* set up on the earth, and its top reached to heaven; and there ᵇthe angels of God were ascending and descending on it. ¹³ªAnd behold, the Lᴏʀᴅ stood above it and said: ᵇ"I *am* the Lᴏʀᴅ God of Abraham your father and the God of Isaac; ᶜthe land on which you lie I will give to you and your descendants. ¹⁴Also your ªdescendants shall be as the dust of the earth; you shall spread abroad ᵇto the west and the east, to the north and the south; and in you and ᶜin your seed all the families of the earth shall be blessed. ¹⁵Behold, ªI *am* with you and will ᵇkeep¹ you wherever you go, and will ᶜbring you back to this land; for ᵈI will not leave you ᵉuntil I have done what I have spoken to you."

¹⁶Then Jacob awoke from his sleep and said, "Surely the Lᴏʀᴅ is in ªthis place, and I did not know *it*." ¹⁷And he was afraid and said, "How awesome *is* this place! This *is* none other than the house of God, and this *is* the gate of heaven!"

¹⁸Then Jacob rose early in the morning, and took the stone that he had put at his head, ªset it up as a pillar, ᵇand poured oil on top of it. ¹⁹And he called the name of ªthat place ¹Bethel; but the name of that city had been Luz previously. ²⁰ªThen Jacob made a vow, saying, "If ᵇGod will be with me, and keep me in this way that I am going, and give me ᶜbread to eat and clothing to put on, ²¹so that ªI come back to my father's house in peace, ᵇthen the Lᴏʀᴅ shall be my God. ²²And this stone which I have set as a pillar ªshall be God's house, ᵇand of all that You give me I will surely give a ¹tenth to You."

JACOB MEETS RACHEL

29 So Jacob went on his journey ªand came to the land of the people of the East. ²And he looked, and saw a ªwell in the field; and behold, there *were* three flocks of sheep lying by it; for out of that well they watered the flocks. A large

28:22 ªGen. 35:7, 14 ᵇGen. 14:20; [Lev. 27:30]; Deut. 14:22   29:1 ªGen. 25:6; Num. 23:7; Judg. 6:3, 33; Hos. 12:12   29:2 ªGen. 24:10, 11; Ex. 2:15, 16

28:15 ¹protect   **28:19** ¹Lit. *House of God*   **28:22** ¹tithe

stone *was* on the well's mouth. ³Now all the flocks would be gathered there; and they would roll the stone from the well's mouth, water the sheep, and put the stone back in its place on the well's mouth.

⁴And Jacob said to them, "My brethren, where *are* you from?"

And they said, "We *are* from ᵃHaran."

⁵Then he said to them, "Do you know ᵃLaban the son of Nahor?"

And they said, "We know him."

⁶So he said to them, ᵃ"Is he well?"

And they said, "*He is* well. And look, his daughter Rachel ᵇis coming with the sheep."

⁷Then he said, "Look, *it is* still ¹high day; *it is* not time for the cattle to be gathered together. Water the sheep, and go and feed *them*."

⁸But they said, "We cannot until all the flocks are gathered together, and they have rolled the stone from the well's mouth; then we water the sheep."

⁹Now while he was still speaking with them, ᵃRachel came with her father's sheep, for she was a shepherdess. ¹⁰And it came to pass, when Jacob saw Rachel the daughter of Laban his mother's brother, and the sheep of Laban his mother's brother, that Jacob went near and ᵃrolled the stone from the well's mouth, and watered the flock of Laban his mother's brother. ¹¹Then Jacob ᵃkissed Rachel, and lifted up his voice and wept. ¹²And Jacob told Rachel that he *was* ᵃher father's relative and that he *was* Rebekah's son. ᵇSo she ran and told her father.

¹³Then it came to pass, when Laban heard the report about Jacob his sister's son, that ᵃhe ran to meet him, and embraced him and kissed him, and brought him to his house. So he told Laban all these things. ¹⁴And Laban said to him, ᵃ"Surely you *are* my bone and my flesh." And he stayed with him for a month.

JACOB MARRIES LEAH AND RACHEL

¹⁵Then Laban said to Jacob, "Because you *are* my relative, should you therefore serve me for nothing? Tell me, ᵃwhat *should* your wages *be*?" ¹⁶Now Laban had two daughters: the name of the elder *was* Leah, and the name of the younger *was* Rachel. ¹⁷Leah's eyes *were* ¹delicate, but Rachel was ᵃbeautiful of form and appearance.

¹⁸Now Jacob loved Rachel; so he said, ᵃ"I will serve you seven years for Rachel your younger daughter."

¹⁹And Laban said, "*It is* better that I give her to you than that I should give her to another man. Stay with me." ²⁰So Jacob ᵃserved seven years for Rachel, and they seemed *only* a few days to him because of the love he had for her.

²¹Then Jacob said to Laban, "Give *me* my wife, for my days are fulfilled, that I may ᵃgo in to her." ²²And Laban gathered together all the men of the place and ᵃmade a feast. ²³Now it came to pass in the evening, that he took Leah his daughter and brought her to Jacob; and he went in to her. ²⁴And Laban gave his maid ᵃZilpah to his daughter Leah *as* a maid. ²⁵So it came to pass in the morning, that behold, it *was* Leah. And he said to Laban, "What is this you have done to me? Was

---

29:4 ᵃGen. 11:31; 28:10

29:5 ᵃGen. 24:24, 29; 28:2

29:6 ᵃGen. 43:27 ᵇGen. 24:11; Ex. 2:16, 17

29:9 ᵃEx. 2:16

29:10 ᵃEx. 2:17

29:11 ᵃGen. 33:4; 45:14, 15

29:12 ᵃGen. 13:8; 14:14, 16; 28:5 ᵇGen. 24:28

29:13 ᵃGen. 24:29–31; Luke 15:20

29:14 ᵃGen. 2:23; 37:27; Judg. 9:2; 2 Sam. 5:1; 19:12, 13

29:15 ᵃGen. 30:28; 31:41

29:17 ᵃGen. 12:11, 14; 26:7

29:18 ᵃGen. 31:41; 2 Sam. 3:14; Hos. 12:12

29:20 ᵃGen. 30:26; Hos. 12:12

29:21 ᵃJudg. 15:1

29:22 ᵃJudg. 14:10; John 2:1, 2

29:24 ᵃGen. 30:9, 10

29:7 ¹early in the day   29:17 ¹Or *weak*

it not for Rachel that I served you? Why then have you ᵃdeceived me?"

²⁶And Laban said, "It must not be done so in our ¹country, to give the younger before the firstborn. ²⁷ᵃFulfill her week, and we will give you this one also for the service which you will serve with me still another seven years."

²⁸Then Jacob did so and fulfilled her week. So he gave him his daughter Rachel as wife also. ²⁹And Laban gave his maid ᵃBilhah to his daughter Rachel as a maid. ³⁰Then *Jacob* also went in to Rachel, and he also ᵃloved Rachel more than Leah. And he served with Laban ᵇstill another seven years.

THE CHILDREN OF JACOB

³¹When the LORD ᵃsaw that Leah *was* ¹unloved, He ᵇopened her womb; but Rachel *was* barren. ³²So Leah conceived and bore a son, and she called his name ¹Reuben; for she said, "The LORD has surely ᵃlooked on my affliction. Now therefore, my husband will love me." ³³Then she conceived again and bore a son, and said, "Because the LORD has heard that I *am* ¹unloved, He has therefore given me this *son* also." And she called his name ²Simeon. ³⁴She conceived again and bore a son, and said, "Now this time my husband will become attached to me, because I have borne him three sons." Therefore his name was called ¹Levi. ³⁵And she conceived again and bore a son, and said, "Now I will praise the LORD." Therefore she called his name ᵃJudah.¹ Then she stopped bearing.

30 Now when Rachel saw that ᵃshe bore Jacob no children, Rachel ᵇenvied her sister, and said to Jacob, "Give me children, ᶜor else I die!"

²And Jacob's anger was aroused against Rachel, and he said, ᵃ"*Am* I in the place of God, who has withheld from you the fruit of the womb?"

³So she said, "Here is ᵃmy maid Bilhah; go in to her, ᵇand she will bear *a child* on my knees, ᶜthat I also may ¹have children by her." ⁴Then she gave him Bilhah her maid ᵃas wife, and Jacob went in to her. ⁵And Bilhah conceived and bore Jacob a son. ⁶Then Rachel said, "God has ᵃjudged my case; and He has also heard my voice and given me a son." Therefore she called his name ¹Dan. ⁷And Rachel's maid Bilhah conceived again and bore Jacob a second son. ⁸Then Rachel said, "With ¹great wrestlings I have wrestled with my sister, *and* indeed I have prevailed." So she called his name ²Naphtali.

⁹When Leah saw that she had stopped bearing, she took Zilpah her maid and ᵃgave her to Jacob as wife. ¹⁰And Leah's maid Zilpah bore Jacob a son. ¹¹Then Leah said, ¹"A troop comes!" So she called his name ²Gad. ¹²And Leah's maid Zilpah bore Jacob a second son. ¹³Then Leah said, "I am happy, for the daughters ᵃwill call me blessed." So she called his name ¹Asher.

¹⁴Now Reuben went in the days of wheat harvest and found mandrakes in the field, and brought them to his mother Leah.

29:25
ᵃGen. 27:35;
31:7;
1 Sam. 28:12

29:27
ᵃGen. 31:41;
Judg. 14:2

29:29
ᵃGen. 30:3–5

29:30
ᵃGen. 29:17–20;
Deut. 21:15–17
ᵇGen. 30:26;
31:41; Hos. 12:12

29:31 ᵃPs. 127:3
ᵇGen. 30:1

29:32
ᵃGen. 16:11;
31:42; Ex. 3:7;
4:31; Deut. 26:7;
Ps. 25:18

29:35
ᵃGen. 49:8;
Matt. 1:2

30:1 ᵃGen. 16:1,
2; 29:31
ᵇGen. 37:11
ᶜ1 Sam. 1:5, 6;
[Job 5:2]

30:2 ᵃGen. 16:2;
1 Sam. 1:5

30:3 ᵃGen. 16:2
ᵇGen. 50:23;
Job 3:12
ᶜGen. 16:2, 3

30:4
ᵃGen. 16:3, 4

30:6
ᵃGen. 18:25;
Ps. 35:24; 43:1;
Lam. 3:59

30:9 ᵃGen. 30:4

30:13
ᵃProv. 31:28;
Luke 1:48

29:26 ¹Lit. *place* **29:31** ¹Lit. *hated* **29:32** ¹Lit. *See, a Son* **29:33** ¹Lit. *hated* ²Lit. *Heard* **29:34** ¹Lit. *Attached* **29:35** ¹Lit. *Praise* **30:3** ¹Lit. *be built up by her* **30:6** ¹Lit. *Judge* **30:8** ¹Lit. *wrestlings of God* ²Lit. *My Wrestling* **30:11** ¹So with Qr., Syr., Tg.; Kt., LXX, Vg. *in fortune* ²Lit. *Troop or Fortune* **30:13** ¹Lit. *Happy*

Then Rachel said to Leah, a"Please give me *some* of your son's mandrakes."

15But she said to her, a"*Is it* a small matter that you have taken away my husband? Would you take away my son's mandrakes also?"

And Rachel said, "Therefore he will lie with you tonight for your son's mandrakes."

16When Jacob came out of the field in the evening, Leah went out to meet him and said, "You must come in to me, for I have surely hired you with my son's mandrakes." And he lay with her that night.

17And God listened to Leah, and she conceived and bore Jacob a fifth son. 18Leah said, "God has given me my wages, because I have given my maid to my husband." So she called his name 1Issachar. 19Then Leah conceived again and bore Jacob a sixth son. 20And Leah said, "God has endowed me *with* a good endowment; now my husband will dwell with me, because I have borne him six sons." So she called his name 1Zebulun. 21Afterward she bore a adaughter, and called her name 1Dinah.

22Then God aremembered Rachel, and God listened to her and bopened her womb. 23And she conceived and bore a son, and said, "God has taken away amy reproach." 24So she called his name 1Joseph, and said, a"The LORD shall add to me another son."

JACOB'S AGREEMENT WITH LABAN

25And it came to pass, when Rachel had borne Joseph, that Jacob said to Laban, a"Send me away, that I may go to bmy own place and to my country. 26Give *me* my wives and my children afor whom I have served you, and let me go; for you know my service which I have done for you."

27And Laban said to him, "Please *stay,* if I have found favor in your eyes, *for* aI have learned by experience that the LORD has blessed me for your sake." 28Then he said, a"Name me your wages, and I will give *it.*"

29So *Jacob* said to him, a"You know how I have served you and how your livestock has been with me. 30For what you had before I *came was* little, and it has increased to a great amount; the LORD has blessed you 1since my coming. And now, when shall I also aprovide for my own house?"

31So he said, "What shall I give you?"

And Jacob said, "You shall not give me anything. If you will do this thing for me, I will again feed and keep your flocks: 32Let me pass through all your flock today, removing from there all the speckled and spotted sheep, and all the brown ones among the lambs, and the spotted and speckled among the goats; and a*these* shall be my wages. 33So my arighteousness will answer for me in time to come, when the subject of my wages comes before you: every one that *is* not speckled and spotted among the goats, and brown among the lambs, will be considered stolen, if *it is* with me."

34And Laban said, "Oh, that it were according to your word!" 35So he removed that day the male goats that were aspeckled and spotted, all the female goats that were speckled

30:14
aGen. 25:30

30:15
a[Num. 16:9, 13]

30:21 aGen. 34:1

30:22
aGen. 19:29;
1 Sam. 1:19, 20
bGen. 29:31

30:23
a1 Sam. 1:6;
Is. 4:1; Luke 1:25

30:24
aGen. 35:16–18

30:25
aGen. 24:54, 56
bGen. 18:33

30:26
aGen. 29:18–20,
27, 30; Hos. 12:12

30:27
aGen. 26:24;
39:3; Is. 61:9

30:28
aGen. 29:15;
31:7, 41

30:29
aGen. 31:6, 38–
40; Matt. 24:45;
Titus 2:10

30:30
a[1 Tim. 5:8]

30:32
aGen. 31:8

30:33 aPs. 37:6

30:35
aGen. 31:9–12

30:18 1Lit. *Wages*   30:20 1Lit. *Dwelling*   30:21 1Lit. *Judgment*   30:24 1Lit. *He Will Add*   30:30 1Lit. *at my foot*

and spotted, every one that had *some* white in it, and all the brown ones among the lambs, and gave *them* into the hand of his sons. ³⁶Then he put three days' journey between himself and Jacob, and Jacob fed the rest of Laban's flocks.

³⁷Now ᵃJacob took for himself rods of green poplar and of the almond and chestnut trees, peeled white strips in them, and exposed the white which *was* in the rods. ³⁸And the rods which he had peeled, he set before the flocks in the gutters, in the watering troughs where the flocks came to drink, so that they should conceive when they came to drink. ³⁹So the flocks conceived before the rods, and the flocks brought forth streaked, speckled, and spotted. ⁴⁰Then Jacob separated the lambs, and made the flocks face toward the streaked and all the brown in the flock of Laban; but he put his own flocks by themselves and did not put them with Laban's flock.

⁴¹And it came to pass, whenever the stronger livestock conceived, that Jacob placed the rods before the eyes of the livestock in the gutters, that they might conceive among the rods. ⁴²But when the flocks were feeble, he did not put *them* in; so the feebler were Laban's and the stronger Jacob's. ⁴³Thus the man ᵃbecame exceedingly prosperous, and ᵇhad large flocks, female and male servants, and camels and donkeys.

JACOB FLEES FROM LABAN

31 Now *Jacob* heard the words of Laban's sons, saying, "Jacob has taken away all that was our father's, and from what was our father's he has acquired all this ᵃwealth." ²And Jacob saw the ᵃcountenance of Laban, and indeed it *was* not ᵇ*favorable* toward him as before. ³Then the LORD said to Jacob, ᵃ"Return to the land of your fathers and to your family, and I will ᵇbe with you."

⁴So Jacob sent and called Rachel and Leah to the field, to his flock, ⁵and said to them, ᵃ"I see your father's ¹countenance, that it *is* not *favorable* toward me as before; but the God of my father ᵇhas been with me. ⁶And ᵃyou know that with all my might I have served your father. ⁷Yet your father has deceived me and ᵃchanged my wages ᵇten times, but God ᶜdid not allow him to hurt me. ⁸If he said thus: ᵃ'The speckled shall be your wages,' then all the flocks bore speckled. And if he said thus: 'The streaked shall be your wages,' then all the flocks bore streaked. ⁹So God has ᵃtaken away the livestock of your father and given *them* to me.

¹⁰"And it happened, at the time when the flocks conceived, that I lifted my eyes and saw in a dream, and behold, the rams which leaped upon the flocks *were* streaked, speckled, and gray-spotted. ¹¹Then ᵃthe Angel of God spoke to me in a dream, saying, 'Jacob.' And I said, 'Here I am.' ¹²And He said, 'Lift your eyes now and see, all the rams which leap on the flocks *are* streaked, speckled, and gray-spotted; for ᵃI have seen all that Laban is doing to you. ¹³I *am* the God of Bethel, ᵃwhere you anointed the pillar *and* where you made a vow to Me. Now ᵇarise, get out of this land, and return to the land of your family.'"

¹⁴Then Rachel and Leah answered and said to him, ᵃ"Is there still any portion or inheritance for us in our father's

---

30:37
ᵃGen. 31:9–12

30:43
ᵃGen. 12:16;
30:30
ᵇGen. 13:2;
24:35; 26:13, 14

31:1 ᵃPs. 49:16

31:2 ᵃGen. 4:5
ᵇDeut. 28:54

31:3 ᵃGen. 28:15,
20, 21; 32:9
ᵇGen. 46:4

31:5
ᵃGen. 31:2, 3
ᵇGen. 21:22;
28:13, 15; 31:29,
42, 53; Is. 41:10;
Heb. 13:5

31:6
ᵃGen. 30:29;
31:38–41

31:7
ᵃGen. 29:25;
31:41
ᵇNum. 14:22;
Neh. 4:12;
Job 19:3;
Zech. 8:23
ᶜGen. 15:1; 20:6;
31:29; Job 1:10;
Ps. 37:28; 105:14

31:8 ᵃGen. 30:32

31:9
ᵃGen. 31:1, 16

31:11
ᵃGen. 16:7–11;
22:11, 15; 31:13;
48:16

31:12
ᵃGen. 31:42;
Ex. 3:7;
Ps. 139:3;
Eccl. 5:8

31:13
ᵃGen. 28:16–22;
35:1, 6, 15
ᵇGen. 31:3; 32:9

31:14 ᵃGen. 2:24

31:5 ¹Lit. *face*

house? ¹⁵Are we not considered strangers by him? For ^ahe has sold us, and also completely consumed our money. ¹⁶For all these riches which God has taken from our father are *really* ours and our children's; now then, whatever God has said to you, do it."

¹⁷Then Jacob rose and set his sons and his wives on camels. ¹⁸And he carried away all his livestock and all his possessions which he had gained, his acquired livestock which he had gained in Padan Aram, to go to his father Isaac in the land of ^aCanaan. ¹⁹Now Laban had gone to shear his sheep, and Rachel had stolen the ^ahousehold¹ idols that were her father's. ²⁰And Jacob stole away, unknown to Laban the Syrian, in that he did not tell him that he intended to flee. ²¹So he fled with all that he had. He arose and crossed the river, and ^aheaded¹ toward the mountains of Gilead.

LABAN PURSUES JACOB

²²And Laban was told on the third day that Jacob had fled. ²³Then he took ^ahis brethren with him and pursued him for seven days' journey, and he overtook him in the mountains of Gilead. ²⁴But God ^ahad come to Laban the Syrian in a dream by night, and said to him, "Be careful that you ^bspeak to Jacob neither good nor bad."

²⁵So Laban overtook Jacob. Now Jacob had pitched his tent in the mountains, and Laban with his brethren pitched in the mountains of Gilead.

²⁶And Laban said to Jacob: "What have you done, that you have stolen away unknown to me, and ^acarried away my daughters like captives *taken* with the sword? ²⁷Why did you flee away secretly, and steal away from me, and not tell me; for I might have sent you away with joy and songs, with timbrel and harp? ²⁸And you did not allow me ^ato kiss my sons and my daughters. Now ^byou have done foolishly in *so* doing. ²⁹It is in my power to do you harm, but the ^aGod of your father spoke to me ^blast night, saying, 'Be careful that you speak to Jacob neither good nor bad.' ³⁰And now you have surely gone because you greatly long for your father's house, *but* why did you ^asteal my gods?"

³¹Then Jacob answered and said to Laban, "Because I was ^aafraid, for I said, 'Perhaps you would take your daughters from me by force.' ³²With whomever you find your gods, ^ado not let him live. In the presence of our brethren, identify what I have of yours and take *it* with you." For Jacob did not know that Rachel had stolen them.

³³And Laban went into Jacob's tent, into Leah's tent, and into the two maids' tents, but he did not find *them*. Then he went out of Leah's tent and entered Rachel's tent. ³⁴Now Rachel had taken the ¹household idols, put them in the camel's saddle, and sat on them. And Laban ²searched all about the tent but did not find *them*. ³⁵And she said to her father, "Let it not displease my lord that I cannot ^arise before you, for the manner of women *is* with me." And he searched but did not find the ¹household idols.

³⁶Then Jacob was angry and rebuked Laban, and Jacob answered and said to Laban: "What *is* my ¹trespass? What *is*

31:15
^aGen. 29:15, 20, 23, 27; Neh. 5:8

31:18 ^aGen. 17:8; 33:18; 35:27

31:19
^aGen. 31:30, 34; 35:2; Judg. 17:5; 1 Sam. 19:13; Hos. 3:4

31:21
^aGen. 46:28; 2 Kin. 12:17; Luke 9:51, 53

31:23 ^aGen. 13:8

31:24
^aGen. 20:3; 31:29; 46:2–4; Job 33:15; Matt. 1:20
^bGen. 24:50; 31:7, 29

31:26
^a1 Sam. 30:2

31:28
^aGen. 31:55; Ruth 1:9, 14; 1 Kin. 19:20; Acts 20:37
^b1 Sam. 13:13

31:29
^aGen. 28:13; 31:5, 24, 42, 53
^bGen. 31:24

31:30
^aGen. 31:19; Josh. 24:2; Judg. 17:5; 18:24

31:31 ^aGen. 26:7; 32:7, 11

31:32 ^aGen. 44:9

31:35 ^aEx. 20:12; Lev. 19:32

31:19 ¹Heb. *teraphim*   31:21 ¹Lit. *set his face toward*   31:34 ¹Heb. *teraphim*
²Lit. *felt*   31:35 ¹Heb. *teraphim*   31:36 ¹*transgression*

my sin, that you have so hotly pursued me? 37Although you have searched all my things, what part of your household things have you found? Set *it* here before my brethren and your brethren, that they may judge between us both! 38These twenty years I *have been* with you; your ewes and your female goats have not miscarried their young, and I have not eaten the rams of your flock. 39aThat which was torn *by beasts* I did not bring to you; I bore the loss of it. bYou required it from my hand, *whether* stolen by day or stolen by night. 40There I was! In the day the drought consumed me, and the frost by night, and my sleep departed from my eyes. 41Thus I have been in your house twenty years; I aserved you fourteen years for your two daughters, and six years for your flock, and byou have changed my wages ten times. 42aUnless the God of my father, the God of Abraham and bthe Fear of Isaac, had been with me, surely now you would have sent me away empty-handed. cGod has seen my affliction and the labor of my hands, and drebuked *you* last night."

LABAN'S COVENANT WITH JACOB

43And Laban answered and said to Jacob, "*These* daughters *are* my daughters, and *these* children *are* my children, and *this* flock *is* my flock; all that you see *is* mine. But what can I do this day to these my daughters or to their children whom they have borne? 44Now therefore, come, alet us make a 1covenant, byou and I, and let it be a witness between you and me."

45So Jacob atook a stone and set it up *as* a pillar. 46Then Jacob said to his brethren, "Gather stones." And they took stones and made a heap, and they ate there on the heap. 47Laban called it 1Jegar Sahadutha, but Jacob called it 2Gal-eed. 48And Laban said, a"This heap *is* a witness between you and me this day." Therefore its name was called Galeed, 49also aMizpah,1 because he said, "May the LORD watch between you and me when we are absent one from another. 50If you afflict my daughters, or if you take *other* wives besides my daugh-ters, *although* no man *is* with us—see, God *is* witness between you and me!"

51Then Laban said to Jacob, "Here is this heap and here is *this* pillar, which I have placed between you and me. 52This heap *is* a witness, and *this* pillar *is* a witness, that I will not pass beyond this heap to you, and you will not pass beyond this heap and this pillar to me, for harm. 53The God of Abra-ham, the God of Nahor, and the God of their father ajudge be-tween us." And Jacob bswore by cthe 1Fear of his father Isaac. 54Then Jacob offered a sacrifice on the mountain, and called his brethren to eat bread. And they ate bread and stayed all night on the mountain. 55And early in the morning Laban arose, and akissed his sons and daughters and bblessed them. Then Laban departed and creturned to his place.

ESAU COMES TO MEET JACOB

32 So Jacob went on his way, and athe angels of God met him. 2When Jacob saw them, he said, "This *is* God's acamp." And he called the name of that place 1Mahanaim.

Cross references (left margin):
31:39 aEx. 22:10
bEx. 22:10–13
31:41 aGen. 29:20, 27–30
bGen. 31:7
31:42 aGen. 31:5, 29, 53; Ps. 124:1, 2
bGen. 31:53; Is. 8:13
cGen. 29:32; Ex. 3:7
dGen. 31:24, 29; 1 Chr. 12:17
31:44 aGen. 21:27, 32; 26:28
bJosh. 24:27
31:45 aGen. 28:18; 35:14; Josh. 24:26, 27
31:48 aJosh. 24:27
31:49 aJudg. 10:17; 11:29; 1 Sam. 7:5, 6
31:53 aGen. 16:5
bGen. 21:23
cGen. 31:42
31:55 aGen. 29:11, 13; 31:28, 43
bGen. 28:1
cGen. 18:33; 30:25; Num. 24:25
32:1 aNum. 22:31; 2 Kin. 6:16, 17; [Ps. 34:7; 91:1; Heb. 1:14]
32:2 aJosh. 5:14; Ps. 103:21; 148:2; Luke 2:13

31:44 1treaty 31:47 1Lit., in Aram., *Heap of Witness* 2Lit., in Heb., *Heap of Witness* 31:49 1Lit. *Watch* 31:53 1A reference to God 32:2 1Lit. *Double Camp*

³Then Jacob sent messengers before him to Esau his brother ᵃin the land of Seir, ᵇthe ¹country of Edom. ⁴And he commanded them, saying, ᵃ"Speak thus to my lord Esau, 'Thus your servant Jacob says: "I have dwelt with Laban and stayed there until now. ⁵ᵃI have oxen, donkeys, flocks, and male and female servants; and I have sent to tell my lord, that ᵇI may find favor in your sight."'"

⁶Then the messengers returned to Jacob, saying, "We came to your brother Esau, and ᵃhe also is coming to meet you, and four hundred men *are* with him." ⁷So Jacob was greatly afraid and ᵃdistressed; and he divided the people that *were* with him, and the flocks and herds and camels, into two companies. ⁸And he said, "If Esau comes to the one company and ¹attacks it, then the other company which is left will escape."

⁹ᵃThen Jacob said, ᵇ"O God of my father Abraham and God of my father Isaac, the Lᴏʀᴅ ᶜwho said to me, 'Return to your country and to your family, and I will deal well with you': ¹⁰I am not worthy of the least of all the ᵃmercies and of all the truth which You have shown Your servant; for I crossed over this Jordan with ᵇmy staff, and now I have become two companies. ¹¹ᵃDeliver me, I pray, from the hand of my brother, from the hand of Esau; for I fear him, lest he come and ¹attack me *and* ᵇthe mother with the children. ¹²For ᵃYou said, 'I will surely treat you well, and make your descendants as the ᵇsand of the sea, which cannot be numbered for multitude.'"

¹³So he lodged there that same night, and took what ¹came to his hand as ᵃa present for Esau his brother: ¹⁴two hundred female goats and twenty male goats, two hundred ewes and twenty rams, ¹⁵thirty milk camels with their colts, forty cows and ten bulls, twenty female donkeys and ten foals. ¹⁶Then he delivered *them* to the hand of his servants, every drove by itself, and said to his servants, "Pass over before me, and put some distance between successive droves." ¹⁷And he commanded the first one, saying, "When Esau my brother meets you and asks you, saying, 'To whom do you belong, and where are you going? Whose *are* these in front of you?' ¹⁸then you shall say, 'They *are* your servant Jacob's. It *is* a present sent to my lord Esau; and behold, he also *is* behind us.'" ¹⁹So he commanded the second, the third, and all who followed the droves, saying, "In this manner you shall speak to Esau when you find him; ²⁰and also say, 'Behold, your servant Jacob *is* behind us.'" For he said, "I will ᵃappease him with the present that goes before me, and afterward I will see his face; perhaps he will accept me." ²¹So the present went on over before him, but he himself lodged that night in the camp.

WRESTLING WITH GOD

²²And he arose that night and took his two wives, his two female servants, and his eleven sons, ᵃand crossed over the ford of Jabbok. ²³He took them, sent them ¹over the brook, and sent over what he had. ²⁴Then Jacob was left alone; and ᵃa Man wrestled with him until the ¹breaking of day. ²⁵Now when He saw that He did not prevail against him, He ¹touched

32:3 ᵃGen. 14:6; 33:14, 16
ᵇGen. 25:30; 36:6–9; Deut. 2:5; Josh. 24:4

32:4 ᵃProv. 15:1

32:5
ᵃGen. 30:43
ᵇGen. 33:8, 15

32:6 ᵃGen. 33:1

32:7 ᵃGen. 32:11; 35:3

32:9 ᵃ[Ps. 50:15]
ᵇGen. 28:13; 31:42 ᶜGen. 31:3, 13

32:10
ᵃGen. 24:27
ᵇJob 8:7

32:11 ᵃPs. 59:1, 2
ᵇHos. 10:14

32:12
ᵃGen. 28:13–15
ᵇGen. 22:17

32:13
ᵃGen. 43:11

32:20
ᵃ[Prov. 21:14]

32:22
ᵃNum. 21:24; Deut. 3:16; Josh. 12:2

32:24
ᵃJosh. 5:13–15; Hos. 12:2–4

32:3 ¹Lit. *field*   32:8 ¹Lit. *strikes*   32:11 ¹Lit. *strike*   32:13 ¹*he had received*
32:23 ¹*across*   32:24 ¹*dawn*   32:25 ¹*struck*

the socket of his hip; and ᵃthe socket of Jacob's hip was out of joint as He wrestled with him. ²⁶And ᵃHe said, "Let Me go, for the day breaks."

But he said, ᵇ"I will not let You go unless You bless me!"

²⁷So He said to him, "What *is* your name?"

He said, "Jacob."

²⁸And He said, ᵃ"Your name shall no longer be called Jacob, but ¹Israel; for you have ᵇstruggled with God and ᶜwith men, and have prevailed."

²⁹Then Jacob asked, saying, "Tell *me* Your name, I pray."

And He said, ᵃ"Why *is* it *that* you ask about My name?" And He ᵇblessed him there.

³⁰So Jacob called the name of the place ¹Peniel: "For ᵃI have seen God face to face, and my life is preserved." ³¹Just as he crossed over ¹Penuel the sun rose on him, and he limped on his hip. ³²Therefore to this day the children of Israel do not eat the muscle that shrank, which *is* on the hip socket, because He ¹touched the socket of Jacob's hip in the muscle that shrank.

JACOB AND ESAU MEET

33 Now Jacob lifted his eyes and looked, and there, ᵃEsau was coming, and with him were four hundred men. So he divided the children among Leah, Rachel, and the two maidservants. ²And he put the maidservants and their children in front, Leah and her children behind, and Rachel and Joseph last. ³Then he crossed over before them and ᵃbowed himself to the ground seven times, until he came near to his brother.

⁴ᵃBut Esau ran to meet him, and embraced him, ᵇand fell on his neck and kissed him, and they wept. ⁵And he lifted his eyes and saw the women and children, and said, "Who *are* these with you?"

So he said, "The children ᵃwhom God has graciously given your servant." ⁶Then the maidservants came near, they and their children, and bowed down. ⁷And Leah also came near with her children, and they bowed down. Afterward Joseph and Rachel came near, and they bowed down.

⁸Then Esau said, "What *do* you *mean by* ᵃall this company which I met?"

And he said, "*These are* ᵇto find favor in the sight of my lord."

⁹But Esau said, "I have enough, my brother; keep what you have for yourself."

¹⁰And Jacob said, "No, please, if I have now found favor in your sight, then receive my present from my hand, inasmuch as I ᵃhave seen your face as though I had seen the face of God, and you were pleased with me. ¹¹Please, take ᵃmy blessing that is brought to you, because God has dealt ᵇgraciously with me, and because I have ¹enough." ᶜSo he urged him, and he took *it*.

¹²Then Esau said, "Let us take our journey; let us go, and I will go before you."

¹³But Jacob said to him, "My lord knows that the children *are* weak, and the flocks and herds which are nursing *are* with me. And if the men should drive them hard one day, all the

---

Cross-references (margin):

32:25 ᵃMatt. 26:41; 2 Cor. 12:7

32:26 ᵃLuke 24:28 ᵇHos. 12:4

32:28 ᵃGen. 35:10; 1 Kin. 18:31; 2 Kin. 17:34 ᵇHos. 12:3, 4 ᶜGen. 25:31; 27:33

32:29 ᵃJudg. 13:17, 18 ᵇGen. 35:9

32:30 ᵃGen. 16:13; Ex. 24:10, 11; 33:20; Num. 12:8; Deut. 5:24; Judg. 6:22; Is. 6:5; [Matt. 5:8; 1 Cor. 13:12]

33:1 ᵃGen. 32:6

33:3 ᵃGen. 18:2; 42:6

33:4 ᵃGen. 32:28 ᵇGen. 45:14, 15

33:5 ᵃGen. 48:9; [Ps. 127:3]; Is. 8:18

33:8 ᵃGen. 32:13–16 ᵇGen. 32:5

33:10 ᵃGen. 43:3; 2 Sam. 3:13; 14:24, 28, 32

33:11 ᵃJudg. 1:15; 1 Sam. 25:27; 30:26 ᵇGen. 30:43; Ex. 33:19 ᶜ2 Kin. 5:23

Footnotes:

32:28 ¹Lit. *Prince with God*   **32:30** ¹Lit. *Face of God*   **32:31** ¹Lit. *Face of God; same as Peniel,* v. 30   **32:32** ¹*struck*   **33:11** ¹Lit. *all*

flock will die. ¹⁴Please let my lord go on ahead before his servant. I will lead on slowly at a pace which the livestock that go before me, and the children, ¹are able to endure, until I come to my lord ªin Seir."

¹⁵And Esau said, "Now let me leave with you *some* of the people who *are* with me."

But he said, "What need is there? ªLet me find favor in the sight of my lord." ¹⁶So Esau returned that day on his way to Seir. ¹⁷And Jacob journeyed to ªSuccoth, built himself a house, and made ¹booths for his livestock. Therefore the name of the place is called ²Succoth.

JACOB COMES TO CANAAN

¹⁸Then Jacob came ¹safely to ªthe city of ᵇShechem, which *is* in the land of Canaan, when he came from Padan Aram; and he pitched his tent before the city. ¹⁹And ªhe bought the parcel of ¹land, where he had pitched his tent, from the children of Hamor, Shechem's father, for one hundred pieces of money. ²⁰Then he erected an altar there and called it ªEl¹ Elohe Israel.

THE DINAH INCIDENT

34 Now ªDinah the daughter of Leah, whom she had borne to Jacob, went out to see the daughters of the land. ²And when Shechem the son of Hamor the Hivite, prince of the country, saw her, he ªtook her and lay with her, and violated her. ³His soul ¹was strongly attracted to Dinah the daughter of Jacob, and he loved the young woman and spoke ²kindly to the young woman. ⁴So Shechem ªspoke to his father Hamor, saying, "Get me this young woman as a wife."

⁵And Jacob heard that he had defiled Dinah his daughter. Now his sons were with his livestock in the field; so Jacob ªheld¹ his peace until they came. ⁶Then Hamor the father of Shechem went out to Jacob to speak with him. ⁷And the sons of Jacob came in from the field when they heard *it;* and the men were grieved and very angry, because he ªhad done a disgraceful thing in Israel by lying with Jacob's daughter, ᵇa thing which ought not to be done. ⁸But Hamor spoke with them, saying, "The soul of my son Shechem longs for your daughter. Please give her to him as a wife. ⁹And make marriages with us; give your daughters to us, and take our daughters to yourselves. ¹⁰So you shall dwell with us, and the land shall be before you. Dwell and trade in it, and acquire possessions for yourselves in it."

¹¹Then Shechem said to her father and her brothers, "Let me find favor in your eyes, and whatever you say to me I will give. ¹²Ask me ever so much ªdowry¹ and gift, and I will give according to what you say to me; but give me the young woman as a wife."

¹³But the sons of Jacob answered Shechem and Hamor his father, and spoke ªdeceitfully, because he had defiled Dinah their sister. ¹⁴And they said to them, "We cannot do this thing, to give our sister to one who is ªuncircumcised, for ᵇthat *would be* a reproach to us. ¹⁵But on this *condition* we will

33:14
ªGen. 32:3;
36:8

33:15
ªGen. 34:11;
47:25; Ruth 2:13

33:17
ªJosh. 13:27;
Judg. 8:5;
Ps. 60:6

33:18
ªJohn 3:23
ᵇGen. 12:6;
35:4; Josh. 24:1;
Judg. 9:1;
Ps. 60:6

33:19
ªJosh. 24:32;
John 4:5

33:20
ªGen. 35:7

34:1 ªGen. 30:21

34:2 ªGen. 20:2

34:4 ªJudg. 14:2

34:5
ª2 Sam. 13:22

34:7
ªDeut. 22:20–
30; Josh. 7:15;
Judg. 20:6
ᵇDeut. 23:17;
2 Sam. 13:12

34:12 ªEx. 22:16,
17; Deut. 22:29

34:13 ªGen. 31:7;
Ex. 8:29

34:14 ªEx. 12:48
ᵇJosh. 5:2–9

33:14 ¹*can stand*   33:17 ¹*shelters*   ²Lit. *Booths*   33:18 ¹Or *to Shalem, a city of*
33:19 ¹Lit. *the field*   33:20 ¹Lit. *God, the God of Israel*   34:3 ¹Lit. *clung to*
²*tenderly*   34:5 ¹*kept silent*   34:12 ¹*bride-price*

consent to you: If you will become as we *are,* if every male of you is circumcised, ¹⁶then we will give our daughters to you, and we will take your daughters to us; and we will dwell with you, and we will become one people. ¹⁷But if you will not heed us and be circumcised, then we will take our daughter and be gone."

¹⁸And their words pleased Hamor and Shechem, Hamor's son. ¹⁹So the young man did not delay to do the thing, because he delighted in Jacob's daughter. He *was* ᵃmore honorable than all the household of his father.

²⁰And Hamor and Shechem his son came to the ᵃgate of their city, and spoke with the men of their city, saying: ²¹"These men *are* at peace with us. Therefore let them dwell in the land and trade in it. For indeed the land *is* large enough for them. Let us take their daughters to us as wives, and let us give them our daughters. ²²Only on this *condition* will the men consent to dwell with us, to be one people: if every male among us is circumcised as they *are* circumcised. ²³*Will* not their livestock, their property, and every animal of theirs *be* ours? Only let us consent to them, and they will dwell with us." ²⁴And all who went out of the gate of his city heeded Hamor and Shechem his son; every male was circumcised, all who ᵃwent out of the gate of his city.

²⁵Now it came to pass on the third day, when they were in pain, that two of the sons of Jacob, ᵃSimeon and Levi, Dinah's brothers, each took his sword and came boldly upon the city and killed all the males. ²⁶And they ᵃkilled Hamor and Shechem his son with the edge of the sword, and took Dinah from Shechem's house, and went out. ²⁷The sons of Jacob came upon the slain, and plundered the city, because their sister had been defiled. ²⁸They took their sheep, their oxen, and their donkeys, what *was* in the city and what *was* in the field, ²⁹and all their wealth. All their little ones and their wives they took captive; and they plundered even all that *was* in the houses.

³⁰Then Jacob said to Simeon and Levi, ᵃ"You have ᵇtroubled me ᶜby making me obnoxious among the inhabitants of the land, among the Canaanites and the Perizzites; ᵈand since I *am* few in number, they will gather themselves together against me and kill me. I shall be destroyed, my household and I."

³¹But they said, "Should he treat our sister like a harlot?"

JACOB'S RETURN TO BETHEL

35 Then God said to Jacob, "Arise, go up to ᵃBethel and dwell there; and make an altar there to God, ᵇwho appeared to you ᶜwhen you fled from the face of Esau your brother."

²And Jacob said to his ᵃhousehold and to all who *were* with him, "Put away ᵇthe foreign gods that *are* among you, ᶜpurify yourselves, and change your garments. ³Then let us arise and go up to Bethel; and I will make an altar there to God, ᵃwho answered me in the day of my distress ᵇand has been with me in the way which I have gone." ⁴So they gave Jacob all the foreign ¹gods which *were* in their hands, and the ᵃearrings which *were* in their ears; and Jacob hid them under ᵇthe terebinth tree which *was* by Shechem.

34:19 ᵃ1 Chr. 4:9

34:20
ᵃGen. 19:1;
23:10; Ruth 4:1,
11; 2 Sam. 15:2

34:24
ᵃGen. 23:10, 18

34:25
ᵃGen. 29:33, 34;
42:24; 49:5–7

34:26
ᵃGen. 49:5, 6

34:30
ᵃGen. 49:6
ᵇJosh. 7:25
ᶜEx. 5:21;
1 Sam. 13:4;
2 Sam. 10:6
ᵈGen. 46:26, 27;
Deut. 4:27;
1 Chr. 16:19;
Ps. 105:12

35:1
ᵃGen. 28:19;
31:13 ᵇGen. 28:13
ᶜGen. 27:43

35:2
ᵃGen. 18:19;
Josh. 24:15
ᵇGen. 31:19, 30,
34; Josh. 24:2,
14, 23 ᶜEx. 19:10,
14; Lev. 13:6

35:3
ᵃGen. 32:7, 24;
Ps. 107:6
ᵇGen. 28:15, 20;
31:3, 42

35:4 ᵃHos. 2:13
ᵇJosh. 24:26;
Judg. 9:6

5And they journeyed, and ªthe terror of God was upon the cities that *were* all around them, and they did not pursue the sons of Jacob. 6So Jacob came to ªLuz (that *is,* Bethel), which *is* in the land of Canaan, he and all the people who *were* with him. 7And he ªbuilt an altar there and called the place 1El Bethel, because bthere God appeared to him when he fled from the face of his brother.

8Now ªDeborah, Rebekah's nurse, died, and she was buried below Bethel under the terebinth tree. So the name of it was called 1Allon Bachuth.

9Then ªGod appeared to Jacob again, when he came from Padan Aram, and bblessed him. 10And God said to him, "Your name *is* Jacob; ªyour name shall not be called Jacob anymore, bbut Israel shall be your name." So He called his name Israel. 11Also God said to him: ª"I *am* God Almighty. bBe fruitful and multiply; ca nation and a company of nations shall proceed from you, and kings shall come from your body. 12The ªland which I gave Abraham and Isaac I give to you; and to your descendants after you I give this land." 13Then God ªwent1 up from him in the place where He talked with him. 14So Jacob ªset up a pillar in the place where He talked with him, a pillar of stone; and he poured a drink offering on it, and he poured oil on it. 15And Jacob called the name of the place where God spoke with him, ªBethel.

DEATH OF RACHEL

16Then they journeyed from Bethel. And when there was but a little distance to go to Ephrath, Rachel labored *in childbirth,* and she had hard labor. 17Now it came to pass, when she was in hard labor, that the midwife said to her, "Do not fear; ªyou will have this son also." 18And so it was, as her soul was departing (for she died), that she called his name 1Ben-Oni; but his father called him 2Benjamin. 19So ªRachel died and was buried on the way to bEphrath (that *is,* Bethlehem). 20And Jacob set a pillar on her grave, which *is* the pillar of Rachel's grave ªto this day.

21Then Israel journeyed and pitched his tent beyond ªthe tower of Eder. 22And it happened, when Israel dwelt in that land, that Reuben went and ªlay with Bilhah his father's concubine; and Israel heard *about it.*

JACOB'S TWELVE SONS

Now the sons of Jacob were twelve: 23the sons of Leah *were* ªReuben, Jacob's firstborn, and Simeon, Levi, Judah, Issachar, and Zebulun; 24the sons of Rachel *were* Joseph and Benjamin; 25the sons of Bilhah, Rachel's maidservant, *were* Dan and Naphtali; 26and the sons of Zilpah, Leah's maidservant, *were* Gad and Asher. These *were* the sons of Jacob who were born to him in Padan Aram.

DEATH OF ISAAC

27Then Jacob came to his father Isaac at ªMamre, or bKirjath Arba1 (that *is,* Hebron), where Abraham and Isaac had dwelt. 28Now the days of Isaac were one hundred and eighty years. 29So Isaac breathed his last and died, and ªwas 1gathered

35:5 ªEx. 15:16; 23:27; [Deut. 2:25; 11:25]; Josh. 2:9; 1 Sam. 14:15

35:6 ªGen. 28:19, 22; 48:3

35:7 ªGen. 33:20; 35:3; Eccl. 5:4 bGen. 28:13

35:8 ªGen. 24:59

35:9 ªJosh. 5:13; Dan. 10:5 bGen. 32:29; Hos. 12:4

35:10 ªGen. 17:5 bGen. 32:28

35:11 ªGen. 17:1; 28:3; 48:3, 4; Ex. 6:3 bGen. 9:1, 7 cGen. 17:5, 6, 16; 28:3; 48:4

35:12 ªGen. 12:7; 13:15; 26:3, 4; 28:13; 48:4; Ex. 32:13

35:13 ªGen. 17:22; 18:33

35:14 ªGen. 28:18, 19; 31:45

35:15 ªGen. 28:19

35:17 ªGen. 30:24; 1 Sam. 4:20

35:19 ªGen. 48:7 bRuth 1:2; 4:11; Mic. 5:2; Matt. 2:6

35:20 ª1 Sam. 10:2

35:21 ªMic. 4:8

35:22 ªGen. 49:4; 1 Chr. 5:1

35:23 ªGen. 29:31–35; 30:18–20; 46:8; Ex. 1:1–4

35:27 ªGen. 13:18; 18:1; 23:19 bJosh. 14:15

35:29 ªGen. 15:15; 25:8; 49:33

35:7 1Lit. *God of the House of God*   35:8 1Lit. *Terebinth of Weeping* 35:13 1*departed*   35:18 1Lit. *Son of My Sorrow*   2Lit. *Son of the Right Hand* 35:27 1Lit. *Town* or *City of Arba*   35:29 1Joined his ancestors

to his people, *being* old and full of days. And [b]his sons Esau and Jacob buried him.

THE FAMILY OF ESAU

(1 Chr. 1:35–42)

36 Now this *is* the genealogy of Esau, [a]who is Edom. [2a]Esau took his wives from the daughters of Canaan: Adah the daughter of Elon the [b]Hittite; [c]Aholibamah[1] the daughter of Anah, the daughter of Zibeon the Hivite; [3]and [a]Basemath, Ishmael's daughter, sister of Nebajoth. [4]Now [a]Adah bore Eliphaz to Esau, and Basemath bore Reuel. [5]And [1]Aholibamah bore Jeush, Jaalam, and Korah. These *were* the sons of Esau who were born to him in the land of Canaan.

[6]Then Esau took his wives, his sons, his daughters, and all the persons of his household, his cattle and all his animals, and all his goods which he had gained in the land of Canaan, and went to a country away from the presence of his brother Jacob. [7a]For their possessions were too great for them to dwell together, and [b]the land where they were strangers could not support them because of their livestock. [8]So Esau dwelt in [a]Mount Seir. [b]Esau *is* Edom.

[9]And this *is* the genealogy of Esau the father of the Edomites in Mount Seir. [10]These *were* the names of Esau's sons: [a]Eliphaz the son of Adah the wife of Esau, and Reuel the son of Basemath the wife of Esau. [11]And the sons of Eliphaz were Teman, Omar, [1]Zepho, Gatam, and Kenaz.

[12]Now Timna was the concubine of Eliphaz, Esau's son, and she bore [a]Amalek to Eliphaz. These *were* the sons of Adah, Esau's wife.

[13]These *were* the sons of Reuel: Nahath, Zerah, Shammah, and Mizzah. These were the sons of Basemath, Esau's wife.

[14]These were the sons of [1]Aholibamah, Esau's wife, the daughter of Anah, the daughter of Zibeon. And she bore to Esau: Jeush, Jaalam, and Korah.

THE CHIEFS OF EDOM

[15]These *were* the chiefs of the sons of Esau. The sons of Eliphaz, the firstborn *son* of Esau, were Chief Teman, Chief Omar, Chief Zepho, Chief Kenaz, [16][1]Chief Korah, Chief Gatam, *and* Chief Amalek. These *were* the chiefs of Eliphaz in the land of Edom. They *were* the sons of Adah.

[17]These *were* the sons of Reuel, Esau's son: Chief Nahath, Chief Zerah, Chief Shammah, and Chief Mizzah. These *were* the chiefs of Reuel in the land of Edom. These *were* the sons of Basemath, Esau's wife.

[18]And these *were* the sons of [1]Aholibamah, Esau's wife: Chief Jeush, Chief Jaalam, and Chief Korah. These *were* the chiefs *who descended* from Aholibamah, Esau's wife, the daughter of Anah. [19]These *were* the sons of Esau, who is Edom, and these *were* their chiefs.

THE SONS OF SEIR

[20a]These *were* the sons of Seir [b]the Horite who inhabited the land: Lotan, Shobal, Zibeon, Anah, [21]Dishon, Ezer, and

---

35:29
[b]Gen. 25:9;
49:31

36:1 [a]Gen. 25:30

36:2
[a]Gen. 26:34;
28:9 [b]2 Kin. 7:6
[c]Gen. 36:25

36:3 [a]Gen. 28:9

36:4 [a]1 Chr. 1:35

36:7 [a]Gen. 13:6,
11 [b]Gen. 17:8;
28:4; Heb. 11:9

36:8 [a]Gen. 32:3;
Deut. 2:5;
Josh. 24:4
[b]Gen. 36:1, 19

36:10
[a]1 Chr. 1:35

36:12
[a]Ex. 17:8–16;
Num. 24:20;
Deut. 25:17–19;
1 Sam. 15:2, 3

36:20
[a]1 Chr. 1:38–42
[b]Gen. 14:6;
Deut. 2:12, 22

36:2 [1]Or *Oholibamah*   36:5 [1]Or *Oholibamah*   36:11 [1]*Zephi,* 1 Chr. 1:36
36:14 [1]Or *Oholibamah*   36:16 [1]Sam. omits *Chief Korah*   36:18 [1]Or *Oholibamah*

Dishan. These *were* the chiefs of the Horites, the sons of Seir, in the land of Edom.

22And the sons of Lotan were Hori and [1]Hemam. Lotan's sister *was* Timna.

23These *were* the sons of Shobal: [1]Alvan, Manahath, Ebal, [2]Shepho, and Onam.

24These *were* the sons of Zibeon: both Ajah and Anah. This *was the* Anah who found the [1]water in the wilderness as he pastured [a]the donkeys of his father Zibeon. 25These *were* the children of Anah: Dishon and [1]Aholibamah the daughter of Anah.

26These *were* the sons of [1]Dishon: [2]Hemdan, Eshban, Ithran, and Cheran. 27These *were* the sons of Ezer: Bilhan, Zaavan, and [1]Akan. 28These *were* the sons of Dishan: [a]Uz and Aran.

29These *were* the chiefs of the Horites: Chief Lotan, Chief Shobal, Chief Zibeon, Chief Anah, 30Chief Dishon, Chief Ezer, and Chief Dishan. These *were* the chiefs of the Horites, according to their chiefs in the land of Seir.

THE KINGS OF EDOM

31[a]Now these *were* the kings who reigned in the land of Edom before any king reigned over the children of Israel: 32Bela the son of Beor reigned in Edom, and the name of his city *was* Dinhabah. 33And when Bela died, Jobab the son of Zerah of Bozrah reigned in his place. 34When Jobab died, Husham of the land of the Temanites reigned in his place. 35And when Husham died, Hadad the son of Bedad, who attacked Midian in the field of Moab, reigned in his place. And the name of his city *was* Avith. 36When Hadad died, Samlah of Masrekah reigned in his place. 37And when Samlah died, Saul of [a]Rehoboth-*by*-the-River reigned in his place. 38When Saul died, Baal-Hanan the son of Achbor reigned in his place. 39And when Baal-Hanan the son of Achbor died, [1]Hadar reigned in his place; and the name of his city *was* [2]Pau. His wife's name *was* Mehetabel, the daughter of Matred, the daughter of Mezahab.

THE CHIEFS OF ESAU

40And these *were* the names of the chiefs of Esau, according to their families and their places, by their names: Chief Timnah, Chief [1]Alvah, Chief Jetheth, 41Chief [1]Aholibamah, Chief Elah, Chief Pinon, 42Chief Kenaz, Chief Teman, Chief Mibzar, 43Chief Magdiel, and Chief Iram. These *were* the chiefs of Edom, according to their dwelling places in the land of their possession. Esau *was* the father of [1]the Edomites.

JOSEPH DREAMS OF GREATNESS

37 Now Jacob dwelt in the land [a]where his father was a [1]stranger, in the land of Canaan. 2This *is* the history of Jacob.

36:24 [a]Lev. 19:19

36:28 [a]Job 1:1

36:31 [a]Gen. 17:6, 16; 35:11; 1 Chr. 1:43

36:37 [a]Gen. 10:11

37:1 [a]Gen. 17:8; 23:4; 28:4; 36:7; Heb. 11:9

36:22 [1]Homam, 1 Chr. 1:39   36:23 [1]Alian, 1 Chr. 1:40   [2]Shephi, 1 Chr. 1:40
36:24 [1]So with MT, Vg. (*hot springs*); LXX *Jamin*; Tg. *mighty men*; Talmud *mules*   36:25 [1]Or *Oholibamah*   36:26 [1]Heb. *Dishan*   [2]*Hamran*, 1 Chr. 1:41
36:27 [1]*Jaakan*, 1 Chr. 1:42   36:39 [1]Sam., Syr. *Hadad* and 1 Chr. 1:50   [2]*Pai*,
1 Chr. 1:50   36:40 [1]*Aliah*, 1 Chr. 1:51   36:41 [1]Or *Oholibamah*   36:43 [1]Heb.
Edom   37:1 [1]*sojourner*, temporary resident

Joseph, *being* seventeen years old, was feeding the flock with his brothers. And the lad *was* with the sons of Bilhah and the sons of Zilpah, his father's wives; and Joseph brought [a]a bad report of them to his father.

3Now Israel loved Joseph more than all his children, because he *was* [a]the son of his old age. Also he [b]made him a tunic of *many* colors. 4But when his brothers saw that their father loved him more than all his brothers, they [a]hated him and could not speak peaceably to him.

5Now Joseph had a dream, and he told *it* to his brothers; and they hated him even more. 6So he said to them, "Please hear this dream which I have dreamed: 7[a]There we were, binding sheaves in the field. Then behold, my sheaf arose and also stood upright; and indeed your sheaves stood all around and bowed down to my sheaf."

8And his brothers said to him, "Shall you indeed reign over us? Or shall you indeed have dominion over us?" So they hated him even more for his dreams and for his words.

9Then he dreamed still another dream and told it to his brothers, and said, "Look, I have dreamed another dream. And this time, [a]the sun, the moon, and the eleven stars bowed down to me."

10So he told *it* to his father and his brothers; and his father rebuked him and said to him, "What *is* this dream that you have dreamed? Shall your mother and I and [a]your brothers indeed come to bow down to the earth before you?" 11And [a]his brothers envied him, but his father [b]kept the matter *in mind*.

JOSEPH SOLD BY HIS BROTHERS

12Then his brothers went to feed their father's flock in [a]Shechem. 13And Israel said to Joseph, "Are not your brothers feeding *the flock* in Shechem? Come, I will send you to them."

So he said to him, "Here I am."

14Then he said to him, "Please go and see if it is well with your brothers and well with the flocks, and bring back word to me." So he sent him out of the Valley of [a]Hebron, and he went to Shechem.

15Now a certain man found him, and there he was, wandering in the field. And the man asked him, saying, "What are you seeking?"

16So he said, "I am seeking my brothers. [a]Please tell me where they are feeding *their flocks.*"

17And the man said, "They have departed from here, for I heard them say, 'Let us go to Dothan.'" So Joseph went after his brothers and found them in [a]Dothan.

18Now when they saw him afar off, even before he came near them, [a]they conspired against him to kill him. 19Then they said to one another, "Look, this ¹dreamer is coming! 20[a]Come therefore, let us now kill him and cast him into some pit; and we shall say, 'Some wild beast has devoured him.' We shall see what will become of his dreams!"

21But [a]Reuben heard *it,* and he delivered him out of their hands, and said, "Let us not kill him." 22And Reuben said to them, "Shed no blood, *but* cast him into this pit which *is* in the wilderness, and do not lay a hand on him"—that he might

---

37:2 [a]Gen. 35:25, 26; 1 Sam. 2:22–24

37:3 [a]Gen. 44:20 [b]Gen. 37:23, 32; Judg. 5:30; 1 Sam. 2:19

37:4 [a]Gen. 27:41; 49:23; 1 Sam. 17:28; John 15:18–20

37:7 [a]Gen. 42:6, 9; 43:26; 44:14

37:9 [a]Gen. 46:29; 47:25

37:10 [a]Gen. 27:29

37:11 [a]Matt. 27:17, 18; Acts 7:9 [b]Dan. 7:28; Luke 2:19, 51

37:12 [a]Gen. 33:18–20

37:14 [a]Gen. 13:18; 23:2, 19; 35:27; Josh. 14:14, 15; Judg. 1:10

37:16 [a]Song 1:7

37:17 [a]2 Kin. 6:13

37:18 [a]1 Sam. 19:1; Ps. 31:13; 37:12, 32; Matt. 21:38; 26:3, 4; 27:1; Mark 14:1; John 11:53; Acts 23:12

37:20 [a]Gen. 37:22; Prov. 1:11

37:21 [a]Gen. 42:22

37:19 ¹Lit. *master of dreams*

deliver him out of their hands, and bring him back to his father.

²³So it came to pass, when Joseph had come to his brothers, that they ᵃstripped Joseph *of* his tunic, the tunic of *many* colors that *was* on him. ²⁴Then they took him and cast him into a pit. And the pit *was* empty; *there was* no water in it.

²⁵ᵃAnd they sat down to eat a meal. Then they lifted their eyes and looked, and there was a company of ᵇIshmaelites, coming from Gilead with their camels, bearing spices, ᶜbalm, and myrrh, on their way to carry *them* down to Egypt. ²⁶So Judah said to his brothers, "What profit *is there* if we kill our brother and ᵃconceal his blood? ²⁷Come and let us sell him to the Ishmaelites, and ᵃlet not our hand be upon him, for he *is* ᵇour brother *and* ᶜour flesh." And his brothers listened. ²⁸Then ᵃMidianite traders passed by; so *the brothers* pulled Joseph up and lifted him out of the pit, ᵇand sold him to the Ishmaelites for ᶜtwenty *shekels* of silver. And they took Joseph to Egypt.

²⁹Then Reuben returned to the pit, and indeed Joseph *was* not in the pit; and he ᵃtore his clothes. ³⁰And he returned to his brothers and said, "The lad ᵃ*is* no *more*; and I, where shall I go?"

³¹So they took ᵃJoseph's tunic, killed a kid of the goats, and dipped the tunic in the blood. ³²Then they sent the tunic of *many* colors, and they brought *it* to their father and said, "We have found this. Do you know whether it *is* your son's tunic or not?"

³³And he recognized it and said, "*It is* my son's tunic. A ᵃwild beast has devoured him. Without doubt Joseph is torn to pieces." ³⁴Then Jacob ᵃtore his clothes, put sackcloth on his waist, and ᵇmourned for his son many days. ³⁵And all his sons and all his daughters ᵃarose to comfort him; but he refused to be comforted, and he said, "For ᵇI shall go down into the grave to my son in mourning." Thus his father wept for him.

³⁶Now ᵃthe ¹Midianites had sold him in Egypt to Potiphar, an officer of Pharaoh *and* captain of the guard.

JUDAH AND TAMAR

38 It came to pass at that time that Judah departed from his brothers, and ᵃvisited a certain Adullamite whose name *was* Hirah. ²And Judah ᵃsaw there a daughter of a certain Canaanite whose name *was* ᵇShua, and he married her and went in to her. ³So she conceived and bore a son, and he called his name ᵃEr. ⁴She conceived again and bore a son, and she called his name ᵃOnan. ⁵And she conceived yet again and bore a son, and called his name ᵃShelah. He was at Chezib when she bore him.

⁶Then Judah ᵃtook a wife for Er his firstborn, and her name *was* ᵇTamar. ⁷But ᵃEr, Judah's firstborn, was wicked in the sight of the LORD, ᵇand the LORD killed him. ⁸And Judah said to Onan, "Go in to ᵃyour brother's wife and marry her, and raise up an heir to your brother." ⁹But Onan knew that the heir would not be ᵃhis; and it came to pass, when he went in to his brother's wife, that he emitted on the ground, lest he should give an heir to his brother. ¹⁰And the thing which he did ¹displeased the LORD; therefore He killed ᵃhim also.

37:23
ᵃMatt. 27:28

37:25
ᵃProv. 30:20
ᵇGen. 16:11, 12; 37:28, 36; 39:1
ᶜJer. 8:22

37:26
ᵃGen. 37:20

37:27
ᵃ1 Sam. 18:17
ᵇGen. 42:21
ᶜGen. 29:14

37:28
ᵃGen. 37:25; Judg. 6:1–3; 8:22, 24
ᵇGen. 45:4, 5; Ps. 105:17; Acts 7:9
ᶜMatt. 27:9

37:29
ᵃGen. 37:34; 44:13; Job 1:20

37:30
ᵃGen. 42:13, 36

37:31
ᵃGen. 37:3, 23

37:33
ᵃGen. 37:20

37:34
ᵃGen. 37:29; 2 Sam. 3:31
ᵇGen. 50:10

37:35
ᵃ2 Sam. 12:17
ᵇGen. 25:8; 35:29; 42:38; 44:29, 31

37:36 ᵃGen. 39:1

38:1 ᵃ2 Kin. 4:8

38:2 ᵃGen. 34:2
ᵇ1 Chr. 2:3

38:3
ᵃGen. 46:12; Num. 26:19

38:4
ᵃGen. 46:12; Num. 26:19

38:5
ᵃNum. 26:20

38:6 ᵃGen. 21:21
ᵇRuth 4:12

38:7
ᵃGen. 46:12; Num. 26:19
ᵇ1 Chr. 2:3

38:8
ᵃDeut. 25:5, 6; Matt. 22:24

38:9
ᵃDeut. 25:6

38:10
ᵃGen. 46:12; Num. 26:19

37:36 ¹MT *Medanites*   38:10 ¹Lit. *was evil in the eyes of*

¹¹Then Judah said to Tamar his daughter-in-law, ᵃ"Remain a widow in your father's house till my son Shelah is grown." For he said, "Lest he also die like his brothers." And Tamar went and dwelt ᵇin her father's house.

¹²Now in the process of time the daughter of Shua, Judah's wife, died; and Judah ᵃwas comforted, and went up to his sheepshearers at Timnah, he and his friend Hirah the Adullamite. ¹³And it was told Tamar, saying, "Look, your father-in-law is going up ᵃto Timnah to shear his sheep." ¹⁴So she took off her widow's garments, covered *herself* with a veil and wrapped herself, and ᵃsat in an open place which *was* on the way to Timnah; for she saw ᵇthat Shelah was grown, and she was not given to him as a wife. ¹⁵When Judah saw her, he thought she *was* a harlot, because she had covered her face. ¹⁶Then he turned to her by the way, and said, "Please let me come in to you"; for he did not know that she *was* his daughter-in-law.

So she said, "What will you give me, that you may come in to me?"

¹⁷And he said, ᵃ"I will send a young goat from the flock."

So she said, ᵇ"Will you give *me* a pledge till you send *it*?"

¹⁸Then he said, "What pledge shall I give you?"

So she said, ᵃ"Your signet and cord, and your staff that *is* in your hand." Then he gave *them* to her, and went in to her, and she conceived by him. ¹⁹So she arose and went away, and ᵃlaid aside her veil and put on the garments of her widowhood.

²⁰And Judah sent the young goat by the hand of his friend the Adullamite, to receive *his* pledge from the woman's hand, but he did not find her. ²¹Then he asked the men of that place, saying, "Where is the harlot who *was* ¹openly by the roadside?"

And they said, "There was no harlot in this *place*."

²²So he returned to Judah and said, "I cannot find her. Also, the men of the place said there was no harlot in this *place*."

²³Then Judah said, "Let her take *them* for herself, lest we be shamed; for I sent this young goat and you have not found her."

²⁴And it came to pass, about three months after, that Judah was told, saying, "Tamar your daughter-in-law has ᵃplayed the harlot; furthermore she is ¹with child by harlotry."

So Judah said, "Bring her out ᵇand let her be burned!"

²⁵When she *was* brought out, she sent to her father-in-law, saying, "By the man to whom these belong, I *am* with child." And she said, ᵃ"Please determine whose these *are*—the signet and cord, and staff."

²⁶So Judah ᵃacknowledged *them* and said, ᵇ"She has been more righteous than I, because ᶜI did not give her to Shelah my son." And he ᵈnever knew her again.

²⁷Now it came to pass, at the time for giving birth, that behold, twins *were* in her womb. ²⁸And so it was, when she was giving birth, that *the one* put out *his* hand; and the midwife took a scarlet *thread* and bound it on his hand, saying, "This one came out first." ²⁹Then it happened, as he drew back his hand, that his brother came out unexpectedly; and she said, "How did you break through? *This* breach *be* upon

38:11
ᵃRuth 1:12, 13
ᵇLev. 22:13

38:12
ᵃ2 Sam. 13:39

38:13
ᵃJosh. 15:10, 57;
Judg. 14:1

38:14 ᵃProv. 7:12
ᵇGen. 38:11, 26

38:17
ᵃJudg. 15:1;
Ezek. 16:33
ᵇGen. 38:20

38:18
ᵃGen. 38:25;
41:42

38:19
ᵃGen. 38:14

38:24
ᵃJudg. 19:2
ᵇLev. 20:14; 21:9;
Deut. 22:21

38:25
ᵃGen. 37:32;
38:18

38:26
ᵃGen. 37:33
ᵇ1 Sam. 24:17
ᶜGen. 38:14
ᵈJob 34:31, 32

you!" Therefore his name was called ªPerez.¹ ³⁰Afterward his brother came out who had the scarlet *thread* on his hand. And his name was called ªZerah.

JOSEPH A SLAVE IN EGYPT

39 Now Joseph had been taken ªdown to Egypt. And ᵇPotiphar, an officer of Pharaoh, captain of the guard, an Egyptian, ᶜbought him from the Ishmaelites who had taken him down there. ²ªThe LORD was with Joseph, and he was a successful man; and he was in the house of his master the Egyptian. ³And his master saw that the LORD *was* with him and that the LORD ªmade all he did ¹to prosper in his hand. ⁴So Joseph ªfound favor in his sight, and served him. Then he made him ᵇoverseer of his house, and all *that* he had he put ¹under his authority. ⁵So it was, from the time *that* he had made him overseer of his house and all that he had, that ªthe LORD blessed the Egyptian's house for Joseph's sake; and the blessing of the LORD was on all that he had in the house and in the field. ⁶Thus he left all that he had in Joseph's ¹hand, and he did not know what he had except for the ²bread which he ate.

Now Joseph ªwas handsome in form and appearance.

⁷And it came to pass after these things that his master's wife ¹cast longing eyes on Joseph, and she said, ª"Lie with me."

⁸But he refused and said to his master's wife, "Look, my master does not know what *is* with me in the house, and he has committed all that he has to my hand. ⁹*There is* no one greater in this house than I, nor has he kept back anything from me but you, because you *are* his wife. ªHow then can I do this great wickedness, and ᵇsin against God?"

¹⁰So it was, as she spoke to Joseph day by day, that he ªdid not heed her, to lie with her *or* to be with her.

¹¹But it happened about this time, when Joseph went into the house to do his work, and none of the men of the house *was* inside, ¹²that she ªcaught him by his garment, saying, "Lie with me." But he left his garment in her hand, and fled and ran outside. ¹³And so it was, when she saw that he had left his garment in her hand and fled outside, ¹⁴that she called to the men of her house and spoke to them, saying, "See, he has brought in to us a ªHebrew to ¹mock us. He came in to me to lie with me, and I cried out with a loud voice. ¹⁵And it happened, when he heard that I lifted my voice and cried out, that he left his garment with me, and fled and went outside."

¹⁶So she kept his garment with her until his master came home. ¹⁷Then she ªspoke to him with words like these, saying, "The Hebrew servant whom you brought to us came in to me to mock me; ¹⁸so it happened, as I lifted my voice and cried out, that he left his garment with me and fled outside."

¹⁹So it was, when his master heard the words which his wife spoke to him, saying, "Your servant did to me after this manner," that his ªanger was aroused. ²⁰Then Joseph's master took him and ªput him into the ᵇprison, a place where the king's prisoners *were* confined. And he was there in the prison. ²¹But the LORD was with Joseph and showed him mercy,

38:29
ªGen. 46:12;
Num. 26:20;
Ruth 4:12;
1 Chr. 2:4;
Matt. 1:3

38:30
ªGen. 46:12;
1 Chr. 2:4;
Matt. 1:3

39:1 ªGen. 12:10;
43:15
ᵇGen. 37:36;
Ps. 105:17
ᶜGen. 37:28;
45:4

39:2
ªGen. 26:24,
28; 28:15; 35:3;
39:3, 21, 23;
1 Sam. 16:18;
18:14, 28;
Acts 7:9

39:3 ªPs. 1:3

39:4 ªGen. 18:3;
19:19; 39:21
ᵇGen. 24:2, 10;
39:8, 22; 41:40

39:5
ªGen. 18:26;
30:27;
2 Sam. 6:11

39:6
ªGen. 29:17;
1 Sam. 16:12

39:7
ª2 Sam. 13:11

39:9
ªLev. 20:10;
Prov. 6:29, 32
ᵇGen. 20:6;
42:18;
2 Sam. 12:13;
Ps. 51:4

39:10 ªProv. 1:10

39:12 ªProv. 7:13

39:14
ªGen. 14:13;
41:12

39:17 ªEx. 23:1;
Ps. 120:3;
Prov. 26:28

39:19
ªProv. 6:34, 35

39:20
ªPs. 105:18;
[1 Pet. 2:19]
ᵇGen. 40:3, 15;
41:14

38:29 ¹Lit. *Breach* or *Breakthrough* **39:3** ¹*to be a success* **39:4** ¹Lit. *in his hand* **39:6** ¹*Care* ²*Food* **39:7** ¹Lit. *lifted up her eyes toward* **39:14** ¹*laugh at*

and He [a]gave[1] him favor in the sight of the keeper of the prison. [22]And the keeper of the prison [a]committed to Joseph's hand all the prisoners who *were* in the prison; whatever they did there, it was his doing. [23]The keeper of the prison did not look into anything *that was* under [1]Joseph's authority, because [a]the LORD was with him; and whatever he did, the LORD made *it* prosper.

THE PRISONERS' DREAMS

40 It came to pass after these things *that* the [a]butler and the baker of the king of Egypt offended their lord, the king of Egypt. [2]And Pharaoh was [a]angry with his two officers, the chief butler and the chief baker. [3][a]So he put them in custody in the house of the captain of the guard, in the prison, the place where Joseph *was* confined. [4]And the captain of the guard charged Joseph with them, and he served them; so they were in custody for a while.

[5]Then the butler and the baker of the king of Egypt, who *were* confined in the prison, [a]had a dream, both of them, each man's dream in one night *and* each man's dream with its *own* interpretation. [6]And Joseph came in to them in the morning and looked at them, and saw that they *were* [1]sad. [7]So he asked Pharaoh's officers who *were* with him in the custody of his lord's house, saying, [a]"Why do you look *so* sad today?"

[8]And they said to him, [a]"We each have had a dream, and *there is* no interpreter of it."

So Joseph said to them, [b]"Do not interpretations belong to God? Tell *them* to me, please."

[9]Then the chief butler told his dream to Joseph, and said to him, "Behold, in my dream a vine *was* before me, [10]and in the vine *were* three branches; it *was* as though it budded, its blossoms shot forth, and its clusters brought forth ripe grapes. [11]Then Pharaoh's cup *was* in my hand; and I took the grapes and pressed them into Pharaoh's cup, and placed the cup in Pharaoh's hand."

[12]And Joseph said to him, [a]"This *is* the interpretation of it: The three branches [b]*are* three days. [13]Now within three days Pharaoh will [a]lift up your head and restore you to your [1]place, and you will put Pharaoh's cup in his hand according to the former manner, when you were his butler. [14]But [a]remember me when it is well with you, and [b]please show kindness to me; make mention of me to Pharaoh, and get me out of this house. [15]For indeed I was [a]stolen away from the land of the Hebrews; [b]and also I have done nothing here that they should put me into the dungeon."

[16]When the chief baker saw that the interpretation was good, he said to Joseph, "I also *was* in my dream, and there *were* three [1]white baskets on my head. [17]In the uppermost basket *were* all kinds of baked goods for Pharaoh, and the birds ate them out of the basket on my head."

[18]So Joseph answered and said, [a]"This *is* the interpretation of it: The three baskets *are* three days. [19][a]Within three days Pharaoh will lift [1]off your head from you and [b]hang you on a tree; and the birds will eat your flesh from you."

39:21
[a]Gen. 39:2;
Ex. 3:21;
Ps. 105:19;
[Prov. 16:7];
Dan. 1:9;
Acts 7:9, 10

39:22
[a]Gen. 39:4;
40:3, 4

39:23
[a]Gen. 39:2, 3

40:1
[a]Gen. 40:11, 13;
Neh. 1:11

40:2 [a]Prov. 16:14

40:3 [a]Gen. 39:1,
20, 23; 41:10

40:5 [a]Gen. 37:5;
41:1

40:7 [a]Neh. 2:2

40:8 [a]Gen. 41:15
[b][Gen. 41:16;
Dan. 2:11, 20–22,
27, 28, 47]

40:12
[a]Gen. 40:18;
41:12, 25;
Judg. 7:14;
Dan. 2:36; 4:18,
19 [b]Gen. 40:18;
42:17

40:13
[a]2 Kin. 25:27;
Ps. 3:3; Jer. 52:31

40:14
[a]1 Sam. 25:31;
Luke 23:42
[b]Gen. 24:49;
47:29;
Josh. 2:12;
1 Sam. 20:14,
15; 2 Sam. 9:1;
1 Kin. 2:7

40:15
[a]Gen. 37:26–28
[b]Gen. 39:20

40:18
[a]Gen. 40:12

40:19
[a]Gen. 40:13
[b]Deut. 21:22

39:21 [1]Caused him to be viewed with favor by   **39:23** [1]Lit. *his hand*
40:6 [1]*dejected*   **40:13** [1]*position*   **40:16** [1]Or *baskets of white bread*
40:19 [1]Lit. *up*

20Now it came to pass on the third day, *which was* Pharaoh's ªbirthday, that he ᵇmade a feast for all his servants; and he ᶜlifted up the head of the chief butler and of the chief baker among his servants. 21Then he ªrestored the chief butler to his butlership again, and ᵇhe placed the cup in Pharaoh's hand. 22But he ªhanged the chief baker, as Joseph had interpreted to them. 23Yet the chief butler did not remember Joseph, but ªforgot him.

PHARAOH'S DREAMS

41 Then it came to pass, at the end of two full years, that ªPharaoh had a dream; and behold, he stood by the river. 2Suddenly there came up out of the river seven cows, fine looking and fat; and they fed in the meadow. 3Then behold, seven other cows came up after them out of the river, ugly and gaunt, and stood by the *other* cows on the bank of the river. 4And the ugly and gaunt cows ate up the seven fine looking and fat cows. So Pharaoh awoke. 5He slept and dreamed a second time; and suddenly seven heads of grain came up on one stalk, plump and good. 6Then behold, seven thin heads, blighted by the ªeast wind, sprang up after them. 7And the seven thin heads devoured the seven plump and full heads. So Pharaoh awoke, and indeed, *it was* a dream. 8Now it came to pass in the morning ªthat his spirit was troubled, and he sent and called for all ᵇthe magicians of Egypt and all its ᶜwise men. And Pharaoh told them his dreams, but *there was* no one who could interpret them for Pharaoh.

9Then the ªchief butler spoke to Pharaoh, saying: "I remember my faults this day. 10When Pharaoh was ªangry with his servants, ᵇand put me in custody in the house of the captain of the guard, *both* me and the chief baker, 11ªwe each had a dream in one night, he and I. Each of us dreamed according to the interpretation of his *own* dream. 12Now there *was* a young ªHebrew man with us there, a ᵇservant of the captain of the guard. And we told him, and he ᶜinterpreted our dreams for us; to each man he interpreted according to his *own* dream. 13And it came to pass, just ªas he interpreted for us, so it happened. He restored me to my office, and he hanged him."

14ªThen Pharaoh sent and called Joseph, and they ᵇbrought him quickly ᶜout of the dungeon; and he shaved, ᵈchanged his clothing, and came to Pharaoh. 15And Pharaoh said to Joseph, "I have had a dream, and *there is* no one who can interpret it. ªBut I have heard it said of you *that* you can understand a dream, to interpret it."

16So Joseph answered Pharaoh, saying, ª"*It is* not in me; ᵇGod will give Pharaoh an answer of peace."

17Then Pharaoh said to Joseph: "Behold, ªin my dream I stood on the bank of the river. 18Suddenly seven cows came up out of the river, fine looking and fat; and they fed in the meadow. 19Then behold, seven other cows came up after them, poor and very ugly and gaunt, such ugliness as I have never seen in all the land of Egypt. 20And the gaunt and ugly cows ate up the first seven, the fat cows. 21When they had eaten them up, no one would have known that they had eaten them, for they *were* just as ugly as at the beginning. So I awoke. 22Also I saw in my dream, and suddenly seven

Cross-references

40:20
ªMatt. 14:6–10
ᵇMark 6:21
ᶜGen. 40:13, 19;
2 Kin. 25:27;
Jer. 52:31;
Matt. 25:19

40:21
ªGen. 40:13
ᵇNeh. 2:1

40:22
ªGen. 40:19;
Deut. 21:23;
Esth. 7:10

40:23
ªJob 19:14;
Ps. 31:12;
Eccl. 9:15,
16; Is. 49:15;
Amos 6:6

41:1 ªGen. 40:5;
Judg. 7:13

41:6 ªEx. 10:13;
Ezek. 17:10

41:8 ªDan. 2:1, 3;
4:5, 19 ᵇEx. 7:11,
22; Is. 29:14;
Dan. 1:20; 2:2;
4:7 ᶜMatt. 2:1

41:9 ªGen. 40:1,
14, 23

41:10
ªGen. 40:2, 3
ᵇGen. 39:20

41:11 ªGen. 40:5;
Judg. 7:15

41:12
ªGen. 39:14;
43:32
ᵇGen. 37:36
ᶜGen. 40:12

41:13
ªGen. 40:21, 22

41:14 ªPs. 105:20
ᵇDan. 2:25
ᶜ[1 Sam. 2:8]
ᵈ2 Kin. 25:27–29

41:15 ªGen. 41:8,
12; Dan. 5:16

41:16
ªDan. 2:30;
Acts 3:12;
[2 Cor. 3:5]
ᵇGen. 40:8;
41:25, 28, 32;
Deut. 29:29;
Dan. 2:22,
28, 47

41:17 ªGen. 41:1

¹heads came up on one stalk, full and good. ²³Then behold, seven heads, withered, thin, *and* blighted by the east wind, sprang up after them. ²⁴And the thin heads devoured the seven good heads. So ᵃI told *this* to the magicians, but *there was* no one who could explain *it* to me."

²⁵Then Joseph said to Pharaoh, "The dreams of Pharaoh *are* one; ᵃGod has shown Pharaoh what He *is* about to do: ²⁶The seven good cows *are* seven years, and the seven good ¹heads *are* seven years; the dreams *are* one. ²⁷And the seven thin and ugly cows which came up after them *are* seven years, and the seven empty heads blighted by the east wind are ᵃseven years of famine. ²⁸ᵃThis *is* the thing which I have spoken to Pharaoh. God has shown Pharaoh what He *is* about to do. ²⁹Indeed ᵃseven years of great plenty will come throughout all the land of Egypt; ³⁰but after them seven years of famine will ᵃarise, and all the plenty will be forgotten in the land of Egypt; and the famine ᵇwill deplete the land. ³¹So the plenty will not be known in the land because of the famine following, for it *will be* very severe. ³²And the dream was repeated to Pharaoh twice because the ᵃthing *is* established by God, and God will shortly bring it to pass.

³³"Now therefore, let Pharaoh select a discerning and wise man, and set him over the land of Egypt. ³⁴Let Pharaoh do *this,* and let him appoint ¹officers over the land, ᵃto collect one-fifth *of the produce* of the land of Egypt in the seven plentiful years. ³⁵And ᵃlet them gather all the food of those good years that are coming, and store up grain under the ¹authority of Pharaoh, and let them keep food in the cities. ³⁶Then that food shall be as a ¹reserve for the land for the seven years of famine which shall be in the land of Egypt, that the land ᵃmay not ²perish during the famine."

JOSEPH'S RISE TO POWER

³⁷So ᵃthe advice was good in the eyes of Pharaoh and in the eyes of all his servants. ³⁸And Pharaoh said to his servants, "Can we find *such a one* as this, a man ᵃin whom *is* the Spirit of God?"

³⁹Then Pharaoh said to Joseph, "Inasmuch as God has shown you all this, *there is* no one as discerning and wise as you. ⁴⁰ᵃYou shall be ¹over my house, and all my people shall be ruled according to your word; only in regard to the throne will I be greater than you." ⁴¹And Pharaoh said to Joseph, "See, I have ᵃset you over all the land of Egypt."

⁴²Then Pharaoh ᵃtook his signet ring off his hand and put it on Joseph's hand; and he ᵇclothed him in garments of fine linen ᶜand put a gold chain around his neck. ⁴³And he had him ride in the second ᵃchariot which he had; ᵇand they cried out before him, "Bow the knee!" So he set him ᶜover all the land of Egypt. ⁴⁴Pharaoh also said to Joseph, "I *am* Pharaoh, and without your consent no man may lift his hand or foot in all the land of Egypt." ⁴⁵And Pharaoh called Joseph's name ¹Zaphnath-Paaneah. And he gave him as a wife ᵃAsenath, the daughter of Poti-Pherah priest of On. So Joseph went out over *all* the land of Egypt.

Cross References

41:24 ᵃGen. 41:8; Ex. 7:11; Is. 8:19; Dan. 4:7

41:25 ᵃGen. 41:28, 32; Dan. 2:28, 29, 45; Rev. 4:1

41:27 ᵃ2 Kin. 8:1

41:28 ᵃ[Gen. 41:25, 32; Dan. 2:28]

41:29 ᵃGen. 41:47

41:30 ᵃGen. 41:54, 56 ᵇGen. 47:13; Ps. 105:16

41:32 ᵃGen. 41:25, 28; Num. 23:19; Is. 46:10, 11

41:34 ᵃ[Prov. 6:6–8]

41:35 ᵃGen. 41:48

41:36 ᵃGen. 47:15, 19

41:37 ᵃPs. 105:19; Acts 7:10

41:38 ᵃNum. 27:18; [Job 32:8; Prov. 2:6]; Dan. 4:8, 9, 18; 5:11, 14; 6:3

41:40 ᵃPs. 105:21; Acts 7:10

41:41 ᵃGen. 42:6; Ps. 105:21; Dan. 6:3; Acts 7:10

41:42 ᵃEsth. 3:10 ᵇEsth. 8:2, 15 ᶜDan. 5:7, 16, 29

41:43 ᵃGen. 46:29 ᵇEsth. 6:9 ᶜGen. 42:6

41:45 ᵃGen. 46:20

41:22 ¹Heads of grain   41:26 ¹Heads of grain   41:34 ¹*overseers*
41:35 ¹Lit. *hand*   41:36 ¹Lit. *supply*   ²*be cut off*   41:40 ¹In charge of
41:45 ¹Probably Egyptian for *God Speaks and He Lives*

46Joseph was thirty years old when he astood before Pharaoh king of Egypt. And Joseph went out from the presence of Pharaoh, and went throughout all the land of Egypt. 47Now in the seven plentiful years the ground brought forth 1abundantly. 48So he gathered up all the food of the seven years which were in the land of Egypt, and laid up the food in the cities; he laid up in every city the food of the fields which surrounded them. 49Joseph gathered very much grain, aas the sand of the sea, until he stopped counting, for *it was* immeasurable.

50aAnd to Joseph were born two sons before the years of famine came, whom Asenath, the daughter of Poti-Pherah priest of On, bore to him. 51Joseph called the name of the firstborn 1Manasseh: "For God has made me forget all my toil and all my afather's house." 52And the name of the second he called 1Ephraim: "For God has caused me to be afruitful in the land of my affliction."

53Then the seven years of plenty which were in the land of Egypt ended, 54aand the seven years of famine began to come, bas Joseph had said. The famine was in all lands, but in all the land of Egypt there was bread. 55So when all the land of Egypt was famished, the people cried to Pharaoh for bread. Then Pharaoh said to all the Egyptians, "Go to Joseph; awhatever he says to you, do." 56The famine was over all the face of the earth, and Joseph opened 1all the storehouses and asold to the Egyptians. And the famine became severe in the land of Egypt. 57aSo all countries came to Joseph in Egypt to bbuy *grain,* because the famine was severe in all lands.

JOSEPH'S BROTHERS GO TO EGYPT

42 When aJacob saw that there was grain in Egypt, Jacob said to his sons, "Why do you look at one another?" 2And he said, "Indeed I have heard that there is grain in Egypt; go down to that place and buy for us there, that we may alive and not die."

3So Joseph's ten brothers went down to buy grain in Egypt. 4But Jacob did not send Joseph's brother Benjamin with his brothers, for he said, a"Lest some calamity befall him." 5And the sons of Israel went to buy *grain* among those who journeyed, for the famine was ain the land of Canaan.

6Now Joseph *was* governor aover the land; and it was he who sold to all the people of the land. And Joseph's brothers came and bbowed down before him with *their* faces to the earth. 7Joseph saw his brothers and recognized them, but he acted as aa stranger to them and spoke 1roughly to them. Then he said to them, "Where do you come from?"

And they said, "From the land of Canaan to buy food."

8So Joseph recognized his brothers, but they did not recognize him. 9Then Joseph aremembered the dreams which he had dreamed about them, and said to them, "You *are* spies! You have come to see the 1nakedness of the land!"

10And they said to him, "No, my lord, but your servants have come to buy food. 11We *are* all one man's sons; we *are* honest *men;* your servants are not spies."

12But he said to them, "No, but you have come to see the nakedness of the land."

41:46
a1 Sam. 16:21;
1 Kin. 12:6, 8;
Dan. 1:19

41:49
aGen. 22:17;
Judg. 7:12;
1 Sam. 13:5

41:50
aGen. 46:20;
48:5

41:51 aPs. 45:10

41:52 aGen. 17:6;
28:3; 49:22

41:54
aPs. 105:16;
Acts 7:11
bGen. 41:30

41:55 aJohn 2:5

41:56 aGen. 42:6

41:57
aEzek. 29:12
bGen. 27:28,
37; 42:3

42:1 aActs 7:12

42:2 aGen. 43:8;
Ps. 33:18, 19;
Is. 38:1

42:4
aGen. 42:38

42:5
aGen. 12:10;
26:1; 41:57;
Acts 7:11

42:6
aGen. 41:41, 55
bGen. 37:7-10;
41:43; Is. 60:14

42:7
aGen. 45:1, 2

42:9
aGen. 37:5-9

41:47 1Lit. *by handfuls*   41:51 1Lit. *Making Forgetful*   41:52 1Lit. *Fruitfulness*
41:56 1Lit. *all that was in them*   42:7 1harshly   42:9 1Exposed parts

¹³And they said, "Your servants *are* twelve brothers, the sons of one man in the land of Canaan; and in fact, the youngest *is* with our father today, and one ᵃ*is* no more."

¹⁴But Joseph said to them, "It *is* as I spoke to you, saying, 'You *are* spies!' ¹⁵In this *manner* you shall be tested: ᵃBy the life of Pharaoh, you shall not leave this place unless your youngest brother comes here. ¹⁶Send one of you, and let him bring your brother; and you shall be ¹kept in prison, that your words may be tested to see whether *there is* any truth in you; or else, by the life of Pharaoh, surely you *are* spies!" ¹⁷So he ¹put them all together in prison ᵃthree days.

¹⁸Then Joseph said to them the third day, "Do this and live, ᵃ*for* I fear God: ¹⁹If you *are* honest *men,* let one of your brothers be confined to your prison house; but you, go and carry grain for the famine of your houses. ²⁰And ᵃbring your youngest brother to me; so your words will be verified, and you shall not die."

And they did so. ²¹Then they said to one another, ᵃ"We *are* truly guilty concerning our brother, for we saw the anguish of his soul when he pleaded with us, and we would not hear; ᵇtherefore this distress has come upon us."

²²And Reuben answered them, saying, ᵃ"Did I not speak to you, saying, 'Do not sin against the boy'; and you would not listen? Therefore behold, his blood is now ᵇrequired of us." ²³But they did not know that Joseph understood *them,* for he spoke to them through an interpreter. ²⁴And he turned himself away from them and ᵃwept. Then he returned to them again, and talked with them. And he took ᵇSimeon from them and bound him before their eyes.

THE BROTHERS RETURN TO CANAAN

²⁵Then Joseph ᵃgave a command to fill their sacks with grain, to ᵇrestore every man's money to his sack, and to give them provisions for the journey. ᶜThus he did for them. ²⁶So they loaded their donkeys with the grain and departed from there. ²⁷But as ᵃone *of them* opened his sack to give his donkey feed at the encampment, he saw his money; and there it was, in the mouth of his sack. ²⁸So he said to his brothers, "My money has been restored, and there it is, in my sack!" Then their hearts ¹failed *them* and they were afraid, saying to one another, "What *is* this *that* God has done to us?"

²⁹Then they went to Jacob their father in the land of Canaan and told him all that had happened to them, saying: ³⁰"The man *who is* lord of the land ᵃspoke ¹roughly to us, and took us for spies of the country. ³¹But we said to him, 'We *are* honest *men;* we are not spies. ³²We *are* twelve brothers, sons of our father; one *is* no *more,* and the youngest *is* with our father this day in the land of Canaan.' ³³Then the man, the lord of the country, said to us, ᵃ'By this I will know that you *are* honest *men:* Leave one of your brothers *here* with me, take *food for* the famine of your households, and be gone. ³⁴And bring your ᵃyoungest brother to me; so I shall know that you *are* not spies, but *that* you *are* honest *men.* I will grant your brother to you, and you may ᵇtrade in the land.'"

³⁵Then it happened as they emptied their sacks, that surprisingly ᵃeach man's bundle of money *was* in his sack; and

---

42:13
ᵃGen. 37:30;
42:32; 44:20;
Lam. 5:7

42:15
ᵃ1 Sam. 1:26;
17:55

42:17
ᵃGen. 40:4, 7, 12

42:18
ᵃGen. 22:12;
39:9; Ex. 1:17;
Lev. 25:43;
Neh. 5:15;
Prov. 1:7; 9:10

42:20
ᵃGen. 42:34;
43:5; 44:23

42:21
ᵃGen. 37:26–28;
44:16; 45:3;
Job 36:8, 9;
Hos. 5:15
ᵇProv. 21:13;
Matt. 7:2

42:22
ᵃGen. 37:21, 22,
29 ᵇGen. 9:5, 6;
1 Kin. 2:32;
2 Chr. 24:22;
Ps. 9:12;
Luke 11:50, 51

42:24
ᵃGen. 43:30;
45:14, 15
ᵇGen. 34:25, 30;
43:14, 23

42:25 ᵃGen. 44:1
ᵇGen. 43:12
ᶜ[Matt. 5:44;
Rom. 12:17, 20,
21; 1 Pet. 3:9]

42:27
ᵃGen. 43:21, 22

42:30
ᵃGen. 42:7

42:33
ᵃGen. 42:15,
19, 20

42:34
ᵃGen. 42:20;
43:3, 5
ᵇGen. 34:10

42:35
ᵃGen. 43:12,
15, 21

42:16 ¹Lit. *bound*   42:17 ¹Lit. *gathered*   42:28 ¹*sank*   42:30 ¹*harshly*

when they and their father saw the bundles of money, they were afraid. ³⁶And Jacob their father said to them, "You have ᵃbereaved me: Joseph is no *more,* Simeon is no *more,* and you want to take ᵇBenjamin. All these things are against me."

³⁷Then Reuben spoke to his father, saying, "Kill my two sons if I do not bring him *back* to you; put him in my hands, and I will bring him back to you."

³⁸But he said, "My son shall not go down with you, for ᵃhis brother is dead, and he is left alone. ᵇIf any calamity should befall him along the way in which you go, then you would ᶜbring down my gray hair with sorrow to the grave."

JOSEPH'S BROTHERS RETURN WITH BENJAMIN

43 Now the famine *was* ᵃsevere in the land. ²And it came to pass, when they had eaten up the grain which they had brought from Egypt, that their father said to them, "Go ᵃback, buy us a little food."

³But Judah spoke to him, saying, "The man solemnly warned us, saying, 'You shall not see my face unless your ᵃbrother *is* with you.' ⁴If you send our brother with us, we will go down and buy you food. ⁵But if you will not send *him,* we will not go down; for the man said to us, 'You shall not see my face unless your brother *is* with you.'"

⁶And Israel said, "Why did you deal *so* ¹wrongfully with me *as* to tell the man whether you had still *another* brother?"

⁷But they said, "The man asked us pointedly about ourselves and our family, saying, '*Is* your father still alive? Have you *another* brother?' And we told him according to these words. Could we possibly have known that he would say, 'Bring your brother down'?"

⁸Then Judah said to Israel his father, "Send the lad with me, and we will arise and go, that we may ᵃlive and not die, both we and you *and* also our little ones. ⁹I myself will be surety for him; from my hand you shall require him. ᵃIf I do not bring him *back* to you and set him before you, then let me bear the blame forever. ¹⁰For if we had not lingered, surely by now we would have returned this second time."

¹¹And their father Israel said to them, "If *it must be* so, then do this: Take some of the best fruits of the land in your vessels and ᵃcarry down a present for the man—a little ᵇbalm and a little honey, spices and myrrh, pistachio nuts and almonds. ¹²Take double money in your hand, and take back in your hand the money ᵃthat was returned in the mouth of your sacks; perhaps it was an oversight. ¹³Take your brother also, and arise, go back to the man. ¹⁴And may God ᵃAlmighty ᵇgive you mercy before the man, that he may release your other brother and Benjamin. ᶜIf I am bereaved, I am bereaved!"

¹⁵So the men took that present and Benjamin, and they took double money in their hand, and arose and went ᵃdown to Egypt; and they stood before Joseph. ¹⁶When Joseph saw Benjamin with them, he said to the ᵃsteward of his house, "Take *these* men to my home, and slaughter ¹an animal and make ready; for *these* men will dine with me at noon." ¹⁷Then the man did as Joseph ordered, and the man brought the men into Joseph's house.

43:6 ¹Lit. *wickedly*   **43:16** ¹Lit. *a slaughter*

42:36
ᵃGen. 43:14
ᵇGen. 35:18;
[Rom. 8:28, 31]

42:38
ᵃGen. 37:22;
42:13; 44:20,
28 ᵇGen. 42:4;
44:29
ᶜGen. 37:35;
44:31

43:1 ᵃGen. 41:54,
57; 42:5; 45:6, 11

43:2 ᵃGen. 42:2;
44:25

43:3
ᵃGen. 42:20;
43:5; 44:23

43:8 ᵃGen. 42:2;
47:19

43:9
ᵃGen. 42:37;
44:32;
Philem. 18, 19

43:11
ᵃGen. 32:20;
33:10; 43:25,
26; [Prov. 18:16]
ᵇGen. 37:25;
Jer. 8:22;
Ezek. 27:17

43:12
ᵃGen. 42:25, 35;
43:21, 22

43:14 ᵃGen. 17:1;
28:3; 35:11; 48:3
ᵇGen. 39:21;
Ps. 106:46
ᶜGen. 42:36;
Esth. 4:16

43:15
ᵃGen. 39:1;
46:3, 6

43:16
ᵃGen. 24:2;
39:4; 44:1

¹⁸Now the men were ªafraid because they were brought into Joseph's house; and they said, "*It is* because of the money, which was returned in our sacks the first time, that we are brought in, so that he may ¹make a case against us and seize us, to take us as slaves with our donkeys."

¹⁹When they drew near to the steward of Joseph's house, they talked with him at the door of the house, ²⁰and said, "O sir, ªwe indeed came down the first time to buy food; ²¹but ªit happened, when we came to the encampment, that we opened our sacks, and there, *each* man's money *was* in the mouth of his sack, our money in full weight; so we have brought it back in our hand. ²²And we have brought down other money in our hands to buy food. We do not know who put our money in our sacks."

²³But he said, "Peace *be* with you, do not be afraid. Your God and the God of your father has given you treasure in your sacks; I had your money." Then he brought ªSimeon out to them.

²⁴So the man brought the men into Joseph's house and ªgave *them* water, and they washed their feet; and he gave their donkeys feed. ²⁵Then they made the present ready for Joseph's coming at noon, for they heard that they would eat bread there.

²⁶And when Joseph came home, they brought him the present which *was* in their hand into the house, and ªbowed down before him to the earth. ²⁷Then he asked them about *their* well-being, and said, "*Is* your father well, the old man ªof whom you spoke? *Is* he still alive?"

²⁸And they answered, "Your servant our father *is* in good health; he *is* still alive." ªAnd they bowed their heads down and prostrated themselves.

²⁹Then he lifted his eyes and saw his brother Benjamin, ªhis mother's son, and said, "*Is* this your younger brother ᵇof whom you spoke to me?" And he said, "God be gracious to you, my son." ³⁰Now ªhis heart yearned for his brother; so Joseph made haste and sought *somewhere* to weep. And he went into *his* chamber and ᵇwept there. ³¹Then he washed his face and came out; and he restrained himself, and said, "Serve the ªbread."

³²So they set him a place by himself, and them by themselves, and the Egyptians who ate with him by themselves; because the Egyptians could not eat food with the ªHebrews, for that *is* ᵇan abomination to the Egyptians. ³³And they sat before him, the firstborn according to his ªbirthright and the youngest according to his youth; and the men looked in astonishment at one another. ³⁴Then he took servings to them from before him, but Benjamin's serving was ªfive times as much as any of theirs. So they drank and were merry with him.

JOSEPH'S CUP

44 And he commanded ¹the ªsteward of his house, saying, ᵇ"Fill the men's sacks with food, as much as they can carry, and put each man's money in the mouth of his sack. ²Also put my cup, the silver cup, in the mouth of the sack of

---

Cross references (margin)

43:18
ªGen. 42:28

43:20
ªGen. 42:3, 10

43:21
ªGen. 42:27, 35

43:23
ªGen. 42:24

43:24
ªGen. 18:4; 19:2; 24:32

43:26
ªGen. 37:7, 10; 42:6; 44:14

43:27
ªGen. 29:6; 42:11, 13; 43:7; 45:3; 2 Kin. 4:26

43:28
ªGen. 37:7, 10

43:29
ªGen. 35:17, 18
ᵇGen. 42:13

43:30
ª1 Kin. 3:26
ᵇGen. 42:24; 45:2, 14, 15; 46:29

43:31
ªGen. 43:25

43:32
ªGen. 41:12; Ex. 1:15
ᵇGen. 46:34; Ex. 8:26

43:33
ªGen. 27:36; 42:7; Deut. 21:16, 17

43:34
ªGen. 35:24; 45:22

44:1 ªGen. 43:16
ᵇGen. 42:25

43:18 ¹Lit. *roll himself upon us*   44:1 ¹Lit. *the one over*

the youngest, and his grain money." So he did according to the word that Joseph had spoken. ³As soon as the morning dawned, the men were sent away, they and their donkeys. ⁴When they had gone out of the city, *and* were not *yet* far off, Joseph said to his steward, "Get up, follow the men; and when you overtake them, say to them, 'Why have you ªrepaid evil for good? ⁵*Is* not this *the one* from which my lord drinks, and with which he indeed practices divination? You have done evil in so doing.'"

⁶So he overtook them, and he spoke to them these same words. ⁷And they said to him, "Why does my lord say these words? Far be it from us that your servants should do such a thing. ⁸Look, we brought back to you from the land of Canaan ªthe money which we found in the mouth of our sacks. How then could we steal silver or gold from your lord's house? ⁹With whomever of your servants it is found, ªlet him die, and we also will be my lord's slaves."

¹⁰And he said, "Now also *let* it *be* according to your words; he with whom it is found shall be my slave, and you shall be blameless." ¹¹Then each man speedily let down his sack to the ground, and each opened his sack. ¹²So he searched. He began with the oldest and ¹left off with the youngest; and the cup was found in Benjamin's sack. ¹³Then they ªtore their clothes, and each man loaded his donkey and returned to the city.

¹⁴So Judah and his brothers came to Joseph's house, and he *was* still there; and they ªfell before him on the ground. ¹⁵And Joseph said to them, "What deed *is* this you have done? Did you not know that such a man as I can certainly practice divination?"

¹⁶Then Judah said, "What shall we say to my lord? What shall we speak? Or how shall we clear ourselves? God has ªfound out the iniquity of your servants; here ᵇwe are, my lord's slaves, both we and *he* also with whom the cup was found."

¹⁷But he said, ª"Far be it from me that I should do so; the man in whose hand the cup was found, he shall be my slave. And as for you, go up in peace to your father."

JUDAH INTERCEDES FOR BENJAMIN

¹⁸Then Judah came near to him and said: "O my lord, please let your servant speak a word in my lord's hearing, and ªdo not let your anger burn against your servant; for you *are* even like Pharaoh. ¹⁹My lord asked his servants, saying, 'Have you a father or a brother?' ²⁰And we said to my lord, 'We have a father, an old man, and ªa child of *his* old age, *who is* young; his brother is ᵇdead, and he ᶜalone is left of his mother's children, and his ᵈfather loves him.' ²¹Then you said to your servants, ª'Bring him down to me, that I may set my eyes on him.' ²²And we said to my lord, 'The lad cannot leave his father, for *if* he should leave his father, *his father* would die.' ²³But you said to your servants, ª'Unless your youngest brother comes down with you, you shall see my face no more.'

²⁴"So it was, when we went up to your servant my father, that we told him the words of my lord. ²⁵And ªour father said,

44:4
ª1 Sam. 25:21

44:8 ªGen. 43:21

44:9 ªGen. 31:32

44:13
ªGen. 37:29, 34; Num. 14:6; 2 Sam. 1:11

44:14
ªGen. 37:7, 10

44:16
ª[Num. 32:23]
ᵇGen. 44:9

44:17 ªProv. 17:15

44:18
ªGen. 18:30, 32; Ex. 32:22

44:20
ªGen. 37:3; 43:8; 44:30
ᵇGen. 42:38
ᶜGen. 46:19
ᵈGen. 42:4

44:21
ªGen. 42:15, 20

44:23
ªGen. 43:3, 5

44:25
ªGen. 43:2

44:12 ¹*finished with*

'Go back *and* buy us a little food.' 26But we said, 'We cannot go down; if our youngest brother is with us, then we will go down; for we may not see the man's face unless our youngest brother *is* with us.' 27Then your servant my father said to us, 'You know that ªmy wife bore me two sons; 28and the one went out from me, and I said, ª"Surely he is torn to pieces"; and I have not seen him since. 29But if you ªtake this one also from me, and calamity befalls him, you shall bring down my gray hair with sorrow to the grave.'

30"Now therefore, when I come to your servant my father, and the lad *is* not with us, since ªhis life is bound up in the lad's life, 31it will happen, when he sees that the lad *is* not *with us*, that he will die. So your servants will bring down the gray hair of your servant our father with sorrow to the grave. 32For your servant became surety for the lad to my father, saying, ª'If I do not bring him *back* to you, then I shall bear the blame before my father forever.' 33Now therefore, please ªlet your servant remain instead of the lad as a slave to my lord, and let the lad go up with his brothers. 34For how shall I go up to my father if the lad *is* not with me, lest perhaps I see the evil that would ¹come upon my father?"

JOSEPH REVEALED TO HIS BROTHERS

45 Then Joseph could not restrain himself before all those who stood by him, and he cried out, "Make everyone go out from me!" So no one stood with him ªwhile Joseph made himself known to his brothers. 2And he ªwept aloud, and the Egyptians and the house of Pharaoh heard *it*.

3Then Joseph said to his brothers, ª"I *am* Joseph; does my father still live?" But his brothers could not answer him, for they were dismayed in his presence. 4And Joseph said to his brothers, "Please come near to me." So they came near. Then he said: "I *am* Joseph your brother, ªwhom you sold into Egypt. 5But now, do not therefore be grieved or angry with yourselves because you sold me here; ªfor God sent me before you to preserve life. 6For these two years the ªfamine *has been* in the land, and *there are* still five years in which *there will be* neither plowing nor harvesting. 7And God ªsent me before you to preserve a ¹posterity for you in the earth, and to save your lives by a great deliverance. 8So now *it was* not you *who* sent me here, but ªGod; and He has made me ªa father to Pharaoh, and lord of all his house, and a ªruler throughout all the land of Egypt.

9"Hurry and go up to my father, and say to him, 'Thus says your son Joseph: "God has made me lord of all Egypt; come down to me, do not ¹tarry. 10ªYou shall dwell in the land of Goshen, and you shall be near to me, you and your children, your children's children, your flocks and your herds, and all that you have. 11There I will ªprovide for you, lest you and your household, and all that you have, come to poverty; for *there are* still five years of famine."'

12"And behold, your eyes and the eyes of my brother Benjamin see that *it is* ªmy mouth that speaks to you. 13So you shall tell my father of all my glory in Egypt, and of all that you have seen; and you shall hurry and ªbring my father down here."

¹⁴Then he fell on his brother Benjamin's neck and wept, and Benjamin wept on his neck. ¹⁵Moreover he ªkissed all his brothers and wept over them, and after that his brothers talked with him.

¹⁶Now the report of it was heard in Pharaoh's house, saying, "Joseph's brothers have come." So it pleased Pharaoh and his servants well. ¹⁷And Pharaoh said to Joseph, "Say to your brothers, 'Do this: Load your animals and depart; go to the land of Canaan. ¹⁸Bring your father and your households and come to me; I will give you the best of the land of Egypt, and you will eat ªthe ¹fat of the land. ¹⁹Now you are commanded—do this: Take carts out of the land of Egypt for your little ones and your wives; bring your father and come. ²⁰Also do not be concerned about your goods, for the best of all the land of Egypt *is* yours.'"

²¹Then the sons of Israel did so; and Joseph gave them ªcarts,¹ according to the command of Pharaoh, and he gave them provisions for the journey. ²²He gave to all of them, to each man, ªchanges of garments; but to Benjamin he gave three hundred *pieces* of silver and ᵇfive changes of garments. ²³And he sent to his father these *things:* ten donkeys loaded with the good things of Egypt, and ten female donkeys loaded with grain, bread, and food for his father for the journey. ²⁴So he sent his brothers away, and they departed; and he said to them, "See that you do not become troubled along the way."

²⁵Then they went up out of Egypt, and came to the land of Canaan to Jacob their father. ²⁶And they told him, saying, "Joseph *is* still alive, and he *is* governor over all the land of Egypt." ªAnd Jacob's heart stood still, because he did not believe them. ²⁷But when they told him all the words which Joseph had said to them, and when he saw the carts which Joseph had sent to carry him, the spirit ªof Jacob their father revived. ²⁸Then Israel said, "*It is* enough. Joseph my son *is* still alive. I will go and see him before I die."

JACOB'S JOURNEY TO EGYPT
(Ex. 6:14–25)

46 So Israel took his journey with all that he had, and came to ªBeersheba, and offered sacrifices ᵇto the God of his father Isaac. ²Then God spoke to Israel ªin the visions of the night, and said, "Jacob, Jacob!"

And he said, "Here I am."

³So He said, "I *am* God, ªthe God of your father; do not fear to go down to Egypt, for I will ᵇmake of you a great nation there. ⁴ªI will go down with you to Egypt, and I will also surely ᵇbring you up *again;* and ᶜJoseph ¹will put his hand on your eyes."

⁵Then ªJacob arose from Beersheba; and the sons of Israel carried their father Jacob, their little ones, and their wives, in the ¹carts ᵇwhich Pharaoh had sent to carry him. ⁶So they took their livestock and their goods, which they had acquired in the land of Canaan, and went to Egypt, ªJacob and all his descendants with him. ⁷His sons and his sons' sons, his

45:15
ªGen. 48:10

45:18
ªGen. 27:28;
47:6;
Deut. 32:9–14

45:21
ªGen. 45:19;
46:5

45:22
ª2 Kin. 5:5
ᵇGen. 43:34

45:26
ªJob 29:24;
Ps. 126:1;
Luke 24:11, 41

45:27
ªJudg. 15:19;
Is. 40:29

46:1 ªGen. 21:31,
33; 26:32,
33; 28:10
ᵇGen. 26:24,
25; 28:13; 31:42;
32:9

46:2 ªGen. 15:1;
22:11; 31:11;
Num. 12:6;
Job 33:14, 15

46:3 ªGen. 17:1;
28:13 ᵇGen. 12:2;
Ex. 1:9; 12:37;
Deut. 26:5

46:4
ªGen. 28:15;
31:3; 48:21;
Ex. 3:12
ᵇGen. 15:16;
50:12, 24,
25; Ex. 3:8
ᶜGen. 50:1

46:5 ªGen. 47:9;
Acts 7:15
ᵇGen. 45:19–21

46:6
ªDeut. 26:5;
Josh. 24:4;
Ps. 105:23;
Is. 52:4;
Acts 7:15

45:18 ¹The choicest produce   45:21 ¹wagons   46:4 ¹Will close your eyes when you die   46:5 ¹wagons

daughters and his sons' daughters, and all his descendants he brought with him to Egypt.

8Now ᵃthese *were* the names of the children of Israel, Jacob and his sons, who went to Egypt: ᵇReuben *was* Jacob's firstborn. 9The ᵃsons of Reuben *were* Hanoch, Pallu, Hezron, and Carmi. 10ᵃThe sons of Simeon *were* ¹Jemuel, Jamin, Ohad, ²Jachin, ³Zohar, and Shaul, the son of a Canaanite woman. 11The sons of ᵃLevi *were* Gershon, Kohath, and Merari. 12The sons of ᵃJudah *were* ᵇEr, Onan, Shelah, Perez, and Zerah (but Er and Onan died in the land of Canaan). ᶜThe sons of Perez were Hezron and Hamul. 13The sons of Issachar *were* Tola, ¹Puvah, ²Job, and Shimron. 14The ᵃsons of Zebulun *were* Sered, Elon, and Jahleel. 15These *were* the ᵃsons of Leah, whom she bore to Jacob in Padan Aram, with his daughter Dinah. All the persons, his sons and his daughters, *were* thirty-three.

16The sons of Gad *were* ¹Ziphion, Haggi, Shuni, ²Ezbon, Eri, ³Arodi, and Areli. 17ᵃThe sons of Asher *were* Jimnah, Ishuah, Isui, Beriah, and Serah, their sister. And the sons of Beriah *were* Heber and Malchiel. 18ᵃThese *were* the sons of Zilpah, ᵇwhom Laban gave to Leah his daughter; and these she bore to Jacob: sixteen persons.

19The ᵃsons of Rachel, ᵇJacob's wife, *were* Joseph and Benjamin. 20ᵃAnd to Joseph in the land of Egypt were born Manasseh and Ephraim, whom Asenath, the daughter of Poti-Pherah priest of On, bore to him. 21ᵃThe sons of Benjamin *were* Belah, Becher, Ashbel, Gera, Naaman, ᵇEhi, Rosh, ᶜMuppim, ¹Huppim, and Ard. 22These *were* the sons of Rachel, who were born to Jacob: fourteen persons in all.

23The son of Dan *was* ¹Hushim. 24ᵃThe sons of Naphtali *were* ¹Jahzeel, Guni, Jezer, and ²Shillem. 25ᵃThese *were* the sons of Bilhah, ᵇwhom Laban gave to Rachel his daughter, and she bore these to Jacob: seven persons in all.

26ᵃAll the persons who went with Jacob to Egypt, who came from his body, ᵇbesides Jacob's sons' wives, *were* sixty-six persons in all. 27And the sons of Joseph who were born to him in Egypt *were* two persons. ᵃAll the persons of the house of Jacob who went to Egypt were seventy.

JACOB SETTLES IN GOSHEN

28Then he sent Judah before him to Joseph, ᵃto point out before him *the way* to Goshen. And they came ᵇto the land of Goshen. 29So Joseph made ready his ᵃchariot and went up to Goshen to meet his father Israel; and he presented himself to him, and ᵇfell on his neck and wept on his neck a good while.

30And Israel said to Joseph, ᵃ"Now let me die, since I have seen your face, because you *are* still alive."

31Then Joseph said to his brothers and to his father's household, ᵃ"I will go up and tell Pharaoh, and say to him, 'My brothers and those of my father's house, who *were* in the land of Canaan, have come to me. 32And the men *are* ᵃshepherds, for their occupation has been to feed livestock; and they have

---

Cross references (left margin):

46:8 ᵃEx. 1:1–4
ᵇNum. 26:4, 5; 1 Chr. 2:1
46:9 ᵃEx. 6:14
46:10 ᵃEx. 6:15; Num. 26:12
46:11 ᵃEx. 6:16, 17; 1 Chr. 6:1, 16
46:12 ᵃNum. 26:19, 20; 1 Chr. 2:3; 4:21 ᵇGen. 38:3, 7, 10 ᶜGen. 38:29
46:14 ᵃNum. 26:26
46:15 ᵃGen. 35:23; 49:31
46:17 ᵃNum. 26:44–47; 1 Chr. 7:30
46:18 ᵃGen. 30:10; 37:2 ᵇGen. 29:24
46:19 ᵃGen. 35:24 ᵇGen. 44:27
46:20 ᵃGen. 41:45, 50–52; 48:1
46:21 ᵃ1 Chr. 7:6; 8:1 ᵇNum. 26:38 ᶜNum. 26:39; 1 Chr. 7:12
46:24 ᵃNum. 26:48
46:25 ᵃGen. 30:5, 7 ᵇGen. 29:29
46:26 ᵃEx. 1:5 ᵇGen. 35:11
46:27 ᵃEx. 1:5; Deut. 10:22; Acts 7:14
46:28 ᵃGen. 31:21 ᵇGen. 47:1
46:29 ᵃGen. 41:43 ᵇGen. 45:14, 15
46:30 ᵃLuke 2:29, 30
46:31 ᵃGen. 47:1
46:32 ᵃGen. 47:3

46:10 ¹*Nemuel,* 1 Chr. 4:24   ²*Jarib,* 1 Chr. 4:24   ³*Zerah,* 1 Chr. 4:24
46:13 ¹*Puah,* Num. 26:23; 1 Chr. 7:1   ²*Jashub,* Num. 26:24; 1 Chr. 7:1
46:16 ¹Sam., LXX *Zephon* and Num. 26:15   ²*Ozni,* Num. 26:16   ³*Arod,* Num. 26:17   46:21 ¹*Hupham,* Num. 26:39   46:23 ¹*Shuham,* Num. 26:42
46:24 ¹*Jahziel,* 1 Chr. 7:13   ²*Shallum,* 1 Chr. 7:13

brought their flocks, their herds, and all that they have.' ³³So it shall be, when Pharaoh calls you and says, ᵃ'What is your occupation?' ³⁴that you shall say, 'Your servants' ᵃoccupation has been with livestock ᵇfrom our youth even till now, both we *and* also our fathers,' that you may dwell in the land of Goshen; for every shepherd *is* ᶜan¹ abomination to the Egyptians."

47 Then Joseph ᵃwent and told Pharaoh, and said, "My father and my brothers, their flocks and their herds and all that they possess, have come from the land of Canaan; and indeed they *are* in ᵇthe land of Goshen." ²And he took five men from among his brothers and ᵃpresented them to Pharaoh. ³Then Pharaoh said to his brothers, ᵃ"What *is* your occupation?"

And they said to Pharaoh, ᵇ"Your servants *are* shepherds, both we *and* also our fathers." ⁴And they said to Pharaoh, ᵃ"We have come to dwell in the land, because your servants have no pasture for their flocks, ᵇfor the famine *is* severe in the land of Canaan. Now therefore, please let your servants ᶜdwell in the land of Goshen."

⁵Then Pharaoh spoke to Joseph, saying, "Your father and your brothers have come to you. ⁶ᵃThe land of Egypt *is* before you. Have your father and brothers dwell in the best of the land; let them dwell ᵇin the land of Goshen. And if you know *any* competent men among them, then make them chief herdsmen over my livestock."

⁷Then Joseph brought in his father Jacob and set him before Pharaoh; and Jacob ᵃblessed Pharaoh. ⁸Pharaoh said to Jacob, "How old *are* you?"

⁹And Jacob said to Pharaoh, ᵃ"The days of the years of my ¹pilgrimage *are* ᵇone hundred and thirty years; ᶜfew and evil have been the days of the years of my life, and ᵈthey have not attained to the days of the years of the life of my fathers in the days of their pilgrimage." ¹⁰So Jacob ᵃblessed Pharaoh, and went out from before Pharaoh.

¹¹And Joseph situated his father and his brothers, and gave them a possession in the land of Egypt, in the best of the land, in the land of ᵃRameses, ᵇas Pharaoh had commanded. ¹²Then Joseph provided ᵃhis father, his brothers, and all his father's household with bread, according to the number in *their* families.

JOSEPH DEALS WITH THE FAMINE

¹³Now *there was* no bread in all the land; for the famine *was* very severe, ᵃso that the land of Egypt and the land of Canaan languished because of the famine. ¹⁴ᵃAnd Joseph gathered up all the money that was found in the land of Egypt and in the land of Canaan, for the grain which they bought; and Joseph brought the money into Pharaoh's house.

¹⁵So when the money failed in the land of Egypt and in the land of Canaan, all the Egyptians came to Joseph and said, "Give us bread, for ᵃwhy should we die in your presence? For the money has failed."

¹⁶Then Joseph said, "Give your livestock, and I will give you *bread* for your livestock, if the money is gone." ¹⁷So they brought their livestock to Joseph, and Joseph gave them

46:33
ᵃGen. 47:2, 3

46:34
ᵃGen. 47:3
ᵇGen. 30:35;
34:5; 37:17
ᶜGen. 43:32;
Ex. 8:26

47:1 ᵃGen. 46:31
ᵇGen. 45:10;
46:28; 50:8

47:2 ᵃActs 7:13

47:3
ᵃGen. 46:33;
Jon. 1:8
ᵇGen. 46:32, 34;
Ex. 2:17, 19

47:4 ᵃGen. 15:13;
Deut. 26:5;
Ps. 105:23
ᵇGen. 43:1;
Acts 7:11
ᶜGen. 46:34

47:6
ᵃGen. 20:15;
45:10, 18; 47:11
ᵇGen. 47:4

47:7
ᵃGen. 47:10;
48:15, 20;
2 Sam. 14:22;
1 Kin. 8:66;
Heb. 7:7

47:9 ᵃPs. 39:12;
[Heb. 11:9, 13]
ᵇGen. 47:28
ᶜ[Job 14:1]
ᵈGen. 5:5; 11:10,
11; 25:7, 8; 35:28

47:10 ᵃGen. 47:7

47:11
ᵃEx. 1:11; 12:37
ᵇGen. 47:6, 27

47:12
ᵃGen. 45:11;
50:21

47:13
ᵃGen. 41:30;
Acts 7:11

47:14
ᵃGen. 41:56;
42:6

47:15
ᵃGen. 47:19

46:34 ¹loathsome   47:9 ¹Lit. *sojourning*

bread *in exchange* for the horses, the flocks, the cattle of the herds, and for the donkeys. Thus he [1]fed them with bread *in exchange* for all their livestock that year.

18When that year had ended, they came to him the next year and said to him, "We will not hide from my lord that our money is gone; my lord also has our herds of livestock. There is nothing left in the sight of my lord but our bodies and our lands. 19Why should we die before your eyes, both we and our land? Buy us and our land for bread, and we and our land will be servants of Pharaoh; give *us* seed, that we may [a]live and not die, that the land may not be desolate."

20Then Joseph [a]bought all the land of Egypt for Pharaoh; for every man of the Egyptians sold his field, because the famine was severe upon them. So the land became Pharaoh's. 21And as for the people, he [1]moved them into the cities, from *one* end of the borders of Egypt to the *other* end. 22[a]Only the land of the [b]priests he did not buy; for the priests had rations *allotted to them* by Pharaoh, and they ate their rations which Pharaoh gave them; therefore they did not sell their lands.

23Then Joseph said to the people, "Indeed I have bought you and your land this day for Pharaoh. Look, *here is* seed for you, and you shall sow the land. 24And it shall come to pass in the harvest that you shall give one-fifth to Pharaoh. Four-fifths shall be your own, as seed for the field and for your food, for those of your households and as food for your little ones."

25So they said, "You have saved [a]our lives; let us find favor in the sight of my lord, and we will be Pharaoh's servants." 26And Joseph made it a law over the land of Egypt to this day, *that* Pharaoh should have one-fifth, [a]except for the land of the priests only, *which* did not become Pharaoh's.

JOSEPH'S VOW TO JACOB

27So Israel [a]dwelt in the land of Egypt, in the country of Goshen; and they had possessions there and [b]grew and multiplied exceedingly. 28And Jacob lived in the land of Egypt seventeen years. So the length of Jacob's life was one hundred and forty-seven years. 29When the time [a]drew near that Israel must die, he called his son Joseph and said to him, "Now if I have found favor in your sight, please [b]put your hand under my thigh, and [c]deal kindly and truly with me. [d]Please do not bury me in Egypt, 30but [a]let me lie with my fathers; you shall carry me out of Egypt and [b]bury me in their burial place."

And he said, "I will do as you have said."

31Then he said, "Swear to me." And he swore to him. So [a]Israel bowed himself on the head of the bed.

JACOB BLESSES JOSEPH'S SONS
(Heb. 11:21)

48 Now it came to pass after these things that Joseph was told, "Indeed your father *is* sick"; and he took with him his two sons, [a]Manasseh and Ephraim. 2And Jacob was told, "Look, your son Joseph is coming to you"; and Israel

47:19 [a]Gen. 43:8
47:20 [a]Jer. 32:43
47:22 [a]Lev. 25:34; Ezra 7:24 [b]Gen. 41:45
47:25 [a]Gen. 33:15
47:26 [a]Gen. 47:22
47:27 [a]Gen. 47:11 [b]Gen. 17:6; 26:4; 35:11; 46:3; Ex. 1:7; Deut. 26:5; Acts 7:17
47:29 [a]Deut. 31:14; 1 Kin. 2:1 [b]Gen. 24:2–4 [c]Gen. 24:49; Josh. 2:14 [d]Gen. 50:25
47:30 [a]2 Sam. 19:37 [b]Gen. 49:29; 50:5–13; Heb. 11:21
47:31 [a]Gen. 48:2; 1 Kin. 1:47; Heb. 11:21
48:1 [a]Gen. 41:51, 56; 46:20; 50:23; Josh. 14:4

47:17 [1]supplied   47:21 [1]So with MT, Tg.; Sam., LXX, Vg. *made the people virtual slaves*

¹strengthened himself and sat up on the bed. ³Then Jacob said to Joseph: "God ªAlmighty appeared to me at ᵇLuz in the land of Canaan and blessed me, ⁴and said to me, 'Behold, I will ªmake you fruitful and multiply you, and I will make of you a multitude of people, and ᵇgive this land to your descendants after you ᶜ*as* an everlasting possession.' ⁵And now your ªtwo sons, Ephraim and Manasseh, who were born to you in the land of Egypt before I came to you in Egypt, *are* mine; as Reuben and Simeon, they shall be mine. ⁶Your ¹offspring ²whom you beget after them shall be yours; they will be called by the name of their brothers in their inheritance. ⁷But as for me, when I came from Padan, ªRachel died beside me in the land of Canaan on the way, when *there was* but a little distance to go to Ephrath; and I buried her there on the way to Ephrath (that is, Bethlehem)."

⁸Then Israel saw Joseph's sons, and said, "Who *are* these?" ⁹Joseph said to his father, "They *are* my sons, whom God has given me in this *place.*"

And he said, "Please bring them to me, and ªI will bless them." ¹⁰Now ªthe eyes of Israel were dim with age, *so that* he could not see. Then Joseph brought them near him, and he ᵇkissed them and embraced them. ¹¹And Israel said to Joseph, ª"I had not thought to see your face; but in fact, God has also shown me your offspring!"

¹²So Joseph brought them from beside his knees, and he bowed down with his face to the earth. ¹³And Joseph took them both, Ephraim with his right hand toward Israel's left hand, and Manasseh with his left hand toward Israel's right hand, and brought *them* near him. ¹⁴Then Israel stretched out his right hand and ªlaid *it* on Ephraim's head, who *was* the younger, and his left hand on Manasseh's head, ᵇguiding his hands knowingly, for Manasseh *was* the ᶜfirstborn. ¹⁵And ªhe blessed Joseph, and said:

> "God, ᵇbefore whom my fathers Abraham and Isaac
>   walked,
> The God who has fed me all my life long to this day,
> 16   The Angel ªwho has redeemed me from all evil,
>   Bless the lads;
>   Let ᵇmy name be named upon them,
>   And the name of my fathers Abraham and Isaac;
>   And let them ᶜgrow into a multitude in the midst of the
>   earth."

¹⁷Now when Joseph saw that his father ªlaid his right hand on the head of Ephraim, it displeased him; so he took hold of his father's hand to remove it from Ephraim's head to Manasseh's head. ¹⁸And Joseph said to his father, "Not so, my father, for this *one is* the firstborn; put your right hand on his head."

¹⁹But his father refused and said, ª"I know, my son, I know. He also shall become a people, and he also shall be great; but truly ᵇhis younger brother shall be greater than he, and his descendants shall become a multitude of nations."

²⁰So he blessed them that day, saying, ª"By you Israel will bless, saying, 'May God make you as Ephraim and as Manasseh!'" And thus he set Ephraim before Manasseh.

48:3
ª Gen. 43:14; 49:25
ᵇ Gen. 28:13, 19; 35:6, 9

48:4 ª Gen. 46:3
ᵇ Gen. 35:12; Ex. 6:8
ᶜ Gen. 17:8

48:5
ª Gen. 41:50; 46:20; 48:8; Josh. 13:7; 14:4

48:7 ª Gen. 35:9, 16, 19, 20

48:9 ª Gen. 27:4; 47:15

48:10
ª Gen. 27:1; 1 Sam. 3:2
ᵇ Gen. 27:27; 45:15; 50:1

48:11
ª Gen. 45:26

48:14
ª Matt. 19:15; Mark 10:16
ᵇ Gen. 48:19
ᶜ Gen. 41:51, 52; Josh. 17:1

48:15 ª Gen. 47:7, 10; 49:24; [Heb. 11:21]
ᵇ Gen. 17:1; 24:40; 2 Kin. 20:3

48:16
ª Gen. 22:11, 15–18; 28:13–15; 31:11; [Ps. 34:22; 121:7]
ᵇ Amos 9:12; Acts 15:17
ᶜ Num. 26:34, 37

48:17
ª Gen. 48:14

48:19
ª Gen. 48:14
ᵇ Num. 1:33, 35; Deut. 33:17

48:20
ª Ruth 4:11, 12

48:2 ¹Collected his strength   **48:6** ¹*children*   ²Who are born to you

21Then Israel said to Joseph, "Behold, I am dying, but aGod will be with you and bring you back to the land of your fathers. 22Moreover aI have given to you one 1portion above your brothers, which I took from the hand bof the Amorite with my sword and my bow."

JACOB'S LAST WORDS TO HIS SONS

49 And Jacob called his sons and said, "Gather together, that I may atell you what shall befall you bin the last days:

2 "Gather together and hear, you sons of Jacob,
   And listen to Israel your father.

3 "Reuben, you are amy firstborn,
   My might and the beginning of my strength,
   The excellency of dignity and the excellency of power.
4 Unstable as water, you shall not excel,
   Because you awent up to your father's bed;
   Then you defiled it—
   He went up to my couch.

5 "Simeon and Levi are brothers;
   Instruments of 1cruelty are in their dwelling place.
6 aLet not my soul enter their council;
   Let not my honor be united bto their assembly;
   cFor in their anger they slew a man,
   And in their self-will they 1hamstrung an ox.
7 Cursed be their anger, for it is fierce;
   And their wrath, for it is cruel!
   aI will divide them in Jacob
   And scatter them in Israel.

8 "Judah,a you are he whom your brothers shall praise;
   bYour hand shall be on the neck of your enemies;
   cYour father's children shall bow down before you.
9 Judah is aa lion's whelp;
   From the prey, my son, you have gone up.
   bHe 1bows down, he lies down as a lion;
   And as a lion, who shall rouse him?
10 aThe 1scepter shall not depart from Judah,
   Nor ba lawgiver from between his feet,
   cUntil Shiloh comes;
   dAnd to Him shall be the obedience of the people.
11 Binding his donkey to the vine,
   And his donkey's colt to the choice vine,
   He washed his garments in wine,
   And his clothes in the blood of grapes.
12 His eyes are darker than wine,
   And his teeth whiter than milk.

13 "Zebuluna shall dwell by the haven of the sea;
   He shall become a haven for ships,
   And his border shall badjoin Sidon.

14 "Issachara is a strong donkey,
   Lying down between two burdens;

48:22 1Lit. shoulder   49:5 1violence   49:6 1lamed   49:9 1couches
49:10 1A symbol of kingship

15 He saw that rest *was* good,
  And that the land *was* pleasant;
  He bowed ªhis shoulder to bear *a burden,*
  And became a band of slaves.

16 "Danª shall judge his people
  As one of the tribes of Israel.
17 ªDan shall be a serpent by the way,
  A viper by the path,
  That bites the horse's heels
  So that its rider shall fall backward.
18 ªI have waited for your salvation, O LORD!

19 "Gad,ª¹ a troop shall ²tramp upon him,
  But he shall triumph at last.

20 "Bread from ªAsher *shall be* rich,
  And he shall yield royal dainties.

21 "Naphtaliª *is* a deer let loose;
  He uses beautiful words.

22 "Joseph *is* a fruitful bough,
  A fruitful bough by a well;
  His branches run over the wall.
23 The archers have ªbitterly grieved him,
  Shot *at him* and hated him.
24 But his ªbow remained in strength,
  And the arms of his hands were ¹made strong
  By the hands of ᵇthe Mighty *God* of Jacob
  ᶜ(From there ᵈ*is* the Shepherd, ᵉthe Stone of Israel),
25 ªBy the God of your father who will help you,
  ᵇAnd by the Almighty ᶜwho will bless you
  With blessings of heaven above,
  Blessings of the deep that lies beneath,
  Blessings of the breasts and of the womb.
26 The blessings of your father
  Have excelled the blessings of my ancestors,
  ªUp to the utmost bound of the everlasting hills.
  ᵇThey shall be on the head of Joseph,
  And on the crown of the head of him who was separate
    from his brothers.

27 "Benjamin is a ªravenous wolf;
  In the morning he shall devour the prey,
  ᵇAnd at night he shall divide the spoil."

28All these *are* the twelve tribes of Israel, and this *is* what their father spoke to them. And he blessed them; he blessed each one according to his own blessing.

JACOB'S DEATH AND BURIAL

29Then he charged them and said to them: "I ªam to be gathered to my people; ᵇbury me with my fathers ᶜin the cave that *is* in the field of Ephron the Hittite, 30in the cave that *is* in the field of Machpelah, which *is* before Mamre in the land of Canaan, ªwhich Abraham bought with the field of Ephron the Hittite as a possession for a burial place. 31ªThere they buried Abraham and Sarah his wife, ᵇthere they buried Isaac and Rebekah his wife, and there I buried Leah. 32The field and

49:15
ª1 Sam. 10:9

49:16
ªGen. 30:6;
Deut. 33:22;
Judg. 18:26, 27

49:17
ªJudg. 18:27

49:18 ªEx. 15:2;
Ps. 25:5; 40:1–3;
119:166, 174;
Is. 25:9; Mic. 7:7

49:19
ªGen. 30:11;
Deut. 33:20;
1 Chr. 5:18

49:20
ªDeut. 33:24;
Josh. 19:24–31

49:21
ªDeut. 33:23

49:23
ªGen. 37:4, 24;
Ps. 118:13

49:24
ªJob 29:20;
Ps. 37:15
ᵇPs. 132:2, 5;
Is. 1:24; 49:26
ᶜGen. 45:11;
47:12 ᵈ[Ps. 23:1;
80:1]
ᵉ[Ps. 118:22];
Is. 28:16;
[1 Pet. 2:6–8]

49:25
ªGen. 28:13;
32:9; 35:3;
43:23; 50:17
ᵇGen. 17:1; 35:11
ᶜDeut. 33:13

49:26
ªDeut. 33:15;
Hab. 3:6
ᵇDeut. 33:16

49:27
ªJudg. 20:21, 25
ᵇNum. 23:24;
Esth. 8:11;
Ezek. 39:10;
Zech. 14:1

49:29
ªGen. 15:15;
25:8; 35:29
ᵇGen. 47:30;
2 Sam. 19:37
ᶜGen. 23:16–20;
50:13

49:30
ªGen. 23:3–20

49:31
ªGen. 23:19,
20; 25:9
ᵇGen. 35:29;
50:13

49:19 ¹Lit. *Troop* ²Lit. *raid* 49:24 ¹Or *supple*

the cave that *is* there *were* purchased from the sons of Heth." 33And when Jacob had finished commanding his sons, he drew his feet up into the bed and breathed his last, and was gathered to his people.

50 Then Joseph ªfell on his father's face and ᵇwept over him, and kissed him. 2And Joseph commanded his servants the physicians to ªembalm his father. So the physicians embalmed Israel. 3Forty days were required for him, for such are the days required for those who are embalmed; and the Egyptians ªmourned¹ for him seventy days.

4Now when the days of his mourning were past, Joseph spoke to ªthe household of Pharaoh, saying, "If now I have found favor in your eyes, please speak in the hearing of Pharaoh, saying, 5ª'My father made me swear, saying, "Behold, I am dying; in my grave ᵇwhich I dug for myself in the land of Canaan, there you shall bury me." Now therefore, please let me go up and bury my father, and I will come back.'"

6And Pharaoh said, "Go up and bury your father, as he made you swear."

7So Joseph went up to bury his father; and with him went up all the servants of Pharaoh, the elders of his house, and all the elders of the land of Egypt, 8as well as all the house of Joseph, his brothers, and his father's house. Only their little ones, their flocks, and their herds they left in the land of Goshen. 9And there went up with him both chariots and horsemen, and it was a very great gathering.

10Then they came to the threshing floor of Atad, which *is* beyond the Jordan, and they ªmourned there with a great and very solemn lamentation. ᵇHe observed seven days of mourning for his father. 11And when the inhabitants of the land, the Canaanites, saw the mourning at the threshing floor of Atad, they said, "This *is* a deep mourning of the Egyptians." Therefore its name was called ¹Abel Mizraim, which *is* beyond the Jordan.

12So his sons did for him just as he had commanded them. 13For ªhis sons carried him to the land of Canaan, and buried him in the cave of the field of Machpelah, before Mamre, which Abraham ᵇbought with the field from Ephron the Hittite as property for a burial place. 14And after he had buried his father, Joseph returned to Egypt, he and his brothers and all who went up with him to bury his father.

JOSEPH REASSURES HIS BROTHERS

15When Joseph's brothers saw that their father was dead, ªthey said, "Perhaps Joseph will hate us, and may ¹actually repay us for all the evil which we did to him." 16So they sent *messengers* to Joseph, saying, "Before your father died he commanded, saying, 17'Thus you shall say to Joseph: "I beg you, please forgive the trespass of your brothers and their sin; ªfor they did evil to you."' Now, please, forgive the trespass of the servants of ᵇthe God of your father." And Joseph wept when they spoke to him.

18Then his brothers also went and ªfell down before his face, and they said, "Behold, we *are* your servants."

19Joseph said to them, ª"Do not be afraid, ᵇfor *am* I in the place of God? 20ªBut as for you, you meant evil against me;

50:1
ªGen. 46:4, 29
ᵇ2 Kin. 13:14

50:2
ªGen. 50:26;
2 Chr. 16:14;
Matt. 26:12;
Mark 16:1;
Luke 24:1;
John 19:39, 40

50:3
ªGen. 37:34;
Num. 20:29;
Deut. 34:8

50:4 ªEsth. 4:2

50:5
ªGen. 47:29–31
ᵇ2 Chr. 16:14;
Is. 22:16;
Matt. 27:60

50:10 ªActs 8:2
ᵇ1 Sam. 31:13;
Job 2:13

50:13
ªGen. 49:29–31;
Acts 7:16
ᵇGen. 23:16–20

50:15
ª[Job 15:21]

50:17
ª[Prov. 28:13]
ᵇGen. 49:25

50:18
ªGen. 37:7–10;
41:43; 44:14

50:19 ªGen. 45:5
ᵇGen. 30:2;
2 Kin. 5:7

50:20
ªGen. 45:5, 7;
Ps. 56:5

50:3 ¹Lit. *wept*   **50:11** ¹Lit. *Mourning of Egypt*   **50:15** ¹*fully*

but ᵇGod meant it for good, in order to bring it about as *it is* this day, to save many people alive. ²¹Now therefore, do not be afraid; ᵃI will provide for you and your little ones." And he comforted them and spoke ¹kindly to them.

DEATH OF JOSEPH
(Heb. 11:22)

²²So Joseph dwelt in Egypt, he and his father's household. And Joseph lived one hundred and ten years. ²³Joseph saw Ephraim's children ᵃto the third *generation.* ᵇThe children of Machir, the son of Manasseh, ᶜwere also brought up on Joseph's knees.

²⁴And Joseph said to his brethren, "I am dying; but ᵃGod will surely visit you, and bring you out of this land to the land ᵇof which He swore to Abraham, to Isaac, and to Jacob." ²⁵Then ᵃJoseph took an oath from the children of Israel, saying, "God will surely ¹visit you, and ᵇyou shall carry up my ᶜbones from here." ²⁶So Joseph died, *being* one hundred and ten years old; and they embalmed him, and he was put in a coffin in Egypt.

50:20
ᵇ[Acts 3:13–15]

50:21
ᵃ[Matt. 5:44]

50:23
ᵃGen. 48:1;
Job 42:16
ᵇNum. 26:29;
32:39
ᶜGen. 30:3

50:24
ᵃGen. 15:14;
46:4; 48:21;
Ex. 3:16, 17;
Josh. 3:17;
Heb. 11:22
ᵇGen. 26:3;
35:12; 46:4;
Ex. 6:8

50:25
ᵃGen. 47:29, 30;
Ex. 13:19;
Josh. 24:32;
Acts 7:15, 16;
Heb. 11:22
ᵇGen. 17:8;
28:13; 35:12;
Deut. 1:8;
30:1–8 ᶜEx. 13:19

50:21 ¹Lit. *to their hearts*   50:25 ¹*give attention to*

THE SECOND BOOK OF MOSES CALLED

EXODUS

1:1
aGen. 46:8–27;
Ex. 6:14–16

1:5 aGen. 46:26,
27; [Deut. 10:22]

1:6 aGen. 50:26;
Acts 7:15

1:7 aGen. 12:2;
28:3; 35:11; 46:3;
47:27; 48:4;
Num. 22:3;
Deut. 1:10, 11;
26:5; Ps. 105:24;
Acts 7:17

1:8 aActs 7:18, 19

1:9 aGen. 26:16

1:10 aPs. 83:3, 4
bPs. 105:25;
[Prov. 16:25];
Acts 7:19

1:11 aGen. 15:13;
Ex. 3:7; 5:6
bEx. 1:14; 2:11;
5:4–9; 6:6
c1 Kin. 9:19;
2 Chr. 8:4
dGen. 47:11

1:13 aGen. 15:13;
Ex. 5:7–19

1:14 aEx. 2:23;
6:9; Num. 20:15;
[Acts 7:19, 34]
bPs. 81:6

1:15 aEx. 2:6

1:16 aMatt. 2:16;
Acts 7:19

1:17 aEx. 1:21;
Prov. 16:6
bDan. 3:16, 18;
Acts 4:18–20;
5:29

1:19 aJosh. 2:4;
2 Sam. 17:19, 20

1:20 aGen. 15:1;
Ruth 2:12;
[Prov. 11:18];
Eccl. 8:12;
[Is. 3:10];
Heb. 6:10

1:21
a1 Sam. 2:35;
2 Sam. 7:11,
13, 27, 29;
1 Kin. 2:24; 11:38;
[Ps. 127:1]

1:22 aActs 7:19

ISRAEL'S SUFFERING IN EGYPT

1 Now athese *are* the names of the children of Israel who came to Egypt; each man and his household came with Jacob: 2Reuben, Simeon, Levi, and Judah; 3Issachar, Zebulun, and Benjamin; 4Dan, Naphtali, Gad, and Asher. 5All those 1who were descendants of Jacob were aseventy2 persons (for Joseph was in Egypt *already*). 6And aJoseph died, all his brothers, and all that generation. 7aBut the children of Israel were fruitful and increased abundantly, multiplied and 1grew exceedingly mighty; and the land was filled with them.

8Now there arose a new king over Egypt, awho did not know Joseph. 9And he said to his people, "Look, the people of the children of Israel *are* more and amightier than we; 10acome, let us bdeal shrewdly with them, lest they multiply, and it happen, in the event of war, that they also join our enemies and fight against us, and *so* go up out of the land." 11Therefore they set taskmasters over them ato afflict them with their bburdens. And they built for Pharaoh csupply cities, Pithom dand Raamses. 12But the more they afflicted them, the more they multiplied and grew. And they were in dread of the children of Israel. 13So the Egyptians made the children of Israel aserve with 1rigor. 14And they amade their lives bitter with hard bondage—bin mortar, in brick, and in all manner of service in the field. All their service in which they made them serve *was* with rigor.

15Then the king of Egypt spoke to the aHebrew midwives, of whom the name of one *was* Shiphrah and the name of the other Puah; 16and he said, "When you do the duties of a midwife for the Hebrew women, and see *them* on the birthstools, if it *is* a ason, then you shall kill him; but if it *is* a daughter, then she shall live." 17But the midwives afeared God, and did not do bas the king of Egypt commanded them, but saved the male children alive. 18So the king of Egypt called for the midwives and said to them, "Why have you done this thing, and saved the male children alive?"

19And athe midwives said to Pharaoh, "Because the Hebrew women *are* not like the Egyptian women; for they 1*are* lively and give birth before the midwives come to them."

20aTherefore God dealt well with the midwives, and the people multiplied and 1grew very mighty. 21And so it was, because the midwives feared God, athat He 1provided households for them.

22So Pharaoh commanded all his people, saying, a"Every son who is 1born you shall cast into the river, and every daughter you shall save alive."

1:5 1Lit. *who came from the loins of*   2DSS, LXX *seventy-five;* cf. Acts 7:14
1:7 1*became very numerous*   **1:13** 1*harshness*   **1:19** 1*have vigor of life,* bear
quickly, easily   **1:20** 1*became very numerous*   **1:21** 1*gave them families*
1:22 1Sam., LXX, Tg. add *to the Hebrews*

MOSES IS BORN
(Heb. 11:23)

2 And [a]a man of the house of Levi went and took *as wife* a daughter of Levi. [2]So the woman conceived and bore a son. And [a]when she saw that he *was* a beautiful *child,* she hid him three months. [3]But when she could no longer hide him, she took an ark of [a]bulrushes for him, daubed it with [b]asphalt and [c]pitch, put the child in it, and laid *it* in the reeds [d]by the river's bank. [4a]And his sister stood afar off, to know what would be done to him.

[5]Then the [a]daughter of Pharaoh came down to bathe at the river. And her maidens walked along the riverside; and when she saw the ark among the reeds, she sent her maid to get it. [6]And when she opened *it,* she saw the child, and behold, the baby wept. So she had compassion on him, and said, "This is one of the Hebrews' children."

[7]Then his sister said to Pharaoh's daughter, "Shall I go and call a nurse for you from the Hebrew women, that she may nurse the child for you?"

[8]And Pharaoh's daughter said to her, "Go." So the maiden went and called the child's mother. [9]Then Pharaoh's daughter said to her, "Take this child away and nurse him for me, and I will give *you* your wages." So the woman took the child and nursed him. [10]And the child grew, and she brought him to Pharaoh's daughter, and he became [a]her son. So she called his name [1]Moses, saying, "Because I drew him out of the water."

MOSES FLEES TO MIDIAN
(Heb. 11:24, 25)

[11]Now it came to pass in those days, [a]when Moses was grown, that he went out to his brethren and looked at their burdens. And he saw an Egyptian beating a Hebrew, one of his brethren. [12]So he looked this way and that way, and when he saw no one, he [a]killed the Egyptian and hid him in the sand. [13]And [a]when he went out the second day, behold, two Hebrew men [b]were fighting, and he said to the one who did the wrong, "Why are you striking your companion?"

[14]Then he said, [a]"Who made you a prince and a judge over us? Do you intend to kill me as you killed the Egyptian?" So Moses [b]feared and said, "Surely this thing is known!" [15]When Pharaoh heard of this matter, he sought to kill Moses. But [a]Moses fled from [1]the face of Pharaoh and dwelt in the land of [b]Midian; and he sat down by [c]a well.

[16a]Now the priest of Midian had seven daughters. [b]And they came and drew water, and they filled the [c]troughs to water their father's flock. [17]Then the [a]shepherds came and [b]drove them away; but Moses stood up and helped them, and [c]watered their flock.

[18]When they came to [a]Reuel[1] their father, [b]he said, "How *is it that* you have come so soon today?"

[19]And they said, "An Egyptian delivered us from the hand of the shepherds, and he also drew enough water for us and watered the flock."

2:1
[a]Ex. 6:16–20; Num. 26:59; 1 Chr. 23:14

2:2 [a]Acts 7:20; Heb. 11:23

2:3 [a]Is. 18:2
[b]Gen. 14:10
[c]Gen. 6:14; Is. 34:9 [d]Is. 19:6

2:4 [a]Ex. 15:20; Num. 26:59

2:5 [a]Ex. 7:15; Acts 7:21

2:10 [a]Acts 7:21

2:11
[a]Acts 7:23, 24; Heb. 11:24–26

2:12
[a]Acts 7:24, 25

2:13
[a]Acts 7:26–28
[b]Prov. 25:8

2:14 [a]Gen. 19:9; Acts 7:27, 28
[b]Judg. 6:27; Heb. 11:27

2:15 [a]Acts 7:29; Heb. 11:27
[b]Ex. 3:1
[c]Gen. 24:11; 29:2; Ex. 15:27

2:16 [a]Ex. 3:1; 4:18; 18:12
[b]Gen. 24:11, 13, 19; 29:6–10; 1 Sam. 9:11
[c]Gen. 30:38

2:17 [a]Gen. 47:3; 1 Sam. 25:7
[b]Gen. 26:19–21
[c]Gen. 29:3, 10

2:18
[a]Num. 10:29
[b]Ex. 3:1; 4:18

2:10 [1]Heb. *Mosheh,* lit. *Drawn Out*   2:15 [1]*the presence of Pharaoh*
2:18 [1]*Jethro,* Ex. 3:1

[20]So he said to his daughters, "And where *is* he? Why *is* it *that* you have left the man? Call him, that he may [a]eat bread."

[21]Then Moses was content to live with the man, and he gave [a]Zipporah his daughter to Moses. [22]And she bore *him* a son. He called his name [a]Gershom,[1] for he said, "I have been [b]a [2]stranger in a foreign land."

[23]Now it happened [a]in the process of time that the king of Egypt died. Then the children of Israel [b]groaned because of the bondage, and they cried out; and [c]their cry came up to God because of the bondage. [24]So God [a]heard their groaning, and God [b]remembered His [c]covenant with Abraham, with Isaac, and with Jacob. [25]And God [a]looked upon the children of Israel, and God [b]acknowledged *them.*

MOSES AT THE BURNING BUSH
(Ex. 6:2—7:7; 11:1–4; 12:35, 36)

3 Now Moses was tending the flock of [a]Jethro his father-in-law, [b]the priest of Midian. And he led the flock to the back of the desert, and came to [c]Horeb, [d]the mountain of God. [2]And [a]the Angel of the LORD appeared to him in a flame of fire from the midst of a bush. So he looked, and behold, the bush was burning with fire, but the bush *was* not consumed. [3]Then Moses said, "I will now turn aside and see this [a]great sight, why the bush does not burn."

[4]So when the LORD saw that he turned aside to look, God called [a]to him from the midst of the bush and said, "Moses, Moses!"

And he said, "Here I am."

[5]Then He said, "Do not draw near this place. [a]Take your sandals off your feet, for the place where you stand *is* holy ground." [6]Moreover He said, [a]"I *am* the God of your father—the God of Abraham, the God of Isaac, and the God of Jacob." And Moses hid his face, for [b]he was afraid to look upon God.

[7]And the LORD said: [a]"I have surely seen the oppression of My people who *are* in Egypt, and have heard their cry [b]because of their taskmasters, [c]for I know their [1]sorrows. [8]So [a]I have come down to [b]deliver them out of the hand of the Egyptians, and to bring them up from that land [c]to a good and large land, to a land [d]flowing with milk and honey, to the place of [e]the Canaanites and the Hittites and the Amorites and the Perizzites and the Hivites and the Jebusites. [9]Now therefore, behold, [a]the cry of the children of Israel has come to Me, and I have also seen the [b]oppression with which the Egyptians oppress them. [10a]Come now, therefore, and I will send you to Pharaoh that you may bring My people, the children of Israel, out of Egypt."

[11]But Moses said to God, [a]"Who *am* I that I should go to Pharaoh, and that I should bring the children of Israel out of Egypt?"

[12]So He said, [a]"I will certainly be with you. And this *shall be* a [b]sign to you that I have sent you: When you have brought the people out of Egypt, you shall serve God on this mountain."

[13]Then Moses said to God, "Indeed, *when* I come to the children of Israel and say to them, 'The God of your fathers

3:10 [a]Gen. 15:13, 14; Ex. 12:40, 41; [Mic. 6:4]; Acts 7:6, 7 3:11 [a]Ex. 4:10; 6:12;
1 Sam. 18:18 3:12 [a]Gen. 31:3; Ex. 4:12, 15; 33:14–16; Deut. 31:23; Josh. 1:5; Is. 43:2;
Rom. 8:31 [b]Ex. 4:8; 19:3

2:22 [1]Lit. *Stranger There* [2]*sojourner,* temporary resident **3:7** [1]*pain*

has sent me to you,' and they say to me, 'What *is* His name?' what shall I say to them?"

¹⁴And God said to Moses, "I AM WHO I AM." And He said, "Thus you shall say to the children of Israel, ᵃ'I AM has sent me to you.'" ¹⁵Moreover God said to Moses, "Thus you shall say to the children of Israel: 'The LORD God of your fathers, the God of Abraham, the God of Isaac, and the God of Jacob, has sent me to you. This *is* ᵃMy name forever, and this *is* My memorial to all generations.' ¹⁶Go and ᵃgather the elders of Israel together, and say to them, 'The LORD God of your fathers, the God of Abraham, of Isaac, and of Jacob, appeared to me, saying, ᵇ"I have surely visited you and *seen* what is done to you in Egypt; ¹⁷and I have said ᵃI will bring you up out of the affliction of Egypt to the land of the Canaanites and the Hittites and the Amorites and the Perizzites and the Hivites and the Jebusites, to a land flowing with milk and honey."' ¹⁸Then ᵃthey will heed your voice; and ᵇyou shall come, you and the elders of Israel, to the king of Egypt; and you shall say to him, 'The LORD God of the Hebrews has ᶜmet with us; and now, please, let us go three days' journey into the wilderness, that we may sacrifice to the LORD our God.' ¹⁹But I am sure that the king of Egypt ᵃwill not let you go, no, not even by a mighty hand. ²⁰So I will ᵃstretch out My hand and strike Egypt with ᵇall My wonders which I will do in its midst; and ᶜafter that he will let you go. ²¹And ᵃI will give this people favor in the sight of the Egyptians; and it shall be, when you go, that you shall not go empty-handed. ²²ᵃBut every woman shall ask of her neighbor, namely, of her who dwells near her house, ᵇarticles of silver, articles of gold, and clothing; and you shall put *them* on your sons and on your daughters. So ᶜyou shall plunder the Egyptians."

MIRACULOUS SIGNS FOR PHARAOH

4 Then Moses answered and said, "But suppose they will not believe me or listen to my voice; suppose they say, 'The LORD has not appeared to you.'"

²So the LORD said to him, "What *is* that in your hand?"

He said, "A rod."

³And He said, "Cast it on the ground." So he cast it on the ground, and it became a serpent; and Moses fled from it. ⁴Then the LORD said to Moses, "Reach out your hand and take *it* by the tail" (and he reached out his hand and caught it, and it became a rod in his hand), ⁵"that they may ᵃbelieve that the ᵇLORD God of their fathers, the God of Abraham, the God of Isaac, and the God of Jacob, has appeared to you."

⁶Furthermore the LORD said to him, "Now put your hand in your bosom." And he put his hand in his bosom, and when he took it out, behold, his hand *was* leprous, ᵃlike snow. ⁷And He said, "Put your hand in your bosom again." So he put his hand in his bosom again, and drew it out of his bosom, and behold, ᵃit was restored like his *other* flesh. ⁸"Then it will be, if they do not believe you, nor heed the message of the ᵃfirst sign, that they may believe the message of the latter sign. ⁹And it shall be, if they do not believe even these two signs, or listen to your voice, that you shall take water from ¹the river and pour *it* on the dry *land.* ᵃThe water which you take from the river will become blood on the dry *land.*"

3:14 ᵃ[Ex. 6:3; John 8:24, 28, 58; Heb. 13:8; Rev. 1:8; 4:8]

3:15 ᵃPs. 30:4; 97:12; 102:12; 135:13; [Hos. 12:5]

3:16 ᵃEx. 4:29 ᵇGen. 50:24; Ex. 2:25; 4:31; Ps. 33:18; Luke 1:68

3:17 ᵃGen. 15:13–21; 46:4; 50:24, 25

3:18 ᵃEx. 4:31 ᵇEx. 5:1, 3 ᶜNum. 23:3, 4, 15, 16

3:19 ᵃEx. 5:2

3:20 ᵃEx. 6:6; 9:15 ᵇDeut. 6:22; Neh. 9:10; Ps. 105:27; 135:9; Jer. 32:20; Acts 7:36 ᶜEx. 11:1; 12:31–37

3:21 ᵃEx. 11:3; 12:36; 1 Kin. 8:50; Ps. 105:37; 106:46; [Prov. 16:7]

3:22 ᵃEx. 11:2 ᵇEx. 33:6 ᶜJob 27:17; Prov. 13:22; [Ezek. 39:10]

4:5 ᵃEx. 4:31; 19:9 ᵇGen. 28:13; 48:15; Ex. 3:6, 15

4:6 ᵃNum. 12:10; 2 Kin. 5:27

4:7 ᵃNum. 12:13–15; Deut. 32:39

4:8 ᵃEx. 7:6–13

4:9 ᵃEx. 7:19, 20

4:9 ¹The Nile

4:10 ªEx. 3:11;
4:1; 6:12; Jer. 1:6

4:11 ªPs. 94:9;
146:8; Matt. 11:5;
Luke 1:20, 64

4:12 ªEx. 4:15,
16; Deut. 18:18;
Is. 50:4; Jer. 1:9;
[Matt. 10:19;
Mark 13:11;
Luke 12:11, 12;
21:14, 15]

4:13 ªJon. 1:3

4:14 ªNum. 11:1,
33 ᵇNum. 26:59
ᶜEx. 4:27;
1 Sam. 10:2, 3, 5

4:15 ªEx. 4:12,
30; 7:1, 2
ᵇNum. 23:5,
12; Deut. 18:18;
2 Sam. 14:3,
19; Is. 51:16;
59:21; Jer. 1:9
ᶜDeut. 5:31

4:16 ªEx. 7:1, 2

4:18 ªEx. 2:21;
3:1; 4:18
ᵇGen. 43:23;
Judg. 18:6

4:19 ªEx. 3:1;
18:1 ᵇGen. 46:3,
6 ᶜEx. 2:15, 23;
Matt. 2:20

4:20 ªEx. 18:2–
5; Acts 7:29
ᵇEx. 4:17; 17:9;
Num. 20:8, 9, 11

4:21 ªEx. 3:20;
11:9, 10 ᵇEx. 7:3,
13; 9:12, 35; 10:1,
20, 27; 14:4, 8;
Deut. 2:30;
Josh. 11:20;
1 Sam. 6:6;
Is. 63:17;
John 12:40;
Rom. 9:18

4:22 ªEx. 5:1
ᵇIs. 63:16;
64:8; Hos. 11:1;
[Rom. 9:4;
2 Cor. 6:16, 18]
ᶜJer. 31:9;
[James 1:18]

4:23 ªEx. 11:5;
12:29; Ps. 105:36;
135:8; 136:10

4:24 ªGen. 42:27
ᵇEx. 3:18; 5:3;
Num. 22:22
ᶜGen. 17:14

4:25 ªEx. 2:21;
18:2 ᵇGen. 17:14;
Josh. 5:2, 3

4:27 ªEx. 4:14
ᵇEx. 3:1; 18:5;
24:13

¹⁰Then Moses said to the LORD, "O my Lord, I *am* not eloquent, neither before nor since You have spoken to Your servant; but ªI *am* slow of speech and ¹slow of tongue."

¹¹So the LORD said to him, ª"Who has made man's mouth? Or who makes the mute, the deaf, the seeing, or the blind? *Have* not I, the LORD? ¹²Now therefore, go, and I will be ªwith your mouth and teach you what you shall say."

¹³But he said, "O my Lord, ªplease send by the hand of whomever *else* You may send."

¹⁴So ªthe anger of the LORD was kindled against Moses, and He said: "Is not Aaron the Levite your ᵇbrother? I know that he can speak well. And look, ᶜhe is also coming out to meet you. When he sees you, he will be glad in his heart. ¹⁵Now ªyou shall speak to him and ᵇput the words in his mouth. And I will be with your mouth and with his mouth, and ᶜI will teach you what you shall do. ¹⁶So he shall be your spokesman to the people. And he himself shall be as a mouth for you, and ªyou shall be to him as God. ¹⁷And you shall take this rod in your hand, with which you shall do the signs."

MOSES GOES TO EGYPT

¹⁸So Moses went and returned to ªJethro his father-in-law, and said to him, "Please let me go and return to my brethren who *are* in Egypt, and see whether they are still alive."

And Jethro said to Moses, ᵇ"Go in peace."

¹⁹Now the LORD said to Moses in ªMidian, "Go, return to ᵇEgypt; for all the men who ᶜsought your life are dead." ²⁰Then Moses ªtook his wife and his sons and set them on a donkey, and he returned to the land of Egypt. And Moses took ᵇthe rod of God in his hand.

²¹And the LORD said to Moses, "When you go back to Egypt, see that you do all those ªwonders before Pharaoh which I have put in your hand. But ᵇI will harden his heart, so that he will not let the people go. ²²Then you shall ªsay to Pharaoh, 'Thus says the LORD: ᵇ"Israel *is* My son, ᶜMy firstborn. ²³So I say to you, let My son go that he may serve Me. But if you refuse to let him go, indeed ªI will kill your son, your firstborn."'"

²⁴And it came to pass on the way, at the ªencampment, that the LORD ᵇmet him and sought to ᶜkill him. ²⁵Then ªZipporah took ᵇa sharp stone and cut off the foreskin of her son and ¹cast *it* at ²*Moses'* feet, and said, "Surely you *are* a husband of blood to me!" ²⁶So He let him go. Then she said, "*You are* a ¹husband of blood!"—because of the circumcision.

²⁷And the LORD said to Aaron, "Go into the wilderness ªto meet Moses." So he went and met him on ᵇthe mountain of God, and kissed him. ²⁸So Moses ªtold Aaron all the words of the LORD who had sent him, and all the ᵇsigns which He had commanded him. ²⁹Then Moses and Aaron ªwent and gathered together all the elders of the children of Israel. ³⁰ªAnd Aaron spoke all the words which the LORD had spoken to Moses. Then he did the signs in the sight of the people. ³¹So the people ªbelieved; and when they heard that the LORD had ᵇvisited the children of Israel and that He ᶜhad looked on their affliction, then ᵈthey bowed their heads and worshiped.

4:28 ªEx. 4:15, 16 ᵇEx. 4:8, 9 4:29 ªEx. 3:16; 12:21 4:30 ªEx. 4:15, 16 4:31 ªEx. 3:18; 4:8, 9; 19:9 ᵇGen. 50:24; Ex. 3:16 ᶜEx. 2:25; 3:7 ᵈGen. 24:26; Ex. 12:27; 1 Chr. 29:20

4:10 ¹*heavy* or *dull of tongue*; *cannot talk very well* 4:25 ¹Lit. *made it touch* ²Lit. *his* 4:26 ¹*bridegroom*

FIRST ENCOUNTER WITH PHARAOH

5 Afterward Moses and Aaron went in and told Pharaoh, "Thus says the LORD God of Israel: 'Let My people go, that they may [1]hold [a]a feast to Me in the wilderness.'"

[2]And Pharaoh said, [a]"Who *is* the LORD, that I should obey His voice to let Israel go? I do not know the LORD, [b]nor will I let Israel go."

[3]So they said, [a]"The God of the Hebrews has [b]met with us. Please, let us go three days' journey into the desert and sacrifice to the LORD our God, lest He fall upon us with [c]pestilence or with the sword."

[4]Then the king of Egypt said to them, "Moses and Aaron, why do you take the people from their work? Get *back* to your [a]labor." [5]And Pharaoh said, "Look, the people of the land *are* [a]many now, and you make them rest from their labor!"

[6]So the same day Pharaoh commanded the [a]taskmasters of the people and their officers, saying, [7]"You shall no longer give the people straw to make [a]brick as before. Let them go and gather straw for themselves. [8]And you shall lay on them the quota of bricks which they made before. You shall not reduce it. For they are idle; therefore they cry out, saying, 'Let us go *and* sacrifice to our God.' [9]Let more work be laid on the men, that they may labor in it, and let them not regard false words."

[10]And the taskmasters of the people and their officers went out and spoke to the people, saying, "Thus says Pharaoh: 'I will not give you straw. [11]Go, get yourselves straw where you can find it; yet none of your work will be reduced.'" [12]So the people were scattered abroad throughout all the land of Egypt to gather stubble instead of straw. [13]And the taskmasters forced *them* to hurry, saying, "Fulfill your work, *your* daily quota, as when there was straw." [14]Also the [a]officers of the children of Israel, whom Pharaoh's taskmasters had set over them, were [b]beaten *and* were asked, "Why have you not fulfilled your task in making brick both yesterday and today, as before?"

[15]Then the officers of the children of Israel came and cried out to Pharaoh, saying, "Why are you dealing thus with your servants? [16]There is no straw given to your servants, and they say to us, 'Make brick!' And indeed your servants *are* beaten, but the fault *is* in your *own* people."

[17]But he said, "You *are* idle! Idle! Therefore you say, 'Let us go *and* sacrifice to the LORD.' [18]Therefore go now *and* work; for no straw shall be given you, yet you shall deliver the quota of bricks." [19]And the officers of the children of Israel saw *that* they *were* in trouble after it was said, "You shall not reduce *any* bricks from your daily quota."

[20]Then, as they came out from Pharaoh, they met Moses and Aaron who stood there to meet them. [21a]And they said to them, "Let the LORD look on you and judge, because you have made [1]us abhorrent in the sight of Pharaoh and in the sight of his servants, to put a sword in their hand to kill us."

ISRAEL'S DELIVERANCE ASSURED
(Ex. 3:1—4:17)

[22]So Moses returned to the LORD and said, "Lord, why have You brought trouble on this people? Why *is* it You have sent

---

5:1 [a]Ex. 3:18; 7:16; 10:9

5:2 [a]2 Kin. 18:35; 2 Chr. 32:14; Job 21:15 [b]Ex. 3:19; 7:14

5:3 [a]Ex. 3:18; 7:16 [b]Ex. 4:24; Num. 23:3 [c]Ex. 9:15

5:4 [a]Ex. 1:11; 2:11; 6:6

5:5 [a]Ex. 1:7, 9

5:6 [a]Ex. 1:11; 3:7; 5:10, 13, 14

5:7 [a]Ex. 1:14

5:14 [a]Ex. 5:6 [b]Is. 10:24

5:21 [a]Ex. 6:9; 14:11; 15:24; 16:2

5:1 [1]*keep a pilgrim-feast*   5:21 [1]Lit. *our scent to stink before*

6:1 ªEx. 3:19
ᵇEx. 12:31, 33, 39
6:3 ªGen. 17:1;
35:9; 48:3
ᵇGen. 28:3; 35:11
ᶜEx. 3:14, 15;
15:3; Ps. 68:4;
83:18; Is. 52:6;
Jer. 16:21;
Ezek. 37:6, 13;
John 8:58
6:4 ªGen. 12:7;
15:18; 17:4, 7, 8;
26:3; 28:4, 13
ᵇGen. 47:9;
Lev. 25:23
ᶜGen. 28:4
6:5 ªEx. 2:24;
[Job 34:28];
Acts 7:34
6:6 ªEx. 13:3, 14;
20:2; Deut. 6:12
ᵇEx. 3:17; 7:4;
12:51; 16:6; 18:1;
Deut. 26:8;
Ps. 136:11
ᶜEx. 15:13;
Deut. 7:8;
1 Chr. 17:21;
Neh. 1:10
6:7 ªEx. 19:5;
Deut. 4:20; 7:6;
2 Sam. 7:24
ᵇGen. 17:7;
Ex. 29:45, 46;
Lev. 26:12, 13,
45; Deut. 29:13;
Rev. 21:7
ᶜEx. 5:4, 5
6:8 ªGen. 15:18;
26:3;
Num. 14:30;
Neh. 9:15;
Ezek. 20:5, 6
6:9 ªEx. 5:21
ᵇEx. 2:23;
Num. 21:4
6:12 ªEx. 4:10;
6:30; Jer. 1:6
6:13
ªNum. 27:19, 23;
Deut. 31:14
6:14 ªGen. 46:9;
Num. 26:5–11;
1 Chr. 5:3
6:15
ªGen. 46:10;
Num. 26:12–14;
1 Chr. 4:24
6:16 ªGen. 46:11;
Num. 3:17;
1 Chr. 6:16–30
6:17 ª1 Chr. 6:17
6:18
ª1 Chr. 6:2, 18
6:19 ª1 Chr. 6:19;
23:21

me? 23For since I came to Pharaoh to speak in Your name, he has done evil to this people; neither have You delivered Your people at all."

6 Then the LORD said to Moses, "Now you shall see what I will do to Pharaoh. For ªwith a strong hand he will let them go, and with a strong hand ᵇhe will drive them out of his land."

2And God spoke to Moses and said to him: "I am ¹the LORD. 3ªI appeared to Abraham, to Isaac, and to Jacob, as ᵇGod Almighty, but by My name ᶜLORD¹ I was not known to them. 4ªI have also ¹established My covenant with them, ᵇto give them the land of Canaan, the land of their ²pilgrimage, ᶜin which they were ³strangers. 5And ªI have also heard the groaning of the children of Israel whom the Egyptians keep in bondage, and I have remembered My covenant. 6Therefore say to the children of Israel: ª'I am the LORD; ᵇI will bring you out from under the burdens of the Egyptians, I will ᶜrescue you from their bondage, and I will redeem you with ¹an outstretched arm and with great judgments. 7I will ªtake you as My people, and ᵇI will be your God. Then you shall know that I am the LORD your God who brings you out ᶜfrom under the burdens of the Egyptians. 8And I will bring you into the land which I ªswore¹ to give to Abraham, Isaac, and Jacob; and I will give it to you as a heritage: I am the LORD.'" 9So Moses spoke thus to the children of Israel; ªbut they did not heed Moses, because of ᵇanguish¹ of spirit and cruel bondage.

10And the LORD spoke to Moses, saying, 11"Go in, tell Pharaoh king of Egypt to let the children of Israel go out of his land."

12And Moses spoke before the LORD, saying, "The children of Israel have not heeded me. How then shall Pharaoh heed me, for ªI am ¹of uncircumcised lips?"

13Then the LORD spoke to Moses and Aaron, and gave them a ªcommand¹ for the children of Israel and for Pharaoh king of Egypt, to bring the children of Israel out of the land of Egypt.

THE FAMILY OF MOSES AND AARON
(Gen. 46:8–27)

14These are the heads of their fathers' houses: ªThe sons of Reuben, the firstborn of Israel, were Hanoch, Pallu, Hezron, and Carmi. These are the families of Reuben. 15ªAnd the sons of Simeon were ¹Jemuel, Jamin, Ohad, Jachin, Zohar, and Shaul the son of a Canaanite woman. These are the families of Simeon. 16These are the names of ªthe sons of Levi according to their generations: Gershon, Kohath, and Merari. And the years of the life of Levi were one hundred and thirty-seven. 17ªThe sons of Gershon were Libni and Shimi according to their families. 18And ªthe sons of Kohath were Amram, Izhar, Hebron, and Uzziel. And the years of the life of Kohath were one hundred and thirty-three. 19ªThe sons of Merari were Mahli and Mushi. These are the families of Levi according to their generations.

6:2 ¹Heb. YHWH   6:3 ¹Heb. YHWH, traditionally Jehovah   6:4 ¹made or ratified   ²sojournings   ³sojourners, temporary residents   6:6 ¹Mighty power   6:8 ¹promised, lit. lifted up My hand   6:9 ¹Lit. shortness   6:12 ¹One who does not speak well   6:13 ¹charge   6:15 ¹Nemuel, Num. 26:12

20Now aAmram took for himself bJochebed, his father's sister, as wife; and she bore him cAaron and Moses. And the years of the life of Amram *were* one hundred and thirty-seven. 21aThe sons of Izhar *were* Korah, Nepheg, and Zichri. 22And athe sons of Uzziel *were* Mishael, Elzaphan, and Zithri. 23Aaron took to himself Elisheba, daughter of aAmminadab, sister of Nahshon, as wife; and she bore him bNadab, Abihu, cEleazar, and Ithamar. 24And athe sons of Korah *were* Assir, Elkanah, and Abiasaph. These are the families of the Korahites. 25Eleazar, Aaron's son, took for himself one of the daughters of Putiel as wife; and ashe bore him Phinehas. These *are* the heads of the fathers' houses of the Levites according to their families.

26These *are the same* Aaron and Moses to whom the LORD said, "Bring out the children of Israel from the land of Egypt according to their aarmies."1 27These *are* the ones who spoke to Pharaoh king of Egypt, ato bring out the children of Israel from Egypt. These *are the same* Moses and Aaron.

AARON IS MOSES' SPOKESMAN

28And it came to pass, on the day the LORD spoke to Moses in the land of Egypt, 29that the LORD spoke to Moses, saying, "I *am* the LORD. aSpeak to Pharaoh king of Egypt all that I say to you."

30But Moses said before the LORD, "Behold, aI *am* 1of uncircumcised lips, and how shall Pharaoh heed me?"

7 So the LORD said to Moses: "See, I have made you a*as* God to Pharaoh, and Aaron your brother shall be byour prophet. 2You ashall speak all that I command you. And Aaron your brother shall tell Pharaoh to send the children of Israel out of his land. 3And aI will harden Pharaoh's heart, and bmultiply My csigns and My wonders in the land of Egypt. 4But aPharaoh will not heed you, so bthat I may lay My hand on Egypt and bring My 1armies *and* My people, the children of Israel, out of the land of Egypt cby great judgments. 5And the Egyptians ashall know that I *am* the LORD, when I bstretch out My hand on Egypt and cbring out the children of Israel from among them."

6Then Moses and Aaron adid *so;* just as the LORD commanded them, so they did. 7And Moses *was* aeighty years old and bAaron eighty-three years old when they spoke to Pharaoh.

AARON'S MIRACULOUS ROD
(Ex. 4:1–5)

8Then the LORD spoke to Moses and Aaron, saying, 9"When Pharaoh speaks to you, saying, a'Show a miracle for yourselves,' then you shall say to Aaron, b'Take your rod and cast *it* before Pharaoh, *and* let it become a serpent.'" 10So Moses and Aaron went in to Pharaoh, and they did so, just aas the LORD commanded. And Aaron cast down his rod before Pharaoh and before his servants, and it bbecame a serpent.

11But Pharaoh also acalled the wise men and bthe 1sorcerers; so the magicians of Egypt, they also cdid in like manner

6:20 aEx. 2:1, 2; Num. 3:19
bNum. 26:59
cNum. 26:59

6:21 aNum. 16:1; 1 Chr. 6:37, 38

6:22 aLev. 10:4

6:23 aRuth 4:19, 20; 1 Chr. 2:10; Matt. 1:4
bLev. 10:1; Num. 3:2; 26:60
cEx. 28:1

6:24
aNum. 26:11

6:25
aNum. 25:7, 11; Josh. 24:33

6:26 aEx. 7:4; 12:17, 51; Num. 33:1

6:27 aEx. 6:13; 32:7; 33:1; Ps. 77:20

6:29 aEx. 6:11; 7:2

6:30 aEx. 4:10; 6:12; Jer. 1:6

7:1 aEx. 4:16; Jer. 1:10
bEx. 4:15, 16

7:2 aEx. 4:15; Deut. 18:18

7:3 aEx. 4:21; 9:12 bEx. 11:9; Acts 7:36
cEx. 4:7; Deut. 4:34

7:4 aEx. 3:19, 20; 10:1; 11:9
bEx. 9:14
cEx. 6:6; 12:12

7:5 aEx. 7:17; 8:22; 14:4, 18; Ps. 9:16 bEx. 9:15
cEx. 3:20; 6:6; 12:51

7:6 aEx. 7:2

7:7 aDeut. 29:5; 31:2; 34:7; Acts 7:23, 30
bNum. 33:39

7:9 aEx. 10:1; Is. 7:11; John 2:18; 6:30
bEx. 4:2, 3, 17

7:10 aEx. 7:9
bEx. 4:3

7:11 aGen. 41:8
bDan. 2:2; 2 Tim. 3:8
cEx. 7:22; 8:7, 18; 2 Tim. 3:9; Rev. 13:13, 14

6:26 1hosts　6:30 1One who does not speak well　7:4 1hosts
7:11 1soothsayers

with their [2]enchantments. [12]For every man threw down his rod, and they became serpents. But Aaron's rod swallowed up their rods. [13]And Pharaoh's heart grew hard, and he did not heed them, as the LORD had said.

THE FIRST PLAGUE: WATERS BECOME BLOOD

[14]So the LORD said to Moses: [a]"Pharaoh's heart *is* hard; he refuses to let the people go. [15]Go to Pharaoh in the morning, when he goes out to the [a]water, and you shall stand by the river's bank to meet him; and [b]the rod which was turned to a serpent you shall take in your hand. [16]And you shall say to him, [a]"The LORD God of the Hebrews has sent me to you, saying, "Let My people go, [b]that they may [1]serve Me in the wilderness"; but indeed, until now you would not hear! [17]Thus says the LORD: "By this [a]you shall know that I *am* the LORD. Behold, I will strike the waters which *are* in the river with the rod that *is* in my hand, and [b]they shall be turned [c]to blood. [18]And the fish that *are* in the river shall die, the river shall stink, and the Egyptians will [a]loathe[1] to drink the water of the river."'"

[19]Then the LORD spoke to Moses, "Say to Aaron, 'Take your rod and [a]stretch out your hand over the waters of Egypt, over their streams, over their rivers, over their ponds, and over all their pools of water, that they may become blood. And there shall be blood throughout all the land of Egypt, both in *buckets of* wood and *pitchers of* stone.'" [20]And Moses and Aaron did so, just as the LORD commanded. So he [a]lifted up the rod and struck the waters that *were* in the river, in the sight of Pharaoh and in the sight of his servants. And all the [b]waters that *were* in the river were turned to blood. [21]The fish that *were* in the river died, the river stank, and the Egyptians [a]could not drink the water of the river. So there was blood throughout all the land of Egypt.

[22][a]Then the magicians of Egypt did [b]so with their [1]enchantments; and Pharaoh's heart grew hard, and he did not heed them, [c]as the LORD had said. [23]And Pharaoh turned and went into his house. Neither was his heart moved by this. [24]So all the Egyptians dug all around the river for water to drink, because they could not drink the water of the river. [25]And seven days passed after the LORD had struck the river.

THE SECOND PLAGUE: FROGS

8 And the LORD spoke to Moses, "Go to Pharaoh and say to him, 'Thus says the LORD: "Let My people go, [a]that they may serve Me. [2]But if you [a]refuse to let *them* go, behold, I will smite all your territory with [b]frogs. [3]So the river shall bring forth frogs abundantly, which shall go up and come into your house, into your [a]bedroom, on your bed, into the houses of your servants, on your people, into your ovens, and into your kneading bowls. [4]And the frogs shall come up on you, on your people, and on all your servants."'"

[5]Then the LORD spoke to Moses, "Say to Aaron, [a]'Stretch out your hand with your rod over the streams, over the rivers, and over the ponds, and cause frogs to come up on the land of Egypt.'" [6]So Aaron stretched out his hand over the waters of Egypt, and [a]the frogs came up and covered the land of Egypt.

Cross-references

7:14 [a]Ex. 8:15; 10:1, 20, 27
7:15 [a]Ex. 2:5; 8:20 [b]Ex. 4:2, 3; 7:10
7:16 [a]Ex. 3:13, 18; 4:22 [b]Ex. 3:12, 18; 4:23; 5:1, 3; 8:1
7:17 [a]Ex. 5:2; 7:5; 10:2; Ps. 9:16; Ezek. 25:17 [b]Ex. 4:9; 7:20 [c]Rev. 11:6; 16:4, 6
7:18 [a]Ex. 7:24
7:19 [a]Ex. 8:5, 6, 16; 9:22; 10:12, 21; 14:21, 26
7:20 [a]Ex. 17:5 [b]Ps. 78:44; 105:29, 30
7:21 [a]Ex. 7:18
7:22 [a]Ex. 7:11 [b]Ex. 8:7 [c]Ex. 3:19; 7:3
8:1 [a]Ex. 3:12, 18; 4:23; 5:1, 3
8:2 [a]Ex. 7:14; 9:2 [b]Rev. 16:13
8:3 [a]Ps. 105:30
8:5 [a]Ex. 7:19
8:6 [a]Ps. 78:45; 105:30

7:11 [2]*secret arts*   7:16 [1]*worship*   7:18 [1]*be weary of drinking*   7:22 [1]*secret arts*

7a And the magicians did so with their ¹enchantments, and brought up frogs on the land of Egypt.

⁸Then Pharaoh called for Moses and Aaron, and said, a"Entreat¹ the LORD that He may take away the frogs from me and from my people; and I will let the people ᵇgo, that they may sacrifice to the LORD."

⁹And Moses said to Pharaoh, "Accept the honor of saying when I shall intercede for you, for your servants, and for your people, to destroy the frogs from you and your houses, *that* they may remain in the river only."

¹⁰So he said, "Tomorrow." And he said, "*Let it be* according to your word, that you may know that ªthere is no one like the LORD our God. ¹¹And the frogs shall depart from you, from your houses, from your servants, and from your people. They shall remain in the river only."

¹²Then Moses and Aaron went out from Pharaoh. And Moses ªcried out to the LORD concerning the frogs which He had brought against Pharaoh. ¹³So the LORD did according to the word of Moses. And the frogs died out of the houses, out of the courtyards, and out of the fields. ¹⁴They gathered them together in heaps, and the land stank. ¹⁵But when Pharaoh saw that there was ªrelief, ᵇhe hardened his heart and did not heed them, as the LORD had said.

THE THIRD PLAGUE: LICE

¹⁶So the LORD said to Moses, "Say to Aaron, 'Stretch out your rod, and strike the dust of the land, so that it may become ¹lice throughout all the land of Egypt.'" ¹⁷And they did so. For Aaron stretched out his hand with his rod and struck the dust of the earth, and ªit became lice on man and beast. All the dust of the land became lice throughout all the land of Egypt.

¹⁸Now ªthe magicians so worked with their ¹enchantments to bring forth lice, but they ᵇcould not. So there were lice on man and beast. ¹⁹Then the magicians said to Pharaoh, "This *is* ªthe¹ finger of God." But Pharaoh's ᵇheart grew hard, and he did not heed them, just as the LORD had said.

THE FOURTH PLAGUE: FLIES

²⁰And the LORD said to Moses, ª"Rise early in the morning and stand before Pharaoh as he comes out to the water. Then say to him, 'Thus says the LORD: ᵇ"Let My people go, that they may serve Me. ²¹Or else, if you will not let My people go, behold, I will send swarms *of flies* on you and your servants, on your people and into your houses. The houses of the Egyptians shall be full of swarms *of flies,* and also the ground on which they *stand.* ²²And in that day ªI will set apart the land of ᵇGoshen, in which My people dwell, that no swarms *of flies* shall be there, in order that you may ᶜknow that I *am* the LORD in the midst of the ᵈland. ²³I will ¹make a difference between My people and your people. Tomorrow this ªsign shall be."'" ²⁴And the LORD did so. ªThick swarms *of flies* came into the house of Pharaoh, *into* his servants' houses, and into all the land of Egypt. The land was corrupted because of the swarms *of flies.*

8:7 ªEx. 7:11, 22

8:8 ªEx. 8:28; 9:28; 10:17; Num. 21:7; 1 Kin. 13:6 ᵇEx. 10:8, 24

8:10 ªEx. 9:14; 15:11; Deut. 4:35, 39; 33:26; 2 Sam. 7:22; 1 Chr. 17:20; Ps. 86:8; Is. 46:9; [Jer. 10:6, 7]

8:12 ªEx. 8:30; 9:33; 10:18; 32:11; [James 5:16–18]

8:15 ªEccl. 8:11 ᵇEx. 7:14, 22; 9:34; 1 Sam. 6:6

8:17 ªPs. 105:31

8:18 ªEx. 7:11, 12; 8:7 ᵇDan. 5:8; 2 Tim. 3:8, 9

8:19 ªEx. 7:5; 10:7; 1 Sam. 6:3, 9; Ps. 8:3; Luke 11:20 ᵇEx. 8:15

8:20 ªEx. 7:15; 9:13 ᵇEx. 3:18; 4:23; 5:1, 3; 8:1

8:22 ªEx. 9:4, 6, 26; 10:23; 11:6, 7; 12:13 ᵇGen. 50:8 ᶜEx. 7:5, 17; 10:2; 14:4 ᵈEx. 9:29

8:23 ªEx. 4:8

8:24 ªPs. 78:45; 105:31

8:7 ¹secret arts   8:8 ¹Pray to, Make supplication to   8:16 ¹gnats
8:18 ¹secret arts   8:19 ¹An act of God   8:23 ¹Lit. *set a ransom,* Ex. 9:4; 11:7

25Then Pharaoh called for Moses and Aaron, and said, "Go, sacrifice to your God in the land."

26And Moses said, "It is not right to do so, for we would be sacrificing ªthe abomination of the Egyptians to the LORD our God. If we sacrifice the abomination of the Egyptians before their eyes, then will they not ¹stone us? 27We will go ªthree days' journey into the wilderness and sacrifice to the LORD our God as ᵇHe will command us."

28So Pharaoh said, "I will let you go, that you may sacrifice to the LORD your God in the wilderness; only you shall not go very far away. ªIntercede for me."

29Then Moses said, "Indeed I am going out from you, and I will entreat the LORD, that the swarms of flies may depart tomorrow from Pharaoh, from his servants, and from his people. But let Pharaoh not ªdeal deceitfully anymore in not letting the people go to sacrifice to the LORD."

30So Moses went out from Pharaoh and ªentreated the LORD. 31And the LORD did according to the word of Moses; He removed the swarms of flies from Pharaoh, from his servants, and from his people. Not one remained. 32But Pharaoh ªhardened his heart at this time also; neither would he let the people go.

THE FIFTH PLAGUE: LIVESTOCK DISEASED

9 Then the LORD said to Moses, ª"Go in to Pharaoh and tell him, 'Thus says the LORD God of the Hebrews: "Let My people go, that they may ᵇserve Me. 2For if you ªrefuse to let them go, and still hold them, 3behold, the ªhand of the LORD will be on your cattle in the field, on the horses, on the donkeys, on the camels, on the oxen, and on the sheep—a very severe pestilence. 4And ªthe LORD will make a difference between the livestock of Israel and the livestock of Egypt. So nothing shall die of all that belongs to the children of Israel."'" 5Then the LORD appointed a set time, saying, "Tomorrow the LORD will do this thing in the land."

6So the LORD did this thing on the next day, and ªall the livestock of Egypt died; but of the livestock of the children of Israel, not one died. 7Then Pharaoh sent, and indeed, not even one of the livestock of the Israelites was dead. But the ªheart of Pharaoh became hard, and he did not let the people go.

THE SIXTH PLAGUE: BOILS

(Deut. 28:27)

8So the LORD said to Moses and Aaron, "Take for yourselves handfuls of ashes from a furnace, and let Moses scatter it toward the heavens in the sight of Pharaoh. 9And it will become fine dust in all the land of Egypt, and it will cause ªboils that break out in sores on man and beast throughout all the land of Egypt." 10Then they took ashes from the furnace and stood before Pharaoh, and Moses scattered them toward heaven. And they caused ªboils that break out in sores on man and beast. 11And the ªmagicians could not stand before Moses because of the ᵇboils, for the boils were on the magicians and on all the Egyptians. 12But the LORD hardened the heart of

---

8:26
ªGen. 43:32;
46:34;
[Deut. 7:25, 26;
12:31]

8:27 ªEx. 3:18;
5:3 ᵇEx. 3:12

8:28 ªEx. 8:8,
15, 29, 32; 9:28;
1 Kin. 13:6

8:29 ªEx. 8:8, 15

8:30 ªEx. 8:12

8:32 ªEx. 4:21;
8:8, 15; Ps. 52:2

9:1 ªEx. 4:23; 8:1
ᵇEx. 7:16

9:2 ªEx. 8:2

9:3 ªEx. 7:4;
1 Sam. 5:6;
Ps. 39:10;
Acts 13:11

9:4 ªEx. 8:22

9:6 ªEx. 9:19,
20, 25;
Ps. 78:48, 50

9:7 ªEx. 7:14;
8:32

9:9
ªDeut. 28:27;
Rev. 16:2

9:10
ªDeut. 28:27

9:11 ª[Ex. 8:18,
19; 2 Tim. 3:9]
ᵇDeut. 28:27;
Job 2:7;
Rev. 16:1, 2

8:26 ¹Put us to death by stoning

Pharaoh; and he ^adid not heed them, just ^bas the LORD had spoken to Moses.

THE SEVENTH PLAGUE: HAIL

¹³Then the LORD said to Moses, ^a"Rise early in the morning and stand before Pharaoh, and say to him, 'Thus says the LORD God of the Hebrews: "Let My people go, that they may ^bserve Me, ¹⁴for at this time I will send all My plagues to your very heart, and on your servants and on your people, ^athat you may know that *there is* none like Me in all the earth. ¹⁵Now if I had ^astretched out My hand and struck you and your people with ^bpestilence, then you would have been cut off from the earth. ¹⁶But indeed for ^athis *purpose* I have raised you up, that I may ^bshow My power *in* you, and that My ^cname may be declared in all the earth. ¹⁷As yet you exalt yourself against My people in that you will not let them go. ¹⁸Behold, tomorrow about this time I will cause very heavy hail to rain down, such as has not been in Egypt since its founding until now. ¹⁹Therefore send now *and* gather your livestock and all that you have in the field, for the hail shall come down on every man and every animal which is found in the field and is not brought home; and they shall die."'"

²⁰He who ^afeared the word of the LORD among the ^bservants of Pharaoh made his servants and his livestock flee to the houses. ²¹But he who did not regard the word of the LORD left his servants and his livestock in the field.

²²Then the LORD said to Moses, "Stretch out your hand toward heaven, that there may be ^ahail in all the land of Egypt—on man, on beast, and on every herb of the field, throughout the land of Egypt." ²³And Moses stretched out his rod toward heaven; and ^athe LORD sent thunder and hail, and fire darted to the ground. And the LORD rained hail on the land of Egypt. ²⁴So there was hail, and fire mingled with the hail, so very heavy that there was none like it in all the land of Egypt since it became a nation. ²⁵And the ^ahail struck throughout the whole land of Egypt, all that *was* in the field, both man and beast; and the hail struck every herb of the field and broke every tree of the field. ^{26a}Only in the land of Goshen, where the children of Israel *were,* there was no hail.

²⁷And Pharaoh sent and ^acalled for Moses and Aaron, and said to them, ^b"I have sinned this time. ^cThe LORD *is* righteous, and my people and I *are* wicked. ^{28a}Entreat¹ the LORD, that there may be no *more* ²mighty thundering and hail, for *it is* enough. I will let you ^bgo, and you shall stay no longer."

²⁹So Moses said to him, "As soon as I have gone out of the city, I will ^aspread out my hands to the LORD; the thunder will cease, and there will be no more hail, that you may know that the ^bearth *is* the LORD's. ³⁰But as for you and your servants, ^aI know that you will not yet fear the LORD God."

³¹Now the flax and the barley were struck, ^afor the barley *was* in the head and the flax *was* in bud. ³²But the wheat and the spelt were not struck, for they *are* ¹late crops.

³³So Moses went out of the city from Pharaoh and ^aspread out his hands to the LORD; then the thunder and the hail ceased, and the rain was not poured on the earth. ³⁴And

---

9:28 ¹*Pray to, Make supplication to*   ²Lit. *voices of God* or *sounds of God*
9:32 ¹Lit. *darkened*

9:12 ^aEx. 7:13
^bEx. 4:21

9:13 ^aEx. 8:20
^bEx. 9:1

9:14 ^aEx. 8:10;
Deut. 3:24;
2 Sam. 7:22;
1 Chr. 17:20;
Ps. 86:8;
Is. 45:5–8; 46:9;
Jer. 10:6, 7

9:15 ^aEx. 3:20;
7:5 ^bEx. 5:3

9:16 ^aEx. 14:17;
Prov. 16:4;
[Rom. 9:17, 18;
1 Pet. 2:8, 9]
^bEx. 7:4, 5;
10:1; 11:9; 14:17
^c1 Kin. 8:43

9:20 ^aEx. 1:17;
14:31;
[Prov. 13:13]
^bEx. 8:19; 10:7

9:22 ^aRev. 16:21

9:23
^aGen. 19:24;
Josh. 10:11;
Ps. 18:13; 78:47;
105:32; 148:8;
Is. 30:30;
Ezek. 38:22;
Rev. 8:7

9:25 ^aEx. 9:19;
Ps. 78:47, 48;
105:32, 33

9:26 ^aEx. 8:22,
23; 9:4, 6;
10:23; 11:7; 12:13;
Is. 32:18, 19

9:27 ^aEx. 8:8
^bEx. 9:34; 10:16,
17 ^c2 Chr. 12:6;
Ps. 129:4; 145:17;
Lam. 1:18

9:28 ^aEx. 8:8,
28; 10:17;
Acts 8:24
^bEx. 8:25;
10:8, 24

9:29
^a1 Kin. 8:22, 38;
Ps. 143:6; Is. 1:15
^bEx. 8:22; 19:5;
20:11; Ps. 24:1;
1 Cor. 10:26, 28

9:30 ^aEx. 8:29;
[Is. 26:10]

9:31 ^aRuth 1:22;
2:23

9:33 ^aEx. 8:12;
9:29

when Pharaoh saw that the rain, the hail, and the thunder had ceased, he sinned yet more; and he hardened his heart, he and his servants. 35So ªthe heart of Pharaoh was hard; neither would he let the children of Israel go, as the LORD had spoken by Moses.

THE EIGHTH PLAGUE: LOCUSTS
(Joel 1:2–4)

10 Now the LORD said to Moses, "Go in to Pharaoh; ªfor I have hardened his heart and the hearts of his servants, ᵇthat I may show these signs of Mine before him, 2and that ªyou may tell in the hearing of your son and your son's son the mighty things I have done in Egypt, and My signs which I have done among them, that you may ᵇknow that I *am* the LORD."

3So Moses and Aaron came in to Pharaoh and said to him, "Thus says the LORD God of the Hebrews: 'How long will you refuse to ªhumble yourself before Me? Let My people go, that they may ᵇserve Me. 4Or else, if you refuse to let My people go, behold, tomorrow I will bring ªlocusts into your territory. 5And they shall cover the face of the earth, so that no one will be able to see the earth; and ªthey shall eat the residue of what is left, which remains to you from the hail, and they shall eat every tree which grows up for you out of the field. 6They shall ªfill your houses, the houses of all your servants, and the houses of all the Egyptians—which neither your fathers nor your fathers' fathers have seen, since the day that they were on the earth to this day.'" And he turned and went out from Pharaoh.

7Then Pharaoh's ªservants said to him, "How long shall this man be ᵇa snare to us? Let the men go, that they may serve the LORD their God. Do you not yet know that Egypt is destroyed?"

8So Moses and Aaron were brought again to Pharaoh, and he said to them, "Go, serve the LORD your God. Who *are* the ones that are going?"

9And Moses said, "We will go with our young and our old; with our sons and our daughters, with our flocks and our herds we will go, for ªwe must hold a feast to the LORD."

10Then he said to them, "The LORD had better be with you when I let you and your little ones go! Beware, for evil is ahead of you. 11Not so! Go now, you *who are* men, and serve the LORD, for that is what you desired." And they were driven ªout from Pharaoh's presence.

12Then the LORD said to Moses, ª"Stretch out your hand over the land of Egypt for the locusts, that they may come upon the land of Egypt, and ᵇeat every herb of the land—all that the hail has left." 13So Moses stretched out his rod over the land of Egypt, and the LORD brought an east wind on the land all that day and all *that* night. When it was morning, the east wind brought the locusts. 14And ªthe locusts went up over all the land of Egypt and rested on all the territory of Egypt. *They were* very severe; ᵇpreviously there had been no such locusts as they, nor shall there be such after them. 15For they ªcovered the face of the whole earth, so that the land was darkened; and they ᵇate every herb of the land and all the fruit of the trees which the hail had left. So there remained nothing

9:35 ªEx. 4:21
10:1 ªEx. 4:21; 7:14; 9:12; 10:27; 11:10; 14:4; Josh. 11:20; John 12:40; Rom. 9:18
ᵇEx. 7:4; 9:16
10:2 ªEx. 12:26; 13:8, 14; Deut. 4:9; 6:7; 11:19; Ps. 44:1; 78:5; Joel 1:3
ᵇEx. 7:5, 17; 8:22
10:3
ª[1 Kin. 21:29; 2 Chr. 34:27]; Job 42:6; [James 4:10]; 1 Pet. 5:6]
ᵇEx. 4:23; 8:1; 9:1
10:4
ªProv. 30:27; Rev. 9:3
10:5 ªEx. 9:32; Joel 1:4; 2:25
10:6 ªEx. 8:3, 21
10:7 ªEx. 7:5; 8:19; 9:20; 12:33
ᵇEx. 23:33; Josh. 23:13; 1 Sam. 18:21; Eccl. 7:26; 1 Cor. 7:35
10:9
ªEx. 5:1; 7:16
10:11 ªEx. 10:28
10:12 ªEx. 7:19
ᵇEx. 10:5, 15
10:14
ªDeut. 28:38; Ps. 78:46; 105:34
ᵇJoel 1:4, 7; 2:1–11; Rev. 9:3
10:15 ªEx. 10:5
ᵇPs. 105:35

green on the trees or on the plants of the field throughout all the land of Egypt.

¹⁶Then Pharaoh called ᵃfor Moses and Aaron in haste, and said, ᵇ"I have sinned against the LORD your God and against you. ¹⁷Now therefore, please forgive my sin only this once, and ᵃentreat¹ the LORD your God, that He may take away from me this death only." ¹⁸So he ᵃwent out from Pharaoh and entreated the LORD. ¹⁹And the LORD turned a very strong west wind, which took the locusts away and blew them ᵃinto the Red Sea. There remained not one locust in all the territory of Egypt. ²⁰But the LORD ᵃhardened Pharaoh's heart, and he did not let the children of Israel go.

THE NINTH PLAGUE: DARKNESS

²¹Then the LORD said to Moses, ᵃ"Stretch out your hand toward heaven, that there may be darkness over the land of Egypt, ¹darkness *which* may even be felt." ²²So Moses stretched out his hand toward heaven, and there was ᵃthick darkness in all the land of Egypt ᵇthree days. ²³They did not see one another; nor did anyone rise from his place for three days. ᵃBut all the children of Israel had light in their dwellings.

²⁴Then Pharaoh called to Moses and ᵃsaid, "Go, serve the LORD; only let your flocks and your herds be kept back. Let your ᵇlittle ones also go with you."

²⁵But Moses said, "You must also give ¹us sacrifices and burnt offerings, that we may sacrifice to the LORD our God. ²⁶Our ᵃlivestock also shall go with us; not a hoof shall be left behind. For we must take some of them to serve the LORD our God, and even we do not know with what we must serve the LORD until we arrive there."

²⁷But the LORD ᵃhardened Pharaoh's heart, and he would not let them go. ²⁸Then Pharaoh said to him, ᵃ"Get away from me! Take heed to yourself and see my face no more! For in the day you see my face you shall die!"

²⁹So Moses said, "You have spoken well. ᵃI will never see your face again."

DEATH OF THE FIRSTBORN ANNOUNCED
(Ex. 3:21, 22; 12:35, 36)

11 And the LORD said to Moses, "I will bring one more plague on Pharaoh and on Egypt. ᵃAfterward he will let you go from here. ᵇWhen he lets *you* go, he will surely drive you out of here altogether. ²Speak now in the hearing of the people, and let every man ask from his neighbor and every woman from her neighbor, ᵃarticles of silver and articles of gold." ³ᵃAnd the LORD gave the people favor in the sight of the Egyptians. Moreover the man ᵇMoses *was* very great in the land of Egypt, in the sight of Pharaoh's servants and in the sight of the people.

⁴Then Moses said, "Thus says the LORD: ᵃ'About midnight I will go out into the midst of Egypt; ⁵and ᵃall the firstborn in the land of Egypt shall die, from the firstborn of Pharaoh who sits on his throne, even to the firstborn of the female servant who *is* behind the handmill, and all the firstborn of

10:16 ᵃEx. 8:8
ᵇEx. 9:27

10:17 ᵃEx. 8:8, 28; 9:28; 1 Kin. 13:6

10:18 ᵃEx. 8:30

10:19 ᵃJoel 2:20

10:20 ᵃEx. 4:21; 10:1; 11:10

10:21 ᵃEx. 9:22

10:22 ᵃPs. 105:28; Rev. 16:10
ᵇEx. 3:18

10:23 ᵃEx. 8:22, 23

10:24 ᵃEx. 8:8, 25; 10:8
ᵇEx. 10:10

10:26 ᵃEx. 10:9

10:27 ᵃEx. 4:21; 10:1, 20; 14:4, 8

10:28 ᵃEx. 10:11

10:29 ᵃEx. 11:8; Heb. 11:27

11:1 ᵃEx. 12:31, 33, 39 ᵇEx. 6:1; 12:39

11:2 ᵃEx. 3:22; 12:35, 36

11:3 ᵃEx. 3:21; 12:36; Ps. 106:46
ᵇDeut. 34:10–12; 2 Sam. 7:9; Esth. 9:4

11:4 ᵃEx. 12:12, 23, 29

11:5 ᵃEx. 4:23; 12:12, 29; Ps. 78:51; 105:36; 135:8; 136:10; Amos 4:10

10:17 ¹*make supplication to*   10:21 ¹Lit. *that one may feel the darkness*
10:25 ¹Lit. *into our hands*

the animals. 6ªThen there shall be a great cry throughout all the land of Egypt, ᵇsuch as was not like it *before,* nor shall be like it again. 7ªBut against none of the children of Israel ᵇshall a dog ¹move its tongue, against man or beast, that you may know that the LORD does make a difference between the Egyptians and Israel.' 8And ªall these your servants shall come down to me and bow down to me, saying, 'Get out, and all the people who follow you!' After that I will go out." ᵇThen he went out from Pharaoh in great anger.

9But the LORD said to Moses, ª"Pharaoh will not heed you, so that ᵇMy wonders may be multiplied in the land of Egypt." 10So Moses and Aaron did all these wonders before Pharaoh; ªand the LORD hardened Pharaoh's heart, and he did not let the children of Israel go out of his land.

THE PASSOVER INSTITUTED
(Num. 9:1–14; Deut. 16:1–8; Ezek. 45:21–25)

12 Now the LORD spoke to Moses and Aaron in the land of Egypt, saying, 2ª"This month *shall be* your beginning of months; it *shall be* the first month of the year to you. 3Speak to all the congregation of Israel, saying: 'On the ªtenth of this month every man shall take for himself a lamb, according to the house of *his* father, a lamb for a household. 4And if the household is too small for the lamb, let him and his neighbor next to his house take *it* according to the number of the persons; according to each man's need you shall make your count for the lamb. 5Your lamb shall be ªwithout¹ blemish, a male ²of the first year. You may take *it* from the sheep or from the goats. 6Now you shall keep it until the ªfourteenth day of the same month. Then the whole assembly of the congregation of Israel shall kill it at twilight. 7And they shall take *some* of the blood and put *it* on the two doorposts and on the lintel of the houses where they eat it. 8Then they shall eat the flesh on that ªnight; ᵇroasted in fire, with ᶜunleavened bread *and* with bitter *herbs* they shall eat it. 9Do not eat it raw, nor boiled at all with water, but ªroasted in fire—its head with its legs and its entrails. 10ªYou shall let none of it remain until morning, and what remains of it until morning you shall burn with fire. 11And thus you shall eat it: ¹*with* a belt on your waist, your sandals on your feet, and your staff in your hand. So you shall eat it in haste. ªIt *is* the LORD's Passover.

12'For I ªwill pass through the land of Egypt on that night, and will strike all the firstborn in the land of Egypt, both man and beast; and ᵇagainst all the gods of Egypt I will execute judgment: ᶜI *am* the LORD. 13Now the blood shall be a sign for you on the houses where you *are.* And when I see the blood, I will pass over you; and the plague shall not be on you to destroy *you* when I strike the land of Egypt.

14'So this day shall be to you ªa memorial; and you shall keep it as a ᵇfeast to the LORD throughout your generations. You shall keep it as a feast ᶜby an everlasting ordinance. 15ªSeven days you shall eat unleavened bread. On the first day you shall remove leaven from your houses. For whoever eats leavened bread from the first day until the seventh day, ᵇthat ¹person shall be ²cut off from Israel. 16On the first day

Cross references (left margin)

11:6 ªEx. 12:30; Amos 5:17
ᵇEx. 10:14
11:7 ªEx. 8:22
ᵇJosh. 10:21
11:8
ªEx. 12:31–33
ᵇEx. 10:29; Heb. 11:27
11:9 ªEx. 3:19; 7:4; 10:1 ᵇEx. 7:3; 9:16
11:10 ªEx. 7:3; 9:12; 10:1, 20, 27; Josh. 11:20; Is. 63:17; John 12:40; Rom. 2:5
12:2 ªEx. 13:4; 23:15; 34:18; Deut. 16:1
12:3 ªJosh. 4:19
12:5
ªLev. 22:18–21; 23:12; Mal. 1:8, 14; [Heb. 9:14; 1 Pet. 1:19]
12:6 ªEx. 12:14, 17; Lev. 23:5; Num. 9:1–3, 11; 28:16; Deut. 16:1, 4, 6
12:8 ªEx. 34:25; Num. 9:12
ᵇDeut. 16:7
ᶜDeut. 16:3, 4; 1 Cor. 5:8
12:9 ªDeut. 16:7
12:10 ªEx. 16:19; 23:18; 34:25
12:11 ªEx. 12:13, 21, 27, 43
12:12
ªEx. 11:4, 5
ᵇNum. 33:4
ᶜEx. 6:2
12:14 ªEx. 13:9
ᵇLev. 23:4, 5; 2 Kin. 23:21
ᶜEx. 12:17, 24; 13:10
12:15
ªEx. 13:6, 7; 23:15; 34:18; Lev. 23:6; Num. 28:17; Deut. 16:3, 8
ᵇGen. 17:14; Ex. 12:19; Num. 9:13

11:7 ¹*sharpen* 12:5 ¹*perfect* or *sound* ²*a year old* 12:11 ¹Made ready to travel 12:15 ¹*soul* ²*Put to death*

there shall be ᵃa holy convocation, and on the seventh day there shall be a holy convocation for you. No manner of work shall be done on them; but *that* which everyone must eat—that only may be prepared by you. ¹⁷So you shall observe *the Feast of* Unleavened Bread, for ᵃon this same day I will have brought your ¹armies ᵇout of the land of Egypt. Therefore you shall observe this day throughout your generations as an everlasting ordinance. ¹⁸ᵃIn the first *month,* on the fourteenth day of the month at evening, you shall eat unleavened bread, until the twenty-first day of the month at evening. ¹⁹For ᵃseven days no leaven shall be found in your houses, since whoever eats what is leavened, that same person shall be cut off from the congregation of Israel, whether *he is* a stranger or a native of the land. ²⁰You shall eat nothing leavened; in all your dwellings you shall eat unleavened bread.'"

²¹Then ᵃMoses called for all the ᵇelders of Israel and said to them, ᶜ"Pick out and take lambs for yourselves according to your families, and kill the Passover *lamb.* ²²ᵃAnd you shall take a bunch of hyssop, dip *it* in the blood that *is* in the basin, and ᵇstrike the lintel and the two doorposts with the blood that *is* in the basin. And none of you shall go out of the door of his house until morning. ²³ᵃFor the LORD will pass through to strike the Egyptians; and when He sees the ᵇblood on the ¹lintel and on the two doorposts, the LORD will pass over the door and ᶜnot allow ᵈthe destroyer to come into your houses to strike *you.* ²⁴And you shall ᵃobserve this thing as an ordinance for you and your sons forever. ²⁵It will come to pass when you come to the land which the LORD will give you, ᵃjust as He promised, that you shall keep this service. ²⁶ᵃAnd it shall be, when your children say to you, 'What do you mean by this service?' ²⁷that you shall say, ᵃ'It *is* the Passover sacrifice of the LORD, who passed over the houses of the children of Israel in Egypt when He struck the Egyptians and delivered our households.'" So the people ᵇbowed their heads and worshiped. ²⁸Then the children of Israel went away and ᵃdid *so;* just as the LORD had commanded Moses and Aaron, so they did.

THE TENTH PLAGUE: DEATH OF THE FIRSTBORN

(Ex. 11:1–10)

²⁹ᵃAnd it came to pass at midnight that ᵇthe LORD struck all the firstborn in the land of Egypt, from the firstborn of Pharaoh who sat on his throne to the firstborn of the captive who *was* ¹in the dungeon, and all the firstborn of ᶜlivestock. ³⁰So Pharaoh rose in the night, he, all his servants, and all the Egyptians; and there was a great cry in Egypt, for *there was* not a house where *there was* not one dead.

THE EXODUS

³¹Then he ᵃcalled for Moses and Aaron by night, and said, "Rise, go out from among my people, ᵇboth you and the children of Israel. And go, serve the LORD as you have ᶜsaid. ³²ᵃAlso take your flocks and your herds, as you have said, and be gone; and bless me also."

³³ᵃAnd the Egyptians ᵇurged the people, that they might send them out of the land in haste. For they said, "We *shall* all

12:16
ᵃLev. 23:2, 7, 8;
Num. 28:18, 25

12:17 ᵃEx. 12:14;
13:3, 10
ᵇNum. 33:1

12:18 ᵃEx. 12:2;
Lev. 23:5–8;
Num. 28:16–25

12:19 ᵃEx. 12:15;
23:15; 34:18

12:21
ᵃ[Heb. 11:28]
ᵇEx. 3:16
ᶜEx. 12:3;
Num. 9:4;
Josh. 5:10;
2 Kin. 23:21;
Ezra 6:20;
Mark 14:12–16

12:22
ᵃHeb. 11:28
ᵇEx. 12:7

12:23 ᵃEx. 11:4;
12:12, 13
ᵇEx. 24:8
ᶜEzek. 9:6;
Rev. 7:3; 9:4
ᵈ1 Cor. 10:10;
Heb. 11:28

12:24 ᵃEx. 12:14,
17; 13:5, 10

12:25 ᵃEx. 3:8, 17

12:26 ᵃEx. 10:2;
13:8, 14, 15;
Deut. 32:7;
Josh. 4:6;
Ps. 78:6

12:27 ᵃEx. 12:11
ᵇEx. 4:31

12:28
ᵃ[Heb. 11:28]

12:29 ᵃEx. 11:4,
5 ᵇNum. 8:17;
33:4; Ps. 135:8;
136:10 ᶜEx. 9:6

12:31 ᵃEx. 10:28,
29 ᵇEx. 8:25; 11:1
ᶜEx. 10:9

12:32
ᵃEx. 10:9, 26

12:33 ᵃEx. 10:7
ᵇEx. 11:8;
Ps. 105:38

12:17 ¹*hosts*   12:23 ¹Crosspiece at top of door   12:29 ¹*in prison*

be dead." ³⁴So the people took their dough before it was leavened, having their kneading bowls bound up in their clothes on their shoulders. ³⁵Now the children of Israel had done according to the word of Moses, and they had asked from the Egyptians ^aarticles of silver, articles of gold, and clothing. ^{36a}And the LORD had given the people favor in the sight of the Egyptians, so that they granted them *what they requested.* Thus ^bthey plundered the Egyptians.

³⁷Then ^athe children of Israel journeyed from ^bRameses to Succoth, about ^csix hundred thousand men on foot, besides children. ³⁸A ^amixed multitude went up with them also, and flocks and herds—a great deal of ^blivestock. ³⁹And they baked unleavened cakes of the dough which they had brought out of Egypt; for it was not leavened, because ^athey were driven out of Egypt and could not wait, nor had they prepared provisions for themselves.

⁴⁰Now the ¹sojourn of the children of Israel who lived in ²Egypt *was* ^afour hundred and thirty years. ⁴¹And it came to pass at the end of the four hundred and thirty years—on that very same day—it came to pass that ^aall the armies of the LORD went out from the land of Egypt. ⁴²It *is* ^aa ¹night of solemn observance to the LORD for bringing them out of the land of Egypt. This *is* that night of the LORD, a solemn observance for all the children of Israel throughout their generations.

PASSOVER REGULATIONS
(Gen. 17:9–14; Ex. 12:1–13)

⁴³And the LORD said to Moses and Aaron, "This *is* ^athe ordinance of the Passover: No foreigner shall eat it. ⁴⁴But every man's servant who is bought for money, when you have ^acircumcised him, then he may eat it. ^{45a}A sojourner and a hired servant shall not eat it. ⁴⁶In one house it shall be eaten; you shall not carry any of the flesh outside the house, ^anor shall you break one of its bones. ^{47a}All the congregation of Israel shall keep it. ⁴⁸And ^awhen a stranger ¹dwells with you *and wants* to keep the Passover to the LORD, let all his males be circumcised, and then let him come near and keep it; and he shall be as a native of the land. For no uncircumcised person shall eat it. ^{49a}One law shall be for the native-born and for the stranger who dwells among you."

⁵⁰Thus all the children of Israel did; as the LORD commanded Moses and Aaron, so they did. ^{51a}And it came to pass, on that very same day, that the LORD brought the children of Israel out of the land of Egypt ^baccording to their armies.

THE FIRSTBORN CONSECRATED

13 Then the LORD spoke to Moses, saying, ^{2a}"Consecrate¹ to Me all the firstborn, whatever opens the womb among the children of Israel, *both* of man and beast; it is Mine."

THE FEAST OF UNLEAVENED BREAD
(Ex. 12:14–20)

³And Moses said to the people: ^a"Remember this day in which you went out of Egypt, out of the house of ¹bondage; for

12:35 ^aEx. 3:21, 22; 11:2, 3; Ps. 105:37
12:36 ^aEx. 3:21 ^bGen. 15:14
12:37 ^aNum. 33:3, 5 ^bGen. 47:11; Ex. 1:11; Num. 33:3, 4 ^cGen. 12:2; Ex. 38:26; Num. 1:46; 2:32; 11:21; 26:51
12:38 ^aNum. 11:4 ^bEx. 17:3; Num. 20:19; 32:1; Deut. 3:19
12:39 ^aEx. 6:1; 11:1; 12:31–33
12:40 ^aGen. 15:13, 16; Acts 7:6; Gal. 3:17
12:41 ^aEx. 3:8, 10; 6:6; 7:4
12:42 ^aEx. 13:10; 34:18; Deut. 16:1, 6
12:43 ^aEx. 12:11; Num. 9:14
12:44 ^aGen. 17:12, 13; Lev. 22:11
12:45 ^aLev. 22:10
12:46 ^aNum. 9:12; Ps. 34:20; [John 19:33, 36]
12:47 ^aEx. 12:6; Num. 9:13, 14
12:48 ^aNum. 9:14
12:49 ^aLev. 24:22; Num. 15:15, 16; [Gal. 3:28]
12:51 ^aEx. 12:41; 20:2 ^bEx. 6:26
13:2 ^aEx. 13:12, 13, 15; 22:29; Lev. 27:26; Num. 3:13; 8:16; 18:15; Deut. 15:19; Luke 2:23
13:3 ^aEx. 12:42; Deut. 16:3

12:40 ¹Length of the stay ²Sam., LXX *Egypt and Canaan* 12:42 ¹*night of vigil* 12:48 ¹As a resident alien 13:2 ¹*Set apart* 13:3 ¹Lit. *slaves*

^bby strength of hand the LORD brought you out of this *place.* ^cNo leavened bread shall be eaten. ^{4a}On this day you are going out, in the month Abib. ⁵And it shall be, when the LORD ^abrings you into the ^bland of the Canaanites and the Hittites and the Amorites and the Hivites and the Jebusites, which He ^cswore to your fathers to give you, a land flowing with milk and honey, ^dthat you shall keep this service in this month. ^{6a}Seven days you shall eat unleavened bread, and on the seventh day *there shall be* a feast to the LORD. ⁷Unleavened bread shall be eaten seven days. And ^ano leavened bread shall be seen among you, nor shall leaven be seen among you in all your quarters. ⁸And you shall ^atell your son in that day, saying, '*This is done* because of what the LORD did for me when I came up from Egypt.' ⁹It shall be as ^aa sign to you on your hand and as a memorial between your eyes, that the LORD's law may be in your mouth; for with a strong hand the LORD has brought you out of Egypt. ^{10a}You shall therefore keep this ¹ordinance in its season from year to year.

THE LAW OF THE FIRSTBORN

¹¹"And it shall be, when the LORD ^abrings you into the land of the ^bCanaanites, as He swore to you and your fathers, and gives it to you, ^{12a}that you shall ¹set apart to the LORD all that open the womb, that is, every firstborn that comes from an animal which you have; the males *shall be* the LORD's. ¹³But ^aevery firstborn of a donkey you shall redeem with a lamb; and if you will not redeem *it,* then you shall break its neck. And all the firstborn of man among your sons ^byou shall redeem. ^{14a}So it shall be, when your son asks you in time to come, saying, 'What *is* this?' that you shall say to him, ^b'By strength of hand the LORD brought us out of Egypt, out of the house of bondage. ¹⁵And it came to pass, when Pharaoh was stubborn about letting us go, that ^athe LORD killed all the firstborn in the land of Egypt, both the firstborn of man and the firstborn of beast. Therefore I sacrifice to the LORD all males that open the womb, but all the firstborn of my sons I redeem.' ¹⁶It shall be as ^aa sign on your hand and as frontlets between your eyes, for by strength of hand the LORD brought us out of Egypt."

THE WILDERNESS WAY

(Ex. 40:34–38; Num. 9:15–23; 1 Kin. 8:10, 11)

¹⁷Then it came to pass, when Pharaoh had let the people go, that God did not lead them *by* way of the land of the Philistines, although that *was* near; for God said, "Lest perhaps the people ^achange their minds when they see war, and ^breturn to Egypt." ¹⁸So God ^aled the people around *by* way of the wilderness of the Red Sea. And the children of Israel went up in orderly ranks out of the land of Egypt.

¹⁹And Moses took the ^abones of ^bJoseph with him, for he had placed the children of Israel under solemn oath, saying, ^c"God will surely ¹visit you, and you shall carry up my bones from here with you."

²⁰So ^athey took their journey from ^bSuccoth and camped in Etham at the edge of the wilderness. ²¹And ^athe LORD went

13:3 ^bEx. 3:20; 6:1 ^cEx. 12:8, 19

13:4 ^aEx. 12:2; 23:15; 34:18; Deut. 16:1

13:5 ^aEx. 3:8, 17; Josh. 24:11 ^bGen. 17:8; Deut. 30:5 ^cEx. 6:8 ^dEx. 12:25, 26

13:6 ^aEx. 12:15–20

13:7 ^aEx. 12:19

13:8 ^aEx. 10:2; 12:26; 13:14; Ps. 44:1

13:9 ^aEx. 12:14; 13:16; 31:13; Deut. 6:8; 11:18; Matt. 23:5

13:10 ^aEx. 12:14, 24

13:11 ^aEx. 13:5 ^bNum. 21:3

13:12 ^aEx. 13:1, 2; 22:29; 34:19; Lev. 27:26; Num. 18:15; Ezek. 44:30; Luke 2:23

13:13 ^aEx. 34:20; Num. 18:15 ^bNum. 3:46, 47; 18:15, 16

13:14 ^aEx. 10:2; 12:26, 27; 13:8; Deut. 6:20; Josh. 4:6, 21 ^bEx. 13:3, 9

13:15 ^aEx. 12:29

13:16 ^aEx. 13:9; Deut. 6:8

13:17 ^aEx. 14:11; Num. 14:1–4 ^bDeut. 17:16

13:18 ^aEx. 14:2; Num. 33:6

13:19 ^aGen. 50:24, 25; Josh. 24:32 ^bEx. 1:6; Deut. 33:13–17 ^cEx. 4:31

13:20 ^aNum. 33:6–8 ^bEx. 12:37

13:21 ^aEx. 14:19, 24; 33:9, 10; Num. 9:15; 14:14; Deut. 1:33; Neh. 9:12; Ps. 78:14; 99:7; 105:39; [Is. 4:5]; 1 Cor. 10:1

13:10 ¹regulation   13:12 ¹Lit. *cause to pass over*   13:19 ¹*give attention to*

before them by day in a pillar of cloud to lead the way, and by night in a pillar of fire to give them light, so as to go by day and night. 22He did not take away the pillar of cloud by day or the pillar of fire by night *from* before the people.

THE RED SEA CROSSING

14 Now the LORD spoke to Moses, saying: 2"Speak to the children of Israel, ᵃthat they turn and camp before ᵇPi Hahiroth, between ᶜMigdol and the sea, opposite Baal Zephon; you shall camp before it by the sea. 3For Pharaoh will say of the children of Israel, ᵃ'They *are* bewildered by the land; the wilderness has closed them in.' 4Then ᵃI will harden Pharaoh's heart, so that he will pursue them; and I ᵇwill gain honor over Pharaoh and over all his army, ᶜthat the Egyptians may know that I *am* the LORD." And they did so.

5Now it was told the king of Egypt that the people had fled, and ᵃthe heart of Pharaoh and his servants was turned against the people; and they said, "Why have we done this, that we have let Israel go from serving us?" 6So he ¹made ready his chariot and took his people with him. 7Also, he took ᵃsix hundred choice chariots, and all the chariots of Egypt with captains over every one of them. 8And the LORD ᵃhardened the heart of Pharaoh king of Egypt, and he pursued the children of Israel; and ᵇthe children of Israel went out with boldness. 9So the ᵃEgyptians pursued them, all the horses *and* chariots of Pharaoh, his horsemen and his army, and overtook them camping by the sea beside Pi Hahiroth, before Baal Zephon.

10And when Pharaoh drew near, the children of Israel lifted their eyes, and behold, the Egyptians marched after them. So they were very afraid, and the children of Israel ᵃcried out to the LORD. 11ᵃThen they said to Moses, "Because *there were* no graves in Egypt, have you taken us away to die in the wilderness? Why have you so dealt with us, to bring us up out of Egypt? 12ᵃIs this not the word that we told you in Egypt, saying, 'Let us alone that we may serve the Egyptians'? For *it would have been* better for us to serve the Egyptians than that we should die in the wilderness."

13And Moses said to the people, ᵃ"Do not be afraid. ᵇStand still, and see the ᶜsalvation¹ of the LORD, which He will accomplish for you today. For the Egyptians whom you see today, you shall ᵈsee again no more forever. 14ᵃThe LORD will fight for you, and you shall ᵇhold¹ your peace."

15And the LORD said to Moses, "Why do you cry to Me? Tell the children of Israel to go forward. 16But ᵃlift up your rod, and stretch out your hand over the sea and divide it. And the children of Israel shall go on dry *ground* through the midst of the sea. 17And I indeed will ᵃharden the hearts of the Egyptians, and they shall follow them. So I will ᵇgain honor over Pharaoh and over all his army, his chariots, and his horsemen. 18Then the Egyptians shall know that I *am* the LORD, when I have gained honor for Myself over Pharaoh, his chariots, and his horsemen."

19And the Angel of God, ᵃwho went before the camp of Israel, moved and went behind them; and the pillar of cloud went from before them and stood behind them. 20So it came

14:2 ᵃEx. 13:18
ᵇNum. 33:7
ᶜJer. 44:1

14:3 ᵃPs. 71:11

14:4 ᵃEx. 4:21;
7:3; 14:17
ᵇEx. 9:16;
14:17, 18, 23;
Rom. 9:17, 22, 23
ᶜEx. 7:5; 14:25

14:5 ᵃPs. 105:25

14:7 ᵃEx. 15:4

14:8 ᵃEx. 14:4
ᵇEx. 6:1; 13:9;
Num. 33:3;
Acts 13:17

14:9 ᵃEx. 15:9;
Josh. 24:6

14:10
ᵃJosh. 24:7;
Neh. 9:9;
Ps. 34:17; 107:6

14:11 ᵃEx. 5:21;
15:24; 16:2; 17:3;
Num. 14:2, 3;
20:3; Ps. 106:7, 8

14:12
ᵃEx. 5:21; 6:9

14:13 ᵃGen. 15:1;
46:3; Ex. 20:20;
2 Chr. 20:15, 17;
Is. 41:10, 13, 14
ᵇPs. 46:10, 11
ᶜEx. 14:30; 15:2
ᵈDeut. 28:68

14:14 ᵃEx. 14:25;
15:3; Deut. 1:30;
3:22; Josh. 10:14,
42; 23:2;
2 Chr. 20:29;
Neh. 4:20;
Is. 31:4
ᵇ[Is. 30:15]

14:16 ᵃEx. 4:17,
20; 7:19; 14:21,
26; 17:5, 6, 9;
Num. 20:8, 9, 11;
Is. 10:26

14:17 ᵃEx. 14:8
ᵇEx. 14:4

14:19
ᵃEx. 13:21, 22;
[Is. 63:9]

14:6 ¹harnessed   14:13 ¹deliverance   14:14 ¹Lit. *be quiet*

between the camp of the Egyptians and the camp of Israel. Thus it was a cloud and darkness *to the one,* and it gave light by night *to the other,* so that the one did not come near the other all that night.

²¹Then Moses stretched out his hand over the sea; and the LORD caused the sea to go *back* by a strong east wind all that night, and ᵃmade the sea into dry *land,* and the waters were ᵇdivided. ²²So ᵃthe children of Israel went into the midst of the sea on the dry *ground,* and the waters *were* ᵇa wall to them on their right hand and on their left. ²³And the Egyptians pursued and went after them into the midst of the sea, all Pharaoh's horses, his chariots, and his horsemen.

²⁴Now it came to pass, in the morning ᵃwatch, that ᵇthe LORD looked down upon the army of the Egyptians through the pillar of fire and cloud, and He ¹troubled the army of the Egyptians. ²⁵And He ¹took off their chariot wheels, so that they drove them with difficulty; and the Egyptians said, "Let us flee from the face of Israel, for the LORD ᵃfights for them against the Egyptians."

²⁶Then the LORD said to Moses, "Stretch out your hand over the sea, that the waters may come back upon the Egyptians, on their chariots, and on their horsemen." ²⁷And Moses stretched out his hand over the sea; and when the morning appeared, the sea ᵃreturned to its full depth, while the Egyptians were fleeing into it. So the LORD ᵇoverthrew¹ the Egyptians in the midst of the sea. ²⁸Then ᵃthe waters returned and covered the chariots, the horsemen, *and* all the army of Pharaoh that came into the sea after them. Not so much as one of them remained. ²⁹But ᵃthe children of Israel had walked on dry *land* in the midst of the sea, and the waters *were* a wall to them on their right hand and on their left.

³⁰So the LORD ᵃsaved¹ Israel that day out of the hand of the Egyptians, and Israel ᵇsaw the Egyptians dead on the seashore. ³¹Thus Israel saw the great ¹work which the LORD had done in Egypt; so the people feared the LORD, and ᵃbelieved the LORD and His servant Moses.

THE SONG OF MOSES
(Ex. 14:13, 14; Ps. 78:12–14)

15 Then ᵃMoses and the children of Israel sang this song to the LORD, and spoke, saying:

"I will ᵇsing to the LORD,
  For He has triumphed gloriously!
  The horse and its rider
  He has thrown into the sea!
2 The LORD *is* my strength and ᵃsong,
  And He has become my salvation;
  He *is* my God, and ᵇI will praise Him;
  My ᶜfather's God, and I ᵈwill exalt Him.
3 The LORD *is* a man of ᵃwar;
  The LORD *is* His ᵇname.
4 ᵃPharaoh's chariots and his army He has cast into the sea;
  ᵇHis chosen captains also are drowned in the Red Sea.

14:21 ᵃPs. 66:6; 106:9; 136:13, 14
ᵇEx. 15:8; Josh. 3:16; 4:23; Neh. 9:11; Ps. 74:13; 78:13; 114:3, 5; Is. 63:12, 13

14:22 ᵃEx. 15:19; Josh. 3:17; 4:22; Neh. 9:11; Ps. 66:6; 78:13; Is. 63:13; 1 Cor. 10:1; Heb. 11:29
ᵇEx. 14:29; 15:8; Hab. 3:10

14:24 ᵃJudg. 7:19
ᵇEx. 13:21

14:25 ᵃEx. 7:5; 14:4, 14, 18

14:27 ᵃJosh. 4:18
ᵇEx. 15:1, 7; Deut. 11:4; Neh. 9:11; Ps. 78:53; Heb. 11:29

14:28 ᵃPs. 78:53; 106:11

14:29 ᵃEx. 14:22; Ps. 66:6; 78:52, 53; Is. 11:15

14:30 ᵃEx. 14:13; Ps. 106:8, 10; Is. 63:8, 11
ᵇPs. 58:10; 59:10

14:31 ᵃEx. 4:31; 19:9; Ps. 106:12; John 2:11; 11:45

15:1 ᵃPs. 106:12; Rev. 15:3
ᵇIs. 12:1–6

15:2 ᵃPs. 18:1, 2; Is. 12:2; Hab. 3:18, 19
ᵇGen. 28:21, 22
ᶜEx. 3:6, 15, 16
ᵈ2 Sam. 22:47; Ps. 99:5; Is. 25:1

15:3 ᵃEx. 14:14; Rev. 19:11
ᵇEx. 3:15; 6:2, 3, 7, 8; Ps. 24:8; 83:18

15:4 ᵃEx. 14:28
ᵇEx. 14:7

14:24 ¹confused **14:25** ¹Sam., LXX, Syr. *bound* **14:27** ¹Lit. *shook off*
14:30 ¹*delivered* **14:31** ¹Lit. *hand with which the LORD worked*

15:5 ᵃEx. 15:10;
Neh. 9:11

15:6 ᵃEx. 3:20;
Ps. 17:7; 118:15

15:7
ᵃDeut. 33:26
ᵇPs. 78:49,
50 ᶜPs. 59:13
ᵈDeut. 4:24;
Is. 5:24;
Heb. 12:29

15:8 ᵃEx. 14:21,
22, 29 ᵇPs. 78:13

15:9 ᵃJudg. 5:30
ᵇIs. 53:12

15:11 ᵃEx. 8:10;
9:14; Deut. 3:24;
2 Sam. 7:22;
1 Kin. 8:23;
Ps. 71:19; 86:8;
Mic. 7:18
ᵇPs. 68:35;
Is. 6:3; Rev. 4:8
ᶜ1 Chr. 16:25
ᵈEx. 3:20;
Ps. 77:11, 14

15:13 ᵃNeh. 9:12;
[Ps. 77:20]
ᵇEx. 15:17;
Deut. 12:5;
Ps. 78:54

15:14 ᵃJosh. 2:9
ᵇPs. 48:6

15:15
ᵃGen. 36:15,
40 ᵇDeut. 2:4
ᶜNum. 22:3,
4 ᵈJosh. 5:1
ᵉJosh. 2:9–11, 24

15:16 ᵃEx. 23:27;
Deut. 2:25;
Josh. 2:9
ᵇ1 Sam. 25:37
ᶜEx. 15:13;
Ps. 74:2; Is. 43:1;
Jer. 31:11;
[Titus 2:14];
2 Pet. 2:1

15:17 ᵃPs. 44:2;
80:8, 15
ᵇPs. 2:6; 78:54,
68 ᶜPs. 68:16;
76:2; 132:13, 14

15:18
ᵃ2 Sam. 7:16;
Ps. 10:16; 29:10;
Is. 57:15

15:19 ᵃEx. 14:23
ᵇEx. 14:28

5 The depths have covered them;
  ᵃThey sank to the bottom like a stone.

6 "Your ᵃright hand, O LORD, has become glorious in power;
  Your right hand, O LORD, has dashed the enemy in
      pieces.

7 And in the greatness of Your ᵃexcellence
  You have overthrown those who rose against You;
  You sent forth ᵇYour wrath;
  It ᶜconsumed them ᵈlike stubble.

8 And ᵃwith the blast of Your nostrils
  The waters were gathered together;
  ᵇThe floods stood upright like a heap;
  The depths ¹congealed in the heart of the sea.

9 ᵃThe enemy said, 'I will pursue,
  I will overtake,
  I will ᵇdivide the spoil;
  My desire shall be satisfied on them.
  I will draw my sword,
  My hand shall destroy them.'

10 You blew with Your wind,
   The sea covered them;
   They sank like lead in the mighty waters.

11 "Whoᵃ is like You, O LORD, among the ¹gods?
   Who is like You, ᵇglorious in holiness,
   Fearful in ᶜpraises, ᵈdoing wonders?

12 You stretched out Your right hand;
   The earth swallowed them.

13 You in Your mercy have ᵃled forth
   The people whom You have redeemed;
   You have guided them in Your strength
   To ᵇYour holy habitation.

14 "The ᵃpeople will hear and be afraid;
   ᵇSorrow¹ will take hold of the inhabitants of Philistia.

15 ᵃThen ᵇthe chiefs of Edom will be dismayed;
   ᶜThe mighty men of Moab,
   Trembling will take hold of them;
   ᵈAll the inhabitants of Canaan will ᵉmelt away.

16 ᵃFear and dread will fall on them;
   By the greatness of Your arm
   They will be ᵇas still as a stone,
   Till Your people pass over, O LORD,
   Till the people pass over
   ᶜWhom You have purchased.

17 You will bring them in and ᵃplant them
   In the ᵇmountain of Your inheritance,
   In the place, O LORD, which You have made
   For Your own dwelling,
   The ᶜsanctuary, O Lord, which Your hands have
       established.

18 "The ᵃ LORD shall reign forever and ever."

19For the ᵃhorses of Pharaoh went with his chariots and
his horsemen into the sea, and ᵇthe LORD brought back the
waters of the sea upon them. But the children of Israel went
on dry land in the midst of the sea.

15:8 ¹became firm   15:11 ¹mighty ones   15:14 ¹Anguish

THE SONG OF MIRIAM
(Num. 26:59)

20Then Miriam ^athe prophetess, ^bthe sister of Aaron, ^ctook the timbrel in her hand; and all the women went out after her ^dwith timbrels and with dances. 21And Miriam ^aanswered them:

^b"Sing to the LORD,
For He has triumphed gloriously!
The horse and its rider
He has thrown into the sea!"

BITTER WATERS MADE SWEET

22So Moses brought Israel from the Red Sea; then they went out into the Wilderness of ^aShur. And they went three days in the wilderness and found no ^bwater. 23Now when they came to ^aMarah, they could not drink the waters of Marah, for they *were* bitter. Therefore the name of it was called ¹Marah. 24And the people ^acomplained against Moses, saying, "What shall we drink?" 25So he cried out to the LORD, and the LORD showed him a tree. ^aWhen he cast *it* into the waters, the waters were made sweet.

There He ^bmade a statute and an ¹ordinance for them, and there ^cHe tested them, 26and said, ^a"If you diligently heed the voice of the LORD your God and do what is right in His sight, give ear to His commandments and keep all His statutes, I will put none of the ^bdiseases on you which I have brought on the Egyptians. For I *am* the LORD ^cwho heals you."

27^aThen they came to Elim, where there *were* twelve wells of water and seventy palm trees; so they camped there by the waters.

BREAD FROM HEAVEN

16 And they ^ajourneyed from Elim, and all the congregation of the children of Israel came to the Wilderness of Sin, which is between Elim and ^bSinai, on the fifteenth day of the second month after they departed from the land of Egypt. 2Then the whole congregation of the children of Israel ^acomplained against Moses and Aaron in the wilderness. 3And the children of Israel said to them, ^a"Oh, that we had died by the hand of the LORD in the land of Egypt, ^bwhen we sat by the pots of meat *and* when we ate bread to the full! For you have brought us out into this wilderness to kill this whole assembly with hunger."

4Then the LORD said to Moses, "Behold, I will rain ^abread from heaven for you. And the people shall go out and gather ¹a certain quota every day, that I may ^btest them, whether they will ^cwalk in My law or not. 5And it shall be on the sixth day that they shall prepare what they bring in, and ^ait shall be twice as much as they gather daily."

6Then Moses and Aaron said to all the children of Israel, ^a"At evening you shall know that the LORD has brought you out of the land of Egypt. 7And in the morning you shall see ^athe glory of the LORD; for He ^bhears your complaints against the LORD. But ^cwhat *are* we, that you complain against us?" 8Also Moses said, *"This shall be seen* when the LORD gives

15:20 ^aJudg. 4:4
^bEx. 2:4;
Num. 26:59;
1 Chr. 6:3;
Mic. 6:4
^c1 Sam. 18:6;
1 Chr. 15:16;
Ps. 68:25; 81:2;
149:3; Jer. 31:4
^dJudg. 11:34;
21:21;
2 Sam. 6:16;
Ps. 30:11; 150:4
15:21 ^a1 Sam. 18:7
^bEx. 15:1

15:22
^aGen. 16:7;
20:1; 25:18;
Num. 33:8
^bEx. 17:1;
Num. 20:2

15:23
^aNum. 33:8;
Ruth 1:20

15:24 ^aEx. 14:11;
16:2; Ps. 106:13

15:25
^a2 Kin. 2:21
^bJosh. 24:25
^cEx. 16:4;
Deut. 8:2, 16;
Judg. 2:22; 3:1,
4; Ps. 66:10

15:26 ^aEx. 19:5,
6; Deut. 7:12, 15
^bDeut. 28:27, 58,
60 ^cEx. 23:25;
Deut. 32:39;
Ps. 41:3, 4; 103:3;
147:3

15:27
^aNum. 33:9

16:1
^aNum. 33:10,
11; Ezek. 30:15
^bEx. 12:6, 51; 19:1

16:2 ^aEx. 14:11;
15:24; Ps. 106:25;
1 Cor. 10:10

16:3 ^aEx. 17:3;
Num. 14:2, 3;
20:3; Lam. 4:9
^bNum. 11:4, 5

16:4 ^aNeh. 9:15;
Ps. 78:23–25;
105:40;
[John 6:31–35];
1 Cor. 10:3
^bEx. 15:25;
Deut. 8:2, 16
^cJudg. 2:22

16:5 ^aEx. 16:22,
29; Lev. 25:21

16:6 ^aEx. 6:7

16:7 ^aEx. 16:10,
12; Is. 35:2; 40:5;
John 11:4, 40
^bNum. 14:27;
17:5 ^cNum. 16:11

15:23 ¹Lit. *Bitter*   15:25 ¹*regulation*   16:4 ¹Lit. *the portion of a day in its day*

you meat to eat in the evening, and in the morning bread to the full; for the LORD hears your complaints which you make against Him. And what *are* we? Your complaints *are* not against us but ªagainst the LORD."

⁹Then Moses spoke to Aaron, "Say to all the congregation of the children of Israel, ª'Come near before the LORD, for He has heard your complaints.'" ¹⁰Now it came to pass, as Aaron spoke to the whole congregation of the children of Israel, that they looked toward the wilderness, and behold, the glory of the LORD ªappeared in the cloud.

¹¹And the LORD spoke to Moses, saying, ¹²ª"I have heard the complaints of the children of Israel. Speak to them, saying, ᵇ'At twilight you shall eat meat, and ᶜin the morning you shall be filled with bread. And you shall know that I *am* the LORD your God.'"

¹³So it was that ªquail came up at evening and covered the camp, and in the morning ᵇthe dew lay all around the camp. ¹⁴And when the layer of dew lifted, there, on the surface of the wilderness, was ªa small round ᵇsubstance, *as* fine as frost on the ground. ¹⁵So when the children of Israel saw *it*, they said to one another, "What is it?" For they did not know what it *was.*

And Moses said to them, ª"This *is* the bread which the LORD has given you to eat. ¹⁶This is the thing which the LORD has commanded: 'Let every man gather it ªaccording to each one's need, one ᵇomer for each person, *according to the* number of persons; let every man take for *those* who *are* in his tent.'"

¹⁷Then the children of Israel did so and gathered, some more, some less. ¹⁸So when they measured *it* by omers, ªhe who gathered much had nothing left over, and he who gathered little had no lack. Every man had gathered according to each one's need. ¹⁹And Moses said, "Let no one ªleave any of it till morning." ²⁰Notwithstanding they did not ¹heed Moses. But some of them left part of it until morning, and it bred worms and stank. And Moses was angry with them. ²¹So they gathered it every morning, every man according to his need. And when the sun became hot, it melted.

²²And so it was, on the sixth day, *that* they gathered twice as much bread, two omers for each one. And all the rulers of the congregation came and told Moses. ²³Then he said to them, "This *is what* the LORD has said: 'Tomorrow *is* ªa Sabbath rest, a holy Sabbath to the LORD. Bake what you will bake *today*, and boil what you will boil; and lay up for yourselves all that remains, to be kept until morning.'" ²⁴So they laid it up till morning, as Moses commanded; and it did not ªstink, nor were there any worms in it. ²⁵Then Moses said, "Eat that today, for today *is* a Sabbath to the LORD; today you will not find it in the field. ²⁶ªSix days you shall gather it, but on the seventh day, the Sabbath, there will be none."

²⁷Now it happened *that some* of the people went out on the seventh day to gather, but they found none. ²⁸And the LORD said to Moses, "How long ªdo you refuse to keep My commandments and My laws? ²⁹See! For the LORD has given you the Sabbath; therefore He gives you on the sixth day bread for two days. Let every man remain in his place; let no man

---

16:8 ª1 Sam. 8:7;
Luke 10:16;
[Rom. 13:2];
1 Thess. 4:8

16:9
ªNum. 16:16

16:10 ªEx. 13:21;
16:7; Num. 16:19;
1 Kin. 8:10

16:12 ªEx. 16:8;
Num. 14:27
ᵇEx. 16:6
ᶜEx. 16:7;
1 Kin. 20:28;
Joel 3:17

16:13
ªNum. 11:31;
Ps. 78:27–29;
105:40
ᵇNum. 11:9

16:14 ªEx. 16:31;
Num. 11:7, 8;
Deut. 8:3;
Neh. 9:15;
Ps. 78:24; 105:40
ᵇPs. 147:16

16:15 ªEx. 16:4;
Neh. 9:15;
Ps. 78:24;
[John 6:31, 49,
58]; 1 Cor. 10:3

16:16 ªEx. 12:4
ᵇEx. 16:32, 36

16:18
ª2 Cor. 8:15

16:19 ªEx. 12:10;
16:23; 23:18

16:23 ªGen. 2:3;
Ex. 20:8–11;
23:12; 31:15;
35:2; Lev. 23:3;
Neh. 9:13, 14

16:24 ªEx. 16:20

16:26
ªEx. 20:9, 10

16:28
ª2 Kin. 17:14;
Ps. 78:10; 106:13

16:20 ¹listen to

go out of his place on the seventh day." [30]So the people rested on the seventh day.

[31]And the house of Israel called its name [1]Manna. And [a]it *was* like white coriander seed, and the taste of it *was* like wafers *made* with honey.

[32]Then Moses said, "This *is* the thing which the LORD has commanded: 'Fill an omer with it, to be kept for your generations, that they may see the bread with which I fed you in the wilderness, when I brought you out of the land of Egypt.'" [33]And Moses said to Aaron, [a]"Take a pot and put an omer of manna in it, and lay it up before the LORD, to be kept for your generations." [34]As the LORD commanded Moses, so Aaron laid it up [a]before the Testimony, to be kept. [35]And the children of Israel [a]ate manna [b]forty years, [c]until they came to an inhabited land; they ate manna until they came to the border of the land of Canaan. [36]Now an omer *is* one-tenth of an ephah.

WATER FROM THE ROCK
(Num. 20:1–13)

17 Then [a]all the congregation of the children of Israel set out on their journey from the Wilderness of [b]Sin, according to the commandment of the LORD, and camped in Rephidim; but *there was* no water for the people to [c]drink. [2a]Therefore the people contended with Moses, and said, "Give us water, that we may drink."

So Moses said to them, "Why do you contend with me? Why do you [b]tempt the LORD?"

[3]And the people thirsted there for water, and the people [a]complained against Moses, and said, "Why *is* it you have brought us up out of Egypt, to kill us and our children and our [b]livestock with thirst?"

[4]So Moses [a]cried out to the LORD, saying, "What shall I do with this people? They are almost ready to [b]stone[1] me!"

[5]And the LORD said to Moses, [a]"Go on before the people, and take with you some of the elders of Israel. Also take in your hand your rod with which [b]you struck the river, and go. [6a]Behold, I will stand before you there on the rock in Horeb; and you shall strike the rock, and water will come out of it, that the people may drink."

And Moses did so in the sight of the elders of Israel. [7]So he called the name of the place [a]Massah[1] and [2]Meribah, because of the contention of the children of Israel, and because they [3]tempted the LORD, saying, "Is the LORD among us or not?"

VICTORY OVER THE AMALEKITES
(Gen. 14:7; Num. 13:29; 14:25)

[8a]Now Amalek came and fought with Israel in Rephidim. [9]And Moses said to Joshua, "Choose us some men and go out, fight with Amalek. Tomorrow I will stand on the top of the hill with [a]the rod of God in my hand." [10]So Joshua did as Moses said to him, and fought with Amalek. And Moses, Aaron, and Hur went up to the top of the hill. [11]And so it was, when Moses [a]held up his hand, that Israel prevailed; and when he let down his hand, Amalek prevailed. [12]But Moses' hands *became*

16:31 [a]Num. 11:7–9; Deut. 8:3, 16

16:33 [a]Heb. 9:4; Rev. 2:17

16:34 [a]Ex. 25:16, 21; 27:21; 40:20; Num. 17:10

16:35 [a]Deut. 8:3, 16 [b]Num. 33:38; John 6:31, 49 [c]Josh. 5:12; Neh. 9:20, 21

17:1 [a]Ex. 16:1 [b]Num. 33:11–15 [c]Ex. 15:22; Num. 20:2

17:2 [a]Ex. 14:11; Num. 20:2, 3, 13 [b][Deut. 6:16]; Ps. 78:18, 41; [Matt. 4:7]; 1 Cor. 10:9

17:3 [a]Ex. 16:2, 3 [b]Ex. 12:38

17:4 [a]Ex. 14:15 [b]John 8:59; 10:31

17:5 [a]Ezek. 2:6 [b]Num. 20:8

17:6 [a]Num. 20:10, 11; Deut. 8:15; Neh. 9:15; Ps. 78:15; 105:41; 114:8; [1 Cor. 10:4]

17:7 [a]Num. 20:13, 24; 27:14; Ps. 81:7

17:8 [a]Gen. 36:12; Num. 24:20; Deut. 25:17–19; 1 Sam. 15:2

17:9 [a]Ex. 4:20

17:11 [a][James 5:16]

16:31 [1]Lit. *What?* Ex. 16:15   **17:4** [1]Put me to death by stoning   **17:7** [1]Lit. *Tempted*   [2]Lit. *Contention*   [3]*tested*

[1]heavy; so they took a stone and put *it* under him, and he sat on it. And Aaron and Hur supported his hands, one on one side, and the other on the other side; and his hands were steady until the going down of the sun. [13]So Joshua defeated Amalek and his people with the edge of the sword.

[14]Then the LORD said to Moses, [a]"Write this *for* a memorial in the book and recount *it* in the hearing of Joshua, that [b]I will utterly blot out the remembrance of Amalek from under heaven." [15]And Moses built an altar and called its name, [1]The-LORD-Is-My-Banner; [16]for he said, "Because [1]the LORD has [a]sworn: the LORD *will have* war with Amalek from generation to generation."

JETHRO'S ADVICE
(Deut. 1:9–18)

18 And [a]Jethro, the priest of Midian, Moses' father-in-law, heard of all that [b]God had done for Moses and for Israel His people—that the LORD had brought Israel out of Egypt. [2]Then Jethro, Moses' father-in-law, took [a]Zipporah, Moses' wife, after he had sent her back, [3]with her [a]two sons, of whom the name of one *was* [1]Gershom (for he said, [b]"I have been a [2]stranger in a foreign land") [4]and the name of the other *was* [1]Eliezer (for *he said,* "The God of my father *was* my [a]help, and delivered me from the sword of Pharaoh"); [5]and Jethro, Moses' father-in-law, came with his sons and his wife to Moses in the wilderness, where he was encamped at [a]the mountain of God. [6]Now he had said to Moses, "I, your father-in-law Jethro, am coming to you with your wife and her two sons with her."

[7]So Moses [a]went out to meet his father-in-law, bowed down, and [b]kissed him. And they asked each other about *their* well-being, and they went into the tent. [8]And Moses told his father-in-law all that the LORD had done to Pharaoh and to the Egyptians for Israel's sake, all the hardship that had come upon them on the way, and *how* the LORD had [a]delivered them. [9]Then Jethro rejoiced for all the [a]good which the LORD had done for Israel, whom He had delivered out of the hand of the Egyptians. [10]And Jethro said, [a]"Blessed *be* the LORD, who has delivered you out of the hand of the Egyptians and out of the hand of Pharaoh, *and* who has delivered the people from under the hand of the Egyptians. [11]Now I know that the LORD *is* [a]greater than all the gods; [b]for in the very thing in which they [1]behaved [c]proudly, *He was* above them." [12]Then Jethro, Moses' father-in-law, [1]took a burnt [a]offering and *other* sacrifices *to offer* to God. And Aaron came with all the elders of Israel [b]to eat bread with Moses' father-in-law before God.

[13]And so it was, on the next day, that Moses [a]sat to judge the people; and the people stood before Moses from morning until evening. [14]So when Moses' father-in-law saw all that he did for the people, he said, "What *is* this thing that you are doing for the people? Why do you alone [1]sit, and all the people stand before you from morning until evening?"

17:14 [a]Ex. 24:4; 34:27; Num. 33:2 [b]Deut. 25:19; 1 Sam. 15:3; 2 Sam. 1:1; 1 Chr. 4:43

17:16 [a]Gen. 22:14–16

18:1 [a]Ex. 2:16, 18; 3:1 [b][Ps. 106:2, 8]

18:2 [a]Ex. 2:21; 4:20–26

18:3 [a]Ex. 2:20; 4:20; Acts 7:29 [b]Ex. 2:22

18:4 [a]Gen. 49:25

18:5 [a]Ex. 3:1, 12; 4:27; 24:13

18:7 [a]Gen. 18:2 [b]Gen. 29:13; Ex. 4:27

18:8 [a]Ex. 15:6, 16; Ps. 81:7

18:9 [a][Is. 63:7–14]

18:10 [a]Gen. 14:20; 2 Sam. 18:28; 1 Kin. 8:56; Ps. 68:19, 20

18:11 [a]Ex. 12:12; 15:11; 2 Chr. 2:5; Ps. 95:3; 97:9; 135:5 [b]Ex. 1:10, 16, 22; 5:2, 7 [c]Luke 1:51

18:12 [a]Ex. 24:5 [b]Gen. 31:54; Deut. 12:7

18:13 [a]Deut. 33:4, 5; Matt. 23:2

17:12 [1]Weary of being held up   **17:15** [1]Heb. *YHWH Nissi*   **17:16** [1]Lit. *a hand is upon the throne of the LORD*   **18:3** [1]Lit. *Stranger There*   [2]*sojourner,* temporary resident   **18:4** [1]Lit. *My God Is Help*   **18:11** [1]*acted presumptuously*   **18:12** [1]So with MT, LXX; Syr., Tg., Vg. *offered*   **18:14** [1]Sit as judge

¹⁵And Moses said to his father-in-law, "Because ᵃthe people come to me to inquire of God. ¹⁶When they have ᵃa ¹difficulty, they come to me, and I judge between one and another; and I make known the statutes of God and His laws."

¹⁷So Moses' father-in-law said to him, "The thing that you do *is* not good. ¹⁸Both you and these people who *are* with you will surely wear yourselves out. For this thing *is* too much for you; ᵃyou are not able to perform it by yourself. ¹⁹Listen now to my voice; I will give you ¹counsel, and God will be with you: Stand ᵃbefore God for the people, so that you may ᵇbring the difficulties to God. ²⁰And you shall ᵃteach them the statutes and the laws, and show them the way in which they must walk and ᵇthe work they must do. ²¹Moreover you shall select from all the people ᵃable men, such as ᵇfear God, ᶜmen of truth, ᵈhating covetousness; and place *such* over them *to be* rulers of thousands, rulers of hundreds, rulers of fifties, and rulers of tens. ²²And let them judge the people at all times. ᵃThen it will be *that* every great matter they shall bring to you, but every small matter they themselves shall judge. So it will be easier for you, for ᵇthey will bear *the burden* with you. ²³If you do this thing, and God *so* commands you, then you will be able to endure, and all this people will also go to their ᵃplace in peace."

²⁴So Moses heeded the voice of his father-in-law and did all that he had said. ²⁵And ᵃMoses chose able men out of all Israel, and made them heads over the people: rulers of thousands, rulers of hundreds, rulers of fifties, and rulers of tens. ²⁶So they judged the people at all times; the ᵃhard¹ cases they brought to Moses, but they judged every small case themselves.

²⁷Then Moses let his father-in-law depart, and ᵃhe went his way to his own land.

ISRAEL AT MOUNT SINAI

19 In the third month after the children of Israel had gone out of the land of Egypt, on the same day, ᵃthey came *to* the Wilderness of Sinai. ²For they had departed from ᵃRephidim, had come *to* the Wilderness of Sinai, and camped in the wilderness. So Israel camped there before ᵇthe mountain.

³And ᵃMoses went up to God, and the LORD ᵇcalled to him from the mountain, saying, "Thus you shall say to the house of Jacob, and tell the children of Israel: ⁴ᵃ'You have seen what I did to the Egyptians, and *how* ᵇI ¹bore you on eagles' wings and brought you to Myself. ⁵Now ᵃtherefore, if you will indeed obey My voice and ᵇkeep My covenant, then ᶜyou shall be a special treasure to Me above all people; for all the earth *is* ᵈMine. ⁶And you shall be to Me a ᵃkingdom of priests and a ᵇholy nation.' These *are* the words which you shall speak to the children of Israel."

⁷So Moses came and called for the ᵃelders of the people, and ¹laid before them all these words which the LORD commanded him. ⁸Then ᵃall the people answered together and said, "All that the LORD has spoken we will do." So Moses brought back the words of the people to the LORD. ⁹And the

---

18:15 ᵃLev. 24:12; Num. 9:6, 8; 27:5; Deut. 17:8–13

18:16 ᵃEx. 24:14; Deut. 19:17

18:18 ᵃNum. 11:14, 17; Deut. 1:12

18:19 ᵃEx. 4:16; 20:19 ᵇNum. 9:8; 27:5

18:20 ᵃDeut. 5:1 ᵇDeut. 1:18

18:21 ᵃEx. 18:24, 25; Deut. 1:13, 15; 2 Chr. 19:5–10; Ps. 15:1–5; Acts 6:3 ᵇGen. 42:18; 2 Sam. 23:3 ᶜEzek. 18:8 ᵈDeut. 16:19

18:22 ᵃLev. 24:11; Deut. 1:17 ᵇNum. 11:17

18:23 ᵃEx. 16:29

18:25 ᵃEx. 18:21; Deut. 1:15

18:26 ᵃJob 29:16

18:27 ᵃNum. 10:29, 30

19:1 ᵃNum. 33:15

19:2 ᵃEx. 17:1 ᵇEx. 3:1, 12; 18:5

19:3 ᵃActs 7:38 ᵇEx. 3:4

19:4 ᵃDeut. 29:2 ᵇDeut. 32:11; Is. 63:9; Rev. 12:14

19:5 ᵃEx. 15:26; 23:22 ᵇDeut. 5:2; Ps. 78:10 ᶜDeut. 4:20; 7:6; 14:2; 26:18; 1 Kin. 8:53; Ps. 135:4; Titus 2:14; 1 Pet. 2:9 ᵈEx. 9:29; Deut. 10:14; Job 41:11; Ps. 50:12; 1 Cor. 10:26

19:6 ᵃDeut. 33:2–4; [1 Pet. 2:5, 9; Rev. 1:6; 5:10] ᵇDeut. 7:6; 14:21; 26:19; Is. 62:12; [1 Cor. 3:17]

19:7 ᵃEx. 4:29, 30

19:8 ᵃEx. 4:31; 24:3, 7; Deut. 5:27; 26:17

18:16 ¹dispute   18:19 ¹advice   18:26 ¹difficult matters   19:4 ¹sustained
19:7 ¹set

L ORD said to Moses, "Behold, I come to you [a]in the thick cloud, [b]that the people may hear when I speak with you, and believe you forever."

So Moses told the words of the people to the L ORD.

[10]Then the L ORD said to Moses, "Go to the people and [a]consecrate them today and tomorrow, and let them wash their clothes. [11]And let them be ready for the third day. For on the third day the L ORD will come down upon Mount Sinai in the sight of all the people. [12]You shall set bounds for the people all around, saying, 'Take heed to yourselves *that* you do *not* go up to the mountain or touch its base. [a]Whoever touches the mountain shall surely be put to death. [13]Not a hand shall touch him, but he shall surely be stoned or shot *with an arrow;* whether man or beast, he shall not live.' When the trumpet sounds long, they shall come near the mountain."

[14]So Moses went down from the mountain to the people and sanctified the people, and they washed their clothes. [15]And he said to the people, "Be ready for the third day; [a]do not come near *your* wives."

[16]Then it came to pass on the third day, in the morning, that there were [a]thunderings and lightnings, and a thick cloud on the mountain; and the sound of the trumpet was very loud, so that all the people who *were* in the camp [b]trembled. [17]And [a]Moses brought the people out of the camp to meet with God, and they stood at the foot of the mountain. [18]Now [a]Mount Sinai *was* completely in smoke, because the L ORD descended upon [b]it in fire. [c]Its smoke ascended like the smoke of a furnace, and [1]the [d]whole mountain quaked greatly. [19]And when the blast of the trumpet sounded long and became louder and louder, [a]Moses spoke, and [b]God answered him by voice. [20]Then the L ORD came down upon Mount Sinai, on the top of the mountain. And the L ORD called Moses to the top of the mountain, and Moses went up.

[21]And the L ORD said to Moses, "Go down and warn the people, lest they break through [a]to gaze at the L ORD, and many of them perish. [22]Also let the [a]priests who come near the L ORD [b]consecrate themselves, lest the L ORD [c]break out against them."

[23]But Moses said to the L ORD, "The people cannot come up to Mount Sinai; for You warned us, saying, [a]'Set bounds around the mountain and consecrate it.'"

[24]Then the L ORD said to him, "Away! Get down and then come up, you and Aaron with you. But do not let the priests and the people break through to come up to the L ORD, lest He break out against them." [25]So Moses went down to the people and spoke to them.

THE TEN COMMANDMENTS
(Deut. 5:1–22)

20 And God spoke [a]all these words, saying:

2 [a]"I *am* the L ORD your God, who brought you out of the land of Egypt, [b]out of the house of [1]bondage.

3 [a]"You shall have no other gods before Me.

4 [a]"You shall not make for yourself a carved image—any likeness *of anything* that *is* in heaven above, or that *is* in the

19:9 [a]Ex. 19:16; 20:21; 24:15; Deut. 4:11; Ps. 99:7; Matt. 17:5 [b]Deut. 4:12, 36; John 12:29, 30
19:10 [a]Lev. 11:44, 45; [Heb. 10:22]
19:12 [a]Ex. 34:3; Heb. 12:20
19:15 [a][1 Cor. 7:5]
19:16 [a]Heb. 12:18, 19 [b]Heb. 12:21
19:17 [a]Deut. 4:10
19:18 [a]Deut. 4:11; Judg. 5:5; Ps. 104:32; 144:5 [b]Ex. 3:2; 24:17; Deut. 5:4; 2 Chr. 7:1–3; Heb. 12:18 [c]Gen. 15:17; 19:28; Rev. 15:8 [d]Ps. 68:8; 1 Kin. 19:12; Jer. 4:24; [Heb. 12:26]
19:19 [a]Heb. 12:21 [b]Neh. 9:13; Ps. 81:7
19:21 [a]1 Sam. 6:19
19:22 [a]Ex. 19:24; 24:5 [b]Lev. 10:3; 21:6–8 [c]2 Sam. 6:7, 8
19:23 [a]Ex. 19:12
20:1 [a]Deut. 5:22
20:2 [a]Hos. 13:4 [b]Ex. 13:3; Deut. 7:8
20:3 [a]Deut. 6:14; 2 Kin. 17:35; Jer. 25:6; 35:15
20:4 [a]Lev. 19:4; 26:1; Deut. 4:15–19; 27:15

19:18 [1]LXX *all the people*   **20:2** [1]*slaves*

earth beneath, or that *is* in the water under the earth; [5a]you shall not bow down to them nor [1]serve them. [b]For I, the LORD your God, *am* a jealous God, [c]visiting[2] the iniquity of the fathers upon the children to the third and fourth *generations* of those who hate Me, [6]but [a]showing mercy to thousands, to those who love Me and keep My commandments.

7 [a]"You shall not take the name of the LORD your God in vain, for the LORD [b]will not hold *him* guiltless who takes His name in vain.

8 [a]"Remember the Sabbath day, to keep it holy. [9a]Six days you shall labor and do all your work, [10]but the [a]seventh day *is* the Sabbath of the LORD your God. *In it* you shall do no work: you, nor your son, nor your daughter, nor your male servant, nor your female servant, nor your cattle, [b]nor your stranger who *is* within your gates. [11]For [a]*in* six days the LORD made the heavens and the earth, the sea, and all that *is* in them, and rested the seventh day. Therefore the LORD blessed the Sabbath day and hallowed it.

12 [a]"Honor your father and your mother, that your days may be [b]long upon the land which the LORD your God is giving you.

13 [a]"You shall not murder.

14 [a]"You shall not commit [b]adultery.

15 [a]"You shall not steal.

16 [a]"You shall not bear false witness against your neighbor.

17 [a]"You shall not covet your neighbor's house; [b]you shall not covet your neighbor's wife, nor his male servant, nor his female servant, nor his ox, nor his donkey, nor anything that *is* your neighbor's."

THE PEOPLE AFRAID OF GOD'S PRESENCE

18Now [a]all the people [b]witnessed the thunderings, the lightning flashes, the sound of the trumpet, and the mountain [c]smoking; and when the people saw *it,* they trembled and stood afar off. 19Then they said to Moses, [a]"You speak with us, and we will hear; but [b]let not God speak with us, lest we die."

20And Moses said to the people, [a]"Do not fear; [b]for God has come to test you, and [c]that His fear may be before you, so that you may not sin." 21So the people stood afar off, but Moses drew near [a]the thick darkness where God *was.*

THE LAW OF THE ALTAR

22Then the LORD said to Moses, "Thus you shall say to the children of Israel: 'You have seen that I have talked with you [a]from heaven. 23You shall not make *anything to be* [a]with Me— gods of silver or gods of gold you shall not make for yourselves. 24An altar of [a]earth you shall make for Me, and you shall sacrifice on it your burnt offerings and your peace offerings, [b]your sheep and your oxen. In every [c]place where I [1]record My name I will come to you, and I will [d]bless you. 25And [a]if you make Me an altar of stone, you shall not build it of hewn stone;

20:18 [a]Heb. 12:18, 19 [b]Rev. 1:10, 12 [c]Ex. 19:16, 18   20:19 [a]Gal. 3:19; Heb. 12:19 [b]Deut. 5:5, 23–27   20:20 [a]Ex. 14:13; [Is. 41:10, 13] [b]Ex. 15:25; [Deut. 13:3] [c]Deut. 4:10; 6:24; Prov. 3:7; 16:6; Is. 8:13   20:21 [a]Ex. 19:16; Deut. 5:22   20:22 [a]Deut. 4:36; 5:24, 26; Neh. 9:13   20:23 [a]Ex. 32:1, 2, 4; Deut. 29:17   20:24 [a]Ex. 20:25; 27:1–8 [b]Ex. 24:5; Lev. 1:2 [c]Deut. 12:5; 16:6, 11; 1 Kin. 9:3; 2 Chr. 6:6 [d]Gen. 12:2   20:25 [a]Deut. 27:5

20:5 [1]worship   [2]punishing   20:24 [1]cause My name to be remembered

20:5
[a]Is. 44:15, 19
[b]Ex. 34:14;
Deut. 4:24;
Josh. 24:19;
Nah. 1:2
[c]Num. 14:18, 33;
Deut. 5:9, 10;
1 Kin. 21:29;
Ps. 79:8;
Jer. 32:18
20:6
[a]Deut. 7:9;
Rom. 11:28
20:7 [a]Lev. 19:12;
Deut. 6:13; 10:20;
[Matt. 5:33–37]
[b]Mic. 6:11
20:8 [a]Ex. 23:12;
31:13–16;
Lev. 26:2;
Deut. 5:12
20:9 [a]Ex. 34:21;
35:2, 3; Lev. 23:3;
Deut. 5:13;
Luke 13:14
20:10
[a]Gen. 2:2, 3
[b]Neh. 13:16–19
20:11
[a]Gen. 2:2, 3;
Ex. 31:17
20:12 [a]Lev. 19:3;
Deut. 27:16;
Matt. 15:4; 19:19;
Mark 7:10; 10:19;
Luke 18:20;
Eph. 6:2
[b]Deut. 5:16, 33;
6:2; 11:8, 9
20:13
[a][Matt. 5:21,
22]; 19:18;
Mark 10:19;
Luke 18:20;
Rom. 13:9;
[1 John 3:15]
20:14
[a]Matt. 5:27;
Mark 10:19;
Luke 18:20;
Rom. 13:9;
James 2:11
[b]Lev. 20:10;
Deut. 5:18
20:15 [a]Ex. 21:16;
Lev. 19:11, 13;
Matt. 19:18;
Rom. 13:9
20:16
[a]Ex. 23:1, 7;
Deut. 5:20;
Matt. 19:18
20:17
[a][Luke 12:15];
Rom. 7:7; 13:9;
[Eph. 5:3, 5];
Heb. 13:5
[b]2 Sam. 11:2;
[Matt. 5:28]

for if you [b]use your tool on it, you have profaned it. [26]Nor shall you go up by steps to My altar, that your [a]nakedness may not be exposed on it.'

THE LAW CONCERNING SERVANTS

(Deut. 15:12–18)

21 "Now these *are* the [1]judgments which you shall [a]set before them: [2a]If you buy a Hebrew servant, he shall serve six years; and in the seventh he shall go out free and pay nothing. [3]If he comes in by himself, he shall go out by himself; if he *comes in* married, then his wife shall go out with him. [4]If his master has given him a wife, and she has borne him sons or daughters, the wife and her children shall be her master's, and he shall go out by himself. [5a]But if the servant plainly says, 'I love my master, my wife, and my children; I will not go out free,' [6]then his master shall bring him to the [a]judges. He shall also bring him to the door, or to the doorpost, and his master shall pierce his ear with an awl; and he shall serve him forever.

[7]"And if a man [a]sells his daughter to be a female slave, she shall not go out as the male slaves do. [8]If she [1]does not please her master, who has betrothed her to himself, then he shall let her be redeemed. He shall have no right to sell her to a foreign people, since he has dealt deceitfully with her. [9]And if he has betrothed her to his son, he shall deal with her according to the custom of daughters. [10]If he takes another *wife,* he shall not diminish her food, her clothing, [a]and her marriage rights. [11]And if he does not do these three for her, then she shall go out free, without *paying* money.

THE LAW CONCERNING VIOLENCE

[12a]"He who strikes a man so that he dies shall surely be put to death. [13]However, [a]if he did not lie in wait, but God [b]delivered *him* into his hand, then [c]I will appoint for you a place where he may flee.

[14]"But if a man acts with [a]premeditation against his neighbor, to kill him by treachery, [b]you shall take him from My altar, that he may die.

[15]"And he who strikes his father or his mother shall surely be put to death.

[16a]"He who kidnaps a man and [b]sells him, or if he is [c]found in his hand, shall surely be put to death.

[17]"And [a]he who curses his father or his mother shall surely be put to death.

[18]"If men contend with each other, and one strikes the other with a stone or with *his* fist, and he does not die but is confined to *his* bed, [19]if he rises again and walks about outside [a]with his staff, then he who struck *him* shall be [1]acquitted. He shall only pay *for* the loss of his time, and shall provide *for him* to be thoroughly healed.

[20]"And if a man beats his male or female servant with a rod, so that he dies under his hand, he shall surely be punished. [21]Notwithstanding, if he remains alive a day or two, he shall not be punished; for he *is* his [a]property.

[22]"If men [1]fight, and hurt a woman with child, so that [2]she gives birth prematurely, yet no harm follows, he shall surely

---

20:25
[b]Josh. 8:30, 31

20:26
[a]Ex. 28:42, 43

21:1 [a]Ex. 24:3, 4;
Deut. 4:14; 6:1

21:2
[a]Lev. 25:39–43;
Deut. 15:12–18;
Jer. 34:14

21:5
[a]Deut. 15:16, 17

21:6 [a]Ex. 12:12;
22:8, 9

21:7 [a]Neh. 5:5

21:10
[a][1 Cor. 7:3, 5]

21:12 [a]Gen. 9:6;
Lev. 24:17;
Num. 35:30;
[Matt. 26:52]

21:13
[a]Deut. 19:4, 5
[b]1 Sam. 24:4, 10,
18 [c]Num. 35:11;
Deut. 19:3;
Josh. 20:2

21:14
[a]Deut. 19:11, 12;
[Heb. 10:26]
[b]1 Kin. 2:28–34

21:16
[a]Deut. 24:7
[b]Gen. 37:28
[c]Ex. 22:4

21:17 [a]Lev. 20:9;
Prov. 20:20;
Matt. 15:4;
Mark 7:10

21:19
[a]2 Sam. 3:29

21:21
[a]Lev. 25:44–46

21:1 [1]*ordinances*   21:8 [1]Lit. *is evil in the eyes of*   21:19 [1]*exempt from punishment*   21:22 [1]*struggle*   [2]Lit. *her children come out*

be punished accordingly as the woman's husband imposes on him; and he shall ªpay as the judges *determine.* 23But if *any* harm follows, then you shall give life for life, 24ªeye for eye, tooth for tooth, hand for hand, foot for foot, 25burn for burn, wound for wound, stripe for stripe.

26"If a man strikes the eye of his male or female servant, and destroys it, he shall let him go free for the sake of his eye. 27And if he knocks out the tooth of his male or female servant, he shall let him go free for the sake of his tooth.

ANIMAL CONTROL LAWS

28"If an ox gores a man or a woman to death, then ªthe ox shall surely be stoned, and its flesh shall not be eaten; but the owner of the ox *shall be* 1acquitted. 29But if the ox 1tended to thrust with its horn in times past, and it has been made known to his owner, and he has not kept it confined, so that it has killed a man or a woman, the ox shall be stoned and its owner also shall be put to death. 30If there is imposed on him a sum of money, then he shall pay ªto redeem his life, whatever is imposed on him. 31Whether it has gored a son or gored a daughter, according to this judgment it shall be done to him. 32If the ox gores a male or female servant, he shall give to their master ªthirty shekels of silver, and the box shall be stoned.

33"And if a man opens a pit, or if a man digs a pit and does not cover it, and an ox or a donkey falls in it, 34the owner of the pit shall make *it* good; he shall give money to their owner, but the dead *animal* shall be his.

35"If one man's ox hurts another's, so that it dies, then they shall sell the live ox and divide the money from it; and the dead *ox* they shall also divide. 36Or if it was known that the ox tended to thrust in time past, and its owner has not kept it confined, he shall surely pay ox for ox, and the dead animal shall be his own.

RESPONSIBILITY FOR PROPERTY

22 "If a man steals an ox or a sheep, and slaughters it or sells it, he shall ªrestore five oxen for an ox and four sheep for a sheep. 2If the thief is found ªbreaking in, and he is struck so that he dies, *there shall be* bno guilt for his bloodshed. 3If the sun has risen on him, *there shall be* guilt for his bloodshed. He should make full restitution; if he has nothing, then he shall be ªsold1 for his theft. 4If the theft is certainly ªfound alive in his hand, whether it is an ox or donkey or sheep, he shall brestore double.

5"If a man causes a field or vineyard to be grazed, and lets loose his animal, and it feeds in another man's field, he shall make restitution from the best of his own field and the best of his own vineyard.

6"If fire breaks out and catches in thorns, so that stacked grain, standing grain, or the field is consumed, he who kindled the fire shall surely make restitution.

7"If a man ªdelivers to his neighbor money or articles to keep, and it is stolen out of the man's house, bif the thief is found, he shall pay double. 8If the thief is not found, then

21:22 ªEx. 18:21, 22; 21:30; Deut. 22:18

21:24 ªLev. 24:20; Deut. 19:21; [Matt. 5:38–44; 1 Pet. 2:19–21]

21:28 ªGen. 9:5

21:30 ªEx. 21:22; Num. 35:31

21:32 ªZech. 11:12, 13; Matt. 26:15; 27:3, 9 bEx. 21:28

22:1 ª2 Sam. 12:6; Prov. 6:31; Luke 19:8

22:2 ªJob 24:16; Matt. 6:19; 24:43; 1 Pet. 4:15 bNum. 35:27

22:3 ªEx. 21:2; Matt. 18:25

22:4 ªEx. 21:16 bProv. 6:31

22:7 ªLev. 6:1–7 bEx. 22:4

21:28 1*exempt from punishment*   21:29 1*was inclined*   22:3 1Sold as a slave

22:8
a Ex. 21:6, 22;
22:28;
Deut. 17:8, 9;
19:17

22:9
a Deut. 25:1;
2 Chr. 19:10

22:11
a Heb. 6:16

22:12
a Gen. 31:39

22:13
a Gen. 31:39

22:16
a Deut. 22:28, 29

22:17
a Gen. 34:12;
1 Sam. 18:25

22:18
a Lev. 19:31;
20:6, 27;
Deut. 18:10, 11;
1 Sam. 28:3–10;
Jer. 27:9, 10

22:19
a Lev. 18:23;
20:15, 16;
Deut. 27:21

22:20 a Ex. 32:8;
34:15; Lev. 17:7;
Num. 25:2;
Deut. 17:2, 3,
5; 1 Kin. 18:40;
2 Kin. 10:25

22:21
a Ex. 23:9;
Deut. 10:19;
Zech. 7:10

22:22
a Deut. 24:17,
18; Prov. 23:10,
11; Jer. 7:6, 7;
[James 1:27]

22:23
a [Luke 18:7]
b Deut. 10:17, 18;
Ps. 18:6

22:24
a Ps. 69:24
b Ps. 109:9

22:25
a Lev. 25:35–37
b Deut. 23:19, 20;
Neh. 5:1–13;
Ps. 15:5;
Ezek. 18:8

22:26
a Deut. 24:6,
10–13; Job 24:3;
Prov. 20:16;
Amos 2:8

22:27
a Ex. 34:6, 7

22:28
a Eccl. 10:20
b Acts 23:5

the master of the house shall be brought to the a judges *to see* whether he has put his hand into his neighbor's goods.

9 "For any kind of trespass, *whether it concerns* an ox, a donkey, a sheep, or clothing, *or* for any kind of lost thing which *another* claims to be his, the a cause of both parties shall come before the judges; *and* whomever the judges condemn shall pay double to his neighbor. 10 If a man delivers to his neighbor a donkey, an ox, a sheep, or any animal to keep, and it dies, is hurt, or driven away, no one seeing *it,* 11 *then* an a oath of the Lord shall be between them both, that he has not put his hand into his neighbor's goods; and the owner of it shall accept *that,* and he shall not make *it* good. 12 But a if, in fact, it is stolen from him, he shall make restitution to the owner of it. 13 If it is a torn to pieces *by a beast, then* he shall bring it as evidence, *and* he shall not make good what was torn.

14 "And if a man borrows *anything* from his neighbor, and it becomes injured or dies, the owner of it not *being* with it, he shall surely make *it* good. 15 If its owner *was* with it, he shall not make *it* good; if it *was* hired, it came for its hire.

MORAL AND CEREMONIAL PRINCIPLES

16 a "If a man entices a virgin who is not betrothed, and lies with her, he shall surely pay the bride-price for her *to be* his wife. 17 If her father utterly refuses to give her to him, he shall pay money according to the a bride-price of virgins.

18 a "You shall not permit a sorceress to live.

19 a "Whoever lies with an animal shall surely be put to death.

20 a "He who sacrifices to *any* god, except to the Lord only, he shall be utterly destroyed.

21 a "You shall neither mistreat a 1 stranger nor oppress him, for you were strangers in the land of Egypt.

22 a "You shall not afflict any widow or fatherless child. 23 If you afflict them in any way, *and* they a cry at all to Me, I will surely b hear their cry; 24 and My a wrath will become hot, and I will kill you with the sword; b your wives shall be widows, and your children fatherless.

25 a "If you lend money to *any of* My people *who are* poor among you, you shall not be like a moneylender to him; you shall not charge him b interest. 26 a If you ever take your neighbor's garment as a pledge, you shall return it to him before the sun goes down. 27 For that *is* his only covering, it *is* his garment for his skin. What will he sleep in? And it will be that when he cries to Me, I will hear, for I *am* a gracious.

28 a "You shall not revile God, nor curse a b ruler of your people.

29 "You shall not delay *to offer* a the first of your ripe produce and your juices. b The firstborn of your sons you shall give to Me. 30 a Likewise you shall do with your oxen *and* your sheep. It shall be with its mother b seven days; on the eighth day you shall give it to Me.

31 "And you shall be a holy men to Me: b you shall not eat meat torn *by beasts* in the field; you shall throw it to the dogs.

22:29 a Ex. 23:16, 19; Deut. 26:2–11; Prov. 3:9 b Ex. 13:2, 12, 15   22:30 a Deut. 15:19
b Lev. 22:27   22:31 a Ex. 19:6; Lev. 11:44; 19:2 b Lev. 7:24; 17:15; Ezek. 4:14

22:21 1 sojourner

JUSTICE FOR ALL

23 "You [a]shall not circulate a false report. Do not put your hand with the wicked to be an [b]unrighteous witness. [2a]You shall not follow a crowd to do evil; [b]nor shall you testify in a dispute so as to turn aside after many to pervert *justice.* [3]You shall not show partiality to a [a]poor man in his dispute.

[4a]"If you meet your enemy's ox or his donkey going astray, you shall surely bring it back to him again. [5a]If you see the donkey of one who hates you lying under its burden, and you would refrain from helping it, you shall surely help him with it.

[6a]"You shall not pervert the judgment of your poor in his dispute. [7a]Keep yourself far from a false matter; [b]do not kill the innocent and righteous. For [c]I will not justify the wicked. [8]And [a]you shall take no bribe, for a bribe blinds the discerning and perverts the words of the righteous.

[9]"Also [a]you shall not oppress a [1]stranger, for you know the heart of a stranger, because you were strangers in the land of Egypt.

THE LAW OF SABBATHS

[10a]"Six years you shall sow your land and gather in its produce, [11]but the seventh *year* you shall let it rest and lie fallow, that the poor of your people may eat; and what they leave, the beasts of the field may eat. In like manner you shall do with your vineyard *and* your [1]olive grove. [12a]Six days you shall do your work, and on the seventh day you shall rest, that your ox and your donkey may rest, and the son of your female servant and the stranger may be refreshed.

[13]"And in all that I have said to you, [a]be circumspect and [b]make no mention of the name of other gods, nor let it be heard from your mouth.

THREE ANNUAL FEASTS
(Ex. 34:18–26; Deut. 16:1–17)

[14a]"Three times you shall keep a feast to Me in the year: [15a]You shall keep the Feast of Unleavened Bread (you shall eat unleavened bread seven days, as I commanded you, at the time appointed in the month of Abib, for in it you came out of Egypt; [b]none shall appear before Me empty); [16a]and the Feast of Harvest, the firstfruits of your labors which you have sown in the field; and [b]the Feast of Ingathering at the end of the year, when you have gathered in *the fruit of* your labors from the field.

[17a]"Three times in the year all your males shall appear before the Lord [1]GOD.

[18a]"You shall not offer the blood of My sacrifice with leavened [b]bread; nor shall the fat of My [1]sacrifice remain until morning. [19a]The first of the firstfruits of your land you shall bring into the house of the LORD your God. [b]You shall not boil a young goat in its mother's milk.

THE ANGEL AND THE PROMISES

[20a]"Behold, I send an Angel before you to keep you in the way and to bring you into the place which I have prepared.

23:20 [a]Ex. 3:2; 13:15; 14:19; Josh. 5:14

23:9 [1]sojourner   23:11 [1]olive yards   23:17 [1]Heb. *YHWH,* usually translated LORD   23:18 [1]feast

23:1 [a]Ex. 20:16; Lev. 19:11; Deut. 5:20; Ps. 101:5; [Prov. 10:18] [b]Deut. 19:16–21; Ps. 35:11; [Prov. 19:5]; Acts 6:11

23:2 [a]Gen. 7:1 [b]Lev. 19:15

23:3 [a]Ex. 23:6; Lev. 19:15; Deut. 1:17; 16:19

23:4 [a][Rom. 12:20]

23:5 [a]Deut. 22:4

23:6 [a]Eccl. 5:8

23:7 [a]Ex. 20:16; Ps. 119:29; Eph. 4:25 [b]Matt. 27:4 [c]Ex. 34:7; Deut. 25:1; Rom. 1:18

23:8 [a]Deut. 10:17; 16:19; Prov. 15:27; 17:8, 23; Is. 5:22, 23

23:9 [a]Ex. 22:21; Lev. 19:33; Deut. 24:17; 27:19

23:10 [a]Lev. 25:1–7

23:12 [a]Luke 13:14

23:13 [a]Deut. 4:9, 23; 1 Tim. 4:16 [b]Josh. 23:7; Ps. 16:4; Hos. 2:17

23:14 [a]Ex. 23:17; 34:22–24; Deut. 16:16

23:15 [a]Ex. 12:14–20; Lev. 23:6–8; Num. 28:16–25 [b]Ex. 22:29; 34:20

23:16 [a]Ex. 34:22; Lev. 23:10; Num. 28:26 [b]Deut. 16:13

23:17 [a]Ex. 23:14; 34:23; Deut. 16:16

23:18 [a]Ex. 34:25; Lev. 2:11 [b]Ex. 12:10; Lev. 7:15; Deut. 16:4

23:19 [a]Ex. 22:29; 34:26; Deut. 26:2, 10; Neh. 10:35; Prov. 3:9 [b]Deut. 14:21

23:21
a Num. 14:11;
Deut. 9:7;
Ps. 78:40, 56
b Deut. 18:19;
1 John 5:16
c Is. 9:6; Jer. 23:6

23:22
a Gen. 12:3;
Num. 24:9;
Deut. 30:7;
Jer. 30:20

23:23
a Ex. 23:20
b Josh. 24:8, 11

23:24 a Ex. 20:5;
23:13, 33
b Deut. 12:30, 31
c Ex. 34:13;
Num. 33:52;
Deut. 7:5; 12:3;
2 Kin. 18:4

23:25
a Deut. 6:13;
[Matt. 4:10]
b Deut. 28:5
c Ex. 15:26;
Deut. 7:15

23:26
a Deut. 7:14;
28:4; Mal. 3:11
b 1 Chr. 23:1

23:27
a Gen. 35:5;
Ex. 15:16;
Deut. 2:25;
Josh. 2:9
b Deut. 7:23

23:28
a Deut. 7:20;
Josh. 24:12

23:29
a Deut. 7:22

23:31
a Gen. 15:18;
Deut. 1:7, 8;
11:24; 1 Kin. 4:21,
24 b Josh. 21:44

23:32 a Ex. 34:12,
15; Deut. 7:2

23:33 a Ex. 34:12;
Deut. 12:30;
Josh. 23:13;
Judg. 2:3;
1 Sam. 18:21;
Ps. 106:36

24:1 a Ex. 6:23;
28:1; Lev. 10:1,
2 b Ex. 1:5;
Num. 11:16

24:3 a Ex. 19:8;
24:7; Deut. 5:27;
[Gal. 3:19]

24:4 a Ex. 17:14;
34:27; Deut. 31:9
b Gen. 28:18

24:5 a Ex. 18:12;
20:24

21Beware of Him and obey His voice; ado not provoke Him, for He will bnot pardon your transgressions; for cMy name is in Him. 22But if you indeed obey His voice and do all that I speak, then aI will be an enemy to your enemies and an adversary to your adversaries. 23aFor My Angel will go before you and bbring you in to the Amorites and the Hittites and the Perizzites and the Canaanites and the Hivites and the Jebusites; and I will 1cut them off. 24You shall not abow down to their gods, nor serve them, bnor do according to their works; cbut you shall utterly overthrow them and completely break down their *sacred* pillars.

25"So you shall aserve the LORD your God, and bHe will bless your bread and your water. And cI will take sickness away from the midst of you. 26aNo one shall suffer miscarriage or be barren in your land; I will bfulfill the number of your days.

27"I will send aMy fear before you, I will bcause confusion among all the people to whom you come, and will make all your enemies turn *their* backs to you. 28And aI will send hornets before you, which shall drive out the Hivite, the Canaanite, and the Hittite from before you. 29aI will not drive them out from before you in one year, lest the land become desolate and the beasts of the field become too numerous for you. 30Little by little I will drive them out from before you, until you have increased, and you inherit the land. 31And aI will set your 1bounds from the Red Sea to the sea, Philistia, and from the desert to the 2River. For I will bdeliver the inhabitants of the land into your hand, and you shall drive them out before you. 32aYou shall make no 1covenant with them, nor with their gods. 33They shall not dwell in your land, lest they make you sin against Me. For *if* you serve their gods, ait will surely be a snare to you."

ISRAEL AFFIRMS THE COVENANT

24 Now He said to Moses, "Come up to the LORD, you and Aaron, aNadab and Abihu, band seventy of the elders of Israel, and worship from afar. 2And Moses alone shall come near the LORD, but they shall not come near; nor shall the people go up with him."

3So Moses came and told the people all the words of the LORD and all the 1judgments. And all the people answered with one voice and said, a"All the words which the LORD has said we will do." 4And Moses awrote all the words of the LORD. And he rose early in the morning, and built an altar at the foot of the mountain, and twelve bpillars according to the twelve tribes of Israel. 5Then he sent young men of the children of Israel, who offered aburnt offerings and sacrificed peace offerings of oxen to the LORD. 6And Moses atook half the blood and put *it* in basins, and half the blood he sprinkled on the altar. 7Then he atook the Book of the Covenant and read in the hearing of the people. And they said, "All that the LORD has said we will do, and be obedient." 8And Moses took the blood, sprinkled *it* on the people, and said, "This is athe blood of the covenant which the LORD has made with you according to all these words."

24:6 a Ex. 29:16, 20; Heb. 9:18   24:7 a Ex. 24:4; Heb. 9:19   24:8 a Zech. 9:11;
[Matt. 26:28; Mark 14:24; Luke 22:20; 1 Cor. 11:25; Heb. 9:19, 20; 13:20; 1 Pet. 1:2]

23:23 1 annihilate them   23:31 1 boundaries   2 Heb. *Nahar,* the Euphrates
23:32 1 treaty   24:3 1 ordinances

ON THE MOUNTAIN WITH GOD

9Then Moses went up, also Aaron, Nadab, and Abihu, and seventy of the elders of Israel, 10and they ªsaw the God of Israel. And *there was* under His feet as it were a paved work of ᵇsapphire stone, and it was like the ᶜvery¹ heavens in *its* clarity. 11But on the nobles of the children of Israel He ªdid not ¹lay His hand. So ᵇthey saw God, and they ᶜate and drank.

12Then the LORD said to Moses, ª"Come up to Me on the mountain and be there; and I will give you ᵇtablets of stone, and the law and commandments which I have written, that you may teach them."

13So Moses arose with ªhis assistant Joshua, and Moses went up to the mountain of God. 14And he said to the elders, "Wait here for us until we come back to you. Indeed, Aaron and ªHur *are* with you. If any man has a difficulty, let him go to them." 15Then Moses went up into the mountain, and ªa cloud covered the mountain.

16Now ªthe glory of the LORD rested on Mount Sinai, and the cloud covered it six days. And on the seventh day He called to Moses out of the midst of the cloud. 17The sight of the glory of the LORD *was* like ªa consuming fire on the top of the mountain in the eyes of the children of Israel. 18So Moses went into the midst of the cloud and went up into the mountain. And ªMoses was on the mountain forty days and forty nights.

OFFERINGS FOR THE SANCTUARY
(Ex. 35:4–9)

25 Then the LORD spoke to Moses, saying: 2"Speak to the children of Israel, that they bring Me an ¹offering. ªFrom everyone who gives it willingly with his heart you shall take My offering. 3And this *is* the offering which you shall take from them: gold, silver, and bronze; 4blue, purple, and scarlet *thread,* fine linen, and goats' *hair;* 5ram skins dyed red, ¹badger skins, and acacia wood; 6ªoil for the light, and ᵇspices for the anointing oil and for the sweet incense; 7onyx stones, and stones to be set in the ªephod and in the breastplate. 8And let them make Me a ªsanctuary,¹ that ᵇI may dwell among them. 9According to all that I show you, *that is,* the pattern of the tabernacle and the pattern of all its furnishings, just so you shall make *it.*

THE ARK OF THE TESTIMONY
(Ex. 37:1–9)

10ª"And they shall make an ark of acacia wood; two and a half cubits *shall be* its length, a cubit and a half its width, and a cubit and a half its height. 11And you shall overlay it with pure gold, inside and out you shall overlay it, and shall make on it a molding of ªgold all around. 12You shall cast four rings of gold for it, and put *them* in its four corners; two rings *shall be* on one side, and two rings on the other side. 13And you shall make poles *of* acacia wood, and overlay them with gold. 14You shall put the poles into the rings on the sides of the ark, that the ark may be carried by them. 15ªThe poles

---

24:10 ªEx. 24:11; Num. 12:8; Is. 6:5; [John 1:18; 6:46]; 1 John 4:12 ᵇEzek. 1:26; Rev. 4:3 ᶜMatt. 17:2

24:11 ªEx. 19:21 ᵇGen. 32:30; Judg. 13:22 ᶜ1 Cor. 10:18

24:12 ªEx. 24:2, 15 ᵇEx. 31:18; 32:15; Deut. 5:22

24:13 ªEx. 32:17

24:14 ªEx. 17:10, 12

24:15 ªEx. 19:9; Matt. 17:5

24:16 ªEx. 16:10; 33:18; Num. 14:10

24:17 ªEx. 3:2; Deut. 4:26, 36; 9:3; Heb. 12:18, 29

24:18 ªEx. 34:28; Deut. 9:9; 10:10

25:2 ªEx. 35:4–9, 21; 1 Chr. 29:3, 5, 9; Ezra 2:68; Neh. 11:2; [2 Cor. 8:11–13; 9:7]

25:6 ªEx. 27:20 ᵇEx. 30:23

25:7 ªEx. 28:4, 6–14

25:8 ªEx. 36:1, 3, 4; Lev. 4:6; 10:4; 21:12; Heb. 9:1, 2 ᵇEx. 29:45; 1 Kin. 6:13; [2 Cor. 6:16; Heb. 3:6; Rev. 2:13]

25:10 ªEx. 37:1–9; Deut. 10:3; Heb. 9:4

25:11 ªEx. 37:2; Heb. 9:4

25:15 ªNum. 4:6; 1 Kin. 8:8

24:10 ¹Lit. *substance of heaven*   24:11 ¹*stretch out His*   25:2 ¹*heave offering*
25:5 ¹Or *dolphin*   25:8 ¹*sacred place*

shall be in the rings of the ark; they shall not be taken from it. ¹⁶And you shall put into the ark ᵃthe Testimony which I will give you.

¹⁷ᵃ"You shall make a mercy seat of pure gold; two and a half cubits *shall be* its length and a cubit and a half its width. ¹⁸And you shall make two cherubim of gold; of hammered work you shall make them at the two ends of the mercy seat. ¹⁹Make one cherub at one end, and the other cherub at the other end; you shall make the cherubim at the two ends of it *of one piece* with the mercy seat. ²⁰And ᵃthe cherubim shall stretch out *their* wings above, covering the mercy seat with their wings, and they shall face one another; the faces of the cherubim *shall be* toward the mercy seat. ²¹ᵃYou shall put the mercy seat on top of the ark, and ᵇin the ark you shall put the Testimony that I will give you. ²²And ᵃthere I will meet with you, and I will speak with you from above the mercy seat, from ᵇbetween the two cherubim which *are* on the ark of the Testimony, about everything which I will give you in commandment to the children of Israel.

THE TABLE FOR THE SHOWBREAD
(Ex. 37:10–16)

²³ᵃ"You shall also make a table of acacia wood; two cubits *shall be* its length, a cubit its width, and a cubit and a half its height. ²⁴And you shall overlay it with pure gold, and make a molding of gold all around. ²⁵You shall make for it a frame of a handbreadth all around, and you shall make a gold molding for the frame all around. ²⁶And you shall make for it four rings of gold, and put the rings on the four corners that *are* at its four legs. ²⁷The rings shall be close to the frame, as holders for the poles to bear the table. ²⁸And you shall make the poles of acacia wood, and overlay them with gold, that the table may be carried with them. ²⁹You shall make ᵃits dishes, its pans, its pitchers, and its bowls for pouring. You shall make them of pure gold. ³⁰And you shall set the ᵃshowbread on the table before Me always.

THE GOLD LAMPSTAND
(Ex. 37:17–24)

³¹ᵃ"You shall also make a lampstand of pure gold; the lampstand shall be of hammered work. Its shaft, its branches, its bowls, its *ornamental* knobs, and flowers shall be *of one piece*. ³²And six branches shall come out of its sides: three branches of the lampstand out of one side, and three branches of the lampstand out of the other side. ³³ᵃThree bowls *shall be* made like almond *blossoms* on one branch, *with* an *ornamental* knob and a flower, and three bowls made like almond *blossoms* on the other branch, *with* an *ornamental* knob and a flower—and so for the six branches that come out of the lampstand. ³⁴ᵃOn the lampstand itself four bowls *shall be* made like almond *blossoms, each with* its *ornamental* knob and flower. ³⁵And *there shall be* a knob under the *first* two branches of the same, a knob under the *second* two branches of the same, and a knob under the *third* two branches of the same, according to the six branches that extend from the lampstand. ³⁶Their knobs and their branches *shall be of one piece*; all of it *shall be* one hammered piece of pure gold.

25:16 ᵃEx. 16:34; 31:18; Deut. 10:2; 31:26; 1 Kin. 8:9; Heb. 9:4

25:17 ᵃEx. 37:6; Heb. 9:5

25:20 ᵃ1 Kin. 8:7; 1 Chr. 28:18; Heb. 9:5

25:21 ᵃEx. 26:34; 40:20 ᵇEx. 25:16

25:22 ᵃEx. 29:42, 43; 30:6, 36; Lev. 16:2; Num. 17:4 ᵇNum. 7:89; 1 Sam. 4:4; 2 Sam. 6:2; 2 Kin. 19:15; Ps. 80:1; Is. 37:16

25:23 ᵃEx. 37:10–16; 1 Kin. 7:48; 2 Chr. 4:8; Heb. 9:2

25:29 ᵃEx. 37:16; Num. 4:7

25:30 ᵃEx. 39:36; 40:23; Lev. 24:5–9

25:31 ᵃEx. 37:17–24; 1 Kin. 7:49; Zech. 4:2; Heb. 9:2; Rev. 1:12

25:33 ᵃEx. 37:19

25:34 ᵃEx. 37:20–22

37You shall make seven lamps for it, and ªthey shall arrange its lamps so that they ᵇgive light in front of it. 38And its wick-trimmers and their trays *shall be* of pure gold. 39It shall be made of a talent of pure gold, with all these utensils. 40And ªsee to it that you make *them* according to the pattern which was shown you on the mountain.

THE TABERNACLE
(Ex. 36:8–38)

26 "Moreover ªyou shall make the tabernacle *with* ten curtains *of* fine woven linen and blue, purple, and scarlet *thread;* with artistic designs of cherubim you shall weave them. 2The length of each curtain *shall be* twenty-eight cubits, and the width of each curtain four cubits. And every one of the curtains shall have ¹the same measurements. 3Five curtains shall be coupled to one another, and *the other* five curtains *shall be* coupled to one another. 4And you shall make loops of blue *yarn* on the edge of the curtain on the selvedge of *one* set, and likewise you shall do on the outer edge of *the other* curtain of the second set. 5Fifty loops you shall make in the one curtain, and fifty loops you shall make on the edge of the curtain that *is* on the end of the second set, that the loops may be clasped to one another. 6And you shall make fifty clasps of gold, and couple the curtains together with the clasps, so that it may be one tabernacle.

7ª"You shall also make curtains of goats' *hair,* to be a tent over the tabernacle. You shall make eleven curtains. 8The length of each curtain *shall be* thirty cubits, and the width of each curtain four cubits; and the eleven curtains shall all have the same measurements. 9And you shall couple five curtains by themselves and six curtains by themselves, and you shall double over the sixth curtain at the forefront of the tent. 10You shall make fifty loops on the edge of the curtain that is outermost in *one* set, and fifty loops on the edge of the curtain of the second set. 11And you shall make fifty bronze clasps, put the clasps into the loops, and couple the tent together, that it may be one. 12The remnant that remains of the curtains of the tent, the half curtain that remains, shall hang over the back of the tabernacle. 13And a cubit on one side and a cubit on the other side, of what remains of the length of the curtains of the tent, shall hang over the sides of the tabernacle, on this side and on that side, to cover it.

14ª"You shall also make a covering of ram skins dyed red for the tent, and a covering of badger skins above that.

15"And for the tabernacle you shall ªmake the boards of acacia wood, standing upright. 16Ten cubits *shall be* the length of a board, and a cubit and a half *shall be* the width of each board. 17Two ¹tenons *shall be* in each board for binding one to another. Thus you shall make for all the boards of the tabernacle. 18And you shall make the boards for the tabernacle, twenty boards for the south side. 19You shall make forty sockets of silver under the twenty boards: two sockets under each of the boards for its two tenons. 20And for the second side of the tabernacle, the north side, *there shall be* twenty boards 21and their forty sockets of silver: two sockets under each of

25:37 ªEx. 27:21;
30:8; Lev. 24:3,
4; 2 Chr. 13:11
ᵇNum. 8:2

25:40 ªEx. 25:9;
26:30;
Num. 8:4;
1 Chr. 28:11,
19; Acts 7:44;
[Heb. 8:5]

26:1
ªEx. 36:8–19

26:7 ªEx. 36:14

26:14 ªEx. 35:7,
23; 36:19

26:15
ªEx. 36:20–34

26:2 ¹Lit. *one measure*   26:17 ¹Projections for joining, lit. *hands*

the boards. ²²For the far side of the tabernacle, westward, you shall make six boards. ²³And you shall also make two boards for the two back corners of the tabernacle. ²⁴They shall be ¹coupled together at the bottom and they shall be coupled together at the top by one ring. Thus it shall be for both of them. They shall be for the two corners. ²⁵So there shall be eight boards with their sockets of silver—sixteen sockets—two sockets under each of the boards.

²⁶"And you shall make bars of acacia wood: five for the boards on one side of the tabernacle, ²⁷five bars for the boards on the other side of the tabernacle, and five bars for the boards of the side of the tabernacle, for the far side westward. ²⁸The ᵃmiddle bar shall pass through the midst of the boards from end to end. ²⁹You shall overlay the boards with gold, make their rings of gold *as* holders for the bars, and overlay the bars with gold. ³⁰And you shall raise up the tabernacle ᵃaccording to its pattern which you were shown on the mountain.

³¹ᵃ"You shall make a veil woven of blue, purple, and scarlet *thread,* and fine woven linen. It shall be woven with an artistic design of cherubim. ³²You shall hang it upon the four pillars of acacia *wood* overlaid with gold. Their hooks *shall be* gold, upon four sockets of silver. ³³And you shall hang the veil from the clasps. Then you shall bring ᵃthe ark of the Testimony in there, behind the veil. The veil shall be a divider for you between ᵇthe holy *place* and the Most Holy. ³⁴ᵃYou shall put the mercy seat upon the ark of the Testimony in the Most Holy. ³⁵ᵃYou shall set the table outside the veil, and ᵇthe lampstand across from the table on the side of the tabernacle toward the south; and you shall put the table on the north side.

³⁶ᵃ"You shall make a screen for the door of the tabernacle, *woven of* blue, purple, and scarlet *thread,* and fine woven linen, made by a weaver. ³⁷And you shall make for the screen ᵃfive pillars of acacia *wood,* and overlay them with gold; their hooks *shall be* gold, and you shall cast five sockets of bronze for them.

THE ALTAR OF BURNT OFFERING
(Ex. 38:1–7)

27 "You shall make ᵃan altar of acacia wood, five cubits long and five cubits wide—the altar shall be square—and its height *shall be* three cubits. ²You shall make its horns on its four corners; its horns shall be of one piece with it. And you shall overlay it with bronze. ³Also you shall make its pans to receive its ashes, and its shovels and its basins and its forks and its firepans; you shall make all its utensils of bronze. ⁴You shall make a grate for it, a network of bronze; and on the network you shall make four bronze rings at its four corners. ⁵You shall put it under the rim of the altar beneath, that the network may be midway up the altar. ⁶And you shall make poles for the altar, poles of acacia wood, and overlay them with bronze. ⁷The poles shall be put in the rings, and the poles shall be on the two sides of the altar to bear it. ⁸You shall make it hollow with boards; ᵃas it was shown you on the mountain, so shall they make *it.*

26:28
ᵃEx. 36:33

26:30 ᵃEx. 25:9, 40; 27:8; 39:32; Num. 8:4; Acts 7:44; [Heb. 8:2, 5]

26:31 ᵃEx. 27:21; 36:35–38; Lev. 16:2; 2 Chr. 3:14; Matt. 27:51; Heb. 9:3; 10:20

26:33 ᵃEx. 25:10–16; 40:21 ᵇLev. 16:2; Heb. 9:2, 3

26:34 ᵃEx. 25:17–22; 40:20; Heb. 9:5

26:35 ᵃEx. 40:22; Heb. 9:2 ᵇEx. 40:24

26:36 ᵃEx. 36:37

26:37 ᵃEx. 36:38

27:1 ᵃEx. 38:1; Ezek. 43:13

27:8 ᵃEx. 25:40; 26:30; Acts 7:44; [Heb. 8:5]

26:24 ¹Lit. *doubled*

THE COURT OF THE TABERNACLE
(Ex. 38:9–20)

9a"You shall also make the court of the tabernacle. For the south side *there shall be* hangings for the court *made of* fine woven linen, one hundred cubits long for one side. 10And its twenty pillars and their twenty sockets *shall be* bronze. The hooks of the pillars and their bands *shall be* silver. 11Likewise along the length of the north side *there shall be* hangings one hundred *cubits* long, with its twenty pillars and their twenty sockets of bronze, and the hooks of the pillars and their bands of silver.

12"And along the width of the court on the west side *shall be* hangings of fifty cubits, with their ten pillars and their ten sockets. 13The width of the court on the east side *shall be* fifty cubits. 14The hangings on *one* side *of the gate shall be* fifteen cubits, *with* their three pillars and their three sockets. 15And on the other side *shall be* hangings of fifteen *cubits, with* their three pillars and their three sockets.

16"For the gate of the court *there shall be* a screen twenty cubits long, *woven of* blue, purple, and scarlet *thread,* and fine woven linen, made by a weaver. It *shall have* four pillars and four sockets. 17All the pillars around the court shall have bands of silver; their ahooks *shall be* of silver and their sockets of bronze. 18The length of the court *shall be* one hundred cubits, the width fifty throughout, and the height five cubits, *made of* fine woven linen, and its sockets of bronze. 19All the utensils of the tabernacle for all its service, all its pegs, and all the pegs of the court, *shall be* of bronze.

THE CARE OF THE LAMPSTAND
(Lev. 24:1–4)

20"And ayou shall command the children of Israel that they bring you pure oil of pressed olives for the light, to cause the lamp to 1burn continually. 21In the tabernacle of meeting, aoutside the veil which *is* before the Testimony, bAaron and his sons shall tend it from evening until morning before the LORD. c*It shall be* a statute forever to their generations on behalf of the children of Israel.

GARMENTS FOR THE PRIESTHOOD
(Ex. 39:1–7)

28 "Now take aAaron your brother, and his sons with him, from among the children of Israel, that he may minister to Me as bpriest, Aaron *and* Aaron's sons: cNadab, Abihu, dEleazar, and Ithamar. 2And ayou shall make 1holy garments for Aaron your brother, for glory and for beauty. 3So ayou shall speak to all *who are* gifted artisans, bwhom I have filled with the spirit of wisdom, that they may make Aaron's garments, to consecrate him, that he may minister to Me as priest. 4And these *are* the garments which they shall make: aa breastplate, ban 1ephod, ca robe, da skillfully woven tunic, a turban, and ea sash. So they shall make holy garments for Aaron your brother and his sons, that he may minister to Me as priest.

27:9
aEx. 38:9–20

27:17 aEx. 38:19

27:20
aEx. 35:8, 28;
Lev. 24:1–4

27:21 aEx. 26:31,
33 bEx. 30:8;
1 Sam. 3:3;
2 Chr. 13:11
cEx. 28:43; 29:9;
Lev. 3:17; 16:34;
Num. 18:23;
19:21;
1 Sam. 30:25

28:1
aNum. 3:10;
18:7 bPs. 99:6;
Heb. 5:4
cEx. 24:1, 9;
Lev. 10:1
dEx. 6:23;
Lev. 10:6, 16

28:2 aEx. 29:5,
29; 31:10;
39:1–31;
Lev. 8:7–9, 30

28:3 aEx. 31:6;
36:1 bEx. 31:3;
35:30, 31; Is. 11:2;
Eph. 1:17

28:4 aEx. 28:15
bEx. 28:6
cEx. 28:31
dEx. 28:39
eLev. 8:7

27:20 1Lit. *ascend*   28:2 1*sacred*   28:4 1Ornamented vest

THE EPHOD

⁵"They shall take the gold, blue, purple, and scarlet *thread,* and the fine linen, ⁶ᵃand they shall make the ephod of gold, blue, purple, *and* scarlet *thread,* and fine woven linen, artistically worked. ⁷It shall have two shoulder straps joined at its two edges, and *so* it shall be joined together. ⁸And the ¹intricately woven band of the ephod, which *is* on it, shall be of the same workmanship, *made of* gold, blue, purple, and scarlet *thread,* and fine woven linen.

⁹"Then you shall take two onyx ᵃstones and engrave on them the names of the sons of Israel: ¹⁰six of their names on one stone and six names on the other stone, in order of their ᵃbirth. ¹¹With the work of an ᵃengraver in stone, *like* the engravings of a signet, you shall engrave the two stones with the names of the sons of Israel. You shall set them in settings of gold. ¹²And you shall put the two stones on the shoulders of the ephod *as* memorial stones for the sons of Israel. So ᵃAaron shall bear their names before the LORD on his two shoulders ᵇas a memorial. ¹³You shall also make settings of gold, ¹⁴and you shall make two chains of pure gold like braided cords, and fasten the braided chains to the settings.

THE BREASTPLATE

(Ex. 39:8–21)

¹⁵ᵃ"You shall make the breastplate of judgment. Artistically woven according to the workmanship of the ephod you shall make it: of gold, blue, purple, and scarlet *thread,* and fine woven linen, you shall make it. ¹⁶It shall be doubled into a square: a span *shall be* its length, and a span *shall be* its width. ¹⁷ᵃAnd you shall put settings of stones in it, four rows of stones: *The first* row *shall be* a ¹sardius, a topaz, and an emerald; *this shall be* the first row; ¹⁸the second row *shall be* a turquoise, a sapphire, and a diamond; ¹⁹the third row, a ¹jacinth, an agate, and an amethyst; ²⁰and the fourth row, a ¹beryl, an ²onyx, and a jasper. They shall be set in gold settings. ²¹And the stones shall have the names of the sons of Israel, twelve according to their names, *like* the engravings of a signet, each one with its own name; they shall be according to the twelve tribes.

²²"You shall make chains for the breastplate at the end, like braided cords of pure gold. ²³And you shall make two rings of gold for the breastplate, and put the two rings on the two ends of the breastplate. ²⁴Then you shall put the two braided *chains* of gold in the two rings which are on the ends of the breastplate; ²⁵and the *other* two ends of the two braided *chains* you shall fasten to the two settings, and put them on the shoulder straps of the ephod in the front.

²⁶"You shall make two rings of gold, and put them on the two ends of the breastplate, on the edge of it, which is on the inner side of the ephod. ²⁷And two *other* rings of gold you shall make, and put them on the two shoulder straps, underneath the ephod toward its front, right at the seam above the ¹intricately woven band of the ephod. ²⁸They shall bind the breastplate by means of its rings to the rings of the ephod, using a blue cord, so that it is above the intricately woven band

---

28:6
ᵃEx. 39:2–7;
Lev. 8:7

28:9 ᵃEx. 35:27

28:10
ᵃGen. 29:31—
30:24; 35:16–18

28:11 ᵃEx. 35:35

28:12
ᵃEx. 28:29,
30; 39:6, 7
ᵇLev. 24:7;
Num. 31:54;
Josh. 4:7;
Zech. 6:14;
1 Cor. 11:24

28:15
ᵃEx. 39:8–21

28:17 ᵃEx. 39:10

28:8 ¹*ingenious work of*   28:17 ¹Or *ruby*   28:19 ¹Or *amber*
28:20 ¹Or *yellow jasper*   ²Or *carnelian*   28:27 ¹*ingenious work of*

of the ephod, and so that the breastplate does not come loose from the ephod. 29"So Aaron shall [a]bear the names of the sons of Israel on the breastplate of judgment over his heart, when he goes into the holy *place,* as a memorial before the LORD continually. 30And [a]you shall put in the breastplate of judgment the [1]Urim and the Thummim, and they shall be over Aaron's heart when he goes in before the LORD. So Aaron shall bear the judgment of the children of Israel over his heart before the LORD continually.

OTHER PRIESTLY GARMENTS

(Ex. 39:22–31)

31[a]"You shall make the robe of the ephod all of blue. 32There shall be an opening for his head in the middle of it; it shall have a woven binding all around its opening, like the opening in a coat of mail, so that it does not tear. 33And upon its hem you shall make pomegranates of blue, purple, and scarlet, all around its hem, and bells of gold between them all around: 34a golden bell and a pomegranate, a golden bell and a pomegranate, upon the hem of the robe all around. 35And it shall be upon Aaron when he ministers, and its sound will be heard when he goes into the holy *place* before the LORD and when he comes out, that he may not die.

36[a]"You shall also make a plate of pure gold and engrave on it, *like* the engraving of a signet:

HOLINESS TO THE LORD.

37And you shall put it on a blue cord, that it may be on the turban; it shall be on the front of the turban. 38So it shall be on Aaron's forehead, that Aaron may [a]bear the iniquity of the holy things which the children of Israel hallow in all their [1]holy gifts; and it shall always be on his forehead, that they may be [b]accepted before the LORD.

39"You shall [a]skillfully weave the tunic of fine linen *thread,* you shall make the turban of fine linen, and you shall make the sash of woven work.

40[a]"For Aaron's sons you shall make tunics, and you shall make sashes for them. And you shall make [1]hats for them, for glory and [b]beauty. 41So you shall put them on Aaron your brother and on his sons with him. You shall [a]anoint them, [b]consecrate them, and [1]sanctify them, that they may minister to Me as priests. 42And you shall make [a]for them linen trousers to cover their [1]nakedness; they shall [2]reach from the waist to the thighs. 43They shall be on Aaron and on his sons when they come into the tabernacle of meeting, or when they come near [a]the altar to minister in the holy *place,* that they [b]do not incur [1]iniquity and die. [c]*It shall be* a statute forever to him and his descendants after him.

AARON AND HIS SONS CONSECRATED

(Lev. 8:1–36)

29 "And this is what you shall do to them to hallow them for ministering to Me as priests: [a]Take one young bull and two rams without blemish, 2and [a]unleavened bread,

28:29 [a]Ex. 28:12

28:30 [a]Lev. 8:8; Num. 27:21; Deut. 33:8; 1 Sam. 28:6; Ezra 2:63; Neh. 7:65

28:31 [a]Ex. 39:22–26

28:36 [a]Ex. 39:30, 31; Lev. 8:9; Zech. 14:20

28:38 [a]Ex. 28:43; Lev. 10:17; 22:9, 16; Num. 18:1; [Is. 53:11]; Ezek. 4:4–6; [John 1:29; Heb. 9:28; 1 Pet. 2:24] [b]Lev. 1:4; 22:27; 23:11; Is. 56:7

28:39 [a]Ex. 35:35; 39:27–29

28:40 [a]Ex. 28:4; 39:27–29, 41; Ezek. 44:17, 18 [b]Ex. 28:2

28:41 [a]Ex. 29:7–9; 30:30; 40:15; Lev. 10:7 [b]Ex. 29:9; Lev. 8; Heb. 7:28

28:42 [a]Ex. 39:28; Lev. 6:10; 16:4; Ezek. 44:18

28:43 [a]Ex. 20:26 [b]Lev. 5:1, 17; 20:19, 20; 22:9; Num. 9:13; 18:22 [c]Ex. 27:21; Lev. 17:7

29:1 [a]Lev. 8; [Heb. 7:26–28]

29:2 [a]Lev. 2:4; 6:19–23

28:30 [1]Lit. *Lights and the Perfections*   28:38 [1]*sacred*   28:40 [1]*headpieces* or *turbans*   28:41 [1]*set them apart*   28:42 [1]*bare flesh*   [2]Lit. *be*   28:43 [1]*guilt*

unleavened cakes mixed with oil, and unleavened wafers anointed with oil (you shall make them of wheat flour). ³You shall put them in one basket and bring them in the basket, with the bull and the two rams.

⁴"And Aaron and his sons you shall bring to the door of the tabernacle of meeting, ᵃand you shall wash them with water. ⁵ᵃThen you shall take the garments, put the tunic on Aaron, and the robe of the ephod, the ephod, and the breastplate, and gird him with ᵇthe intricately woven band of the ephod. ⁶ᵃYou shall put the turban on his head, and put the holy crown on the turban. ⁷And you shall take the anointing ᵃoil, pour *it* on his head, and anoint him. ⁸Then ᵃyou shall bring his sons and put tunics on them. ⁹And you shall gird them with sashes, Aaron and his sons, and put the hats on them. ᵃThe priesthood shall be theirs for a perpetual statute. So you shall ᵇconsecrate Aaron and his sons.

¹⁰"You shall also have the bull brought before the tabernacle of meeting, and ᵃAaron and his sons shall put their hands on the head of the bull. ¹¹Then you shall kill the bull before the LORD, *by* the door of the tabernacle of meeting. ¹²You shall take *some* of the blood of the bull and put *it* on ᵃthe horns of the altar with your finger, and ᵇpour all the blood beside the base of the altar. ¹³And ᵃyou shall take all the fat that covers the entrails, the fatty lobe *attached* to the liver, and the two kidneys and the fat that *is* on them, and burn *them* on the altar. ¹⁴But ᵃthe flesh of the bull, with its skin and its offal, you shall burn with fire outside the camp. It *is* a sin offering.

¹⁵ᵃ"You shall also take one ram, and Aaron and his sons shall ᵇput their hands on the head of the ram; ¹⁶and you shall kill the ram, and you shall take its blood and ᵃsprinkle *it* all around on the altar. ¹⁷Then you shall cut the ram in pieces, wash its entrails and its legs, and put *them* with its pieces and with its head. ¹⁸And you shall burn the whole ram on the altar. It *is* a ᵃburnt offering to the LORD; it *is* a sweet aroma, an offering made by fire to the LORD.

¹⁹ᵃ"You shall also take the other ram, and Aaron and his sons shall put their hands on the head of the ram. ²⁰Then you shall kill the ram, and take some of its blood and put *it* on the tip of the right ear of Aaron and on the tip of the right ear of his sons, on the thumb of their right hand and on the big toe of their right foot, and sprinkle the blood all around on the altar. ²¹And you shall take some of the blood that is on the altar, and some of ᵃthe anointing oil, and sprinkle *it* on Aaron and on his garments, on his sons and on the garments of his sons with him; and ᵇhe and his garments shall be hallowed, and his sons and his sons' garments with him.

²²"Also you shall take the fat of the ram, the fat tail, the fat that covers the entrails, the fatty lobe *attached to* the liver, the two kidneys and the fat on them, the right thigh (for it *is* a ram of consecration), ²³ᵃone loaf of bread, one cake *made with* oil, and one wafer from the basket of the unleavened bread that *is* before the LORD; ²⁴and you shall put all these in the hands of Aaron and in the hands of his sons, and you shall ᵃwave them *as* a wave offering before the LORD. ²⁵ᵃYou shall receive them back from their hands and burn *them* on the altar as a burnt offering, as a sweet aroma before the LORD. It *is* an offering made by fire to the LORD.

29:4 ᵃEx. 40:12; Lev. 8:6; [Heb. 10:22]

29:5 ᵃEx. 28:2; Lev. 8:7 ᵇEx. 28:8

29:6 ᵃEx. 28:36, 37; Lev. 8:9

29:7 ᵃEx. 25:6; 30:25–31; Lev. 8:12; 10:7; 21:10; Num. 35:25; Ps. 133:2

29:8 ᵃEx. 28:39, 40; Lev. 8:13

29:9 ᵃEx. 40:15; Num. 3:10; 18:7; 25:13; Deut. 18:5 ᵇEx. 28:41; Lev. 8

29:10 ᵃLev. 1:4; 8:14

29:12 ᵃLev. 8:15 ᵇEx. 27:2; 30:2; Lev. 4:7

29:13 ᵃLev. 1:8; 3:3, 4

29:14 ᵃLev. 4:11, 12, 21; Heb. 13:11

29:15 ᵃLev. 8:18 ᵇLev. 1:4–9

29:16 ᵃEx. 24:6; Lev. 1:5, 11

29:18 ᵃEx. 20:24

29:19 ᵃLev. 8:22

29:21 ᵃEx. 30:25, 31; Lev. 8:30 ᵇEx. 28:41; 29:1; [Heb. 9:22]

29:23 ᵃLev. 8:26

29:24 ᵃLev. 7:30; 10:14

29:25 ᵃLev. 8:28

26"Then you shall take ªthe breast of the ram of Aaron's consecration and wave it *as* a wave offering before the LORD; and it shall be your portion. 27And from the ram of the consecration you shall consecrate ªthe breast of the wave offering which is waved, and the thigh of the heave offering which is raised, of *that* which *is* for Aaron and of *that* which is for his sons. 28It shall be from the children of Israel *for* Aaron and his sons ªby a statute forever. For it is a heave offering; ᵇit shall be a heave offering from the children of Israel from the sacrifices of their peace offerings, *that is,* their heave offering to the LORD.

29"And the ªholy garments of Aaron ᵇshall be his sons' after him, ᶜto be anointed in them and to be consecrated in them. 30ªThat son who becomes priest in his place shall put them on for ᵇseven days, when he enters the tabernacle of meeting to minister in the ¹holy *place.*

31"And you shall take the ram of the consecration and ªboil its flesh in the holy place. 32Then Aaron and his sons shall eat the flesh of the ram, and the ªbread that *is* in the basket, *by* the door of the tabernacle of meeting. 33ªThey shall eat those things with which the atonement was made, to consecrate *and* to sanctify them; ᵇbut an outsider shall not eat *them,* because they *are* holy. 34And if any of the flesh of the consecration offerings, or of the bread, remains until the morning, then ªyou shall burn the remainder with fire. It shall not be eaten, because it *is* holy.

35"Thus you shall do to Aaron and his sons, according to all that I have commanded you. ªSeven days you shall consecrate them. 36And you ªshall offer a bull every day *as* a sin offering for atonement. ᵇYou shall cleanse the altar when you make atonement for it, and you shall anoint it to sanctify it. 37Seven days you shall make atonement for the altar and sanctify it. And the altar shall be most holy. ªWhatever touches the altar must be holy.

THE DAILY OFFERINGS
(Num. 28:1–8)

38"Now this *is* what you shall offer on the altar: ªtwo lambs of the first year, ᵇday by day continually. 39One lamb you shall offer ªin the morning, and the other lamb you shall offer ¹at twilight. 40With the one lamb shall be one-tenth *of an ephah* of flour mixed with one-fourth of a hin of pressed oil, and one-fourth of a hin of wine *as* a drink offering. 41And the other lamb you shall ªoffer ¹at twilight; and you shall offer with it the grain offering and the drink offering, as in the morning, for a sweet aroma, an offering made by fire to the LORD. 42*This shall be* ªa continual burnt offering throughout your generations *at* the door of the tabernacle of meeting before the LORD, ᵇwhere I will meet you to speak with you. 43And there I will meet with the children of Israel, and *the tabernacle* ªshall be sanctified by My glory. 44So I will consecrate the tabernacle of meeting and the altar. I will also ªconsecrate both Aaron and his sons to minister to Me as priests. 45ªI will dwell among the children of Israel and will ᵇbe their God. 46And they shall

---

29:26 ªLev. 7:31, 34; 8:29
29:27 ªLev. 7:31, 34; Num. 18:11, 18; Deut. 18:3
29:28 ªLev. 10:15 ᵇLev. 3:1; 7:34
29:29 ªEx. 28:2 ᵇNum. 20:26, 28 ᶜEx. 28:41; 30:30; Num. 18:8
29:30 ªNum. 20:28 ᵇLev. 8:35
29:31 ªLev. 8:31
29:32 ªMatt. 12:4
29:33 ªLev. 10:14, 15, 17 ᵇEx. 12:43; Lev. 22:10
29:34 ªEx. 12:10; 23:18; 34:25; Lev. 7:18; 8:32
29:35 ªLev. 8:33–35
29:36 ªHeb. 10:11 ᵇEx. 30:26–29; 40:10, 11
29:37 ªNum. 4:15; Hag. 2:11–13; Matt. 23:19
29:38 ªNum. 28:3–31; 29:6–38; 1 Chr. 16:40; Ezra 3:3 ᵇDan. 12:11
29:39 ªEzek. 46:13–15
29:41 ª1 Kin. 18:29, 36; 2 Kin. 16:15; Ezra 9:4, 5; Ps. 141:2
29:42 ªEx. 30:8 ᵇEx. 25:22; 33:7, 9; Num. 17:4
29:43 ªEx. 40:34; 1 Kin. 8:11; 2 Chr. 5:14; Ezek. 43:5; Hag. 2:7, 9
29:44 ªLev. 21:15
29:45 ªEx. 25:8; Lev. 26:12; Num. 5:3; Deut. 12:11; Zech. 2:10; [John 14:17, 23; Rev. 21:3] ᵇGen. 17:8; Lev. 11:45

29:30 ¹*sanctuary*   **29:39** ¹Lit. *between the two evenings*   **29:41** ¹Lit. *between the two evenings*

know that ªI *am* the LORD their God, who ᵇbrought them up out of the land of Egypt, that I may dwell among them. I *am* the LORD their God.

THE ALTAR OF INCENSE
(Ex. 37:25–28)

30 "You shall make ªan altar to burn incense on; you shall make it of acacia wood. ²A cubit *shall be* its length and a cubit its width—it shall be square—and two cubits *shall be* its height. Its horns *shall be* of one piece with it. ³And you shall overlay its top, its sides all around, and its horns with pure gold; and you shall make for it a ¹molding of gold all around. ⁴Two gold rings you shall make for it, under the molding on both its sides. You shall place *them* on its two sides, and they will be holders for the poles with which to bear it. ⁵You shall make the poles of acacia wood, and overlay them with gold. ⁶And you shall put it before the ªveil that *is* before the ark of the Testimony, before the ᵇmercy seat that *is* over the Testimony, where I will meet with you.

⁷"Aaron shall burn on it ªsweet incense every morning; when ᵇhe tends the lamps, he shall burn incense on it. ⁸And when Aaron lights the lamps ¹at twilight, he shall burn incense on it, a perpetual incense before the LORD throughout your generations. ⁹You shall not offer ªstrange incense on it, or a burnt offering, or a grain offering; nor shall you pour a drink offering on it. ¹⁰And ªAaron shall make atonement upon its horns once a year with the blood of the sin offering of atonement; once a year he shall make atonement upon it throughout your generations. It *is* most holy to the LORD."

THE RANSOM MONEY

¹¹Then the LORD spoke to Moses, saying: ¹²ª"When you take the census of the children of Israel for their number, then every man shall give ᵇa¹ ransom for himself to the LORD, when you number them, that there may be no ᶜplague among them when *you* number them. ¹³ªThis is what everyone among those who are numbered shall give: half a shekel according to the shekel of the sanctuary ᵇ(a shekel *is* twenty gerahs). ᶜThe half-shekel *shall be* an offering to the LORD. ¹⁴Everyone included among those who are numbered, from twenty years old and above, shall give an ¹offering to the LORD. ¹⁵The ªrich shall not give more and the poor shall not give less than half a shekel, when *you* give an offering to the LORD, to make atonement for yourselves. ¹⁶And you shall take the atonement money of the children of Israel, and ªshall ¹appoint it for the service of the tabernacle of meeting, that it may be ᵇa memorial for the children of Israel before the LORD, to make atonement for yourselves."

THE BRONZE LAVER

¹⁷Then the LORD spoke to Moses, saying: ¹⁸ª"You shall also make a ¹laver of bronze, with its base also of bronze, for washing. You shall ᵇput it between the tabernacle of meeting and the altar. And you shall put water in it, ¹⁹for Aaron and his

---

Cross references (margin):

29:46 ªEx. 16:12; 20:2; Deut. 4:35
ᵇLev. 11:45

30:1 ªEx. 37:25–29

30:6 ªEx. 26:31–35
ᵇEx. 25:21, 22

30:7 ªEx. 30:34; 1 Sam. 2:28; 1 Chr. 23:13; Luke 1:9
ᵇEx. 27:20, 21

30:9 ªLev. 10:1

30:10 ªLev. 16:3–34

30:12 ªEx. 38:25, 26; Num. 1:2; 26:2; 2 Sam. 24:2
ᵇNum. 31:50; [Matt. 20:28; 1 Pet. 1:18, 19]
ᶜ2 Sam. 24:15

30:13 ªMatt. 17:24
ᵇLev. 27:25; Num. 3:47; Ezek. 45:12
ᶜEx. 38:26

30:15 ªJob 34:19; Prov. 22:2; [Eph. 6:9]

30:16 ªEx. 38:25–31
ᵇNum. 16:40

30:18 ªEx. 38:8; 1 Kin. 7:38
ᵇEx. 40:30

30:3 ¹*border*   30:8 ¹Lit. *between the two evenings*   30:12 ¹*the price of a life*
30:14 ¹*contribution*   30:16 ¹*give*   30:18 ¹*basin*

sons ªshall wash their hands and their feet in water from it. ²⁰When they go into the tabernacle of meeting, or when they come near the altar to minister, to burn an offering made by fire to the LORD, they shall wash with water, lest they die. ²¹So they shall wash their hands and their feet, lest they die. And ªit shall be a ¹statute forever to them—to him and his descendants throughout their generations."

THE HOLY ANOINTING OIL
(Ex. 37:29)

²²Moreover the LORD spoke to Moses, saying: ²³"Also take for yourself ªquality spices—five hundred *shekels* of liquid ᵇmyrrh, half as much sweet-smelling cinnamon (two hundred and fifty *shekels*), two hundred and fifty *shekels* of sweet-smelling ᶜcane, ²⁴five hundred *shekels* of ªcassia, according to the shekel of the sanctuary, and a ᵇhin of olive oil. ²⁵And you shall make from these a holy anointing oil, an ointment compounded according to the art of the perfumer. It shall be ªa holy anointing oil. ²⁶ªWith it you shall anoint the tabernacle of meeting and the ark of the Testimony; ²⁷the table and all its utensils, the lampstand and its utensils, and the altar of incense; ²⁸the altar of burnt offering with all its utensils, and the laver and its base. ²⁹You shall consecrate them, that they may be most holy; ªwhatever touches them must be holy. ³⁰And you shall anoint Aaron and his sons, and consecrate them, that *they* may minister to Me as priests.

³¹"And you shall speak to the children of Israel, saying: 'This shall be a holy anointing oil to Me throughout your generations. ³²It shall not be poured on man's flesh; nor shall you make *any other* like it, according to its composition. ªIt *is* holy, *and* it shall be holy to you. ³³ªWhoever ¹compounds *any* like it, or whoever puts *any* of it on an outsider, ᵇshall be ²cut off from his people.' "

THE INCENSE
(Ex. 37:29)

³⁴And the LORD said to Moses: ª"Take sweet spices, stacte and onycha and galbanum, and pure frankincense with *these* sweet spices; there shall be equal amounts of each. ³⁵You shall make of these an incense, a compound ªaccording to the art of the perfumer, salted, pure, *and* holy. ³⁶And you shall beat *some* of it very fine, and put some of it before the Testimony in the tabernacle of meeting ªwhere I will meet with you. ᵇIt shall be most holy to you. ³⁷But *as for* the incense which you shall make, ªyou shall not make any for yourselves, according to its ¹composition. It shall be to you holy for the LORD. ³⁸ªWhoever makes *any* like it, to smell it, he shall be cut off from his people."

ARTISANS FOR BUILDING THE TABERNACLE
(Ex. 35:30—36:1)

31 Then the LORD spoke to Moses, saying: ²ª"See, I have called by name Bezalel the ᵇson of Uri, the son of Hur, of the tribe of Judah. ³And I have ªfilled him with the Spirit

---

30:19 ªEx. 40:31, 32; Ps. 26:6; Is. 52:11; John 13:8, 10; Heb. 10:22

30:21 ªEx. 28:43

30:23 ªSong 4:14; Ezek. 27:22 ᵇPs. 45:8; Prov. 7:17 ᶜSong 4:14; Jer. 6:20

30:24 ªPs. 45:8 ᵇEx. 29:40

30:25 ªEx. 37:29; 40:9; Lev. 8:10; Num. 35:25; Ps. 89:20; 133:2

30:26 ªEx. 40:9; Lev. 8:10; Num. 7:1

30:29 ªEx. 29:37; Num. 4:15; Hag. 2:11–13

30:30 ªEx. 29:7; Lev. 8:12

30:32 ªEx. 30:25, 37

30:33 ªEx. 30:38 ᵇGen. 17:14; Ex. 12:15; Lev. 7:20, 21

30:34 ªEx. 25:6; 37:29

30:35 ªEx. 30:25

30:36 ªEx. 29:42; Lev. 16:2 ᵇ[Ex. 29:37; 30:32]; Lev. 2:3

30:37 ªEx. 30:32

30:38 ªEx. 30:33

31:2 ªEx. 35:30—36:1 ᵇ1 Chr. 2:20

31:3 ªEx. 28:3; 35:31; 1 Kin. 7:14; Eph. 1:17

30:21 ¹*requirement*   **30:33** ¹*mixes*   ²Put to death   **30:37** ¹Lit. *proportion*

of God, in wisdom, in understanding, in knowledge, and in all *manner of* workmanship, [4]to design artistic works, to work in gold, in silver, in bronze, [5]in cutting jewels for setting, in carving wood, and to work in all *manner of* workmanship.

[6]"And I, indeed I, have appointed with him [a]Aholiab the son of Ahisamach, of the tribe of Dan; and I have put wisdom in the hearts of all the [b]gifted artisans, that they may make all that I have commanded you: [7a]the tabernacle of meeting, [b]the ark of the Testimony and [c]the mercy seat that *is* on it, and all the furniture of the tabernacle— [8a]the table and its utensils, [b]the pure *gold* lampstand with all its utensils, the altar of incense, [9a]the altar of burnt offering with all its utensils, and [b]the laver and its base— [10a]the [1]garments of ministry, the holy garments for Aaron the priest and the garments of his sons, to minister as priests, [11a]and the anointing oil and [b]sweet incense for the holy *place*. According to all that I have commanded you they shall do."

THE SABBATH LAW

[12]And the LORD spoke to Moses, saying, [13]"Speak also to the children of Israel, saying: [a]'Surely My Sabbaths you shall keep, for it *is* a sign between Me and you throughout your generations, that *you* may know that I *am* the LORD who [b]sanctifies[1] you. [14a]You shall keep the Sabbath, therefore, for *it is* holy to you. Everyone who [1]profanes it shall surely be put to death; for [b]whoever does *any* work on it, that person shall be cut off from among his people. [15]Work shall be done for [a]six days, but the [b]seventh *is* the Sabbath of rest, holy to the LORD. Whoever does *any* work on the Sabbath day, he shall surely be put to death. [16]Therefore the children of Israel shall keep the Sabbath, to observe the Sabbath throughout their generations *as* a perpetual covenant. [17]It *is* [a]a sign between Me and the children of Israel forever; for [b]*in* six days the LORD made the heavens and the earth, and on the seventh day He rested and was refreshed.'"

[18]And when He had made an end of speaking with him on Mount Sinai, He gave Moses [a]two tablets of the Testimony, tablets of stone, written with the finger of God.

THE GOLD CALF
(Deut. 9:6–29)

32 Now when the people saw that Moses [a]delayed coming down from the mountain, the people [b]gathered together to Aaron, and said to him, [c]"Come, make us [1]gods that shall [d]go before us; for *as for* this Moses, the man who [e]brought us up out of the land of Egypt, we do not know what has become of him."

[2]And Aaron said to them, "Break off the [a]golden earrings which *are* in the ears of your wives, your sons, and your daughters, and bring *them* to me." [3]So all the people broke off the golden earrings which *were* in their ears, and brought *them* to Aaron. [4a]And he received *the gold* from their hand, and he fashioned it with an engraving tool, and made a molded calf.

31:6 [a]Ex. 35:34
[b]Ex. 28:3; 35:10, 35; 36:1
31:7 [a]Ex. 36:8
[b]Ex. 37:1–5
[c]Ex. 37:6–9
31:8 [a]Ex. 37:10–16 [b]Ex. 37:17–24; Lev. 24:4
31:9 [a]Ex. 38:1–7
[b]Ex. 38:8
31:10
[a]Ex. 39:1, 41
31:11
[a]Ex. 30:23–33
[b]Ex. 30:34–38
31:13 [a]Ex. 31:17; Lev. 19:3, 30; 26:2; Ezek. 20:12, 20
[b]Lev. 20:8
31:14 [a]Ex. 20:8; Deut. 5:12
[b]Ex. 31:15; 35:2; Num. 15:32–36; John 7:23
31:15
[a]Ex. 20:9–11; Lev. 23:3; Deut. 5:12–14
[b]Gen. 2:2; Ex. 16:23; 20:8; 35:2
31:17 [a]Ex. 31:13; Ezek. 20:12
[b]Gen. 1:31; 2:2, 3; Ex. 20:11
31:18 [a][Ex. 24:12; 32:15, 16; Deut. 4:13; 5:22; 2 Cor. 3:3]
32:1 [a]Ex. 24:18; Deut. 9:9–12
[b]Ex. 17:1–3
[c]Acts 7:40
[d]Ex. 13:21
[e]Ex. 32:8
32:2 [a]Ex. 11:2; 35:22; Judg. 8:24–27
32:4
[a]Ex. 20:3, 4, 23; Deut. 9:16; Judg. 17:3, 4; 1 Kin. 12:28; Neh. 9:18; Ps. 106:19; Acts 7:41

31:10 [1]Or *woven garments*   31:13 [1]*consecrates*   31:14 [1]*defiles*
32:1 [1]Or *a god*

Then they said, "This *is* your god, O Israel, that ᵇbrought you out of the land of Egypt!"

⁵So when Aaron saw *it,* he built an altar before it. And Aaron made a ᵃproclamation and said, "Tomorrow *is* a feast to the LORD." ⁶Then they rose early on the next day, offered burnt offerings, and brought peace offerings; and the people ᵃsat down to eat and drink, and rose up to play.

⁷And the LORD said to Moses, ᵃ"Go, get down! For your people whom you brought out of the land of Egypt ᵇhave corrupted *themselves.* ⁸They have turned aside quickly out of the way which ᵃI commanded them. They have made themselves a molded calf, and worshiped it and sacrificed to it, and said, ᵇ'This *is* your god, O Israel, that brought you out of the land of Egypt!'" ⁹And the LORD said to Moses, ᵃ"I have seen this people, and indeed it *is* a ¹stiff-necked people! ¹⁰Now therefore, ᵃlet Me alone, that ᵇMy wrath may burn hot against them and I may ¹consume them. And ᶜI will make of you a great nation."

¹¹ᵃThen Moses pleaded with ¹the LORD his God, and said: "LORD, why does Your wrath burn hot against Your people whom You have brought out of the land of Egypt with great power and with a mighty hand? ¹²ᵃWhy should the Egyptians speak, and say, 'He brought them out to harm them, to kill them in the mountains, and to consume them from the face of the earth'? Turn from Your fierce wrath, and ᵇrelent from this harm to Your people. ¹³Remember Abraham, Isaac, and Israel, Your servants, to whom You ᵃswore by Your own self, and said to them, ᵇ'I will multiply your descendants as the stars of heaven; and all this land that I have spoken of I give to your descendants, and they shall inherit *it* forever.'" ¹⁴So the LORD ᵃrelented from the harm which He said He would do to His people.

¹⁵And ᵃMoses turned and went down from the mountain, and the two tablets of the Testimony *were* in his hand. The tablets *were* written on both sides; on the one *side* and on the other they were written. ¹⁶Now the ᵃtablets *were* the work of God, and the writing *was* the writing of God engraved on the tablets.

¹⁷And when Joshua heard the noise of the people as they shouted, he said to Moses, "*There is* a noise of war in the camp."

¹⁸But he said:

"*It is* not the noise of the shout of victory,
Nor the noise of the cry of defeat,
But the sound of singing I hear."

¹⁹So it was, as soon as he came near the camp, that ᵃhe saw the calf *and* the dancing. So Moses' anger became hot, and he cast the tablets out of his hands and broke them at the foot of the mountain. ²⁰ᵃThen he took the calf which they had made, burned *it* in the fire, and ground *it* to powder; and he scattered *it* on the water and made the children of Israel drink *it.* ²¹And Moses said to Aaron, ᵃ"What did this people do to you that you have brought *so* great a sin upon them?"

²²So Aaron said, "Do not let the anger of my lord become hot. ᵃYou know the people, that they *are set* on evil. ²³For they

32:4
ᵇEx. 29:45, 46

32:5
ᵃLev. 23:2, 4, 21, 37; 2 Kin. 10:20; 2 Chr. 30:5

32:6 ᵃEx. 32:17–19; Num. 25:2; 1 Cor. 10:7

32:7
ᵃDeut. 9:8–21; Dan. 9:14
ᵇGen. 6:11, 12

32:8 ᵃEx. 20:3, 4, 23; Deut. 32:17
ᵇ1 Kin. 12:28

32:9
ᵃEx. 33:3, 5; 34:9; Deut. 9:6; 2 Chr. 30:8; Is. 48:4; [Acts 7:51]

32:10
ᵃDeut. 9:14, 19 ᵇEx. 22:24
ᶜNum. 14:12

32:11
ᵃDeut. 9:18, 26–29

32:12
ᵃNum. 14:13–19; Deut. 9:28; Josh. 7:9
ᵇEx. 32:14

32:13
ᵃGen. 22:16–18; [Heb. 6:13]
ᵇGen. 12:7; 13:15; 15:7, 18; 22:17; 26:4; 35:11, 12; Ex. 13:5, 11; 33:1

32:14
ᵃ2 Sam. 24:16

32:15
ᵃDeut. 9:15

32:16 ᵃEx. 31:18

32:19
ᵃDeut. 9:16, 17

32:20
ᵃNum. 5:17, 24; Deut. 9:21

32:21
ᵃGen. 26:10

32:22 ᵃEx. 14:11; Deut. 9:24

32:9 ¹stubborn   **32:10** ¹*destroy*   **32:11** ¹Lit. *the face of the LORD*

said to me, 'Make us gods that shall go before us; *as for* this Moses, the man who brought us out of the land of Egypt, we do not know what has become of him.' 24And I said to them, 'Whoever has any gold, let them break *it* off.' So they gave *it* to me, and I cast it into the fire, and this calf came out."

25Now when Moses saw that the people *were* ªunrestrained (for Aaron ᵇhad not restrained them, to *their* shame among their enemies), 26then Moses stood in the entrance of the camp, and said, "Whoever *is* on the Lord's side—*come* to me!" And all the sons of Levi gathered themselves together to him. 27And he said to them, "Thus says the Lord God of Israel: 'Let every man put his sword on his side, and go in and out from entrance to entrance throughout the camp, and ªlet every man kill his brother, every man his companion, and every man his neighbor.' " 28So the sons of Levi did according to the word of Moses. And about three thousand men of the people fell that day. 29ªThen Moses said, ¹"Consecrate yourselves today to the Lord, that He may bestow on you a blessing this day, for every man has opposed his son and his brother."

30Now it came to pass on the next day that Moses said to the people, ª"You have committed a great sin. So now I will go up to the Lord; ᵇperhaps I can ᶜmake atonement for your sin." 31Then Moses ªreturned to the Lord and said, "Oh, these people have committed a great sin, and have ᵇmade for themselves a god of gold! 32Yet now, if You will forgive their sin— but if not, I pray, ªblot me ᵇout of Your book which You have written."

33And the Lord said to Moses, ª"Whoever has sinned against Me, I will ᵇblot him out of My book. 34Now therefore, go, lead the people to *the place* of which I have ªspoken to you. ᵇBehold, My Angel shall go before you. Nevertheless, ᶜin the day when I ᵈvisit for punishment, I will visit punishment upon them for their sin."

35So the Lord plagued the people because of ªwhat they did with the calf which Aaron made.

THE COMMAND TO LEAVE SINAI

33 Then the Lord said to Moses, "Depart *and* go up from here, you ªand the people whom you have brought out of the land of Egypt, to the land of which I swore to Abraham, Isaac, and Jacob, saying, ᵇ'To your descendants I will give it.' 2ªAnd I will send *My* Angel before you, ᵇand I will drive out the Canaanite and the Amorite and the Hittite and the Perizzite and the Hivite and the Jebusite. 3*Go up* ªto a land flowing with milk and honey; for I will not go up in your midst, lest ᵇI ¹consume you on the way, for you *are* a ᶜstiff-necked² people."

4And when the people heard this bad news, ªthey mourned, ᵇand no one put on his ornaments. 5For the Lord had said to Moses, "Say to the children of Israel, 'You *are* a stiff-necked people. I could come up into your midst in one moment and consume you. Now therefore, take off your ¹ornaments, that I may ªknow what to do to you.' " 6So the children of Israel stripped themselves of their ornaments by Mount Horeb.

32:25 ªEx. 33:4, 5 ᵇ2 Chr. 28:19
32:27 ªNum. 25:5–13
32:29 ªEx. 28:41; 1 Sam. 15:18, 22; Prov. 21:3; Zech. 13:3
32:30 ª1 Sam. 12:20, 23 ᵇ2 Sam. 16:12 ᶜNum. 25:13
32:31 ªDeut. 9:18 ᵇEx. 20:23
32:32 ªPs. 69:28; Is. 4:3; Mal. 3:16; Rom. 9:3 ᵇDan. 12:1; Phil. 4:3; Rev. 3:5; 21:27
32:33 ªLev. 23:30; [Ezek. 18:4; 33:2, 14, 15] ᵇEx. 17:14; Deut. 29:20; Ps. 9:5; Rev. 3:5; 21:27
32:34 ªEx. 3:17 ᵇEx. 23:20; Josh. 5:14 ᶜDeut. 32:35; Rom. 2:5, 6 ᵈPs. 89:32
32:35 ªNeh. 9:18
33:1 ªEx. 32:1, 7, 13; Josh. 3:17 ᵇGen. 12:7
33:2 ªEx. 32:34; Josh. 5:14 ᵇEx. 23:27–31; Josh. 24:11
33:3 ªEx. 3:8 ᵇNum. 16:21, 45 ᶜEx. 32:9; 33:5
33:4 ªNum. 14:1, 39 ᵇEzra 9:3; Esth. 4:1, 4; Ezek. 24:17, 23
33:5 ª[Ps. 139:23]

32:29 ¹Lit. *Fill your hand*   33:3 ¹destroy   ²stubborn   33:5 ¹jewelry

MOSES MEETS WITH THE LORD

[7]Moses took his tent and pitched it outside the camp, far from the camp, and [a]called it the tabernacle of meeting. And it came to pass *that* everyone who [b]sought the LORD went out to the tabernacle of meeting which *was* outside the camp. [8]So it was, whenever Moses went out to the tabernacle, *that* all the people rose, and each man stood [a]at his tent door and watched Moses until he had gone into the tabernacle. [9]And it came to pass, when Moses entered the tabernacle, that the pillar of cloud descended and stood *at* the door of the tabernacle, and *the* LORD [a]talked with Moses. [10]All the people saw the pillar of cloud standing *at* the tabernacle door, and all the people rose and [a]worshiped, each man *in* his tent door. [11]So [a]the LORD spoke to Moses face to face, as a man speaks to his friend. And he would return to the camp, but [b]his servant Joshua the son of Nun, a young man, did not depart from the tabernacle.

THE PROMISE OF GOD'S PRESENCE

[12]Then Moses said to the LORD, "See, [a]You say to me, 'Bring up this people.' But You have not let me know whom You will send with me. Yet You have said, [b]'I know you by name, and you have also found grace in My sight.' [13]Now therefore, I pray, [a]if I have found grace in Your sight, [b]show me now Your way, that I may know You and that I may find grace in Your sight. And consider that this nation *is* [c]Your people."

[14]And He said, [a]"My Presence will go *with you,* and I will give you [b]rest."

[15]Then he said to Him, [a]"If Your Presence does not go *with us,* do not bring us up from here. [16]For how then will it be known that Your people and I have found grace in Your sight, [a]except You go with us? So we [b]shall be separate, Your people and I, from all the people who *are* upon the face of the earth."

[17]So the LORD said to Moses, [a]"I will also do this thing that you have spoken; for you have found grace in My sight, and I know you by name."

[18]And he said, "Please, show me [a]Your glory."

[19]Then He said, "I will make all My [a]goodness pass before you, and I will proclaim the name of the LORD before you. [b]I will be gracious to whom I will be [c]gracious, and I will have compassion on whom I will have compassion." [20]But He said, "You cannot see My face; for [a]no man shall see Me, and live." [21]And the LORD said, "Here is a place by Me, and you shall stand on the rock. [22]So it shall be, while My glory passes by, that I will put you [a]in the cleft of the rock, and will [b]cover you with My hand while I pass by. [23]Then I will take away My hand, and you shall see My back; but My face shall [a]not be seen."

MOSES MAKES NEW TABLETS

(Deut. 10:1–5)

34 And the LORD said to Moses, [a]"Cut two tablets of stone like the first *ones,* and [b]I will write on *these* tablets the words that were on the first tablets which you broke. [2]So be ready in the morning, and come up in the morning to Mount Sinai, and present yourself to Me there [a]on the top of the mountain. [3]And no man shall [a]come up with you, and let no

33:7 [a]Ex. 29:42, 43 [b]Deut. 4:29

33:8 [a]Num. 16:27

33:9 [a]Ex. 25:22; 31:18; Ps. 99:7

33:10 [a]Ex. 4:31

33:11 [a]Num. 12:8; Deut. 34:10 [b]Ex. 24:13

33:12 [a]Ex. 3:10; 32:34 [b]Ex. 33:17; John 10:14, 15; 2 Tim. 2:19

33:13 [a]Ex. 34:9 [b]Ps. 25:4; 27:11; 86:11; 119:33 [c]Ex. 3:7, 10; 5:1; 32:12, 14; Deut. 9:26, 29

33:14 [a]Ex. 3:12; Deut. 4:37; Is. 63:9 [b]Deut. 12:10; 25:19; Josh. 21:44; 22:4

33:15 [a]Ex. 33:3

33:16 [a]Num. 14:14 [b]Ex. 34:10; Deut. 4:7, 34

33:17 [a][James 5:16]

33:18 [a]Ex. 24:16, 17; [1 Tim. 6:16]

33:19 [a]Ex. 34:6, 7 [b][Rom. 9:15, 16, 18] [c][Rom. 4:4, 16]

33:20 [a][Gen. 32:30]

33:22 [a]Song 2:14; Is. 2:21 [b]Ps. 91:1, 4; Is. 49:2; 51:16

33:23 [a]Ex. 33:20; [John 1:18]

34:1 [a][Ex. 24:12; 31:18; 32:15, 16, 19; Deut. 4:13] [b]Deut. 10:2, 4

34:2 [a]Ex. 19:11, 18, 20

34:3 [a]Ex. 19:12, 13; 24:9–11

34:5 aEx. 19:9
bEx. 33:19

34:6
aNum. 14:18;
Deut. 4:31;
Neh. 9:17;
Joel 2:13
bRom. 2:4
cPs. 108:4

34:7 aEx. 20:6
bPs. 103:3, 4;
Dan. 9:9;
Eph. 4:32;
1 John 1:9
cJosh. 24:19;
Job 10:14;
Mic. 6:11;
Nah. 1:3

34:8 aEx. 4:31

34:9 aEx. 33:12–
16 bEx. 33:3
cPs. 33:12; 94:14

34:10 aEx. 34:27,
28; Deut. 5:2
bDeut. 4:32;
Ps. 77:14
cPs. 145:6

34:11 aDeut. 6:25
bEx. 23:20–33;
33:2; Josh. 11:23

34:12
aEx. 23:32, 33

34:13 aEx. 23:24;
Deut. 12:3
bDeut. 16:21;
Judg. 6:25,
26; 2 Kin. 18:4;
2 Chr. 34:3, 4

34:14
a[Ex. 20:3–5]
b[Is. 9:6; 57:15]
c[Ex. 20:5;
Deut. 4:24]

34:15 aJudg. 2:17
bNum. 25:1, 2;
Deut. 32:37, 38
c1 Cor. 8:4, 7, 10

34:16
aGen. 28:1;
Deut. 7:3;
Josh. 23:12,
13; 1 Kin. 11:2;
Ezra 9:2;
Neh. 13:25
bNum. 25:1, 2;
1 Kin. 11:4

34:17 aEx. 20:4,
23; 32:8;
Lev. 19:4;
Deut. 5:8

34:18 aEx. 12:15,
16 bEx. 12:2; 13:4

34:19 aEx. 13:2;
22:29

34:20 aEx. 13:13
bEx. 22:29;
23:15;
Deut. 16:16

man be seen throughout all the mountain; let neither flocks nor herds feed before that mountain."

4So he cut two tablets of stone like the first *ones.* Then Moses rose early in the morning and went up Mount Sinai, as the LORD had commanded him; and he took in his hand the two tablets of stone.

5Now the LORD descended in the acloud and stood with him there, and bproclaimed the name of the LORD. 6And the LORD passed before him and proclaimed, "The LORD, the LORD aGod, merciful and gracious, longsuffering, and abounding in bgoodness and ctruth, 7akeeping mercy for thousands, bforgiving iniquity and transgression and sin, cby no means clearing *the guilty,* visiting the iniquity of the fathers upon the children and the children's children to the third and the fourth generation."

8So Moses made haste and abowed his head toward the earth, and worshiped. 9Then he said, "If now I have found grace in Your sight, O Lord, alet my Lord, I pray, go among us, even though we *are* a bstiff-necked¹ people; and pardon our iniquity and our sin, and take us as cYour inheritance."

THE COVENANT RENEWED
(Ex. 23:14–19; Deut. 7:1–6; 16:1–17)

10And He said: "Behold, aI make a covenant. Before all your people I will bdo ¹marvels such as have not been done in all the earth, nor in any nation; and all the people among whom you *are* shall see the work of the LORD. For it *is* can awesome thing that I will do with you. 11aObserve what I command you this day. Behold, bI am driving out from before you the Amorite and the Canaanite and the Hittite and the Perizzite and the Hivite and the Jebusite. 12aTake heed to yourself, lest you make a covenant with the inhabitants of the land where you are going, lest it be a snare in your midst. 13But you shall adestroy their altars, break their *sacred* pillars, and bcut down their wooden images 14(for you shall worship ano other god, for the LORD, whose bname *is* Jealous, *is* a cjealous God), 15lest you make a covenant with the inhabitants of the land, and they aplay the harlot with their gods and make sacrifice to their gods, and *one of them* binvites you and you ceat of his sacrifice, 16and you take of ahis daughters for your sons, and his daughters bplay the harlot with their gods and make your sons play the harlot with their gods.

17a"You shall make no molded gods for yourselves.

18"The Feast of aUnleavened Bread you shall keep. Seven days you shall eat unleavened bread, as I commanded you, in the appointed time of the month of Abib; for in the bmonth of Abib you came out from Egypt.

19a"All ¹that open the womb *are* Mine, and every male firstborn among your livestock, *whether* ox or sheep. 20But athe firstborn of a donkey you shall redeem with a lamb. And if you will not redeem *him,* then you shall break his neck. All the firstborn of your sons you shall redeem.

"And none shall appear before Me bempty-handed.

21a"Six days you shall work, but on the seventh day you shall rest; in plowing time and in harvest you shall rest.

34:21 aEx. 20:9; 23:12; 31:15; 35:2; Lev. 23:3; Deut. 5:13

34:9 ¹*stubborn*   **34:10** ¹*wonderful acts*   **34:19** ¹*the firstborn*

22"And you shall observe the Feast of Weeks, of the first-fruits of wheat harvest, and the Feast of Ingathering at the year's end.

23a"Three times in the year all your men shall appear before the Lord, the LORD God of Israel. 24For I will acast out the nations before you and enlarge your borders; neither will any man covet your land when you go up to appear before the LORD your God three times in the year.

25"You shall not offer the blood of My sacrifice with leaven, anor shall the sacrifice of the Feast of the Passover be left until morning.

26a"The first of the firstfruits of your land you shall bring to the house of the LORD your God. You shall not boil a young goat in its mother's milk."

27Then the LORD said to Moses, "Write athese words, for according to the tenor of these words I have made a covenant with you and with Israel." 28aSo he was there with the LORD forty days and forty nights; he neither ate bread nor drank water. And bHe wrote on the tablets the words of the covenant, the 1Ten Commandments.

THE SHINING FACE OF MOSES

29Now it was so, when Moses came down from Mount Sinai (and the atwo tablets of the Testimony were in Moses' hand when he came down from the mountain), that Moses did not know that bthe skin of his face shone while he talked with Him. 30So when Aaron and all the children of Israel saw Moses, behold, the skin of his face shone, and they were afraid to come near him. 31Then Moses called to them, and Aaron and all the rulers of the congregation returned to him; and Moses talked with them. 32Afterward all the children of Israel came near, aand he gave them as commandments all that the LORD had spoken with him on Mount Sinai. 33And when Moses had finished speaking with them, he put aa veil on his face. 34But awhenever Moses went in before the LORD to speak with Him, he would take the veil off until he came out; and he would come out and speak to the children of Israel whatever he had been commanded. 35And whenever the children of Israel saw the face of Moses, that the skin of Moses' face shone, then Moses would put the veil on his face again, until he went in to speak with Him.

SABBATH REGULATIONS

35 Then Moses gathered all the congregation of the children of Israel together, and said to them, a"These are the words which the LORD has commanded you to do: 2Work shall be done for asix days, but the seventh day shall be a holy day for you, a Sabbath of rest to the LORD. Whoever does any work on it shall be put to bdeath. 3aYou shall kindle no fire throughout your dwellings on the Sabbath day."

OFFERINGS FOR THE TABERNACLE
(Ex. 25:1–9; 39:32–43)

4And Moses spoke to all the congregation of the children of Israel, saying, a"This is the thing which the LORD

34:23
aEx. 23:14–17

34:24
a[Ex. 33:2];
Josh. 11:23;
1 Kin. 4:21;
2 Chr. 36:14–16;
Ps. 78:55

34:25 aEx. 12:10

34:26
aEx. 23:19;
Deut. 26:2

34:27 aEx. 17:14;
24:4; Deut. 31:9

34:28 aEx. 24:18
bEx. 34:1, 4;
Deut. 4:31;
10:2, 4

34:29 aEx. 32:15
bMatt. 17:2;
2 Cor. 3:7

34:32 aEx. 24:3

34:33
a[2 Cor. 3:13, 14]

34:34
a[2 Cor. 3:13–16]

35:1 aEx. 34:32

35:2 aEx. 20:9,
10; Lev. 23:3;
Deut. 5:13
bNum. 15:32–36

35:3 aEx. 12:16;
16:23

35:4 aEx. 25:1, 2

34:28 1Lit. *Ten Words*

commanded, saying: ⁵"Take from among you an offering to the LORD. ᵃWhoever *is* of a willing heart, let him bring it as an offering to the LORD: ᵇgold, silver, and bronze; ⁶ᵃblue, purple, and scarlet *thread,* fine linen, and ᵇgoats' *hair;* ⁷ram skins dyed red, badger skins, and acacia wood; ⁸oil for the light, ᵃand spices for the anointing oil and for the sweet incense; ⁹onyx stones, and stones to be set in the ephod and in the breastplate.

ARTICLES OF THE TABERNACLE

¹⁰ᵃ"All *who are* gifted artisans among you shall come and make all that the LORD has commanded: ¹¹ᵃthe tabernacle, its tent, its covering, its clasps, its boards, its bars, its pillars, and its sockets; ¹²ᵃthe ark and its poles, *with* the mercy seat, and the veil of the covering; ¹³the ᵃtable and its poles, all its utensils, ᵇand the showbread; ¹⁴also ᵃthe lampstand for the light, its utensils, its lamps, and the oil for the light; ¹⁵ᵃthe incense altar, its poles, ᵇthe anointing oil, ᶜthe sweet incense, and the screen for the door at the entrance of the tabernacle; ¹⁶ᵃthe altar of burnt offering with its bronze grating, its poles, all its utensils, *and* the laver and its base; ¹⁷ᵃthe hangings of the court, its pillars, their sockets, and the screen for the gate of the court; ¹⁸the pegs of the tabernacle, the pegs of the court, and their cords; ¹⁹ᵃthe ¹garments of ministry, for ministering in the holy *place*—the holy garments for Aaron the priest and the garments of his sons, to minister as priests.'"

THE TABERNACLE OFFERINGS PRESENTED

²⁰And all the congregation of the children of Israel departed from the presence of Moses. ²¹Then everyone came ᵃwhose heart ¹was stirred, and everyone whose spirit was willing, *and* they ᵇbrought the LORD's offering for the work of the tabernacle of meeting, for all its service, and for the holy garments. ²²They came, both men and women, as many as had a willing heart, *and* brought ᵃearrings and nose rings, rings and necklaces, all ᵇjewelry of gold, that is, every man who *made* an offering of gold to the LORD. ²³And ᵃevery man, with whom was found blue, purple, and scarlet *thread,* fine linen, and goats' *hair,* red skins of rams, and ¹badger skins, brought *them.* ²⁴Everyone who offered an offering of silver or bronze brought the LORD's offering. And everyone with whom was found acacia wood for any work of the service, brought *it.* ²⁵All the women *who were* ᵃgifted artisans spun yarn with their hands, and brought what they had spun, of blue, purple, *and* scarlet, and fine linen. ²⁶And all the women whose hearts ¹stirred with wisdom spun yarn of goats' *hair.* ²⁷ᵃThe rulers brought onyx stones, and the stones to be set in the ephod and in the breastplate, ²⁸and ᵃspices and oil for the light, for the anointing oil, and for the sweet incense. ²⁹The children of Israel brought a ᵃfreewill offering to the LORD, all the men and women whose hearts were willing to bring *material* for all kinds of work which the LORD, by the hand of Moses, had commanded to be done.

35:5 ᵃEx. 25:2; 1 Chr. 29:14; Mark 12:41–44; 2 Cor. 8:10–12; 9:7 ᵇEx. 38:24
35:6 ᵃEx. 36:8 ᵇEx. 36:14
35:8 ᵃEx. 25:6; 30:23–25
35:10 ᵃEx. 31:2–6; 36:1, 2
35:11 ᵃEx. 26:1, 2; 36:14
35:12 ᵃEx. 25:10–22
35:13 ᵃEx. 25:23 ᵇEx. 25:30; Lev. 24:5, 6
35:14 ᵃEx. 25:31
35:15 ᵃEx. 30:1 ᵇEx. 30:25 ᶜEx. 30:34–38
35:16 ᵃEx. 27:1–8
35:17 ᵃEx. 27:9–18
35:19 ᵃEx. 31:10; 39:1, 41
35:21 ᵃEx. 25:2; 35:5, 22, 26, 29; 36:2 ᵇEx. 35:24
35:22 ᵃEx. 32:2, 3 ᵇEx. 11:2
35:23 ᵃ1 Chr. 29:8
35:25 ᵃEx. 28:3; 31:6; 36:1
35:27 ᵃ1 Chr. 29:6; Ezra 2:68
35:28 ᵃEx. 30:23
35:29 ᵃEx. 35:5, 21; 36:3; 1 Chr. 29:9

35:19 ¹Or *woven garments*   35:21 ¹Lit. *lifted him up*   35:23 ¹Or *dolphin*   35:26 ¹Lit. *lifted them up*

THE ARTISANS CALLED BY GOD
(Ex. 31:1–11)

³⁰And Moses said to the children of Israel, "See, ^athe LORD has called by name Bezalel the son of Uri, the son of Hur, of the tribe of Judah; ³¹and He has filled him with the Spirit of God, in wisdom and understanding, in knowledge and all manner of workmanship, ³²to design artistic works, to work in gold and silver and bronze, ³³in cutting jewels for setting, in carving wood, and to work in all manner of artistic workmanship.

³⁴"And He has put in his heart the ability to teach, *in* him and ^aAholiab the son of Ahisamach, of the tribe of Dan. ³⁵He has ^afilled them with skill to do all manner of work of the engraver and the designer and the tapestry maker, in blue, purple, and scarlet *thread,* and fine linen, and of the weaver— those who do every work and those who design artistic works.

36 "And Bezalel and Aholiab, and every ^agifted artisan in whom the LORD has put wisdom and understanding, to know how to do all manner of work for the service of the ^bsanctuary,¹ shall do according to all that the LORD has commanded."

THE PEOPLE GIVE MORE THAN ENOUGH

²Then Moses called Bezalel and Aholiab, and every gifted artisan in whose heart the LORD had put wisdom, everyone ^awhose heart ¹was stirred, to come and do the work. ³And they received from Moses all the ^aoffering which the children of Israel ^bhad brought for the work of the service of making the sanctuary. So they continued bringing to him freewill offerings every morning. ⁴Then all the craftsmen who were doing all the work of the sanctuary came, each from the work he was doing, ⁵and they spoke to Moses, saying, ^a"The people bring much more than enough for the service of the work which the LORD commanded *us* to do."

⁶So Moses gave a commandment, and they caused it to be proclaimed throughout the camp, saying, "Let neither man nor woman do any more work for the offering of the sanctuary." And the people were restrained from bringing, ⁷for the material they had was sufficient for all the work to be done— indeed too ^amuch.

BUILDING THE TABERNACLE
(Ex. 26:1–37)

^{8a}Then all the gifted artisans among them who worked on the tabernacle made ten curtains woven of fine linen, and of blue, purple, and scarlet *thread; with* artistic designs of cherubim they made them. ⁹The length of each curtain *was* twenty-eight cubits, and the width of each curtain four cubits; the curtains *were* all the same size. ¹⁰And he coupled five curtains to one another, and *the other* five curtains he coupled to one another. ¹¹He made loops of blue *yarn* on the edge of the curtain on the selvedge of one set; likewise he did on the outer edge of *the other* curtain of the second set. ^{12a}Fifty loops he made on one curtain, and fifty loops he made on the edge of the curtain on the end of the second set; the loops held

35:30
^aEx. 31:1–6

35:34 ^aEx. 31:6

35:35
^aEx. 31:3, 6;
35:31; 1 Kin. 7:14;
2 Chr. 2:14;
Is. 28:26

36:1 ^aEx. 28:3;
31:6; 35:10, 35
^bEx. 25:8

36:2 ^aEx. 35:21,
26; 1 Chr. 29:5,
9, 17

36:3 ^aEx. 35:5
^bEx. 35:27

36:5
^a2 Chr. 24:14;
31:6–10;
[2 Cor. 8:2, 3]

36:7 ^a1 Kin. 8:64

36:8
^aEx. 26:1–14

36:12 ^aEx. 26:5

36:1 ¹*holy place*   36:2 ¹*lifted him up*

one *curtain* to another. ¹³And he made fifty clasps of gold, and coupled the curtains to one another with the clasps, that it might be one tabernacle.

¹⁴ᵃHe made curtains of goats' *hair* for the tent over the tabernacle; he made eleven curtains. ¹⁵The length of each curtain *was* thirty cubits, and the width of each curtain four cubits; the eleven curtains *were* the same size. ¹⁶He coupled five curtains by themselves and six curtains by themselves. ¹⁷And he made fifty loops on the edge of the curtain that is outermost in one set, and fifty loops he made on the edge of the curtain of the second set. ¹⁸He also made fifty bronze clasps to couple the tent together, that it might be one. ¹⁹ᵃThen he made a covering for the tent of ram skins dyed red, and a covering of ¹badger skins above *that.*

²⁰For the tabernacle ᵃhe made boards of acacia wood, standing upright. ²¹The length of each board *was* ten cubits, and the width of each board a cubit and a half. ²²Each board had two ¹tenons ᵃfor binding one to another. Thus he made for all the boards of the tabernacle. ²³And he made boards for the tabernacle, twenty boards for the south side. ²⁴Forty sockets of silver he made to go under the twenty boards: two sockets under each of the boards for its two tenons. ²⁵And for the other side of the tabernacle, the north side, he made twenty boards ²⁶and their forty sockets of silver: two sockets under each of the boards. ²⁷For the west side of the tabernacle he made six boards. ²⁸He also made two boards for the two back corners of the tabernacle. ²⁹And they were coupled at the bottom and ¹coupled together at the top by one ring. Thus he made both of them for the two corners. ³⁰So there were eight boards and their sockets—sixteen sockets of silver—two sockets under each of the boards.

³¹And he made ᵃbars of acacia wood: five for the boards on one side of the tabernacle, ³²five bars for the boards on the other side of the tabernacle, and five bars for the boards of the tabernacle on the far side westward. ³³And he made the middle bar to pass through the boards from one end to the other. ³⁴He overlaid the boards with gold, made their rings of gold *to be* holders for the bars, and overlaid the bars with gold.

³⁵And he made ᵃa veil of blue, purple, and scarlet *thread,* and fine woven linen; it was worked *with* an artistic design of cherubim. ³⁶He made for it four pillars of acacia *wood,* and overlaid them with gold, with their hooks of gold; and he cast four sockets of silver for them.

³⁷He also made a ᵃscreen for the tabernacle door, of blue, purple, and scarlet *thread,* and fine woven linen, made by a ¹weaver, ³⁸and its five pillars with their hooks. And he overlaid their capitals and their rings with gold, but their five sockets *were* bronze.

MAKING THE ARK OF THE TESTIMONY
(Ex. 25:10–22)

37 Then ᵃBezalel made ᵇthe ark of acacia wood; two and a half cubits *was* its length, a cubit and a half its width, and a cubit and a half its height. ²He overlaid it with pure gold inside and outside, and made a molding of gold all around

36:14 ᵃEx. 26:7
36:19 ᵃEx. 26:14
36:20
ᵃEx. 26:15–29
36:22 ᵃEx. 26:17
36:31
ᵃEx. 26:26–29
36:35
ᵃEx. 26:31–37
36:37 ᵃEx. 26:36
37:1
ᵃEx. 35:30; 36:1
ᵇEx. 25:10–20

36:19 ¹Or *dolphin*   **36:22** ¹Projections for joining, lit. *hands*   **36:29** ¹Lit. *doubled*   **36:37** ¹Lit. *variegator,* a weaver in colors

it. ³And he cast for it four rings of gold *to be set* in its four corners: two rings on one side, and two rings on the other side of it. ⁴He made poles of acacia wood, and overlaid them with gold. ⁵And he put the poles into the rings at the sides of the ark, to bear the ark. ⁶He also made the ᵃmercy seat of pure gold; two and a half cubits *was* its length and a cubit and a half its width. ⁷He made two cherubim of beaten gold; he made of one piece at the two ends of the mercy seat: ⁸one cherub at one end on this side, and the other cherub at the *other* end on that side. He made the cherubim at the two ends *of one piece* with the mercy seat. ⁹The cherubim spread out *their* wings above, *and* covered the ᵃmercy seat with their wings. They faced one another; the faces of the cherubim were toward the mercy seat.

MAKING THE TABLE FOR THE SHOWBREAD
(Ex. 25:23–30)

¹⁰He made ᵃthe table of acacia wood; two cubits *was* its length, a cubit its width, and a cubit and a half its height. ¹¹And he overlaid it with pure gold, and made a molding of gold all around it. ¹²Also he made a frame of a handbreadth all around it, and made a molding of gold for the frame all around it. ¹³And he cast for it four rings of gold, and put the rings on the four corners that *were* at its four legs. ¹⁴The rings were close to the frame, as holders for the poles to bear the table. ¹⁵And he made the poles of acacia wood to bear the table, and overlaid them with gold. ¹⁶He made of pure gold the utensils which were on the table: its ᵃdishes, its cups, its bowls, and its pitchers for pouring.

MAKING THE GOLD LAMPSTAND
(Ex. 25:31–40)

¹⁷He also made the ᵃlampstand of pure gold; of hammered work he made the lampstand. Its shaft, its branches, its bowls, its *ornamental* knobs, and its flowers were of the same piece. ¹⁸And six branches came out of its sides: three branches of the lampstand out of one side, and three branches of the lampstand out of the other side. ¹⁹There were three bowls made like almond *blossoms* on one branch, with an *ornamental* knob and a flower, and three bowls made like almond *blossoms* on the other branch, with an *ornamental* knob and a flower—and so for the six branches coming out of the lampstand. ²⁰And on the lampstand itself *were* four bowls made like almond *blossoms, each with* its *ornamental* knob and flower. ²¹*There was* a knob under the *first* two branches of the same, a knob under the *second* two branches of the same, and a knob under the *third* two branches of the same, according to the six branches extending from it. ²²Their knobs and their branches were of one piece; all of it *was* one hammered piece of pure gold. ²³And he made its seven lamps, its ᵃwick-trimmers, and its trays of pure gold. ²⁴Of a talent of pure gold he made it, with all its utensils.

MAKING THE ALTAR OF INCENSE
(Ex. 30:1–5)

²⁵ᵃHe made the incense altar of acacia wood. Its length *was* a cubit and its width a cubit—*it was* square—and two cubits

37:6 ᵃEx. 25:17
37:9 ᵃEx. 25:20
37:10
ᵃEx. 25:23–29
37:16 ᵃEx. 25:29
37:17
ᵃEx. 25:31–39
37:23
ᵃNum. 4:9
37:25
ᵃEx. 30:1–5

was its height. Its horns were *of one piece* with it. ²⁶And he overlaid it with pure gold: its top, its sides all around, and its horns. He also made for it a molding of gold all around it. ²⁷He made two rings of gold for it under its molding, by its two corners on both sides, as holders for the poles with which to bear it. ²⁸And he ªmade the poles of acacia wood, and overlaid them with gold.

MAKING THE ANOINTING OIL AND THE INCENSE
(Ex. 30:22–38)

²⁹He also made ªthe holy anointing oil and the pure incense of sweet spices, according to the work of the perfumer.

MAKING THE ALTAR OF BURNT OFFERING
(Ex. 27:1–8)

38 He made ªthe altar of burnt offering of acacia wood; five cubits *was* its length and five cubits its width—*it was* square—and its height *was* three cubits. ²He made its horns on its four corners; the horns were *of one piece* with it. And he overlaid it with bronze. ³He made all the utensils for the altar: the pans, the shovels, the basins, the forks, and the firepans; all its utensils he made of bronze. ⁴And he made a grate of bronze network for the altar, under its rim, midway from the bottom. ⁵He cast four rings for the four corners of the bronze grating, *as* holders for the poles. ⁶And he made the poles of acacia wood, and overlaid them with bronze. ⁷Then he put the poles into the rings on the sides of the altar, with which to bear it. He made the altar hollow with boards.

MAKING THE BRONZE LAVER

⁸He made ªthe laver of bronze and its base of bronze, from the bronze mirrors of the serving women who assembled at the door of the tabernacle of meeting.

MAKING THE COURT OF THE TABERNACLE
(Ex. 27:9–19)

⁹Then he made ªthe court on the south side; the hangings of the court *were of* fine woven linen, one hundred cubits long. ¹⁰There *were* twenty pillars for them, with twenty bronze sockets. The hooks of the pillars and their bands *were* silver. ¹¹On the north side *the hangings were* one hundred cubits *long,* with twenty pillars and their twenty bronze sockets. The hooks of the pillars and their bands *were* silver. ¹²And on the west side *there were* hangings of fifty cubits, with ten pillars and their ten sockets. The hooks of the pillars and their bands *were* silver. ¹³For the east side *the hangings were* fifty cubits. ¹⁴The hangings of one side *of the gate were* fifteen cubits *long, with* their three pillars and their three sockets, ¹⁵and the same for the other side of the court gate; on this side and that *were* hangings of fifteen cubits, *with* their three pillars and their three sockets. ¹⁶All the hangings of the court all around *were of* fine woven linen. ¹⁷The sockets for the pillars *were* bronze, the hooks of the pillars and their bands *were* silver, and the overlay of their capitals *was* silver; and all the pillars of the court had bands of silver. ¹⁸The screen for

37:28 ªEx. 30:5
37:29
ªEx. 30:23–25
38:1 ªEx. 27:1–8
38:8 ªEx. 30:18
38:9
ªEx. 27:9–19

the gate of the court *was* woven of blue, purple, and scarlet *thread,* and of fine woven linen. The length *was* twenty cubits, and the height along its width *was* five cubits, corresponding to the hangings of the court. ¹⁹And *there were* four pillars *with* their four sockets of bronze; their sockets *were* silver, and the overlay of their capitals and their bands *was* silver. ²⁰All the ªpegs of the tabernacle, and of the court all around, *were* bronze.

MATERIALS OF THE TABERNACLE

²¹¹This is the inventory of the tabernacle, ªthe tabernacle of the Testimony, which was counted according to the commandment of Moses, for the service of the Levites, ᵇby the hand of ᶜIthamar, son of Aaron the priest.

²²ªBezalel the son of Uri, the son of Hur, of the tribe of Judah, made all that the Lᴏʀᴅ had commanded Moses. ²³And with him *was* ªAholiab the son of Ahisamach, of the tribe of Dan, an engraver and ¹designer, a weaver of blue, purple, and scarlet *thread,* and of fine linen.

²⁴All the gold that was used in all the work of the holy *place,* that is, the gold of the ªoffering, was twenty-nine talents and seven hundred and thirty shekels, according to ᵇthe shekel of the sanctuary. ²⁵And the silver from those who were ªnumbered of the congregation *was* one hundred talents and one thousand seven hundred and seventy-five shekels, according to the shekel of the sanctuary: ²⁶ªa bekah for ¹each man (*that is,* half a shekel, according to the shekel of the sanctuary), for everyone included in the numbering from twenty years old and above, for ᵇsix hundred and three thousand, five hundred and fifty *men.* ²⁷And from the hundred talents of silver were cast ªthe sockets of the sanctuary and the bases of the veil: one hundred sockets from the hundred talents, one talent for each socket. ²⁸Then from the one thousand seven hundred and seventy-five *shekels* he made hooks for the pillars, overlaid their capitals, and ªmade bands for them.

²⁹The offering of bronze *was* seventy talents and two thousand four hundred shekels. ³⁰And with it he made the sockets for the door of the tabernacle of meeting, the bronze altar, the bronze grating for it, and all the utensils for the altar, ³¹the sockets for the court all around, the bases for the court gate, all the pegs for the tabernacle, and all the pegs for the court all around.

MAKING THE GARMENTS OF THE PRIESTHOOD
(Ex. 28:1–43)

39 Of the ªblue, purple, and scarlet *thread* they made ᵇgarments¹ of ministry, for ministering in the ²holy *place,* and made the holy garments for Aaron, ᶜas the Lᴏʀᴅ had commanded Moses.

MAKING THE EPHOD

²ªHe made the ᵇephod of gold, blue, purple, and scarlet *thread,* and of fine woven linen. ³And they beat the gold

---

38:20 ªEx. 27:19

38:21
ªNum. 1:50, 53;
9:15; 10:11; 17:7,
8; 2 Chr. 24:6;
Acts 7:44
ᵇNum. 4:28,
33 ᶜEx. 28:1;
Lev. 10:6, 16

38:22
ªEx. 31:2, 6;
1 Chr. 2:18–20

38:23
ªEx. 31:6; 36:1

38:24 ªEx. 35:5,
22 ᵇEx. 30:13,
24; Lev. 5:15;
27:3, 25;
Num. 3:47;
18:16

38:25
ªEx. 30:11–16;
Num. 1:2

38:26
ªEx. 30:13, 15
ᵇEx. 12:37;
Num. 1:46;
26:51

38:27
ªEx. 26:19, 21,
25, 32

38:28 ªEx. 27:17

39:1 ªEx. 25:4;
35:23 ᵇEx. 31:10;
35:19 ᶜEx. 28:4

39:2
ªEx. 28:6–14
ᵇLev. 8:7

38:21 ¹Lit. *These are the things appointed for*   38:23 ¹*skillful workman*
38:26 ¹Lit. *a head*   39:1 ¹Or *woven garments*   ²*sanctuary*

into thin sheets and cut *it into* threads, to work *it* in *with* the blue, purple, and scarlet *thread,* and the fine linen, *into* artistic designs. 4They made shoulder straps for it to couple *it* together; it was coupled together at its two edges. 5And the intricately woven band of his ephod that *was* on it *was* of the same workmanship, *woven of* gold, blue, purple, and scarlet *thread,* and *of* fine woven linen, as the LORD had commanded Moses.

6aAnd they set onyx stones, enclosed in ¹settings of gold; they were engraved, as signets are engraved, with the names of the sons of Israel. 7He put them on the shoulders of the ephod *as* ªmemorial stones for the sons of Israel, as the LORD had commanded Moses.

MAKING THE BREASTPLATE

8aAnd he made the breastplate, artistically woven like the workmanship of the ephod, of gold, blue, purple, and scarlet *thread,* and of fine woven linen. 9They made the breastplate square by doubling it; a span *was* its length and a span its width when doubled. 10aAnd they set in it four rows of stones: a row with a sardius, a topaz, and an emerald was the first row; 11the second row, a turquoise, a sapphire, and a diamond; 12the third row, a jacinth, an agate, and an amethyst; 13the fourth row, a beryl, an onyx, and a jasper. *They were* enclosed in settings of gold in their mountings. 14*There were* ªtwelve stones according to the names of the sons of Israel: according to their names, *engraved like* a signet, each one with its own name according to the twelve tribes. 15And they made chains for the breastplate at the ends, like braided cords of pure gold. 16They also made two settings of gold and two gold rings, and put the two rings on the two ends of the breastplate. 17And they put the two braided *chains* of gold in the two rings on the ends of the breastplate. 18The two ends of the two braided *chains* they fastened in the two settings, and put them on the shoulder straps of the ephod in the front. 19And they made two rings of gold and put *them* on the two ends of the breastplate, on the edge of it, which *was* on the inward side of the ephod. 20They made two *other* gold rings and put them on the two shoulder straps, underneath the ephod toward its front, right at the seam above the intricately woven band of the ephod. 21And they bound the breastplate by means of its rings to the rings of the ephod with a blue cord, so that it would be above the intricately woven band of the ephod, and that the breastplate would not come loose from the ephod, as the LORD had commanded Moses.

MAKING THE OTHER PRIESTLY GARMENTS

22aHe made the bʳobe of the ephod of woven work, all of blue. 23And *there was* an opening in the middle of the robe, like the opening in a coat of mail, *with* a woven binding all around the opening, so that it would not tear. 24They made on the hem of the robe pomegranates of blue, purple, and scarlet, and of fine woven *linen.* 25And they made ªbells of pure gold, and put the bells between the pomegranates on

39:6
ªEx. 28:9–11

39:7 ªEx. 28:12, 29; Josh. 4:7

39:8
ªEx. 28:15–30

39:10 ªEx. 28:17

39:14 ªRev. 21:12

39:22
ªEx. 28:31–35
ᵇEx. 29:5;
Lev. 8:7

39:25 ªEx. 28:33

39:6 ¹*plaited work*

the hem of the robe all around between the pomegranates: [26]a bell and a pomegranate, a bell and a pomegranate, all around the hem of the robe to [1]minister in, as the LORD had commanded Moses.

[27a]They made tunics, artistically woven of fine linen, for Aaron and his sons, [28a]a turban of fine linen, exquisite hats of fine linen, [b]short trousers of fine woven linen, [29a]and a sash of fine woven linen with blue, purple, and scarlet *thread,* made by a weaver, as the LORD had commanded Moses.

[30a]Then they made the plate of the holy crown of pure gold, and wrote on it an inscription *like* the engraving of a signet:

[b]HOLINESS TO THE LORD.

[31]And they tied to it a blue cord, to fasten *it* above on the turban, as the LORD had commanded Moses.

THE WORK COMPLETED

(*Ex. 35:10–19*)

[32]Thus all the work of the tabernacle of the tent of meeting was [a]finished. And the children of Israel did [b]according to all that the LORD had commanded Moses; so they did. [33]And they brought the tabernacle to Moses, the tent and all its furnishings: its clasps, its boards, its bars, its pillars, and its sockets; [34]the covering of ram skins dyed red, the covering of badger skins, and the veil of the covering; [35]the ark of the Testimony with its poles, and the mercy seat; [36]the table, all its utensils, and the [a]showbread; [37]the pure *gold* lampstand with its lamps (the lamps set in order), all its utensils, and the oil for light; [38]the gold altar, the anointing oil, and the sweet incense; the screen for the tabernacle door; [39]the bronze altar, its grate of bronze, its poles, and all its utensils; the laver with its base; [40]the hangings of the court, its pillars and its sockets, the screen for the court gate, its cords, and its pegs; all the utensils for the service of the tabernacle, for the tent of meeting; [41]and the [1]garments of ministry, to [2]minister in the holy *place:* the holy garments for Aaron the priest, and his sons' garments, to minister as priests.

[42]According to all that the LORD had commanded Moses, so the children of Israel [a]did all the work. [43]Then Moses looked over all the work, and indeed they had done it; as the LORD had commanded, just so they had done it. And Moses [a]blessed them.

THE TABERNACLE ERECTED AND ARRANGED

40 Then the LORD [a]spoke to Moses, saying: [2]"On the first day of the [a]first month you shall set up [b]the tabernacle of the tent of meeting. [3a]You shall put in it the ark of the Testimony, and [1]partition off the ark with the veil. [4a]You shall bring in the table and [b]arrange the things that are to be set in order on it; [c]and you shall bring in the lampstand and [1]light its lamps. [5a]You shall also set the altar of gold for the incense before the ark of the Testimony, and put up the screen for the door of the tabernacle. [6]Then you shall set the [a]altar of the burnt offering before the door of the tabernacle

39:27
[a]Ex. 28:39, 40

39:28 [a]Ex. 28:4, 39; Lev. 8:9; Ezek. 44:18
[b]Ex. 28:42; Lev. 6:10

39:29
[a]Ex. 28:39

39:30
[a]Ex. 28:36, 37
[b]Zech. 14:20

39:32 [a]Ex. 40:17
[b]Ex. 25:40; 39:42, 43

39:36
[a]Ex. 25:23–30

39:42 [a]Ex. 35:10

39:43
[a]Lev. 9:22, 23; Num. 6:23–26; Josh. 22:6; 2 Sam. 6:18; 1 Kin. 8:14; 2 Chr. 30:27

40:1
[a]Ex. 25:1—31:18

40:2 [a]Ex. 12:2; 13:4 [b]Ex. 26:1, 30; 40:17

40:3 [a]Ex. 26:33; 40:21; Lev. 16:2; Num. 4:5

40:4 [a]Ex. 26:35; 40:22
[b]Ex. 25:30; 40:23
[c]Ex. 40:24, 25

40:5 [a]Ex. 40:26

40:6 [a]Ex. 39:39

39:26 [1]*serve*   39:41 [1]*Or woven garments*   [2]*serve*   40:3 [1]*screen*   40:4 [1]*set up*

of the tent of meeting. [7]And [a]you shall set the laver between the tabernacle of meeting and the altar, and put water in it. [8]You shall set up the court all around, and hang up the screen at the court gate.

[9]"And you shall take the anointing oil, and [a]anoint the tabernacle and all that *is* in it; and you shall hallow it and all its utensils, and it shall be holy. [10]You shall [a]anoint the altar of the burnt offering and all its utensils, and consecrate the altar. [b]The altar shall be most holy. [11]And you shall anoint the laver and its base, and consecrate it.

[12a]"Then you shall bring Aaron and his sons to the door of the tabernacle of meeting and wash them with water. [13]You shall put the holy [a]garments on Aaron, [b]and anoint him and consecrate him, that he may minister to Me as priest. [14]And you shall bring his sons and clothe them with tunics. [15]You shall anoint them, as you anointed their father, that they may minister to Me as priests; for their anointing shall surely be [a]an everlasting priesthood throughout their generations."

[16]Thus Moses did; according to all that the LORD had commanded him, so he did.

[17]And it came to pass in the first month of the second year, on the first *day* of the month, *that* the [a]tabernacle was [1]raised up. [18]So Moses raised up the tabernacle, fastened its sockets, set up its boards, put in its bars, and raised up its pillars. [19]And he spread out the tent over the tabernacle and put the covering of the tent on top of it, as the LORD had commanded Moses. [20]He took [a]the Testimony and put *it* into the ark, inserted the poles through the rings of the ark, and put the mercy seat on top of the ark. [21]And he brought the ark into the tabernacle, [a]hung up the veil of the covering, and partitioned off the ark of the Testimony, as the LORD had commanded Moses.

[22a]He put the table in the tabernacle of meeting, on the north side of the tabernacle, outside the veil; [23a]and he set the bread in order upon it before the LORD, as the LORD had commanded Moses. [24a]He put the lampstand in the tabernacle of meeting, across from the table, on the south side of the tabernacle; [25]and [a]he lit the lamps before the LORD, as the LORD had commanded Moses. [26a]He put the gold altar in the tabernacle of meeting in front of the veil; [27a]and he burned sweet incense on it, as the LORD had commanded Moses. [28a]He hung up the screen *at* the door of the tabernacle. [29a]And he put the altar of burnt offering *before* the door of the tabernacle of the tent of meeting, and [b]offered upon it the burnt offering and the grain offering, as the LORD had commanded Moses. [30a]He set the laver between the tabernacle of meeting and the altar, and put water there for washing; [31]and Moses, Aaron, and his sons would [a]wash their hands and their feet *with water* from it. [32]Whenever they went into the tabernacle of meeting, and when they came near the altar, they washed, [a]as the LORD had commanded Moses. [33a]And he raised up the court all around the tabernacle and the altar, and hung up the screen of the court gate. So Moses [b]finished the work.

40:7 [a]Ex. 30:18; 40:30
40:9 [a]Ex. 30:26; Lev. 8:10
40:10 [a]Ex. 30:26–30 [b]Ex. 29:36, 37
40:12 [a]Ex. 29:4–9; Lev. 8:1–13
40:13 [a]Ex. 29:5; 39:1, 41 [b][Ex. 28:41]; Lev. 8:12
40:15 [a]Ex. 29:9; Num. 25:13
40:17 [a]Ex. 40:2; Num. 7:1
40:20 [a]Ex. 25:16; Deut. 10:5; 1 Kin. 8:9; 2 Chr. 5:10; Heb. 9:4
40:21 [a]Ex. 26:33
40:22 [a]Ex. 26:35
40:23 [a]Ex. 40:4; Lev. 24:5, 6
40:24 [a]Ex. 26:35
40:25 [a]Ex. 25:37; 30:7, 8; 40:4; Lev. 24:3, 4
40:26 [a]Ex. 30:1, 6; 40:5
40:27 [a]Ex. 30:7
40:28 [a]Ex. 26:36; 40:5
40:29 [a]Ex. 40:6 [b]Ex. 29:38–42
40:30 [a]Ex. 30:18; 40:7
40:31 [a]Ex. 30:19, 20; John 13:8
40:32 [a]Ex. 30:19
40:33 [a]Ex. 27:9–18; 40:8 [b][Heb. 3:2–5]

40:17 [1]erected

THE CLOUD AND THE GLORY
(Ex. 13:21, 22; Num. 9:15–23)

34[a]Then the [b]cloud covered the tabernacle of meeting, and the [c]glory of the LORD filled the tabernacle. 35And Moses [a]was not able to enter the tabernacle of meeting, because the cloud rested above it, and the glory of the LORD filled the tabernacle. 36[a]Whenever the cloud was taken up from above the tabernacle, the children of Israel would [1]go onward in all their journeys. 37But [a]if the cloud was not taken up, then they did not journey till the day that it was taken up. 38For [a]the cloud of the LORD *was* above the tabernacle by day, and fire was over it by night, in the sight of all the house of Israel, throughout all their journeys.

40:34
[a]Ex. 29:43;
Lev. 16:2;
Num. 9:15;
2 Chr. 5:13;
Is. 6:4
[b]1 Kin. 8:10, 11
[c]Lev. 9:6, 23

40:35
[a][Lev. 16:2];
1 Kin. 8:11;
2 Chr. 5:13, 14

40:36 [a]Ex. 13:21, 22; Num. 9:17; Neh. 9:19

40:37
[a]Num. 9:19–22

40:38 [a]Ex. 13:21; Num. 9:15; Ps. 78:14; Is. 4:5

THE THIRD BOOK OF MOSES CALLED
LEVITICUS

THE BURNT OFFERING

1 Now the LORD ᵃcalled to Moses, and spoke to him ᵇfrom the tabernacle of meeting, saying, 2"Speak to the children of Israel, and say to them: ᵃ'When any one of you brings an offering to the LORD, you shall bring your offering of the livestock—of the herd and of the flock.

3'If his offering *is* a burnt sacrifice of the herd, let him offer a male ᵃwithout blemish; he shall offer it of his own free will at the door of the tabernacle of meeting before the LORD. 4ᵃThen he shall put his hand on the head of the burnt offering, and it will be ᵇaccepted on his behalf ᶜto make atonement for him. 5He shall kill the ᵃbull before the LORD; ᵇand the priests, Aaron's sons, shall bring the blood ᶜand sprinkle the blood all around on the altar that *is by* the door of the tabernacle of meeting. 6And he shall ᵃskin the burnt offering and cut it into its pieces. 7The sons of Aaron the priest shall put ᵃfire on the altar, and ᵇlay the wood in order on the fire. 8Then the priests, Aaron's sons, shall lay the parts, the head, and the fat in order on the wood that *is* on the fire upon the altar; 9but he shall wash its entrails and its legs with water. And the priest shall burn all on the altar as a burnt sacrifice, an offering made by fire, a ᵃsweet¹ aroma to the LORD.

10'If his offering *is* of the flocks—of the sheep or of the goats—as a burnt sacrifice, he shall bring a male ᵃwithout blemish. 11ᵃHe shall kill it on the north side of the altar before the LORD; and the priests, Aaron's sons, shall sprinkle its blood all around on the altar. 12And he shall cut it into its pieces, with its head and its fat; and the priest shall lay them in order on the wood that *is* on the fire upon the altar; 13but he shall wash the entrails and the legs with water. Then the priest shall bring *it* all and burn *it* on the altar; it *is* a burnt sacrifice, an ᵃoffering made by fire, a sweet aroma to the LORD.

14'And if the burnt sacrifice of his offering to the LORD *is* of birds, then he shall bring his offering of ᵃturtledoves or young pigeons. 15The priest shall bring it to the altar, ¹wring off its head, and burn *it* on the altar; its blood shall be drained out at the side of the altar. 16And he shall remove its crop with its feathers and cast it ᵃbeside the altar on the east side, into the place for ashes. 17Then he shall split it at its wings, *but* ᵃshall not divide *it* completely; and the priest shall burn it on the altar, on the wood that *is* on the fire. ᵇIt *is* a burnt sacrifice, an offering made by fire, a ¹sweet aroma to the LORD.

THE GRAIN OFFERING

2 'When anyone offers ᵃa grain offering to the LORD, his offering shall be *of* fine flour. And he shall pour oil on it,

Cross references (side column)

1:1 ᵃEx. 19:3; 25:22; Num. 7:89 ᵇEx. 40:34

1:2 ᵃLev. 22:18, 19

1:3 ᵃEx. 12:5; Lev. 22:20–24; Deut. 15:21; Eph. 5:27; Heb. 9:14; 1 Pet. 1:19

1:4 ᵃEx. 29:10, 15, 19; Lev. 3:2, 8, 13; 4:15 ᵇ[Rom. 12:1]; Phil. 4:18 ᶜLev. 4:20, 26, 31; 2 Chr. 29:23, 24

1:5 ᵃMic. 6:6 ᵇ2 Chr. 35:11 ᶜLev. 1:11; 3:2, 8, 13; [Heb. 12:24; 1 Pet. 1:2]

1:6 ᵃLev. 7:8

1:7 ᵃLev. 6:8–13; Mal. 1:10 ᵇGen. 22:9

1:9 ᵃGen. 8:21; [Ezek. 20:28, 41; 2 Cor. 2:15]

1:10 ᵃEx. 12:5; Lev. 1:3; Ezek. 43:22; [1 Pet. 1:19]

1:11 ᵃEx. 24:6; 40:22; Lev. 1:5; Ezek. 8:5

1:13 ᵃNum. 15:4–7; 28:12–14

1:14 ᵃGen. 15:9; Lev. 5:7, 11; 12:8; Luke 2:24

1:16 ᵃLev. 6:10

1:17 ᵃGen. 15:10; Lev. 5:8 ᵇLev. 1:9, 13

2:1 ᵃLev. 6:14; 9:17; Num. 15:4

1:9 ¹*soothing* or *pleasing aroma*   **1:15** ¹Lit. *nip* or *chop off*   **1:17** ¹*soothing* or *pleasing aroma*

and put ᵇfrankincense on it. ²He shall bring it to Aaron's sons, the priests, one of whom shall take from it his handful of fine flour and oil with all the frankincense. And the priest shall burn ᵃ*it as* a memorial on the altar, an offering made by fire, a sweet aroma to the LORD. ³ᵃThe rest of the grain offering *shall be* Aaron's and his ᵇsons'. ᶜ*It is* most holy of the offerings to the LORD made by fire.

⁴'And if you bring as an offering a grain offering baked in the oven, *it shall be* unleavened cakes of fine flour mixed with oil, or unleavened wafers ᵃanointed¹ with oil. ⁵But if your offering *is* a grain offering *baked* in a ¹pan, *it shall be of* fine flour, unleavened, mixed with oil. ⁶You shall break it in pieces and pour oil on it; it *is* a grain offering.

⁷'If your offering *is* a grain offering *baked* in a ᵃcovered pan, it shall be made *of* fine flour with oil. ⁸You shall bring the grain offering that is made of these things to the LORD. And when it is presented to the priest, he shall bring it to the altar. ⁹Then the priest shall take from the grain offering ᵃa memorial portion, and burn *it* on the altar. *It is* an ᵇoffering made by fire, a sweet aroma to the LORD. ¹⁰And ᵃwhat is left of the grain offering *shall be* Aaron's and his sons'. *It is* most holy of the offerings to the LORD made by fire.

¹¹'No grain offering which you bring to the LORD shall be made with ᵃleaven, for you shall burn no leaven nor any honey in any offering to the LORD made by fire. ¹²ᵃAs for the offering of the firstfruits, you shall offer them to the LORD, but they shall not be burned on the altar for a sweet aroma. ¹³And every offering of your grain offering ᵃyou shall season with salt; you shall not allow ᵇthe salt of the covenant of your God to be lacking from your grain offering. ᶜWith all your offerings you shall offer salt.

¹⁴'If you offer a grain offering of your firstfruits to the LORD, ᵃyou shall offer for the grain offering of your firstfruits green heads of grain roasted on the fire, grain beaten from ᵇfull heads. ¹⁵And ᵃyou shall put oil on it, and lay frankincense on it. It *is* a grain offering. ¹⁶Then the priest shall burn ᵃthe memorial portion: *part* of its beaten grain and *part* of its oil, with all the frankincense, as an offering made by fire to the LORD.

THE PEACE OFFERING

3 'When his offering *is* a ᵃsacrifice of a peace offering, if he offers *it* of the herd, whether male or female, he shall offer it ᵇwithout ¹blemish before the LORD. ²And ᵃhe shall lay his hand on the head of his offering, and kill it *at* the door of the tabernacle of meeting; and Aaron's sons, the priests, shall ᵇsprinkle the blood all around on the altar. ³Then he shall offer from the sacrifice of the peace offering an offering made by fire to the LORD. ᵃThe fat that covers the entrails and all the fat that *is* on the entrails, ⁴the two kidneys and the fat that *is* on them by the flanks, and the fatty lobe *attached* to the liver above the kidneys, he shall remove; ⁵and Aaron's sons ᵃshall burn it on the altar upon the ᵇburnt sacrifice, which *is* on the wood that *is* on the fire, *as* an ᶜoffering made by fire, a ᵈsweet aroma to the LORD.

⁶'If his offering as a sacrifice of a peace offering to the LORD *is* of the flock, *whether* male or female, ᵃhe shall offer

2:1 ᵇLev. 5:11

2:2 ᵃLev. 2:9; 5:12; 6:15; 24:7; Acts 10:4

2:3 ᵃLev. 7:9 ᵇLev. 6:6; 10:12, 13 ᶜEx. 29:37; Num. 18:9

2:4 ᵃEx. 29:2

2:7 ᵃLev. 7:9

2:9 ᵃLev. 2:2, 16; 5:12; 6:15 ᵇEx. 29:18

2:10 ᵃLev. 2:3; 6:16

2:11 ᵃEx. 23:18; 34:25; Lev. 6:16, 17; [Matt. 16:12; Mark 8:15; Luke 12:1; 1 Cor. 5:8; Gal. 5:9]

2:12 ᵃEx. 22:29; 34:22; Lev. 23:10, 11, 17, 18

2:13 ᵃ[Mark 9:49, 50; Col. 4:6] ᵇNum. 18:19; 2 Chr. 13:5 ᶜEzek. 43:24

2:14 ᵃLev. 23:10, 14 ᵇ2 Kin. 4:42

2:15 ᵃLev. 2:1

2:16 ᵃLev. 2:2

3:1 ᵃLev. 7:11, 29 ᵇLev. 1:3; 22:20–24

3:2 ᵃEx. 29:10, 11, 16, 20; Lev. 1:4, 5; 16:21 ᵇLev. 1:5

3:3 ᵃEx. 29:13, 22; Lev. 1:8; 3:16; 4:8, 9

3:5 ᵃEx. 29:13; Lev. 6:12; 7:28–34 ᵇ2 Chr. 35:14 ᶜNum. 28:3–10 ᵈNum. 15:8–10

3:6 ᵃLev. 3:1; 22:20–24

it without blemish. [7]If he offers a [a]lamb as his offering, then he shall [b]offer it [c]before the LORD. [8]And he shall lay his hand on the head of his offering, and kill it before the tabernacle of meeting; and Aaron's sons shall sprinkle its blood all around on the altar.

[9]"Then he shall offer from the sacrifice of the peace offering, as an offering made by fire to the LORD, its fat *and* the whole fat tail which he shall remove close to the backbone. And the fat that covers the entrails and all the fat that *is* on the entrails, [10]the two kidneys and the fat that *is* on them by the flanks, and the fatty lobe *attached* to the liver above the kidneys, he shall remove; [11]and the priest shall burn *them* on the altar *as* [a]food, an offering made by fire to the LORD.

[12]"And if his [a]offering *is* a goat, then [b]he shall offer it before the LORD. [13]He shall lay his hand on its head and kill it before the tabernacle of meeting; and the sons of Aaron shall sprinkle its blood all around on the altar. [14]Then he shall offer from it his offering, as an offering made by fire to the LORD. The fat that covers the entrails and all the fat that *is* on the entrails, [15]the two kidneys and the fat that *is* on them by the flanks, and the fatty lobe *attached* to the liver above the kidneys, he shall remove; [16]and the priest shall burn them on the altar *as* food, an offering made by fire for a sweet aroma; [a]all the fat *is* the LORD's.

[17]"This shall be a [a]perpetual[1] statute throughout your generations in all your dwellings: you shall eat neither fat nor [b]blood.'"

THE SIN OFFERING

4 Now the LORD spoke to Moses, saying, [2]"Speak to the children of Israel, saying: [a]'If a person sins [1]unintentionally against any of the commandments of the LORD *in anything* which ought not to be done, and does any of them, [3a]if the anointed priest sins, bringing guilt on the people, then let him offer to the LORD for his sin which he has sinned [b]a young bull without blemish as a [c]sin offering. [4]He shall bring the bull [a]to the door of the tabernacle of meeting before the LORD, lay his hand on the bull's head, and kill the bull before the LORD. [5]Then the anointed priest [a]shall take some of the bull's blood and bring it to the tabernacle of meeting. [6]The priest shall dip his finger in the blood and sprinkle some of the blood seven times before the LORD, in front of the [a]veil of the sanctuary. [7]And the priest shall [a]put some of the blood on the horns of the altar of sweet incense before the LORD, which is in the tabernacle of meeting; and he shall pour [b]the remaining blood of the bull at the base of the altar of the burnt offering, which is at the door of the tabernacle of meeting. [8]He shall take from it all the fat of the bull as the sin offering. The fat that covers the entrails and all the fat which *is* on the entrails, [9]the two kidneys and the fat that *is* on them by the flanks, and the fatty lobe *attached* to the liver above the kidneys, he shall remove, [10a]as it was taken from the bull of the sacrifice of the peace offering; and the priest shall burn them on the altar of the burnt offering. [11a]But the bull's hide and all its flesh, with its head and legs, its entrails and offal— [12]the whole bull he shall carry outside the camp

---

3:7 [a]Num. 15:4, 5 [b]1 Kin. 8:62 [c]Lev. 17:8, 9

3:11 [a]Lev. 21:6, 8, 17, 21, 22; 22:25; Num. 28:2; [Ezek. 44:7; Mal. 1:7, 12]

3:12 [a]Num. 15:6–11 [b]Lev. 3:1, 7

3:16 [a]Lev. 7:23–25; 1 Sam. 2:15; 2 Chr. 7:7

3:17 [a]Lev. 6:18; 7:36; 17:7; 23:14 [b]Gen. 9:4; Lev. 7:23, 26; 17:10, 14; 1 Sam. 14:33

4:2 [a]Lev. 5:15–18; Num. 15:22–30; 1 Sam. 14:27; Acts 3:17

4:3 [a]Ex. 40:15; Lev. 8:12 [b]Lev. 3:1; 9:2 [c]Lev. 9:7

4:4 [a]Lev. 1:3, 4; 4:15; Num. 8:12

4:5 [a]Lev. 16:14; Num. 19:4

4:6 [a]Ex. 40:21, 26

4:7 [a]Lev. 4:18, 25, 30, 34; 8:15; 9:9; 16:18 [b]Ex. 40:5, 6; Lev. 5:9

4:10 [a]Lev. 3:3–5

4:11 [a]Ex. 29:14; Lev. 9:11; Num. 19:5

3:17 [1]everlasting or *never-ending* 4:2 [1]through error

to a clean place, ^awhere the ashes are poured out, and ^bburn it on wood with fire; where the ashes are poured out it shall be burned.

¹³'Now ^aif the whole congregation of Israel sins unintentionally, ^band the thing is hidden from the eyes of the assembly, and they have done *something against* any of the commandments of the LORD *in anything* which should not be done, and are guilty; ¹⁴when the sin which they have committed becomes known, then the assembly shall offer a young bull for the sin, and bring it before the tabernacle of meeting. ¹⁵And the elders of the congregation ^ashall lay their hands on the head of the bull before the LORD. Then the bull shall be killed before the LORD. ^{16a}The anointed priest shall bring some of the bull's blood to the tabernacle of meeting. ¹⁷Then the priest shall dip his finger in the blood and sprinkle *it* seven times before the LORD, in front of the veil. ¹⁸And he shall put *some* of the blood on the horns of the altar which *is* before the LORD, which *is* in the tabernacle of meeting; and he shall pour the remaining blood at the base of the altar of burnt offering, which is at the door of the tabernacle of meeting. ¹⁹He shall take all the fat from it and burn *it* on the altar. ²⁰And he shall do ^awith the bull as he did with the bull as a sin offering; thus he shall do with it. ^bSo the priest shall make ¹atonement for them, and it shall be forgiven them. ²¹Then he shall carry the bull outside the camp, and burn it as he burned the first bull. It *is* a sin offering for the assembly.

²²'When a ¹ruler has sinned, and ^adone *something* unintentionally *against* any of the commandments of the LORD his God *in anything* which should not be done, and is guilty; ²³or ^aif his sin in which he has committed ¹comes to his knowledge, he shall bring as his offering a kid of the goats, a male without blemish. ²⁴And ^ahe shall lay his hand on the head of the goat, and kill it at the place where they kill the burnt offering before the LORD. It *is* a sin offering. ^{25a}The priest shall take some of the blood of the sin offering with his finger, put *it* on the horns of the altar of burnt offering, and pour its blood at the base of the altar of burnt offering. ²⁶And he shall burn all its fat on the altar, like ^athe fat of the sacrifice of the peace offering. ^bSo the priest shall make ¹atonement for him concerning his sin, and it shall be forgiven him.

^{27a}'If ¹anyone of the ²common people sins unintentionally by doing *something against* any of the commandments of the LORD *in anything* which ought not to be done, and is guilty; ²⁸or ^aif his sin which he has committed comes to his knowledge, then he shall bring as his offering a kid of the goats, a female without blemish, for his sin which he has committed. ^{29a}And he shall lay his hand on the head of the sin offering, and kill the sin offering at the place of the burnt offering. ³⁰Then the priest shall take *some* of its blood with his finger, put *it* on the horns of the altar of burnt offering, and pour all *the remaining* blood at the base of the altar. ^{31a}He shall remove all its fat, ^bas fat is removed from the sacrifice of the peace offering; and the priest shall burn it on the altar for a ^csweet aroma to the LORD. ^dSo the priest shall make atonement for him, and it shall be forgiven him.

4:12 ^aLev. 4:21; 6:10, 11; 16:27
^b[Heb. 13:11, 12]

4:13
^aNum. 15:24–26; Josh. 7:11
^bLev. 5:2–4, 17

4:15 ^aLev. 1:3, 4

4:16 ^aLev. 4:5; [Heb. 9:12–14]

4:20 ^aLev. 4:3
^bLev. 1:4; Num. 15:25

4:22
^aLev. 4:2, 13, 27

4:23 ^aLev. 4:14; 5:4

4:24 ^aLev. 4:4; [Is. 53:6]

4:25 ^aLev. 4:7, 18, 30, 34

4:26
^aLev. 3:3–5
^bLev. 4:20; Num. 15:28

4:27 ^aLev. 4:2; Num. 15:27

4:28 ^aLev. 4:23

4:29 ^aLev. 1:4; 4:4, 24

4:31 ^aLev. 3:14
^bLev. 3:3, 4
^cGen. 8:21; Ex. 29:18; Lev. 1:9, 13; 3:2, 2, 9, 12 ^dLev. 4:26

32'If he brings a lamb as his sin offering, [a]he shall bring a female without blemish. 33Then he shall [a]lay his hand on the head of the sin offering, and kill it as a sin offering at the place where they kill the burnt offering. 34The priest shall take *some* of the blood of the sin offering with his finger, put *it* on the horns of the altar of burnt offering, and pour all *the remaining* blood at the base of the altar. 35He shall remove all its fat, as the fat of the lamb is removed from the sacrifice of the peace offering. Then the priest shall burn it on the altar, [a]according to the offerings made by fire to the LORD. [b]So the priest shall make atonement for his sin that he has committed, and it shall be forgiven him.

THE TRESPASS OFFERING

5 'If a person sins in [a]hearing the utterance of an oath, and *is* a witness, whether he has seen or known *of the matter*— if he does not tell *it*, he [b]bears [1]guilt.

2'Or [a]if a person touches any unclean thing, whether *it is* the carcass of an unclean beast, or the carcass of unclean livestock, or the carcass of unclean creeping things, and he is unaware of it, he also shall be unclean and [b]guilty. 3Or if he touches [a]human uncleanness—whatever uncleanness with which a man may be defiled, and he is unaware of it—when he realizes *it*, then he shall be guilty.

4'Or if a person [1]swears, speaking thoughtlessly with *his* lips [a]to do evil or [b]to do good, whatever *it is* that a man may pronounce by an oath, and he is unaware of it—when he realizes *it*, then he shall be guilty in any of these *matters*.

5'And it shall be, when he is guilty in any of these *matters*, that he shall [a]confess that he has sinned in that *thing;* 6and he shall bring his trespass offering to the LORD for his sin which he has committed, a female from the flock, a lamb or a kid of the goats as a sin offering. So the priest shall make atonement for him concerning his sin.

7[a]'If he is not able to bring a lamb, then he shall bring to the LORD, for his trespass which he has committed, two [b]turtledoves or two young pigeons: one as a sin offering and the other as a burnt offering. 8And he shall bring them to the priest, who shall offer *that* which *is* for the sin offering first, and [a]wring off its head from its neck, but shall not divide *it* [1]completely. 9Then he shall sprinkle *some* of the blood of the sin offering on the side of the altar, and the [a]rest of the blood shall be drained out at the base of the altar. It *is* a sin offering. 10And he shall offer the second *as* a burnt offering according to the [a]prescribed manner. So [b]the priest shall make atonement on his behalf for his sin which he has committed, and it shall be forgiven him.

11'But if he is [a]not able to bring two turtledoves or two young pigeons, then he who sinned shall bring for his offering one-tenth of an ephah of fine flour as a sin offering. [b]He shall put no oil on it, nor shall he put frankincense on it, for it *is* a sin offering. 12Then he shall bring it to the priest, and the priest shall take his handful of it [a]as a memorial portion, and burn *it* on the altar [b]according to the offerings made by fire to the LORD. It *is* a sin offering. 13[a]The priest shall make

Cross references (left margin)

4:32 [a]Lev. 4:28

4:33 [a]Lev. 1:4; Num. 8:12

4:35 [a]Lev. 3:5 [b]Lev. 4:26, 31

5:1 [a]Prov. 29:24; [Jer. 23:10] [b]Lev. 5:17; 7:18; 17:16; 19:8; 20:17; Num. 9:13

5:2 [a]Lev. 11:24, 28, 31, 39; Num. 19:11–16; Deut. 14:8 [b]Lev. 5:17

5:3 [a]Lev. 5:12, 13, 15

5:4 [a]1 Sam. 25:22; Acts 23:12 [b][Matt. 5:33–37]; Mark 6:23; [James 5:12]

5:5 [a]Lev. 16:21; 26:40; Num. 5:7; Ezra 10:11, 12; Ps. 32:5; Prov. 28:13

5:7 [a]Lev. 12:6, 8; 14:21 [b]Lev. 1:14

5:8 [a]Lev. 1:15–17

5:9 [a]Lev. 4:7, 18, 30, 34

5:10 [a]Lev. 1:14–17 [b]Lev. 4:20, 26; 5:13, 16

5:11 [a]Lev. 14:21–32 [b]Lev. 2:1, 2; 6:15; Num. 5:15

5:12 [a]Lev. 2:2 [b]Lev. 4:35

5:13 [a]Lev. 4:26

5:1 [1]*his iniquity*   5:4 [1]*vows*   5:8 [1]Lit. *apart*

atonement for him, [1]for his sin that he has committed in any of these matters; and it shall be forgiven him. [b]*The rest* shall be the priest's as a grain offering.'"

OFFERINGS WITH RESTITUTION

[14]Then the LORD spoke to Moses, saying: [15a]"If a person commits a trespass, and sins unintentionally in regard to the holy things of the LORD, then [b]he shall bring to the LORD as his trespass offering a ram without blemish from the flocks, with your valuation in shekels of silver according to [c]the shekel of the sanctuary, as a trespass offering. [16]And he shall make restitution for the harm that he has done in regard to the holy thing, [a]and shall add one-fifth to it and give it to the priest. [b]So the priest shall make atonement for him with the ram of the trespass offering, and it shall be forgiven him.

[17]"If a person sins, and commits any of these things which are forbidden to be done by the commandments of the LORD, [a]though he does not know *it*, yet he is [b]guilty and shall bear his [1]iniquity. [18a]And he shall bring to the priest a ram without blemish from the flock, with your valuation, as a trespass offering. So the priest shall make atonement for him regarding his ignorance in which he erred and did not know *it*, and it shall be forgiven him. [19]It is a trespass offering; [a]he has certainly trespassed against the LORD."

6 And the LORD spoke to Moses, saying: [2]"If a person sins and [a]commits a trespass against the LORD by [b]lying[1] to his neighbor about [c]what was delivered to him for safekeeping, or about [2]a pledge, or about a robbery, or if he has [d]extorted from his neighbor, [3]or if he [a]has found what was lost and lies concerning it, and [b]swears falsely—in any one of these things that a man may do in which he sins: [4]then it shall be, because he has sinned and is guilty, that he shall [1]restore [a]what he has stolen, or the thing which he has extorted, or what was delivered to him for safekeeping, or the lost thing which he found, [5]or all that about which he has sworn falsely. He shall [a]restore its full value, add one-fifth more to it, *and* give it to whomever it belongs, on the day of his trespass offering. [6]And he shall bring his trespass offering to the LORD, [a]a ram without blemish from the flock, with your [1]valuation, as a trespass offering, to the priest. [7a]So the priest shall make atonement for him before the LORD, and he shall be forgiven for any one of these things that he may have done in which he trespasses."

THE LAW OF THE BURNT OFFERING

[8]Then the LORD spoke to Moses, saying, [9]"Command Aaron and his sons, saying, 'This *is* the [a]law of the burnt offering: The burnt offering *shall be* on the hearth upon the altar all night until morning, and the fire of the altar shall be kept burning on it. [10a]And the priest shall put on his linen garment, and his linen trousers he shall put on his body, and take up the ashes of the burnt offering which the fire has consumed on the altar, and he shall put them [b]beside the altar. [11]Then [a]he shall take off his garments, put on other garments, and carry the ashes outside the camp [b]to a clean place. [12]And

5:13 [b]Lev. 2:3; 6:17, 26

5:15 [a]Lev. 4:2; 22:14; Num. 5:5–8 [b]Ezra 10:19 [c]Ex. 30:13; Lev. 27:25

5:16 [a]Lev. 6:5; 22:14; 27:13, 15, 27, 31; Num. 5:7 [b]Lev. 4:26

5:17 [a]Lev. 4:2, 13, 22, 27 [b]Lev. 5:1, 2

5:18 [a]Lev. 5:15

5:19 [a]Ezra 10:2

6:2 [a]Num. 5:6 [b]Lev. 19:11; Acts 5:4; Col. 3:9 [c]Ex. 22:7, 10 [d]Prov. 24:28

6:3 [a]Ex. 23:4; Deut. 22:1–4 [b]Ex. 22:11; Lev. 19:12; Jer. 7:9; Zech. 5:4

6:4 [a]Lev. 24:18, 21

6:5 [a]Lev. 5:16; Num. 5:7, 8; 2 Sam. 12:6

6:6 [a]Lev. 1:3; 5:15

6:7 [a]Lev. 4:26

6:9 [a]Ex. 29:38–42; Num. 28:3–10

6:10 [a]Ex. 28:39–43; Lev. 16:4; Ezek. 44:17, 18 [b]Lev. 1:16

6:11 [a]Ezek. 44:19 [b]Lev. 4:12

5:13 [1]*concerning his sin*   5:17 [1]*punishment*   6:2 [1]*deceiving his associate*
[2]*an entrusted security*   6:4 [1]*return*   6:6 [1]*appraisal*

the fire on the altar shall be kept burning on it; it shall not be put out. And the priest shall burn wood on it every morning, and lay the burnt offering in order on it; and he shall burn on it [a]the fat of the peace offerings. [13]A fire shall always be burning on the [a]altar; it shall never go out.

THE LAW OF THE GRAIN OFFERING

[14]"This *is* the law of the grain offering: The sons of Aaron shall offer it on the altar before the Lord. [15]He shall take from it his handful of the fine flour of the grain offering, with its oil, and all the frankincense which *is* on the grain offering, and shall burn *it* on the altar *for* a sweet aroma, as a memorial to the Lord. [16]And the remainder of it Aaron and his sons shall eat; with unleavened bread it shall be eaten in a holy place; in the court of the tabernacle of meeting they shall eat it. [17]It shall not be baked with leaven. I have given it *as* their [1]portion of My offerings made by fire; it *is* most holy, like the sin offering and the [a]trespass offering. [18a]All the males among the children of Aaron may eat it. [b]*It shall be* a statute forever in your generations concerning the offerings made by fire to the Lord. [c]Everyone who touches them must be holy.' "

[19]And the Lord spoke to Moses, saying, [20a]"This *is* the offering of Aaron and his sons, which they shall offer to the Lord, *beginning* on the day when he is anointed: one-tenth of an [b]ephah of fine flour as a daily grain offering, half of it in the morning and half of it at night. [21]It shall be made in a [a]pan with oil. *When it is* mixed, you shall bring it in. The baked pieces of the grain offering you shall offer *for* a [1]sweet aroma to the Lord. [22]The priest from among his sons, [a]who is anointed in his place, shall offer it. *It is* a statute forever to the Lord. [b]It shall be [1]wholly burned. [23]For every grain offering for the priest shall be wholly burned. It shall not be eaten."

THE LAW OF THE SIN OFFERING

[24]Also the Lord spoke to Moses, saying, [25]"Speak to Aaron and to his sons, saying, 'This *is* the law of the sin offering: [a]In the place where the burnt offering is killed, the sin offering shall be killed before the Lord. It *is* most holy. [26a]The priest who offers it for sin shall eat it. In a holy place it shall be eaten, in the court of the tabernacle of meeting. [27a]Everyone who touches its flesh [1]must be holy. And when its blood is sprinkled on any garment, you shall wash that on which it was sprinkled, in a holy place. [28]But the earthen vessel in which it is boiled [a]shall be broken. And if it is boiled in a bronze pot, it shall be both scoured and rinsed in water. [29]All the males among the priests may eat it. It *is* most holy. [30a]But no sin offering from which *any* of the blood is brought into the tabernacle of meeting, to make atonement in [1]the holy [b]*place*, shall be [c]eaten. It shall be [d]burned in the fire.

THE LAW OF THE TRESPASS OFFERING

7 'Likewise [a]this *is* the law of the trespass offering (it *is* most holy): [2]In the place where they kill the burnt offering they shall kill the trespass offering. And its blood he shall sprinkle

6:12 [a]Lev. 3:3, 5, 9, 14
6:13 [a]Lev. 1:7
6:17 [a]Lev. 7:7
6:18 [a]Lev. 6:29; 7:6; Num. 18:10; 1 Cor. 9:13
[b]Lev. 3:17
[c]Ex. 29:37; Lev. 22:3–7; Num. 4:15; Hag. 2:11–13
6:20 [a]Ex. 29:2
[b]Ex. 16:36
6:21 [a]Lev. 2:5; 7:9
6:22 [a]Lev. 4:3
[b]Ex. 29:25
6:25 [a]Lev. 1:1, 3, 5, 11
6:26 [a][Lev. 10:17, 18]; Num. 18:9, 10; [Ezek. 44:28, 29]
6:27 [a]Ex. 29:37; Num. 4:15; Hag. 2:11–13
6:28 [a]Lev. 11:33; 15:12
6:30 [a]Lev. 4:7, 11, 12, 18, 21; 10:18; 16:27; [Heb. 13:11, 12]
[b]Ex. 26:33
[c]Lev. 6:16, 23, 26
[d]Lev. 16:27
7:1 [a]Lev. 5:14—6:7

6:17 [1]share   6:21 [1]pleasing   6:22 [1]completely   6:27 [1]Lit. shall   6:30 [1]The Most Holy Place when capitalized

all around on the altar. ³And he shall offer from it all its fat. The fat tail and the fat that covers the entrails, ⁴the two kidneys and the fat that *is* on them by the flanks, and the fatty lobe *attached* to the liver above the kidneys, he shall remove; ⁵and the priest shall burn them on the altar *as* an offering made by fire to the LORD. It *is* a trespass offering. ⁶ªEvery male among the priests may eat it. It shall be eaten in a holy place. ᵇIt *is* most holy. ⁷ªThe trespass offering *is* like the sin offering; *there is* one law for them both: the priest who makes atonement with it shall have *it*. ⁸And the priest who offers anyone's burnt offering, that priest shall have for himself the skin of the burnt offering which he has offered. ⁹Also ªevery grain offering that is baked in the oven and all that is prepared in the covered pan, or ¹in a pan, shall be the priest's who offers it. ¹⁰Every grain offering, *whether* mixed with oil or dry, shall belong to all the sons of Aaron, to one *as much* as the other.

THE LAW OF PEACE OFFERINGS

¹¹ª"This *is* the law of the sacrifice of peace offerings which he shall offer to the LORD: ¹²If he offers it for a thanksgiving, then he shall offer, with the sacrifice of thanksgiving, unleavened cakes mixed with oil, unleavened wafers ªanointed with oil, or cakes of blended flour mixed with oil. ¹³Besides the cakes, *as* his offering he shall offer ªleavened bread with the sacrifice of thanksgiving of his peace offering. ¹⁴And from it he shall offer one cake from each offering *as* a heave offering to the LORD. ªIt shall belong to the priest who sprinkles the blood of the peace offering.

¹⁵ª"The flesh of the sacrifice of his peace offering for thanksgiving shall be eaten the same day it is offered. He shall not leave any of it until morning. ¹⁶But ªif the sacrifice of his offering *is* a vow or a voluntary offering, it shall be eaten the same day that he offers his sacrifice; but on the next day the remainder of it also may be eaten; ¹⁷the remainder of the flesh of the sacrifice on the third day must be burned with fire. ¹⁸And if *any* of the flesh of the sacrifice of his peace offering is eaten at all on the third day, it shall not be accepted, nor shall it be ªimputed to him; it shall be an ᵇabomination *to* him who offers it, and the person who eats of it shall bear ¹guilt.

¹⁹"The flesh that touches any unclean thing shall not be eaten. It shall be burned with fire. And as for the *clean* flesh, all who are ¹clean may eat of it. ²⁰But the person who eats the flesh of the sacrifice of the peace offering that *belongs* to the ªLORD, ᵇwhile he is unclean, that person ᶜshall be cut off from his people. ²¹Moreover the person who touches any unclean thing, *such as* ªhuman uncleanness, *an* ᵇunclean animal, or any ᶜabominable¹ unclean thing, and who eats the flesh of the sacrifice of the peace offering that *belongs* to the LORD, that person ᵈshall be cut off from his people.'"

FAT AND BLOOD MAY NOT BE EATEN

²²And the LORD spoke to Moses, saying, ²³"Speak to the children of Israel, saying: ª'You shall not eat any fat, of ox or sheep or goat. ²⁴And the fat of an animal that dies *naturally*,

7:6
ªLev. 6:16–18, 29; Num. 18:9
ᵇLev. 2:3

7:7
ªLev. 6:24–30; 14:13

7:9 ªLev. 2:3, 10; Num. 18:9; Ezek. 44:29

7:11 ªLev. 3:1; 22:18, 21; Ezek. 45:15

7:12 ªLev. 2:4; Num. 6:15

7:13 ªLev. 2:12; 23:17, 18; Amos 4:5

7:14 ªNum. 18:8, 11, 19

7:15
ªLev. 22:29, 30

7:16 ªLev. 19:5–8

7:18
ªNum. 18:27
ᵇLev. 11:10, 11, 41; 19:7; [Prov. 15:8]

7:20
ª[Heb. 2:17]
ᵇLev. 5:3; 15:3; 22:3–7; Num. 19:13; [1 Cor. 11:28]
ᶜGen. 17:14; Ex. 31:14

7:21
ªLev. 5:2, 3, 5
ᵇLev. 11:24, 28
ᶜEzek. 4:14
ᵈLev. 7:20

7:23 ªLev. 3:17; 17:10–15; Deut. 14:21; Ezek. 4:14; 44:31

7:9 ¹*on a griddle*　7:18 ¹*his iniquity*　7:19 ¹*pure*　7:21 ¹So with MT, LXX, Vg.; Sam., Syr., Tg. *swarming thing* (cf. 5:2)

and the fat of what is torn by wild beasts, may be used in any other way; but you shall by no means eat it. 25For whoever eats the fat of the animal of which men offer an offering made by fire to the LORD, the person who eats *it* shall be cut off from his people. 26aMoreover you shall not eat any blood in any of your dwellings, *whether* of bird or beast. 27Whoever eats any blood, that person shall be cut off from his people.'"

THE PORTION OF AARON AND HIS SONS

28Then the LORD spoke to Moses, saying, 29"Speak to the children of Israel, saying: a'He who offers the sacrifice of his peace offering to the LORD shall bring his offering to the LORD from the sacrifice of his peace offering. 30aHis own hands shall bring the offerings made by fire to the LORD. The fat with the breast he shall bring, that the bbreast may be waved *as* a wave offering before the LORD. 31aAnd the priest shall burn the fat on the altar, but the bbreast shall be Aaron's and his sons'. 32aAlso the right thigh you shall give to the priest *as* a heave offering from the sacrifices of your peace offerings. 33He among the sons of Aaron, who offers the blood of the peace offering and the fat, shall have the right thigh for *his* part. 34For athe breast of the wave offering and the thigh of the heave offering I have taken from the children of Israel, from the sacrifices of their peace offerings, and I have given them to Aaron the priest and to his sons from the children of Israel by a statute forever.'"

35This *is* the consecrated portion for Aaron and his sons, from the offerings made by fire to the LORD, on the day when *Moses* presented them to 1minister to the LORD as priests. 36The LORD commanded this to be given to them by the children of Israel, aon the day that He anointed them, *by* a statute forever throughout their generations.

37This *is* the law aof the burnt offering, bthe grain offering, cthe sin offering, dthe trespass offering, ethe consecrations, and fthe sacrifice of the peace offering, 38which the LORD commanded Moses on Mount Sinai, on the day when He commanded the children of Israel ato offer their offerings to the LORD in the Wilderness of Sinai.

AARON AND HIS SONS CONSECRATED
(Ex. 29:1–37)

8 And the LORD spoke to Moses, saying: 2a"Take Aaron and his sons with him, and bthe garments, cthe anointing oil, a dbull as the sin offering, two erams, and a basket of unleavened bread; 3and gather all the congregation together at the door of the tabernacle of meeting."

4So Moses did as the LORD commanded him. And the congregation was gathered together at the door of the tabernacle of meeting. 5And Moses said to the congregation, "This *is* what the LORD commanded to be done."

6Then Moses brought Aaron and his sons and awashed them with water. 7And he aput the tunic on him, girded him with the sash, clothed him with the robe, and put the ephod on him; and he girded him with the intricately woven band of the ephod, and with it tied *the ephod* on him. 8Then he put the

7:26 aGen. 9:4; Lev. 3:17; 17:10–16; 19:26; Deut. 12:23; 1 Sam. 14:33; Ezek. 33:25; Acts 15:20, 29

7:29 aLev. 3:1; 22:21; Ezek. 45:15

7:30 aLev. 3:3, 4, 9, 14 bEx. 29:24, 27; Lev. 8:27; 9:21; Num. 6:20

7:31 aLev. 3:5, 11, 16 bNum. 18:11; Deut. 18:3

7:32 aEx. 29:27; Lev. 7:34; 9:21; Num. 6:20

7:34 aEx. 29:28; Lev. 10:14, 15; Num. 18:18, 19; Deut. 18:3

7:36 aEx. 40:13–15; Lev. 8:12, 30

7:37 aLev. 6:9 bLev. 6:14 cLev. 6:25 dLev. 7:1 eEx. 29:1; Lev. 6:20 fLev. 7:11

7:38 aLev. 1:1, 2; Deut. 4:5

8:2 aEx. 29:1–3 bEx. 28:2, 4 cEx. 30:24, 25 dEx. 29:10 eEx. 29:15, 19

8:6 aEx. 30:20; Heb. 10:22

8:7 aEx. 39:1–31

breastplate on him, and he [a]put the [1]Urim and the Thummim in the breastplate. [9a]And he put the turban on his head. Also on the turban, on its front, he put the golden plate, the holy crown, as the LORD had commanded Moses.

[10a]Also Moses took the anointing oil, and anointed the tabernacle and all that *was* in it, and consecrated them. [11]He sprinkled some of it on the altar seven times, anointed the altar and all its utensils, and the laver and its base, to [1]consecrate them. [12]And he [a]poured some of the anointing oil on Aaron's head and anointed him, to consecrate him.

[13a]Then Moses brought Aaron's sons and put tunics on them, girded them with sashes, and put [1]hats on them, as the LORD had commanded Moses.

[14a]And he brought the bull for the sin offering. Then Aaron and his sons [b]laid their hands on the head of the bull for the sin offering, [15]and Moses killed *it*. [a]Then he took the blood, and put *some* on the horns of the altar all around with his finger, and purified the altar. And he poured the blood at the base of the altar, and consecrated it, to make [1]atonement for it. [16a]Then he took all the fat that *was* on the entrails, the fatty lobe *attached to* the liver, and the two kidneys with their fat, and Moses burned *them* on the altar. [17]But the bull, its hide, its flesh, and its offal, he burned with fire outside the camp, as the LORD [a]had commanded Moses.

[18a]Then he brought the ram as the burnt offering. And Aaron and his sons laid their hands on the head of the ram, [19]and Moses killed *it*. Then he sprinkled the blood all around on the altar. [20]And he cut the ram into pieces; and Moses [a]burned the head, the pieces, and the fat. [21]Then he washed the entrails and the legs in water. And Moses burned the whole ram on the altar. It *was* a burnt sacrifice for a [1]sweet aroma, an offering made by fire to the LORD, [a]as the LORD had commanded Moses.

[22]And [a]he brought the second ram, the ram of consecration. Then Aaron and his sons laid their hands on the head of the ram, [23]and Moses killed *it*. Also he took *some* of [a]its blood and put it on the tip of Aaron's right ear, on the thumb of his right hand, and on the big toe of his right foot. [24]Then he brought Aaron's sons. And Moses put *some* of the [a]blood on the tips of their right ears, on the thumbs of their right hands, and on the big toes of their right feet. And Moses sprinkled the blood all around on the altar. [25a]Then he took the fat and the fat tail, all the fat that *was* on the entrails, the fatty lobe *attached to* the liver, the two kidneys and their fat, and the right thigh; [26a]and from the basket of unleavened bread that was before the LORD he took one unleavened cake, a cake of bread *anointed with* oil, and one wafer, and put *them* on the fat and on the right thigh; [27]and he put all *these* [a]in Aaron's hands and in his sons' hands, and waved them *as* a wave offering before the LORD. [28a]Then Moses took them from their hands and burned *them* on the altar, on the burnt offering. They *were* consecration offerings for a sweet aroma. That *was* an offering made by fire to the LORD. [29]And [a]Moses took the [b]breast and waved it *as* a wave offering before the LORD. It was Moses' [c]part of the ram of consecration, as the LORD had commanded Moses.

8:8 [a]Ex. 28:30; Num. 27:21; Deut. 33:8; 1 Sam. 28:6; Ezra 2:63; Neh. 7:65

8:9 [a]Ex. 28:36, 37; 29:6

8:10 [a]Ex. 30:26–29; 40:10, 11; Lev. 8:2

8:12 [a]Ex. 29:7; 30:30; Lev. 21:10, 12; Ps. 133:2

8:13 [a]Ex. 29:8, 9

8:14 [a]Ex. 29:10; Ps. 66:15; Ezek. 43:19 [b]Lev. 4:4

8:15 [a]Ex. 29:12, 36; Lev. 4:7; Ezek. 43:20, 26; [Heb. 9:22]

8:16 [a]Ex. 29:13; Lev. 4:8

8:17 [a]Ex. 29:14; Lev. 4:11, 12

8:18 [a]Ex. 29:15

8:20 [a]Lev. 1:8

8:21 [a]Ex. 29:18

8:22 [a]Ex. 29:19, 31; Lev. 8:2

8:23 [a]Ex. 29:20, 21; Lev. 14:14

8:24 [a][Heb. 9:13, 14, 18–23]

8:25 [a]Ex. 29:22

8:26 [a]Ex. 29:23

8:27 [a]Ex. 29:24; Lev. 7:30, 34

8:28 [a]Ex. 29:25

8:29 [a]Ps. 99:6 [b]Ex. 29:27 [c]Ex. 29:26

8:8 [1]Lit. *Lights and the Perfections,* Ex. 28:30   8:11 [1]*set them apart* for the LORD   8:13 [1]*headpieces*   8:15 [1]Lit. *covering*   8:21 [1]*pleasing*

30Then aMoses took some of the anointing oil and some of the blood which *was* on the altar, and sprinkled *it* on Aaron, on his garments, on his sons, and on the garments of his sons with him; and he consecrated Aaron, his garments, his sons, and the garments of his sons with him.

31And Moses said to Aaron and his sons, a"Boil the flesh *at* the door of the tabernacle of meeting, and eat it there with the bread that *is* in the basket of consecration offerings, as I commanded, saying, 'Aaron and his sons shall eat it.' 32aWhat remains of the flesh and of the bread you shall burn with fire. 33And you shall not go outside the door of the tabernacle of meeting *for* seven days, until the days of your consecration are ended. For aseven days he shall consecrate you. 34aAs he has done this day, *so* the LORD has commanded to do, to make atonement for you. 35Therefore you shall stay *at* the door of the tabernacle of meeting day and night for seven days, and akeep the 1charge of the LORD, so that you may not die; for so I have been commanded." 36So Aaron and his sons did all the things that the LORD had commanded by the hand of Moses.

THE PRIESTLY MINISTRY BEGINS

9 It came to pass on the aeighth day that Moses called Aaron and his sons and the elders of Israel. 2And he said to Aaron, "Take for yourself a young abull as a sin offering and a ram as a burnt offering, without blemish, and offer *them* before the LORD. 3And to the children of Israel you shall speak, saying, a'Take a kid of the goats as a sin offering, and a calf and a lamb, *both* of the first year, without blemish, as a burnt offering, 4also a bull and a ram as peace offerings, to sacrifice before the LORD, and aa grain offering mixed with oil; for bto-day the LORD will appear to you.'"

5So they brought what Moses commanded before the tabernacle of meeting. And all the congregation drew near and stood 1before the LORD. 6Then Moses said, "This *is* the thing which the LORD commanded you to do, and the glory of the LORD will appear to you." 7And Moses said to Aaron, "Go to the altar, aoffer your sin offering and your burnt offering, and make atonement for yourself and for the people. bOffer the offering of the people, and make atonement for them, as the LORD commanded."

8Aaron therefore went to the altar and killed the calf of the sin offering, which *was* for himself. 9Then the sons of Aaron brought the blood to him. And he dipped his finger in the blood, put *it* on the horns of the altar, and poured the blood at the base of the altar. 10aBut the fat, the kidneys, and the fatty lobe from the liver of the sin offering he burned on the altar, as the LORD had commanded Moses. 11aThe flesh and the hide he burned with fire outside the camp.

12And he killed the burnt offering; and Aaron's sons presented to him the blood, awhich he sprinkled all around on the altar. 13aThen they presented the burnt offering to him, with its pieces and head, and he burned *them* on the altar. 14aAnd he washed the entrails and the legs, and burned *them* with the burnt offering on the altar.

8:30 aEx. 29:21; 30:30; Num. 3:3
8:31 aEx. 29:31, 32
8:32 aEx. 29:34
8:33 aEx. 29:30, 35; Lev. 10:7; Ezek. 43:25, 26
8:34 a[Heb. 7:16]
8:35 aNum. 1:53; 3:7; 9:19; Deut. 11:1; 1 Kin. 2:3; Ezek. 48:11
9:1 aEzek. 43:27
9:2 aEx. 29:21; Lev. 4:1–12
9:3 aLev. 4:23, 28; Ezra 6:17; 10:19
9:4 aLev. 2:4 bEx. 29:43; Lev. 9:6, 23
9:7 aLev. 4:3; 1 Sam. 3:14; [Heb. 5:3–5; 7:27] bLev. 4:16, 20; Heb. 5:1
9:10 aEx. 23:18; Lev. 8:16
9:11 aLev. 4:11, 12; 8:17
9:12 aLev. 1:5; 8:19
9:13 aLev. 8:20
9:14 aLev. 8:21

8:35 1office   9:5 1in the presence of

^{15a}Then he brought the people's offering, and took the goat, which *was* the sin offering for the people, and killed it and offered it for sin, like the first one. ¹⁶And he brought the burnt offering and offered it ^aaccording to the ¹prescribed manner. ¹⁷Then he brought the grain offering, took a handful of it, and burned *it* on the altar, ^abesides the burnt sacrifice of the morning.

¹⁸He also killed the bull and the ram *as* ^asacrifices of peace offerings, which *were* for the people. And Aaron's sons presented to him the blood, which he sprinkled all around on the altar, ¹⁹and the fat from the bull and the ram—the fatty tail, what covers *the entrails* and the kidneys, and the fatty lobe *attached to* the liver; ²⁰and they put the fat on the breasts. ^aThen he burned the fat on the altar; ²¹but the breasts and the right thigh Aaron waved ^a*as* a wave offering before the LORD, as Moses had commanded.

²²Then Aaron lifted his hand toward the people, ^ablessed them, and came down from offering the sin offering, the burnt offering, and peace offerings. ²³And Moses and Aaron went into the tabernacle of meeting, and came out and blessed the people. Then the glory of the LORD appeared to all the people, ²⁴and ^afire came out from before the LORD and consumed the burnt offering and the fat on the altar. When all the people saw *it*, they ^bshouted and fell on their ^cfaces.

THE PROFANE FIRE OF NADAB AND ABIHU

10 Then ^aNadab and Abihu, the sons of Aaron, ^beach took his censer and put fire in it, put incense on it, and offered ^cprofane fire before the LORD, which He had not commanded them. ²So ^afire went out from the LORD and devoured them, and they died before the LORD. ³And Moses said to Aaron, "This is what the LORD spoke, saying:

'By those ^awho come near Me
I must be regarded as holy;
And before all the people
I must be glorified.'"

So Aaron held his peace.

⁴Then Moses called Mishael and Elzaphan, the sons of Uzziel the uncle of Aaron, and said to them, "Come near, ^acarry your brethren from ¹before the sanctuary out of the camp." ⁵So they went near and carried them by their tunics out of the camp, as Moses had said.

⁶And Moses said to Aaron, and to Eleazar and Ithamar, his sons, "Do not ¹uncover your heads nor tear your clothes, lest you die, and ^awrath come upon all the people. But let your brethren, the whole house of Israel, ²bewail the burning which the LORD has kindled. ^{7a}You shall not go out from the door of the tabernacle of meeting, lest you die, ^bfor the anointing oil of the LORD *is* upon you." And they did according to the word of Moses.

CONDUCT PRESCRIBED FOR PRIESTS

⁸Then the LORD spoke to Aaron, saying: ^{9a}"Do not drink wine or intoxicating drink, you, nor your sons with you, when

---

9:15 ^a[Is. 53:10;
Heb. 2:17; 5:3]

9:16 ^aLev. 1:1–13

9:17
^aEx. 29:38, 39

9:18 ^aLev. 3:1–11

9:20
^aLev. 3:5, 16

9:21 ^aEx. 29:24,
26, 27;
Lev. 7:30–34

9:22
^aNum. 6:22–26;
Deut. 21:5;
Luke 24:50

9:24 ^aGen. 4:4;
Judg. 6:21;
2 Chr. 7:1;
Ps. 20:3
^bEzra 3:11
^c1 Kin. 18:38, 39

10:1 ^aEx. 24:1, 9;
Num. 3:2–4;
1 Chr. 24:2
^bLev. 16:12
^cEx. 30:9;
1 Sam. 2:17

10:2
^aGen. 19:24;
Num. 11:1; 16:35;
Rev. 20:9

10:3 ^aEx. 19:22;
Lev. 21:6;
Is. 52:11;
Ezek. 20:41

10:4
^aActs 5:6, 10

10:6 ^aNum. 1:53;
16:22, 46; 18:5;
Josh. 7:1; 22:18,
20; 2 Sam. 24:1

10:7 ^aLev. 8:33;
21:12 ^bLev. 8:30

10:9 ^aGen. 9:21;
[Prov. 20:1;
31:5]; Is. 28:7;
Ezek. 44:21;
Hos. 4:11;
Luke 1:15;
[Eph. 5:18];
1 Tim. 3:3;
Titus 1:7

9:16 ¹*ordinance*   10:4 ¹*in front of*   10:6 ¹*An act of mourning*   ²*weep bitterly*

you go into the tabernacle of meeting, lest you die. *It shall be* a statute forever throughout your generations, [10]that you may [a]distinguish between holy and unholy, and between unclean and clean, [11a]and that you may teach the children of Israel all the statutes which the LORD has spoken to them by the hand of Moses."

[12]And Moses spoke to Aaron, and to Eleazar and Ithamar, his sons who were left: [a]"Take the grain offering that remains of the offerings made by fire to the LORD, and eat it without leaven beside the altar; [b]for it *is* most holy. [13]You shall eat it in a [a]holy place, because it *is* your [1]due and your sons' due, of the sacrifices made by fire to the LORD; for [b]so I have been commanded. [14a]The breast of the wave offering and the thigh of the heave offering you shall eat in a clean place, you, your sons, and your [b]daughters with you; for *they are* your due and your sons' [c]due, *which* are given from the sacrifices of peace offerings of the children of Israel. [15a]The thigh of the heave offering and the breast of the wave offering they shall bring with the offerings of fat made by fire, to offer *as* a wave offering before the LORD. And it shall be yours and your sons' with you, by a statute forever, as the LORD has commanded."

[16]Then Moses made careful inquiry about [a]the goat of the sin offering, and there it was—burned up. And he was angry with Eleazar and Ithamar, the sons of Aaron *who were* left, saying, [17a]"Why have you not eaten the sin offering in a holy place, since it *is* most holy, and *God* has given it to you to bear [b]the guilt of the congregation, to make atonement for them before the LORD? [18]See! [a]Its blood was not brought inside [1]the holy *place*; indeed you should have eaten it in a holy *place*, [b]as I commanded."

[19]And Aaron said to Moses, "Look, [a]this day they have offered their sin offering and their burnt offering before the LORD, and such things have befallen me! *If* I had eaten the sin offering today, [b]would it have been accepted in the sight of the LORD?" [20]So when Moses heard *that*, he was content.

FOODS PERMITTED AND FORBIDDEN
(Deut. 14:3–21)

11 Now the LORD spoke to Moses and Aaron, saying to them, [2]"Speak to the children of Israel, saying, [a]"These *are* the animals which you may eat among all the animals that *are* on the earth: [3]Among the animals, whatever divides the hoof, having cloven hooves *and* chewing the cud—that you may eat. [4]Nevertheless these you shall [a]not eat among those that chew the cud or those that have cloven hooves: the camel, because it chews the cud but does not have cloven hooves, is [1]unclean to you; [5]the [1]rock hyrax, because it chews the cud but does not have cloven hooves, *is* [2]unclean to you; [6]the hare, because it chews the cud but does not have cloven hooves, *is* unclean to you; [7]and the swine, though it divides the hoof, having cloven hooves, yet does not chew the cud, [a]*is* unclean to you. [8]Their flesh you shall not eat, and their carcasses you shall not touch. [a]They *are* unclean to you.

10:10 [a]Lev. 11:47; 20:25; Ezek. 22:26; 44:23

10:11 [a]Deut. 24:8; Neh. 8:2, 8; Jer. 18:18; Mal. 2:7

10:12 [a]Num. 18:9 [b]Lev. 21:22

10:13 [a]Num. 18:10 [b]Lev. 2:3; 6:16

10:14 [a]Ex. 29:24, 26, 27; Lev. 7:30–34; Num. 18:11 [b]Lev. 22:13 [c]Num. 18:10

10:15 [a]Lev. 7:29, 30, 34

10:16 [a]Lev. 9:3, 15

10:17 [a]Lev. 6:24–30 [b]Ex. 28:38; Lev. 22:16; Num. 18:1

10:18 [a]Lev. 6:30 [b]Lev. 6:26, 30

10:19 [a]Lev. 9:8, 12 [b][Is. 1:11–15]; Jer. 6:20; 14:12; Hos. 9:4; [Mal. 1:10, 13; 3:1–4]

11:2 [a]Deut. 14:4; Ezek. 4:14; Dan. 1:8; [Matt. 15:11]; Acts 10:12, 14; [Rom. 14:14]; Heb. 9:10; 13:9]

11:4 [a]Acts 10:14

11:7 [a]Is. 65:4; 66:3, 17; Mark 5:1–17

11:8 [a]Is. 52:11; [Mark 7:2, 15, 18]; Acts 10:14, 15; 15:29

10:13 [1]*portion*   **10:18** [1]The Most Holy Place when capitalized   **11:4** [1]*impure*
11:5 [1]*rock badger*   [2]*impure*

9a"These you may eat of all that *are* in the water: whatever in the water has fins and scales, whether in the seas or in the rivers—that you may eat. 10But all in the seas or in the rivers that do not have fins and scales, all that move in the water or any living thing which *is* in the water, they *are* ¹an ᵃabomination to you. 11They shall be an abomination to you; you shall not eat their flesh, but you shall regard their carcasses as an abomination. 12Whatever in the water does not have fins or scales—that *shall be* an abomination to you.

13a'And these you shall regard as an abomination among the birds; they shall not be eaten, they *are* an abomination: the eagle, the vulture, the buzzard, 14the kite, and the falcon after its kind; 15every raven after its kind, 16the ostrich, the short-eared owl, the sea gull, and the hawk after its kind; 17the little owl, the fisher owl, and the screech owl; 18the white owl, the jackdaw, and the carrion vulture; 19the stork, the heron after its kind, the hoopoe, and the bat.

20'All flying insects that creep on *all* fours *shall be* an abomination to you. 21Yet these you may eat of every flying insect that creeps on *all* fours: those which have jointed legs above their feet with which to leap on the earth. 22These you may eat: ᵃthe locust after its kind, the destroying locust after its kind, the cricket after its kind, and the grasshopper after its kind. 23But all *other* flying insects which have four feet *shall be* an abomination to you.

UNCLEAN ANIMALS

24'By these you shall become ¹unclean; whoever touches the carcass of any of them shall be unclean until evening; 25whoever carries part of the carcass of any of them ᵃshall wash his clothes and be unclean until evening: 26*The carcass* of any animal which divides the foot, but is not cloven-hoofed or does not chew the cud, *is* unclean to you. Everyone who touches it shall be unclean. 27And whatever goes on its paws, among all kinds of animals that go on *all* fours, those *are* unclean to you. Whoever touches any such carcass shall be unclean until evening. 28Whoever carries *any such* carcass shall wash his clothes and be unclean until evening. It *is* unclean to you.

29'These also *shall be* unclean to you among the creeping things that creep on the earth: the mole, ᵃthe mouse, and the large lizard after its kind; 30the gecko, the monitor lizard, the sand reptile, the sand lizard, and the chameleon. 31These *are* unclean to you among all that creep. Whoever ᵃtouches them when they are dead shall be unclean until evening. 32Anything on which *any* of them falls, when they are dead shall be ¹unclean, whether *it is* any item of wood or clothing or skin or sack, whatever item *it is*, in which *any* work is done, ᵃit must be put in water. And it shall be unclean until evening; then it shall be clean. 33Any ᵃearthen vessel into which *any* of them falls ᵇyou shall break; and whatever *is* in it shall be unclean: 34in such a vessel, any edible food upon which water falls becomes unclean, and any drink that may be drunk from it becomes unclean. 35And everything on which *a part* of *any such* carcass falls shall be unclean; *whether it is* an oven or cooking stove, it shall be broken down; *for* they *are* unclean, and

11:9 ᵃDeut. 14:9

11:10
ᵃLev. 7:18, 21;
Deut. 14:3

11:13
ᵃDeut. 14:12–19;
Is. 66:17

11:22 ᵃMatt. 3:4;
Mark 1:6

11:25 ᵃLev. 14:8;
15:5; Num. 19:10,
21, 22; 31:24;
Zech. 13:1;
[Heb. 9:10;
10:22; Rev. 7:14]

11:29 ᵃIs. 66:17

11:31 ᵃHag. 2:13

11:32 ᵃLev. 15:12

11:33 ᵃLev. 6:28
ᵇLev. 15:12;
Ps. 2:9;
Jer. 48:38;
[2 Tim. 2:21];
Rev. 2:27

11:10 ¹*detestable*　　11:24 ¹*impure*　　11:32 ¹*impure*

shall be unclean to you. 36Nevertheless a spring or a cistern, *in which there is* plenty of water, shall be clean, but whatever touches any such carcass becomes unclean. 37And if a part of *any such* carcass falls on any planting seed which is to be sown, it *remains* clean. 38But if water is put on the seed, and if *a part* of *any such* carcass falls on it, it *becomes* ¹unclean to you.

39'And if any animal which you may eat dies, he who touches its carcass shall be ªunclean until evening. 40ªHe who eats of its carcass shall wash his clothes and be unclean until evening. He also who carries its carcass shall wash his clothes and be unclean until evening.

41'And every creeping thing that creeps on the earth *shall be* ¹an abomination. It shall not be eaten. 42Whatever crawls on its belly, whatever goes on *all* fours, or whatever has many feet among all creeping things that creep on the earth—these you shall not eat, for they *are* an abomination. 43ªYou shall not make ¹yourselves ²abominable with any creeping thing that creeps; nor shall you make yourselves unclean with them, lest you be defiled by them. 44For I *am* the LORD your ªGod. You shall therefore consecrate yourselves, and ᵇyou shall be holy; for I *am* holy. Neither shall you defile yourselves with any creeping thing that creeps on the earth. 45ªFor I *am* the LORD who brings you up out of the land of Egypt, to be your God. ᵇYou shall therefore be holy, for I *am* holy.

46'This *is* the law ¹of the animals and the birds and every living creature that moves in the waters, and of every creature that creeps on the earth, 47ªto distinguish between the unclean and the clean, and between the animal that may be eaten and the animal that may not be eaten.'"

THE RITUAL AFTER CHILDBIRTH
(cf. Luke 2:22–24)

12 Then the LORD spoke to Moses, saying, 2"Speak to the children of Israel, saying: 'If a ªwoman has conceived, and borne a male child, then ᵇshe shall be ¹unclean seven days; ᶜas in the days of her customary impurity she shall be unclean. 3And on the ªeighth day the flesh of his foreskin shall be circumcised. 4She shall then continue in the blood of *her* purification thirty-three days. She shall not touch any ¹hallowed thing, nor come into the sanctuary until the days of her purification are fulfilled.

5'But if she bears a female child, then she shall be unclean two weeks, as in her customary impurity, and she shall continue in the blood of *her* purification sixty-six days.

6ª'When the days of her purification are fulfilled, whether for a son or a daughter, she shall bring to the priest a ᵇlamb ¹of the first year as a burnt offering, and a young pigeon or a turtledove as a ᶜsin offering, to the door of the tabernacle of meeting. 7Then he shall offer it before the LORD, and make ¹atonement for her. And she shall be clean from the flow of her blood. This *is* the law for her who has borne a male or a female.

8ª'And if she is not able to bring a lamb, then she may bring two turtledoves or two young pigeons—one as a burnt

Cross References
11:39
ªHag. 2:11–13

11:40 ªEx. 22:31;
Lev. 17:15; 22:8;
Deut. 14:21;
Ezek. 4:14; 44:31

11:43 ªLev. 20:25

11:44 ªEx. 6:7;
Lev. 22:33;
25:38; 26:45
ᵇEx. 19:6;
Lev. 19:2; 20:7,
26; [Amos 3:3];
Matt. 5:48;
1 Thess. 4:7;
1 Pet. 1:15, 16;
[Rev. 22:11, 14]

11:45 ªEx. 6:7;
20:2; Lev. 22:33;
25:38; 26:45;
Ps. 105:43–45;
Hos. 11:1
ᵇLev. 11:44

11:47 ªLev. 10:10;
Ezek. 44:23;
Mal. 3:18

12:2 ªLev. 15:19;
[Job 14:4;
Ps. 51:5]
ᵇEx. 22:30;
Lev. 8:33; 13:4;
Luke 2:22
ᶜLev. 18:19

12:3 ªGen. 17:12;
Luke 1:59; 2:21;
John 7:22, 23;
Gal. 5:3

12:6 ªLuke 2:22
ᵇ[John 1:29];
1 Pet. 1:18, 19]
ᶜLev. 5:7

12:8 ªLev. 5:7;
Luke 2:22–24

Footnotes
11:38 ¹impure   11:41 ¹detestable   11:43 ¹Lit. *your souls*   ²impure
11:46 ¹concerning   12:2 ¹impure   12:4 ¹consecrated   12:6 ¹Lit. *a son of his year*   12:7 ¹Lit. *covering*

offering and the other as a sin offering. ᵇSo the priest shall make atonement for her, and she will be ¹clean.' "

THE LAW CONCERNING LEPROSY

13 And the LORD spoke to Moses and Aaron, saying: ²"When a man has on the skin of his body a swelling, ᵃa scab, or a bright spot, and it becomes on the skin of his body *like* a ¹leprous sore, ᵇthen he shall be brought to Aaron the priest or to one of his sons the priests. ³The priest shall examine the sore on the skin of the body; and if the hair on the sore has turned white, and the sore appears *to be* deeper than the skin of his body, it *is* a leprous sore. Then the priest shall examine him, and pronounce him ¹unclean. ⁴But if the bright spot *is* white on the skin of his body, and does not appear *to be* deeper than the skin, and its hair has not turned white, then the priest shall isolate *the one who has* the sore ᵃseven days. ⁵And the priest shall examine him on the seventh day; and indeed *if* the sore appears to be as it was, *and* the sore has not spread on the skin, then the priest shall isolate him another seven days. ⁶Then the priest shall examine him again on the seventh day; and indeed *if* the sore has faded, *and* the sore has not spread on the skin, then the priest shall pronounce him clean; it *is only* a scab, and he ᵃshall wash his clothes and be clean. ⁷But if the scab should at all spread over the skin, after he has been seen by the priest for his cleansing, he shall be seen by the priest again. ⁸And *if* the priest sees that the scab has indeed spread on the skin, then the priest shall pronounce him ¹unclean. It *is* leprosy.

⁹"When the leprous sore is on a person, then he shall be brought to the priest. ¹⁰ᵃAnd the priest shall examine *him;* and indeed *if* the swelling on the skin *is* white, and it has turned the hair white, and *there is* a spot of raw flesh in the swelling, ¹¹it *is* an old leprosy on the skin of his body. The priest shall pronounce him ¹unclean, and shall not isolate him, for he *is* unclean.

¹²"And if leprosy breaks out all over the skin, and the leprosy covers all the skin of *the one who has* the sore, from his head to his foot, wherever the priest looks, ¹³then the priest shall consider; and indeed *if* the leprosy has covered all his body, he shall pronounce *him* clean *who has* the sore. It has all turned ᵃwhite. He *is* clean. ¹⁴But when raw flesh appears on him, he shall be unclean. ¹⁵And the priest shall examine the raw flesh and pronounce him to be unclean; *for* the raw flesh *is* unclean. It *is* leprosy. ¹⁶Or if the raw flesh changes and turns white again, he shall come to the priest. ¹⁷And the priest shall examine him; and indeed *if* the sore has turned white, then the priest shall pronounce *him* clean *who has* the sore. He *is* clean.

¹⁸"If the body develops a ᵃboil in the skin, and it is healed, ¹⁹and in the place of the boil there comes a white swelling or a bright spot, reddish-white, then it shall be shown to the priest; ²⁰and *if,* when the priest sees it, it indeed appears deeper than the skin, and its hair has turned white, the priest shall pronounce him unclean. It *is* a leprous sore which has broken out of the boil. ²¹But if the priest examines it, and indeed *there are*

12:8 ᵇLev. 4:26

13:2
ᵃDeut. 28:27;
Is. 3:17
ᵇDeut. 17:8, 9;
24:8; Mal. 2:7;
Luke 17:14

13:4 ᵃLev. 14:8

13:6
ᵃLev. 11:25; 14:8;
[John 13:8, 10]

13:10
ᵃNum. 12:10,
12; 2 Kin. 5:27;
2 Chr. 26:19, 20

13:13 ᵃEx. 4:6

13:18 ᵃEx. 9:9;
15:26

12:8 ¹*pure*   13:2 ¹Heb. *saraath,* disfiguring skin diseases, including leprosy, and so in vv. 2–46 and 14:2–32   13:3 ¹*defiled*   13:8 ¹*defiled*   13:11 ¹*defiled*

no white hairs in it, and it *is* not deeper than the skin, but has faded, then the priest shall isolate him seven days; [22]and if it should at all spread over the skin, then the priest shall pronounce him unclean. It *is* a [1]leprous sore. [23]But if the bright spot stays in one place, *and* has not spread, it *is* the scar of the boil; and the priest shall pronounce him clean.

[24]"Or if the body receives a [a]burn on its skin by fire, and the raw *flesh* of the burn becomes a bright spot, reddish-white or white, [25]then the priest shall examine it; and indeed *if* the hair of the bright spot has turned white, and it appears deeper than the skin, it *is* leprosy broken out in the burn. Therefore the priest shall pronounce him unclean. It *is* a leprous sore. [26]But if the priest examines it, and indeed *there are* no white hairs in the bright spot, and it *is* not deeper than the skin, but has faded, then the priest shall isolate him seven days. [27]And the priest shall examine him on the seventh day. If it has at all spread over the skin, then the priest shall pronounce him unclean. It *is* a leprous sore. [28]But if the bright spot stays in one place, *and* has not spread on the skin, but has faded, it *is* a swelling from the burn. The priest shall pronounce him clean, for it *is* the scar from the burn.

[29]"If a man or woman has a sore on the head or the beard, [30]then the priest shall examine the sore; and indeed if it appears deeper than the skin, *and there is* in it thin yellow hair, then the priest shall pronounce him unclean. It *is* a scaly leprosy of the head or beard. [31]But if the priest examines the scaly sore, and indeed it does not appear deeper than the skin, and *there is* no black hair in it, then the priest shall isolate *the one who has* the scale seven days. [32]And on the seventh day the priest shall examine the sore; and indeed *if* the scale has not spread, and there is no yellow hair in it, and the scale does not appear deeper than the skin, [33]he shall shave himself, but the scale he shall not shave. And the priest shall isolate *the one who has* the scale another seven days. [34]On the seventh day the priest shall examine the scale; and indeed *if* the scale has not spread over the skin, and does not appear deeper than the skin, then the priest shall pronounce him clean. He shall wash his clothes and be clean. [35]But if the scale should at all spread over the skin after his cleansing, [36]then the priest shall examine him; and indeed *if* the scale has spread over the skin, the priest need not seek for yellow hair. He *is* unclean. [37]But if the scale appears to be at a standstill, and there is black hair grown up in it, the scale has healed. He *is* clean, and the priest shall pronounce him clean.

[38]"If a man or a woman has bright spots on the skin of the body, *specifically* white bright spots, [39]then the priest shall look; and indeed *if* the bright spots on the skin of the body *are* dull white, it *is* a white spot *that* grows on the skin. He *is* clean.

[40]"As for the man whose hair has fallen from his head, he *is* bald, *but* he *is* clean. [41]He whose hair has fallen from his forehead, he *is* bald on the forehead, *but* he *is* clean. [42]And if there is on the bald head or bald [a]forehead a reddish-white sore, it *is* leprosy breaking out on his bald head or his bald forehead. [43]Then the priest shall examine it; and indeed *if* the swelling of the sore *is* reddish-white on his bald head or on his bald forehead, as the appearance of leprosy on the skin

13:24 [a]Is. 3:24
13:42
[a]2 Chr. 26:19

13:22 [1]infection

of the body, [44]he is a leprous man. He *is* unclean. The priest shall surely pronounce him [1]unclean; his sore *is* on his [a]head.

[45]"Now the leper on whom the sore *is*, his clothes shall be torn and his head [a]bare; and he shall [b]cover his mustache, and cry, [c]'Unclean! Unclean!' [46]He shall be unclean. All the days he has the sore he shall be unclean. He *is* unclean, and he shall [1]dwell alone; his dwelling *shall be* [a]outside the camp.

THE LAW CONCERNING LEPROUS GARMENTS

[47]"Also, if a garment has a [1]leprous plague in it, *whether it is* a woolen garment or a linen garment, [48]whether *it is* in the warp or woof of linen or wool, whether in leather or in anything made of leather, [49]and if the plague is greenish or reddish in the garment or in the leather, whether in the warp or in the woof, or in anything made of leather, it *is* a leprous [1]plague and shall be shown to the priest. [50]The priest shall examine the plague and isolate *that which has* the plague seven days. [51]And he shall examine the plague on the seventh day. If the plague has spread in the garment, either in the warp or in the woof, in the leather *or* in anything made of leather, the plague *is* [a]an active leprosy. It *is* unclean. [52]He shall therefore burn that garment in which is the plague, whether warp or woof, in wool or in linen, or anything of leather, for it *is* an active leprosy; *the garment* shall be burned in the fire.

[53]"But if the priest examines *it*, and indeed the plague has not spread in the garment, either in the warp or in the woof, or in anything made of leather, [54]then the priest shall command that they wash *the thing* in which *is* the plague; and he shall isolate it another seven days. [55]Then the priest shall examine the plague after it has been washed; and indeed *if* the plague has not changed its color, though the plague has not spread, it *is* unclean, and you shall burn it in the fire; it continues eating away, *whether* the damage *is* outside or inside. [56]If the priest examines *it*, and indeed the plague has faded after washing it, then he shall tear it out of the garment, whether out of the warp or out of the woof, or out of the leather. [57]But if it appears again in the garment, either in the warp or in the woof, or in anything made of leather, it *is* a spreading *plague;* you shall burn with fire that in which is the plague. [58]And if you wash the garment, either warp or woof, or whatever is made of leather, if the plague has disappeared from it, then it shall be washed a second time, and shall be clean.

[59]"This *is* the law of the leprous plague in a garment of wool or linen, either in the warp or woof, or in anything made of leather, to pronounce it clean or to pronounce it unclean."

THE RITUAL FOR CLEANSING HEALED LEPERS
(cf. Matt. 8:1–4; Luke 5:12–14)

14 Then the LORD spoke to Moses, saying, [2]"This shall be the law of the [1]leper for the day of his cleansing: He [a]shall be brought to the priest. [3]And the priest shall go out of the camp, and the priest shall examine *him;* and indeed, *if* the [1]leprosy is healed in the leper, [4]then the priest shall command

13:44 [a]Is. 1:5

13:45
[a]Lev. 10:6; 21:10
[b]Ezek. 24:17, 22;
Mic. 3:7 [c]Is. 6:5;
64:6; Lam. 4:15;
Luke 5:8

13:46
[a]Num. 5:1–4;
12:14;
2 Kin. 7:3; 15:5;
2 Chr. 26:21;
Ps. 38:11;
Luke 17:12

13:51 [a]Lev. 14:44

14:2
[a]Matt. 8:2, 4;
Mark 1:40, 44;
Luke 5:12, 14;
17:14

13:44 [1]*altogether defiled*   13:46 [1]*live alone*   13:47 [1]A mold, fungus, or similar infestation, and so in vv. 47–59   13:49 [1]*mark*   14:2 [1]See note at 13:2   14:3 [1]Heb. *saraath,* disfiguring skin diseases, including leprosy, and so in vv. 2–32

to take for him who is to be cleansed two living *and* clean birds, [a]cedar wood, [b]scarlet, and [c]hyssop. [5]And the priest shall command that one of the birds be killed in an earthen vessel over running water. [6]As for the living bird, he shall take it, the cedar wood and the scarlet and the hyssop, and dip them and the living bird in the blood of the bird *that was* killed over the running water. [7]And he shall [a]sprinkle it [b]seven times on him who is to be cleansed from the leprosy, and shall pronounce him clean, and shall let the living bird loose in the open field. [8]He who is to be cleansed [a]shall wash his clothes, shave off all his hair, and [b]wash himself in water, that he may be clean. After that he shall come into the camp, and [c]shall stay outside his tent seven days. [9]But on the [a]seventh day he shall shave all the hair off his head and his beard and his eyebrows—all his hair he shall shave off. He shall wash his clothes and wash his body in water, and he shall be clean.

[10]"And on the eighth day [a]he shall take two male lambs without blemish, one ewe lamb of the first year without blemish, three-tenths *of an ephah* of fine flour mixed with oil as [b]a grain offering, and one log of oil. [11]Then the priest who makes *him* clean shall present the man who is to be made clean, and those things, before the LORD, *at* the door of the tabernacle of meeting. [12]And the priest shall take one male lamb and [a]offer it as a trespass offering, and the log of oil, and [b]wave them *as* a wave offering before the LORD. [13]Then he shall kill the lamb [a]in the place where he kills the sin offering and the burnt offering, in a holy place; for [b]as the sin offering *is* the priest's, so *is* the trespass offering. [c]It *is* most holy. [14]The priest shall take *some* of the blood of the trespass offering, and the priest shall put *it* [a]on the tip of the right ear of him who is to be cleansed, on the thumb of his right hand, and on the big toe of his right foot. [15]And the priest shall take *some* of the log of oil, and pour *it* into the palm of his own left hand. [16]Then the priest shall dip his right finger in the oil that *is* in his left hand, and shall [a]sprinkle some of the oil with his finger seven times before the LORD. [17]And of the rest of the oil in his hand, the priest shall put *some* on the tip of the right ear of him who is to be cleansed, on the thumb of his right hand, and on the big toe of his right foot, on the blood of the trespass offering. [18]The rest of the oil that *is* in the priest's hand he shall put on the head of him who is to be cleansed. [a]So the priest shall make [1]atonement for him before the LORD.

[19]"Then the priest shall offer [a]the sin offering, and make atonement for him who is to be cleansed from his uncleanness. Afterward he shall kill the burnt offering. [20]And the priest shall offer the burnt offering and the grain offering on the altar. So the priest shall make atonement for him, and he shall be [a]clean.

[21]"But [a]if he *is* poor and cannot afford it, then he shall take one male lamb *as* a trespass offering to be waved, to make atonement for him, [1]one-tenth *of an ephah* of fine flour mixed with oil as a grain offering, a log of oil, [22a]and two turtledoves or two young pigeons, such as he is able to afford: one shall be a sin offering and the other a burnt offering. [23a]He shall bring them to the priest on the eighth day for his cleansing, to the door of the tabernacle of meeting, before the LORD.

14:4 [a]Lev. 14:6, 49, 51, 52; Num. 19:6; Heb. 9:19 [b]Ex. 25:4 [c]Ex. 12:22; Ps. 51:7

14:7 [a]Num. 19:18, 19; [Heb. 9:13, 21; 12:24] [b]2 Kin. 5:10, 14; Ps. 51:2

14:8 [a]Lev. 11:25; 13:6; Num. 8:7 [b]Lev. 11:25; [Eph. 5:26; Heb. 10:22; Rev. 1:5, 6] [c]Lev. 13:5; Num. 5:2, 3; 12:14, 15; 2 Chr. 26:21

14:9 [a]Num. 19:19

14:10 [a]Matt. 8:4; Mark 1:44; Luke 5:14 [b]Lev. 2:1; Num. 15:4

14:12 [a]Lev. 5:6, 18; 6:6; 14:19 [b]Ex. 29:22–24, 26

14:13 [a]Ex. 29:11; Lev. 1:5, 11; 4:4, 24 [b]Lev. 6:24–30; 7:7 [c]Lev. 2:3; 7:6; 21:22

14:14 [a]Ex. 29:20; Lev. 8:23, 24

14:16 [a]Lev. 4:6

14:18 [a]Lev. 4:26; 5:6; Num. 15:28; [Heb. 2:17]

14:19 [a]Lev. 5:1, 6; 12:7; [2 Cor. 5:21]

14:20 [a]Lev. 14:8, 9

14:21 [a]Lev. 5:7, 11; 12:8; 27:8

14:22 [a]Lev. 12:8; 15:14, 15

14:23 [a]Lev. 14:10, 11

14:18 [1]Lit. *covering*   14:21 [1]Approximately two dry quarts

24a And the priest shall take the lamb of the trespass offering and the log of oil, and the priest shall wave them *as* a wave offering before the LORD. 25Then he shall kill the lamb of the trespass offering, ᵃand the priest shall take *some* of the blood of the trespass offering and put *it* on the tip of the right ear of him who is to be cleansed, on the thumb of his right hand, and on the big toe of his right foot. 26And the priest shall pour some of the oil into the palm of his own left hand. 27Then the priest shall sprinkle with his right finger *some* of the oil that *is* in his left hand seven times before the LORD. 28And the priest shall put *some* of the oil that *is* in his hand on the tip of the right ear of him who is to be cleansed, on the thumb of the right hand, and on the big toe of his right foot, on the place of the blood of the trespass offering. 29The rest of the oil that *is* in the priest's hand he shall put on the head of him who is to be cleansed, to make atonement for him before the LORD. 30And he shall offer one of ᵃthe turtledoves or young pigeons, such as he can afford— 31such as he is able to afford, the one *as* a sin offering and the other *as* a burnt offering, with the grain offering. So the priest shall make atonement for him who is to be cleansed before the LORD. 32This *is* the law *for one* who had a leprous sore, who cannot afford ᵃthe usual cleansing."

THE LAW CONCERNING LEPROUS HOUSES

33And the LORD spoke to Moses and Aaron, saying: 34a"When you have come into the land of Canaan, which I give you as a possession, and ᵇI put the ¹leprous plague in a house in the land of your possession, 35and he who owns the house comes and tells the priest, saying, 'It seems to me that *there is* ᵃsome plague in the house,' 36then the priest shall command that they empty the house, before the priest goes *into it* to examine the plague, that all that *is* in the house may not be made unclean; and afterward the priest shall go in to examine the house. 37And he shall examine the plague; and indeed *if* the plague *is* on the walls of the house with ingrained streaks, greenish or reddish, which appear to be ¹deep in the wall, 38then the priest shall go out of the house, to the door of the house, and ¹shut up the house seven days. 39And the priest shall come again on the seventh day and look; and indeed *if* the plague has spread on the walls of the house, 40then the priest shall command that they take away the stones in which *is* the plague, and they shall cast them into an unclean place outside the city. 41And he shall cause the house to be scraped inside, all around, and the dust that they scrape off they shall pour out in an unclean place outside the city. 42Then they shall take other stones and put *them* in the place of *those* stones, and he shall take other mortar and plaster the house.

43"Now if the plague comes back and breaks out in the house, after he has taken away the stones, after he has scraped the house, and after it is plastered, 44then the priest shall come and look; and indeed *if* the plague has spread in the house, it *is* ᵃan active leprosy in the house. It *is* unclean. 45And he shall break down the house, its stones, its timber, and all the plaster

14:24 ᵃLev. 14:12
14:25
ᵃLev. 14:14, 17
14:30
ᵃLev. 14:22;
15:14, 15
14:32 ᵃLev. 14:10
14:34 ᵃGen. 12:7;
13:17; 17:8;
Num. 32:22;
Deut. 7:1; 32:49
ᵇ[Prov. 3:33]
14:35 ᵃ[Ps. 91:9,
10; Prov. 3:33;
Zech. 5:4]
14:44 ᵃLev. 13:51;
[Zech. 5:4]

14:34 ¹Decomposition by mildew, mold, dry rot, etc., and so in vv. 34–53
14:37 ¹Lit. *lower than the wall*   14:38 ¹*quarantine*

of the house, and he shall carry *them* outside the city to an unclean place. 46Moreover he who goes into the house at all while it is shut up shall be ¹unclean ªuntil evening. 47And he who lies down in the house shall ªwash his clothes, and he who eats in the house shall wash his clothes.

48"But if the priest comes in and examines *it,* and indeed the plague has not spread in the house after the house was plastered, then the priest shall pronounce the house clean, because the plague is healed. 49And ªhe shall take, to cleanse the house, two birds, cedar wood, scarlet, and hyssop. 50Then he shall kill one of the birds in an earthen vessel over running water; 51and he shall take the cedar wood, the hyssop, the scarlet, and the living bird, and dip them in the blood of the slain bird and in the running water, and sprinkle the house seven times. 52And he shall ¹cleanse the house with the blood of the bird and the running water and the living bird, with the cedar wood, the hyssop, and the scarlet. 53Then he shall let the living bird loose outside the city in the open field, and ªmake atonement for the house, and it shall be clean.

54"This *is* the law for any ªleprous sore and scale, 55for the ªleprosy of a garment ᵇand of a house, 56ªfor a swelling and a scab and a bright spot, 57to ªteach when *it is* unclean and when *it is* clean. This *is* the law of leprosy."

THE LAW CONCERNING BODILY DISCHARGES

15 And the Lᴏʀᴅ spoke to Moses and Aaron, saying, 2"Speak to the children of Israel, and say to them: ª'When any man has a discharge from his body, his discharge *is* unclean. 3And this shall be his uncleanness in regard to his discharge—whether his body runs with his discharge, or his body is stopped up by his discharge, it *is* his uncleanness. 4Every bed is ¹unclean on which he who has the discharge lies, and everything on which he sits shall be unclean. 5And whoever ªtouches his bed shall ᵇwash his clothes and ᶜbathe in water, and be unclean until evening. 6He who sits on anything on which he who has the ªdischarge sat shall wash his clothes and bathe in water, and be unclean until evening. 7And he who touches the body of him who has the discharge shall wash his clothes and bathe in water, and be unclean until evening. 8If he who has the discharge ªspits on him who is clean, then he shall wash his clothes and bathe in water, and be unclean until evening. 9Any saddle on which he who has the discharge rides shall be unclean. 10Whoever touches anything that was under him shall be unclean until evening. He who carries *any of* those things shall wash his clothes and bathe in water, and be unclean until evening. 11And whomever the one who has the discharge touches, and has not rinsed his hands in water, he shall wash his clothes and bathe in water, and be unclean until evening. 12The ªvessel of earth that he who has the discharge touches shall be broken, and every vessel of wood shall be rinsed in water.

13'And when he who has a discharge is cleansed of his discharge, then ªhe shall count for himself seven days for his cleansing, wash his clothes, and bathe his body in running water; then he shall be clean. 14On the eighth day he shall take

14:46
ªLev. 11:24; 15:5

14:47 ªLev. 14:8

14:49 ªLev. 14:4

14:53 ªLev. 14:20

14:54
ªLev. 13:30;
26:21

14:55
ªLev. 13:47–52
ᵇLev. 14:34

14:56 ªLev. 13:2

14:57 ªLev. 11:47;
20:25;
Deut. 24:8;
Ezek. 44:23

15:2 ªLev. 22:4;
Num. 5:2;
2 Sam. 3:29

15:5
ªLev. 5:2; 14:46
ᵇLev. 14:8, 47
ᶜLev. 11:25; 17:15

15:6 ªLev. 15:10;
Deut. 23:10

15:8 ªNum. 12:14

15:12 ªLev. 6:28;
11:32, 33

15:13 ªLev. 14:8;
15:28;
Num. 19:11, 12

14:46 ¹defiled   14:52 ¹ceremonially cleanse   15:4 ¹defiled

for himself [a]two turtledoves or two young pigeons, and come before the LORD, to the door of the tabernacle of meeting, and give them to the priest. [15]Then the priest shall offer them, [a]the one *as* a sin offering and the other *as* a burnt offering. [b]So the priest shall make [1]atonement for him before the LORD because of his discharge.

[16a]'If any man has an emission of semen, then he shall wash all his body in water, and be unclean until evening. [17]And any garment and any leather on which there is semen, it shall be washed with water, and be unclean until evening. [18]Also, when a woman lies with a man, and *there is* an emission of semen, they shall bathe in water, and [a]be unclean until evening.

[19a]'If a woman has a discharge, *and* the discharge from her body is blood, she shall be [1]set apart seven days; and whoever touches her shall be unclean until evening. [20]Everything that she lies on during her impurity shall be unclean; also everything that she sits on shall be unclean. [21]Whoever touches her bed shall wash his clothes and bathe in water, and be unclean until evening. [22]And whoever touches anything that she sat on shall wash his clothes and bathe in water, and be unclean until evening. [23]If *anything* is on *her* bed or on anything on which she sits, when he touches it, he shall be unclean until evening. [24]And [a]if any man lies with her at all, so that her impurity is on him, he shall be [1]unclean seven days; and every bed on which he lies shall be unclean.

[25]'If [a]a woman has a discharge of blood for many days, other than at the time of her *customary* impurity, or if it runs beyond her *usual time of* impurity, all the days of her unclean discharge shall be as the days of her *customary* impurity. She *shall be* unclean. [26]Every bed on which she lies all the days of her discharge shall be to her as the bed of her impurity; and whatever she sits on shall be unclean, as the uncleanness of her impurity. [27]Whoever touches those things shall be unclean; he shall wash his clothes and bathe in water, and be unclean until evening.

[28]'But [a]if she is cleansed of her discharge, then she shall count for herself seven days, and after that she shall be clean. [29]And on the eighth day she shall take for herself two turtledoves or two young pigeons, and bring them to the priest, to the door of the tabernacle of meeting. [30]Then the priest shall offer the one *as* a sin offering and the other *as* a [a]burnt offering, and the priest shall make atonement for her before the LORD for the discharge of her uncleanness.

[31]'Thus you shall [a]separate the children of Israel from their uncleanness, lest they die in their uncleanness when they [b]defile My tabernacle that *is* among them. [32a]This *is* the law for one who has a discharge, [b]and *for him* who emits semen and is unclean thereby, [33a]and for her who is indisposed because of her *customary* impurity, and for one who has a discharge, either man [b]or woman, [c]and for him who lies with her who is unclean.' "

THE DAY OF ATONEMENT

16 Now the LORD spoke to Moses after [a]the death of the two sons of Aaron, when they offered *profane fire* before the LORD, and died; [2]and the LORD said to Moses: "Tell

15:14 [a]Lev. 14:22, 23, 30, 31

15:15 [a]Lev. 14:30, 31 [b]Lev. 14:19, 31

15:16 [a]Lev. 22:4; Deut. 23:10, 11

15:18 [a][Ex. 19:15; 1 Sam. 21:4; 1 Cor. 6:18]

15:19 [a]Lev. 12:2

15:24 [a]Lev. 18:19; 20:18

15:25 [a]Matt. 9:20; Mark 5:25; Luke 8:43

15:28 [a]Lev. 15:13–15

15:30 [a]Lev. 5:7

15:31 [a]Lev. 11:47; 14:57; 22:2; Deut. 24:8; Ezek. 44:23; [Heb. 12:15] [b]Lev. 20:3; Num. 5:3; 19:13, 20; Ezek. 5:11; 23:38; 36:17

15:32 [a]Lev. 15:2 [b]Lev. 15:16

15:33 [a]Lev. 15:19 [b]Lev. 15:25 [c]Lev. 15:24

16:1 [a]Lev. 10:1, 2; 2 Sam. 6:6–8

Aaron your brother [a]not to come at *just* any time into the Holy *Place* inside the veil, before the mercy seat which *is* on the ark, lest he die; for [b]I will appear in the cloud above the mercy seat.

31"Thus Aaron shall [a]come into the Holy *Place*: [b]with *the blood of* a young bull as a sin offering, and *of* a ram as a burnt offering. 4He shall put the [a]holy linen tunic and the linen trousers on his body; he shall be girded with a linen sash, and with the linen turban he shall be attired. These *are* holy garments. Therefore [b]he shall wash his body in water, and put them on. 5And he shall take from [a]the congregation of the children of Israel two kids of the goats as a sin offering, and one ram as a burnt offering.

6"Aaron shall offer the bull as a sin offering, which *is* for himself, and [a]make atonement for himself and for his house. 7He shall take the two goats and present them before the LORD *at* the door of the tabernacle of meeting. 8Then Aaron shall cast lots for the two goats: one lot for the LORD and the other lot for the scapegoat. 9And Aaron shall bring the goat on which the LORD's lot fell, and offer it *as* a sin offering. 10But the goat on which the lot fell to be the scapegoat shall be presented alive before the LORD, to make [a]atonement upon it, *and* to let it go as the scapegoat into the wilderness.

11"And Aaron shall bring the bull of the sin offering, which is for [a]himself, and make atonement for himself and for his house, and shall kill the bull as the sin offering which *is* for himself. 12Then he shall take [a]a censer full of burning coals of fire from the altar before the LORD, with his hands full of [b]sweet incense beaten fine, and bring *it* inside the veil. 13[a]And he shall put the incense on the fire before the LORD, that the cloud of incense may cover the [b]mercy seat that *is* on the Testimony, lest he [c]die. 14[a]He shall take some of the blood of the bull and [b]sprinkle *it* with his finger on the mercy seat on the east *side;* and before the mercy seat he shall sprinkle some of the blood with his finger seven times.

15[a]"Then he shall kill the goat of the sin offering, which *is* for the people, bring its blood [b]inside the veil, do with that blood as he did with the blood of the bull, and sprinkle it on the mercy seat and before the mercy seat. 16So he shall [a]make atonement for the Holy *Place*, because of the uncleanness of the children of Israel, and because of their transgressions, for all their sins; and so he shall do for the tabernacle of meeting which remains among them in the midst of their uncleanness. 17There shall be [a]no man in the tabernacle of meeting when he goes in to make atonement in the Holy *Place*, until he comes out, that he may make atonement for himself, for his household, and for all the assembly of Israel. 18And he shall go out to the altar that *is* before the LORD, and make atonement for [a]it, and shall take some of the blood of the bull and some of the blood of the goat, and put it on the horns of the altar all around. 19Then he shall sprinkle some of the blood on it with his finger seven times, cleanse it, and [a]consecrate[1] it from the [2]uncleanness of the children of Israel.

20"And when he has made an end of atoning for the Holy *Place*, the tabernacle of meeting, and the altar, he shall bring the live goat. 21Aaron shall lay both his hands on the head of

16:2 [a]Ex. 30:10; Lev. 16:34; 23:27; [Heb. 6:19; 9:7, 8, 12; 10:19] [b]Ex. 25:21, 22; 40:34; 1 Kin. 8:10–12

16:3 [a]Lev. 4:1–12; 16:6; [Heb. 9:7, 12, 24, 25] [b]Lev. 4:3

16:4 [a]Ex. 28:39, 42, 43; Lev. 6:10; Ezek. 44:17, 18 [b]Ex. 30:20; Lev. 8:6, 7

16:5 [a]Lev. 4:14; Num. 29:11; 2 Chr. 29:21; Ezra 6:17; Ezek. 45:22, 23

16:6 [a]Lev. 9:7; [Heb. 5:3; 7:27, 28; 9:7]

16:10 [a][Is. 53:5, 6; Rom. 3:25; Heb. 7:27; 9:23, 24; 1 John 2:2]

16:11 [a][Heb. 7:27; 9:7]

16:12 [a]Lev. 10:1; Num. 16:7, 18; Is. 6:6, 7; Rev. 8:5 [b]Ex. 30:34–38

16:13 [a]Ex. 30:7, 8; Num. 16:7, 18, 46 [b]Ex. 25:21 [c]Ex. 28:43; Lev. 22:9; Num. 4:15, 20

16:14 [a]Lev. 4:5; [Heb. 9:25; 10:4] [b]Lev. 4:6, 17

16:15 [a][Heb. 2:17] [b][Heb. 6:19; 7:27; 9:3, 7, 12]

16:16 [a]Ex. 29:36; 30:10; Ezek. 45:18; [Heb. 9:22–24]

16:17 [a]Ex. 34:3; Luke 1:10

16:18 [a]Ex. 29:36

16:19 [a]Lev. 16:14; Ezek. 43:20

16:3 [1]Lit. *With this*   16:19 [1]*set it apart*   [2]*impurity*

the live goat, ᵃconfess over it all the iniquities of the children of Israel, and all their transgressions, concerning all their sins, ᵇputting them on the head of the goat, and shall send *it* away into the wilderness by the hand of a suitable man. ²²The goat ¹shall ᵃbear on itself all their iniquities to an ²uninhabited land; and he shall ᵇrelease the goat in the wilderness.

²³"Then Aaron shall come into the tabernacle of meeting, ᵃshall take off the linen garments which he put on when he went into the Holy *Place*, and shall leave them there. ²⁴And he shall wash his body with water in a holy place, put on his garments, come out and offer his burnt offering and the burnt offering of the people, and make ¹atonement for himself and for the people. ²⁵ᵃThe fat of the sin offering he shall burn on the altar. ²⁶And he who released the goat as the scapegoat shall wash his clothes ᵃand bathe his body in water, and afterward he may come into the camp. ²⁷ᵃThe bull *for* the sin offering and the goat *for* the sin offering, whose blood was brought in to make atonement in the Holy *Place*, shall be carried outside the camp. And they shall burn in the fire their skins, their flesh, and their offal. ²⁸Then he who burns them shall wash his clothes and bathe his body in water, and afterward he may come into the camp.

²⁹"*This* shall be a statute forever for you: ᵃIn the seventh month, on the tenth *day* of the month, you shall ¹afflict your souls, and do no work at all, *whether* a native of your own country or a stranger who ²dwells among you. ³⁰For on that day *the priest* shall make ¹atonement for you, to ᵃcleanse you, *that* you may be clean from all your sins before the LORD. ³¹It *is* a sabbath of solemn rest for you, and you shall afflict your souls. *It is* a statute forever. ³²ᵃAnd the priest, who is anointed and ᵇconsecrated to minister as priest in his father's place, shall make atonement, and put on the linen clothes, the holy garments; ³³then he shall make ¹atonement for ²the Holy Sanctuary, and he shall make atonement for the tabernacle of meeting and for the altar, and he shall make atonement for the priests and for all the people of the assembly. ³⁴ᵃThis shall be an everlasting statute for you, to make atonement for the children of Israel, for all their sins, ᵇonce a year." And he did as the LORD commanded Moses.

THE SANCTITY OF BLOOD

17 And the LORD spoke to Moses, saying, ²"Speak to Aaron, to his sons, and to all the children of Israel, and say to them, 'This *is* the thing which the LORD has commanded, saying: ³"Whatever man of the house of Israel who ᵃkills an ox or lamb or goat in the camp, or who kills *it* outside the camp, ⁴and does not bring it to the door of the tabernacle of meeting to offer an offering to the LORD before the tabernacle of the LORD, the guilt of bloodshed shall be ᵃimputed to that man. He has shed blood; and that man shall be ¹cut off from among his people, ⁵to the end that the children of Israel may bring their sacrifices ᵃwhich they offer in the open field, that they may bring them to the LORD at the door of the tabernacle of meeting, to the priest, and offer them *as* peace offerings to

---

16:21 ᵃLev. 5:5; 26:40 ᵇ[Is. 53:6]

16:22 ᵃLev. 8:14; [Is. 53:6, 11, 12; John 1:29; Heb. 9:28; 1 Pet. 2:24] ᵇLev. 14:7

16:23 ᵃLev. 6:11; 16:4; Ezek. 42:14; 44:19

16:25 ᵃLev. 1:8; 4:10

16:26 ᵃLev. 15:5

16:27 ᵃLev. 4:12, 21; 6:30; Heb. 13:11

16:29 ᵃEx. 30:10; Lev. 23:27–32; Num. 29:7

16:30 ᵃPs. 51:2; Jer. 33:8; [Eph. 5:26; Heb. 9:13, 14; 1 John 1:7, 9]

16:31 ᵃLev. 23:27, 32; Ezra 8:21; Is. 58:3, 5; Dan. 10:12

16:32 ᵃLev. 4:3, 5, 16; 21:10 ᵇEx. 29:29, 30; Num. 20:26, 28

16:34 ᵃLev. 23:31; Num. 29:7 ᵇEx. 30:10; [Heb. 9:7, 25, 28]

17:3 ᵃDeut. 12:5, 15, 21

17:4 ᵃRom. 5:13

17:5 ᵃGen. 21:33; 22:2; 31:54; Deut. 12:1–27; Ezek. 20:28

16:22 ¹shall carry   ²solitary land   16:24 ¹Lit. *covering*   16:29 ¹humble yourselves   ²As a resident alien   16:30 ¹Lit. *covering*   16:33 ¹Lit. *covering* ²The Most Holy Place   17:4 ¹Put to death

the LORD. 6And the priest ashall sprinkle the blood on the altar of the LORD *at* the door of the tabernacle of meeting, and bburn the fat for a sweet aroma to the LORD. 7They shall no more offer their sacrifices ato 1demons, after whom they bhave played the harlot. This shall be a statute forever for them throughout their generations."'

8"Also you shall say to them: 'Whatever man of the house of Israel, or of the strangers who dwell among you, awho offers a burnt offering or sacrifice, 9and does not abring it to the door of the tabernacle of meeting, to offer it to the LORD, that man shall be 1cut off from among his people.

10a'And whatever man of the house of Israel, or of the strangers who dwell among you, who eats any blood, bI will set My face against that person who eats blood, and will cut him off from among his people. 11For the alife of the flesh *is* in the blood, and I have given it to you upon the altar bto make atonement for your souls; for cit *is* the blood *that* makes atonement for the soul.' 12Therefore I said to the children of Israel, 'No one among you shall eat blood, nor shall any stranger who dwells among you eat blood.'

13"Whatever man of the children of Israel, or of the strangers who dwell among you, who ahunts and catches any animal or bird that may be eaten, he shall bpour out its blood and ccover it with dust; 14afor *it is* the life of all flesh. Its blood sustains its life. Therefore I said to the children of Israel, 'You shall not eat the blood of any flesh, for the life of all flesh is its blood. Whoever eats it shall be cut off.'

15a"And every person who eats what died *naturally* or what was torn *by beasts, whether he is* a native of your own country or a stranger, bhe shall both wash his clothes and cbathe in water, and be unclean until evening. Then he shall be clean. 16But if he does not wash *them* or bathe his body, then ahe shall bear his 1guilt."

LAWS OF SEXUAL MORALITY

18 Then the LORD spoke to Moses, saying, 2"Speak to the children of Israel, and say to them: a'I am the LORD your God. 3aAccording to 1the doings of the land of Egypt, where you dwelt, you shall not do; and baccording to the doings of the land of Canaan, where I am bringing you, you shall not do; nor shall you walk in their 2ordinances. 4aYou shall observe My judgments and keep My ordinances, to walk in them: I *am* the LORD your God. 5You shall therefore keep My statutes and My judgments, which if a man does, he shall live by them: I *am* the LORD.

6'None of you shall approach anyone who is near of kin to him, to uncover his nakedness: I *am* the LORD. 7The nakedness of your father or the nakedness of your mother you shall not uncover. She *is* your mother; you shall not uncover her nakedness. 8The nakedness of your afather's wife you shall not uncover; it *is* your father's nakedness. 9aThe nakedness of your sister, the daughter of your father, or the daughter of your mother, *whether* born at home or elsewhere, their nakedness you shall not uncover. 10The nakedness of your son's daughter or your daughter's daughter, their nakedness you

17:7 1Having the form of a goat or satyr   17:9 1Put to death   17:16 1iniquity
18:3 1what is done in   2statutes

shall not uncover; for theirs *is* your own nakedness. ¹¹The nakedness of your father's wife's daughter, begotten by your father—she *is* your sister—you shall not uncover her nakedness. ¹²ªYou shall not uncover the nakedness of your father's sister; she *is* near of kin to your father. ¹³You shall not uncover the nakedness of your mother's sister, for she *is* near of kin to your mother. ¹⁴ªYou shall not uncover the nakedness of your father's brother. You shall not approach his wife; she *is* your aunt. ¹⁵You shall not uncover the nakedness of your daughter-in-law—she *is* your son's wife—you shall not uncover her nakedness. ¹⁶You shall not uncover the nakedness of your brother's wife; it *is* your brother's nakedness. ¹⁷You shall not uncover the nakedness of a woman and her ªdaughter, nor shall you take her son's daughter or her daughter's daughter, to uncover her nakedness. They *are* near of kin to her. It *is* wickedness. ¹⁸Nor shall you take a woman ªas a rival to her sister, to uncover her nakedness while the other is alive.

¹⁹'Also you shall not approach a woman to uncover her nakedness as ªlong as she is in her ᵇ*customary* impurity. ²⁰ªMoreover you shall not lie carnally with your ᵇneighbor's wife, to defile yourself with her. ²¹And you shall not let any of your descendants ªpass through ᵇ*the fire* to ᶜMolech, nor shall you profane the name of your God: I *am* the LORD. ²²You shall not lie with ªa male as with a woman. It *is* an abomination. ²³Nor shall you mate with any ªanimal, to defile yourself with it. Nor shall any woman stand before an animal to mate with it. It *is* perversion.

²⁴ª'Do not defile yourselves with any of these things; ᵇfor by all these the nations are defiled, which I am casting out before you. ²⁵For ªthe land is defiled; therefore I ᵇvisit¹ the punishment of its iniquity upon it, and the land ᶜvomits out its inhabitants. ²⁶ªYou shall therefore ¹keep My statutes and My judgments, and shall not commit *any* of these abominations, *either* any of your own nation or any stranger who dwells among you ²⁷(for all these abominations the men of the land have done, who *were* before you, and thus the land is defiled), ²⁸lest ªthe land vomit you out also when you defile it, as it vomited out the nations that *were* before you. ²⁹For whoever commits any of these abominations, the persons who commit *them* shall be ¹cut off from among their people.

³⁰'Therefore you shall keep My ¹ordinance, so ªthat *you* do not commit *any* of these abominable customs which were committed before you, and that you do not defile yourselves by them: ᵇI *am* the LORD your God.' "

MORAL AND CEREMONIAL LAWS

19 And the LORD spoke to Moses, saying, ²"Speak to all the congregation of the children of Israel, and say to them: ª'You shall be holy, for I the LORD your God *am* holy.

³ª'Every one of you shall revere his mother and his father, and ᵇkeep My Sabbaths: I *am* the LORD your God.

⁴ª'Do not turn to idols, ᵇnor make for yourselves ¹molded gods: I *am* the LORD your God.

⁵'And ªif you offer a sacrifice of a peace offering to the LORD, you shall offer it of your own free will. ⁶It shall be

---

18:12 ªLev. 20:19

18:14
ªLev. 20:20

18:17 ªLev. 20:14

18:18
ª1 Sam. 1:6, 8

18:19 ªEzek. 18:6
ᵇLev. 15:24;
20:18

18:20
ª[Prov. 6:25–33]
ᵇEx. 20:14;
Lev. 20:10;
[Matt. 5:27,
28; 1 Cor. 6:9;
Heb. 13:4]

18:21
ªLev. 20:2–5;
Deut. 12:31
ᵇ2 Kin. 16:3
ᶜ1 Kin. 11:7, 33;
Acts 7:43

18:22
ªLev. 20:13;
Rom. 1:27

18:23 ªEx. 22:19;
Lev. 20:15, 16;
Deut. 27:21

18:24
ªMatt. 15:18–20;
1 Cor. 3:17
ᵇLev. 18:3;
20:23;
Deut. 18:12

18:25
ªNum. 35:33,
34; Ezek. 36:17
ᵇIs. 26:21;
Jer. 5:9
ᶜLev. 18:28;
20:22

18:26
ªLev. 18:5, 30

18:28 ªJer. 9:19

18:30 ªLev. 18:3;
22:9 ᵇLev. 18:2

19:2 ªEx. 19:6;
Lev. 11:44; 20:7,
26; [Eph. 1:4];
1 Pet. 1:16

19:3 ªEx. 20:12;
Deut. 5:16;
Matt. 15:4;
Eph. 6:2
ᵇEx. 16:23; 20:8;
31:13

19:4
ªEx. 20:4;
Ps. 96:5;
115:4–7;
1 Cor. 10:14;
[Col. 3:5]
ᵇEx. 34:17

19:5 ªLev. 7:16

18:25 ¹bring judgment for   18:26 ¹obey   18:29 ¹Put to death
18:30 ¹charge   19:4 ¹molten

eaten the same day you offer *it,* and on the next day. And if any remains until the third day, it shall be burned in the fire. [7]And if it is eaten at all on the third day, it *is* an abomination. It shall not be accepted. [8]Therefore *everyone* who eats it shall bear his iniquity, because he has profaned the hallowed *offering* of the LORD; and that person shall be cut off from his people.

[9a]'When you reap the harvest of your land, you shall not wholly reap the corners of your field, nor shall you gather the gleanings of your harvest. [10]And you shall not glean your vineyard, nor shall you gather *every* grape of your vineyard; you shall leave them for the poor and the stranger: I *am* the LORD your God.

[11a]'You shall not steal, nor deal falsely, [b]nor lie to one another. [12]And you shall not [a]swear by My name falsely, [b]nor shall you profane the name of your God: I *am* the LORD.

[13a]'You shall not cheat your neighbor, nor rob *him.* [b]The wages of him who is hired shall not remain with you all night until morning. [14]You shall not curse the deaf, [a]nor put a stumbling block before the blind, but shall fear your God: I *am* the LORD.

[15]'You shall do no injustice in [a]judgment. You shall not [b]be partial to the poor, nor honor the person of the mighty. In righteousness you shall judge your neighbor. [16]You shall not go about *as* a [a]talebearer among your people; nor shall you [b]take a stand against the life of your neighbor: I *am* the LORD.

[17a]'You shall not hate your brother in your heart. [b]You shall surely [1]rebuke your neighbor, and not bear sin because of him. [18a]You shall not take vengeance, nor bear any grudge against the children of your people, [b]but you shall love your neighbor as yourself: I *am* the LORD.

[19]'You shall keep My statutes. You shall not let your livestock breed with another kind. You shall not sow your field with mixed seed. Nor shall a garment of mixed linen and wool come upon you.

[20]'Whoever lies carnally with a woman who *is* [a]betrothed to a man as a concubine, and who has not at all been redeemed nor given her freedom, for this there shall be [1]scourging; *but* they shall not be put to death, because she was not free. [21]And he shall bring his trespass offering to the LORD, to the door of the tabernacle of meeting, a ram as a trespass offering. [22]The priest shall make [1]atonement for him with the ram of the trespass offering before the LORD for his sin which he has committed. And the sin which he has committed shall be forgiven him.

[23]'When you come into the land, and have planted all kinds of trees for food, then you shall count their fruit as [1]uncircumcised. Three years it shall be as uncircumcised to you. *It* shall not be eaten. [24]But in the fourth year all its fruit shall be holy, a praise to the LORD. [25]And in the fifth year you may eat its fruit, that it may yield to you its increase: I *am* the LORD your God.

[26]'You shall not eat *anything* with the blood, nor shall you practice divination or soothsaying. [27]You shall not shave around the sides of your head, nor shall you disfigure the

---

19:9 [a]Lev. 23:22;
Deut. 24:19–22

19:11 [a]Ex. 20:15,
16 [b]Jer. 9:3–5;
Eph. 4:25

19:12 [a]Ex. 20:7;
Deut. 5:11;
[Matt. 5:33–37;
James 5:12]
[b]Lev. 18:21

19:13
[a]Ex. 22:7–15,
21–27;
Mark 10:19
[b]Deut. 24:15;
Mal. 3:5;
James 5:4

19:14
[a]Deut. 27:18

19:15
[a]Deut. 16:19
[b]Ex. 23:3, 6;
Deut. 1:17; 10:17;
Ps. 82:2

19:16
[a]Prov. 11:13; 18:8;
20:19 [b]Ex. 23:7;
Deut. 27:25;
1 Kin. 21:7–19

19:17
[a][1 John 2:9,
11; 3:15]
[b]Matt. 18:15;
[Luke 17:3];
Eph. 5:11

19:18
[a][Deut. 32:35;
1 Sam. 24:12;
Rom. 12:19;
Heb. 10:30]
[b]Matt. 5:43;
19:19;
Mark 12:31;
Luke 10:27;
[Rom. 13:9;
Gal. 5:14];
James 2:8

19:20
[a]Deut. 22:23–27

19:17 [1]*reprove*   19:20 [1]*punishment*   19:22 [1]Lit. *covering*   19:23 [1]*unclean*

edges of your beard. [28]You shall not [a]make any cuttings in your flesh for the dead, nor tattoo any marks on you: I *am* the LORD.

[29a]'Do not prostitute your daughter, to cause her to be a harlot, lest the land fall into harlotry, and the land become full of wickedness.

[30]'You shall [1]keep My Sabbaths and [a]reverence My sanctuary: I *am* the LORD.

[31]'Give no regard to mediums and familiar spirits; do not seek after [a]them, to be defiled by them: I *am* the LORD your God.

[32a]'You shall [1]rise before the gray headed and honor the presence of an old man, and [b]fear your God: I *am* the LORD.

[33]'And [a]if a stranger dwells with you in your land, you shall not mistreat him. [34a]The stranger who dwells among you shall be to you as [1]one born among you, and [b]you shall love him as yourself; for you were strangers in the land of Egypt: I *am* the LORD your God.

[35]'You shall do no injustice in judgment, in measurement of length, weight, or volume. [36]You shall have [a]honest scales, honest weights, an honest ephah, and an honest hin: I *am* the LORD your God, who brought you out of the land of Egypt.

[37a]'Therefore you shall observe all My statutes and all My judgments, and perform them: I *am* the LORD.'"

PENALTIES FOR BREAKING THE LAW

20 Then the LORD spoke to Moses, saying, [2a]"Again, you shall say to the children of Israel: [b]'Whoever of the children of Israel, or of the strangers who [1]dwell in Israel, who gives *any* of his descendants to Molech, he shall surely be put to death. The people of the land shall [c]stone him with stones. [3a]I will set My face against that man, and will [1]cut him off from his people, because he has given *some* of his descendants to Molech, to defile My sanctuary and profane My holy name. [4]And if the people of the land should in any way [1]hide their eyes from the man, when he gives *some* of his descendants to Molech, and they do not kill him, [5]then I will set My face against that man and against his family; and I will cut him off from his people, and all who prostitute themselves with him to commit harlotry with Molech.

[6]'And [a]the person who turns to mediums and familiar spirits, to prostitute himself with them, I will set My face against that person and cut him off from his people. [7a]Consecrate[1] yourselves therefore, and be holy, for I *am* the LORD your God. [8]And you shall keep [a]My statutes, and perform them: [b]I *am* the LORD who [1]sanctifies you.

[9]'For [a]everyone who curses his father or his mother shall surely be put to death. He has cursed his father or his mother. [b]His blood *shall be* upon him.

[10a]'The man who commits adultery with *another* man's wife, *he* who commits adultery with his neighbor's wife, the adulterer and the adulteress, shall surely be put to death. [11]The man who lies with his [a]father's wife has uncovered his father's nakedness; both of them shall surely be put to

---

19:28
[a]1 Kin. 18:28;
Jer. 16:6

19:29 [a]Lev. 21:9;
Deut. 22:21;
23:17, 18

19:30 [a]Lev. 26:2;
Eccl. 5:1

19:31 [a]Lev. 20:6,
27; Deut. 18:11;
1 Sam. 28:3;
Is. 8:19

19:32
[a]Prov. 23:22;
Lam. 5:12;
1 Tim. 5:1
[b]Lev. 19:14

19:33 [a]Ex. 22:21;
Deut. 24:17, 18

19:34 [a]Ex. 12:48
[b]Deut. 10:19

19:36
[a]Deut. 25:13–15;
Prov. 20:10

19:37 [a]Lev. 18:4,
5; Deut. 4:5, 6;
5:1; 6:25

20:2 [a]Lev. 18:2
[b]Lev. 18:21;
2 Kin. 23:10;
2 Chr. 33:6;
Jer. 7:31
[c]Deut. 17:2–5

20:3 [a]Lev. 17:10

20:6 [a]Lev. 19:31;
1 Sam. 28:7–25

20:7 [a]Lev. 19:2;
Heb. 12:14

20:8 [a]Lev. 19:19,
37 [b]Ex. 31:13;
Deut. 14:2;
Ezek. 37:28

20:9 [a]Ex. 21:17;
Deut. 27:16;
Prov. 20:20;
Matt. 15:4
[b]2 Sam. 1:16

20:10
[a]Ex. 20:14;
Lev. 18:20;
Deut. 5:18;
22:22;
John 8:4, 5

20:11
[a]Lev. 18:7, 8;
Deut. 27:20

19:30 [1]*observe*   19:32 [1]*rise to give honor*   19:34 [1]*native among you*
20:2 [1]As resident aliens   20:3 [1]Put him to death   20:4 [1]*disregard*
20:7 [1]*Set yourselves apart* for the LORD   20:8 [1]*sets you apart*

death. Their blood *shall be* upon them. [12]If a man lies with his [a]daughter-in-law, both of them shall surely be put to death. They have committed perversion. Their blood *shall be* upon them. [13a]If a man lies with a male as he lies with a woman, both of them have committed an abomination. They shall surely be put to death. Their blood *shall be* upon them. [14]If a man marries a woman and her [a]mother, it *is* wickedness. They shall be burned with fire, both he and they, that there may be no wickedness among you. [15]If a man mates with an [a]animal, he shall surely be put to death, and you shall kill the animal. [16]If a woman approaches any animal and mates with it, you shall kill the woman and the animal. They shall surely be put to death. Their blood *is* upon them.

[17]'If a man takes his [a]sister, his father's daughter or his mother's daughter, and sees her nakedness and she sees his nakedness, it *is* a wicked thing. And they shall be [1]cut off in the sight of their people. He has uncovered his sister's nakedness. He shall bear his [2]guilt. [18a]If a man lies with a woman during her [1]sickness and uncovers her nakedness, he has [2]exposed her flow, and she has uncovered the flow of her blood. Both of them shall be [3]cut off from their people.

[19]'You shall not uncover the nakedness of your [a]mother's sister nor of your [b]father's sister, for that would uncover his near of kin. They shall bear their guilt. [20]If a man lies with his [a]uncle's wife, he has uncovered his uncle's nakedness. They shall bear their sin; they shall die childless. [21]If a man takes his [a]brother's wife, it *is* an [1]unclean thing. He has uncovered his brother's nakedness. They shall be childless.

[22]'You shall therefore keep all My [a]statutes and all My judgments, and perform them, that the land where I am bringing you to dwell [b]may not vomit you out. [23a]And you shall not walk in the statutes of the nation which I am casting out before you; for they commit all these things, and [b]therefore I abhor them. [24]But [a]I have said to you, "You shall inherit their land, and I will give it to you to possess, a land flowing with milk and honey." I *am* the LORD your God, [b]who has separated you from the peoples. [25a]You shall therefore distinguish between clean animals and unclean, between unclean birds and clean, [b]and you shall not make yourselves [1]abominable by beast or by bird, or by any kind of living thing that creeps on the ground, which I have separated from you as [2]unclean. [26]And you shall be holy to Me, [a]for I the LORD *am* holy, and have separated you from the peoples, that you should be Mine.

[27a]'A man or a woman who is a medium, or who has familiar spirits, shall surely be put to death; they shall stone them with stones. Their blood *shall be* upon them.' "

REGULATIONS FOR CONDUCT OF PRIESTS
(cf. Ezek. 44:15–31)

21 And the LORD said to Moses, "Speak to the priests, the sons of Aaron, and say to them: [a]'None shall defile himself for the dead among his people, [2]except for his relatives who are nearest to him: his mother, his father, his son, his

20:17 [1]Put to death   [2]iniquity   20:18 [1]Or *customary impurity*   [2]Lit. *made bare*   [3]*put to death*   20:21 [1]*indecent, impure*   20:25 [1]*detestable* or *loathsome*   [2]*defiled*

daughter, and his brother; ³also his virgin sister who is near to him, who has had no husband, for her he may defile himself. ⁴*Otherwise* he shall not defile himself, *being* a ¹chief man among his people, to profane himself.

⁵ᵃ'They shall not make any bald *place* on their heads, nor shall they shave the edges of their beards nor make any cuttings in their flesh. ⁶They shall be ᵃholy to their God and not profane the name of their God, for they offer the offerings of the LORD made by fire, *and* the ᵇbread of their God; ᶜtherefore they shall be holy. ⁷ᵃThey shall not take a wife *who is* a harlot or a defiled woman, nor shall they take a woman ᵇdivorced from her husband; for ¹*the priest* is holy to his God. ⁸Therefore you shall ¹consecrate him, for he offers the bread of your God. He shall be holy to you, for ᵃI the LORD, who ᵇsanctify you, *am* holy. ⁹The daughter of any priest, if she profanes herself by playing the harlot, she profanes her father. She shall be ᵃburned with fire.

¹⁰'*He who is* the high priest among his brethren, on whose head the anointing oil was ᵃpoured and who is consecrated to wear the garments, shall not ᵇuncover¹ his head nor tear his clothes; ¹¹nor shall he go ᵃnear any dead body, nor defile himself for his father or his mother; ¹²ᵃnor shall he go out of the sanctuary, nor profane the sanctuary of his God; for the ᵇconsecration of the anointing oil of his God *is* upon him: I *am* the LORD. ¹³And he shall take a wife in her virginity. ¹⁴A widow or a divorced woman or a defiled woman *or* a harlot— these he shall not marry; but he shall take a virgin of his own people as wife. ¹⁵Nor shall he profane his posterity among his people, for I the LORD sanctify him.'"

¹⁶And the LORD spoke to Moses, saying, ¹⁷"Speak to Aaron, saying: 'No man of your descendants in *succeeding* generations, who has *any* defect, may approach to offer the bread of his God. ¹⁸For any man who has a ᵃdefect shall not approach: a man blind or lame, who has a marred *face* or any *limb* ᵇtoo long, ¹⁹a man who has a broken foot or broken hand, ²⁰or is a hunchback or a dwarf, or *a man* who has a defect in his eye, or eczema or scab, or is a eunuch. ²¹No man of the descendants of Aaron the priest, who has a defect, shall come near to offer the offerings made by fire to the LORD. He has a defect; he shall not come near to offer the bread of his God. ²²He may eat the bread of his God, *both* the most holy and the holy; ²³only he shall not go near the ᵃveil or approach the altar, because he has a defect, lest ᵇhe profane My sanctuaries; for I the LORD sanctify them.'"

²⁴And Moses told *it* to Aaron and his sons, and to all the children of Israel.

22

Then the LORD spoke to Moses, saying, ²"Speak to Aaron and his sons, that they ᵃseparate¹ themselves from the holy things of the children of Israel, and that they ᵇdo not profane My holy name *by* what they ᶜdedicate to Me: I *am* the LORD. ³Say to them: 'Whoever of all your descendants throughout your generations, who goes near the holy things which the children of Israel dedicate to the LORD, ᵃwhile he has ¹uncleanness upon him, that person shall be cut off from My presence: I *am* the LORD.

21:5 ᵃLev. 19:27; Deut. 14:1; Ezek. 44:20

21:6 ᵃEx. 22:31 ᵇLev. 3:11 ᶜIs. 52:11

21:7 ᵃEzek. 44:22 ᵇDeut. 24:1, 2

21:8 ᵃLev. 11:44, 45 ᵇLev. 8:12, 30

21:9 ᵃDeut. 22:21

21:10 ᵃLev. 8:12 ᵇLev. 10:6, 7

21:11 ᵃNum. 19:14

21:12 ᵃLev. 10:7 ᵇEx. 29:6, 7

21:18 ᵃLev. 22:19–25 ᵇLev. 22:23

21:23 ᵃLev. 16:2 ᵇLev. 21:12

22:2 ᵃNum. 6:3 ᵇLev. 18:21 ᶜEx. 28:38; Lev. 16:19; 25:10; Num. 18:32; Deut. 15:19

22:3 ᵃLev. 7:20, 21; Num. 19:13

21:4 ¹Lit. *master* or *husband*   21:7 ¹Lit. *he*   21:8 ¹*set him apart*   21:10 ¹In mourning   22:2 ¹*keep themselves apart from*   22:3 ¹*defilement*

⁴'Whatever man of the descendants of Aaron, who *is* a ᵃleper or has ᵇa discharge, shall not eat the holy offerings ᶜuntil he is clean. And ᵈwhoever touches anything made unclean *by* a corpse, or ᵉa man who has had an emission of semen, ⁵or ᵃwhoever touches any creeping thing by which he would be made unclean, or ᵇany person by whom he would become unclean, whatever his uncleanness may be— ⁶the person who has touched any such thing shall be unclean until evening, and shall not eat the holy *offerings* unless he ᵃwashes his body with water. ⁷And when the sun goes down he shall be clean; and afterward he may eat the holy *offerings*, because ᵃit *is* his food. ⁸ᵃWhatever dies *naturally* or is torn *by beasts* he shall not eat, to defile himself with it: I *am* the LORD.

⁹'They shall therefore keep ᵃMy ¹ordinance, ᵇlest they bear sin for it and die thereby, if they profane it: I the LORD sanctify them.

¹⁰ᵃ'No outsider shall eat the holy *offering;* one who ¹dwells with the priest, or a hired servant, shall not eat the holy thing. ¹¹But if the priest ᵃbuys a person with his money, he may eat it; and one who is born in his house may eat his food. ¹²If the priest's daughter is married to an outsider, she may not eat of the holy offerings. ¹³But if the priest's daughter is a widow or divorced, and has no child, and has returned to her father's house as in her youth, she may eat her father's food; but no outsider shall eat it.

¹⁴'And if a man eats the holy *offering* unintentionally, then he shall restore a holy *offering* to the priest, and add one-fifth to it. ¹⁵They shall not profane the ᵃholy *offerings* of the children of Israel, which they offer to the LORD, ¹⁶or allow them to bear the guilt of trespass when they eat their holy *offerings;* for I the LORD sanctify them.'"

OFFERINGS ACCEPTED AND NOT ACCEPTED

¹⁷And the LORD spoke to Moses, saying, ¹⁸"Speak to Aaron and his sons, and to all the children of Israel, and say to them: ᵃ'Whatever man of the house of Israel, or of the strangers in Israel, who ¹offers his sacrifice for any of his vows or for any of his freewill offerings, which they offer to the LORD as a burnt offering— ¹⁹ᵃ*you shall offer* of your own free will a male without blemish from the cattle, from the sheep, or from the goats. ²⁰ᵃWhatever has a defect, you shall not offer, for it shall not be acceptable on your behalf. ²¹And ᵃwhoever offers a sacrifice of a peace offering to the LORD, ᵇto fulfill *his* vow, or a freewill offering from the cattle or the sheep, it must be perfect to be accepted; there shall be no defect in it. ²²ᵃThose *that are* blind or broken or maimed, or have an ¹ulcer or eczema or scabs, you shall not offer to the LORD, nor make ᵇan offering by fire of them on the altar to the LORD. ²³Either a bull or a lamb that has any limb ᵃtoo long or too short you may offer *as* a freewill offering, but for a vow it shall not be accepted.

²⁴'You shall not offer to the LORD what is bruised or crushed, or torn or cut; nor shall you make *any offering of them* in your land. ²⁵Nor ᵃfrom a foreigner's hand shall you offer any of these as ᵇthe bread of your God, because their

22:4 ᵃNum. 5:2
ᵇLev. 15:2
ᶜLev. 14:2; 15:13
ᵈLev. 11:24–28, 39, 40; Num. 19:11
ᵉLev. 15:16, 17

22:5 ᵃLev. 11:23–28
ᵇLev. 15:7, 19

22:6 ᵃLev. 15:5

22:7 ᵃLev. 21:22; Num. 18:11, 13

22:8 ᵃEx. 22:31; Lev. 7:24; 11:39, 40; 17:15; Ezek. 44:31

22:9 ᵃLev. 18:30
ᵇEx. 28:43; Lev. 22:16; Num. 18:22

22:10 ᵃEx. 29:33; Lev. 22:13; Num. 3:10

22:11 ᵃEx. 12:44

22:15 ᵃNum. 18:32

22:18 ᵃLev. 1:2, 3, 10

22:19 ᵃLev. 1:3; Deut. 15:21

22:20 ᵃDeut. 15:21; 17:1; Mal. 1:8, 14; [Eph. 5:27; Heb. 9:14; 1 Pet. 1:19]

22:21 ᵃLev. 3:1, 6
ᵇNum. 15:3, 8; Ps. 61:8; 65:1; Eccl. 5:4, 5

22:22 ᵃLev. 22:20; Mal. 1:8
ᵇLev. 1:9, 13; 3:3, 5

22:23 ᵃLev. 21:18

22:25 ᵃNum. 15:15, 16
ᵇLev. 21:6, 17

22:9 ¹*charge*   **22:10** ¹As a visitor   **22:18** ¹*brings his offering*
22:22 ¹*running sore*

^ccorruption *is* in them, *and* defects *are* in them. They shall not be accepted on your behalf.' "

²⁶And the LORD spoke to Moses, saying: ^{27a}"When a bull or a sheep or a goat is born, it shall be seven days with its mother; and from the eighth day and thereafter it shall be accepted as an offering made by fire to the LORD. ²⁸*Whether it is* a cow or ewe, do not kill both her ^aand her young on the same day. ²⁹And when you ^aoffer a sacrifice of thanksgiving to the LORD, offer *it* of your own free will. ³⁰On the same day it shall be eaten; you shall leave ^anone of it until morning: I *am* the LORD.

^{31a}"Therefore you shall keep My commandments, and perform them: I *am* the LORD. ^{32a}You shall not profane My holy name, but ^bI will be ¹hallowed among the children of Israel. I *am* the LORD who ^csanctifies you, ^{33a}who brought you out of the land of Egypt, to be your God: I *am* the LORD."

FEASTS OF THE LORD

23 And the LORD spoke to Moses, saying, ²"Speak to the children of Israel, and say to them: 'The feasts of the LORD, which you shall proclaim *to be* ^aholy convocations, these *are* My feasts.

THE SABBATH

^{3a}'Six days shall work be done, but the seventh day *is* a Sabbath of solemn rest, a holy convocation. You shall do no work *on it;* it *is* the Sabbath of the LORD in all your dwellings.

THE PASSOVER AND UNLEAVENED BREAD
(Num. 28:16–25)

^{4a}'These *are* the feasts of the LORD, holy convocations which you shall proclaim at their appointed times. ^{5a}On the fourteenth *day* of the first month at twilight *is* the LORD's Passover. ⁶And on the fifteenth day of the same month *is* the Feast of Unleavened Bread to the LORD; seven days you must eat unleavened bread. ^{7a}On the first day you shall have a holy convocation; you shall do no ¹customary work on it. ⁸But you shall offer an offering made by fire to the LORD for seven days. The seventh day *shall be* a holy convocation; you shall do no customary work *on it.*' "

THE FEAST OF FIRSTFRUITS

⁹And the LORD spoke to Moses, saying, ¹⁰"Speak to the children of Israel, and say to them: ^a'When you come into the land which I give to you, and reap its harvest, then you shall bring a sheaf of ^bthe firstfruits of your harvest to the priest. ¹¹He shall ^awave the sheaf before the LORD, to be accepted on your behalf; on the day after the Sabbath the priest shall wave it. ¹²And you shall offer on that day, when you wave the sheaf, a male lamb of the first year, without blemish, as a burnt offering to the LORD. ¹³Its grain offering *shall be* two-tenths *of an ephah* of fine flour mixed with oil, an offering made by fire to the LORD, for a ¹sweet aroma; and its drink offering *shall be* of wine, one-fourth of a hin. ¹⁴You shall eat neither bread nor parched grain nor fresh grain until the

22:25 ^cMal. 1:14

22:27 ^aEx. 22:30

22:28
^aDeut. 22:6, 7

22:29 ^aLev. 7:12;
Ps. 107:22;
116:17; Amos 4:5

22:30 ^aLev. 7:15

22:31
^aLev. 19:37;
Num. 15:40;
Deut. 4:40

22:32 ^aLev. 18:21
^bLev. 10:3;
Matt. 6:9;
Luke 11:2
^cLev. 20:8

22:33
^aLev. 19:36, 37;
Num. 15:40;
Deut. 4:40

23:2 ^aEx. 12:16

23:3 ^aEx. 20:9;
23:12; 31:15;
Lev. 19:3;
Deut. 5:13, 14;
Luke 13:14

23:4
^aEx. 23:14–16;
Lev. 23:2, 37

23:5
^aEx. 12:1–28;
Num. 9:1–5;
28:16–25;
Deut. 16:1–8;
Josh. 5:10

23:7 ^aEx. 12:16;
Num. 28:18, 25

23:10
^aEx. 23:19; 34:26
^b[Rom. 11:16];
James 1:18;
Rev. 14:4

23:11 ^aEx. 29:24

22:32 ¹*treated as holy* 23:7 ¹*occupational* 23:13 ¹*pleasing*

same day that you have brought an offering to your God; *it shall be* a statute forever throughout your generations in all your dwellings.

THE FEAST OF WEEKS
(Ex. 34:22; Num. 28:26–31; Deut. 16:9, 10)

15'And you shall count for yourselves from the day after the Sabbath, from the day that you brought the sheaf of the wave offering: seven Sabbaths shall be completed. 16Count ^afifty days to the day after the seventh Sabbath; then you shall offer ^ba new grain offering to the LORD. 17You shall bring from your dwellings two wave *loaves* of two-tenths *of an ephah.* They shall be of fine flour; they shall be baked with leaven. *They are* ^athe firstfruits to the LORD. 18And you shall offer with the bread seven lambs of the first year, without blemish, one young bull, and two rams. They shall be *as* a burnt offering to the LORD, with their grain offering and their drink offerings, an offering made by fire for a sweet aroma to the LORD. 19Then you shall sacrifice ^aone kid of the goats as a sin offering, and two male lambs of the first year as a sacrifice of a ^bpeace offering. 20The priest shall wave them with the bread of the firstfruits *as* a wave offering before the LORD, with the two lambs. ^aThey shall be holy to the LORD for the priest. 21And you shall proclaim on the same day *that* it is a holy convocation to you. You shall do no customary work *on it. It shall be* a statute forever in all your dwellings throughout your generations.

22a'When you reap the harvest of your land, you shall not wholly reap the corners of your field when you reap, nor shall you gather any gleaning from your harvest. You shall leave them for the poor and for the stranger: I *am* the LORD your God.'"

THE FEAST OF TRUMPETS
(Num. 29:1–6)

23Then the LORD spoke to Moses, saying, 24"Speak to the children of Israel, saying: 'In the ^aseventh month, on the first *day* of the month, you shall have a sabbath-*rest,* ^ba memorial of blowing of trumpets, a holy convocation. 25You shall do no customary work *on it;* and you shall offer an offering made by fire to the LORD.'"

THE DAY OF ATONEMENT
(Num. 29:7–11)

26And the LORD spoke to Moses, saying: 27a"Also the tenth *day* of this seventh month *shall be* the Day of Atonement. It shall be a holy convocation for you; you shall afflict your souls, and offer an offering made by fire to the LORD. 28And you shall do no work on that same day, for it *is* the Day of Atonement, ^ato make atonement for you before the LORD your God. 29For any person who is not ^aafflicted *in soul* on that same day ^bshall be cut off from his people. 30And any person who does any work on that same day, ^athat person I will destroy from among his people. 31You shall do no manner of work; *it shall be* a statute forever throughout your generations in all your dwellings. 32It *shall be* to you a sabbath of

23:16 ^aActs 2:1
^bNum. 28:26

23:17
^aEx. 23:16, 19;
Num. 15:17–21

23:19
^aLev. 4:23, 28;
Num. 28:30;
[2 Cor. 5:21]
^bLev. 3:1

23:20
^aLev. 14:13;
Num. 18:12;
Deut. 18:4

23:22 ^aLev. 19:9,
10; Deut. 24:19–
22; Ruth 2:2, 15

23:24
^aNum. 29:1
^bLev. 25:9

23:27
^aLev. 16:1–34;
25:9; Num. 29:7

23:28
^aLev. 16:34

23:29 ^aIs. 22:12;
Jer. 31:9;
Ezek. 7:16
^bGen. 17:14;
Lev. 13:46;
Num. 5:2

23:30
^aLev. 20:3–6

solemn rest, and you shall ¹afflict your souls; on the ninth *day* of the month at evening, from evening to evening, you shall ²celebrate your sabbath."

THE FEAST OF TABERNACLES
(Num. 29:12–40; Deut. 16:13–17)

³³Then the LORD spoke to Moses, saying, ³⁴"Speak to the children of Israel, saying: ᵃ'The fifteenth day of this seventh month *shall be* the Feast of Tabernacles *for* seven days to the LORD. ³⁵On the first day *there shall be* a holy convocation. You shall do no customary work *on it.* ³⁶*For* seven days you shall offer an ᵃoffering made by fire to the LORD. ᵇOn the eighth day you shall have a holy convocation, and you shall offer an offering made by fire to the LORD. It *is* a ᶜsacred¹ assembly, *and* you shall do no customary work *on it.*

³⁷ᵃ'These *are* the feasts of the LORD which you shall proclaim *to be* holy convocations, to offer an offering made by fire to the LORD, a burnt offering and a grain offering, a sacrifice and drink offerings, everything on its day— ³⁸ᵃbesides the Sabbaths of the LORD, besides your gifts, besides all your vows, and besides all your freewill offerings which you give to the LORD.

³⁹'Also on the fifteenth day of the seventh month, when you have ᵃgathered in the fruit of the land, you shall keep the feast of the LORD *for* seven days; on the first day *there shall be* a sabbath-*rest,* and on the eighth day a sabbath-*rest.* ⁴⁰And ᵃyou shall take for yourselves on the first day the ¹fruit of beautiful trees, branches of palm trees, the boughs of leafy trees, and willows of the brook; ᵇand you shall rejoice before the LORD your God for seven days. ⁴¹ᵃYou shall keep it as a feast to the LORD for seven days in the year. *It shall be* a statute forever in your generations. You shall celebrate it in the seventh month. ⁴²ᵃYou shall dwell in ¹booths for seven days. ᵇAll who are native Israelites shall dwell in booths, ⁴³ᵃthat your generations may ᵇknow that I made the children of Israel dwell in booths when ᶜI brought them out of the land of Egypt: I *am* the LORD your God.' "

⁴⁴So Moses ᵃdeclared to the children of Israel the feasts of the LORD.

CARE OF THE TABERNACLE LAMPS
(Ex. 27:20, 21)

24 Then the LORD spoke to Moses, saying: ²ᵃ"Command the children of Israel that they bring to you pure oil of pressed olives for the light, to make the lamps burn continually. ³Outside the veil of the Testimony, in the tabernacle of meeting, Aaron shall be in charge of it from evening until morning before the LORD continually; *it shall be* a statute forever in your generations. ⁴He shall ¹be in charge of the lamps on ᵃthe pure *gold* lampstand before the LORD continually.

THE BREAD OF THE TABERNACLE

⁵"And you shall take fine flour and bake twelve ᵃcakes with it. Two-tenths *of an ephah* shall be in each cake. ⁶You shall set

23:34
ᵃEx. 23:16;
Num. 29:12;
Deut. 16:13–
16; Ezra 3:4;
Neh. 8:14;
Zech. 14:16–19;
John 7:2

23:36
ᵃNum. 29:12–34
ᵇNum. 29:35–
38; Neh. 8:18;
John 7:37
ᶜDeut. 16:8;
2 Chr. 7:8

23:37
ᵃLev. 23:2, 4

23:38
ᵃNum. 29:39

23:39
ᵃEx. 23:16;
Deut. 16:13

23:40
ᵃNeh. 8:15
ᵇDeut. 12:7;
16:14, 15

23:41
ᵃNum. 29:12;
Neh. 8:18

23:42 ᵃ[Is. 4:6]
ᵇNeh. 8:14–16

23:43 ᵃEx. 13:14;
Deut. 31:13;
Ps. 78:5
ᵇEx. 10:2
ᶜLev. 22:33

23:44 ᵃLev. 23:2

24:2
ᵃEx. 27:20, 21

24:4 ᵃEx. 25:31;
31:8; 37:17

24:5 ᵃEx. 25:30;
39:36; 40:23

23:32 ¹*humble yourselves*   ²*observe your sabbath*   23:36 ¹*solemn*
23:40 ¹*foliage*   23:42 ¹*tabernacles;* shelters made of boughs
24:4 ¹*arrange* or set in order

them in two rows, six in a row, [a]on the pure *gold* table before the LORD. [7]And you shall put pure frankincense on *each* row, that it may be on the bread for a [a]memorial, an offering made by fire to the LORD. [8a]Every Sabbath he shall set it in order before the LORD continually, *being taken* from the children of Israel by an everlasting covenant. [9]And [a]it shall be for Aaron and his sons, [b]and they shall eat it in a holy place; for it *is* most holy to him from the offerings of the LORD made by fire, by a perpetual statute."

THE PENALTY FOR BLASPHEMY

[10]Now the son of an Israelite woman, whose father *was* an Egyptian, went out among the children of Israel; and this Israelite *woman's* son and a man of Israel fought each other in the camp. [11]And the Israelite woman's son [a]blasphemed the name *of the LORD* and [b]cursed; and so they [c]brought him to Moses. (His mother's name *was* Shelomith the daughter of Dibri, of the tribe of Dan.) [12]Then they [a]put him [1]in custody, [b]that [2]the mind of the LORD might be shown to them.

[13]And the LORD spoke to Moses, saying, [14]"Take outside the camp him who has cursed; then let all who heard *him* [a]lay their hands on his head, and let all the congregation stone him.

[15]"Then you shall speak to the children of Israel, saying: 'Whoever curses his God [a]shall [1]bear his sin. [16]And whoever [a]blasphemes the name of the LORD shall surely be put to death. All the congregation shall certainly stone him, the stranger as well as him who is born in the land. When he blasphemes the name *of the LORD*, he shall be put to death.

[17a]'Whoever kills any man shall surely be put to death. [18a]Whoever kills an animal shall make it good, animal for animal.

[19]'If a man causes disfigurement of his neighbor, as [a]he has done, so shall it be done to him— [20]fracture for [a]fracture, [b]eye for eye, tooth for tooth; as he has caused disfigurement of a man, so shall it be done to him. [21]And whoever kills an animal shall restore it; but whoever kills a man shall be put to death. [22]You shall have [a]the[1] same law for the stranger and for one from your own country; for I *am* the LORD your God.'"

[23]Then Moses spoke to the children of Israel; and they took outside the camp him who had cursed, and stoned him with stones. So the children of Israel did as the LORD commanded Moses.

THE SABBATH OF THE SEVENTH YEAR
(Deut. 15:1–11)

25 And the LORD spoke to Moses on Mount [a]Sinai, saying, [2]"Speak to the children of Israel, and say to them: 'When you come into the land which I give you, then the land shall [a]keep a sabbath to the LORD. [3]Six years you shall sow your field, and six years you shall prune your vineyard, and gather its fruit; [4]but in the [a]seventh year there shall be a sabbath of solemn [b]rest for the land, a sabbath to the LORD. You shall neither sow your field nor prune your vineyard. [5a]What

24:6 [a]Ex. 25:23, 24; 1 Kin. 7:48; 2 Chr. 4:19; 13:11; Heb. 9:2

24:7 [a]Lev. 2:2, 9, 16

24:8 [a]Num. 4:7; 1 Chr. 9:32; 2 Chr. 2:4; Matt. 12:4, 5

24:9 [a]1 Sam. 21:6; Matt. 12:4; Mark 2:26; Luke 6:4 [b]Ex. 29:33; Lev. 8:31

24:11 [a]Ex. 22:28 [b]Job 1:5, 11, 22; Is. 8:21 [c]Ex. 18:22, 26

24:12 [a]Num. 15:34 [b]Num. 27:5

24:14 [a]Deut. 13:9; 17:7

24:15 [a]Lev. 20:17; Num. 9:13

24:16 [a]Ex. 20:7; 1 Kin. 21:10, 13; [Matt. 12:31; Mark 3:28, 29]

24:17 [a]Gen. 9:6; Ex. 21:12; Num. 35:30, 31; Deut. 19:11, 12; 27:24

24:18 [a]Lev. 24:21

24:19 [a]Ex. 21:24

24:20 [a]Ex. 21:23; Deut. 19:21 [b][Matt. 5:38, 39]

24:22 [a]Ex. 12:49; Lev. 19:33–37; Num. 9:14; 15:15, 16, 29

25:1 [a]Lev. 26:46

25:2 [a]Lev. 26:34, 35

25:4 [a]Deut. 15:1; Neh. 10:31 [b][Heb. 4:9]

25:5 [a]2 Kin. 19:29

24:12 [1]*under guard* [2]Lit. *it might be declared to them from the mouth of the LORD* 24:15 [1]*be responsible for* 24:22 [1]*one standard of judgment*

grows of its own accord of your harvest you shall not reap, nor gather the grapes of your untended vine, *for* it is a year of rest for the land. 6And the sabbath *produce* of the land shall be food for you: for you, your male and female servants, your hired man, and the stranger who dwells with you, 7for your livestock and the beasts that *are* in your land—all its produce shall be for food.

THE YEAR OF JUBILEE

8'And you shall count seven sabbaths of years for yourself, seven times seven years; and the time of the seven sabbaths of years shall be to you forty-nine years. 9Then you shall cause the trumpet of the Jubilee to sound on the tenth *day* of the seventh month; aon the Day of Atonement you shall make the trumpet to sound throughout all your land. 10And you shall consecrate the fiftieth year, and aproclaim liberty throughout *all* the land to all its inhabitants. It shall be a Jubilee for you; band each of you shall return to his possession, and each of you shall return to his family. 11That fiftieth year shall be a Jubilee to you; in it ayou shall neither sow nor reap what grows of its own accord, nor gather *the grapes* of your untended vine. 12For it *is* the Jubilee; it shall be holy to you; ayou shall eat its produce from the field.

13a'In this Year of Jubilee, each of you shall return to his possession. 14And if you sell anything to your neighbor or buy from your neighbor's hand, you shall not aoppress one another. 15aAccording to the number of years after the Jubilee you shall buy from your neighbor, and according to the number of years of crops he shall sell to you. 16According to the multitude of years you shall increase its price, and according to the fewer number of years you shall diminish its price; for he sells to you *according* to the number *of the years* of the crops. 17Therefore ayou shall not 1oppress one another, bbut you shall fear your God; for I *am* the LORD your God.

PROVISIONS FOR THE SEVENTH YEAR

18a'So you shall observe My statutes and keep My judgments, and perform them; band you will dwell in the land in safety. 19Then the land will yield its fruit, and ayou will eat your fill, and dwell there in safety.

20'And if you say, a"What shall we eat in the seventh year, since bwe shall not sow nor gather in our produce?" 21Then I will acommand My blessing on you in the bsixth year, and it will bring forth produce enough for three years. 22aAnd you shall sow in the eighth year, and eat bold produce until the ninth year; until its produce comes in, you shall eat *of* the old *harvest.*

REDEMPTION OF PROPERTY

23'The land shall not be sold permanently, for athe land *is* Mine; for you *are* bstrangers and sojourners with Me. 24And in all the land of your possession you shall grant redemption of the land.

25a'If one of your brethren becomes poor, and has sold *some* of his possession, and if bhis redeeming relative comes to redeem it, then he may redeem what his brother sold. 26Or

25:17 1*mistreat*

25:9
aLev. 23:24, 27

25:10
aIs. 61:2; 63:4;
Jer. 34:8, 15,
17; [Luke 4:19]
bLev. 25:13, 28,
54; Num. 36:4

25:11 aLev. 25:5

25:12
aLev. 25:6, 7

25:13
aLev. 25:10;
27:24;
Num. 36:4

25:14 aLev. 19:13

25:15
aLev. 27:18, 23

25:17
aLev. 25:14;
Prov. 14:31;
22:22; Jer. 7:5,
6; 1 Thess. 4:6
bLev. 19:14, 32;
25:43

25:18 aLev. 19:37
bLev. 26:5;
Deut. 12:10;
Ps. 4:8; Jer. 23:6

25:19 aLev. 26:5;
Ezek. 34:25

25:20
aMatt. 6:25, 31
bLev. 25:4, 5

25:21
aDeut. 28:8
bEx. 16:29

25:22
a2 Kin. 19:29
bLev. 26:10;
Josh. 5:11

25:23 aEx. 19:5;
2 Chr. 7:20
bGen. 23:4;
Ex. 6:4;
1 Chr. 29:15;
Ps. 39:12;
Heb. 11:13;
1 Pet. 2:11

25:25
aRuth 2:20; 4:4,
6 bNum. 5:8;
Ruth 3:2, 9, 12;
[Job 19:25];
Jer. 32:7, 8

if the man has no one to redeem it, but he himself becomes able to redeem it, ²⁷then ^alet him count the years since its sale, and restore the remainder to the man to whom he sold it, that he may return to his possession. ²⁸But if he is not able to have *it* restored to himself, then what was sold shall remain in the hand of him who bought it until the Year of Jubilee; ^aand in the Jubilee it shall be released, and he shall return to his possession.

²⁹'If a man sells a house in a walled city, then he may redeem it within a whole year after it is sold; *within* a full year he may redeem it. ³⁰But if it is not redeemed within the space of a full year, then the house in the walled city shall belong permanently to him who bought it, throughout his generations. It shall not be released in the Jubilee. ³¹However the houses of villages which have no wall around them shall be counted as the fields of the country. They may be redeemed, and they shall be released in the Jubilee. ³²Nevertheless ^athe cities of the Levites, *and* the houses in the cities of their possession, the Levites may redeem at any time. ³³And if a man purchases a house from the Levites, then the house that was sold in the city of his possession shall be released in the Jubilee; for the houses in the cities of the Levites *are* their possession among the children of Israel. ³⁴But ^athe field of the common-land of their cities may not be ^bsold, for it *is* their perpetual possession.

LENDING TO THE POOR

³⁵'If one of your brethren becomes poor, and ¹falls into poverty among you, then you shall ^ahelp him, like a stranger or a sojourner, that he may live with you. ^{36a}Take no usury or interest from him; but ^bfear your God, that your brother may live with you. ³⁷You shall not lend him your money for usury, nor lend him your food at a profit. ^{38a}I *am* the LORD your God, who brought you out of the land of Egypt, to give you the land of Canaan *and* to be your God.

THE LAW CONCERNING SLAVERY

³⁹'And if *one of* your brethren *who dwells* by you becomes poor, and sells himself to you, you shall not compel him to serve as a slave. ⁴⁰As a hired servant *and* a sojourner he shall be with you, *and* shall serve you until the Year of Jubilee. ⁴¹And *then* he shall depart from you—he and his children ^awith him—and shall return to his own family. He shall return to the possession of his fathers. ⁴²For they *are* ^aMy servants, whom I brought out of the land of Egypt; they shall not be sold as slaves. ^{43a}You shall not rule over him ^bwith ¹rigor, but you ^cshall fear your God. ⁴⁴And as for your male and female slaves whom you may have—from the nations that are around you, from them you may buy male and female slaves. ⁴⁵Moreover you may buy ^athe children of the strangers who dwell among you, and their families who are with you, which they beget in your land; and they shall become your property. ⁴⁶And ^ayou may take them as an inheritance for your children after you, to inherit *them as* a possession; they shall be your permanent slaves. But regarding your brethren, the children of Israel, you shall not rule over one another with rigor.

25:27
^aLev. 25:50–52

25:28
^aLev. 25:10, 13

25:32
^aNum. 35:1–8;
Josh. 21:2

25:34
^aNum. 35:2–5
^bActs 4:36, 37

25:35
^aDeut. 15:7–11;
24:14, 15;
Luke 6:35;
1 John 3:17

25:36
^aEx. 22:25;
Deut. 23:19, 20
^bNeh. 5:9

25:38
^aLev. 11:45;
22:32, 33

25:41 ^aEx. 21:3

25:42
^aLev. 25:55;
[Rom. 6:22;
1 Cor. 7:22, 23]

25:43 ^aEph. 6:9;
Col. 4:1 ^bEx. 1:13,
14; Lev. 25:46,
53; Ezek. 34:4
^cEx. 1:17;
Deut. 25:18;
Mal. 3:5

25:45
^a[Is. 56:3, 6, 7]

25:46 ^aIs. 14:2

25:35 ¹Lit. *his hand fails*   **25:43** ¹*severity*

⁴⁷'Now if a sojourner or stranger close to you becomes rich, and *one of* your brethren *who dwells* by him becomes poor, and sells himself to the stranger *or* sojourner close to you, or to a member of the stranger's family, ⁴⁸after he is sold he may be redeemed again. One of his brothers may redeem him; ⁴⁹or his uncle or his uncle's son may redeem him; or *anyone* who is near of kin to him in his family may redeem him; or if he is able he may redeem himself. ⁵⁰Thus he shall reckon with him who bought him: The price of his release shall be according to the number of years, from the year that he was sold to him until the Year of Jubilee; *it shall be* ᵃaccording to the time of a hired servant for him. ⁵¹If *there are* still many years *remaining*, according to them he shall repay the price of his redemption from the money with which he was bought. ⁵²And if there remain but a few years until the Year of Jubilee, then he shall reckon with him, *and* according to his years he shall repay him the price of his redemption. ⁵³He shall be with him as a yearly hired servant, and he shall not rule with rigor over him in your sight. ⁵⁴And if he is not redeemed in these *years*, then he shall be released in the Year of Jubilee—he and his children with him. ⁵⁵For the children of Israel *are* servants to Me; they *are* My servants whom I brought out of the land of Egypt: I *am* the LORD your God.

PROMISE OF BLESSING AND RETRIBUTION
(Deut. 7:12–24; 28:1–68)

26 'You shall ᵃnot make idols for yourselves;
　　neither a carved image nor a *sacred* pillar shall you
　　　rear up for yourselves;
　　nor shall you set up an engraved stone in your land, to
　　　bow down to it;
　　for I *am* the LORD your God.
2　ᵃYou shall ¹keep My Sabbaths and reverence My sanctuary:
　　I *am* the LORD.

3　ᵃ'If you walk in My statutes and keep My commandments,
　　　and perform them,
4　ᵃthen I will give you rain in its season, ᵇthe land shall yield
　　　its produce, and the trees of the field shall yield their
　　　fruit.
5　ᵃYour threshing shall last till the time of vintage, and the
　　　vintage shall last till the time of sowing;
　　you shall eat your bread to the full, and ᵇdwell in your land
　　　safely.
6　ᵃI will give peace in the land, and ᵇyou shall lie down, and
　　　none will make *you* afraid;
　　I will rid the land of ᶜevil¹ beasts,
　　and ᵈthe sword will not go through your land.
7　You will chase your enemies, and they shall fall by the
　　　sword before you.
8　ᵃFive of you shall chase a hundred, and a hundred of you
　　　shall put ten thousand to flight;
　　your enemies shall fall by the sword before you.

9　'For I will ᵃlook on you favorably and ᵇmake you fruitful,
　　　multiply you and confirm My ᶜcovenant with you.

25:50 ᵃJob 7:1;
Is. 16:14

26:1
ᵃEx. 20:4, 5;
Deut. 4:15–18;
5:8

26:2 ᵃLev. 19:30

26:3
ᵃDeut. 28:1–14

26:4 ᵃIs. 30:23
ᵇPs. 67:6

26:5
ᵃDeut. 11:15;
Joel 2:19, 26;
Amos 9:13
ᵇLev. 25:18, 19;
Ezek. 34:25

26:6 ᵃIs. 45:7
ᵇJob 11:19;
Ps. 4:8;
Zeph. 3:13
ᶜ2 Kin. 17:25;
Hos. 2:18
ᵈEzek. 14:17

26:8
ᵃDeut. 32:30;
Judg. 7:7–12

26:9 ᵃEx. 2:25;
2 Kin. 13:23
ᵇGen. 17:6,
7; Ps. 107:38
ᶜGen. 17:1–7

26:2 ¹*observe*　26:6 ¹*wild beasts*

10 You shall eat the ᵃold harvest, and clear out the old because of the new.

11 ᵃI will set My ¹tabernacle among you, and My soul shall not abhor you.

12 ᵃI will walk among you and be your God, and you shall be My people.

13 I *am* the Lᴏʀᴅ your God, who brought you out of the land of Egypt, that *you* should not be their slaves;
I have broken the bands of your ᵃyoke and made you walk ¹upright.

14 'But if you do not obey Me, and do not observe all these commandments,

15 and if you despise My statutes, or if your soul abhors My judgments, so that you do not perform all My commandments, *but* break My covenant,

16 I also will do this to you:
I will even appoint terror over you, ᵃwasting disease and fever which shall ᵇconsume the eyes and ᶜcause sorrow of heart.
And ᵈyou shall sow your seed ¹in vain, for your enemies shall eat it.

17 I will ¹set ᵃMy face against you, and ᵇyou shall be defeated by your enemies.
ᶜThose who hate you shall reign over you, and you shall ᵈflee when no one pursues you.

18 'And after all this, if you do not obey Me, then I will punish you ᵃseven times more for your sins.

19 I will ᵃbreak the pride of your power;
I ᵇwill make your heavens like iron and your earth like bronze.

20 And your ᵃstrength shall be spent in vain;
for your ᵇland shall not yield its produce, nor shall the trees of the land yield their fruit.

21 'Then, if you walk contrary to Me, and are not willing to obey Me, I will bring on you seven times more plagues, according to your sins.

22 ᵃI will also send wild beasts among you, which shall rob you of your children, destroy your livestock, and make you few in number;
and ᵇyour highways shall be desolate.

23 'And if ᵃby these things you are not reformed by Me, but walk contrary to Me,

24 ᵃthen I also will walk contrary to you, and I will punish you yet seven times for your sins.

25 And ᵃI will bring a sword against you that will execute the vengeance of the covenant;
when you are gathered together within your cities ᵇI will send pestilence among you;
and you shall be delivered into the hand of the enemy.

26 ᵃWhen I have cut off your supply of bread, ten women shall bake your bread in one oven, and they shall bring back your bread by weight, ᵇand you shall eat and not be satisfied.

26:10
ᵃLev. 25:22

26:11 ᵃEx. 25:8;
29:45, 46;
Josh. 22:19;
Ps. 76:2;
Ezek. 37:26;
Rev. 21:3

26:12
ᵃDeut. 23:14;
[2 Cor. 6:16]

26:13
ᵃGen. 27:40

26:16
ᵃDeut. 28:22
ᵇ1 Sam. 2:33
ᶜEzek. 24:23;
33:10
ᵈJudg. 6:3–6;
Job 31:8;
Mic. 6:15

26:17 ᵃPs. 34:16
ᵇDeut. 28:25;
1 Sam. 4:10;
31:1 ᶜPs. 106:41
ᵈProv. 28:1

26:18
ᵃ1 Sam. 2:5

26:19 ᵃIs. 25:11
ᵇDeut. 28:23

26:20 ᵃPs. 127:1;
Is. 17:10, 11;
49:4; Jer. 12:13
ᵇGen. 4:12;
Deut. 11:17

26:22
ᵃDeut. 32:24;
Ezek. 14:21
ᵇJudg. 5:6;
2 Chr. 15:5;
Zech. 7:14

26:23
ᵃJer. 2:30;
Amos 4:6–12

26:24
ᵃLev. 26:28, 41;
Ps. 18:26

26:25
ᵃEzek. 5:17
ᵇNum. 16:49;
Deut. 28:21;
2 Sam. 24:15

26:26
ᵃPs. 105:16;
Is. 3:1;
Ezek. 4:16, 17;
5:16 ᵇMic. 6:14;
Hag. 1:6

26:11 ¹*dwelling place*   26:13 ¹*erect*   26:16 ¹*without profit*
26:17 ¹*oppose you*

27 'And after all this, if you do not obey Me, but walk contrary to Me,

28 then I also will walk contrary to you in fury; and I, even I, will chastise you seven times for your sins.

29 [a]You[1] shall eat the flesh of your sons, and you shall eat the flesh of your daughters.

30 [a]I will destroy your high places, cut down your incense altars, and cast your carcasses on the lifeless forms of your idols;
and My soul shall abhor you.

31 I will lay your [a]cities waste and [b]bring your sanctuaries to desolation, and I will not [c]smell the fragrance of your [1]sweet aromas.

32 [a]I will bring the land to desolation, and your enemies who dwell in it shall be astonished at it.

33 [a]I will scatter you among the nations and draw out a sword after you;
your land shall be desolate and your cities waste.

34 [a]Then the land shall enjoy its sabbaths as long as it lies desolate and you *are* in your enemies' land;
then the land shall rest and enjoy its sabbaths.

35 As long as *it* lies desolate it shall rest—
for the time it did not rest on your [a]sabbaths when you dwelt in it.

36 'And as for those of you who are left, I will send [a]faintness[1] into their hearts in the lands of their enemies;
the sound of a shaken leaf shall cause them to flee;
they shall flee as though fleeing from a sword, and they shall fall when no one pursues.

37 [a]They shall stumble over one another, as it were before a sword, when no one pursues;
and [b]you shall have no *power* to stand before your enemies.

38 You shall [a]perish among the nations, and the land of your enemies shall eat you up.

39 And those of you who are left [a]shall [1]waste away in their iniquity in your enemies' lands;
also in their [b]fathers' iniquities, which are with them, they shall waste away.

40 '*But* [a]if they confess their iniquity and the iniquity of their fathers, with their unfaithfulness in which they were unfaithful to Me, and that they also have walked contrary to Me,

41 and *that* I also have walked contrary to them and have brought them into the land of their enemies;
if their [a]uncircumcised hearts are [b]humbled, and they [c]accept their guilt—

42 then I will [a]remember My covenant with Jacob, and My covenant with Isaac and My covenant with Abraham I will remember;
I will [b]remember the land.

43 [a]The land also shall be left empty by them, and will enjoy its sabbaths while it lies desolate without them;
they will accept their guilt, because they [b]despised My judgments and because their soul abhorred My statutes.

26:29 [a]Deut. 28:53; 2 Kin. 6:28, 29

26:30 [a]1 Kin. 13:2; 2 Chr. 34:3; Is. 27:9; Ezek. 6:3–6, 13

26:31 [a]2 Kin. 25:4, 10 [b]2 Chr. 36:19; Ps. 74:7 [c]Is. 1:11–15

26:32 [a]Jer. 9:11; 18:16

26:33 [a]Deut. 4:27; Ps. 44:11; Ezek. 12:15; 20:23; 22:15; Zech. 7:14

26:34 [a]Lev. 26:43; 2 Chr. 36:21

26:35 [a]Lev. 25:2

26:36 [a]Is. 30:17; Lam. 1:3, 6; 4:19; Ezek. 21:7, 12, 15

26:37 [a]Judg. 7:22; 1 Sam. 14:15, 16; Is. 10:4 [b]Josh. 7:12, 13; Judg. 2:14

26:38 [a]Deut. 4:26

26:39 [a]Deut. 28:65; Ezek. 4:17; 33:10; Zech. 10:9 [b]Ex. 34:7

26:40 [a]Num. 5:7; 1 Kin. 8:33, 34; Neh. 9:2; Luke 15:18; [1 John 1:9]

26:41 [a]Acts 7:51; Rom. 2:29 [b]2 Chr. 12:6, 7, 12; 1 Pet. 5:5, 6 [c]Ps. 39:9; 51:3, 4; Dan. 9:7

26:42 [a]Ex. 2:24; 6:5; Ps. 106:45; Ezek. 16:60 [b]Ps. 136:23

26:43 [a]Lev. 26:34, 35 [b]Lev. 26:15

26:29 [1]In time of famine   26:31 [1]pleasing   26:36 [1]fear   26:39 [1]rot away

44 Yet for all that, when they are in the land of their enemies, [a]I will not cast them away, nor shall I abhor them, to utterly destroy them and break My covenant with them; for I *am* the LORD their God.

45 But [a]for their sake I will remember the covenant of their ancestors, [b]whom I brought out of the land of Egypt [c]in the sight of the nations, that I might be their God: I *am* the LORD.'"

46[a]These *are* the statutes and judgments and laws which the LORD made between Himself and the children of Israel [b]on Mount Sinai by the hand of Moses.

REDEEMING PERSONS AND PROPERTY DEDICATED TO GOD

27 Now the LORD spoke to Moses, saying, 2"Speak to the children of Israel, and say to them: [a]'When a man [1]consecrates by a vow certain persons to the LORD, according to your [2]valuation, 3if your valuation is of a male from twenty years old up to sixty years old, then your valuation shall be fifty shekels of silver, [a]according to the shekel of the sanctuary. 4If it *is* a female, then your valuation shall be thirty shekels; 5and if from five years old up to twenty years old, then your valuation for a male shall be twenty shekels, and for a female ten shekels; 6and if from a month old up to five years old, then your valuation for a male shall be five shekels of silver, and for a female your valuation shall be three shekels of silver; 7and if from sixty years old and above, if *it is* a male, then your valuation shall be fifteen shekels, and for a female ten shekels.

8'But if he is too poor to pay your valuation, then he shall present himself before the priest, and the priest shall set a value for [a]him; according to the ability of him who vowed, the priest shall value him.

9'If *it is* an animal that men may bring as an offering to the LORD, all that *anyone* gives to the LORD shall be holy. 10He shall not substitute it or exchange it, good for bad or bad for good; and if he at all exchanges animal for animal, then both it and the one exchanged for it shall be [a]holy. 11If *it is* an unclean animal which they do not offer as a sacrifice to the LORD, then he shall present the animal before the priest; 12and the priest shall set a value for it, whether it is good or bad; as you, the priest, value it, so it shall be. 13[a]But if he *wants* at all *to* redeem it, then he must add one-fifth to your valuation.

14'And when a man [1]dedicates his house *to be* holy to the LORD, then the priest shall set a value for it, whether it is good or bad; as the priest values it, so it shall stand. 15If he who dedicated it *wants to* [1]redeem his house, then he must add one-fifth of the money of your valuation to it, and it shall be his.

16'If a man [1]dedicates to the LORD *part* of a field of his possession, then your valuation shall be according to the seed for it. A homer of barley seed *shall be valued* at fifty shekels of silver. 17If he dedicates his field from the Year of Jubilee, according to your valuation it shall stand. 18But if he dedicates his field after the Jubilee, then the priest shall [a]reckon to him the money due according to the years that remain till the Year

---

26:44
[a]Deut. 4:31;
2 Kin. 13:23;
Jer. 30:11;
[Rom. 11:1–36]

26:45
[a][Rom. 11:28]
[b]Lev. 22:33;
25:38 [c]Ps. 98:2;
Ezek. 20:9,
14, 22

26:46
[a]Lev. 27:34;
Deut. 6:1; 12:1;
[John 1:17]
[b]Lev. 25:1

27:2 [a]Lev. 7:16;
Num. 6:2;
Deut. 23:21–23;
Judg. 11:30,
31, 39

27:3 [a]Ex. 30:13;
Lev. 27:25;
Num. 3:47;
18:16

27:8 [a]Lev. 5:11;
14:21–24

27:10
[a]Lev. 27:33

27:13 [a]Lev. 6:5;
22:14; 27:15, 19

27:18
[a]Lev. 25:15,
16, 28

27:2 [1]Or *makes a difficult* or *extraordinary vow* [2]*appraisal* 27:14 [1]*sets apart* 27:15 [1]*buy back* 27:16 [1]*sets apart*

of Jubilee, and it shall be deducted from your valuation. ¹⁹And if he who dedicates the field ever wishes to redeem it, then he must add one-fifth of the money of your valuation to it, and it shall belong to him. ²⁰But if he does not want to redeem the field, or if he has sold the field to another man, it shall not be redeemed anymore; ²¹but the field, ᵃwhen it is released in the Jubilee, shall be holy to the LORD, as a ᵇdevoted field; it shall be ᶜthe possession of the priest.

²²'And if a man dedicates to the LORD a field which he has bought, which is not the field of ᵃhis possession, ²³then the priest shall reckon to him the worth of your valuation, up to the Year of Jubilee, and he shall give your valuation on that day *as* a holy *offering* to the LORD. ²⁴ᵃIn the Year of Jubilee the field shall return to him from whom it was bought, to the one who *owned* the land as a possession. ²⁵And all your valuations shall be according to the shekel of the sanctuary: ᵃtwenty gerahs to the shekel.

²⁶'But the ᵃfirstborn of the animals, which should be the LORD's firstborn, no man shall dedicate; whether *it is* an ox or sheep, it *is* the LORD's. ²⁷And if *it is* an unclean animal, then he shall redeem *it* according to your valuation, and ᵃshall add one-fifth to it; or if it is not redeemed, then it shall be sold according to your valuation.

²⁸ᵃ'Nevertheless no ¹devoted *offering* that a man may devote to the LORD of all that he has, *both* man and beast, or the field of his possession, shall be sold or redeemed; every devoted *offering is* most holy to the LORD. ²⁹ᵃNo person under the ban, who may become doomed to destruction among men, shall be redeemed, *but* shall surely be put to death. ³⁰And ᵃall the tithe of the land, *whether* of the seed of the land *or* of the fruit of the tree, *is* the LORD's. It *is* holy to the LORD. ³¹ᵃIf a man wants at all to redeem *any* of his tithes, he shall add one-fifth to it. ³²And concerning the tithe of the herd or the flock, of whatever ᵃpasses under the rod, the tenth one shall be holy to the LORD. ³³He shall not inquire whether it is good or bad, ᵃnor shall he exchange it; and if he exchanges it at all, then both it and the one exchanged for it shall be holy; it shall not be redeemed.'"

³⁴ᵃThese *are* the commandments which the LORD commanded Moses for the children of Israel on Mount ᵇSinai.

27:21
ᵃLev. 25:10, 28, 31 ᵇLev. 27:28
ᶜNum. 18:14; Ezek. 44:29

27:22
ᵃLev. 25:10, 25

27:24
ᵃLev. 25:10–13, 28

27:25
ᵃEx. 30:13; Lev. 27:3; Num. 3:47; 18:16; Ezek. 45:12

27:26 ᵃEx. 13:2, 12; 22:30

27:27
ᵃLev. 27:11, 12

27:28
ᵃLev. 27:21; Num. 18:14; Josh. 6:17–19

27:29
ᵃNum. 21:2

27:30
ᵃGen. 28:22; Num. 18:21, 24; 2 Chr. 31:5, 6, 12; Neh. 13:12; Mal. 3:8

27:31 ᵃLev. 27:13

27:32
ᵃJer. 33:13; Ezek. 20:37; Mic. 7:14

27:33
ᵃLev. 27:10

27:34
ᵃLev. 26:46; Deut. 4:5; Mal. 4:4
ᵇEx. 19:1–6, 25; [Heb. 12:18–29]

27:28 ¹Given exclusively and irrevocably

NUMBERS

THE FIRST CENSUS OF ISRAEL
(cf. 2 Sam. 24:1–9; 1 Chr. 21:1–6)

1 Now the LORD spoke to Moses ᵃin the Wilderness of Sinai, ᵇin the tabernacle of meeting, on the ᶜfirst *day* of the second month, in the second year after they had come out of the land of Egypt, saying: ²ᵃ"Take a census of all the congregation of the children of Israel, by their families, by their fathers' houses, according to the number of names, every male ᵇindividually, ³from ᵃtwenty years old and above—all who *are able to* go to war in Israel. You and Aaron shall number them by their armies. ⁴And with you there shall be a man from every tribe, each one the head of his father's house.

⁵"These are the names of the men who shall stand with you: from Reuben, Elizur the son of Shedeur; ⁶from Simeon, Shelumiel the son of Zurishaddai; ⁷from Judah, Nahshon the son of Amminadab; ⁸from Issachar, Nethanel the son of Zuar; ⁹from Zebulun, Eliab the son of Helon; ¹⁰from the sons of Joseph: from Ephraim, Elishama the son of Ammihud; from Manasseh, Gamaliel the son of Pedahzur; ¹¹from Benjamin, Abidan the son of Gideoni; ¹²from Dan, Ahiezer the son of Ammishaddai; ¹³from Asher, Pagiel the son of Ocran; ¹⁴from Gad, Eliasaph the son of ᵃDeuel;¹ ¹⁵from Naphtali, Ahira the son of Enan." ¹⁶ᵃThese *were* ᵇchosen¹ from the congregation, leaders of their fathers' tribes, ᶜheads of the divisions in Israel.

¹⁷Then Moses and Aaron took these men who had been ¹mentioned ᵃby name, ¹⁸and they assembled all the congregation together on the first *day* of the second month; and they recited their ᵃancestry by families, by their fathers' houses, according to the number of names, from twenty years old and above, each one individually. ¹⁹As the LORD commanded Moses, so he numbered them in the Wilderness of Sinai.

²⁰Now the ᵃchildren of Reuben, Israel's oldest son, their genealogies by their families, by their fathers' house, according to the number of names, every male individually, from twenty years old and above, all who *were able to* go to war: ²¹those who were numbered of the tribe of Reuben *were* forty-six thousand five hundred.

²²From the ᵃchildren of Simeon, their genealogies by their families, by their fathers' house, of those who were numbered, according to the number of names, every male individually, from twenty years old and above, all who *were able to* go to war: ²³those who were numbered of the tribe of Simeon *were* fifty-nine thousand three hundred.

²⁴From the ᵃchildren of Gad, their genealogies by their families, by their fathers' house, according to the number of

Cross-references (margin)

1:1 ᵃEx. 19:1; Num. 10:11, 12 ᵇEx. 25:22 ᶜEx. 40:2, 17; Num. 9:1; 10:11

1:2 ᵃEx. 30:12; Num. 26:2, 63, 64; 2 Sam. 24:2; 1 Chr. 21:2 ᵇEx. 30:12, 13; 38:26

1:3 ᵃEx. 30:14; 38:26

1:14 ᵃNum. 7:42

1:16 ᵃEx. 18:21; Num. 7:2; 1 Chr. 27:16–22 ᵇNum. 16:2 ᶜEx. 18:21, 25; Jer. 5:5; Mic. 3:1, 9; 5:2

1:17 ᵃIs. 43:1

1:18 ᵃEzra 2:59; Heb. 7:3

1:20 ᵃNum. 2:10, 11; 26:5–11; 32:6, 15, 21, 29

1:22 ᵃNum. 2:12, 13; 26:12–14

1:24 ᵃGen. 30:11; Num. 26:15–18; Josh. 4:12; Jer. 49:1

names, from twenty years old and above, all who *were able to* go to war: ²⁵those who were numbered of the tribe of Gad *were* forty-five thousand six hundred and fifty.

²⁶From the ᵃchildren of Judah, their genealogies by their families, by their fathers' house, according to the number of names, from twenty years old and above, all who *were able to* go to war: ²⁷those who were numbered of the tribe of Judah *were* ᵃseventy-four thousand six hundred.

²⁸From the ᵃchildren of Issachar, their genealogies by their families, by their fathers' house, according to the number of names, from twenty years old and above, all who *were able to* go to war: ²⁹those who were numbered of the tribe of Issachar *were* fifty-four thousand four hundred.

³⁰From the ᵃchildren of Zebulun, their genealogies by their families, by their fathers' house, according to the number of names, from twenty years old and above, all who *were able to* go to war: ³¹those who were numbered of the tribe of Zebulun *were* fifty-seven thousand four hundred.

³²From the sons of Joseph, the ᵃchildren of Ephraim, their genealogies by their families, by their fathers' house, according to the number of names, from twenty years old and above, all who *were able to* go to war: ³³those who were numbered of the tribe of Ephraim *were* forty thousand five hundred.

³⁴From the ᵃchildren of Manasseh, their genealogies by their families, by their fathers' house, according to the number of names, from twenty years old and above, all who *were able to* go to war: ³⁵those who were numbered of the tribe of Manasseh *were* thirty-two thousand two hundred.

³⁶From the ᵃchildren of Benjamin, their genealogies by their families, by their fathers' house, according to the number of names, from twenty years old and above, all who *were able to* go to war: ³⁷those who were numbered of the tribe of Benjamin *were* thirty-five thousand four hundred.

³⁸From the ᵃchildren of Dan, their genealogies by their families, by their fathers' house, according to the number of names, from twenty years old and above, all who *were able to* go to war: ³⁹those who were numbered of the tribe of Dan *were* sixty-two thousand seven hundred.

⁴⁰From the ᵃchildren of Asher, their genealogies by their families, by their fathers' house, according to the number of names, from twenty years old and above, all who *were able to* go to war: ⁴¹those who were numbered of the tribe of Asher *were* forty-one thousand five hundred.

⁴²From the children of Naphtali, their genealogies by their families, by their fathers' house, according to the number of names, from twenty years old and above, all who *were able to* go to war: ⁴³those who were numbered of the tribe of Naphtali *were* fifty-three thousand four hundred.

⁴⁴ᵃThese are the ones who were numbered, whom Moses and Aaron numbered, with the leaders of Israel, twelve men, each one representing his father's house. ⁴⁵So all who were numbered of the children of Israel, by their fathers' houses, from twenty years old and above, all who *were able to* go to war in Israel— ⁴⁶all who were numbered were ᵃsix hundred and three thousand five hundred and fifty.

⁴⁷But ᵃthe Levites were not numbered among them by their fathers' tribe; ⁴⁸for the LORD had spoken to Moses, saying:

1:26
ᵃGen. 29:35;
Num. 26:19–22;
2 Sam. 24:9;
Ps. 78:68;
Matt. 1:2

1:27 ᵃ2 Chr. 17:14

1:28
ᵃNum. 2:5, 6

1:30 ᵃNum. 2:7,
8; 26:26, 27

1:32
ᵃGen. 48:1–22;
Num. 26:28–37;
Deut. 33:13–17;
Jer. 7:15;
Obad. 19

1:34
ᵃNum. 2:20, 21;
26:28–34

1:36
ᵃGen. 49:27;
Num. 26:38–41;
2 Chr. 17:17;
Rev. 7:8

1:38 ᵃGen. 30:6;
46:23;
Num. 2:25, 26;
26:42, 43

1:40 ᵃNum. 2:27,
28; 26:44–47

1:44
ᵃNum. 26:64

1:46 ᵃEx. 12:37;
38:26;
Num. 2:32;
26:51, 63;
Heb. 11:12;
Rev. 7:4–8

1:47
ᵃNum. 2:33;
3:14–22;
26:57–62;
1 Chr. 6:1–47;
21:6

⁴⁹ᵃ"Only the tribe of Levi you shall not number, nor take a census of them among the children of Israel; ⁵⁰ᵃbut you shall appoint the Levites over the tabernacle of the Testimony, over all its furnishings, and over all things that belong to it; they shall carry the tabernacle and all its furnishings; they shall attend to it ᵇand camp around the tabernacle. ⁵¹ᵃAnd when the tabernacle is to go forward, the Levites shall take it down; and when the tabernacle is to be set up, the Levites shall set it ᵇup. ᶜThe outsider who comes near shall be put to death. ⁵²The children of Israel shall pitch their tents, ᵃeveryone by his own camp, everyone by his own standard, according to their armies; ⁵³ᵃbut the Levites shall camp around the tabernacle of the Testimony, that there may be no ᵇwrath on the congregation of the children of Israel; and the Levites shall ᶜkeep¹ charge of the tabernacle of the Testimony."

⁵⁴Thus the children of Israel did; according to all that the LORD commanded Moses, so they did.

THE TRIBES AND LEADERS BY ARMIES

2 And the LORD spoke to Moses and Aaron, saying: ²ᵃ"Everyone of the children of Israel shall camp by his own ¹standard, beside the emblems of his father's house; they shall camp ᵇsome distance from the tabernacle of meeting. ³On the ᵃeast side, toward the rising of the sun, those of the standard of the forces with Judah shall camp according to their armies; and ᵇNahshon the son of Amminadab *shall be* the leader of the children of Judah." ⁴And his army was numbered at seventy-four thousand six hundred.

⁵"Those who camp next to him *shall be* the tribe of Issachar, and Nethanel the son of Zuar *shall be* the leader of the children of Issachar." ⁶And his army was numbered at fifty-four thousand four hundred.

⁷"Then *comes* the tribe of Zebulun, and Eliab the son of Helon *shall be* the leader of the children of Zebulun." ⁸And his army was numbered at fifty-seven thousand four hundred. ⁹"All who were numbered according to their armies of the forces with Judah, one hundred and eighty-six thousand four hundred—ᵃthese shall ¹break camp first.

¹⁰"On the ᵃsouth side *shall be* the standard of the forces with Reuben according to their armies, and the leader of the children of Reuben *shall be* Elizur the son of Shedeur." ¹¹And his army was numbered at forty-six thousand five hundred.

¹²"Those who camp next to him *shall be* the tribe of Simeon, and the leader of the children of Simeon *shall be* Shelumiel the son of Zurishaddai." ¹³And his army was numbered at fifty-nine thousand three hundred.

¹⁴"Then *comes* the tribe of Gad, and the leader of the children of Gad *shall be* Eliasaph the son of ¹Reuel." ¹⁵And his army was numbered at forty-five thousand six hundred and fifty. ¹⁶"All who were numbered according to their armies of the forces with Reuben, one hundred and fifty-one thousand four hundred and fifty—ᵃthey shall ¹be the second to break camp.

¹⁷ᵃ"And the tabernacle of meeting shall move out with the ¹camp of the Levites ᵇin the middle of the ²camps; as they

1:49
ᵃNum. 2:33;
26:62

1:50 ᵃEx. 38:21;
Num. 3:7, 8;
4:15, 25–27, 33
ᵇNum. 3:23, 29,
35, 38

1:51
ᵃNum. 4:5–15;
10:17, 21
ᵇNum. 10:21
ᶜNum. 3:10,
38; 4:15, 19, 20;
18:22

1:52 ᵃNum. 2:2,
34; 24:2

1:53 ᵃNum. 1:50
ᵇLev. 10:6;
Num. 8:19;
16:46; 18:5;
1 Sam. 6:19
ᶜNum. 8:24;
18:2–4;
1 Chr. 23:32

2:2 ᵃNum. 1:52;
24:2 ᵇJosh. 3:4

2:3 ᵃNum. 10:5
ᵇNum. 1:7; 7:12;
10:14; Ruth 4:20;
1 Chr. 2:10;
Matt. 1:4;
Luke 3:32, 33

2:9 ᵃNum. 10:14

2:10 ᵃNum. 10:6

2:16
ᵃNum. 10:18

2:17
ᵃNum. 10:17, 21
ᵇNum. 1:53

1:53 ¹*have in their care*   2:2 ¹*banner*   2:9 ¹Lit. *set forth*   2:14 ¹*Deuel,* Num. 1:14; 7:42   2:16 ¹Lit. *set forth second*   2:17 ¹*company*   ²*whole company*

camp, so they shall move out, everyone in his place, by their [3]standards.

[18]"On the west side *shall be* the standard of the forces with Ephraim according to their armies, and the leader of the children of Ephraim *shall be* Elishama the son of Ammihud." [19]And his army was numbered at forty thousand five hundred.

[20]"Next to him *comes* the tribe of Manasseh, and the leader of the children of Manasseh *shall be* Gamaliel the son of Pedahzur." [21]And his army was numbered at thirty-two thousand two hundred.

[22]"Then *comes* the tribe of Benjamin, and the leader of the children of Benjamin *shall be* Abidan the son of Gideoni." [23]And his army was numbered at thirty-five thousand four hundred. [24]"All who were numbered according to their armies of the forces with Ephraim, one hundred and eight thousand one hundred—[a]they shall [1]be the third to break camp.

[25]"The [1]standard of the forces with Dan *shall be* on the north side according to their armies, and the leader of the children of Dan *shall be* Ahiezer the son of Ammishaddai." [26]And his army was numbered at sixty-two thousand seven hundred.

[27]"Those who camp next to him *shall be* the tribe of Asher, and the leader of the children of Asher *shall be* Pagiel the son of Ocran." [28]And his army was numbered at forty-one thousand five hundred.

[29]"Then *comes* the tribe of Naphtali, and the leader of the children of Naphtali *shall be* Ahira the son of Enan." [30]And his army was numbered at fifty-three thousand four hundred. [31]"All who were numbered of the forces with Dan, one hundred and fifty-seven thousand six hundred—[a]they shall [1]break camp last, with their [2]standards."

[32]These *are* the ones who were numbered of the children of Israel by their fathers' houses. [a]All who were numbered according to their armies of the forces *were* six hundred and three thousand five hundred and fifty. [33]But [a]the Levites were not numbered among the children of Israel, just as the LORD commanded Moses.

[34]Thus the children of Israel [a]did according to all that the LORD commanded Moses; [b]so they camped by their [1]standards and so they broke camp, each one by his family, according to their fathers' houses.

THE SONS OF AARON
(Lev. 10:1–7)

3 Now these *are* the [a]records[1] of Aaron and Moses when the LORD spoke with Moses on Mount Sinai. [2]And these *are* the names of the sons of Aaron: Nadab, the [a]firstborn, and [b]Abihu, Eleazar, and Ithamar. [3]These *are* the names of the sons of Aaron, [a]the anointed priests, [1]whom he consecrated to minister as priests. [4][a]Nadab and Abihu had died before the LORD when they offered profane fire before the LORD in the Wilderness of Sinai; and they had no children. So Eleazar and

2:24
[a]Num. 10:22

2:31
[a]Num. 10:25

2:32 [a]Ex. 38:26;
Num. 1:46; 11:21

2:33
[a]Num. 1:47;
26:57–62

2:34 [a]Num. 1:54
[b]Num. 24:2,
5, 6

3:1 [a]Ex. 6:16–27

3:2 [a]Ex. 6:23
[b]Lev. 10:1, 2;
Num. 26:60, 61;
1 Chr. 24:2

3:3 [a]Ex. 28:41;
Lev. 8

3:4 [a]Lev. 10:1, 2;
Num. 26:61;
1 Chr. 24:2

2:17 [3]banners   2:24 [1]Lit. *set forth third*   2:25 [1]banner   2:31 [1]Lit. *set forth last*   [2]banners   2:34 [1]banners   3:1 [1]Lit. *generations*   3:3 [1]Lit. *whose hands he filled*

Ithamar ministered as priests in the presence of Aaron their father.

THE LEVITES SERVE IN THE TABERNACLE

5And the LORD spoke to Moses, saying: 6a"Bring the tribe of Levi near, and present them before Aaron the priest, that they may serve him. 7And they shall attend to his needs and the needs of the whole congregation before the tabernacle of meeting, to do athe work of the tabernacle. 8Also they shall attend to all the furnishings of the tabernacle of meeting, and to the needs of the children of Israel, to do the work of the tabernacle. 9And ayou shall give the Levites to Aaron and his sons; they *are* given entirely to 1him from among the children of Israel. 10So you shall appoint Aaron and his sons, aand they shall attend to their priesthood; bbut the outsider who comes near shall be put to death."

11Then the LORD spoke to Moses, saying: 12"Now behold, aI Myself have taken the Levites from among the children of Israel instead of every firstborn who opens the womb among the children of Israel. Therefore the Levites shall be bMine, 13because aall the firstborn *are* Mine. bOn the day that I struck all the firstborn in the land of Egypt, I sanctified to Myself all the firstborn in Israel, both man and beast. They shall be Mine: I *am* the LORD."

CENSUS OF THE LEVITES COMMANDED

(*cf. Num.* 1:47–54)

14Then the LORD spoke to Moses in the Wilderness of Sinai, saying: 15"Number the children of Levi by their fathers' houses, by their families; you shall number aevery male from a month old and above."

16So Moses numbered them according to the 1word of the LORD, as he was commanded. 17aThese were the sons of Levi by their names: Gershon, Kohath, and Merari. 18And these *are* the names of the sons of aGershon by their families: bLibni and Shimei. 19And the sons of aKohath by their families: bAmram, Izehar, Hebron, and Uzziel. 20aAnd the sons of Merari by their families: Mahli and Mushi. These *are* the families of the Levites by their fathers' houses.

21From Gershon *came* the family of the Libnites and the family of the Shimites; these *were* the families of the Gershonites. 22Those who were numbered, according to the number of all the males from a month old and above—of those who were numbered *there were* seven thousand five hundred. 23aThe families of the Gershonites were to camp behind the tabernacle westward. 24And the leader of the father's house of the Gershonites *was* Eliasaph the son of Lael. 25aThe duties of the children of Gershon in the tabernacle of meeting *included* bthe tabernacle, cthe tent with dits covering, ethe screen for the door of the tabernacle of meeting, 26athe screen for the door of the court, bthe hangings of the court which *are* around the tabernacle and the altar, and ctheir cords, according to all the work relating to them.

27aFrom Kohath *came* the family of the Amramites, the family of the Izharites, the family of the Hebronites, and the

3:6
aNum. 8:6–22;
18:1–7;
Deut. 10:8;
33:8–11

3:7 aNum. 1:50;
8:11, 15, 24, 26

3:9 aNum. 8:19;
18:6, 7

3:10 aEx. 29:9;
Num. 18:7
bNum. 1:51;
3:38; 16:40

3:12 aNum. 3:41;
8:16; 18:6
bEx. 13:2;
Num. 3:45; 8:14

3:13 aEx. 13:2;
Lev. 27:26;
Num. 8:16, 17;
Neh. 10:36;
Luke 2:23
bEx. 13:12, 15;
Num. 8:17

3:15
aNum. 3:39;
26:62

3:17 aGen. 46:11;
Ex. 6:16–22;
Num. 26:57;
1 Chr. 6:1, 16;
23:6

3:18
aNum. 4:38–41
bEx. 6:17

3:19
aNum. 4:34–37
bEx. 6:18

3:20 aEx. 6:19;
Num. 4:42–45

3:23 aNum. 1:53

3:25
aNum. 4:24–26
bEx. 25:9
cEx. 26:1
dEx. 26:7, 14
eEx. 26:36

3:26 aEx. 27:9,
12, 14, 15
bEx. 27:16
cEx. 35:18

3:27
a1 Chr. 26:23

3:9 1Sam., LXX *Me*   3:16 1Lit. *mouth*

family of the Uzzielites; these *were* the families of the Kohathites. 28According to the number of all the males, from a month old and above, *there were* eight thousand [1]six hundred [2]keeping charge of the sanctuary. 29aThe families of the children of Kohath were to camp on the south side of the tabernacle. 30And the leader of the fathers' house of the families of the Kohathites *was* Elizaphan the son of aUzziel. 31aTheir duty *included* bthe ark, cthe table, dthe lampstand, ethe altars, the utensils of the sanctuary with which they ministered, fthe screen, and all the work relating to them.

32And Eleazar the son of Aaron the priest *was to be* chief over the leaders of the Levites, *with* oversight of those who kept charge of the sanctuary.

33From Merari *came* the family of the Mahlites and the family of the Mushites; these *were* the families of Merari. 34And those who were numbered, according to the number of all the males from a month old and above, *were* six thousand two hundred. 35The leader of the fathers' house of the families of Merari *was* Zuriel the son of Abihail. aThese *were* to camp on the north side of the tabernacle. 36And athe appointed duty of the children of Merari *included* the boards of the tabernacle, its bars, its pillars, its sockets, its utensils, all the work relating to them, 37and the pillars of the court all around, with their sockets, their pegs, and their cords.

38aMoreover those who were to camp before the tabernacle on the east, before the tabernacle of meeting, *were* Moses, Aaron, and his sons, bkeeping charge of the sanctuary, cto meet the needs of the children of Israel; but dthe outsider who came near was to be put to death. 39aAll who were numbered of the Levites, whom Moses and Aaron numbered at the commandment of the LORD, by their families, all the males from a month old and above, *were* twenty-two thousand.

LEVITES DEDICATED INSTEAD OF THE FIRSTBORN

40Then the LORD said to Moses: a"Number[1] all the firstborn males of the children of Israel from a month old and above, and take the number of their names. 41aAnd you shall take the Levites for Me—I *am* the LORD—instead of all the firstborn among the children of Israel, and the livestock of the Levites instead of all the firstborn among the livestock of the children of Israel." 42So Moses numbered all the firstborn among the children of Israel, as the LORD commanded him. 43And all the firstborn males, according to the number of names from a month old and above, of those who were numbered of them, were twenty-two thousand two hundred and seventy-three.

44Then the LORD spoke to Moses, saying: 45a"Take the Levites instead of all the firstborn among the children of Israel, and the livestock of the Levites instead of their livestock. The Levites shall be Mine: I *am* the LORD. 46And for athe redemption of the two hundred and seventy-three of the firstborn of the children of Israel, bwho are more than the number of the Levites, 47you shall take afive shekels for each one bindividually; you shall take *them* in the currency of the shekel of the sanctuary, cthe shekel of twenty gerahs. 48And you shall

3:29 aEx. 6:18; Num. 1:53

3:30 aLev. 10:4

3:31 aNum. 4:15
bEx. 25:10
cEx. 25:23
dEx. 25:31
eEx. 27:1; 30:1
fEx. 26:31–33

3:35 aNum. 1:53; 2:25

3:36 aNum. 4:31, 32

3:38 aNum. 1:53
bNum. 18:5
cNum. 3:7, 8
dNum. 3:10

3:39 aNum. 3:43; 4:48; 26:62

3:40 aNum. 3:15

3:41 aNum. 3:12, 45

3:45 aNum. 3:12, 41

3:46 aEx. 13:13, 15; Num. 18:15, 16
bNum. 3:39, 43

3:47 aLev. 27:6; Num. 18:16
bNum. 1:2, 18, 20 cEx. 30:13

3:28 [1]Some LXX mss. *three* [2]*taking care of* 3:40 [1]*Take a census of*

give the money, with which the excess number of them is redeemed, to Aaron and his sons."

⁴⁹So Moses took the redemption money from those who were over and above those who were redeemed by the Levites. ⁵⁰From the firstborn of the children of Israel he took the money, ᵃone thousand three hundred and sixty-five *shekels,* according to the shekel of the sanctuary. ⁵¹And Moses ᵃgave their redemption money to Aaron and his sons, according to the word of the LORD, as the LORD commanded Moses.

DUTIES OF THE SONS OF KOHATH

4 Then the LORD spoke to Moses and Aaron, saying: ²"Take a census of the sons of ᵃKohath from among the children of Levi, by their families, by their fathers' house, ³ᵃfrom thirty years old and above, even to fifty years old, all who enter the service to do the work in the tabernacle of meeting.

⁴ᵃ"This *is* the service of the sons of Kohath in the tabernacle of meeting, *relating to* ᵇthe most holy things: ⁵When the camp prepares to journey, Aaron and his sons shall come, and they shall take down ᵃthe covering veil and cover the ᵇark of the Testimony with it. ⁶Then they shall put on it a covering of badger skins, and spread over *that* a cloth entirely of ᵃblue; and they shall insert ᵇits poles.

⁷"On the ᵃtable of showbread they shall spread a blue cloth, and put on it the dishes, the pans, the bowls, and the ¹pitchers for pouring; and the ᵇshowbread² shall be on it. ⁸They shall spread over them a scarlet cloth, and cover the same with a covering of badger skins; and they shall insert its poles. ⁹And they shall take a blue cloth and cover the ᵃlampstand of the light, ᵇwith its lamps, its wick-trimmers, its trays, and all its oil vessels, with which they service it. ¹⁰Then they shall put it with all its utensils in a covering of badger skins, and put *it* on a carrying beam.

¹¹"Over ᵃthe golden altar they shall spread a blue cloth, and cover it with a covering of badger skins; and they shall insert its poles. ¹²Then they shall take all the ᵃutensils of service with which they minister in the sanctuary, put *them* in a blue cloth, cover them with a covering of badger skins, and put *them* on a carrying beam. ¹³Also they shall take away the ashes from the altar, and spread a purple cloth over it. ¹⁴They shall put on it all its implements with which they minister there—the firepans, the forks, the shovels, the ¹basins, and all the utensils of the altar—and they shall spread on it a covering of badger skins, and insert its poles. ¹⁵And when Aaron and his sons have finished covering the sanctuary and all the furnishings of the sanctuary, when the camp is set to go, then ᵃthe sons of Kohath shall come to carry *them;* ᵇbut they shall not touch any holy thing, lest they die.

"ᶜThese *are* the things in the tabernacle of meeting which the sons of Kohath are to carry.

¹⁶"The appointed duty of Eleazar the son of Aaron the priest *is* ᵃthe oil for the light, the ᵇsweet incense, ᶜthe daily grain offering, the ᵈanointing oil, the oversight of all the tabernacle, of all that *is* in it, with the sanctuary and its furnishings."

3:50
ᵃNum. 3:46, 47
3:51 ᵃNum. 3:48
4:2
ᵃNum. 3:27–32
4:3 ᵃNum. 4:23, 30, 35; 8:24; 1 Chr. 23:3, 24, 27; Ezra 3:8
4:4 ᵃNum. 4:15 ᵇNum. 4:19
4:5 ᵃEx. 26:31; Heb. 9:3 ᵇEx. 25:10, 16
4:6 ᵃEx. 39:1 ᵇEx. 25:13; 1 Kin. 8:7, 8
4:7 ᵃEx. 25:23, 29, 30 ᵇLev. 24:5–9
4:9 ᵃEx. 25:31 ᵇEx. 25:37, 38
4:11 ᵃEx. 30:1–5
4:12 ᵃEx. 25:9; 1 Chr. 9:29
4:15 ᵃNum. 7:9; 10:21; Deut. 31:9; Josh. 4:10; 2 Sam. 6:13; 1 Chr. 15:2, 15 ᵇ2 Sam. 6:6, 7; 1 Chr. 13:9, 10 ᶜNum. 3:31
4:16 ᵃEx. 25:6; Lev. 24:2 ᵇEx. 30:34 ᶜEx. 29:38 ᵈEx. 30:23–25

4:7 ¹*jars for the drink offering*   ²Lit. *continual bread*   4:14 ¹*bowls*

¹⁷Then the LORD spoke to Moses and Aaron, saying: ¹⁸"Do not cut off the tribe of the families of the Kohathites from among the Levites; ¹⁹but do this in regard to them, that they may live and not die when they approach ᵃthe most holy things: Aaron and his sons shall go in and ¹appoint each of them to his service and his task. ²⁰ᵃBut they shall not go in to watch while the holy things are being covered, lest they die."

DUTIES OF THE SONS OF GERSHON

²¹Then the LORD spoke to Moses, saying: ²²"Also take a census of the sons of ᵃGershon, by their fathers' house, by their families. ²³ᵃFrom thirty years old and above, even to fifty years old, you shall number them, all who enter to perform the service, to do the work in the tabernacle of meeting. ²⁴This *is* the ᵃservice of the families of the Gershonites, in serving and carrying: ²⁵ᵃThey shall carry the ᵇcurtains of the tabernacle and the tabernacle of meeting *with* its covering, the covering of ᶜbadger skins that *is* on it, the screen for the door of the tabernacle of meeting, ²⁶the screen for the door of the gate of the court, the hangings of the court which *are* around the tabernacle and altar, and their cords, all the furnishings for their service and all that is made for these things: so shall they serve.

²⁷"Aaron and his sons shall ¹assign all the service of the sons of the Gershonites, all their tasks and all their service. And you shall ²appoint to them all their tasks as their duty. ²⁸This *is* the service of the families of the sons of Gershon in the tabernacle of meeting. And their duties *shall be* ᵃunder the ¹authority of Ithamar the son of Aaron the priest.

DUTIES OF THE SONS OF MERARI

²⁹"*As for* the sons of ᵃMerari, you shall number them by their families and by their fathers' house. ³⁰ᵃFrom thirty years old and above, even to fifty years old, you shall number them, everyone who enters the service to do the work of the tabernacle of meeting. ³¹And ᵃthis *is* ᵇwhat they must carry as all their service for the tabernacle of meeting: ᶜthe boards of the tabernacle, its bars, its pillars, its sockets, ³²and the pillars around the court with their sockets, pegs, and cords, with all their furnishings and all their service; and you shall ᵃassign *to* each *man* by name the items he must carry. ³³This *is* the service of the families of the sons of Merari, as all their service for the tabernacle of meeting, under the ¹authority of Ithamar the son of Aaron the priest."

CENSUS OF THE LEVITES

³⁴ᵃAnd Moses, Aaron, and the leaders of the congregation numbered the sons of the Kohathites by their families and by their fathers' house, ³⁵from thirty ᵃyears old and above, even to fifty years old, everyone who entered the service for work in the tabernacle of meeting; ³⁶and those who were numbered by their families were two thousand seven hundred and fifty. ³⁷These *were* the ones who were numbered of the families of the Kohathites, all who might serve in the tabernacle of meeting, whom Moses and Aaron numbered

4:19 ᵃNum. 4:4

4:20 ᵃEx. 19:21; 1 Sam. 6:19

4:22 ᵃNum. 3:22

4:23 ᵃNum. 4:3; 1 Chr. 23:3, 24, 27

4:24 ᵃNum. 7:7

4:25 ᵃNum. 3:25, 26 ᵇEx. 36:8 ᶜEx. 26:14

4:28 ᵃNum. 4:33

4:29 ᵃNum. 3:33–37

4:30 ᵃNum. 4:3; 8:24–26

4:31 ᵃNum. 3:36, 37 ᵇNum. 7:8 ᶜEx. 26:15

4:32 ᵃEx. 25:9; 38:21

4:34 ᵃNum. 4:2

4:35 ᵃNum. 4:47

4:19 ¹*assign*　4:27 ¹*command*　²*assign*　4:28 ¹Lit. *hand*　4:33 ¹Lit. *hand*

according to the commandment of the LORD by the hand of Moses.

38And those who were numbered of the sons of Gershon, by their families and by their fathers' house, 39from thirty years old and above, even to fifty years old, everyone who entered the service for work in the tabernacle of meeting— 40those who were numbered by their families, by their fathers' house, were two thousand six hundred and thirty. 41aThese *are* the ones who were numbered of the families of the sons of Gershon, of all who might serve in the tabernacle of meeting, whom Moses and Aaron numbered according to the commandment of the LORD.

42Those of the families of the sons of Merari who were numbered, by their families, by their fathers' [1]house, 43from thirty years old and above, even to fifty years old, everyone who entered the service for work in the tabernacle of meeting— 44those who were numbered by their families were three thousand two hundred. 45These *are* the ones who were numbered of the families of the sons of Merari, whom Moses and Aaron numbered aaccording to the word of the LORD by the hand of Moses.

46All who were anumbered of the Levites, whom Moses, Aaron, and the leaders of Israel numbered, by their families and by their fathers' houses, 47afrom thirty years old and above, even to fifty years old, everyone who came to do the work of service and the work of bearing burdens in the tabernacle of meeting— 48those who were numbered were eight thousand five hundred and eighty.

49According to the commandment of the LORD they were numbered by the hand of Moses, aeach according to his service and according to his task; thus were they numbered by him, bas the LORD commanded Moses.

CEREMONIALLY UNCLEAN PERSONS ISOLATED
(cf. Lev. 15:1–33)

5 And the LORD spoke to Moses, saying: 2"Command the children of Israel that they put out of the camp every aleper, everyone who has a bdischarge, and whoever becomes cdefiled [1]by a corpse. 3You shall put out both male and female; you shall put them outside the camp, that they may not defile their camps ain the midst of which I dwell." 4And the children of Israel did so, and put them outside the camp; as the LORD spoke to Moses, so the children of Israel did.

CONFESSION AND RESTITUTION
(Lev. 6:1–7)

5Then the LORD spoke to Moses, saying, 6"Speak to the children of Israel: a'When a man or woman commits any sin that men commit in unfaithfulness against the LORD, and that person is guilty, 7athen he shall confess the sin which he has committed. He shall make restitution for his trespass bin full, plus one-fifth of it, and give *it* to the one he has wronged. 8But if the man has no [1]relative to whom restitution may be made for the wrong, the restitution for the wrong *must go* to the LORD for the priest, in addition to athe

---

4:41 aNum. 4:22
4:45 aNum. 4:29
4:46 aNum. 3:39; 26:57–62; 1 Chr. 23:3–23
4:47 aNum. 4:3, 23, 30
4:49 aNum. 4:15, 24, 31 bNum. 4:1, 21
5:2 aLev. 13:3, 8, 46; Num. 12:10, 14, 15 bLev. 15:2 cLev. 21:1; Num. 9:6, 10; 19:11, 13; 31:19
5:3 aLev. 26:11, 12; Num. 35:34; [2 Cor. 6:16]
5:6 aLev. 5:14—6:7
5:7 aLev. 5:5; 26:40, 41; Josh. 7:19; Ps. 32:5; 1 John 1:9 bLev. 6:4, 5
5:8 aLev. 5:15; 6:6, 7; 7:7

4:42 [1]household   5:2 [1]by contact with   5:8 [1]redeemer, Heb. *goel*

ram of the atonement with which atonement is made for him. 9Every ᵃoffering¹ of all the holy things of the children of Israel, which they bring to the priest, shall be ᵇhis. 10And every man's ¹holy things shall be his; whatever any man gives the priest shall be ᵃhis.'"

CONCERNING UNFAITHFUL WIVES

11And the LORD spoke to Moses, saying, 12"Speak to the children of Israel, and say to them: 'If any man's wife goes astray and behaves unfaithfully toward him, 13and a man ᵃlies with her carnally, and it is hidden from the eyes of her husband, and it is concealed that she has defiled herself, and *there was* no witness against her, nor was she ᵇcaught— 14if the spirit of jealousy comes upon him and he becomes ᵃjealous of his wife, who has defiled herself; or if the spirit of jealousy comes upon him and he becomes jealous of his wife, although she has not defiled herself— 15then the man shall bring his wife to the priest. He shall ᵃbring the offering required for her, one-tenth of an ephah of barley meal; he shall pour no oil on it and put no frankincense on it, because it *is* a grain offering of jealousy, an offering for remembering, for ᵇbringing iniquity to remembrance.

16'And the priest shall bring her near, and set her before the LORD. 17The priest shall take holy water in an earthen vessel, and take some of the dust that is on the floor of the tabernacle and put *it* into the water. 18Then the priest shall stand the woman before the ᵃLORD, uncover the woman's head, and put the offering for remembering in her hands, which *is* the grain offering of jealousy. And the priest shall have in his hand the bitter water that brings a curse. 19And the priest shall put her under oath, and say to the woman, "If no man has lain with you, and if you have not gone astray to uncleanness *while* under your husband's *authority,* be free from this bitter water that brings a curse. 20But if you have gone astray *while* under your husband's *authority,* and if you have defiled yourself and some man other than your husband has lain with you"— 21then the priest shall ᵃput the woman under the oath of the curse, and he shall say to the woman—ᵇ"the LORD make you a curse and an oath among your people, when the LORD makes your thigh ¹rot and your belly swell; 22and may this water that causes the curse ᵃgo into your stomach, and make *your* belly swell and *your* thigh rot."

'ᵇThen the woman shall say, "Amen, so be it."

23'Then the priest shall write these curses in a book, and he shall scrape *them* off into the bitter water. 24And he shall make the woman drink the bitter water that brings a curse, and the water that brings the curse shall enter her *to become* bitter. 25ᵃThen the priest shall take the grain offering of jealousy from the woman's hand, shall ᵇwave the offering before the LORD, and bring it to the altar; 26and the priest shall take a handful of the offering, ᵃas its memorial portion, burn *it* on the altar, and afterward make the woman drink the water. 27When he has made her drink the water, then it shall be, if she has defiled herself and behaved unfaithfully toward her husband, that the water that brings a ᵃcurse will enter her *and become* bitter, and her belly will swell, her thigh will rot, and

5:9 ᵃEx. 29:28; Lev. 6:17, 18, 26; 7:6–14
ᵇLev. 7:32–34; 10:14, 15

5:10 ᵃLev. 10:13

5:13 ᵃLev. 18:20; 20:10 ᵇJohn 8:4

5:14 ᵃProv. 6:34; Song 8:6

5:15 ᵃLev. 5:11
ᵇ1 Kin. 17:18; Ezek. 29:16; Heb. 10:3

5:18 ᵃHeb. 13:4

5:21 ᵃJosh. 6:26; 1 Sam. 14:24; Neh. 10:29
ᵇJer. 29:22

5:22 ᵃPs. 109:18
ᵇDeut. 27:15–26

5:25 ᵃLev. 8:27
ᵇLev. 2:2, 9

5:26 ᵃLev. 2:2, 9

5:27
ᵃDeut. 28:37; Is. 65:15; Jer. 24:9; 29:18, 22; 42:18

5:9 ¹heave offering   5:10 ¹consecrated   5:21 ¹Lit. fall away

the woman [b]will become a curse among her people. [28]But if the woman has not defiled herself, and is clean, then she shall be free and may conceive children.

[29]'This *is* the law of jealousy, when a wife, *while* under her husband's *authority,* [a]goes astray and defiles herself, [30]or when the spirit of jealousy comes upon a man, and he becomes jealous of his wife; then he shall stand the woman before the LORD, and the priest shall execute all this law upon her. [31]Then the man shall be free from [1]iniquity, but that woman [a]shall bear her [2]guilt.'"

THE LAW OF THE NAZIRITE

6 Then the LORD spoke to Moses, saying, [2]"Speak to the children of Israel, and say to them: 'When either a man or woman [1]consecrates an offering to take the vow of a Nazirite, [a]to separate himself to the LORD, [3a]he shall separate himself from wine and *similar* drink; he shall drink neither vinegar made from wine nor vinegar made from *similar* drink; neither shall he drink any grape juice, nor eat fresh grapes or raisins. [4]All the days of his [1]separation he shall eat nothing that is produced by the grapevine, from seed to skin.

[5]'All the days of the vow of his separation no [a]razor shall come upon his head; until the days are fulfilled for which he separated himself to the LORD, he shall be holy. *Then* he shall let the locks of the hair of his head grow. [6]All the days that he separates himself to the LORD [a]he shall not go near a dead body. [7a]He shall not [1]make himself unclean even for his father or his mother, for his brother or his sister, when they die, because his separation to God *is* on his head. [8a]All the days of his separation he shall be holy to the LORD.

[9]'And if anyone dies very suddenly beside him, and he defiles his consecrated head, then he shall [a]shave his head on the day of his cleansing; on the seventh day he shall shave it. [10]Then [a]on the eighth day he shall bring two turtledoves or two young pigeons to the priest, to the door of the tabernacle of meeting; [11]and the priest shall offer one as a sin offering and *the* other as a burnt offering, and make atonement for him, because he sinned in regard to the corpse; and he shall sanctify his head that same day. [12]He shall consecrate to the LORD the days of his separation, and bring a male lamb in its first year [a]as a trespass offering; but the former days shall be [1]lost, because his separation was defiled.

[13]'Now this *is* the law of the Nazirite: [a]When the days of his separation are fulfilled, he shall be brought to the door of the tabernacle of meeting. [14]And he shall present his offering to the LORD: one male lamb in its first year without blemish as a burnt offering, one ewe lamb in its first year without blemish [a]as a sin offering, one ram without blemish [b]as a peace offering, [15]a basket of unleavened bread, [a]cakes of fine flour mixed with oil, unleavened wafers [b]anointed with oil, and their grain offering with their [c]drink offerings.

[16]'Then the priest shall bring *them* before the LORD and offer his sin offering and his burnt offering; [17]and he shall offer the ram as a sacrifice of a peace offering to the LORD, with the basket of unleavened bread; the priest shall also offer its

---

5:27 [b]Num. 5:21

5:29 [a]Num. 5:19

5:31 [a]Lev. 20:17, 19, 20

6:2 [a]Lev. 27:2; Judg. 13:5; [Lam. 4:7; Amos 2:11, 12]; Acts 21:23; Rom. 1:1

6:3 [a]Lev. 10:9; Amos 2:12; Luke 1:15

6:5 [a]Judg. 13:5; 16:17; 1 Sam. 1:11

6:6 [a]Lev. 21:1–3, 11; Num. 19:11–22

6:7 [a]Lev. 21:1, 2, 11; Num. 9:6

6:8 [a][2 Cor. 6:17, 18]

6:9 [a]Lev. 14:8, 9; Acts 18:18; 21:24

6:10 [a]Lev. 5:7; 14:22; 15:14, 29

6:12 [a]Lev. 5:6

6:13 [a]Acts 21:26

6:14 [a]Lev. 4:2, 27, 32 [b]Lev. 3:6

6:15 [a]Lev. 2:4 [b]Ex. 29:2 [c]Num. 15:5, 7, 10

5:31 [1]*guilt*   [2]*iniquity*   **6:2** [1]Or *makes a difficult vow*   **6:4** [1]*Separation as a Nazirite*   **6:7** [1]*By touching a dead body*   **6:12** [1]*void*

grain offering and its drink offering. [18a]Then the Nazirite shall shave his consecrated head *at* the door of the tabernacle of meeting, and shall take the hair from his consecrated head and put *it* on the fire which is under the sacrifice of the peace offering.

[19]'And the priest shall take the [a]boiled shoulder of the ram, one [b]unleavened cake from the basket, and one unleavened wafer, and [c]put *them* upon the hands of the Nazirite after he has shaved his consecrated *hair,* [20]and the priest shall wave them as a wave offering before the LORD; [a]they *are* holy for the priest, together with the breast of the wave offering and the thigh of the heave offering. After that the Nazirite may drink wine.'

[21]"This is the law of the Nazirite who vows to the LORD the offering for his separation, and besides that, whatever else his hand is able to provide; according to the vow which he takes, so he must do according to the law of his separation."

THE PRIESTLY BLESSING

[22]And the LORD spoke to Moses, saying: [23]"Speak to Aaron and his sons, saying, 'This is the way you shall bless the children of Israel. Say to them:

[24] "The LORD [a]bless you and [b]keep you;
[25]   The LORD [a]make His face shine upon you,
      And [b]be gracious to you;
[26] [a]The LORD [1]lift up His countenance upon you,
      And [b]give you peace."'

[27a]"So they shall [1]put My name on the children of Israel, and [b]I will bless them."

OFFERINGS OF THE LEADERS

7 Now it came to pass, when Moses had finished [a]setting up the tabernacle, that he [b]anointed it and consecrated it and all its furnishings, and the altar and all its utensils; so he anointed them and consecrated them. [2]Then [a]the leaders of Israel, the heads of their fathers' houses, who *were* the leaders of the tribes [1]and over those who were numbered, made an offering. [3]And they brought their offering before the LORD, six covered carts and twelve oxen, a cart for *every* two of the leaders, and for each one an ox; and they presented them before the tabernacle.

[4]Then the LORD spoke to Moses, saying, [5]"Accept *these* from them, that they may be used in doing the work of the tabernacle of meeting; and you shall give them to the Levites, *to* every man according to his service." [6]So Moses took the carts and the oxen, and gave them to the Levites. [7]Two carts and four oxen [a]he gave to the sons of Gershon, according to their service; [8a]and four carts and eight oxen he gave to the sons of Merari, according to their service, under the [1]authority of Ithamar the son of Aaron the priest. [9]But to the sons of Kohath he gave none, because theirs *was* [a]the service of the holy things, [b]*which* they carried on their shoulders.

[10]Now the leaders offered [a]the dedication *offering* for the altar when it was anointed; so the leaders offered their offering

6:18 [a]Num. 6:9; Acts 21:23, 24

6:19 [a]1 Sam. 2:15
[b]Ex. 29:23, 24
[c]Lev. 7:30

6:20
[a]Ex. 29:27, 28

6:24
[a]Deut. 28:3–6
[b]Ps. 121:7;
John 7:11

6:25 [a]Ps. 31:16;
67:1; 80:3, 7, 19;
119:135; Dan. 9:17
[b]Gen. 43:29;
Ex. 33:19;
Mal. 1:9

6:26 [a]Ps. 4:6;
89:15 [b]Lev. 26:6;
Is. 26:3, 12;
John 14:27;
Phil. 4:7

6:27
[a]Deut. 28:10;
2 Sam. 7:23;
2 Chr. 7:14;
Is. 43:7;
Dan. 9:18, 19
[b]Ex. 20:24;
Num. 23:20;
Ps. 5:12; 67:7;
115:12, 13;
Eph. 1:3

7:1 [a]Ex. 40:17–33
[b]Lev. 8:10, 11

7:2 [a]Num. 1:4

7:7
[a]Num. 4:24–28

7:8
[a]Num. 4:29–33

7:9 [a]Num. 4:15
[b]Num. 4:6–14

7:10 [a]Num. 7:1;
Deut. 20:5;
1 Kin. 8:63;
2 Chr. 7:5, 9;
Ezra 6:16;
Neh. 12:27

6:26 [1]Look upon you with favor   6:27 [1]invoke   7:2 [1]Lit. *who stood over*
7:8 [1]Lit. *hand*

before the altar. ¹¹For the LORD said to Moses, "They shall offer their offering, one leader each day, for the dedication of the altar."

¹²And the one who offered his offering on the first day *was* ªNahshon the son of Amminadab, from the tribe of Judah. ¹³His offering *was* one silver platter, the weight of which *was* one hundred and thirty *shekels,* and one silver bowl of seventy shekels, according to ªthe shekel of the sanctuary, both of them full of fine flour mixed with oil as a ᵇgrain offering; ¹⁴one gold pan of ten *shekels,* full of ªincense; ¹⁵ªone young bull, one ram, and one male lamb ᵇin its first year, as a burnt offering; ¹⁶one kid of the goats as a ªsin offering; ¹⁷and for ªthe sacrifice of peace offerings: two oxen, five rams, five male goats, and five male lambs in their first year. This *was* the offering of Nahshon the son of Amminadab.

¹⁸On the second day Nethanel the son of Zuar, leader of Issachar, presented *an offering.* ¹⁹*For* his offering he offered one silver platter, the weight of which *was* one hundred and thirty *shekels,* and one silver bowl of seventy shekels, according to the shekel of the sanctuary, both of them full of fine flour mixed with oil as a grain offering; ²⁰one gold pan of ten *shekels,* full of incense; ²¹one young bull, one ram, and one male lamb in its first year, as a burnt offering; ²²one kid of the goats as a sin offering; ²³and as the sacrifice of peace offerings: two oxen, five rams, five male goats, and five male lambs in their first year. This *was* the offering of Nethanel the son of Zuar.

²⁴On the third day Eliab the son of Helon, leader of the children of Zebulun, *presented an offering.* ²⁵His offering *was* one silver platter, the weight of which *was* one hundred and thirty *shekels,* and one silver bowl of seventy shekels, according to the shekel of the sanctuary, both of them full of fine flour mixed with oil as a grain offering; ²⁶one gold pan of ten *shekels,* full of incense; ²⁷one young bull, one ram, and one male lamb in its first year, as a burnt offering; ²⁸one kid of the goats as a sin offering; ²⁹and for the sacrifice of peace offerings: two oxen, five rams, five male goats, and five male lambs in their first year. This *was* the offering of Eliab the son of Helon.

³⁰On the fourth day ªElizur the son of Shedeur, leader of the children of Reuben, *presented an offering.* ³¹His offering *was* one silver platter, the weight of which *was* one hundred and thirty *shekels,* and one silver bowl of seventy shekels, according to the shekel of the sanctuary, both of them full of fine flour mixed with oil as a grain offering; ³²one gold pan of ten *shekels,* full of incense; ³³one young bull, one ram, and one male lamb in its first year, as a burnt offering; ³⁴one kid of the goats as a sin offering; ³⁵and as the sacrifice of peace offerings: two oxen, five rams, five male goats, and five male lambs in their first year. This *was* the offering of Elizur the son of Shedeur.

³⁶On the fifth day ªShelumiel the son of Zurishaddai, leader of the children of Simeon, *presented an offering.* ³⁷His offering *was* one silver platter, the weight of which *was* one hundred and thirty *shekels,* and one silver bowl of seventy shekels, according to the shekel of the sanctuary, both of them full of fine flour mixed with oil as a grain offering; ³⁸one gold pan of ten *shekels,* full of incense; ³⁹one young bull, one

7:12 ªNum. 2:3
7:13 ªEx. 30:13
ᵇLev. 2:1
7:14
ªEx. 30:34, 35
7:15 ªLev. 1:2
ᵇEx. 12:5
7:16 ªLev. 4:23
7:17 ªLev. 3:1
7:30 ªNum. 1:5;
2:10
7:36 ªNum. 1:6;
2:12; 7:41

ram, and one male lamb in its first year, as a burnt offering; ⁴⁰one kid of the goats as a sin offering; ⁴¹and as the sacrifice of peace offerings: two oxen, five rams, five male goats, and five male lambs in their first year. This *was* the offering of Shelumiel the son of Zurishaddai.

⁴²On the sixth day ᵃEliasaph the son of ¹Deuel, leader of the children of Gad, *presented an offering.* ⁴³His offering *was* one silver platter, the weight of which *was* one hundred and thirty *shekels,* and one silver bowl of seventy shekels, according to the shekel of the sanctuary, both of them full of fine flour mixed with oil as a grain offering; ⁴⁴one gold pan of ten *shekels,* full of incense; ⁴⁵one young bull, one ram, and one male lamb in its first year, as ᵃa burnt offering; ⁴⁶one kid of the goats as a sin offering; ⁴⁷and as the sacrifice of peace offerings: two oxen, five rams, five male goats, and five male lambs in their first year. This *was* the offering of Eliasaph the son of Deuel.

⁴⁸On the seventh day ᵃElishama the son of Ammihud, leader of the children of Ephraim, *presented an offering.* ⁴⁹His offering *was* one silver platter, the weight of which *was* one hundred and thirty *shekels,* and one silver bowl of seventy shekels, according to the shekel of the sanctuary, both of them full of fine flour mixed with oil as a grain offering; ⁵⁰one gold pan of ten *shekels,* full of incense; ⁵¹one young bull, one ram, and one male lamb in its first year, as a burnt offering; ⁵²one kid of the goats as a sin offering; ⁵³and as the sacrifice of peace offerings: two oxen, five rams, five male goats, and five male lambs in their first year. This *was* the offering of Elishama the son of Ammihud.

⁵⁴On the eighth day ᵃGamaliel the son of Pedahzur, leader of the children of Manasseh, *presented an offering.* ⁵⁵His offering *was* one silver platter, the weight of which *was* one hundred and thirty *shekels,* and one silver bowl of seventy shekels, according to the shekel of the sanctuary, both of them full of fine flour mixed with oil as a grain offering; ⁵⁶one gold pan of ten *shekels,* full of incense; ⁵⁷one young bull, one ram, and one male lamb in its first year, as a burnt offering; ⁵⁸one kid of the goats as a sin offering; ⁵⁹and as the sacrifice of peace offerings: two oxen, five rams, five male goats, and five male lambs in their first year. This *was* the offering of Gamaliel the son of Pedahzur.

⁶⁰On the ninth day ᵃAbidan the son of Gideoni, leader of the children of Benjamin, *presented an offering.* ⁶¹His offering *was* one silver platter, the weight of which *was* one hundred and thirty *shekels,* and one silver bowl of seventy shekels, according to the shekel of the sanctuary, both of them full of fine flour mixed with oil as a grain offering; ⁶²one gold pan of ten *shekels,* full of incense; ⁶³one young bull, one ram, and one male lamb in its first year, as a burnt offering; ⁶⁴one kid of the goats as a sin offering; ⁶⁵and as the sacrifice of peace offerings: two oxen, five rams, five male goats, and five male lambs in their first year. This *was* the offering of Abidan the son of Gideoni.

⁶⁶On the tenth day ᵃAhiezer the son of Ammishaddai, leader of the children of Dan, *presented an offering.* ⁶⁷His offering *was* one silver platter, the weight of which *was* one hundred and thirty *shekels,* and one silver bowl of seventy

7:42 ᵃNum. 1:14; 2:14; 10:20

7:45 ᵃPs. 40:6

7:48 ᵃNum. 1:10; 2:18; 1 Chr. 7:26

7:54 ᵃNum. 1:10; 2:20

7:60 ᵃNum. 1:11; 2:22

7:66 ᵃNum. 1:12; 2:25

7:42 ¹*Reuel,* Num. 2:14

shekels, according to the shekel of the sanctuary, both of them full of fine flour mixed with oil as a grain offering; 68one gold pan of ten *shekels,* full of incense; 69one young bull, one ram, and one male lamb in its first year, as a burnt offering; 70one kid of the goats as a sin offering; 71and as the sacrifice of peace offerings: two oxen, five rams, five male goats, and five male lambs in their first year. This *was* the offering of Ahiezer the son of Ammishaddai.

72On the eleventh day aPagiel the son of Ocran, leader of the children of Asher, *presented an offering.* 73His offering *was* one silver platter, the weight of which *was* one hundred and thirty *shekels,* and one silver bowl of seventy shekels, according to the shekel of the sanctuary, both of them full of fine flour mixed with oil as a grain offering; 74one gold pan of ten *shekels,* full of incense; 75one young bull, one ram, and one male lamb in its first year, as a burnt offering; 76one kid of the goats as a sin offering; 77and as the sacrifice of peace offerings: two oxen, five rams, five male goats, and five male lambs in their first year. This *was* the offering of Pagiel the son of Ocran.

78On the twelfth day aAhira the son of Enan, leader of the children of Naphtali, *presented an offering.* 79His offering *was* one silver platter, the weight of which *was* one hundred and thirty *shekels,* and one silver bowl of seventy shekels, according to the shekel of the sanctuary, both of them full of fine flour mixed with oil as a grain offering; 80one gold pan of ten *shekels,* full of incense; 81one young bull, one ram, and one male lamb in its first year, as a burnt offering; 82one kid of the goats as a sin offering; 83and as the sacrifice of peace offerings: two oxen, five rams, five male goats, and five male lambs in their first year. This *was* the offering of Ahira the son of Enan.

84"This *was* athe dedication *offering* for the altar from the leaders of Israel, when it was anointed: twelve silver platters, twelve silver bowls, and twelve gold pans. 85Each silver platter *weighed* one hundred and thirty *shekels* and each bowl seventy *shekels.* All the silver of the vessels *weighed* two thousand four hundred *shekels,* according to the shekel of the sanctuary. 86The twelve gold pans full of incense *weighed* ten *shekels* apiece, according to the shekel of the sanctuary; all the gold of the pans *weighed* one hundred and twenty *shekels.* 87All the oxen for the burnt offering *were* twelve young bulls, the rams twelve, the male lambs in their first year twelve, with their grain offering, and the kids of the goats as a sin offering twelve. 88And all the oxen for the sacrifice of peace offerings were twenty-four bulls, the rams sixty, the male goats sixty, and the lambs in their first year sixty. This *was* the dedication *offering* for the altar after it was aanointed.

89Now when Moses went into the tabernacle of meeting ato speak with Him, he heard bthe voice of One speaking to him from above the mercy seat that *was* on the ark of the Testimony, from cbetween the two cherubim; thus He spoke to him.

ARRANGEMENT OF THE LAMPS
(Ex. 25:31–40)

8 And the LORD spoke to Moses, saying: 2"Speak to Aaron, and say to him, 'When you aarrange the lamps, the seven blamps shall give light in front of the lampstand.'" 3And

---

7:72
aNum. 1:13; 2:27

7:78
aNum. 1:15; 2:29

7:84 aNum. 7:10

7:88
aNum. 7:1, 10

7:89
a[Ex. 33:9, 11];
Num. 12:8
bEx. 25:21, 22
cPs. 80:1; 99:1

8:2
aLev. 24:2–4
bEx. 25:37;
40:25

Aaron did so; he arranged the lamps to face toward the front of the lampstand, as the LORD commanded Moses. 4aNow this workmanship of the lampstand *was* hammered gold; from its shaft to its flowers it *was* bhammered work. cAccording to the pattern which the LORD had shown Moses, so he made the lampstand.

CLEANSING AND DEDICATION OF THE LEVITES

5Then the LORD spoke to Moses, saying: 6"Take the Levites from among the children of Israel and cleanse them *ceremonially.* 7Thus you shall do to them to cleanse them: Sprinkle awater of purification on them, and blet1 them shave all their body, and let them wash their clothes, and *so* make themselves clean. 8Then let them take a young bull with aits grain offering of fine flour mixed with oil, and you shall take another young bull as a sin offering. 9aAnd you shall bring the Levites before the tabernacle of meeting, band you shall gather together the whole congregation of the children of Israel. 10So you shall bring the Levites before the LORD, and the children of Israel ashall lay their hands on the Levites; 11and Aaron shall 1offer the Levites before the LORD *like* a awave offering from the children of Israel, that they may perform the work of the LORD. 12aThen the Levites shall lay their hands on the heads of the young bulls, and you shall offer one as a sin offering and the other as a burnt offering to the LORD, to make atonement for the Levites.

13"And you shall stand the Levites before Aaron and his sons, and then offer them *like* a wave offering to the LORD. 14Thus you shall aseparate the Levites from among the children of Israel, and the Levites shall be bMine. 15After that the Levites shall go in to service the tabernacle of meeting. So you shall cleanse them and aoffer them *like* a wave offering. 16For they *are* awholly given to Me from among the children of Israel; I have taken them for Myself binstead of all who open the womb, the firstborn of all the children of Israel. 17aFor all the firstborn among the children of Israel *are* Mine, *both* man and beast; on the day that I struck all the firstborn in the land of Egypt I 1sanctified them to Myself. 18I have taken the Levites instead of all the firstborn of the children of Israel. 19And aI have given the Levites as a gift to Aaron and his sons from among the children of Israel, to do the work for the children of Israel in the tabernacle of meeting, and to make atonement for the children of Israel, bthat there be no plague among the children of Israel when the children of Israel come near the sanctuary."

20Thus Moses and Aaron and all the congregation of the children of Israel did to the Levites; according to all that the LORD commanded Moses concerning the Levites, so the children of Israel did to them. 21aAnd the Levites purified themselves and washed their clothes; then Aaron presented them *like* a wave offering before the LORD, and Aaron made atonement for them to cleanse them. 22aAfter that the Levites went in to do their work in the tabernacle of meeting before Aaron and his sons; bas the LORD commanded Moses concerning the Levites, so they did to them.

8:4 aEx. 25:31
bEx. 25:18
cEx. 25:40;
Acts 7:44

8:7 aNum. 19:9,
13, 17, 20;
Ps. 51:2, 7;
[Heb. 9:13, 14]
bLev. 14:8, 9

8:8 aLev. 2:1;
Num. 15:8–10

8:9 aEx. 29:4;
40:12 bLev. 8:3

8:10 aLev. 1:4

8:11 aNum. 18:6

8:12 aEx. 29:10

8:14 aNum. 16:9
bNum. 3:12,
45; 16:9

8:15
aNum. 8:11, 13

8:16 aNum. 3:9
bEx. 13:2;
Num. 3:12, 45

8:17 aEx. 12:2,
12, 13, 15;
Num. 3:13;
Luke 2:23

8:19 aNum. 3:9
bNum. 1:53;
16:46; 18:5;
2 Chr. 26:16

8:21 aNum. 8:7

8:22 aNum. 8:15
bNum. 8:5

8:7 1Heb. *let them cause a razor to pass over*   8:11 1*present*   8:17 1*set them apart*

23Then the LORD spoke to Moses, saying, 24"This *is* what *pertains* to the Levites: aFrom twenty-five years old and above one may enter to perform service in the work of the tabernacle of meeting; 25and at the age of fifty years they must cease performing this work, and shall work no more. 26They may minister with their brethren in the tabernacle of meeting, ato attend to needs, but they *themselves* shall do no work. Thus you shall do to the Levites regarding their duties."

THE SECOND PASSOVER
(*Ex. 12:1–20*)

9 Now the LORD spoke to Moses in the Wilderness of Sinai, in the first month of the second year after they had come out of the land of Egypt, saying: 2"Let the children of Israel keep athe Passover at its appointed btime. 3On the fourteenth day of this month, 1at twilight, you shall 2keep it at its appointed time. According to all its 3rites and ceremonies you shall keep it." 4So Moses told the children of Israel that they should keep the Passover. 5And athey kept the Passover on the fourteenth day of the first month, at twilight, in the Wilderness of Sinai; according to all that the LORD commanded Moses, so the children of Israel did.

6Now there were *certain* men who were adefiled by a human corpse, so that they could not keep the Passover on that day; band they came before Moses and Aaron that day. 7And those men said to him, "We *became* defiled by a human corpse. Why are we kept from presenting the offering of the LORD at its appointed time among the children of Israel?"

8And Moses said to them, "Stand still, that aI may hear what the LORD will command concerning you."

9Then the LORD spoke to Moses, saying, 10"Speak to the children of Israel, saying: 'If anyone of you or your 1posterity is unclean because of a corpse, or *is* far away on a journey, he may still keep the LORD's Passover. 11On athe fourteenth day of the second month, at twilight, they may keep it. They shall beat it with unleavened bread and bitter herbs. 12aThey shall leave none of it until morning, bnor break one of its bones. cAccording to all the 1ordinances of the Passover they shall keep it. 13But the man who *is* clean and is not on a journey, and ceases to keep the Passover, that same person ashall be cut off from among his people, because he bdid not bring the offering of the LORD at its appointed time; that man shall cbear his sin.

14'And if a stranger 1dwells among you, and would keep the LORD's Passover, he must do so according to the rite of the Passover and according to its ceremony; ayou shall have one 2ordinance, both for the stranger and the native of the land.'"

THE CLOUD AND THE FIRE
(*Ex. 13:21, 22; 40:34–38*)

15Now aon the day that the tabernacle was raised up, the cloud bcovered the tabernacle, the tent of the Testimony; cfrom evening until morning it was above the tabernacle like the appearance of fire. 16So it was always: the cloud covered

Cross-references

8:24 aNum. 4:3; 1 Chr. 23:3, 24, 27
8:26 aNum. 1:53
9:2 aEx. 12:1–16; Lev. 23:5; Num. 28:16; Deut. 16:1, 2 b2 Chr. 30:1–15; Luke 22:7; [1 Cor. 5:7, 8]
9:5 aJosh. 5:10
9:6 aNum. 5:2; 19:11–22; John 18:28 bEx. 18:15, 19, 26; Num. 27:2
9:8 aEx. 18:22; Num. 27:5
9:11 a2 Chr. 30:2, 15 bEx. 12:8
9:12 aEx. 12:10 bEx. 12:46; [John 19:36] cEx. 12:43
9:13 aGen. 17:14; Ex. 12:15, 47 bNum. 9:7 cNum. 5:31
9:14 aEx. 12:49; Lev. 24:22; Num. 15:15, 16, 29
9:15 aEx. 40:33, 34; Neh. 9:12, 19; Ps. 78:14 bIs. 4:5 cEx. 13:21, 22; 40:38

9:3 1Lit. *between the evenings* 2*observe* 3*statutes* 9:10 1*descendants*
9:12 1*statutes* 9:14 1As a resident alien 2*statute*

it *by day,* and the appearance of fire by night. ¹⁷Whenever the cloud ᵃwas ¹taken up from above the tabernacle, after that the children of Israel would journey; and in the place where the cloud settled, there the children of Israel would pitch their tents. ¹⁸At the ¹command of the LORD the children of Israel would journey, and at the command of the LORD they would camp; ᵃas long as the cloud stayed above the tabernacle they remained encamped. ¹⁹Even when the cloud continued long, many days above the tabernacle, the children of Israel ᵃkept the charge of the LORD and did not journey. ²⁰So it was, when the cloud was above the tabernacle a few days: according to the command of the LORD they would remain encamped, and according to the command of the LORD they would journey. ²¹So it was, when the cloud remained only from evening until morning: when the cloud was taken up in the morning, then they would journey; whether by day or by night, whenever the cloud was taken up, they would journey. ²²*Whether it was* two days, a month, or a year that the cloud remained above the tabernacle, the children of Israel ᵃwould remain encamped and not journey; but when it was taken up, they would journey. ²³At the command of the LORD they remained encamped, and at the command of the LORD they journeyed; they ᵃkept the charge of the LORD, at the command of the LORD by the hand of Moses.

TWO SILVER TRUMPETS

10 And the LORD spoke to Moses, saying: ²"Make two silver trumpets for yourself; you shall make them of hammered work; you shall use them for ᵃcalling the congregation and for directing the movement of the camps. ³When ᵃthey blow both of them, all the congregation shall gather before you at the door of the tabernacle of meeting. ⁴But if they blow *only* one, then the leaders, the ᵃheads of the divisions of Israel, shall gather to you. ⁵When you sound the ᵃadvance, ᵇthe camps that lie on the east side shall then begin their journey. ⁶When you sound the advance the second time, then the camps that lie ᵃon the south side shall begin their journey; they shall sound the call for them to begin their journeys. ⁷And when the assembly is to be gathered together, ᵃyou shall blow, but not ᵇsound the advance. ⁸ᵃThe sons of Aaron, the priests, shall blow the trumpets; and these shall be to you as an ¹ordinance forever throughout your generations.

⁹ᵃ"When you go to war in your land against the enemy who ᵇoppresses you, then you shall sound an alarm with the trumpets, and you will be ᶜremembered before the LORD your God, and you will be saved from your enemies. ¹⁰Also ᵃin the day of your gladness, in your appointed feasts, and at the beginning of your months, you shall blow the trumpets over your burnt offerings and over the sacrifices of your peace offerings; and they shall be ᵇa memorial for you before your God: I *am* the LORD your God."

DEPARTURE FROM SINAI

¹¹Now it came to pass on the twentieth *day* of the second

9:17
ᵃEx. 40:36–38;
Num. 10:11, 12,
33, 34; Ps. 80:1

9:18 ᵃ1 Cor. 10:1

9:19
ᵃNum. 1:53; 3:8

9:22
ᵃEx. 40:36, 37

9:23 ᵃNum. 9:19

10:2 ᵃIs. 1:13

10:3 ᵃJer. 4:5;
Joel 2:15

10:4 ᵃEx. 18:21;
Num. 1:16; 7:2

10:5 ᵃJoel 2:1
ᵇNum. 2:3

10:6 ᵃNum. 2:10

10:7 ᵃNum. 10:3
ᵇJoel 2:1

10:8
ᵃNum. 31:6;
Josh. 6:4;
1 Chr. 15:24;
2 Chr. 13:12

10:9
ᵃNum. 31:6;
Josh. 6:5;
2 Chr. 13:14
ᵇJudg. 2:18; 4:3;
6:9; 10:8, 12
ᶜGen. 8:1;
Ps. 106:4

10:10
ᵃLev. 23:24;
Num. 29:1;
1 Chr. 15:24;
2 Chr. 5:12;
Ps. 81:3
ᵇLev. 23:24;
Num. 10:9

9:17 ¹*lifted up*   9:18 ¹Lit. *mouth*   10:8 ¹*statute*

month, in the second year, that the cloud ªwas taken up from above the tabernacle of the Testimony. ¹²And the children of Israel set out from the ªWilderness of Sinai on ᵇtheir journeys; then the cloud settled down in the ᶜWilderness of Paran. ¹³So they started out for the first time ªaccording to the command of the LORD by the hand of Moses.

¹⁴The ¹standard of the camp of the children of Judah ªset out first according to their armies; over their army was ᵇNahshon the son of Amminadab. ¹⁵Over the army of the tribe of the children of Issachar *was* Nethanel the son of Zuar. ¹⁶And over the army of the tribe of the children of Zebulun *was* Eliab the son of Helon.

¹⁷Then ªthe tabernacle was taken down; and the sons of Gershon and the sons of Merari set out, ᵇcarrying the tabernacle.

¹⁸And ªthe standard of the camp of Reuben set out according to their armies; over their army *was* Elizur the son of Shedeur. ¹⁹Over the army of the tribe of the children of Simeon *was* Shelumiel the son of Zurishaddai. ²⁰And over the army of the tribe of the children of Gad *was* Eliasaph the son of Deuel.

²¹Then the Kohathites set out, carrying the ªholy things. (The tabernacle would be ¹prepared for their arrival.)

²²And ªthe standard of the camp of the children of Ephraim set out according to their armies; over their army *was* Elishama the son of Ammihud. ²³Over the army of the tribe of the children of Manasseh *was* Gamaliel the son of Pedahzur. ²⁴And over the army of the tribe of the children of Benjamin *was* Abidan the son of Gideoni.

²⁵Then ªthe standard of the camp of the children of Dan (the rear guard of all the camps) set out according to their armies; over their army *was* Ahiezer the son of Ammishaddai. ²⁶Over the army of the tribe of the children of Asher *was* Pagiel the son of Ocran. ²⁷And over the army of the tribe of the children of Naphtali *was* Ahira the son of Enan.

²⁸ªThus *was* the order of march of the children of Israel, according to their armies, when they began their journey.

²⁹Now Moses said to ªHobab the son of ᵇReuel¹ the Midianite, Moses' father-in-law, "We are setting out for the place of which the LORD said, ᶜ'I will give it to you.' Come with us, and ᵈwe will treat you well; for ᵉthe LORD has promised good things to Israel."

³⁰And he said to him, "I will not go, but I will depart to my *own* land and to my relatives."

³¹So *Moses* said, "Please do not leave, inasmuch as you know how we are to camp in the wilderness, and you can ¹be our ªeyes. ³²And it shall be, if you go with us—indeed it shall be—that ªwhatever good the LORD will do to us, the same we will do to you."

³³So they departed from ªthe mountain of the LORD on a journey of three days; and the ark of the covenant of the LORD ᵇwent before them for the three days' journey, to search out a resting place for them. ³⁴And ªthe cloud of the LORD *was* above them by day when they went out from the camp.

³⁵So it was, whenever the ark set out, that Moses said:

10:11 ªNum. 9:17

10:12 ªEx. 19:1; Num. 1:1; 9:5
ᵇEx. 40:36
ᶜGen. 21:21; Num. 12:16; Deut. 1:1

10:13
ªNum. 10:5, 6

10:14
ªNum. 2:3–9
ᵇNum. 1:7

10:17 ªNum. 1:51
ᵇNum. 4:21–32; 7:7–9

10:18
ªNum. 2:10–16

10:21
ªNum. 4:4–20; 7:9

10:22
ªNum. 2:18–24

10:25
ªNum. 2:25–31; Josh. 6:9

10:28
ªNum. 2:34

10:29 ªJudg. 4:11
ᵇEx. 2:18; 3:1;
18:12 ᶜGen. 12:7; Ex. 6:4–8
ᵈJudg. 1:16
ᵉGen. 32:12; Ex. 3:8

10:31 ªJob 29:15

10:32 ªEx. 18:9; Lev. 19:34; Judg. 1:16

10:33 ªEx. 3:1; Deut. 1:6
ᵇDeut. 1:33; Josh. 3:3–6; Ezek. 20:6

10:34 ªEx. 13:21; Neh. 9:12, 19

10:14 ¹*banner*   **10:21** ¹Prepared by the Gershonites and the Merarites
10:29 ¹*Jethro*, Ex. 3:1; LXX *Raguel*   **10:31** ¹Act as our guide

a"Rise up, O LORD!
Let Your enemies be scattered,
And let those who hate You flee before You."

36And when it rested, he said:

"Return, O LORD,
To the many thousands of Israel."

THE PEOPLE COMPLAIN

11 Now a*when* the people complained, it displeased the LORD; bfor the LORD heard *it,* and His anger was aroused. So the cfire of the LORD burned among them, and consumed *some* in the outskirts of the camp. 2Then the people acried out to Moses, and when Moses bprayed to the LORD, the fire was 1quenched. 3So he called the name of the place 1Taberah, because the fire of the LORD had burned among them.

4Now the amixed multitude who were among them 1yielded to bintense craving; so the children of Israel also wept again and said: c"Who will give us meat to eat? 5aWe remember the fish which we ate freely in Egypt, the cucumbers, the melons, the leeks, the onions, and the garlic; 6but now aour whole being *is* dried up; *there is* nothing at all except this manna *before* our eyes!"

7Now athe manna *was* like coriander seed, and its color like the color of bdellium. 8The people went about and gathered *it,* ground *it* on millstones or beat *it* in the mortar, cooked *it* in pans, and made cakes of it; and aits taste was like the taste of pastry prepared with oil. 9And awhen the dew fell on the camp in the night, the manna fell on it.

10Then Moses heard the people weeping throughout their families, everyone at the door of his tent; and athe anger of the LORD was greatly aroused; Moses also was displeased. 11aSo Moses said to the LORD, "Why have You afflicted Your servant? And why have I not found favor in Your sight, that You have laid the 1burden of all these people on me? 12Did I conceive all these people? Did I beget them, that You should say to me, a'Carry them in your bosom, as a bguardian carries a nursing child,' to the land which You cswore1 to their fathers? 13aWhere am I to get meat to give to all these people? For they weep all over me, saying, 'Give us meat, that we may eat.' 14aI am not able to bear all these people alone, because the burden *is* too heavy for me. 15If You treat me like this, please kill me here and now—if I have found favor in Your sight—and ado not let me see my wretchedness!"

THE SEVENTY ELDERS

16So the LORD said to Moses: "Gather to Me aseventy men of the elders of Israel, whom you know to be the elders of the people and bofficers over them; bring them to the tabernacle of meeting, that they may stand there with you. 17Then I will come down and talk with you there. aI will take of the Spirit that *is* upon you and will put *the same* upon them; and they shall bear the burden of the people with you, that you may not bear *it* yourself alone. 18Then you shall say to the people, 1'Consecrate yourselves for tomorrow, and you shall eat meat;

10:35
aPs. 68:1, 2;
132:8; Is. 17:12–14

11:1 aNum. 14:2;
16:11; 17:5;
Deut. 9:22
bPs. 78:21
cLev. 10:2;
2 Kin. 1:12

11:2 aNum. 12:11,
13; 21:7
b[James 5:16]

11:4 aEx. 12:38
b1 Cor. 10:6
c[Ps. 78:18]

11:5 aEx. 16:3

11:6 aNum. 21:5

11:7 aEx. 16:14, 31

11:8 aEx. 16:31

11:9 aEx. 16:13, 14

11:10 aPs. 78:21

11:11 aEx. 5:22;
Deut. 1:12

11:12 aIs. 40:11
bIs. 49:23;
1 Thess. 2:7
cGen. 26:3

11:13
aMatt. 15:33;
Mark 8:4

11:14 aEx. 18:18;
Deut. 1:12

11:15 aRev. 3:17

11:16 aEx. 18:25;
24:1, 9
bDeut. 16:18

11:17
a1 Sam. 10:6;
2 Kin. 2:15;
[Joel 2:28]

11:2 1extinguished   11:3 1Lit. *Burning*   11:4 1Lit. *lusted intensely*
11:11 1responsibility   11:12 1solemnly promised   11:18 1Set yourselves apart

for you have wept [a]in the hearing of the LORD, saying, "Who will give us meat to eat? For *it was* well with us in Egypt." Therefore the LORD will give you meat, and you shall eat. [19]You shall eat, not one day, nor two days, nor five days, nor ten days, nor twenty days, [20a]but *for* a whole month, until it comes out of your nostrils and becomes loathsome to you, because you have [b]despised the LORD who is among you, and have wept before Him, saying, [c]"Why did we ever come up out of Egypt?"'"

[21]And Moses said, [a]"The people whom I *am* among *are* six hundred thousand men on foot; yet You have said, 'I will give them meat, that they may eat *for* a whole month.' [22a]Shall flocks and herds be slaughtered for them, to provide enough for them? Or shall all the fish of the sea be gathered together for them, to provide enough for them?"

[23]And the LORD said to Moses, [a]"Has[1] the LORD's arm been shortened? Now you shall see whether [b]what I say will happen to you or not."

[24]So Moses went out and told the people the words of the LORD, and he [a]gathered the seventy men of the elders of the people and placed them around the tabernacle. [25]Then the LORD came down in the cloud, and spoke to him, and took of the Spirit that *was* upon him, and placed *the same* upon the seventy elders; and it happened, [a]when the Spirit rested upon them, that [b]they prophesied, [1]although they never did so again.

[26]But two men had remained in the camp: the name of one *was* Eldad, and the name of the other Medad. And the Spirit rested upon them. Now they *were* among those listed, but who [a]had not gone out to the tabernacle; yet they prophesied in the camp. [27]And a young man ran and told Moses, and said, "Eldad and Medad are prophesying in the camp."

[28]So Joshua the son of Nun, Moses' assistant, *one* of his choice men, answered and said, "Moses my lord, [a]forbid them!"

[29]Then Moses said to him, "Are you [1]zealous for my sake? [a]Oh, that all the LORD's people were prophets *and* that the LORD would put His Spirit upon them!" [30]And Moses returned to the camp, he and the elders of Israel.

THE LORD SENDS QUAIL

[31]Now a [a]wind went out from the LORD, and it brought quail from the sea and left *them* fluttering near the camp, about a day's journey on this side and about a day's journey on the other side, all around the camp, and about two cubits above the surface of the ground. [32]And the people stayed up all that day, all night, and all the next day, and gathered the quail (he who gathered least gathered ten [a]homers); and they spread *them* out for themselves all around the camp. [33]But while the [a]meat *was* still between their teeth, before it was chewed, the wrath of the LORD was aroused against the people, and the LORD struck the people with a very great plague. [34]So he called the name of that place [1]Kibroth Hattaavah, because there they buried the people who had yielded to craving.

11:18 [a]Ex. 16:7
11:20 [a]Ps. 78:29; 106:15
[b]1 Sam. 10:19
[c]Num. 21:5
11:21 [a]Gen. 12:2; Ex. 12:37; Num. 1:46; 2:32
11:22 [a]2 Kin. 7:2
11:23 [a]Is. 50:2; 59:1
[b]Num. 23:19
11:24 [a]Num. 11:16
11:25 [a]2 Kin. 2:15
[b]1 Sam. 10:5, 6, 10; Joel 2:28; Acts 2:17, 18; 1 Cor. 14:1
11:26 [a]Jer. 36:5
11:28 [a][Mark 9:38–40; Luke 9:49]
11:29 [a]1 Cor. 14:5
11:31 [a]Ex. 16:13; Ps. 78:26–28; 105:40
11:32 [a]Ex. 16:36; Ezek. 45:11
11:33 [a]Ps. 78:29–31; 106:15

11:23 [1]Is the LORD's power limited?　11:25 [1]Tg., Vg. *and they did not cease*
11:29 [1]*jealous*　11:34 [1]Lit. *Graves of Craving*

35aFrom Kibroth Hattaavah the people moved to Hazeroth, and camped at Hazeroth.

DISSENSION OF AARON AND MIRIAM

12 Then aMiriam and Aaron 1spoke bagainst Moses because of the 2Ethiopian woman whom he had married; for che had married an Ethiopian woman. 2So they said, "Has the LORD indeed spoken only through aMoses? bHas He not spoken through us also?" And the LORD cheard it. 3(Now the man Moses *was* very humble, more than all men who *were* on the face of the earth.)

4aSuddenly the LORD said to Moses, Aaron, and Miriam, "Come out, you three, to the tabernacle of meeting!" So the three came out. 5aThen the LORD came down in the pillar of cloud and stood *in* the door of the tabernacle, and called Aaron and Miriam. And they both went forward. 6Then He said,

"Hear now My words:
If there is a prophet among you,
I, the LORD, make Myself known to him ain a vision;
I speak to him bin a dream.
7   Not so with aMy servant Moses;
bHe *is* faithful in all cMy house.
8   I speak with him aface to face,
Even bplainly,1 and not in 2dark sayings;
And he sees cthe form of the LORD.
Why then dwere you not afraid
To speak against My servant Moses?"

9So the anger of the LORD was aroused against them, and He departed. 10And when the cloud departed from above the tabernacle, asuddenly Miriam *became* bleprous, *as white as* snow. Then Aaron turned toward Miriam, and there she was, a leper. 11So Aaron said to Moses, "Oh, my lord! Please ado not lay 1*this* sin on us, in which we have done foolishly and in which we have sinned. 12Please ado not let her be as one dead, whose flesh is half consumed when he comes out of his mother's womb!"

13So Moses cried out to the LORD, saying, "Please aheal her, O God, I pray!"

14Then the LORD said to Moses, "If her father had but aspit in her face, would she not be shamed seven days? Let her be bshut1 out of the camp seven days, and afterward she may be received *again*." 15aSo Miriam was shut out of the camp seven days, and the people did not journey till Miriam was brought in *again*. 16And afterward the people moved from aHazeroth and camped in the Wilderness of Paran.

SPIES SENT INTO CANAAN
(Deut. 1:19–33)

13 And the LORD spoke to Moses, saying, 2a"Send men to spy out the land of Canaan, which I am giving to the children of Israel; from each tribe of their fathers you shall send a man, every one a leader among them."

3So Moses sent them afrom the Wilderness of Paran according to the command of the LORD, all of them men who

---

12:1 1criticized   2Cushite   12:8 1appearing   2riddles   12:11 1the penalty for this   12:14 1exiled

11:35
aNum. 33:17

12:1 aEx. 15:20, 21; Num. 20:1
bNum. 11:1
cEx. 2:21

12:2 aNum. 16:3
bEx. 15:20;
Mic. 6:4
cGen. 29:33;
Num. 11:1;
2 Kin. 19:4;
Is. 37:4;
Ezek. 35:12, 13

12:4 a[Ps. 76:9]

12:5 aEx. 19:9; 34:5;
Num. 11:25; 16:19

12:6 aGen. 46:2;
1 Sam. 3:15;
Job 33:15;
Ezek. 1:1;
Dan. 8:2;
Luke 1:11;
Acts 10:11, 17; 22:17, 18
bGen. 31:10;
1 Kin. 3:5, 15;
Matt. 1:20

12:7 aJosh. 1:1;
Ps. 105:26
bHeb. 3:2, 5
c1 Tim. 1:12

12:8 aEx. 33:11;
Deut. 34:10;
Hos. 12:13
b[1 Cor. 13:12]
cEx. 33:19–23
d2 Pet. 2:10;
Jude 8

12:10
aDeut. 24:9
bEx. 4:6;
2 Kin. 5:27; 15:5;
2 Chr. 26:19, 20

12:11
a2 Sam. 19:19;
24:10

12:12 aPs. 88:4

12:13 aPs. 103:3

12:14
aDeut. 25:9;
Job 30:10;
Is. 50:6
bLev. 13:46;
Num. 5:1–4

12:15
aDeut. 24:9;
2 Chr. 26:20, 21

12:16
aNum. 11:35;
33:17, 18

13:2
aNum. 32:8;
Deut. 1:22; 9:23

13:3 aNum. 12:16;
32:8; Deut. 1:19;
9:23

were heads of the children of Israel. ⁴Now these *were* their names: from the tribe of Reuben, Shammua the son of Zaccur; ⁵from the tribe of Simeon, Shaphat the son of Hori; ⁶ᵃfrom the tribe of Judah, ᵇCaleb the son of Jephunneh; ⁷from the tribe of Issachar, Igal the son of Joseph; ⁸from the tribe of Ephraim, ¹Hoshea the son of Nun; ⁹from the tribe of Benjamin, Palti the son of Raphu; ¹⁰from the tribe of Zebulun, Gaddiel the son of Sodi; ¹¹from the tribe of Joseph, *that is,* from the tribe of Manasseh, Gaddi the son of Susi; ¹²from the tribe of Dan, Ammiel the son of Gemalli; ¹³from the tribe of Asher, Sethur the son of Michael; ¹⁴from the tribe of Naphtali, Nahbi the son of Vophsi; ¹⁵from the tribe of Gad, Geuel the son of Machi.

¹⁶These *are* the names of the men whom Moses sent to ¹spy out the land. And Moses called ᵃHoshea² the son of Nun, Joshua.

¹⁷Then Moses sent them to spy out the land of Canaan, and said to them, "Go up this *way* into the South, and go up to ᵃthe mountains, ¹⁸and see what the land is like: whether the people who dwell in it *are* strong or weak, few or many; ¹⁹whether the land they dwell in *is* good or bad; whether the cities they inhabit *are* like camps or strongholds; ²⁰whether the land *is* ¹rich or poor; and whether there are forests there or not. ᵃBe of good courage. And bring some of the fruit of the land." Now the time *was* the season of the first ripe grapes.

²¹So they went up and spied out the land ᵃfrom the Wilderness of Zin as far as ᵇRehob, near the entrance of ᶜHamath. ²²And they went up through the South and came to ᵃHebron; Ahiman, Sheshai, and Talmai, the descendants of ᵇAnak, *were* there. (Now Hebron was built seven years before Zoan in Egypt.) ²³ᵃThen they came to the ¹Valley of Eshcol, and there cut down a branch with one cluster of grapes; they carried it between two of them on a pole. *They* also *brought* some of the pomegranates and figs. ²⁴The place was called the Valley of ¹Eshcol, because of the cluster which the men of Israel cut down there. ²⁵And they returned from spying out the land after forty days.

²⁶Now they departed and came back to Moses and Aaron and all the congregation of the children of Israel in the Wilderness of Paran, at ᵃKadesh; they brought back word to them and to all the congregation, and showed them the fruit of the land. ²⁷Then they told him, and said: "We went to the land where you sent us. It truly ¹flows with ᵃmilk and honey, ᵇand this *is* its fruit. ²⁸Nevertheless the ᵃpeople who dwell in the land *are* strong; the cities *are* fortified *and* very large; moreover we saw the descendants of ᵇAnak there. ²⁹ᵃThe Amalekites dwell in the land of the South; the Hittites, the Jebusites, and the Amorites dwell in the mountains; and the Canaanites dwell by the sea and along the banks of the Jordan."

³⁰Then ᵃCaleb quieted the people before Moses, and said, "Let us go up at once and take possession, for we are well able to overcome it."

³¹ᵃBut the men who had gone up with him said, "We are not able to go up against the people, for they *are* stronger

---

13:6
ᵃNum. 34:19
ᵇNum. 14:6, 30; Josh. 14:6, 7; Judg. 1:12; 1 Chr. 4:15

13:16 ᵃEx. 17:9; Deut. 32:44

13:17 ᵃJudg. 1:9

13:20
ᵃDeut. 31:6, 7, 23

13:21
ᵃNum. 20:1; 27:14; 33:36; Josh. 15:1
ᵇJosh. 19:28
ᶜNum. 34:8; Josh. 13:5

13:22
ᵃJosh. 15:13, 14; Judg. 1:10
ᵇJosh. 11:21, 22

13:23
ᵃGen. 14:13; Num. 13:24; 32:9; Deut. 1:24, 25

13:26
ᵃNum. 20:1, 16; 32:8; 33:36; Deut. 1:19; Josh. 14:6

13:27
ᵃEx. 3:8, 17; 13:5; 33:3 ᵇDeut. 1:25

13:28
ᵃDeut. 1:28; 9:1, 2
ᵇJosh. 11:21, 22

13:29 ᵃEx. 17:8; Judg. 6:3

13:30
ᵃNum. 14:6, 24

13:31
ᵃNum. 32:9; Deut. 1:28; 9:1–3; Josh. 14:8

13:8 ¹LXX, Vg. *Oshea*   13:16 ¹*secretly search*   ²LXX, Vg. *Oshea*
13:20 ¹*fertile or barren*   13:23 ¹*Wadi*   13:24 ¹Lit. *Cluster*   13:27 ¹Has an abundance of food

than we." ³²And they ^agave the children of Israel a bad report of the land which they had spied out, saying, "The land through which we have gone as spies *is* a land that devours its inhabitants, and ^ball the people whom we saw in it *are* men of *great* stature. ³³There we saw the ¹giants (^athe descendants of Anak came from the giants); and we were ^blike² grasshoppers in our own sight, and so we were ^cin their sight."

ISRAEL REFUSES TO ENTER CANAAN

14 So all the congregation lifted up their voices and cried, and the people ^awept that night. ^{2a}And all the children of Israel complained against Moses and Aaron, and the whole congregation said to them, "If only we had died in the land of Egypt! Or if only we had died in this wilderness! ³Why has the LORD brought us to this land to ¹fall by the sword, that our wives and ^achildren should become victims? Would it not be better for us to return to Egypt?" ⁴So they said to one another, ^a"Let us select a leader and ^breturn to Egypt."

⁵Then Moses and Aaron ¹fell on their faces before all the assembly of the congregation of the children of Israel.

⁶But Joshua the son of Nun and Caleb the son of Jephunneh, *who were* among those who had spied out the land, tore their clothes; ⁷and they spoke to all the congregation of the children of Israel, saying: ^a"The land we passed through to spy out *is* an exceedingly good land. ⁸If the LORD ^adelights in us, then He will bring us into this land and give it to us, ^b'a land which flows with milk and honey.' ⁹Only ^ado not rebel against the LORD, ^bnor fear the people of the land, for ^cthey¹ *are* our bread; their protection has departed from them, ^dand the LORD *is* with us. Do not fear them."

^{10a}And all the congregation said to stone them with stones. Now ^bthe glory of the LORD appeared in the tabernacle of meeting before all the children of Israel.

MOSES INTERCEDES FOR THE PEOPLE

¹¹Then the LORD said to Moses: "How long will these people ^areject¹ Me? And how long will they not ^bbelieve Me, with all the ²signs which I have performed among them? ¹²I will strike them with the pestilence and disinherit them, and I will ^amake of you a nation greater and mightier than they."

¹³And ^aMoses said to the LORD: ^b"Then the Egyptians will hear *it,* for by Your might You brought these people up from among them, ¹⁴and they will tell *it* to the inhabitants of this land. They have ^aheard that You, LORD, *are* among these people; that You, LORD, are seen face to face and Your cloud stands above them, and You go before them in a pillar of cloud by day and in a pillar of fire by night. ¹⁵Now *if* You kill these people as one man, then the nations which have heard of Your fame will speak, saying, ¹⁶'Because the LORD was not ^aable to bring this people to the land which He swore to give them, therefore He killed them in the wilderness.' ¹⁷And now, I pray, let the power of my Lord be great, just as You have spoken, saying, ^{18a}'The LORD is longsuffering and abundant in mercy, forgiving iniquity and transgression; but He by no means clears *the*

13:33 ¹Heb. *nephilim* ²As mere insects 14:3 ¹*be killed in battle* 14:5 ¹*prostrated themselves* 14:9 ¹They shall be as food for our consumption. 14:11 ¹*despise* ²*miraculous signs*

13:32
^aNum. 14:36, 37; Ps. 106:24
^bAmos 2:9

13:33
^aDeut. 1:28; 9:2; Josh. 11:21
^bIs. 40:22
^c1 Sam. 17:42

14:1 ^aNum. 11:4; Deut. 1:45

14:2 ^aEx. 16:2; 17:3; Num. 16:41; Ps. 106:25; 1 Cor. 10:10

14:3
^aNum. 14:31; Deut. 1:39

14:4 ^aNeh. 9:17
^bDeut. 17:16; Acts 7:39

14:7
^aNum. 13:27; Deut. 1:25

14:8
^aDeut. 10:15; 2 Sam. 15:25, 26; 1 Kin. 10:9; Ps. 147:11
^bEx. 3:8; Num. 13:27

14:9 ^aDeut. 1:26; 9:7, 23, 24; 1 Sam. 15:23
^bDeut. 7:18
^cNum. 24:8
^dGen. 48:21; Ex. 33:16; Deut. 20:1, 3, 4; 31:6–8; Josh. 1:5; Judg. 1:22; 2 Chr. 13:12; Ps. 46:7, 11; Zech. 8:23; Matt. 28:20; Heb. 13:5

14:10 ^aEx. 17:4
^bEx. 16:10; Lev. 9:23

14:11 ^aPs. 95:8; Heb. 3:8
^bDeut. 9:23; [John 12:37]

14:12 ^aEx. 32:10

14:13 ^aPs. 106:23
^bEx. 32:12; Deut. 9:26–28; 32:27

14:14
^aDeut. 2:25

14:16
^aDeut. 9:28

14:18
^aEx. 34:6, 7; Deut. 5:10; 7:9; Ps. 103:8; 145:8; Jon. 4:2

14:18 ᵇEx. 20:5;
Deut. 5:9

14:19 ªEx. 32:32;
34:9 ᵇPs. 51:1;
106:45 ᶜPs. 78:38

14:20
ª2 Sam. 12:13;
Mic. 7:18–20;
[1 John 5:14–16]

14:21 ªPs. 72:19;
Is. 6:3; 66:18, 19;
Hab. 2:14

14:22
ªDeut. 1:35;
1 Cor. 10:5;
Heb. 3:17
ᵇGen. 31:7

14:23
ªNum. 26:65;
32:11; Heb. 3:18

14:24 ªJosh. 14:6,
8, 9 ᵇNum. 32:12

14:25
ªNum. 21:4;
Deut. 1:40

14:27 ªEx. 16:28
ᵇEx. 16:12

14:28
ªDeut. 1:35; 2:14,
15; Heb. 3:16–19

14:29
ªNum. 1:45, 46;
26:64; Josh. 5:6

14:30
ªNum. 26:65;
32:12;
Deut. 1:36–38;
Josh. 14:6–15

14:31 ªNum. 14:3;
Deut. 1:39
ᵇPs. 106:24

14:32
ªNum. 26:64,
65; 32:13;
1 Cor. 10:5

14:33
ªNum. 32:13;
Ps. 107:40
ᵇDeut. 2:14
ᶜEzek. 23:35

14:34
ªNum. 13:25
ᵇPs. 95:10;
Ezek. 4:6
ᶜ1 Kin. 8:56;
[Heb. 4:1]

14:35
ªNum. 23:19
ᵇ1 Cor. 10:5

14:37
ªNum. 16:49;
[1 Cor. 10:10];
Heb. 3:17, 18

14:38
ªJosh. 14:6, 10

14:39 ªEx. 33:4

guilty, ᵇvisiting the iniquity of the fathers on the children to the third and fourth *generation.'* ¹⁹ªPardon the iniquity of this people, I pray, ᵇaccording to the greatness of Your mercy, just ᶜas You have forgiven this people, from Egypt even until now."

²⁰Then the LORD said: "I have pardoned, ªaccording to your word; ²¹but truly, as I live, ªall the earth shall be filled with the glory of the LORD— ²²ªbecause all these men who have seen My glory and the signs which I did in Egypt and in the wilderness, and have put Me to the test now ᵇthese ten times, and have not heeded My voice, ²³they certainly shall not ªsee the land of which I ¹swore to their fathers, nor shall any of those who rejected Me see it. ²⁴But My servant ªCaleb, because he has a different spirit in him and ᵇhas followed Me fully, I will bring into the land where he went, and his descendants shall inherit it. ²⁵Now the Amalekites and the Canaanites dwell in the valley; tomorrow turn and ªmove out into the wilderness by the Way of the Red Sea."

DEATH SENTENCE ON THE REBELS

²⁶And the LORD spoke to Moses and Aaron, saying, ²⁷ª"How long *shall I bear with* this evil congregation who complain against Me? ᵇI have heard the complaints which the children of Israel make against Me. ²⁸Say to them, ª'As I live,' says the LORD, 'just as you have spoken in My hearing, so I will do to you: ²⁹The carcasses of you who have complained against Me shall fall in this wilderness, ªall of you who were numbered, according to your entire number, from twenty years old and above. ³⁰ªExcept for Caleb the son of Jephunneh and Joshua the son of Nun, you shall by no means enter the land which I ¹swore I would make you dwell in. ³¹ªBut your little ones, whom you said would be victims, I will bring in, and they shall ¹know the land which ᵇyou have despised. ³²But *as for* you, ªyour¹ carcasses shall fall in this wilderness. ³³And your sons shall ªbe ¹shepherds in the wilderness ᵇforty years, and ᶜbear the brunt of your infidelity, until your carcasses are consumed in the wilderness. ³⁴ªAccording to the number of the days in which you spied out the land, ᵇforty days, for each day you shall bear your ¹guilt one year, *namely* forty years, ᶜand you shall know My ²rejection. ³⁵ªI the LORD have spoken this. I will surely do so to all ᵇthis evil congregation who are gathered together against Me. In this wilderness they shall be consumed, and there they shall die.'"

³⁶Now the men whom Moses sent to spy out the land, who returned and made all the congregation complain against him by bringing a bad report of the land, ³⁷those very men who brought the evil report about the land, ªdied by the plague before the LORD. ³⁸ªBut Joshua the son of Nun and Caleb the son of Jephunneh remained alive, of the men who went to spy out the land.

A FUTILE INVASION ATTEMPT
(Deut. 1:41–45)

³⁹Then Moses told these words to all the children of Israel, ªand the people mourned greatly. ⁴⁰And they rose early

in the morning and went up to the top of the mountain, saying, [a]"Here we are, and we will go up to the place which the LORD has promised, for we have sinned!"

41And Moses said, "Now why do you [1]transgress the command of the LORD? For this will not succeed. 42a Do not go up, lest you be defeated by your enemies, for the LORD *is* not among you. 43For the Amalekites and the Canaanites *are* there before you, and you shall fall by the sword; [a]because you have turned away from the LORD, the LORD will not be with you."

44a But they presumed to go up to the mountaintop. Nevertheless, neither the ark of the covenant of the LORD nor Moses departed from the camp. 45Then the Amalekites and the Canaanites who dwelt in that mountain came down and attacked them, and drove them back as far as [a]Hormah.

LAWS OF GRAIN AND DRINK OFFERINGS

15 And the LORD spoke to Moses, saying, 2a"Speak to the children of Israel, and say to them: 'When you have come into the land you are to inhabit, which I am giving to you, 3and you [a]make an offering by fire to the LORD, a burnt offering or a sacrifice, [b]to fulfill a vow or as a freewill offering or [c]in your appointed feasts, to make a [d]sweet[1] aroma to the LORD, from the herd or the flock, 4then [a]he who presents his offering to the LORD shall bring [b]a grain offering of one-tenth *of an ephah* of fine flour mixed [c]with one-fourth of a hin of oil; 5aand one-fourth of a hin of wine as a drink offering you shall prepare with the burnt offering or the sacrifice, for each [b]lamb. 6a Or for a ram you shall prepare as a grain offering two-tenths *of an ephah* of fine flour mixed with one-third of a hin of oil; 7and as a drink offering you shall offer one-third of a hin of wine as a sweet aroma to the LORD. 8And when you prepare a young bull as a burnt offering, or as a sacrifice to fulfill a vow, or as a [a]peace offering to the LORD, 9then shall be offered [a]with the young bull a grain offering of three-tenths *of an ephah* of fine flour mixed with half a hin of oil; 10and you shall bring as the drink offering half a hin of wine as an offering made by fire, a sweet aroma to the LORD.

11a"Thus it shall be done for each young bull, for each ram, or for each lamb or young goat. 12According to the number that you prepare, so you shall do with everyone according to their number. 13All who are native-born shall do these things in this manner, in presenting an offering made by fire, a sweet aroma to the LORD. 14And if a stranger [1]dwells with you, or whoever *is* among you throughout your generations, and would present an offering made by fire, a sweet aroma to the LORD, just as you do, so shall he do. 15a One [1]ordinance *shall be* for you of the assembly and for the stranger who dwells *with you,* an ordinance forever throughout your generations; as you are, so shall the stranger be before the LORD. 16One law and one custom shall be for you and for the stranger who dwells with you.' "

17Again the LORD spoke to Moses, saying, 18a"Speak to the children of Israel, and say to them: 'When you come into the land to which I bring you, 19then it will be, when you eat of

14:40
[a]Deut. 1:41–44

14:42
[a]Deut. 1:42;
31:17

14:43
[a]2 Chr. 15:2

14:44
[a]Deut. 1:43

14:45
[a]Num. 21:3

15:2 [a]Lev. 23:10;
Num. 15:18;
Deut. 7:1

15:3 [a]Lev. 1:2, 3
[b]Lev. 7:16; 22:18,
21 [c]Lev. 23:2,
8, 12, 38;
Num. 28:18, 19,
27; Deut. 16:10
[d]Gen. 8:21;
Ex. 29:18;
Lev. 1:9

15:4 [a]Lev. 2:1;
6:14 [b]Ex. 29:40;
Lev. 23:13
[c]Lev. 14:10;
Num. 28:5

15:5
[a]Num. 28:7, 14
[b]Lev. 1:10; 3:6;
Num. 15:11;
28:4, 5

15:6
[a]Num. 28:12, 14

15:8 [a]Lev. 7:11

15:9
[a]Num. 28:12, 14

15:11 [a]Num. 28

15:15 [a]Ex. 12:49;
Num. 9:14;
15:29

15:18
[a]Num. 15:2;
Deut. 26:1

ᵃthe bread of the land, that you shall offer up a heave offering to the LORD. ²⁰ᵃYou shall offer up a cake of the first of your ground meal *as* a heave offering; as ᵇa heave offering of the threshing floor, so shall you offer it up. ²¹Of the first of your ground meal you shall give to the LORD a heave offering throughout your generations.

LAWS CONCERNING UNINTENTIONAL SIN

²²ᵃ'If you sin unintentionally, and do not observe all these commandments which the LORD has spoken to Moses— ²³all that the LORD has commanded you by the hand of Moses, from the day the LORD gave commandment and onward throughout your generations— ²⁴then it will be, ᵃif it is unintentionally committed, ¹without the knowledge of the congregation, that the whole congregation shall offer one young bull as a burnt offering, as a sweet aroma to the LORD, ᵇwith its grain offering and its drink offering, according to the ordinance, and ᶜone kid of the goats as a sin offering. ²⁵ᵃSo the priest shall make atonement for the whole congregation of the children of Israel, and it shall be forgiven them, for it was unintentional; they shall bring their offering, an offering made by fire to the LORD, and their sin offering before the LORD, for their unintended sin. ²⁶It shall be forgiven the whole congregation of the children of Israel and the stranger who dwells among them, because all the people *did it* unintentionally.

²⁷'And ᵃif a person sins unintentionally, then he shall bring a female goat in its first year as a sin offering. ²⁸ᵃSo the priest shall make atonement for the person who sins unintentionally, when he sins unintentionally before the LORD, to make atonement for him; and it shall be forgiven him. ²⁹ᵃYou shall have one law for him who sins unintentionally, *for* him who is native-born among the children of Israel and for the stranger who dwells among them.

LAW CONCERNING PRESUMPTUOUS SIN

³⁰ᵃ'But the person who does *anything* ¹presumptuously, *whether he is* native-born or a stranger, that one ²brings reproach on the LORD, and he shall be ³cut off from among his people. ³¹Because he has ᵃdespised the word of the LORD, and has broken His commandment, that person shall be completely cut off; his ¹guilt *shall be* upon him.'"

PENALTY FOR VIOLATING THE SABBATH
(*Ex. 31:12–17*)

³²Now while the children of Israel were in the wilderness, ᵃthey found a man gathering sticks on the Sabbath day. ³³And those who found him gathering sticks brought him to Moses and Aaron, and to all the congregation. ³⁴They put him ᵃunder guard, because it had not been explained what should be done to him.

³⁵Then the LORD said to Moses, ᵃ"The man must surely be put to death; all the congregation shall ᵇstone him with stones outside the camp." ³⁶So, as the LORD commanded Moses, all the congregation brought him outside the camp and stoned him with stones, and he died.

15:19
ᵃJosh. 5:11, 12

15:20
ᵃEx. 34:26;
Lev. 23:10, 14, 17;
Deut. 26:2, 10;
Prov. 3:9, 10
ᵇLev. 2:14;
23:10, 16

15:22 ᵃLev. 4:2

15:24 ᵃLev. 4:13
ᵇNum. 15:8–10
ᶜLev. 4:23

15:25 ᵃLev. 4:20;
[Heb. 2:17]

15:27
ᵃLev. 4:27–31

15:28 ᵃLev. 4:35

15:29
ᵃNum. 15:15

15:30
ᵃNum. 14:40–44;
Deut. 1:43;
17:12; Ps. 19:13;
Heb. 10:26

15:31
ᵃ2 Sam. 12:9;
Prov. 13:13

15:32 ᵃEx. 31:14,
15; 35:2, 3

15:34 ᵃLev. 24:12

15:35 ᵃEx. 31:14,
15 ᵇLev. 24:14;
Deut. 21:21;
1 Kin. 21:13;
Acts 7:58

15:24 ¹Lit. *away from the eyes*   15:30 ¹*defiantly*, lit. *with a high hand*
²*blasphemes*   ³Put to death   15:31 ¹*iniquity*

TASSELS ON GARMENTS

37Again the LORD spoke to Moses, saying, 38"Speak to the children of Israel: Tell ᵃthem to make tassels on the corners of their garments throughout their generations, and to put a blue thread in the tassels of the corners. 39And you shall have the tassel, that you may look upon it and ᵃremember all the commandments of the LORD and do them, and that you ᵇ*may* not ᶜfollow the harlotry to which your own heart and your own eyes are inclined, 40and that you may remember and do all My commandments, and be ᵃholy for your God. 41I *am* the LORD your God, who brought you out of the land of Egypt, to be your God: I *am* the LORD your God."

REBELLION AGAINST MOSES AND AARON

16 Now ᵃKorah the son of Izhar, the son of Kohath, the son of Levi, with ᵇDathan and Abiram the sons of Eliab, and On the son of Peleth, sons of Reuben, took *men;* 2and they rose up before Moses with some of the children of Israel, two hundred and fifty leaders of the congregation, ᵃrepresentatives of the congregation, men of renown. 3ᵃThey gathered together against Moses and Aaron, and said to them, "*You* ¹*take* too much upon yourselves, for ᵇall the congregation *is* holy, every one of them, ᶜand the LORD *is* among them. Why then do you exalt yourselves above the assembly of the LORD?"

4So when Moses heard *it,* he ᵃfell on his face; 5and he spoke to Korah and all his company, saying, "Tomorrow morning the LORD will show who *is* ᵃHis and *who is* ᵇholy,¹ and will cause *him* to come near to Him. That one whom He chooses He will cause to ᶜcome near to Him. 6Do this: Take censers, Korah and all your company; 7put fire in them and put incense in them before the LORD tomorrow, and it shall be *that* the man whom the LORD chooses *is* the holy one. *You take* too much upon yourselves, you sons of Levi!"

8Then Moses said to Korah, "Hear now, you sons of Levi: 9*Is it* ᵃa small thing to you that the God of Israel has ᵇseparated you from the congregation of Israel, to bring you near to Himself, to do the work of the tabernacle of the LORD, and to stand before the congregation to serve them; 10and that He has brought you near *to Himself,* you and all your brethren, the sons of Levi, with you? And are you seeking the priesthood also? 11Therefore you and all your company *are* gathered together against the LORD. ᵃAnd what *is* Aaron that you complain against him?"

12And Moses sent to call Dathan and Abiram the sons of Eliab, but they said, "We will not come up! 13*Is it* a small thing that you have brought us up out of ᵃa land flowing with milk and honey, to kill us in the wilderness, that you should ᵇkeep acting like a prince over us? 14Moreover ᵃyou have not brought us into ᵇa land flowing with milk and honey, nor given us inheritance of fields and vineyards. Will you put out the eyes of these men? We will not come up!"

15Then Moses was very angry, and said to the LORD, ᵃ"Do not ¹respect their offering. ᵇI have not taken one donkey from them, nor have I hurt one of them."

15:38
ᵃDeut. 22:12;
Matt. 23:5

15:39 ᵃPs. 103:18
ᵇDeut. 29:19
ᶜPs. 73:27;
106:39;
James 4:4

15:40
ᵃ[Lev. 11:44, 45;
Rom. 12:1;
Col. 1:22;
1 Pet. 1:15, 16]

16:1 ᵃEx. 6:21
ᵇNum. 26:9;
Deut. 11:6

16:2 ᵃNum. 1:16;
26:9

16:3 ᵃNum. 12:2;
14:2; Ps. 106:16
ᵇEx. 19:6
ᶜEx. 29:45

16:4 ᵃNum. 14:5;
20:6

16:5
ᵃ[2 Tim. 2:19]
ᵇLev. 21:6–8, 12
ᶜEzek. 40:46;
44:15, 16

16:9
ᵃ1 Sam. 18:23;
Is. 7:13
ᵇNum. 3:41,
45; 8:13–16;
Deut. 10:8

16:11 ᵃEx. 16:7, 8

16:13 ᵃEx. 16:3;
Num. 11:4–6
ᵇEx. 2:14;
Acts 7:27, 35

16:14
ᵃNum. 14:1–4
ᵇEx. 3:8;
Lev. 20:24

16:15
ᵃGen. 4:4, 5
ᵇ1 Sam. 12:3;
Acts 20:33

16:3 ¹*assume too much for*   16:5 ¹*set aside* for His use only
16:15 ¹*graciously regard*

¹⁶And Moses said to Korah, "Tomorrow, you and all your company be present ᵃbefore the LORD—you and they, as well as Aaron. ¹⁷Let each take his censer and put incense in it, and each of you bring his censer before the LORD, two hundred and fifty censers; both you and Aaron, each *with* his censer." ¹⁸So every man took his censer, put fire in it, laid incense on it, and stood at the door of the tabernacle of meeting with Moses and Aaron. ¹⁹And Korah gathered all the congregation against them at the door of the tabernacle of meeting. Then ᵃthe glory of the LORD appeared to all the congregation.

²⁰And the LORD spoke to Moses and Aaron, saying, ²¹ᵃ"Separate yourselves from among this congregation, that I may ᵇconsume them in a moment."

²²Then they ᵃfell¹ on their faces, and said, "O God, ᵇthe God of the spirits of all flesh, shall one man sin, and You be angry with all the ᶜcongregation?"

²³So the LORD spoke to Moses, saying, ²⁴"Speak to the congregation, saying, 'Get away from the tents of Korah, Dathan, and Abiram.'"

²⁵Then Moses rose and went to Dathan and Abiram, and the elders of Israel followed him. ²⁶And he spoke to the congregation, saying, ᵃ"Depart now from the tents of these wicked men! Touch nothing of theirs, lest you be consumed in all their sins." ²⁷So they got away from around the tents of Korah, Dathan, and Abiram; and Dathan and Abiram came out and stood at the door of their tents, with their wives, their sons, and their little ᵃchildren.

²⁸And Moses said: ᵃ"By this you shall know that the LORD has sent me to do all these works, for *I have* not *done them* ᵇof my own will. ²⁹If these men die naturally like all men, or if they are ᵃvisited by the common fate of all men, *then* the LORD has not sent me. ³⁰But if the LORD creates ᵃa new thing, and the earth opens its mouth and swallows them up with all that belongs to them, and they ᵇgo down alive into the pit, then you will understand that these men have rejected the LORD."

³¹ᵃNow it came to pass, as he finished speaking all these words, that the ground split apart under them, ³²and the earth opened its mouth and swallowed them up, with their households and ᵃall the men with Korah, with all *their* goods. ³³So they and all those with them went down alive into the pit; the earth closed over them, and they perished from among the assembly. ³⁴Then all Israel who *were* around them fled at their cry, for they said, "Lest the earth swallow us up *also!*"

³⁵And ᵃa fire came out from the LORD and consumed the two hundred and fifty men who were offering incense.

³⁶Then the LORD spoke to Moses, saying: ³⁷"Tell Eleazar, the son of Aaron the priest, to pick up the censers out of the blaze, for ᵃthey are holy, and scatter the fire some distance away. ³⁸The censers of ᵃthese men who sinned ¹against their own souls, let them be made into hammered plates as a covering for the altar. Because they presented them before the LORD, therefore they are holy; ᵇand they shall be a sign to the children of Israel." ³⁹So Eleazar the priest took the bronze censers, which those who were burned up had presented, and they were hammered out as a covering on the altar, ⁴⁰*to be* a

---

16:16
ᵃ1 Sam. 12:3, 7

16:19 ᵃEx. 16:7,
10; Lev. 9:6, 23;
Num. 14:10

16:21
ᵃGen. 19:17;
Jer. 51:6
ᵇEx. 32:10; 33:5

16:22
ᵃNum. 14:5
ᵇNum. 27:16;
Job 12:10;
Eccl. 12:7;
Heb. 12:9
ᶜGen. 18:23–32;
20:4

16:26
ᵃGen. 19:12, 14,
15, 17

16:27 ᵃEx. 20:5;
Num. 26:11

16:28 ᵃEx. 3:12;
John 5:36
ᵇNum. 24:13;
John 5:30

16:29 ᵃEx. 20:5;
Job 35:15;
Is. 10:3

16:30 ᵃJob 31:3;
Is. 28:21
ᵇ[Ps. 55:15]

16:31
ᵃNum. 26:10;
Ps. 106:17

16:32
ᵃNum. 26:11;
1 Chr. 6:22, 37

16:35 ᵃLev. 10:2;
Num. 11:1–3;
26:10; Ps. 106:18

16:37
ᵃLev. 27:28

16:38
ᵃProv. 20:2;
Hab. 2:10
ᵇNum. 17:10;
Ezek. 14:8

16:22 ¹*prostrated themselves*   16:38 ¹Or *at the cost of their own lives*

¹memorial to the children of Israel ᵃthat no outsider, who *is* not a descendant of Aaron, should come near to offer incense before the LORD, that he might not become like Korah and his companions, just as the LORD had said to him through Moses.

COMPLAINTS OF THE PEOPLE

⁴¹On the next day ᵃall the congregation of the children of Israel complained against Moses and Aaron, saying, "You have killed the people of the LORD." ⁴²Now it happened, when the congregation had gathered against Moses and Aaron, that they turned toward the tabernacle of meeting; and suddenly ᵃthe cloud covered it, and the glory of the LORD appeared. ⁴³Then Moses and Aaron came before the tabernacle of meeting.

⁴⁴And the LORD spoke to Moses, saying, ⁴⁵"Get away from among this congregation, that I may consume them in a moment."

And they fell on their faces.

⁴⁶So Moses said to Aaron, "Take a censer and put fire in it from the altar, put incense *on it,* and take it quickly to the congregation and make ¹atonement for them; ᵃfor wrath has gone out from the LORD. The plague has begun." ⁴⁷Then Aaron took *it* as Moses commanded, and ran into the midst of the assembly; and already the plague had begun among the people. So he put in the incense and made atonement for the people. ⁴⁸And he stood between the dead and the living; so ᵃthe plague was stopped. ⁴⁹Now those who died in the plague were fourteen thousand seven hundred, besides those who died in the Korah incident. ⁵⁰So Aaron returned to Moses at the door of the tabernacle of meeting, for the plague had stopped.

THE BUDDING OF AARON'S ROD

17 And the LORD spoke to Moses, saying: ²"Speak to the children of Israel, and get from them a rod from each father's house, all their leaders according to their fathers' houses—twelve rods. Write each man's name on his rod. ³And you shall write Aaron's name on the rod of Levi. For there shall be one rod for the head of *each* father's house. ⁴Then you shall place them in the tabernacle of meeting before ᵃthe Testimony, ᵇwhere I meet with you. ⁵And it shall be *that* the rod of the man ᵃwhom I choose will blossom; thus I will rid Myself of the complaints of the children of Israel, ᵇwhich they make against you."

⁶So Moses spoke to the children of Israel, and each of their leaders gave him a rod apiece, for each leader according to their fathers' houses, twelve rods; and the rod of Aaron *was* among their rods. ⁷And Moses placed the rods before the LORD in ᵃthe tabernacle of witness.

⁸Now it came to pass on the next day that Moses went into the tabernacle of witness, and behold, the ᵃrod of Aaron, of the house of Levi, had sprouted and put forth buds, had produced blossoms and yielded ripe almonds. ⁹Then Moses brought out all the rods from before the LORD to all the children of Israel; and they looked, and each man took his rod.

16:40
ᵃNum. 3:10;
2 Chr. 26:18

16:41
ᵃNum. 14:2;
Ps. 106:25

16:42 ᵃEx. 40:34

16:46 ᵃLev. 10:6;
Num. 18:5

16:48
ᵃNum. 25:8;
Ps. 106:30

17:4 ᵃEx. 25:16
ᵇEx. 25:22;
29:42, 43; 30:36;
Num. 17:7

17:5 ᵃNum. 16:5
ᵇNum. 16:11

17:7 ᵃEx. 38:21;
Num. 1:50,
51; 9:15; 18:2;
Acts 7:44

17:8
ᵃ[Ezek. 17:24];
Heb. 9:4

16:40 ¹reminder   16:46 ¹Lit. *covering*

¹⁰And the LORD said to Moses, "Bring ^aAaron's rod back before the Testimony, to be kept ^bas a sign against the rebels, ^cthat you may put their complaints away from Me, lest they die." ¹¹Thus did Moses; just as the LORD had commanded him, so he did.

¹²So the children of Israel spoke to Moses, saying, "Surely we die, we perish, we all perish! ^{13a}Whoever even comes near the tabernacle of the LORD must die. Shall we all utterly die?"

DUTIES OF PRIESTS AND LEVITES

18 Then the LORD said to Aaron: ^a"You and your sons and your father's house with you shall ^bbear the ¹iniquity *related to* the sanctuary, and you and your sons with you shall bear the iniquity *associated with* your priesthood. ²Also bring with you your brethren of the ^atribe of Levi, the tribe of your father, that they may be ^bjoined with you and serve you while you and your sons *are* with you before the tabernacle of ¹witness. ³They shall attend to your ¹needs and ^aall the needs of the tabernacle; ^bbut they shall not come near the articles of the sanctuary and the altar, ^clest they die—they and you also. ⁴They shall be joined with you and attend to the needs of the tabernacle of meeting, for all the work of the tabernacle; ^abut an outsider shall not come near you. ⁵And you shall attend to ^athe duties of the sanctuary and the duties of the altar, ^bthat there *may* be no more wrath on the children of Israel. ⁶Behold, I Myself have ^ataken your brethren the Levites from among the children of Israel; ^bthey *are* a gift to you, given by the LORD, to do the work of the tabernacle of meeting. ⁷Therefore ^ayou and your sons with you shall attend to your priesthood for everything at the altar and ^bbehind the veil; and you shall serve. I give your priesthood *to you* as a ^cgift for service, but the outsider who comes near shall be put to death."

OFFERINGS FOR SUPPORT OF THE PRIESTS

⁸And the LORD spoke to Aaron: "Here, ^aI Myself have also given you ¹charge of My heave offerings, all the holy gifts of the children of Israel; I have given them ^bas a portion to you and your sons, as an ordinance forever. ⁹This shall be yours of the most holy things *reserved* from the fire: every offering of theirs, every ^agrain offering and every ^bsin offering and every ^ctrespass offering which they render to Me, *shall be* most holy for you and your sons. ^{10a}In a most holy *place* you shall eat it; every male shall eat it. It shall be holy to you.

¹¹"This also *is* yours: ^athe heave offering of their gift, with all the wave offerings of the children of Israel; I have given them to you, and your sons and daughters with you, as an ordinance forever. ^bEveryone who is ¹clean in your house may eat it.

^{12a}"All the ¹best of the oil, all the best of the new wine and the grain, ^btheir firstfruits which they offer to the LORD, I have given them to you. ¹³Whatever first ripe fruit is in their land, ^awhich they bring to the LORD, shall be yours. Everyone who is clean in your house may eat it.

^{14a}"Every ¹devoted thing in Israel shall be yours.

17:10 ^aHeb. 9:4
^bNum. 16:38;
Deut. 9:7, 24
^cNum. 17:5

17:13 ^aNum. 1:51,
53; 18:4, 7

18:1 ^aNum. 17:13
^bEx. 28:38;
Lev. 10:17; 22:16

18:2
^aGen. 29:34;
Num. 1:47
^bNum. 3:5–10

18:3
^aNum. 3:25, 31,
36 ^bNum. 16:40
^cNum. 4:15

18:4 ^aNum. 3:10

18:5 ^aEx. 27:21;
30:7; Lev. 24:3
^bNum. 8:19;
16:46

18:6 ^aNum. 3:12,
45 ^bNum. 3:9

18:7 ^aNum. 3:10;
18:5 ^bHeb. 9:3, 6
^cMatt. 10:8;
1 Pet. 5:2, 3

18:8
^aLev. 6:16, 18;
7:28–34;
Num. 5:9
^bEx. 29:29;
40:13, 15

18:9 ^aLev. 2:2,
3; 10:12, 13
^bLev. 6:25,
26 ^cLev. 7:7;
Num. 5:8–10

18:10
^aLev. 6:16, 26

18:11 ^aEx. 29:27,
28; Deut. 18:3–5
^bLev. 22:1–16

18:12 ^aEx. 23:19;
Neh. 10:35, 36
^bEx. 22:29;
Lev. 23:20

18:13 ^aEx. 22:29;
23:19; 34:26

18:14
^aLev. 27:1–33

18:1 ¹*guilt*   **18:2** ¹*testimony*   **18:3** ¹*service*   **18:8** ¹*custody*   **18:11** ¹*purified*
18:12 ¹Lit. *fat*   **18:14** ¹*consecrated*

15"Everything that first opens ªthe womb of all flesh, which they bring to the LORD, whether man or beast, shall be yours; nevertheless ᵇthe firstborn of man you shall surely redeem, and the firstborn of unclean animals you shall redeem. 16And those redeemed of the devoted things you shall redeem when one month old, ªaccording to your valuation, for five shekels of silver, according to the shekel of the sanctuary, which *is* ᵇtwenty gerahs. 17ªBut the firstborn of a cow, the firstborn of a sheep, or the firstborn of a goat you shall not redeem; they *are* holy. ᵇYou shall sprinkle their blood on the altar, and burn their fat *as* an offering made by fire for a sweet aroma to the LORD. 18And their flesh shall be yours, just as the ªwave¹ breast and the right thigh are yours.

19"All the heave offerings of the holy things, which the children of Israel offer to the LORD, I have given to you and your sons and daughters with you as an ordinance forever; ªit *is* a covenant of salt forever before the LORD with you and your descendants with you."

20Then the LORD said to Aaron: "You shall have ªno inheritance in their land, nor shall you have any portion among them; ᵇI *am* your portion and your inheritance among the children of Israel.

TITHES FOR SUPPORT OF THE LEVITES

21"Behold, ªI have given the children of Levi all the tithes in Israel as ¹an inheritance in return for the work which they perform, ᵇthe work of the tabernacle of meeting. 22ªHereafter the children of Israel shall not come near the tabernacle of meeting, ᵇlest they bear sin and die. 23But the Levites shall perform the work of the tabernacle of meeting, and they shall bear their iniquity; *it shall be* a statute forever, throughout your generations, that among the children of Israel they shall have no inheritance. 24For the tithes of the children of Israel, which they offer up *as* a heave offering to the LORD, I have given to the Levites ¹as an inheritance; therefore I have said to them, 'Among the children of Israel they shall have no inheritance.'"

THE TITHE OF THE LEVITES

25Then the LORD spoke to Moses, saying, 26"Speak thus to the Levites, and say to them: 'When you take from the children of Israel the tithes which I have given you from them as your inheritance, then you shall offer up a heave offering of it to the LORD, ªa tenth of the tithe. 27And your heave offering shall be reckoned to you as though *it were* the grain of the ªthreshing floor and as the fullness of the winepress. 28Thus you shall also offer a heave offering to the LORD from all your tithes which you receive from the children of Israel, and you shall give the LORD's heave offering from it to Aaron the priest. 29Of all your gifts you shall offer up every heave offering due to the LORD, from all the ¹best of them, the consecrated part of them.' 30Therefore you shall say to them: 'When you have lifted up the best of it, then *the rest* shall be accounted to the Levites as the produce of the threshing floor and as the produce of the winepress. 31You may eat it in any

18:15 ªEx. 13:2
ᵇEx. 13:12–15;
Num. 3:46;
Luke 2:22–24

18:16 ªLev. 27:6
ᵇEx. 30:13

18:17
ªDeut. 15:19
ᵇLev. 3:2, 5

18:18
ªEx. 29:26–28;
Lev. 7:31–36

18:19 ªLev. 2:13;
2 Chr. 13:5;
[Mark 9:49, 50]

18:20
ªDeut. 10:8, 9;
12:12; 14:27–29;
18:1, 2;
Josh. 13:14,
33 ᵇPs. 16:5;
Ezek. 44:28

18:21
ªLev. 27:30–33;
Deut. 14:22–29;
Neh. 10:37;
12:44;
Mal. 3:8–10;
[Heb. 7:4–10]
ᵇNum. 3:7, 8

18:22 ªNum. 1:51
ᵇLev. 22:9

18:26
ªNeh. 10:38

18:27
ªNum. 15:20;
[2 Cor. 8:12]

18:18 ¹*breast of the wave offering*   18:21 ¹*a possession*   18:24 ¹*for a possession*   18:29 ¹Lit. *fat*

place, you and your households, for it *is* ᵃyour ¹reward for your work in the tabernacle of meeting. ³²And you shall ᵃbear no sin because of it, when you have lifted up the best of it. But you shall not ᵇprofane the holy gifts of the children of Israel, lest you die.' "

LAWS OF PURIFICATION

19 Now the LORD spoke to Moses and Aaron, saying, ²"This *is* the ¹ordinance of the law which the LORD has commanded, saying: 'Speak to the children of Israel, that they bring you a red heifer without ²blemish, in which there *is* no ᵃdefect ᵇ*and* on which a yoke has never come. ³You shall give it to Eleazar the priest, that he may take it ᵃoutside the camp, and it shall be slaughtered before him; ⁴and Eleazar the priest shall take some of its blood with his finger, and ᵃsprinkle some of its blood seven times directly in front of the tabernacle of meeting. ⁵Then the heifer shall be burned in his sight: ᵃits hide, its flesh, its blood, and its offal shall be burned. ⁶And the priest shall take ᵃcedar wood and ᵇhyssop and scarlet, and cast *them* into the midst of the fire burning the heifer. ⁷ᵃThen the priest shall wash his clothes, he shall bathe in water, and afterward he shall come into the camp; the priest shall be unclean until evening. ⁸And the one who burns it shall wash his clothes in water, bathe in water, and shall be unclean until evening. ⁹Then a man *who is* clean shall gather up ᵃthe ashes of the heifer, and store *them* outside the camp in a clean place; and they shall be kept for the congregation of the children of Israel ᵇfor the water of ¹purification; it *is* for purifying from sin. ¹⁰And the one who gathers the ashes of the heifer shall wash his clothes, and be unclean until evening. It shall be a statute forever to the children of Israel and to the stranger who dwells among them.

¹¹ᵃ'He who touches the dead ¹body of anyone shall be unclean seven days. ¹²ᵃHe shall purify himself with the water on the third day and on the seventh day; *then* he will be clean. But if he does not purify himself on the third day and on the seventh day, he will not be clean. ¹³Whoever touches the body of anyone who has died, and ᵃdoes not purify himself, ᵇdefiles the tabernacle of the LORD. That person shall be cut off from Israel. He shall be unclean, because ᶜthe water of purification was not sprinkled on him; ᵈhis uncleanness *is* still on him.

¹⁴"This *is* the law when a man dies in a tent: All who come into the tent and all who *are* in the tent shall be unclean seven days; ¹⁵and every ᵃopen vessel, which has no cover fastened on it, *is* unclean. ¹⁶ᵃWhoever in the open field touches one who is slain by a sword or who has died, or a bone of a man, or a grave, shall be unclean seven days.

¹⁷'And for an unclean *person* they shall take some of the ᵃashes of the heifer burnt for purification from sin, and ¹running water shall be put on them in a vessel. ¹⁸A clean person shall take ᵃhyssop and dip *it* in the water, sprinkle *it* on the tent, on all the vessels, on the persons who were there, or on the one who touched a bone, the slain, the dead, or a grave. ¹⁹The clean *person* shall sprinkle the unclean on the third day and on the seventh day; ᵃand on the seventh day he shall

18:31 ᵃ[Matt. 10:10; Luke 10:7]; 1 Cor. 9:13; [1 Tim. 5:18]
18:32 ᵃLev. 19:8; 22:16; Ezek. 22:26 ᵇLev. 22:2, 15
19:2 ᵃLev. 22:20–25 ᵇDeut. 21:3; 1 Sam. 6:7
19:3 ᵃLev. 4:12, 21; Num. 19:9; Heb. 13:11
19:4 ᵃLev. 4:6; Heb. 9:13
19:5 ᵃEx. 29:14; Lev. 4:11, 12; 9:11
19:6 ᵃLev. 14:4, 6, 49 ᵇEx. 12:22; 1 Kin. 4:33
19:7 ᵃLev. 11:25; 15:5; 16:26, 28
19:9 ᵃ[Heb. 9:13, 14] ᵇNum. 19:13, 20, 21
19:11 ᵃLev. 21:1, 11; Num. 5:2; 6:6; 9:6, 10; 31:19; Lam. 4:14; Hag. 2:13
19:12 ᵃNum. 19:19; 31:19
19:13 ᵃLev. 22:3–7 ᵇLev. 15:31 ᶜNum. 8:7; 19:9 ᵈLev. 7:20; 22:3
19:15 ᵃLev. 11:32; Num. 31:20
19:16 ᵃNum. 19:11; 31:19
19:17 ᵃNum. 19:9
19:18 ᵃPs. 51:7
19:19 ᵃLev. 14:9

purify himself, wash his clothes, and bathe in water; and at evening he shall be clean. ²⁰'But the man who is unclean and does not purify himself, that person shall be cut off from among the assembly, because he has ªdefiled the sanctuary of the LORD. The water of purification has not been sprinkled on him; he *is* unclean. ²¹It shall be a perpetual statute for them. He who sprinkles the water of purification shall wash his clothes; and he who touches the water of purification shall be unclean until evening. ²²ªWhatever the unclean *person* touches shall be unclean; and ᵇthe person who touches *it* shall be unclean until evening.'"

MOSES' ERROR AT KADESH
(Ex. 17:1–7)

20 Thenª the children of Israel, the whole congregation, came into the Wilderness of Zin in the first month, and the people stayed in ᵇKadesh; and ᶜMiriam died there and was buried there.

²ªNow there was no water for the congregation; ᵇso they gathered together against Moses and Aaron. ³And the people ªcontended with Moses and spoke, saying: "If only we had died ᵇwhen our brethren died before the LORD! ⁴ªWhy have you brought up the assembly of the LORD into this wilderness, that we and our animals should die here? ⁵And why have you made us come up out of Egypt, to bring us to this evil place? It *is* not a place of grain or figs or vines or pomegranates; nor *is* there any water to drink." ⁶So Moses and Aaron went from the presence of the assembly to the door of the tabernacle of meeting, and ªthey ¹fell on their faces. And ᵇthe glory of the LORD appeared to them.

⁷Then the LORD spoke to Moses, saying, ⁸ª"Take the rod; you and your brother Aaron gather the congregation together. Speak to the rock before their eyes, and it will yield its water; thus ᵇyou shall bring water for them out of the rock, and give drink to the congregation and their animals." ⁹So Moses took the rod ªfrom before the LORD as He commanded him.

¹⁰And Moses and Aaron gathered the assembly together before the rock; and he said to them, ª"Hear now, you rebels! Must we bring water for you out of this rock?" ¹¹Then Moses lifted his hand and struck the rock twice with his rod; ªand water came out abundantly, and the congregation and their animals drank.

¹²Then the LORD spoke to Moses and Aaron, "Because ªyou did not believe Me, to ᵇhallow Me in the eyes of the children of Israel, therefore you shall not bring this assembly into the land which I have given them."

¹³ªThis *was* the water of ¹Meribah, because the children of Israel contended with the LORD, and He was hallowed among them.

PASSAGE THROUGH EDOM REFUSED

¹⁴ªNow Moses sent messengers from Kadesh to the king of ᵇEdom. ᶜ"Thus says your brother Israel: 'You know all the hardship that has befallen us, ¹⁵ªhow our fathers went down

---

19:20
ª Num. 19:13

19:22
ª Hag. 2:11–13
ᵇ Lev. 15:5

20:1
ª Num. 13:21;
33:36
ᵇ Num. 13:26
ᶜ Ex. 15:20;
Num. 26:59

20:2 ª Ex. 17:1
ᵇ Num. 16:19, 42

20:3 ª Ex. 17:2;
Num. 14:2
ᵇ Num. 11:1, 33;
14:37; 16:31–
35, 49

20:4 ª Ex. 17:3

20:6
ª Num. 14:5;
16:4, 22, 45
ᵇ Num. 14:10

20:8 ª Ex. 4:17,
20; 17:5, 6
ᵇ Neh. 9:15;
Ps. 78:15,
16; 105:41;
Is. 43:20; 48:21;
[1 Cor. 10:4]

20:9
ª Num. 17:10

20:10
ª Ps. 106:33

20:11 ª Ex. 17:6;
Deut. 8:15;
Ps. 78:16;
Is. 48:21;
[1 Cor. 10:4]

20:12
ª Num. 20:28;
27:14; Deut. 1:37;
3:26, 27; 34:5
ᵇ Lev. 10:3;
Ezek. 20:41;
36:23; 1 Pet. 3:15

20:13
ª Deut. 33:8;
Ps. 106:32

20:14
ª Judg. 11:16, 17
ᵇ Gen. 36:31–39
ᶜ Deut. 2:4;
Obad. 10–12

20:15
ª Gen. 46:6;
Acts 7:15

20:6 ¹*prostrated themselves*   20:13 ¹Lit. *Contention*

to Egypt, [b]and we dwelt in Egypt a long time, [c]and the Egyptians [1]afflicted us and our fathers. [16a]When we cried out to the LORD, He heard our voice and [b]sent the Angel and brought us up out of Egypt; now here we are in Kadesh, a city on the edge of your border. [17]Please [a]let us pass through your country. We will not pass through fields or vineyards, nor will we drink water from wells; we will go along the King's Highway; we will not turn aside to the right hand or to the left until we have passed through your territory.'"

[18]Then [a]Edom said to him, "You shall not pass through my *land,* lest I come out against you with the sword."

[19]So the children of Israel said to him, "We will go by the Highway, and if I or my livestock drink any of your water, [a]then I will pay for it; let me only pass through on foot, nothing *more.*"

[20]Then he said, [a]"You shall not pass through." So Edom came out against them with many men and with a strong hand. [21]Thus Edom [a]refused to give Israel passage through his territory; so Israel [b]turned away from him.

DEATH OF AARON

[22]Now the children of Israel, the whole congregation, journeyed from [a]Kadesh [b]and came to Mount Hor. [23]And the LORD spoke to Moses and Aaron in Mount Hor by the border of the land of Edom, saying: [24]"Aaron shall [1]be [a]gathered to his people, for he shall not enter the land which I have given to the children of Israel, because you rebelled against My word at the water of Meribah. [25a]Take Aaron and Eleazar his son, and bring them up to Mount Hor; [26]and strip Aaron of his garments and put them on Eleazar his son; for Aaron shall be gathered *to his people* and die there." [27]So Moses did just as the LORD commanded, and they went up to Mount Hor in the sight of all the congregation. [28a]Moses stripped Aaron of his garments and put them on Eleazar his son; and [b]Aaron died there on the top of the mountain. Then Moses and Eleazar came down from the mountain. [29]Now when all the congregation saw that Aaron was dead, all the house of Israel mourned for Aaron [a]thirty days.

CANAANITES DEFEATED AT HORMAH

21 The [a]king of Arad, the Canaanite, who dwelt in the South, heard that Israel was coming on the road to Atharim. Then he fought against Israel and took *some* of them prisoners. [2a]So Israel made a vow to the LORD, and said, "If You will indeed deliver this people into my hand, then [b]I will utterly destroy their cities." [3]And the LORD listened to the voice of Israel and delivered up the Canaanites, and they utterly destroyed them and their cities. So the name of that place was called [1]Hormah.

THE BRONZE SERPENT

[4]Then they journeyed from Mount Hor by the Way of the Red Sea, to [a]go around the land of Edom; and the soul of the people became very [1]discouraged on the way. [5]And the people [a]spoke against God and against Moses: "Why have you

20:15 [b]Ex. 12:40
[c]Ex. 1:11;
Deut. 26:6;
Acts 7:19

20:16 [a]Ex. 2:23;
3:7 [b]Ex. 3:2;
14:19

20:17
[a]Num. 21:22

20:18
[a]Num. 24:18;
Ps. 137:7;
Ezek. 25:12, 13;
Obad. 10–15

20:19
[a]Deut. 2:6, 28

20:20
[a]Judg. 11:17

20:21
[a]Deut. 2:27,
30 [b]Deut. 2:8;
Judg. 11:18

20:22
[a]Num. 33:37
[b]Num. 21:4

20:24
[a]Gen. 25:8;
Deut. 32:50

20:25
[a]Num. 33:38;
Deut. 32:50

20:28
[a]Ex. 29:29,
30; Deut. 10:6
[b]Num. 33:38

20:29
[a]Gen. 50:3, 10;
Deut. 34:8

21:1
[a]Num. 33:40;
Josh. 12:14;
Judg. 1:16

21:2
[a]Gen. 28:20;
Judg. 11:30
[b]Deut. 2:34

21:4 [a]Judg. 11:18

21:5
[a]Num. 20:4, 5

20:15 [1]*did evil to*   20:24 [1]Die and join his ancestors   21:3 [1]Lit. *Utter Destruction*   21:4 [1]*impatient*

brought us up out of Egypt to die in the wilderness? For *there is* no food and no water, and our soul ¹loathes this worthless bread." ⁶So ªthe LORD sent ᵇfiery serpents among the people, and they bit the people; and many of the people of Israel died.

⁷ªTherefore the people came to Moses, and said, "We have ᵇsinned, for we have spoken against the LORD and against you; ᶜpray to the LORD that He take away the serpents from us." So Moses prayed for the people.

⁸Then the LORD said to Moses, ª"Make a ᵇfiery *serpent,* and set it on a pole; and it shall be that everyone who is bitten, when he looks at it, shall live." ⁹So ªMoses made a bronze serpent, and put it on a pole; and so it was, if a serpent had bitten anyone, when he looked at the bronze serpent, he lived.

FROM MOUNT HOR TO MOAB

¹⁰Now the children of Israel moved on and ªcamped in Oboth. ¹¹And they journeyed from Oboth and camped at ¹Ije Abarim, in the wilderness which *is* east of Moab, toward the sunrise. ¹²ªFrom there they moved and camped in the Valley of Zered. ¹³From there they moved and camped on the other side of the Arnon, which *is* in the wilderness that extends from the border of the Amorites; for ªthe Arnon *is* the border of Moab, between Moab and the Amorites. ¹⁴Therefore it is said in the Book of the Wars of the LORD:

¹"Waheb in Suphah,
The brooks of the Arnon,
15 And the slope of the brooks
That reaches to the dwelling of ªAr,
And lies on the border of Moab."

¹⁶From there *they went* ªto Beer, which *is* the well where the LORD said to Moses, "Gather the people together, and I will give them water." ¹⁷ªThen Israel sang this song:

"Spring up, O well!
All of you sing to it—
18 The well the leaders sank,
Dug by the nation's nobles,
By the ªlawgiver, with their staves."

And from the wilderness *they went* to Mattanah, ¹⁹from Mattanah to Nahaliel, from Nahaliel to Bamoth, ²⁰and from Bamoth, *in* the valley that *is* in the ¹country of Moab, to the top of Pisgah which looks ªdown on the ²wasteland.

KING SIHON DEFEATED
(Deut. 2:26–37)

²¹Then ªIsrael sent messengers to Sihon king of the Amorites, saying, ²²ª"Let me pass through your land. We will not turn aside into fields or vineyards; we will not drink water from wells. We will go by the King's Highway until we have passed through your territory." ²³ªBut Sihon would not allow Israel to pass through his territory. So Sihon gathered all his people together and ¹went out against Israel in the wilderness,

21:6 ª1 Cor. 10:9
ᵇDeut. 8:15

21:7 ªNum. 11:2;
Ps. 78:34;
Is. 26:16;
Hos. 5:15
ᵇLev. 26:40
ᶜEx. 8:8;
1 Sam. 12:19;
1 Kin. 13:6;
Acts 8:24

21:8 ª[John 3:14,
15] ᵇIs. 14:29;
30:6

21:9 ª2 Kin. 18:4;
John 3:14, 15

21:10
ªNum. 33:43, 44

21:12 ªDeut. 2:13

21:13
ªNum. 22:36;
Judg. 11:18

21:15
ªNum. 21:28;
Deut. 2:9, 18, 29

21:16 ªJudg. 9:21

21:17 ªEx. 15:1

21:18 ªIs. 33:22

21:20
ªNum. 23:28

21:21
ªNum. 32:33;
Deut. 2:26–37;
Judg. 11:19

21:22
ªNum. 20:16, 17

21:23
ªDeut. 29:7

21:5 ¹detests   21:11 ¹Lit. *The Heaps of Abarim*   21:14 ¹Ancient unknown places; Vg. *What He did in the Red Sea*   21:20 ¹Lit. *field*   ²Heb. *Jeshimon*
21:23 ¹attacked

21:23
ᵇDeut. 2:32;
Judg. 11:20

21:24
ᵃDeut. 2:33;
Josh. 12:1;
Neh. 9:22;
Ps. 135:10;
136:19;
Amos 2:9

21:25
ᵃAmos 2:10

21:28
ᵃJer. 48:45, 46
ᵇDeut. 2:9,
18; Is. 15:1
ᶜNum. 22:41;
33:52

21:29
ᵃJer. 48:46
ᵇJudg. 11:24;
1 Kin. 11:33;
2 Kin. 23:13
ᶜIs. 15:2, 5
ᵈIs. 16:2

21:30
ᵃNum. 32:3, 34;
Jer. 48:18, 22
ᵇIs. 15:2

21:32
ᵃNum. 32:1, 3,
35; Jer. 48:32

21:33
ᵃDeut. 29:7
ᵇDeut. 3:1
ᶜJosh. 13:13

21:34 ᵃDeut. 3:2
ᵇNum. 21:24;
Ps. 135:10;
136:20

21:35
ᵃDeut. 3:3, 4;
29:7; Josh. 13:12

22:1
ᵃNum. 33:48, 49

22:2
ᵃJosh. 24:9;
Judg. 11:25;
Mic. 6:5;
Rev. 2:14

22:3 ᵃEx. 15:15

22:4
ᵃNum. 25:15–18;
31:1–3;
Josh. 13:21

22:5
ᵃNum. 31:8, 16;
Deut. 23:4;
Josh. 13:22;
24:9; Neh. 13:1,
2; Mic. 6:5;
2 Pet. 2:15;
Jude 11; Rev. 2:14
ᵇDeut. 23:4

ᵇand he came to Jahaz and fought against Israel. ²⁴Then ᵃIsrael defeated him with the edge of the sword, and took possession of his land from the Arnon to the Jabbok, as far as the people of Ammon; for the border of the people of Ammon *was* fortified. ²⁵So Israel took all these cities, and Israel ᵃdwelt in all the cities of the Amorites, in Heshbon and in all its villages. ²⁶For Heshbon *was* the city of Sihon king of the Amorites, who had fought against the former king of Moab, and had taken all his land from his hand as far as the Arnon. ²⁷Therefore those who speak in ¹proverbs say:

"Come to Heshbon, let it be built;
Let the city of Sihon be repaired.

28 "For ᵃfire went out from Heshbon,
A flame from the city of Sihon;
It consumed ᵇAr of Moab,
The lords of the ᶜheights of the Arnon.

29 Woe to you, ᵃMoab!
You have perished, O people of ᵇChemosh!
He has given his ᶜsons as fugitives,
And his ᵈdaughters into captivity,
To Sihon king of the Amorites.

30 "But we have shot at them;
Heshbon has perished ᵃas far as Dibon.
Then we laid waste as far as Nophah,
Which *reaches* to ᵇMedeba."

³¹Thus Israel dwelt in the land of the Amorites. ³²Then Moses sent to ¹spy out ᵃJazer; and they took its villages and drove out the Amorites who *were* there.

KING OG DEFEATED
(Deut. 3:1–22)

³³ᵃAnd they turned and went up by the way to ᵇBashan. So Og king of Bashan went out against them, he and all his people, to battle ᶜat Edrei. ³⁴Then the LORD said to Moses, ᵃ"Do not fear him, for I have ¹delivered him into your hand, with all his people and his land; and ᵇyou shall do to him as you did to Sihon king of the Amorites, who dwelt at Heshbon." ³⁵ᵃSo they defeated him, his sons, and all his people, until there was no survivor left him; and they took possession of his land.

BALAK SENDS FOR BALAAM

22 Then ᵃthe children of Israel moved, and camped in the plains of Moab on the side of the Jordan *across from* Jericho.

²Now ᵃBalak the son of Zippor saw all that Israel had done to the Amorites. ³And ᵃMoab was exceedingly afraid of the people because they *were* many, and Moab was sick with dread because of the children of Israel. ⁴So Moab said to ᵃthe elders of Midian, "Now this company will ¹lick up everything around us, as an ox licks up the grass of the field." And Balak the son of Zippor *was* king of the Moabites at that time. ⁵Then ᵃhe sent messengers to Balaam the son of Beor at ᵇPethor, which *is* near ¹the River in the land of ²the sons of his people,

to call him, saying: "Look, a people has come from Egypt. See, they cover the face of the earth, and are settling next to me! 6aTherefore please come at once, bcurse this people for me, for they *are* too mighty for me. Perhaps I shall be able to defeat them and drive them out of the land, for I know that he whom you bless *is* blessed, and he whom you curse is cursed."

7So the elders of Moab and the elders of Midian departed with athe diviner's fee in their hand, and they came to Balaam and spoke to him the words of Balak. 8And he said to them, a"Lodge here tonight, and I will bring back word to you, as the LORD speaks to me." So the princes of Moab stayed with Balaam.

9aThen God came to Balaam and said, "Who *are* these men with you?"

10So Balaam said to God, "Balak the son of Zippor, king of Moab, has sent to me, *saying*, 11'Look, a people has come out of Egypt, and they cover the face of the earth. Come now, curse them for me; perhaps I shall be able to overpower them and drive them out.'"

12And God said to Balaam, "You shall not go with them; you shall not curse the people, for athey *are* blessed."

13So Balaam rose in the morning and said to the princes of Balak, "Go back to your land, for the LORD has refused to give me permission to go with you."

14And the princes of Moab rose and went to Balak, and said, "Balaam refuses to come with us."

15Then Balak again sent princes, more numerous and more ¹honorable than they. 16And they came to Balaam and said to him, "Thus says Balak the son of Zippor: 'Please let nothing hinder you from coming to me; 17for I will certainly ahonor you greatly, and I will do whatever you say to me. bTherefore please come, curse this people for me.'"

18Then Balaam answered and said to the servants of Balak, a"Though Balak were to give me his house full of silver and gold, bI could not go beyond the word of the LORD my God, to do less or more. 19Now therefore, please, you also astay here tonight, that I may know what more the LORD will say to me."

20aAnd God came to Balaam at night and said to him, "If the men come to call you, rise *and* go with them; but bonly the word which I speak to you—that you shall do." 21So Balaam rose in the morning, saddled his donkey, and went with the princes of Moab.

BALAAM, THE DONKEY, AND THE ANGEL

22Then God's anger was aroused because he went, aand the Angel of the LORD took His stand in the way as an adversary against him. And he was riding on his donkey, and his two servants *were* with him. 23Now athe donkey saw the Angel of the LORD standing in the way with His drawn sword in His hand, and the donkey turned aside out of the way and went into the field. So Balaam struck the donkey to turn her back onto the road. 24Then the Angel of the LORD stood in a narrow path between the vineyards, *with* a wall on this side and a wall on that side. 25And when the donkey saw the Angel of

22:6
aNum. 22:17;
23:7, 8
bNum. 22:12;
24:9

22:7
a1 Sam. 9:7, 8

22:8
aNum. 22:19

22:9 aGen. 20:3

22:12
aNum. 23:20;
[Rom. 11:28]

22:17
aNum. 24:11
bNum. 22:6

22:18
aNum. 22:38;
24:13
b1 Kin. 22:14;
2 Chr. 18:13

22:19
aNum. 22:8

22:20
aNum. 22:9
bNum. 22:35;
23:5, 12, 16, 26;
24:13

22:22 aEx. 4:24

22:23
aJosh. 5:13;
2 Kin. 6:17;
Dan. 10:7;
Acts 22:9

22:15 ¹*distinguished*

the LORD, she pushed herself against the wall and crushed Balaam's foot against the wall; so he struck her again. [26]Then the Angel of the LORD went further, and stood in a narrow place where there *was* no way to turn either to the right hand or to the left. [27]And when the donkey saw the Angel of the LORD, she lay down under Balaam; so Balaam's anger was aroused, and he struck the donkey with his staff.

[28]Then the LORD [a]opened the mouth of the donkey, and she said to Balaam, "What have I done to you, that you have struck me these three times?"

[29]And Balaam said to the donkey, "Because you have [1]abused me. I wish there were a sword in my hand, [a]for now I would kill you!"

[30a]So the donkey said to Balaam, "*Am* I not your donkey on which you have ridden, ever since *I became* yours, to this day? Was I ever [1]disposed to do this to you?"

And he said, "No."

[31]Then the LORD [a]opened Balaam's eyes, and he saw the Angel of the LORD standing in the way with His drawn sword in His hand; and he bowed his head and fell flat on his face. [32]And the Angel of the LORD said to him, "Why have you struck your donkey these three times? Behold, I have come out [1]to stand against you, because *your* way is [a]perverse[2] before Me. [33]The donkey saw Me and turned aside from Me these three times. If she had not turned aside from Me, surely I would also have killed you by now, and let her live."

[34]And Balaam said to the Angel of the LORD, [a]"I have sinned, for I did not know You stood in the way against me. Now therefore, if it [1]displeases You, I will turn back."

[35]Then the Angel of the LORD said to Balaam, "Go with the men, [a]but only the word that I speak to you, that you shall speak." So Balaam went with the princes of Balak.

[36]Now when Balak heard that Balaam was coming, [a]he went out to meet him at the city of Moab, [b]which *is* on the border at the Arnon, the boundary of the territory. [37]Then Balak said to Balaam, "Did I not earnestly send to you, calling for you? Why did you not come to me? Am I not able [a]to honor you?"

[38]And Balaam said to Balak, "Look, I have come to you! Now, have I any power at all to say anything? [a]The word that God puts in my mouth, that I must speak." [39]So Balaam went with Balak, and they came to Kirjath Huzoth. [40]Then Balak offered oxen and sheep, and he sent *some* to Balaam and to the princes who *were* with him.

BALAAM'S FIRST PROPHECY

[41]So it was, the next day, that Balak took Balaam and brought him up to the [a]high places of Baal, that from there he might observe [1]the extent of the people.

23 Then Balaam said to Balak, [a]"Build seven altars for me here, and prepare for me here seven bulls and seven rams."

[2]And Balak did just as Balaam had spoken, and Balak and Balaam [a]offered a bull and a ram on *each* altar. [3]Then Balaam said to Balak, [a]"Stand by your burnt offering, and I will go;

22:28
[a]2 Pet. 2:16

22:29
[a][Prov. 12:10;
Matt. 15:19]

22:30
[a]2 Pet. 2:16

22:31
[a]Gen. 21:19;
2 Kin. 6:17;
Luke 24:16, 31

22:32
[a][2 Pet. 2:14, 15]

22:34
[a]1 Sam. 15:24,
30; 26:21;
2 Sam. 12:13

22:35
[a]Num. 22:20

22:36
[a]Gen. 14:17
[b]Num. 21:13

22:37
[a]Num. 22:17;
24:11

22:38
[a]Num. 23:26;
24:13;
1 Kin. 22:14;
2 Chr. 18:13

22:41
[a]Num. 21:28;
Deut. 12:2

23:1
[a]Num. 23:29

23:2
[a]Num. 23:14, 30

23:3
[a]Num. 23:15

22:29 [1]mocked   **22:30** [1]accustomed   **22:32** [1]as an adversary   [2]contrary
22:34 [1]Lit. *is evil in your eyes*   **22:41** [1]the farthest extent

perhaps the LORD will come [b]to meet me, and whatever He shows me I will tell you." So he went to a desolate height. [4a]And God met Balaam, and he said to Him, "I have prepared the seven altars, and I have offered on *each* altar a bull and a ram."

[5]Then the LORD [a]put a word in Balaam's mouth, and said, "Return to Balak, and thus you shall speak." [6]So he returned to him, and there he was, standing by his burnt offering, he and all the princes of Moab.

[7]And he [a]took up his [1]oracle and said:

"Balak the king of Moab has brought me from Aram,
From the mountains of the east.
[b]'Come, curse Jacob for me,
And come, [c]denounce Israel!'

8 "How[a] shall I curse whom God has not cursed?
And how shall I denounce *whom* the LORD has not
denounced?
9 For from the top of the rocks I see him,
And from the hills I behold him;
There! [a]A people dwelling alone,
[b]Not reckoning itself among the nations.

10 "Who[a] can count the [1]dust of Jacob,
Or number one-fourth of Israel?
Let me die [b]the death of the righteous,
And let my end be like his!"

[11]Then Balak said to Balaam, "What have you done to me? [a]I took you to curse my enemies, and look, you have blessed *them* bountifully!"

[12]So he answered and said, [a]"Must I not take heed to speak what the LORD has put in my mouth?"

BALAAM'S SECOND PROPHECY

[13]Then Balak said to him, "Please come with me to another place from which you may see them; you shall see only the outer part of them, and shall not see them all; curse them for me from there." [14]So he brought him to the field of Zophim, to the top of Pisgah, [a]and built seven altars, and offered a bull and a ram on *each* altar.

[15]And he said to Balak, "Stand here by your burnt offering while I [1]meet *the LORD* over there."

[16]Then the LORD met Balaam, and [a]put a word in his mouth, and said, "Go back to Balak, and thus you shall speak." [17]So he came to him, and there he was, standing by his burnt offering, and the princes of Moab were with him. And Balak said to him, "What has the LORD spoken?"

[18]Then he took up his oracle and said:

[a]"Rise up, Balak, and hear!
Listen to me, son of Zippor!

19 "God[a] *is* not a man, that He should lie,
Nor a son of man, that He should repent.
Has He [b]said, and will He not do?
Or has He spoken, and will He not make it good?

23:3
[b]Num. 23:4, 16

23:4
[a]Num. 23:16

23:5
[a]Num. 22:20, 35, 38; 23:16; Deut. 18:18; Jer. 1:9

23:7
[a]Deut. 23:4; Job 27:1; 29:1; Ps. 78:2
[b]Num. 22:6, 11, 17 [c]1 Sam. 17:10

23:8
[a]Num. 22:12

23:9
[a]Deut. 32:8; 33:28; Josh. 11:23
[b]Ex. 33:16; Ezra 9:2; [Eph. 2:14]

23:10
[a]Gen. 13:16; 22:17; 28:14; 2 Chr. 1:9
[b]Ps. 116:15

23:11
[a]Num. 22:11

23:12
[a]Num. 22:38

23:14
[a]Num. 23:1, 2

23:16
[a]Num. 22:35; 23:5

23:18
[a]Judg. 3:20

23:19
[a]1 Sam. 15:29; Mal. 3:6; James 1:17
[b]Num. 11:23; 1 Kin. 8:56

23:7 [1]*prophetic discourse* 23:10 [1]Or *dust cloud* 23:15 [1]So with MT, Tg., Vg.; Syr. *call;* LXX *go and ask God*

20 Behold, I have received *a command* to bless;
ᵃHe has blessed, and I cannot reverse it.

21 "Heᵃ has not observed iniquity in Jacob,
Nor has He seen ¹wickedness in Israel.
The LORD his God *is* with him,
ᵇAnd the shout of a King *is* among them.
22 ᵃGod brings them out of Egypt;
He has ᵇstrength like a wild ox.

23 "For *there is* no ¹sorcery against Jacob,
Nor any ²divination against Israel.
It now must be said of Jacob
And of Israel, 'Oh, ᵃwhat God has done!'
24 Look, a people rises ᵃlike a lioness,
And lifts itself up like a lion;
ᵇIt shall not lie down until it devours the prey,
And drinks the blood of the slain."

25Then Balak said to Balaam, "Neither curse them at all, nor bless them at all!"

26So Balaam answered and said to Balak, "Did I not tell you, saying, ᵃ'All that the LORD speaks, that I must do'?"

BALAAM'S THIRD PROPHECY

27Then Balak said to Balaam, "Please come, I will take you to another place; perhaps it will please God that you may curse them for me from there." 28So Balak took Balaam to the top of Peor, that ᵃoverlooks the ¹wasteland. 29Then Balaam said to Balak, "Build for me here seven altars, and prepare for me here seven bulls and seven rams." 30And Balak did as Balaam had said, and offered a bull and a ram on *every* altar.

24 Now when Balaam saw that it pleased the LORD to bless Israel, he did not go as at ᵃother times, to seek to use ¹sorcery, but he set his face toward the wilderness. 2And Balaam raised his eyes, and saw Israel ᵃencamped according to their tribes; and ᵇthe Spirit of God came upon him.
3ᵃThen he took up his oracle and said:

"The utterance of Balaam the son of Beor,
The utterance of the man whose eyes are opened,
4 The utterance of him who hears the words of
God,
Who sees the vision of the Almighty,
Who ᵃfalls down, with eyes wide open:

5 "How lovely are your tents, O Jacob!
Your dwellings, O Israel!
6 Like valleys that stretch out,
Like gardens by the riverside,
ᵃLike aloes ᵇplanted by the LORD,
Like cedars beside the waters.
7 He shall pour water from his buckets,
And his seed *shall be* ᵃin many waters.

"His king shall be higher than ᵇAgag,
And his ᶜkingdom shall be exalted.

23:20
ᵃGen. 12:2; 22:17;
Num. 22:12

23:21 ᵃPs. 32:2;
[Rom. 4:7, 8]
ᵇPs. 89:15–18

23:22
ᵃNum. 24:8
ᵇDeut. 33:17;
Job 39:10

23:23 ᵃPs. 31:19;
44:1

23:24
ᵃGen. 49:9
ᵇGen. 49:27;
Josh. 11:23

23:26
ᵃNum. 22:38

23:28
ᵃNum. 21:20

24:1
ᵃNum. 23:3, 15

24:2 ᵃNum. 2:2,
34 ᵇNum. 11:25;
1 Sam. 10:10;
19:20, 23;
2 Chr. 15:1

24:3
ᵃNum. 23:7, 18

24:4 ᵃEzek. 1:28

24:6 ᵃPs. 1:3;
Jer. 17:8
ᵇPs. 104:16

24:7 ᵃJer. 51:13;
Rev. 17:1, 15
ᵇ1 Sam. 15:8, 9
ᶜ2 Sam. 5:12;
1 Chr. 14:2

23:21 ¹trouble   23:23 ¹enchantment   ²fortune-telling   23:28 ¹Heb.
Jeshimon   24:1 ¹enchantments

8 "God[a] brings him out of Egypt;
  He has strength like a wild ox;
  He shall [b]consume the nations, his enemies;
  He shall [c]break their bones
  And [d]pierce *them* with his arrows.
9 'He[a] bows down, he lies down as a lion;
  And as a lion, who shall rouse him?'

[b]"Blessed *is* he who blesses you,
  And cursed *is* he who curses you."

10Then Balak's anger was aroused against Balaam, and he [a]struck his hands together; and Balak said to Balaam, [b]"I called you to curse my enemies, and look, you have bountifully blessed *them* these three times! 11Now therefore, flee to your place. [a]I said I would greatly honor you, but in fact, the LORD has kept you back from honor."

12So Balaam said to Balak, "Did I not also speak to your messengers whom you sent to me, saying, 13'If Balak were to give me his house full of silver and gold, I could not go beyond the word of the LORD, to do good or bad of my own will. What the LORD says, that I must speak'? 14And now, indeed, I am going to my people. Come, [a]I will advise you what this people will do to your people in the [b]latter days."

BALAAM'S FOURTH PROPHECY

15So he took up his oracle and said:

"The utterance of Balaam the son of Beor,
  And the utterance of the man whose eyes are
    opened;
16 The utterance of him who hears the words of God,
  And has the knowledge of the Most High,
  Who sees the vision of the Almighty,
  Who falls down, with eyes wide open:

17 "I[a] see Him, but not now;
  I behold Him, but not near;
  [b]A Star shall come out of Jacob;
  [c]A Scepter shall rise out of Israel,
  And [1]batter the brow of Moab,
  And destroy all the sons of [2]tumult.

18 "And [a]Edom shall be a possession;
  Seir also, his enemies, shall be a possession,
  While Israel does [1]valiantly.
19 [a]Out of Jacob One [1]shall have dominion,
  And destroy the remains of the city."

20Then he looked on Amalek, and he took up his oracle and said:

"Amalek *was* first among the nations,
  But *shall be* last until he perishes."

21Then he looked on the Kenites, and he took up his oracle and said:

"Firm is your dwelling place,
  And your nest is set in the rock;

24:8
[a]Num. 23:22
[b]Num. 14:9;
23:24 [c]Ps. 2:9;
Jer. 50:17
[d]Ps. 45:5

24:9 [a]Gen. 49:9;
Num. 23:24
[b]Gen. 12:3;
27:29

24:10
[a]Ezek. 21:14, 17
[b]Num. 23:11;
Neh. 13:2

24:11
[a]Num. 22:17, 37

24:14
[a][Mic. 6:5]
[b]Gen. 49:1;
Deut. 4:30;
Dan. 2:28

24:17 [a]Rev. 1:7;
Matt. 1:2;
Luke 3:34
[b]Matt. 2:2
[c]Gen. 49:10

24:18
[a]2 Sam. 8:14

24:19
[a]Gen. 49:10;
Amos 9:11, 12

24:17 [1]*shatter the forehead*   [2]Heb. *Sheth,* Jer. 48:45   24:18 [1]*mightily*
24:19 [1]*shall rule*

22 Nevertheless Kain shall be burned.
How long until Asshur carries you away captive?"

23Then he took up his oracle and said:

"Alas! Who shall live when God does this?
24 But ships *shall come* from the coasts of [a]Cyprus,[1]
And they shall afflict Asshur and afflict [b]Eber,
And so shall [2]*Amalek*, until he perishes."

25So Balaam rose and departed and [a]returned to his place;
Balak also went his way.

ISRAEL'S HARLOTRY IN MOAB

25 Now Israel remained in [a]Acacia Grove,[1] and the [b]people began to commit harlotry with the women of Moab. 2[a]They invited the people to [b]the sacrifices of their gods, and the people ate and [c]bowed down to their gods. 3So Israel was joined to Baal of Peor, and [a]the anger of the LORD was aroused against Israel.

4Then the LORD said to Moses, [a]"Take all the leaders of the people and hang the offenders before the LORD, out in the sun, [b]that the fierce anger of the LORD may turn away from Israel."

5So Moses said to [a]the judges of Israel, [b]"Every one of you kill his men who were joined to Baal of Peor."

6And indeed, one of the children of Israel came and presented to his brethren a Midianite woman in the sight of Moses and in the sight of all the congregation of the children of Israel, [a]who *were* weeping at the door of the tabernacle of meeting. 7Now [a]when Phinehas [b]the son of Eleazar, the son of Aaron the priest, saw *it*, he rose from among the congregation and took a javelin in his hand; 8and he went after the man of Israel into the tent and thrust both of them through, the man of Israel, and the woman through her body. So [a]the plague was [b]stopped among the children of Israel. 9And [a]those who died in the plague were twenty-four thousand.

10Then the LORD spoke to Moses, saying: 11[a]"Phinehas the son of Eleazar, the son of Aaron the priest, has turned back My wrath from the children of Israel, because he was zealous with My zeal among them, so that I did not consume the children of Israel in [b]My zeal. 12Therefore say, [a]'Behold, I give to him My [b]covenant of peace; 13and it shall be to him and [a]his descendants after him a covenant of [b]an everlasting priesthood, because he was [c]zealous for his God, and [d]made [1]atonement for the children of Israel.'"

14Now the name of the Israelite who was killed, who was killed with the Midianite woman, *was* Zimri the son of Salu, a leader of a father's house among the Simeonites. 15And the name of the Midianite woman who was killed *was* Cozbi the daughter of [a]Zur; he *was* head of the people of a father's house in Midian.

16Then the LORD spoke to Moses, saying: 17[a]"Harass the Midianites, and [1]attack them; 18for they harassed you with their [a]schemes[1] by which they seduced you in the matter of Peor and in the matter of Cozbi, the daughter of a leader of

Cross references (margin)

24:24 [a]Gen. 10:4; Ezek. 27:6; Dan. 11:30 [b]Gen. 10:21, 25
24:25 [a]Num. 22:5; 31:8
25:1 [a]Num. 33:49; Josh. 2:1 [b]Rev. 2:14
25:2 [a]Josh. 22:17; Hos. 9:10 [b]Ex. 34:15; Deut. 32:38; 1 Cor. 10:20 [c]Ex. 20:5
25:3 [a]Ps. 106:28, 29
25:4 [a]Deut. 4:3 [b]Num. 25:11; Deut. 13:17
25:5 [a]Ex. 18:21 [b]Deut. 13:6, 9
25:6 [a]Joel 2:17
25:7 [a]Ps. 106:30 [b]Ex. 6:25
25:8 [a]Ps. 106:30 [b]Num. 16:46–48
25:9 [a]Deut. 4:3
25:11 [a]Ps. 106:30 [b][Ex. 20:5]; Deut. 32:16, 21; 1 Kin. 14:22; Ps. 78:58; Ezek. 16:38
25:12 [a][Mal. 2:4, 5; 3:1] [b]Is. 54:10; Ezek. 34:25; 37:26; Mal. 2:5
25:13 [a]1 Chr. 6:4–15 [b]Ex. 40:15 [c]Acts 22:3; Rom. 10:2 [d][Heb. 2:17]
25:15 [a]Num. 31:8; Josh. 13:21
25:17 [a]Num. 31:1–3
25:18 [a]Num. 31:16; Rev. 2:14

24:24 [1]Heb. *Kittim* [2]Lit. *he* or *that one* 25:1 [1]Heb. *Shittim* 25:13 [1]Lit. *covering* 25:17 [1]*be hostile toward* 25:18 [1]*tricks*

Midian, their sister, who was killed in the day of the plague because of Peor."

THE SECOND CENSUS OF ISRAEL

26 And it came to pass, after the [a]plague, that the LORD spoke to Moses and Eleazar the son of Aaron the priest, saying: 2[a]"Take a census of all the congregation of the children of Israel [b]from twenty years old and above, by their fathers' houses, all who are able to go to war in Israel." 3So Moses and Eleazar the priest spoke with them [a]in the plains of Moab by the Jordan, *across from* Jericho, saying: 4"*Take a census of the people* from twenty years old and above, just as the LORD [a]commanded Moses and the children of Israel who came out of the land of Egypt."

5[a]Reuben *was* the firstborn of Israel. The children of Reuben *were: of* Hanoch, the family of the Hanochites; *of* Pallu, the family of the Palluites; 6*of* Hezron, the family of the Hezronites; *of* Carmi, the family of the Carmites. 7These *are* the families of the Reubenites: those who were numbered of them were forty-three thousand seven hundred and thirty. 8And the son of Pallu *was* Eliab. 9The sons of Eliab *were* Nemuel, Dathan, and Abiram. These *are* the Dathan and Abiram, [a]representatives of the congregation, who contended against Moses and Aaron in the company of Korah, when they contended against the LORD; 10[a]and the earth opened its mouth and swallowed them up together with Korah when that company died, when the fire devoured two hundred and fifty men; [b]and they became a sign. 11Nevertheless [a]the children of Korah did not die.

12The sons of Simeon according to their families *were: of* [1]Nemuel, the family of the Nemuelites; *of* Jamin, the family of the Jaminites; *of* [2]Jachin, the family of the Jachinites; 13*of* [1]Zerah, the family of the Zarhites; *of* Shaul, the family of the Shaulites. 14These *are* the families of the Simeonites: twenty-two thousand two hundred.

15The sons of Gad according to their families *were: of* [1]Zephon, the family of the Zephonites; *of* Haggi, the family of the Haggites; *of* Shuni, the family of the Shunites; 16*of* [1]Ozni, the family of the Oznites; *of* Eri, the family of the Erites; 17*of* [1]Arod, the family of the Arodites; *of* Areli, the family of the Arelites. 18These *are* the families of the sons of Gad according to those who were numbered of them: forty thousand five hundred.

19[a]The sons of Judah *were* Er and Onan; and Er and Onan died in the land of Canaan. 20And [a]the sons of Judah according to their families were: *of* Shelah, the family of the Shelanites; *of* Perez, the family of the Parzites; *of* Zerah, the family of the Zarhites. 21And the sons of Perez were: *of* Hezron, the family of the Hezronites; *of* Hamul, the family of the Hamulites. 22These *are* the families of Judah according to those who were numbered of them: seventy-six thousand five hundred.

23The sons of Issachar according to their families *were: of* Tola, the family of the Tolaites; *of* [1]Puah, the family of the [2]Punites; 24*of* [1]Jashub, the family of the Jashubites; *of* Shimron,

26:1 [a]Num. 25:9

26:2 [a]Ex. 30:12; 38:25, 26; Num. 1:2; 14:29 [b]Num. 1:3

26:3 [a]Num. 22:1; 31:12; 33:48; 35:1

26:4 [a]Num. 1:1

26:5 [a]Gen. 46:8; Ex. 6:14; 1 Chr. 5:1–3

26:9 [a]Num. 1:16; 16:1, 2

26:10 [a]Num. 16:32–35 [b]Num. 16:38–40; 1 Cor. 10:6; 2 Pet. 2:6

26:11 [a]Ex. 6:24; 1 Chr. 6:22, 23

26:19 [a]Gen. 38:2; 46:12

26:20 [a]1 Chr. 2:3

the family of the Shimronites. ²⁵These *are* the families of Issachar according to those who were numbered of them: sixty-four thousand three hundred.

^{26a}The sons of Zebulun according to their families *were:* of Sered, the family of the Sardites; of Elon, the family of the Elonites; of Jahleel, the family of the Jahleelites. ²⁷These *are* the families of the Zebulunites according to those who were numbered of them: sixty thousand five hundred.

^{28a}The sons of Joseph according to their families, by Manasseh and Ephraim, *were:* ²⁹The sons of ^aManasseh: of ^bMachir, the family of the Machirites; and Machir begot Gilead; of Gilead, the family of the Gileadites. ³⁰These *are* the sons of Gilead: of ¹Jeezer, the family of the Jeezerites; of Helek, the family of the Helekites; ³¹of Asriel, the family of the Asrielites; *of* Shechem, the family of the Shechemites; ³²*of* Shemida, the family of the Shemidaites; *of* Hepher, the family of the Hepherites. ³³Now ^aZelophehad the son of Hepher had no sons, but daughters; and the names of the daughters of Zelophehad *were* Mahlah, Noah, Hoglah, Milcah, and Tirzah. ³⁴These *are* the families of Manasseh; and those who were numbered of them *were* fifty-two thousand seven hundred.

³⁵These *are* the sons of Ephraim according to their families: of Shuthelah, the family of the Shuthalhites; of ¹Becher, the family of the Bachrites; of Tahan, the family of the Tahanites. ³⁶And these *are* the sons of Shuthelah: of Eran, the family of the Eranites. ³⁷These *are* the families of the sons of Ephraim according to those who were numbered of them: thirty-two thousand five hundred.

These *are* the sons of Joseph according to their families.

^{38a}The sons of Benjamin according to their families were: of Bela, the family of the Belaites; of Ashbel, the family of the Ashbelites; of ^bAhiram, the family of the Ahiramites; ³⁹of ^aShupham,¹ the family of the Shuphamites; of ²Hupham, the family of the Huphamites. ⁴⁰And the sons of Bela were ¹Ard and Naaman: ^a*of Ard,* the family of the Ardites; of Naaman, the family of the Naamites. ⁴¹These *are* the sons of Benjamin according to their families; and those who were numbered of them *were* forty-five thousand six hundred.

⁴²These *are* the sons of Dan according to their families: of ¹Shuham, the family of the Shuhamites. These *are* the families of Dan according to their families. ⁴³All the families of the Shuhamites, according to those who were numbered of them, *were* sixty-four thousand four hundred.

^{44a}The sons of Asher according to their families *were:* of Jimna, the family of the Jimnites; of Jesui, the family of the Jesuites; of Beriah, the family of the Beriites. ⁴⁵Of the sons of Beriah: of Heber, the family of the Heberites; of Malchiel, the family of the Malchielites. ⁴⁶And the name of the daughter of Asher *was* Serah. ⁴⁷These *are* the families of the sons of Asher according to those who were numbered of them: fifty-three thousand four hundred.

^{48a}The sons of Naphtali according to their families *were:* of ¹Jahzeel, the family of the Jahzeelites; of Guni, the family of the Gunites; ⁴⁹of Jezer, the family of the Jezerites; of ^aShillem,

---

26:26 ^aGen. 46:14
26:28 ^aGen. 46:20; Deut. 33:16
26:29 ^aJosh. 17:1 ^b1 Chr. 7:14, 15
26:33 ^aNum. 27:1; 36:11
26:38 ^aGen. 46:21; 1 Chr. 7:6 ^bGen. 46:21; 1 Chr. 8:1, 2
26:39 ^a1 Chr. 7:12
26:40 ^a1 Chr. 8:3
26:44 ^aGen. 46:17; 1 Chr. 7:30
26:48 ^aGen. 46:24; 1 Chr. 7:13
26:49 ^a1 Chr. 7:13

26:30 ¹*Abiezer,* Josh. 17:2   26:35 ¹*Bered,* 1 Chr. 7:20   26:39 ¹MT *Shephupham; Shephuphan,* 1 Chr. 8:5   ²*Huppim,* Gen. 46:21   26:40 ¹*Addar,* 1 Chr. 8:3   26:42 ¹*Hushim,* Gen. 46:23   26:48 ¹*Jahziel,* 1 Chr. 7:13

the family of the Shillemites. 50These *are* the families of Naphtali according to their families; and those who were numbered of them *were* forty-five thousand four hundred.

51aThese *are* those who were numbered of the children of Israel: six hundred and one thousand seven hundred and thirty.

52Then the LORD spoke to Moses, saying: 53a"To these the land shall be bdivided as an inheritance, according to the number of names. 54aTo a large *tribe* you shall give a larger inheritance, and to a small *tribe* you shall give a smaller inheritance. Each shall be given its inheritance according to those who were numbered of them. 55But the land shall be adivided by lot; they shall inherit according to the names of the tribes of their fathers. 56According to the lot their inheritance shall be divided between the larger and the smaller."

57aAnd these *are* those who were numbered of the Levites according to their families: of Gershon, the family of the Gershonites; of Kohath, the family of the Kohathites; of Merari, the family of the Merarites. 58These *are* the families of the Levites: the family of the Libnites, the family of the Hebronites, the family of the Mahlites, the family of the Mushites, and the family of the Korathites. And Kohath begot Amram. 59The name of Amram's wife *was* aJochebed the daughter of Levi, who was born to Levi in Egypt; and to Amram she bore Aaron and Moses and their sister Miriam. 60aTo Aaron were born Nadab and Abihu, Eleazar and Ithamar. 61And aNadab and Abihu died when they offered profane fire before the LORD.

62aNow those who were numbered of them were twenty-three thousand, every male from a month old and above; bfor they were not numbered among the other children of Israel, because there was cno inheritance given to them among the children of Israel.

63These *are* those who were numbered by Moses and Eleazar the priest, who numbered the children of Israel ain the plains of Moab by the Jordan, *across from* Jericho. 64aBut among these there was not a man of those who were numbered by Moses and Aaron the priest when they numbered the children of Israel in the bWilderness of Sinai. 65For the LORD had said of them, "They ashall surely die in the wilderness." So there was not left a man of them, bexcept Caleb the son of Jephunneh and Joshua the son of Nun.

INHERITANCE LAWS

27 Then came the daughters of aZelophehad the son of Hepher, the son of Gilead, the son of Machir, the son of Manasseh, from the families of Manasseh the son of Joseph; and these *were* the names of his daughters: Mahlah, Noah, Hoglah, Milcah, and Tirzah. 2And they stood before Moses, before Eleazar the priest, and before the leaders and all the congregation, *by* the doorway of the tabernacle of meeting, saying: 3"Our father adied in the wilderness; but he was not in the company of those who gathered together against the LORD, bin company with Korah, but he died in his own sin; and he had no sons. 4Why should the name of our father be aremoved1 from among his family because

26:51 aEx. 12:37; 38:26; Num. 1:46; 11:21

26:53 aJosh. 11:23; 14:1 bNum. 33:54

26:54 aNum. 33:54

26:55 aNum. 33:54; 34:13; Josh. 11:23; 14:2

26:57 aGen. 46:11; Ex. 6:16–19; Num. 3:15; 1 Chr. 6:1, 16

26:59 aEx. 2:1, 2; 6:20

26:60 aNum. 3:2

26:61 aLev. 10:1, 2; Num. 3:3, 4; 1 Chr. 24:2

26:62 aNum. 3:39 bNum. 1:49 cNum. 18:20, 23, 24

26:63 aNum. 26:3

26:64 aNum. 14:29–35; Deut. 2:14–16; Heb. 3:17 bNum. 1:1–46

26:65 aNum. 14:26–35; [1 Cor. 10:5, 6] bNum. 14:30

27:1 aNum. 26:33; 36:1, 11; Josh. 17:3

27:3 aNum. 14:35; 26:64, 65 bNum. 16:1, 2

27:4 aDeut. 25:6

27:4 1withdrawn

he had no son? ᵇGive us a ²possession among our father's brothers."

⁵So Moses ᵃbrought their case before the LORD.

⁶And the LORD spoke to Moses, saying: ⁷"The daughters of Zelophehad speak *what is* right; ᵃyou shall surely give them a possession of inheritance among their father's brothers, and cause the inheritance of their father to pass to them. ⁸And you shall speak to the children of Israel, saying: 'If a man dies and has no son, then you shall cause his inheritance to pass to his daughter. ⁹If he has no daughter, then you shall give his inheritance to his brothers. ¹⁰If he has no brothers, then you shall give his inheritance to his father's brothers. ¹¹And if his father has no brothers, then you shall give his inheritance to the relative closest to him in his family, and he shall possess it.'" And it shall be to the children of Israel ᵃa statute of judgment, just as the LORD commanded Moses.

JOSHUA THE NEXT LEADER OF ISRAEL
(Deut. 31:1–8)

¹²Now the LORD said to Moses: ᵃ"Go up into this Mount Abarim, and see the land which I have given to the children of Israel. ¹³And when you have seen it, you also ᵃshall ¹be gathered to your people, as Aaron your brother was gathered. ¹⁴For in the Wilderness of Zin, during the strife of the congregation, you ᵃrebelled against My command to hallow Me at the waters before their eyes." (These *are* the ᵇwaters of Meribah, at Kadesh in the Wilderness of Zin.)

¹⁵Then Moses spoke to the LORD, saying: ¹⁶"Let the LORD, ᵃthe God of the spirits of all flesh, set a man over the congregation, ¹⁷ᵃwho may go out before them and go in before them, who may lead them out and bring them in, that the congregation of the LORD may not be ᵇlike sheep which have no shepherd."

¹⁸And the LORD said to Moses: "Take Joshua the son of Nun with you, a man ᵃin whom *is* the Spirit, and ᵇlay your hand on him; ¹⁹set him before Eleazar the priest and before all the congregation, and ᵃinaugurate¹ him in their sight. ²⁰And ᵃyou shall give *some* of your authority to him, that all the congregation of the children of Israel ᵇmay be obedient. ²¹ᵃHe shall stand before Eleazar the priest, who shall inquire before the LORD for him ᵇby the judgment of the Urim. ᶜAt his word they shall go out, and at his word they shall come in, he and all the children of Israel with him—all the congregation."

²²So Moses did as the LORD commanded him. He took Joshua and set him before Eleazar the priest and before all the congregation. ²³And he laid his hands on him ᵃand ¹inaugurated him, just as the LORD commanded by the hand of Moses.

DAILY OFFERINGS
(Ex. 29:38–46)

28 Now the LORD spoke to Moses, saying, ²"Command the children of Israel, and say to them, 'My offering, ᵃMy food for My offerings made by fire as a sweet aroma to

---

27:4 ᵇJosh. 17:4
27:5
ᵃEx. 18:13–26
27:7
ᵃNum. 36:2;
Josh. 17:4
27:11
ᵃNum. 35:29
27:12
ᵃNum. 33:47;
Deut. 3:23–27;
32:48–52;
34:1–4
27:13
ᵃNum. 20:12,
24, 28; 31:2;
Deut. 10:6;
34:5, 6
27:14
ᵃNum. 20:12,
24; Deut. 1:37;
32:51; Ps. 106:32,
33 ᵇEx. 17:7
27:16
ᵃNum. 16:22;
Heb. 12:9
27:17
ᵃDeut. 31:2;
1 Sam. 8:20;
18:13; 2 Chr. 1:10
ᵇ1 Kin. 22:17;
Zech. 10:2;
Matt. 9:36;
Mark 6:34
27:18
ᵃGen. 41:38;
Judg. 3:10;
1 Sam. 16:13, 18
ᵇDeut. 34:9
27:19
ᵃDeut. 3:28;
31:3, 7, 8, 23
27:20
ᵃNum. 11:17
ᵇJosh. 1:16–18
27:21
ᵃJudg. 20:18, 23,
26; 1 Sam. 23:9;
30:7 ᵇEx. 28:30;
1 Sam. 28:6
ᶜJosh. 9:14;
1 Sam. 22:10
27:23
ᵃDeut. 3:28;
31:7, 8
28:2
ᵃLev. 3:11; 21:6, 8;
[Mal. 1:7, 12]

27:4 ²*inheritance*   27:13 ¹Die and join your ancestors   27:19 ¹*commission*
27:23 ¹*commissioned*

Me, you shall be careful to offer to Me at their appointed time.'

3"And you shall say to them, ªThis *is* the offering made by fire which you shall offer to the LORD: two male lambs in their first year without blemish, day by day, as a regular burnt offering. 4The one lamb you shall offer in the morning, the other lamb you shall offer in the evening, 5and ªone-tenth of an ephah of fine flour as a bgrain offering mixed with one-fourth of a hin of pressed oil. 6*It is* ªa regular burnt offering which was ordained at Mount Sinai for a sweet aroma, an offering made by fire to the LORD. 7And its drink offering *shall be* one-fourth of a hin for each lamb; ªin a holy *place* you shall pour out the drink to the LORD as an offering. 8The other lamb you shall offer in the evening; as the morning grain offering and its drink offering, you shall offer *it* as an offering made by fire, a ¹sweet aroma to the LORD.

SABBATH OFFERINGS

9'And on the Sabbath day two lambs in their first year, without blemish, and two-tenths *of an ephah* of fine flour as a grain offering, mixed with oil, with its drink offering— 10*this is* ªthe burnt offering for every Sabbath, besides the regular burnt offering with its drink offering.

MONTHLY OFFERINGS

11ª'At the beginnings of your months you shall present a burnt offering to the LORD: two young bulls, one ram, and seven lambs in their first year, without blemish; 12ªthree-tenths *of an ephah* of fine flour as a grain offering, mixed with oil, for each bull; two-tenths *of an ephah* of fine flour as a grain offering, mixed with oil, for the one ram; 13and one-tenth *of an ephah* of fine flour, mixed with oil, as a grain offering for each lamb, as a burnt offering of sweet aroma, an offering made by fire to the LORD. 14Their drink offering shall be half a hin of wine for a bull, one-third of a hin for a ram, and one-fourth of a hin for a lamb; this *is* the burnt offering for each month throughout the months of the year. 15Also ªone kid of the goats as a sin offering to the LORD shall be offered, besides the regular burnt offering and its drink offering.

OFFERINGS AT PASSOVER
(*Lev. 23:5–14*)

16ª'On the fourteenth day of the first month *is* the Passover of the LORD. 17ªAnd on the fifteenth day of this month *is* the feast; unleavened bread shall be eaten for seven days. 18On the ªfirst day *you shall have* a holy ¹convocation. You shall do no ²customary work. 19And you shall present an offering made by fire as a burnt offering to the LORD: two young bulls, one ram, and seven lambs in their first year. ªBe sure they are without blemish. 20Their grain offering shall be of fine flour mixed with oil: three-tenths *of an ephah* you shall offer for a bull, and two-tenths for a ram; 21you shall offer one-tenth *of an ephah* for each of the seven lambs; 22also ªone goat *as* a sin offering, to make ¹atonement for you. 23You shall offer these besides

28:3
ªEx. 29:38–42

28:5 ªEx. 16:36;
Num. 15:4
bLev. 2:1

28:6 ªEx. 29:42;
Amos 5:25

28:7 ªEx. 29:42

28:10
ªEzek. 46:4

28:11
ªNum. 10:10;
1 Sam. 20:5;
1 Chr. 23:31;
2 Chr. 2:4;
Ezra 3:5;
Neh. 10:33;
Is. 1:13, 14;
Ezek. 45:17;
46:6, 7;
Hos. 2:11;
Col. 2:16

28:12
ªNum. 15:4–12

28:15
ªNum. 15:24;
28:3, 22

28:16
ªEx. 12:1–20;
Lev. 23:5–8;
Num. 9:2–5;
Deut. 16:1–8;
Ezek. 45:21

28:17 ªLev. 23:6

28:18 ªEx. 12:16;
Lev. 23:7

28:19
ªLev. 22:20;
Num. 28:31;
29:8; Deut. 15:21

28:22
ªNum. 28:15

28:8 ¹*pleasing*   28:18 ¹*assembly* or *gathering*   ²*occupational*   28:22 ¹Lit. *covering*

the burnt offering of the morning, which *is* for a regular burnt offering. 24In this manner you shall offer the food of the offering made by fire daily for seven days, as a sweet aroma to the LORD; it shall be offered besides the regular burnt offering and its drink offering. 25And aon the seventh day you shall have a holy convocation. You shall do no customary work.

OFFERINGS AT THE FEAST OF WEEKS
(*Lev. 23:15–22*)

26‘Also aon the day of the firstfruits, when you bring a new grain offering to the LORD at your *Feast of* Weeks, you shall have a holy convocation. You shall do no customary work. 27You shall present a burnt offering as a sweet aroma to the LORD: atwo young bulls, one ram, and seven lambs in their first year, 28with their grain offering of fine flour mixed with oil: three-tenths *of an ephah* for each bull, two-tenths for the one ram, 29and one-tenth for each of the seven lambs; 30*also* one kid of the goats, to make ¹atonement for you. 31aBe sure they are without ¹blemish. You shall present *them* with their drink offerings, besides the regular burnt offering with its grain offering.

OFFERINGS AT THE FEAST OF TRUMPETS
(*Lev. 23:23–25*)

29 ‘And in the seventh month, on the first *day* of the month, you shall have a holy convocation. You shall do no customary work. For you ait is a day of blowing the trumpets. 2You shall offer a burnt offering as a sweet aroma to the LORD: one young bull, one ram, *and* seven lambs in their first year, without blemish. 3Their grain offering *shall be* fine flour mixed with oil: three-tenths *of an ephah* for the bull, two-tenths for the ram, 4and one-tenth for each of the seven lambs; 5also one kid of the goats *as* a sin offering, to make atonement for you; 6besides athe burnt offering with its grain offering for the New Moon, bthe regular burnt offering with its grain offering, and their drink offerings, caccording to their ordinance, as a sweet aroma, an offering made by fire to the LORD.

OFFERINGS ON THE DAY OF ATONEMENT
(*Lev. 23:26–32*)

7a‘On the tenth *day* of this seventh month you shall have a holy convocation. You shall baffict your souls; you shall not do any work. 8You shall present a burnt offering to the LORD as a sweet aroma: one young bull, one ram, *and* seven lambs in their first year. aBe sure they are without blemish. 9Their grain offering *shall be of* fine flour mixed with oil: three-tenths *of an ephah* for the bull, two-tenths for the one ram, 10and one-tenth for each of the seven lambs; 11also one kid of the goats *as* a sin offering, besides athe sin offering for atonement, the regular burnt offering with its grain offering, and their drink offerings.

OFFERINGS AT THE FEAST OF TABERNACLES
(*Lev. 23:33–44*)

12a‘On the fifteenth day of the seventh month you shall have a holy convocation. You shall do no customary work,

28:25 aEx. 12:16; 13:6; Lev. 23:8
28:26 aEx. 23:16; 34:22; Lev. 23:10–21; Deut. 16:9–12; Acts 2:1
28:27 aLev. 23:18, 19
28:31 aNum. 28:3, 19
29:1 aEx. 23:16; 34:22; Lev. 23:23–25
29:6 aNum. 28:11–15 bNum. 28:3 cNum. 15:11, 12
29:7 aLev. 16:29–34; 23:26–32 bPs. 35:13; Is. 58:5
29:8 aNum. 28:19
29:11 aLev. 16:3, 5
29:12 aLev. 23:33–35; Deut. 16:13–15; Ezek. 45:25

28:30 ¹Lit. *covering*   28:31 ¹*defect*

and you shall keep a feast to the LORD seven days. [13a]You shall present a burnt offering, an offering made by fire as a sweet aroma to the LORD: thirteen young bulls, two rams, *and* fourteen lambs in their first year. They shall be without blemish. [14]Their grain offering *shall be of* fine flour mixed with oil: three-tenths *of an ephah* for each of the thirteen bulls, two-tenths for each of the two rams, [15]and one-tenth for each of the fourteen lambs; [16]also one kid of the goats *as* a sin offering, besides the regular burnt offering, its grain offering, and its drink offering.

[17]'On the [a]second day *present* twelve young bulls, two rams, fourteen lambs in their first year without blemish, [18]and their grain offering and their drink offerings for the bulls, for the rams, and for the lambs, by their number, [a]according to the ordinance; [19]also one kid of the goats *as* a sin offering, besides the regular burnt offering with its grain offering, and their drink offerings.

[20]'On the third day *present* eleven bulls, two rams, fourteen lambs in their first year without blemish, [21]and their grain offering and their drink offerings for the bulls, for the rams, and for the lambs, by their number, [a]according to the ordinance; [22]also one goat *as* a sin offering, besides the regular burnt offering, its grain offering, and its drink offering.

[23]'On the fourth day *present* ten bulls, two rams, *and* fourteen lambs in their first year, without blemish, [24]and their grain offering and their drink offerings for the bulls, for the rams, and for the lambs, by their number, according to the ordinance; [25]also one kid of the goats *as* a sin offering, besides the regular burnt offering, its grain offering, and its drink offering.

[26]'On the fifth day *present* nine bulls, two rams, *and* fourteen lambs in their first year without blemish, [27]and their grain offering and their drink offerings for the bulls, for the rams, and for the lambs, by their number, according to the ordinance; [28]also one goat *as* a sin offering, besides the regular burnt offering, its grain offering, and its drink offering.

[29]'On the sixth day *present* eight bulls, two rams, *and* fourteen lambs in their first year without blemish, [30]and their grain offering and their drink offerings for the bulls, for the rams, and for the lambs, by their number, according to the ordinance; [31]also one goat *as* a sin offering, besides the regular burnt offering, its grain offering, and its drink offering.

[32]'On the seventh day *present* seven bulls, two rams, *and* fourteen lambs in their first year without blemish, [33]and their grain offering and their drink offerings for the bulls, for the rams, and for the lambs, by their number, according to the ordinance; [34]also one goat *as* a sin offering, besides the regular burnt offering, its grain offering, and its drink offering.

[35]'On the eighth day you shall have a [a]sacred[1] assembly. You shall do no customary work. [36]You shall present a burnt offering, an offering made by fire as a sweet aroma to the LORD: one bull, one ram, seven lambs in their first year without blemish, [37]and their grain offering and their drink offerings for the bull, for the ram, and for the lambs, by their number, according to the ordinance; [38]also one goat *as* a sin

29:13 [a]Ezra 3:4
29:17
[a]Lev. 23:36
29:18
[a]Num. 15:12; 28:7, 14; 29:3, 4, 9, 10
29:21
[a]Num. 29:18
29:35
[a]Lev. 23:36

29:35 [1]solemn

offering, besides the regular burnt offering, its grain offering, and its drink offering. ³⁹"These you shall present to the LORD at your ᵃappointed feasts (besides your ᵇvowed offerings and your freewill offerings) as your burnt offerings and your grain offerings, as your drink offerings and your peace offerings.'"

⁴⁰So Moses told the children of Israel everything, just as the LORD commanded Moses.

THE LAW CONCERNING VOWS

30 Then Moses spoke to ᵃthe heads of the tribes concerning the children of Israel, saying, "This *is* the thing which the LORD has commanded: ²ᵃIf a man makes a vow to the LORD, or ᵇswears an oath to bind himself by some agreement, he shall not break his word; he shall ᶜdo according to all that proceeds out of his mouth.

³"Or if a woman makes a vow to the LORD, and binds *herself* by some agreement while in her father's house in her youth, ⁴and her father hears her vow and the agreement by which she has bound herself, and her father ¹holds his peace, then all her vows shall stand, and every agreement with which she has bound herself shall stand. ⁵But if her father overrules her on the day that he hears, then none of her vows nor her agreements by which she has bound herself shall stand; and the LORD will release her, because her father overruled her.

⁶"If indeed she takes a husband, while bound by her vows or by a rash utterance from her lips by which she bound herself, ⁷and her husband hears *it,* and makes no response to her on the day that he hears, then her vows shall stand, and her agreements by which she bound herself shall stand. ⁸But if her husband ᵃoverrules her on the day that he hears *it,* he shall make void her vow which she took and what she uttered with her lips, by which she bound herself, and the LORD will release her.

⁹"Also any vow of a widow or a divorced woman, by which she has bound herself, shall stand against her.

¹⁰"If she vowed in her husband's house, or bound herself by an agreement with an oath, ¹¹and her husband heard *it,* and made no response to her *and* did not overrule her, then all her vows shall stand, and every agreement by which she bound herself shall stand. ¹²But if her husband truly made them void on the day he heard *them,* then whatever proceeded from her lips concerning her vows or concerning the agreement binding her, it shall not stand; her husband has made them ¹void, and the LORD will release her. ¹³Every vow and every binding oath to afflict her soul, her husband may confirm it, or her husband may make it void. ¹⁴Now if her husband makes no response whatever to her from day to day, then he confirms all her vows or all the agreements that bind her; he confirms them, because he made no response to her on the day that he heard *them.* ¹⁵But if he does make them void after he has heard *them,* then he shall bear her guilt."

¹⁶These *are* the statutes which the LORD commanded Moses, between a man and his wife, and between a father and his daughter in her youth in her father's house.

29:39
ᵃLev. 23:1–44;
1 Chr. 23:31;
2 Chr. 31:3;
Ezra 3:5;
Neh. 10:33;
Is. 1:14 ᵇLev. 7:16;
22:18, 21, 23;
23:38

30:1
ᵃNum. 1:4, 16;
7:2

30:2 ᵃLev. 27:2;
Deut. 23:21–23;
Judg. 11:30, 31,
35; Eccl. 5:4
ᵇLev. 5:4;
Matt. 14:9;
Acts 23:14
ᶜJob 22:27;
Ps. 22:25;
50:14; 66:13, 14;
Nah. 1:15

30:8
ᵃ[Gen. 3:16]

30:4 ¹*says nothing* to interfere   **30:12** ¹*annulled* or *invalidated*

VENGEANCE ON THE MIDIANITES

31 And the LORD spoke to Moses, saying: 2a"Take vengeance on the Midianites for the children of Israel. Afterward you shall bbe gathered to your people."

3So Moses spoke to the people, saying, "Arm some of yourselves for war, and let them go against the Midianites to take vengeance for the LORD on aMidian. 4A thousand from each tribe of all the tribes of Israel you shall send to the war."

5So there were recruited from the divisions of Israel one thousand from *each* tribe, twelve thousand armed for war. 6Then Moses sent them to the war, one thousand from *each* tribe; he sent them to the war with Phinehas the son of Eleazar the priest, with the holy articles and athe signal trumpets in his hand. 7And they warred against the Midianites, just as the LORD commanded Moses, and athey killed all the bmales. 8They killed the kings of Midian with *the rest of* those who were killed—aEvi, Rekem, bZur, Hur, and Reba, the five kings of Midian. cBalaam the son of Beor they also killed with the sword.

9And the children of Israel took the women of Midian captive, with their little ones, and took as spoil all their cattle, all their flocks, and all their goods. 10They also burned with fire all the cities where they dwelt, and all their forts. 11And athey took all the spoil and all the booty—of man and beast.

RETURN FROM THE WAR

12Then they brought the captives, the booty, and the spoil to Moses, to Eleazar the priest, and to the congregation of the children of Israel, to the camp in the plains of Moab by the Jordan, *across from* Jericho. 13And Moses, Eleazar the priest, and all the leaders of the congregation, went to meet them outside the camp. 14But Moses was angry with the officers of the army, *with* the captains over thousands and captains over hundreds, who had come from the battle.

15And Moses said to them: "Have you kept aall the women alive? 16Look, athese *women* caused the children of Israel, through the bcounsel of Balaam, to trespass against the LORD in the incident of Peor, and cthere was a plague among the congregation of the LORD. 17Now therefore, akill every male among the little ones, and kill every woman who has known a man intimately. 18But keep alive afor yourselves all the young girls who have not known a man intimately. 19And as for you, aremain outside the camp seven days; whoever has killed any person, and bwhoever has touched any slain, purify yourselves and your captives on the third day and on the seventh day. 20Purify every garment, everything made of leather, everything woven of goats' *hair,* and everything made of wood."

21Then Eleazar the priest said to the men of war who had gone to the battle, "This *is* the ¹ordinance of the law which the LORD commanded Moses: 22Only the gold, the silver, the bronze, the iron, the tin, and the lead, 23everything that can endure fire, you shall put through the fire, and it shall be clean; and it shall be purified awith the water of purification. But all that cannot endure fire you shall put through water.

31:2
aNum. 25:17
bNum. 27:12, 13

31:3 aJosh. 13:21

31:6 aNum. 10:9

31:7
aDeut. 20:13;
Judg. 21:11;
1 Sam. 27:9;
1 Kin. 11:15, 16
bGen. 34:25

31:8 aJosh. 13:21
bNum. 25:15
cNum. 31:16;
Josh. 13:22

31:11
aDeut. 20:14

31:15
aDeut. 20:14

31:16
aNum. 25:2
bNum. 24:14;
2 Pet. 2:15;
Rev. 2:14
cNum. 25:9

31:17 aDeut. 7:2;
20:16–18;
Judg. 21:11

31:18
aDeut. 21:10–14

31:19 aNum. 5:2
bNum. 19:11–22

31:23
aNum. 19:9, 17

31:21 ¹*statute*

²⁴ªAnd you shall wash your clothes on the seventh day and be clean, and afterward you may come into the camp."

DIVISION OF THE PLUNDER

²⁵Now the LORD spoke to Moses, saying: ²⁶"Count up the plunder that was ¹taken—of man and beast—you and Eleazar the priest and the chief fathers of the congregation; ²⁷and ªdivide the plunder into two parts, between those who took part in the war, who went out to battle, and all the congregation. ²⁸And levy a ¹tribute for the LORD on the men of war who went out to battle: ªone of every five hundred of the persons, the cattle, the donkeys, and the sheep; ²⁹take *it* from their half, and ªgive *it* to Eleazar the priest as a heave offering to the LORD. ³⁰And from the children of Israel's half you shall take ªone of every fifty, drawn from the persons, the cattle, the donkeys, and the sheep, from all the livestock, and give them to the Levites ᵇwho ¹keep charge of the tabernacle of the LORD." ³¹So Moses and Eleazar the priest did as the LORD commanded Moses.

³²The booty remaining from the plunder, which the men of war had taken, was six hundred and seventy-five thousand sheep, ³³seventy-two thousand cattle, ³⁴sixty-one thousand donkeys, ³⁵and thirty-two thousand persons in all, of women who had not known a man intimately. ³⁶And the half, the portion for those who had gone out to war, was in number three hundred and thirty-seven thousand five hundred sheep; ³⁷and the LORD's ¹tribute of the sheep was six hundred and seventy-five. ³⁸The cattle *were* thirty-six thousand, of which the LORD's tribute *was* seventy-two. ³⁹The donkeys *were* thirty thousand five hundred, of which the LORD's tribute *was* sixty-one. ⁴⁰The persons *were* sixteen thousand, of which the LORD's tribute *was* thirty-two persons. ⁴¹So Moses gave the tribute *which was* the LORD's heave offering to Eleazar the priest, ªas the LORD commanded Moses.

⁴²And from the children of Israel's half, which Moses separated from the men who fought— ⁴³now the half belonging to the congregation was three hundred and thirty-seven thousand five hundred sheep, ⁴⁴thirty-six thousand cattle, ⁴⁵thirty thousand five hundred donkeys, ⁴⁶and sixteen thousand persons— ⁴⁷and ªfrom the children of Israel's half Moses took one of every fifty, drawn from man and beast, and gave them to the Levites, who kept charge of the tabernacle of the LORD, as the LORD commanded Moses.

⁴⁸Then the officers who *were* over thousands of the army, the captains of thousands and captains of hundreds, came near to Moses; ⁴⁹and they said to Moses, "Your servants have taken a count of the men of war who *are* under our command, and not a man of us is missing. ⁵⁰Therefore we have brought an offering for the LORD, what every man found of ornaments of gold: armlets and bracelets and signet rings and earrings and necklaces, ªto make ¹atonement for ourselves before the LORD." ⁵¹So Moses and Eleazar the priest received the gold from them, all the fashioned ornaments. ⁵²And all the gold of the offering that they offered to the LORD, from the captains of thousands and captains of hundreds, was sixteen thousand

31:24 ªLev. 11:25

31:27
ªJosh. 22:8;
1 Sam. 30:24

31:28
ªNum. 31:30, 47

31:29
ªDeut. 18:1–5

31:30
ªNum. 31:42–47
ᵇNum. 3:7, 8, 25, 31, 36; 18:3, 4

31:41 ªNum. 5:9, 10; 18:8, 19

31:47
ªNum. 31:30

31:50
ªEx. 30:12–16

31:26 ¹captured   31:28 ¹tax   31:30 ¹perform the service   31:37 ¹tax
31:50 ¹Lit. covering

seven hundred and fifty shekels. 53a(The men of war had taken spoil, every man for himself.) 54And Moses and Eleazar the priest received the gold from the captains of thousands and of hundreds, and brought it into the tabernacle of meeting aas a memorial for the children of Israel before the LORD.

THE TRIBES SETTLING EAST OF THE JORDAN
(Deut. 3:12–22)

32 Now the children of Reuben and the children of Gad had a very great multitude of livestock; and when they saw the land of aJazer and the land of bGilead, that indeed the region *was* a place for livestock, 2the children of Gad and the children of Reuben came and spoke to Moses, to Eleazar the priest, and to the leaders of the congregation, saying, 3"Ataroth, Dibon, Jazer, aNimrah, bHeshbon, Elealeh, cShebam, Nebo, and dBeon, 4the country awhich the LORD defeated before the congregation of Israel, *is* a land for livestock, and your servants have livestock." 5Therefore they said, "If we have found favor in your sight, let this land be given to your servants as a possession. Do not take us over the Jordan."

6And Moses said to the children of Gad and to the children of Reuben: "Shall your brethren go to war while you sit here? 7Now why will you adiscourage the heart of the children of Israel from going over into the land which the LORD has given them? 8Thus your fathers did awhen I sent them away from Kadesh Barnea bto see the land. 9For awhen they went up to the Valley of Eshcol and saw the land, they discouraged the heart of the children of Israel, so that they did not go into the land which the LORD had given them. 10aSo the LORD's anger was aroused on that day, and He swore an oath, saying, 11"Surely none of the men who came up from Egypt, afrom twenty years old and above, shall see the land of which I swore to Abraham, Isaac, and Jacob, because bthey have not wholly followed Me, 12except Caleb the son of Jephunneh, the Kenizzite, and Joshua the son of Nun, afor they have wholly followed the LORD.' 13So the LORD's anger was aroused against Israel, and He made them awander in the wilderness forty years, until ball the generation that had done evil in the sight of the LORD was gone. 14And look! You have risen in your fathers' place, a brood of sinful men, to increase still more the afierce anger of the LORD against Israel. 15For if you aturn away from following Him, He will once again leave them in the wilderness, and you will destroy all these people."

16Then they came near to him and said: "We will build sheepfolds here for our livestock, and cities for our little ones, 17but awe ourselves will be armed, ready *to go* before the children of Israel until we have brought them to their place; and our little ones will dwell in the fortified cities because of the inhabitants of the land. 18aWe will not return to our homes until every one of the children of Israel has 1received his inheritance. 19For we will not inherit with them on the other side of the Jordan and beyond, abecause our inheritance has fallen to us on this eastern side of the Jordan."

20Then aMoses said to them: "If you do this thing, if you arm yourselves before the LORD for the war, 21and all your

31:53
aNum. 31:32;
Deut. 20:14

31:54 aEx. 30:16

32:1
aNum. 21:32;
Josh. 13:25;
2 Sam. 24:5
bDeut. 3:13

32:3
aNum. 32:36
bJosh. 13:17, 26
cNum. 32:38
dNum. 32:38

32:4
aNum. 21:24,
34, 35

32:7
aNum. 13:27—
14:4

32:8
aNum. 13:3, 26
bDeut. 1:19–25

32:9
aNum. 13:24, 31;
Deut. 1:24, 28

32:10
aNum. 14:11;
Deut. 1:34–36

32:11
aNum. 14:28,
29; 26:63–65;
Deut. 1:35
bNum. 14:24, 30

32:12
aNum. 14:6–9,
24, 30;
Deut. 1:36;
Josh. 14:8, 9

32:13
aNum. 14:33–35
bNum. 26:64,
65

32:14
aNum. 11:1;
Deut. 1:34

32:15
aDeut. 30:17, 18;
Josh. 22:16–18;
2 Chr. 7:19; 15:2

32:17
aJosh. 4:12, 13

32:18
aJosh. 22:1–4

32:19
aJosh. 12:1; 13:8

32:20
aDeut. 3:18;
Josh. 1:14

32:18 1possessed

armed men cross over the Jordan before the LORD until He has driven out His enemies from before Him, 22and ªthe land is subdued before the LORD, then afterward ᵇyou may return and be blameless before the LORD and before Israel; and ᶜthis land shall be your possession before the LORD. 23But if you do not do so, then take note, you have sinned against the LORD; and be sure ªyour sin will find you out. 24ªBuild cities for your little ones and folds for your sheep, and do ¹what has proceeded out of your mouth."

25And the children of Gad and the children of Reuben spoke to Moses, saying: "Your servants will do as my lord commands. 26ªOur little ones, our wives, our flocks, and all our livestock will be there in the cities of Gilead; 27ªbut your servants will cross over, every man armed for war, before the LORD to battle, just as my lord says."

28So Moses gave command ªconcerning them to Eleazar the priest, to Joshua the son of Nun, and to the chief fathers of the tribes of the children of Israel. 29And Moses said to them: "If the children of Gad and the children of Reuben cross over the Jordan with you, every man armed for battle before the LORD, and the land is subdued before you, then you shall give them the land of Gilead as a possession. 30But if they do not cross over armed with you, they shall have possessions among you in the land of Canaan."

31Then the children of Gad and the children of Reuben answered, saying: "As the LORD has said to your servants, so we will do. 32We will cross over armed before the LORD into the land of Canaan, but the possession of our inheritance *shall remain* with us on this side of the Jordan."

33So ªMoses gave to the children of Gad, to the children of Reuben, and to half the tribe of Manasseh the son of Joseph, ᵇthe kingdom of Sihon king of the Amorites and the kingdom of Og king of Bashan, the land with its cities within the borders, the cities of the surrounding country. 34And the children of Gad built ªDibon and Ataroth and ᵇAroer, 35Atroth and Shophan and ªJazer and Jogbehah, 36ªBeth Nimrah and Beth Haran, ᵇfortified cities, and folds for sheep. 37And the children of Reuben built ªHeshbon and Elealeh and Kirjathaim, 38ªNebo and ᵇBaal Meon ᶜ(*their* names being changed) and Shibmah; and they gave *other* names to the cities which they built.

39And the children of ªMachir the son of Manasseh went to Gilead and took it, and ¹dispossessed the Amorites who *were* in it. 40So Moses ªgave Gilead to Machir the son of Manasseh, and he dwelt in it. 41Also ªJair the son of Manasseh went and took its small towns, and called them ᵇHavoth Jair.¹ 42Then Nobah went and took Kenath and its villages, and he called it Nobah, after his own name.

ISRAEL'S JOURNEY FROM EGYPT REVIEWED

33 These *are* the journeys of the children of Israel, who went out of the land of Egypt by their armies under the ªhand of Moses and Aaron. 2Now Moses wrote down the starting points of their journeys at the command of the LORD. And these *are* their journeys according to their starting points:

32:22
ªDeut. 3:20;
Josh. 11:23
ᵇJosh. 22:4
ᶜDeut. 3:12, 15,
16, 18; Josh. 1:15;
13:8, 32; 22:4, 9

32:23
ªGen. 4:7; 44:16;
Josh. 7:1–26;
Is. 59:12;
[Gal. 6:7]

32:24
ªNum. 32:16

32:26
ªJosh. 1:14

32:27
ªJosh. 4:12

32:28
ªJosh. 1:13

32:33
ªDeut. 3:8–17;
29:8;
Josh. 12:1–6;
13:8–31; 22:4
ᵇNum. 21:24,
33, 35

32:34
ªNum. 33:45, 46
ᵇDeut. 2:36

32:35
ªNum. 32:1, 3

32:36
ªNum. 32:3
ᵇNum. 32:24

32:37
ªNum. 21:27

32:38 ªIs. 46:1
ᵇEzek. 25:9
ᶜEx. 23:13;
Josh. 23:7

32:39
ªGen. 50:23;
Num. 27:1; 36:1

32:40
ªDeut. 3:12, 13,
15; Josh. 13:31

32:41
ªDeut. 3:14;
Josh. 13:30
ᵇJudg. 10:4;
1 Kin. 4:13

33:1 ªPs. 77:20

32:24 ¹*what you said you would do*   **32:39** ¹*drove out*   **32:41** ¹Lit. *Towns of Jair*

3They ^adeparted from Rameses in ^bthe first month, on the fifteenth day of the first month; on the day after the Passover the children of Israel went out ^cwith boldness in the sight of all the Egyptians. 4For the Egyptians were burying all *their* firstborn, ^awhom the LORD had killed among them. Also ^bon their gods the LORD had executed judgments.

5^aThen the children of Israel moved from Rameses and camped at Succoth. 6They departed from ^aSuccoth and camped at Etham, which *is* on the edge of the wilderness. 7^aThey moved from Etham and turned back to Pi Hahiroth, which *is* east of Baal Zephon; and they camped near Migdol. 8They departed ¹from before Hahiroth and ^apassed through the midst of the sea into the wilderness, went three days' journey in the Wilderness of Etham, and camped at Marah. 9They moved from Marah and ^acame to Elim. At Elim *were* twelve springs of water and seventy palm trees; so they camped there.

10They moved from Elim and camped by the Red Sea. 11They moved from the Red Sea and camped in the ^aWilderness of Sin. 12They journeyed from the Wilderness of Sin and camped at Dophkah. 13They departed from Dophkah and camped at Alush. 14They moved from Alush and camped at ^aRephidim, where there was no water for the people to drink.

15They departed from Rephidim and camped in the ^aWilderness of Sinai. 16They moved from the Wilderness of Sinai and camped ^aat ¹Kibroth Hattaavah. 17They departed from Kibroth Hattaavah and ^acamped at Hazeroth. 18They departed from Hazeroth and camped at ^aRithmah. 19They departed from Rithmah and camped at Rimmon Perez. 20They departed from Rimmon Perez and camped at Libnah. 21They moved from Libnah and camped at Rissah. 22They journeyed from Rissah and camped at Kehelathah. 23They went from Kehelathah and camped at Mount Shepher. 24They moved from Mount Shepher and camped at Haradah. 25They moved from Haradah and camped at Makheloth. 26They moved from Makheloth and camped at Tahath. 27They departed from Tahath and camped at Terah. 28They moved from Terah and camped at Mithkah. 29They went from Mithkah and camped at Hashmonah. 30They departed from Hashmonah and ^acamped at Moseroth. 31They departed from Moseroth and camped at Bene Jaakan. 32They moved from ^aBene Jaakan and ^bcamped at Hor Hagidgad. 33They went from Hor Hagidgad and camped at Jotbathah. 34They moved from Jotbathah and camped at Abronah. 35They departed from Abronah ^aand camped at Ezion Geber. 36They moved from Ezion Geber and camped in the ^aWilderness of Zin, which *is* Kadesh. 37They moved from ^aKadesh and camped at Mount Hor, on the boundary of the land of Edom.

38Then ^aAaron the priest went up to Mount Hor at the command of the LORD, and died there in the fortieth year after the children of Israel had come out of the land of Egypt, on the first *day* of the fifth month. 39Aaron *was* one hundred and twenty-three years old when he died on Mount Hor.

40Now ^athe king of Arad, the Canaanite, who dwelt in the South in the land of Canaan, heard of the coming of the children of Israel.

33:3 ^aEx. 12:37
^bEx. 12:2; 13:4
^cEx. 14:8

33:4 ^aEx. 12:29
^b[Ex. 12:12; 18:11]; Is. 19:1

33:5 ^aEx. 12:37

33:6 ^aEx. 13:20

33:7
^aEx. 14:1, 2, 9

33:8 ^aEx. 14:22; 15:22, 23

33:9 ^aEx. 15:27

33:11 ^aEx. 16:1

33:14 ^aEx. 17:1; 19:2

33:15 ^aEx. 16:1; 19:1, 2

33:16
^aNum. 11:34

33:17
^aNum. 11:35

33:18
^aNum. 12:16

33:30
^aDeut. 10:6

33:32
^aDeut. 10:6
^bDeut. 10:7

33:35
^aDeut. 2:8; 1 Kin. 9:26; 22:48

33:36
^aNum. 20:1; 27:14

33:37
^aNum. 20:22, 23; 21:4

33:38
^aNum. 20:25, 28; Deut. 10:6; 32:50

33:40
^aNum. 21:1

33:8 ¹Many Heb. mss., Sam., Syr., Tg., Vg. *from Pi Hahiroth;* cf. Num. 33:7
33:16 ¹Lit. *Graves of Craving*

33:43
a Num. 21:10

33:44
a Num. 21:11

33:45
a Num. 32:34

33:46
a Jer. 48:22;
Ezek. 6:14

33:47
a Num. 21:20;
Deut. 32:49

33:48
a Num. 22:1;
31:12; 35:1

33:49
a Num. 25:1;
Josh. 2:1

33:51
a Deut. 7:1, 2; 9:1;
Josh. 3:17

33:52
a Ex. 23:24,
33; 34:13;
Deut. 7:2, 5;
12:3; Judg. 2:2;
Ps. 106:34–36

33:53
a Deut. 11:31;
Josh. 21:43

33:54
a Num. 26:53–56

33:55
a Josh. 23:13;
Judg. 2:3

34:2 a Gen. 17:8;
Deut. 1:7, 8;
Ps. 78:54, 55;
105:11

34:3
a Josh. 15:1–3;
Ezek. 47:13,
19 b Gen. 14:3;
Josh. 15:2

34:4 a Josh. 15:3;
b Num. 13:26;
32:8
c Josh. 15:3, 4

34:5 a Gen. 15:18;
Josh. 15:4, 47;
1 Kin. 8:65;
Is. 27:12

34:6 a Ex. 23:31;
Josh. 15:12;
Ezek. 47:20

34:7
a Num. 33:37

34:8
a Num. 13:21;
Josh. 13:5;
2 Kin. 14:25
b Ezek. 47:15

34:9
a Ezek. 47:17

[41]So they departed from Mount Hor and camped at Zalmonah. [42]They departed from Zalmonah and camped at Punon. [43]They departed from Punon and [a]camped at Oboth. [44a]They departed from Oboth and camped at Ije Abarim, at the border of Moab. [45]They departed from [1]Ijim and camped [a]at Dibon Gad. [46]They moved from Dibon Gad and camped at [a]Almon Diblathaim. [47]They moved from Almon Diblathaim [a]and camped in the mountains of Abarim, before Nebo. [48]They departed from the mountains of Abarim and [a]camped in the plains of Moab by the Jordan, *across from* Jericho. [49]They camped by the Jordan, from Beth Jesimoth as far as the [a]Abel Acacia Grove[1] in the plains of Moab.

INSTRUCTIONS FOR THE CONQUEST OF CANAAN

[50]Now the LORD spoke to Moses in the plains of Moab by the Jordan, *across from* Jericho, saying, [51]"Speak to the children of Israel, and say to them: [a]'When you have crossed the Jordan into the land of Canaan, [52a]then you shall drive out all the inhabitants of the land from before you, destroy all their engraved stones, destroy all their molded images, and demolish all their [1]high places; [53]you shall dispossess *the inhabitants of* the land and dwell in it, for I have given you the land to [a]possess. [54]And [a]you shall divide the land by lot as an inheritance among your families; to the larger you shall give a larger inheritance, and to the smaller you shall give a smaller inheritance; there everyone's *inheritance* shall be whatever falls to him by lot. You shall inherit according to the tribes of your fathers. [55]But if you do not drive out the inhabitants of the land from before you, then it shall be that those whom you let remain *shall be* [a]irritants in your eyes and thorns in your sides, and they shall harass you in the land where you dwell. [56]Moreover it shall be *that* I will do to you as I thought to do to them.'"

THE APPOINTED BOUNDARIES OF CANAAN

34 Then the LORD spoke to Moses, saying, [2]"Command the children of Israel, and say to them: 'When you come into [a]the land of Canaan, this *is* the land that shall fall to you as an inheritance—the land of Canaan to its boundaries. [3a]Your southern border shall be from the Wilderness of Zin along the border of Edom; then your southern border shall extend eastward to the end of [b]the Salt Sea; [4]your border shall turn from the southern side of [a]the Ascent of Akrabbim, continue to Zin, and be on the south of [b]Kadesh Barnea; then it shall go on to [c]Hazar Addar, and continue to Azmon; [5]the border shall turn from Azmon [a]to the Brook of Egypt, and it shall end at the Sea.

[6]'As for the [a]western border, you shall have the Great Sea for a border; this shall be your western border.

[7]'And this shall be your northern border: From the Great Sea you shall mark out your *border* line to [a]Mount Hor; [8]from Mount Hor you shall mark out *your border* [a]to the entrance of Hamath; then the direction of the border shall be toward [b]Zedad; [9]the border shall proceed to Ziphron, and it shall end at [a]Hazar Enan. This shall be your northern border.

33:45 [1]Same as *Ije Abarim*, v. 44   **33:49** [1]Heb. *Abel Shittim*   **33:52** [1]Places for pagan worship

10'You shall mark out your eastern border from Hazar Enan to Shepham; 11the border shall go down from Shepham ato Riblah on the east side of Ain; the border shall go down and reach to the eastern 1side of the Sea bof Chinnereth; 12the border shall go down along the Jordan, and it shall end at athe Salt Sea. This shall be your land with its surrounding boundaries.'"

13Then Moses commanded the children of Israel, saying: a"This *is* the land which you shall inherit by lot, which the LORD has commanded to give to the nine tribes and to the half-tribe. 14aFor the tribe of the children of Reuben according to the house of their fathers, and the tribe of the children of Gad according to the house of their fathers, have received *their inheritance;* and the half-tribe of Manasseh has received its inheritance. 15The two tribes and the half-tribe have received their inheritance on this side of the Jordan, *across from* Jericho eastward, toward the sunrise."

THE LEADERS APPOINTED TO DIVIDE THE LAND

16And the LORD spoke to Moses, saying, 17"These *are* the names of the men who shall divide the land among you as an inheritance: aEleazar the priest and Joshua the son of Nun. 18And you shall take one aleader of every tribe to divide the land for the inheritance. 19These *are* the names of the men: from the tribe of Judah, Caleb the son of Jephunneh; 20from the tribe of the children of Simeon, Shemuel the son of Ammihud; 21from the tribe of Benjamin, Elidad the son of Chislon; 22a leader from the tribe of the children of Dan, Bukki the son of Jogli; 23from the sons of Joseph: a leader from the tribe of the children of Manasseh, Hanniel the son of Ephod, 24and a leader from the tribe of the children of Ephraim, Kemuel the son of Shiphtan; 25a leader from the tribe of the children of Zebulun, Elizaphan the son of Parnach; 26a leader from the tribe of the children of Issachar, Paltiel the son of Azzan; 27a leader from the tribe of the children of Asher, Ahihud the son of Shelomi; 28and a leader from the tribe of the children of Naphtali, Pedahel the son of Ammihud."

29These *are* the ones the LORD commanded to 1divide the inheritance among the children of Israel in the land of Canaan.

CITIES FOR THE LEVITES

35 And the LORD spoke to Moses in athe plains of Moab by the Jordan *across from* Jericho, saying: 2a"Command the children of Israel that they give the Levites cities to dwell in from the inheritance of their possession, and you shall *also* give the Levites bcommon-land around the cities. 3They shall have the cities to dwell in; and their common-land shall be for their cattle, for their herds, and for all their animals. 4The common-land of the cities which you will give the Levites *shall extend* from the wall of the city outward a thousand cubits all around. 5And you shall measure outside the city on the east side two thousand cubits, on the south side two thousand cubits, on the west side two thousand cubits, and on the north side two thousand cubits. The city *shall*

34:11
a 2 Kin. 23:33;
Jer. 39:5, 6
b Deut. 3:17;
Josh. 11:2; 12:3;
13:27; 19:35;
Matt. 14:34;
Luke 5:1

34:12
a Num. 34:3

34:13
a Gen. 15:18;
Num. 26:52–56;
Deut. 11:24;
Josh. 14:1–5

34:14
a Num. 32:33

34:17 a Josh. 14:1, 2; 19:51

34:18
a Num. 1:4, 16

35:1
a Num. 33:50

35:2 a Josh. 14:3, 4; 21:2, 3; Ezek. 45:1; 48:10–20
b Lev. 25:32–34

34:11 1Lit. *shoulder*   34:29 1*apportion*

be in the middle. This shall belong to them as common-land for the cities.

6"Now among the cities which you will give to the Levites *you shall appoint* [a]six cities of refuge, to which a manslayer may flee. And to these you shall add forty-two cities. 7So all the cities you will give to the Levites *shall be* [a]forty-eight; these *you shall give* with their common-land. 8And the cities which you will give *shall be* [a]from the possession of the children of Israel; [b]from the larger *tribe* you shall give many, from the smaller you shall give few. Each shall give some of its cities to the Levites, in proportion to the inheritance that each receives."

CITIES OF REFUGE
(Deut. 19:1–13; Josh. 20:1–9)

9Then the LORD spoke to Moses, saying, 10"Speak to the children of Israel, and say to them: [a]'When you cross the Jordan into the land of Canaan, 11then [a]you shall appoint cities to be cities of refuge for you, that the manslayer who kills any person accidentally may flee there. 12[a]They shall be cities of refuge for you from the avenger, that the manslayer may not die until he stands before the congregation in judgment. 13And of the cities which you give, you shall have [a]six cities of refuge. 14[a]You shall appoint three cities on this side of the Jordan, and three cities you shall appoint in the land of Canaan, *which* will be cities of refuge. 15These six cities shall be for refuge for the children of Israel, [a]for the stranger, and for the sojourner among them, that anyone who kills a person accidentally may flee there.

16[a]'But if he strikes him with an iron implement, so that he dies, he *is* a murderer; the murderer shall surely be put to death. 17And if he strikes him with a stone in the hand, by which one could die, and he does die, he *is* a murderer; the murderer shall surely be put to death. 18Or *if* he strikes him with a wooden hand weapon, by which one could die, and he does die, he *is* a murderer; the murderer shall surely be put to death. 19[a]The[1] avenger of blood himself shall put the murderer to death; when he meets him, he shall put him to death. 20[a]If he pushes him out of hatred or, [b]while lying in wait, hurls something at him so that he dies, 21or in enmity he strikes him with his hand so that he dies, the one who struck *him* shall surely be put to death. He *is* a murderer. The avenger of blood shall put the murderer to death when he meets him.

22'However, if he pushes him suddenly [a]without enmity, or throws anything at him without lying in wait, 23or uses a stone, by which a man could die, throwing *it* at him without seeing *him,* so that he dies, while he was not his enemy or seeking his harm, 24then [a]the congregation shall judge between the manslayer and the avenger of blood according to these judgments. 25So the congregation shall deliver the manslayer from the hand of the avenger of blood, and the congregation shall return him to the city of refuge where he had fled, and [a]he shall remain there until the death of the high priest [b]who was anointed with the holy oil. 26But if the manslayer at

---

35:6 [a]Deut. 4:41; Josh. 20:2, 7, 8; 21:3, 13

35:7 [a]Josh. 21:41

35:8 [a]Josh. 21:3 [b]Num. 26:54; 33:54

35:10 [a]Deut. 19:2; Josh. 20:1–9

35:11 [a]Ex. 21:13; Num. 35:22–25; Deut. 19:1–13

35:12 [a]Deut. 19:6; Josh. 20:3, 5, 6

35:13 [a]Num. 35:6

35:14 [a]Deut. 4:41; Josh. 20:8

35:15 [a]Num. 15:16

35:16 [a]Ex. 21:12, 14; Lev. 24:17; Deut. 19:11, 12

35:19 [a]Num. 35:21, 24, 27; Deut. 19:6, 12

35:20 [a]Gen. 4:8; 2 Sam. 3:27; 20:10; 1 Kin. 2:31, 32 [b]Ex. 21:14; Deut. 19:11, 12

35:22 [a]Ex. 21:13

35:24 [a]Num. 35:12; Josh. 20:6

35:25 [a]Josh. 20:6 [b]Ex. 29:7; Lev. 4:3; 21:10

35:19 [1]A family member who is to avenge the victim

any time goes outside the limits of the city of refuge where he fled, [27]and the avenger of blood finds him outside the limits of his city of refuge, and the avenger of blood kills the manslayer, he shall not be guilty of [1]blood, [28]because he should have remained in his city of refuge until the death of the high priest. But after the death of the high priest the manslayer may return to the land of his possession.

[29]'And these *things* shall be [a]a statute of judgment to you throughout your generations in all your dwellings. [30]Whoever kills a person, the murderer shall be put to death on the [a]testimony of witnesses; but one witness is not *sufficient* testimony against a person for the death *penalty.* [31]Moreover you shall take no ransom for the life of a murderer who *is* guilty of death, but he shall surely be put to death. [32]And you shall take no ransom for him who has fled to his city of refuge, that he may return to dwell in the land before the death of the priest. [33]So you shall not pollute the land where you *are*; for blood [a]defiles the land, and no [1]atonement can be made for the land, for the blood that is shed on it, except [b]by the blood of him who shed it. [34]Therefore [a]do not defile the land which you inhabit, in the midst of which I dwell; for [b]I the LORD dwell among the children of Israel.'"

MARRIAGE OF FEMALE HEIRS

36 Now the chief fathers of the families of the [a]children of Gilead the son of Machir, the son of Manasseh, of the families of the sons of Joseph, came near and [b]spoke before Moses and before the leaders, the chief fathers of the children of Israel. [2]And they said: [a]"The LORD commanded my lord *Moses* to give the land as an inheritance by lot to the children of Israel, and [b]my lord was commanded by the LORD to give the inheritance of our brother Zelophehad to his daughters. [3]Now if they are married to any of the sons of the *other* tribes of the children of Israel, then their inheritance will be [a]taken from the inheritance of our fathers, and it will be added to the inheritance of the tribe into which they marry; so it will be taken from the lot of our inheritance. [4]And when [a]the Jubilee of the children of Israel comes, then their inheritance will be added to the inheritance of the tribe into which they marry; so their inheritance will be taken away from the inheritance of the tribe of our fathers."

[5]Then Moses commanded the children of Israel according to the word of the LORD, saying: [a]"What the tribe of the sons of Joseph speaks is right. [6]This *is* what the LORD commands concerning the daughters of Zelophehad, saying, 'Let them [1]marry whom they think best, [a]but they may marry only within the family of their father's tribe.' [7]So the inheritance of the children of Israel shall not change hands from tribe to tribe, for every one of the children of Israel shall [a]keep the inheritance of the tribe of his fathers. [8]And [a]every daughter who possesses an inheritance in any tribe of the children of Israel shall be the wife of one of the family of her father's tribe, so that the children of Israel each may possess the inheritance of his fathers. [9]Thus no inheritance shall change hands from *one* tribe to another, but every tribe of the children of Israel shall keep its own inheritance."

35:29
[a]Num. 27:11

35:30
[a]Deut. 17:6;
19:15;
Matt. 18:16;
John 7:51; 8:17,
18; 2 Cor. 13:1;
Heb. 10:28

35:33
[a]Deut. 21:7,
8; Ps. 106:38
[b]Gen. 9:6

35:34
[a]Lev. 18:24, 25;
Deut. 21:23
[b]Ex. 29:45, 46

36:1
[a]Num. 26:29
[b]Num. 27:1–11

36:2
[a]Num. 26:55;
33:54; Josh. 17:4
[b]Num. 27:1, 5–7

36:3 [a]Num. 27:4

36:4 [a]Lev. 25:10

36:5 [a]Num. 27:7

36:6
[a]Num. 36:11, 12

36:7 [a]1 Kin. 21:3

36:8
[a]1 Chr. 23:22

35:27 [1]Murder   35:33 [1]Lit. *covering*   36:6 [1]Lit. *be wives to*

¹⁰Just as the LORD commanded Moses, so did the daughters of Zelophehad; ¹¹ᵃfor Mahlah, Tirzah, Hoglah, Milcah, and Noah, the daughters of Zelophehad, were married to the sons of their father's brothers. ¹²They were married into the families of the children of Manasseh the son of Joseph, and their inheritance remained in the tribe of their father's family.

¹³These *are* the commandments and the judgments which the LORD commanded the children of Israel by the hand of Moses ᵃin the plains of Moab by the Jordan, *across from* Jericho.

36:11
ᵃNum. 26:33;
27:1
36:13
ᵃNum. 26:3;
33:50

DEUTERONOMY

THE PREVIOUS COMMAND TO ENTER CANAAN

1 These *are* the words which Moses spoke to all Israel [a]on this side of the Jordan in the wilderness, in the [1]plain opposite [2]Suph, between Paran, Tophel, Laban, Hazeroth, and Dizahab. [2]*It is* eleven days' *journey* from Horeb by way of Mount Seir [a]to Kadesh Barnea. [3]Now it came to pass [a]in the fortieth year, in the eleventh month, on the first *day* of the month, *that* Moses spoke to the children of Israel according to all that the LORD had given him as commandments to them, [4a]after he had killed Sihon king of the Amorites, who dwelt in Heshbon, and Og king of Bashan, who dwelt at Ashtaroth [b]in[1] Edrei.

[5]On this side of the Jordan in the land of Moab, Moses began to explain this law, saying, [6]"The LORD our God spoke to us [a]in Horeb, saying: 'You have dwelt long [b]enough at this mountain. [7]Turn and take your journey, and go to the mountains of the Amorites, to all the neighboring *places* in the [1]plain, in the mountains and in the lowland, in the South and on the seacoast, to the land of the Canaanites and to Lebanon, as far as the great river, the River Euphrates. [8]See, I have set the land before you; go in and possess the land which the LORD [1]swore to your fathers—to [a]Abraham, Isaac, and Jacob—to give to them and their descendants after them.'

TRIBAL LEADERS APPOINTED

(Ex. 18:13–27)

[9]"And [a]I spoke to you at that time, saying: 'I [1]alone am not able to bear you. [10]The LORD your God has multiplied you, [a]and here you *are* today, as the stars of heaven in multitude. [11a]May the LORD God of your fathers make you a thousand times more numerous than you are, and bless you [b]as He has promised you! [12a]How can I alone bear your problems and your burdens and your complaints? [13]Choose wise, understanding, and knowledgeable men from among your tribes, and I will make them [1]heads over you.' [14]And you answered me and said, 'The thing which you have told *us* to do *is* good.' [15]So I took [a]the heads of your tribes, wise and knowledgeable men, and [1]made them heads over you, leaders of thousands, leaders of hundreds, leaders of fifties, leaders of tens, and officers for your tribes.

[16]"Then I commanded your judges at that time, saying, 'Hear *the cases* between your brethren, and [a]judge righteously between a man and his [b]brother or the stranger who is with him. [17a]You shall not show partiality in judgment; you shall hear the small as well as the great; you shall not be afraid in

1:1
[a]Deut. 4:44–46;
Josh. 9:1, 10

1:2 [a]Num. 13:26;
32:8; Deut. 9:23

1:3 [a]Num. 33:38

1:4 [a]Num. 21:23,
24, 33–35;
Deut. 2:26–35;
Josh. 13:10;
Neh. 9:22
[b]Josh. 13:12

1:6 [a]Ex. 3:1, 12
[b]Ex. 19:1, 2

1:8 [a]Gen. 12:7;
15:5; 22:17; 26:3;
28:13; Ex. 33:1;
Num. 14:23;
32:11

1:9
[a]Ex. 18:18, 24;
Num. 11:14, 24

1:10 [a]Gen. 15:5;
22:17; Ex. 32:13;
Deut. 7:7; 10:22;
26:5; 28:62

1:11 [a]2 Sam. 24:3
[b]Gen. 15:5

1:12 [a]1 Kin. 3:8, 9

1:15 [a]Ex. 18:25

1:16
[a]Deut. 16:18;
John 7:24
[b]Lev. 24:22

1:17 [a]Lev. 19:15;
Deut. 10:17;
16:19; 24:17;
1 Sam. 16:7;
Prov. 24:23–26;
Acts 10:34;
James 2:1, 9

any man's presence, for ^bthe judgment *is* God's. The case that is too hard for you, ^cbring to me, and I will hear it.' ¹⁸And I commanded you at that time all the things which you should do.

ISRAEL'S REFUSAL TO ENTER THE LAND
(Num. 13:1–33)

¹⁹"So we departed from Horeb, ^aand went through all that great and terrible wilderness which you saw on the way to the mountains of the Amorites, as the LORD our God had commanded us. Then ^bwe came to Kadesh Barnea. ²⁰And I said to you, 'You have come to the mountains of the Amorites, which the LORD our God is giving us. ²¹Look, the LORD your God has set the land before you; go up *and* possess *it,* as the LORD God of your fathers has spoken to you; ^ado not fear or be discouraged.'

²²"And every one of you came near to me and said, 'Let us send men before us, and let them search out the land for us, and bring back word to us of the way by which we should go up, and of the cities into which we shall come.'

²³"The plan pleased me well; so ^aI took twelve of your men, one man from *each* tribe. ^{24a}And they departed and went up into the mountains, and came to the Valley of Eshcol, and spied it out. ²⁵They also took *some* of the fruit of the land in their hands and brought *it* down to us; and they brought back word to us, saying, '*It is* a ^agood land which the LORD our God is giving us.'

^{26a}"Nevertheless you would not go up, but rebelled against the command of the LORD your God; ²⁷and you ^acomplained in your tents, and said, 'Because the LORD ^bhates us, He has brought us out of the land of Egypt to deliver us into the hand of the Amorites, to destroy us. ²⁸Where can we go up? Our brethren have ¹discouraged our hearts, saying, ^a"The people *are* greater and taller than we; the cities *are* great and fortified up to heaven; moreover we have seen the sons of the ^bAnakim there."'

²⁹"Then I said to you, 'Do not be terrified, ^aor afraid of them. ^{30a}The LORD your God, who goes before you, He will fight for you, according to all He did for you in Egypt before your eyes, ³¹and in the wilderness where you saw how the LORD your God carried you, as a ^aman carries his son, in all the way that you went until you came to this place.' ³²Yet, for all that, ^ayou did not believe the LORD your God, ^{33a}who went in the way before you ^bto search out a place for you to pitch your tents, to show you the way you should go, in the fire by night and in the cloud by day.

THE PENALTY FOR ISRAEL'S REBELLION
(Num. 14:20–45)

³⁴"And the LORD heard the sound of your words, and was angry, ^aand took an oath, saying, ^{35a}'Surely not one of these men of this evil generation shall see that good land of which I ¹swore to give to your fathers, ^{36a}except Caleb the son of Jephunneh; he shall see it, and to him and his children I am giving the land on which he walked, because ^bhe ¹wholly

---

1:17 ^b2 Chr. 19:6
^cEx. 18:22, 26
1:19
^aNum. 10:12;
Deut. 2:7; 8:15;
32:10; Jer. 2:6
^bNum. 13:26
1:21 ^aJosh. 1:6, 9
1:23
^aNum. 13:2, 3
1:24
^aNum. 13:21–25
1:25
^aNum. 13:27
1:26
^aNum. 14:1–4;
Ps. 106:24
1:27 ^aPs. 106:25
^bDeut. 9:28
1:28
^aNum. 13:28,
31–33;
Deut. 9:1, 2
^bNum. 13:28
1:29 ^aNum. 14:9;
Deut. 7:18
1:30 ^aEx. 14:14;
Deut. 3:22;
20:4; Neh. 4:20
1:31
^aDeut. 32:10–12;
Is. 46:3, 4; 63:9;
Hos. 11:3
1:32 ^aNum. 14:11;
20:12;
Ps. 106:24;
Heb. 3:9, 10,
16–19; 4:1, 2;
Jude 5
1:33 ^aEx. 13:21;
Num. 9:15–23;
Neh. 9:12;
Ps. 78:14
^bNum. 10:33;
Ezek. 20:6
1:34
^aDeut. 2:14, 15
1:35
^aNum. 14:22, 23;
Ps. 95:10, 11
1:36
^aNum. 14:24;
[Josh. 14:9]
^bNum. 32:11, 12

1:28 ¹Lit. *melted*   **1:35** ¹*promised*   **1:36** ¹*fully*

followed the LORD.' [37a]The LORD was also angry with me for your sakes, saying, 'Even you shall not go in there. [38a]Joshua the son of Nun, [b]who stands before you, he shall go in there. [c]Encourage him, for he shall cause Israel to inherit it.

[39a]'Moreover your little ones and your children, who [b]you say will be victims, who today [c]have no knowledge of good and evil, they shall go in there; to them I will give it, and they shall possess it. [40a]But *as for* you, turn and take your journey into the wilderness by the Way of the Red Sea.'

[41]"Then you answered and said to me, [a]'We have sinned against the LORD; we will go up and fight, just as the LORD our God commanded us.' And when everyone of you had girded on his weapons of war, you were ready to go up into the mountain.

[42]"And the LORD said to me, 'Tell them, [a]"Do not go up nor fight, for I *am* not among you; lest you be defeated before your enemies."' [43]So I spoke to you; yet you would not listen, but [a]rebelled against the command of the LORD, and [b]presumptuously[1] went up into the mountain. [44]And the Amorites who dwelt in that mountain came out against you and chased you [a]as bees do, and drove you back from Seir to Hormah. [45]Then you returned and wept before the LORD, but the LORD would not listen to your voice nor give ear to you.

[46a]"So you remained in Kadesh many days, according to the days that you spent *there.*

THE DESERT YEARS

2 "Then we turned and [a]journeyed into the wilderness of the Way of the Red Sea, [b]as the LORD spoke to me, and we [1]skirted Mount Seir for many days.

[2]"And the LORD spoke to me, saying: [3]'You have skirted this mountain [a]long enough; turn northward. [4]And command the people, saying, [a]"You *are about to* pass through the territory of [b]your brethren, the descendants of Esau, who live in Seir; and they will be afraid of you. Therefore watch yourselves carefully. [5]Do not meddle with them, for I will not give you *any* of their land, no, not so much as one footstep, [a]because I have given Mount Seir to Esau *as* a possession. [6]You shall buy food from them with money, that you may eat; and you shall also buy water from them with money, that you may drink.

[7]"For the LORD your God has blessed you in all the work of your hand. He knows your [1]trudging through this great wilderness. [a]These forty years the LORD your God *has been* with you; you have lacked nothing."'

[8]"And when we passed beyond our brethren, the descendants of Esau who dwell in Seir, away from the road of the plain, away from [a]Elath and Ezion Geber, we [b]turned and passed by way of the Wilderness of Moab. [9]Then the LORD said to me, 'Do not harass Moab, nor contend with them in battle, for I will not give you *any* of their land *as* a possession, because I have given [a]Ar to [b]the descendants of Lot *as* a possession.'"

[10a](The Emim had dwelt there in times past, a people as great and numerous and tall as [b]the Anakim. [11]They were also regarded as [1]giants, like the Anakim, but the Moabites

1:37
[a]Num. 20:12; 27:14; Deut. 3:26; 4:21; 34:4; Ps. 106:32

1:38
[a]Num. 14:30
[b]Ex. 24:13; 33:11; 1 Sam. 16:22
[c]Num. 27:18, 19; Deut. 31:7, 23; Josh. 11:23

1:39 [a]Num. 14:31
[b]Num. 14:3
[c]Is. 7:15, 16

1:40
[a]Num. 14:25

1:41 [a]Num. 14:40

1:42
[a]Num. 14:41–43

1:43
[a]Num. 14:44
[b]Deut. 17:12, 13

1:44
[a]Num. 14:45; Ps. 118:12

1:46
[a]Num. 13:25; 20:1, 22; Deut. 2:7, 14

2:1 [a]Deut. 1:40
[b]Num. 14:25

2:3
[a]Deut. 2:7, 14

2:4
[a]Num. 20:14–21
[b]Deut. 23:7

2:5 [a]Gen. 36:8; Josh. 24:4

2:7
[a]Deut. 8:2–4; [Matt. 6:8, 32]

2:8 [a]Judg. 11:18; 1 Kin. 9:26
[b]Num. 21:4

2:9
[a]Num. 21:15, 28; Deut. 2:18, 29
[b]Gen. 19:36–38

2:10 [a]Gen. 14:5
[b]Num. 13:22, 33; Deut. 9:2

call them Emim. ¹²ᵃThe Horites formerly dwelt in Seir, but the descendants of Esau dispossessed them and destroyed them from before them, and dwelt in their ¹place, just as Israel did to the land of their possession which the LORD gave them.)

¹³"'Now rise and cross over ᵃthe ¹Valley of the Zered.' So we crossed over the Valley of the Zered. ¹⁴And the time we took to come ᵃfrom Kadesh Barnea until we crossed over the Valley of the Zered *was* thirty-eight years, ᵇuntil all the generation of the men of war ¹was consumed from the midst of the camp, ᶜjust as the LORD had sworn to them. ¹⁵For indeed the hand of the LORD was against them, to destroy them from the midst of the camp until they ¹were consumed.

¹⁶"So it was, when all the men of war had finally perished from among the people, ¹⁷that the LORD spoke to me, saying: ¹⁸"This day you are to cross over at Ar, the boundary of Moab. ¹⁹And *when* you come near the people of Ammon, do not harass them or meddle with them, for I will not give you *any* of the land of the people of Ammon *as* a possession, because I have given it to ᵃthe descendants of Lot *as* a possession.'"

²⁰(That was also regarded as a land of ¹giants; giants formerly dwelt there. But the Ammonites call them ᵃZamzummim, ²¹ᵃa people as great and numerous and tall as the Anakim. But the LORD destroyed them before them, and they dispossessed them and dwelt in their place, ²²just as He had done for the descendants of Esau, ᵃwho dwelt in Seir, when He destroyed ᵇthe Horites from before them. They dispossessed them and dwelt in their place, even to this day. ²³And ᵃthe Avim, who dwelt in villages as far as Gaza—ᵇthe Caphtorim, who came from Caphtor, destroyed them and dwelt in their place.)

²⁴"'Rise, take your journey, and ᵃcross over the River Arnon. Look, I have given into your hand ᵇSihon the Amorite, king of Heshbon, and his land. Begin ¹to possess *it,* and engage him in battle. ²⁵ᵃThis day I will begin to put the dread and fear of you upon the nations ¹under the whole heaven, who shall hear the report of you, and shall ᵇtremble and be in anguish because of you.'

KING SIHON DEFEATED
(Num. 21:21–32)

²⁶"And I ᵃsent messengers from the Wilderness of Kedemoth to Sihon king of Heshbon, ᵇwith words of peace, saying, ²⁷ᵃ'Let me pass through your land; I will keep strictly to the road, and I will turn neither to the right nor to the left. ²⁸You shall sell me food for money, that I may eat, and give me water for money, that I may drink; ᵃonly let me pass through on foot, ²⁹ᵃjust as the descendants of Esau who dwell in Seir and the Moabites who dwell in Ar did for me, until I cross the Jordan to the land which the LORD our God is giving us.' ³⁰ᵃ"But Sihon king of Heshbon would not let us pass through, for ᵇthe LORD your God ᶜhardened his spirit and made his heart obstinate, that He might deliver him into your hand, as *it is* this day.

2:12 ᵃGen. 14:6; 36:20; Deut. 2:22
2:13 ᵃNum. 21:12
2:14 ᵃNum. 13:26 ᵇNum. 14:33; 26:64; Deut. 1:34, 35 ᶜNum. 14:35; Ezek. 20:15
2:19 ᵃGen. 19:38; Num. 21:24
2:20 ᵃGen. 14:5
2:21 ᵃDeut. 2:10
2:22 ᵃGen. 36:8; Deut. 2:5 ᵇGen. 14:6; 36:20–30
2:23 ᵃJosh. 13:3 ᵇGen. 10:14; 1 Chr. 1:12; Jer. 47:4; Amos 9:7
2:24 ᵃNum. 21:13, 14; Judg. 11:18 ᵇDeut. 1:4
2:25 ᵃEx. 23:27; Deut. 11:25; Josh. 2:9 ᵇEx. 15:14–16
2:26 ᵃNum. 21:21–32; Deut. 1:4; Judg. 11:19–21 ᵇDeut. 20:10
2:27 ᵃNum. 21:21, 22; Judg. 11:19
2:28 ᵃNum. 20:19
2:29 ᵃNum. 20:18; Deut. 23:3, 4; Judg. 11:17
2:30 ᵃNum. 21:23 ᵇJosh. 11:20 ᶜEx. 4:21

2:12 ¹stead   2:13 ¹Wadi or Brook   2:14 ¹perished   2:15 ¹perished
2:20 ¹Heb. *rephaim*   2:24 ¹to take possession   2:25 ¹everywhere under the heavens

31"And the LORD said to me, 'See, I have begun to ᵃgive Sihon and his land over to you. Begin to possess *it,* that you may inherit his land.' 32ᵃThen Sihon and all his people came out against us to fight at Jahaz. 33And ᵃthe LORD our God delivered him ¹over to us; so ᵇwe defeated him, his sons, and all his people. 34We took all his cities at that time, and we ᵃutterly destroyed the men, women, and little ones of every city; we left none remaining. 35We took only the livestock as plunder for ourselves, with the spoil of the cities which we took. 36ᵃFrom Aroer, which *is* on the bank of the River Arnon, and *from* ᵇthe city that *is* in the ravine, as far as Gilead, there was not one city too strong for us; ᶜthe LORD our God delivered all to us. 37Only you did not go near the land of the people of Ammon—anywhere along the River ᵃJabbok, or to the cities of the mountains, or ᵇwherever the LORD our God had forbidden us.

KING OG DEFEATED
(Num. 21:33–35)

3 "Then we turned and went up the road to Bashan; and ᵃOg king of Bashan came out against us, he and all his people, to battle ᵇat Edrei. 2And the LORD said to me, 'Do not fear him, for I have delivered him and all his people and his land into your hand; you shall do to him as you did to ᵃSihon king of the Amorites, who dwelt at Heshbon.'

3"So the LORD our God also delivered into our hands Og king of Bashan, with all his people, and we ¹attacked him until he had no survivors remaining. 4And we took all his cities at that time; there was not a city which we did not take from them: sixty cities, ᵃall the region of Argob, the kingdom of Og in Bashan. 5All these cities *were* fortified with high walls, gates, and bars, besides a great many rural towns. 6And we utterly destroyed them, as we did to Sihon king ᵃof Heshbon, utterly destroying the men, women, and children of every city. 7But all the livestock and the spoil of the cities we took as booty for ourselves.

8"And at that time we took the ᵃland from the hand of the two kings of the Amorites who *were* on this side of the Jordan, from the River Arnon to Mount ᵇHermon 9(the Sidonians call ᵃHermon Sirion, and the Amorites call it Senir), 10ᵃall the cities of the plain, all Gilead, and ᵇall Bashan, as far as Salcah and Edrei, cities of the kingdom of Og in Bashan.

11ᵃ"For only Og king of Bashan remained of the remnant of ᵇthe ¹giants. Indeed his bedstead *was* an iron bedstead. (*Is* it not in ᶜRabbah of the people of Ammon?) Nine cubits *is* its length and four cubits its width, according to the standard cubit.

THE LAND EAST OF THE JORDAN DIVIDED
(Num. 32:25–41)

12"And this ᵃland, *which* we possessed at that time, ᵇfrom Aroer, which *is* by the River Arnon, and half the mountains of Gilead and ᶜits cities, I gave to the Reubenites and the Gadites. 13ᵃThe rest of Gilead, and all Bashan, the kingdom of Og, I gave to half the tribe of Manasseh. (All the region of Argob, with all

2:31
ᵃDeut. 1:3, 8

2:32
ᵃNum. 21:23

2:33 ᵃEx. 23:31;
Deut. 7:2
ᵇNum. 21:24

2:34 ᵃLev. 27:28

2:36
ᵃDeut. 3:12;
4:48; Josh. 13:9
ᵇJosh. 13:9, 16
ᶜPs. 44:3

2:37
ᵃGen. 32:22;
Num. 21:24;
Deut. 3:16
ᵇDeut. 2:5, 9, 19

3:1
ᵃNum. 21:33–35;
Deut. 29:7
ᵇDeut. 1:4

3:2
ᵃNum. 21:34;
Josh. 13:21

3:4
ᵃDeut. 3:13, 14

3:6 ᵃDeut. 2:24,
34, 35

3:8
ᵃNum. 32:33;
Josh. 12:6;
13:8–12
ᵇDeut. 4:48;
1 Chr. 5:23

3:9 ᵃ1 Chr. 5:23

3:10 ᵃDeut. 4:49
ᵇJosh. 12:5; 13:11

3:11 ᵃAmos 2:9
ᵇGen. 14:5;
Deut. 2:11, 20
ᶜ2 Sam. 12:26;
Jer. 49:2;
Ezek. 21:20

3:12
ᵃNum. 32:33;
Josh. 12:6;
13:8–12
ᵇDeut. 2:36;
Josh. 12:2
ᶜNum. 34:14

3:13
ᵃJosh. 13:29–31;
17:1

2:33 ¹Lit. *before us*　　3:3 ¹*struck*　　3:11 ¹Heb. *rephaim*

3:14 [a]1 Chr. 2:22
[b]Josh. 13:13;
2 Sam. 3:3; 10:6
[c]Num. 32:41

3:15
[a]Num. 32:39, 40

3:16
[a]2 Sam. 24:5
[b]Num. 21:24;
Deut. 2:37;
Josh. 12:2

3:17
[a]Num. 34:11,
12; Deut. 4:49;
Josh. 12:3
[b]Gen. 14:3;
Josh. 3:16

3:18
[a]Num. 32:20;
Josh. 4:12, 13

3:20
[a]Deut. 12:9, 10
[b]Josh. 22:4

3:21
[a][Num. 27:22,
23]; Josh. 11:23

3:22 [a]Ex. 14:14;
Deut. 1:30; 20:4;
Neh. 4:20

3:23
[a][2 Cor. 12:8, 9]

3:24
[a]Deut. 5:24; 11:2
[b]Ex. 8:10; 15:11;
2 Sam. 7:22;
Ps. 71:19; 86:8

3:25 [a]Ex. 3:8;
Deut. 4:22

3:26
[a]Num. 20:12;
27:14; Deut. 1:37;
31:2; 32:51, 52;
34:4

3:27
[a]Num. 23:14;
27:12

3:28
[a]Num. 27:18,
23; Deut. 31:3,
7, 8, 23

3:29
[a]Deut. 4:46;
34:6

4:1 [a]Lev. 19:37;
20:8; 22:31;
Deut. 5:1; 8:1;
Ezek. 20:11;
[Rom. 10:5]

4:2 [a]Deut. 12:32;
[Josh. 1:7];
Prov. 30:6;
[Rev. 22:18, 19]

4:3 [a]Num. 25:1–
9; Josh. 22:17;
Ps. 106:28

Bashan, was called the land of the [1]giants. [14a]Jair the son of Manasseh took all the region of Argob, [b]as far as the border of the Geshurites and the Maachathites, and [c]called Bashan after his own name, [1]Havoth Jair, to this day.)

[15]"Also I gave [a]Gilead to Machir. [16]And to the Reubenites [a]and the Gadites I gave from Gilead as far as the River Arnon, the middle of the river as *the* border, as far as the River Jabbok, [b]the border of the people of Ammon; [17]the plain also, with the Jordan as *the* border, from Chinnereth [a]as far as the east side of the Sea of the Arabah [b](the Salt Sea), below the slopes of Pisgah.

[18]"Then I commanded you at that time, saying: 'The LORD your God has given you this land to possess. [a]All you men of valor shall cross over armed before your brethren, the children of Israel. [19]But your wives, your little ones, and your livestock (I know that you have much livestock) shall stay in your cities which I have given you, [20]until the LORD has given [a]rest to your brethren as to you, and they also possess the land which the LORD your God is giving them beyond the Jordan. Then each of you may [b]return to his possession which I have given you.'

[21]"And [a]I commanded Joshua at that time, saying, 'Your eyes have seen all that the LORD your God has done to these two kings; so will the LORD do to all the kingdoms through which you pass. [22]You must not fear them, for [a]the LORD your God Himself fights for you.'

MOSES FORBIDDEN TO ENTER THE LAND

[23]"Then [a]I pleaded with the LORD at that time, saying: [24]'O Lord GOD, You have begun to show Your servant [a]Your greatness and Your [1]mighty hand, for [b]what god *is there* in heaven or on earth who can do *anything* like Your works and Your mighty *deeds?* [25]I pray, let me cross over and see [a]the good land beyond the Jordan, those pleasant mountains, and Lebanon.'

[26]"But the LORD [a]was angry with me on your account, and would not listen to me. So the LORD said to me: 'Enough of that! Speak no more to Me of this matter. [27a]Go up to the top of Pisgah, and lift your eyes toward the west, the north, the south, and the east; behold *it* with your eyes, for you shall not cross over this Jordan. [28]But [a]command[1] Joshua, and encourage him and strengthen him; for he shall go over before this people, and he shall cause them to inherit the land which you will see.'

[29]"So we stayed in [a]the valley opposite Beth Peor.

MOSES COMMANDS OBEDIENCE

4 "Now, O Israel, listen to [a]the statutes and the judgments which I teach you to observe, that you may live, and go in and [1]possess the land which the LORD God of your fathers is giving you. [2a]You shall not add to the word which I command you, nor take from it, that you may keep the commandments of the LORD your God which I command you. [3]Your eyes have seen what the LORD did at [a]Baal Peor; for the LORD your God has destroyed from among you all the men who followed Baal

---

3:13 [1]Heb. *rephaim*   3:14 [1]Lit. *Towns of Jair*   3:24 [1]*strong*   3:28 [1]*charge*
4:1 [1]*take possession of*

of Peor. [4]But you who held fast to the LORD your God *are* alive today, every one of you.

[5]"Surely I have taught you statutes and judgments, just as the LORD my God commanded me, that you should act according *to them* in the land which you go to possess. [6]Therefore be careful to observe *them;* for this *is* [a]your wisdom and your understanding in the sight of the peoples who will hear all these statutes, and say, 'Surely this great nation *is* a wise and understanding people.'

[7]"For [a]what great nation *is there* that has [b]God[1] *so* near to it, as the LORD our God *is* to us, for whatever *reason* we may call upon Him? [8]And what great nation *is there* that has *such* statutes and righteous judgments as are in all this law which I set before you this day? [9]Only take heed to yourself, and diligently [a]keep yourself, lest you [b]forget the things your eyes have seen, and lest they depart from your heart all the days of your life. And [c]teach them to your children and your grandchildren, [10]*especially concerning* [a]the day you stood before the LORD your God in Horeb, when the LORD said to me, 'Gather the people to Me, and I will let them hear My words, that they may learn to fear Me all the days they live on the earth, and *that* they may teach their children.'

[11]"Then you came near and stood at the foot of the mountain, and the mountain burned with fire to the midst of heaven, with darkness, cloud, and thick darkness. [12a]And the LORD spoke to you out of the midst of the fire. You heard the sound of the words, but saw no [1]form; [b]*you* only *heard* a voice. [13a]So He declared to you His covenant which He commanded you to perform, [b]the Ten Commandments; and [c]He wrote them on two tablets of stone. [14]And [a]the LORD commanded me at that time to teach you statutes and judgments, that you might [1]observe them in the land which you cross over to possess.

BEWARE OF IDOLATRY

[15a]"Take careful heed to yourselves, for you saw no [b]form when the LORD spoke to you at Horeb out of the midst of the fire, [16]lest you [a]act corruptly and [b]make for yourselves a carved image in the [1]form of any figure: [c]the likeness of male or female, [17]the likeness of any animal that *is* on the earth or the likeness of any winged bird that flies in the air, [18]the likeness of anything that creeps on the ground or the likeness of any fish that *is* in the water beneath the earth. [19]And *take heed,* lest you [a]lift your eyes to heaven, and *when* you see the sun, the moon, and the stars, [b]all the host of heaven, you feel driven to [c]worship them and serve them, which the LORD your God has [1]given to all the peoples under the whole heaven as a heritage. [20]But the LORD has taken you and [a]brought you out of Egypt, out of the iron furnace, to be [b]His people, an inheritance, as you are this day. [21]Furthermore [a]the LORD was angry with me for your sakes, and swore that [b]I would not cross over the Jordan, and that I would not enter the good land which the LORD your God is giving you as an inheritance. [22]But [a]I must die in this land, [b]I must not cross over the Jordan; but you shall cross over and [1]possess [c]that good land. [23]Take heed to yourselves, lest you forget the covenant of the

4:6 [a]Deut. 30:19, 20; 32:46, 47; Job 28:28; Ps. 19:7; 111:10; Prov. 1:7; [2 Tim. 3:15]

4:7 [a][Deut. 4:32–34; 2 Sam. 7:23] [b][Ps. 46:1; Is. 55:6]

4:9 [a]Prov. 4:23 [b]Deut. 29:2–8 [c]Gen. 18:19; Deut. 4:10; 6:7, 20–25; Ps. 78:5, 6; Prov. 22:6; Eph. 6:4

4:10 [a]Ex. 19:9, 16, 17

4:12 [a]Deut. 5:4, 22 [b]Ex. 19:17–19; 20:22; 1 Kin. 19:11–18

4:13 [a]Deut. 9:9, 11 [b]Ex. 34:28; Deut. 10:4 [c]Ex. 24:12

4:14 [a]Ex. 21:1

4:15 [a]Josh. 23:11 [b]Is. 40:18

4:16 [a]Ex. 32:7; Deut. 9:12; 31:29 [b]Ex. 20:4, 5 [c]Rom. 1:23

4:19 [a]Deut. 17:3; Job 31:26–28 [b]2 Kin. 21:3 [c][Rom. 1:25]

4:20 [a]1 Kin. 8:51; Jer. 11:4 [b]Deut. 7:6; 27:9; [Titus 2:14]

4:21 [a]Num. 20:12; Deut. 1:37; 3:26 [b]Num. 27:13, 14

4:22 [a]2 Pet. 1:13–15 [b]Deut. 3:27 [c]Deut. 3:25

4:7 [1]Or *a god* 4:12 [1]*similitude* 4:14 [1]*do* or *perform* 4:16 [1]*similitude*
4:19 [1]*divided* 4:22 [1]*take possession of*

4:23
a Ex. 20:4, 5;
Deut. 4:16

4:24 a Ex. 24:17;
Deut. 9:3;
Is. 33:14;
Heb. 12:29
b Ex. 20:5; 34:14

4:25 a 2 Kin. 17:17

4:26
a Deut. 30:18, 19;
2 Chr. 36:14–20;
Is. 1:2; Mic. 6:2

4:27 a Lev. 26:33;
Deut. 28:62;
Neh. 1:8

4:28
a Deut. 28:64;
1 Sam. 26:19;
Jer. 16:13
b Ps. 115:4–7;
135:15–17;
Is. 44:9; 46:7

4:29
a [Lev. 26:39–45;
Deut. 30:1–3;
2 Chr. 15:4;
Neh. 1:9]

4:30 a Gen. 49:1;
Deut. 31:29;
Jer. 23:20;
Hos. 3:5
b Joel 2:12;
Heb. 1:2

4:31 a Lev. 26:44;
Jer. 30:11

4:32 a Deut. 32:7;
Job 8:8
b Deut. 28:64;
Matt. 24:31

4:33
a Ex. 20:22; 24:11;
Deut. 5:24–26

4:34 a Deut. 7:19
b Ex. 7:3 c Ex. 13:3
d Ex. 6:6
e Deut. 26:8

4:35
a Ex. 8:10; 9:14;
[Deut. 4:39;
32:12, 39;
1 Sam. 2:2;
Is. 43:10–12;
44:6–8; 45:5–7];
Mark 12:32

4:36
a Ex. 19:9, 19;
20:18, 22;
Deut. 4:33;
Neh. 9:13;
Heb. 12:19, 25

4:37 a Deut. 7:7,
8; 10:15; 33:3
b Ex. 13:3, 9, 14

4:38 a Deut. 7:1

4:39
a Deut. 4:35;
Josh. 2:11

Lord your God which He made with you, [a]and make for yourselves a carved image in the form of anything which the Lord your God has forbidden you. [24]For [a]the Lord your God *is* a consuming fire, [b]a jealous God.

[25]"When you beget children and grandchildren and have grown old in the land, and act corruptly and make a carved image in the form of anything, and [a]do evil in the sight of the Lord your God to provoke Him to anger, [26a]I call heaven and earth to witness against you this day, that you will soon utterly perish from the land which you cross over the Jordan to possess; you will not [1]prolong *your* days in it, but will be utterly destroyed. [27]And the Lord [a]will scatter you among the peoples, and you will be left few in number among the nations where the Lord will drive you. [28]And [a]there you will serve gods, the work of men's hands, wood and stone, [b]which neither see nor hear nor eat nor smell. [29a]But from there you will seek the Lord your God, and you will find *Him* if you seek Him with all your heart and with all your soul. [30]When you are in [1]distress, and all these things come upon you in the [a]latter days, when you [b]turn to the Lord your God and obey His voice [31](for the Lord your God *is* a merciful God), He will not forsake you nor [a]destroy you, nor forget the covenant of your fathers which He swore to them.

[32]"For [a]ask now concerning the days that are past, which were before you, since the day that God created man on the earth, and *ask* [b]from one end of heaven to the other, whether *any* great *thing* like this has happened, or *anything* like it has been heard. [33a]Did *any* people *ever* hear the voice of God speaking out of the midst of the fire, as you have heard, and live? [34]Or did God *ever* try to go *and* take for Himself a nation from the midst of *another* nation, [a]by trials, [b]by signs, by wonders, by war, [c]by a mighty hand and [d]an outstretched arm, [e]and by great [1]terrors, according to all that the Lord your God did for you in Egypt before your eyes? [35]To you it was shown, that you might know that the Lord Himself *is* God; [a]there is none other besides Him. [36a]Out of heaven He let you hear His voice, that He might instruct you; on earth He showed you His great fire, and you heard His words out of the midst of the fire. [37]And because [a]He loved your fathers, therefore He chose their [1]descendants after them; and [b]He brought you out of Egypt with His Presence, with His mighty power, [38a]driving out from before you nations greater and mightier than you, to bring you in, to give you their land *as* an inheritance, as *it is* this day. [39]Therefore know this day, and consider *it* in your heart, that [a]the Lord Himself *is* God in heaven above and on the earth beneath; *there is* no other. [40a]You shall therefore keep His statutes and His commandments which I command you today, that [1]it may go well with you and with your children after you, and that you may [2]prolong *your* days in the land which the Lord your God is giving you for all time."

CITIES OF REFUGE EAST OF THE JORDAN

[41]Then Moses [a]set apart three cities on this side of the Jordan, toward the rising of the sun, [42a]that the manslayer might

4:40 a Lev. 22:31; Deut. 5:16; 32:46, 47   4:41 a Num. 35:6; Deut. 19:2–13; Josh. 20:7–9
4:42 a Deut. 19:4

4:26 [1]*live long on it*   4:30 [1]*tribulation*   4:34 [1]*calamities*   4:37 [1]Lit. *seed*
4:40 [1]*you may prosper*   [2]*live long*

flee there, who kills his neighbor unintentionally, without having hated him in time past, and that by fleeing to one of these cities he might live: ⁴³ᵃBezer in the wilderness on the plateau for the Reubenites, Ramoth in Gilead for the Gadites, and Golan in Bashan for the Manassites.

INTRODUCTION TO GOD'S LAW

⁴⁴Now this *is* the law which Moses set before the children of Israel. ⁴⁵These *are* the testimonies, the statutes, and the judgments which Moses spoke to the children of Israel after they came out of Egypt, ⁴⁶on this side of the Jordan, ᵃin the valley opposite Beth Peor, in the land of Sihon king of the Amorites, who dwelt at Heshbon, whom Moses and the children of Israel ᵇdefeated¹ after they came out of Egypt. ⁴⁷And they took possession of his land and the land ᵃof Og king of Bashan, two kings of the Amorites, who *were* on this side of the Jordan, toward the ¹rising of the sun, ⁴⁸ᵃfrom Aroer, which *is* on the bank of the River Arnon, even to Mount ¹Sion (that is, ᵇHermon), ⁴⁹and all the plain on the east side of the Jordan as far as the Sea of the Arabah, below the ᵃslopes of Pisgah.

THE TEN COMMANDMENTS REVIEWED
(Ex. 20:1–17)

5 And Moses called all Israel, and said to them: "Hear, O Israel, the statutes and judgments which I speak in your hearing today, that you may learn them and be careful to observe them. ²ᵃThe LORD our God made a covenant with us in Horeb. ³The LORD ᵃdid not make this covenant with our fathers, but with us, those who *are* here today, all of us who *are* alive. ⁴ᵃThe LORD talked with you face to face on the mountain from the midst of the fire. ⁵ᵃI stood between the LORD and you at that time, to declare to you the word of the LORD; for ᵇyou were afraid because of the fire, and you did not go up the mountain. *He* said:

6 ᵃ'I *am* the LORD your God who brought you out of the land of Egypt, out of the house of ¹bondage.

7 ᵃ'You shall have no other gods ¹before Me.

8 ᵃ'You shall not make for yourself a carved image—any likeness *of anything* that *is* in heaven above, or that *is* in the earth beneath, or that *is* in the water under the earth; ⁹you shall not ᵃbow¹ down to them nor serve them. For I, the LORD your God, *am* a jealous God, ²visiting the iniquity of the fathers upon the children to the third and fourth *generations* of those who hate Me, ¹⁰ᵃbut showing mercy to thousands, to those who love Me and ¹keep My commandments.

11 ᵃ'You shall not take the name of the LORD your God in vain, for the LORD will not hold *him* ¹guiltless who takes His name in vain.

12 ᵃ'Observe the Sabbath day, to ¹keep it holy, as the LORD your God commanded you. ¹³ᵃSix days you shall labor and do all your work, ¹⁴but the seventh day *is* the ᵃSabbath of the LORD your God. *In it* you shall do no work: you, nor your son, nor your daughter, nor your male servant,

---

4:43 ᵃJosh. 20:8

4:46
ᵃDeut. 3:29
ᵇNum. 21:24;
Deut. 1:4

4:47
ᵃNum. 21:33–35

4:48
ᵃDeut. 2:36;
3:12 ᵇDeut. 3:9;
Ps. 133:3

4:49 ᵃDeut. 3:17

5:2 ᵃEx. 19:5;
Deut. 4:23;
Mal. 4:4

5:3 ᵃJer. 31:32;
Matt. 13:17;
Heb. 8:9

5:4 ᵃEx. 19:9

5:5 ᵃEx. 20:21;
Gal. 3:19
ᵇEx. 19:16

5:6
ᵃEx. 20:2–17;
Lev. 26:1;
Deut. 6:4;
Ps. 81:10

5:7 ᵃEx. 20:2, 3;
23:13; Hos. 13:4

5:8 ᵃEx. 20:4

5:9 ᵃEx. 34:7,
14–16;
Num. 14:18;
Deut. 7:10

5:10
ᵃNum. 14:18;
Deut. 7:9;
Jer. 32:18;
Dan. 9:4

5:11 ᵃEx. 20:7;
Lev. 19:12;
Deut. 6:13;
10:20;
Matt. 5:33

5:12 ᵃEx. 20:8;
Ezek. 20:12;
Mark 2:27

5:13 ᵃEx. 23:12;
35:2

5:14 ᵃ[Gen. 2:2];
Ex. 16:29;
[Heb. 4:4]

4:46 ¹*struck* 4:47 ¹*east* 4:48 ¹Syr. *Sirion* 5:6 ¹*slavery* 5:7 ¹*besides*
5:9 ¹*worship them* ²*punishing* 5:10 ¹*observe* 5:11 ¹*innocent*
5:12 ¹*sanctify it*

5:15 ªDeut. 15:15
ᵇDeut. 4:34, 37

5:16 ªEx. 20:12;
Lev. 19:3;
Matt. 15:4;
Eph. 6:2, 3;
Col. 3:20
ᵇDeut. 6:2
ᶜDeut. 4:40

5:17 ªEx. 20:13;
Matt. 5:21

5:18 ªEx. 20:14;
Mark 10:19;
Luke 18:20;
[Rom. 13:9];
James 2:11

5:19 ªEx. 20:15;
Lev. 19:11;
[Rom. 13:9]

5:20 ªEx. 20:16;
23:1; Matt. 19:18

5:21 ªEx. 20:17;
[Rom. 7:7; 13:9]

5:22 ªEx. 24:12;
31:18; Deut. 4:13

5:23
ªEx. 20:18, 19

5:24 ªEx. 19:19
ᵇDeut. 4:33;
Judg. 13:22

5:25
ªEx. 20:18, 19;
Deut. 18:16

5:26 ªDeut. 4:33

5:27 ªEx. 20:19;
Heb. 12:19

5:28
ªDeut. 18:17

5:29
ªDeut. 32:29;
Ps. 81:13;
Is. 48:18
ᵇDeut. 11:1
ᶜDeut. 4:40

5:31 ª[Gal. 3:19]

5:32
ªDeut. 17:20;
28:14; Josh. 1:7;
23:6; Prov. 4:27

nor your female servant, nor your ox, nor your donkey, nor any of your cattle, nor your stranger who *is* within your gates, that your male servant and your female servant may rest as well as you. 15ªAnd remember that you were a slave in the land of Egypt, and the Lᴏʀᴅ your God brought you out from there ᵇby a mighty hand and by an outstretched arm; therefore the Lᴏʀᴅ your God commanded you to keep the Sabbath day.

16 ª'Honor your father and your mother, as the Lᴏʀᴅ your God has commanded you, ᵇthat your days may be long, and that it may be well with ᶜyou in the land which the Lᴏʀᴅ your God is giving you.

17 ª'You shall not murder.

18 ª'You shall not commit adultery.

19 ª'You shall not steal.

20 ª'You shall not bear false witness against your neighbor.

21 ª'You shall not covet your neighbor's wife; and you shall not desire your neighbor's house, his field, his male servant, his female servant, his ox, his donkey, or anything that *is* your neighbor's.'

22"These words the Lᴏʀᴅ spoke to all your assembly, in the mountain from the midst of the fire, the cloud, and the thick darkness, with a loud voice; and He added no more. And ªHe wrote them on two tablets of stone and gave them to me.

THE PEOPLE AFRAID OF GOD'S PRESENCE
(Ex. 20:18–21)

23ª"So it was, when you heard the voice from the midst of the darkness, while the mountain was burning with fire, that you came near to me, all the heads of your tribes and your elders. 24And you said: 'Surely the Lᴏʀᴅ our God has shown us His glory and His greatness, and ªwe have heard His voice from the midst of the fire. We have seen this day that God speaks with man; yet he ᵇ*still* lives. 25Now therefore, why should we die? For this great fire will consume us; ªif we hear the voice of the Lᴏʀᴅ our God anymore, then we shall die. 26ªFor who *is there* of all flesh who has heard the voice of the living God speaking from the midst of the fire, as we *have,* and lived? 27You go near and hear all that the Lᴏʀᴅ our God may say, and ªtell us all that the Lᴏʀᴅ our God says to you, and we will hear and do *it.*'

28"Then the Lᴏʀᴅ heard the voice of your words when you spoke to me, and the Lᴏʀᴅ said to me: 'I have heard the voice of the words of this people which they have spoken to you. ªThey are right *in* all that they have spoken. 29ªOh, that they had such a heart in them that they would fear Me and ᵇalways keep all My commandments, ᶜthat it might be well with them and with their children forever! 30Go and say to them, "Return to your tents." 31But as for you, stand here by Me, ªand I will speak to you all the commandments, the statutes, and the judgments which you shall teach them, that they may observe *them* in the land which I am giving them to possess.'

32"Therefore you shall ¹be careful to do as the Lᴏʀᴅ your God has commanded you; ªyou shall not turn aside to the

---

5:32 ¹*observe*

right hand or to the left. [33]You shall walk in [a]all the ways which the LORD your God has commanded you, that you may live [b]and *that it may be* well with you, and *that* you may prolong *your* days in the land which you shall possess.

THE GREATEST COMMANDMENT

6 "Now this *is* [a]the commandment, *and these are* the statutes and judgments which the LORD your God has commanded to teach you, that you may observe *them* in the land which you are crossing over to possess, [2a]that you may fear the LORD your God, to keep all His statutes and His commandments which I command you, you and your son and your grandson, all the days of your life, [b]and that your days may be prolonged. [3]Therefore hear, O Israel, and [1]be careful to observe *it,* that it may be well with you, and that you may [a]multiply greatly [b]as the LORD God of your fathers has promised you—[c]'a land flowing with milk and honey.'

[4a]"Hear, O Israel: [1]The LORD our God, the LORD *is* one! [5a]You shall love the LORD your God with all your heart, [b]with all your soul, and with all your strength.

[6]"And [a]these words which I command you today shall be in your heart. [7a]You shall teach them diligently to your children, and shall talk of them when you sit in your house, when you walk by the way, when you lie down, and when you rise up. [8a]You shall bind them as a sign on your hand, and they shall be as frontlets between your eyes. [9a]You shall write them on the doorposts of your house and on your gates.

CAUTION AGAINST DISOBEDIENCE

[10]"So it shall be, when the LORD your God brings you into the land of which He [1]swore to your fathers, to Abraham, Isaac, and Jacob, to give you large and beautiful cities [a]which you did not build, [11]houses full of all good things, which you did not fill, hewn-out wells which you did not dig, vineyards and olive trees which you did not plant—[a]when you have eaten and are full— [12]then beware, lest you forget the [a]LORD who brought you out of the land of Egypt, from the house of bondage. [13]You shall [a]fear the LORD your God and serve Him, and [b]shall take oaths in His name. [14]You shall not go after other gods, [a]the gods of the peoples who *are* all around you [15](for [a]the LORD your God *is* a jealous God [b]among you), lest the anger of the LORD your God be aroused against you and destroy you from the face of the earth.

[16a]"You shall not [1]tempt the LORD your God [b]as you [2]tempted *Him* in Massah. [17]You shall [a]diligently keep the commandments of the LORD your God, His testimonies, and His statutes which He has commanded you. [18]And you [a]shall do *what is* right and good in the sight of the LORD, that it may be well with you, and that you may go in and possess the good land of which the LORD swore to your fathers, [19a]to cast out all your enemies from before you, as the LORD has spoken.

[20a]"When your son asks you in time to come, saying, 'What *is the meaning of* the testimonies, the statutes, and the judgments which the LORD our God has commanded you?' [21]then you shall say to your son: 'We were slaves of Pharaoh in Egypt,

---

6:3 [1]Lit. *observe to do*   6:4 [1]Or *The LORD is our God, the LORD alone,* i.e., the only one   6:10 [1]*promised*   6:16 [1]*test*   [2]*tested*

5:33
[a]Deut. 10:12;
Ps. 119:3;
Jer. 7:23;
Luke 1:6
[b]Deut. 4:40;
Eph. 6:3

6:1 [a]Deut. 12:1

6:2 [a]Ex. 20:20;
Deut. 10:12, 13;
[Ps. 111:10; 128:1;
Eccl. 12:13]
[b]Deut. 4:40

6:3 [a]Deut. 7:13
[b]Gen. 22:17
[c]Ex. 3:8, 17

6:4 [a]Deut. 4:35;
Mark 12:29;
John 17:3;
[1 Cor. 8:4, 6]

6:5
[a]Matt. 22:37;
Mark 12:30;
Luke 10:27
[b]2 Kin. 23:25

6:6
[a]Deut. 11:18–20;
Ps. 119:11, 98

6:7 [a]Deut. 4:9;
11:19; [Eph. 6:4]

6:8 [a]Ex. 12:14;
13:9, 16;
Deut. 11:18;
Prov. 3:3; 6:21;
7:3

6:9 [a]Deut. 11:20;
Is. 57:8

6:10 [a]Deut. 9:1;
19:1; Josh. 24:13;
Ps. 105:44

6:11 [a]Deut. 8:10;
11:15; 14:29

6:12
[a]Deut. 8:11–18

6:13 [a]Deut. 13:4;
Matt. 4:10;
Luke 4:8
[b]Deut. 5:11;
[Is. 45:23;
Jer. 4:2]

6:14 [a]Deut. 13:7

6:15 [a]Ex. 20:5;
Deut. 4:24
[b]Ex. 33:3

6:16 [a]Matt. 4:7;
Luke 4:12
[b][1 Cor. 10:9]

6:17
[a]Deut. 11:22;
Ps. 119:4

6:18 [a]Ex. 15:26;
Deut. 8:7–10

6:19
[a]Num. 33:52, 53

6:20 [a]Ex. 13:8, 14

and the LORD brought us out of Egypt ^awith a mighty hand; ²²and the LORD showed signs and wonders before our eyes, great and severe, against Egypt, Pharaoh, and all his household. ²³Then He brought us out from there, that He might bring us in, to give us the land of which He ¹swore to our fathers. ²⁴And the LORD commanded us to ¹observe all these ²statutes, ^ato fear the LORD our God, ^bfor our good always, that ^cHe might preserve us alive, as *it is* ³this day. ²⁵Then ^ait will be righteousness for us, if we are careful to observe all these commandments before the LORD our God, as He has commanded us.'

A CHOSEN PEOPLE
(Ex. 34:10–16)

7 "When the LORD your God brings you into the land which you go to ^apossess, and has cast out many ^bnations before you, ^cthe Hittites and the Girgashites and the Amorites and the Canaanites and the Perizzites and the Hivites and the Jebusites, seven nations greater and mightier than you, ²and when the LORD your God delivers ^athem over to you, you shall conquer them *and* utterly destroy them. ^bYou shall make no covenant with them nor show mercy to them. ^{3a}Nor shall you make marriages with them. You shall not give your daughter to their son, nor take their daughter for your son. ⁴For they will turn your sons away from following Me, to serve other gods; ^aso the anger of the LORD will be aroused against you and destroy you suddenly. ⁵But thus you shall deal with them: you shall ^adestroy their altars, and break down their *sacred* pillars, and cut down their ¹wooden images, and burn their carved images with fire.

⁶"For you *are* a ¹holy people to the LORD your God; ^athe LORD your God has chosen you to be a people for Himself, a special treasure above all the peoples on the face of the earth. ⁷The LORD did not set His ^alove on you nor choose you because you were more in number than any other people, for you were ^bthe least of all peoples; ⁸but ^abecause the LORD loves you, and because He would keep ^bthe oath which He swore to your fathers, ^cthe LORD has brought you out with a mighty hand, and redeemed you from the house of ¹bondage, from the hand of Pharaoh king of Egypt.

⁹"Therefore know that the LORD your God, He *is* God, ^athe faithful God ^bwho keeps covenant and mercy for a thousand generations with those who love Him and keep His commandments; ¹⁰and He repays those who hate Him to their face, to destroy them. He will not ¹be ^aslack with him who hates Him; He will repay him to his face. ¹¹Therefore you shall keep the commandment, the statutes, and the judgments which I command you today, to observe them.

BLESSINGS OF OBEDIENCE
(Lev. 26:1–13; Deut. 28:1–14)

¹²"Then it shall come to pass, because you listen to these judgments, and keep and do them, that the LORD your God will keep with you the covenant and the mercy which He

---

6:21 ^aEx. 13:3
6:24 ^aDeut. 6:2
^bDeut. 10:12, 13; Job 35:7, 8; Jer. 32:39
^cDeut. 4:1
6:25 ^aDeut. 24:13; [Rom. 10:3, 5]
7:1 ^aDeut. 6:10 ^bGen. 15:19–21 ^cEx. 33:2
7:2 ^aNum. 31:17; Deut. 20:16–18 ^bEx. 23:32, 33; Josh. 2:14
7:3 ^aEx. 34:15, 16; Josh. 23:12; 1 Kin. 11:2; Ezra 9:2
7:4 ^aDeut. 6:15
7:5 ^aEx. 23:24; 34:13; Deut. 12:3
7:6 ^aEx. 19:5, 6; Amos 3:2; 1 Pet. 2:9
7:7 ^aDeut. 4:37 ^bDeut. 10:22
7:8 ^aDeut. 10:15 ^bLuke 1:55, 72, 73 ^cEx. 13:3, 14
7:9 ^a1 Cor. 1:9; 2 Thess. 3:3; 2 Tim. 2:13 ^bEx. 20:6; Deut. 5:10; Neh. 1:5; Dan. 9:4
7:10 ^a[2 Pet. 3:9, 10]

6:23 ¹*promised*   6:24 ¹*do*   ²*ordinances*   ³*today*   7:5 ¹Heb. *Asherim,* Canaanite deities   7:6 ¹*set-apart*   7:8 ¹*slavery*   7:10 ¹*delay*

swore to your fathers. [13]And He will [a]love you and bless you and [1]multiply you; [b]He will also bless the fruit of your womb and the fruit of your land, your grain and your new wine and your oil, the increase of your cattle and the offspring of your flock, in the land of which He [2]swore to your fathers to give you. [14]You shall be blessed above all peoples; there shall not be a male or female [a]barren among you or among your livestock. [15]And the LORD will take away from you all sickness, and will afflict you with none of the [a]terrible diseases of Egypt which you have known, but will lay *them* on all those who hate you. [16]Also you shall [1]destroy all the peoples whom the LORD your God delivers over to you; your eye shall have no pity on them; nor shall you serve their gods, for that *will* [a]*be* a snare to you.

[17]"If you should say in your heart, 'These nations are greater than I; how can I dispossess them?'— [18]you shall not be afraid of them, *but* you shall [a]remember well what the LORD your God did to Pharaoh and to all Egypt: [19][a]the great trials which your eyes saw, the signs and the wonders, the mighty hand and the outstretched arm, by which the LORD your God brought you out. So shall the LORD your God do to all the peoples of whom you are afraid. [20][a]Moreover the LORD your God will send the hornet among them until those who are left, who hide themselves from you, are destroyed. [21]You shall not be terrified of them; for the LORD your God, the great and awesome God, *is* among you. [22]And the LORD your God will drive out those nations before you [a]little by little; you will be unable to [1]destroy them at once, lest the beasts of the field become *too* numerous for you. [23]But the LORD your God will deliver them over to you, and will inflict defeat upon them until they are destroyed. [24]And [a]He will deliver their kings into your hand, and you will destroy their name from under heaven; [b]no one shall be able to stand [1]against you until you have destroyed them. [25]You shall burn the carved images of their gods with fire; you shall not [a]covet[1] the silver or gold *that is* on them, nor take *it* for yourselves, lest you be snared by it; for it *is* an abomination to the LORD your God. [26]Nor shall you bring an abomination into your house, lest you be doomed to destruction like it. You shall utterly detest it and utterly abhor it, [a]for it *is* an [1]accursed thing.

REMEMBER THE LORD YOUR GOD

8 "Every commandment which I command you today [a]you must [1]be careful to observe, that you may live and [b]multiply,[2] and go in and possess the land of which the LORD [3]swore to your fathers. [2]And you shall remember that the LORD your God [a]led you all the way these forty years in the wilderness, to humble you *and* [b]test you, [c]to know what *was* in your heart, whether you would keep His commandments or not. [3]So He humbled you, [a]allowed you to hunger, and [b]fed you with manna which you did not know nor did your fathers know, that He might make you know that man shall [c]not live by bread alone; but man lives by every *word* that proceeds from the mouth of the LORD. [4][a]Your garments did not wear out on you, nor did

Cross references

7:13 [a]Ps. 146:8; Prov. 15:9; John 14:21 [b]Deut. 28:4

7:14 [a]Ex. 23:26

7:15 [a]Ex. 9:14; 15:26; Deut. 28:27, 60

7:16 [a]Ex. 23:33; Judg. 8:27; Ps. 106:36

7:18 [a]Ps. 105:5

7:19 [a]Deut. 4:34; 29:3

7:20 [a]Ex. 23:28; Josh. 24:12

7:22 [a]Ex. 23:29, 30

7:24 [a]Josh. 10:24, 42; 12:1–24 [b]Josh. 23:9

7:25 [a]Prov. 23:6

7:26 [a]Deut. 13:17

8:1 [a]Deut. 4:1; 6:24 [b]Deut. 30:16

8:2 [a]Deut. 1:3; 2:7; 29:5; Ps. 136:16; Amos 2:10 [b]Ex. 16:4 [c][John 2:25]

8:3 [a]Ex. 16:2, 3 [b]Ex. 16:12, 14, 35 [c]Matt. 4:4; Luke 4:4

8:4 [a]Deut. 29:5; Neh. 9:21

7:13 [1]*cause you to increase*   [2]*promised*   7:16 [1]*consume*   7:22 [1]*consume*
7:24 [1]*before*   7:25 [1]*desire*   7:26 [1]*devoted* or *banned*   8:1 [1]*observe to do*
[2]*increase in number*   [3]*promised*

your foot swell these forty years. ⁵ᵃYou should ¹know in your heart that as a man chastens his son, *so* the LORD your God chastens you.

⁶"Therefore you shall keep the commandments of the LORD your God, ᵃto walk in His ways and to fear Him. ⁷For the LORD your God is bringing you into a good land, ᵃa land of brooks of water, of fountains and springs, that flow out of valleys and hills; ⁸a land of wheat and barley, of vines and fig trees and pomegranates, a land of olive oil and honey; ⁹a land in which you will eat bread without scarcity, in which you will lack nothing; a land whose stones *are* iron and out of whose hills you can dig copper. ¹⁰ᵃWhen you have eaten and are full, then you shall bless the LORD your God for the good land which He has given you.

¹¹"Beware that you do not forget the LORD your God by not keeping His commandments, His judgments, and His statutes which I command you today, ¹²ᵃlest—*when* you have eaten and are ¹full, and have built beautiful houses and dwell *in them;* ¹³and *when* your herds and your flocks multiply, and your silver and your gold are ¹multiplied, and all that you have is multiplied; ¹⁴ᵃwhen your heart ¹is lifted up, and you ᵇforget the LORD your God who brought you out of the land of Egypt, from the house of bondage; ¹⁵who ᵃled you through that great and terrible wilderness, ᵇ*in which were* fiery serpents and scorpions and thirsty land where there was no water; ᶜwho brought water for you out of the flinty rock; ¹⁶who fed you in the wilderness with ᵃmanna, which your fathers did not know, that He might humble you and that He might test you, ᵇto do you good in the end— ¹⁷then you say in your heart, 'My power and the might of my hand have gained me this wealth.'

¹⁸"And you shall remember the LORD your God, ᵃfor *it is* He who gives you power to get wealth, ᵇthat He may ¹establish His covenant which He swore to your fathers, as *it is* this day. ¹⁹Then it shall be, if you by any means forget the LORD your God, and follow other gods, and serve them and worship them, ᵃI testify against you this day that you shall surely perish. ²⁰As the nations which the LORD destroys before you, ᵃso you shall perish, because you would not be obedient to the voice of the LORD your God.

ISRAEL'S REBELLIONS REVIEWED
(Ex. 32:1–35)

9 "Hear, O Israel: You *are* to cross over the Jordan today, and go in to dispossess nations greater and mightier than yourself, cities great and fortified up to heaven, ²a people great and tall, the ᵃdescendants of the Anakim, whom you know, and *of whom* you heard *it said,* 'Who can stand before the descendants of Anak?' ³Therefore understand today that the LORD your God *is* He who ᵃgoes over before you *as a* ᵇconsuming fire. ᶜHe will destroy them and bring them down before you; ᵈso you shall drive them out and destroy them quickly, as the LORD has said to you.

⁴ᵃ"Do not think in your heart, after the LORD your God has cast them out before you, saying, 'Because of my righteousness the LORD has brought me in to possess this land'; but *it*

8:5 ᵃ2 Sam. 7:14;
Ps. 89:30–33;
Prov. 3:11, 12;
Heb. 12:5–11;
Rev. 3:19

8:6
ᵃ[Deut. 5:33]

8:7
ᵃDeut. 11:9–12;
Jer. 2:7

8:10
ᵃDeut. 6:11, 12

8:12
ᵃDeut. 28:47;
Prov. 30:9;
Hos. 13:6

8:14 ᵃ1 Cor. 4:7
ᵇDeut. 8:11;
Ps. 106:21

8:15
ᵃIs. 63:12–14
ᵇNum. 21:6
ᶜEx. 17:6;
Num. 20:11

8:16 ᵃEx. 16:15
ᵇJer. 24:5, 6;
[Heb. 12:11]

8:18
ᵃProv. 10:22;
Hos. 2:8
ᵇDeut. 7:8, 12

8:19
ᵃDeut. 4:26;
30:18

8:20
ᵃ[Dan. 9:11, 12]

9:2
ᵃNum. 13:22, 28,
33; Josh. 11:21, 22

9:3 ᵃDeut. 1:33;
31:3; Josh. 3:11;
5:14; John 10:4
ᵇDeut. 4:24;
Heb. 12:29
ᶜDeut. 7:24
ᵈEx. 23:31

9:4 ᵃDeut. 8:17;
[Rom. 11:6, 20;
1 Cor. 4:4, 7]

8:5 ¹*consider* 8:12 ¹*satisfied* 8:13 ¹*increased* 8:14 ¹*becomes proud*
8:18 ¹*confirm*

is ᵇbecause of the wickedness of these nations *that* the LORD is driving them out from before you. ⁵ᵃ*It is* not because of your righteousness or the uprightness of your heart *that* you go in to possess their land, but because of the wickedness of these nations *that* the LORD your God drives them out from before you, and that He may ¹fulfill the ᵇword which the LORD swore to your fathers, to Abraham, Isaac, and Jacob. ⁶Therefore understand that the LORD your God is not giving you this good land to possess because of your righteousness, for you *are* a ᵃstiff-necked¹ people.

⁷"Remember! Do not forget how you ᵃprovoked the LORD your God to wrath in the wilderness. ᵇFrom the day that you departed from the land of Egypt until you came to this place, you have been rebellious against the LORD. ⁸Also ᵃin Horeb you provoked the LORD to wrath, so that the LORD was angry *enough* with you to have destroyed you. ⁹ᵃWhen I went up into the mountain to receive the tablets of stone, the tablets of the covenant which the LORD made with you, then I stayed on the mountain forty days and ᵇforty nights. I neither ate bread nor drank water. ¹⁰ᵃThen the LORD delivered to me two tablets of stone written with the finger of God, and on them *were* all the words which the LORD had spoken to you on the mountain from the midst of the fire ᵇin¹ the day of the assembly. ¹¹And it came to pass, at the end of forty days and forty nights, *that* the LORD gave me the two tablets of stone, the tablets of the covenant.

¹²"Then the LORD said to me, ᵃ'Arise, go down quickly from here, for your people whom you brought out of Egypt have acted corruptly; they have ᵇquickly turned aside from the way which I commanded them; they have made themselves a molded image.'

¹³"Furthermore ᵃthe LORD spoke to me, saying, 'I have seen this people, and indeed ᵇthey are a ¹stiff-necked people. ¹⁴ᵃLet Me alone, that I may destroy them and ᵇblot out their name from under heaven; ᶜand I will make of you a nation mightier and greater than they.'

¹⁵ᵃ"So I turned and came down from the mountain, and ᵇthe mountain burned with fire; and the two tablets of the covenant *were* in my two hands. ¹⁶And ᵃI looked, and behold, you had sinned against the LORD your God—had made for yourselves a molded calf! You had turned aside quickly from the way which the LORD had commanded you. ¹⁷Then I took the two tablets and threw them out of my two hands and ᵃbroke them before your eyes. ¹⁸And I ᵃfell¹ down before the LORD, as at the first, forty days and forty nights; I neither ate bread nor drank water, because of all your sin which you committed in doing wickedly in the sight of the LORD, to provoke Him to anger. ¹⁹ᵃFor I was afraid of the anger and hot displeasure with which the LORD was angry with you, to destroy you. ᵇBut the LORD listened to me at that time also. ²⁰And the LORD was very angry with Aaron *and* would have destroyed him; so I prayed for Aaron also at the same time. ²¹Then I took your sin, the calf which you had made, and burned it with fire and crushed it *and* ground *it* very small, until it was as fine as dust; and I ᵃthrew its dust into the brook that descended from the mountain.

9:4
ᵇGen. 15:16;
Lev. 18:3,
24–30;
Deut. 12:31;
18:9–14

9:5 ᵃ[Titus 3:5]
ᵇGen. 50:24

9:6 ᵃEx. 34:9;
Deut. 31:27

9:7 ᵃNum. 14:22
ᵇEx. 14:11

9:8 ᵃEx. 32:1–8;
Ps. 106:19

9:9 ᵃEx. 24:12,
15; Deut. 5:2–22
ᵇEx. 24:18

9:10 ᵃEx. 31:18;
Deut. 4:13
ᵇEx. 19:17

9:12 ᵃEx. 32:7, 8
ᵇDeut. 31:29

9:13 ᵃEx. 32:9
ᵇDeut. 9:6

9:14 ᵃEx. 32:10
ᵇDeut. 29:20
ᶜNum. 14:12

9:15
ᵃEx. 32:15–19
ᵇEx. 19:18

9:16 ᵃEx. 32:19

9:17 ᵃEx. 32:19

9:18 ᵃEx. 34:28;
Ps. 106:23

9:19
ᵃEx. 32:10, 11;
Heb. 12:21
ᵇEx. 32:14

9:21 ᵃEx. 32:20

9:5 ¹*perform*   9:6 ¹*stubborn* or *rebellious*   9:10 ¹*when you were all gathered together*   9:13 ¹*stubborn* or *rebellious*   9:18 ¹*prostrated myself*

22"Also at [a]Taberah and [b]Massah and [c]Kibroth Hattaavah you [1]provoked the LORD to wrath. 23Likewise, [a]when the LORD sent you from Kadesh Barnea, saying, 'Go up and possess the land which I have given you,' then you rebelled against the commandment of the LORD your God, and [b]you did not believe Him nor obey His voice. 24[a]You have been rebellious against the LORD from the day that I knew you.

25[a]"Thus I [1]prostrated myself before the LORD; forty days and forty nights I kept prostrating myself, because the LORD had said He would destroy you. 26Therefore I prayed to the LORD, and said: 'O Lord GOD, do not destroy Your people and [a]Your inheritance whom You have redeemed through Your greatness, whom You have brought out of Egypt with a mighty hand. 27Remember Your servants, Abraham, Isaac, and Jacob; do not look on the stubbornness of this people, or on their wickedness or their sin, 28lest the land from which You brought us should say, "Because the LORD was not able to bring them to the land which He promised them, and because He hated them, He has brought them out to kill them in the wilderness." 29Yet they *are* Your people and Your inheritance, whom You brought out by Your mighty power and by Your outstretched arm.'

THE SECOND PAIR OF TABLETS
(Ex. 34:1–9)

10 "At that time the LORD said to me, [1]'Hew for yourself two tablets of stone like the first, and come up to Me on the mountain and make yourself an [a]ark of wood. 2And I will write on the tablets the words that were on the first tablets, which you broke; and [a]you shall put them in the ark.'

3"So I made an ark of acacia wood, hewed two tablets of stone like the first, and went up the mountain, having the two tablets in my hand. 4And He wrote on the tablets according to the first writing, the Ten [1]Commandments, [a]which the LORD had spoken to you in the mountain from the midst of the fire in the day of the assembly; and the LORD gave them to me. 5Then I turned and [a]came down from the mountain, and [b]put the tablets in the ark which I had made; [c]and there they are, just as the LORD commanded me."

6(Now the children of Israel journeyed from the wells of Bene Jaakan to Moserah, where Aaron [a]died, and where he was buried; and Eleazar his son ministered as priest in his [1]stead. 7[a]From there they journeyed to Gudgodah, and from Gudgodah to Jotbathah, a land of [1]rivers of water. 8At that time [a]the LORD [1]separated the tribe of Levi [b]to bear the ark of the covenant of the LORD, [c]to stand before the LORD to minister to Him and [d]to bless in His name, to this day. 9[a]Therefore Levi has no portion nor inheritance with his brethren; the LORD *is* his inheritance, just as the LORD your God promised him.)

10"As at the first time, [a]I stayed in the mountain forty days and forty nights; [b]the LORD also heard me at that time, *and* the LORD chose not to destroy you. 11[a]Then the LORD said to me, 'Arise, begin *your* journey before the people, that they

---

9:22 [a]Num. 11:1, 3 [b]Ex. 17:7 [c]Num. 11:4, 34
9:23 [a]Num. 13:3 [b]Ps. 106:24, 25
9:24 [a]Deut. 9:7; 31:27
9:25 [a]Deut. 9:18
9:26 [a]Deut. 32:9
10:1 [a]Ex. 25:10
10:2 [a]Ex. 25:16, 21
10:4 [a]Ex. 20:1; 34:28
10:5 [a]Ex. 34:29 [b]Ex. 40:20 [c]1 Kin. 8:9
10:6 [a]Num. 20:25–28; 33:38
10:7 [a]Num. 33:32–34
10:8 [a]Num. 3:6 [b]Num. 4:5, 15; 10:21 [c]Deut. 18:5 [d]Num. 6:23
10:9 [a]Num. 18:20, 24; Deut. 18:1, 2; Ezek. 44:28
10:10 [a]Ex. 34:28; Deut. 9:18 [b]Ex. 32:14
10:11 [a]Ex. 33:1

9:22 [1]*caused the LORD to be angry*   9:25 [1]*fell down*   10:1 [1]*Cut out*
10:4 [1]Lit. *Words*   10:6 [1]*place*   10:7 [1]*brooks*   10:8 [1]*set apart*

may go in and possess the land which I swore to their fathers to give them.'

THE ESSENCE OF THE LAW

12"And now, Israel, ªwhat does the LORD your God require of you, but to fear the LORD your God, to walk in all His ways and to ᵇlove Him, to serve the LORD your God with all your heart and with all your soul, 13*and* to keep the commandments of the LORD and His statutes which I command you today ªfor your ¹good? 14Indeed heaven and the highest heavens belong to the ªLORD your God, *also* the earth with all that *is* in it. 15The LORD delighted only in your fathers, to love them; and He chose their ¹descendants after them, you above all peoples, as *it is* this day. 16Therefore circumcise the foreskin of your ªheart, and be ᵇstiff-necked¹ no longer. 17For the LORD your God *is* ªGod of gods and ᵇLord of lords, the great God, ᶜmighty and awesome, who ᵈshows no partiality nor takes a bribe. 18ªHe administers justice for the fatherless and the widow, and loves the stranger, giving him food and clothing. 19Therefore love the stranger, for you were strangers in the land of Egypt. 20ªYou shall fear the LORD your God; you shall serve Him, and to Him you shall hold fast, and take oaths in His name. 21He *is* your praise, and He *is* your God, who has done for you these great and awesome things which your eyes have seen. 22Your fathers went down to Egypt with seventy persons, and now the LORD your God has made you as the stars of heaven in multitude.

LOVE AND OBEDIENCE REWARDED

11 "Therefore you shall love the LORD your God, and keep His charge, His statutes, His judgments, and His commandments always. 2Know today that *I do* not *speak* with your children, who have not known and who have not seen the ¹chastening of the LORD your God, His greatness and His mighty hand and His outstretched arm— 3His signs and His acts which He did in the midst of Egypt, to Pharaoh king of Egypt, and to all his land; 4what He did to the army of Egypt, to their horses and their chariots: ªhow He made the waters of the Red Sea overflow them as they pursued you, and *how* the LORD has destroyed them to this day; 5what He did for you in the wilderness until you came to this place; 6and ªwhat He did to Dathan and Abiram the sons of Eliab, the son of Reuben: how the earth opened its mouth and swallowed them up, their households, their tents, and all the substance that *was* ¹in their possession, in the midst of all Israel— 7but your eyes have ªseen every great ¹act of the LORD which He did.

8"Therefore you shall keep every commandment which I command you today, that you may ªbe strong, and go in and possess the land which you cross over to possess, 9and ªthat you may prolong *your* days in the land ᵇwhich the LORD ¹swore to give your fathers, to them and their descendants, ᶜ'a land flowing with milk and honey.' 10For the land which you go to possess *is* not like the land of Egypt from which you have come, where you sowed your seed and watered *it* by foot, as a vegetable garden; 11ªbut the land which you cross over

10:12 ªMic. 6:8
ᵇDeut. 6:5;
Matt. 22:37;
1 Tim. 1:5

10:13
ªDeut. 6:24

10:14
ª[Neh. 9:6;
Ps. 68:33;
115:16]

10:16
ªLev. 26:41;
Deut. 30:6;
Jer. 4:4;
Rom. 2:28, 29
ᵇDeut. 9:6, 13

10:17
ªDeut. 4:35, 39;
Is. 44:8; 46:9;
Dan. 2:47;
1 Cor. 8:5, 6
ᵇRev. 19:16
ᶜDeut. 7:21
ᵈActs 10:34

10:18
ªEx. 22:22–24;
Ps. 68:5; 146:9

10:20
ªMatt. 4:10

11:4 ªEx. 14:28;
Ps. 106:11

11:6
ªNum. 16:1–35;
Ps. 106:16–18

11:7 ªDeut. 10:21;
29:2

11:8 ªDeut. 31:6,
7, 23; Josh. 1:6, 7

11:9 ªDeut. 4:40;
5:16, 33; 6:2;
Prov. 10:27
ᵇDeut. 9:5
ᶜEx. 3:8

11:11 ªDeut. 8:7

10:13 ¹*benefit* or *welfare*   10:15 ¹Lit. *seed*   10:16 ¹*rebellious*
11:2 ¹*discipline*   11:6 ¹*at their feet*   11:7 ¹*work*   11:9 ¹*promised*

to possess *is* a land of hills and valleys, which drinks water from the rain of heaven, [12]a land for which the LORD your God cares; [a]the eyes of the LORD your God *are* always on it, from the beginning of the year to the very end of the year.

[13]'And it shall be that if you earnestly [1]obey My commandments which I command you today, to love the LORD your God and serve Him with all your heart and with all your soul, [14]then [a]I[1] will give *you* the rain for your land in its season, [b]the early rain and the latter rain, that you may gather in your grain, your new wine, and your oil. [15a]And I will send grass in your fields for your livestock, that you may [b]eat and be [1]filled.' [16]Take heed to yourselves, [a]lest your heart be deceived, and you turn aside and [b]serve other gods and worship them, [17]lest [a]the LORD's anger be aroused against you, and He [b]shut up the heavens so that there be no rain, and the land yield no produce, and [c]you perish quickly from the good land which the LORD is giving you.

[18]"Therefore [a]you shall [1]lay up these words of mine in your heart and in your [b]soul, and [c]bind them as a sign on your hand, and they shall be as frontlets between your eyes. [19a]You shall teach them to your children, speaking of them when you sit in your house, when you walk by the way, when you lie down, and when you rise up. [20a]And you shall write them on the doorposts of your house and on your gates, [21]that [a]your days and the days of your children may be multiplied in the land of which the LORD swore to your fathers to give them, like [b]the days of the heavens above the earth.

[22]"For if [a]you carefully keep all these commandments which I command you to do—to love the LORD your God, to walk in all His ways, and [b]to hold fast to Him— [23]then the LORD will [a]drive out all these nations from before you, and you will [b]dispossess greater and mightier nations than yourselves. [24a]Every place on which the sole of your foot treads shall be yours: [b]from the wilderness and Lebanon, from the river, the River Euphrates, even to the [1]Western Sea, shall be your territory. [25]No man shall be able to [a]stand [1]against you; the LORD your God will put the [b]dread of you and the fear of you upon all the land where you tread, just as He has said to you.

[26a]"Behold, I set before you today a blessing and a curse: [27a]the blessing, if you obey the commandments of the LORD your God which I command you today; [28]and the [a]curse, if you do not obey the commandments of the LORD your God, but turn aside from the way which I command you today, to go after other gods which you have not known. [29]Now it shall be, when the LORD your God has brought you into the land which you go to possess, that you shall put the [a]blessing on Mount Gerizim and the [b]curse on Mount Ebal. [30]*Are* they not on the other side of the Jordan, toward the setting sun, in the land of the Canaanites who dwell in the plain opposite Gilgal, [a]beside the terebinth trees of Moreh? [31]For you will cross over the Jordan and go in to possess the land which the LORD your God is giving you, and you will possess it and dwell in it. [32]And you shall be careful to observe all the statutes and judgments which I set before you today.

11:12 [a]1 Kin. 9:3

11:14 [a]Lev. 26:4; Deut. 28:12 [b]Joel 2:23; James 5:7

11:15 [a]Ps. 104:14 [b]Deut. 6:11; Joel 2:19

11:16 [a]Deut. 29:18; Job 31:27 [b]Deut. 8:19

11:17 [a]Deut. 6:15; 9:19 [b]Deut. 28:24; 1 Kin. 8:35; 2 Chr. 6:26; 7:13 [c]Deut. 4:26; 2 Chr. 36:14–20

11:18 [a]Deut. 6:6–9 [b]Ps. 119:2, 34 [c]Deut. 6:8

11:19 [a]Deut. 4:9, 10; 6:7; Prov. 22:6

11:20 [a]Deut. 6:9

11:21 [a]Deut. 4:40 [b]Ps. 72:5; 89:29; Prov. 3:2; 4:10; 9:11

11:22 [a]Deut. 11:1 [b]Deut. 10:20

11:23 [a]Deut. 4:38 [b]Deut. 9:1

11:24 [a]Josh. 1:3; 14:9 [b]Gen. 15:18; Ex. 23:31; Deut. 1:7, 8

11:25 [a]Deut. 7:24 [b]Ex. 23:27; Deut. 2:25; Josh. 2:9–11

11:26 [a]Deut. 30:1, 15, 19

11:27 [a]Deut. 28:1–14

11:28 [a]Deut. 28:15–68

11:29 [a]Deut. 27:12, 13; Josh. 8:33 [b]Deut. 27:13–26

11:30 [a]Gen. 12:6

11:13 [1]Lit. *listen to*   11:14 [1]So with MT, Tg.; Sam., LXX, Vg. *He*
11:15 [1]*satisfied*   11:18 [1]Lit. *put*   11:24 [1]Mediterranean   11:25 [1]*before*

A PRESCRIBED PLACE OF WORSHIP

12 "These [a]*are* the statutes and judgments which you shall be careful to observe in the land which the LORD God of your fathers is giving you to possess, [b]all[1] the days that you live on the earth. [2][a]You shall utterly destroy all the places where the nations which you shall dispossess served their gods, [b]on the high mountains and on the hills and under every green tree. [3]And [a]you shall destroy their altars, break their *sacred* pillars, and burn their [1]wooden images with fire; you shall cut down the carved images of their gods and destroy their names from that place. [4]You shall not [a]worship the LORD your God *with* such *things*.

[5]"But you shall seek the [a]place where the LORD your God chooses, out of all your tribes, to put His name for His [b]dwelling[1] place; and there you shall go. [6][a]There you shall take your burnt offerings, your sacrifices, your tithes, the heave offerings of your hand, your vowed offerings, your freewill offerings, and the [b]firstborn of your herds and flocks. [7]And [a]there you shall eat before the LORD your God, and [b]you shall rejoice in [1]all to which you have put your hand, you and your households, in which the LORD your God has blessed you.

[8]"You shall not at all do as we are doing here today—[a]every man doing whatever *is* right in his own eyes— [9]for as yet you have not come to the [a]rest[1] and the inheritance which the LORD your God is giving you. [10]But *when* you cross over the Jordan and dwell in the land which the LORD your God is giving you to inherit, and He gives you [a]rest from all your enemies round about, so that you dwell in safety, [11]then there will be the place where the LORD your God chooses to make His name abide. There you shall bring all that I command you: your burnt offerings, your sacrifices, your tithes, the heave offerings of your hand, and all your choice offerings which you vow to the LORD. [12]And [a]you shall rejoice before the LORD your God, you and your sons and your daughters, your male and female servants, and the [b]Levite who *is* within your gates, since he has no portion nor inheritance with you. [13]Take heed to yourself that you do not offer your burnt offerings in every place that you see; [14]but in the place which the LORD chooses, in one of your tribes, there you shall offer your burnt offerings, and there you shall do all that I command you.

[15]"However, [a]you may slaughter and eat meat within all your gates, whatever your heart desires, according to the blessing of the LORD your God which He has given you; [b]the unclean and the clean may eat of it, [c]of the gazelle and the deer alike. [16][a]Only you shall not eat the blood; you shall pour it on the earth like water. [17]You may not eat within your gates the tithe of your grain or your new wine or your oil, of the firstborn of your herd or your flock, of any of your offerings which you vow, of your freewill offerings, or of the [1]heave offering of your hand. [18]But you must eat them before the LORD your God in the place which the LORD your God chooses, you and your son and your daughter, your male servant and your female servant, and the Levite who *is* within your gates; and you shall rejoice before the LORD your God in [1]all

---

12:1 [a]Deut. 6:1
[b]Deut. 4:9, 10;
1 Kin. 8:40

12:2 [a]Ex. 34:13
[b]2 Kin. 16:4;
17:10, 11

12:3
[a]Num. 33:52;
Deut. 7:5;
Judg. 2:2

12:4 [a]Deut. 12:31

12:5 [a]Ex. 20:24
[b]Ex. 15:13;
1 Sam. 2:29

12:6 [a]Lev. 17:3, 4
[b]Deut. 14:23

12:7
[a]Deut. 14:26
[b]Deut. 12:12, 18

12:8 [a]Judg. 17:6;
21:25

12:9
[a]Deut. 3:20;
25:19; Ps. 95:11

12:10
[a]Josh. 11:23

12:12
[a]Deut. 12:18;
26:11
[b]Deut. 10:9;
14:29

12:15
[a]Deut. 12:21
[b]Deut. 12:22
[c]Deut. 14:5

12:16
[a]Gen. 9:4;
Lev. 7:26;
17:10–12;
1 Sam. 14:33;
Acts 15:20, 29

12:1 [1]As long as   12:3 [1]Heb. *Asherim*   12:5 [1]*home*   12:7 [1]*all that you undertake*   12:9 [1]Or *place of rest*   12:17 [1]*contribution*   12:18 [1]*all your undertakings*

to which you put your hands. [19]¹Take heed to yourself that you do not forsake the Levite as long as you live in your land.

[20]"When the LORD your God ªenlarges your border as He has promised you, and you say, 'Let me eat meat,' because you long to eat meat, you may eat as much meat as your heart desires. [21]If the place where the LORD your God chooses to put His name is too far from ªyou, then you may slaughter from your herd and from your flock which the LORD has given you, just as I have commanded you, and you may eat within your gates as much as your heart desires. [22]Just as the gazelle and the deer are eaten, so you may eat them; the unclean and the clean alike may eat them. [23]Only be sure that you do not eat the blood, ªfor the blood *is* the life; you may not eat the life with the meat. [24]You shall not eat it; you shall pour it on the earth like water. [25]You shall not eat it, ªthat it may go well with you and your children after you, ᵇwhen you do *what is* right in the sight of the LORD. [26]Only the ªholy things which you have, and your vowed offerings, you shall take and go to the place which the LORD chooses. [27]And ªyou shall offer your burnt offerings, the meat and the blood, on the altar of the LORD your God; and the blood of your sacrifices shall be poured out on the altar of the LORD your God, and you shall eat the meat. [28]Observe and obey all these words which I command you, ªthat it may go well with you and your children after you forever, when you do *what is* good and right in the sight of the LORD your God.

BEWARE OF FALSE GODS

[29]"When ªthe LORD your God cuts off from before you the nations which you go to dispossess, and you displace them and dwell in their land, [30]take heed to yourself that you are not ensnared to follow them, after they are destroyed from before you, and that you do not inquire after their gods, saying, 'How did these nations serve their gods? I also will do likewise.' [31]ªYou shall not worship the LORD your God in that way; for every ¹abomination to the LORD which He hates they have done to their gods; for ᵇthey burn even their sons and daughters in the fire to their gods.

[32]"Whatever I command you, be careful to observe it; ªyou shall not add to it nor take away from it.

PUNISHMENT OF APOSTATES

13 "If there arises among you a prophet or a ªdreamer of dreams, ᵇand he gives you a sign or a wonder, [2]and ªthe sign or the wonder comes to pass, of which he spoke to you, saying, 'Let us go after other gods'—which you have not known—'and let us serve them,' [3]you shall not listen to the words of that prophet or that dreamer of dreams, for the LORD your God ªis testing you to know whether you love the LORD your God with all your heart and with all your soul. [4]You shall ªwalk¹ after the LORD your God and fear Him, and keep His commandments and obey His voice; you shall serve Him and ᵇhold fast to Him. [5]But ªthat prophet or that dreamer of dreams shall be put to death, because he has spoken in order to turn *you* away from the LORD your God, who brought you

Cross references (margin)

12:20 ªGen. 15:18; Ex. 34:24; Deut. 11:24; 19:8

12:21 ªDeut. 14:24

12:23 ªGen. 9:4; Lev. 17:10–14; Deut. 12:16

12:25 ªDeut. 4:40; 6:18; Is. 3:10 ᵇEx. 15:26; 1 Kin. 11:38

12:26 ªNum. 5:9, 10; 18:19

12:27 ªLev. 1:5, 9, 13, 17

12:28 ªDeut. 12:25

12:29 ªEx. 23:23; Deut. 19:1; Josh. 23:4

12:31 ªLev. 18:3, 26, 30; 20:1, 2 ᵇDeut. 18:10; Ps. 106:37; Jer. 32:35

12:32 ªDeut. 4:2; 13:18; Josh. 1:7; Prov. 30:6; Rev. 22:18, 19

13:1 ªNum. 12:6; Jer. 23:28; Zech. 10:2 ᵇMatt. 24:24; 2 Thess. 2:9

13:2 ªDeut. 18:22

13:3 ªEx. 20:20; Deut. 8:2, 16

13:4 ªDeut. 10:12, 20; 2 Kin. 23:3 ᵇDeut. 30:20

13:5 ªDeut. 18:20; Jer. 14:15

12:19 ¹*Be careful*   12:31 ¹*detestable action*   13:4 ¹*follow the LORD*

out of the land of Egypt and redeemed you from the house of bondage, to entice you from the way in which the LORD your God commanded you to walk. [b]So you shall [1]put away the evil from your midst.

6a"If your brother, the son of your mother, your son or your daughter, [b]the wife [1]of your bosom, or your friend [c]who is as your own soul, secretly entices you, saying, 'Let us go and serve other gods,' which you have not known, neither you nor your fathers, 7of the gods of the people which *are* all around you, near to you or far off from you, from *one* end of the earth to the *other* end of the earth, 8you shall [a]not [1]consent to him or listen to him, nor shall your eye pity him, nor shall you spare him or conceal him; 9but you shall surely kill him; your hand shall be first against him to put him to [a]death, and afterward the hand of all the people. 10And you shall stone him with stones until he dies, because he sought to entice you away from the LORD your God, who brought you out of the land of Egypt, from the house of bondage. 11So all Israel shall hear and [a]fear, and not again do such wickedness as this among you.

12a"If you hear someone in one of your cities, which the LORD your God gives you to dwell in, saying, 13[1]'Corrupt men have gone out from among you and enticed the inhabitants of their city, saying, "Let us go and serve other gods" '—which you have not known— 14then you shall inquire, search out, and ask diligently. And *if it is* indeed true *and* certain *that* such an [1]abomination was committed among you, 15you shall surely strike the inhabitants of that city with the edge of the sword, utterly destroying it, all that is in it and its livestock— with the edge of the sword. 16And you shall gather all its plunder into the middle of the street, and [1]completely [a]burn with fire the city and all its plunder, for the LORD your God. It shall be [b]a [2]heap forever; it shall not be built again. 17aSo none of the accursed things shall remain in your hand, that the LORD may [b]turn from the fierceness of His anger and show you mercy, have compassion on you and [1]multiply you, just as He swore to your fathers, 18because you have listened to the voice of the LORD your God, [a]to keep all His commandments which I command you today, to do *what is* right in the eyes of the LORD your God.

IMPROPER MOURNING

14 "You *are* [a]the children of the LORD your God; [b]you shall not cut yourselves nor [1]shave the front of your head for the dead. 2aFor you *are* a holy people to the LORD your God, and the LORD has chosen you to be a people for Himself, a special treasure above all the peoples who *are* on the face of the earth.

CLEAN AND UNCLEAN MEAT
(*Lev. 11:1–47*)

3a"You shall not eat any [1]detestable thing. 4aThese *are* the animals which you may eat: the ox, the sheep, the goat, 5the

---

13:5
[b]Deut. 17:5, 7;
1 Cor. 5:13

13:6 [a]Deut. 17:2
[b]Gen. 16:5
[c]1 Sam. 18:1, 3

13:8 [a]Deut. 7:16;
Prov. 1:10

13:9 [a]Lev. 24:14;
Deut. 17:7

13:11 [a]Deut. 17:13

13:12
[a]Judg. 20:1–48

13:16
[a]Josh. 6:24
[b]Josh. 8:28;
Is. 17:1; 25:2;
Jer. 49:2

13:17 [a]Josh. 6:18
[b]Josh. 7:26

13:18
[a]Deut. 12:25,
28, 32

14:1
[a][Rom. 8:16;
Gal. 3:26]
[b]Lev. 19:28;
21:1–5

14:2 [a]Lev. 20:26;
Deut. 7:6;
[Rom. 12:1]

14:3 [a]Ezek. 4:14

14:4
[a]Lev. 11:2–45

13:5 [1]*exterminate*   13:6 [1]*Whom you cherish*   13:8 [1]*yield*   13:13 [1]Lit. *Sons of Belial*   13:14 [1]*detestable action*   13:16 [1]Or *as a whole-offering*   [2]Lit. *mound* or *ruin*   13:17 [1]*increase*   14:1 [1]*make any baldness between your eyes*   14:3 [1]*abominable*

deer, the gazelle, the roe deer, the wild goat, the [1]mountain goat, the antelope, and the mountain sheep. [6]And you may eat every animal with cloven hooves, having the hoof split into two parts, *and that* chews the cud, among the animals. [7]Nevertheless, of those that chew the cud or have cloven hooves, you shall not eat, *such as* these: the camel, the hare, and the rock hyrax; for they chew the cud but do not have cloven hooves; they *are* unclean for you. [8]Also the swine is unclean for you, because it has cloven hooves, yet *does* not *chew* the cud; you shall not eat their flesh [a]or touch their dead carcasses.

[9a]"These you may eat of all that *are* in the waters: you may eat all that have fins and scales. [10]And whatever does not have fins and scales you shall not eat; it *is* unclean for you.

[11]"All clean birds you may eat. [12a]But these you shall not eat: the eagle, the vulture, the buzzard, [13]the red kite, the falcon, and the kite after their kinds; [14]every raven after its kind; [15]the ostrich, the short-eared owl, the sea gull, and the hawk after their kinds; [16]the little owl, the screech owl, the white owl, [17]the jackdaw, the carrion vulture, the fisher owl, [18]the stork, the heron after its kind, and the hoopoe and the bat.

[19]"Also [a]every [1]creeping thing that flies is unclean for you; [b]they shall not be eaten.

[20]"You may eat all clean birds.

[21a]"You shall not eat anything that dies *of itself;* you may give it to the alien who *is* within your gates, that he may eat it, or you may sell it to a foreigner; [b]for you *are* a holy people to the LORD your God.

"[c]You shall not boil a young goat in its mother's milk.

TITHING PRINCIPLES

[22a]"You shall truly tithe all the increase of your grain that the field produces year by year. [23a]And you shall eat before the LORD your God, in the place where He chooses to make His name abide, the tithe of your grain and your new wine and your oil, of [b]the firstborn of your herds and your flocks, that you may learn to fear the LORD your God always. [24]But if the journey is too long for you, so that you are not able to carry *the tithe,* or [a]if the place where the LORD your God chooses to put His name is too far from you, when the LORD your God has blessed you, [25]then you shall exchange *it* for money, take the money in your hand, and go to the place which the LORD your God chooses. [26]And you shall spend that money for whatever your heart desires: for oxen or sheep, for wine or similar drink, for whatever your heart desires; you shall eat there before the LORD your God, and you shall [a]rejoice, you and your household. [27]You shall not [1]forsake the [a]Levite who *is* within your gates, for he has no part nor inheritance with you.

[28a]"At the end of *every* third year you shall bring out the [b]tithe of your produce of that year and store *it* up within your gates. [29]And the Levite, because he has no portion nor inheritance with you, and the stranger and the fatherless and the widow who *are* within your gates, may come and eat and be satisfied, that the LORD your God may bless you in all the work of your hand which you do.

Cross references

14:8 [a]Lev. 11:26, 27

14:9 [a]Lev. 11:9

14:12 [a]Lev. 11:13

14:19 [a]Lev. 11:20
[b]Lev. 11:23

14:21 [a]Lev. 17:15; 22:8; Ezek. 4:14; 44:31 [b]Deut. 14:2 [c]Ex. 23:19; 34:26

14:22 [a]Lev. 27:30; Deut. 12:6, 17; Neh. 10:37

14:23 [a]Deut. 12:5–7 [b]Deut. 15:19, 20

14:24 [a]Deut. 12:5, 21

14:26 [a]Deut. 12:7

14:27 [a]Deut. 12:12

14:28 [a]Deut. 26:12; Amos 4:4 [b]Num. 18:21–24

14:5 [1]Or *addax*　14:19 [1]*swarming*　14:27 [1]*neglect*

DEBTS CANCELED EVERY SEVEN YEARS
(Ex. 21:1–11; Lev. 25:1–7)

15 "At the end of [a]*every* seven years you shall grant a [1]release *of debts.* [2]And this *is* the form of the release: Every creditor who has lent *anything* to his neighbor shall [1]release *it;* he shall not [2]require *it* of his neighbor or his brother, because it is called the LORD's release. [3]Of a foreigner you may require *it;* but you shall give up your claim to what is owed by your brother, [4]except when there may be no poor among you; for the LORD will greatly [a]bless you in the land which the LORD your God is giving you to possess *as* an inheritance— [5]only if you carefully obey the voice of the LORD your God, to observe with care all these commandments which I command you today. [6]For the LORD your God will bless you just as He promised you; [a]you shall lend to many nations, but you shall not borrow; you shall reign over many nations, but they shall not reign over you.

GENEROSITY TO THE POOR

[7]"If there is among you a poor man of your brethren, within any of the [1]gates in your land which the LORD your God is giving you, [a]you shall not harden your heart nor shut your hand from your poor brother, [8]but [a]you shall [1]open your hand wide to him and willingly lend him sufficient for his need, whatever he needs. [9]Beware lest there be a wicked thought in your heart, saying, 'The seventh year, the year of release, is at hand,' and your [a]eye be evil against your poor brother and you give him nothing, and [b]he cry out to the LORD against you, and [c]it become sin among you. [10]You shall surely give to him, and [a]your heart should not be grieved when you give to him, because [b]for this thing the LORD your God will bless you in all your works and in all to which you put your hand. [11]For [a]the poor will never cease from the land; therefore I command you, saying, 'You shall [1]open your hand wide to your brother, to your poor and your needy, in your land.'

THE LAW CONCERNING BONDSERVANTS

[12][a]"If your brother, a Hebrew man, or a Hebrew woman, is [b]sold to you and serves you six years, then in the seventh year you shall let him go free from you. [13]And when you [1]send him away free from you, you shall not let him go away empty-handed; [14]you shall supply him liberally from your flock, from your threshing floor, and from your winepress. *From what* the LORD your God has [a]blessed you with, you shall give to him. [15][a]You shall remember that you were a slave in the land of Egypt, and the LORD your God redeemed you; therefore I command you this thing today. [16]And [a]if it happens that he says to you, 'I will not go away from you,' because he loves you and your house, since he prospers with you, [17]then you shall take an awl and thrust *it* through his ear to the door, and he shall be your servant forever. Also to your female servant you shall do likewise. [18]It shall not seem hard to you when you send him away free from you; for he has been worth [a]a

15:1 [a]Ex. 21:2; 23:10, 11; Lev. 25:4; Jer. 34:14

15:4 [a]Deut. 7:13

15:6 [a]Deut. 28:12, 44

15:7 [a]Ex. 23:6; Lev. 25:35–37; Deut. 24:12–14; [1 John 3:17]

15:8 [a]Matt. 5:42; Gal. 2:10

15:9 [a]Deut. 28:54, 56 [b]Ex. 22:23; Deut. 24:15; Job 34:28; Ps. 12:5; James 5:4 [c][Matt. 25:41, 42]

15:10 [a]2 Cor. 9:5, 7 [b]Deut. 14:29; Ps. 41:1; Prov. 22:9

15:11 [a]Matt. 26:11; Mark 14:7; John 12:8

15:12 [a]Ex. 21:2–6; Jer. 34:14 [b]Lev. 25:39–46

15:14 [a]Prov. 10:22

15:15 [a]Deut. 5:15

15:16 [a]Ex. 21:5, 6

15:18 [a]Is. 16:14

15:1 [1]*remission* 15:2 [1]*cancel the debt* [2]*exact it* 15:7 [1]*towns* 15:8 [1]*freely open* 15:11 [1]*freely open* 15:13 [1]*set him free*

double hired servant in serving you six years. Then the Lord your God will bless you in all that you do.

THE LAW CONCERNING FIRSTBORN ANIMALS

19a"All the firstborn males that come from your herd and your flock you shall ¹sanctify to the Lord your God; you shall do no work with the firstborn of your herd, nor shear the firstborn of your flock. 20aYou and your household shall eat *it* before the Lord your God year by year in the place which the Lord chooses. 21aBut if there is a defect in it, *if it is* lame or blind *or has* any serious defect, you shall not sacrifice it to the Lord your God. 22You may eat it within your gates; ªthe unclean and the clean *person* alike *may eat it,* as *if it were* a gazelle or a deer. 23Only you shall not eat its blood; you shall pour it on the ground like water.

THE PASSOVER REVIEWED

(Ex. 12:1–20; 23:14–19; 34:18–26)

16 "Observe the ªmonth of Abib, and keep the Passover to the Lord your God, for ᵇin the month of Abib the Lord your God brought you out of Egypt by night. 2Therefore you shall sacrifice the Passover to the Lord your God, from the flock and ªthe herd, in the ᵇplace where the Lord chooses to put His name. 3You shall eat no leavened bread with it; ªseven days you shall eat unleavened bread with it, *that is,* the bread of affliction (for you came out of the land of Egypt in haste), that you may ᵇremember the day in which you came out of the land of Egypt all the days of your life. 4aAnd no leaven shall be seen among you in all your territory for seven days, nor shall *any* of the meat which you sacrifice the first day at twilight remain overnight until ᵇmorning.

5"You may not sacrifice the Passover within any of your gates which the Lord your God gives you; 6but at the place where the Lord your God chooses to make His name abide, there you shall sacrifice the Passover ªat twilight, at the going down of the sun, at the time you came out of Egypt. 7And you shall roast and eat *it* ªin the place which the Lord your God chooses, and in the morning you shall turn and go to your tents. 8Six days you shall eat unleavened bread, and ªon the seventh day there *shall be* a ¹sacred assembly to the Lord your God. You shall do no work *on it.*

THE FEAST OF WEEKS REVIEWED

(Ex. 34:22; Lev. 23:15–21; Num. 28:26–31)

9"You shall count seven weeks for yourself; begin to count the seven weeks from *the time* you begin *to put* the sickle to the grain. 10Then you shall keep the ªFeast of Weeks to the Lord your God with the tribute of a freewill offering from your hand, which you shall give ᵇas the Lord your God blesses you. 11aYou shall rejoice before the Lord your God, you and your son and your daughter, your male servant and your female servant, the Levite who *is* within your gates, the stranger and the fatherless and the widow who *are* among you, at the place where the Lord your God chooses to make His name abide. 12aAnd you shall remember that you were

---

15:19
aEx. 13:2, 12

15:20
aLev. 7:15–18;
Deut. 12:5; 14:23

15:21
aLev. 22:19–25;
Deut. 17:1

15:22
aDeut. 12:15,
16, 22

16:1 aEx. 12:2
bEx. 13:4

16:2
aNum. 28:19
bDeut. 12:5, 26;
15:20

16:3
aNum. 29:12
bEx. 13:3;
Deut. 4:9

16:4 aEx. 13:7
bNum. 9:12

16:6 aEx. 12:7–10

16:7
a2 Kin. 23:23

16:8
aEx. 12:16; 13:6;
Lev. 23:8, 36

16:10 aEx. 34:22;
Lev. 23:15, 16;
Num. 28:26
b1 Cor. 16:2

16:11
aDeut. 16:14

16:12
aDeut. 15:15

15:19 ¹*set apart* or *consecrate*   **16:8** ¹Lit. *restraint*

a slave in Egypt, and you shall be careful to observe these statutes.

THE FEAST OF TABERNACLES REVIEWED
(Lev. 23:33–43; Num. 29:12–40)

13a"You shall observe the Feast of Tabernacles seven days, when you have gathered from your threshing floor and from your winepress. 14And ayou shall rejoice in your feast, you and your son and your daughter, your male servant and your female servant and the Levite, the stranger and the fatherless and the widow, who *are* within your 1gates. 15aSeven days you shall keep a sacred feast to the LORD your God in the place which the LORD chooses, because the LORD your God will bless you in all your produce and in all the work of your hands, so that you surely rejoice.

16a"Three times a year all your males shall appear before the LORD your God in the place which He chooses: at the Feast of Unleavened Bread, at the Feast of Weeks, and at the Feast of Tabernacles; and bthey shall not appear before the LORD empty-handed. 17Every man *shall give* as he is able, aaccording to the blessing of the LORD your God which He has given you.

JUSTICE MUST BE ADMINISTERED

18"You shall appoint ajudges and officers in all your 1gates, which the LORD your God gives you, according to your tribes, and they shall judge the people with just judgment. 19aYou shall not pervert justice; byou shall not 1show partiality, cnor take a bribe, for a bribe blinds the eyes of the wise and 2twists the words of the righteous. 20You shall follow what is altogether just, that you may alive and inherit the land which the LORD your God is giving you.

21a"You shall not plant for yourself any tree, as a 1wooden image, near the altar which you build for yourself to the LORD your God. 22aYou shall not set up a *sacred* pillar, which the LORD your God hates.

17 "You ashall not sacrifice to the LORD your God a bull or sheep which has any 1blemish *or* defect, for that *is* an 2abomination to the LORD your God.

2a"If there is found among you, within any of your 1gates which the LORD your God gives you, a man or a woman who has been wicked in the sight of the LORD your God, bin transgressing His covenant, 3who has gone and served other gods and worshiped them, either athe sun or moon or any of the host of heaven, bwhich I have not commanded, 4aand it is told you, and you hear *of it,* then you shall inquire diligently. And if *it is* indeed true *and* certain that such an 1abomination has been committed in Israel, 5then you shall bring out to your gates that man or woman who has committed that wicked thing, and ashall stone bto death that man or woman with stones. 6Whoever is deserving of death shall be put to death on the testimony of two or three awitnesses; he shall not be put to death on the testimony of one witness. 7The hands of the witnesses shall be the first against him to put him to

16:13 aEx. 23:16

16:14 aNeh. 8:9

16:15
aLev. 23:39–41

16:16
aEx. 23:14–17;
34:22–24
bEx. 23:15

16:17
aLev. 14:30, 31;
Deut. 16:10

16:18
aEx. 23:1–8;
Deut. 1:16, 17;
John 7:24

16:19
aEx. 23:2, 6
bDeut. 1:17
cEx. 23:8

16:20
aEzek. 18:5–9

16:21 aEx. 34:13

16:22 aLev. 26:1

17:1 aDeut. 15:21;
Mal. 1:8, 13

17:2 aDeut. 13:6
bJosh. 7:11

17:3 aDeut. 4:19
bJer. 7:22

17:4
aDeut. 13:12, 14

17:5
aLev. 24:14–16;
Josh. 7:25
bDeut. 13:6–18

17:6
aNum. 35:30;
Deut. 19:15;
Matt. 18:16;
John 8:17;
2 Cor. 13:1;
1 Tim. 5:19;
Heb. 10:28

16:14 1*towns*   16:18 1*towns*   16:19 1Lit. *regard faces*   2*perverts*
16:21 1Or *Asherah*   17:1 1Lit. *evil thing*   2*detestable thing*   17:2 1*towns*
17:4 1*detestable thing*

death, and afterward the hands of all the people. So you shall put away the evil from among ^ayou.

8^a"If a matter arises which is too hard for you to judge, between degrees of guilt for bloodshed, between one judgment or another, or between one punishment or another, matters of controversy within your gates, then you shall arise and go up to the ^bplace which the LORD your God chooses. ⁹And ^ayou shall come to the priests, the Levites, and ^bto the judge *there* in those days, and inquire *of them;* ^cthey shall pronounce upon you the sentence of judgment. ¹⁰You shall do according to the sentence which they pronounce upon you in that place which the LORD chooses. And you shall be careful to do according to all that they order you. ¹¹According to the sentence of the law in which they instruct you, according to the judgment which they tell you, you shall do; you shall not turn aside *to* the right hand or *to* the left from the sentence which they pronounce upon you. ¹²Now ^athe man who acts presumptuously and will not heed the priest who stands to minister there before the LORD your God, or the judge, that man shall die. So you shall put away the evil from Israel. ^{13a}And all the people shall hear and fear, and no longer act presumptuously.

PRINCIPLES GOVERNING KINGS

¹⁴"When you come to the land which the LORD your God is giving you, and possess it and dwell in it, and say, ^a'I will set a king over me like all the nations that *are* around me,' ¹⁵you shall surely set a king over you ^awhom the LORD your God chooses; *one* ^bfrom among your brethren you shall set as king over you; you may not set a foreigner over you, who *is* not your brother. ¹⁶But he shall not multiply ^ahorses for himself, nor cause the people ^bto return to Egypt to multiply horses, for ^cthe LORD has said to you, ^d'You shall not return that way again.' ¹⁷Neither shall he multiply wives for himself, lest his heart turn away; nor shall he greatly multiply silver and ^agold for himself.

¹⁸"Also it shall be, when he sits on the throne of his kingdom, that he shall write for himself a copy of this law in a book, from *the one* ^abefore the priests, the Levites. ¹⁹And ^ait shall be with him, and he shall read it all the days of his life, that he may learn to fear the LORD his God and be careful to observe all the words of this law and these statutes, ²⁰that his heart may not ¹be lifted above his brethren, that he ^amay not turn aside from the commandment *to* the right hand or *to* the left, and that he may ²prolong *his* days in his kingdom, he and his children in the midst of Israel.

THE PORTION OF THE PRIESTS AND LEVITES

18 "The priests, the Levites—all the tribe of Levi—shall have ¹no part nor ^ainheritance with Israel; they shall eat the offerings of the LORD made by fire, and His portion. ²Therefore they shall have no inheritance among their brethren; the LORD is their inheritance, as He said to them.

³"And this shall be the priest's ^adue¹ from the people, from those who offer a sacrifice, whether *it is* bull or sheep: they shall give to the priest the shoulder, the cheeks, and the stomach.

17:7 ^aDeut. 13:5; 19:19; 1 Cor. 5:13

17:8 ^aDeut. 1:17; 2 Chr. 19:10 ^bDeut. 12:5; 16:2

17:9 ^aJer. 18:18 ^bDeut. 19:17–19 ^cEzek. 44:24

17:12 ^aNum. 15:30; Deut. 1:43

17:13 ^aDeut. 13:11

17:14 ^a1 Sam. 8:5, 19, 20; 10:19

17:15 ^a1 Sam. 9:15, 16; 10:24; 16:12, 13; 1 Chr. 22:8–10; Hos. 8:4 ^bJer. 30:21

17:16 ^a1 Kin. 4:26; 10:26–29; Ps. 20:7 ^bIs. 31:1; Ezek. 17:15 ^cEx. 13:17, 18; Hos. 11:5 ^dDeut. 28:68

17:17 ^a1 Kin. 10:14

17:18 ^aDeut. 31:24–26

17:19 ^aPs. 119:97, 98

17:20 ^aDeut. 5:32; 1 Kin. 15:5

18:1 ^aDeut. 10:9; 1 Cor. 9:13

18:3 ^aLev. 7:32–34; Num. 18:11, 12; 1 Sam. 2:13–16, 29

17:20 ¹*become proud* ²*continue long in his kingdom* **18:1** ¹*no portion*
18:3 ¹*right*

[4] [a]The firstfruits of your grain and your new wine and your oil, and the first of the fleece of your sheep, you shall give him. [5]For [a]the LORD your God has chosen him out of all your tribes [b]to stand to minister in the name of the LORD, him and his sons forever.

[6]"So if a Levite comes from any of your [1]gates, from where he [a]dwells among all Israel, and comes with all the desire of his mind [b]to the place which the LORD chooses, [7]then he may serve in the name of the LORD his God [a]as all his brethren the Levites *do*, who stand there before the LORD. [8]They shall have equal [a]portions to eat, besides what comes from the sale of his inheritance.

AVOID WICKED CUSTOMS

[9]"When you come into the land which the LORD your God is giving you, [a]you shall not learn to follow the [1]abominations of those nations. [10]There shall not be found among you *anyone* who makes his son or his daughter [a]pass[1] through the fire, [b]*or one* who practices witchcraft, *or* a soothsayer, or one who interprets omens, or a sorcerer, [11][a]or one who conjures spells, or a medium, or a spiritist, or [b]one who calls up the dead. [12]For all who do these things *are* [1]an abomination to the LORD, and [a]because of these abominations the LORD your God drives them out from before you. [13]You shall be [1]blameless before the LORD your God. [14]For these nations which you will dispossess listened to soothsayers and diviners; but as for you, the LORD your God has not [1]appointed such for you.

A NEW PROPHET LIKE MOSES

[15][a]"The LORD your God will raise up for you a Prophet like me from your midst, from your brethren. Him you shall hear, [16]according to all you desired of the LORD your God in Horeb [a]in the day of the assembly, saying, [b]'Let me not hear again the voice of the LORD my God, nor let me see this great fire anymore, lest I die.'

[17]"And the LORD said to me: [a]'What they have spoken is good. [18][a]I will raise up for them a Prophet like you from among their brethren, and [b]will put My words in His mouth, [c]and He shall speak to them all that I command Him. [19][a]And it shall be *that* whoever will not hear My words, which He speaks in My name, I will require *it* of him. [20]But [a]the prophet who presumes to speak a word in My name, which I have not commanded him to speak, or [b]who speaks in the name of other gods, that prophet shall die.' [21]And if you say in your heart, 'How shall we know the word which the LORD has not spoken?'— [22][a]when a prophet speaks in the name of the LORD, [b]if the thing does not happen or come to pass, that *is* the thing which the LORD has not spoken; the prophet has spoken it [c]presumptuously; you shall not be afraid of him.

THREE CITIES OF REFUGE

(Num. 35:9–28; Josh. 20:1–9)

19 "When the LORD your God [a]has cut off the nations whose land the LORD your God is giving you, and you dispossess them and dwell in their cities and in their houses,

---

18:4 [a]Ex. 22:29

18:5 [a]Ex. 28:1
[b]Deut. 10:8

18:6 [a]Num. 35:2
[b]Deut. 12:5;
14:23

18:7 [a]Num. 1:50;
2 Chr. 31:2

18:8
[a]Lev. 27:30–33;
Num. 18:21–24;
2 Chr. 31:4;
Neh. 12:44

18:9 [a]Lev. 18:26,
27, 30;
Deut. 12:29, 30;
20:16–18

18:10 [a]Lev. 18:21;
Deut. 12:31
[b]Ex. 22:18;
Lev. 19:26, 31;
20:6, 27; Is. 8:19

18:11 [a]Lev. 20:27
[b]1 Sam. 28:7

18:12
[a]Lev. 18:24;
Deut. 9:4

18:15
[a]Matt. 21:11;
Luke 1:76;
2:25–34; 7:16;
24:19; Acts 3:22

18:16
[a]Deut. 5:23–27
[b]Ex. 20:18, 19;
Heb. 12:19

18:17
[a]Deut. 5:28

18:18
[a]Deut. 34:10;
John 1:45;
Acts 3:22
[b]Num. 23:5;
Is. 49:2; 51:16;
John 17:8
[c][John 4:25;
8:28]

18:19 [a]Acts 3:23;
[Heb. 12:25]

18:20
[a]Deut. 13:5;
Jer. 14:14, 15;
Zech. 13:2–5
[b]Deut. 13:1–3;
Jer. 2:8

18:22 [a]Jer. 28:9
[b]Deut. 13:2
[c]Deut. 18:20

19:1 [a]Deut. 12:29

18:6 [1]*towns*　18:9 [1]*detestable acts*　18:10 [1]Be burned as an offering to an idol　18:12 [1]*detestable*　18:13 [1]Lit. *perfect*　18:14 [1]*allowed you to do so*

²ᵃyou shall separate three cities for yourself in the midst of your land which the LORD your God is giving you to possess. ³You shall prepare roads for yourself, and divide into three parts the territory of your land which the LORD your God is giving you to inherit, that any manslayer may flee there.

⁴"And ᵃthis *is* the case of the manslayer who flees there, that he may live: Whoever kills his neighbor ¹unintentionally, not having hated him in time past— ⁵as when *a man* goes to the woods with his neighbor to cut timber, and his hand swings a stroke with the ax to cut down the tree, and the head slips from the handle and strikes his neighbor so that he dies—he shall flee to one of these cities and live; ⁶ᵃlest the avenger of blood, while his anger is hot, pursue the manslayer and overtake him, because the way is long, and kill him, though he *was* not deserving of death, since he had not hated the victim in time past. ⁷Therefore I command you, saying, 'You shall separate three cities for yourself.'

⁸"Now if the LORD your God ᵃenlarges your territory, as He swore to ᵇyour fathers, and gives you the land which He promised to give to your fathers, ⁹and if you keep all these commandments and do them, which I command you today, to love the LORD your God and to walk always in His ways, ᵃthen you shall add three more cities for yourself besides these three, ¹⁰ᵃlest innocent blood be shed in the midst of your land which the LORD your God is giving you *as* an inheritance, and *thus* guilt of bloodshed be upon you.

¹¹"But ᵃif anyone hates his neighbor, lies in wait for him, rises against him and strikes him mortally, so that he dies, and he flees to one of these cities, ¹²then the elders of his city shall send and bring him from there, and deliver him over to the hand of the avenger of blood, that he may die. ¹³ᵃYour eye shall not pity him, ᵇbut you shall ¹put away *the guilt of* innocent blood from Israel, that it may go well with you.

PROPERTY BOUNDARIES

¹⁴ᵃ"You shall not remove your neighbor's landmark, which the men of old have set, in your inheritance which you will inherit in the land that the LORD your God is giving you to possess.

THE LAW CONCERNING WITNESSES

¹⁵ᵃ"One witness shall not rise against a man concerning any iniquity or any sin that he commits; by the mouth of two or three witnesses the matter shall be established. ¹⁶If a false witness ᵃrises against any man to testify against him of wrongdoing, ¹⁷then both men in the controversy shall stand before the LORD, ᵃbefore the priests and the judges who serve in those days. ¹⁸And the judges shall make careful inquiry, and indeed, *if* the witness *is* a false witness, who has testified falsely against his brother, ¹⁹ᵃthen you shall do to him as he thought to have done to his brother; so ᵇyou shall put away the evil from among you. ²⁰ᵃAnd those who remain shall hear and fear, and hereafter they shall not again commit such evil among you. ²¹ᵃYour eye shall not pity: ᵇlife *shall be* for life, eye for eye, tooth for tooth, hand for hand, foot for foot.

19:2 ᵃEx. 21:13; Num. 35:10–15; Deut. 4:41; Josh. 20:2

19:4 ᵃNum. 35:9–34; Deut. 4:42

19:6 ᵃNum. 35:12

19:8 ᵃDeut. 12:20 ᵇGen. 15:18–21

19:9 ᵃJosh. 20:7–9

19:10 ᵃNum. 35:33; Deut. 21:1–9

19:11 ᵃNum. 35:16, 24; Deut. 27:24; [1 John 3:15]

19:13 ᵃDeut. 13:8 ᵇNum. 35:33, 34; 1 Kin. 2:31

19:14 ᵃDeut. 27:17; Job 24:2; Prov. 22:28; Hos. 5:10

19:15 ᵃNum. 35:30; Deut. 17:6; Matt. 18:16; John 8:17; 2 Cor. 13:1; 1 Tim. 5:19; Heb. 10:28

19:16 ᵃEx. 23:1; Ps. 27:12; 35:11

19:17 ᵃDeut. 17:8–11; 21:5

19:19 ᵃProv. 19:5; Dan. 6:24 ᵇDeut. 13:5; 17:7; 21:21; 22:21

19:20 ᵃDeut. 17:13; 21:21

19:21 ᵃDeut. 19:13 ᵇEx. 21:23, 24; Lev. 24:20; Matt. 5:38, 39

19:4 ¹*ignorantly,* lit. *without knowledge*   19:13 ¹*purge the blood of the innocent*

PRINCIPLES GOVERNING WARFARE

20 "When you go out to battle against your enemies, and see [a]horses and chariots *and* people more numerous than you, do not be [b]afraid of them; for the LORD your God *is* [c]with you, who brought you up from the land of Egypt. ²So it shall be, when you are on the verge of battle, that the priest shall approach and speak to the people. ³And he shall say to them, 'Hear, O Israel: Today you are on the verge of battle with your enemies. Do not let your heart faint, do not be afraid, and do not tremble or be terrified because of them; ⁴for the LORD your God *is* He who goes with you, [a]to fight for you against your enemies, to save you.'

⁵"Then the officers shall speak to the people, saying: 'What man *is there* who has built a new house and has not [a]dedicated it? Let him go and return to his house, lest he die in the battle and another man dedicate it. ⁶Also what man *is there* who has planted a vineyard and has not eaten of it? Let him go and return to his house, lest he die in the battle and another man eat of it. ⁷[a]And what man *is there* who is betrothed to a woman and has not married her? Let him go and return to his house, lest he die in the battle and another man marry her.'

⁸"The officers shall speak further to the people, and say, [a]'What man *is there who is* fearful and fainthearted? Let him go and return to his house, [1]lest the heart of his brethren faint like his heart.' ⁹And so it shall be, when the officers have finished speaking to the people, that they shall make captains of the armies to lead the people.

¹⁰"When you go near a city to fight against it, [a]then proclaim an offer of peace to it. ¹¹And it shall be that if they accept your offer of peace, and open to you, then all the people *who are* found in it shall be placed under tribute to you, and serve you. ¹²Now if *the city* will not make peace with you, but war against you, then you shall besiege it. ¹³And when the LORD your God delivers it into your hands, [a]you shall strike every male in it with the edge of the sword. ¹⁴But the women, the little ones, [a]the livestock, and all that is in the city, all its spoil, you shall plunder for yourself; and [b]you shall eat the enemies' plunder which the LORD your God gives you. ¹⁵Thus you shall do to all the cities *which are* very far from you, which *are* not of the cities of these nations.

¹⁶"But [a]of the cities of these peoples which the LORD your God gives you *as* an inheritance, you shall let nothing that breathes remain alive, ¹⁷but you shall utterly destroy them: the Hittite and the Amorite and the Canaanite and the Perizzite and the Hivite and the Jebusite, just as the LORD your God has commanded you, ¹⁸lest [a]they teach you to do according to all their [1]abominations which they have done for their gods, and you [b]sin against the LORD your God.

¹⁹"When you besiege a city for a long time, while making war against it to take it, you shall not destroy its trees by wielding an ax against them; if you can eat of them, do not cut them down to use in the siege, for the tree of the field *is* man's *food*. ²⁰Only the trees which you know *are* not trees for food you may destroy and cut down, to build siegeworks against the city that makes war with you, until it is subdued.

20:1 [a]Ps. 20:7; Is. 31:1
[b]Deut. 7:18
[c]Num. 23:21; Deut. 5:6; 31:6, 8; 2 Chr. 13:12; 32:7, 8; Ps. 23:4; Is. 41:10
20:4 [a]Deut. 1:30; 3:22; Josh. 23:10
20:5 [a]Neh. 12:27
20:7 [a]Deut. 24:5
20:8 [a]Judg. 7:3
20:10 [a]2 Sam. 10:19
20:13 [a]Num. 31:7
20:14 [a]Josh. 8:2
[b]1 Sam. 14:30
20:16 [a]Ex. 23:31–33; Num. 21:2, 3; Deut. 7:1–5; Josh. 11:14
20:18 [a]Ex. 34:12–16; Deut. 7:4; 12:30; 18:9 [b]Ex. 23:33; 2 Kin. 21:3–15; Ps. 106:34–41

20:8 [1]So with MT, Tg.; Sam., LXX, Syr., Vg. *lest he make his brother's heart faint* **20:18** [1]*detestable things*

THE LAW CONCERNING UNSOLVED MURDER

21 "If *anyone* is found slain, lying in the field in the land which the LORD your God is giving you to possess, *and* it is not known who killed him, [2]then your elders and your judges shall go out and measure *the distance* from the slain man to the surrounding cities. [3]And it shall be *that* the elders of the city nearest to the slain man will take a heifer which has not been worked *and* which has not pulled with a [a]yoke. [4]The elders of that city shall bring the heifer down to a valley with flowing water, which is neither plowed nor sown, and they shall break the heifer's neck there in the valley. [5]Then the priests, the sons of Levi, shall come near, for [a]the LORD your God has chosen them to minister to Him and to bless in the name of the LORD; [b]by their word every controversy and every [1]assault shall be *settled*. [6]And all the elders of that city nearest to the slain *man* [a]shall wash their hands over the heifer whose neck was broken in the valley. [7]Then they shall answer and say, 'Our hands have not shed this blood, nor have our eyes seen *it*. [8]Provide atonement, O LORD, for Your people Israel, whom You have redeemed, [a]and do not lay innocent blood to the charge of Your people Israel.' And atonement shall be provided on their behalf for the blood. [9]So [a]you shall put away the *guilt of* innocent blood from among you when you do *what is* right in the sight of the LORD.

FEMALE CAPTIVES

[10]"When you go out to war against your enemies, and the LORD your God delivers them into your hand, and you take them captive, [11]and you see among the captives a beautiful woman, and desire her and would take her for your [a]wife, [12]then you shall bring her home to your house, and she shall [a]shave her head and trim her nails. [13]She shall put off the clothes of her captivity, remain in your house, and [a]mourn her father and her mother a full month; after that you may go in to her and be her husband, and she shall be your wife. [14]And it shall be, if you have no delight in her, then you shall set her free, but you certainly shall not sell her for money; you shall not treat her brutally, because you have [a]humbled her.

FIRSTBORN INHERITANCE RIGHTS

[15]"If a man has two wives, one loved [a]and the other unloved, and they have borne him children, *both* the loved and the unloved, and *if* the firstborn son is of her who is unloved, [16]then it shall be, [a]on the day he bequeaths his possessions to his sons, *that* he must not bestow firstborn status on the son of the loved wife in preference to the son of the unloved, the *true* firstborn. [17]But he shall acknowledge the son of the unloved wife *as* the firstborn [a]by giving him a double portion of all that he has, for he [b]*is* the beginning of his strength; [c]the right of the firstborn *is* his.

THE REBELLIOUS SON

[18]"If a man has a stubborn and rebellious son who will not obey the voice of his father or the voice of his mother, and *who*, when they have chastened him, will not heed them,

21:3 [a]Num. 19:2

21:5 [a]Deut. 10:8; 1 Chr. 23:13
[b]Deut. 17:8, 9

21:6 [a]Ps. 19:12; 26:6; Matt. 27:24

21:8 [a]Deut. 19:10, 13; Jon. 1:14

21:9 [a]Deut. 19:13

21:11 [a]Num. 31:18

21:12 [a]Lev. 14:8, 9; Num. 6:9

21:13 [a]Ps. 45:10

21:14 [a]Gen. 34:2; Deut. 22:29; Judg. 19:24

21:15 [a]Gen. 29:33

21:16 [a]1 Chr. 5:2; 26:10

21:17 [a]2 Kin. 2:9
[b]Gen. 49:3
[c]Gen. 25:31, 33

21:5 [1]Lit. *stroke*

¹⁹then his father and his mother shall take hold of him and bring him out to the elders of his city, to the gate of his city. ²⁰And they shall say to the elders of his city, 'This son of ours is stubborn and rebellious; he will not obey our voice; he is a glutton and a drunkard.' ²¹Then all the men of his city shall stone him to death with stones; ᵃso you shall put away the evil from among you, ᵇand all Israel shall hear and fear.

MISCELLANEOUS LAWS

²²"If a man has committed a sin ᵃdeserving of death, and he is put to death, and you hang him on a tree, ²³ᵃhis body shall not remain overnight on the tree, but you shall surely bury him that day, so that ᵇyou do not defile the land which the LORD your God is giving you *as* an inheritance; for ᶜhe who is hanged *is* accursed of God.

22 "You ᵃshall not see your brother's ox or his sheep going astray, and ¹hide yourself from them; you shall certainly bring them back to your brother. ²And if your brother *is* not near you, or if you do not know him, then you shall bring it to your own house, and it shall remain with you until your brother seeks it; then you shall restore it to him. ³You shall do the same with his donkey, and so shall you do with his garment; with any lost thing of your brother's, which he has lost and you have found, you shall do likewise; you ¹must not hide yourself.

⁴ᵃ"You shall not see your brother's donkey or his ox fall down along the road, and hide yourself from them; you shall surely help him lift *them* up again.

⁵"A woman shall not wear anything that pertains to a man, nor shall a man put on a woman's garment, for all who do so *are* ¹an abomination to the LORD your God.

⁶"If a bird's nest happens to be before you along the way, in any tree or on the ground, with young ones or eggs, with the mother sitting on the young or on the eggs, ᵃyou shall not take the mother with the young; ⁷you shall surely let the mother go, and take the young for yourself, ᵃthat it may be well with you and *that* you may prolong *your* days.

⁸"When you build a new house, then you shall make a parapet for your roof, that you may not bring guilt of bloodshed on your household if anyone falls from it.

⁹ᵃ"You shall not sow your vineyard with different kinds of seed, lest the yield of the seed which you have sown and the fruit of your vineyard be defiled.

¹⁰ᵃ"You shall not plow with an ox and a donkey together.

¹¹ᵃ"You shall not wear a garment of different sorts, *such as* wool and linen mixed together.

¹²"You shall make ᵃtassels on the four corners of the clothing with which you cover *yourself.*

LAWS OF SEXUAL MORALITY

¹³"If any man takes a wife, and goes in to her, and ᵃdetests her, ¹⁴and charges her with shameful conduct, and brings a bad name on her, and says, 'I took this woman, and when I came to her I found she *was* not a virgin,' ¹⁵then the father and mother of the young woman shall take and bring out *the evidence of* the young woman's virginity to the elders of the city

21:21
ᵃDeut. 13:5;
19:19, 20; 22:21,
24 ᵇDeut. 13:11

21:22
ᵃDeut. 22:26;
Matt. 26:66;
Mark 14:64;
Acts 23:29

21:23
ᵃJosh. 8:29;
10:26, 27;
John 19:31
ᵇLev. 18:25;
Num. 35:34
ᶜGal. 3:13

22:1 ᵃEx. 23:4

22:4 ᵃEx. 23:5

22:6 ᵃLev. 22:28

22:7
ᵃDeut. 4:40

22:9 ᵃLev. 19:19

22:10
ᵃ[2 Cor. 6:14–16]

22:11 ᵃLev. 19:19

22:12
ᵃNum. 15:37–41;
Matt. 23:5

22:13
ᵃDeut. 21:15;
24:3

22:1 ¹*ignore them*   22:3 ¹*may not avoid responsibility*   22:5 ¹*detestable*

at the gate. ¹⁶And the young woman's father shall say to the elders, 'I gave my daughter to this man as wife, and he detests her. ¹⁷Now he has charged her with shameful conduct, saying, "I found your daughter *was* not a virgin," and yet these *are the evidences of* my daughter's virginity.' And they shall spread the cloth before the elders of the city. ¹⁸Then the elders of that city shall take that man and punish him; ¹⁹and they shall fine him one hundred *shekels* of silver and give *them* to the father of the young woman, because he has brought a bad name on a virgin of Israel. And she shall be his wife; he cannot divorce her all his days.

²⁰"But if the thing is true, *and evidences of* virginity are not found for the young woman, ²¹then they shall bring out the young woman to the door of her father's house, and the men of her city shall stone her to death with ^astones, because she has ^bdone a disgraceful thing in Israel, to play the harlot in her father's house. ^cSo you shall ¹put away the evil from among you.

^{22a}"If a man is found lying with a woman married to a husband, then both of them shall die—the man that lay with the woman, and the woman; so you shall put away the evil from Israel.

²³"If a young woman *who is* a virgin is ^abetrothed to a husband, and a man finds her in the city and lies with her, ²⁴then you shall bring them both out to the gate of that city, and you shall stone them to death with stones, the young woman because she did not cry out in the city, and the man because he ^ahumbled his neighbor's wife; ^bso you shall put away the evil from among you.

²⁵"But if a man finds a betrothed young woman in the countryside, and the man forces her and lies with her, then only the man who lay with her shall die. ²⁶But you shall do nothing to the young woman; *there is* in the young woman no sin *deserving* of death, for just as when a man rises against his neighbor and kills him, even so *is* this matter. ²⁷For he found her in the countryside, *and* the betrothed young woman cried out, but *there was* no one to save her.

^{28a}"If a man finds a young woman *who is* a virgin, who is not betrothed, and he seizes her and lies with her, and they are found out, ²⁹then the man who lay with her shall give to the young woman's father ^afifty *shekels* of silver, and she shall be his wife ^bbecause he has humbled her; he shall not be permitted to divorce her all his days.

^{30a}"A man shall not take his father's wife, nor ^buncover his father's bed.

THOSE EXCLUDED FROM THE CONGREGATION

23 "He who is emasculated by crushing or mutilation shall ^anot enter the assembly of the LORD.

²"One of illegitimate birth shall not enter the assembly of the LORD; even to the tenth generation none of his *descendants* shall enter the assembly of the LORD.

^{3a}"An Ammonite or Moabite shall not enter the assembly of the LORD; even to the tenth generation none of his *descendants* shall enter the assembly of the LORD forever, ^{4a}because they did not meet you with bread and water on the

22:21
^aDeut. 21:21
^bGen. 34:7;
Judg. 20:5–10;
2 Sam. 13:12, 13
^cDeut. 13:5

22:22
^aLev. 20:10;
Num. 5:22–27;
Ezek. 16:38;
[Matt. 5:27, 28];
John 8:5;
[1 Cor. 6:9;
Heb. 13:4]

22:23
^aLev. 19:20–22;
Matt. 1:18, 19

22:24
^aDeut. 21:14
^bDeut. 22:21, 22;
1 Cor. 5:2, 13

22:28
^aEx. 22:16, 17

22:29
^aEx. 22:16, 17
^bDeut. 22:24

22:30
^aLev. 18:8; 20:11;
Deut. 27:20;
1 Cor. 5:1
^bRuth 3:9;
Ezek. 16:8

23:1 ^aLev. 21:20;
22:24

23:3
^aNeh. 13:1, 2

23:4
^aDeut. 2:27–30

22:21 ¹*purge the evil person*

road when you came out of Egypt, and ^bbecause they hired against you Balaam the son of Beor from Pethor of [1]Mesopotamia, to curse you. ⁵Nevertheless the LORD your God would not listen to Balaam, but the LORD your God turned the curse into a blessing for you, because the LORD your God ^aloves you. ^{6a}You shall not seek their peace nor their prosperity all your days forever.

⁷"You shall not abhor an Edomite, ^afor he *is* your brother. You shall not abhor an Egyptian, because ^byou were an alien in his land. ⁸The children of the third generation born to them may enter the assembly of the LORD.

CLEANLINESS OF THE CAMPSITE

⁹"When the army goes out against your enemies, then keep yourself from every wicked thing. ^{10a}If there is any man among you who becomes unclean by some occurrence in the night, then he shall go outside the camp; he shall not come inside the camp. ¹¹But it shall be, when evening comes, that ^ahe shall wash with water; and when the sun sets, he may come into the camp.

¹²"Also you shall have a place outside the camp, where you may go out; ¹³and you shall have an implement among your equipment, and when you sit down outside, you shall dig with it and turn and cover your refuse. ¹⁴For the LORD your God ^awalks in the midst of your camp, to deliver you and give your enemies over to you; therefore your camp shall be holy, that He may see no unclean thing among you, and turn away from you.

MISCELLANEOUS LAWS

^{15a}"You shall not give back to his master the slave who has escaped from his master to you. ¹⁶He may dwell with you in your midst, in the place which he chooses within one of your gates, where it [1]seems best to him; ^ayou shall not oppress him.

¹⁷"There shall be no *ritual* [1]harlot ^aof the daughters of Israel, or a ^bperverted[2] one of the sons of Israel. ¹⁸You shall not bring the wages of a harlot or the price of a dog to the house of the LORD your God for any vowed offering, for both of these *are* [1]an abomination to the LORD your God.

^{19a}"You shall not charge interest to your brother—interest on money *or* food *or* anything that is lent out at interest. ^{20a}To a foreigner you may charge interest, but to your brother you shall not charge interest, ^bthat the LORD your God may bless you in all to which you set your hand in the land which you are entering to possess.

^{21a}"When you make a vow to the LORD your God, you shall not delay to pay it; for the LORD your God will surely require it of you, and it would be sin to you. ²²But if you abstain from vowing, it shall not be sin to you. ^{23a}That which has gone from your lips you shall keep and perform, for you voluntarily vowed to the LORD your God what you have promised with your mouth.

²⁴"When you come into your neighbor's vineyard, you may eat your fill of grapes at your pleasure, but you shall

23:4
^bNum. 22:5, 6;
23:7; Josh. 24:9;
2 Pet. 2:15;
Jude 11

23:5 ^aDeut. 4:37

23:6 ^aEzra 9:12

23:7
^aGen. 25:24–26;
Deut. 2:4, 8;
Amos 1:11;
Obad. 10, 12
^bEx. 22:21;
23:9; Lev. 19:34;
Deut. 10:19

23:10 ^aLev. 15:16

23:11 ^aLev. 15:5

23:14
^aLev. 26:12;
Deut. 7:21

23:15
^a1 Sam. 30:15

23:16 ^aEx. 22:21;
Prov. 22:22

23:17
^aLev. 19:29;
Deut. 22:21
^bGen. 19:5;
2 Kin. 23:7

23:19
^aEx. 22:25;
Lev. 25:35–37;
Neh. 5:2–7;
Ps. 15:5

23:20
^aDeut. 15:3
^bDeut. 15:10

23:21
^aNum. 30:1,
2; Job 22:27;
Ps. 61:8;
Eccl. 5:4, 5;
Matt. 5:33

23:23
^aNum. 30:2;
Ps. 66:13, 14

23:4 [1]Heb. *Aram Naharaim*   23:16 [1]*pleases him best*   23:17 [1]Heb. *qedeshah,* fem. of *qadesh* (next note)   [2]Heb. *qadesh,* one practicing sodomy and prostitution in religious rituals   23:18 [1]*detestable*

not put *any* in your container. [25]When you come into your neighbor's standing grain, [a]you may pluck the heads with your hand, but you shall not use a sickle on your neighbor's standing grain.

LAW CONCERNING DIVORCE

24 "When a [a]man takes a wife and marries her, and it happens that she finds no favor in his eyes because he has found some [1]uncleanness in her, and he writes her a [b]certificate of divorce, puts *it* in her hand, and sends her out of his house, [2]when she has departed from his house, and goes and becomes another man's *wife*, [3]*if* the latter husband detests her and writes her a certificate of divorce, puts *it* in her hand, and sends her out of his house, or if the latter husband dies who took her as his wife, [4a]*then* her former husband who divorced her must not take her back to be his wife after she has been defiled; for that *is* [1]an abomination before the LORD, and you shall not bring sin on the land which the LORD your God is giving you *as* an inheritance.

MISCELLANEOUS LAWS

[5a]"When a man has taken a new wife, he shall not go out to war or be charged with any business; he shall be free at home one year, and [b]bring happiness to his wife whom he has taken.

[6]"No man shall take the lower or the upper millstone in pledge, for he takes [1]*one's* living in pledge.

[7]"If a man is [a]found [1]kidnapping any of his brethren of the children of Israel, and mistreats him or sells him, then that kidnapper shall die; [b]and you shall put away the evil from among you.

[8]"Take heed in [a]an outbreak of leprosy, that you carefully observe and do according to all that the priests, the Levites, shall teach you; just as I commanded them, *so* you shall be careful to do. [9a]Remember what the LORD your God did [b]to Miriam on the way when you came out of Egypt!

[10]"When you [a]lend your brother anything, you shall not go into his house to get his pledge. [11]You shall stand outside, and the man to whom you lend shall bring the pledge out to you. [12]And if the man *is* poor, you shall not [1]keep his pledge overnight. [13a]You shall in any case return the pledge to him again when the sun goes down, that he may sleep in his own garment and [b]bless you; and [c]it shall be righteousness to you before the LORD your God.

[14]"You shall not [a]oppress a hired servant *who is* poor and needy, *whether* one of your brethren or one of the aliens who *is* in your land within your gates. [15]Each day [a]you shall give *him* his wages, and not let the sun go down on it, for he *is* poor and has set his heart on it; [b]lest he cry out against you to the LORD, and it be sin to you.

[16a]"Fathers shall not be put to death for *their* children, nor shall children be put to death for *their* fathers; a person shall be put to death for his own sin.

[17a]"You shall not pervert justice due the stranger or the fatherless, [b]nor take a widow's garment as a pledge. [18]But [a]you shall remember that you were a slave in Egypt, and the LORD

Cross references (margin)

23:25
[a]Matt. 12:1;
Mark 2:23;
Luke 6:1

24:1
[a][Matt. 5:31;
19:7; Mark 10:4]
[b][Jer. 3:8]

24:4 [a][Jer. 3:1]

24:5 [a]Deut. 20:7
[b]Prov. 5:18

24:7 [a]Ex. 21:16
[b]Deut. 19:19

24:8
[a]Lev. 13:2; 14:2

24:9
[a][1 Cor. 10:6]
[b]Num. 12:10

24:10
[a]Matt. 5:42

24:13
[a]Ex. 22:26;
Ezek. 18:7
[b]Job 29:11;
2 Tim. 1:18
[c]Deut. 6:25;
Ps. 106:31;
Dan. 4:27

24:14 [a]Lev. 19:13;
Deut. 15:7–18;
[Prov. 14:31];
Amos 4:1;
[Mal. 3:5];
1 Tim. 5:18]

24:15 [a]Lev. 19:13;
Jer. 22:13
[b]Ex. 22:23;
Deut. 15:9;
Job 35:9;
James 5:4

24:16
[a]2 Kin. 14:6;
2 Chr. 25:4;
Jer. 31:29, 30;
Ezek. 18:20

24:17 [a]Ex. 23:6
[b]Ex. 22:26

24:18
[a]Deut. 24:22

24:1 [1]indecency, lit. *nakedness of a thing*   24:4 [1]*a detestable thing*
24:6 [1]*life*   24:7 [1]Lit. *stealing*   24:12 [1]Lit. *sleep with his pledge*

your God redeemed you from there; therefore I command you to do this thing.

19a"When you reap your harvest in your field, and forget a sheaf in the field, you shall not go back to get it; it shall be for the stranger, the fatherless, and the widow, that the LORD your God may bbless you in all the work of your hands. 20When you beat your olive trees, you shall not go over the boughs again; it shall be for the stranger, the fatherless, and the widow. 21When you gather the grapes of your vineyard, you shall not glean *it* afterward; it shall be for the stranger, the fatherless, and the widow. 22And you shall remember that you were a slave in the land of Egypt; therefore I command you to do this thing.

25 "If there is a adispute between men, and they come to 1court, that *the judges* may judge them, and they bjustify the righteous and condemn the wicked, 2then it shall be, if the wicked man adeserves to be beaten, that the judge will cause him to lie down band be beaten in his presence, according to his guilt, with a certain number of blows. 3aForty blows he may give him *and* no more, lest he should exceed this and beat him with many blows above these, and your brother bbe humiliated in your sight.

4a"You shall not muzzle an ox while it 1treads out *the grain.*

MARRIAGE DUTY OF THE SURVIVING BROTHER

5a"If brothers dwell together, and one of them dies and has no son, the widow of the dead man shall not be *married* to a stranger outside *the family;* her husband's brother shall go in to her, take her as his wife, and perform the duty of a husband's brother to her. 6And it shall be *that* the firstborn son which she bears awill succeed to the name of his dead brother, that bhis name may not be blotted out of Israel. 7But if the man does not want to take his brother's wife, then let his brother's wife go up to the agate to the elders, and say, 'My husband's brother refuses to raise up a name to his brother in Israel; he will not perform the duty of my husband's brother.' 8Then the elders of his city shall call him and speak to him. But *if* he stands firm and says, a'I do not want to take her,' 9then his brother's wife shall come to him in the presence of the elders, aremove his sandal from his foot, spit in his face, and answer and say, 'So shall it be done to the man who will not bbuild up his brother's house.' 10And his name shall be called in Israel, 'The house of him who had his sandal removed.'

MISCELLANEOUS LAWS

11"If *two* men fight together, and the wife of one draws near to rescue her husband from the hand of the one attacking him, and puts out her hand and seizes him by the genitals, 12then you shall cut off her hand; ayour eye shall not pity *her.*

13a"You shall not have in your bag differing weights, a heavy and a light. 14You shall not have in your house differing measures, a large and a small. 15You shall have a perfect and just weight, a perfect and just measure, athat your days may be lengthened in the land which the LORD your God is giving you.

24:19 aLev. 19:9, 10 bDeut. 15:10; Ps. 41:1; Prov. 19:17

25:1 aDeut. 17:8–13; 19:17; Ezek. 44:24 bProv. 17:15

25:2 aProv. 19:29; Luke 12:48 bMatt. 10:17

25:3 a2 Cor. 11:24 bJob 18:3

25:4 a[Prov. 12:10; 1 Cor. 9:9; 1 Tim. 5:18]

25:5 aMatt. 22:24; Mark 12:19; Luke 20:28

25:6 aGen. 38:9 bRuth 4:5, 10

25:7 aRuth 4:1, 2

25:8 aRuth 4:6

25:9 aRuth 4:7, 8 bRuth 4:11

25:12 aDeut. 7:2; 19:13

25:13 aLev. 19:35–37; Prov. 11:1; 20:23; Ezek. 45:10; Mic. 6:11

25:15 aEx. 20:12

25:1 1Lit. *the judgment*   25:4 1*threshes*

¹⁶For ªall who do such things, all who behave unrighteously, *are* ¹an abomination to the LORD your God.

DESTROY THE AMALEKITES

¹⁷ª"Remember what Amalek did to you on the way as you were coming out of Egypt, ¹⁸how he met you on the way and attacked your rear ranks, all the stragglers at your rear, when you *were* tired and weary; and he ªdid not fear God. ¹⁹Therefore it shall be, ªwhen the LORD your God has given you rest from your enemies all around, in the land which the LORD your God is giving you to possess *as* an inheritance, *that* you will ᵇblot out the remembrance of Amalek from under heaven. You shall not forget.

OFFERINGS OF FIRSTFRUITS AND TITHES

26 "And it shall be, when you come into the land which the LORD your God is giving you *as* an inheritance, and you possess it and dwell in it, ²ªthat you shall take some of the first of all the produce of the ground, which you shall bring from your land that the LORD your God is giving you, and put *it* in a basket and ᵇgo to the place where the LORD your God chooses to make His name abide. ³And you shall go to the one who is priest in those days, and say to him, 'I declare today to the LORD ¹your God that I have come to the country which the LORD swore to our fathers to give us.'

⁴"Then the priest shall take the basket out of your hand and set it down before the altar of the LORD your God. ⁵And you shall answer and say before the LORD your God: 'My father *was* ªa ¹Syrian, ᵇabout to perish, and ᶜhe went down to Egypt and ²dwelt there, ᵈfew in number; and there he became a nation, ᵉgreat, mighty, and populous. ⁶But the ªEgyptians mistreated us, afflicted us, and laid hard bondage on us. ⁷ªThen we cried out to the LORD God of our fathers, and the LORD heard our voice and looked on our affliction and our labor and our oppression. ⁸So ªthe LORD brought us out of Egypt with a mighty hand and with an outstretched arm, ᵇwith great terror and with signs and wonders. ⁹He has brought us to this place and has given us this land, ª"a land flowing with milk and honey"; ¹⁰and now, behold, I have brought the firstfruits of the land which you, O LORD, have given me.'

"Then you shall set it before the LORD your God, and worship before the LORD your God. ¹¹So ªyou shall rejoice in every good *thing* which the LORD your God has given to you and your house, you and the Levite and the stranger who *is* among you.

¹²"When you have finished laying aside all the ªtithe of your increase in the third year—ᵇthe year of tithing—and have given *it* to the Levite, the stranger, the fatherless, and the widow, so that they may eat within your gates and be filled, ¹³then you shall say before the LORD your God: 'I have removed the ¹holy *tithe* from *my* house, and also have given them to the Levite, the stranger, the fatherless, and the widow, according to all Your commandments which You have commanded me; I have not transgressed Your commandments, ªnor have I forgotten *them*. ¹⁴ªI have not eaten any of

25:16 ªProv. 11:1;
[1 Thess. 4:6]

25:17
ªEx. 17:8–16;
1 Sam. 15:1–3

25:18
ª[Ps. 36:1];
Rom. 3:18

25:19
ª1 Sam. 15:3
ᵇEx. 17:14

26:2 ªEx. 22:29;
23:16, 19;
Num. 18:13;
Deut. 16:10;
Prov. 3:9
ᵇDeut. 12:5

26:5
ªGen. 25:20;
Hos. 12:12
ᵇGen. 43:1,
2; 45:7, 11
ᶜGen. 46:1,
6; Acts 7:15
ᵈGen. 46:27;
Deut. 10:22
ᵉDeut. 1:10

26:6
ªEx. 1:8–11, 14

26:7
ªEx. 2:23–25;
3:9; 4:31

26:8 ªEx. 12:37,
51; 13:3, 14, 16;
Deut. 5:15
ᵇDeut. 4:34;
34:11, 12

26:9 ªEx. 3:8, 17

26:11
ªDeut. 12:7;
16:11; Eccl. 3:12,
13; 5:18–20

26:12
ªLev. 27:30;
Num. 18:24
ᵇDeut. 14:28, 29

26:13
ªPs. 119:141,
153, 176

26:14 ªLev. 7:20;
Jer. 16:7;
Hos. 9:4

25:16 ¹detestable   26:3 ¹LXX *my*   26:5 ¹Or *Aramean*   ²As a resident alien
26:13 ¹*hallowed things*

it [1]when in mourning, nor have I removed *any* of it [2]for an unclean *use,* nor given *any* of it for the dead. I have obeyed the voice of the LORD my God, and have done according to all that You have commanded me. [15a]Look down from Your holy [1]habitation, from heaven, and bless Your people Israel and the land which You have given us, just as You swore to our fathers, [b]"a land flowing with milk and honey."'

A SPECIAL PEOPLE OF GOD

[16]"This day the LORD your God commands you to observe these statutes and judgments; therefore you shall be careful to observe them with all your heart and with all your soul. [17]Today you have [a]proclaimed the LORD to be your God, and that you will walk in His ways and keep His statutes, His commandments, and His judgments, and that you will [b]obey His voice. [18]Also today [a]the LORD has proclaimed you to be His special people, just as He promised you, that *you* should keep all His commandments, [19]and that He will set you [a]high above all nations which He has made, in praise, in name, and in honor, and that you may be [b]a [1]holy people to the LORD your God, just as He has spoken."

THE LAW INSCRIBED ON STONES

27 Now Moses, with the elders of Israel, commanded the people, saying: "Keep all the commandments which I command you today. [2]And it shall be, on the day [a]when you cross over the Jordan to the land which the LORD your God is giving you, that [b]you shall set up for yourselves large stones, and whitewash them with lime. [3]You shall write on them all the words of this law, when you have crossed over, that you may enter the land which the LORD your God is giving you, [a]'a land flowing with milk and honey,' just as the LORD God of your fathers promised you. [4]Therefore it shall be, when you have crossed over the Jordan, *that* [a]on Mount Ebal you shall set up these stones, which I command you today, and you shall whitewash them with lime. [5]And there you shall build an altar to the LORD your God, an altar of stones; [a]you shall not use an iron *tool* on them. [6]You shall build with [1]whole stones the altar of the LORD your God, and offer burnt offerings on it to the LORD your God. [7]You shall offer peace offerings, and shall eat there, and [a]rejoice before the LORD your God. [8]And you shall [a]write very plainly on the stones all the words of this law."

[9]Then Moses and the priests, the Levites, spoke to all Israel, saying, "Take heed and listen, O Israel: [a]This day you have become the people of the LORD your God. [10]Therefore you shall obey the voice of the LORD your God, and observe His commandments and His statutes which I command you today."

CURSES PRONOUNCED FROM MOUNT EBAL

[11]And Moses commanded the people on the same day, saying, [12]"These shall stand [a]on Mount Gerizim to bless the people, when you have crossed over the Jordan: Simeon, Levi, Judah, Issachar, Joseph, and Benjamin; [13]and [a]these shall

26:15 [a]Ps. 80:14;
Is. 63:15;
Zech. 2:13
[b]Ex. 3:8

26:17 [a]Ex. 20:19
[b]Deut. 15:5

26:18 [a]Ex. 6:7;
19:5; Deut. 7:6;
14:2; 28:9;
[Titus 2:14;
1 Pet. 2:9]

26:19
[a]Deut. 4:7, 8;
28:1 [b]Ex. 19:6;
Deut. 7:6;
28:9; Is. 62:12;
[1 Pet. 2:9]

27:2 [a]Josh. 4:1
[b]Josh. 8:32

27:3 [a]Ex. 3:8

27:4
[a]Deut. 11:29;
Josh. 8:30, 31

27:5 [a]Ex. 20:25;
Josh. 8:31

27:7 [a]Deut. 26:11

27:8 [a]Josh. 8:32

27:9
[a]Deut. 26:18

27:12
[a]Deut. 11:29;
Josh. 8:33;
Judg. 9:7

27:13
[a]Deut. 11:29;
Josh. 8:33

26:14 [1]Lit. *in my mourning* [2]Or *while I was unclean* 26:15 [1]*home*
26:19 [1]*consecrated* 27:6 [1]*uncut*

stand on Mount Ebal to curse: Reuben, Gad, Asher, Zebulun, Dan, and Naphtali.

14"And [a]the Levites shall speak with a loud voice and say to all the men of Israel: 15a'Cursed *is* the one who makes a carved or molded image, [1]an abomination to the LORD, the work of the hands of the craftsman, and sets *it* up in secret.'

[b]"And all the people shall answer and say, 'Amen!'

16a'Cursed *is* the one who treats his father or his mother with contempt.'

"And all the people shall say, 'Amen!'

17a'Cursed *is* the one who moves his neighbor's landmark.'

"And all the people shall say, 'Amen!'

18a'Cursed *is* the one who makes the blind to wander off the road.'

"And all the people shall say, 'Amen!'

19a'Cursed *is* the one who perverts the justice due the stranger, the fatherless, and widow.'

"And all the people shall say, 'Amen!'

20a'Cursed *is* the one who lies with his father's wife, because he has uncovered his father's bed.'

"And all the people shall say, 'Amen!'

21a'Cursed *is* the one who lies with any kind of animal.'

"And all the people shall say, 'Amen!'

22a'Cursed *is* the one who lies with his sister, the daughter of his father or the daughter of his mother.'

"And all the people shall say, 'Amen!'

23a'Cursed *is* the one who lies with his mother-in-law.'

"And all the people shall say, 'Amen!'

24a'Cursed *is* the one who attacks his neighbor secretly.'

"And all the people shall say, 'Amen!'

25a'Cursed *is* the one who takes a bribe to slay an innocent person.'

"And all the people shall say, 'Amen!'

26a'Cursed *is* the one who does not confirm *all* the words of this law by observing them.'

"And all the people shall say, 'Amen!' "

BLESSINGS ON OBEDIENCE
(Lev. 26:1–13; Deut. 7:12–24)

28 "Now it shall come to pass, [a]if you diligently obey the voice of the LORD your God, to observe carefully all His commandments which I command you today, that the LORD your God [b]will set you high above all nations of the earth. 2And all these blessings shall come upon you and [a]overtake you, because you obey the voice of the LORD your God:

3a"Blessed *shall* you *be* in the city, and blessed *shall* you *be* [b]in the country.

4"Blessed *shall be* [a]the [1]fruit of your body, the produce of your ground and the increase of your herds, the increase of your cattle and the offspring of your flocks.

5"Blessed *shall be* your basket and your kneading bowl.

6a"Blessed *shall* you *be* when you come in, and blessed *shall* you *be* when you go out.

7"The LORD [a]will cause your enemies who rise against you

27:14
[a]Deut. 33:10;
Josh. 8:33;
Dan. 9:11

27:15 [a]Ex. 20:4,
23; 34:17;
Lev. 19:4; 26:1;
Deut. 4:16,
23; Is. 44:9;
Hos. 13:2
[b]Num. 5:22;
Jer. 11:5;
1 Cor. 14:16

27:16 [a]Ex. 20:12;
Lev. 19:3; 20:9;
Deut. 5:16;
21:18–21;
Ezek. 22:7

27:17
[a]Deut. 19:14;
Prov. 22:28

27:18 [a]Lev. 19:14

27:19 [a]Ex. 22:21,
22; 23:9;
Lev. 19:33;
Deut. 10:18;
24:17

27:20
[a]Lev. 18:8; 20:11;
Deut. 22:30;
1 Cor. 5:1

27:21 [a]Ex. 22:19;
Lev. 18:23;
20:15, 16

27:22 [a]Lev. 18:9

27:23
[a]Lev. 18:17;
20:14

27:24
[a]Ex. 20:13;
21:12; Lev. 24:17;
Num. 35:30, 31

27:25 [a]Ex. 23:7;
Ps. 15:5;
Ezek. 22:12

27:26
[a]Ps. 119:21;
Jer. 11:3;
Gal. 3:10

28:1 [a]Ex. 15:26;
Lev. 26:3–13;
Deut. 7:12–
26; 11:13
[b]Deut. 26:19;
1 Chr. 14:2

28:2
[a]Deut. 28:15

28:3
[a]Ps. 128:1, 4
[b]Gen. 39:5

28:4 [a]Gen. 22:17

28:6 [a]Ps. 121:8

28:7
[a]Lev. 26:7, 8

27:15 [1]*a detestable thing*   28:4 [1]*offspring*

to be defeated before your face; they shall come out against you one way and flee before you seven ways.

8"The LORD will ªcommand the blessing on you in your storehouses and in all to which you bset your hand, and He will bless you in the land which the LORD your God is giving you.

9ª"The LORD will establish you as a holy people to Himself, just as He has sworn to you, if you keep the commandments of the LORD your God and walk in His ways. 10Then all peoples of the earth shall see that you are ªcalled by the name of the LORD, and they shall be bafraid of you. 11And ªthe LORD will grant you plenty of goods, in the fruit of your body, in the increase of your livestock, and in the produce of your ground, in the land of which the LORD 1swore to your fathers to give you. 12The LORD will open to you His good 1treasure, the heavens, ªto give the rain to your land in its season, and bto bless all the work of your hand. cYou shall lend to many nations, but you shall not borrow. 13And the LORD will make ªyou the head and not the tail; you shall be above only, and not be beneath, if you 1heed the commandments of the LORD your God, which I command you today, and are careful to observe *them*. 14ªSo you shall not turn aside from any of the words which I command you this day, *to* the right or the left, to go after other gods to serve them.

CURSES ON DISOBEDIENCE
(Lev. 26:14–46)

15"But it shall come to pass, ªif you do not obey the voice of the LORD your God, to observe carefully all His commandments and His statutes which I command you today, that all these curses will come upon you and overtake you:

16"Cursed *shall* you *be* in the city, and cursed *shall* you *be* in the country.

17"Cursed *shall be* your basket and your kneading bowl.

18"Cursed *shall be* the 1fruit of your body and the produce of your land, the increase of your cattle and the offspring of your flocks.

19"Cursed *shall* you *be* when you come in, and cursed *shall* you *be* when you go out.

20"The LORD will send on you ªcursing, bconfusion, and crebuke in all that you set your hand to do, until you are destroyed and until you perish quickly, because of the wickedness of your doings in which you have forsaken Me. 21The LORD will make the 1plague cling to you until He has consumed you from the land which you are going to possess. 22ªThe LORD will strike you with consumption, with fever, with inflammation, with severe burning fever, with the sword, with bscorching,1 and with mildew; they shall pursue you until you perish. 23And ªyour heavens which *are* over your head shall be bronze, and the earth which is under you *shall be* iron. 24The LORD will change the rain of your land to powder and dust; from the heaven it shall come down on you until you are destroyed.

25ª"The LORD will cause you to be defeated before your

28:8 ªLev. 25:21
bDeut. 15:10
28:9 ªEx. 19:5, 6
28:10
ªNum. 6:27;
2 Chr. 7:14;
Is. 63:19;
Dan. 9:18, 19
bDeut. 11:25
28:11
ªDeut. 30:9
28:12 ªLev. 26:4;
Deut. 11:14
bDeut. 14:29
cDeut. 15:6
28:13
ª[Is. 9:14, 15]
28:14
ªDeut. 5:32;
Josh. 1:7
28:15
ªLev. 26:14–39;
Josh. 23:15;
Dan. 9:10–14;
Mal. 2:2
28:20 ªMal. 2:2
bIs. 65:14
cPs. 80:16;
Is. 30:17
28:22
ªLev. 26:16
bAmos 4:9
28:23
ªLev. 26:19
28:25
ªDeut. 32:30

28:11 1promised 28:12 1storehouse 28:13 1listen to 28:18 1offspring
28:21 1pestilence 28:22 1blight

enemies; you shall go out one way against them and flee seven ways before them; and you shall become ¹troublesome to all the kingdoms of the earth. ²⁶ᵃYour carcasses shall be food for all the birds of the air and the beasts of the earth, and no one shall frighten *them* away. ²⁷The LORD will strike you with ᵃthe boils of Egypt, with ᵇtumors, with the scab, and with the itch, from which you cannot be healed. ²⁸The LORD will strike you with madness and blindness and ᵃconfusion of heart. ²⁹And you shall ᵃgrope at noonday, as a blind man gropes in darkness; you shall not prosper in your ways; you shall be only oppressed and plundered continually, and no one shall save *you*.

³⁰ᵃ"You shall betroth a wife, but another man shall lie with her; ᵇyou shall build a house, but you shall not dwell in it; ᶜyou shall plant a vineyard, but shall not gather its grapes. ³¹Your ox *shall be* slaughtered before your eyes, but you shall not eat of it; your donkey *shall be* violently taken away from before you, and shall not be restored to you; your sheep *shall be* given to your enemies, and you shall have no one to rescue *them*. ³²Your sons and your daughters *shall be* given to ᵃanother people, and your eyes shall look and ᵇfail *with longing* for them all day long; and *there shall be* ¹no strength in your ᶜhand. ³³A nation whom you have not known shall eat ᵃthe fruit of your land and the produce of your labor, and you shall be only oppressed and crushed continually. ³⁴So you shall be driven mad because of the sight which your eyes see. ³⁵The LORD will strike you in the knees and on the legs with severe boils which cannot be healed, and from the sole of your foot to the top of your head.

³⁶"The LORD will ᵃbring you and the king whom you set over you to a nation which neither you nor your fathers have known, and ᵇthere you shall serve other gods—wood and stone. ³⁷And you shall become ᵃan¹ astonishment, a proverb, ᵇand a byword among all nations where the LORD will drive you.

³⁸ᵃ"You shall carry much seed out to the field but gather little in, for ᵇthe locust shall ¹consume it. ³⁹You shall plant vineyards and tend *them,* but you shall neither drink *of* the ᵃwine nor gather the *grapes;* for the worms shall eat them. ⁴⁰You shall have olive trees throughout all your territory, but you shall not anoint *yourself* with the oil; for your olives shall drop off. ⁴¹You shall beget sons and daughters, but they shall not be yours; for ᵃthey shall go into captivity. ⁴²Locusts shall ¹consume all your trees and the produce of your land.

⁴³"The alien who *is* among you shall rise higher and higher above you, and you shall come down lower and lower. ⁴⁴He shall lend to you, but you shall not lend to him; he shall be the head, and you shall be the tail.

⁴⁵"Moreover all these curses shall come upon you and pursue and overtake you, until you are destroyed, because you ¹did not obey the voice of the LORD your God, to keep His commandments and His statutes which He commanded you. ⁴⁶And they shall be upon ᵃyou for a sign and a wonder, and on your descendants forever.

⁴⁷ᵃ"Because you did not serve the LORD your God with joy and gladness of heart, ᵇfor the abundance of everything,

---

28:26 ᵃ1 Sam. 17:44; Ps. 79:2
28:27 ᵃEx. 15:26 ᵇ1 Sam. 5:6
28:28 ᵃJer. 4:9
28:29 ᵃJob 5:14
28:30 ᵃ2 Sam. 12:11; Job 31:10; Jer. 8:10 ᵇAmos 5:11; Zeph. 1:13 ᶜDeut. 20:6; Job 31:8; Jer. 12:13; Mic. 6:15
28:32 ᵃ2 Chr. 29:9 ᵇPs. 119:82 ᶜNeh. 5:5
28:33 ᵃLev. 26:16; Jer. 5:15, 17
28:36 ᵃ2 Kin. 17:4, 6; 24:12, 14; 25:7, 11; 2 Chr. 36:1–21; Jer. 39:1–9 ᵇDeut. 4:28; Jer. 16:13
28:37 ᵃ1 Kin. 9:7, 8; Jer. 24:9; 25:9 ᵇPs. 44:14
28:38 ᵃMic. 6:15; Hag. 1:6 ᵇEx. 10:4; Joel 1:4
28:39 ᵃZeph. 1:13
28:41 ᵃLam. 1:5
28:46 ᵃNum. 26:10; Is. 8:18; Ezek. 14:8
28:47 ᵃDeut. 12:7; Neh. 9:35–37 ᵇDeut. 32:15

28:25 ¹a terror   **28:32** ¹nothing you can do   **28:37** ¹a thing of horror
28:38 ¹devour   **28:42** ¹possess   **28:45** ¹did not listen to

48therefore you shall serve your enemies, whom the LORD will send against you, in ahunger, in thirst, in nakedness, and in need of everything; and He bwill put a yoke of iron on your neck until He has destroyed you. 49aThe LORD will bring a nation against you from afar, from the end of the earth, bas swift as the eagle flies, a nation whose language you will not understand, 50a nation of fierce countenance, awhich does not respect the elderly nor show favor to the young. 51And they shall eat the increase of your livestock and the produce of your land, until you are destroyed; they shall not leave you grain or new wine or oil, or the increase of your cattle or the offspring of your flocks, until they have destroyed you.

52"They shall abesiege you at all your gates until your high and fortified walls, in which you trust, come down throughout all your land; and they shall besiege you at all your gates throughout all your land which the LORD your God has given you. 53aYou shall eat the 1fruit of your own body, the flesh of your sons and your daughters whom the LORD your God has given you, in the siege and desperate straits in which your enemy shall distress you. 54The 1sensitive and very refined man among you awill2 be hostile toward his brother, toward bthe wife of his bosom, and toward the rest of his children whom he leaves behind, 55so that he will not give any of them the flesh of his children whom he will eat, because he has nothing left in the siege and desperate straits in which your enemy shall distress you at all your gates. 56The 1tender and 2delicate woman among you, who would not venture to set the sole of her foot on the ground because of her delicateness and sensitivity, 3will refuse to the husband of her bosom, and to her son and her daughter, 57her 1placenta which comes out afrom between her feet and her children whom she bears; for she will eat them secretly for lack of everything in the siege and desperate straits in which your enemy shall distress you at all your gates.

58"If you do not carefully observe all the words of this law that are written in this book, that you may fear athis glorious and awesome name, THE LORD YOUR GOD, 59then the LORD will bring upon you and your descendants aextraordinary plagues—great and prolonged plagues—and serious and prolonged sicknesses. 60Moreover He will bring back on you all athe diseases of Egypt, of which you were afraid, and they shall cling to you. 61Also every sickness and every plague, which is not written in this Book of the Law, will the LORD bring upon you until you are destroyed. 62You ashall be left few in number, whereas you were bas the stars of heaven in multitude, because you would not obey the voice of the LORD your God. 63And it shall be, that just as the LORD arejoiced over you to do you good and multiply you, so the LORD bwill rejoice over you to destroy you and bring you to nothing; and you shall be cplucked1 from off the land which you go to possess.

64"Then the LORD awill scatter you among all peoples, from one end of the earth to the other, and bthere you shall serve other gods, which neither you nor your fathers have known—wood and stone. 65And aamong those nations you

28:48
aLam. 4:4–6
bJer. 28:13, 14

28:49
aIs. 5:26–30;
7:18–20; Jer. 5:15
bJer. 48:40;
49:22;
Lam. 4:19;
Hos. 8:1

28:50
a2 Chr. 36:17

28:52
a2 Kin. 25:1, 2, 4

28:53
aLev. 26:29;
2 Kin. 6:28,
29; Jer. 19:9;
Lam. 2:20; 4:10

28:54
aDeut. 15:9
bDeut. 13:6

28:57
aGen. 49:10

28:58 aEx. 6:3

28:59
aDan. 9:12

28:60
aDeut. 7:15

28:62
aDeut. 4:27
bDeut. 10:22;
Neh. 9:23

28:63
aDeut. 30:9;
Jer. 32:41
bProv. 1:26;
[Is. 1:24]
cJer. 12:14; 45:4

28:64
aLev. 26:33;
Deut. 4:27, 28;
Neh. 1:8;
Jer. 16:13;
Amos 9:9
bDeut. 28:36

28:65 aLam. 1:3;
Amos 9:4

28:53 1offspring   28:54 1Lit. tender   2Lit. his eye shall be evil toward
28:56 1sensitive   2refined   3Lit. her eye shall be evil toward
28:57 1afterbirth   28:63 1torn

shall find no rest, nor shall the sole of your foot have a resting place; [b]but there the LORD will give you a [1]trembling heart, failing eyes, and [c]anguish of soul. [66]Your life shall hang in doubt before you; you shall fear day and night, and have no assurance of life. [67a]In the morning you shall say, 'Oh, that it were evening!' And at evening you shall say, 'Oh, that it were morning!' because of the fear which terrifies your heart, and [b]because of the sight which your eyes see.

[68]"And the LORD [a]will take you back to Egypt in ships, by the way of which I said to you, [b]'You shall never see it again.' And there you shall be offered for sale to your enemies as male and female slaves, but no one will buy *you*."

THE COVENANT RENEWED IN MOAB

29 These *are* the words of the covenant which the LORD commanded Moses to make with the children of Israel in the land of Moab, besides the [a]covenant which He made with them in Horeb.

[2]Now Moses called all Israel and said to them: [a]"You have seen all that the LORD did before your eyes in the land of Egypt, to Pharaoh and to all his servants and to all his land— [3a]the great trials which your eyes have seen, the signs, and those great wonders. [4]Yet [a]the LORD has not given you a heart to [1]perceive and eyes to see and ears to hear, to this *very* day. [5a]And I have led you forty years in the wilderness. [b]Your clothes have not worn out on you, and your sandals have not worn out on your feet. [6a]You have not eaten bread, nor have you drunk wine or *similar* drink, that you may know that I *am* the LORD your God. [7]And when you came to this place, [a]Sihon king of Heshbon and Og king of Bashan came out against us to battle, and we conquered them. [8]We took their land and [a]gave it as an inheritance to the Reubenites, to the Gadites, and to half the tribe of Manasseh. [9]Therefore [a]keep the words of this covenant, and do them, that you may [b]prosper in all that you do.

[10]"All of you stand today before the LORD your God: your leaders and your tribes and your elders and your officers, all the men of Israel, [11]your little ones and your wives—also the stranger who *is* in your camp, from [a]the one who cuts your wood to the one who draws your water— [12]that you may enter into covenant with the LORD your God, and [a]into His oath, which the LORD your God makes with you today, [13]that He may [a]establish you today as a people for Himself, and *that* He may be God to you, [b]just as He has spoken to you, and [c]just as He has sworn to your fathers, to Abraham, Isaac, and Jacob.

[14]"I make this covenant and this oath, [a]not with you alone, [15]but with *him* who stands here with us today before the LORD our God, [a]as well as with *him* who *is* not here with us today [16](for you know that we dwelt in the land of Egypt and that we came through the nations which you passed by, [17]and you saw their [1]abominations and their idols which *were* among them—wood and stone and silver and gold); [18]so that there may not be among you man or woman or family or tribe, [a]whose heart turns away today from the LORD our God, to go *and* serve the gods of these nations, [b]and that there may not be among you a root bearing [c]bitterness or wormwood; [19]and

---

28:65
[b]Lev. 26:36
[c]Lev. 26:16

28:67 [a]Job 7:4
[b]Deut. 28:34

28:68 [a]Jer. 43:7;
Hos. 8:13
[b]Deut. 17:16

29:1 [a]Lev. 26:46;
Deut. 5:2, 3

29:2 [a]Ex. 19:4;
Deut. 11:7

29:3
[a]Deut. 4:34;
7:19

29:4
[a][Is. 6:9, 10;
Ezek. 12:2];
Matt. 13:14;
[Acts 28:26, 27];
Rom. 11:8;
[Eph. 4:18]

29:5 [a]Deut. 1:3;
8:2 [b]Deut. 8:4

29:6 [a]Ex. 16:12;
Deut. 8:3

29:7
[a]Num. 21:23, 24;
Deut. 2:26—3:3

29:8
[a]Num. 32:33;
Deut. 3:12, 13

29:9 [a]Deut. 4:6;
1 Kin. 2:3
[b]Josh. 1:7

29:11
[a]Josh. 9:21,
23, 27

29:12
[a]Neh. 10:29

29:13
[a]Deut. 28:9
[b]Ex. 6:7
[c]Gen. 17:7, 8

29:14
[a][Jer. 31:31;
Heb. 8:7, 8]

29:15 [a]Acts 2:39

29:18
[a]Deut. 11:16
[b]Heb. 12:15
[c]Deut. 32:32;
Acts 8:23

28:65 [1]anxious   29:4 [1]understand or know   29:17 [1]detestable things

so it may not happen, when he hears the words of this curse, that he blesses himself in his heart, saying, 'I shall have peace, even though I [1]follow the [a]dictates of my heart'—[b]as though the drunkard could be included with the sober.

20[a]"The LORD would not spare him; for then [b]the anger of the LORD and [c]His jealousy would burn against that man, and every curse that is written in this book would settle on him, and the LORD [d]would blot out his name from under heaven. 21And the LORD [a]would separate him from all the tribes of Israel for adversity, according to all the curses of the covenant that are written in this Book of the [b]Law, 22so that the coming generation of your children who rise up after you, and the foreigner who comes from a far land, would say, when they [a]see the plagues of that land and the sicknesses which the LORD has laid on it:

23"The whole land is brimstone, [a]salt, and burning; it is not sown, nor does it bear, nor does any grass grow there, [b]like the overthrow of Sodom and Gomorrah, Admah, and Zeboiim, which the LORD overthrew in His anger and His wrath.' 24All nations would say, [a]'Why has the LORD done so to this land? What does the heat of this great anger mean?' 25Then people would say: 'Because they have forsaken the covenant of the LORD God of their fathers, which He made with them when He brought them out of the land of Egypt; 26for they went and served other gods and worshiped them, gods that they did not know and that He had not given to them. 27Then the anger of the LORD was aroused against this land, [a]to bring on it every curse that is written in this book. 28And the LORD [a]uprooted them from their land in anger, in wrath, and in great indignation, and cast them into another land, as it is this day.'

29"The secret things belong to the LORD our God, but those things which are revealed belong to us and to our children forever, that we may do all the words of this law.

THE BLESSING OF RETURNING TO GOD

30 "Now [a]it shall come to pass, when [b]all these things come upon you, the blessing and the [c]curse which I have set before you, and [d]you [1]call them to mind among all the nations where the LORD your God drives you, 2and you [a]return to the LORD your God and obey His voice, according to all that I command you today, you and your children, with all your heart and with all your soul, 3[a]that the LORD your God will bring you back from captivity, and have compassion on you, and [b]gather you again from all the nations where the LORD your God has scattered you. 4[a]If any of you are driven out to the farthest parts under heaven, from there the LORD your God will gather you, and from there He will bring you. 5Then the LORD your God will bring you to the land which your fathers possessed, and you shall possess it. He will prosper you and multiply you more than your fathers. 6And [a]the LORD your God will circumcise your heart and the heart of your descendants, to love the LORD your God with all your heart and with all your soul, that you may live.

7"Also the LORD your God will put all these [a]curses on your enemies and on those who hate you, who persecuted

---

29:19 [a]Jer. 3:17; 7:24 [b]Is. 30:1
29:20 [a]Ezek. 14:7 [b]Ps. 74:1 [c]Ps. 79:5; Ezek. 23:25 [d]Ex. 32:33; Deut. 9:14; 2 Kin. 14:27
29:21 [a][Matt. 24:51] [b]Deut. 30:10
29:22 [a]Jer. 19:8; 49:17; 50:13
29:23 [a]Jer. 17:6; Zeph. 2:9 [b]Gen. 19:24, 25; Is. 1:9; Jer. 20:16; Hos. 11:8
29:24 [a]1 Kin. 9:8; Jer. 22:8
29:27 [a]Dan. 9:11
29:28 [a]1 Kin. 14:15; 2 Chr. 7:20; Ps. 52:5; Prov. 2:22
30:1 [a]Lev. 26:40 [b]Deut. 28:2 [c]Deut. 28:15–45 [d]Deut. 4:29, 30
30:2 [a]Deut. 4:29, 30; Neh. 1:9; Is. 55:7; Lam. 3:40; Joel 2:12
30:3 [a]Ps. 106:45; Jer. 29:14; Lam. 3:22, 32 [b]Ps. 147:2; Jer. 32:37; Ezek. 34:13
30:4 [a]Deut. 28:64; Neh. 1:9; Is. 62:11
30:6 [a]Deut. 10:16; Jer. 32:39; Ezek. 11:19
30:7 [a]Is. 54:15–17; Jer. 30:16, 20

29:19 [1]walk in the stubbornness or imagination   30:1 [1]Lit. cause them to return to your heart

you. [8]And you will [a]again obey the voice of the LORD and do all His commandments which I command you today. [9a]The LORD your God will make you abound in all the work of your hand, in the [1]fruit of your body, in the increase of your livestock, and in the produce of your land for good. For the LORD will again [b]rejoice over you for good as He rejoiced over your fathers, [10]if you obey the voice of the LORD your God, to keep His commandments and His statutes which are written in this Book of the Law, *and* if you turn to the LORD your God with all your heart and with all your soul.

THE CHOICE OF LIFE OR DEATH

[11]"For this commandment which I command you today [a]*is* [1]not *too* mysterious for you, nor *is* it far off. [12a]It *is* not in heaven, that you should say, 'Who will ascend into heaven for us and bring it to us, that we may hear it and do it?' [13]Nor *is* it beyond the sea, that you should say, 'Who will go over the sea for us and bring it to us, that we may hear it and do it?' [14]But the word *is* very near you, [a]in your mouth and in your heart, that you may do it.

[15]"See, [a]I have set before you today life and good, death and evil, [16]in that I command you today to love the LORD your God, to walk in His ways, and to keep His commandments, His statutes, and His judgments, that you may live and multiply; and the LORD your God will bless you in the land which you go to possess. [17]But if your heart turns away so that you do not hear, and are drawn away, and worship other gods and serve them, [18a]I announce to you today that you shall surely perish; you shall not prolong *your* days in the land which you cross over the Jordan to go in and possess. [19a]I call heaven and earth as witnesses today against you, *that* [b]I have set before you life and death, blessing and cursing; therefore choose life, that both you and your descendants may live; [20]that you may love the LORD your God, that you may obey His voice, and that you may cling to Him, for He *is* your [a]life and the length of your days; and that you may dwell in the land which the LORD swore to your fathers, to Abraham, Isaac, and Jacob, to give them."

JOSHUA THE NEW LEADER OF ISRAEL
(Num. 27:12–23)

31 Then Moses went and spoke these words to all Israel. [2]And he said to them: "I [a]*am* one hundred and twenty years old today. I can no longer [b]go out and come in. Also the LORD has said to me, [c]'You shall not cross over this Jordan.' [3]The LORD your God [a]Himself crosses over before you; He will destroy these nations from before you, and you shall dispossess them. [b]Joshua himself crosses over before you, just [c]as the LORD has said. [4a]And the LORD will do to them [b]as He did to Sihon and Og, the kings of the Amorites and their land, when He destroyed them. [5a]The LORD will give them over to you, that you may do to them according to every commandment which I have commanded you. [6a]Be strong and of good courage, [b]do not fear nor be afraid of them; for the LORD your God, [c]He *is* the One who goes with you. [d]He will not leave you nor forsake you."

Cross references (margin)

30:8
[a]Zeph. 3:20

30:9
[a]Deut. 28:11
[b]Deut. 28:63;
Jer. 32:41

30:11 [a]Is. 45:19

30:12
[a]Prov. 30:4;
Rom. 10:6–8

30:14
[a]Rom. 10:8

30:15
[a]Deut. 30:1, 19

30:18
[a]Deut. 4:26;
8:19

30:19
[a]Deut. 4:26
[b]Deut. 30:15

30:20 [a]Ps. 27:1;
[John 11:25; 14:6;
Col. 3:4]

31:2 [a]Ex. 7:7;
Deut. 34:7
[b]Num. 27:17;
1 Kin. 3:7
[c]Num. 20:12

31:3 [a]Deut. 9:3;
Josh. 11:23
[b]Num. 27:18
[c]Num. 27:21

31:4 [a]Deut. 3:21
[b]Num. 21:24, 33

31:5 [a]Deut. 7:2;
20:10–20

31:6
[a]Josh. 10:25;
1 Chr. 22:13
[b]Deut. 1:29
[c]Deut. 20:4
[d]Josh. 1:5;
Heb. 13:5

30:9 [1]offspring   **30:11** [1]*not hidden from*

7Then Moses called Joshua and said to him in the sight of all Israel, a"Be strong and of good courage, for you must go with this people to the land which the LORD has sworn to their fathers to give them, and you shall cause them to inherit it. 8And the LORD, aHe *is* the One who goes before you. bHe will be with you, He will not leave you nor forsake you; do not fear nor be dismayed."

THE LAW TO BE READ EVERY SEVEN YEARS

9So Moses wrote this law aand delivered it to the priests, the sons of Levi, bwho bore the ark of the covenant of the LORD, and to all the elders of Israel. 10And Moses commanded them, saying: "At the end of *every* seven years, at the appointed time in the ayear of release, bat the Feast of Tabernacles, 11when all Israel comes to aappear before the LORD your God in the bplace which He chooses, cyou shall read this law before all Israel in their hearing. 12aGather the people together, men and women and little ones, and the stranger who *is* within your gates, that they may hear and that they may learn to fear the LORD your God and carefully observe all the words of this law, 13and *that* their children, awho have not known it, bmay hear and learn to fear the LORD your God as long as you live in the land which you cross the Jordan to possess."

PREDICTION OF ISRAEL'S REBELLION

14Then the LORD said to Moses, a"Behold, the days approach when you must die; call Joshua, and present yourselves in the tabernacle of meeting, that bI may 1inaugurate him."

So Moses and Joshua went and presented themselves in the tabernacle of meeting. 15Now athe LORD appeared at the tabernacle in a pillar of cloud, and the pillar of cloud stood above the door of the tabernacle.

16And the LORD said to Moses: "Behold, you will 1rest with your fathers; and this people will arise and bplay the harlot with the gods of the foreigners of the land, where they go *to be* among them, and they will cforsake Me and dbreak My covenant which I have made with them. 17Then My anger shall be aaroused against them in that day, and bI will forsake them, and I will chide My face from them, and they shall be 1devoured. And many evils and troubles shall befall them, so that they will say in that day, d'Have not these evils come upon us because our God *is* enot among us?' 18And aI will surely hide My face in that day because of all the evil which they have done, in that they have turned to other gods.

19"Now therefore, write down this song for yourselves, and teach it to the children of Israel; put it in their mouths, that this song may be aa witness for Me against the children of Israel. 20When I have brought them to the land flowing with milk and honey, of which I swore to their fathers, and they have eaten and filled themselves aand grown fat, bthen they will turn to other gods and serve them; and they will provoke Me and break My covenant. 21Then it shall be, awhen many evils and troubles have come upon them, that this song will testify against them as a witness; for it will not be forgotten in the mouths of their descendants, for bI know the inclination

---

31:7
aNum. 27:19;
Deut. 31:23;
Josh. 1:6

31:8 aEx. 13:21
bDeut. 31:6;
Josh. 1:5;
1 Chr. 28:20;
Heb. 13:5

31:9
aDeut. 17:18;
31:25, 26
bNum. 4:5, 6,
15; Deut. 10:8;
31:25, 26;
Josh. 3:3

31:10
aDeut. 15:1, 2
bLev. 23:34;
Deut. 16:13

31:11
aDeut. 16:16
bDeut. 12:5
cJosh. 8:34;
2 Kin. 23:2

31:12 aDeut. 4:10

31:13 aDeut. 11:2
bPs. 78:6, 7

31:14
aNum. 27:13
bNum. 27:19;
Deut. 3:28

31:15 aEx. 33:9

31:16
aDeut. 29:22
bEx. 34:15;
Deut. 4:25–28;
Judg. 2:11, 12,
17 cDeut. 32:15
dJudg. 2:20

31:17
aJudg. 2:14; 6:13
b2 Chr. 15:2
cDeut. 32:20
dJudg. 6:13
eNum. 14:42

31:18
aDeut. 31:17;
[Is. 1:15, 16]

31:19
aDeut. 31:22, 26

31:20
aDeut. 32:15–17
bDeut. 31:16

31:21
aDeut. 31:17
bHos. 5:3

31:14 1commission   31:16 1Die and join your ancestors   31:17 1consumed

^cof their behavior today, even before I have brought them to the land of which I swore *to give them.*"

²²Therefore Moses wrote this song the same day, and taught it to the children of Israel. ^{23a}Then He inaugurated Joshua the son of Nun, and said, ^b"Be strong and of good courage; for you shall bring the children of Israel into the land of which I swore to them, and I will be with you."

²⁴So it was, when Moses had completed writing the words of this law in a book, when they were finished, ²⁵that Moses commanded the Levites, who bore the ark of the covenant of the LORD, saying: ²⁶"Take this Book of the Law, ^aand put it beside the ark of the covenant of the LORD your God, that it may be there ^bas a witness against you; ^{27a}for I know your rebellion and your ^bstiff neck. *If* today, while I am yet alive with you, you have been rebellious against the LORD, then how much more after my death? ²⁸Gather to me all the elders of your tribes, and your officers, that I may speak these words in their hearing ^aand call heaven and earth to witness against them. ²⁹For I know that after my death you will ^abecome utterly corrupt, and turn aside from the way which I have commanded you. And ^bevil will befall you ^cin the latter days, because you will do evil in the sight of the LORD, to provoke Him to anger through the work of your hands."

THE SONG OF MOSES

³⁰Then Moses spoke in the hearing of all the assembly of Israel the words of this song until they were ended:

32 "Give ^aear, O heavens, and I will speak;
And hear, O ^bearth, the words of my mouth.
2   Let ^amy ¹teaching drop as the rain,
     My speech distill as the dew,
     ^bAs raindrops on the tender herb,
     And as showers on the grass.
3   For I proclaim the ^aname of the LORD:
     ^bAscribe greatness to our God.
4   *He is* ^athe Rock, ^bHis work *is* perfect;
     For all His ways *are* justice,
     ^cA God of truth and ^dwithout injustice;
     Righteous and upright *is* He.

5   "They^a have corrupted themselves;
     They are not His children,
     Because of their blemish:
     A ^bperverse and crooked generation.
6   Do you thus ^adeal¹ with the LORD,
     O foolish and unwise people?
     Is He not ^byour Father, *who* ^cbought you?
     Has He not ^dmade you and established you?

7   "Remember^a the days of old,
     Consider the years of many generations.
     ^bAsk your father, and he will show you;
     Your elders, and they will tell you:
8   When the Most High ^adivided their inheritance to the
          nations,
     When He ^bseparated the sons of Adam,

31:21
^cAmos 5:25, 26

31:23
^aNum. 27:23;
Deut. 31:14
^bDeut. 31:7

31:26
^a2 Kin. 22:8
^bDeut. 31:19

31:27
^aDeut. 9:7, 24
^bEx. 32:9;
Deut. 9:6, 13

31:28
^aDeut. 30:19

31:29
^aDeut. 32:5;
Judg. 2:19;
[Acts 20:29, 30]
^bDeut. 28:15
^cGen. 49:1;
Deut. 4:30

32:1
^aDeut. 4:26;
Ps. 50:4; Is. 1:2
^bJer. 6:19

32:2
^aIs. 55:10, 11
^bPs. 72:6

32:3
^aDeut. 28:58
^b1 Chr. 29:11

32:4
^aDeut. 32:15,
18, 30; Ps. 18:2
^b2 Sam. 22:31
^cDeut. 7:9;
Is. 65:16;
Jer. 10:10
^dJob 34:10

32:5
^aDeut. 4:25;
31:29 ^bPhil. 2:15

32:6 ^aPs. 116:12
^bEx. 4:22;
Deut. 1:31;
Is. 63:16
^cPs. 74:2
^dDeut. 32:15

32:7 ^aPs. 44:1
^bEx. 12:26; 13:14;
Ps. 78:5–8

32:8 ^aActs 17:26
^bGen. 11:8

32:2 ¹*doctrine*   **32:6** ¹*repay the*

He set the boundaries of the peoples
According to the number of the [1]children of Israel.
9 For [a]the LORD's portion *is* His people;
Jacob *is* the place of His inheritance.

10 "He found him [a]in a desert land
And in the wasteland, a howling wilderness;
He encircled him, He instructed him,
He [b]kept him as the [1]apple of His eye.
11 [a]As an eagle stirs up its nest,
Hovers over its young,
Spreading out its wings, taking them up,
Carrying them on its wings,
12 *So* the LORD alone led him,
And *there was* no foreign god with him.

13 "He[a] made him ride in the heights of the earth,
That he might eat the produce of the fields;
He made him draw honey from the rock,
And oil from the flinty rock;
14 Curds from the cattle, and milk of the flock,
[a]With fat of lambs;
And rams of the breed of Bashan, and goats,
With the choicest wheat;
And you drank wine, the [b]blood of the grapes.

15 "But Jeshurun grew fat and kicked;
[a]You grew fat, you grew thick,
You are obese!
Then he [b]forsook God *who* [c]made him,
And scornfully esteemed the [d]Rock of his salvation.
16 [a]They provoked Him to jealousy with foreign *gods;*
With [1]abominations they provoked Him to anger.
17 [a]They sacrificed to demons, not to God,
To gods they did not know,
To new *gods,* new arrivals
That your fathers did not fear.
18 [a]Of the Rock *who* begot you, you are unmindful,
And have [b]forgotten the God who fathered you.

19 "And[a] when the LORD saw *it,* He spurned *them,*
Because of the provocation of His sons and His
daughters.
20 And He said: 'I will hide My face from them,
I will see what their end *will be,*
For they *are* a perverse generation,
[a]Children in whom *is* no faith.
21 [a]They have provoked Me to jealousy by *what* is not God;
They have moved Me to anger [b]by their [1]foolish idols.
But [c]I will provoke them to jealousy by *those who are* not
a nation;
I will move them to anger by a foolish nation.
22 For [a]a fire is kindled in My anger,
And shall burn to the [1]lowest [2]hell;
It shall consume the earth with her increase,
And set on fire the foundations of the mountains.

32:9 [a]Ex. 19:5
32:10 [a]Jer. 2:6;
Hos. 13:5
[b]Ps. 17:8;
Prov. 7:2;
Zech. 2:8
32:11 [a]Is. 31:5
32:13 [a]Is. 58:14
32:14 [a]Ps. 81:16
[b]Gen. 49:11
32:15
[a]Deut. 31:20
[b]Is. 1:4 [c]Is. 51:13
[d]Ps. 95:1
32:16
[a]Ps. 78:58;
1 Cor. 10:22
32:17 [a]Rev. 9:20
32:18 [a]Is. 17:10
[b]Jer. 2:32
32:19
[a]Judg. 2:14
32:20
[a]Matt. 17:17
32:21 [a]Ps. 78:58
[b]Ps. 31:6
[c]Rom. 10:19
32:22
[a]Num. 16:33–35;
Ps. 18:7, 8;
Lam. 4:11

32:8 [1]LXX, DSS *angels of God;* Symmachus, Lat. *sons of God*   32:10 [1]*pupil*
32:16 [1]*detestable acts*   32:21 [1]*foolishness,* lit. *vanities*   32:22 [1]*lowest part
of*   [2]Or *Sheol*

23 'I will ªheap disasters on them;
    ᵇI will spend My arrows on them.
24 *They shall be* wasted with hunger,
    Devoured by pestilence and bitter destruction;
    I will also send against them the ªteeth of beasts,
    With the poison of serpents of the dust.
25 The sword shall destroy outside;
    There shall be terror within
    For the young man and virgin,
    The nursing child with the man of gray hairs.

32:23
ªEx. 32:12;
Deut. 29:21, 24
ᵇPs. 7:12, 13

32:24
ªLev. 26:22

32:26
ªEzek. 20:23

32:27
ªIs. 10:12–15

32:29 ªPs. 81:13;
[Luke 19:42]
ᵇDeut. 31:29

32:30
ªJudg. 2:14;
Ps. 44:12

32:31
ª[1 Sam. 4:7, 8;
Jer. 40:2, 3]

32:32 ªIs. 1:8–10

32:33 ªPs. 58:4
ᵇRom. 3:13

32:34
ª[Jer. 2:22]

32:35 ªPs. 94:1;
Rom. 12:19;
Heb. 10:30
ᵇ2 Pet. 2:3

32:36
ªPs. 135:14;
Heb. 10:30
ᵇPs. 106:45;
Jer. 31:20
ᶜ2 Kin. 14:26

32:37
ªJudg. 10:14;
Jer. 2:28

32:39
ªIs. 41:4; 43:10
ᵇDeut. 32:12;
Is. 45:5
ᶜ1 Sam. 2:6;
Ps. 68:20

26 ªI would have said, "I will dash them in pieces,
    I will make the memory of them to cease from among
        men,"
27 Had I not feared the wrath of the enemy,
    Lest their adversaries should misunderstand,
    Lest they should say, ª"Our hand *is* high;
    And it is not the LORD who has done all this."'

28 "For they *are* a nation void of counsel,
    Nor *is there any* understanding in them.
29 ªOh, that they were wise, *that* they understood this,
    That they would consider their ᵇlatter end!
30 How could one chase a thousand,
    And two put ten thousand to flight,
    Unless their Rock ªhad sold them,
    And the LORD had surrendered them?
31 For their rock *is* not like our Rock,
    ªEven our enemies themselves *being* judges.
32 For ªtheir vine *is* of the vine of Sodom
    And of the fields of Gomorrah;
    Their grapes *are* grapes of gall,
    Their clusters *are* bitter.
33 Their wine *is* ªthe poison of serpents,
    And the cruel ᵇvenom of cobras.

34 '*Is* this not ªlaid up in store with Me,
    Sealed up among My treasures?
35 ªVengeance is Mine, and recompense;
    Their foot shall slip in *due* time;
    ᵇFor the day of their calamity *is* at hand,
    And the things to come hasten upon them.'

36 "Forª the LORD will judge His people
    ᵇAnd have compassion on His servants,
    When He sees that *their* power is gone,
    And ᶜ*there is* no one *remaining,* bond or free.
37 He will say: ª'Where *are* their gods,
    The rock in which they sought refuge?
38 Who ate the fat of their sacrifices,
    And drank the wine of their drink offering?
    Let them rise and help you,
    And be your refuge.

39 'Now see that ªI, *even* I, *am* He,
    And ᵇ*there is* no God besides Me;
    ᶜI kill and I make alive;
    I wound and I heal;
    Nor *is there any* who can deliver from My hand.
40 For I raise My hand to heaven,
    And say, "*As* I live forever,

41 [a]If I [1]whet My glittering sword,
And My hand takes hold on judgment,
I will render vengeance to My enemies,
And repay those who hate Me.
42 I will make My arrows drunk with blood,
And My sword shall devour flesh,
With the blood of the slain and the captives,
From the heads of the leaders of the enemy.' "

43 "Rejoice,[a] O Gentiles, *with* His [1]people;
For He will [b]avenge the blood of His servants,
And render vengeance to His adversaries;
He [c]will provide atonement for His land *and* His people."

[44]So Moses came with [1]Joshua the son of Nun and spoke all the words of this song in the hearing of the people. [45]Moses finished speaking all these words to all Israel, [46]and he said to them: [a]"Set your hearts on all the words which I testify among you today, which you shall command your [b]children to be careful to observe—all the words of this law. [47]For it *is* not a [1]futile thing for you, because it *is* your [a]life, and by this word you shall prolong *your* days in the land which you cross over the Jordan to possess."

MOSES TO DIE ON MOUNT NEBO

[48]Then the LORD spoke to Moses that very same day, saying: [49a]"Go up this mountain of the Abarim, Mount Nebo, which *is* in the land of Moab, across from Jericho; view the land of Canaan, which I give to the children of Israel as a possession; [50]and die on the mountain which you ascend, and be [1]gathered to your people, just as [a]Aaron your brother died on Mount Hor and was gathered to his people; [51]because [a]you trespassed against Me among the children of Israel at the waters of [1]Meribah Kadesh, in the Wilderness of Zin, because you [b]did not hallow Me in the midst of the children of Israel. [52a]Yet you shall see the land before *you,* though you shall not go there, into the land which I am giving to the children of Israel."

MOSES' FINAL BLESSING ON ISRAEL

33 Now this *is* [a]the blessing with which Moses [b]the man of God blessed the children of Israel before his death. [2]And he said:

[a]"The LORD came from Sinai,
And dawned on them from [b]Seir;
He shone forth from [c]Mount Paran,
And He came with [d]ten thousands of saints;
From His right hand
Came a fiery law for them.
3 Yes, [a]He loves the people;
[b]All His saints *are* in Your hand;
They [c]sit down at Your feet;
Everyone [d]receives Your words.
4 [a]Moses [1]commanded a law for us,
[b]A heritage of the congregation of Jacob.

32:41 [a]Is. 1:24;
66:16;
Jer. 50:28–32

32:43
[a]Rom. 15:10
[b]2 Kin. 9:7;
Rev. 6:10; 19:2
[c]Ps. 65:3; 79:9;
85:1

32:46
[a]Ezek. 40:4;
44:5 [b]Deut. 11:19

32:47
[a]Deut. 8:3;
30:15–20

32:49
[a]Num. 27:12–14;
Deut. 3:27

32:50
[a]Num. 20:25,
28; 33:38

32:51
[a]Num. 20:11–13
[b]Lev. 10:3

32:52
[a]Num. 27:12;
Deut. 34:1–5

33:1 [a]Gen. 49:28
[b]Ps. 90

33:2 [a]Ex. 19:18,
20; Ps. 68:8,
17; Hab. 3:3
[b]Deut. 2:1, 4
[c]Num. 10:12
[d]Dan. 7:10;
Acts 7:53;
Rev. 5:11

33:3 [a]Ps. 47:4;
Hos. 11:1
[b]1 Sam. 2:9
[c][Luke 10:39]
[d]Prov. 2:1

33:4 [a]Deut. 4:2;
John 1:17; 7:19
[b]Ps. 119:111

32:41 [1]*sharpen*   32:43 [1]DSS fragment adds *And let all the gods (angels) worship Him;* cf. LXX and Heb. 1:6   32:44 [1]Heb. *Hoshea,* Num. 13:8, 16   32:47 [1]*vain*   32:50 [1]Join your ancestors   32:51 [1]Lit. *Contention at Kadesh*   33:4 [1]*charged us with*

5 And He was ᵃKing in ᵇJeshurun,
　When the leaders of the people were gathered,
　All the tribes of Israel together.

6 "Let ᵃReuben live, and not die,
　Nor let his men be few."

7And this he said of ᵃJudah:

"Hear, LORD, the voice of Judah,
　And bring him to his people;
ᵇLet his hands be sufficient for him,
　And may You be ᶜa help against his enemies."

8And of ᵃLevi he said:

ᵇ"*Let* Your ¹Thummim and Your Urim *be* with Your holy one,
ᶜWhom You tested at Massah,
　And with whom You contended at the waters of Meribah,
9 ᵃWho says of his father and mother,
　'I have not ᵇseen them';
ᶜNor did he acknowledge his brothers,
　Or know his own children;
For ᵈthey have observed Your word
　And kept Your covenant.
10 ᵃThey shall teach Jacob Your judgments,
　And Israel Your law.
　They shall put incense before You,
ᵇAnd a whole burnt sacrifice on Your altar.
11 Bless his substance, LORD,
　And ᵃaccept the work of his hands;
　Strike the loins of those who rise against him,
　And of those who hate him, that they rise not again."

12Of Benjamin he said:

"The beloved of the LORD shall dwell in safety by Him,
　Who shelters him all the day long;
　And he shall dwell between His shoulders."

13And of Joseph he said:

ᵃ"Blessed of the LORD *is* his land,
　With the precious things of heaven, with the ᵇdew,
　And the deep lying beneath,
14 With the precious fruits of the sun,
　With the precious produce of the months,
15 With the best things of ᵃthe ancient mountains,
　With the precious things ᵇof the everlasting hills,
16 With the precious things of the earth and its fullness,
　And the favor of ᵃHim who dwelt in the bush.
　Let *the blessing* come ᵇ'on the head of Joseph,
　And on the crown of the head of him *who was* separate
　　from his brothers.'
17 His glory *is like* a ᵃfirstborn bull,
　And his horns *like* the ᵇhorns of the wild ox;
　Together with them
ᶜHe shall push the peoples
　To the ends of the earth;
ᵈThey *are* the ten thousands of Ephraim,
　And they *are* the thousands of Manasseh."

33:8 ¹Lit. *Perfections and Your Lights*

Cross references (left margin):

33:5 ᵃEx. 15:18
ᵇDeut. 32:15

33:6
ᵃGen. 49:3, 4

33:7
ᵃGen. 49:8–12
ᵇGen. 49:8
ᶜPs. 146:5

33:8 ᵃGen. 49:5
ᵇEx. 28:30;
Lev. 8:8
ᶜNum. 20:2–13;
Deut. 6:2, 3, 16;
Ps. 81:7

33:9
ᵃ[Num. 25:5–8;
Matt. 10:37;
19:29]
ᵇ[Gen. 29:32]
ᶜEx. 32:26–28
ᵈMal. 2:5, 6

33:10 ᵃLev. 10:11;
Deut. 31:9–13;
Mal. 2:7
ᵇLev. 1:9;
Ps. 51:19

33:11
ᵃ2 Sam. 24:23;
Ezek. 20:40

33:13
ᵃGen. 49:22–26
ᵇGen. 27:28

33:15
ᵃGen. 49:26
ᵇHab. 3:6

33:16
ᵃEx. 3:2–4;
Acts 7:30–35
ᵇGen. 49:26

33:17 ᵃ1 Chr. 5:1
ᵇNum. 23:22
ᶜ1 Kin. 22:11;
Ps. 44:5
ᵈGen. 48:19

18And of Zebulun he said:

a"Rejoice, Zebulun, in your going out,
And Issachar in your tents!

19 They shall acall the peoples *to* the mountain;
There bthey shall offer sacrifices of righteousness;
For they shall partake *of* the abundance of the seas
And *of* treasures hidden in the sand."

20And of Gad he said:

"Blessed *is* he who aenlarges Gad;
He dwells as a lion,
And tears the arm and the crown of his head.

21 aHe provided the first *part* for himself,
Because a lawgiver's portion was reserved there.
bHe came *with* the heads of the people;
He administered the justice of the LORD,
And His judgments with Israel."

22And of Dan he said:

"Dan *is* a lion's whelp;
aHe shall leap from Bashan."

23And of Naphtali he said:

"O Naphtali, asatisfied with favor,
And full of the blessing of the LORD,
bPossess the west and the south."

24And of Asher he said:

a"Asher *is* most blessed of sons;
Let him be favored by his brothers,
And let him bdip his foot in oil.

25 Your sandals *shall be* airon and bronze;
As your days, *so shall* your strength *be*.

26 "*There is* ano one like the God of bJeshurun,
cWho rides the heavens to help you,
And in His excellency on the clouds.

27 The eternal God *is your* arefuge,
And underneath *are* the everlasting arms;
bHe will thrust out the enemy from before you,
And will say, 'Destroy!'

28 Then aIsrael shall dwell in safety,
bThe fountain of Jacob calone,
In a land of grain and new wine;
His dheavens shall also drop dew.

29 aHappy *are* you, O Israel!
bWho *is* like you, a people saved by the LORD,
cThe shield of your help
And the sword of your majesty!
Your enemies dshall submit to you,
And eyou shall tread down their 1high places."

MOSES DIES ON MOUNT NEBO

34 Then Moses went up from the plains of Moab ato Mount Nebo, to the top of Pisgah, which is across from Jericho. And the LORD showed him all the land of Gilead as far

33:18
aGen. 49:13–15
33:19 aEx. 15:17;
Ps. 2:6; Is. 2:3
bPs. 4:5; 51:19
33:20
a1 Chr. 12:8
33:21
aNum. 32:16, 17
bJosh. 4:12
33:22
aGen. 49:16, 17;
Josh. 19:47
33:23
aGen. 49:21
bJosh. 19:32
33:24
aGen. 49:20
bJob 29:6
33:25
aDeut. 8:9
33:26 aEx. 15:11;
Deut. 4:35;
Ps. 86:8;
Jer. 10:6
bDeut. 32:15
cDeut. 10:14;
Ps. 68:3, 33, 34;
104:3
33:27 a[Ps. 90:1;
91:2, 9]
bDeut. 9:3–5
33:28
aDeut. 33:12;
Jer. 23:6; 33:16
bDeut. 8:7, 8
cNum. 23:9
dGen. 27:28
33:29 aPs. 144:15
bDeut. 4:32–34;
2 Sam. 7:23
cGen. 15:1;
Ps. 115:9
dPs. 18:44; 66:3
eNum. 33:52
34:1
aNum. 27:12;
Deut. 32:49

33:29 1Places for pagan worship

as Dan, ²all Naphtali and the land of Ephraim and Manasseh, all the land of Judah as far as the ¹Western Sea, ³the South, and the plain of the Valley of Jericho, ᵃthe city of palm trees, as far as Zoar. ⁴Then the LORD said to him, ᵃ"This *is* the land of which I swore to give Abraham, Isaac, and Jacob, saying, 'I will give it to your descendants.' ᵇI have caused you to see *it* with your eyes, but you shall not cross over there."

⁵ᵃSo Moses the servant of the LORD died there in the land of Moab, according to the word of the LORD. ⁶And He buried him in a valley in the land of Moab, opposite Beth Peor; but ᵃno one knows his grave to this day. ⁷ᵃMoses *was* one hundred and twenty years old when he died. ᵇHis ¹eyes were not dim nor his natural vigor ²diminished. ⁸And the children of Israel wept for Moses in the plains of Moab ᵃthirty days. So the days of weeping *and* mourning for Moses ended.

⁹Now Joshua the son of Nun was full of the ᵃspirit of wisdom, for ᵇMoses had laid his hands on him; so the children of Israel heeded him, and did as the LORD had commanded Moses.

¹⁰But since then there ᵃhas not arisen in Israel a prophet like Moses, ᵇwhom the LORD knew face to face, ¹¹in all ᵃthe signs and wonders which the LORD sent him to do in the land of Egypt, before Pharaoh, before all his servants, and in all his land, ¹²and by all that mighty power and all the great terror which Moses performed in the sight of all Israel.

34:3
ᵃ2 Chr. 28:15

34:4 ᵃGen. 12:7
ᵇDeut. 3:27

34:5
ᵃNum. 20:12;
Deut. 32:50;
Josh. 1:1, 2

34:6 ᵃJude 9

34:7 ᵃDeut. 31:2
ᵇGen. 27:1;
48:10

34:8
ᵃGen. 50:3, 10

34:9 ᵃIs. 11:2
ᵇNum. 27:18, 23

34:10
ᵃDeut. 18:15,
18 ᵇEx. 33:11;
Num. 12:8;
Deut. 5:4

34:11 ᵃDeut. 7:19

34:2 ¹Mediterranean   34:7 ¹eyesight was not weakened   ²reduced

THE BOOK OF
JOSHUA

GOD'S COMMISSION TO JOSHUA

1 After the death of Moses the servant of the LORD, it came to pass that the LORD spoke to Joshua the son of Nun, Moses' ªassistant, saying: 2ª"Moses My servant is dead. Now therefore, arise, go over this Jordan, you and all this people, to the land which I am giving to them—the children of Israel. 3ªEvery place that the sole of your foot will tread upon I have given you, as I said to Moses. 4ªFrom the wilderness and this Lebanon as far as the great river, the River Euphrates, all the land of the Hittites, and to the Great Sea toward the going down of the sun, shall be your territory. 5ªNo man shall *be able to* stand before you all the days of your life; ᵇas I was with Moses, *so* ᶜI will be with you. ᵈI will not leave you nor forsake you. 6ªBe strong and of good courage, for to this people you shall ¹divide as an inheritance the land which I swore to their fathers to give them. 7Only be strong and very courageous, that you may observe to do according to all the law ªwhich Moses My servant commanded you; ᵇdo not turn from it to the right hand or to the left, that you may ¹prosper wherever you go. 8ªThis Book of the Law shall not depart from your mouth, but ᵇyou¹ shall meditate in it day and night, that you may observe to do according to all that is written in it. For then you will make your way prosperous, and then you will have good success. 9ªHave I not commanded you? Be strong and of good courage; ᵇdo not be afraid, nor be dismayed, for the LORD your God *is* with you wherever you go."

THE ORDER TO CROSS THE JORDAN

10Then Joshua commanded the officers of the people, saying, 11"Pass through the camp and command the people, saying, 'Prepare provisions for yourselves, for ªwithin three days you will cross over this Jordan, to go in to possess the land which the LORD your God is giving you to possess.'"

12And to the Reubenites, the Gadites, and half the tribe of Manasseh Joshua spoke, saying, 13"Remember ªthe word which Moses the servant of the LORD commanded you, saying, 'The LORD your God is giving you rest and is giving you this land.' 14Your wives, your little ones, and your livestock shall remain in the land which Moses gave you on this side of the Jordan. But you shall ¹pass before your brethren armed, all your mighty men of valor, and help them, 15until the LORD has given your brethren rest, as He *gave* you, and they also have taken possession of the land which the LORD your God is giving them. ªThen you shall return to the land of your possession and enjoy it, which Moses the LORD's servant gave you on this side of the Jordan toward the sunrise."

1:1 ªEx. 24:13;
Num. 13:16;
14:6, 29, 30, 37,
38; Deut. 1:38;
Acts 7:45

1:2 ªNum. 12:7;
Deut. 34:5

1:3 ªDeut. 11:24;
Josh. 11:23

1:4 ªGen. 15:18;
Ex. 23:31;
Num. 34:3–12

1:5 ªDeut. 7:24
ᵇEx. 3:12
ᶜDeut. 31:8, 23
ᵈDeut. 31:6, 7;
Heb. 13:5

1:6
ªDeut. 31:7, 23

1:7 ªNum. 27:23;
Deut. 31:7;
Josh. 11:15
ᵇDeut. 5:32

1:8
ªDeut. 17:18, 19;
31:24, 26;
Josh. 8:34
ᵇDeut. 29:9;
Ps. 1:1–3

1:9 ªDeut. 31:7
ᵇPs. 27:1

1:11 ªDeut. 9:1;
Josh. 3:17

1:13
ªNum. 32:20–28

1:15
ªJosh. 22:1–4

1:6 ¹*give as a possession* 1:7 ¹*have success* or *act wisely* 1:8 ¹*you shall be constantly in* 1:14 ¹*cross over ahead of*

[16]So they answered Joshua, saying, "All that you command us we will do, and wherever you send us we will go. [17]Just as we heeded Moses in all things, so we will heed you. Only the LORD your God [a]be with you, as He was with Moses. [18]Whoever rebels against your command and does not heed your words, in all that you command him, shall be put to death. Only be strong and of good courage."

RAHAB HIDES THE SPIES
(Heb. 11:31)

2 Now Joshua the son of Nun sent out two men [a]from [1]Acacia Grove to spy secretly, saying, "Go, view the land, especially Jericho."

So they went, and [b]came to the house of a harlot named [c]Rahab, and [2]lodged there. [2]And [a]it was told the king of Jericho, saying, "Behold, men have come here tonight from the children of Israel to search out the country."

[3]So the king of Jericho sent to Rahab, saying, "Bring out the men who have come to you, who have entered your house, for they have come to search out all the country."

[4a]Then the woman took the two men and hid them. So she said, "Yes, the men came to me, but I did not know where they *were* from. [5]And it happened as the gate was being shut, when it was dark, that the men went out. Where the men went I do not know; pursue them quickly, for you may overtake them." [6](But [a]she had brought them up to the roof and hidden them with the stalks of flax, which she had laid in order on the roof.) [7]Then the men pursued them by the road to the Jordan, to the fords. And as soon as those who pursued them had gone out, they shut the gate.

[8]Now before they lay down, she came up to them on the roof, [9]and said to the men: [a]"I know that the LORD has given you the land, that [b]the terror of you has fallen on us, and that all the inhabitants of the land [c]are fainthearted because of you. [10]For we have heard how the LORD [a]dried up the water of the Red Sea for you when you came out of Egypt, and [b]what you did to the two kings of the Amorites who *were* on the other side of the Jordan, Sihon and Og, whom you [c]utterly destroyed. [11]And as soon as we [a]heard *these things,* [b]our hearts melted; neither did there remain any more courage in anyone because of you, for [c]the LORD your God, He *is* God in heaven above and on earth beneath. [12]Now therefore, I beg you, [a]swear to me by the LORD, since I have shown you kindness, that you also will show kindness to [b]my father's house, and [c]give me [1]a true token, [13]and [a]spare my father, my mother, my brothers, my sisters, and all that they have, and deliver our lives from death."

[14]So the men answered her, "Our lives for yours, if none of you tell this business of ours. And it shall be, when the LORD has given us the land, that [a]we will deal kindly and truly with you."

[15]Then she [a]let them down by a rope through the window, for her house *was* on the city wall; she dwelt on the wall. [16]And she said to them, "Get to the mountain, lest the pursuers meet you. Hide there three days, until the pursuers have returned. Afterward you may go your way."

1:17
[a]1 Sam. 20:13; 1 Kin. 1:37

2:1 [a]Num. 25:1; Josh. 3:1
[b]Heb. 11:31; James 2:25
[c]Matt. 1:5

2:2 [a]Josh. 2:22

2:4
[a]2 Sam. 17:19, 20

2:6 [a]Ex. 1:17; 2 Sam. 17:19

2:9 [a]Deut. 1:8
[b]Gen. 35:5; Ex. 23:27; Deut. 2:25; 11:25; Josh. 9:9, 10 [c]Ex. 15:15; Josh. 5:1

2:10 [a]Ex. 14:21; Josh. 4:23
[b]Num. 21:21–35
[c]Deut. 20:17; Josh. 6:21

2:11 [a]Ex. 15:14, 15
[b]Josh. 5:1; 7:5; Ps. 22:14; Is. 13:7
[c]Deut. 4:39

2:12
[a]1 Sam. 20:14, 15, 17 [b]1 Tim. 5:8
[c]Ex. 12:13; Josh. 2:18

2:13
[a]Josh. 6:23–25

2:14
[a]Gen. 47:29; Judg. 1:24; [Matt. 5:7]

2:15 [a]Acts 9:25

2:1 [1]Heb. *Shittim*   [2]Lit. *lay down*   **2:12** [1]*a pledge of truth*

[17]So the men said to her: "We *will be* [a]blameless[1] of this oath of yours which you have made us swear, [18][a]unless, *when* we come into the land, you bind this line of scarlet cord in the window through which you let us down, [b]and unless you [1]bring your father, your mother, your brothers, and all your father's household to your own home. [19]So it shall be *that* whoever goes outside the doors of your house into the street, his blood *shall be* on his own head, and we *will be* [1]guiltless. And whoever is with you in the house, [a]his [2]blood *shall be* on our head if a hand is laid on him. [20]And if you tell this business of ours, then we will be [1]free from your oath which you made us swear."

[21]Then she said, "According to your words, so *be* it." And she sent them away, and they departed. And she bound the scarlet cord in the window.

[22]They departed and went to the mountain, and stayed there three days until the pursuers returned. The pursuers sought *them* all along the way, but did not find *them*. [23]So the two men returned, descended from the mountain, and crossed over; and they came to Joshua the son of Nun, and told him all that had befallen them. [24]And they said to Joshua, "Truly [a]the LORD has delivered all the land into our hands, for indeed all the inhabitants of the country are fainthearted because of us."

ISRAEL CROSSES THE JORDAN

3 Then Joshua rose early in the morning; and they set out [a]from [1]Acacia Grove and came to the Jordan, he and all the children of Israel, and lodged there before they crossed over. [2]So it was, [a]after three days, that the officers went through the camp; [3]and they commanded the people, saying, [a]"When you see the ark of the covenant of the LORD your God, [b]and the priests, the Levites, [1]bearing it, then you shall set out from your place and go after it. [4][a]Yet there shall be a space between you and it, about two thousand cubits by measure. Do not come near it, that you may know the way by which you must go, for you have not passed *this* way before."

[5]And Joshua said to the people, [a]"Sanctify[1] yourselves, for tomorrow the LORD will do wonders among you." [6]Then Joshua spoke to the priests, saying, [a]"Take up the ark of the covenant and cross over before the people."

So they took up the ark of the covenant and went before the people.

[7]And the LORD said to Joshua, "This day I will begin to [a]exalt[1] you in the sight of all Israel, that they may know that, [b]as I was with Moses, *so* I will be with you. [8]You shall command [a]the priests who bear the ark of the covenant, saying, 'When you have come to the edge of the water of the Jordan, [b]you shall stand in the Jordan.'"

[9]So Joshua said to the children of Israel, "Come here, and hear the words of the LORD your God." [10]And Joshua said, "By this you shall know that [a]the living God *is* among you, and *that* He will without fail [b]drive out from before you the [c]Canaanites and the Hittites and the Hivites and the Perizzites and

2:17 [a]Ex. 20:7

2:18 [a]Josh. 2:12
[b]Josh. 6:23

2:19 [a]1 Kin. 2:32;
Matt. 27:25

2:24 [a]Ex. 23:31;
Josh. 6:2; 21:44

3:1 [a]Josh. 2:1

3:2
[a]Josh. 1:10, 11

3:3 [a]Num. 10:33
[b]Deut. 31:9, 25

3:4 [a]Ex. 19:12

3:5 [a]Ex. 19:10,
14, 15; Lev. 20:7;
Num. 11:18;
Josh. 7:13;
1 Sam. 16:5;
Job 1:5; Joel 2:16

3:6 [a]Num. 4:15

3:7 [a]Josh. 4:14;
1 Chr. 29:25;
2 Chr. 1:1
[b]Josh. 1:5, 9

3:8 [a]Josh. 3:3
[b]Josh. 3:17

3:10
[a]Deut. 5:26;
Josh. 11:23;
1 Sam. 17:26;
2 Kin. 19:4;
Hos. 1:10;
Matt. 16:16;
1 Thess. 1:9
[b]Ex. 33:2;
Deut. 7:1;
18:12; Ps. 44:2
[c]Acts 13:19

2:17 [1]*free from obligation to this oath*   2:18 [1]Lit. *gather*   2:19 [1]*free from obligation*   [2]*guilt of bloodshed*   2:20 [1]*free from obligation to*   3:1 [1]Heb. *Shittim*   3:3 [1]*carrying*   3:5 [1]*Consecrate*   3:7 [1]*make you great*

the Girgashites and the Amorites and the Jebusites: ¹¹Behold, the ark of the covenant of ᵃthe Lord of all the earth is crossing over before you into the Jordan. ¹²Now therefore, ᵃtake for yourselves twelve men from the tribes of Israel, one man from every tribe. ¹³And it shall come to pass, ᵃas soon as the soles of the feet of the priests who bear the ark of the LORD, ᵇthe Lord of all the earth, shall rest in the waters of the Jordan, *that* the waters of the Jordan shall be cut off, the waters that come down from upstream, and they ᶜshall stand as a heap."

¹⁴So it was, when the people set out from their camp to cross over the Jordan, with the priests bearing the ᵃark of the covenant before the people, ¹⁵and as those who bore the ark came to the Jordan, and ᵃthe feet of the priests who bore the ark dipped in the edge of the water (for the ᵇJordan overflows all its banks ᶜduring the whole time of harvest), ¹⁶that the waters which came down from upstream stood *still, and* rose in a heap very far away ¹at Adam, the city that *is* beside ᵃZaretan. So the waters that went down ᵇinto the Sea of the Arabah, ᶜthe Salt Sea, failed, *and* were cut off; and the people crossed over opposite Jericho. ¹⁷Then the priests who bore the ark of the covenant of the LORD stood firm on dry ground in the midst of the Jordan; ᵃand all Israel crossed over on dry ground, until all the people had crossed completely over the Jordan.

THE MEMORIAL STONES

4 And it came to pass, when all the people had completely crossed ᵃover the Jordan, that the LORD spoke to Joshua, saying: ²ᵃ"Take for yourselves twelve men from the people, one man from every tribe, ³and command them, saying, 'Take for yourselves twelve stones from here, out of the midst of the Jordan, from the place where ᵃthe priests' feet stood firm. You shall carry them over with you and leave them in ᵇthe lodging place where you lodge tonight.'"

⁴Then Joshua called the twelve men whom he had appointed from the children of Israel, one man from every tribe; ⁵and Joshua said to them: "Cross over before the ark of the LORD your God into the midst of the Jordan, and each one of you take up a stone on his shoulder, according to the number of the tribes of the children of Israel, ⁶that this may be ᵃa sign among you ᵇwhen your children ask in time to come, saying, 'What do these stones *mean* to you?' ⁷Then you shall answer them that ᵃthe waters of the Jordan were cut off before the ark of the covenant of the LORD; when it crossed over the Jordan, the waters of the Jordan were cut off. And these stones shall be for ᵇa memorial to the children of Israel forever."

⁸And the children of Israel did so, just as Joshua commanded, and took up twelve stones from the midst of the Jordan, as the LORD had spoken to Joshua, according to the number of the tribes of the children of Israel, and carried them over with them to the place where they lodged, and laid them down there. ⁹Then Joshua set up twelve stones in the midst of the Jordan, in the place where the feet of the priests who bore the ark of the covenant stood; and they are there to this day.

3:11 ᵃJosh. 3:13;
Job 41:11;
Ps. 24:1;
Mic. 4:13;
Zech. 4:14; 6:5

3:12
ᵃJosh. 4:2, 4

3:13
ᵃJosh. 3:15, 16
ᵇJosh. 3:11
ᶜPs. 78:13; 114:3

3:14 ᵃPs. 132:8;
Acts 7:44, 45

3:15 ᵃJosh. 3:13
ᵇ1 Chr. 12:15;
Jer. 12:5; 49:19
ᶜJosh. 4:18;
5:10, 12

3:16 ᵃ1 Kin. 4:12;
7:46 ᵇDeut. 3:17
ᶜGen. 14:3;
Num. 34:3

3:17
ᵃGen. 50:24;
Ex. 3:8; 6:1–8;
14:21, 22, 29;
33:1; Deut. 6:10;
Heb. 11:29

4:1 ᵃDeut. 27:2;
Josh. 3:17

4:2 ᵃJosh. 3:12

4:3 ᵃJosh. 3:13
ᵇJosh. 4:19, 20

4:6 ᵃDeut. 27:2;
Ps. 103:2
ᵇEx. 12:26; 13:14;
Deut. 6:20

4:7
ᵃJosh. 3:13, 16
ᵇEx. 12:14;
Num. 16:40

3:16 ¹Qr., many mss. and vss. *from Adam*

¹⁰So the priests who bore the ark stood in the midst of the Jordan until everything was finished that the LORD had commanded Joshua to speak to the people, according to all that Moses had commanded Joshua; and the people hurried and crossed over. ¹¹Then it came to pass, when all the people had completely crossed over, that the ᵃark of the LORD and the priests crossed over in the presence of the people. ¹²And ᵃthe men of Reuben, the men of Gad, and half the tribe of Manasseh crossed over armed before the children of Israel, as Moses had spoken to them. ¹³About forty thousand ¹prepared for war crossed over before the LORD for battle, to the plains of Jericho. ¹⁴On that day the LORD ᵃexalted¹ Joshua in the sight of all Israel; and they feared him, as they had feared Moses, all the days of his life.

¹⁵Then the LORD spoke to Joshua, saying, ¹⁶"Command the priests who bear ᵃthe ark of the Testimony to come up from the Jordan." ¹⁷Joshua therefore commanded the priests, saying, "Come up from the Jordan." ¹⁸And it came to pass, when the priests who bore the ark of the covenant of the LORD had come from the midst of the Jordan, *and* the soles of the priests' feet touched the dry land, that the waters of the Jordan returned to their place ᵃand overflowed all its banks as before.

¹⁹Now the people came up from the Jordan on the tenth *day* of the first month, and they camped ᵃin Gilgal on the east border of Jericho. ²⁰And ᵃthose twelve stones which they took out of the Jordan, Joshua set up in Gilgal. ²¹Then he spoke to the children of Israel, saying: ᵃ"When your children ask their fathers in time to come, saying, 'What *are* these stones?' ²²then you shall let your children know, saying, ᵃ'Israel crossed over this Jordan on ᵇdry land'; ²³for the LORD your God dried up the waters of the Jordan before you until you had crossed over, as the LORD your God did to the Red Sea, ᵃwhich He dried up before us until we had crossed over, ²⁴ᵃthat all the peoples of the earth may know the hand of the LORD, that it *is* ᵇmighty, that you may ᶜfear the LORD your God ¹forever."

THE SECOND GENERATION CIRCUMCISED

5 So it was, when all the kings of the Amorites who *were* on the west side of the Jordan, and all the kings of the Canaanites ᵃwho *were* by the sea, ᵇheard that the LORD had dried up the waters of the Jordan from before the children of Israel until ¹we had crossed over, that ²their heart melted; ᶜand there was no spirit in them any longer because of the children of Israel.

²At that time the LORD said to Joshua, "Make ᵃflint knives for yourself, and circumcise the sons of Israel again the second time." ³So Joshua made flint knives for himself, and circumcised the sons of Israel at ¹the hill of the foreskins. ⁴And this *is* the reason why Joshua circumcised them: ᵃAll the people who came out of Egypt *who were* males, all the men of war, had died in the wilderness on the way, after they had come out of Egypt. ⁵For all the people who came out had

4:11
ᵃJosh. 3:11; 6:11

4:12
ᵃNum. 32:17, 20, 27, 28; Josh. 1:14

4:14 ᵃJosh. 3:7; 1 Chr. 29:25

4:16
ᵃEx. 25:16, 22

4:18 ᵃJosh. 3:15; 1 Chr. 12:15

4:19 ᵃJosh. 5:9

4:20
ᵃDeut. 11:30; Josh. 4:3; 5:9, 10

4:21 ᵃJosh. 4:6

4:22 ᵃEx. 12:26, 27; 13:8–14; Deut. 26:5–9
ᵇJosh. 3:17

4:23 ᵃEx. 14:21

4:24
ᵃ1 Kin. 8:42; 2 Kin. 19:19; Ps. 106:8
ᵇEx. 15:16; 1 Chr. 29:12; Ps. 89:13
ᶜEx. 14:31; Deut. 6:2; Ps. 76:7; Jer. 10:7

5:1 ᵃNum. 13:29
ᵇEx. 15:14, 15
ᶜJosh. 2:10, 11; 9:9; 1 Kin. 10:5

5:2 ᵃEx. 4:25

5:4
ᵃNum. 14:29; 26:64, 65; Deut. 2:14–16

been circumcised, but all the people born in the wilderness, on the way as they came out of Egypt, had not been circumcised. 6For the children of Israel walked ᵃforty years in the wilderness, till all the people *who were* men of war, who came out of Egypt, were ¹consumed, because they did not obey the voice of the LORD—to whom the LORD swore that ᵇHe would not show them the land which the LORD had sworn to their fathers that He would give us, ᶜ"a land flowing with milk and honey." 7Then Joshua circumcised ᵃtheir sons *whom* He raised up in their place; for they were uncircumcised, because they had not been circumcised on the way.

8So it was, when they had finished circumcising all the people, that they stayed in their places in the camp ᵃtill they were healed. 9Then the LORD said to Joshua, "This day I have rolled away ᵃthe reproach of Egypt from you." Therefore the name of the place is called ᵇGilgal¹ to this day.

10Now the children of Israel camped in Gilgal, and kept the Passover ᵃon the fourteenth day of the month at twilight on the plains of Jericho. 11And they ate of the produce of the land on the day after the Passover, unleavened bread and ¹parched grain, on the very same day. 12Then ᵃthe manna ceased on the day after they had eaten the produce of the land; and the children of Israel no longer had manna, but they ate the food of the land of Canaan that year.

THE COMMANDER OF THE ARMY OF THE LORD

13And it came to pass, when Joshua was by Jericho, that he lifted his eyes and looked, and behold, ᵃa Man stood opposite him ᵇwith His sword drawn in His hand. And Joshua went to Him and said to Him, "*Are* You for us or for our adversaries?"

14So He said, "No, but *as* Commander of the army of the LORD I have now come."

And Joshua ᵃfell on his face to the earth and ᵇworshiped, and said to Him, "What does my Lord say to His servant?"

15Then the Commander of the LORD's army said to Joshua, ᵃ"Take your sandal off your foot, for the place where you stand *is* holy." And Joshua did so.

THE DESTRUCTION OF JERICHO

6 Now ᵃJericho was securely shut up because of the children of Israel; none went out, and none came in. 2And the LORD said to Joshua: "See! ᵃI have given Jericho into your hand, its ᵇking, *and* the mighty men of valor. 3You shall march around the city, all *you* men of war; you shall go all around the city once. This you shall do six days. 4And seven priests shall bear seven ᵃtrumpets of rams' horns before the ark. But the seventh day you shall march around the city ᵇseven times, and ᶜthe priests shall blow the trumpets. 5It shall come to pass, when they make a long *blast* with the ram's horn, *and* when you hear the sound of the trumpet, that all the people shall shout with a great shout; then the wall of the city will fall down flat. And the people shall go up every man straight before him."

6Then Joshua the son of Nun called the priests and said to them, "Take up the ark of the covenant, and let seven

5:6
ᵃNum. 14:33;
Deut. 1:3; 29:5
ᵇNum. 14:23,
29–35;
26:23–65;
Heb. 3:11
ᶜEx. 3:8

5:7 ᵃNum. 14:31;
Deut. 1:39

5:8 ᵃGen. 34:25

5:9 ᵃGen. 34:14
ᵇJosh. 4:19

5:10 ᵃEx. 12:6;
Num. 9:5

5:12 ᵃEx. 16:35

5:13
ᵃGen. 18:1, 2;
32:24, 30;
Ex. 23:23;
Num. 22:31;
Zech. 1:8;
Acts 1:10
ᵇNum. 22:23;
1 Chr. 21:16

5:14 ᵃGen. 17:3;
Num. 20:6
ᵇEx. 34:8

5:15 ᵃEx. 3:5;
Acts 7:33

6:1 ᵃJosh. 2:1

6:2 ᵃJosh. 2:9,
24; 8:1
ᵇDeut. 7:24

6:4 ᵃLev. 25:9;
Judg. 7:16, 22
ᵇ1 Kin. 18:43;
2 Kin. 4:35; 5:10
ᶜNum. 10:8

5:6 ¹destroyed   **5:9** ¹Lit. *Rolling*   **5:11** ¹roasted

priests bear seven trumpets of rams' horns before the ark of the LORD." [7]And he said to the people, "Proceed, and march around the city, and let him who is armed advance before the ark of the LORD."

[8]So it was, when Joshua had spoken to the people, that the seven priests bearing the seven trumpets of rams' horns before the LORD advanced and blew the trumpets, and the ark of the covenant of the LORD followed them. [9]The armed men went before the priests who blew the trumpets, [a]and the rear guard came after the ark, while *the priests* continued blowing the trumpets. [10]Now Joshua had commanded the people, saying, "You shall not shout or make any noise with your voice, nor shall a word proceed out of your mouth, until the day I say to you, 'Shout!' Then you shall shout." [11]So he had [a]the ark of the LORD circle the city, going around *it* once. Then they came into the camp and [1]lodged in the camp.

[12]And Joshua rose early in the morning, [a]and the priests took up the ark of the LORD. [13]Then seven priests bearing seven trumpets of rams' horns before the ark of the LORD went on continually and blew with the trumpets. And the armed men went before them. But the rear guard came after the ark of the LORD, while *the priests* continued blowing the trumpets. [14]And the second day they marched around the city once and returned to the camp. So they did six days.

[15]But it came to pass on the seventh day that they rose early, about the dawning of the day, and marched around the city seven times in the same manner. On that day only they marched around the city seven times. [16]And the seventh time it happened, when the priests blew the trumpets, that Joshua said to the people: "Shout, for the LORD has given you the city! [17]Now the city shall be [a]doomed by the LORD to destruction, it and all who *are* in it. Only [b]Rahab the harlot shall live, she and all who *are* with her in the house, because [c]she hid the messengers that we sent. [18]And you, [a]by all means abstain from the accursed things, lest you become accursed when you take of the accursed things, and make the camp of Israel a curse, [b]and trouble it. [19]But all the silver and gold, and vessels of bronze and iron, *are* [1]consecrated to the LORD; they [2]shall come into the treasury of the LORD."

[20]So the people shouted when *the priests* blew the trumpets. And it happened when the people heard the sound of the trumpet, and the people shouted with a great shout, that [a]the wall fell down flat. Then the people went up into the city, every man straight before him, and they took the city. [21]And they [a]utterly destroyed all that *was* in the city, both man and woman, young and old, ox and sheep and donkey, with the edge of the sword.

[22]But Joshua had said to the two men who had spied out the country, "Go into the harlot's house, and from there bring out the woman and all that she has, [a]as you swore to her." [23]And the young men who had been spies went in and brought out Rahab, [a]her father, her mother, her brothers, and all that she had. So they brought out all her relatives and left them outside the camp of Israel. [24]But they burned the city and all that *was* in it with fire. Only the silver and gold, and the vessels of bronze and iron, they put into the treasury of

6:9 [a]Num. 10:25
6:11 [a]Josh. 4:11
6:12 [a]Deut. 31:25
6:17 [a]Deut. 13:17; Josh. 7:1; [b]Josh. 2:1; Matt. 1:5; [c]Josh. 2:4, 6
6:18 [a]Deut. 7:26 [b]Josh. 7:1, 12, 25; 1 Kin. 18:17, 18; [Jon. 1:12]
6:20 [a]Heb. 11:30
6:21 [a]Deut. 7:2; 20:16, 17
6:22 [a]Josh. 2:12–19; Heb. 11:31
6:23 [a]Josh. 2:13

6:11 [1]spent the night   6:19 [1]set apart   [2]shall go

the house of the LORD. [25]And Joshua spared Rahab the harlot, her father's household, and all that she had. So [a]she dwells in Israel to this day, because she hid the messengers whom Joshua sent to spy out Jericho.

[26]Then Joshua [1]charged *them* at that time, saying, [a]"Cursed *be* the man before the LORD who rises up and builds this city Jericho; he shall lay its foundation with his firstborn, and with his youngest he shall set up its gates."

[27]So the LORD was with Joshua, and his fame spread throughout all the country.

DEFEAT AT AI

7 But the children of Israel [1]committed a [a]trespass regarding the [b]accursed[2] things, for [c]Achan the son of Carmi, the son of [3]Zabdi, the son of Zerah, of the tribe of Judah, took of the accursed things; so the anger of the LORD burned against the children of Israel.

[2]Now Joshua sent men from Jericho to Ai, which *is* beside Beth Aven, on the east side of Bethel, and spoke to them, saying, "Go up and spy out the country." So the men went up and spied out Ai. [3]And they returned to Joshua and said to him, "Do not let all the people go up, but let about two or three thousand men go up and attack Ai. Do not weary all the people there, for *the people of Ai are* few." [4]So about three thousand men went up there from the people, [a]but they fled before the men of Ai. [5]And the men of Ai struck down about thirty-six men, for they chased them *from* before the gate as far as Shebarim, and struck them down on the descent; therefore [a]the[1] hearts of the people melted and became like water.

[6]Then Joshua [a]tore his clothes, and fell to the earth on his face before the ark of the LORD until evening, he and the elders of Israel; and they [b]put dust on their heads. [7]And Joshua said, "Alas, Lord [1]GOD, [a]why have You brought this people over the Jordan at all—to deliver us into the hand of the Amorites, to destroy us? Oh, that we had been content, and dwelt on the other side of the Jordan! [8]O Lord, what shall I say when Israel turns its [1]back before its enemies? [9]For the Canaanites and all the inhabitants of the land will hear *it,* and surround us, and [a]cut off our name from the earth. Then [b]what will You do for Your great name?"

THE SIN OF ACHAN

[10]So the LORD said to Joshua: "Get up! Why do you lie thus on your face? [11]Israel has sinned, and they have also transgressed My covenant which I commanded them. [a]For they have even taken some of the [1]accursed things, and have both stolen and [b]deceived; and they have also put *it* among their own stuff. [12][a]Therefore the children of Israel could not stand before their enemies, *but* turned *their* backs before their enemies, because [b]they have become doomed to destruction. Neither will I be with you anymore, unless you destroy the accursed from among you. [13]Get up, [a]sanctify[1] the people, and say, [b]'Sanctify yourselves for tomorrow, because thus says the LORD God of Israel: "*There is* an accursed thing in your midst,

---

6:25 [a][Matt. 1:5]

6:26
[a]1 Kin. 16:34

7:1 [a]Josh. 7:20, 21 [b]Josh. 6:17–19 [c]Josh. 22:20

7:4 [a]Lev. 26:17; Deut. 28:25

7:5 [a]Lev. 26:36; Josh. 2:9, 11

7:6
[a]Gen. 37:29, 34 [b]1 Sam. 4:12

7:7 [a]Ex. 17:3; Num. 21:5

7:9 [a]Deut. 32:26 [b]Ex. 32:12; Num. 14:13

7:11
[a]Josh. 6:17–19 [b]Acts 5:1, 2

7:12 [a]Judg. 2:14 [b]Deut. 7:26; [Hag. 2:13, 14]

7:13 [a]Ex. 19:10 [b]Josh. 3:5

6:26 [1]*warned*   7:1 [1]*acted unfaithfully*   [2]*devoted*   [3]*Zimri,* 1 Chr. 2:6
7:5 [1]*the people's courage failed*   7:7 [1]Heb. *YHWH,* LORD   7:8 [1]Lit. *neck*
7:11 [1]*devoted*   7:13 [1]*set apart*

O Israel; you cannot stand before your enemies until you take away the accursed thing from among you." [14]In the morning therefore you shall be brought according to your tribes. And it shall be *that* the tribe which [a]the LORD takes shall come according to families; and the family which the LORD takes shall come by households; and the household which the LORD takes shall come man by man. [15a]Then it shall be *that* he who is taken with the accursed thing shall be burned with fire, he and all that he has, because he has [b]transgressed[1] the covenant of the LORD, and because he [c]has done a disgraceful thing in Israel.'"

[16]So Joshua rose early in the morning and brought Israel by their tribes, and the tribe of Judah was taken. [17]He brought the clan of Judah, and he took the family of the Zarhites; and he brought the family of the Zarhites man by man, and Zabdi was taken. [18]Then he brought his household man by man, and Achan the son of Carmi, the son of Zabdi, the son of Zerah, of the tribe of Judah, [a]was taken.

[19]Now Joshua said to Achan, "My son, I beg you, [a]give glory to the LORD God of Israel, [b]and make confession to Him, and [c]tell me now what you have done; do not hide *it* from me."

[20]And Achan answered Joshua and said, "Indeed [a]I have sinned against the LORD God of Israel, and this is what I have done: [21]When I saw among the spoils a beautiful Babylonian garment, two hundred shekels of silver, and a wedge of gold weighing fifty shekels, I [1]coveted them and took them. And there they are, hidden in the earth in the midst of my tent, with the silver under it."

[22]So Joshua sent messengers, and they ran to the tent; and there it was, hidden in his tent, with the silver under it. [23]And they took them from the midst of the tent, brought them to Joshua and to all the children of Israel, and laid them out before the LORD. [24]Then Joshua, and all Israel with him, took Achan the son of Zerah, the silver, the garment, the wedge of gold, his sons, his daughters, his oxen, his donkeys, his sheep, his tent, and [a]all that he had, and they brought them to [b]the Valley of Achor. [25]And Joshua said, [a]"Why have you troubled us? The LORD will trouble you this day." [b]So all Israel stoned him with stones; and they burned them with fire after they had stoned them with stones.

[26]Then they [a]raised over him a great heap of stones, still there to this day. So [b]the LORD turned from the fierceness of His anger. Therefore the name of that place has been called [c]the Valley of [1]Achor to this day.

THE FALL OF AI

8 Now the LORD said to Joshua: [a]"Do not be afraid, nor be dismayed; take all the people of war with you, and arise, go up to Ai. See, [b]I have given into your hand the king of Ai, his people, his city, and his land. [2]And you shall do to Ai and its king as you did to [a]Jericho and its king. Only [b]its spoil and its cattle you shall take as booty for yourselves. Lay an ambush for the city behind it."

[3]So Joshua arose, and all the people of war, to go up against Ai; and Joshua chose thirty thousand mighty men of valor and sent them away by night. [4]And he commanded

7:14
[a][Prov. 16:33]

7:15
[a]1 Sam. 14:38, 39
[b]Josh. 7:11
[c]Gen. 34:7;
Judg. 20:6

7:18
[a]1 Sam. 14:42

7:19 [a]1 Sam. 6:5;
Jer. 13:16;
John 9:24
[b]Num. 5:6, 7;
2 Chr. 30:22;
Ezra 10:10, 11;
Ps. 32:5;
Prov. 28:13;
Jer. 3:12, 13;
Dan. 9:4
[c]1 Sam. 14:43

7:20
[a]Num. 22:34;
1 Sam. 15:24

7:24
[a]Num. 16:32, 33;
Dan. 6:24
[b]Josh. 7:26; 15:7

7:25 [a]Josh. 6:18;
1 Chr. 2:7;
[Gal. 5:12]
[b]Deut. 17:5

7:26
[a]Josh. 8:29;
2 Sam. 18:17;
Lam. 3:53
[b]Deut. 13:17
[c]Josh. 7:24;
Is. 65:10;
Hos. 2:15

8:1 [a]Deut. 1:21;
7:18; 31:8;
Josh. 1:9; 10:8
[b]Josh. 6:2

8:2 [a]Josh. 6:21
[b]Deut. 20:14;
Josh. 8:27

7:15 [1]overstepped   **7:21** [1]desired   **7:26** [1]Lit. *Trouble*

them, saying: "Behold, [a]you shall lie in ambush against the city, behind the city. Do not go very far from the city, but all of you be ready. [5]Then I and all the people who *are* with me will approach the city; and it will come about, when they come out against us as at the first, that [a]we shall flee before them. [6]For they will come out after us till we have drawn them from the city, for they will say, '*They are* fleeing before us as at the first.' Therefore we will flee before them. [7]Then you shall rise from the ambush and seize the city, for the LORD your God will deliver it into your hand. [8]And it will be, when you have taken the city, *that* you shall set the city on fire. According to the commandment of the LORD you shall do. [a]See, I have commanded you."

[9]Joshua therefore sent them out; and they went to lie in ambush, and stayed between Bethel and Ai, on the west side of Ai; but Joshua lodged that night among the people. [10]Then Joshua rose up early in the morning and mustered the people, and went up, he and the elders of Israel, before the people to Ai. [11][a]And all the people of war who *were* with him went up and drew near; and they came before the city and camped on the north side of Ai. Now a valley *lay* between them and Ai. [12]So he took about five thousand men and set them in ambush between Bethel and Ai, on the west side of [1]the city. [13]And when they had set the people, all the army that *was* on the north of the city, and its rear guard on the west of the city, Joshua went that night into the midst of the valley.

[14]Now it happened, when the king of Ai saw *it,* that the men of the city hurried and rose early and went out against Israel to battle, he and all his people, at an appointed place before the plain. But he [a]did not know that *there was* an ambush against him behind the city. [15]And Joshua and all Israel [a]made as if they were beaten before them, and fled by the way of the wilderness. [16]So all the people who *were* in Ai were called together to pursue them. And they pursued Joshua and were drawn away from the city. [17]There was not a man left in Ai or Bethel who did not go out after Israel. So they left the city open and pursued Israel.

[18]Then the LORD said to Joshua, "Stretch out the spear that *is* in your hand toward Ai, for I will give it into your hand." And Joshua stretched out the spear that *was* in his hand toward the city. [19]So *those in* ambush arose quickly out of their place; they ran as soon as he had stretched out his hand, and they entered the city and took it, and hurried to set the city on fire. [20]And when the men of Ai looked behind them, they saw, and behold, the smoke of the city ascended to heaven. So they had no power to flee this way or that way, and the people who had fled to the wilderness turned back on the pursuers. [21]Now when Joshua and all Israel saw that the ambush had taken the city and that the smoke of the city ascended, they turned back and struck down the men of Ai. [22]Then the others came out of the city against them; so they were *caught* in the midst of Israel, some on this side and some on that side. And they struck them down, so that they [a]let none of them remain or escape. [23]But the king of Ai they took alive, and brought him to Joshua.

8:4
[a]Judg. 20:29

8:5 [a]Josh. 7:5;
Judg. 20:32

8:8
[a]2 Sam. 13:28

8:11 [a]Josh. 8:5

8:14
[a]Judg. 20:34;
Eccl. 9:12

8:15
[a]Judg. 20:36

8:22 [a]Deut. 7:2

8:12 [1]Ai

²⁴And it came to pass when Israel had made an end of slaying all the inhabitants of Ai in the field, in the wilderness where they pursued them, and when they all had fallen by the edge of the sword until they were consumed, that all the Israelites returned to Ai and struck it with the edge of the sword. ²⁵So it was *that* all who fell that day, both men and women, *were* twelve thousand—all the people of Ai. ²⁶For Joshua did not draw back his hand, with which he stretched out the spear, until he had ᵃutterly destroyed all the inhabitants of Ai. ²⁷ᵃOnly the livestock and the spoil of that city Israel took as booty for themselves, according to the word of the LORD which He had ᵇcommanded Joshua. ²⁸So Joshua burned Ai and made it ᵃa heap forever, a desolation to this day. ²⁹ᵃAnd the king of Ai he hanged on a tree until evening. ᵇAnd as soon as the sun was down, Joshua commanded that they should take his corpse down from the tree, cast it at the entrance of the gate of the city, and ᶜraise over it a great heap of stones *that remains* to this day.

JOSHUA RENEWS THE COVENANT
(cf. Deut. 27:4, 5)

³⁰Now Joshua built an altar to the LORD God of Israel ᵃin Mount Ebal, ³¹as Moses the servant of the LORD had commanded the children of Israel, as it is written in the Book of the Law of Moses: ᵃ"an altar of whole stones over which no man has wielded an iron *tool*." And ᵇthey offered on it burnt offerings to the LORD, and sacrificed peace offerings. ³²And there, in the presence of the children of Israel, ᵃhe wrote on the stones a copy of the law of Moses, which he had written. ³³Then all Israel, with their elders and officers and judges, stood on either side of the ark before the priests, the Levites, ᵃwho bore the ark of the covenant of the LORD, ᵇthe stranger as well as he who was born among them. Half of them *were* in front of Mount Gerizim and half of them in front of Mount Ebal, ᶜas Moses the servant of the LORD had commanded before, that they should bless the people of Israel. ³⁴And afterward ᵃhe read all the words of the law, ᵇthe blessings and the cursings, according to all that is written in the ᶜBook of the Law. ³⁵There was not a word of all that Moses had commanded which Joshua did not read before all the assembly of Israel, ᵃwith the women, the little ones, ᵇand the strangers who were living among them.

THE TREATY WITH THE GIBEONITES

9 And it came to pass when ᵃall the kings who *were* on this side of the Jordan, in the hills and in the lowland and in all the coasts of ᵇthe Great Sea toward Lebanon—ᶜthe Hittite, the Amorite, the Canaanite, the Perizzite, the Hivite, and the Jebusite—heard *about it,* ²that they ᵃgathered together to fight with Joshua and Israel with one ¹accord.

³But when the inhabitants of ᵃGibeon ᵇheard what Joshua had done to Jericho and Ai, ⁴they worked craftily, and went and ¹pretended to be ambassadors. And they took old sacks on their donkeys, old wineskins torn and ²mended, ⁵old and patched sandals on their feet, and old garments on themselves; and all

8:26 ᵃJosh. 6:21

8:27
ᵃNum. 31:22, 26
ᵇJosh. 8:2

8:28
ᵃDeut. 13:16

8:29
ᵃJosh. 10:26
ᵇDeut. 21:22, 23;
Josh. 10:27
ᶜJosh. 7:26;
10:27

8:30
ᵃDeut. 27:4–8

8:31 ᵃEx. 20:25;
Deut. 27:5, 6
ᵇEx. 20:24

8:32
ᵃDeut. 27:2, 3, 8

8:33
ᵃDeut. 31:9, 25
ᵇDeut. 31:12
ᶜDeut. 11:29;
27:12

8:34
ᵃDeut. 31:11;
Neh. 8:3
ᵇDeut. 28:2, 15,
45; 29:20, 21;
30:19 ᶜJosh. 1:8

8:35 ᵃEx. 12:38;
Deut. 31:12
ᵇJosh. 8:33

9:1 ᵃNum. 13:29;
Josh. 3:10
ᵇNum. 34:6
ᶜEx. 3:17; 23:23

9:2 ᵃJosh. 10:5;
Ps. 83:3, 5

9:3
ᵃJosh. 9:17, 22;
10:2; 21:17;
2 Sam. 21:1, 2
ᵇJosh. 6:27

9:2 ¹Lit. *mouth*   9:4 ¹*acted as envoys*   ²Lit. *tied up*

the bread of their provision was dry *and* moldy. 6And they went to Joshua, ato the camp at Gilgal, and said to him and to the men of Israel, "We have come from a far country; now therefore, make a 1covenant with us."

7Then the men of Israel said to the aHivites, "Perhaps you dwell among us; so bhow can we make a covenant with you?"

8But they said to Joshua, a"We *are* your servants."

And Joshua said to them, "Who *are* you, and where do you come from?"

9So they said to him: a"From a very far country your servants have come, because of the name of the LORD your God; for we have bheard of His fame, and all that He did in Egypt, 10and aall that He did to the two kings of the Amorites who *were* beyond the Jordan—to Sihon king of Heshbon, and Og king of Bashan, who was at Ashtaroth. 11Therefore our elders and all the inhabitants of our country spoke to us, saying, 'Take provisions with you for the journey, and go to meet them, and say to them, "We *are* your servants; now therefore, make a covenant with us." ' 12This bread of ours we took hot *for* our provision from our houses on the day we departed to come to you. But now look, it is dry and moldy. 13And these wineskins which we filled *were* new, and see, they are torn; and these our garments and our sandals have become old because of the very long journey."

14Then the men of Israel took some of their provisions; abut they 1did not ask counsel of the LORD. 15So Joshua amade peace with them, and made a covenant with them to let them live; and the rulers of the congregation swore to them.

16And it happened at the end of three days, after they had made a covenant with them, that they heard that they *were* their neighbors who dwelt near them. 17Then the children of Israel journeyed and came to their cities on the third day. Now their cities *were* aGibeon, Chephirah, Beeroth, and Kirjath Jearim. 18But the children of Israel did not 1attack them, abecause the rulers of the congregation had sworn to them by the LORD God of Israel. And all the congregation complained against the rulers.

19Then all the rulers said to all the congregation, "We have sworn to them by the LORD God of Israel; now therefore, we may not touch them. 20This we will do to them: We will let them live, lest awrath be upon us because of the oath which we swore to them." 21And the rulers said to them, "Let them live, but let them be awoodcutters and water carriers for all the congregation, as the rulers had bpromised them."

22Then Joshua called for them, and he spoke to them, saying, "Why have you deceived us, saying, a'We *are* very far from you,' when byou dwell near us? 23Now therefore, you *are* acursed, and none of you shall be freed from being slaves— woodcutters and water carriers for the house of my God."

24So they answered Joshua and said, "Because your servants were clearly told that the LORD your God acommanded His servant Moses to give you all the land, and to destroy all the inhabitants of the land from before you; therefore bwe were very much afraid for our lives because of you, and have done this thing. 25And now, here we are, ain your hands; do with us as it seems good and right to do to us." 26So he did to

9:6 aJosh. 5:10
9:7 aJosh. 9:1;
11:19 bEx. 23:32;
Deut. 7:2
9:8 aDeut. 20:11;
2 Kin. 10:5
9:9 aDeut. 20:15
bEx. 15:14;
Josh. 2:9, 10; 5:1
9:10
aNum. 21:24, 33
9:14
aNum. 27:21;
Is. 30:1
9:15
a2 Sam. 21:2
9:17 aJosh. 18:25
9:18 aPs. 15:4
9:20
a2 Sam. 21:1, 2, 6;
Ezek. 17:13, 15
9:21 aDeut. 29:11
bJosh. 9:15
9:22
aJosh. 9:6, 9
bJosh. 9:16
9:23 aGen. 9:25
9:24
aEx. 23:31–33;
Deut. 7:1, 2
bEx. 15:14
9:25 aGen. 16:6

them, and delivered them out of the hand of the children of Israel, so that they did not kill them. [27]And that day Joshua made them [a]woodcutters and water carriers for the congregation and for the altar of the LORD, [b]in the place which He would choose, even to this day.

THE SUN STANDS STILL

10 Now it came to pass when Adoni-Zedek king of Jerusalem [a]heard how Joshua had taken [b]Ai and had utterly destroyed it—[c]as he had done to Jericho and its king, so he had done to [d]Ai and its king—and [e]how the inhabitants of Gibeon had made peace with Israel and were among them, [2]that they [a]feared greatly, because Gibeon *was* a great city, like one of the royal cities, and because it *was* greater than Ai, and all its men *were* mighty. [3]Therefore Adoni-Zedek king of Jerusalem sent to Hoham king of Hebron, Piram king of Jarmuth, Japhia king of Lachish, and Debir king of Eglon, saying, [4]"Come up to me and help me, that we may attack Gibeon, for [a]it has made peace with Joshua and with the children of Israel." [5]Therefore the five kings of the [a]Amorites, the king of Jerusalem, the king of Hebron, the king of Jarmuth, the king of Lachish, *and* the king of Eglon, [b]gathered together and went up, they and all their armies, and camped before Gibeon and made war against it.

[6]And the men of Gibeon sent to Joshua at the camp [a]at Gilgal, saying, "Do not forsake your servants; come up to us quickly, save us and help us, for all the kings of the Amorites who dwell in the mountains have gathered together against us." [7]So Joshua ascended from Gilgal, he and [a]all the people of war with him, and all the mighty men of valor. [8]And the LORD said to Joshua, [a]"Do not fear them, for I have delivered them into your hand; [b]not a man of them shall [c]stand before you." [9]Joshua therefore came upon them suddenly, having marched all night from Gilgal. [10]So the LORD [a]routed them before Israel, killed them with a great slaughter at Gibeon, chased them along the road that goes [b]to Beth Horon, and struck them down as far as [c]Azekah and Makkedah. [11]And it happened, as they fled before Israel *and* were on the descent of Beth Horon, [a]that the LORD cast down large hailstones from heaven on them as far as Azekah, and they died. *There were* more who died from the hailstones than the children of Israel killed with the sword.

[12]Then Joshua spoke to the LORD in the day when the LORD delivered up the Amorites before the children of Israel, and he said in the sight of Israel:

[a]"Sun, stand still over Gibeon;
And Moon, in the Valley of [b]Aijalon."
[13] So the sun stood still,
And the moon stopped,
Till the people had revenge
Upon their enemies.

[a]*Is* this not written in the Book of Jasher? So the sun stood still in the midst of heaven, and did not hasten to go *down* for about a whole day. [14]And there has been [a]no day like that, before it or after it, that the LORD heeded the voice of a man; for [b]the LORD fought for Israel.

9:27
[a]Josh. 9:21, 23
[b]Deut. 12:5

10:1 [a]Josh. 9:1
[b]Josh. 8:1
[c]Josh. 6:21
[d]Josh. 8:22, 26, 28 [e]Josh. 9:15

10:2
[a]Ex. 15:14–16;
Deut. 11:25;
1 Chr. 14:17

10:4
[a]Josh. 9:15; 10:1

10:5
[a]Num. 13:29
[b]Josh. 9:2

10:6
[a]Josh. 5:10; 9:6

10:7 [a]Josh. 8:1

10:8 [a]Josh. 11:6;
Judg. 4:14
[b]Josh. 1:5, 9
[c]Josh. 21:44

10:10
[a]Judg. 4:15;
1 Sam. 7:10, 12;
Is. 28:21
[b]Josh. 16:3, 5
[c]Josh. 15:35

10:11 [a]Is. 30:30;
Rev. 16:21

10:12 [a]Is. 28:21;
Hab. 3:11
[b]Judg. 12:12

10:13
[a]2 Sam. 1:18

10:14
[a]Is. 38:7, 8
[b]Ex. 14:14;
Deut. 1:30; 20:4;
Josh. 10:42;
23:3

15a Then Joshua returned, and all Israel with him, to the camp at Gilgal.

THE AMORITE KINGS EXECUTED

16But these five kings had fled and hidden themselves in a cave at Makkedah. **17**And it was told Joshua, saying, "The five kings have been found hidden in the cave at Makkedah."

18So Joshua said, "Roll large stones against the mouth of the cave, and set men by it to guard them. **19**And do not stay *there* yourselves, *but* pursue your enemies, and attack their rear *guard.* Do not allow them to enter their cities, for the LORD your God has delivered them into your hand." **20**Then it happened, while Joshua and the children of Israel made an end of slaying them with a very great slaughter, till they had finished, that those who escaped entered fortified cities. **21**And all the people returned to the camp, to Joshua at Makkedah, in peace. **a**No one **1**moved his tongue against any of the children of Israel.

22Then Joshua said, "Open the mouth of the cave, and bring out those five kings to me from the cave." **23**And they did so, and brought out those five kings to him from the cave: the king of Jerusalem, the king of Hebron, the king of Jarmuth, the king of Lachish, *and* the king of Eglon.

24So it was, when they brought out those kings to Joshua, that Joshua called for all the men of Israel, and said to the captains of the men of war who went with him, "Come near, put your feet on the necks of these kings." And they drew near and **a**put their feet on their necks. **25**Then Joshua said to **1**them, **a**"Do not be afraid, nor be dismayed; be strong and of good courage, for **b**thus the LORD will do to all your enemies against whom you fight." **26**And afterward Joshua struck **1**them and killed them, and hanged them on five trees; and they **a**were hanging on the trees until evening. **27**So it was at the time of the going down of the sun *that* Joshua commanded, and they **a**took them down from the trees, cast them into the cave where they had been hidden, and laid large stones against the cave's mouth, *which remain* until this very day.

CONQUEST OF THE SOUTHLAND

28On that day Joshua took Makkedah, and struck it and its king with the edge of the sword. He utterly **a**destroyed **1**them—all the people who *were* in it. He let none remain. He also did to the king of Makkedah **b**as he had done to the king of Jericho.

29Then Joshua passed from Makkedah, and all Israel with him, to **a**Libnah; and they fought against Libnah. **30**And the LORD also delivered it and its king into the hand of Israel; he struck it and all the people who *were* in it with the edge of the sword. He let none remain in it, but did to its king as he had done to the king of Jericho.

31Then Joshua passed from Libnah, and all Israel with him, to Lachish; and they encamped against it and fought

---

10:15
a Josh. 10:43

10:21 a Ex. 11:7

10:24
a Ps. 107:40;
Is. 26:5, 6;
Mal. 4:3

10:25
a Deut. 31:6–8;
Josh. 1:9
b Deut. 3:21; 7:19

10:26
a Josh. 8:29;
2 Sam. 21:9

10:27
a Deut. 21:22, 23;
Josh. 8:29

10:28
a Deut. 7:2, 16
b Josh. 6:21

10:29
a Josh. 15:42;
21:13;
2 Kin. 8:22; 19:8

10:21 **1***criticized,* lit. *sharpened his tongue* **10:25** **1**The captains **10:26** **1**The kings **10:28** **1**So with MT and most authorities; many Heb. mss., some LXX mss., and some Tg. mss. *it*

against it. 32And the LORD delivered Lachish into the hand of Israel, who took it on the second day, and struck it and all the people who *were* in it with the edge of the sword, according to all that he had done to Libnah. 33Then Horam king of Gezer came up to help Lachish; and Joshua struck him and his people, until he left him none remaining.

34From Lachish Joshua passed to Eglon, and all Israel with him; and they encamped against it and fought against it. 35They took it on that day and struck it with the edge of the sword; all the people who *were* in it he utterly destroyed that day, according to all that he had done to Lachish.

36So Joshua went up from Eglon, and all Israel with him, to aHebron; and they fought against it. 37And they took it and struck it with the edge of the sword—its king, all its cities, and all the people who *were* in it; he left none remaining, according to all that he had done to Eglon, but utterly destroyed it and all the people who *were* in it.

38Then Joshua returned, and all Israel with him, to aDebir; and they fought against it. 39And he took it and its king and all its cities; they struck them with the edge of the sword and utterly destroyed all the people who *were* in it. He left none remaining; as he had done to Hebron, so he did to Debir and its king, as he had done also to Libnah and its king.

40So Joshua conquered all the land: the amountain country and the 1South and the lowland and the wilderness slopes, and ball their kings; he left none remaining, but cutterly destroyed all that breathed, as the LORD God of Israel had commanded. 41And Joshua conquered them from aKadesh Barnea as far as bGaza, cand all the country of Goshen, even as far as Gibeon. 42All these kings and their land Joshua took at one time, abecause the LORD God of Israel fought for Israel. 43Then Joshua returned, and all Israel with him, to the camp at Gilgal.

THE NORTHERN CONQUEST

11 And it came to pass, when Jabin king of Hazor heard *these things*, that he asent to Jobab king of Madon, to the king bof Shimron, to the king of Achshaph, 2and to the kings who *were* from the north, in the mountains, in the plain south of aChinneroth, in the lowland, and in the heights bof Dor on the west, 3to the Canaanites in the east and in the west, the aAmorite, the Hittite, the Perizzite, the Jebusite in the mountains, band the Hivite below cHermon din the land of Mizpah. 4So they went out, they and all their armies with them, *as* many people a*as* the sand that *is* on the seashore in multitude, with very many horses and chariots. 5And when all these kings had 1met together, they came and camped together at the waters of Merom to fight against Israel.

6But the LORD said to Joshua, a"Do not be afraid because of them, for tomorrow about this time I will deliver all of them slain before Israel. You shall bhamstring their horses and burn their chariots with fire." 7So Joshua and all the people of war with him came against them suddenly by the waters of Merom, and they attacked them. 8And the LORD delivered them into the hand of Israel, who defeated them and chased

10:36
aNum. 13:22;
Josh. 14:13–15;
15:13; Judg. 1:10,
20; 2 Sam. 5:1, 3,
5, 13; 2 Chr. 11:10

10:38
aJosh. 15:15;
Judg. 1:11;
1 Chr. 6:58

10:40 aDeut. 1:7
bDeut. 7:24
cDeut. 20:16, 17

10:41
aNum. 13:26;
Deut. 9:23
bGen. 10:19;
Josh. 11:22
cJosh. 11:16;
15:51

10:42
aJosh. 10:14

11:1 aJosh. 10:3
bJosh. 19:15

11:2 aNum. 34:11
bJosh. 17:11;
Judg. 1:27;
1 Kin. 4:11

11:3 aJosh. 9:1
bDeut. 7:1;
Judg. 3:3, 5;
1 Kin. 9:20
cJosh. 11:17;
13:5, 11
dGen. 31:49

11:4 aGen. 22:17;
32:12; Judg. 7:12;
1 Sam. 13:5

11:6 aJosh. 10:8
b2 Sam. 8:4

10:40 1Heb. *Negev,* and so throughout the book **11:5** 1Lit. *assembled by appointment*

them to [1]Greater [a]Sidon, to the [2]Brook [b]Misrephoth, and to the Valley of Mizpah eastward; they attacked them until they left none of them remaining. [9]So Joshua did to them as the LORD had told him: he hamstrung their horses and burned their chariots with fire.

[10]Joshua turned back at that time and took Hazor, and struck its king with the sword; for Hazor was formerly the head of all those kingdoms. [11]And they struck all the people who *were* in it with the edge of the sword, [a]utterly destroying *them.* There was none left [b]breathing. Then he burned Hazor with fire.

[12]So all the cities of those kings, and all their kings, Joshua took and struck with the edge of the sword. He utterly destroyed them, [a]as Moses the servant of the LORD had commanded. [13]But *as for* the cities that stood on their [1]mounds, Israel burned none of them, except Hazor only, *which* Joshua burned. [14]And all the [a]spoil of these cities and the livestock, the children of Israel took as booty for themselves; but they struck every man with the edge of the sword until they had destroyed them, and they left none breathing. [15a]As the LORD had commanded Moses His servant, so [b]Moses commanded Joshua, and [c]so Joshua did. [1]He left nothing undone of all that the LORD had commanded Moses.

SUMMARY OF JOSHUA'S CONQUESTS

[16]Thus Joshua took all this land: [a]the mountain country, all the South, [b]all the land of Goshen, the lowland, and the Jordan [1]plain—the mountains of Israel and its lowlands, [17a]from [1]Mount Halak and the ascent to Seir, even as far as Baal Gad in the Valley of Lebanon below Mount Hermon. He captured [b]all their kings, and struck them down and killed them. [18]Joshua made war a long time with all those kings. [19]There was not a city that made peace with the children of Israel, except [a]the Hivites, the inhabitants of Gibeon. All *the others* they took in battle. [20]For [a]it was of the LORD [1]to harden their hearts, that they should come against Israel in battle, that He might utterly destroy them, *and* that they might receive no mercy, but that He might destroy them, [b]as the LORD had commanded Moses.

[21]And at that time Joshua came and cut off [a]the Anakim from the mountains: from Hebron, from Debir, from Anab, from all the mountains of Judah, and from all the mountains of Israel; Joshua utterly destroyed them with their cities. [22]None of the Anakim were left in the land of the children of Israel; they remained only [a]in Gaza, in Gath, [b]and in Ashdod.

[23]So Joshua took the whole land, [a]according to all that the LORD had said to Moses; and Joshua gave it as an inheritance to Israel [b]according to their divisions by their tribes. Then the land [c]rested from war.

THE KINGS CONQUERED BY MOSES
(cf. Num. 21:21–35)

12 These *are* the kings of the land whom the children of Israel defeated, and whose land they possessed on the

---

11:8 [a]Gen. 49:13
[b]Josh. 13:6

11:11
[a]Deut. 20:16
[b]Josh. 10:40

11:12
[a]Num. 33:50–56; Deut. 7:2; 20:16

11:14
[a]Deut. 20:14–18

11:15
[a]Ex. 34:10–17
[b]Deut. 31:7, 8
[c]Josh. 1:7

11:16 [a]Josh. 12:8
[b]Josh. 10:40, 41

11:17 [a]Josh. 12:7
[b]Deut. 7:24

11:19
[a]Josh. 9:3–7

11:20
[a]Deut. 2:30
[b]Deut. 20:16, 17

11:21
[a]Num. 13:22, 33; Deut. 1:28; 9:2; Josh. 15:13, 14

11:22
[a]1 Sam. 17:4
[b]Josh. 15:46; 1 Sam. 5:1; Is. 20:1

11:23 [a]Ex. 33:2; Num. 34:2–15
[b]Num. 26:53; Josh. 14; 15
[c]Deut. 12:9, 10; 25:19; [Heb. 4:8]

11:8 [1]Heb. *Sidon Rabbah*   [2]Heb. *Misrephoth Maim,* lit. *Burnings of Water*
11:13 [1]Heb. *tel,* a heap of successive city ruins   11:15 [1]Lit. *He turned aside from nothing*   11:16 [1]Heb. *arabah*   11:17 [1]Lit. *The Smooth* or *Bald Mountain*
11:20 [1]Lit. *to make strong*

other side of the Jordan toward the rising of the sun, [a]from the River Arnon [b]to Mount Hermon, and all the eastern Jordan plain: [2]*One king was* [a]Sihon king of the Amorites, who dwelt in Heshbon *and* ruled half of Gilead, from Aroer, which is on the bank of the River Arnon, from the middle of that river, even as far as the River Jabbok, *which is* the border of the Ammonites, [3]and [a]the eastern Jordan plain from the [1]Sea of Chinneroth as far as the [2]Sea of the Arabah (the Salt Sea), [b]the road to Beth Jeshimoth, and [3]southward below [c]the[4] slopes of Pisgah. [4]*The other king was* [a]Og king of Bashan and his territory, *who was* of [b]the remnant of the giants, [c]who dwelt at Ashtaroth and at Edrei, [5]and reigned over [a]Mount Hermon, [b]over Salcah, over all Bashan, [c]as far as the border of the Geshurites and the Maachathites, and over half of Gilead *to* the border of Sihon king of Heshbon.

[6][a]These Moses the servant of the LORD and the children of Israel had conquered; and [b]Moses the servant of the LORD had given it *as* a possession to the Reubenites, the Gadites, and half the tribe of Manasseh.

THE KINGS CONQUERED BY JOSHUA

[7]And these *are* the kings of the country [a]which Joshua and the children of Israel conquered on this side of the Jordan, on the west, from Baal Gad in the Valley of Lebanon as far as [1]Mount Halak and the ascent to [b]Seir, which Joshua [c]gave to the tribes of Israel *as* a possession according to their divisions, [8][a]in the mountain country, in the lowlands, in the *Jordan* plain, in the slopes, in the wilderness, and in the South—[b]the Hittites, the Amorites, the Canaanites, the Perizzites, the Hivites, and the Jebusites: [9][a]the king of Jericho, one; [b]the king of Ai, which *is* beside Bethel, one; [10][a]the king of Jerusalem, one; the king of Hebron, one; [11]the king of Jarmuth, one; the king of Lachish, one; [12]the king of Eglon, one; [a]the king of Gezer, one; [13][a]the king of Debir, one; the king of Geder, one; [14]the king of Hormah, one; the king of Arad, one; [15][a]the king of Libnah, one; the king of Adullam, one; [16][a]the king of Makkedah, one; [b]the king of Bethel, one; [17]the king of Tappuah, one; [a]the king of Hepher, one; [18]the king of Aphek, one; the king of [1]Lasharon, one; [19]the king of Madon, one; [a]the king of Hazor, one; [20]the king of [a]Shimron Meron, one; the king of Achshaph, one; [21]the king of Taanach, one; the king of Megiddo, one; [22][a]the king of Kedesh, one; the king of Jokneam in Carmel, one; [23]the king of Dor in the [a]heights of Dor, one; the king of [b]the people of Gilgal, one; [24]the king of Tirzah, one—[a]all the kings, thirty-one.

REMAINING LAND TO BE CONQUERED

13 Now Joshua [a]was old, advanced in years. And the LORD said to him: "You are old, advanced in years, and there remains very much land yet to be possessed. [2][a]This is the land that yet remains: [b]all the territory of the Philistines and all [c]*that of* the Geshurites, [3][a]from Sihor, which *is* east of Egypt, as far as the border of Ekron northward (*which* is counted as Canaanite); the [b]five lords of the Philistines—the Gazites,

13:3 [a]1 Chr. 13:5; Jer. 2:18 [b]Judg. 3:3

12:3 [1]Sea of Galilee   [2]Lit. *Sea of the Plain,* the Dead Sea   [3]Or *Teman*
[4]Or *Ashdoth Pisgah*   12:7 [1]Lit. *The Bald Mountain*   12:18 [1]Or *Sharon*

12:1 [a]Num. 21:24
[b]Deut. 3:8

12:2
[a]Num. 21:24;
Deut. 2:24–27

12:3 [a]Deut. 3:17
[b]Josh. 13:20
[c]Deut. 3:17;
4:49

12:4
[a]Num. 21:33;
Deut. 3:4, 10
[b]Deut. 3:11;
Josh. 13:12
[c]Deut. 1:4

12:5 [a]Deut. 3:8
[b]Deut. 3:10;
Josh. 13:11;
1 Chr. 5:11
[c]Deut. 3:14;
1 Sam. 27:8

12:6
[a]Num. 21:24, 35
[b]Num. 32:29–
33; Deut. 3:12;
Josh. 13:8

12:7 [a]Josh. 11:17
[b]Gen. 14:6; 32:3;
Deut. 2:1, 4
[c]Josh. 11:23

12:8
[a]Josh. 10:40;
11:16 [b]Ex. 3:8;
23:23; Josh. 9:1

12:9 [a]Josh. 6:2
[b]Josh. 8:29

12:10
[a]Josh. 10:23

12:12
[a]Josh. 10:33

12:13
[a]Josh. 10:38, 39

12:15
[a]Josh. 10:29, 30

12:16
[a]Josh. 10:28
[b]Josh. 8:17;
Judg. 1:22

12:17 [a]1 Kin. 4:10

12:19 [a]Josh. 11:10

12:20 [a]Josh. 11:1;
19:15

12:22
[a]Josh. 19:37;
20:7; 21:32

12:23 [a]Josh. 11:2
[b]Gen. 14:1, 2;
Is. 9:1

12:24
[a]Deut. 7:24

13:1 [a]Josh. 14:10;
23:1, 2

13:2
[a]Judg. 3:1–3
[b]Joel 3:4
[c]Josh. 13:13;
2 Sam. 3:3

the Ashdodites, the Ashkelonites, the Gittites, and the Ekronites; also [c]the Avites; [4]from the south, all the land of the Canaanites, and Mearah that belongs to the Sidonians [a]as far as Aphek, to the border of [b]the Amorites; [5]the land of [a]the [1]Gebalites, and all Lebanon, toward the sunrise, [b]from Baal Gad below Mount Hermon as far as the entrance to Hamath; [6]all the inhabitants of the mountains from Lebanon as far as [a]the [1]Brook Misrephoth, *and* all the Sidonians—them [b]I will drive out from before the children of Israel; only [c]divide[2] it by lot to Israel as an inheritance, as I have commanded you. [7]Now therefore, divide this land as an inheritance to the nine tribes and half the tribe of Manasseh."

THE LAND DIVIDED EAST OF THE JORDAN

[8]With the other half-tribe the Reubenites and the Gadites received their inheritance, [a]which Moses had given them, [b]beyond the Jordan eastward, as Moses the servant of the LORD had given them: [9]from Aroer which *is* on the bank of the River Arnon, and the town that *is* in the midst of the ravine, [a]and all the plain of Medeba as far as Dibon; [10a]all the cities of Sihon king of the Amorites, who reigned in Heshbon, as far as the border of the children of Ammon; [11a]Gilead, and the border of the Geshurites and Maachathites, all Mount Hermon, and all Bashan as far as Salcah; [12]all the kingdom of Og in Bashan, who reigned in Ashtaroth and Edrei, who remained of [a]the remnant of the giants; [b]for Moses had [1]defeated and [2]cast out these.

[13]Nevertheless the children of Israel [a]did not drive out the Geshurites or the Maachathites, but the Geshurites and the Maachathites dwell among the Israelites until this day.

[14a]Only to the tribe of Levi he had given [1]no inheritance; the sacrifices of the LORD God of Israel made by fire *are* their inheritance, [b]as He said to them.

THE LAND OF REUBEN

[15a]And Moses had given to the tribe of the children of Reuben *an inheritance* according to their families. [16]Their territory was [a]from Aroer, which *is* on the bank of the River Arnon, [b]and the city that *is* in the midst of the ravine, [c]and all the plain by Medeba; [17a]Heshbon and all its cities that *are* in the plain: Dibon, Bamoth Baal, Beth Baal Meon, [18a]Jahaza, Kedemoth, Mephaath, [19a]Kirjathaim, [b]Sibmah, Zereth Shahar on the mountain of the valley, [20]Beth Peor, [a]the slopes of Pisgah, and Beth Jeshimoth— [21a]all the cities of the plain and all the kingdom of Sihon king of the Amorites, who reigned in Heshbon, [b]whom Moses had struck [c]with the princes of Midian: Evi, Rekem, Zur, Hur, and Reba, who *were* princes of Sihon dwelling in the country. [22]The children of Israel also killed with the sword [a]Balaam the son of Beor, the [1]soothsayer, among those who were killed by them. [23]And the border of the children of Reuben was the bank of the Jordan. This *was* the inheritance of the children of Reuben according to their families, the cities and their villages.

13:3 [c]Deut. 2:23
13:4 [a]Josh. 12:18; 19:30; 1 Sam. 4:1; 1 Kin. 20:26, 30 [b]Judg. 1:34
13:5 [a]1 Kin. 5:18; Ezek. 27:9 [b]Josh. 12:7
13:6 [a]Josh. 11:8 [b]Josh. 23:13; Judg. 2:21, 23 [c]Josh. 14:1, 2
13:8 [a]Num. 32:33; Deut. 3:12, 13; Josh. 22:4 [b]Josh. 12:1–6
13:9 [a]Num. 21:30; Josh. 13:16
13:10 [a]Num. 21:24, 25
13:11 [a]Num. 32:1; Josh. 12:5
13:12 [a]Deut. 3:11; Josh. 12:4 [b]Num. 21:24, 34, 35
13:13 [a]Josh. 13:11
13:14 [a]Num. 18:20, 23, 24; Deut. 18:1; Josh. 14:3, 4 [b]Josh. 13:33
13:15 [a]Num. 34:14; Josh. 13:15–23
13:16 [a]Josh. 12:2 [b]Num. 21:28 [c]Num. 21:30; Josh. 13:9
13:17 [a]Num. 21:28, 30
13:18 [a]Num. 21:23; Judg. 11:20; Is. 15:4; Jer. 48:34
13:19 [a]Num. 32:37; Jer. 48:1, 23; Ezek. 25:9 [b]Num. 32:38
13:20 [a]Deut. 3:17; Josh. 12:3
13:21 [a]Deut. 3:10 [b]Num. 21:24 [c]Num. 31:8
13:22 [a]Num. 22:5; 31:8

13:5 [1]Or *Giblites*   13:6 [1]Heb. *Misrephoth Maim,* lit. *Burnings of Water* [2]*apportion*   13:12 [1]Lit. *struck* [2]*dispossessed*   13:14 [1]*no land as a possession*   13:22 [1]*diviner*

THE LAND OF GAD

[24a]Moses also had given *an inheritance* to the tribe of Gad, to the children of Gad according to their families. [25a]Their territory was Jazer, and all the cities of Gilead, [b]and half the land of the Ammonites as far as Aroer, which *is* before [c]Rabbah, [26]and from Heshbon to Ramath Mizpah and Betonim, and from Mahanaim to the border of Debir, [27]and in the valley [a]Beth Haram, Beth Nimrah, [b]Succoth, and Zaphon, the rest of the kingdom of Sihon king of Heshbon, with the Jordan as *its* border, as far as the edge [c]of the [1]Sea of Chinnereth, on the other side of the Jordan eastward. [28]This *is* the inheritance of the children of Gad according to their families, the cities and their villages.

HALF THE TRIBE OF MANASSEH (EAST)

[29a]Moses also had given *an inheritance* to half the tribe of Manasseh; it was for half the tribe of the children of Manasseh according to their families: [30]Their territory was from Mahanaim, all Bashan, all the kingdom of Og king of Bashan, and [a]all the towns of Jair which are in Bashan, sixty cities; [31]half of Gilead, and [a]Ashtaroth and Edrei, cities of the kingdom of Og in Bashan, *were* for the [b]children of Machir the son of Manasseh, for half of the children of Machir according to their families.

[32]These *are the areas* which Moses had [1]distributed as an inheritance in the plains of Moab on the other side of the Jordan, by Jericho eastward. [33a]But to the tribe of Levi Moses had given no inheritance; the LORD God of Israel *was* their inheritance, [b]as He had said to them.

THE LAND DIVIDED WEST OF THE JORDAN

14 These *are the areas* which the children of Israel inherited in the land of Canaan, [a]which Eleazar the priest, Joshua the son of Nun, and the heads of the fathers of the tribes of the children of Israel distributed as an inheritance to them. [2]Their inheritance *was* [a]by lot, as the LORD had commanded by the hand of Moses, for the nine tribes and the half-tribe. [3a]For Moses had given the inheritance of the two tribes and the half-tribe on the other side of the Jordan; but to the Levites he had given no inheritance among them. [4]For [a]the children of Joseph were two tribes: Manasseh and Ephraim. And they gave no part to the Levites in the land, except [b]cities to dwell *in,* with their common-lands for their livestock and their property. [5a]As the LORD had commanded Moses, so the children of Israel did; and they divided the land.

CALEB INHERITS HEBRON

[6]Then the children of Judah came to Joshua in Gilgal. And Caleb the son of Jephunneh the [a]Kenizzite said to him: "You know [b]the word which the LORD said to Moses the man of God concerning [c]you and me in Kadesh Barnea. [7]I *was* forty years old when Moses the servant of the LORD [a]sent me from Kadesh Barnea to spy out the land, and I brought back word to him as *it was* in my heart. [8]Nevertheless [a]my brethren who went up with me made the [1]heart of the people melt, but I

13:24
[a]Num. 34:14;
1 Chr. 5:11

13:25
[a]Num. 32:1, 35
[b]Judg. 11:13, 15
[c]Deut. 3:11;
2 Sam. 11:1;
12:26

13:27
[a]Num. 32:36
[b]Gen. 33:17;
1 Kin. 7:46
[c]Num. 34:11;
Deut. 3:17

13:29
[a]Num. 34:14;
1 Chr. 5:23

13:30
[a]Num. 32:41;
1 Chr. 2:23

13:31
[a]Josh. 9:10; 12:4;
13:12; 1 Chr. 6:71
[b]Num. 32:39,
40; Josh. 17:1

13:33
[a]Deut. 18:1;
Josh. 13:14; 18:7
[b]Num. 18:20;
Deut. 10:9;
18:1, 2

14:1
[a]Num. 34:16–29

14:2
[a]Num. 26:55;
33:54; 34:13;
Ps. 16:5

14:3
[a]Num. 32:33;
Josh. 13:8,
32, 33

14:4 [a]Gen. 41:51;
46:20; 48:1, 5;
Num. 26:28;
2 Chr. 30:1
[b]Num. 35:2–8;
Josh. 21:1–42

14:5
[a]Num. 35:2;
Josh. 21:2

14:6
[a]Num. 32:11, 12
[b]Num. 14:24, 30
[c]Num. 13:26

14:7 [a]Num. 13:6,
17; 14:6

14:8
[a]Num. 13:31, 32;
Deut. 1:28

wholly ᵇfollowed the LORD my God. ⁹So Moses swore on that day, saying, ᵃ'Surely the land ᵇwhere your foot has trodden shall be your inheritance and your children's forever, because you have wholly followed the LORD my God.' ¹⁰And now, behold, the LORD has kept me ᵃalive, ᵇas He said, these forty-five years, ever since the LORD spoke this word to Moses while Israel ¹wandered in the wilderness; and now, here I am this day, eighty-five years old. ¹¹ᵃAs yet I *am as* strong this day as on the day that Moses sent me; just as my strength *was* then, so now *is* my strength for war, both ᵇfor going out and for coming in. ¹²Now therefore, give me this mountain of which the LORD spoke in that day; for you heard in that day how ᵃthe Anakim *were* there, and *that* the cities *were* great *and* fortified. ᵇIt may be that the LORD *will be* with me, and ᶜI shall be able to drive them out as the LORD said."

¹³And Joshua ᵃblessed him, ᵇand gave Hebron to Caleb the son of Jephunneh as an inheritance. ¹⁴ᵃHebron therefore became the inheritance of Caleb the son of Jephunneh the Kenizzite to this day, because he ᵇwholly followed the LORD God of Israel. ¹⁵And ᵃthe name of Hebron formerly was Kirjath Arba (*Arba was* the greatest man among the Anakim).

ᵇThen the land had rest from war.

THE LAND OF JUDAH

15 So *this* was the ¹lot of the tribe of the children of Judah according to their families:

ᵃThe border of Edom at the ᵇWilderness of Zin southward *was* the extreme southern boundary. ²And their ᵃsouthern border began at the shore of the Salt Sea, from the bay that faces southward. ³Then it went out to the southern side of ᵃthe Ascent of Akrabbim, passed along to Zin, ascended on the south side of Kadesh Barnea, passed along to Hezron, went up to Adar, and went around to Karkaa. ⁴*From there* it passed ᵃtoward Azmon and went out to the Brook of Egypt; and the border ended at the sea. This shall be your southern border.

⁵The east border *was* the Salt Sea as far as the mouth of the Jordan.

And the ᵃborder on the northern quarter *began* at the bay of the sea at the mouth of the Jordan. ⁶The border went up to ᵃBeth Hoglah and passed north of Beth Arabah; and the border went up ᵇto the stone of Bohan the son of Reuben. ⁷Then the border went up toward ᵃDebir from ᵇthe Valley of Achor, and it turned northward toward Gilgal, which *is* before the Ascent of Adummim, which *is* on the south side of the valley. The border continued toward the waters of En Shemesh and ended at ᶜEn Rogel. ⁸And the border went up ᵃby the Valley of the Son of Hinnom to the southern slope of the ᵇJebusite *city* (which *is* Jerusalem). The border went up to the top of the mountain that *lies* before the Valley of Hinnom westward, which *is* at the end of the Valley ᶜof ¹Rephaim northward. ⁹Then the border went around from the top of the hill to ᵃthe fountain of the water of Nephtoah, and extended to the cities of Mount Ephron. And the border went around ᵇto Baalah (which *is* ᶜKirjath Jearim). ¹⁰Then the border ¹turned westward from Baalah to Mount Seir, passed along to the

Cross references (margin)

14:8 ᵇNum. 14:24; Deut. 1:36

14:9 ᵃNum. 14:23, 24; ᵇNum. 13:22; Deut. 1:36

14:10 ᵃNum. 14:24, 30, 38 ᵇJosh. 5:6; Neh. 9:21

14:11 ᵃDeut. 34:7 ᵇDeut. 31:2

14:12 ᵃNum. 13:28, 33 ᵇRom. 8:31 ᶜJosh. 15:14; Judg. 1:20

14:13 ᵃJosh. 22:6 ᵇJosh. 10:37; 15:13

14:14 ᵃJosh. 21:12 ᵇJosh. 14:8, 9

14:15 ᵃGen. 23:2; Josh. 15:13 ᵇJosh. 11:23

15:1 ᵃNum. 34:3 ᵇNum. 33:36

15:2 ᵃNum. 34:3, 4

15:3 ᵃNum. 34:4

15:4 ᵃNum. 34:5

15:5 ᵃJosh. 18:15–19

15:6 ᵃJosh. 18:19, 21 ᵇJosh. 18:17

15:7 ᵃJosh. 13:26 ᵇJosh. 7:26 ᶜ2 Sam. 17:17; 1 Kin. 1:9

15:8 ᵃJosh. 18:16; 2 Kin. 23:10; Jer. 19:2, 6 ᵇJosh. 15:63; 18:28; Judg. 1:21; 19:10 ᶜJosh. 18:16

15:9 ᵃJosh. 18:15 ᵇ1 Chr. 13:6 ᶜJudg. 18:12

14:10 ¹Lit. *walked*   15:1 ¹*allotment*   15:8 ¹Lit. *Giants*   15:10 ¹*turned around*

side of Mount Jearim on the north (which *is* Chesalon), went down to Beth Shemesh, and passed on to ᵃTimnah. ¹¹And the border went out to the side of ᵃEkron northward. Then the border went around to Shicron, passed along to Mount Baalah, and extended to Jabneel; and the border ended at the sea.

¹²The west border *was* ᵃthe coastline of the Great Sea. This *is* the boundary of the children of Judah all around according to their families.

CALEB OCCUPIES HEBRON AND DEBIR
(Judg. 1:11–15)

¹³ᵃNow to Caleb the son of Jephunneh he gave a share among the children of ᵇJudah, according to the commandment of the LORD to Joshua, *namely,* ᶜKirjath Arba, which *is* Hebron (*Arba was* the father of Anak). ¹⁴Caleb drove out ᵃthe three sons of Anak from there: ᵇSheshai, Ahiman, and Talmai, the children of Anak. ¹⁵Then ᵃhe went up from there to the inhabitants of Debir (formerly the name of Debir *was* Kirjath Sepher).

¹⁶ᵃAnd Caleb said, "He who ¹attacks Kirjath Sepher and takes it, to him I will give Achsah my daughter as wife." ¹⁷So ᵃOthniel the ᵇson of Kenaz, the brother of Caleb, took it; and he gave him ᶜAchsah his daughter as wife. ¹⁸ᵃNow it was so, when she came *to him,* that she persuaded him to ask her father for a field. So ᵇshe dismounted from *her* donkey, and Caleb said to her, "What do you wish?" ¹⁹She answered, "Give me a ᵃblessing; since you have given me land in the South, give me also springs of water." So he gave her the upper springs and the lower springs.

THE CITIES OF JUDAH

²⁰This *was* the inheritance of the tribe of the children of Judah according to their families:

²¹The cities at the limits of the tribe of the children of Judah, toward the border of Edom in the South, were Kabzeel, ᵃEder, Jagur, ²²Kinah, Dimonah, Adadah, ²³Kedesh, Hazor, Ithnan, ²⁴ᵃZiph, Telem, Bealoth, ²⁵Hazor, Hadattah, Kerioth, Hezron (which *is* Hazor), ²⁶Amam, Shema, Moladah, ²⁷Hazar Gaddah, Heshmon, Beth Pelet, ²⁸Hazar Shual, ᵃBeersheba, Bizjothjah, ²⁹Baalah, Ijim, Ezem, ³⁰Eltolad, Chesil, ᵃHormah, ³¹ᵃZiklag, Madmannah, Sansannah, ³²Lebaoth, Shilhim, Ain, and ᵃRimmon: all the cities *are* twenty-nine, with their villages.

³³In the lowland: ᵃEshtaol, Zorah, Ashnah, ³⁴Zanoah, En Gannim, Tappuah, Enam, ³⁵Jarmuth, ᵃAdullam, Socoh, Azekah, ³⁶Sharaim, Adithaim, Gederah, and Gederothaim: fourteen cities with their villages; ³⁷Zenan, Hadashah, Migdal Gad, ³⁸Dilean, Mizpah, ᵃJoktheel, ³⁹ᵃLachish, Bozkath, ᵇEglon, ⁴⁰Cabbon, ¹Lahmas, Kithlish, ⁴¹Gederoth, Beth Dagon, Naamah, and Makkedah: sixteen cities with their villages; ⁴²ᵃLibnah, Ether, Ashan, ⁴³Jiphtah, Ashnah, Nezib, ⁴⁴Keilah, Achzib, and Mareshah: nine cities with their villages; ⁴⁵Ekron, with its towns and villages; ⁴⁶from Ekron to the sea, all that *lay* near ᵃAshdod, with their villages; ⁴⁷Ashdod with its towns and villages, Gaza with

15:10
ᵃGen. 38:13;
Judg. 14:1

15:11
ᵃJosh. 19:43

15:12
ᵃNum. 34:6, 7;
Josh. 15:47

15:13
ᵃJosh. 14:13
ᵇNum. 13:6
ᶜJosh. 14:15

15:14 ᵃJudg. 1:10,
20 ᵇNum. 13:22

15:15
ᵃJosh. 10:38;
Judg. 1:11

15:16 ᵃJudg. 1:12

15:17
ᵃJudg. 1:13; 3:9
ᵇNum. 32:12;
Josh. 14:6
ᶜJudg. 1:12

15:18 ᵃJudg. 1:14
ᵇGen. 24:64;
1 Sam. 25:23

15:19 ᵃGen. 33:11

15:21
ᵃGen. 35:21

15:24
ᵃ1 Sam. 23:14

15:28
ᵃGen. 21:31;
Josh. 19:2

15:30
ᵃJosh. 19:4

15:31
ᵃJosh. 19:5;
1 Sam. 27:6; 30:1

15:32
ᵃJudg. 20:45, 47

15:33
ᵃJudg. 13:25;
16:31

15:35
ᵃ1 Sam. 22:1

15:38
ᵃ2 Kin. 14:7

15:39
ᵃ2 Kin. 14:19
ᵇJosh. 10:3

15:42
ᵃJosh. 21:13

15:46
ᵃJosh. 11:22

its towns and villages—as far as [a]the Brook of Egypt and [b]the Great Sea with *its* coastline.

[48]And in the mountain country: Shamir, Jattir, Sochoh, [49]Dannah, Kirjath Sannah (which *is* Debir), [50]Anab, Eshtemoh, Anim, [51a]Goshen, Holon, and Giloh: eleven cities with their villages; [52]Arab, Dumah, Eshean, [53]Janum, Beth Tappuah, Aphekah, [54]Humtah, [a]Kirjath Arba (which *is* Hebron), and Zior: nine cities with their villages; [55a]Maon, Carmel, Ziph, Juttah, [56]Jezreel, Jokdeam, Zanoah, [57]Kain, Gibeah, and Timnah: ten cities with their villages; [58]Halhul, Beth Zur, Gedor, [59]Maarath, Beth Anoth, and Eltekon: six cities with their villages; [60a]Kirjath Baal (which *is* Kirjath Jearim) and Rabbah: two cities with their villages.

[61]In the wilderness: Beth Arabah, Middin, Secacah, [62]Nibshan, the City of Salt, and [a]En Gedi: six cities with their villages.

[63]As for the Jebusites, the inhabitants of Jerusalem, [a]the children of Judah could not drive them out; [b]but the Jebusites dwell with the children of Judah at Jerusalem to this day.

EPHRAIM AND WEST MANASSEH

16 The lot [1]fell to the children of Joseph from the Jordan, by Jericho, to the waters of Jericho on the east, to the [a]wilderness that goes up from Jericho through the mountains to [2]Bethel, [2]then went out [1]from [a]Bethel to Luz, passed along to the border of the Archites at Ataroth, [3]and went down westward to the boundary of the Japhletites, [a]as far as the boundary of Lower Beth Horon to [b]Gezer; and [1]it ended at the sea. [4a]So the children of Joseph, Manasseh and Ephraim, took their [1]inheritance.

THE LAND OF EPHRAIM

[5a]The border of the children of Ephraim, according to their families, was *thus:* The border of their inheritance on the east side was [b]Ataroth Addar [c]as far as Upper Beth Horon. [6]And the border went out toward the sea on the north side of [a]Michmethath; then the border went around eastward to Taanath Shiloh, and passed by it on the east of Janohah. [7]Then it went down from Janohah to Ataroth and [1]Naarah, reached to Jericho, and came out at the Jordan.

[8]The border went out from [a]Tappuah westward to the [b]Brook Kanah, and [1]it ended at the sea. This *was* the inheritance of the tribe of the children of Ephraim according to their families. [9a]The separate cities for the children of Ephraim *were* among the inheritance of the children of Manasseh, all the cities with their villages.

[10a]And they did not drive out the Canaanites who dwelt in Gezer; but the Canaanites dwell among the Ephraimites to this day and have become forced laborers.

THE OTHER HALF-TRIBE OF MANASSEH (WEST)

17 There was also a lot for the tribe of Manasseh, for he *was* the [a]firstborn of Joseph: *namely* for [b]Machir the firstborn of Manasseh, the father of Gilead, because he was a man

---

15:47 [a]Josh. 15:4
[b]Num. 34:6

15:51
[a]Josh. 10:41;
11:16

15:54
[a]Josh. 14:15

15:55
[a]1 Sam. 23:24, 25

15:60
[a]Josh. 18:14;
1 Sam. 7:1, 2

15:62
[a]1 Sam. 23:29;
Ezek. 47:10

15:63
[a]Judg. 1:8, 21;
2 Sam. 5:6;
1 Chr. 11:4
[b]Judg. 1:21

16:1 [a]Josh. 8:15;
18:12

16:2
[a]Josh. 18:13;
Judg. 1:26

16:3
[a]Josh. 18:13;
1 Kin. 9:17;
2 Chr. 8:5
[b]Josh. 21:21;
1 Kin. 9:15;
1 Chr. 7:28

16:4 [a]Josh. 17:14

16:5 [a]Judg. 1:29;
1 Chr. 7:28, 29
[b]Josh. 18:13
[c]2 Chr. 8:5

16:6 [a]Josh. 17:7

16:8 [a]Josh. 17:8
[b]Josh. 17:9

16:9 [a]Josh. 17:9

16:10
[a]Josh. 15:63;
17:12, 13;
Judg. 1:29;
1 Kin. 9:16

17:1 [a]Gen. 41:51;
46:20; 48:18
[b]Gen. 50:23;
Judg. 5:14

16:1 [1]Lit. *went out*   [2]LXX *Bethel Luz*   16:2 [1]LXX *to Bethel*,   16:3 [1]Lit. *the goings out of it were at the sea*   16:4 [1]*possession*   16:7 [1]*Naaran,* 1 Chr. 7:28
16:8 [1]Lit. *the goings out of it were at the sea*

of war; therefore he was given [c]Gilead and Bashan. [2]And there was *a lot* for [a]the rest of the children of Manasseh according to their families: [b]for the children of [1]Abiezer, the children of Helek, [c]the children of Asriel, the children of Shechem, [d]the children of Hepher, and the children of Shemida; these *were* the male children of Manasseh the son of Joseph according to their families.

[3]But [a]Zelophehad the son of Hepher, the son of Gilead, the son of Machir, the son of Manasseh, had no sons, but only daughters. And these *are* the names of his daughters: Mahlah, Noah, Hoglah, Milcah, and Tirzah. [4]And they came near before [a]Eleazar the priest, before Joshua the son of Nun, and before the rulers, saying, [b]"The LORD commanded Moses to give us an [1]inheritance among our brothers." Therefore, according to the commandment of the LORD, he gave them an inheritance among their father's brothers. [5]Ten shares fell to [a]Manasseh, besides the land of Gilead and Bashan, which *were* on the other side of the Jordan, [6]because the daughters of Manasseh received an inheritance among his sons; and the rest of Manasseh's sons had the land of Gilead.

[7]And the territory of Manasseh was from Asher to [a]Michmethath, that *lies* east of Shechem; and the border went along south to the inhabitants of En Tappuah. [8]Manasseh had the land of Tappuah, but [a]Tappuah on the border of Manasseh *belonged* to the children of Ephraim. [9]And the [1]border descended to the [2]Brook Kanah, southward to the brook. [a]These cities of Ephraim *are* among the cities of Manasseh. The border of Manasseh *was* on the north side of the brook; and it ended at the sea.

[10]Southward *it was* Ephraim's, northward *it was* Manasseh's, and the sea was its border. Manasseh's territory was adjoining Asher on the north and Issachar on the east. [11]And in Issachar and in Asher, [a]Manasseh had [b]Beth Shean and its towns, Ibleam and its towns, the inhabitants of Dor and its towns, the inhabitants of En Dor and its towns, the inhabitants of Taanach and its towns, and the inhabitants of Megiddo and its towns—three hilly regions. [12]Yet [a]the children of Manasseh could not drive out *the inhabitants of* those cities, but the Canaanites were determined to dwell in that land. [13]And it happened, when the children of Israel grew strong, that they put the Canaanites to [a]forced labor, but did not utterly drive them out.

MORE LAND FOR EPHRAIM AND MANASSEH

[14a]Then the children of Joseph spoke to Joshua, saying, "Why have you given us *only* [b]one [1]lot and one share to inherit, since we *are* [c]a great people, inasmuch as the LORD has blessed us until now?"

[15]So Joshua answered them, "If you *are* a great people, *then* go up to the forest *country* and clear a place for yourself there in the land of the Perizzites and the giants, since the mountains of Ephraim are too confined for you."

[16]But the children of Joseph said, "The mountain country is not enough for us; and all the Canaanites who dwell in the

---

17:1 [c]Deut. 3:15

17:2
[a]Num. 26:29–33
[b]1 Chr. 7:18
[c]Num. 26:31
[d]Num. 26:32

17:3
[a]Num. 26:33;
27:1; 36:2

17:4 [a]Josh. 14:1
[b]Num. 27:2–11

17:5 [a]Josh. 22:7

17:7 [a]Josh. 16:6

17:8 [a]Josh. 16:8

17:9 [a]Josh. 16:9

17:11 [a]1 Chr. 7:29
[b]Judg. 1:27;
1 Sam. 31:10;
1 Kin. 4:12

17:12 [a]Judg. 1:19,
27, 28

17:13
[a]Josh. 16:10

17:14 [a]Josh. 16:4
[b]Gen. 48:22
[c]Gen. 48:19;
Num. 26:34, 37

17:2 [1]*Jeezer,* Num. 26:30   17:4 [1]*possession*   17:9 [1]*boundary*   [2]*Wadi*
17:14 [1]*allotment*

land of the valley have ᵃchariots of iron, *both those* who *are* of Beth Shean and its towns and *those* who *are* ᵇof the Valley of Jezreel."

¹⁷And Joshua spoke to the house of Joseph—to Ephraim and Manasseh—saying, "You *are* a great people and have great power; you shall not have *only* one ¹lot, ¹⁸but the mountain country shall be yours. Although it *is* wooded, you shall cut it down, and its ¹farthest extent shall be yours; for you shall drive out the Canaanites, ᵃthough they have iron chariots *and* are strong."

THE REMAINDER OF THE LAND DIVIDED

18 Now the whole congregation of the children of Israel assembled together ᵃat Shiloh, and ᵇset up the tabernacle of meeting there. And the land was subdued before them. ²But there remained among the children of Israel seven tribes which had not yet received their inheritance.

³Then Joshua said to the children of Israel: ᵃ"How long will you neglect to go and possess the land which the LORD God of your fathers has given you? ⁴Pick out from among you three men for *each* tribe, and I will send them; they shall rise and go through the land, survey it according to their inheritance, and come *back* to me. ⁵And they shall divide it into seven parts. ᵃJudah shall remain in their territory on the south, and the ᵇhouse of Joseph shall remain in their territory on the north. ⁶You shall therefore ¹survey the land in seven parts and bring *the survey* here to me, ᵃthat I may cast lots for you here before the LORD our God. ⁷ᵃBut the Levites have no part among you, for the priesthood of the LORD *is* their inheritance. ᵇAnd Gad, Reuben, and half the tribe of Manasseh have received their inheritance beyond the Jordan on the east, which Moses the servant of the LORD gave them."

⁸Then the men arose to go away; and Joshua charged those who went to ¹survey the land, saying, "Go, walk ᵃthrough the land, survey it, and come back to me, that I may cast lots for you here before the LORD in Shiloh." ⁹So the men went, passed through the land, and ¹wrote the survey in a book in seven parts by cities; and they came to Joshua at the camp in Shiloh. ¹⁰Then Joshua cast ᵃlots for them in Shiloh before the LORD, and there ᵇJoshua divided the land to the children of Israel according to their ¹divisions.

THE LAND OF BENJAMIN

¹¹ᵃNow the lot of the tribe of the children of Benjamin came up according to their families, and the territory of their lot came out between the children of Judah and the children of Joseph. ¹²ᵃTheir border on the north side began at the Jordan, and the border went up to the side of Jericho on the north, and went up through the mountains westward; it ended at the Wilderness of Beth Aven. ¹³The border went over from there toward Luz, to the side of Luz ᵃ(which *is* Bethel) southward; and the border descended to Ataroth Addar, near the hill that *lies* on the south side ᵇof Lower Beth Horon.

17:16
ᵃJosh. 17:18;
Judg. 1:19; 4:3
ᵇJosh. 19:18;
1 Kin. 4:12

17:18 ᵃDeut. 20:1

18:1 ᵃJosh. 19:51;
21:2; 22:9;
Jer. 7:12
ᵇJudg. 18:31;
1 Sam. 1:3, 24;
4:3, 4

18:3 ᵃJudg. 18:9

18:5 ᵃJosh. 15:1
ᵇJosh. 16:1—
17:18

18:6 ᵃJosh. 14:2;
18:10

18:7
ᵃNum. 18:7, 20;
Josh. 13:33
ᵇJosh. 13:8

18:8 ᵃGen. 13:17

18:10 ᵃActs 13:19
ᵇNum. 34:16–29;
Josh. 19:51

18:11 ᵃJudg. 1:21

18:12 ᵃJosh. 16:1

18:13
ᵃGen. 28:19;
Josh. 16:2;
Judg. 1:23
ᵇJosh. 16:3

17:17 ¹*allotment*   17:18 ¹Lit. *goings out*   18:6 ¹*describe in writing*
18:8 ¹*describe in writing*   18:9 ¹*described it in writing*   18:10 ¹*portions*

[14]Then the border extended around the west side to the south, from the hill that *lies* before Beth Horon southward; and [1]it ended at [a]Kirjath Baal (which *is* Kirjath Jearim), a city of the children of Judah. This *was* the west side.

[15]The south side *began* at the end of Kirjath Jearim, and the border extended on the west and went out to [a]the spring of the waters of Nephtoah. [16]Then the border came down to the end of the mountain that *lies* before [a]the Valley of the Son of Hinnom, which *is* in the Valley of the [1]Rephaim on the north, descended to the Valley of Hinnom, to the side of the Jebusite *city* on the south, and descended to [b]En Rogel. [17]And it went around from the north, went out to En Shemesh, and extended toward Geliloth, which is before the Ascent of Adummim, and descended to [a]the stone of Bohan the son of Reuben. [18]Then it passed along toward the north side of [1]Arabah, and went down to Arabah. [19]And the border passed along to the north side of Beth Hoglah; then [1]the border ended at the north bay at the [a]Salt Sea, at the south end of the Jordan. This *was* the southern boundary.

[20]The Jordan was its border on the east side. This *was* the inheritance of the children of Benjamin, according to its boundaries all around, according to their families.

[21]Now the cities of the tribe of the children of Benjamin, according to their families, were Jericho, Beth Hoglah, Emek Keziz, [22]Beth Arabah, Zemaraim, Bethel, [23]Avim, Parah, Ophrah, [24]Chephar Haammoni, Ophni, and Gaba: twelve cities with their villages; [25][a]Gibeon, [b]Ramah, Beeroth, [26]Mizpah, Chephirah, Mozah, [27]Rekem, Irpeel, Taralah, [28]Zelah, Eleph, [a]Jebus (which *is* Jerusalem), Gibeath, *and* Kirjath: fourteen cities with their villages. This was the inheritance of the children of Benjamin according to their families.

SIMEON'S INHERITANCE WITH JUDAH

19 The [a]second lot came out for Simeon, for the tribe of the children of Simeon according to their families. [b]And their inheritance was within the inheritance of the children of Judah. [2][a]They had in their inheritance Beersheba (Sheba), Moladah, [3]Hazar Shual, Balah, Ezem, [4]Eltolad, Bethul, Hormah, [5]Ziklag, Beth Marcaboth, Hazar Susah, [6]Beth Lebaoth, and Sharuhen: thirteen cities and their villages; [7]Ain, Rimmon, Ether, and Ashan: four cities and their villages; [8]and all the villages that *were* all around these cities as far as Baalath Beer, [a]Ramah of the South. This *was* the inheritance of the tribe of the children of Simeon according to their families.

[9]The inheritance of the children of Simeon *was included* in the share of the children of Judah, for the share of the children of Judah was [1]too much for them. [a]Therefore the children of Simeon had *their* inheritance within the inheritance of [2]that people.

THE LAND OF ZEBULUN

[10]The third lot came out for the children of Zebulun according to their families, and the border of their inheritance was as far as Sarid. [11][a]Their border went toward the west and

18:14 [a]Josh. 15:9
18:15 [a]Josh. 15:9
18:16 [a]Josh. 15:8 [b]Josh. 15:7
18:17 [a]Josh. 15:6
18:19 [a]Josh. 15:2, 5
18:25 [a]Josh. 11:19; 21:17; 1 Kin. 3:4, 5 [b]Jer. 31:15
18:28 [a]Josh. 15:8, 63
19:1 [a]Judg. 1:3 [b]Josh. 19:9
19:2 [a]1 Chr. 4:28
19:8 [a]1 Sam. 30:27
19:9 [a]Josh. 19:1
19:11 [a]Gen. 49:13

18:14 [1]Lit. *its goings out were*   18:16 [1]Lit. *Giants*   18:18 [1]*Beth Arabah,* Josh. 15:6; 18:22   18:19 [1]Lit. *the goings out of the border were*   19:9 [1]*too large* [2]Lit. *them*

to Maralah, went to Dabbasheth, and extended along the brook that is [b]east of Jokneam. [12]Then from Sarid it went eastward toward the sunrise along the border of Chisloth Tabor, and went out toward [a]Daberath, bypassing Japhia. [13]And from there it passed along on the east of [a]Gath Hepher, toward Eth Kazin, and extended to Rimmon, which borders on Neah. [14]Then the border went around it on the north side of Hannathon, and [1]it ended in the Valley of Jiphthah El. [15]Included were Kattath, Nahallal, Shimron, Idalah, and Bethlehem: twelve cities with their villages. [16]This *was* the inheritance of the children of Zebulun according to their families, these cities with their villages.

THE LAND OF ISSACHAR

[17]The fourth lot came out to Issachar, for the children of Issachar according to their families. [18]And their territory went to Jezreel, and *included* Chesulloth, Shunem, [19]Haphraim, Shion, Anaharath, [20]Rabbith, Kishion, Abez, [21]Remeth, En Gannim, En Haddah, and Beth Pazzez. [22]And the border reached to Tabor, Shahazimah, and [a]Beth Shemesh; their border ended at the Jordan: sixteen cities with their villages. [23]This *was* the inheritance of the tribe of the children of Issachar according to their families, the cities and their villages.

THE LAND OF ASHER

[24a]The fifth lot came out for the tribe of the children of Asher according to their families. [25]And their territory included Helkath, Hali, Beten, Achshaph, [26]Alammelech, Amad, and Mishal; it reached to [a]Mount Carmel westward, along *the Brook* Shihor Libnath. [27]It turned toward the sunrise to Beth Dagon; and it reached to Zebulun and to the Valley of Jiphthah El, then northward beyond Beth Emek and Neiel, bypassing [a]Cabul *which was* on the left, [28]including [1]Ebron, Rehob, Hammon, and Kanah, [a]as far as Greater Sidon. [29]And the border turned to Ramah and to the fortified city of Tyre; then the border turned to Hosah, and ended at the sea by the region of [a]Achzib. [30]Also Ummah, Aphek, and Rehob *were included:* twenty-two cities with their villages. [31]This *was* the inheritance of the tribe of the children of Asher according to their families, these cities with their villages.

THE LAND OF NAPHTALI

[32a]The sixth lot came out to the children of Naphtali, for the children of Naphtali according to their families. [33]And their border began at Heleph, enclosing the territory from the terebinth tree in Zaanannim, Adami Nekeb, and Jabneel, as far as Lakkum; [1]it ended at the Jordan. [34a]From Heleph the border extended westward to Aznoth Tabor, and went out from there toward Hukkok; it adjoined Zebulun on the south side and Asher on the west side, and ended at Judah by the Jordan toward the sunrise. [35]And the fortified cities *are* Ziddim, Zer, Hammath, Rakkath, Chinnereth, [36]Adamah, Ramah, Hazor, [37a]Kedesh, Edrei, En Hazor, [38]Iron, Migdal El, Horem, Beth Anath, and Beth Shemesh: nineteen cities with

19:11
[b]Josh. 12:22
19:12 [a]1 Chr. 6:72
19:13
[a]2 Kin. 14:25
19:22
[a]Josh. 15:10;
Judg. 1:33
19:24
[a]Judg. 1:31, 32
19:26
[a]1 Sam. 15:12;
1 Kin. 18:20;
Is. 33:9; 35:2;
Jer. 46:18
19:27 [a]1 Kin. 9:13
19:28
[a]Gen. 10:19;
Josh. 11:8;
Judg. 1:31;
Acts 27:3
19:29 [a]Judg. 1:31
19:32
[a]Josh. 19:32–39;
Judg. 1:33
19:34
[a]Deut. 33:23
19:37
[a]Josh. 20:7

19:14 [1]Lit. *the goings out of it were*   19:28 [1]So with MT, Tg., Vg.; a few Heb. mss. *Abdon* (cf. 21:30 and 1 Chr. 6:74)   19:33 [1]Lit. *its goings out were*

their villages. ³⁹This *was* the inheritance of the tribe of the children of Naphtali according to their families, the cities and their villages.

THE LAND OF DAN

⁴⁰ᵃThe seventh lot came out for the tribe of the children of Dan according to their families. ⁴¹And the territory of their inheritance was Zorah, ᵃEshtaol, Ir Shemesh, ⁴²ᵃShaalabbin, ᵇAijalon, Jethlah, ⁴³Elon, Timnah, ᵃEkron, ⁴⁴Eltekeh, Gibbethon, Baalath, ⁴⁵Jehud, Bene Berak, Gath Rimmon, ⁴⁶Me Jarkon, and Rakkon, with the region ¹near ²Joppa. ⁴⁷And the ᵃborder of the children of Dan went beyond these, because the children of Dan went up to fight against Leshem and took it; and they struck it with the edge of the sword, took possession of it, and dwelt in it. They called Leshem, ᵇDan, after the name of Dan their father. ⁴⁸This *is* the inheritance of the tribe of the children of Dan according to their families, these cities with their villages.

JOSHUA'S INHERITANCE

⁴⁹When they had ¹made an end of dividing the land as an inheritance according to their borders, the children of Israel gave an inheritance among them to Joshua the son of Nun. ⁵⁰According to the word of the LORD they gave him the city which he asked for, ᵃTimnath ᵇSerah in the mountains of Ephraim; and he built the city and dwelt in it.

⁵¹ᵃThese *were* the inheritances which Eleazar the priest, Joshua the son of Nun, and the heads of the fathers of the tribes of the children of Israel divided as an inheritance by lot ᵇin Shiloh before the LORD, at the door of the tabernacle of meeting. So they made an end of dividing the country.

THE CITIES OF REFUGE
(Num. 35:9–28; Deut. 19:1–13)

20 The LORD also spoke to Joshua, saying, ²"Speak to the children of Israel, saying: ᵃ'Appoint¹ for yourselves cities of refuge, of which I spoke to you through Moses, ³that the slayer who kills a person accidentally *or* unintentionally may flee there; and they shall be your refuge from the avenger of blood. ⁴And when he flees to one of those cities, and stands at the entrance of the gate of the city, and ¹declares his case in the hearing of the elders of that city, they shall take him into the city as one of them, and give him a place, that he may dwell among them. ⁵ᵃThen if the avenger of blood pursues him, they shall not deliver the slayer into his hand, because he struck his neighbor unintentionally, but did not hate him beforehand. ⁶And he shall dwell in that city ᵃuntil he stands before the congregation for judgment, *and* until the death of the one who is high priest in those days. Then the slayer may return and come to his own city and his own house, to the city from which he fled.'"

⁷So they appointed ᵃKedesh in Galilee, in the mountains of Naphtali, ᵇShechem in the mountains of Ephraim, and ᶜKirjath Arba (which *is* Hebron) in ᵈthe mountains of Judah.

19:40
ᵃJosh. 19:40–48;
Judg. 1:34–36

19:41
ᵃJosh. 15:33

19:42
ᵃJudg. 1:35;
1 Kin. 4:9
ᵇJosh. 10:12;
21:24

19:43
ᵃJosh. 15:11;
Judg. 1:18

19:47 ᵃJudg. 18
ᵇJudg. 18:29

19:50
ᵃJosh. 24:30
ᵇ1 Chr. 7:24

19:51
ᵃNum. 34:17;
Josh. 14:1
ᵇJosh. 18:1, 10

20:2 ᵃEx. 21:13;
Num. 35:6–34;
Deut. 19:2, 9

20:5
ᵃNum. 35:12

20:6
ᵃNum. 35:12,
24, 25

20:7
ᵃJosh. 21:32;
1 Chr. 6:76
ᵇJosh. 21:21;
2 Chr. 10:1
ᶜJosh. 14:15;
21:11, 13
ᵈLuke 1:39

19:46 ¹*over against*   ²Heb. *Japho*   19:49 ¹*finished*   20:2 ¹*Designate*
20:4 ¹*states*

8And on the other side of the Jordan, by Jericho eastward, they assigned ᵃBezer in the wilderness on the plain, from the tribe of Reuben, ᵇRamoth in Gilead, from the tribe of Gad, and ᶜGolan in Bashan, from the tribe of Manasseh. 9ᵃThese were the cities appointed for all the children of Israel and for the stranger who ¹dwelt among them, that whoever killed a person accidentally might flee there, and not die by the hand of the avenger of blood ᵇuntil he stood before the congregation.

CITIES OF THE LEVITES
(1 Chr. 6:54–81)

21 Then the heads of the fathers' *houses* of the ᵃLevites came near to ᵇEleazar the priest, to Joshua the son of Nun, and to the heads of the fathers' *houses* of the tribes of the children of Israel. 2And they spoke to them at ᵃShiloh in the land of Canaan, saying, ᵇ"The LORD commanded through Moses to give us cities to dwell in, with their common-lands for our livestock." 3So the children of Israel gave to the Levites from their inheritance, at the commandment of the LORD, these cities and their common-lands:

4Now the lot came out for the families of the Kohathites. And ᵃthe children of Aaron the priest, *who were* of the Levites, ᵇhad thirteen cities by lot from the tribe of Judah, from the tribe of Simeon, and from the tribe of Benjamin. 5ᵃThe rest of the children of Kohath had ten cities by lot from the families of the tribe of Ephraim, from the tribe of Dan, and from the half-tribe of Manasseh.

6And ᵃthe children of Gershon had thirteen cities by lot from the families of the tribe of Issachar, from the tribe of Asher, from the tribe of Naphtali, and from the half-tribe of Manasseh in Bashan.

7ᵃThe children of Merari according to their families had twelve cities from the tribe of Reuben, from the tribe of Gad, and from the tribe of Zebulun.

8ᵃAnd the children of Israel gave these cities with their common-lands by lot to the Levites, ᵇas the LORD had commanded by the hand of Moses.

9So they gave from the tribe of the children of Judah and from the tribe of the children of Simeon these cities which are ¹designated by name, 10which were for the children of Aaron, one of the families of the Kohathites, *who were* of the children of Levi; for the lot was theirs first. 11ᵃAnd they gave them ¹Kirjath Arba (*Arba was* the father of ᵇAnak), ᶜwhich *is* Hebron, in the mountains of Judah, with the common-land surrounding it. 12But ᵃthe fields of the city and its villages they gave to Caleb the son of Jephunneh as his possession.

13Thus ᵃto the children of Aaron the priest they gave ᵇHebron with its common-land (a city of refuge for the slayer), ᶜLibnah with its common-land, 14ᵃJattir with its common-land, ᵇEshtemoa with its common-land, 15ᵃHolon with its common-land, ᵇDebir with its common-land, 16ᵃAin with its common-land, ᵇJuttah with its common-land, and ᶜBeth Shemesh with its common-land: nine cities from those two tribes; 17and from the tribe of Benjamin, ᵃGibeon with its

---

Cross references (margin):

20:8
ᵃDeut. 4:43;
Josh. 21:36;
1 Chr. 6:78
ᵇJosh. 21:38;
1 Kin. 22:3
ᶜJosh. 21:27

20:9
ᵃNum. 35:15
ᵇJosh. 20:6

21:1
ᵃNum. 35:1–8
ᵇNum. 34:16–29;
Josh. 14:1; 17:4

21:2 ᵃJosh. 18:1
ᵇNum. 35:2

21:4
ᵃJosh. 21:8, 19
ᵇJosh. 19:51

21:5 ᵃJosh. 21:20

21:6 ᵃJosh. 21:27

21:7 ᵃJosh. 21:34

21:8 ᵃJosh. 21:3
ᵇNum. 35:2

21:11
ᵃJosh. 20:7;
1 Chr. 6:55
ᵇJosh. 14:15;
15:13, 14
ᶜJosh. 20:7;
Luke 1:39

21:12
ᵃJosh. 14:14;
1 Chr. 6:56

21:13 ᵃ1 Chr. 6:57
ᵇJosh. 15:54;
20:2, 7
ᶜJosh. 15:42;
2 Kin. 8:22

21:14
ᵃJosh. 15:48
ᵇJosh. 15:50

21:15
ᵃ1 Chr. 6:58
ᵇJosh. 15:49

21:16
ᵃ1 Chr. 6:59
ᵇJosh. 15:55
ᶜJosh. 15:10

21:17
ᵃJosh. 18:25

---

common-land, [b]Geba with its common-land, [18]Anathoth with its common-land, and [a]Almon with its common-land: four cities. [19]All the cities of the children of Aaron, the priests, *were* thirteen cities with their common-lands.

[20a]And the families of the children of Kohath, the Levites, the rest of the children of Kohath, even they had the cities of their [1]lot from the tribe of Ephraim. [21]For they gave them [a]Shechem with its common-land in the mountains of Ephraim (a city of refuge for the slayer), [b]Gezer with its common-land, [22]Kibzaim with its common-land, and Beth Horon with its common-land: four cities; [23]and from the tribe of Dan, Eltekeh with its common-land, Gibbethon with its common-land, [24a]Aijalon with its common-land, *and* Gath Rimmon with its common-land: four cities; [25]and from the half-tribe of Manasseh, Tanach with its common-land and Gath Rimmon with its common-land: two cities. [26]All the ten cities with their common-lands were for the rest of the families of the children of Kohath.

[27a]Also to the children of Gershon, of the families of the Levites, from the *other* half-tribe of Manasseh, *they gave* [b]Golan in Bashan with its common-land (a city of refuge for the slayer), and Be Eshterah with its common-land: two cities; [28]and from the tribe of Issachar, Kishion with its common-land, Daberath with its common-land, [29]Jarmuth with its common-land, *and* En Gannim with its common-land: four cities; [30]and from the tribe of Asher, Mishal with its common-land, Abdon with its common-land, [31]Helkath with its common-land, and Rehob with its common-land: four cities; [32]and from the tribe of Naphtali, [a]Kedesh in Galilee with its common-land (a city of refuge for the slayer), Hammoth Dor with its common-land, and Kartan with its common-land: three cities. [33]All the cities of the Gershonites according to their families *were* thirteen cities with their common-lands.

[34a]And to the families of the children of Merari, the rest of the Levites, from the tribe of Zebulun, Jokneam with its common-land, Kartah with its common-land, [35]Dimnah with its common-land, *and* Nahalal with its common-land: four cities; [36][1]and from the tribe of Reuben, [a]Bezer with its common-land, Jahaz with its common-land, [37]Kedemoth with its common-land, and Mephaath with its common-land: four cities; [38]and from the tribe of Gad, [a]Ramoth in Gilead with its common-land (a city of refuge for the slayer), Mahanaim with its common-land, [39]Heshbon with its common-land, *and* Jazer with its common-land: four cities in all. [40]So all the cities for the children of Merari according to their families, the rest of the families of the Levites, were *by* their lot twelve cities.

[41a]All the cities of the Levites within the possession of the children of Israel *were* forty-eight cities with their common-lands. [42]Every one of these cities had its common-land surrounding it; thus *were* all these cities.

THE PROMISE FULFILLED

[43]So the LORD gave to Israel [a]all the land of which He had sworn to give to their fathers, and they [b]took possession of it

---

21:17
[b]Josh. 18:24

21:18
[a]1 Chr. 6:60

21:20
[a]1 Chr. 6:66

21:21
[a]Josh. 20:7
[b]Judg. 1:29

21:24
[a]Josh. 10:12

21:27
[a]Josh. 21:6;
1 Chr. 6:71
[b]Josh. 20:8

21:32
[a]Josh. 20:7

21:34
[a]Josh. 21:7;
1 Chr. 6:77–81

21:36
[a]Deut. 4:43;
Josh. 20:8

21:38
[a]Josh. 20:8

21:41
[a]Num. 35:7

21:43 [a]Gen. 12:7;
26:3, 4; 28:4, 13,
14 [b]Num. 33:53;
Josh. 1:11

21:20 [1]*allotment*   21:36 [1]So with LXX, Vg. (cf. 1 Chr. 6:78, 79); MT, Bg., Tg. omit vv. 36, 37

and dwelt in it. [44a]The LORD gave them [b]rest all around, according to all that He had sworn to their fathers. And [c]not a man of all their enemies stood against them; the LORD delivered all their enemies into their hand. [45a]Not a word failed of any good thing which the LORD had spoken to the house of Israel. All came to pass.

EASTERN TRIBES RETURN TO THEIR LANDS

22 Then Joshua called the Reubenites, the Gadites, and half the tribe of Manasseh, [2]and said to them: "You have kept [a]all that Moses the servant of the LORD commanded you, [b]and have obeyed my voice in all that I commanded you. [3]You have not [1]left your brethren these many days, up to this day, but have kept the charge of the commandment of the LORD your God. [4]And now the LORD your God has given [a]rest to your brethren, as He promised them; now therefore, return and go to your tents *and* to the land of your possession, [b]which Moses the servant of the LORD gave you on the other side of the Jordan. [5]But [a]take[1] careful heed to do the commandment and the law which Moses the servant of the LORD commanded you, [b]to love the LORD your God, to walk in all His ways, to keep His commandments, to hold fast to Him, and to serve Him with all your heart and with all your soul." [6]So Joshua [a]blessed them and sent them away, and they went to their tents.

[7]Now to half the tribe of Manasseh Moses had given a possession in Bashan, [a]but to the *other* half of it Joshua gave *a possession* among their brethren on this side of the Jordan, westward. And indeed, when Joshua sent them away to their tents, he blessed them, [8]and spoke to them, saying, "Return with much riches to your tents, with very much livestock, with silver, with gold, with bronze, with iron, and with very much clothing. [a]Divide the [1]spoil of your enemies with your brethren."

[9]So the children of Reuben, the children of Gad, and half the tribe of Manasseh returned, and departed from the children of Israel at Shiloh, which *is* in the land of Canaan, to go to [a]the country of Gilead, to the land of their possession, which they had obtained according to the word of the LORD by the hand of Moses.

AN ALTAR BY THE JORDAN

[10]And when they came to the region of the Jordan which *is* in the land of Canaan, the children of Reuben, the children of Gad, and half the tribe of Manasseh built an altar there by the Jordan—a great, impressive altar. [11]Now the children of Israel [a]heard *someone* say, "Behold, the children of Reuben, the children of Gad, and half the tribe of Manasseh have built an altar on the [1]frontier of the land of Canaan, in the region of the Jordan—on the children of Israel's side." [12]And when the children of Israel heard *of it,* [a]the whole congregation of the children of Israel gathered together at Shiloh to go to war against them.

[13]Then the children of Israel [a]sent [b]Phinehas the son of Eleazar the priest to the children of Reuben, to the children of Gad, and to half the tribe of Manasseh, into the land of Gilead,

---

21:44 [a]Deut. 7:23, 24; Josh. 11:23; 22:4 [b]Josh. 1:13, 15; 11:23 [c]Deut. 7:24
21:45 [a][Num. 23:19]; Josh. 23:14; 1 Kin. 8:56
22:2 [a]Num. 32:20–22; Deut. 3:18 [b]Josh. 1:12–18
22:4 [a]Josh. 21:44 [b]Num. 32:33
22:5 [a]Deut. 6:6, 17; 11:22; Jer. 12:16 [b]Deut. 10:12; 11:13, 22
22:6 [a]Gen. 47:7; Ex. 39:43; Josh. 14:13; 2 Sam. 6:18; Luke 24:50
22:7 [a]Josh. 17:1–13
22:8 [a]Num. 31:27; 1 Sam. 30:24
22:9 [a]Num. 32:1, 26, 29
22:11 [a]Deut. 13:12–18; Judg. 20:12, 13
22:12 [a]Josh. 18:1; Judg. 20:1
22:13 [a]Deut. 13:14; Judg. 20:12 [b]Ex. 6:25; Num. 25:7, 11–13

22:3 [1]forsaken   **22:5** [1]be very careful to do   **22:8** [1]plunder   **22:11** [1]Lit. *front*

¹⁴and with him ten rulers, one ruler each from the chief house of every tribe of Israel; and ᵃeach one *was* the head of the house of his father among the ¹divisions of Israel. ¹⁵Then they came to the children of Reuben, to the children of Gad, and to half the tribe of Manasseh, to the land of Gilead, and they spoke with them, saying, ¹⁶"Thus says the whole congregation of the LORD: 'What ᵃtreachery¹ *is* this that you have committed against the God of Israel, to turn away this day from following the LORD, in that you have built for yourselves an altar, ᵇthat you might rebel this day against the LORD? ¹⁷*Is* the iniquity ᵃof Peor not enough for us, from which we are not cleansed till this day, although there was a plague in the congregation of the LORD, ¹⁸but that you must turn away this day from following the LORD? And it shall be, if you rebel today against the LORD, that tomorrow ᵃHe will be angry with the whole congregation of Israel. ¹⁹¹Nevertheless, if the land of your possession *is* unclean, *then* cross over to the land of the possession of the LORD, ᵃwhere the LORD's tabernacle stands, and take possession among us; but do not rebel against the LORD, nor rebel against us, by building yourselves an altar besides the altar of the LORD our God. ²⁰ᵃDid not Achan the son of Zerah ¹commit a trespass in the ²accursed thing, and wrath fell on all the congregation of Israel? And that man did not perish alone in his iniquity.'"

²¹Then the children of Reuben, the children of Gad, and half the tribe of Manasseh answered and said to the heads of the ¹divisions of Israel: ²²"The LORD ᵃGod of gods, the LORD God of gods, He ᵇknows, and let Israel itself know— if *it is* in rebellion, or if in treachery against the LORD, do not save us this day. ²³If we have built ourselves an altar to turn from following the LORD, or if to offer on it burnt offerings or grain offerings, or if to offer peace offerings on it, let the LORD Himself ᵃrequire *an account*. ²⁴But in fact we have done it ¹for fear, for a reason, saying, 'In time to come your descendants may speak to our descendants, saying, "What have you to do with the LORD God of Israel? ²⁵For the LORD has made the Jordan a border between you and us, *you* children of Reuben and children of Gad. You have no part in the LORD." So your descendants would make our descendants cease fearing the LORD.' ²⁶Therefore we said, 'Let us now prepare to build ourselves an altar, not for burnt offering nor for sacrifice, ²⁷but *that* it *may be* ᵃa ¹witness between you and us and our generations after us, that we may ᵇperform the service of the LORD before Him with our burnt offerings, with our sacrifices, and with our peace offerings; that your descendants may not say to our descendants in time to come, "You have no part in the LORD."' ²⁸Therefore we said that it will be, when they say *this* to us or to our generations in time to come, that we may say, 'Here is the replica of the altar of the LORD which our fathers made, though not for burnt offerings nor for sacrifices; but it *is* a witness between you and us.' ²⁹Far be it from us that we should rebel against the LORD, and turn from following the LORD this day, ᵃto build an altar for burnt offerings, for grain offerings, or

22:14 ᵃNum. 1:4
22:16
ᵃDeut. 12:5–14
ᵇLev. 17:8, 9
22:17
ᵃNum. 25:1–9;
Deut. 4:3
22:18
ᵃNum. 16:22
22:19 ᵃJosh. 18:1
22:20
ᵃJosh. 7:1–26
22:22
ᵃDeut. 4:35;
10:17; Is. 44:8;
45:5; 46:9;
[1 Cor. 8:5, 6]
ᵇ[Job 10:7;
23:10; Jer. 12:3;
2 Cor. 11:11, 31]
22:23
ᵃDeut. 18:19;
1 Sam. 20:16
22:27
ᵃGen. 31:48;
Josh. 22:34;
24:27
ᵇDeut. 12:5, 14
22:29
ᵃDeut. 12:13, 14

22:14 ¹Lit. *thousands*   22:16 ¹*unfaithful act*   22:19 ¹*However*   22:20 ¹*act unfaithfully*   ²*devoted thing*   22:21 ¹Lit. *thousands*   22:24 ¹Lit. *from fear*
22:27 ¹*testimony*

for sacrifices, besides the altar of the LORD our God which *is* before His tabernacle."

30Now when Phinehas the priest and the rulers of the congregation, the heads of the [1]divisions of Israel who *were* with him, heard the words that the children of Reuben, the children of Gad, and the children of Manasseh spoke, it pleased them. 31Then Phinehas the son of Eleazar the priest said to the children of Reuben, the children of Gad, and the children of Manasseh, "This day we perceive that the LORD *is* [a]among us, because you have not committed this treachery against the LORD. Now you have delivered the children of Israel out of the hand of the LORD."

32And Phinehas the son of Eleazar the priest, and the rulers, returned from the children of Reuben and the children of Gad, from the land of Gilead to the land of Canaan, to the children of Israel, and brought back word to them. 33So the thing pleased the children of Israel, and the children of Israel [a]blessed God; they spoke no more of going against them in battle, to destroy the land where the children of Reuben and Gad dwelt.

34The children of Reuben and the children of [1]Gad called the altar, *Witness*, "For *it is* a witness between us that the LORD *is* God."

JOSHUA'S FAREWELL ADDRESS

23 Now it came to pass, a long time after the LORD [a]had given rest to Israel from all their enemies round about, that Joshua [b]was old, advanced in age. 2And Joshua [a]called for all Israel, for their elders, for their heads, for their judges, and for their officers, and said to them:

"I am old, advanced in age. 3You have seen all that the [a]LORD your God has done to all these nations because of you, for the [b]LORD your God *is* He who has fought for you. 4See, [a]I have divided to you by lot these nations that remain, to be an inheritance for your tribes, from the Jordan, with all the nations that I have cut off, as far as the Great Sea westward. 5And the LORD your God [a]will expel them from before you and drive them out of your sight. So you shall possess their land, [b]as the LORD your God promised you. 6[a]Therefore be very courageous to keep and to do all that is written in the Book of the Law of Moses, [b]lest you turn aside from it to the right hand or to the left, 7*and* lest you [a]go[1] among these nations, these who remain among you. You shall not [b]make mention of the name of their gods, nor cause *anyone* to [c]swear *by them;* you shall not [d]serve them nor bow down to them, 8but you shall [a]hold fast to the LORD your God, as you have done to this day. 9[a]For the LORD has [1]driven out from before you great and strong nations; but *as for* you, no one has been able to stand against you to this day. 10[a]One man of you shall chase a thousand, for the LORD your God *is* He who fights for you, [b]as He promised you. 11[a]Therefore take careful heed to yourselves, that you love the LORD your God. 12Or else, if indeed you do [a]go back, and cling to the remnant of these nations—these that remain among you—and [b]make marriages with them, and go in to them and they to you, 13know for certain that [a]the LORD your

---

22:31 [a]Ex. 25:8;
Lev. 26:11, 12;
2 Chr. 15:2;
Zech. 8:23

22:33
[a]1 Chr. 29:20;
Neh. 8:6;
Dan. 2:19;
Luke 2:28

23:1
[a]Josh. 21:44;
22:4 [b]Josh. 13:1;
24:29

23:2
[a]Deut. 31:28

23:3 [a]Ps. 44:3
[b]Ex. 14:14;
Deut. 1:30;
Josh. 10:14, 42

23:4
[a]Josh. 13:2, 6;
18:10

23:5
[a]Ex. 23:30; 33:2
[b]Num. 33:53

23:6 [a]Josh. 1:7
[b]Deut. 5:32

23:7 [a]Ex. 23:33;
Deut. 7:2, 3;
[Prov. 4:14;
Eph. 5:11]
[b]Ex. 23:13;
Ps. 16:4; Jer. 5:7;
Hos. 2:17
[c]Deut. 6:13;
10:20 [d]Ex. 20:5

23:8
[a]Deut. 10:20

23:9
[a]Deut. 7:24;
11:23; Josh. 1:5

23:10
[a]Lev. 26:8;
Deut. 28:7;
Is. 30:17
[b]Ex. 14:14

23:11 [a]Josh. 22:5

23:12
[a][2 Pet. 2:20, 21]
[b]Deut. 7:3, 4;
Ezra 9:2;
Neh. 13:25

23:13 [a]Judg. 2:3

22:30 [1]Lit. *thousands*   22:34 [1]LXX adds *and half the tribe of Manasseh*
23:7 [1]*associate with*   23:9 [1]*dispossessed*

God will no longer drive out these nations from before you. [b]But they shall be snares and traps to you, and scourges on your sides and thorns in your eyes, until you perish from this good land which the LORD your God has given you.

14"Behold, this day [a]I[1] *am* going the way of all the earth. And you know in all your hearts and in all your souls that [b]not one thing has failed of all the good things which the LORD your God spoke concerning you. All have come to pass for you; not one word of them has failed. 15[a]Therefore it shall come to pass, that as all the good things have come upon you which the LORD your God promised you, so the LORD will bring upon you [b]all harmful things, until He has destroyed you from this good land which the LORD your God has given you. 16[1]When you have transgressed the covenant of the LORD your God, which He commanded you, and have gone and served other gods, and bowed down to them, then the [a]anger of the LORD will burn against you, and you shall perish quickly from the good land which He has given you."

THE COVENANT AT SHECHEM
(cf. Ex. 24:9–18)

24 Then Joshua gathered all the tribes of Israel to [a]Shechem and [b]called for the elders of Israel, for their heads, for their judges, and for their officers; and they [c]presented themselves before God. 2And Joshua said to all the people, "Thus says the LORD God of Israel: [a]'Your fathers, *including* Terah, the father of Abraham and the father of Nahor, dwelt on the other side of [1]the River in old times; and [b]they served other gods. 3[a]Then I took your father Abraham from the other side of [1]the River, led him throughout all the land of Canaan, and multiplied his [2]descendants and [b]gave him Isaac. 4To Isaac I gave [a]Jacob and Esau. To [b]Esau I gave the mountains of Seir to possess, [c]but Jacob and his children went down to Egypt. 5[a]Also I sent Moses and Aaron, and [b]I plagued Egypt, according to what I did among them. Afterward I brought you out.

6'Then I [a]brought your fathers out of Egypt, and you came to the sea; and the Egyptians pursued your fathers with chariots and horsemen to the Red Sea. 7So they cried out to the LORD; and He put [a]darkness between you and the Egyptians, brought the sea upon them, and covered them. And [b]your eyes saw what I did in Egypt. Then you dwelt in the wilderness [c]a long time. 8And I brought you into the land of the Amorites, who dwelt on the other side of the Jordan, [a]and they fought with you. But I gave them into your hand, that you might possess their land, and I destroyed them from before you. 9Then [a]Balak the son of Zippor, king of Moab, arose to make war against Israel, and [b]sent and called Balaam the son of Beor to curse you. 10[a]But I would not listen to Balaam; [b]therefore he continued to bless you. So I delivered you out of his hand. 11Then [a]you went over the Jordan and came to Jericho. And [b]the men of Jericho fought against you—*also* the Amorites, the Perizzites, the Canaanites, the Hittites, the Girgashites, the Hivites, and the Jebusites. But I delivered them into your hand. 12[a]I sent the hornet before you which drove

23:13
[b]Ex. 23:33; 34:12; Deut. 7:16
23:14 [a]1 Kin. 2:2
[b]Josh. 21:45; [Luke 21:33]
23:15
[a]Deut. 28:63
[b]Lev. 26:14–39; Deut. 28:15–68
23:16
[a]Deut. 4:24–28
24:1 [a]Gen. 35:4
[b]Josh. 23:2
[c]1 Sam. 10:19
24:2
[a]Gen. 11:7–32
[b]Josh. 24:14
24:3 [a]Gen. 12:1; Acts 7:2, 3
[b]Gen. 21:1–8; [Ps. 127:3]
24:4
[a]Gen. 25:24–26
[b]Gen. 36:8; Deut. 2:5
[c]Gen. 46:1, 3, 6
24:5 [a]Ex. 3:10
[b]Ex. 7—10
24:6 [a]Ex. 12:37, 51; 14:2–31
24:7 [a]Ex. 14:20
[b]Deut. 4:34
[c]Josh. 5:6
24:8
[a]Num. 21:21–35
24:9
[a]Judg. 11:25
[b]Num. 22:2–14
24:10
[a]Deut. 23:5
[b]Num. 23:11, 20; 24:10
24:11
[a]Josh. 3:14, 17
[b]Josh. 6:1; 10:1
24:12
[a]Ex. 23:28; Deut. 7:20

23:14 [1]I am going to die.   23:16 [1]Or *if ever*   24:2 [1]The Euphrates
24:3 [1]The Euphrates   [2]Lit. *seed*

them out from before you, *also* the two kings of the Amorites, *but* [b]not with your sword or with your bow. [13]I have given you a land for which you did not labor, and [a]cities which you did not build, and you dwell in them; you eat of the vineyards and olive groves which you did not plant.'

[14a]"Now therefore, fear the LORD, serve Him in [b]sincerity and in truth, and [c]put away the gods which your fathers served on the other side of [1]the River and [d]in Egypt. Serve the LORD! [15]And if it seems evil to you to serve the LORD, [a]choose for yourselves this day whom you will serve, whether [b]the gods which your fathers served that *were* on the other side of [1]the River, or [c]the gods of the Amorites, in whose land you dwell. [d]But as for me and my house, we will serve the LORD."

[16]So the people answered and said: "Far be it from us that we should forsake the LORD to serve other gods; [17]for the LORD our God *is* He who brought us and our fathers up out of the land of Egypt, from the house of bondage, who did those great signs in our sight, and preserved us in all the way that we went and among all the people through whom we passed. [18]And the LORD drove out from before us all the people, including the Amorites who dwelt in the land. [a]We also will serve the LORD, for He *is* our God."

[19]But Joshua said to the people, [a]"You cannot serve the LORD, for He *is* a [b]holy God. He *is* [c]a jealous God; [d]He will not forgive your transgressions nor your sins. [20a]If you forsake the LORD and serve foreign gods, [b]then He will turn and do you harm and consume you, after He has done you good."

[21]And the people said to Joshua, "No, but we will serve the LORD!"

[22]So Joshua said to the people, "You *are* witnesses against yourselves that [a]you have chosen the LORD for yourselves, to serve Him."

And they said, "*We are* witnesses!"

[23]"Now therefore," *he said,* [a]"put away the foreign gods which *are* among you, and [b]incline your heart to the LORD God of Israel."

[24]And the people [a]said to Joshua, "The LORD our God we will serve, and His voice we will obey!"

[25]So Joshua [a]made[1] a covenant with the people that day, and made for them a statute and an ordinance [b]in Shechem. [26]Then Joshua [a]wrote these words in the Book of the Law of God. And he took [b]a large stone, and [c]set it up there [d]under the oak that *was* by the sanctuary of the LORD. [27]And Joshua said to all the people, "Behold, this stone shall be [a]a witness to us, for [b]it has heard all the words of the LORD which He spoke to us. It shall therefore be a witness to you, lest you deny your God." [28]So [a]Joshua let the people depart, each to his own inheritance.

DEATH OF JOSHUA AND ELEAZAR

[29a]Now it came to pass after these things that Joshua the son of Nun, the servant of the LORD, died, *being* one hundred and ten years old. [30]And they buried him within the border of his inheritance at [a]Timnath Serah, which *is* in the mountains of Ephraim, on the north side of Mount Gaash.

24:12 [b]Ps. 44:3
24:13 [a]Deut. 6:10, 11
24:14 [a]Deut. 10:12, 13; 1 Sam. 12:24 [b]2 Cor. 1:12 [c]Josh. 24:2, 23; Ezek. 20:18 [d]Ezek. 20:7, 8
24:15 [a]Ruth 1:15; 1 Kin. 18:21 [b]Josh. 24:2; Ezek. 20:39 [c]Ex. 23:24, 32 [d]Gen. 18:19; Ps. 101:2; [1 Tim. 3:4, 5]
24:18 [a]Ps. 116:16
24:19 [a]Matt. 6:24 [b]Lev. 11:44, 45; 1 Sam. 6:20 [c]Ex. 20:5 [d]Ex. 23:21
24:20 [a]1 Chr. 28:9; Ezra 8:22; Is. 1:28; 63:10; 65:11, 12; Jer. 17:13 [b]Deut. 4:24–26; Josh. 23:15
24:22 [a]Ps. 119:173
24:23 [a]Gen. 35:2; Josh. 24:14; Judg. 10:15, 16; 1 Sam. 7:3 [b]1 Kin. 8:57, 58; Ps. 119:36; 141:4
24:24 [a]Ex. 19:8; 24:3, 7; Deut. 5:24–27
24:25 [a]Ex. 15:25 [b]Josh. 24:1
24:26 [a]Deut. 31:24 [b]Judg. 9:6 [c]Gen. 28:18 [d]Gen. 35:4
24:27 [a]Gen. 31:48 [b]Deut. 32:1
24:28 [a]Judg. 2:6, 7
24:29 [a]Judg. 2:8
24:30 [a]Josh. 19:50; Judg. 2:9

24:14 [1]The Euphrates   24:15 [1]The Euphrates   24:25 [1]Lit. *cut a covenant*

31aIsrael served the LORD all the days of Joshua, and all the days of the elders who outlived Joshua, who had bknown all the works of the LORD which He had done for Israel.

32aThe bones of Joseph, which the children of Israel had brought up out of Egypt, they buried at Shechem, in the plot of ground bwhich Jacob had bought from the sons of Hamor the father of Shechem for one hundred ¹pieces of silver, and which had become an inheritance of the children of Joseph.

33And aEleazar the son of Aaron died. They buried him in a hill *belonging to* bPhinehas his son, which was given to him in the mountains of Ephraim.

24:31 aJudg. 2:7
bDeut. 11:2

24:32
aGen. 50:25;
Ex. 13:19;
Heb. 11:22
bGen. 33:19;
John 4:5

24:33 aEx. 28:1;
Num. 20:28;
Josh. 14:1
bEx. 6:25

24:32 ¹Heb. *qesitah,* an unknown ancient measure of weight

THE BOOK OF
JUDGES

THE CONTINUING CONQUEST OF CANAAN
(Josh. 15:13–19)

1 Now after the ^adeath of Joshua it came to pass that the children of Israel ^basked the LORD, saying, "Who shall be first to go up for us against the ^cCanaanites to fight against them?"

²And the LORD said, ^a"Judah shall go up. Indeed I have delivered the land into his hand."

³So Judah said to ^aSimeon his brother, "Come up with me to my allotted territory, that we may fight against the Canaanites; and ^bI will likewise go with you to your allotted territory." And Simeon went with him. ⁴Then Judah went up, and the LORD delivered the Canaanites and the Perizzites into their hand; and they killed ten thousand men at ^aBezek. ⁵And they found Adoni-Bezek in Bezek, and fought against him; and they defeated the Canaanites and the Perizzites. ⁶Then Adoni-Bezek fled, and they pursued him and caught him and cut off his thumbs and big toes. ⁷And Adoni-Bezek said, "Seventy kings with their thumbs and big toes cut off used to gather *scraps* under my table; ^aas I have done, so God has repaid me." Then they brought him to Jerusalem, and there he died.

⁸Now ^athe children of Judah fought against Jerusalem and took it; they struck it with the edge of the sword and set the city on fire. ^{9a}And afterward the children of Judah went down to fight against the Canaanites who dwelt in the mountains, in the ¹South, and in the lowland. ¹⁰Then Judah ¹went against the Canaanites who dwelt in ^aHebron. (Now the name of Hebron *was* formerly ^bKirjath Arba.) And they killed Sheshai, Ahiman, and Talmai.

^{11a}From there they went against the inhabitants of Debir. (The name of Debir *was* formerly Kirjath Sepher.) ^{12a}Then Caleb said, "Whoever attacks Kirjath Sepher and takes it, to him I will give my daughter Achsah as wife." ¹³And Othniel the son of Kenaz, ^aCaleb's younger brother, took it; so he gave him his daughter Achsah as wife. ^{14a}Now it happened, when she came *to him,* that ¹she urged him to ask her father for a field. And she dismounted from *her* donkey, and Caleb said to her, "What do you wish?" ¹⁵So she said to him, ^a"Give me a blessing; since you have given me land in the South, give me also springs of water."

And Caleb gave her the upper springs and the lower springs.

^{16a}Now the children of the Kenite, Moses' father-in-law, went up ^bfrom the City of Palms with the children of Judah into the Wilderness of Judah, which *lies* in the South *near* ^cArad; ^dand they went and dwelt among the people. ^{17a}And Judah went with his brother Simeon, and they attacked the Canaanites who inhabited Zephath, and utterly destroyed it.

^{1:1} ^aJosh. 24:29
^bNum. 27:21;
Judg. 20:18
^cJosh. 17:12, 13

^{1:2}
^aGen. 49:8, 9;
Rev. 5:5

^{1:3} ^aJosh. 19:1
^bJudg. 1:17

^{1:4} ^a1 Sam. 11:8

^{1:7} ^aLev. 24:19;
1 Sam. 15:33;
[James 2:13]

^{1:8} ^aJosh. 15:63;
Judg. 1:21

^{1:9} ^aJosh. 10:36;
11:21; 15:13

^{1:10}
^aJosh. 15:13–19
^bJosh. 14:15

^{1:11} ^aJosh. 15:15

^{1:12}
^aJosh. 15:16, 17

^{1:13} ^aJudg. 3:9

^{1:14}
^aJosh. 15:18, 19

^{1:15} ^aGen. 33:11

^{1:16}
^aNum. 10:29–32;
Judg. 4:11, 17;
1 Sam. 15:6;
1 Chr. 2:55
^bDeut. 34:3;
Judg. 3:13
^cJosh. 12:14
^d1 Sam. 15:6

^{1:17} ^aJudg. 1:3

1:9 ¹Heb. *Negev,* and so throughout the book   **1:10** ¹*attacked*   **1:14** ¹LXX, Vg. *he urged her*

So the name of the city was called [b]Hormah. [18]Also Judah took [a]Gaza with its territory, Ashkelon with its territory, and Ekron with its territory. [19]So the LORD was with Judah. And they drove out the mountaineers, but they could not drive out the inhabitants of the lowland, because they had [a]chariots of iron. [20a]And they gave Hebron to Caleb, as Moses had said. Then he [1]expelled from there the [b]three sons of Anak. [21a]But the children of Benjamin did not drive out the Jebusites who inhabited Jerusalem; so the Jebusites dwell with the children of Benjamin in Jerusalem to this day.

[22]And the [1]house of Joseph also went up against Bethel, [a]and the LORD was with them. [23]So the [1]house of Joseph [a]sent men to spy out Bethel. (The name of the city was formerly [b]Luz.) [24]And when the spies saw a man coming out of the city, they said to him, "Please show us the entrance to the city, and [a]we will show you mercy." [25]So he showed them the entrance to the city, and they struck the city with the edge of the sword; but they let the man and all his family go. [26]And the man went to the land of the Hittites, built a city, and called its name Luz, which is its name to this day.

INCOMPLETE CONQUEST OF THE LAND

[27a]However, Manasseh did not drive out the inhabitants of Beth Shean and its villages, or [b]Taanach and its villages, or the inhabitants of [c]Dor and its villages, or the inhabitants of Ibleam and its villages, or the inhabitants of Megiddo and its villages; for the Canaanites were determined to dwell in that land. [28]And it came to pass, when Israel was strong, that they put the Canaanites [1]under tribute, but did not completely drive them out.

[29a]Nor did Ephraim drive out the Canaanites who dwelt in Gezer; so the Canaanites dwelt in Gezer among them.

[30]Nor did [a]Zebulun drive out the inhabitants of Kitron or the inhabitants of Nahalol; so the Canaanites dwelt among them, and [1]were put under tribute.

[31a]Nor did Asher drive out the inhabitants of Acco or the inhabitants of Sidon, or of Ahlab, Achzib, Helbah, Aphik, or Rehob. [32]So the Asherites [a]dwelt among the Canaanites, the inhabitants of the land; for they did not drive them out.

[33a]Nor did Naphtali drive out the inhabitants of Beth Shemesh or the inhabitants of Beth Anath; but they dwelt among the Canaanites, the inhabitants of the land. Nevertheless the inhabitants of Beth Shemesh and Beth Anath were put under tribute to them.

[34]And the Amorites forced the children of Dan into the mountains, for they would not allow them to come down to the valley; [35]and the Amorites were determined to dwell in Mount Heres, [a]in Aijalon, and in [1]Shaalbim; yet when the strength of the house of Joseph became greater, they [2]were put under tribute.

[36]Now the boundary of the Amorites was [a]from the Ascent of Akrabbim, from Sela, and upward.

ISRAEL'S DISOBEDIENCE

2 Then the Angel of the LORD came up from Gilgal to Bochim, and said: [a]"I led you up from Egypt and [b]brought

Cross References

1:17 [b]Num. 21:3; Josh. 19:4

1:18 [a]Josh. 11:22

1:19 [a]Josh. 17:16, 18; Judg. 4:3, 13

1:20 [a]Num. 14:24; Josh. 14:9, 14 [b]Josh. 15:14; Judg. 1:10

1:21 [a]Josh. 15:63; Judg. 1:8

1:22 [a]Judg. 1:19

1:23 [a]Josh. 2:1; 7:2 [b]Gen. 28:19

1:24 [a]Josh. 2:12, 14

1:27 [a]Josh. 17:11–13 [b]Josh. 21:25 [c]Josh. 17:11

1:29 [a]Josh. 16:10; 1 Kin. 9:16

1:30 [a]Josh. 19:10–16

1:31 [a]Josh. 19:24–31

1:32 [a]Ps. 106:34, 35

1:33 [a]Josh. 19:32–39

1:35 [a]Josh. 19:42

1:36 [a]Num. 34:4; Josh. 15:3

2:1 [a]Ex. 20:2; Judg. 6:8, 9 [b]Deut. 1:8

1:20 [1]drove out from there   1:22 [1]family   1:23 [1]family   1:28 [1]to forced labor   1:30 [1]became forced laborers   1:35 [1]Shaalbbin, Josh. 19:42 [2]became forced laborers

you to the land of which I swore to your fathers; and ^cI said, 'I will never break My covenant with you. ²And ^ayou shall make no ¹covenant with the inhabitants of this land; ^byou shall tear down their altars.' ^cBut you have not obeyed My voice. Why have you done this? ³Therefore I also said, 'I will not drive them out before you; but they shall be ^a*thorns*¹ in your side, and ^btheir gods shall ²be a ^csnare to you.'" ⁴So it was, when the Angel of the LORD spoke these words to all the children of Israel, that the people lifted up their voices and wept.

⁵Then they called the name of that place ¹Bochim; and they sacrificed there to the LORD. ⁶And when ^aJoshua had dismissed the people, the children of Israel went each to his own inheritance to possess the land.

DEATH OF JOSHUA
(Josh. 24:29–31)

^{7a}So the people served the LORD all the days of Joshua, and all the days of the elders who outlived Joshua, who had seen all the great works of the LORD which He had done for Israel. ⁸Now ^aJoshua the son of Nun, the servant of the LORD, died *when he was* one hundred and ten years old. ^{9a}And they buried him within the border of his inheritance at ^bTimnath Heres, in the mountains of Ephraim, on the north side of Mount Gaash. ¹⁰When all that generation had ¹been gathered to their fathers, another generation arose after them who ^adid not know the LORD nor the work which He had done for Israel.

ISRAEL'S UNFAITHFULNESS

¹¹Then the children of Israel did ^aevil in the sight of the LORD, and served the Baals; ¹²and they ^aforsook the LORD God of their fathers, who had brought them out of the land of Egypt; and they followed ^bother gods from *among* the gods of the people who *were* all around them, and they ^cbowed down to them; and they provoked the LORD to anger. ¹³They forsook the LORD ^aand served ¹Baal and the ²Ashtoreths. ^{14a}And the anger of the LORD was hot against Israel. So He ^bdelivered them into the hands of plunderers who despoiled them; and ^cHe sold them into the hands of their enemies all around, so that they ^dcould no longer stand before their enemies. ¹⁵Wherever they went out, the hand of the LORD was against them for calamity, as the LORD had said, and as the LORD had ^asworn to them. And they were greatly distressed.

¹⁶Nevertheless, ^athe LORD raised up judges who delivered them out of the hand of those who plundered them. ¹⁷Yet they would not listen to their judges, but they ^aplayed the harlot with other gods, and bowed down to them. They turned quickly from the way in which their fathers walked, in obeying the commandments of the LORD; they did not do so. ¹⁸And when the LORD raised up judges for them, ^athe LORD was with the judge and delivered them out of the hand of their enemies all the days of the judge; ^bfor the LORD was moved to pity by their groaning because of those who oppressed them and harassed them. ¹⁹And it came to pass, ^awhen the judge was dead,

Cross-references

2:1 ^cGen. 17:7, 8; Lev. 26:42, 44; Deut. 7:9; Ps. 89:34

2:2 ^aEx. 23:32; Deut. 7:2 ^bEx. 34:12, 13; Deut. 12:3 ^cPs. 106:34

2:3 ^aNum. 33:55; Josh. 23:13 ^bJudg. 3:6 ^cEx. 23:33; Deut. 7:16; Ps. 106:36

2:6 ^aJosh. 22:6; 24:28–31

2:7 ^aJosh. 24:31

2:8 ^aJosh. 24:29

2:9 ^aJosh. 24:30 ^bJosh. 19:49, 50

2:10 ^aEx. 5:2; 1 Sam. 2:12; Gal. 4:8; [Titus 1:16]

2:11 ^aJudg. 3:7, 12; 4:1; 6:1

2:12 ^aDeut. 31:16; Judg. 8:33; 10:6 ^bDeut. 6:14 ^cEx. 20:5

2:13 ^aJudg. 10:6; Ps. 106:36

2:14 ^aDeut. 31:17; Judg. 3:8; Ps. 106:40–42 ^b2 Kin. 17:20 ^cIs. 50:1 ^dLev. 26:37; Josh. 7:12, 13

2:15 ^aLev. 26:14–26; Deut. 28:15–68

2:16 ^aJudg. 3:9, 10, 15; Ps. 106:43–45

2:17 ^aEx. 34:15

2:18 ^aJosh. 1:5 ^bGen. 6:6

2:19 ^aJudg. 3:12

Footnotes

2:2 ¹treaty   2:3 ¹LXX, Tg., Vg. *enemies to you*   ²*entrap you*   2:5 ¹Lit. *Weeping*   2:10 ¹Died and joined their ancestors   2:13 ¹A Canaanite god   ²Canaanite goddesses

that they reverted and behaved more corruptly than their fathers, by following other gods, to serve them and bow down to them. They did not cease from their own doings nor from their stubborn way.

20Then the anger of the LORD was hot against Israel; and He said, "Because this nation has atransgressed My covenant which I commanded their fathers, and has not heeded My voice, 21I also will no longer drive out before them any of the nations which Joshua aleft when he died, 22so athat through them I may btest Israel, whether they will keep the ways of the LORD, to walk in them as their fathers kept *them,* or not." 23Therefore the LORD left those nations, without driving them out immediately; nor did He deliver them into the hand of Joshua.

THE NATIONS REMAINING IN THE LAND

3 Now these *are* athe nations which the LORD left, that He might test Israel by them, *that is,* all who had not 1known any of the wars in Canaan 2(*this was* only so that the generations of the children of Israel might be taught to know war, at least those who had not formerly known it), 3*namely,* afive lords of the Philistines, all the Canaanites, the Sidonians, and the Hivites who dwelt in Mount Lebanon, from Mount Baal Hermon to the entrance of Hamath. 4And they were *left, that He might* test Israel by them, to 1know whether they would obey the commandments of the LORD, which He had commanded their fathers by the hand of Moses.

5aThus the children of Israel dwelt among the Canaanites, the Hittites, the Amorites, the Perizzites, the Hivites, and the Jebusites. 6And athey took their daughters to be their wives, and gave their daughters to their sons; and they served their gods.

OTHNIEL

7So the children of Israel did aevil in the sight of the LORD. They bforgot the LORD their God, and served the Baals and 1Asherahs. 8Therefore the anger of the LORD was hot against Israel, and He asold them into the hand of bCushan-Rishathaim king of Mesopotamia; and the children of Israel served Cushan-Rishathaim eight years. 9When the children of Israel acried out to the LORD, the LORD braised up a deliverer for the children of Israel, who delivered them: cOthniel the son of Kenaz, Caleb's younger brother. 10aThe Spirit of the LORD came upon him, and he judged Israel. He went out to war, and the LORD delivered Cushan-Rishathaim king of Mesopotamia into his hand; and his hand prevailed over Cushan-Rishathaim. 11So the land had rest for forty years. Then Othniel the son of Kenaz died.

EHUD

12aAnd the children of Israel again did evil in the sight of the LORD. So the LORD strengthened bEglon king of Moab against Israel, because they had done evil in the sight of the LORD. 13Then he gathered to himself the people of Ammon and aAmalek, went and 1defeated Israel, and took possession

2:20
a[Josh. 23:16]

2:21 aJosh. 23:4, 5, 13

2:22
aJudg. 3:1, 4
bDeut. 8:2, 16; 13:3

3:1 aJudg. 1:1; 2:21, 22

3:3 aJosh. 13:3

3:5 aPs. 106:35

3:6 aEx. 34:15, 16; Deut. 7:3, 4; Josh. 23:12

3:7 aJudg. 2:11
bDeut. 32:18

3:8
aDeut. 32:30; Judg. 2:14
bHab. 3:7

3:9 aJudg. 3:15
bJudg. 2:16
cJudg. 1:13

3:10
aNum. 27:18; 1 Sam. 11:6; 2 Chr. 15:1

3:12 aJudg. 2:19
b1 Sam. 12:9

3:13 aJudg. 5:14

3:1 1*experienced*   3:4 1*find out*   3:7 1Name or symbol for Canaanite goddesses   3:13 1*struck*

of [b]the City of Palms. [14]So the children of Israel [a]served Eglon king of Moab eighteen years.

[15]But when the children of Israel [a]cried out to the LORD, the LORD raised up a deliverer for them: Ehud the son of Gera, the Benjamite, a [b]left-handed man. By him the children of Israel sent tribute to Eglon king of Moab. [16]Now Ehud made himself a dagger (it was double-edged and a cubit in length) and fastened it under his clothes on his right thigh. [17]So he brought the tribute to Eglon king of Moab. (Now Eglon *was* a very fat man.) [18]And when he had finished presenting the tribute, he sent away the people who had carried the tribute. [19]But he himself turned back [a]from the [1]stone images that *were* at Gilgal, and said, "I have a secret message for you, O king."

He said, "Keep silence!" And all who attended him went out from him.

[20]So Ehud came to him (now he was sitting upstairs in his cool private chamber). Then Ehud said, "I have a message from God for you." So he arose from *his* seat. [21]Then Ehud reached with his left hand, took the dagger from his right thigh, and thrust it into his belly. [22]Even the [1]hilt went in after the blade, and the fat closed over the blade, for he did not draw the dagger out of his belly; and his entrails came out. [23]Then Ehud went out through the porch and shut the doors of the upper room behind him and locked them.

[24]When he had gone out, [1]Eglon's servants came to look, and *to their* surprise, the doors of the upper room were locked. So they said, "He is probably [a]attending[2] to his needs in the cool chamber." [25]So they waited till they were [a]embarrassed, and still he had not opened the doors of the upper room. Therefore they took the key and opened *them*. And there was their master, fallen dead on the floor.

[26]But Ehud had escaped while they delayed, and passed beyond the [1]stone images and escaped to Seirah. [27]And it happened, when he arrived, that [a]he blew the trumpet in the [b]mountains of Ephraim, and the children of Israel went down with him from the mountains; and [1]he led them. [28]Then he said to them, "Follow *me*, for [a]the LORD has delivered your enemies the Moabites into your hand." So they went down after him, seized the [b]fords of the Jordan leading to Moab, and did not allow anyone to cross over. [29]And at that time they killed about ten thousand men of Moab, all stout men of valor; not a man escaped. [30]So Moab was subdued that day under the hand of Israel. And [a]the land had rest for eighty years.

SHAMGAR

[31]After him was [a]Shamgar the son of Anath, who killed six hundred men of the Philistines [b]with an ox goad; [c]and he also delivered [d]Israel.

DEBORAH

4 When Ehud was dead, [a]the children of Israel again did [b]evil in the sight of the LORD. [2]So the LORD [a]sold them into the hand of Jabin king of Canaan, who reigned in [b]Hazor.

3:13
[b]Deut. 34:3;
Judg. 1:16;
2 Chr. 28:15

3:14
[a]Deut. 28:48

3:15 [a]Ps. 78:34
[b]Judg. 20:16

3:19 [a]Josh. 4:20

3:24
[a]1 Sam. 24:3

3:25
[a]2 Kin. 2:17; 8:11

3:27
[a]Judg. 6:34;
1 Sam. 13:3
[b]Josh. 17:15

3:28
[a]Judg. 7:9, 15;
1 Sam. 17:47
[b]Josh. 2:7;
Judg. 12:5

3:30 [a]Judg. 3:11

3:31 [a]Judg. 5:6
[b]1 Sam. 17:47
[c]Judg. 2:16
[d]1 Sam. 4:1

4:1 [a]Judg. 2:19
[b]Judg. 2:11

4:2 [a]Judg. 2:14
[b]Josh. 11:1, 10

3:19 [1]Tg. *quarries*   **3:22** [1]*handle*   **3:24** [1]Lit. *his*   [2]Lit. *covering his feet*
3:26 [1]Tg. *quarries*   **3:27** [1]Lit. *he went before them*

The commander of his army *was* ^cSisera, who dwelt in ^dHarosheth Hagoyim. ³And the children of Israel cried out to the LORD; for Jabin had nine hundred ^achariots of iron, and for twenty years ^bhe had harshly oppressed the children of Israel.

⁴Now Deborah, a prophetess, the wife of Lapidoth, was judging Israel at that time. ^{5a}And she would sit under the palm tree of Deborah between Ramah and Bethel in the mountains of Ephraim. And the children of Israel came up to her for judgment. ⁶Then she sent and called for ^aBarak the son of Abinoam from ^bKedesh in Naphtali, and said to him, "Has not the LORD God of Israel commanded, 'Go and ¹deploy *troops* at Mount ^cTabor; take with you ten thousand men of the sons of Naphtali and of the sons of Zebulun; ⁷and against you ^aI will deploy Sisera, the commander of Jabin's army, with his chariots and his multitude at the ^bRiver Kishon; and I will ¹deliver him into your hand'?"

⁸And Barak said to her, "If you will go with me, then I will go; but if you will not go with me, I will not go!"

⁹So she said, "I will surely go with you; nevertheless there will be no glory for you in the journey you are taking, for the LORD will ^asell Sisera into the hand of a woman." Then Deborah arose and went with Barak to Kedesh. ¹⁰And Barak called ^aZebulun and Naphtali to Kedesh; he went up with ten thousand men ^bunder¹ his command, and Deborah went up with him.

¹¹Now Heber ^athe Kenite, of the children of ^bHobab the father-in-law of Moses, had separated himself from the Kenites and pitched his tent near the terebinth tree at Zaanaim, ^cwhich *is* beside Kedesh.

¹²And they reported to Sisera that Barak the son of Abinoam had gone up to Mount Tabor. ¹³So Sisera gathered together all his chariots, nine hundred chariots of iron, and all the people who *were* with him, from Harosheth Hagoyim to the River Kishon.

¹⁴Then Deborah said to Barak, ¹"Up! For this *is* the day in which the LORD has delivered Sisera into your hand. ^aHas not the LORD gone out before you?" So Barak went down from Mount Tabor with ten thousand men following him. ¹⁵And the LORD routed Sisera and all *his* chariots and all *his* army with the edge of the sword before Barak; and Sisera alighted from *his* chariot and fled away on foot. ¹⁶But Barak pursued the chariots and the army as far as Harosheth Hagoyim, and all the army of Sisera fell by the edge of the sword; not a man was ^aleft.

¹⁷However, Sisera had fled away on foot to the tent of ^aJael, the wife of Heber the Kenite; for *there was* peace between Jabin king of Hazor and the house of Heber the Kenite. ¹⁸And Jael went out to meet Sisera, and said to him, "Turn aside, my lord, turn aside to me; do not fear." And when he had turned aside with her into the tent, she covered him with a ¹blanket.

¹⁹Then he said to her, "Please give me a little water to drink, for I am thirsty." So she opened ^aa jug of milk, gave him a drink, and covered him. ²⁰And he said to her, "Stand at the door of the tent, and if any man comes and inquires of you, and says, 'Is there any man here?' you shall say, 'No.'"

4:2 ^c1 Sam. 12:9;
Ps. 83:9
^dJudg. 4:13, 16

4:3 ^aDeut. 20:1;
Judg. 1:19
^bPs. 106:42

4:5 ^aGen. 35:8

4:6 ^aHeb. 11:32
^bJosh. 19:37;
21:32 ^cJudg. 8:18

4:7 ^aEx. 14:4
^bJudg. 5:21;
1 Kin. 18:40;
Ps. 83:9, 10

4:9 ^aJudg. 2:14

4:10 ^aJudg. 5:18
^bEx. 11:8;
1 Kin. 20:10

4:11 ^aJudg. 1:16
^bNum. 10:29
^cJudg. 4:6

4:14
^aDeut. 9:3; 31:3;
2 Sam. 5:24;
Ps. 68:7;
Is. 52:12

4:16 ^aEx. 14:28;
Ps. 83:9

4:17 ^aJudg. 5:6

4:19
^aJudg. 5:24–27

²¹Then Jael, Heber's wife, ᵃtook a tent peg and took a hammer in her hand, and went softly to him and drove the peg into his temple, and it went down into the ground; for he was fast asleep and weary. So he died. ²²And then, as Barak pursued Sisera, Jael came out to meet him, and said to him, "Come, I will show you the man whom you seek." And when he went into her *tent*, there lay Sisera, dead with the peg in his temple.

²³So on that day God subdued Jabin king of Canaan in the presence of the children of Israel. ²⁴And the hand of the children of Israel grew stronger and stronger against Jabin king of Canaan, until they had destroyed Jabin king of Canaan.

THE SONG OF DEBORAH

5 Then Deborah and Barak the son of Abinoam ᵃsang on that day, saying:

2 "When¹ leaders ᵃlead in Israel,
　　ᵇWhen the people ²willingly offer themselves,
　　Bless the LORD!

3 "Hear,ᵃ O kings! Give ear, O princes!
　　I, *even* ᵇI, will sing to the LORD;
　　I will sing praise to the LORD God of Israel.

4 "LORD, ᵃwhen You went out from Seir,
　　When You marched from ᵇthe field of Edom,
　　The earth trembled and the heavens poured,
　　The clouds also poured water;

5 ᵃThe mountains ¹gushed before the LORD,
　　ᵇThis Sinai, before the LORD God of Israel.

6 "In the days of ᵃShamgar, son of Anath,
　　In the days of ᵇJael,
　　ᶜThe highways were deserted,
　　And the travelers walked along the byways.

7 Village life ceased, it ceased in Israel,
　　Until I, Deborah, arose,
　　Arose a mother in Israel.

8 They chose ᵃnew gods;
　　Then *there was* war in the gates;
　　Not a shield or spear was seen among forty thousand in Israel.

9 My heart *is* with the rulers of Israel
　　Who offered themselves willingly with the people.
　　Bless the LORD!

10 "Speak, you who ride on white ᵃdonkeys,
　　Who sit in judges' attire,
　　And who walk along the road.

11 Far from the noise of the archers, among the watering places,
　　There they shall recount the righteous acts of the LORD,
　　The righteous acts *for* His villagers in Israel;
　　Then the people of the LORD shall go down to the gates.

12 "Awake,ᵃ awake, Deborah!
　　Awake, awake, sing a song!
　　Arise, Barak, and lead your captives away,
　　O son of Abinoam!

4:21
ᵃJudg. 5:24–27
5:1 ᵃEx. 15:1;
Judg. 4:4
5:2 ᵃPs. 18:47
ᵇ2 Chr. 17:16
5:3
ᵃDeut. 32:1, 3
ᵇPs. 27:6
5:4 ᵃDeut. 33:2;
Ps. 68:7
ᵇPs. 68:8
5:5 ᵃPs. 97:5
ᵇEx. 19:18
5:6 ᵃJudg. 3:31
ᵇJudg. 4:17
ᶜIs. 33:8
5:8 ᵃDeut. 32:17
5:10 ᵃJudg. 10:4;
12:14
5:12 ᵃPs. 57:8

5:2 ¹Or *When locks are loosed*　　²volunteer　　5:5 ¹*flowed*

13 "Then the survivors came down, the people against the
    nobles;
    The LORD came down for me against the mighty.
14 From Ephraim *were* those whose roots were in ᵃAmalek.
    After you, Benjamin, with your peoples,
    From Machir rulers came down,
    And from Zebulun those who bear the recruiter's staff.
15 And ¹the princes of Issachar *were* with Deborah;
    As Issachar, so *was* Barak
    Sent into the valley ²under his command;
    Among the divisions of Reuben
    There were great resolves of heart.
16 Why did you sit among the sheepfolds,
    To hear the pipings for the flocks?
    The divisions of Reuben have great searchings of heart.
17 ᵃGilead stayed beyond the Jordan,
    And why did Dan remain ¹on ships?
    ᵇAsher continued at the seashore,
    And stayed by his inlets.
18 ᵃZebulun *is* a people *who* jeopardized their lives to the
    point of death,
    Naphtali also, on the heights of the battlefield.

19 "The kings came *and* fought,
    Then the kings of Canaan fought
    In ᵃTaanach, by the waters of Megiddo;
    They took no spoils of silver.
20 They fought from the heavens;
    The stars from their courses fought against Sisera.
21 ᵃThe torrent of Kishon swept them away,
    That ancient torrent, the torrent of Kishon.
    O my soul, march on in strength!
22 Then the horses' hooves pounded,
    The galloping, galloping of his steeds.
23 'Curse Meroz,' said the ¹angel of the LORD,
    'Curse its inhabitants bitterly,
    Because they did not come to the help of the LORD,
    To the help of the LORD against the mighty.'

24 "Most blessed among women is Jael,
    The wife of Heber the Kenite;
    ᵃBlessed is she among women in tents.
25 He asked for water, she gave milk;
    She brought out cream in a lordly bowl.
26 She stretched her hand to the tent peg,
    Her right hand to the workmen's hammer;
    She pounded Sisera, she pierced his head,
    She split and struck through his temple.
27 At her feet he sank, he fell, he lay still;
    At her feet he sank, he fell;
    Where he sank, there he fell ᵃdead.

28 "The mother of Sisera looked through the window,
    And cried out through the lattice,
    'Why is his chariot *so* long in coming?
    Why tarries the clatter of his chariots?'

5:14 ᵃJudg. 3:13

5:17 ᵃJosh. 22:9
ᵇJosh. 19:29, 31

5:18
ᵃJudg. 4:6, 10

5:19 ᵃJudg. 1:27

5:21 ᵃJudg. 4:7

5:24
ᵃ[Luke 1:28]

5:27
ᵃJudg. 4:18–21

5:15 ¹So with LXX, Syr., Tg., Vg.; MT *And my princes in Issachar*   ²Lit. *at his feet*   5:17 ¹Or *at ease*   5:23 ¹Or *Angel*

29 Her wisest [1]ladies answered her,
   Yes, she [2]answered herself,
30 'Are they not finding and dividing the spoil:
   To every man a girl *or* two;
   For Sisera, plunder of dyed garments,
   Plunder of garments embroidered and dyed,
   Two pieces of dyed embroidery for the neck of the
      looter?'

31 "Thus let all Your enemies [a]perish, O LORD!
   But *let* those who love Him *be* [b]like the [c]sun
   When it comes out in full [d]strength."

So the land had rest for forty years.

MIDIANITES OPPRESS ISRAEL

6 Then the children of Israel did [a]evil in the sight of the LORD. So the LORD delivered them into the hand of [b]Midian for seven years, 2and the hand of Midian prevailed against Israel. Because of the Midianites, the children of Israel made for themselves the dens, [a]the caves, and the strongholds which *are* in the mountains. 3So it was, whenever Israel had sown, Midianites would come up; also Amalekites and the [a]people of the East would come up against them. 4Then they would encamp against them and [a]destroy the produce of the earth as far as Gaza, and leave no sustenance for Israel, neither sheep nor ox nor [b]donkey. 5For they would come up with their livestock and their tents, coming in as numerous as locusts; both they and their camels were [1]without number; and they would enter the land to destroy it. 6So Israel was greatly impoverished because of the Midianites, and the children of Israel [a]cried out to the LORD.

7And it came to pass, when the children of Israel cried out to the LORD because of the Midianites, 8that the LORD sent a prophet to the children of Israel, who said to them, "Thus says the LORD God of Israel: 'I brought you up from Egypt and brought you out of the [a]house of [1]bondage; 9and I delivered you out of the hand of the Egyptians and out of the hand of all who oppressed you, and [a]drove them out before you and gave you their land. 10Also I said to you, "I *am* the LORD your God; [a]do not fear the gods of the Amorites, in whose land you dwell." But you have not obeyed My [b]voice.'"

GIDEON

11Now the Angel of the LORD came and sat under the terebinth tree which *was* in Ophrah, which *belonged* to Joash [a]the Abiezrite, while his son [b]Gideon threshed wheat in the winepress, in order to hide *it* from the Midianites. 12And the [a]Angel of the LORD appeared to him, and said to him, "The LORD *is* [b]with you, you mighty man of valor!"

13Gideon said to Him, "O [1]my lord, if the LORD is with us, why then has all this happened to us? And [a]where *are* all His miracles [b]which our fathers told us about, saying, 'Did not the LORD bring us up from Egypt?' But now the LORD has [c]forsaken us and delivered us into the hands of the Midianites."

5:31 [a]Ps. 92:9
[b]2 Sam. 23:4
[c]Ps. 37:6;
89:36, 37
[d]Ps. 19:5

6:1 [a]Judg. 2:11
[b]Num. 22:4;
31:1–3

6:2 [a]1 Sam. 13:6;
Heb. 11:38

6:3 [a]Judg. 7:12

6:4 [a]Lev. 26:16
[b]Deut. 28:31

6:6 [a]Ps. 50:15;
Hos. 5:15

6:8 [a]Josh. 24:17

6:9 [a]Ps. 44:2, 3

6:10
[a]2 Kin. 17:35,
37, 38; Jer. 10:2
[b]Judg. 2:1, 2

6:11 [a]Josh. 17:2;
Judg. 6:15
[b]Judg. 7:1;
Heb. 11:32

6:12 [a]Judg. 13:3;
Luke 1:11, 28
[b]Josh. 1:5

6:13 [a][Is. 59:1]
[b]Josh. 4:6,
21; Ps. 44:1
[c]Deut. 31:17;
2 Chr. 15:2;
Ps. 44:9–16

5:29 [1]*princesses*   [2]Lit. *repeats her words to herself*   6:5 [1]*innumerable*
6:8 [1]*slavery*   6:13 [1]Heb. *adoni,* used of man

¹⁴Then the LORD turned to him and said, ᵃ"Go in this might of yours, and you shall save Israel from the hand of the Midianites. ᵇHave I not sent you?"

¹⁵So he said to Him, "O ¹my Lord, how can I save Israel? Indeed ᵃmy clan *is* the weakest in Manasseh, and I *am* the least in my father's house."

¹⁶And the LORD said to him, ᵃ"Surely I will be with you, and you shall ¹defeat the Midianites as one man."

¹⁷Then he said to Him, "If now I have found favor in Your sight, then ᵃshow me a sign that it is You who talk with me. ¹⁸ᵃDo not depart from here, I pray, until I come to You and bring out my offering and set *it* before You."

And He said, "I will wait until you come back."

¹⁹ᵃSo Gideon went in and prepared a young goat, and unleavened bread from an ephah of flour. The meat he put in a basket, and he put the broth in a pot; and he brought *them* out to Him under the terebinth tree and presented *them*. ²⁰The Angel of God said to him, "Take the meat and the unleavened bread and ᵃlay *them* on this rock, and ᵇpour out the broth." And he did so.

²¹Then the Angel of the LORD put out the end of the staff that *was* in His hand, and touched the meat and the unleavened bread; and ᵃfire rose out of the rock and consumed the meat and the unleavened bread. And the Angel of the LORD departed out of his sight.

²²Now Gideon ᵃperceived that He *was* the Angel of the LORD. So Gideon said, "Alas, O Lord GOD! ᵇFor I have seen the Angel of the LORD face to face."

²³Then the LORD said to him, ᵃ"Peace *be* with you; do not fear, you shall not die." ²⁴So Gideon built an altar there to the LORD, and called it ¹The-LORD-*Is*-Peace. To this day it *is* still ᵃin Ophrah of the Abiezrites.

²⁵Now it came to pass the same night that the LORD said to him, "Take your father's young bull, the second bull of seven years old, and ᵃtear down the altar of ᵇBaal that your father has, and ᶜcut down the ¹wooden image that *is* beside it; ²⁶and build an altar to the LORD your God on top of this ¹rock in the proper arrangement, and take the second bull and offer a burnt sacrifice with the wood of the image which you shall cut down." ²⁷So Gideon took ten men from among his servants and did as the LORD had said to him. But because he feared his father's household and the men of the city too much to do *it* by day, he did *it* by night.

GIDEON DESTROYS THE ALTAR OF BAAL

²⁸And when the men of the city arose early in the morning, there was the altar of Baal, torn down; and the wooden image that *was* beside it was cut down, and the second bull was being offered on the altar *which had been* built. ²⁹So they said to one another, "Who has done this thing?" And when they had inquired and asked, they said, "Gideon the son of Joash has done this thing." ³⁰Then the men of the city said to Joash, "Bring out your son, that he may die, because he has torn down the altar of Baal, and because he has cut down the wooden image that *was* beside it."

6:14 ᵃ1 Sam. 12:11
ᵇJosh. 1:9

6:15 ᵃ1 Sam. 9:21

6:16 ᵃEx. 3:12;
Josh. 1:5

6:17
ᵃJudg. 6:36, 37;
2 Kin. 20:8;
Ps. 86:17; Is. 7:11;
38:7, 8

6:18
ᵃGen. 18:3, 5

6:19
ᵃGen. 18:6–8

6:20
ᵃJudg. 13:19
ᵇ1 Kin. 18:33, 34

6:21 ᵃLev. 9:24

6:22
ᵃGen. 32:30;
Ex. 33:20;
Judg. 13:21, 22
ᵇGen. 16:13

6:23 ᵃDan. 10:19

6:24
ᵃJudg. 8:32

6:25 ᵃJudg. 2:2
ᵇJudg. 3:7
ᶜEx. 34:13;
Deut. 7:5

6:15 ¹Heb. *Adonai,* used of God   6:16 ¹Lit. *strike*   6:24 ¹Heb. *YHWH Shalom*   6:25 ¹Heb. *Asherah,* a Canaanite goddess   6:26 ¹*stronghold*

31But Joash said to all who stood against him, "Would you 1plead for Baal? Would you save him? Let the one who would plead for him be put to death by morning! If he *is* a god, let him plead for himself, because his altar has been torn down!" 32Therefore on that day he called him aJerubbaal,1 saying, "Let Baal plead against him, because he has torn down his altar."

33Then all athe Midianites and Amalekites, the people of the East, gathered together; and they crossed over and encamped in bthe Valley of Jezreel. 34But athe Spirit of the LORD came upon Gideon; then he bblew the trumpet, and the Abiezrites gathered behind him. 35And he sent messengers throughout all Manasseh, who also gathered behind him. He also sent messengers to aAsher, bZebulun, and Naphtali; and they came up to meet them.

THE SIGN OF THE FLEECE

36So Gideon said to God, "If You will save Israel by my hand as You have said— 37alook, I shall put a fleece of wool on the threshing floor; if there is dew on the fleece only, and *it is* dry on all the ground, then I shall know that You will save Israel by my hand, as You have said." 38And it was so. When he rose early the next morning and squeezed the fleece together, he wrung the dew out of the fleece, a bowlful of water. 39Then Gideon said to God, a"Do not be angry with me, but let me speak just once more: Let me test, I pray, just once more with the fleece; let it now be dry only on the fleece, but on all the ground let there be dew." 40And God did so that night. It was dry on the fleece only, but there was dew on all the ground.

GIDEON'S VALIANT THREE HUNDRED

7 Then aJerubbaal (that *is,* Gideon) and all the people who *were* with him rose early and encamped beside the well of Harod, so that the camp of the Midianites was on the north side of them by the hill of Moreh in the valley.

2And the LORD said to Gideon, "The people who *are* with you *are* too many for Me to give the Midianites into their hands, lest Israel aclaim glory for itself against Me, saying, 'My own hand has saved me.' 3Now therefore, proclaim in the hearing of the people, saying, a'Whoever *is* fearful and afraid, let him turn and depart at once from Mount Gilead.' " And twenty-two thousand of the people returned, and ten thousand remained.

4But the LORD said to Gideon, "The people *are* still *too* many; bring them down to the water, and I will test them for you there. Then it will be, *that* of whom I say to you, 'This one shall go with you,' the same shall go with you; and of whomever I say to you, 'This one shall not go with you,' the same shall not go." 5So he brought the people down to the water. And the LORD said to Gideon, "Everyone who laps from the water with his tongue, as a dog laps, you shall set apart by himself; likewise everyone who gets down on his knees to drink." 6And the number of those who lapped, *putting* their hand to their mouth, was three hundred men; but all the rest of the people got down on their knees to drink water. 7Then

6:32 aJudg. 7:1;
1 Sam. 12:11;
2 Sam. 11:21
6:33 aJudg. 6:3
bJosh. 17:16;
Hos. 1:5
6:34
aJudg. 3:10;
1 Chr. 12:18;
2 Chr. 24:20
bNum. 10:3;
Judg. 3:27
6:35
aJudg. 5:17; 7:23
bJudg. 4:6, 10;
5:18
6:37
a[Ex. 4:3–7]
6:39 aGen. 18:32
7:1 aJudg. 6:32
7:2 aDeut. 8:17;
Is. 10:13
7:3 aDeut. 20:8

6:31 1contend   6:32 1Lit. *Let Baal Plead*

the LORD said to Gideon, a"By the three hundred men who lapped I will save you, and deliver the Midianites into your hand. Let all the *other* people go, every man to his ¹place." 8So the people took provisions and their trumpets in their hands. And he sent away all *the rest of* Israel, every man to his tent, and retained those three hundred men. Now the camp of Midian was below him in the valley.

9It happened on the same ªnight that the LORD said to him, "Arise, go down against the camp, for I have delivered it into your hand. 10But if you are afraid to go down, go down to the camp with Purah your servant, 11and you shall ªhear what they say; and afterward ¹your hands shall be strengthened to go down against the camp." Then he went down with Purah his servant to the outpost of the armed men who *were* in the camp. 12Now the Midianites and Amalekites, ªall the people of the East, were lying in the valley bas numerous as locusts; and their camels *were* ¹without number, as the sand by the seashore in multitude.

13And when Gideon had come, there was a man telling a dream to his companion. He said, "I have had a dream: *To my* surprise, a loaf of barley bread tumbled into the camp of Midian; it came to a tent and struck it so that it fell and overturned, and the tent collapsed."

14Then his companion answered and said, "This *is* nothing else but the sword of Gideon the son of Joash, a man of Israel! Into his hand ªGod has delivered Midian and the whole camp."

15And so it was, when Gideon heard the telling of the dream and its interpretation, that he worshiped. He returned to the camp of Israel, and said, "Arise, for the LORD has delivered the camp of Midian into your hand." 16Then he divided the three hundred men *into* three companies, and he put a trumpet into every man's hand, with empty pitchers, and torches inside the pitchers. 17And he said to them, "Look at me and do likewise; watch, and when I come to the edge of the camp you shall do as I do: 18When I blow the trumpet, I and all who *are* with me, then you also blow the trumpets on every side of the whole camp, and say, '*The sword of* the LORD and of Gideon!'"

19So Gideon and the hundred men who *were* with him came to the outpost of the camp at the beginning of the middle watch, just as they had posted the watch; and they blew the trumpets and broke the pitchers that *were* in their hands. 20Then the three companies blew the trumpets and broke the pitchers—they held the torches in their left hands and the trumpets in their right hands for blowing—and they cried, "The sword of the LORD and of Gideon!" 21And ªevery man stood in his place all around the camp; band the whole army ran and cried out and fled. 22When the three hundred ªblew the trumpets, bthe LORD set cevery man's sword against his companion throughout the whole camp; and the army fled to ¹Beth Acacia, toward Zererah, as far as the border of dAbel Meholah, by Tabbath.

23And the men of Israel gathered together from ªNaphtali, Asher, and all Manasseh, and pursued the Midianites.

7:7 ª1 Sam. 14:6

7:9
ªGen. 46:2, 3;
Judg. 6:25

7:11 ªGen. 24:14;
1 Sam. 14:9, 10

7:12
ªJudg. 6:3, 33;
8:10 bJudg. 6:5

7:14
ªJudg. 6:14, 16

7:21
ªEx. 14:13, 14;
2 Chr. 20:17
b2 Kin. 7:7

7:22 ªJosh. 6:4,
16, 20 bPs. 83:9;
Is. 9:4
c1 Sam. 14:20;
2 Chr. 20:23
d1 Kin. 4:12

7:23 ªJudg. 6:35

7:7 ¹home   7:11 ¹you shall be encouraged   7:12 ¹innumerable   7:22 ¹Heb. *Beth Shittah*

24Then Gideon sent messengers throughout all the [a]mountains of Ephraim, saying, "Come down against the Midianites, and seize from them the watering places as far as Beth Barah and the Jordan." Then all the men of Ephraim gathered together and [b]seized the watering places as far as [c]Beth Barah and the Jordan. 25And they captured [a]two princes of the Midianites, [b]Oreb and Zeeb. They killed Oreb at the rock of Oreb, and Zeeb they killed at the winepress of Zeeb. They pursued Midian and brought the heads of Oreb and Zeeb to Gideon on the [c]other side of the Jordan.

GIDEON SUBDUES THE MIDIANITES

8 Now [a]the men of Ephraim said to him, "Why have you done this to us by not calling us when you went to fight with the Midianites?" And they reprimanded him sharply.

2So he said to them, "What have I done now in comparison with you? Is not the [1]gleaning of the grapes of Ephraim better than [2]the vintage of [a]Abiezer? 3[a]God has delivered into your hands the princes of Midian, Oreb and Zeeb. And what was I able to do in comparison with you?" Then their [b]anger toward him subsided when he said that.

4When Gideon came [a]to the Jordan, he and [b]the three hundred men who were with him crossed over, exhausted but still in pursuit. 5Then he said to the men of [a]Succoth, "Please give loaves of bread to the people who follow me, for they are exhausted, and I am pursuing Zebah and Zalmunna, kings of Midian."

6And the leaders of Succoth said, [a]"Are[1] the hands of Zebah and Zalmunna now in your hand, that [b]we should give bread to your army?"

7So Gideon said, "For this cause, when the LORD has delivered Zebah and Zalmunna into my hand, [a]then I will tear your flesh with the thorns of the wilderness and with briers!" 8Then he went up from there [a]to Penuel and spoke to them in the same way. And the men of Penuel answered him as the men of Succoth had answered. 9So he also spoke to the men of Penuel, saying, "When I [a]come back in peace, [b]I will tear down this tower!"

10Now Zebah and Zalmunna were at Karkor, and their armies with them, about fifteen thousand, all who were left of [a]all the army of the people of the East; for [b]one hundred and twenty thousand men who drew the sword had fallen. 11Then Gideon went up by the road of those who dwell in tents on the east of [a]Nobah and Jogbehah; and he [1]attacked the army while the camp felt [b]secure. 12When Zebah and Zalmunna fled, he pursued them; and he [a]took the two kings of Midian, Zebah and Zalmunna, and routed the whole army.

13Then Gideon the son of Joash returned from battle, from the Ascent of Heres. 14And he caught a young man of the men of Succoth and interrogated him; and he wrote down for him the leaders of Succoth and its elders, seventy-seven men. 15Then he came to the men of Succoth and said, "Here are Zebah and Zalmunna, about whom you [a]ridiculed me, saying, 'Are the hands of Zebah and Zalmunna now in your hand, that we should give bread to your weary men?' " 16[a]And he took

---

7:24 [a]Judg. 3:27
[b]Judg. 3:28
[c]John 1:28

7:25 [a]Judg. 8:3
[b]Ps. 83:11;
Is. 10:26
[c]Judg. 8:4

8:1 [a]Judg. 12:1;
2 Sam. 19:41

8:2 [a]Judg. 6:11

8:3
[a]Judg. 7:24, 25
[b]Prov. 15:1

8:4 [a]Judg. 7:25
[b]Judg. 7:6

8:5 [a]Gen. 33:17;
Ps. 60:6

8:6 [a]1 Kin. 20:11;
Judg. 8:15
[b]1 Sam. 25:11

8:7 [a]Judg. 8:16

8:8
[a]Gen. 32:30, 31;
1 Kin. 12:25

8:9 [a]1 Kin. 22:27
[b]Judg. 8:17

8:10 [a]Judg. 7:12
[b]Judg. 6:5

8:11
[a]Num. 32:35, 42
[b]Judg. 18:27;
[1 Thess. 5:3]

8:12 [a]Ps. 83:11

8:15 [a]Judg. 8:6

8:16 [a]Judg. 8:7

8:2 [1]Few grapes left after the harvest   [2]The whole harvest   8:6 [1]Lit. Is the palm   8:11 [1]Lit. struck

the elders of the city, and thorns of the wilderness and briers, and with them he ¹taught the men of Succoth. ¹⁷ᵃThen he tore down the tower of ᵇPenuel and killed the men of the city.

¹⁸And he said to Zebah and Zalmunna, "What kind of men *were they* whom you killed at ᵃTabor?"

So they answered, "As you *are*, so *were* they; each one resembled the son of a king."

¹⁹Then he said, "They *were* my brothers, the sons of my mother. *As* the LORD lives, if you had let them live, I would not kill you." ²⁰And he said to Jether his firstborn, "Rise, kill them!" But the youth would not draw his sword; for he was afraid, because he *was* still a youth.

²¹So Zebah and Zalmunna said, "Rise yourself, and kill us; for as a man *is, so is* his strength." So Gideon arose and ᵃkilled Zebah and Zalmunna, and took the crescent ornaments that *were* on their camels' necks.

GIDEON'S EPHOD

²²Then the men of Israel said to Gideon, ᵃ"Rule over us, both you and your son, and your grandson also; for you have ᵇdelivered us from the hand of Midian."

²³But Gideon said to them, "I will not rule over you, nor shall my son rule over you; ᵃthe LORD shall rule over you." ²⁴Then Gideon said to them, "I would like to ¹make a request of you, that each of you would give me the earrings from his plunder." For they had golden earrings, ᵃbecause they *were* Ishmaelites.

²⁵So they answered, "We will gladly give *them*." And they spread out a garment, and each man threw into it the earrings from his plunder. ²⁶Now the weight of the gold earrings that he requested was one thousand seven hundred *shekels* of gold, besides the crescent ornaments, pendants, and purple robes which *were* on the kings of Midian, and besides the chains that *were* around their camels' necks. ²⁷Then Gideon ᵃmade it into an ephod and set it up in his city, ᵇOphrah. And all Israel ᶜplayed the harlot with it there. It became ᵈa snare to Gideon and to his house.

²⁸Thus Midian was subdued before the children of Israel, so that they lifted their heads no more. ᵃAnd the country was quiet for forty years in the days of Gideon.

DEATH OF GIDEON

²⁹Then ᵃJerubbaal the son of Joash went and dwelt in his own house. ³⁰Gideon had ᵃseventy sons who were his own offspring, for he had many wives. ³¹ᵃAnd his concubine who *was* in Shechem also bore him a son, whose name he called Abimelech. ³²Now Gideon the son of Joash died ᵃat a good old age, and was buried in the tomb of Joash his father, ᵇin Ophrah of the Abiezrites.

³³So it was, ᵃas soon as Gideon was dead, that the children of Israel again ᵇplayed the harlot with the Baals, ᶜand made Baal-Berith their god. ³⁴Thus the children of Israel ᵃdid not remember the LORD their God, who had delivered them from the hands of all their enemies on every side; ³⁵ᵃnor did they show kindness to the house of Jerubbaal (Gideon) in accordance with the good he had done for Israel.

8:17 ᵃJudg. 8:9
ᵇ1 Kin. 12:25

8:18 ᵃJudg. 4:6;
Ps. 89:12

8:21 ᵃPs. 83:11

8:22
ᵃ[Judg. 9:8]
ᵇJudg. 3:9; 9:17

8:23
ᵃ1 Sam. 8:7;
10:19; 12:12;
Ps. 10:16

8:24
ᵃGen. 37:25, 28

8:27 ᵃJudg. 17:5
ᵇJudg. 6:11, 24
ᶜ[Ps. 106:39]
ᵈDeut. 7:16

8:28 ᵃJudg. 5:31

8:29
ᵃJudg. 6:32; 7:1

8:30
ᵃJudg. 9:2, 5

8:31 ᵃJudg. 9:1

8:32 ᵃGen. 25:8;
Job 5:26
ᵇJudg. 6:24;
8:27

8:33 ᵃJudg. 2:19
ᵇJudg. 2:17
ᶜJudg. 9:4, 46

8:34 ᵃDeut. 4:9;
Judg. 3:7;
Ps. 78:11, 42;
106:13, 21

8:35
ᵃJudg. 9:16–18

8:16 ¹*disciplined*   8:24 ¹Lit. *request a request*

ABIMELECH'S CONSPIRACY

9 Then Abimelech the son of Jerubbaal went to Shechem, to [a]his mother's brothers, and spoke with them and with all the family of the house of his mother's father, saying, 2"Please speak in the hearing of all the men of Shechem: 'Which is better for you, that all [a]seventy of the sons of Jerubbaal reign over you, or that one reign over you?' Remember that I *am* your own flesh and [b]bone."

3And his mother's brothers spoke all these words concerning him in the hearing of all the men of Shechem; and their heart was inclined to follow Abimelech, for they said, "He is our [a]brother." 4So they gave him seventy *shekels* of silver from the temple of [a]Baal-Berith, with which Abimelech hired [b]worthless and reckless men; and they followed him. 5Then he went to his father's house [a]at Ophrah and [b]killed his brothers, the seventy sons of Jerubbaal, on one stone. But Jotham the youngest son of Jerubbaal was left, because he hid himself. 6And all the men of Shechem gathered together, all of Beth Millo, and they went and made Abimelech king beside the terebinth tree at the pillar that *was* in Shechem.

THE PARABLE OF THE TREES

7Now when they told Jotham, he went and stood on top of [a]Mount Gerizim, and lifted his voice and cried out. And he said to them:

"Listen to me, you men of Shechem,
That God may listen to you!

8 "The[a] trees once went forth to anoint a king over them.
And they said to the olive tree,
[b]'Reign over us!'
9 But the olive tree said to them,
'Should I cease giving my oil,
[a]With which they honor God and men,
And go to sway over trees?'

10 "Then the trees said to the fig tree,
'You come *and* reign over us!'
11 But the fig tree said to them,
'Should I cease my sweetness and my good fruit,
And go to sway over trees?'

12 "Then the trees said to the vine,
'You come *and* reign over us!'
13 But the vine said to them,
'Should I cease my new wine,
[a]Which cheers *both* God and men,
And go to sway over trees?'

14 "Then all the trees said to the bramble,
'You come *and* reign over us!'
15 And the bramble said to the trees,
'If in truth you anoint me as king over you,
Then come *and* take shelter in my [a]shade;
But if not, [b]let fire come out of the bramble
And devour the [c]cedars of Lebanon!'

16"Now therefore, if you have acted in truth and sincerity in making Abimelech king, and if you have dealt well with

---

9:1
[a]Judg. 8:31, 35
9:2 [a]Judg. 8:30;
9:5, 18
[b]Gen. 29:14
9:3 [a]Gen. 29:15
9:4 [a]Judg. 8:33
[b]Judg. 11:3;
2 Chr. 13:7;
Acts 17:5
9:5 [a]Judg. 6:24
[b]Judg. 8:30;
9:2, 18;
2 Kin. 11:1, 2
9:7 [a]Deut. 11:29;
27:12;
Josh. 8:33;
John 4:20
9:8 [a]2 Kin. 14:9
[b]Judg. 8:22, 23
9:9 [a][John 5:23]
9:13 [a]Ps. 104:15
9:15 [a]Is. 30:2;
Dan. 4:12;
Hos. 14:7
[b]Num. 21:28;
Judg. 9:20;
Ezek. 19:14
[c]2 Kin. 14:9;
Is. 2:13;
Ezek. 31:3

Jerubbaal and his house, and have done to him [a]as[1] he deserves— [17]for my [a]father fought for you, risked his life, and [b]delivered you out of the hand of Midian; [18a]but you have risen up against my father's house this day, and killed his seventy sons on one stone, and made Abimelech, the son of his [b]female servant, king over the men of Shechem, because he is your brother— [19]if then you have acted in truth and sincerity with Jerubbaal and with his house this day, *then* [a]rejoice in Abimelech, and let him also rejoice in you. [20]But if not, [a]let fire come from Abimelech and devour the men of Shechem and Beth Millo; and let fire come from the men of Shechem and from Beth Millo and devour Abimelech!" [21]And Jotham ran away and fled; and he went to [a]Beer and dwelt there, for fear of Abimelech his brother.

DOWNFALL OF ABIMELECH

[22]After Abimelech had reigned over Israel three years, [23a]God sent a [b]spirit of ill will between Abimelech and the men of Shechem; and the men of Shechem [c]dealt treacherously with Abimelech, [24a]that the crime *done* to the seventy sons of Jerubbaal might be settled and their [b]blood be laid on Abimelech their brother, who killed them, and on the men of Shechem, who aided him in the killing of his brothers. [25]And the men of Shechem set [1]men in ambush against him on the tops of the mountains, and they robbed all who passed by them along that way; and it was told Abimelech.

[26]Now Gaal the son of Ebed came with his brothers and went over to Shechem; and the men of Shechem put their confidence in him. [27]So they went out into the fields, and gathered *grapes* from their vineyards and trod *them,* and [1]made merry. And they went into [a]the house of their god, and ate and drank, and cursed Abimelech. [28]Then Gaal the son of Ebed said, [a]"Who *is* Abimelech, and who *is* Shechem, that we should serve him? *Is he* not the son of Jerubbaal, and *is not* Zebul his officer? Serve the men of [b]Hamor the father of Shechem; but why should we serve him? [29a]If only this people were under my [1]authority! Then I would remove Abimelech." So [2]he said to Abimelech, "Increase your army and come out!"

[30]When Zebul, the ruler of the city, heard the words of Gaal the son of Ebed, his anger was aroused. [31]And he sent messengers to Abimelech secretly, saying, "Take note! Gaal the son of Ebed and his brothers have come to Shechem; and here they are, fortifying the city against you. [32]Now therefore, get up by night, you and the people who *are* with you, and [1]lie in wait in the field. [33]And it shall be, as soon as the sun is up in the morning, *that* you shall rise early and rush upon the city; and *when* he and the people who are with him come out against you, you may then do to them [1]as you find opportunity."

[34]So Abimelech and all the people who *were* with him rose by night, and [1]lay in wait against Shechem in four companies. [35]When Gaal the son of Ebed went out and stood in the entrance to the city gate, Abimelech and the people who *were*

9:16 [a] Judg. 8:35

9:17 [a] Judg. 7
[b] Judg. 8:22

9:18
[a] Judg. 8:30, 35;
9:2, 5, 6
[b] Judg. 8:31

9:19 [a] Is. 8:6;
[Phil. 3:3]

9:20
[a] Judg. 9:15, 45,
56, 57

9:21 [a] Num. 21:16

9:23
[a] 1 Kin. 12:15;
Is. 19:14
[b] 1 Sam. 16:14;
18:9, 10;
1 Kin. 22:22;
2 Chr. 18:22
[c] Is. 33:1

9:24
[a] 1 Kin. 2:32;
Esth. 9:25;
Matt. 23:35, 36
[b] Num. 35:33

9:27 [a] Judg. 9:4

9:28
[a] 1 Sam. 25:10;
1 Kin. 12:16
[b] Gen. 34:2, 6;
Josh. 24:32

9:29
[a] 2 Sam. 15:4

9:16 [1]Lit. *according to the doing of his hands*   9:25 [1]Lit. *liers-in-wait for*
9:27 [1]*rejoiced*   9:29 [1]Lit. *hand*   [2]So with MT, Tg.; DSS *they*; LXX *I*
9:32 [1]Set up an ambush   9:33 [1]Lit. *as your hand can find*   9:34 [1]Set up an ambush

with him rose from lying in wait. ³⁶And when Gaal saw the people, he said to Zebul, "Look, people are coming down from the tops of the mountains!"

But Zebul said to him, "You see the shadows of the mountains as *if they were* men."

³⁷So Gaal spoke again and said, "See, people are coming down from the center of the land, and another company is coming from the ¹Diviners' Terebinth Tree."

³⁸Then Zebul said to him, "Where indeed *is* your mouth now, with which you ᵃsaid, 'Who is Abimelech, that we should serve him?' *Are* not these the people whom you despised? Go out, if you will, and fight with them now."

³⁹So Gaal went out, leading the men of Shechem, and fought with Abimelech. ⁴⁰And Abimelech chased him, and he fled from him; and many fell wounded, to the *very* entrance of the gate. ⁴¹Then Abimelech dwelt at Arumah, and Zebul ¹drove out Gaal and his brothers, so that they would not dwell in Shechem.

⁴²And it came about on the next day that the people went out into the field, and they told Abimelech. ⁴³So he took his people, divided them into three companies, and lay in wait in the field. And he looked, and there were the people, coming out of the city; and he rose against them and ¹attacked them. ⁴⁴Then Abimelech and the company that *was* with him rushed forward and stood at the entrance of the gate of the city; and the *other* two companies rushed upon all who *were* in the fields and killed them. ⁴⁵So Abimelech fought against the city all that day; ᵃhe took the city and killed the people who *were* in it; and he ᵇdemolished the city and sowed it with salt.

⁴⁶Now when all the men of the tower of Shechem had heard *that*, they entered the ¹stronghold of the temple ᵃof the god Berith. ⁴⁷And it was told Abimelech that all the men of the tower of Shechem were gathered together. ⁴⁸Then Abimelech went up to Mount ᵃZalmon, he and all the people who *were* with him. And Abimelech took an ax in his hand and cut down a bough from the trees, and took it and laid *it* on his shoulder; then he said to the people who were with him, "What you have seen me do, make haste *and* do as I *have done*." ⁴⁹So each of the people likewise cut down his own bough and followed Abimelech, put *them* against the ¹stronghold, and set the stronghold on fire above them, so that all the people of the tower of Shechem died, about a thousand men and women.

⁵⁰Then Abimelech went to Thebez, and he ¹encamped against Thebez and took it. ⁵¹But there was a strong tower in the city, and all the men and women—all the people of the city—fled there and shut themselves in; then they went up to the top of the tower. ⁵²So Abimelech came as far as the tower and fought against it; and he drew near the door of the tower to burn it with fire. ⁵³But a certain woman ᵃdropped an upper millstone on Abimelech's head and crushed his skull. ⁵⁴Then ᵃhe called quickly to the young man, his armorbearer, and said to him, "Draw your sword and kill me, lest men say of me, 'A woman killed him.'" So his young man thrust him

---

9:38
ᵃ Judg. 9:28, 29

9:45
ᵃ Judg. 9:20
ᵇ Deut. 29:23;
2 Kin. 3:25

9:46
ᵃ Judg. 8:33

9:48 ᵃ Ps. 68:14

9:53
ᵃ 2 Sam. 11:21

9:54
ᵃ 1 Sam. 31:4

9:37 ¹Heb. *Meonenim*   **9:41** ¹*exiled*   **9:43** ¹Lit. *struck*   **9:46** ¹*fortified room*
9:49 ¹*fortified room*   **9:50** ¹*besieged*

through, and he died. ⁵⁵And when the men of Israel saw that Abimelech was dead, they departed, every man to his ¹place.

⁵⁶ᵃThus God repaid the wickedness of Abimelech, which he had done to his father by killing his seventy brothers. ⁵⁷And all the evil of the men of Shechem God returned on their own heads, and on them came ᵃthe curse of Jotham the son of Jerubbaal.

TOLA

10 After Abimelech there ᵃarose to save Israel Tola the son of Puah, the son of Dodo, a man of Issachar; and he dwelt in Shamir in the mountains of Ephraim. ²He judged Israel twenty-three years; and he died and was buried in Shamir.

JAIR

³After him arose Jair, a Gileadite; and he judged Israel twenty-two years. ⁴Now he had thirty sons who ᵃrode on thirty donkeys; they also had thirty towns, ᵇwhich are called ¹"Havoth Jair" to this day, which *are* in the land of Gilead. ⁵And Jair died and was buried in Camon.

ISRAEL OPPRESSED AGAIN

⁶Then ᵃthe children of Israel again did evil in the sight of the LORD, and ᵇserved the Baals and the Ashtoreths, ᶜthe gods of Syria, the gods of ᵈSidon, the gods of Moab, the gods of the people of Ammon, and the gods of the Philistines; and they forsook the LORD and did not serve Him. ⁷So the anger of the LORD was hot against Israel; and He ᵃsold them into the hands of the ᵇPhilistines and into the hands of the people of ᶜAmmon. ⁸From that year they ¹harassed and oppressed the children of Israel for eighteen years—all the children of Israel who *were* on the other side of the Jordan in the ᵃland of the Amorites, in Gilead. ⁹Moreover the people of Ammon crossed over the Jordan to fight against Judah also, against Benjamin, and against the house of Ephraim, so that Israel was severely distressed.

¹⁰ᵃAnd the children of Israel cried out to the LORD, saying, "We have ᵇsinned against You, because we have both forsaken our God and served the Baals!"

¹¹So the LORD said to the children of Israel, "*Did I* not *deliver you* ᵃfrom the Egyptians and ᵇfrom the Amorites and ᶜfrom the people of Ammon and ᵈfrom the Philistines? ¹²Also ᵃthe Sidonians ᵇand Amalekites and ¹Maonites ᶜoppressed you; and you cried out to Me, and I delivered you from their hand. ¹³ᵃYet you have forsaken Me and served other gods. Therefore I will deliver you no more. ¹⁴"Go and ᵃcry out to the gods which you have chosen; let them deliver you in your time of distress."

¹⁵And the children of Israel said to the LORD, "We have sinned! ᵃDo to us whatever seems best to You; only deliver us this day, we pray." ¹⁶ᵃSo they put away the foreign gods from among them and served the LORD. And ᵇHis soul could no longer endure the misery of Israel.

¹⁷Then the people of Ammon gathered together and encamped in Gilead. And the children of Israel assembled

9:56
ᵃJudg. 9:24;
Job 31:3;
Prov. 5:22

9:57
ᵃJudg. 9:20

10:1 ᵃJudg. 2:16

10:4 ᵃJudg. 5:10;
12:14 ᵇDeut. 3:14

10:6 ᵃJudg. 2:11;
3:7; 6:1; 13:1
ᵇJudg. 2:13
ᶜJudg. 2:12
ᵈ1 Kin. 11:33;
Ps. 106:36

10:7
ᵃJudg. 2:14; 4:2;
1 Sam. 12:9
ᵇJudg. 13:1
ᶜJudg. 3:13

10:8
ᵃNum. 32:33

10:10
ᵃJudg. 6:6;
1 Sam. 12:10
ᵇDeut. 1:41

10:11
ᵃEx. 14:30
ᵇNum. 21:21,
24, 25
ᶜJudg. 3:12, 13
ᵈJudg. 3:31

10:12
ᵃJudg. 1:31; 5:19
ᵇJudg. 6:3; 7:12
ᶜPs. 106:42, 43

10:13
ᵃ[Deut. 32:15;
Judg. 2:12;
Jer. 2:13]

10:14
ᵃDeut. 32:37, 38

10:15
ᵃ1 Sam. 3:18;
2 Sam. 15:26

10:16
ᵃ2 Chr. 7:14;
Jer. 18:7, 8
ᵇPs. 106:44, 45;
Is. 63:9

9:55 ¹home   10:4 ¹Lit. *Towns of Jair*, Num. 32:41; Deut. 3:14   10:8 ¹Lit. shattered   10:12 ¹LXX mss. *Midianites*

together and encamped in ᵃMizpah. ¹⁸And the people, the leaders of Gilead, said to one another, "Who *is* the man who will begin the fight against the people of Ammon? He shall ᵃbe head over all the inhabitants of Gilead."

JEPHTHAH

11 Now ᵃJephthah the Gileadite was ᵇa mighty man of valor, but he *was* the son of a harlot; and Gilead begot Jephthah. ²Gilead's wife bore sons; and when his wife's sons grew up, they drove Jephthah out, and said to him, "You shall have ᵃno inheritance in our father's house, for you *are* the son of another woman." ³Then Jephthah fled from his brothers and dwelt in the land of ᵃTob; and ᵇworthless men banded together with Jephthah and went out *raiding* with him.

⁴It came to pass after a time that the ᵃpeople of Ammon made war against Israel. ⁵And so it was, when the people of Ammon made war against Israel, that the elders of Gilead went to get Jephthah from the land of Tob. ⁶Then they said to Jephthah, "Come and be our commander, that we may fight against the people of Ammon."

⁷So Jephthah said to the elders of Gilead, ᵃ"Did you not hate me, and expel me from my father's house? Why have you come to me now when you are in ¹distress?"

⁸ᵃAnd the elders of Gilead said to Jephthah, "That is why we have ᵇturned¹ again to you now, that you may go with us and fight against the people of Ammon, and be ᶜour head over all the inhabitants of Gilead."

⁹So Jephthah said to the elders of Gilead, "If you take me back home to fight against the people of Ammon, and the LORD delivers them to me, shall I be your head?"

¹⁰And the elders of Gilead said to Jephthah, ᵃ"The LORD will be a witness between us, if we do not do according to your words." ¹¹Then Jephthah went with the elders of Gilead, and the people made him ᵃhead and commander over them; and Jephthah spoke all his words ᵇbefore the LORD in Mizpah.

¹²Now Jephthah sent messengers to the king of the people of Ammon, saying, ᵃ"What do you have against me, that you have come to fight against me in my land?"

¹³And the king of the people of Ammon answered the messengers of Jephthah, ᵃ"Because Israel took away my land when they came up out of Egypt, from ᵇthe Arnon as far as ᶜthe Jabbok, and to the Jordan. Now therefore, restore those *lands* peaceably."

¹⁴So Jephthah again sent messengers to the king of the people of Ammon, ¹⁵and said to him, "Thus says Jephthah: ᵃ'Israel did not take away the land of Moab, nor the land of the people of Ammon; ¹⁶for when Israel came up from Egypt, they walked through the wilderness as far as the Red Sea and ᵃcame to Kadesh. ¹⁷Then ᵃIsrael sent messengers to the king of Edom, saying, "Please let me pass through your land." ᵇBut the king of Edom would not heed. And in like manner they sent to the ᶜking of Moab, but he would not *consent*. So Israel ᵈremained in Kadesh. ¹⁸And they ᵃwent along through the wilderness and ᵇbypassed the land of Edom and the land of Moab, came to the east side of the land of Moab, and encamped on the other side of the Arnon. But they did not enter

---

10:17 ᵃGen. 31:49; Judg. 11:11, 29
10:18 ᵃJudg. 11:8, 11
11:1 ᵃHeb. 11:32 ᵇJudg. 6:12; 2 Kin. 5:1
11:2 ᵃGen. 21:10; Deut. 23:2
11:3 ᵃ2 Sam. 10:6, 8 ᵇ1 Sam. 22:2
11:4 ᵃJudg. 10:9, 17
11:7 ᵃGen. 26:27
11:8 ᵃJudg. 10:18 ᵇ[Luke 17:4] ᶜJudg. 10:18
11:10 ᵃGen. 31:49, 50; Jer. 29:23; 42:5
11:11 ᵃJudg. 11:8 ᵇJudg. 10:17; 20:1; 1 Sam. 10:17
11:12 ᵃ2 Sam. 16:10
11:13 ᵃNum. 21:24–26 ᵇJosh. 13:9 ᶜGen. 32:22
11:15 ᵃDeut. 2:9, 19
11:16 ᵃNum. 13:26; 20:1
11:17 ᵃNum. 20:14 ᵇNum. 20:14–21 ᶜJosh. 24:9 ᵈNum. 20:1
11:18 ᵃDeut. 2:9, 18, 19 ᵇNum. 21:4

11:7 ¹trouble   11:8 ¹returned

the border of Moab, for the Arnon *was* the border of Moab. 19Then ^aIsrael sent messengers to Sihon king of the Amorites, king of Heshbon; and Israel said to him, "Please ^blet us pass through your land into our place." 20^aBut Sihon did not trust Israel to pass through his territory. So Sihon gathered all his people together, encamped in Jahaz, and fought against Israel. 21And the LORD God of Israel ^adelivered Sihon and all his people into the hand of Israel, and they ^bdefeated¹ them. Thus Israel gained possession of all the land of the Amorites, who inhabited that country. 22They took possession of ^aall the territory of the Amorites, from the Arnon to the Jabbok and from the wilderness to the Jordan.

23'And now the LORD God of Israel has ¹dispossessed the Amorites from before His people Israel; should you then possess it? 24Will you not possess whatever ^aChemosh your god gives you to possess? So whatever ^bthe LORD our God takes possession of before us, we will possess. 25And now, *are* you any better than ^aBalak the son of Zippor, king of Moab? Did he ever strive against Israel? Did he ever fight against them? 26While Israel dwelt in ^aHeshbon and its villages, in ^bAroer and its villages, and in all the cities along the banks of the Arnon, for three hundred years, why did you not recover *them* within that time? 27Therefore I have not sinned against you, but you wronged me by fighting against me. May the LORD, ^athe Judge, ^brender judgment this day between the children of Israel and the people of Ammon.'" 28However, the king of the people of Ammon did not heed the words which Jephthah sent him.

JEPHTHAH'S VOW AND VICTORY

29Then ^athe Spirit of the LORD came upon Jephthah, and he passed through Gilead and Manasseh, and passed through Mizpah of Gilead; and from Mizpah of Gilead he advanced *toward* the people of Ammon. 30And Jephthah ^amade a vow to the LORD, and said, "If You will indeed deliver the people of Ammon into my hands, 31then it will be that whatever comes out of the doors of my house to meet me, when I return in peace from the people of Ammon, ^ashall surely be the LORD's, ^band I will offer it up as a burnt offering."

32So Jephthah advanced toward the people of Ammon to fight against them, and the LORD delivered them into his hands. 33And he ¹defeated them from Aroer as far as ^aMinnith—twenty cities—and to ²Abel Keramim, with a very great slaughter. Thus the people of Ammon were subdued before the children of Israel.

JEPHTHAH'S DAUGHTER

34When Jephthah came to his house at ^aMizpah, there was ^bhis daughter, coming out to meet him with timbrels and dancing; and she *was his* only child. Besides her he had neither son nor daughter. 35And it came to pass, when he saw her, that he ^atore his clothes, and said, "Alas, my daughter! You have brought me very low! You are among those who trouble me! For I ^bhave ¹given my word to the LORD, and ^cI cannot ²go back on it."

11:19
^aNum. 21:21;
Deut. 2:26–36
^bNum. 21:22;
Deut. 2:27

11:20
^aNum. 21:23;
Deut. 2:27

11:21 ^aJosh. 24:8
^bNum. 21:24, 25

11:22
^aDeut. 2:36, 37

11:24
^aNum. 21:29;
1 Kin. 11:7;
Jer. 48:7
^b[Deut. 9:4, 5;
Josh. 3:10]

11:25
^aNum. 22:2;
Josh. 24:9;
Mic. 6:5

11:26
^aNum. 21:25, 26
^bDeut. 2:36

11:27 ^aGen. 18:25
^bGen. 16:5;
31:53;
[1 Sam. 24:12, 15]

11:29
^aJudg. 3:10

11:30
^aGen. 28:20;
Num. 30:2;
1 Sam. 1:11

11:31
^aLev. 27:2, 3, 28;
1 Sam. 1:11
^bPs. 66:13

11:33
^aEzek. 27:17

11:34
^aJudg. 10:17;
11:11 ^bEx. 15:20;
1 Sam. 18:6;
Ps. 68:25;
Jer. 31:4

11:35
^aGen. 37:29, 34
^bEccl. 5:2, 4, 5
^cNum. 30:2

11:21 ¹Lit. *struck*   11:23 ¹*driven out*   11:33 ¹Lit. *struck*   ²Lit. *Plain of Vineyards*   11:35 ¹Lit. *opened my mouth*   ²Lit. *take it back*

³⁶So she said to him, "My father, *if* you have given your word to the LORD, ᵃdo to me according to what has gone out of your mouth, because ᵇthe LORD has avenged you of your enemies, the people of Ammon." ³⁷Then she said to her father, "Let this thing be done for me: let me alone for two months, that I may go and wander on the mountains and ¹bewail my virginity, my ²friends and I."

³⁸So he said, "Go." And he sent her away *for* two months; and she went with her friends, and bewailed her virginity on the mountains. ³⁹And it was so at the end of two months that she returned to her father, and he ᵃcarried out his vow with her which he had vowed. She ¹knew no man.

And it became a custom in Israel ⁴⁰*that* the daughters of Israel went four days each year to ¹lament the daughter of Jephthah the Gileadite.

JEPHTHAH'S CONFLICT WITH EPHRAIM

12 Then ᵃthe men of Ephraim ¹gathered together, crossed over toward Zaphon, and said to Jephthah, "Why did you cross over to fight against the people of Ammon, and did not call us to go with you? We will burn your house down on you with fire!"

²And Jephthah said to them, "My people and I were in a great struggle with the people of Ammon; and when I called you, you did not deliver me out of their hands. ³So when I saw that you would not deliver *me,* I ᵃtook my life in my hands and crossed over against the people of Ammon; and the LORD delivered them into my hand. Why then have you come up to me this day to fight against me?" ⁴Now Jephthah gathered together all the men of Gilead and fought against Ephraim. And the men of Gilead defeated Ephraim, because they said, "You Gileadites ᵃ*are* fugitives of Ephraim among the Ephraimites *and* among the Manassites." ⁵The Gileadites ᵃseized the fords of the Jordan before the Ephraimites *arrived.* And when *any* Ephraimite who escaped said, "Let me cross over," the men of Gilead would say to him, "*Are* you an Ephraimite?" If he said, "No," ⁶then they would say to him, "Then say, ᵃ'Shibboleth'!"¹ And he would say, "Sibboleth," for he could not ²pronounce *it* right. Then they would take him and kill him at the fords of the Jordan. There fell at that time forty-two thousand Ephraimites.

⁷And Jephthah judged Israel six years. Then Jephthah the Gileadite died and was buried among the cities of Gilead.

IBZAN, ELON, AND ABDON

⁸After him, Ibzan of Bethlehem judged Israel. ⁹He had thirty sons. And he gave away thirty daughters in marriage, and brought in thirty daughters from elsewhere for his sons. He judged Israel seven years. ¹⁰Then Ibzan died and was buried at Bethlehem.

¹¹After him, Elon the Zebulunite judged Israel. He judged Israel ten years. ¹²And Elon the Zebulunite died and was buried at Aijalon in the country of Zebulun.

¹³After him, Abdon the son of Hillel the Pirathonite judged Israel. ¹⁴He had forty sons and thirty grandsons, who ᵃrode on

11:36
ᵃNum. 30:2
ᵇ2 Sam. 18:19, 31
11:39 ᵃJudg. 11:31
12:1 ᵃJudg. 8:1
12:3
ᵃ1 Sam. 19:5;
28:21; Job 13:14
12:4
ᵃ1 Sam. 25:10
12:5 ᵃJosh. 22:11
12:6
ᵃPs. 69:2, 15
12:14
ᵃJudg. 5:10; 10:4

11:37 ¹*lament*   ²*companions*   11:39 ¹Remained a virgin
11:40 ¹*commemorate*   12:1 ¹were summoned   12:6 ¹Lit. *a flowing stream;*
used as a test of dialect   ²Lit. *speak so*

seventy young donkeys. He judged Israel eight years. ¹⁵Then Abdon the son of Hillel the Pirathonite died and was buried in Pirathon in the land of Ephraim, ᵃin the mountains of the Amalekites.

THE BIRTH OF SAMSON
(cf. Num. 6:1–21)

13 Again the children of Israel ᵃdid evil in the sight of the LORD, and the LORD delivered them ᵇinto the hand of the Philistines for forty years.

²Now there was a certain man from ᵃZorah, of the family of the Danites, whose name *was* Manoah; and his wife *was* barren and had no children. ³And the ᵃAngel of the LORD appeared to the woman and said to her, "Indeed now, you are barren and have borne no children, but you shall conceive and bear a son. ⁴Now therefore, please be careful ᵃnot to drink wine or *similar* drink, and not to eat anything unclean. ⁵For behold, you shall conceive and bear a son. And no ᵃrazor shall come upon his head, for the child shall be ᵇa Nazirite to God from the womb; and he shall ᶜbegin to deliver Israel out of the hand of the Philistines."

⁶So the woman came and told her husband, saying, ᵃ"A Man of God came to me, and His ᵇcountenance¹ *was* like the countenance of the Angel of God, very awesome; but I ᶜdid not ask Him where He *was* from, and He did not tell me His name. ⁷And He said to me, 'Behold, you shall conceive and bear a son. Now drink no wine or *similar* drink, nor eat anything unclean, for the child shall be a Nazirite to God from the womb to the day of his death.'"

⁸Then Manoah prayed to the LORD, and said, "O my Lord, please let the Man of God whom You sent come to us again and teach us what we shall do for the child who will be born."

⁹And God listened to the voice of Manoah, and the Angel of God came to the woman again as she was sitting in the field; but Manoah her husband *was* not with her. ¹⁰Then the woman ran in haste and told her husband, and said to him, "Look, the Man who came to me the *other* day has just now appeared to me!"

¹¹So Manoah arose and followed his wife. When he came to the Man, he said to Him, "Are You the Man who spoke to this woman?"

And He said, "I *am*."

¹²Manoah said, "Now let Your words come *to pass!* What will be the boy's rule of life, and his work?"

¹³So the Angel of the LORD said to Manoah, "Of all that I said to the woman let her be careful. ¹⁴She may not eat anything that comes from the vine, ᵃnor may she drink wine or *similar* drink, nor eat anything unclean. All that I commanded her let her observe."

¹⁵Then Manoah said to the Angel of the LORD, "Please ᵃlet us detain You, and we will prepare a young goat for You."

¹⁶And the Angel of the LORD said to Manoah, "Though you detain Me, I will not eat your food. But if you offer a burnt offering, you must offer it to the LORD." (For Manoah did not know He *was* the Angel of the LORD.)

12:15
ᵃ Judg. 3:13, 27; 5:14

13:1 ᵃJudg. 2:11
ᵇJudg. 10:7; 1 Sam. 12:9

13:2
ᵃJosh. 19:41; Judg. 16:31

13:3 ᵃJudg. 6:12

13:4
ᵃNum. 6:2, 3, 20; Judg. 13:4; Luke 1:15

13:5 ᵃNum. 6:5; 1 Sam. 1:11
ᵇNum. 6:2
ᶜ1 Sam. 7:13; 2 Sam. 8:1; 1 Chr. 18:1

13:6
ᵃGen. 32:24–30
ᵇMatt. 28:3; Luke 9:29; Acts 6:15
ᶜJudg. 13:17, 18

13:14
ᵃNum. 6:3, 4; Judg. 13:4

13:15 ᵃGen. 18:5; Judg. 6:18

13:6 ¹appearance

[17]Then Manoah said to the Angel of the LORD, "What *is* Your name, that when Your words come *to pass* we may honor You?"

[18]And the Angel of the LORD said to him, [a]"Why do you ask My name, seeing it *is* wonderful?"

[19]So Manoah took the young goat with the grain offering, [a]and offered it upon the rock to the LORD. And He did a wondrous thing while Manoah and his wife looked on— [20]it happened as the flame went up toward heaven from the altar—the Angel of the LORD ascended in the flame of the altar! When Manoah and his wife saw *this,* they [a]fell on their faces to the ground. [21]When the Angel of the LORD appeared no more to Manoah and his wife, [a]then Manoah knew that He *was* the Angel of the LORD.

[22]And Manoah said to his wife, [a]"We shall surely die, because we have seen God!"

[23]But his wife said to him, "If the LORD had desired to kill us, He would not have accepted a burnt offering and a grain offering from our hands, nor would He have shown us all these *things,* nor would He have told us *such things* as these at this time."

[24]So the woman bore a son and called his name [a]Samson; and [b]the child grew, and the LORD blessed him. [25a]And the Spirit of the LORD began to move upon him at [1]Mahaneh Dan [b]between Zorah and [c]Eshtaol.

SAMSON'S PHILISTINE WIFE

14 Now Samson went down [a]to Timnah, and [b]saw a woman in Timnah of the daughters of the Philistines. [2]So he went up and told his father and mother, saying, "I have seen a woman in Timnah of the daughters of the Philistines; now therefore, [a]get her for me as a wife."

[3]Then his father and mother said to him, "*Is there* no woman among the daughters of [a]your brethren, or among all my people, that you must go and get a wife from the [b]uncircumcised Philistines?"

And Samson said to his father, "Get her for me, for [1]she pleases me well."

[4]But his father and mother did not know that it was [a]of the LORD—that He was seeking an occasion to move against the Philistines. For at that time [b]the Philistines had dominion over Israel.

[5]So Samson went down to Timnah with his father and mother, and came to the vineyards of Timnah.

Now *to his* surprise, a young lion *came* roaring against him. [6]And [a]the Spirit of the LORD came mightily upon him, and he tore the lion apart as one would have torn apart a young goat, though *he had* nothing in his hand. But he did not tell his father or his mother what he had done.

[7]Then he went down and talked with the woman; and she pleased Samson well. [8]After some time, when he returned to get her, he turned aside to see the carcass of the lion. And behold, a swarm of bees and honey *were* in the carcass of the lion. [9]He took some of it in his hands and went along, eating. When he came to his father and mother, he gave *some* to

---

13:18
[a]Gen. 32:29

13:19
[a]Judg. 6:19–21

13:20 [a]Lev. 9:24;
1 Chr. 21:16;
Ezek. 1:28;
Matt. 17:6

13:21
[a]Judg. 6:22

13:22
[a]Gen. 32:30;
Ex. 33:20;
Deut. 5:26;
Judg. 6:22, 23

13:24
[a]Heb. 11:32
[b]1 Sam. 3:19;
Luke 1:80

13:25
[a]Judg. 3:10;
1 Sam. 11:6;
Matt. 4:1
[b]Josh. 15:33;
Judg. 18:11
[c]Judg. 16:31

14:1 [a]Gen. 38:13;
Josh. 15:10, 57
[b]Gen. 34:2

14:2 [a]Gen. 21:21

14:3
[a]Gen. 24:3, 4
[b]Gen. 34:14;
Ex. 34:16;
Deut. 7:3

14:4
[a]Josh. 11:20;
1 Kin. 12:15;
2 Kin. 6:33;
2 Chr. 10:15
[b]Deut. 28:48;
Judg. 13:1

14:6 [a]Judg. 3:10

13:25 [1]Lit. *Camp of Dan,* Judg. 18:12   14:3 [1]Lit. *she is right in my eyes*

them, and they also ate. But he did not tell them that he had taken the honey out of the [a]carcass of the lion.

[10]So his father went down to the woman. And Samson gave a feast there, for young men used to do so. [11]And it happened, when they saw him, that they brought thirty companions to be with him.

[12]Then Samson said to them, "Let me [a]pose a riddle to you. If you can correctly solve and explain it to me [b]within the seven days of the feast, then I will give you thirty linen garments and thirty [c]changes of clothing. [13]But if you cannot explain *it* to me, then you shall give me thirty linen garments and thirty changes of clothing."

And they said to him, [a]"Pose your riddle, that we may hear it."

[14]So he said to them:

"Out of the eater came something to eat,
And out of the strong came something sweet."

Now for three days they could not explain the riddle.

[15]But it came to pass on the [1]seventh day that they said to Samson's wife, [a]"Entice your husband, that he may explain the riddle to us, [b]or else we will burn you and your father's house with fire. Have you invited us in order to take what is ours? *Is that* not *so?*"

[16]Then Samson's wife wept on him, and said, [a]"You only hate me! You do not love me! You have posed a riddle to the sons of my people, but you have not explained *it* to me."

And he said to her, "Look, I have not explained *it* to my father or my mother; so should I explain *it* to you?" [17]Now she had wept on him the seven days while their feast lasted. And it happened on the seventh day that he told her, because she pressed him so much. Then she explained the riddle to the sons of her people. [18]So the men of the city said to him on the seventh day before the sun went down:

"What *is* sweeter than honey?
And what *is* stronger than a lion?"

And he said to them:

"If you had not plowed with my heifer,
You would not have solved my riddle!"

[19]Then [a]the Spirit of the LORD came upon him mightily, and he went down to Ashkelon and killed thirty of their men, took their apparel, and gave the changes *of clothing* to those who had explained the riddle. So his anger was aroused, and he went back up to his father's house. [20]And Samson's wife [a]was *given* to his companion, who had been [b]his best man.

SAMSON DEFEATS THE PHILISTINES

15 After a while, in the time of wheat harvest, it happened that Samson visited his wife with a [a]young goat. And he said, "Let me go in to my wife, into *her* room." But her father would not permit him to go in.

[2]Her father said, "I really thought that you thoroughly [a]hated her; therefore I gave her to your companion. *Is* not her younger sister better than she? Please, take her instead."

14:9 [a]Lev. 11:27

14:12 [a]1 Kin. 10:1; Ezek. 17:2
[b]Gen. 29:27
[c]Gen. 45:22; 2 Kin. 5:22

14:13 [a]Ezek. 17:2

14:15 [a]Judg. 16:5
[b]Judg. 15:6

14:16 [a]Judg. 16:15

14:19 [a]Judg. 3:10; 13:25

14:20 [a]Judg. 15:2
[b]John 3:29

15:1 [a]Gen. 38:17

15:2 [a]Judg. 14:20

3And Samson said to them, "This time I shall be blameless regarding the Philistines if I harm them!" 4Then Samson went and caught three hundred foxes; and he took torches, turned *the foxes* tail to tail, and put a torch between each pair of tails. 5When he had set the torches on fire, he let *the foxes* go into the standing grain of the Philistines, and burned up both the shocks and the standing grain, as well as the vineyards *and* olive groves.

6Then the Philistines said, "Who has done this?"

And they answered, "Samson, the son-in-law of the Timnite, because he has taken his wife and given her to his companion." aSo the Philistines came up and burned her and her father with fire.

7Samson said to them, "Since you would do a thing like this, I will surely take revenge on you, and after that I will cease." 8So he attacked them hip and thigh with a great slaughter; then he went down and dwelt in the cleft of the rock of aEtam.

9Now the Philistines went up, encamped in Judah, and deployed themselves aagainst Lehi. 10And the men of Judah said, "Why have you come up against us?"

So they answered, "We have come up to 1arrest Samson, to do to him as he has done to us."

11Then three thousand men of Judah went down to the cleft of the rock of Etam, and said to Samson, "Do you not know that the Philistines arule over us? What *is* this you have done to us?"

And he said to them, "As they did to me, so I have done to them."

12But they said to him, "We have come down to arrest you, that we may deliver you into the hand of the Philistines."

Then Samson said to them, "Swear to me that you will not kill me yourselves."

13So they spoke to him, saying, "No, but we will tie you securely and deliver you into their hand; but we will surely not kill you." And they bound him with two anew ropes and brought him up from the rock.

14When he came to Lehi, the Philistines came shouting against him. Then athe Spirit of the LORD came mightily upon him; and the ropes that *were* on his arms became like flax that is burned with fire, and his bonds 1broke loose from his hands. 15He found a fresh jawbone of a donkey, reached out his hand and took it, and akilled a thousand men with it. 16Then Samson said:

"With the jawbone of a donkey,
Heaps upon heaps,
With the jawbone of a donkey
I have slain a thousand men!"

17And so it was, when he had finished speaking, that he threw the jawbone from his hand, and called that place 1Ramath Lehi.

18Then he became very thirsty; so he cried out to the LORD and said, a"You have given this great deliverance by the hand of Your servant; and now shall I die of thirst and fall into the hand of the uncircumcised?" 19So God split the hollow place

15:6 aJudg. 14:15
15:8 a2 Chr. 11:6
15:9 aJudg. 15:19
15:11 aLev. 26:25; Deut. 28:43; Judg. 13:1; 14:4; Ps. 106:40–42
15:13 aJudg. 16:11, 12
15:14 aJudg. 3:10; 14:6
15:15 aLev. 26:8; Josh. 23:10; Judg. 3:31
15:18 aPs. 3:7

15:10 1Lit. *bind*   15:14 1Lit. *were melted*   15:17 1Lit. *Jawbone Height*

that *is* in ¹Lehi, and water came out, and he drank; and ᵃhis spirit returned, and he revived. Therefore he called its name ²En Hakkore, which is in Lehi to this day. ²⁰And ᵃhe judged Israel ᵇtwenty years ᶜin the days of the Philistines.

SAMSON AND DELILAH

16 Now Samson went to ᵃGaza and saw a harlot there, and went in to her. ²*When* the Gazites *were told,* "Samson has come here!" they ᵃsurrounded *the place* and lay in wait for him all night at the gate of the city. They were quiet all night, saying, "In the morning, when it is daylight, we will kill him." ³And Samson lay *low* till midnight; then he arose at midnight, took hold of the doors of the gate of the city and the two gateposts, pulled them up, bar and all, put *them* on his shoulders, and carried them to the top of the hill that faces Hebron.

⁴Afterward it happened that he loved a woman in the Valley of Sorek, whose name *was* Delilah. ⁵And the ᵃlords of the Philistines came up to her and said to her, ᵇ"Entice him, and find out where his great strength *lies,* and by what *means* we may overpower him, that we may bind him to afflict him; and every one of us will give you eleven hundred *pieces* of silver."

⁶So Delilah said to Samson, "Please tell me where your great strength *lies,* and with what you may be bound to afflict you."

⁷And Samson said to her, "If they bind me with seven fresh bowstrings, not yet dried, then I shall become weak, and be like any *other* man."

⁸So the lords of the Philistines brought up to her seven fresh bowstrings, not yet dried, and she bound him with them. ⁹Now *men were* lying in wait, staying with her in the room. And she said to him, "The Philistines *are* upon you, Samson!" But he broke the bowstrings as a strand of yarn breaks when it touches fire. So the secret of his strength was not known.

¹⁰Then Delilah said to Samson, "Look, you have mocked me and told me lies. Now, please tell me what you may be bound with."

¹¹So he said to her, "If they bind me securely with ᵃnew ropes ¹that have never been used, then I shall become weak, and be like any *other* man."

¹²Therefore Delilah took new ropes and bound him with them, and said to him, "The Philistines *are* upon you, Samson!" And *men were* lying in wait, staying in the room. But he broke them off his arms like a thread.

¹³Delilah said to Samson, "Until now you have mocked me and told me lies. Tell me what you may be bound with."

And he said to her, "If you weave the seven locks of my head into the web of the loom"—

¹⁴So she wove *it* tightly with the batten of the loom, and said to him, "The Philistines *are* upon you, Samson!" But he awoke from his sleep, and pulled out the batten and the web from the loom.

¹⁵Then she said to him, ᵃ"How can you say, 'I love you,' when your heart *is* not with me? You have mocked me these

15:19
ᵃGen. 45:27;
Is. 40:29

15:20
ᵃJudg. 10:2;
12:7–14
ᵇJudg. 16:31
ᶜJudg. 13:1

16:1 ᵃJosh. 15:47

16:2
ᵃ1 Sam. 23:26;
Ps. 118:10–12

16:5 ᵃJosh. 13:3
ᵇJudg. 14:15

16:11 ᵃJudg. 15:13

16:15
ᵃJudg. 14:16

15:19 ¹Lit. *Jawbone,* Judg. 15:14   ²Lit. *Spring of the Caller*   16:11 ¹Lit. *with which work has never been done*

three times, and have not told me where your great strength *lies*." ¹⁶And it came to pass, when she pestered him daily with her words and pressed him, *so* that his soul was ¹vexed to death, ¹⁷that he ᵃtold her all his heart, and said to her, ᵇ"No razor has ever come upon my head, for I *have been* a Nazirite to God from my mother's womb. If I am shaven, then my strength will leave me, and I shall become weak, and be like any *other* man."

¹⁸When Delilah saw that he had told her all his heart, she sent and called for the lords of the Philistines, saying, "Come up once more, for he has told me all his heart." So the lords of the Philistines came up to her and brought the money in their hand. ¹⁹ᵃThen she lulled him to sleep on her knees, and called for a man and had him shave off the seven locks of his head. Then ¹she began to torment him, and his strength left him. ²⁰And she said, "The Philistines *are* upon you, Samson!" So he awoke from his sleep, and said, "I will go out as before, at other times, and shake myself free!" But he did not know that the LORD ᵃhad departed from him.

²¹Then the Philistines took him and ¹put out his ᵃeyes, and brought him down to Gaza. They bound him with bronze fetters, and he became a grinder in the prison. ²²However, the hair of his head began to grow again after it had been shaven.

SAMSON DIES WITH THE PHILISTINES

²³Now the lords of the Philistines gathered together to offer a great sacrifice to ᵃDagon their god, and to rejoice. And they said:

"Our god has delivered into our hands
  Samson our enemy!"

²⁴When the people saw him, they ᵃpraised their god; for they said:

"Our god has delivered into our hands our enemy,
  The destroyer of our land,
  And the one who multiplied our dead."

²⁵So it happened, when their hearts were ᵃmerry, that they said, "Call for Samson, that he may perform for us." So they called for Samson from the prison, and he performed for them. And they stationed him between the pillars. ²⁶Then Samson said to the lad who held him by the hand, "Let me feel the pillars which support the temple, so that I can lean on them." ²⁷Now the temple was full of men and women. All the lords of the Philistines *were* there—about three thousand men and women on the ᵃroof watching while Samson performed.

²⁸Then Samson called to the LORD, saying, "O Lord GOD, ᵃremember me, I pray! Strengthen me, I pray, just this once, O God, that I may with one *blow* take vengeance on the Philistines for my two eyes!" ²⁹And Samson took hold of the two middle pillars which supported the temple, and he braced himself against them, one on his right and the other on his left. ³⁰Then Samson said, "Let me die with the Philistines!"

16:17 ᵃ[Mic. 7:5]
ᵇNum. 6:5;
Judg. 13:5
16:19
ᵃProv. 7:26, 27
16:20
ᵃNum. 14:9, 42,
43; [Josh. 7:12];
1 Sam. 16:14;
18:12; 28:15, 16;
2 Chr. 15:2
16:21
ᵃ2 Kin. 25:7
16:23
ᵃ1 Sam. 5:2
16:24 ᵃDan. 5:4
16:25
ᵃJudg. 9:27
16:27
ᵃDeut. 22:8
16:28 ᵃJer. 15:15

16:16 ¹Lit. *impatient to the point of*   16:19 ¹So with MT, Tg., Vg.; LXX *he began to be weak,*   16:21 ¹Lit. *bored out*

And he pushed with *all his* might, and the temple fell on the lords and all the people who *were* in it. So the dead that he killed at his death were more than he had killed in his life.

³¹And his brothers and all his father's household came down and took him, and brought *him* up and ªburied him between Zorah and Eshtaol in the tomb of his father Manoah. He had judged Israel ᵇtwenty years.

MICAH'S IDOLATRY

17 Now there was a man from the mountains of Ephraim, whose name *was* ªMicah. ²And he said to his mother, "The eleven hundred *shekels* of silver that were taken from you, and on which you ªput a curse, even saying it in my ears—here *is* the silver with me; I took it."

And his mother said, ᵇ"May you be blessed by the LORD, my son!" ³So when he had returned the eleven hundred *shekels* of silver to his mother, his mother said, "I had wholly dedicated the silver from my hand to the LORD for my son, to ªmake a carved image and a molded image; now therefore, I will return it to you." ⁴Thus he returned the silver to his mother. Then his mother ªtook two hundred *shekels* of silver and gave them to the silversmith, and he made it into a carved image and a molded image; and they were in the house of Micah.

⁵The man Micah had a ªshrine, and made an ᵇephod and ᶜhousehold¹ idols; and he consecrated one of his sons, who became his priest. ⁶ªIn those days *there was* no king in Israel; ᵇeveryone did *what was* right in his own eyes.

⁷Now there was a young man from ªBethlehem in Judah, of the family of Judah; he *was* a Levite, and ᵇwas staying there. ⁸The man departed from the city of Bethlehem in Judah to stay wherever he could find *a place.* Then he came to the mountains of Ephraim, to the house of Micah, as he journeyed. ⁹And Micah said to him, "Where do you come from?"

So he said to him, "I *am* a Levite from Bethlehem in Judah, and I am on my way to find *a place* to stay."

¹⁰Micah said to him, "Dwell with me, ªand be a ᵇfather and a priest to me, and I will give you ten *shekels* of silver per year, a suit of clothes, and your sustenance." So the Levite went in. ¹¹Then the Levite was content to dwell with the man; and the young man became like one of his sons to him. ¹²So Micah ªconsecrated¹ the Levite, and the young man ᵇbecame his priest, and lived in the house of Micah. ¹³Then Micah said, "Now I know that the LORD will be good to me, since I have a Levite as ªpriest!"

THE DANITES ADOPT MICAH'S IDOLATRY

18 In ªthose days *there was* no king in Israel. And in those days ᵇthe tribe of the Danites was seeking an inheritance for itself to dwell in; for until that day *their* inheritance among the tribes of Israel had not fallen to them. ²So the children of Dan sent five men of their family from their territory, men of valor from ªZorah and Eshtaol, ᵇto spy out the land and search it. They said to them, "Go, search the land." So they went to the mountains of Ephraim, to the ᶜhouse of Micah, and lodged there. ³While they *were* at the house of Micah,

16:31
ª Judg. 13:25
ᵇ Judg. 15:20

17:1 ª Judg. 18:2

17:2 ª Lev. 5:1
ᵇ Gen. 14:19

17:3 ª Ex. 20:4, 23; 34:17;
Lev. 19:4

17:4 ª Is. 46:6

17:5 ª Judg. 18:24
ᵇ Judg. 8:27;
18:14 ᶜ Gen. 31:19, 30; Hos. 3:4

17:6 ª Judg. 18:1;
19:1 ᵇ Deut. 12:8;
Judg. 21:25

17:7 ª Josh. 19:15;
Judg. 19:1;
Ruth 1:1, 2;
Mic. 5:2;
Matt. 2:1, 5, 6
ᵇ Deut. 18:6

17:10
ª Judg. 18:19
ᵇ Gen. 45:8;
Job 29:16

17:12 ª Judg. 17:5
ᵇ Judg. 18:30

17:13 ª Judg. 18:4

18:1 ª Judg. 17:6;
19:1; 21:25
ᵇ Josh. 19:40–48

18:2
ª Judg. 13:25
ᵇ Num. 13:17;
Josh. 2:1;
ᶜ Judg. 17:1

they recognized the voice of the young Levite. They turned aside and said to him, "Who brought you here? What are you doing in this *place?* What do you have here?"

⁴He said to them, "Thus and so Micah did for me. He has ᵃhired me, and I have become his priest."

⁵So they said to him, "Please ᵃinquire ᵇof God, that we may know whether the journey on which we go will be prosperous."

⁶And the priest said to them, ᵃ"Go in peace. ¹The presence of the LORD *be* with you on your way."

⁷So the five men departed and went to ᵃLaish. They saw the people who *were* there, ᵇhow they dwelt safely, in the manner of the Sidonians, quiet and secure. *There were* no rulers in the land who might put *them* to shame for anything. They *were* far from the ᶜSidonians, and they had no ties ¹with anyone.

⁸Then *the spies* came back to their brethren at ᵃZorah and Eshtaol, and their brethren said to them, "What *is* your *report?*"

⁹So they said, ᵃ"Arise, let us go up against them. For we have seen the land, and indeed it *is* very good. *Would* you ᵇ*do* nothing? Do not hesitate to go, *and* enter to possess the land. ¹⁰When you go, you will come to a ᵃsecure people and a large land. For God has given it into your hands, ᵇa place where *there is* no lack of anything that *is* on the earth."

¹¹And six hundred men of the family of the Danites went from there, from Zorah and Eshtaol, armed with weapons of war. ¹²Then they went up and encamped in ᵃKirjath Jearim in Judah. (Therefore they call that place ᵇMahaneh Dan¹ to this day. There *it is,* west of Kirjath Jearim.) ¹³And they passed from there to the mountains of Ephraim, and came to ᵃthe house of Micah.

¹⁴ᵃThen the five men who had gone to spy out the country of Laish answered and said to their brethren, "Do you know that ᵇthere are in these houses an ephod, household idols, a carved image, and a molded image? Now therefore, consider what you should do." ¹⁵So they turned aside there, and came to the house of the young Levite man—to the house of Micah—and greeted him. ¹⁶The ᵃsix hundred men armed with their weapons of war, who *were* of the children of Dan, stood by the entrance of the gate. ¹⁷Then ᵃthe five men who had gone to spy out the land went up. Entering there, they took ᵇthe carved image, the ephod, the household idols, and the molded image. The priest stood at the entrance of the gate with the six hundred men *who were* armed with weapons of war.

¹⁸When these went into Micah's house and took the carved image, the ephod, the household idols, and the molded image, the priest said to them, "What are you doing?"

¹⁹And they said to him, "Be quiet, ᵃput your hand over your mouth, and come with us; ᵇbe a father and a priest to us. *Is it* better for you to be a priest to the household of one man, or that you be a priest to a tribe and a family in Israel?" ²⁰So the priest's heart was glad; and he took the ephod, the household idols, and the carved image, and took his place among the people.

18:4
ᵃ Judg. 17:10, 12

18:5 ᵃ1 Kin. 22:5;
[Is. 30:1];
Hos. 4:12
ᵇ Judg. 1:1; 17:5;
18:14

18:6 ᵃ1 Kin. 22:6

18:7 ᵃJosh. 19:47
ᵇ Judg. 18:27–29
ᶜJudg. 10:12

18:8 ᵃJudg. 18:2

18:9
ᵃNum. 13:30;
Josh. 2:23, 24
ᵇ1 Kin. 22:3

18:10
ᵃ Judg. 18:7, 27
ᵇDeut. 8:9

18:12
ᵃ Josh. 15:60
ᵇJudg. 13:25

18:13 ᵃJudg. 18:2

18:14
ᵃ1 Sam. 14:28
ᵇJudg. 17:5

18:16
ᵃJudg. 18:11

18:17
ᵃJudg. 18:2, 14
ᵇJudg. 17:4, 5

18:19 ᵃJob 21:5;
29:9; 40:4;
Mic. 7:16
ᵇJudg. 17:10

18:6 ¹Lit. *The LORD is before the way in which you go*   18:7 ¹So with MT, Tg., Vg.; LXX *with Syria*   18:12 ¹Lit. *Camp of Dan*

21Then they turned and departed, and put the little ones, the livestock, and the goods in front of them. 22When they were a good way from the house of Micah, the men who *were* in the houses near Micah's house gathered together and overtook the children of Dan. 23And they called out to the children of Dan. So they turned around and said to Micah, a"What ails you, that you have gathered such a company?"

24So he said, "You have ataken away my 1gods which I made, and the priest, and you have gone away. Now what more do I have? How can you say to me, 'What ails you?'"

25And the children of Dan said to him, "Do not let your voice be heard among us, lest 1angry men fall upon you, and you lose your life, with the lives of your household!" 26Then the children of Dan went their way. And when Micah saw that they *were* too strong for him, he turned and went back to his house.

DANITES SETTLE IN LAISH

27So they took *the things* Micah had made, and the priest who had belonged to him, and went to Laish, to a people quiet and secure; aand they struck them with the edge of the sword and burned the city with fire. 28*There was* no deliverer, because it *was* afar from Sidon, and they had no ties with anyone. It was in the valley that belongs bto Beth Rehob. So they rebuilt the city and dwelt there. 29And athey called the name of the city bDan, after the name of Dan their father, who was born to Israel. However, the name of the city formerly *was* Laish.

30Then the children of Dan set up for themselves the carved image; and Jonathan the son of Gershom, the son of 1Manasseh, and his sons were priests to the tribe of Dan auntil the day of the captivity of the land. 31So they set up for themselves Micah's carved image which he made, aall the time that the house of God was in Shiloh.

THE LEVITE'S CONCUBINE

19 And it came to pass in those days, awhen *there was* no king in Israel, that there was a certain Levite staying in the remote mountains of Ephraim. He took for himself a concubine from bBethlehem in Judah. 2But his concubine played the harlot against him, and went away from him to her father's house at Bethlehem in Judah, and was there four whole months. 3Then her husband arose and went after her, to aspeak 1kindly to her *and* bring her back, having his servant and a couple of donkeys with him. So she brought him into her father's house; and when the father of the young woman saw him, he was glad to meet him. 4Now his father-in-law, the young woman's father, detained him; and he stayed with him three days. So they ate and drank and lodged there.

5Then it came to pass on the fourth day that they arose early in the morning, and he stood to depart; but the young woman's father said to his son-in-law, a"Refresh your heart with a morsel of bread, and afterward go your way."

6So they sat down, and the two of them ate and drank

18:23
a2 Kin. 6:28

18:24
aGen. 31:30;
Judg. 17:5

18:27
aJosh. 19:47

18:28
aJudg. 18:7
bNum. 13:21;
2 Sam. 10:6

18:29
aJosh. 19:47
bJudg. 20:1;
1 Kin. 12:29, 30;
15:20

18:30
a2 Kin. 15:29

18:31
aDeut. 12:1–32;
Josh. 18:1, 8;
Judg. 19:18;
21:12

19:1 aJudg. 17:6;
18:1; 21:25
bJudg. 17:7;
Ruth 1:1

19:3 aGen. 34:3;
50:21

19:5 aGen. 18:5;
Judg. 19:8;
Ps. 104:15

18:24 1*idols*   18:25 1Lit. *bitter of soul*   18:30 1LXX, Vg. *Moses*   19:3 1Lit. *to her heart*

together. Then the young woman's father said to the man, "Please be content to stay all night, and let your heart be merry." [7]And when the man stood to depart, his father-in-law urged him; so he lodged there again. [8]Then he arose early in the morning on the fifth day to depart, but the young woman's father said, "Please refresh your heart." So they delayed until afternoon; and both of them ate.

[9]And when the man stood to depart—he and his concubine and his servant—his father-in-law, the young woman's father, said to him, "Look, the day is now drawing toward evening; please spend the night. See, the day is coming to an end; lodge here, that your heart may be merry. Tomorrow go your way early, so that you may get [1]home."

[10]However, the man was not willing to spend that night; so he rose and departed, and came opposite [a]Jebus (that is, Jerusalem). With him were the two saddled donkeys; his concubine was also with him. [11]They were near Jebus, and the day was far spent; and the servant said to his master, "Come, please, and let us turn aside into this city [a]of the Jebusites and lodge in it."

[12]But his master said to him, "We will not turn aside here into a city of foreigners, who are not of the children of Israel; we will go on [a]to Gibeah." [13]So he said to his servant, "Come, let us draw near to one of these places, and spend the night in Gibeah or in [a]Ramah." [14]And they passed by and went their way; and the sun went down on them near Gibeah, which belongs to Benjamin. [15]They turned aside there to go in to lodge in Gibeah. And when he went in, he sat down in the open square of the city, for no one would [a]take them into his house to spend the night.

[16]Just then an old man came in from [a]his work in the field at evening, who also was from the mountains of Ephraim; he was staying in Gibeah, whereas the men of the place were Benjamites. [17]And when he raised his eyes, he saw the traveler in the open square of the city; and the old man said, "Where are you going, and where do you come from?"

[18]So he said to him, "We are passing from Bethlehem in Judah toward the remote mountains of Ephraim; I am from there. I went to Bethlehem in Judah; now I am going to [a]the house of the LORD. But there is no one who will take me into his house, [19]although we have both straw and fodder for our donkeys, and bread and wine for myself, for your female servant, and for the young man who is with your servant; there is no lack of anything."

[20]And the old man said, [a]"Peace be with you! However, let all your needs be my responsibility; [b]only do not spend the night in the open square." [21][a]So he brought him into his house, and gave fodder to the donkeys. [b]And they washed their feet, and ate and drank.

GIBEAH'S CRIME

[22]As they were [a]enjoying themselves, suddenly [b]certain men of the city, [c]perverted[1] men, surrounded the house and beat on the door. They spoke to the master of the house, the old man, saying, [d]"Bring out the man who came to your house, that we may know him carnally!"

19:10 [a]Josh. 18:28; 1 Chr. 11:4, 5

19:11 [a]Josh. 15:8, 63; Judg. 1:21; 2 Sam. 5:6

19:12 [a]Josh. 18:28

19:13 [a]Josh. 18:25

19:15 [a]Matt. 25:43

19:16 [a]Ps. 104:23

19:18 [a]Josh. 18:1; Judg. 18:31; 20:18; 1 Sam. 1:3, 7

19:20 [a]Gen. 43:23; Judg. 6:23; 1 Sam. 25:6 [b]Gen. 19:2

19:21 [a]Gen. 24:32; 43:24 [b]Gen. 18:4; John 13:5

19:22 [a]Judg. 16:25; 19:6, 9 [b]Gen. 19:4, 5; Judg. 20:5; Hos. 9:9; 10:9 [c]Deut. 13:13; 1 Sam. 2:12; 1 Kin. 21:10; [2 Cor. 6:15] [d]Gen. 19:5; [Rom. 1:26, 27]

19:9 [1]Lit. to your tent   **19:22** [1]Lit. sons of Belial

23But athe man, the master of the house, went out to them and said to them, "No, my brethren! I beg you, do not act *so* wickedly! Seeing this man has come into my house, bdo not commit this outrage. 24aLook, *here is* my virgin daughter and 1*the man's* concubine; let me bring them out now. bHumble them, and do with them as you please; but to this man do not do such a vile thing!" 25But the men would not heed him. So the man took his concubine and brought *her* out to them. And they aknew her and abused her all night until morning; and when the day began to break, they let her go.

26Then the woman came as the day was dawning, and fell down at the door of the man's house where her master *was*, till it was light.

27When her master arose in the morning, and opened the doors of the house and went out to go his way, there was his concubine, fallen *at* the door of the house with her hands on the threshold. 28And he said to her, "Get up and let us be going." But athere was no answer. So the man lifted her onto the donkey; and the man got up and went to his place.

29When he entered his house he took a knife, laid hold of his concubine, and adivided her into twelve pieces, 1limb by limb, and sent her throughout all the territory of Israel. 30And so it was that all who saw it said, "No such deed has been done or seen from the day that the children of Israel came up from the land of Egypt until this day. Consider it, aconfer, and speak up!"

ISRAEL'S WAR WITH THE BENJAMITES

20 So aall the children of Israel came out, from bDan to cBeersheba, as well as from the land of Gilead, and the congregation gathered together as one man before the LORD dat Mizpah. 2And the leaders of all the people, all the tribes of Israel, presented themselves in the assembly of the people of God, four hundred thousand foot soldiers awho drew the sword. 3(Now the children of Benjamin heard that the children of Israel had gone up to Mizpah.)

Then the children of Israel said, "Tell *us*, how did this wicked deed happen?"

4So the Levite, the husband of the woman who was murdered, answered and said, "My concubine and aI went into Gibeah, which belongs to Benjamin, to spend the night. 5aAnd the men of Gibeah rose against me, and surrounded the house at night because of me. They intended to kill me, bbut instead they ravished my concubine so that she died. 6So aI took hold of my concubine, cut her in pieces, and sent her throughout all the territory of the inheritance of Israel, because they bcommitted lewdness and outrage in Israel. 7Look! All of you *are* children of Israel; agive your advice and counsel here and now!"

8So all the people arose as one man, saying, "None *of us* will go to his tent, nor will any turn back to his house; 9but now this *is* the thing which we will do to Gibeah: *We will go up* aagainst it by lot. 10We will take ten men out of *every* hundred throughout all the tribes of Israel, a hundred out of *every* thousand, and a thousand out of *every* ten thousand, to make provisions for the people, that when they come to Gibeah in

19:23
aGen. 19:6, 7
bGen. 34:7;
Deut. 22:21;
Judg. 20:6, 10;
2 Sam. 13:12

19:24 aGen. 19:8
bGen. 34:2;
Deut. 21:14

19:25 aGen. 4:1

19:28
aJudg. 20:5

19:29
aJudg. 20:6;
1 Sam. 11:7

19:30
aJudg. 20:7;
Prov. 13:10

20:1
aJosh. 22:12;
Judg. 20:11; 21:5
bJudg. 18:29;
1 Sam. 3:20;
2 Sam. 3:10;
24:2 cJosh. 19:2
dJudg. 10:17;
1 Sam. 7:5

20:2 aJudg. 8:10

20:4
aJudg. 19:15

20:5
aJudg. 19:22
bJudg. 19:25, 26

20:6
aJudg. 19:29
bJosh. 7:15

20:7
aJudg. 19:30

20:9 aJudg. 1:3

19:24 1Lit. *his*   19:29 1Lit. *with her bones*

Benjamin, they may repay all the vileness that they have done in Israel." ¹¹So all the men of Israel were gathered against the city, united together as one man.

¹²ᵃThen the tribes of Israel sent men through all the tribe of Benjamin, saying, "What *is* this wickedness that has occurred among you? ¹³Now therefore, deliver up the men, ᵃthe ¹perverted men who *are* in Gibeah, that we may put them to death and ᵇremove the evil from Israel!" But the children of Benjamin would not listen to the voice of their brethren, the children of Israel. ¹⁴Instead, the children of Benjamin gathered together from their cities to Gibeah, to go to battle against the children of Israel. ¹⁵And from their cities at that time ᵃthe children of Benjamin numbered twenty-six thousand men who drew the sword, besides the inhabitants of Gibeah, who numbered seven hundred select men. ¹⁶Among all this people *were* seven hundred select men *who were* ᵃleft-handed; every one could sling a stone at a hair's *breadth* and not miss. ¹⁷Now besides Benjamin, the men of Israel numbered four hundred thousand men who drew the sword; all of these *were* men of war.

¹⁸Then the children of Israel arose and ᵃwent up to ¹the house of God to ᵇinquire of God. They said, "Which of us shall go up first to battle against the children of Benjamin?"

The LORD said, ᶜ"Judah first!"

¹⁹So the children of Israel rose in the morning and encamped against Gibeah. ²⁰And the men of Israel went out to battle against Benjamin, and the men of Israel put themselves in battle array to fight against them at Gibeah. ²¹Then ᵃthe children of Benjamin came out of Gibeah, and on that day cut down to the ground twenty-two thousand men of the Israelites. ²²And the people, that is, the men of Israel, encouraged themselves and again formed the battle line at the place where they had put themselves in array on the first day. ²³ᵃThen the children of Israel went up and wept before the LORD until evening, and asked counsel of the LORD, saying, "Shall I again draw near for battle against the children of my brother Benjamin?"

And the LORD said, "Go up against him."

²⁴So the children of Israel approached the children of Benjamin on the second day. ²⁵And ᵃBenjamin went out against them from Gibeah on the second day, and cut down to the ground eighteen thousand more of the children of Israel; all these drew the sword.

²⁶Then all the children of Israel, that is, all the people, ᵃwent up and came to ¹the house of God and wept. They sat there before the LORD and fasted that day until evening; and they offered burnt offerings and peace offerings before the LORD. ²⁷So the children of Israel inquired of the LORD (ᵃthe ark of the covenant of God *was* there in those days, ²⁸ᵃand Phinehas the son of Eleazar, the son of Aaron, ᵇstood before it in those days), saying, "Shall I yet again go out to battle against the children of my brother Benjamin, or shall I cease?"

And the LORD said, "Go up, for tomorrow I will deliver them into your hand."

²⁹Then Israel ᵃset men in ambush all around Gibeah. ³⁰And the children of Israel went up against the children of

---

20:12
ᵃDeut. 13:14;
Josh. 22:13, 16

20:13
ᵃDeut. 13:13;
Judg. 19:22
ᵇDeut. 17:12;
1 Cor. 5:13

20:15
ᵃNum. 1:36, 37;
2:23; 26:41

20:16
ᵃJudg. 3:15;
1 Chr. 12:2

20:18
ᵃJudg. 20:23,
26 ᵇNum. 27:21
ᶜJudg. 1:1, 2

20:21
ᵃ[Gen. 49:27]

20:23
ᵃJudg. 20:26, 27

20:25
ᵃJudg. 20:21

20:26
ᵃJudg. 20:18,
23; 21:2

20:27
ᵃJosh. 18:1;
1 Sam. 1:3; 3:3;
4:3, 4

20:28
ᵃNum. 25:7, 13;
Josh. 24:33
ᵇDeut. 10:8;
18:5

20:29
ᵃJosh. 8:4

20:13 ¹Lit. *sons of Belial* **20:18** ¹Or *Bethel* **20:26** ¹Or *Bethel*

Benjamin on the third day, and put themselves in battle array against Gibeah as at the other times. [31]So the children of Benjamin went out against the people, *and* were drawn away from the city. They began to strike down *and* kill some of the people, as at the other times, in the highways [a](one of which goes up to Bethel and the other to Gibeah) and in the field, about thirty men of Israel. [32]And the children of Benjamin said, "They *are* defeated before us, as at first."

But the children of Israel said, "Let us flee and draw them away from the city to the highways." [33]So all the men of Israel rose from their place and put themselves in battle array at Baal Tamar. Then Israel's men in ambush burst forth from their position in the plain of Geba. [34]And ten thousand select men from all Israel came against Gibeah, and the battle was fierce. [a]But [1]*the Benjamites* did not know that disaster *was* upon them. [35]The LORD [1]defeated Benjamin before Israel. And the children of Israel destroyed that day twenty-five thousand one hundred Benjamites; all these drew the sword.

[36]So the children of Benjamin saw that they were defeated. [a]The men of Israel had given ground to the Benjamites, because they relied on the men in ambush whom they had set against Gibeah. [37][a]And the men in ambush quickly rushed upon Gibeah; the men in ambush spread out and struck the whole city with the edge of the sword. [38]Now the appointed signal between the men of Israel and the men in ambush was that they would make a great cloud of [a]smoke rise up from the city, [39]whereupon the men of Israel would turn in battle. Now Benjamin had begun [1]to strike *and* kill about thirty of the men of Israel. For they said, "Surely they are defeated before us, as *in* the first battle." [40]But when the cloud began to rise from the city in a column of smoke, the Benjamites [a]looked behind them, and there was the whole city going up *in smoke* to heaven. [41]And when the men of Israel turned back, the men of Benjamin panicked, for they saw that disaster had come upon them. [42]Therefore they [1]turned *their backs* before the men of Israel in the direction of the wilderness; but the battle overtook them, and whoever *came* out of the cities they destroyed in their midst. [43]They surrounded the Benjamites, chased them, *and* easily trampled them down as far as the front of Gibeah toward the east. [44]And eighteen thousand men of Benjamin fell; all these *were* men of valor. [45]Then [1]they turned and fled toward the wilderness to the rock of [a]Rimmon; and they cut down five thousand of them on the highways. Then they pursued them relentlessly up to Gidom, and killed two thousand of them. [46]So all who fell of Benjamin that day were twenty-five thousand men who drew the sword; all these *were* [1]men of valor.

[47][a]But six hundred men turned and fled toward the wilderness to the rock of Rimmon, and they stayed at the rock of Rimmon for four months. [48]And the men of Israel turned back against the children of Benjamin, and struck them down with the edge of the sword—from *every* city, men and beasts, all who were found. They also set fire to all the cities they came to.

20:31
[a] Judg. 21:19

20:34
[a] Josh. 8:14;
Job 21:13;
Is. 47:11

20:36
[a] Josh. 8:15

20:37
[a] Josh. 8:19

20:38
[a] Josh. 8:20

20:40
[a] Josh. 8:20

20:45
[a] Josh. 15:32;
1 Chr. 6:77;
Zech. 14:10

20:47
[a] Judg. 21:13

20:34 [1]Lit. *they*   20:35 [1]Lit. *struck*   20:39 [1]Lit. *to strike the slain ones*
20:42 [1]*fled*   20:45 [1]LXX *the rest*   20:46 [1]*valiant warriors*

WIVES PROVIDED FOR THE BENJAMITES

21 Now ^athe men of Israel had sworn an oath at Mizpah, saying, "None of us shall give his daughter to Benjamin as a wife." ²Then the people came ^ato ¹the house of God, and remained there before God till evening. They lifted up their voices and wept bitterly, ³and said, "O LORD God of Israel, why has this come to pass in Israel, that today there should be one tribe *missing* in Israel?"

⁴So it was, on the next morning, that the people rose early and ^abuilt an altar there, and offered burnt offerings and peace offerings. ⁵The children of Israel said, "Who *is there* among all the tribes of Israel who did not come up with the assembly to the LORD?" ^aFor they had made a great oath concerning anyone who had not come up to the LORD at Mizpah, saying, "He shall surely be put to death." ⁶And the children of Israel grieved for Benjamin their brother, and said, "One tribe is cut off from Israel today. ⁷What shall we do for wives for those who remain, seeing we have sworn by the LORD that we will not give them our daughters as wives?"

⁸And they said, "What one *is there* from the tribes of Israel who did not come up to Mizpah to the LORD?" And, in fact, no one had come to the camp from ^aJabesh Gilead to the assembly. ⁹For when the people were counted, indeed, not one of the inhabitants of Jabesh Gilead *was* there. ¹⁰So the congregation sent out there twelve thousand of their most valiant men, and commanded them, saying, ^a"Go and strike the inhabitants of Jabesh Gilead with the edge of the sword, including the women and children. ¹¹And this *is* the thing that you shall do: ^aYou shall utterly destroy every male, and every woman who has known a man intimately." ¹²So they found among the inhabitants of Jabesh Gilead four hundred young virgins who had not known a man intimately; and they brought them to the camp at ^aShiloh, which is in the land of Canaan.

¹³Then the whole congregation sent *word* to the children of Benjamin ^awho *were* at the rock of Rimmon, and announced peace to them. ¹⁴So Benjamin came back at that time, and they gave them the women whom they had saved alive of the women of Jabesh Gilead; and yet they had not found enough for them.

¹⁵And the people ^agrieved for Benjamin, because the LORD had made a void in the tribes of Israel.

¹⁶Then the elders of the congregation said, "What shall we do for wives for those who remain, since the women of Benjamin have been destroyed?" ¹⁷And they said, "*There must be* an inheritance for the survivors of Benjamin, that a tribe may not be destroyed from Israel. ¹⁸However, we cannot give them wives from our daughters, ^afor the children of Israel have sworn an oath, saying, 'Cursed *be* the one who gives a wife to Benjamin.'" ¹⁹Then they said, "In fact, *there is* a yearly ^afeast of the LORD in ^bShiloh, which *is* north of Bethel, on the east side of the ^chighway that goes up from Bethel to Shechem, and south of Lebonah."

²⁰Therefore they instructed the children of Benjamin, saying, "Go, lie in wait in the vineyards, ²¹and watch; and just

---

21:1 ^aJudg. 20:1

21:2
^aJudg. 20:18, 26

21:4 ^aDeut. 12:5;
2 Sam. 24:25

21:5
^aJudg. 20:1–3

21:8
^a1 Sam. 11:1; 31:11

21:10
^aNum. 31:17;
Judg. 5:23;
1 Sam. 11:7

21:11
^aNum. 31:17;
Deut. 20:13, 14

21:12 ^aJosh. 18:1;
Judg. 18:31

21:13
^aJudg. 20:47

21:15 ^aJudg. 21:6

21:18
^aJudg. 11:35; 21:1

21:19 ^aLev. 23:2
^bDeut. 12:5;
Josh. 18:1;
Judg. 18:31;
1 Sam. 1:3
^cJudg. 20:31

21:2 ¹Or *Bethel*

when the daughters of Shiloh come out [a]to perform their dances, then come out from the vineyards, and every man catch a wife for himself from the daughters of Shiloh; then go to the land of Benjamin. [22]Then it shall be, when their fathers or their brothers come to us to complain, that we will say to them, 'Be kind to them for our sakes, because we did not take a wife for any of them in the war; for *it is* not *as though* you have given the *women* to them at this time, making yourselves guilty of your oath.' "

[23]And the children of Benjamin did so; they took enough wives for their number from those who danced, whom they caught. Then they went and returned to their inheritance, and they [a]rebuilt the cities and dwelt in them. [24]So the children of Israel departed from there at that time, every man to his tribe and family; they went out from there, every man to his inheritance.

[25a]In those days *there was* no king in Israel; [b]everyone did *what was* right in his own eyes.

21:21 [a]Ex. 15:20; Judg. 11:34; 1 Sam. 18:6

21:23 [a]Judg. 20:48

21:25 [a]Judg. 17:6; 18:1; 19:1 [b]Deut. 12:8; Judg. 17:6

THE BOOK OF
RUTH

ELIMELECH'S FAMILY GOES TO MOAB

1 Now it came to pass, in the days when ᵃthe judges ¹ruled, that there was ᵇa famine in the land. And a certain man of ᶜBethlehem, Judah, went to ²dwell in the country of ᵈMoab, he and his wife and his two sons. ²The name of the man *was* Elimelech, the name of his wife *was* Naomi, and the names of his two sons *were* Mahlon and Chilion—ᵃEphrathites of Bethlehem, Judah. And they went ᵇto the country of Moab and remained there. ³Then Elimelech, Naomi's husband, died; and she was left, and her two sons. ⁴Now they took wives of the women of Moab: the name of the one *was* Orpah, and the name of the other Ruth. And they ¹dwelt there about ten years. ⁵Then both Mahlon and Chilion also died; so the woman survived her two sons and her husband.

NAOMI RETURNS WITH RUTH

⁶Then she arose with her daughters-in-law that she might return from the country of Moab, for she had heard in the country of Moab that the LORD had ᵃvisited¹ His people by ᵇgiving them bread. ⁷Therefore she went out from the place where she was, and her two daughters-in-law with her; and they went on the way to return to the land of Judah. ⁸And Naomi said to her two daughters-in-law, ᵃ"Go, return each to her mother's house. ᵇThe LORD deal kindly with you, as you have dealt ᶜwith the dead and with me. ⁹The LORD grant that you may find ᵃrest, each in the house of her husband."

So she kissed them, and they lifted up their voices and wept. ¹⁰And they said to her, "Surely we will return with you to your people."

¹¹But Naomi said, "Turn back, my daughters; why will you go with me? *Are* there still sons in my womb, ᵃthat they may be your husbands? ¹²Turn back, my daughters, go—for I am too old to have a husband. If I should say I have hope, *if* I should have a husband tonight and should also bear sons, ¹³would you wait for them till they were grown? Would you restrain yourselves from having husbands? No, my daughters; for it grieves me very much for your sakes that ᵃthe hand of the LORD has gone out against me!"

¹⁴Then they lifted up their voices and wept again; and Orpah kissed her mother-in-law, but Ruth ᵃclung to her.

¹⁵And she said, "Look, your sister-in-law has gone back to ᵃher people and to her gods; ᵇreturn after your sister-in-law."

¹⁶But Ruth said:

ᵃ"Entreat¹ me not to leave you,

Or to turn back from following after you;

1:1
ᵃ Judg. 2:16–18
ᵇ Gen. 12:10;
26:1; 2 Kin. 8:1
ᶜ Judg. 17:8;
Mic. 5:2
ᵈ Gen. 19:37

1:2 ᵃ Gen. 35:19;
1 Sam. 1:1;
1 Kin. 11:26
ᵇ Judg. 3:30

1:6 ᵃ Ex. 3:16;
4:31; Jer. 29:10;
Zeph. 2:7;
Luke 1:68
ᵇ Ps. 132:15;
Matt. 6:11

1:8 ᵃ Josh. 24:15
ᵇ 2 Tim. 1:16–18
ᶜ Ruth 2:20

1:9 ᵃ Ruth 3:1

1:11 ᵃ Gen. 38:11;
Deut. 25:5

1:13 ᵃ Judg. 2:15;
Job 19:21;
Ps. 32:4; 38:2

1:14
ᵃ [Prov. 17:17]

1:15 ᵃ Judg. 11:24
ᵇ Josh. 1:15

1:16
ᵃ 2 Kin. 2:2, 4, 6

1:1 ¹Lit. *judged*   ²As a resident alien   **1:4** ¹*lived*   **1:6** ¹*attended to*
1:16 ¹*Urge me not*

For wherever you go, I will go;
And wherever you lodge, I will lodge;
[b]Your people *shall be* my people,
And your God, my God.
17 Where you die, I will die,
And there will I be buried.
[a]The LORD do so to me, and more also,
If *anything but* death parts you and me."

18[a]When she saw that she [1]was determined to go with her, she stopped speaking to her.

19Now the two of them went until they came to Bethlehem. And it happened, when they had come to Bethlehem, that [a]all the city was excited because of them; and the women said, [b]"*Is* this Naomi?"

20But she said to them, "Do not call me [1]Naomi; call me [2]Mara, for the Almighty has dealt very bitterly with me. 21I went out full, [a]and the LORD has brought me home again empty. Why do you call me Naomi, since the LORD has testified against me, and [1]the Almighty has afflicted me?"

22So Naomi returned, and Ruth the Moabitess her daughter-in-law with her, who returned from the country of Moab. Now they came to Bethlehem [a]at the beginning of barley harvest.

RUTH MEETS BOAZ

2 There was a [a]relative of Naomi's husband, a man of great wealth, of the family of [b]Elimelech. His name *was* [c]Boaz. 2So Ruth the Moabitess said to Naomi, "Please let me go to the [a]field, and glean heads of grain after *him* in whose sight I may find favor."

And she said to her, "Go, my daughter."

3Then she left, and went and gleaned in the field after the reapers. And she happened to come to the part of the field *belonging* to Boaz, who *was* of the family of Elimelech.

4Now behold, Boaz came from [a]Bethlehem, and said to the reapers, [b]"The LORD *be* with you!"

And they answered him, "The LORD bless you!"

5Then Boaz said to his servant who was in charge of the reapers, "Whose young woman *is* this?"

6So the servant who was in charge of the reapers answered and said, "It *is* the young Moabite woman [a]who came back with Naomi from the country of Moab. 7And she said, 'Please let me glean and gather after the reapers among the sheaves.' So she came and has continued from morning until now, though she rested a little in the house."

8Then Boaz said to Ruth, "You will listen, my daughter, will you not? Do not go to glean in another field, nor go from here, but stay close by my young women. 9*Let* your eyes *be* on the field which they reap, and go after them. Have I not commanded the young men not to touch you? And when you are thirsty, go to the vessels and drink from what the young men have drawn."

10So she [a]fell on her face, bowed down to the ground, and said to him, "Why have I found [b]favor in your eyes, that you should take notice of me, since I *am* a foreigner?"

1:16
[b]Ruth 2:11, 12

1:17 [a]1 Sam. 3:17;
2 Sam. 19:13;
2 Kin. 6:31

1:18 [a]Acts 21:14

1:19 [a]Matt. 21:10
[b]Is. 23:7;
Lam. 2:15

1:21 [a]Job 1:21

1:22 [a]Ruth 2:23;
2 Sam. 21:9

2:1
[a]Ruth 3:2, 12
[b]Ruth 1:2
[c]Ruth 4:21

2:2
[a]Lev. 19:9, 10;
23:22;
Deut. 24:19

2:4 [a]Ruth 1:1
[b]Ps. 129:7, 8;
Luke 1:28;
2 Thess. 3:16

2:6 [a]Ruth 1:22

2:10
[a]1 Sam. 25:23
[b]1 Sam. 1:18

1:18 [1]Lit. *made herself strong to go*   1:20 [1]Lit. *Pleasant*   [2]Lit. *Bitter*
1:21 [1]Heb. *Shaddai*

[11]And Boaz answered and said to her, "It has been fully reported to me, [a]all that you have done for your mother-in-law since the death of your husband, and *how* you have left your father and your mother and the land of your birth, and have come to a people whom you did not know before. [12][a]The LORD repay your work, and a full reward be given you by the LORD God of Israel, [b]under whose wings you have come for refuge."

[13]Then she said, [a]"Let me find favor in your sight, my lord; for you have comforted me, and have spoken [1]kindly to your maidservant, [b]though I am not like one of your maidservants."

[14]Now Boaz said to her at mealtime, "Come here, and eat of the bread, and dip your piece of bread in the vinegar." So she sat beside the reapers, and he passed parched *grain* to her; and she ate and [a]was satisfied, and kept some back. [15]And when she rose up to [1]glean, Boaz commanded his young men, saying, "Let her glean even among the sheaves, and do not [2]reproach her. [16]Also let *grain* from the bundles fall purposely for her; leave *it* that she may glean, and do not rebuke her."

[17]So she gleaned in the field until evening, and beat out what she had gleaned, and it was about an ephah of [a]barley. [18]Then she took *it* up and went into the city, and her mother-in-law saw what she had gleaned. So she brought out and gave to her [a]what she had kept back after she had been satisfied.

[19]And her mother-in-law said to her, "Where have you gleaned today? And where did you work? Blessed be the one who [a]took notice of you."

So she told her mother-in-law with whom she had worked, and said, "The man's name with whom I worked today *is* Boaz."

[20]Then Naomi said to her daughter-in-law, [a]"Blessed *be* he of the LORD, who [b]has not forsaken His kindness to the living and the dead!" And Naomi said to her, "This man *is* a relation of ours, [c]one of [1]our close relatives."

[21]Ruth the Moabitess said, "He also said to me, 'You shall stay close by my young men until they have finished all my harvest.'"

[22]And Naomi said to Ruth her daughter-in-law, "*It is* good, my daughter, that you go out with his young women, and that people do not [1]meet you in any other field." [23]So she stayed close by the young women of Boaz, to glean until the end of barley harvest and wheat harvest; and she dwelt with her mother-in-law.

RUTH'S REDEMPTION ASSURED

3 Then Naomi her mother-in-law said to her, "My daughter, [a]shall I not seek [b]security[1] for you, that it may be well with you? [2]Now Boaz, [a]whose young women you were with, *is he* not our relative? In fact, he is winnowing barley tonight at the threshing floor. [3]Therefore wash yourself and [a]anoint yourself, put on your *best* garment and go down to the threshing floor; *but* do not make yourself known to the man until he has finished eating and drinking. [4]Then it shall be, when he lies down, that you shall notice the place where he lies; and you shall go in, uncover his feet, and lie down; and he will tell you what you should do."

2:11
[a]Ruth 1:14–18

2:12
[a]1 Sam. 24:19;
Ps. 58:11
[b]Ruth 1:16;
Ps. 17:8; 36:7;
57:1; 61:4;
63:7; 91:4

2:13 [a]Gen. 33:15;
1 Sam. 1:18
[b]1 Sam. 25:41

2:14 [a]Ruth 2:18

2:17 [a]Ruth 1:22

2:18 [a]Ruth 2:14

2:19 [a]Ruth 2:10;
[Ps. 41:1]

2:20 [a]Ruth 3:10;
2 Sam. 2:5
[b]Prov. 17:17
[c]Ruth 3:9;
4:4, 6

3:1 [a]1 Cor. 7:36;
1 Tim. 5:8
[b]Ruth 1:9

3:2 [a]Ruth 2:3, 8

3:3 [a]2 Sam. 14:2

2:13 [1]Lit. *to the heart of*   **2:15** [1]Gather after the reapers   [2]*rebuke*
2:20 [1]*our redeemers,* Heb. *goalenu*   **2:22** [1]*encounter*   **3:1** [1]Lit. *rest*

[5]And she said to her, "All that you say to me I will do."

[6]So she went down to the threshing floor and did according to all that her mother-in-law instructed her. [7]And after Boaz had eaten and drunk, and [a]his heart was cheerful, he went to lie down at the end of the heap of grain; and she came softly, uncovered his feet, and lay down.

[8]Now it happened at midnight that the man was startled, and turned himself; and there, a woman was lying at his feet. [9]And he said, "Who *are* you?"

So she answered, "I *am* Ruth, your maidservant. [a]Take[1] your maidservant under your wing, for you are [b]a [2]close relative."

[10]Then he said, [a]"Blessed *are* you of the LORD, my daughter! For you have shown more kindness at the end than [b]at the beginning, in that you did not go after young men, whether poor or rich. [11]And now, my daughter, do not fear. I will do for you all that you request, for all the people of my town know that you *are* a [a]virtuous woman. [12]Now it is true that I *am* a [a]close relative; however, [b]there is a relative closer than I. [13]Stay this night, and in the morning it shall be *that* if he will [a]perform the duty of a close relative for you—good; let him do it. But if he does not want to perform the duty for you, then I will perform the duty for you, [b]*as* the LORD lives! Lie down until morning."

[14]So she lay at his feet until morning, and she arose before one could recognize another. Then he said, [a]"Do not let it be known that the woman came to the threshing floor." [15]Also he said, "Bring the [1]shawl that *is* on you and hold it." And when she held it, he measured six *ephahs* of barley, and laid *it* on her. Then [2]she went into the city.

[16]When she came to her mother-in-law, she said, [1]"*Is* that you, my daughter?"

Then she told her all that the man had done for her. [17]And she said, "These six *ephahs* of barley he gave me; for he said to me, 'Do not go empty-handed to your mother-in-law.'"

[18]Then she said, [a]"Sit still, my daughter, until you know how the matter will turn out; for the man will not rest until he has concluded the matter this day."

BOAZ REDEEMS RUTH

4 Now Boaz went up to the gate and sat down there; and behold, [a]the close relative of whom Boaz had spoken came by. So Boaz said, "Come aside, [1]friend, sit down here." So he came aside and sat down. [2]And he took ten men of [a]the elders of the city, and said, "Sit down here." So they sat down. [3]Then he said to the close relative, "Naomi, who has come back from the country of Moab, sold the piece of land [a]which *belonged* to our brother Elimelech. [4]And I thought to [1]inform you, saying, [a]'Buy *it* back [b]in the presence of the inhabitants and the elders of my people. If you will redeem *it,* redeem *it*; but if [2]you will not redeem *it, then* tell me, that I may know; [c]for *there is* no one but you to redeem *it,* and I *am* next after you.'"

3:7
[a]Judg. 19:6, 9, 22; 2 Sam. 13:28; Esth. 1:10

3:9 [a]Ezek. 16:8
[b]Ruth 2:20; 3:12

3:10 [a]Ruth 2:20
[b]Ruth 1:8

3:11 [a]Prov. 12:4; 31:10–31

3:12 [a]Ruth 3:9
[b]Ruth 4:1

3:13
[a]Deut. 25:5–10; Ruth 4:5, 10; Matt. 22:24
[b]Judg. 8:19; Jer. 4:2; 12:16

3:14
[a][Rom. 12:17; 14:16; 1 Cor. 10:32; 2 Cor. 8:21; 1 Thess. 5:22]

3:18
[a][Ps. 37:3, 5]

4:1 [a]Ruth 3:12

4:2 [a]1 Kin. 21:8; Prov. 31:23

4:3 [a]Lev. 25:25

4:4
[a]Jer. 32:7, 8
[b]Gen. 23:18
[c]Lev. 25:25

3:9 [1]Or *Spread the corner of your garment over your maidservant*
[2]*redeemer,* Heb. *goel*   3:15 [1]*cloak*   [2]Many Heb. mss., Syr., Vg. *she*; MT, LXX, Tg. *he*   3:16 [1]Or *How are you,*   4:1 [1]Heb. *peloni almoni,* lit. *so and so*
4:4 [1]Lit. *uncover your ear*   [2]So with many Heb. mss., LXX, Syr., Tg., Vg.; MT *he*

And he said, "I will redeem *it.*"

⁵Then Boaz said, "On the day you buy the field from the hand of Naomi, you must also buy *it* from Ruth the Moabitess, the wife of the dead, ᵃto ¹perpetuate the name of the dead through his inheritance."

⁶ᵃAnd the close relative said, "I cannot redeem *it* for myself, lest I ruin my own inheritance. You redeem my right of redemption for yourself, for I cannot redeem *it.*"

⁷ᵃNow this *was the custom* in former times in Israel concerning redeeming and exchanging, to confirm anything: one man took off his sandal and gave *it* to the other, and this *was* a confirmation in Israel.

⁸Therefore the close relative said to Boaz, "Buy *it* for yourself." So he took off his sandal. ⁹And Boaz said to the elders and all the people, "You *are* witnesses this day that I have bought all that was Elimelech's, and all that *was* Chilion's and Mahlon's, from the hand of Naomi. ¹⁰Moreover, Ruth the Moabitess, the widow of Mahlon, I have acquired as my wife, to perpetuate the name of the dead through his inheritance, ᵃthat the name of the dead may not be cut off from among his brethren and from ¹his position at the gate. You *are* witnesses this day."

¹¹And all the people who *were* at the gate, and the elders, said, "*We are* witnesses. ᵃThe LORD make the woman who is coming to your house like Rachel and Leah, the two who ᵇbuilt the house of Israel; and may you prosper in ᶜEphrathah and be famous in ᵈBethlehem. ¹²May your house be like the house of ᵃPerez, ᵇwhom Tamar bore to Judah, because of ᶜthe offspring which the LORD will give you from this young woman."

DESCENDANTS OF BOAZ AND RUTH
(Matt. 1:2–6)

¹³So Boaz ᵃtook Ruth and she became his wife; and when he went in to her, ᵇthe LORD gave her conception, and she bore a son. ¹⁴Then ᵃthe women said to Naomi, "Blessed *be* the LORD, who has not left you this day without a ¹close relative; and may his name be famous in Israel! ¹⁵And may he be to you a restorer of life and a ¹nourisher of your old age; for your daughter-in-law, who loves you, who is ᵃbetter to you than seven sons, has borne him." ¹⁶Then Naomi took the child and laid him on her bosom, and became a nurse to him. ¹⁷ᵃAlso the neighbor women gave him a name, saying, "There is a son born to Naomi." And they called his name Obed. He *is* the father of Jesse, the father of David.

¹⁸ᵃNow this *is* the genealogy of Perez: ᵇPerez begot Hezron; ¹⁹Hezron begot Ram, and Ram begot Amminadab; ²⁰Amminadab begot ᵃNahshon, and Nahshon begot ᵇSalmon;¹ ²¹Salmon begot Boaz, and Boaz begot Obed; ²²Obed begot Jesse, and Jesse begot ᵃDavid.

4:5 ᵃGen. 38:8;
Deut. 25:5, 6;
Ruth 3:13;
Matt. 22:24

4:6
ᵃRuth 3:12, 13;
Job 19:14

4:7
ᵃDeut. 25:7–10

4:10 ᵃDeut. 25:6

4:11
ᵃPs. 127:3; 128:3
ᵇGen. 29:25–30;
Deut. 25:9
ᶜGen. 35:16–18
ᵈ1 Sam. 16:4–13;
Mic. 5:2;
Matt. 2:1–8

4:12 ᵃ1 Chr. 2:4;
Matt. 1:3
ᵇGen. 38:6–29
ᶜ1 Sam. 2:20

4:13 ᵃRuth 3:11
ᵇGen. 29:31;
33:5; Matt. 1:5

4:14 ᵃLuke 1:58;
[Rom. 12:15]

4:15 ᵃ1 Sam. 1:8

4:17 ᵃLuke 1:58

4:18
ᵃ1 Chr. 2:4, 5;
Matt. 1:1–7
ᵇNum. 26:20, 21

4:20 ᵃNum. 1:7
ᵇMatt. 1:4

4:22 ᵃ1 Chr. 2:15;
Matt. 1:6

4:5 ¹Lit. *raise up*   4:10 ¹Probably his civic office   4:14 ¹*redeemer,* Heb. *goel*
4:15 ¹*sustainer*   4:20 ¹Heb. *Salmah*

THE FIRST BOOK OF
SAMUEL

THE FAMILY OF ELKANAH

1 Now there was a certain man of Ramathaim Zophim, of the ªmountains of Ephraim, and his name *was* ᵇElkanah the son of Jeroham, the son of ¹Elihu, the son of ²Tohu, the son of Zuph, ᶜan Ephraimite. ²And he had ªtwo wives: the name of one *was* Hannah, and the name of the other Peninnah. Peninnah had children, but Hannah had no children. ³This man went up from his city ªyearly ᵇto worship and sacrifice to the LORD of hosts in ᶜShiloh. Also the two sons of Eli, Hophni and Phinehas, the priests of the LORD, *were* there. ⁴And whenever the time came for Elkanah to make an ªoffering, he would give portions to Peninnah his wife and to all her sons and daughters. ⁵But to Hannah he would give a double portion, for he loved Hannah, ªalthough the LORD had closed her womb. ⁶And her rival also ªprovoked her severely, to make her miserable, because the LORD had closed her womb. ⁷So it was, year by year, when she went up to the house of the LORD, that she provoked her; therefore she wept and did not eat.

HANNAH'S VOW

⁸Then Elkanah her husband said to her, "Hannah, why do you weep? Why do you not eat? And why is your heart grieved? *Am* I not ªbetter to you than ten sons?"

⁹So Hannah arose after they had finished eating and drinking in Shiloh. Now Eli the priest was sitting on the seat by the doorpost of ªthe ¹tabernacle of the LORD. ¹⁰ªAnd she *was* in bitterness of soul, and prayed to the LORD and ¹wept in anguish. ¹¹Then she ªmade a vow and said, "O LORD of hosts, if You will indeed ᵇlook on the affliction of Your maidservant and ᶜremember me, and not forget Your maidservant, but will give Your maidservant a male child, then I will give him to the LORD all the days of his life, and ᵈno razor shall come upon his head."

¹²And it happened, as she continued praying before the LORD, that Eli watched her mouth. ¹³Now Hannah spoke in her heart; only her lips moved, but her voice was not heard. Therefore Eli thought she was drunk. ¹⁴So Eli said to her, "How long will you be drunk? Put your wine away from you!"

¹⁵But Hannah answered and said, "No, my lord, I *am* a woman of sorrowful spirit. I have drunk neither wine nor intoxicating drink, but have ªpoured out my soul before the LORD. ¹⁶Do not consider your maidservant a ªwicked¹ woman, for out of the abundance of my complaint and grief I have spoken until now."

¹⁷Then Eli answered and said, ª"Go in peace, and ᵇthe God of Israel grant your petition which you have asked of Him."

1:1
ªJosh. 17:17, 18; 24:33
ᵇ1 Chr. 6:27, 33–38 ᶜRuth 1:2
1:2
ªDeut. 21:15–17
1:3 ªEx. 34:14, 23; Judg. 21:19; 1 Sam. 1:21; Luke 2:41
ᵇDeut. 12:5–7; 16:16 ᶜJosh. 18:1
1:4
ªDeut. 12:17, 18
1:5 ªGen. 16:1; 30:1, 2
1:6 ªJob 24:21
1:8 ªRuth 4:15
1:9 ª1 Sam. 3:3
1:10 ªJob 7:11
1:11 ªGen. 28:20; Num. 30:6–11
ᵇPs. 25:18
ᶜGen. 8:1
ᵈNum. 6:5; Judg. 13:5
1:15 ªJob 30:16; Ps. 42:4; 62:8; Lam. 2:19
1:16 ªDeut. 13:13
1:17 ªJudg. 18:6; 1 Sam. 25:35; 2 Kin. 5:19; Mark 5:34; Luke 7:50
ᵇPs. 20:3–5

1:1 ¹*Eliel,* 1 Chr. 6:34   ²*Toah,* 1 Chr. 6:34   **1:9** ¹*palace* or *temple,* Heb. *heykal*
1:10 ¹Lit. *wept greatly*   **1:16** ¹Lit. *daughter of Belial*

18And she said, a"Let your maidservant find favor in your sight." So the woman bwent her way and ate, and her face was no longer *sad*.

SAMUEL IS BORN AND DEDICATED

19Then they rose early in the morning and worshiped before the LORD, and returned and came to their house at Ramah. And Elkanah aknew Hannah his wife, and the LORD bremembered her. 20So it came to pass in the process of time that Hannah conceived and bore a son, and called his name 1Samuel, *saying*, "Because I have asked for him from the LORD."

21Now the man Elkanah and all his house awent up to offer to the LORD the yearly sacrifice and his vow. 22But Hannah did not go up, for she said to her husband, "*Not* until the child is weaned; then I will atake him, that he may appear before the LORD and bremain there cforever."

23So aElkanah her husband said to her, "Do what seems best to you; wait until you have weaned him. Only let the LORD 1establish 2His word." Then the woman stayed and nursed her son until she had weaned him.

24Now when she had weaned him, she atook him up with her, with 1three bulls, one ephah of flour, and a skin of wine, and brought him to bthe house of the LORD in Shiloh. And the child *was* young. 25Then they slaughtered a bull, and abrought the child to Eli. 26And she said, "O my lord! aAs your soul lives, my lord, I *am* the woman who stood by you here, praying to the LORD. 27aFor this child I prayed, and the LORD has granted me my petition which I asked of Him. 28Therefore I also have lent him to the LORD; as long as he lives he shall be 1lent to the LORD." So they aworshiped the LORD there.

HANNAH'S PRAYER
(cf. Luke 1:46–55)

2 And Hannah aprayed and said:

b"My heart rejoices in the LORD;
  cMy 1horn is exalted in the LORD.
  2I smile at my enemies,
    Because I drejoice in Your salvation.

2 "Noa one is holy like the LORD,
  For *there is* bnone besides You,
  Nor *is there* any crock like our God.

3 "Talk no more so very proudly;
  aLet no arrogance come from your mouth,
  For the LORD *is* the God of bknowledge;
  And by Him actions are weighed.

4 "Thea bows of the mighty men *are* broken,
  And those who stumbled are girded with strength.
5 *Those who were* full have hired themselves out for bread,
  And the hungry have ceased *to hunger*.
  Even athe barren has borne seven,
  And bshe who has many children has become feeble.

1:18 aGen. 33:15; Ruth 2:13 bProv. 15:13; Eccl. 9:7; Rom. 15:13

1:19 aGen. 4:1 bGen. 21:1; 30:22

1:21 aDeut. 12:11; 1 Sam. 1:3

1:22 aLuke 2:22 b1 Sam. 1:11, 28 cEx. 21:6

1:23 aNum. 30:7, 10, 11

1:24 aNum. 15:9, 10; Deut. 12:5, 6 bJosh. 18:1; 1 Sam. 4:3, 4

1:25 aLuke 2:22

1:26 a2 Kin. 2:2, 4, 6; 4:30

1:27 a[Matt. 7:7]

1:28 aGen. 24:26, 52

2:1 aPhil. 4:6 b1 Sam. 2:1–10; Ps. 97:11, 12; Luke 1:46–55 cPs. 75:10; 89:17, 24; 92:10; 112:9 dPs. 9:14; 13:5; 35:9; Is. 12:2, 3

2:2 aEx. 15:11; Ps. 86:8; Rev. 15:4 bDeut. 4:35 cDeut. 32:4, 30, 31; 2 Sam. 22:32; Ps. 18:2

2:3 aPs. 94:4 b1 Sam. 16:7

2:4 aPs. 37:15; 46:9

2:5 aPs. 113:9 bIs. 54:1; Jer. 15:9

1:20 1Lit. *Heard by God*   1:23 1confirm   2So with MT, Tg., Vg.; DSS, LXX, Syr. *your*   1:24 1DSS, LXX, Syr. *a three-year-old bull*   1:28 1granted
2:1 1Strength   2Lit. *My mouth is enlarged*

6 "The[a] LORD kills and makes alive;
   He brings down to the grave and brings up.
7 The LORD [a]makes poor and makes rich;
   [b]He brings low and lifts up.
8 [a]He raises the poor from the dust
   And lifts the beggar from the ash heap,
   [b]To set *them* among princes
   And make them inherit the throne of glory.

   [c]"For the pillars of the earth *are* the LORD's,
   And He has set the world upon them.
9 [a]He will guard the feet of His saints,
   But the [b]wicked shall be silent in darkness.

   "For by strength no man shall prevail.
10 The adversaries of the LORD shall be [a]broken in
      pieces;
   [b]From heaven He will thunder against them.
   [c]The LORD will judge the ends of the earth.

   [d]"He will give [e]strength to His king,
   And [f]exalt the [1]horn of His anointed."

11Then Elkanah went to his house at Ramah. But the child [1]ministered to the LORD before Eli the priest.

THE WICKED SONS OF ELI

12Now the sons of Eli *were* [a]corrupt;[1] [b]they did not know the LORD. 13And the priests' custom with the people *was that* when any man offered a sacrifice, the priest's servant would come with a three-pronged fleshhook in his hand while the meat was boiling. 14Then he would thrust *it* into the pan, or kettle, or caldron, or pot; and the priest would take for himself all that the fleshhook brought up. So they did in [a]Shiloh to all the Israelites who came there. 15Also, before they [a]burned the fat, the priest's servant would come and say to the man who sacrificed, "Give meat for roasting to the priest, for he will not take boiled meat from you, but raw."

16And *if* the man said to him, "They should really burn the fat first; *then* you may take *as much* as your heart desires," he would then answer him, "*No,* but you must give *it* now; and if not, I will take *it* by force."

17Therefore the sin of the young men was very great [a]before the LORD, for men [b]abhorred[1] the offering of the LORD.

SAMUEL'S CHILDHOOD MINISTRY

18[a]But Samuel ministered before the LORD, *even as* a child, [b]wearing a linen ephod. 19Moreover his mother used to make him a little robe, and bring *it* to him year by year when she [a]came up with her husband to offer the yearly sacrifice. 20And Eli [a]would bless Elkanah and his wife, and say, "The LORD give you descendants from this woman for the [1]loan that was [b]given to the LORD." Then they would go to their own home.

21And the LORD [a]visited[1] Hannah, so that she conceived and bore three sons and two daughters. Meanwhile the child Samuel [b]grew before the LORD.

2:6
[a]Deut. 32:39;
2 Kin. 5:7;
Job 5:18;
[Rev. 1:18]

2:7 [a]Deut. 8:17,
18; Job 1:21
[b] Job 5:11;
Ps. 75:7;
James 4:10

2:8
[a]Job 42:10–12;
Ps. 75:7; 113:7;
Luke 1:52
[b]Job 36:7;
Ps. 113:8
[c]Job 38:4–6;
Ps. 75:3; 104:5

2:9 [a]Ps. 37:23,
24; 91:11, 12;
94:18; 121:3;
Prov. 3:26;
[1 Pet. 1:5]
[b][Rom. 3:19]

2:10 [a]Ex. 15:6;
Ps. 2:9
[b]1 Sam. 7:10;
2 Sam. 22:14, 15;
Ps. 18:13, 14
[c]Ps. 96:13; 98:9;
[Matt. 25:31, 32]
[d][Matt. 28:18]
[e]Ps. 21:1, 7
[f]Ps. 89:24

2:12 [a]Deut. 13:13
[b]Judg. 2:10;
[Rom. 1:28]

2:14 [a]1 Sam. 1:3

2:15
[a]Lev. 3:3–5, 16

2:17 [a]Gen. 6:11
[b][Mal. 2:7–9]

2:18 [a]1 Sam. 2:11;
3:1 [b]Ex. 28:4

2:19
[a]1 Sam. 1:3, 21

2:20 [a]Gen. 14:19
[b]1 Sam. 1:11,
27, 28

2:21 [a]Gen. 21:1
[b]Judg. 13:24;
1 Sam. 2:26;
3:19–21;
Luke 1:80; 2:40

2:10 [1]Strength   2:11 [1]*served*   2:12 [1]Lit. *sons of Belial*   2:17 [1]*despised*
2:20 [1]*gift*   2:21 [1]*attended to*

PROPHECY AGAINST ELI'S HOUSEHOLD

²²Now Eli was very old; and he heard everything his sons did to all Israel, ¹and how they lay with ᵃthe women who assembled at the door of the tabernacle of meeting. ²³So he said to them, "Why do you do such things? For I hear of your evil dealings from all the people. ²⁴No, my sons! For *it is* not a good report that I hear. You make the LORD's people transgress. ²⁵If one man sins against another, ᵃGod¹ will judge him. But if a man ᵇsins against the LORD, who will intercede for him?" Nevertheless they did not heed the voice of their father, ᶜbecause the LORD desired to kill them.

²⁶And the child Samuel ᵃgrew in stature, and ᵇin favor both with the LORD and men.

²⁷Then a ᵃman of God came to Eli and said to him, "Thus says the LORD: ᵇ'Did I not clearly reveal Myself to the house of your father when they were in Egypt in Pharaoh's house? ²⁸Did I not ᵃchoose him out of all the tribes of Israel *to be* My priest, to offer upon My altar, to burn incense, and to wear an ephod before Me? And ᵇdid I not give to the house of your father all the offerings of the children of Israel made by fire? ²⁹Why do you ᵃkick at My sacrifice and My offering which I have commanded *in My* ᵇdwelling place, and honor your sons more than ᶜMe, to make yourselves fat with the best of all the offerings of Israel My people?' ³⁰Therefore the LORD God of Israel says: ᵃ'I said indeed *that* your house and the house of your father would walk before Me forever.' But now the LORD says: ᵇ'Far be it from Me; for those who honor Me I will honor, and ᶜthose who despise Me shall be lightly esteemed. ³¹Behold, ᵃthe days are coming that I will cut off your ¹arm and the arm of your father's house, so that there will not be an old man in your house. ³²And you will see an enemy *in My* dwelling place, *despite* all the good which God does for Israel. And there shall not be ᵃan old man in your house forever. ³³But any of your men *whom* I do not cut off from My altar shall consume your eyes and grieve your heart. And all the descendants of your house shall die in the flower of their age. ³⁴Now this *shall be* ᵃa sign to you that will come upon your two sons, on Hophni and Phinehas: ᵇin one day they shall die, both of them. ³⁵Then ᵃI will raise up for Myself a faithful priest *who* shall do according to what *is* in My heart and in My mind. ᵇI will build him a sure house, and he shall walk before ᶜMy anointed forever. ³⁶ᵃAnd it shall come to pass that everyone who is left in your house will come *and* bow down to him for a piece of silver and a morsel of bread, and say, "Please, ¹put me in one of the priestly positions, that I may eat a piece of bread."'"

SAMUEL'S FIRST PROPHECY

3 Now ᵃthe boy Samuel ministered to the LORD before Eli. And ᵇthe word of the LORD was rare in those days; *there was* no widespread revelation. ²And it came to pass at that time, while Eli *was* lying down in his place, and when his eyes had begun to grow ᵃso dim that he could not see, ³and before ᵃthe lamp of God went out in the ¹tabernacle of the LORD where the ark of God *was,* and while Samuel was lying down,

2:22 ᵃEx. 38:8

2:25 ᵃDeut. 1:17;
25:1, 2
ᵇNum. 15:30
ᶜJosh. 11:20

2:26
ᵃ1 Sam. 2:21
ᵇProv. 3:4

2:27 ᵃDeut. 33:1;
Judg. 13:6;
1 Sam. 9:6;
1 Kin. 13:1
ᵇEx. 4:14–16; 12:1

2:28
ᵃEx. 28:1, 4;
Num. 16:5
ᵇLev. 2:3, 10;
6:16; 7:7, 8, 34,
35; Num. 5:9

2:29
ᵃDeut. 32:15
ᵇDeut. 12:5;
Ps. 26:8
ᶜMatt. 10:37

2:30 ᵃEx. 29:9;
Num. 25:13
ᵇJer. 18:9, 10
ᶜPs. 91:14;
Mal. 2:9–12

2:31
ᵃ1 Sam. 4:11–18;
22:18, 19;
1 Kin. 2:27, 35

2:32 ᵃZech. 8:4

2:34
ᵃ1 Sam. 10:7–9;
1 Kin. 13:3
ᵇ1 Sam. 4:11, 17

2:35
ᵃ1 Sam. 2:35;
Ezek. 44:15;
[Heb. 2:17;
7:26–28]
ᵇ2 Sam. 7:11, 27;
1 Kin. 11:38
ᶜPs. 18:50

2:36 ᵃ1 Kin. 2:27

3:1
ᵃ1 Sam. 2:11, 18
ᵇPs. 74:9;
Ezek. 7:26;
Amos 8:11, 12

3:2 ᵃGen. 27:1;
48:10;
1 Sam. 4:15

3:3
ᵃEx. 27:20, 21

2:22 ¹So with MT, Tg., Vg.; DSS, LXX omit rest of verse   2:25 ¹Tg. *the Judge*
2:31 ¹*strength*   2:36 ¹*assign*   3:3 ¹*palace* or *temple*

[4]that the LORD called Samuel. And he answered, "Here I am!" [5]So he ran to Eli and said, "Here I am, for you called me."

And he said, "I did not call; lie down again." And he went and lay down.

[6]Then the LORD called yet again, "Samuel!"

So Samuel arose and went to Eli, and said, "Here I am, for you called me." He answered, "I did not call, my son; lie down again." [7](Now Samuel [a]did not yet know the LORD, nor was the word of the LORD yet revealed to him.)

[8]And the LORD called Samuel again the third time. So he arose and went to Eli, and said, "Here I am, for you did call me."

Then Eli perceived that the LORD had called the boy. [9]Therefore Eli said to Samuel, "Go, lie down; and it shall be, if He calls you, that you must say, [a]'Speak, LORD, for Your servant hears.'" So Samuel went and lay down in his place.

[10]Now the LORD came and stood and called as at other times, "Samuel! Samuel!"

And Samuel answered, "Speak, for Your servant hears."

[11]Then the LORD said to Samuel: "Behold, I will do something in Israel [a]at which both ears of everyone who hears it will tingle. [12]In that day I will perform against Eli [a]all that I have spoken concerning his house, from beginning to end. [13a]For I have told him that I will [b]judge his house forever for the iniquity which he knows, because [c]his sons made themselves vile, and he [d]did not [1]restrain them. [14]And therefore I have sworn to the house of Eli that the iniquity of Eli's house [a]shall not be atoned for by sacrifice or offering forever."

[15]So Samuel lay down until [1]morning, and opened the doors of the house of the LORD. And Samuel was afraid to tell Eli the vision. [16]Then Eli called Samuel and said, "Samuel, my son!"

He answered, "Here I am."

[17]And he said, "What is the word that the LORD spoke to you? Please do not hide it from me. [a]God do so to you, and more also, if you hide anything from me of all the things that He said to you." [18]Then Samuel told him everything, and hid nothing from him. And he said, [a]"It is the LORD. Let Him do what seems good to Him."

[19]So Samuel [a]grew, and [b]the LORD was with him [c]and let none of his words [1]fall to the ground. [20]And all Israel [a]from Dan to Beersheba knew that Samuel had been [1]established as a prophet of the LORD. [21]Then the LORD appeared again in Shiloh. For the LORD revealed Himself to Samuel in Shiloh by [a]the word of the LORD.

4

And the word of Samuel came to all [1]Israel.

THE ARK OF GOD CAPTURED

Now Israel went out to battle against the Philistines, and encamped beside [a]Ebenezer; and the Philistines encamped in Aphek. [2]Then the [a]Philistines put themselves in battle array against Israel. And when they joined battle, Israel was [1]defeated by the Philistines, who killed about four thousand men of

3:7 [a]1 Sam. 2:12; Acts 19:2; 1 Cor. 13:11

3:9 [a]1 Kin. 2:17

3:11 [a]2 Kin. 21:12; Jer. 19:3

3:12 [a]1 Sam. 2:27–36; Ezek. 12:25; Luke 21:33

3:13 [a]1 Sam. 2:29–31 [b]1 Sam. 2:22; Ezek. 7:3; 18:30 [c]1 Sam. 2:12, 17, 22 [d]1 Sam. 2:23, 25

3:14 [a]Num. 15:30, 31; Is. 22:14; Heb. 10:4, 26–31

3:17 [a]Ruth 1:17

3:18 [a]Gen. 24:50; Ex. 34:5–7; Lev. 10:3; Is. 39:8; Acts 5:39

3:19 [a]1 Sam. 2:21 [b]Gen. 21:22; 28:15; 39:2, 21, 23 [c]1 Sam. 9:6

3:20 [a]Judg. 20:1

3:21 [a]1 Sam. 3:1, 4

4:1 [a]1 Sam. 7:12

4:2 [a]1 Sam. 12:9

3:13 [1]Lit. rebuke 3:15 [1]So with MT, Tg., Vg.; LXX adds and he arose in the morning 3:19 [1]fail 3:20 [1]confirmed 4:1 [1]So with MT, Tg.; LXX, Vg. add And it came to pass in those days that the Philistines gathered themselves together to fight; LXX adds further against Israel 4:2 [1]Lit. struck

the army in the field. ³And when the people had come into the camp, the elders of Israel said, "Why has the LORD defeated us today before the Philistines? ᵃLet us bring the ark of the covenant of the LORD from Shiloh to us, that when it comes among us it may save us from the hand of our enemies." ⁴So the people sent to Shiloh, that they might bring from there the ark of the covenant of the LORD of hosts, ᵃwho dwells *between* ᵇthe cherubim. And the ᶜtwo sons of Eli, Hophni and Phinehas, *were* there with the ark of the covenant of God.

⁵And when the ark of the covenant of the LORD came into the camp, all Israel shouted so loudly that the earth shook. ⁶Now when the Philistines heard the noise of the shout, they said, "What *does* the sound of this great shout in the camp of the Hebrews *mean?*" Then they understood that the ark of the LORD had come into the camp. ⁷So the Philistines were afraid, for they said, "God has come into the camp!" And they said, ᵃ"Woe to us! For such a thing has never happened before. ⁸Woe to us! Who will deliver us from the hand of these mighty gods? These *are* the gods who struck the Egyptians with all the plagues in the wilderness. ⁹ᵃBe strong and conduct yourselves like men, you Philistines, that you do not become servants of the Hebrews, ᵇas they have been to you. ¹Conduct yourselves like men, and fight!"

¹⁰So the Philistines fought, and ᵃIsrael was ¹defeated, and every man fled to his tent. There was a very great slaughter, and there fell of Israel thirty thousand foot soldiers. ¹¹Also ᵃthe ark of God was captured; and ᵇthe two sons of Eli, Hophni and Phinehas, died.

DEATH OF ELI

¹²Then a man of Benjamin ran from the battle line the same day, and ᵃcame to Shiloh with his clothes torn and ᵇdirt on his head. ¹³Now when he came, there was Eli, sitting on ᵃa seat ¹by the wayside watching, for his heart ²trembled for the ark of God. And when the man came into the city and told *it,* all the city cried out. ¹⁴When Eli heard the noise of the outcry, he said, "What *does* the sound of this tumult *mean?*" And the man came quickly and told Eli. ¹⁵Eli was ninety-eight years old, and ᵃhis eyes were so ¹dim that he could not see.

¹⁶Then the man said to Eli, "I *am* he who came from the battle. And I fled today from the battle line."

And he said, ᵃ"What happened, my son?"

¹⁷So the messenger answered and said, "Israel has fled before the Philistines, and there has been a great slaughter among the people. Also your two sons, Hophni and Phinehas, are dead; and the ark of God has been captured."

¹⁸Then it happened, when he made mention of the ark of God, that Eli fell off the seat backward by the side of the gate; and his neck was broken and he died, for the man was old and heavy. And he had judged Israel forty years.

ICHABOD

¹⁹Now his daughter-in-law, Phinehas' wife, was with child, *due* to be delivered; and when she heard the news that the ark of God was captured, and that her father-in-law and her

4:3 ᵃNum. 10:35; Josh. 6:6–21
4:4 ᵃEx. 25:18–21; 1 Sam. 6:2; Ps. 80:1 ᵇNum. 7:89 ᶜ1 Sam. 2:12
4:7 ᵃEx. 15:14
4:9 ᵃ1 Cor. 16:13 ᵇJudg. 13:1; 1 Sam. 14:21
4:10 ᵃLev. 26:17; Deut. 28:15, 25; 1 Sam. 4:2; 2 Sam. 18:17; 19:8; 2 Kin. 14:12; 2 Chr. 25:22
4:11 ᵃ1 Sam. 2:32; Ps. 78:60, 61 ᵇ1 Sam. 2:34; Ps. 78:64
4:12 ᵃ2 Sam. 1:2 ᵇJosh. 7:6; 2 Sam. 13:19; 15:32; Neh. 9:1; Job 2:12
4:13 ᵃ1 Sam. 1:9; 4:18
4:15 ᵃ1 Sam. 3:2; 1 Kin. 14:4
4:16 ᵃ2 Sam. 1:4

4:9 ¹Lit. *Be men* **4:10** ¹Lit. *struck down* **4:13** ¹So with MT, Vg.; LXX *beside the gate watching the road* ²*trembled with anxiety* **4:15** ¹*fixed*

husband were dead, she bowed herself and gave birth, for her labor pains came upon her. [20]And about the time of her death [a]the women who stood by her said to her, "Do not fear, for you have borne a son." But she did not answer, nor did she [1]regard it. [21]Then she named the child [a]Ichabod,[1] saying, [b]"The glory has departed from Israel!" because the ark of God had been captured and because of her father-in-law and her husband. [22]And she said, "The glory has departed from Israel, for the ark of God has been captured."

THE PHILISTINES AND THE ARK

5 Then the Philistines took the ark of God and brought it [a]from Ebenezer to Ashdod. [2]When the Philistines took the ark of God, they brought it into the house of [a]Dagon[1] and set it by Dagon. [3]And when the people of Ashdod arose early in the morning, there was Dagon, [a]fallen on its face to the earth before the ark of the LORD. So they took Dagon and [b]set it in its place again. [4]And when they arose early the next morning, there was Dagon, fallen on its face to the ground before the ark of the LORD. [a]The head of Dagon and both the palms of its hands *were* broken off on the threshold; only [1]Dagon's *torso* was left of it. [5]Therefore neither the priests of Dagon nor any who come into Dagon's house [a]tread on the threshold of Dagon in Ashdod to this day.

[6]But the [a]hand of the LORD was heavy on the people of Ashdod, and He [b]ravaged them and struck them with [c]tumors,[1] *both* Ashdod and its [d]territory. [7]And when the men of Ashdod saw how *it was,* they said, "The ark of the [a]God of Israel must not remain with us, for His hand is harsh toward us and Dagon our god." [8]Therefore they sent and gathered to themselves all the [a]lords of the Philistines, and said, "What shall we do with the ark of the God of Israel?"

And they answered, "Let the ark of the God of Israel be carried away to [b]Gath." So they carried the ark of the God of Israel away. [9]So it was, after they had carried it away, that [a]the hand of the LORD was against the city with a very great destruction; and He struck the men of the city, both small and great, [1]and tumors broke out on them.

[10]Therefore they sent the ark of God to Ekron. So it was, as the ark of God came to Ekron, that the Ekronites cried out, saying, "They have brought the ark of the God of Israel to us, to kill us and our people!" [11]So they sent and gathered together all the lords of the Philistines, and said, "Send away the ark of the God of Israel, and let it go back to its own place, so that it does not kill us and our people." For there was a deadly destruction throughout all the city; the hand of God was very heavy there. [12]And the men who did not die were stricken with the tumors, and the [a]cry of the city went up to heaven.

THE ARK RETURNED TO ISRAEL

6 Now the ark of the LORD was in the country of the Philistines seven months. [2]And the Philistines [a]called for the

---

4:20
[a]Gen. 35:16–19

4:21 [a]1 Sam. 14:3
[b]Ps. 26:8; 78:61;
[Jer. 2:11]

5:1 [a]1 Sam. 4:1;
7:12

5:2
[a]Judg. 16:23–30;
1 Chr. 10:8–10

5:3 [a]Is. 19:1;
46:1, 2 [b]Is. 46:7

5:4 [a]Jer. 50:2;
Ezek. 6:4, 6;
Mic. 1:7

5:5 [a]Zeph. 1:9

5:6 [a]Ex. 9:3;
Deut. 2:15;
1 Sam. 5:7;
7:13; Ps. 32:4;
145:20; 147:6
[b]1 Sam. 6:5
[c]Deut. 28:27;
Ps. 78:66
[d]Josh. 15:46, 47

5:7 [a]1 Sam. 6:5

5:8 [a]1 Sam. 6:4
[b]Josh. 11:22

5:9 [a]Deut. 2:15;
1 Sam. 5:11; 7:13;
12:15

5:12
[a]1 Sam. 9:16;
Jer. 14:2

6:2 [a]Gen. 41:8;
Ex. 7:11; Is. 2:6;
47:13; Dan. 2:2;
5:7

4:20 [1]*pay any attention to*   **4:21** [1]Lit. *Inglorious*   **5:2** [1]A Philistine idol
5:4 [1]So with LXX, Syr., Tg., Vg.; MT *Dagon*   **5:6** [1]Probably bubonic plague.
LXX, Vg. add *And in the midst of their land rats sprang up, and there was a great death panic in the city.*   **5:9** [1]Vg. *and they had tumors in their secret parts*

priests and the diviners, saying, "What shall we do with the ark of the LORD? Tell us how we should send it to its place."

3So they said, "If you send away the ark of the God of Israel, do not send it ªempty; but by all means return *it* to Him *with* ᵇa trespass offering. Then you will be healed, and it will be known to you why His hand is not removed from you."

4Then they said, "What *is* the trespass offering which we shall return to Him?"

They answered, ª"Five golden tumors and five golden rats, *according to* the number of the lords of the Philistines. For the same plague *was* on all of ¹you and on your lords. 5Therefore you shall make images of your tumors and images of your rats that ªravage the land, and you shall ᵇgive glory to the God of Israel; perhaps He will ᶜlighten¹ His hand from you, from ᵈyour gods, and from your land. 6Why then do you harden your hearts ªas the Egyptians and Pharaoh hardened their hearts? When He did mighty things among them, ᵇdid they not let the people go, that they might depart? 7Now therefore, make ªa new cart, take two milk cows ᵇwhich have never been yoked, and hitch the cows to the cart; and take their calves home, away from them. 8Then take the ark of the LORD and set it on the cart; and put ªthe articles of gold which you are returning to Him *as* a trespass offering in a chest by its side. Then send it away, and let it go. 9And watch: if it goes up the road to its own territory, to ªBeth Shemesh, *then* He has done ¹us this great evil. But if not, then ᵇwe shall know that *it is* not His hand *that* struck us—it happened to us by chance."

10Then the men did so; they took two milk cows and hitched them to the cart, and shut up their calves at home. 11And they set the ark of the LORD on the cart, and the chest with the gold rats and the images of their tumors. 12Then the cows headed straight for the road to Beth Shemesh, *and* went along the ªhighway, lowing as they went, and did not turn aside to the right hand or the left. And the lords of the Philistines went after them to the border of Beth Shemesh.

13Now *the people of* Beth Shemesh *were* reaping their ªwheat harvest in the valley; and they lifted their eyes and saw the ark, and rejoiced to see *it.* 14Then the cart came into the field of Joshua of Beth Shemesh, and stood there; a large stone *was* there. So they split the wood of the cart and offered the cows as a burnt offering to the LORD. 15The Levites took down the ark of the LORD and the chest that *was* with it, in which *were* the articles of gold, and put *them* on the large stone. Then the men of Beth Shemesh offered burnt offerings and made sacrifices the same day to the LORD. 16So when ªthe five lords of the Philistines had seen *it,* they returned to Ekron the same day.

17ªThese *are* the golden tumors which the Philistines returned *as* a trespass offering to the LORD: one for Ashdod, one for Gaza, one for Ashkelon, one for ᵇGath, one for Ekron; 18and the golden rats, *according to* the number of all the cities of the Philistines *belonging* to the five lords, *both* fortified cities and country villages, even as far as the large *stone of* Abel on which they set the ark of the LORD, *which stone remains* to this day in the field of Joshua of Beth Shemesh.

6:3 ªEx. 23:15;
Deut. 16:16
ᵇLev. 5:15, 16

6:4 ª1 Sam. 5:6,
9, 12; 6:17

6:5 ª1 Sam. 5:6
ᵇJosh. 7:19;
1 Chr. 16:28, 29;
Is. 42:12;
Jer. 13:16;
Mal. 2:2;
Rev. 14:7
ᶜ1 Sam. 5:6, 11;
Ps. 39:10
ᵈ1 Sam. 5:3, 4, 7

6:6 ªEx. 7:13;
8:15; 9:34; 14:17
ᵇEx. 12:31

6:7 ª2 Sam. 6:3
ᵇNum. 19:2;
Deut. 21:3, 4

6:8
ª1 Sam. 6:4, 5

6:9 ªJosh. 15:10;
21:16 ᵇ1 Sam. 6:3

6:12
ªNum. 20:19

6:13
ª1 Sam. 12:17

6:16 ªJosh. 13:3;
Judg. 3:3

6:17 ª1 Sam. 6:4
ᵇ1 Sam. 5:8

¹⁹Then ᵃHe struck the men of Beth Shemesh, because they had looked into the ark of the LORD. ¹He ᵇstruck fifty thousand and seventy men of the people, and the people lamented because the LORD had struck the people with a great slaughter.

THE ARK AT KIRJATH JEARIM

²⁰And the men of Beth Shemesh said, ᵃ"Who is able to stand before this holy LORD God? And to whom shall it go up from us?" ²¹So they sent messengers to the inhabitants of ᵃKirjath Jearim, saying, "The Philistines have brought back the ark of the LORD; come down *and* take it up with you."

7 Then the men of ᵃKirjath Jearim came and took the ark of the LORD, and brought it into the house of ᵇAbinadab on the hill, and ᶜconsecrated Eleazar his son to keep the ark of the LORD.

SAMUEL JUDGES ISRAEL

²So it was that the ark remained in Kirjath Jearim a long time; it was there twenty years. And all the house of Israel lamented after the LORD.

³Then Samuel spoke to all the house of Israel, saying, "If you ᵃreturn to the LORD with all your hearts, *then* ᵇput away the foreign gods and the ᶜAshtoreths¹ from among you, and ᵈprepare your hearts for the LORD, and ᵉserve Him only; and He will deliver you from the hand of the Philistines." ⁴So the children of Israel put away the ᵃBaals and the ¹Ashtoreths, and served the LORD only.

⁵And Samuel said, ᵃ"Gather all Israel to Mizpah, and ᵇI will pray to the LORD for you." ⁶So they gathered together at Mizpah, ᵃdrew water, and poured *it* out before the LORD. And they ᵇfasted that day, and said there, ᶜ"We have sinned against the LORD." And Samuel judged the children of Israel at Mizpah.

⁷Now when the Philistines heard that the children of Israel had gathered together at Mizpah, the lords of the Philistines went up against Israel. And when the children of Israel heard *of it,* they were afraid of the Philistines. ⁸So the children of Israel said to Samuel, ᵃ"Do not cease to cry out to the LORD our God for us, that He may save us from the hand of the Philistines."

⁹And Samuel took a ᵃsuckling lamb and offered *it as a* whole burnt offering to the LORD. Then ᵇSamuel cried out to the LORD for Israel, and the LORD answered him. ¹⁰Now as Samuel was offering up the burnt offering, the Philistines drew near to battle against Israel. ᵃBut the LORD thundered with a loud thunder upon the Philistines that day, and so confused them that they were overcome before Israel. ¹¹And the men of Israel went out of Mizpah and pursued the Philistines, and ¹drove them back as far as below Beth Car. ¹²Then Samuel ᵃtook a stone and set *it* up between Mizpah and Shen, and called its name ¹Ebenezer, saying, "Thus far the LORD has helped us."

¹³ᵃSo the Philistines were subdued, and they ᵇdid not come anymore into the territory of Israel. And the hand of the LORD was against the Philistines all the days of Samuel.

6:19 ᵃEx. 19:21; Num. 4:5, 15, 16, 20 ᵇ2 Sam. 6:7

6:20 ᵃLev. 11:44, 45; Ps. 24:3, 4; Mal. 3:2; Rev. 6:17

6:21 ᵃJosh. 9:17; 15:9, 60; 18:14; Judg. 18:12; 1 Chr. 13:5, 6

7:1 ᵃ1 Sam. 6:21; Ps. 132:6 ᵇ2 Sam. 6:3, 4 ᶜLev. 21:8

7:3 ᵃDeut. 30:2–10; 1 Kin. 8:48; Is. 55:7; Hos. 6:1; Joel 2:12–14 ᵇGen. 35:2; Josh. 24:14, 23; Judg. 10:16 ᶜJudg. 2:13; 1 Sam. 31:10 ᵈ2 Chr. 30:19; Job 11:13 ᵉDeut. 6:13; 10:20; 13:4; Josh. 24:14; Matt. 4:10; Luke 4:8

7:4 ᵃJudg. 2:11; 10:16

7:5 ᵃJudg. 10:17; 20:1; 1 Sam. 10:17 ᵇ1 Sam. 12:17–19

7:6 ᵃ2 Sam. 14:14 ᵇJudg. 20:26; Neh. 9:1, 2; Dan. 9:3–5; Joel 2:12 ᶜJudg. 10:10; 1 Sam. 12:10; 1 Kin. 8:47; Ps. 106:6

7:8 ᵃ1 Sam. 12:19–24; Is. 37:4

7:9 ᵃLev. 22:27 ᵇ1 Sam. 12:18; Ps. 99:6; Jer. 15:1

7:10 ᵃJosh. 10:10; 2 Sam. 22:14, 15; Ps. 18:13, 14

7:12 ᵃGen. 28:18; 35:14; Josh. 4:9; 24:26

7:13 ᵃJudg. 13:1 ᵇ1 Sam. 13:5

6:19 ¹Or *He struck seventy men of the people and fifty oxen of a man*
7:3 ¹Images of Canaanite goddesses   7:4 ¹Images of Canaanite goddesses
7:11 ¹*struck them down*   7:12 ¹Lit. *Stone of Help*

¹⁴Then the cities which the Philistines had taken from Israel were restored to Israel, from Ekron to Gath; and Israel recovered its territory from the hands of the Philistines. Also there was peace between Israel and the Amorites.

¹⁵And Samuel ᵃjudged Israel all the days of his life. ¹⁶He went from year to year on a circuit to Bethel, Gilgal, and Mizpah, and judged Israel in all those places. ¹⁷But ᵃhe always returned to Ramah, for his home *was* there. There he judged Israel, and there he ᵇbuilt an altar to the LORD.

ISRAEL DEMANDS A KING

8 Now it came to pass when Samuel was ᵃold that he ᵇmade his ᶜsons judges over Israel. ²The name of his firstborn was Joel, and the name of his second, Abijah; *they were* judges in Beersheba. ³But his sons ᵃdid not walk in his ways; they turned aside ᵇafter dishonest gain, ᶜtook bribes, and perverted justice.

⁴Then all the elders of Israel gathered together and came to Samuel at Ramah, ⁵and said to him, "Look, you are old, and your sons do not walk in your ways. Now ᵃmake us a king to judge us like all the nations."

⁶But the thing ᵃdispleased Samuel when they said, "Give us a king to judge us." So Samuel ᵇprayed to the LORD. ⁷And the LORD said to Samuel, "Heed the voice of the people in all that they say to you; for ᵃthey have not rejected you, but ᵇthey have rejected Me, that I should not reign over them. ⁸According to all the works which they have done since the day that I brought them up out of Egypt, even to this day—with which they have forsaken Me and served other gods—so they are doing to you also. ⁹Now therefore, heed their voice. However, you shall solemnly forewarn them, and ᵃshow them the behavior of the king who will reign over them."

¹⁰So Samuel told all the words of the LORD to the people who asked him for a king. ¹¹And he said, ᵃ"This will be the behavior of the king who will reign over you: He will take your ᵇsons and appoint *them* for his own ᶜchariots and *to be* his horsemen, and *some* will run before his chariots. ¹²He will ᵃappoint captains over his thousands and captains over his fifties, *will set some* to plow his ground and reap his harvest, and *some* to make his weapons of war and equipment for his chariots. ¹³He will take your daughters *to be* perfumers, cooks, and bakers. ¹⁴And ᵃhe will take the best of your fields, your vineyards, and your olive groves, and give *them* to his servants. ¹⁵He will take a tenth of your grain and your vintage, and give it to his officers and servants. ¹⁶And he will take your male servants, your female servants, your finest ¹young men, and your donkeys, and put *them* to his work. ¹⁷He will take a tenth of your sheep. And you will be his servants. ¹⁸And you will cry out in that day because of your king whom you have chosen for yourselves, and the LORD ᵃwill not hear you in that day."

¹⁹Nevertheless the people ᵃrefused to obey the voice of Samuel; and they said, "No, but we will have a king over us, ²⁰that we also may be ᵃlike all the nations, and that our king may judge us and go out before us and fight our battles."

²¹And Samuel heard all the words of the people, and he

7:15 ᵃ1 Sam. 12:11
7:17 ᵃ1 Sam. 8:4
ᵇJudg. 21:4
8:1 ᵃ1 Sam. 12:2
ᵇDeut. 16:18, 19;
2 Chr. 19:5
ᶜJudg. 10:4
8:3
ᵃJer. 22:15–17
ᵇEx. 18:21
ᶜEx. 23:6–8;
Deut. 16:19;
1 Sam. 12:3
8:5
ᵃDeut. 17:14, 15;
Hos. 13:10, 11;
Acts 13:21
8:6 ᵃ1 Sam. 12:17
ᵇ1 Sam. 7:9
8:7 ᵃEx. 16:8
ᵇ1 Sam. 10:19
8:9
ᵃ1 Sam. 8:11–18
8:11
ᵃDeut. 17:14–20
ᵇ1 Sam. 14:52
ᶜ2 Sam. 15:1
8:12
ᵃ1 Sam. 22:7
8:14 ᵃ1 Kin. 21:7;
[Ezek. 46:18]
8:18
ᵃProv. 1:25–28;
Is. 1:15; Mic. 3:4
8:19 ᵃIs. 66:4;
Jer. 44:16
8:20 ᵃ1 Sam. 8:5

8:16 ¹LXX *cattle*

repeated them in the hearing of the LORD. [22]So the LORD said to Samuel, [a]"Heed their voice, and make them a king."

And Samuel said to the men of Israel, "Every man go to his city."

SAUL CHOSEN TO BE KING

9 There was a man of Benjamin whose name *was* [a]Kish the son of Abiel, the son of Zeror, the son of Bechorath, the son of Aphiah, a Benjamite, a mighty man of [1]power. [2]And he had a choice and handsome son whose name *was* Saul. *There was* not a more handsome person than he among the children of Israel. [a]From his shoulders upward *he was* taller than any of the people.

[3]Now the donkeys of Kish, Saul's father, were lost. And Kish said to his son Saul, "Please take one of the servants with you, and arise, go and look for the donkeys." [4]So he passed through the mountains of Ephraim and through the land of [a]Shalisha, but they did not find *them.* Then they passed through the land of Shaalim, and *they were* not *there.* Then he passed through the land of the Benjamites, but they did not find *them.*

[5]When they had come to the land of [a]Zuph, Saul said to his servant who *was* with him, "Come, let [b]us return, lest my father cease *caring* about the donkeys and become worried about us."

[6]And he said to him, "Look now, *there is* in this city [a]a man of God, and *he is* an honorable man; [b]all that he says surely comes to pass. So let us go there; perhaps he can show us the way that we should go."

[7]Then Saul said to his servant, "But look, *if* we go, [a]what shall we bring the man? For the bread in our vessels is all gone, and *there is* no present to bring to the man of God. What do we have?"

[8]And the servant answered Saul again and said, "Look, I have here at hand one-fourth of a shekel of silver. I will give *that* to the man of God, to tell us our way." [9](Formerly in Israel, when a man [a]went [1]to inquire of God, he spoke thus: "Come, let us go to the seer"; for *he who is* now *called* a prophet was formerly called [b]a seer.)

[10]Then Saul said to his servant, [1]"Well said; come, let us go." So they went to the city where the man of God *was.*

[11]As they went up the hill to the city, [a]they met some young women going out to draw water, and said to them, "Is the seer here?"

[12]And they answered them and said, "Yes, there he is, just ahead of you. Hurry now; for today he came to this city, because [a]there is a sacrifice of the people today [b]on the high place. [13]As soon as you come into the city, you will surely find him before he goes up to the high place to eat. For the people will not eat until he comes, because he must bless the sacrifice; afterward those who are invited will eat. Now therefore, go up, for about this time you will find him." [14]So they went up to the city. As they were coming into the city, there was Samuel, coming out toward them on his way up to the high place.

[15a]Now the LORD had told Samuel in his ear the day before Saul came, saying, [16]"Tomorrow about this time [a]I will send

8:22
[a]1 Sam. 8:7;
Hos. 13:11

9:1 [a]1 Sam. 14:51;
1 Chr. 8:33;
9:36–39

9:2
[a]1 Sam. 10:23

9:4 [a]2 Kin. 4:42

9:5 [a]1 Sam. 1:1
[b]1 Sam. 10:2

9:6 [a]Deut. 33:1;
1 Kin. 13:1;
2 Kin. 5:8
[b]1 Sam. 3:19

9:7 [a]Judg. 6:18;
13:17; 1 Kin. 14:3;
2 Kin. 4:42; 8:8

9:9 [a]Gen. 25:22
[b]2 Sam. 24:11;
2 Kin. 17:13;
1 Chr. 26:28;
29:29;
2 Chr. 16:7, 10;
Is. 30:10;
Amos 7:12

9:11
[a]Gen. 24:11, 15;
29:8, 9; Ex. 2:16

9:12 [a]Gen. 31:54;
1 Sam. 16:2
[b]1 Sam. 7:17;
10:5; 1 Kin. 3:2

9:15 [a]1 Sam. 15:1

9:16 [a]Deut. 17:15

9:1 [1]*wealth*   **9:9** [1]Lit. *to seek God*   **9:10** [1]Lit. *Your word is good*

you a man from the land of Benjamin, ᵇand you shall anoint him ¹commander over My people Israel, that he may save My people from the hand of the Philistines; for I have ᶜlooked upon My people, because their cry has come to Me."

¹⁷So when Samuel saw Saul, the Lᴏʀᴅ said to him, ᵃ"There he is, the man of whom I spoke to you. This one shall reign over My people." ¹⁸Then Saul drew near to Samuel in the gate, and said, "Please tell me, where *is* the seer's house?"

¹⁹Samuel answered Saul and said, "I *am* the seer. Go up before me to the high place, for you shall eat with me today; and tomorrow I will let you go and will tell you all that *is* in your heart. ²⁰But as for ᵃyour donkeys that were lost three days ago, do not be anxious about them, for they have been found. And ¹on whom ᵇ*is* all the desire of Israel? *Is it* not on you and on all your father's house?"

²¹And Saul answered and said, ᵃ"*Am* I not a Benjamite, of the ᵇsmallest of the tribes of Israel, and ᶜmy family the least of all the families of the ¹tribe of Benjamin? Why then do you speak like this to me?"

²²Now Samuel took Saul and his servant and brought them into the hall, and had them sit in the place of honor among those who were invited; there *were* about thirty persons. ²³And Samuel said to the cook, "Bring the portion which I gave you, of which I said to you, 'Set it apart.'" ²⁴So the cook took up ᵃthe thigh with its upper part and set *it* before Saul. And *Samuel* said, "Here it is, what was kept back. *It* was set apart for you. Eat; for until this time it has been kept for you, since I said I invited the people." So Saul ate with Samuel that day.

²⁵When they had come down from the high place into the city, ¹*Samuel* spoke with Saul on ᵃthe top of the house. ²⁶They arose early; and it was about the dawning of the day that Samuel called to Saul on the top of the house, saying, "Get up, that I may send you on your way." And Saul arose, and both of them went outside, he and Samuel.

SAUL ANOINTED KING

²⁷As they were going down to the outskirts of the city, Samuel said to Saul, "Tell the servant to go on ahead of us." And he went on. "But you stand here ¹awhile, that I may announce to you the word of God."

10 Then ᵃSamuel took a flask of oil and poured *it* on his head, ᵇand kissed him and said: "*Is it* not because ᶜthe Lᴏʀᴅ has anointed you commander over ᵈHis ¹inheritance? ²When you have departed from me today, you will find two men by ᵃRachel's tomb in the territory of Benjamin ᵇat Zelzah; and they will say to you, 'The donkeys which you went to look for have been found. And now your father has ceased caring about the donkeys and is worrying about ᶜyou, saying, "What shall I do about my son?"' ³Then you shall go on forward from there and come to the terebinth tree of Tabor. There three

---

9:16 ᵇ1 Sam. 10:1
ᶜEx. 2:23–25;
3:7, 9
9:17
ᵃ1 Sam. 16:12;
Hos. 13:11
9:20 ᵃ1 Sam. 9:3
ᵇ1 Sam. 8:5, 19;
12:13
9:21
ᵃ1 Sam. 15:17
ᵇJudg. 20:46–
48; Ps. 68:27
ᶜJudg. 6:15
9:24
ᵃEx. 29:22, 27;
Lev. 7:32, 33;
Num. 18:18;
Ezek. 24:4
9:25
ᵃDeut. 22:8;
2 Sam. 11:2;
Luke 5:19;
Acts 10:9
10:1
ᵃEx. 30:23–33;
1 Sam. 9:16;
16:13;
2 Kin. 9:3, 6
ᵇPs. 2:12
ᶜ2 Sam. 5:2;
Acts 13:21
ᵈEx. 34:9;
Deut. 32:9;
Ps. 78:71
10:2
ᵃGen. 35:16–20;
48:7
ᵇJosh. 18:28
ᶜ1 Sam. 9:3–5

9:16 ¹*prince* or *ruler*   9:20 ¹*for whom*   9:21 ¹Lit. *tribes*   9:25 ¹So with MT, Tg.; LXX omits *He spoke with Saul on the top of the house*; LXX, Vg. afterward add *And he prepared a bed for Saul on the top of the house, and he slept.* 9:27 ¹*now*   10:1 ¹So with MT, Tg., Vg.; LXX *people Israel; and you shall rule the people of the Lord*; LXX, Vg. add *And you shall deliver His people from the hands of their enemies all around them. And this shall be a sign to you, that God has anointed you to be a prince.*

men going up ^ato God at Bethel will meet you, one carrying three young goats, another carrying three loaves of bread, and another carrying a skin of wine. ⁴And they will ¹greet you and give you two *loaves* of bread, which you shall receive from their hands. ⁵After that you shall come to the hill of God ^awhere the Philistine garrison *is*. And it will happen, when you have come there to the city, that you will meet a group of prophets coming down ^bfrom the high place with a stringed instrument, a tambourine, a flute, and a harp before them; ^cand they will be prophesying. ⁶Then ^athe Spirit of the LORD will come upon you, and ^byou will prophesy with them and be turned into another man. ⁷And let it be, when these ^asigns come to you, *that* you do as the occasion demands; for ^bGod *is* with you. ⁸You shall go down before me ^ato Gilgal; and surely I will come down to you to offer burnt offerings *and* make sacrifices of peace offerings. ^bSeven days you shall wait, till I come to you and show you what you should do."

⁹So it was, when he had turned his back to go from Samuel, that God ¹gave him another heart; and all those signs came to pass that day. ^{10a}When they came there to the hill, there was ^ba group of prophets to meet him; then the Spirit of God came upon him, and he prophesied among them. ¹¹And it happened, when all who knew him formerly saw that he indeed prophesied among the prophets, that the people said to one another, "What *is* this *that* has come upon the son of Kish? ^a*Is* Saul also among the prophets?" ¹²Then a man from there answered and said, "But ^awho *is* their father?" Therefore it became a proverb: "*Is* Saul also among the prophets?" ¹³And when he had finished prophesying, he went to the high place.

¹⁴Then Saul's ^auncle said to him and his servant, "Where did you go?"

So he said, "To look for the donkeys. When we saw that *they were* nowhere *to be found,* we went to Samuel."

¹⁵And Saul's uncle said, "Tell me, please, what Samuel said to you."

¹⁶So Saul said to his uncle, "He told us plainly that the donkeys had been ^afound." But about the matter of the kingdom, he did not tell him what Samuel had said.

SAUL PROCLAIMED KING

¹⁷Then Samuel called the people together ^ato the LORD ^bat Mizpah, ¹⁸and said to the children of Israel, ^a"Thus says the LORD God of Israel: 'I brought up Israel out of Egypt, and delivered you from the hand of the Egyptians *and* from the hand of all kingdoms and from those who oppressed you.' ^{19a}But you have today rejected your God, who Himself saved you from all your adversities and your tribulations; and you have said to Him, 'No, set a king over us!' Now therefore, present yourselves before the LORD by your tribes and by your ¹clans."

²⁰And when Samuel had ^acaused all the tribes of Israel to come near, the tribe of Benjamin was chosen. ²¹When he had caused the tribe of Benjamin to come near by their families, the family of Matri was chosen. And Saul the son of Kish was chosen. But when they sought him, he could not be found.

10:3
^aGen. 28:22; 35:1, 3, 7

10:5
^a1 Sam. 13:2, 3
^b1 Sam. 19:12, 20; 2 Kin. 2:3, 5, 15
^cEx. 15:20, 21; 2 Kin. 3:15; 1 Chr. 25:1–6; 1 Cor. 14:1

10:6
^aNum. 11:25, 29; Judg. 14:6; 1 Sam. 16:13
^b1 Sam. 10:10; 19:23, 24

10:7 ^aEx. 4:8; Luke 2:12
^bJosh. 1:5; Judg. 6:12; 1 Sam. 3:19; [Heb. 13:5]

10:8
^a1 Sam. 11:14, 15; 13:8
^b1 Sam. 13:8–10

10:10
^a1 Sam. 10:5
^b1 Sam. 19:20

10:11
^a1 Sam. 19:24; Amos 7:14, 15; Matt. 13:54–57; John 7:15; Acts 4:13

10:12
^aJohn 5:30, 36

10:14
^a1 Sam. 14:50

10:16
^a1 Sam. 9:20

10:17 ^aJudg. 20:1
^b1 Sam. 7:5, 6

10:18
^aJudg. 6:8, 9; 1 Sam. 8:8; 12:6, 8

10:19
^a1 Sam. 8:7, 19; 12:12

10:20
^aActs 1:24, 26

10:4 ¹*ask you about your welfare*   **10:9** ¹*changed his heart*   **10:19** ¹Lit. *thousands*

²²Therefore they ^ainquired of the LORD further, "Has the man come here yet?"

And the LORD answered, "There he is, hidden among the equipment."

²³So they ran and brought him from there; and when he stood among the people, ^ahe was taller than any of the people from his shoulders upward. ²⁴And Samuel said to all the people, "Do you see him ^awhom the LORD has chosen, that *there is* no one like him among all the people?"

So all the people shouted and said, ^b"Long¹ live the king!"

²⁵Then Samuel explained to the people ^athe behavior of royalty, and wrote *it* in a book and laid *it* up before the LORD. And Samuel sent all the people away, every man to his house. ²⁶And Saul also went home ^ato Gibeah; and valiant *men* went with him, whose hearts God had touched. ^{27a}But some ^brebels said, "How can this man save us?" So they despised him, ^cand brought him no presents. But he ¹held his peace.

SAUL SAVES JABESH GILEAD

11 Then ^aNahash the Ammonite came up and ¹encamped against ^bJabesh Gilead; and all the men of Jabesh said to Nahash, ^c"Make a covenant with us, and we will serve you."

²And Nahash the Ammonite answered them, "On this *condition* I will make *a covenant* with you, that I may put out all your right eyes, and bring ^areproach on all Israel."

³Then the elders of Jabesh said to him, "Hold off for seven days, that we may send messengers to all the territory of Israel. And then, if *there is* no one to ¹save us, we will come out to you."

⁴So the messengers came ^ato Gibeah of Saul and told the news in the hearing of the people. And ^ball the people lifted up their voices and wept. ⁵Now there was Saul, coming behind the herd from the field; and Saul said, "What *troubles* the people, that they weep?" And they told him the words of the men of Jabesh. ^{6a}Then the Spirit of God came upon Saul when he heard this news, and his anger was greatly aroused. ⁷So he took a yoke of oxen and ^acut them in pieces, and sent *them* throughout all the territory of Israel by the hands of messengers, saying, ^b"Whoever does not go out with Saul and Samuel to battle, so it shall be done to his oxen."

And the fear of the LORD fell on the people, and they came out ¹with one consent. ⁸When he numbered them in ^aBezek, the children ^bof Israel were three hundred thousand, and the men of Judah thirty thousand. ⁹And they said to the messengers who came, "Thus you shall say to the men of Jabesh Gilead: 'Tomorrow, by *the time* the sun is hot, you shall have help.'" Then the messengers came and reported *it* to the men of Jabesh, and they were glad. ¹⁰Therefore the men of Jabesh said, "Tomorrow we will come out to you, and you may do with us whatever seems good to you."

¹¹So it was, on the next day, that ^aSaul put the people ^bin three companies; and they came into the midst of the camp in the morning watch, and killed Ammonites until the heat of the day. And it happened that those who survived were scattered, so that no two of them were left together.

10:22
^a1 Sam. 23:2, 4, 10, 11

10:23
^a1 Sam. 9:2

10:24
^aDeut. 17:15; 1 Sam. 9:16; 2 Sam. 21:6
^b1 Kin. 1:25, 39

10:25
^aDeut. 17:14–20; 1 Sam. 8:11–18

10:26
^aJudg. 20:14

10:27
^a1 Sam. 11:12
^bDeut. 13:13; 1 Sam. 25:17
^c2 Sam. 8:2; 1 Kin. 4:21; 10:25; 2 Chr. 17:5; Matt. 2:11

11:1 ^a1 Sam. 12:12
^bJudg. 21:8; 1 Sam. 31:11
^cGen. 26:28; 1 Kin. 20:34; Job 41:4; Ezek. 17:13

11:2 ^aGen. 34:14; 1 Sam. 17:26; Ps. 44:13

11:4
^a1 Sam. 10:26; 15:34; 2 Sam. 21:6
^bGen. 27:38; Judg. 2:4; 20:23, 26; 21:2; 1 Sam. 30:4

11:6 ^aJudg. 3:10; 6:34; 11:29; 13:25; 14:6; 1 Sam. 10:10; 16:13

11:7 ^aJudg. 19:29
^bJudg. 21:5, 8, 10

11:8 ^aJudg. 1:5
^b2 Sam. 24:9

11:11 ^a1 Sam. 31:11
^bJudg. 7:16, 20

10:24 ¹Lit. *May the king live*   **10:27** ¹*kept silent*   **11:1** ¹*besieged*
11:3 ¹*deliver*   **11:7** ¹Lit. *as one man*

[12]Then the people said to Samuel, [a]"Who *is* he who said, 'Shall Saul reign over us?' [b]Bring the men, that we may put them to death."

[13]But Saul said, [a]"Not a man shall be put to death this day, for today [b]the LORD has accomplished salvation in Israel."

[14]Then Samuel said to the people, "Come, let us go [a]to Gilgal and renew the kingdom there." [15]So all the people went to Gilgal, and there they made Saul king [a]before the LORD in Gilgal. [b]There they made sacrifices of peace offerings before the LORD, and there Saul and all the men of Israel rejoiced greatly.

SAMUEL'S ADDRESS AT SAUL'S CORONATION

12 Now Samuel said to all Israel: "Indeed I have [1]heeded [a]your voice in all that you said to me, and [b]have made a king over you. [2]And now here is the king, [a]walking before you; [b]and I am old and grayheaded, and look, my sons *are* with you. I have walked before you from my childhood to this day. [3]Here I am. Witness against me before the LORD and before [a]His anointed: [b]Whose ox have I taken, or whose donkey have I taken, or whom have I cheated? Whom have I oppressed, or from whose hand have I received *any* [c]bribe with which to [d]blind my eyes? I will restore *it* to you."

[4]And they said, [a]"You have not cheated us or oppressed us, nor have you taken anything from any man's hand."

[5]Then he said to them, "The LORD *is* witness against you, and His anointed *is* witness this day, [a]that you have not found anything [b]in my hand."

And they answered, "*He is* witness."

[6]Then Samuel said to the people, [a]"*It is* the LORD who raised up Moses and Aaron, and who brought your fathers up from the land of Egypt. [7]Now therefore, stand still, that I may [a]reason with you before the LORD concerning all the [b]righteous acts of the LORD which He did to you and your fathers: [8a]When Jacob had gone into [1]Egypt, and your fathers [b]cried out to the LORD, then the LORD [c]sent Moses and Aaron, who brought your fathers out of Egypt and made them dwell in this place. [9]And when they [a]forgot the LORD their God, He sold them into the hand of [b]Sisera, commander of the army of Hazor, into the hand of the [c]Philistines, and into the hand of the king of [d]Moab; and they fought against them. [10]Then they cried out to the LORD, and said, [a]'We have sinned, because we have forsaken the LORD [b]and served the Baals and [1]Ashtoreths; but now deliver us from the hand of our enemies, and we will serve You.' [11]And the LORD sent [1]Jerubbaal, [2]Bedan, [a]Jephthah, and [b]Samuel,[3] and delivered you out of the hand of your enemies on every side; and you dwelt in safety. [12]And when you saw that [a]Nahash king of the Ammonites came against you, [b]you said to me, 'No, but a king shall reign over us,' when [c]the LORD your God *was* your king.

[13]"Now therefore, [a]here is the king [b]whom you have chosen *and* whom you have desired. And take note, [c]the LORD has set a king over you. [14]If you [a]fear the LORD and serve Him

---

11:12
[a]1 Sam. 10:27
[b]Luke 19:27

11:13
[a]1 Sam. 10:27;
2 Sam. 19:22
[b]Ex. 14:13, 30;
1 Sam. 19:5

11:14 [a]1 Sam. 7:16;
10:8

11:15
[a]1 Sam. 10:17
[b]Josh. 8:31;
1 Sam. 10:8

12:1 [a]1 Sam. 8:5,
7, 9, 20, 22
[b]1 Sam. 10:24;
11:14, 15

12:2
[a]Num. 27:17;
1 Sam. 8:20
[b]1 Sam. 8:1, 5

12:3 [a]1 Sam. 10:1;
24:6; 2 Sam. 1:14,
16 [b]Num. 16:15;
Acts 20:33;
1 Thess. 2:5
[c]Ex. 23:8
[d]Deut. 16:19

12:4 [a]Lev. 19:13

12:5
[a]John 18:38;
Acts 23:9; 24:20
[b]Ex. 22:4

12:6 [a]Ex. 6:26;
Mic. 6:4

12:7 [a]Is. 1:18;
Ezek. 20:35;
Mic. 6:1–5
[b]Judg. 5:11;
Ps. 103:6

12:8 [a]Gen. 46:5,
6; Ps. 105:23
[b]Ex. 2:23–25
[c]Ex. 3:10; 4:14–16

12:9
[a]Deut. 32:18;
Judg. 3:7
[b]Judg. 4:2
[c]Judg. 3:31; 10:7;
13:1 [d]Judg. 3:12–
30

12:10
[a]Judg. 10:10
[b]Judg. 2:13; 3:7

12:11 [a]Judg. 11:1
[b]1 Sam. 7:13

12:12 [a]1 Sam. 11:1,
2 [b]1 Sam. 8:5, 19,
20 [c]Judg. 8:23;
1 Sam. 8:7;
Ps. 59:13

12:13
[a]1 Sam. 10:24
[b]1 Sam. 8:5; 12:17,
19 [c]Hos. 13:11

12:14 [a]Josh. 24:14

12:1 [1]*listened to*   12:8 [1]So with MT, Tg., Vg.; LXX adds *and the Egyptians afflicted them*   12:10 [1]Images of Canaanite goddesses   12:11 [1]Gideon, cf. Judg. 6:25–32; Syr. *Deborah;* Tg. *Gideon*   [2]LXX, Syr. *Barak;* Tg. *Simson*
[3]Syr. *Simson*

and obey His voice, and do not rebel against the commandment of the LORD, then both you and the king who reigns over you will continue following the LORD your God. 15However, if you do ᵃnot obey the voice of the LORD, but ᵇrebel against the commandment of the LORD, then the hand of the LORD will be against you, as *it was* against your fathers.

16"Now therefore, ᵃstand and see this great thing which the LORD will do before your eyes: 17*Is* today not the ᵃwheat harvest? ᵇI will call to the LORD, and He will send thunder and ᶜrain, that you may perceive and see that ᵈyour wickedness *is* great, which you have done in the sight of the LORD, in asking a king for yourselves."

18So Samuel called to the LORD, and the LORD sent thunder and rain that day; and ᵃall the people greatly feared the LORD and Samuel.

19And all the people said to Samuel, ᵃ"Pray for your servants to the LORD your God, that we may not die; for we have added to all our sins the evil of asking a king for ourselves."

20Then Samuel said to the people, "Do not fear. You have done all this wickedness; ᵃyet do not turn aside from following the LORD, but serve the LORD with all your heart. 21And ᵃdo not turn aside; ᵇfor *then you would go* after empty things which cannot profit or deliver, for they *are* nothing. 22For ᵃthe LORD will not forsake ᵇHis people, ᶜfor His great name's sake, because ᵈit has pleased the LORD to make you His people. 23Moreover, as for me, far be it from me that I should sin against the LORD ᵃin ceasing to pray for you; but ᵇI will teach you the ᶜgood and the right way. 24ᵃOnly fear the LORD, and serve Him in truth with all your heart; for ᵇconsider what ᶜgreat things He has done for you. 25But if you still do wickedly, ᵃyou shall be swept away, ᵇboth you and your king."

SAUL'S UNLAWFUL SACRIFICE

13 Saul ¹reigned one year; and when he had reigned two years over Israel, 2Saul chose for himself three thousand *men* of Israel. Two thousand were with Saul in ᵃMichmash and in the mountains of Bethel, and a thousand were with ᵇJonathan in ᶜGibeah of Benjamin. The rest of the people he sent away, every man to his tent.

3And Jonathan attacked ᵃthe garrison of the Philistines that *was* in ᵇGeba, and the Philistines heard *of it.* Then Saul blew the trumpet throughout all the land, saying, "Let the Hebrews hear!" 4Now all Israel heard it said *that* Saul had attacked a garrison of the Philistines, and *that* Israel had also become ¹an abomination to the Philistines. And the people were called together to Saul at Gilgal.

5Then the Philistines gathered together to fight with Israel, ¹thirty thousand chariots and six thousand horsemen, and people ᵃas the sand which *is* on the seashore in multitude. And they came up and encamped in Michmash, to the east of ᵇBeth Aven. 6When the men of Israel saw that they were in danger (for the people were distressed), then the people ᵃhid in caves, in thickets, in rocks, in holes, and in pits. 7And *some of* the Hebrews crossed over the Jordan to the ᵃland of Gad and Gilead.

12:15
ᵃDeut. 28:15
ᵇLev. 26:14, 15;
Josh. 24:20;
Is. 1:20

12:16
ᵃEx. 14:13, 31

12:17
ᵃGen. 30:14
ᵇJosh. 10:12;
1 Sam. 7:9, 10;
[James 5:16–18]
ᶜEzra 10:9
ᵈ1 Sam. 8:7

12:18 ᵃEx. 14:31

12:19 ᵃEx. 9:28;
1 Sam. 7:8;
[James 5:15;
1 John 5:16]

12:20
ᵃDeut. 11:16

12:21
ᵃ2 Chr. 25:15
ᵇIs. 41:29;
Jer. 16:19;
Hab. 2:18;
1 Cor. 8:4

12:22
ᵃDeut. 31:6;
1 Kin. 6:13
ᵇIs. 43:21
ᶜEx. 32:12;
Num. 14:13;
Josh. 7:9;
Ps. 106:8;
Jer. 14:21
ᵈDeut. 7:6–11;
1 Pet. 2:9

12:23 ᵃActs 12:5;
Rom. 1:9;
Col. 1:9;
2 Tim. 1:3
ᵇPs. 34:11;
Prov. 4:11
ᶜ1 Kin. 8:36

12:24
ᵃEccl. 12:13
ᵇIs. 5:12
ᶜDeut. 10:21

12:25
ᵃJosh. 24:20
ᵇDeut. 28:36

13:2
ᵃ1 Sam. 14:5, 31
ᵇ1 Sam. 14:1
ᶜ1 Sam. 10:26

13:3 ᵃ1 Sam. 10:5
ᵇ2 Sam. 5:25

13:5 ᵃJudg. 7:12
ᵇJosh. 7:2;
1 Sam. 14:23

13:6 ᵃJudg. 6:2;
1 Sam. 14:11

13:7
ᵃNum. 32:1–42

13:1 ¹Heb. is difficult; cf. 2 Sam. 5:4; 2 Kin. 14:2; see also 2 Sam. 2:10; Acts 13:21   13:4 ¹*odious*   13:5 ¹So with MT, LXX, Tg., Vg.; Syr. and some mss. of LXX *three thousand*

As for Saul, he *was* still in Gilgal, and all the people followed him trembling. [8a]Then he waited seven days, according to the time set by Samuel. But Samuel did not come to Gilgal; and the people were scattered from him. [9]So Saul said, "Bring a burnt offering and peace offerings here to me." And he offered the burnt offering. [10]Now it happened, as soon as he had finished presenting the burnt offering, that Samuel came; and Saul went out to meet him, that he might [1]greet him.

[11]And Samuel said, "What have you done?"

Saul said, "When I saw that the people were scattered from me, and *that* you did not come within the days appointed, and *that* the Philistines gathered together at Michmash, [12]then I said, 'The Philistines will now come down on me at Gilgal, and I have not made supplication to the LORD.' Therefore I felt compelled, and offered a burnt offering."

[13]And Samuel said to Saul, [a]"You have done foolishly. [b]You have not kept the commandment of the LORD your God, which He commanded you. For now the LORD would have established your kingdom over Israel forever. [14a]But now your kingdom shall not continue. [b]The LORD has sought for Himself a man [c]after His own heart, and the LORD has commanded him *to be* commander over His people, because you have [d]not kept what the LORD commanded you."

[15]Then Samuel arose and went up from Gilgal to Gibeah of [1]Benjamin. And Saul numbered the people present with him, [a]about six hundred men.

NO WEAPONS FOR THE ARMY

[16]Saul, Jonathan his son, and the people present with them remained in [1]Gibeah of Benjamin. But the Philistines encamped in Michmash. [17]Then raiders came out of the camp of the Philistines in three companies. One company turned onto the road to [a]Ophrah, to the land of Shual, [18]another company turned to the road *to* [a]Beth Horon, and another company turned *to* the road of the border that overlooks the Valley of [b]Zeboim toward the wilderness.

[19]Now [a]there was no blacksmith to be found throughout all the land of Israel, for the Philistines said, "Lest the Hebrews make swords or spears." [20]But all the Israelites would go down to the Philistines to sharpen each man's plowshare, his mattock, his ax, and his sickle; [21]and the charge for a sharpening was a [1]pim for the plowshares, the mattocks, the forks, and the axes, and to set the points of the goads. [22]So it came about, on the day of battle, that [a]there was neither sword nor spear found in the hand of any of the people who *were* with Saul and Jonathan. But they were found with Saul and Jonathan his son.

[23a]And the garrison of the Philistines went out to the pass of Michmash.

JONATHAN DEFEATS THE PHILISTINES

14 Now it happened one day that Jonathan the son of Saul said to the young man who [1]bore his armor, "Come, let us go over to the Philistines' garrison that *is* on the other

Cross-references

13:8 [a]1 Sam. 10:8

13:13
[a]2 Chr. 16:9
[b]1 Sam. 15:11, 22, 28

13:14
[a]1 Sam. 15:28; 31:6 [b]1 Sam. 16:1
[c]Ps. 89:20; Acts 7:46; 13:22
[d]1 Sam. 15:11, 19

13:15
[a]1 Sam. 13:2, 6, 7; 14:2

13:17
[a]Josh. 18:23

13:18
[a]Josh. 16:3; 18:13, 14
[b]Gen. 14:2; Neh. 11:34

13:19 [a]Judg. 5:8; 2 Kin. 24:14; Jer. 24:1; 29:2

13:22 [a]Judg. 5:8

13:23
[a]1 Sam. 14:1, 4

13:10 [1]Lit. *bless him*   **13:15** [1]So with MT, Tg.; LXX, Vg. add *And the rest of the people went up after Saul to meet the people who fought against them, going from Gilgal to Gibeah in the hill of Benjamin.*   **13:16** [1]Heb. *Geba*
13:21 [1]About two-thirds shekel weight   **14:1** [1]*carried*

side." But he did not tell his father. ²And Saul was sitting in the outskirts of ªGibeah under a pomegranate tree which *is* in Migron. The people who *were* with him *were* about six hundred men. ³ªAhijah the son of Ahitub, ᵇIchabod's brother, the son of Phinehas, the son of Eli, the LORD's priest in Shiloh, was ᶜwearing an ephod. But the people did not know that Jonathan had gone.

⁴Between the passes, by which Jonathan sought to go over ªto the Philistines' garrison, *there was* a sharp rock on one side and a sharp rock on the other side. And the name of one *was* Bozez, and the name of the other Seneh. ⁵The front of one faced northward opposite Michmash, and the other southward opposite Gibeah.

⁶Then Jonathan said to the young man who bore his armor, "Come, let us go over to the garrison of these ªuncircumcised; it may be that the LORD will work for us. For nothing restrains the LORD ᵇfrom saving by many or by few."

⁷So his armorbearer said to him, "Do all that is in your heart. Go then; here I am with you, according to your heart."

⁸Then Jonathan said, "Very well, let us cross over to *these* men, and we will show ourselves to them. ⁹If they say thus to us, 'Wait until we come to you,' then we will stand still in our place and not go up to them. ¹⁰But if they say thus, 'Come up to us,' then we will go up. For the LORD has delivered them into our hand, and ªthis *will be* a sign to us."

¹¹So both of them showed themselves to the garrison of the Philistines. And the Philistines said, "Look, the Hebrews are coming out of the holes where they have ªhidden." ¹²Then the men of the garrison called to Jonathan and his armorbearer, and said, "Come up to us, and we will ¹show you something."

Jonathan said to his armorbearer, "Come up after me, for the LORD has delivered them into the hand of Israel." ¹³And Jonathan climbed up on his hands and knees with his armorbearer after him; and they ªfell before Jonathan. And as he came after him, his armorbearer killed them. ¹⁴That first slaughter which Jonathan and his armorbearer made was about twenty men within about ¹half an acre of land.

¹⁵And ªthere was ¹trembling in the camp, in the field, and among all the people. The garrison and ᵇthe raiders also trembled; and the earth quaked, so that it was ᶜa very great trembling. ¹⁶Now the watchmen of Saul in Gibeah of Benjamin looked, and *there* was the multitude, melting away; and they ªwent here and there. ¹⁷Then Saul said to the people who *were* with him, "Now call the roll and see who has gone from us." And when they had called the roll, surprisingly, Jonathan and his armorbearer *were* not *there*. ¹⁸And Saul said to Ahijah, "Bring the ¹ark of God here" (for at that time the ark of God was with the children of Israel). ¹⁹Now it happened, while Saul ªtalked to the priest, that the noise which *was* in the camp of the Philistines continued to increase; so Saul said to the priest, "Withdraw your hand." ²⁰Then Saul and all the people who *were* with him assembled, and they went to the battle; and indeed ªevery man's sword was against his neighbor, *and* there was very great confusion. ²¹Moreover the Hebrews *who*

Cross references (margin)

14:2
ª1 Sam. 13:15, 16

14:3
ª1 Sam. 22:9, 11, 20 ᵇ1 Sam. 4:21 ᶜ1 Sam. 2:28

14:4
ª1 Sam. 13:23

14:6
ª1 Sam. 17:26, 36; Jer. 9:25, 26 ᵇJudg. 7:4, 7; 1 Sam. 17:46, 47; 2 Chr. 14:11; [Ps. 115:3; 135:6; Zech. 4:6; Matt. 19:26; Rom. 8:31]

14:10
ªGen. 24:14; Judg. 6:36–40

14:11
ª1 Sam. 13:6; 14:22

14:13 ªLev. 26:8; Josh. 23:10

14:15
ªDeut. 28:7; 2 Kin. 7:6, 7; Job 18:11 ᵇ1 Sam. 13:17 ᶜGen. 35:5

14:16
ª1 Sam. 14:20

14:19
ªNum. 27:21

14:20
ªJudg. 7:22; 2 Chr. 20:23

14:12 ¹*teach*   14:14 ¹Lit. *half the area plowed by a yoke* of oxen in a day
14:15 ¹*terror*   14:18 ¹So with MT, Tg., Vg.; LXX *ephod*

were with the Philistines before that time, who went up with them into the camp *from the* surrounding *country,* they also joined the Israelites who *were* with Saul and Jonathan. 22Likewise all the men of Israel who ªhad hidden in the mountains of Ephraim, *when* they heard that the Philistines fled, they also followed hard after them in the battle. 23ªSo the LORD saved Israel that day, and the battle shifted ᵇto Beth Aven.

SAUL'S RASH OATH

24And the men of Israel were distressed that day, for Saul had ªplaced the people under oath, saying, "Cursed *is* the man who eats *any* food until evening, before I have taken vengeance on my enemies." So none of the people tasted food. 25ªNow all *the people* of the land came to a forest; and there was ᵇhoney on the ground. 26And when the people had come into the woods, there was the honey, dripping; but no one put his hand to his mouth, for the people feared the oath. 27But Jonathan had not heard his father charge the people with the oath; therefore he stretched out the end of the rod that *was* in his hand and dipped it in a honeycomb, and put his hand to his mouth; and his ¹countenance brightened. 28Then one of the people said, "Your father strictly charged the people with an oath, saying, 'Cursed *is* the man who eats food this day.'" And the people were faint.

29But Jonathan said, "My father has troubled the land. Look now, how my countenance has brightened because I tasted a little of this honey. 30How much better if the people had eaten freely today of the spoil of their enemies which they found! For now would there not have been a much greater slaughter among the Philistines?"

31Now they had ¹driven back the Philistines that day from Michmash to Aijalon. So the people were very faint. 32And the people rushed on the ¹spoil, and took sheep, oxen, and calves, and slaughtered *them* on the ground; and the people ate *them* ªwith the blood. 33Then they told Saul, saying, "Look, the people are sinning against the LORD by eating with the blood!"

So he said, "You have dealt treacherously; roll a large stone to me this day." 34Then Saul said, "Disperse yourselves among the people, and say to them, 'Bring me here every man's ox and every man's sheep, slaughter *them* here, and eat; and do not sin against the LORD by eating with the blood.'" So every one of the people brought his ox with him that night, and slaughtered *it* there. 35Then Saul ªbuilt an altar to the LORD. This was the first altar that he built to the LORD.

36Now Saul said, "Let us go down after the Philistines by night, and plunder them until the morning light; and let us not leave a man of them."

And they said, "Do whatever seems good to you."

Then the priest said, "Let us draw near to God here."

37So Saul ªasked counsel of God, "Shall I go down after the Philistines? Will You deliver them into the hand of Israel?" But ᵇHe did not answer him that day. 38And Saul said, ª"Come over here, all you chiefs of the people, and know and see what this sin was today. 39For ªas the LORD lives, who saves Israel, though it be in Jonathan my son, he shall surely die." But not a man among all the people answered him. 40Then he said to

14:22
ª1 Sam. 13:6

14:23 ªEx. 14:30;
2 Chr. 32:22;
Hos. 1:7
ᵇ1 Sam. 13:5

14:24
ªJosh. 6:26

14:25
ªDeut. 9:28;
Matt. 3:5
ᵇEx. 3:8;
Num. 13:27;
Matt. 3:4

14:32 ªGen. 9:4;
Lev. 3:17;
17:10–14; 19:26;
Deut. 12:16, 23,
24; Acts 15:20

14:35
ª1 Sam. 7:12, 17;
2 Sam. 24:25

14:37
ªJudg. 20:18
ᵇ1 Sam. 28:6

14:38
ªJosh. 7:14;
1 Sam. 10:19

14:39
ª1 Sam. 14:24,
44; 2 Sam. 12:5

14:27 ¹Lit. *eyes*   14:31 ¹Lit. *struck*   14:32 ¹*plunder*

all Israel, "You be on one side, and my son Jonathan and I will be on the other side."

And the people said to Saul, "Do what seems good to you."

[41]Therefore Saul said to the LORD God of Israel, [a]"Give[1] a perfect *lot*." [b]So Saul and Jonathan were taken, but the people escaped. [42]And Saul said, "Cast *lots* between my son Jonathan and me." So Jonathan was taken. [43]Then Saul said to Jonathan, [a]"Tell me what you have done."

And Jonathan told him, and said, [b]"I only tasted a little honey with the end of the rod that *was* in my hand. So now I must die!"

[44]Saul answered, [a]"God do so and more also; [b]for you shall surely die, Jonathan."

[45]But the people said to Saul, "Shall Jonathan die, who has accomplished this great deliverance in Israel? Certainly not! [a]As the LORD lives, not one hair of his head shall fall to the ground, for he has worked [b]with God this day." So the people rescued Jonathan, and he did not die.

[46]Then Saul returned from pursuing the Philistines, and the Philistines went to their own place.

SAUL'S CONTINUING WARS

[47]So Saul established his sovereignty over Israel, and fought against all his enemies on every side, against Moab, against the people of [a]Ammon, against Edom, against the kings of [b]Zobah, and against the Philistines. Wherever he turned, he [1]harassed *them*. [48]And he gathered an army and [a]attacked[1] the Amalekites, and delivered Israel from the hands of those who plundered them.

[49a]The sons of Saul were Jonathan, [1]Jishui, and Malchishua. And the names of his two daughters *were these:* the name of the firstborn Merab, and the name of the younger [b]Michal. [50]The name of Saul's wife *was* Ahinoam the daughter of Ahimaaz. And the name of the commander of his army *was* Abner the son of Ner, Saul's [a]uncle. [51a]Kish *was* the father of Saul, and Ner the father of Abner *was* the son of Abiel.

[52]Now there was fierce war with the Philistines all the days of Saul. And when Saul saw any strong man or any valiant man, [a]he took him for himself.

SAUL SPARES KING AGAG

15 Samuel also said to Saul, [a]"The LORD sent me to anoint you king over His people, over Israel. Now therefore, heed the voice of the words of the LORD. [2]Thus says the LORD of hosts: 'I will punish Amalek *for* what he did to Israel, [a]how he ambushed him on the way when he came up from Egypt. [3]Now go and [a]attack[1] Amalek, and [b]utterly destroy all that they have, and do not spare them. But kill both man and woman, infant and nursing child, ox and sheep, camel and donkey.'"

[4]So Saul gathered the people together and numbered them in Telaim, two hundred thousand foot soldiers and ten

Cross references (margin)

14:41
[a]Prov. 16:33;
Acts 1:24–26
[b]Josh. 7:16;
1 Sam. 10:20, 21

14:43 [a]Josh. 7:19
[b]1 Sam. 14:27

14:44 [a]Ruth 1:17;
1 Sam. 25:22
[b]1 Sam. 14:39

14:45
[a]2 Sam. 14:11;
1 Kin. 1:52;
Luke 21:18;
Acts 27:34
[b][2 Cor. 6:1;
Phil. 2:12, 13]

14:47
[a]1 Sam. 11:1–13
[b]2 Sam. 10:6

14:48 [a]Ex. 17:16;
1 Sam. 15:3–7

14:49
[a]1 Sam. 31:2;
1 Chr. 8:33
[b]1 Sam. 18:17–20,
27; 19:12

14:50
[a]1 Sam. 10:14

14:51
[a]1 Sam. 9:1, 21

14:52
[a]1 Sam. 8:11

15:1 [a]1 Sam. 9:16;
10:1

15:2
[a]Ex. 17:8, 14;
Num. 24:20;
Deut. 25:17–19

15:3
[a]Deut. 25:19
[b]Lev. 27:28, 29;
Num. 24:20;
Deut. 20:16–18;
Josh. 6:17–21

14:41 [1]So with MT, Tg.; LXX, Vg. *Why do You not answer Your servant today? If the injustice is with me or Jonathan my son, O LORD God of Israel, give proof; and if You say it is with Your people Israel, give holiness.* 14:47 [1]LXX, Vg. *prospered* 14:48 [1]Lit. *struck* 14:49 [1]*Abinadab*, 1 Chr. 8:33; 9:39 15:3 [1]Lit. *strike*

thousand men of Judah. [5]And Saul came to a city of Amalek, and lay in wait in the valley.

[6]Then Saul said to [a]the Kenites, [b]"Go, depart, get down from among the Amalekites, lest I destroy you with them. For [c]you showed kindness to all the children of Israel when they came up out of Egypt." So the Kenites departed from among the Amalekites. [7a]And Saul attacked the Amalekites, from [b]Havilah all the way to [c]Shur, which is east of Egypt. [8a]He also took Agag king of the Amalekites alive, and [b]utterly destroyed all the people with the edge of the sword. [9]But Saul and the people [a]spared Agag and the best of the sheep, the oxen, the fatlings, the lambs, and all *that was* good, and were unwilling to utterly destroy them. But everything despised and worthless, that they utterly destroyed.

SAUL REJECTED AS KING

[10]Now the word of the LORD came to Samuel, saying, [11a]"I greatly regret that I have set up Saul *as* king, for he has [b]turned back from following Me, [c]and has not performed My commandments." And it [d]grieved Samuel, and he cried out to the LORD all night. [12]So when Samuel rose early in the morning to meet Saul, it was told Samuel, saying, "Saul went to [a]Carmel, and indeed, he set up a monument for himself; and he has gone on around, passed by, and gone down to Gilgal." [13]Then Samuel went to Saul, and Saul said to him, [a]"Blessed *are* you of the LORD! I have performed the commandment of the LORD."

[14]But Samuel said, "What then *is* this bleating of the sheep in my ears, and the lowing of the oxen which I hear?"

[15]And Saul said, "They have brought them from the Amalekites; [a]for the people spared the best of the sheep and the oxen, to sacrifice to the LORD your God; and the rest we have utterly destroyed."

[16]Then Samuel said to Saul, "Be quiet! And I will tell you what the LORD said to me last night."

And he said to him, "Speak on."

[17]So Samuel said, [a]"When you *were* little in your own eyes, *were* you not head of the tribes of Israel? And did not the LORD anoint you king over Israel? [18]Now the LORD sent you on a mission, and said, 'Go, and utterly destroy the sinners, the Amalekites, and fight against them until they are [1]consumed.' [19]Why then did you not obey the voice of the LORD? Why did you swoop down on the [1]spoil, and do evil in the sight of the LORD?"

[20]And Saul said to Samuel, [a]"But I have obeyed the voice of the LORD, and gone on the mission on which the LORD sent me, and brought back Agag king of Amalek; I have utterly destroyed the Amalekites. [21a]But the people took of the plunder, sheep and oxen, the best of the things which should have been utterly destroyed, to sacrifice to the LORD your God in Gilgal."

[22]So Samuel said:

[a]"Has the LORD *as great* delight in burnt offerings and
     sacrifices,
As in obeying the voice of the LORD?
Behold, [b]to obey is better than sacrifice,
And to heed than the fat of rams.

15:6
[a]Num. 24:21;
Judg. 1:16;
4:11–22;
1 Chr. 2:55
[b]Gen. 18:25;
19:12, 14;
Rev. 18:4
[c]Ex. 18:10, 19;
Num. 10:29, 32

15:7
[a]1 Sam. 14:48
[b]Gen. 2:11; 25:17,
18 [c]Gen. 16:7;
Ex. 15:22;
1 Sam. 27:8

15:8
[a]1 Sam. 15:32, 33
[b]1 Sam. 27:8, 9

15:9
[a]1 Sam. 15:3,
15, 19

15:11
[a]Gen. 6:6, 7;
1 Sam. 15:35;
2 Sam. 24:16
[b]Josh. 22:16;
1 Kin. 9:6
[c]1 Sam. 13:13;
15:3, 9
[d]1 Sam. 15:35;
16:1

15:12
[a]Josh. 15:55;
1 Sam. 25:2

15:13
[a]Gen. 14:19;
Judg. 17:2;
Ruth 3:10;
2 Sam. 2:5

15:15
[a][Gen. 3:12, 13;
Ex. 32:22, 23];
1 Sam. 15:9, 21;
[Prov. 28:13]

15:17
[a]1 Sam. 9:21;
10:22

15:20
[a]1 Sam. 15:13;
[Prov. 28:13]

15:21
[a]1 Sam. 15:15

15:22
[a]Ps. 50:8, 9;
51:16, 17;
[Prov. 21:3;
Is. 1:11–17;
Jer. 7:22, 23;
Mic. 6:6–8;
Heb. 10:4–10]
[b][Eccl. 5:1;
Hos. 6:6;
Matt. 5:24; 9:13;
12:7; Mark 12:33]

15:18 [1]*exterminated*   15:19 [1]*plunder*

23 For rebellion *is as* the sin of [1]witchcraft,
And stubbornness *is as* iniquity and idolatry.
Because you have rejected the word of the LORD,
[a]He also has rejected you from *being* king."

24[a]Then Saul said to Samuel, "I have sinned, for I have transgressed the commandment of the LORD and your words, because I [b]feared the people and obeyed their voice. 25Now therefore, please pardon my sin, and return with me, that I may worship the LORD."

26But Samuel said to Saul, "I will not return with you, [a]for you have rejected the word of the LORD, and the LORD has rejected you from being king over Israel."

27And as Samuel turned around to go away, [a]*Saul* seized the edge of his robe, and it tore. 28So Samuel said to him, [a]"The LORD has torn the kingdom of Israel from you today, and has given it to a neighbor of yours, *who is* better than you. 29And also the Strength of Israel [a]will not lie nor relent. For He *is* not a man, that He should relent."

30Then he said, "I have sinned; *yet* [a]honor me now, please, before the elders of my people and before Israel, and return with me, that I may worship the LORD your God." 31So Samuel turned back after Saul, and Saul worshiped the LORD.

32Then Samuel said, "Bring Agag king of the Amalekites here to me." So Agag came to him cautiously.

And Agag said, "Surely the bitterness of death is past."

33But Samuel said, [a]"As your sword has made women childless, so shall your mother be childless among women." And Samuel hacked Agag in pieces before the LORD in Gilgal.

34Then Samuel went to [a]Ramah, and Saul went up to his house at [b]Gibeah of Saul. 35And [a]Samuel went no more to see Saul until the day of his death. Nevertheless Samuel mourned for Saul, and the LORD regretted that He had made Saul king over Israel.

DAVID ANOINTED KING

16 Now the LORD said to Samuel, [a]"How long will you mourn for Saul, seeing I have rejected him from reigning over Israel? [b]Fill your horn with oil, and go; I am sending you to [c]Jesse the Bethlehemite. For [d]I have [1]provided Myself a king among his sons."

2And Samuel said, "How can I go? If Saul hears *it*, he will kill me."

But the LORD said, "Take a heifer with you, and say, [a]'I have come to sacrifice to the LORD.' 3Then invite Jesse to the sacrifice, and I will show you what you shall do; you shall anoint for Me the one I name to you."

4So Samuel did what the LORD said, and went to Bethlehem. And the elders of the town [a]trembled at his coming, and said, [b]"Do you come peaceably?"

5And he said, "Peaceably; I have come to sacrifice to the LORD. [a]Sanctify[1] yourselves, and come with me to the sacrifice." Then he consecrated Jesse and his sons, and invited them to the sacrifice.

6So it was, when they came, that he looked at [a]Eliab and [b]said, "Surely the LORD's anointed *is* before Him!"

15:23
[a]1 Sam. 13:14;
16:1

15:24
[a]Num. 22:34;
Josh. 7:20;
1 Sam. 26:21;
2 Sam. 12:13;
Ps. 51:4
[b][Ex. 23:2;
Prov. 29:25;
Is. 51:12, 13]

15:26
[a]1 Sam. 2:30

15:27
[a]1 Kin. 11:30, 31

15:28
[a]1 Sam. 28:17, 18;
1 Kin. 11:31

15:29
[a]Num. 23:19;
Ezek. 24:14;
2 Tim. 2:13;
Titus 1:2

15:30
[a][John 5:44;
12:43]

15:33
[a][Gen. 9:6];
Num. 14:45;
Judg. 1:7;
[Matt. 7:2]

15:34
[a]1 Sam. 7:17
[b]1 Sam. 11:4

15:35
[a]1 Sam. 19:24

16:1
[a]1 Sam. 15:23, 35
[b]1 Sam. 9:16;
10:1; 2 Kin. 9:1
[c]Ruth 4:18–22
[d]Ps. 78:70, 71;
Acts 13:22

16:2 [a]1 Sam. 9:12

16:4 [a]1 Sam. 21:1
[b]1 Kin. 2:13;
2 Kin. 9:22

16:5 [a]Gen. 35:2;
Ex. 19:10

16:6
[a]1 Sam. 17:13, 28
[b]1 Kin. 12:26

15:23 [1]*divination* **16:1** [1]Lit. *seen* **16:5** [1]*Consecrate*

7But the LORD said to Samuel, a"Do not look at his appearance or at his physical stature, because I have 1refused him. bFor2 *the LORD does* not *see* as man sees; for man clooks at the outward appearance, but the LORD looks at the dheart."

8So Jesse called Abinadab, and made him pass before Samuel. And he said, "Neither has the LORD chosen this one." 9Then Jesse made Shammah pass by. And he said, "Neither has the LORD chosen this one." 10Thus Jesse made seven of his sons pass before Samuel. And Samuel said to Jesse, "The LORD has not chosen these." 11And Samuel said to Jesse, "Are all the young men here?" Then he said, "There remains yet the youngest, and there he is, keeping the asheep."

And Samuel said to Jesse, "Send and bring him. For we will not 1sit down till he comes here." 12So he sent and brought him in. Now he *was* aruddy, bwith 1bright eyes, and good-looking. cAnd the LORD said, "Arise, anoint him; for this *is* the one!" 13Then Samuel took the horn of oil and anointed him in the midst of his brothers; and athe Spirit of the LORD came upon David from that day forward. So Samuel arose and went to Ramah.

A DISTRESSING SPIRIT TROUBLES SAUL

14aBut the Spirit of the LORD departed from Saul, and ba distressing spirit from the LORD troubled him. 15And Saul's servants said to him, "Surely, a distressing spirit from God is troubling you. 16Let our master now command your servants, *who are* before you, to seek out a man *who is* a skillful player on the harp. And it shall be that he will aplay it with his hand when the 1distressing spirit from God is upon you, and you shall be well."

17So Saul said to his servants, 1"Provide me now a man who can play well, and bring *him* to me."

18Then one of the servants answered and said, "Look, I have seen a son of Jesse the Bethlehemite, *who is* skillful in playing, a mighty man of valor, a man of war, prudent in speech, and a handsome person; and athe LORD *is* with him."

19Therefore Saul sent messengers to Jesse, and said, "Send me your son David, who *is* with the sheep." 20And Jesse atook a donkey *loaded with* bread, a skin of wine, and a young goat, and sent *them* by his son David to Saul. 21So David came to Saul and astood before him. And he loved him greatly, and he became his armorbearer. 22Then Saul sent to Jesse, saying, "Please let David stand before me, for he has found favor in my sight." 23And so it was, whenever the spirit from God was upon Saul, that David would take a harp and play *it* with his hand. Then Saul would become refreshed and well, and the distressing spirit would depart from him.

DAVID AND GOLIATH

17 Now the Philistines gathered their armies together to battle, and were gathered at aSochoh, which *belongs* to Judah; they encamped between Sochoh and Azekah, in Ephes Dammim. 2And Saul and the men of Israel were gathered

16:7 aPs. 147:10
bIs. 55:8, 9
c2 Cor. 10:7
d1 Kin. 8:39

16:11
a2 Sam. 7:8;
Ps. 78:70–72

16:12
a1 Sam. 17:42
bGen. 39:6;
Ex. 2:2;
Acts 7:20
c1 Sam. 9:17

16:13
aNum. 27:18;
1 Sam. 10:6, 9, 10

16:14
aJudg. 16:20;
1 Sam. 11:6;
18:12; 28:15
bJudg. 9:23;
1 Sam. 16:15, 16;
18:10; 19:9;
1 Kin. 22:19–22

16:16
a1 Sam. 18:10;
19:9; 2 Kin. 3:15

16:18
a1 Sam. 3:19;
18:12, 14

16:20
a1 Sam. 10:4, 27;
Prov. 18:16

16:21
aGen. 41:46;
Prov. 22:29

17:1 aJosh. 15:35;
2 Chr. 28:18

together, and they encamped in the Valley of Elah, and drew up in battle array against the Philistines. ³The Philistines stood on a mountain on one side, and Israel stood on a mountain on the other side, with a valley between them.

⁴And a champion went out from the camp of the Philistines, named ªGoliath, from ᵇGath, whose height *was* six cubits and a span. ⁵*He had* a bronze helmet on his head, and he *was* ¹armed with a coat of mail, and the weight of the coat *was* five thousand shekels of bronze. ⁶And *he had* bronze armor on his legs and a bronze javelin between his shoulders. ⁷Now the staff of his spear *was* like a weaver's beam, and his iron spearhead *weighed* six hundred shekels; and a shield-bearer went before him. ⁸Then he stood and cried out to the armies of Israel, and said to them, "Why have you come out to line up for battle? *Am* I not a Philistine, and you the ªservants of Saul? Choose a man for yourselves, and let him come down to me. ⁹If he is able to fight with me and kill me, then we will be your servants. But if I prevail against him and kill him, then you shall be our servants and ªserve us." ¹⁰And the Philistine said, "I ªdefy the armies of Israel this day; give me a man, that we may fight together." ¹¹When Saul and all Israel heard these words of the Philistine, they were dismayed and greatly afraid.

¹²Now David *was* ªthe son of that ᵇEphrathite of Bethlehem Judah, whose name *was* Jesse, and who had ᶜeight sons. And the man was old, advanced *in years,* in the days of Saul. ¹³The three oldest sons of Jesse had gone to follow Saul to the battle. The ªnames of his three sons who went to the battle *were* Eliab the firstborn, next to him Abinadab, and the third Shammah. ¹⁴David *was* the youngest. And the three oldest followed Saul. ¹⁵But David occasionally went and returned from Saul ªto feed his father's sheep at Bethlehem.

¹⁶And the Philistine drew near and presented himself forty days, morning and evening.

¹⁷Then Jesse said to his son David, "Take now for your brothers an ephah of this dried *grain* and these ten loaves, and run to your brothers at the camp. ¹⁸And carry these ten cheeses to the captain of *their* thousand, and ªsee how your brothers fare, and bring back news of them." ¹⁹Now Saul and they and all the men of Israel *were* in the Valley of Elah, fighting with the Philistines.

²⁰So David rose early in the morning, left the sheep with a keeper, and took *the things* and went as Jesse had commanded him. And he came to the camp as the army was going out to the fight and shouting for the battle. ²¹For Israel and the Philistines had drawn up in battle array, army against army. ²²And David left his supplies in the hand of the supply keeper, ran to the army, and came and greeted his brothers. ²³Then as he talked with them, there was the champion, the Philistine of Gath, Goliath by name, coming up from the armies of the Philistines; and he spoke ªaccording to the same words. So David heard *them.* ²⁴And all the men of Israel, when they saw the man, fled from him and were dreadfully afraid. ²⁵So the men of Israel said, "Have you seen this man who has come up? Surely he has come up to defy Israel; and it shall be *that* the man who kills him the king will enrich with great riches, ªwill

17:4
ª2 Sam. 21:19
ᵇJosh. 11:21, 22

17:8 ª1 Sam. 8:17

17:9 ª1 Sam. 11:1

17:10
ª1 Sam. 17:26,
36, 45;
2 Sam. 21:21

17:12
ªRuth 4:22;
1 Sam. 16:1,
18; 17:58
ᵇGen. 35:19
ᶜ1 Sam. 16:10, 11;
1 Chr. 2:13–15

17:13
ª1 Sam. 16:6, 8, 9;
1 Chr. 2:13

17:15
ª1 Sam. 16:11, 19;
2 Sam. 7:8

17:18
ªGen. 37:13, 14

17:23
ª1 Sam. 17:8–10

17:25
ªJosh. 15:16

17:5 ¹*clothed with scaled body armor*

give him his daughter, and give his father's house exemption *from taxes* in Israel."

26Then David spoke to the men who stood by him, saying, "What shall be done for the man who kills this Philistine and takes away ªthe reproach from Israel? For who *is* this ᵇuncircumcised Philistine, that he should ᶜdefy the armies of ᵈthe living God?"

27And the people answered him in this manner, saying, ª"So shall it be done for the man who kills him."

28Now Eliab his oldest brother heard when he spoke to the men; and Eliab's ªanger was aroused against David, and he said, "Why did you come down here? And with whom have you left those few sheep in the wilderness? I know your pride and the insolence of your heart, for you have come down to see the battle."

29And David said, "What have I done now? *Is¹ there* not a cause?" 30Then he turned from him toward another and ªsaid the same thing; and these people answered him as the first ones *did.*

31Now when the words which David spoke were heard, they reported *them* to Saul; and he sent for him. 32Then David said to Saul, ª"Let no man's heart fail because of him; ᵇyour servant will go and fight with this Philistine."

33And Saul said to David, ª"You are not able to go against this Philistine to fight with him; for you *are* a youth, and he a man of war from his youth."

34But David said to Saul, "Your servant used to keep his father's sheep, and when a ªlion or a bear came and took a lamb out of the flock, 35I went out after it and struck it, and delivered *the lamb* from its mouth; and when it arose against me, I caught *it* by its beard, and struck and killed it. 36Your servant has killed both lion and bear; and this uncircumcised Philistine will be like one of them, seeing he has defied the armies of the living God." 37Moreover David said, ª"The LORD, who delivered me from the paw of the lion and from the paw of the bear, He will deliver me from the hand of this Philistine."

And Saul said to David, ᵇ"Go, and the LORD be with you!"

38So Saul clothed David with his ¹armor, and he put a bronze helmet on his head; he also clothed him with a coat of mail. 39David fastened his sword to his armor and tried to walk, for he had not tested *them.* And David said to Saul, "I cannot walk with these, for I have not tested *them.*" So David took them off.

40Then he took his staff in his hand; and he chose for himself five smooth stones from the brook, and put them in a shepherd's bag, in a pouch which he had, and his sling was in his hand. And he drew near to the Philistine. 41So the Philistine came, and began drawing near to David, and the man who bore the shield *went* before him. 42And when the Philistine looked about and saw David, he ªdisdained¹ him; for he was *only* a youth, ᵇruddy and goodlooking. 43So the Philistine ªsaid to David, "*Am* I a dog, that you come to me with sticks?" And the Philistine cursed David by his gods. 44And the Philistine ªsaid to David, "Come to me, and I will give your flesh to the birds of the air and the beasts of the field!"

17:26
ª1 Sam. 11:2
ᵇ1 Sam. 14:6;
17:36; Jer. 9:25,
26 ᶜ1 Sam. 17:10
ᵈDeut. 5:26;
2 Kin. 19:4;
Jer. 10:10

17:27
ª1 Sam. 17:25

17:28
ªGen. 37:4,
8–36;
[Prov. 18:19;
Matt. 10:36]

17:29
ª1 Sam. 17:17

17:30
ª1 Sam. 17:26, 27

17:32
ªDeut. 20:1–4
ᵇ1 Sam. 16:18

17:33
ªNum. 13:31;
Deut. 9:2

17:34 ªJudg. 14:5

17:37
ª[2 Cor. 1:10;
2 Tim. 4:17, 18]
ᵇ1 Sam. 20:13;
1 Chr. 22:11, 16

17:42
ª[Ps. 123:4;
Prov. 16:18;
1 Cor. 1:27, 28]
ᵇ1 Sam. 16:12

17:43
ª1 Sam. 24:14;
2 Sam. 3:8; 9:8;
16:9; 2 Kin. 8:13

17:44
ª1 Sam. 17:46;
1 Kin. 20:10, 11

17:29 ¹Lit. *Is it not a word?* or *matter?* **17:38** ¹Lit. *clothes* **17:42** ¹*belittled*

⁴⁵Then David said to the Philistine, "You come to me with a sword, with a spear, and with a javelin. ^aBut I come to you in the name of the LORD of hosts, the God of the armies of Israel, whom you have ^bdefied. ⁴⁶This day the LORD will deliver you into my hand, and I will strike you and take your head from you. And this day I will give ^athe carcasses of the camp of the Philistines to the birds of the air and the wild beasts of the earth, ^bthat all the earth may know that there is a God in Israel. ⁴⁷Then all this assembly shall know that the LORD ^adoes not save with sword and spear; for ^bthe battle *is* the LORD's, and He will give you into our hands."

⁴⁸So it was, when the Philistine arose and came and drew near to meet David, that David hurried and ^aran toward the army to meet the Philistine. ⁴⁹Then David put his hand in his bag and took out a stone; and he slung *it* and struck the Philistine in his forehead, so that the stone sank into his forehead, and he fell on his face to the earth. ⁵⁰So David prevailed over the Philistine with a ^asling and a stone, and struck the Philistine and killed him. But *there was* no sword in the hand of David. ⁵¹Therefore David ran and stood over the Philistine, took his ^asword and drew it out of its sheath and killed him, and cut off his head with it.

And when the Philistines saw that their champion was dead, ^bthey fled. ⁵²Now the men of Israel and Judah arose and shouted, and pursued the Philistines as far as the entrance of ¹the valley and to the gates of Ekron. And the wounded of the Philistines fell along the road to ^aShaaraim, even as far as Gath and Ekron. ⁵³Then the children of Israel returned from chasing the Philistines, and they plundered their tents. ⁵⁴And David took the head of the Philistine and brought it to Jerusalem, but he put his armor in his tent.

⁵⁵When Saul saw David going out against the Philistine, he said to ^aAbner, the commander of the army, "Abner, ^bwhose son *is* this youth?"

And Abner said, "As your soul lives, O king, I do not know."

⁵⁶So the king said, "Inquire whose son this young man *is*."

⁵⁷Then, as David returned from the slaughter of the Philistine, Abner took him and brought him before Saul ^awith the head of the Philistine in his hand. ⁵⁸And Saul said to him, "Whose son *are* you, young man?"

So David answered, ^a"*I am* the son of your servant Jesse the Bethlehemite."

SAUL RESENTS DAVID

18 Now when he had finished speaking to Saul, ^athe ¹soul of Jonathan was knit to the soul of David, ^band Jonathan loved him as his own soul. ²Saul took him that day, ^aand would not let him go home to his father's house anymore. ³Then Jonathan and David made a ^acovenant, because he loved him as his own soul. ⁴And Jonathan took off the robe that *was* on him and gave it to David, with his armor, even to his sword and his bow and his belt.

⁵So David went out wherever Saul sent him, *and* ¹behaved wisely. And Saul set him over the men of war, and he was accepted in the sight of all the people and also in the sight of

17:45
^a2 Sam. 22:33, 35; 2 Chr. 32:8; Ps. 124:8; [2 Cor. 10:4]; Heb. 11:33, 34
^b1 Sam. 17:10

17:46
^aDeut. 28:26
^bJosh. 4:24; 1 Kin. 8:43; 18:36; 2 Kin. 19:19; Is. 52:10

17:47
^a1 Sam. 14:6; 2 Chr. 14:11; 20:15; Ps. 44:6; Hos. 1:7; Zech. 4:6
^b2 Chr. 20:15

17:48 ^aPs. 27:3

17:50
^aJudg. 3:31; 15:15; 20:16

17:51
^a1 Sam. 21:9; 2 Sam. 23:21
^bHeb. 11:34

17:52
^aJosh. 15:36

17:55
^a1 Sam. 14:50
^b1 Sam. 16:21, 22

17:57
^a1 Sam. 17:54

17:58
^a1 Sam. 17:12

18:1 ^aGen. 44:30
^bDeut. 13:6; 1 Sam. 20:17; 2 Sam. 1:26

18:2
^a1 Sam. 17:15

18:3
^a1 Sam. 20:8–17

17:52 ¹So with MT, Syr., Tg., Vg.; LXX *Gath*   18:1 ¹*life of Jonathan was bound up with the life of*   18:5 ¹Or *prospered*

Saul's servants. [6]Now it had happened as they were coming *home,* when David was returning from the slaughter of the [1]Philistine, that [a]the women had come out of all the cities of Israel, singing and dancing, to meet King Saul, with tambourines, with joy, and with musical instruments. [7]So the women [a]sang as they danced, and said:

> [b]"Saul has slain his thousands,
> And David his ten thousands."

[8]Then Saul was very angry, and the saying [a]displeased him; and he said, "They have ascribed to David ten thousands, and to me they have ascribed *only* thousands. Now *what* more can he have but [b]the kingdom?" [9]So Saul [1]eyed David from that day forward.

[10]And it happened on the next day that [a]the distressing spirit from God came upon Saul, [b]and he prophesied inside the house. So David [c]played *music* with his hand, as at other times; [d]but *there was* a spear in Saul's hand. [11]And Saul [a]cast the spear, for he said, "I will pin David to the wall!" But David escaped his presence twice.

[12]Now Saul was [a]afraid of David, because [b]the LORD was with him, but had [c]departed from Saul. [13]Therefore Saul removed him from [1]his presence, and made him his captain over a thousand; and [a]he went out and came in before the people. [14]And David behaved wisely in all his ways, and [a]the LORD *was* with him. [15]Therefore, when Saul saw that he behaved very wisely, he was afraid of him. [16]But [a]all Israel and Judah loved David, because he went out and came in before them.

DAVID MARRIES MICHAL

[17]Then Saul said to David, "Here is my older daughter Merab; [a]I will give her to you as a wife. Only be valiant for me, and fight [b]the LORD's battles." For Saul thought, [c]"Let my hand not be against him, but let the hand of the Philistines be against him."

[18]So David said to Saul, [a]"Who *am* I, and what *is* my life *or* my father's family in Israel, that I should be son-in-law to the king?" [19]But it happened at the time when Merab, Saul's daughter, should have been given to David, that she was given to [a]Adriel the [b]Meholathite as a wife.

[20][a]Now Michal, Saul's daughter, loved David. And they told Saul, and the thing pleased him. [21]So Saul said, "I will give her to him, that she may [1]be a snare to him, and that [a]the hand of the Philistines may be against him." Therefore Saul said to David a second time, [b]"You shall be my son-in-law today."

[22]And Saul commanded his servants, "Communicate with David secretly, and say, 'Look, the king has delight in you, and all his servants love you. Now therefore, become the king's son-in-law.'"

[23]So Saul's servants spoke those words in the hearing of David. And David said, "Does it seem to you *a* light *thing* to be a king's son-in-law, seeing I *am* a poor and lightly esteemed man?" [24]And the servants of Saul told him, saying, [1]"In this manner David spoke."

18:6
[a]Ex. 15:20, 21; Judg. 11:34; Ps. 68:25; 149:3
18:7 [a]Ex. 15:21
[b]1 Sam. 21:11; 29:5
18:8 [a]Eccl. 4:4
[b]1 Sam. 15:28
18:10
[a]1 Sam. 16:14
[b]1 Sam. 19:24; 1 Kin. 18:29; Acts 16:16
[c]1 Sam. 16:23
[d]1 Sam. 19:9, 10
18:11
[a]1 Sam. 19:10; 20:33
18:12
[a]1 Sam. 18:15, 29
[b]1 Sam. 16:13, 18
[c]1 Sam. 16:14; 28:15
18:13
[a]Num. 27:17; 1 Sam. 18:16; 29:6; 2 Sam. 5:2
18:14
[a]Gen. 39:2, 3, 23; Josh. 6:27; 1 Sam. 16:18
18:16
[a]Num. 27:16, 17; 1 Sam. 18:5; 2 Sam. 5:2; 1 Kin. 3:7
18:17
[a]1 Sam. 14:49; 17:25
[b]Num. 32:20, 27, 29; 1 Sam. 25:28
[c]1 Sam. 18:21, 25; 2 Sam. 12:9
18:18
[a]1 Sam. 9:21; 18:23; 2 Sam. 7:18
18:19
[a]2 Sam. 21:8
[b]Judg. 7:22; 2 Sam. 21:8; 1 Kin. 19:16
18:20
[a]1 Sam. 18:28
18:21
[a]1 Sam. 18:17
[b]1 Sam. 18:26

18:6 [1]Philistines   **18:9** [1]Viewed with suspicion   **18:13** [1]Lit. *himself*
18:21 [1]*be bait for*   **18:24** [1]Lit. *According to these words*

25Then Saul said, "Thus you shall say to David: 'The king does not desire any ᵃdowry but one hundred foreskins of the Philistines, to take ᵇvengeance on the king's enemies.'" But Saul ᶜthought to make David fall by the hand of the Philistines. 26So when his servants told David these words, it pleased David well to become the king's son-in-law. Now ᵃthe days had not expired; 27therefore David arose and went, he and ᵃhis men, and killed two hundred men of the Philistines. And ᵇDavid brought their foreskins, and they gave them in full count to the king, that he might become the king's son-in-law. Then Saul gave him Michal his daughter as a wife.

28Thus Saul saw and knew that the LORD *was* with David, and *that* Michal, Saul's daughter, loved him; 29and Saul was still more afraid of David. So Saul became David's enemy ¹continually. 30Then the princes of the Philistines ᵃwent out *to war.* And so it was, whenever they went out, *that* David ᵇbehaved more wisely than all the servants of Saul, so that his name became highly esteemed.

SAUL PERSECUTES DAVID

19 Now Saul spoke to Jonathan his son and to all his servants, that they should kill ᵃDavid; but Jonathan, Saul's son, ᵇdelighted greatly in David. 2So Jonathan told David, saying, "My father Saul seeks to kill you. Therefore please be on your guard until morning, and stay in a secret *place* and hide. 3And I will go out and stand beside my father in the field where you *are,* and I will speak with my father about you. Then what I observe, I will tell ᵃyou."

4Thus Jonathan ᵃspoke well of David to Saul his father, and said to him, "Let not the king ᵇsin against his servant, against David, because he has not sinned against you, and because his works *have been* very good toward you. 5For he took his ᵃlife in his hands and ᵇkilled the Philistine, and ᶜthe LORD brought about a great deliverance for all Israel. You saw *it* and rejoiced. ᵈWhy then will you ᵉsin against innocent blood, to kill David without a cause?"

6So Saul heeded the voice of Jonathan, and Saul swore, "*As* the LORD lives, he shall not be killed." 7Then Jonathan called David, and Jonathan told him all these things. So Jonathan brought David to Saul, and he was in his presence ᵃas in times past.

8And there was war again; and David went out and fought with the Philistines, ᵃand struck them with a mighty blow, and they fled from him.

9Now ᵃthe distressing spirit from the LORD came upon Saul as he sat in his house with his spear in his hand. And David was playing *music* with *his* hand. 10Then Saul sought to pin David to the wall with the spear, but he slipped away from Saul's presence; and he drove the spear into the wall. So David fled and escaped that night.

11ᵃSaul also sent messengers to David's house to watch him and to kill him in the morning. And Michal, David's wife, told him, saying, "If you do not save your life tonight, tomorrow you will be killed." 12So Michal ᵃlet David down through a window. And he went and fled and escaped. 13And Michal took ¹an image and laid *it* in the bed, put a cover of goats' *hair*

18:25 ᵃGen. 34:12; Ex. 22:17 ᵇ1 Sam. 14:24 ᶜ1 Sam. 18:17

18:26 ᵃ1 Sam. 18:21

18:27 ᵃ1 Sam. 18:13 ᵇ2 Sam. 3:14

18:30 ᵃ2 Sam. 11:1 ᵇ1 Sam. 18:5

19:1 ᵃ1 Sam. 8:8, 9 ᵇ1 Sam. 18:1

19:3 ᵃ1 Sam. 20:8–13

19:4 ᵃ1 Sam. 20:32; [Prov. 31:8, 9] ᵇGen. 42:22; [Prov. 17:13]; Jer. 18:20

19:5 ᵃJudg. 9:17; 12:3 ᵇ1 Sam. 17:49, 50 ᶜ1 Sam. 11:13; 1 Chr. 11:14 ᵈ1 Sam. 20:32 ᵉ[Deut. 19:10–13]

19:7 ᵃ1 Sam. 16:21; 18:2, 10, 13

19:8 ᵃ1 Sam. 18:27; 23:5

19:9 ᵃ1 Sam. 16:14; 18:10, 11

19:11 ᵃJudg. 16:2; Ps. 59:title

19:12 ᵃJosh. 2:15; Acts 9:25; 2 Cor. 11:33

18:29 ¹*all the days*   **19:13** ¹*household idols,* Heb. teraphim

for his head, and covered *it* with clothes. ¹⁴So when Saul sent messengers to take David, she said, "He *is* sick."

¹⁵Then Saul sent the messengers *back* to see David, saying, "Bring him up to me in the bed, that I may kill him." ¹⁶And when the messengers had come in, there was the image in the bed, with a cover of goats' *hair* for his head. ¹⁷Then Saul said to Michal, "Why have you deceived me like this, and sent my enemy away, so that he has escaped?"

And Michal answered Saul, "He said to me, 'Let me go! ᵃWhy should I kill you?'"

¹⁸So David fled and escaped, and went to ᵃSamuel at ᵇRamah, and told him all that Saul had done to him. And he and Samuel went and stayed in Naioth. ¹⁹Now it was told Saul, saying, "Take note, David *is* at Naioth in Ramah!" ²⁰Then ᵃSaul sent messengers to take David. ᵇAnd when they saw the group of prophets prophesying, and Samuel standing *as* leader over them, the Spirit of God came upon the messengers of Saul, and they also ᶜprophesied. ²¹And when Saul was told, he sent other messengers, and they prophesied likewise. Then Saul sent messengers again the third time, and they prophesied also. ²²Then he also went to Ramah, and came to the great well that *is* at Sechu. So he asked, and said, "Where *are* Samuel and David?"

And *someone* said, "Indeed *they are* at Naioth in Ramah." ²³So he went there to Naioth in Ramah. Then ᵃthe Spirit of God was upon him also, and he went on and prophesied until he came to Naioth in Ramah. ²⁴ᵃAnd he also stripped off his clothes and prophesied before Samuel in like manner, and lay down ᵇnaked all that day and all that night. Therefore they say, ᶜ"*Is* Saul also among the prophets?"

JONATHAN'S LOYALTY TO DAVID

20 Then David fled from Naioth in Ramah, and went and said to Jonathan, "What have I done? What *is* my iniquity, and what *is* my sin before your father, that he seeks my life?"

²So Jonathan said to him, "By no means! You shall not die! Indeed, my father will do nothing either great or small without first telling me. And why should my father hide this thing from me? It *is* not *so!*"

³Then David took an oath again, and said, "Your father certainly knows that I have found favor in your eyes, and he has said, 'Do not let Jonathan know this, lest he be grieved.' But ᵃtruly, *as* the LORD lives and *as* your soul lives, *there is* but a step between me and death."

⁴So Jonathan said to David, "Whatever you yourself desire, I will do *it* for you."

⁵And David said to Jonathan, "Indeed tomorrow *is* the ᵃNew Moon, and I should not fail to sit with the king to eat. But let me go, that I may ᵇhide in the field until the third *day* at evening. ⁶If your father misses me at all, then say, 'David earnestly asked *permission* of me that he might run over ᵃto Bethlehem, his city, for *there is* a yearly sacrifice there for all the family.' ⁷ᵃIf he says thus: '*It is* well,' your servant will be safe. But if he is very angry, be sure that ᵇevil is determined by him. ⁸Therefore you shall ᵃdeal kindly with your servant, for ᵇyou have brought your servant into a covenant of the

19:17
ᵃ2 Sam. 2:22

19:18
ᵃ1 Sam. 16:13
ᵇ1 Sam. 7:17

19:20
ᵃ1 Sam. 19:11, 14; John 7:32
ᵇ1 Sam. 10:5, 6, 10; [1 Cor. 14:3, 24, 25]
ᶜNum. 11:25; Joel 2:28

19:23
ᵃ1 Sam. 10:10

19:24 ᵃIs. 20:2
ᵇMic. 1:8
ᶜ1 Sam. 10:10–12

20:3
ᵃ1 Sam. 27:1; 2 Kin. 2:6

20:5
ᵃNum. 10:10; 28:11–15
ᵇ1 Sam. 19:2, 3

20:6
ᵃ1 Sam. 16:4; 17:12; John 7:42

20:7
ᵃDeut. 1:23; 2 Sam. 17:4
ᵇ1 Sam. 25:17; Esth. 7:7

20:8 ᵃJosh. 2:14
ᵇ1 Sam. 18:3; 20:16; 23:18

LORD with you. Nevertheless, ᶜif there is iniquity in me, kill me yourself, for why should you bring me to your father?"

⁹But Jonathan said, "Far be it from you! For if I knew certainly that evil was determined by my father to come upon you, then would I not tell you?"

¹⁰Then David said to Jonathan, "Who will tell me, or what *if* your father answers you roughly?"

¹¹And Jonathan said to David, "Come, let us go out into the field." So both of them went out into the field. ¹²Then Jonathan said to David: "The LORD God of Israel *is witness!* When I have ¹sounded out my father sometime tomorrow, *or* the third *day,* and indeed *there is* good toward David, and I do not send to you and tell you, ¹³may ᵃthe LORD do so and much more to Jonathan. But if it pleases my father *to do* you evil, then I will report it to you and send you away, that you may go in safety. And ᵇthe LORD be with you as He has ᶜbeen with my father. ¹⁴And you shall not only show me the kindness of the LORD while I still live, that I may not die; ¹⁵but ᵃyou shall not ¹cut off your kindness from my ²house forever, no, not when the LORD has cut off every one of the enemies of David from the face of the earth." ¹⁶So Jonathan made *a covenant* with the ¹house of David, *saying,* ᵃ"Let the LORD require *it* at the hand of David's enemies."

¹⁷Now Jonathan again caused David to vow, because he loved him; ᵃfor he loved him as he loved his own soul. ¹⁸Then Jonathan said to David, ᵃ"Tomorrow *is* the New Moon; and you will be missed, because your seat will be empty. ¹⁹And *when* you have stayed three days, go down quickly and come to ᵃthe place where you hid on the day of the deed; and remain by the stone Ezel. ²⁰Then I will shoot three arrows to the side, as though I shot at a target; ²¹and there I will send a lad, *saying,* 'Go, find the arrows.' If I expressly say to the lad, 'Look, the arrows *are* on this side of you; get them and come'—then, ᵃas the LORD lives, *there is* safety for you and no harm. ²²But if I say thus to the young man, 'Look, the arrows *are* beyond you'—go your way, for the LORD has sent you away. ²³And as for ᵃthe matter which you and I have spoken of, indeed the LORD *be* between you and me forever."

²⁴Then David hid in the field. And when the New Moon had come, the king sat down to eat the feast. ²⁵Now the king sat on his seat, as at other times, on a seat by the wall. And ¹Jonathan arose, and Abner sat by Saul's side, but David's place was empty. ²⁶Nevertheless Saul did not say anything that day, for he thought, "Something has happened to him; he *is* unclean, surely he *is* ᵃunclean." ²⁷And it happened the next day, the second *day* of the month, that David's place was empty. And Saul said to Jonathan his son, "Why has the son of Jesse not come to eat, either yesterday or today?"

²⁸So Jonathan ᵃanswered Saul, "David earnestly asked *permission* of me *to go* to Bethlehem. ²⁹And he said, 'Please let me go, for our family has a sacrifice in the city, and my brother has commanded me *to be there.* And now, if I have found favor in your eyes, please let me get away and see my brothers.' Therefore he has not come to the king's table."

³⁰Then Saul's anger was aroused against Jonathan, and he

20:8
ᶜ2 Sam. 14:32

20:13 ᵃRuth 1:17;
1 Sam. 3:17
ᵇ Josh. 1:5;
1 Sam. 17:37;
18:12; 1 Chr. 22:11,
16 ᶜ1 Sam. 10:7

20:15
ᵃ1 Sam. 24:21;
2 Sam. 9:1, 3,
7; 21:7

20:16
ᵃDeut. 23:21;
1 Sam. 25:22;
31:2; 2 Sam. 4:7;
21:8

20:17
ᵃ1 Sam. 18:1

20:18
ᵃ1 Sam. 20:5, 24

20:19
ᵃ1 Sam. 19:2

20:21 ᵃJer. 4:2

20:23
ᵃ1 Sam. 20:14, 15

20:26
ᵃLev. 7:20, 21;
15:5

20:28
ᵃ1 Sam. 20:6

20:12 ¹*searched out*   **20:15** ¹*stop being kind*   ²*family*   **20:16** ¹*family*
20:25 ¹So with MT, Syr., Tg., Vg.; LXX *he sat across from Jonathan*

said to him, "You son of a perverse, rebellious *woman!* Do I not know that you have chosen the son of Jesse to your own shame and to the shame of your mother's nakedness? ³¹For as long as the son of Jesse lives on the earth, you shall not be established, nor your kingdom. Now therefore, send and bring him to me, for he ¹shall surely die."

³²And Jonathan answered Saul his father, and said to him, ᵃ"Why should he be killed? What has he done?" ³³Then Saul ᵃcast a spear at him to ¹kill him, ᵇby which Jonathan knew that it was determined by his father to kill David.

³⁴So Jonathan arose from the table in fierce anger, and ate no food the second day of the month, for he was grieved for David, because his father had treated him shamefully.

³⁵And so it was, in the morning, that Jonathan went out into the field at the time appointed with David, and a little lad *was* with him. ³⁶Then he said to his lad, "Now run, find the arrows which I shoot." As the lad ran, he shot an arrow beyond him. ³⁷When the lad had come to the place where the arrow was which Jonathan had shot, Jonathan cried out after the lad and said, "*Is* not the arrow beyond you?" ³⁸And Jonathan cried out after the lad, "Make haste, hurry, do not delay!" So Jonathan's lad gathered up the arrows and came back to his master. ³⁹But the lad did not know anything. Only Jonathan and David knew of the matter. ⁴⁰Then Jonathan gave his ¹weapons to his lad, and said to him, "Go, carry *them* to the city."

⁴¹As soon as the lad had gone, David arose from *a place* toward the south, fell on his face to the ground, and bowed down three times. And they kissed one another; and they wept together, but David more so. ⁴²Then Jonathan said to David, ᵃ"Go in peace, since we have both sworn in the name of the LORD, saying, 'May the LORD be between you and me, and between your descendants and my descendants, forever.'" So he arose and departed, and Jonathan went into the city.

DAVID AND THE HOLY BREAD

21 Now David came to Nob, to Ahimelech the priest. And ᵃAhimelech was ᵇafraid when he met David, and said to him, "Why *are* you alone, and no one is with you?"

²So David said to Ahimelech the priest, "The king has ordered me on some business, and said to me, 'Do not let anyone know anything about the business on which I send you, or what I have commanded you.' And I have directed *my* young men to such and such a place. ³Now therefore, what have you on hand? Give *me* five *loaves of* bread in my hand, or whatever can be found."

⁴And the priest answered David and said, "*There is* no ¹common bread on hand; but there is ᵃholy² bread, ᵇif the young men have at least kept themselves from women."

⁵Then David answered the priest, and said to him, "Truly, women *have been* kept from us about three days since I came out. And ¹the ᵃvessels of the young men are holy, and *the bread is* in effect common, even though it was consecrated ᵇin the vessel this day."

20:32 ᵃGen. 31:36; 1 Sam. 19:5; [Prov. 31:9]; Matt. 27:23; Luke 23:22

20:33 ᵃ1 Sam. 18:11; 19:10 ᵇ1 Sam. 20:7

20:42 ᵃ1 Sam. 1:17

21:1 ᵃ1 Sam. 14:3; Mark 2:26 ᵇ1 Sam. 16:4

21:4 ᵃEx. 25:30; Lev. 24:5–9; Matt. 12:4 ᵇEx. 19:15

21:5 ᵃEx. 19:14, 15; 1 Thess. 4:4 ᵇLev. 8:26

20:31 ¹Lit. *is a son of death*   **20:33** ¹*strike him down*   **20:40** ¹*equipment*
21:4 ¹*ordinary*   ²*consecrated*   **21:5** ¹The young men are ceremonially undefiled

6So the priest ^agave him holy *bread;* for there was no bread there but the showbread ^bwhich had been taken from before the LORD, in order to put hot bread *in its place* on the day when it was taken away.

7Now a certain man of the servants of Saul *was* there that day, detained before the LORD. And his name *was* ^aDoeg, an Edomite, the chief of the herdsmen who *belonged* to Saul.

8And David said to Ahimelech, "Is there not here on hand a spear or a sword? For I have brought neither my sword nor my weapons with me, because the king's business required haste."

9So the priest said, "The sword of Goliath the Philistine, whom you killed in ^athe Valley of Elah, ^bthere it is, wrapped in a cloth behind the ephod. If you will take that, take *it.* For *there is* no other except that one here."

And David said, "*There is* none like it; give it to me."

DAVID FLEES TO GATH

10Then David arose and fled that day from before Saul, and went to Achish the king of Gath. 11And ^athe servants of Achish said to him, "*Is* this not David the king of the land? Did they not sing of him to one another in dances, saying:

^b'Saul has slain his thousands,
And David his ten thousands'?"

12Now David ^atook these words [1]to heart, and was very much afraid of Achish the king of Gath. 13So ^ahe changed his behavior before them, pretended [1]madness in their hands, [2]scratched on the doors of the gate, and let his saliva fall down on his beard. 14Then Achish said to his servants, "Look, you see the man is insane. Why have you brought him to me? 15Have I need of madmen, that you have brought this *fellow* to play the madman in my presence? Shall this *fellow* come into my house?"

DAVID'S FOUR HUNDRED MEN
(1 Chr. 12:16–18)

22 David therefore departed from there and ^aescaped ^bto the cave of Adullam. So when his brothers and all his father's house heard *it,* they went down there to him. 2aAnd everyone *who was* in distress, everyone who *was* in debt, and everyone *who was* [1]discontented gathered to him. So he became captain over them. And there were about ^bfour hundred men with him.

3Then David went from there to Mizpah of ^aMoab; and he said to the king of Moab, "Please let my father and mother come here with you, till I know what God will do for me." 4So he brought them before the king of Moab, and they dwelt with him all the time that David was in the stronghold.

5Now the prophet ^aGad said to David, "Do not stay in the stronghold; depart, and go to the land of Judah." So David departed and went into the forest of Hereth.

SAUL MURDERS THE PRIESTS

6When Saul heard that David and the men who *were* with him had been discovered—now Saul was staying in ^aGibeah

Cross references:
21:6 ^aMatt. 12:3, 4; Mark 2:25, 26; Luke 6:3, 4 ^bLev. 24:8, 9
21:7 ^a1 Sam. 14:47; 22:9; Ps. 52:title
21:9 ^a1 Sam. 17:2, 50 ^b1 Sam. 31:10
21:11 ^aPs. 56:title ^b1 Sam. 18:6–8; 29:5
21:12 ^aLuke 2:19
21:13 ^aPs. 34:title
22:1 ^aPs. 57:title; 142:title ^bJosh. 12:15; 15:35; 2 Sam. 23:13
22:2 ^aJudg. 11:3 ^b1 Sam. 25:13
22:3 ^a2 Sam. 8:2
22:5 ^a2 Sam. 24:11; 1 Chr. 21:9; 29:29; 2 Chr. 29:25
22:6 ^a1 Sam. 15:34

under a tamarisk tree in Ramah, with his spear in his hand, and all his servants standing about him— [7]then Saul said to his servants who stood about him, "Hear now, you Benjamites! Will the son of Jesse [a]give every one of you fields and vineyards, *and* make you all captains of thousands and captains of hundreds? [8]All of you have conspired against me, and *there is* no one who reveals to me that [a]my son has made a covenant with the son of Jesse; and *there is* not one of you who is sorry for me or reveals to me that my son has stirred up my servant against me, to lie in wait, as *it is* this day."

[9]Then answered [a]Doeg the Edomite, who was set over the servants of Saul, and said, "I saw the son of Jesse going to Nob, to [b]Ahimelech the son of [c]Ahitub. [10a]And he inquired of the LORD for him, [b]gave him provisions, and gave him the sword of Goliath the Philistine."

[11]So the king sent to call Ahimelech the priest, the son of Ahitub, and all his father's house, the priests who *were* in Nob. And they all came to the king. [12]And Saul said, "Hear now, son of Ahitub!"

He answered, "Here I am, my lord."

[13]Then Saul said to him, "Why have you conspired against me, you and the son of Jesse, in that you have given him bread and a sword, and have inquired of God for him, that he should rise against me, to lie in wait, as it is this day?"

[14]So Ahimelech answered the king and said, "And who among all your servants *is as* [a]faithful as David, who is the king's son-in-law, who goes at your bidding, and is honorable in your house? [15]Did I then begin to inquire of God for him? Far be it from me! Let not the king impute anything to his servant, *or* to any in the house of my father. For your servant knew nothing of all this, little or much."

[16]And the king said, "You shall surely die, Ahimelech, you and all [a]your father's house!" [17]Then the king said to the guards who stood about him, "Turn and kill the priests of the LORD, because their hand also *is* with David, and because they knew when he fled and did not tell it to me." But the servants of the king [a]would not lift their hands to strike the priests of the LORD. [18]And the king said to Doeg, "You turn and kill the priests!" So Doeg the Edomite turned and [1]struck the priests, and [a]killed on that day eighty-five men who wore a linen ephod. [19a]Also Nob, the city of the priests, he struck with the edge of the sword, both men and women, children and nursing infants, oxen and donkeys and sheep—with the edge of the sword.

[20a]Now one of the sons of Ahimelech the son of Ahitub, named Abiathar, [b]escaped and fled after David. [21]And Abiathar told David that Saul had killed the LORD's priests. [22]So David said to Abiathar, "I knew that day, when Doeg the Edomite *was* there, that he would surely tell Saul. I have caused *the death* of all the persons of your father's [1]house. [23]Stay with me; do not fear. [a]For he who seeks my life seeks your life, but with me you *shall be* safe."

DAVID SAVES THE CITY OF KEILAH

23 Then they told David, saying, "Look, the Philistines are fighting against [a]Keilah, and they are robbing the threshing floors."

22:7
[a]1 Sam. 8:14

22:8
[a]1 Sam. 18:3;
20:16, 30

22:9
[a]1 Sam. 21:7;
22:22;
Ps. 52:title
[b]1 Sam. 21:1
[c]1 Sam. 14:3

22:10
[a]Num. 27:21;
1 Sam. 10:22
[b]1 Sam. 21:6, 9

22:14
[a]1 Sam. 19:4, 5;
20:32; 24:11

22:16
[a]Deut. 24:16

22:17 [a]Ex. 1:17

22:18
[a]1 Sam. 2:31

22:19
[a]Josh. 21:1–45;
1 Sam. 22:9, 11

22:20
[a]1 Sam. 23:6, 9;
30:7; 1 Kin. 2:26,
27 [b]1 Sam. 2:33

22:23
[a]1 Kin. 2:26

23:1
[a]Josh. 15:44;
Neh. 3:17, 18

22:18 [1]*attacked*   22:22 [1]*family*

2Therefore David ainquired of the LORD, saying, "Shall I go and 1attack these Philistines?"

And the LORD said to David, "Go and attack the Philistines, and save Keilah."

3But David's men said to him, "Look, we are afraid here in Judah. How much more then if we go to Keilah against the armies of the Philistines?" 4Then David inquired of the LORD once again.

And the LORD answered him and said, "Arise, go down to Keilah. For I will deliver the Philistines into your hand." 5And David and his men went to Keilah and afought with the Philistines, struck them with a mighty blow, and took away their livestock. So David saved the inhabitants of Keilah.

6Now it happened, when Abiathar the son of Ahimelech afled to David at Keilah, *that* he went down *with* an ephod in his hand.

7And Saul was told that David had gone to Keilah. So Saul said, "God has delivered him into my hand, for he has shut himself in by entering a town that has gates and bars." 8Then Saul called all the people together for war, to go down to Keilah to besiege David and his men.

9When David knew that Saul plotted evil against him, ahe said to Abiathar the priest, "Bring the ephod here." 10Then David said, "O LORD God of Israel, Your servant has certainly heard that Saul seeks to come to Keilah ato destroy the city for my sake. 11Will the men of Keilah deliver me into his hand? Will Saul come down, as Your servant has heard? O LORD God of Israel, I pray, tell Your servant."

And the LORD said, "He will come down."

12Then David said, "Will the men of Keilah 1deliver me and my men into the hand of Saul?"

And the LORD said, "They will deliver *you*."

13So David and his men, aabout six hundred, arose and departed from Keilah and went wherever they could go. Then it was told Saul that David had escaped from Keilah; so he halted the expedition.

DAVID IN WILDERNESS STRONGHOLDS

14And David stayed in strongholds in the wilderness, and remained in athe mountains in the Wilderness of bZiph. Saul csought him every day, but God did not deliver him into his hand. 15So David saw that Saul had come out to seek his life. And David *was* in the Wilderness of Ziph 1in a forest. 16Then Jonathan, Saul's son, arose and went to David in the woods and 1strengthened his hand in God. 17And he said to him, a"Do not fear, for the hand of Saul my father shall not find you. You shall be king over Israel, and I shall be next to you. bEven my father Saul knows that." 18So the two of them amade a covenant before the LORD. And David stayed in the woods, and Jonathan went to his own house.

19Then the Ziphites acame up to Saul at Gibeah, saying, "Is David not hiding with us in strongholds in the woods, in the hill of Hachilah, which *is* on the south of Jeshimon? 20Now therefore, O king, come down according to all the desire of your soul to come down; and aour part *shall be* to deliver him into the king's hand."

23:2
a1 Sam. 22:10;
23:4, 6, 9;
28:6; 30:8;
2 Sam. 5:19, 23

23:5
a1 Sam. 19:8;
2 Sam. 5:20

23:6
a1 Sam. 22:20

23:9
aNum. 27:21;
1 Sam. 23:6;
30:7

23:10
a1 Sam. 22:19

23:13
a1 Sam. 22:2;
25:13

23:14 aPs. 11:1
bJosh. 15:55;
2 Chr. 11:8
cPs. 32:7; 54:3, 4

23:17
a[Ps. 27:1–3;
Heb. 13:6]
b1 Sam. 20:31;
24:20

23:18
a1 Sam. 18:3;
20:12–17, 42;
2 Sam. 9:1; 21:7

23:19
a1 Sam. 26:1;
Ps. 54:title

23:20 aPs. 54:3

23:2 1Lit. *strike* 23:12 1Lit. *shut up* 23:15 1Or *in Horesh*
23:16 1*encouraged him*

21And Saul said, "Blessed *are* you of the LORD, for you have compassion on me. 22Please go and find out for sure, and see the place where his hideout is, *and* who has seen him there. For I am told he is very crafty. 23See therefore, and take knowledge of all the lurking places where he hides; and come back to me with certainty, and I will go with you. And it shall be, if he is in the land, that I will search for him throughout all the ¹clans of Judah."

24So they arose and went to Ziph before Saul. But David and his men *were* in the Wilderness ᵃof Maon, in the plain on the south of Jeshimon. 25When Saul and his men went to seek *him,* they told David. Therefore he went down ¹to the rock, and stayed in the Wilderness of Maon. And when Saul heard *that,* he pursued David in the Wilderness of Maon. 26Then Saul went on one side of the mountain, and David and his men on the other side of the mountain. ᵃSo David made haste to get away from Saul, for Saul and his men ᵇwere encircling David and his men to take them.

27ᵃBut a messenger came to Saul, saying, "Hurry and come, for the Philistines have invaded the land!" 28Therefore Saul returned from pursuing David, and went against the Philistines; so they called that place ¹the Rock of Escape. 29Then David went up from there and dwelt in strongholds at ᵃEn Gedi.

DAVID SPARES SAUL

24 Now it happened, ᵃwhen Saul had returned from following the Philistines, that it was told him, saying, "Take note! David *is* in the Wilderness of En Gedi." 2Then Saul took three thousand chosen men from all Israel, and ᵃwent to seek David and his men on the Rocks of the Wild Goats. 3So he came to the sheepfolds by the road, where there *was* a cave; and ᵃSaul went in to ᵇattend to his needs. (ᶜDavid and his men were staying in the recesses of the cave.) 4ᵃThen the men of David said to him, "This is the day of which the LORD said to you, 'Behold, I will deliver your enemy into your hand, that you may do to him as it seems good to you.'" And David arose and secretly cut off a corner of Saul's robe. 5Now it happened afterward that ᵃDavid's heart troubled him because he had cut Saul's robe. 6And he said to his men, ᵃ"The LORD forbid that I should do this thing to my master, the LORD's anointed, to stretch out my hand against him, seeing he *is* the anointed of the LORD." 7So David ᵃrestrained his servants with *these* words, and did not allow them to rise against Saul. And Saul got up from the cave and went on *his* way.

8David also arose afterward, went out of the cave, and called out to Saul, saying, "My lord the king!" And when Saul looked behind him, David stooped with his face to the earth, and bowed down. 9And David said to Saul: ᵃ"Why do you listen to the words of men who say, 'Indeed David seeks your harm'? 10Look, this day your eyes have seen that the LORD delivered you today into my hand in the cave, and *someone* urged *me* to kill you. But *my eye* spared you, and I said, 'I will not stretch out my hand against my lord, for he *is* the LORD's

23:24
ᵃJosh. 15:55;
1 Sam. 25:2

23:26 ᵃPs. 31:22
ᵇPs. 17:9

23:27
ᵃ2 Kin. 19:9

23:29
ᵃJosh. 15:62;
2 Chr. 20:2

24:1
ᵃ1 Sam. 23:19,
28, 29

24:2
ᵃ1 Sam. 26:2;
Ps. 38:12

24:3
ᵃ1 Sam. 24:10
ᵇJudg. 3:24
ᶜPs. 57:title;
142:title

24:4
ᵃ1 Sam. 26:8–11

24:5
ᵃ2 Sam. 24:10

24:6
ᵃ1 Sam. 26:11

24:7 ᵃPs. 7:4;
[Matt. 5:44;
Rom. 12:17, 19]

24:9 ᵃPs. 141:6;
[Prov. 16:28;
17:9]

23:23 ¹Lit. *thousands*   23:25 ¹Or *from the rock*   23:28 ¹Heb. *Sela Hammahlekoth*

anointed.' ¹¹Moreover, my father, see! Yes, see the corner of your robe in my hand! For in that I cut off the corner of your robe, and did not kill you, know and see that *there is* ᵃneither evil nor rebellion in my hand, and I have not sinned against you. Yet you ᵇhunt my life to take it. ¹²ᵃLet the LORD judge between you and me, and let the LORD avenge me on you. But my hand shall not be against you. ¹³As the proverb of the ancients says, ᵃ'Wickedness proceeds from the wicked.' But my hand shall not be against you. ¹⁴After whom has the king of Israel come out? Whom do you pursue? ᵃA dead dog? ᵇA flea? ¹⁵ᵃTherefore let the LORD be judge, and judge between you and me, and ᵇsee and ᶜplead my case, and deliver me out of your hand."

¹⁶So it was, when David had finished speaking these words to Saul, that Saul said, ᵃ"Is this your voice, my son David?" And Saul lifted up his voice and wept. ¹⁷ᵃThen he said to David: "You *are* ᵇmore righteous than I; for ᶜyou have rewarded me with good, whereas I have rewarded you with evil. ¹⁸And you have shown this day how you have dealt well with me; for when ᵃthe LORD delivered me into your hand, you did not kill me. ¹⁹For if a man finds his enemy, will he let him get away safely? Therefore may the LORD reward you with good for what you have done to me this day. ²⁰And now ᵃI know indeed that you shall surely be king, and that the kingdom of Israel shall be established in your hand. ²¹ᵃTherefore swear now to me by the LORD ᵇthat you will not cut off my descendants after me, and that you will not destroy my name from my father's house."

²²So David swore to Saul. And Saul went home, but David and his men went up to ᵃthe stronghold.

DEATH OF SAMUEL

25 Then ᵃSamuel died; and the Israelites gathered together and ᵇlamented for him, and buried him at his home in Ramah. And David arose and went down ᶜto the Wilderness of ¹Paran.

DAVID AND THE WIFE OF NABAL

²Now *there was* a man ᵃin Maon whose business *was* in ᵇCarmel, and the man *was* very rich. He had three thousand sheep and a thousand goats. And he was shearing his sheep in Carmel. ³The name of the man *was* Nabal, and the name of his wife Abigail. And *she was* a woman of good understanding and beautiful appearance; but the man *was* harsh and evil in *his* doings. He *was of the house of* ᵃCaleb.

⁴When David heard in the wilderness that Nabal was ᵃshearing his sheep, ⁵David sent ten young men; and David said to the young men, "Go up to Carmel, go to Nabal, and greet him in my name. ⁶And thus you shall say to him who lives *in prosperity:* ᵃ'Peace *be* to you, peace to your house, and peace to all that you have! ⁷Now I have heard that you have shearers. Your shepherds were with us, and we did not hurt them, ᵃnor was there anything missing from them all the while they were in Carmel. ⁸Ask your young men, and they will tell you. Therefore ¹let *my* young men find favor in your

24:11 ᵃJudg. 11:27; Ps. 7:3; 35:7 ᵇ1 Sam. 26:20
24:12 ᵃGen. 16:5; Judg. 11:27; 1 Sam. 26:10–23; Job 5:8
24:13 ᵃ[Matt. 7:16–20]
24:14 ᵃ1 Sam. 17:43; 2 Sam. 9:8 ᵇ1 Sam. 26:20
24:15 ᵃ1 Sam. 24:12 ᵇ2 Chr. 24:22 ᶜPs. 35:1; 43:1; 119:154; Mic. 7:9
24:16 ᵃ1 Sam. 26:17
24:17 ᵃ1 Sam. 26:21 ᵇGen. 38:26 ᶜ[Matt. 5:44]
24:18 ᵃ1 Sam. 26:23
24:20 ᵃ1 Sam. 23:17
24:21 ᵃGen. 21:23; 1 Sam. 20:14–17 ᵇ2 Sam. 21:6–8
24:22 ᵃ1 Sam. 23:29
25:1 ᵃ1 Sam. 28:3 ᵇNum. 20:29; Deut. 34:8 ᶜGen. 21:21; Num. 10:12; 13:3
25:2 ᵃ1 Sam. 23:24 ᵇJosh. 15:55
25:3 ᵃJosh. 15:13; 1 Sam. 30:14
25:4 ᵃGen. 38:13; 2 Sam. 13:23
25:6 ᵃJudg. 19:20; 1 Chr. 12:18; Ps. 122:7; Luke 10:5
25:7 ᵃ1 Sam. 25:15, 21

25:1 ¹So with MT, Syr., Tg., Vg.; LXX *Maon* 25:8 ¹*be gracious to the young men*

eyes, for we come on ᵃa feast day. Please give whatever comes to your hand to your servants and to your son David.'"

⁹So when David's young men came, they spoke to Nabal according to all these words in the name of David, and waited.

¹⁰Then Nabal answered David's servants, and said, ᵃ"Who *is* David, and who *is* the son of Jesse? There are many servants nowadays who break away each one from his master. ¹¹ᵃShall I then take my bread and my water and my ¹meat that I have killed for my shearers, and give *it* to men when I do not know where they *are* from?"

¹²So David's young men turned on their heels and went back; and they came and told him all these words. ¹³Then David said to his men, "Every man gird on his sword." So every man girded on his sword, and David also girded on his sword. And about four hundred men went with David, and two hundred ᵃstayed with the supplies.

¹⁴Now one of the young men told Abigail, Nabal's wife, saying, "Look, David sent messengers from the wilderness to greet our master; and he ¹reviled them. ¹⁵But the men *were* very good to us, and ᵃwe were not hurt, nor did we miss anything as long as we accompanied them, when we were in the fields. ¹⁶They were ᵃa wall to us both by night and day, all the time we were with them keeping the sheep. ¹⁷Now therefore, know and consider what you will do, for ᵃharm is determined against our master and against all his household. For he *is* such a ᵇscoundrel¹ that *one* cannot speak to him."

¹⁸Then Abigail made haste and ᵃtook two hundred *loaves* of bread, two skins of wine, five sheep already dressed, five seahs of roasted *grain,* one hundred clusters of raisins, and two hundred cakes of figs, and loaded *them* on donkeys. ¹⁹And she said to her servants, ᵃ"Go on before me; see, I am coming after you." But she did not tell her husband Nabal.

²⁰So it was, *as* she rode on the donkey, that she went down under cover of the hill; and there were David and his men, coming down toward her, and she met them. ²¹Now David had said, "Surely in vain I have protected all that this *fellow* has in the wilderness, so that nothing was missed of all that *belongs* to him. And he has ᵃrepaid me evil for good. ²²ᵃMay God do so, and more also, to the enemies of David, if I ᵇleave ᶜone male of all who *belong* to him by morning light."

²³Now when Abigail saw David, she ᵃdismounted quickly from the donkey, fell on her face before David, and bowed down to the ground. ²⁴So she fell at his feet and said: "On me, my lord, *on* me *let* this iniquity *be!* And please let your maidservant ¹speak in your ears, and hear the words of your maidservant. ²⁵Please, let not my lord ¹regard this scoundrel Nabal. For as his name *is,* so *is* he: ²Nabal *is* his name, and folly *is* with him! But I, your maidservant, did not see the young men of my lord whom you sent. ²⁶Now therefore, my lord, ᵃ*as* the LORD lives and *as* your soul lives, since the LORD has ᵇheld you back from coming to bloodshed and from ᶜavenging¹ yourself with your own hand, now then, ᵈlet your enemies and those who seek harm for my lord be as Nabal. ²⁷And now ᵃthis present which your maidservant has brought to my lord,

25:8
ᵃNeh. 8:10–12; Esth. 8:17; 9:19, 22

25:10
ᵃJudg. 9:28

25:11
ᵃJudg. 8:6, 15

25:13
ᵃ1 Sam. 30:24

25:15
ᵃ1 Sam. 25:7, 21

25:16 ᵃEx. 14:22; Job 1:10

25:17
ᵃ1 Sam. 20:7
ᵇDeut. 13:13; Judg. 19:22

25:18
ᵃGen. 32:13; [Prov. 18:16; 21:14]

25:19
ᵃGen. 32:16, 20

25:21
ᵃ1 Sam. 24:17; Ps. 109:5; [Prov. 17:13]

25:22
ᵃRuth 1:17; 1 Sam. 3:17; 20:13, 16
ᵇ1 Sam. 25:34
ᶜ1 Kin. 14:10; 21:21; 2 Kin. 9:8

25:23
ᵃJosh. 15:18; Judg. 1:14

25:26
ᵃ2 Kin. 2:2
ᵇGen. 20:6; 1 Sam. 25:33
ᶜ[Rom. 12:19]
ᵈ2 Sam. 18:32

25:27
ᵃGen. 33:11; 1 Sam. 30:26; 2 Kin. 5:15

25:11 ¹Lit. *slaughter*   25:14 ¹*scolded* or *scorned at*   25:17 ¹Lit. *son of Belial*   25:24 ¹*speak to you*   25:25 ¹*pay attention to*   ²Lit. *Fool*   25:26 ¹Lit. *saving yourself*

let it be given to the young men who follow my lord. [28]Please forgive the trespass of your maidservant. For [a]the LORD will certainly make for my lord an enduring house, because my lord [b]fights the battles of the LORD, [c]and evil is not found in you throughout your days. [29]Yet a man has risen to pursue you and seek your life, but the life of my lord shall be [a]bound in the bundle of the living with the LORD your God; and the lives of your enemies He shall [b]sling out, *as from* the pocket of a sling. [30]And it shall come to pass, when the LORD has done for my lord according to all the good that He has spoken concerning you, and has appointed you [a]ruler over Israel, [31]that this will be no grief to you, nor offense of heart to my lord, either that you have shed blood without cause, or that my lord has avenged himself. But when the LORD has dealt well with my lord, then remember your maidservant."

[32]Then David said to Abigail: [a]"Blessed *is* the LORD God of Israel, who sent you this day to meet me! [33]And blessed *is* your advice and blessed *are* you, because you have [a]kept me this day from coming to bloodshed and from avenging myself with my own hand. [34]For indeed, *as* the LORD God of Israel lives, who has [a]kept me back from hurting you, unless you had hurried and come to meet me, surely [b]by morning light no males would have been left to Nabal!" [35]So David received from her hand what she had brought him, and said to her, [a]"Go up in peace to your house. See, I have heeded your voice and [b]respected your person."

[36]Now Abigail went to Nabal, and there he was, [a]holding a feast in his house, like the feast of a king. And Nabal's heart *was* merry within him, for he *was* very drunk; therefore she told him nothing, little or much, until morning light. [37]So it was, in the morning, when the wine had gone from Nabal, and his wife had told him these things, that his heart died within him, and he became *like* a stone. [38]Then it happened, *after* about ten days, that the LORD [a]struck Nabal, and he died.

[39]So when David heard that Nabal was dead, he said, [a]"Blessed *be* the LORD, who has [b]pleaded the cause of my reproach from the hand of Nabal, and has [c]kept His servant from evil! For the LORD has [d]returned the wickedness of Nabal on his own head."

And David sent and proposed to Abigail, to take her as his wife. [40]When the servants of David had come to Abigail at Carmel, they spoke to her saying, "David sent us to you, to ask you to become his wife."

[41]Then she arose, bowed her face to the earth, and said, "Here is your maidservant, a servant to [a]wash the feet of the servants of my lord." [42]So Abigail rose in haste and rode on a donkey, [1]attended by five of her maidens; and she followed the messengers of David, and became his wife. [43]David also took Ahinoam [a]of Jezreel, [b]and so both of them were his wives.

[44]But Saul had given [a]Michal his daughter, David's wife, to [1]Palti the son of Laish, who *was* from [b]Gallim.

DAVID SPARES SAUL A SECOND TIME

26 Now the Ziphites came to Saul at Gibeah, saying, [a]"Is David not hiding in the hill of Hachilah, opposite Jeshimon?" [2]Then Saul arose and went down to the Wilderness of

---

25:28
[a]2 Sam. 7:11–16, 27; 1 Kin. 9:5; 1 Chr. 17:10, 25
[b]1 Sam. 18:17
[c]1 Sam. 24:11; Ps. 7:3

25:29
[a][Ps. 66:9; Col. 3:3]
[b]Jer. 10:18

25:30
[a]1 Sam. 13:14; 15:28

25:32
[a]Gen. 24:27; Ex. 18:10; 1 Kin. 1:48; Ps. 41:13; 72:18; 106:48; Luke 1:68

25:33
[a]1 Sam. 25:26

25:34
[a]1 Sam. 25:26
[b]1 Sam. 25:22

25:35
[a]1 Sam. 20:42; 2 Sam. 15:9; 2 Kin. 5:19; Luke 7:50; 8:48
[b]Gen. 19:21

25:36
[a]2 Sam. 13:28; Prov. 20:1; Is. 5:11; Dan. 5:1; [Hos. 4:11]

25:38
[a]1 Sam. 26:10; 2 Sam. 6:7; Ps. 104:29

25:39
[a]1 Sam. 25:32
[b]1 Sam. 24:15; Prov. 22:23
[c]1 Sam. 25:26, 34 [d]1 Kin. 2:44

25:41
[a][Prov. 15:33]; Luke 7:38, 44

25:43
[a]Josh. 15:56
[b]1 Sam. 27:3; 30:5

25:44
[a]1 Sam. 18:20; 2 Sam. 3:14
[b]Is. 10:30

26:1
[a]1 Sam. 23:19; Ps. 54:title

25:42 [1]Lit. *with five of her maidens at her feet*   25:44 [1]*Paltiel*, 2 Sam. 3:15

Ziph, having [a]three thousand chosen men of Israel with him, to seek David in the Wilderness of Ziph. [3]And Saul encamped in the hill of Hachilah, which *is* opposite Jeshimon, by the road. But David stayed in the wilderness, and he saw that Saul came after him into the wilderness. [4]David therefore sent out spies, and understood that Saul had indeed come.

[5]So David arose and came to the place where Saul had encamped. And David saw the place where Saul lay, and [a]Abner the son of Ner, the commander of his army. Now Saul lay within the camp, with the people encamped all around him. [6]Then David answered, and said to Ahimelech the Hittite and to Abishai [a]the son of Zeruiah, brother of [b]Joab, saying, "Who will [c]go down with me to Saul in the camp?"

And [d]Abishai said, "I will go down with you."

[7]So David and Abishai came to the people by night; and there Saul lay sleeping within the camp, with his spear stuck in the ground by his head. And Abner and the people lay all around him. [8]Then Abishai said to David, [a]"God has delivered your enemy into your hand this day. Now therefore, please, let me strike him [1]at once with the spear, right to the earth; and I will not *have to strike* him a second time!"

[9]But David said to Abishai, "Do not destroy him; [a]for who can stretch out his hand against the LORD's anointed, and be guiltless?" [10]David said furthermore, "*As* the LORD lives, [a]the LORD shall strike him, or [b]his day shall come to die, or he shall [c]go out to battle and perish. [11a]The LORD forbid that I should stretch out my hand against the LORD's anointed. But please, take the spear and the jug of water that *are* by his head, and let us go." [12]So David took the spear and the jug of water *by* Saul's head, and they got away; and no man saw or knew *it* or awoke. For they *were* all asleep, because [a]a deep sleep from the LORD had fallen on them.

[13]Now David went over to the other side, and stood on the top of a hill afar off, a great distance *being* between them. [14]And David called out to the people and to Abner the son of Ner, saying, "Do you not answer, Abner?"

Then Abner answered and said, "Who *are* you, calling out to the king?"

[15]So David said to Abner, "*Are* you not a man? And who *is* like you in Israel? Why then have you not guarded your lord the king? For one of the people came in to destroy your lord the king. [16]This thing that you have done *is* not good. *As* the LORD lives, you deserve to die, because you have not guarded your master, the LORD's anointed. And now see where the king's spear *is*, and the jug of water that *was* by his head."

[17]Then Saul knew David's voice, and said, [a]"*Is* that your voice, my son David?"

David said, "*It is* my voice, my lord, O king." [18]And he said, [a]"Why does my lord thus pursue his servant? For what have I done, or what evil *is* in my hand? [19]Now therefore, please, let my lord the king hear the words of his servant: If the LORD has [a]stirred you up against me, let Him accept an offering. But if *it is* the children of men, *may* they *be* cursed before the LORD, [b]for they have driven me out this day from sharing in the [c]inheritance of the LORD, saying, 'Go, serve other gods.' [20]So now, do not let my blood fall to the earth before the face

26:2
[a]1 Sam. 13:2;
24:2

26:5
[a]1 Sam. 14:50,
51; 17:55

26:6 [a]1 Chr. 2:16
[b]2 Sam. 2:13
[c]Judg. 7:10, 11
[d]2 Sam. 2:18, 24

26:8
[a]1 Sam. 24:4

26:9
[a]1 Sam. 24:6, 7;
2 Sam. 1:14, 16

26:10
[a][Deut. 32:35];
1 Sam. 25:26, 38;
[Luke 18:7;
Rom. 12:19;
Heb. 10:30]
[b]Gen. 47:29;
Deut. 31:14;
[Job 7:1; 14:5];
Ps. 37:13
[c]1 Sam. 31:6

26:11
[a]1 Sam. 24:6–12;
[Rom. 12:17, 19]

26:12
[a]Gen. 2:21; 15:12;
Is. 29:10

26:17
[a]1 Sam. 24:16

26:18
[a]1 Sam. 24:9,
11–14

26:19
[a]2 Sam. 16:11;
24:1 [b]Deut. 4:27,
28 [c]2 Sam. 14:16;
20:19

26:8 [1]Or *one time*

of the LORD. For the king of Israel has come out to seek ᵃa flea, as when one hunts a partridge in the mountains."

²¹Then Saul said, ᵃ"I have sinned. Return, my son David. For I will harm you no more, because my life was precious in your eyes this day. Indeed I have played the fool and erred exceedingly."

²²And David answered and said, "Here is the king's spear. Let one of the young men come over and get it. ²³ᵃMay the LORD ᵇrepay every man *for* his righteousness and his faithfulness; for the LORD delivered you into *my* hand today, but I would not stretch out my hand against the LORD's anointed. ²⁴And indeed, as your life was valued much this day in my eyes, so let my life be valued much in the eyes of the LORD, and let Him deliver me out of all tribulation."

²⁵Then Saul said to David, "*May* you *be* blessed, my son David! You shall both do great things and also still ᵃprevail."

So David went on his way, and Saul returned to his place.

DAVID ALLIED WITH THE PHILISTINES

27 And David said in his heart, "Now I shall perish someday by the hand of Saul. *There is* nothing better for me than that I should speedily escape to the land of the Philistines; and Saul will ¹despair of me, to seek me anymore in any part of Israel. So I shall escape out of his hand." ²Then David arose ᵃand went over with the six hundred men who *were* with him ᵇto Achish the son of Maoch, king of Gath. ³So David dwelt with Achish at Gath, he and his men, each man with his household, *and* David ᵃwith his two wives, Ahinoam the Jezreelitess, and Abigail the Carmelitess, Nabal's widow. ⁴And it was told Saul that David had fled to Gath; so he sought him no more.

⁵Then David said to Achish, "If I have now found favor in your eyes, let them give me a place in some town in the country, that I may dwell there. For why should your servant dwell in the royal city with you?" ⁶So Achish gave him Ziklag that day. Therefore ᵃZiklag has belonged to the kings of Judah to this day. ⁷Now ¹the time that David ᵃdwelt in the country of the Philistines was one full year and four months.

⁸And David and his men went up and raided ᵃthe Geshurites, ᵇthe ¹Girzites, and the ᶜAmalekites. For those *nations* were the inhabitants of the land from ²of old, ᵈas you go to Shur, even as far as the land of Egypt. ⁹Whenever David ¹attacked the land, he left neither man nor woman alive, but took away the sheep, the oxen, the donkeys, the camels, and the apparel, and returned and came to Achish. ¹⁰Then Achish would say, "Where have you made a raid today?" And David would say, "Against the southern *area* of Judah, or against the southern *area* of ᵃthe Jerahmeelites, or against the southern *area* of ᵇthe Kenites." ¹¹David would save neither man nor woman alive, to bring *news* to Gath, saying, "Lest they should inform on us, saying, 'Thus David did.'" And thus *was* his behavior all the time he dwelt in the country of the Philistines. ¹²So Achish believed David, saying, "He has made his people Israel utterly abhor him; therefore he will be my servant forever."

26:20
ᵃ1 Sam. 24:14

26:21 ᵃEx. 9:27;
1 Sam. 15:24,
30; 24:17;
2 Sam. 12:13

26:23
ᵃ1 Sam. 24:19;
Ps. 7:8;
18:20; 62:12
ᵇ2 Sam. 22:21

26:25
ᵃGen. 32:28;
1 Sam. 24:20

27:2
ᵃ1 Sam. 25:13
ᵇ1 Sam. 21:10;
1 Kin. 2:39

27:3
ᵃ1 Sam. 25:42, 43

27:6
ᵃJosh. 15:31;
19:5; 1 Chr. 12:1;
Neh. 11:28

27:7
ᵃ1 Sam. 29:3

27:8
ᵃJosh. 13:2, 13
ᵇJosh. 16:10;
Judg. 1:29
ᶜEx. 17:8, 16;
1 Sam. 15:7, 8
ᵈGen. 25:18;
Ex. 15:22

27:10
ᵃ1 Chr. 2:9, 25
ᵇJudg. 1:16

27:1 ¹*despair of searching for*   27:7 ¹Lit. *the number of days*   27:8 ¹Or *Gezrites*   ²*ancient times*   27:9 ¹Lit. *struck*

28 Now [a]it happened in those days that the Philistines gathered their armies together for war, to fight with Israel. And Achish said to David, "You assuredly know that you will go out with me to battle, you and your men."

[2]So David said to Achish, "Surely you know what your servant can do."

And Achish said to David, "Therefore I will make you one of my chief guardians forever."

SAUL CONSULTS A MEDIUM

(cf. Deut. 18:9–14)

[3]Now [a]Samuel had died, and all Israel had lamented for him and buried him in [b]Ramah, in his own city. And Saul had put [c]the mediums and the spiritists out of the land.

[4]Then the Philistines gathered together, and came and encamped at [a]Shunem. So Saul gathered all Israel together, and they encamped at [b]Gilboa. [5]When Saul saw the army of the Philistines, he was [a]afraid, and his heart trembled greatly. [6]And when Saul inquired of the LORD, [a]the LORD did not answer him, either by [b]dreams or [c]by Urim or by the prophets.

[7]Then Saul said to his servants, "Find me a woman who is a medium, [a]that I may go to her and inquire of her."

And his servants said to him, "In fact, *there is* a woman who is a medium at En Dor."

[8]So Saul disguised himself and put on other clothes, and he went, and two men with him; and they came to the woman by night. And [a]he said, "Please conduct a séance for me, and bring up for me the one I shall name to you."

[9]Then the woman said to him, "Look, you know what Saul has done, how he has [a]cut off the mediums and the spiritists from the land. Why then do you lay a snare for my life, to cause me to die?"

[10]And Saul swore to her by the LORD, saying, "*As* the LORD lives, no punishment shall come upon you for this thing."

[11]Then the woman said, "Whom shall I bring up for you?"

And he said, "Bring up Samuel for me."

[12]When the woman saw Samuel, she cried out with a loud voice. And the woman spoke to Saul, saying, "Why have you deceived me? For you *are* Saul!"

[13]And the king said to her, "Do not be afraid. What did you see?"

And the woman said to Saul, "I saw [a]a[1] spirit ascending out of the earth."

[14]So he said to her, "What *is* his form?"

And she said, "An old man is coming up, and he *is* covered with [a]a mantle." And Saul perceived that it *was* Samuel, and he stooped with *his* face to the ground and bowed down.

[15]Now Samuel said to Saul, "Why have you [a]disturbed me by bringing me up?"

And Saul answered, "I am deeply distressed; for the Philistines make war against me, and [b]God has departed from me and [c]does not answer me anymore, neither by prophets nor by dreams. Therefore I have called you, that you may reveal to me what I should do."

28:13 [1]Heb. *elohim*

28:1
[a]1 Sam. 29:1, 2

28:3
[a]1 Sam. 25:1
[b]1 Sam. 1:19
[c]Ex. 22:18;
Lev. 19:31; 20:27;
Deut. 18:10, 11;
1 Sam. 15:23;
28:9

28:4
[a]Josh. 19:18;
1 Sam. 28:4;
1 Kin. 1:3;
2 Kin. 4:8
[b]1 Sam. 31:1

28:5 [a]Job 18:11;
[Is. 57:20]

28:6
[a]1 Sam. 14:37;
Prov. 1:28;
Lam. 2:9
[b]Num. 12:6;
Joel 2:28
[c]Ex. 28:30;
Num. 27:21;
Deut. 33:8

28:7 [a]1 Chr. 10:13

28:8
[a]Deut. 18:10, 11;
1 Chr. 10:13;
Is. 8:19

28:9
[a]1 Sam. 28:3

28:13
[a]Ex. 22:28;
Ps. 138:1

28:14
[a]1 Sam. 15:27;
2 Kin. 2:8, 13

28:15 [a]Is. 14:9
[b]1 Sam. 16:14;
18:12
[c]1 Sam. 28:6

[16]Then Samuel said: "So why do you ask me, seeing the LORD has departed from you and has become your enemy? [17]And the LORD has done for [1]Himself [a]as He spoke by me. For the LORD has torn the kingdom out of your hand and given it to your neighbor, David. [18a]Because you did not obey the voice of the LORD nor execute His fierce wrath upon [b]Amalek, therefore the LORD has done this thing to you this day. [19]Moreover the LORD will also deliver Israel with you into the hand of the Philistines. And tomorrow you and your sons *will be* with [a]me. The LORD will also deliver the army of Israel into the hand of the Philistines."

[20]Immediately Saul fell full length on the ground, and was dreadfully afraid because of the words of Samuel. And there was no strength in him, for he had eaten no food all day or all night.

[21]And the woman came to Saul and saw that he was severely troubled, and said to him, "Look, your maidservant has obeyed your voice, and I have [a]put my life in my hands and heeded the words which you spoke to me. [22]Now therefore, please, heed also the voice of your maidservant, and let me set a piece of bread before you; and eat, that you may have strength when you go on *your* way."

[23]But he refused and said, "I will not eat."

So his servants, together with the woman, urged him; and he heeded their voice. Then he arose from the ground and sat on the bed. [24]Now the woman had a fatted calf in the house, and she hastened to kill it. And she took flour and kneaded *it*, and baked unleavened bread from it. [25]So she brought *it* before Saul and his servants, and they ate. Then they rose and went away that night.

THE PHILISTINES REJECT DAVID

29 Then [a]the Philistines gathered together all their armies [b]at Aphek, and the Israelites encamped by a fountain which *is* in Jezreel. [2]And the [a]lords of the Philistines [1]passed in review by hundreds and by thousands, but [b]David and his men passed in review at the rear with Achish. [3]Then the princes of the Philistines said, "What *are* these Hebrews *doing here?*"

And Achish said to the princes of the Philistines, "*Is* this not David, the servant of Saul king of Israel, who has been with me [a]these days, or these years? And to this day I have [b]found no fault in him since he defected *to me.*"

[4]But the princes of the Philistines were angry with him; so the princes of the Philistines said to him, [a]"Make this fellow return, that he may go back to the place which you have appointed for him, and do not let him go down with us to [b]battle, lest [c]in the battle he become our adversary. For with what could he reconcile himself to his master, if not with the heads of these [d]men? [5]*Is* this not David, [a]of whom they sang to one another in dances, saying:

[b]'Saul has slain his thousands,
And David his ten thousands'?"

[6]Then Achish called David and said to him, "Surely, *as* the LORD lives, you have been upright, and [a]your going out

---

28:17
[a]1 Sam. 15:28

28:18
[a]1 Sam. 13:9–13; 15:1–26; 1 Kin. 20:42; 1 Chr. 10:13; Jer. 48:10
[b]1 Sam. 15:3–9

28:19
[a]1 Sam. 31:1–6; Job 3:17–19

28:21
[a]Judg. 12:3; 1 Sam. 19:5; Job 13:14

29:1 [a]1 Sam. 28:1
[b]Josh. 12:18; 19:30; 1 Sam. 4:1; 1 Kin. 20:30

29:2
[a]1 Sam. 6:4; 7:7
[b]1 Sam. 28:1, 2

29:3
[a]1 Sam. 27:7
[b]1 Sam. 27:1–6; 1 Chr. 12:19, 20; Dan. 6:5

29:4
[a]1 Sam. 27:6
[b]1 Sam. 14:21
[c]1 Sam. 29:9
[d]1 Chr. 12:19, 20

29:5
[a]1 Sam. 21:11
[b]1 Sam. 18:7

29:6
[a]2 Sam. 3:25; 2 Kin. 19:27

28:17 [1]Or *him,* i.e., David   **29:2** [1]*passed on in the rear*

and your coming in with me in the army *is* good in my sight. For to this day [b]I have not found evil in you since the day of your coming to me. Nevertheless the lords do not favor you. [7]Therefore return now, and go in peace, that you may not displease the lords of the Philistines."

[8]So David said to Achish, "But what have I done? And to this day what have you found in your servant as long as I have been with you, that I may not go and fight against the enemies of my lord the king?"

[9]Then Achish answered and said to David, "I know that you *are* as good in my sight [a]as an angel of God; nevertheless [b]the princes of the Philistines have said, 'He shall not go up with us to the battle.' [10]Now therefore, rise early in the morning with your master's servants [a]who have come with [1]you. And as soon as you are up early in the morning and have light, depart."

[11]So David and his men rose early to depart in the morning, to return to the land of the Philistines. [a]And the Philistines went up to Jezreel.

DAVID'S CONFLICT WITH THE AMALEKITES

30 Now it happened, when David and his men came to [a]Ziklag, on the third day, that the [b]Amalekites had invaded the South and Ziklag, attacked Ziklag and burned it with fire, [2]and had taken captive the [a]women and those who *were* there, from small to great; they did not kill anyone, but carried *them* away and went their way. [3]So David and his men came to the city, and there it was, burned with fire; and their wives, their sons, and their daughters had been taken captive. [4]Then David and the people who *were* with him lifted up their voices and wept, until they had no more power to weep. [5]And David's two [a]wives, Ahinoam the Jezreelitess, and Abigail the widow of Nabal the Carmelite, had been taken captive. [6]Now David was greatly distressed, for [a]the people spoke of stoning him, because the soul of all the people was [1]grieved, every man for his sons and his daughters. [b]But David strengthened himself in the LORD his God.

[7a]Then David said to Abiathar the priest, Ahimelech's son, "Please bring the ephod here to me." And [b]Abiathar brought the ephod to David. [8a]So David inquired of the LORD, saying, "Shall I pursue this troop? Shall I overtake them?"

And He answered him, "Pursue, for you shall surely overtake *them* and without fail recover *all*."

[9]So David went, he and the six hundred men who *were* with him, and came to the Brook Besor, where those stayed who were left behind. [10]But David pursued, he and four hundred men; [a]for two hundred stayed *behind*, who were so weary that they could not cross the Brook Besor.

[11]Then they found an Egyptian in the field, and brought him to David; and they gave him bread and he ate, and they let him drink water. [12]And they gave him a piece of [a]a cake of figs and two clusters of raisins. So [b]when he had eaten, his strength came back to him; for he had eaten no bread nor drunk water for three days and three nights. [13]Then David

29:6
[b]1 Sam. 29:3

29:9
[a]2 Sam. 14:17, 20; 19:27
[b]1 Sam. 29:4

29:10
[a]1 Chr. 12:19, 22

29:11
[a]2 Sam. 4:4

30:1
[a]1 Sam. 27:6
[b]1 Sam. 15:7; 27:8

30:2
[a]1 Sam. 27:2, 3

30:5
[a]1 Sam. 25:42, 43

30:6 [a]Ex. 17:4; John 8:59
[b]1 Sam. 23:16; Is. 25:4; Hab. 3:17–19

30:7
[a]1 Sam. 23:2–9
[b]1 Sam. 23:6

30:8
[a]1 Sam. 23:2, 4; Ps. 50:15; 91:15

30:10
[a]1 Sam. 30:9, 21

30:12
[a]1 Sam. 25:18; 1 Kin. 20:7
[b]Judg. 15:19; 1 Sam. 14:27

29:10 [1]So with MT, Tg., Vg.; LXX adds *and go to the place which I have selected for you there; and set no bothersome word in your heart, for you are good before me. And rise on your way*   **30:6** [1]Lit. *bitter*

said to him, "To whom do you *belong*, and where *are* you from?"

And he said, "I *am* a young man from Egypt, servant of an Amalekite; and my master left me behind, because three days ago I fell sick. [14]We made an invasion of the southern *area* of [a]the Cherethites, in the *territory* which *belongs* to Judah, and of the southern *area* [b]of Caleb; and we burned Ziklag with fire."

[15]And David said to him, "Can you take me down to this troop?"

So he said, "Swear to me by God that you will neither kill me nor deliver me into the hands of my [a]master, and I will take you down to this troop."

[16]And when he had brought him down, there they were, spread out over all the land, [a]eating and drinking and dancing, because of all the great spoil which they had taken from the land of the Philistines and from the land of Judah. [17]Then David attacked them from twilight until the evening of the next day. Not a man of them escaped, except four hundred young men who rode on camels and fled. [18]So David recovered all that the Amalekites had carried away, and David rescued his two wives. [19]And nothing of theirs was lacking, either small or great, sons or daughters, spoil or anything which they had taken from them; [a]David recovered all. [20]Then David took all the flocks and herds they had driven before those *other* livestock, and said, "This *is* David's spoil."

[21]Now David came to the [a]two hundred men who had been so weary that they could not follow David, whom they also had made to stay at the Brook Besor. So they went out to meet David and to meet the people who *were* with him. And when David came near the people, he [1]greeted them. [22]Then all the wicked and [a]worthless[1] men of those who went with David answered and said, "Because they did not go with us, we will not give them *any* of the spoil that we have recovered, except for every man's wife and children, that they may lead *them* away and depart."

[23]But David said, "My brethren, you shall not do so with what the LORD has given us, who has preserved us and delivered into our hand the troop that came against us. [24]For who will heed you in this matter? But [a]as his part *is* who goes down to the battle, so *shall* his part *be* who stays by the supplies; they shall share alike." [25]So it was, from that day forward; he made it a statute and an ordinance for Israel to this day.

[26]Now when David came to Ziklag, he sent *some* of the [1]spoil to the elders of Judah, to his friends, saying, "Here is a present for you from the spoil of the enemies of the LORD"— [27]to those who *were* in Bethel, *those* who *were* in [a]Ramoth of the South, *those* who *were* in [b]Jattir, [28]*those* who *were* in [a]Aroer, *those* who *were* in [b]Siphmoth, *those* who *were* in [c]Eshtemoa, [29]*those* who *were* in Rachal, *those* who *were* in the cities of [a]the Jerahmeelites, *those* who *were* in the cities of the [b]Kenites, [30]*those* who *were* in [a]Hormah, *those* who *were* in [1]Chorashan, *those* who *were* in Athach, [31]*those* who *were* in [a]Hebron, and to all the places where David himself and his men were accustomed to [b]rove.

30:14
[a]2 Sam. 8:18;
1 Kin. 1:38, 44;
Ezek. 25:16;
Zeph. 2:5
[b]Josh. 14:13;
15:13

30:15
[a]Deut. 23:15

30:16
[a]1 Thess. 5:3

30:19
[a]1 Sam. 30:8

30:21
[a]1 Sam. 30:10

30:22
[a]Deut. 13:13;
Judg. 19:22

30:24
[a]Num. 31:27;
Josh. 22:8

30:27
[a]Josh. 19:8
[b]Josh. 15:48;
21:14

30:28
[a]Josh. 13:16
[b]1 Chr. 27:27
[c]Josh. 15:50

30:29
[a]1 Sam. 27:10
[b]Judg. 1:16;
1 Sam. 15:6;
27:10

30:30
[a]Num. 14:45;
21:3; Josh. 12:14;
15:30; 19:4;
Judg. 1:17

30:31
[a]Num. 13:22;
Josh. 14:13–15;
21:11–13;
2 Sam. 2:1
[b]1 Sam. 23:22

30:21 [1]*asked them concerning their welfare*   **30:22** [1]Lit. *men of Belial*
30:26 [1]*booty*   **30:30** [1]Or *Borashan*

THE TRAGIC END OF SAUL AND HIS SONS
(1 Chr. 10:1–14)

31 Now [a]the Philistines fought against Israel; and the men of Israel fled from before the Philistines, and fell slain on Mount [b]Gilboa. [2]Then the Philistines followed hard after Saul and his sons. And the Philistines killed [a]Jonathan, Abinadab, and Malchishua, Saul's sons. [3a]The battle became fierce against Saul. The archers [1]hit him, and he was severely wounded by the archers.

[4a]Then Saul said to his armorbearer, "Draw your sword, and thrust me through with it, lest [b]these uncircumcised men come and thrust me through and [1]abuse me."

But his armorbearer would not, [c]for he was greatly afraid. Therefore Saul took a sword and [d]fell on it. [5]And when his armorbearer saw that Saul was dead, he also fell on his sword, and died with him. [6]So Saul, his three sons, his armorbearer, and all his men died together that same day.

[7]And when the men of Israel who *were* on the other side of the valley, and *those* who *were* on the other side of the Jordan, saw that the men of Israel had fled and that Saul and his sons were dead, they forsook the cities and fled; and the Philistines came and dwelt in them. [8]So it happened the next day, when the Philistines came to strip the slain, that they found Saul and his three sons fallen on Mount Gilboa. [9]And they cut off his head and stripped off his armor, and sent *word* throughout the land of the Philistines, to [a]proclaim *it in* the temple of their idols and among the people. [10a]Then they put his armor in the temple of the [b]Ashtoreths, and [c]they fastened his body to the wall of [d]Beth[1] Shan.

[11a]Now when the inhabitants of Jabesh Gilead heard what the Philistines had done to Saul, [12a]all the valiant men arose and traveled all night, and took the body of Saul and the bodies of his sons from the wall of Beth Shan; and they came to Jabesh and [b]burned them there. [13]Then they took their bones and [a]buried *them* under the tamarisk tree at Jabesh, [b]and fasted seven days.

31:1
[a]1 Chr. 10:1–12
[b]1 Sam. 28:4

31:2
[a]1 Sam. 14:49;
1 Chr. 8:33

31:3 [a]2 Sam. 1:6

31:4
[a]Judg. 9:54;
1 Chr. 10:4
[b]Judg. 14:3;
1 Sam. 14:6;
17:26, 36
[c]2 Sam. 1:14
[d]2 Sam. 1:6, 10

31:9
[a]Judg. 16:23, 24;
2 Sam. 1:20

31:10
[a]1 Sam. 21:9
[b]Judg. 2:13;
1 Sam. 7:3
[c]2 Sam. 21:12
[d]Judg. 1:27

31:11
[a]1 Sam. 11:1–13

31:12
[a]1 Sam. 11:1–11;
2 Sam. 2:4–7
[b]2 Chr. 16:14;
Jer. 34:5;
Amos 6:10

31:13
[a]2 Sam. 2:4, 5;
21:12–14
[b]Gen. 50:10

31:3 [1]Lit. *found him*   31:4 [1]torture   31:10 [1]*Beth Shean*, Josh. 17:11

THE SECOND BOOK OF
SAMUEL

THE REPORT OF SAUL'S DEATH

1 Now it came to pass after the ^adeath of Saul, when David had returned from ^bthe slaughter of the Amalekites, and David had stayed two days in Ziklag, ²on the third day, behold, it happened that ^aa man came from Saul's camp ^bwith his clothes ¹torn and dust on his head. So it was, when he came to David, that he ^cfell to the ground and prostrated himself.

³And David said to him, "Where have you come from?"

So he said to him, "I have escaped from the camp of Israel."

⁴Then David said to him, ^a"How did the matter go? Please tell me."

And he answered, "The people have fled from the battle, many of the people are fallen and dead, and Saul and ^bJonathan his son are dead also."

⁵So David said to the young man who told him, "How do you know that Saul and Jonathan his son are dead?"

⁶Then the young man who told him said, "As I happened by chance *to be* on ^aMount Gilboa, there was ^bSaul, leaning on his spear; and indeed the chariots and horsemen followed hard after him. ⁷Now when he looked behind him, he saw me and called to me. And I answered, 'Here I am.' ⁸And he said to me, 'Who *are* you?' So I answered him, 'I *am* an Amalekite.' ⁹He said to me again, 'Please stand over me and kill me, for ¹anguish has come upon me, but my life still *remains* in me.' ¹⁰So I stood over him and ^akilled him, because I was sure that he could not live after he had fallen. And I took the crown that *was* on his head and the bracelet that *was* on his arm, and have brought them here to my lord."

¹¹Therefore David took hold of his own clothes and ^atore them, and *so did* all the men who *were* with him. ¹²And they ^amourned and wept and ^bfasted until evening for Saul and for Jonathan his son, for the ^cpeople of the LORD and for the house of Israel, because they had fallen by the sword.

¹³Then David said to the young man who told him, "Where *are* you from?"

And he answered, "I *am* the son of an alien, an Amalekite."

¹⁴So David said to him, "How ^awas it you were not ^bafraid to ^cput forth your hand to destroy the LORD's anointed?" ¹⁵Then ^aDavid called one of the young men and said, "Go near, *and* execute him!" And he struck him so that he died. ¹⁶So David said to him, ^a"Your blood *is* on your own head, for ^byour own mouth has testified against you, saying, 'I have killed the LORD's anointed.'"

THE SONG OF THE BOW

¹⁷Then David lamented with this lamentation over Saul and over Jonathan his son, ^{18a}and he told *them* to teach the

1:1 ^a1 Sam. 31:6
^b1 Sam. 30:1, 17, 26
1:2 ^a2 Sam. 4:10
^b1 Sam. 4:12
^c1 Sam. 25:23
1:4 ^a1 Sam. 4:16; 31:3 ^b1 Sam. 31:2
1:6 ^a1 Sam. 31:1
^b1 Sam. 31:2–4
1:10 ^aJudg. 9:54; 2 Kin. 11:12
1:11 ^a2 Sam. 3:31; 13:31
1:12 ^a2 Sam. 3:31
^b1 Sam. 31:13
^c2 Sam. 6:21
1:14 ^aNum. 12:8
^b1 Sam. 31:4
^c1 Sam. 24:6; 26:9
1:15
^a2 Sam. 4:10, 12
1:16
^a1 Sam. 26:9; 2 Sam. 3:28; 1 Kin. 2:32–37
^b2 Sam. 1:10; Luke 19:22
1:18 ^a1 Sam. 31:3

1:2 ¹To show grief   1:9 ¹agony

children of Judah *the Song of* the Bow; indeed *it is* written ᵇin the Book ¹of Jasher:

19 "The beauty of Israel is slain on your high places!
ᵃHow the mighty have fallen!
20 ᵃTell *it* not in Gath,
Proclaim *it* not in the streets of ᵇAshkelon—
Lest ᶜthe daughters of the Philistines rejoice,
Lest the daughters of ᵈthe uncircumcised triumph.

21 "O ᵃmountains of Gilboa,
ᵇLet *there be* no dew nor rain upon you,
Nor fields of offerings.
For the shield of the mighty is ¹cast away there!
The shield of Saul, not ᶜanointed with oil.
22 From the blood of the slain,
From the fat of the mighty,
ᵃThe bow of Jonathan did not turn back,
And the sword of Saul did not return empty.

23 "Saul and Jonathan *were* beloved and pleasant in their
lives,
And in their ᵃdeath they were not divided;
They were swifter than eagles,
They were ᵇstronger than lions.

24 "O daughters of Israel, weep over Saul,
Who clothed you in scarlet, with luxury;
Who put ornaments of gold on your apparel.

25 "How the mighty have fallen in the midst of the battle!
Jonathan *was* slain in your high places.
26 I am distressed for you, my brother Jonathan;
You have been very pleasant to me;
ᵃYour love to me was wonderful,
Surpassing the love of women.

27 "Howᵃ the mighty have fallen,
And the weapons of war perished!"

DAVID ANOINTED KING OF JUDAH

2 It happened after this that David ᵃinquired of the LORD, saying, "Shall I go up to any of the cities of Judah?"
And the LORD said to him, "Go up."
David said, "Where shall I go up?"
And He said, "To ᵇHebron."
²So David went up there, and his ᵃtwo wives also, Ahinoam the Jezreelitess, and Abigail the widow of Nabal the Carmelite. ³And David brought up ᵃthe men who *were* with him, every man with his household. So they dwelt in the cities of Hebron.
⁴ᵃThen the men of Judah came, and there they ᵇanointed David king over the house of Judah. And they told David, saying, ᶜ"The men of Jabesh Gilead *were the ones* who buried Saul." ⁵So David sent messengers to the men of Jabesh Gilead, and said to them, ᵃ"You *are* blessed of the LORD, for you have shown this kindness to your lord, to Saul, and have buried him. ⁶And now may ᵃthe LORD show kindness and truth to you. I also will repay you this kindness, because you have done this thing. ⁷Now therefore, let your hands be strengthened, and be

1:18 ᵇJosh. 10:13
1:19 ᵃ2 Sam. 1:27
1:20
ᵃ1 Sam. 27:2;
31:8–13; Mic. 1:10
ᵇ1 Sam. 6:17;
Jer. 25:20
ᶜEx. 15:20;
Judg. 11:34;
1 Sam. 18:6
ᵈ1 Sam. 31:4

1:21 ᵃ1 Sam. 31:1
ᵇEzek. 31:15
ᶜ1 Sam. 10:1
1:22
ᵃDeut. 32:42;
1 Sam. 18:4
1:23
ᵃ1 Sam. 31:2–4
ᵇJudg. 14:18
1:26
ᵃ1 Sam. 18:1–4;
19:2; 20:17
1:27
ᵃ2 Sam. 1:19, 25

2:1 ᵃJudg. 1:1;
1 Sam. 23:2,
4, 9; 30:7, 8
ᵇ1 Sam. 30:31;
2 Sam. 2:11;
5:1–3; 1 Kin. 2:11
2:2
ᵃ1 Sam. 25:42,
43; 30:5
2:3 ᵃ1 Sam. 27:2,
3; 30:1; 1 Chr. 12:1
2:4
ᵃ1 Sam. 30:26;
2 Sam. 2:11; 5:5;
19:14, 41–43
ᵇ1 Sam. 16:13;
2 Sam. 5:3
ᶜ1 Sam. 31:11–13
2:5 ᵃRuth 2:20;
3:10
2:6 ᵃEx. 34:6;
2 Tim. 1:16, 18

valiant; for your master Saul is dead, and also the house of Judah has anointed me king over them."

ISHBOSHETH MADE KING OF ISRAEL

8But aAbner the son of Ner, commander of Saul's army, took 1Ishbosheth the son of Saul and brought him over to bMahanaim; 9and he made him king over aGilead, over the bAshurites, over cJezreel, over Ephraim, over Benjamin, and over all Israel. 10Ishbosheth, Saul's son, *was* forty years old when he began to reign over Israel, and he reigned two years. Only the house of Judah followed David. 11And athe 1time that David was king in Hebron over the house of Judah was seven years and six months.

ISRAEL AND JUDAH AT WAR

12Now Abner the son of Ner, and the servants of Ishbosheth the son of Saul, went out from Mahanaim to aGibeon. 13And aJoab the son of Zeruiah, and the servants of David, went out and met them by bthe pool of Gibeon. So they sat down, one on one side of the pool and the other on the other side of the pool. 14Then Abner said to Joab, "Let the young men now arise and compete before us."

And Joab said, "Let them arise."

15So they arose and went over by number, twelve from Benjamin, *followers* of Ishbosheth the son of Saul, and twelve from the servants of David. 16And each one grasped his opponent by the head and *thrust* his sword in his opponent's side; so they fell down together. Therefore that place was called 1the Field of Sharp Swords, which *is* in Gibeon. 17So there was a very fierce battle that day, and Abner and the men of Israel were beaten before the servants of David.

18Now the athree sons of Zeruiah were there: Joab and Abishai and Asahel. And Asahel *was* bas fleet of foot cas a wild gazelle. 19So Asahel pursued Abner, and in going he did not turn to the right hand or to the left from following Abner.

20Then Abner looked behind him and said, "*Are* you Asahel?"

He answered, "I *am*."

21And Abner said to him, "Turn aside to your right hand or to your left, and lay hold on one of the young men and take his armor for yourself." But Asahel would not turn aside from following him. 22So Abner said again to Asahel, "Turn aside from following me. Why should I strike you to the ground? How then could I face your brother Joab?" 23However, he refused to turn aside. Therefore Abner struck him ain the stomach with the blunt end of the spear, so that the spear came out of his back; and he fell down there and died on the spot. So it was *that* as many as came to the place where Asahel fell down and died, stood bstill.

24Joab and Abishai also pursued Abner. And the sun was going down when they came to the hill of Ammah, which *is* before Giah by the road to the Wilderness of Gibeon. 25Now the children of Benjamin gathered together behind Abner and became 1a unit, and took their stand on top of a hill. 26Then Abner called to Joab and said, "Shall the sword devour

2:8
a1 Sam. 14:50;
2 Sam. 3:6
bGen. 32:2;
Josh. 21:38;
2 Sam. 17:24

2:9 aJosh. 22:9
bJudg. 1:32
c1 Sam. 29:1

2:11 a2 Sam. 5:5;
1 Kin. 2:11

2:12
aJosh. 10:2–12;
18:25

2:13
a1 Sam. 26:6;
2 Sam. 8:16;
1 Chr. 2:16; 11:6
bJer. 41:12

2:18 a1 Chr. 2:16
b1 Chr. 12:8;
Hab. 3:19
cPs. 18:33

2:23
a2 Sam. 3:27;
4:6; 20:10
b2 Sam. 20:12

2:8 1*Esh-Baal,* 1 Chr. 8:33; 9:39   **2:11** 1Lit. *number of days*   **2:16** 1Heb. *Helkath Hazzurim*   **2:25** 1*one band*

forever? Do you not know that it will be bitter in the latter end? How long will it be then until you tell the people to return from pursuing their brethren?"

27And Joab said, "*As* God lives, [1]unless [a]you had spoken, surely then by morning all the people would have given up pursuing their brethren." 28So Joab blew a trumpet; and all the people stood still and did not pursue Israel anymore, nor did they fight anymore. 29Then Abner and his men went on all that night through the plain, crossed over the Jordan, and went through all Bithron; and they came to Mahanaim.

30So Joab returned from pursuing Abner. And when he had gathered all the people together, there were missing of David's servants nineteen men and Asahel. 31But the servants of David had struck down, of Benjamin and Abner's men, three hundred and sixty men who died. 32Then they took up Asahel and buried him in his father's tomb, which *was in* [a]Bethlehem. And Joab and his men went all night, and they came to Hebron at daybreak.

3 Now there was a long [a]war between the house of Saul and the house of David. But David grew stronger and stronger, and the house of Saul grew weaker and weaker.

SONS OF DAVID

2Sons were born [a]to David in Hebron: His firstborn was Amnon [b]by Ahinoam the Jezreelitess; 3his second, [1]Chileab, by Abigail the widow of Nabal the Carmelite; the third, [a]Absalom the son of Maacah, the daughter of Talmai, king [b]of Geshur; 4the fourth, [a]Adonijah the son of Haggith; the fifth, Shephatiah the son of Abital; 5and the sixth, Ithream, by David's wife Eglah. These were born to David in Hebron.

ABNER JOINS FORCES WITH DAVID

6Now it was so, while there was war between the house of Saul and the house of David, that Abner was strengthening *his hold* on the house of Saul.

7And Saul had a concubine, whose name *was* [a]Rizpah, the daughter of Aiah. So *Ishbosheth* said to Abner, "Why have you [b]gone in to my father's concubine?"

8Then Abner became very angry at the words of Ishbosheth, and said, "*Am* I [a]a dog's head that belongs to Judah? Today I show loyalty to the house of Saul your father, to his brothers, and to his friends, and have not delivered you into the hand of David; and you charge me today with a fault concerning this woman? 9aMay God do so to Abner, and more also, if I do not do for David [b]as the Lord has sworn to him— 10to transfer the kingdom from the [1]house of Saul, and set up the throne of David over Israel and over Judah, [a]from Dan to Beersheba." 11And he could not answer Abner another word, because he feared him.

12Then Abner sent messengers on his behalf to David, saying, "Whose *is* the land?" saying *also*, "Make your covenant with me, and indeed my hand *shall be* with you to bring all Israel to you."

13And *David* said, "Good, I will make a covenant with you. But one thing I require of you: [a]you shall not see my face unless you first bring [b]Michal, Saul's daughter, when you come

2:27
[a]2 Sam. 2:14

2:32
[a]1 Sam. 20:6

3:1 [a]1 Kin. 14:30;
[Ps. 46:9]

3:2 [a]1 Chr. 3:1–4
[b]1 Sam. 25:42,
43

3:3
[a]2 Sam. 15:1–10
[b]Josh. 13:13;
1 Sam. 27:8;
2 Sam. 13:37;
14:32; 15:8

3:4 [a]1 Kin. 1:5

3:7
[a]2 Sam. 21:8–11
[b]2 Sam. 16:21

3:8
[a]Deut. 23:18;
1 Sam. 24:14;
2 Sam. 9:8; 16:9

3:9 [a]Ruth 1:17;
1 Kin. 19:2
[b]1 Sam. 15:28;
16:1, 12; 28:17;
1 Chr. 12:23

3:10 [a]Judg. 20:1;
1 Sam. 3:20;
2 Sam. 17:11;
1 Kin. 4:25

3:13 [a]Gen. 43:3
[b]1 Sam. 18:20;
19:11; 25:44;
2 Sam. 6:16

---

to see my face." ¹⁴So David sent messengers to ᵃIshbosheth, Saul's son, saying, "Give *me* my wife Michal, whom I betrothed to myself ᵇfor a hundred foreskins of the Philistines." ¹⁵And Ishbosheth sent and took her from *her* husband, from ¹Paltiel the son of Laish. ¹⁶Then her husband went along with her to ᵃBahurim, ¹weeping behind her. So Abner said to him, "Go, return!" And he returned.

¹⁷Now Abner had communicated with the elders of Israel, saying, "In time past you were seeking for David *to be* king over you. ¹⁸Now then, do *it!* ᵃFor the LORD has spoken of David, saying, 'By the hand of My servant David, ¹I will save My people Israel from the hand of the Philistines and the hand of all their enemies.'" ¹⁹And Abner also spoke in the hearing of ᵃBenjamin. Then Abner also went to speak in the hearing of David in Hebron all that seemed good to Israel and the whole house of Benjamin.

²⁰So Abner and twenty men with him came to David at Hebron. And David made a feast for Abner and the men who *were* with him. ²¹Then Abner said to David, "I will arise and go, and ᵃgather all Israel to my lord the king, that they may make a covenant with you, and that you may ᵇreign over all that your heart desires." So David sent Abner away, and he went in peace.

JOAB MURDERS ABNER

²²At that moment the servants of David and Joab came from a raid and brought much ¹spoil with them. But Abner *was* not with David in Hebron, for he had sent him away, and he had gone in peace. ²³When Joab and all the troops that *were* with him had come, they told Joab, saying, "Abner the son of Ner came to the king, and he sent him away, and he has gone in peace." ²⁴Then Joab came to the king and said, "What have you done? Look, Abner came to you; why *is* it *that* you sent him away, and he has already gone? ²⁵Surely you realize that Abner the son of Ner came to deceive you, to know ᵃyour going out and your coming in, and to know all that you are doing."

²⁶And when Joab had gone from David's presence, he sent messengers after Abner, who brought him back from the well of Sirah. But David did not know *it*. ²⁷Now when Abner had returned to Hebron, Joab ᵃtook him aside in the gate to speak with him privately, and there ¹stabbed him ᵇin the stomach, so that he died for the blood of ᶜAsahel his brother.

²⁸Afterward, when David heard *it*, he said, "My kingdom and I *are* ¹guiltless before the LORD forever of the blood of Abner the son of Ner. ²⁹ᵃLet it rest on the head of Joab and on all his father's house; and let there never fail to be in the ¹house of Joab one ᵇwho has a discharge or is a leper, who leans on a staff or falls by the sword, or who lacks bread." ³⁰So Joab and Abishai his brother killed Abner, because he had killed their brother ᵃAsahel at Gibeon in the battle.

DAVID'S MOURNING FOR ABNER

³¹Then David said to Joab and to all the people who were with him, ᵃ"Tear your clothes, ᵇgird yourselves with sackcloth,

---

3:14
ᵃ2 Sam. 2:10
ᵇ1 Sam. 18:25–27

3:16
ᵃ2 Sam. 16:5;
19:16

3:18 ᵃ2 Sam. 3:9

3:19
ᵃ1 Sam. 10:20,
21; 1 Chr. 12:29

3:21
ᵃ2 Sam. 3:10, 12
ᵇ1 Kin. 11:37

3:25
ᵃDeut. 28:6;
1 Sam. 29:6;
Is. 37:28

3:27
ᵃ2 Sam. 20:9,
10; 1 Kin. 2:5
ᵇ2 Sam. 4:6
ᶜ2 Sam. 2:23

3:29
ᵃDeut. 21:6–9;
1 Kin. 2:32, 33
ᵇLev. 15:2

3:30
ᵃ2 Sam. 2:23

3:31 ᵃJosh. 7:6;
2 Sam. 1:2, 11
ᵇGen. 37:34

3:15 ¹*Palti,* 1 Sam. 25:44 **3:16** ¹Lit. *going and weeping* **3:18** ¹So with many Heb. mss., LXX, Syr., Tg.; MT *he* **3:22** ¹*booty* **3:27** ¹Lit. *struck* **3:28** ¹*innocent* **3:29** ¹*family*

and mourn for Abner." And King David followed the coffin. [32]So they buried Abner in Hebron; and the king lifted up his voice and wept at the grave of Abner, and all the people wept. [33]And the king sang *a lament* over Abner and said:

"Should Abner die as a [a]fool dies?
[34]   Your hands were not bound
       Nor your feet put into fetters;
       As a man falls before wicked men, *so* you fell."

Then all the people wept over him again.

[35]And when all the people came [a]to persuade David to eat food while it was still day, David took an oath, saying, [b]"God do so to me, and more also, if I taste bread or anything else [c]till the sun goes down!" [36]Now all the people took note *of it,* and it pleased them, since whatever the king did pleased all the people. [37]For all the people and all Israel understood that day that it had not been the king's *intent* to kill Abner the son of Ner. [38]Then the king said to his servants, "Do you not know that a prince and a great man has fallen this day in Israel? [39]And I *am* weak today, though anointed king; and these men, the sons of Zeruiah, [a]*are* too harsh for me. [b]The LORD shall repay the evildoer according to his wickedness."

ISHBOSHETH IS MURDERED

4 When Saul's [1]son heard that Abner had died in Hebron, [a]he[2] lost heart, and all Israel was [b]troubled. [2]Now Saul's son *had* two men *who were* captains of troops. The name of one *was* Baanah and the name of the other Rechab, the sons of Rimmon the Beerothite, of the children of Benjamin. (For [a]Beeroth also was [1]*part* of Benjamin, [3]because the Beerothites fled to [a]Gittaim and have been sojourners there until this day.)

[4a]Jonathan, Saul's son, had a son *who was* lame in *his* feet. He was five years old when the news about Saul and Jonathan came [b]from Jezreel; and his nurse took him up and fled. And it happened, as she made haste to flee, that he fell and became lame. His name *was* [c]Mephibosheth.[1]

[5]Then the sons of Rimmon the Beerothite, Rechab and Baanah, set out and came at about the heat of the day to the [a]house of Ishbosheth, who was lying on his bed at noon. [6]And they came there, all the way into the house, *as though* to get wheat, and they [1]stabbed him [a]in the stomach. Then Rechab and Baanah his brother escaped. [7]For when they came into the house, he was lying on his bed in his bedroom; then they struck him and killed him, beheaded him and took his head, and were all night escaping through the plain. [8]And they brought the head of Ishbosheth to David at Hebron, and said to the king, "Here is the head of Ishbosheth, the son of Saul your enemy, [a]who sought your life; and the LORD has avenged my lord the king this day of Saul and his descendants."

[9]But David answered Rechab and Baanah his brother, the sons of Rimmon the Beerothite, and said to them, "*As the* LORD lives, [a]who has redeemed my life from all adversity, [10]when [a]someone told me, saying, 'Look, Saul is dead,' thinking

3:33
[a]2 Sam. 13:12, 13

3:35
[a]2 Sam. 12:17;
Jer. 16:7, 8
[b]Ruth 1:17
[c]Judg. 20:26;
2 Sam. 1:12

3:39
[a]2 Sam. 19:5–7
[b]1 Kin. 2:5,
6, 32–34;
2 Tim. 4:14

4:1 [a]Ezra 4:4;
Is. 13:7
[b]Matt. 2:3

4:2 [a]Josh. 18:25

4:3 [a]Neh. 11:33

4:4 [a]2 Sam. 9:3
[b]1 Sam. 29:1, 11
[c]2 Sam. 9:6

4:5
[a]2 Sam. 2:8, 9

4:6
[a]2 Sam. 2:23;
20:10

4:8 [a]1 Sam. 19:2,
10, 11; 23:15;
25:29

4:9 [a]Gen. 48:16;
1 Kin. 1:29;
Ps. 31:7

4:10
[a]2 Sam. 1:2–16

4:1 [1]Ishbosheth   [2]Lit. *his hands dropped*   4:2 [1]*considered part of*
4:4 [1]*Merib-Baal,* 1 Chr. 8:34; 9:40   4:6 [1]Lit. *struck*

to have brought good news, I arrested him and had him executed in Ziklag—the one who *thought* I would give him a reward for *his* news. ¹¹How much more, when wicked men have killed a righteous person in his own house on his bed? Therefore, shall I not now ᵃrequire his ¹blood at your hand and ²remove you from the earth?" ¹²So David ᵃcommanded his young men, and they executed them, cut off their hands and feet, and hanged *them* by the pool in Hebron. But they took the head of Ishbosheth and buried *it* in the ᵇtomb of Abner in Hebron.

DAVID REIGNS OVER ALL ISRAEL
(1 Chr. 11:1–3)

5 Then all the tribes of Israel ᵃcame to David at Hebron and spoke, saying, "Indeed ᵇwe *are* your bone and your flesh. ²Also, in time past, when Saul was king over us, ᵃyou were the one who led Israel out and brought them in; and the LORD said to you, ᵇ'You shall shepherd My people Israel, and be ruler over Israel.' " ³ᵃTherefore all the elders of Israel came to the king at Hebron, ᵇand King David made a covenant with them at Hebron ᶜbefore the LORD. And they anointed David king over Israel. ⁴David *was* ᵃthirty years old when he began to reign, *and* ᵇhe reigned forty years. ⁵In Hebron he reigned over Judah ᵃseven years and six months, and in Jerusalem he reigned thirty-three years over all Israel and Judah.

THE CONQUEST OF JERUSALEM
(1 Chr. 11:4–9; 14:1–7)

⁶ᵃAnd the king and his men went to Jerusalem against ᵇthe Jebusites, the inhabitants of the land, who spoke to David, saying, "You shall not come in here; but the blind and the lame will repel you," thinking, "David cannot come in here." ⁷Nevertheless David took the stronghold of Zion ᵃ(that *is*, the City of David).

⁸Now David said on that day, "Whoever climbs up by way of the water shaft and defeats the Jebusites (the lame and the blind, *who are* hated by David's soul), ᵃhe shall be chief and captain." Therefore they say, "The blind and the lame shall not come into the house."

⁹Then David dwelt in the stronghold, and called it ᵃthe City of David. And David built all around from ¹the Millo and inward. ¹⁰So David went on and became great, and ᵃthe LORD God of hosts *was* with ᵇhim.

¹¹Then ᵃHiram ᵇking of Tyre sent messengers to David, and cedar trees, and carpenters and masons. And they built David a house. ¹²So David knew that the LORD had established him as king over Israel, and that He had ᵃexalted His kingdom ᵇfor the sake of His people Israel.

¹³And ᵃDavid took more concubines and wives from Jerusalem, after he had come from Hebron. Also more sons and daughters were born to David. ¹⁴Now ᵃthese *are* the names of those who were born to him in Jerusalem: ¹Shammua, Shobab, Nathan, ᵇSolomon, ¹⁵Ibhar, ¹Elishua, Nepheg, Japhia, ¹⁶Elishama, Eliada, and Eliphelet.

Cross-references (margin)

4:11 ᵃ[Gen. 9:5, 6; Ps. 9:12]
4:12 ᵃ2 Sam. 1:15
ᵇ2 Sam. 3:32

5:1 ᵃ1 Chr. 11:1–3
ᵇGen. 29:14;
Judg. 9:2;
2 Sam. 19:12, 13
5:2 ᵃ1 Sam. 18:5, 13, 16
ᵇ1 Sam. 16:1
5:3 ᵃ2 Sam. 3:17;
1 Chr. 11:3
ᵇ2 Sam. 2:4;
3:21; 2 Kin. 11:17
ᶜJudg. 11:11;
1 Sam. 23:18
5:4 ᵃGen. 41:46;
Num. 4:3;
Luke 3:23
ᵇ1 Kin. 2:11;
1 Chr. 26:31;
29:27
5:5 ᵃ2 Sam. 2:11;
1 Chr. 3:4; 29:27
5:6 ᵃJudg. 1:21
ᵇJosh. 15:63;
Judg. 1:8;
19:11, 12
5:7
ᵃ2 Sam. 6:12, 16;
1 Kin. 2:10; 8:1;
9:24
5:8
ᵃ1 Chr. 11:6–9
5:9 ᵃ2 Sam. 5:7;
1 Kin. 9:15, 24
5:10
ᵃ1 Sam. 17:45
ᵇ1 Sam. 18:12, 28
5:11
ᵃ1 Kin. 5:1–18
ᵇ1 Chr. 14:1
5:12 ᵃNum. 24:7
ᵇIs. 45:4
5:13
ᵃ[Deut. 17:17];
1 Chr. 3:9
5:14
ᵃ1 Chr. 3:5–8
ᵇ2 Sam. 12:24

4:11 ¹Or *bloodshed* ²Lit. *consume you* 5:9 ¹Lit. *The Landfill*
5:14 ¹*Shimea*, 1 Chr. 3:5 5:15 ¹*Elishama*, 1 Chr. 3:6

THE PHILISTINES DEFEATED
(1 Chr. 14:8–17)

17aNow when the Philistines heard that they had anointed David king over Israel, all the Philistines went up to search for David. And David heard *of it* band went down to the stronghold. 18The Philistines also went and deployed themselves in athe Valley of Rephaim. 19So David ainquired of the LORD, saying, "Shall I go up against the Philistines? Will You deliver them into my hand?"

And the LORD said to David, "Go up, for I will doubtless deliver the Philistines into your hand."

20So David went to aBaal Perazim, and David defeated them there; and he said, "The LORD has broken through my enemies before me, like a breakthrough of water." Therefore he called the name of that place 1Baal Perazim. 21And they left their 1images there, and David and his men acarried them away.

22aThen the Philistines went up once again and deployed themselves in the Valley of Rephaim. 23Therefore aDavid inquired of the LORD, and He said, "You shall not go up; circle around behind them, and come upon them in front of the mulberry trees. 24And it shall be, when you ahear the sound of marching in the tops of the mulberry trees, then you shall advance quickly. For then bthe LORD will go out before you to strike the camp of the Philistines." 25And David did so, as the LORD commanded him; and he drove back the Philistines from aGeba1 as far as bGezer.

THE ARK BROUGHT TO JERUSALEM
(1 Chr. 13:1–14; 15:25—16:3)

6 Again David gathered all *the* choice *men* of Israel, thirty thousand. 2And aDavid arose and went with all the people who *were* with him from 1Baale Judah to bring up from there the ark of God, whose name is called 2by the Name, the LORD of Hosts, bwho dwells *between* the cherubim. 3So they set the ark of God on a new cart, and brought it out of the house of Abinadab, which *was* on athe hill; and Uzzah and Ahio, the sons of Abinadab, drove the new 1cart. 4And they brought it out of athe house of Abinadab, which *was* on the hill, accompanying the ark of God; and Ahio went before the ark. 5Then David and all the house of Israel aplayed *music* before the LORD on all kinds of *instruments of* fir wood, on harps, on stringed instruments, on tambourines, on sistrums, and on cymbals.

6And when they came to aNachon's threshing floor, Uzzah put out *his* bhand to the ark of God and 1took hold of it, for the oxen stumbled. 7Then the anger of the LORD was aroused against Uzzah, and God struck him there for *his* 1error; and he died there by the ark of God. 8And David became angry because of the LORD's outbreak against Uzzah; and he called the name of the place 1Perez Uzzah to this day.

9aDavid was afraid of the LORD that day; and he said, "How can the ark of the LORD come to me?" 10So David would not move the ark of the LORD with him into the aCity of David; but

5:17 a1 Chr. 11:16
b2 Sam. 23:14

5:18 aGen. 14:5;
Josh. 15:8;
1 Chr. 11:15;
Is. 17:5

5:19
a1 Sam. 23:2;
2 Sam. 2:1

5:20
a1 Chr. 14:11;
Is. 28:21

5:21
aDeut. 7:5, 25

5:22 a1 Chr. 14:13

5:23
a2 Sam. 5:19

5:24 a2 Kin. 7:6;
1 Chr. 14:15
bJudg. 4:14

5:25 a1 Chr. 14:16
bJosh. 16:10

6:2
a1 Chr. 13:5, 6
bEx. 25:22;
1 Sam. 4:4;
Ps. 80:1

6:3 a1 Sam. 26:1

6:4 a1 Sam. 7:1;
1 Chr. 13:7

6:5
a1 Sam. 18:6, 7

6:6 a1 Chr. 13:9
bNum. 4:15,
19, 20

6:9 aDeut. 9:19;
Ps. 119:120;
Luke 5:8

6:10 a2 Sam. 5:7

5:20 1Lit. *Master of Breakthroughs*   5:21 1*idols*   5:25 1So with MT, Tg., Vg.; LXX *Gibeon*   6:2 1*Baalah, Kirjath Jearim*, Josh. 15:9; 1 Chr. 13:6   2LXX, Tg., Vg. omit *by the Name*; many Heb. mss., Syr. *there*   6:3 1LXX adds *with the ark*   6:6 1*held it*   6:7 1Or *irreverence*   6:8 1Lit. *Outburst Against Uzzah*

David took it aside into the house of Obed-Edom the ᵇGittite. ¹¹ᵃThe ark of the LORD remained in the house of Obed-Edom the Gittite three months. And the LORD ᵇblessed Obed-Edom and all his household.

¹²Now it was told King David, saying, "The LORD has blessed the house of Obed-Edom and all that *belongs* to him, because of the ark of God." ᵃSo David went and brought up the ark of God from the house of Obed-Edom to the City of David with gladness. ¹³And so it was, when ᵃthose bearing the ark of the LORD had gone six paces, that he sacrificed ᵇoxen and fatted sheep. ¹⁴Then David ᵃdanced¹ before the LORD with all *his* might; and David *was* wearing ᵇa linen ephod. ¹⁵ᵃSo David and all the house of Israel brought up the ark of the LORD with shouting and with the sound of the trumpet.

¹⁶Now as the ark of the LORD came into the City of David, ᵃMichal, Saul's daughter, looked through a window and saw King David leaping and whirling before the LORD; and she despised him in her heart. ¹⁷So ᵃthey brought the ark of the LORD, and set it in ᵇits place in the midst of the tabernacle that David had erected for it. Then David ᶜoffered burnt offerings and peace offerings before the LORD. ¹⁸And when David had finished offering burnt offerings and peace offerings, ᵃhe blessed the people in the name of the LORD of hosts. ¹⁹ᵃThen he distributed among all the people, among the whole multitude of Israel, both the women and the men, to everyone a loaf of bread, a piece *of meat,* and a cake of raisins. So all the people departed, everyone to his house.

²⁰ᵃThen David returned to bless his household. And Michal the daughter of Saul came out to meet David, and said, "How glorious was the king of Israel today, ᵇuncovering himself today in the eyes of the maids of his servants, as one of the ᶜbase fellows ¹shamelessly uncovers himself!"

²¹So David said to Michal, "*It was* before the LORD, ᵃwho chose me instead of your father and all his house, to appoint me ruler over the ᵇpeople of the LORD, over Israel. Therefore I will play *music* before the LORD. ²²And I will be even more undignified than this, and will be humble in my own sight. But as for the maidservants of whom you have spoken, by them I will be held in honor."

²³Therefore Michal the daughter of Saul had no children ᵃto the day of her death.

GOD'S COVENANT WITH DAVID
(1 Chr. 17:1–15)

7 Now it came to pass ᵃwhen the king was dwelling in his house, and the LORD had given him rest from all his enemies all around, ²that the king said to Nathan the prophet, "See now, I dwell in ᵃa house of cedar, ᵇbut the ark of God dwells inside tent ᶜcurtains."

³Then Nathan said to the king, "Go, do all that *is* in your ᵃheart, for the LORD *is* with you."

⁴But it happened that night that the word of the LORD came to Nathan, saying, ⁵"Go and tell My servant David, 'Thus says the LORD: ᵃ"Would you build a house for Me to dwell in? ⁶For I have not dwelt in a house ᵃsince the time that I brought the

---

6:10
ᵇ1 Chr. 13:13; 26:4–8

6:11 ᵃ1 Chr. 13:14
ᵇGen. 30:27; 39:5

6:12
ᵃ1 Chr. 15:25—16:3

6:13 ᵃNum. 4:15; Josh. 3:3; 1 Sam. 6:15; 2 Sam. 15:24; 1 Chr. 15:2, 15
ᵇ1 Kin. 8:5

6:14 ᵃPs. 30:11; 149:3
ᵇ1 Sam. 2:18, 28

6:15 ᵃ1 Chr. 15:28

6:16
ᵃ2 Sam. 3:14

6:17 ᵃ1 Chr. 16:1
ᵇ1 Chr. 15:1; 2 Chr. 1:4
ᶜ1 Kin. 8:5, 62, 63

6:18 ᵃ1 Kin. 8:14, 15, 55

6:19 ᵃ1 Chr. 16:3

6:20
ᵃPs. 30:title
ᵇ2 Sam. 6:14, 16
ᶜJudg. 9:4

6:21
ᵃ1 Sam. 13:14; 15:28
ᵇ2 Kin. 11:17

6:23
ᵃ1 Sam. 15:35; Is. 22:14

7:1
ᵃ1 Chr. 17:1–27

7:2 ᵃ2 Sam. 5:11
ᵇActs 7:46
ᶜEx. 26:1

7:3
ᵃ1 Kin. 8:17, 18; 1 Chr. 22:7

7:5 ᵃ1 Kin. 5:3, 4; 8:19; 1 Chr. 22:8

7:6 ᵃJosh. 18:1; 1 Kin. 8:16

6:14 ¹*whirled about* 6:20 ¹*openly*

children of Israel up from Egypt, even to this day, but have moved about in [b]a tent and in a tabernacle. 7Wherever I have [a]moved about with all the children of Israel, have I ever spoken a word to anyone from the tribes of Israel, whom I commanded [b]to shepherd My people Israel, saying, 'Why have you not built Me a house of cedar?' " ' 8Now therefore, thus shall you say to My servant David, 'Thus says the LORD of hosts: [a]"I took you from the sheepfold, from following the sheep, to be ruler over My people, over Israel. 9And [a]I have been with you wherever you have gone, [b]and have [1]cut off all your enemies from before you, and have made you a great name, like the name of the great men who *are* on the earth. 10Moreover I will appoint a place for My people Israel, and will [a]plant them, that they may dwell in a place of their own and move no more; [b]nor shall the sons of wickedness oppress them anymore, as previously, 11a since the time that I commanded judges *to be* over My people Israel, and have caused you to rest from all your enemies. Also the LORD [1]tells you [b]that He will make you a [2]house.

12a"When your days are fulfilled and you [b]rest with your fathers, [c]I will set up your seed after you, who will come from your body, and I will establish his kingdom. 13a He shall build a house for My name, and I will [b]establish the throne of his kingdom forever. 14a I will be his Father, and he shall be [b]My son. If he commits iniquity, I will chasten him with the rod of men and with the [1]blows of the sons of men. 15But My mercy shall not depart from him, [a]as I took *it* from Saul, whom I removed from before you. 16And [a]your house and your kingdom shall be established forever before [1]you. Your throne shall be established forever." ' "

17According to all these words and according to all this vision, so Nathan spoke to David.

DAVID'S THANKSGIVING TO GOD
(1 Chr. 17:16–27)

18Then King David went in and sat before the LORD; and he said: [a]"Who *am* I, O Lord GOD? And what is my house, that You have brought me this far? 19And yet this was a small thing in Your sight, O Lord GOD; and You have also spoken of Your servant's house for a great while to come. [a]*Is* this the manner of man, O Lord GOD? 20Now what more can David say to You? For You, Lord GOD, [a]know Your servant. 21For Your word's sake, and according to Your own heart, You have done all these great things, to make Your servant know *them*. 22There-fore [a]You are great, [1]O Lord GOD. For [b]*there is* none like You, nor *is there any* God besides You, according to all that we have heard with our [c]ears. 23And who *is* like Your people, like Israel, [a]the one nation on the earth whom God went to redeem for Himself as a people, to make for Himself a name—and to do for Yourself great and awesome deeds for Your land—before [b]Your people whom You redeemed for Yourself from Egypt, the nations, and their gods? 24For [a]You have made Your people Israel Your very own people forever; [b]and You, LORD, have become their God.

25"Now, O LORD God, the word which You have spoken concerning Your servant and concerning his house, establish *it*

7:6 [b]Ex. 40:18, 34

7:7 [a]Lev. 26:11, 12 [b]2 Sam. 5:2; [Acts 20:28]

7:8 [a]1 Sam. 16:11, 12; Ps. 78:70, 71

7:9 [a]1 Sam. 18:14; 2 Sam. 5:10 [b]1 Sam. 31:6

7:10 [a]Ex. 15:17; Ps. 44:2; 80:8; Jer. 24:6 [b]Ps. 89:22, 23; Is. 60:18

7:11 [a]Judg. 2:14–16 [b]Ex. 1:21; 1 Sam. 25:28; 2 Sam. 7:27

7:12 [a]1 Kin. 2:1 [b]Deut. 31:16; Acts 13:36 [c]1 Kin. 8:20; Ps. 132:11; Matt. 1:6; Luke 3:31

7:13 [a]1 Kin. 5:5; 8:19; 2 Chr. 6:2 [b]2 Sam. 7:16; [Is. 9:7; 49:8]

7:14 [a][Heb. 1:5] [b][Ps. 2:7; 89:26, 27, 30]; Matt. 3:17

7:15 [a]1 Sam. 15:23, 28; 16:14

7:16 [a]2 Sam. 7:13; Ps. 89:36, 37; Matt. 25:31; John 12:34

7:18 [a]Gen. 32:10; Ex. 3:11; 1 Sam. 18:18

7:19 [a][Is. 55:8, 9]

7:20 [a][1 Sam. 16:7]; Ps. 139:1; John 21:17

7:22 [a]Deut. 10:17; 1 Chr. 16:25; 2 Chr. 2:5; Ps. 86:10; Jer. 10:6 [b]Ex. 15:11; Deut. 3:24; 4:35; 32:39 [c]Ex. 10:2; Ps. 44:1

7:23 [a]Ps. 147:20 [b]Deut. 9:26; 33:29

7:24 [a]Gen. 17:7, 8; Ex. 6:7; [Deut. 26:18] [b]Ps. 48:14

7:9 [1]destroyed   7:11 [1]declares to you   [2]Royal dynasty   7:14 [1]strokes
7:16 [1]LXX Me   7:22 [1]Tg., Syr. *O LORD God*

forever and do as You have said. ²⁶So let Your name be magnified forever, saying, 'The Lᴏʀᴅ of hosts *is* the God over Israel.' And let the house of Your servant David be established before You. ²⁷For You, O Lᴏʀᴅ of hosts, God of Israel, have revealed *this* to Your servant, saying, 'I will build you a house.' Therefore Your servant has found it in his heart to pray this prayer to You.

²⁸"And now, O Lord Gᴏᴅ, You are God, and ᵃYour words are true, and You have promised this goodness to Your servant. ²⁹Now therefore, let it please You to bless the house of Your servant, that it may continue before You forever; for You, O Lord Gᴏᴅ, have spoken *it,* and with Your blessing let the house of Your servant be blessed ᵃforever."

DAVID'S FURTHER CONQUESTS
(1 Chr. 18:1–13)

8 After this it came to pass that David ¹attacked the Philistines and subdued them. And David took ²Metheg Ammah from the hand of the Philistines.

²Then ᵃhe defeated Moab. Forcing them down to the ground, he measured them off with a line. With two lines he measured off those to be put to death, and with one full line those to be kept alive. So the Moabites became David's ᵇservants, *and* ᶜbrought tribute.

³David also defeated Hadadezer the son of Rehob, king of ᵃZobah, as he went to recover ᵇhis territory at the River Euphrates. ⁴David took from him one thousand *chariots,* ¹seven hundred horsemen, and twenty thousand foot soldiers. Also David ᵃhamstrung all the chariot *horses,* except that he spared *enough* of them for one hundred chariots.

⁵ᵃWhen the Syrians of Damascus came to help Hadadezer king of Zobah, David killed twenty-two thousand of the Syrians. ⁶Then David put garrisons in Syria of Damascus; and the Syrians became David's servants, *and* brought tribute. So ᵃthe Lᴏʀᴅ preserved David wherever he went. ⁷And David took ᵃthe shields of gold that had belonged to the servants of Hadadezer, and brought them to Jerusalem. ⁸Also from ¹Betah and from ᵃBerothai,² cities of Hadadezer, King David took a large amount of bronze.

⁹When ¹Toi king of ᵃHamath heard that David had defeated all the army of Hadadezer, ¹⁰then Toi sent ¹Joram his son to King David, to ²greet him and bless him, because he had fought against Hadadezer and defeated him (for Hadadezer had been at war with Toi); and *Joram* brought with him articles of silver, articles of gold, and articles of bronze. ¹¹King David also ᵃdedicated these to the Lᴏʀᴅ, along with the silver and gold that he had dedicated from all the nations which he had subdued— ¹²from ¹Syria, from Moab, from the people of Ammon, from the ᵃPhilistines, from Amalek, and from the spoil of Hadadezer the son of Rehob, king of Zobah.

¹³And David made *himself* a ᵃname when he returned from killing ᵇeighteen thousand ¹Syrians in ᶜthe Valley of Salt. ¹⁴He also put garrisons in Edom; throughout all Edom he

---

7:28 ᵃEx. 34:6;
Josh. 21:45;
John 17:17

7:29
ᵃ2 Sam. 22:51

8:2 ᵃNum. 24:17
ᵇ2 Sam. 12:31
ᶜ1 Sam. 10:27;
1 Kin. 4:21

8:3
ᵃ1 Sam. 14:47;
2 Sam. 10:16, 19
ᵇGen. 15:18;
2 Sam. 10:15–19

8:4 ᵃJosh. 11:6, 9

8:5
ᵃ1 Kin. 11:23–25

8:6 ᵃ2 Sam. 7:9;
8:14

8:7 ᵃ1 Kin. 10:16

8:8 ᵃEzek. 47:16

8:9 ᵃ1 Kin. 8:65;
2 Kin. 14:28;
2 Chr. 8:4

8:11 ᵃ1 Kin. 7:51

8:12
ᵃ2 Sam. 5:17–25

8:13 ᵃ2 Sam. 7:9
ᵇ2 Kin. 14:7
ᶜ1 Chr. 18:12;
Ps. 60:title

8:1 ¹Lit. *struck*   ²Lit. *The Bridle of the Mother City*   8:4 ¹*seven thousand,* 1 Chr. 18:4   8:8 ¹*Tibhath,* 1 Chr. 18:8   ²*Chun,* 1 Chr. 18:8   8:9 ¹*Tou,* 1 Chr. 18:9   8:10 ¹*Hadoram,* 1 Chr. 18:10   ²Lit. *ask him of his welfare*   8:12 ¹LXX, Syr., Heb. mss. *Edom*   8:13 ¹LXX, Syr., Heb. mss. *Edomites* and 1 Chr. 18:12

put garrisons, and [a]all the Edomites became David's servants. And the LORD preserved David wherever he went.

DAVID'S ADMINISTRATION
(1 Chr. 18:14–17)

[15]So David reigned over all Israel; and David administered judgment and justice to all his people. [16a]Joab the son of Zeruiah *was* over the army; [b]Jehoshaphat the son of Ahilud *was* recorder; [17a]Zadok the son of Ahitub and Ahimelech the son of Abiathar *were* the priests; [1]Seraiah *was* the [2]scribe; [18a]Benaiah the son of Jehoiada *was over* both the [b]Cherethites and the Pelethites; and David's sons were [1]chief ministers.

DAVID'S KINDNESS TO MEPHIBOSHETH

9 Now David said, "Is there still anyone who is left of the house of Saul, that I may [a]show him [1]kindness for Jonathan's sake?"

[2]And *there was* a servant of the house of Saul whose name *was* [a]Ziba. So when they had called him to David, the king said to him, "*Are* you Ziba?"

He said, "At your service!"

[3]Then the king said, "*Is* there not still someone of the house of Saul, to whom I may show [a]the kindness of God?"

And Ziba said to the king, "There is still a son of Jonathan *who is* [b]lame in *his* feet."

[4]So the king said to him, "Where *is* he?"

And Ziba said to the king, "Indeed he *is* in the house of [a]Machir the son of Ammiel, in Lo Debar."

[5]Then King David sent and brought him out of the house of Machir the son of Ammiel, from Lo Debar.

[6]Now when [a]Mephibosheth[1] the son of Jonathan, the son of Saul, had come to David, he fell on his face and prostrated himself. Then David said, "Mephibosheth?"

And he answered, "Here is your servant!"

[7]So David said to him, "Do not fear, for I will surely show you kindness for Jonathan your father's sake, and will restore to you all the land of Saul your grandfather; and you shall eat bread at my table continually."

[8]Then he bowed himself, and said, "What *is* your servant, that you should look upon such [a]a dead dog as I?"

[9]And the king called to Ziba, Saul's servant, and said to him, [a]"I have given to your master's son all that belonged to Saul and to all his house. [10]You therefore, and your sons and your servants, shall work the land for him, and you shall bring in *the harvest,* that your master's son may have food to eat. But Mephibosheth your master's son [a]shall eat bread at my table always." Now Ziba had [b]fifteen sons and twenty servants.

[11]Then Ziba said to the king, "According to all that my lord the king has commanded his servant, so will your servant do."

"As for Mephibosheth," *said the king,* "he shall eat at [1]my table like one of the king's sons." [12]Mephibosheth had a young son [a]whose name *was* Micha. And all who dwelt in the house of Ziba *were* servants of Mephibosheth. [13]So Mephibosheth dwelt in Jerusalem, [a]for he ate continually at the king's table. And he [b]was lame in both his feet.

8:14
[a]Gen. 27:29, 37–40;
Num. 24:18;
1 Kin. 11:15

8:16
[a]2 Sam. 19:13; 20:23; 1 Chr. 11:6
[b]1 Kin. 4:3

8:17
[a]1 Chr. 6:4–8; 24:3

8:18 [a]1 Kin. 1:8;
1 Chr. 18:17
[b]1 Sam. 30:14;
1 Kin. 1:38

9:1 [a]1 Sam. 18:3;
20:14–16;
2 Sam. 21:7;
[Prov. 27:10]

9:2
[a]2 Sam. 16:1–4;
19:17, 29

9:3
[a]1 Sam. 20:14
[b]2 Sam. 4:4

9:4
[a]2 Sam. 17:27–29

9:6
[a]2 Sam. 16:4;
19:24–30

9:8 [a]2 Sam. 16:9

9:9
[a]2 Sam. 16:4;
19:29

9:10 [a]2 Sam. 9:7, 11, 13; 19:28
[b]2 Sam. 19:17

9:12 [a]1 Chr. 8:34

9:13 [a]2 Sam. 9:7, 10, 11; 1 Kin. 2:7;
2 Kin. 25:29
[b]2 Sam. 9:3

8:17 [1]*Shavsha,* 1 Chr. 18:16 [2]*secretary* 8:18 [1]Lit. *priests* 9:1 [1]*covenant faithfulness* 9:6 [1]Or *Merib-Baal* 9:11 [1]LXX *David's table*

THE AMMONITES AND SYRIANS DEFEATED
(1 Chr. 19:1–19)

10 It happened after this that the [a]king of the people of Ammon died, and Hanun his son reigned in his place. [2]Then David said, "I will show [a]kindness to Hanun the son of [b]Nahash, as his father showed kindness to me."

So David sent by the hand of his servants to comfort him concerning his father. And David's servants came into the land of the people of Ammon. [3]And the princes of the people of Ammon said to Hanun their lord, "Do you think that David really honors your father because he has sent comforters to you? Has David not *rather* sent his servants to you to search the city, to spy it out, and to overthrow it?"

[4]Therefore Hanun took David's servants, shaved off half of their beards, cut off their garments in the middle, [a]at their buttocks, and sent them away. [5]When they told David, he sent to meet them, because the men were greatly [1]ashamed. And the king said, "Wait at Jericho until your beards have grown, and *then* return."

[6]When the people of Ammon saw that they [a]had made themselves repulsive to David, the people of Ammon sent and hired [b]the Syrians of [c]Beth Rehob and the Syrians of Zoba, twenty thousand foot soldiers; and from the king of [d]Maacah one thousand men, and from [e]Ish-Tob twelve thousand men. [7]Now when David heard *of it,* he sent Joab and all the army of [a]the mighty men. [8]Then the people of Ammon came out and put themselves in battle array at the entrance of the gate. And [a]the Syrians of Zoba, Beth Rehob, Ish-Tob, and Maacah *were* by themselves in the field.

[9]When Joab saw that the battle line was against him before and behind, he chose some of Israel's best and put *them* in battle array against the Syrians. [10]And the rest of the people he put under the command of [a]Abishai his brother, that he might set *them* in battle array against the people of Ammon. [11]Then he said, "If the Syrians are too strong for me, then you shall help me; but if the people of Ammon are too strong for you, then I will come and help you. [12a]Be of good courage, and let us [b]be strong for our people and for the cities of our God. And may [c]the LORD do *what is* good in His sight."

[13]So Joab and the people who *were* with him drew near for the battle against the Syrians, and they fled before him. [14]When the people of Ammon saw that the Syrians were fleeing, they also fled before Abishai, and entered the city. So Joab returned from the people of Ammon and went to [a]Jerusalem.

[15]When the Syrians saw that they had been defeated by Israel, they gathered together. [16]Then [1]Hadadezer sent and brought out the Syrians who *were* beyond [2]the River, and they came to Helam. And [3]Shobach the commander of Hadadezer's army *went* before them. [17]When it was told David, he gathered all Israel, crossed over the Jordan, and came to Helam. And the Syrians set themselves in battle array against David and fought with him. [18]Then the Syrians fled before Israel; and David killed seven hundred charioteers and forty thousand [a]horsemen of the Syrians, and struck Shobach the

Cross references (margin)
10:1 [a]2 Sam. 11:1; 1 Chr. 19:1
10:2 [a]2 Sam. 9:1; 1 Kin. 2:7 [b]1 Sam. 11:1
10:4 [a]Is. 20:4; 47:2
10:6 [a]Gen. 34:30; Ex. 5:21 [b]2 Sam. 8:3, 5 [c]Judg. 18:28 [d]Deut. 3:14; Josh. 13:11, 13 [e]Judg. 11:3, 5
10:7 [a]2 Sam. 23:8
10:8 [a]2 Sam. 10:6
10:10 [a]1 Sam. 26:6; 2 Sam. 3:30
10:12 [a]Deut. 31:6; Josh. 1:6, 7, 9; Neh. 4:14 [b]1 Sam. 4:9; 1 Cor. 16:13 [c]1 Sam. 3:18
10:14 [a]2 Sam. 11:1
10:18 [a]1 Chr. 19:18

Footnotes
10:5 [1]humiliated   10:16 [1]Heb. *Hadarezer*   [2]The Euphrates   [3]*Shophach,* 1 Chr. 19:16

commander of their army, who died there. 19And when all the kings *who were* servants to 1Hadadezer saw that they were defeated by Israel, they made peace with Israel and ªserved them. So the Syrians were afraid to help the people of Ammon anymore.

DAVID, BATHSHEBA, AND URIAH

11 It happened in the spring of the year, at the ªtime when kings go out *to battle*, that ᵇDavid sent Joab and his servants with him, and all Israel; and they destroyed the people of Ammon and besieged ᶜRabbah. But David remained at Jerusalem.

2Then it happened one evening that David arose from his bed ªand walked on the roof of the king's house. And from the roof he ᵇsaw a woman bathing, and the woman *was* very beautiful to behold. 3So David sent and inquired about the woman. And *someone* said, "*Is* this not 1Bathsheba, the daughter of 2Eliam, the wife ªof Uriah the ᵇHittite?" 4Then David sent messengers, and took her; and she came to him, and ªhe lay with her, for she was ᵇcleansed from her impurity; and she returned to her house. 5And the woman conceived; so she sent and told David, and said, "I *am* with child."

6Then David sent to Joab, *saying*, "Send me Uriah the Hittite." And Joab sent Uriah to David. 7When Uriah had come to him, David asked how Joab was doing, and how the people were doing, and how the war prospered. 8And David said to Uriah, "Go down to your house and ªwash your feet." So Uriah departed from the king's house, and a gift *of food* from the king followed him. 9But Uriah slept at the ªdoor of the king's house with all the servants of his lord, and did not go down to his house. 10So when they told David, saying, "Uriah did not go down to his house," David said to Uriah, "Did you not come from a journey? Why did you not go down to your house?"

11And Uriah said to David, ª"The ark and Israel and Judah are dwelling in tents, and ᵇmy lord Joab and the servants of my lord are encamped in the open fields. Shall I then go to my house to eat and drink, and to lie with my wife? *As* you live, and *as* your soul lives, I will not do this thing."

12Then David said to Uriah, "Wait here today also, and tomorrow I will let you depart." So Uriah remained in Jerusalem that day and the next. 13Now when David called him, he ate and drank before him; and he made him ªdrunk. And at evening he went out to lie on his bed ᵇwith the servants of his lord, but he did not go down to his house.

14In the morning it happened that David ªwrote a letter to Joab and sent *it* by the hand of Uriah. 15And he wrote in the letter, saying, "Set Uriah in the forefront of the 1hottest battle, and retreat from him, that he may ªbe struck down and die." 16So it was, while Joab besieged the city, that he assigned Uriah to a place where he knew there *were* valiant men. 17Then the men of the city came out and fought with Joab. And *some* of the people of the servants of David fell; and Uriah the Hittite died also.

18Then Joab sent and told David all the things concerning the war, 19and charged the messenger, saying, "When you

10:19
ª2 Sam. 8:6

11:1
ª1 Kin. 20:22–26
ᵇ1 Chr. 20:1
ᶜ2 Sam. 12:26;
Jer. 49:2, 3;
Amos 1:14

11:2 ªDeut. 22:8;
1 Sam. 9:25;
Matt. 24:17;
Acts 10:9
ᵇGen. 34:2;
[Ex. 20:17];
Job 31:1;
[Matt. 5:28]

11:3
ª2 Sam. 23:39
ᵇ1 Sam. 26:6

11:4 ª[Lev. 20:10;
Deut. 22:22];
Ps. 51:title;
[James 1:14, 15]
ᵇLev. 15:19, 28

11:8
ªGen. 18:4; 19:2

11:9
ª1 Kin. 14:27, 28

11:11
ª2 Sam. 7:2, 6
ᵇ2 Sam. 20:6–22

11:13
ªGen. 19:33, 35
ᵇ2 Sam. 11:9

11:14
ª1 Kin. 21:8, 9

11:15
ª2 Sam. 12:9

10:19 1Heb. *Hadarezer*   11:3 1*Bathshua*, 1 Chr. 3:5   2*Ammiel*, 1 Chr. 3:5
11:15 1*fiercest*

have finished telling the matters of the war to the king, 20if it happens that the king's wrath rises, and he says to you: 'Why did you approach so near to the city when you fought? Did you not know that they would shoot from the wall? 21Who struck aAbimelech the son of 1Jerubbesheth? Was it not a woman who cast a piece of a millstone on him from the wall, so that he died in Thebez? Why did you go near the wall?'—then you shall say, 'Your servant Uriah the Hittite is dead also.'"

22So the messenger went, and came and told David all that Joab had sent by him. 23And the messenger said to David, "Surely the men prevailed against us and came out to us in the field; then we drove them back as far as the entrance of the gate. 24The archers shot from the wall at your servants; and *some* of the king's servants are dead, and your servant Uriah the Hittite is dead also."

25Then David said to the messenger, "Thus you shall say to Joab: 'Do not let this thing 1displease you, for the sword devours one as well as another. Strengthen your attack against the city, and overthrow it.' So encourage him."

26When the wife of Uriah heard that Uriah her husband was dead, she mourned for her husband. 27And when her mourning was over, David sent and brought her to his house, and she abecame his wife and bore him a son. But the thing that David had done bdispleased1 the LORD.

NATHAN'S PARABLE AND DAVID'S CONFESSION

12 Then the LORD sent Nathan to David. And ahe came to him, and bsaid to him: "There were two men in one city, one rich and the other poor. 2The rich *man* had exceedingly many flocks and herds. 3But the poor *man* had nothing, except one little ewe lamb which he had bought and nourished; and it grew up together with him and with his children. It ate of his own food and drank from his own cup and lay in his bosom; and it was like a daughter to him. 4And a traveler came to the rich man, who refused to take from his own flock and from his own herd to prepare one for the wayfaring man who had come to him; but he took the poor man's lamb and prepared it for the man who had come to him."

5So David's anger was greatly aroused against the man, and he said to Nathan, "*As* the LORD lives, the man who has done this 1shall surely die! 6And he shall restore afourfold for the lamb, because he did this thing and because he had no pity."

7Then Nathan said to David, "You *are* the man! Thus says the LORD God of Israel: 'I aanointed you king over Israel, and I delivered you from the hand of Saul. 8I gave you your master's house and your master's wives into your keeping, and gave you the house of Israel and Judah. And if *that had been* too little, I also would have given you much more! 9aWhy have you bdespised the commandment of the LORD, to do evil in His sight? cYou have killed Uriah the Hittite with the sword; you have taken his wife *to be* your wife, and have killed him with the sword of the people of Ammon. 10Now therefore, athe sword shall never depart from your house, because you have despised Me, and have taken the wife of Uriah the Hittite to

---

11:21
aJudg. 9:50–54

11:27
a2 Sam. 12:9
b1 Chr. 21:7;
[Heb. 13:4]

12:1 aPs. 51:title
b1 Kin. 20:35–41

12:6 a[Ex. 22:1];
Luke 19:8

12:7
a1 Sam. 16:13;
2 Sam. 5:3

12:9
a1 Sam. 15:19
bNum. 15:31
c2 Sam. 11:14–
17, 27

12:10
a2 Sam. 13:28;
18:14; 1 Kin. 2:25;
[Amos 7:9]

11:21 1*Jerubbaal* (Gideon), Judg. 6:32ff.   11:25 1Lit. *be evil in your sight*
11:27 1Lit. *was evil in the eyes of*   12:5 1*deserves to die*, lit. *is a son of death*

be your wife.' 11Thus says the LORD: 'Behold, I will raise up adversity against you from your own house; and I will ªtake your wives before your eyes and give *them* to your neighbor, and he shall lie with your wives in the sight of this sun. 12For you did *it* secretly, ªbut I will do this thing before all Israel, before the sun.'"

13ªSo David said to Nathan, b"I have sinned against the LORD."

And Nathan said to David, "The LORD also has cput away your sin; you shall not die. 14However, because by this deed you have given great occasion to the enemies of the LORD ªto blaspheme, the child also *who is* born to you shall surely die." 15Then Nathan departed to his house.

THE DEATH OF DAVID'S SON

And the ªLORD struck the child that Uriah's wife bore to David, and it became ill. 16David therefore pleaded with God for the child, and David fasted and went in and ªlay all night on the ground. 17So the elders of his house arose *and went* to him, to raise him up from the ground. But he would not, nor did he eat food with them. 18Then on the seventh day it came to pass that the child died. And the servants of David were afraid to tell him that the child was dead. For they said, "Indeed, while the child was alive, we spoke to him, and he would not heed our voice. How can we tell him that the child is dead? He may do some harm!"

19When David saw that his servants were whispering, David perceived that the child was dead. Therefore David said to his servants, "Is the child dead?"

And they said, "He is dead."

20So David arose from the ground, washed and ªanointed himself, and changed his clothes; and he went into the house of the LORD and bworshiped. Then he went to his own house; and when he requested, they set food before him, and he ate. 21Then his servants said to him, "What *is* this that you have done? You fasted and wept for the child *while he was* alive, but when the child died, you arose and ate food."

22And he said, "While the child was alive, I fasted and wept; ªfor I said, 'Who can tell *whether* 1the LORD will be gracious to me, that the child may live?' 23But now he is dead; why should I fast? Can I bring him back again? I shall go ªto him, but bhe shall not return to me."

SOLOMON IS BORN

24Then David comforted Bathsheba his wife, and went in to her and lay with her. So ªshe bore a son, and bhe1 called his name Solomon. Now the LORD loved him, 25and He sent *word* by the hand of Nathan the prophet: So 1he called his name 2Jedidiah, because of the LORD.

RABBAH IS CAPTURED
(1 Chr. 20:1–3)

26Now ªJoab fought against bRabbah of the people of Ammon, and took the royal city. 27And Joab sent messengers to

---

12:11
ªDeut. 28:30;
2 Sam. 16:21, 22

12:12
ª2 Sam. 16:22

12:13
ª1 Sam. 15:24
b2 Sam. 24:10;
Job 7:20; Ps. 51;
Luke 18:13
c2 Sam. 24:10;
Job 7:21;
[Ps. 32:1–5;
Prov. 28:13;
Mic. 7:18];
Zech. 3:4

12:14 ªIs. 52:5;
[Ezek. 36:20,
23]; Rom. 2:24

12:15
ª1 Sam. 25:38

12:16
ª2 Sam. 13:31

12:20 ªRuth 3:3;
Matt. 6:17
bJob 1:20

12:22
ªIs. 38:1–5;
Joel 2:14;
Jon. 3:9

12:23
ªGen. 37:35
bJob 7:8–10

12:24 ªMatt. 1:6
b1 Chr. 22:9

12:26
ª1 Chr. 20:1
bDeut. 3:11;
2 Sam. 11:1

12:22 1Heb. mss., Syr. *God*   12:24 1So with Kt., LXX, Vg.; Qr., a few Heb. mss., Syr., Tg. *she*   12:25 1Qr., some Heb. mss., Syr., Tg. *she*   2Lit. *Beloved of the LORD*

David, and said, "I have fought against Rabbah, and I have taken the city's water *supply.* 28Now therefore, gather the rest of the people together and encamp against the city and take it, lest I take the city and it be called after my name." 29So David gathered all the people together and went to Rabbah, fought against it, and took it. 30aThen he took their king's crown from his head. Its weight *was* a talent of gold, with precious stones. And it was *set* on David's head. Also he brought out the 1spoil of the city in great abundance. 31And he brought out the people who *were* in it, and put *them to work* with saws and iron picks and iron axes, and made them cross over to the brick works. So he did to all the cities of the people of Ammon. Then David and all the people returned to Jerusalem.

AMNON AND TAMAR

13 After this aAbsalom the son of David had a lovely sister, whose name *was* bTamar; and cAmnon the son of David loved her. 2Amnon was so distressed over his sister Tamar that he became sick; for she *was* a virgin. And it was improper for Amnon to do anything to her. 3But Amnon had a friend whose name *was* Jonadab athe son of Shimeah, David's brother. Now Jonadab *was* a very crafty man. 4And he said to him, "Why *are* you, the king's son, becoming thinner day after day? Will you not tell me?"

Amnon said to him, "I love Tamar, my brother Absalom's sister."

5So Jonadab said to him, "Lie down on your bed and pretend to be ill. And when your father comes to see you, say to him, 'Please let my sister Tamar come and give me food, and prepare the food in my sight, that I may see *it* and eat it from her hand.'" 6Then Amnon lay down and pretended to be ill; and when the king came to see him, Amnon said to the king, "Please let Tamar my sister come and amake a couple of cakes for me in my sight, that I may eat from her hand."

7And David sent home to Tamar, saying, "Now go to your brother Amnon's house, and prepare food for him." 8So Tamar went to her brother Amnon's house; and he was lying down. Then she took flour and kneaded *it,* made cakes in his sight, and baked the cakes. 9And she took the pan and placed *them* out before him, but he refused to eat. Then Amnon said, a"Have everyone go out from me." And they all went out from him. 10Then Amnon said to Tamar, "Bring the food into the bedroom, that I may eat from your hand." And Tamar took the cakes which she had made, and brought *them* to Amnon her brother in the bedroom. 11Now when she had brought *them* to him to eat, ahe took hold of her and said to her, "Come, lie with me, my sister."

12But she answered him, "No, my brother, do not 1force me, for ano such thing should be done in Israel. Do not do this bdisgraceful thing! 13And I, where could I take my shame? And as for you, you would be like one of the fools in Israel. Now therefore, please speak to the king; afor he will not withhold me from you." 14However, he would not heed her voice; and being stronger than she, he aforced her and lay with her.

15Then Amnon hated her 1exceedingly, so that the hatred

12:30
a1 Chr. 20:2

13:1
a2 Sam. 3:2, 3;
1 Chr. 3:2
b1 Chr. 3:9
c2 Sam. 3:2

13:3 a1 Sam. 16:9

13:6 aGen. 18:6

13:9 aGen. 45:1

13:11
aGen. 39:12;
[Deut. 27:22];
Ezek. 22:11

13:12
a[Lev. 18:9–
11; 20:17]
bGen. 34:7;
Judg. 19:23;
20:6

13:13
aGen. 20:12

13:14 aDeut. 22:9;
[Deut. 22:25;
27:22];
2 Sam. 12:11

12:30 1*plunder*   13:12 1Lit. *humble me*   13:15 1*with a very great hatred*

with which he hated her *was* greater than the love with which he had loved her. And Amnon said to her, "Arise, be gone!"

16So she said to him, "No, indeed! This evil of sending me away *is* worse than the other that you did to me."

But he would not listen to her. 17Then he called his servant who attended him, and said, "Here! Put this *woman* out, away from me, and bolt the door behind her." 18Now she had on ᵃa robe of many colors, for the king's virgin daughters wore such apparel. And his servant put her out and bolted the door behind her.

19Then Tamar put ᵃashes on her head, and tore her robe of many colors that *was* on her, and ᵇlaid her hand on her head and went away crying bitterly. 20And Absalom her brother said to her, "Has Amnon your brother been with you? But now hold your peace, my sister. He *is* your brother; do not take this thing to heart." So Tamar remained desolate in her brother Absalom's house.

21But when King David heard of all these things, he was very angry. 22And Absalom spoke to his brother Amnon ᵃneither good nor bad. For Absalom ᵇhated Amnon, because he had forced his sister Tamar.

ABSALOM MURDERS AMNON

23And it came to pass, after two full years, that Absalom ᵃhad sheepshearers in Baal Hazor, which *is* near Ephraim; so Absalom invited all the king's sons. 24Then Absalom came to the king and said, "Kindly note, your servant has sheepshearers; please, let the king and his servants go with your servant."

25But the king said to Absalom, "No, my son, let us not all go now, lest we be a burden to you." Then he urged him, but he would not go; and he blessed him.

26Then Absalom said, "If not, please let my brother Amnon go with us."

And the king said to him, "Why should he go with you?" 27But Absalom urged him; so he let Amnon and all the king's sons go with him.

28Now Absalom had commanded his servants, saying, "Watch now, when Amnon's ᵃheart is merry with wine, and when I say to you, 'Strike Amnon!' then kill him. Do not be afraid. Have I not commanded you? Be courageous and ¹valiant." 29So the servants of Absalom ᵃdid to Amnon as Absalom had commanded. Then all the king's sons arose, and each one got on ᵇhis mule and fled.

30And it came to pass, while they were on the way, that news came to David, saying, "Absalom has killed all the king's sons, and not one of them is left!" 31So the king arose and ᵃtore his garments and ᵇlay on the ground, and all his servants stood by with their clothes torn. 32Then ᵃJonadab the son of Shimeah, David's brother, answered and said, "Let not my lord suppose they have killed all the young men, the king's sons, for only Amnon is dead. For by the command of Absalom this has been determined from the day that he forced his sister Tamar. 33Now therefore, ᵃlet not my lord the king take the thing to his heart, to think that all the king's sons are dead. For only Amnon is dead."

13:18 ᵃGen. 37:3; Judg. 5:30; Ps. 45:13, 14

13:19 ᵃJosh. 7:6; 2 Sam. 1:2; Job 2:12; 42:6 ᵇJer. 2:37

13:22 ᵃGen. 24:50; 31:24 ᵇ[Lev. 19:17, 18; 1 John 2:9, 11; 3:10, 12, 15]

13:23 ᵃGen. 38:12, 13; 1 Sam. 25:4

13:28 ᵃJudg. 19:6, 9, 22; Ruth 3:7; 1 Sam. 25:36; Esth. 1:10

13:29 ᵃ2 Sam. 12:10 ᵇ2 Sam. 18:9; 1 Kin. 1:33, 38

13:31 ᵃ2 Sam. 1:11 ᵇ2 Sam. 12:16

13:32 ᵃ2 Sam. 13:3–5

13:33 ᵃ2 Sam. 19:19

13:28 ¹Lit. *sons of valor*

ABSALOM FLEES TO GESHUR

34aThen Absalom fled. And the young man who was keeping watch lifted his eyes and looked, and there, many people were coming from the road on the hillside behind [1]him. 35And Jonadab said to the king, "Look, the king's sons are coming; as your servant said, so it is." 36So it was, as soon as he had finished speaking, that the king's sons indeed came, and they lifted up their voice and wept. Also the king and all his servants wept very bitterly.

37But Absalom fled and went to aTalmai the son of Ammihud, king of Geshur. And *David* mourned for his son every day. 38So Absalom fled and went to aGeshur, and was there three years. 39And [1]King David [2]longed to go to Absalom. For he had been acomforted concerning Amnon, because he was dead.

ABSALOM RETURNS TO JERUSALEM

14 So Joab the son of Zeruiah perceived that the king's heart *was* concerned aabout Absalom. 2And Joab sent to aTekoa and brought from there a wise woman, and said to her, "Please pretend to be a mourner, band put on mourning apparel; do not anoint yourself with oil, but act like a woman who has been mourning a long time for the dead. 3Go to the king and speak to him in this manner." So Joab aput the words in her mouth.

4And when the woman of Tekoa [1]spoke to the king, she afell on her face to the ground and prostrated herself, and said, b"Help, O king!"

5Then the king said to her, "What troubles you?"

And she answered, a"Indeed I *am* a widow, my husband is dead. 6Now your maidservant had two sons; and the two fought with each other in the field, and *there was* no one to part them, but the one struck the other and killed him. 7And now the whole family has risen up against your maidservant, and they said, 'Deliver him who struck his brother, that we may execute him afor the life of his brother whom he killed; and we will destroy the heir also.' So they would extinguish my ember that is left, and leave to my husband *neither* name nor remnant on the earth."

8Then the king said to the woman, "Go to your house, and I will give orders concerning you."

9And the woman of Tekoa said to the king, "My lord, O king, *let* athe [1]iniquity *be* on me and on my father's house, band the king and his throne *be* guiltless."

10So the king said, "Whoever says *anything* to you, bring him to me, and he shall not touch you anymore."

11Then she said, "Please let the king remember the LORD your God, and do not permit athe avenger of blood to destroy anymore, lest they destroy my son."

And he said, b"As the LORD lives, not one hair of your son shall fall to the ground."

12Therefore the woman said, "Please, let your maidservant speak *another* word to my lord the king."

13:34
a2 Sam. 13:37, 38

13:37
a2 Sam. 3:3;
1 Chr. 3:2

13:38
a2 Sam. 14:23,
32; 15:8

13:39
aGen. 38:12;
2 Sam. 12:19, 23

14:1
a2 Sam. 13:39

14:2
a2 Sam. 23:26;
2 Chr. 11:6;
Amos 1:1
bRuth 3:3

14:3 aEx. 4:15;
2 Sam. 14:19

14:4
a1 Sam. 20:41;
25:23; 2 Sam. 1:2
b2 Kin. 6:26, 28

14:5
a[Zech. 7:10]

14:7
aNum. 35:19;
Deut. 19:12, 13

14:9 aGen. 27:13;
43:9;
1 Sam. 25:24;
Matt. 27:25
b2 Sam. 3:28, 29;
1 Kin. 2:33

14:11
aNum. 35:19, 21;
[Deut. 19:4–10]
b1 Sam. 14:45;
1 Kin. 1:52;
Matt. 10:30;
Acts 27:34

13:34 [1]LXX adds *And the watchman went and told the king, and said, "I see men from the way of Horonaim, from the regions of the mountains."*
13:39 [1]So with MT, Syr., Vg.; LXX *the spirit of the king;* Tg. *the soul of King David* [2]So with MT, Tg.; LXX, Vg. *ceased to pursue after* **14:4** [1]Many Heb. mss., LXX, Syr., Vg. *came* **14:9** [1]*guilt*

And he said, "Say on."

13So the woman said: "Why then have you schemed such a thing against ᵃthe people of God? For the king speaks this thing as one who is guilty, *in that* the king does not bring ᵇhis banished one home again. 14For we ᵃwill surely die and *become* like water spilled on the ground, which cannot be gathered up again. Yet God does not ᵇtake away a life; but He ᶜdevises means, so that His banished ones are not ¹expelled from Him. 15Now therefore, I have come to speak of this thing to my lord the king because the people have made me afraid. And your maidservant said, 'I will now speak to the king; it may be that the king will perform the request of his maidservant. 16For the king will hear and deliver his maidservant from the hand of the man *who would* destroy me and my son together from the ᵃinheritance of God.' 17Your maidservant said, 'The word of my lord the king will now be comforting; for ᵃas the angel of God, so *is* my lord the king in ᵇdiscerning good and evil. And may the Lᴏʀᴅ your God be with you.'"

18Then the king answered and said to the woman, "Please do not hide from me anything that I ask you."

And the woman said, "Please, let my lord the king speak."

19So the king said, "*Is* the hand of Joab with you in all this?" And the woman answered and said, "*As* you live, my lord the king, no one can turn to the right hand or to the left from anything that my lord the king has spoken. For your servant Joab commanded me, and ᵃhe put all these words in the mouth of your maidservant. 20To bring about this change of affairs your servant Joab has done this thing; but my lord *is* wise, ᵃaccording to the wisdom of the angel of God, to know everything that *is* in the earth."

21And the king said to Joab, "All right, I have granted this thing. Go therefore, bring back the young man Absalom."

22Then Joab fell to the ground on his face and bowed himself, and ¹thanked the king. And Joab said, "Today your servant knows that I have found favor in your sight, my lord, O king, in that the king has fulfilled the request of his servant." 23So Joab arose ᵃand went to Geshur, and brought Absalom to Jerusalem. 24And the king said, "Let him return to his own house, but ᵃdo not let him see my face." So Absalom returned to his own house, but did not see the king's face.

DAVID FORGIVES ABSALOM

25Now in all Israel there was no one who was praised as much as Absalom for his good looks. ᵃFrom the sole of his foot to the crown of his head there was no blemish in him. 26And when he cut the hair of his head—at the end of every year he cut *it* because it was heavy on him—when he cut it, he weighed the hair of his head at two hundred shekels according to the king's standard. 27ᵃTo Absalom were born three sons, and one daughter whose name *was* Tamar. She was a woman of beautiful appearance.

28And Absalom dwelt two full years in Jerusalem, ᵃbut did not see the king's face. 29Therefore Absalom sent for Joab, to send him to the king, but he would not come to him. And when he sent again the second time, he would not come. 30So he said to his servants, "See, Joab's field is near mine, and he

14:13
ᵃJudg. 20:2
ᵇ2 Sam. 13:37, 38

14:14
ᵃJob 30:23;
34:15;
[Heb. 9:27]
ᵇJob 34:19;
Matt. 22:16;
Acts 10:34;
Rom. 2:11
ᶜNum. 35:15

14:16
ᵃDeut. 32:9;
1 Sam. 26:19;
2 Sam. 20:19

14:17
ᵃ1 Sam. 29:9;
2 Sam. 19:27
ᵇ1 Kin. 3:9

14:19
ᵃ2 Sam. 14:3

14:20
ᵃ2 Sam. 14:17;
19:27

14:23
ᵃ2 Sam. 13:37, 38

14:24
ᵃGen. 43:3;
2 Sam. 3:13

14:25
ᵃDeut. 28:35;
Job 2:7; Is. 1:6

14:27
ᵃ2 Sam. 13:1;
18:18

14:28
ᵃ2 Sam. 14:24

14:14 ¹cast out   14:22 ¹Lit. *blessed*

has barley there; go and set it on fire." And Absalom's servants set the field on fire.

31Then Joab arose and came to Absalom's house, and said to him, "Why have your servants set my field on fire?"

32And Absalom answered Joab, "Look, I sent to you, saying, 'Come here, so that I may send you to the king, to say, "Why have I come from Geshur? *It would be* better for me *to be* there still."' Now therefore, let me see the king's face; but ªif there is iniquity in me, let him execute me."

33So Joab went to the king and told him. And when he had called for Absalom, he came to the king and bowed himself on his face to the ground before the king. Then the king ªkissed Absalom.

ABSALOM'S TREASON

15 After this ªit happened that Absalom ᵇprovided himself with chariots and horses, and fifty men to run before him. 2Now Absalom would rise early and stand beside the way to the gate. *So* it was, whenever anyone who had a ªlawsuit¹ came to the king for a decision, that Absalom would call to him and say, "What city *are* you from?" And he would say, "Your servant *is* from such and such a tribe of Israel." 3Then Absalom would say to him, "Look, your ¹case *is* good and right; but *there is* no ²deputy of the king to hear you." 4Moreover Absalom would say, ª"Oh, that I were made judge in the land, and everyone who has any suit or cause would come to me; then I would give him justice." 5And *so* it was, whenever anyone came near to bow down to him, that he would put out his hand and take him and ªkiss him. 6In this manner Absalom acted toward all Israel who came to the king for judgment. ªSo Absalom stole the hearts of the men of Israel.

7Now it came to pass ªafter ¹forty years that Absalom said to the king, "Please, let me go to ᵇHebron and pay the vow which I made to the LORD. 8ªFor your servant ᵇtook a vow ᶜwhile I dwelt at Geshur in Syria, saying, 'If the LORD indeed brings me back to Jerusalem, then I will serve the LORD.'"

9And the king said to him, "Go in peace." So he arose and went to Hebron.

10Then Absalom sent spies throughout all the tribes of Israel, saying, "As soon as you hear the sound of the trumpet, then you shall say, 'Absalom ªreigns in Hebron!'" 11And with Absalom went two hundred men ªinvited from Jerusalem, and they ᵇwent along innocently and did not know anything. 12Then Absalom sent for Ahithophel the Gilonite, ªDavid's counselor, from his city—from ᵇGiloh—while he offered sacrifices. And the conspiracy grew strong, for the people with Absalom ᶜcontinually increased in number.

DAVID ESCAPES FROM JERUSALEM

13Now a messenger came to David, saying, ª"The hearts of the men of Israel are ¹with Absalom."

14So David said to all his servants who *were* with him at Jerusalem, "Arise, and let us ªflee, or we shall not escape from Absalom. Make haste to depart, lest he overtake us suddenly

---

14:32
ª1 Sam. 20:8;
[Prov. 28:13]

14:33
ªGen. 33:4;
45:15;
Luke 15:20

15:1 ª2 Sam. 12:11
ᵇ1 Kin. 1:5

15:2 ªDeut. 19:17

15:4 ªJudg. 9:29

15:5
ª2 Sam. 14:33;
20:9

15:6
ª[Rom. 16:18]

15:7
ª[Deut. 23:21]
ᵇ2 Sam. 3:2, 3

15:8 ª1 Sam. 16:2
ᵇGen. 28:20, 21
ᶜ2 Sam. 13:38

15:10
ª1 Kin. 1:34;
2 Kin. 9:13

15:11
ª1 Sam. 16:3, 5
ᵇGen. 20:5

15:12
ª2 Sam. 16:15;
1 Chr. 27:33;
Ps. 41:9; 55:12–14
ᵇJosh. 15:51
ᶜPs. 3:1

15:13 ªJudg. 9:3;
2 Sam. 15:6

15:14
ª2 Sam. 12:11;
Ps. 3:title

15:2 ¹Lit. *controversy*   15:3 ¹Lit. *words*   ²Lit. *listener*   15:7 ¹LXX mss., Syr., Josephus *four*   15:13 ¹Lit. *after*

and bring disaster upon us, and strike the city with the edge of the sword."

15And the king's servants said to the king, "We *are* your servants, *ready to do* whatever my lord the king commands." 16Then ªthe king went out with all his household after him. But the king left ᵇten women, concubines, to keep the house. 17And the king went out with all the people after him, and stopped at the outskirts. 18Then all his servants passed ¹before him; ªand all the Cherethites, all the Pelethites, and all the Gittites, ᵇsix hundred men who had followed him from Gath, passed before the king.

19Then the king said to ªIttai the Gittite, "Why are you also going with us? Return and remain with the king. For you *are* a foreigner and also an exile from your own place. 20In fact, you came *only* yesterday. Should I make you wander up and down with us today, since I go ªI know not where? Return, and take your brethren back. Mercy and truth *be* with you."

21But Ittai answered the king and said, ª"*As* the LORD lives, and *as* my lord the king lives, surely in whatever place my lord the king shall be, whether in death or life, even there also your servant will be."

22So David said to Ittai, "Go, and cross over." Then Ittai the Gittite and all his men and all the little ones who *were* with him crossed over. 23And all the country wept with a loud voice, and all the people crossed over. The king himself also crossed over the Brook Kidron, and all the people crossed over toward the way of the ªwilderness.

24There was ªZadok also, and all the Levites with him, bearing the ᵇark of the covenant of God. And they set down the ark of God, and ᶜAbiathar went up until all the people had finished crossing over from the city. 25Then the king said to Zadok, "Carry the ark of God back into the city. If I find favor in the eyes of the LORD, He ªwill bring me back and show me *both* it and ᵇHis dwelling place. 26But if He says thus: 'I have no ªdelight in you,' here I am, ᵇlet Him do to me as seems good to Him." 27The king also said to Zadok the priest, "*Are* you *not* a ªseer?¹ Return to the city in peace, and ᵇyour two sons with you, Ahimaaz your son, and Jonathan the son of Abiathar. 28See, ªI will wait in the plains of the wilderness until word comes from you to inform me." 29Therefore Zadok and Abiathar carried the ark of God back to Jerusalem. And they remained there.

30So David went up by the Ascent of the *Mount of* Olives, and wept as he went up; and he ªhad his head covered and went ᵇbarefoot. And all the people who *were* with him ᶜcovered their heads and went up, ᵈweeping as they went up. 31Then *someone* told David, saying, ª"Ahithophel *is* among the conspirators with Absalom." And David said, "O LORD, I pray, ᵇturn the counsel of Ahithophel into foolishness!"

32Now it happened when David had come to the top *of the mountain,* where he worshiped God—there was Hushai the ªArchite coming to meet him ᵇwith his robe torn and dust on his head. 33David said to him, "If you go on with me, then you will become ªa burden to me. 34But if you return to the city, and say to Absalom, ª'I will be your servant, O king; *as* I *was* your father's servant previously, so I *will* now also *be* your

15:16 ªPs. 3:title
ᵇ2 Sam. 12:11;
16:21, 22

15:18
ª2 Sam. 8:18
ᵇ1 Sam. 23:13;
25:13; 30:1, 9

15:19
ª2 Sam. 18:2

15:20
ª1 Sam. 23:13

15:21
ªRuth 1:16, 17;
[Prov. 17:17]

15:23
ª2 Sam. 15:28;
16:2

15:24
ª2 Sam. 8:17
ᵇNum. 4:15;
1 Sam. 4:4
ᶜ1 Sam. 22:20

15:25 ª[Ps. 43:3]
ᵇEx. 15:13;
Jer. 25:30

15:26
ªNum. 14:8;
2 Sam. 22:20;
1 Kin. 10:9;
2 Chr. 9:8;
Is. 62:4
ᵇ1 Sam. 3:18

15:27
ª1 Sam. 9:6–9
ᵇ2 Sam. 17:17–20

15:28
ªJosh. 5:10;
2 Sam. 17:16

15:30
ª2 Sam. 19:4;
Esth. 6:12;
Ezek. 24:17, 23
ᵇIs. 20:2–4
ᶜJer. 14:3, 4
ᵈ[Ps. 126:6]

15:31 ªPs. 3:1, 2;
55:12
ᵇ2 Sam. 16:23;
17:14, 23

15:32 ªJosh. 16:2
ᵇ2 Sam. 1:2

15:33
ª2 Sam. 19:35

15:34
ª2 Sam. 16:19

15:18 ¹Lit. *by his hand*   15:27 ¹*prophet*

servant,' then you may defeat the counsel of Ahithophel for me. [35]And *do* you not *have* Zadok and Abiathar the priests with you there? Therefore it will be *that* whatever you hear from the king's house, you shall tell to [a]Zadok and Abiathar the priests. [36]Indeed *they have* there [a]with them their two sons, Ahimaaz, Zadok's *son,* and Jonathan, Abiathar's *son;* and by them you shall send me everything you hear."

[37]So Hushai, [a]David's friend, went into the city. [b]And Absalom came into Jerusalem.

MEPHIBOSHETH'S SERVANT

16 When[a] David was a little past the top *of the mountain,* there was [b]Ziba the servant of Mephibosheth, who met him with a couple of saddled donkeys, and on them two hundred *loaves* of bread, one hundred clusters of raisins, one hundred summer fruits, and a skin of wine. [2]And the king said to Ziba, "What do you mean to do with these?"

So Ziba said, "The donkeys *are* for the king's household to ride on, the bread and summer fruit for the young men to eat, and the wine for [a]those who are faint in the wilderness to drink."

[3]Then the king said, "And where *is* your [a]master's son?"

[b]And Ziba said to the king, "Indeed he is staying in Jerusalem, for he said, 'Today the house of Israel will restore the kingdom of my father to me.'"

[4]So the king said to Ziba, "Here, all that *belongs* to Mephibosheth *is* yours."

And Ziba said, "I humbly bow before you, *that* I may find favor in your sight, my lord, O king!"

SHIMEI CURSES DAVID

[5]Now when King David came to [a]Bahurim, there was a man from the family of the house of Saul, whose name *was* [b]Shimei the son of Gera, coming from there. He came out, cursing continuously as he came. [6]And he threw stones at David and at all the servants of King David. And all the people and all the mighty men *were* on his right hand and on his left. [7]Also Shimei said thus when he cursed: "Come out! Come out! You [1]bloodthirsty man, [a]you [2]rogue! [8]The LORD has [a]brought upon you all [b]the blood of the house of Saul, in whose place you have reigned; and the LORD has delivered the kingdom into the hand of Absalom your son. So now you *are caught* in your own evil, because you are a [1]bloodthirsty man!"

[9]Then Abishai the son of Zeruiah said to the king, "Why should this [a]dead dog [b]curse my lord the king? Please, let me go over and take off his head!"

[10]But the king said, [a]"What have I to do with you, you sons of Zeruiah? So let him curse, because [b]the LORD has said to him, 'Curse David.' [c]Who then shall say, 'Why have you done so?'"

[11]And David said to Abishai and all his servants, "See how [a]my son who [b]came from my own body seeks my life. How much more now *may this* Benjamite? Let him alone, and let him curse; for so the LORD has ordered him. [12]It may be that the LORD will look on [1]my affliction, and that the LORD will [a]repay me with [b]good for his cursing this day." [13]And as David

---

Cross references (left margin):

15:35 [a]2 Sam. 17:15, 16

15:36 [a]2 Sam. 15:27

15:37 [a]2 Sam. 16:16; 1 Chr. 27:33 [b]2 Sam. 16:15

16:1 [a]2 Sam. 15:30, 32 [b]2 Sam. 9:2; 19:17, 29

16:2 [a]2 Sam. 15:23; 17:29

16:3 [a]2 Sam. 9:9, 10 [b]2 Sam. 19:27

16:5 [a]2 Sam. 3:16 [b]2 Sam. 19:21; 1 Kin. 2:8, 9, 44–46

16:7 [a]Deut. 13:13

16:8 [a]Judg. 9:24, 56, 57; 1 Kin. 2:32, 33 [b]2 Sam. 1:16; 3:28, 29; 4:11, 12

16:9 [a]1 Sam. 24:14; 2 Sam. 9:8 [b]Ex. 22:28

16:10 [a]2 Sam. 3:39; 19:22; [1 Pet. 2:23] [b]2 Kin. 18:25; [Lam. 3:38] [c][Rom. 9:20]

16:11 [a]2 Sam. 12:11 [b]Gen. 15:4

16:12 [a]Deut. 23:5; Neh. 13:2; Prov. 20:22 [b]Deut. 23:5; [Rom. 8:28]; Heb. 12:10, 11]

16:7 [1]Lit. *man of bloodshed*   [2]*worthless man*   **16:8** [1]Lit. *man of bloodshed*
16:12 [1]So with Kt., LXX, Syr., Vg.; Qr. *my eyes;* Tg. *tears of my eyes*

and his men went along the road, Shimei went along the hillside opposite him and cursed as he went, threw stones at him and [1]kicked up dust. [14]Now the king and all the people who *were* with him became weary; so they refreshed themselves there.

THE ADVICE OF AHITHOPHEL

[15]Meanwhile [a]Absalom and all the people, the men of Israel, came to Jerusalem; and Ahithophel *was* with him. [16]And so it was, when Hushai the Archite, [a]David's friend, came to Absalom, that [b]Hushai said to Absalom, "*Long* live the king! *Long* live the king!"

[17]So Absalom said to Hushai, "*Is* this your loyalty to your friend? [a]Why did you not go with your friend?"

[18]And Hushai said to Absalom, "No, but whom the LORD and this people and all the men of Israel choose, his I will be, and with him I will remain. [19]Furthermore, [a]whom should I serve? *Should I* not *serve* in the presence of his son? As I have served in your father's presence, so will I be in your presence."

[20]Then Absalom said to [a]Ahithophel, "Give advice as to what we should do."

[21]And Ahithophel said to Absalom, "Go in to your father's [a]concubines, whom he has left to keep the house; and all Israel will hear that you [b]are abhorred by your father. Then [c]the hands of all who are with you will be strong." [22]So they pitched a tent for Absalom on the top of the house, and Absalom went in to his father's concubines [a]in the sight of all Israel.

[23]Now the advice of Ahithophel, which he gave in those days, *was* as if one had inquired at the oracle of God. So *was* all the advice of Ahithophel [a]both with David and with Absalom.

17 Moreover Ahithophel said to Absalom, "Now let me choose twelve thousand men, and I will arise and pursue David tonight. [2]I will come upon him while he *is* [a]weary and weak, and make him [1]afraid. And all the people who *are* with him will flee, and I will [b]strike only the king. [3]Then I will bring back all the people to you. When all return except the man whom you seek, all the people will be at peace." [4]And the saying pleased Absalom and all the [a]elders of Israel.

THE ADVICE OF HUSHAI

[5]Then Absalom said, "Now call Hushai the Archite also, and let us hear what he [a]says too." [6]And when Hushai came to Absalom, Absalom spoke to him, saying, "Ahithophel has spoken in this manner. Shall we do as he says? If not, speak up."

[7]So Hushai said to Absalom: "The advice that Ahithophel has given *is* not good at this time. [8]For," said Hushai, "you know your father and his men, that they *are* mighty men, and they *are* enraged in their minds, like [a]a bear robbed of her cubs in the field; and your father *is* a man of war, and will not camp with the people. [9]Surely by now he is hidden in some pit, or in some *other* place. And it will be, when some of them are overthrown at the first, that whoever hears *it* will say, 'There is a slaughter among the people who follow Absalom.' [10]And even he *who is* valiant, whose heart *is* like the heart of a lion, will [a]melt completely. For all Israel knows that your

---

16:15
[a]2 Sam. 15:12, 37

16:16
[a]2 Sam. 15:37
[b]2 Sam. 15:34

16:17
[a]2 Sam. 19:25;
[Prov. 17:17]

16:19
[a]2 Sam. 15:34

16:20
[a]2 Sam. 15:12

16:21
[a]2 Sam. 15:16;
20:3
[b]Gen. 34:30;
1 Sam. 13:4
[c]2 Sam. 2:7;
Zech. 8:13

16:22
[a]2 Sam. 12:11, 12

16:23
[a]2 Sam. 15:12

17:2
[a]Deut. 25:18;
2 Sam. 16:14
[b]Zech. 13:7

17:4 [a]2 Sam. 5:3;
19:11

17:5
[a]2 Sam. 15:32–34

17:8 [a]Hos. 13:8

17:10 [a]Josh. 2:11

16:13 [1]Lit. *dusted him with dust*   17:2 [1]*tremble with fear*

father *is* a mighty man, and *those* who *are* with him *are* valiant men. [11]Therefore I advise that all Israel be fully gathered to you, [a]from Dan to Beersheba, [b]like the sand that *is* by the sea for multitude, and that you go to battle in person. [12]So we will come upon him in some place where he may be found, and we will fall on him as the dew falls on the ground. And of him and all the men who *are* with him there shall not be left so much as one. [13]Moreover, if he has withdrawn into a city, then all Israel shall bring ropes to that city; and we will [a]pull it into the river, until there is not one small stone found there."

[14]So Absalom and all the men of Israel said, "The advice of Hushai the Archite *is* better than the advice of Ahithophel." For [a]the LORD had purposed to defeat the good advice of Ahithophel, to the intent that the LORD might bring disaster on Absalom.

HUSHAI WARNS DAVID TO ESCAPE

[15a]Then Hushai said to Zadok and Abiathar the priests, "Thus and so Ahithophel advised Absalom and the elders of Israel, and thus and so I have advised. [16]Now therefore, send quickly and tell David, saying, 'Do not spend this night [a]in the plains of the wilderness, but speedily cross over, lest the king and all the people who *are* with him be swallowed up.'" [17a]Now Jonathan and Ahimaaz [b]stayed at [c]En Rogel, for they dared not be seen coming into the city; so a female servant would come and tell them, and they would go and tell King David. [18]Nevertheless a lad saw them, and told Absalom. But both of them went away quickly and came to a man's house [a]in Bahurim, who had a well in his court; and they went down into it. [19a]Then the woman took and spread a covering over the well's mouth, and spread ground grain on it; and the thing was not known. [20]And when Absalom's servants came to the woman at the house, they said, "Where *are* Ahimaaz and Jonathan?"

So [a]the woman said to them, "They have gone over the water brook."

And when they had searched and could not find *them,* they returned to Jerusalem. [21]Now it came to pass, after they had departed, that they came up out of the well and went and told King David, and said to David, [a]"Arise and cross over the water quickly. For thus has Ahithophel advised against you." [22]So David and all the people who *were* with him arose and crossed over the Jordan. By morning light not one of them was left who had not gone over the Jordan.

[23]Now when Ahithophel saw that his advice was not followed, he saddled a donkey, and arose and went home to [a]his house, to his city. Then he [1]put his [b]household in order, and [c]changed himself, and died; and he was buried in his father's tomb.

[24]Then David went to [a]Mahanaim. And Absalom crossed over the Jordan, he and all the men of Israel with him. [25]And Absalom made [a]Amasa captain of the army instead of Joab. This Amasa *was* the son of a man whose name *was* [1]Jithra, an [2]Israelite, who had gone in to [b]Abigail the daughter of Nahash,

17:11 [a]Judg. 20:1;
2 Sam. 3:10
[b]Gen. 22:17;
Josh. 11:4;
1 Kin. 20:10

17:13 [a]Mic. 1:6

17:14
[a]2 Sam. 15:31, 34

17:15
[a]2 Sam. 15:35, 36

17:16
[a]2 Sam. 15:28

17:17
[a]2 Sam. 15:27, 36;
1 Kin. 1:42, 43
[b]Josh. 2:4–6
[c]Josh. 15:7;
18:16

17:18
[a]2 Sam. 3:16;
16:5

17:19
[a]Josh. 2:4–6

17:20 [a]Ex. 1:19;
[Lev. 19:11];
Josh. 2:3–5

17:21
[a]2 Sam. 17:15, 16

17:23
[a]2 Sam. 15:12
[b]2 Kin. 20:1
[c]Matt. 27:5

17:24
[a]Gen. 32:2;
Josh. 13:26;
2 Sam. 2:8;
19:32

17:25
[a]2 Sam. 19:13;
20:9–12;
1 Kin. 2:5, 32
[b]1 Chr. 2:16

17:23 [1]Lit. *gave charge concerning his house* 17:25 [1]*Jether,* 1 Chr. 2:17 [2]So with MT, some LXX mss., Tg.; some LXX mss. *Ishmaelite* (cf. 1 Chr. 2:17); Vg. *of Jezrael*

sister of Zeruiah, Joab's mother. [26]So Israel and Absalom encamped in the land of Gilead.

[27]Now it happened, when David had come to Mahanaim, that [a]Shobi the son of Nahash from Rabbah of the people of Ammon, [b]Machir the son of Ammiel from Lo Debar, and [c]Barzillai the Gileadite from Rogelim, [28]brought beds and basins, earthen vessels and wheat, barley and flour, parched *grain* and beans, lentils and parched *seeds,* [29]honey and curds, sheep and cheese of the herd, for David and the people who *were* with him to eat. For they said, "The people are hungry and weary and thirsty [a]in the wilderness."

ABSALOM'S DEFEAT AND DEATH

18 And David [1]numbered the people who *were* with him, and [a]set captains of thousands and captains of hundreds over them. [2]Then David sent out one third of the people under the hand of Joab, [a]one third under the hand of Abishai the son of Zeruiah, Joab's brother, and one third under the hand of [b]Ittai the Gittite. And the king said to the people, "I also will surely go out with you myself."

[3a]But the people answered, "You shall not go out! For if we flee away, they will not care about us; nor if half of us die, will they care about us. But *you are* worth ten thousand of us now. For you are now more help to us in the city."

[4]Then the king said to them, "Whatever seems best to you I will do." So the king stood beside the gate, and all the people went out by hundreds and by thousands. [5]Now the king had commanded Joab, Abishai, and Ittai, saying, "*Deal* gently for my sake with the young man Absalom." [a]And all the people heard when the king gave all the captains orders concerning Absalom.

[6]So the people went out into the field of battle against Israel. And the battle was in the [a]woods of Ephraim. [7]The people of Israel were overthrown there before the servants of David, and a great slaughter of twenty thousand took place there that day. [8]For the battle there was scattered over the face of the whole countryside, and the woods devoured more people that day than the sword devoured.

[9]Then Absalom met the servants of David. Absalom rode on a mule. The mule went under the thick boughs of a great terebinth tree, and [a]his head caught in the terebinth; so he was left hanging between heaven and earth. And the mule which *was* under him went on. [10]Now a certain man saw *it* and told Joab, and said, "I just saw Absalom hanging in a terebinth tree!"

[11]So Joab said to the man who told him, "You just saw *him!* And why did you not strike him there to the ground? I would have given you ten *shekels* of silver and a belt."

[12]But the man said to Joab, "Though I were to receive a thousand *shekels* of silver in my hand, I would not raise my hand against the king's son. [a]For in our hearing the king commanded you and Abishai and Ittai, saying, [1]'Beware lest anyone *touch* the young man Absalom!' [13]Otherwise I would have dealt falsely against my own life. For there is nothing hidden from the king, and you yourself would have set yourself against *me.*"

17:27
[a]1 Sam. 11:1;
2 Sam. 10:1;
12:29
[b]2 Sam. 9:4
[c]2 Sam. 19:31,
32; 1 Kin. 2:7

17:29
[a]2 Sam. 16:2, 14

18:1 [a]Ex. 18:25;
Num. 31:14;
1 Sam. 22:7

18:2 [a]Judg. 7:16;
1 Sam. 11:11
[b]2 Sam. 15:19–22

18:3
[a]2 Sam. 21:17

18:5
[a]2 Sam. 18:12

18:6 [a]Josh. 17:15,
18; 2 Sam. 17:26

18:9
[a]2 Sam. 14:26

18:12
[a]2 Sam. 18:5

18:1 [1]Lit. *attended to*   18:12 [1]Vss. *'Protect the young man Absalom for me!'*

¹⁴Then Joab said, "I cannot linger with you." And he took three spears in his hand and thrust them through Absalom's heart, while he was *still* alive in the midst of the terebinth tree. ¹⁵And ten young men who bore Joab's armor surrounded Absalom, and struck and killed him.

¹⁶So Joab blew the trumpet, and the people returned from pursuing Israel. For Joab held back the people. ¹⁷And they took Absalom and cast him into a large pit in the woods, and ªlaid a very large heap of stones over him. Then all Israel ᵇfled, everyone to his tent.

¹⁸Now Absalom in his lifetime had taken and set up a ¹pillar for himself, which *is* in ªthe King's Valley. For he said, ᵇ"I have no son to keep my name in remembrance." He called the pillar after his own name. And to this day it is called Absalom's Monument.

DAVID HEARS OF ABSALOM'S DEATH

¹⁹Then ªAhimaaz the son of Zadok said, "Let me run now and take the news to the king, how the LORD has ¹avenged him of his enemies."

²⁰And Joab said to him, "You shall not take the news this day, for you shall take the news another day. But today you shall take no news, because the king's son is dead." ²¹Then Joab said to the Cushite, "Go, tell the king what you have seen." So the Cushite bowed himself to Joab and ran.

²²And Ahimaaz the son of Zadok said again to Joab, "But ¹whatever happens, please let me also run after the Cushite."

So Joab said, "Why will you run, my son, since you have no news ready?"

²³"But whatever happens," *he said,* "let me run."

So he said to him, "Run." Then Ahimaaz ran by way of the plain, and outran the Cushite.

²⁴Now David was sitting between the ªtwo gates. And the watchman went up to the roof over the gate, to the wall, lifted his eyes and looked, and there was a man, running alone. ²⁵Then the watchman cried out and told the king. And the king said, "If he *is* alone, *there is* news in his mouth." And he came rapidly and drew near.

²⁶Then the watchman saw *another* man running, and the watchman called to the gatekeeper and said, "There is *another* man, running alone!"

And the king said, "He also brings news."

²⁷So the watchman said, ¹"I think the running of the first is like the running of Ahimaaz the son of Zadok."

And the king said, "He *is* a good man, and comes with ªgood news."

²⁸So Ahimaaz called out and said to the king, ¹"All is well!" Then he bowed down with his face to the earth before the king, and said, ª"Blessed *be* the LORD your God, who has delivered up the men who raised their hand against my lord the king!"

²⁹The king said, "Is the young man Absalom safe?"

Ahimaaz answered, "When Joab sent the king's servant and *me* your servant, I saw a great tumult, but I did not know what *it was* about."

18:17
ªDeut. 21:20, 21; Josh. 7:26; 8:29
ᵇ2 Sam. 19:8; 20:1, 22

18:18 ªGen. 14:17
ᵇ2 Sam. 14:27

18:19
ª2 Sam. 15:36; 17:17

18:24
ªJudg. 5:11; 2 Sam. 13:34; 2 Kin. 9:17

18:27 ª1 Kin. 1:42

18:28
ª2 Sam. 16:12

18:18 ¹monument   18:19 ¹vindicated   18:22 ¹Lit. *be what may*   18:27 ¹Lit. *I see the running*   18:28 ¹*Peace be to you*

³⁰And the king said, "Turn aside *and* stand here." So he turned aside and stood still.

³¹Just then the Cushite came, and the Cushite said, "There is good news, my lord the king! For the LORD has avenged you this day of all those who rose against you."

³²And the king said to the Cushite, "Is the young man Absalom safe?"

So the Cushite answered, "May the enemies of my lord the king, and all who rise against you to do harm, be like *that* young man!"

DAVID'S MOURNING FOR ABSALOM

³³Then the king was deeply moved, and went up to the chamber over the gate, and wept. And as he went, he said thus: ᵃ"O my son Absalom—my son, my son Absalom—if only I had died in your place! O Absalom my son, ᵇmy son!"

19 And Joab was told, "Behold, the king is weeping and ᵃmourning for Absalom." ²So the victory that day was *turned* into ᵃmourning for all the people. For the people heard it said that day, "The king is grieved for his son." ³And the people ¹stole back ᵃinto the city that day, as people who are ashamed steal away when they flee in battle. ⁴But the king ᵃcovered his face, and the king cried out with a loud voice, ᵇ"O my son Absalom! O Absalom, my son, my son!"

⁵Then ᵃJoab came into the house to the king, and said, "Today you have disgraced all your servants who today have saved your life, the lives of your sons and daughters, the lives of your wives and the lives of your concubines, ⁶in that you love your enemies and hate your friends. For you have declared today that you ¹regard neither princes nor servants; for today I perceive that if Absalom had lived and all of us had died today, then it would have pleased you well. ⁷Now therefore, arise, go out and speak ¹comfort to your servants. For I swear by the LORD, if you do not go out, not one will stay with you this night. And that will be worse for you than all the evil that has befallen you from your youth until now." ⁸Then the king arose and sat in the ᵃgate. And they told all the people, saying, "There is the king, sitting in the gate." So all the people came before the king.

For everyone of Israel had ᵇfled to his tent.

DAVID RETURNS TO JERUSALEM

⁹Now all the people were in a dispute throughout all the tribes of Israel, saying, "The king saved us from the hand of our ᵃenemies, he delivered us from the hand of the ᵇPhilistines, and now he has ᶜfled from the land because of Absalom. ¹⁰But Absalom, whom we anointed over us, has died in battle. Now therefore, why do you say nothing about bringing back the king?"

¹¹So King David sent to ᵃZadok and Abiathar the priests, saying, "Speak to the elders of Judah, saying, 'Why are you the last to bring the king back to his house, since the words of all Israel have come to the king, to his *very* house? ¹²You *are* my brethren, you *are* ᵃmy bone and my flesh. Why then are you the last to bring back the king?' ¹³ᵃAnd say to Amasa, '*Are* you not my bone and my flesh? ᵇGod do so to me, and

18:33
ᵃ2 Sam. 12:10
ᵇ2 Sam. 19:4

19:1 ᵃJer. 14:2

19:2 ᵃEsth. 4:3

19:3
ᵃ2 Sam. 17:24, 27; 19:32

19:4
ᵃ2 Sam. 15:30
ᵇ2 Sam. 18:33

19:5
ᵃ2 Sam. 18:14

19:8
ᵃ2 Sam. 15:2; 18:24
ᵇ2 Sam. 18:17

19:9
ᵃ2 Sam. 8:1–14
ᵇ2 Sam. 3:18
ᶜ2 Sam. 15:14

19:11
ᵃ2 Sam. 15:24

19:12
ᵃ2 Sam. 5:1; 1 Chr. 11:1

19:13
ᵃ2 Sam. 17:25; 1 Chr. 2:17
ᵇRuth 1:17

19:3 ¹*went by stealth*   **19:6** ¹*have no respect for*   **19:7** ¹*Lit. to the heart of*

more also, if you are not commander of the army before me [1]continually in place of Joab.'" [14]So he swayed the hearts of all the men of Judah, [a]just as *the heart of* one man, so that they sent *this word* to the king: "Return, you and all your servants!"

[15]Then the king returned and came to the Jordan. And Judah came to [a]Gilgal, to go to meet the king, to escort the king [b]across the Jordan. [16]And [a]Shimei the son of Gera, a Benjamite, who *was* from Bahurim, hurried and came down with the men of Judah to meet King David. [17]*There were* a thousand men of [a]Benjamin with him, and [b]Ziba the servant of the house of Saul, and his fifteen sons and his twenty servants with him; and they went over the Jordan before the king. [18]Then a ferryboat went across to carry over the king's household, and to do what he thought good.

DAVID'S MERCY TO SHIMEI

Now Shimei the son of Gera fell down before the king when he had crossed the Jordan. [19]Then he said to the king, [a]"Do not let my lord [1]impute iniquity to me, or remember what [b]wrong your servant did on the day that my lord the king left Jerusalem, that the king should [c]take *it* to heart. [20]For I, your servant, know that I have sinned. Therefore here I am, the first to come today of all [a]the house of Joseph to go down to meet my lord the king."

[21]But Abishai the son of Zeruiah answered and said, "Shall not Shimei be put to death for this, [a]because he [b]cursed the LORD's anointed?"

[22]And David said, [a]"What have I to do with you, you sons of Zeruiah, that you should be adversaries to me today? [b]Shall any man be put to death today in Israel? For do I not know that today I *am* king over Israel?" [23]Therefore [a]the king said to Shimei, "You shall not die." And the king swore to him.

DAVID AND MEPHIBOSHETH MEET

[24]Now [a]Mephibosheth the son of Saul came down to meet the king. And he had not cared for his feet, nor trimmed his mustache, nor washed his clothes, from the day the king departed until the day he returned in peace. [25]So it was, when he had come to Jerusalem to meet the king, that the king said to him, [a]"Why did you not go with me, Mephibosheth?"

[26]And he answered, "My lord, O king, my servant deceived me. For your servant said, 'I will saddle a donkey for myself, that I may ride on it and go to the king,' because your servant *is* lame. [27]And [a]he has slandered your servant to my lord the king, [b]but my lord the king *is* like the angel of God. Therefore do *what is* good in your eyes. [28]For all my father's house were but dead men before my lord the king. [a]Yet you set your servant among those who eat at your own table. Therefore what right have I still to [1]cry out anymore to the king?"

[29]So the king said to him, "Why do you speak anymore of your matters? I have said, 'You and Ziba divide the land.'"

[30]Then Mephibosheth said to the king, "Rather, let him take it all, inasmuch as my lord the king has come back in peace to his own house."

19:14 [a]Judg. 20:1

19:15 [a]Josh. 5:9; 1 Sam. 11:14, 15 [b]2 Sam. 17:22

19:16 [a]2 Sam. 16:5; 1 Kin. 2:8

19:17 [a]2 Sam. 3:19; 1 Kin. 12:21 [b]2 Sam. 9:2, 10; 16:1, 2

19:19 [a]1 Sam. 22:15 [b]2 Sam. 16:5, 6 [c]2 Sam. 13:33

19:20 [a]Judg. 1:22; 1 Kin. 11:28

19:21 [a][Ex. 22:28] [b][1 Sam. 26:9]

19:22 [a]2 Sam. 3:39; 16:10 [b]1 Sam. 11:13

19:23 [a]1 Kin. 2:8, 9, 37, 46

19:24 [a]2 Sam. 9:6; 21:7

19:25 [a]2 Sam. 16:17

19:27 [a]2 Sam. 16:3, 4 [b]2 Sam. 14:17, 20

19:28 [a]2 Sam. 9:7–13

19:13 [1]*permanently*　19:19 [1]*charge me with iniquity*　19:28 [1]*complain*

DAVID'S KINDNESS TO BARZILLAI

31And aBarzillai the Gileadite came down from Rogelim and went across the Jordan with the king, to escort him across the Jordan. 32Now Barzillai was a very aged man, eighty years old. And ahe had provided the king with supplies while he stayed at Mahanaim, for he *was* a very rich man. 33And the king said to Barzillai, "Come across with me, and I will provide for you while you are with me in Jerusalem."

34But Barzillai said to the king, "How long have I to live, that I should go up with the king to Jerusalem? 35I *am* today aeighty years old. Can I discern between the good and bad? Can your servant taste what I eat or what I drink? Can I hear any longer the voice of singing men and singing women? Why then should your servant be a further burden to my lord the king? 36Your servant will go a little way across the Jordan with the king. And why should the king repay me *with* such a reward? 37Please let your servant turn back again, that I may die in my own city, near the grave of my father and mother. But here is your servant aChimham; let him cross over with my lord the king, and do for him what seems good to you."

38And the king answered, "Chimham shall cross over with me, and I will do for him what seems good to you. Now whatever you request of me, I will do for you." 39Then all the people went over the Jordan. And when the king had crossed over, the king akissed Barzillai and blessed him, and he returned to his own place.

THE QUARREL ABOUT THE KING

40Now the king went on to Gilgal, and 1Chimham went on with him. And all the people of Judah escorted the king, and also half the people of Israel. 41Just then all the men of Israel came to the king, and said to the king, "Why have our brethren, the men of Judah, stolen you away and abrought the king, his household, and all David's men with him across the Jordan?"

42So all the men of Judah answered the men of Israel, "Because the king *is* aa close relative of ours. Why then are you angry over this matter? Have we ever eaten at the king's *expense*? Or has he given us any gift?"

43And the men of Israel answered the men of Judah, and said, "We have aten shares in the king; therefore we also have more *right* to David than you. Why then do you despise us— were we not the first to advise bringing back our king?"

Yet bthe words of the men of Judah were 1fiercer than the words of the men of Israel.

THE REBELLION OF SHEBA

20 And there happened to be there a 1rebel, whose name *was* Sheba the son of Bichri, a Benjamite. And he blew a trumpet, and said:

a"We have no share in David,
   Nor do we have inheritance in the son of Jesse;
   bEvery man to his tents, O Israel!"

2So every man of Israel deserted David, *and* followed Sheba the son of Bichri. But the amen of Judah, from the Jordan as far as Jerusalem, remained loyal to their king.

19:31
a2 Sam. 17:27–29; 1 Kin. 2:7

19:32
a2 Sam. 17:27–29

19:35 aPs. 90:10

19:37
a2 Sam. 19:40; Jer. 41:17

19:39
aGen. 31:55; Ruth 1:14; 2 Sam. 14:33

19:41
a2 Sam. 19:15

19:42
a2 Sam. 19:12

19:43
a1 Kin. 11:30, 31
bJudg. 8:1; 12:1

20:1
a2 Sam. 19:43; 1 Kin. 12:16
b1 Sam. 13:2; 2 Sam. 18:17; 2 Chr. 10:16

20:2
a2 Sam. 19:14

19:40 1MT *Chimham*   19:43 1*harsher*   20:1 1Lit. *man of Belial*

3Now David came to his house at Jerusalem. And the king took the ten women, ªhis concubines whom he had left to keep the house, and put them in seclusion and supported them, but did not go in to them. So they were shut up to the day of their death, living in widowhood.

4And the king said to Amasa, ª"Assemble the men of Judah for me within three days, and be present here yourself." 5So Amasa went to assemble *the men of* Judah. But he delayed longer than the set time which David had appointed him. 6And David said to ªAbishai, "Now Sheba the son of Bichri will do us more harm than Absalom. Take ᵇyour lord's servants and pursue him, lest he find for himself fortified cities, and escape us." 7So Joab's men, with the ªCherethites, the Pelethites, and ᵇall the mighty men, went out after him. And they went out of Jerusalem to pursue Sheba the son of Bichri. 8When they *were* at the large stone which *is* in Gibeon, Amasa came before them. Now Joab was dressed in battle armor; on it was a belt *with* a sword fastened in its sheath at his hips; and as he was going forward, it fell out. 9Then Joab said to Amasa, "*Are* you in health, my brother?" ªAnd Joab took Amasa by the beard with his right hand to kiss him. 10But Amasa did not notice the sword that *was* in Joab's hand. And ªhe struck him with it ᵇin the stomach, and his entrails poured out on the ground; and he did not *strike* him again. Thus he died.

Then Joab and Abishai his brother pursued Sheba the son of Bichri. 11Meanwhile one of Joab's men stood near Amasa, and said, "Whoever favors Joab and whoever *is* for David—follow Joab!" 12But Amasa wallowed in *his* blood in the middle of the highway. And when the man saw that all the people stood still, he moved Amasa from the highway to the field and threw a garment over him, when he saw that everyone who came upon him halted. 13When he was removed from the highway, all the people went on after Joab to pursue Sheba the son of Bichri.

14And he went through all the tribes of Israel to ªAbel and Beth Maachah and all the Berites. So they were gathered together and also went after ¹*Sheba.* 15Then they came and besieged him in Abel of Beth Maachah; and they ªcast up a siege mound against the city, and it stood by the rampart. And all the people who *were* with Joab battered the wall to throw it down.

16Then a wise woman cried out from the city, "Hear, hear! Please say to Joab, 'Come nearby, that I may speak with you.'" 17When he had come near to her, the woman said, "*Are* you Joab?"

He answered, "I *am.*"

Then she said to him, "Hear the words of your maidservant."

And he answered, "I am listening."

18So she spoke, saying, "They used to talk in former times, saying, 'They shall surely seek *guidance* at Abel,' and so they would end *disputes.* 19I *am among the* peaceable *and* faithful in Israel. You seek to destroy a city and a mother in Israel. Why would you swallow up ªthe inheritance of the LORD?"

20And Joab answered and said, "Far be it, far be it from me, that I should swallow up or destroy! 21That *is* not so. But a

---

20:3
ª2 Sam. 15:16;
16:21, 22

20:4
ª2 Sam. 17:25;
19:13

20:6
ª2 Sam. 21:17
ᵇ2 Sam. 11:11;
1 Kin. 1:33

20:7
ª2 Sam. 8:18;
1 Kin. 1:38, 44
ᵇ2 Sam. 15:18

20:9
ªMatt. 26:49;
Luke 22:47

20:10
ª2 Sam. 3:27;
1 Kin. 2:5
ᵇ2 Sam. 2:23

20:14
ª1 Kin. 15:20;
2 Kin. 15:29;
2 Chr. 16:4

20:15
ª2 Kin. 19:32;
Ezek. 4:2

20:19
ª1 Sam. 26:19;
2 Sam. 14:16;
21:3

20:14 ¹Lit. *him*

man from the mountains of Ephraim, Sheba the son of Bichri by name, has raised his hand against the king, against David. Deliver him only, and I will depart from the city."

So the woman said to Joab, "Watch, his head will be thrown to you over the wall." 22Then the woman ain her wisdom went to all the people. And they cut off the head of Sheba the son of Bichri, and threw *it* out to Joab. Then he blew a trumpet, and they withdrew from the city, every man to his tent. So Joab returned to the king at Jerusalem.

DAVID'S GOVERNMENT OFFICERS

23And aJoab *was* over all the army of Israel; Benaiah the son of Jehoiada *was* over the Cherethites and the Pelethites; 24Adoram *was* ain charge of revenue; bJehoshaphat the son of Ahilud *was* recorder; 25Sheva *was* scribe; aZadok and Abiathar *were* the priests; 26aand Ira the Jairite was 1a chief minister under David.

DAVID AVENGES THE GIBEONITES

21 Now there was a famine in the days of David for three years, year after year; and David ainquired of the LORD. And the LORD answered, "*It is* because of Saul and *his* 1bloodthirsty house, because he killed the Gibeonites." 2So the king called the Gibeonites and spoke to them. Now the Gibeonites *were* not of the children of Israel, but aof the remnant of the Amorites; the children of Israel had sworn protection to them, but Saul had sought to kill them bin his zeal for the children of Israel and Judah.

3Therefore David said to the Gibeonites, "What shall I do for you? And with what shall I make atonement, that you may bless athe inheritance of the LORD?"

4And the Gibeonites said to him, "We will have no silver or gold from Saul or from his house, nor shall you kill any man in Israel for us."

So he said, "Whatever you say, I will do for you."

5Then they answered the king, "As for the man who consumed us and plotted against us, *that* we should be destroyed from remaining in any of the territories of Israel, 6let seven men of his descendants be delivered ato us, and we will hang them before the LORD bin Gibeah of Saul, cwhom the LORD chose."

And the king said, "I will give *them*."

7But the king spared aMephibosheth the son of Jonathan, the son of Saul, because of bthe LORD's oath that *was* between them, between David and Jonathan the son of Saul. 8So the king took Armoni and Mephibosheth, the two sons of aRizpah the daughter of Aiah, whom she bore to Saul, and the five sons of 1Michal the daughter of Saul, whom she 2brought up for Adriel the son of Barzillai the Meholathite; 9and he delivered them into the hands of the Gibeonites, and they hanged them on the hill abefore the LORD. So they fell, *all* seven together, and were put to death in the days of harvest, in the first *days,* in the beginning of barley harvest.

10Now aRizpah the daughter of Aiah took sackcloth and spread it for herself on the rock, bfrom the beginning of harvest until the late rains poured on them from heaven. And

20:22
a2 Sam. 20:16;
[Eccl. 9:13–16]

20:23
a2 Sam. 8:16–18;
1 Kin. 4:3–6

20:24 a1 Kin. 4:6
b2 Sam. 8:16;
1 Kin. 4:3

20:25
a2 Sam. 8:17;
1 Kin. 4:4

20:26
a2 Sam. 8:18

21:1
aNum. 27:21;
2 Sam. 5:19

21:2 aJosh. 9:3,
15–20
b[Ex. 34:11–16]

21:3
a1 Sam. 26:19;
2 Sam. 20:19

21:6 aNum. 25:4
b1 Sam. 10:26
c1 Sam. 10:24;
[Hos. 13:11]

21:7 a2 Sam. 4:4;
9:10
b1 Sam. 18:3;
20:12–17; 23:18;
2 Sam. 9:1–7

21:8 a2 Sam. 3:7

21:9
a2 Sam. 6:17

21:10
a2 Sam. 3:7; 21:8
bDeut. 21:23

20:26 1Or *David's priest*   21:1 1Lit. *house of bloodshed*   21:8 1*Merab,* 1 Sam. 18:19; 25:44; 2 Sam. 3:14; 6:23   2Lit. *bore to Adriel*

she did not allow the birds of the air to rest on them by day nor the beasts of the field by night.

[11]And David was told what Rizpah the daughter of Aiah, the concubine of Saul, had done. [12]Then David went and took the bones of Saul, and the bones of Jonathan his son, from the men of [a]Jabesh Gilead who had stolen them from the street of [1]Beth Shan, where the [b]Philistines had hung them up, after the Philistines had struck down Saul in Gilboa. [13]So he brought up the bones of Saul and the bones of Jonathan his son from there; and they gathered the bones of those who had been hanged. [14]They buried the bones of Saul and Jonathan his son in the country of Benjamin in [a]Zelah, in the tomb of Kish his father. So they performed all that the king commanded. And after that [b]God heeded the prayer for the land.

PHILISTINE GIANTS DESTROYED
(1 Chr. 20:4–8)

[15]When the Philistines were at war again with Israel, David and his servants with him went down and fought against the Philistines; and David grew faint. [16]Then Ishbi-Benob, who *was* one of the sons of [1]the [a]giant, the weight of whose bronze spear *was* three hundred *shekels,* who was bearing a new *sword,* thought he could kill David. [17]But [a]Abishai the son of Zeruiah came to his aid, and struck the Philistine and killed him. Then the men of David swore to him, saying, [b]"You shall go out no more with us to battle, lest you quench the [c]lamp of Israel."

[18a]Now it happened afterward that there was again a battle with the Philistines at Gob. Then [b]Sibbechai the Hushathite killed [1]Saph, who *was* one of the sons of [2]the giant. [19]Again there was war at Gob with the Philistines, where [a]Elhanan the son of [1]Jaare-Oregim the Bethlehemite killed [b]*the brother of* Goliath the Gittite, the shaft of whose spear *was* like a weaver's beam.

[20]Yet again [a]there was war at Gath, where there was a man of *great* stature, who had six fingers on each hand and six toes on each foot, twenty-four in number; and he also was born to [1]the giant. [21]So when he [a]defied Israel, Jonathan the son of [1]Shimea, David's brother, killed him.

[22a]These four were born to [1]the giant in Gath, and fell by the hand of David and by the hand of his servants.

PRAISE FOR GOD'S DELIVERANCE
(Ps. 18:1–50)

22 Then David [a]spoke to the Lord the words of this song, on the day when the Lord had [b]delivered him from the hand of all his enemies, and from the hand of Saul. [2]And he [a]said:

[b]"The Lord *is* my rock and my [c]fortress and my deliverer;
3   The God of my strength, [a]in whom I will trust;
     My [b]shield and the [c]horn[1] of my salvation,
     My [d]stronghold and my [e]refuge;
     My Savior, You save me from violence.

21:12 [a]1 Sam. 31:11–13
[b]1 Sam. 31:8

21:14 [a]Josh. 18:28
[b]Josh. 7:26;
2 Sam. 24:25

21:16 [a]Num. 13:22, 28; Josh. 15:14;
2 Sam. 21:18–22

21:17 [a]2 Sam. 20:6–10
[b]2 Sam. 18:3
[c]2 Sam. 22:29;
1 Kin. 11:36

21:18 [a]1 Chr. 20:4–8
[b]1 Chr. 11:29;
27:11

21:19 [a]2 Sam. 23:24
[b]1 Sam. 17:4;
1 Chr. 20:5

21:20 [a]1 Chr. 20:6

21:21 [a]1 Sam. 17:10

21:22 [a]1 Chr. 20:8

22:1 [a]Ex. 15:1;
Deut. 31:30;
Judg. 5:1
[b]Ps. 18:title;
34:19

22:2 [a]Ps. 18
[b]Deut. 32:4;
1 Sam. 2:2
[c]Ps. 91:2

22:3 [a]Ps. 7:1;
Heb. 2:13
[b]Gen. 15:1;
Deut. 33:29;
Ps. 84:11
[c]Luke 1:69
[d]Prov. 18:10
[e]Ps. 9:9; 46:1, 7, 11; Jer. 16:19

21:12 [1]*Beth Shean,* Josh. 17:11   21:16 [1]Or *Rapha*   21:18 [1]*Sippai,* 1 Chr. 20:4
[2]Or *Rapha*   21:19 [1]*Jair,* 1 Chr. 20:5   21:20 [1]Or *Rapha*   21:21 [1]*Shammah,*
1 Sam. 16:9 and elsewhere   21:22 [1]Or *Rapha*   22:3 [1]Strength

4   I will call upon the LORD, *who is worthy* to be
        praised;
    So shall I be saved from my enemies.

5   "When the waves of death surrounded me,
    The floods of ungodliness ¹made me afraid.
6   The ªsorrows of Sheol surrounded me;
    The snares of death confronted me.
7   In my distress ªI called upon the LORD,
    And cried out to my God;
    He ᵇheard my voice from His temple,
    And my cry *entered* His ears.

8   "Then ªthe earth shook and trembled;
    ᵇThe foundations of ¹heaven quaked and were shaken,
    Because He was angry.
9   Smoke went up from His nostrils,
    And devouring ªfire from His mouth;
    Coals were kindled by it.
10 He ªbowed the heavens also, and came down
    With ᵇdarkness under His feet.
11 He rode upon a cherub, and flew;
    And He ¹was seen ªupon the wings of the wind.
12 He made ªdarkness canopies around Him,
    Dark waters *and* thick clouds of the skies.
13 From the brightness before Him
    Coals of fire were kindled.

14 "The LORD ªthundered from heaven,
    And the Most High uttered His voice.
15 He sent out ªarrows and scattered them;
    Lightning bolts, and He vanquished them.
16 Then the channels of the sea ªwere seen,
    The foundations of the world were uncovered,
    At the ᵇrebuke of the LORD,
    At the blast of the breath of His nostrils.

17 "Heª sent from above, He took me,
    He drew me out of many waters.
18 He delivered me from my strong enemy,
    From those who hated me;
    For they were too strong for me.
19 They confronted me in the day of my calamity,
    But the LORD was my ªsupport.
20 ªHe also brought me out into a broad place;
    He delivered me because He ᵇdelighted in me.

21 "Theª LORD rewarded me according to my
        righteousness;
    According to the ᵇcleanness of my hands
    He has recompensed me.
22 For I have ªkept the ways of the LORD,
    And have not wickedly departed from my God.
23 For all His ªjudgments *were* before me;
    And *as for* His statutes, I did not depart from them.
24 I was also ªblameless before Him,
    And I kept myself from my iniquity.

22:6 ªPs. 116:3

22:7 ªPs. 116:4;
120:1 ᵇEx. 3:7;
Ps. 34:6, 15

22:8 ªJudg. 5:4;
Ps. 77:18; 97:4
ᵇJob 26:11

22:9
ªDeut. 32:22;
Ps. 97:3, 4;
Heb. 12:29

22:10
ªEx. 19:16–20;
Is. 64:1
ᵇEx. 20:21

22:11 ªPs. 104:3

22:12
ªJob 36:29;
Ps. 97:2

22:14
ª1 Sam. 2:10;
Job 37:2–5;
Ps. 29:3

22:15
ªDeut. 32:23;
Josh. 10:10;
1 Sam. 7:10;
Ps. 7:13

22:16 ªNah. 1:4
ᵇEx. 15:8

22:17 ªPs. 144:7;
Is. 43:2

22:19 ªIs. 10:20

22:20
ªPs. 31:8; 118:5
ᵇ2 Sam. 15:26

22:21
ª1 Sam. 26:23;
[Ps. 7:8]
ᵇ[Job 17:9];
Ps. 24:4

22:22
ªGen. 18:19;
2 Chr. 34:33;
Ps. 119:3

22:23
ª[Deut. 6:6–9;
7:12]; Ps. 119:30,
102

22:24
ªGen. 6:9;
7:1; Job 1:1;
[Eph. 1:4;
Col. 1:21, 22]

22:5 ¹Or *overwhelmed*   22:8 ¹So with MT, LXX, Tg.; Syr., Vg. *hills* (cf. Ps. 18:7)
22:11 ¹So with MT, LXX; many Heb. mss., Syr., Vg. *flew* (cf. Ps. 18:10); Tg.
spoke with power

25 Therefore ^athe LORD has ¹recompensed me according to
   my righteousness,
   According to ²my cleanness in His eyes.

26 "With ^athe merciful You will show Yourself merciful;
   With a blameless man You will show Yourself
   blameless;

27 With the pure You will show Yourself pure;
   And ^awith the devious You will show Yourself shrewd.

28 You will save the ^ahumble¹ people;
   But Your eyes *are* on ^bthe haughty, *that* You may bring
   them down.

29 "For You *are* my ^alamp, O LORD;
   The LORD shall enlighten my darkness.

30 For by You I can run against a troop;
   By my God I can leap over a ^awall.

31 *As for* God, ^aHis way *is* perfect;
   ^bThe word of the LORD *is* proven;
   He *is* a shield to all who trust in Him.

32 "For ^awho *is* God, except the LORD?
   And who *is* a rock, except our God?

33 ¹God *is* my ^astrength *and* power,
   And He ^bmakes ²my way ^cperfect.

34 He makes ¹my feet ^alike the *feet* of deer,
   And ^bsets me on my high places.

35 He teaches my hands ¹to make war,
   So that my arms can bend a bow of bronze.

36 "You have also given me the shield of Your salvation;
   Your gentleness has made me great.

37 You ^aenlarged my path under me;
   So my feet did not slip.

38 "I have pursued my enemies and destroyed them;
   Neither did I turn back again till they were destroyed.

39 And I have destroyed them and wounded them,
   So that they could not rise;
   They have fallen ^aunder my feet.

40 For You have ^aarmed me with strength for the battle;
   You have ¹subdued under me ^bthose who rose against me.

41 You have also ¹given me the ^anecks of my enemies,
   So that I destroyed those who hated me.

42 They looked, but *there was* none to save;
   Even ^ato the LORD, but He did not answer them.

43 Then I beat them as fine ^aas the dust of the earth;
   I trod them ^blike dirt in the streets,
   And I ¹spread them out.

44 "You^a have also delivered me from the ¹strivings of my
   people;
   You have kept me as the ^bhead of the nations.
   ^cA people I have not known shall serve me.

22:25
^a2 Sam. 22:21

22:26
^a[Matt. 5:7]

22:27
^a[Lev. 26:23, 24;
Rom. 1:28]

22:28 ^aPs. 72:12
^bJob 40:11

22:29
^aPs. 119:105;
132:17

22:30
^a2 Sam. 5:6–8

22:31
^a[Deut. 32:4];
Dan. 4:37;
[Matt. 5:48];
^bPs. 12:6;
[Prov. 30:5]

22:32
^aIs. 45:5, 6

22:33 ^aPs. 27:1
^b[Heb. 13:21]
^cPs. 101:2, 6

22:34
^a2 Sam. 2:18;
Hab. 3:19
^bIs. 33:16

22:37
^a2 Sam. 22:20;
Prov. 4:12

22:39 ^aMal. 4:3

22:40
^a[Ps. 18:32]
^b[Ps. 44:5]

22:41
^aGen. 49:8;
Josh. 10:24

22:42
^a1 Sam. 28:6;
Prov. 1:28; Is. 1:15

22:43
^a2 Kin. 13:7;
Ps. 18:42
^bIs. 10:6

22:44
^a2 Sam. 3:1
^bDeut. 28:13
^c[Is. 55:5]

22:25 ¹*rewarded*   ²LXX, Syr., Vg. *the cleanness of my hands in His sight* (cf. Ps. 18:24); Tg. *my cleanness before His word*   22:28 ¹*afflicted*   22:33 ¹DSS, LXX, Syr., Vg. *It is God who arms me with strength* (cf. Ps. 18:32); Tg. *It is God who sustains me with strength*   ²So with Qr., LXX, Syr., Tg., Vg. (cf. Ps. 18:32); Kt. *His*   22:34 ¹So with Qr., LXX, Syr., Tg., Vg. (cf. Ps. 18:33); Kt. *His*   22:35 ¹Lit. *for the war*   22:40 ¹Lit. *caused to bow down*   22:41 ¹*given me victory over*   22:43 ¹*scattered*   22:44 ¹*contentions*

45 The foreigners submit to me;
   As soon as they hear, they obey me.
46 The foreigners fade away,
   And ¹come frightened ᵃfrom their hideouts.

47 "The LORD lives!
   Blessed *be* my Rock!
   Let God be exalted,
   The ᵃRock of my salvation!
48 *It is* God who avenges me,
   And ᵃsubdues the peoples under me;
49 He delivers me from my enemies.
   You also lift me up above those who rise against me;
   You have delivered me from the ᵃviolent man.
50 Therefore I will give thanks to You, O LORD, among ᵃthe
      Gentiles,
   And sing praises to Your ᵇname.

51 "Heᵃ *is* the tower of salvation to His king,
   And shows mercy to His ᵇanointed,
   To David and ᶜhis descendants forevermore."

DAVID'S LAST WORDS

23 Now these *are* the last words of David.

   Thus says David the son of Jesse;
   Thus says ᵃthe man raised up on high,
   ᵇThe anointed of the God of Jacob,
   And the sweet psalmist of Israel:

2 "Theᵃ Spirit of the LORD spoke by me,
   And His word *was* on my tongue.
3 The God of Israel said,
   ᵃThe Rock of Israel spoke to me:
   'He who rules over men *must be* just,
   Ruling ᵇin the fear of God.
4 And ᵃhe shall *be* like the light of the morning *when* the
      sun rises,
   A morning without clouds,
   Like the tender grass *springing* out of the earth,
   By clear shining after rain.'

5 "Although my house *is* not so with God,
   ᵃYet He has made with me an everlasting covenant,
   Ordered in all *things* and secure.
   For *this is* all my salvation and all *my* desire;
   Will He not make *it* increase?
6 But *the sons* of rebellion *shall* all *be* as thorns thrust away,
   Because they cannot be taken with hands.
7 But the man *who* touches them
   Must be ¹armed with iron and the shaft of a spear,
   And they shall be utterly burned with fire in *their* place."

DAVID'S MIGHTY MEN
(1 Chr. 11:10–47)

⁸These *are* the names of the mighty men whom David
had: ¹Josheb-Basshebeth the Tachmonite, chief among ²the

22:46
ᵃ1 Sam. 14:11;
[Mic. 7:17]

22:47
ᵃ[2 Sam. 22:3];
Ps. 89:26

22:48
ᵃ1 Sam. 24:12;
Ps. 144:2

22:49 ᵃPs. 140:1,
4, 11

22:50
ᵃ2 Sam. 8:1–14
ᵇPs. 57:7;
Rom. 15:9

22:51 ᵃPs. 144:10
ᵇPs. 89:20
ᶜ2 Sam. 7:12–16;
Ps. 89:29

23:1
ᵃ2 Sam. 7:8, 9;
Ps. 78:70, 71
ᵇ1 Sam. 16:12, 13;
Ps. 89:20

23:2
ᵃMatt. 22:43;
[2 Pet. 1:21]

23:3
ᵃ[Deut. 32:4]
ᵇEx. 18:21;
[Is. 11:1–5]

23:4 ᵃPs. 89:36;
Is. 60:1

23:5
ᵃ2 Sam. 7:12;
Ps. 89:29;
Is. 55:3

22:46 ¹So with LXX, Tg., Vg. (cf. Ps. 18:45); MT *gird themselves*   23:7 ¹Lit.
filled   23:8 ¹Lit. *One Who Sits in the Seat* (1 Chr. 11:11)   ²So with MT, Tg.;
LXX, Vg. *the three*

captains. He was called Adino the Eznite, because he had killed eight hundred men at one time. 9And after him *was* [a]Eleazar the son of [1]Dodo, the Ahohite, *one* of the three mighty men with David when they defied the Philistines *who* were gathered there for battle, and the men of Israel had retreated. 10He arose and attacked the Philistines until his hand was [a]weary, and his hand stuck to the sword. The LORD brought about a great victory that day; and the people returned after him only to [b]plunder. 11And after him *was* [a]Shammah the son of Agee the Hararite. [b]The Philistines had gathered together into a troop where there was a piece of ground full of lentils. So the people fled from the Philistines. 12But he stationed himself in the middle of the field, defended it, and killed the Philistines. So the LORD brought about a great victory.

13Then [a]three of the thirty chief men went down at harvest time and came to David at [b]the cave of Adullam. And the troop of Philistines encamped in [c]the Valley of Rephaim. 14David *was* then in [a]the stronghold, and the garrison of the Philistines *was* then *in* Bethlehem. 15And David said with longing, "Oh, that someone would give me a drink of the water from the well of Bethlehem, which *is* by the gate!" 16So the three mighty men broke through the camp of the Philistines, drew water from the well of Bethlehem that *was* by the gate, and took it and brought *it* to David. Nevertheless he would not drink it, but poured it out to the LORD. 17And he said, "Far be it from me, O LORD, that I should do this! Is *this not* [a]the blood of the men who went in *jeopardy of* their lives?" Therefore he would not drink it.

These things were done by the three mighty men.

18Now [a]Abishai the brother of Joab, the son of Zeruiah, was chief of [1]*another* three. He lifted his spear against three hundred *men*, killed *them*, and won a name among *these* three. 19Was he not the most honored of three? Therefore he became their captain. However, he did not attain to the *first* three.

20Benaiah *was* the son of Jehoiada, the son of a valiant man from [a]Kabzeel, [1]who had done many deeds. [b]He had killed two lion-like heroes of Moab. He also had gone down and killed a lion in the midst of a pit on a snowy day. 21And he killed an Egyptian, [1]a spectacular man. The Egyptian *had* a spear in his hand; so he went down to him with a staff, wrested the spear out of the Egyptian's hand, and killed him with his own spear. 22These *things* Benaiah the son of Jehoiada did, and won a name among three mighty men. 23He was more honored than the thirty, but he did not attain to the *first* three. And David appointed him [a]over his guard.

24[a]Asahel the brother of Joab *was* one of the thirty; Elhanan the son of Dodo of Bethlehem, 25[a]Shammah the Harodite, Elika the Harodite, 26Helez the Paltite, Ira the son of Ikkesh the Tekoite, 27Abiezer the Anathothite, Mebunnai the Hushathite, 28Zalmon the Ahohite, Maharai the Netophathite, 29Heleb the son of Baanah (the Netophathite), Ittai the son of Ribai from Gibeah of the children of Benjamin, 30Benaiah a Pirathonite, Hiddai from the brooks of [a]Gaash, 31Abi-Albon the Arbathite, Azmaveth the Barhumite, 32Eliahba the Shaalbonite (of the

Cross-references (margin):

23:9
[a]1 Chr. 11:12; 27:4

23:10 [a]Judg. 8:4
[b]1 Sam. 30:24, 25

23:11 [a]1 Chr. 11:27
[b]1 Chr. 11:13, 14

23:13
[a]1 Chr. 11:15
[b]1 Sam. 22:1
[c]2 Sam. 5:18

23:14
[a]1 Sam. 22:4, 5

23:17
[a][Lev. 17:10]

23:18
[a]2 Sam. 21:17;
1 Chr. 11:20

23:20
[a]Josh. 15:21
[b]Ex. 15:15

23:23
[a]2 Sam. 8:18;
20:23

23:24
[a]2 Sam. 2:18;
1 Chr. 27:7

23:25
[a]1 Chr. 11:27

23:30
[a]Judg. 2:9

23:9 [1]*Dodai,* 1 Chr. 27:4   23:18 [1]So with MT, LXX, Vg.; some Heb. mss., Syr. *thirty;* Tg. *the mighty men*   23:20 [1]Lit. *great of acts*   23:21 [1]Lit. *a man of appearance*

sons of Jashen), Jonathan, 33aShammah the 1Hararite, Ahiam the son of Sharar the Hararite, 34Eliphelet the son of Ahasbai, the son of the Maachathite, Eliam the son of aAhithophel the Gilonite, 351Hezrai the Carmelite, Paarai the Arbite, 36Igal the son of Nathan of aZobah, Bani the Gadite, 37Zelek the Ammonite, Naharai the Beerothite (armorbearer of Joab the son of Zeruiah), 38aIra the Ithrite, Gareb the Ithrite, 39and aUriah the Hittite: thirty-seven in all.

DAVID'S CENSUS OF ISRAEL AND JUDAH
(1 Chr. 21:1–6)

24 Again athe anger of the LORD was aroused against Israel, and He moved David against them to say, b"Go, 1number Israel and Judah."

2So the king said to Joab the commander of the army who *was* with him, "Now go throughout all the tribes of Israel, afrom Dan to Beersheba, and count the people, that bI may know the number of the people."

3And Joab said to the king, "Now may the LORD your God aadd to the people a hundred times more than there are, and may the eyes of my lord the king see *it*. But why does my lord the king desire this thing?" 4Nevertheless the king's word 1prevailed against Joab and against the captains of the army. Therefore Joab and the captains of the army went out from the presence of the king to count the people of Israel.

5And they crossed over the Jordan and camped in aAroer, on the right side of the town which *is* in the midst of the ravine of Gad, and toward bJazer. 6Then they came to Gilead and to the land of Tahtim Hodshi; they came to aDan Jaan and around to bSidon; 7and they came to the stronghold of aTyre and to all the cities of the bHivites and the Canaanites. Then they went out to South Judah *as far as* Beersheba. 8So when they had gone through all the land, they came to Jerusalem at the end of nine months and twenty days. 9Then Joab gave the sum of the number of the people to the king. aAnd there were in Israel eight hundred thousand valiant men who drew the sword, and the men of Judah were five hundred thousand men.

THE JUDGMENT ON DAVID'S SIN
(1 Chr. 21:7–17)

10And aDavid's heart condemned him after he had numbered the people. So bDavid said to the LORD, c"I have sinned greatly in what I have done; but now, I pray, O LORD, take away the iniquity of Your servant, for I have ddone very foolishly."

11Now when David arose in the morning, the word of the LORD came to the prophet aGad, David's bseer, saying, 12"Go and tell David, 'Thus says the LORD: "I offer you three *things;* choose one of them for yourself, that I may do *it* to you."'" 13So Gad came to David and told him; and he said to him, "Shall aseven1 years of famine come to you in your land? Or shall you flee three months before your enemies, while they pursue you? Or shall there be three days' plague in your land? Now consider and see what answer I should take back to Him who sent me."

23:33
a 2 Sam. 23:11

23:34
a 2 Sam. 15:12

23:36
a 2 Sam. 8:3

23:38
a 1 Chr. 2:53

23:39
a 2 Sam. 11:3, 6

24:1
a 2 Sam. 21:1, 2
b Num. 26:2;
1 Chr. 27:23, 24

24:2
a Judg. 20:1;
2 Sam. 3:10
b [Jer. 17:5]

24:3 a Deut. 1:11

24:5
a Deut. 2:36;
Josh. 13:9, 16
b Num. 32:1, 3

24:6
a Josh. 19:47;
Judg. 18:29
b Josh. 19:28;
Judg. 18:28

24:7
a Josh. 19:29
b Josh. 11:3;
Judg. 3:3

24:9 a 1 Chr. 21:5

24:10
a 1 Sam. 24:5
b 2 Sam. 23:1
c 2 Sam. 12:13
d 1 Sam. 13:13;
[2 Chr. 16:9]

24:11
a 1 Sam. 22:5
b 1 Sam. 9:9;
1 Chr. 29:29

24:13
a Ezek. 14:21

23:33 1Or Ararite   23:35 1Hezro, 1 Chr. 11:37   24:1 1take a census of
24:4 1overruled   24:13 1So with MT, Syr., Tg., Vg.; LXX three (cf. 1 Chr. 21:12)

[14]And David said to Gad, "I am in great distress. Please let us fall into the hand of the LORD, [a]for His mercies *are* great; but [b]do not let me fall into the hand of man."

[15]So [a]the LORD sent a plague upon Israel from the morning till the appointed time. From Dan to Beersheba seventy thousand men of the people died. [16a]And when the [1]angel stretched out His hand over Jerusalem to destroy it, [b]the LORD relented from the destruction, and said to the angel who was destroying the people, "It is enough; now restrain your hand." And the angel of the LORD was by the threshing floor of [2]Araunah the Jebusite.

[17]Then David spoke to the LORD when he saw the angel who was striking the people, and said, "Surely [a]I have sinned, and I have done wickedly; but these sheep, what have they done? Let Your hand, I pray, be against me and against my father's house."

THE ALTAR ON THE THRESHING FLOOR

(1 Chr. 21:18–27)

[18]And Gad came that day to David and said to him, [a]"Go up, erect an altar to the LORD on the threshing floor of Araunah the Jebusite." [19]So David, according to the word of Gad, went up as the LORD commanded. [20]Now Araunah looked, and saw the king and his servants coming toward him. So Araunah went out and bowed before the king with his face to the ground.

[21]Then Araunah said, "Why has my lord the king come to his servant?"

[a]And David said, "To buy the threshing floor from you, to build an altar to the LORD, that [b]the plague may be withdrawn from the people."

[22]Now Araunah said to David, "Let my lord the king take and offer up whatever *seems* good to him. [a]Look, *here are* oxen for burnt sacrifice, and threshing implements and the yokes of the oxen for wood. [23]All these, O king, Araunah has given to the king."

And Araunah said to the king, "May the LORD your God [a]accept you."

[24]Then the king said to Araunah, "No, but I will surely buy *it* from you for a price; nor will I offer burnt offerings to the LORD my God with that which costs me nothing." So [a]David bought the threshing floor and the oxen for fifty shekels of silver. [25]And David built there an altar to the LORD, and offered burnt offerings and peace offerings. [a]So the LORD heeded the prayers for the land, and [b]the plague was withdrawn from Israel.

24:14 [a][Ps. 51:1; 103:8, 13, 14; 119:156; 130:4, 7] [b][Is. 47:6; Zech. 1:15]

24:15 [a]1 Chr. 21:14

24:16 [a]Ex. 12:23; 2 Kin. 19:35; Acts 12:23 [b]Gen. 6:6; 1 Sam. 15:11

24:17 [a]2 Sam. 7:8; 1 Chr. 21:17; Ps. 74:1

24:18 [a]1 Chr. 21:18

24:21 [a]Gen. 23:8–16 [b]Num. 16:48, 50

24:22 [a]1 Sam. 6:14; 1 Kin. 19:21

24:23 [a][Ezek. 20:40, 41]

24:24 [a]1 Chr. 21:24, 25

24:25 [a]2 Sam. 21:14 [b]2 Sam. 24:21

24:16 [1]Or *Angel*   [2]*Ornan,* 1 Chr. 21:15

THE FIRST BOOK OF THE
KINGS

ADONIJAH PRESUMES TO BE KING

1 Now King David was ᵃold, ¹advanced in years; and they put covers on him, but he could not get warm. ²Therefore his servants said to him, "Let a young woman, a virgin, be sought for our lord the king, and let her ¹stand before the king, and let her care for him; and let her lie in your bosom, that our lord the king may be warm." ³So they sought for a lovely young woman throughout all the territory of Israel, and found ᵃAbishag the ᵇShunammite, and brought her to the king. ⁴The young woman *was* very lovely; and she cared for the king, and served him; but the king did not know her.

⁵Then ᵃAdonijah the ¹son of Haggith exalted himself, saying, "I will ²be king"; and ᵇhe prepared for himself chariots and horsemen, and fifty men to run before him. ⁶(And his father had not ¹rebuked him at any time by saying, "Why have you done so?" He *was* also very good-looking. ᵃ*His mother* had borne him after Absalom.) ⁷Then he conferred with ᵃJoab the son of Zeruiah and with ᵇAbiathar the priest, and ᶜthey followed and helped Adonijah. ⁸But ᵃZadok the priest, ᵇBenaiah the son of Jehoiada, ᶜNathan the prophet, ᵈShimei, Rei, and ᵉthe mighty men who *belonged* to David were not with Adonijah.

⁹And Adonijah sacrificed sheep and oxen and fattened cattle by the stone of ¹Zoheleth, which *is* by ᵃEn Rogel;² he also invited all his brothers, the king's sons, and all the men of Judah, the king's servants. ¹⁰But he did not invite Nathan the prophet, Benaiah, the mighty men, or ᵃSolomon his brother.

¹¹So Nathan spoke to Bathsheba the mother of Solomon, saying, "Have you not heard that Adonijah the son of ᵃHaggith has become king, and David our lord does not know *it*? ¹²Come, please, let me now give you advice, that you may save your own life and the life of your son Solomon. ¹³Go immediately to King David and say to him, 'Did you not, my lord, O king, swear to your maidservant, saying, ᵃ"Assuredly your son Solomon shall reign after me, and he shall sit on my throne"? Why then has Adonijah become king?' ¹⁴Then, while you are still talking there with the king, I also will come in after you and confirm your words."

¹⁵So Bathsheba went into the chamber to the king. (Now the king was very old, and Abishag the Shunammite was serving the king.) ¹⁶And Bathsheba bowed and did homage to the king. Then the king said, "What is your wish?"

¹⁷Then she said to him, "My lord, ᵃyou swore by the LORD your God to your maidservant, *saying,* 'Assuredly Solomon your son shall reign after me, and he shall sit on my throne.'

1:1 ᵃ1 Chr. 23:1

1:3 ᵃ1 Kin. 2:17
ᵇJosh. 19:18;
1 Sam. 28:4

1:5 ᵃ2 Sam. 3:4
ᵇ2 Sam. 15:1

1:6
ᵃ2 Sam. 3:3, 4;
1 Chr. 3:2

1:7 ᵃ1 Chr. 11:6
ᵇ2 Sam. 20:25
ᶜ1 Kin. 2:22, 28

1:8 ᵃ1 Kin. 2:35
ᵇ1 Kin. 2:25;
2 Sam. 8:18
ᶜ2 Sam. 12:1
ᵈ1 Kin. 4:18
ᵉ2 Sam. 23:8

1:9 ᵃJosh. 15:7;
18:16;
2 Sam. 17:17

1:10
ᵃ2 Sam. 12:24

1:11 ᵃ2 Sam. 3:4

1:13 ᵃ1 Kin. 1:30;
1 Chr. 22:9–13

1:17
ᵃ1 Kin. 1:13, 30

1:1 ¹Seventy years   1:2 ¹Or *serve*   1:5 ¹The fourth son   ²Lit. *reign*
1:6 ¹Lit. *pained*   1:9 ¹Lit. *Serpent*   ²A spring south of Jerusalem in the Kidron Valley

[18]So now, look! Adonijah has become king; and now, my lord the king, you do not know about *it.* [19a]He has sacrificed oxen and fattened cattle and sheep in abundance, and has invited all the sons of the king, Abiathar the priest, and Joab the commander of the army; but Solomon your servant he has not invited. [20]And as for you, my lord, O king, the eyes of all Israel *are* on you, that you should tell them who will sit on the throne of my lord the king after him. [21]Otherwise it will happen, when my lord the king [a]rests with his fathers, that I and my son Solomon will be counted as offenders."

[22]And just then, while she was still talking with the king, Nathan the prophet also came in. [23]So they told the king, saying, "Here is Nathan the prophet." And when he came in before the king, he bowed down before the king with his face to the ground. [24]And Nathan said, "My lord, O king, have you said, 'Adonijah shall reign after me, and he shall sit on my throne'? [25a]For he has gone down today, and has sacrificed oxen and fattened cattle and sheep in abundance, and has invited all the king's sons, and the commanders of the army, and Abiathar the priest; and look! They are eating and drinking before him; and they say, [b]'*Long*[1] live King Adonijah!' [26]But he has not invited me—me your servant—nor Zadok the priest, nor Benaiah the son of Jehoiada, nor your servant Solomon. [27]Has this thing been done by my lord the king, and you have not told your servant who should sit on the throne of my lord the king after him?"

DAVID PROCLAIMS SOLOMON KING
(1 Chr. 29:22–25)

[28]Then King David answered and said, "Call Bathsheba to me." So she came into the king's presence and stood before the king. [29]And the king took an oath and said, [a]"*As* the LORD lives, who has redeemed my life from every distress, [30a]just as I swore to you by the LORD God of Israel, saying, 'Assuredly Solomon your son shall be king after me, and he shall sit on my throne in my place,' so I certainly will do this day." [31]Then Bathsheba bowed with *her* face to the earth, and paid homage to the king, and said, [a]"Let my lord King David live forever!"

[32]And King David said, "Call to me Zadok the priest, Nathan the prophet, and Benaiah the son of Jehoiada." So they came before the king. [33]The king also said to them, [a]"Take with you the servants of your lord, and have Solomon my son ride on my own [b]mule, and take him down to [c]Gihon.[1] [34]There let Zadok the priest and Nathan the prophet [a]anoint him king over Israel; and [b]blow the horn, and say, [1]'*Long* live King Solomon!' [35]Then you shall come up after him, and he shall come and sit on my throne, and he shall be king in my place. For I have appointed him to be ruler over Israel and Judah."

[36]Benaiah the son of Jehoiada answered the king and said, [a]"Amen! May the LORD God of my lord the king say so *too.* [37a]As the LORD has been with my lord the king, even so may He be with Solomon, and [b]make his throne greater than the throne of my lord King David."

Cross references
1:19 [a]1 Kin. 1:7–9, 25
1:21 [a]Deut. 31:16; 2 Sam. 7:12; 1 Kin. 2:10
1:25 [a]1 Kin. 1:9, 19 [b]1 Sam. 10:24
1:29 [a]2 Sam. 4:9; 12:5
1:30 [a]1 Kin. 1:13, 17
1:31 [a]Neh. 2:3; Dan. 2:4; 3:9
1:33 [a]2 Sam. 20:6 [b]Esth. 6:8 [c]2 Chr. 32:30; 33:14
1:34 [a]1 Sam. 10:1; 16:3, 12; 2 Sam. 2:4; 5:3; 1 Kin. 19:16; 2 Kin. 9:3; 11:12; 1 Chr. 29:22 [b]2 Sam. 15:10; 2 Kin. 9:13; 11:14
1:36 [a]Jer. 28:6
1:37 [a]Josh. 1:5, 17; 1 Sam. 20:13 [b]1 Kin. 1:47

1:25 [1]Lit. *Let King Adonijah live*   1:33 [1]A spring east of Jerusalem in the Kidron Valley   1:34 [1]Lit. *Let King Solomon live*

³⁸So Zadok the priest, Nathan the prophet, ªBenaiah the son of Jehoiada, the ᵇCherethites, and the Pelethites went down and had Solomon ride on King David's mule, and took him to Gihon. ³⁹Then Zadok the priest took a horn of ªoil from the tabernacle and ᵇanointed Solomon. And they blew the horn, ᶜand all the people said, ¹"*Long* live King Solomon!" ⁴⁰And all the people went up after him; and the people played the flutes and rejoiced with great joy, so that the earth *seemed to* split with their sound.

⁴¹Now Adonijah and all the guests who *were* with him heard *it* as they finished eating. And when Joab heard the sound of the horn, he said, "Why *is* the city in such a noisy uproar?" ⁴²While he was still speaking, there came ªJonathan, the son of Abiathar the priest. And Adonijah said to him, "Come in, for ᵇyou *are* a prominent man, and bring good news."

⁴³Then Jonathan answered and said to Adonijah, "No! Our lord King David has made Solomon king. ⁴⁴The king has sent with him Zadok the priest, Nathan the prophet, Benaiah the son of Jehoiada, the Cherethites, and the Pelethites; and they have made him ride on the king's mule. ⁴⁵So Zadok the priest and Nathan the prophet have anointed him king at Gihon; and they have gone up from there rejoicing, so that the city is in an uproar. This *is* the noise that you have heard. ⁴⁶Also Solomon ªsits on the throne of the kingdom. ⁴⁷And moreover the king's servants have gone to bless our lord King David, saying, ª'May God make the name of Solomon better than your name, and may He make his throne greater than your throne.' ᵇThen the king bowed himself on the bed. ⁴⁸Also the king said thus, 'Blessed *be* the LORD God of Israel, who has ªgiven *one* to sit on my throne this day, while my eyes see ᵇ*it!* '"

⁴⁹So all the guests who were with Adonijah were afraid, and arose, and each one went his way.

⁵⁰Now Adonijah was afraid of Solomon; so he arose, and went and ªtook hold of the horns of the altar. ⁵¹And it was told Solomon, saying, "Indeed Adonijah is afraid of King Solomon; for look, he has taken hold of the horns of the altar, saying, 'Let King Solomon swear to me today that he will not put his servant to death with the sword.'"

⁵²Then Solomon said, "If he proves himself a worthy man, ªnot one hair of him shall fall to the earth; but if wickedness is found in him, he shall die." ⁵³So King Solomon sent them to bring him down from the altar. And he came and fell down before King Solomon; and Solomon said to him, "Go to your house."

DAVID'S INSTRUCTIONS TO SOLOMON

2 Now ªthe days of David drew near that he should die, and he ¹charged Solomon his son, saying: ²ª"I go the way of all the earth; ᵇbe strong, therefore, and prove yourself a man. ³And keep the charge of the LORD your God: to walk in His ways, to keep His statutes, His commandments, His judgments, and His testimonies, as it is written in the Law of Moses, that you may ªprosper in all that you do and wherever you turn; ⁴that the LORD may ªfulfill His word which He spoke concerning me, saying, ᵇ'If your sons take heed to their way, to ᶜwalk before Me in truth with all their heart and with all

---

1:38
ª2 Sam. 8:18;
23:20–23
ᵇ2 Sam. 20:7;
1 Chr. 18:17

1:39 ªEx. 30:23,
25, 32; Ps. 89:20
ᵇ1 Chr. 29:22
ᶜ1 Sam. 10:24

1:42
ª2 Sam. 17:17, 20
ᵇ2 Sam. 18:27

1:46 ª1 Kin. 2:12;
1 Chr. 29:23

1:47 ª1 Kin. 1:37
ᵇGen. 47:31

1:48 ª1 Kin. 3:6;
[Ps. 132:11, 12]
ᵇ2 Sam. 7:12

1:50 ªEx. 27:2;
30:10; 1 Kin. 2:28

1:52
ª1 Sam. 14:45;
2 Sam. 14:11;
Acts 27:34

2:1 ªGen. 47:29;
Deut. 31:14

2:2 ªJosh. 23:14
ᵇDeut. 31:7, 23;
1 Chr. 22:13

2:3
ª[Deut. 29:9;
Josh. 1:7];
1 Chr. 22:12, 13

2:4 ª2 Sam. 7:25
ᵇ[Ps. 132:12]
ᶜ2 Kin. 20:3

1:39 ¹Lit. *Let King Solomon live*   2:1 ¹commanded

their soul,' He said, ᵈ'you shall not lack a man on the throne of Israel.'

⁵"Moreover you know also what Joab the son of Zeruiah ᵃdid to me, *and* what he did to the two commanders of the armies of Israel, to ᵇAbner the son of Ner and ᶜAmasa the son of Jether, whom he killed. And he shed the blood of war in peacetime, and put the blood of war on his belt that *was* around his waist, and on his sandals that *were* on his feet. ⁶Therefore do ᵃaccording to your wisdom, and do not let his gray hair go down to the grave in peace.

⁷"But show kindness to the sons of ᵃBarzillai the Gileadite, and let them be among those who ᵇeat at your table, for so ᶜthey came to me when I fled from Absalom your brother.

⁸"And see, *you have* with you ᵃShimei the son of Gera, a Benjamite from Bahurim, who cursed me with a malicious curse in the day when I went to Mahanaim. But ᵇhe came down to meet me at the Jordan, and ᶜI swore to him by the LORD, saying, 'I will not put you to death with the sword.' ⁹Now therefore, ᵃdo not hold him guiltless, for you *are* a wise man and know what you ought to do to him; but ᵇbring his gray hair down to the grave with blood."

DEATH OF DAVID
(1 Chr. 3:4; 29:26–28)

¹⁰So ᵃDavid ¹rested with his fathers, and was buried in ᵇthe City of David. ¹¹The period that David ᵃreigned over Israel *was* forty years; seven years he reigned in Hebron, and in Jerusalem he reigned thirty-three years. ¹²ᵃThen Solomon sat on the throne of his father David; and his kingdom was ᵇfirmly established.

SOLOMON EXECUTES ADONIJAH

¹³Now Adonijah the son of Haggith came to Bathsheba the mother of Solomon. So she said, ᵃ"Do you come peaceably?"

And he said, "Peaceably." ¹⁴Moreover he said, "I have something *to say* to you."

And she said, "Say it."

¹⁵Then he said, "You know that the kingdom was ᵃmine, and all Israel had set their expectations on me, that I should reign. However, the kingdom has been turned over, and has become my brother's; for ᵇit was his from the LORD. ¹⁶Now I ask one petition of you; do not ¹deny me."

And she said to him, "Say it."

¹⁷Then he said, "Please speak to King Solomon, for he will not refuse you, that he may give me ᵃAbishag the Shunammite as wife."

¹⁸So Bathsheba said, "Very well, I will speak for you to the king."

¹⁹Bathsheba therefore went to King Solomon, to speak to him for Adonijah. And the king rose up to meet her and ᵃbowed down to her, and sat down on his throne and had a throne set for the king's mother; ᵇso she sat at his right hand. ²⁰Then she said, "I desire one small petition of you; do not ¹refuse me."

2:4
ᵈ2 Sam. 7:12, 13;
1 Kin. 8:25

2:5
ᵃ2 Sam. 3:39;
18:5, 12, 14
ᵇ2 Sam. 3:27;
1 Kin. 2:32
ᶜ2 Sam. 20:10

2:6 ᵃ1 Kin. 2:9;
Prov. 20:26

2:7
ᵃ2 Sam. 19:31–39
ᵇ2 Sam. 9:7,
10; 19:28
ᶜ2 Sam. 17:17–29

2:8
ᵃ2 Sam. 16:5–13
ᵇ2 Sam. 19:18
ᶜ2 Sam. 19:23

2:9 ᵃEx. 20:7;
Job 9:28
ᵇGen. 42:38;
44:31

2:10 ᵃ1 Kin. 1:21;
Acts 2:29; 13:36
ᵇ2 Sam. 5:7;
1 Kin. 3:1

2:11
ᵃ2 Sam. 5:4, 5;
1 Chr. 3:4;
29:26, 27

2:12 ᵃ1 Kin. 1:46;
1 Chr. 29:23
ᵇ1 Kin. 2:46;
2 Chr. 1:1

2:13
ᵃ1 Sam. 16:4, 5

2:15
ᵃ1 Kin. 1:11, 18
ᵇ1 Chr. 22:9,
10; 28:5–7;
[Dan. 2:21]

2:17 ᵃ1 Kin. 1:3, 4

2:19 ᵃ[Ex. 20:12]
ᵇPs. 45:9

2:10 ¹Died and joined his ancestors 2:16 ¹Lit. *turn away the face*
2:20 ¹Lit. *turn away the face*

And the king said to her, "Ask it, my mother, for I will not refuse you."

²¹So she said, "Let Abishag the Shunammite be given to Adonijah your brother as wife."

²²And King Solomon answered and said to his mother, "Now why do you ask Abishag the Shunammite for Adonijah? Ask for him the kingdom also—for he *is* my ᵃolder brother—for him, and for ᵇAbiathar the priest, and for Joab the son of Zeruiah." ²³Then King Solomon swore by the Lᴏʀᴅ, saying, ᵃ"May God do so to me, and more also, if Adonijah has not spoken this word against his own life! ²⁴Now therefore, *as* the Lᴏʀᴅ lives, who has confirmed me and set me on the throne of David my father, and who has established a ¹house for me, as He ᵃpromised, Adonijah shall be put to death today!"

²⁵So King Solomon sent by the hand of ᵃBenaiah the son of Jehoiada; and he struck him down, and he died.

ABIATHAR EXILED, JOAB EXECUTED

²⁶And to Abiathar the priest the king said, "Go to ᵃAnathoth, to your own fields, for ¹you *are* deserving of death; but I will not put you to death at this time, ᵇbecause you carried the ark of the Lord Gᴏᴅ before my father David, and because you were afflicted every time my father was afflicted." ²⁷So Solomon removed Abiathar from being priest to the Lᴏʀᴅ, that he might ᵃfulfill the word of the Lᴏʀᴅ which He spoke concerning the house of Eli at Shiloh.

²⁸Then news came to Joab, for Joab ᵃhad defected to Adonijah, though he had not defected to Absalom. So Joab fled to the tabernacle of the Lᴏʀᴅ, and ᵇtook hold of the horns of the altar. ²⁹And King Solomon was told, "Joab has fled to the tabernacle of the Lᴏʀᴅ; there *he is,* by the altar." Then Solomon sent Benaiah the son of Jehoiada, saying, "Go, ᵃstrike him down." ³⁰So Benaiah went to the tabernacle of the Lᴏʀᴅ, and said to him, "Thus says the king, ᵃ'Come out!'"

And he said, "No, but I will die here." And Benaiah brought back word to the king, saying, "Thus said Joab, and thus he answered me."

³¹Then the king said to him, ᵃ"Do as he has said, and strike him down and bury him, ᵇthat you may take away from me and from the house of my father the innocent blood which Joab shed. ³²So the Lᴏʀᴅ ᵃwill return his ¹blood on his head, because he struck down two men more righteous ᵇand better than he, and killed them with the sword—ᶜAbner the son of Ner, the commander of the army of Israel, and ᵈAmasa the son of Jether, the commander of the army of Judah—though my father David did not know *it*. ³³Their blood shall therefore return upon the head of Joab and ᵃupon the head of his descendants forever. ᵇBut upon David and his descendants, upon his house and his throne, there shall be peace forever from the Lᴏʀᴅ."

³⁴So Benaiah the son of Jehoiada went up and struck and killed him; and he was buried in his own house in the wilderness. ³⁵The king put Benaiah the son of Jehoiada in his place over the army, and the king put ᵃZadok the priest in the place of ᵇAbiathar.

2:22 ᵃ1 Kin. 1:6; 2:15; 1 Chr. 3:2, 5
ᵇ1 Kin. 1:7

2:23 ᵃRuth 1:17

2:24
ᵃ2 Sam. 7:11, 13; 1 Chr. 22:10

2:25
ᵃ2 Sam. 8:18; 1 Kin. 4:4

2:26
ᵃJosh. 21:18; Jer. 1:1
ᵇ1 Sam. 22:23; 23:6;
2 Sam. 15:14, 29

2:27
ᵃ1 Sam. 2:31–35

2:28 ᵃ1 Kin. 1:7
ᵇ1 Kin. 1:50

2:29
ᵃ1 Kin. 2:5, 6

2:30 ᵃ[Ex. 21:14]

2:31 ᵃ[Ex. 21:14]
ᵇ[Num. 35:33; Deut. 19:13; 21:8, 9]

2:32
ᵃ[Gen. 9:6]; Judg. 9:24, 57
ᵇ2 Chr. 21:13, 14
ᶜ2 Sam. 3:27
ᵈ2 Sam. 20:9, 10

2:33
ᵃ2 Sam. 3:29
ᵇ[Prov. 25:5]

2:35
ᵃ1 Sam. 2:35; 1 Kin. 4:4; 1 Chr. 6:53; 24:3; 29:22
ᵇ1 Kin. 2:27

2:24 ¹Royal dynasty   2:26 ¹Lit. *you are a man of death*   2:32 ¹Or *bloodshed*

SHIMEI EXECUTED

[36] Then the king sent and called for [a]Shimei, and said to him, "Build yourself a house in Jerusalem and dwell there, and do not go out from there anywhere. [37]For it shall be, on the day you go out and cross [a]the Brook Kidron, know for certain you shall surely die; [b]your [1]blood shall be on your own head."

[38]And Shimei said to the king, "The saying *is* good. As my lord the king has said, so your servant will do." So Shimei dwelt in Jerusalem many days.

[39]Now it happened at the end of three years, that two slaves of Shimei ran away to [a]Achish the son of Maachah, king of Gath. And they told Shimei, saying, "Look, your slaves *are* in Gath!" [40]So Shimei arose, saddled his donkey, and went to Achish at Gath to seek his slaves. And Shimei went and brought his slaves from Gath. [41]And Solomon was told that Shimei had gone from Jerusalem to Gath and had come back. [42]Then the king sent and called for Shimei, and said to him, "Did I not make you swear by the LORD, and warn you, saying, 'Know for certain that on the day you go out and travel anywhere, you shall surely die'? And you said to me, 'The word I have heard *is* good.' [43]Why then have you not kept the oath of the LORD and the commandment that I gave you?" [44]The king said moreover to Shimei, "You know, as your heart acknowledges, [a]all the wickedness that you did to my father David; therefore the LORD will [b]return your wickedness on your own head. [45]But King Solomon *shall be* blessed, and [a]the throne of David shall be established before the LORD forever."

[46]So the king commanded Benaiah the son of Jehoiada; and he went out and struck him down, and he died. Thus the [a]kingdom was established in the hand of Solomon.

SOLOMON REQUESTS WISDOM

(2 Chr. 1:2–13)

3 Now [a]Solomon made [1]a treaty with Pharaoh king of Egypt, and married Pharaoh's daughter; then he brought her [b]to the City of David until he had finished building his [c]own house, and [d]the house of the LORD, and [e]the wall all around Jerusalem. [2a]Meanwhile the people sacrificed at the high places, because there was no house built for the name of the LORD until those days. [3]And Solomon [a]loved the LORD, [b]walking in the statutes of his father David, except that he sacrificed and burned incense at the high places.

[4]Now [a]the king went to Gibeon to sacrifice there, [b]for that *was* the great high place: Solomon offered a thousand burnt offerings on that altar. [5a]At Gibeon the LORD appeared to Solomon [b]in a dream by night; and God said, "Ask! What shall I give you?"

[6a]And Solomon said: "You have shown great mercy to Your servant David my father, because he [b]walked before You in truth, in righteousness, and in uprightness of heart with You; You have continued this great kindness for him, and You [c]have given him a son to sit on his throne, as *it is* this day. [7]Now, O LORD my God, You have made Your servant king instead of my father David, but I *am* a [a]little child; I do not know

2:36
[a]2 Sam. 16:5–13;
1 Kin. 2:8

2:37
[a]2 Sam. 15:23;
2 Kin. 23:6;
John 18:1
[b]Lev. 20:9;
Josh. 2:19;
2 Sam. 1:16;
Ezek. 18:13

2:39
[a]1 Sam. 27:2

2:44
[a]2 Sam. 16:5–13
[b]1 Sam. 25:39;
2 Kin. 11:1,
12–16; Ps. 7:16;
Ezek. 17:19

2:45
[a]2 Sam. 7:13;
[Prov. 25:5]

2:46 [a]1 Kin. 2:12;
2 Chr. 1:1

3:1 [a]1 Kin. 7:8;
9:24 [b]2 Sam. 5:7
[c]1 Kin. 7:1
[d]1 Kin. 6
[e]1 Kin. 9:15, 19

3:2
[a][Deut. 12:2–5,
13, 14;] 1 Kin. 11:7;
22:43

3:3
[a][Rom. 8:28]
[b][1 Kin. 3:6, 14]

3:4 [a]1 Kin. 9:2;
2 Chr. 1:3
[b]1 Chr. 16:39;
21:29

3:5 [a]1 Kin. 9:2;
11:9; 2 Chr. 1:7
[b]Num. 12:6;
Matt. 1:20; 2:13

3:6 [a]2 Chr. 1:8
[b]1 Kin. 2:4; 9:4;
2 Kin. 20:3
[c]2 Sam. 7:8–17;
1 Kin. 1:48

3:7 [a]1 Chr. 22:5;
Jer. 1:6, 7

2:37 [1]Or *bloodshed*   **3:1** [1]*an alliance*

how ᵇto go out or come in. ⁸And Your servant *is* in the midst of Your people whom You ᵃhave chosen, a great people, ᵇtoo numerous to be numbered or counted. ⁹ᵃTherefore give to Your servant an ¹understanding heart ᵇto judge Your people, that I may ᶜdiscern between good and evil. For who is able to judge this great people of Yours?"

¹⁰The speech pleased the Lord, that Solomon had asked this thing. ¹¹Then God said to him: "Because you have asked this thing, and have ᵃnot asked long life for yourself, nor have asked riches for yourself, nor have asked the life of your enemies, but have asked for yourself understanding to discern justice, ¹²ᵃbehold, I have done according to your words; ᵇsee, I have given you a wise and understanding heart, so that there has not been anyone like you before you, nor shall any like you arise after you. ¹³And I have also ᵃgiven you what you have not asked: both ᵇriches and honor, so that there shall not be anyone like you among the kings all your days. ¹⁴So ᵃif you walk in My ways, to keep My statutes and My commandments, ᵇas your father David walked, then I will ᶜlengthen¹ your days."

¹⁵Then Solomon ᵃawoke; and indeed it had been a dream. And he came to Jerusalem and stood before the ark of the covenant of the Lᴏʀᴅ, offered up burnt offerings, offered peace offerings, and ᵇmade a feast for all his servants.

SOLOMON'S WISE JUDGMENT

¹⁶Now two women *who were* harlots came to the king, and ᵃstood before him. ¹⁷And one woman said, "O my lord, this woman and I dwell in the same house; and I gave birth while she *was* in the house. ¹⁸Then it happened, the third day after I had given birth, that this woman also gave birth. And we *were* together; ¹no one *was* with us in the house, except the two of us in the house. ¹⁹And this woman's son died in the night, because she lay on him. ²⁰So she arose in the middle of the night and took my son from my side, while your maidservant slept, and laid him in her bosom, and laid her dead child in my bosom. ²¹And when I rose in the morning to nurse my son, there he was, dead. But when I had examined him in the morning, indeed, he was not my son whom I had borne."

²²Then the other woman said, "No! But the living one *is* my son, and the dead one *is* your son."

And the first woman said, "No! But the dead one *is* your son, and the living one *is* my son."

Thus they spoke before the king.

²³And the king said, "The one says, 'This *is* my son, who lives, and your son *is* the dead one'; and the other says, 'No! But your son *is* the dead one, and my son *is* the living one.'" ²⁴Then the king said, "Bring me a sword." So they brought a sword before the king. ²⁵And the king said, "Divide the living child in two, and give half to one, and half to the other."

²⁶Then the woman whose son *was* living spoke to the king, for ᵃshe yearned with compassion for her son; and she said, "O my lord, give her the living child, and by no means kill him!"

But the other said, "Let him be neither mine nor yours, *but* divide *him*."

3:7 ᵇNum. 27:17; 2 Sam. 5:2

3:8 ᵃ[Ex. 19:6; Deut. 7:6] ᵇGen. 13:6; 15:5; 22:17

3:9 ᵃ2 Chr. 1:10; [James 1:5] ᵇPs. 72:1, 2 ᶜ2 Sam. 14:17; Is. 7:15; [Heb. 5:14]

3:11 ᵃ[James 4:3]

3:12 ᵃ[1 John 5:14, 15] ᵇ1 Kin. 4:29–31; 5:12; 10:24; Eccl. 1:16

3:13 ᵃ[Matt. 6:33; Eph. 3:20] ᵇ1 Kin. 4:21, 24; 10:23; 1 Chr. 29:12

3:14 ᵃ[1 Kin. 6:12] ᵇ1 Kin. 15:5 ᶜPs. 91:16; Prov. 3:2

3:15 ᵃGen. 41:7 ᵇGen. 40:20; 1 Kin. 8:65; Esth. 1:3; Dan. 5:1; Mark 6:21

3:16 ᵃNum. 27:2

3:26 ᵃGen. 43:30; Is. 49:15; Jer. 31:20; Hos. 11:8

27So the king answered and said, "Give the first woman the living child, and by no means kill him; she *is* his mother."

28And all Israel heard of the judgment which the king had rendered; and they feared the king, for they saw that the ᵃwisdom of God *was* in him to administer justice.

SOLOMON'S ADMINISTRATION

4 So King Solomon was king over all Israel. 2And these *were* his officials: Azariah the son of Zadok, the priest; 3Elihoreph and Ahijah, the sons of Shisha, ¹scribes; ᵃJehoshaphat the son of Ahilud, the recorder; 4ᵃBenaiah the son of Jehoiada, over the army; Zadok and ᵇAbiathar, the priests; 5Azariah the son of Nathan, over ᵃthe officers; Zabud the son of Nathan, ᵇa priest *and* ᶜthe king's friend; 6Ahishar, over the household; and ᵃAdoniram the son of Abda, over the labor force.

7And Solomon had twelve governors over all Israel, who provided food for the king and his household; each one made provision for one month of the year. 8These *are* their names: ¹Ben-Hur, in the mountains of Ephraim; 9¹Ben-Deker, in Makaz, Shaalbim, Beth Shemesh, and Elon Beth Hanan; 10¹Ben-Hesed, in Arubboth; to him *belonged* Sochoh and all the land of Hepher; 11¹Ben-Abinadab, *in* all the regions of Dor; he had Taphath the daughter of Solomon as wife; 12Baana the son of Ahilud, *in* Taanach, Megiddo, and all Beth Shean, which *is* beside Zaretan below Jezreel, from Beth Shean to Abel Meholah, as far as the other side of Jokneam; 13¹Ben-Geber, in Ramoth Gilead; to him *belonged* ᵃthe towns of Jair the son of Manasseh, in Gilead; to him *also belonged* ᵇthe region of Argob in Bashan—sixty large cities with walls and bronze gatebars; 14Ahinadab the son of Iddo, *in* Mahanaim; 15ᵃAhimaaz, in Naphtali; he also took Basemath the daughter of Solomon as wife; 16Baanah the son of ᵃHushai, in Asher and Aloth; 17Jehoshaphat the son of Paruah, in Issachar; 18ᵃShimei the son of Elah, in Benjamin; 19Geber the son of Uri, in the land of Gilead, *in* ᵃthe country of Sihon king of the Amorites, and of Og king of Bashan. *He was* the only governor who *was* in the land.

PROSPERITY AND WISDOM OF SOLOMON'S REIGN

20Judah and Israel *were* as numerous ᵃas the sand by the sea in multitude, ᵇeating and drinking and rejoicing. 21So ᵃSolomon reigned over all kingdoms from ᵇthe¹ River *to* the land of the Philistines, as far as the border of Egypt. ᶜ*They* brought tribute and served Solomon all the days of his life.

22ᵃNow Solomon's ¹provision for one day was thirty ²kors of fine flour, sixty kors of meal, 23ten fatted oxen, twenty oxen from the pastures, and one hundred sheep, besides deer, gazelles, roebucks, and fatted fowl.

24For he had dominion over all *the region* on this side of ¹the River from Tiphsah even to Gaza, namely over ᵃall the kings on this side of the River; and ᵇhe had peace on every side all around him. 25And Judah and Israel ᵃdwelt¹ safely, ᵇeach man under his vine and his fig tree, ᶜfrom Dan as far as Beersheba, all the days of Solomon.

3:28 ᵃ1 Kin. 3:9, 11, 12; 2 Chr. 1:12; Dan. 1:17; [Col. 2:2, 3]

4:3 ᵃ2 Sam. 8:16; 20:24

4:4 ᵃ1 Kin. 2:35 ᵇ1 Kin. 2:27

4:5 ᵃ1 Kin. 4:7 ᵇ2 Sam. 8:18; 20:26 ᶜ2 Sam. 15:37; 16:16; 1 Chr. 27:33

4:6 ᵃ1 Kin. 5:14

4:13 ᵃNum. 32:41; 1 Chr. 2:22 ᵇDeut. 3:4

4:15 ᵃ2 Sam. 15:27

4:16 ᵃ2 Sam. 15:32; 1 Chr. 27:33

4:18 ᵃ1 Kin. 1:8

4:19 ᵃDeut. 3:8–10

4:20 ᵃGen. 22:17; 32:12; 1 Kin. 3:8; [Prov. 14:28] ᵇPs. 72:3, 7; Mic. 4:4

4:21 ᵃEx. 34:24; 2 Chr. 9:26; Ps. 72:8 ᵇGen. 15:18; Josh. 1:4 ᶜPs. 68:29

4:22 ᵃNeh. 5:18

4:24 ᵃPs. 72:11 ᵇ1 Kin. 5:4; 1 Chr. 22:9

4:25 ᵃ[Jer. 23:6] ᵇ[Mic. 4:4; Zech. 3:10] ᶜJudg. 20:1

4:3 ¹*secretaries* 4:8 ¹Lit. *Son of Hur* 4:9 ¹Lit. *Son of Deker* 4:10 ¹Lit. *Son of Hesed* 4:11 ¹Lit. *Son of Abinadab* 4:13 ¹Lit. *Son of Geber* 4:21 ¹The Euphrates 4:22 ¹Lit. *bread* ²Each about 5 bushels 4:24 ¹The Euphrates 4:25 ¹*lived in safety*

26aSolomon had 1forty thousand stalls of bhorses for his chariots, and twelve thousand horsemen. 27And athese governors, each man in his month, provided food for King Solomon and for all who came to King Solomon's table. There was no lack in their supply. 28They also brought barley and straw to the proper place, for the horses and steeds, each man according to his charge.

29And aGod gave Solomon wisdom and exceedingly great understanding, and largeness of heart like the sand on the seashore. 30Thus Solomon's wisdom excelled the wisdom of all the men aof the East and all bthe wisdom of Egypt. 31For he was awiser than all men—bthan Ethan the Ezrahite, cand Heman, Chalcol, and Darda, the sons of Mahol; and his fame was in all the surrounding nations. 32aHe spoke three thousand proverbs, and his bsongs were one thousand and five. 33Also he spoke of trees, from the cedar tree of Lebanon even to the hyssop that springs out of the wall; he spoke also of animals, of birds, of creeping things, and of fish. 34And men of all nations, from all the kings of the earth who had heard of his wisdom, acame to hear the wisdom of Solomon.

SOLOMON PREPARES TO BUILD THE TEMPLE
(2 Chr. 2:1–18)

5 Now aHiram king of Tyre sent his servants to Solomon, because he heard that they had anointed him king in place of his father, bfor Hiram had always loved David. 2Then aSolomon sent to Hiram, saying:

3   aYou know how my father David could not build a house for the name of the LORD his God bbecause of the wars which were fought against him on every side, until the LORD put 1his foes under the soles of his feet.

4   But now the LORD my God has given me arest1 on every side; there is neither adversary nor 2evil occurrence.

5   aAnd behold, 1I propose to build a house for the name of the LORD my God, bas the LORD spoke to my father David, saying, "Your son, whom I will set on your throne in your place, he shall build the house for My name."

6   Now therefore, command that they cut down acedars for me from Lebanon; and my servants will be with your servants, and I will pay you wages for your servants according to whatever you say. For you know there is none among us who has skill to cut timber like the Sidonians.

7So it was, when Hiram heard the words of Solomon, that he rejoiced greatly and said,

Blessed be the LORD this day, for He has given David a wise son over this great people!

8Then Hiram sent to Solomon, saying:

I have considered the message which you sent me, and I will do all you desire concerning the cedar and cypress logs.

9   My servants shall bring them down afrom Lebanon to the sea; I will float them in rafts by sea to the place you

4:26
a1 Kin. 10:26;
2 Chr. 1:14
b[Deut. 17:16]

4:27 a1 Kin. 4:7

4:29 a1 Kin. 3:12

4:30 aGen. 25:6
bIs. 19:11, 12;
Acts 7:22

4:31 a1 Kin. 3:12
b1 Chr. 15:19;
Ps. 89:title
c1 Chr. 2:6;
Ps. 88:title

4:32 aProv. 1:1;
10:1; 25:1;
Eccl. 12:9
bSong 1:1

4:34 a1 Kin. 10:1;
2 Chr. 9:1, 23

5:1 a1 Kin. 5:10,
18; 2 Chr. 2:3
b2 Sam. 5:11;
1 Chr. 14:1

5:2 a2 Chr. 2:3

5:3 a1 Chr. 28:2,
3 b1 Chr. 22:8;
28:3

5:4 a1 Kin. 4:24;
1 Chr. 22:9

5:5 a2 Chr. 2:4
b2 Sam. 7:12, 13;
1 Kin. 6:38;
1 Chr. 17:12;
22:10; 28:6;
2 Chr. 6:2

5:6
a2 Chr. 2:8, 10

5:9 aEzra 3:7

4:26 1So with MT, most other authorities; some LXX mss. four thousand; cf. 2 Chr. 9:25   5:3 1Lit. them   5:4 1peace   2misfortune   5:5 1Lit. I am saying

indicate to me, and will have them broken apart there; then you can take *them* away. And you shall fulfill my desire [b]by giving food for my household.

[10]Then Hiram gave Solomon cedar and cypress logs *according to* all his desire. [11a]And Solomon gave Hiram twenty thousand [1]kors of wheat *as* food for his household, and [2]twenty kors of pressed oil. Thus Solomon gave to Hiram year by year.

[12]So the Lord gave Solomon wisdom, [a]as He had promised him; and there was peace between Hiram and Solomon, and the two of them made a treaty together.

[13]Then King Solomon raised up a labor force out of all Israel; and the labor force was thirty thousand men. [14]And he sent them to Lebanon, ten thousand a month in shifts: they were one month in Lebanon *and* two months at home; [a]Adoniram *was* in charge of the labor force. [15a]Solomon had seventy thousand who carried burdens, and eighty thousand who quarried *stone* in the mountains, [16]besides three thousand [1]three hundred from the [a]chiefs of Solomon's deputies, who supervised the people who labored in the work. [17]And the king commanded them to quarry large stones, costly stones, *and* [a]hewn stones, to lay the foundation of the [1]temple. [18]So Solomon's builders, Hiram's builders, and the Gebalites quarried *them;* and they prepared timber and stones to build the [1]temple.

SOLOMON BUILDS THE TEMPLE
(2 Chr. 3:1–14)

6 And [a]it came to pass in the four hundred and [1]eightieth year after the children of Israel had come out of the land of Egypt, in the fourth year of Solomon's reign over Israel, in the month of [2]Ziv, which *is* the second month, [b]that he began to build the house of the Lord. [2]Now [a]the house which King Solomon built for the Lord, its length *was* sixty cubits, its width twenty, and its height thirty cubits. [3]The vestibule in front of the [1]sanctuary of the house *was* [2]twenty cubits long across the width of the house, *and* the width of [3]*the vestibule* extended [4]ten cubits from the front of the house. [4]And he made for the house [a]windows with beveled frames.

[5]Against the wall of the [1]temple he built [a]chambers all around, *against* the walls of the temple, all around the sanctuary [b]and the [2]inner sanctuary. Thus he made side chambers all around it. [6]The lowest chamber *was* five cubits wide, the middle *was* six cubits wide, and the third *was* seven cubits wide; for he made narrow ledges around the outside of the temple, so that *the support beams* would not be fastened into the walls of the [1]temple. [7]And [a]the temple, when it was being built, was built with stone finished at the quarry, so that no hammer or chisel *or* any iron tool was heard in the temple

5:9 [b]Ezek. 27:17; Acts 12:20

5:11 [a]2 Chr. 2:10

5:12 [a]1 Kin. 3:12

5:14 [a]1 Kin. 12:18

5:15 [a]1 Kin. 9:20–22; 2 Chr. 2:17, 18

5:16 [a]1 Kin. 9:23

5:17 [a]1 Kin. 6:7; 1 Chr. 22:2

6:1 [a]2 Chr. 3:1, 2 [b]Acts 7:47

6:2 [a]Ezek. 41:1

6:4 [a]Ezek. 40:16; 41:16

6:5 [a]Ezek. 41:6 [b]1 Kin. 6:16, 19–21, 31

6:7 [a]Ex. 20:25; Deut. 27:5, 6

5:11 [1]Each about 5 bushels   [2]So with MT, Tg., Vg.; LXX, Syr. *twenty thousand kors*   5:16 [1]So with MT, Tg., Vg.; LXX *six hundred*   5:17 [1]Lit. *house*   5:18 [1]Lit. *house*   6:1 [1]So with MT, Tg., Vg.; LXX *fortieth*   [2]Or *Ayyar,* April or May   6:3 [1]Heb. *heykal;* here the main room of the temple; elsewhere called the holy place, Ex. 26:33; Ezek. 41:1   [2]About 30 feet   [3]Lit. *it*   [4]About 15 feet   6:5 [1]Lit. *house*   [2]Heb. *debir;* here the inner room of the temple; elsewhere called the Most Holy Place, v. 16   6:6 [1]Lit. *house*

while it was being built. ⁸The doorway for the ¹middle story *was* on the right side of the temple. They went up by stairs to the middle *story,* and from the middle to the third.

^{9a}So he built the ¹temple and finished it, and he paneled the temple with beams and boards of cedar. ¹⁰And he built side chambers against the entire temple, each five cubits high; they were attached to the temple with cedar beams.

¹¹Then the word of the LORD came to Solomon, saying: ¹²"*Concerning* this ¹temple which you are building, ^aif you walk in My statutes, execute My judgments, keep all My commandments, and walk in them, then I will perform My ²word with you, ^bwhich I spoke to your father David. ¹³And ^aI will dwell among the children of Israel, and will not ^bforsake My people Israel."

¹⁴So Solomon built the temple and finished it. ¹⁵And he built the inside walls of the temple with cedar boards; from the floor of the temple to the ceiling he paneled the inside with wood; and he covered the floor of the temple with planks of cypress. ¹⁶Then he built the twenty-cubit room at the rear of the temple, from floor to ceiling, with cedar boards; he built *it* inside as the inner sanctuary, as the ^aMost Holy *Place.* ¹⁷And in front of it the temple sanctuary was forty cubits *long.* ¹⁸The inside of the temple was cedar, carved with ornamental buds and open flowers. All *was* cedar; there was no stone *to be* seen.

¹⁹And he prepared the ¹inner sanctuary inside the temple, to set the ark of the covenant of the LORD there. ²⁰The inner sanctuary *was* twenty cubits long, twenty cubits wide, and twenty cubits high. He overlaid it with pure gold, and overlaid the altar of cedar. ²¹So Solomon overlaid the inside of the temple with pure gold. He stretched gold chains across the front of the inner sanctuary, and overlaid it with gold. ²²The whole temple he overlaid with gold, until he had finished all the temple; also he overlaid with gold ^athe entire altar that *was* by the inner sanctuary.

²³Inside the inner sanctuary ^ahe made two cherubim *of* olive wood, *each* ten cubits high. ²⁴One wing of the cherub *was* five cubits, and the other wing of the cherub five cubits: ten cubits from the tip of one wing to the tip of the other. ²⁵And the other cherub *was* ten cubits; both cherubim *were* of the same size and shape. ²⁶The height of one cherub *was* ten cubits, and so *was* the other cherub. ²⁷Then he set the cherubim inside the inner ¹room; and ^athey stretched out the wings of the cherubim so that the wing of the one touched *one* wall, and the wing of the other cherub touched the other wall. And their wings touched each other in the middle of the room. ²⁸Also he overlaid the cherubim with gold.

²⁹Then he carved all the walls of the temple all around, both the inner and outer *sanctuaries,* with carved ^afigures of cherubim, palm trees, and open flowers. ³⁰And the floor of the temple he overlaid with gold, both the inner and outer *sanctuaries.*

³¹For the entrance of the inner sanctuary he made doors *of* olive wood; the lintel *and* doorposts *were* ¹one-fifth *of the wall.* ³²The two doors *were of* olive wood; and he carved on

6:9
^a1 Kin. 6:14, 38

6:12
^a1 Kin. 2:4; 9:4
^b[2 Sam. 7:13;
1 Chr. 22:10]

6:13 ^aEx. 25:8;
Lev. 26:11;
[2 Cor. 6:16;
Rev. 21:3]
^b[Deut. 31:6]

6:16 ^aEx. 26:33;
Lev. 16:2;
1 Kin. 8:6;
2 Chr. 3:8;
Ezek. 45:3;
Heb. 9:3

6:22
^aEx. 30:1, 3, 6

6:23
^aEx. 37:7–9;
2 Chr. 3:10–12

6:27 ^aEx. 25:20;
37:9; 1 Kin. 8:7;
2 Chr. 5:8

6:29
^aEx. 36:8, 35

6:8 ¹So with MT, Vg.; LXX *upper story;* Tg. *ground story*   6:9 ¹Lit. *house*
6:12 ¹Lit. *house*   ²*promise*   6:19 ¹The Most Holy Place   6:27 ¹Lit. *house*
6:31 ¹Or *five-sided*

them figures of cherubim, palm trees, and open flowers, and overlaid *them* with gold; and he spread gold on the cherubim and on the palm trees. ³³So for the door of the ¹sanctuary he also made doorposts *of* olive wood, ²one-fourth *of the wall.* ³⁴And the two doors *were of* cypress wood; ᵃtwo panels *comprised* one folding door, and two panels *comprised* the other folding door. ³⁵Then he carved cherubim, palm trees, and open flowers *on them,* and overlaid *them* with gold applied evenly on the carved work.

³⁶And he built the ᵃinner court with three rows of hewn stone and a row of cedar beams.

³⁷ᵃIn the fourth year the foundation of the house of the LORD was laid, in the month of ¹Ziv. ³⁸And in the eleventh year, in the month of ¹Bul, which is the eighth month, the house was finished in all its details and according to all its plans. So he was ᵃseven years in building it.

SOLOMON'S OTHER BUILDINGS

7 But Solomon took ᵃthirteen years to build his own house; so he finished all his house.

²He also built the ᵃHouse of the Forest of Lebanon; its length *was* ¹one hundred cubits, its width ²fifty cubits, and its height thirty cubits, with four rows of cedar pillars, and cedar beams on the pillars. ³And *it was* paneled with cedar above the beams that *were* on forty-five pillars, fifteen *to* a row. ⁴*There were* windows *with beveled frames in* three rows, and window *was* opposite window *in* three tiers. ⁵And all the doorways and doorposts *had* rectangular frames; and window *was* opposite window *in* three tiers.

⁶He also made the Hall of Pillars: its length *was* fifty cubits, and its width thirty cubits; and in front of them *was* a portico with pillars, and a canopy *was* in front of them.

⁷Then he made a hall for the throne, the Hall of Judgment, where he might judge; and *it was* paneled with cedar from floor to ¹ceiling.

⁸And the house where he dwelt *had* another court inside the hall, of like workmanship. Solomon also made a house like this hall for Pharaoh's daughter, ᵃwhom he had taken *as wife.*

⁹All these *were of* costly stones cut to size, trimmed with saws, inside and out, from the foundation to the eaves, and also on the outside to the great court. ¹⁰The foundation *was* of costly stones, large stones, some ten cubits and some eight cubits. ¹¹And above *were* costly stones, hewn to size, and cedar wood. ¹²The great court *was* enclosed with three rows of hewn stones and a row of cedar beams. So were the ᵃinner court of the house of the LORD ᵇand the vestibule of the temple.

HIRAM THE CRAFTSMAN

¹³Now King Solomon sent and brought ¹Huram from Tyre. ¹⁴ᵃHe *was* the son of a widow from the tribe of Naphtali, and ᵇhis father *was* a man of Tyre, a bronze worker; ᶜhe was filled with wisdom and understanding and skill in working with all kinds of bronze work. So he came to King Solomon and did all his work.

6:34
ᵃEzek. 41:23–25
6:36 ᵃ1 Kin. 7:12;
Jer. 36:10
6:37 ᵃ1 Kin. 6:1
6:38
ᵃ2 Sam. 7:13;
1 Kin. 5:5; 6:1;
8:19
7:1 ᵃ1 Kin. 3:1;
9:10; 2 Chr. 8:1
7:2
ᵃ1 Kin. 10:17, 21;
2 Chr. 9:16
7:8 ᵃ1 Kin. 3:1;
9:24; 11:1;
2 Chr. 8:11
7:12 ᵃ1 Kin. 6:36
ᵇJohn 10:23;
Acts 3:11
7:14 ᵃ2 Chr. 2:14
ᵇ2 Chr. 4:16
ᶜEx. 31:3; 36:1

6:33 ¹*temple*   ²Or *four-sided*   **6:37** ¹Or *Ayyar,* April or May   **6:38** ¹Or *Heshvan,* October or November   **7:2** ¹About 150 feet   ²About 75 feet
7:7 ¹Lit. *floor* of the upper level   **7:13** ¹Heb. *Hiram;* cf. 2 Chr. 2:13, 14

THE BRONZE PILLARS FOR THE TEMPLE
(2 Chr. 3:15–17)

15And he ¹cast ᵃtwo pillars of bronze, each one eighteen cubits high, and a line of twelve cubits measured the circumference of each. 16Then he made two capitals *of* cast bronze, to set on the tops of the pillars. The height of one capital *was* five cubits, and the height of the other capital *was* five cubits. 17*He made* a lattice network, with wreaths of chainwork, for the capitals which *were* on top of the pillars: seven chains for one capital and seven for the other capital. 18So he made the pillars, and two rows of pomegranates above the network all around to cover the capitals that *were* on top; and thus he did for the other capital.

19The capitals which *were* on top of the pillars in the hall *were* in the shape of lilies, four cubits. 20The capitals on the two pillars also *had pomegranates* above, by the convex surface which *was* next to the network; and there *were* ᵃtwo hundred such pomegranates in rows on each of the capitals all around.

21ᵃThen he set up the pillars by the vestibule of the temple; he set up the pillar on the right and called its name ¹Jachin, and he set up the pillar on the left and called its name ²Boaz. 22The tops of the pillars were in the shape of lilies. So the work of the pillars was finished.

THE SEA AND THE OXEN

23And he made ᵃthe Sea of cast bronze, ten cubits from one brim to the other; *it was* completely round. Its height *was* five cubits, and a line of thirty cubits measured its circumference. 24Below its brim *were* ornamental buds encircling it all around, ten to a cubit, ᵃall the way around the Sea. The ornamental buds *were* cast in two rows when it was cast. 25It stood on ᵃtwelve oxen: three looking toward the north, three looking toward the west, three looking toward the south, and three looking toward the east; the Sea *was set* upon them, and all their back parts *pointed* inward. 26It *was* a handbreadth thick; and its brim was shaped like the brim of a cup, *like* a lily blossom. It contained ¹two thousand baths.

THE CARTS AND THE LAVERS

27He also made ten ¹carts of bronze; four cubits *was* the length of each cart, four cubits its width, and three cubits its height. 28And this *was* the design of the carts: They had panels, and the panels *were* between frames; 29on the panels that *were* between the frames *were* lions, oxen, and cherubim. And on the frames *was* a pedestal on top. Below the lions and oxen *were* wreaths of plaited work. 30Every cart had four bronze wheels and axles of bronze, and its four feet had supports. Under the laver *were* supports of cast *bronze* beside each wreath. 31Its opening inside the crown at the top *was* one cubit in diameter; and the opening *was* round, shaped *like* a pedestal, one and a half cubits in outside diameter; and also on the opening *were* engravings, but the panels were square, not round. 32Under the panels *were* the four wheels, and the axles of the wheels *were joined* to the cart. The height of a wheel *was* one

7:15
ᵃ2 Kin. 25:17;
2 Chr. 3:15; 4:12;
Jer. 52:21

7:20
ᵃ2 Chr. 3:16;
4:13; Jer. 52:23

7:21 ᵃ2 Chr. 3:17

7:23
ᵃ2 Kin. 25:13;
2 Chr. 4:2;
Jer. 52:17

7:24 ᵃ2 Chr. 4:3

7:25
ᵃ2 Chr. 4:4, 5;
Jer. 52:20

7:15 ¹*fashioned*   7:21 ¹Lit. *He Shall Establish*   ²Lit. *In It Is Strength*
7:26 ¹About 12,000 gallons; *three thousand,* 2 Chr. 4:5   7:27 ¹Or *stands*

and a half cubits. ³³The workmanship of the wheels *was* like the workmanship of a chariot wheel; their axle pins, their rims, their spokes, and their hubs *were* all of cast *bronze.* ³⁴And *there were* four supports at the four corners of each cart; its supports *were* part of the cart itself. ³⁵On the top of the cart, at the height of half a cubit, *it was* perfectly round. And on the top of the cart, its flanges and its panels *were* of the same casting. ³⁶On the plates of its flanges and on its panels he engraved cherubim, lions, and palm trees, wherever there was a clear space on each, with wreaths all around. ³⁷Thus he made the ten carts. All of them were of ¹the same mold, one measure, *and* one shape.

³⁸Then ᵃhe made ten lavers of bronze; each laver contained ¹forty baths, *and* each laver *was* four cubits. On each of the ten carts *was* a laver. ³⁹And he put five carts on the right side of the house, and five on the left side of the house. He set the Sea on the right side of the house, toward the southeast.

FURNISHINGS OF THE TEMPLE
(2 Chr. 4:11–18)

⁴⁰ᵃHuram¹ made the lavers and the shovels and the bowls. So Huram finished doing all the work that he was to do for King Solomon *for* the house of the LORD: ⁴¹the two pillars, the *two* bowl-shaped capitals that *were* on top of the two pillars; the two ᵃnetworks covering the two bowl-shaped capitals which *were* on top of the pillars; ⁴²ᵃfour hundred pomegranates for the two networks (two rows of pomegranates for each network, to cover the two bowl-shaped capitals that *were* on top of the pillars); ⁴³the ten carts, and ten lavers on the carts; ⁴⁴one Sea, and twelve oxen under the Sea; ⁴⁵ᵃthe pots, the shovels, and the bowls.

All these articles which ¹Huram made for King Solomon *for* the house of the LORD *were of* burnished bronze. ⁴⁶ᵃIn the plain of Jordan the king had them cast in clay molds, between ᵇSuccoth and ᶜZaretan. ⁴⁷And Solomon did not weigh all the articles, because *there were* so many; the weight of the bronze was not ᵃdetermined.

⁴⁸Thus Solomon had all the furnishings made for the house of the LORD: ᵃthe altar of gold, and ᵇthe table of gold on which *was* ᶜthe showbread; ⁴⁹the lampstands of pure gold, five on the right *side* and five on the left in front of the inner sanctuary, with the flowers and the lamps and the wick-trimmers of gold; ⁵⁰the basins, the trimmers, the bowls, the ladles, and the ¹censers of pure gold; and the hinges of gold, *both* for the doors of the inner room (the Most Holy *Place*) *and* for the doors of the main hall of the temple.

⁵¹So all the work that King Solomon had done for the house of the LORD was finished; and Solomon brought in the things ᵃwhich his father David had dedicated: the silver and the gold and the furnishings. He put them in the treasuries of the house of the LORD.

THE ARK BROUGHT INTO THE TEMPLE
(2 Chr. 5:2—6:2)

8 Now ᵃSolomon assembled the elders of Israel and all the heads of the tribes, the chief fathers of the children of Israel, to King Solomon in Jerusalem, ᵇthat they might bring

Cross references
7:38 ᵃEx. 30:18;
2 Chr. 4:6

7:40
ᵃ2 Chr. 4:11—5:1

7:41
ᵃ1 Kin. 7:17, 18

7:42 ᵃ1 Kin. 7:20

7:45 ᵃEx. 27:3;
2 Chr. 4:16

7:46 ᵃ2 Chr. 4:17
ᵇGen. 33:17;
Josh. 13:27
ᶜJosh. 3:16

7:47
ᵃ1 Chr. 22:3, 14

7:48
ᵃEx. 37:25, 26;
2 Chr. 4:8
ᵇEx. 37:10, 11
ᶜLev. 24:5–8

7:51
ᵃ2 Sam. 8:11;
1 Chr. 18:11;
2 Chr. 5:1

8:1
ᵃNum. 1:4; 7:2;
2 Chr. 5:2–14
ᵇ2 Sam. 6:12–17;
1 Chr. 15:25–29

Footnotes
7:37 ¹one   7:38 ¹About 240 gallons   7:40 ¹Heb. *Hiram;* cf. 2 Chr. 2:13, 14   7:45 ¹Heb. *Hiram;* cf. 2 Chr. 2:13, 14   7:50 ¹*firepans*

[c]up the ark of the covenant of the LORD from the City of David, which *is* Zion. [2]Therefore all the men of Israel assembled with King Solomon at the [a]feast in the month of [1]Ethanim, which *is* the seventh month. [3]So all the elders of Israel came, [a]and the priests took up the ark. [4]Then they brought up the ark of the LORD, [a]the [1]tabernacle of meeting, and all the holy furnishings that *were* in the tabernacle. The priests and the Levites brought them up. [5]Also King Solomon, and all the congregation of Israel who were assembled with him, *were* with him before the ark, [a]sacrificing sheep and oxen that could not be counted or numbered for multitude. [6]Then the priests [a]brought in the ark of the covenant of the LORD to [b]its place, into the inner sanctuary of the temple, to the Most Holy *Place,* [c]under the wings of the cherubim. [7]For the cherubim spread *their* two wings over the place of the ark, and the cherubim overshadowed the ark and its poles. [8]The poles [a]extended so that the [1]ends of the poles could be seen from the holy *place,* in front of the inner sanctuary; but they could not be seen from outside. And they are there to this day. [9a]Nothing *was* in the ark [b]except the two tablets of stone which Moses [c]put there at Horeb, [d]when the LORD made *a covenant* with the children of Israel, when they came out of the land of Egypt.

[10]And it came to pass, when the priests came out of the holy *place,* that the cloud [a]filled the house of the LORD, [11]so that the priests could not continue ministering because of the cloud; for the [a]glory of the LORD filled the house of the LORD.

[12a]Then Solomon spoke:

"The LORD said He would dwell [b]in the dark cloud.
[13]   [a]I have surely built You an exalted house,
   [b]And a place for You to dwell in forever."

SOLOMON'S SPEECH AT COMPLETION OF THE WORK
(2 Chr. 6:3–11)

[14]Then the king turned around and [a]blessed the whole assembly of Israel, while all the assembly of Israel was standing. [15]And he said: [a]"Blessed *be* the LORD God of Israel, who [b]spoke with His mouth to my father David, and with His hand has fulfilled *it,* saying, [16]'Since the day that I brought My people Israel out of Egypt, I have chosen no city from any tribe of Israel *in* which to build a house, that [a]My name might be there; but I chose [b]David to be over My people Israel.' [17]Now [a]it was in the heart of my father David to build a [1]temple for the name of the LORD God of Israel. [18a]But the LORD said to my father David, 'Whereas it was in your heart to build a temple for My name, you did well that it was in your heart. [19]Nevertheless [a]you shall not build the temple, but your son who will come from your body, he shall build the temple for My name.' [20]So the LORD has fulfilled His word which He spoke; and I have [1]filled the position of my father David, and sit on the throne of Israel, [a]as the LORD promised; and I have built a temple for the name of the LORD God of Israel. [21]And there I have made a place for the ark, in which *is* [a]the covenant of the LORD which He made with our fathers, when He brought them out of the land of Egypt."

8:1 [c]2 Sam. 5:7; 6:12, 16

8:2 [a]Lev. 23:34; 1 Kin. 8:65; 2 Chr. 7:8–10

8:3 [a]Num. 4:15; 7:9; Deut. 31:9; Josh. 3:3, 6

8:4 [a]1 Kin. 3:4; 2 Chr. 1:3

8:5 [a]2 Sam. 6:13; 2 Chr. 1:6

8:6 [a]2 Sam. 6:17 [b]Ex. 26:33, 34; 1 Kin. 6:19 [c]1 Kin. 6:27

8:8 [a]Ex. 25:13–15; 37:4, 5

8:9 [a]Ex. 25:21; Deut. 10:2 [b]Ex. 25:16; Deut. 10:5; Heb. 9:4 [c]Ex. 24:7, 8; 40:20; Deut. 4:13 [d]Ex. 34:27, 28

8:10 [a]Ex. 40:34, 35; 2 Chr. 7:1, 2

8:11 [a]2 Chr. 7:1, 2

8:12 [a]2 Chr. 6:1 [b]Lev. 16:2; Ps. 18:11; 97:2

8:13 [a]2 Sam. 7:13 [b][Ex. 15:17]; Ps. 132:14

8:14 [a]2 Sam. 6:18; 1 Kin. 8:55

8:15 [a]1 Chr. 29:10, 20; Neh. 9:5; Luke 1:68 [b]2 Sam. 7:2, 12, 13, 25; 1 Chr. 22:10

8:16 [a]Deut. 12:5; 1 Kin. 8:29 [b]1 Sam. 16:1; 2 Sam. 7:8; 1 Chr. 28:4

8:17 [a]2 Sam. 7:2, 3; 1 Chr. 17:1, 2

8:18 [a]2 Chr. 6:8, 9

8:19 [a]2 Sam. 7:5, 12, 13; 1 Kin. 5:3, 5; 6:38; 1 Chr. 17:11, 12; 22:8–10; 2 Chr. 6:2

8:20 [a]1 Chr. 28:5, 6

8:21 [a]Deut. 31:26; 1 Kin. 8:9

SOLOMON'S PRAYER OF DEDICATION
(2 Chr. 6:12–39)

²²Then Solomon stood before ᵃthe altar of the LORD in the presence of all the assembly of Israel, and ᵇspread out his hands toward heaven; ²³and he said: "LORD God of Israel, ᵃ*there is* no God in heaven above or on earth below like You, ᵇwho keep *Your* covenant and mercy with Your servants who ᶜwalk before You with all their hearts. ²⁴You have kept what You promised Your servant David my father; You have both spoken with Your mouth and fulfilled *it* with Your hand, as *it is* this day. ²⁵Therefore, LORD God of Israel, now keep what You promised Your servant David my father, saying, ᵃ'You shall not fail to have a man sit before Me on the throne of Israel, only if your sons take heed to their way, that they walk before Me as you have walked before Me.' ²⁶ᵃAnd now I pray, O God of Israel, let Your word come true, which You have spoken to Your servant David my father.

²⁷"But ᵃwill God indeed dwell on the earth? Behold, heaven and the ᵇheaven of heavens cannot contain You. How much less this temple which I have built! ²⁸Yet regard the prayer of Your servant and his supplication, O LORD my God, and listen to the cry and the prayer which Your servant is praying before You today: ²⁹that Your eyes may be open toward this ¹temple night and day, toward the place of which You said, ᵃ'My name shall be ᵇthere,' that You may hear the prayer which Your servant makes ᶜtoward this place. ³⁰ᵃAnd may You hear the supplication of Your servant and of Your people Israel, when they pray toward this place. Hear in heaven Your dwelling place; and when You hear, forgive.

³¹"When anyone sins against his neighbor, and is forced to take ᵃan oath, and comes *and* takes an oath before Your altar in this temple, ³²then hear in heaven, and act, and judge Your servants, ᵃcondemning the wicked, bringing his way on his head, and justifying the righteous by giving him according to his righteousness.

³³ᵃ"When Your people Israel are defeated before an enemy because they have sinned against You, and ᵇwhen they turn back to You and confess Your name, and pray and make supplication to You in this temple, ³⁴then hear in heaven, and forgive the sin of Your people Israel, and bring them back to the land which You gave to their ᵃfathers.

³⁵ᵃ"When the heavens are shut up and there is no rain because they have sinned against You, when they pray toward this place and confess Your name, and turn from their sin because You afflict them, ³⁶then hear in heaven, and forgive the sin of Your servants, Your people Israel, that You may ᵃteach them ᵇthe good way in which they should walk; and send rain on Your land which You have given to Your people as an inheritance.

³⁷ᵃ"When there is famine in the land, pestilence *or* blight *or* mildew, locusts *or* grasshoppers; when their enemy besieges them in the land of their ¹cities; whatever plague or whatever sickness *there is;* ³⁸whatever prayer, whatever supplication is made by anyone, *or* by all Your people Israel, when each one knows the plague of his own heart, and spreads out his hands

8:22
ᵃ1 Kin. 8:54;
2 Chr. 6:12
ᵇEx. 9:33;
Ezra 9:5

8:23 ᵃEx. 15:11;
2 Sam. 7:22
ᵇ[Deut. 7:9;
Neh. 1:5;
Dan. 9:4]
ᶜ[Gen. 17:1;
1 Kin. 3:6];
2 Kin. 20:3

8:25
ᵃ2 Sam. 7:12, 16;
1 Kin. 2:4; 9:5

8:26
ᵃ2 Sam. 7:25

8:27
ᵃ[2 Chr. 2:6;
Is. 66:1;
Acts 7:49; 17:24]
ᵇ2 Cor. 12:2

8:29 ᵃDeut. 12:11
ᵇ1 Kin. 9:3;
2 Chr. 7:15
ᶜDan. 6:10

8:30 ᵃNeh. 1:6

8:31 ᵃEx. 22:8–11

8:32 ᵃDeut. 25:1

8:33 ᵃLev. 26:17;
Deut. 28:25
ᵇLev. 26:39, 40

8:34
ᵃ[Lev. 26:40–42;
Deut. 30:1–3]

8:35 ᵃLev. 26:19;
Deut. 28:23

8:36 ᵃPs. 25:4;
27:11; 94:12
ᵇ1 Sam. 12:23

8:37 ᵃLev. 26:16,
25, 26;
Deut. 28:21, 22,
27, 38, 42, 52

8:29 ¹Lit. *house*   8:37 ¹Lit. *gates*

toward this temple: [39]then hear in heaven Your dwelling place, and forgive, and act, and give to everyone according to all his ways, whose heart You know (for You alone [a]know the hearts of all the sons of men), [40a]that they may fear You all the days that they live in the land which You gave to our fathers.

[41]"Moreover, concerning a foreigner, who *is* not of Your people Israel, but has come from a far country for Your name's sake [42](for they will hear of Your great name and Your [a]strong hand and Your outstretched arm), when he comes and prays toward this temple, [43]hear in heaven Your dwelling place, and do according to all for which the foreigner calls to You, [a]that all peoples of the earth may know Your name and [b]fear You, as *do* Your people Israel, and that they may know that this temple which I have built is called by Your name.

[44]"When Your people go out to battle against their enemy, wherever You send them, and when they pray to the LORD toward the city which You have chosen and the temple which I have built for Your name, [45]then hear in heaven their prayer and their supplication, and maintain their [1]cause.

[46]"When they sin against You [a](for *there is* no one who does not sin), and You become angry with them and deliver them to the enemy, and they take them captive [b]to the land of the enemy, far or near; [47a]*yet* when they [1]come to themselves in the land where they were carried captive, and repent, and make supplication to You in the land of those who took them captive, [b]saying, 'We have sinned and done wrong, we have committed wickedness'; [48]and *when* they [a]return to You with all their heart and with all their soul in the land of their enemies who led them away captive, and [b]pray to You toward their land which You gave to their fathers, the city which You have chosen and the temple which I have built for Your name: [49]then hear in heaven Your dwelling place their prayer and their supplication, and maintain their [1]cause, [50]and forgive Your people who have sinned against You, and all their transgressions which they have transgressed against You; and [a]grant them compassion before those who took them captive, that they may have compassion on them [51](for [a]they *are* Your people and Your inheritance, whom You brought out of Egypt, [b]out of the iron furnace), [52a]that Your eyes may be open to the supplication of Your servant and the supplication of Your people Israel, to listen to them whenever they call to You. [53]For You separated them from among all the peoples of the earth *to be* Your inheritance, [a]as You spoke by Your servant Moses, when You brought our fathers out of Egypt, O Lord GOD."

SOLOMON BLESSES THE ASSEMBLY
(2 Chr. 6:40–42)

[54a]And so it was, when Solomon had finished praying all this prayer and supplication to the LORD, that he arose from before the altar of the LORD, from kneeling on his knees with his hands spread up to heaven. [55]Then he stood [a]and blessed all the assembly of Israel with a loud voice, saying: [56]"Blessed *be* the LORD, who has given [a]rest[1] to His people Israel, according to all that He promised. [b]There has not failed one word of

8:39
[a][1 Sam. 16:7;
1 Chr. 28:9;
Jer. 17:10];
Acts 1:24

8:40
[a][Ps. 130:4]

8:42 [a]Ex. 13:3;
Deut. 3:24

8:43 [a][Ex. 9:16;
1 Sam. 17:46;
2 Kin. 19:19]
[b]Ps. 102:15

8:46
[a]2 Chr. 6:36;
Ps. 130:3;
Prov. 20:9;
Eccl. 7:20;
[Rom. 3:23;
1 John 1:8, 10]
[b]Lev. 26:34, 44;
Deut. 28:36, 64;
2 Kin. 17:6, 18;
25:21

8:47
[a][Lev. 26:40–42];
Neh. 9:2
[b]Ezra 9:6,
7; Neh. 1:6;
Ps. 106:6;
Dan. 9:5

8:48
[a]Jer. 29:12–14
[b]Dan. 6:10;
Jon. 2:4

8:50
[a][2 Chr. 30:9];
Ezra 7:6;
Ps. 106:46;
Acts 7:10

8:51
[a]Ex. 32:11, 12;
Deut. 9:26–29;
Neh. 1:10;
[Rom. 11:28, 29]
[b]Deut. 4:20;
Jer. 11:4

8:52 [a]1 Kin. 8:29

8:53 [a]Ex. 19:5, 6

8:54 [a]2 Chr. 7:1

8:55
[a]Num. 6:23–26;
2 Sam. 6:18;
1 Kin. 8:14

8:56
[a]1 Chr. 22:18
[b]Deut. 12:10;
Josh. 21:45;
23:14

8:45 [1]justice   8:47 [1]Lit. *bring back to their heart*   8:49 [1]justice   8:56 [1]peace

all His good promise, which He promised through His servant Moses. [57]May the LORD our God be with us, as He was with our fathers. [a]May He not leave us nor forsake us, [58]that He may [a]incline our hearts to Himself, to walk in all His ways, and to keep His commandments and His statutes and His judgments, which He commanded our fathers. [59]And may these words of mine, with which I have made supplication before the LORD, be near the LORD our God day and night, that He may maintain the cause of His servant and the cause of His people Israel, as each day may require, [60a]that all the peoples of the earth may know that [b]the LORD *is* God; *there is* no other. [61]Let your [a]heart therefore be [1]loyal to the LORD our God, to walk in His statutes and keep His commandments, as at this day."

SOLOMON DEDICATES THE TEMPLE
(2 Chr. 7:4–11)

[62]Then [a]the king and all Israel with him offered sacrifices before the LORD. [63]And Solomon offered a sacrifice of peace offerings, which he offered to the LORD, twenty-two thousand bulls and one hundred and twenty thousand sheep. So the king and all the children of Israel dedicated the house of the LORD. [64]On [a]the same day the king consecrated the middle of the court that *was* in front of the house of the LORD; for there he offered burnt offerings, grain offerings, and the fat of the peace offerings, because the [b]bronze altar that *was* before the LORD *was* too small to receive the burnt offerings, the grain offerings, and the fat of the peace offerings.

[65]At that time Solomon held [a]a feast, and all Israel with him, a great assembly from [b]the entrance of Hamath to [c]the Brook of Egypt, before the LORD our God, [d]seven days and seven *more* days—fourteen days. [66a]On the eighth day he sent the people away; and they [1]blessed the king, and went to their tents joyful and glad of heart for all the good that the LORD had done for His servant David, and for Israel His people.

GOD'S SECOND APPEARANCE TO SOLOMON
(2 Chr. 7:12–22)

9 And [a]it came to pass, when Solomon had finished building the house of the LORD [b]and the king's house, and [c]all Solomon's desire which he wanted to do, [2]that the LORD appeared to Solomon the second time, [a]as He had appeared to him at Gibeon. [3]And the LORD said to him: [a]"I have heard your prayer and your supplication that you have made before Me; I have consecrated this house which you have built [b]to put My name there forever, [c]and My eyes and My heart will be there perpetually. [4]Now if you [a]walk before Me [b]as your father David walked, in integrity of heart and in uprightness, to do according to all that I have commanded you, *and* if you [c]keep My statutes and My judgments, [5]then I will establish the throne of your kingdom over Israel forever, [a]as I promised David your father, saying, 'You shall not fail to have a man on the throne of Israel.' [6a]*But* if you or your sons at all [1]turn from following Me, and do not keep My commandments *and* My statutes which I have set before you, but go and serve other

---

8:57 [a]Deut. 31:6; Josh. 1:5; 1 Sam. 12:22; [Rom. 8:31–37]; Heb. 13:5

8:58 [a]Ps. 119:36; Jer. 31:33

8:60 [a]Josh. 4:24; 1 Sam. 17:46; 1 Kin. 8:43; 2 Kin. 19:19 [b]Deut. 4:35, 39; 1 Kin. 18:39; [Jer. 10:10–12]

8:61 [a]Deut. 18:13; 1 Kin. 11:4; 15:3, 14; 2 Kin. 20:3

8:62 [a]2 Chr. 7:4–10

8:64 [a]2 Chr. 7:7 [b]2 Chr. 4:1

8:65 [a]Lev. 23:34; 1 Kin. 8:2 [b]Num. 34:8; Josh. 13:5; Judg. 3:3; 2 Kin. 14:25 [c]Gen. 15:18; Ex. 23:31; Num. 34:5 [d]2 Chr. 7:8

8:66 [a]2 Chr. 7:9

9:1 [a]2 Chr. 7:11 [b]1 Kin. 7:1 [c]2 Chr. 8:6

9:2 [a]1 Kin. 3:5; 11:9; 2 Chr. 1:7

9:3 [a]2 Kin. 20:5; Ps. 10:17 [b]1 Kin. 8:29 [c]Deut. 11:12

9:4 [a]Gen. 17:1 [b]1 Kin. 11:4, 6; 15:5 [c]1 Kin. 8:61

9:5 [a]2 Sam. 7:12, 16; 1 Kin. 2:4; 6:12; 8:25; 1 Chr. 22:10; Matt. 1:6; 25:31

9:6 [a]2 Sam. 7:14–16; 2 Chr. 7:19, 20; Ps. 89:30

8:61 [1]Lit. *at peace with*   **8:66** [1]*thanked*   **9:6** [1]*turn back*

gods and worship them, [7a]then I will [1]cut off Israel from the land which I have given them; and this house which I have consecrated [b]for My name I will cast out of My sight. [c]Israel will be a proverb and a byword among all peoples. [8]And *as for* [a]this house, *which* is exalted, everyone who passes by it will be astonished and will hiss, and say, [b]'Why has the LORD done thus to this land and to this house?' [9]Then they will answer, 'Because they forsook the LORD their God, who brought their fathers out of the land of Egypt, and have embraced other gods, and worshiped them and served them; therefore the LORD has brought all this [a]calamity on them.'"

SOLOMON AND HIRAM EXCHANGE GIFTS

[10]Now [a]it happened at the end of twenty years, when Solomon had built the two houses, the house of the LORD and the king's house [11a](Hiram the king of Tyre had supplied Solomon with cedar and cypress and gold, as much as he desired), *that* King Solomon then gave Hiram twenty cities in the land of Galilee. [12]Then Hiram went from Tyre to see the cities which Solomon had given him, but they did not please him. [13]So he said, "What *kind of* cities *are* these which you have given me, my brother?" [a]And he called them the land of [1]Cabul, as they are to this day. [14]Then Hiram sent the king one hundred and twenty talents of gold.

SOLOMON'S ADDITIONAL ACHIEVEMENTS
(2 *Chr.* 8:3–16)

[15]And this *is* the reason for [a]the labor force which King Solomon raised: to build the house of the LORD, his own house, [1]the [b]Millo, the wall of Jerusalem, [c]Hazor, [d]Megiddo, and [e]Gezer. [16](Pharaoh king of Egypt had gone up and taken Gezer and burned it with fire, [a]had killed the Canaanites who dwelt in the city, and had given it *as* a dowry to his daughter, Solomon's wife.) [17]And Solomon built Gezer, Lower [a]Beth Horon, [18a]Baalath, and Tadmor in the wilderness, in the land *of Judah,* [19]all the storage cities that Solomon had, cities for [a]his chariots and cities for his [b]cavalry, and whatever Solomon [c]desired to build in Jerusalem, in Lebanon, and in all the land of his dominion.

[20a]All the people *who were* left of the Amorites, Hittites, Perizzites, Hivites, and Jebusites, who *were* not of the children of Israel— [21]that is, their descendants [a]who were left in the land after them, [b]whom the children of Israel had not been able to destroy completely—[c]from these Solomon raised [d]forced labor, as it is to this day. [22]But of the children of Israel Solomon [a]made no forced laborers, because they *were* men of war and his servants: his officers, his captains, commanders of his chariots, and his cavalry.

[23]Others *were* chiefs of the officials who *were* over Solomon's work: [a]five hundred and fifty, who ruled over the people who did the work.

[24]But [a]Pharaoh's daughter came up from the City of David to [b]her house which [1]*Solomon* had built for her. [c]Then he built the Millo.

9:7
[a][Lev. 18:24–29];
Deut. 4:26;
2 Kin. 17:23;
25:21
[b][Jer. 7:4–14]
[c]Deut. 28:37;
Ps. 44:14;
Jer. 24:9

9:8 [a]2 Chr. 7:21
[b][Deut. 29:24–26]; Jer. 22:8, 9

9:9
[a][Deut. 29:25–28]

9:10 [a]1 Kin. 6:37, 38; 7:1; 2 Chr. 8:1

9:11 [a]1 Kin. 5:1

9:13 [a]Josh. 19:27

9:15 [a]1 Kin. 5:13
[b]2 Sam. 5:9;
1 Kin. 9:24
[c]Josh. 11:1; 19:36
[d]Josh. 17:11
[e]Josh. 16:10

9:16
[a]Josh. 16:10;
Judg. 1:29

9:17
[a]Josh. 10:10;
16:3; 21:22;
2 Chr. 8:5

9:18
[a]Josh. 19:44;
2 Chr. 8:4

9:19
[a]1 Kin. 10:26;
2 Chr. 1:14
[b]1 Kin. 4:26
[c]1 Kin. 9:1

9:20 [a]2 Chr. 8:7

9:21
[a]Judg. 1:21–36;
3:1 [b]Josh. 15:63;
17:12, 13
[c]Judg. 1:28, 35
[d]Ezra 2:55, 58;
Neh. 7:57

9:22
[a][Lev. 25:39]

9:23 [a]2 Chr. 8:10

9:24 [a]1 Kin. 3:1
[b]1 Kin. 7:8
[c]2 Sam. 5:9;
1 Kin. 11:27;
2 Chr. 32:5

9:7 [1]*destroy*   9:13 [1]Lit. *Good for Nothing*   9:15 [1]Lit. *The Landfill*   9:24 [1]Lit. *he;* cf. 2 Chr. 8:11

25aNow three times a year Solomon offered burnt offerings and peace offerings on the altar which he had built for the LORD, and he burned incense with them *on the altar* that *was* before the LORD. So he finished the temple.

26aKing Solomon also built a fleet of ships at bEzion Geber, which *is* near 1Elath on the shore of the Red Sea, in the land of Edom. 27aThen Hiram sent his servants with the fleet, seamen who knew the sea, to work with the servants of Solomon. 28And they went to aOphir, and acquired four hundred and twenty talents of gold from there, and brought *it* to King Solomon.

THE QUEEN OF SHEBA'S PRAISE OF SOLOMON
(2 Chr. 9:1–28)

10 Now when the aqueen of Sheba heard of the fame of Solomon concerning the name of the LORD, she came bto test him with hard questions. 2She came to Jerusalem with a very great 1retinue, with camels that bore spices, very much gold, and precious stones; and when she came to Solomon, she spoke with him about all that was in her heart. 3So Solomon answered all her questions; there was nothing 1so difficult for the king that he could not explain *it* to her. 4And when the queen of Sheba had seen all the wisdom of Solomon, the house that he had built, 5the food on his table, the seating of his servants, the service of his waiters and their apparel, his cupbearers, aand his entryway by which he went up to the house of the LORD, there was no more spirit in her. 6Then she said to the king: "It was a true report which I heard in my own land about your words and your wisdom. 7However I did not believe the words until I came and saw with my own eyes; and indeed the half was not told me. Your wisdom and prosperity exceed the fame of which I heard. 8aHappy *are* your men and happy *are* these your servants, who stand continually before you *and* hear your wisdom! 9aBlessed be the LORD your God, who bdelighted in you, setting you on the throne of Israel! Because the LORD has loved Israel forever, therefore He made you king, cto do justice and righteousness."

10Then she agave the king one hundred and twenty talents of gold, spices in great quantity, and precious stones. There never again came such abundance of spices as the queen of Sheba gave to King Solomon. 11aAlso, the ships of Hiram, which brought gold from Ophir, brought great quantities of 1almug wood and precious stones from Ophir. 12aAnd the king made 1steps of the almug wood for the house of the LORD and for the king's house, also harps and stringed instruments for singers. There never again came such balmug wood, nor has the like been seen to this day.

13Now King Solomon gave the queen of Sheba all she desired, whatever she asked, besides what Solomon had given her according to the royal generosity. So she turned and went to her own country, she and her servants.

SOLOMON'S GREAT WEALTH

14The weight of gold that came to Solomon yearly was six hundred and sixty-six talents of gold, 15besides *that* from the

---

9:25
aEx. 23:14–17;
Deut. 16:16;
2 Chr. 8:12, 13

9:26
a2 Chr. 8:17, 18
bNum. 33:35;
Deut. 2:8;
1 Kin. 22:48

9:27 a1 Kin. 5:6, 9; 10:11

9:28 aJob 22:24

10:1 a2 Chr. 9:1;
Matt. 12:42;
Luke 11:31
bJudg. 14:12;
Ps. 49:4;
Prov. 1:6

10:5
a1 Chr. 26:16;
2 Chr. 9:4

10:8 aProv. 8:34

10:9 a1 Kin. 5:7
b2 Sam. 22:20
c2 Sam. 8:15;
Ps. 72:2;
[Prov. 8:15]

10:10
aPs. 72:10, 15

10:11
a1 Kin. 9:27, 28;
Job 22:24

10:12 a2 Chr. 9:11
b2 Chr. 9:10

9:26 1Heb. *Eloth* **10:2** 1*company* **10:3** 1*too* **10:11** 1*algum,* 2 Chr. 9:10, 11
10:12 1Or *supports*

ᵃtraveling merchants, from the income of traders, ᵇfrom all the kings of Arabia, and from the governors of the country.

¹⁶And King Solomon made two hundred large shields *of* hammered gold; six hundred *shekels* of gold went into each shield. ¹⁷He also *made* ᵃthree hundred shields *of* hammered gold; three minas of gold went into each shield. The king put them in the ᵇHouse of the Forest of Lebanon.

¹⁸ᵃMoreover the king made a great throne of ivory, and overlaid it with pure gold. ¹⁹The throne had six steps, and the top of the throne *was* round at the back; *there were* armrests on either side of the place of the seat, and two lions stood beside the armrests. ²⁰Twelve lions stood there, one on each side of the six steps; nothing like *this* had been made for any *other* kingdom.

²¹ᵃAll King Solomon's drinking vessels *were* gold, and all the vessels of the House of the Forest of Lebanon *were* pure gold. Not *one was* silver, for this was accounted as nothing in the days of Solomon. ²²For the king had ᵃmerchant¹ ships at sea with the fleet of Hiram. Once every three years the merchant ᵇships came bringing gold, silver, ivory, apes, and ²monkeys. ²³So ᵃKing Solomon surpassed all the kings of the earth in riches and wisdom.

²⁴Now all the earth sought the presence of Solomon to hear his wisdom, which God had put in his heart. ²⁵Each man brought his present: articles of silver and gold, garments, armor, spices, horses, and mules, at a set rate year by year.

²⁶ᵃAnd Solomon ᵇgathered chariots and horsemen; he had one thousand four hundred chariots and twelve thousand horsemen, whom he ¹stationed in the chariot cities and with the king at Jerusalem. ²⁷ᵃThe king made silver *as common* in Jerusalem as stones, and he made cedar trees as abundant as the sycamores which *are* in the lowland.

²⁸ᵃAlso Solomon had horses imported from Egypt and Keveh; the king's merchants bought them in Keveh at the *current* price. ²⁹Now a chariot that was imported from Egypt cost six hundred *shekels* of silver, and a horse one hundred and fifty; ᵃand ¹thus, through their agents, they exported *them* to all the kings of the Hittites and the kings of Syria.

SOLOMON'S HEART TURNS FROM THE LORD

11 But ᵃKing Solomon loved ᵇmany foreign women, as well as the daughter of Pharaoh: women of the Moabites, Ammonites, Edomites, Sidonians, *and* Hittites— ²from the nations of whom the LORD had said to the children of Israel, ᵃ"You shall not intermarry with them, nor they with you. Surely they will turn away your hearts after their gods." Solomon clung to these in love. ³And he had seven hundred wives, princesses, and three hundred concubines; and his wives turned away his heart. ⁴For it was so, when Solomon was old, ᵃthat his wives turned his heart after other gods; and his ᵇheart was not ¹loyal to the LORD his God, ᶜas *was* the heart of his father David. ⁵For Solomon went after ᵃAshtoreth the goddess of the Sidonians, and after ᵇMilcom¹ the abomination of the ᶜAmmonites. ⁶Solomon did evil in the sight of

Cross references

10:15 ᵃ2 Chr. 1:16
ᵇ2 Chr. 9:24;
Ps. 72:10

10:17
ᵃ1 Kin. 14:26
ᵇ1 Kin. 7:2

10:18
ᵃ1 Kin. 10:22;
2 Chr. 9:17;
Ps. 45:8

10:21
ᵃ2 Chr. 9:20

10:22
ᵃGen. 10:4;
2 Chr. 20:36
ᵇ1 Kin. 9:26–28;
22:48; Ps. 72:10

10:23
ᵃ1 Kin. 3:12, 13;
4:30; 2 Chr. 1:12

10:26
ᵃ1 Kin. 4:26;
2 Chr. 1:14; 9:25
ᵇ[Deut. 17:16];
1 Kin. 9:19

10:27
ᵃ[Deut. 17:17];
2 Chr. 1:15–17

10:28
ᵃ[Deut. 17:16];
2 Chr. 1:16; 9:28

10:29 ᵃJosh. 1:4;
2 Kin. 7:6, 7

11:1
ᵃ[Neh. 13:26]
ᵇ[Deut. 17:17];
1 Kin. 3:1

11:2 ᵃEx. 34:16;
[Deut. 7:3, 4]

11:4
ᵃ[Deut. 17:17;
Neh. 13:26]
ᵇ1 Kin. 8:61
ᶜ1 Kin. 9:4

11:5 ᵃJudg. 2:13;
1 Kin. 11:33
ᵇ[Lev. 20:2–5]
ᶜ2 Kin. 23:13

10:22 ¹Lit. *ships of Tarshish,* deep-sea vessels   ²Or *peacocks*   10:26 ¹So with LXX, Syr., Tg., Vg. (cf. 2 Chr. 9:25); MT *led*   10:29 ¹Lit. *by their hands*   11:4 ¹Lit. *at peace with*   11:5 ¹Or *Molech*

the LORD, and did not fully follow the LORD, as *did* his father David. ⁷ªThen Solomon built a ¹high place for ᵇChemosh the abomination of Moab, on ᶜthe hill that *is* east of Jerusalem, and for Molech the abomination of the people of Ammon. ⁸And he did likewise for all his foreign wives, who burned incense and sacrificed to their gods.

⁹So the LORD became angry with Solomon, because his heart had turned from the LORD God of Israel, ªwho had appeared to him twice, ¹⁰and ªhad commanded him concerning this thing, that he should not go after other gods; but he did not keep what the LORD had commanded. ¹¹Therefore the LORD said to Solomon, "Because you have done this, and have not kept My covenant and My statutes, which I have commanded you, ªI will surely tear the kingdom away from you and give it to your ᵇservant. ¹²Nevertheless I will not do it in your days, for the sake of your father David; I will tear it out of the hand of your son. ¹³ªHowever I will not tear away the whole kingdom; I will give ᵇone tribe to your son ᶜfor the sake of My servant David, and for the sake of Jerusalem ᵈwhich I have chosen."

ADVERSARIES OF SOLOMON

¹⁴Now the LORD ªraised up an adversary against Solomon, Hadad the Edomite; he *was* a descendant of the king in Edom. ¹⁵ªFor it happened, when David was in Edom, and Joab the commander of the army had gone up to bury the slain, ᵇafter he had killed every male in Edom ¹⁶(because for six months Joab remained there with all Israel, until he had cut down every male in Edom), ¹⁷that Hadad fled to go to Egypt, he and certain Edomites of his father's servants with him. Hadad *was* still a little child. ¹⁸Then they arose from Midian and came to Paran; and they took men with them from Paran and came to Egypt, to Pharaoh king of Egypt, who gave him a house, apportioned food for him, and gave him land. ¹⁹And Hadad found great favor in the sight of Pharaoh, so that he gave him as wife the sister of his own wife, that is, the sister of Queen Tahpenes. ²⁰Then the sister of Tahpenes bore him Genubath his son, whom Tahpenes weaned in Pharaoh's house. And Genubath was in Pharaoh's household among the sons of Pharaoh.

²¹ªSo when Hadad heard in Egypt that David ¹rested with his fathers, and that Joab the commander of the army was dead, Hadad said to Pharaoh, ²"Let me depart, that I may go to my own country."

²²Then Pharaoh said to him, "But what have you lacked with me, that suddenly you seek to go to your own country?"

So he answered, "Nothing, but do let me go anyway."

²³And God raised up *another* adversary against him, Rezon the son of Eliadah, who had fled from his lord, ªHadadezer king of Zobah. ²⁴So he gathered men to him and became captain over a band *of raiders,* ªwhen David killed those *of Zobah.* And they went to Damascus and dwelt there, and reigned in Damascus. ²⁵He was an adversary of Israel all the days of Solomon (besides the trouble that Hadad *caused*); and he abhorred Israel, and reigned over Syria.

Cross references (margin)

11:7
ªNum. 33:52
ᵇNum. 21:29;
Judg. 11:24
ᶜ2 Kin. 23:13

11:9
ª1 Kin. 3:5; 9:2

11:10 ª1 Kin. 6:12;
9:6, 7

11:11 ª1 Kin. 11:31;
12:15, 16
ᵇ1 Kin. 11:31, 37

11:13
ª2 Sam. 7:15;
1 Chr. 17:13;
Ps. 89:33
ᵇ1 Kin. 12:20
ᶜ2 Sam. 7:15, 16
ᵈDeut. 12:11;
1 Kin. 9:3; 14:21

11:14 ª1 Chr. 5:26

11:15
ª2 Sam. 8:14;
1 Chr. 18:12, 13
ᵇNum. 24:18, 19;
[Deut. 20:13]

11:21
ª1 Kin. 2:10, 34

11:23
ª2 Sam. 8:3;
10:16

11:24
ª2 Sam. 8:3;
10:8, 18

11:7 ¹A place for pagan worship   11:21 ¹Died and joined his ancestors
²Lit. *Send me away*

JEROBOAM'S REBELLION

26Then Solomon's servant, aJeroboam the son of Nebat, an Ephraimite from Zereda, whose mother's name *was* Zeruah, a widow, balso crebelled against the king.

27And this *is* what caused him to rebel against the king: aSolomon had built the Millo *and* 1repaired the damages to the City of David his father. 28The man Jeroboam *was* a mighty man of valor; and Solomon, seeing that the young man was aindustrious, made him the officer over all the labor force of the house of Joseph.

29Now it happened at that time, when Jeroboam went out of Jerusalem, that the prophet aAhijah the Shilonite met him on the way; and he had clothed himself with a new garment, and the two *were* alone in the field. 30Then Ahijah took hold of the new garment that *was* on him, and atore it *into* twelve pieces. 31And he said to Jeroboam, "Take for yourself ten pieces, for athus says the LORD, the God of Israel: 'Behold, I will tear the kingdom out of the hand of Solomon and will give ten tribes to you 32(but he shall have one tribe for the sake of My servant David, and for the sake of Jerusalem, the city which I have chosen out of all the tribes of Israel), 33abecause 1they have forsaken Me, and worshiped Ashtoreth the goddess of the Sidonians, Chemosh the god of the Moabites, and Milcom the god of the people of Ammon, and have not walked in My ways to do *what is* right in My eyes and *keep* My statutes and My judgments, as *did* his father David. 34However I will not take the whole kingdom out of his hand, because I have made him ruler all the days of his life for the sake of My servant David, whom I chose because he kept My commandments and My statutes. 35But aI will take the kingdom out of his son's hand and give it to you—ten tribes. 36And to his son I will give one tribe, that aMy servant David may always have a lamp before Me in Jerusalem, the city which I have chosen for Myself, to put My name there. 37So I will take you, and you shall reign over all your heart desires, and you shall be king over Israel. 38Then it shall be, if you heed all that I command you, walk in My ways, and do *what is* right in My sight, to keep My statutes and My commandments, as My servant David did, then aI will be with you and bbuild for you an enduring house, as I built for David, and will give Israel to you. 39And I will afflict the descendants of David because of this, but not forever.'"

40Solomon therefore sought to kill Jeroboam. But Jeroboam arose and fled to Egypt, to aShishak king of Egypt, and was in Egypt until the death of Solomon.

DEATH OF SOLOMON
(2 Chr. 9:29–31)

41Now athe rest of the acts of Solomon, all that he did, and his wisdom, *are* they not written in the book of the acts of Solomon? 42aAnd the period that Solomon reigned in Jerusalem over all Israel *was* forty years. 43aThen Solomon 1rested with his fathers, and was buried in the City of David his father. And Rehoboam his son reigned in his bplace.

11:26 a1 Kin. 12:2
b1 Kin. 11:11;
2 Chr. 13:6
c2 Sam. 20:21

11:27
a1 Kin. 9:15, 24

11:28
a[Prov. 22:29]

11:29
a1 Kin. 12:15;
14:2; 2 Chr. 9:29

11:30
a1 Sam. 15:27,
28; 24:5

11:31
a1 Kin. 11:11, 13

11:33
a1 Sam. 7:3;
1 Kin. 11:5–8

11:35
a1 Kin. 12:16, 17

11:36
a[1 Kin. 15:4;
2 Kin. 8:19]

11:38
aDeut. 31:8;
Josh. 1:5
b2 Sam. 7:11, 27

11:40
a1 Kin. 11:17;
14:25;
2 Chr. 12:2–9

11:41 a2 Chr. 9:29

11:42
a2 Chr. 9:30

11:43
a1 Kin. 2:10;
2 Chr. 9:31
b1 Kin. 14:21;
2 Chr. 10:1

11:27 1Lit. *closed up the breaches*   11:33 1So with MT, Tg.; LXX, Syr., Vg. *he has*   11:43 1Died and joined his ancestors

THE REVOLT AGAINST REHOBOAM
(*2 Chr. 10:1–19; 11:1–4*)

12 And ªRehoboam went to ᵇShechem, for all Israel had gone to Shechem to make him king. ²So it happened, when ªJeroboam the son of Nebat heard *it* (he was still in ᵇEgypt, for he had fled from the presence of King Solomon and had been dwelling in Egypt), ³that they sent and called him. Then Jeroboam and the whole assembly of Israel came and spoke to Rehoboam, saying, ⁴"Your father made our ªyoke ¹heavy; now therefore, lighten the burdensome service of your father, and his heavy yoke which he put on us, and we will serve you."

⁵So he said to them, "Depart *for* three days, then come back to me." And the people departed.

⁶Then King Rehoboam consulted the elders who stood before his father Solomon while he still lived, and he said, "How do you advise *me* to answer these people?"

⁷And they spoke to him, saying, ª"If you will be a servant to these people today, and serve them, and answer them, and speak good words to them, then they will be your servants forever."

⁸But he rejected the advice which the elders had given him, and consulted the young men who had grown up with him, who stood before him. ⁹And he said to them, "What advice do you give? How should we answer this people who have spoken to me, saying, 'Lighten the yoke which your father put on us'?"

¹⁰Then the young men who had grown up with him spoke to him, saying, "Thus you should speak to this people who have spoken to you, saying, 'Your father made our yoke heavy, but you make *it* lighter on us'—thus you shall say to them: 'My little *finger* shall be thicker than my father's waist! ¹¹And now, whereas my father put a heavy yoke on you, I will add to your yoke; my father chastised you with whips, but I will chastise you with ¹scourges!' "

¹²So Jeroboam and all the people came to Rehoboam the third day, as the king had directed, saying, "Come back to me the third day." ¹³Then the king answered the people ¹roughly, and rejected the advice which the elders had given him; ¹⁴and he spoke to them according to the advice of the young men, saying, "My father made your yoke heavy, but I will add to your yoke; my father chastised you with whips, but I will chastise you with ¹scourges!" ¹⁵So the king did not listen to the people; for ªthe turn *of events* was from the Lᴏʀᴅ, that He might fulfill His word, which the Lᴏʀᴅ had ᵇspoken by Ahijah the Shilonite to Jeroboam the son of Nebat.

¹⁶Now when all Israel saw that the king did not listen to them, the people answered the king, saying:

ª"What share have we in David?
We have no inheritance in the son of Jesse.
To your tents, O Israel!
Now, see to your own house, O David!"

So Israel departed to their tents. ¹⁷But Rehoboam reigned over ªthe children of Israel who dwelt in the cities of Judah.

12:1 ª2 Chr. 10:1
ᵇ Judg. 9:6
12:2 ª1 Kin. 11:26
ᵇ1 Kin. 11:40
12:4
ª1 Sam. 8:11–18;
1 Kin. 4:7;
5:13–15
12:7 ª2 Chr. 10:7;
[Prov. 15:1]
12:15
ªDeut. 2:30;
Judg. 14:4;
1 Kin. 12:24;
2 Chr. 10:15
ᵇ1 Kin. 11:11,
29, 31
12:16
ª2 Sam. 20:1
12:17
ª1 Kin. 11:13, 36;
2 Chr. 11:14–17

12:4 ¹*hard*   12:11 ¹Scourges with points or barbs, lit. *scorpions*
12:13 ¹*harshly*   12:14 ¹Lit. *scorpions*

[18]Then King Rehoboam [a]sent Adoram, who *was* in charge of the revenue; but all Israel stoned him with stones, and he died. Therefore King Rehoboam mounted his chariot in haste to flee to Jerusalem. [19]So [a]Israel has been in rebellion against the house of David to this day.

[20]Now it came to pass when all Israel heard that Jeroboam had come back, they sent for him and called him to the congregation, and made him king over all [a]Israel. There was none who followed the house of David, but the tribe of Judah [b]only.

[21]And when [a]Rehoboam came to Jerusalem, he assembled all the house of Judah with the tribe of [b]Benjamin, one hundred and eighty thousand chosen *men* who were warriors, to fight against the house of Israel, that he might restore the kingdom to Rehoboam the son of Solomon. [22]But [a]the word of God came to Shemaiah the man of God, saying, [23]"Speak to Rehoboam the son of Solomon, king of Judah, to all the house of Judah and Benjamin, and to the rest of the people, saying, [24]'Thus says the LORD: "You shall not go up nor fight against your brethren the children of Israel. Let every man return to his house, [a]for this thing is from Me."'" Therefore they obeyed the word of the LORD, and turned back, according to the word of the LORD.

JEROBOAM'S GOLD CALVES

[25]Then Jeroboam [a]built[1] Shechem in the mountains of Ephraim, and dwelt there. Also he went out from there and built [b]Penuel. [26]And Jeroboam said in his heart, "Now the kingdom may return to the house of David: [27]If these people [a]go up to offer sacrifices in the house of the LORD at Jerusalem, then the heart of this people will turn back to their lord, Rehoboam king of Judah, and they will kill me and go back to Rehoboam king of Judah."

[28]Therefore the king asked advice, [a]made two calves of gold, and said to the people, "It is too much for you to go up to Jerusalem. [b]Here are your gods, O Israel, which brought you up from the land of Egypt!" [29]And he set up one in [a]Bethel, and the other he put in [b]Dan. [30]Now this thing became [a]a sin, for the people went *to worship* before the one as far as Dan. [31]He made [1]shrines on the high places, [a]and made priests from every class of people, who were not of the sons of Levi.

[32]Jeroboam [1]ordained a feast on the fifteenth day of the eighth month, like [a]the feast that *was* in Judah, and offered sacrifices on the altar. So he did at Bethel, sacrificing to the calves that he had made. [b]And at Bethel he installed the priests of the high places which he had made. [33]So he made offerings on the altar which he had made at Bethel on the fifteenth day of the eighth month, in the month which he had [a]devised in his own heart. And he [1]ordained a feast for the children of Israel, and offered sacrifices on the altar and [b]burned incense.

THE MESSAGE OF THE MAN OF GOD

13 And behold, [a]a man of God went from Judah to Bethel [1]by the word of the LORD, [b]and Jeroboam stood by the altar to burn incense. [2]Then he cried out against the altar [1]by

Cross references

12:18
[a]1 Kin. 4:6; 5:14

12:19
[a]2 Kin. 17:21

12:20
[a]2 Kin. 17:21
[b]1 Kin. 11:13, 32, 36

12:21
[a]2 Chr. 11:1–4
[b]2 Sam. 19:17

12:22
[a]2 Chr. 11:2; 12:5–7

12:24
[a]1 Kin. 12:15

12:25
[a]Gen. 12:6; Judg. 9:45–49; 1 Kin. 12:1
[b]Gen. 32:30, 31; Judg. 8:8, 17

12:27
[a][Deut. 12:5–7, 14]

12:28
[a]2 Kin. 10:29; 17:16; [Hos. 8:4–7]
[b]Ex. 32:4, 8

12:29
[a]Gen. 28:19
[b]Judg. 18:26–31

12:30
[a]1 Kin. 13:34; 2 Kin. 17:21

12:31
[a][Num. 3:10; 17:1–11]; Judg. 17:5; 1 Kin. 13:33; 2 Kin. 17:32; 2 Chr. 11:14, 15

12:32
[a]Lev. 23:33, 34; Num. 29:12; 1 Kin. 8:2, 5
[b]Amos 7:10–13

12:33
[a]Num. 15:39
[b]1 Kin. 13:1

13:1
[a]2 Kin. 23:17
[b]1 Kin. 12:32, 33

12:25 [1]fortified   12:31 [1]Lit. *a house;* cf. 1 Kin. 13:32, lit. *houses*
12:32 [1]instituted   12:33 [1]instituted   13:1 [1]at the LORD's command
13:2 [1]at the LORD's command

the word of the LORD, and said, "O altar, altar! Thus says the LORD: 'Behold, a child, ªJosiah by name, shall be born to the house of David; and on you he shall sacrifice the priests of the high places who burn incense on you, and men's bones shall be ᵇburned on you.'" ³And he gave ªa sign the same day, saying, "This *is* the sign which the LORD has spoken: Surely the altar shall split apart, and the ashes on it shall be poured out."

⁴So it came to pass when King Jeroboam heard the saying of the man of God, who cried out against the altar in Bethel, that he stretched out his hand from the altar, saying, "Arrest him!" Then his hand, which he stretched out toward him, withered, so that he could not pull it back to himself. ⁵The altar also was split apart, and the ashes poured out from the altar, according to the sign which the man of God had given by the word of the LORD. ⁶Then the king answered and said to the man of God, "Please ªentreat the favor of the LORD your God, and pray for me, that my hand may be restored to me."

So the man of God entreated the LORD, and the king's hand was restored to him, and became as before. ⁷Then the king said to the man of God, "Come home with me and refresh yourself, and ªI will give you a reward."

⁸But the man of God said to the king, ª"If you were to give me half your house, I would not go in with you; nor would I eat bread nor drink water in this place. ⁹For so it was commanded me by the word of the LORD, saying, ª'You shall not eat bread, nor drink water, nor return by the same way you came.'" ¹⁰So he went another way and did not return by the way he came to Bethel.

DEATH OF THE MAN OF GOD

¹¹Now an ªold prophet dwelt in Bethel, and his ¹sons came and told him all the works that the man of God had done that day in Bethel; they also told their father the words which he had spoken to the king. ¹²And their father said to them, "Which way did he go?" For his sons ¹had seen which way the man of God went who came from Judah. ¹³Then he said to his sons, "Saddle the donkey for me." So they saddled the donkey for him; and he rode on it, ¹⁴and went after the man of God, and found him sitting under an oak. Then he said to him, "*Are* you the man of God who came from Judah?"

And he said, "I *am*."

¹⁵Then he said to him, "Come home with me and eat bread."

¹⁶And he said, ª"I cannot return with you nor go in with you; neither can I eat bread nor drink water with you in this place. ¹⁷For ¹I have been told ªby the word of the LORD, 'You shall not eat bread nor drink water there, nor return by going the way you came.'"

¹⁸He said to him, "I too *am* a prophet as you *are,* and an angel spoke to me by the word of the LORD, saying, 'Bring him back with you to your house, that he may eat bread and drink water.'" (He was lying to him.)

¹⁹So he went back with him, and ate bread in his house, and drank water.

²⁰Now it happened, as they sat at the table, that the word of the LORD came to the prophet who had brought him back;

13:2
ª2 Kin. 23:15, 16
ᵇ[Lev. 26:30]

13:3 ªEx. 4:1–5;
Judg. 6:17;
Is. 7:14; 38:7;
John 2:18;
1 Cor. 1:22

13:6 ªEx. 8:8;
9:28; 10:17;
Num. 21:7;
Jer. 37:3;
Acts 8:24;
[James 5:16]

13:7 ª1 Sam. 9:7;
2 Kin. 5:15

13:8
ªNum. 22:18;
24:13;
1 Kin. 13:16, 17

13:9 ª[1 Cor. 5:11]

13:11 ª1 Kin. 13:25

13:16
ª1 Kin. 13:8, 9

13:17
ª1 Kin. 20:35;
1 Thess. 4:15

---

²¹and he cried out to the man of God who came from Judah, saying, "Thus says the LORD: 'Because you have disobeyed the word of the LORD, and have not kept the commandment which the LORD your God commanded you, ²²but you came back, ate bread, and drank water in the ᵃplace of which *the* LORD said to you, "Eat no bread and drink no water," your corpse shall not come to the tomb of your fathers.'"

²³So it was, after he had eaten bread and after he had drunk, that he saddled the donkey for him, the prophet whom he had brought back. ²⁴When he was gone, ᵃa lion met him on the road and killed him. And his corpse was thrown on the road, and the donkey stood by it. The lion also stood by the corpse. ²⁵And there, men passed by and saw the corpse thrown on the road, and the lion standing by the corpse. Then they went and told *it* in the city where the old prophet dwelt.

²⁶Now when the prophet who had brought him back from the way heard *it,* he said, "It *is* the man of God who was disobedient to the word of the LORD. Therefore the LORD has delivered him to the lion, which has torn him and killed him, according to the word of the LORD which He spoke to him." ²⁷And he spoke to his sons, saying, "Saddle the donkey for me." So they saddled *it.* ²⁸Then he went and found his corpse thrown on the road, and the donkey and the lion standing by the corpse. The lion had not eaten the corpse nor torn the donkey. ²⁹And the prophet took up the corpse of the man of God, laid it on the donkey, and brought it back. So the old prophet came to the city to mourn, and to bury him. ³⁰Then he laid the corpse in his own tomb; and they mourned over him, *saying,* ᵃ"Alas, my brother!" ³¹So it was, after he had buried him, that he spoke to his sons, saying, "When I am dead, then bury me in the tomb where the man of God *is* buried; ᵃlay my bones beside his bones. ³²ᵃFor the ¹saying which he cried out by the word of the LORD against the altar in Bethel, and against all the ²shrines on the high places which *are* in the cities of ᵇSamaria, will surely come to pass."

³³ᵃAfter this event Jeroboam did not turn from his evil way, but again he made priests from every class of people for the high places; whoever wished, he consecrated him, and he became *one* of the priests of the high places. ³⁴ᵃAnd this thing was the sin of the house of Jeroboam, so as ᵇto exterminate and destroy *it* from the face of the earth.

JUDGMENT ON THE HOUSE OF JEROBOAM

14 At that time Abijah the son of Jeroboam became sick. ²And Jeroboam said to his wife, "Please arise, and disguise yourself, that they may not recognize you as the wife of Jeroboam, and go to Shiloh. Indeed, Ahijah the prophet *is* there, who told me that ᵃI *would be* king over this people. ³ᵃAlso take ¹with you ten loaves, *some* cakes, and a jar of honey, and go to him; he will tell you what will become of the child." ⁴And Jeroboam's wife did so; she arose ᵃand went to Shiloh, and came to the house of Ahijah. But Ahijah could not see, for his eyes were ¹glazed by reason of his age.

⁵Now the LORD had said to Ahijah, "Here is the wife of Jeroboam, coming to ask you something about her son, for he *is*

13:22
ᵃ1 Kin. 13:9

13:24
ᵃ1 Kin. 20:36

13:30 ᵃJer. 22:18

13:31 ᵃRuth 1:17;
2 Kin. 23:17, 18

13:32
ᵃ1 Kin. 13:2;
2 Kin. 23:16, 19
ᵇ1 Kin. 16:24;
John 4:5;
Acts 8:14

13:33
ᵃ1 Kin. 12:31, 32;
2 Chr. 11:15; 13:9

13:34
ᵃ1 Kin. 12:30;
2 Kin. 17:21
ᵇ[1 Kin. 14:10;
15:29, 30]

14:2
ᵃ1 Kin. 11:29–31

14:3
ᵃ1 Sam. 9:7, 8;
1 Kin. 13:7;
2 Kin. 4:42

14:4 ᵃ1 Kin. 11:29

13:32 ¹Lit. *word*   ²Lit. *houses*   14:3 ¹Lit. *in your hand*   14:4 ¹Lit. *set*

sick. Thus and thus you shall say to her; for it will be, when she comes in, that she will pretend *to be* another *woman.*"

6And so it was, when Ahijah heard the sound of her footsteps as she came through the door, he said, "Come in, wife of Jeroboam. Why do you pretend *to be* another *person?* For I *have been* sent to you *with* bad *news.* 7Go, tell Jeroboam, 'Thus says the LORD God of Israel: a"Because I exalted you from among the people, and made you ruler over My people Israel, 8and atore the kingdom away from the house of David, and gave it to you; and *yet* you have not been as My servant David, bwho kept My commandments and who followed Me with all his heart, to do only *what was* right in My eyes; 9but you have done more evil than all who were before you, afor you have gone and made for yourself other gods and molded images to provoke Me to anger, and bhave cast Me behind your back— 10therefore behold! aI will bring disaster on the house of Jeroboam, and bwill cut off from Jeroboam every male in Israel, cbond and free; I will take away the remnant of the house of Jeroboam, as one takes away refuse until it is all gone. 11The dogs shall eat awhoever belongs to Jeroboam and dies in the city, and the birds of the air shall eat whoever dies in the field; for the LORD has spoken!"' 12Arise therefore, go to your own house. aWhen your feet enter the city, the child shall die. 13And all Israel shall mourn for him and bury him, for he is the only one of Jeroboam who shall 1come to the grave, because in him athere is found something good toward the LORD God of Israel in the house of Jeroboam.

14a"Moreover the LORD will raise up for Himself a king over Israel who shall cut off the house of Jeroboam; 1this is the day. What? Even now! 15For the LORD will strike Israel, as a reed is shaken in the water. He will auproot Israel from this bgood land which He gave to their fathers, and will scatter them cbeyond 1the River, dbecause they have made their 2wooden images, provoking the LORD to anger. 16And He will give Israel up because of the sins of Jeroboam, awho sinned and who made Israel sin."

17Then Jeroboam's wife arose and departed, and came to aTirzah. bWhen she came to the threshold of the house, the child died. 18And they buried him; and all Israel mourned for him, aaccording to the word of the LORD which He spoke through His servant Ahijah the prophet.

DEATH OF JEROBOAM

19Now the rest of the acts of Jeroboam, how he amade war and how he reigned, indeed they *are* written in the book of the chronicles of the kings of Israel. 20The period that Jeroboam reigned *was* twenty-two years. So he rested with his fathers. Then aNadab his son reigned in his place.

REHOBOAM REIGNS IN JUDAH
(2 Chr. 11:5—12:16)

21And Rehoboam the son of Solomon reigned in Judah. aRehoboam *was* forty-one years old when he became king. He reigned seventeen years in Jerusalem, the city bwhich the LORD had chosen out of all the tribes of Israel, to put His

---

14:7
a2 Sam. 12:7, 8;
1 Kin. 16:2

14:8 a1 Kin. 11:31
b1 Kin. 11:33,
38; 15:5

14:9
a1 Kin. 12:28;
2 Chr. 11:15
b2 Chr. 29:6;
Neh. 9:26;
Ps. 50:17

14:10
a1 Kin. 15:29
b1 Kin. 21:21;
2 Kin. 9:8
cDeut. 32:36;
2 Kin. 14:26

14:11 a1 Kin. 16:4;
21:24

14:12 a1 Kin. 14:17

14:13
a2 Chr. 12:12;
19:3

14:14
a1 Kin. 15:27–29

14:15
aDeut. 29:28;
2 Kin. 17:6;
Ps. 52:5
b[Josh. 23:15, 16]
c2 Kin. 15:29
d[Ex. 34:13, 14;
Deut. 12:3]

14:16
a1 Kin. 12:30;
13:34; 15:30,
34; 16:2

14:17
a1 Kin. 15:21, 33;
16:6, 8, 15, 23;
Song 6:4
b1 Kin. 14:12

14:18
a1 Kin. 14:13

14:19
a1 Kin. 14:30;
2 Chr. 13:2–20

14:20
a1 Kin. 15:25

14:21
a2 Chr. 12:13
b1 Kin. 11:32, 36

14:13 1Be buried   14:14 1Or *this day and from now on*   14:15 1The Euphrates   2Heb. *Asherim,* Canaanite deities

name there. ᶜHis mother's name *was* Naamah, an Ammonitess. 22ᵃNow Judah did evil in the sight of the LORD, and they ᵇprovoked Him to jealousy with their sins which they committed, more than all that their fathers had done. 23For they also built for themselves ᵃhigh¹ places, ᵇ*sacred* pillars, and ᶜwooden images on every high hill and ᵈunder every green tree. 24ᵃAnd there were also ¹perverted persons in the land. They did according to all the ᵇabominations of the nations which the LORD had cast out before the children of ᶜIsrael.

25ᵃIt happened in the fifth year of King Rehoboam *that* Shishak king of Egypt came up against Jerusalem. 26ᵃAnd he took away the treasures of the house of the LORD and the treasures of the king's house; he took away everything. He also took away all the gold shields ᵇwhich Solomon had made. 27Then King Rehoboam made bronze shields in their place, and ¹committed *them* to the hands of the captains of the ²guard, who guarded the doorway of the king's house. 28And whenever the king entered the house of the LORD, the guards carried them, then brought them back into the guardroom.

29ᵃNow the rest of the acts of Rehoboam, and all that he did, *are* they not written in the book of the chronicles of the kings of Judah? 30And there was ᵃwar between Rehoboam and Jeroboam all *their* days. 31ᵃSo Rehoboam ¹rested with his fathers, and was buried with his fathers in the City of David. ᵇHis mother's name *was* Naamah, an Ammonitess. Then ᶜAbijam² his son reigned in his place.

ABIJAM REIGNS IN JUDAH
(2 *Chr.* 13:1—14:1)

15 ᵃIn the eighteenth year of King Jeroboam the son of Nebat, Abijam became king over Judah. 2He reigned three years in Jerusalem. ᵃHis mother's name *was* ᵇMaachah the granddaughter of ᶜAbishalom. 3And he walked in all the sins of his father, which he had done before him; ᵃhis heart was not ¹loyal to the LORD his God, as was the heart of his father David. 4Nevertheless ᵃfor David's sake the LORD his God gave him a lamp in Jerusalem, by setting up his son after him and by establishing Jerusalem; 5because David ᵃdid *what was* right in the eyes of the LORD, and had not turned aside from anything that He commanded him all the days of his life, ᵇexcept in the matter of Uriah the Hittite. 6ᵃAnd there was war between ¹Rehoboam and Jeroboam all the days of his life. 7ᵃNow the rest of the acts of Abijam, and all that he did, *are* they not written in the book of the chronicles of the kings of Judah? And there was war between Abijam and Jeroboam.

8ᵃSo Abijam ¹rested with his fathers, and they buried him in the City of David. Then Asa his son reigned in his place.

ASA REIGNS IN JUDAH
(2 *Chr.* 14:1—16:14)

9In the twentieth year of Jeroboam king of Israel, Asa became king over Judah. 10And he reigned forty-one years in

---

14:21
ᶜ1 Kin. 14:31

14:22
ᵃ2 Chr. 12:1, 14
ᵇDeut. 32:21;
Ps. 78:58;
1 Cor. 10:22

14:23
ᵃDeut. 12:2;
Ezek. 16:24, 25
ᵇ[Deut. 16:22]
ᶜ[2 Kin. 17:9, 10]
ᵈIs. 57:5;
Jer. 2:20

14:24
ᵃGen. 19:5;
Deut. 23:17;
1 Kin. 15:12;
22:46;
2 Kin. 23:7
ᵇDeut. 20:18
ᶜ[Deut. 9:4, 5]

14:25
ᵃ1 Kin. 11:40;
2 Chr. 12:2

14:26
ᵃ1 Kin. 15:18;
2 Chr. 12:9–11
ᵇ1 Kin. 10:17

14:29
ᵃ2 Chr. 12:15, 16

14:30
ᵃ1 Kin. 12:21–24;
15:6

14:31
ᵃ2 Chr. 12:16
ᵇ1 Kin. 14:21
ᶜ2 Chr. 12:16

15:1 ᵃ2 Chr. 13:1

15:2
ᵃ2 Chr. 11:20–22
ᵇ2 Chr. 13:2
ᶜ2 Chr. 11:21

15:3 ᵃ1 Kin. 11:4;
Ps. 119:80

15:4
ᵃ2 Sam. 21:17;
1 Kin. 11:32, 36;
2 Chr. 21:7

15:5 ᵃ1 Kin. 9:4;
14:8; Luke 1:6
ᵇ2 Sam. 11:3,
15–17; 12:9, 10

15:6
ᵃ1 Kin. 14:30;
2 Chr. 12:15—
13:20

15:7
ᵃ2 Chr. 13:2–22

15:8 ᵃ2 Chr. 14:1

14:23 ¹Places for pagan worship   14:24 ¹Heb. *qadesh,* one practicing sodomy and prostitution in religious rituals   14:27 ¹*entrusted*   ²Lit. *runners*   14:31 ¹Died and joined his ancestors   ²*Abijah,* 2 Chr. 12:16ff   15:3 ¹Lit. *at peace with*   15:6 ¹So with MT, LXX, Tg., Vg.; some Heb. mss., Syr. *Abijam*   15:8 ¹Died and joined his ancestors

Jerusalem. His grandmother's name *was* Maachah the grand-daughter of Abishalom. [11a]Asa did *what was* right in the eyes of the LORD, as *did* his father David. [12a]And he banished the [1]perverted persons from the land, and removed all the idols that his fathers had made. [13]Also he removed [a]Maachah his grandmother from *being* queen mother, because she had made an obscene image of [1]Asherah. And Asa cut down her obscene image and [b]burned *it* by the Brook Kidron. [14a]But the [1]high places were not removed. Nevertheless Asa's [b]heart was loyal to the LORD all his days. [15]He also brought into the house of the LORD the things which his father [a]had dedicated, and the things which he himself had dedicated: silver and gold and utensils.

[16]Now there was war between Asa and Baasha king of Israel all their days. [17]And [a]Baasha king of Israel came up against Judah, and built [b]Ramah, [c]that he might let none go out or come in to Asa king of Judah. [18]Then Asa took all the silver and gold *that was* left in the treasuries of the house of the LORD and the treasuries of the king's house, and delivered them into the hand of his servants. And King Asa sent them to [a]Ben-Hadad the son of Tabrimmon, the son of Hezion, king of Syria, who dwelt in [b]Damascus, saying, [19]"*Let there be* a treaty between you and me, as there was between my father and your father. See, I have sent you a present of silver and gold. Come and break your treaty with Baasha king of Israel, so that he will withdraw from me."

[20]So Ben-Hadad heeded King Asa, and [a]sent the captains of his armies against the cities of Israel. He attacked [b]Ijon, [c]Dan, [d]Abel Beth Maachah, and all Chinneroth, with all the land of Naphtali. [21]Now it happened, when Baasha heard *it*, that he stopped building Ramah, and remained in [a]Tirzah.

[22a]Then King Asa made a proclamation throughout all Judah; none *was* exempted. And they took away the stones and timber of Ramah, which Baasha had used for building; and with them King Asa built [b]Geba of Benjamin, and [c]Mizpah.

[23]The rest of all the acts of Asa, all his might, all that he did, and the cities which he built, *are* they not written in the book of the chronicles of the kings of Judah? But [a]in the time of his old age he was diseased in his feet. [24]So Asa [1]rested with his fathers, and was buried with his fathers in the City of David his father. [a]Then [b]Jehoshaphat his son reigned in his place.

NADAB REIGNS IN ISRAEL

[25]Now [a]Nadab the son of Jeroboam became king over Israel in the second year of Asa king of Judah, and he reigned over Israel two years. [26]And he did evil in the sight of the LORD, and walked in the way of his father, and in [a]his sin by which he had made Israel sin.

[27a]Then Baasha the son of Ahijah, of the house of Issachar, conspired against him. And Baasha killed him at [b]Gibbethon, which *belonged* to the Philistines, while Nadab and all Israel laid siege to Gibbethon. [28]Baasha killed him in the third year of Asa king of Judah, and reigned in his place. [29]And it was so, when he became king, *that* he killed all the

---

15:11 [a]2 Chr. 14:2

15:12
[a]Deut. 23:17;
1 Kin. 14:24;
22:46

15:13
[a]2 Chr. 15:16–18
[b]Ex. 32:20

15:14 [a]1 Kin. 3:2;
22:43;
2 Kin. 12:3;
2 Chr. 15:17, 18
[b][1 Sam. 16:7];
1 Kin. 8:61; 15:3

15:15 [a]1 Kin. 7:51

15:17
[a]2 Chr. 16:1–6
[b]Josh. 18:25;
1 Kin. 15:21, 22
[c]1 Kin. 12:26–29

15:18
[a]2 Kin. 12:17, 18;
2 Chr. 16:2
[b]Gen. 14:15;
1 Kin. 11:23, 24

15:20
[a]1 Kin. 20:1
[b]2 Kin. 15:29
[c]Judg. 18:29;
1 Kin. 12:29
[d]2 Sam. 20:14, 15

15:21
[a]1 Kin. 14:17;
16:15–18

15:22
[a]2 Chr. 16:6
[b]Josh. 21:17
[c]Josh. 18:26

15:23
[a]2 Chr. 16:11–14

15:24 [a]2 Chr. 17:1
[b]1 Kin. 22:41–44;
Matt. 1:8

15:25
[a]1 Kin. 14:20

15:26
[a]1 Kin. 12:28–33;
14:16

15:27
[a]1 Kin. 14:14
[b]Josh. 19:44;
21:23; 1 Kin. 16:15

15:12 [1]Heb. *qedeshim,* those practicing sodomy and prostitution in religious rituals   15:13 [1]A Canaanite goddess   15:14 [1]Places for pagan worship
15:24 [1]Died and joined his ancestors

house of Jeroboam. He did not leave to Jeroboam anyone that breathed, until he had destroyed him, according to [a]the word of the LORD which He had spoken by His servant Ahijah the Shilonite, [30a]because of the sins of Jeroboam, which he had sinned and by which he had made Israel sin, because of his provocation with which he had provoked the LORD God of Israel to anger.

[31]Now the rest of the acts of Nadab, and all that he did, *are* they not written in the book of the chronicles of the kings of Israel? [32a]And there was war between Asa and Baasha king of Israel all their days.

BAASHA REIGNS IN ISRAEL

[33]In the third year of Asa king of Judah, Baasha the son of Ahijah became king over all Israel in Tirzah, and *reigned* twenty-four years. [34]He did evil in the sight of the LORD, and walked in [a]the way of Jeroboam, and in his sin by which he had made Israel sin.

16 Then the word of the LORD came to [a]Jehu the son of [b]Hanani, against [c]Baasha, saying: [2a]"Inasmuch as I lifted you out of the dust and made you ruler over My people Israel, and [b]you have walked in the way of Jeroboam, and have made My people Israel sin, to provoke Me to anger with their sins, [3]surely I will [a]take[1] away the posterity of Baasha and the posterity of his house, and I will make your house like [b]the house of Jeroboam the son of Nebat. [4]The dogs shall eat [a]whoever belongs to Baasha and dies in the city, and the birds of the air shall eat whoever dies in the fields."

[5]Now the rest of the acts of Baasha, what he did, and his might, [a]*are* they not written in the book of the chronicles of the kings of Israel? [6]So Baasha [1]rested with his fathers and was buried in [a]Tirzah. Then Elah his son reigned in his place.

[7]And also the word of the LORD came by the prophet [a]Jehu the son of Hanani against Baasha and his house, because of all the evil that he did in the sight of the LORD in provoking Him to anger with the work of his hands, in being like the house of Jeroboam, and because [b]he killed them.

ELAH REIGNS IN ISRAEL

[8]In the twenty-sixth year of Asa king of Judah, Elah the son of Baasha became king over Israel, *and reigned* two years in Tirzah. [9a]Now his servant Zimri, commander of half *his* chariots, conspired against him as he was in Tirzah drinking himself drunk in the house of Arza, [b]steward[1] of *his* house in Tirzah. [10]And Zimri went in and struck him and killed him in the twenty-seventh year of Asa king of Judah, and reigned in his place.

[11]Then it came to pass, when he began to reign, as soon as he was seated on his throne, *that* he killed all the household of Baasha; he [a]did not leave him one male, neither of his relatives nor of his friends. [12]Thus Zimri destroyed all the household of Baasha, [a]according to the word of the LORD, which He spoke against Baasha by Jehu the prophet, [13]for all the sins of Baasha and the sins of Elah his son, by which they had sinned

15:29
[a]1 Kin. 14:10–14

15:30
[a]1 Kin. 14:9, 16

15:32
[a]1 Kin. 15:16

15:34
[a]1 Kin. 13:33; 14:16

16:1 [a]1 Kin. 16:7; 2 Chr. 19:2; 20:34
[b]2 Chr. 16:7–10
[c]1 Kin. 15:27

16:2 [a]1 Sam. 2:8; 1 Kin. 14:7
[b]1 Kin. 12:25–33; 15:34

16:3 [a]1 Kin. 16:11; 21:21
[b]1 Kin. 14:10; 15:29

16:4 [a]1 Kin. 14:11; 21:24

16:5 [a]2 Chr. 16:11

16:6 [a]1 Kin. 14:17; 15:21

16:7 [a]1 Kin. 16:1
[b]1 Kin. 15:27, 29

16:9
[a]2 Kin. 9:30–33
[b]Gen. 24:2; 39:4; 1 Kin. 18:3

16:11
[a]1 Sam. 25:22

16:12 [a]1 Kin. 16:3

16:3 [1]consume   16:6 [1]Died and joined his ancestors   16:9 [1]Lit. *who was over the house*

and by which they had made Israel sin, in provoking the LORD God of Israel to anger [a]with their [1]idols.

[14]Now the rest of the acts of Elah, and all that he did, *are* they not written in the book of the chronicles of the kings of Israel?

ZIMRI REIGNS IN ISRAEL

[15]In the twenty-seventh year of Asa king of Judah, Zimri had reigned in Tirzah seven days. And the people *were* encamped [a]against Gibbethon, which *belonged* to the Philistines. [16]Now the people *who were* encamped heard it said, "Zimri has conspired and also has killed the king." So all Israel made Omri, the commander of the army, king over Israel that day in the camp. [17]Then Omri and all Israel with him went up from Gibbethon, and they besieged Tirzah. [18]And it happened, when Zimri saw that the city was [1]taken, that he went into the citadel of the king's house and burned the king's house [2]down upon himself with fire, and died, [19]because of the sins which he had committed in doing evil in the sight of the LORD, [a]in walking in the [b]way of Jeroboam, and in his sin which he had committed to make Israel sin.

[20]Now the rest of the acts of Zimri, and the treason he committed, *are* they not written in the book of the chronicles of the kings of Israel?

OMRI REIGNS IN ISRAEL

[21]Then the people of Israel were divided into two parts: half of the people followed Tibni the son of Ginath, to make him king, and half followed Omri. [22]But the people who followed Omri prevailed over the people who followed Tibni the son of Ginath. So Tibni died and Omri reigned. [23]In the thirty-first year of Asa king of Judah, Omri became king over Israel, *and reigned* twelve years. Six years he reigned in [a]Tirzah. [24]And he bought the hill of Samaria from Shemer for two talents of silver; then he built on the hill, and called the name of the city which he built, [a]Samaria,[1] after the name of Shemer, owner of the hill. [25a]Omri did evil in the eyes of the LORD, and did worse than all who *were* before him. [26]For he [a]walked in all the ways of Jeroboam the son of Nebat, and in his sin by which he had made Israel sin, provoking the LORD God of Israel to anger with their [b]idols.[1]

[27]Now the rest of the acts of Omri which he did, and the might that he showed, *are* they not written in the book of the chronicles of the kings of Israel?

[28]So Omri rested with his fathers and was buried in Samaria. Then Ahab his son reigned in his place.

AHAB REIGNS IN ISRAEL

[29]In the thirty-eighth year of Asa king of Judah, Ahab the son of Omri became king over Israel; and Ahab the son of Omri reigned over Israel in Samaria twenty-two years. [30]Now Ahab the son of Omri did evil in the sight of the LORD, more than all who *were* before him. [31]And it came to pass, as though it had been a trivial thing for him to walk in the sins of Jeroboam the son of Nebat, [a]that he took as wife Jezebel the

---

16:13
[a]Deut. 32:21;
1 Sam. 12:21;
[Is. 41:29;
Jon. 2:8;
1 Cor. 8:4; 10:19]

16:15
[a]1 Kin. 15:27

16:19
[a]1 Kin. 15:26, 34
[b]1 Kin. 12:25–33

16:23
[a]1 Kin. 15:21;
2 Kin. 15:14

16:24
[a]1 Kin. 13:32;
2 Kin. 17:24;
John 4:4

16:25 [a]Mic. 6:16

16:26
[a]1 Kin. 16:19
[b]1 Kin. 16:13

16:31 [a]Deut. 7:3

16:13 [1]Lit. *vanities*   16:18 [1]*captured*   [2]Lit. *over him*   16:24 [1]Heb. *Shomeron*   16:26 [1]Lit. *vanities*

daughter of Ethbaal, king of the ᵇSidonians; ᶜand he went and served Baal and worshiped him. ³²Then he set up an altar for Baal in ᵃthe temple of Baal, which he had built in Samaria. ³³ᵃAnd Ahab made a ¹wooden image. Ahab ᵇdid more to provoke the LORD God of Israel to anger than all the kings of Israel who were before him. ³⁴In his days Hiel of Bethel built Jericho. He laid its foundation ¹with Abiram his firstborn, and with his youngest *son* Segub he set up its gates, ᵃaccording to the word of the LORD, which He had spoken through Joshua the son of Nun.

ELIJAH PROCLAIMS A DROUGHT

17 And Elijah the Tishbite, of the ᵃinhabitants of Gilead, said to Ahab, ᵇ"As the LORD God of Israel lives, ᶜbefore whom I stand, ᵈthere shall not be dew nor rain ᵉthese years, except at my word."

²Then the word of the LORD came to him, saying, ³"Get away from here and turn eastward, and hide by the Brook Cherith, which flows into the Jordan. ⁴And it will be *that* you shall drink from the brook, and I have commanded the ᵃravens to feed you there."

⁵So he went and did according to the word of the LORD, for he went and stayed by the Brook Cherith, which flows into the Jordan. ⁶The ravens brought him bread and meat in the morning, and bread and meat in the evening; and he drank from the brook. ⁷And it happened after a while that the brook dried up, because there had been no rain in the land.

ELIJAH AND THE WIDOW

⁸Then the word of the LORD came to him, saying, ⁹"Arise, go to ᵃZarephath, which *belongs* to ᵇSidon, and dwell there. See, I have commanded a widow there to provide for you." ¹⁰So he arose and went to Zarephath. And when he came to the gate of the city, indeed a widow *was* there gathering sticks. And he called to her and said, "Please bring me a little water in a cup, that I may drink." ¹¹And as she was going to get *it,* he called to her and said, "Please bring me a morsel of bread in your hand."

¹²So she said, "As the LORD your God lives, I do not have bread, only a handful of flour in a bin, and a little oil in a ¹jar; and see, I *am* gathering a couple of sticks that I may go in and prepare it for myself and my son, that we may eat it, and ᵃdie."

¹³And Elijah said to her, "Do not fear; go *and* do as you have said, but make me a small cake from it first, and bring *it* to me; and afterward make *some* for yourself and your son. ¹⁴For thus says the LORD God of Israel: 'The bin of flour shall not be used up, nor shall the jar of oil run dry, until the day the LORD sends rain on the earth.'"

¹⁵So she went away and did according to the word of Elijah; and she and he and her household ate for *many* days. ¹⁶The bin of flour was not used up, nor did the jar of oil run dry, according to the word of the LORD which He spoke by Elijah.

ELIJAH REVIVES THE WIDOW'S SON

¹⁷Now it happened after these things *that* the son of the woman who owned the house became sick. And his sickness

---

16:31
ᵇ Judg. 18:7;
1 Kin. 11:1–5
ᶜ1 Kin. 21:25,
26; 2 Kin. 10:18;
17:16

16:32
ᵃ2 Kin. 10:21,
26, 27

16:33
ᵃ2 Kin. 13:6
ᵇ1 Kin. 14:9;
16:29, 30; 21:25

16:34
ᵃJosh. 6:26

17:1 ᵃJudg. 12:4
ᵇ1 Kin. 18:10;
22:14;
2 Kin. 3:14; 5:20
ᶜDeut. 10:8
ᵈ1 Kin. 18:1;
James 5:17
ᵉLuke 4:25

17:4 ᵃJob 38:41

17:9 ᵃObad. 20;
Luke 4:25, 26
ᵇ2 Sam. 24:6

17:12
ᵃDeut. 28:23, 24

16:33 ¹Heb. *Asherah,* a Canaanite goddess   16:34 ¹At the cost of the life of
17:12 ¹Lit. *pitcher* or *water jar*

was so [1]serious that [2]there was no breath left in him. [18]So she said to Elijah, [a]"What have I to do with you, O man of God? Have you come to me to bring my sin to remembrance, and to kill my son?"

[19]And he said to her, "Give me your son." So he took him out of her arms and carried him to the upper room where he was staying, and laid him on his own bed. [20]Then he cried out to the LORD and said, "O LORD my God, have You also brought tragedy on the widow with whom I lodge, by killing her son?" [21a]And he stretched himself out on the child three times, and cried out to the LORD and said, "O LORD my God, I pray, let this child's soul come back to him." [22]Then the LORD heard the voice of Elijah; and the soul of the child came back to him, and he [a]revived.

[23]And Elijah took the child and brought him down from the upper room into the house, and gave him to his mother. And Elijah said, "See, your son lives!"

[24]Then the woman said to Elijah, "Now by this [a]I know that you *are* a man of God, *and* that the word of the LORD in your mouth *is* the truth."

ELIJAH'S MESSAGE TO AHAB

18 And it came to pass *after* [a]many days that the word of the LORD came to Elijah, in the third year, saying, "Go, present yourself to Ahab, and [b]I will send rain on the earth."

[2]So Elijah went to present himself to Ahab; and *there was* a severe famine in Samaria. [3]And Ahab had called Obadiah, who *was* [1]in charge of *his* house. (Now Obadiah feared the LORD greatly. [4]For so it was, while Jezebel [1]massacred the prophets of the LORD, that Obadiah had taken one hundred prophets and hidden them, fifty to a cave, and had fed them with bread and water.) [5]And Ahab had said to Obadiah, "Go into the land to all the springs of water and to all the brooks; perhaps we may find grass to keep the horses and mules alive, so that we will not have to kill any livestock." [6]So they divided the land between them to explore it; Ahab went one way by himself, and Obadiah went another way by himself.

[7]Now as Obadiah was on his way, suddenly Elijah met him; and he [a]recognized him, and fell on his face, and said, "*Is that* you, my lord Elijah?"

[8]And he answered him, "*It is* I. Go, tell your master, 'Elijah *is here.*' "

[9]So he said, "How have I sinned, that you are delivering your servant into the hand of Ahab, to kill me? [10]*As the* LORD your God lives, there is no nation or kingdom where my master has not sent someone to hunt for you; and when they said, '*He is* not *here,*' he took an oath from the kingdom or nation that they could not find you. [11]And now you say, 'Go, tell your master, "Elijah *is here*"'! [12]And it shall come to pass, *as soon as* I am gone from you, that [a]the Spirit of the LORD will carry you to a place I do not know; so when I go and tell Ahab, and he cannot find you, he will kill me. But I your servant have feared the LORD from my youth. [13]Was it not reported to my lord what I did when Jezebel killed the prophets of the LORD, how I hid one hundred men of the LORD's prophets, fifty to a cave, and fed them with bread and water? [14]And now you say, 'Go, tell your master, "Elijah *is here.*"' He will kill me!"

17:18 [a]Luke 5:8

17:21 [a]2 Kin. 4:34, 35; Acts 20:10

17:22 [a]Luke 7:14, 15; Heb. 11:35

17:24 [a]John 2:11; 3:2; 16:30

18:1 [a]1 Kin. 17:1; Luke 4:25; James 5:17 [b]Deut. 28:12

18:7 [a]2 Kin. 1:6–8

18:12 [a]2 Kin. 2:16; Ezek. 3:12, 14; Matt. 4:1; Acts 8:39

17:17 [1]*severe*   [2]*He died.*   18:3 [1]Lit. *over the house*   18:4 [1]Lit. *cut off*

15Then Elijah said, "As the LORD of hosts lives, before whom I stand, I will surely present myself to him today."

16So Obadiah went to meet Ahab, and told him; and Ahab went to meet Elijah.

17Then it happened, when Ahab saw Elijah, that Ahab said to him, a"Is that you, O btroubler of Israel?"

18And he answered, "I have not troubled Israel, but you and your father's house have, ain that you have forsaken the commandments of the LORD and have followed the Baals. 19Now therefore, send and gather all Israel to me on aMount Carmel, the four hundred and fifty prophets of Baal, band the four hundred prophets of 1Asherah, who 2eat at Jezebel's table."

ELIJAH'S MOUNT CARMEL VICTORY

20So Ahab sent for all the children of Israel, and agathered the prophets together on Mount Carmel. 21And Elijah came to all the people, and said, a"How long will you falter between two opinions? If the LORD is God, follow Him; but if Baal, bfollow him." But the people answered him not a word. 22Then Elijah said to the people, a"I alone am left a prophet of the LORD; bbut Baal's prophets are four hundred and fifty men. 23Therefore let them give us two bulls; and let them choose one bull for themselves, cut it in pieces, and lay it on the wood, but put no fire under it; and I will prepare the other bull, and lay it on the wood, but put no fire under it. 24Then you call on the name of your gods, and I will call on the name of the LORD; and the God who aanswers by fire, He is God."

So all the people answered and said, 1"It is well spoken."

25Now Elijah said to the prophets of Baal, "Choose one bull for yourselves and prepare it first, for you are many; and call on the name of your god, but put no fire under it."

26So they took the bull which was given them, and they prepared it, and called on the name of Baal from morning even till noon, saying, "O Baal, 1hear us!" But there was ano voice; no one answered. Then they 2leaped about the altar which they had made.

27And so it was, at noon, that Elijah mocked them and said, "Cry 1aloud, for he is a god; either he is meditating, or he is busy, or he is on a journey, or perhaps he is sleeping and must be awakened." 28So they cried aloud, and acut themselves, as was their custom, with 1knives and lances, until the blood gushed out on them. 29And when midday was past, athey prophesied until the time of the offering of the evening sacrifice. But there was bno voice; no one answered, no one paid attention.

30Then Elijah said to all the people, "Come near to me." So all the people came near to him. aAnd he repaired the altar of the LORD that was broken down. 31And Elijah took twelve stones, according to the number of the tribes of the sons of Jacob, to whom the word of the LORD had come, saying, a"Israel shall be your name." 32Then with the stones he built an altar ain the name of the LORD; and he made a trench around

18:17
a1 Kin. 21:20
bJosh. 7:25;
Acts 16:20

18:18
a1 Kin. 16:30–33;
[2 Chr. 15:2]

18:19
aJosh. 19:26;
2 Kin. 2:25
b1 Kin. 16:33

18:20
a1 Kin. 22:6

18:21
a2 Kin. 17:41;
[Matt. 6:24]
bJosh. 24:15

18:22
a1 Kin. 19:10, 14
b1 Kin. 18:19

18:24
a1 Kin. 18:38;
1 Chr. 21:26

18:26 aPs. 115:5;
Jer. 10:5;
[1 Cor. 8:4]

18:28
a[Lev. 19:28;
Deut. 14:1]

18:29
aEx. 29:39, 41
b1 Kin. 18:26

18:30
a1 Kin. 19:10, 14;
2 Chr. 33:16

18:31
aGen. 32:28;
35:10;
2 Kin. 17:34

18:32
a[Ex. 20:25;
Col. 3:17]

18:19 1A Canaanite goddess   2Are provided for by Jezebel   18:24 1Lit. The word is good   18:26 1answer   2Lit. limped about, leaped in dancing around   18:27 1with a loud voice   18:28 1swords

the altar large enough to hold two seahs of seed. ³³And he ᵃput the wood in order, cut the bull in pieces, and laid *it* on the wood, and said, "Fill four waterpots with water, and ᵇpour *it* on the burnt sacrifice and on the wood." ³⁴Then he said, "Do *it* a second time," and they did *it* a second time; and he said, "Do *it* a third time," and they did *it* a third time. ³⁵So the water ran all around the altar; and he also filled ᵃthe trench with water.

³⁶And it came to pass, at *the time of* the offering of the *evening* sacrifice, that Elijah the prophet came near and said, "Lᴏʀᴅ ᵃGod of Abraham, Isaac, and Israel, ᵇlet it be known this day that You *are* God in Israel and I *am* Your servant, and *that* ᶜI have done all these things at Your word. ³⁷Hear me, O Lᴏʀᴅ, hear me, that this people may know that You *are* the Lᴏʀᴅ God, and *that* You have turned their hearts back *to You* again."

³⁸Then ᵃthe fire of the Lᴏʀᴅ fell and consumed the burnt sacrifice, and the wood and the stones and the dust, and it licked up the water that *was* in the trench. ³⁹Now when all the people saw *it,* they fell on their faces; and they said, ᵃ"The Lᴏʀᴅ, He *is* God! The Lᴏʀᴅ, He *is* God!"

⁴⁰And Elijah said to them, ᵃ"Seize the prophets of Baal! Do not let one of them escape!" So they seized them; and Elijah brought them down to the Brook ᵇKishon and ᶜexecuted them there.

THE DROUGHT ENDS

⁴¹Then Elijah said to Ahab, "Go up, eat and drink; for *there is* the sound of abundance of rain." ⁴²So Ahab went up to eat and drink. And Elijah went up to the top of Carmel; ᵃthen he bowed down on the ground, and put his face between his knees, ⁴³and said to his servant, "Go up now, look toward the sea."

So he went up and looked, and said, "*There is* nothing." And seven times he said, "Go again."

⁴⁴Then it came to pass the seventh *time,* that he said, "There is a cloud, as small as a man's hand, rising out of the sea!" So he said, "Go up, say to Ahab, ¹'Prepare *your chariot,* and go down before the rain stops you.'"

⁴⁵Now it happened in the meantime that the sky became black with clouds and wind, and there was a heavy rain. So Ahab rode away and went to Jezreel. ⁴⁶Then the ᵃhand of the Lᴏʀᴅ came upon Elijah; and he ᵇgirded¹ up his loins and ran ahead of Ahab to the entrance of Jezreel.

ELIJAH ESCAPES FROM JEZEBEL

19 And Ahab told Jezebel all that Elijah had done, also how he had ᵃexecuted all the prophets with the sword. ²Then Jezebel sent a messenger to Elijah, saying, ᵃ"So let the gods do *to me,* and more also, if I do not make your life as the life of one of them by tomorrow about this time." ³And when he saw *that,* he arose and ran for his life, and went to Beersheba, which *belongs* to Judah, and left his servant there.

⁴But he himself went a day's journey into the wilderness, and came and sat down under a ¹broom tree. And he ᵃprayed

---

18:33
ᵃGen. 22:9;
Lev. 1:6–8
ᵇJudg. 6:20

18:35
ᵃ1 Kin. 18:32, 38

18:36
ᵃGen. 28:13;
Ex. 3:6; 4:5;
[Matt. 22:32]
ᵇ1 Kin. 8:43;
2 Kin. 19:19
ᶜNum. 16:28

18:38
ᵃGen. 15:17;
Lev. 9:24; 10:1, 2;
Judg. 6:21;
2 Kin. 1:12;
1 Chr. 21:26;
2 Chr. 7:1;
Job 1:16

18:39
ᵃ1 Kin. 18:21, 24

18:40
ᵃ2 Kin. 10:25
ᵇJudg. 4:7; 5:21
ᶜ[Deut. 13:5;
18:20]

18:42
ᵃJames 5:17, 18

18:46
ᵃ2 Kin. 3:15;
Is. 8:11;
Ezek. 3:14
ᵇ2 Kin. 4:29;
9:1; Jer. 1:17;
1 Pet. 1:13

19:1 ᵃ1 Kin. 18:40

19:2 ᵃRuth 1:17;
1 Kin. 20:10;
2 Kin. 6:31

19:4 ᵃNum. 11:15;
Jer. 20:14–18;
Jon. 4:3, 8

18:44 ¹Lit. *Bind* or *Harness*   **18:46** ¹Tucked the skirts of his robe in his belt in preparation for quick travel   **19:4** ¹*juniper*

that he might die, and said, "It is enough! Now, LORD, take my life, for I *am* no better than my fathers!"

[5]Then as he lay and slept under a broom tree, suddenly an [1]angel touched him, and said to him, "Arise *and* eat." [6]Then he looked, and there by his head *was* a cake baked on [1]coals, and a jar of water. So he ate and drank, and lay down again. [7]And the [1]angel of the LORD came back the second time, and touched him, and said, "Arise *and* eat, because the journey *is* too great for you." [8]So he arose, and ate and drank; and he went in the strength of that food forty days and [a]forty nights as far as [b]Horeb, the mountain of God.

[9]And there he went into a cave, and spent the night in that place; and behold, the word of the LORD *came* to him, and He said to him, "What are you doing here, Elijah?"

[10]So he said, [a]"I have been very [b]zealous for the LORD God of hosts; for the children of Israel have forsaken Your covenant, torn down Your altars, and [c]killed Your prophets with the sword. [d]I alone am left; and they seek to take my life."

GOD'S REVELATION TO ELIJAH

[11]Then He said, "Go out, and stand [a]on the mountain before the LORD." And behold, the LORD [b]passed by, and [c]a great and strong wind tore into the mountains and broke the rocks in pieces before the LORD, *but* the LORD *was* not in the wind; and after the wind an earthquake, *but* the LORD *was* not in the earthquake; [12]and after the earthquake a fire, *but* the LORD *was* not in the fire; and after the fire [1]a still small voice.

[13]So it was, when Elijah heard *it,* that [a]he wrapped his face in his mantle and went out and stood in the entrance of the cave. [b]Suddenly a voice *came* to him, and said, "What are you doing here, Elijah?"

[14][a]And he said, "I have been very zealous for the LORD God of hosts; because the children of Israel have forsaken Your covenant, torn down Your altars, and killed Your prophets with the sword. I alone am left; and they seek to take my life."

[15]Then the LORD said to him: "Go, return on your way to the Wilderness of Damascus; [a]and when you arrive, anoint Hazael *as* king over Syria. [16]Also you shall anoint [a]Jehu the son of Nimshi *as* king over Israel. And [b]Elisha the son of Shaphat of Abel Meholah you shall anoint *as* prophet in your place. [17][a]It shall be *that* whoever escapes the sword of Hazael, Jehu will [b]kill; and whoever escapes the sword of Jehu, [c]Elisha will kill. [18][a]Yet I have reserved seven thousand in Israel, all whose knees have not bowed to Baal, [b]and every mouth that has not kissed him."

ELISHA FOLLOWS ELIJAH

[19]So he departed from there, and found Elisha the son of Shaphat, who *was* plowing *with* twelve yoke *of oxen* before him, and he was with the twelfth. Then Elijah passed by him and threw his [a]mantle on him. [20]And he left the oxen and ran after Elijah, and said, [a]"Please let me kiss my father and my mother, and *then* I will follow you."

19:8 [a]Ex. 24:18;
34:28;
Deut. 9:9–11, 18;
Matt. 4:2
[b]Ex. 3:1; 4:27

19:10 [a]Rom. 11:3
[b]Num. 25:11, 13;
Ps. 69:9
[c]1 Kin. 18:4
[d]1 Kin. 18:22;
Rom. 11:3

19:11 [a]Ex. 19:20;
24:12, 18
[b]Ex. 33:21, 22
[c]Ezek. 1:4; 37:7

19:13 [a]Ex. 3:6;
Is. 6:2
[b]1 Kin. 19:9

19:14
[a]1 Kin. 19:10

19:15
[a]2 Kin. 8:8–15

19:16
[a]2 Kin. 9:1–10
[b]1 Kin. 19:19–21;
2 Kin. 2:9–15

19:17
[a]2 Kin. 8:12;
13:3, 22
[b]2 Kin. 9:14–
10:28
[c][Hos. 6:5]

19:18 [a]Rom. 11:4
[b]Hos. 13:2

19:19
[a]1 Sam. 28:14;
2 Kin. 2:8, 13, 14

19:20
[a][Matt. 8:21, 22;
Luke 9:61, 62];
Acts 20:37

19:5 [1]Or *Angel* **19:6** [1]*hot stones* **19:7** [1]Or *Angel* **19:12** [1]*a delicate whispering voice*

And he said to him, "Go back again, for what have I done to you?"

21So *Elisha* turned back from him, and took a yoke of oxen and slaughtered them and aboiled their flesh, using the oxen's equipment, and gave it to the people, and they ate. Then he arose and followed Elijah, and became his servant.

AHAB DEFEATS THE SYRIANS

20 Now aBen-Hadad the king of Syria gathered all his forces together; thirty-two kings *were* with him, with horses and chariots. And he went up and besieged bSamaria, and made war against it. 2Then he sent messengers into the city to Ahab king of Israel, and said to him, "Thus says Ben-Hadad: 3'Your silver and your gold *are* mine; your loveliest wives and children are mine.'"

4And the king of Israel answered and said, "My lord, O king, just as you say, I and all that I have *are* yours."

5Then the messengers came back and said, "Thus speaks Ben-Hadad, saying, 'Indeed I have sent to you, saying, "You shall deliver to me your silver and your gold, your wives and your children"; 6but I will send my servants to you tomorrow about this time, and they shall search your house and the houses of your servants. And it shall be, *that* whatever is 1pleasant in your eyes, they will put *it* in their hands and take *it*.'"

7So the king of Israel called all the elders of the land, and said, "Notice, please, and see how this *man* seeks trouble, for he sent to me for my wives, my children, my silver, and my gold; and I did not deny him."

8And all the elders and all the people said to him, "Do not listen or consent."

9Therefore he said to the messengers of Ben-Hadad, "Tell my lord the king, 'All that you sent for to your servant the first time I will do, but this thing I cannot do.'"

And the messengers departed and brought back word to him.

10Then Ben-Hadad sent to him and said, a"The gods do so to me, and more also, if enough dust is left of Samaria for a handful for each of the people 1who follow me."

11So the king of Israel answered and said, "Tell *him*, 'Let not the one who puts on *his armor* aboast like the one who takes *it off*.'"

12And it happened when *Ben-Hadad* heard this message, as he and the kings *were* adrinking at the 1command post, that he said to his servants, "Get ready." And they got ready to attack the city.

13Suddenly a prophet approached Ahab king of Israel, saying, "Thus says the LORD: 'Have you seen all this great multitude? Behold, aI will deliver it into your hand today, and you shall know that I *am* the LORD.'"

14So Ahab said, "By whom?"

And he said, "Thus says the LORD: 'By the young leaders of the provinces.'"

Then he said, "Who will set the battle in order?"

And he answered, "You."

15Then he mustered the young leaders of the provinces, and there were two hundred and thirty-two; and after them

19:21
a2 Sam. 24:22

20:1
a1 Kin. 15:18, 20;
2 Kin. 6:24
b1 Kin. 16:24;
2 Kin. 6:24

20:10
a1 Kin. 19:2;
2 Kin. 6:31

20:11 aProv. 27:1;
[Eccl. 7:8]

20:12
a1 Kin. 20:16

20:13
a1 Kin. 20:28

20:6 1pleasing   20:10 1Lit. *at my feet*   20:12 1Lit. *booths* or *shelters*

he mustered all the people, all the children of Israel—seven thousand.

16So they went out at noon. Meanwhile Ben-Hadad and the thirty-two kings helping him were ªgetting drunk at the command post. 17The young leaders of the provinces went out first. And Ben-Hadad sent out *a patrol,* and they told him, saying, "Men are coming out of Samaria!" 18So he said, "If they have come out for peace, take them alive; and if they have come out for war, take them alive."

19Then these young leaders of the provinces went out of the city with the army which followed them. 20And each one killed his man; so the Syrians fled, and Israel pursued them; and Ben-Hadad the king of Syria escaped on a horse with the cavalry. 21Then the king of Israel went out and attacked the horses and chariots, and killed the Syrians with a great slaughter.

22And the prophet came to the king of Israel and said to him, "Go, strengthen yourself; take note, and see what you should do, ªfor 1in the spring of the year the king of Syria will come up against you."

THE SYRIANS AGAIN DEFEATED

23Then the servants of the king of Syria said to him, "Their gods *are* gods of the hills. Therefore they were stronger than we; but if we fight against them in the plain, surely we will be stronger than they. 24So do this thing: Dismiss the kings, each from his position, and put captains in their 1places; 25and you shall muster an army like the army 1that you have lost, horse for horse and chariot for chariot. Then we will fight against them in the plain; surely we will be stronger than they."

And he listened to their voice and did so.

26So it was, in the spring of the year, that Ben-Hadad mustered the Syrians and went up to ªAphek to fight against Israel. 27And the children of Israel were mustered and given provisions, and they went against them. Now the children of Israel encamped before them like two little flocks of goats, while the Syrians filled the ªcountryside.

28Then a ªman of God came and spoke to the king of Israel, and said, "Thus says the LORD: 'Because the Syrians have said, "The LORD *is* God of the hills, but He *is* not God of the valleys," therefore bI will deliver all this great multitude into your hand, and you shall know that I *am* the LORD.' " 29And they encamped opposite each other for seven days. So it was that on the seventh day the battle was joined; and the children of Israel killed one hundred thousand foot soldiers *of* the Syrians in one day. 30But the rest fled to Aphek, into the city; then a wall fell on twenty-seven thousand of the men *who were* left.

And Ben-Hadad fled and went into the city, into an inner chamber.

AHAB'S TREATY WITH BEN-HADAD

31Then his servants said to him, "Look now, we have heard that the kings of the house of Israel *are* merciful kings.

20:16
ª1 Kin. 16:9;
20:12;
[Prov. 20:1]

20:22
ª2 Sam. 11:1;
1 Kin. 20:26

20:26
ªJosh. 13:4;
2 Kin. 13:17

20:27
ªJudg. 6:3–5;
1 Sam. 13:5–8

20:28
ª1 Kin. 17:18
b1 Kin. 20:13

20:22 1Lit. *at the return*   20:24 1*positions*   20:25 1Lit. *that fell from you*

Please, let us ªput sackcloth around our waists and ropes around our heads, and go out to the king of Israel; perhaps he will spare your life." ³²So they wore sackcloth around their waists and *put* ropes around their heads, and came to the king of Israel and said, "Your servant Ben-Hadad says, 'Please let me live.'"

And he said, "*Is* he still alive? He *is* my brother."

³³Now the men were watching closely to see whether *any sign of mercy would come* from him; and they quickly grasped *at this word* and said, "Your brother Ben-Hadad."

So he said, "Go, bring him." Then Ben-Hadad came out to him; and he had him come up into the chariot.

³⁴So *Ben-Hadad* said to him, ª"The cities which my father took from your father I will restore; and you may set up marketplaces for yourself in Damascus, as my father did in Samaria."

Then *Ahab said,* "I will send you away with this treaty." So he made a treaty with him and sent him away.

AHAB CONDEMNED

³⁵Now a certain man of ªthe sons of the prophets said to his neighbor ᵇby the word of the LORD, "Strike me, please." And the man refused to strike him. ³⁶Then he said to him, "Because you have not obeyed the voice of the LORD, surely, as soon as you depart from me, a lion shall kill you." And as soon as he left him, ªa lion found him and killed him.

³⁷And he found another man, and said, "Strike me, please." So the man struck him, inflicting a wound. ³⁸Then the prophet departed and waited for the king by the road, and disguised himself with a bandage over his eyes. ³⁹Now ªas the king passed by, he cried out to the king and said, "Your servant went out into the midst of the battle; and there, a man came over and brought a man to me, and said, 'Guard this man; if by any means he is missing, ᵇyour life shall be for his life, or else you shall ¹pay a talent of silver.' ⁴⁰While your servant was busy here and there, he was gone."

Then the king of Israel said to him, "So *shall* your judgment *be;* you yourself have decided *it.*"

⁴¹And he hastened to take the bandage away from his eyes; and the king of Israel recognized him as one of the prophets. ⁴²Then he said to him, "Thus says the LORD: ª'Because you have let slip out of *your* hand a man whom I appointed to utter destruction, therefore your life shall go for his life, and your people for his people.'"

⁴³So the king of Israel ªwent to his house sullen and displeased, and came to Samaria.

NABOTH IS MURDERED FOR HIS VINEYARD

21 And it came to pass after these things *that* Naboth the Jezreelite had a vineyard which *was* in ªJezreel, next to the palace of Ahab king of Samaria. ²So Ahab spoke to Naboth, saying, "Give me your ªvineyard, that I may have it for a vegetable garden, because it *is* near, next to my house; and for it I will give you a vineyard better than it. *Or,* if it seems good to you, I will give you its worth in money."

20:31
ªGen. 37:34;
2 Sam. 3:31
20:34
ª1 Kin. 15:20
20:35
ª2 Kin. 2:3, 5, 7,
15 ᵇ1 Kin. 13:17, 18
20:36
ª1 Kin. 13:24
20:39
ª2 Sam. 12:1
ᵇ2 Kin. 10:24
20:42
ª1 Kin. 22:31–37
20:43
ª1 Kin. 21:4
21:1 ªJudg. 6:33;
1 Kin. 18:45, 46
21:2 ª1 Sam. 8:14

³But Naboth said to Ahab, "The LORD forbid ᵃthat I should give the inheritance of my fathers to you!"

⁴So Ahab went into his house sullen and displeased because of the word which Naboth the Jezreelite had spoken to him; for he had said, "I will not give you the inheritance of my fathers." And he lay down on his bed, and turned away his face, and would eat no food. ⁵But ᵃJezebel his wife came to him, and said to him, "Why is your spirit so sullen that you eat no food?"

⁶He said to her, "Because I spoke to Naboth the Jezreelite, and said to him, 'Give me your vineyard for money; or else, if it pleases you, I will give you *another* vineyard for it.' And he answered, 'I will not give you my vineyard.'"

⁷Then Jezebel his wife said to him, "You now exercise authority over Israel! Arise, eat food, and let your heart be cheerful; I will give you the vineyard of Naboth the Jezreelite."

⁸And she wrote letters in Ahab's name, sealed *them* with his seal, and sent the letters to the elders and the nobles who *were* dwelling in the city with Naboth. ⁹She wrote in the letters, saying,

Proclaim a fast, and seat Naboth ¹with high honor among the people; ¹⁰and seat two men, scoundrels, before him to bear witness against him, saying, "You have ᵃblasphemed God and the king." *Then* take him out, and ᵇstone him, that he may die.

¹¹So the men of his city, the elders and nobles who were inhabitants of his city, did as Jezebel had sent to them, as it *was* written in the letters which she had sent to them. ¹²ᵃThey proclaimed a fast, and seated Naboth with high honor among the people. ¹³And two men, scoundrels, came in and sat before him; and the scoundrels ᵃwitnessed against him, against Naboth, in the presence of the people, saying, "Naboth has blasphemed God and the king!" ᵇThen they took him outside the city and stoned him with stones, so that he died. ¹⁴Then they sent to Jezebel, saying, "Naboth has been stoned and is dead."

¹⁵And it came to pass, when Jezebel heard that Naboth had been stoned and was dead, that Jezebel said to Ahab, "Arise, take possession of the vineyard of Naboth the Jezreelite, which he refused to give you for money; for Naboth is not alive, but dead." ¹⁶So it was, when Ahab heard that Naboth was dead, that Ahab got up and went down to take possession of the vineyard of Naboth the Jezreelite.

THE LORD CONDEMNS AHAB

¹⁷ᵃThen the word of the LORD came to ᵇElijah the Tishbite, saying, ¹⁸"Arise, go down to meet Ahab king of Israel, ᵃwho *lives* in Samaria. There *he is,* in the vineyard of Naboth, where he has gone down to take possession of it. ¹⁹You shall speak to him, saying, 'Thus says the LORD: "Have you murdered and also taken possession?"' And you shall speak to him, saying, 'Thus says the LORD: ᵃ"In the place where dogs licked the blood of Naboth, dogs shall lick your blood, even yours."'"

21:3 ᵃ[Lev. 25:23; Num. 36:7; Ezek. 46:18]
21:5 ᵃ1 Kin. 19:1, 2
21:10 ᵃ[Ex. 22:28; Lev. 24:15, 16]; Acts 6:11 ᵇ[Lev. 24:14]
21:12 ᵃIs. 58:4
21:13 ᵃ[Ex. 20:16; 23:1, 7] ᵇ2 Kin. 9:26; 2 Chr. 24:21; Acts 7:58, 59; Heb. 11:37
21:17 ᵃ[Ps. 9:12] ᵇ1 Kin. 19:1
21:18 ᵃ1 Kin. 13:32; 2 Chr. 22:9
21:19 ᵃ1 Kin. 22:38; 2 Kin. 9:26

²⁰So Ahab said to Elijah, ª"Have you found me, O my enemy?"

And he answered, "I have found *you*, because ᵇyou have sold yourself to do evil in the sight of the LORD: ²¹'Behold, ªI will bring calamity on you. I will take away your ᵇposterity, and will cut off from Ahab ᶜevery male in Israel, both ᵈbond and free. ²²I will make your house like the house of ªJeroboam the son of Nebat, and like the house of ᵇBaasha the son of Ahijah, because of the provocation with which you have provoked *Me* to anger, and made Israel sin.' ²³And ªconcerning Jezebel the LORD also spoke, saying, 'The dogs shall eat Jezebel by the ¹wall of Jezreel.' ²⁴The dogs shall eat ªwhoever belongs to Ahab and dies in the city, and the birds of the air shall eat whoever dies in the field."

²⁵But ªthere was no one like Ahab who sold himself to do wickedness in the sight of the LORD, ᵇbecause Jezebel his wife ¹stirred him up. ²⁶And he behaved very abominably in following idols, according to all ª*that* the Amorites had done, whom the LORD had cast out before the children of Israel.

²⁷So it was, when Ahab heard those words, that he tore his clothes and ªput sackcloth on his body, and fasted and lay in sackcloth, and went about mourning.

²⁸And the word of the LORD came to Elijah the Tishbite, saying, ²⁹"See how Ahab has humbled himself before Me? Because he ªhas humbled himself before Me, I will not bring the calamity in his days. ᵇIn the days of his son I will bring the calamity on his house."

MICAIAH WARNS AHAB
(2 Chr. 18:1–27)

22 Now three years passed without war between Syria and Israel. ²Then it came to pass, in the third year, that ªJehoshaphat the king of Judah went down to *visit* the king of Israel.

³And the king of Israel said to his servants, "Do you know that ªRamoth in Gilead *is* ours, but we hesitate to take it out of the hand of the king of Syria?" ⁴So he said to Jehoshaphat, "Will you go with me to fight at Ramoth Gilead?"

Jehoshaphat said to the king of Israel, ª"I *am* as you *are*, my people as your people, my horses as your horses." ⁵Also Jehoshaphat said to the king of Israel, ª"Please inquire for the word of the LORD today."

⁶Then the king of Israel ªgathered ¹the prophets together, about four hundred men, and said to them, "Shall I go against Ramoth Gilead to fight, or shall I refrain?"

So they said, "Go up, for the Lord will deliver *it* into the hand of the king."

⁷And ªJehoshaphat said, "*Is there* not still a prophet of the LORD here, that we may inquire of ¹Him?"

⁸So the king of Israel said to Jehoshaphat, "*There is* still one man, Micaiah the son of Imlah, by whom we may inquire of the LORD; but I hate him, because he does not prophesy good concerning me, but evil."

And Jehoshaphat said, "Let not the king say such things!"

21:20
ª1 Kin. 18:17
ᵇ1 Kin. 21:25;
2 Kin. 17:17;
[Rom. 7:14]

21:21
ª1 Kin. 14:10;
2 Kin. 9:8
ᵇ2 Kin. 10:10
ᶜ1 Sam. 25:22
ᵈ1 Kin. 14:10

21:22
ª1 Kin. 15:29
ᵇ1 Kin. 16:3, 11

21:23
ª2 Kin. 9:10,
30–37

21:24
ª1 Kin. 14:11; 16:4

21:25
ª1 Kin. 16:30–
33; 21:20
ᵇ1 Kin. 16:31

21:26
ªGen. 15:16;
[Lev. 18:25–30];
2 Kin. 21:11

21:27
ªGen. 37:34;
2 Sam. 3:31;
2 Kin. 6:30

21:29
ª[2 Kin. 22:19]
ᵇ2 Kin. 9:25;
10:11, 17

22:2
ª1 Kin. 15:24;
2 Chr. 18:2

22:3
ªDeut. 4:43;
Josh. 21:38;
1 Kin. 4:13

22:4 ª2 Kin. 3:7

22:5 ª2 Kin. 3:11

22:6
ª1 Kin. 18:19

22:7 ª2 Kin. 3:11

21:23 ¹So with MT, LXX; some Heb. mss., Syr., Tg., Vg. *plot of ground* instead of *wall* (cf. 2 Kin. 9:36)   **21:25** ¹*incited him*   **22:6** ¹The false prophets   **22:7** ¹Or *him*

⁹Then the king of Israel called an officer and said, "Bring Micaiah the son of Imlah quickly!"

¹⁰The king of Israel and Jehoshaphat the king of Judah, having put on *their* robes, sat each on his throne, at a threshing floor at the entrance of the gate of Samaria; and all the prophets prophesied before them. ¹¹Now Zedekiah the son of Chenaanah had made ᵃhorns of iron for himself; and he said, "Thus says the LORD: 'With these you shall ᵇgore the Syrians until they are destroyed.'" ¹²And all the prophets prophesied so, saying, "Go up to Ramoth Gilead and prosper, for the LORD will deliver *it* into the king's hand."

¹³Then the messenger who had gone to call Micaiah spoke to him, saying, "Now listen, the words of the prophets with one accord encourage the king. Please, let your word be like the word of one of them, and speak encouragement."

¹⁴And Micaiah said, "*As* the LORD lives, ᵃwhatever the LORD says to me, that I will speak."

¹⁵Then he came to the king; and the king said to him, "Micaiah, shall we go to war against Ramoth Gilead, or shall we refrain?"

And he answered him, "Go and prosper, for the LORD will deliver *it* into the hand of the king!"

¹⁶So the king said to him, "How many times shall I make you swear that you tell me nothing but the truth in the name of the LORD?"

¹⁷Then he said, "I saw all Israel ᵃscattered on the mountains, as sheep that have no shepherd. And the LORD said, 'These have no master. Let each return to his house in peace.'"

¹⁸And the king of Israel said to Jehoshaphat, "Did I not tell you he would not prophesy good concerning me, but evil?"

¹⁹Then *Micaiah* said, "Therefore hear the word of the LORD: ᵃI saw the LORD sitting on His throne, ᵇand all the host of heaven standing by, on His right hand and on His left. ²⁰And the LORD said, 'Who will persuade Ahab to go up, that he may fall at Ramoth Gilead?' So one spoke in this manner, and another spoke in that manner. ²¹Then a spirit came forward and stood before the LORD, and said, 'I will persuade him.' ²²The LORD said to him, 'In what way?' So he said, 'I will go out and be a lying spirit in the mouth of all his prophets.' And the LORD said, ᵃ'You shall persuade *him,* and also prevail. Go out and do so.' ²³ᵃTherefore look! The LORD has put a lying spirit in the mouth of all these prophets of yours, and the LORD has declared disaster against you."

²⁴Now Zedekiah the son of Chenaanah went near and ᵃstruck Micaiah on the cheek, and said, ᵇ"Which way did the spirit from the LORD go from me to speak to you?"

²⁵And Micaiah said, "Indeed, you shall see on that day when you go into an ᵃinner chamber to hide!"

²⁶So the king of Israel said, "Take Micaiah, and return him to Amon the governor of the city and to Joash the king's son; ²⁷and say, 'Thus says the king: "Put this *fellow* in ᵃprison, and feed him with bread of affliction and water of affliction, until I come in peace."'"

²⁸But Micaiah said, "If you ever return in peace, ᵃthe LORD has not spoken by me." And he said, "Take heed, all you people!"

22:11
ᵃZech. 1:18–21
ᵇDeut. 33:17

22:14
ᵃNum. 22:38;
24:13

22:17
ᵃNum. 27:17;
1 Kin. 22:34–36;
2 Chr. 18:16;
Matt. 9:36;
Mark 6:34

22:19 ᵃIs. 6:1;
Ezek. 1:26–28;
Dan. 7:9
ᵇJob 1:6; 2:1;
Ps. 103:20;
Dan. 7:10;
Zech. 1:10;
[Matt. 18:10;
Heb. 1:7, 14]

22:22
ᵃJudg. 9:23;
1 Sam. 16:14;
18:10; 19:9;
Job 12:16;
[Ezek. 14:9;
2 Thess. 2:11]

22:23
ᵃ[Ezek. 14:9]

22:24 ᵃJer. 20:2
ᵇ2 Chr. 18:23

22:25
ᵃ1 Kin. 20:30

22:27
ᵃ2 Chr. 16:10;
18:25–27

22:28
ᵃNum. 16:29;
Deut. 18:20–22

AHAB DIES IN BATTLE
(2 Chr. 18:28–34)

²⁹So the king of Israel and Jehoshaphat the king of Judah went up to Ramoth Gilead. ³⁰And the king of Israel said to Jehoshaphat, "I will disguise myself and go into battle; but you put on your robes." So the king of Israel ᵃdisguised himself and went into battle.

³¹Now the ᵃking of Syria had commanded the thirty-two ᵇcaptains of his chariots, saying, "Fight with no one small or great, but only with the king of Israel." ³²So it was, when the captains of the chariots saw Jehoshaphat, that they said, "Surely it *is* the king of Israel!" Therefore they turned aside to fight against him, and Jehoshaphat ᵃcried out. ³³And it happened, when the captains of the chariots saw that it *was* not the king of Israel, that they turned back from pursuing him. ³⁴Now a *certain* man drew a bow at random, and struck the king of Israel between the joints of his armor. So he said to the driver of his chariot, "Turn around and take me out of the battle, for I am wounded."

³⁵The battle increased that day; and the king was propped up in his chariot, facing the Syrians, and died at evening. The blood ran out from the wound onto the floor of the chariot. ³⁶Then, as the sun was going down, a shout went throughout the army, saying, "Every man to his city, and every man to his own country!"

³⁷So the king died, and was brought to Samaria. And they buried the king in Samaria. ³⁸Then *someone* washed the chariot at a pool in Samaria, and the dogs licked up his blood while ¹the harlots bathed, according ᵃto the word of the LORD which He had spoken.

³⁹Now the rest of the acts of Ahab, and all that he did, ᵃthe ivory house which he built and all the cities that he built, *are* they not written in the book of the chronicles of the kings of Israel? ⁴⁰So Ahab ¹rested with his fathers. Then ᵃAhaziah his son reigned in his place.

JEHOSHAPHAT REIGNS IN JUDAH
(2 Chr. 20:31—21:1)

⁴¹ᵃJehoshaphat the son of Asa had become king over Judah in the fourth year of Ahab king of Israel. ⁴²Jehoshaphat *was* thirty-five years old when he became king, and he reigned twenty-five years in Jerusalem. His mother's name *was* Azubah the daughter of Shilhi. ⁴³And ᵃhe walked in all the ways of his father Asa. He did not turn aside from them, doing *what was* right in the eyes of the LORD. Nevertheless ᵇthe high places were not taken away, *for* the people offered sacrifices and burned incense on the high places. ⁴⁴Also ᵃJehoshaphat made ᵇpeace with the king of Israel.

⁴⁵Now the rest of the acts of Jehoshaphat, the might that he showed, and how he made war, *are* they not written ᵃin the book of the chronicles of the kings of Judah? ⁴⁶And the rest of the ¹perverted persons, who remained in the days of his father Asa, he banished from the land. ⁴⁷ᵃ*There was* then no king in Edom, only a deputy of the king.

22:30 ᵃ2 Chr. 35:22

22:31 ᵃ1 Kin. 20:1 ᵇ1 Kin. 20:24; 2 Chr. 18:30

22:32 ᵃ2 Chr. 18:31

22:38 ᵃ1 Kin. 21:19

22:39 ᵃPs. 45:8; Amos 3:15

22:40 ᵃ2 Kin. 1:2, 18

22:41 ᵃ2 Chr. 20:31

22:43 ᵃ2 Chr. 17:3; 20:32, 33 ᵇ1 Kin. 14:23; 15:14; 2 Kin. 12:3

22:44 ᵃ2 Chr. 19:2 ᵇ2 Chr. 18:1

22:45 ᵃ2 Chr. 20:34

22:46 ᵃGen. 19:5; Deut. 23:17; 1 Kin. 14:24; 15:12; 2 Kin. 23:7; Jude 7

22:47 ᵃ2 Sam. 8:14; 2 Kin. 3:9; 8:20

22:38 ¹Tg., Syr. *they washed his armor*   **22:40** ¹Died and joined his ancestors   **22:46** ¹Heb. *qadesh,* one practicing sodomy and prostitution in religious rituals

48aJehoshaphat bmade ¹merchant ships to go to cOphir for gold; dbut they never sailed, for the ships were wrecked at eEzion Geber. 49Then Ahaziah the son of Ahab said to Jehoshaphat, "Let my servants go with your servants in the ships." But Jehoshaphat would not.

50And aJehoshaphat ¹rested with his fathers, and was buried with his fathers in the City of David his father. Then Jehoram his son reigned in his place.

AHAZIAH REIGNS IN ISRAEL

51aAhaziah the son of Ahab became king over Israel in Samaria in the seventeenth year of Jehoshaphat king of Judah, and reigned two years over Israel. 52He did evil in the sight of the LORD, and awalked in the way of his father and in the way of his mother and in the way of Jeroboam the son of Nebat, who had made Israel sin; 53for ahe served Baal and worshiped him, and provoked the LORD God of Israel to anger, baccording¹ to all that his father had done.

22:48
a2 Chr. 20:35–37
b1 Kin. 10:22
c1 Kin. 9:28
d2 Chr. 20:37
e1 Kin. 9:26

22:50
a2 Chr. 21:1

22:51
a1 Kin. 22:40

22:52
a1 Kin. 15:26;
21:25

22:53
aJudg. 2:11
b1 Kin. 16:30–32

22:48 ¹Or *ships of Tarshish*   22:50 ¹Died and joined his ancestors
22:53 ¹In the same way that

THE SECOND BOOK OF THE
KINGS

GOD JUDGES AHAZIAH

1 Moab ^arebelled against Israel ^bafter the death of Ahab. ²Now ^aAhaziah fell through the lattice of his upper room in Samaria, and was injured; so he sent messengers and said to them, "Go, inquire of ^bBaal-Zebub,¹ the god of ^cEkron, whether I shall recover from this injury." ³But the ¹angel of the LORD said to Elijah the Tishbite, "Arise, go up to meet the messengers of the king of Samaria, and say to them, '*Is it* because *there is* no God in Israel *that* you are going to inquire of Baal-Zebub, the god of Ekron?' ⁴Now therefore, thus says the LORD: 'You shall not come down from the bed to which you have gone up, but you shall surely die.'" So Elijah departed.

⁵And when the messengers returned to ¹him, he said to them, "Why have you come back?"

⁶So they said to him, "A man came up to meet us, and said to us, 'Go, return to the king who sent you, and say to him, "Thus says the LORD: '*Is it* because *there is* no God in Israel *that* you are sending to inquire of Baal-Zebub, the god of Ekron? Therefore you shall not come down from the bed to which you have gone up, but you shall surely die.'"'"

⁷Then he said to them, "What kind of man *was it* who came up to meet you and told you these words?"

⁸So they answered him, ^a"A hairy man wearing a leather belt around his waist."

And he said, ^b"It *is* Elijah the Tishbite."

⁹Then the king sent to him a captain of fifty with his fifty men. So he went up to him; and there he was, sitting on the top of a hill. And he spoke to him: "Man of God, the king has said, 'Come down!'"

¹⁰So Elijah answered and said to the captain of fifty, "If I *am* a man of God, then ^alet fire come down from heaven and consume you and your fifty men." And fire came down from heaven and consumed him and his fifty. ¹¹Then he sent to him another captain of fifty with his fifty men.

And he answered and said to him: "Man of God, thus has the king said, 'Come down quickly!'"

¹²So Elijah answered and said to them, "If I *am* a man of God, let fire come down from heaven and consume you and your fifty men." And the fire of God came down from heaven and consumed him and his fifty.

¹³Again, he sent a third captain of fifty with his fifty men. And the third captain of fifty went up, and came and ¹fell on his knees before Elijah, and pleaded with him, and said to him: "Man of God, please let my life and the life of these fifty servants of yours ^abe precious in your sight. ¹⁴Look, fire has come down from heaven and burned up the first two captains of fifties with their fifties. But let my life now be precious in your sight."

1:1 ^a2 Sam. 8:2
^b2 Kin. 3:5

1:2 ^a1 Kin. 22:40
^b2 Kin. 1:3, 6, 16; Matt. 10:25; Mark 3:22
^c1 Sam. 5:10

1:8 ^aZech. 13:4; Matt. 3:4; Mark 1:6
^b1 Kin. 18:7

1:10
^a1 Kin. 18:36–38; Luke 9:54

1:13
^a1 Sam. 26:21; Ps. 72:14

¹⁵And the ¹angel of the LORD said to Elijah, "Go down with him; do not be afraid of him." So he arose and went down with him to the king. ¹⁶Then he said to him, "Thus says the LORD: 'Because you have sent messengers to inquire of Baal-Zebub, the god of Ekron, *is it* because *there is* no God in Israel to inquire of His word? Therefore you shall not come down from the bed to which you have gone up, but you shall surely die.'"

¹⁷So *Ahaziah* died according to the word of the LORD which Elijah had spoken. Because he had no son, ªJehoram¹ became king in his place, in the second year of Jehoram the son of Jehoshaphat, king of Judah.

¹⁸Now the rest of the acts of Ahaziah which he did, *are* they not written in the book of the chronicles of the kings of Israel?

ELIJAH ASCENDS TO HEAVEN

2 And it came to pass, when the LORD was about to ªtake up Elijah into heaven by a whirlwind, that Elijah went with ᵇElisha from Gilgal. ²Then Elijah said to Elisha, ª"Stay here, please, for the LORD has sent me on to Bethel."

But Elisha said, "*As* the LORD lives, and ᵇ*as* your soul lives, I will not leave you!" So they went down to Bethel.

³Now ªthe sons of the prophets who *were* at Bethel came out to Elisha, and said to him, "Do you know that the LORD will take away your master ¹from over you today?"

And he said, "Yes, I know; keep silent!"

⁴Then Elijah said to him, "Elisha, stay here, please, for the LORD has sent me on to Jericho."

But he said, "*As* the LORD lives, and *as* your soul lives, I will not leave you!" So they came to Jericho.

⁵Now the sons of the prophets who *were* at Jericho came to Elisha and said to him, "Do you know that the LORD will take away your master from over you today?"

So he answered, "Yes, I know; keep silent!"

⁶Then Elijah said to him, "Stay here, please, for the LORD has sent me on to the Jordan."

But he said, "*As* the LORD lives, and *as* your soul lives, I will not leave you!" So the two of them went on. ⁷And fifty men of the sons of the prophets went and stood facing *them* at a distance, while the two of them stood by the Jordan. ⁸Now Elijah took his mantle, rolled *it* up, and struck the water; and ªit was divided this way and that, so that the two of them crossed over on dry ᵇground.

⁹And so it was, when they had crossed over, that Elijah said to Elisha, "Ask! What may I do for you, before I am taken away from you?"

Elisha said, "Please let a double portion of your spirit be upon me."

¹⁰So he said, "You have asked a hard thing. *Nevertheless,* if you see me *when I am* taken from you, it shall be so for you; but if not, it shall not be *so.*" ¹¹Then it happened, as they continued on and talked, that suddenly ªa chariot of fire *appeared* with horses of fire, and separated the two of them; and Elijah ᵇwent up by a whirlwind into heaven.

¹²And Elisha saw *it,* and he cried out, ª"My father, my father, the chariot of Israel and its horsemen!" So he saw him

1:17
ª1 Kin. 22:50;
2 Kin. 8:16;
Matt. 1:8

2:1 ªGen. 5:24;
[Heb. 11:5]
ᵇ1 Kin. 19:16–21

2:2
ªRuth 1:15, 16
ᵇ1 Sam. 1:26;
2 Kin. 2:4, 6;
4:30

2:3
ª1 Kin. 20:35;
2 Kin. 2:5, 7, 15;
4:1, 38; 9:1

2:8
ªEx. 14:21, 22;
Josh. 3:16;
2 Kin. 2:14
ᵇJosh. 3:17

2:11 ª2 Kin. 6:17;
Ps. 104:4
ᵇGen. 5:24;
Heb. 11:5

2:12 ª2 Kin. 13:14

1:15 ¹Or *Angel*   **1:17** ¹The son of Ahab king of Israel, 2 Kin. 3:1   **2:3** ¹Lit. *from your head*

no more. And he took hold of his own clothes and tore them into two pieces. ¹³He also took up the mantle of Elijah that had fallen from him, and went back and stood by the bank of the Jordan. ¹⁴Then he took the mantle of Elijah that had fallen from him, and struck the water, and said, "Where *is* the LORD God of Elijah?" And when he also had struck the water, ᵃit was divided this way and that; and Elisha crossed over.

¹⁵Now when the sons of the prophets who *were* ᵃfrom¹ Jericho saw him, they said, "The spirit of Elijah rests on Elisha." And they came to meet him, and bowed to the ground before him. ¹⁶Then they said to him, "Look now, there are fifty strong men with your servants. Please let them go and search for your master, ᵃlest perhaps the Spirit of the LORD has taken him up and cast him upon some mountain or into some valley."

And he said, "You shall not send anyone."

¹⁷But when they urged him till he was ᵃashamed, he said, "Send *them!*" Therefore they sent fifty men, and they searched for three days but did not find him. ¹⁸And when they came back to him, for he had stayed in Jericho, he said to them, "Did I not say to you, 'Do not go'?"

ELISHA PERFORMS MIRACLES

¹⁹Then the men of the city said to Elisha, "Please notice, the situation of this city *is* pleasant, as my lord sees; but the water *is* bad, and the ground barren."

²⁰And he said, "Bring me a new bowl, and put salt in it." So they brought *it* to him. ²¹Then he went out to the source of the water, and ᵃcast in the salt there, and said, "Thus says the LORD: 'I have ¹healed this water; from it there shall be no more death or barrenness.' " ²²So the water remains ᵃhealed to this day, according to the word of Elisha which he spoke.

²³Then he went up from there to Bethel; and as he was going up the road, some youths came from the city and mocked him, and said to him, "Go up, you baldhead! Go up, you baldhead!"

²⁴So he turned around and looked at them, and ᵃpronounced a curse on them in the name of the LORD. And two female bears came out of the woods and mauled forty-two of the youths.

²⁵Then he went from there to ᵃMount Carmel, and from there he returned to Samaria.

MOAB REBELS AGAINST ISRAEL

3 Now ᵃJehoram the son of Ahab became king over Israel at Samaria in the eighteenth year of Jehoshaphat king of Judah, and reigned twelve years. ²And he did evil in the sight of the LORD, but not like his father and mother; for he put away the *sacred* pillar of Baal ᵃthat his father had made. ³Nevertheless he persisted in ᵃthe sins of Jeroboam the son of Nebat, who had made Israel sin; he did not depart from them.

⁴Now Mesha king of Moab was a sheepbreeder, and he ᵃregularly paid the king of Israel one hundred thousand ᵇlambs and the wool of one hundred thousand rams. ⁵But it happened, when ᵃAhab died, that the king of Moab rebelled against the king of Israel.

⁶So King Jehoram went out of Samaria at that time and mustered all Israel. ⁷Then he went and sent to Jehoshaphat

king of Judah, saying, "The king of Moab has rebelled against me. Will you go with me to fight against Moab?"

And he said, "I will go up; ᵃI *am* as you *are,* my people as your people, my horses as your horses." ⁸Then he said, "Which way shall we go up?"

And he answered, "By way of the Wilderness of Edom."

⁹So the king of Israel went with the king of Judah and the king of Edom, and they marched on that roundabout route seven days; and there was no water for the army, nor for the animals that followed them. ¹⁰And the king of Israel said, "Alas! For the LORD has called these three kings together to deliver them into the hand of Moab."

¹¹But ᵃJehoshaphat said, "*Is there* no prophet of the LORD here, that we may inquire of the LORD by him?"

So one of the servants of the king of Israel answered and said, "Elisha the son of Shaphat *is* here, who ᵇpoured¹ water on the hands of Elijah."

¹²And Jehoshaphat said, "The word of the LORD is with him." So the king of Israel and Jehoshaphat and the king of Edom ᵃwent down to him.

¹³Then Elisha said to the king of Israel, ᵃ"What have I to do with you? ᵇGo to ᶜthe prophets of your father and the ᵈprophets of your mother."

But the king of Israel said to him, "No, for the LORD has called these three kings *together* to deliver them into the hand of Moab."

¹⁴And Elisha said, ᵃ"As the LORD of hosts lives, before whom I stand, surely were it not that I regard the presence of Jehoshaphat king of Judah, I would not look at you, nor see you. ¹⁵But now bring me ᵃa musician."

Then it happened, when the musician ᵇplayed, that ᶜthe hand of the LORD came upon him. ¹⁶And he said, "Thus says the LORD: ᵃ'Make this valley full of ¹ditches.' ¹⁷For thus says the LORD: 'You shall not see wind, nor shall you see rain; yet that valley shall be filled with water, so that you, your cattle, and your animals may drink.' ¹⁸And this is a simple matter in the sight of the LORD; He will also deliver the Moabites into your hand. ¹⁹Also you shall attack every fortified city and every choice city, and shall cut down every good tree, and stop up every spring of water, and ruin every good piece of land with stones."

²⁰Now it happened in the morning, when ᵃthe grain offering was offered, that suddenly water came by way of Edom, and the land was filled with water.

²¹And when all the Moabites heard that the kings had come up to fight against them, all who were able to bear arms and older were ¹gathered; and they stood at the border. ²²Then they rose up early in the morning, and the sun was shining on the water; and the Moabites saw the water on the other side *as* red as blood. ²³And they said, "This is blood; the kings have surely struck swords and have killed one another; now therefore, Moab, to the spoil!"

²⁴So when they came to the camp of Israel, Israel rose up and attacked the Moabites, so that they fled before them; and they entered *their* land, killing the Moabites. ²⁵Then they destroyed the cities, and each man threw a stone on every

3:7 ᵃ1 Kin. 22:4

3:11 ᵃ1 Kin. 22:7
ᵇ1 Kin. 19:21;
[John 13:4, 5,
13, 14]

3:12 ᵃ2 Kin. 2:25

3:13
ᵃ[Ezek. 14:3]
ᵇJudg. 10:14;
Ruth 1:15
ᶜ1 Kin. 22:6–11
ᵈ1 Kin. 18:19

3:14 ᵃ1 Kin. 17:1;
2 Kin. 5:16

3:15 ᵃ1 Sam. 10:5
ᵇ1 Sam. 16:16,
23; 1 Chr. 25:1
ᶜEzek. 1:3; 3:14,
22; 8:1

3:16 ᵃJer. 14:3

3:20
ᵃEx. 29:39, 40

3:11 ¹Was the personal servant of   3:16 ¹*water canals*   3:21 ¹*summoned*

good piece of land and filled it; and they stopped up all the springs of water and cut down all the good trees. But they left the stones of ᵃKir Haraseth *intact.* However the slingers surrounded and attacked it.

²⁶And when the king of Moab saw that the battle was too fierce for him, he took with him seven hundred men who drew swords, to break through to the king of Edom, but they could not. ²⁷Then ᵃhe took his eldest son who would have reigned in his place, and offered him *as* a burnt offering upon the wall; and there was great ¹indignation against Israel. ᵇSo they departed from him and returned to *their own* land.

ELISHA AND THE WIDOW'S OIL
(cf. 1 Kin. 17:14–16)

4 A certain woman of the wives of ᵃthe sons of the prophets cried out to Elisha, saying, "Your servant my husband is dead, and you know that your servant feared the LORD. And the creditor is coming ᵇto take my two sons to be his slaves."

²So Elisha said to her, "What shall I do for you? Tell me, what do you have in the house?" And she said, "Your maidservant has nothing in the house but a jar of oil."

³Then he said, "Go, borrow vessels from everywhere, from all your neighbors—empty vessels; ᵃdo not gather just a few. ⁴And when you have come in, you shall shut the door behind you and your sons; then pour it into all those vessels, and set aside the full ones."

⁵So she went from him and shut the door behind her and her sons, who brought *the vessels* to her; and she poured *it* out. ⁶Now it came to pass, when the vessels were full, that she said to her son, "Bring me another vessel."

And he said to her, "*There is* not another vessel." So the oil ceased. ⁷Then she came and told the man of God. And he said, "Go, sell the oil and pay your debt; and you *and* your sons live on the rest."

ELISHA RAISES THE SHUNAMMITE'S SON
(cf. 1 Kin. 17:17–24)

⁸Now it happened one day that Elisha went to ᵃShunem, where there *was* a ¹notable woman, and she ²persuaded him to eat some food. So it was, as often as he passed by, he would turn in there to eat some food. ⁹And she said to her husband, "Look now, I know that this *is* a holy man of God, who passes by us regularly. ¹⁰Please, let us make ¹a small upper room on the wall; and let us put a bed for him there, and a table and a chair and a lampstand; so it will be, whenever he comes to us, he can turn in there."

¹¹And it happened one day that he came there, and turned in to the upper room and lay down there. ¹²Then he said to ᵃGehazi his servant, "Call this Shunammite woman." When he had called her, she stood before him. ¹³And he said to him, "Say now to her, 'Look, you have been concerned for us with all this care. What *can I* do for you? Do you want me to speak on your behalf to the king or to the commander of the army?'"

3:25 ᵃIs. 16:7, 11; Jer. 48:31, 36

3:27 ᵃ[Deut. 18:10; Amos 2:1; Mic. 6:7] ᵇ2 Kin. 8:20

4:1 ᵃ1 Kin. 20:35; 2 Kin. 2:3 ᵇ[Lev. 25:39–41, 48]; 1 Sam. 22:2; Neh. 5:2–5; Matt. 18:25

4:3 ᵃ2 Kin. 3:16

4:8 ᵃJosh. 19:18

4:12 ᵃ2 Kin. 4:29–31; 5:20–27; 8:4, 5

3:27 ¹*wrath* 4:8 ¹Lit. *great* ²Lit. *laid hold on him* 4:10 ¹Or *a small walled upper chamber*

She answered, "I dwell among my own people."

¹⁴So he said, "What then *is* to be done for her?"

And Gehazi answered, "Actually, she has no son, and her husband is old."

¹⁵So he said, "Call her." When he had called her, she stood in the doorway. ¹⁶Then he said, ¹"About this time next year you shall embrace a son."

And she said, "No, my lord. Man of God, ᵃdo not lie to your maidservant!"

¹⁷But the woman conceived, and bore a son when the appointed time had come, of which Elisha had told her.

¹⁸And the child grew. Now it happened one day that he went out to his father, to the reapers. ¹⁹And he said to his father, "My head, my head!"

So he said to a servant, "Carry him to his mother." ²⁰When he had taken him and brought him to his mother, he sat on her knees till noon, and *then* died. ²¹And she went up and laid him on the bed of the man of God, shut *the door* upon him, and went out. ²²Then she called to her husband, and said, "Please send me one of the young men and one of the donkeys, that I may run to the man of God and come back."

²³So he said, "Why are you going to him today? *It is* neither the ᵃNew Moon nor the Sabbath."

And she said, ¹"*It is* well." ²⁴Then she saddled a donkey, and said to her servant, "Drive, and go forward; do not slacken the pace for me unless I tell you." ²⁵And so she departed, and went to the man of God ᵃat Mount Carmel.

So it was, when the man of God saw her afar off, that he said to his servant Gehazi, "Look, the Shunammite woman! ²⁶Please run now to meet her, and say to her, '*Is it* well with you? *Is it* well with your husband? *Is it* well with the child?'"

And she answered, "*It is* well." ²⁷Now when she came to the man of God at the hill, she caught him by the feet, but Gehazi came near to push her away. But the man of God said, "Let her alone; for her soul *is* in deep distress, and the LORD has hidden *it* from me, and has not told me."

²⁸So she said, "Did I ask a son of my lord? ᵃDid I not say, 'Do not deceive me'?"

²⁹Then he said to Gehazi, ᵃ"Get¹ yourself ready, and take my staff in your hand, and be on your way. If you meet anyone, ᵇdo not greet him; and if anyone greets you, do not answer him; but ᶜlay my staff on the face of the child."

³⁰And the mother of the child said, ᵃ"As the LORD lives, and *as* your soul lives, I will not ᵇleave you." So he arose and followed her. ³¹Now Gehazi went on ahead of them, and laid the staff on the face of the child; but *there was* neither voice nor hearing. Therefore he went back to meet him, and told him, saying, "The child has ᵃnot awakened."

³²When Elisha came into the house, there was the child, lying dead on his bed. ³³He ᵃwent in therefore, shut the door behind the two of them, and ᵇprayed to the LORD. ³⁴And he went up and lay on the child, and put his mouth on his mouth, his eyes on his eyes, and his hands on his hands; and ᵃhe stretched himself out on the child, and the flesh of the child became

4:16 ᵃ2 Kin. 4:28

4:23
ᵃNum. 10:10;
28:11; 1 Chr. 23:31

4:25 ᵃ2 Kin. 2:25

4:28 ᵃ2 Kin. 4:16

4:29
ᵃ1 Kin. 18:46;
2 Kin. 9:1
ᵇLuke 10:4
ᶜEx. 7:19; 14:16;
2 Kin. 2:8, 14;
Acts 19:12

4:30 ᵃ2 Kin. 2:2
ᵇ2 Kin. 2:4

4:31 ᵃJohn 11:11

4:33 ᵃ2 Kin. 4:4;
[Matt. 6:6];
Luke 8:51
ᵇ1 Kin. 17:20

4:34
ᵃ1 Kin. 17:21–23;
Acts 20:10

499 | 2 KINGS 5:6

warm. 35He returned and walked back and forth in the house, and again went up ^aand stretched himself out on him; then ^bthe child sneezed seven times, and the child opened his eyes. 36And he called Gehazi and said, "Call this Shunammite woman." So he called her. And when she came in to him, he said, "Pick up your son." 37So she went in, fell at his feet, and bowed to the ground; then she ^apicked up her son and went out.

ELISHA PURIFIES THE POT OF STEW

38And Elisha returned to ^aGilgal, and *there was* a ^bfamine in the land. Now the sons of the prophets *were* ^csitting before him; and he said to his servant, "Put on the large pot, and boil stew for the sons of the prophets." 39So one went out into the field to gather herbs, and found a wild vine, and gathered from it a lapful of wild gourds, and came and sliced *them* into the pot of stew, though they did not know *what they were.* 40Then they served it to the men to eat. Now it happened, as they were eating the stew, that they cried out and said, "Man of God, *there is* ^adeath in the pot!" And they could not eat *it.*

41So he said, "Then bring some flour." And ^ahe put *it* into the pot, and said, "Serve *it* to the people, that they may eat." And there was nothing harmful in the pot.

ELISHA FEEDS ONE HUNDRED MEN
(cf. Matt. 14:13–21; 15:32–39)

42Then a man came from ^aBaal Shalisha, ^band brought the man of God bread of the firstfruits, twenty loaves of barley bread, and newly ripened grain in his knapsack. And he said, "Give *it* to the people, that they may eat."

43But his servant said, ^a"What? Shall I set this before one hundred men?"

He said again, "Give it to the people, that they may eat; for thus says the LORD: ^b'They shall eat and have *some* left over.'" 44So he set *it* before them; and they ate ^aand had *some* left over, according to the word of the LORD.

NAAMAN'S LEPROSY HEALED

5 Now ^aNaaman, commander of the army of the king of Syria, was ^ba great and honorable man in the eyes of his master, because by him the LORD had given victory to Syria. He was also a mighty man of valor, *but* a leper. 2And the Syrians had gone out ^aon¹ raids, and had brought back captive a young girl from the land of Israel. She ²waited on Naaman's wife. 3Then she said to her mistress, "If only my master *were* with the prophet who *is* in Samaria! For he would heal him of his leprosy." 4And *Naaman* went in and told his master, saying, "Thus and thus said the girl who *is* from the land of Israel."

5Then the king of Syria said, "Go now, and I will send a letter to the king of Israel."

So he departed and ^atook with him ten talents of silver, six thousand *shekels* of gold, and ten changes of clothing. 6Then he brought the letter to the king of Israel, which said,

Now be advised, when this letter comes to you, that I have sent Naaman my servant to you, that you may heal him of his leprosy.

4:35 ^a1 Kin. 17:21
^b2 Kin. 8:1, 5
4:37
^a1 Kin. 17:23;
[Heb. 11:35]
4:38 ^a2 Kin. 2:1
^b2 Kin. 8:1
^cLuke 10:39;
Acts 22:3
4:40 ^aEx. 10:17
4:41 ^aEx. 15:25;
2 Kin. 2:21
4:42 ^a1 Sam. 9:4
^b1 Sam. 9:7;
[1 Cor. 9:11;
Gal. 6:6]
4:43 ^aLuke 9:13;
John 6:9
^bLuke 9:17;
John 6:11
4:44
^aMatt. 14:20;
15:37; John 6:13
5:1 ^aLuke 4:27
^bEx. 11:3
5:2 ^a2 Kin. 6:23;
13:20
5:5 ^a1 Sam. 9:8;
2 Kin. 8:8, 9

5:2 ¹Or *in bands*   ²Served, lit. *was before*

7And it happened, when the king of Israel read the letter, that he tore his clothes and said, "*Am* I ªGod, to kill and make alive, that this man sends a man to me to heal him of his leprosy? Therefore please consider, and see how he seeks a quarrel with me."

8So it was, when Elisha the man of God heard that the king of Israel had torn his clothes, that he sent to the king, saying, "Why have you torn your clothes? Please let him come to me, and he shall know that there is a prophet in Israel."

9Then Naaman went with his horses and chariot, and he stood at the door of Elisha's house. 10And Elisha sent a messenger to him, saying, "Go and ªwash in the Jordan seven times, and your flesh shall be restored to you, and *you shall* be clean." 11But Naaman became furious, and went away and said, "Indeed, I said to myself, 'He will surely come out *to me,* and stand and call on the name of the LORD his God, and wave his hand over the place, and heal the leprosy.' 12*Are* not the ¹Abanah and the Pharpar, the rivers of Damascus, better than all the waters of Israel? Could I not wash in them and be clean?" So he turned and went away in a rage. 13And his ªservants came near and spoke to him, and said, "My father, *if* the prophet had told you *to do* something great, would you not have done *it*? How much more then, when he says to you, 'Wash, and be clean'?" 14So he went down and dipped seven times in the Jordan, according to the saying of the man of God; and his ªflesh was restored like the flesh of a little child, and ᵇhe was clean.

15And he returned to the man of God, he and all his aides, and came and stood before him; and he said, "Indeed, now I know that *there is* ªno God in all the earth, except in Israel; now therefore, please take ᵇa gift from your servant."

16But he said, ª"*As* the LORD lives, before whom I stand, ᵇI will receive nothing." And he urged him to take *it,* but he refused.

17So Naaman said, "Then, if not, please let your servant be given two mule-loads of earth; for your servant will no longer offer either burnt offering or sacrifice to other gods, but to the LORD. 18Yet in this thing may the LORD pardon your servant: when my master goes into the temple of Rimmon to worship there, and ªhe leans on my hand, and I bow down in the temple of Rimmon—when I bow down in the temple of Rimmon, may the LORD please pardon your servant in this thing."

19Then he said to him, "Go in peace." So he departed from him a short distance.

GEHAZI'S GREED

20But ªGehazi, the servant of Elisha the man of God, said, "Look, my master has spared Naaman this Syrian, while not receiving from his hands what he brought; but *as* the LORD lives, I will run after him and take something from him." 21So Gehazi pursued Naaman. When Naaman saw *him* running after him, he got down from the chariot to meet him, and said, "*Is* all well?"

22And he said, "All *is* ªwell. My master has sent me, saying, 'Indeed, just now two young men of the sons of the prophets have come to me from the mountains of Ephraim. Please give them a talent of silver and two changes of garments.'"

5:7 ª[Gen. 30:2; Deut. 32:39; 1 Sam. 2:6]

5:10 ª2 Kin. 4:41; John 9:7

5:13 ª1 Sam. 28:23

5:14 ª2 Kin. 5:10; Job 33:25 ᵇLuke 4:27; 5:13

5:15 ªDan. 2:47; 3:29; 6:26, 27 ᵇGen. 33:11

5:16 ª2 Kin. 3:14 ᵇGen. 14:22, 23; 2 Kin. 5:20, 26; [Matt. 10:8]; Acts 8:18, 20

5:18 ª2 Kin. 7:2, 17

5:20 ª2 Kin. 4:12; 8:4, 5

5:22 ª2 Kin. 4:26

5:12 ¹So with Kt., LXX, Vg.; Qr., Syr., Tg. *Amanah*

²³So Naaman said, "Please, take two talents." And he urged him, and bound two talents of silver in two bags, with two changes of garments, and handed *them* to two of his servants; and they carried *them* on ahead of him. ²⁴When he came to ¹the citadel, he took *them* from their hand, and stored *them* away in the house; then he let the men go, and they departed. ²⁵Now he went in and stood before his master. Elisha said to him, "Where *did you go*, Gehazi?"

And he said, "Your servant did not go anywhere."

²⁶Then he said to him, "Did not my heart go *with you* when the man turned back from his chariot to meet you? *Is it* ªtime to receive money and to receive clothing, olive groves and vineyards, sheep and oxen, male and female servants? ²⁷Therefore the leprosy of Naaman ªshall cling to you and your descendants forever." And he went out from his presence ᵇleprous, *as white* as snow.

THE FLOATING AX HEAD

6 And ªthe sons of the prophets said to Elisha, "See now, the place where we dwell with you is too small for us. ²Please, let us go to the Jordan, and let every man take a beam from there, and let us make there a place where we may dwell."

So he answered, "Go."

³Then one said, ª"Please consent to go with your servants."

And he answered, "I will go." ⁴So he went with them. And when they came to the Jordan, they cut down trees. ⁵But as one was cutting down a tree, the iron *ax head* fell into the water; and he cried out and said, "Alas, master! For it was ªborrowed."

⁶So the man of God said, "Where did it fall?" And he showed him the place. So ªhe cut off a stick, and threw *it* in there; and he made the iron float. ⁷Therefore he said, "Pick *it* up for yourself." So he reached out his hand and took it.

THE BLINDED SYRIANS CAPTURED

⁸Now the ªking of Syria was making war against Israel; and he consulted with his servants, saying, "My camp *will be* in such and such a place." ⁹And the man of God sent to the king of Israel, saying, "Beware that you do not pass this place, for the Syrians are coming down there." ¹⁰Then the king of Israel sent *someone* to the place of which the man of God had told him. Thus he warned him, and he was watchful there, not just once or twice.

¹¹Therefore the heart of the king of Syria was greatly troubled by this thing; and he called his servants and said to them, "Will you not show me which of us *is* for the king of Israel?"

¹²And one of his servants said, "None, my lord, O king; but Elisha, the prophet who *is* in Israel, tells the king of Israel the words that you speak in your bedroom."

¹³So he said, "Go and see where he *is*, that I may send and get him."

And it was told him, saying, "Surely *he is* in ªDothan."

¹⁴Therefore he sent horses and chariots and a great army there, and they came by night and surrounded the city. ¹⁵And when the servant of the man of God arose early and went out, there was an army, surrounding the city with horses and

---

5:26
ª[Eccl. 3:1, 6]

5:27
ª[1 Tim. 6:10]
ᵇEx. 4:6;
Num. 12:10;
2 Kin. 15:5

6:1 ª2 Kin. 4:38

6:3 ª2 Kin. 5:23

6:5 ª[Ex. 22:14]

6:6 ªEx. 15:25;
2 Kin. 2:21; 4:41

6:8
ª2 Kin. 8:28, 29

6:13 ªGen. 37:17

5:24 ¹Lit. *the hill*

chariots. And his servant said to him, "Alas, my master! What shall we do?"

16So he answered, a"Do not fear, for bthose who *are* with us *are* more than those who *are* with them." 17And Elisha prayed, and said, "LORD, I pray, open his eyes that he may see." Then the LORD aopened the eyes of the young man, and he saw. And behold, the mountain *was* full of bhorses and chariots of fire all around Elisha. 18So when *the Syrians* came down to him, Elisha prayed to the LORD, and said, "Strike this people, I pray, with blindness." And aHe struck them with blindness according to the word of Elisha.

19Now Elisha said to them, "This *is* not the way, nor *is* this the city. Follow me, and I will bring you to the man whom you seek." But he led them to Samaria.

20So it was, when they had come to Samaria, that Elisha said, "LORD, open the eyes of these *men,* that they may see." And the LORD opened their eyes, and they saw; and there *they were,* inside Samaria!

21Now when the king of Israel saw them, he said to Elisha, "My afather, shall I kill *them?* Shall I kill *them?*"

22But he answered, "You shall not kill *them.* Would you kill those whom you have taken captive with your sword and your bow? aSet food and water before them, that they may eat and drink and go to their master." 23Then he prepared a great feast for them; and after they ate and drank, he sent them away and they went to their master. So athe bands of Syrian *raiders* came no more into the land of Israel.

SYRIA BESIEGES SAMARIA IN FAMINE

24And it happened after this that aBen-Hadad king of Syria gathered all his army, and went up and besieged Samaria. 25And there was a great afamine in Samaria; and indeed they besieged it until a donkey's head was *sold* for eighty *shekels* of silver, and one-fourth of a 1kab of dove droppings for five *shekels* of silver.

26Then, as the king of Israel was passing by on the wall, a woman cried out to him, saying, "Help, my lord, O king!"

27And he said, "If the LORD does not help you, where can I find help for you? From the threshing floor or from the winepress?" 28Then the king said to her, "What is troubling you?"

And she answered, "This woman said to me, 'Give your son, that we may eat him today, and we will eat my son tomorrow.' 29So awe boiled my son, and ate him. And I said to her on the next day, 'Give your son, that we may eat him'; but she has hidden her son."

30Now it happened, when the king heard the words of the woman, that he atore his clothes; and as he passed by on the wall, the people looked, and there underneath *he had* sackcloth on his body. 31Then he said, a"God do so to me and more also, if the head of Elisha the son of Shaphat remains on him today!"

32But Elisha was sitting in his house, and athe elders were sitting with him. And *the king* sent a man ahead of him, but before the messenger came to him, he said to the elders, b"Do you see how this son of ca murderer has sent someone to take away my head? Look, when the messenger comes, shut the

6:16 aEx. 14:13;
1 Kin. 17:13
b2 Chr. 32:7;
Ps. 55:18;
[Rom. 8:31]

6:17
aNum. 22:31;
Luke 24:31
b2 Kin. 2:11;
Ps. 34:7; 68:17;
Zech. 1:8; 6:1–7

6:18 aGen. 19:11;
Acts 13:11

6:21 a2 Kin. 2:12;
5:13; 8:9

6:22
a[Rom. 12:20]

6:23 a2 Kin. 5:2;
6:8, 9

6:24 a1 Kin. 20:1

6:25
a2 Kin. 4:38; 8:1

6:29
aLev. 26:27–29;
Deut. 28:52–57;
Lam. 4:10

6:30
a1 Kin. 21:27

6:31 aRuth 1:17;
1 Kin. 19:2

6:32 aEzek. 8:1;
14:1; 20:1
bLuke 13:32
c1 Kin. 18:4, 13,
14; 21:10, 13

6:25 1Approximately 1 pint

door, and hold him fast at the door. *Is* not the sound of his master's feet behind him?" [33]And while he was still talking with them, there was the messenger, coming down to him; and then *the king* said, "Surely this calamity *is* from the LORD; [a]why should I wait for the LORD any longer?"

7 Then Elisha said, "Hear the word of the LORD. Thus says the LORD: [a]"Tomorrow about this time a [1]seah of fine flour *shall be sold* for a shekel, and two seahs of barley for a shekel, at the gate of Samaria.'"

[2a]So an officer on whose hand the king leaned answered the man of God and said, "Look, [b]*if* the LORD would make windows in heaven, could this thing be?"

And he said, "In fact, you shall see *it* with your eyes, but you shall not eat of it."

THE SYRIANS FLEE

[3]Now there were four leprous men [a]at the entrance of the gate; and they said to one another, "Why are we sitting here until we die? [4]If we say, 'We will enter the city,' the famine *is* in the city, and we shall die there. And if we sit here, we die also. Now therefore, come, let us surrender to the [a]army of the Syrians. If they keep us alive, we shall live; and if they kill us, we shall only die." [5]And they rose at twilight to go to the camp of the Syrians; and when they had come to the outskirts of the Syrian camp, to their surprise no one *was* there. [6]For the Lord had caused the army of the Syrians [a]to hear the noise of chariots and the noise of horses—the noise of a great army; so they said to one another, "Look, the king of Israel has hired against us [b]the kings of the Hittites and the kings of the Egyptians to attack us!" [7]Therefore they [a]arose and fled at twilight, and left the camp intact—their tents, their horses, and their donkeys—and they fled for their lives. [8]And when these lepers came to the outskirts of the camp, they went into one tent and ate and drank, and carried from it silver and gold and clothing, and went and hid *them;* then they came back and entered another tent, and carried *some* from there *also,* and went and hid *it.*

[9]Then they said to one another, "We are not doing right. This day *is* a day of good news, and we remain silent. If we wait until morning light, some [1]punishment will come upon us. Now therefore, come, let us go and tell the king's household." [10]So they went and called to the gatekeepers of the city, and told them, saying, "We went to the Syrian camp, and surprisingly no one *was* there, not a human sound—only horses and donkeys tied, and the tents intact." [11]And the gatekeepers called out, and they told *it* to the king's household inside.

[12]So the king arose in the night and said to his servants, "Let me now tell you what the Syrians have done to us. They know that we *are* [a]hungry; therefore they have gone out of the camp to [1]hide themselves in the field, saying, 'When they come out of the city, we shall catch them alive, and get into the city.'"

[13]And one of his servants answered and said, "Please, let several *men* take five of the remaining horses which are left in the city. Look, they *may either become* like all the multitude of

---

6:33 [a]Job 2:9

7:1
[a]2 Kin. 7:18, 19

7:2 [a]2 Kin. 5:18;
7:17, 19, 20
[b]Gen. 7:11;
Mal. 3:10

7:3 [a][Lev. 13:45,
46; Num. 5:2–4;
12:10–14]

7:4 [a]2 Kin. 6:24

7:6
[a]2 Sam. 5:24;
2 Kin. 19:7;
Job 15:21
[b]1 Kin. 10:29

7:7 [a]Ps. 48:4–6;
[Prov. 28:1]

7:12
[a]2 Kin. 6:24–29

7:1 [1]A third of an ephah, or about 8 gallons   7:9 [1]Calamity   7:12 [1]Hide themselves in ambush

Israel that are left in it; or indeed, *I say,* they *may become* like all the multitude of Israel left from those who are consumed; so let us send them and see." ¹⁴Therefore they took two chariots with horses; and the king sent them in the direction of the Syrian army, saying, "Go and see." ¹⁵And they went after them to the Jordan; and indeed all the road *was* full of garments and weapons which the Syrians had thrown away in their haste. So the messengers returned and told the king. ¹⁶Then the people went out and plundered the tents of the Syrians. So a seah of fine flour was *sold* for a shekel, and two seahs of barley for a shekel, ᵃaccording to the word of the LORD.

¹⁷Now the king had appointed the officer on whose hand he leaned to have charge of the gate. But the people trampled him in the gate, and he died, just ᵃas the man of God had said, who spoke when the king came down to him. ¹⁸So it happened just as the man of God had spoken to the king, saying, ᵃ"Two seahs of barley for a shekel, and a seah of fine flour for a shekel, shall be *sold* tomorrow about this time in the gate of Samaria."

¹⁹Then that officer had answered the man of God, and said, "Now look, *if* the LORD would make windows in heaven, could such a thing be?"

And he had said, "In fact, you shall see *it* with your eyes, but you shall not eat of it." ²⁰And so it happened to him, for the people trampled him in the gate, and he died.

THE KING RESTORES THE SHUNAMMITE'S LAND

8 Then Elisha spoke to the woman ᵃwhose son he had restored to life, saying, "Arise and go, you and your household, and stay wherever you can; for the LORD ᵇhas called for a ᶜfamine, and furthermore, it will come upon the land for seven years." ²So the woman arose and did according to the saying of the man of God, and she went with her household and dwelt in the land of the Philistines seven years.

³It came to pass, at the end of seven years, that the woman returned from the land of the Philistines; and she went to make an appeal to the king for her house and for her land. ⁴Then the king talked with ᵃGehazi, the servant of the man of God, saying, "Tell me, please, all the great things Elisha has done." ⁵Now it happened, as he was telling the king how he had restored the dead to life, that there was the woman whose son he had ᵃrestored to life, appealing to the king for her house and for her land. And Gehazi said, "My lord, O king, this *is* the woman, and this *is* her son whom Elisha restored to life." ⁶And when the king asked the woman, she told him.

So the king appointed a certain officer for her, saying, "Restore all that *was* hers, and all the proceeds of the field from the day that she left the land until now."

DEATH OF BEN-HADAD

⁷Then Elisha went to Damascus, and ᵃBen-Hadad king of Syria was sick; and it was told him, saying, "The man of God has come here." ⁸And the king said to ᵃHazael, ᵇ"Take a present in your hand, and go to meet the man of God, and ᶜinquire of the LORD by him, saying, 'Shall I recover from this disease?'" ⁹So ᵃHazael went to meet him and took a present with him, of every good thing of Damascus, forty camel-loads;

7:16 ᵃ2 Kin. 7:1

7:17 ᵃ2 Kin. 6:32; 7:2

7:18 ᵃ2 Kin. 7:1

8:1 ᵃ2 Kin. 4:18, 31–35
ᵇPs. 105:16; Hag. 1:11
ᶜ2 Sam. 21:1; 1 Kin. 18:2; 2 Kin. 4:38; 6:25

8:4 ᵃ2 Kin. 4:12; 5:20–27

8:5 ᵃ2 Kin. 4:35

8:7 ᵃ2 Kin. 6:24

8:8 ᵃ1 Kin. 19:15
ᵇ1 Sam. 9:7; 1 Kin. 14:3; 2 Kin. 5:5
ᶜ2 Kin. 1:2

8:9 ᵃ1 Kin. 19:15

and he came and stood before him, and said, "Your son Ben-Hadad king of Syria has sent me to you, saying, 'Shall I recover from this disease?'"

¹⁰And Elisha said to him, "Go, say to him, 'You shall certainly recover.' However the LORD has shown me that ᵃhe will really die." ¹¹Then he ¹set his countenance in a stare until he was ashamed; and the man of God ᵃwept. ¹²And Hazael said, "Why is my lord weeping?"

He answered, "Because I know ᵃthe evil that you will do to the children of Israel: Their strongholds you will set on fire, and their young men you will kill with the sword; and you ᵇwill dash their children, and rip open their women with child."

¹³So Hazael said, "But what ᵃis your servant—a dog, that he should do this gross thing?"

And Elisha answered, ᵇ"The LORD has shown me that you *will become* king over Syria."

¹⁴Then he departed from Elisha, and came to his master, who said to him, "What did Elisha say to you?" And he answered, "He told me you would surely recover." ¹⁵But it happened on the next day that he took a thick cloth and dipped *it* in water, and spread *it* over his face so that he died; and Hazael reigned in his place.

JEHORAM REIGNS IN JUDAH
(2 Chr. 21:1–20)

¹⁶Now ᵃin the fifth year of Joram the son of Ahab, king of Israel, Jehoshaphat *having been* king of Judah, ᵇJehoram the son of Jehoshaphat began to reign as ¹king of Judah. ¹⁷He was ᵃthirty-two years old when he became king, and he reigned eight years in Jerusalem. ¹⁸And he walked in the way of the kings of Israel, just as the house of Ahab had done, for ᵃthe daughter of Ahab was his wife; and he did evil in the sight of the LORD. ¹⁹Yet the LORD would not destroy Judah, for the sake of His servant David, ᵃas He promised him to give a lamp to him *and* his sons forever.

²⁰In his days ᵃEdom revolted against Judah's authority, ᵇand made a king over themselves. ²¹So ¹Joram went to Zair, and all his chariots with him. Then he rose by night and attacked the Edomites who had surrounded him and the captains of the chariots; and the troops fled to their tents. ²²Thus Edom has been in revolt against Judah's authority to this day. ᵃAnd Libnah revolted at that time.

²³Now the rest of the acts of Joram, and all that he did, *are* they not written in the book of the chronicles of the kings of Judah? ²⁴So Joram ¹rested with his fathers, and was buried with his fathers in the City of David. Then ᵃAhaziah² his son reigned in his place.

AHAZIAH REIGNS IN JUDAH
(2 Chr. 22:1–6)

²⁵In the twelfth year of Joram the son of Ahab, king of Israel, Ahaziah the son of Jehoram, king of Judah, began to reign. ²⁶Ahaziah *was* ᵃtwenty-two years old when he became

---

8:10 ᵃ2 Kin. 8:15
8:11 ᵃLuke 19:41
8:12
ᵃ2 Kin. 10:32;
12:17; 13:3, 7;
Amos 1:3, 4
ᵇ2 Kin. 15:16;
Hos. 13:16;
Amos 1:13;
Nah. 3:10
8:13
ᵃ1 Sam. 17:43;
2 Sam. 9:8
ᵇ1 Kin. 19:15
8:16
ᵃ2 Kin. 1:17; 3:1
ᵇ2 Chr. 21:3
8:17
ᵃ2 Chr. 21:5–10
8:18
ᵃ2 Kin. 8:26, 27
8:19
ᵃ2 Sam. 7:13;
1 Kin. 11:36; 15:4;
2 Chr. 21:7
8:20
ᵃGen. 27:40;
2 Chr. 21:8–10
ᵇ1 Kin. 22:47
8:22
ᵃJosh. 21:13;
2 Kin. 19:8;
2 Chr. 21:10
8:24
ᵃ2 Chr. 22:1, 7
8:26
ᵃ2 Chr. 22:2

8:11 ¹*fixed his gaze*   **8:16** ¹Co-regent with his father   **8:21** ¹*Jehoram*, v. 16
8:24 ¹Died and joined his ancestors   ²Or *Azariah* or *Jehoahaz*

king, and he reigned one year in Jerusalem. His mother's name *was* Athaliah the granddaughter of Omri, king of Israel. [27a]And he walked in the way of the house of Ahab, and did evil in the sight of the Lord, like the house of Ahab, for he *was* the son-in-law of the house of Ahab.

[28]Now he went [a]with Joram the son of Ahab to war against Hazael king of Syria at [b]Ramoth Gilead; and the Syrians wounded Joram. [29]Then [a]King Joram went back to Jezreel to recover from the wounds which the Syrians had inflicted on him at [1]Ramah, when he fought against Hazael king of Syria. [b]And Ahaziah the son of Jehoram, king of Judah, went down to see Joram the son of Ahab in Jezreel, because he was sick.

JEHU ANOINTED KING OF ISRAEL

9 And Elisha the prophet called one of [a]the sons of the prophets, and said to him, [b]"Get[1] yourself ready, take this flask of oil in your hand, [c]and go to Ramoth Gilead. [2]Now when you arrive at that place, look there for Jehu the son of Jehoshaphat, the son of Nimshi, and go in and make him rise up from among [a]his associates, and take him to an inner room. [3]Then [a]take the flask of oil, and pour *it* on his head, and say, 'Thus says the Lord: "I have anointed you king over Israel."' Then open the door and flee, and do not delay."

[4]So the young man, the servant of the prophet, went to Ramoth Gilead. [5]And when he arrived, there *were* the captains of the army sitting; and he said, "I have a message for you, Commander."

Jehu said, "For which *one* of us?"

And he said, "For you, Commander." [6]Then he arose and went into the house. And he poured the oil on his head, and said to him, [a]"Thus says the Lord God of Israel: 'I have anointed you king over the people of the Lord, over Israel. [7]You shall strike down the house of Ahab your master, that I may [a]avenge the blood of My servants the prophets, and the blood of all the servants of the Lord, [b]at the hand of Jezebel. [8]For the whole house of Ahab shall perish; and [a]I will cut off from Ahab all [b]the males in Israel, both [c]bond and free. [9]So I will make the house of Ahab like the house of [a]Jeroboam the son of Nebat, and like the house of [b]Baasha the son of Ahijah. [10a]The dogs shall eat Jezebel on the plot *of ground* at Jezreel, and *there shall be* none to bury *her.*'" And he opened the door and fled.

[11]Then Jehu came out to the servants of his master, and *one* said to him, "*Is* all well? Why did [a]this madman come to you?"

And he said to them, "You know the man and his babble."

[12]And they said, "A lie! Tell us now."

So he said, "Thus and thus he spoke to me, saying, 'Thus says the Lord: "I have anointed you king over Israel."'"

[13]Then each man hastened [a]to take his garment and put *it* [1]under him on the top of the steps; and they blew trumpets, saying, "Jehu is king!"

JORAM OF ISRAEL KILLED

[14]So Jehu the son of Jehoshaphat, the son of Nimshi, conspired against [a]Joram. (Now Joram had been defending Ramoth Gilead, he and all Israel, against Hazael king of Syria.

8:27
[a]2 Chr. 22:3, 4

8:28
[a]2 Chr. 22:5
[b]1 Kin. 22:3, 29

8:29 [a]2 Kin. 9:15
[b]2 Kin. 9:16;
2 Chr. 22:6, 7

9:1 [a]1 Kin. 20:35
[b]2 Kin. 4:29;
Jer. 1:17
[c]2 Kin. 8:28, 29

9:2
[a]2 Kin. 9:5, 11

9:3 [a]1 Kin. 19:16

9:6
[a]1 Sam. 2:7, 8;
1 Kin. 19:16;
2 Kin. 9:3;
2 Chr. 22:7

9:7
[a][Deut. 32:35, 41]
[b]1 Kin. 18:4;
21:15

9:8 [a]1 Kin. 14:10;
21:21; 2 Kin. 10:17
[b]1 Sam. 25:22
[c]Deut. 32:36;
2 Kin. 14:26

9:9 [a]1 Kin. 14:10;
15:29; 21:22
[b]1 Kin. 16:3, 11

9:10
[a]1 Kin. 21:23;
2 Kin. 9:35, 36

9:11 [a]Jer. 29:26;
Hos. 9:7;
Mark 3:21;
John 10:20;
Acts 26:24;
[1 Cor. 4:10]

9:13
[a]Matt. 21:7, 8;
Mark 11:7, 8

9:14 [a]2 Kin. 8:28

15But aKing 1Joram had returned to Jezreel to recover from the wounds which the Syrians had inflicted on him when he fought with Hazael king of Syria.) And Jehu said, "If you are so minded, let no one leave *or* escape from the city to go and tell *it* in Jezreel." 16So Jehu rode in a chariot and went to Jezreel, for Joram was laid up there; aand Ahaziah king of Judah had come down to see Joram.

17Now a watchman stood on the tower in Jezreel, and he saw the company of Jehu as he came, and said, "I see a company of men."

And Joram said, "Get a horseman and send him to meet them, and let him say, 1'*Is it* peace?'"

18So the horseman went to meet him, and said, "Thus says the king: '*Is it* peace?'"

And Jehu said, "What have you to do with peace? 1Turn around and follow me."

So the watchman reported, saying, "The messenger went to them, but is not coming back."

19Then he sent out a second horseman who came to them, and said, "Thus says the king: '*Is it* peace?'"

And Jehu answered, "What have you to do with peace? Turn around and follow me."

20So the watchman reported, saying, "He went up to them and is not coming back; and the driving *is* like the driving of Jehu the son of Nimshi, for he drives furiously!"

21Then Joram said, 1"Make ready." And his chariot was made ready. Then aJoram king of Israel and Ahaziah king of Judah went out, each in his chariot; and they went out to meet Jehu, and 2met him bon the property of Naboth the Jezreelite. 22Now it happened, when Joram saw Jehu, that he said, "*Is it* peace, Jehu?"

So he answered, "What peace, as long as the harlotries of your mother Jezebel and her witchcraft *are so* many?"

23Then Joram turned around and fled, and said to Ahaziah, "Treachery, Ahaziah!" 24Now Jehu 1drew his bow with full strength and shot Jehoram between his arms; and the arrow came out at his heart, and he sank down in his chariot. 25Then *Jehu* said to Bidkar his captain, "Pick *him* up, *and* throw him into the tract of the field of Naboth the Jezreelite; for remember, when you and I were riding together behind Ahab his father, that athe LORD laid this bburden upon him: 26'Surely I saw yesterday the blood of Naboth and the blood of his sons,' says the LORD, a'and I will repay you 1in this plot,' says the LORD. Now therefore, take *and* throw him on the plot *of ground,* according to the word of the LORD."

AHAZIAH OF JUDAH KILLED
(2 Chr. 22:7–9)

27But when Ahaziah king of Judah saw *this,* he fled by the road to 1Beth Haggan. So Jehu pursued him, and said, 2"Shoot him also in the chariot." *And they shot him* at the Ascent of Gur, which is by Ibleam. Then he fled to aMegiddo, and died there. 28And his servants carried him in the chariot to Jerusalem, and buried him in his tomb with his fathers in the City of

9:15 a2 Kin. 8:29
9:16 a2 Kin. 8:29
9:21 a1 Kin. 19:17; 2 Chr. 22:7
b1 Kin. 21:1–14
9:25 a1 Kin. 21:19, 24–29
bIs. 13:1
9:26 a1 Kin. 21:13, 19
9:27 a2 Chr. 22:7, 9

9:15 1*Jehoram,* v. 24   9:17 1Are you peaceful?   9:18 1Lit. *Turn behind me*
9:21 1*Harness up*   2Lit. *found*   9:24 1Lit. *filled his hand*   9:26 1*on this property*   9:27 1Lit. *The Garden House*   2Lit. *Strike*

David. [29]In the eleventh year of Joram the son of Ahab, Ahaziah had become king over Judah.

JEZEBEL'S VIOLENT DEATH

[30]Now when Jehu had come to Jezreel, Jezebel heard *of it;* [a]and she put paint on her eyes and adorned her head, and looked through a window. [31]Then, as Jehu entered at the gate, she said, [a]*"Is it* peace, Zimri, murderer of your master?"

[32]And he looked up at the window, and said, "Who *is* on my side? Who?" So two *or* three eunuchs looked out at him. [33]Then he said, "Throw her down." So they threw her down, and *some* of her blood spattered on the wall and on the horses; and he trampled her underfoot. [34]And when he had gone in, he ate and drank. Then he said, "Go now, see to this accursed *woman,* and bury her, for [a]she was a king's daughter." [35]So they went to bury her, but they found no more of her than the skull and the feet and the palms of *her* hands. [36]Therefore they came back and told him. And he said, "This *is* the word of the LORD, which He spoke by His servant Elijah the Tishbite, saying, [a]'On the plot *of ground* at Jezreel dogs shall eat the flesh of Jezebel; [37]and the corpse of Jezebel shall be [a]as refuse on the surface of the field, in the plot at Jezreel, so that they shall not say, "Here *lies* Jezebel."'"

AHAB'S SEVENTY SONS KILLED

10 Now Ahab had seventy sons in Samaria. And Jehu wrote and sent letters to Samaria, to the rulers of [1]Jezreel, to the elders, and to [2]those who reared Ahab's *sons,* saying:

2   Now as soon as this letter comes to you, since your master's sons *are* with you, and you have chariots and horses, a fortified city also, and weapons, [3]choose the [1]best qualified of your master's sons, set *him* on his father's throne, and fight for your master's house.

[4]But they were exceedingly afraid, and said, "Look, [a]two kings could not [1]stand up to him; how then can we stand?" [5]And he who *was* in charge of the house, and he who *was* in charge of the city, the elders also, and those who reared *the sons,* sent to Jehu, saying, "We *are* your servants, we will do all you tell us; but we will not make anyone king. Do *what is* good in your sight." [6]Then he wrote a second letter to them, saying:

If you *are* for me and will obey my voice, take the heads of the men, your master's sons, and come to me at Jezreel by this time tomorrow.

Now the king's sons, seventy persons, *were* with the great men of the city, *who* were rearing them. [7]So it was, when the letter came to them, that they took the king's sons and [a]slaughtered seventy persons, put their heads in baskets and sent *them* to him at Jezreel.

[8]Then a messenger came and told him, saying, "They have brought the heads of the king's sons."

And he said, "Lay them in two heaps at the entrance of the gate until morning."

9:30 [a][Jer. 4:30]; Ezek. 23:40
9:31 [a]1 Kin. 16:9–20; 2 Kin. 9:18–22
9:34 [a][Ex. 22:28]; 1 Kin. 16:31
9:36 [a]1 Kin. 21:23
9:37 [a]Ps. 83:10
10:4 [a]2 Kin. 9:24, 27
10:7 [a]Judg. 9:5; 1 Kin. 21:21; 2 Kin. 11:1

10:1 [1]So with MT, Syr., Tg.; LXX *Samaria;* Vg. *city*   [2]*the guardians of*
10:3 [1]*most upright*   10:4 [1]Lit. *stand before*

9So it was, in the morning, that he went out and stood, and said to all the people, "You *are* righteous. Indeed aI conspired against my master and killed him; but who killed all these? 10Know now that nothing shall afall to the earth of the word of the LORD which the LORD spoke concerning the house of Ahab; for the LORD has done what He spoke bby His servant Elijah." 11So Jehu killed all who remained of the house of Ahab in Jezreel, and all his great men and his close acquaintances and his priests, until he left him none remaining.

AHAZIAH'S FORTY-TWO BROTHERS KILLED

12And he arose and departed and went to Samaria. On the way, at 1Beth Eked of the Shepherds, 13aJehu met with the brothers of Ahaziah king of Judah, and said, "Who *are* you?"

So they answered, "We *are* the brothers of Ahaziah; we have come down to greet the sons of the king and the sons of the queen mother."

14And he said, "Take them alive!" So they took them alive, and akilled them at the well of 1Beth Eked, forty-two men; and he left none of them.

THE REST OF AHAB'S FAMILY KILLED

15Now when he departed from there, he 1met aJehonadab the son of bRechab, *coming* to meet him; and he greeted him and said to him, "Is your heart right, as my heart *is* toward your heart?"

And Jehonadab answered, "It is."

Jehu said, "If it is, cgive *me* your hand." So he gave *him* his hand, and he took him up to him into the chariot. 16Then he said, "Come with me, and see my azeal for the LORD." So they had him ride in his chariot. 17And when he came to Samaria, ahe killed all who remained to Ahab in Samaria, till he had destroyed them, according to the word of the LORD bwhich He spoke to Elijah.

WORSHIPERS OF BAAL KILLED

18Then Jehu gathered all the people together, and said to them, a"Ahab served Baal a little, Jehu will serve him much. 19Now therefore, call to me all the aprophets of Baal, all his servants, and all his priests. Let no one be missing, for I have a great sacrifice for Baal. Whoever is missing shall not live." But Jehu acted deceptively, with the intent of destroying the worshipers of Baal. 20And Jehu said, 1"Proclaim a solemn assembly for Baal." So they proclaimed *it.* 21Then Jehu sent throughout all Israel; and all the worshipers of Baal came, so that there was not a man left who did not come. So they came into the 1temple of Baal, and the atemple of Baal was full from one end to the other. 22And he said to the one in charge of the wardrobe, "Bring out vestments for all the worshipers of Baal." So he brought out vestments for them. 23Then Jehu and Jehonadab the son of Rechab went into the temple of Baal, and said to the worshipers of Baal, "Search and see that no servants of the LORD are here with you, but only the worshipers of Baal." 24So they went in to offer sacrifices and burnt offerings. Now Jehu had appointed for himself eighty men

10:9
a2 Kin. 9:14–24

10:10
a1 Sam. 3:19;
1 Kin. 8:56;
Jer. 44:28
b1 Kin. 21:17–24, 29

10:13
a2 Chr. 22:8

10:14
a2 Chr. 22:8

10:15 aJer. 35:6
b1 Chr. 2:55
cEzra 10:19;
Ezek. 17:18

10:16
a1 Kin. 19:10

10:17 a2 Kin. 9:8;
2 Chr. 22:8
b1 Kin. 21:21, 29

10:18
a1 Kin. 16:31, 32

10:19
a1 Kin. 18:19;
22:6

10:21
a1 Kin. 16:32;
2 Kin. 11:18

10:12 1Or *The Shearing House*   10:14 1Or *The Shearing House*   10:15 1Lit. *found*   10:20 1Consecrate   10:21 1Lit. *house*

on the outside, and had said, "*If* any of the men whom I have brought into your hands escapes, *whoever lets him escape, it shall be* ᵃhis life for the life of the other."

²⁵Now it happened, as soon as he had made an end of offering the burnt offering, that Jehu said to the guard and to the captains, "Go in *and* kill them; let no one come out!" And they killed them with the edge of the sword; then the guards and the officers threw *them* out, and went into the ¹inner room of the temple of Baal. ²⁶And they brought the ᵃsacred pillars out of the temple of Baal and burned them. ²⁷Then they broke down the *sacred* pillar of Baal, and tore down the ¹temple of Baal and ᵃmade it a refuse dump to this day. ²⁸Thus Jehu destroyed Baal from Israel.

²⁹However Jehu did not turn away from the sins of Jeroboam the son of Nebat, who had made Israel sin, *that is,* from ᵃthe golden calves that *were* at Bethel and Dan. ³⁰And the LORD ᵃsaid to Jehu, "Because you have done well in doing *what is* right in My sight, *and* have done to the house of Ahab all that *was* in My heart, ᵇyour sons shall sit on the throne of Israel to the fourth *generation.*" ³¹But Jehu ¹took no heed to walk in the law of the LORD God of Israel with all his heart; for he did not depart from ᵃthe sins of Jeroboam, who had made Israel sin.

DEATH OF JEHU

³²In those days the LORD began to cut off *parts* of Israel; and ᵃHazael conquered them in all the territory of Israel ³³from the Jordan eastward: all the land of Gilead—Gad, Reuben, and Manasseh—from ᵃAroer, which *is* by the River Arnon, including ᵇGilead and Bashan.

³⁴Now the rest of the acts of Jehu, all that he did, and all his might, *are* they not written in the book of the chronicles of the kings of Israel? ³⁵So Jehu ¹rested with his fathers, and they buried him in Samaria. Then ᵃJehoahaz his son reigned in his place. ³⁶And the period that Jehu reigned over Israel in Samaria *was* twenty-eight years.

ATHALIAH REIGNS IN JUDAH
(2 Chr. 22:10–12)

11 When ᵃAthaliah ᵇthe mother of Ahaziah saw that her son was ᶜdead, she arose and destroyed all the royal heirs. ²But ¹Jehosheba, the daughter of King Joram, sister of ᵃAhaziah, took ²Joash the son of Ahaziah, and stole him away from among the king's sons *who were* being murdered; and they hid him and his nurse in the bedroom, from Athaliah, so that he was not killed. ³So he was hidden with her in the house of the LORD for six years, while Athaliah reigned over the land.

JOASH CROWNED KING OF JUDAH
(2 Chr. 23:1–11)

⁴In ᵃthe seventh year Jehoiada sent and brought the captains of hundreds—of the bodyguards and the ¹escorts—and brought them into the house of the LORD to him. And he made a covenant with them and took an oath from them

---

10:24
ᵃ1 Kin. 20:39

10:26
ᵃ[Deut. 7:5, 25]; 1 Kin. 14:23; 2 Kin. 3:2

10:27 ᵃEzra 6:11; Dan. 2:5; 3:29

10:29
ᵃ1 Kin. 12:28–30; 13:33, 34

10:30
ᵃ2 Kin. 9:6, 7
ᵇ2 Kin. 13:1, 10; 14:23; 15:8, 12

10:31
ᵃ1 Kin. 14:16

10:32
ᵃ1 Kin. 19:17; 2 Kin. 8:12; 13:22

10:33
ᵃDeut. 2:36
ᵇAmos 1:3–5

10:35 ᵃ2 Kin. 13:1

11:1 ᵃ2 Chr. 22:10
ᵇ2 Kin. 8:26
ᶜ2 Kin. 9:27

11:2 ᵃ2 Kin. 8:25

11:4 ᵃ2 Kin. 12:2; 2 Chr. 23:1

10:25 ¹Lit. *city*   10:27 ¹Lit. *house*   10:31 ¹*was not careful*   10:35 ¹Died and joined his ancestors   11:2 ¹*Jehoshabeath,* 2 Chr. 22:11   ²Or *Jehoash*   11:4 ¹*guards*

in the house of the LORD, and showed them the king's son. ⁵Then he commanded them, saying, "This *is* what you shall do: One-third of you who ¹come on duty ªon the Sabbath shall be keeping watch over the king's house, ⁶one-third *shall be* at the gate of Sur, and one-third at the gate behind the escorts. You shall keep the watch of the house, lest it be broken down. ⁷The two ¹contingents of you who go off duty on the Sabbath shall keep the watch of the house of the LORD for the king. ⁸But you shall surround the king on all sides, every man with his weapons in his hand; and whoever comes within range, let him be put to death. You are to be with the king as he goes out and as he comes in."

⁹ªSo the captains of the hundreds did according to all that Jehoiada the priest commanded. Each of them took his men who were to be on duty on the Sabbath, with those who were going off duty on the Sabbath, and came to Jehoiada the priest. ¹⁰And the priest gave the captains of hundreds the spears and shields which *had belonged* to King David, ªthat were in the temple of the LORD. ¹¹Then the escorts stood, every man with his weapons in his hand, all around the king, from the right ¹side of the temple to the left side of the temple, by the altar and the house. ¹²And he brought out the king's son, put the crown on him, and *gave him* the ªTestimony;¹ they made him king and anointed him, and they clapped their hands and said, ᵇ"Long live the king!"

DEATH OF ATHALIAH
(2 Chr. 23:12—24:1)

¹³ªNow when Athaliah heard the noise of the escorts *and* the people, she came to the people *in* the temple of the LORD. ¹⁴When she looked, there was the king standing by ªa pillar according to custom; and the leaders and the trumpeters were by the king. All the people of the land were rejoicing and blowing trumpets. So Athaliah tore her clothes and cried out, "Treason! Treason!"

¹⁵And Jehoiada the priest commanded the captains of the hundreds, the officers of the army, and said to them, "Take her outside ¹under guard, and slay with the sword whoever follows her." For the priest had said, "Do not let her be killed in the house of the LORD." ¹⁶So they seized her; and she went by way of the horses' entrance *into* the king's house, and there she was killed.

¹⁷ªThen Jehoiada ᵇmade a covenant between the LORD, the king, and the people, that they should be the LORD's people, and *also* ᶜbetween the king and the people. ¹⁸And all the people of the land went to the ªtemple of Baal, and tore it down. They thoroughly ᵇbroke in pieces its altars and ¹images, and ᶜkilled Mattan the priest of Baal before the altars. And ᵈthe priest appointed ²officers over the house of the LORD. ¹⁹Then he took the captains of hundreds, the bodyguards, the escorts, and all the people of the land; and they brought the king down from the house of the LORD, and went by way of the gate of the escorts to the king's house. Then he sat on the throne of the kings. ²⁰So all the people of the land rejoiced; and the city was quiet, for they had slain Athaliah with the

---

11:5 ª1 Chr. 9:25
11:9 ª2 Chr. 23:8
11:10
ª2 Sam. 8:7;
1 Chr. 18:7
11:12 ªEx. 25:16;
31:18
ᵇ1 Sam. 10:24
11:13
ª2 Kin. 8:26;
2 Chr. 23:12
11:14
ª2 Kin. 23:3;
2 Chr. 34:31
11:17
ª2 Chr. 23:16
ᵇJosh. 24:24, 25;
2 Chr. 15:12–15
ᶜ2 Sam. 5:3
11:18
ª2 Kin. 10:26, 27
ᵇ[Deut. 12:3]
ᶜ1 Kin. 18:40;
2 Kin. 10:11
ᵈ2 Chr. 23:18

11:5 ¹Lit. *enter in*   **11:7** ¹*companies*   **11:11** ¹Lit. *shoulder*   **11:12** ¹*Law*, Ex. 25:16, 21; Deut. 31:9   **11:15** ¹Lit. *between ranks*   **11:18** ¹*Idols*   ²Lit. *offices*

sword *in* the king's house. [21]Jehoash *was* [a]seven years old when he became king.

JEHOASH REPAIRS THE TEMPLE
(2 Chr. 24:1–14)

12 In the seventh year of Jehu, [a]Jehoash[1] became king, and he reigned forty years in Jerusalem. His mother's name *was* Zibiah of Beersheba. [2]Jehoash did *what was* right in the sight of the LORD all the days in which [a]Jehoiada the priest instructed him. [3]But [a]the [1]high places were not taken away; the people still sacrificed and burned incense on the high places.

[4]And Jehoash said to the priests, [a]"All the money of the dedicated gifts that are brought into the house of the LORD— each man's [b]census[1] money, each man's [c]assessment money— *and* all the money that [2]a man [d]purposes in his heart to bring into the house of the LORD, [5]let the priests take *it* themselves, each from his constituency; and let them repair the [1]damages of the temple, wherever any dilapidation is found."

[6]Now it was so, by the twenty-third year of King Jehoash, [a]*that* the priests had not repaired the damages of the temple. [7a]So King Jehoash called Jehoiada the priest and the *other* priests, and said to them, "Why have you not repaired the damages of the temple? Now therefore, do not take *more* money from your constituency, but deliver it for repairing the damages of the temple." [8]And the priests agreed that they would neither receive *more* money from the people, nor repair the damages of the temple.

[9]Then Jehoiada the priest took [a]a chest, bored a hole in its lid, and set it beside the altar, on the right side as one comes into the house of the LORD; and the priests who [1]kept the door put [b]there all the money brought into the house of the LORD. [10]So it was, whenever they saw that *there was* much money in the chest, that the king's [a]scribe[1] and the high priest came up and [2]put it in bags, and counted the money that was found in the house of the LORD. [11]Then they gave the money, which had been apportioned, into the hands of those who did the work, who had the oversight of the house of the LORD; and they [1]paid it out to the carpenters and builders who worked on the house of the LORD, [12]and to masons and stonecutters, and for buying timber and hewn stone, to [a]repair the damage of the house of the LORD, and for all that was paid out to repair the temple. [13]However [a]there were not made for the house of the LORD basins of silver, trimmers, sprinkling-bowls, trumpets, any articles of gold or articles of silver, from the money brought into the house of the LORD. [14]But they gave that to the workmen, and they repaired the house of the LORD with it. [15]Moreover [a]they did not require an account from the men into whose hand they delivered the money to be paid to workmen, for they dealt faithfully. [16a]The money from the trespass offerings and the money from the sin offerings was not brought into the house of the LORD. [b]It belonged to the priests.

11:21
[a]2 Chr. 24:1–14

12:1 [a]2 Chr. 24:1

12:2 [a]2 Kin. 11:4

12:3 [a]1 Kin. 15:14; 22:43;
2 Kin. 14:4; 15:35

12:4 [a]2 Kin. 22:4
[b]Ex. 30:13–16
[c]Lev. 27:2–28
[d]Ex. 35:5;
1 Chr. 29:3–9

12:6 [a]2 Chr. 24:5

12:7 [a]2 Chr. 24:6

12:9 [a]2 Chr. 23:1; 24:8
[b]Mark 12:41;
Luke 21:1

12:10
[a]2 Sam. 8:17;
2 Kin. 19:2; 22:3, 4, 12

12:12
[a]2 Kin. 22:5, 6

12:13
[a]2 Chr. 24:14

12:15
[a]2 Kin. 22:7;
[1 Cor. 4:2];
2 Cor. 8:20

12:16
[a][Lev. 5:15, 18]
[b][Lev. 7:7;
Num. 18:9]

12:1 [1]*Joash,* 2 Kin. 11:2ff.   **12:3** [1]Places for pagan worship   **12:4** [1]Lit. *the money coming over*   [2]*any man's heart prompts him to bring*   **12:5** [1]Lit. *breaches*   **12:9** [1]*guarded at the door*   **12:10** [1]*secretary*   [2]*tied it up*   **12:11** [1]Lit. *weighed*

HAZAEL THREATENS JERUSALEM

17aHazael king of Syria went up and fought against Gath, and took it; then bHazael set his face to 1go up to Jerusalem. 18And Jehoash king of Judah atook all the sacred things that his fathers, Jehoshaphat and Jehoram and Ahaziah, kings of Judah, had dedicated, and his own sacred things, and all the gold found in the treasuries of the house of the LORD and in the king's house, and sent *them* to Hazael king of Syria. Then he went away from Jerusalem.

DEATH OF JOASH
(2 Chr. 24:23–27)

19Now the rest of the acts of 1Joash, and all that he did, *are* they not written in the book of the chronicles of the kings of Judah?

20And ahis servants arose and formed a conspiracy, and killed Joash in the house of 1the Millo, which goes down to Silla. 21For 1Jozachar the son of Shimeath and Jehozabad the son of 2Shomer, his servants, struck him. So he died, and they buried him with his fathers in the City of David. Then aAmaziah his son reigned in his place.

JEHOAHAZ REIGNS IN ISRAEL

13 In the twenty-third year of aJoash1 the son of Ahaziah, king of Judah, bJehoahaz the son of Jehu became king over Israel in Samaria, *and reigned* seventeen years. 2And he did evil in the sight of the LORD, and followed the asins of Jeroboam the son of Nebat, who had made Israel sin. He did not 1depart from them.

3Then athe anger of the LORD was aroused against Israel, and He delivered them into the hand of bHazael king of Syria, and into the hand of cBen-Hadad the son of Hazael, all *their* days. 4So Jehoahaz apleaded with the LORD, and the LORD listened to him; for bHe saw the oppression of Israel, because the king of Syria oppressed them. 5aThen the LORD gave Israel a deliverer, so that they escaped from under the hand of the Syrians; and the children of Israel dwelt in their tents as before. 6Nevertheless they did not depart from the sins of the house of Jeroboam, who had made Israel sin, *but* walked in them; aand the 1wooden image also remained in Samaria. 7For He left of the army of Jehoahaz only fifty horsemen, ten chariots, and ten thousand foot soldiers; for the king of Syria had destroyed them aand made them blike the dust at threshing.

8Now the rest of the acts of Jehoahaz, all that he did, and his might, *are* they not written in the book of the chronicles of the kings of Israel? 9So Jehoahaz 1rested with his fathers, and they buried him in Samaria. Then 2Joash his son reigned in his place.

JEHOASH REIGNS IN ISRAEL

10In the thirty-seventh year of Joash king of Judah, 1Jehoash the son of Jehoahaz became king over Israel in Samaria,

---

12:17 a2 Kin. 8:12
b2 Chr. 24:23

12:18
a1 Kin. 15:18;
2 Kin. 16:8;
18:15, 16

12:20
a2 Kin. 14:5;
2 Chr. 24:25

12:21
a2 Chr. 24:27

13:1 a2 Kin. 12:1
b2 Kin. 10:35

13:2
a1 Kin. 12:26–33

13:3 aJudg. 2:14
b2 Kin. 8:12
cAmos 1:4

13:4 a[Ps. 78:34]
b[Ex. 3:7, 9;
Judg. 2:18];
2 Kin. 14:26

13:5
a2 Kin. 13:25;
14:25, 27;
Neh. 9:27

13:6 a1 Kin. 16:33

13:7
a2 Kin. 10:32
b[Amos 1:3]

12:17 1Advance upon   12:19 1Jehoash, vv. 1–18   12:20 1Lit. The Landfill
12:21 1Zabad, 2 Chr. 24:26   2Shimrith, 2 Chr. 24:26   13:1 1Jehoash, 2 Kin.
12:1–18   13:2 1Lit. turn   13:6 1Heb. Asherah, a Canaanite goddess
13:9 1Died and joined his ancestors   2Or Jehoash   13:10 1Joash, v. 9

and reigned sixteen years. ¹¹And he did evil in the sight of the LORD. He did not depart from all the sins of Jeroboam the son of Nebat, who made Israel sin, *but* walked in them.

¹²ᵃNow the rest of the acts of Joash, ᵇall that he did, and ᶜhis might with which he fought against Amaziah king of Judah, *are* they not written in the book of the chronicles of the kings of Israel? ¹³So Joash ᵃrested¹ with his fathers. Then Jeroboam sat on his throne. And Joash was buried in Samaria with the kings of Israel.

DEATH OF ELISHA

¹⁴Elisha had become sick with the illness of which he would die. Then Joash the king of Israel came down to him, and wept over his face, and said, "O my father, my father, ᵃthe chariots of Israel and their horsemen!"

¹⁵And Elisha said to him, "Take a bow and some arrows." So he took himself a bow and some arrows. ¹⁶Then he said to the king of Israel, "Put your hand on the bow." So he put his hand *on it*, and Elisha put his hands on the king's hands. ¹⁷And he said, "Open the east window"; and he opened *it*. Then Elisha said, "Shoot"; and he shot. And he said, "The arrow of the LORD's deliverance and the arrow of deliverance from Syria; for you must strike the Syrians at ᵃAphek till you have destroyed *them*." ¹⁸Then he said, "Take the arrows"; so he took *them*. And he said to the king of Israel, "Strike the ground"; so he struck three times, and stopped. ¹⁹And the man of God was angry with him, and said, "You should have struck five or six times; then you would have struck Syria till you had destroyed *it!* ᵃBut now you will strike Syria *only* three times."

²⁰Then Elisha ¹died, and they buried him. And the ᵃ*raiding* bands from Moab invaded the land in the spring of the year. ²¹So it was, as they were burying a man, that suddenly they spied a band *of raiders;* and they put the man in the tomb of Elisha; and when the man was let down and touched the bones of Elisha, he revived and stood on his feet.

ISRAEL RECAPTURES CITIES FROM SYRIA

²²And ᵃHazael king of Syria oppressed Israel all the days of Jehoahaz. ²³But the LORD was ᵃgracious to them, had compassion on them, and ᵇregarded them, ᶜbecause of His covenant with Abraham, Isaac, and Jacob, and would not yet destroy them or cast them from His presence.

²⁴Now Hazael king of Syria died. Then Ben-Hadad his son reigned in his place. ²⁵And ¹Jehoash the son of Jehoahaz recaptured from the hand of Ben-Hadad, the son of Hazael, the cities which he had taken out of the hand of Jehoahaz his father by war. ᵃThree times Joash defeated him and recaptured the cities of Israel.

AMAZIAH REIGNS IN JUDAH
(2 Chr. 25:1—26:2)

14 In ᵃthe second year of Joash the son of Jehoahaz, king of Israel, ᵇAmaziah the son of Joash, king of Judah, became king. ²He was twenty-five years old when he became king, and he reigned twenty-nine years in Jerusalem. His

---

13:12
ᵃ 2 Kin. 14:8–15
ᵇ 2 Kin. 13:14–19, 25 ᶜ 2 Kin. 14:9; 2 Chr. 25:17–25

13:13
ᵃ 2 Kin. 14:16

13:14 ᵃ 2 Kin. 2:12

13:17
ᵃ 1 Kin. 20:26

13:19
ᵃ 2 Kin. 13:25

13:20
ᵃ 2 Kin. 3:5; 24:2

13:22
ᵃ 2 Kin. 8:12, 13

13:23
ᵃ 2 Kin. 14:27
ᵇ [Ex. 2:24, 25]
ᶜ Gen. 13:16, 17; 17:2–7; Ex. 32:13

13:25
ᵃ 2 Kin. 13:18, 19

14:1 ᵃ 2 Kin. 13:10
ᵇ 2 Chr. 25:1, 2

13:13 ¹Died and joined his ancestors   13:20 ¹Having prophesied at least 55 years   13:25 ¹*Joash*, vv. 12–14, 25

mother's name was Jehoaddan of Jerusalem. ³And he did *what was* right in the sight of the LORD, yet not like his father David; he did everything ᵃas his father Joash had done. ⁴ᵃHowever the ¹high places were not taken away, and the people still sacrificed and burned incense on the high places.

⁵Now it happened, as soon as the kingdom was established in his hand, that he executed his servants ᵃwho had murdered his father the king. ⁶But the children of the murderers he did not execute, according to what is written in the Book of the Law of Moses, in which the LORD commanded, saying, ᵃ"Fathers shall not be put to death for their children, nor shall children be put to death for their fathers; but a person shall be put to death for his own sin."

⁷ᵃHe killed ten thousand Edomites in ᵇthe Valley of Salt, and took ¹Sela by war, ᶜand called its name Joktheel to this day.

⁸ᵃThen Amaziah sent messengers to ¹Jehoash the son of Jehoahaz, the son of Jehu, king of Israel, saying, "Come, let us face one another *in battle*." ⁹And Jehoash king of Israel sent to Amaziah king of Judah, saying, ᵃ"The thistle that *was* in Lebanon sent to the ᵇcedar that *was* in Lebanon, saying, 'Give your daughter to my son as wife'; and a wild beast that *was* in Lebanon passed by and trampled the thistle. ¹⁰You have indeed defeated Edom, and ᵃyour heart has ¹lifted you up. Glory *in that,* and stay at home; for why should you meddle with trouble so that you fall—you and Judah with you?"

¹¹But Amaziah would not heed. Therefore Jehoash king of Israel went out; so he and Amaziah king of Judah faced one another at ᵃBeth Shemesh, which *belongs* to Judah. ¹²And Judah was defeated by Israel, and every man fled to his tent. ¹³Then Jehoash king of Israel captured Amaziah king of Judah, the son of Jehoash, the son of Ahaziah, at Beth Shemesh; and he went to Jerusalem, and broke down the wall of Jerusalem from ᵃthe Gate of Ephraim to ᵇthe Corner Gate—¹four hundred cubits. ¹⁴And he took all ᵃthe gold and silver, all the articles that were found in the house of the LORD and in the treasuries of the king's house, and hostages, and returned to Samaria.

¹⁵ᵃNow the rest of the acts of Jehoash which he did—his might, and how he fought with Amaziah king of Judah—*are* they not written in the book of the chronicles of the kings of Israel? ¹⁶So Jehoash ¹rested with his fathers, and was buried in Samaria with the kings of Israel. Then Jeroboam his son reigned in his place.

¹⁷ᵃAmaziah the son of Joash, king of Judah, lived fifteen years after the death of Jehoash the son of Jehoahaz, king of Israel. ¹⁸Now the rest of the acts of Amaziah, *are* they not written in the book of the chronicles of the kings of Judah? ¹⁹And ᵃthey formed a conspiracy against him in Jerusalem, and he fled to ᵇLachish; but they sent after him to Lachish and killed him there. ²⁰Then they brought him on horses, and he was buried at Jerusalem with his fathers in the City of David.

²¹And all the people of Judah took ᵃAzariah,¹ who *was* sixteen years old, and made him king instead of his father Amaziah. ²²He built ᵃElath¹ and restored it to Judah, after ²the king rested with his fathers.

14:3 ᵃ2 Kin. 12:2
14:4 ᵃ2 Kin. 12:3
14:5 ᵃ2 Kin. 12:20
14:6 ᵃDeut. 24:16; [Jer. 31:30; Ezek. 18:4, 20]
14:7 ᵃ2 Chr. 25:5–16 ᵇ2 Sam. 8:13; 1 Chr. 18:12; Ps. 60:title ᶜJosh. 15:38
14:8 ᵃ2 Chr. 25:17, 18
14:9 ᵃJudg. 9:8–15 ᵇ1 Kin. 4:33
14:10 ᵃDeut. 8:14; 2 Chr. 32:25; [Ezek. 28:2, 5, 17; Hab. 2:4]
14:11 ᵃJosh. 19:38; 21:16
14:13 ᵃNeh. 8:16; 12:39 ᵇJer. 31:38; Zech. 14:10
14:14 ᵃ1 Kin. 7:51; 2 Kin. 12:18; 16:8
14:15 ᵃ2 Kin. 13:12, 13
14:17 ᵃ2 Chr. 25:25–28
14:19 ᵃ2 Chr. 25:27 ᵇJosh. 10:31
14:21 ᵃ2 Kin. 15:13; 2 Chr. 26:1
14:22 ᵃ1 Kin. 9:26; 2 Kin. 16:6; 2 Chr. 8:17

14:4 ¹Places for pagan worship   **14:7** ¹Lit. *The Rock;* the city of Petra
14:8 ¹*Joash,* 2 Kin. 13:9, 12–14, 25; 2 Chr. 25:17ff.   **14:10** ¹Made you proud
14:13 ¹About 600 feet   **14:16** ¹Died and joined his ancestors
14:21 ¹*Uzziah,* 2 Chr. 26:1ff.; Is. 6:1; etc.   **14:22** ¹Heb. *Eloth*   ²Amaziah died and joined his ancestors.

JEROBOAM II REIGNS IN ISRAEL

23In the fifteenth year of Amaziah the son of Joash, king of Judah, Jeroboam the son of Joash, king of Israel, became king in Samaria, *and reigned* forty-one years. 24And he did evil in the sight of the LORD; he did not depart from all the asins of Jeroboam the son of Nebat, who had made Israel sin. 25He arestored the 1territory of Israel bfrom the entrance of Hamath to cthe2 Sea of the Arabah, according to the word of the LORD God of Israel, which He had spoken through His servant dJonah the son of Amittai, the prophet who *was* from eGath Hepher. 26For the LORD asaw *that* the affliction of Israel *was* very bitter; and whether bond or free, bthere was no helper for Israel. 27aAnd the LORD did not say that He would blot out the name of Israel from under heaven; but He saved them by the hand of Jeroboam the son of Joash.

28Now the rest of the acts of Jeroboam, and all that he did—his might, how he made war, and how he recaptured for Israel, from aDamascus and Hamath, b*what had belonged* to Judah—*are* they not written in the book of the chronicles of the kings of Israel? 29So Jeroboam 1rested with his fathers, the kings of Israel. Then aZechariah his son reigned in his place.

AZARIAH REIGNS IN JUDAH
(2 Chr. 26:3–23)

15 In the twenty-seventh year of Jeroboam king of Israel, aAzariah the son of Amaziah, king of Judah, bbecame king. 2He was sixteen years old when he became king, and he reigned fifty-two years in Jerusalem. His mother's name *was* Jecholiah of Jerusalem. 3And he did *what was* right in the sight of the LORD, according to all that his father Amaziah had done, 4aexcept that the 1high places were not removed; the people still sacrificed and burned incense on the high places. 5Then the LORD astruck the king, so that he was a leper until the day of his bdeath; so he cdwelt in an isolated house. And Jotham the king's son *was* over the *royal* house, judging the people of the land.

6Now the rest of the acts of Azariah, and all that he did, *are* they not written in the book of the chronicles of the kings of Judah? 7So Azariah 1rested with his fathers, and athey buried him with his fathers in the City of David. Then Jotham his son reigned in his place.

ZECHARIAH REIGNS IN ISRAEL

8In the thirty-eighth year of Azariah king of Judah, aZechariah the son of Jeroboam reigned over Israel in Samaria six months. 9And he did evil in the sight of the LORD, aas his fathers had done; he did not depart from the sins of Jeroboam the son of Nebat, who had made Israel sin. 10Then Shallum the son of Jabesh conspired against him, and astruck and killed him in front of the people; and he reigned in his place.

11Now the rest of the acts of Zechariah, indeed they *are* written in the book of the chronicles of the kings of Israel.

12This *was* the word of the LORD which He spoke to Jehu, saying, a"Your sons shall sit on the throne of Israel to the fourth *generation.*" And so it was.

14:24
a1 Kin. 12:26–33

14:25
a2 Kin. 10:32;
13:5, 25
bNum. 13:21;
34:8; 1 Kin. 8:65
cDeut. 3:17
dJon. 1:1;
Matt. 12:39, 40
eJosh. 19:13

14:26 aEx. 3:7;
2 Kin. 13:4;
Ps. 106:44
bDeut. 32:36

14:27
a[2 Kin. 13:5, 23]

14:28
a1 Kin. 11:24
b2 Sam. 8:6;
1 Kin. 11:24;
2 Chr. 8:3

14:29
a2 Kin. 15:8

15:1
a2 Kin. 15:13, 30
b2 Kin. 14:21;
2 Chr. 26:1, 3, 4

15:4 a2 Kin. 12:3;
14:4; 15:35

15:5
a2 Chr. 26:19–23;
Ps. 78:31 bIs. 6:1
c[Lev. 13:46];
Num. 12:14

15:7
a2 Chr. 26:23

15:8
a2 Kin. 14:29

15:9
a2 Kin. 14:24

15:10 aAmos 7:9

15:12
a2 Kin. 10:30

14:25 1*border*   2The Dead Sea   14:29 1Died and joined his ancestors
15:4 1Places for pagan worship   15:7 1Died and joined his ancestors

SHALLUM REIGNS IN ISRAEL

13Shallum the son of Jabesh became king in the thirty-ninth year of ¹Uzziah king of Judah; and he reigned a full month in Samaria. 14For Menahem the son of Gadi went up from ªTirzah, came to Samaria, and struck Shallum the son of Jabesh in Samaria and killed him; and he reigned in his place.

15Now the rest of the acts of Shallum, and the conspiracy which he ¹led, indeed they *are* written in the book of the chronicles of the kings of Israel. 16Then from Tirzah, Menahem attacked ªTiphsah, all who *were* there, and its territory. Because they did not surrender, therefore he attacked *it.* All ᵇthe women there who were with child he ripped open.

MENAHEM REIGNS IN ISRAEL

17In the thirty-ninth year of Azariah king of Judah, Menahem the son of Gadi became king over Israel, *and reigned* ten years in Samaria. 18And he did evil in the sight of the LORD; he did not depart all his days from the sins of Jeroboam the son of Nebat, who had made Israel sin. 19ªPul¹ king of Assyria came against the land; and Menahem gave Pul a thousand talents of silver, that his ²hand might be with him to ᵇstrengthen the kingdom under his control. 20And Menahem ªexacted¹ the money from Israel, from all the very wealthy, from each man fifty shekels of silver, to give to the king of Assyria. So the king of Assyria turned back, and did not stay there in the land.

21Now the rest of the acts of Menahem, and all that he did, *are* they not written in the book of the chronicles of the kings of Israel? 22So Menahem ¹rested with his fathers. Then Pekahiah his son reigned in his place.

PEKAHIAH REIGNS IN ISRAEL

23In the fiftieth year of Azariah king of Judah, Pekahiah the son of Menahem became king over Israel in Samaria, *and reigned* two years. 24And he did evil in the sight of the LORD; he did not depart from the sins of Jeroboam the son of Nebat, who had made Israel sin. 25Then Pekah the son of Remaliah, an officer of his, conspired against him and ¹killed him in Samaria, in the ªcitadel of the king's house, along with Argob and Arieh; and with him were fifty men of Gilead. He killed him and reigned in his place.

26Now the rest of the acts of Pekahiah, and all that he did, indeed they *are* written in the book of the chronicles of the kings of Israel.

PEKAH REIGNS IN ISRAEL

27In the fifty-second year of Azariah king of Judah, ªPekah the son of Remaliah became king over Israel in Samaria, *and reigned* twenty years. 28And he did evil in the sight of the LORD; he did not depart from the sins of Jeroboam the son of Nebat, who had made Israel sin. 29In the days of Pekah king of Israel, ¹Tiglath-Pileser king of Assyria ªcame and took ᵇIjon, Abel Beth Maachah, Janoah, Kedesh, Hazor, Gilead, and Galilee, all the land of Naphtali; and he ᶜcarried them captive to Assyria. 30Then Hoshea the son of Elah led a conspiracy

15:14
ª1 Kin. 14:17;
Song 6:4
15:16 ª1 Kin. 4:24
ᵇ2 Kin. 8:12;
Hos. 13:16
15:19
ª1 Chr. 5:26;
Is. 66:19;
Hos. 8:9
ᵇ2 Kin. 14:5
15:20
ª2 Kin. 23:35
15:25
ª1 Kin. 16:18
15:27
ª2 Chr. 28:6;
Is. 7:1
15:29
ª2 Kin. 16:7, 10;
1 Chr. 5:26
ᵇ1 Kin. 15:20
ᶜ2 Kin. 17:6

15:13 ¹*Azariah,* 2 Kin. 14:21ff.; 15:1ff. **15:15** ¹Lit. *conspired* **15:19** ¹Tiglath-Pileser III, v. 29 ²Support **15:20** ¹*took* **15:22** ¹Died and joined his ancestors **15:25** ¹Lit. *struck* **15:29** ¹A later name of *Pul,* v. 19

against Pekah the son of Remaliah, and struck and killed him; so he ᵃreigned in his place in the twentieth year of Jotham the son of Uzziah.

31Now the rest of the acts of Pekah, and all that he did, indeed they *are* written in the book of the chronicles of the kings of Israel.

JOTHAM REIGNS IN JUDAH
(2 Chr. 27:1–9)

32In the second year of Pekah the son of Remaliah, king of Israel, ᵃJotham the son of Uzziah, king of Judah, began to reign. 33He was twenty-five years old when he became king, and he reigned sixteen years in Jerusalem. His mother's name *was* ¹Jerusha the daughter of Zadok. 34And he did *what was* right in the sight of the LORD; he did ᵃaccording to all that his father Uzziah had done. 35ᵃHowever the ¹high places were not removed; the people still sacrificed and burned incense on the high places. ᵇHe built the Upper Gate of the house of the LORD.

36Now the rest of the acts of Jotham, and all that he did, *are* they not written in the book of the chronicles of the kings of Judah? 37In those days the LORD began to send ᵃRezin king of Syria and ᵇPekah the son of Remaliah against Judah. 38So Jotham ¹rested with his fathers, and was buried with his fathers in the City of David his father. Then Ahaz his son reigned in his place.

AHAZ REIGNS IN JUDAH
(2 Chr. 28:1–27)

16 In the seventeenth year of Pekah the son of Remaliah, Ahaz the son of Jotham, king of Judah, began to reign. 2Ahaz *was* twenty years old when he became king, and he reigned sixteen years in Jerusalem; and he did not do *what was* right in the sight of the LORD his God, as his father David *had done.* 3But he walked in the way of the kings of Israel; indeed ᵃhe made his son pass through the fire, according to the ᵇabominations of the nations whom the LORD had cast out from before the children of Israel. 4And he sacrificed and burned incense on the ᵃhigh places, ᵇon the hills, and under every green tree.

5ᵃThen Rezin king of Syria and Pekah the son of Remaliah, king of Israel, came up to Jerusalem to *make* war; and they besieged Ahaz but could not overcome *him.* 6At that time Rezin king of Syria ᵃcaptured ¹Elath for Syria, and drove the men of Judah from Elath. Then the ²Edomites went to Elath, and dwell there to this day.

7So Ahaz sent messengers to ᵃTiglath-Pileser¹ king of Assyria, saying, "I *am* your servant and your son. Come up and save me from the hand of the king of Syria and from the hand of the king of Israel, who rise up against me." 8And Ahaz ᵃtook the silver and gold that was found in the house of the LORD, and in the treasuries of the king's house, and sent *it as* a present to the king of Assyria. 9So the king of Assyria heeded him; for the king of Assyria went up against ᵃDamascus and ᵇtook it, carried *its people* captive to ᶜKir, and killed Rezin.

15:30 ᵃ2 Kin. 17:1; [Hos. 10:3, 7, 15]
15:32 ᵃ2 Chr. 27:1
15:34 ᵃ2 Kin. 15:3, 4; 2 Kin. 26:4, 5
15:35 ᵃ2 Kin. 15:4; ᵇ2 Chr. 23:20; 27:3
15:37 ᵃ2 Kin. 16:5–9; Is. 7:1–17; ᵇ2 Kin. 15:26, 27
16:3 ᵃ[Lev. 18:21]; 2 Kin. 17:17; 2 Chr. 28:3; Ps. 106:37, 38; Is. 1:1; ᵇ[Deut. 12:31]; 2 Kin. 21:2, 11
16:4 ᵃ2 Kin. 15:34, 35; ᵇ[Deut. 12:2]; 1 Kin. 14:23
16:5 ᵃ2 Kin. 15:37; Is. 7:1, 4
16:6 ᵃ2 Kin. 14:22; 2 Chr. 26:2
16:7 ᵃ2 Kin. 15:29; 1 Chr. 5:26; 2 Chr. 28:20
16:8 ᵃ2 Kin. 12:17, 18; 2 Chr. 28:21
16:9 ᵃ2 Kin. 14:28; ᵇAmos 1:5; ᶜIs. 22:6; Amos 9:7

¹⁰Now King Ahaz went to Damascus to meet Tiglath-Pileser king of Assyria, and saw an altar that *was* at Damascus; and King Ahaz sent to Urijah the priest the design of the altar and its pattern, according to all its workmanship. ¹¹Then ^aUrijah the priest built an altar according to all that King Ahaz had sent from Damascus. So Urijah the priest made *it* before King Ahaz came back from Damascus. ¹²And when the king came back from Damascus, the king saw the altar; and ^athe king approached the altar and made offerings on it. ¹³So he burned his burnt offering and his grain offering; and he poured his drink offering and sprinkled the blood of his peace offerings on the altar. ¹⁴He also brought ^athe bronze altar which *was* before the LORD, from the front of the ¹temple—from between the *new* altar and the house of the LORD—and put it on the north side of the *new* altar. ¹⁵Then King Ahaz commanded Urijah the priest, saying, "On the great *new* altar burn ^athe morning burnt offering, the evening grain offering, the king's burnt sacrifice, and his grain offering, with the burnt offering of all the people of the land, their grain offering, and their drink offerings; and sprinkle on it all the blood of the burnt offering and all the blood of the sacrifice. And the bronze altar shall be for me to inquire *by*." ¹⁶Thus did Urijah the priest, according to all that King Ahaz commanded.

^{17a}And King Ahaz cut off ^bthe panels of the carts, and removed the lavers from them; and he took down ^cthe Sea from the bronze oxen that *were* under it, and put it on a pavement of stones. ¹⁸Also he removed the Sabbath pavilion which they had built in the temple, and he removed the king's outer entrance from the house of the LORD, on account of the king of Assyria.

¹⁹Now the rest of the acts of Ahaz which he did, *are* they not written in the book of the chronicles of the kings of Judah? ²⁰So Ahaz rested with his fathers, and ^awas buried with his fathers in the City of David. Then Hezekiah his son reigned in his place.

HOSHEA REIGNS IN ISRAEL

17 In the twelfth year of Ahaz king of Judah, ^aHoshea the son of Elah became king of Israel in Samaria, *and he reigned* nine years. ²And he did evil in the sight of the LORD, but not as the kings of Israel who were before him. ^{3a}Shalmaneser king of Assyria came up against him; and Hoshea ^bbecame his vassal, and paid him tribute money. ⁴And the king of Assyria uncovered a conspiracy by Hoshea; for he had sent messengers to So, king of Egypt, and brought no tribute to the king of Assyria, as *he had done* year by year. Therefore the king of Assyria shut him up, and bound him in prison.

ISRAEL CARRIED CAPTIVE TO ASSYRIA

(2 Kin. 18:9–12)

⁵Now ^athe king of Assyria went throughout all the land, and went up to Samaria and besieged it for three years. ^{6a}In the ninth year of Hoshea, the king of Assyria took Samaria and ^bcarried Israel away to Assyria, ^cand placed them in Halah and by the Habor, the River of Gozan, and in the cities of the Medes.

16:11 ^aIs. 8:2
16:12
^a2 Chr. 26:16, 19
16:14 ^aEx. 27:1, 2; 40:6, 29; 2 Chr. 4:1
16:15
^aEx. 29:39–41
16:17
^a2 Chr. 28:24
^b1 Kin. 7:27–29
^c1 Kin. 7:23–25
16:20
^a2 Chr. 28:27
17:1 ^a2 Kin. 15:30
17:3
^a2 Kin. 18:9–12
^b2 Kin. 24:1
17:5 ^a2 Kin. 18:9; Hos. 13:16
17:6
^a2 Kin. 18:10, 11; Is. 7:7–9; Hos. 1:4; 13:16; Amos 4:2
^bLev. 26:32, 33; [Deut. 28:36, 64; 29:27, 28]
^c1 Chr. 5:26

16:14 ¹Lit. *house*

7For aso it was that the children of Israel had sinned against the LORD their God, who had brought them up out of the land of Egypt, from under the hand of Pharaoh king of Egypt; and they had bfeared other gods, 8and ahad walked in the statutes of the nations whom the LORD had cast out from before the children of Israel, and of the kings of Israel, which they had made. 9Also the children of Israel secretly did against the LORD their God things that *were* not right, and they built for themselves 1high places in all their cities, afrom watchtower to fortified city. 10aThey set up for themselves *sacred* pillars and bwooden images1 con every high hill and under every green tree. 11There they burned incense on all the high places, like the nations whom the LORD had carried away before them; and they did wicked things to provoke the LORD to anger, 12for they served idols, aof which the LORD had said to them, b"You shall not do this thing."

13Yet the LORD testified against Israel and against Judah, by all of His aprophets, bevery seer, saying, c"Turn from your evil ways, and keep My commandments *and* My statutes, according to all the law which I commanded your fathers, and which I sent to you by My servants the prophets." 14Nevertheless they would not hear, but astiffened their necks, like the necks of their fathers, who bdid not believe in the LORD their God. 15And they arejected His statutes band His covenant that He had made with their fathers, and His testimonies which He had testified against them; they followed cidols, dbecame idolaters, and *went* after the nations who *were* all around them, *concerning* whom the LORD had charged them that they should enot do like them. 16So they left all the commandments of the LORD their God, amade for themselves a molded image *and* two calves, bmade a wooden image and worshiped all the chost of heaven, dand served Baal. 17aAnd they caused their sons and daughters to pass through the fire, bpracticed witchcraft and soothsaying, and csold themselves to do evil in the sight of the LORD, to provoke Him to anger. 18Therefore the LORD was very angry with Israel, and removed them from His sight; there was none left abut the tribe of Judah alone.

19Also aJudah did not keep the commandments of the LORD their God, but walked in the statutes of Israel which they made. 20And the LORD rejected all the descendants of Israel, afflicted them, and adelivered them into the hand of plunderers, until He had cast them from His bsight. 21For aHe tore Israel from the house of David, and bthey made Jeroboam the son of Nebat king. Then Jeroboam drove Israel from following the LORD, and made them commit a great sin. 22For the children of Israel walked in all the sins of Jeroboam which he did; they did not depart from them, 23until the LORD removed Israel out of His sight, aas He had said by all His servants the prophets. bSo Israel was carried away from their own land to Assyria, *as it is* to this day.

ASSYRIA RESETTLES SAMARIA

24aThen the king of Assyria brought *people* from Babylon, Cuthah, bAva, Hamath, and from Sepharvaim, and placed *them* in the cities of Samaria instead of the children of Israel;

17:24 aEzra 4:2, 10 b2 Kin. 18:34

17:9 1Places for pagan worship   17:10 1Heb. *Asherim,* Canaanite deities

17:7
a[Josh. 23:16]
bJudg. 6:10

17:8
a[Lev. 18:3;
Deut. 18:9];
2 Kin. 16:3

17:9 a2 Kin. 18:8

17:10
a1 Kin. 14:23;
Is. 57:5
b[Ex. 34:12–14;
Deut. 16:21];
Mic. 5:14
c[Deut. 12:2];
2 Kin. 16:4

17:12
a[Ex. 20:3–5;
Lev. 26:1;
Deut. 5:7, 8]
b[Deut. 4:19]

17:13
aNeh. 9:29,
30 b1 Sam. 9:9
c[Jer. 18:11;
25:5; 35:15;
Ezek. 18:31]

17:14 aEx. 32:9;
33:3; Deut. 31:27;
[Prov. 29:1;
Acts 7:51]
bDeut. 9:23;
Ps. 78:22

17:15 aJer. 44:3
bEx. 24:6–8;
Deut. 29:25
cDeut. 32:21;
1 Kin. 16:31;
[1 Cor. 8:4]
d2 Chr. 13:7;
Jer. 2:5;
[Rom. 1:21–23]
e[Deut. 12:30, 31]

17:16 aEx. 32:8;
1 Kin. 12:28
b[1 Kin. 14:15]
c[Deut. 4:19]
d1 Kin. 16:31;
22:53

17:17
a[Lev. 18:21];
2 Kin. 16:3;
Ezek. 23:37
b[Lev. 19:26;
Deut. 18:10–12]
c1 Kin. 21:20

17:18
a1 Kin. 11:13, 32

17:19 aJer. 3:8

17:20
aJudg. 2:14;
2 Kin. 13:3; 15:29
b2 Kin. 24:20

17:21
a1 Kin. 11:11, 31
b1 Kin. 12:20, 28

17:23
a1 Kin. 14:16;
Is. 8:4
b2 Kin. 17:6

and they took possession of Samaria and dwelt in its cities. 25And it was so, at the beginning of their dwelling there, *that* they did not fear the LORD; therefore the LORD sent lions among them, which killed *some* of them. 26So they spoke to the king of Assyria, saying, "The nations whom you have removed and placed in the cities of Samaria do not know the rituals of the God of the land; therefore He has sent lions among them, and indeed, they are killing them because they do not know the rituals of the God of the land." 27Then the king of Assyria commanded, saying, "Send there one of the priests whom you brought from there; let him go and dwell there, and let him teach them the rituals of the God of the land." 28Then one of the priests whom they had carried away from Samaria came and dwelt in Bethel, and taught them how they should fear the LORD.

29However every nation continued to make gods of its own, and put *them* ªin the shrines on the high places which the Samaritans had made, *every* nation in the cities where they dwelt. 30The men of ªBabylon made Succoth Benoth, the men of Cuth made Nergal, the men of Hamath made Ashima, 31ªand the Avites made Nibhaz and Tartak; and the Sepharvites ᵇburned their children in fire to Adrammelech and Anammelech, the gods of Sepharvaim. 32So they feared the LORD, ªand from every class they appointed for themselves priests of the ¹high places, who sacrificed for them in the shrines of the high places. 33ªThey feared the LORD, yet served their own gods—according to the rituals of the nations from among whom they were carried away.

34To this day they continue practicing the former rituals; they do not fear the LORD, nor do they follow their statutes or their ordinances, or the law and commandment which the LORD had commanded the children of Jacob, ªwhom He named Israel, 35with whom the LORD had made a covenant and charged them, saying: ª"You shall not fear other gods, nor ᵇbow down to them nor serve them nor sacrifice to them; 36but the LORD, who ªbrought you up from the land of Egypt with great power and ᵇan outstretched arm, ᶜHim you shall fear, Him you shall worship, and to Him you shall offer sacrifice. 37And the statutes, the ordinances, the law, and the commandment which He wrote for you, ªyou shall be careful to observe forever; you shall not fear other gods. 38And the covenant that I have made with you, ªyou shall not forget, nor shall you fear other gods. 39But the LORD your God you shall fear; and He will deliver you from the hand of all your enemies." 40However they did not obey, but they followed their former rituals. 41ªSo these nations feared the LORD, yet served their carved images; also their children and their children's children have continued doing as their fathers did, even to this day.

HEZEKIAH REIGNS IN JUDAH
(2 Chr. 29:1, 2; 31:1)

18 Now it came to pass in the third year of ªHoshea the son of Elah, king of Israel, *that* ᵇHezekiah the son of Ahaz, king of Judah, began to reign. 2He was twenty-five years old when he became king, and he reigned twenty-nine years

---

17:29
ª1 Kin. 12:31;
13:32

17:30
ª2 Kin. 17:24

17:31 ªEzra 4:9
ᵇ[Lev. 18:21;
Deut. 12:31]

17:32
ª1 Kin. 12:31;
13:33

17:33 ªZeph. 1:5

17:34
ªGen. 32:28;
35:10

17:35
ªJudg. 6:10
ᵇ[Ex. 20:5]

17:36
ªEx. 14:15–30
ᵇEx. 6:6; 9:15
ᶜ[Deut. 10:20]

17:37
ªDeut. 5:32

17:38
ªDeut. 4:23;
6:12

17:41
ª2 Kin. 17:32, 33

18:1 ª2 Kin. 17:1
ᵇ2 Chr. 28:27;
29:1

17:32 ¹Places for pagan worship

in Jerusalem. His mother's name *was* [a]Abi[1] the daughter of Zechariah. [3]And he did *what was* right in the sight of the Lord, according to all that his father David had done.

[4a]He removed the [1]high places and broke the *sacred* pillars, cut down the [2]wooden image and broke in pieces the [b]bronze serpent that Moses had made; for until those days the children of Israel burned incense to it, and called it [3]Nehushtan. [5]He [a]trusted in the Lord God of Israel, [b]so that after him was none like him among all the kings of Judah, nor who were before him. [6]For he [a]held fast to the Lord; he did not depart from following Him, but kept His commandments, which the Lord had commanded Moses. [7]The Lord [a]was with him; he [b]prospered wherever he went. And he [c]rebelled against the king of Assyria and did not serve him. [8a]He [1]subdued the Philistines, as far as Gaza and its territory, [b]from watchtower to fortified city.

[9]Now [a]it came to pass in the fourth year of King Hezekiah, which *was* the seventh year of Hoshea the son of Elah, king of Israel, *that* Shalmaneser king of Assyria came up against Samaria and besieged it. [10]And at the end of three years they took it. In the sixth year of Hezekiah, that *is,* [a]the ninth year of Hoshea king of Israel, Samaria was taken. [11a]Then the king of Assyria carried Israel away captive to Assyria, and put them [b]in Halah and by the Habor, the River of Gozan, and in the cities of the Medes, [12]because they [a]did not obey the voice of the Lord their God, but transgressed His covenant *and* all that Moses the servant of the Lord had commanded; and they would neither hear nor do *them.*

[13]And [a]in the fourteenth year of King Hezekiah, Sennacherib king of Assyria came up against all the fortified cities of Judah and took them. [14]Then Hezekiah king of Judah sent to the king of Assyria at Lachish, saying, "I have done wrong; turn away from me; whatever you impose on me I will pay." And the king of Assyria assessed Hezekiah king of Judah three hundred talents of silver and thirty talents of gold. [15]So Hezekiah [a]gave *him* all the silver that was found in the house of the Lord and in the treasuries of the king's house. [16]At that time Hezekiah stripped *the gold from* the doors of the temple of the Lord, and *from* the pillars which Hezekiah king of Judah had overlaid, and gave [1]it to the king of Assyria.

SENNACHERIB BOASTS AGAINST THE LORD
(Is. 36:2–22; 2 Chr. 32:9–15)

[17]Then the king of Assyria sent *the* [1]Tartan, *the* [2]Rabsaris, *and the* [3]Rabshakeh from Lachish, with a great army against Jerusalem, to King Hezekiah. And they went up and came to Jerusalem. When they had come up, they went and stood by the [a]aqueduct from the upper pool, [b]which *was* on the highway to the Fuller's Field. [18]And when they had called to the king, [a]Eliakim the son of Hilkiah, who *was* over the household, Shebna the [1]scribe, and Joah the son of Asaph, the recorder, came out to them. [19]Then *the* Rabshakeh said to them,

18:2 [a]Is. 38:5

18:4 [a]2 Chr. 31:1
[b]Num. 21:5–9

18:5
[a]2 Kin. 19:10;
[Job 13:15;
Ps. 13:5]
[b]2 Kin. 23:25

18:6
[a]Deut. 10:20;
Josh. 23:8

18:7
[a][2 Chr. 15:2]
[b]Gen. 39:2, 3;
1 Sam. 18:5, 14;
Ps. 60:12
[c]2 Kin. 16:7

18:8 [a]1 Chr. 4:41;
2 Chr. 28:18;
Is. 14:29
[b]2 Kin. 17:9

18:9 [a]2 Kin. 17:3

18:10
[a]2 Kin. 17:6

18:11
[a]2 Kin. 17:6;
Hos. 1:4;
Amos 4:2
[b]1 Chr. 5:26

18:12
[a]2 Kin. 17:7–18

18:13
[a]2 Chr. 32:1;
Is. 36:1—39:8

18:15
[a]1 Kin. 15:18, 19;
2 Kin. 12:18; 16:8

18:17
[a]2 Kin. 20:20
[b]Is. 7:3

18:18
[a]2 Kin. 19:2;
Is. 22:20

18:2 [1]*Abijah,* 2 Chr. 29:1ff.   18:4 [1]Places for pagan worship   [2]Heb. *Asherah,* a Canaanite goddess   [3]Lit. *Bronze Thing,* also similar to Heb. *nahash, serpent*   18:8 [1]Lit. *struck*   18:16 [1]Lit. *them*   18:17 [1]A title, probably *Commander in Chief*   [2]A title, probably *Chief Officer*   [3]A title, probably *Chief of Staff* or *Governor*   18:18 [1]*secretary*

"Say now to Hezekiah, 'Thus says the great king, the king of Assyria: a"What confidence *is* this in which you trust? 20You speak of *having* plans and power for war; but *they are* 1mere words. And in whom do you trust, that you rebel against me? 21aNow look! You are trusting in the staff of this broken reed, Egypt, on which if a man leans, it will go into his hand and pierce it. So *is* Pharaoh king of Egypt to all who trust in him. 22But if you say to me, 'We trust in the LORD our God,' *is* it not He awhose 1high places and whose altars Hezekiah has taken away, and said to Judah and Jerusalem, 'You shall worship before this altar in Jerusalem'?" ' 23Now therefore, I urge you, give a pledge to my master the king of Assyria, and I will give you two thousand horses—if you are able on your part to put riders on them! 24How then will you repel one captain of the least of my master's servants, and put your trust in Egypt for chariots and horsemen? 25Have I now come up without the LORD against this place to destroy it? The LORD said to me, 'Go up against this land, and destroy it.' "

26aThen Eliakim the son of Hilkiah, Shebna, and Joah said to *the* Rabshakeh, "Please speak to your servants in bAramaic, for we understand *it;* and do not speak to us in 1Hebrew in the hearing of the people who *are* on the wall."

27But *the* Rabshakeh said to them, "Has my master sent me to your master and to you to speak these words, and not to the men who sit on the wall, who will eat and drink their own waste with you?"

28Then *the* Rabshakeh stood and called out with a loud voice in 1Hebrew, and spoke, saying, "Hear the word of the great king, the king of Assyria! 29Thus says the king: a'Do not let Hezekiah deceive you, for he shall not be able to deliver you from his hand; 30nor let Hezekiah make you trust in the LORD, saying, "The LORD will surely deliver us; this city shall not be given into the hand of the king of Assyria." ' 31Do not listen to Hezekiah; for thus says the king of Assyria: 'Make *peace* with me 1by a present and come out to me; and every one of you eat from his own avine and every one from his own fig tree, and every one of you drink the waters of his own cistern; 32until I come and take you away to a land like your own land, aa land of grain and new wine, a land of bread and vineyards, a land of olive groves and honey, that you may live and not die. But do not listen to Hezekiah, lest he persuade you, saying, "The LORD will deliver us." 33aHas any of the gods of the nations at all delivered its land from the hand of the king of Assyria? 34Where *are* the gods of aHamath and Arpad? Where *are* the gods of Sepharvaim and Hena and bIvah? Indeed, have they delivered Samaria from my hand? 35Who among all the gods of the lands have delivered their countries from my hand, athat the LORD should deliver Jerusalem from my hand?' "

36But the people held their peace and answered him not a word; for the king's commandment was, "Do not answer him." 37Then Eliakim the son of Hilkiah, who *was* over the household, Shebna the scribe, and Joah the son of Asaph, the recorder, came to Hezekiah awith *their* clothes torn, and told him the words of *the* Rabshakeh.

18:19
a2 Chr. 32:10;
[Ps. 118:8, 9]

18:21
aIs. 30:2–7;
Ezek. 29:6, 7

18:22
a2 Kin. 18:4;
2 Chr. 31:1; 32:12

18:26
aIs. 36:11—39:8
bEzra 4:7;
Dan. 2:4

18:29
a2 Chr. 32:15

18:31
a1 Kin. 4:20, 25

18:32
aDeut. 8:7–9;
11:12

18:33
a2 Kin. 19:12;
Is. 10:10, 11

18:34
a2 Kin. 19:13
b2 Kin. 17:24

18:35 aDan. 3:15

18:37 aIs. 33:7

18:20 1Lit. *a word of the lips* **18:22** 1Places for pagan worship **18:26** 1Lit. *Judean* **18:28** 1Lit. *Judean* **18:31** 1By paying tribute

ISAIAH ASSURES DELIVERANCE
(Is. 37:1-7)

19 And [a]so it was, when King Hezekiah heard *it,* that he tore his clothes, covered himself with [b]sackcloth, and went into the house of the LORD. [2]Then he sent Eliakim, who *was* over the household, Shebna the scribe, and the elders of the priests, covered with sackcloth, to Isaiah the prophet, the son of Amoz. [3]And they said to him, "Thus says Hezekiah: 'This day *is* a day of trouble, and rebuke, and blasphemy; for the children have come to birth, but *there is* no strength to [1]bring them forth. [4a]It may be that the LORD your God will hear all the words of *the* Rabshakeh, whom his master the king of Assyria has sent to [b]reproach the living God, and will [c]rebuke the words which the LORD your God has heard. Therefore lift up *your* prayer for the remnant that is left.' "

[5]So the servants of King Hezekiah came to Isaiah. [6a]And Isaiah said to them, "Thus you shall say to your master, 'Thus says the LORD: "Do not be [b]afraid of the words which you have heard, with which the [c]servants of the king of Assyria have blasphemed Me. [7]Surely I will send [a]a spirit upon him, and he shall hear a rumor and return to his own land; and I will cause him to fall by the sword in his own land." ' "

SENNACHERIB'S THREAT AND HEZEKIAH'S PRAYER
(Is. 37:8-20)

[8]Then *the* Rabshakeh returned and found the king of Assyria warring against Libnah, for he heard that he had departed [a]from Lachish. [9]And [a]the king heard concerning Tirhakah king of Ethiopia, "Look, he has come out to make war with you." So he again sent messengers to Hezekiah, saying, [10]"Thus you shall speak to Hezekiah king of Judah, saying: 'Do not let your God [a]in whom you trust deceive you, saying, "Jerusalem shall not be given into the hand of the king of Assyria." [11]Look! You have heard what the kings of Assyria have done to all lands by utterly destroying them; and shall you be delivered? [12a]Have the gods of the nations delivered those whom my fathers have destroyed, Gozan and Haran and Rezeph, and the people of [b]Eden who *were* in Telassar? [13a]Where *is* the king of Hamath, the king of Arpad, and the king of the city of Sepharvaim, Hena, and Ivah?' "

[14a]And Hezekiah received the letter from the hand of the messengers, and read it; and Hezekiah went up to the house of the LORD, and spread it before the LORD. [15]Then Hezekiah prayed before the LORD, and said: "O LORD God of Israel, *the* One [a]who dwells *between* the cherubim, [b]You are God, You alone, of all the kingdoms of the earth. You have made heaven and earth. [16a]Incline Your ear, O LORD, and hear; [b]open Your eyes, O LORD, and see; and hear the words of Sennacherib, [c]which he has sent to reproach the living God. [17]Truly, LORD, the kings of Assyria have laid waste the nations and their lands, [18]and have cast their gods into the fire; for they *were* [a]not gods, but [b]the work of men's hands—wood and stone. Therefore they destroyed them. [19]Now therefore, O LORD our God, I pray, save us from his hand, [a]that all the kingdoms of the earth may [b]know that You *are* the LORD God, You alone."

19:1
[a]2 Kin. 18:13;
2 Chr. 32:20–22;
Is. 37:1 [b]Ps. 69:11

19:4
[a]2 Sam. 16:12
[b]2 Kin. 18:35
[c]Ps. 50:21

19:6 [a]Is. 37:6
[b][Ps. 112:7]
[c]2 Kin. 18:17

19:7
[a]2 Kin. 19:35–37;
Jer. 51:1

19:8
[a]2 Kin. 18:14, 17

19:9
[a]1 Sam. 23:27;
Is. 37:9

19:10
[a]2 Kin. 18:5

19:12
[a]2 Kin. 18:33, 34
[b]Ezek. 27:23

19:13
[a]2 Kin. 18:34

19:14 [a]Is. 37:14

19:15 [a]Ex. 25:22;
Ps. 80:1; Is. 37:16
[b][Is. 44:6]

19:16 [a]Ps. 31:2;
Is. 37:17
[b]1 Kin. 8:29;
2 Chr. 6:40
[c]2 Kin. 19:4

19:18
[a][Is. 44:9–20;
Jer. 10:3–5]
[b]Ps. 115:4;
Jer. 10:3;
[Acts 17:29]

19:19 [a]Ps. 83:18
[b]1 Kin. 8:42, 43

19:3 [1]*give birth*

THE WORD OF THE LORD CONCERNING SENNACHERIB
(Is. 37:21–35)

20Then Isaiah the son of Amoz sent to Hezekiah, saying, "Thus says the LORD God of Israel: a'Because you have prayed to Me against Sennacherib king of Assyria, bI have heard.' 21This *is* the word which the LORD has spoken concerning him:

'The virgin, athe daughter of Zion,
    Has despised you, laughed you to scorn;
    The daughter of Jerusalem
    bHas shaken *her* head behind your back!

22 'Whom have you reproached and blasphemed?
    Against whom have you raised *your* voice,
    And lifted up your eyes on high?
    Against athe Holy *One* of Israel.
23 aBy your messengers you have reproached the Lord,
    And said: b"By the multitude of my chariots
    I have come up to the height of the mountains,
    To the limits of Lebanon;
    I will cut down its tall cedars
    And its choice cypress trees;
    I will enter the extremity of its borders,
    To its fruitful forest.
24 I have dug and drunk strange water,
    And with the soles of my feet I have adried up
    All the brooks of defense."

25 'Did you not hear long ago
    How aI made it,
    From ancient times that I formed it?
    Now I have brought it to pass,
    That byou should be
    For crushing fortified cities *into* heaps of ruins.
26 Therefore their inhabitants had little power;
    They were dismayed and confounded;
    They were *as* the grass of the field
    And the green herb,
    As athe grass on the housetops
    And *grain* blighted before it is grown.

27 'But aI know your dwelling place,
    Your going out and your coming in,
    And your rage against Me.
28 Because your rage against Me and your tumult
    Have come up to My ears,
    Therefore aI will put My hook in your nose
    And My bridle in your lips,
    And I will turn you back
    bBy the way which you came.

29"This *shall be* a asign to you:

'You shall eat this year such as grows 1of itself,
    And in the second year what springs from the same;
    Also in the third year sow and reap,
    Plant vineyards and eat the fruit of them.

19:20 aIs. 37:21
    b2 Kin. 20:5;
    Ps. 65:2
19:21 aJer. 14:17;
    Lam. 2:13
    bPs. 22:7, 8
19:22 aJer. 51:5
19:23
    a2 Kin. 18:17
    bPs. 20:7
19:24 aIs. 19:6
19:25 a[Is. 45:7]
    bIs. 10:5, 6
19:26 aPs. 129:6
19:27 aPs. 139:1–
    3; Is. 37:28
19:28 aJob 41:2;
    Ezek. 29:4;
    38:4; Amos 4:2
    b2 Kin. 19:33, 36
19:29 aEx. 3:12;
    1 Sam. 2:34;
    2 Kin. 20:8, 9;
    Is. 7:11–14;
    Luke 2:12

19:29 1Without cultivation

30 aAnd the remnant who have escaped of the house of
   Judah
Shall again take root downward,
And bear fruit upward.
31 For out of Jerusalem shall go a remnant,
And those who escape from Mount Zion.
aThe zeal of the LORD 1of hosts will do this.'

32"Therefore thus says the LORD concerning the king of
Assyria:

'He shall anot come into this city,
Nor shoot an arrow there,
Nor come before it with shield,
Nor build a siege mound against it.
33 By the way that he came,
By the same shall he return;
And he shall not come into this city,'
Says the LORD.
34 'For aI will bdefend this city, to save it
For My own sake and cfor My servant David's sake.'"

SENNACHERIB'S DEFEAT AND DEATH
(Is. 37:36–38; 2 Chr. 32:20–23)

35And ait came to pass on a certain night that the 1angel
of the LORD went out, and killed in the camp of the Assyrians one hundred and eighty-five thousand; and when *people*
arose early in the morning, there were the corpses—all dead.
36So Sennacherib king of Assyria departed and went away,
returned *home,* and remained at aNineveh. 37Now it came to
pass, as he was worshiping in the temple of Nisroch his god,
that his sons aAdrammelech and Sharezer bstruck him down
with the sword; and they escaped into the land of Ararat. Then
cEsarhaddon his son reigned in his place.

HEZEKIAH'S LIFE EXTENDED
(2 Chr. 32:24–26; Is. 38:1–8)

20 In athose days Hezekiah was sick and near death. And
Isaiah the prophet, the son of Amoz, went to him and
said to him, "Thus says the LORD: 'Set your house in order, for
you shall die, and not live.'"
2Then he turned his face toward the wall, and prayed to the
LORD, saying, 3a"Remember now, O LORD, I pray, how I have
walked before You in truth and with a loyal heart, and have
done *what was* good in Your sight." And Hezekiah wept bitterly.
4And it happened, before Isaiah had gone out into the
middle court, that the word of the LORD came to him, saying,
5"Return and tell Hezekiah athe leader of My people, 'Thus
says the LORD, the God of David your father: b"I have heard
your prayer, I have seen cyour tears; surely I will heal you.
On the third day you shall go up to the house of the LORD.
6And I will add to your days fifteen years. I will deliver you
and this city from the hand of the king of Assyria; and aI will
defend this city for My own sake, and for the sake of My servant David."'"

19:30
a2 Kin. 19:4;
2 Chr. 32:22, 23

19:31
a2 Kin. 25:26;
Is. 9:7

19:32 aIs. 8:7–10

19:34
a2 Kin. 20:6;
2 Chr. 32:21
bIs. 31:5
c1 Kin. 11:12, 13

19:35 aEx. 12:29;
Is. 10:12–19;
37:36; Hos. 1:7

19:36 aGen. 10:11

19:37
a2 Kin. 17:31
b2 Kin. 19:7;
2 Chr. 32:21
cEzra 4:2

20:1
a2 Kin. 18:13;
2 Chr. 32:24;
Is. 38:1–22

20:3
a2 Kin. 18:3–6;
Neh. 13:22

20:5
a1 Sam. 9:16; 10:1
b2 Kin. 19:20;
Ps. 65:2
cPs. 39:12; 56:8

20:6
a2 Kin. 19:34;
2 Chr. 32:21

19:31 1So with many Heb. mss. and ancient vss. (cf. Is. 37:32); MT omits *of
hosts* 19:35 1Or *Angel*

7Then [a]Isaiah said, "Take a lump of figs." So they took and laid *it* on the boil, and he recovered.

8And Hezekiah said to Isaiah, [a]"What *is* the sign that the LORD will heal me, and that I shall go up to the house of the LORD the third day?"

9Then Isaiah said, [a]"This is the sign to you from the LORD, that the LORD will do the thing which He has spoken: *shall* the shadow go forward ten degrees or go backward ten degrees?"

10And Hezekiah answered, "It is an easy thing for the shadow to go down ten [1]degrees; no, but let the shadow go backward ten degrees."

11So Isaiah the prophet cried out to the LORD, and [a]He brought the shadow ten [1]degrees backward, by which it had gone down on the sundial of Ahaz.

THE BABYLONIAN ENVOYS

(Is. 39:1–8)

12[a]At that time [1]Berodach-Baladan the son of Baladan, king of Babylon, sent letters and a present to Hezekiah, for he heard that Hezekiah had been sick. 13And [a]Hezekiah was attentive to them, and showed them all the house of his treasures—the silver and gold, the spices and precious ointment, and [1]all [2]his armory—all that was found among his treasures. There was nothing in his house or in all his dominion that Hezekiah did not show them.

14Then Isaiah the prophet went to King Hezekiah, and said to him, "What did these men say, and from where did they come to you?"

So Hezekiah said, "They came from a far country, from Babylon."

15And he said, "What have they seen in your house?"

So Hezekiah answered, [a]"They have seen all that *is* in my house; there is nothing among my treasures that I have not shown them."

16Then Isaiah said to Hezekiah, "Hear the word of the LORD: 17'Behold, the days are coming when all that *is* in your house, and what your fathers have accumulated until this day, [a]shall be carried to Babylon; nothing shall be left,' says the LORD. 18'And [a]they shall take away some of your sons who will [1]descend from you, whom you will beget; [b]and they shall be [c]eunuchs in the palace of the king of Babylon.'"

19So Hezekiah said to Isaiah, [a]"The word of the LORD which you have spoken *is* good!" For he said, "Will there not be peace and truth at least in my days?"

DEATH OF HEZEKIAH

(2 Chr. 32:32, 33)

20[a]Now the rest of the acts of Hezekiah—all his might, and how he [b]made a [c]pool and a [1]tunnel and [d]brought water into the city—*are* they not written in the book of the chronicles of the kings of Judah? 21So [a]Hezekiah [1]rested with his fathers. Then Manasseh his son reigned in his place.

20:7 [a]Is. 38:21
20:8 [a]Judg. 6:17, 37, 39; Is. 7:11, 14; 38:22
20:9 [a]Num. 23:19; Is. 38:7, 8
20:11 [a]Josh. 10:12–14; Is. 38:8
20:12 [a]2 Kin. 8:8, 9; 2 Chr. 32:31; Is. 39:1–8
20:13 [a]2 Kin. 16:9; 2 Chr. 32:27, 31
20:15 [a]2 Kin. 20:13
20:17 [a]2 Kin. 24:13; 25:13–15; 2 Chr. 36:10; Jer. 27:21, 22; 52:17
20:18 [a]2 Kin. 24:12; 2 Chr. 33:11 [b]Dan. 1:3–7 [c]Dan. 1:11, 18
20:19 [a]1 Sam. 3:18
20:20 [a]2 Chr. 32:32 [b]Neh. 3:16 [c]2 Kin. 18:17; Is. 7:3 [d]2 Chr. 32:3, 30
20:21 [a]2 Kin. 16:20; 2 Chr. 32:33

20:10 [1]Lit. *steps*   **20:11** [1]Lit. *steps*   **20:12** [1]*Merodach-Baladan,* Is. 39:1   **20:13** [1]So with many Heb. mss., Syr., Tg.; MT omits *all*   [2]Lit. *the house of his armor*   **20:18** [1]*be born from*   **20:20** [1]*aqueduct*   **20:21** [1]Died and joined his ancestors

MANASSEH REIGNS IN JUDAH
(2 Chr. 33:1–20)

21 Manasseh [a]*was* twelve years old when he became king, and he reigned fifty-five years in Jerusalem. His mother's name *was* Hephzibah. [2]And he did evil in the sight of the LORD, [a]according to the abominations of the nations whom the LORD had cast out before the children of Israel. [3]For he rebuilt the [1]high places [a]which Hezekiah his father had destroyed; he raised up altars for Baal, and made a [2]wooden image, [b]as Ahab king of Israel had done; and he [c]worshiped all [3]the host of heaven and served them. [4][a]He also built altars in the house of the LORD, of which the LORD had said, [b]"In Jerusalem I will put My name." [5]And he built altars for all the host of heaven in the [a]two courts of the house of the LORD. [6][a]Also he made his son pass through the fire, practiced [b]soothsaying, used witchcraft, and consulted spiritists and mediums. He did much evil in the sight of the LORD, to provoke *Him* to anger. [7]He even set a carved image of [1]Asherah that he had made, in the [2]house of which the LORD had said to David and to Solomon his son, [a]"In this house and in Jerusalem, which I have chosen out of all the tribes of Israel, I will put My name forever; [8]and I will not make the feet of Israel wander anymore from the land which I gave their fathers—only if they are careful to do according to all that I have commanded them, and according to all the law that My servant Moses commanded them." [9]But they paid no attention, and Manasseh [a]seduced them to do more evil than the nations whom the LORD had destroyed before the children of Israel.

[10]And the LORD spoke [a]by His servants the prophets, saying, [11][a]"Because Manasseh king of Judah has done these abominations ([b]he has acted more wickedly than all the [c]Amorites who *were* before him, and [d]has also made Judah sin with his idols), [12]therefore thus says the LORD God of Israel: 'Behold, *I* am bringing *such* calamity upon Jerusalem and Judah, that whoever hears of it, both [a]his ears will tingle. [13]And I will stretch over Jerusalem [a]the measuring line of Samaria and the plummet of the house of Ahab; [b]I will wipe Jerusalem as *one* wipes a dish, wiping *it* and turning *it* upside down. [14]So I will forsake the [a]remnant of My inheritance and deliver them into the hand of their enemies; and they shall become victims of plunder to all their enemies, [15]because they have done evil in My sight, and have provoked Me to anger since the day their fathers came out of Egypt, even to this day.'"

[16][a]Moreover Manasseh shed very much innocent blood, till he had filled Jerusalem from one end to another, besides his sin by which he made Judah sin, in doing evil in the sight of the LORD.

[17]Now [a]the rest of the acts of [b]Manasseh—all that he did, and the sin that he committed—*are* they not written in the book of the chronicles of the kings of Judah? [18]So [a]Manasseh [1]rested with his fathers, and was buried in the garden of his own house, in the garden of Uzza. Then his son Amon reigned in his place.

Cross references

21:1
[a]2 Chr. 33:1–9

21:2 [a]2 Kin. 16:3

21:3
[a]2 Kin. 18:4, 22
[b]1 Kin. 16:31–33
[c][Deut. 4:19;
17:2–5];
2 Kin. 17:16; 23:5

21:4 [a]Jer. 7:30;
32:34
[b]1 Kin. 11:13

21:5 [a]1 Kin. 6:36;
7:12; 2 Kin. 23:12

21:6 [a][Lev. 18:21;
20:2];
2 Kin. 16:3; 17:17
[b]Lev. 19:26, 31;
[Deut. 18:10–14];
2 Kin. 17:17

21:7
[a]2 Sam. 7:13;
1 Kin. 8:29; 9:3;
2 Kin. 23:27;
2 Chr. 7:12, 16;
Jer. 32:34

21:8
[a]2 Sam. 7:10;
[2 Kin. 18:11, 12]

21:9
[a][Prov. 29:12]

21:10
[a]2 Kin. 17:13

21:11
[a]2 Kin. 23:26,
27; 24:3, 4
[b]1 Kin. 21:26
[c]Gen. 15:16
[d]2 Kin. 21:9

21:12
[a]1 Sam. 3:11;
Jer. 19:3

21:13 [a]Lam. 2:8;
Amos 7:7, 8
[b]2 Kin. 22:16–19;
25:4–11

21:14 [a]Jer. 6:9

21:16
[a]2 Kin. 24:4

21:17
[a]2 Chr. 33:11–19
[b]2 Kin. 20:21

21:18
[a]2 Chr. 33:20

21:3 [1]Places for pagan worship   [2]Heb. *Asherah,* a Canaanite goddess
[3]The gods of the Assyrians   21:7 [1]A Canaanite goddess   [2]Temple
21:18 [1]Died and joined his ancestors

AMON'S REIGN AND DEATH
(2 Chr. 33:21–25)

19ªAmon *was* twenty-two years old when he became king, and he reigned two years in Jerusalem. His mother's name *was* Meshullemeth the daughter of Haruz of Jotbah. 20And he did evil in the sight of the LORD, ªas his father Manasseh had done. 21So he walked in all the ways that his father had walked; and he served the idols that his father had served, and worshiped them. 22He ªforsook the LORD God of his fathers, and did not walk in the way of the LORD.

23ªThen the servants of Amon ᵇconspired against him, and killed the king in his own house. 24But the people of the land ªexecuted all those who had conspired against King Amon. Then the people of the land made his son Josiah king in his place.

25Now the rest of the acts of Amon which he did, *are* they not written in the book of the chronicles of the kings of Judah? 26And he was buried in his tomb in the garden of Uzza. Then Josiah his son reigned in his place.

JOSIAH REIGNS IN JUDAH
(2 Chr. 34:1, 2)

22 Josiah ªwas eight years old when he became king, and he reigned thirty-one years in Jerusalem. His mother's name *was* Jedidah the daughter of Adaiah of ᵇBozkath. 2And he did *what was* right in the sight of the LORD, and walked in all the ways of his father David; he ªdid not turn aside to the right hand or to the left.

HILKIAH FINDS THE BOOK OF THE LAW
(2 Chr. 34:8–28)

3ªNow it came to pass, in the eighteenth year of King Josiah, *that* the king sent Shaphan the scribe, the son of Azaliah, the son of Meshullam, to the house of the LORD, saying: 4"Go up to Hilkiah the high priest, that he may count the money which has been ªbrought into the house of the LORD, which ᵇthe doorkeepers have gathered from the people. 5And let them ªdeliver it into the hand of those doing the work, who are the overseers in the house of the LORD; let them give it to those who *are* in the house of the LORD doing the work, to repair the damages of the house— 6to carpenters and builders and masons—and to buy timber and hewn stone to repair the house. 7However ªthere need be no accounting made with them of the money delivered into their hand, because they deal faithfully."

8Then Hilkiah the high priest said to Shaphan the scribe, ª"I have found the Book of the Law in the house of the LORD." And Hilkiah gave the book to Shaphan, and he read it. 9So Shaphan the scribe went to the king, bringing the king word, saying, "Your servants have ¹gathered the money that was found in the house, and have delivered it into the hand of those who do the work, who oversee the house of the LORD." 10Then Shaphan the scribe showed the king, saying, "Hilkiah the priest has given me a book." And Shaphan read it before the king.

21:19
ª2 Chr. 33:21–23

21:20
ª2 Kin. 21:2–6, 11, 16

21:22
ªJudg. 2:12, 13; 1 Kin. 11:33; 1 Chr. 28:9

21:23
ª1 Chr. 3:14; 2 Chr. 33:24, 25; Matt. 1:10
ᵇ2 Kin. 12:20; 14:19

21:24
ª2 Kin. 14:5

22:1 ª1 Kin. 13:2; 2 Chr. 34:1
ᵇJosh. 15:39

22:2
ªDeut. 5:32; Josh. 1:7

22:3
ª2 Chr. 34:8

22:4 ª2 Kin. 12:4
ᵇ2 Kin. 12:9, 10

22:5
ª2 Kin. 12:11–14

22:7
ª2 Kin. 12:15; [1 Cor. 4:2]

22:8
ªDeut. 31:24–26; 2 Chr. 34:14

22:9 ¹Lit. *poured out*

[11]Now it happened, when the king heard the words of the Book of the Law, that he tore his clothes. [12]Then the king commanded Hilkiah the priest, [a]Ahikam the son of Shaphan, [1]Achbor the son of Michaiah, Shaphan the scribe, and Asaiah a servant of the king, saying, [13]"Go, inquire of the LORD for me, for the people and for all Judah, concerning the words of this book that has been found; for great *is* [a]the wrath of the LORD that is aroused against us, because our fathers have not obeyed the words of this book, to do according to all that is written concerning us."

[14]So Hilkiah the priest, Ahikam, Achbor, Shaphan, and Asaiah went to Huldah the prophetess, the wife of Shallum the son of [a]Tikvah, the son of Harhas, keeper of the wardrobe. (She dwelt in Jerusalem in the Second Quarter.) And they spoke with her. [15]Then she said to them, "Thus says the LORD God of Israel, 'Tell the man who sent you to Me, [16]"Thus says the LORD: 'Behold, [a]I will bring calamity on this place and on its inhabitants—all the words of the book which the king of Judah has read— [17a]because they have forsaken Me and burned incense to other gods, that they might provoke Me to anger with all the works of their hands. Therefore My wrath shall be aroused against this place and shall not be quenched.'"' [18]But as for [a]the king of Judah, who sent you to inquire of the LORD, in this manner you shall speak to him, 'Thus says the LORD God of Israel: "*Concerning* the words which you have heard— [19]because your [a]heart was tender, and you [b]humbled yourself before the LORD when you heard what I spoke against this place and against its inhabitants, that they would become [c]a desolation and [d]a curse, and you tore your clothes and wept before Me, I also have heard *you*," says the LORD. [20]"Surely, therefore, I will [1]gather you to your fathers, and you [a]shall [2]be gathered to your grave in peace; and your eyes shall not see all the calamity which I will bring on this place."'" So they brought back word to the king.

JOSIAH RESTORES TRUE WORSHIP
(2 Chr. 34:29—35:19)

23 Now [a]the king sent them to gather all the elders of Judah and Jerusalem to him. [2]The king went up to the house of the LORD with all the men of Judah, and with him all the inhabitants of Jerusalem—the priests and the prophets and all the people, both small and great. And he [a]read in their hearing all the words of the Book of the Covenant [b]which had been found in the house of the LORD.

[3]Then the king [a]stood by a pillar and made a [b]covenant before the LORD, to follow the LORD and to keep His commandments and His testimonies and His statutes, with all *his* heart and all *his* soul, to perform the words of this covenant that were written in this book. And all the people took a stand for the covenant. [4]And the king commanded Hilkiah the high priest, the [a]priests of the second order, and the doorkeepers, to bring [b]out of the temple of the LORD all the articles that were made for Baal, for [1]Asherah, and for all [2]the host of heaven; and he burned them outside Jerusalem in the

22:12
[a]2 Kin. 25:22;
Jer. 26:24

22:13
[a][Deut. 29:23–28; 31:17, 18]

22:14
[a]2 Chr. 34:22

22:16
[a]Deut. 29:27;
[Dan. 9:11–14]

22:17
[a]Deut. 29:25–27;
2 Kin. 21:22

22:18
[a]2 Chr. 34:26

22:19
[a]1 Sam. 24:5;
[Ps. 51:17];
Is. 57:15]
[b]Ex. 10:3;
1 Kin. 21:29;
[2 Chr. 7:14]
[c]Lev. 26:31, 32
[d]Jer. 26:6;
44:22

22:20
[a]2 Kin. 23:30;
[Ps. 37:37;
Is. 57:1, 2]

23:1
[a]2 Sam. 19:11;
2 Chr. 34:29, 30

23:2
[a]Deut. 31:10–13
[b]2 Kin. 22:8

23:3 [a]2 Kin. 11:14
[b]2 Kin. 11:17

23:4
[a]2 Kin. 25:18;
Jer. 52:24
[b]2 Kin. 21:3–7

22:12 [1]*Abdon the son of Micah,* 2 Chr. 34:20   **22:20** [1]Cause you to join your ancestors in death   [2]Die a natural death   **23:4** [1]A Canaanite goddess   [2]The gods of the Assyrians

fields of Kidron, and carried their ashes to Bethel. 5Then he removed the idolatrous priests whom the kings of Judah had ordained to burn incense on the high places in the cities of Judah and in the places all around Jerusalem, and those who burned incense to Baal, to the sun, to the moon, to the 1constellations, and to aall the host of heaven. 6And he brought out the awooden1 image from the house of the LORD, to the Brook Kidron outside Jerusalem, burned it at the Brook Kidron and ground *it* to bashes, and threw its ashes on cthe graves of the common people. 7Then he tore down the *ritual* 1booths aof the 2perverted persons that *were* in the house of the LORD, bwhere the cwomen wove hangings for the wooden image. 8And he brought all the priests from the cities of Judah, and defiled the high places where the priests had burned incense, from aGeba to Beersheba; also he broke down the high places at the gates which *were* at the entrance of the Gate of Joshua the governor of the city, which *were* to the left of the city gate. 9aNevertheless the priests of the high places did not come up to the altar of the LORD in Jerusalem, bbut they ate unleavened bread among their brethren.

10And he defiled aTopheth, which *is* in bthe Valley of the 1Son of Hinnom, cthat no man might make his son or his daughter dpass through the fire to Molech. 11Then he removed the horses that the kings of Judah had 1dedicated to the sun, at the entrance to the house of the LORD, by the chamber of Nathan-Melech, the officer who *was* in the court; and he burned the chariots of the sun with fire. 12The altars that *were* aon the roof, the upper chamber of Ahaz, which the kings of Judah had made, and the altars which bManasseh had made in the two courts of the house of the LORD, the king broke down and pulverized there, and threw their dust into the Brook Kidron. 13Then the king defiled the 1high places that *were* east of Jerusalem, which *were* on the 2south of 3the Mount of Corruption, which aSolomon king of Israel had built for Ashtoreth the abomination of the Sidonians, for Chemosh the abomination of the Moabites, and for Milcom the abomination of the people of Ammon. 14And he abroke in pieces the *sacred* pillars and cut down the wooden images, and filled their places with the bones of men.

15Moreover the altar that *was* at Bethel, *and* the 1high place awhich Jeroboam the son of Nebat, who made Israel sin, had made, both that altar and the high place he broke down; and he burned the high place *and* crushed *it* to powder, and burned the wooden image. 16As Josiah turned, he saw the tombs that *were* there on the mountain. And he sent and took the bones out of the tombs and burned *them* on the altar, and defiled it according to the aword of the LORD which the man of God proclaimed, who proclaimed these words. 17Then he said, "What gravestone *is* this that I see?"

So the men of the city told him, "*It is* athe tomb of the man of God who came from Judah and proclaimed these things which you have done against the altar of Bethel."

23:5 a2 Kin. 21:3

23:6 a2 Kin. 21:7
bEx. 32:20
c2 Chr. 34:4

23:7
a1 Kin. 14:24;
15:12 bEx. 35:25,
26; Ezek. 16:16
cEx. 38:8

23:8
aJosh. 21:17;
1 Kin. 15:22

23:9
a[Ezek. 44:10–14]
b1 Sam. 2:36

23:10 aIs. 30:33;
Jer. 7:31, 32
bJosh. 15:8
c[Lev. 18:21;
Deut. 18:10];
Ezek. 23:37–39
d2 Kin. 21:6

23:12 aJer. 19:13;
Zeph. 1:5
b2 Kin. 21:5;
2 Chr. 33:5

23:13
a1 Kin. 11:5–7

23:14
a[Ex. 23:24;
Deut. 7:5–25]

23:15
a1 Kin. 12:28–33

23:16 a1 Kin. 13:2

23:17 a1 Kin. 13:1,
30, 31

23:5 1Of the Zodiac **23:6** 1Heb. *Asherah,* a Canaanite goddess **23:7** 1Lit. *houses* 2Heb. *qedeshim,* those practicing sodomy and prostitution in religious rituals **23:10** 1Kt. *Sons* **23:11** 1*given* **23:13** 1Places for pagan worship 2Lit. *right of* 3The Mount of Olives **23:15** 1A place for pagan worship

18And he said, "Let him alone; let no one move his bones." So they let his bones alone, with the bones of ᵃthe prophet who came from Samaria.

19Now Josiah also took away all the ¹shrines of the ²high places that *were* ᵃin the cities of Samaria, which the kings of Israel had made to provoke ³the LORD to anger; and he did to them according to all the deeds he had done in Bethel. 20ᵃHe ᵇexecuted all the priests of the ¹high places who *were* there, on the altars, and ᶜburned men's bones on them; and he returned to Jerusalem.

21Then the king commanded all the people, saying, ᵃ"Keep the Passover to the LORD your God, ᵇas *it is* written in this Book of the Covenant." 22ᵃSuch a Passover surely had never been held since the days of the judges who judged Israel, nor in all the days of the kings of Israel and the kings of Judah. 23But in the eighteenth year of King Josiah this Passover was held before the LORD in Jerusalem. 24Moreover Josiah put away those who consulted mediums and spiritists, the household gods and idols, all the abominations that were seen in the land of Judah and in Jerusalem, that he might perform the words of ᵃthe law which were written in the book ᵇthat Hilkiah the priest found in the house of the LORD. 25ᵃNow before him there was no king like him, who turned to the LORD with all his heart, with all his soul, and with all his might, according to all the Law of Moses; nor after him did *any* arise like him.

IMPENDING JUDGMENT ON JUDAH

26Nevertheless the LORD did not turn from the fierceness of His great wrath, with which His anger was aroused against Judah, ᵃbecause of all the provocations with which Manasseh had provoked Him. 27And the LORD said, "I will also remove Judah from My sight, as ᵃI have removed Israel, and will cast off this city Jerusalem which I have chosen, and the house of which I said, ᵇ'My name shall be there.'"

JOSIAH DIES IN BATTLE
(2 Chr. 35:20—36:1)

28Now the rest of the acts of Josiah, and all that he did, *are* they not written in the book of the chronicles of the kings of Judah? 29ᵃIn his days Pharaoh Necho king of Egypt went ¹to the aid of the king of Assyria, to the River Euphrates; and King Josiah went against him. And *Pharaoh Necho* killed him at ᵇMegiddo when he ᶜconfronted him. 30ᵃThen his servants moved his body in a chariot from Megiddo, brought him to Jerusalem, and buried him in his own tomb. And ᵇthe people of the land took Jehoahaz the son of Josiah, anointed him, and made him king in his father's place.

THE REIGN AND CAPTIVITY OF JEHOAHAZ
(2 Chr. 36:1–4)

31ᵃJehoahaz *was* twenty-three years old when he became king, and he reigned three months in Jerusalem. His mother's

23:18
ᵃ1 Kin. 13:11, 31

23:19
ᵃ2 Chr. 34:6, 7

23:20
ᵃ1 Kin. 13:2
ᵇ[Ex. 22:20];
1 Kin. 18:40;
2 Kin. 10:25; 11:18
ᶜ2 Chr. 34:5

23:21
ᵃNum. 9:5;
Josh. 5:10;
2 Chr. 35:1
ᵇEx. 12:3;
Lev. 23:5;
Num. 9:2;
Deut. 16:2–8

23:22
ᵃ2 Chr. 35:18, 19

23:24
ᵃ[Lev. 19:31;
20:27];
Deut. 18:11
ᵇ2 Kin. 22:8

23:25
ᵃ2 Kin. 18:5

23:26
ᵃ2 Kin. 21:11, 12;
24:3, 4; Jer. 15:4

23:27
ᵃ2 Kin. 17:18,
20; 18:11; 21:13
ᵇ1 Kin. 8:29; 9:3;
2 Kin. 21:4, 7

23:29
ᵃ2 Chr. 35:20;
Jer. 2:16; 46:2
ᵇJudg. 5:19;
Zech. 12:11
ᶜ2 Kin. 14:8

23:30
ᵃ2 Chr. 35:24;
2 Kin. 22:20
ᵇ2 Chr. 36:1–4

23:31
ᵃ1 Chr. 3:15;
Jer. 22:11

23:19 ¹Lit. *houses* ²Places for pagan worship ³So with LXX, Syr., Vg.; MT, Tg. omit *the LORD* **23:20** ¹Places for pagan worship **23:29** ¹Or *to attack,* Heb. *al* can mean *together with* or *against*

name *was* [b]Hamutal the daughter of Jeremiah of Libnah. [32]And he did evil in the sight of the LORD, according to all that his fathers had done. [33]Now Pharaoh Necho put him in prison [a]at Riblah in the land of Hamath, that he might not reign in Jerusalem; and he imposed on the land a tribute of one hundred talents of silver and a talent of gold. [34]Then [a]Pharaoh Necho made Eliakim the son of Josiah king in place of his father Josiah, and [b]changed his name to [c]Jehoiakim. And *Pharaoh* took Jehoahaz [d]and went to Egypt, and [1]he died there.

JEHOIAKIM REIGNS IN JUDAH
(2 Chr. 36:5–8)

[35]So Jehoiakim gave [a]the silver and gold to Pharaoh; but he taxed the land to give money according to the command of Pharaoh; he exacted the silver and gold from the people of the land, from every one according to his assessment, to give *it* to Pharaoh Necho. [36a]Jehoiakim *was* twenty-five years old when he became king, and he reigned eleven years in Jerusalem. His mother's name *was* Zebudah the daughter of Pedaiah of Rumah. [37]And he did evil in the sight of the LORD, according to all that his fathers had done.

JUDAH OVERRUN BY ENEMIES

24 In [a]his days Nebuchadnezzar king of [b]Babylon came up, and Jehoiakim became his vassal *for* three years. Then he turned and rebelled against him. [2a]And the LORD sent against him *raiding* [1]bands of Chaldeans, bands of Syrians, bands of Moabites, and bands of the people of Ammon; He sent them against Judah to destroy it, [b]according to the word of the LORD which He had spoken by His servants the prophets. [3]Surely at the commandment of the LORD *this* came upon Judah, to remove *them* from His sight [a]because of the sins of Manasseh, according to all that he had done, [4a]and also because of the innocent blood that he had shed; for he had filled Jerusalem with innocent blood, which the LORD would not pardon.

[5]Now the rest of the acts of Jehoiakim, and all that he did, *are* they not written in the book of the chronicles of the kings of Judah? [6a]So Jehoiakim rested with his fathers. Then Jehoiachin his son reigned in his place.

[7]And [a]the king of Egypt did not come out of his land anymore, for [b]the king of Babylon had taken all that belonged to the king of Egypt from the Brook of Egypt to the River Euphrates.

THE REIGN AND CAPTIVITY OF JEHOIACHIN
(2 Chr. 36:9, 10)

[8a]Jehoiachin[1] *was* eighteen years old when he became king, and he reigned in Jerusalem three months. His mother's name *was* Nehushta the daughter of Elnathan of Jerusalem. [9]And he did evil in the sight of the LORD, according to all that his father had done.

[10a]At that time the servants of Nebuchadnezzar king of Babylon came up against Jerusalem, and the city [1]was besieged.

Cross-references (margin)
23:31
[b]2 Kin. 24:18

23:33
[a]2 Kin. 25:6;
Jer. 52:27

23:34
[a]2 Chr. 36:4
[b]2 Kin. 24:17;
Dan. 1:7
[c]Matt. 1:11
[d]Jer. 22:11, 12;
Ezek. 19:3, 4

23:35
[a]2 Kin. 23:33

23:36
[a]2 Chr. 36:5;
Jer. 22:18, 19;
26:1

24:1
[a]2 Chr. 36:6;
Jer. 25:1,
9; Dan. 1:1
[b]2 Kin. 20:14

24:2 [a]Jer. 25:9;
32:28; 35:11;
Ezek. 19:8
[b]2 Kin. 20:17;
21:12–14; 23:27

24:3
[a]2 Kin. 21:2, 11;
23:26

24:4
[a]2 Kin. 21:16

24:6
[a]2 Chr. 36:6, 8;
Jer. 22:18, 19

24:7 [a]Jer. 37:5–7
[b]Jer. 46:2

24:8 [a]1 Chr. 3:16;
2 Chr. 36:9

24:10 [a]Dan. 1:1

23:34 [1]Jehoahaz   24:2 [1]troops   24:8 [1]Jeconiah, 1 Chr. 3:16; Jer. 24:1; or Coniah, Jer. 22:24, 28   24:10 [1]Lit. *came into siege*

¹¹And Nebuchadnezzar king of Babylon came against the city, as his servants were besieging it. ¹²ᵃThen Jehoiachin king of Judah, his mother, his servants, his princes, and his officers went out to the king of Babylon; and the king of Babylon, ᵇin the eighth year of his reign, took him prisoner.

THE CAPTIVITY OF JERUSALEM

¹³ᵃAnd he carried out from there all the treasures of the house of the LORD and the treasures of the king's house, and he ᵇcut in pieces all the articles of gold which Solomon king of Israel had made in the temple of the LORD, ᶜas the LORD had said. ¹⁴Also ᵃhe carried into captivity all Jerusalem: all the captains and all the mighty men of valor, ᵇten thousand captives, and ᶜall the craftsmen and smiths. None remained except ᵈthe poorest people of the land. ¹⁵And ᵃhe carried Jehoiachin captive to Babylon. The king's mother, the king's wives, his officers, and the mighty of the land he carried into captivity from Jerusalem to Babylon. ¹⁶ᵃAll the valiant men, seven thousand, and craftsmen and smiths, one thousand, all *who were* strong *and* fit for war, these the king of Babylon brought captive to Babylon.

ZEDEKIAH REIGNS IN JUDAH
(2 Chr. 36:11–14; Jer. 52:1–3)

¹⁷Then ᵃthe king of Babylon made Mattaniah, ᵇ*Jehoiachin's¹* uncle, king in his place, and ᶜchanged his name to Zedekiah.
¹⁸ᵃZedekiah *was* twenty-one years old when he became king, and he reigned eleven years in Jerusalem. His mother's name *was* ᵇHamutal the daughter of Jeremiah of Libnah. ¹⁹ᵃHe also did evil in the sight of the LORD, according to all that Jehoiakim had done. ²⁰For because of the anger of the LORD *this* happened in Jerusalem and Judah, that He finally cast them out from His presence. ᵃThen Zedekiah rebelled against the king of Babylon.

THE FALL AND CAPTIVITY OF JUDAH
(2 Chr. 36:15–21; Jer. 52:4–30)

25 Now it came to pass ᵃin the ninth year of his reign, in the tenth month, on the tenth *day* of the month, *that* Nebuchadnezzar king of Babylon and all his army came against Jerusalem and encamped against it; and they built a siege wall against it all around. ²So the city was besieged until the eleventh year of King Zedekiah. ³By the ninth *day* of the ᵃ*fourth* month the famine had become so severe in the city that there was no food for the people of the land.
⁴Then ᵃthe city wall was broken through, and all the men of war *fled* at night by way of the gate between two walls, which was by the king's garden, even though the Chaldeans *were* still encamped all around against the city. And ᵇ*the king¹* went by way of the ²plain. ⁵But the army of the Chaldeans pursued the king, and they overtook him in the plains of Jericho. All his army was scattered from him. ⁶So they took the king and brought him up to the king of Babylon ᵃat Riblah, and they pronounced judgment on him. ⁷Then they killed the sons

24:12 ᵃJer. 22:24–30; 24:1; 29:1, 2; Ezek. 17:12 ᵇ2 Chr. 36:10
24:13 ᵃ2 Kin. 20:17; Is. 39:6 ᵇDan. 5:2, 3 ᶜJer. 20:5
24:14 ᵃIs. 3:2, 3; Jer. 24:1 ᵇ2 Kin. 24:16; Jer. 52:28 ᶜ1 Sam. 13:19 ᵈ2 Kin. 25:12
24:15 ᵃ2 Chr. 36:10; Esth. 2:6; Jer. 22:24–28; Ezek. 17:12
24:16 ᵃJer. 52:28
24:17 ᵃJer. 37:1 ᵇ1 Chr. 3:15; 2 Chr. 36:10 ᶜ2 Chr. 36:4
24:18 ᵃ2 Chr. 36:11; Jer. 52:1 ᵇ2 Kin. 23:31
24:19 ᵃ2 Chr. 36:12
24:20 ᵃ2 Chr. 36:13; Ezek. 17:15
25:1 ᵃ2 Chr. 36:17; Jer. 6:6; 34:2; Ezek. 4:2; 24:1, 2; Hab. 1:6
25:3 ᵃ2 Kin. 6:24, 25; Is. 3:1; Jer. 39:2; Lam. 4:9, 10
25:4 ᵃJer. 39:2 ᵇJer. 39:4–7; Ezek. 12:12
25:6 ᵃ2 Kin. 23:33; Jer. 52:9

24:17 ¹Lit. *his*   25:4 ¹Lit. *he*   ²Or *Arabah*, the Jordan Valley

of Zedekiah before his eyes, ᵃput¹ out the eyes of Zedekiah, bound him with bronze fetters, and took him to Babylon.

⁸And in the fifth month, ᵃon the seventh *day* of the month (which *was* ᵇthe nineteenth year of King Nebuchadnezzar king of Babylon), ᶜNebuzaradan the captain of the guard, a servant of the king of Babylon, came to Jerusalem. ⁹ᵃHe burned the house of the LORD ᵇand the king's house; all the houses of Jerusalem, that is, all the houses of the great, ᶜhe burned with fire. ¹⁰And all the army of the Chaldeans who *were with* the captain of the guard ᵃbroke down the walls of Jerusalem all around.

¹¹Then Nebuzaradan the captain of the guard carried away captive ᵃthe rest of the people *who* remained in the city and the defectors who had deserted to the king of Babylon, with the rest of the multitude. ¹²But the captain of the guard ᵃleft *some* of the poor of the land as vinedressers and farmers. ¹³ᵃThe bronze ᵇpillars that *were* in the house of the LORD, and ᶜthe carts and ᵈthe bronze Sea that *were* in the house of the LORD, the Chaldeans broke in pieces, and ᵉcarried their bronze to Babylon. ¹⁴They also took away ᵃthe pots, the shovels, the trimmers, the spoons, and all the bronze utensils with which the priests ministered. ¹⁵The firepans and the basins, the things of solid gold and solid silver, the captain of the guard took away. ¹⁶The two pillars, one Sea, and the carts, which Solomon had made for the house of the LORD, ᵃthe bronze of all these articles was beyond measure. ¹⁷ᵃThe height of one pillar *was* ¹eighteen cubits, and the capital on it *was* of bronze. The height of the capital was three cubits, and the network and pomegranates all around the capital were all of bronze. The second pillar was the same, with a network.

¹⁸ᵃAnd the captain of the guard took ᵇSeraiah the chief priest, ᶜZephaniah the second priest, and the three doorkeepers. ¹⁹He also took out of the city an officer who had charge of the men of war, ᵃfive men of ¹the king's close associates who were found in the city, the chief recruiting officer of the army, who mustered the people of the land, and sixty men of the people of the land *who were* found in the city. ²⁰So Nebuzaradan, captain of the guard, took these and brought them to the king of Babylon at Riblah. ²¹Then the king of Babylon struck them and put them to death at Riblah in the land of Hamath. ᵃThus Judah was carried away captive from its own land.

GEDALIAH MADE GOVERNOR OF JUDAH
(Jer. 40:5—41:18)

²²Then he made Gedaliah the son of ᵃAhikam, the son of Shaphan, governor over ᵇthe people who remained in the land of Judah, whom Nebuchadnezzar king of Babylon had left. ²³Now when all the ᵃcaptains of the armies, they and *their* men, heard that the king of Babylon had made Gedaliah governor, they came to Gedaliah at Mizpah—Ishmael the son of Nethaniah, Johanan the son of Careah, Seraiah the son of Tanhumeth the Netophathite, and ¹Jaazaniah the son of a Maachathite, they and their men. ²⁴And Gedaliah took an oath before them and their men, and said to them, "Do not

25:7 ᵃJer. 39:7;
Ezek. 17:16

25:8 ᵃJer. 52:12
ᵇ2 Kin. 24:12
ᶜJer. 39:9

25:9
ᵃ2 Kin. 25:13;
2 Chr. 36:19;
Ps. 79:1; Jer. 7:14
ᵇJer. 39:8
ᶜJer. 17:27

25:10
ᵃ2 Kin. 14:13;
Neh. 1:3

25:11 ᵃIs. 1:9;
Jer. 5:19; 39:9

25:12
ᵃ2 Kin. 24:14;
Jer. 39:10; 40:7;
52:16

25:13 ᵃJer. 52:17
ᵇ1 Kin. 7:15
ᶜ1 Kin. 7:27
ᵈ1 Kin. 7:23
ᵉ2 Kin. 20:17;
Jer. 27:19–22

25:14 ᵃEx. 27:3;
1 Kin. 7:45

25:16
ᵃ1 Kin. 7:47

25:17
ᵃ1 Kin. 7:15–22;
Jer. 52:21

25:18
ᵃJer. 39:9–13;
52:12–16, 24
ᵇ1 Chr. 6:14;
Ezra 7:1
ᶜJer. 21:1; 29:25,
29

25:19 ᵃEsth. 1:14;
Jer. 52:25

25:21
ᵃLev. 26:33;
Deut. 28:36, 64;
2 Kin. 23:27

25:22
ᵃ2 Kin. 22:12
ᵇIs. 1:9; Jer. 40:5

25:23
ᵃJer. 40:7–9

25:7 ¹*blinded*   25:17 ¹*About 27 feet*   25:19 ¹Lit. *those seeing the king's face*
25:23 ¹*Jezaniah,* Jer. 40:8

be afraid of the servants of the Chaldeans. Dwell in the land and serve the king of Babylon, and it shall be well with you."

25But ait happened in the seventh month that Ishmael the son of Nethaniah, the son of Elishama, of the royal family, came with ten men and struck and killed Gedaliah, the Jews, as well as the Chaldeans who were with him at Mizpah. 26And all the people, small and great, and the captains of the armies, arose aand went to Egypt; for they were afraid of the Chaldeans.

JEHOIACHIN RELEASED FROM PROSION

(Jer. 52:31–34)

27aNow it came to pass in the thirty-seventh year of the captivity of Jehoiachin king of Judah, in the twelfth month, on the twenty-seventh *day* of the month, *that* 1Evil-Merodach king of Babylon, in the year that he began to reign, breleased Jehoiachin king of Judah from prison. 28He spoke kindly to him, and gave him a more prominent seat than those of the kings who *were* with him in Babylon. 29So Jehoiachin changed from his prison garments, and he aate 1bread regularly before the king all the days of his life. 30And as for his 1provisions, *there was* a 2regular ration given him by the king, a portion for each day, all the days of his life.

25:25
aJer. 41:1–3

25:26
a2 Kin. 19:31;
Jer. 43:4–7

25:27
a2 Kin. 24:12,
15; Jer. 52:31–34
bGen. 40:13, 20

25:29
a2 Sam. 9:7

25:27 1Lit. *Man of Marduk*   25:29 1Food   25:30 1Lit. *allowance*   2Lit. *allowance*

THE FIRST BOOK OF THE
CHRONICLES

THE FAMILY OF ADAM—SETH TO ABRAHAM
(Gen. 5:1–32; 10:1–32; 11:10–26; Luke 3:34–38)

1 Adam,[a] [b]Seth, Enosh, [2]Cainan, Mahalalel, Jared, [3]Enoch, Methuselah, Lamech, [4a]Noah,[1] Shem, Ham, and Japheth.

[5a]The sons of Japheth *were* Gomer, Magog, Madai, Javan, Tubal, Meshech, and Tiras. [6]The sons of Gomer *were* Ashkenaz, [1]Diphath, and Togarmah. [7]The sons of Javan *were* Elishah, [1]Tarshishah, Kittim, and [2]Rodanim.

[8a]The sons of Ham *were* Cush, Mizraim, Put, and Canaan. [9]The sons of Cush *were* Seba, Havilah, [1]Sabta, [2]Raama, and Sabtecha. The sons of Raama *were* Sheba and Dedan. [10]Cush [a]begot Nimrod; he began to be a mighty one on the earth. [11]Mizraim begot Ludim, Anamim, Lehabim, Naphtuhim, [12]Pathrusim, Casluhim (from whom came the Philistines and the [a]Caphtorim). [13a]Canaan begot Sidon, his firstborn, and Heth; [14]the Jebusite, the Amorite, and the Girgashite; [15]the Hivite, the Arkite, and the Sinite; [16]the Arvadite, the Zemarite, and the Hamathite.

[17]The sons of [a]Shem *were* Elam, Asshur, [b]Arphaxad, Lud, Aram, Uz, Hul, Gether, and [1]Meshech. [18]Arphaxad begot Shelah, and Shelah begot Eber. [19]To Eber were born two sons: the name of one *was* [1]Peleg, for in his days the [2]earth was divided; and his brother's name *was* Joktan. [20a]Joktan begot Almodad, Sheleph, Hazarmaveth, Jerah, [21]Hadoram, Uzal, Diklah, [22][1]Ebal, Abimael, Sheba, [23]Ophir, Havilah, and Jobab. All these *were* the sons of Joktan.

[24a]Shem, Arphaxad, Shelah, [25a]Eber, Peleg, Reu, [26]Serug, Nahor, Terah, [27]and [a]Abram, who *is* Abraham. [28a]The sons of Abraham *were* [b]Isaac and [c]Ishmael.

THE FAMILY OF ISHMAEL
(Gen. 25:12–16)

[29]These *are* their genealogies: The [a]firstborn of Ishmael *was* Nebajoth; then Kedar, Adbeel, Mibsam, [30]Mishma, Dumah, Massa, [1]Hadad, Tema, [31]Jetur, Naphish, and Kedemah. These *were* the sons of Ishmael.

THE FAMILY OF KETURAH
(Gen. 25:1–4)

[32]Now [a]the sons born to Keturah, Abraham's concubine, *were* Zimran, Jokshan, Medan, Midian, Ishbak, and Shuah. The sons of Jokshan *were* Sheba and Dedan. [33]The sons of Midian *were* Ephah, Epher, Hanoch, Abida, and Eldaah. All these were the children of Keturah.

1:1 [a]Gen. 1:27; 2:7; 5:1, 2, 5 [b]Gen. 4:25, 26; 5:3–9
1:4 [a]Gen. 5:28—10:1
1:5 [a]Gen. 10:2–4
1:8 [a]Gen. 10:6
1:10 [a]Gen. 10:8–10, 13
1:12 [a]Deut. 2:23
1:13 [a]Gen. 9:18, 25–27; 10:15
1:17 [a]Gen. 10:22–29; 11:10 [b]Luke 3:36
1:20 [a]Gen. 10:26
1:24 [a]Gen. 11:10–26; Luke 3:34–36
1:25 [a]Gen. 11:15
1:27 [a]Gen. 17:5
1:28 [a]Gen. 21:2, 3 [b]Gen. 21:2 [c]Gen. 16:11, 15
1:29 [a]Gen. 25:13–16
1:32 [a]Gen. 25:1–4

1:4 [1]So with MT, Vg.; LXX adds *the sons of Noah*   1:6 [1]*Riphath,* Gen. 10:3
1:7 [1]*Tarshish,* Gen. 10:4   [2]*Dodanim,* Gen. 10:4   1:9 [1]*Sabtah,* Gen. 10:7
[2]*Raamah,* Gen. 10:7   1:17 [1]*Mash,* Gen. 10:23   1:19 [1]Lit. *Division,* Gen. 10:25
[2]Or *land*   1:22 [1]*Obal,* Gen. 10:28   1:30 [1]*Hadar,* Gen. 25:15

THE FAMILY OF ISAAC
(Gen. 36:10–14)

[34]And [a]Abraham begot Isaac. [b]The sons of Isaac *were* Esau and Israel. [35]The sons of [a]Esau *were* Eliphaz, Reuel, Jeush, Jaalam, and Korah. [36]And the sons of Eliphaz *were* Teman, Omar, [1]Zephi, Gatam, *and* Kenaz; and *by* [a]Timna, Amalek. [37]The sons of Reuel *were* Nahath, Zerah, Shammah, and Mizzah.

THE FAMILY OF SEIR
(Gen. 36:20–28)

[38][a]The sons of Seir *were* Lotan, Shobal, Zibeon, Anah, Dishon, Ezer, and Dishan. [39]And the sons of Lotan *were* Hori and [1]Homam; Lotan's sister *was* Timna. [40]The sons of Shobal *were* [1]Alian, Manahath, Ebal, [2]Shephi, and Onam. The sons of Zibeon *were* Ajah and Anah. [41]The son of Anah *was* [a]Dishon. The sons of Dishon *were* [1]Hamran, Eshban, Ithran, and Cheran. [42]The sons of Ezer *were* Bilhan, Zaavan, *and* [1]Jaakan. The sons of Dishan *were* Uz and Aran.

THE KINGS OF EDOM
(Gen. 36:31–43)

[43]Now these *were* the [a]kings who reigned in the land of Edom before a king reigned over the children of Israel: Bela the son of Beor, and the name of his city was Dinhabah. [44]And when Bela died, Jobab the son of Zerah of Bozrah reigned in his place. [45]When Jobab died, Husham of the land of the Temanites reigned in his place. [46]And when Husham died, Hadad the son of Bedad, who [1]attacked Midian in the field of Moab, reigned in his place. The name of his city *was* Avith. [47]When Hadad died, Samlah of Masrekah reigned in his place. [48][a]And when Samlah died, Saul of Rehoboth-by-the-River reigned in his place. [49]When Saul died, Baal-Hanan the son of Achbor reigned in his place. [50]And when Baal-Hanan died, [1]Hadad reigned in his place; and the name of his city was [2]Pai. His wife's name was Mehetabel the daughter of Matred, the daughter of Mezahab. [51]Hadad died also. And the chiefs of Edom were Chief Timnah, Chief [1]Aliah, Chief Jetheth, [52]Chief Aholibamah, Chief Elah, Chief Pinon, [53]Chief Kenaz, Chief Teman, Chief Mibzar, [54]Chief Magdiel, and Chief Iram. These *were* the chiefs of Edom.

THE FAMILY OF ISRAEL
(Gen. 35:23–26; 46:8–25)

2 These *were* the [a]sons of [1]Israel: [b]Reuben, Simeon, Levi, Judah, Issachar, Zebulun, [2]Dan, Joseph, Benjamin, Naphtali, Gad, and Asher.

FROM JUDAH TO DAVID
(Ruth 4:18–22; Matt. 1:2–6; Luke 3:31–33)

[3]The sons of [a]Judah *were* Er, Onan, and Shelah. *These* three were born to him by the daughter of [b]Shua, the Canaanitess.

1:34 [a]Gen. 21:2
[b]Gen. 25:9, 25, 26, 29; 32:28
1:35 [a]Gen. 36:10–19
1:36 [a]Gen. 36:12
1:38 [a]Gen. 36:20–28
1:41 [a]Gen. 36:25
1:43 [a]Gen. 36:31–43
1:48 [a]Gen. 36:37
2:1 [a]Gen. 29:32–35; 35:23, 26; 46:8–27
[b]Gen. 29:32; 35:22
2:3 [a]Gen. 38:3–5; 46:12; Num. 26:19
[b]Gen. 38:2

1:36 [1]*Zepho,* Gen. 36:11   1:39 [1]*Hemam* or *Heman,* Gen. 36:22   1:40 [1]*Alvan,* Gen. 36:23   [2]*Shepho,* Gen. 36:23   1:41 [1]*Hemdan,* Gen. 36:26   1:42 [1]*Akan,* Gen. 36:27   1:46 [1]Lit. *struck*   1:50 [1]*Hadar,* Gen. 36:39   [2]*Pau,* Gen. 36:39   1:51 [1]*Alvah,* Gen. 36:40   2:1 [1]*Jacob,* Gen. 32:28

^cEr, the firstborn of Judah, was wicked in the sight of the LORD; so He killed him. ⁴And ^aTamar, his daughter-in-law, ^bbore him Perez and Zerah. All the sons of Judah *were* five.

⁵The sons of ^aPerez *were* Hezron and Hamul. ⁶The sons of Zerah *were* ¹Zimri, ^aEthan, Heman, Calcol, and ²Dara—five of them in all.

⁷The son of ^aCarmi *was* ¹Achar, the troubler of Israel, who transgressed in the ^baccursed² thing.

⁸The son of Ethan *was* Azariah.

⁹Also the sons of Hezron who were born to him *were* Jerahmeel, ¹Ram, and ²Chelubai. ¹⁰Ram ^abegot Amminadab, and Amminadab begot Nahshon, ^bleader of the children of Judah; ¹¹Nahshon begot ¹Salma, and Salma begot Boaz; ¹²Boaz begot Obed, and Obed begot Jesse; ^{13a}Jesse begot Eliab his firstborn, Abinadab the second, ¹Shimea the third, ¹⁴Nethanel the fourth, Raddai the fifth, ¹⁵Ozem the sixth, *and* David the ^aseventh.

¹⁶Now their sisters *were* Zeruiah and Abigail. ^aAnd the sons of Zeruiah *were* Abishai, Joab, and Asahel—three. ¹⁷Abigail bore Amasa; and the father of Amasa *was* ¹Jether the Ishmaelite.

THE FAMILY OF HEZRON

¹⁸Caleb the son of Hezron had children by Azubah, *his* wife, and by Jerioth. Now these were her sons: Jesher, Shobab, and Ardon. ¹⁹When Azubah died, Caleb ¹took ^aEphrath² as his wife, who bore him Hur. ²⁰And Hur begot Uri, and Uri begot ^aBezalel.

²¹Now afterward Hezron went in to the daughter of ^aMachir the father of Gilead, whom he married when he *was* sixty years old; and she bore him Segub. ²²Segub begot ^aJair,¹ who had twenty-three cities in the land of Gilead. ^{23a}(Geshur and Syria took from them the towns of Jair, with Kenath and its towns—sixty towns.) All these *belonged to* the sons of Machir the father of Gilead. ²⁴After Hezron died in Caleb Ephrathah, Hezron's wife Abijah bore him ^aAshhur the father of Tekoa.

THE FAMILY OF JERAHMEEL

²⁵The sons of Jerahmeel, the firstborn of Hezron, *were* Ram, the firstborn, and Bunah, Oren, Ozem, *and* Ahijah. ²⁶Jerahmeel had another wife, whose name was Atarah; she was the mother of Onam. ²⁷The sons of Ram, the firstborn of Jerahmeel, were Maaz, Jamin, and Eker. ²⁸The sons of Onam were Shammai and Jada. The sons of Shammai *were* Nadab and Abishur.

²⁹And the name of the wife of Abishur *was* Abihail, and she bore him Ahban and Molid. ³⁰The sons of Nadab *were* Seled and Appaim; Seled died without children. ³¹The son of Appaim *was* Ishi, the son of Ishi *was* Sheshan, and ^aSheshan's son *was* Ahlai. ³²The sons of Jada, the brother of Shammai, *were* Jether and Jonathan; Jether died without children. ³³The sons of Jonathan *were* Peleth and Zaza. These were the sons of Jerahmeel.

Cross-references (margin)

2:3 ^cGen. 38:7
2:4 ^aGen. 38:6; ^bMatt. 1:3
2:5 ^aGen. 46:12; Ruth 4:18
2:6 ^a1 Kin. 4:31
2:7 ^a1 Chr. 4:1; ^bJosh. 6:18
2:10 ^aRuth 4:19–22; Matt. 1:4; ^bNum. 1:7; 2:3
2:13 ^a1 Sam. 16:6
2:15 ^a1 Sam. 16:10, 11; 17:12
2:16 ^a2 Sam. 2:18
2:19 ^a1 Chr. 2:50
2:20 ^aEx. 31:2; 38:22
2:21 ^aNum. 27:1; Judg. 5:14; 1 Chr. 7:14
2:22 ^aJudg. 10:3
2:23 ^aNum. 32:41; Deut. 3:14; Josh. 13:30
2:24 ^a1 Chr. 4:5
2:31 ^a1 Chr. 2:34, 35

Footnotes

2:6 ¹*Zabdi,* Josh. 7:1 ²*Darda,* 1 Kin. 4:31 2:7 ¹*Achan,* Josh. 7:1 ²*banned* or *devoted* 2:9 ¹*Aram,* Matt. 1:3, 4 ²*Caleb,* vv. 18, 42 2:11 ¹*Salmon,* Ruth 4:21; Luke 3:32 2:13 ¹*Shammah,* 1 Sam. 16:9 2:17 ¹*Jithra the Israelite,* 2 Sam. 17:25 2:19 ¹Lit. *took to himself* ²Or *Ephrathah* 2:22 ¹Reckoned to Manasseh through the daughter of Machir, Num. 32:41; Deut. 3:14; 25:5, 6; 1 Kin. 4:13; 1 Chr. 7:14

34Now Sheshan had no sons, only daughters. And Sheshan had an Egyptian servant whose name *was* Jarha. 35Sheshan gave his daughter to Jarha his servant as wife, and she bore him Attai. 36Attai begot Nathan, and Nathan begot aZabad; 37Zabad begot Ephlal, and Ephlal begot aObed; 38Obed begot Jehu, and Jehu begot Azariah; 39Azariah begot Helez, and Helez begot Eleasah; 40Eleasah begot Sismai, and Sismai begot Shallum; 41Shallum begot Jekamiah, and Jekamiah begot Elishama.

THE FAMILY OF CALEB

42The descendants of Caleb the brother of Jerahmeel *were* Mesha, his firstborn, who was the father of Ziph, and the sons of Mareshah the father of Hebron. 43The sons of Hebron *were* Korah, Tappuah, Rekem, and Shema. 44Shema begot Raham the father of Jorkoam, and Rekem begot Shammai. 45And the son of Shammai *was* Maon, and Maon *was* the father of Beth Zur.

46Ephah, Caleb's concubine, bore Haran, Moza, and Gazez; and Haran begot Gazez. 47And the sons of Jahdai *were* Regem, Jotham, Geshan, Pelet, Ephah, and Shaaph.

48Maachah, Caleb's concubine, bore Sheber and Tirhanah. 49She also bore Shaaph the father of Madmannah, Sheva the father of Machbenah and the father of Gibea. And the daughter of Caleb *was* aAchsah.[1]

50These were the descendants of Caleb: The sons of aHur, the firstborn of [1]Ephrathah, *were* Shobal the father of bKirjath Jearim, 51Salma the father of Bethlehem, *and* Hareph the father of Beth Gader.

52And Shobal the father of Kirjath Jearim had descendants: [1]Haroeh, *and* half of the [2]*families of* Manuhoth. 53The families of Kirjath Jearim *were* the Ithrites, the Puthites, the Shumathites, and the Mishraites. From these came the Zorathites and the Eshtaolites.

54The sons of Salma *were* Bethlehem, the Netophathites, [1]Atroth Beth Joab, half of the Manahethites, and the Zorites.

55And the families of the scribes who dwelt at Jabez *were* the Tirathites, the Shimeathites, *and* the Suchathites. These *were* the aKenites who came from Hammath, the father of the house of bRechab.

THE FAMILY OF DAVID

(*Matt. 1:6*)

3 Now these were the sons of David who were born to him in Hebron: The firstborn *was* aAmnon, by bAhinoam the cJezreelitess; the second, [1]Daniel, by dAbigail the Carmelitess; 2the third, aAbsalom the son of Maacah, the daughter of Talmai, king of Geshur; the fourth, bAdonijah the son of Haggith; 3the fifth, Shephatiah, by Abital; the sixth, Ithream, by his wife aEglah.

4*These* six were born to him in Hebron. aThere he reigned seven years and six months, and bin Jerusalem he reigned thirty-three years. 5aAnd these were born to him in Jerusalem: [1]Shimea, Shobab, Nathan, and bSolomon—four by [2]Bathshua

---

2:36 a1 Chr. 11:41
2:37 a2 Chr. 23:1
2:49 aJosh. 15:17
2:50 a1 Chr. 4:4
bJosh. 9:17;
18:14
2:55 aJudg. 1:16
b2 Kin. 10:15;
Jer. 35:2
3:1
a2 Sam. 3:2–5
b1 Sam. 25:43
cJosh. 15:56
d1 Sam. 25:39–
42
3:2
a2 Sam. 13:37;
15:1 b1 Kin. 1:5
3:3 a2 Sam. 3:5
3:4 a2 Sam. 2:11
b2 Sam. 5:5
3:5
a1 Chr. 14:4–7
b2 Sam. 12:24,
25

2:49 [1]Or *Achsa* 2:50 [1]*Ephrath,* v. 19 2:52 [1]*Reaiah,* 1 Chr. 4:2 [2]Or *Manuhothites,* same as *Manahethites,* v. 54 2:54 [1]Or *Ataroth of the house of Joab* 3:1 [1]*Chileab,* 2 Sam. 3:3 3:5 [1]*Shammua,* 1 Chr. 14:4; 2 Sam. 5:14 [2]*Bathsheba,* 2 Sam. 11:3

the daughter of [3]Ammiel. [6]Also *there* were Ibhar, [1]Elishama, [2]Eliphelet, [7]Nogah, Nepheg, Japhia, [8]Elishama, [1]Eliada, and Eliphelet—[a]nine *in all.* [9]*These were* all the sons of David, besides the sons of the concubines, and [a]Tamar their sister.

THE FAMILY OF SOLOMON
(Matt. 1:7–11)

[10]Solomon's son *was* [a]Rehoboam; [1]Abijah *was* his son, Asa his son, Jehoshaphat his son, [1][11]Joram his son, [2]Ahaziah his son, [3]Joash his son, [12]Amaziah his son, [1]Azariah his son, Jotham his son, [13]Ahaz his son, Hezekiah his son, Manasseh his son, [14]Amon his son, *and* Josiah his son. [15]The sons of Josiah *were* Johanan the firstborn, the second [1]Jehoiakim, the third Zedekiah, and the fourth [2]Shallum. [16]The sons of [a]Jehoiakim *were* [1]Jeconiah his son *and* [2]Zedekiah his son.

THE FAMILY OF JECONIAH

[17]And the sons of [1]Jeconiah [2]*were* Assir, Shealtiel [a]his son, [18]*and* Malchiram, Pedaiah, Shenazzar, Jecamiah, Hoshama, and Nedabiah. [19]The sons of Pedaiah *were* Zerubbabel and Shimei. The sons of Zerubbabel *were* Meshullam, Hananiah, Shelomith their sister, [20]and Hashubah, Ohel, Berechiah, Hasadiah, and Jushab-Hesed—five *in all.*

[21]The sons of Hananiah *were* Pelatiah and Jeshaiah, the sons of Rephaiah, the sons of Arnan, the sons of Obadiah, and the sons of Shechaniah. [22]The son of Shechaniah was Shemaiah. The sons of Shemaiah *were* [a]Hattush, Igal, Bariah, Neariah, and Shaphat—six *in all.* [23]The sons of Neariah *were* Elioenai, Hezekiah, and Azrikam—three *in all.* [24]The sons of Elioenai *were* Hodaviah, Eliashib, Pelaiah, Akkub, Johanan, Delaiah, and Anani—seven *in all.*

THE FAMILY OF JUDAH

4 The sons of Judah *were* [a]Perez, Hezron, [1]Carmi, Hur, and Shobal. [2]And [1]Reaiah the son of Shobal begot Jahath, and Jahath begot Ahumai and Lahad. These *were* the families of the Zorathites. [3]These *were the sons of* the father of Etam: Jezreel, Ishma, and Idbash; and the name of their sister *was* Hazelelponi; [4]and Penuel *was* the father of Gedor, and Ezer *was the* father of Hushah.

These *were* the sons of [a]Hur, the firstborn of Ephrathah the father of Bethlehem.

[5]And [a]Ashhur the father of Tekoa had two wives, Helah and Naarah. [6]Naarah bore him Ahuzzam, Hepher, Temeni, and Haahashtari. These *were* the sons of Naarah. [7]The sons of Helah *were* Zereth, Zohar, and Ethnan; [8]and Koz begot Anub, Zobebah, and the families of Aharhel the son of Harum.

[9]Now Jabez was [a]more honorable than his brothers, and his mother called his name [1]Jabez, saying, "Because I bore *him* in pain." [10]And Jabez called on the God of Israel saying,

---

3:8
[a]2 Sam. 5:14–16
3:9 [a]2 Sam. 13:1
3:10
[a]1 Kin. 11:43; Matt. 1:7–10
3:16 [a]Matt. 1:11
3:17 [a]Matt. 1:12
3:22 [a]Ezra 8:2
4:1 [a]Gen. 38:29; 46:12
4:4 [a]Ex. 31:2; 1 Chr. 2:50
4:5 [a]1 Chr. 2:24
4:9 [a]Gen. 34:19

3:5 [3]*Eliam,* 2 Sam. 11:3   3:6 [1]*Elishua,* 1 Chr. 14:5; 2 Sam. 5:15   [2]*Elpelet,* 1 Chr. 14:5   3:8 [1]*Beeliada,* 1 Chr. 14:7   3:10 [1]*Abijam,* 1 Kin. 15:1
3:11 [1]*Jehoram,* 2 Kin. 1:17; 8:16   [2]Or *Azariah* or *Jehoahaz*   [3]*Jehoash,* 2 Kin. 12:1   3:12 [1]*Uzziah,* Is. 6:1   3:15 [1]*Eliakim,* 2 Kin. 23:34   [2]*Jehoahaz,* 2 Kin. 23:31   3:16 [1]*Jehoiachin,* 2 Kin. 24:8, or *Coniah,* Jer. 22:24   [2]*Mattaniah,* 2 Kin. 24:17   3:17 [1]*Jehoiachin,* 2 Kin. 24:8, or *Coniah,* Jer. 22:24   [2]Or *the captive were Shealtiel*   4:1 [1]*Chelubai,* 1 Chr. 2:9 or *Caleb,* 1 Chr. 2:18
4:2 [1]*Haroeh,* 1 Chr. 2:52   4:9 [1]Lit. *He Will Cause Pain*

"Oh, that You would bless me indeed, and enlarge my [1]territory, that Your hand would be with me, and that You would keep *me* from evil, that I may not cause pain!" So God granted him what he requested.

[11]Chelub the brother of [a]Shuhah begot Mehir, who *was* the father of Eshton. [12]And Eshton begot Beth-Rapha, Paseah, and Tehinnah the father of [1]Ir-Nahash. These *were* the men of Rechah.

[13]The sons of Kenaz *were* [a]Othniel and Seraiah. The sons of Othniel *were* [1]Hathath, [14]and Meonothai *who* begot Ophrah. Seraiah begot Joab the father of [a]Ge Harashim,[1] for they were craftsmen. [15]The sons of [a]Caleb the son of Jephunneh *were* Iru, Elah, and Naam. The son of Elah *was* [1]Kenaz. [16]The sons of Jehallelel *were* Ziph, Ziphah, Tiria, and Asarel. [17]The sons of Ezrah *were* Jether, Mered, Epher, and Jalon. And [1]*Mered's wife* bore Miriam, Shammai, and Ishbah the father of Eshtemoa. [18]([1]His wife Jehudijah bore Jered the father of Gedor, Heber the father of Sochoh, and Jekuthiel the father of Zanoah.) And these were the sons of Bithiah the daughter of Pharaoh, whom Mered took.

[19]The sons of Hodiah's wife, the sister of Naham, *were* the fathers of Keilah the Garmite and of Eshtemoa the [a]Maachathite. [20]And the sons of Shimon *were* Amnon, Rinnah, Ben-Hanan, and Tilon. And the sons of Ishi *were* Zoheth and Ben-Zoheth.

[21]The sons of [a]Shelah [b]the son of Judah *were* Er the father of Lecah, Laadah the father of Mareshah, and the families of the house of the linen workers of the house of Ashbea; [22]also Jokim, the men of Chozeba, and Joash; Saraph, who ruled in Moab, and Jashubi-Lehem. Now the [1]records are ancient. [23]These *were* the potters and those who dwell at [1]Netaim and [2]Gederah; there they dwelt with the king for his work.

THE FAMILY OF SIMEON
(Gen. 46:10)

[24]The [a]sons of Simeon *were* [1]Nemuel, Jamin, [2]Jarib, [3]Zerah, *and* Shaul, [25]Shallum his son, Mibsam his son, and Mishma his son. [26]And the sons of Mishma *were* Hamuel his son, Zacchur his son, and Shimei his son. [27]Shimei had sixteen sons and six daughters; but his brothers did not have many children, [a]nor did any of their families multiply as much as the children of Judah.

[28]They dwelt at Beersheba, Moladah, Hazar Shual, [29][1]Bilhah, Ezem, [2]Tolad, [30]Bethuel, Hormah, Ziklag, [31]Beth Marcaboth, [1]Hazar Susim, Beth Biri, and at Shaaraim. These *were* their cities until the reign of David. [32]And their villages *were* [1]Etam, Ain, Rimmon, Tochen, and Ashan—five cities— [33]and all the villages that *were* around these cities as far as [1]Baal. These *were* their dwelling places, and they maintained their genealogy: [34]Meshobab, Jamlech, and Joshah the son of Amaziah; [35]Joel, and Jehu the son of Joshibiah, the son of Seraiah,

4:11 [a]Job 8:1

4:13 [a]Josh. 15:17; Judg. 3:9, 11

4:14 [a]Neh. 11:35

4:15 [a]Josh. 14:6, 14; 15:13, 17; 1 Chr. 6:56

4:19 [a]2 Kin. 25:23

4:21 [a]Gen. 38:11, 14 [b]Gen. 38:1–5; 46:12

4:24 [a]Num. 26:12–14

4:27 [a]Num. 2:9

4:10 [1]*border*   4:12 [1]Lit. *City of Nahash*   4:13 [1]LXX, Vg. add *and Meonothai*   4:14 [1]Lit. *Valley of Craftsmen*   4:15 [1]Or *Uknaz*   4:17 [1]Lit. *she*   4:18 [1]Or *His Judean wife*   4:22 [1]Lit. *words*   4:23 [1]Lit. *Plants*   [2]Lit. *Hedges*
4:24 [1]*Jemuel*, Gen. 46:10; Ex. 6:15; Num. 26:12   [2]*Jachin*, Gen. 46:10; Num. 26:12   [3]*Zohar*, Gen. 46:10; Ex. 6:15   4:29 [1]*Balah*, Josh. 19:3   [2]*Eltolad*, Josh. 19:4   4:31 [1]*Hazar Susah*, Josh. 19:5   4:32 [2]*Ether*, Josh. 19:7   4:33 [1]*Baalath Beer*, Josh. 19:8

the son of Asiel; 36Elioenai, Jaakobah, Jeshohaiah, Asaiah, Adiel, Jesimiel, and Benaiah; 37Ziza the son of Shiphi, the son of Allon, the son of Jedaiah, the son of Shimri, the son of Shemaiah— 38these mentioned by name *were* leaders in their families, and their father's house increased greatly.

39So they went to the entrance of Gedor, as far as the east side of the valley, to seek pasture for their flocks. 40And they found rich, good pasture, and the land *was* broad, quiet, and peaceful; for some Hamites formerly lived there.

41These recorded by name came in the days of Hezekiah king of Judah; and they ªattacked[1] their tents and the Meunites who were found there, and butterly destroyed them, as it is to this day. So they dwelt in their place, because *there was* pasture for their flocks there. 42Now *some* of them, five hundred men of the sons of Simeon, went to Mount Seir, having as their captains Pelatiah, Neariah, Rephaiah, and Uzziel, the sons of Ishi. 43And they [1]defeated ªthe rest of the Amalekites who had escaped. They have dwelt there to this day.

THE FAMILY OF REUBEN

(Gen. 46:8, 9)

5 Now the sons of Reuben the firstborn of Israel—ªhe *was* indeed the firstborn, but because he bdefiled his father's bed, chis birthright was given to the sons of Joseph, the son of Israel, so that the genealogy is not listed according to the birthright; 2yet ªJudah prevailed over his brothers, and from him *came* a bruler, although [1]the birthright was Joseph's— 3the sons of ªReuben the firstborn of Israel were Hanoch, Pallu, Hezron, and Carmi.

4The sons of Joel *were* Shemaiah his son, Gog his son, Shimei his son, 5Micah his son, Reaiah his son, Baal his son, 6and Beerah his son, whom [1]Tiglath-Pileser king of Assyria ªcarried into captivity. He *was* leader of the Reubenites. 7And his brethren by their families, ªwhen the genealogy of their generations was registered: the chief, Jeiel, and Zechariah, 8and Bela the son of Azaz, the son of Shema, the son of Joel, who dwelt in ªAroer, as far as Nebo and Baal Meon. 9Eastward they settled as far as the [1]entrance of the wilderness this side of the River Euphrates, because their cattle had [2]multiplied ªin the land of Gilead.

10Now in the days of Saul they made war ªwith the Hagrites, who fell by their hand; and they dwelt in their tents throughout the entire *area* east of Gilead.

THE FAMILY OF GAD

11And the ªchildren of Gad dwelt next to them in the land of bBashan as far as cSalcah: 12Joel *was* the chief, Shapham the next, then Jaanai and Shaphat in Bashan, 13and their brethren of their father's house: Michael, Meshullam, Sheba, Jorai, Jachan, Zia, and Eber—seven *in all.* 14These *were* the children of Abihail the son of Huri, the son of Jaroah, the son of Gilead, the son of Michael, the son of Jeshishai, the son of Jahdo, the son of Buz; 15Ahi the son of Abdiel, the son of Guni, *was* chief of their father's house. 16And *the Gadites* dwelt in Gilead, in Bashan and in its villages, and in all the [1]common-lands of

4:41 ª2 Kin. 18:8
b2 Kin. 19:11
4:43 ªEx. 17:14;
1 Sam. 15:8;
30:17
5:1 ªGen. 29:32;
49:3
bGen. 35:22;
49:4
cGen. 48:15, 22
5:2 ªGen. 49:8, 10;
Ps. 60:7; 108:8
bMic. 5:2;
Matt. 2:6
5:3 ªGen. 46:9;
Ex. 6:14;
Num. 26:5
5:6 ª2 Kin. 18:11
5:7 ª1 Chr. 5:17
5:8 ªNum. 32:34;
Josh. 12:2;
13:15, 16
5:9 ªJosh. 22:8, 9
5:10 ªGen. 25:12
5:11 ªNum. 26:15–18
bJosh. 13:11, 24–28 cDeut. 3:10

4:41 [1]Lit. *struck*   4:43 [1]Lit. *struck*   5:2 [1]*the right of the firstborn*   5:6 [1]Heb. *Tilgath-Pileser*   5:9 [1]*beginning*   [2]*increased*   5:16 [1]*open lands*

[a]Sharon within their borders. [17]All these were registered by genealogies in the days of [a]Jotham king of Judah, and in the days of [b]Jeroboam king of Israel.

[18]The sons of Reuben, the Gadites, and half the tribe of Manasseh *had* forty-four thousand seven hundred and sixty valiant men, men able to bear shield and sword, to shoot with the bow, and skillful in war, who went to war. [19]They made war with the Hagrites, [a]Jetur, Naphish, and Nodab. [20]And [a]they were helped against them, and the Hagrites were delivered into their hand, and all who *were* with them, for they [b]cried out to God in the battle. He [1]heeded their prayer, because they [c]put their trust in Him. [21]Then they took away their livestock—fifty thousand of their camels, two hundred and fifty thousand of their sheep, and two thousand of their donkeys—also one hundred thousand of their men; [22]for many fell dead, because the war [a]*was* God's. And they dwelt in their place until [b]the captivity.

THE FAMILY OF MANASSEH (EAST)

[23]So the children of the half-tribe of Manasseh dwelt in the land. Their *numbers* increased from Bashan to Baal Hermon, that is, to [a]Senir, or Mount Hermon. [24]These *were* the heads of their fathers' houses: Epher, Ishi, Eliel, Azriel, Jeremiah, Hodaviah, and Jahdiel. They were mighty men of valor, famous men, *and* heads of their fathers' houses.

[25]And they were unfaithful to the God of their fathers, and [a]played the harlot after the gods of the peoples of the land, whom God had destroyed before them. [26]So the God of Israel stirred up the spirit of [a]Pul king of Assyria, that is, [b]Tiglath-Pileser[1] king of Assyria. He carried the Reubenites, the Gadites, and the half-tribe of Manasseh into captivity. He took them to [c]Halah, Habor, Hara, and the river of Gozan to this day.

THE FAMILY OF LEVI

(Gen. 46:11)

6 The sons of Levi *were* [a]Gershon,[1] Kohath, and Merari. [2]The sons of Kohath *were* Amram, [a]Izhar, Hebron, and Uzziel. [3]The children of Amram *were* Aaron, Moses, and Miriam. And the sons of Aaron *were* [a]Nadab, Abihu, Eleazar, and Ithamar. [4]Eleazar begot Phinehas, *and* Phinehas begot Abishua; [5]Abishua begot Bukki, and Bukki begot Uzzi; [6]Uzzi begot Zerahiah, and Zerahiah begot Meraioth; [7]Meraioth begot Amariah, and Amariah begot Ahitub; [8a]Ahitub begot [b]Zadok, and Zadok begot Ahimaaz; [9]Ahimaaz begot Azariah, and Azariah begot Johanan; [10]Johanan begot Azariah (it was he [a]who ministered as priest in the [b]temple[1] that Solomon built in Jerusalem); [11a]Azariah begot [b]Amariah, and Amariah begot Ahitub; [12]Ahitub begot Zadok, and Zadok begot [1]Shallum; [13]Shallum begot Hilkiah, and Hilkiah begot Azariah; [14]Azariah begot [a]Seraiah, and Seraiah begot Jehozadak. [15]Jehozadak went *into captivity* [a]when the LORD carried Judah and Jerusalem into captivity by the hand of Nebuchadnezzar.

[16]The sons of Levi *were* [a]Gershon,[1] Kohath, and Merari. [17]These are the names of the sons of Gershon: Libni and

5:16 [a]1 Chr. 27:29; Song 2:1; Is. 35:2; 65:10

5:17 [a]2 Kin. 15:5, 32 [b]2 Kin. 14:16, 28

5:19 [a]Gen. 25:15; 1 Chr. 1:31

5:20 [a][1 Chr. 5:22] [b]2 Chr. 14:11–13 [c]Ps. 9:10; 20:7, 8; 22:4, 5

5:22 [a][Josh. 23:10; 2 Chr. 32:8; Rom. 8:31] [b]2 Kin. 15:29; 17:6

5:23 [a]Deut. 3:9

5:25 [a]2 Kin. 17:7

5:26 [a]2 Kin. 15:19 [b]2 Kin. 15:29 [c]2 Kin. 17:6; 18:11

6:1 [a]Gen. 46:11; Ex. 6:16; Num. 26:57; 1 Chr. 23:6

6:2 [a]1 Chr. 6:18, 22

6:3 [a]Lev. 10:1, 2

6:8 [a]2 Sam. 8:17 [b]2 Sam. 15:27

6:10 [a]2 Chr. 26:17, 18 [b]1 Kin. 6:1; 2 Chr. 3:1

6:11 [a]Ezra 7:3 [b]2 Chr. 19:11

6:14 [a]2 Kin. 25:18–21; Neh. 11:11

6:15 [a]2 Kin. 25:21

6:16 [a]Gen. 46:11; Ex. 6:16

5:20 [1]Lit. *was entreated for them*   **5:26** [1]Heb. *Tilgath-Pilneser*   **6:1** [1]Or *Gershom*, v. 16   **6:10** [1]Lit. *house*   **6:12** [1]*Meshullam*, 1 Chr. 9:11   **6:16** [1]Heb. *Gershom*, an alternate spelling for *Gershon*, vv. 1, 17, 20, 43, 62, 71

Shimei. 18The sons of Kohath *were* Amram, Izhar, Hebron, and Uzziel. 19The sons of Merari *were* Mahli and Mushi. Now these *are* the families of the Levites according to their fathers: 20Of Gershon *were* Libni his son, Jahath his son, ªZimmah his son, 21¹Joah his son, ²Iddo his son, Zerah his son, *and* ³Jeatherai his son. 22The sons of Kohath *were* ¹Amminadab his son, ªKorah his son, Assir his son, 23Elkanah his son, Ebiasaph his son, Assir his son, 24Tahath his son, Uriel his son, Uzziah his son, and Shaul his son. 25The sons of Elkanah *were* ªAmasai and Ahimoth. 26*As for* Elkanah, the sons of Elkanah *were* ¹Zophai his son, ²Nahath his son, 27¹Eliab his son, Jeroham his son, *and* Elkanah his son. 28The sons of Samuel *were* ¹Joel the firstborn, and Abijah ²the second. 29The sons of Merari *were* Mahli, Libni his son, Shimei his son, Uzzah his son, 30Shimea his son, Haggiah his son, *and* Asaiah his son.

MUSICIANS IN THE HOUSE OF THE LORD

31Now these are ªthe men whom David appointed over the service of song in the house of the LORD, after the ᵇark came to rest. 32They were ministering with music before the dwelling place of the tabernacle of meeting, until Solomon had built the house of the LORD in Jerusalem, and they served in their office according to their order.

33And these *are* the ones who ¹ministered with their sons: Of the sons of the ªKohathites *were* Heman the singer, the son of Joel, the son of Samuel, 34the son of Elkanah, the son of Jeroham, the son of ¹Eliel, the son of ²Toah, 35the son of Zuph, the son of Elkanah, the son of Mahath, the son of Amasai, 36the son of Elkanah, the son of Joel, the son of Azariah, the son of Zephaniah, 37the son of Tahath, the son of Assir, the son of ªEbiasaph, the son of Korah, 38the son of Izhar, the son of Kohath, the son of Levi, the son of Israel. 39And his brother ªAsaph, who stood at his right hand, *was* Asaph the son of Berachiah, the son of Shimea, 40the son of Michael, the son of Baaseiah, the son of Malchijah, 41the son of ªEthni, the son of Zerah, the son of Adaiah, 42the son of Ethan, the son of Zimmah, the son of Shimei, 43the son of Jahath, the son of Gershon, the son of Levi.

44Their brethren, the sons of Merari, on the left hand, *were* ¹Ethan the son of ²Kishi, the son of Abdi, the son of Malluch, 45the son of Hashabiah, the son of Amaziah, the son of Hilkiah, 46the son of Amzi, the son of Bani, the son of Shamer, 47the son of Mahli, the son of Mushi, the son of Merari, the son of Levi.

48And their brethren, the Levites, *were* appointed to every ªkind of service of the tabernacle of the house of God.

THE FAMILY OF AARON

49ªBut Aaron and his sons offered sacrifices ᵇon the altar of burnt offering and ᶜon the altar of incense, for all the work of the Most Holy *Place*, and to make atonement for Israel, according to all that Moses the servant of God had commanded. 50Now these *are* the ªsons of Aaron: Eleazar his son, Phinehas

6:20 ª1 Chr. 6:42
6:22 ªNum. 16:1
6:25
ª1 Chr. 6:35, 36
6:31
ª1 Chr. 15:16–22, 27; 16:4–6
ᵇ2 Sam. 6:17; 1 Kin. 8:4; 1 Chr. 15:25—16:1
6:33
ªNum. 26:57
6:37 ªEx. 6:24
6:39 ª2 Chr. 5:12
6:41 ª1 Chr. 6:21
6:48
ª1 Chr. 9:14–34
6:49 ªEx. 28:1; [Num. 18:1–8]
ᵇLev. 1:8, 9
ᶜEx. 30:7
6:50
ª1 Chr. 6:4–8; Ezra 7:5

6:21 ¹*Ethan,* v. 42   ²*Adaiah,* v. 41   ³*Ethni,* v. 41   6:22 ¹*Izhar,* vv. 2, 18   6:26 ¹*Zuph,* v. 35; 1 Sam. 1:1   ²*Toah,* v. 34   6:27 ¹*Eliel,* v. 34   6:28 ¹So with LXX, Syr., Arab.; cf. v. 33 and 1 Sam. 8:2   ²Heb. *Vasheni*   6:33 ¹Lit. *stood with*   6:34 ¹*Elihu,* 1 Sam. 1:1   ²*Tohu,* 1 Sam. 1:1   6:44 ¹*Jeduthun,* 1 Chr. 9:16; 25:1, 3, 6; 2 Chr. 35:15; Ps. 62:title   ²Or *Kushaiah*

his son, Abishua his son, [51]Bukki his son, Uzzi his son, Zerahiah his son, [52]Meraioth his son, Amariah his son, Ahitub his son, [53]Zadok his son, *and* Ahimaaz his son.

DWELLING PLACES OF THE LEVITES
(Josh. 21:1–42)

[54a]Now these *are* their dwelling places throughout their settlements in their territory, for they were *given* by lot to the sons of Aaron, of the family of the Kohathites: [55a]They gave them Hebron in the land of Judah, with its surrounding [1]common-lands. [56a]But the fields of the city and its villages they gave to Caleb the son of Jephunneh. [57]And [a]to the sons of Aaron they gave *one of* the cities of refuge, Hebron; also Libnah with its common-lands, Jattir, Eshtemoa with its common-lands, [58][1]Hilen with its common-lands, Debir with its common-lands, [59][1]Ashan with its common-lands, and Beth Shemesh with its common-lands. [60]And from the tribe of Benjamin: Geba with its common-lands, [1]Alemeth with its common-lands, and Anathoth with its common-lands. All their cities among their families *were* thirteen.

[61a]To the rest of the family of the tribe of the Kohathites *they gave* [b]by lot ten cities from half the tribe of Manasseh. [62]And to the sons of Gershon, throughout their families, *they gave* thirteen cities from the tribe of Issachar, from the tribe of Asher, from the tribe of Naphtali, and from the tribe of Manasseh in Bashan. [63]To the sons of Merari, throughout their families, *they gave* [a]twelve cities from the tribe of Reuben, from the tribe of Gad, and from the tribe of Zebulun. [64]So the children of Israel gave *these* cities with their [1]common-lands to the Levites. [65]And they gave by lot from the tribe of the children of Judah, from the tribe of the children of Simeon, and from the tribe of the children of Benjamin these cities which are called by *their* names.

[66]Now [a]some of the families of the sons of Kohath *were given* cities as their territory from the tribe of Ephraim. [67a]And they gave them *one of* the cities of refuge, Shechem with its common-lands, in the mountains of Ephraim, also Gezer with its common-lands, [68a]Jokmeam with its common-lands, Beth Horon with its common-lands, [69]Aijalon with its common-lands, and Gath Rimmon with its common-lands. [70]And from the half-tribe of Manasseh: Aner with its common-lands and Bileam with its common-lands, for the rest of the family of the sons of Kohath.

[71]From the family of the half-tribe of Manasseh the sons of Gershon *were given* Golan in Bashan with its common-lands and [1]Ashtaroth with its common-lands. [72]And from the tribe of Issachar: [1]Kedesh with its common-lands, Daberath with its common-lands, [73]Ramoth with its common-lands, and Anem with its common-lands. [74]And from the tribe of Asher: Mashal with its common-lands, Abdon with its common-lands, [75]Hukok with its common-lands, and Rehob with its common-lands. [76]And from the tribe of Naphtali: Kedesh in Galilee with its common-lands, Hammon with its common-lands, and Kirjathaim with its common-lands.

6:54 [a]Josh. 21
6:55 [a]Josh. 14:13; 21:11, 12
6:56 [a]Josh. 14:13; 15:13
6:57 [a]Josh. 21:13, 19
6:61 [a]1 Chr. 6:66–70 [b]Josh. 21:5
6:63 [a]Josh. 21:7, 34–40
6:66 [a]1 Chr. 6:61
6:67 [a]Josh. 21:21
6:68 [a]Josh. 21:22

6:55 [1]*open lands*   6:58 [1]*Holon,* Josh. 21:15   6:59 [1]*Ain,* Josh. 21:16
6:60 [1]*Almon,* Josh. 21:18   6:64 [1]*open lands*   6:71 [1]*Beeshterah,* Josh. 21:27
6:72 [1]*Kishon,* Josh. 21:28

77From the tribe of Zebulun the rest of the children of Merari *were given* [1]Rimmon with its common-lands and Tabor with its common-lands. 78And on the other side of the Jordan, across from Jericho, on the east side of the Jordan, *they were given* from the tribe of Reuben: Bezer in the wilderness with its common-lands, Jahzah with its common-lands, 79Kedemoth with its common-lands, and Mephaath with its common-lands. 80And from the tribe of Gad: Ramoth in Gilead with its common-lands, Mahanaim with its common-lands, 81Heshbon with its common-lands, and Jazer with its common-lands.

THE FAMILY OF ISSACHAR
(Gen. 46:13)

7 The sons of Issachar *were* [a]Tola, [1]Puah, [2]Jashub, and Shimron—four *in all.* 2The sons of Tola *were* Uzzi, Rephaiah, Jeriel, Jahmai, Jibsam, and Shemuel, heads of their father's house. *The sons* of Tola *were* mighty men of valor in their generations; [a]their number in the days of David *was* twenty-two thousand six hundred. 3The son of Uzzi *was* Izrahiah, and the sons of Izrahiah *were* Michael, Obadiah, Joel, and Ishiah. All five of them *were* chief men. 4And with them, by their generations, according to their fathers' houses, *were* thirty-six thousand troops ready for war; for they had many wives and sons.

5Now their brethren among all the families of Issachar *were* mighty men of valor, listed by their genealogies, eighty-seven thousand in all.

THE FAMILY OF BENJAMIN
(Gen. 46:21)

6*The sons* of [a]Benjamin *were* Bela, Becher, and Jediael—three *in all.* 7The sons of Bela were Ezbon, Uzzi, Uzziel, Jerimoth, and Iri—five *in all.* They *were* heads of *their* fathers' houses, and they were listed by their genealogies, twenty-two thousand and thirty-four mighty men of valor.

8The sons of Becher *were* Zemirah, Joash, Eliezer, Elioenai, Omri, Jerimoth, Abijah, Anathoth, and Alemeth. All these *are* the sons of Becher. 9And they were recorded by genealogy according to their generations, heads of their fathers' houses, twenty thousand two hundred mighty men of valor. 10The son of Jediael *was* Bilhan, and the sons of Bilhan *were* Jeush, Benjamin, Ehud, Chenaanah, Zethan, Tharshish, and Ahishahar.

11All these sons of Jediael *were* heads of their fathers' houses; *there were* seventeen thousand two hundred mighty men of valor fit to go out for war *and* battle. 12[1]Shuppim and [2]Huppim *were* the sons of [3]Ir, *and* Hushim *was* the son of [4]Aher.

THE FAMILY OF NAPHTALI
(Gen. 46:24)

13The [a]sons of Naphtali *were* [1]Jahziel, Guni, Jezer, and [2]Shallum, the sons of Bilhah.

7:1
[a]Num. 26:23–25

7:2
[a]2 Sam. 24:1–9;
1 Chr. 27:1

7:6 [a]Gen. 46:21;
Num. 26:38–41;
1 Chr. 8:1

7:13
[a]Num. 26:48–50

6:77 [1]Heb. *Rimmono,* an alternate spelling of *Rimmon,* 1 Chr. 4:32
7:1 [1]*Puvah,* Gen. 46:13   [2]*Job,* Gen. 46:13   7:12 [1]*Shupham,* Num. 26:39
[2]*Hupham,* Num. 26:39   [3]*Iri,* v. 7   [4]*Ahiram,* Num. 26:38   7:13 [1]*Jahzeel,*
Gen. 46:24   [2]*Shillem,* Gen. 46:24

THE FAMILY OF MANASSEH (WEST)

14The ^a^descendants of Manasseh: his Syrian concubine bore him ^b^Machir the father of Gilead, the father of Asriel. 15Machir took as his wife *the sister* of ^1^Huppim and ^2^Shuppim, whose name *was* Maachah. The name of *Gilead's* ^3^grandson *was* ^a^Zelophehad, but Zelophehad begot only daughters. 16(Maachah the wife of Machir bore a son, and she called his name Peresh. The name of his brother *was* Sheresh, and his sons *were* Ulam and Rakem. 17The son of Ulam *was* ^a^Bedan.) These *were* the descendants of Gilead the son of Machir, the son of Manasseh.

18His sister Hammoleketh bore Ishhod, ^1^Abiezer, and Mahlah.

19And the sons of Shemida were Ahian, Shechem, Likhi, and Aniam.

THE FAMILY OF EPHRAIM

20^a^The sons of Ephraim *were* Shuthelah, Bered his son, Tahath his son, Eladah his son, Tahath his son, 21Zabad his son, Shuthelah his son, and Ezer and Elead. The men of Gath who were born in *that* land killed *them* because they came down to take away their cattle. 22Then Ephraim their father mourned many days, and his brethren came to comfort him.

23And when he went in to his wife, she conceived and bore a son; and he called his name ^1^Beriah, because tragedy had come upon his house. 24Now his daughter *was* Sheerah, who built Lower and Upper ^a^Beth Horon and Uzzen Sheerah; 25and Rephah *was* his son, *as well* as Resheph, and Telah his son, Tahan his son, 26Laadan his son, Ammihud his son, ^a^Elishama his son, 27^1^Nun his son, and ^a^Joshua his son.

28Now their ^a^possessions and dwelling places *were* Bethel and its towns: to the east ^1^Naaran, to the west Gezer and its towns, and Shechem and its towns, as far as ^2^Ayyah and its towns; 29and by the borders of the children of ^a^Manasseh *were* Beth Shean and its towns, Taanach and its towns, ^b^Megiddo and its towns, Dor and its towns. In these dwelt the children of Joseph, the son of Israel.

THE FAMILY OF ASHER
(Gen. 46:17)

30^a^The sons of Asher *were* Imnah, Ishvah, Ishvi, Beriah, and their sister Serah. 31The sons of Beriah *were* Heber and Malchiel, who was the father of ^1^Birzaith. 32And Heber begot Japhlet, ^1^Shomer, ^2^Hotham, and their sister Shua. 33The sons of Japhlet *were* Pasach, Bimhal, and Ashvath. These *were* the children of Japhlet. 34The sons of ^a^Shemer *were* Ahi, Rohgah, Jehubbah, and Aram. 35And the sons of his brother Helem *were* Zophah, Imna, Shelesh, and Amal. 36The sons of Zophah *were* Suah, Harnepher, Shual, Beri, Imrah, 37Bezer, Hod, Shamma, Shilshah, ^1^Jithran, and Beera. 38The sons of Jether *were* Jephunneh, Pispah, and Ara. 39The sons of Ulla *were* Arah, Haniel, and Rizia.

7:14 ^a^Num. 26:29–34 ^b^1 Chr. 2:21
7:15 ^a^Num. 26:30–33; 27:1
7:17 ^a^1 Sam. 12:11
7:20 ^a^Num. 26:35–37
7:24 ^a^Josh. 16:3, 5; 2 Chr. 8:5
7:26 ^a^Num. 10:22
7:27 ^a^Ex. 17:9, 14; 24:13; 33:11
7:28 ^a^Josh. 16:1–10
7:29 ^a^Gen. 41:51; Josh. 17:7 ^b^Josh. 17:11
7:30 ^a^Gen. 46:17; Num. 26:44–47
7:34 ^a^1 Chr. 7:32

7:15 ^1^*Hupham*, v. 12; Num. 26:39 ^2^*Shupham*, v. 12; Num. 26:39 ^3^Lit. *the second* 7:18 ^1^*Jeezer*, Num. 26:30 7:23 ^1^Lit. *In Tragedy* 7:27 ^1^Heb. *Non* 7:28 ^1^*Naarath*, Josh. 16:7 ^2^Many Heb. mss., Bg., LXX, Tg., Vg. *Gazza* 7:31 ^1^Or *Birzavith* or *Birzoth* 7:32 ^1^*Shemer*, 1 Chr. 7:34 ^2^*Helem*, 1 Chr. 7:35 7:37 ^1^*Jether*, v. 38

40All these *were* the children of Asher, heads of *their* fathers' houses, choice men, mighty men of valor, chief leaders. And they were recorded by genealogies among the army fit for battle; their number *was* twenty-six thousand.

THE FAMILY TREE OF KING SAUL OF BENJAMIN
(Gen. 46:21)

8 Now Benjamin begot ªBela his firstborn, Ashbel the second, ¹Aharah the third, ²Nohah the fourth, and Rapha the fifth. ³The sons of Bela *were* ¹Addar, Gera, Abihud, ⁴Abishua, Naaman, Ahoah, ⁵Gera, ¹Shephuphan, and Huram.

⁶These *are* the sons of Ehud, who were the heads of the fathers' *houses* of the inhabitants of ªGeba, and who forced them to move to ᵇManahath: ⁷Naaman, Ahijah, and Gera who forced them to move. He begot Uzza and Ahihud.

⁸Also Shaharaim had children in the country of Moab, after he had sent away Hushim and Baara his wives. ⁹By Hodesh his wife he begot Jobab, Zibia, Mesha, Malcam, ¹⁰Jeuz, Sachiah, and Mirmah. These *were* his sons, heads of their fathers' *houses.*

¹¹And by Hushim he begot Abitub and Elpaal. ¹²The sons of Elpaal *were* Eber, Misham, and Shemed, who built Ono and Lod with its towns; ¹³and Beriah and ªShema, who *were* heads of their fathers' *houses* of the inhabitants of Aijalon, who drove out the inhabitants of Gath. ¹⁴Ahio, Shashak, Jeremoth, ¹⁵Zebadiah, Arad, Eder, ¹⁶Michael, Ispah, and Joha *were* the sons of Beriah. ¹⁷Zebadiah, Meshullam, Hizki, Heber, ¹⁸Ishmerai, Jizliah, and Jobab *were* the sons of Elpaal. ¹⁹Jakim, Zichri, Zabdi, ²⁰Elienai, Zillethai, Eliel, ²¹Adaiah, Beraiah, and Shimrath *were* the sons of ¹Shimei. ²²Ishpan, Eber, Eliel, ²³Abdon, Zichri, Hanan, ²⁴Hananiah, Elam, Antothijah, ²⁵Iphdeiah, and Penuel *were* the sons of Shashak. ²⁶Shamsherai, Shehariah, Athaliah, ²⁷Jaareshiah, Elijah, and Zichri *were* the sons of Jeroham.

²⁸These *were* heads of the fathers' *houses* by their generations, chief men. These dwelt in Jerusalem.

²⁹Now ¹the father of Gibeon, whose ªwife's name *was* Maacah, dwelt at Gibeon. ³⁰And his firstborn son *was* Abdon, then Zur, Kish, Baal, Nadab, ³¹Gedor, Ahio, ¹Zecher, ³²and Mikloth, *who* begot ¹Shimeah. They also dwelt ²alongside their ³relatives in Jerusalem, with their brethren. ³³ªNer¹ begot Kish, Kish begot Saul, and Saul begot Jonathan, Malchishua, ²Abinadab, and ³Esh-Baal. ³⁴The son of Jonathan *was* ¹Merib-Baal, and Merib-Baal begot ªMicah. ³⁵The sons of Micah *were* Pithon, Melech, ¹Tarea, and Ahaz. ³⁶And Ahaz begot ¹Jehoaddah; Jehoaddah begot Alemeth, Azmaveth, and Zimri; and Zimri begot Moza. ³⁷Moza begot Binea, ¹Raphah his son, Eleasah his son, *and* Azel his son.

³⁸Azel had six sons whose names *were* these: Azrikam, Bocheru, Ishmael, Sheariah, Obadiah, and Hanan. All these *were* the sons of Azel. ³⁹And the sons of Eshek his brother *were* Ulam his firstborn, Jeush the second, and Eliphelet the third.

8:1 ªGen. 46:21;
Num. 26:38;
1 Chr. 7:6

8:6 ª1 Chr. 6:60
ᵇ1 Chr. 2:52

8:13 ª1 Chr. 8:21

8:29

ª1 Chr. 9:35–38

8:33

ª1 Sam. 14:51

8:34

ª2 Sam. 9:12

8:1 ¹*Ahiram,* Num. 26:38   8:3 ¹*Ard,* Num. 26:40   8:5 ¹*Shupham,* Num. 26:39,
or *Shuppim,* 1 Chr. 7:12   8:21 ¹*Shema,* 1 Chr. 7:13   8:29 ¹*Jeiel,* 1 Chr. 9:35
8:31 ¹*Zechariah,* 1 Chr. 9:37   8:32 ¹*Shimeam,* 1 Chr. 9:38   ²Lit. *opposite*
³*brethren*   8:33 ¹Also the son of Gibeon, 1 Chr. 9:36, 39   ²*Jishui,* 1 Sam. 14:49
³*Ishbosheth,* 2 Sam. 2:8   8:34 ¹*Mephibosheth,* 2 Sam. 4:4   8:35 ¹*Tahrea,* 1 Chr.
9:41   8:36 ¹*Jarah,* 1 Chr. 9:42   8:37 ¹*Raphaiah,* 1 Chr. 9:43

⁴⁰The sons of Ulam were mighty men of valor—archers. *They* had many sons and grandsons, one hundred and fifty *in all.* These *were* all sons of Benjamin.

9 So ªall Israel was ¹recorded by genealogies, and indeed, they *were* inscribed in the book of the kings of Israel. But Judah was carried away captive to Babylon because of their unfaithfulness. ²ªAnd the first inhabitants who *dwelt* in their possessions in their cities *were* Israelites, priests, Levites, and ᵇthe Nethinim.

DWELLERS IN JERUSALEM

³Now in ªJerusalem the children of Judah dwelt, and some of the children of Benjamin, and of the children of Ephraim and Manasseh: ⁴Uthai the son of Ammihud, the son of Omri, the son of Imri, the son of Bani, of the descendants of Perez, the son of Judah. ⁵Of the Shilonites: Asaiah the firstborn and his sons. ⁶Of the sons of Zerah: Jeuel, and their brethren—six hundred and ninety. ⁷Of the sons of Benjamin: Sallu the son of Meshullam, the son of Hodaviah, the son of Hassenuah; ⁸Ibneiah the son of Jeroham; Elah the son of Uzzi, the son of Michri; Meshullam the son of Shephatiah, the son of Reuel, the son of Ibnijah; ⁹and their brethren, according to their generations—nine hundred and fifty-six. All these men *were* heads of a father's *house* in their fathers' houses.

THE PRIESTS AT JERUSALEM

¹⁰ªOf the priests: Jedaiah, Jehoiarib, and Jachin; ¹¹Azariah the son of Hilkiah, the son of Meshullam, the son of Zadok, the son of Meraioth, the son of Ahitub, the ªofficer over the house of God; ¹²Adaiah the son of Jeroham, the son of Pashur, the son of Malchijah; Maasai the son of Adiel, the son of Jahzerah, the son of Meshullam, the son of Meshillemith, the son of Immer; ¹³and their brethren, heads of their fathers' houses—one thousand seven hundred and sixty. *They were* ¹very able men for the work of the service of the house of God.

THE LEVITES AT JERUSALEM

¹⁴Of the Levites: Shemaiah the son of Hasshub, the son of Azrikam, the son of Hashabiah, of the sons of Merari; ¹⁵Bakbakkar, Heresh, Galal, and Mattaniah the son of Micah, the son of ªZichri, the son of Asaph; ¹⁶ªObadiah the son of ᵇShemaiah, the son of Galal, the son of Jeduthun; and Berechiah the son of Asa, the son of Elkanah, who lived in the villages of the Netophathites.

THE LEVITE GATEKEEPERS

¹⁷And the gatekeepers *were* Shallum, Akkub, Talmon, Ahiman, and their brethren. Shallum *was* the chief. ¹⁸Until then *they had been* gatekeepers for the camps of the children of Levi at the King's Gate on the east.

¹⁹Shallum the son of Kore, the son of Ebiasaph, the son of Korah, and his brethren, from his father's house, the Korahites, *were* in charge of the work of the service, ¹gatekeepers of the tabernacle. Their fathers had been keepers of the entrance to the camp of the LORD. ²⁰And ªPhinehas the son

9:1 ªEzra 2:59

9:2 ªEzra 2:70; Neh. 7:73
ᵇEzra 2:43; 8:20

9:3 ªNeh. 11:1, 2

9:10 ªNeh. 11:10–14

9:11 ª2 Chr. 31:13; Jer. 20:1

9:15 ªNeh. 11:17

9:16 ªNeh. 11:17 ᵇNeh. 11:17

9:20 ªNum. 25:6–13; 31:6

9:1 ¹enrolled   9:11 ¹Seraiah, Neh. 11:11   9:13 ¹Lit. *mighty men of strength*
9:19 ¹Lit. *thresholds*

of Eleazar had been the officer over them in time past; the LORD *was* with him. [21a]Zechariah the son of Meshelemiah *was* [1]keeper of the door of the tabernacle of meeting.

[22]All those chosen as gatekeepers *were* two hundred and twelve. [a]They were recorded by their genealogy, in their villages. David and Samuel [b]the seer had appointed them to their trusted office. [23]So they and their children *were* in charge of the gates of the house of the LORD, the house of the tabernacle, by assignment. [24]The gatekeepers were assigned to the four directions: the east, west, north, and south. [25]And their brethren in their villages *had* to come with them from time to time [a]for seven days. [26]For in this trusted office *were* four chief gatekeepers; they were Levites. And they had charge over the chambers and treasuries of the house of God. [27]And they lodged *all* around the house of God because [1]they *had* the [a]responsibility, and they *were* in charge of opening *it* every morning.

OTHER LEVITE RESPONSIBILITIES

[28]Now *some* of them were in charge of the serving vessels, for they brought them in and took them out by count. [29]*Some* of them *were* appointed over the furnishings and over all the implements of the sanctuary, and over the [a]fine flour and the wine and the oil and the incense and the spices. [30]And *some* of the sons of the priests made [a]the ointment of the spices.

[31]Mattithiah of the Levites, the firstborn of Shallum the Korahite, had the trusted office [a]over the things that were baked in the pans. [32]And some of their brethren of the sons of the Kohathites [a]*were* in charge of preparing the showbread for every Sabbath.

[33]These are [a]the singers, heads of the fathers' *houses* of the Levites, *who* lodged in the chambers, *and were* free *from other duties;* for they were employed in *that* work day and night. [34]These heads of the fathers' *houses* of the Levites *were* heads throughout their generations. They dwelt at Jerusalem.

THE FAMILY OF KING SAUL

[35]Jeiel the father of Gibeon, whose wife's name *was* [a]Maacah, dwelt at Gibeon. [36]His firstborn son *was* Abdon, then Zur, Kish, Baal, Ner, Nadab, [37]Gedor, Ahio, [1]Zechariah, and Mikloth. [38]And Mikloth begot [1]Shimeam. They also dwelt alongside their relatives in Jerusalem, with their brethren. [39a]Ner begot Kish, Kish begot Saul, and Saul begot Jonathan, Malchishua, Abinadab, and Esh-Baal. [40]The son of Jonathan *was* Merib-Baal, and Merib-Baal begot Micah. [41]The sons of Micah *were* Pithon, Melech, [1]Tahrea, [a]and[2] Ahaz. [42]And Ahaz begot [1]Jarah; Jarah begot Alemeth, Azmaveth, and Zimri; and Zimri begot Moza; [43]Moza begot Binea, [1]Rephaiah his son, Eleasah his son, and Azel his son.

[44]And Azel had six sons whose names *were* these: Azrikam, Bocheru, Ishmael, Sheariah, Obadiah, and Hanan; these *were* the sons of Azel.

Cross references

9:21 [a]1 Chr. 26:2, 14

9:22 [a]1 Chr. 26:1, 2; [b]1 Sam. 9:9

9:25 [a]2 Kin. 11:4–7; 2 Chr. 23:8

9:27 [a]1 Chr. 23:30–32

9:29 [a]1 Chr. 23:29

9:30 [a]Ex. 30:22–25

9:31 [a]Lev. 2:5; 6:21

9:32 [a]Lev. 24:5–8

9:33 [a]1 Chr. 6:31; 25:1

9:35 [a]1 Chr. 8:29–32

9:39 [a]1 Chr. 8:33–38

9:41 [a]1 Chr. 8:35

9:21 [1]*gatekeeper*   **9:27** [1]*the watch was committed to them*   **9:37** [1]*Zecher,* 1 Chr. 8:31   **9:38** [1]*Shimeah,* 1 Chr. 8:32   **9:41** [1]*Tarea,* 1 Chr. 8:35   [2]So with Arab., Syr., Tg., Vg. (cf. 8:35); MT, LXX omit *and Ahaz*   **9:42** [1]*Jehoaddah,* 1 Chr. 8:36   **9:43** [1]*Raphah,* 1 Chr. 8:37

TRAGIC END OF SAUL AND HIS SONS
(1 Sam. 31:1–13)

10 Now ªthe Philistines fought against Israel; and the men of Israel fled from before the Philistines, and fell slain on Mount Gilboa. ²Then the Philistines followed hard after Saul and his sons. And the Philistines killed Jonathan, ¹Abinadab, and Malchishua, Saul's sons. ³The battle became fierce against Saul. The archers hit him, and he was wounded by the archers. ⁴Then Saul said to his armorbearer, "Draw your sword, and thrust me through with it, lest these uncircumcised men come and abuse me." But his armorbearer would not, for he was greatly afraid. Therefore Saul took a sword and fell on it. ⁵And when his armorbearer saw that Saul was dead, he also fell on his sword and died. ⁶So Saul and his three sons died, and all his house died together. ⁷And when all the men of Israel who *were* in the valley saw that they had fled and that Saul and his sons were dead, they forsook their cities and fled; then the Philistines came and dwelt in them.

⁸So it happened the next day, when the Philistines came to ¹strip the slain, that they found Saul and his sons fallen on Mount Gilboa. ⁹And they stripped him and took his head and his armor, and sent word throughout the land of the Philistines to proclaim the news *in the temple* of their idols and among the people. ¹⁰ªThen they put his armor in the ¹temple of their gods, and fastened his head in the temple of Dagon.

¹¹And when all Jabesh Gilead heard all that the Philistines had done to Saul, ¹²all the ªvaliant men arose and took the body of Saul and the bodies of his sons; and they brought them to ᵇJabesh, and buried their bones under the tamarisk tree at Jabesh, and fasted seven days.

¹³So Saul died for his unfaithfulness which he had ¹committed against the LORD, ªbecause he did not keep the word of the LORD, and also because ᵇhe consulted a medium for guidance. ¹⁴But *he* did not inquire of the LORD; therefore He killed him, and ªturned the kingdom over to David the son of Jesse.

DAVID MADE KING OVER ALL ISRAEL
(2 Sam. 5:1–3)

11 Then ªall Israel came together to David at Hebron, saying, "Indeed we *are* your bone and your flesh. ²Also, in time past, even when Saul was king, you *were* the one who led Israel out and brought them in; and the LORD your ªGod said to you, 'You shall ᵇshepherd My people Israel, and be ruler over My people Israel.'" ³Therefore all the elders of Israel came to the king at Hebron, and David made a covenant with them at Hebron before the LORD. And ªthey anointed David king over Israel, according to the word of the LORD ¹by ᵇSamuel.

THE CITY OF DAVID
(2 Sam. 5:6–10)

⁴And David and all Israel ªwent to Jerusalem, which is Jebus, ᵇwhere the Jebusites *were,* the inhabitants of the land. ⁵But the inhabitants of Jebus said to David, "You shall not come in here!" Nevertheless David took the stronghold of Zion (that is,

10:1
ª1 Sam. 31:1, 2

10:10
ª1 Sam. 31:10

10:12
ª1 Sam. 14:52
ᵇ2 Sam. 21:12

10:13
ª1 Sam. 13:13, 14;
15:22–26
ᵇ[Lev. 19:31;
20:6];
1 Sam. 28:7

10:14
ª1 Sam. 15:28;
2 Sam. 3:9, 10;
5:3; 1 Chr. 12:23

11:1 ª2 Sam. 5:1

11:2
ª1 Sam. 16:1–3;
Ps. 78:70–72
ᵇ2 Sam. 7:7

11:3 ª2 Sam. 5:3
ᵇ1 Sam. 16:1, 4,
12, 13

11:4 ª2 Sam. 5:6
ᵇ Josh. 15:8, 63;
Judg. 1:21;
19:10, 11

10:2 ¹*Jishui,* 1 Sam. 14:49   10:8 ¹*plunder*   10:10 ¹Lit. *house*   10:13 ¹Lit. *transgressed*   11:3 ¹Lit. *by the hand of Samuel*

the City of David). 6Now David said, "Whoever attacks the Jebusites first shall be 1chief and captain." And Joab the son of Zeruiah went up first, and became chief. 7Then David dwelt in the stronghold; therefore they called it 1the City of David. 8And he built the city around it, from 1the Millo to the surrounding area. Joab 2repaired the rest of the city. 9So David awent on and became great, and the LORD of hosts was with bhim.

THE MIGHTY MEN OF DAVID
(2 Sam. 23:8–39)

10Now athese were the heads of the mighty men whom David had, who strengthened themselves with him in his kingdom, with all Israel, to make him king, according to bthe word of the LORD concerning Israel.

11And this is the number of the mighty men whom David had: aJashobeam the son of a Hachmonite, bchief of 1the captains; he had lifted up his spear against three hundred, killed by him at one time.

12After him was Eleazar the son of aDodo, the Ahohite, who was one of the three mighty men. 13He was with David at 1Pasdammim. Now there the Philistines were gathered for battle, and there was a piece of ground full of barley. So the people fled from the Philistines. 14But they 1stationed themselves in the middle of that field, defended it, and killed the Philistines. So the LORD brought about a great victory.

15Now three of the thirty chief men awent down to the rock to David, into the cave of Adullam; and the army of the Philistines encamped bin the Valley of 1Rephaim. 16David was then in the stronghold, and the garrison of the Philistines was then in Bethlehem. 17And David said with longing, "Oh, that someone would give me a drink of water from the well of Bethlehem, which is by the gate!" 18So the three broke through the camp of the Philistines, drew water from the well of Bethlehem that was by the gate, and took it and brought it to David. Nevertheless David would not drink it, but poured it out to the LORD. 19And he said, "Far be it from me, O my God, that I should do this! Shall I drink the blood of these men who have put their lives in jeopardy? For at the risk of their lives they brought it." Therefore he would not drink it. These things were done by the three mighty men.

20aAbishai the brother of Joab was chief of another 1three. He had lifted up his spear against three hundred men, killed them, and won a name among these three. 21aOf the three he was more honored than the other two men. Therefore he became their captain. However he did not attain to the first three.

22Benaiah was the son of Jehoiada, the son of a valiant man from Kabzeel, who 1had done many deeds. aHe had killed two lion-like heroes of Moab. He also had gone down and killed a lion in the midst of a pit on a snowy day. 23And he killed an Egyptian, a man of great height, 1five cubits tall. In the Egyptian's hand there was a spear like a weaver's beam; and he went down to him with a staff, wrested the spear out

11:9 a2 Sam. 3:1 b1 Sam. 16:18
11:10 a2 Sam. 23:8 b1 Sam. 16:1, 12
11:11 a1 Chr. 27:2 b1 Chr. 12:18
11:12 a1 Chr. 27:4
11:15 a2 Sam. 23:13 b2 Sam. 5:18; 1 Chr. 14:9
11:20 a2 Sam. 23:18; 1 Chr. 18:12
11:21 a2 Sam. 23:19
11:22 a2 Sam. 23:20

11:6 1Lit. head   11:7 1Zion, 2 Sam. 5:7   11:8 1Lit. The Landfill   2Lit. revived
11:11 1So with Qr.; Kt., LXX, Vg. the thirty (cf. 2 Sam. 23:8)   11:13 1Ephes Dammim, 1 Sam. 17:1   11:14 1Lit. took their stand   11:15 1Lit. Giants
11:20 1So with MT, LXX, Vg.; Syr. thirty   11:22 1was great in deeds
11:23 1About 7 1/2 feet

of the Egyptian's hand, and killed him with his own spear. 24These *things* Benaiah the son of Jehoiada did, and won a name among three mighty men. 25Indeed he was more honored than the thirty, but he did not attain to the *first* three. And David appointed him over his guard.

26Also the mighty warriors *were* aAsahel the brother of Joab, Elhanan the son of Dodo of Bethlehem, 271Shammoth the Harorite, aHelez the 2Pelonite, 28aIra the son of Ikkesh the Tekoite, bAbiezer the Anathothite, 291Sibbechai the Hushathite, 2Ilai the Ahohite, 30aMaharai the Netophathite, 1Heled the son of Baanah the Netophathite, 311Ithai the son of Ribai of Gibeah, of the sons of Benjamin, aBenaiah the Pirathonite, 321Hurai of the brooks of Gaash, 2Abiel the Arbathite, 33Azmaveth the 1Baharumite, Eliahba the Shaalbonite, 34the sons of 1Hashem the Gizonite, Jonathan the son of Shageh the Hararite, 35Ahiam the son of 1Sacar the Hararite, 2Eliphal the son of 3Ur, 36Hepher the Mecherathite, Ahijah the Pelonite, 371Hezro the Carmelite, 2Naarai the son of Ezbai, 38Joel the brother of Nathan, Mibhar the son of Hagri, 39Zelek the Ammonite, Naharai the 1Berothite (the armorbearer of Joab the son of Zeruiah), 40Ira the Ithrite, Gareb the Ithrite, 41aUriah the Hittite, 1Zabad the son of Ahlai, 42Adina the son of Shiza the Reubenite (a chief of the Reubenites) and thirty with him, 43Hanan the son of Maachah, Joshaphat the Mithnite, 44Uzzia the Ashterathite, Shama and Jeiel the sons of Hotham the Aroerite, 45Jediael the son of Shimri, and Joha his brother, the Tizite, 46Eliel the Mahavite, Jeribai and Joshaviah the sons of Elnaam, Ithmah the Moabite, 47Eliel, Obed, and Jaasiel the Mezobaite.

THE GROWTH OF DAVID'S ARMY
(1 Sam. 22:1, 2)

12 Now athese *were* the men who came to David at bZiklag while he was still a fugitive from Saul the son of Kish; and they *were* among the mighty men, helpers in the war, 2armed with bows, using both the right hand and athe left in *hurling* stones and *shooting* arrows with the bow. *They were* of Benjamin, Saul's brethren.

3The chief *was* Ahiezer, then Joash, the sons of 1Shemaah the Gibeathite; Jeziel and Pelet the sons of Azmaveth; Berachah, and Jehu the Anathothite; 4Ishmaiah the Gibeonite, a mighty man among the thirty, and over the thirty; Jeremiah, Jahaziel, Johanan, and Jozabad the Gederathite; 5Eluzai, Jerimoth, Bealiah, Shemariah, and Shephatiah the Haruphite; 6Elkanah, Jisshiah, Azarel, Joezer, and Jashobeam, the Korahites; 7and Joelah and Zebadiah the sons of Jeroham of Gedor.

8*Some* Gadites 1joined David at the stronghold in the wilderness, mighty men of valor, men trained for battle, who could handle shield and spear, whose faces *were like* the faces of lions, and *were* aas swift as gazelles on the mountains:

11:26
a2 Sam. 23:24

11:27
a2 Sam. 23:26;
1 Chr. 27:10

11:28 a1 Chr. 27:9
b1 Chr. 27:12

11:30
a1 Chr. 27:13

11:31 a1 Chr. 27:14

11:41 a2 Sam. 11

12:1 a1 Sam. 27:2
b1 Sam. 27:6

12:2 aJudg. 3:15;
20:16

12:8
a2 Sam. 2:18

11:27 1*Shammah the Harodite*, 2 Sam. 23:25   2*Paltite*, 2 Sam. 23:26
11:29 1*Mebunnai*, 2 Sam. 23:27   2*Zalmon*, 2 Sam. 23:28   11:30 1*Heleb*,
2 Sam. 23:29, or *Heldai*, 1 Chr. 27:15   11:31 1*Ittai*, 2 Sam. 23:29
11:32 1*Hiddai*, 2 Sam. 23:30   2*Abi-Albon*, 2 Sam. 23:31   11:33 1*Barhumite*,
2 Sam. 23:31   11:34 1*Jashen*, 2 Sam. 23:32   11:35 1*Sharar*, 2 Sam. 23:33
2*Eliphelet*, 2 Sam. 23:34   3*Ahasbai*, 2 Sam. 23:34   11:37 1*Hezrai*, 2 Sam.
23:38   2*Paarai the Arbite*, 2 Sam. 23:35   11:39 1*Beerothite*, 2 Sam. 23:37
11:41 1The last sixteen are not added in 2 Sam. 23.   12:3 1Or *Hasmaah*
12:8 1Lit. *separated themselves to*

9Ezer the first, Obadiah the second, Eliab the third, 10Mishmannah the fourth, Jeremiah the fifth, 11Attai the sixth, Eliel the seventh, 12Johanan the eighth, Elzabad the ninth, 13Jeremiah the tenth, and Machbanai the eleventh. 14These *were* from the sons of Gad, captains of the army; the least was over a hundred, and the greatest was over a ªthousand. 15These *are* the ones who crossed the Jordan in the first month, when it had overflowed all its ªbanks; and they put to flight all *those* in the valleys, to the east and to the west.

16Then some of the sons of Benjamin and Judah came to David at the stronghold. 17And David went out 1to meet them, and answered and said to them, "If you have come peaceably to me to help me, my heart will be united with you; but if to betray me to my enemies, since *there is* no 2wrong in my hands, may the God of our fathers look and bring judgment." 18Then the Spirit 1came upon ªAmasai, chief of the captains, *and he said:*

> "*We are* yours, O David;
> We *are* on your side, O son of Jesse!
> Peace, peace to you,
> And peace to your helpers!
> For your God helps you."

So David received them, and made them captains of the troop.

19And *some* from Manasseh defected to David ªwhen he was going with the Philistines to battle against Saul; but they did not help them, for the lords of the Philistines sent him away by agreement, saying, b"He may defect to his master Saul *and endanger* our heads." 20When he went to Ziklag, those of Manasseh who defected to him were Adnah, Jozabad, Jediael, Michael, Jozabad, Elihu, and Zillethai, captains of the thousands who *were* from Manasseh. 21And they helped David against ªthe bands *of raiders,* for they *were* all mighty men of valor, and they were captains in the army. 22For at *that* time they came to David day by day to help him, until *it was* a great army, ªlike the army of God.

DAVID'S ARMY AT HEBRON

23Now these *were* the numbers of the 1divisions *that were* equipped for war, *and* ªcame to David at bHebron to cturn *over* the kingdom of Saul to him, daccording to the word of the LORD: 24of the sons of Judah bearing shield and spear, six thousand eight hundred 1armed for war; 25of the sons of Simeon, mighty men of valor fit for war, seven thousand one hundred; 26of the sons of Levi four thousand six hundred; 27Jehoiada, the leader of the Aaronites, and with him three thousand seven hundred; 28ªZadok, a young man, a valiant warrior, and from his father's house twenty-two captains; 29of the sons of Benjamin, relatives of Saul, three thousand (until then ªthe greatest part of them had remained loyal to the house of Saul); 30of the sons of Ephraim twenty thousand eight hundred, mighty men of valor, 1famous men throughout their father's house; 31of the half-tribe of Manasseh eighteen thousand, who were designated by name to come and make David king; 32of the sons of Issachar ªwho had understanding

12:14
ª1 Sam. 18:13

12:15
ªJosh. 3:15;
4:18, 19

12:18
ª2 Sam. 17:25

12:19
ª1 Sam. 29:2
b1 Sam. 29:4

12:21
ª1 Sam. 30:1,
9, 10

12:22
ªGen. 32:2;
Josh. 5:13–15

12:23
ª2 Sam. 2:1–4
b1 Chr. 11:1
c1 Chr. 10:14
d1 Sam. 16:1–4

12:28
ª2 Sam. 8:17;
1 Chr. 6:8, 53

12:29
ª2 Sam. 2:8, 9

12:32 ªEsth. 1:13

12:17 1Lit. *before them* 2Lit. *violence* 12:18 1Lit. *clothed* 12:23 1Lit. *heads of those* 12:24 1*equipped* 12:30 1Lit. *men of names*

of the times, to know what Israel ought to do, their chiefs were two hundred; and all their brethren were at their command; 33of Zebulun there were fifty thousand who went out to battle, expert in war with all weapons of war, astouthearted men who could keep ranks; 34of Naphtali one thousand captains, and with them thirty-seven thousand with shield and spear; 35of the Danites who could keep battle formation, twenty-eight thousand six hundred; 36of Asher, those who could go out to war, able to keep battle formation, forty thousand; 37of the Reubenites and the Gadites and the half-tribe of Manasseh, from the other side of the Jordan, one hundred and twenty thousand armed for battle with every *kind* of weapon of war.

38All these men of war, who could keep ranks, came to Hebron with a loyal heart, to make David king over all Israel; and all the rest of Israel *were* of aone mind to make David king. 39And they were there with David three days, eating and drinking, for their brethren had prepared for them. 40Moreover those who were near to them, from as far away as Issachar and Zebulun and Naphtali, were bringing food on donkeys and camels, on mules and oxen—provisions of flour and cakes of figs and cakes of raisins, wine and oil and oxen and sheep abundantly, for *there was* joy in Israel.

THE ARK BROUGHT FROM KIRJATH JEARIM
(2 Sam. 6:1–11)

13 Then David consulted with the acaptains of thousands and hundreds, *and* with every leader. 2And David said to all the assembly of Israel, "If *it seems* good to you, and if it is of the LORD our God, let us send out to our brethren everywhere *who are* aleft in all the land of Israel, and with them to the priests and Levites *who are* in their cities *and* their common-lands, that they may gather together to us; 3and let us bring the ark of our God back to us, afor we have not inquired at it since the days of Saul." 4Then all the assembly said that they would do so, for the thing was right in the eyes of all the people.

5So aDavid gathered all Israel together, from bShihor in Egypt to as far as the entrance of Hamath, to bring the ark of God cfrom Kirjath Jearim. 6And David and all Israel went up to aBaalah,1 to Kirjath Jearim, which belonged to Judah, to bring up from there the ark of God the LORD, bwho dwells *between* the cherubim, where *His* name is proclaimed. 7So they 1carried the ark of God aon a new cart bfrom the house of Abinadab, and Uzza and Ahio drove the cart. 8Then aDavid and all Israel played *music* before God with all *their* might, with 1singing, on harps, on stringed instruments, on tambourines, on cymbals, and with trumpets.

9And when they came to 1Chidon's threshing floor, Uzza put out his hand to hold the ark, for the oxen 2stumbled. 10Then the anger of the LORD was aroused against Uzza, and He struck him abecause he put his hand to the ark; and he bdied there before God. 11And David became angry because of the LORD's outbreak against Uzza; therefore that place is called 1Perez Uzza to this day. 12David was afraid of God that day, saying, "How can I bring the ark of God to me?"

12:33 aPs. 12:2; [James 1:8]

12:38 a2 Chr. 30:12

13:1 a1 Chr. 11:15; 12:34

13:2 a1 Sam. 31:1; Is. 37:4

13:3 a1 Sam. 7:1, 2

13:5 a1 Sam. 7:5 bJosh. 13:3 c1 Sam. 6:21; 7:1, 2

13:6 aJosh. 15:9, 60 bEx. 25:22; 1 Sam. 4:4; 2 Kin. 19:15

13:7 aNum. 4:15; 1 Sam. 6:7 b1 Sam. 7:1

13:8 a2 Sam. 6:5

13:10 a[Num. 4:15]; 1 Chr. 15:13, 15 bLev. 10:2

13:6 1*Baale Judah*, 2 Sam. 6:2   13:7 1Lit. *caused the ark of God to ride*
13:8 1*songs*   13:9 1*Nachon*, 2 Sam. 6:6   2Or *let it go off*   13:11 1Lit. *Outburst Against Uzza*

¹³So David would not move the ark with him into the City of David, but took it aside into the house of Obed-Edom the Gittite. ¹⁴ᵃThe ark of God remained with the family of Obed-Edom in his house three months. And the LORD blessed ᵇthe house of Obed-Edom and all that he had.

DAVID ESTABLISHED AT JERUSALEM
(2 Sam. 5:11–16)

14 Now ᵃHiram king of Tyre sent messengers to David, and cedar trees, with masons and carpenters, to build him a house. ²So David knew that the LORD had established him as king over Israel, for his kingdom was ᵃhighly exalted for the sake of His people Israel.

³Then David took more wives in Jerusalem, and David begot more sons and daughters. ⁴And ᵃthese are the names of his children whom he had in Jerusalem: ¹Shammua, Shobab, Nathan, Solomon, ⁵Ibhar, ¹Elishua, ²Elpelet, ⁶Nogah, Nepheg, Japhia, ⁷Elishama, ¹Beeliada, and Eliphelet.

THE PHILISTINES DEFEATED
(2 Sam. 5:17–25)

⁸Now when the Philistines heard that ᵃDavid had been anointed king over all Israel, all the Philistines went up to search for David. And David heard *of it* and went out against them. ⁹Then the Philistines went and made a raid ᵃon the Valley of ¹Rephaim. ¹⁰And David ᵃinquired of God, saying, "Shall I go up against the Philistines? Will You deliver them into my hand?"

The LORD said to him, "Go up, for I will deliver them into your hand."

¹¹So they went up to Baal Perazim, and David defeated them there. Then David said, "God has broken through my enemies by my hand like a breakthrough of water." Therefore they called the name of that place ¹Baal Perazim. ¹²And when they left their gods there, David gave a commandment, and they were burned with fire.

¹³ᵃThen the Philistines once again made a raid on the valley. ¹⁴Therefore David inquired again of God, and God said to him, "You shall not go up after them; circle around them, ᵃand come upon them in front of the mulberry trees. ¹⁵And it shall be, when you hear a sound of marching in the tops of the mulberry trees, then you shall go out to battle, for God has gone out before you to strike the camp of the Philistines." ¹⁶So David did as God commanded him, and they drove back the army of the Philistines from ¹Gibeon as far as Gezer. ¹⁷Then ᵃthe fame of David went out into all lands, and the LORD ᵇbrought the fear of him upon all nations.

THE ARK BROUGHT TO JERUSALEM
(2 Sam. 6:12–16)

15 *David* built houses for himself in the City of David; and he prepared a place for the ark of God, ᵃand pitched a tent for it. ²Then David said, "No one may carry the ᵃark of

---

13:14
ᵃ2 Sam. 6:11
ᵇ[Gen. 30:27];
1 Chr. 26:4–8

14:1 ᵃ2 Sam. 5:11;
1 Kin. 5:1

14:2 ᵃNum. 24:7

14:4
ᵃ1 Chr. 3:5–8

14:8
ᵃ2 Sam. 5:17–21

14:9 ᵃJosh. 17:15;
18:16; 1 Chr. 11:15;
14:13

14:10
ᵃ1 Sam. 23:2, 4;
30:8; 2 Sam. 2:1;
5:19, 23; 21:1

14:13
ᵃ2 Sam. 5:22–25

14:14
ᵃ2 Sam. 5:23

14:17
ᵃJosh. 6:27;
2 Chr. 26:8
ᵇ[Ex. 15:14–16];
Deut. 2:25;
11:25];
2 Chr. 20:29

15:1 ᵃ1 Chr. 16:1

15:2
ᵃ[Num. 4:15];
2 Sam. 6:1–11

14:4 ¹*Shimea,* 1 Chr. 3:5   14:5 ¹*Elishama,* 1 Chr. 3:6   ²*Eliphelet,* 1 Chr. 3:6
14:7 ¹*Eliada,* 2 Sam. 5:6; 1 Chr. 3:8   14:9 ¹Lit. *Giants*   14:11 ¹Lit. *Master of Breakthroughs*   14:16 ¹*Geba,* 2 Sam. 5:25

God but the Levites, for [b]the LORD has chosen them to carry the ark of God and to minister before Him forever." 3And David [a]gathered all Israel together at Jerusalem, to bring up the ark of the LORD to its place, which he had prepared for it. 4Then David assembled the children of Aaron and the Levites: 5of the sons of Kohath, Uriel the chief, and one hundred and twenty of his [1]brethren; 6of the sons of Merari, Asaiah the chief, and two hundred and twenty of his brethren; 7of the sons of Gershom, Joel the chief, and one hundred and thirty of his brethren; 8of the sons of [a]Elizaphan, Shemaiah the chief, and two hundred of his brethren; 9of the sons of [a]Hebron, Eliel the chief, and eighty of his brethren; 10of the sons of Uzziel, Amminadab the chief, and one hundred and twelve of his brethren.

11And David called for [a]Zadok and [b]Abiathar the priests, and for the Levites: for Uriel, Asaiah, Joel, Shemaiah, Eliel, and Amminadab. 12He said to them, "You *are* the heads of the fathers' *houses* of the Levites; [1]sanctify yourselves, you and your brethren, that you may bring up the ark of the LORD God of Israel to *the place* I have prepared for it. 13For [a]because you *did* not *do it* the first *time,* [b]the LORD our God broke out against us, because we did not consult Him [1]about the proper order."

14So the priests and the Levites [1]sanctified themselves to bring up the ark of the LORD God of Israel. 15And the children of the Levites bore the ark of God on their shoulders, by its poles, as [a]Moses had commanded according to the word of the LORD.

16Then David spoke to the leaders of the Levites to appoint their brethren *to be* the singers accompanied by instruments of music, stringed instruments, harps, and cymbals, by raising the voice with resounding joy. 17So the Levites appointed [a]Heman the son of Joel; and of his brethren, [b]Asaph the son of Berechiah; and of their brethren, the sons of Merari, [c]Ethan the son of Kushaiah; 18and with them their brethren of the second *rank*: Zechariah, [1]Ben, Jaaziel, Shemiramoth, Jehiel, Unni, Eliab, Benaiah, Maaseiah, Mattithiah, Elipheleh, Mikneiah, Obed-Edom, and Jeiel, the gatekeepers; 19the singers, Heman, Asaph, and Ethan, *were* to sound the cymbals of bronze; 20Zechariah, [1]Aziel, Shemiramoth, Jehiel, Unni, Eliab, Maaseiah, and Benaiah, with strings according to [a]Alamoth; 21Mattithiah, Elipheleh, Mikneiah, Obed-Edom, Jeiel, and Azaziah, to direct with harps on the [a]Sheminith; 22Chenaniah, leader of the Levites, was instructor *in charge of* the music, because he *was* skillful; 23Berechiah and Elkanah *were* doorkeepers for the ark; 24Shebaniah, Joshaphat, Nethanel, Amasai, Zechariah, Benaiah, and Eliezer, the priests, [a]were to blow the trumpets before the ark of God; and [b]Obed-Edom and Jehiah, doorkeepers for the ark.

25So [a]David, the elders of Israel, and the captains over thousands went to bring up the ark of the covenant of the LORD from the house of Obed-Edom with joy. 26And so it was, when God helped the Levites who bore the ark of the covenant of the LORD, that they offered seven bulls and seven rams. 27David was clothed with a robe of fine [a]linen, as were all the Levites who bore the ark, the singers, and Chenaniah the music master

15:2
[b]Num. 4:2–15;
Deut. 10:8; 31:9

15:3
[a]Ex. 40:20, 21;
2 Sam. 6:12;
1 Kin. 8:1;
1 Chr. 13:5

15:8 [a]Ex. 6:22

15:9 [a]Ex. 6:18

15:11
[a]2 Sam. 8:17;
15:24–29, 35,
36; 18:19, 22,
27; 19:11; 20:25;
1 Chr. 12:28
[b]1 Sam. 22:20–
23; 23:6; 30:7;
1 Kin. 2:22, 26,
27; Mark 2:6

15:13
[a]2 Sam. 6:3
[b]1 Chr. 13:7–11

15:15 [a]Ex. 25:14;
Num. 4:15; 7:9

15:17
[a]1 Chr. 6:33; 25:1
[b]1 Chr. 6:39
[c]1 Chr. 6:44

15:20
[a]Ps. 46:title

15:21 [a]Ps. 6:title

15:24
[a][Num. 10:8];
Ps. 81:3
[b]1 Chr. 13:13, 14

15:25
[a]2 Sam. 6:12, 13;
1 Kin. 8:1

15:27
[a]1 Sam. 2:18, 28

15:5 [1]*kinsmen*   15:12 [1]*consecrate*   15:13 [1]*regarding the ordinance*
15:14 [1]*consecrated*   15:18 [1]So with MT, Vg.; LXX omits *Ben*
15:20 [1]*Jaaziel,* v. 18

with the singers. David also wore a linen ephod. 28ªThus all Israel brought up the ark of the covenant of the Lᴏʀᴅ with shouting and with the sound of the horn, with trumpets and with cymbals, making music with stringed instruments and harps.

29And it happened, ª*as* the ark of the covenant of the Lᴏʀᴅ came to the City of David, that Michal, Saul's daughter, looked through a window and saw King David whirling and playing music; and she despised him in her heart.

THE ARK PLACED IN THE TABERNACLE
(2 Sam. 6:17–19)

16 So ªthey brought the ark of God, and set it in the midst of the tabernacle that David had erected for it. Then they offered burnt offerings and peace offerings before God. 2And when David had finished offering the burnt offerings and the peace offerings, ªhe blessed the people in the name of the Lᴏʀᴅ. 3Then he distributed to everyone of Israel, both man and woman, to everyone a loaf of bread, a piece *of meat,* and a cake of raisins.

4And he appointed some of the Levites to minister before the ark of the Lᴏʀᴅ, to ªcommemorate, to thank, and to praise the Lᴏʀᴅ God of Israel: 5Asaph the chief, and next to him Zechariah, *then* ªJeiel, Shemiramoth, Jehiel, Mattithiah, Eliab, Benaiah, and Obed-Edom: Jeiel with stringed instruments and harps, but Asaph made music with cymbals; 6Benaiah and Jahaziel the priests regularly *blew* the trumpets before the ark of the covenant of God.

DAVID'S SONG OF THANKSGIVING
(Ps. 96:1–13; 105:1–15; 106:1, 47, 48)

7On that day ªDavid ᵇfirst delivered *this psalm* into the hand of Asaph and his brethren, to thank the Lᴏʀᴅ:

8   ªOh, give thanks to the Lᴏʀᴅ!
Call upon His name;
Make known His deeds among the peoples!
9   Sing to Him, sing psalms to Him;
Talk of all His wondrous works!
10 Glory in His holy name;
Let the hearts of those rejoice who seek the Lᴏʀᴅ!
11 Seek the Lᴏʀᴅ and His strength;
Seek His face evermore!
12 Remember His marvelous works which He has done,
His wonders, and the judgments of His mouth,
13 O seed of Israel His servant,
You children of Jacob, His chosen ones!

14 He *is* the Lᴏʀᴅ our God;
His ªjudgments *are* in all the earth.
15 Remember His covenant forever,
The word which He commanded, for a thousand
generations,
16 The ªcovenant which He made with Abraham,
And His oath to Isaac,
17 And ªconfirmed it to ᵇJacob for a statute,
To Israel *for* an everlasting covenant,
18 Saying, "To you I will give the land of Canaan
As the allotment of your inheritance,"

Cross references (margin)

15:28
ªNum. 23:21;
Josh. 6:20;
1 Chr. 13:8;
Zech. 4:7;
1 Thess. 4:16

15:29
ª1 Sam. 18:20,
27; 19:11–17;
2 Sam. 3:13, 14;
6:16, 20–23

16:1
ª2 Sam. 6:17;
1 Chr. 15:1

16:2 ª1 Kin. 8:14

16:4
ªPs. 38:title;
70:title

16:5 ª1 Chr. 15:18

16:7
ª2 Sam. 22:1;
23:1 ᵇPs. 105:1–15

16:8 ª1 Chr. 17:19,
20; Ps. 105:1–15

16:14 ªPs. 48:10;
[Is. 26:9]

16:16 ªGen. 17:2;
26:3; 28:13; 35:11

16:17
ªGen. 35:11, 12
ᵇGen. 28:10–15

19 When you were ᵃfew in number,
Indeed very few, and strangers in it.
20 When they went from one nation to another,
And from *one* kingdom to another people,
21 He permitted no man to do them wrong;
Yes, He ᵃrebuked kings for their sakes,
22 *Saying,* ᵃ"Do not touch My anointed ones,
And do My prophets no harm."

23 ᵃSing to the LORD, all the earth;
Proclaim the good news of His salvation from day to day.
24 Declare His glory among the nations,
His wonders among all peoples.

25 For the LORD *is* great and greatly to be praised;
He *is* also to be feared above all gods.
26 For all the gods ᵃof the peoples *are* ¹idols,
But the LORD made the heavens.
27 Honor and majesty *are* before Him;
Strength and gladness are in His place.

28 Give to the LORD, O families of the peoples,
Give to the LORD glory and strength.
29 Give to the LORD the glory *due* His name;
Bring an offering, and come before Him.
Oh, worship the LORD in the beauty of holiness!
30 Tremble before Him, all the earth.
The world also is firmly established,
It shall not be moved.

31 Let the heavens rejoice, and let the earth be glad;
And let them say among the nations, "The LORD reigns."
32 Let the sea roar, and all its fullness;
Let the field rejoice, and all that *is* in it.
33 Then the ᵃtrees of the woods shall rejoice before the LORD,
For He is ᵇcoming to judge the earth.

34 ᵃOh, give thanks to the LORD, for *He is* good!
For His mercy *endures* forever.

35 ᵃAnd say, "Save us, O God of our salvation;
Gather us together, and deliver us from the Gentiles,
To give thanks to Your holy name,
To triumph in Your praise."

36 ᵃBlessed *be* the LORD God of Israel
From everlasting to everlasting!

And all ᵇthe people said, "Amen!" and praised the LORD.

REGULAR WORSHIP MAINTAINED

37So he left ᵃAsaph and his brothers there before the ark of the covenant of the LORD to minister before the ark regularly, as every day's work ᵇrequired; 38and ᵃObed-Edom with his sixty-eight brethren, including Obed-Edom the son of Jeduthun, and Hosah, *to be* gatekeepers; 39and Zadok the priest and his brethren the priests, ᵃbefore the tabernacle of the LORD ᵇat the ¹high place that *was* at Gibeon, 40to offer burnt offerings to the LORD on the altar of burnt offering regularly ᵃmorning and evening, and *to do* according to all that is

16:19
ᵃGen. 34:30;
Deut. 7:7

16:21
ᵃGen. 12:17;
20:3; Ex. 7:15–18

16:22
ᵃGen. 20:7;
Ps. 105:15

16:23
ᵃPs. 96:1–13

16:26 ᵃLev. 19:4;
[1 Cor. 8:5, 6]

16:33
ᵃIs. 55:12, 13
ᵇ[Joel 3:1–14];
Zech. 14:1–14;
[Matt. 25:31–46]

16:34
ᵃ2 Chr. 5:13;
7:3; Ezra 3:11;
Ps. 106:1; 107:1;
118:1; 136:1;
Jer. 33:11

16:35
ᵃPs. 106:47, 48

16:36
ᵃ1 Kin. 8:15, 56;
Ps. 72:18
ᵇDeut. 27:15;
Neh. 8:6

16:37
ᵃ1 Chr. 16:4, 5
ᵇ2 Chr. 8:14;
Ezra 3:4

16:38
ᵃ1 Chr. 13:14

16:39
ᵃ1 Chr. 21:29;
2 Chr. 1:3
ᵇ1 Kin. 3:4

16:40
ᵃ[Ex. 29:38–42;
Num. 28:3, 4]

16:26 ¹*worthless things*   16:39 ¹Place for pagan worship

written in the Law of the LORD which He commanded Israel; ⁴¹and with them Heman and Jeduthun and the rest who were chosen, who were designated by name, to give thanks to the LORD, ^abecause His mercy *endures* forever; ⁴²and with them Heman and Jeduthun, to sound aloud with trumpets and cymbals and the musical instruments of God. Now the sons of Jeduthun *were* gatekeepers.

^{43a}Then all the people departed, every man to his house; and David returned to bless his house.

GOD'S COVENANT WITH DAVID
(2 Sam. 7:1–29)

17 Now ^ait came to pass, when David was dwelling in his house, that David said to Nathan the prophet, "See now, I dwell in a house of cedar, but the ark of the covenant of the LORD *is* under tent curtains."

²Then Nathan said to David, "Do all that *is* in your heart, for God *is* with you."

³But it happened that night that the word of God came to Nathan, saying, ⁴"Go and tell My servant David, 'Thus says the LORD: "You shall ^anot build Me a house to dwell in. ⁵For I have not dwelt in a house since the time that I brought up Israel, even to this day, but have gone from tent to tent, and from *one* tabernacle *to another.* ⁶Wherever I have moved about with all Israel, have I ever spoken a word to any of the judges of Israel, whom I commanded to shepherd My people, saying, 'Why have you not built Me a house of cedar?' " ' ⁷Now therefore, thus shall you say to My servant David, 'Thus says the LORD of hosts: "I took you ^afrom the sheepfold, from following the sheep, to be ¹ruler over My people Israel. ⁸And I have been with you wherever you have gone, and have cut off all your enemies from before you, and have ¹made you a name like the name of the great men who *are* on the earth. ⁹Moreover I will appoint a place for My people Israel, and will ^aplant them, that they may dwell in a place of their own and move no more; nor shall the sons of wickedness oppress them anymore, as previously, ¹⁰since the time that I commanded judges *to be* over My people Israel. Also I will subdue all your enemies. Furthermore I tell you that the LORD will build you a ¹house. ¹¹And it shall be, when your days are ^afulfilled, when you must ¹go *to be* with your fathers, that I will set up your ^bseed after you, who will be of your sons; and I will establish his kingdom. ^{12a}He shall build Me a house, and I will establish his throne forever. ^{13a}I will be his Father, and he shall be My son; and I will not take My mercy away from him, ^bas I took *it* from *him* who was before you. ¹⁴And ^aI will establish him in My house and in My kingdom forever; and his throne shall be established forever." ' "

¹⁵According to all these words and according to all this vision, so Nathan spoke to David.

^{16a}Then King David went in and sat before the LORD; and he said: "Who *am* I, O LORD God? And what is my house, that You have brought me this far? ¹⁷And *yet* this was a small thing in Your sight, O God; and You have *also* spoken of Your servant's house for a great while to come, and have regarded me according to the rank of a man of high degree, O LORD God.

16:41
^a1 Chr. 25:1–6;
2 Chr. 5:13;
7:3; Ezra 3:11;
Jer. 33:11

16:43
^a2 Sam. 6:18–20

17:1 ^a2 Sam. 7:1;
1 Chr. 14:1

17:4
^a[1 Chr. 28:2, 3]

17:7
^a1 Sam. 16:11–13

17:9
^a[Deut. 30:1–9;
Jer. 16:14–16;
23:5–8; 24:6;
Ezek. 37:21–27];
Amos 9:14

17:11 ^a1 Kin. 2:10;
1 Chr. 29:28
^b1 Kin. 5:5;
6:12; 8:19–21;
[1 Chr. 22:9–13;
28:20];
Matt. 1:6;
Luke 3:31

17:12
^a1 Kin. 6:38;
2 Chr. 6:2;
[Ps. 89:20–37]

17:13
^a2 Sam. 7:14, 15;
Matt. 3:17;
Mark 1:11;
Luke 3:22;
2 Cor. 6:18;
Heb. 1:5
^b[1 Sam. 15:23–28]; 1 Chr. 10:14

17:14
^aPs. 89:3, 4;
Matt. 19:28;
25:31;
[Luke 1:31–33]

17:16
^a2 Sam. 7:18

17:7 ¹leader   17:8 ¹*given you prestige*   17:10 ¹Royal dynasty   17:11 ¹Die and join your ancestors

18What more can David *say* to You for the honor of Your servant? For You know Your servant. 19O LORD, for Your servant's sake, and according to Your own heart, You have done all this greatness, in making known all these great things. 20O LORD, *there is* none like You, nor *is there any* God besides You, according to all that we have heard with our ears. 21aAnd who *is* like Your people Israel, the one nation on the earth whom God went to redeem for Himself *as* a people—to make for Yourself a name by great and awesome deeds, by driving out nations from before Your people whom You redeemed from Egypt? 22For You have made Your people Israel Your very own people forever; and You, LORD, have become their God.

23"And now, O LORD, the word which You have spoken concerning Your servant and concerning his house, *let it* be established forever, and do as You have said. 24So let it be established, that Your name may be magnified forever, saying, 'The LORD of hosts, the God of Israel, *is* Israel's God.' And let the house of Your servant David be established before You. 25For You, O my God, 1have revealed to Your servant that You will build him a house. Therefore Your servant has found it *in his heart* to pray before You. 26And now, LORD, 1You are God, and have promised this goodness to Your servant. 27Now You have been pleased to bless the house of Your servant, that it may continue before You forever; for You have blessed it, O LORD, and *it shall be* blessed forever."

DAVID'S FURTHER CONQUESTS
(2 Sam. 8:1–14)

18 After this ait came to pass that David 1attacked the Philistines, subdued them, and took Gath and its towns from the hand of the Philistines. 2Then he 1defeated aMoab, and the Moabites became David's bservants, *and* brought tribute.

3And aDavid 1defeated 2Hadadezer king of Zobah *as far as* Hamath, as he went to establish his power by the River Euphrates. 4David took from him one thousand chariots, 1seven thousand horsemen, and twenty thousand foot soldiers. Also David 2hamstrung all the chariot *horses,* except that he spared enough of them for one hundred chariots.

5When the aSyrians of Damascus came to help Hadadezer king of Zobah, David killed twenty-two thousand of the Syrians. 6Then David put *garrisons* in Syria of Damascus; and the Syrians became David's servants, *and* brought tribute. So the LORD preserved David wherever he went. 7And David took the shields of gold that were on the servants of Hadadezer, and brought them to Jerusalem. 8Also from 1Tibhath and from 2Chun, cities of 3Hadadezer, David brought a large amount of abronze, with which bSolomon made the bronze 4Sea, the pillars, and the articles of bronze.

9Now when 1Tou king of Hamath heard that David had 2defeated all the army of Hadadezer king of Zobah, 10he sent 1Hadoram his son to King David, to greet him and bless him, because he had fought against Hadadezer and 2defeated

17:21
a[Deut. 4:6–8, 33–38];
Ps. 147:20

18:1
a2 Sam. 8:1–18

18:2
a2 Sam. 8:2;
Zeph. 2:9
bPs. 60:8

18:3 a2 Sam. 8:3

18:5
a2 Sam. 8:5, 6;
1 Kin. 11:23–25

18:8 a2 Sam. 8:8
b1 Kin. 7:15, 23; 2 Chr. 4:12, 15, 16

17:25 1Lit. *have uncovered the ear of*   17:26 1Or *You alone are*   18:1 1Lit. *struck*   18:2 1Lit. *struck*   18:3 1Lit. *struck*   2Heb. *Hadarezer*   18:4 1*seven hundred,* 2 Sam. 8:4   2*crippled*   18:8 1*Betah,* 2 Sam. 8:8   2*Berothai,* 2 Sam. 8:8   3Heb. *Hadarezer*   4Great laver or basin   18:9 1*Toi,* 2 Sam. 8:9, 10   2Lit. *struck*   18:10 1*Joram,* 2 Sam. 8:10   2Lit. *struck*

him (for Hadadezer had been at war with Tou); and *Hadoram brought with him* all kinds of ᵃarticles of gold, silver, and bronze. ¹¹King David also dedicated these to the LORD, along with the silver and gold that he had brought from all *these* nations—from Edom, from Moab, from the ᵃpeople of Ammon, from the ᵇPhilistines, and from ᶜAmalek.

¹²Moreover ᵃAbishai the son of Zeruiah killed ᵇeighteen thousand ¹Edomites in the Valley of Salt. ¹³ᵃHe also put garrisons in Edom, and all the Edomites became David's servants. And the LORD preserved David wherever he went.

DAVID'S ADMINISTRATION
(2 Sam. 8:15–18)

¹⁴So David reigned over all Israel, and administered judgment and justice to all his people. ¹⁵Joab the son of Zeruiah *was* over the army; Jehoshaphat the son of Ahilud *was* recorder; ¹⁶Zadok the son of Ahitub and ¹Abimelech the son of Abiathar *were* the priests; ²Shavsha *was* the scribe; ¹⁷ᵃBenaiah the son of Jehoiada *was* over the Cherethites and the Pelethites; and David's sons *were* ¹chief ministers at the king's side.

THE AMMONITES AND SYRIANS DEFEATED
(2 Sam. 10:1–19)

19 Itᵃ happened after this that Nahash the king of the people of Ammon died, and his son reigned in his place. ²Then David said, "I will show kindness to Hanun the son of Nahash, because his father showed kindness to me." So David sent messengers to comfort him concerning his father. And David's servants came to Hanun in the land of the people of Ammon to comfort him.

³And the princes of the people of Ammon said to Hanun, ¹"Do you think that David really honors your father because he has sent comforters to you? Did his servants not come to you to search and to overthrow and to spy out the land?"

⁴Therefore Hanun took David's servants, shaved them, and cut off their garments ¹in the middle, at their ᵃbuttocks, and sent them away. ⁵Then *some* went and told David about the men; and he sent to meet them, because the men were greatly ashamed. And the king said, "Wait at Jericho until your beards have grown, and *then* return."

⁶When the people of Ammon saw that they had made themselves repulsive to David, Hanun and the people of Ammon sent a thousand talents of silver to hire for themselves chariots and horsemen from ¹Mesopotamia, from Syrian Maacah, ᵃand from ²Zobah. ⁷So they hired for themselves thirty-two thousand chariots, with the king of Maacah and his people, who came and encamped before Medeba. Also the people of Ammon gathered together from their cities, and came to battle.

⁸Now when David heard *of it*, he sent Joab and all the army of the mighty men. ⁹Then the people of Ammon came out and put themselves in battle array before the gate of the city, and the kings who had come *were* by themselves in the field. ¹⁰When Joab saw that the battle line was against him

---

18:10
ᵃ2 Sam. 8:10–12

18:11
ᵃ2 Sam. 10:14
ᵇ2 Sam. 5:17–25
ᶜ2 Sam. 1:1

18:12
ᵃ2 Sam. 23:18;
1 Chr. 2:16
ᵇ2 Sam. 8:13

18:13
ᵃGen. 27:29–40;
Num. 24:18;
2 Sam. 8:14

18:17
ᵃ2 Sam. 8:18

19:1 ᵃ1 Sam. 11:1;
2 Sam. 10:1–19

19:4 ᵃIs. 20:4

19:6
ᵃ1 Chr. 18:5, 9

18:12 ¹*Syrians,* 2 Sam. 8:13   18:16 ¹*Ahimelech,* 2 Sam. 8:17   ²*Seraiah,* 2 Sam. 8:17, or *Shisha,* 1 Kin. 4:3   18:17 ¹Lit. *at the hand of the king*
19:3 ¹Lit. *In your eyes is David honoring your father because*   19:4 ¹*in half*
19:6 ¹Heb. *Aram Naharaim*   ²*Zoba,* 2 Sam. 10:6

before and behind, he chose some of Israel's best and put *them* in battle array against the Syrians. ¹¹And the rest of the people he put under the command of Abishai his brother, and they set *themselves* in battle array against the people of Ammon. ¹²Then he said, "If the Syrians are too strong for me, then you shall help me; but if the people of Ammon are too strong for you, then I will help you. ¹³Be of good courage, and let us be strong for our people and for the cities of our God. And may the LORD do *what is* good in His sight."

¹⁴So Joab and the people who *were* with him drew near for the battle against the Syrians, and they fled before him. ¹⁵When the people of Ammon saw that the Syrians were fleeing, they also fled before Abishai his brother, and entered the city. So Joab went to Jerusalem.

¹⁶Now when the Syrians saw that they had been defeated by Israel, they sent messengers and brought the Syrians who were beyond ¹the River, and ²Shophach the commander of Hadadezer's army *went* before them. ¹⁷When it was told David, he gathered all Israel, crossed over the Jordan and came upon them, and set up in battle array against them. So when David had set up in battle array against the Syrians, they fought with him. ¹⁸Then the Syrians fled before Israel; and David killed ¹seven thousand charioteers and forty thousand ²foot soldiers of the Syrians, and killed Shophach the commander of the army. ¹⁹And when the servants of Hadadezer saw that they were defeated by Israel, they made peace with David and became his servants. So the Syrians were not willing to help the people of Ammon anymore.

RABBAH IS CONQUERED
(2 Sam. 11:1; 12:26–31)

20 It^a happened ¹in the spring of the year, at the time kings go out *to battle,* that Joab led out the armed forces and ravaged the country of the people of Ammon, and came and besieged Rabbah. But ^bDavid stayed at Jerusalem. And ^cJoab defeated Rabbah and overthrew it. ²Then David ^atook their king's crown from his head, and found it to weigh a talent of gold, and *there were* precious stones in it. And it was set on David's head. Also he brought out the ¹spoil of the city in great abundance. ³And he brought out the people who *were* in it, and ¹put *them* to work with saws, with iron picks, and with axes. So David did to all the cities of the people of Ammon. Then David and all the people returned *to* Jerusalem.

PHILISTINE GIANTS DESTROYED
(2 Sam. 21:15–22)

⁴Now it happened afterward ^athat war broke out at ¹Gezer with the Philistines, at which time ^bSibbechai the Hushathite killed ²Sippai, *who was one* of the sons of ³the giant. And they were subdued.

⁵Again there was war with the Philistines, and Elhanan the son of ¹Jair killed Lahmi the brother of Goliath the Gittite, the shaft of whose spear *was* like a weaver's ^abeam.

20:1 ^a2 Sam. 11:1
^b2 Sam. 11:2—
12:25
^c2 Sam. 12:26

20:2
^a2 Sam. 12:30, 31

20:4
^a2 Sam. 21:18
^b1 Chr. 11:29

20:5
^a1 Sam. 17:7;
1 Chr. 11:23

19:16 ¹The Euphrates   ²Zoba, 2 Sam. 10:6, or Shobach, 2 Sam. 10:16
19:18 ¹seven hundred, 2 Sam. 10:18   ²horsemen, 2 Sam. 10:18   20:1 ¹Lit. at
the return of the year   20:2 ¹plunder   20:3 ¹LXX cut them with
20:4 ¹Gob, 2 Sam. 21:18   ²Saph, 2 Sam. 21:18   ³Or Raphah   20:5 ¹Jaare-
Oregim, 2 Sam. 21:19

6Yet again [a]there was war at Gath, where there was a man of *great* stature, with twenty-four fingers and toes, six *on each hand* and six *on each foot;* and he also was born to [1]the giant. 7So when he defied Israel, Jonathan the son of [1]Shimea, David's brother, killed him.

8These were born to the giant in Gath, and they fell by the hand of David and by the hand of his servants.

THE CENSUS OF ISRAEL AND JUDAH
(2 Sam. 24:1–25)

21 Now [a]Satan stood up against Israel, and moved David to [1]number Israel. 2So David said to Joab and to the leaders of the people, "Go, number Israel from Beersheba to Dan, [a]and bring the number of them to me that I may know *it.*"

3And Joab answered, "May the LORD make His people a hundred times more than they are. But, my lord the king, *are* they not all my lord's servants? Why then does my lord require this thing? Why should he be a cause of guilt in Israel?"

4Nevertheless the king's word prevailed against Joab. Therefore Joab departed and went throughout all Israel and came to Jerusalem. 5Then Joab gave the sum of the number of the people to David. All Israel *had* one million one hundred thousand men who drew the sword, and Judah *had* four hundred and seventy thousand men who drew the sword. 6[a]But he did not count Levi and Benjamin among them, for the king's [1]word was abominable to Joab.

7And [1]God was displeased with this thing; therefore He struck Israel. 8So David said to God, [a]"I have sinned greatly, because I have done this thing; [b]but now, I pray, take away the iniquity of Your servant, for I have done very foolishly."

9Then the LORD spoke to Gad, David's [a]seer, saying, 10"Go and tell David, [a]saying, 'Thus says the LORD: "I offer you three *things;* choose one of them for yourself, that I may do *it* to you."'"

11So Gad came to David and said to him, "Thus says the LORD: 'Choose for yourself, 12[a]either [1]three years of famine, or three months to be defeated by your foes with the sword of your enemies overtaking *you,* or else for three days the sword of the LORD—the plague in the land, with the [2]angel of the LORD destroying throughout all the territory of Israel.' Now consider what answer I should take back to Him who sent me."

13And David said to Gad, "I am in great distress. Please let me fall into the hand of the LORD, for His [a]mercies *are* very great; but do not let me fall into the hand of man."

14So the LORD sent a [a]plague upon Israel, and seventy thousand men of Israel fell. 15And God sent [1]an [a]angel to Jerusalem to destroy it. As [2]he was destroying, the LORD looked and [b]relented of the disaster, and said to the angel who was destroying, "It is enough; now restrain [3]your hand." And the angel of the LORD stood by the [c]threshing floor of [4]Ornan the Jebusite.

16Then David lifted his eyes and [a]saw the angel of the LORD standing between earth and heaven, having in his hand a drawn sword stretched out over Jerusalem. So David and the

---

20:6
[a]1 Sam. 5:8;
2 Sam. 21:20

21:1
[a]2 Sam. 24:1–25;
Job 1:6

21:2
[a]1 Chr. 27:23, 24

21:6
[a]1 Chr. 27:24

21:8
[a]2 Sam. 24:10
[b]2 Sam. 12:13

21:9 [a]1 Sam. 9:9;
2 Kin. 17:13;
1 Chr. 29:29;
2 Chr. 16:7, 10;
Is. 30:9, 10;
Amos 7:12, 13

21:10
[a]2 Sam. 24:12–14

21:12
[a]2 Sam. 24:13

21:13 [a]Ps. 51:1;
130:4, 7

21:14
[a]1 Chr. 27:24

21:15
[a]2 Sam. 24:16
[b]Gen. 6:6
[c]2 Chr. 3:1

21:16
[a]Josh. 5:13;
2 Chr. 3:1

20:6 [1]Or *Raphah*   **20:7** [1]*Shammah,* 1 Sam. 16:9 or *Shimeah,* 2 Sam. 21:21
21:1 [1]*take a census of*   **21:6** [1]*command*   **21:7** Lit. *it was evil in the eyes of God*   **21:12** [1]*seven,* 2 Sam. 24:13   [2]Or *Angel,* and so throughout the chapter   **21:15** [1]Or *the Angel*   [2]Or *He*   [3]Or *Your*   [4]*Araunah,* 2 Sam. 24:16, 18–24

elders, clothed in sackcloth, fell on their faces. [17]And David said to God, "Was it not I who commanded the people to be numbered? I am the one who has sinned and done evil indeed; but these [a]sheep, what have they done? Let Your hand, I pray, O Lord my God, be against me and my father's house, but not against Your people that they should be plagued."

[18]Therefore, the [a]angel of the Lord commanded Gad to say to David that David should go and erect an altar to the Lord on the threshing floor of Ornan the Jebusite. [19]So David went up at the word of Gad, which he had spoken in the name of the Lord. [20]Now Ornan turned and saw the angel; and his four sons *who were* with him hid themselves, but Ornan continued threshing wheat. [21]So David came to Ornan, and Ornan looked and saw David. And he went out from the threshing floor, and bowed before David with *his* face to the ground. [22]Then David said to Ornan, [1]"Grant me the place of *this* threshing floor, that I may build an altar on it to the Lord. You shall grant it to me at the full price, that the plague may be withdrawn from the people."

[23]But Ornan said to David, "Take *it* to yourself, and let my lord the king do *what is* good in his eyes. Look, I *also* give *you* the oxen for burnt offerings, the threshing implements for wood, and the wheat for the grain offering; I give *it* all."

[24]Then King David said to Ornan, "No, but I will surely buy *it* for the full price, for I will not take what is yours for the Lord, nor offer burnt offerings with *that which* costs *me* nothing." [25]So [a]David gave Ornan six hundred shekels of gold by weight for the place. [26]And David built there an altar to the Lord, and offered burnt offerings and peace offerings, and called on the Lord; and [a]He answered him from heaven by fire on the altar of burnt offering.

[27]So the Lord commanded the angel, and he returned his sword to its sheath.

[28]At that time, when David saw that the Lord had answered him on the threshing floor of Ornan the Jebusite, he sacrificed there. [29a]For the tabernacle of the Lord and the altar of the burnt offering, which Moses had made in the wilderness, *were* at that time at the high place in [b]Gibeon. [30]But David could not go before it to inquire of God, for he was afraid of the sword of the angel of the Lord.

DAVID PREPARES TO BUILD THE TEMPLE

22 Then David said, [a]"This *is* the house of the Lord God, and this *is* the altar of burnt offering for Israel." [2]So David commanded to gather the [a]aliens who *were* in the land of Israel; and he appointed masons to [b]cut hewn stones to build the house of God. [3]And David prepared iron in abundance for the nails of the doors of the gates and for the joints, and bronze in abundance [a]beyond measure, [4]and cedar trees in abundance; for the [a]Sidonians and those from Tyre brought much cedar wood to David.

[5]Now David said, [a]"Solomon my son *is* young and inexperienced, and the house to be built for the Lord *must be* exceedingly magnificent, famous and glorious throughout all countries. I will now make preparation for it." So David made abundant preparations before his death.

21:17
[a]2 Sam. 7:8;
Ps. 74:1

21:18
[a]1 Chr. 21:11, 12;
2 Chr. 3:1

21:25
[a]2 Sam. 24:24

21:26 [a]Lev. 9:24;
Judg. 6:21;
1 Kin. 18:36–38;
2 Chr. 3:1; 7:1

21:29 [a]1 Kin. 3:4;
2 Chr. 1:3
[b]1 Chr. 16:39

22:1 [a]Deut. 12:5;
2 Sam. 24:18;
1 Chr. 21:18, 19,
26, 28; 2 Chr. 3:1

22:2
[a]1 Kin. 9:20, 21;
2 Chr. 2:17, 18
[b]1 Kin. 5:17, 18

22:3 [a]1 Kin. 7:47;
1 Chr. 22:14

22:4
[a]1 Kin. 5:6–10

22:5 [a]1 Kin. 3:7;
1 Chr. 29:1, 2

21:22 [1]Lit. *Give*

22:7 ᵃ2 Sam. 7:1,
2; 1 Kin. 8:17;
1 Chr. 17:1; 28:2
ᵇDeut. 12:5, 11

22:8
ᵃ2 Sam. 7:5–13;
1 Kin. 5:3;
1 Chr. 28:3

22:9 ᵃ1 Chr. 28:5
ᵇ1 Kin. 4:20,
25; 5:4

22:10
ᵃ2 Sam. 7:13;
1 Kin. 5:5; 6:38;
1 Chr. 17:12, 13;
28:6; 2 Chr. 6:2
ᵇHeb. 1:5

22:11
ᵃ1 Chr. 22:16

22:12
ᵃ1 Kin. 3:9–12;
2 Chr. 1:10

22:13
ᵃ[Josh. 1:7, 8];
1 Chr. 28:7
ᵇ[Deut. 31:7, 8;
Josh. 1:6, 7, 9];
1 Chr. 28:20]

22:14
ᵃ1 Chr. 22:3

22:16
ᵃ1 Chr. 22:11

22:17
ᵃ1 Chr. 28:1–6

22:18
ᵃDeut. 12:10;
Josh. 22:4;
2 Sam. 7:1;
[1 Kin. 5:4; 8:56]

22:19
ᵃ1 Kin. 8:1–11;
2 Chr. 5:2–14
ᵇ1 Kin. 5:3

23:1
ᵃ1 Kin. 1:33–40;
1 Chr. 28:4, 5

23:3
ᵃNum. 4:1–3

23:4
ᵃ2 Chr. 2:2, 18;
Ezra 3:8, 9
ᵇDeut. 16:18–20

23:5 ᵃ1 Chr. 15:16
ᵇ2 Chr. 29:25–27

23:6 ᵃEx. 6:16;
Num. 26:57;
2 Chr. 8:14

23:7
ᵃ1 Chr. 26:21

⁶Then he called for his son Solomon, and ¹charged him to build a house for the LORD God of Israel. ⁷And David said to Solomon: "My son, as for me, ᵃit was in my mind to build a house ᵇto the name of the LORD my God; ⁸but the word of the LORD came to me, saying, ᵃ'You have shed much blood and have made great wars; you shall not build a house for My name, because you have shed much blood on the earth in My sight. ⁹ᵃBehold, a son shall be born to you, who shall be a man of rest; and I will give him ᵇrest from all his enemies all around. His name shall be ¹Solomon, for I will give peace and quietness to Israel in his days. ¹⁰ᵃHe shall build a house for My name, and ᵇhe shall be My son, and I *will be* his Father; and I will establish the throne of his kingdom over Israel forever.' ¹¹Now, my son, may ᵃthe LORD be with you; and may you prosper, and build the house of the LORD your God, as He has said to you. ¹²Only may the LORD ᵃgive you wisdom and understanding, and give you charge concerning Israel, that you may keep the law of the LORD your God. ¹³ᵃThen you will prosper, if you take care to fulfill the statutes and judgments with which the LORD ¹charged Moses concerning Israel. ᵇBe strong and of good courage; do not fear nor be dismayed. ¹⁴Indeed I have taken much trouble to prepare for the house of the LORD one hundred thousand talents of gold and one million talents of silver, and bronze and iron ᵃbeyond measure, for it is so abundant. I have prepared timber and stone also, and you may add to them. ¹⁵Moreover *there are* workmen with you in abundance: woodsmen and stonecutters, and all types of skillful men for every kind of work. ¹⁶Of gold and silver and bronze and iron *there is* no limit. Arise and begin working, and ᵃthe LORD be with you."

¹⁷David also commanded all the ᵃleaders of Israel to help Solomon his son, *saying*, ¹⁸"*Is* not the LORD your God with you? ᵃAnd has He *not* given you rest on every side? For He has given the inhabitants of the land into my hand, and the land is subdued before the LORD and before His people. ¹⁹Now set your heart and your soul to seek the LORD your God. Therefore arise and build the sanctuary of the LORD God, to ᵃbring the ark of the covenant of the LORD and the holy articles of God into the house that is to be built ᵇfor the name of the LORD."

THE DIVISIONS OF THE LEVITES

23 So when David was old and full of days, he made his son ᵃSolomon king over Israel.

²And he gathered together all the leaders of Israel, with the priests and the Levites. ³Now the Levites were numbered from the age of ᵃthirty years and above; and the number of individual males was thirty-eight thousand. ⁴Of these, twenty-four thousand *were* to ᵃlook after the work of the house of the LORD, six thousand *were* ᵇofficers and judges, ⁵four thousand *were* gatekeepers, and four thousand ᵃpraised the LORD with *musical* instruments, ᵇ"which I made," *said David*, "for giving praise."

⁶Also ᵃDavid separated them into ¹divisions among the sons of Levi: Gershon, Kohath, and Merari.

⁷Of the ᵃGershonites: ¹Laadan and Shimei. ⁸The sons of Laadan: the first Jehiel, then Zetham and Joel—three *in all*.

22:6 ¹commanded 22:9 ¹Lit. Peaceful 22:13 ¹commanded 23:6 ¹groups
23:7 ¹Libni, Ex. 6:17

⁹The sons of Shimei: Shelomith, Haziel, and Haran—three *in all.* These were the heads of the fathers' *houses* of Laadan. ¹⁰And the sons of Shimei: Jahath, ¹Zina, Jeush, and Beriah. These *were* the four sons of Shimei. ¹¹Jahath was the first and Zizah the second. But Jeush and Beriah did not have many sons; therefore they were assigned as one father's house.

¹²ᵃThe sons of Kohath: Amram, Izhar, Hebron, and Uzziel—four *in all.* ¹³The sons of ᵃAmram: Aaron and Moses; and ᵇAaron was set apart, he and his sons forever, that he should ¹sanctify the most holy things, ᶜto burn incense before the LORD, ᵈto minister to Him, and ᵉto give the blessing in His name forever. ¹⁴Now ᵃthe sons of Moses the man of God were reckoned to the tribe of Levi. ¹⁵ᵃThe sons of Moses *were* ¹Gershon and Eliezer. ¹⁶Of the sons of Gershon, ᵃShebuel¹ *was* the first. ¹⁷Of the descendants of Eliezer, ᵃRehabiah was the first. And Eliezer had no other sons, but the sons of Rehabiah were very many. ¹⁸Of the sons of Izhar, ᵃShelomith *was* the first. ¹⁹ᵃOf the sons of Hebron, Jeriah *was* the first, Amariah the second, Jahaziel the third, and Jekameam the fourth. ²⁰Of the sons of Uzziel, Michah *was* the first and Jesshiah the second.

²¹ᵃThe sons of Merari *were* Mahli and Mushi. The sons of Mahli *were* Eleazar and ᵇKish. ²²And Eleazar died, and ᵃhad no sons, but only daughters; and their ¹brethren, the sons of Kish, ᵇtook them *as wives.* ²³ᵃThe sons of Mushi *were* Mahli, Eder, and Jeremoth—three *in all.*

²⁴These *were* the sons of ᵃLevi by their fathers' houses—the heads of the fathers' *houses* as they were counted individually by the number of their names, who did the work for the service of the house of the LORD, from the age of ᵇtwenty years and above.

²⁵For David said, "The LORD God of Israel ᵃhas given rest to His people, that they may dwell in Jerusalem forever"; ²⁶and also to the Levites, "They shall no longer ᵃcarry the tabernacle, or any of the articles for its service." ²⁷For by the ᵃlast words of David the Levites *were* numbered from twenty years old and above; ²⁸because their duty *was* to help the sons of Aaron in the service of the house of the LORD, in the courts and in the chambers, in the purifying of all holy things and the work of the service of the house of God, ²⁹both with ᵃthe showbread and ᵇthe fine flour for the grain offering, with ᶜthe unleavened cakes and ᵈ*what is baked in* the pan, with what is mixed and with all kinds of ᵉmeasures and sizes; ³⁰to stand every morning to thank and praise the LORD, and likewise at evening; ³¹and at every presentation of a burnt offering to the LORD ᵃon the Sabbaths and on the New Moons and on the ᵇset¹ feasts, by number according to the ordinance governing them, regularly before the LORD; ³²and that they should ᵃattend to the ᵇneeds of the tabernacle of meeting, the needs of the holy *place,* and the ᶜneeds of the sons of Aaron their brethren in the work of the house of the LORD.

THE DIVISIONS OF THE PRIESTS

24 Now *these are* the divisions of the sons of Aaron. ᵃThe sons of Aaron *were* Nadab, Abihu, Eleazar, and Ithamar. ²And ᵃNadab and Abihu died before their father, and

---

23:12 ᵃEx. 6:18

23:13 ᵃEx. 6:20
ᵇEx. 28:1;
Heb. 5:4
ᶜEx. 30:7;
1 Sam. 2:28
ᵈ[Deut. 21:5]
ᵉNum. 6:23

23:14
ᵃ1 Chr. 26:20–24

23:15
ᵃEx. 18:3, 4

23:16
ᵃ1 Chr. 26:24

23:17
ᵃ1 Chr. 26:25

23:18
ᵃ1 Chr. 24:22

23:19
ᵃ1 Chr. 24:23

23:21
ᵃ1 Chr. 24:26
ᵇ1 Chr. 24:29

23:22
ᵃ1 Chr. 24:28
ᵇNum. 36:6

23:23
ᵃ1 Chr. 24:30

23:24
ᵃNum. 10:17, 21 ᵇNum. 1:3; Ezra 3:8

23:25
ᵃ1 Chr. 22:18

23:26
ᵃNum. 4:5, 15; 7:9; Deut. 10:8

23:27
ᵃ2 Sam. 23:1

23:29
ᵃEx. 25:30
ᵇLev. 6:20
ᶜLev. 2:1, 4
ᵈLev. 2:5, 7
ᵉLev. 19:35

23:31
ᵃNum. 10:10
ᵇLev. 23:2–4

23:32
ᵃ2 Chr. 13:10, 11
ᵇ[Num. 1:53];
1 Chr. 9:27
ᶜNum. 3:6–9, 38

24:1
ᵃLev. 10:1–6;
Num. 26:60, 61;
1 Chr. 6:3

24:2
ᵃNum. 3:1–4;
26:61

23:10 ¹LXX, Vg. *Zizah* and v. 11   23:13 ¹*consecrate*   23:15 ¹Heb. *Gershom,* 1 Chr. 6:16   23:16 ¹*Shubael,* 1 Chr. 24:20   23:22 ¹*kinsmen* 23:31 ¹*appointed feasts*

had no children; therefore Eleazar and Ithamar ministered as priests. ³Then David with Zadok of the sons of Eleazar, and ᵃAhimelech of the sons of Ithamar, divided them according to the schedule of their service.

⁴There were more leaders found of the sons of Eleazar than of the sons of Ithamar, and *thus* they were divided. Among the sons of Eleazar *were* sixteen heads of *their* fathers' houses, and eight heads of their fathers' houses among the sons of Ithamar. ⁵Thus they were divided by lot, one group as another, for there were officials of the sanctuary and officials *of the house* of God, from the sons of Eleazar and from the sons of Ithamar. ⁶And the scribe, Shemaiah the son of Nethanel, *one of* the Levites, wrote them down before the king, the leaders, Zadok the priest, Ahimelech the son of Abiathar, and the heads of the fathers' *houses* of the priests and Levites, one father's house taken for Eleazar and *one* for Ithamar.

⁷Now the first lot fell to Jehoiarib, the second to Jedaiah, ⁸the third to Harim, the fourth to Seorim, ⁹the fifth to Malchijah, the sixth to Mijamin, ¹⁰the seventh to Hakkoz, the eighth to ᵃAbijah, ¹¹the ninth to Jeshua, the tenth to Shecaniah, ¹²the eleventh to Eliashib, the twelfth to Jakim, ¹³the thirteenth to Huppah, the fourteenth to Jeshebeab, ¹⁴the fifteenth to Bilgah, the sixteenth to Immer, ¹⁵the seventeenth to Hezir, the eighteenth to ¹Happizzez, ¹⁶the nineteenth to Pethahiah, the twentieth to ¹Jehezekel, ¹⁷the twenty-first to Jachin, the twenty-second to Gamul, ¹⁸the twenty-third to Delaiah, the twenty-fourth to Maaziah.

¹⁹This *was* the schedule of their service ᵃfor coming into the house of the LORD according to their ordinance by the hand of Aaron their father, as the LORD God of Israel had commanded him.

OTHER LEVITES

²⁰And the rest of the sons of Levi: of the sons of Amram, ¹Shubael; of the sons of Shubael, Jehdeiah. ²¹Concerning ᵃRehabiah, of the sons of Rehabiah, the first *was* Isshiah. ²²Of the Izharites, ¹Shelomoth; of the sons of Shelomoth, Jahath. ²³Of the sons ¹of ᵃHebron, Jeriah *was the first,* Amariah the second, Jahaziel the third, *and* Jekameam the fourth. ²⁴*Of* the sons of Uzziel, Michah; of the sons of Michah, Shamir. ²⁵The brother of Michah, Isshiah; of the sons of Isshiah, Zechariah. ²⁶ᵃThe sons of Merari *were* Mahli and Mushi; the son of Jaaziah, Beno. ²⁷The sons of Merari by Jaaziah *were* Beno, Shoham, Zaccur, and Ibri. ²⁸Of Mahli: Eleazar, ᵃwho had no sons. ²⁹Of Kish: the son of Kish, Jerahmeel.

³⁰Also ᵃthe sons of Mushi *were* Mahli, Eder, and Jerimoth. These *were* the sons of the Levites according to their fathers' houses.

³¹These also cast lots just as their brothers the sons of Aaron did, in the presence of King David, Zadok, Ahimelech, and the heads of the fathers' *houses* of the priests and Levites. The chief fathers *did* just as their younger brethren.

THE MUSICIANS

25 Moreover David and the captains of the army separated for the service *some* of the sons of ᵃAsaph, of

24:3 ᵃ1 Chr. 18:16

24:10
ᵃNeh. 12:4, 17;
Luke 1:5

24:19
ᵃ1 Chr. 9:25

24:21
ᵃ1 Chr. 23:17

24:23
ᵃ1 Chr. 23:19;
26:31

24:26 ᵃEx. 6:19;
1 Chr. 23:21

24:28
ᵃ1 Chr. 23:22

24:30
ᵃ1 Chr. 23:23

25:1 ᵃ1 Chr. 6:30,
33, 39, 44;
2 Chr. 5:12

24:15 ¹LXX, Vg. *Aphses*   24:16 ¹MT *Jehezkel*   24:20 ¹*Shebuel*, 1 Chr. 23:16
24:22 ¹*Shelomith*, 1 Chr. 23:18   24:23 ¹Supplied from 23:19 (following some Heb. mss. and LXX mss.)

Heman, and of Jeduthun, who *should* prophesy with harps, stringed instruments, and cymbals. And the number of the skilled men performing their service was: [2]Of the sons of Asaph: Zaccur, Joseph, Nethaniah, and [1]Asharelah; the sons of Asaph *were* [2]under the direction of Asaph, who prophesied according to the order of the king. [3]Of [a]Jeduthun, the sons of Jeduthun: Gedaliah, [1]Zeri, Jeshaiah, [2]*Shimei*, Hashabiah, and Mattithiah, [3]six, under the direction of their father Jeduthun, who prophesied with a harp to give thanks and to praise the LORD. [4]Of Heman, the sons of Heman: Bukkiah, Mattaniah, [1]Uzziel, [2]Shebuel, [3]Jerimoth, Hananiah, Hanani, Eliathah, Giddalti, Romamti-Ezer, Joshbekashah, Mallothi, Hothir, *and* Mahazioth. [5]All these *were* the sons of Heman the king's seer in the words of God, to [1]exalt his [a]horn. For God gave Heman fourteen sons and three daughters.

[6]All these *were* under the direction of their father for the music *in* the house of the LORD, with cymbals, stringed instruments, and [a]harps, for the service of the house of God. Asaph, Jeduthun, and Heman *were* [b]under the authority of the king. [7]So the [a]number of them, with their brethren who were instructed in the songs of the LORD, all who were skillful, *was* two hundred and eighty-eight.

[8]And they cast lots for their duty, the small as well as the great, [a]the teacher with the student.

[9]Now the first lot for Asaph came out for Joseph; the second for Gedaliah, him with his brethren and sons, twelve; [10]the third for Zaccur, his sons and his brethren, twelve; [11]the fourth for [1]Jizri, his sons and his brethren, twelve; [12]the fifth for Nethaniah, his sons and his brethren, twelve; [13]the sixth for Bukkiah, his sons and his brethren, twelve; [14]the seventh for [1]Jesharelah, his sons and his brethren, twelve; [15]the eighth for Jeshaiah, his sons and his brethren, twelve; [16]the ninth for Mattaniah, his sons and his brethren, twelve; [17]the tenth for Shimei, his sons and his brethren, twelve; [18]the eleventh for [1]Azarel, his sons and his brethren, twelve; [19]the twelfth for Hashabiah, his sons and his brethren, twelve; [20]the thirteenth for [1]Shubael, his sons and his brethren, twelve; [21]the fourteenth for Mattithiah, his sons and his brethren, twelve; [22]the fifteenth for [1]Jeremoth, his sons and his brethren, twelve; [23]the sixteenth for Hananiah, his sons and his brethren, twelve; [24]the seventeenth for Joshbekashah, his sons and his brethren, twelve; [25]the eighteenth for Hanani, his sons and his brethren, twelve; [26]the nineteenth for Mallothi, his sons and his brethren, twelve; [27]the twentieth for Eliathah, his sons and his brethren, twelve; [28]the twenty-first for Hothir, his sons and his brethren, twelve; [29]the twenty-second for Giddalti, his sons and his brethren, twelve; [30]the twenty-third for Mahazioth, his sons and his brethren, twelve; [31]the twenty-fourth for Romamti-Ezer, his sons and his brethren, twelve.

THE GATEKEEPERS

26 Concerning the divisions of the gatekeepers: of the Korahites, [1]Meshelemiah the son of [a]Kore, of the sons

Cross references

25:3
[a]1 Chr. 16:41, 42

25:5
[a]1 Chr. 16:42

25:6 [a]1 Chr. 15:16
[b]1 Chr. 15:19;
25:2

25:7 [a]1 Chr. 23:5

25:8
[a]2 Chr. 23:13

26:1 [a]Ps. 42:title

25:2 [1]*Jesharelah*, v. 14   [2]Lit. *at the hands of*   25:3 [1]*Jizri*, v. 11   [2]So with one Heb. ms., LXX mss.   [3]*Shimei* is the sixth, v. 17   25:4 [1]*Azarel*, v. 18   [2]*Shubael*, v. 20   [3]*Jeremoth*, v. 22   25:5 [1]Increase his power or influence   25:11 [1]*Zeri*, v. 3   25:14 [1]*Asharelah*, v. 2   25:18 [1]*Uzziel*, v. 4   25:20 [1]*Shebuel*, v. 4   25:22 [1]*Jerimoth*, v. 4   26:1 [1]*Shelemiah*, v. 14

of [2]Asaph. [2]And the sons of Meshelemiah *were* [a]Zechariah the firstborn, Jediael the second, Zebadiah the third, Jathniel the fourth, [3]Elam the fifth, Jehohanan the sixth, Eliehoenai the seventh.

[4]Moreover the sons of [a]Obed-Edom *were* Shemaiah the firstborn, Jehozabad the second, Joah the third, Sacar the fourth, Nethanel the fifth, [5]Ammiel the sixth, Issachar the seventh, Peulthai the eighth; for God blessed him.

[6]Also to Shemaiah his son were sons born who governed their fathers' houses, because they *were* men of great ability. [7]The sons of Shemaiah *were* Othni, Rephael, Obed, and Elzabad, whose brothers Elihu and Semachiah *were* able men.

[8]All these *were* of the sons of Obed-Edom, they and their sons and their brethren, [a]able men with strength for the work: sixty-two of Obed-Edom.

[9]And Meshelemiah had sons and brethren, eighteen able men.

[10]Also [a]Hosah, of the children of Merari, had sons: Shimri the first (for *though* he was not the firstborn, his father made him the first), [11]Hilkiah the second, Tebaliah the third, Zechariah the fourth; all the sons and brethren of Hosah *were* thirteen.

[12]Among these *were* the divisions of the gatekeepers, among the chief men, *having* duties just like their brethren, to serve in the house of the LORD. [13]And they [a]cast lots for each gate, the small as well as the great, according to their father's house. [14]The lot for the East *Gate* fell to [1]Shelemiah. Then they cast lots *for* his son Zechariah, a wise counselor, and his lot came out for the North Gate; [15]to Obed-Edom the South Gate, and to his sons the [1]storehouse. [16]To Shuppim and Hosah *the lot came out* for the West Gate, with the Shallecheth Gate on the [a]ascending highway—watchman opposite watchman. [17]On the east *were* six Levites, on the north four each day, on the south four each day, and for the [1]storehouse two by two. [18]As for the [1]Parbar on the west, *there were* four on the highway *and* two at the Parbar. [19]These were the divisions of the gatekeepers among the sons of Korah and among the sons of Merari.

THE TREASURIES AND OTHER DUTIES

[20]Of the Levites, Ahijah *was* [a]over the treasuries of the house of God and over the treasuries of the [b]dedicated[1] things. [21]The sons of [1]Laadan, the descendants of the Gershonites of Laadan, heads of their fathers' *houses,* of Laadan the Gershonite: [2]Jehieli. [22]The sons of Jehieli, Zetham and Joel his brother, *were* over the treasuries of the house of the LORD. [23]Of the [a]Amramites, the Izharites, the Hebronites, and the Uzzielites: [24][a]Shebuel the son of Gershom, the son of Moses, *was* overseer of the treasuries. [25]And his brethren by Eliezer *were* Rehabiah his son, Jeshaiah his son, Joram his son, Zichri his son, and [a]Shelomith his son.

[26]This Shelomith and his brethren *were* over all the treasuries of the dedicated things [a]which King David and the heads of fathers' *houses,* the captains over thousands and hundreds, and the captains of the army, had dedicated. [27]Some of the [1]spoils won in battles they dedicated to maintain the

26:2 [a]1 Chr. 9:21
26:4 [a]1 Chr. 15:18, 21
26:8 [a]1 Chr. 9:13
26:10 [a]1 Chr. 16:38
26:13 [a]1 Chr. 24:5, 31; 25:8
26:16 [a]1 Kin. 10:5; 2 Chr. 9:4
26:20 [a]1 Chr. 9:26 [b]2 Sam. 8:11; 1 Chr. 26:22, 24, 26; 28:12; Ezra 2:69
26:23 [a]Ex. 6:18; Num. 3:19
26:24 [a]1 Chr. 23:16
26:25 [a]1 Chr. 23:18
26:26 [a]2 Sam. 8:11

26:1 [2]*Ebiasaph,* 1 Chr. 6:37; 9:19   26:14 [1]*Meshelemiah,* v. 1   26:15 [1]Heb. *asuppim*   26:17 [1]Heb. *asuppim*   26:18 [1]Probably a court or colonnade extending west of the temple   26:20 [1]*holy things*   26:21 [1]*Libni,* 1 Chr. 6:17 [2]*Jehiel,* 1 Chr. 23:8; 29:8   26:27 [1]*plunder*

house of the LORD. ²⁸And all that Samuel ªthe seer, Saul the son of Kish, Abner the son of Ner, and Joab the son of Zeruiah had dedicated, every dedicated *thing,* was under the hand of Shelomith and his brethren.

²⁹Of the Izharites, Chenaniah and his sons ªperformed duties as ᵇofficials and judges over Israel outside Jerusalem.

³⁰Of the Hebronites, ªHashabiah and his brethren, one thousand seven hundred able men, had the oversight of Israel on the west side of the Jordan for all the business of the LORD, and in the service of the king. ³¹Among the Hebronites, ªJerijah *was* head of the Hebronites according to his genealogy of the fathers. In the fortieth year of the reign of David they were sought, and there were found among them capable men ᵇat Jazer of Gilead. ³²And his brethren *were* two thousand seven hundred able men, heads of fathers' *houses,* whom King David made officials over the Reubenites, the Gadites, and the half-tribe of Manasseh, for every matter pertaining to God and the ªaffairs of the king.

THE MILITARY DIVISIONS

27 And the children of Israel, according to their number, the heads of fathers' *houses,* the captains of thousands and hundreds and their officers, served the king in every matter of the *military* divisions. *These divisions* came in and went out month by month throughout all the months of the year, each division *having* twenty-four thousand.

²Over the first division for the first month *was* ªJashobeam the son of Zabdiel, and in his division *were* twenty-four thousand; ³he *was* of the children of Perez, and the chief of all the captains of the army for the first month. ⁴Over the division of the second month *was* ¹Dodai an Ahohite, and of his division Mikloth also *was* the leader; in his division *were* twenty-four thousand. ⁵The third captain of the army for the third month *was* ªBenaiah, the son of Jehoiada the priest, who was chief; in his division *were* twenty-four thousand. ⁶This was the Benaiah *who was* ªmighty *among* the thirty, and was over the thirty; in his division *was* Ammizabad his son. ⁷The fourth *captain* for the fourth month *was* ªAsahel the brother of Joab, and Zebadiah his son after him; in his division *were* twenty-four thousand. ⁸The fifth captain for the fifth month *was* ¹Shamhuth the Izrahite; in his division were twenty-four thousand. ⁹The sixth *captain* for the sixth month *was* ªIra the son of Ikkesh the Tekoite; in his division *were* twenty-four thousand. ¹⁰The seventh *captain* for the seventh month *was* ªHelez the Pelonite, of the children of Ephraim; in his division *were* twenty-four thousand. ¹¹The eighth *captain* for the eighth month *was* ªSibbechai the Hushathite, of the Zarhites; in his division *were* twenty-four thousand. ¹²The ninth *captain* for the ninth month *was* ªAbiezer the Anathothite, of the Benjamites; in his division *were* twenty-four thousand. ¹³The tenth *captain* for the tenth month *was* ªMaharai the Netophathite, of the Zarhites; in his division *were* twenty-four thousand. ¹⁴The eleventh *captain* for the eleventh month *was* ªBenaiah the Pirathonite, of the children of Ephraim; in his division *were* twenty-four thousand. ¹⁵The twelfth *captain* for the twelfth month *was* ¹Heldai the Netophathite, of Othniel; in his division *were* twenty-four thousand.

26:28
ª1 Sam. 9:9

26:29
ªNeh. 11:16
ᵇ1 Chr. 23:4

26:30
ª1 Chr. 27:17

26:31
ª1 Chr. 23:19
ᵇJosh. 21:39

26:32
ª2 Chr. 19:11

27:2 ª1 Chr. 11:11

27:5 ª1 Chr. 18:17

27:6
ª2 Sam. 23:20–23

27:7
ª2 Sam. 23:24;
1 Chr. 11:26

27:9 ª1 Chr. 11:28

27:10
ª1 Chr. 11:27

27:11
ª2 Sam. 21:18;
1 Chr. 11:29; 20:4

27:12
ª1 Chr. 11:28

27:13
ª2 Sam. 23:28;
1 Chr. 11:30

27:14 ª1 Chr. 11:31

LEADERS OF TRIBES

16Furthermore, over the tribes of Israel: the officer over the Reubenites *was* Eliezer the son of Zichri; over the Simeonites, Shephatiah the son of Maachah; 17*over* the Levites, aHashabiah the son of Kemuel; over the Aaronites, Zadok; 18*over* Judah, aElihu, *one* of David's brothers; *over* Issachar, Omri the son of Michael; 19*over* Zebulun, Ishmaiah the son of Obadiah; *over* Naphtali, Jerimoth the son of Azriel; 20*over* the children of Ephraim, Hoshea the son of Azaziah; *over* the half-tribe of Manasseh, Joel the son of Pedaiah; 21*over* the half-*tribe* of Manasseh in Gilead, Iddo the son of Zechariah; *over* Benjamin, Jaasiel the son of Abner; 22*over* Dan, Azarel the son of Jeroham. These *were* the leaders of the tribes of Israel.

23But David did not take the number of those twenty years old and under, because athe LORD had said He would multiply Israel like the bstars of the heavens. 24Joab the son of Zeruiah began a census, but he did not finish, for awrath came upon Israel because of this census; nor was the number recorded in the account of the chronicles of King David.

OTHER STATE OFFICIALS

25And Azmaveth the son of Adiel *was* over the king's treasuries; and Jehonathan the son of Uzziah was over the storehouses in the field, in the cities, in the villages, and in the fortresses. 26Ezri the son of Chelub was over those who did the work of the field for tilling the ground. 27And Shimei the Ramathite *was* over the vineyards, and Zabdi the Shiphmite was over the produce of the vineyards for the supply of wine. 28Baal-Hanan the Gederite was over the olive trees and the sycamore trees that *were* in the lowlands, and Joash *was* over the store of oil. 29And Shitrai the Sharonite *was* over the herds that fed in Sharon, and Shaphat the son of Adlai was over the herds *that were* in the valleys. 30Obil the Ishmaelite *was* over the camels, Jehdeiah the Meronothite *was* over the donkeys, 31and Jaziz the aHagrite *was* over the flocks. All these *were* the officials over King David's property.

32Also Jehonathan, David's uncle, *was* a counselor, a wise man, and a 1scribe; and Jehiel the 2son of Hachmoni *was* with the king's sons. 33aAhithophel *was* the king's counselor, and bHushai the Archite *was* the king's companion. 34After Ahithophel *was* Jehoiada the son of Benaiah, then aAbiathar. And the general of the king's army *was* bJoab.

SOLOMON INSTRUCTED TO BUILD THE TEMPLE

28 Now David assembled at Jerusalem all athe leaders of Israel: the officers of the tribes and bthe captains of the divisions who served the king, the captains over thousands and captains over hundreds, and cthe stewards over all the substance and 1possessions of the king and of his sons, with the officials, the valiant men, and all dthe mighty men of valor.

2Then King David rose to his feet and said, "Hear me, my brethren and my people: aI *had* it in my heart to build a house of rest for the ark of the covenant of the LORD, and for bthe footstool of our God, and had made preparations to build it. 3But God said to me, a"You shall not build a house for My name,

27:17
a1 Chr. 26:30

27:18
a1 Sam. 16:6

27:23
a[Deut. 6:3]
bGen. 15:5;
22:17; 26:4;
Ex. 32:13;
Deut. 1:10

27:24
a2 Sam. 24:12–15;
1 Chr. 21:1–7

27:31 a1 Chr. 5:10

27:33
a2 Sam. 15:12
b2 Sam. 15:32–37

27:34 a1 Kin. 1:7
b1 Chr. 11:6

28:1 a1 Chr. 27:16
b1 Chr. 27:1, 2
c1 Chr. 27:25
d2 Sam. 23:8–39;
1 Chr. 11:10–47

28:2 a2 Sam. 7:2
bPs. 99:5; 132:7;
[Is. 66:1]

28:3
a2 Sam. 7:5, 13;
1 Kin. 5:3

27:32 1secretary   2Or *Hachmonite*   28:1 1Or *livestock*

because you *have been* a man of war and have shed [b]blood.' [4]However the Lord God of Israel [a]chose me above all the house of my father to be king over Israel forever, for He has chosen [b]Judah *to be* the ruler. And of the house of Judah, [c]the house of my father, and [d]among the sons of my father, He was pleased with me to make *me* king over all Israel. [5a]And of all my sons (for the Lord has given me many sons) [b]He has chosen my son Solomon to sit on the throne of the kingdom of the Lord over Israel. [6]Now He said to me, 'It is [a]your son Solomon *who* shall build My house and My courts; for I have chosen him *to be* My son, and I will be his Father. [7]Moreover I will establish his kingdom forever, [a]if he is steadfast to observe My commandments and My judgments, as it is this day.' [8]Now therefore, in the sight of all Israel, the assembly of the Lord, and in the hearing of our God, be careful to seek out all the commandments of the Lord your God, that you may possess this good land, and leave *it* as an inheritance for your children after you forever.

[9]"As for you, my son Solomon, [a]know the God of your father, and serve Him [b]with a loyal heart and with a willing mind; for [c]the Lord searches all hearts and understands all the intent of the thoughts. [d]If you seek Him, He will be found by you; but if you forsake Him, He will [e]cast you off forever. [10]Consider now, [a]for the Lord has chosen you to build a house for the sanctuary; be strong, and do it."

[11]Then David gave his son Solomon [a]the plans for the vestibule, its houses, its treasuries, its upper chambers, its inner chambers, and the place of the mercy seat; [12]and the [a]plans for all that he had by the Spirit, of the courts of the house of the Lord, of all the chambers all around, [b]of the treasuries of the house of God, and of the treasuries for the dedicated things; [13]also for the division of the priests and the [a]Levites, for all the work of the service of the house of the Lord, and for all the articles of service in the house of the Lord. [14]*He gave* gold by weight for *things* of gold, for all articles used in every kind of service; also *silver* for all articles of silver by weight, for all articles used in every kind of service; [15]the weight for the [a]lampstands of gold, and their lamps of gold, by weight for each lampstand and its lamps; for the lampstands of silver by weight, for the lampstand and its lamps, according to the use of each lampstand. [16]And by weight *he gave* gold for the tables of the showbread, for each [a]table, and silver for the tables of silver; [17]also pure gold for the forks, the basins, the pitchers of pure gold, and the golden bowls—*he gave gold* by weight for every bowl; and for the silver bowls, *silver* by weight for every bowl; [18]and refined gold by weight for the [a]altar of incense, and for the construction of the chariot, that is, the gold [b]cherubim that spread *their wings* and overshadowed the ark of the covenant of the Lord. [19]"All *this*," said David, [a]"the Lord made me understand in writing, by *His* hand upon me, all the [1]works of these plans."

[20]And David said to his son Solomon, [a]"Be strong and of good courage, and do *it;* do not fear nor be dismayed, for the Lord God—my God—*will be* with you. [b]He will not leave you nor forsake you, until you have finished all the work for the service of the house of the Lord. [21]Here are [a]the divisions of the priests and the Levites for all the service of the house of

28:19 [1]details

28:3
[b][1 Chr. 17:4; 22:8]

28:4
[a]1 Sam. 16:6–13
[b]Gen. 49:8–10;
1 Chr. 5:2;
Ps. 60:7
[c]1 Sam. 16:1
[d]1 Sam. 13:14;
16:12, 13;
Acts 13:22

28:5
[a]1 Chr. 3:1–9;
14:3–7; 23:1
[b]1 Chr. 22:9;
29:1

28:6
[a]2 Sam. 7:13, 14;
1 Kin. 6:38;
1 Chr. 22:9, 10;
2 Chr. 1:9; 6:2

28:7
[a]1 Chr. 22:13

28:9
[a][1 Sam. 12:24];
Jer. 9:24;
Hos. 4:1;
[John 17:3]
[b]2 Kin. 20:3
[c][1 Sam. 16:7;
1 Kin. 8:39;
1 Chr. 29:17];
Jer. 11:20; 17:10;
20:12; Rev. 2:23
[d]2 Chr. 15:2;
[Jer. 29:13]
[e]Deut. 31:17

28:10
[a]1 Chr. 22:13;
28:6

28:11 [a]1 Kin. 6:3;
1 Chr. 28:19

28:12
[a]Ex. 25:40;
Heb. 8:5
[b]1 Chr. 26:20, 28

28:13
[a]1 Chr. 23:6

28:15
[a]Ex. 25:31–39;
1 Kin. 7:49

28:16
[a]1 Kin. 7:48

28:18
[a]Ex. 30:1–10
[b]Ex. 25:18–22;
1 Sam. 4:4;
1 Kin. 6:23

28:19
[a]Ex. 25:40;
1 Chr. 28:11, 12

28:20
[a]Deut. 31:6, 7;
[Josh. 1:6–9];
1 Chr. 22:13
[b]Josh. 1:5;
Heb. 13:5

28:21
[a]1 Chr. 24—26

God; and [b]every willing craftsman *will be* with you for all manner of workmanship, for every kind of service; also the leaders and all the people *will be* completely at your command."

OFFERINGS FOR BUILDING THE TEMPLE

29 Furthermore King David said to all the assembly: "My son Solomon, whom alone God has [a]chosen, *is* [b]young and inexperienced; and the work *is* great, because the [1]temple *is* not for man but for the LORD God. [2]Now for the house of my God I have prepared with all my might: gold for *things to be made of* gold, silver for *things of* silver, bronze for *things of* bronze, iron for *things of* iron, wood for *things of* wood, [a]onyx stones, *stones* to be set, glistening stones of various colors, all kinds of precious stones, and marble slabs in abundance. [3]Moreover, because I have set my affection on the house of my God, I have given to the house of my God, over and above all that I have prepared for the holy house, my own special treasure of gold and silver: [4]three thousand talents of gold, of the gold of [a]Ophir, and seven thousand talents of refined silver, to overlay the walls of the houses; [5]the gold for *things of* gold and the silver for *things of* silver, and for all kinds of work *to be done* by the hands of craftsmen. Who *then* is [a]willing to [1]consecrate himself this day to the LORD?"

[6]Then [a]the leaders of the fathers' *houses,* leaders of the tribes of Israel, the captains of thousands and of hundreds, with [b]the officers over the king's work, [c]offered willingly. [7]They gave for the work of the house of God five thousand talents and ten thousand darics of gold, ten thousand talents of silver, eighteen thousand talents of bronze, and one hundred thousand talents of iron. [8]And whoever had *precious* stones gave *them* to the treasury of the house of the LORD, into the hand of [a]Jehiel[1] the Gershonite. [9]Then the people rejoiced, for they had offered willingly, because with a loyal heart they had [a]offered willingly to the LORD; and King David also rejoiced greatly.

DAVID'S PRAISE TO GOD

[10]Therefore David blessed the LORD before all the assembly; and David said:

"Blessed are You, LORD God of Israel, our Father, forever
     and ever.
[11] [a]Yours, O LORD, *is* the greatness,
     The power and the glory,
     The victory and the majesty;
     For all *that is* in heaven and in earth *is Yours;*
     Yours *is* the kingdom, O LORD,
     And You are exalted as head over all.
[12] [a]Both riches and honor *come* from You,
     And You reign over all.
     In Your hand *is* power and might;
     In Your hand *it is* to make great
     And to give strength to all.
[13] "Now therefore, our God,
     We thank You
     And praise Your glorious name.

28:21
[b]Ex. 35:25–35;
36:1, 2;
2 Chr. 2:13, 14

29:1 [a]1 Chr. 28:5
[b]1 Kin. 3:7;
1 Chr. 22:5;
Prov. 4:3

29:2 [a]Is. 54:11,
12; Rev. 21:18

29:4 [a]1 Kin. 9:28

29:5
[a]2 Chr. 29:31;
[2 Cor. 8:5, 12]

29:6
[a]1 Chr. 27:1; 28:1
[b]1 Chr. 27:25–31
[c]Ex. 35:21–35

29:8 [a]1 Chr. 23:8

29:9 [a]Ex. 25:2;
1 Kin. 8:61;
2 Cor. 9:7

29:11
[a]Matt. 6:13;
1 Tim. 1:17;
Rev. 5:13

29:12
[a]Rom. 11:36

29:1 [1]Lit. *palace*   29:5 [1]Lit. *fill his hand*   29:8 [1]Possibly the same as *Jehieli,* 1 Chr. 26:21, 22

14 But who *am* I, and who *are* my people,
That we should be able to offer so willingly as this?
For all things *come* from You,
And [1]of Your own we have given You.
15 For [a]we *are* [1]aliens and [2]pilgrims before You,
As *were* all our fathers;
[b]Our days on earth *are* as a shadow,
And without hope.

16"O LORD our God, all this abundance that we have prepared to build You a house for Your holy name is from Your hand, and *is* all Your own. 17I know also, my God, that You [a]test the heart and [b]have pleasure in uprightness. As for me, in the uprightness of my heart I have willingly offered all these *things;* and now with joy I have seen Your people, who are present here to offer willingly to You. 18O LORD God of Abraham, Isaac, and Israel, our fathers, keep this forever in the intent of the thoughts of the heart of Your people, and fix their heart toward You. 19And [a]give my son Solomon a loyal heart to keep Your commandments and Your testimonies and Your statutes, to do all *these things,* and to build the [1]temple for which [b]I have made provision."

20Then David said to all the assembly, "Now bless the LORD your God." So all the assembly blessed the LORD God of their fathers, and bowed their heads and prostrated themselves before the LORD and the king.

SOLOMON ANOINTED KING
(1 Kin. 1:38–40; 2:12)

21And they made sacrifices to the LORD and offered burnt offerings to the LORD on the next day: a thousand bulls, a thousand rams, a thousand lambs, with their drink offerings, and [a]sacrifices in abundance for all Israel. 22So they ate and drank before the LORD with great gladness on that day. And they made Solomon the son of David king the second time, and [a]anointed *him* before the LORD *to be* the leader, and Zadok *to be* priest. 23Then Solomon sat on the throne of the LORD as king instead of David his father, and prospered; and all Israel obeyed him. 24All the leaders and the mighty men, and also all the sons of King David, [a]submitted[1] themselves to King Solomon. 25So the LORD exalted Solomon exceedingly in the sight of all Israel, and [a]bestowed on him *such* royal majesty as had not been on any king before him in Israel.

THE CLOSE OF DAVID'S REIGN

26Thus David the son of Jesse reigned over all Israel. 27[a]And the period that he reigned over Israel *was* forty years; [b]seven years he reigned in Hebron, and thirty-three *years* he reigned in Jerusalem. 28So he [a]died in a good old age, [b]full of days and riches and honor; and Solomon his son reigned in his place. 29Now the acts of King David, first and last, indeed they *are* written in the [1]book of Samuel the seer, in the book of Nathan the prophet, and in the book of Gad the seer, 30with all his reign and his might, [a]and the events that happened to him, to Israel, and to all the kingdoms of the lands.

29:15
[a]Lev. 25:23;
Ps. 39:12;
Heb. 11:13,
14; 1 Pet. 2:11
[b]Job 14:2;
Ps. 90:9

29:17
[a][1 Sam. 16:7;
1 Chr. 28:9]
[b]Prov. 11:20

29:19
[a][1 Chr. 28:9];
Ps. 72:1
[b]1 Chr. 29:1, 2

29:21
[a]1 Kin. 8:62, 63

29:22
[a]1 Kin. 1:32–35,
39; 1 Chr. 23:1

29:24 [a]Eccl. 8:2

29:25
[a]1 Kin. 3:13;
2 Chr. 1:12;
Eccl. 2:9

29:27
[a]2 Sam. 5:4;
1 Kin. 2:11
[b]2 Sam. 5:5

29:28
[a]Gen. 25:8
[b]1 Chr. 23:1

29:30
[a]Dan. 2:21;
4:23, 25

29:14 [1]Lit. *of Your hand*   29:15 [1]*sojourners,* temporary residents
[2]*transients,* temporary residents in an even more temporary sense
29:19 [1]Lit. *palace*   29:24 [1]Lit. *gave the hand*   29:29 [1]Lit. *words*

THE SECOND BOOK OF THE
CHRONICLES

SOLOMON REQUESTS WISDOM
(1 Kin. 3:1–15)

1 Now ᵃSolomon the son of David was strengthened in his kingdom, and ᵇthe LORD his God *was* with him and ᶜexalted him exceedingly.

2 And Solomon spoke to all Israel, to ᵃthe captains of thousands and of hundreds, to the judges, and to every leader in all Israel, the heads of the fathers' *houses*. 3 Then Solomon, and all the assembly with him, went to ¹the high place that *was* at ᵃGibeon; for the tabernacle of meeting with God was there, which Moses the servant of the LORD had ᵇmade in the wilderness. 4ᵃBut David had brought up the ark of God from Kirjath Jearim to *the place* David had prepared for it, for he had pitched a tent for it at Jerusalem. 5 Now ᵃthe bronze altar that ᵇBezalel the son of Uri, the son of Hur, had made, ¹he put before the tabernacle of the LORD; Solomon and the assembly sought Him *there*. 6 And Solomon went up there to the bronze altar before the LORD, which *was* at the tabernacle of meeting, and ᵃoffered a thousand burnt offerings on it.

7ᵃOn that night God appeared to Solomon, and said to him, "Ask! What shall I give you?"

8 And Solomon said to God: "You have shown great ᵃmercy to David my father, and have made me ᵇking in his place. 9 Now, O LORD God, let Your promise to David my father be established, ᵃfor You have made me king over a people like the ᵇdust of the earth in multitude. 10ᵃNow give me wisdom and knowledge, that I may ᵇgo out and come in before this people; for who can judge this great people of Yours?"

11ᵃThen God said to Solomon: "Because this was in your heart, and you have not asked riches or wealth or honor or the life of your enemies, nor have you asked long life—but have asked wisdom and knowledge for yourself, that you may judge My people over whom I have made you king— 12 wisdom and knowledge *are* granted to you; and I will give you riches and wealth and honor, such as ᵃnone of the kings have had who *were* before you, nor shall any after you have the like."

SOLOMON'S MILITARY AND ECONOMIC POWER
(1 Kin. 10:26–29; 2 Chr. 9:25–28)

13 So Solomon came to Jerusalem from ¹the high place that *was* at Gibeon, from before the tabernacle of meeting, and reigned over Israel. 14ᵃAnd Solomon gathered chariots and horsemen; he had one thousand four hundred chariots and twelve thousand horsemen, whom he stationed in the

---

1:3 ¹Place for worship   1:5 ¹Some authorities *it was there*   1:13 ¹Place for worship

chariot cities and with the king in Jerusalem. [15a]Also the king made silver and gold as common in Jerusalem as stones, and he made cedars as abundant as the sycamores which *are* in the lowland. [16a]And Solomon had horses imported from Egypt and Keveh; the king's merchants bought them in Keveh at the *current* price. [17]They also acquired and imported from Egypt a chariot for six hundred *shekels* of silver, and a horse for one hundred and fifty; thus, [1]through their agents, they exported them to all the kings of the Hittites and the kings of Syria.

SOLOMON PREPARES TO BUILD THE TEMPLE
(1 Kin. 5:1–18)

2 Then Solomon [a]determined to build a temple for the name of the LORD, and a royal house for himself. [2a]Solomon selected seventy thousand men to bear burdens, eighty thousand to quarry *stone* in the mountains, and three thousand six hundred to oversee them.

[3]Then Solomon sent to [1]Hiram king of Tyre, saying:

[a]As you have dealt with David my father, and sent him cedars to build himself a house to dwell in, *so deal with me.* [4]Behold, [a]I am building a temple for the name of the LORD my God, to dedicate *it* to Him, [b]to burn before Him [1]sweet incense, for [c]the continual showbread, for [d]the burnt offerings morning and evening, on the [e]Sabbaths, on the New Moons, and on the [2]set feasts of the LORD our God. This *is an ordinance* forever to Israel.

5   And the temple which I build *will be* great, for [a]our God is greater than all gods. [6a]But who is able to build Him a temple, since heaven and the heaven of heavens cannot contain Him? Who *am* I then, that I should build Him a temple, except to burn sacrifice before Him?

7   Therefore send me at once a man skillful to work in gold and silver, in bronze and iron, in purple and crimson and blue, who has skill to engrave with the skillful men who are with me in Judah and Jerusalem, [a]whom David my father provided. [8a]Also send me cedar and cypress and algum logs from Lebanon, for I know that your servants have skill to cut timber in Lebanon; and indeed my servants *will be* with your servants, [9]to prepare timber for me in abundance, for the [1]temple which I am about to build *shall be* great and wonderful.

10   [a]And indeed I will give to your servants, the woodsmen who cut timber, twenty thousand kors of ground wheat, twenty thousand kors of barley, twenty thousand baths of wine, and twenty thousand baths of oil.

[11]Then Hiram king of Tyre answered in writing, which he sent to Solomon:

[a]Because the LORD loves His people, He has made you king over them.

[12][1]Hiram also said:

[a]Blessed *be* the LORD God of Israel, [b]who made heaven and earth, for He has given King David a wise son,

---

1:15 [a]1 Kin. 10:27; 2 Chr. 9:27; Job 22:24

1:16 [a]1 Kin. 10:28; 22:36; 2 Chr. 9:28

2:1 [a]1 Kin. 5:5

2:2 [a]1 Kin. 5:15, 16; 2 Chr. 2:18

2:3 [a]1 Chr. 14:1

2:4 [a]2 Chr. 2:1 [b]Ex. 30:7 [c]Ex. 25:30; Lev. 24:8 [d]Ex. 29:38–42 [e]Num. 28:3, 9–11

2:5 [a]Ps. 135:5; [1 Cor. 8:5, 6]

2:6 [a]1 Kin. 8:27; 2 Chr. 6:18; Is. 66:1

2:7 [a]1 Chr. 22:15

2:8 [a]1 Kin. 5:6

2:10 [a]1 Kin. 5:11

2:11 [a]1 Kin. 10:9; 2 Chr. 9:8

2:12 [a]1 Kin. 5:7 [b]Gen. 1; 2; Acts 4:24; 14:15; Rev. 10:6

1:17 [1]Lit. *by their hands*   2:3 [1]Heb. *Huram;* cf. 1 Kin. 5:1   2:4 [1]Lit. *incense of spices*   [2]*appointed*   2:9 [1]Lit. *house*   2:12 [1]Heb. *Huram;* cf. 1 Kin. 5:1

endowed with prudence and understanding, who will build a temple for the LORD and a royal house for himself!

13 And now I have sent a skillful man, endowed with understanding, [1]Huram my [2]master *craftsman* [14a](the son of a woman of the daughters of Dan, and his father was a man of Tyre), skilled to work in gold and silver, bronze and iron, stone and wood, purple and blue, fine linen and crimson, and to make any engraving and to accomplish any plan which may be given to him, with your skillful men and with the skillful men of my lord David your father.

15 Now therefore, the wheat, the barley, the oil, and the wine which [a]my lord has spoken of, let him send to his servants. [16a]And we will cut wood from Lebanon, as much as you need; we will bring it to you in rafts by sea to [1]Joppa, and you will carry it up to Jerusalem.

[17a]Then Solomon numbered all the aliens who *were* in the land of Israel, after the census in which [b]David his father had numbered them; and there were found to be one hundred and fifty-three thousand six hundred. [18]And he made [a]seventy thousand of them bearers of burdens, eighty thousand stonecutters in the mountain, and three thousand six hundred overseers to make the people work.

SOLOMON BUILDS THE TEMPLE
(1 Kin. 6:1–22)

3 Now [a]Solomon began to build the house of the LORD at [b]Jerusalem on Mount Moriah, where [1]the LORD had appeared to his father David, at the place that David had prepared on the threshing floor of [c]Ornan[2] the Jebusite. [2]And he began to build on the second *day* of the second month in the fourth year of his reign.

[3]This is the foundation [a]which Solomon laid for building the house of God: The length *was* sixty cubits (by cubits according to the former measure) and the width twenty cubits. [4]And the [a]vestibule that *was* in front *of* [1]the sanctuary was twenty cubits long across the width of the house, and the height *was* [2]one hundred and twenty. He overlaid the inside with pure gold. [5a]The larger [1]room he [b]paneled with cypress which he overlaid with fine gold, and he carved palm trees and chainwork on it. [6]And he decorated the house with precious stones for beauty, and the gold *was* gold from Parvaim. [7]He also overlaid the house—the beams and doorposts, its walls and doors—with gold; and he carved cherubim on the walls.

[8]And he made the [a]Most Holy Place. Its length was according to the width of the house, twenty cubits, and its width twenty cubits. He overlaid it with six hundred talents of fine gold. [9]The weight of the nails *was* fifty shekels of gold; and he overlaid the upper [a]area with gold. [10a]In the Most Holy Place he made two cherubim, fashioned by carving, and overlaid

2:14
[a]1 Kin. 7:13, 14

2:15 [a]2 Chr. 2:10

2:16
[a]1 Kin. 5:8, 9

2:17 [a]1 Kin. 5:13;
2 Chr. 8:7, 8
[b]1 Chr. 22:2

2:18 [a]2 Chr. 2:2

3:1 [a]1 Kin. 6:1
[b]Gen. 22:2–14
[c]1 Chr. 21:18; 22:1

3:3 [a]1 Kin. 6:2;
1 Chr. 28:11–19

3:4 [a]1 Kin. 6:3;
1 Chr. 28:11

3:5 [a]1 Kin. 6:17
[b]1 Kin. 6:15;
Jer. 22:14

3:8 [a]Ex. 26:33;
1 Kin. 6:16

3:9 [a]1 Chr. 28:11

3:10
[a]Ex. 25:18–20;
1 Kin. 6:23–28

2:13 [1]*Hiram,* 1 Kin. 7:13 [2]Lit. *father,* 1 Kin. 7:13, 14 2:16 [1]Heb. *Japho*
3:1 [1]Lit. *He,* following MT, Vg.; LXX *the LORD;* Tg. *the* Angel of the LORD
[2]*Araunah,* 2 Sam. 24:16ff 3:4 [1]The holy place, the main room of the temple, 1 Kin. 6:3 [2]So with MT, LXX, Vg.; Arab., some LXX mss., Syr. *twenty* 3:5 [1]Lit. *house*

them with gold. ¹¹The wings of the cherubim *were* twenty cubits in *overall* length: one wing *of the one cherub was* five cubits, touching the wall of the room, and the other wing *was* five cubits, touching the wing of the other cherub; ¹²one wing of the other cherub *was* five cubits, touching the wall of the room, and the other wing *also was* five cubits, touching the wing of the other cherub. ¹³The wings of these cherubim spanned twenty cubits overall. They stood on their feet, and they faced inward. ¹⁴And he made the ªveil of blue, purple, crimson, and fine linen, and wove cherubim into it.

¹⁵Also he made in front of the ¹temple ªtwo pillars ²thirty-five cubits ³high, and the capital that *was* on the top of each of *them* was five cubits. ¹⁶He made wreaths of chainwork, as in the inner sanctuary, and put *them* on top of the pillars; and he made ªone hundred pomegranates, and put *them* on the wreaths of chainwork. ¹⁷Then he ªset up the pillars before the temple, one on the right hand and the other on the left; he called the name of the one on the right hand ¹Jachin, and the name of the one on the left ²Boaz.

FURNISHINGS OF THE TEMPLE
(1 Kin. 6:23–38; 7:13–51)

4 Moreover he made ªa bronze altar: twenty cubits was its length, twenty cubits its width, and ten cubits its height. ²ªThen he made the ¹Sea of cast *bronze,* ten cubits from one brim to the other; *it was* completely round. Its height *was* five cubits, and a line of thirty cubits measured its circumference. ³ªAnd under it *was* the likeness of oxen encircling it all around, ten to a cubit, all the way around the Sea. The oxen *were* cast in two rows, when it was cast. ⁴It stood on twelve ªoxen: three looking toward the north, three looking toward the west, three looking toward the south, and three looking toward the east; the Sea *was set* upon them, and all their back parts *pointed* inward. ⁵It *was* a handbreadth thick; and its brim was shaped like the brim of a cup, *like* a lily blossom. It contained ¹three thousand baths.

⁶He also made ªten lavers, and put five on the right side and five on the left, to wash in them; such things as they offered for the burnt offering they would wash in them, but the ¹Sea *was* for the ᵇpriests to wash in. ⁷ªAnd he made ten lampstands of gold ᵇaccording to their design, and set *them* in the temple, five on the right side and five on the left. ⁸ªHe also made ten tables, and placed *them* in the temple, five on the right side and five on the left. And he made one hundred ᵇbowls of gold.

⁹Furthermore ªhe made the court of the priests, and the ᵇgreat court and doors for the court; and he overlaid these doors with bronze. ¹⁰ªHe set the Sea on the right side, toward the southeast.

¹¹Then ªHuram made the pots and the shovels and the bowls. So Huram finished doing the work that he was to do for King Solomon for the house of God: ¹²the two pillars and ªthe bowl-shaped capitals *that were* on top of the two pillars; the two networks covering the two bowl-shaped capitals which

3:14 ªEx. 26:31;
Matt. 27:51;
Heb. 9:3

3:15
ª1 Kin. 7:15–20;
Jer. 52:21

3:16 ª1 Kin. 7:20

3:17 ª1 Kin. 7:21

4:1 ªEx. 27:1,
2; 2 Kin. 16:14;
Ezek. 43:13, 16

4:2
ªEx. 30:17–21;
1 Kin. 7:23–26

4:3
ª1 Kin. 7:24–26

4:4 ª1 Kin. 7:25

4:6 ª1 Kin. 7:38,
40 ᵇEx. 30:19–21

4:7 ª1 Kin. 7:49
ᵇEx. 25:31;
1 Chr. 28:12, 19

4:8 ª1 Kin. 7:48
ᵇ1 Chr. 28:17

4:9 ª1 Kin. 6:36
ᵇ2 Kin. 21:5

4:10 ª1 Kin. 7:39

4:11
ª1 Kin. 7:40–51

4:12 ª1 Kin. 7:41

3:15 ¹Lit. *house*   ²*eighteen,* 1 Kin. 7:15; 2 Kin. 25:17; Jer. 52:21   ³Lit. *long*
3:17 ¹Lit. *He Shall Establish*   ²Lit. *In It Is Strength*   4:2 ¹Great laver or basin
4:5 ¹About 8,000 gallons; *two thousand,* 1 Kin. 7:26   4:6 ¹Great basin

were on top of the pillars; [13a]four hundred pomegranates for the two networks (two rows of pomegranates for each network, to cover the two bowl-shaped capitals that *were* on the pillars); [14]he also made [a]carts and the lavers on the carts; [15]one Sea and twelve oxen under it; [16]also the pots, the shovels, the forks—and all their articles [a]Huram his [1]master *craftsman* made of burnished bronze for King Solomon for the house of the LORD.

[17]In the plain of Jordan the king had them cast in clay molds, between Succoth and [1]Zeredah. [18a]And Solomon had all these articles made in such great abundance that the weight of the bronze was not determined.

[19]Thus [a]Solomon had all the furnishings made for the house of God: the altar of gold and the tables on which *was* [b]the showbread; [20]the lampstands with their lamps of pure gold, to burn [a]in the prescribed manner in front of the inner sanctuary, [21]with [a]the flowers and the lamps and the wick-trimmers of gold, of purest gold; [22]the trimmers, the bowls, the ladles, and the censers of pure gold. As for the entry of the [1]sanctuary, its inner doors to the Most Holy *Place,* and the doors of the main hall of the temple, *were* gold.

5 So [a]all the work that Solomon had done for the house of the LORD was finished; and Solomon brought in the things which his father David had dedicated: the silver and the gold and all the furnishings. And he put *them* in the treasuries of the house of God.

THE ARK BROUGHT INTO THE TEMPLE
(1 Kin. 8:1–13)

[2a]Now Solomon assembled the elders of Israel and all the heads of the tribes, the chief fathers of the children of Israel, in Jerusalem, that they might bring the ark of the covenant of the LORD up [b]from the City of David, which *is* Zion. [3a]Therefore all the men of Israel assembled with the king [b]at the feast, which *was* in the seventh month. [4]So all the elders of Israel came, and the [a]Levites took up the ark. [5]Then they brought up the ark, the tabernacle of meeting, and all the holy furnishings that *were* in the tabernacle. The priests and the Levites brought them up. [6]Also King Solomon, and all the congregation of Israel who were assembled with him before the ark, were sacrificing sheep and oxen that could not be counted or numbered for multitude. [7]Then the priests brought in the ark of the covenant of the LORD to its place, into the [a]inner sanctuary of the [1]temple, to the Most Holy *Place,* under the wings of the cherubim. [8]For the cherubim spread *their* wings over the place of the ark, and the cherubim overshadowed the ark and its poles. [9]The poles extended so that the ends of the [a]poles of the ark could be seen from *the holy place,* in front of the inner sanctuary; but they could not be seen from outside. And [1]they are there to this day. [10]Nothing was in the ark except the two tablets which Moses [a]put *there* at Horeb, [1]when the LORD made *a covenant* with the children of Israel, when they had come out of Egypt.

[11]And it came to pass when the priests came out of the *Most* Holy *Place* (for all the priests who *were* present had

4:13 [a1] Kin. 7:20
4:14
[a1] Kin. 7:27, 43
4:16 [a1] Kin. 7:45;
2 Chr. 2:13
4:18 [a1] Kin. 7:47
4:19
[a1] Kin. 7:48–50
[b] Ex. 25:30
4:20
[a] Ex. 27:20, 21
4:21 [a] Ex. 25:31
5:1 [a1] Kin. 7:51
5:2
[a1] Kin. 8:1–9;
Ps. 47:9
[b] 2 Sam. 6:12
5:3 [a1] Kin. 8:2
[b] Lev. 23:34;
2 Chr. 7:8–10
5:4
[a1] Chr. 15:2, 15
5:7 [a] 2 Chr. 4:20
5:9 [a] Ex. 25:13–15
5:10 [a] Ex. 25:16;
Deut. 10:2, 5;
2 Chr. 6:11;
Heb. 9:4

4:16 [1]Lit. *father*   4:17 [1]*Zaretan,* 1 Kin. 7:46   4:22 [1]Lit. *house*   5:7 [1]Lit. *house*
5:9 [1]Lit. *it is*   5:10 [1]Or *where*

¹sanctified themselves, without keeping to their ªdivisions), ¹²ªand the Levites *who were* the singers, all those of Asaph and Heman and Jeduthun, with their sons and their brethren, stood at the east end of the altar, clothed in white linen, having cymbals, stringed instruments and harps, ᵇand with them one hundred and twenty priests sounding with trumpets— ¹³indeed it came to pass, when the trumpeters and singers *were* as one, to make one sound to be heard in praising and thanking the LORD, and when they lifted up their voice with the trumpets and cymbals and instruments of music, and praised the LORD, *saying:*

ª"*For He is* good,
For His mercy *endures* forever,"

that the house, the house of the LORD, was filled with a cloud, ¹⁴so that the priests could not ¹continue ministering because of the cloud; ªfor the glory of the LORD filled the house of God.

6 Then ªSolomon spoke:

"The LORD said He would dwell in the ᵇdark cloud.
2 I have surely built You an exalted house,
And ªa place for You to dwell in forever."

SOLOMON'S SPEECH UPON COMPLETION OF THE WORK
(1 Kin. 8:14–21)

³Then the king turned around and ªblessed the whole assembly of Israel, while all the assembly of Israel was standing. ⁴And he said: "Blessed *be* the LORD God of Israel, who has fulfilled with His hands *what* He spoke with His mouth to my father David, ªsaying, ⁵'Since the day that I brought My people out of the land of Egypt, I have chosen no city from any tribe of Israel *in which* to build a house, that My name might be there, nor did I choose any man to be a ruler over My people Israel. ⁶ªYet I have chosen Jerusalem, that My name may be there, and I ᵇhave chosen David to be over My people Israel.' ⁷Now ªit was in the heart of my father David to build a ¹temple for the name of the LORD God of Israel. ⁸But the LORD said to my father David, 'Whereas it was in your heart to build a temple for My name, you did well in that it was in your heart. ⁹Nevertheless you shall not build the temple, but your son who will come from your body, he shall build the temple for My ªname.' ¹⁰So the LORD has fulfilled His word which He spoke, and I have filled the position of my father David, and ªsit on the throne of Israel, as the LORD promised; and I have built the temple for the name of the LORD God of Israel. ¹¹And there I have put the ark, ªin which *is* the covenant of the LORD which He made with the children of Israel."

SOLOMON'S PRAYER OF DEDICATION
(1 Kin. 8:22–53)

¹²ªThen ¹Solomon stood before the altar of the LORD in the presence of all the assembly of Israel, and spread out his hands ¹³(for Solomon had made a bronze platform five cubits long, five cubits wide, and three cubits high, and had set it in the midst of the court; and he stood on it, knelt down

---

5:11
ª1 Chr. 24:1–5

5:12 ªEx. 32:26;
1 Chr. 25:1–7
ᵇ1 Chr. 13:8;
15:16, 24

5:13
ª1 Chr. 16:34, 41;
2 Chr. 7:3;
Ezra 3:11;
Ps. 100:5; 106:1;
Ps. 136; Jer. 33:11

5:14 ªEx. 40:35;
1 Kin. 8:11;
2 Chr. 7:2;
Ezek. 43:5

6:1 ªEx. 19:9;
20:21;
1 Kin. 8:12–21
ᵇ[Lev. 16:2];
Ps. 97:2

6:2 ª2 Sam. 7:13;
1 Chr. 17:12;
2 Chr. 7:12

6:3 ª2 Sam. 6:18

6:4 ª1 Chr. 17:5

6:6
ªDeut. 12:5–7;
2 Chr. 12:13;
Zech. 2:12
ᵇ1 Sam. 16:7–13;
1 Chr. 28:4

6:7 ª2 Sam. 7:2;
1 Chr. 17:1; 28:2;
Ps. 132:1–5

6:9
ª1 Chr. 28:3–6

6:10
ª1 Kin. 2:12; 10:9

6:11
ª2 Chr. 5:7–10

6:12 ª1 Kin. 8:22;
2 Chr. 7:7–9

5:11 ¹consecrated   5:14 ¹Lit. *stand to minister*   6:7 ¹Lit. *house,* and so in vv. 8–10   6:12 ¹Lit. *he*

on his knees before all the assembly of Israel, and spread out his hands toward heaven); [14]and he said: "LORD God of Israel, [a]*there is* no God in heaven or on earth like You, who keep *Your* [b]covenant and mercy with Your servants who walk before You with all their hearts. [15a]You have kept what You promised Your servant David my father; You have both spoken with Your mouth and fulfilled *it* with Your hand, as *it is* this day. [16]Therefore, LORD God of Israel, now keep what You promised Your servant David my father, saying, [a]'You shall not fail to have a man sit before Me on the throne of Israel, [b]only if your sons take heed to their way, that they walk in My law as you have walked before Me.' [17]And now, O LORD God of Israel, let Your word come true, which You have spoken to Your servant David.

[18]"But will God indeed dwell with men on the earth? [a]Behold, heaven and the heaven of heavens cannot contain You. How much less this [1]temple which I have built! [19]Yet regard the prayer of Your servant and his supplication, O LORD my God, and listen to the cry and the prayer which Your servant is praying before You: [20]that Your eyes may be [a]open toward this temple day and night, toward the place where *You* said *You would* put Your name, that You may hear the prayer which Your servant makes [b]toward this place. [21]And may You hear the supplications of Your servant and of Your people Israel, when they pray toward this place. Hear from heaven Your dwelling place, and when You hear, [a]forgive.

[22]"If anyone sins against his neighbor, and is forced to take an [a]oath, and comes *and* takes an oath before Your altar in this temple, [23]then hear from heaven, and act, and judge Your servants, bringing retribution on the wicked by bringing his way on his own head, and justifying the righteous by giving him according to his [a]righteousness.

[24]"Or if Your people Israel are defeated before an [a]enemy because they have sinned against You, and return and confess Your name, and pray and make supplication before You in this temple, [25]then hear from heaven and forgive the sin of Your people Israel, and bring them back to the land which You gave to them and their fathers.

[26]"When the [a]heavens are shut up and there is no rain because they have sinned against You, when they pray toward this place and confess Your name, and turn from their sin because You afflict them, [27]then hear *in* heaven, and forgive the sin of Your servants, Your people Israel, that You may teach them the good way in which they should walk; and send rain on Your land which You have given to Your people as an inheritance.

[28]"When there [a]is famine in the land, pestilence or blight or mildew, locusts or grasshoppers; when their enemies besiege them in the land of their cities; whatever plague or whatever [b]sickness *there is;* [29]whatever prayer, whatever supplication is *made* by anyone, or by all Your people Israel, when each one knows his own burden and his own grief, and spreads out his hands to this temple: [30]then hear from heaven Your dwelling place, and forgive, and give to everyone according to all his ways, whose heart You know (for You alone [a]know the [b]hearts of the sons of men), [31]that they may

6:14 [a][Ex. 15:11; Deut. 4:39] [b][Deut. 7:9]

6:15 [a]1 Chr. 22:9, 10

6:16 [a]2 Sam. 7:12, 16; 1 Kin. 2:4; 6:12; 2 Chr. 7:18 [b]Ps. 132:12

6:18 [a][2 Chr. 2:6; Is. 66:1; Acts 7:49]

6:20 [a]2 Chr. 7:15 [b]Ps. 5:7; Dan. 6:10

6:21 [a][Is. 43:25; 44:22; Mic. 7:18]

6:22 [a]Ex. 22:8–11

6:23 [a][Job 34:11]

6:24 [a]2 Kin. 21:14, 15

6:26 [a]Deut. 28:23, 24; 1 Kin. 17:1

6:28 [a]2 Chr. 20:9 [b][Mic. 6:13]

6:30 [a][1 Chr. 28:9; Prov. 21:2; 24:12] [b][1 Sam. 16:7]

6:18 [1]Lit. *house*

fear You, to walk in Your ways as long as they live in the land which You gave to our fathers.

32"Moreover, concerning a foreigner, ^awho is not of Your people Israel, but has come from a far country for the sake of Your great name and Your mighty hand and Your outstretched arm, when they come and pray in this temple; 33then hear from heaven Your dwelling place, and do according to all for which the foreigner calls to You, that all peoples of the earth may know Your name and fear You, as *do* Your people Israel, and that they may know that ¹this temple which I have built is called by Your name.

34"When Your people go out to battle against their enemies, wherever You send them, and when they pray to You toward this city which You have chosen and the temple which I have built for Your name, 35then hear from heaven their prayer and their supplication, and maintain their cause.

36"When they sin against You (for *there is* ^ano one who does not sin), and You become angry with them and deliver them to the enemy, and they take them ^bcaptive to a land far or near; 37*yet* when they ¹come to themselves in the land where they were carried captive, and repent, and make supplication to You in the land of their captivity, saying, 'We have sinned, we have done wrong, and have committed wickedness'; 38and *when* they return to You with all their heart and with all their soul in the land of their captivity, where they have been carried captive, and pray toward their land which You gave to their fathers, the ^acity which You have chosen, and toward the temple which I have built for Your name: 39then hear from heaven Your dwelling place their prayer and their supplications, and maintain their cause, and forgive Your people who have sinned against You. 40Now, my God, I pray, let Your eyes be ^aopen and *let* Your ears *be* attentive to the prayer *made* in this place.

41 "Now^a therefore,
    Arise, O LORD God, to Your ^bresting place,
    You and the ark of Your strength.
    Let Your priests, O LORD God, be clothed with salvation,
    And let Your saints ^crejoice in goodness.

42 "O LORD God, do not turn away the face of Your Anointed;
    ^aRemember the mercies of Your servant David."

SOLOMON DEDICATES THE TEMPLE
(1 Kin. 8:62–66)

7 When ^aSolomon had finished praying, ^bfire came down from heaven and consumed the burnt offering and the sacrifices; and ^cthe glory of the LORD filled the ¹temple. 2^aAnd the priests could not enter the house of the LORD, because the glory of the LORD had filled the LORD's house. 3When all the children of Israel saw how the fire came down, and the glory of the LORD on the temple, they bowed their faces to the ground on the pavement, and worshiped and praised the LORD, *saying:*

    ^a"For *He is* good,
        ^bFor His mercy *endures* forever."

6:32
^aJohn 12:20;
Acts 8:27

6:36
^aProv. 20:9;
Eccl. 7:20;
[Rom. 3:9, 19;
5:12; Gal. 3:10];
James 3:2;
1 John 1:8
^bDeut. 28:63–68

6:38 ^aDan. 6:10

6:40
^a2 Chr. 6:20

6:41
^aPs. 132:8–10, 16
^b1 Chr. 28:2
^cNeh. 9:25

6:42
^a2 Sam. 7:15;
Ps. 89:49; 132:1,
8–10; Is. 55:3

7:1 ^a1 Kin. 8:54
^bLev. 9:24;
Judg. 6:21;
1 Kin. 18:38;
1 Chr. 21:26
^c1 Kin. 8:10, 11

7:2 ^a2 Chr. 5:14

7:3 ^a2 Chr. 5:13;
Ps. 106:1; 136:1
^b1 Chr. 16:41;
2 Chr. 20:21

6:33 ¹Lit. *Your name is called upon this house*   6:37 ¹Lit. *bring back to their hearts*   7:1 ¹Lit. *house*

[4a]Then the king and all the people offered sacrifices before the LORD. [5]King Solomon offered a sacrifice of twenty-two thousand bulls and one hundred and twenty thousand sheep. So the king and all the people dedicated the house of God. [6a]And the priests attended to their services; the Levites also with instruments of the music of the LORD, which King David had made to praise the LORD, saying, "For His mercy *endures* forever," whenever David offered praise by their [1]ministry. [b]The priests sounded trumpets opposite them, while all Israel stood.

[7]Furthermore [a]Solomon consecrated the middle of the court that *was* in front of the house of the LORD; for there he offered burnt offerings and the fat of the peace offerings, because the bronze altar which Solomon had made was not able to receive the burnt offerings, the grain offerings, and the fat.

[8a]At that time Solomon kept the feast seven days, and all Israel with him, a very great assembly [b]from the entrance of Hamath to [c]the[1] Brook of Egypt. [9]And on the eighth day they held a [a]sacred assembly, for they observed the dedication of the altar seven days, and the feast seven days. [10a]On the twenty-third day of the seventh month he sent the people away to their tents, joyful and glad of heart for the good that the LORD had done for David, for Solomon, and for His people Israel. [11]Thus [a]Solomon finished the house of the LORD and the king's house; and Solomon successfully accomplished all that came into his heart to make in the house of the LORD and in his own house.

GOD'S SECOND APPEARANCE TO SOLOMON
(1 *Kin.* 9:1–9)

[12]Then the LORD [a]appeared to Solomon by night, and said to him: "I have heard your prayer, [b]and have chosen this [c]place for Myself as a house of sacrifice. [13a]When I shut up heaven and there is no rain, or command the locusts to devour the land, or send pestilence among My people, [14]if My people who are [a]called by My name will [b]humble themselves, and pray and seek My face, and turn from their wicked ways, [c]then I will hear from heaven, and will forgive their sin and heal their land. [15]Now [a]My eyes will be open and My ears attentive to prayer *made* in this place. [16]For now [a]I have chosen and [1]sanctified this house, that My name may be there forever; and [2]My eyes and [3]My heart will be there perpetually. [17a]As for you, if you walk before Me as your father David walked, and do according to all that I have commanded you, and if you keep My statutes and My judgments, [18]then I will establish the throne of your kingdom, as I covenanted with David your father, saying, [a]'You shall not fail *to have* a man as ruler in Israel.'

[19a]"But if you turn away and forsake My statutes and My commandments which I have set before you, and go and serve other gods, and worship them, [20a]then I will uproot them from My land which I have given them; and this house which I have [1]sanctified for My name I will cast out of My sight, and will make it a proverb and a [b]byword among all peoples.

7:4
[a]1 Kin. 8:62, 63

7:6 [a]1 Chr. 15:16
[b]2 Chr. 5:12

7:7
[a]1 Kin. 8:64–66;
9:3

7:8 [a]1 Kin. 8:65
[b]1 Kin. 4:21, 24;
2 Kin. 14:25
[c]Josh. 13:3

7:9 [a]Lev. 23:36

7:10 [a]1 Kin. 8:66

7:11 [a]1 Kin. 9:1

7:12
[a]1 Kin. 3:5; 11:9
[b]Deut. 12:5, 11
[c]2 Chr. 6:20

7:13
[a]Deut. 28:23, 24;
1 Kin. 17:1;
2 Chr. 6:26–28

7:14
[a]Deut. 28:10;
[Is. 43:7]
[b]2 Chr. 12:6, 7;
[James 4:10]
[c]2 Chr. 6:27, 30

7:15
[a]2 Chr. 6:20, 40

7:16 [a]1 Kin. 9:3;
2 Chr. 6:6

7:17 [a]1 Kin. 9:4

7:18
[a]2 Sam. 7:12–16;
1 Kin. 2:4;
2 Chr. 6:16

7:19
[a]Lev. 26:14, 33;
[Deut. 28:15, 36]

7:20
[a]Deut. 28:63–
68; 2 Kin. 25:1–7
[b]Ps. 44:14

7:6 [1]Lit. *hand*   7:8 [1]The Shihor, 1 Chr. 13:5   7:16 [1]*set apart*   [2]My attention
[3]My concern   7:20 [1]*set apart*

21"And *as for* [a]this [1]house, which [2]is exalted, everyone who passes by it will be [b]astonished and say, [c]'Why has the LORD done thus to this land and this house?' 22Then they will answer, 'Because they forsook the LORD God of their fathers, who brought them out of the land of Egypt, and embraced other gods, and worshiped them and served them; therefore He has brought all this calamity on them.'"

SOLOMON'S ADDITIONAL ACHIEVEMENTS
(1 Kin. 9:10–28)

8 It [a]came to pass at the end of [b]twenty years, when Solomon had built the house of the LORD and his own house, 2that the cities which [1]Hiram had given to Solomon, Solomon built them; and he settled the children of Israel there. 3And Solomon went to Hamath Zobah and seized it. 4[a]He also built Tadmor in the wilderness, and all the storage cities which he built in [b]Hamath. 5He built Upper Beth Horon and [a]Lower Beth Horon, fortified cities *with* walls, gates, and bars, 6also Baalath and all the storage cities that Solomon had, and all the chariot cities and the cities of the cavalry, and all that Solomon [a]desired to build in Jerusalem, in Lebanon, and in all the land of his dominion.

7[a]All the people *who were* left of the Hittites, Amorites, Perizzites, Hivites, and Jebusites, who *were* not of Israel— 8that is, their descendants who were left in the land after them, whom the children of Israel did not destroy—from these Solomon raised forced labor, as it is to this day. 9But Solomon did not make the children of Israel [1]servants for his work. Some *were* men of war, captains of his officers, captains of his chariots, and his cavalry. 10And others *were* chiefs of the officials of King Solomon: [a]two hundred and fifty, who ruled over the people.

11Now Solomon [a]brought the daughter of Pharaoh up from the City of David to the house he had built for her, for he said, "My wife shall not dwell in the house of David king of Israel, because the *places* to which the ark of the LORD has come are holy."

12Then Solomon offered burnt offerings to the LORD on the altar of the LORD which he had built before the vestibule, 13according to the [a]daily rate, offering according to the commandment of Moses, for the Sabbaths, the New Moons, and the [b]three appointed yearly [c]feasts—the Feast of Unleavened Bread, the Feast of Weeks, and the Feast of Tabernacles. 14And, according to the [1]order of David his father, he appointed the [a]divisions of the priests for their service, [b]the Levites for their duties (to praise and serve before the priests) as the duty of each day required, and the [c]gatekeepers by their divisions at each gate; for so David the man of God had commanded. 15They did not depart from the command of the king to the priests and Levites concerning any matter or concerning the [a]treasuries.

16Now all the work of Solomon was well-ordered [1]from the day of the foundation of the house of the LORD until it was finished. So the house of the LORD was completed.

7:21 [a]2 Kin. 25:9
[b]2 Chr. 29:8
[c][Deut. 29:24, 25; Jer. 22:8, 9]

8:1
[a]1 Kin. 9:10–14
[b]1 Kin. 6:38—7:1

8:4
[a]1 Kin. 9:17, 18
[b]1 Chr. 18:3, 9

8:5 [a]1 Chr. 7:24

8:6 [a]2 Chr. 7:11

8:7
[a]Gen. 15:18–21;
1 Kin. 9:20

8:10 [a]1 Kin. 9:23

8:11 [a]1 Kin. 3:1;
7:8; 9:24; 11:1

8:13
[a]Ex. 29:38–42;
Num. 28:3, 9,
11, 26; 29:1
[b]Ex. 23:14–17;
34:22, 23;
Deut. 16:16
[c]Lev. 23:1–44

8:14 [a]1 Chr. 24:3
[b]1 Chr. 25:1
[c]1 Chr. 9:17; 26:1

8:15
[a]1 Chr. 26:20–28

7:21 [1]Temple   [2]Or *was*   8:2 [1]Heb. *Huram,* 2 Chr. 2:3   8:9 [1]*slaves*
8:14 [1]*ordinance*   8:16 [1]So with LXX, Syr., Vg.; MT *as far as*

[17]Then Solomon went to [a]Ezion Geber and [1]Elath on the seacoast, in the land of Edom. [18a]And Hiram sent him ships by the hand of his servants, and servants who knew the sea. They went with the servants of Solomon to [b]Ophir, and acquired four hundred and fifty talents of gold from there, and brought it to King Solomon.

THE QUEEN OF SHEBA'S PRAISE OF SOLOMON
(1 Kin. 10:1–13)

9 Now [a]when the queen of Sheba heard of the fame of Solomon, she came to Jerusalem to test Solomon with hard questions, *having* a very great retinue, camels that bore spices, gold in abundance, and precious stones; and when she came to Solomon, she spoke with him about all that was in her heart. [2]So Solomon answered all her questions; there was nothing so difficult for Solomon that he could not explain it to her. [3]And when the queen of Sheba had seen the wisdom of Solomon, the house that he had built, [4]the food on his table, the seating of his servants, the service of his waiters and their apparel, his [a]cupbearers and their apparel, and his entryway by which he went up to the house of the LORD, there was no more spirit in her.

[5]Then she said to the king: "*It was* a true report which I heard in my own land about your words and your wisdom. [6]However I did not believe their words until I came and saw with my own eyes; and indeed the half of the greatness of your wisdom was not told me. You exceed the fame of which I heard. [7]Happy *are* your men and happy *are* these your servants, who stand continually before you and hear your wisdom! [8]Blessed be the LORD your God, who delighted in you, setting you on His throne *to be* king for the LORD your God! Because your God has [a]loved Israel, to establish them forever, therefore He made you king over them, to do justice and righteousness."

[9]And she gave the king one hundred and twenty talents of gold, spices in great abundance, and precious stones; there never were any spices such as those the queen of Sheba gave to King Solomon.

[10]Also, the servants of Hiram and the servants of Solomon, [a]who brought gold from Ophir, brought [1]algum wood and precious stones. [11]And the king made walkways *of* the [1]algum wood for the house of the LORD and for the king's house, also harps and stringed instruments for singers; and there were none such *as these* seen before in the land of Judah.

[12]Now King Solomon gave to the queen of Sheba all she desired, whatever she asked, *much more* than she had brought to the king. So she turned and went to her own country, she and her servants.

SOLOMON'S GREAT WEALTH
(1 Kin. 10:14–29; 2 Chr. 1:14–17)

[13a]The weight of gold that came to Solomon yearly was six hundred and sixty-six talents of gold, [14]besides *what* the traveling merchants and traders brought. And all the kings of

8:17 [a]1 Kin. 9:26; 2 Chr. 20:36

8:18 [a]1 Kin. 9:27; 2 Chr. 9:10, 13 [b]1 Chr. 29:4

9:1 [a]1 Kin. 10:1; Ps. 72:10; [Matt. 12:42; Luke 11:31]

9:4 [a]Neh. 1:11

9:8 [a]Deut. 7:8; 2 Chr. 2:11; [Ps. 44:3]

9:10 [a]2 Chr. 8:18

9:13 [a]1 Kin. 10:14–29

8:17 [1]Heb. *Eloth,* 2 Kin. 14:22   9:10 [1]*almug,* 1 Kin. 10:11, 12   9:11 [1]*almug,* 1 Kin. 10:11, 12

Arabia and governors of the country brought gold and silver to Solomon. ¹⁵And King Solomon made two hundred large shields of hammered gold; six hundred *shekels* of hammered gold went into each shield. ¹⁶He also *made* three hundred shields of hammered gold; ¹three hundred *shekels* of gold went into each shield. The king put them in the ᵃHouse of the Forest of Lebanon.

¹⁷Moreover the king made a great throne of ivory, and overlaid it with pure gold. ¹⁸The throne *had* six steps, with a footstool of gold, *which were* fastened to the throne; there were ¹armrests on either side of the place of the seat, and two lions stood beside the armrests. ¹⁹Twelve lions stood there, one on each side of the six steps; nothing like *this* had been made for any *other* kingdom.

²⁰All King Solomon's drinking vessels *were* gold, and all the vessels of the House of the Forest of Lebanon *were* pure gold. Not *one was* silver, for this was accounted as nothing in the days of Solomon. ²¹For the king's ships went to ᵃTarshish with the servants of ¹Hiram. Once every three years the ²merchant ships came, bringing gold, silver, ivory, apes, and ³monkeys.

²²So King Solomon surpassed all the kings of the earth in riches and wisdom. ²³And all the kings of the earth sought the presence of Solomon to hear his wisdom, which God had put in his heart. ²⁴Each man brought his present: articles of silver and gold, garments, ᵃarmor, spices, horses, and mules, at a set rate year by year.

²⁵Solomon ᵃhad four thousand stalls for horses and chariots, and twelve thousand horsemen whom he stationed in the chariot cities and with the king at Jerusalem.

²⁶ᵃSo he reigned over all the kings ᵇfrom ¹the River to the land of the Philistines, as far as the border of Egypt. ²⁷ᵃThe king made silver *as common* in Jerusalem as stones, and he made cedar trees ᵇas abundant as the sycamores which *are* in the lowland. ²⁸ᵃAnd they brought horses to Solomon from Egypt and from all lands.

DEATH OF SOLOMON
(1 Kin. 11:41–43)

²⁹ᵃNow the rest of the acts of Solomon, first and last, *are* they not written in the book of Nathan the prophet, in the prophecy of ᵇAhijah the Shilonite, and in the visions of ᶜIddo the seer concerning Jeroboam the son of Nebat? ³⁰ᵃSolomon reigned in Jerusalem over all Israel forty years. ³¹Then Solomon ¹rested with his fathers, and was buried in the City of David his father. And Rehoboam his son reigned in his place.

THE REVOLT AGAINST REHOBOAM
(1 Kin. 12:1–19)

10 And ᵃRehoboam went to Shechem, for all Israel had gone to Shechem to make him king. ²So it happened, when Jeroboam the son of Nebat heard *it* (he was in Egypt, ᵃwhere he had fled from the presence of King Solomon), that

9:16 ᵃ1 Kin. 7:2
9:21
ᵃ2 Chr. 20:36, 37; Ps. 72:10
9:24 ᵃ1 Kin. 20:11
9:25
ᵃDeut. 17:16;
1 Kin. 4:26;
10:26; 2 Chr. 1:14;
Is. 2:7
9:26 ᵃ1 Kin. 4:21
ᵇGen. 15:18;
Ps. 72:8
9:27
ᵃ1 Kin. 10:27
ᵇ2 Chr. 1:15–17
9:28
ᵃ1 Kin. 10:28;
2 Chr. 1:16
9:29 ᵃ1 Kin. 11:41
ᵇ1 Kin. 11:29
ᶜ2 Chr. 12:15;
13:22
9:30 ᵃ1 Kin. 4:21;
11:42, 43;
1 Chr. 29:28
10:1
ᵃ1 Kin. 12:1–20
10:2 ᵃ1 Kin. 11:40

9:16 ¹*three minas,* 1 Kin. 10:17   9:18 ¹Lit. *hands*   9:21 ¹Heb. *Huram;* cf.
1 Kin. 10:22   ²Lit. *ships of Tarshish,* deep-sea vessels   ³Or *peacocks*
9:26 ¹The Euphrates   9:31 ¹Died and joined his ancestors

Jeroboam returned from Egypt. ³Then they sent for him and called him. And Jeroboam and all Israel came and spoke to Rehoboam, saying, ⁴"Your father made our yoke heavy; now therefore, lighten the burdensome service of your father and his heavy yoke which he put on us, and we will serve you."

⁵So he said to them, "Come back to me after three days." And the people departed.

⁶Then King Rehoboam consulted the elders who stood before his father Solomon while he still lived, saying, "How do you advise *me* to answer these people?"

⁷And they spoke to him, saying, "If you are kind to these people, and please them, and speak good words to them, they will be your servants forever."

⁸ªBut he rejected the advice which the elders had given him, and consulted the young men who had grown up with him, who stood before him. ⁹And he said to them, "What advice do you give? How should we answer this people who have spoken to me, saying, 'Lighten the yoke which your father put on us'?"

¹⁰Then the young men who had grown up with him spoke to him, saying, "Thus you should speak to the people who have spoken to you, saying, 'Your father made our yoke heavy, but you make *it* lighter on us'—thus you shall say to them: 'My little *finger* shall be thicker than my father's waist! ¹¹And now, whereas my father put a heavy yoke on you, I will add to your yoke; my father chastised you with whips, but I *will chastise you* with ¹scourges!'"

¹²So ªJeroboam and all the people came to Rehoboam on the third day, as the king had directed, saying, "Come back to me the third day." ¹³Then the king answered them roughly. King Rehoboam rejected the advice of the elders, ¹⁴and he spoke to them according to the advice of the young men, saying, ¹"My father made your yoke heavy, but I will add to it; my father chastised you with whips, but I *will chastise you* with ²scourges!" ¹⁵So the king did not listen to the people; ªfor the turn *of events* was from God, that the LORD might fulfill His ᵇword, which He had spoken by the hand of Ahijah the Shilonite to Jeroboam the son of Nebat.

¹⁶Now when all Israel *saw* that the king did not listen to them, the people answered the king, saying:

"What share have we in David?
We have no inheritance in the son of Jesse.
Every man to your tents, O Israel!
Now see to your own house, O David!"

So all Israel departed to their tents. ¹⁷But Rehoboam reigned over the children of Israel who dwelt in the cities of Judah.

¹⁸Then King Rehoboam sent Hadoram, who *was* in charge of revenue; but the children of Israel stoned him with stones, and he died. Therefore King Rehoboam mounted *his* chariot in haste to flee to Jerusalem. ¹⁹ªSo Israel has been in rebellion against the house of David to this day.

11 Now ªwhen Rehoboam came to Jerusalem, he assembled from the house of Judah and Benjamin one hundred and eighty thousand chosen *men* who were warriors,

10:8
ª1 Kin. 12:8–11

10:12
ª1 Kin. 12:12–14

10:15
ª Judg. 14:4;
1 Chr. 5:22;
2 Chr. 11:4; 22:7
ᵇ1 Kin. 11:29–39

10:19
ª1 Kin. 12:19

11:1
ª1 Kin. 12:21–24

10:11 ¹Scourges with points or barbs, lit. *scorpions*   10:14 ¹So with many Heb. mss., LXX, Syr., Vg. (cf. v. 10; 1 Kin. 12:14); MT *I*   ²Lit. *scorpions*

to fight against Israel, that he might restore the kingdom to Rehoboam.

2But the word of the LORD came ato Shemaiah the man of God, saying, 3"Speak to Rehoboam the son of Solomon, king of Judah, and to all Israel in Judah and Benjamin, saying, 4'Thus says the LORD: "You shall not go up or fight against your brethren! Let every man return to his house, for this thing is from Me." ' " Therefore they obeyed the words of the LORD, and turned back from attacking Jeroboam.

REHOBOAM FORTIFIES THE CITIES

5So Rehoboam dwelt in Jerusalem, and built cities for defense in Judah. 6And he built Bethlehem, Etam, Tekoa, 7Beth Zur, Sochoh, Adullam, 8Gath, Mareshah, Ziph, 9Adoraim, Lachish, Azekah, 10Zorah, Aijalon, and Hebron, which are in Judah and Benjamin, fortified cities. 11And he fortified the strongholds, and put captains in them, and stores of food, oil, and wine. 12Also in every city *he put* shields and spears, and made them very strong, having Judah and Benjamin on his side.

PRIESTS AND LEVITES MOVE TO JUDAH
(1 Kin. 14:21–24)

13And from all their territories the priests and the Levites who *were* in all Israel took their stand with him. 14For the Levites left atheir common-lands and their possessions and came to Judah and Jerusalem, for bJeroboam and his sons had rejected them from serving as priests to the LORD. 15aThen he appointed for himself priests for the 1high places, for bthe demons, and cthe calf idols which he had made. 16aAnd 1after *the* Levites *left,* those from all the tribes of Israel, such as set their heart to seek the LORD God of Israel, bcame to Jerusalem to sacrifice to the LORD God of their fathers. 17So they astrengthened the kingdom of Judah, and made Rehoboam the son of Solomon strong for three years, because they walked in the way of David and Solomon for three years.

THE FAMILY OF REHOBOAM

18Then Rehoboam took for himself as wife Mahalath the daughter of Jerimoth the son of David, *and of* Abihail the daughter of aEliah the son of Jesse. 19And she bore him children: Jeush, Shamariah, and Zaham. 20After her he took aMaachah the 1granddaughter of bAbsalom; and she bore him cAbijah, Attai, Ziza, and Shelomith. 21Now Rehoboam loved Maachah the granddaughter of Absalom more than all his awives and his concubines; for he took eighteen wives and sixty concubines, and begot twenty-eight sons and sixty daughters. 22And Rehoboam aappointed bAbijah the son of Maachah as chief, *to be* leader among his brothers; for he *intended* to make him king. 23He dealt wisely, and 1dispersed some of his sons throughout all the territories of Judah and Benjamin, to every afortified city; and he gave them provisions in abundance. He also sought many wives *for them.*

11:2 a1 Chr. 12:5;
2 Chr. 12:15

11:14
aNum. 35:2–5
b1 Kin. 12:28–33;
2 Chr. 13:9

11:15
a1 Kin. 12:31;
13:33; 14:9;
[Hos. 13:2]
b[Lev. 17:7;
1 Cor. 10:20]
c1 Kin. 12:28

11:16 a2 Chr. 14:7
b2 Chr. 15:9, 10;
30:11, 18

11:17
a2 Chr. 12:1, 13

11:18
a1 Sam. 16:6

11:20
a2 Chr. 13:2
b1 Kin. 15:2
c1 Kin. 14:31

11:21 aDeut. 17:17

11:22
aDeut. 21:15–17
b2 Chr. 13:1

11:23 a2 Chr. 11:5

11:15 1Places for pagan worship   11:16 1Lit. *after them*   11:20 1Lit. *daughter,* but in the broader sense of granddaughter   11:23 1*distributed*

EGYPT ATTACKS JUDAH
(1 Kin. 14:25–28)

12 Now [a]it came to pass, when Rehoboam had established the kingdom and had strengthened himself, that [b]he forsook the law of the LORD, and all Israel along with him. [2a]And it happened in the fifth year of King Rehoboam *that* Shishak king of Egypt came up against Jerusalem, because they had transgressed against the LORD, [3]with twelve hundred chariots, sixty thousand horsemen, and people without number who came with him out of Egypt—[a]the Lubim and the Sukkiim and the Ethiopians. [4]And he took the fortified cities of Judah and came to Jerusalem.

[5]Then [a]Shemaiah the prophet came to Rehoboam and the leaders of Judah, who were gathered together in Jerusalem because of Shishak, and said to them, "Thus says the LORD: 'You have forsaken Me, and therefore I also have left you in the hand of Shishak.'"

[6]So the leaders of Israel and the king [a]humbled themselves; and they said, [b]"The LORD *is* righteous."

[7]Now when the LORD saw that they humbled themselves, [a]the word of the LORD came to Shemaiah, saying, "They have humbled themselves; *therefore* I will not destroy them, but I will grant them some deliverance. My wrath shall not be poured out on Jerusalem by the hand of Shishak. [8]Nevertheless [a]they will be his servants, that they may distinguish [b]My service from the service of the kingdoms of the nations."

[9a]So Shishak king of Egypt came up against Jerusalem, and took away the treasures of the house of the LORD and the treasures of the king's house; he took everything. He also carried away the gold shields which Solomon had [b]made. [10]Then King Rehoboam made bronze shields in their place, and committed *them* [a]to the hands of the captains of the guard, who guarded the doorway of the king's house. [11]And whenever the king entered the house of the LORD, the guard would go and bring them out; then they would take them back into the guardroom. [12]When he humbled himself, the wrath of the LORD turned from him, so as not to destroy *him* completely; and things also went well in Judah.

THE END OF REHOBOAM'S REIGN
(1 Kin. 14:21, 22, 29–31)

[13]Thus King Rehoboam strengthened himself in Jerusalem and reigned. Now [a]Rehoboam *was* forty-one years old when he became king; and he reigned seventeen years in Jerusalem, [b]the city which the LORD had chosen out of all the tribes of Israel, to put His name there. His mother's name *was* Naamah, an [c]Ammonitess. [14]And he did evil, because he did not prepare his heart to seek the LORD.

[15]The acts of Rehoboam, first and last, *are* they not written in the book of Shemaiah the prophet, [a]and of Iddo the seer concerning genealogies? [b]And *there were* wars between Rehoboam and Jeroboam all their days. [16]So Rehoboam [1]rested with his fathers, and was buried in the City of David. Then [a]Abijah[2] his son reigned in his place.

12:1 [a]2 Chr. 11:17
[b]1 Kin. 14:22–24

12:2
[a]1 Kin. 11:40;
14:25

12:3 [a]2 Chr. 16:8;
Nah. 3:9

12:5 [a]2 Chr. 11:2

12:6
[a][James 4:10]
[b]Ex. 9:27;
[Dan. 9:14]

12:7
[a]1 Kin. 21:28, 29

12:8 [a]Is. 26:13
[b][Deut. 28:47, 48]

12:9
[a]1 Kin. 14:25, 26
[b]1 Kin. 10:16, 17;
2 Chr. 9:15, 16

12:10
[a]1 Kin. 14:27

12:13
[a]1 Kin. 14:21
[b]2 Chr. 6:6
[c]1 Kin. 11:1, 5

12:15
[a]2 Chr. 9:29;
13:22
[b]1 Kin. 14:30

12:16
[a]2 Chr. 11:20–22

12:16 [1]Died and joined his ancestors   [2]*Abijam,* 1 Kin. 14:31

ABIJAH REIGNS IN JUDAH
(1 Kin. 15:1–8)

13 In ᵃthe eighteenth year of King Jeroboam, Abijah became king over ᵇJudah. ²He reigned three years in Jerusalem. His mother's name *was* ¹Michaiah the daughter of Uriel of Gibeah.

And there was war between Abijah and Jeroboam. ³Abijah set the battle in order with an army of valiant warriors, four hundred thousand choice men. Jeroboam also drew up in battle formation against him with eight hundred thousand choice men, mighty men of valor.

⁴Then Abijah stood on Mount ᵃZemaraim, which *is* in the mountains of Ephraim, and said, "Hear me, Jeroboam and all Israel: ⁵Should you not know that the LORD God of Israel ᵃgave the dominion over Israel to David forever, to him and his sons, ᵇby a covenant of salt? ⁶Yet Jeroboam the son of Nebat, the servant of Solomon the son of David, rose up and ᵃrebelled against his lord. ⁷Then ᵃworthless rogues gathered to him, and strengthened themselves against Rehoboam the son of Solomon, when Rehoboam was ᵇyoung and inexperienced and could not withstand them. ⁸And now you think to withstand the kingdom of the LORD, which is in the hand of the sons of David; and you *are* a great multitude, and with you are the gold calves which Jeroboam ᵃmade for you as gods. ⁹ᵃHave you not cast out the priests of the LORD, the sons of Aaron, and the Levites, and made for yourselves priests, like the peoples of *other* lands, ᵇso that whoever comes to consecrate himself with a young bull and seven rams may be a priest of ᶜ*things that are* not gods? ¹⁰But as for us, the LORD *is* our ᵃGod, and we have not forsaken Him; and the priests who minister to the LORD *are* the sons of Aaron, and the Levites *attend* to *their* duties. ¹¹ᵃAnd they burn to the LORD every morning and every evening burnt sacrifices and sweet incense; *they* also *set* the ᵇshowbread *in order on* the pure *gold* table, and the lampstand of gold with its lamps ᶜto burn every evening; for we keep the command of the LORD our God, but you have forsaken Him. ¹²Now look, God Himself is with us as *our* ᵃhead, ᵇand His priests with sounding trumpets to sound the alarm against you. O children of Israel, do not fight against the LORD God of your fathers, for you shall not prosper!"

¹³But Jeroboam caused an ambush to go around behind them; so they were in front of Judah, and the ambush *was* behind them. ¹⁴And when Judah looked around, to their surprise the battle line *was* at both front and rear; and they ᵃcried out to the LORD, and the priests sounded the trumpets. ¹⁵Then the men of Judah gave a shout; and as the men of Judah shouted, it happened that God ᵃstruck Jeroboam and all Israel before Abijah and Judah. ¹⁶And the children of Israel fled before Judah, and God delivered them into their hand. ¹⁷Then Abijah and his people struck them with a great slaughter; so five hundred thousand choice men of Israel fell slain. ¹⁸Thus the children of Israel were subdued at that time; and the children of Judah prevailed, ᵃbecause they relied on the LORD God of their fathers.

13:1 ᵃ1 Kin. 15:1
ᵇ1 Kin. 12:17

13:4 ᵃJosh. 18:22

13:5
ᵃ2 Sam. 7:8–16
ᵇLev. 2:13;
Num. 18:19

13:6
ᵃ1 Kin. 11:28;
12:20

13:7 ᵃJudg. 9:4
ᵇ2 Chr. 12:13

13:8
ᵃ1 Kin. 12:28;
14:9; 2 Chr. 11:15;
[Hos. 8:4–6]

13:9
ᵃ2 Chr. 11:13–15
ᵇEx. 29:29–33
ᶜJer. 2:11; 5:7

13:10
ᵃJosh. 24:15

13:11 ᵃEx. 29:38;
2 Chr. 2:4
ᵇEx. 25:30;
Lev. 24:5–9
ᶜEx. 27:20, 21;
Lev. 24:2, 3

13:12
ᵃJosh. 5:13–15;
[Heb. 2:10]
ᵇ[Num. 10:8–10]

13:14
ᵃJosh. 24:7;
2 Chr. 6:34, 35;
14:11

13:15
ᵃ1 Kin. 14:14;
2 Chr. 14:12

13:18
ᵃ1 Chr. 5:20;
2 Chr. 14:11;
[Ps. 22:5]

13:2 ¹*Maachah*, 1 Kin. 15:2; 2 Chr. 11:20, 21

¹⁹And Abijah pursued Jeroboam and took cities from him: Bethel with its villages, Jeshanah with its villages, and ªEphrain¹ with its villages. ²⁰So Jeroboam did not recover strength again in the days of Abijah; and the LORD ªstruck him, and ᵇhe died.

²¹But Abijah grew mighty, married fourteen wives, and begot twenty-two sons and sixteen daughters. ²²Now the rest of the acts of Abijah, his ways, and his sayings *are* written in ªthe ¹annals of the prophet Iddo.

14 So Abijah rested with his fathers, and they buried him in the City of David. Then ªAsa his son reigned in his place. In his days the land was quiet for ten years.

ASA REIGNS IN JUDAH
(1 Kin. 15:9–15)

²Asa did *what was* good and right in the eyes of the LORD his God, ³for he removed the altars of the foreign *gods* and ªthe ¹high places, and ᵇbroke down the *sacred* pillars ᶜand cut down the wooden images. ⁴He commanded Judah to ªseek the LORD God of their fathers, and to observe the law and the commandment. ⁵He also removed the ¹high places and the incense altars from all the cities of Judah, and the kingdom was quiet under him. ⁶And he built fortified cities in Judah, for the land had rest; he had no war in those years, because the LORD had given him ªrest. ⁷Therefore he said to Judah, "Let us build these cities and make walls around *them,* and towers, gates, and bars, *while* the land *is* yet before us, because we have sought the LORD our God; we have sought *Him,* and He has given us rest on every side." So they built and prospered. ⁸And Asa had an army of three hundred thousand from Judah who carried ¹shields and spears, and from Benjamin two hundred and eighty thousand men who carried shields and drew ªbows; all these *were* mighty men of ᵇvalor.

⁹ªThen Zerah the Ethiopian came out against them with an army of a million men and three hundred chariots, and he came to ᵇMareshah. ¹⁰So Asa went out against him, and they set the troops in battle array in the Valley of Zephathah at Mareshah. ¹¹And Asa ªcried out to the LORD his God, and said, "LORD, *it is* ᵇnothing for You to help, whether with many or with those who have no power; help us, O LORD our God, for we rest on You, and ᶜin Your name we go against this multitude. O LORD, You *are* our God; do not let man prevail against You!"

¹²So the LORD ªstruck the Ethiopians before Asa and Judah, and the Ethiopians fled. ¹³And Asa and the people who *were* with him pursued them to ªGerar. So the Ethiopians were overthrown, and they could not recover, for they were broken before the LORD and His army. And they carried away very much ¹spoil. ¹⁴Then they defeated all the cities around Gerar, for ªthe fear of the LORD came upon them; and they plundered all the cities, for there was exceedingly much ¹spoil in them. ¹⁵They also ¹attacked the livestock enclosures, and carried off sheep and camels in abundance, and returned to Jerusalem.

13:19 ªJosh. 15:9
13:20
ª1 Sam. 2:6;
25:38; Acts 12:23
ᵇ1 Kin. 14:20
13:22
ª2 Chr. 9:29
14:1 ª1 Kin. 15:8
14:3 ª1 Kin. 15:14;
2 Chr. 15:17
ᵇ[Ex. 34:13]
ᶜ1 Kin. 11:7
14:4
ª[2 Chr. 7:14]
14:6 ª2 Chr. 15:15
14:8 ª1 Chr. 12:2
ᵇ2 Chr. 13:3
14:9 ª2 Chr. 12:2,
3; 16:8
ᵇJosh. 15:44
14:11 ªEx. 14:10;
2 Chr. 13:14;
[Ps. 22:5]
ᵇ[1 Sam. 14:6]
ᶜ1 Sam. 17:45;
[Prov. 18:10]
14:12
ª2 Chr. 13:15
14:13
ªGen. 10:19; 20:1
14:14 ªGen. 35:5;
Deut. 11:25;
Josh. 2:9;
2 Chr. 17:10

13:19 ¹Or *Ephron*   13:22 ¹Or *commentary,* Heb. *midrash*   14:3 ¹Places for pagan worship   14:5 ¹Places for pagan worship   14:8 ¹*large shields*
14:13 ¹*plunder*   14:14 ¹*plunder*   14:15 ¹Lit. *struck*

THE REFORMS OF ASA

15 Now [a]the Spirit of God came upon Azariah the son of Oded. [2]And he went out [1]to meet Asa, and said to him: "Hear me, Asa, and all Judah and Benjamin. [a]The LORD *is* with you while you are with Him. [b]If you seek Him, He will be found by you; but [c]if you forsake Him, He will forsake you. [3a]For a long time Israel *has been* without the true God, without a [b]teaching priest, and without [c]law; [4]but [a]when in their trouble they turned to the LORD God of Israel, and sought Him, He was found by them. [5]And in those times *there was* no peace to the one who went out, nor to the one who came in, but great turmoil *was* on all the inhabitants of the lands. [6]So nation was [1]destroyed by nation, and city by city, for God troubled them with every adversity. [7]But you, be strong and do not let your hands be weak, for your work shall be rewarded!"

[8]And when Asa heard these words and the prophecy of [1]Oded the prophet, he took courage, and removed the abominable idols from all the land of Judah and Benjamin and from the cities [a]which he had taken in the mountains of Ephraim; and he restored the altar of the LORD that *was* before the vestibule of the LORD. [9]Then he gathered all Judah and Benjamin, and [a]those who dwelt with them from Ephraim, Manasseh, and Simeon, for they came over to him in great numbers from Israel when they saw that the LORD his God was with him.

[10]So they gathered together at Jerusalem in the third month, in the fifteenth year of the reign of Asa. [11a]And they offered to the LORD [1]at that time seven hundred bulls and seven thousand sheep from the [2]spoil they had brought. [12]Then they [a]entered into a covenant to seek the LORD God of their fathers with all their heart and with all their soul; [13a]and whoever would not seek the LORD God of Israel [b]was to be put to death, whether small or great, whether man or woman. [14]Then they took an oath before the LORD with a loud voice, with shouting and trumpets and rams' horns. [15]And all Judah rejoiced at the oath, for they had sworn with all their heart and [a]sought Him with all their soul; and He was found by them, and the LORD gave them [b]rest all around.

[16]Also he removed [a]Maachah, the [1]mother of Asa the king, from *being* queen mother, because she had made an obscene image of [2]Asherah; and Asa cut down her obscene image, then crushed and burned *it* by the Brook Kidron. [17]But [a]the [1]high places were not removed from Israel. Nevertheless the heart of Asa was loyal all his days. [18]He also brought into the house of God the things that his father had dedicated and that he himself had dedicated: silver and gold and utensils. [19]And there was no war until the thirty-fifth year of the reign of Asa.

ASA'S TREATY WITH SYRIA
(1 Kin. 15:16–22)

16 In the thirty-sixth year of the reign of Asa, [a]Baasha king of Israel came up against Judah and built Ramah, [b]that he might let none go out or come in to Asa king of Judah.

Cross references (margin)

15:1 [a]Num. 24:2; Judg. 3:10; 2 Chr. 20:14; 24:20

15:2 [a][James 4:8] [b][1 Chr. 28:9]; 2 Chr. 14:4; 33:12, 13; [Jer. 29:13]; Matt. 7:7] [c]2 Chr. 24:20

15:3 [a]Hos. 3:4 [b]2 Kin. 12:2 [c]Lev. 10:11; 2 Chr. 17:8, 9

15:4 [a][Deut. 4:29]

15:6 [a]Matt. 24:7

15:8 [a]2 Chr. 13:19

15:9 [a]2 Chr. 11:16

15:11 [a]2 Chr. 14:13–15

15:12 [a]2 Kin. 23:3; 2 Chr. 23:16; 34:31; Neh. 10:29

15:13 [a]Ex. 22:20 [b]Deut. 13:5–15

15:15 [a]2 Chr. 15:2 [b]2 Chr. 14:7

15:16 [a]1 Kin. 15:2, 10, 13

15:17 [a]1 Kin. 15:14; 2 Chr. 14:3, 5

16:1 [a]1 Kin. 15:17–22 [b]2 Chr. 15:9

15:2 [1]Lit. *before* 15:6 [1]Lit. *beaten in pieces* 15:8 [1]So with MT, LXX; Syr., Vg. *Azariah the son of Oded* (cf. v. 1) 15:11 [1]Lit. *in that day* [2]*plunder* 15:16 [1]Or *grandmother* [2]A Canaanite deity 15:17 [1]Places for pagan worship

2Then Asa brought silver and gold from the treasuries of the house of the LORD and of the king's house, and sent to Ben-Hadad king of Syria, who dwelt in Damascus, saying, 3"*Let there be* a treaty between you and me, as there was between my father and your father. See, I have sent you silver and gold; come, break your treaty with Baasha king of Israel, so that he will withdraw from me."

4So Ben-Hadad heeded King Asa, and sent the captains of his armies against the cities of Israel. They attacked Ijon, Dan, Abel Maim, and all the storage cities of Naphtali. 5Now it happened, when Baasha heard *it*, that he stopped building Ramah and ceased his work. 6Then King Asa took all Judah, and they carried away the stones and timber of Ramah, which Baasha had used for building; and with them he built Geba and Mizpah.

HANANI'S MESSAGE TO ASA

7And at that time aHanani the seer came to Asa king of Judah, and said to him: b"Because you have relied on the king of Syria, and have not relied on the LORD your God, therefore the army of the king of Syria has escaped from your hand. 8Were athe Ethiopians and bthe Lubim not a huge army with very many chariots and horsemen? Yet, because you relied on the LORD, He delivered them into your chand. 9aFor the eyes of the LORD run to and fro throughout the whole earth, to show Himself strong on behalf of *those* whose heart *is* loyal to Him. In this byou have done foolishly; therefore from now on cyou shall have wars." 10Then Asa was angry with the seer, and aput him in prison, for *he was* enraged at him because of this. And Asa oppressed *some* of the people at that time.

ILLNESS AND DEATH OF ASA
(1 Kin. 15:23, 24)

11aNote that the acts of Asa, first and last, are indeed written in the book of the kings of Judah and Israel. 12And in the thirty-ninth year of his reign, Asa became diseased in his feet, and his malady was severe; yet in his disease he adid not seek the LORD, but the physicians. 13aSo Asa 1rested with his fathers; he died in the forty-first year of his reign. 14They buried him in his own tomb, which he had 1made for himself in the City of David; and they laid him in the bed which was filled awith spices and various ingredients prepared in a mixture of ointments. They made ba very great burning for him.

JEHOSHAPHAT REIGNS IN JUDAH

17 Then aJehoshaphat his son reigned in his place, and strengthened himself against Israel. 2And he placed troops in all the fortified cities of Judah, and set garrisons in the land of aJudah and in the cities of Ephraim bwhich Asa his father had taken. 3Now the LORD was with Jehoshaphat, because he walked in the former ways of his father David; he did not seek the Baals, 4but sought 1the God of his father, and walked in His commandments and not according to athe acts

---

16:7 a1 Kin. 16:1;
2 Chr. 19:2
b2 Chr. 32:8–10;
Ps. 118:9;
[Is. 31:1; Jer. 17:5]

16:8 a2 Chr. 14:9
b2 Chr. 12:3
c2 Chr. 13:16, 18

16:9 aJob 34:21;
[Prov. 5:21; 15:3;
Jer. 16:17; 32:19];
Zech. 4:10
b1 Sam. 13:13
c1 Kin. 15:32

16:10
a2 Chr. 18:26;
Jer. 20:2;
Matt. 14:3

16:11
a1 Kin. 15:23, 24;
2 Chr. 14:2

16:12 a[Jer. 17:5]

16:13
a1 Kin. 15:24

16:14
aGen. 50:2;
Mark 16:1;
John 19:39, 40
b2 Chr. 21:19;
Jer. 34:5

17:1 a1 Kin. 15:24;
2 Chr. 20:31

17:2 a2 Chr. 11:5
b2 Chr. 15:8

17:4 a1 Kin. 12:28

16:13 1Died and joined his ancestors   16:14 1Lit. *dug*   17:4 1LXX *the LORD God*

of Israel. ⁵Therefore the LORD established the kingdom in his hand; and all Judah ᵃgave presents to Jehoshaphat, ᵇand he had riches and honor in abundance. ⁶And his heart took delight in the ways of the LORD; moreover ᵃhe removed the ¹high places and wooden images from Judah.

⁷Also in the third year of his reign he sent his leaders, Ben-Hail, Obadiah, Zechariah, Nethanel, and Michaiah, ᵃto teach in the cities of Judah. ⁸And with them *he sent* Levites: Shemaiah, Nethaniah, Zebadiah, Asahel, Shemiramoth, Jehonathan, Adonijah, Tobijah, and Tobadonijah—the Levites; and with them Elishama and Jehoram, the priests. ⁹ᵃSo they taught in Judah, and *had* the Book of the Law of the LORD with them; they went throughout all the cities of Judah and taught the people.

¹⁰And ᵃthe fear of the LORD fell on all the kingdoms of the lands that *were* around Judah, so that they did not make war against Jehoshaphat. ¹¹Also *some* of the Philistines ᵃbrought Jehoshaphat presents and silver as tribute; and the Arabians brought him flocks, seven thousand seven hundred rams and seven thousand seven hundred male goats.

¹²So Jehoshaphat became increasingly powerful, and he built fortresses and storage cities in Judah. ¹³He had much property in the cities of Judah; and the men of war, mighty men of valor, *were* in Jerusalem.

¹⁴These *are* their numbers, according to their fathers' houses. Of Judah, the captains of thousands: Adnah the captain, and with him three hundred thousand mighty men of valor; ¹⁵and next to him *was* Jehohanan the captain, and with him two hundred and eighty thousand; ¹⁶and next to him *was* Amasiah the son of Zichri, ᵃwho willingly offered himself to the LORD, and with him two hundred thousand mighty men of valor. ¹⁷Of Benjamin: Eliada a mighty man of valor, and with him two hundred thousand men armed with bow and shield; ¹⁸and next to him *was* Jehozabad, and with him one hundred and eighty thousand prepared for war. ¹⁹These served the king, besides ᵃthose the king put in the fortified cities throughout all Judah.

MICAIAH WARNS AHAB
(1 Kin. 22:1–28)

18 Jehoshaphat ᵃhad riches and honor in abundance; and by marriage he ᵇallied himself with ᶜAhab. ²ᵃAfter some years he went down to *visit* Ahab in Samaria; and Ahab killed sheep and oxen in abundance for him and the people who were with him, and persuaded him to go up *with him* to Ramoth Gilead. ³So Ahab king of Israel said to Jehoshaphat king of Judah, "Will you go with me *against* Ramoth Gilead?"

And he answered him, "I *am* as you *are,* and my people as your people; *we will be* with you in the war."

⁴Also Jehoshaphat said to the king of Israel, ᵃ"Please inquire for the word of the LORD today."

⁵Then the king of Israel gathered the prophets together, four hundred men, and said to them, "Shall we go to war against Ramoth Gilead, or shall I refrain?"

So they said, "Go up, for God will deliver it into the king's hand."

17:5
ᵃ1 Sam. 10:27;
1 Kin. 10:25
ᵇ2 Chr. 18:1

17:6
ᵃ1 Kin. 22:43;
2 Chr. 15:17; 19:3;
20:33

17:7 ᵃ2 Chr. 15:3;
35:3

17:9
ᵃDeut. 6:4–9;
2 Chr. 35:3;
Neh. 8:3, 7

17:10 ᵃGen. 35:5;
2 Chr. 14:14

17:11
ᵃ2 Sam. 8:2;
2 Chr. 9:14; 26:8

17:16 ᵃJudg. 5:2,
9; 1 Chr. 29:9

17:19 ᵃ2 Chr. 17:2

18:1 ᵃ2 Chr. 17:5
ᵇ1 Kin. 22:44;
2 Kin. 8:18
ᶜ1 Kin. 22:40

18:2 ᵃ[Ex. 23:2];
1 Kin. 22:2

18:4
ᵃ1 Sam. 23:2, 4,
9; 2 Sam. 2:1

17:6 ¹Places for pagan worship

6But Jehoshaphat said, "Is there not still a prophet of the LORD here, that we may inquire of aHim?"[1]

7So the king of Israel said to Jehoshaphat, "There is still one man by whom we may inquire of the LORD; but I hate him, because he never prophesies good concerning me, but always evil. He is Micaiah the son of Imla."

And Jehoshaphat said, "Let not the king say such things!"

8Then the king of Israel called one of his officers and said, "Bring Micaiah the son of Imla quickly!"

9The king of Israel and Jehoshaphat king of Judah, clothed in their robes, sat each on his throne; and they sat at a threshing floor at the entrance of the gate of Samaria; and all the prophets prophesied before them. 10Now Zedekiah the son of Chenaanah had made ahorns of iron for himself; and he said, "Thus says the LORD: 'With these you shall gore the Syrians until they are destroyed.'"

11And all the prophets prophesied so, saying, "Go up to Ramoth Gilead and prosper, for the LORD will deliver it into the king's hand."

12Then the messenger who had gone to call Micaiah spoke to him, saying, "Now listen, the words of the prophets with one accord encourage the king. Therefore please let your word be like the word of one of them, and speak encouragement."

13And Micaiah said, "As the LORD lives, awhatever my God says, that I will speak."

14Then he came to the king; and the king said to him, "Micaiah, shall we go to war against Ramoth Gilead, or shall I refrain?"

And he said, "Go and prosper, and they shall be delivered into your hand!"

15So the king said to him, "How many times shall I make you swear that you tell me nothing but the truth in the name of the LORD?"

16Then he said, "I saw all Israel ascattered on the mountains, as sheep that have no bshepherd. And the LORD said, 'These have no master. Let each return to his house in peace.'"

17And the king of Israel said to Jehoshaphat, "Did I not tell you he would not prophesy good concerning me, but evil?"

18Then Micaiah said, "Therefore hear the word of the LORD: I saw the LORD sitting on His athrone, and all the host of heaven standing on His right hand and His left. 19And the LORD said, 'Who will persuade Ahab king of Israel to go up, that he may fall at Ramoth Gilead?' So one spoke in this manner, and another spoke in that manner. 20Then a aspirit came forward and stood before the LORD, and said, 'I will persuade him.' The LORD said to him, 'In what way?' 21So he said, 'I will go out and be a lying spirit in the mouth of all his prophets.' And the LORD said, 'You shall persuade him and also prevail; go out and do so.' 22Therefore look! aThe LORD has put a lying spirit in the mouth of these prophets of yours, and the LORD has declared disaster against you."

23Then Zedekiah the son of Chenaanah went near and astruck Micaiah on the cheek, and said, "Which way did the spirit from the LORD go from me to speak to you?"

24And Micaiah said, "Indeed you shall see on that day when you go into an inner chamber to hide!"

18:6 ª2 Kin. 3:11

18:10
ªZech. 1:18–21

18:13
ªNum. 22:18–20, 35; 23:12, 26; 1 Kin. 22:14

18:16
ª[Jer. 23:1–8; 31:10]
bNum. 27:17; 1 Kin. 22:17; [Ezek. 34:5–8]; Matt. 9:36; Mark 6:34

18:18 ªIs. 6:1–5; Dan. 7:9, 10

18:20 ªJob 1:6; 2 Thess. 2:9

18:22
ªJob 12:16, 17; Is. 19:12–14; Ezek. 14:9

18:23 ªJer. 20:2; Mark 14:65; Acts 23:2

18:6 [1]Or him

25Then the king of Israel said, "Take Micaiah, and return him to Amon the governor of the city and to Joash the king's son; 26and say, 'Thus says the king: a"Put this *fellow* in prison, and feed him with bread of affliction and water of affliction, until I return in peace."'"

27But Micaiah said, "If you ever return in peace, the LORD has not spoken by ame." And he said, "Take heed, all you people!"

AHAB DIES IN BATTLE
(1 Kin. 22:29–40)

28So the king of Israel and Jehoshaphat the king of Judah went up to Ramoth Gilead. 29And the king of Israel said to Jehoshaphat, "I will adisguise myself and go into battle; but you put on your robes." So the king of Israel disguised himself, and they went into battle.

30Now the king of Syria had commanded the captains of the chariots who *were* with him, saying, "Fight with no one small or great, but only with the king of Israel."

31So it was, when the captains of the chariots saw Jehoshaphat, that they said, "It *is* the king of Israel!" Therefore they surrounded him to attack; but Jehoshaphat acried out, and the LORD helped him, and God diverted them from him. 32For so it was, when the captains of the chariots saw that it was not the king of Israel, that they turned back from pursuing him. 33Now a certain man drew a bow at random, and struck the king of Israel between the ¹joints of his armor. So he said to the driver of his chariot, "Turn around and take me out of the battle, for I am wounded." 34The battle increased that day, and the king of Israel propped *himself* up in *his* chariot facing the Syrians until evening; and about the time of sunset he died.

19 Then Jehoshaphat the king of Judah returned safely to his house in Jerusalem. 2And Jehu the son of Hanani athe seer went out to meet him, and said to King Jehoshaphat, "Should you help the wicked and blove those who hate the LORD? Therefore the cwrath of the LORD *is* upon you. 3Nevertheless agood things are found in you, in that you have removed the ¹wooden images from the land, and have bprepared your heart to seek God."

THE REFORMS OF JEHOSHAPHAT

4So Jehoshaphat dwelt at Jerusalem; and he went out again among the people from Beersheba to the mountains of Ephraim, and brought them back to the LORD God of their afathers. 5Then he set ajudges in the land throughout all the fortified cities of Judah, city by city, 6and said to the judges, "Take heed to what you are doing, for ayou do not judge for man but for the LORD, bwho *is* with you ¹in the judgment. 7Now therefore, let the fear of the LORD be upon you; take care and do *it*, for athere is no iniquity with the LORD our God, no bpartiality, nor taking of bribes."

8Moreover in Jerusalem, for the judgment of the LORD and for controversies, Jehoshaphat aappointed some of the Levites and priests, and some of the chief fathers of Israel,

18:26
a2 Chr. 16:10

18:27
aDeut. 18:22

18:29
a2 Chr. 35:22

18:31
a2 Chr. 13:14, 15

19:2 a1 Sam. 9:9;
1 Kin. 16:1;
2 Chr. 20:34
bPs. 139:21
c2 Chr. 32:25

19:3
a2 Chr. 17:4, 6
b2 Chr. 30:19

19:4
a2 Chr. 15:8–13

19:5
a[Deut. 16:18–20]

19:6 a[Lev. 19:15;
Deut. 1:17];
Ps. 58:1
bPs. 82:1;
[Eccl. 5:8]

19:7
a[Gen. 18:25;
Deut. 32:4];
Rom. 9:17
b[Deut. 10:17,
18; Job 34:19];
Acts 10:34;
Rom. 2:11;
Gal. 2:6;
[Eph. 6:9;
Col. 3:25]

19:8
aDeut. 16:18;
2 Chr. 17:8

18:33 ¹Or *scale armor and the breastplate*   19:3 ¹Or *Asherim*, Heb. *Asheroth*
19:6 ¹Lit. *in the matter of the judgment*

¹when they returned to Jerusalem. ⁹And he commanded them, saying, "Thus you shall act ᵃin the fear of the LORD, faithfully and with a loyal heart: ¹⁰ᵃWhatever case comes to you from your brethren who dwell in their cities, whether of bloodshed or offenses against law or commandment, against statutes or ordinances, you shall warn them, lest they trespass against the LORD and ᵇwrath come upon ᶜyou and your brethren. Do this, and you will not be guilty. ¹¹And take notice: ᵃAmariah the chief priest *is* over you ᵇin all matters of the LORD; and Zebadiah the son of Ishmael, the ruler of the house of Judah, for all the king's matters; also the Levites *will be* officials before you. Behave courageously, and the LORD will be ᶜwith the good."

AMMON, MOAB, AND MOUNT SEIR DEFEATED

20 It happened after this *that* the people of ᵃMoab with the people of ᵇAmmon, and *others* with them besides the ᶜAmmonites,¹ came to battle against Jehoshaphat. ²Then some came and told Jehoshaphat, saying, "A great multitude is coming against you from beyond the sea, from ¹Syria; and they are ᵃin Hazazon Tamar" (which *is* ᵇEn Gedi). ³And Jehoshaphat feared, and set ¹himself to ᵃseek the LORD, and ᵇproclaimed a fast throughout all Judah. ⁴So Judah gathered together to ask ᵃ*help* from the LORD; and from all the cities of Judah they came to seek the LORD.

⁵Then Jehoshaphat stood in the assembly of Judah and Jerusalem, in the house of the LORD, before the new court, ⁶and said: "O LORD God of our fathers, *are* You not ᵃGod in heaven, and ᵇdo You *not* rule over all the kingdoms of the nations, and ᶜin Your hand *is there not* power and might, so that no one is able to withstand You? ⁷Are You not ᵃour God, *who* ᵇdrove out the inhabitants of this land before Your people Israel, and gave it to the descendants of Abraham ᶜYour friend forever? ⁸And they dwell in it, and have built You a sanctuary in it for Your name, saying, ⁹ᵃ'If disaster comes upon us— sword, judgment, pestilence, or famine—we will stand before this temple and in Your presence (for Your ᵇname *is* in this temple), and cry out to You in our affliction, and You will hear and save.' ¹⁰And now, here are the people of Ammon, Moab, and Mount Seir—whom You ᵃwould not let Israel invade when they came out of the land of Egypt, but ᵇthey turned from them and did not destroy them— ¹¹here they are, rewarding us ᵃby coming to throw us out of Your possession which You have given us to inherit. ¹²O our God, will You not ᵃjudge them? For we have no power against this great multitude that is coming against us; nor do we know what to do, but ᵇour eyes *are* upon You."

¹³Now all Judah, with their little ones, their wives, and their children, stood before the LORD. ¹⁴Then ᵃthe Spirit of the LORD came upon Jahaziel the son of Zechariah, the son of Benaiah, the son of Jeiel, the son of Mattaniah, a Levite of the sons of Asaph, in the midst of the assembly. ¹⁵And he said, "Listen, all you of Judah and you inhabitants of Jerusalem, and you, King Jehoshaphat! Thus says

---

19:9
ᵃ[2 Sam. 23:3]

19:10 ᵃDeut. 17:8
ᵇNum. 16:46
ᶜ[Ezek. 3:18]

19:11 ᵃEzra 7:3
ᵇ1 Chr. 26:30
ᶜ[2 Chr. 15:2;
20:17]

20:1 ᵃ1 Chr. 18:2
ᵇ1 Chr. 19:15
ᶜ2 Chr. 26:7

20:2 ᵃGen. 14:7
ᵇJosh. 15:62

20:3 ᵃ2 Chr. 19:3
ᵇ1 Sam. 7:6;
Ezra 8:21;
Jer. 36:9;
Jon. 3:5

20:4 ᵃ2 Chr. 14:11

20:6
ᵃDeut. 4:39;
Josh. 2:11;
[1 Kin. 8:23];
Matt. 6:9
ᵇPs. 22:28;
47:2, 8;
Dan. 4:17, 25, 32
ᶜ1 Chr. 29:12;
2 Chr. 25:8;
Ps. 62:11;
Matt. 6:13

20:7
ᵃGen. 13:14–17;
17:7; Ex. 6:7
ᵇPs. 44:2
ᶜIs. 41:8;
James 2:23

20:9
ᵃ1 Kin. 8:33, 37;
2 Chr. 6:28–30
ᵇ2 Chr. 6:20

20:10
ᵃDeut. 2:4, 9, 19
ᵇNum. 20:21

20:11
ᵃPs. 83:1–18

20:12
ᵃJudg. 11:27;
[1 Sam. 3:13]
ᵇPs. 25:15;
121:1, 2;
123:1, 2; 141:8

20:14
ᵃNum. 11:25, 26;
24:2; 2 Chr. 15:1;
24:20

19:8 ¹LXX, Vg. *for the inhabitants of Jerusalem*   **20:1** ¹So with MT, Vg.; LXX *Meunites* (cf. 2 Chr. 26:7)   **20:2** ¹So with MT, LXX, Vg.; Heb. mss., Old Lat. *Edom*   **20:3** ¹Lit. *his face*

the LORD to you: ^a'Do not be afraid nor dismayed because of this great multitude, ^bfor the battle *is* not yours, but God's. ¹⁶Tomorrow go down against them. They will surely come up by the Ascent of Ziz, and you will find them at the end of the ¹brook before the Wilderness of Jeruel. ^{17a}You will not *need* to fight in this *battle*. Position yourselves, stand still and see the salvation of the LORD, who is with you, O Judah and Jerusalem!' Do not fear or be dismayed; tomorrow go out against them, ^bfor the LORD *is* with you."

¹⁸And Jehoshaphat ^abowed his head with *his* face to the ground, and all Judah and the inhabitants of Jerusalem bowed before the LORD, worshiping the LORD. ¹⁹Then the Levites of the children of the Kohathites and of the children of the Korahites stood up to praise the LORD God of Israel with voices loud and high.

²⁰So they rose early in the morning and went out into the Wilderness of Tekoa; and as they went out, Jehoshaphat stood and said, "Hear me, O Judah and you inhabitants of Jerusalem: ^aBelieve in the LORD your God, and you shall be established; believe His prophets, and you shall prosper." ²¹And when he had consulted with the people, he appointed those who should sing to the LORD, ^aand who should praise the beauty of holiness, as they went out before the army and were saying:

^b"Praise the LORD,
^cFor His mercy *endures* forever."

²²Now when they began to sing and to praise, ^athe LORD set ambushes against the people of Ammon, Moab, and Mount Seir, who had come against Judah; and they were defeated. ²³For the people of Ammon and Moab stood up against the inhabitants of Mount Seir to utterly kill and destroy *them*. And when they ¹had made an end of the inhabitants of Seir, ^athey helped to destroy one another.

²⁴So when Judah came to a place overlooking the wilderness, they looked toward the multitude; and there *were* their dead bodies, fallen on the earth. No one had escaped.

²⁵When Jehoshaphat and his people came to take away their spoil, they found among them an abundance of valuables on the ¹dead bodies, and precious jewelry, which they stripped off for themselves, more than they could carry away; and they were three days gathering the spoil because there was so much. ²⁶And on the fourth day they assembled in the Valley of ¹Berachah, for there they blessed the LORD; therefore the name of that place was called The Valley of Berachah until this day. ²⁷Then they returned, every man of Judah and Jerusalem, with Jehoshaphat in front of them, to go back to Jerusalem with joy, for the LORD had ^amade them rejoice over their enemies. ²⁸So they came to Jerusalem, with stringed instruments and harps and trumpets, to the house of the LORD. ²⁹And ^athe fear of God was on all the kingdoms of *those* countries when they heard that the LORD had fought against the enemies of Israel. ³⁰Then the realm of Jehoshaphat was quiet, for his ^aGod gave him rest all around.

20:15
^aEx. 14:13, 14;
[Deut. 1:29, 30;
31:6, 8];
2 Chr. 32:7
^b1 Sam. 17:47;
Zech. 14:3

20:17
^aEx. 14:13, 14
^bNum. 14:9;
[2 Chr. 15:2;
32:8]

20:18 ^aEx. 4:31;
2 Chr. 7:3; 29:28

20:20 ^aIs. 7:9

20:21
^a1 Chr. 16:29;
Ps. 29:2; 90:17;
96:9; 110:3
^b1 Chr. 16:34;
Ps. 106:1; 136:1
^c1 Chr. 16:41;
2 Chr. 5:13

20:22
^aJudg. 7:22;
1 Sam. 14:20

20:23
^aJudg. 7:22;
1 Sam. 14:20

20:27
^aNeh. 12:43

20:29
^a2 Chr. 14:14;
17:10

20:30
^a1 Kin. 22:41–43;
2 Chr. 14:6, 7;
15:15; Job 34:29

20:16 ¹*streambed* or *wadi*   20:23 ¹*had finished*   20:25 ¹A few Heb. mss.,
Old Lat., Vg. *garments*; LXX *armor*   20:26 ¹Lit. *Blessing*

THE END OF JEHOSHAPHAT'S REIGN
(1 Kin. 22:41–50)

31aSo Jehoshaphat was king over Judah. *He was* thirty-five years old when he became king, and he reigned twenty-five years in Jerusalem. His mother's name *was* Azubah the daughter of Shilhi. 32And he walked in the way of his father aAsa, and did not turn aside from it, doing *what was* right in the sight of the LORD. 33Nevertheless athe ¹high places were not taken away, for as yet the people had not bdirected their hearts to the God of their fathers.

34Now the rest of the acts of Jehoshaphat, first and last, indeed they *are* written in the book of Jehu the son of Hanani, awhich *is* mentioned in the book of the kings of Israel.

35After this aJehoshaphat king of Judah allied himself with Ahaziah king of Israel, bwho acted very cwickedly. 36And he allied himself with him ato make ships to go to Tarshish, and they made the ships in Ezion Geber. 37But Eliezer the son of Dodavah of Mareshah prophesied against Jehoshaphat, saying, "Because you have allied yourself with Ahaziah, the LORD has destroyed your works." aThen the ships were wrecked, so that they were not able to go bto Tarshish.

JEHORAM REIGNS IN JUDAH
(1 Kin. 22:50; 2 Kin. 8:16–24)

21 And aJehoshaphat ¹rested with his fathers, and was buried with his fathers in the City of David. Then Jehoram his son reigned in his place. 2He had brothers, the sons of Jehoshaphat: Azariah, Jehiel, Zechariah, Azaryahu, Michael, and Shephatiah; all these *were* the sons of Jehoshaphat king of Israel. 3Their father gave them great gifts of silver and gold and precious things, with fortified cities in Judah; but he gave the kingdom to Jehoram, because he *was* the firstborn.

4Now when Jehoram ¹was established over the kingdom of his father, he strengthened himself and killed all his brothers with the sword, and also *others* of the princes of Israel.

5aJehoram *was* thirty-two years old when he became king, and he reigned eight years in Jerusalem. 6And he walked in the way of the kings of Israel, just as the house of Ahab had done, for he had the daughter of aAhab as a wife; and he did evil in the sight of the LORD. 7Yet the LORD would not destroy the house of David, because of the acovenant that He had made with David, and since He had promised to give a lamp to him and to his bsons forever.

8aIn his days Edom revolted against Judah's authority, and made a king over themselves. 9So Jehoram went out with his officers, and all his chariots with him. And he rose by night and attacked the Edomites who had surrounded him and the captains of the chariots. 10Thus Edom has been in revolt against Judah's authority to this day. At that time Libnah revolted against his rule, because he had forsaken the LORD God of his fathers. 11Moreover he made ¹high places in the mountains of Judah, and caused the inhabitants of Jerusalem to acommit harlotry, and led Judah astray.

Cross references (margin)
20:31 a[1 Kin. 22:41–43]
20:32 a2 Chr. 14:2
20:33 a2 Chr. 15:17; 17:6 b2 Chr. 12:14; 19:3
20:34 a1 Kin. 16:1, 7
20:35 a2 Chr. 18:1 b1 Kin. 22:48–53 c[2 Chr. 19:2]
20:36 a1 Kin. 9:26; 10:22
20:37 a1 Kin. 22:48 b2 Chr. 9:21
21:1 a1 Kin. 22:50
21:5 a2 Kin. 8:17–22
21:6 a2 Chr. 18:1
21:7 a2 Sam. 7:8–17 b1 Kin. 11:36; 2 Kin. 8:19; Ps. 132:11
21:8 a2 Kin. 8:20; 14:7, 10; 2 Chr. 25:14, 19
21:11 a[Lev. 20:5]

20:33 ¹Places for pagan worship   21:1 ¹Died and joined his ancestors
21:4 ¹Lit. *arose*   21:11 ¹Places for pagan worship

¹²And a letter came to him from Elijah the prophet, saying,

Thus says the LORD God of your father David:
Because you have not walked in the ways of Jehoshaphat your father, or in the ways of Asa king of Judah, ¹³but have walked in the way of the kings of Israel, and have ᵃmade Judah and the inhabitants of Jerusalem to ᵇplay the harlot like the ᶜharlotry of the house of Ahab, and also have ᵈkilled your brothers, those of your father's household, *who were* better than yourself, ¹⁴behold, the LORD will strike your people with a serious affliction— your children, your wives, and all your possessions; ¹⁵and you *will become* very sick with a ᵃdisease of your intestines, until your intestines come out by reason of the sickness, day by day.

¹⁶Moreover the ᵃLORD ᵇstirred up against Jehoram the spirit of the Philistines and the ᶜArabians who *were* near the Ethiopians. ¹⁷And they came up into Judah and invaded it, and carried away all the possessions that were found in the king's house, and also ᵃhis sons and his wives, so that there was not a son left to him except ¹Jehoahaz, the youngest of his sons.

¹⁸After all this the LORD struck him ᵃin his intestines with an incurable disease. ¹⁹Then it happened in the course of time, after the end of two years, that his intestines came out because of his sickness; so he died in severe pain. And his people made no ¹burning for him, like ᵃthe burning for his fathers.

²⁰He was thirty-two years old when he became king. He reigned in Jerusalem eight years and, to no one's sorrow, departed. However they buried him in the City of David, but not in the tombs of the kings.

AHAZIAH REIGNS IN JUDAH
(2 Kin. 8:25–29; 9:14–16, 27–29)

22 Then the inhabitants of Jerusalem made ᵃAhaziah his youngest son king in his place, for the raiders who came with the ᵇArabians into the camp had killed all the ᶜolder *sons.* So Ahaziah the son of Jehoram, king of Judah, reigned. ²Ahaziah *was* ¹forty-two years old when he became king, and he reigned one year in Jerusalem. His mother's name *was* ᵃAthaliah the ²granddaughter of Omri. ³He also walked in the ways of the house of Ahab, for his mother advised him to do wickedly. ⁴Therefore he did evil in the sight of the LORD, like the house of Ahab; for they were his counselors after the death of his father, to his destruction. ⁵He also followed their advice, and went with ¹Jehoram the son of Ahab king of Israel to war against Hazael king of Syria at Ramoth Gilead; and the Syrians wounded Joram. ⁶ᵃThen he returned to Jezreel to recover from the wounds which he had received at Ramah, when he fought against Hazael king of Syria. And ¹Azariah the son of Jehoram, king of Judah, went down to see Jehoram the son of Ahab in Jezreel, because he was sick.

21:13
ᵃ2 Chr. 21:11
ᵇ[Ex. 34:15];
Deut. 31:16
ᶜ1 Kin. 16:31–33;
2 Kin. 9:22
ᵈ1 Kin. 2:32;
2 Chr. 21:4

21:15
ᵃ2 Chr. 21:18, 19

21:16
ᵃ2 Chr. 33:11;
[Jer. 51:11]
ᵇ1 Kin. 11:14, 23
ᶜ2 Chr. 17:11

21:17
ᵃ2 Chr. 24:7

21:18
ᵃ2 Chr. 13:20;
21:15; Acts 12:23

21:19
ᵃ2 Chr. 16:14

22:1
ᵃ2 Chr. 21:17;
22:6
ᵇ2 Chr. 21:16
ᶜ2 Chr. 21:17

22:2 ᵃ2 Chr. 21:6

22:6 ᵃ2 Kin. 9:15

21:17 ¹*Ahaziah* or *Azariah,* 2 Chr. 22:1   21:19 ¹Burning of spices
22:2 ¹*twenty-two,* 2 Kin. 8:26   ²Lit. *daughter*   22:5 ¹*Joram,* v. 7; 2 Kin. 8:28
22:6 ¹Heb. mss., LXX, Syr., Vg. *Ahaziah* and 2 Kin. 8:29

7His going to Joram ªwas God's occasion for Ahaziah's
¹downfall; for when he arrived, ᵇhe went out with ²Jehoram
against Jehu the son of Nimshi, ᶜwhom the LORD had anointed to ³cut off the house of Ahab. 8And it happened, when Jehu
was ªexecuting judgment on the house of Ahab, and ᵇfound
the princes of Judah and the sons of Ahaziah's brothers who
served Ahaziah, that he killed them. 9ªThen he searched for
Ahaziah; and they caught him (he was hiding in Samaria), and
brought him to Jehu. When they had killed him, they buried
him, "because," they said, "he is the son of ᵇJehoshaphat, who
ᶜsought the LORD with all his heart."

So the house of Ahaziah had no one to assume power over
the kingdom.

ATHALIAH REIGNS IN JUDAH
(2 Kin. 11:1–3)

10ªNow when Athaliah the mother of Ahaziah saw that her
son was dead, she arose and destroyed all the royal heirs of
the house of Judah. 11But ¹Jehoshabeath, the daughter of the
king, took ªJoash the son of Ahaziah, and stole him away from
among the king's sons who were being murdered, and put
him and his nurse in a bedroom. So Jehoshabeath, the daughter of King Jehoram, the wife of Jehoiada the priest (for she
was the sister of Ahaziah), hid him from Athaliah so that she
did not kill him. 12And he was hidden with them in the house
of God for six years, while Athaliah reigned over the land.

JOASH CROWNED KING OF JUDAH
(2 Kin. 11:4–12)

23 In ªthe seventh year ᵇJehoiada strengthened himself,
and made a covenant with the captains of hundreds:
Azariah the son of Jeroham, Ishmael the son of Jehohanan,
Azariah the son of ᶜObed, Maaseiah the son of Adaiah, and
Elishaphat the son of Zichri. 2And they went throughout Judah and gathered the Levites from all the cities of Judah, and
the ªchief fathers of Israel, and they came to Jerusalem.

3Then all the assembly made a covenant with the king in
the house of God. And he said to them, "Behold, the king's son
shall reign, as the LORD has ªsaid of the sons of David. 4This *is*
what you shall do: One-third of you ªentering on the Sabbath,
of the priests and the Levites, *shall be* keeping watch over the
doors; 5one-third *shall be* at the king's house; and one-third
at the Gate of the Foundation. All the people *shall be* in the
courts of the house of the LORD. 6But let no one come into
the house of the LORD except the priests and ªthose of the
Levites who serve. They may go in, for they *are* holy; but all
the people shall keep the watch of the LORD. 7And the Levites
shall surround the king on all sides, every man with his weapons in his hand; and whoever comes into the house, let him
be put to death. You are to be with the king when he comes in
and when he goes out."

8So the Levites and all Judah did according to all that Jehoiada the priest commanded. And each man took his men
who were to be on duty on the Sabbath, with those who were

22:7 ªJudg. 14:4;
1 Kin. 12:15;
2 Chr. 10:15
ᵇ2 Kin. 9:21–24
ᶜ2 Kin. 9:6, 7

22:8
ª2 Kin. 9:22–24
ᵇ2 Kin. 10:10–14;
Hos. 1:4

22:9
ª[2 Kin. 9:27]
ᵇ1 Kin. 15:24
ᶜ2 Chr. 17:4;
20:3, 4

22:10
ª2 Kin. 11:1–3

22:11
ª2 Kin. 12:18

23:1 ª2 Kin. 11:4
ᵇ2 Kin. 12:2
ᶜ1 Chr. 2:37, 38

23:2 ªEzra 1:5

23:3
ª2 Sam. 7:12;
1 Kin. 2:4; 9:5;
2 Chr. 6:16; 7:18;
21:7

23:4 ª1 Chr. 9:25

23:6
ª1 Chr. 23:28–32

22:7 ¹Lit. *crushing* ²*Joram*, vv. 5, 7; 2 Kin. 8:28 ³*destroy*
22:11 ¹*Jehosheba*, 2 Kin. 11:2

going *off duty* on the Sabbath; for Jehoiada the priest had not dismissed ᵃthe divisions. ⁹And Jehoiada the priest gave to the captains of hundreds the spears and the large and small ᵃshields which *had belonged* to King David, that *were* in the temple of God. ¹⁰Then he set all the people, every man with his weapon in his hand, from the right side of the temple to the left side of the temple, along by the altar and by the temple, all around the king. ¹¹And they brought out the king's son, put the crown on him, ᵃ*gave him* the ¹Testimony, and made him king. Then Jehoiada and his sons anointed him, and said, "*Long* live the king!"

DEATH OF ATHALIAH
(2 Kin. 11:13–20)

¹²Now when ᵃAthaliah heard the noise of the people running and praising the king, she came to the people *in* the temple of the LORD. ¹³*When* she looked, there was the king standing by his pillar at the entrance; and the leaders and the trumpeters *were* by the king. All the people of the land were rejoicing and blowing trumpets, also the singers with musical instruments, and ᵃthose who led in praise. So Athaliah tore her clothes and said, ᵇ"Treason! Treason!"

¹⁴And Jehoiada the priest brought out the captains of hundreds who were set over the army, and said to them, "Take her outside under guard, and slay with the sword whoever follows her." For the priest had said, "Do not kill her in the house of the LORD."

¹⁵So they seized her; and she went by way of the entrance ᵃof the Horse Gate *into* the king's house, and they killed her there.

¹⁶Then Jehoiada made a ᵃcovenant between himself, the people, and the king, that they should be the LORD's people. ¹⁷And all the people went to the ¹temple of Baal, and tore it down. They broke in pieces its altars and images, and ᵃkilled Mattan the priest of Baal before the altars. ¹⁸Also Jehoiada appointed the oversight of the house of the LORD to the hand of the priests, the Levites, whom David had ᵃassigned in the house of the LORD, to offer the burnt offerings of the LORD, as *it is* written in the ᵇLaw of Moses, with rejoicing and with singing, *as it was established* by David. ¹⁹And he set the ᵃgatekeepers at the gates of the house of the LORD, so that no one *who was* in any way unclean should enter.

²⁰ᵃThen he took the captains of hundreds, the nobles, the governors of the people, and all the people of the land, and brought the king down from the house of the LORD; and they went through the Upper Gate to the king's house, and set the king on the throne of the kingdom. ²¹So all the people of the land rejoiced; and the city was quiet, for they had slain Athaliah with the sword.

JOASH REPAIRS THE TEMPLE
(2 Kin. 11:21—12:16)

24 Joash ᵃ*was* seven years old when he became king, and he reigned forty years in Jerusalem. His mother's name *was* Zibiah of Beersheba. ²Joash ᵃdid *what was* right

---

23:8
ᵃ1 Chr. 24:1–31

23:9
ᵃ2 Sam. 8:7

23:11
ᵃDeut. 17:18

23:12
ᵃ2 Chr. 22:10

23:13
ᵃ1 Chr. 25:6–8
ᵇ2 Kin. 9:23

23:15
ᵃNeh. 3:28;
Jer. 31:40

23:16
ᵃJosh. 24:24, 25;
2 Chr. 15:12–15

23:17
ᵃDeut. 13:6–9;
1 Kin. 18:40

23:18
ᵃ1 Chr. 23:6,
30, 31; 24:1
ᵇNum. 28:2

23:19
ᵃ1 Chr. 26:1–19

23:20
ᵃ1 Kin. 9:22;
2 Kin. 11:19

24:1 ᵃ2 Kin. 11:21;
12:1–15

24:2
ᵃ2 Chr. 26:4, 5

in the sight of the LORD all the days of Jehoiada the priest. ³And Jehoiada took two wives for him, and he had sons and daughters.

⁴Now it happened after this *that* Joash set his heart on repairing the house of the LORD. ⁵Then he gathered the priests and the Levites, and said to them, "Go out to the cities of Judah, and ᵃgather from all Israel money to repair the house of your God from year to year, and see that you do it quickly."

However the Levites did not do it quickly. ⁶ᵃSo the king called Jehoiada the chief *priest,* and said to him, "Why have you not required the Levites to bring in from Judah and from Jerusalem the collection, *according to the commandment* of ᵇMoses the servant of the LORD and of the assembly of Israel, for the ᶜtabernacle of witness?" ⁷For ᵃthe sons of Athaliah, that wicked woman, had broken into the house of God, and had also presented all the ᵇdedicated things of the house of the LORD to the Baals.

⁸Then at the king's command ᵃthey made a chest, and set it outside at the gate of the house of the LORD. ⁹And they made a proclamation throughout Judah and Jerusalem to bring to the LORD ᵃthe collection *that* Moses the servant of God *had imposed* on Israel in the wilderness. ¹⁰Then all the leaders and all the people rejoiced, brought their contributions, and put *them* into the chest until all had given. ¹¹So it was, at that time, when the chest was brought to the king's official by the hand of the Levites, and ᵃwhen they saw that *there was* much money, that the king's scribe and the high priest's officer came and emptied the chest, and took it and returned it to its place. Thus they did day by day, and gathered money in abundance.

¹²The king and Jehoiada gave it to those who did the work of the service of the house of the LORD; and they hired masons and carpenters to ᵃrepair the house of the LORD, and also those who worked in iron and bronze to restore the house of the LORD. ¹³So the workmen labored, and the work was completed by them; they restored the house of God to its original condition and reinforced it. ¹⁴When they had finished, they brought the rest of the money before the king and Jehoiada; ᵃthey made from it articles for the house of the LORD, articles for serving and offering, spoons and vessels of gold and silver. And they offered burnt offerings in the house of the LORD continually all the days of Jehoiada.

APOSTASY OF JOASH

¹⁵But Jehoiada grew old and was full of days, and he died; *he was* one hundred and thirty years old when he died. ¹⁶And they buried him in the City of David among the kings, because he had done good in Israel, both toward God and His house.

¹⁷Now after the death of Jehoiada the leaders of Judah came and bowed down to the king. And the king listened to them. ¹⁸Therefore they left the house of the LORD God of their fathers, and served ᵃwooden images and idols; and ᵇwrath came upon Judah and Jerusalem because of their trespass. ¹⁹Yet He ᵃsent prophets to them, to bring them back to the LORD; and they testified against them, but they would not listen.

24:5 ᵃ2 Kin. 12:4

24:6 ᵃ2 Kin. 12:7
ᵇEx. 30:12–16
ᶜNum. 1:50;
Acts 7:44

24:7 ᵃ2 Chr. 21:17
ᵇ2 Kin. 12:4

24:8 ᵃ2 Kin. 12:9

24:9
ᵃ2 Chr. 24:6

24:11
ᵃ2 Kin. 12:10

24:12
ᵃ2 Chr. 30:12

24:14
ᵃ2 Kin. 12:13

24:18
ᵃ1 Kin. 14:23
ᵇ[Ex. 34:12–14];
Judg. 5:8;
2 Chr. 19:2;
28:13; 29:8;
32:25

24:19
ᵃ2 Kin. 17:13;
21:10–15;
2 Chr. 36:15, 16;
Jer. 7:25, 26;
25:4

20Then the Spirit of God 1came upon aZechariah the son of Jehoiada the priest, who stood above the people, and said to them, "Thus says God: b'Why do you transgress the commandments of the LORD, so that you cannot prosper? cBecause you have forsaken the LORD, He also has forsaken you.'" 21So they conspired against him, and at the command of the king they astoned him with stones in the court of the house of the LORD. 22Thus Joash the king did not remember the kindness which Jehoiada his 1father had done to him, but killed his son; and as he died, he said, "The LORD look on it, and arepay!"

DEATH OF JOASH
(2 Kin. 12:19–21)

23So it happened in the spring of the year that athe army of Syria came up against him; and they came to Judah and Jerusalem, and destroyed all the leaders of the people from among the people, and sent all their 1spoil to the king of Damascus. 24For the army of the Syrians acame with a small company of men; but the LORD bdelivered a very great army into their hand, because they had forsaken the LORD God of their fathers. So they cexecuted judgment against Joash. 25And when they had withdrawn from him (for they left him severely wounded), ahis own servants conspired against him because of the blood of the 1sons of Jehoiada the priest, and killed him on his bed. So he died. And they buried him in the City of David, but they did not bury him in the tombs of the kings.

26These are the ones who conspired against him: 1Zabad the son of Shimeath the Ammonitess, and Jehozabad the son of 2Shimrith the Moabitess. 27Now concerning his sons, and athe many oracles about him, and the repairing of the house of God, indeed they are written in the 1annals of the book of the kings. bThen Amaziah his son reigned in his place.

AMAZIAH REIGNS IN JUDAH
(2 Kin. 14:1–6)

25 Amaziah awas twenty-five years old when he became king, and he reigned twenty-nine years in Jerusalem. His mother's name was Jehoaddan of Jerusalem. 2And he did what was right in the sight of the LORD, abut not with a loyal heart.

3aNow it happened, as soon as the kingdom was established for him, that he executed his servants who had murdered his father the king. 4However he did not execute their children, but did as it is written in the Law in the Book of Moses, where the LORD commanded, saying, a"The fathers shall not be put to death for their children, nor shall the children be put to death for their fathers; but a person shall die for his own sin."

THE WAR AGAINST EDOM
(2 Kin. 14:7)

5Moreover Amaziah gathered Judah together and set over them captains of thousands and captains of hundreds,

24:20 aJudg. 6:34; Matt. 23:35 bNum. 14:41; [Prov. 28:13] c[2 Chr. 15:2]

24:21 a[Neh. 9:26]; Matt. 23:35; Acts 7:58, 59

24:22 a[Gen. 9:5]

24:23 a2 Kin. 12:17; Is. 7:2

24:24 aLev. 26:8; [Deut. 32:30]; Is. 30:17 bLev. 26:25; [Deut. 28:25] c2 Chr. 22:8; Is. 10:5

24:25 a2 Kin. 12:20, 21; 2 Chr. 25:3

24:27 a2 Kin. 12:18 b2 Kin. 12:21

25:1 a2 Kin. 14:1–6

25:2 a2 Kin. 14:4; 2 Chr. 25:14

25:3 a2 Kin. 14:5; 2 Chr. 24:25

25:4 aDeut. 24:16; 2 Kin. 14:6; Jer. 31:30; [Ezek. 18:20]

24:20 1Lit. clothed   24:22 1Foster father   24:23 1plunder   24:25 1LXX, Vg. son and vv. 20–22   24:26 1Jozachar, 2 Kin. 12:21   2Shomer, 2 Kin. 12:21
24:27 1Or commentary, Heb. midrash

according to *their* fathers' houses, throughout all Judah and Benjamin; and he numbered them [a]from twenty years old and above, and found them to be three hundred thousand choice *men, able* to go to war, who could handle spear and shield. [6]He also hired one hundred thousand mighty men of valor from Israel for one hundred talents of silver. [7]But a [a]man of God came to him, saying, "O king, do not let the army of Israel go with you, for the LORD *is* not with Israel—*not with* any of the children of Ephraim. [8]But if you go, be gone! Be strong in battle! *Even so,* God shall make you fall before the enemy; for God has [a]power to help and to overthrow."

[9]Then Amaziah said to the man of God, "But what *shall we* do about the hundred talents which I have given to the troops of Israel?"

And the man of God answered, [a]"The LORD is able to give you much more than this." [10]So Amaziah discharged the troops that had come to him from Ephraim, to go back home. Therefore their anger was greatly aroused against Judah, and they returned home in great anger.

[11]Then Amaziah strengthened himself, and leading his people, he went to [a]the Valley of Salt and killed ten thousand of the people of Seir. [12]Also the children of Judah took captive ten thousand alive, brought them to the top of the rock, and cast them down from the top of the rock, so that they all were dashed in pieces.

[13]But as for the soldiers of the army which Amaziah had discharged, so that they would not go with him to battle, they raided the cities of Judah from Samaria to Beth Horon, killed three thousand in them, and took much [1]spoil.

[14]Now it was so, after Amaziah came from the slaughter of the Edomites, that [a]he brought the gods of the people of Seir, set them up *to be* [b]his gods, and bowed down before them and burned incense to them. [15]Therefore the anger of the LORD was aroused against Amaziah, and He sent him a prophet who said to him, "Why have you sought [a]the gods of the people, which [b]could not rescue their own people from your hand?"

[16]So it was, as he talked with him, that *the king* said to him, "Have we made you the king's counselor? Cease! Why should you be killed?"

Then the prophet ceased, and said, "I know that God has [a]determined to destroy you, because you have done this and have not heeded my advice."

ISRAEL DEFEATS JUDAH
(2 Kin. 14:8–14)

[17]Now [a]Amaziah king of Judah asked advice and sent to [1]Joash the son of Jehoahaz, the son of Jehu, king of Israel, saying, "Come, let us face one another *in battle.*"

[18]And Joash king of Israel sent to Amaziah king of Judah, saying, "The thistle that *was* in Lebanon sent to the cedar that was in Lebanon, saying, 'Give your daughter to my son as wife'; and a wild beast that *was* in Lebanon passed by and trampled the thistle. [19]Indeed you say that you have defeated the Edomites, and your heart is lifted up to [a]boast. Stay

25:5 [a]Num. 1:3
25:7 [a]2 Chr. 11:2
25:8
[a]2 Chr. 14:11;
20:6
25:9
[a][Deut. 8:18];
Prov. 10:22
25:11 [a]2 Kin. 14:7
25:14
[a]2 Chr. 28:23
[b][Ex. 20:3, 5]
25:15 [a][Ps. 96:5]
[b]2 Chr. 25:11
25:16
[a][1 Sam. 2:25]
25:17
[a]2 Kin. 14:8–14
25:19
[a]2 Chr. 26:16;
32:25;
[Prov. 16:18]

25:13 [1]*plunder* 25:17 [1]*Jehoash,* 2 Kin. 14:8ff.

at home now; why should you meddle with trouble, that you should fall—you and Judah with you?"

20But Amaziah would not heed, for ªit *came* from God, that He might give them into the hand *of their enemies,* because they ᵇsought the gods of Edom. 21So Joash king of Israel went out; and he and Amaziah king of Judah faced one another at ªBeth Shemesh, which *belongs* to Judah. 22And Judah was defeated by Israel, and every man fled to his tent. 23Then Joash the king of Israel captured Amaziah king of Judah, the son of Joash, the son of ªJehoahaz, at Beth Shemesh; and he brought him to Jerusalem, and broke down the wall of Jerusalem from the Gate of Ephraim to the Corner Gate—four hundred cubits. 24And *he took* all the gold and silver, all the articles that were found in the house of God with ªObed-Edom, the treasures of the king's house, and hostages, and returned to Samaria.

DEATH OF AMAZIAH
(2 Kin. 14:17–20)

25ªAmaziah the son of Joash, king of Judah, lived fifteen years after the death of Joash the son of Jehoahaz, king of Israel. 26Now the rest of the acts of Amaziah, from first to last, indeed *are* they not written in the book of the kings of Judah and Israel? 27After the time that Amaziah turned away from following the LORD, they made a conspiracy against him in Jerusalem, and he fled to Lachish; but they sent after him to Lachish and killed him there. 28Then they brought him on horses and buried him with his fathers in ¹the City of Judah.

UZZIAH REIGNS IN JUDAH
(2 Kin. 14:21, 22; 15:1–3)

26 Now all the people of Judah took ¹Uzziah, who *was* sixteen years old, and made him king instead of his father Amaziah. 2He built ¹Elath and restored it to Judah, after the king rested with his fathers.

3Uzziah *was* sixteen years old when he became king, and he reigned fifty-two years in Jerusalem. His mother's name was Jecholiah of Jerusalem. 4And he did *what was* ªright in the sight of the LORD, according to all that his father Amaziah had done. 5ªHe sought God in the days of Zechariah, who ᵇhad understanding in the ¹visions of God; and as long as he sought the LORD, God made him ᶜprosper.

6Now he went out and ªmade war against the Philistines, and broke down the wall of Gath, the wall of Jabneh, and the wall of Ashdod; and he built cities *around* Ashdod and among the Philistines. 7God helped him against ªthe Philistines, against the Arabians who lived in Gur Baal, and against the Meunites. 8Also the Ammonites ªbrought tribute to Uzziah. His fame spread as far as the entrance of Egypt, for he became exceedingly strong.

9And Uzziah built towers in Jerusalem at the ªCorner Gate, at the Valley Gate, and at the corner buttress of the wall; then he fortified them. 10Also he built towers in the desert. He dug many wells, for he had much livestock, both in the lowlands

25:20
ª1 Kin. 12:15;
2 Chr. 22:7
ᵇ2 Chr. 25:14

25:21
ªJosh. 19:38

25:23
ª2 Chr. 21:17;
22:1, 6

25:24
ª1 Chr. 26:15

25:25
ª2 Kin. 14:17–22

26:4
ª2 Chr. 24:2

26:5
ª2 Chr. 24:2
ᵇGen. 41:15;
Dan. 1:17; 10:1
ᶜ[2 Chr. 15:2;
20:20; 31:21]

26:6 ªIs. 14:29

26:7
ª2 Chr. 21:16

26:8
ª2 Sam. 8:2;
2 Chr. 17:11

26:9
ª2 Kin. 14:13;
2 Chr. 25:23;
Neh. 3:13, 19, 32;
Zech. 14:10

25:28 ¹The City of David   26:1 ¹*Azariah*, 2 Kin. 14:21ff.   26:2 ¹Heb. *Eloth*
26:5 ¹Heb. mss., LXX, Syr., Tg., Arab. *fear*

and in the plains; *he also had* farmers and vinedressers in the mountains and in [1]Carmel, for he loved the soil. [11]Moreover Uzziah had an army of fighting men who went out to war by companies, according to the number on their roll as prepared by Jeiel the scribe and Maaseiah the officer, under the hand of Hananiah, *one* of the king's captains. [12]The total number of [1]chief officers of the mighty men of valor *was* two thousand six hundred. [13]And under their authority *was* an army of three hundred and seven thousand five hundred, that made war with mighty power, to help the king against the enemy. [14]Then Uzziah prepared for them, for the entire army, shields, spears, helmets, body armor, bows, and slings *to cast* stones. [15]And he made devices in Jerusalem, invented by [a]skillful men, to be on the towers and the corners, to shoot arrows and large stones. So his fame spread far and wide, for he was marvelously helped till he became strong.

THE PENALTY FOR UZZIAH'S PRIDE
(2 Kin. 15:4–7)

[16]But [a]when he was strong his heart was [b]lifted up, to *his* destruction, for he transgressed against the LORD his God [c]by entering the temple of the LORD to burn incense on the altar of incense. [17]So [a]Azariah the priest went in after him, and with him were eighty priests of the LORD—valiant men. [18]And they withstood King Uzziah, and said to him, "*It* [a]*is* not for you, Uzziah, to burn incense to the LORD, but for the [b]priests, the sons of Aaron, who are consecrated to burn incense. Get out of the sanctuary, for you have trespassed! You *shall have* no honor from the LORD God."

[19]Then Uzziah became furious; and he *had* a censer in his hand to burn incense. And while he was angry with the priests, [a]leprosy broke out on his forehead, before the priests in the house of the LORD, beside the incense altar. [20]And Azariah the chief priest and all the priests looked at him, and there, on his forehead, he *was* leprous; so they thrust him out of that place. Indeed he also [a]hurried to get out, because the LORD had struck him.

[21]aKing Uzziah was a leper until the day of his death. He dwelt in an [b]isolated house, because he was a leper; for he was cut off from the house of the LORD. Then Jotham his son *was* over the king's house, judging the people of the land.

[22]Now the rest of the acts of Uzziah, from first to last, the prophet [a]Isaiah the son of Amoz wrote. [23]aSo Uzziah [1]rested with his fathers, and they buried him with his fathers in the field of burial which *belonged* to the kings, for they said, "He is a leper." Then Jotham his son reigned in his place.

JOTHAM REIGNS IN JUDAH
(2 Kin. 15:32–38)

27 Jotham [a]*was* twenty-five years old when he became king, and he reigned sixteen years in Jerusalem. His mother's name *was* [1]Jerushah the daughter of Zadok. [2]And he did *what was* right in the sight of the LORD, according to

---

26:15
[a]Ex. 39:3, 8

26:16
[a][Deut. 32:15]
[b]Deut. 8:14;
2 Chr. 25:19
[c]1 Kin. 13:1–4;
2 Kin. 16:12, 13

26:17
[a]1 Chr. 6:10

26:18
[a][Num. 3:10;
16:39, 40; 18:7]
[b]Ex. 30:7, 8;
Heb. 7:14

26:19
[a]Lev. 13:42;
Num. 12:10;
2 Kin. 5:25–27

26:20
[a]Esth. 6:12

26:21
[a]2 Kin. 15:5
[b][Lev. 13:46;
Num. 5:2]

26:22
[a]2 Kin. 20:1;
2 Chr. 32:20, 32;
Is. 1:1

26:23
[a]2 Kin. 15:7;
2 Chr. 21:20;
28:27; Is. 6:1

27:1
[a]2 Kin. 15:32–35

26:10 [1]Or *the fertile fields*   26:12 [1]Lit. *chief fathers*   26:23 [1]Died and joined his ancestors   27:1 [1]*Jerusha,* 2 Kin. 15:33

all that his father Uzziah had done (although he did not enter the temple of the LORD). But still ᵃthe people acted corruptly.

³He built the Upper Gate of the house of the LORD, and he built extensively on the wall of ᵃOphel. ⁴Moreover he built cities in the mountains of Judah, and in the forests he built fortresses and towers. ⁵He also fought with the king of the ᵃAmmonites and defeated them. And the people of Ammon gave him in that year one hundred talents of silver, ten thousand kors of wheat, and ten thousand of barley. The people of Ammon paid this to him in the second and third years also. ⁶So Jotham became mighty, ᵃbecause he prepared his ways before the LORD his God.

⁷Now the rest of the acts of Jotham, and all his wars and his ways, indeed they *are* written in the book of the kings of Israel and Judah. ⁸He was twenty-five years old when he became king, and he reigned sixteen years in Jerusalem. ⁹ᵃSo Jotham ¹rested with his fathers, and they buried him in the City of David. Then ᵇAhaz his son reigned in his place.

AHAZ REIGNS IN JUDAH
(2 Kin. 16:1–4)

28 Ahaz ᵃ*was* twenty years old when he became king, and he reigned sixteen years in Jerusalem; and he did not do *what was* right in the sight of the LORD, as his father David *had done.* ²For he walked in the ways of the kings of Israel, and made ᵃmolded images for ᵇthe Baals. ³He burned incense in ᵃthe Valley of the Son of Hinnom, and burned ᵇhis children in the ᶜfire, according to the abominations of the nations whom the LORD had ᵈcast out before the children of Israel. ⁴And he sacrificed and burned incense on the ¹high places, on the hills, and under every green tree.

SYRIA AND ISRAEL DEFEAT JUDAH
(2 Kin. 16:5, 6; Is. 7:1)

⁵Therefore ᵃthe LORD his God delivered him into the hand of the king of Syria. They ᵇdefeated him, and carried away a great multitude of them as captives, and brought *them* to Damascus. Then he was also delivered into the hand of the king of Israel, who defeated him with a great slaughter. ⁶For ᵃPekah the son of Remaliah killed one hundred and twenty thousand in Judah in one day, all valiant men, ᵇbecause they had forsaken the LORD God of their fathers. ⁷Zichri, a mighty man of Ephraim, killed Maaseiah the king's son, Azrikam the officer over the house, and Elkanah *who was* second to the king. ⁸And the children of Israel carried away captive of their ᵃbrethren two hundred thousand women, sons, and daughters; and they also took away much ¹spoil from them, and brought the spoil to Samaria.

ISRAEL RETURNS THE CAPTIVES

⁹But a ᵃprophet of the LORD was there, whose name *was* Oded; and he went out before the army that came to Samaria, and said to them: "Look, ᵇbecause the LORD God of your fathers was angry with Judah, He has delivered them into your

27:2
ᵃ2 Kin. 15:35;
Ezek. 20:44;
30:13

27:3
ᵃ2 Chr. 33:14;
Neh. 3:26

27:5
ᵃ2 Chr. 26:8

27:6
ᵃ2 Chr. 26:5

27:9
ᵃ2 Kin. 15:38
ᵇIs. 1:1; Hos. 1:1;
Mic. 1:1

28:1
ᵃ2 Kin. 16:2–4

28:2 ᵃEx. 34:17;
Lev. 19:4
ᵇJudg. 2:11

28:3 ᵃJosh. 15:8
ᵇ2 Kin. 23:10
ᶜ[Lev. 18:21];
2 Kin. 16:3;
2 Chr. 33:6
ᵈ[Lev. 18:24–30]

28:5 ᵃ[Is. 10:5]
ᵇ2 Kin. 16:5, 6;
[2 Chr. 24:24];
Is. 7:1, 17

28:6
ᵃ2 Kin. 15:27
ᵇ[2 Chr. 29:8]

28:8
ᵃDeut. 28:25, 41;
2 Chr. 11:4

28:9
ᵃ2 Chr. 25:15
ᵇPs. 69:26;
[Is. 10:5; 47:6];
Ezek. 25:12, 15;
26:2; Obad. 10;
[Zech. 1:15]

hand; but you have killed them in a rage *that* [c]reaches up to heaven. [10]And now you propose to force the children of Judah and Jerusalem to be your [a]male and female slaves; *but are* you not also guilty before the LORD your God? [11]Now hear me, therefore, and return the captives, whom you have taken captive from your brethren, [a]for the fierce wrath of the LORD *is* upon you."

[12]Then some of the heads of the children of Ephraim, Azariah the son of Johanan, Berechiah the son of Meshillemoth, Jehizkiah the son of Shallum, and Amasa the son of Hadlai, stood up against those who came from the war, [13]and said to them, "You shall not bring the captives here, for we *already* have offended the LORD. You intend to add to our sins and to our guilt; for our guilt is great, and *there is* fierce wrath against Israel." [14]So the armed men left the captives and the [1]spoil before the leaders and all the assembly. [15]Then the men [a]who were designated by name rose up and took the captives, and from the [1]spoil they clothed all who were naked among them, dressed them and gave them sandals, [b]gave them food and drink, and anointed them; and they let all the feeble ones ride on donkeys. So they brought them to their brethren at Jericho, [c]the city of palm trees. Then they returned to Samaria.

ASSYRIA REFUSES TO HELP JUDAH
(2 Kin. 16:7–9)

[16a]At the same time King Ahaz sent to the [1]kings of Assyria to help him. [17]For again the [a]Edomites had come, attacked Judah, and carried away captives. [18a]The Philistines also had invaded the cities of the lowland and of the South of Judah, and had taken Beth Shemesh, Aijalon, Gederoth, Sochoh with its villages, Timnah with its villages, and Gimzo with its villages; and they dwelt there. [19]For the LORD [1]brought Judah low because of Ahaz king of [a]Israel, for he had [b]encouraged moral decline in Judah and had been continually unfaithful to the LORD. [20]Also [a]Tiglath-Pileser[1] king of Assyria came to him and distressed him, and did not assist him. [21]For Ahaz took part *of the treasures* from the house of the LORD, from the house of the king, and from the leaders, and he gave *it* to the king of Assyria; but he did not help him.

APOSTASY AND DEATH OF AHAZ
(2 Kin. 16:12–20)

[22]Now in the time of his distress King Ahaz became increasingly unfaithful to the LORD. This *is that* King Ahaz. [23]For [a]he sacrificed to the gods of Damascus which had defeated him, saying, "Because the gods of the kings of Syria help them, I will sacrifice to them [b]that they may help me." But they were the ruin of him and of all Israel. [24]So Ahaz gathered the articles of the house of God, cut in pieces the articles of the house of God, [a]shut up the doors of the house of the LORD, and made for himself altars in every corner of Jerusalem. [25]And in every single city of Judah he made [1]high places to burn incense to other gods, and provoked to anger the LORD God of his fathers.

Cross References (margin)

28:9 [c]Ezra 9:6; Rev. 18:5

28:10 [a][Lev. 25:39, 42, 43, 46]

28:11 [a]Ps. 78:49; James 2:13

28:15 [a]2 Chr. 28:12; [b][Prov. 25:21, 22; Luke 6:27; Rom. 12:20]; [c]Deut. 34:3; Judg. 1:16

28:16 [a]2 Kin. 16:7

28:17 [a]2 Chr. 21:10; Obad. 10–14

28:18 [a]2 Chr. 21:16, 17; Ezek. 16:27, 57

28:19 [a]2 Kin. 16:2; 2 Chr. 21:2; [b]Ex. 32:25

28:20 [a]2 Kin. 15:29; 16:7–9; 1 Chr. 5:26

28:23 [a]2 Chr. 25:14; [b]Jer. 44:17, 18

28:24 [a]2 Chr. 29:3, 7

Footnotes

28:14 [1]*plunder*   28:15 [1]*plunder*   28:16 [1]LXX, Syr., Vg. *king* (cf. v. 20)
28:19 [1]*humbled Judah*   28:20 [1]Heb. *Tilgath-Pilneser*   28:25 [1]Places for pagan worship

26a Now the rest of his acts and all his ways, from first to last, indeed they *are* written in the book of the kings of Judah and Israel. 27So Ahaz 1rested with his fathers, and they buried him in the city, in Jerusalem; but they a did not bring him into the tombs of the kings of Israel. Then Hezekiah his son reigned in his place.

HEZEKIAH REIGNS IN JUDAH
(2 Kin. 18:1–3)

29 Hezekiah a became king *when he was* twenty-five years old, and he reigned twenty-nine years in Jerusalem. His mother's name *was* 1Abijah the daughter of Zechariah. 2And he did *what was* right in the sight of the LORD, according to all that his father David had done.

HEZEKIAH CLEANSES THE TEMPLE

3In the first year of his reign, in the first month, he a opened the doors of the house of the LORD and repaired them. 4Then he brought in the priests and the Levites, and gathered them in the East Square, 5and said to them: "Hear me, Levites! Now 1sanctify yourselves, a sanctify the house of the LORD God of your fathers, and carry out the rubbish from the holy *place*. 6For our fathers have trespassed and done evil in the eyes of the LORD our God; they have forsaken Him, have a turned their faces away from the 1dwelling place of the LORD, and turned *their* backs *on Him*. 7a They have also shut up the doors of the vestibule, put out the lamps, and have not burned incense or offered burnt offerings in the holy *place* to the God of Israel. 8Therefore the a wrath of the LORD fell upon Judah and Jerusalem, and He has b given them up to trouble, to desolation, and to c jeering, as you see with your d eyes. 9For indeed, because of this a our fathers have fallen by the sword; and our sons, our daughters, and our wives *are* in captivity.

10"Now *it is* in my heart to make a a covenant with the LORD God of Israel, that His fierce wrath may turn away from us. 11My sons, do not be negligent now, for the LORD has a chosen you to stand before Him, to serve Him, and that you should minister to Him and burn incense."

12Then these Levites arose: a Mahath the son of Amasai and Joel the son of Azariah, of the sons of the b Kohathites; of the sons of Merari, Kish the son of Abdi and Azariah the son of Jehallelel; of the Gershonites, Joah the son of Zimmah and Eden the son of Joah; 13of the sons of Elizaphan, Shimri and Jeiel; of the sons of Asaph, Zechariah and Mattaniah; 14of the sons of Heman, Jehiel and Shimei; and of the sons of Jeduthun, Shemaiah and Uzziel.

15And they gathered their brethren, a sanctified1 themselves, and went according to the commandment of the king, at the words of the LORD, b to cleanse the house of the LORD. 16Then the priests went into the inner part of the house of the LORD to cleanse *it,* and brought out all the debris that they found in the temple of the LORD to the court of the house of the LORD. And the Levites took *it* out and carried *it* to the Brook a Kidron.

28:26
a 2 Kin. 16:19, 20

28:27
a 2 Chr. 21:20; 24:25

29:1 a 2 Kin. 18:1; 2 Chr. 32:22, 33

29:3
a 2 Chr. 28:24; 29:7

29:5
a 1 Chr. 15:12; 2 Chr. 29:15, 34; 35:6

29:6 a [Is. 1:4]; Jer. 2:27; Ezek. 8:16

29:7
a 2 Chr. 28:24

29:8
a 2 Chr. 24:18
b 2 Chr. 28:5
c 1 Kin. 9:8; Jer. 18:16; 19:8; 25:9, 18; 29:18
d Deut. 28:32

29:9
a Deut. 28:25; 2 Chr. 28:5–8, 17

29:10
a 2 Chr. 15:12; 23:16

29:11
a Num. 3:6; 8:14; 18:2, 6; 2 Chr. 30:16, 17

29:12
a 2 Chr. 31:13
b Num. 3:19, 20

29:15
a 2 Chr. 29:5
b 1 Chr. 23:28

29:16
a 2 Chr. 15:16; 30:14

28:27 1Died and joined his ancestors   29:1 1Abi, 2 Kin. 18:2
29:5 1consecrate   29:6 1Temple   29:15 1consecrated

[17]Now they began to [1]sanctify on the first *day* of the first month, and on the eighth day of the month they came to the vestibule of the LORD. So they sanctified the house of the LORD in eight days, and on the sixteenth day of the first month they finished.

[18]Then they went in to King Hezekiah and said, "We have cleansed all the house of the LORD, the altar of burnt offerings with all its articles, and the table of the showbread with all its articles. [19]Moreover all the articles which King Ahaz in his reign had [a]cast aside in his transgression we have prepared and [1]sanctified; and there they *are,* before the altar of the LORD."

HEZEKIAH RESTORES TEMPLE WORSHIP

[20]Then King Hezekiah rose early, gathered the rulers of the city, and went up to the house of the LORD. [21]And they brought seven bulls, seven rams, seven lambs, and seven male goats for a [a]sin offering for the kingdom, for the sanctuary, and for Judah. Then he commanded the priests, the sons of Aaron, to offer *them* on the altar of the LORD. [22]So they killed the bulls, and the priests received the blood and [a]sprinkled *it* on the altar. Likewise they killed the rams and sprinkled the blood on the altar. They also killed the lambs and sprinkled the blood on the altar. [23]Then they brought out the male goats *for* the sin offering before the king and the assembly, and they laid their [a]hands on them. [24]And the priests killed them; and they presented their blood on the altar as a sin offering [a]to make an atonement for all Israel, for the king commanded *that* the burnt offering and the sin offering *be made* for all Israel.

[25a]And he stationed the Levites in the house of the LORD with cymbals, with stringed instruments, and with harps, [b]according to the commandment of David, of [c]Gad the king's seer, and of Nathan the prophet; [d]for thus *was* the commandment of the LORD by His prophets. [26]The Levites stood with the instruments [a]of David, and the priests with [b]the trumpets. [27]Then Hezekiah commanded *them* to offer the burnt offering on the altar. And when the burnt offering began, [a]the song of the LORD *also* began, with the trumpets and with the instruments of David king of Israel. [28]So all the assembly worshiped, the singers sang, and the trumpeters sounded; all *this* continued until the burnt offering was finished. [29]And when they had finished offering, [a]the king and all who were present with him bowed and worshiped. [30]Moreover King Hezekiah and the leaders commanded the Levites to sing praise to the LORD with the words of David and of Asaph the seer. So they sang praises with gladness, and they bowed their heads and worshiped.

[31]Then Hezekiah answered and said, "Now *that* you have consecrated yourselves to the LORD, come near, and bring sacrifices and [a]thank offerings into the house of the LORD." So the assembly brought in sacrifices and thank offerings, and as many as were of a [b]willing heart *brought* burnt offerings. [32]And the number of the burnt offerings which the assembly brought was seventy bulls, one hundred rams, *and* two hundred lambs; all these *were* for a burnt offering to the LORD.

29:19
[a]2 Chr. 28:24

29:21
[a]Lev. 4:3–14

29:22 [a]Lev. 8:14, 15, 19, 24; Heb. 9:21

29:23 [a]Lev. 4:15, 24; 8:14

29:24
[a]Lev. 14:20

29:25
[a]1 Chr. 16:4; 25:6
[b]1 Chr. 23:5; 25:1; 2 Chr. 8:14
[c]2 Sam. 24:11
[d]2 Chr. 30:12

29:26
[a]1 Chr. 23:5; Amos 6:5
[b]Num. 10:8, 10; 1 Chr. 15:24; 16:6; 2 Chr. 5:12

29:27
[a]2 Chr. 23:18

29:29
[a]2 Chr. 20:18

29:31 [a]Lev. 7:12
[b]Ex. 35:5, 22

29:17 [1]*consecrate*   29:19 [1]*consecrated*

³³The consecrated things *were* six hundred bulls and three thousand sheep. ³⁴But the priests were too few, so that they could not skin all the burnt offerings; therefore ᵃtheir brethren the Levites helped them until the work was ended and until the *other* priests had ¹sanctified themselves, ᵇfor the Levites were ᶜmore diligent in ᵈsanctifying themselves than the priests. ³⁵Also the burnt offerings *were* in abundance, with ᵃthe fat of the peace offerings and *with* ᵇthe drink offerings for *every* burnt offering.

So the service of the house of the LORD was set in order. ³⁶Then Hezekiah and all the people rejoiced that God had prepared the people, since the events took place so suddenly.

HEZEKIAH KEEPS THE PASSOVER

30 And Hezekiah sent to all Israel and Judah, and also wrote letters to Ephraim and Manasseh, that they should come to the house of the LORD at Jerusalem, to keep the Passover to the LORD God of Israel. ²For the king and his leaders and all the assembly in Jerusalem had agreed to keep the Passover in the second ᵃmonth. ³For they could not keep it ᵃat ¹the regular time, ᵇbecause a sufficient number of priests had not consecrated themselves, nor had the people gathered together at Jerusalem. ⁴And the matter pleased the king and all the assembly. ⁵So they ¹resolved to make a proclamation throughout all Israel, from Beersheba to Dan, that they should come to keep the Passover to the LORD God of Israel at Jerusalem, since they had not done *it* for a long *time* in the *prescribed* manner.

⁶Then the ᵃrunners went throughout all Israel and Judah with the letters from the king and his leaders, and spoke according to the command of the king: "Children of Israel, ᵇreturn to the LORD God of Abraham, Isaac, and Israel; then He will return to the remnant of you who have escaped from the hand of ᶜthe kings of ᵈAssyria. ⁷And do not be ᵃlike your fathers and your brethren, who trespassed against the LORD God of their fathers, so that He ᵇgave them up to ᶜdesolation, as you see. ⁸Now do not be ᵃstiff-necked,¹ as your fathers *were, but* yield yourselves to the LORD; and enter His sanctuary, which He has sanctified forever, and serve the LORD your God, ᵇthat the fierceness of His wrath may turn away from you. ⁹For if you return to the LORD, your brethren and your children *will be treated* with ᵃcompassion by those who lead them captive, so that they may come back to this land; for the LORD your God *is* ᵇgracious and merciful, and will not turn *His* face from you if you ᶜreturn to Him."

¹⁰So the runners passed from city to city through the country of Ephraim and Manasseh, as far as Zebulun; but ᵃthey laughed at them and mocked them. ¹¹Nevertheless ᵃsome from Asher, Manasseh, and Zebulun humbled themselves and came to Jerusalem. ¹²Also ᵃthe hand of God was on Judah to give them singleness of heart to obey the command of the king and the leaders, ᵇat the word of the LORD.

¹³Now many people, a very great assembly, gathered at Jerusalem to keep the Feast of ᵃUnleavened Bread in the second month. ¹⁴They arose and took away the ᵃaltars that *were*

Cross references

29:34
ᵃ2 Chr. 35:11
ᵇ2 Chr. 30:3
ᶜPs. 7:10
ᵈ2 Chr. 29:5

29:35
ᵃLev. 3:15, 16
ᵇNum. 15:5–10

30:2
ᵃNum. 9:10, 11;
2 Chr. 30:13, 15

30:3
ᵃEx. 12:6, 18
ᵇ2 Chr. 29:17, 34

30:6 ᵃEsth. 8:14;
Job 9:25;
Jer. 51:31
ᵇ[Jer. 4:1;
Joel 2:13]
ᶜ2 Kin. 15:19, 29
ᵈ2 Chr. 28:20

30:7
ᵃEzek. 20:18
ᵇIs. 1:9
ᶜ2 Chr. 29:8

30:8 ᵃEx. 32:9;
Deut. 10:16;
Acts 7:51
ᵇ2 Chr. 29:10

30:9 ᵃPs. 106:46
ᵇ[Ex. 34:6;
Mic. 7:18]
ᶜ[Is. 55:7]

30:10
ᵃ2 Chr. 36:16

30:11
ᵃ2 Chr. 11:16;
30:18, 21

30:12
ᵃ[2 Cor. 3:5;
Phil. 2:13;
Heb. 13:20, 21]
ᵇ2 Chr. 29:25

30:13 ᵃLev. 23:6;
Num. 9:11

30:14
ᵃ2 Chr. 28:24

29:34 ¹*consecrated* **30:3** ¹The first month, Lev. 23:5; lit. *that time*
30:5 ¹*established a decree to* **30:8** ¹Rebellious

in Jerusalem, and they took away all the incense altars and cast *them* into the Brook ᵇKidron. ¹⁵Then they slaughtered the Passover *lambs* on the fourteenth *day* of the second month. The priests and the Levites ¹were ᵃashamed, and ²sanctified themselves, and brought the burnt offerings to the house of the LORD. ¹⁶They stood in their ᵃplace ¹according to their custom, according to the Law of Moses the man of God; the priests sprinkled the blood *received* from the hand of the Levites. ¹⁷For *there were* many in the assembly who had not ¹sanctified themselves; ᵃtherefore the Levites had charge of the slaughter of the Passover *lambs* for everyone *who was* not clean, to sanctify *them* to the LORD. ¹⁸For a multitude of the people, ᵃmany from Ephraim, Manasseh, Issachar, and Zebulun, had not cleansed themselves, ᵇyet they ate the Passover contrary to what was written. But Hezekiah prayed for them, saying, "May the good LORD provide atonement for everyone ¹⁹*who* ᵃprepares his heart to seek God, the LORD God of his fathers, though *he is* not *cleansed* according to the purification of the sanctuary." ²⁰And the LORD listened to Hezekiah and healed the people.

²¹So the children of Israel who were present at Jerusalem kept ᵃthe Feast of Unleavened Bread seven days with great gladness; and the Levites and the priests praised the LORD day by day, *singing* to the LORD, accompanied by loud instruments. ²²And Hezekiah gave encouragement to all the Levites ᵃwho taught the good knowledge of the LORD; and they ate throughout the feast seven days, offering peace offerings and ᵇmaking confession to the LORD God of their fathers.

²³Then the whole assembly agreed to keep *the feast* ᵃanother seven days, and they kept it *another* seven days with gladness. ²⁴For Hezekiah king of Judah ᵃgave to the assembly a thousand bulls and seven thousand sheep, and the leaders gave to the assembly a thousand bulls and ten thousand sheep; and a great number of priests ᵇsanctified¹ themselves. ²⁵The whole assembly of Judah rejoiced, also the priests and Levites, all the assembly that came from Israel, the sojourners ᵃwho came from the land of Israel, and those who dwelt in Judah. ²⁶So there was great joy in Jerusalem, for since the time of ᵃSolomon the son of David, king of Israel, *there had* been nothing like this in Jerusalem. ²⁷Then the priests, the Levites, arose and ᵃblessed the people, and their voice was heard; and their prayer came *up* to ᵇHis holy dwelling place, to heaven.

THE REFORMS OF HEZEKIAH
(2 Kin. 18:4)

31 Now when all this was finished, all Israel who were present went out to the cities of Judah and ᵃbroke the *sacred* pillars in pieces, cut down the wooden images, and threw down the ¹high places and the altars—from all Judah, Benjamin, Ephraim, and Manasseh—until they had utterly destroyed them all. Then all the children of Israel returned to their own cities, every man to his possession.

²And Hezekiah appointed ᵃthe divisions of the priests and

Cross-references (margin)

30:14
ᵇ2 Chr. 29:16

30:15
ᵃ2 Chr. 29:34

30:16
ᵃ2 Chr. 35:10, 15

30:17
ᵃ2 Chr. 29:34

30:18
ᵃ2 Chr. 30:1,
11, 25
ᵇEx. 12:43–49;
[Num. 9:10]

30:19
ᵃ2 Chr. 19:3

30:21 ᵃEx. 12:15;
13:6; 1 Kin. 8:65

30:22
ᵃ[Deut. 33:10];
2 Chr. 17:9; 35:3
ᵇEzra 10:11

30:23
ᵃ1 Kin. 8:65;
2 Chr. 35:17, 18

30:24
ᵃ2 Chr. 35:7, 8
ᵇ2 Chr. 29:34

30:25
ᵃ2 Chr. 30:11, 18

30:26
ᵃ2 Chr. 7:8–10

30:27
ᵃNum. 6:23
ᵇDeut. 26:15;
Ps. 68:5

31:1 ᵃ2 Kin. 18:4

31:2 ᵃ1 Chr. 23:6;
24:1

30:15 ¹*humbled themselves*   ²*set themselves apart*   30:16 ¹Or *in their proper order*   30:17 ¹*consecrated*   30:24 ¹*consecrated*   31:1 ¹Places for pagan worship

the Levites according to their divisions, each man according to his service, the priests and Levites [b]for burnt offerings and peace offerings, to serve, to give thanks, and to praise in the gates of the [1]camp of the LORD. [3]The king also *appointed* a [1]portion of his [a]possessions[2] for the burnt offerings: for the morning and evening burnt offerings, the burnt offerings for the Sabbaths and the New Moons and the set feasts, as *it is* written in the [b]Law of the LORD.

[4]Moreover he commanded the people who dwelt in Jerusalem to contribute [a]support[1] for the priests and the Levites, that they might devote themselves to [b]the Law of the LORD.

[5]As soon as the commandment was circulated, the children of Israel brought in abundance [a]the firstfruits of grain and wine, oil and honey, and of all the produce of the field; and they brought in abundantly the [b]tithe of everything. [6]And the children of Israel and Judah, who dwelt in the cities of Judah, brought the tithe of oxen and sheep; also the [a]tithe of holy things which were consecrated to the LORD their God they laid in heaps.

[7]In the third month they began laying them in heaps, and they finished in the seventh month. [8]And when Hezekiah and the leaders came and saw the heaps, they blessed the LORD and His people Israel. [9]Then Hezekiah questioned the priests and the Levites concerning the heaps. [10]And Azariah the chief priest, from the [a]house of Zadok, answered him and said, [b]"Since *the people* began to bring the offerings into the house of the LORD, we have had enough to eat and have plenty left, for the LORD has blessed His people; and what is left *is* this great [c]abundance."

[11]Now Hezekiah commanded *them* to prepare [a]rooms[1] in the house of the LORD, and they prepared them. [12]Then they faithfully brought in the offerings, the tithes, and the dedicated things; [a]Cononiah the Levite had charge of them, and Shimei his brother *was* the next. [13]Jehiel, Azaziah, Nahath, Asahel, Jerimoth, Jozabad, Eliel, Ismachiah, Mahath, and Benaiah *were* overseers under the hand of Cononiah and Shimei his brother, at the commandment of Hezekiah the king and Azariah the [a]ruler of the house of God. [14]Kore the son of Imnah the Levite, the keeper of the East Gate, *was* over the [a]freewill offerings to God, to distribute the offerings of the LORD and the most holy things. [15]And under him *were* [a]Eden, Miniamin, Jeshua, Shemaiah, Amariah, and Shecaniah, *his* faithful assistants in [b]the cities of the priests, to distribute [c]allotments to their brethren by divisions, to the great as well as the small.

[16]Besides those males from three years old and up who were written in the genealogy, they distributed to everyone who entered the house of the LORD his daily portion for the work of his service, by his division, [17]and to the priests who were written in the genealogy according to their father's house, and to the Levites [a]from twenty years old and up according to their work, by their divisions, [18]and to all who were written in the genealogy—their little ones and their wives, their sons and daughters, the whole company of them—for in their faithfulness they [1]sanctified themselves in holiness.

31:2 [b]1 Chr. 23:30, 31
31:3 [a]2 Chr. 35:7 [b]Num. 28:1—29:40
31:4 [a]Num. 18:8; 2 Kin. 12:16; Neh. 13:10; Ezek. 44:29 [b]Mal. 2:7
31:5 [a]Ex. 22:29; Neh. 13:12 [b][Lev. 27:30]; Deut. 14:28; 26:12, 13
31:6 [a][Lev. 27:30]; Deut. 14:28
31:10 [a]1 Chr. 6:8, 9 [b][Mal. 3:10] [c]Ex. 36:5
31:11 [a]1 Kin. 6:5–8
31:12 [a]2 Chr. 35:9; Neh. 13:13
31:13 [a]1 Chr. 9:11; Jer. 20:1
31:14 [a]Deut. 23:23; 2 Chr. 35:8
31:15 [a]2 Chr. 29:12 [b]Josh. 21:1–3, 9 [c]1 Chr. 9:26
31:17 [a]1 Chr. 23:24, 27

31:2 [1]Temple 31:3 [1]share [2]property 31:4 [1]the portion due
31:11 [1]storerooms 31:18 [1]consecrated

¹⁹Also for the sons of Aaron the priests, *who were* in ^athe fields of the common-lands of their cities, in every single city, *there were* men who were ^bdesignated by name to distribute portions to all the males among the priests and to all who were listed by genealogies among the Levites.

²⁰Thus Hezekiah did throughout all Judah, and he ^adid what *was* good and right and true before the LORD his God. ²¹And in every work that he began in the service of the house of God, in the law and in the commandment, to seek his God, he did *it* with all his heart. So he ^aprospered.

SENNACHERIB BOASTS AGAINST THE LORD
(2 Kin. 18:13—19:34; Is. 36:1–22)

32 After ^athese deeds of faithfulness, Sennacherib king of Assyria came and entered Judah; he encamped against the fortified cities, thinking to win them over to himself. ²And when Hezekiah saw that Sennacherib had come, and that his purpose was to make war against Jerusalem, ³he consulted with his leaders and ¹commanders to stop the water from the springs which *were* outside the city; and they helped him. ⁴Thus many people gathered together who stopped all the ^asprings and the brook that ran through the land, saying, "Why should the ¹kings of Assyria come and find much water?" ⁵And ^ahe strengthened himself, ^bbuilt up all the wall that was broken, raised *it* up to the towers, and *built* another wall outside; also he repaired ¹the ^cMillo *in* the City of David, and made ²weapons and shields in abundance. ⁶Then he set military captains over the people, gathered them together to him in the open square of the city gate, and ^agave them encouragement, saying, ^{7a}"Be strong and courageous; ^bdo not be afraid nor dismayed before the king of Assyria, nor before all the multitude that *is* with him; for ^c*there are* more with us than with him. ⁸With him *is* an ^aarm of flesh; but ^bwith us *is* the LORD our God, to help us and to fight our battles." And the people were strengthened by the words of Hezekiah king of Judah.

^{9a}After this Sennacherib king of Assyria sent his servants to Jerusalem (but he and all the forces with him *laid siege* against Lachish), to Hezekiah king of Judah, and to all Judah who *were* in Jerusalem, saying, ^{10a}"Thus says Sennacherib king of Assyria: 'In what do you trust, that you remain under siege in Jerusalem? ¹¹Does not Hezekiah persuade you to give yourselves over to die by famine and by thirst, saying, ^a"The LORD our God will deliver us from the hand of the king of Assyria"? ^{12a}Has not the same Hezekiah taken away His high places and His altars, and commanded Judah and Jerusalem, saying, "You shall worship before one altar and burn incense on ^bit"? ¹³Do you not know what I and my fathers have done to all the peoples of *other* lands? ^aWere the gods of the nations of those lands in any way able to deliver their lands out of my hand? ¹⁴Who *was there* among all the gods of those nations that my fathers utterly destroyed that could deliver his people from my hand, that your God should be able to deliver you from my ^ahand? ¹⁵Now therefore, ^ado not let Hezekiah deceive

31:19
^aLev. 25:34;
Num. 35:1–4
^b2 Chr. 31:12–15

31:20
^a2 Kin. 20:3;
22:2

31:21
^a2 Chr. 26:5;
32:30; Ps. 1:3

32:1
^a2 Kin. 18:13—
19:37; Is. 36:1—
37:38

32:4
^a2 Kin. 20:20

32:5
^aIs. 22:9, 10
^b2 Kin. 25:4;
2 Chr. 25:23
^c2 Sam. 5:9;
1 Kin. 9:15,
24; 11:27;
2 Kin. 12:20;
1 Chr. 11:8

32:6
^a2 Chr. 30:22;
Is. 40:2

32:7
^a[Deut. 31:6]
^b2 Chr. 20:15
^c2 Cor. 6:16;
[Rom. 8:31]

32:8 ^a[Jer. 17:5;
1 John 4:4]
^bEx. 14:13;
[1 Sam. 17:45–
47]; 2 Chr. 13:12;
20:17;
[Rom. 8:31]

32:9
^a2 Kin. 18:17

32:10
^a2 Kin. 18:19

32:11
^a2 Kin. 18:30

32:12
^a2 Kin. 18:22
^b2 Chr. 31:1, 2

32:13
^a2 Kin. 18:33–35

32:14
^a[Is. 10:5–12]

32:15
^a2 Kin. 18:29

32:3 ¹Lit. *mighty men*   **32:4** ¹So with MT, Vg.; Arab., LXX, Syr. *king*
32:5 ¹Lit. *The Landfill*   ²*javelins*

you or persuade you like this, and do not believe him; for no god of any nation or kingdom was able to deliver his people from my hand or the hand of my fathers. How much less will your God deliver you from my hand?'"

16Furthermore, his servants spoke against the LORD God and against His servant Hezekiah.

17He also wrote letters to revile the LORD God of Israel, and to speak against Him, saying, a"As the gods of the nations of *other* lands have not delivered their people from my hand, so the God of Hezekiah will not deliver His people from my bhand." 18aThen they called out with a loud voice in 1Hebrew to the people of Jerusalem who *were* on the wall, to frighten them and trouble them, that they might take the city. 19And they spoke against the God of Jerusalem, as against the gods of the people of the earth—athe work of men's hands.

SENNACHERIB'S DEFEAT AND DEATH
(2 Kin. 19:35–37)

20aNow because of this King Hezekiah and bthe prophet Isaiah, the son of Amoz, prayed and cried out to heaven. 21aThen the LORD sent an angel who cut down every mighty man of valor, leader, and captain in the camp of the king of Assyria. So he returned bshamefaced to his own land. And when he had gone into the temple of his god, some of his own offspring struck him down with the sword there.

22Thus the LORD saved Hezekiah and the inhabitants of Jerusalem from the hand of Sennacherib the king of Assyria, and from the hand of all *others*, and 1guided them on every side. 23And many brought gifts to the LORD at Jerusalem, and apresents1 to Hezekiah king of Judah, so that he was bexalted in the sight of all nations thereafter.

HEZEKIAH HUMBLES HIMSELF
(2 Kin. 20:1–11; Is. 38:1–8)

24aIn those days Hezekiah was sick and near death, and he prayed to the LORD; and He spoke to him and gave him a sign. 25But Hezekiah adid not repay according to the favor *shown* him, for bhis heart was lifted up; ctherefore wrath was looming over him and over Judah and Jerusalem. 26aThen Hezekiah humbled himself for the pride of his heart, he and the inhabitants of Jerusalem, so that the wrath of the LORD did not come upon them bin the days of Hezekiah.

HEZEKIAH'S WEALTH AND HONOR
(2 Kin. 20:12–21; Is. 39:1–8)

27Hezekiah had very great riches and honor. And he made himself treasuries for silver, for gold, for precious stones, for spices, for shields, and for all kinds of desirable items; 28storehouses for the harvest of grain, wine, and oil; and stalls for all kinds of livestock, and 1folds for flocks. 29Moreover he provided cities for himself, and possessions of flocks and herds in abundance; for aGod had given him very much property. 30aThis same Hezekiah also stopped the

32:17
a2 Kin. 19:9;
[1 Cor. 8:5, 6]
b2 Kin. 19:12;
Dan. 3:15

32:18
a2 Kin. 18:28;
Ps. 59:6

32:19
a2 Kin. 19:18;
[Ps. 96:5;
115:4–8]

32:20
a2 Kin. 19:15
b2 Kin. 19:2

32:21
a2 Kin. 19:35;
Is. 10:12–19;
Zech. 14:3
bPs. 44:7

32:23
a2 Sam. 8:10;
2 Chr. 17:5;
26:8; Ps. 45:12
b2 Chr. 1:1

32:24
a2 Kin. 20:1–11;
Is. 38:1–8

32:25 aPs. 116:12
b2 Chr. 26:16;
[Hab. 2:4]
c2 Chr. 24:18

32:26
aJer. 26:18, 19
b2 Kin. 20:19

32:29
a1 Chr. 29:12

32:30
aIs. 22:9–11

32:18 1Lit. *Judean*   32:22 1LXX *gave them rest*; Vg. *gave them treasures*
32:23 1Lit. *precious things*   32:28 1So with LXX, Vg.; Arab., Syr. omit *folds for flocks*; MT *flocks for sheepfolds*

water outlet of Upper Gihon, and ¹brought the water by tunnel to the west side of the City of David. Hezekiah ᵇprospered in all his works.

³¹However, *regarding* the ambassadors of the princes of Babylon, whom they ᵃsent to him to inquire about the wonder that was *done* in the land, God withdrew from him, in order to ᵇtest him, that He might know all *that was* in his heart.

DEATH OF HEZEKIAH

³²Now the rest of the acts of Hezekiah, and his goodness, indeed they *are* written in ᵃthe vision of Isaiah the prophet, the son of Amoz, *and* in the ᵇbook of the kings of Judah and Israel. ³³ᵃSo Hezekiah ¹rested with his fathers, and they buried him in the upper tombs of the sons of David; and all Judah and the inhabitants of Jerusalem ᵇhonored him at his death. Then Manasseh his son reigned in his place.

MANASSEH REIGNS IN JUDAH

(2 Kin. 21:1–9)

33 Manasseh ᵃ*was* twelve years old when he became king, and he reigned fifty-five years in Jerusalem. ²But he did evil in the sight of the LORD, according to the ᵃabominations of the nations whom the LORD had cast out before the children of Israel. ³For he rebuilt the ¹high places which Hezekiah his father had ᵃbroken down; he raised up altars for the Baals, and ᵇmade wooden images; and he worshiped ᶜall ²the host of heaven and served them. ⁴He also built altars in the house of the LORD, of which the LORD had said, ᵃ"In Jerusalem shall My name be forever." ⁵And he built altars for all the host of heaven ᵃin the two courts of the house of the LORD. ⁶ᵃAlso he caused his sons to pass through the fire in the Valley of the Son of Hinnom; he practiced ᵇsoothsaying, used witchcraft and sorcery, and ᶜconsulted mediums and spiritists. He did much evil in the sight of the LORD, to provoke Him to anger. ⁷ᵃHe even set a carved image, the idol which he had made, in the ¹house of God, of which God had said to David and to Solomon his son, ᵇ"In this house and in Jerusalem, which I have chosen out of all the tribes of Israel, I will put My name forever; ⁸ᵃand I will not again remove the foot of Israel from the land which I have appointed for your fathers—only if they are careful to do all that I have commanded them, according to the whole law and the statutes and the ordinances by the hand of Moses." ⁹So Manasseh seduced Judah and the inhabitants of Jerusalem to do more evil than the nations whom the LORD had destroyed before the children of Israel.

MANASSEH RESTORED AFTER REPENTANCE

¹⁰And the LORD spoke to Manasseh and his people, but they would not ¹listen. ¹¹ᵃTherefore the LORD brought upon them the captains of the army of the king of Assyria, who took Manasseh with ¹hooks, ᵇbound him with ²bronze *fetters,* and carried him off to Babylon. ¹²Now when he was in affliction, he implored the LORD his God, and ᵃhumbled himself greatly

Cross-references

32:30
ᵇ2 Chr. 31:21

32:31
ᵃ2 Kin. 20:12;
Is. 39:1
ᵇ[Deut. 8:2, 16]

32:32
ᵃIs. 36—39
ᵇ2 Kin. 18—20

32:33
ᵃ1 Kin. 1:21;
2 Kin. 20:21
ᵇPs. 112:6;
Prov. 10:7

33:1
ᵃ2 Kin. 21:1–9

33:2
ᵃ[Deut. 18:9–12];
2 Chr. 28:3;
[Jer. 15:4]

33:3
ᵃ2 Kin. 18:4;
2 Chr. 30:14; 31:1
ᵇDeut. 16:21;
2 Kin. 23:5, 6
ᶜDeut. 17:3

33:4
ᵃDeut. 12:11;
1 Kin. 8:29; 9:3;
2 Chr. 6:6; 7:16

33:5 ᵃ2 Chr. 4:9

33:6
ᵃ[Lev. 18:21];
Deut. 18:10;
2 Kin. 23:10;
2 Chr. 28:3;
Ezek. 23:37, 39
ᵇDeut. 18:11;
2 Kin. 17:17
ᶜ[Lev. 19:31;
20:27];
2 Kin. 21:6

33:7 ᵃ2 Kin. 21:7;
2 Chr. 25:14
ᵇPs. 132:14

33:8
ᵃ2 Sam. 7:10

33:11
ᵃDeut. 28:36
ᵇ2 Chr. 36:6;
Job 36:8;
Ps. 107:10, 11

33:12
ᵃ2 Chr. 7:14;
32:26;
[1 Pet. 5:6]

32:30 ¹Lit. *brought it straight to* (cf. 2 Kin. 20:20)   **32:33** ¹Died and joined his ancestors   **33:3** ¹Places for pagan worship   ²The gods of the Assyrians   **33:7** ¹Temple   **33:10** ¹obey   **33:11** ¹Nose hooks, 2 Kin. 19:28 ²*chains*

before the God of his fathers, [13]and prayed to Him; and He [a]received his entreaty, heard his supplication, and brought him back to Jerusalem into his kingdom. Then Manasseh [b]knew that the LORD *was* God.

[14]After this he built a wall outside the City of David on the west side of [a]Gihon, in the valley, as far as the entrance of the Fish Gate; and *it* [b]enclosed Ophel, and he raised it to a very great height. Then he put military captains in all the fortified cities of Judah. [15]He took away [a]the foreign gods and the idol from the house of the LORD, and all the altars that he had built in the mount of the house of the LORD and in Jerusalem; and he cast *them* out of the city. [16]He also repaired the altar of the LORD, sacrificed peace offerings and [a]thank offerings on it, and commanded Judah to serve the LORD God of Israel. [17a]Nevertheless the people still sacrificed on the [1]high places, *but* only to the LORD their God.

DEATH OF MANASSEH
(2 Kin. 21:17, 18)

[18]Now the rest of the acts of Manasseh, his prayer to his God, and the words of [a]the seers who spoke to him in the name of the LORD God of Israel, indeed they *are written* in the [1]book of the kings of Israel. [19]Also his prayer and *how God* received his entreaty, and all his sin and trespass, and the sites where he built [1]high places and set up wooden images and carved images, before he was humbled, indeed they *are* written among the sayings of [2]Hozai. [20a]So Manasseh rested with his fathers, and they buried him in his own house. Then his son Amon reigned in his place.

AMON'S REIGN AND DEATH
(2 Kin. 21:19–26)

[21a]Amon *was* twenty-two years old when he became king, and he reigned two years in Jerusalem. [22]But he did evil in the sight of the LORD, as his father Manasseh had done; for Amon sacrificed to all the carved images which his father Manasseh had made, and served them. [23]And he did not humble himself before the LORD, [a]as his father Manasseh had humbled himself; but Amon trespassed more and more.

[24a]Then his servants conspired against him, and [b]killed him in his own house. [25]But the people of the land executed all those who had conspired against King Amon. Then the people of the land made his son Josiah king in his place.

JOSIAH REIGNS IN JUDAH
(2 Kin. 22:1, 2)

34 Josiah [a]*was* eight years old when he became king, and he reigned thirty-one years in Jerusalem. [2]And he did *what was* right in the sight of the LORD, and walked in the ways of his father David; *he* did *not* turn aside to the right hand or to the left.

[3]For in the eighth year of his reign, while he was still [a]young, he began to [b]seek the God of his father David; and in the twelfth year he began [c]to purge Judah and Jerusalem

33:13
[a]1 Chr. 5:20;
Ezra 8:23
[b]1 Kin. 20:13;
Ps. 9:16;
Dan. 4:25

33:14 [a]1 Kin. 1:33
[b]2 Chr. 27:3

33:15
[a]2 Chr. 33:3, 5, 7

33:16 [a]Lev. 7:12

33:17
[a]2 Chr. 32:12

33:18
[a]1 Sam. 9:9

33:20
[a]1 Kin. 1:21;
2 Kin. 21:18

33:21
[a]2 Kin. 21:19–24;
1 Chr. 3:14

33:23
[a]2 Chr. 33:12, 19

33:24
[a]2 Kin. 21:23, 24;
2 Chr. 24:25
[b]2 Chr. 25:27

34:1 [a]2 Kin. 22:1,
2; Jer. 1:2; 3:6

34:3 [a]Eccl. 12:1
[b]2 Chr. 15:2;
[Prov. 8:17]
[c]1 Kin. 13:2

33:17 [1]Places for pagan worship   33:18 [1]Lit. *words*   33:19 [1]Places for pagan worship   [2]LXX *the seers*

dof the ¹high places, the wooden images, the carved images, and the molded images. ⁴ªThey broke down the altars of the Baals in his presence, and the incense altars which *were* above them he cut down; and the wooden images, the carved images, and the molded images he broke in pieces, and made dust of them ᵇand scattered *it* on the graves of those who had sacrificed to them. ⁵He also ªburned the bones of the priests on their ᵇaltars, and cleansed Judah and Jerusalem. ⁶And *so he did* in the cities of Manasseh, Ephraim, and Simeon, as far as Naphtali and all around, with ¹axes. ⁷When he had broken down the altars and the wooden images, had ªbeaten the carved images into powder, and cut down all the incense altars throughout all the land of Israel, he returned to Jerusalem.

HILKIAH FINDS THE BOOK OF THE LAW
(2 Kin. 22:3–20)

⁸ªIn the eighteenth year of his reign, when he had purged the land and the ¹temple, he sent ᵇShaphan the son of Azaliah, Maaseiah the ᶜgovernor of the city, and Joah the son of Joahaz the recorder, to repair the house of the LORD his God. ⁹When they came to Hilkiah the high priest, they delivered ªthe money that was brought into the house of God, which the Levites who kept the doors had gathered from the hand of Manasseh and Ephraim, from all the ᵇremnant of Israel, from all Judah and Benjamin, and *which* they had brought back to Jerusalem. ¹⁰Then they put *it* in the hand of the foremen who had the oversight of the house of the LORD; and they gave it to the workmen who worked in the house of the LORD, to repair and restore the house. ¹¹They gave *it* to the craftsmen and builders to buy hewn stone and timber for beams, and to floor the houses which the kings of Judah had destroyed. ¹²And the men did the work faithfully. Their overseers *were* Jahath and Obadiah the Levites, of the sons of Merari, and Zechariah and Meshullam, of the sons of the Kohathites, to supervise. *Others of* the Levites, all of whom were skillful with instruments of music, ¹³*were* ªover the burden bearers and *were* overseers of all who did work in any kind of service. ᵇAnd *some* of the Levites *were* scribes, officers, and gatekeepers.

¹⁴Now when they brought out the money that was brought into the house of the LORD, Hilkiah the priest ªfound the Book of the Law of the LORD *given* by Moses. ¹⁵Then Hilkiah answered and said to Shaphan the scribe, "I have found the Book of the Law in the house of the LORD." And Hilkiah gave the ªbook to Shaphan. ¹⁶So Shaphan carried the book to the king, bringing the king word, saying, "All that was committed to your servants they are doing. ¹⁷And they have ¹gathered the money that was found in the house of the LORD, and have delivered it into the hand of the overseers and the workmen." ¹⁸Then Shaphan the scribe told the king, saying, "Hilkiah the priest has given me a book." And Shaphan read it before the king.

¹⁹Thus it happened, when the king heard the words of the Law, that he tore his clothes. ²⁰Then the king commanded

Cross-references (margin)

34:3
d2 Chr. 33:17–19, 22

34:4
aLev. 26:30;
2 Kin. 23:4
b2 Kin. 23:6

34:5 a1 Kin. 13:2
b2 Kin. 23:20

34:7 aDeut. 9:21

34:8
a2 Kin. 22:3–20
b2 Kin. 25:22
c2 Chr. 18:25

34:9 a2 Kin. 12:4
b2 Chr. 30:6

34:13
a2 Chr. 8:10
b1 Chr. 23:4, 5

34:14
a2 Kin. 22:8

34:15
aDeut. 31:24, 26

34:3 ¹Places for pagan worship   34:6 ¹Lit. *swords*   34:8 ¹Lit. *house*
34:17 ¹Lit. *poured out*

Hilkiah, ᵃAhikam the son of Shaphan, ¹Abdon the son of Micah, Shaphan the scribe, and Asaiah a servant of the king, saying, ²¹"Go, inquire of the LORD for me, and for those who are left in Israel and Judah, concerning the words of the book that is found; for great *is* the wrath of the LORD that is poured out on us, because our fathers have not ᵃkept the word of the LORD, to do according to all that is written in this book."

²²So Hilkiah and those the king *had appointed* went to Huldah the prophetess, the wife of Shallum the son of ¹Tokhath, the son of ²Hasrah, keeper of the wardrobe. (She dwelt in Jerusalem in the Second Quarter.) And they spoke to her to that *effect*.

²³Then she answered them, "Thus says the LORD God of Israel, 'Tell the man who sent you to Me, ²⁴"Thus says the LORD: 'Behold, I will ᵃbring calamity on this place and on its inhabitants, all the curses that are written in the ᵇbook which they have read before the king of Judah, ²⁵because they have forsaken Me and burned incense to other gods, that they might provoke Me to anger with all the works of their hands. Therefore My wrath will be poured out on this place, and not be quenched.' " ' ²⁶But as for the king of Judah, who sent you to inquire of the LORD, in this manner you shall speak to him, 'Thus says the LORD God of Israel: "*Concerning* the words which you have heard— ²⁷because your heart was tender, and you humbled yourself before God when you heard His words against this place and against its inhabitants, and you humbled yourself before Me, and you tore your clothes and wept before Me, I also have heard *you*," says the ᵃLORD. ²⁸"Surely I will gather you to your fathers, and you shall be gathered to your grave in peace; and your eyes shall not see all the calamity which I will bring on this place and its inhabitants." ' " So they brought back word to the king.

JOSIAH RESTORES TRUE WORSHIP
(2 Kin. 23:1–20)

²⁹ᵃThen the king sent and gathered all the elders of Judah and Jerusalem. ³⁰The king went up to the house of the LORD, with all the men of Judah and the inhabitants of Jerusalem— the priests and the Levites, and all the people, great and small. And he ᵃread in their hearing all the words of the Book of the Covenant which had been found in the house of the LORD. ³¹Then the king ᵃstood in ᵇhis place and made a ᶜcovenant before the LORD, to follow the LORD, and to keep His commandments and His testimonies and His statutes with all his heart and all his soul, to perform the words of the covenant that were written in this book. ³²And he made all who were present in Jerusalem and Benjamin take a stand. So the inhabitants of Jerusalem did according to the covenant of God, the God of their fathers. ³³Thus Josiah removed all the ᵃabominations from all the country that *belonged* to the children of Israel, and made all who were present in Israel ¹diligently serve the LORD their God. ᵇAll his days they did not depart from following the LORD God of their fathers.

34:20
ᵃJer. 26:24

34:21
ᵃ2 Kin. 17:15–19

34:24
ᵃ2 Chr. 36:14–20
ᵇDeut. 28:15–68

34:27
ᵃ2 Kin. 22:19;
2 Chr. 12:7; 30:6;
33:12, 13

34:29
ᵃ2 Kin. 23:1–3

34:30
ᵃNeh. 8:1–3

34:31
ᵃ2 Chr. 6:13
ᵇ2 Kin. 11:14;
23:3;
2 Chr. 30:16
ᶜ2 Chr. 23:16;
29:10

34:33
ᵃ1 Kin. 11:5;
2 Chr. 33:2
ᵇJer. 3:10

34:20 ¹*Achbor the son of Michaiah*, 2 Kin. 22:12   34:22 ¹*Tikvah*, 2 Kin. 22:14
²*Harhas*, 2 Kin. 22:14   34:33 ¹Lit. *serve to serve*

JOSIAH KEEPS THE PASSOVER
(2 Kin. 23:21–23)

35 Now [a]Josiah kept a Passover to the LORD in Jerusalem, and they slaughtered the Passover *lambs* on the [b]fourteenth *day* of the first month. [2]And he set the priests in their [a]duties and [b]encouraged them for the service of the house of the LORD. [3]Then he said to the Levites [a]who taught all Israel, who were holy to the LORD: [b]"Put the holy ark [c]in the house which Solomon the son of David, king of Israel, built. [d]*It shall* no longer *be* a burden on *your* shoulders. Now serve the LORD your God and His people Israel. [4]Prepare *yourselves* [a]according to your fathers' [1]houses, according to your divisions, following the [b]written instruction of David king of Israel and the [c]written instruction of Solomon his son. [5]And [a]stand in the holy *place* according to the divisions of the fathers' houses of your brethren the *lay* people, and *according to* the division of the father's house of the Levites. [6]So slaughter the Passover *offerings,* [a]consecrate yourselves, and prepare *them* for your brethren, that *they* may do according to the word of the LORD by the hand of Moses."

[7]Then Josiah [a]gave the *lay* people lambs and young goats from the flock, all for Passover *offerings* for all who were present, to the number of thirty thousand, as well as three thousand cattle; these *were* from the king's [b]possessions. [8]And his [a]leaders gave willingly to the people, to the priests, and to the Levites. Hilkiah, Zechariah, and Jehiel, rulers of the house of God, gave to the priests for the Passover *offerings* two thousand six hundred *from the flock,* and three hundred cattle. [9]Also [a]Conaniah, his brothers Shemaiah and Nethanel, and Hashabiah and Jeiel and Jozabad, chief of the Levites, gave to the Levites for Passover *offerings* five thousand *from the flock* and five hundred cattle.

[10]So the service was prepared, and the priests [a]stood in their places, and the [b]Levites in their divisions, according to the king's command. [11]And they slaughtered the Passover *offerings;* and the priests [a]sprinkled *the blood* with their hands, while the Levites [b]skinned *the animals.* [12]Then they removed the burnt offerings that *they* might give them to the divisions of the fathers' houses of the *lay* people, to offer to the LORD, as *it is* written [a]in the Book of Moses. And so *they did* with the cattle. [13]Also they [a]roasted the Passover *offerings* with fire according to the ordinance; but the *other* holy *offerings* they [b]boiled in pots, in caldrons, and in pans, and divided *them* quickly among all the *lay* people. [14]Then afterward they prepared portions for themselves and for the priests, because the priests, the sons of Aaron, *were busy* in offering burnt offerings and fat until night; therefore the Levites prepared portions for themselves and for the priests, the sons of Aaron. [15]And the singers, the sons of Asaph, *were* in their places, according to the [a]command of David, Asaph, Heman, and Jeduthun the king's seer. Also the gatekeepers [b]were at each gate; they did not have to leave their position, because their brethren the Levites prepared portions for them.

[16]So all the service of the LORD was prepared the same day, to keep the Passover and to offer burnt offerings on the altar

---

35:1
[a]2 Kin. 23:21, 22
[b]Ex. 12:6;
Num. 9:3;
Ezra 6:19

35:2
[a]2 Chr. 23:18;
Ezra 6:18
[b]2 Chr. 29:5–15

35:3
[a]Deut. 33:10;
2 Chr. 17:8, 9;
Neh. 8:7
[b]2 Chr. 34:14
[c]Ex. 40:21;
2 Chr. 5:7
[d]1 Chr. 23:26

35:4
[a]1 Chr. 9:10–13
[b]1 Chr. 23—26
[c]2 Chr. 8:14

35:5 [a]Ps. 134:1

35:6
[a]2 Chr. 29:5, 15

35:7
[a]2 Chr. 30:24
[b]2 Chr. 31:3

35:8 [a]Num. 7:2

35:9
[a]2 Chr. 31:12

35:10
[a]Ezra 6:18;
Heb. 9:6
[b]2 Chr. 5:12; 7:6;
8:14, 15; 13:10;
29:25–34

35:11 [a]Ex. 12:22;
2 Chr. 29:22
[b]2 Chr. 29:34

35:12 [a]Lev. 3:3;
Ezra 6:18

35:13
[a]Ex. 12:8, 9;
Deut. 16:7
[b]1 Sam. 2:13–15

35:15
[a]1 Chr. 25:1–6
[b]1 Chr. 9:17, 18

35:4 [1]households

of the LORD, according to the command of King Josiah. ¹⁷And the children of Israel who were present kept the Passover at that time, and the Feast of ªUnleavened Bread for seven days. ¹⁸ªThere had been no Passover kept in Israel like that since the days of Samuel the prophet; and none of the kings of Israel had kept such a Passover as Josiah kept, with the priests and the Levites, all Judah and Israel who were present, and the inhabitants of Jerusalem. ¹⁹In the eighteenth year of the reign of Josiah this Passover was kept.

JOSIAH DIES IN BATTLE
(2 Kin. 23:28–30)

²⁰ªAfter all this, when Josiah had prepared the temple, Necho king of Egypt came up to fight against ᵇCarchemish by the Euphrates; and Josiah went out against him. ²¹But he sent messengers to him, saying, "What have I to do with you, king of Judah? *I have* not *come* against you this day, but against the house with which I have war; for God commanded me to make haste. Refrain *from meddling with* God, who *is* with me, lest He destroy you." ²²Nevertheless Josiah would not turn his face from him, but ªdisguised himself so that he might fight with him, and did not heed the words of Necho from the mouth of God. So he came to fight in the Valley of Megiddo.

²³And the archers shot King Josiah; and the king said to his servants, "Take me away, for I am severely wounded." ²⁴ªHis servants therefore took him out of that chariot and put him in the second chariot that he had, and they brought him to Jerusalem. So he died, and was buried in *one of* the tombs of his fathers. And ᵇall Judah and Jerusalem mourned for Josiah.

²⁵Jeremiah also ªlamented for ᵇJosiah. And to this day ᶜall the singing men and the singing women speak of Josiah in their lamentations. ᵈThey made it a custom in Israel; and indeed they *are* written in the Laments.

²⁶Now the rest of the acts of Josiah and his goodness, according to *what was* written in the Law of the LORD, ²⁷and his deeds from first to last, indeed they *are* written in the book of the kings of Israel and Judah.

THE REIGN AND CAPTIVITY OF JEHOAHAZ
(2 Kin. 23:31–33)

36 Then ªthe people of the land took Jehoahaz the son of Josiah, and made him king in his father's place in Jerusalem. ²Jehoahaz *was* twenty-three years old when he became king, and he reigned three months in Jerusalem. ³Now the king of Egypt deposed him at Jerusalem; and he imposed on the land a tribute of one hundred talents of silver and a talent of gold. ⁴Then the king of Egypt made ¹*Jehoahaz's* brother Eliakim king over Judah and Jerusalem, and changed his name to Jehoiakim. And Necho took ²Jehoahaz his brother and carried him off to Egypt.

THE REIGN AND CAPTIVITY OF JEHOIAKIM
(2 Kin. 23:34—24:7)

⁵ªJehoiakim *was* twenty-five years old when he became king, and he reigned eleven years in Jerusalem. And he did

35:17 ªEx. 12:15; 13:6; 2 Chr. 30:21

35:18 ª2 Kin. 23:22, 23

35:20 ª2 Kin. 23:29 ᵇIs. 10:9; Jer. 46:2

35:22 ª1 Kin. 22:30; 2 Chr. 18:29

35:24 ª2 Kin. 23:30 ᵇ1 Kin. 14:18; Zech. 12:11

35:25 ªLam. 4:20 ᵇJer. 22:10, 11 ᶜMatt. 9:23 ᵈJer. 22:20

36:1 ª2 Kin. 23:30–34

36:5 ª2 Kin. 23:36, 37; 1 Chr. 3:15

36:2 ¹MT *Joahaz*   36:4 ¹Lit. *his*   ²MT *Joahaz*

^bevil in the sight of the LORD his God. ^{6a}Nebuchadnezzar king of Babylon came up against him, and bound him in ¹bronze *fetters* to ^bcarry him off to Babylon. ^{7a}Nebuchadnezzar also carried off *some* of the articles from the house of the LORD to Babylon, and put them in his temple at Babylon. ⁸Now the rest of the acts of Jehoiakim, the abominations which he did, and what was found against him, indeed they *are* written in the book of the kings of Israel and Judah. Then ¹Jehoiachin his son reigned in his place.

THE REIGN AND CAPTIVITY OF JEHOIACHIN
(2 Kin. 24:8–17)

^{9a}Jehoiachin *was* ¹eight years old when he became king, and he reigned in Jerusalem three months and ten days. And he did evil in the sight of the LORD. ¹⁰At the turn of the year ^aKing Nebuchadnezzar summoned *him* and took him to Babylon, ^bwith the costly articles from the house of the LORD, and made ^cZedekiah,¹ ²*Jehoiakim's* brother, king over Judah and Jerusalem.

ZEDEKIAH REIGNS IN JUDAH
(2 Kin. 24:18–20; Jer. 52:1–3)

^{11a}Zedekiah *was* twenty-one years old when he became king, and he reigned eleven years in Jerusalem. ¹²He did evil in the sight of the LORD his God, *and* ^adid not humble himself before Jeremiah the prophet, *who spoke* from the mouth of the LORD. ¹³And he also ^arebelled against King Nebuchadnezzar, who had made him swear *an oath* by God; but he ^bstiffened his neck and hardened his heart against turning to the LORD God of Israel. ¹⁴Moreover all the leaders of the priests and the people transgressed more and more, *according* to all the abominations of the nations, and defiled the house of the LORD which He had consecrated in Jerusalem.

THE FALL OF JERUSALEM
(2 Kin. 25:1–21; Jer. 52:4–30)

^{15a}And the LORD God of their fathers sent *warnings* to them by His messengers, rising up early and sending *them,* because He had compassion on His people and on His dwelling place. ¹⁶But ^athey mocked the messengers of God, ^bdespised His words, and ^cscoffed at His prophets, until the ^dwrath of the LORD arose against His people, till *there was* no remedy.

^{17a}Therefore He brought against them the king of the Chaldeans, who ^bkilled their young men with the sword in the house of their sanctuary, and had no compassion on young man or virgin, on the aged or the weak; He gave *them* all into his hand. ^{18a}And all the articles from the house of God, great and small, the treasures of the house of the LORD, and the treasures of the king and of his leaders, all *these* he took to Babylon. ^{19a}Then they burned the house of God, broke down the wall of Jerusalem, burned all its palaces with fire, and destroyed all its precious possessions. ²⁰And ^athose who escaped from the sword he carried away to Babylon, ^bwhere they became servants to him and his sons until the rule of

---

36:5
^b[Jer. 22:13–19]
36:6
^a2 Kin. 24:1;
Hab. 1:6
^b[Deut. 29:22–29]; 2 Chr. 33:11;
Jer. 36:30
36:7
^a2 Kin. 24:13;
Dan. 1:1, 2
36:9
^a2 Kin. 24:8–17
36:10
^a2 Kin. 24:10–17
^bDan. 1:1, 2
^cJer. 37:1
36:11
^a2 Kin. 24:18–20; Jer. 52:1
36:12 ^aJer. 21:3–7; 44:10
36:13 ^aJer. 52:3;
Ezek. 17:15
^b2 Kin. 17:14;
[2 Chr. 30:8]
36:15 ^aJer. 7:13;
25:3, 4
36:16
^a2 Chr. 30:10;
Jer. 5:12, 13
^b[Prov. 1:24–32] ^cJer. 38:6;
Matt. 23:34
^d2 Chr. 34:25;
Ps. 79:5
36:17
^aNum. 33:56;
Deut. 4:26;
28:49;
2 Kin. 25:1;
Ezra 9:7; Is. 3:8
^bPs. 74:20
36:18
^a2 Kin. 25:13–15;
2 Chr. 36:7, 10
36:19
^a2 Kin. 25:9;
Ps. 79:1, 7; Is. 1:7, 8; Jer. 52:13
36:20
^a2 Kin. 25:11;
Jer. 5:19;
Mic. 4:10
^bJer. 17:4; 27:7

36:6 ¹*chains*   **36:8** ¹Or *Jeconiah*   **36:9** ¹Heb. mss., LXX, Syr. *eighteen* and 2 Kin. 24:8   **36:10** ¹Or *Mattaniah*   ²Lit. *his brother,* 2 Kin. 24:17

the kingdom of Persia, [21]to fulfill the word of the LORD by the mouth of [a]Jeremiah, until the land [b]had enjoyed her Sabbaths. As long as she lay desolate [c]she kept Sabbath, to fulfill seventy years.

THE PROCLAMATION OF CYRUS
(Ezra 1:1–4)

[22][a]Now in the first year of Cyrus king of Persia, that the word of the LORD by the mouth of [b]Jeremiah might be fulfilled, the LORD stirred up the spirit of [c]Cyrus king of Persia, so that he made a proclamation throughout all his kingdom, and also *put it* in writing, saying,

23 [a]Thus says Cyrus king of Persia:
All the kingdoms of the earth the LORD God of heaven has given me. And He has commanded me to build Him a [1]house at Jerusalem which is in Judah. Who *is* among you of all His people? May the LORD his God *be* with him, and let him go up!

36:21
[a]Jer. 25:9–12;
27:6–8; 29:10
[b]Lev. 26:34–43;
Dan. 9:2
[c]Lev. 25:4, 5

36:22
[a]Ezra 1:1–3
[b]Jer. 29:10
[c]Is. 44:28; 45:1

36:23
[a]Ezra 1:2, 3

36:23 [1]Temple

THE BOOK OF
EZRA

END OF THE BABYLONIAN CAPTIVITY
(2 Chr. 36:22, 23)

1 Now in the first year of Cyrus king of Persia, that the word of the LORD ᵃby the mouth of Jeremiah might be fulfilled, the LORD stirred up the spirit of Cyrus king of Persia, ᵇso that he made a proclamation throughout all his kingdom, and also *put it* in writing, saying,

2   Thus says Cyrus king of Persia:
All the kingdoms of the earth the LORD God of heaven has given me. And He has ᵃcommanded me to build Him a ¹house at Jerusalem which *is* in Judah. ³Who *is* among you of all His people? May his God be with him, and let him go up to Jerusalem which *is* in Judah, and build the house of the LORD God of Israel ᵃ(He *is* God), which *is* in Jerusalem. ⁴And whoever is left in any place where he dwells, let the men of his place help him with silver and gold, with goods and livestock, besides the freewill offerings for the house of God which *is* in Jerusalem.

⁵Then the heads of the fathers' *houses* of Judah and Benjamin, and the priests and the Levites, with all whose spirits ᵃGod ¹had moved, arose to go up and build the house of the LORD which *is* in Jerusalem. ⁶And all those who *were* around them ¹encouraged them with articles of silver and gold, with goods and livestock, and with precious things, besides all *that* was ᵃwillingly offered.

⁷ᵃKing Cyrus also brought out the articles of the house of the LORD, ᵇwhich Nebuchadnezzar had taken from Jerusalem and put in the ¹temple of his gods; ⁸and Cyrus king of Persia brought them out by the hand of Mithredath the treasurer, and counted them out to ᵃSheshbazzar the prince of Judah. ⁹This *is* the number of them: thirty gold platters, one thousand silver platters, twenty-nine knives, ¹⁰thirty gold basins, four hundred and ten silver basins of a similar *kind, and* one thousand other articles. ¹¹All the articles of gold and silver *were* five thousand four hundred. All *these* Sheshbazzar took with the captives who were brought from Babylon to Jerusalem.

THE CAPTIVES WHO RETURNED TO JERUSALEM
(Neh. 7:6–73)

2 Now ᵃthese *are* the people of the province who came back from the captivity, of those who had been carried away, ᵇwhom Nebuchadnezzar the king of Babylon had carried away to Babylon, and who returned to Jerusalem and Judah, everyone to his *own* city.

1:1
ᵃ2 Chr. 36:22, 23;
Jer. 25:12; 29:10
ᵇEzra 5:13, 14;
Is. 44:28—45:13
1:2 ᵃIs. 44:28;
45:1, 13
1:3 ᵃ1 Kin. 8:23;
18:39; Is. 37:16;
Dan. 6:26
1:5 ᵃ[Phil. 2:13]
1:6 ᵃEzra 2:68
1:7 ᵃEzra 5:14;
6:5; Dan. 1:2;
5:2, 3
ᵇ2 Kin. 24:13;
2 Chr. 36:7, 18
1:8 ᵃEzra 5:14, 16
2:1 ᵃNeh. 7:6–
73; Jer. 32:15;
50:5; Ezek. 14:22
ᵇ2 Kin. 24:14–
16; 25:11;
2 Chr. 36:20

1:2 ¹Temple   1:5 ¹stirred up   1:6 ¹Lit. *strengthened their hands*   1:7 ¹Lit. *house*

²*Those* who came with Zerubbabel *were* Jeshua, Nehemiah, ¹Seraiah, ²Reelaiah, Mordecai, Bilshan, ³Mispar, Bigvai, ⁴Rehum, *and* Baanah. The number of the men of the people of Israel: ³the people of Parosh, two thousand one hundred and seventy-two; ⁴the people of Shephatiah, three hundred and seventy-two; ⁵the people of Arah, ᵃseven hundred and seventy-five; ⁶the people of ᵃPahath-Moab, of the people of Jeshua *and* Joab, two thousand eight hundred and twelve; ⁷the people of Elam, one thousand two hundred and fifty-four; ⁸the people of Zattu, nine hundred and forty-five; ⁹the people of Zaccai, seven hundred and sixty; ¹⁰the people of ¹Bani, six hundred and forty-two; ¹¹the people of Bebai, six hundred and twenty-three; ¹²the people of Azgad, one thousand two hundred and twenty-two; ¹³the people of Adonikam, six hundred and sixty-six; ¹⁴the people of Bigvai, two thousand and fifty-six; ¹⁵the people of Adin, four hundred and fifty-four; ¹⁶the people of Ater of Hezekiah, ninety-eight; ¹⁷the people of Bezai, three hundred and twenty-three; ¹⁸the people of ¹Jorah, one hundred and twelve; ¹⁹the people of Hashum, two hundred and twenty-three; ²⁰the people of ¹Gibbar, ninety-five; ²¹the people of Bethlehem, one hundred and twenty-three; ²²the men of Netophah, fifty-six; ²³the men of Anathoth, one hundred and twenty-eight; ²⁴the people of ¹Azmaveth, forty-two; ²⁵the people of ¹Kirjath Arim, Chephirah, and Beeroth, seven hundred and forty-three; ²⁶the people of Ramah and Geba, six hundred and twenty-one; ²⁷the men of Michmas, one hundred and twenty-two; ²⁸the men of Bethel and Ai, two hundred and twenty-three; ²⁹the people of Nebo, fifty-two; ³⁰the people of Magbish, one hundred and fifty-six; ³¹the people of the other ᵃElam, one thousand two hundred and fifty-four; ³²the people of Harim, three hundred and twenty; ³³the people of Lod, Hadid, and Ono, seven hundred and twenty-five; ³⁴the people of Jericho, three hundred and forty-five; ³⁵the people of Senaah, three thousand six hundred and thirty.

³⁶The priests: the sons of ᵃJedaiah, of the house of Jeshua, nine hundred and seventy-three; ³⁷the sons of ᵃImmer, one thousand and fifty-two; ³⁸the sons of ᵃPashhur, one thousand two hundred and forty-seven; ³⁹the sons of ᵃHarim, one thousand and seventeen.

⁴⁰The Levites: the sons of Jeshua and Kadmiel, of the sons of ¹Hodaviah, seventy-four.

⁴¹The singers: the sons of Asaph, one hundred and twenty-eight.

⁴²The sons of the gatekeepers: the sons of Shallum, the sons of Ater, the sons of Talmon, the sons of Akkub, the sons of Hatita, and the sons of Shobai, one hundred and thirty-nine *in* all.

⁴³ᵃThe Nethinim: the sons of Ziha, the sons of Hasupha, the sons of Tabbaoth, ⁴⁴the sons of Keros, the sons of ¹Siaha, the sons of Padon, ⁴⁵the sons of Lebanah, the sons of Hagabah, the sons of Akkub, ⁴⁶the sons of Hagab, the sons of Shalmai, the sons of Hanan, ⁴⁷the sons of Giddel, the sons of Gahar, the sons of Reaiah, ⁴⁸the sons of Rezin, the sons of Nekoda, the sons of Gazzam, ⁴⁹the sons of Uzza, the sons of Paseah, the sons of Besai, ⁵⁰the sons of Asnah, the sons of Meunim, the

2:5 ᵃNeh. 7:10

2:6 ᵃNeh. 7:11

2:31 ᵃEzra 2:7

2:36 ᵃ1 Chr. 24:7–18

2:37 ᵃ1 Chr. 24:14

2:38 ᵃ1 Chr. 9:12

2:39 ᵃ1 Chr. 24:8

2:43 ᵃ1 Chr. 9:2; Ezra 7:7

2:2 ¹*Azariah,* Neh. 7:7   ²*Raamiah,* Neh. 7:7   ³*Mispereth,* Neh. 7:7
⁴*Nehum,* Neh. 7:7   2:10 ¹*Binnui,* Neh. 7:15   2:18 ¹*Hariph,* Neh. 7:24
2:20 ¹*Gibeon,* Neh. 7:25   2:24 ¹*Beth Azmaveth,* Neh. 7:28   2:25 ¹*Kirjath Jearim,* Neh. 7:29   2:40 ¹*Judah,* Ezra 3:9, or *Hodevah,* Neh. 7:43   2:44 ¹*Sia,* Neh. 7:47

sons of [1]Nephusim, [51]the sons of Bakbuk, the sons of Hakupha, the sons of Harhur, [52]the sons of [1]Bazluth, the sons of Mehida, the sons of Harsha, [53]the sons of Barkos, the sons of Sisera, the sons of Tamah, [54]the sons of Neziah, and the sons of Hatipha.

[55]The sons of [a]Solomon's servants: the sons of Sotai, the sons of [b]Sophereth, the sons of [1]Peruda, [56]the sons of Jaala, the sons of Darkon, the sons of Giddel, [57]the sons of Shephatiah, the sons of Hattil, the sons of Pochereth of Zebaim, and the sons of [1]Ami. [58]All the [a]Nethinim and the children of [b]Solomon's servants were three hundred and ninety-two.

[59]And these *were* the ones who came up from Tel Melah, Tel Harsha, Cherub, [1]Addan, and Immer; but they could not [2]identify their father's house or their [3]genealogy, whether they *were* of Israel: [60]the sons of Delaiah, the sons of Tobiah, and the sons of Nekoda, six hundred and fifty-two; [61]and of the sons of the priests: the sons of [a]Habaiah, the sons of [1]Koz, and the sons of [b]Barzillai, who took a wife of the daughters of Barzillai the Gileadite, and was called by their name. [62]These sought their listing *among* those who were registered by genealogy, but they were not found; [a]therefore they *were* excluded from the priesthood as defiled. [63]And the [1]governor said to them that they [a]should not eat of the most holy things till a priest could consult with the [b]Urim and Thummim.

[64][a]The whole assembly together *was* forty-two thousand three hundred *and* sixty, [65]besides their male and female servants, of whom *there were* seven thousand three hundred and thirty-seven; and they had two hundred men and women singers. [66]Their horses *were* seven hundred and thirty-six, their mules two hundred and forty-five, [67]their camels four hundred and thirty-five, and *their* donkeys six thousand seven hundred and twenty.

[68][a]*Some* of the heads of the fathers' *houses,* when they came to the house of the LORD which *is* in Jerusalem, offered freely for the house of God, to erect it in its place: [69]According to their ability, they gave to the [a]treasury for the work sixty-one thousand gold drachmas, five thousand minas of silver, and one hundred priestly garments.

[70][a]So the priests and the Levites, *some* of the people, the singers, the gatekeepers, and the Nethinim, dwelt in their cities, and all Israel in their cities.

WORSHIP RESTORED AT JERUSALEM

3 And when the [a]seventh month had come, and the children of Israel *were* in the cities, the people gathered together as one man to Jerusalem. [2]Then [1]Joshua the son of [a]Jozadak[2] and his brethren the priests, [b]and Zerubbabel the son of [c]Shealtiel and his brethren, arose and built the altar of the God of Israel, to offer burnt offerings on it, as *it is* [d]written in the Law of Moses the man of God. [3]Though fear *had come* upon them because of the people of those countries, they set the altar on its [1]bases; and they offered [a]burnt offerings on it to the LORD, *both* the morning and evening burnt offerings. [4][a]They also kept the Feast of Tabernacles, [b]as *it is* written, and [c]*offered* the daily burnt offerings in the number required by

Cross-references (margin)

2:55 [a]1 Kin. 9:21
[b]Neh. 7:57–60

2:58 [a]Josh. 9:21, 27; 1 Chr. 9:2
[b]1 Kin. 9:21

2:61 [a]Neh. 7:63
[b]2 Sam. 17:27; 1 Kin. 2:7

2:62 [a]Num. 3:10

2:63 [a]Lev. 22:2, 10, 15, 16
[b]Ex. 28:30; Num. 27:21

2:64 [a]Neh. 7:66; Is. 10:22

2:68
[a]Ezra 1:6; 3:5; Neh. 7:70

2:69
[a]1 Chr. 26:20; Ezra 8:25–35

2:70
[a]Ezra 6:16, 17; Neh. 7:73

3:1 [a]Neh. 7:73; 8:1, 2

3:2
[a]1 Chr. 6:14, 15; Ezra 4:3; Neh. 12:1, 8; Hag. 1:1; 2:2
[b]Ezra 2:2; 4:2, 3; 5:2 [c]1 Chr. 3:17
[d]Deut. 12:5, 6

3:3 [a]Num. 28:3

3:4
[a]Lev. 23:33–43; Neh. 8:14–18; Zech. 14:16
[b]Ex. 23:16
[c]Num. 29:12, 13

Footnotes

2:50 [1]*Nephishesim,* Neh. 7:52   2:52 [1]*Bazlith,* Neh. 7:54   2:55 [1]*Perida,* Neh. 7:57   2:57 [1]*Amon,* Neh. 7:59   2:59 [1]Or *Addon,* Neh. 7:61   [2]Lit. *tell*   [3]Lit. *seed*   2:61 [1]Or *Hakkoz*   2:63 [1]Heb. *Tirshatha*   3:2 [1]Or *Joshua*   [2]*Jehozadak,* 1 Chr. 6:14   3:3 [1]*foundations*

ordinance for each day. [5]Afterwards *they offered* the [a]regular burnt offering, and *those* for New Moons and for all the appointed feasts of the LORD that were consecrated, and *those* of everyone who willingly offered a freewill offering to the LORD. [6]From the first day of the seventh month they began to offer burnt offerings to the LORD, although the foundation of the temple of the LORD had not been laid. [7]They also gave money to the masons and the carpenters, and [a]food, drink, and oil to the people of Sidon and Tyre to bring cedar logs from Lebanon to the sea, to [b]Joppa, [c]according to the permission which they had from Cyrus king of Persia.

RESTORATION OF THE TEMPLE BEGINS

[8]Now in the second month of the second year of their coming to the house of God at Jerusalem, [a]Zerubbabel the son of Shealtiel, Jeshua the son of [1]Jozadak, and the rest of their brethren the priests and the Levites, and all those who had come out of the captivity to Jerusalem, began *work* [b]and appointed the Levites from twenty years old and above to oversee the work of the house of the LORD. [9]Then Jeshua *with* his sons and brothers, Kadmiel *with* his sons, and the sons of [1]Judah, arose as one to oversee those working on the house of God: the sons of Henadad *with* their sons and their brethren the Levites.

[10]When the builders laid the foundation of the temple of the LORD, [a]the[1] priests stood in their apparel with trumpets, and the Levites, the sons of Asaph, with cymbals, to praise the LORD, according to the [b]ordinance[2] of David king of Israel. [11a]And they sang responsively, praising and giving thanks to the LORD:

[b]"For *He is* good,
[c]For His mercy *endures* forever toward Israel."

Then all the people shouted with a great shout, when they praised the LORD, because the foundation of the house of the LORD was laid.

[12]But many of the priests and Levites and [a]heads of the fathers' *houses,* old men who had seen the first temple, wept with a loud voice when the foundation of this temple was laid before their eyes. Yet many shouted aloud for joy, [13]so that the people could not discern the noise of the shout of joy from the noise of the weeping of the people, for the people shouted with a loud shout, and the sound was heard afar off.

RESISTANCE TO REBUILDING THE TEMPLE

4 Now when [a]the [1]adversaries of Judah and Benjamin heard that the descendants of the captivity were building the temple of the LORD God of Israel, [2]they came to Zerubbabel and the heads of the fathers' *houses,* and said to them, "Let us build with you, for we seek your God as you *do;* and we have sacrificed to Him [a]since the days of Esarhaddon king of Assyria, who brought us here." [3]But Zerubbabel and Jeshua and the rest of the heads of the fathers' *houses* of Israel said to them, [a]"You may do nothing with us to build a [1]house for our God; but we alone will build to the LORD God of Israel,

3:5 [a]Ex. 29:38; Num. 28:3, 11, 19, 26; Ezra 1:4; 2:68; 7:15, 16; 8:28

3:7 [a]1 Kin. 5:6, 9; 2 Chr. 2:10; Acts 12:20 [b]2 Chr. 2:16; Acts 9:36 [c]Ezra 1:2; 6:3

3:8 [a]Ezra 3:2; 4:3 [b]1 Chr. 23:4, 24

3:10 [a]1 Chr. 16:5, 6 [b]1 Chr. 6:31; 16:4; 25:1

3:11 [a]Ex. 15:21; 2 Chr. 7:3; Neh. 12:24 [b]1 Chr. 16:34; Ps. 136:1 [c]1 Chr. 16:41; Jer. 33:11

3:12 [a]Ezra 2:68

4:1 [a]Ezra 4:7-9

4:2 [a]2 Kin. 17:24; 19:37; Ezra 4:10

4:3 [a]Neh. 2:20

3:8 [1]*Jehozadak,* 1 Chr. 6:14   3:9 [1]*Hodaviah,* Ezra 2:40   3:10 [1]So with LXX, Syr., Vg.; MT *they stationed the priests*   [2]Lit. *hands*   4:1 [1]*enemies*
4:3 [1]*Temple*

as [b]King Cyrus the king of Persia has commanded us." [4]Then [a]the people of the land tried to discourage the people of Judah. They troubled them in building, [5]and hired counselors against them to frustrate their purpose all the days of Cyrus king of Persia, even until the reign of [a]Darius king of Persia.

REBUILDING OF JERUSALEM OPPOSED

[6]In the reign of Ahasuerus, in the beginning of his reign, they wrote an accusation against the inhabitants of Judah and Jerusalem.

[7]In the days of [a]Artaxerxes also, [1]Bishlam, Mithredath, Tabel, and the rest of their companions wrote to Artaxerxes king of Persia; and the letter *was* written in [b]Aramaic script, and translated into the Aramaic language. [8][1]Rehum the commander and Shimshai the scribe wrote a letter against Jerusalem to King Artaxerxes in this fashion:

9   [1]From Rehum the commander, Shimshai the scribe,
     and the rest of their companions—*representatives* of
     [a]the Dinaites, the Apharsathchites, the Tarpelites, the
     people of Persia and Erech and Babylon and [2]Shushan,
     the Dehavites, the Elamites, [10a]and the rest of the nations
     whom the great and noble Osnapper took captive and
     settled in the cities of Samaria and the remainder
     beyond [1]the River—[b]and[2] so forth.

[11](This *is* a copy of the letter that they sent him.)

To King Artaxerxes from your servants, the men *of the region* beyond the River, [1]and so forth:

12   Let it be known to the king that the Jews who came
     up from you have come to us at Jerusalem, and are
     building the [a]rebellious and evil city, and are finishing
     its [b]walls and repairing the foundations. [13]Let it now be
     known to the king that, if this city is built and the walls
     completed, they will not pay [a]tax, tribute, or custom, and
     the king's treasury will be diminished. [14]Now because
     we receive support from the palace, it was not proper
     for us to see the king's dishonor; therefore we have sent
     and informed the king, [15]that search may be made in
     the book of the records of your fathers. And you will
     find in the book of the records and know that this city
     is a rebellious city, harmful to kings and provinces, and
     that they have incited sedition within the city in former
     times, for which cause this city was destroyed.

16   We inform the king that if this city is rebuilt and its walls
     are completed, the result will be that you will have no
     dominion beyond the River.

[17]The king sent an answer:

To Rehum the commander, *to* Shimshai the scribe, *to* the rest of their companions who dwell in Samaria, and *to* the remainder beyond the River:

Peace, [1]and so forth.

4:3 [b]Ezra 1:1–4
4:4 [a]Ezra 3:3
    4:5
[a]Ezra 5:5; 6:1
    4:7
[a]Ezra 7:1, 7, 21
[b]2 Kin. 18:26
    4:9
[a]2 Kin. 17:30, 31
    4:10
[a]2 Kin. 17:24;
    Ezra 4:1
[b]Ezra 4:11, 17;
    7:12
    4:12
[a]2 Chr. 36:13
[b]Ezra 5:3, 9
4:13 [a]Ezra 4:20;
    7:24

4:7 [1]Or *in peace*   4:8 [1]The original language of Ezra 4:8 through 6:18 is Aramaic.   4:9 [1]Lit. *Then*   [2]Or *Susa*   4:10 [1]The Euphrates   [2]Lit. *and now*   4:11 [1]Lit. *and now*   4:17 [1]Lit. *and now*

18 The letter which you sent to us has been clearly read before me. [19]And [1]I gave the command, and a search has been made, and it was found that this city in former times has revolted against kings, and rebellion and sedition have been fostered in it. [20]There have also been mighty kings over Jerusalem, who have [a]ruled over all *the region* [b]beyond the River; and tax, tribute, and custom were paid to them. [21]Now [1]give the command to make these men cease, that this city may not be built until the command is given by me.

22 Take heed now that you do not fail to do this. Why should damage increase to the hurt of the kings?

[23]Now when the copy of King Artaxerxes' letter *was* read before Rehum, Shimshai the scribe, and their companions, they went up in haste to Jerusalem against the Jews, and by force of arms made them cease. [24]Thus the work of the house of God which *is* at Jerusalem ceased, and it was discontinued until the second year of the reign of Darius king of Persia.

RESTORATION OF THE TEMPLE RESUMED
(Hab. 1:1; Zech. 1:1)

5 Then the prophet [a]Haggai and [b]Zechariah the son of Iddo, prophets, prophesied to the Jews who *were* in Judah and Jerusalem, in the name of the God of Israel, *who was* over them. [2]So [a]Zerubbabel the son of Shealtiel and Jeshua the son of [1]Jozadak rose up and began to build the house of God which *is* in Jerusalem; and [b]the prophets of God *were* with them, helping them.

[3]At the same time [a]Tattenai the governor of *the region* beyond [1]the River and Shethar-Boznai and their companions came to them and spoke thus to them: [b]"Who has commanded you to build this [2]temple and finish this wall?" [4a]Then, accordingly, we told them the names of the men who were constructing this building. [5]But [a]the eye of their God was upon the elders of the Jews, so that they could not make them cease till a report could go to Darius. Then a [b]written answer was returned concerning this *matter*. [6]This is a copy of the letter that Tattenai sent:

The governor of *the region* beyond the River, and Shethar-Boznai, [a]and his companions, the Persians who *were in the region* beyond the River, to Darius the king.

[7](They sent a letter to him, in which was written thus.)

To Darius the king:

All peace.

8 Let it be known to the king that we went into the province of Judea, to the [1]temple of the great God, which is being built with [2]heavy stones, and timber is being laid in the walls; and this work goes on diligently and prospers in their hands.

4:20 [a]1 Kin. 4:21;
1 Chr. 18:3;
Ps. 72:8
[b]Gen. 15:18;
Josh. 1:4

5:1 [a]Hag. 1:1
[b]Zech. 1:1

5:2 [a]Ezra 3:2;
Hag. 1:12
[b]Ezra 6:14;
Hag. 2:4

5:3
[a]Ezra 5:6; 6:6
[b]Ezra 1:3; 5:9

5:4 [a]Ezra 5:10

5:5 [a]2 Chr. 16:9;
Ezra 7:6, 28;
Ps. 33:18
[b]Ezra 6:6

5:6 [a]Ezra 4:7–10

4:19 [1]Lit. *by me a decree has been put forth*   4:21 [1]*put forth a decree*
5:2 [1]*Jehozadak,* 1 Chr. 6:14   5:3 [1]The Euphrates   [2]Lit. *house*   5:8 [1]Lit. *house*   [2]Lit. *stones of rolling,* stones too heavy to be carried

9 Then we asked those elders, *and* spoke thus to them: a"Who commanded you to build this temple and to finish these walls?" 10We also asked them their names to inform you, that we might write the names of the men who *were* chief among them.

11 And thus they returned us an answer, saying: "We are the servants of the God of heaven and earth, and we are rebuilding the 1temple that was built many years ago, which a great king of Israel built aand completed. 12But abecause our fathers provoked the God of heaven to wrath, He gave them into the hand of bNebuchadnezzar king of Babylon, the Chaldean, *who* destroyed this temple and ccarried the people away to Babylon. 13However, in the first year of aCyrus king of Babylon, King Cyrus issued a decree to build this 1house of God. 14Also, athe gold and silver articles of the house of God, which Nebuchadnezzar had taken from the temple that *was* in Jerusalem and carried into the temple of Babylon—those King Cyrus took from the temple of Babylon, and they were given to bone named Sheshbazzar, whom he had made governor. 15And he said to him, 'Take these articles; go, carry them to the temple *site* that *is* in Jerusalem, and let the house of God be rebuilt on its former site.' 16Then the same Sheshbazzar came *and* alaid the foundation of the house of God which *is* in Jerusalem; but from that time even until now it has been under construction, and bit is not finished."

17 Now therefore, if *it seems* good to the king, alet a search be made in the king's treasure house, which *is* there in Babylon, whether it is *so* that a decree was issued by King Cyrus to build this house of God at Jerusalem, and let the king send us his pleasure concerning this *matter*.

THE DECREE OF DARIUS

6 Then King Darius issued a decree, aand a search was made in the 1archives, where the treasures were stored in Babylon. 2And at 1Achmetha, in the palace that *is* in the province of aMedia, a scroll was found, and in it a record *was* written thus:

3 In the first year of King Cyrus, King Cyrus issued a adecree *concerning* the house of God at Jerusalem: "Let the house be rebuilt, the place where they offered sacrifices; and let the foundations of it be firmly laid, its height sixty cubits *and* its width sixty cubits, 4awith three rows of heavy stones and one row of new timber. Let the bexpenses be paid from the king's treasury. 5Also let athe gold and silver articles of the house of God, which Nebuchadnezzar took from the temple which *is* in Jerusalem and brought to Babylon, be restored and taken back to the temple which *is* in Jerusalem, *each* to its place; and deposit *them* in the house of God"—

6 aNow *therefore*, Tattenai, governor of *the region* beyond the River, and Shethar-Boznai, and your companions the

Cross references (margin)

5:9 aEzra 5:3, 4
5:11 a1 Kin. 6:1, 38
5:12 a2 Chr. 34:25; 36:16, 17 b2 Kin. 24:2; 25:8–11; 2 Chr. 36:17; Jer. 52:12–15 cJer. 13:19
5:13 aEzra 1:1
5:14 aEzra 1:7, 8; 6:5; Dan. 5:2 bHag. 1:14; 2:2, 21
5:16 aEzra 3:8–10; Hag. 2:18 bEzra 6:15
5:17 aEzra 6:1, 2
6:1 aEzra 5:17
6:2 a2 Kin. 17:6
6:3 aEzra 1:1; 5:13
6:4 a1 Kin. 6:36 bEzra 3:7
6:5 a1 Kin. 1:7, 8; 5:14
6:6 aEzra 5:3, 6

5:11 1Lit. *house*   5:13 1Temple   6:1 1Lit. *house of the scrolls*   6:2 1Probably *Ecbatana*, the ancient capital of Media

Persians who *are* beyond the River, keep yourselves far from there. 7Let the work of this house of God alone; let the governor of the Jews and the elders of the Jews build this house of God on its site.

8 Moreover I issue a decree *as to* what you shall do for the elders of these Jews, for the building of this ¹house of God: Let the cost be paid at the king's expense from taxes *on the region* beyond the River; this is to be given immediately to these men, so that they are not hindered. 9And whatever they need—young bulls, rams, and lambs for the burnt offerings of the God of heaven, wheat, salt, wine, and oil, according to the request of the priests who *are* in Jerusalem—let it be given them day by day without fail, 10ᵃthat they may offer sacrifices of sweet aroma to the God of heaven, and pray for the life of the king and his sons.

11 Also I issue a decree that whoever alters this edict, let a timber be pulled from his house and erected, and let him be hanged on it; ᵃand let his house be made a refuse heap because of this. 12And may the God who causes His ᵃname to dwell there destroy any king or people who put their hand to alter it, or to destroy this ¹house of God which is in Jerusalem. I Darius issue a decree; let it be done diligently.

THE TEMPLE COMPLETED AND DEDICATED

13Then Tattenai, governor of *the region* beyond the River, Shethar-Boznai, and their companions diligently did according to what King Darius had sent. 14ᵃSo the elders of the Jews built, and they prospered through the prophesying of Haggai the prophet and Zechariah the son of Iddo. And they built and finished *it,* according to the commandment of the God of Israel, and according to the ¹command of ᵇCyrus, ᶜDarius, and ᵈArtaxerxes king of Persia. 15Now the temple was finished on the third day of the month of Adar, which was in the sixth year of the reign of King Darius. 16Then the children of Israel, the priests and the Levites and the rest of the descendants of the captivity, celebrated ᵃthe dedication of this ¹house of God with joy. 17And they ᵃoffered sacrifices at the dedication of this house of God, one hundred bulls, two hundred rams, four hundred lambs, and as a sin offering for all Israel twelve male goats, according to the number of the tribes of Israel. 18They assigned the priests to their ᵃdivisions and the Levites to their ᵇdivisions, over the service of God in Jerusalem, ᶜas it is written in the Book of Moses.

THE PASSOVER CELEBRATED

(cf. Deut. 16:1–8)

19¹And the descendants of the captivity kept the Passover ᵃon the fourteenth *day* of the first month. 20For the priests and the Levites had ᵃpurified themselves; all of them *were ritually* clean. And they ᵇslaughtered the Passover *lambs* for all the descendants of the captivity, for their brethren the priests, and for themselves. 21Then the children of Israel who

6:10 ᵃEzra 7:23;
[Jer. 29:7;
1 Tim. 2:1, 2]

6:11 ᵃDan. 2:5;
3:29

6:12 ᵃDeut. 12:5,
11; 1 Kin. 9:3

6:14
ᵃEzra 5:1, 2
ᵇEzra 1:1; 5:13;
6:3 ᶜEzra 4:24;
6:12 ᵈEzra 7:1, 11;
Neh. 2:1

6:16
ᵃ1 Kin. 8:63;
2 Chr. 7:5

6:17 ᵃEzra 8:35

6:18 ᵃ1 Chr. 24:1;
2 Chr. 35:5
ᵇ1 Chr. 23:6
ᶜNum. 3:6; 8:9

6:19 ᵃEx. 12:6

6:20
ᵃ2 Chr. 29:34;
30:15
ᵇ2 Chr. 35:11

6:8 ¹Temple   6:12 ¹Temple   6:14 ¹*decree*   6:16 ¹Temple   6:19 ¹The Hebrew language resumes in Ezra 6:19 and continues through 7:11.

had returned from the captivity ate together with all who had separated themselves from the [a]filth[1] of the nations of the land in order to seek the LORD God of Israel. [22]And they kept the [a]Feast of Unleavened Bread seven days with joy; for the LORD made them joyful, and [b]turned the heart [c]of the king of Assyria toward them, to strengthen their hands in the work of the house of God, the God of Israel.

THE ARRIVAL OF EZRA

7 Now after these things, in the reign of [a]Artaxerxes king of Persia, Ezra the [b]son of Seraiah, [c]the son of Azariah, the son of [d]Hilkiah, [2]the son of Shallum, the son of Zadok, the son of Ahitub, [3]the son of Amariah, the son of Azariah, the son of Meraioth, [4]the son of Zerahiah, the son of Uzzi, the son of Bukki, [5]the son of Abishua, the son of Phinehas, the son of Eleazar, the son of Aaron the chief priest— [6]this Ezra came up from Babylon; and he *was* [a]a skilled scribe in the Law of Moses, which the LORD God of Israel had given. The king granted him all his request, [b]according to the hand of the LORD his God upon him. [7a]*Some* of the children of Israel, the priests, [b]the Levites, the singers, the gatekeepers, and [c]the Nethinim came up to Jerusalem in the seventh year of King Artaxerxes. [8]And Ezra came to Jerusalem in the fifth month, which *was* in the seventh year of the king. [9]On the first *day* of the first month he began *his* journey from Babylon, and on the first *day* of the fifth month he came to Jerusalem, [a]according to the good hand of his God upon him. [10]For Ezra had prepared his heart to [a]seek[1] the Law of the LORD, and to do *it*, and to [b]teach statutes and ordinances in Israel.

THE LETTER OF ARTAXERXES TO EZRA

[11]This *is* a copy of the letter that King Artaxerxes gave Ezra the priest, the scribe, expert in the words of the commandments of the LORD, and of His statutes to Israel:

12 [1]Artaxerxes, [a]king of kings,

To Ezra the priest, a scribe of the Law of the God of heaven:

Perfect *peace*, [b]and[2] so forth.

13 I issue a decree that all those of the people of Israel and the priests and Levites in my realm, who volunteer to go up to Jerusalem, may go with you. [14]And whereas you are being sent [1]by the king and his [a]seven counselors to inquire concerning Judah and Jerusalem, with regard to the Law of your God which *is* in your hand; [15]and *whereas you are* to carry the silver and gold which the king and his counselors have freely offered to the God of Israel, [a]whose dwelling *is* in Jerusalem; [16a]and *whereas* all the silver and gold that you may find in all the province of Babylon, along with the freewill offering of the people and the priests, *are to be* [b]freely offered for the [1]house of their God in Jerusalem— [17]now therefore, be careful to buy with this money bulls, rams, and lambs, with their [a]grain offerings and their drink

---

6:21 [a]Ezra 9:11
6:22 [a]Ex. 12:15;
  13:6, 7;
  2 Chr. 30:21;
  35:17 [b]Ezra 7:27;
  [Prov. 21:1]
  [c]2 Kin. 23:29;
  2 Chr. 33:11;
  Ezra 1:1; 6:1
7:1 [a]Neh. 2:1
  [b]1 Chr. 6:14
  [c]Jer. 52:24
  [d]2 Chr. 35:8
7:6 [a]Ezra 7:11,
12, 21 [b]Ezra 7:9,
  28; 8:22
7:7
[a]Ezra 8:1–14
[b]Ezra 8:15
[c]Ezra 2:43; 8:20
7:9 [a]Ezra 7:6;
  Neh. 2:8, 18
7:10 [a]Ps. 119:45
  [b]Deut. 33:10;
  Ezra 7:6, 25;
  Neh. 8:1–8;
  [Mal. 2:7]
7:12 [a]Ezek. 26:7;
  Dan. 2:37
  [b]Ezra 4:10
7:14 [a]Esth. 1:14
7:15 [a]2 Chr. 6:2;
  Ezra 6:12;
  Ps. 135:21
7:16 [a]Ezra 8:25
  [b]1 Chr. 29:6, 9
7:17
[a]Num. 15:4–13

6:21 [1]*uncleanness*   7:10 [1]*Study*   7:12 [1]The original language of Ezra 7:12–26 is Aramaic.   [2]Lit. *and now*   7:14 [1]*from before*   7:16 [1]*Temple*

offerings, and [b]offer them on the altar of the house of your God in Jerusalem.

18 And whatever seems good to you and your brethren to do with the rest of the silver and the gold, do it according to the will of your God. [19]Also the articles that are given to you for the service of the house of your God, deliver in full before the God of Jerusalem. [20]And whatever more may be needed for the house of your God, which you may have occasion to provide, pay *for it* from the king's treasury.

21 And I, *even* I, Artaxerxes the king, issue a decree to all the treasurers who *are in the region* beyond the River, that whatever Ezra the priest, the scribe of the Law of the God of heaven, may require of you, let it be done diligently, [22]up to one hundred talents of silver, one hundred kors of wheat, one hundred baths of wine, one hundred baths of oil, and salt without prescribed limit. [23]Whatever [1]is commanded by the God of heaven, let it diligently be done for the [2]house of the God of heaven. For why should there be wrath against the realm of the king and his sons?

24 Also we inform you that it shall not be lawful to impose tax, tribute, or custom on any of the priests, Levites, singers, gatekeepers, Nethinim, or servants of this house of God. [25]And you, Ezra, according to your God-given wisdom, [a]set magistrates and judges who may judge all the people who *are in the region* beyond the River, all such as know the laws of your God; and [b]teach those who do not know *them.* [26]Whoever will not observe the law of your God and the law of the king, let judgment be executed speedily on him, whether *it be* death, or [1]banishment, or confiscation of goods, or imprisonment.

[27a]Blessed[1] *be* the LORD God of our fathers, [b]who has put *such a thing* as this in the king's heart, to beautify the house of the LORD which *is* in Jerusalem, [28]and [a]has extended mercy to me before the king and his counselors, and before all the king's mighty princes.

So I was encouraged, as [b]the hand of the LORD my God *was* upon me; and I gathered leading men of Israel to go up with me.

HEADS OF FAMILIES WHO RETURNED WITH EZRA

8 These *are* the heads of their fathers' *houses,* and *this is* the genealogy of those who went up with me from Babylon, in the reign of King Artaxerxes: [2]of the sons of Phinehas, Gershom; of the sons of Ithamar, Daniel; of the sons of David, [a]Hattush; [3]of the sons of Shecaniah, of the sons of [a]Parosh, Zechariah; and registered with him *were* one hundred and fifty males; [4]of the sons of [a]Pahath-Moab, Eliehoenai the son of Zerahiah, and with him two hundred males; [5]of [1]the sons of Shechaniah, Ben-Jahaziel, and with him three hundred males; [6]of the sons of Adin, Ebed the son of Jonathan, and

7:17
[b]Deut. 12:5–11

7:25
[a]Ex. 18:21, 22;
Deut. 16:18
[b]2 Chr. 17:7;
Ezra 7:10;
[Mal. 2:7;
Col. 1:28]

7:27
[a]1 Chr. 29:10
[b]Ezra 6:22;
[Prov. 21:1]

7:28 [a]Ezra 9:9
[b]Ezra 5:5; 7:6, 9;
8:18

8:2 [a]1 Chr. 3:22;
Ezra 2:68

8:3 [a]Ezra 2:3

8:4 [a]Ezra 10:30

7:23 [1]Lit. *is from the decree*　[2]Temple　7:26 [1]Lit. *rooting out*　7:27 [1]The Hebrew language resumes in Ezra 7:27.　8:5 [1]So with MT, Vg.; LXX *the sons of Zatho, Shechaniah*

with him fifty males; [7]of the sons of Elam, Jeshaiah the son of Athaliah, and with him seventy males; [8]of the sons of Shephatiah, Zebadiah the son of Michael, and with him eighty males; [9]of the sons of Joab, Obadiah the son of Jehiel, and with him two hundred and eighteen males; [10]of [1]the sons of Shelomith, Ben-Josiphiah, and with him one hundred and sixty males; [11]of the sons of [a]Bebai, Zechariah the son of Bebai, and with him twenty-eight males; [12]of the sons of Azgad, Johanan [1]the son of Hakkatan, and with him one hundred and ten males; [13]of the last sons of Adonikam, whose names *are* these— Eliphelet, Jeiel, and Shemaiah—and with them sixty males; [14]also of the sons of Bigvai, Uthai and [1]Zabbud, and with them seventy males.

SERVANTS FOR THE TEMPLE

[15]Now I gathered them by the river that flows to Ahava, and we camped there three days. And I looked among the people and the priests, and found none of the [a]sons of Levi there. [16]Then I sent for Eliezer, Ariel, Shemaiah, Elnathan, Jarib, Elnathan, Nathan, Zechariah, and [a]Meshullam, leaders; also for Joiarib and Elnathan, men of understanding. [17]And I gave them a command for Iddo the chief man at the place Casiphia, and [1]I told them what they should say to [2]Iddo *and* his brethren the Nethinim at the place Casiphia—that they should bring us servants for the house of our God. [18]Then, by the good hand of our God upon us, they [a]brought us a man of understanding, of the sons of Mahli the son of Levi, the son of Israel, namely Sherebiah, with his sons and brothers, eighteen men; [19]and [a]Hashabiah, and with him Jeshaiah of the sons of Merari, his brothers and their sons, twenty men; [20a]also of the Nethinim, whom David and the leaders had appointed for the service of the Levites, two hundred and twenty Nethinim. All of them were designated by name.

FASTING AND PRAYER FOR PROTECTION

[21]Then I [a]proclaimed a fast there at the river of Ahava, that we might [b]humble ourselves before our God, to seek from Him the [c]right way for us and our little ones and all our possessions. [22]For [a]I was ashamed to request of the king an escort of soldiers and horsemen to help us against the enemy on the road, because we had spoken to the king, saying, [b]"The hand of our God *is* upon all those for [c]good who seek Him, but His power and His wrath *are* [d]against all those who [e]forsake Him." [23]So we fasted and entreated our God for this, and He [a]answered our prayer.

GIFTS FOR THE TEMPLE

[24]And I separated twelve of the leaders of the priests— Sherebiah, Hashabiah, and ten of their brethren with them— [25]and weighed out to them [a]the silver, the gold, and the articles, the offering for the house of our God which the king and his counselors and his princes, and all Israel *who were* present, had offered. [26]I weighed into their hand six hundred and fifty talents of silver, silver articles *weighing* one hundred

8:11 [a]Ezra 10:28

8:15
[a]Ezra 7:7; 8:2

8:16 [a]Ezra 10:15

8:18
[a]2 Chr. 30:22;
Neh. 8:7

8:19 [a]Neh. 12:24

8:20
[a]Ezra 2:43; 7:7

8:21 [a]1 Sam. 7:6;
2 Chr. 20:3
[b]Lev. 16:29;
23:29; Is. 58:3, 5
[c]Ps. 5:8

8:22 [a]1 Cor. 9:15
[b]Ezra 7:6, 9, 28
[c][Ps. 33:18,
19; 34:15, 22;
Rom. 8:28]
[d][Ps. 34:16]
[e][2 Chr. 15:2]

8:23
[a][1 Chr. 5:20];
2 Chr. 33:13;
Is. 19:22

8:25
[a]Ezra 7:15, 16

8:10 [1]So with MT, Vg.; LXX *the sons of Banni, Shelomith*   8:12 [1]Or *the youngest son,*   8:14 [1]Or *Zakkur*   8:17 [1]Lit. *I put words in their mouths to say* [2]So with Vg.; MT *to Iddo his brother;* LXX *to their brethren*

talents, one hundred talents of gold, ²⁷twenty gold basins *worth* a thousand drachmas, and two vessels of fine polished bronze, precious as gold. ²⁸And I said to them, "You *are* ^aholy¹ to the LORD; the articles *are* ^bholy also; and the silver and the gold *are* a freewill offering to the LORD God of your fathers. ²⁹Watch and keep *them* until you weigh *them* before the leaders of the priests and the Levites and ^aheads of the fathers' *houses* of Israel in Jerusalem, *in* the chambers of the house of the LORD." ³⁰So the priests and the Levites received the silver and the gold and the articles by weight, to bring *them* to Jerusalem to the house of our God.

THE RETURN TO JERUSALEM

³¹Then we departed from the river of Ahava on the twelfth *day* of the first month, to go to Jerusalem. And ^athe hand of our God was upon us, and He delivered us from the hand of the enemy and from ambush along the road. ³²So we ^acame to Jerusalem, and stayed there three days.

³³Now on the fourth day the silver and the gold and the articles were ^aweighed in the house of our God by the hand of Meremoth the son of Uriah the priest, and with him *was* Eleazar the son of Phinehas; with them *were* the Levites, ^bJozabad the son of Jeshua and Noadiah the son of Binnui, ³⁴with the number *and* weight of everything. All the weight was written down at that time.

³⁵The children of those who had been ^acarried away captive, who had come from the captivity, ^boffered burnt offerings to the God of Israel: twelve bulls for all Israel, ninety-six rams, seventy-seven lambs, and twelve male goats *as* a sin offering. All *this was* a burnt offering to the LORD.

³⁶And they delivered the king's ^aorders to the king's satraps and the governors *in the region* beyond ¹the River. So they gave support to the people and the ²house of God.

INTERMARRIAGE WITH PAGANS

9 When these things were done, the leaders came to me, saying, "The people of Israel and the priests and the Levites have not ^aseparated themselves from the peoples of the lands, ^bwith respect to the abominations of the Canaanites, the Hittites, the Perizzites, the Jebusites, the Ammonites, the Moabites, the Egyptians, and the Amorites. ²For they have ^ataken some of their daughters *as wives* for themselves and their sons, so that the ^bholy seed is ^cmixed with the peoples of *those* lands. Indeed, the hand of the leaders and rulers has been foremost in this ¹trespass." ³So when I heard this thing, ^aI tore my garment and my robe, and plucked out some of the hair of my head and beard, and sat down ^bastonished. ⁴Then everyone who ^atrembled at the words of the God of Israel assembled to me, because of the transgression of those who had been carried away captive, and I sat astonished until the ^bevening sacrifice.

⁵At the evening sacrifice I arose from my fasting; and having torn my garment and my robe, I fell on my knees and ^aspread out my hands to the LORD my God. ⁶And I said: "O my God, I am too ^aashamed and humiliated to lift up my face to

8:28
^aLev. 21:6–9;
Deut. 33:8
^bLev. 22:2, 3;
Num. 4:4, 15,
19, 20

8:29 ^aEzra 4:3

8:31
^aEzra 7:6, 9, 28

8:32 ^aNeh. 2:11

8:33 ^aEzra 8:26,
30 ^bNeh. 11:16

8:35 ^aEzra 2:1
^bEzra 6:17

8:36
^aEzra 7:21–24

9:1 ^aEzra 6:21;
Neh. 9:2
^bDeut. 12:30, 31

9:2 ^aEx. 34:16;
[Deut. 7:3];
Ezra 10:2;
Neh. 13:23
^bEx. 22:31;
[Deut. 7:6]
^c[2 Cor. 6:14]

9:3 ^aJob 1:20
^bPs. 143:4

9:4 ^aEzra 10:3;
Is. 66:2
^bEx. 29:39

9:5 ^aEx. 9:29

9:6 ^aDan. 9:7, 8

8:28 ¹*consecrated*   **8:36** ¹The Euphrates   ²Temple   **9:2** ¹*unfaithfulness*

You, my God; for ᵇour iniquities have risen higher than *our* heads, and our guilt has ᶜgrown up to the heavens. ⁷Since the days of our fathers to this day ᵃwe *have been* very guilty, and for our iniquities ᵇwe, our kings, *and* our priests have been delivered into the hand of the kings of the lands, to the ᶜsword, to captivity, to plunder, and to ᵈhumiliation,¹ as *it is* this day. ⁸And now for a little while grace has been *shown* from the LORD our God, to leave us a remnant to escape, and to give us a peg in His holy place, that our God may ᵃenlighten our eyes and give us a measure of revival in our bondage. ⁹ᵃFor we *were* slaves. ᵇYet our God did not forsake us in our bondage; but ᶜHe extended mercy to us in the sight of the kings of Persia, to revive us, to repair the house of our God, to rebuild its ruins, and to give us ᵈa wall in Judah and Jerusalem. ¹⁰And now, O our God, what shall we say after this? For we have forsaken Your commandments, ¹¹which You commanded by Your servants the prophets, saying, 'The land which you are entering to possess is an unclean land, with the ᵃuncleanness of the peoples of the lands, with their abominations which have filled it from one end to another with their impurity. ¹²Now therefore, ᵃdo not give your daughters as wives for their sons, nor take their daughters to your sons; and ᵇnever seek their peace or prosperity, that you may be strong and eat the good of the land, and ᶜleave *it* as an inheritance to your children forever.' ¹³And after all that has come upon us for our evil deeds and for our great guilt, since You our God ᵃhave punished us less than our iniquities *deserve,* and have given us *such* deliverance as this, ¹⁴should we ᵃagain break Your commandments, and ᵇjoin in marriage with the people *committing* these abominations? Would You not be ᶜangry with us until You had ¹consumed *us,* so that *there would be* no remnant or survivor? ¹⁵O LORD God of Israel, ᵃYou *are* righteous, for we are left as a remnant, as *it is* this day. ᵇHere we *are* before You, ᶜin our guilt, though no one can stand before You because of this!"

CONFESSION OF IMPROPER MARRIAGES

10 Now ᵃwhile Ezra was praying, and while he was confessing, weeping, and bowing down ᵇbefore the house of God, a very large assembly of men, women, and children gathered to him from Israel; for the people wept very ᶜbitterly. ²And Shechaniah the son of Jehiel, *one* of the sons of Elam, spoke up and said to Ezra, "We have ᵃtrespassed¹ against our God, and have taken pagan wives from the peoples of the land; yet now there is hope in Israel in spite of this. ³Now therefore, let us make ᵃa covenant with our God to put away all these wives and those who have been born to them, according to the advice of my master and of those who ᵇtremble at ᶜthe commandment of our God; and let it be done according to the ᵈlaw. ⁴Arise, for *this* matter *is* your *responsibility.* We also *are* with you. ᵃBe of good courage, and do *it.*"

⁵Then Ezra arose, and made the leaders of the priests, the Levites, and all Israel ᵃswear an oath that they would do according to this word. So they swore an oath. ⁶Then Ezra rose up from before the house of God, and went into the chamber

9:6 ᵇPs. 38:4; ᶜ2 Chr. 28:9; [Ezra 9:13, 15]; Rev. 18:5
9:7 ᵃ2 Chr. 36:14–17; Ps. 106:6; Dan. 9:5, 6; ᵇDeut. 28:36; Neh. 9:30; ᶜDeut. 32:25; ᵈDan. 9:7, 8
9:8 ᵃPs. 34:5
9:9 ᵃNeh. 9:36; Esth. 7:4; ᵇNeh. 9:17; Ps. 136:23; ᶜEzra 7:28; ᵈIs. 5:2
9:11 ᵃEzra 6:21
9:12 ᵃ[Ex. 23:32; 34:15, 16; Deut. 7:3, 4]; Ezra 9:2; ᵇDeut. 23:6; ᶜ[Prov. 13:22; 20:7]
9:13 ᵃ[Ps. 103:10]
9:14 ᵃ[John 5:14; 2 Pet. 2:20]; ᵇNeh. 13:23; ᶜDeut. 9:8
9:15 ᵃNeh. 9:33; Dan. 9:14; ᵇ[Rom. 3:19]; ᶜ1 Cor. 15:17
10:1 ᵃDan. 9:4, 20; ᵇ2 Chr. 20:9; ᶜNeh. 8:1–9
10:2 ᵃEzra 10:10, 13, 14, 17, 18; Neh. 13:23–27
10:3 ᵃ2 Chr. 34:31; ᵇEzra 9:4; ᶜDeut. 7:2, 3; ᵈDeut. 24:1, 2
10:4 ᵃ1 Chr. 28:10
10:5 ᵃEzra 10:12, 19; Neh. 5:12; 13:25

9:7 ¹Lit. *shame of faces*   9:14 ¹*destroyed*   10:2 ¹*been unfaithful to*

of Jehohanan the son of Eliashib; and *when* he came there, he [a]ate no bread and drank no water, for he mourned because of the guilt of those from the captivity.

[7]And they issued a proclamation throughout Judah and Jerusalem to all the descendants of the captivity, that they must gather at Jerusalem, [8]and that whoever would not come within three days, according to the instructions of the leaders and elders, all his property would be confiscated, and he himself would be separated from the assembly of those from the captivity.

[9]So all the men of Judah and Benjamin gathered at Jerusalem within three days. It *was* the ninth month, on the twentieth of the month; and [a]all the people sat in the open square of the house of God, trembling because of *this* matter and because of heavy rain. [10]Then Ezra the priest stood up and said to them, "You have [1]transgressed and [2]have taken pagan wives, adding to the guilt of Israel. [11]Now therefore, [a]make confession to the LORD God of your fathers, and do His will; [b]separate yourselves from the peoples of the land, and from the pagan wives."

[12]Then all the assembly answered and said with a loud voice, "Yes! As you have said, so we must do. [13]But *there are* many people; *it is* the season for heavy rain, and we are not able to stand outside. Nor *is this* the work of one or two days, for *there are* many of us who have transgressed in this matter. [14]Please, let the leaders of our entire assembly stand; and let all those in our cities who have taken pagan wives come at appointed times, together with the elders and judges of their cities, until [a]the fierce wrath of our God is turned away from us in this matter." [15]Only Jonathan the son of Asahel and Jahaziah the son of Tikvah opposed this, and [a]Meshullam and Shabbethai the Levite gave them support.

[16]Then the descendants of the captivity did so. And Ezra the priest, *with* certain [a]heads of the fathers' *households,* were set apart by the fathers' households, each of them by name; and they sat down on the first day of the tenth month to examine the matter. [17]By the first day of the first month they finished *questioning* all the men who had taken pagan wives.

PAGAN WIVES PUT AWAY

[18]And among the sons of the priests who had taken pagan wives *the following* were found of the sons of [a]Jeshua the son of [1]Jozadak, and his brothers: Maaseiah, Eliezer, Jarib, and Gedaliah. [19]And they [a]gave their promise that they would put away their wives; and *being* [b]guilty, *they presented* a ram of the flock as their [c]trespass offering.

[20]Also of the sons of Immer: Hanani and Zebadiah; [21]of the sons of Harim: Maaseiah, Elijah, Shemaiah, Jehiel, and Uzziah; [22]of the sons of Pashhur: Elioenai, Maaseiah, Ishmael, Nethanel, Jozabad, and Elasah.

[23]Also of the Levites: Jozabad, Shimei, Kelaiah (the same *is* Kelita), Pethahiah, Judah, and Eliezer.

[24]Also of the singers: Eliashib; and of the gatekeepers: Shallum, Telem, and Uri.

[25]And others of Israel: of the [a]sons of Parosh: Ramiah,

10:6 [a]Deut. 9:18

10:9
[a]1 Sam. 12:18;
Ezra 9:4; 10:3

10:11
[a][Lev. 26:40–42];
Josh. 7:19;
[Prov. 28:13]
[b]Ezra 10:3

10:14
[a]2 Kin. 23:26;
2 Chr. 28:11–13;
29:10; 30:8

10:15 [a]Ezra 8:16;
Neh. 3:4

10:16 [a]Ezra 4:3

10:18 [a]Ezra 5:2;
Hag. 1:1, 12; 2:4;
Zech. 3:1; 6:11

10:19
[a]2 Kin. 10:15
[b]Lev. 6:4, 6
[c]Lev. 5:6, 15

10:25 [a]Ezra 2:3;
8:3; Neh. 7:8

10:10 [1]*acted unfaithfully*   [2]Heb. *have caused to dwell* or *have brought back*
10:18 [1]*Jehozadak,* 1 Chr. 6:14

Jeziah, Malchiah, Mijamin, Eleazar, Malchijah, and Benaiah; 26of the sons of Elam: Mattaniah, Zechariah, Jehiel, Abdi, Jeremoth, and Eliah; 27of the sons of Zattu: Elioenai, Eliashib, Mattaniah, Jeremoth, Zabad, and Aziza; 28of the asons of Bebai: Jehohanan, Hananiah, Zabbai, *and* Athlai; 29of the sons of Bani: Meshullam, Malluch, Adaiah, Jashub, Sheal, *and* 1Ramoth; 30of the asons of Pahath-Moab: Adna, Chelal, Benaiah, Maaseiah, Mattaniah, Bezalel, Binnui, and Manasseh; 31*of* the sons of Harim: Eliezer, Ishijah, Malchijah, Shemaiah, Shimeon, 32Benjamin, Malluch, *and* Shemariah; 33of the sons of Hashum: Mattenai, Mattattah, Zabad, Eliphelet, Jeremai, Manasseh, *and* Shimei; 34of the sons of Bani: Maadai, Amram, Uel, 35Benaiah, Bedeiah, 1Cheluh, 36Vaniah, Meremoth, Eliashib, 37Mattaniah, Mattenai, 1Jaasai, 38Bani, Binnui, Shimei, 39Shelemiah, Nathan, Adaiah, 40Machnadebai, Shashai, Sharai, 41Azarel, Shelemiah, Shemariah, 42Shallum, Amariah, *and* Joseph; 43of the sons of Nebo: Jeiel, Mattithiah, Zabad, Zebina, 1Jaddai, Joel, *and* Benaiah.

44All these had taken pagan wives, and *some* of them had wives *by whom* they had children.

10:28 aEzra 8:11
10:30 aEzra 8:4

10:29 1Or *Jeremoth*   10:35 1Or *Cheluhi* or *Cheluhu*   10:37 1Or *Jaasu*
10:43 1Or *Jaddu*

THE BOOK OF
NEHEMIAH

NEHEMIAH PRAYS FOR HIS PEOPLE

1 The words of ᵃNehemiah the son of Hachaliah.

It came to pass in the month of Chislev, *in* the ᵇtwentieth year, as I was in ᶜShushan¹ the ²citadel, ²that ᵃHanani one of my brethren came with men from Judah; and I asked them concerning the Jews who had escaped, who had survived the captivity, and concerning Jerusalem. ³And they said to me, "The survivors who are left from the captivity in the ᵃprovince *are* there in great distress and ᵇreproach. ᶜThe wall of Jerusalem ᵈ*is* also broken down, and its gates are burned with fire."

⁴So it was, when I heard these words, that I sat down and wept, and mourned *for many* days; I was fasting and praying before the God of heaven.

⁵And I said: "I pray, ᵃLᴏʀᴅ God of heaven, O great and ᵇawesome God, ᶜ*You* who keep *Your* covenant and mercy with those who love ¹You and observe ²Your commandments, ⁶please let Your ear be attentive and ᵃYour eyes open, that You may hear the prayer of Your servant which I pray before You now, day and night, for the children of Israel Your servants, and ᵇconfess the sins of the children of Israel which we have sinned against You. Both my father's house and I have sinned. ⁷ᵃWe have acted very corruptly against You, and have ᵇnot kept the commandments, the statutes, nor the ordinances which You commanded Your servant Moses. ⁸Remember, I pray, the word that You commanded Your servant Moses, saying, ᵃ'*If* you ¹are unfaithful, I will scatter you among the nations; ⁹ᵃbut *if* you return to Me, and keep My commandments and do them, ᵇthough some of you were cast out to the farthest part of the heavens, *yet* I will gather them from there, and bring them to the place which I have chosen as a dwelling for My name.' ¹⁰ᵃNow these *are* Your servants and Your people, whom You have redeemed by Your great power, and by Your strong hand. ¹¹O Lord, I pray, please ᵃlet Your ear be attentive to the prayer of Your servant, and to the prayer of Your servants who ᵇdesire to fear Your name; and let Your servant prosper this day, I pray, and grant him mercy in the sight of this man."

For I was the king's ᶜcupbearer.

NEHEMIAH SENT TO JUDAH

2 And it came to pass in the month of Nisan, in the twentieth year of ᵃKing ¹Artaxerxes, *when* wine *was* before him, that ᵇI took the wine and gave it to the king. Now I had never been sad in his presence before. ²Therefore the king said to me, "Why *is* your face sad, since you *are* not sick? This *is* nothing but ᵃsorrow of heart."

1:1 ᵃNeh. 10:1
ᵇNeh. 2:1
ᶜEsth. 1:1, 2, 5;
Dan. 8:2

1:2 ᵃNeh. 7:2

1:3 ᵃNeh. 7:6
ᵇNeh. 2:17
ᶜNeh. 2:17
ᵈ2 Kin. 25:10

1:5 ᵃDan. 9:4
ᵇNeh. 4:14
ᶜ[Ex. 20:6; 34:6, 7]; Ps. 89:2, 3

1:6 ᵃ1 Kin. 8:28, 29; 2 Chr. 6:40; Dan. 9:17, 18
ᵇEzra 10:1;
Neh. 9:2;
Dan. 9:20

1:7 ᵃPs. 106:6;
Dan. 9:5
ᵇDeut. 28:15

1:8 ᵃLev. 26:33;
Deut. 4:25–27;
28:63–67

1:9 ᵃLev. 26:39;
[Deut. 4:29–31; 30:2–5]
ᵇDeut. 30:4

1:10 ᵃEx. 32:11;
Deut. 9:29;
Dan. 9:15

1:11 ᵃNeh. 1:6
ᵇIs. 26:8;
[Heb. 13:18]
ᶜGen. 40:21;
Neh. 2:1

2:1 ᵃEzra 7:1
ᵇNeh. 1:11

2:2 ᵃProv. 15:13

So I became [1]dreadfully afraid, [3]and said to the king, [a]"May the king live forever! Why should my face not be sad, when [b]the city, the place of my fathers' tombs, *lies* waste, and its gates are burned with [c]fire?"

[4]Then the king said to me, "What do you request?"

So I [a]prayed to the God of heaven. [5]And I said to the king, "If it pleases the king, and if your servant has found favor in your sight, I ask that you send me to Judah, to the city of my fathers' tombs, that I may rebuild it."

[6]Then the king said to me (the queen also sitting beside him), "How long will your journey be? And when will you return?" So it pleased the king to send me; and I set him [a]a time.

[7]Furthermore I said to the king, "If it pleases the king, let letters be given to me for the [a]governors *of the region* beyond [1]the River, that they must permit me to pass through till I come to Judah, [8]and a letter to Asaph the keeper of the king's forest, that he must give me timber to make beams for the gates of the [1]citadel which *pertains* [a]to the [2]temple, for the city wall, and for the house that I will occupy." And the king granted *them* to me [b]according to the good hand of my God upon me.

[9]Then I went to the governors *in the region* beyond the River, and gave them the king's letters. Now the king had sent captains of the army and horsemen with me. [10]When [a]Sanballat the Horonite and Tobiah the Ammonite [1]official heard *of it*, they were deeply disturbed that a man had come to seek the well-being of the children of Israel.

NEHEMIAH VIEWS THE WALL OF JERUSALEM

[11]So I [a]came to Jerusalem and was there three days. [12]Then I arose in the night, I and a few men with me; I told no one what my God had put in my heart to do at Jerusalem; nor was there any animal with me, except the one on which I rode. [13]And I went out by night [a]through the Valley Gate to the Serpent Well and the [1]Refuse Gate, and [2]viewed the walls of Jerusalem which were [b]broken down and its gates which were burned with fire. [14]Then I went on to the [a]Fountain Gate and to the [b]King's Pool, but *there was* no room for the animal under me to pass. [15]So I went up in the night by the [a]valley,[1] and [2]viewed the wall; then I turned back and entered by the Valley Gate, and so returned. [16]And the officials did not know where I had gone or what I had done; I had not yet told the Jews, the priests, the nobles, the officials, or the others who did the work.

[17]Then I said to them, "You see the distress that we *are* in, how Jerusalem *lies* [1]waste, and its gates are burned with fire. Come and let us build the wall of Jerusalem, that we may no longer be [a]a reproach." [18]And I told them of [a]the hand of my God which had been good upon me, and also of the king's words that he had spoken to me.

So they said, "Let us rise up and build." Then they [b]set[1] their hands to *this* good *work*.

[19]But when Sanballat the Horonite, Tobiah the Ammonite official, and Geshem the Arab heard *of it*, they laughed at us

---

2:3 [a]1 Kin. 1:31; Dan. 2:4; 5:10; 6:6, 21
[b]2 Kin. 25:8–10; 2 Chr. 36:19; Jer. 52:12–14
[c]2 Kin. 24:10; Neh. 1:3

2:4 [a]Neh. 1:4

2:6 [a]Neh. 5:14; 13:6

2:7 [a]Ezra 7:21; 8:36

2:8 [a]Neh. 3:7
[b]Ezra 5:5; 7:6, 9, 28; Neh. 2:18

2:10 [a]Neh. 2:19; 4:1

2:11 [a]Ezra 8:32

2:13 [a]2 Chr. 26:9; Neh. 3:13
[b]Neh. 1:3; 2:17

2:14 [a]Neh. 3:15
[b]2 Kin. 20:20

2:15 [a]2 Sam. 15:23; Jer. 31:40

2:17 [a]Neh. 1:3; Ps. 44:13; 79:4; Jer. 24:9; Ezek. 5:14, 15; 22:4

2:18 [a]Neh. 2:8
[b]2 Sam. 2:7

2:2 [1]Lit. *very much*   2:7 [1]The Euphrates   2:8 [1]*palace*   [2]Lit. *house*
2:10 [1]Lit. *servant*   2:13 [1]*Dung*   [2]*examined*   2:15 [1]*torrent valley, wadi*
[2]*examined*   2:17 [1]*desolate*   2:18 [1]Lit. *strengthened*

and despised us, and said, "What *is* this thing that you are doing? [a]Will you rebel against the king?"

20So I answered them, and said to them, "The God of heaven Himself will prosper us; therefore we His servants will arise and build, [a]but you have no heritage or right or memorial in Jerusalem."

REBUILDING THE WALL

3 Then [a]Eliashib the high priest rose up with his brethren the priests [b]and built the Sheep Gate; they consecrated it and hung its doors. They built [c]as far as the Tower of [1]the Hundred, *and* consecrated it, then as far as the Tower of [d]Hananel. 21Next to *Eliashib* [a]the men of Jericho built. And next to them Zaccur the son of Imri built.

3Also the sons of Hassenaah built [a]the Fish Gate; they laid its beams and [b]hung its doors with its bolts and bars. 4And next to them [a]Meremoth the son of Urijah, the son of [1]Koz, made repairs. Next to them [b]Meshullam the son of Berechiah, the son of Meshezabel, made repairs. Next to them Zadok the son of Baana made repairs. 5Next to them the Tekoites made repairs; but their nobles did not put their [1]shoulders to [a]the work of their Lord.

6Moreover Jehoiada the son of Paseah and Meshullam the son of Besodeiah repaired [a]the Old Gate; they laid its beams and hung its doors, with its bolts and bars. 7And next to them Melatiah the Gibeonite, Jadon the Meronothite, the [a]men of Gibeon and Mizpah, repaired the [b]residence[1] of the governor *of the region* [2]beyond the River. 8Next to him Uzziel the son of Harhaiah, one of the goldsmiths, made repairs. Also next to him Hananiah, [1]one of the perfumers, made repairs; and they [2]fortified Jerusalem as far as the [a]Broad Wall. 9And next to them Rephaiah the son of Hur, leader of half the district of Jerusalem, made repairs. 10Next to them Jedaiah the son of Harumaph made repairs in front of his house. And next to him Hattush the son of Hashabniah made repairs.

11Malchijah the son of Harim and Hashub the son of Pahath-Moab repaired another section, [a]as well as the Tower of the Ovens. 12And next to him was Shallum the son of Hallohesh, leader of half the district of Jerusalem; he and his daughters made repairs.

13Hanun and the inhabitants of Zanoah repaired [a]the Valley Gate. They built it, hung its doors with its bolts and bars, and *repaired* a thousand cubits of the wall as far as [b]the Refuse Gate.

14Malchijah the son of Rechab, leader of the district of [a]Beth Haccerem, repaired the Refuse Gate; he built it and hung its doors with its bolts and bars.

15Shallun the son of Col-Hozeh, leader of the district of Mizpah, repaired [a]the Fountain Gate; he built it, covered it, hung its doors with its bolts and bars, and repaired the wall of the Pool of [b]Shelah[1] by the [c]King's Garden, as far as the stairs that go down from the City of David. 16After him Nehemiah the son of Azbuk, leader of half the district of Beth Zur, made repairs as far as *the place* in front of the [1]tombs

2:19 [a]Neh. 6:6

2:20 [a]Ezra 4:3; Neh. 6:16

3:1 [a]Neh. 3:20; 12:10; 13:4, 7, 28
[b]John 5:2
[c]Neh. 12:39
[d]Jer. 31:38; Zech. 14:10

3:2 [a]Ezra 2:34; Neh. 7:36

3:3
[a]2 Chr. 33:14; Neh. 12:39; Zeph. 1:10
[b]Neh. 6:1; 7:1

3:4 [a]Ezra 8:33
[b]Ezra 10:15

3:5
[a][Judg. 5:23]

3:6 [a]Neh. 12:39

3:7 [a]Neh. 7:25
[b]Ezra 8:36; Neh. 2:7–9

3:8 [a]Neh. 12:38

3:11 [a]Neh. 12:38

3:13
[a]Neh. 2:13, 15
[b]Neh. 2:13

3:14 [a]Jer. 6:1

3:15 [a]Neh. 2:14
[b]Is. 8:6; John 9:7
[c]2 Kin. 25:4

3:1 [1]Heb. *Hammeah*   3:2 [1]Lit. *On his hand*   3:4 [1]Or *Hakkoz*   3:5 [1]Lit. *necks*   3:7 [1]Lit. *throne*   [2]West of the Euphrates   3:8 [1]Lit. *the son* [2]restored   3:15 [1]Or *Shiloah*   3:16 [1]LXX, Syr., Vg. *tomb*

of David, to the [a]man-made pool, and as far as the House of the Mighty.

[17]After him the Levites, *under* Rehum the son of Bani, made repairs. Next to him Hashabiah, leader of half the district of Keilah, made repairs for his district. [18]After him their brethren, *under* [1]Bavai the son of Henadad, leader of the *other* half of the district of Keilah, made repairs. [19]And next to him Ezer the son of Jeshua, the leader of Mizpah, repaired another section in front of the Ascent to the Armory at the [a]buttress.[1] [20]After him Baruch the son of [1]Zabbai carefully repaired the other section, from the [2]buttress to the door of the house of Eliashib the high priest. [21]After him Meremoth the son of Urijah, the son of [1]Koz, repaired another section, from the door of the house of Eliashib to the end of the house of Eliashib.

[22]And after him the priests, the men of the plain, made repairs. [23]After him Benjamin and Hasshub made repairs opposite their house. After them Azariah the son of Maaseiah, the son of Ananiah, made repairs by his house. [24]After him [a]Binnui the son of Henadad repaired another section, from the house of Azariah to [b]the [1]buttress, even as far as the corner. [25]Palal the son of Uzai *made repairs* opposite the [1]buttress, and on the tower which projects from the king's upper house that *was* by the [a]court of the prison. After him Pedaiah the son of Parosh *made repairs.*

[26]Moreover [a]the Nethinim who dwelt in [b]Ophel *made repairs* as far as *the place* in front of [c]the Water Gate toward the east, and on the projecting tower. [27]After them the Tekoites repaired another section, next to the great projecting tower, and as far as the wall of Ophel.

[28]Beyond the [a]Horse Gate the priests made repairs, each in front of his *own* house. [29]After them Zadok the son of Immer made repairs in front of his *own* house. After him Shemaiah the son of Shechaniah, the keeper of the East Gate, made repairs. [30]After him Hananiah the son of Shelemiah, and Hanun, the sixth son of Zalaph, repaired another section. After him Meshullam the son of Berechiah made repairs in front of his [1]dwelling. [31]After him Malchijah, [1]one of the goldsmiths, made repairs as far as the house of the Nethinim and of the merchants, in front of the [2]Miphkad Gate, and as far as the upper room at the corner. [32]And between the upper room at the corner, as far as the [a]Sheep Gate, the goldsmiths and the merchants made repairs.

THE WALL DEFENDED AGAINST ENEMIES

4 But it so happened, [a]when Sanballat heard that we were rebuilding the wall, that he was furious and very indignant, and mocked the Jews. [2]And he spoke before his brethren and the army of Samaria, and said, "What are these feeble Jews doing? Will they fortify themselves? Will they offer sacrifices? Will they complete it in a day? Will they revive the stones from the heaps of rubbish—*stones* that are burned?"

[3]Now [a]Tobiah the Ammonite *was* beside him, and he said,

3:16
[a]2 Kin. 20:20;
Is. 7:3; 22:11

3:19 [a]2 Chr. 26:9

3:24 [a]Ezra 8:33
[b]Neh. 3:19

3:25 [a]Jer. 32:2;
33:1; 37:21

3:26 [a]Ezra 2:43;
Neh. 11:21
[b]2 Chr. 27:3
[c]Neh. 8:1, 3;
12:37

3:28
[a]2 Kin. 11:16;
2 Chr. 23:15;
Jer. 31:40

3:32
[a]Neh. 3:1; 12:39

4:1
[a]Neh. 2:10, 19

4:3
[a]Neh. 2:10, 19

3:18 [1]So with MT, Vg.; some Heb. mss., LXX, Syr. *Binnui* (cf. v. 24)   3:19 [1]Lit. *turning*   3:20 [1]A few Heb. mss., Syr., Vg. *Zaccai*   [2]Lit. *turning*   3:21 [1]Or *Hakkoz*   3:24 [1]Lit. *turning*   3:25 [1]Lit. *turning*   3:30 [1]Lit. *room*   3:31 [1]Lit. *a son of the goldsmiths*   [2]Lit. *Inspection* or *Recruiting*

"Whatever they build, if even a fox goes up *on it,* he will break down their stone wall."

[4]a Hear, O our God, for we are despised; b turn their reproach on their own heads, and give them as plunder to a land of captivity! [5]a Do not cover their iniquity, and do not let their sin be blotted out from before You; for they have provoked *You* to anger before the builders.

[6] So we built the wall, and the entire wall was joined together up to half its *height,* for the people had a mind to work.

[7] Now it happened, a when Sanballat, Tobiah, b the Arabs, the Ammonites, and the Ashdodites heard that the walls of Jerusalem were being restored and the [1]gaps were beginning to be closed, that they became very angry, [8] and all of them a conspired together to come *and* attack Jerusalem and create confusion. [9] Nevertheless a we made our prayer to our God, and because of them we set a watch against them day and night.

[10] Then Judah said, "The strength of the laborers is failing, and *there is* so much rubbish that we are not able to build the wall."

[11] And our adversaries said, "They will neither know nor see anything, till we come into their midst and kill them and cause the work to cease."

[12] So it was, when the Jews who dwelt near them came, that they told us ten times, "From whatever place you turn, *they will be* upon us."

[13] Therefore I positioned *men* behind the lower parts of the wall, at the openings; and I set the people according to their families, with their swords, their spears, and their bows. [14] And I looked, and arose and said to the nobles, to the leaders, and to the rest of the people, a "Do not be afraid of them. Remember the Lord, b great and awesome, and c fight for your brethren, your sons, your daughters, your wives, and your houses."

[15] And it happened, when our enemies heard that it was known to us, and a *that* God had brought their plot to nothing, that all of us returned to the wall, everyone to his work. [16] So it was, from that time on, *that* half of my servants worked at construction, while the other half held the spears, the shields, the bows, and *wore* armor; and the leaders [1]*were* behind all the house of Judah. [17] Those who built on the wall, and those who carried burdens, loaded themselves so that with one hand they worked at construction, and with the other held a weapon. [18] Every one of the builders had his sword girded at his side as he built. And the one who sounded the trumpet *was* beside me.

[19] Then I said to the nobles, the rulers, and the rest of the people, "The work *is* great and extensive, and we are separated far from one another on the wall. [20] Wherever you hear the sound of the trumpet, rally to us there. a Our God will fight for us."

[21] So we labored in the work, and half of [1]*the men* held the spears from daybreak until the stars appeared. [22] At the same time I also said to the people, "Let each man and his servant stay at night in Jerusalem, that they may be our guard by night and a working party by day." [23] So neither I, my brethren, my servants, nor the men of the guard who followed me

4:4
a Ps. 123:3, 4
b Ps. 79:12;
Prov. 3:34
4:5
a Ps. 69:27, 28;
109:14, 15;
Jer. 18:23
4:7 a Neh. 4:1
b Neh. 2:19
4:8 a Ps. 83:3–5
4:9 a [Ps. 50:15]
4:14
a [Num. 14:9];
Deut. 1:29
b [Deut. 10:17]
c 2 Sam. 10:12
4:15 a Job 5:12
4:20
a Ex. 14:14, 25;
Deut. 1:30;
3:22; 20:4;
Josh. 23:10;
2 Chr. 20:29

4:7 [1]Lit. *breaks*   4:16 [1]Supported   4:21 [1]Lit. *them*

took off our clothes, *except* that everyone took them off for washing.

NEHEMIAH DEALS WITH OPPRESSION

5 And there was a great ᵃoutcry of the people and their wives against their ᵇJewish brethren. ²For there were those who said, "We, our sons, and our daughters *are* many; therefore let us get grain, that we may eat and live."

³There were also *some* who said, "We have mortgaged our lands and vineyards and houses, that we might buy grain because of the famine."

⁴There were also those who said, "We have borrowed money for the king's tax *on* our lands and vineyards. ⁵Yet now ᵃour flesh *is* as the flesh of our brethren, our children as their children; and indeed we ᵇare forcing our sons and our daughters to be slaves, and *some* of our daughters have been brought into slavery. *It is* not in our power *to redeem them,* for other men have our lands and vineyards."

⁶And I became very angry when I heard their outcry and these words. ⁷After serious thought, I rebuked the nobles and rulers, and said to them, ᵃ"Each of you is ¹exacting usury from his brother." So I ²called a great assembly against them. ⁸And I said to them, "According to our ability we have ᵃredeemed our Jewish brethren who were sold to the nations. Now indeed, will you even sell your brethren? Or should they be sold to us?"

Then they were silenced and found nothing *to say.* ⁹Then I said, "What you are doing *is* not good. Should you not walk ᵃin the fear of our God ᵇbecause of the reproach of the nations, our enemies? ¹⁰I also, *with* my brethren and my servants, am lending them money and grain. Please, let us stop this ¹usury! ¹¹Restore now to them, even this day, their lands, their vineyards, their olive groves, and their houses, also a hundredth of the money and the grain, the new wine and the oil, that you have charged them."

¹²So they said, "We will restore *it,* and will require nothing from them; we will do as you say."

Then I called the priests, ᵃand required an oath from them that they would do according to this promise. ¹³Then ᵃI shook out ¹the fold of my garment and said, "So may God shake out each man from his house, and from his property, who does not perform this promise. Even thus may he be shaken out and emptied."

And all the assembly said, "Amen!" and praised the LORD. ᵇThen the people did according to this promise.

THE GENEROSITY OF NEHEMIAH

¹⁴Moreover, from the time that I was appointed to be their governor in the land of Judah, from the twentieth year ᵃuntil the thirty-second year of King Artaxerxes, twelve years, neither I nor my brothers ᵇate the governor's provisions. ¹⁵But the former governors who *were* before me laid burdens on the people, and took from them bread and wine, besides forty shekels of silver. Yes, even their servants bore rule over the people, but ᵃI did not do so, because of the ᵇfear of God.

5:1
ᵃLev. 25:35–37;
Neh. 5:7, 8
ᵇDeut. 15:7

5:5 ᵃIs. 58:7
ᵇEx. 21:7;
[Lev. 25:39]

5:7 ᵃ[Ex. 22:25;
Lev. 25:36;
Deut. 23:19, 20];
Ezek. 22:12

5:8 ᵃLev. 25:48

5:9 ᵃLev. 25:36
ᵇ2 Sam. 12:14;
Rom. 2:24;
[1 Pet. 2:12]

5:12 ᵃEzra 10:5;
Jer. 34:8, 9

5:13
ᵃMatt. 10:14;
Acts 13:51; 18:6
ᵇ2 Kin. 23:3

5:14
ᵃNeh. 2:1; 13:6
ᵇ[1 Cor. 9:4–15]

5:15 ᵃ2 Cor. 11:9;
12:13 ᵇNeh. 5:9

5:7 ¹*charging interest*   ²Lit. *held*   **5:10** ¹*interest*   **5:13** ¹Lit. *my lap*

¹⁶Indeed, I also continued the ᵃwork on this wall, and ¹we did not buy any land. All my servants *were* gathered there for the work.

¹⁷And ᵃat my table *were* one hundred and fifty Jews and rulers, besides those who came to us from the nations around us. ¹⁸Now *that* ᵃwhich was prepared daily *was* one ox *and* six choice sheep. Also fowl were prepared for me, and once every ten days an abundance of all kinds of wine. Yet in spite of this ᵇI did not demand the governor's provisions, because the bondage was heavy on this people.

¹⁹ᵃRemember me, my God, for good, *according to* all that I have done for this people.

CONSPIRACY AGAINST NEHEMIAH

6 Now it happened ᵃwhen Sanballat, Tobiah, ¹Geshem the Arab, and the rest of our enemies heard that I had rebuilt the wall, and *that* there were no breaks left in it ᵇ(though at that time I had not hung the doors in the gates), ²that Sanballat and ¹Geshem ᵃsent to me, saying, "Come, let us meet together ²among the villages in the plain of ᵇOno." But they ᶜthought to do me harm.

³So I sent messengers to them, saying, "I *am* doing a great work, so that I cannot come down. Why should the work cease while I leave it and go down to you?"

⁴But they sent me this message four times, and I answered them in the same manner.

⁵Then Sanballat sent his servant to me as before, the fifth time, with an open letter in his hand. ⁶In it *was* written:

It is reported among the nations, and ¹Geshem says, *that* you and the Jews plan to rebel; therefore, according to these rumors, you are rebuilding the wall, ᵃthat you may be their king. ⁷And you have also appointed prophets to proclaim concerning you at Jerusalem, saying, "*There is* a king in Judah!" Now these matters will be reported to the king. So come, therefore, and let us consult together.

⁸Then I sent to him, saying, "No such things as you say are being done, but you invent them in your own heart."

⁹For they all *were trying to* make us afraid, saying, "Their hands will be weakened in the work, and it will not be done."

Now therefore, *O God*, strengthen my hands.

¹⁰Afterward I came to the house of Shemaiah the son of Delaiah, the son of Mehetabel, who *was* a secret informer; and he said, "Let us meet together in the house of God, within the ¹temple, and let us close the doors of the temple, for they are coming to kill you; indeed, at night they will come to kill you."

¹¹And I said, "Should such a man as I flee? And who *is there* such as I who would go into the temple to save his life? I will not go in!" ¹²Then I perceived that God had not sent him at all, but that ᵃhe pronounced *this* prophecy against me because Tobiah and Sanballat had hired him. ¹³For this reason he *was* hired, that I should be afraid and act that way and sin, so *that* they might have *cause* for an evil report, that they might reproach me.

5:16
ᵃNeh. 4:1; 6:1

5:17 ᵃ2 Sam. 9:7;
1 Kin. 18:19

5:18 ᵃ1 Kin. 4:22
ᵇNeh. 5:14, 15

5:19
ᵃ2 Kin. 20:3;
Neh. 13:14,
22, 31

6:1
ᵃNeh. 2:10, 19;
4:1, 7; 13:28
ᵇNeh. 3:1, 3

6:2
ᵃProv. 26:24, 25
ᵇ1 Chr. 8:12;
Neh. 11:35
ᶜPs. 37:12, 32

6:6 ᵃNeh. 2:19

6:12 ᵃEzek. 13:22

5:16 ¹So with MT; LXX, Syr., Vg. I 6:1 ¹Or *Gashmu* 6:2 ¹Or *Gashmu* ²Or *in Kephirim*, exact location unknown 6:6 ¹Heb. *Gashmu* 6:10 ¹Lit. *house*

[14a]My God, remember Tobiah and Sanballat, according to these their works, and the [b]prophetess Noadiah and the rest of the prophets who would have made me afraid.

THE WALL COMPLETED

[15]So the wall was finished on the twenty-fifth *day* of Elul, in fifty-two days. [16]And it happened, [a]when all our enemies heard *of it*, and all the nations around us saw *these things*, that they were very disheartened in their own eyes; for [b]they perceived that this work was done by our God.

[17]Also in those days the nobles of Judah sent many letters to Tobiah, and *the letters of* Tobiah came to them. [18]For many in Judah were pledged to him, because he was the [a]son-in-law of Shechaniah the son of Arah, and his son Jehohanan had married the daughter of [b]Meshullam the son of Berechiah. [19]Also they reported his good deeds before me, and reported my [1]words to him. Tobiah sent letters to frighten me.

7 Then it was, when the wall was built and I had [a]hung the doors, when the gatekeepers, the singers, and the Levites had been appointed, [2]that I gave the charge of Jerusalem to my brother [a]Hanani, and Hananiah the leader [b]of the [1]citadel, for he *was* a faithful man and [c]feared God more than many.

[3]And I said to them, "Do not let the gates of Jerusalem be opened until the sun is hot; and while they stand *guard,* let them shut and bar the doors; and appoint guards from among the inhabitants of Jerusalem, one at his watch station and another in front of his own house."

THE CAPTIVES WHO RETURNED TO JERUSALEM
(Ezra 2:1–70)

[4]Now the city *was* large and spacious, but the people in it *were* [a]few, and the houses *were* not rebuilt. [5]Then my God put it into my heart to gather the nobles, the rulers, and the people, that they might be registered by genealogy. And I found a register of the genealogy of those who had come up in the first *return,* and found written in it:

6   [a]These *are* the people of the province who came back from the captivity, of those who had been carried away, whom Nebuchadnezzar the king of Babylon had carried away, and who returned to Jerusalem and Judah, everyone to his city.

7   Those who came with [a]Zerubbabel *were* Jeshua, Nehemiah, [1]Azariah, Raamiah, Nahamani, Mordecai, Bilshan, [2]Mispereth, Bigvai, Nehum, and Baanah.

The number of the men of the people of Israel: [8]the sons of Parosh, two thousand one hundred and seventy-two; [9]the sons of Shephatiah, three hundred and seventy-two; [10]the sons of Arah, six hundred and fifty-two; [11]the sons of Pahath-Moab, of the sons of Jeshua and Joab, two thousand eight hundred and eighteen; [12]the sons of Elam, one thousand two hundred and fifty-four; [13]the sons of Zattu, eight hundred and forty-five; [14]the sons of Zaccai, seven hundred and sixty;

6:14 [a]Neh. 13:29
[b]Ezek. 13:17

6:16
[a]Neh. 2:10, 20; 4:1, 7; 6:1
[b]Ps. 126:2

6:18
[a]Neh. 13:4, 28
[b]Ezra 10:15; Neh. 3:4

7:1 [a]Neh. 6:1, 15

7:2 [a]Neh. 1:2
[b]Neh. 2:8; 10:23
[c]Ex. 18:21

7:4 [a]Deut. 4:27

7:6 [a]Ezra 2:1–70

7:7 [a]Ezra 5:2; Neh. 12:1, 47; Matt. 1:12, 13

6:19 [1]Or *affairs*   7:2 [1]*palace*   7:7 [1]*Seraiah,* Ezra 2:2   [2]*Mispar,* Ezra 2:2

¹⁵the sons of ¹Binnui, six hundred and forty-eight;

¹⁶the sons of Bebai, six hundred and twenty-eight;

¹⁷the sons of Azgad, two thousand three hundred and twenty-two;

¹⁸the sons of Adonikam, six hundred and sixty-seven;

¹⁹the sons of Bigvai, two thousand and sixty-seven;

²⁰the sons of Adin, six hundred and fifty-five;

²¹the sons of Ater of Hezekiah, ninety-eight;

²²the sons of Hashum, three hundred and twenty-eight;

²³the sons of Bezai, three hundred and twenty-four;

²⁴the sons of ¹Hariph, one hundred and twelve;

²⁵the sons of ¹Gibeon, ninety-five;

²⁶the men of Bethlehem and Netophah, one hundred and eighty-eight;

²⁷the men of Anathoth, one hundred and twenty-eight;

²⁸the men of ¹Beth Azmaveth, forty-two;

²⁹the men of ¹Kirjath Jearim, Chephirah, and Beeroth, seven hundred and forty-three;

³⁰the men of Ramah and Geba, six hundred and twenty-one;

³¹the men of Michmas, one hundred and twenty-two;

³²the men of Bethel and Ai, one hundred and twenty-three;

³³the men of the other Nebo, fifty-two;

³⁴the sons of the other ªElam, one thousand two hundred and fifty-four;

³⁵the sons of Harim, three hundred and twenty;

³⁶the sons of Jericho, three hundred and forty-five;

³⁷the sons of Lod, Hadid, and Ono, seven hundred and twenty-one;

³⁸the sons of Senaah, three thousand nine hundred and thirty.

39 The priests: the sons of ªJedaiah, of the house of Jeshua, nine hundred and seventy-three;

⁴⁰the sons of ªImmer, one thousand and fifty-two;

⁴¹the sons of ªPashhur, one thousand two hundred and forty-seven;

⁴²the sons of ªHarim, one thousand and seventeen.

43 The Levites: the sons of Jeshua, of Kadmiel, *and* of the sons of ¹Hodevah, seventy-four.

44 The singers: the sons of Asaph, one hundred and forty-eight.

45 The gatekeepers: the sons of Shallum,
the sons of Ater,
the sons of Talmon,
the sons of Akkub,
the sons of Hatita,
the sons of Shobai, one hundred and thirty-eight.

46 The Nethinim: the sons of Ziha,
the sons of Hasupha,
the sons of Tabbaoth,
⁴⁷the sons of Keros,

7:34 ªNeh. 7:12
7:39 ª1 Chr. 24:7
7:40 ª1 Chr. 9:12
7:41 ªEzra 2:38; 10:22
7:42 ª1 Chr. 24:8

7:15 ¹*Bani,* Ezra 2:10   7:24 ¹*Jorah,* Ezra 2:18   7:25 ¹*Gibbar,* Ezra 2:20
7:28 ¹*Azmaveth,* Ezra 2:24   7:29 ¹*Kirjath Arim,* Ezra 2:25   7:43 ¹*Hodaviah,*
Ezra 2:40; or *Judah,* Ezra 3:9

the sons of [1]Sia,
the sons of Padon,
48the sons of [1]Lebana,
the sons of [2]Hagaba,
the sons of [3]Salmai,
49the sons of Hanan,
the sons of Giddel,
the sons of Gahar,
50the sons of Reaiah,
the sons of Rezin,
the sons of Nekoda,
51the sons of Gazzam,
the sons of Uzza,
the sons of Paseah,
52the sons of Besai,
the sons of Meunim,
the sons of [1]Nephishesim,
53the sons of Bakbuk,
the sons of Hakupha,
the sons of Harhur,
54the sons of [1]Bazlith,
the sons of Mehida,
the sons of Harsha,
55the sons of Barkos,
the sons of Sisera,
the sons of Tamah,
56the sons of Neziah,
and the sons of Hatipha.

57 The sons of Solomon's servants: the sons of Sotai,
the sons of Sophereth,
the sons of [1]Perida,
58the sons of Jaala,
the sons of Darkon,
the sons of Giddel,
59the sons of Shephatiah,
the sons of Hattil,
the sons of Pochereth of Zebaim,
and the sons of [1]Amon.
60All the Nethinim, and the sons of Solomon's servants,
were three hundred and ninety-two.

61 And these *were* the ones who came up from Tel Melah,
Tel Harsha, Cherub, [1]Addon, and Immer, but they could
not identify their father's house nor their lineage,
whether they *were* of Israel: 62the sons of Delaiah,
the sons of Tobiah,
the sons of Nekoda, six hundred and forty-two;
63and of the priests: the sons of Habaiah,
the sons of [1]Koz,
the sons of Barzillai, who took a wife of the daughters of
Barzillai the Gileadite, and was called by their name.
64These sought their listing *among* those who were
registered by genealogy, but it was not found; therefore

7:47 [1]*Siaha*, Ezra 2:44 7:48 [1]MT *Lebanah* [2]MT *Hogabah* [3]*Shalmai*, Ezra
2:46; or *Shamlai* 7:52 [1]*Nephusim*, Ezra 2:50 7:54 [1]*Bazluth*, Ezra 2:52
7:57 [1]*Peruda*, Ezra 2:55 7:59 [1]*Ami*, Ezra 2:57 7:61 [1]*Addan*, Ezra 2:59
7:63 [1]Or *Hakkoz*

they were excluded from the priesthood as defiled. [65]And the [1]governor said to them that they should not eat of the most holy things till a priest could consult with the Urim and Thummim.

[66] Altogether the whole assembly *was* forty-two thousand three hundred and sixty, [67]besides their male and female servants, of whom *there were* seven thousand three hundred and thirty-seven; and they had two hundred and forty-five men and women singers. [68]Their horses were seven hundred and thirty-six, their mules two hundred and forty-five, [69]*their* camels four hundred and thirty-five, *and* donkeys six thousand seven hundred and twenty.

[70] And some of the heads of the fathers' *houses* gave to the work. [a]The [1]governor gave to the treasury one thousand gold drachmas, fifty basins, and five hundred and thirty priestly garments. [71]Some of the heads of the fathers' *houses* gave to the treasury of the work [a]twenty thousand gold drachmas, and two thousand two hundred silver minas. [72]And that which the rest of the people gave *was* twenty thousand gold drachmas, two thousand silver minas, and sixty-seven priestly garments.

[73]So the priests, the Levites, the gatekeepers, the singers, *some* of the people, the Nethinim, and all Israel dwelt in their cities.

EZRA READS THE LAW

[a]When the seventh month came, the children of Israel *were* in their cities.

8 Now all [a]the people gathered together as one man in the open square that *was* [b]in front of the Water Gate; and they told Ezra the [c]scribe to bring the Book of the Law of Moses, which the LORD had commanded Israel. [2]So Ezra the priest brought [a]the Law before the assembly of men and women and all who *could* hear with understanding [b]on the first day of the seventh month. [3]Then he [a]read from it in the open square that *was* in front of the Water Gate [1]from morning until midday, before the men and women and those who could understand; and the ears of all the people *were attentive* to the Book of the Law.

[4]So Ezra the scribe stood on a platform of wood which they had made for the purpose; and beside him, at his right hand, stood Mattithiah, Shema, Anaiah, Urijah, Hilkiah, and Maaseiah; and at his left hand Pedaiah, Mishael, Malchijah, Hashum, Hashbadana, Zechariah, *and* Meshullam. [5]And Ezra opened the book in the sight of all the people, for he was *standing* above all the people; and when he opened it, all the people [a]stood up. [6]And Ezra blessed the LORD, the great God.

Then all the people [a]answered, "Amen, Amen!" while [b]lifting up their hands. And they [c]bowed their heads and worshiped the LORD with *their* faces to the ground.

[7]Also Jeshua, Bani, Sherebiah, Jamin, Akkub, Shabbethai, Hodijah, Maaseiah, Kelita, Azariah, Jozabad, Hanan, Pelaiah, and the Levites, [a]helped the people to understand the Law; and the people [b]stood in their place. [8]So they read distinctly

7:70 [a]Neh. 8:9

7:71 [a]Ezra 2:69

7:73 [a]Ezra 3:1

8:1 [a]Ezra 3:1
[b]Neh. 3:26
[c]Ezra 7:6

8:2
[a][Deut. 31:11, 12];
Neh. 8:9
[b]Lev. 23:24;
Num. 29:1–6

8:3
[a]Deut. 31:9–11;
2 Kin. 23:2

8:5 [a]Judg. 3:20;
1 Kin. 8:12–14

8:6 [a]Neh. 5:13;
[1 Cor. 14:16]
[b]Ps. 28:2;
Lam. 3:41;
1 Tim. 2:8
[c]Ex. 4:31; 12:27;
2 Chr. 20:18

8:7 [a]Lev. 10:11;
Deut. 33:10;
2 Chr. 17:7;
[Mal. 2:7]
[b]Neh. 9:3

7:65 [1]Heb. *Tirshatha*   7:70 [1]Heb. *Tirshatha*   8:3 [1]Lit. *from the light*

from the book, in the Law of God; and they gave the sense, and helped *them* to understand the reading.

9 [a]And Nehemiah, who *was* the [1]governor, Ezra the priest *and* scribe, and the Levites who taught the people said to all the people, [b]"This day *is* holy to the LORD your God; [c]do not mourn nor weep." For all the people wept, when they heard the words of the Law.

10 Then he said to them, "Go your way, eat the fat, drink the sweet, [a]and send portions to those for whom nothing is prepared; for *this* day *is* holy to our Lord. Do not sorrow, for the joy of the LORD is your strength."

11 So the Levites quieted all the people, saying, "Be still, for the day *is* holy; do not be grieved." 12 And all the people went their way to eat and drink, to [a]send portions and rejoice greatly, because they [b]understood the words that were declared to them.

THE FEAST OF TABERNACLES
(cf. Lev. 23:33–43)

13 Now on the second day the heads of the fathers' *houses* of all the people, with the priests and Levites, were gathered to Ezra the scribe, in order to understand the words of the Law. 14 And they found written in the Law, which the LORD had commanded by Moses, that the children of Israel should dwell in [a]booths[1] during the feast of the seventh month, 15 and [a]that they should announce and proclaim in all their cities and [b]in Jerusalem, saying, "Go out to the mountain, and [c]bring olive branches, branches of oil trees, myrtle branches, palm branches, and branches of leafy trees, to make booths, as *it is* written."

16 Then the people went out and brought *them* and made themselves booths, each one on the [a]roof of his house, or in their courtyards or the courts of the house of God, and in the open square of the [b]Water Gate [c]and in the open square of the Gate of Ephraim. 17 So the whole assembly of those who had returned from the captivity made [1]booths and sat under the booths; for since the days of Joshua the son of Nun until that day the children of Israel had not done so. And there was very [a]great gladness. 18 Also [a]day by day, from the first day until the last day, he read from the Book of the Law of God. And they kept the feast [b]seven days; and on the [c]eighth day *there was* a sacred assembly, according to the *prescribed* manner.

THE PEOPLE CONFESS THEIR SINS

9 Now on the twenty-fourth day of [a]this month the children of Israel were assembled with fasting, in sackcloth, [b]and with [1]dust on their heads. 2 Then [a]those of Israelite lineage separated themselves from all foreigners; and they stood and [b]confessed their sins and the iniquities of their fathers. 3 And they stood up in their place and [a]read from the Book of the Law of the LORD their God *for one*-fourth of the day; and *for another* fourth they confessed and worshiped the LORD their God.

4 Then Jeshua, Bani, Kadmiel, Shebaniah, Bunni, Sherebiah, Bani, *and* Chenani stood on the [1]stairs of the Levites and

8:9 [a]Ezra 2:63; Neh. 7:65, 70; 10:1 [b]Lev. 23:24; Num. 29:1 [c]Deut. 16:14; Eccl. 3:4
8:10 [a][Deut. 26:11–13]; Esth. 9:19, 22; Rev. 11:10
8:12 [a]Neh. 8:10 [b]Neh. 8:7, 8
8:14 [a]Lev. 23:34, 40, 42; Deut. 16:13
8:15 [a]Lev. 23:4 [b]Deut. 16:16 [c]Lev. 23:40
8:16 [a]Deut. 22:8 [b]Neh. 12:37 [c]2 Kin. 14:13; Neh. 12:39
8:17 [a]2 Chr. 30:21
8:18 [a]Deut. 31:11 [b]Lev. 23:36 [c]Num. 29:35
9:1 [a]Neh. 8:2 [b]Josh. 7:6; 1 Sam. 4:12; 2 Sam. 1:2; Job 2:12
9:2 [a]Ezra 10:11; Neh. 13:3, 30 [b]Neh. 1:6
9:3 [a]Neh. 8:7, 8

8:9 [1]Heb. *Tirshatha*   8:14 [1]Temporary shelters   8:17 [1]Temporary shelters
9:1 [1]Lit. *earth on them*   9:4 [1]Lit. *ascent*

cried out with a loud voice to the LORD their God. ⁵And the Levites, Jeshua, Kadmiel, Bani, Hashabniah, Sherebiah, Hodijah, Shebaniah, *and* Pethahiah, said:

> "Stand up *and* bless the LORD your God
> Forever and ever!

> "Blessed be ᵃYour glorious name,
> Which is exalted above all blessing and praise!

6   ᵃYou alone *are* the LORD;
> ᵇYou have made heaven,
> ᶜThe heaven of heavens, with ᵈall their host,
> The earth and everything on it,
> The seas and all that is in them,
> And You ᵉpreserve them all.
> The host of heaven worships You.

7   "You *are* the LORD God,
> Who chose ᵃAbram,
> And brought him out of Ur of the Chaldeans,
> And gave him the name ᵇAbraham;

8   You found his heart ᵃfaithful before You,
> And made a ᵇcovenant with him
> To give the land of the Canaanites,
> The Hittites, the Amorites,
> The Perizzites, the Jebusites,
> And the Girgashites—
> To give *it* to his descendants.
> You ᶜhave performed Your words,
> For You *are* righteous.

9   "Youᵃ saw the affliction of our fathers in Egypt,
> And ᵇheard their cry by the Red Sea.

10   You ᵃshowed signs and wonders against Pharaoh,
> Against all his servants,
> And against all the people of his land.
> For You knew that they ᵇacted ¹proudly against them.
> So You ᶜmade a name for Yourself, as *it is* this day.

11   ᵃAnd You divided the sea before them,
> So that they went through the midst of the sea on the dry
> land;
> And their persecutors You threw into the deep,
> ᵇAs a stone into the mighty waters.

12   Moreover You ᵃled them by day with a cloudy pillar,
> And by night with a pillar of fire,
> To give them light on the road
> Which they should travel.

13   "Youᵃ came down also on Mount Sinai,
> And spoke with them from heaven,
> And gave them ᵇjust ordinances and true laws,
> Good statutes and commandments.

14   You made known to them Your ᵃholy Sabbath,
> And commanded them precepts, statutes and laws,
> By the hand of Moses Your servant.

15   You ᵃgave them bread from heaven for their hunger,
> And ᵇbrought them water out of the rock for their thirst,
> And told them to ᶜgo in to possess the land
> Which You had ¹sworn to give them.

9:5 ᵃ1 Chr. 29:13

9:6 ᵃDeut. 6:4;
2 Kin. 19:15, 19;
[Ps. 86:10];
Is. 37:16, 20
ᵇGen. 1:1;
Ex. 20:11;
Rev. 14:7
ᶜ[Deut. 10:14];
1 Kin. 8:27
ᵈGen. 2:1
ᵉ[Ps. 36:6]

9:7 ᵃGen. 11:31
ᵇGen. 17:5

9:8 ᵃGen. 15:6;
22:1–3;
[James 2:21–23]
ᵇGen. 15:18
ᶜJosh. 23:14

9:9
ᵃEx. 2:25; 3:7
ᵇEx. 14:10

9:10
ᵃEx. 7—14
ᵇEx. 18:11
ᶜJer. 32:20

9:11
ᵃEx. 14:20–28
ᵇEx. 15:1, 5

9:12
ᵃEx. 13:21, 22

9:13
ᵃEx. 20:1–18
ᵇ[Rom. 7:12]

9:14 ᵃGen. 2:3;
Ex. 16:23; 20:8;
23:12

9:15
ᵃEx. 16:14–17;
John 6:31
ᵇEx. 17:6;
Num. 20:8;
[1 Cor. 10:4]
ᶜDeut. 1:8

9:10 ¹*presumptuously* or *insolently*   9:15 ¹Lit. *raised Your hand to*

16 "But[a] they and our fathers acted [1]proudly,
　　[b]Hardened[2] their necks,
　　And did not heed Your commandments.
17 They refused to obey,
　　And [a]they were not mindful of Your wonders
　　That You did among them.
　　But they hardened their necks,
　　And [1]in their rebellion
　　They appointed [b]a leader
　　To return to their bondage.
　　But You *are* God,
　　Ready to pardon,
　　[c]Gracious and merciful,
　　Slow to anger,
　　Abundant in kindness,
　　And did not forsake them.

18 "Even [a]when they made a molded calf for themselves,
　　And said, 'This *is* your god
　　That brought you up out of Egypt,'
　　And worked great provocations,
19 Yet in Your [a]manifold mercies
　　You did not forsake them in the wilderness.
　　The [b]pillar of the cloud did not depart from them by
　　　　day,
　　To lead them on the road;
　　Nor the pillar of fire by night,
　　To show them light,
　　And the way they should go.
20 You also gave Your [a]good Spirit to instruct them,
　　And did not withhold Your [b]manna from their mouth,
　　And gave them [c]water for their thirst.
21 [a]Forty years You sustained them in the wilderness;
　　They lacked nothing;
　　Their [b]clothes did not wear out
　　And their feet did not swell.

22 "Moreover You gave them kingdoms and nations,
　　And divided them into [1]districts.
　　So they took possession of the land of [a]Sihon,
　　[2]The land of the king of Heshbon,
　　And the land of Og king of Bashan.
23 You also multiplied [a]their children as the stars of
　　　　heaven,
　　And brought them into the land
　　Which You had told their fathers
　　To go in and possess.
24 So [a]the [1]people went in
　　And possessed the land;
　　[b]You subdued before them the inhabitants of the land,
　　The Canaanites,
　　And gave them into their hands,
　　With their kings
　　And the people of the land,
　　That they might do with them as they wished.

9:16 [a]Ps. 106:6
[b]Deut. 1:26–33;
31:27; Neh. 9:29
9:17
[a]Ps. 78:11, 42–45
[b]Num. 14:4;
Acts 7:39
[c]Joel 2:13
9:18
[a]Ex. 32:4–8, 31
9:19 [a]Ps. 106:45
[b]Ex. 13:20–22;
1 Cor. 10:1
9:20 [a]Num. 11:17
[b]Ex. 16:14–16
[c]Ex. 17:6
9:21 [a]Deut. 2:7
[b]Deut. 8:4; 29:5
9:22
[a]Num. 21:21–35
9:23 [a]Gen. 15:5;
22:17; Heb. 11:12
9:24
[a]Josh. 1:2–4
[b]Josh. 18:1;
[Ps. 44:2, 3]

9:16 [1]*presumptuously*　[2]*Stiffened their necks,* became stubborn　9:17 [1]So
with MT, Vg.; LXX *in Egypt*　9:22 [1]Lit. *corners*　[2]So with MT, Vg.; LXX
omits *The land of*　9:24 [1]Lit. *sons*

25 And they took strong cities and a [a]rich land,
And possessed [b]houses full of all goods,
Cisterns *already* dug, vineyards, olive groves,
And [1]fruit trees in abundance.
So they ate and were filled and [c]grew fat,
And delighted themselves in Your great [d]goodness.

26 "Nevertheless they [a]were disobedient
And rebelled against You,
[b]Cast Your law behind their backs
And killed Your [c]prophets, who [1]testified against
them
To turn them to Yourself;
And they worked great provocations.

27 [a]Therefore You delivered them into the hand of their
enemies,
Who oppressed them;
And in the time of their trouble,
When they cried to You,
You [b]heard from heaven;
And according to Your abundant mercies
[c]You gave them deliverers who saved them
From the hand of their enemies.

28 "But after they had rest,
[a]They again did evil before You.
Therefore You left them in the hand of their enemies,
So that they had dominion over them;
Yet when they returned and cried out to You,
You heard from heaven;
And [b]many times You delivered them according to Your
mercies,

29 And [1]testified against them,
That You might bring them back to Your law.
Yet they acted [2]proudly,
And did not heed Your commandments,
But sinned against Your judgments,
[a]'Which if a man does, he shall live by them.'
And they shrugged their shoulders,
[3]Stiffened their necks,
And would not hear.

30 Yet for many years You had patience with them,
And [1]testified [a]against them by Your Spirit [b]in Your
prophets.
Yet they would not listen;
[c]Therefore You gave them into the hand of the peoples of
the lands.

31 Nevertheless in Your great mercy
[a]You did not utterly consume them nor forsake them;
For You *are* God, gracious and merciful.

32 "Now therefore, our God,
The great, the [a]mighty, and awesome God,
Who keeps covenant and mercy:
Do not let all the [1]trouble seem small before You
That has come upon us,

9:25
[a]Num. 13:27
[b]Deut. 6:11;
Josh. 24:13
[c][Deut. 32:15]
[d]Hos. 3:5

9:26 [a]Judg. 2:11
[b]1 Kin. 14:9;
Ps. 50:17
[c]1 Kin. 18:4;
19:10;
Matt. 23:37;
Acts 7:52

9:27 [a]Judg. 2:14;
Ps. 106:41
[b]Ps. 106:44
[c]Judg. 2:18

9:28 [a]Judg. 3:12
[b]Ps. 106:43

9:29 [a]Lev. 18:5;
Rom. 10:5;
[Gal. 3:12]

9:30
[a]2 Kin. 17:13–18;
2 Chr. 36:11–
20; Jer. 7:25
[b][Acts 7:51];
1 Pet. 1:11 [c]Is. 5:5

9:31 [a]Jer. 4:27;
[Rom. 11:2–5]

9:32
[a][Ex. 34:6, 7]

9:25 [1]Lit. *trees for eating*   9:26 [1]*admonished* or *warned them*
9:29 [1]*admonished them*   [2]*presumptuously*   [3]*Became stubborn*
9:30 [1]*admonished* or *warned them*   9:32 [1]*hardship*

Our kings and our princes,
Our priests and our prophets,
Our fathers and on all Your people,
[b]From the days of the kings of Assyria until this day.

33 However [a]You *are* just in all that has befallen us;
For You have dealt faithfully,
But [b]we have done wickedly.

34 Neither our kings nor our princes,
Our priests nor our fathers,
Have kept Your law,
Nor heeded Your commandments and Your testimonies,
With which You testified against them.

35 For they have [a]not served You in their kingdom,
Or in the many good *things* that You gave them,
Or in the large and rich land which You set before them;
Nor did they turn from their wicked works.

36 "Here [a]we *are*, servants today!
And the land that You gave to our fathers,
To eat its fruit and its bounty,
Here we *are*, servants in it!

37 And [a]it yields much increase to the kings
You have set over us,
Because of our sins;
Also they have [b]dominion over our bodies and our cattle
At their pleasure;
And we *are* in great distress.

38 "And because of all this,
We [a]make a sure *covenant* and write *it*;
Our leaders, our Levites, *and* our priests [b]seal *it*."

THE PEOPLE WHO SEALED THE COVENANT

10 Now those who placed *their* seal on *the document were:* Nehemiah the [1]governor, [a]the son of Hacaliah, and Zedekiah, [2a]Seraiah, Azariah, Jeremiah, [3]Pashhur, Amariah, Malchijah, [4]Hattush, Shebaniah, Malluch, [5]Harim, Meremoth, Obadiah, [6]Daniel, Ginnethon, Baruch, [7]Meshullam, Abijah, Mijamin, [8]Maaziah, Bilgai, *and* Shemaiah. These *were* the priests.

[9]The Levites: Jeshua the son of Azaniah, Binnui of the sons of Henadad, *and* Kadmiel.

[10]Their brethren: Shebaniah, Hodijah, Kelita, Pelaiah, Hanan, [11]Micha, Rehob, Hashabiah, [12]Zaccur, Sherebiah, Shebaniah, [13]Hodijah, Bani, *and* Beninu.

[14]The leaders of the people: [a]Parosh, Pahath-Moab, Elam, Zattu, Bani, [15]Bunni, Azgad, Bebai, [16]Adonijah, Bigvai, Adin, [17]Ater, Hezekiah, Azzur, [18]Hodijah, Hashum, Bezai, [19]Hariph, Anathoth, Nebai, [20]Magpiash, Meshullam, Hezir, [21]Meshezabel, Zadok, Jaddua, [22]Pelatiah, Hanan, Anaiah, [23]Hoshea, Hananiah, Hasshub, [24]Hallohesh, Pilha, Shobek, [25]Rehum, Hashabnah, Maaseiah, [26]Ahijah, Hanan, Anan, [27]Malluch, Harim, *and* Baanah.

THE COVENANT THAT WAS SEALED

[28a]Now the rest of the people—the priests, the Levites, the gatekeepers, the singers, the Nethinim, [b]and all those who

---

Margin references:

9:32
[b]2 Kin. 15:19;
17:3–6;
Ezra 4:2, 10

9:33
[a]Ps. 119:137;
[Dan. 9:14]
[b]Ps. 106:6;
[Dan. 9:5, 6, 8]

9:35
[a]Deut. 28:47

9:36
[a]Deut. 28:48;
Ezra 9:9

9:37
[a]Deut. 28:33, 51
[b]Deut. 28:48

9:38
[a]2 Kin. 23:3;
2 Chr. 29:10;
Ezra 10:3
[b]Neh. 10:1

10:1 [a]Neh. 1:1

10:2
[a]Neh. 12:1–21

10:14 [a]Ezra 2:3

10:28
[a]Ezra 2:36–43
[b]Ezra 9:1;
Neh. 13:3

10:1 [1]Heb. *Tirshatha*

had separated themselves from the peoples of the lands to the Law of God, their wives, their sons, and their daughters, everyone who had knowledge and understanding— [29]these joined with their brethren, their nobles, [a]and entered into a curse and an oath [b]to walk in God's Law, which was given by Moses the servant of God, and to observe and do all the commandments of the LORD our Lord, and His ordinances and His statutes: [30]We would not give [a]our daughters as wives to the peoples of the land, nor take their daughters for our sons; [31][a]if the peoples of the land brought [1]wares or any grain to sell on the Sabbath day, we would not buy it from them on the Sabbath, or on a holy day; and we would forego the [b]seventh year's *produce* and the [c]exacting[2] of every debt.

[32]Also we made ordinances for ourselves, to exact from ourselves yearly [a]one-third of a shekel for the service of the house of our God: [33]for [a]the showbread, for the regular grain offering, for the [b]regular burnt offering of the Sabbaths, the New Moons, and the set feasts; for the holy things, for the sin offerings to make atonement for Israel, and all the work of the house of our God. [34]We cast lots among the priests, the Levites, and the people, [a]for bringing the wood offering into the house of our God, according to our fathers' houses, at the appointed times year by year, to burn on the altar of the LORD our God [b]as *it is* written in the Law.

[35]And *we made ordinances* [a]to bring the firstfruits of our ground and the firstfruits of all fruit of all trees, year by year, to the house of the LORD; [36]to bring the [a]firstborn of our sons and our cattle, as *it is* written in the Law, and the firstborn of our herds and our flocks, to the house of our God, to the priests who minister in the house of our God; [37][a]to bring the firstfruits of our dough, our offerings, the fruit from all kinds of trees, *the* new wine and oil, to the priests, to the storerooms of the [1]house of our God; and to bring [b]the tithes of our land to the Levites, for the Levites should receive the tithes in all our farming communities. [38]And the priest, the descendant of Aaron, shall be with the Levites [a]when the Levites receive tithes; and the Levites shall bring up a tenth of the tithes to the house of our God, to [b]the rooms of the storehouse.

[39]For the children of Israel and the children of Levi [a]shall bring the offering of the grain, of the new wine and the oil, to the storerooms where the articles of the sanctuary *are, where* the priests who minister and the gatekeepers [b]and the singers *are;* and we will not [c]neglect the house of our God.

THE PEOPLE DWELLING IN JERUSALEM

11 Now the leaders of the people dwelt at Jerusalem; the rest of the people cast lots to bring one out of ten to dwell in Jerusalem, [a]the holy city, and nine-tenths *were to dwell* in *other* cities. [2]And the people blessed all the men who [a]willingly offered themselves to dwell at Jerusalem.

[3][a]These *are* the heads of the province who dwelt in Jerusalem. (But in the cities of Judah everyone dwelt in his own possession in their cities—Israelites, priests, Levites, [b]Nethinim, and [c]descendants of Solomon's servants.) [4]Also [a]in Jerusalem dwelt *some* of the children of Judah and of the children of Benjamin.

Cross-references

10:29
[a]Deut. 29:12;
Neh. 5:12;
Ps. 119:106
[b]2 Kin. 23:3;
2 Chr. 34:31

10:30 [a]Ex. 34:16;
Deut. 7:3;
[Ezra 9:12]

10:31 [a]Ex. 20:10;
Lev. 23:3;
Deut. 5:12
[b]Ex. 23:10, 11;
Lev. 25:4;
Jer. 34:14
[c][Deut. 15:1, 2];
Neh. 5:12

10:32
[a]Ex. 30:11–16;
38:25, 26;
2 Chr. 24:6, 9;
Matt. 17:24

10:33 [a]Lev. 24:5;
2 Chr. 2:4
[b]Num. 28; 29

10:34
[a]Neh. 13:31;
[Is. 40:16]
[b]Lev. 6:12

10:35 [a]Ex. 23:19;
34:26;
Lev. 19:23;
Num. 18:12;
Deut. 26:1, 2

10:36
[a]Ex. 13:2, 12, 13;
Lev. 27:26, 27;
Num. 18:15, 16

10:37
[a]Lev. 23:17;
Num. 15:19;
18:12; Deut. 18:4;
26:2 [b]Lev. 27:30;
Num. 18:21;
Mal. 3:10

10:38
[a]Num. 18:26
[b]1 Chr. 9:26;
2 Chr. 31:11

10:39
[a]Deut. 12:6, 11;
2 Chr. 31:12;
Neh. 13:12
[b]Neh. 13:10, 11
[c][Heb. 10:25]

11:1 [a]Neh. 10:18;
Matt. 4:5; 5:35;
27:53

11:2 [a]Judg. 5:9;
2 Chr. 17:16

11:3 [a]1 Chr. 9:2, 3
[b]Ezra 2:43
[c]Ezra 2:55

11:4 [a]1 Chr. 9:3

10:31 [1]merchandise   [2]collection   10:37 [1]Temple

The children of Judah: Athaiah the son of Uzziah, the son of Zechariah, the son of Amariah, the son of Shephatiah, the son of Mahalalel, of the children of [b]Perez; 5and Maaseiah the son of Baruch, the son of Col-Hozeh, the son of Hazaiah, the son of Adaiah, the son of Joiarib, the son of Zechariah, the son of Shiloni. 6All the sons of Perez who dwelt at Jerusalem *were* four hundred and sixty-eight valiant men.

7And these are the sons of Benjamin: Sallu the son of Meshullam, the son of Joed, the son of Pedaiah, the son of Kolaiah, the son of Maaseiah, the son of Ithiel, the son of Jeshaiah; 8and after him Gabbai *and* Sallai, nine hundred and twenty-eight. 9Joel the son of Zichri *was* their overseer, and Judah the son of [1]Senuah *was* second over the city.

10[a]Of the priests: Jedaiah the son of Joiarib, and Jachin; 11Seraiah the son of Hilkiah, the son of Meshullam, the son of Zadok, the son of Meraioth, the son of Ahitub, *was* the leader of the house of God. 12Their brethren who did the work of the house *were* eight hundred and twenty-two; and Adaiah the son of Jeroham, the son of Pelaliah, the son of Amzi, the son of Zechariah, the son of Pashhur, the son of Malchijah, 13and his brethren, heads of the fathers' *houses, were* two hundred and forty-two; and Amashai the son of Azarel, the son of Ahzai, the son of Meshillemoth, the son of Immer, 14and their brethren, mighty men of valor, *were* one hundred and twenty-eight. Their overseer *was* Zabdiel [1]the son of *one of* the great men.

15Also of the Levites: Shemaiah the son of Hasshub, the son of Azrikam, the son of Hashabiah, the son of Bunni; 16[a]Shabbethai and [b]Jozabad, of the heads of the Levites, *had* the oversight of [c]the business outside of the [1]house of God; 17Mattaniah the son of [1]Micha, the son of Zabdi, the son of Asaph, the leader *who* began the thanksgiving with prayer; Bakbukiah, the second among his brethren; and Abda the son of Shammua, the son of Galal, the son of Jeduthun. 18All the Levites in [a]the holy city *were* two hundred and eighty-four.

19Moreover the gatekeepers, Akkub, Talmon, and their brethren who kept the gates, *were* one hundred and seventy-two.

20And the rest of Israel, of the priests *and* Levites, *were* in all the cities of Judah, everyone in his inheritance. 21[a]But the Nethinim dwelt in Ophel. And Ziha and Gishpa *were* over the Nethinim.

22Also the overseer of the Levites at Jerusalem *was* Uzzi the son of Bani, the son of Hashabiah, the son of Mattaniah, the son of Micha, of the sons of Asaph, the singers in charge of the [1]service of the [2]house of God. 23For [a]*it was* the king's command concerning them that a [1]certain portion should be for the singers, a quota day by day. 24Pethahiah the son of Meshezabel, of the children of [a]Zerah the son of Judah, *was* [b]the[1] king's deputy in all matters concerning the people.

THE PEOPLE DWELLING OUTSIDE JERUSALEM

25And as for the villages with their fields, *some* of the children of Judah dwelt in [a]Kirjath Arba and its villages, Dibon

---

11:4 [b]Gen. 38:29

11:10 [a]1 Chr. 9:10

11:16 [a]Ezra 10:15
[b]Ezra 8:33
[c]1 Chr. 26:29

11:18 [a]Neh. 11:1

11:21
[a]2 Chr. 27:3;
Neh. 3:26

11:23 [a]Ezra 6:8,
9; 7:20

11:24
[a]Gen. 38:30
[b]1 Chr. 18:17

11:25
[a]Josh. 14:15

11:9 [1]Or *Hassenuah*   11:14 [1]Or *the son of Haggedolim*   11:16 [1]Temple
11:17 [1]Or *Michah*   11:22 [1]*work*   [2]Temple   11:23 [1]*fixed share*   11:24 [1]Lit. *at the king's hand*

and its villages, Jekabzeel and its villages; [26]in Jeshua, Moladah, Beth Pelet, [27]Hazar Shual, and Beersheba and its villages; [28]in Ziklag and Meconah and its villages; [29]in En Rimmon, Zorah, Jarmuth, [30]Zanoah, Adullam, and their villages; in Lachish and its fields; in Azekah and its villages. They dwelt from Beersheba to the Valley of Hinnom.

[31]Also the children of Benjamin from Geba *dwelt* in Michmash, Aija, and Bethel, and their villages; [32]in Anathoth, Nob, Ananiah; [33]in Hazor, Ramah, Gittaim; [34]in Hadid, Zeboim, Neballat; [35]in Lod, Ono, *and* [a]the Valley of Craftsmen. [36]Some of the Judean divisions of Levites *were* in Benjamin.

THE PRIESTS AND LEVITES
(cf. Ezra 2:36–40)

12 Now these *are* the [a]priests and the Levites who came up with [b]Zerubbabel the son of Shealtiel, and Jeshua: [c]Seraiah, Jeremiah, Ezra, [2]Amariah, [1]Malluch, Hattush, [31]Shechaniah, [2]Rehum, [3]Meremoth, [4]Iddo, [1]Ginnethoi, [a]Abijah, [51]Mijamin, [2]Maadiah, Bilgah, [6]Shemaiah, Joiarib, Jedaiah, [71]Sallu, Amok, Hilkiah, *and* Jedaiah.

These *were* the heads of the priests and their brethren in the days of [a]Jeshua.

[8]Moreover the Levites *were* Jeshua, Binnui, Kadmiel, Sherebiah, Judah, *and* Mattaniah [a]*who led* the thanksgiving *psalms,* he and his brethren. [9]Also Bakbukiah and Unni, their brethren, *stood* across from them in *their* duties.

[10]Jeshua begot Joiakim, Joiakim begot Eliashib, Eliashib begot Joiada, [11]Joiada begot Jonathan, and Jonathan begot Jaddua.

[12]Now in the days of Joiakim, the priests, the [a]heads of the fathers' *houses were:* of Seraiah, Meraiah; of Jeremiah, Hananiah; [13]of Ezra, Meshullam; of Amariah, Jehohanan; [14]of [1]Melichu, Jonathan; of [2]Shebaniah, Joseph; [15]of [1]Harim, Adna; of [2]Meraioth, Helkai; [16]of Iddo, Zechariah; of Ginnethon, Meshullam; [17]of Abijah, Zichri; *the son* of [1]Minjamin; of [2]Moadiah, Piltai; [18]of Bilgah, Shammua; of Shemaiah, Jehonathan; [19]of Joiarib, Mattenai; of Jedaiah, Uzzi; [20]of [1]Sallai, Kallai; of Amok, Eber; [21]of Hilkiah, Hashabiah; *and* of Jedaiah, Nethanel.

[22]During the reign of Darius the Persian, a record *was also kept* of the Levites and priests *who had been* [a]heads of their fathers' *houses* in the days of Eliashib, Joiada, Johanan, and Jaddua. [23]The sons of Levi, the heads of the fathers' *houses* until the days of Johanan the son of Eliashib, *were* written in the book of the [a]chronicles.

[24]And the heads of the Levites *were* Hashabiah, Sherebiah, and Jeshua the son of Kadmiel, with their brothers across from them, to [a]praise *and* give thanks, [b]group[1] alternating with group, [c]according to the command of David the man of God. [25]Mattaniah, Bakbukiah, Obadiah, Meshullam, Talmon, and Akkub *were* gatekeepers keeping the watch at the storerooms of the gates. [26]These *lived* in the days of Joiakim the

11:35 [a]1 Chr. 4:14

12:1
[a]Ezra 2:1, 2;
7:7 [b]Neh. 7:7;
Matt. 1:12, 13
[c]Neh. 10:2–8

12:4 [a]Luke 1:5

12:7 [a]Ezra 3:2;
Hag. 1:1;
Zech. 3:1

12:8 [a]Neh. 11:17

12:12
[a]Neh. 7:70, 71;
8:13; 11:13

12:22
[a]1 Chr. 24:6

12:23
[a]1 Chr. 9:14–22

12:24 [a]Neh. 11:17
[b]Ezra 3:11
[c]1 Chr. 23—26

12:2 [1]*Melichu,* v. 14   12:3 [1]*Shebaniah,* v. 14   [2]*Harim,* v. 15   [3]*Meraioth,* v. 15
12:4 [1]*Ginnethon,* v. 16   12:5 [1]*Minjamin,* v. 17   [2]*Moadiah,* v. 17   12:7 [1]*Sallai,*
v. 20   12:14 [1]*Malluch,* v. 2   [2]*Shechaniah,* v. 3   12:15 [1]*Rehum,* v. 3
[2]*Meremoth,* v. 3   12:17 [1]*Mijamin,* v. 5   [2]*Maadiah,* v. 5   12:20 [1]*Sallu,* v. 7
12:24 [1]Lit. *watch by watch*

son of Jeshua, the son of [1]Jozadak, and in the days of Nehemiah [a]the governor, and of Ezra the priest, [b]the scribe.

NEHEMIAH DEDICATES THE WALL

[27]Now at [a]the dedication of the wall of Jerusalem they sought out the Levites in all their places, to bring them to Jerusalem to celebrate the dedication with gladness, [b]both with thanksgivings and singing, *with* cymbals and stringed instruments and harps. [28]And the sons of the singers gathered together from the countryside around Jerusalem, from the [a]villages of the Netophathites, [29]from the house of Gilgal, and from the fields of Geba and Azmaveth; for the singers had built themselves villages all around Jerusalem. [30]Then the priests and Levites [a]purified themselves, and purified the people, the gates, and the wall.

[31]So I brought the leaders of Judah up on the wall, and appointed two large thanksgiving choirs. [a]*One* went to the right hand on the wall [b]toward the Refuse Gate. [32]After them went Hoshaiah and half of the leaders of Judah, [33]and Azariah, Ezra, Meshullam, [34]Judah, Benjamin, Shemaiah, Jeremiah, [35]and some of the priests' sons [a]with trumpets—Zechariah the son of Jonathan, the son of Shemaiah, the son of Mattaniah, the son of Michaiah, the son of Zaccur, the son of Asaph, [36]and his brethren, Shemaiah, Azarel, Milalai, Gilalai, Maai, Nethanel, Judah, *and* Hanani, with [a]the musical [b]instruments of David the man of God. And Ezra the scribe *went* before them. [37][a]By the Fountain Gate, in front of them, they went up [b]the stairs of the [c]City of David, on the stairway of the wall, beyond the house of David, as far as [d]the Water Gate eastward.

[38][a]The other thanksgiving choir went the opposite *way*, and I *was* behind them with half of the people on the wall, going past the [b]Tower of the Ovens as far as [c]the Broad Wall, [39][a]and above the Gate of Ephraim, above [b]the Old Gate, above [c]the Fish Gate, [d]the Tower of Hananel, the Tower of [1]the Hundred, as far as [e]the Sheep Gate; and they stopped by [f]the Gate of the Prison.

[40]So the two thanksgiving choirs stood in the house of God, likewise I and the half of the rulers with me; [41]and the priests, Eliakim, Maaseiah, [1]Minjamin, Michaiah, Elioenai, Zechariah, *and* Hananiah, with trumpets; [42]also Maaseiah, Shemaiah, Eleazar, Uzzi, Jehohanan, Malchijah, Elam, and Ezer. The singers [1]sang loudly with Jezrahiah the director.

[43]Also that day they offered great sacrifices, and rejoiced, for God had made them rejoice with great joy; the women and the children also rejoiced, so that the joy of Jerusalem was heard [a]afar off.

TEMPLE RESPONSIBILITIES

[44][a]And at the same time some were appointed over the rooms of the storehouse for the offerings, the firstfruits, and the [b]tithes, to gather into them from the fields of the cities the portions specified by the Law for the priests and Levites; for Judah rejoiced over the priests and Levites who [1]ministered. [45]Both the singers and the gatekeepers kept the charge of their God and the charge of the purification, [a]according to

12:26 [a]Neh. 8:9 [b]Ezra 7:6, 11
12:27 [a]Deut. 20:5; Neh. 7:1; Ps. 30:title [b]1 Chr. 25:6; 2 Chr. 5:13; 7:6
12:28 [a]1 Chr. 9:16
12:30 [a]Ezra 6:20; Neh. 13:22, 30
12:31 [a]Neh. 12:38 [b]Neh. 2:13; 3:13
12:35 [a]Num. 10:2, 8
12:36 [a]1 Chr. 23:5 [b]2 Chr. 29:26, 27
12:37 [a]Neh. 2:14; 3:15 [b]Neh. 3:15 [c]2 Sam. 5:7–9 [d]Neh. 3:26; 8:1, 3, 16
12:38 [a]Neh. 12:31 [b]Neh. 3:11 [c]Neh. 3:8
12:39 [a]2 Kin. 14:13; Neh. 8:16 [b]Neh. 3:6 [c]Neh. 3:3 [d]Neh. 3:1 [e]Neh. 3:32 [f]Jer. 32:2
12:43 [a]Ezra 3:13
12:44 [a]2 Chr. 31:11, 12; Neh. 13:5, 12, 13 [b]Neh. 10:37–39
12:45 [a]1 Chr. 25; 26

12:26 [1]*Jehozadak*, 1 Chr. 6:14   12:39 [1]Heb. *Hammeah*   12:41 [1]Or *Mijamin*, v. 5
12:42 [1]Lit. *made their voice to be heard*   12:44 [1]Lit. *stood*

the command of David *and* Solomon his son. [46]For in the days of David [a]and Asaph of old *there were* chiefs of the singers, and songs of praise and thanksgiving to God. [47]In the days of Zerubbabel and in the days of Nehemiah all Israel gave the portions for the singers and the gatekeepers, a portion for [a]each day. [b]They also [1]consecrated *holy things* for the Levites, [c]and the Levites consecrated *them* for the children of Aaron.

PRINCIPLES OF SEPARATION
(Num. 22:1—24:25)

13 On that day [a]they read from the Book of Moses in the hearing of the people, and in it was found written [b]that no Ammonite or Moabite should ever come into the assembly of God, [2]because they had not met the children of Israel with bread and water, but [a]hired Balaam against them to curse them. [b]However, our God turned the curse into a blessing. [3]So it was, when they had heard the Law, [a]that they separated all the mixed multitude from Israel.

THE REFORMS OF NEHEMIAH

[4]Now before this, [a]Eliashib the priest, having authority over the storerooms of the house of our God, *was* allied with [b]Tobiah. [5]And he had prepared for him a large room, [a]where previously they had stored the grain offerings, the frankincense, the articles, the tithes of grain, the new wine and oil, [b]which were commanded *to be given* to the Levites and singers and gatekeepers, and the offerings for the priests. [6]But during all this I was not in Jerusalem, [a]for in the thirty-second year of Artaxerxes king of Babylon I had returned to the king. Then after certain days I obtained leave from the king, [7]and I came to Jerusalem and discovered the evil that Eliashib had done for Tobiah, in [a]preparing a room for him in the courts of the [1]house of God. [8]And it grieved me bitterly; therefore I threw all the household goods of Tobiah out of the room. [9]Then I commanded them to [a]cleanse the rooms; and I brought back into them the articles of the house of God, with the grain offering and the frankincense.

[10]I also realized that the portions for the Levites had [a]not been given *them;* for each of the Levites and the singers who did the work had gone back to [b]his field. [11]So [a]I contended with the rulers, and said, [b]"Why is the house of God forsaken?" And I gathered them together and set them in their place. [12a]Then all Judah brought the tithe of the grain and the new wine and the oil to the storehouse. [13a]And I appointed as treasurers over the storehouse Shelemiah the priest and Zadok the scribe, and of the Levites, Pedaiah; and next to them *was* Hanan the son of Zaccur, the son of Mattaniah; for they were considered [b]faithful, and their task *was* to distribute to their brethren.

[14a]Remember me, O my God, concerning this, and do not wipe out my good deeds that I have done for the house of my God, and for its services!

[15]In those days I saw *people* in Judah treading winepresses [a]on the Sabbath, and bringing in sheaves, and loading donkeys with wine, grapes, figs, and all *kinds of* burdens,

12:46
[a1] Chr. 25:1;
2 Chr. 29:30

12:47 [a]Neh. 11:23
[b]Num. 18:21, 24
[c]Num. 18:26

13:1
[a][Deut. 31:11, 12]; 2 Kin. 23:2; Neh. 8:3, 8; 9:3; Is. 34:16
[b]Deut. 23:3, 4

13:2
[a]Num. 22:5; Josh. 24:9, 10
[b]Num. 23:1; 24:10; Deut. 23:5

13:3 [a]Neh. 9:2; 10:28

13:4 [a]Neh. 12:10
[b]Neh. 2:10; 4:3; 6:1

13:5 [a]Neh. 12:44
[b]Num. 18:21, 24

13:6
[a]Neh. 5:14–16

13:7 [a]Neh. 13:1, 5

13:9
[a]2 Chr. 29:5, 15, 16

13:10
[a]Neh. 10:37; Mal. 3:8
[b]Num. 35:2

13:11 [a]Neh. 13:17, 25 [b]Neh. 10:39

13:12
[a]Neh. 10:38; 12:44

13:13
[a]2 Chr. 31:12
[b]1 Cor. 4:2

13:14 [a]Neh. 5:19; 13:22, 31

13:15
[a][Ex. 20:10]

[b]which they brought into Jerusalem on the Sabbath day. And I warned *them* about the day on which they were selling provisions. [16]Men of Tyre dwelt there also, who brought in fish and all kinds of goods, and sold *them* on the Sabbath to the children of Judah, and in Jerusalem.

[17]Then I contended with the nobles of Judah, and said to them, "What evil thing *is* this that you do, by which you profane the Sabbath day? [18a]Did not your fathers do thus, and did not our God bring all this disaster on us and on this city? Yet you bring added wrath on Israel by profaning the Sabbath."

[19]So it was, at the gates of Jerusalem, as it [a]began to be dark before the Sabbath, that I commanded the gates to be shut, and charged that they must not be opened till after the Sabbath. [b]Then I posted *some* of my servants at the gates, *so that* no burdens would be brought in on the Sabbath day. [20]Now the merchants and sellers of all kinds of [1]wares [2]lodged outside Jerusalem once or twice.

[21]Then I warned them, and said to them, "Why do you spend the night [1]around the wall? If you do *so* again, I will lay hands on you!" From that time on they came no *more* on the Sabbath. [22]And I commanded the Levites that [a]they should cleanse themselves, and that they should go and guard the gates, to sanctify the Sabbath day.

Remember me, O my God, *concerning* this also, and spare me according to the greatness of Your mercy!

[23]In those days I also saw Jews *who* [a]had married women of [b]Ashdod, Ammon, *and* Moab. [24]And half of their children spoke the language of Ashdod, and could not speak the language of Judah, but spoke according to the language of one or the other people.

[25]So I [a]contended with them and [1]cursed them, struck some of them and pulled out their hair, and made them [b]swear by God, *saying,* "You shall not give your daughters as wives to their sons, nor take their daughters for your sons or yourselves. [26a]Did not Solomon king of Israel sin by these things? Yet among many nations there was no king like him, [b]who was beloved of his God; and God made him king over all Israel. [c]Nevertheless pagan women caused even him to sin. [27]Should we then hear of your doing all this great evil, [a]transgressing against our God by marrying pagan women?"

[28]And *one* of the sons [a]of Joiada, the son of Eliashib the high priest, *was* a son-in-law of [b]Sanballat the Horonite; therefore I drove him from me.

[29a]Remember them, O my God, because they have defiled the priesthood and [b]the covenant of the priesthood and the Levites.

[30a]Thus I cleansed them of everything pagan. I also [b]assigned duties to the priests and the Levites, each to his service, [31]and *to bringing* [a]the wood offering and the firstfruits at appointed times.

[b]Remember me, O my God, for good!

13:15
[b]Neh. 10:31;
[Jer. 17:21]

13:18 [a]Ezra 9:13;
[Jer. 17:21]

13:19 [a]Lev. 23:32
[b]Jer. 17:21, 22

13:22
[a]1 Chr. 15:12;
Neh. 12:30

13:23
[a][Ex. 34:16;
Deut. 7:3, 4];
Ezra 9:2;
Neh. 10:30
[b]Neh. 4:7

13:25
[a]Prov. 28:4
[b]Ezra 10:5;
Neh. 10:29, 30

13:26
[a]1 Kin. 11:1, 2
[b]2 Sam. 12:24, 25
[c]1 Kin. 11:4–8

13:27
[a][Ezra 10:2];
Neh. 13:23

13:28
[a]Neh. 12:10, 12
[b]Neh. 4:1, 7;
6:1, 2

13:29 [a]Neh. 6:14
[b]Mal. 2:4, 11, 12

13:30
[a]Neh. 10:30
[b]Neh. 12:1

13:31
[a]Neh. 10:34
[b]Neh. 13:14, 22

13:20 [1]*merchandise* [2]*spent the night* 13:21 [1]Lit. *before*
13:25 [1]*pronounced them cursed*

THE BOOK OF
ESTHER

THE KING DETHRONES QUEEN VASHTI

1 Now it came to pass in the days of ᵃAhasuerus¹ (this *was* the Ahasuerus who reigned ᵇover one hundred and twenty-seven provinces, ᶜfrom India to Ethiopia), ²in those days when King Ahasuerus ᵃsat on the throne of his kingdom, which *was* in ᵇShushan¹ the ²citadel, ³*that* in the third year of his reign he ᵃmade a feast for all his officials and servants— the powers of Persia and Media, the nobles, and the princes of the provinces *being* before him— ⁴when he showed the riches of his glorious kingdom and the splendor of his excellent majesty for many days, one hundred and eighty days *in all.*

⁵And when these days were completed, the king made a feast lasting seven days for all the people who were present in ¹Shushan the ²citadel, from great to small, in the court of the garden of the king's palace. ⁶*There were* white and blue linen *curtains* fastened with cords of fine linen and purple on silver rods and marble pillars; *and the* ᵃcouches *were* of gold and silver on a *mosaic* pavement of alabaster, turquoise, and white and black marble. ⁷And they served drinks in golden vessels, each vessel being different from the other, with royal wine in abundance, ᵃaccording to the ¹generosity of the king. ⁸In accordance with the law, the drinking was not compulsory; for so the king had ordered all the officers of his household, that they should do according to each man's pleasure.

⁹Queen Vashti also made a feast for the women *in* the royal palace which *belonged* to King Ahasuerus.

¹⁰On the seventh day, when the heart of the king was merry with wine, he commanded Mehuman, Biztha, ᵃHarbona, Bigtha, Abagtha, Zethar, and Carcas, seven eunuchs who served in the presence of King Ahasuerus, ¹¹to bring Queen Vashti before the king, *wearing* her royal crown, in order to show her beauty to the people and the officials, for she *was* beautiful to behold. ¹²But Queen Vashti refused to come at the king's command *brought* by *his* eunuchs; therefore the king was furious, and his anger burned within him.

¹³Then the king said to the ᵃwise men ᵇwho understood the times (for this *was* the king's manner toward all who knew law and justice, ¹⁴those closest to him *being* Carshena, Shethar, Admatha, Tarshish, Meres, Marsena, and Memucan, the ᵃseven princes of Persia and Media, ᵇwho had access to the king's presence, *and* who ¹ranked highest in the kingdom): ¹⁵"What *shall we* do to Queen Vashti, according to law, because she did not obey the command of King Ahasuerus *brought to her* by the eunuchs?"

1:1 ᵃEzra 4:6;
Dan. 9:1
ᵇEsth. 8:9
ᶜDan. 6:1

1:2 ᵃ1 Kin. 1:46
ᵇNeh. 1:1;
Dan. 8:2

1:3 ᵃGen. 40:20;
Esth. 2:18

1:6 ᵃEsth. 7:8;
Ezek. 23:41;
Amos 2:8; 6:4

1:7 ᵃEsth. 2:18

1:10 ᵃEsth. 7:9

1:13 ᵃJer. 10:7;
Dan. 2:12;
Matt. 2:1
ᵇ1 Chr. 12:32

1:14 ᵃEzra 7:14
ᵇ2 Kin. 25:19;
[Matt. 18:10]

1:1 ¹Generally identified with Xerxes I (485–464 B.C.)   1:2 ¹Or *Susa*   ²Or *fortified palace,* and so elsewhere in the book   1:5 ¹Or *Susa*   ²*palace* 1:7 ¹Lit. *hand*   1:14 ¹Lit. *sat in first place*

¹⁶And Memucan answered before the king and the princes: "Queen Vashti has not only wronged the king, but also all the princes, and all the people who *are* in all the provinces of King Ahasuerus. ¹⁷For the queen's behavior will become known to all women, so that they will ^adespise their husbands in their eyes, when they report, 'King Ahasuerus commanded Queen Vashti to be brought in before him, but she did not come.' ¹⁸This very day the *noble* ladies of Persia and Media will say to all the king's officials that they have heard of the behavior of the queen. Thus *there will be* excessive contempt and wrath. ¹⁹If it pleases the king, let a royal ¹decree go out from him, and let it be recorded in the laws of the Persians and the Medes, so that it will ^anot ²be altered, that Vashti shall come no more before King Ahasuerus; and let the king give her royal position to another who is better than she. ²⁰When the king's decree which he will make is proclaimed throughout all his empire (for it is great), all wives will ^ahonor their husbands, both great and small."

²¹And the reply pleased the king and the princes, and the king did according to the word of Memucan. ²²Then he sent letters to all the king's provinces, ^ato each province in its own script, and to every people in their own language, that each man should ^bbe master in his own house, and speak in the language of his own people.

ESTHER BECOMES QUEEN

2 After these things, when the wrath of King Ahasuerus subsided, he remembered Vashti, ^awhat she had done, and what had been decreed against her. ²Then the king's servants who attended him said: "Let beautiful young virgins be sought for the king; ³and let the king appoint officers in all the provinces of his kingdom, that they may gather all the beautiful young virgins to ¹Shushan the ²citadel, into the women's quarters, under the custody of ³Hegai the king's eunuch, custodian of the women. And let beauty preparations be given *them*. ⁴Then let the young woman who pleases the king be queen instead of Vashti."

This thing pleased the king, and he did so.

⁵In ¹Shushan the ²citadel there was a certain Jew whose name *was* Mordecai the son of Jair, the son of Shimei, the son of ^aKish, a Benjamite. ^{6a}Kish¹ had been carried away from Jerusalem with the captives who had been captured with ²Jeconiah king of Judah, whom Nebuchadnezzar the king of Babylon had carried away. ⁷And *Mordecai* had brought up Hadassah, that *is*, Esther, ^ahis uncle's daughter, for she had neither father nor mother. The young woman *was* lovely and beautiful. When her father and mother died, Mordecai took her as his own daughter.

⁸So it was, when the king's command and decree were heard, and when many young women were ^agathered at ¹Shushan the ²citadel, *under* the custody of Hegai, that Esther also was taken to the king's palace, into the care of Hegai the custodian of the women. ⁹Now the young woman pleased him, and she obtained his favor; so he readily gave ^abeauty

1:17 ^a[Eph. 5:33]
1:19 ^aEsth. 8:8; Dan. 6:8
1:20 ^a[Eph. 5:33; Col. 3:18; 1 Pet. 3:1]
1:22 ^aEsth. 3:12, 8:9 ^b[Eph. 5:22–24; 1 Tim. 2:12]
2:1 ^aEsth. 1:19, 20
2:5 ^a1 Sam. 9:1
2:6 ^a2 Kin. 24:14, 15; 2 Chr. 36:10, 20; Jer. 24:1
2:7 ^aEsth. 2:15
2:8 ^aEsth. 2:3
2:9 ^aEsth. 2:3, 12

1:19 ¹Lit. *word* ²*pass away* 2:3 ¹Or *Susa* ²*palace* ³Heb. *Hege* 2:5 ¹Or *Susa* ²*palace* 2:6 ¹Lit. *Who* ²*Jehoiachin,* 2 Kin. 24:6 2:8 ¹Or *Susa* ²*palace*

preparations to her, besides [1]her allowance. Then seven choice maidservants were provided for her from the king's palace, and he moved her and her maidservants to the best *place* in the house of the women.

[10a]Esther had not [1]revealed her people or family, for Mordecai had charged her not to reveal *it.* [11]And every day Mordecai paced in front of the court of the women's quarters, to learn of Esther's welfare and what was happening to her.

[12]Each young woman's turn came to go in to King Ahasuerus after she had completed twelve months' preparation, according to the regulations for the women, for thus were the days of their preparation apportioned: six months with oil of myrrh, and six months with perfumes and preparations for beautifying women. [13]Thus *prepared, each* young woman went to the king, and she was given whatever she desired to take with her from the women's quarters to the king's palace. [14]In the evening she went, and in the morning she returned to the second house of the women, to the custody of Shaashgaz, the king's eunuch who kept the concubines. She would not go in to the king again unless the king delighted in her and called for her by name.

[15]Now when the turn came for Esther [a]the daughter of Abihail the uncle of Mordecai, who had taken her as his daughter, to go in to the king, she requested nothing but what Hegai the king's eunuch, the custodian of the women, advised. And Esther [b]obtained favor in the sight of all who saw her. [16]So Esther was taken to King Ahasuerus, into his royal palace, in the tenth month, which *is* the month of Tebeth, in the seventh year of his reign. [17]The king loved Esther more than all the *other* women, and she obtained grace and favor in his sight more than all the virgins; so he set the royal [a]crown upon her head and made her queen instead of Vashti. [18]Then the king [a]made a great feast, the Feast of Esther, for all his officials and servants; and he proclaimed a holiday in the provinces and gave gifts according to the [1]generosity of a king.

MORDECAI DISCOVERS A PLOT

[19]When virgins were gathered together a second time, Mordecai sat within the king's gate. [20a]*Now* Esther had not revealed her family and her people, just as Mordecai had charged her, for Esther obeyed the command of Mordecai as when she was brought up by him.

[21]In those days, while Mordecai sat within the king's gate, two of the king's eunuchs, [1]Bigthan and Teresh, doorkeepers, became furious and sought to lay hands on King Ahasuerus. [22]So the matter became known to Mordecai, [a]who told Queen Esther, and Esther informed the king in Mordecai's name. [23]And when an inquiry was made into the matter, it was confirmed, and both were hanged on a gallows; and it was written in [a]the book of the chronicles in the presence of the king.

HAMAN'S CONSPIRACY AGAINST THE JEWS

3 After these things King Ahasuerus promoted Haman, the son of Hammedatha the [a]Agagite, and [b]advanced him and set his seat above all the princes who *were* with him. [2]And

2:10 [a]Esth. 2:20

2:15
[a]Esth. 2:7, 9:29
[b]Esth. 5:2, 8

2:17 [a]Esth. 1:11

2:18 [a]Esth. 1:3

2:20 [a]Esth. 2:10;
[Prov. 22:6]

2:22
[a]Esth. 6:1, 2

2:23 [a]Esth. 6:1

3:1 [a]Num. 24:7;
1 Sam. 15:8
[b]Esth. 5:11

2:9 [1]Lit. *her portions*   2:10 [1]Revealed the identity of   2:18 [1]Lit. *hand*
2:21 [1]*Bigthana*, Esth. 6:2

all the king's servants who *were* ᵃwithin the king's gate bowed and paid homage to Haman, for so the king had commanded concerning him. But Mordecai ᵇwould not bow or pay homage. ³Then the king's servants who *were* within the king's gate said to Mordecai, "Why do you transgress the ᵃking's command?" ⁴Now it happened, when they spoke to him daily and he would not listen to them, that they told *it* to Haman, to see whether Mordecai's words would stand; for *Mordecai* had told them that he *was* a Jew. ⁵When Haman saw that Mordecai ᵃdid not bow or pay him homage, Haman was ᵇfilled with wrath. ⁶But he disdained to lay hands on Mordecai alone, for they had told him of the people of Mordecai. Instead, Haman ᵃsought to destroy all the Jews who *were* throughout the whole kingdom of Ahasuerus—the people of Mordecai.

⁷In the first month, which is the month of Nisan, in the twelfth year of King Ahasuerus, ᵃthey cast Pur (that *is,* the lot), before Haman ¹to determine the day and the ²month, ³until *it fell on the* twelfth *month,* which *is* the month of Adar.

⁸Then Haman said to King Ahasuerus, "There is a certain people scattered and dispersed among the people in all the provinces of your kingdom; ᵃtheir laws *are* different from all *other* people's, and they do not keep the king's laws. Therefore it *is* not fitting for the king to let them remain. ⁹If it pleases the king, let *a decree* be written that they be destroyed, and I will pay ten thousand talents of silver into the hands of those who do the work, to bring *it* into the king's treasuries."

¹⁰So the king ᵃtook ᵇhis signet ring from his hand and gave it to Haman, the son of Hammedatha the Agagite, the ᶜenemy of the Jews. ¹¹And the king said to Haman, "The money and the people *are* given to you, to do with them as seems good to you."

¹²ᵃThen the king's scribes were called on the thirteenth day of the first month, and *a decree* was written according to all that Haman commanded—to the king's satraps, to the governors who *were* over each province, to the officials of all people, to every province ᵇaccording to its script, and to every people in their language. ᶜIn the name of King Ahasuerus it was written, and sealed with the king's signet ring. ¹³And the letters were ᵃsent by couriers into all the king's provinces, to destroy, to kill, and to annihilate all the Jews, both young and old, little children and women, ᵇin one day, on the thirteenth *day* of the twelfth month, which *is* the month of Adar, and ᶜto plunder their ¹possessions. ¹⁴ᵃA copy of the document was to be issued as law in every province, being published for all people, that they should be ready for that day. ¹⁵The couriers went out, hastened by the king's command; and the decree was proclaimed in ¹Shushan the ²citadel. So the king and Haman sat down to drink, but ᵃthe city of Shushan was ³perplexed.

ESTHER AGREES TO HELP THE JEWS

4 When Mordecai learned all that had happened, ¹he ᵃtore his clothes and put on sackcloth ᵇand ashes, and went

Cross references (margin)

3:2 ᵃEsth. 2:19, 21, 5:9
ᵇEsth. 3:5; Ps. 15:4
3:3 ᵃEsth. 3:2
3:5 ᵃEsth. 3:2, 5:9 ᵇDan. 3:19
3:6 ᵃPs. 83:4; [Rev. 12:1–17]
3:7 ᵃEsth. 9:24–26
3:8 ᵃEzra 4:12–15; Acts 16:20, 21
3:10 ᵃGen. 41:42 ᵇEsth. 8:2, 8 ᶜEsth. 7:6
3:12 ᵃEsth. 8:9 ᵇEsth. 1:22 ᶜ1 Kin. 21:8; Esth. 8:8–10
3:13 ᵃ2 Chr. 30:6; Esth. 8:10, 14 ᵇEsth. 8:12 ᶜEsth. 8:11, 9:10
3:14 ᵃEsth. 8:13, 14
3:15 ᵃEsth. 8:15; [Prov. 29:2]
4:1 ᵃ2 Sam. 1:11; Esth. 3:8–10; Jon. 3:5, 6 ᵇJosh. 7:6; Ezek. 27:30

3:7 ¹Lit. *from day to day and month to month*   ²LXX adds *to destroy the people of Mordecai in one day;* Vg. adds *the nation of the Jews should be destroyed*   ³So with MT, Vg.; LXX *and the lot fell on the fourteenth of the month*   3:13 ¹LXX adds the text of the letter here   3:15 ¹Or *Susa*   ²*palace*   ³*in confusion*   4:1 ¹Lit. *Mordecai*

out into the midst of the city. He ^ccried out with a loud and bitter cry. ²He went as far as the front of the king's gate, for no one *might* enter the king's gate clothed with sackcloth. ³And in every province where the king's command and decree arrived, *there was* great mourning among the Jews, with fasting, weeping, and wailing; and many lay in sackcloth and ashes.

⁴So Esther's maids and eunuchs came and told her, and the queen was deeply distressed. Then she sent garments to clothe Mordecai and take his sackcloth away from him, but he would not accept *them.* ⁵Then Esther called Hathach, *one* of the king's eunuchs whom he had appointed to attend her, and she gave him a command concerning Mordecai, to learn what and why this *was.* ⁶So Hathach went out to Mordecai in the city square that *was* in front of the king's gate. ⁷And Mordecai told him all that had happened to him, and ^athe sum of money that Haman had promised to pay into the king's treasuries to destroy the Jews. ⁸He also gave him ^aa copy of the written decree for their destruction, which was given at ¹Shushan, that he might show it to Esther and explain it to her, and that he might command her to go in to the king to make supplication to him and plead before him for her people. ⁹So Hathach returned and told Esther the words of Mordecai.

¹⁰Then Esther spoke to Hathach, and gave him a command for Mordecai: ¹¹"All the king's servants and the people of the king's provinces know that any man or woman who goes into ^athe inner court to the king, who has not been called, ^bhe has but one law: put *all* to death, except the one ^cto whom the king holds out the golden scepter, that he may live. Yet I myself have not been ^dcalled to go in to the king these thirty days." ¹²So they told Mordecai Esther's words.

¹³And Mordecai told *them* to answer Esther: "Do not think in your heart that you will escape in the king's palace any more than all the other Jews. ¹⁴For if you remain completely silent at this time, relief and deliverance will arise for the Jews from another place, but you and your father's house will perish. Yet who knows whether you have come to the kingdom for *such* a time as this?"

¹⁵Then Esther told *them* to reply to Mordecai: ¹⁶"Go, gather all the Jews who are present in ¹Shushan, and fast for me; neither eat nor drink for ^athree days, night or day. My maids and I will fast likewise. And so I will go to the king, which *is* against the law; ^band if I perish, I perish!"

¹⁷So Mordecai went his way and did according to all that Esther commanded ¹him.

ESTHER'S BANQUET

5 Now it happened ^aon the third day that Esther put on *her* royal *robes* and stood in ^bthe inner court of the king's palace, across from the king's house, while the king sat on his royal throne in the royal house, facing the entrance of the ¹house. ²So it was, when the king saw Queen Esther standing in the court, *that* ^ashe found favor in his sight, and ^bthe king held out to Esther the golden scepter that *was* in his hand. Then Esther went near and touched the top of the scepter.

4:1 ^cGen. 27:34

4:7 ^aEsth. 3:9

4:8
^aEsth. 3:14, 15

4:11 ^aEsth. 5:1,
6:4 ^bDan. 2:9
^cEsth. 5:2, 8:4
^dEsth. 2:14

4:16 ^aEsth. 5:1
^bGen. 43:14

5:1 ^aEsth. 4:16
^bEsth. 4:11, 6:4

5:2 ^a[Prov. 21:1]
^bEsth. 4:11, 8:4

4:8 ¹Or *Susa*   4:16 ¹Or *Susa*   4:17 ¹LXX adds a prayer of Mordecai here
5:1 ¹LXX adds many extra details in vv. 1, 2

³And the king said to her, "What do you wish, Queen Esther? What *is* your request? ^aIt shall be given to you—up to half the kingdom!"

⁴So Esther answered, "If it pleases the king, let the king and Haman come today to the banquet that I have prepared for him."

⁵Then the king said, "Bring Haman quickly, that he may do as Esther has said." So the king and Haman went to the banquet that Esther had prepared.

⁶At the banquet of wine ^athe king said to Esther, ^b"What *is* your petition? It shall be granted you. What *is* your request, up to half the kingdom? It shall be done!"

⁷Then Esther answered and said, "My petition and request *is this:* ⁸If I have found favor in the sight of the king, and if it pleases the king to grant my petition and ¹fulfill my request, then let the king and Haman come to the ^abanquet which I will prepare for them, and tomorrow I will do as the king has said."

HAMAN'S PLOT AGAINST MORDECAI

⁹So Haman went out that day ^ajoyful and with a glad heart; but when Haman saw Mordecai in the king's gate, and ^bthat he did not stand or tremble before him, he was filled with indignation against Mordecai. ¹⁰Nevertheless Haman ^arestrained himself and went home, and he sent and called for his friends and his wife Zeresh. ¹¹Then Haman told them of his great riches, ^athe multitude of his children, everything in which the king had promoted him, and how he had ^badvanced him above the officials and servants of the king.

¹²Moreover Haman said, "Besides, Queen Esther invited no one but me to come in with the king to the banquet that she prepared; and tomorrow I am again invited by her, along with the king. ¹³Yet all this avails me nothing, so long as I see Mordecai the Jew sitting at the king's gate."

¹⁴Then his wife Zeresh and all his friends said to him, "Let a ^agallows¹ be made, ²fifty cubits high, and in the morning ^bsuggest to the king that Mordecai be hanged on it; then go merrily with the king to the banquet."

And the thing pleased Haman; so he had ^cthe gallows made.

THE KING HONORS MORDECAI

6 That night ¹the king could not sleep. So one was commanded to bring ^athe book of the records of the chronicles; and they were read before the king. ²And it was found written that Mordecai had told of ¹Bigthana and Teresh, two of the king's eunuchs, the doorkeepers who had sought to lay hands on King Ahasuerus. ³Then the king said, "What honor or dignity has been bestowed on Mordecai for this?"

And the king's servants who attended him said, "Nothing has been done for him."

⁴So the king said, "Who *is* in the court?" Now Haman had *just* entered ^athe outer court of the king's palace ^bto suggest that the king hang Mordecai on the gallows that he had prepared for him.

Cross-refs: 5:3 ^aEsth. 7:2; Mark 6:23; 5:6 ^aEsth. 7:2 ^bEsth. 9:12; 5:8 ^aEsth. 6:14; 5:9 ^a[Job 20:5; Luke 6:25] ^bEsth. 3:5; 5:10 ^a2 Sam. 13:22; 5:11 ^aEsth. 9:7–10 ^bEsth. 3:1; 5:14 ^aEsth. 7:9 ^bEsth. 6:4 ^cEsth. 7:10; 6:1 ^aEsth. 2:23, 10:2; 6:4 ^aEsth. 5:1 ^bEsth. 5:14

⁵The king's servants said to him, "Haman is there, standing in the court."

And the king said, "Let him come in."

⁶So Haman came in, and the king asked him, "What shall be done for the man whom the king delights to honor?"

Now Haman thought in his heart, "Whom would the king delight to honor more than ᵃme?" ⁷And Haman answered the king, "*For* the man whom the king delights to honor, ⁸let a royal robe be brought which the king has worn, and ᵃa horse on which the king has ridden, which has a royal ¹crest placed on its head. ⁹Then let this robe and horse be delivered to the hand of one of the king's most noble princes, that he may array the man whom the king delights to honor. Then ¹parade him on horseback through the city square, ᵃand proclaim before him: 'Thus shall it be done to the man whom the king delights to honor!'"

¹⁰Then the king said to Haman, "Hurry, take the robe and the horse, as you have suggested, and do so for Mordecai the Jew who sits within the king's gate! Leave nothing undone of all that you have spoken."

¹¹So Haman took the robe and the horse, arrayed Mordecai and led him on horseback through the city square, and proclaimed before him, "Thus shall it be done to the man whom the king delights to honor!"

¹²Afterward Mordecai went back to the king's gate. But Haman ᵃhurried to his house, mourning ᵇand with his head covered. ¹³When Haman told his wife Zeresh and all his friends everything that had happened to him, his wise men and his wife Zeresh said to him, "If Mordecai, before whom you have begun to fall, is of Jewish descent, you will not prevail against ᵃhim but will surely fall before him."

¹⁴While they *were* still talking with him, the king's eunuchs came, and hastened to bring Haman to ᵃthe banquet which Esther had prepared.

HAMAN HANGED INSTEAD OF MORDECAI

7 So the king and Haman went to dine with Queen Esther. ²And on the second day, ᵃat the banquet of wine, the king again said to Esther, "What *is* your petition, Queen Esther? It shall be granted you. And what *is* your request, up to half the kingdom? It shall be done!"

³Then Queen Esther answered and said, "If I have found favor in your sight, O king, and if it pleases the king, let my life be given me at my petition, and my people at my request. ⁴For we have been ᵃsold, my people and I, to be destroyed, to be killed, and to be annihilated. Had we been sold as ᵇmale and female slaves, I would have held my tongue, although the enemy could never compensate for the king's loss."

⁵So King Ahasuerus answered and said to Queen Esther, "Who is he, and where is he, who would dare presume in his heart to do such a thing?"

⁶And Esther said, "The adversary and ᵃenemy *is* this wicked Haman!"

So Haman was terrified before the king and queen.

⁷Then the king arose in his wrath from the banquet of wine *and went* into the palace garden; but Haman stood before

6:6 ᵃ[Prov. 16:18; 18:12]
6:8 ᵃ1 Kin. 1:33
6:9 ᵃGen. 41:43
6:12 ᵃ2 Chr. 26:20 ᵇ2 Sam. 15:30; Jer. 14:3, 4
6:13 ᵃ[Gen. 12:3]; Zech. 2:8
6:14 ᵃEsth. 5:8
7:2 ᵃEsth. 5:6
7:4 ᵃEsth. 3:9, 4:7 ᵇDeut. 28:68
7:6 ᵃEsth. 3:10

6:8 ¹crown   6:9 ¹Lit. *cause him to ride*

Queen Esther, pleading for his life, for he saw that evil was determined against him by the king. [8]When the king returned from the palace garden to the place of the banquet of wine, Haman had fallen across [a]the couch where Esther *was*. Then the king said, "Will he also assault the queen while I *am* in the house?"

As the word left the king's mouth, they [b]covered Haman's face. [9]Now [a]Harbonah, one of the eunuchs, said to the king, "Look! [b]The [1]gallows, fifty cubits high, which Haman made for Mordecai, who spoke [c]good on the king's behalf, is standing at the house of Haman."

Then the king said, "Hang him on it!"

[10]So [a]they [b]hanged Haman on the gallows that he had prepared for Mordecai. Then the king's wrath subsided.

ESTHER SAVES THE JEWS

8 On that day King Ahasuerus gave Queen Esther the house of Haman, the [a]enemy of the Jews. And Mordecai came before the king, for Esther had told [b]how he *was related* to her. [2]So the king took off [a]his signet ring, which he had taken from Haman, and gave it to Mordecai; and Esther appointed Mordecai over the house of Haman.

[3]Now Esther spoke again to the king, fell down at his feet, and implored him with tears to counteract the evil of Haman the Agagite, and the scheme which he had devised against the Jews. [4]And [a]the king held out the golden scepter toward Esther. So Esther arose and stood before the king, [5]and said, "If it pleases the king, and if I have found favor in his sight and the thing *seems* right to the king and I am pleasing in his eyes, let it be written to revoke the [a]letters devised by Haman, the son of Hammedatha the Agagite, which he wrote to annihilate the Jews who *are* in all the king's provinces. [6]For how can I endure to see [a]the evil that will come to my people? Or how can I endure to see the destruction of my countrymen?"

[7]Then King Ahasuerus said to Queen Esther and Mordecai the Jew, "Indeed, [a]I have given Esther the house of Haman, and they have hanged him on the gallows because he *tried to* lay his hand on the Jews. [8]You yourselves write *a decree* concerning the Jews, [1]as you please, in the king's name, and seal *it* with the king's signet ring; for whatever is written in the king's name and sealed with the king's signet ring [a]no one can revoke."

[9a]So the king's scribes were called at that time, in the third month, which *is* the month of Sivan, on the twenty-third *day*; and it was written, according to all that Mordecai commanded, to the Jews, the satraps, the governors, and the princes of the provinces [b]from India to Ethiopia, one hundred and twenty-seven provinces *in all*, to every province [c]in its own script, to every people in their own language, and to the Jews in their own script and language. [10a]And he wrote in the name of King Ahasuerus, sealed *it* with the king's signet ring, and sent letters by couriers on horseback, riding on royal horses [1]bred from swift steeds.

[11]By these letters the king permitted the Jews who *were* in every city to [a]gather together and protect their lives—to

---

7:8 [a]Esth. 1:6
[b]Job 9:24

7:9 [a]Esth. 1:10
[b]Esth. 5:14;
[Ps. 7:16;
Prov. 11:5, 6]
[c]Esth. 6:2

7:10
[a][Ps. 7:16; 94:23;
Prov. 11:5, 6]
[b]Ps. 37:35, 36;
Dan. 6:24

8:1 [a]Esth. 7:6
[b]Esth. 2:7, 15

8:2 [a]Esth. 3:10

8:4
[a]Esth. 4:11, 5:2

8:5 [a]Esth. 3:13

8:6 [a]Neh. 2:3;
Esth. 7:4, 9:1

8:7 [a]Esth. 8:1;
Prov. 13:22

8:8 [a]Esth. 1:19;
Dan. 6:8, 12, 15

8:9 [a]Esth. 3:12
[b]Esth. 1:1
[c]Esth. 1:22, 3:12

8:10 [a]1 Kin. 21:8;
Esth. 3:12, 13

8:11 [a]Esth. 9:2

7:9 [1]Lit. *tree* or *wood*   8:8 [1]Lit. *as is good in your eyes*   8:10 [1]Lit. *sons of the swift horses*

ᵇdestroy, kill, and annihilate all the forces of any people or province that would assault them, *both* little children and women, and to plunder their possessions, ¹²ᵃon one day in all the provinces of King Ahasuerus, on the thirteenth *day* of the twelfth month, which *is* the month of ¹Adar. ¹³ᵃA copy of the document was to be issued as a decree in every province and published for all people, so that the Jews would be ready on that day to avenge themselves on their enemies. ¹⁴The couriers who rode on royal horses went out, hastened and pressed on by the king's command. And the decree was issued in ¹Shushan the ²citadel.

¹⁵So Mordecai went out from the presence of the king in royal apparel of ¹blue and white, with a great crown of gold and a garment of fine linen and purple; and ᵃthe city of ²Shushan rejoiced and was glad. ¹⁶The Jews had ᵃlight and gladness, joy and honor. ¹⁷And in every province and city, wherever the king's command and decree came, the Jews had joy and gladness, a feast ᵃand a holiday. Then many of the people of the land ᵇbecame Jews, because ᶜfear of the Jews fell upon them.

THE JEWS DESTROY THEIR TORMENTORS

9 Now ᵃin the twelfth month, that *is,* the month of Adar, on the thirteenth day, ᵇ*the time* came for the king's command and his decree to be executed. On the day that the enemies of the Jews had hoped to overpower them, the opposite occurred, in that the Jews themselves ᶜoverpowered those who hated them. ²The Jews ᵃgathered together in their cities throughout all the provinces of King Ahasuerus to lay hands on those who ᵇsought their harm. And no one could withstand them, ᶜbecause fear of them fell upon all people. ³And all the officials of the provinces, the satraps, the governors, and all those doing the king's work, helped the Jews, because the fear of Mordecai fell upon them. ⁴For Mordecai *was* great in the king's palace, and his fame spread throughout all the provinces; for this man Mordecai ᵃbecame increasingly prominent. ⁵Thus the Jews defeated all their enemies with the stroke of the sword, with slaughter and destruction, and did what they pleased with those who hated them.

⁶And in ᵃShushan¹ the ²citadel the Jews killed and destroyed five hundred men. ⁷Also Parshandatha, Dalphon, Aspatha, ⁸Poratha, Adalia, Aridatha, ⁹Parmashta, Arisai, Aridai, and Vajezatha— ¹⁰ᵃthe ten sons of Haman the son of Hammedatha, the enemy of the Jews—they killed; ᵇbut they did not lay a hand on the ¹plunder.

¹¹On that day the number of those who were killed in ¹Shushan the ²citadel ³was brought to the king. ¹²And the king said to Queen Esther, "The Jews have killed and destroyed five hundred men in Shushan the citadel, and the ten sons of Haman. What have they done in the rest of the king's provinces? Now ᵃwhat *is* your petition? It shall be granted to you. Or what *is* your further request? It shall be done."

¹³Then Esther said, "If it pleases the king, let it be granted to the Jews who *are* in Shushan to do again tomorrow ᵃaccording to today's decree, and let Haman's ten sons ᵇbe hanged on the gallows."

8:11 ᵇEsth. 9:10, 15, 16

8:12 ᵃEsth. 3:13, 9:1

8:13 ᵃEsth. 3:14, 15

8:15 ᵃEsth. 3:15; Prov. 29:2

8:16 ᵃPs. 97:11; 112:4

8:17 ᵃ1 Sam. 25:8; Esth. 9:19 ᵇPs. 18:43 ᶜGen. 35:5; Ex. 15:16; Deut. 2:25; 11:25; 1 Chr. 14:17; Esth. 9:2

9:1 ᵃEsth. 8:12 ᵇEsth. 3:13 ᶜ2 Sam. 22:41

9:2 ᵃEsth. 8:11; 9:15–18 ᵇPs. 71:13, 14 ᶜEsth. 8:17

9:4 ᵃ2 Sam. 3:1; 1 Chr. 11:9; [Prov. 4:18]

9:6 ᵃEsth. 1:2; 3:15; 4:16

9:10 ᵃEsth. 5:11; 9:7–10; Job 18:19; 27:13–15; Ps. 21:10 ᵇEsth. 8:11

9:12 ᵃEsth. 5:6, 7:2

9:13 ᵃEsth. 8:11, 9:15 ᵇ2 Sam. 21:6, 9

8:12 ¹LXX adds the text of the letter here   8:14 ¹Or *Susa*   ²*palace*
8:15 ¹*violet*   ²Or *Susa*   9:6 ¹Or *Susa*   ²*palace*   9:10 ¹*spoil*   9:11 ¹Or *Susa*
²*palace*   ³Lit. *came*

[14]So the king commanded this to be done; the decree was issued in Shushan, and they hanged Haman's ten sons.

[15]And the Jews who *were* in [1]Shushan [a]gathered together again on the fourteenth day of the month of Adar and killed three hundred men at Shushan; [b]but they did not lay a hand on the plunder.

[16]The remainder of the Jews in the king's provinces [a]gathered together and protected their lives, had rest from their enemies, and killed seventy-five thousand of their enemies; [b]but they did not lay a hand on the plunder. [17]*This was* on the thirteenth day of the month of Adar. And on the fourteenth of [1]*the month* they rested and made it a day of feasting and gladness.

THE FEAST OF PURIM

[18]But the Jews who *were* at [1]Shushan assembled together [a]on the thirteenth *day*, as well as on the fourteenth; and on the fifteenth of [2]*the month* they rested, and made it a day of feasting and gladness. [19]Therefore the Jews of the villages who dwelt in the unwalled towns celebrated the fourteenth day of the month of Adar [a]*with* gladness and feasting, [b]as a holiday, and for [c]sending presents to one another.

[20]And Mordecai wrote these things and sent letters to all the Jews, near and far, who *were* in all the provinces of King Ahasuerus, [21]to establish among them that they should celebrate yearly the fourteenth and fifteenth days of the month of Adar, [22]as the days on which the Jews had rest from their enemies, as the month which was turned from sorrow to joy for them, and from mourning to a holiday; that they should make them days of feasting and joy, of [a]sending presents to one another and gifts to the [b]poor. [23]So the Jews accepted the custom which they had begun, as Mordecai had written to them, [24]because Haman, the son of Hammedatha the Agagite, the enemy of all the Jews, [a]had plotted against the Jews to annihilate them, and had cast Pur (that *is*, the lot), to consume them and destroy them; [25]but [a]when [1]*Esther* came before the king, he commanded by letter that [2]this wicked plot which *Haman* had devised against the Jews should [b]return on his own head, and that he and his sons should be hanged on the gallows.

[26]So they called these days Purim, after the name [1]Pur. Therefore, because of all the words of [a]this letter, what they had seen concerning this matter, and what had happened to them, [27]the Jews established and imposed it upon themselves and their descendants and all who would [a]join them, that without fail they should celebrate these two days every year, according to the written *instructions* and according to the *prescribed* time, [28]that these days *should be* remembered and kept throughout every generation, every family, every province, and every city, that these days of Purim should not fail *to be observed* among the Jews, and *that* the memory of them should not perish among their descendants.

[29]Then Queen Esther, [a]the daughter of Abihail, with Mordecai the Jew, wrote with full authority to confirm this [b]second letter about Purim. [30]And *Mordecai* sent letters to all the

---

9:15 [a]Esth. 8:11,
9:2 [b]Esth. 9:10

9:16 [a]Esth. 9:2
[b]Esth. 8:11

9:18
[a]Esth. 9:11, 15

9:19 [a]Deut. 16:11,
14 [b]Esth. 8:16, 17
[c]Neh. 8:10, 12;
Esth. 9:22

9:22 [a]Neh. 8:10;
Esth. 9:19
[b][Deut. 15:7–11];
Job 29:16

9:24
[a]Esth. 3:6, 7,
9:26

9:25
[a]Esth. 7:4–10;
8:3; 9:13, 14
[b]Esth. 7:10

9:26 [a]Esth. 9:20

9:27 [a]Esth. 8:17;
[Is. 56:3, 6];
Zech. 2:11

9:29 [a]Esth. 2:15;
[b]Esth. 8:10;
9:20, 21

9:15 [1]Or *Susa*   9:17 [1]Lit. *it*   9:18 [1]Or *Susa*   [2]Lit. *it*   9:25 [1]Lit. *she* or *it*
[2]Lit. *his*   9:26 [1]Lit. *Lot*

Jews, to ªthe one hundred and twenty-seven provinces of the kingdom of Ahasuerus, *with* words of peace and truth, ³¹to confirm these days of Purim at their *appointed* time, as Mordecai the Jew and Queen Esther had prescribed for them, and as they had decreed for themselves and their descendants concerning matters of their ªfasting and lamenting. ³²So the decree of Esther confirmed these matters of Purim, and it was written in the book.

MORDECAI'S ADVANCEMENT

10 And King Ahasuerus imposed tribute on the land and *on* ªthe islands of the sea. ²Now all the acts of his power and his might, and the account of the greatness of Mordecai, ªto which the king ¹advanced him, *are* they not written in the book of the ᵇchronicles of the kings of Media and Persia? ³For Mordecai the Jew *was* ªsecond to King Ahasuerus, and was great among the Jews and well received by the multitude of his brethren, ᵇseeking the good of his people and speaking peace to all his ¹countrymen.

9:30 ªEsth. 1:1

9:31
ªEsth. 4:3, 16

10:1 ªGen. 10:5;
Ps. 72:10; Is. 11:11;
24:15

10:2 ªEsth. 8:15,
9:4 ᵇEsth. 6:1

10:3
ªGen. 41:40, 43,
44; 2 Chr. 28:7
ᵇNeh. 2:10;
Ps. 122:8, 9

10:2 ¹Lit. *made him great*   10:3 ¹Lit. *seed.* LXX, Vg. add a dream of Mordecai here; Vg. adds six more chapters

THE BOOK OF
JOB

JOB AND HIS FAMILY IN UZ

1 There was a man ᵃin the land of Uz, whose name *was* ᵇJob; and that man was ᶜblameless and upright, and one who ᵈfeared God and ¹shunned evil. ²And seven sons and three daughters were born to him. ³Also, his possessions were seven thousand sheep, three thousand camels, five hundred yoke of oxen, five hundred female donkeys, and a very large household, so that this man was the greatest of all the ¹people of the East.

⁴And his sons would go and feast *in their* houses, each on his *appointed* day, and would send and invite their three sisters to eat and drink with them. ⁵So it was, when the days of feasting had run their course, that Job would send and ¹sanctify them, and he would rise early in the morning ᵃand offer burnt offerings *according to* the number of them all. For Job said, "It may be that my sons have sinned and ᵇcursed² God in their hearts." Thus Job did regularly.

SATAN ATTACKS JOB'S CHARACTER

⁶Now ᵃthere was a day when the sons of God came to present themselves before the LORD, and ¹Satan also came among them. ⁷And the LORD said to ¹Satan, "From where do you come?"

So Satan answered the LORD and said, "From ᵃgoing to and fro on the earth, and from walking back and forth on it."

⁸Then the LORD said to Satan, "Have you ¹considered My servant Job, that *there is* none like him on the earth, a blameless and upright man, one who fears God and ²shuns evil?"

⁹So Satan answered the LORD and said, "Does Job fear God for nothing? ¹⁰ᵃHave You not ¹made a hedge around him, around his household, and around all that he has on every side? ᵇYou have blessed the work of his hands, and his possessions have increased in the land. ¹¹ᵃBut now, stretch out Your hand and touch all that he has, and he will surely ᵇcurse¹ You to Your face!"

¹²And the LORD said to Satan, "Behold, all that he has *is* in your ¹power; only do not lay a hand on his *person*."

So Satan went out from the presence of the LORD.

JOB LOSES HIS PROPERTY AND CHILDREN

¹³Now there was a day ᵃwhen his sons and daughters *were* eating and drinking wine in their oldest brother's house; ¹⁴and a messenger came to Job and said, "The oxen were plowing

---

1:1 ᵃ1 Chr. 1:17
ᵇEzek. 14:14, 20;
James 5:11
ᶜGen. 6:9; 17:1;
[Deut. 18:13]
ᵈ[Prov. 16:6]

1:5 ᵃGen. 8:20;
[Job 42:8]
ᵇ1 Kin. 21:10, 13

1:6 ᵃJob 2:1

1:7 ᵃ[1 Pet. 5:8]

1:10
ᵃJob 29:2–6;
Ps. 34:7; Is. 5:2
ᵇ[Ps. 128:1, 2;
Prov. 10:22]

1:11 ᵃJob 2:5;
19:21 ᵇIs. 8:21;
Mal. 3:13, 14

1:13 ᵃ[Eccl. 9:12]

1:1 ¹Lit. *turned away from*   1:3 ¹Lit. *sons*   1:5 ¹*consecrate*   ²Lit. *blessed,* but in an evil sense; cf. Job 1:11; 2:5, 9   1:6 ¹Lit. *the Adversary*   1:7 ¹Lit. *the Adversary*   1:8 ¹Lit. *set your heart on*   ²Lit. *turns away from*   1:10 ¹*Protected him*   1:11 ¹Lit. *bless,* but in an evil sense; cf. Job 1:5   1:12 ¹Lit. *hand*

and the donkeys feeding beside them, [15]when the [1]Sabeans [2]raided *them* and took them away—indeed they have killed the servants with the edge of the sword; and I alone have escaped to tell you!"

[16]While he *was* still speaking, another also came and said, "The fire of God fell from heaven and burned up the sheep and the servants, and [1]consumed them; and I alone have escaped to tell you!"

[17]While he *was* still speaking, another also came and said, "The Chaldeans formed three bands, raided the camels and took them away, yes, and killed the servants with the edge of the sword; and I alone have escaped to tell you!"

[18]While he *was* still speaking, another also came and said, [a]"Your sons and daughters *were* eating and drinking wine in their oldest brother's house, [19]and suddenly a great wind came from [1]across the wilderness and struck the four corners of the house, and it fell on the young people, and they are dead; and I alone have escaped to tell you!"

[20]Then Job arose, [a]tore his robe, and shaved his head; and he [b]fell to the ground and worshiped. [21]And he said:

[a]"Naked I came from my mother's womb,
And naked shall I return there.
The LORD [b]gave, and the LORD has [c]taken away;
[d]Blessed be the name of the LORD."

[22][a]In all this Job did not sin nor charge God with wrong.

SATAN ATTACKS JOB'S HEALTH

2 Again [a]there was a day when the sons of God came to present themselves before the LORD, and Satan came also among them to present himself before the LORD. [2]And the LORD said to Satan, "From where do you come?"

[a]Satan answered the LORD and said, "From going to and fro on the earth, and from walking back and forth on it."

[3]Then the LORD said to Satan, "Have you considered My servant Job, that *there is* none like him on the earth, [a]a blameless and upright man, one who fears God and shuns evil? And still he [b]holds fast to his integrity, although you incited Me against him, [c]to [1]destroy him without cause."

[4]So Satan answered the LORD and said, "Skin for skin! Yes, all that a man has he will give for his life. [5a]But stretch out Your hand now, and touch his [b]bone and his flesh, and he will surely [1]curse You to Your face!"

[6a]And the LORD said to Satan, "Behold, he *is* in your hand, but spare his life."

[7]So Satan went out from the presence of the LORD, and struck Job with painful boils [a]from the sole of his foot to the crown of his head. [8]And he took for himself a potsherd with which to scrape himself [a]while he sat in the midst of the ashes.

[9]Then his wife said to him, "Do you still hold fast to your integrity? [1]Curse God and die!"

[10]But he said to her, "You speak as one of the foolish women speaks. [a]Shall we indeed accept good from God, and shall

1:18 [a]Job 1:4, 13
1:20
[a]Gen. 37:29, 34; Josh. 7:6; Ezra 9:3
[b][1 Pet. 5:6]
1:21 [a][Ps. 49:17; Eccl. 5:15]; 1 Tim. 6:7
[b]Eccl. 5:19; [James 1:17]
[c]Gen. 31:16; [1 Sam. 2:6]
[d]Eph. 5:20; [1 Thess. 5:18]
1:22 [a]Job 2:10
2:1 [a]Job 1:6–8
2:2 [a]Job 1:7
2:3 [a]Job 1:1, 8
[b]Job 27:5, 6
[c]Job 9:17
2:5 [a]Job 1:11
[b]Job 19:20
2:6 [a]Job 1:12
2:7 [a]Is. 1:6
2:8 [a]Job 42:6; Jer. 6:26; Ezek. 27:30; Jon. 3:6; Matt. 11:21
2:10
[a]Job 1:21, 22; [Heb. 12:6; James 5:10, 11]

1:15 [1]Lit. *Sheba;* cf. Job 6:19   [2]Lit. *fell upon*   1:16 [1]*destroyed*   1:19 [1]LXX omits *across*   2:3 [1]Lit. *consume*   2:5 [1]Lit. *bless,* but in an evil sense; cf. Job 1:5   2:9 [1]Lit. *Bless,* but in an evil sense; cf. Job 1:5

we not accept adversity?" ᵇIn all this Job did not ᶜsin with his lips.

JOB'S THREE FRIENDS

¹¹Now when Job's three friends heard of all this adversity that had come upon him, each one came from his own place—Eliphaz the ᵃTemanite, Bildad the ᵇShuhite, and Zophar the Naamathite. For they had made an appointment together to come ᶜand mourn with him, and to comfort him. ¹²And when they raised their eyes from afar, and did not recognize him, they lifted their voices and wept; and each one tore his robe and ᵃsprinkled dust on his head toward heaven. ¹³So they sat down with him on the ground ᵃseven days and seven nights, and no one spoke a word to him, for they saw that *his* grief was very great.

JOB DEPLORES HIS BIRTH

3 After this Job opened his mouth and cursed the day of his birth. ²And Job ¹spoke, and said:

3 "Mayᵃ the day perish on which I was born,
  And the night *in which* it was said,
  'A male child is conceived.'

4 May that day be darkness;
  May God above not seek it,
  Nor the light shine upon it.

5 May darkness and ᵃthe shadow of death claim it;
  May a cloud settle on it;
  May the blackness of the day terrify it.

6 *As for* that night, may darkness seize it;
  May it not ¹rejoice among the days of the year,
  May it not come into the number of the months.

7 Oh, may that night be barren!
  May no joyful shout come into it!

8 May those curse it who curse the day,
  Those ᵃwho are ready to arouse Leviathan.

9 May the stars of its morning be dark;
  May it look for light, but *have* none,
  And not see the ¹dawning of the day;

10 Because it did not shut up the doors of my *mother's* womb,
   Nor hide sorrow from my eyes.

11 "Whyᵃ did I not die at birth?
   Why did I *not* ¹perish when I came from the womb?

12 ᵃWhy did the knees receive me?
   Or why the breasts, that I should nurse?

13 For now I would have lain still and been quiet,
   I would have been asleep;
   Then I would have been at rest

14 With kings and counselors of the earth,
   Who ᵃbuilt ruins for themselves,

15 Or with princes who had gold,
   Who filled their houses *with* silver;

16 Or *why* was I not hidden ᵃlike a stillborn child,
   Like infants who never saw light?

2:10 ᵇJob 1:22;
[James 1:12]
ᶜPs. 39:1

2:11 ᵃGen. 36:11;
1 Chr. 1:36;
Job 6:19;
Jer. 49:7;
Obad. 9
ᵇGen. 25:2;
1 Chr. 1:32
ᶜJob 42:11;
Rom. 12:15

2:12 ᵃJosh. 7:6;
Neh. 9:1;
Lam. 2:10;
Ezek. 27:30

2:13
ᵃGen. 50:10;
Ezek. 3:15

3:3
ᵃJob 10:18, 19;
Jer. 20:14–18

3:5
ᵃJob 10:21,
22; Jer. 13:16;
Amos 5:8

3:8 ᵃJer. 9:17

3:11
ᵃJob 10:18, 19

3:12 ᵃGen. 30:3

3:14 ᵃJob 15:28;
Is. 58:12

3:16 ᵃPs. 58:8

3:2 ¹Lit. *answered*   3:6 ¹LXX, Syr., Tg., Vg. *be joined*   3:9 ¹*eyelids of the dawn*   3:11 ¹*expire*

17 There the wicked cease *from* troubling,
And there the ¹weary are at ªrest.
18 *There* the prisoners ¹rest together;
ªThey do not hear the voice of the oppressor.
19 The small and great are there,
And the servant *is* free from his master.
20 "Whyª is light given to him who is in misery,
And life to the ᵇbitter of soul,
21 Who ªlong¹ for death, but it does not *come*,
And search for it more than ᵇhidden treasures;
22 Who rejoice exceedingly,
And are glad when they can find the ªgrave?
23 *Why is light given* to a man whose way is hidden,
ªAnd whom God has hedged in?
24 For my sighing comes before ¹I eat,
And my groanings pour out like water.
25 For the thing I greatly ªfeared has come upon me,
And what I dreaded has happened to me.
26 I am not at ease, nor am I quiet;
I have no rest, for trouble comes."

ELIPHAZ: JOB HAS SINNED

4 Then Eliphaz the Temanite answered and said:

2 "*If* one attempts a word with you, will you become
weary?
But who can withhold himself from speaking?
3 Surely you have instructed many,
And you ªhave strengthened weak hands.
4 Your words have upheld him who was stumbling,
And you ªhave strengthened the ¹feeble knees;
5 But now it comes upon you, and you are weary;
It touches you, and you are troubled.
6 *Is* not ªyour reverence ᵇyour confidence?
And the integrity of your ways your hope?

7 "Remember now, ªwho *ever* perished being innocent?
Or where were the upright *ever* cut off?
8 Even as I have seen,
ªThose who plow iniquity
And sow trouble reap the same.
9 By the blast of God they perish,
And by the breath of His anger they are consumed.
10 The roaring of the lion,
The voice of the fierce lion,
And ªthe teeth of the young lions are broken.
11 ªThe old lion perishes for lack of prey,
And the cubs of the lioness are scattered.

12 "Now a word was secretly brought to me,
And my ear received a whisper of it.
13 ªIn disquieting thoughts from the visions of the night,
When deep sleep falls on men,
14 Fear came upon me, and ªtrembling,
Which made all my bones shake.

3:17 ªJob 17:16
3:18 ªJob 39:7
3:20 ªJer. 20:18
ᵇ2 Kin. 4:27
3:21 ªRev. 9:6
ᵇProv. 2:4
3:22
ªJob 7:15, 16
3:23 ªJob 19:8;
Ps. 88:8;
Lam. 3:7
3:25 ª[Job 9:28;
30:15]
4:3 ªIs. 35:3
4:4 ªIs. 35:3
4:6 ªJob 1:1
ᵇProv. 3:26
4:7 ª[Job 8:20;
36:6, 7;
Ps. 37:25]
4:8
ª[Job 15:31, 35;
Prov. 22:8;
Hos. 10:13;
Gal. 6:7]
4:10 ªJob 5:15;
Ps. 58:6
4:11 ªJob 29:17;
Ps. 34:10
4:13 ªJob 33:15
4:14 ªHab. 3:16

3:17 ¹Lit. *weary of strength*   3:18 ¹*are at ease*   3:21 ¹Lit. *wait*   3:24 ¹Lit.
my bread   4:4 ¹Lit. *bending*

15 Then a spirit passed before my face;
The hair on my body stood up.
16 It stood still,
But I could not discern its appearance.
A form *was* before my eyes;
There was silence;
Then I heard a voice *saying:*
17 'Can a mortal be more righteous than God?
Can a man be more pure than his Maker?
18 If He aputs no trust in His servants,
If He charges His angels with error,
19 How much more those who dwell in houses of clay,
Whose foundation is in the dust,
Who are crushed before a moth?
20 aThey are broken in pieces from morning till evening;
They perish forever, with no one regarding.
21 Does not their own excellence go away?
They die, even without wisdom.'

ELIPHAZ: JOB IS CHASTENED BY GOD

5 "Call out now;
Is there anyone who will answer you?
And to which of the holy ones will you turn?
2 For wrath kills a foolish man,
And envy slays a simple one.
3 aI have seen the foolish taking root,
But suddenly I cursed his dwelling place.
4 His sons are afar from safety,
They are crushed in the gate,
And bthere is no deliverer.
5 Because the hungry eat up his harvest,
1Taking it even from the thorns,
2And a snare snatches their 3substance.
6 For affliction does not come from the dust,
Nor does trouble spring from the ground;
7 Yet man is aborn to 1trouble,
As the sparks fly upward.
8 "But as for me, I would seek God,
And to God I would commit my cause—
9 Who does great things, and unsearchable,
Marvelous things without number.
10 aHe gives rain on the earth,
And sends waters on the fields.
11 aHe sets on high those who are lowly,
And those who mourn are lifted to safety.
12 aHe frustrates the devices of the crafty,
So that their hands cannot carry out their plans.
13 He catches the awise in their own craftiness,
And the counsel of the cunning comes quickly upon them.
14 They meet with darkness in the daytime,
And grope at noontime as in the night.
15 But aHe saves the needy from the sword,
From the mouth of the mighty,
And from their hand.

4:18 aJob 15:15
4:20
aPs. 90:5, 6
5:3
a[Ps. 37:35, 36];
Jer. 12:1–3
5:4 aPs. 119:155
bPs. 109:12
5:7 aJob 14:1
5:10
a[Job 36:27–29;
37:6–11; 38:26]
5:11 aPs. 113:7
5:12 aNeh. 4:15
5:13 a[Job 37:24;
1 Cor. 3:19]
5:15
aJob 4:10, 11;
Ps. 35:10

5:5 1LXX *They shall not be taken from evil men;* Vg. *And the armed man shall take him by violence* 2LXX *The might shall draw them off;* Vg. *And the thirsty shall drink up their riches* 3*wealth* 5:7 1*labor*

16 ^aSo the poor have hope,
And injustice shuts her mouth.

17 "Behold,^a happy *is* the man whom God corrects;
Therefore do not despise the chastening of the Almighty.

18 ^aFor He bruises, but He binds up;
He wounds, but His hands make whole.

19 ^aHe shall deliver you in six troubles,
Yes, in seven ^bno evil shall touch you.

20 ^aIn famine He shall redeem you from death,
And in war from the ¹power of the sword.

21 ^aYou shall be hidden from the scourge of the tongue,
And you shall not be afraid of destruction when it
comes.

22 You shall laugh at destruction and famine,
And ^ayou shall not be afraid of the ^bbeasts of the earth.

23 ^aFor you shall have a covenant with the stones of the field,
And the beasts of the field shall be at peace with you.

24 You shall know that your tent *is* in peace;
You shall visit your dwelling and find nothing amiss.

25 You shall also know that ^ayour descendants *shall be*
many,
And your offspring ^blike the grass of the earth.

26 ^aYou shall come to the grave at a full age,
As a sheaf of grain ripens in its season.

27 Behold, this we have ^asearched out;
It *is* true.
Hear it, and know for yourself."

JOB: MY COMPLAINT IS JUST

6 Then Job answered and said:

2 "Oh, that my grief were fully weighed,
And my calamity laid with it on the scales!

3 For then it would be heavier than the sand of the sea—
Therefore my words have been rash.

4 ^aFor the arrows of the Almighty *are* within me;
My spirit drinks in their poison;
^bThe terrors of God are arrayed ^cagainst me.

5 Does the ^awild donkey bray when it has grass,
Or does the ox low over its fodder?

6 Can flavorless food be eaten without salt?
Or is there *any* taste in the white of an egg?

7 My soul refuses to touch them;
They *are* as loathsome food to me.

8 "Oh, that I might have my request,
That God would grant *me* the thing that I long for!

9 That it would please God to crush me,
That He would loose His hand and ^acut me off!

10 Then I would still have comfort;
Though in anguish I would exult,
He will not spare;
For ^aI have not concealed the words of ^bthe Holy One.

11 "What strength do I have, that I should hope?
And what *is* my end, that I should prolong my life?

5:16 ^a1 Sam. 2:8;
Ps. 107:41, 42

5:17 ^aPs. 94:12;
[Prov. 3:11, 12;
Heb. 12:5, 6;
Rev. 3:19]

5:18
^a[Deut. 32:39;
1 Sam. 2:6, 7];
Is. 30:26;
Hos. 6:1

5:19 ^aPs. 34:19;
91:3;
[1 Cor. 10:13]
^bPs. 91:10;
[Prov. 24:16]

5:20 ^aPs. 33:19,
20; 37:19

5:21 ^aJob 5:15;
Ps. 31:20

5:22 ^aPs. 91:13;
Is. 11:9;
35:9; 65:25;
Ezek. 34:25
^bHos. 2:18

5:23 ^aPs. 91:12

5:25 ^aPs. 112:2
^bPs. 72:16

5:26
^a[Prov. 9:11;
10:27]

5:27 ^aPs. 111:2

6:4 ^aJob 16:13;
Ps. 38:2
^bPs. 88:15, 16
^cJob 30:15

6:5 ^aJob 39:5–8

6:9
^aNum. 11:15;
1 Kin. 19:4;
Job 7:16; 9:21;
10:1

6:10
^aActs 20:20
^b[Lev. 19:2;
Is. 57:15]

5:20 ¹Lit. *hand*

12 *Is* my strength the strength of stones?
Or is my flesh bronze?
13 *Is* my help not within me?
And is success driven from me?

14 "To[a] him who is [1]afflicted, kindness *should be shown* by his friend,
Even though he forsakes the fear of the Almighty.
15 [a]My brothers have dealt deceitfully like a brook,
[b]Like the streams of the brooks that pass away,
16 Which are dark because of the ice,
And into which the snow vanishes.
17 When it is warm, they cease to flow;
When it is hot, they vanish from their place.
18 The paths of their way turn aside,
They go nowhere and perish.
19 The caravans of [a]Tema look,
The travelers of [b]Sheba hope for them.
20 They are [a]disappointed[1] because they were confident;
They come there and are confused.
21 For now [a]you are nothing,
You see terror and [b]are afraid.
22 Did I ever say, 'Bring *something* to me'?
Or, 'Offer a bribe for me from your wealth'?
23 Or, 'Deliver me from the enemy's hand'?
Or, 'Redeem me from the hand of oppressors'?

24 "Teach me, and I will hold my tongue;
Cause me to understand wherein I have erred.
25 How forceful are right words!
But what does your arguing prove?
26 Do you intend to rebuke *my* words,
And the speeches of a desperate one, *which are* as wind?
27 Yes, you overwhelm the fatherless,
And you [a]undermine your friend.
28 Now therefore, be pleased to look at me;
For I would never lie to your face.
29 [a]Yield now, let there be no injustice!
Yes, concede, my [b]righteousness [1]still stands!
30 Is there injustice on my tongue?
Cannot my [1]taste discern the unsavory?

JOB: MY SUFFERING IS COMFORTLESS

7 "Is *there* not [a]a time of hard service for man on earth?
Are not his days also like the days of a hired man?
2 Like a servant who [1]earnestly desires the shade,
And like a hired man who eagerly looks for his wages,
3 So I have been allotted [a]months of futility,
And wearisome nights have been appointed to me.
4 [a]When I lie down, I say, 'When shall I arise,
And the night be ended?'
For I have had my fill of tossing till dawn.
5 My flesh is [a]caked with worms and dust,
My skin is cracked and breaks out afresh.

6 "My[a] days are swifter than a weaver's shuttle,
And are spent without hope.

6:14
a[Prov. 17:17]

6:15 aPs. 38:11
bJer. 15:18

6:19 aGen. 25:15;
Is. 21:14;
Jer. 25:23
b1 Kin. 10:1;
Ps. 72:10;
Ezek. 27:22, 23

6:20 aJer. 14:3

6:21 aJob 13:4
bPs. 38:11

6:27 aPs. 57:6

6:29 aJob 17:10
bJob 27:5, 6;
34:5

7:1
a[Job 14:5, 13,
14]; Ps. 39:4

7:3 a[Job 15:31]

7:4
aDeut. 28:67;
Job 7:13, 14

7:5 aIs. 14:11

7:6 aJob 9:25;
16:22; 17:11;
Is. 38:12;
[James 4:14]

6:14 [1]Or *despairing*   6:20 [1]Lit. *ashamed*   6:29 [1]Lit. *is in it*   6:30 [1]*palate*
7:2 [1]Lit. *pants for*

7 Oh, remember that ᵃmy life *is* a breath!
My eye will never again see good.
8 ᵃThe eye of him who sees me will see me no *more;*
While your eyes *are* upon me, I shall no longer *be.*
9 *As* the cloud disappears and vanishes away,
So ᵃhe who goes down to the grave does not come up.
10 He shall never return to his house,
ᵃNor shall his place know him anymore.

11 "Therefore I will ᵃnot restrain my mouth;
I will speak in the anguish of my spirit;
I will ᵇcomplain in the bitterness of my soul.
12 *Am* I a sea, or a sea serpent,
That You set a guard over me?
13 ᵃWhen I say, 'My bed will comfort me,
My couch will ease my complaint,'
14 Then You scare me with dreams
And terrify me with visions,
15 So that my soul chooses strangling
And death rather than ¹my body.
16 ᵃI loathe *my life;*
I would not live forever.
ᵇLet me alone,
For ᶜmy days *are but* ¹a breath.

17 "Whatᵃ *is* man, that You should exalt him,
That You should set Your heart on him,
18 That You should ¹visit him every morning,
And test him every moment?
19 How long?
Will You not look away from me,
And let me alone till I swallow my saliva?
20 Have I sinned?
What have I done to You, ᵃO watcher of men?
Why ᵇhave You set me as Your target,
So that I am a burden ¹to myself?
21 Why then do You not pardon my transgression,
And take away my iniquity?
For now I will lie down in the dust,
And You will seek me diligently,
But I *will* no longer *be.*"

BILDAD: JOB SHOULD REPENT

8 Then Bildad the Shuhite answered and said:

2 "How long will you speak these *things,*
And the words of your mouth *be like* a strong wind?
3 ᵃDoes God subvert judgment?
Or does the Almighty pervert justice?
4 If ᵃyour sons have sinned against Him,
He has cast them away ¹for their transgression.
5 ᵃIf you would earnestly seek God
And make your supplication to the Almighty,
6 If you *were* pure and upright,
Surely now He would ¹awake for you,
And prosper your rightful dwelling place.

7:7 ᵃJob 7:16;
Ps. 78:39; 89:47
7:8
ᵃJob 8:18; 20:9
7:9
ᵃ2 Sam. 12:23
7:10 ᵃPs. 103:16
7:11 ᵃPs. 39:1, 9
ᵇ1 Sam. 1:10
7:13 ᵃJob 9:27
7:16 ᵃJob 10:1
ᵇJob 14:6
ᶜPs. 62:9
7:17 ᵃJob 22:2;
Ps. 8:4; 144:3;
Heb. 2:6
7:20 ᵃPs. 36:6
ᵇPs. 21:12
8:3 ᵃGen. 18:25;
[Deut. 32:4;
2 Chr. 19:7;
Job 34:10, 12;
36:23; 37:23];
Rom. 3:5
8:4 ᵃJob 1:5,
18, 19
8:5
ᵃ[Job 5:17–27;
11:13]

7:15 ¹Lit. *my bones*   7:16 ¹Without substance, futile   7:18 ¹*attend to*
7:20 ¹So with MT, Tg., Vg.; LXX, Jewish tradition *to You*   8:4 ¹Lit. *into the
hand of their transgression*   8:6 ¹*arise*

7 Though your beginning was small,
Yet your latter end would [a]increase abundantly.

8 "For[a] inquire, please, of the former age,
And consider the things discovered by their fathers;
9 For [a]we *were born* yesterday, and know [1]nothing,
Because our days on earth *are* a shadow.
10 Will they not teach you and tell you,
And utter words from their heart?

11 "Can the papyrus grow up without a marsh?
Can the reeds flourish without water?
12 [a]While it *is* yet green *and* not cut down,
It withers before any *other* plant.
13 So *are* the paths of all who [a]forget God;
And the hope of the [b]hypocrite shall perish,
14 Whose confidence shall be cut off,
And whose trust *is* [1]a spider's web.
15 [a]He leans on his house, but it does not stand.
He holds it fast, but it does not endure.
16 He grows green in the sun,
And his branches spread out in his garden.
17 His roots wrap around the rock heap,
And look for a place in the stones.
18 [a]If he is destroyed from his place,
Then *it* will deny him, *saying*, 'I have not seen you.'

19 "Behold, this is the joy of His way,
And [a]out of the earth others will grow.
20 Behold, [a]God will not [1]cast away the blameless,
Nor will He uphold the evildoers.
21 He will yet fill your mouth with laughing,
And your lips with [1]rejoicing.
22 Those who hate you will be [a]clothed with shame,
And the dwelling place of the wicked [1]will come to
nothing."

JOB: THERE IS NO MEDIATOR

9 Then Job answered and said:

2 "Truly I know *it is* so,
But how can a [a]man be [b]righteous before God?
3 If one wished to [1]contend with Him,
He could not answer Him one time out of a thousand.
4 [a]*God is* wise in heart and mighty in strength.
Who has hardened *himself* against Him and prospered?
5 He removes the mountains, and they do not know
When He overturns them in His anger;
6 He [a]shakes the earth out of its place,
And its [b]pillars tremble;
7 He commands the sun, and it does not rise;
He seals off the stars;
8 [a]He alone spreads out the heavens,
And [1]treads on the [2]waves of the sea;
9 [a]He made [1]the Bear, Orion, and the Pleiades,
And the chambers of the south;

8:7 [a]Job 42:12
8:8 [a]Deut. 4:32;
32:7; Job 15:18;
20:4
8:9 [a]Gen. 47:9;
[1 Chr. 29:15];
Job 7:6;
[Ps. 39:5; 102:11;
144:4]
8:12 [a]Ps. 129:6
8:13 [a]Ps. 9:17
[b]Job 11:20; 18:14;
27:8; Ps. 112:10;
[Prov. 10:28]
8:15 [a]Job 8:22;
27:18; Ps. 49:11
8:18 [a]Job 7:10
8:19 [a]Ps. 113:7
8:20 [a]Job 4:7
8:22 [a]Ps. 35:26;
109:29
9:2 [a][Job 4:17;
15:14–16;
Ps. 143:2;
Rom. 3:20]
[b][Hab. 2:4;
Rom. 1:17;
Gal. 3:11;
Heb. 10:38]
9:4 [a]Job 36:5
9:6
[a]Is. 2:19, 21;
Hag. 2:6;
Heb. 12:26
[b]Job 26:11
9:8 [a]Gen. 1:6;
Job 37:18;
Ps. 104:2, 3;
Is. 40:22
9:9 [a]Gen. 1:16;
Job 38:31;
Amos 5:8

8:9 [1]Lit. *not*   8:14 [1]Lit. *a spider's house*   8:20 [1]reject   8:21 [1]Lit. *shouts of
joy*   8:22 [1]Lit. *will not be*   9:3 [1]*argue*   9:8 [1]*walks*   [2]Lit. *heights*
9:9 [1]Heb. *Ash, Kesil,* and *Kimah*

10 ^aHe does great things past finding out,
Yes, wonders without number.

11 ^aIf He goes by me, I do not see *Him;*
If He moves past, I do not perceive Him;

12 ^aIf He takes away, ¹who can hinder Him?
Who can say to Him, 'What are You doing?'

13 God will not withdraw His anger,
^aThe allies of ¹the proud lie prostrate beneath Him.

14 "How then can I answer Him,
And choose my words *to reason* with Him?

15 ^aFor though I were righteous, I could not answer Him;
I would beg mercy of my Judge.

16 If I called and He answered me,
I would not believe that He was listening to my voice.

17 For He crushes me with a tempest,
And multiplies my wounds ^awithout cause.

18 He will not allow me to catch my breath,
But fills me with bitterness.

19 If *it is a matter* of strength, indeed *He is* strong;
And if of justice, who will appoint my day *in court?*

20 Though I were righteous, my own mouth would
condemn me;
Though I *were* blameless, it would prove me
perverse.

21 "I am blameless, yet I do not know myself;
I despise my life.

22 It *is* all one *thing;*
Therefore I say, ^a'He destroys the blameless and the
wicked.'

23 If the scourge slays suddenly,
He laughs at the plight of the innocent.

24 The earth is given into the hand of the wicked.
He covers the faces of its judges.
If it is not *He,* who else could it be?

25 "Now ^amy days are swifter than a runner;
They flee away, they see no good.

26 They pass by like ¹swift ships,
^aLike an eagle swooping on its prey.

27 ^aIf I say, 'I will forget my complaint,
I will put off my sad face and wear a smile,'

28 ^aI am afraid of all my sufferings;
I know that You ^bwill not hold me innocent.

29 *If* I am condemned,
Why then do I labor in vain?

30 ^aIf I wash myself with snow water,
And cleanse my hands with ¹soap,

31 Yet You will plunge me into the pit,
And my own clothes will ¹abhor me.

32 "For ^a*He is* not a man, as I *am,*
That I may answer Him,
And that we should go to court together.

33 ^aNor is there any mediator between us,
Who may lay his hand on us both.

9:10 ^aJob 5:9
9:11
^a[Job 23:8, 9;
35:14]
9:12 ^a[Is. 45:9;
Dan. 4:35;
Rom. 9:20]
9:13 ^aJob 26:12
9:15 ^aJob 10:15;
23:1–7
9:17 ^aJob 2:3
9:22
^a[Eccl. 9:2, 3];
Ezek. 21:3
9:25 ^aJob 7:6, 7
9:26
^aJob 39:29;
Hab. 1:8
9:27 ^aJob 7:13
9:28 ^aPs. 119:120
^bEx. 20:7
9:30 ^a[Jer. 2:22]
9:32 ^aEccl. 6:10;
[Is. 45:9;
Jer. 49:19;
Rom. 9:20]
9:33
^a[1 Sam. 2:25];
Job 9:19; Is. 1:18

9:12 ¹Lit. *who can turn Him back?*   9:13 ¹Heb. *rahab*   9:26 ¹Lit. *ships of
reeds*   9:30 ¹*lye*   9:31 ¹*loathe*

34 ᵃLet Him take His rod away from me,
And do not let dread of Him terrify me.
35 *Then* I would speak and not fear Him,
But it is not so with me.

JOB: I WOULD PLEAD WITH GOD

10 "My ᵃsoul loathes my life;
I will ¹give free course to my complaint,
ᵇI will speak in the bitterness of my soul.
2 I will say to God, 'Do not condemn me;
Show me why You contend with me.
3 *Does it* seem good to You that You should oppress,
That You should despise the work of Your hands,
And smile on the counsel of the wicked?
4 Do You have eyes of flesh?
Or ᵃdo You see as man sees?
5 *Are* Your days like the days of a mortal man?
Are Your years like the days of a mighty man,
6 That You should seek for my iniquity
And search out my sin,
7 Although You know that I am not wicked,
And *there is* no one who can deliver from Your hand?

8 'Yourᵃ hands have made me and fashioned me,
An intricate unity;
Yet You would ᵇdestroy me.
9 Remember, I pray, ᵃthat You have made me like clay.
And will You turn me into dust again?
10 ᵃDid You not pour me out like milk,
And curdle me like cheese,
11 Clothe me with skin and flesh,
And knit me together with bones and sinews?
12 You have granted me life and favor,
And Your care has preserved my spirit.

13 'And these *things* You have hidden in Your heart;
I know that this *was* with You:
14 If I sin, then ᵃYou mark me,
And will not acquit me of my iniquity.
15 If I am wicked, ᵃwoe to me;
ᵇEven *if* I am righteous, I ¹cannot lift up my head.
I am full of disgrace;
ᶜSee my misery!
16 If *my head* is exalted,
ᵃYou hunt me like a fierce lion,
And again You show Yourself awesome against me.
17 You renew Your witnesses against me,
And increase Your indignation toward me;
Changes and war are *ever* with me.

18 'Whyᵃ then have You brought me out of the womb?
Oh, that I had perished and no eye had seen me!
19 I would have been as though I had not been.
I would have been carried from the womb to the grave.
20 ᵃAre not my days few?
Cease! ᵇLeave me alone, that I may take a little comfort,
21 Before I go *to the place from which* I shall not return,
ᵃTo the land of darkness ᵇand the shadow of death,

9:34
ᵃJob 13:20, 21;
Ps. 39:10

10:1 ᵃ1 Kin. 19:4;
Job 7:16;
Jon. 4:3
ᵇJob 7:11

10:4
ᵃ[1 Sam. 16:7;
Job 28:24;
34:21]

10:8 ᵃJob 10:3;
Ps. 119:73
ᵇ[Job 9:22]

10:9 ᵃGen. 2:7;
Job 33:6

10:10
ᵃ[Ps. 139:14–16]

10:14 ᵃJob 7:20;
Ps. 139:1

10:15 ᵃJob 10:7;
Is. 3:11
ᵇ[Job 9:12, 15]
ᶜPs. 25:18

10:16 ᵃIs. 38:13;
Lam. 3:10;
Hos. 13:7

10:18
ᵃJob 3:11–13

10:20 ᵃPs. 39:5
ᵇJob 7:16, 19

10:21 ᵃPs. 88:12
ᵇPs. 23:4

10:1 ¹Lit. *leave on myself*   **10:15** ¹Lit. *will not*

22 A land as dark as darkness *itself,*
  As the shadow of death, without any order,
  Where even the light *is* like darkness.'"

ZOPHAR URGES JOB TO REPENT

11 Then Zophar the Naamathite answered and said:

2 "Should not the multitude of words be answered?
  And should ¹a man full of talk be vindicated?
3 Should your empty talk make men ¹hold their peace?
  And when you mock, should no one rebuke you?
4 For you have said,
 ᵃ'My doctrine *is* pure,
  And I am clean in your eyes.'
5 But oh, that God would speak,
  And open His lips against you,
6 That He would show you the secrets of wisdom!
  For *they would* double *your* prudence.
  Know therefore that ᵃGod ¹exacts from you
  Less than your iniquity *deserves.*

7 "Canᵃ you search out the deep things of God?
  Can you find out the limits of the Almighty?
8 *They are* higher than heaven—what can you do?
  Deeper than ¹Sheol—what can you know?
9 Their measure *is* longer than the earth
  And broader than the sea.

10 "Ifᵃ He passes by, imprisons, and gathers *to judgment,*
  Then who can ¹hinder Him?
11 For ᵃHe knows deceitful men;
  He sees wickedness also.
  Will He not then consider *it?*
12 For an ᵃempty-headed man will be wise,
  When a wild donkey's colt is born a man.

13 "If you would ᵃprepare your heart,
  And ᵇstretch out your hands toward Him;
14 If iniquity *were* in your hand, *and you* put it far away,
  And ᵃwould not let wickedness dwell in your tents;
15 ᵃThen surely you could lift up your face without spot;
  Yes, you could be steadfast, and not fear;
16 Because you would ᵃforget *your* misery,
  And remember *it* as waters *that have* passed away,
17 And *your* life ᵃwould be brighter than noonday.
  Though you were dark, you would be like the
    morning.
18 And you would be secure, because there is hope;
  Yes, you would dig *around you, and* ᵃtake your rest in
    safety.
19 You would also lie down, and no one would make *you*
    afraid;
  Yes, many would court your favor.
20 But ᵃthe eyes of the wicked will fail,
  And they shall not escape,
  And ᵇtheir hope—¹loss of life!"

11:4 ᵃJob 6:30
11:6 ᵃ[Ezra 9:13]
11:7
ᵃJob 33:12, 13;
36:26;
[Eccl. 3:11;
Rom. 11:33]
11:10 ᵃJob 9:12;
[Rev. 3:7]
11:11 ᵃ[Ps. 10:14]
11:12 ᵃ[Ps. 39:5];
Rom. 1:22
11:13
ᵃ[1 Sam. 7:3]
ᵇPs. 88:9
11:14 ᵃPs. 101:3
11:15 ᵃJob 22:26;
Ps. 119:6;
[1 John 3:21]
11:16 ᵃIs. 65:16
11:17 ᵃPs. 37:6;
Prov. 4:18;
Is. 58:8, 10
11:18
ᵃLev. 26:5, 6;
Ps. 3:5;
Prov. 3:24
11:20
ᵃLev. 26:16;
Deut. 28:65;
Job 17:5
ᵇJob 18:14;
[Prov. 11:7]

11:2 ¹Lit. *a man of lips* 11:3 ¹Lit. *be silent* 11:6 ¹Lit. *forgets some of your iniquity for you* 11:8 ¹The abode of the dead 11:10 ¹*restrain* 11:20 ¹Lit. *the breathing out of life*

JOB ANSWERS HIS CRITICS

12 Then Job answered and said:

2 "No doubt you *are* the people,
  And wisdom will die with you!
3 But I have [1]understanding as well as you;
  I *am* not [a]inferior to you.
  Indeed, who does not *know* such things as these?

4 "I[a] am one mocked by his friends,
  Who [b]called on God, and He answered him,
  The just and blameless *who is* ridiculed.
5 A [1]lamp is despised in the thought of one who is at ease;
  It is made ready for [a]those whose feet slip.
6 [a]The tents of robbers prosper,
  And those who provoke God are secure—
  In what God provides by His hand.

7 "But now ask the beasts, and they will teach you;
  And the birds of the air, and they will tell you;
8 Or speak to the earth, and it will teach you;
  And the fish of the sea will explain to you.
9 Who among all these does not know
  That the hand of the LORD has done this,
10 [a]In whose hand *is* the [1]life of every living thing,
  And the [b]breath of [2]all mankind?
11 Does not the ear test words
  And the [1]mouth taste its food?
12 Wisdom *is* with aged men,
  And with [1]length of days, understanding.

13 "With Him *are* [a]wisdom and strength,
  He has counsel and understanding.
14 If [a]He breaks *a thing* down, it cannot be rebuilt;
  If He imprisons a man, there can be no release.
15 If He [a]withholds the waters, they dry up;
  If He [b]sends them out, they overwhelm the earth.
16 With Him *are* strength and prudence.
  The deceived and the deceiver *are* His.
17 He leads counselors away plundered,
  And makes fools of the judges.
18 He loosens the bonds of kings,
  And binds their waist with a belt.
19 He leads [1]princes away plundered,
  And overthrows the mighty.
20 [a]He deprives the trusted ones of speech,
  And takes away the discernment of the elders.
21 [a]He pours contempt on princes,
  And [1]disarms the mighty.
22 He [a]uncovers deep things out of darkness,
  And brings the shadow of death to light.
23 [a]He makes nations great, and destroys them;
  He [1]enlarges nations, and guides them.
24 He takes away the [1]understanding of the chiefs of the
    people of the earth,
  And [a]makes them wander in a pathless wilderness.

12:3 [a]Job 13:2
12:4 [a]Job 21:3
  [b]Ps. 91:15
12:5 [a]Prov. 14:2
12:6 [a][Job 9:24;
  21:6–16;
  Ps. 73:12;
  Jer. 12:1;
  Mal. 3:15]
12:10
  [a][Acts 17:28]
  [b]Job 27:3; 33:4
12:13
  [a]Job 9:4; 36:5
12:14 [a]Job 11:10;
  Is. 25:2
12:15
  [a]Deut. 11:17;
  [1 Kin. 8:35, 36]
  [b]Gen. 7:11–24
12:20 [a]Job 32:9
12:21
  [a][Job 34:19];
  Ps. 107:40;
  [Dan. 2:21]
12:22
  [a]Dan. 2:22;
  [1 Cor. 4:5]
12:23
  [a]Is. 9:3; 26:15
12:24 [a]Ps. 107:4

12:3 [1]Lit. *a heart*   12:5 [1]Or *disaster*   12:10 [1]Or *soul*   [2]Lit. *all flesh of men*
12:11 [1]*palate*   12:12 [1]Long life   12:19 [1]Lit. *priests*, but not in a technical
sense   12:21 [1]*loosens the belt of*   12:23 [1]Lit. *spreads out*   12:24 [1]Lit. *heart*

25 [a]They grope in the dark without light,
And He makes them [b]stagger like a drunken *man*.

13

"Behold, my eye has seen all *this*,
My ear has heard and understood it.

2 [a]What you know, I also know;
I *am* not inferior to you.

3 [a]But I would speak to the Almighty,
And I desire to reason with God.

4 But you forgers of lies,
[a]You *are* all worthless physicians.

5 Oh, that you would be silent,
And [a]it would be your wisdom!

6 Now hear my reasoning,
And heed the pleadings of my lips.

7 [a]Will you speak [1]wickedly for God,
And talk deceitfully for Him?

8 Will you show partiality for Him?
Will you contend for God?

9 Will it be well when He searches you out?
Or can you mock Him as one mocks a man?

10 He will surely rebuke you
If you secretly show partiality.

11 Will not His [1]excellence make you afraid,
And the dread of Him fall upon you?

12 Your platitudes *are* proverbs of ashes,
Your defenses are defenses of clay.

13 "Hold[1] your peace with me, and let me speak,
Then let come on me what *may!*

14 Why [a]do I take my flesh in my teeth,
And put my life in my hands?

15 [a]Though He slay me, yet will I trust Him.
[b]Even so, I will defend my own ways before Him.

16 He also *shall* be my salvation,
For a [a]hypocrite could not come before Him.

17 Listen carefully to my speech,
And to my declaration with your ears.

18 See now, I have prepared *my* case,
I know that I shall be [a]vindicated.

19 [a]Who *is* he *who* will contend with me?
If now I hold my tongue, I perish.

JOB'S DESPONDENT PRAYER

20 "Only[a] two *things* do not do to me,
Then I will not hide myself from You:

21 [a]Withdraw Your hand far from me,
And let not the dread of You make me afraid.

22 Then call, and I will [a]answer;
Or let me speak, then You respond to me.

23 How many *are* my iniquities and sins?
Make me know my transgression and my sin.

24 [a]Why do You hide Your face,
And [b]regard me as Your enemy?

25 [a]Will You frighten a leaf driven to and fro?
And will You pursue dry stubble?

26 For You write bitter things against me,
And [a]make me inherit the iniquities of my youth.

12:25 [a]Job 5:14;
15:30; 18:18
[b]Ps. 107:27
13:2 [a]Job 12:3
13:3
[a]Job 23:3; 31:35
13:4 [a]Job 6:21;
[Jer. 23:32]
13:5 [a]Job 13:13;
21:5; Prov. 17:28
13:7
[a]Job 27:4; 36:4
13:14 [a]Job 18:4
13:15 [a]Ps. 23:4;
[Prov. 14:32]
[b]Job 27:5
13:16 [a]Job 8:13
13:18
[a][Rom. 8:34]
13:19 [a]Job 7:21;
10:8; Is. 50:8
13:20 [a]Job 9:34
13:21 [a]Job 9:34;
Ps. 39:10
13:22
[a]Job 9:16; 14:15
13:24
[a][Deut. 32:20];
Ps. 13:1
[b]Lam. 2:5
13:25 [a]Is. 42:3
13:26 [a]Job 20:11

13:7 [1]unrighteously   13:11 [1]Lit. *exaltation*   13:13 [1]*Be silent*

27 ^aYou put my feet in the stocks,
And watch closely all my paths.
You ¹set a limit for the ²soles of my feet.

28 "*Man*¹ decays like a rotten thing,
Like a garment that is moth-eaten.

14 "Man *who is* born of woman
Is of few days and ^afull of ¹trouble.

2 ^aHe comes forth like a flower and fades away;
He flees like a shadow and does not continue.

3 And ^ado You open Your eyes on such a one,
And ^bbring ¹me to judgment with Yourself?

4 Who ^acan bring a clean *thing* out of an unclean?
No one!

5 ^aSince his days *are* determined,
The number of his months *is* with You;
You have appointed his limits, so that he cannot pass.

6 ^aLook away from him that he may ¹rest,
Till ^blike a hired man he finishes his day.

7 "For there is hope for a tree,
If it is cut down, that it will sprout again,
And that its tender shoots will not cease.

8 Though its root may grow old in the earth,
And its stump may die in the ground,

9 *Yet* at the scent of water it will bud
And bring forth branches like a plant.

10 But man dies and ¹is laid away;
Indeed he ²breathes his last
And where *is* ^ahe?

11 *As* water disappears from the sea,
And a river becomes parched and dries up,

12 So man lies down and does not rise.
^aTill the heavens *are* no more,
They will not awake
Nor be roused from their sleep.

13 "Oh, that You would hide me in the grave,
That You would conceal me until Your wrath is past,
That You would appoint me a set time, and remember me!

14 If a man dies, shall he live *again?*
All the days of my hard service ^aI will wait,
Till my change comes.

15 ^aYou shall call, and I will answer You;
You shall desire the work of Your hands.

16 For now ^aYou number my steps,
But do not watch over my sin.

17 ^aMy transgression *is* sealed up in a bag,
And You ¹cover my iniquity.

18 "But *as* a mountain falls *and* crumbles away,
And *as* a rock is moved from its place;

19 *As* water wears away stones,
And *as* torrents wash away the soil of the earth;
So You destroy the hope of man.

13:27 ^aJob 33:11
14:1 ^aJob 5:7; Eccl. 2:23
14:2 ^aJob 8:9; Ps. 90:5, 6, 9; 102:11; 103:15; 144:4; Is. 40:6; James 1:10, 11; 1 Pet. 1:24
14:3 ^aPs. 8:4; 144:3 ^b[Ps. 143:2]
14:4 ^a[Job 15:14; 25:4; Ps. 51:2, 5, 10; John 3:6; Rom. 5:12; Eph. 2:3]
14:5 ^aJob 7:1; 21:21; Heb. 9:27
14:6 ^aJob 7:16, 19; Ps. 39:13 ^bJob 7:1
14:10 ^aJob 10:21, 22
14:12 ^aPs. 102:25, 26; [Is. 51:6; 65:17; 66:22]; Acts 3:21; [2 Pet. 3:7, 10, 11; Rev. 20:11; 21:1]
14:14 ^aJob 13:15
14:15 ^aJob 13:22
14:16 ^aJob 10:6, 14; 13:27; 31:4; 34:21; Ps. 56:8; 139:1–3; Prov. 5:21; [Jer. 32:19]
14:17 ^aDeut. 32:32–34

13:27 ¹Lit. *inscribe a print* ²Lit. *roots* 13:28 ¹Lit. *He* 14:1 ¹*turmoil*
14:3 ¹LXX, Syr., Vg. *him* 14:6 ¹Lit. *cease* 14:10 ¹*lies prostrate* ²*expires*
14:17 ¹Lit. *plaster over*

20 You prevail forever against him, and he passes on;
  You change his countenance and send him away.
21 His sons come to honor, and ªhe does not know *it;*
  They are brought low, and he does not perceive *it.*
22 But his flesh will be in pain over it,
  And his soul will mourn over it."

ELIPHAZ ACCUSES JOB OF FOLLY

15 Then ªEliphaz the Temanite answered and said:

2 "Should a wise man answer with empty knowledge,
  And fill ¹himself with the east wind?
3 Should he reason with unprofitable talk,
  Or by speeches with which he can do no good?
4 Yes, you cast off fear,
  And restrain ¹prayer before God.
5 For your iniquity teaches your mouth,
  And you choose the tongue of the crafty.
6 ªYour own mouth condemns you, and not I;
  Yes, your own lips testify against you.

7 "*Are* you the first man *who* was born?
  ªOr were you made before the hills?
8 ªHave you heard the counsel of God?
  Do you limit wisdom to yourself?
9 ªWhat do you know that we do not know?
  What do you understand that *is* not in us?
10 ªBoth the gray-haired and the aged *are* among us,
  Much older than your father.
11 *Are* the consolations of God too small for you,
  And the word *spoken* ¹gently with you?
12 Why does your heart carry you away,
  And ¹what do your eyes wink at,
13 That you turn your spirit against God,
  And let *such* words go out of your mouth?

14 "Whatª *is* man, that he could be pure?
  And *he who is* born of a woman, that he could be
    righteous?
15 ªIf *God* puts no trust in His saints,
  And the heavens are not pure in His sight,
16 ªHow much less man, *who is* abominable and filthy,
  ᵇWho drinks iniquity like water!

17 "I will tell you, hear me;
  What I have seen I will declare,
18 What wise men have told,
  Not hiding *anything received* ªfrom their fathers,
19 To whom alone the ¹land was given,
  And ªno alien passed among them:
20 The wicked man writhes with pain all *his* days,
  ªAnd the number of years is hidden from the oppressor.
21 ¹Dreadful sounds *are* in his ears;
  ªIn prosperity the destroyer comes upon him.
22 He does not believe that he will ªreturn from darkness,
  For a sword is waiting for him.

14:21 ªEccl. 9:5;
Is. 63:16

15:1 ªJob 4:1

15:6 ªJob 9:20;
[Luke 19:22]

15:7
ªJob 38:4, 21;
Ps. 90:2;
Prov. 8:25

15:8 ªJob 29:4;
Rom. 11:34;
[1 Cor. 2:11]

15:9
ªJob 12:3; 13:2

15:10
ªJob 8:8–10;
12:12; 32:6, 7

15:14 ªJob 14:4;
Prov. 20:9;
[Eccl. 7:20;
1 John 1:8, 10]

15:15
ªJob 4:18; 25:5

15:16 ªJob 4:19;
Ps. 14:3; 53:3
ᵇJob 34:7;
Prov. 19:28

15:18
ªJob 8:8; 20:4

15:19 ªJoel 3:17

15:20 ªPs. 90:12

15:21 ªJob 20:21;
1 Thess. 5:3

15:22
ªJob 14:10–12

15:2 ¹Lit. *his belly* 15:4 ¹*meditation* or *complaint* 15:11 ¹Or *a secret thing*
15:12 ¹Or *why do your eyes flash* 15:19 ¹Or *earth* 15:21 ¹*Terrifying*

23 He ᵃwanders about for bread, *saying,* 'Where *is it?'*
   He knows ᵇthat a day of darkness is ready at his
      hand.
24 Trouble and anguish make him afraid;
   They overpower him, like a king ready for ¹battle.
25 For he stretches out his hand against God,
   And acts defiantly against the Almighty,
26 Running stubbornly against Him
   With his strong, embossed shield.

27 "Thoughᵃ he has covered his face with his fatness,
   And made *his* waist heavy with fat,
28 He dwells in desolate cities,
   In houses which no one inhabits,
   Which are destined to become ruins.
29 He will not be rich,
   Nor will his wealth ᵃcontinue,
   Nor will his possessions overspread the earth.
30 He will not depart from darkness;
   The flame will dry out his branches,
   And ᵃby the breath of His mouth he will go away.
31 Let him not ᵃtrust in futile *things,* deceiving himself,
   For futility will be his reward.
32 It will be accomplished ᵃbefore his time,
   And his branch will not be green.
33 He will shake off his unripe grape like a vine,
   And cast off his blossom like an olive tree.
34 For the company of hypocrites *will be* barren,
   And fire will consume the tents of bribery.
35 ᵃThey conceive trouble and bring forth futility;
   Their womb prepares deceit."

JOB REPROACHES HIS PITILESS FRIENDS

16 Then Job answered and said:

2 "I have heard many such things;
   ᵃMiserable¹ comforters *are* you all!
3 Shall ¹words of wind have an end?
   Or what provokes you that you answer?
4 I also could speak as you *do,*
   If your soul were in my soul's place.
   I could heap up words against you,
   And ᵃshake my head at you;
5 *But* I would strengthen you with my mouth,
   And the comfort of my lips would relieve *your grief.*

6 "Though I speak, my grief is not relieved;
   And *if* I remain silent, how am I eased?
7 But now He has ᵃworn me out;
   You ᵇhave made desolate all my company.
8 You have shriveled me up,
   And it is a ᵃwitness *against me;*
   My leanness rises up against me
   And bears witness to my face.
9 ᵃHe tears *me* in His wrath, and hates me;
   He gnashes at me with His teeth;
   ᵇMy adversary sharpens His gaze on me.

15:23 ᵃPs. 59:15;
109:10 ᵇJob 18:12

15:27 ᵃPs. 17:10;
73:7; 119:70

15:29
ᵃJob 20:28;
27:16, 17

15:30 ᵃJob 4:9

15:31 ᵃJob 35:13;
Is. 59:4

15:32
ᵃJob 22:16;
Ps. 55:23;
Eccl. 7:17

15:35 ᵃPs. 7:14;
Is. 59:4;
[Hos. 10:13]

16:2 ᵃJob 13:4;
21:34

16:4 ᵃPs. 22:7;
109:25;
Lam. 2:15;
Zeph. 2:15;
Matt. 27:39

16:7 ᵃJob 7:3
ᵇJob 16:20;
19:13–15

16:8 ᵃJob 10:17

16:9
ᵃJob 10:16, 17;
19:11; Hos. 6:1
ᵇJob 13:24;
33:10

15:24 ¹attack   16:2 ¹Troublesome   16:3 ¹Empty words

10 They ªgape at me with their mouth,
They ᵇstrike me reproachfully on the cheek,
They gather together against me.
11 God ªhas delivered me to the ungodly,
And turned me over to the hands of the wicked.
12 I was at ease, but He has ªshattered me;
He also has taken *me* by my neck, and shaken me to
pieces;
He has ᵇset me up for His target,
13 His archers surround me.
He pierces my ¹heart and does not pity;
He pours out my gall on the ground.
14 He breaks me with wound upon wound;
He runs at me like a ¹warrior.

15 "I have sewn sackcloth over my skin,
And ªlaid my ¹head in the dust.
16 My face is ¹flushed from weeping,
And on my eyelids *is* the shadow of death;
17 Although no violence *is* in my hands,
And my prayer *is* pure.

18 "O earth, do not cover my blood,
And ªlet my cry have no *resting* place!
19 Surely even now ªmy witness *is* in heaven,
And my evidence *is* on high.
20 My friends scorn me;
My eyes pour out *tears* to God.
21 ªOh, that one might plead for a man with God,
As a man *pleads* for his ¹neighbor!
22 For when a few years are finished,
I shall ªgo the way of no return.

JOB PRAYS FOR RELIEF

17 "My spirit is broken,
My days are extinguished,
ªThe grave *is ready* for me.
2 *Are* not mockers with me?
And does not my eye ¹dwell on their ªprovocation?

3 "Now put down a pledge for me with Yourself.
Who *is* he *who* ªwill shake hands with me?
4 For You have hidden their heart from ªunderstanding;
Therefore You will not exalt *them*.
5 He who speaks flattery to *his* friends,
Even the eyes of his children will ªfail.

6 "But He has made me ªa byword of the people,
And I have become one in whose face men spit.
7 ªMy eye has also grown dim because of sorrow,
And all my members *are* like shadows.
8 Upright *men* are astonished at this,
And the innocent stirs himself up against the
hypocrite.
9 Yet the righteous will hold to his ªway,
And he who has ᵇclean hands will be stronger and
stronger.

16:10
ªPs. 22:13; 35:21
ᵇIs. 50:6;
Lam. 3:30;
Mic. 5:1;
Matt. 26:67;
Mark 14:65;
Luke 22:63;
Acts 23:2

16:11 ªJob 1:15, 17

16:12 ªJob 9:17
ᵇJob 7:20;
Lam. 3:12

16:15
ªJob 30:19;
Ps. 7:5

16:18 ªJob 27:9;
[Ps. 66:18]

16:19
ªGen. 31:50;
Rom. 1:9;
Phil. 1:8;
1 Thess. 2:5

16:21 ªJob 31:35;
Eccl. 6:10;
[Is. 45:9;
Rom. 9:20]

16:22 ªJob 10:21;
Eccl. 12:5

17:1 ªPs. 88:3, 4

17:2 ª1 Sam. 1:6;
Job 12:4; 17:6;
30:1, 9; 34:7

17:3 ªProv. 6:1;
17:18; 22:26

17:4
ªJob 12:20; 32:9

17:5 ªJob 11:20

17:6 ªJob 30:9

17:7
ªPs. 6:7; 31:9

17:9 ªProv. 4:18
ᵇPs. 24:4

16:13 ¹Lit. *kidneys*   16:14 ¹Vg. *giant*   16:15 ¹Lit. *horn*   16:16 ¹Lit. *red*
16:21 ¹*friend*   17:2 ¹Lit. *lodge*

10 "But please, ᵃcome back again, ¹all of you,
For I shall not find *one* wise *man* among you.
11 ᵃMy days are past,
My purposes are broken off,
Even the ¹thoughts of my heart.
12 They change the night into day;
'The light *is* near,' *they say,* in the face of darkness.
13 If I wait *for* the grave *as* my house,
If I make my bed in the darkness,
14 If I say to corruption, 'You *are* my father,'
And to the worm, 'You *are* my mother and my
sister,'
15 Where then *is* my ᵃhope?
As for my hope, who can see it?
16 *Will* they go down ᵃto the gates of ¹Sheol?
Shall *we have* ᵇrest together in the dust?"

BILDAD: THE WICKED ARE PUNISHED

18 Then ᵃBildad the Shuhite answered and said:

2 "How long *till* you put an end to words?
Gain understanding, and afterward we will speak.
3 Why are we counted ᵃas beasts,
And regarded as stupid in your sight?
4 ᵃYou¹ who tear yourself in anger,
Shall the earth be forsaken for you?
Or shall the rock be removed from its place?

5 "Theᵃ light of the wicked indeed goes out,
And the flame of his fire does not shine.
6 The light is dark in his tent,
ᵃAnd his lamp beside him is put out.
7 The steps of his strength are shortened,
And ᵃhis own counsel casts him down.
8 For ᵃhe is cast into a net by his own feet,
And he walks into a snare.
9 The net takes *him* by the heel,
And ᵃa snare lays hold of him.
10 A noose *is* hidden for him on the ground,
And a trap for him in the road.
11 ᵃTerrors frighten him on every side,
And drive him to his feet.
12 His strength is starved,
And ᵃdestruction *is* ready at his side.
13 It devours patches of his skin;
The firstborn of death devours his ¹limbs.
14 He is uprooted from ᵃthe shelter of his tent,
And they parade him before the king of terrors.
15 They dwell in his tent *who are* none of his;
Brimstone is scattered on his dwelling.
16 ᵃHis roots are dried out below,
And his branch withers above.
17 ᵃThe memory of him perishes from the earth,
And he has no name ¹among the renowned.

17:10 ᵃJob 6:29
17:11 ᵃJob 7:6
17:15 ᵃJob 7:6;
13:15; 14:19; 19:10
17:16 ᵃJon. 2:6
ᵇJob 3:17–19;
21:33
18:1 ᵃJob 8:1
18:3 ᵃPs. 73:22
18:4 ᵃJob 13:14
18:5 ᵃJob 21:17;
Prov. 13:9;
20:20; 24:20
18:6 ᵃJob 21:17;
Ps. 18:28
18:7
ᵃJob 5:12, 13;
15:6
18:8 ᵃJob 22:10;
Ps. 9:15; 35:8;
Is. 24:17, 18
18:9 ᵃJob 5:5
18:11 ᵃJob 20:25;
Jer. 6:25
18:12 ᵃJob 15:23
18:14 ᵃJob 11:20
18:16 ᵃJob 29:19
18:17
ᵃJob 24:20;
[Ps. 34:16];
Prov. 10:7

17:10 ¹So with some Heb. mss., LXX, Syr., Vg.; MT, Tg. *all of them*
17:11 ¹*desires*   17:16 ¹The abode of the dead   18:4 ¹Lit. *one who tears his
soul*   18:13 ¹*parts*   18:17 ¹Lit. *before the outside,* i.e., the distinguished or
famous

18 ¹He is driven from light into darkness,
And chased out of the world.
19 ªHe has neither son nor posterity among his people,
Nor any remaining in his dwellings.
20 Those ¹in the west are astonished ªat his day,
As those ²in the east are frightened.
21 Surely such *are* the dwellings of the wicked,
And this *is* the place *of him who* ªdoes not know God."

JOB TRUSTS IN HIS REDEEMER

19

Then Job answered and said:

2 "How long will you torment my soul,
And break me in pieces with words?
3 These ten times you have ¹reproached me;
You are not ashamed *that* you ²have wronged me.
4 And if indeed I have erred,
My error remains with me.
5 If indeed you ªexalt *yourselves* against me,
And plead my disgrace against me,
6 Know then that ªGod has wronged me,
And has surrounded me with His net.

7 "If I cry out concerning ¹wrong, I am not heard.
If I cry aloud, *there is* no justice.
8 ªHe has ¹fenced up my way, so that I cannot pass;
And He has set darkness in my paths.
9 ªHe has stripped me of my glory,
And taken the crown *from* my head.
10 He breaks me down on every side,
And I am gone;
My ªhope He has uprooted like a tree.
11 He has also kindled His wrath against me,
And ªHe counts me as *one of* His enemies.
12 His troops come together
And build up their road against me;
They encamp all around my tent.

13 "Heª has removed my brothers far from me,
And my acquaintances are completely estranged from me.
14 My relatives have failed,
And my close friends have forgotten me.
15 Those who dwell in my house, and my maidservants,
Count me as a stranger;
I am an alien in their sight.
16 I call my servant, but he gives no answer;
I beg him with my mouth.
17 My breath is offensive to my wife,
And I am ¹repulsive to the children of my own body.
18 Even ªyoung children despise me;
I arise, and they speak against me.
19 ªAll my close friends abhor me,
And those whom I love have turned against me.
20 ªMy bone clings to my skin and to my flesh,
And I have escaped by the skin of my teeth.

18:19
ªJob 27:14, 15;
Is. 14:22

18:20 ªPs. 37:13;
Jer. 50:27;
Obad. 12

18:21 ªJer. 9:3;
1 Thess. 4:5

19:5 ªPs. 35:26;
38:16; 55:12, 13

19:6 ªJob 16:11

19:8 ªJob 3:23;
Ps. 88:8;
Lam. 3:7, 9

19:9
ªJob 12:17, 19;
Ps. 89:44

19:10
ªJob 17:14–16

19:11
ªJob 13:24; 33:10

19:13
ªJob 16:20;
Ps. 31:11; 38:11;
69:8; 88:8, 18

19:18
ª2 Kin. 2:23;
Job 17:6

19:19 ªPs. 38:11;
55:12, 13

19:20 ªJob 16:8;
33:21; Ps. 102:5;
Lam. 4:8

18:18 ¹Or *They drive him*   18:20 ¹Lit. *who came after*   ²Lit. *who have gone before*   19:3 ¹*shamed* or *disgraced*   ²A Jewish tradition *make yourselves strange to me*   19:7 ¹*violence*   19:8 ¹*walled off my way*   19:17 ¹Lit. *strange*

21 "Have pity on me, have pity on me, O you my friends,
   For the hand of God has struck me!
22 Why do you ªpersecute me as God *does,*
   And are not satisfied with my flesh?

23 "Oh, that my words were written!
   Oh, that they were inscribed in a book!
24 That they were engraved on a rock
   With an iron pen and lead, forever!
25 For I know *that* my Redeemer lives,
   And He shall stand at last on the earth;
26 And after my skin is ¹destroyed, this *I know,*
   That ªin my flesh I shall see God,
27 Whom I shall see for myself,
   And my eyes shall behold, and not another.
   How my ¹heart yearns within me!
28 If you should say, 'How shall we persecute him?'—
   Since the root of the matter is found in me,
29 Be afraid of the sword for yourselves;
   For wrath *brings* the punishment of the sword,
   That you may know *there is* a judgment."

ZOPHAR'S SERMON ON THE WICKED MAN

20 Then ªZophar the Naamathite answered and said:

2 "Therefore my anxious thoughts make me answer,
   Because of the turmoil within me.
3 I have heard the rebuke ¹that reproaches me,
   And the spirit of my understanding causes me to answer.

4 "Do you *not* know this of ªold,
   Since man was placed on earth,
5 ªThat the triumphing of the wicked is short,
   And the joy of the hypocrite is *but* for a ᵇmoment?
6 ªThough his haughtiness mounts up to the heavens,
   And his head reaches to the clouds,
7 *Yet* he will perish forever like his own refuse;
   Those who have seen him will say, 'Where is he?'
8 He will fly away ªlike a dream, and not be found;
   Yes, he ᵇwill be chased away like a vision of the night.
9 The eye *that* saw him will *see him* no more,
   Nor will his place behold him anymore.
10 His children will seek the favor of the poor,
   And his hands will restore his wealth.
11 His bones are full of ªhis youthful vigor,
   ᵇBut it will lie down with him in the dust.

12 "Though evil is sweet in his mouth,
   And he hides it under his tongue,
13 *Though* he spares it and does not forsake it,
   But still keeps it in his ¹mouth,
14 *Yet* his food in his stomach turns sour;
   It becomes cobra venom within him.
15 He swallows down riches
   And vomits them up again;
   God casts them out of his belly.

19:22 ªJob 13:24, 25; 16:11; 19:6; Ps. 69:26
19:26 ª[Ps. 17:15]; Matt. 5:8; 1 Cor. 13:12; [1 John 3:2]
20:1 ªJob 11:1
20:4 ªJob 8:8; 15:10
20:5 ªPs. 37:35, 36 ᵇ[Job 8:13; 13:16; 15:34; 27:8]
20:6 ªIs. 14:13, 14
20:8 ªPs. 73:20; 90:5 ᵇJob 18:18; 27:21–23
20:11 ªJob 13:26 ᵇJob 21:26

16 He will suck the poison of cobras;
The viper's tongue will slay him.
17 He will not see ᵃthe streams,
The rivers flowing with honey and cream.
18 He will restore that for which he labored,
And will not swallow *it* down;
From the proceeds of business
He will get no enjoyment.
19 For he has ¹oppressed *and* forsaken the poor,
He has violently seized a house which he did not build.

20 "Becauseᵃ he knows no quietness in his ¹heart,
He will not save anything he desires.
21 Nothing is left for him to eat;
Therefore his well-being will not last.
22 In his self-sufficiency he will be in distress;
Every hand of ¹misery will come against him.
23 *When* he is about to fill his stomach,
God will cast on him the fury of His wrath,
And will rain *it* on him while he is eating.
24 ᵃHe will flee from the iron weapon;
A bronze bow will pierce him through.
25 It is drawn, and comes out of the body;
Yes, ᵃthe glittering *point comes* out of his ¹gall.
ᵇTerrors *come* upon him;
26 Total darkness *is* reserved for his treasures.
ᵃAn unfanned fire will consume him;
It shall go ill with him who is left in his tent.
27 The heavens will reveal his iniquity,
And the earth will rise up against him.
28 The increase of his house will depart,
And his goods will flow away in the day of His ᵃwrath.
29 ᵃThis *is* the portion from God for a wicked man,
The heritage appointed to him by God."

JOB'S DISCOURSE ON THE WICKED

21 Then Job answered and said:

2 "Listen carefully to my speech,
And let this be your ¹consolation.
3 Bear with me that I may speak,
And after I have spoken, keep ᵃmocking.

4 "As for me, *is* my complaint against man?
And if *it were,* why should I not be impatient?
5 Look at me and be astonished;
ᵃPut *your* hand over *your* mouth.
6 Even when I remember I am terrified,
And trembling takes hold of my flesh.
7 ᵃWhy do the wicked live *and* become old,
Yes, become mighty in power?
8 Their descendants are established with them in their sight,
And their offspring before their eyes.
9 Their houses *are* safe from fear,
ᵃNeither *is* ¹the rod of God upon them.

20:17 ᵃPs. 36:8;
Jer. 17:8

20:20
ᵃEccl. 5:13–15

20:24 ᵃIs. 24:18;
Amos 5:19

20:25 ᵃJob 16:13
ᵇJob 18:11, 14

20:26 ᵃPs. 21:9

20:28
ᵃJob 20:15;
21:30

20:29
ᵃJob 27:13;
31:2, 3

21:3 ᵃJob 16:10

21:5
ᵃJudg. 18:19;
Job 13:5; 29:9;
40:4

21:7 ᵃJob 12:6;
Ps. 17:10, 14;
73:3, 12;
[Jer. 12:1];
Hab. 1:13, 16

21:9 ᵃPs. 73:5

20:19 ¹*crushed*   20:20 ¹Lit. *belly*   20:22 ¹Or *the wretched* or *sufferer*
20:25 ¹*Gallbladder*   21:2 ¹*comfort*   21:9 ¹The rod of God's chastisement

10 Their bull breeds without failure;
 Their cow calves ᵃwithout miscarriage.
11 They send forth their little ones like a flock,
 And their children dance.
12 They sing to the tambourine and harp,
 And rejoice to the sound of the flute.
13 They ᵃspend their days in wealth,
 And ¹in a moment go down to the ²grave.
14 ᵃYet they say to God, 'Depart from us,
 For we do not desire the knowledge of Your ways.
15 ᵃWho *is* the Almighty, that we should serve Him?
 And ᵇwhat profit do we have if we pray to Him?'
16 Indeed ¹their prosperity *is* not in their hand;
 ᵃThe counsel of the wicked is far from me.

17 "How often is the lamp of the wicked put out?
 How often does their destruction come upon them,
 The sorrows God ᵃdistributes in His anger?
18 ᵃThey are like straw before the wind,
 And like chaff that a storm ¹carries away.
19 *They say,* 'God ¹lays up ²one's iniquity ᵃfor his
 children';
 Let Him recompense him, that he may know *it.*
20 Let his eyes see his destruction,
 And ᵃlet him drink of the wrath of the Almighty.
21 For what does he care about his household after him,
 When the number of his months is cut in half?

22 "Canᵃ *anyone* teach God knowledge,
 Since He judges those on high?
23 One dies in his full strength,
 Being wholly at ease and secure;
24 His ¹pails are full of milk,
 And the marrow of his bones is moist.
25 Another man dies in the bitterness of his soul,
 Never having eaten with pleasure.
26 They ᵃlie down alike in the dust,
 And worms cover them.

27 "Look, I know your thoughts,
 And the schemes *with which* you would wrong me.
28 For you say,
 'Where *is* the house of the prince?
 And where *is* ¹the tent,
 The dwelling place of the wicked?'
29 Have you not asked those who travel the road?
 And do you not know their signs?
30 ᵃFor the wicked are reserved for the day of doom;
 They shall be brought out on the day of wrath.
31 Who condemns his way to his face?
 And who repays him *for what* he has done?
32 Yet he shall be brought to the grave,
 And a vigil kept over the tomb.
33 The clods of the valley shall be sweet to him;
 ᵃEveryone shall follow him,
 As countless *have gone* before him.

21:10 ᵃEx. 23:26
21:13
ᵃJob 21:23; 36:11
21:14 ᵃJob 22:17
21:15 ᵃEx. 5:2;
Job 22:17; 34:9
 ᵇJob 35:3;
Mal. 3:14
21:16 ᵃJob 22:18;
Ps. 1:1; Prov. 1:10
21:17
ᵃ[Job 31:2, 3;
Luke 12:46]
21:18 ᵃPs. 1:4;
35:5; Is. 17:13;
Hos. 13:3
21:19
ᵃ[Ex. 20:5];
Jer. 31:29;
Ezek. 18:2
21:20 ᵃPs. 75:8;
Is. 51:17;
Jer. 25:15;
Rev. 14:10; 19:15
21:22 ᵃJob 35:11;
36:22; [Is. 40:13;
45:9; Rom. 11:34;
1 Cor. 2:16]
21:26 ᵃJob 3:13;
20:11; Eccl. 9:2
21:30
ᵃJob 20:29;
[Prov. 16:4;
2 Pet. 2:9]
21:33 ᵃHeb. 9:27

21:13 ¹Without lingering ²Or *Sheol* 21:16 ¹Lit. *their goal* 21:18 ¹*steals*
away 21:19 ¹*stores up* ²Lit. *his* 21:24 ¹LXX, Vg. *bowels;* Syr. *sides;* Tg.
breasts 21:28 ¹Vg. omits *the tent*

34 How then can you comfort me with empty words,
Since [1]falsehood remains in your answers?"

ELIPHAZ ACCUSES JOB OF WICKEDNESS

22 Then [a]Eliphaz the Temanite answered and said:

2 "Can[a] a man be profitable to God,
Though he who is wise may be profitable to himself?

3 *Is it* any pleasure to the Almighty that you are righteous?
Or *is it* gain *to Him* that you make your ways blameless?

4 "Is it because of your fear of Him that He corrects you,
And enters into judgment with you?

5 *Is* not your wickedness great,
And your iniquity without end?

6 For you have [a]taken pledges from your brother for no
reason,
And stripped the naked of their clothing.

7 You have not given the weary water to drink,
And you [a]have withheld bread from the hungry.

8 But the [1]mighty man possessed the land,
And the honorable man dwelt in it.

9 You have sent widows away empty,
And the [1]strength of the fatherless was crushed.

10 Therefore snares *are* all around you,
And sudden fear troubles you,

11 Or darkness *so that* you cannot see;
And an abundance of [a]water covers you.

12 "Is not God in the height of heaven?
And see the highest stars, how lofty they are!

13 And you say, [a]'What does God know?
Can He judge through the deep darkness?

14 [a]Thick clouds cover Him, so that He cannot see,
And He walks above the circle of heaven.'

15 Will you keep to the old way
Which wicked men have trod,

16 Who [a]were cut down before their time,
Whose foundations were swept away by a flood?

17 [a]They said to God, 'Depart from us!
What can the Almighty do to [1]them?'

18 Yet He filled their houses with good *things*;
But the counsel of the wicked is far from me.

19 "The[a] righteous see *it* and are glad,
And the innocent laugh at them:

20 'Surely our [1]adversaries are cut down,
And the fire consumes their remnant.'

21 "Now acquaint yourself with Him, and [a]be at peace;
Thereby good will come to you.

22 Receive, please, [a]instruction from His mouth,
And [b]lay up His words in your heart.

23 If you return to the Almighty, you will be built up;
You will remove iniquity far from your tents.

24 Then you will [a]lay your gold in the dust,
And the *gold* of Ophir among the stones of the brooks.

22:1 [a]Job 4:1;
15:1; 42:9

22:2 [a]Job 35:7;
[Ps. 16:2;
Luke 17:10]

22:6
[a][Ex. 22:26, 27];
Deut. 24:6, 10,
17; Job 24:3, 9;
Ezek. 18:16

22:7 [a]Deut. 15:7;
Job 31:17;
Is. 58:7;
Ezek. 18:7;
Matt. 25:42

22:11
[a]Job 38:34;
Ps. 69:1, 2; 124:5;
Lam. 3:54

22:13 [a]Ps. 73:11

22:14
[a]Ps. 139:11, 12

22:16 [a]Job 14:19;
15:32; Ps. 90:5;
Is. 28:2;
Matt. 7:26, 27

22:17
[a]Job 21:14, 15

22:19 [a]Ps. 52:6;
58:10; 107:42

22:21
[a][Ps. 34:10];
Is. 27:5

22:22 [a]Job 6:10;
23:12; Prov. 2:6
[b][Ps. 119:11]

22:24
[a]2 Chr. 1:15

21:34 [1]*faithlessness*   22:8 [1]Lit. *man of arm*   22:9 [1]Lit. *arms*   22:17 [1]LXX,
Syr. *us*   22:20 [1]LXX *substance is*

25 Yes, the Almighty will be your ¹gold
    And your precious silver;
26 For then you will have your ᵃdelight in the Almighty,
    And lift up your face to God.
27 ᵃYou will make your prayer to Him,
    He will hear you,
    And you will pay your vows.
28 You will also declare a thing,
    And it will be established for you;
    So light will shine on your ways.
29 When they cast *you* down, and you say, 'Exaltation *will*
        come!'
    Then ᵃHe will save the humble *person.*
30 He will *even* deliver one who is not innocent;
    Yes, he will be delivered by the purity of your hands."

JOB PROCLAIMS GOD'S RIGHTEOUS JUDGMENTS

23 Then Job answered and said:

2 "Even today my ᵃcomplaint is bitter;
    ¹My hand is listless because of my groaning.
3 ᵃOh, that I knew where I might find Him,
    That I might come to His seat!
4 I would present *my* case before Him,
    And fill my mouth with arguments.
5 I would know the words *which* He would answer me,
    And understand what He would say to me.
6 ᵃWould He contend with me in His great power?
    No! But He would take *note* of me.
7 There the upright could reason with Him,
    And I would be delivered forever from my Judge.

8 "Look,ᵃ I go forward, but He is not *there,*
    And backward, but I cannot perceive Him;
9 When He works on the left hand, I cannot behold *Him;*
    When He turns to the right hand, I cannot see *Him.*
10 But ᵃHe knows the way that I take;
    When ᵇHe has tested me, I shall come forth as gold.
11 ᵃMy foot has held fast to His steps;
    I have kept His way and not turned aside.
12 I have not departed from the ᵃcommandment of His
        lips;
    ᵇI have treasured the words of His mouth
    More than my ¹necessary *food.*

13 "But He *is* unique, and who can make Him change?
    And *whatever* ᵃHis soul desires, *that* He does.
14 For He performs *what is* ᵃappointed for me,
    And many such *things are* with Him.
15 Therefore I am terrified at His presence;
    When I consider *this,* I am afraid of Him.
16 For God ᵃmade my heart weak,
    And the Almighty terrifies me;
17 Because I was not ᵃcut off ¹from the presence of
        darkness,
    And He did *not* hide deep darkness from my face.

22:26
ᵃJob 27:10;
Ps. 37:4; Is. 58:14

22:27
ᵃJob 11:13; 33:26;
[Is. 58:9–11]

22:29 ᵃJob 5:11;
[Matt. 23:12;
James 4:6;
1 Pet. 5:5]

23:2 ᵃJob 7:11

23:3
ᵃJob 13:3, 18;
16:21; 31:35

23:6 ᵃIs. 57:16

23:8
ᵃJob 9:11; 35:14

23:10 ᵃ[Ps. 1:6;
139:1–3]
ᵇ[Ps. 17:3; 66:10;
James 1:12]

23:11 ᵃJob 31:7;
Ps. 17:5

23:12 ᵃJob 6:10;
22:22 ᵇPs. 44:18

23:13
ᵃ[Ps. 115:3]

23:14
ᵃ[1 Thess. 3:2–4]

23:16 ᵃPs. 22:14

23:17
ᵃJob 10:18, 19

22:25 ¹Ancient vss. suggest *defense;* MT *gold,* as in v. 24   **23:2** ¹So with MT,
Tg., Vg.; LXX, Syr. *His*   **23:12** ¹Lit. *appointed portion*   **23:17** ¹Or *by* or *before*

JOB COMPLAINS OF VIOLENCE ON THE EARTH

24 "Since [a]times are not hidden from the Almighty,
Why do those who know Him see not His [b]days?

2 "*Some* remove [a]landmarks;
They seize flocks violently and feed *on them;*

3 They drive away the donkey of the fatherless;
They [a]take the widow's ox as a pledge.

4 They push the needy off the road;
All the [a]poor of the land are forced to hide.

5 Indeed, *like* wild donkeys in the desert,
They go out to their work, searching for food.
The wilderness *yields* food for them *and* for *their*
children.

6 They gather their fodder in the field
And glean in the vineyard of the wicked.

7 They [a]spend the night naked, without clothing,
And have no covering in the cold.

8 They are wet with the showers of the mountains,
And [a]huddle around the rock for want of shelter.

9 "*Some* snatch the fatherless from the breast,
And take a pledge from the poor.

10 They cause *the poor* to go naked, without [a]clothing;
And they take away the sheaves from the hungry.

11 They press out oil within their walls,
And tread winepresses, yet suffer thirst.

12 The dying groan in the city,
And the souls of the wounded cry out;
Yet God does not charge *them* with wrong.

13 "There are those who rebel against the light;
They do not know its ways
Nor abide in its paths.

14 [a]The murderer rises with the light;
He kills the poor and needy;
And in the night he is like a thief.

15 [a]The eye of the adulterer waits for the twilight,
[b]Saying, 'No eye will see me';
And he [1]disguises *his* face.

16 In the dark they break into houses
Which they marked for themselves in the daytime;
[a]They do not know the light.

17 For the morning is the same to them as the shadow of
death;
If *someone* recognizes *them,*
They are in the terrors of the shadow of death.

18 "They *should be* swift on the face of the waters,
Their portion *should be* cursed in the earth,
So that no *one would* turn into the way of their
vineyards.

19 As drought and heat [1]consume the snow waters,
So [2]the grave *consumes those who* have sinned.

20 The womb *should* forget him,
The worm *should* feed sweetly on him;
[a]He *should* be remembered no more,
And wickedness *should* be broken like a tree.

24:1 [a][Acts 1:7]
[b][Is. 2:12];
Jer. 46:10;
[Obad. 15];
Zeph. 1:7

24:2
[a][Deut. 19:14;
27:17];
Prov. 22:28;
23:10; Hos. 5:10

24:3
[a][Deut. 24:6,
10, 12, 17];
Job 22:6, 9

24:4 [a]Job 29:16;
Prov. 28:28

24:7
[a]Ex. 22:26, 27;
[Deut. 24:12, 13];
Job 22:6;
[James 2:15, 16]

24:8 [a]Lam. 4:5

24:10 [a]Job 31:19

24:14 [a]Ps. 10:8

24:15
[a]Prov. 7:7–10
[b]Ps. 10:11

24:16
[a][John 3:20]

24:20
[a]Job 18:17;
Ps. 34:16;
Prov. 10:7

24:15 [1]Lit. *puts a covering on his face*   24:19 [1]Lit. *seize*   [2]Or *Sheol*

21 For he ¹preys on the barren *who* do not bear,
And does no good for the widow.

22 "But *God* draws the mighty away with His power;
He rises up, but no *man* is sure of life.

23 He gives them security, and they rely *on it;*
Yet ᵃHis eyes *are* on their ways.

24 They are exalted for a little while,
Then they are gone.
They are brought low;
They are ¹taken out of the way like all *others;*
They dry out like the heads of grain.

25 "Now if *it is* not *so,* who will prove me a liar,
And make my speech worth nothing?"

BILDAD: HOW CAN MAN BE RIGHTEOUS?

25 Then ᵃBildad the Shuhite answered and said:

2 "Dominion and fear *belong* to Him;
He makes peace in His high places.

3 ¹Is there any number to His armies?
Upon whom does ᵃHis light not rise?

4 ᵃHow then can man be righteous before God?
Or how can he be ᵇpure *who is* born of a woman?

5 If even the moon does not shine,
And the stars are not pure in His ᵃsight,

6 How much less man, *who is* ᵃa maggot,
And a son of man, *who is* a worm?"

JOB: MAN'S FRAILTY AND GOD'S MAJESTY

26 But Job answered and said:

2 "How have you helped *him who is* without power?
How have you saved the arm *that has* no strength?

3 How have you counseled *one who has* no wisdom?
And *how* have you declared sound advice to many?

4 To whom have you uttered words?
And whose spirit came from you?

5 "The dead tremble,
Those under the waters and those inhabiting them.

6 ᵃSheol *is* naked before Him,
And Destruction has no covering.

7 ᵃHe stretches out the north over empty space;
He hangs the earth on nothing.

8 ᵃHe binds up the water in His thick clouds,
Yet the clouds ¹are not broken under it.

9 He covers the face of *His* throne,
And spreads His cloud over it.

10 ᵃHe drew a circular horizon on the face of the waters,
At the boundary of light and darkness.

11 The pillars of heaven tremble,
And are ¹astonished at His rebuke.

12 ᵃHe stirs up the sea with His power,
And by His understanding He breaks up ¹the storm.

24:23 ᵃPs. 11:4;
[Prov. 15:3]

25:1
ᵃJob 8:1; 18:1

25:3 ᵃJames 1:17

25:4 ᵃJob 4:17;
15:14; Ps. 130:3;
143:2 ᵇ[Job 14:4]

25:5 ᵃJob 15:15

25:6 ᵃPs. 22:6

26:6
ᵃ[Ps. 139:8];
Prov. 15:11;
[Heb. 4:13]

26:7 ᵃJob 9:8;
Ps. 24:2; 104:2

26:8 ᵃJob 37:11;
Prov. 30:4

26:10
ᵃ[Job 38:1–11];
Ps. 33:7; 104:9;
Prov. 8:29;
Jer. 5:22

26:12 ᵃEx. 14:21;
Job 9:13;
Is. 51:15;
[Jer. 31:35]

24:21 ¹Lit. *feeds on* 24:24 ¹Lit. *gathered up* 25:3 ¹Can His armies be
counted? 26:8 ¹*do not break* 26:11 ¹*amazed* 26:12 ¹Heb. *rahab*

13 [a]By His Spirit He adorned the heavens;
His hand pierced [b]the fleeing serpent.
14 Indeed these *are* the mere edges of His ways,
And how small a whisper we hear of Him!
But the thunder of His power who can understand?"

JOB MAINTAINS HIS INTEGRITY

27 Moreover Job continued his discourse, and said:

2 "As God lives, [a]*who* has taken away my justice,
And the Almighty, *who* has made my soul bitter,
3 As long as my breath *is* in me,
And the breath of God in my nostrils,
4 My lips will not speak wickedness,
Nor my tongue utter deceit.
5 Far be it from me
That I should say you are right;
Till I die [a]I will not put away my integrity from me.
6 My righteousness I [a]hold fast, and will not let it go;
[b]My heart shall not [1]reproach *me* as long as I live.

7 "May my enemy be like the wicked,
And he who rises up against me like the
unrighteous.
8 [a]For what is the hope of the hypocrite,
Though he may gain *much*,
If God takes away his life?
9 [a]Will God hear his cry
When trouble comes upon him?
10 [a]Will he delight himself in the Almighty?
Will he always call on God?

11 "I will teach you [1]about the hand of God;
What *is* with the Almighty I will not conceal.
12 Surely all of you have seen *it*;
Why then do you behave with complete nonsense?

13 "This[a] is the portion of a wicked man with God,
And the heritage of oppressors, received from the
Almighty:
14 [a]If his children are multiplied, *it is* for the sword;
And his offspring shall not be satisfied with bread.
15 Those who survive him shall be buried in death,
And [a]their[1] widows shall not weep,
16 Though he heaps up silver like dust,
And piles up clothing like clay—
17 He may pile *it* up, but [a]the just will wear *it*,
And the innocent will divide the silver.
18 He builds his house like a [1]moth,
[a]Like a [2]booth *which* a watchman makes.
19 The rich man will lie down,
[1]But not be gathered *up*;
He opens his eyes,
And he *is* [a]no more.
20 [a]Terrors overtake him like a flood;
A tempest steals him away in the night.

26:13
[a][Job 9:8];
Ps. 33:6 [b]Is. 27:1

27:2 [a]Job 34:5

27:5
[a]Job 2:9; 13:15

27:6 [a]Job 2:3;
33:9 [b]Acts 24:16

27:8
[a]Matt. 16:26;
Luke 12:20

27:9
[a]Job 35:12, 13;
Ps. 18:41;
Prov. 1:28;
28:9; [Is. 1:15];
Jer. 14:12;
Ezek. 8:18;
[Mic. 3:4;
John 9:31;
James 4:3]

27:10
[a]Job 22:26,
27; [Ps. 37:4;
Is. 58:14]

27:13
[a]Job 20:29

27:14
[a]Deut. 28:41;
Esth. 9:10;
Hos. 9:13

27:15 [a]Ps. 78:64

27:17
[a]Prov. 28:8;
[Eccl. 2:26]

27:18 [a]Is. 1:8;
Lam. 2:6

27:19 [a]Job 7:8,
21; 20:7

27:20 [a]Job 18:11

27:6 [1]*reprove*   27:11 [1]*Or by*   27:15 [1]Lit. *his*   27:18 [1]So with MT, Vg.; LXX,
Syr. *spider* (cf. 8:14); Tg. *decay*   [2]Temporary shelter   27:19 [1]So with MT,
Tg.; LXX, Syr. *But shall not add* (i.e., do it again); Vg. *But take away nothing*

21 The east wind carries him away, and he is gone;
   It sweeps him out of his place.
22 It hurls against him and does not ªspare;
   He flees desperately from its ¹power.
23 *Men* shall clap their hands at him,
   And shall hiss him out of his place.

JOB'S DISCOURSE ON WISDOM

28 "Surely there is a mine for silver,
     And a place *where* gold is refined.
2 Iron is taken from the ¹earth,
   And copper *is* smelted *from* ore.
3 *Man* puts an end to darkness,
   And searches every recess
   For ore in the darkness and the shadow of death.
4 He breaks open a shaft away from people;
   In places forgotten by feet
   They hang far away from men;
   They swing to and fro.
5 *As for* the earth, from it comes bread,
   But underneath it is turned up as by fire;
6 Its stones *are* the source of sapphires,
   And it contains gold dust.
7 *That* path no bird knows,
   Nor has the falcon's eye seen it.
8 The ¹proud lions have not trodden it,
   Nor has the fierce lion passed over it.
9 He puts his hand on the flint;
   He overturns the mountains ¹at the roots.
10 He cuts out channels in the rocks,
   And his eye sees every precious thing.
11 He dams up the streams from trickling;
   What is hidden he brings forth to light.

12 "But ª where can wisdom be found?
   And where *is* the place of understanding?
13 Man does not know its ªvalue,
   Nor is it found in the land of the living.
14 ªThe deep says, '*It is* not in me';
   And the sea says, '*It is* not with me.'
15 It ªcannot be purchased for gold,
   Nor can silver be weighed *for* its price.
16 It cannot be valued in the gold of Ophir,
   In precious onyx or sapphire.
17 Neither ªgold nor crystal can equal it,
   Nor can it be exchanged for ¹jewelry of fine gold.
18 No mention shall be made of ¹coral or quartz,
   For the price of wisdom *is* above ªrubies.
19 The topaz of Ethiopia cannot equal it,
   Nor can it be valued in pure ªgold.

20 "From ª where then does wisdom come?
   And where *is* the place of understanding?
21 It is hidden from the eyes of all living,
   And concealed from the birds of the ¹air.

27:22 ªJer. 13:14;
Ezek. 5:11; 24:14
28:12 ªEccl. 7:24
28:13 ªProv. 3:15
28:14
ªJob 28:22
28:15
ªProv. 3:13–15;
8:10, 11, 19
28:17
ªProv. 8:10;
16:16
28:18
ªProv. 3:15; 8:11
28:19 ªProv. 8:19
28:20
ªJob 28:12;
[Ps. 111:10;
Prov. 1:7; 9:10]

27:22 ¹Lit. *hand*   28:2 ¹Lit. *dust*   28:8 ¹Lit. *sons of pride*, figurative of the great lions   28:9 ¹At the base   28:17 ¹*vessels*   28:18 ¹Heb. *ramoth*
28:21 ¹*heaven*

22 ^aDestruction[1] and Death say,
   'We have heard a report about it with our ears.'
23 God understands its way,
   And He knows its place.
24 For He looks to the ends of the earth,
   And ^asees under the whole heavens,
25 ^aTo establish a weight for the wind,
   And apportion the waters by measure.
26 When He ^amade a law for the rain,
   And a path for the thunderbolt,
27 Then He saw [1]*wisdom* and declared it;
   He prepared it, indeed, He searched it out.
28 And to man He said,
   'Behold, ^athe fear of the Lord, that *is* wisdom,
   And to depart from evil *is* understanding.'"

JOB'S SUMMARY DEFENSE

29 Job further continued his discourse, and said:

2 "Oh, that I were as *in* months ^apast,
   As *in* the days *when* God ^bwatched over me;
3 ^aWhen His lamp shone upon my head,
   And when by His light I walked *through* darkness;
4 Just as I was in the days of my prime,
   When ^athe friendly counsel of God *was* over my
     tent;
5 When the Almighty *was* yet with me,
   When my children *were* around me;
6 When ^amy steps were bathed with [1]cream,
   And ^bthe rock poured out rivers of oil for me!

7 "When I went out to the gate by the city,
   When I took my seat in the open square,
8 The young men saw me and hid,
   And the aged arose *and* stood;
9 The princes refrained from talking,
   And ^aput *their* hand on their mouth;
10 The voice of nobles was hushed,
   And their ^atongue stuck to the roof of their mouth.
11 When the ear heard, then it blessed me,
   And when the eye saw, then it approved me;
12 Because ^aI delivered the poor who cried out,
   The fatherless and *the one who* had no helper.
13 The blessing of a perishing *man* came upon me,
   And I caused the widow's heart to sing for joy.
14 ^aI put on righteousness, and it clothed me;
   My justice *was* like a robe and a turban.
15 I *was* ^aeyes to the blind,
   And I *was* feet to the lame.
16 I *was* a father to the poor,
   And ^aI searched out the case *that* I did not know.
17 I broke ^athe fangs of the wicked,
   And plucked the victim from his teeth.

18 "Then I said, ^a'I shall die in my nest,
   And multiply *my* days as the sand.

28:22
^aJob 28:14

28:24 ^a[Ps. 11:4;
33:13, 14; 66:7;
Prov. 15:3]

28:25 ^aPs. 135:7

28:26
^aJob 37:3; 38:25

28:28
^a[Deut. 4:6;
Ps. 111:10;
Prov. 1:7; 9:10;
Eccl. 12:13]

29:2 ^aJob 1:1–5
^bJob 1:10

29:3 ^aJob 18:6

29:4 ^aJob 15:8;
[Ps. 25:14;
Prov. 3:32]

29:6
^aGen. 49:11;
Deut. 32:14;
Job 20:17
^bDeut. 32:13;
Ps. 81:16

29:9 ^aJob 21:5

29:10 ^aPs. 137:6

29:12
^aJob 31:16–23;
[Ps. 72:12;
Prov. 21:13;
24:11]

29:14
^aDeut. 24:13;
Job 27:5, 6;
Ps. 132:9;
[Is. 59:17; 61:10;
Eph. 6:14]

29:15
^aNum. 10:31

29:16
^aProv. 29:7

29:17 ^aPs. 58:6;
Prov. 30:14

29:18 ^aPs. 30:6

28:22 [1]Heb. *Abaddon*   **28:27** [1]Lit. *it*   **29:6** [1]So with ancient vss. and a few
Heb. mss. (cf. Job 20:17); MT *wrath*

19 ^aMy root *is* spread out ^bto the waters,
    And the dew lies all night on my branch.
20 My glory *is* fresh within me,
    And my ^abow is renewed in my hand.'
21 "*Men* listened to me and waited,
    And kept silence for my counsel.
22 After my words they did not speak again,
    And my speech settled on them *as dew.*
23 They waited for me *as* for the rain,
    And they opened their mouth wide *as* for ^athe spring
       rain.
24 *If* I mocked at them, they did not believe *it,*
    And the light of my countenance they did not cast down.
25 I chose the way for them, and sat as chief;
    So I dwelt as a king in the army,
    As one *who* comforts mourners.

30

"But now they mock at me, *men* ¹younger than I,
    Whose fathers I disdained to put with the dogs of
       my flock.
2   Indeed, what *profit* is the strength of their hands to me?
    Their vigor has perished.
3   *They are* gaunt from want and famine,
    Fleeing late to the wilderness, desolate and waste,
4   Who pluck ¹mallow by the bushes,
    And broom tree roots *for* their food.
5   They were driven out from among *men,*
    They shouted at them as *at* a thief.
6   *They had* to live in the clefts of the ¹valleys,
    In ²caves of the earth and the rocks.
7   Among the bushes they brayed,
    Under the nettles they nestled.
8   *They were* sons of fools,
    Yes, sons of vile men;
    They were scourged from the land.
9   "And^a now I am their taunting song;
    Yes, I am their byword.
10 They abhor me, they keep far from me;
    They do not hesitate ^ato spit in my face.
11 Because ^aHe has loosed ¹my bowstring and afflicted me,
    They have cast off restraint before me.
12 At *my* right *hand* the rabble arises;
    They push away my feet,
    And ^athey raise against me their ways of destruction.
13 They break up my path,
    They promote my calamity;
    They have no helper.
14 They come as broad breakers;
    Under the ruinous storm they roll along.
15 Terrors are turned upon me;
    They pursue my honor as the wind,
    And my prosperity has passed like a cloud.
16 "And^a now my soul is ^bpoured out because of my *plight;*
    The days of affliction take hold of me.

29:19 ^aJob 18:16
    ^bPs. 1:3;
    [Jer. 17:7, 8]
29:20
^aGen. 49:24;
    Ps. 18:34
29:23
^a[Zech. 10:1]
30:9 ^aJob 17:6;
    Ps. 69:12;
    Lam. 3:14, 63
30:10
^aNum. 12:14;
    Deut. 25:9;
    Job 17:6;
    Is. 50:6;
    Matt. 26:67;
    27:30
30:11 ^aJob 12:18
30:12 ^aJob 19:12
30:16 ^aPs. 42:4
    ^bPs. 22:14;
    Is. 53:12

30:1 ¹Lit. *of fewer days*   **30:4** ¹A plant of the salty marshes   **30:6** ¹*wadis*
²Lit. *holes*   **30:11** ¹So with MT, Syr., Tg.; LXX, Vg. *His*

17 My bones are pierced in me at night,
And my gnawing pains take no rest.
18 By great force my garment is disfigured;
It binds me about as the collar of my coat.
19 He has cast me into the mire,
And I have become like dust and ashes.

20 "I ᵃcry out to You, but You do not answer me;
I stand up, and You regard me.
21 *But* You have become cruel to me;
With the strength of Your hand You ᵃoppose me.
22 You lift me up to the wind and cause me to ride *on it;*
You spoil my success.
23 For I know *that* You will bring me *to* death,
And *to* the house ᵃappointed for all living.

24 "Surely He would not stretch out *His* hand against a heap
of ruins,
If they cry out when He destroys *it.*
25 ᵃHave I not wept for him who was in trouble?
Has *not* my soul grieved for the poor?
26 ᵃBut when I looked for good, evil came *to me;*
And when I waited for light, then came darkness.
27 ¹My heart is in turmoil and cannot rest;
Days of affliction confront me.
28 ᵃI go about mourning, but not in the sun;
I stand up in the assembly *and* cry out for help.
29 ᵃI am a brother of jackals,
And a companion of ostriches.
30 ᵃMy skin grows black and falls from me;
ᵇMy bones burn with fever.
31 My harp is *turned* to mourning,
And my flute to the voice of those who weep.

31 "I have made a covenant with my eyes;
Why then should I ¹look upon a ᵃyoung woman?
2 For what *is* the ᵃallotment of God from above,
And the inheritance of the Almighty from on high?
3 *Is* it not destruction for the wicked,
And disaster for the workers of iniquity?
4 ᵃDoes He not see my ways,
And count all my steps?

5 "If I have walked with falsehood,
Or if my foot has hastened to deceit,
6 ¹Let me be weighed on honest scales,
That God may know my ᵃintegrity.
7 If my step has turned from the way,
Or ᵃmy heart walked after my eyes,
Or if any spot adheres to my hands,
8 *Then* ᵃlet me sow, and another eat;
Yes, let my harvest be ¹rooted out.

9 "If my heart has been enticed by a woman,
Or *if* I have lurked at my neighbor's door,
10 *Then* let my wife grind for ᵃanother,
And let others bow down over her.

30:20 ᵃJob 19:7
30:21 ᵃJob 10:3;
16:9, 14; 19:6, 22
30:23
ᵃ[Heb. 9:27]
30:25
ᵃPs. 35:13, 14;
Rom. 12:15
30:26
ᵃJob 3:25, 26;
Jer. 8:15
30:28
ᵃJob 30:31;
Ps. 38:6; 42:9;
43:2
30:29
ᵃPs. 44:19;
102:6; Mic. 1:8
30:30
ᵃPs. 119:83;
Lam. 4:8; 5:10
ᵇPs. 102:3
31:1
ᵃ[Matt. 5:28]
31:2 ᵃJob 20:29
31:4
ᵃ[2 Chr. 16:9];
Job 24:23;
28:24; 34:21;
36:7; [Prov. 5:21;
15:3; Jer. 32:19]
31:6 ᵃJob 23:10;
27:5, 6
31:7
ᵃNum. 15:39;
[Eccl. 11:9];
Ezek. 6:9;
[Matt. 5:29]
31:8 ᵃLev. 26:16;
Deut. 28:30,
38; Job 20:18;
Mic. 6:15
31:10
ᵃDeut. 28:30;
2 Sam. 12:11;
Jer. 8:10

30:27 ¹*I seethe inside*　31:1 ¹*look intently* or *gaze*　31:6 ¹Lit. *Let Him
weigh me*　31:8 ¹*uprooted*

11 For that *would be* wickedness;
　　Yes, [a]it *would be* iniquity *deserving of* judgment.
12 For that *would be* a fire *that* consumes to destruction,
　　And would root out all my increase.

13 "If I have [a]despised the cause of my male or female
　　　　servant
　　When they complained against me,
14 What then shall I do when [a]God rises up?
　　When He punishes, how shall I answer Him?
15 [a]Did not He who made me in the womb make them?
　　Did not the same One fashion us in the womb?

16 "If I have kept the poor from *their* desire,
　　Or caused the eyes of the widow to [a]fail,
17 Or eaten my morsel by myself,
　　So that the fatherless could not eat of it
18 (But from my youth I reared him as a father,
　　And from my mother's womb I guided [1]*the widow*);
19 If I have seen anyone perish for lack of clothing,
　　Or any poor *man* without covering;
20 If his [1]heart has not [a]blessed me,
　　And *if* he was *not* warmed with the fleece of my sheep;
21 If I have raised my hand [a]against the fatherless,
　　When I saw I had help in the gate;
22 *Then* let my arm fall from my shoulder,
　　Let my arm be torn from the socket.
23 For [a]destruction *from* God *is* a terror to me,
　　And because of His magnificence I cannot endure.

24 "If[a] I have made gold my hope,
　　Or said to fine gold, '*You are* my confidence';
25 [a]If I have rejoiced because my wealth *was* great,
　　And because my hand had gained much;
26 [a]If I have observed the [1]sun when it shines,
　　Or the moon moving *in* brightness,
27 So that my heart has been secretly enticed,
　　And my mouth has kissed my hand;
28 This also *would be* an iniquity *deserving of* judgment,
　　For I would have denied God *who is* above.

29 "If[a] I have rejoiced at the destruction of him who hated
　　　　me,
　　Or lifted myself up when evil found him
30 [a](Indeed I have not allowed my mouth to sin
　　By asking for a curse on his [1]soul);
31 If the men of my tent have not said,
　　'Who is there that has not been satisfied with his
　　　　meat?'
32 [a](*But* no sojourner had to lodge in the street,
　　For I have opened my doors to the [1]traveler);
33 If I have covered my transgressions [a]as[1] Adam,
　　By hiding my iniquity in my bosom,
34 Because I feared the great [a]multitude,
　　And dreaded the contempt of families,
　　So that I kept silence
　　And did not go out of the door—

31:11
[a]Gen. 38:24;
[Lev. 20:10;
Deut. 22:22];
Job 31:28

31:13
[a][Deut. 24:14, 15]

31:14 [a][Ps. 44:21]

31:15 [a]Job 34:19;
Prov. 14:31; 22:2;
[Mal. 2:10]

31:16 [a]Job 29:12

31:20
[a][Deut. 24:13]

31:21 [a]Job 22:9

31:23 [a]Is. 13:6

31:24
[a][Matt. 6:19, 20;
Mark 10:23–25]

31:25 [a]Job 1:3,
10; Ps. 62:10

31:26
[a][Deut. 4:19;
17:3]; Ezek. 8:16

31:29
[a][Prov. 17:5;
24:17]; Obad. 12

31:30
[a][Matt. 5:44]

31:32
[a]Gen. 19:2, 3

31:33
[a]Gen. 3:10;
[Prov. 28:13]

31:34 [a]Ex. 23:2

31:18 [1]Lit. *her*　**31:20** [1]Lit. *loins*　**31:26** [1]Lit. *light*　**31:30** [1]Or *life*
31:32 [1]So with LXX, Syr., Tg., Vg.; MT *road*　**31:33** [1]Or *as men do*

35 ªOh, that I had one to hear me!
  Here is my mark.
  Oh, ᵇ*that* the Almighty would answer me,
  That my ¹Prosecutor had written a book!
36 Surely I would carry it on my shoulder,
  And bind it on me *like* a crown;
37 I would declare to Him the number of my steps;
  Like a prince I would approach Him.

38 "If my land cries out against me,
  And its furrows weep together;
39 If ªI have eaten its ¹fruit without money,
  Or ᵇcaused its owners to lose their lives;
40 *Then* let ªthistles grow instead of wheat,
  And weeds instead of barley."

The words of Job are ended.

ELIHU CONTRADICTS JOB'S FRIENDS

32 So these three men ceased answering Job, because he *was* ªrighteous in his own eyes. ²Then the wrath of Elihu, the son of Barachel the ªBuzite, of the family of Ram, was aroused against Job; his wrath was aroused because he ᵇjustified himself rather than God. ³Also against his three friends his wrath was aroused, because they had found no answer, and *yet* had condemned Job.

⁴Now because they *were* years older than he, Elihu had waited ¹to speak to Job. ⁵When Elihu saw that *there was* no answer in the mouth of these three men, his wrath was aroused.

⁶So Elihu, the son of Barachel the Buzite, answered and said:

"I *am* ªyoung in years, and you *are* very old;
  Therefore I was afraid,
  And dared not declare my opinion to you.
7 I said, ¹'Age should speak,
  And multitude of years should teach wisdom.'
8 But *there is* a spirit in man,
  And ªthe breath of the Almighty gives him
    understanding.
9 ªGreat¹ men are not *always* wise,
  Nor do the aged *always* understand justice.

10 "Therefore I say, 'Listen to me,
  I also will declare my opinion.'
11 Indeed I waited for your words,
  I listened to your reasonings, while you searched out
    what to say.
12 I paid close attention to you;
  And surely not one of you convinced Job,
  Or answered his words—
13 ªLest you say,
  'We have found wisdom';
  God will vanquish him, not man.
14 Now he has not ¹directed *his* words against me;
  So I will not answer him with your words.

31:35 ªJob 19:7;
30:20, 24, 28
ᵇJob 13:22, 24;
33:10
31:39 ªJob 24:6,
10–12;
[James 5:4]
ᵇ1 Kin. 21:19
31:40 ªGen. 3:18
32:1 ªJob 6:29;
31:6; 33:9
32:2 ªGen. 22:21
ᵇJob 27:5, 6
32:6 ªLev. 19:32
32:8 ª1 Kin. 3:12;
4:29; [Job 35:11;
38:36; Prov. 2:6;
Eccl. 2:26;
Dan. 1:17; 2:21;
Matt. 11:25;
James 1:5]
32:9
ª[1 Cor. 1:26]
32:13
ª[Jer. 9:23;
1 Cor. 1:29]

31:35 ¹Lit. *Accuser*   **31:39** ¹Lit. *strength*   **32:4** ¹Vg. *till Job had spoken*
32:7 ¹Lit. *Days,* i.e., years   **32:9** ¹Or *Men of many years*   **32:14** ¹ordered

15 "They are dismayed and answer no more;
　　Words escape them.
16 And I have waited, because they did not speak,
　　Because they stood still *and* answered no more.
17 I also will answer my part,
　　I too will declare my opinion.
18 For I am full of words;
　　The spirit within me compels me.
19 Indeed my ¹belly *is* like wine *that* has no ²vent;
　　It is ready to burst like new wineskins.
20 I will speak, that I may find relief;
　　I must open my lips and answer.
21 Let me not, I pray, show partiality to anyone;
　　Nor let me flatter any man.
22 For I do not know how to flatter,
　　Else my Maker would soon take me ᵃaway.

ELIHU CONTRADICTS JOB

33 "But please, Job, hear my speech,
　　And listen to all my words.
2 Now, I open my mouth;
　　My tongue speaks in my mouth.
3 My words *come* from my upright heart;
　　My lips utter pure knowledge.
4 ᵃThe Spirit of God has made me,
　　And the breath of the Almighty gives me life.
5 If you can answer me,
　　Set *your words* in order before me;
　　Take your stand.
6 ᵃTruly I *am* ¹as your spokesman before God;
　　I also have been formed out of clay.
7 ᵃSurely no fear of me will terrify you,
　　Nor will my hand be heavy on you.
8 "Surely you have spoken ¹in my hearing,
　　And I have heard the sound of *your* words, *saying,*
9 'Iᵃ *am* pure, without transgression;
　　I *am* innocent, and *there is* no iniquity in me.
10 Yet He finds occasions against me,
　　ᵃHe counts me as His enemy;
11 ᵃHe puts my feet in the stocks,
　　He watches all my paths.'
12 "Look, *in* this you are not righteous.
　　I will answer you,
　　For God is greater than man.
13 Why do you ᵃcontend with Him?
　　For He does not give an accounting of any of His words.
14 ᵃFor God may speak in one way, or in another,
　　Yet man does not perceive it.
15 ᵃIn a dream, in a vision of the night,
　　When deep sleep falls upon men,
　　While slumbering on their beds,
16 ᵃThen He opens the ears of men,
　　And seals their instruction.
17 In order to turn man *from his* deed,
　　And conceal pride from man,

32:22 ᵃJob 27:8
33:4
ᵃ[Gen. 2:7];
Job 32:8
33:6 ᵃJob 4:19
33:7 ᵃJob 9:34
33:9 ᵃJob 10:7
33:10
ᵃJob 13:24; 16:9
33:11
ᵃJob 13:27; 19:8
33:13 ᵃJob 40:2;
[Is. 45:9]
33:14
ᵃJob 33:29;
40:5; Ps. 62:11
33:15
ᵃ[Num. 12:6]
33:16
ᵃ[Job 36:10, 15]

32:19 ¹bosom　²opening　**33:6** ¹Lit. *as your mouth*　**33:8** ¹Lit. *in my ears*

18 He keeps back his soul from the Pit,
And his life from ¹perishing by the sword.

19 "*Man* is also chastened with pain on his ᵃbed,
And with strong *pain* in many of his bones,

20 ᵃSo that his life abhors ᵇbread,
And his soul ¹succulent food.

21 His flesh wastes away from sight,
And his bones stick out *which once* were not seen.

22 Yes, his soul draws near the Pit,
And his life to the executioners.

23 "If there is a messenger for him,
A mediator, one among a thousand,
To show man His uprightness,

24 Then He is gracious to him, and says,
'Deliver him from going down to the Pit;
I have found ¹a ransom';

25 His flesh shall be young like a child's,
He shall return to the days of his youth.

26 He shall pray to God, and He will delight in him,
He shall see His face with joy,
For He restores to man His righteousness.

27 Then he looks at men and ᵃsays,
'I have sinned, and perverted *what was* right,
And it ᵇdid not profit me.'

28 He will ᵃredeem ¹his soul from going down to the Pit,
And his life shall see the light.

29 "Behold, God works all these *things*,
Twice, *in fact,* three *times* with a man,

30 ᵃTo bring back his soul from the Pit,
That he may be enlightened with the light of life.

31 "Give ear, Job, listen to me;
Hold your peace, and I will speak.

32 If you have anything to say, answer me;
Speak, for I desire to justify you.

33 If not, ᵃlisten to me;
¹Hold your peace, and I will teach you wisdom."

ELIHU PROCLAIMS GOD'S JUSTICE

34 Elihu further answered and said:

2 "Hear my words, you wise *men;*
Give ear to me, you who have knowledge.

3 ᵃFor the ear tests words
As the palate tastes food.

4 Let us choose justice for ourselves;
Let us know among ourselves what *is* good.

5 "For Job has said, ᵃ'I am righteous,
But ᵇGod has taken away my justice;

6 ᵃShould I lie concerning my right?
My ¹wound *is* incurable, *though I am* without
transgression.'

7 What man *is* like Job,
ᵃWho drinks ¹scorn like water,

33:19 ᵃJob 30:17
33:20
ᵃPs. 107:18
ᵇJob 3:24; 6:7
33:27
ᵃ[2 Sam. 12:13;
Prov. 28:13;
Luke 15:21;
1 John 1:9]
ᵇ[Rom. 6:21]
33:28 ᵃIs. 38:17
33:30 ᵃPs. 56:13
33:33 ᵃPs. 34:11
34:3
ᵃJob 6:30; 12:11
34:5 ᵃJob 13:18;
33:9 ᵇJob 27:2
34:6
ᵃJob 6:4; 9:17
34:7 ᵃJob 15:16

33:18 ¹Lit. *passing*   33:20 ¹*desirable*   33:24 ¹*an atonement*   33:28 ¹Kt.
my   33:33 ¹*Keep silent*   34:6 ¹Lit. *arrow*   34:7 ¹*derision*

8   Who goes in company with the workers of iniquity,
    And walks with wicked men?
9   For ªhe has said, 'It profits a man nothing
    That he should delight in God.'

34:9 ªMal. 3:14

10 "Therefore listen to me, you ¹men of understanding:
    ªFar be it from God *to do* wickedness,
    And *from* the Almighty to *commit* iniquity.
11 ªFor He repays man *according to* his work,
    And makes man to find a reward according to *his* way.
12 Surely God will never do wickedly,
    Nor will the Almighty ªpervert justice.
13 Who gave Him charge over the earth?
    Or who appointed *Him over* the whole world?
14 If He should set His heart on it,
    If He should ªgather to Himself His Spirit and His breath,
15 ªAll flesh would perish together,
    And man would return to dust.

34:10
ª[Gen. 18:25;
Deut. 32:4;
2 Chr. 19:7];
Job 8:3; 36:23;
Ps. 92:15;
Rom. 9:14

34:11
ªJob 34:25;
Ps. 62:12;
[Prov. 24:12;
Jer. 32:19];
Ezek. 33:20;
[Matt. 16:27];
Rom. 2:6;
[2 Cor. 5:10;
Rev. 22:12]

34:12 ªJob 8:3

34:14 ªJob 12:10;
Ps. 104:29;
[Eccl. 12:7]

34:15
ª[Gen. 3:19];
Job 10:9;
[Eccl. 12:7]

16 "If *you have* understanding, hear this;
    Listen to the sound of my words:
17 ªShould one who hates justice govern?
    Will you ᵇcondemn *Him who is* most just?
18 ª*Is it fitting* to say to a king, 'You are worthless,'
    And to nobles, '*You are* wicked'?
19 Yet He ªis not partial to princes,
    Nor does He regard the rich more than the poor;
    For ᵇthey *are* all the work of His hands.
20 In a moment they die, ªin the middle of the night;
    The people are shaken and pass away;
    The mighty are taken away without a hand.

34:17
ª2 Sam. 23:3;
Job 34:30
ᵇJob 40:8

34:18 ªEx. 22:28

34:19
ª[Deut. 10:17;
Acts 10:34;
Rom. 2:11, 12]
ᵇJob 31:15

34:20
ªEx. 12:29;
Job 34:25; 36:20

21 "Forª His eyes *are* on the ways of man,
    And He sees all his steps.
22 ªThere is no darkness nor shadow of death
    Where the workers of iniquity may hide themselves.
23 For He need not further consider a man,
    That he should go before God in judgment.
24 ªHe breaks in pieces mighty men without inquiry,
    And sets others in their place.
25 Therefore He knows their works;
    He overthrows *them* in the night,
    And they are crushed.
26 He strikes them as wicked *men*
    In the open sight of others,
27 Because they ªturned back from Him,
    And ᵇwould not consider any of His ways,
28 So that they ªcaused the cry of the poor to come to Him;
    For He ᵇhears the cry of the afflicted.
29 When He gives quietness, who then can make trouble?
    And when He hides *His* face, who then can see Him,
    Whether *it is* against a nation or a man alone?—
30 That the hypocrite should not reign,
    Lest the people be ensnared.

34:21
ª[2 Chr. 16:9];
Job 31:4;
Ps. 34:15;
[Prov. 5:21; 15:3;
Jer. 16:17; 32:19]

34:22
ª[Ps. 139:11, 12;
Amos 9:2, 3]

34:24
ªJob 12:19;
[Dan. 2:21]

34:27
ª1 Sam. 15:11
ᵇPs. 28:5;
Is. 5:12

34:28
ªJob 35:9;
James 5:4
ᵇ[Ex. 22:23];
Job 22:27

31 "For has *anyone* said to God,
    'I have borne *chastening;*
    I will offend no more;

32 Teach me *what* I do not see;
If I have done iniquity, I will do no more'?
33 Should He repay *it* according to your *terms,*
Just because you disavow it?
You must choose, and not I;
Therefore speak what you know.

34 "Men of understanding say to me,
Wise men who listen to me:
35 'Job[a] speaks without knowledge,
His words *are* without wisdom.'
36 Oh, that Job were tried to the utmost,
Because *his* answers *are like* those of wicked men!
37 For he adds [a]rebellion to his sin;
He claps *his hands* among us,
And multiplies his words against God."

ELIHU CONDEMNS SELF-RIGHTEOUSNESS

35 Moreover Elihu answered and said:

2 "Do you think this is right?
Do you say,
'My righteousness is more than God's'?
3 For [a]you say,
'What advantage will it be to You?
What profit shall I have, more than *if* I had sinned?'

4 "I will answer you,
And [a]your companions with you.
5 [a]Look to the heavens and see;
And behold the clouds—
They are higher than you.
6 If you sin, what do you accomplish [a]against Him?
Or, *if* your transgressions are multiplied, what do you do to Him?
7 [a]If you are righteous, what do you give Him?
Or what does He receive from your hand?
8 Your wickedness affects a man such as you,
And your righteousness a son of man.

9 "Because[a] of the multitude of oppressions they cry out;
They cry out for help because of the arm of the mighty.
10 But no one says, [a]'Where *is* God my Maker,
[b]Who gives songs in the night,
11 Who [a]teaches us more than the beasts of the earth,
And makes us wiser than the birds of heaven?'
12 [a]There they cry out, but He does not answer,
Because of the pride of evil men.
13 [a]Surely God will not listen to empty *talk,*
Nor will the Almighty regard it.
14 [a]Although you say you do not see Him,
Yet justice *is* before Him, and [b]you must wait for Him.
15 And now, because He has not [a]punished in His anger,
Nor taken much notice of folly,
16 [a]Therefore Job opens his mouth in vain;
He multiplies words without knowledge."

34:35 [a]Job 35:16; 38:2
34:37 [a]Job 7:11; 10:1
35:3 [a]Job 21:15; 34:9
35:4 [a]Job 34:8
35:5 [a]Gen. 15:5; [Job 22:12; Ps. 8:3]
35:6 [a]Job 7:20; [Prov. 8:36; Jer. 7:19]
35:7 [a]Job 22:2; Ps. 16:2; Prov. 9:12; [Luke 17:10]; Rom. 11:35
35:9 [a]Job 34:28
35:10 [a]Is. 51:13 [b]Job 8:21; Ps. 42:8; 77:6; 149:5; Acts 16:25
35:11 [a]Job 36:22; Ps. 94:12; [Is. 48:17]; Jer. 32:33; [1 Cor. 2:13]
35:12 [a]Prov. 1:28
35:13 [a]Job 27:9; [Prov. 15:29; Is. 1:15]; Jer. 11:11; [Mic. 3:4]
35:14 [a]Job 9:11 [b][Ps. 37:5, 6]
35:15 [a]Ps. 89:32
35:16 [a]Job 34:35; 38:2

ELIHU PROCLAIMS GOD'S GOODNESS

36 Elihu also proceeded and said:

2 "Bear with me a little, and I will show you
  That *there are* yet words to speak on God's behalf.
3 I will fetch my knowledge from afar;
  I will ascribe righteousness to my Maker.
4 For truly my words *are* not false;
  One who is perfect in knowledge *is* with you.

5 "Behold, God *is* mighty, but despises *no one*;
  ªHe *is* mighty in strength ¹of understanding.
6 He does not preserve the life of the wicked,
  But gives justice to the ªoppressed.
7 ªHe does not withdraw His eyes from the righteous;
  But ᵇ*they are* on the throne with kings,
  For He has seated them forever,
  And they are exalted.
8 And ªif *they are* bound in ¹fetters,
  Held in the cords of affliction,
9 Then He tells them their work and their transgressions—
  That they have acted ¹defiantly.
10 ªHe also opens their ear to ¹instruction,
  And commands that they turn from iniquity.
11 If they obey and serve *Him*,
  They shall ªspend their days in prosperity,
  And their years in pleasures.
12 But if they do not obey,
  They shall perish by the sword,
  And they shall die ¹without ªknowledge.

13 "But the hypocrites in heart ªstore up wrath;
  They do not cry for help when He binds them.
14 ªThey¹ die in youth,
  And their life *ends* among the ²perverted persons.
15 He delivers the poor in their affliction,
  And opens their ears in oppression.

16 "Indeed He would have brought you out of dire distress,
  ªInto a broad place where *there is* no restraint;
  And ᵇwhat is set on your table *would be* full of ᶜrichness.
17 But you are filled with the judgment due the ªwicked;
  Judgment and justice take hold *of you*.
18 Because *there is* wrath, *beware* lest He take you away with
    one blow;
  For ªa large ransom would not help you avoid *it*.
19 ªWill your riches,
  Or all the mighty forces,
  Keep you from distress?
20 Do not desire the night,
  When people are cut off in their place.
21 Take heed, ªdo not turn to iniquity,
  For ᵇyou have chosen this rather than affliction.

22 "Behold, God is exalted by His power;
  Who teaches like Him?

Cross references (margin):

36:5 ªJob 12:13, 16; 37:23; [Ps. 99:2–5]
36:6 ªJob 5:15
36:7 ª[Ps. 33:18; 34:15] ᵇJob 5:11; Ps. 113:8
36:8 ªPs. 107:10
36:10 ªJob 33:16; 36:15
36:11 ªJob 21:13; [Is. 1:19, 20]
36:12 ªJob 4:21
36:13 ª[Rom. 2:5]
36:14 ªPs. 55:23
36:16 ªPs. 18:19; 31:8; 118:5 ᵇPs. 23:5 ᶜPs. 36:8
36:17 ªJob 22:5, 10, 11
36:18 ªPs. 49:7
36:19 ª[Prov. 11:4]
36:21 ªJob 36:10; [Ps. 31:6; 66:18] ᵇJob 36:8, 15; [Heb. 11:25]

36:5 ¹of heart 36:8 ¹chains 36:9 ¹proudly 36:10 ¹discipline 36:12 ¹MT *as one without knowledge* 36:14 ¹Lit. *Their soul dies* ²Heb. *qedeshim*, those practicing sodomy or prostitution in religious rituals

23 ᵃWho has assigned Him His way,
Or who has said, 'You have done ᵇwrong'?

ELIHU PROCLAIMS GOD'S MAJESTY

24 "Remember to ᵃmagnify His work,
Of which men have sung.
25 Everyone has seen it;
Man looks on *it* from afar.

26 "Behold, God *is* great, and we ᵃdo not know *Him;*
ᵇNor can the number of His years *be* discovered.
27 For He ᵃdraws up drops of water,
Which distill as rain from the mist,
28 ᵃWhich the clouds drop down
And pour abundantly on man.
29 Indeed, can *anyone* understand the spreading of
clouds,
The thunder from His canopy?
30 Look, He ᵃscatters His light upon it,
And covers the depths of the sea.
31 For ᵃby these He judges the peoples;
He ᵇgives food in abundance.
32 ᵃHe covers *His* hands with lightning,
And commands it to ¹strike.
33 ᵃHis thunder declares it,
The cattle also, concerning ¹the rising *storm.*

37 "At this also my heart trembles,
And leaps from its place.
2 Hear attentively the thunder of His voice,
And the rumbling *that* comes from His mouth.
3 He sends it forth under the whole heaven,
His ¹lightning to the ends of the earth.
4 After it ᵃa voice roars;
He thunders with His majestic voice,
And He does not restrain them when His voice is
heard.
5 God thunders marvelously with His voice;
ᵃHe does great things which we cannot comprehend.
6 For ᵃHe says to the snow, 'Fall *on* the earth';
Likewise to the ¹gentle rain and the heavy rain of His
strength.
7 He seals the hand of every man,
ᵃThat ᵇall men may know His work.
8 The beasts ᵃgo into dens,
And remain in their lairs.
9 From the chamber *of the south* comes the
whirlwind,
And cold from the scattering winds *of the north.*
10 ᵃBy the breath of God ice is given,
And the broad waters are frozen.
11 Also with moisture He saturates the thick clouds;
He scatters His ¹bright clouds.
12 And they swirl about, being turned by His guidance,
That they may ᵃdo whatever He commands them
On the face of ¹the whole earth.

36:23
ᵃJob 34:13;
[Is. 40:13, 14]
ᵇ[Deut. 32:4];
Job 8:3

36:24
ᵃ[Ps. 92:5;
Rev. 15:3]

36:26
ᵃJob 11:7–9;
37:23;
[1 Cor. 13:12]
ᵇJob 10:5;
[Ps. 90:2;
102:24, 27];
Heb. 1:12

36:27 ᵃJob 5:10;
37:6, 11; 38:28;
Ps. 147:8

36:28
ᵃ[Prov. 3:20]

36:30 ᵃJob 37:3

36:31
ᵃ[Acts 14:17]
ᵇGen. 9:3;
Ps. 104:14, 15

36:32 ᵃPs. 147:8

36:33
ᵃ1 Kin. 18:41;
Job 37:2

37:4 ᵃPs. 29:3

37:5 ᵃJob 5:9;
9:10; 36:26;
Rev. 15:3

37:6
ᵃPs. 147:16, 17

37:7 ᵃPs. 109:27
ᵇPs. 19:3, 4

37:8
ᵃJob 38:40;
Ps. 104:21, 22

37:10
ᵃJob 38:29, 30;
Ps. 147:17, 18

37:12
ᵃJob 36:32;
Ps. 148:8

36:32 ¹*strike the mark* 36:33 ¹Lit. *what is rising* 37:3 ¹Or *light* 37:6 ¹Lit.
shower of rain 37:11 ¹*clouds of light* 37:12 ¹Lit. *the world of the earth*

13 ^aHe causes it to come,
Whether for ¹correction,
Or ^bfor His land,
Or ^cfor mercy.

14 "Listen to this, O Job;
Stand still and ^aconsider the wondrous works of God.

15 Do you know when God ¹dispatches them,
And causes the light of His cloud to shine?

16 ^aDo you know how the clouds are balanced,
Those wondrous works of ^bHim who is perfect in
knowledge?

17 Why *are* your garments hot,
When He quiets the earth by the south *wind?*

18 With Him, have you ^aspread out the ^bskies,
Strong as a cast metal mirror?

19 "Teach us what we should say to Him,
For we can prepare nothing because of the darkness.

20 Should He be told that I *wish to* speak?
If a man were to speak, surely he would be
swallowed up.

21 Even now *men* cannot look at the light *when it is* bright
in the skies,
When the wind has passed and cleared them.

22 He comes from the north *as* golden *splendor;*
With God *is* awesome majesty.

23 *As for* the Almighty, ^awe cannot find Him;
^b*He is* excellent in power,
In judgment and abundant justice;
He does not oppress.

24 Therefore men ^afear Him;
He shows no partiality to any *who are* ^bwise of heart."

THE LORD REVEALS HIS OMNIPOTENCE TO JOB

(Gen. 1:1–10)

38 Then the LORD answered Job ^aout of the whirlwind,
and said:

2 "Who^a *is* this who darkens counsel
By ^bwords without knowledge?

3 ^aNow ¹prepare yourself like a man;
I will question you, and you shall answer Me.

4 "Where^a were you when I laid the foundations of the
earth?
Tell *Me,* if you have understanding.

5 Who determined its measurements?
Surely you know!
Or who stretched the ¹line upon it?

6 To what were its foundations fastened?
Or who laid its cornerstone,

7 When the morning stars sang together,
And all ^athe sons of God shouted for joy?

8 "Or^a *who* shut in the sea with doors,
When it burst forth *and* issued from the womb;

37:13
^aEx. 9:18, 23;
1 Sam. 12:18, 19
^bJob 38:26, 27
^c1 Kin. 18:41–46

37:14 ^aPs. 111:2

37:16
^aJob 36:29
^bJob 36:4

37:18 ^aGen. 1:6;
[Is. 44:24]
^bJob 9:8;
Ps. 104:2;
[Is. 45:12];
Jer. 10:12;
Zech. 12:1]

37:23
^a[Job 11:7, 8;
Rom. 11:33, 34;
1 Tim. 6:16]
^b[Job 9:4; 36:5]

37:24
^a[Matt. 10:28]
^b[Job 5:13;
Matt. 11:25];
1 Cor. 1:26

38:1 ^aEx. 19:16;
Job 40:6

38:2 ^aJob 34:35;
42:3 ^b1 Tim. 1:7

38:3 ^aJob 40:7

38:4 ^aJob 15:7;
Ps. 104:5

38:7 ^aJob 1:6

38:8 ^aGen. 1:9;
Ps. 33:7; 104:9;
Prov. 8:29;
[Jer. 5:22]

37:13 ¹Lit. *a rod*   **37:15** ¹*places them*   **38:3** ¹Lit. *gird up your loins like*
38:5 ¹*measuring line*

9   When I made the clouds its garment,
    And thick darkness its swaddling band;
10 When ᵃI fixed My limit for it,
    And set bars and doors;
11 When I said,
    'This far you may come, but no farther,
    And here your proud waves ᵃmust stop!'

12 "Have you ᵃcommanded the morning since your days
      began,
    And caused the dawn to know its place,
13 That it might take hold of the ends of the earth,
    And ᵃthe wicked be shaken out of it?
14 It takes on form like clay *under* a seal,
    And stands out like a garment.
15 From the wicked their ᵃlight is withheld,
    And ᵇthe ¹upraised arm is broken.

16 "Have you ᵃentered the springs of the sea?
    Or have you walked in search of the depths?
17 Have ᵃthe gates of death been ¹revealed to you?
    Or have you seen the doors of the shadow of death?
18 Have you comprehended the breadth of the earth?
    Tell *Me*, if you know all this.

19 "Where *is* the way *to* the dwelling of light?
    And darkness, where *is* its place,
20 That you may take it to its territory,
    That you may know the paths *to* its home?
21 Do you know *it*, because you were born then,
    Or *because* the number of your days *is* great?

22 "Have you entered ᵃthe treasury of snow,
    Or have you seen the treasury of hail,
23 ᵃWhich I have reserved for the time of trouble,
    For the day of battle and war?
24 By what way is light ¹diffused,
    Or the east wind scattered over the earth?

25 "Who ᵃhas divided a channel for the overflowing *water*,
    Or a path for the thunderbolt,
26 To cause it to rain on a land *where there is* no one,
    A wilderness in which *there is* no man;
27 ᵃTo satisfy the desolate waste,
    And cause to spring forth the growth of tender grass?
28 ᵃHas the rain a father?
    Or who has begotten the drops of dew?
29 From whose womb comes the ice?
    And the ᵃfrost of heaven, who gives it birth?
30 The waters harden like stone,
    And the surface of the deep is ᵃfrozen.¹

31 "Can you bind the cluster of the ᵃPleiades,¹
    Or loose the belt of Orion?
32 Can you bring out ¹Mazzaroth in its season?
    Or can you guide ²the Great Bear with its cubs?
33 Do you know ᵃthe ordinances of the heavens?
    Can you set their dominion over the earth?

38:10
ᵃJob 26:10

38:11
ᵃ[Ps. 89:9; 93:4]

38:12
ᵃ[Ps. 74:16;
148:5]

38:13
ᵃJob 34:25;
Ps. 104:35

38:15 ᵃJob 18:5;
[Prov. 13:9]
ᵇ[Num. 15:30];
Ps. 10:15; 37:17

38:16
ᵃ[Ps. 77:19];
Prov. 8:24

38:17 ᵃPs. 9:13

38:22 ᵃPs. 135:7

38:23 ᵃEx. 9:18;
Josh. 10:11;
Is. 30:30;
Ezek. 13:11, 13;
Rev. 16:21

38:25
ᵃJob 28:26

38:27
ᵃPs. 104:13, 14;
107:35

38:28
ᵃJob 36:27,
28; [Ps. 147:8;
Jer. 14:22]

38:29
ᵃ[Job 37:10];
Ps. 147:16, 17

38:30
ᵃ[Job 37:10]

38:31 ᵃJob 9:9;
Amos 5:8

38:33
ᵃ[Ps. 148:6];
Jer. 31:35, 36

38:15 ¹Lit. *high*   38:17 ¹Lit. *opened*   38:24 ¹Lit. *divided*   38:30 ¹Lit.
imprisoned   38:31 ¹Or *the Seven Stars*   38:32 ¹Lit. *Constellations*   ²Or
Arcturus

34 "Can you lift up your voice to the clouds,
   That an abundance of water may cover you?
35 Can you send out lightnings, that they may go,
   And say to you, 'Here we *are!*'?
36 [a]Who has put wisdom in [1]the mind?
   Or who has given understanding to the heart?
37 Who can number the clouds by wisdom?
   Or who can pour out the bottles of heaven,
38 When the dust hardens in clumps,
   And the clods cling together?

39 "Can[a] you hunt the prey for the lion,
   Or satisfy the appetite of the young lions,
40 When they crouch in *their* dens,
   Or lurk in their lairs to lie in wait?
41 [a]Who provides food for the raven,
   When its young ones cry to God,
   And wander about for lack of food?

39 "Do you know the time when the wild [a]mountain
      goats bear young?
   Or can you mark when [b]the deer gives birth?
2 Can you number the months *that* they fulfill?
   Or do you know the time when they bear young?
3 They bow down,
   They bring forth their young,
   They deliver their [1]offspring.
4 Their young ones are healthy,
   They grow strong with grain;
   They depart and do not return to them.

5 "Who set the wild donkey free?
   Who loosed the bonds of the [1]onager,
6 [a]Whose home I have made the wilderness,
   And the [1]barren land his dwelling?
7 He scorns the tumult of the city;
   He does not heed the shouts of the driver.
8 The range of the mountains *is* his pasture,
   And he searches after [a]every green thing.

9 "Will the [a]wild ox be willing to serve you?
   Will he bed by your manger?
10 Can you bind the wild ox in the furrow with ropes?
   Or will he plow the valleys behind you?
11 Will you trust him because his strength *is* great?
   Or will you leave your labor to him?
12 Will you trust him to bring home your [1]grain,
   And gather it to your threshing floor?

13 "The wings of the ostrich wave proudly,
   But are her wings and pinions *like the* kindly stork's?
14 For she leaves her eggs on the ground,
   And warms them in the dust;
15 She forgets that a foot may crush them,
   Or that a wild beast may break them.
16 She [a]treats her young harshly, as though *they were* not
      hers;
   Her labor is in vain, without [1]concern,

38:36
[a][Job 9:4; 32:8;
Ps. 51:6;
Eccl. 2:26;
James 1:5]
38:39
[a]Ps. 104:21
38:41 [a]Ps. 147:9;
[Matt. 6:26;
Luke 12:24]
39:1 [a]Deut. 14:5;
1 Sam. 24:2;
Ps. 104:18
[b]Ps. 29:9
39:6 [a]Job 24:5;
Jer. 2:24;
Hos. 8:9
39:8 [a]Gen. 1:29
39:9
[a]Num. 23:22;
Deut. 33:17;
Ps. 22:21; 29:6;
92:10; Is. 34:7
39:16 [a]Lam. 4:3

38:36 [1]Lit. *the inward parts*   39:3 [1]Lit. *pangs*   39:5 [1]A species of wild
donkey   39:6 [1]Lit. *salt land*   39:12 [1]Lit. *seed*   39:16 [1]Lit. *fear*

17 Because God deprived her of wisdom,
   And did not ªendow her with understanding.
18 When she lifts herself on high,
   She scorns the horse and its rider.

19 "Have you given the horse strength?
   Have you clothed his neck with ¹thunder?
20 Can you ¹frighten him like a locust?
   His majestic snorting strikes terror.
21 He paws in the valley, and rejoices in *his* strength;
   ªHe gallops into the clash of arms.
22 He mocks at fear, and is not frightened;
   Nor does he turn back from the sword.
23 The quiver rattles against him,
   The glittering spear and javelin.
24 He devours the distance with fierceness and rage;
   Nor does he come to a halt because the trumpet *has*
      sounded.
25 At *the blast of* the trumpet he says, 'Aha!'
   He smells the battle from afar,
   The thunder of captains and shouting.

26 "Does the hawk fly by your wisdom,
   And spread its wings toward the south?
27 Does the ªeagle mount up at your command,
   And ᵇmake its nest on high?
28 On the rock it dwells and resides,
   On the crag of the rock and the stronghold.
29 From there it spies out the prey;
   Its eyes observe from afar.
30 Its young ones suck up blood;
   And ªwhere the slain *are*, there it *is*."

40

Moreover the LORD ªanswered Job, and said:

2 "Shall ªthe one who contends with the Almighty correct
      Him?
   He who ᵇrebukes God, let him answer it."

JOB'S RESPONSE TO GOD

3 Then Job answered the LORD and said:

4 "Behold,ª I am vile;
   What shall I answer You?
   ᵇI lay my hand over my mouth.
5 Once I have spoken, but I will not answer;
   Yes, twice, but I will proceed no further."

GOD'S CHALLENGE TO JOB

6 ªThen the LORD answered Job out of the whirlwind, and
said:

7 "Nowª ¹prepare yourself like a man;
   ᵇI will question you, and you shall answer Me:

8 "Wouldª you indeed ¹annul My judgment?
   Would you condemn Me that you may be justified?
9 Have you an arm like God?
   Or can you thunder with ªa voice like His?

39:17 ªJob 35:11
39:21 ªJer. 8:6
39:27
ªProv. 30:18, 19
ᵇJer. 49:16;
Obad. 4
39:30
ªMatt. 24:28;
Luke 17:37
40:1 ªJob 38:1
40:2 ªJob 9:3;
10:2; 33:13
ᵇJob 13:3; 23:4
40:4 ªEzra 9:6;
Job 42:6
ᵇJob 29:9;
Ps. 39:9
40:6 ªJob 38:1
40:7 ªJob 38:3
ᵇJob 42:4
40:8 ªJob 16:11;
19:6; [Ps. 51:4;
Rom. 3:4]
40:9 ªJob 37:4;
[Ps. 29:3, 4]

39:19 ¹Or *a mane*   39:20 ¹*make him spring*   40:7 ¹Lit. *gird up your loins*
40:8 ¹*nullify*

10 aThen adorn yourself *with* majesty and splendor,
  And array yourself with glory and beauty.
11 Disperse the rage of your wrath;
  Look on everyone *who is* proud, and humble him.
12 Look on everyone *who is* aproud, *and* bring him low;
  Tread down the wicked in their place.
13 Hide them in the dust together,
  Bind their faces in hidden *darkness.*
14 Then I will also confess to you
  That your own right hand can save you.

15 "Look now at the ¹behemoth, which I made *along* with
    you;
  He eats grass like an ox.
16 See now, his strength *is* in his hips,
  And his power *is* in his stomach muscles.
17 He moves his tail like a cedar;
  The sinews of his thighs are tightly knit.
18 His bones *are like* beams of bronze,
  His ribs like bars of iron.
19 He *is* the first of the aways of God;
  Only He who made him can bring near His sword.
20 Surely the mountains ayield food for him,
  And all the beasts of the field play there.
21 He lies under the lotus trees,
  In a covert of reeds and marsh.
22 The lotus trees cover him *with* their shade;
  The willows by the brook surround him.
23 Indeed the river may rage,
  Yet he is not disturbed;
  He is confident, though the Jordan gushes into his
    mouth,
24 *Though* he takes it in his eyes,
  Or one pierces *his* nose with a snare.

41 "Can you draw out aLeviathan¹ with a hook,
  Or *snare* his tongue with a line *which* you lower?
2 Can you aput a reed through his nose,
  Or pierce his jaw with a ¹hook?
3 Will he make many supplications to you?
  Will he speak softly to you?
4 Will he make a covenant with you?
  Will you take him as a servant forever?
5 Will you play with him as *with* a bird,
  Or will you leash him for your maidens?
6 Will *your* companions ¹make a banquet of him?
  Will they apportion him among the merchants?
7 Can you fill his skin with harpoons,
  Or his head with fishing spears?
8 Lay your hand on him;
  Remember the battle—
  Never do it again!
9 Indeed, *any* hope of *overcoming* him is false;
  Shall *one* not be overwhelmed at the sight of him?
10 No one *is* so fierce that he would dare stir him up.
  Who then is able to stand against Me?

40:10
aPs. 93:1; 104:1
40:12
a1 Sam. 2:7;
[Is. 2:12; 13:11];
Dan. 4:37
40:19 aJob 26:14
40:20
aPs. 104:14
41:1 aPs. 74:14;
104:26; Is. 27:1
41:2
a2 Kin. 19:28;
Is. 37:29

40:15 ¹A large animal, exact identity unknown   41:1 ¹A large sea creature,
exact identity unknown   41:2 ¹thorn   41:6 ¹Or *bargain over him*

11 ᵃWho has preceded Me, that I should pay *him?*
   ᵇEverything under heaven is Mine.

12 "I will not ¹conceal his limbs,
   His mighty power, or his graceful proportions.

13 Who can ¹remove his outer coat?
   Who can approach *him* with a double bridle?

14 Who can open the doors of his face,
   With his terrible teeth all around?

15 *His* rows of ¹scales are *his* pride,
   Shut up tightly *as with* a seal;

16 One is so near another
   That no air can come between them;

17 They are joined one to another,
   They stick together and cannot be parted.

18 His sneezings flash forth light,
   And his eyes *are* like the eyelids of the morning.

19 Out of his mouth go burning lights;
   Sparks of fire shoot out.

20 Smoke goes out of his nostrils,
   As *from* a boiling pot and burning rushes.

21 His breath kindles coals,
   And a flame goes out of his mouth.

22 Strength dwells in his neck,
   And ¹sorrow dances before him.

23 The folds of his flesh are joined together;
   They are firm on him and cannot be moved.

24 His heart is as hard as stone,
   Even as hard as the lower *millstone.*

25 When he raises himself up, the mighty are afraid;
   Because of his crashings they ¹are beside themselves.

26 *Though* the sword reaches him, it cannot avail;
   Nor does spear, dart, or javelin.

27 He regards iron as straw,
   And bronze as rotten wood.

28 The arrow cannot make him flee;
   Slingstones become like stubble to him.

29 Darts are regarded as straw;
   He laughs at the threat of javelins.

30 His undersides *are* like sharp potsherds;
   He spreads pointed *marks* in the mire.

31 He makes the deep boil like a pot;
   He makes the sea like a pot of ointment.

32 He leaves a shining wake behind him;
   One would think the deep had white hair.

33 On earth there is nothing like him,
   Which is made without fear.

34 He beholds every high *thing;*
   He *is* king over all the children of pride."

JOB'S REPENTANCE AND RESTORATION

42 Then Job answered the LORD and said:

2 "I know that You ᵃcan do everything,
   And that no purpose *of Yours* can be withheld from You.

41:11
ᵃ[Rom. 11:35]
ᵇEx. 19:5;
[Deut. 10:14;
Job 9:5–10;
26:6–14];
Ps. 24:1; 50:12;
1 Cor. 10:26, 28

42:2
ᵃGen. 18:14;
[Matt. 19:26;
Mark 10:27;
14:36;
Luke 18:27]

41:12 ¹Lit. *keep silent about*   41:13 ¹Lit. *take off the face of his garment*
41:15 ¹Lit. *shields*   41:22 ¹*despair*   41:25 ¹Or *purify themselves*

3   *You asked,* a'Who *is* this who hides counsel without
    knowledge?'
    Therefore I have uttered what I did not understand,
    bThings too wonderful for me, which I did not know.
4   Listen, please, and let me speak;
    You said, a'I will question you, and you shall answer Me.'

5   "I have aheard of You by the hearing of the ear,
    But now my eye sees You.
6   Therefore I aabhor[1] *myself,*
    And repent in dust and ashes."

7And so it was, after the Lord had spoken these words to Job, that the Lord said to Eliphaz the Temanite, "My wrath is aroused against you and your two friends, for you have not spoken of Me *what is* right, as My servant Job *has.* 8Now therefore, take for yourselves aseven bulls and seven rams, bgo to My servant Job, and offer up for yourselves a burnt offering; and My servant Job shall cpray for you. For I will accept [1]him, lest I deal with you *according to your* folly; because you have not spoken of Me *what is* right, as My servant Job *has.*"

9So Eliphaz the Temanite and Bildad the Shuhite *and* Zophar the Naamathite went and did as the Lord commanded them; for the Lord had [1]accepted Job. 10aAnd the Lord [1]restored Job's losses when he prayed for his friends. Indeed the Lord gave Job btwice as much as he had before. 11Then aall his brothers, all his sisters, and all those who had been his acquaintances before, came to him and ate food with him in his house; and they consoled him and comforted him for all the adversity that the Lord had brought upon him. Each one gave him a piece of silver and each a ring of gold.

12Now the Lord blessed athe latter *days* of Job more than his beginning; for he had bfourteen thousand sheep, six thousand camels, one thousand yoke of oxen, and one thousand female donkeys. 13aHe also had seven sons and three daughters. 14And he called the name of the first [1]Jemimah, the name of the second [2]Keziah, and the name of the third [3]Keren-Happuch. 15In all the land were found no women *so* beautiful as the daughters of Job; and their father gave them an inheritance among their brothers.

16After this Job alived one hundred and forty years, and saw his children and grandchildren *for* four generations. 17So Job died, old and afull of days.

42:3 aJob 38:2
bPs. 40:5; 131:1;
139:6
42:4 aJob 38:3;
40:7
42:5 aJob 26:14;
[Rom. 10:17]
42:6 aEzra 9:6;
Job 40:4
42:8 aNum. 23:1
b[Matt. 5:24]
cGen. 20:17;
[James 5:15, 16];
1 John 5:16]
42:10
aDeut. 30:3;
Ps. 14:7; 85:1–3;
126:1 bIs. 40:2
42:11 aJob 19:13
42:12 aJob 1:10;
8:7; James 5:11
bJob 1:3
42:13 aJob 1:2
42:16 aJob 5:26;
Prov. 3:16
42:17
aGen. 15:15;
25:8; Job 5:26

42:6 [1]*despise*   42:8 [1]Lit. *his face*   42:9 [1]Lit. *lifted up the face of Job*
42:10 [1]Lit. *turned the captivity of Job,* what was captured from Job
42:14 [1]Lit. *Handsome as the Day*   [2]*Cassia,* a fragrance   [3]Lit. *The Horn of Color* or *The Colorful Ray*

THE BOOK OF
PSALMS

BOOK ONE
Psalms 1–41

PSALM 1

THE WAY OF THE RIGHTEOUS AND THE END OF THE UNGODLY

1 BLESSED ^a*is* the man
Who walks not in the counsel of the ¹ungodly,
　Nor stands in the path of sinners,
^bNor sits in the seat of the scornful;
2 But ^ahis delight *is* in the law of the LORD,
^bAnd in His law he ¹meditates day and night.
3 He shall be like a tree
^aPlanted by the ¹rivers of water,
　That brings forth its fruit in its season,
　Whose leaf also shall not wither;
And whatever he does shall ^bprosper.

4 The ungodly *are* not so,
But *are* ^alike the chaff which the wind drives away.
5 Therefore the ungodly shall not stand in the judgment,
Nor sinners in the congregation of the righteous.

6 For ^athe LORD knows the way of the righteous,
But the way of the ungodly shall perish.

PSALM 2

THE MESSIAH'S TRIUMPH AND KINGDOM
(Acts 4:23–31)

1 WHY ^ado the ¹nations ²rage,
And the people plot a ³vain thing?
2 The kings of the earth set themselves,
And the ^arulers take counsel together,
Against the LORD and against His ^bAnointed,¹ *saying,*
3 "Let ^aus break Their bonds in pieces
And cast away Their cords from us."

4 He who sits in the heavens ^ashall laugh;
The Lord shall hold them in derision.
5 Then He shall speak to them in His wrath,
And distress them in His deep displeasure:
6 "Yet I have ¹set My King
²On My holy hill of Zion."

7 "I will declare the ¹decree:

1:1 ^aProv. 4:14
^bPs. 26:4, 5;
Jer. 15:17

1:2
^aPs. 119:14, 16, 35
^b[Josh. 1:8]

1:3
^a[Ps. 92:12–14];
Jer. 17:8;
Ezek. 19:10
^bGen. 39:2, 3,
23; Ps. 128:2

1:4 ^aJob 21:18;
Ps. 35:5; Is. 17:13

1:6 ^aPs. 37:18;
[Nah. 1:7;
John 10:14;
2 Tim. 2:19]

2:1
^aActs 4:25, 26

2:2
^a[Matt. 12:14;
26:3, 4, 59–66;
27:1, 2;
Mark 3:6; 11:18]
^b[John 1:41]

2:3 ^aLuke 19:14

2:4 ^aPs. 37:13

1:1 ¹*wicked*　1:2 ¹*ponders* by talking to himself　1:3 ¹*channels*　2:1 ¹*Gentiles*
²*throng tumultuously*　³*worthless* or *empty*　2:2 ¹*Christ,* Commissioned
One, Heb. *Messiah*　2:6 ¹Lit. *installed*　²Lit. *Upon Zion, the hill of My holiness*
2:7 ¹Or *decree of the LORD: He said to Me*

The LORD has said to Me,
  a'You *are* My Son,
  Today I have begotten You.
8 Ask of Me, and I will give *You*
  The nations *for* Your inheritance,
  And the ends of the earth *for* Your possession.
9 aYou shall ¹break them with a rod of iron;
  You shall dash them to pieces like a potter's vessel.' "

10 Now therefore, be wise, O kings;
  Be instructed, you judges of the earth.
11 Serve the LORD with fear,
  And rejoice with trembling.
12 ¹Kiss the Son, lest ²He be angry,
  And you perish *in* the way,
  When aHis wrath is kindled but a little.
  bBlessed *are* all those who put their trust in Him.

PSALM 3

THE LORD HELPS HIS TROUBLED PEOPLE

A Psalm of David awhen he fled from Absalom his son.

1 LORD, how they have increased who trouble me!
  Many *are* they who rise up against me.
2 Many *are* they who say of me,
  "*There is* no help for him in God."   *Selah*

3 But You, O LORD, *are* aa shield ¹for me,
  My glory and bthe One who lifts up my head.
4 I cried to the LORD with my voice,
  And aHe heard me from His bholy hill.   *Selah*

5 aI lay down and slept;
  I awoke, for the LORD sustained me.
6 aI will not be afraid of ten thousands of people
  Who have set *themselves* against me all around.

7 Arise, O LORD;
  Save me, O my God!
  aFor You have struck all my enemies on the cheekbone;
  You have broken the teeth of the ungodly.
8 aSalvation *belongs* to the LORD.
  Your blessing *is* upon Your people.   *Selah*

PSALM 4

THE SAFETY OF THE FAITHFUL

To the ¹Chief Musician. With stringed
instruments. A Psalm of David.

1 HEAR me when I call, O God of my righteousness!
  You have relieved me in *my* distress;
  ¹Have mercy on me, and hear my prayer.

2 How long, O you sons of men,
  Will you turn my glory to shame?
  How long will you love worthlessness
  And seek falsehood?   *Selah*

2:7 aMatt. 3:17;
Mark 1:1, 11;
Luke 3:22;
John 1:18;
Acts 13:33;
[Heb. 1:5; 5:5]

2:9 aPs. 89:23;
110:5, 6;
[Rev. 2:26, 27;
12:5; 19:15]

2:12
a[Rev. 6:16, 17]
b[Ps. 5:11; 34:22]

3:title
a2 Sam. 15:13–17

3:3
aPs. 5:12; 28:7
bPs. 9:13; 27:6

3:4 aPs. 4:3;
34:4 bPs. 2:6;
15:1; 43:3

3:5 aLev. 26:6;
Ps. 4:8;
Prov. 3:24

3:6
aPs. 23:4; 27:3

3:7 aJob 16:10

3:8 aPs. 28:8;
35:3; [Is. 43:11]

2:9 ¹So with MT, Tg.; LXX, Syr., Vg. *rule* (cf. Rev. 2:27)   2:12 ¹LXX, Vg.
Embrace discipline; Tg. *Receive instruction*   ²LXX *the LORD*   3:3 ¹Lit.
around   4:title ¹*Choir Director*   4:1 ¹*Be gracious to me*

3 But know that ᵃthe LORD has ¹set apart for Himself him
    who is godly;
  The LORD will hear when I call to Him.

4 ᵃBe¹ angry, and do not sin.
  ᵇMeditate within your heart on your bed, and be still.
                             Selah

5 Offer ᵃthe sacrifices of righteousness,
  And ᵇput your trust in the LORD.

6 *There are* many who say,
  "Who will show us *any* good?"
  ᵃLORD, lift up the light of Your countenance upon us.

7 You have put ᵃgladness in my heart,
  More than in the season that their grain and wine
    increased.

8 ᵃI will both lie down in peace, and sleep;
  ᵇFor You alone, O LORD, make me dwell in safety.

PSALM 5

A PRAYER FOR GUIDANCE

To the Chief Musician. With ¹flutes. A Psalm of David.

1 GIVE ᵃear to my words, O LORD,
  Consider my ¹meditation.
2 Give heed to the voice of my cry,
  My King and my God,
  For to You I will pray.
3 My voice You shall hear in the morning, O LORD;
  ᵃIn the morning I will direct *it* to You,
  And I will look up.

4 For You *are* not a God who takes pleasure in wickedness,
  Nor shall evil ¹dwell with You.
5 The ᵃboastful shall not ᵇstand in Your sight;
  You hate all workers of iniquity.
6 You shall destroy those who speak falsehood;
  The LORD abhors the ᵃbloodthirsty and deceitful man.

7 But as for me, I will come into Your house in the
    multitude of Your mercy;
  In fear of You I will worship toward ¹Your holy temple.
8 ᵃLead me, O LORD, in Your righteousness because of my
    enemies;
  Make Your way straight before my face.

9 For *there is* no ¹faithfulness in their mouth;
  Their inward part *is* destruction;
  ᵃTheir throat *is* an open tomb;
  They flatter with their tongue.
10 Pronounce them guilty, O God!
  Let them fall by their own counsels;
  Cast them out in the multitude of their transgressions,
  For they have rebelled against You.

11 But let all those rejoice who put their trust in You;
  Let them ever shout for joy, because You ¹defend them;

4:3
ᵃ[2 Tim. 2:19]

4:4 ᵃ[Ps. 119:11;
Eph. 4:26]
ᵇPs. 77:6

4:5
ᵃDeut. 33:19;
Ps. 51:19
ᵇPs. 37:3, 5;
62:8

4:6 ᵃNum. 6:26;
Ps. 80:3, 7, 19

4:7 ᵃPs. 97:11, 12;
Is. 9:3; Acts 14:17

4:8 ᵃJob 11:19;
Ps. 3:5
ᵇ[Lev. 25:18];
Deut. 12:10

5:1 ᵃPs. 4:1

5:3 ᵃPs. 55:17;
88:13

5:5 ᵃ[Hab. 1:13]
ᵇPs. 1:5

5:6 ᵃPs. 55:23

5:8 ᵃPs. 25:4, 5;
27:11; 31:3

5:9 ᵃRom. 3:13

4:3 ¹Many Heb. mss., LXX, Tg., Vg. *made wonderful*   4:4 ¹Lit. *Tremble* or *Be
agitated*   5:title ¹Heb. *nehiloth*   5:1 ¹Lit. *groaning*   5:4 ¹Lit. *sojourn*
5:7 ¹Lit. *the temple of Your holiness*   5:9 ¹*uprightness*   5:11 ¹*protect,* lit. *cover*

Let those also who love Your name
Be joyful in You.
12 For You, O LORD, will bless the righteous;
With favor You will surround him as *with* a shield.

PSALM 6

A PRAYER OF FAITH IN TIME OF DISTRESS

To the Chief Musician. With stringed instruments.
[a]On [1]an eight-stringed harp. A Psalm of David.

1 O LORD, [a]do not rebuke me in Your anger,
Nor chasten me in Your hot displeasure.
2 Have mercy on me, O LORD, for I *am* weak;
O LORD, [a]heal me, for my bones are troubled.
3 My soul also is greatly [a]troubled;
But You, O LORD—how long?

4 Return, O LORD, deliver me!
Oh, save me for Your mercies' sake!
5 [a]For in death *there is* no remembrance of You;
In the grave who will give You thanks?

6 I am weary with my groaning;
[1]All night I make my bed swim;
I drench my couch with my tears.
7 [a]My eye wastes away because of grief;
It grows old because of all my enemies.

8 [a]Depart from me, all you workers of iniquity;
For the LORD has [b]heard the voice of my weeping.
9 The LORD has heard my supplication;
The LORD will receive my prayer.
10 Let all my enemies be ashamed and greatly troubled;
Let them turn back *and* be ashamed suddenly.

PSALM 7

PRAYER AND PRAISE FOR DELIVERANCE FROM ENEMIES

A [a]Meditation[1] of David, which he sang to the LORD
[b]concerning the words of Cush, a Benjamite.

1 O LORD my God, in You I put my trust;
[a]Save me from all those who persecute me;
And deliver me,
2 [a]Lest they tear me like a lion,
[b]Rending *me* in pieces, while *there is* none to deliver.

3 O LORD my God, [a]if I have done this:
If there is [b]iniquity in my hands,
4 If I have repaid evil to him who was at peace with me,
Or [a]have plundered my enemy without cause,
5 Let the enemy pursue me and overtake *me*;
Yes, let him trample my life to the earth,
And lay my honor in the dust.   *Selah*

6 Arise, O LORD, in Your anger;
[a]Lift Yourself up because of the rage of my enemies;
[b]Rise up [1]for me *to* the judgment You have commanded!

6:title
[a]Ps. 12:title

6:1 [a]Ps. 38:1;
118:18;
[Jer. 10:24]

6:2 [a]Ps. 41:4;
147:3; [Hos. 6:1]

6:3 [a]Ps. 88:3;
John 12:27

6:5 [a]Ps. 30:9;
88:10–12; 115:17;
[Eccl. 9:10];
Is. 38:18

6:7 [a]Job 17:7;
Ps. 31:9

6:8
[a][Matt. 25:41]
[b]Ps. 3:4; 28:6

7:title [a]Hab. 3:1
[b]2 Sam. 16

7:1 [a]Ps. 31:15

7:2 [a]Ps. 57:4;
Is. 38:13
[b]Ps. 50:22

7:3 [a]2 Sam. 16:7
[b]1 Sam. 24:11

7:4 [a]1 Sam. 24:7;
26:9

7:6 [a]Ps. 94:2
[b]Ps. 35:23;
44:23

6:title [1]Heb. *Sheminith*   6:6 [1]Or *Every night*   7:title [1]Heb. *Shiggaion*
7:6 [1]So with MT, Tg., Vg.; LXX *O LORD my God*

7 So the congregation of the peoples shall surround You;
For their sakes, therefore, return on high.
8 The LORD shall judge the peoples;
aJudge me, O LORD, baccording to my righteousness,
And according to my integrity within me.

9 Oh, let the wickedness of the wicked come to an end,
But establish the just;
aFor the righteous God tests the hearts and 1minds.
10 1My defense *is* of God,
Who saves the aupright in heart.

11 God *is* a just judge,
And God is angry *with the wicked* every day.
12 If he does not turn back,
He will asharpen His sword;
He bends His bow and makes it ready.
13 He also prepares for Himself instruments of death;
He makes His arrows into fiery shafts.

14 aBehold, *the wicked* brings forth iniquity;
Yes, he conceives trouble and brings forth falsehood.
15 He made a pit and dug it out,
aAnd has fallen into the ditch *which* he made.
16 aHis trouble shall return upon his own head,
And his violent dealing shall come down on 1his own crown.

17 I will praise the LORD according to His righteousness,
And will sing praise to the name of the LORD Most High.

PSALM 8

THE GLORY OF THE LORD IN CREATION

*To the Chief Musician. 1On the instrument
of Gath. A Psalm of David.*

1 O LORD, our Lord,
How aexcellent *is* Your name in all the earth,
Who have bset Your glory above the heavens!

2 aOut of the mouth of babes and nursing infants
You have 1ordained strength,
Because of Your enemies,
That You may silence bthe enemy and the avenger.

3 When I aconsider Your heavens, the work of Your fingers,
The moon and the stars, which You have ordained,
4 aWhat is man that You are mindful of him,
And the son of man that You bvisit1 him?
5 For You have made him a little lower than 1the angels,
And You have crowned him with glory and honor.

6 aYou have made him to have dominion over the works of
Your hands;
bYou have put all *things* under his feet,
7 All sheep and oxen—
Even the beasts of the field,

7:8 aPs. 26:1;
35:24; 43:1
bPs. 18:20;
35:24
7:9
a[1 Sam. 16:7]
7:10
aPs. 97:10, 11;
125:4
7:12 aDeut. 32:41
7:14 aJob 15:35;
Is. 59:4;
[James 1:15]
7:15 a[Job 4:8];
Ps. 57:6
7:16 aEsth. 9:25;
Ps. 140:9
8:1 aPs. 148:13
bPs. 113:4
8:2 aMatt. 21:16;
[1 Cor. 1:27]
bPs. 44:16
8:3 aPs. 111:2
8:4 aJob 7:17, 18;
[Heb. 2:6–8]
b[Job 10:12]
8:6
a[Gen. 1:26, 28]
b[1 Cor. 15:27;
Eph. 1:22;
Heb. 2:8]

7:9 1Lit. *kidneys,* the most secret part of man   7:10 1Lit. *My shield is upon God*   7:16 1The crown of his own head   8:title 1Heb. *Al Gittith*
8:2 1*established*   8:4 1*give attention to* or *care for*   8:5 1Heb. *Elohim, God;* LXX, Syr., Tg., Jewish tradition *angels*

8   The birds of the air,
And the fish of the sea
That pass through the paths of the seas.

9   ªO LORD, our Lord,
How excellent *is* Your name in all the earth!

PSALM 9

PRAYER AND THANKSGIVING FOR THE LORD'S RIGHTEOUS JUDGMENTS

To the Chief Musician. To *the tune of* ¹"Death
of the Son." A Psalm of David.

1   I WILL praise *You,* O LORD, with my whole heart;
I will tell of all Your marvelous works.
2   I will be glad and ªrejoice in You;
I will sing praise to Your name, ᵇO Most High.

3   When my enemies turn back,
They shall fall and perish at Your presence.
4   For You have maintained my right and my cause;
You sat on the throne judging in righteousness.
5   You have rebuked the ¹nations,
You have destroyed the wicked;
You have ªblotted out their name forever and ever.

6   O enemy, destructions are finished forever!
And you have destroyed cities;
Even their memory has ªperished.
7   ªBut the LORD shall endure forever;
He has prepared His throne for judgment.
8   ªHe shall judge the world in righteousness,
And He shall administer judgment for the peoples in
uprightness.

9   The LORD also will be a ªrefuge¹ for the oppressed,
A refuge in times of trouble.
10   And those who ªknow Your name will put their trust in
You;
For You, LORD, have not forsaken those who seek You.

11   Sing praises to the LORD, who dwells in Zion!
ªDeclare His deeds among the people.
12   ªWhen He avenges blood, He remembers them;
He does not forget the cry of the ¹humble.

13   Have mercy on me, O LORD!
Consider my trouble from those who hate me,
You who lift me up from the gates of death,
14   That I may tell of all Your praise
In the gates of ¹the daughter of Zion.
I will ªrejoice in Your salvation.

15   ªThe ¹nations have sunk down in the pit *which* they made;
In the net which they hid, their own foot is caught.
16   The LORD is ªknown *by* the judgment He executes;
The wicked is snared in the work of his own hands.
ᵇMeditation.¹   *Selah*

8:9 ªPs. 8:1
9:2 ªPs. 5:11;
104:34
ᵇ[Ps. 83:18; 92:1]
9:5 ªProv. 10:7
9:6 ª[Ps. 34:16]
9:7 ªPs. 102:12,
26; Heb. 1:11
9:8 ª[Ps. 96:13;
98:9; Acts 17:31]
9:9 ªPs. 32:7;
46:1; 91:2
9:10 ªPs. 91:14
9:11 ªPs. 66:16;
107:22
9:12 ª[Gen. 9:5;
Ps. 72:14]
9:14 ªPs. 13:5;
20:5; 35:9
9:15 ªPs. 7:15, 16
9:16 ªEx. 7:5
ᵇPs. 92:3

9:title ¹Heb. *Muth Labben*   9:5 ¹*Gentiles*   9:9 ¹Lit. *secure height*
9:12 ¹*afflicted*   9:14 ¹Jerusalem   9:15 ¹*Gentiles*   9:16 ¹Heb. *Higgaion*

17 The wicked shall be turned into hell,
And all the ¹nations ᵃthat forget God.
18 ᵃFor the needy shall not always be forgotten;
ᵇThe expectation of the poor shall *not* perish forever.

19 Arise, O LORD,
Do not let man prevail;
Let the ¹nations be judged in Your sight.
20 Put them in fear, O LORD,
That the ¹nations may know themselves *to be but* men.

Selah

PSALM 10

A SONG OF CONFIDENCE IN GOD'S TRIUMPH OVER EVIL

1 WHY do You stand afar off, O LORD?
Why do You hide in times of trouble?
2 The wicked in *his* pride ¹persecutes the poor;
ᵃLet them be caught in the plots which they have devised.

3 For the wicked ᵃboasts of his heart's desire;
¹He ᵇblesses the greedy *and* renounces the LORD.
4 The wicked in his proud countenance does not seek *God;*
¹God *is* in none of his ᵃthoughts.

5 His ways ¹are always prospering;
Your judgments *are* far above, out of his sight;
As for all his enemies, he sneers at them.
6 ᵃHe has said in his heart, "I shall not be moved;
ᵇI shall never be in adversity."
7 ᵃHis mouth is full of cursing and ᵇdeceit and oppression;
Under his tongue *is* trouble and iniquity.

8 He sits in the lurking places of the villages;
In the secret places he murders the innocent;
His eyes are secretly fixed on the helpless.
9 He lies in wait secretly, as a lion in his den;
He lies in wait to catch the poor;
He catches the poor when he draws him into his net.
10 So ¹he crouches, he lies low,
That the helpless may fall by his ²strength.
11 He has said in his heart,
"God has forgotten;
He hides His face;
He will never see."

12 Arise, O LORD!
O God, ᵃlift up Your hand!
Do not forget the ᵇhumble.
13 Why do the wicked renounce God?
He has said in his heart,
"You will not require *an account*."

14 But You have ᵃseen, for You observe trouble and grief,
To repay *it* by Your hand.
The helpless ᵇcommits¹ himself to You;
ᶜYou are the helper of the fatherless.

9:17 ᵃJob 8:13;
Ps. 50:22
9:18 ᵃPs. 9:12;
12:5 ᵇ[Ps. 62:5;
71:5]; Prov. 23:18
10:2
ᵃPs. 7:16; 9:16
10:3
ᵃPs. 49:6; 94:3, 4
ᵇProv. 28:4
10:4
ᵃPs. 14:1; 36:1
10:6 ᵃPs. 49:11;
[Eccl. 8:11]
ᵇRev. 18:7
10:7
ᵃ[Rom. 3:14]
ᵇPs. 55:10, 11
10:12 ᵃPs. 17:7;
94:2; Mic. 5:9
ᵇPs. 9:12
10:14 ᵃ[Ps. 11:4]
ᵇ[2 Tim. 1:12]
ᶜPs. 68:5;
Hos. 14:3

9:17 ¹Gentiles   9:19 ¹Gentiles   9:20 ¹Gentiles   10:2 ¹hotly pursues
10:3 ¹Or *The greedy man curses and spurns the LORD*   10:4 ¹Or *All his
thoughts are, "There is no God"*   10:5 ¹Lit. *are strong*   10:10 ¹Or *he is
crushed, is bowed*   ²Or *mighty ones*   10:14 ¹Lit. *leaves, entrusts*

15 Break the arm of the wicked and the evil *man;*
Seek out his wickedness *until* You find none.

16 ªThe LORD *is* King forever and ever;
The nations have perished out of His land.

17 LORD, You have heard the desire of the humble;
You will prepare their heart;
You will cause Your ear to hear,

18 To ¹do justice to the fatherless and the oppressed,
That the man of the earth may ²oppress no more.

PSALM 11

FAITH IN THE LORD'S RIGHTEOUSNESS

To the Chief Musician. *A Psalm* of David.

1 IN ªthe LORD I put my trust;
How can you say to my soul,
"Flee *as* a bird to your mountain"?

2 For look! ªThe wicked bend *their* bow,
They make ready their arrow on the string,
That they may shoot ¹secretly at the upright in heart.

3 ªIf the foundations are destroyed,
What can the righteous do?

4 The LORD *is* in His holy temple,
The LORD's ªthrone *is* in heaven;
ᵇHis eyes behold,
His eyelids test the sons of men.

5 The LORD ªtests the righteous,
But the wicked and the one who loves violence His soul
hates.

6 Upon the wicked He will rain coals;
Fire and brimstone and a burning wind
ª*Shall be* ¹the portion of their cup.

7 For the LORD *is* righteous,
He ªloves righteousness;
¹His countenance beholds the upright.

PSALM 12

MAN'S TREACHERY AND GOD'S CONSTANCY

To the Chief Musician. ªOn ¹an eight-stringed
harp. A Psalm of David.

1 HELP,¹ LORD, for the godly man ªceases!
For the faithful disappear from among the sons of men.

2 ªThey speak idly everyone with his neighbor;
With flattering lips *and* ¹a double heart they speak.

3 May the LORD ¹cut off all flattering lips,
And the tongue that speaks ²proud things,

4 Who have said,
"With our tongue we will prevail;
Our lips *are* our own;
Who *is* lord over us?"

10:16 ªPs. 29:10

11:1 ªPs. 56:11

11:2 ªPs. 64:3, 4

11:3 ªPs. 82:5;
87:1; 119:152

11:4 ªPs. 2:4;
[Is. 66:1];
Matt. 5:34;
23:22;
[Acts 7:49];
Rev. 4:2
ᵇ[Ps. 33:18;
34:15, 16]

11:5 ªGen. 22:1;
[James 1:12]

11:6 ª1 Sam. 1:4;
Ps. 75:8;
Ezek. 38:22

11:7
ªPs. 33:5; 45:7

12:title
ªPs. 6:title

12:1 ª[Is. 57:1];
Mic. 7:2

12:2
ªPs. 10:7; 41:6

10:18 ¹*vindicate*   ²*terrify*   11:2 ¹Lit. *in darkness*   11:6 ¹Their allotted
portion or serving   11:7 ¹Or *The upright beholds His countenance*
12:title ¹Heb. *Sheminith*   12:1 ¹*Save*   12:2 ¹An inconsistent mind
12:3 ¹*destroy*   ²*great*

5 "For the oppression of the poor, for the sighing of the
      needy,
   Now I will arise," says the LORD;
   "I will set *him* in the safety for which he yearns."

6 The words of the LORD *are* [a]pure words,
   Like silver tried in a furnace of earth,
   Purified seven times.
7 You shall keep them, O LORD,
   You shall preserve them from this generation forever.

8 The wicked prowl on every side,
   When vileness is exalted among the sons of men.

PSALM 13

TRUST IN THE SALVATION OF THE LORD

To the Chief Musician. A Psalm of David.

1 HOW long, O LORD? Will You forget me forever?
   [a]How long will You hide Your face from me?
2 How long shall I take counsel in my soul,
   Having sorrow in my heart daily?
   How long will my enemy be exalted over me?

3 Consider *and* hear me, O LORD my God;
   [a]Enlighten my eyes,
   [b]Lest I sleep the *sleep of* death;
4 Lest my enemy say,
   "I have prevailed against him";
   Lest those who trouble me rejoice when I am moved.

5 But I have trusted in Your mercy;
   My heart shall rejoice in Your salvation.
6 I will sing to the LORD,
   Because He has dealt bountifully with me.

PSALM 14

FOLLY OF THE GODLESS, AND GOD'S FINAL TRIUMPH

(Ps. 53:1–6)

To the Chief Musician. *A Psalm* of David.

1 THE [a]fool has said in his heart,
   "There is no God."
   They are corrupt,
   They have done abominable works,
   There is none who does good.

2 [a]The LORD looks down from heaven upon the children of
      men,
   To see if there are any who understand, who seek
      God.
3 [a]They have all turned aside,
   They have together become corrupt;
   There is none who does good,
   No, not one.

4 Have all the workers of iniquity no knowledge,
   Who eat up my people *as* they eat bread,
   And [a]do not call on the LORD?

12:6
[a]2 Sam. 22:31;
Ps. 18:30;
119:140;
Prov. 30:5

13:1 [a]Job 13:24;
Ps. 89:46

13:3
[a]1 Sam. 14:29;
Ezra 9:8;
Job 33:30;
Ps. 18:28
[b]Jer. 51:39

14:1
[a]Ps. 10:4; 53:1

14:2
[a]Ps. 33:13, 14;
102:19; Rom. 3:11

14:3 [a]Rom. 3:12

14:4 [a]Ps. 79:6;
Is. 64:7;
Jer. 10:25;
Amos 8:4;
Mic. 3:3

5 There they are in great fear,
For God *is* with the generation of the righteous.
6 You shame the counsel of the poor,
But the LORD *is* his [a]refuge.

7 [a]Oh,[1] that the salvation of Israel *would come* out of Zion!
[b]When the LORD brings back [2]the captivity of His people,
Let Jacob rejoice *and* Israel be glad.

PSALM 15

THE CHARACTER OF THOSE WHO MAY DWELL
WITH THE LORD

A Psalm of David.

1 LORD, [a]who may [1]abide in Your tabernacle?
Who may dwell in Your holy hill?

2 He who walks uprightly,
And works righteousness,
And speaks the [a]truth in his heart;
3 He *who* [a]does not backbite with his tongue,
Nor does evil to his neighbor,
[b]Nor does he [1]take up a reproach against his friend;
4 [a]In whose eyes a vile person is despised,
But he honors those who fear the LORD;
He *who* [b]swears to his own hurt and does not change;
5 He *who* does not put out his money at usury,
Nor does he take a bribe against the innocent.

He who does these *things* [a]shall never be moved.

PSALM 16

THE HOPE OF THE FAITHFUL, AND THE MESSIAH'S VICTORY

A [a]Michtam of David.

1 PRESERVE[1] me, O God, for in You I put my trust.

2 *O my soul,* you have said to the LORD,
"You *are* my Lord,
[a]My goodness is nothing apart from You."
3 As for the saints who *are* on the earth,
"They are the excellent ones, in [a]whom is all my delight."

4 Their sorrows shall be multiplied who hasten *after*
another *god;*
Their drink offerings of [a]blood I will not offer,
[b]Nor take up their names on my lips.

5 O LORD, *You are* the portion of my inheritance and my
cup;
You [1]maintain my lot.
6 The lines have fallen to me in pleasant *places;*
Yes, I have a good inheritance.

7 I will bless the LORD who has given me counsel;
My [1]heart also instructs me in the night seasons.

14:6 [a]Ps. 9:9;
40:17; 46:1; 142:5

14:7 [a]Ps. 53:6;
[Rom. 11:25–27]
[b]Deut. 30:3;
Job 42:10

15:1 [a]Ps. 24:3–5

15:2 [a]Zech. 8:16;
[Eph. 4:25]

15:3
[a][Lev. 19:16–18]
[b]Ex. 23:1

15:4 [a]Esth. 3:2
[b]Lev. 5:4

15:5 [a]2 Pet. 1:10

16:title
[a]Ps. 56—60

16:2 [a]Job 35:7

16:3 [a]Ps. 119:63

16:4
[a]Ps. 106:37, 38
[b][Ex. 23:13];
Josh. 23:7

14:7 [1]Lit. *Who will give out of Zion the salvation of Israel?*   [2]Or *His captive people*   15:1 [1]*sojourn*   15:3 [1]*receive*   16:1 [1]*Watch over*   16:5 [1]Lit. *uphold*
16:7 [1]Mind, lit. *kidneys*

8 ^aI have set the LORD always before me;
  Because *He is* at my right hand I shall not be moved.

9 Therefore my heart is glad, and my glory rejoices;
  My flesh also will ¹rest in hope.

10 ^aFor You will not leave my soul in ¹Sheol,
   Nor will You allow Your Holy One to ²see corruption.

11 You will show me the ^apath of life;
   In Your presence *is* fullness of joy;
   At Your right hand *are* pleasures forevermore.

PSALM 17

PRAYER WITH CONFIDENCE IN FINAL SALVATION

A Prayer of David.

1 HEAR a just cause, O LORD,
  Attend to my cry;
  Give ear to my prayer *which is* not from deceitful lips.

2 Let my vindication come from Your presence;
  Let Your eyes look on the things that are upright.

3 You have tested my heart;
  You have visited *me* in the night;
  ^aYou have ¹tried me and have found ²nothing;
  I have purposed that my mouth shall not ^btransgress.

4 Concerning the works of men,
  By the word of Your lips,
  I have kept away from the paths of the destroyer.

5 ^aUphold my steps in Your paths,
  That my footsteps may not slip.

6 ^aI have called upon You, for You will hear me, O God;
  Incline Your ear to me, *and* hear my speech.

7 Show Your marvelous lovingkindness by Your right
     hand,
  O You who ¹save those who trust *in You*
  From those who rise up *against them*.

8 Keep me as the ¹apple of Your eye;
  Hide me under the shadow of Your wings,

9 From the wicked who oppress me,
  From my deadly enemies who surround me.

10 They have closed up their ^afat *hearts;*
   With their mouths they ^bspeak proudly.

11 They have now surrounded us in our steps;
   They have set their eyes, crouching down to the earth,

12 As a lion is eager to tear his prey,
   And like a young lion lurking in secret places.

13 Arise, O LORD,
   Confront him, cast him down;
   Deliver my life from the wicked with Your sword,

14 With Your hand from men, O LORD,
   From men of the world *who have* their portion in *this* life,
   And whose belly You fill with Your hidden treasure.
   They are satisfied with children,
   And leave the rest of their *possession* for their babes.

16:8
^a[Acts 2:25–28]

16:10 ^aPs. 49:15;
86:13; Acts 2:31,
32; Heb. 13:20

16:11 ^aPs. 139:24;
[Matt. 7:14]

17:3 ^aJob 23:10;
Ps. 66:10;
Zech. 13:9;
[1 Pet. 1:7]
^bPs. 39:1

17:5 ^aJob 23:11;
Ps. 44:18; 119:133

17:6
^aPs. 86:7; 116:2

17:10
^aEzek. 16:49
^b[1 Sam. 2:3]

16:9 ¹Or *dwell securely*   16:10 ¹The abode of the dead   ²*undergo*
17:3 ¹*examined*   ²Nothing evil   17:7 ¹*deliver*   17:8 ¹*pupil*

15 As for me, [a]I will see Your face in righteousness;
[b]I shall be satisfied when I [c]awake in Your likeness.

PSALM 18

GOD THE SOVEREIGN SAVIOR

(2 Sam. 22:1–51)

To the Chief Musician. *A Psalm* of David [a]the servant of the
Lord, who spoke to the Lord the words of [b]this song on
the day that the Lord delivered him from the hand of all
his enemies and from the hand of Saul. And he said:

1 I [a]WILL love You, O Lord, my strength.

2 The Lord is my rock and my fortress and my deliverer;
My God, my [1]strength, [a]in whom I will trust;
My shield and the [2]horn of my salvation, my stronghold.

3 I will call upon the Lord, [a]*who is worthy* to be praised;
So shall I be saved from my enemies.

4 [a]The pangs of death surrounded me,
And the floods of [1]ungodliness made me afraid.

5 The sorrows of Sheol surrounded me;
The snares of death confronted me.

6 In my distress I called upon the Lord,
And cried out to my God;
He heard my voice from His temple,
And my cry came before Him, *even* to His ears.

7 [a]Then the earth shook and trembled;
The foundations of the hills also quaked and were
    shaken,
Because He was angry.

8 Smoke went up from His nostrils,
And devouring fire from His mouth;
Coals were kindled by it.

9 [a]He bowed the heavens also, and came down
With darkness under His feet.

10 [a]And He rode upon a cherub, and flew;
[b]He flew upon the wings of the wind.

11 He made darkness His secret place;
[a]His canopy around Him *was* dark waters
And thick clouds of the skies.

12 [a]From the brightness before Him,
His thick clouds passed with hailstones and coals of fire.

13 The Lord thundered from heaven,
And the Most High uttered [a]His voice,
[1]Hailstones and coals of fire.

14 [a]He sent out His arrows and scattered [1]the foe,
Lightnings in abundance, and He vanquished them.

15 Then the channels of the sea were seen,
The foundations of the world were uncovered
At Your rebuke, O Lord,
At the blast of the breath of Your nostrils.

16 [a]He sent from above, He took me;
He drew me out of many waters.

17:15
[a][1 John 3:2]
[b]Ps. 4:6, 7; 16:11
[c][Is. 26:19]

18:title
[a]Ps. 36:title
[b]2 Sam. 22

18:1 [a]Ps. 144:1

18:2 [a]Heb. 2:13

18:3 [a]Ps. 76:4; Rev. 5:12

18:4 [a]Ps. 116:3

18:7 [a]Acts 4:31

18:9 [a]Ps. 144:5

18:10 [a]Ps. 80:1; 99:1 [b][Ps. 104:3]

18:11 [a]Ps. 97:2

18:12 [a]Ps. 97:3; 140:10; Hab. 3:11

18:13 [a][Ps. 29:3–9; 104:7]

18:14 [a]Josh. 10:10; Ps. 144:6; Is. 30:30; Hab. 3:11

18:16 [a]Ps. 144:7

18:2 [1]Lit. *rock*   [2]Strength   **18:4** [1]Lit. *Belial*   **18:13** [1]So with MT, Tg., Vg.; a few Heb. mss., LXX omit *Hailstones and coals of fire*   **18:14** [1]Lit. *them*

17 He delivered me from my strong enemy,
From those who hated me,
For they were too strong for me.
18 They confronted me in the day of my calamity,
But the LORD was my support.
19 ªHe also brought me out into a broad place;
He delivered me because He delighted in me.
20 ªThe LORD rewarded me according to my righteousness;
According to the cleanness of my hands
He has recompensed me.
21 For I have kept the ways of the LORD,
And have not wickedly departed from my God.
22 For all His judgments *were* before me,
And I did not put away His statutes from me.
23 I was also blameless ¹before Him,
And I kept myself from my iniquity.
24 ªTherefore the LORD has recompensed me according to
my righteousness,
According to the cleanness of my hands in His sight.

25 ªWith the merciful You will show Yourself merciful;
With a blameless man You will show Yourself blameless;
26 With the pure You will show Yourself pure;
And ªwith the devious You will show Yourself shrewd.
27 For You will save the humble people,
But will bring down ªhaughty looks.

28 ªFor You will light my lamp;
The LORD my God will enlighten my darkness.
29 For by You I can ¹run against a troop,
By my God I can leap over a wall.
30 *As for* God, ªHis way *is* perfect;
ᵇThe word of the LORD is ¹proven;
He *is* a shield ᶜto all who trust in Him.

31 ªFor who *is* God, except the LORD?
And who *is* a rock, except our God?
32 *It is* God who ªarms me with strength,
And makes my way perfect.
33 ªHe makes my feet like the *feet of* deer,
And ᵇsets me on my high places.
34 ªHe teaches my hands to make war,
So that my arms can bend a bow of bronze.
35 You have also given me the shield of Your salvation;
Your right hand has held me up,
Your gentleness has made me great.
36 You enlarged my path under me,
ªSo my feet did not slip.

37 I have pursued my enemies and overtaken them;
Neither did I turn back again till they were destroyed.
38 I have wounded them,
So that they could not rise;
They have fallen under my feet.
39 For You have armed me with strength for the battle;
You have ¹subdued under me those who rose up against
me.

18:19 ªPs. 4:1;
31:8; 118:5

18:20
ª1 Sam. 24:19;
[Job 33:26];
Ps. 7:8

18:24
ª1 Sam. 26:23;
Ps. 18:20

18:25
ª[1 Kin. 8:32;
Ps. 62:12];
Matt. 5:7

18:26
ª[Lev. 26:23–28];
Prov. 3:34

18:27
ª[Ps. 101:5];
Prov. 6:17

18:28
ª1 Kin. 15:4;
Job 18:6;
[Ps. 119:105]

18:30
ª[Deut. 32:4];
Rev. 15:3
ᵇPs. 12:6;
119:140;
[Prov. 30:5]
ᶜ[Ps. 17:7]

18:31
ª[Deut. 32:31,
39; 1 Sam. 2:2;
Ps. 86:8–10;
Is. 45:5]

18:32 ª[Ps. 91:2]

18:33
ª2 Sam. 2:18;
Hab. 3:19
ᵇDeut. 32:13;
33:29

18:34 ªPs. 144:1

18:36 ªPs. 66:9;
Prov. 4:12

18:23 ¹*with*   **18:29** ¹Or *run through*   **18:30** ¹Lit. *refined*   **18:39** ¹Lit. *caused
to bow*

40   You have also given me the necks of my enemies,
      So that I destroyed those who hated me.
41   They cried out, but *there was* none to save;
      [a]*Even* to the LORD, but He did not answer them.
42   Then I beat them as fine as the dust before the wind;
      I [a]cast them out like dirt in the streets.

43   You have delivered me from the strivings of the people;
      [a]You have made me the head of the [1]nations;
      [b]A people I have not known shall serve me.
44   As soon as they hear of me they obey me;
      The foreigners [1]submit to me.
45   [a]The foreigners fade away,
      And come frightened from their hideouts.

46   The LORD lives!
      Blessed *be* my Rock!
      Let the God of my salvation be exalted.
47   *It is* God who avenges me,
      [a]And subdues the peoples under me;
48   He delivers me from my enemies.
      [a]You also lift me up above those who rise against me;
      You have delivered me from the violent man.
49   [a]Therefore I will give thanks to You, O LORD, among the
         [1]Gentiles,
      And sing praises to Your name.

50   [a]Great deliverance He gives to His king,
      And shows mercy to His anointed,
      To David and his [1]descendants forevermore.

PSALM 19

THE PERFECT REVELATION OF THE LORD

To the Chief Musician. A Psalm of David.

1   THE [a]heavens declare the glory of God;
      And the [b]firmament[1] shows [2]His handiwork.
2   Day unto day utters speech,
      And night unto night reveals knowledge.
3   *There is* no speech nor language
      Where their voice is not heard.
4   [a]Their [1]line has gone out through all the earth,
      And their words to the end of the world.

      In them He has set a [2]tabernacle for the sun,
5   Which *is* like a bridegroom coming out of his chamber,
      [a]*And* rejoices like a strong man to run its race.
6   Its rising *is* from one end of heaven,
      And its circuit to the other end;
      And there is nothing hidden from its heat.

7   [a]The law of the LORD *is* perfect, [1]converting the soul;
      The testimony of the LORD *is* sure, making [b]wise the
         simple;
8   The statutes of the LORD *are* right, rejoicing the heart;
      The commandment of the LORD *is* pure, enlightening
         the eyes;

18:41 [a]Job 27:9;
Prov. 1:28;
Is. 1:15;
Ezek. 8:18;
Zech. 7:13

18:42
[a]Zech. 10:5

18:43 [a]2 Sam. 8;
Ps. 89:27
[b]Is. 52:15

18:45 [a]Mic. 7:17

18:47 [a]Ps. 47:3

18:48
[a]Ps. 27:6; 59:1

18:49
[a]2 Sam. 22:50;
Rom. 15:9

18:50
[a]2 Sam. 7:12;
Ps. 21:1; 144:10

19:1 [a]Is. 40:22;
[Rom. 1:19, 20]
[b]Gen. 1:6, 7

19:4 [a]Rom. 10:18

19:5 [a]Eccl. 1:5

19:7 [a]Ps. 111:7;
[Rom. 7:12]
[b]Ps. 119:130

18:43 [1]*Gentiles*   18:44 [1]*feign submission*   18:49 [1]*nations*   18:50 [1]*Lit. seed*
19:1 [1]*expanse* of heaven   [2]*the work of His hands*   19:4 [1]*LXX, Syr., Vg.*
sound; Tg. *business*   [2]*tent*   19:7 [1]*restoring*

9   The fear of the LORD *is* clean, enduring forever;
    The judgments of the LORD *are* true *and* righteous
        altogether.
10 More to be desired *are they* than ᵃgold,
    Yea, than much fine gold;
    Sweeter also than honey and the ¹honeycomb.
11 Moreover by them Your servant is warned,
    And in keeping them *there is* great reward.

12 Who can understand *his* errors?
    ᵃCleanse me from secret *faults.*
13 Keep back Your servant also from ᵃpresumptuous *sins;*
    Let them not have ᵇdominion over me.
    Then I shall be blameless,
    And I shall be innocent of ¹great transgression.

14 ᵃLet the words of my mouth and the meditation of my
        heart
    Be acceptable in Your sight,
    O LORD, my ¹strength and my ᵇRedeemer.

PSALM 20

THE ASSURANCE OF GOD'S SAVING WORK

To the Chief Musician. A Psalm of David.

1   MAY the LORD answer you in the day of trouble;
    May the name of the God of Jacob ¹defend you;
2   May He send you help from the sanctuary,
    And strengthen you out of Zion;
3   May He remember all your offerings,
    And accept your burnt sacrifice.   *Selah*

4   May He grant you according to your heart's *desire,*
    And ᵃfulfill all your ¹purpose.
5   We will rejoice in your salvation,
    And in the name of our God we will set up *our* banners!
    May the LORD fulfill all your petitions.

6   Now I know that the LORD saves His ¹anointed;
    He will answer him from His holy heaven
    With the saving strength of His right hand.

7   Some *trust* in chariots, and some in ᵃhorses;
    But we will remember the name of the LORD our God.
8   They have bowed down and fallen;
    But we have risen and stand upright.

9   Save, LORD!
    May the King answer us when we call.

PSALM 21

JOY IN THE SALVATION OF THE LORD

To the Chief Musician. A Psalm of David.

1   THE king shall have joy in Your strength, O LORD;
    And in Your salvation how greatly shall he rejoice!

19:10
ᵃPs. 119:72, 127;
Prov. 8:10, 11, 19
19:12
ᵃ[Ps. 51:1, 2]
19:13
ᵃNum. 15:30
ᵇPs. 119:133;
[Rom. 6:12–14]
19:14 ᵃPs. 51:15
ᵇPs. 31:5; Is. 47:4
20:4 ᵃPs. 21:2
20:7
ᵃDeut. 20:1;
Ps. 33:16, 17;
Prov. 21:31;
Is. 31:1

19:10 ¹*honey in the combs*   19:13 ¹Or *much*   19:14 ¹Lit. *set*
you on high   20:4 ¹*counsel*   20:6 ¹Commissioned one, Heb. *messiah*

2   You have given him his heart's desire,
      And have not withheld the [a]request of his lips.   *Selah*

3   For You meet him with the blessings of goodness;
      You set a crown of pure gold upon his head.

4   [a]He asked life from You, *and* You gave *it* to him—
      Length of days forever and ever.

5   His glory *is* great in Your salvation;
      Honor and majesty You have placed upon him.

6   For You have made him most blessed forever;
      [a]You have made him [1]exceedingly glad with Your
         presence.

7   For the king trusts in the LORD,
      And through the mercy of the Most High he shall not be
         [1]moved.

8   Your hand will find all Your enemies;
      Your right hand will find those who hate You.

9   You shall make them as a fiery oven in the time of Your
         anger;
      The LORD shall swallow them up in His wrath,
      And the fire shall devour them.

10   Their offspring You shall destroy from the earth,
      And their [1]descendants from among the sons of men.

11   For they intended evil against You;
      They devised a plot *which* they are not able *to*
         [a]*perform.*

12   Therefore You will make them turn their back;
      You will make ready *Your arrows* on Your string toward
         their faces.

13   Be exalted, O LORD, in Your own strength!
      We will sing and praise Your power.

PSALM 22

THE SUFFERING, PRAISE, AND POSTERITY
OF THE MESSIAH

To the Chief Musician. Set to [1]"The Deer
of the Dawn." A Psalm of David.

1   MY [a]God, My God, why have You forsaken Me?
      Why are You so far from helping Me,
      And from the words of My groaning?

2   O My God, I cry in the daytime, but You do not hear;
      And in the night season, and am not silent.

3   But You *are* holy,
      Enthroned in the [a]praises of Israel.

4   Our fathers trusted in You;
      They trusted, and You delivered them.

5   They cried to You, and were delivered;
      [a]They trusted in You, and were not ashamed.

6   But I *am* [a]a worm, and no man;
      [b]A reproach of men, and despised by the people.

7   [a]All those who see Me ridicule Me;
      They [1]shoot out the lip, they shake the head, *saying,*

21:2
[a]2 Sam. 7:26–29

21:4
[a]Ps. 61:5, 6;
133:3

21:6
[a]Ps. 16:11; 45:7

21:11 [a]Ps. 2:1–4

22:1
[a][Matt. 27:46;
Mark 15:34]

22:3
[a]Deut. 10:21;
Ps. 148:14

22:5 [a]Is. 49:23

22:6 [a]Job 25:6;
Is. 41:14
[b]Ps. 109:25;
[Is. 53:3];
Matt. 27:39–44

22:7
[a]Matt. 27:39;
Mark 15:29

21:6 [1]Lit. *joyful with gladness*   **21:7** [1]*shaken*   **21:10** [1]Lit. *seed*
22:title [1]Heb. *Aijeleth Hashahar*   **22:7** [1]Show contempt with their mouth

8 "He[a] [1]trusted in the LORD, let Him rescue Him;
   [b]Let Him deliver Him, since He delights in Him!"

9 [a]But You *are* He who took Me out of the womb;
   You made Me trust *while* on My mother's breasts.
10 I was cast upon You from birth.
   From My mother's womb
   [a]You *have been* My God.
11 Be not far from Me,
   For trouble *is* near;
   For *there is* none to help.

12 [a]Many bulls have surrounded Me;
   Strong *bulls* of [b]Bashan have encircled Me.
13 [a]They [1]gape at Me *with* their mouths,
   Like a raging and roaring lion.

14 I am poured out like water,
   [a]And all My bones are out of joint;
   My heart is like wax;
   It has melted [1]within Me.
15 [a]My strength is dried up like a potsherd,
   And [b]My tongue clings to My jaws;
   You have brought Me to the dust of death.

16 For dogs have surrounded Me;
   The congregation of the wicked has enclosed Me.
   [a]They[1] pierced My hands and My feet;
17 I can count all My bones.
   [a]They look *and* stare at Me.
18 [a]They divide My garments among them,
   And for My clothing they cast lots.

19 But You, O LORD, do not be far from Me;
   O My Strength, hasten to help Me!
20 Deliver Me from the sword,
   [a]My[1] precious *life* from the power of the dog.
21 [a]Save Me from the lion's mouth
   And from the horns of the wild oxen!

   [b]You have answered Me.

22 [a]I will declare Your name to [b]My brethren;
   In the midst of the assembly I will praise You.
23 [a]You who fear the LORD, praise Him!
   All you [1]descendants of Jacob, glorify Him,
   And fear Him, all you offspring of Israel!
24 For He has not despised nor abhorred the affliction of
      the afflicted;
   Nor has He hidden His face from Him;
   But [a]when He cried to Him, He heard.

25 [a]My praise *shall be* of You in the great assembly;
   [b]I will pay My vows before those who fear Him.
26 The poor shall eat and be satisfied;
   Those who seek Him will praise the LORD.
   Let your heart live forever!

22:8
[a]Matt. 27:43;
Luke 23:35
[b]Ps. 91:14

22:9
[a][Ps. 71:5, 6]

22:10
[a][Is. 46:3; 49:1];
Luke 1:35

22:12 [a]Ps. 22:21;
68:30
[b]Deut. 32:14

22:13
[a]Job 16:10;
Ps. 35:21;
Lam. 2:16; 3:46

22:14 [a]Ps. 31:10;
Dan. 5:6

22:15
[a]Prov. 17:22
[b]John 19:28

22:16 [a]Is. 53:7;
Matt. 27:35;
John 20:25

22:17
[a]Luke 23:27, 35

22:18
[a]Matt. 27:35;
Mark 15:24;
Luke 23:34;
John 19:24

22:20 [a]Ps. 35:17

22:21
[a]2 Tim. 4:17
[b]Is. 34:7

22:22
[a]Matt. 4:23;
Mark 1:21, 39;
Heb. 2:12
[b][Rom. 8:29]

22:23
[a]Ps. 135:19, 20

22:24 [a]Ps. 31:22;
Heb. 5:7

22:25
[a]Ps. 35:18;
40:9, 10
[b]Ps. 61:8;
Eccl. 5:4

22:8 [1]LXX, Syr., Vg. *hoped;* Tg. *praised*   22:13 [1]Lit. *have opened their mouths at Me*   22:14 [1]Lit. *in the midst of My bowels*   22:16 [1]So with some Heb. mss., LXX, Syr., Vg.; MT *Like a lion* instead of *They pierced*   22:20 [1]Lit. *My only one*   22:23 [1]Lit. *seed*

27 All the ends of the world
   Shall remember and turn to the LORD,
   And all the families of the ¹nations
   Shall worship before ²You.
28 ᵃFor the kingdom *is* the LORD's,
   And He rules over the nations.

29 ᵃAll the prosperous of the earth
   Shall eat and worship;
   ᵇAll those who go down to ¹the dust
   Shall bow before Him,
   Even he who cannot keep himself alive.

30 A posterity shall serve Him.
   It will be recounted of the Lord to the *next* generation,
31 They will come and declare His righteousness to a
   people who will be born,
   That He has done *this.*

PSALM 23

THE LORD THE SHEPHERD OF HIS PEOPLE

A Psalm of David.

1 THE LORD *is* ᵃmy shepherd;
   ᵇI shall not ¹want.
2 ᵃHe makes me to lie down in ¹green pastures;
   ᵇHe leads me beside the ²still waters.
3 He restores my soul;
   ᵃHe leads me in the paths of righteousness
   For His name's sake.
4 Yea, though I walk through the valley of ᵃthe shadow of
   death,
   ᵇI will fear no evil;
   ᶜFor You *are* with me;
   Your rod and Your staff, they comfort me.
5 You ᵃprepare a table before me in the presence of my
   enemies;
   You ᵇanoint my head with oil;
   My cup runs over.
6 Surely goodness and mercy shall follow me
   All the days of my life;
   And I will ¹dwell in the house of the LORD
   ²Forever.

PSALM 24

THE KING OF GLORY AND HIS KINGDOM

A Psalm of David.

1 THE ᵃearth *is* the LORD's, and all its fullness,
   The world and those who dwell therein,
2 For He has ᵃfounded it upon the seas,
   And established it upon the ¹waters.

22:28
ᵃ[Ps. 47:7];
Obad. 21;
[Zech. 14:9];
Matt. 6:13

22:29 ᵃPs. 17:10;
45:12; Hab. 1:16
ᵇPs. 28:1;
[Is. 26:19]

23:1 ᵃPs. 78:52;
80:1; [Is. 40:11];
Ezek. 34:11, 12;
[John 10:11;
1 Pet. 2:25;
Rev. 7:16, 17]
ᵇ[Ps. 34:9, 10;
Phil. 4:19]

23:2
ᵃPs. 65:11–13;
Ezek. 34:14
ᵇ[Rev. 7:17]

23:3
ᵃPs. 5:8; 31:3;
Prov. 8:20

23:4 ᵃJob 3:5;
10:21, 22;
24:17; Ps. 44:19
ᵇ[Ps. 3:6;
27:1] ᶜPs. 16:8;
[Is. 43:2]

23:5 ᵃPs. 104:15
ᵇPs. 92:10;
Luke 7:46

24:1
ᵃ1 Cor. 10:26, 28

24:2 ᵃPs. 89:11

22:27 ¹*Gentiles*   ²So with MT, LXX, Tg.; Arab., Syr., Vg. *Him*   **22:29** ¹Death
23:1 ¹*lack*   **23:2** ¹Lit. *pastures of tender grass*   ²Lit. *waters of rest*
23:6 ¹So with LXX, Syr., Tg., Vg.; MT *return*   ²Or *To the end of my days,* lit.
For length of days   **24:2** ¹Lit. *rivers*

3 ^aWho may ascend into the hill of the LORD?
   Or who may stand in His holy place?
4 He who has ^aclean hands and ^ba pure heart,
   Who has not lifted up his soul to an idol,
   Nor ^csworn deceitfully.
5 He shall receive blessing from the LORD,
   And righteousness from the God of his salvation.
6 This *is* Jacob, the generation of those who ^aseek Him,
   Who seek Your face. *Selah*

7 ^aLift up your heads, O you gates!
   And be lifted up, you everlasting doors!
   ^bAnd the King of glory shall come in.
8 Who *is* this King of glory?
   The LORD strong and mighty,
   The LORD mighty in ^abattle.
9 Lift up your heads, O you gates!
   Lift up, you everlasting doors!
   And the King of glory shall come in.
10 Who is this King of glory?
   The LORD of hosts,
   He *is* the King of glory. *Selah*

PSALM 25

A PLEA FOR DELIVERANCE AND FORGIVENESS

A Psalm of David.

1 TO ^aYou, O LORD, I lift up my soul.
2 O my God, I ^atrust in You;
   Let me not be ashamed;
   ^bLet not my enemies triumph over me.
3 Indeed, let no one who ¹waits on You be ashamed;
   Let those be ashamed who deal treacherously without
      cause.

4 ^aShow me Your ways, O LORD;
   Teach me Your paths.
5 Lead me in Your truth and teach me,
   For You *are* the God of my salvation;
   On You I wait all the day.

6 Remember, O LORD, ^aYour tender mercies and Your
      lovingkindnesses,
   For they *are* from of old.
7 Do not remember ^athe sins of my youth, nor my
      transgressions;
   ^bAccording to Your mercy remember me,
   For Your goodness' sake, O LORD.

8 Good and upright *is* the LORD;
   Therefore He teaches sinners in the way.
9 The humble He guides in justice,
   And the humble He teaches His way.
10 All the paths of the LORD *are* mercy and truth,
   To such as keep His covenant and His testimonies.
11 ^aFor Your name's sake, O LORD,
   Pardon my iniquity, for it *is* great.

25:3 ¹Waits for You in faith

24:3 ^aPs. 15:1–5
24:4 ^a[Job 17:9];
Ps. 26:6
^bPs. 51:10; 73:1;
[Matt. 5:8]
^cPs. 15:4

24:6 ^aPs. 27:4, 8
24:7 ^aPs. 118:20;
Is. 26:2
^bPs. 29:2, 9;
97:6; Hag. 2:7;
Acts 7:2;
[1 Cor. 2:8]
24:8
^aRev. 19:13–16
25:1 ^aPs. 86:4;
143:8
25:2 ^aPs. 34:8
^bPs. 13:4; 41:11
25:4 ^aEx. 33:13;
Ps. 5:8; 27:11;
86:11; 119:27;
143:8
25:6
^aPs. 103:17; 106:1
25:7 ^aJob 13:26;
[Jer. 3:25]
^bPs. 51:1
25:11 ^aPs. 31:3;
79:9; 109:21;
143:11

12 Who *is* the man that fears the LORD?
 ªHim shall ¹He teach in the way He chooses.
13 ªHe himself shall dwell in ¹prosperity,
 And ᵇhis descendants shall inherit the earth.
14 ªThe secret of the LORD *is* with those who fear Him,
 And He will show them His covenant.
15 ªMy eyes *are* ever toward the LORD,
 For He shall ¹pluck my feet out of the net.

16 ªTurn Yourself to me, and have mercy on me,
 For I *am* ¹desolate and afflicted.
17 The troubles of my heart have enlarged;
 Bring me out of my distresses!
18 ªLook on my affliction and my pain,
 And forgive all my sins.
19 Consider my enemies, for they are many;
 And they hate me with ¹cruel hatred.
20 Keep my soul, and deliver me;
 Let me not be ashamed, for I put my trust in You.
21 Let integrity and uprightness preserve me,
 For I wait for You.

22 ªRedeem Israel, O God,
 Out of all their troubles!

PSALM 26

A PRAYER FOR DIVINE SCRUTINY AND REDEMPTION

A Psalm of David.

1 VINDICATE ªme, O LORD,
 For I have ᵇwalked in my integrity.
 ᶜI have also trusted in the LORD;
 I shall not slip.
2 ªExamine me, O LORD, and ¹prove me;
 Try my mind and my heart.
3 For Your lovingkindness *is* before my eyes,
 And ªI have walked in Your truth.
4 I have not ªsat with idolatrous mortals,
 Nor will I go in with hypocrites.
5 I have ªhated the assembly of evildoers,
 And will not sit with the wicked.
6 I will wash my hands in innocence;
 So I will go about Your altar, O LORD,
7 That I may proclaim with the voice of thanksgiving,
 And tell of all Your wondrous works.
8 LORD, ªI have loved the habitation of Your house,
 And the place ¹where Your glory dwells.

9 ªDo¹ not gather my soul with sinners,
 Nor my life with bloodthirsty men,
10 In whose hands *is* a sinister scheme,
 And whose right hand is full of ªbribes.

11 But as for me, I will walk in my integrity;
 Redeem me and be merciful to me.

25:12
ª[Ps. 25:8; 37:23]

25:13
ª[Prov. 19:23]
ᵇPs. 37:11; 69:36;
Matt. 5:5

25:14
ª[Prov. 3:32;
John 7:17]

25:15
ª[Ps. 123:2;
141:8]

25:16 ªPs. 69:16

25:18
ª2 Sam. 16:12;
Ps. 31:7

25:22
ª[Ps. 130:8]

26:1 ªPs. 7:8
ᵇ2 Kin. 20:3;
[Prov. 20:7]
ᶜ[Ps. 13:5; 28:7]

26:2
ªPs. 17:3; 139:23

26:3
ª2 Kin. 20:3;
Ps. 86:11

26:4 ªPs. 1:1;
Jer. 15:17

26:5 ªPs. 31:6;
139:21

26:8 ªPs. 27:4;
84:1–4, 10

26:9 ªPs. 28:3

26:10
ª1 Sam. 8:3

25:12 ¹Or he   25:13 ¹Lit. *goodness*   25:15 ¹Lit. *bring out*   25:16 ¹*lonely*
25:19 ¹*violent hatred*   26:2 ¹*test me*   26:8 ¹Lit. *of the tabernacle of Your
glory*   26:9 ¹*Do not take away*

12 ᵃMy foot stands in an even place;
In the congregations I will bless the LORD.

PSALM 27

AN EXUBERANT DECLARATION OF FAITH

A Psalm of David.

1 THE LORD *is* my ᵃlight and my salvation;
Whom shall I fear?
The ᵇLORD *is* the strength of my life;
Of whom shall I be afraid?

2 When the wicked came against me
To ᵃeat¹ up my flesh,
My enemies and foes,
They stumbled and fell.

3 ᵃThough an army may encamp against me,
My heart shall not fear;
Though war may rise against me,
In this I *will be* confident.

4 ᵃOne *thing* I have desired of the LORD,
That will I seek:
That I may ᵇdwell in the house of the LORD
All the days of my life,
To behold the ¹beauty of the LORD,
And to inquire in His temple.

5 For ᵃin the time of trouble
He shall hide me in His pavilion;
In the secret place of His tabernacle
He shall hide me;
He shall ᵇset me high upon a rock.

6 And now ᵃmy head shall be ¹lifted up above my enemies
all around me;
Therefore I will offer sacrifices of ²joy in His tabernacle;
I will sing, yes, I will sing praises to the LORD.

7 Hear, O LORD, *when* I cry with my voice!
Have mercy also upon me, and answer me.

8 *When You said,* "Seek My face,"
My heart said to You, "Your face, LORD, I will seek."

9 ᵃDo not hide Your face from me;
Do not turn Your servant away in anger;
You have been my help;
Do not leave me nor forsake me,
O God of my salvation.

10 ᵃWhen my father and my mother forsake me,
Then the LORD will take care of me.

11 ᵃTeach me Your way, O LORD,
And lead me in a smooth path, because of my enemies.

12 Do not deliver me to the will of my adversaries;
For ᵃfalse witnesses have risen against me,
And such as breathe out violence.

13 *I would have lost heart,* unless I had believed
That I would see the goodness of the LORD
ᵃIn the land of the living.

26:12 ᵃPs. 40:2

27:1 ᵃPs. 18:28;
84:11; [Is. 60:19,
20; Mic. 7:8]
ᵇEx. 15:2;
Ps. 62:7; 118:14;
Is. 12:2; 33:2

27:2 ᵃPs. 14:4

27:3 ᵃPs. 3:6

27:4 ᵃPs. 26:8;
65:4 ᵇLuke 2:37

27:5
ᵃPs. 31:20; 91:1
ᵇPs. 40:2

27:6 ᵃPs. 3:3

27:9
ᵃPs. 69:17; 143:7

27:10 ᵃIs. 49:15

27:11 ᵃPs. 25:4;
86:11; 119:33

27:12
ᵃDeut. 19:18;
Ps. 35:11;
Matt. 26:60;
Mark 14:56;
John 19:33

27:13
ᵃJob 28:13;
Ps. 52:5; 116:9;
142:5; Is. 38:11;
Jer. 11:19;
Ezek. 26:20

27:2 ¹*devour*   27:4 ¹*delightfulness*   27:6 ¹Lifted up in honor   ²*joyous shouts*

14 ^aWait[1] on the LORD;
  Be of good courage,
  And He shall strengthen your heart;
  Wait, I say, on the LORD!

PSALM 28

REJOICING IN ANSWERED PRAYER

A Psalm of David.

1 TO You I will cry, O LORD my Rock:
  ^aDo not be silent to me,
  ^bLest, if You *are* silent to me,
  I become like those who go down to the pit.
2 Hear the voice of my supplications
  When I cry to You,
  ^aWhen I lift up my hands ^btoward Your holy sanctuary.
3 Do not [1]take me away with the wicked
  And with the workers of iniquity,
  ^aWho speak peace to their neighbors,
  But evil *is* in their hearts.
4 ^aGive them according to their deeds,
  And according to the wickedness of their endeavors;
  Give them according to the work of their hands;
  Render to them what they deserve.
5 Because ^athey do not regard the works of the LORD,
  Nor the operation of His hands,
  He shall destroy them
  And not build them up.
6 Blessed *be* the LORD,
  Because He has heard the voice of my supplications!
7 The LORD *is* ^amy strength and my shield;
  My heart ^btrusted in Him, and I am helped;
  Therefore my heart greatly rejoices,
  And with my song I will praise Him.
8 The LORD *is* [1]their strength,
  And He *is* the ^asaving refuge of His [2]anointed.
9 Save Your people,
  And bless ^aYour inheritance;
  Shepherd them also,
  ^bAnd bear them up forever.

PSALM 29

PRAISE TO GOD IN HIS HOLINESS AND MAJESTY

A Psalm of David.

1 GIVE[1] ^aunto the LORD, O you mighty ones,
  Give unto the LORD glory and strength.
2 [1]Give unto the LORD the glory [2]due to His name;
  Worship the LORD in ^athe [3]beauty of holiness.
3 The voice of the LORD *is* over the waters;
  ^aThe God of glory thunders;
  The LORD *is* over many waters.

Cross references (margin)

27:14 ^aPs. 25:3; 37:34; 40:1; 62:5; 130:5; Prov. 20:22; Is. 25:9; [Hab. 2:3]

28:1 ^aPs. 35:22; 39:12; 83:1 ^bPs. 88:4; 143:7; Prov. 1:12

28:2 ^aPs. 5:7 ^bPs. 138:2

28:3 ^aPs. 12:2; 55:21; 62:4; Jer. 9:8

28:4 ^a[Ps. 62:12]; 2 Tim. 4:14; [Rev. 18:6; 22:12]

28:5 ^aIs. 5:12

28:7 ^aPs. 18:2; 59:17 ^bPs. 13:5; 112:7

28:8 ^aPs. 20:6

28:9 ^a[Deut. 9:29]; 32:9; 1 Kin. 8:51; Ps. 33:12]; 106:40 ^bDeut. 1:31; Is. 63:9

29:1 ^a1 Chr. 16:28, 29

29:2 ^a2 Chr. 20:21; Ps. 110:3

29:3 ^a[Job 37:4, 5]; Ps. 18:13; Acts 7:2

27:14 [1]Wait in faith 28:3 [1]*drag* 28:8 [1]So with MT, Tg.; LXX, Syr., Vg. *the strength of His people* [2]Commissioned one, Heb. *messiah* 29:1 [1]*Ascribe* 29:2 [1]*Ascribe* [2]Lit. *of His name* [3]*majesty*

4 The voice of the LORD *is* powerful;
The voice of the LORD *is* full of majesty.

5 The voice of the LORD breaks ªthe cedars,
Yes, the LORD splinters the cedars of Lebanon.

6 ªHe makes them also skip like a calf,
Lebanon and ᵇSirion like a young wild ox.

7 The voice of the LORD ¹divides the flames of fire.

8 The voice of the LORD shakes the wilderness;
The LORD shakes the Wilderness of ªKadesh.

9 The voice of the LORD makes the ªdeer give birth,
And strips the forests bare;
And in His temple everyone says, "Glory!"

10 The ªLORD sat *enthroned* at the Flood,
And ᵇthe LORD sits as King forever.

11 ªThe LORD will give strength to His people;
The LORD will bless His people with peace.

PSALM 30

THE BLESSEDNESS OF ANSWERED PRAYER

A Psalm. A Song ªat the dedication of the house of David.

1 I WILL extol You, O LORD, for You have ªlifted me up,
And have not let my foes ᵇrejoice over me.

2 O LORD my God, I cried out to You,
And You ªhealed me.

3 O LORD, ªYou brought my soul up from the grave;
You have kept me alive, ¹that I should not go down to
the pit.

4 ªSing praise to the LORD, you saints of His,
And give thanks at the remembrance of ¹His holy name.

5 For ªHis anger *is but for* a moment,
ᵇHis favor *is for* life;
Weeping may endure for a night,
But ¹joy *comes* in the morning.

6 Now in my prosperity I said,
"I shall never be ¹moved."

7 LORD, by Your favor You have made my mountain stand
strong;
ªYou hid Your face, *and* I was troubled.

8 I cried out to You, O LORD;
And to the LORD I made supplication:

9 "What profit *is there* in my blood,
When I go down to the pit?
ªWill the dust praise You?
Will it declare Your truth?

10 Hear, O LORD, and have mercy on me;
LORD, be my helper!"

11 ªYou have turned for me my mourning into dancing;
You have put off ¹my sackcloth and clothed me with
gladness,

29:5 ªJudg. 9:15; 1 Kin. 5:6; Ps. 104:16; Is. 2:13; 14:8

29:6 ªPs. 114:4 ᵇDeut. 3:9

29:8 ªNum. 13:26

29:9 ªJob 39:1

29:10 ªGen. 6:17; Job 38:8, 25 ᵇPs. 10:16

29:11 ªPs. 28:8; 68:35; [Is. 40:29]

30:title ªDeut. 20:5

30:1 ªPs. 28:9 ᵇPs. 25:2

30:2 ªPs. 6:2; 103:3; [Is. 53:5]

30:3 ªPs. 86:13

30:4 ªPs. 97:12

30:5 ªPs. 103:9; Is. 26:20; 54:7, 8 ᵇPs. 63:3

30:7 ª[Deut. 31:17; Ps. 104:29; 143:7]

30:9 ª[Ps. 6:5]

30:11 ªEccl. 3:4; Is. 61:3; Jer. 31:4

29:7 ¹*stirs up*, lit. *hews out* 30:3 ¹So with Qr., Tg.; Kt., LXX, Syr., Vg. *from those who descend to the pit* 30:4 ¹Or *His holiness* 30:5 ¹*a shout of joy* 30:6 ¹*shaken* 30:11 ¹The sackcloth of my mourning

12 To the end that *my* ¹glory may sing praise to You and not
be silent.
O LORD my God, I will give thanks to You forever.

PSALM 31

THE LORD A FORTRESS IN ADVERSITY

To the Chief Musician. A Psalm of David.

1 IN ᵃYou, O LORD, I ¹put my trust;
Let me never be ashamed;
Deliver me in Your righteousness.
2 ᵃBow down Your ear to me,
Deliver me speedily;
Be my rock of ¹refuge,
A ²fortress of defense to save me.
3 ᵃFor You *are* my rock and my fortress;
Therefore, ᵇfor Your name's sake,
Lead me and guide me.
4 Pull me out of the net which they have secretly laid for
me,
For You *are* my strength.
5 ᵃInto Your hand I commit my spirit;
You have redeemed me, O LORD God of ᵇtruth.
6 I have hated those ᵃwho regard useless idols;
But I trust in the LORD.
7 I will be glad and rejoice in Your mercy,
For You have considered my trouble;
You have ᵃknown my soul in ¹adversities,
8 And have not ᵃshut¹ me up into the hand of the enemy;
ᵇYou have set my feet in a wide place.

9 Have mercy on me, O LORD, for I am in trouble;
ᵃMy eye wastes away with grief,
Yes, my soul and my ¹body!
10 For my life is spent with grief,
And my years with sighing;
My strength fails because of my iniquity,
And my bones waste away.
11 ᵃI am a ¹reproach among all my enemies,
But ᵇespecially among my neighbors,
And *am* repulsive to my acquaintances;
ᶜThose who see me outside flee from me.
12 ᵃI am forgotten like a dead man, out of mind;
I am like a ¹broken vessel.
13 ᵃFor I hear the slander of many;
ᵇFear *is* on every side;
While they ᶜtake counsel together against me,
They scheme to take away my life.

14 But as for me, I trust in You, O LORD;
I say, "You *are* my God."
15 My times *are* in Your ᵃhand;
Deliver me from the hand of my enemies,
And from those who persecute me.

31:1 ᵃPs. 22:5

31:2 ᵃPs. 17:6;
71:2; 86:1; 102:2

31:3 ᵃ[Ps. 18:2]
ᵇPs. 23:3; 25:11

31:5 ᵃLuke 23:46
ᵇ[Deut. 32:4];
Ps. 71:22

31:6 ᵃJon. 2:8

31:7
ᵃ[John 10:27]

31:8
ᵃ[Deut. 32:30];
Ps. 37:33
ᵇ[Ps. 4:1; 18:19]

31:9 ᵃPs. 6:7

31:11 ᵃ[Is. 53:4]
ᵇJob 19:13;
Ps. 38:11;
88:8, 18
ᶜPs. 64:8

31:12
ᵃPs. 88:4, 5

31:13 ᵃPs. 50:20;
Jer. 20:10
ᵇLam. 2:22
ᶜPs. 62:4;
Matt. 27:1

31:15
ᵃ[Job 14:5; 24:1]

30:12 ¹*soul*   31:1 ¹*have taken refuge*   31:2 ¹*strength*   ²Lit. *house of
fortresses*   31:7 ¹*troubles*   31:8 ¹*given me over*   31:9 ¹Lit. *belly*
31:11 ¹*despised thing*   31:12 ¹Lit. *perishing*

16 ^aMake Your face shine upon Your servant;
   Save me for Your mercies' sake.
17 ^aDo not let me be ashamed, O LORD, for I have called
      upon You;
   Let the wicked be ashamed;
   ^bLet them be silent in the grave.
18 ^aLet the lying lips be put to silence,
   Which ^bspeak insolent things proudly and
      contemptuously against the righteous.

19 ^aOh, how great *is* Your goodness,
   Which You have laid up for those who fear You,
   Which You have prepared for those who trust in You
   In the presence of the sons of men!
20 ^aYou shall hide them in the secret place of Your presence
   From the plots of man;
   ^bYou shall keep them secretly in a ¹pavilion
   From the strife of tongues.

21 Blessed *be* the LORD,
   For ^aHe has shown me His marvelous kindness in a
      ¹strong city!
22 For I said in my haste,
   "I am cut off from before Your eyes";
   Nevertheless You heard the voice of my supplications
   When I cried out to You.

23 Oh, love the LORD, all you His saints!
   For the LORD preserves the faithful,
   And fully repays the proud person.
24 ^aBe of good courage,
   And He shall strengthen your heart,
   All you who hope in the LORD.

PSALM 32

THE JOY OF FORGIVENESS

A Psalm of David. A ¹Contemplation.

1 BLESSED *is he whose* ^atransgression *is* forgiven,
   Whose sin *is* covered.
2 Blessed *is* the man to whom the LORD ^adoes not ¹impute
      iniquity,
   And ^bin whose spirit *there is* no deceit.

3 When I kept silent, my bones grew old
   Through my groaning all the day long.
4 For day and night Your ^ahand was heavy upon me;
   My vitality was turned into the drought of summer. *Selah*
5 I acknowledged my sin to You,
   And my iniquity I have not hidden.
   ^aI said, "I will confess my transgressions to the LORD,"
   And You forgave the iniquity of my sin. *Selah*

6 ^aFor this cause everyone who is godly shall ^bpray to You
   In a time when You may be found;
   Surely in a flood of great waters
   They shall not come near him.

31:16
^aPs. 4:6; 80:3

31:17
^aPs. 25:2, 20
^b[1 Sam. 2:9];
Ps. 94:17; 115:17

31:18
^aPs. 109:2; 120:2
^b[1 Sam. 2:3];
Ps. 94:4;
[Jude 15]

31:19 ^aPs. 145:7;
[Rom. 2:4;
11:22]

31:20
^a[Ps. 27:5; 32:7]
^bJob 5:21

31:21 ^a[Ps. 17:7]

31:24
^a[Ps. 27:14]

32:1
^a[Ps. 85:2;
103:3];
Rom. 4:7, 8

32:2
^a[2 Cor. 5:19]
^bJohn 1:47

32:4
^a1 Sam. 5:6;
Ps. 38:2; 39:10

32:5
^a2 Sam. 12:13;
Ps. 38:18;
[Prov. 28:13;
1 John 1:9]

32:6
^a[1 Tim. 1:16]
^bPs. 69:13;
Is. 55:6

31:20 ¹shelter   31:21 ¹fortified   32:title ¹Heb. *Maschil*   32:2 ¹*charge his*
account with

7 [a]You *are* my hiding place;
   You shall preserve me from trouble;
   You shall surround me with [b]songs of deliverance. *Selah*

8 I will instruct you and teach you in the way you
       should go;
   I will guide you with My eye.

9 Do not be like the [a]horse *or* like the mule,
   Which have no understanding,
   Which must be harnessed with bit and bridle,
   Else they will not come near you.

10 [a]Many sorrows *shall be* to the wicked;
    But [b]he who trusts in the LORD, mercy shall surround
        him.

11 [a]Be glad in the LORD and rejoice, you righteous;
    And shout for joy, all *you* upright in heart!

PSALM 33

THE SOVEREIGNTY OF THE LORD IN CREATION
AND HISTORY

1 REJOICE [a]in the LORD, O you righteous!
   For praise from the upright is beautiful.

2 Praise the LORD with the harp;
   [1]Make melody to Him with an instrument of ten strings.

3 Sing to Him a new song;
   Play skillfully with a shout of joy.

4 For the word of the LORD *is* right,
   And all His work *is done* in truth.

5 He loves righteousness and justice;
   The earth is full of the goodness of the LORD.

6 [a]By the word of the LORD the heavens were made,
   And all the [b]host of them [c]by the breath of His mouth.

7 [a]He gathers the waters of the sea together [1]as a heap;
   He lays up the deep in storehouses.

8 Let all the earth fear the LORD;
   Let all the inhabitants of the world stand in awe of Him.

9 For [a]He spoke, and it was *done;*
   He commanded, and it stood fast.

10 [a]The LORD brings the counsel of the nations to nothing;
    He makes the plans of the peoples of no effect.

11 [a]The counsel of the LORD stands forever,
    The plans of His heart to all generations.

12 Blessed *is* the nation whose God *is* the LORD,
    The people He has [a]chosen as His own inheritance.

13 [a]The LORD looks from heaven;
    He sees all the sons of men.

14 From the place of His dwelling He looks
    On all the inhabitants of the earth;

15 He fashions their hearts individually;
    [a]He [1]considers all their works.

16 [a]No king *is* saved by the multitude of an army;
    A mighty man is not delivered by great strength.

32:7 [a]Ps. 9:9
[b]Ex. 15:1;
Judg. 5:1;
[Ps. 40:3]
32:9 [a]Prov. 26:3
32:10 [a]Ps. 16:4;
[Prov. 13:21;
Rom. 2:9]
[b][Ps. 5:11, 12];
Prov. 16:20
32:11 [a]Ps. 64:10;
68:3; 97:12
33:1
[a]Ps. 32:11; 97:12;
Phil. 3:1; 4:4
33:6
[a]Gen. 1:6, 7;
Ps. 148:5;
[Heb. 11:3;
2 Pet. 3:5]
[b]Gen. 2:1
[c][Job 26:13]
33:7 [a]Gen. 1:9;
Job 26:10; 38:8
33:9 [a]Gen. 1:3;
Ps. 148:5
33:10
[a][Ps. 2:1–3];
Is. 8:10; 19:3
33:11
[a][Job 23:13];
Prov. 19:21]
33:12 [a][Ex. 19:5;
Deut. 7:6];
Ps. 28:9
33:13
[a]Job 28:24;
[Ps. 14:2]
33:15
[a][2 Chr. 16:9];
Job 34:21;
[Jer. 32:19]
33:16
[a]Ps. 44:6; 60:11;
[Jer. 9:23, 24]

33:2 [1]Lit. *Sing to Him*   33:7 [1]LXX, Tg., Vg. *in a vessel*   33:15 [1]*understands*

17 ᵃA horse *is* a ¹vain hope for safety;
    Neither shall it deliver *any* by its great strength.

18 ᵃBehold, the eye of the LORD *is* on those who fear Him,
    On those who hope in His mercy,
19 To deliver their soul from death,
    And ᵃto keep them alive in famine.

20 Our soul waits for the LORD;
    He *is* our help and our shield.
21 For our heart shall rejoice in Him,
    Because we have trusted in His holy name.
22 Let Your mercy, O LORD, be upon us,
    Just as we hope in You.

PSALM 34

THE HAPPINESS OF THOSE WHO TRUST IN GOD

A Psalm of David ᵃwhen he pretended madness before
Abimelech, who drove him away, and he departed.

1 I WILL ᵃbless the LORD at all times;
    His praise *shall* continually *be* in my mouth.
2 My soul shall make its boast in the LORD;
    The humble shall hear *of it* and be glad.
3 Oh, magnify the LORD with me,
    And let us exalt His name together.

4 I ᵃsought the LORD, and He heard me,
    And delivered me from all my fears.
5 They looked to Him and were radiant,
    And their faces were not ashamed.
6 This poor man cried out, and the LORD heard *him*,
    And saved him out of all his troubles.
7 ᵃThe ¹angel of the LORD ᵇencamps all around those who
        fear Him,
    And delivers them.

8 Oh, ᵃtaste and see that the LORD *is* good;
    ᵇBlessed *is* the man *who* trusts in Him!
9 Oh, fear the LORD, you His saints!
    There is no ¹want to those who fear Him.
10 The young lions lack and suffer hunger;
    ᵃBut those who seek the LORD shall not lack any good
        thing.

11 Come, you children, listen to me;
    ᵃI will teach you the fear of the LORD.
12 ᵃWho *is* the man *who* desires life,
    And loves *many* days, that he may see good?
13 Keep your tongue from evil,
    And your lips from speaking ᵃdeceit.
14 ᵃDepart from evil and do good;
    ᵇSeek peace and pursue it.

15 ᵃThe eyes of the LORD *are* on the righteous,
    And His ears *are open* to their cry.
16 ᵃThe face of the LORD *is* against those who do evil,
    ᵇTo ¹cut off the remembrance of them from the earth.

33:17 ᵃ[Ps. 20:7;
147:10;
Prov. 21:31]

33:18
ᵃ[Job 36:7];
Ps. 32:8; 34:15;
[1 Pet. 3:12]

33:19 ᵃJob 5:20;
Ps. 37:19

34:title
ᵃ1 Sam. 21:10–15

34:1
ᵃ[Eph. 5:20;
1 Thess. 5:18]

34:4
ᵃ[2 Chr. 15:2;
Ps. 9:10;
Matt. 7:7;
Luke 11:9]

34:7 ᵃ[Ps. 91:11];
Dan. 6:22
ᵇ2 Kin. 6:17

34:8
ᵃPs. 119:103;
[Heb. 6:5];
1 Pet. 2:3
ᵇPs. 2:12

34:10
ᵃ[Ps. 84:11]

34:11 ᵃPs. 32:8

34:12
ᵃ[1 Pet. 3:10–12]

34:13
ᵃ[Eph. 4:25]

34:14 ᵃPs. 37:27;
Is. 1:16, 17
ᵇ[Rom. 14:19;
Heb. 12:14]

34:15 ᵃJob 36:7;
[Ps. 33:18]

34:16 ᵃLev. 17:10;
Jer. 44:11;
Amos 9:4
ᵇJob 18:17;
Ps. 9:6; 109:15;
[Prov. 10:7]

33:17 ¹*false*   34:7 ¹*Or Angel*   34:9 ¹*lack*   34:16 ¹*destroy*

17 *The righteous* cry out, and ᵃthe LORD hears,
And delivers them out of all their troubles.
18 ᵃThe LORD *is* near ᵇto those who have a broken heart,
And saves such as ¹have a contrite spirit.

19 ᵃMany *are* the afflictions of the righteous,
ᵇBut the LORD delivers him out of them all.
20 He guards all his bones;
ᵃNot one of them is broken.
21 ᵃEvil shall slay the wicked,
And those who hate the righteous shall be ¹condemned.
22 The LORD ᵃredeems the soul of His servants,
And none of those who trust in Him shall be condemned.

PSALM 35

THE LORD THE AVENGER OF HIS PEOPLE

A Psalm of David.

1 PLEAD¹ *my cause*, O LORD, with those who strive with me;
Fight against those who fight against me.
2 Take hold of shield and ¹buckler,
And stand up for my help.
3 Also draw out the spear,
And stop those who pursue me.
Say to my soul,
"I *am* your salvation."

4 ᵃLet those be put to shame and brought to dishonor
Who seek after my life;
Let those be ᵇturned back and brought to confusion
Who plot my hurt.
5 ᵃLet them be like chaff before the wind,
And let the ¹angel of the LORD chase *them*.
6 Let their way be ᵃdark and slippery,
And let the angel of the LORD pursue them.
7 For without cause they have ᵃhidden their net for me *in* a pit,
Which they have dug without cause for my life.
8 ¹Let ᵃdestruction come upon him unexpectedly,
And let his net that he has hidden catch himself;
Into that very destruction let him fall.

9 And my soul shall be joyful in the LORD;
It shall rejoice in His salvation.
10 ᵃAll my bones shall say,
"LORD, ᵇwho *is* like You,
Delivering the poor from him who is too strong for him,
Yes, the poor and the needy from him who plunders him?"

11 Fierce witnesses rise up;
They ask me *things* that I do not know.
12 ᵃThey reward me evil for good,
To the sorrow of my soul.

34:17 ᵃPs. 34:6; 145:19
34:18 ᵃ[Ps. 145:18] ᵇPs. 51:17; [Is. 57:15]
34:19 ᵃProv. 24:16 ᵇPs. 34:4, 6, 17
34:20 ᵃJohn 19:33, 36
34:21 ᵃPs. 94:23; 140:11; Prov. 24:16
34:22 ᵃ1 Kin. 1:29
35:4 ᵃPs. 40:14, 15; 70:2, 3 ᵇPs. 129:5
35:5 ᵃJob 21:18; Ps. 83:13; Is. 29:5
35:6 ᵃPs. 73:18; Jer. 23:12
35:7 ᵃPs. 9:15
35:8 ᵃ[Ps. 55:23]; Is. 47:11; [1 Thess. 5:3]
35:10 ᵃPs. 51:8 ᵇ[Ex. 15:11]; Ps. 71:19; 86:8; [Mic. 7:18]
35:12 ᵃPs. 38:20; 109:5; Jer. 18:20; John 10:32

34:18 ¹*are crushed in spirit* 34:21 ¹*held guilty* 35:1 ¹*Contend for me* 35:2 ¹*A small shield* 35:5 ¹*Or Angel* 35:8 ¹Lit. *Let destruction he does not know come upon him,*

13 But as for me, ^awhen they were sick,
My clothing *was* sackcloth;
I humbled myself with fasting;
And my prayer would return to my own ¹heart.
14 I paced about as though *he were* my friend *or* brother;
I bowed down ¹heavily, as one who mourns *for his*
mother.

15 But in my ¹adversity they rejoiced
And gathered together;
Attackers gathered against me,
And I did not know *it;*
They tore *at me* and did not cease;
16 With ungodly mockers at feasts
They gnashed at me with their teeth.

17 Lord, how long will You ^alook on?
Rescue me from their destructions,
My precious *life* from the lions.
18 I will give You thanks in the great assembly;
I will praise You among ¹many people.

19 ^aLet them not rejoice over me who are wrongfully my
enemies;
Nor let them wink with the eye who hate me without a
cause.
20 For they do not speak peace,
But they devise deceitful matters
Against *the* quiet ones in the land.
21 They also opened their mouth wide against me,
And said, "Aha, aha!
Our eyes have seen *it.*"

22 *This* You have seen, O LORD;
Do not keep silence.
O Lord, do not be far from me.
23 Stir up Yourself, and awake to my vindication,
To my cause, my God and my Lord.
24 Vindicate me, O LORD my God, according to Your
righteousness;
And let them not rejoice over me.
25 Let them not say in their hearts, "Ah, so we would
have it!"
Let them not say, "We have swallowed him up."

26 Let them be ashamed and brought to mutual
confusion
Who rejoice at my hurt;
Let them be ^aclothed with shame and dishonor
Who exalt themselves against me.

27 ^aLet them shout for joy and be glad,
Who favor my righteous cause;
And let them say continually,
"Let the LORD be magnified,
Who has pleasure in the prosperity of His servant."
28 And my tongue shall speak of Your righteousness
And of Your praise all the day long.

35:13
^aJob 30:25

35:17 ^aPs. 13:1;
[Hab. 1:13]

35:19 ^aPs. 69:4;
109:3;
Lam. 3:52;
[John 15:25]

35:26
^aPs. 109:29

35:27
^aRom. 12:15

35:13 ¹Lit. *bosom*   35:14 ¹*in mourning*   35:15 ¹*limping, stumbling*
35:18 ¹*a mighty*

PSALM 36

MAN'S WICKEDNESS AND GOD'S PERFECTIONS

*To the Chief Musician. A Psalm of David
the servant of the LORD.*

1 AN oracle within my heart concerning the transgression
　　of the wicked:
　ᵃ*There is* no fear of God before his eyes.
2 For he flatters himself in his own eyes,
　　When he finds out his iniquity *and* when he hates.
3 The words of his mouth *are* wickedness and deceit;
　ᵃHe has ceased to be wise *and* to do good.
4 ᵃHe devises wickedness on his bed;
　　He sets himself ᵇin a way *that is* not good;
　　He does not ¹abhor ᶜevil.

5 Your mercy, O LORD, *is* in the heavens;
　　Your faithfulness *reaches* to the clouds.
6 Your righteousness *is* like the ¹great mountains;
　ᵃYour judgments *are* a great deep;
　　O LORD, You preserve man and beast.

7 How precious *is* Your lovingkindness, O God!
　　Therefore the children of men ᵃput their trust under the
　　　shadow of Your wings.
8 ᵃThey are abundantly satisfied with the fullness of Your
　　　house,
　　And You give them drink from ᵇthe river of Your
　　　pleasures.
9 ᵃFor with You *is* the fountain of life;
　ᵇIn Your light we see light.

10 Oh, continue Your lovingkindness to those who know
　　　You,
　　And Your righteousness to the upright in heart.
11 Let not the foot of pride come against me,
　　And let not the hand of the wicked drive me away.
12 There the workers of iniquity have fallen;
　　They have been cast down and are not able to rise.

PSALM 37

THE HERITAGE OF THE RIGHTEOUS AND
THE CALAMITY OF THE WICKED

A Psalm of David.

1 DOᵃ not fret because of evildoers,
　　Nor be envious of the workers of iniquity.
2 For they shall soon be cut down ᵃlike the grass,
　　And wither as the green herb.

3 Trust in the LORD, and do good;
　　Dwell in the land, and feed on His faithfulness.
4 ᵃDelight yourself also in the LORD,
　　And He shall give you the desires of your ᵇheart.

5 ᵃCommit¹ your way to the LORD,
　　Trust also in Him,
　　And He shall bring *it* to pass.

36:1 ᵃRom. 3:18
36:3 ᵃPs. 94:8;
Jer. 4:22
36:4 ᵃProv. 4:16;
[Mic. 2:1]
ᵇIs. 65:2
ᶜ[Ps. 52:3;
Rom. 12:9]
36:6 ᵃJob 11:8;
Ps. 77:19;
[Rom. 11:33]
36:7 ᵃRuth 2:12;
Ps. 17:8; 57:1;
91:4
36:8 ᵃPs. 63:5;
65:4; Is. 25:6;
Jer. 31:12–14
ᵇPs. 46:4;
Rev. 22:1
36:9 ᵃ[Jer. 2:13;
John 4:10, 14]
ᵇ[1 Pet. 2:9]
37:1 ᵃPs. 73:3;
[Prov. 23:17;
24:19]
37:2 ᵃJob 14:2;
Ps. 90:5, 6; 92:7;
James 1:11
37:4 ᵃJob 22:26;
Ps. 94:19;
Is. 58:14
ᵇPs. 21:2; 145:19;
[Matt. 7:7, 8]
37:5 ᵃ[Ps. 55:22;
Prov. 16:3;
1 Pet. 5:7]

36:4 ¹*reject, loathe*　36:6 ¹Lit. *mountains of God*　37:5 ¹Lit. *Roll off onto*

6 aHe shall bring forth your righteousness as the light,
And your justice as the noonday.

7 Rest in the LORD, aand wait patiently for Him;
Do not fret because of him who bprospers in his way,
Because of the man who brings wicked schemes to pass.
8 aCease from anger, and forsake wrath;
bDo not fret—it only *causes* harm.

9 For evildoers shall be 1cut off;
But those who wait on the LORD,
They shall ainherit the earth.
10 For ayet a little while and the wicked *shall be* no *more;*
Indeed, byou will look carefully for his place,
But it *shall be* no *more.*
11 aBut the meek shall inherit the earth,
And shall delight themselves in the abundance of
peace.

12 The wicked plots against the just,
aAnd gnashes at him with his teeth.
13 aThe Lord laughs at him,
For He sees that bhis day is coming.
14 The wicked have drawn the sword
And have bent their bow,
To cast down the poor and needy,
To slay those who are of upright conduct.
15 Their sword shall enter their own heart,
And their bows shall be broken.

16 aA little that a righteous man has
Is better than the riches of many wicked.
17 For the arms of the wicked shall be broken,
But the LORD upholds the righteous.

18 The LORD knows the days of the upright,
And their inheritance shall be forever.
19 They shall not be ashamed in the evil time,
And in the days of famine they shall be satisfied.
20 But the wicked shall perish;
And the enemies of the LORD,
Like the splendor of the meadows, shall vanish.
Into smoke they shall vanish away.

21 The wicked borrows and does not repay,
But athe righteous shows mercy and gives.
22 aFor *those* blessed by Him shall inherit the earth,
But *those* cursed by Him shall be 1cut off.

23 aThe steps of a *good* man are 1ordered by the LORD,
And He delights in his way.
24 aThough he fall, he shall not be utterly cast down;
For the LORD upholds *him with* His hand.

25 I have been young, and *now* am old;
Yet I have not seen the righteous forsaken,
Nor his descendants begging bread.
26 aHe is 1ever merciful, and lends;
And his descendants *are* blessed.

37:6 aJob 11:17;
[Is. 58:8, 10]

37:7 aPs. 40:1;
62:5;
[Lam. 3:26]
b[Ps. 73:3–12]

37:8
a[Eph. 4:26]
bPs. 73:3

37:9 aPs. 25:13;
Prov. 2:21;
[Is. 57:13; 60:21;
Matt. 5:5]

37:10
a[Heb. 10:37]
bJob 7:10;
Ps. 37:35, 36

37:11
a[Matt. 5:5]

37:12 aPs. 35:16

37:13
aPs. 2:4; 59:8
b1 Sam. 26:10;
Job 18:20

37:16
aProv. 15:16;
16:8; [1 Tim. 6:6]

37:21
aPs. 112:5, 9

37:22
a[Prov. 3:33]

37:23
a[1 Sam. 2:9];
Ps. 40:2; 66:9;
119:5

37:24
aProv. 24:16

37:26
a[Deut. 15:8];
Ps. 37:21

37:9 1destroyed   37:22 1destroyed   37:23 1established   37:26 1Lit. all
the day

27 Depart from evil, and do good;
  And dwell forevermore.
28 For the LORD loves justice,
  And does not forsake His saints;
  They are preserved forever,
  But the descendants of the wicked shall be cut off.
29 ªThe righteous shall inherit the land,
  And dwell in it forever.

30 ªThe mouth of the righteous speaks wisdom,
  And his tongue talks of justice.
31 The law of his God *is* in his heart;
  None of his steps shall ¹slide.

32 The wicked ªwatches the righteous,
  And seeks to slay him.
33 The LORD ªwill not leave him in his hand,
  Nor condemn him when he is judged.

34 ªWait on the LORD,
  And keep His way,
  And He shall exalt you to inherit the land;
  When the wicked are cut off, you shall see *it.*
35 I have seen the wicked in great power,
  And spreading himself like a native green tree.
36 Yet ¹he passed away, and behold, he *was* no *more;*
  Indeed I sought him, but he could not be found.

37 Mark the blameless *man,* and observe the upright;
  For the future of *that* man *is* peace.
38 ªBut the transgressors shall be destroyed together;
  The future of the wicked shall be cut off.
39 But the salvation of the righteous *is* from the LORD;
  He is their strength ªin the time of trouble.
40 And ªthe LORD shall help them and deliver them;
  He shall deliver them from the wicked,
  And save them,
  ᵇBecause they trust in Him.

PSALM 38

PRAYER IN TIME OF CHASTENING

A Psalm of David. ªTo bring to remembrance.

1 O LORD, do not ªrebuke me in Your wrath,
  Nor chasten me in Your hot displeasure!
2 For Your arrows pierce me deeply,
  And Your hand presses me down.

3 *There is* no soundness in my flesh
  Because of Your anger,
  Nor *any* health in my bones
  Because of my sin.
4 For my iniquities have gone over my head;
  Like a heavy burden they are too heavy for me.
5 My wounds are foul *and* festering
  Because of my foolishness.

37:29 ªPs. 37:9; Prov. 2:21
37:30 ª[Matt. 12:35]
37:32 ªPs. 10:8; 17:11
37:33 ªPs. 31:8; [2 Pet. 2:9]
37:34 ªPs. 27:14; 37:9
37:38 ª[Ps. 1:4–6; 37:20, 28]
37:39 ªPs. 9:9; 37:19
37:40 ªPs. 22:4; Is. 31:5; Dan. 3:17; 6:23 ᵇ1 Chr. 5:20; Ps. 34:22
38:title ªPs. 70:title
38:1 ªPs. 6:1

37:31 ¹slip   37:36 ¹So with MT, LXX, Tg.; Syr., Vg. *I passed by*

6 I am ¹troubled, I am bowed down greatly;
  I go mourning all the day long.
7 For my loins are full of inflammation,
  And *there is* no soundness in my flesh.
8 I am feeble and severely broken;
  I groan because of the turmoil of my heart.

9 Lord, all my desire *is* before You;
  And my sighing is not hidden from You.
10 My heart pants, my strength fails me;
   As for the light of my eyes, it also has gone from me.

11 My loved ones and my friends ᵃstand aloof from my
     plague,
   And my relatives stand afar off.
12 Those also who seek my life lay snares *for me;*
   Those who seek my hurt speak of destruction,
   And plan deception all the day long.

13 But I, like a deaf *man,* do not hear;
   And *I am* like a mute *who* does not open his mouth.
14 Thus I am like a man who does not hear,
   And in whose mouth *is* no response.

15 For ¹in You, O LORD, ᵃI hope;
   You will ²hear, O Lord my God.
16 For I said, "*Hear me,* lest they rejoice over me,
   Lest, when my foot slips, they exalt *themselves* against me."

17 ᵃFor I *am* ready to fall,
   And my sorrow *is* continually before me.
18 For I will ᵃdeclare my iniquity;
   I will be ᵇin ¹anguish over my sin.
19 But my enemies *are* vigorous, *and* they are strong;
   And those who hate me wrongfully have multiplied.
20 Those also ᵃwho render evil for good,
   They are my adversaries, because I follow *what is* good.

21 Do not forsake me, O LORD;
   O my God, ᵃbe not far from me!
22 Make haste to help me,
   O Lord, my salvation!

PSALM 39

PRAYER FOR WISDOM AND FORGIVENESS

To the Chief Musician. To Jeduthun. A Psalm of David.

1 I SAID, "I will guard my ways,
  Lest I sin with my ᵃtongue;
  I will restrain my mouth with a muzzle,
  While the wicked are before me."
2 ᵃI was mute with silence,
  I held my peace *even* from good;
  And my sorrow was stirred up.
3 My heart was hot within me;
  While I was ¹musing, the fire burned.
  Then I spoke with my tongue:

38:11
ᵃPs. 31:11; 88:18
38:15 ᵃ[Ps. 39:7]
38:17 ᵃPs. 51:3
38:18 ᵃPs. 32:5
ᵇ[2 Cor. 7:9, 10]
38:20 ᵃPs. 35:12
38:21
ᵃPs. 22:19; 35:22
39:1 ᵃJob 2:10;
Ps. 34:13;
[James 3:5–12]
39:2 ᵃPs. 38:13

38:6 ¹Lit. *bent down*   38:15 ¹*I wait for You, O LORD*   ²*answer*
38:18 ¹*anxiety*   39:3 ¹*meditating*

4 "LORD, ᵃmake me to know my end,
   And what *is* the measure of my days,
   That I may know how frail I *am*.
5 Indeed, You have made my days *as* handbreadths,
   And my age *is* as nothing before You;
   Certainly every man at his best state *is* but ᵃvapor.   *Selah*
6 Surely every man walks about like a shadow;
   Surely they ¹busy themselves in vain;
   He heaps up *riches,*
   And does not know who will gather them.

7 "And now, Lord, what do I wait for?
   My ᵃhope *is* in You.
8 Deliver me from all my transgressions;
   Do not make me ᵃthe reproach of the foolish.
9 ᵃI was mute, I did not open my mouth,
   Because it was ᵇYou who did *it.*
10 ᵃRemove Your plague from me;
   I am consumed by the blow of Your hand.
11 When with rebukes You correct man for iniquity,
   You make his beauty ᵃmelt away like a moth;
   Surely every man *is* vapor.   *Selah*

12 "Hear my prayer, O LORD,
   And give ear to my cry;
   Do not be silent at my tears;
   For I *am* a stranger with You,
   A sojourner, ᵃas all my fathers *were.*
13 ᵃRemove Your gaze from me, that I may regain strength,
   Before I go away and ᵇam no more."

PSALM 40

FAITH PERSEVERING IN TRIAL

(Ps. 70:1–5)

To the Chief Musician. A Psalm of David.

1 I ᵃWAITED patiently for the LORD;
   And He inclined to me,
   And heard my cry.
2 He also brought me up out of a horrible pit,
   Out of ᵃthe miry clay,
   And ᵇset my feet upon a rock,
   And established my steps.
3 ᵃHe has put a new song in my mouth—
   Praise to our God;
   Many will see *it* and fear,
   And will trust in the LORD.

4 ᵃBlessed *is* that man who makes the LORD his trust,
   And does not respect the proud, nor such as turn aside
      to lies.
5 ᵃMany, O LORD my God, *are* Your wonderful works
   Which You have done;
   ᵇAnd Your thoughts toward us
   Cannot be recounted to You in order;
   If I would declare and speak *of them,*
   They are more than can be numbered.

39:4
ᵃPs. 90:12; 119:84
39:5 ᵃPs. 62:9;
[Eccl. 6:12]
39:7 ᵃPs. 38:15
39:8 ᵃPs. 44:13;
79:4; 119:22
39:9 ᵃPs. 39:2
ᵇ2 Sam. 16:10;
Job 2:10
39:10
ᵃJob 9:34; 13:21
39:11 ᵃJob 13:28;
[Ps. 90:7];
Is. 50:9
39:12
ᵃGen. 47:9;
Lev. 25:23;
1 Chr. 29:15;
Ps. 119:19;
Heb. 11:13;
1 Pet. 2:11
39:13 ᵃJob 7:19;
10:20, 21; 14:6;
Ps. 102:24
ᵇ[Job 14:10]
40:1 ᵃPs. 25:5;
27:14; 37:7
40:2
ᵃPs. 69:2, 14;
Jer. 38:6
ᵇPs. 27:5
40:3
ᵃPs. 32:7; 33:3
40:4
ᵃPs. 34:8; 84:12
40:5 ᵃJob 9:10
ᵇPs. 139:17;
[Is. 55:8]

39:6 ¹*make an uproar for nothing*

6 [a]Sacrifice and offering You did not desire;
My ears You have opened.
Burnt offering and sin offering You did not require.
7 Then I said, "Behold, I come;
In the scroll of the book *it is* written of me.
8 [a]I delight to do Your will, O my God,
And Your law *is* [b]within my heart."

9 [a]I have proclaimed the good news of righteousness
In the great assembly;
Indeed, [b]I do not restrain my lips,
O LORD, You Yourself know.
10 [a]I have not hidden Your righteousness within my heart;
I have declared Your faithfulness and Your salvation;
I have not concealed Your lovingkindness and Your truth
From the great assembly.

11 Do not withhold Your tender mercies from me, O LORD;
[a]Let Your lovingkindness and Your truth continually
preserve me.
12 For innumerable evils have surrounded me;
[a]My iniquities have overtaken me, so that I am not able
to look up;
They are more than the hairs of my head;
Therefore my heart fails me.

13 [a]Be pleased, O LORD, to deliver me;
O LORD, make haste to help me!
14 [a]Let them be ashamed and brought to mutual confusion
Who seek to destroy my [1]life;
Let them be driven backward and brought to dishonor
Who wish me evil.
15 Let them be [a]confounded because of their shame,
Who say to me, "Aha, aha!"

16 [a]Let all those who seek You rejoice and be glad in You;
Let such as love Your salvation [b]say continually,
"The LORD be magnified!"
17 [a]But I *am* poor and needy;
[b]*Yet* the LORD thinks upon me.
You *are* my help and my deliverer;
Do not delay, O my God.

PSALM 41

THE BLESSING AND SUFFERING OF THE GODLY

To the Chief Musician. A Psalm of David.

1 BLESSED *is* he who considers the [1]poor;
The LORD will deliver him in time of trouble.
2 The LORD will preserve him and keep him alive,
And he will be blessed on the earth;
[a]You will not deliver him to the will of his enemies.
3 The LORD will strengthen him on his bed of illness;
You will [1]sustain him on his sickbed.

4 I said, "LORD, be merciful to me;
[a]Heal my soul, for I have sinned against You."
5 My enemies speak evil of me:
"When will he die, and his name perish?"

40:6
[a][1 Sam. 15:22];
Ps. 51:16; Is. 1:11;
[Jer. 6:20; 7:22,
23]; Amos 5:22;
[Mic. 6:6–8;
Heb. 10:5–9]

40:8
[a][Matt. 26:39;
John 4:34;
6:38]; Heb. 10:7
[b][Ps. 37:31;
Jer. 31:33;
2 Cor. 3:3]

40:9
[a]Ps. 22:22, 25
[b]Ps. 119:13

40:10
[a]Acts 20:20, 27

40:11 [a]Ps. 61:7;
Prov. 20:28

40:12 [a]Ps. 38:4;
65:3

40:13 [a]Ps. 70:1

40:14 [a]Ps. 35:4,
26; 70:2; 71:13

40:15 [a]Ps. 73:19

40:16 [a]Ps. 70:4
[b]Ps. 35:27

40:17 [a]Ps. 70:5;
86:1; 109:22
[b]Ps. 40:5;
1 Pet. 5:7

41:2 [a]Ps. 27:12

41:4 [a]Ps. 6:2;
103:3; 147:3

40:14 [1]Lit. *soul*   **41:1** [1]*helpless* or *powerless*   **41:3** [1]*restore*

6 And if he comes to see *me,* he speaks [1]lies;
His heart gathers iniquity to itself;
When he goes out, he tells *it.*

7 All who hate me whisper together against me;
Against me they [1]devise my hurt.

8 "An[1] evil disease," *they say,* "clings to him.
And *now* that he lies down, he will rise up no more."

9 [a]Even my own familiar friend in whom I trusted,
[b]Who ate my bread,
Has [1]lifted up *his* heel against me.

10 But You, O LORD, be merciful to me, and raise me up,
That I may repay them.

11 By this I know that You are well pleased with me,
Because my enemy does not triumph over me.

12 As for me, You uphold me in my integrity,
And [a]set me before Your face forever.

13 [a]Blessed *be* the LORD God of Israel
From everlasting to everlasting!
Amen and Amen.

BOOK TWO

Psalms 42–72

PSALM 42

YEARNING FOR GOD IN THE MIDST OF DISTRESSES

To the Chief Musician. A [1]Contemplation
of the sons of Korah.

1 AS the deer [1]pants for the water brooks,
So pants my soul for You, O God.

2 [a]My soul thirsts for God, for the [b]living God.
When shall I come and [1]appear before God?

3 [a]My tears have been my food day and night,
While they continually say to me,
[b]"Where *is* your God?"

4 When I remember these *things,*
[a]I pour out my soul within me.
For I used to go with the multitude;
[b]I went with them to the house of God,
With the voice of joy and praise,
With a multitude that kept a pilgrim feast.

5 [a]Why are you [1]cast down, O my soul?
And *why* are you disquieted within me?
[b]Hope in God, for I shall yet praise Him
[2]*For* the help of His countenance.

6 [1]O my God, my soul is cast down within me;
Therefore I will remember You from the land of the
Jordan,

41:9
[a]2 Sam. 15:12;
Job 19:13, 19
[b]Ps. 55:12–14,
20; Jer. 20:10;
Obad. 7;
[Mic. 7:5];
Matt. 26:14–16,
21–25, 47–50;
John 13:18,
21–30;
Acts 1:16, 17

41:12 [a][Job 36:7;
Ps. 21:6; 34:15]

41:13
[a]Ps. 72:18, 19;
89:52; 106:48;
150:6

42:2 [a]Ps. 63:1;
84:2; 143:6;
[Jer. 10:10]
[b]Rom. 9:26;
1 Thess. 1:9

42:3 [a]Ps. 80:5;
102:9 [b]Ps. 79:10;
115:2; Joel 2:17;
Mic. 7:10

42:4
[a]1 Sam. 1:15;
Job 30:16
[b]Ps. 55:14; 122:1;
Is. 30:29

42:5
[a]Ps. 42:11; 43:5
[b]Ps. 71:14;
Lam. 3:24

41:6 [1]*empty words*   41:7 [1]*plot*   41:8 [1]Lit. *A thing of Belial*   41:9 [1]Acted as a
traitor   42:title [1]Heb. *Maschil*   42:1 [1]Lit. *longs for*   42:2 [1]So with MT, Vg.;
some Heb. mss., LXX, Syr., Tg. *I see the face of God*   42:5 [1]Lit. *bowed down*
[2]So with MT, Tg.; a few Heb. mss., LXX, Syr., Vg. *The help of my countenance,
my God*   42:6 [1]So with MT, Tg.; a few Heb. mss., LXX, Syr., Vg. put *my God*
at the end of v. 5

And from the heights of Hermon,
From ²the Hill Mizar.
7 Deep calls unto deep at the noise of Your waterfalls;
ᵃAll Your waves and billows have gone over me.
8 The LORD will ᵃcommand His lovingkindness in the
daytime,
And ᵇin the night His song *shall be* with me—
A prayer to the God of my life.

9 I will say to God my Rock,
ᵃ"Why have You forgotten me?
Why do I go mourning because of the oppression of the
enemy?"
10 *As* with a ¹breaking of my bones,
My enemies ²reproach me,
ᵃWhile they say to me all day long,
"Where *is* your God?"

11 ᵃWhy are you cast down, O my soul?
And why are you disquieted within me?
Hope in God;
For I shall yet praise Him,
The ¹help of my countenance and my God.

PSALM 43

PRAYER TO GOD IN TIME OF TROUBLE

1 VINDICATE ᵃme, O God,
And ᵇplead my cause against an ungodly nation;
Oh, deliver me from the deceitful and unjust man!
2 For You *are* the God of my strength;
Why do You cast me off?
ᵃWhy do I go mourning because of the oppression of the
enemy?
3 ᵃOh, send out Your light and Your truth!
Let them lead me;
Let them bring me to ᵇYour holy hill
And to Your ¹tabernacle.
4 Then I will go to the altar of God,
To God my exceeding joy;
And on the harp I will praise You,
O God, my God.

5 ᵃWhy are you cast down, O my soul?
And why are you disquieted within me?
Hope in God;
For I shall yet praise Him,
The ¹help of my countenance and my God.

PSALM 44

REDEMPTION REMEMBERED IN PRESENT DISHONOR

To the Chief Musician. A ᵃContemplation¹
of the sons of Korah.

1 WE have heard with our ears, O God,
ᵃOur fathers have told us,

42:7 ᵃPs. 69:1, 2;
88:7; Jon. 2:3

42:8
ᵃDeut. 28:8
ᵇJob 35:10;
Ps. 149:5

42:9 ᵃPs. 38:6

42:10 ᵃPs. 42:3;
Joel 2:17;
Mic. 7:10

42:11 ᵃPs. 43:5

43:1 ᵃ[Ps. 26:1;
35:24]
ᵇ1 Sam. 24:15;
Ps. 35:1

43:2 ᵃPs. 42:9

43:3 ᵃ[Ps. 40:11]
ᵇPs. 3:4

43:5 ᵃPs. 42:5, 11

44:title
ᵃPs. 42:title

44:1 ᵃ[Ex. 12:26,
27; Deut. 6:20];
Judg. 6:13;
Ps. 78:3

42:6 ²Or *Mount*   42:10 ¹Lit. *shattering*   ²*revile*   42:11 ¹Lit. *salvation*
43:3 ¹*dwelling places*   43:5 ¹Lit. *salvation*   44:title ¹Heb. *Maschil*

The deeds You did in their days,
In days of old:

2 [a]You drove out the [1]nations with Your hand,
But them You planted;
You afflicted the peoples, and cast them out.

3 For [a]they did not gain possession of the land by their
own sword,
Nor did their own arm save them;
But it was Your right hand, Your arm, and the light of
Your countenance,
[b]Because You favored them.

4 [a]You are my King, [1]O God;
[2]Command victories for Jacob.

5 Through You [a]we will push down our enemies;
Through Your name we will trample those who rise up
against us.

6 For [a]I will not trust in my bow,
Nor shall my sword save me.

7 But You have saved us from our enemies,
And have put to shame those who hated us.

8 [a]In God we boast all day long,
And praise Your name forever.   *Selah*

9 But [a]You have cast *us* off and put us to shame,
And You do not go out with our armies.

10 You make us [a]turn back from the enemy,
And those who hate us have taken [1]spoil for themselves.

11 [a]You have given us up like sheep *intended* for food,
And have [b]scattered us among the nations.

12 [a]You sell Your people for *next to* nothing,
And are not enriched by selling them.

13 [a]You make us a reproach to our neighbors,
A scorn and a derision to those all around us.

14 [a]You make us a byword among the nations,
[b]A shaking of the head among the peoples.

15 My dishonor *is* continually before me,
And the shame of my face has covered me,

16 Because of the voice of him who reproaches and
reviles,
[a]Because of the enemy and the avenger.

17 [a]All this has come upon us;
But we have not forgotten You,
Nor have we dealt falsely with Your covenant.

18 Our heart has not turned back,
[a]Nor have our steps departed from Your way;

19 But You have severely broken us in [a]the place of jackals,
And covered us [b]with the shadow of death.

20 If we had forgotten the name of our God,
Or [a]stretched[1] out our hands to a foreign god,

21 [a]Would not God search this out?
For He knows the secrets of the heart.

22 [a]Yet for Your sake we are killed all day long;
We are accounted as sheep for the slaughter.

44:2 [a]Ex. 15:17;
2 Sam. 7:10;
Jer. 24:6;
Amos 9:15

44:3
[a][Deut. 8:17, 18];
Josh. 24:12
[b][Deut. 4:37;
7:7, 8]

44:4 [a][Ps. 74:12]

44:5
[a]Deut. 33:17;
[Dan. 8:4]

44:6
[a][1 Sam. 17:47];
Ps. 33:16;
[Hos. 1:7]

44:8 [a]Ps. 34:2;
[Jer. 9:24]

44:9 [a]Ps. 60:1

44:10
[a]Lev. 26:17;
Josh. 7:8, 12;
Ps. 89:43

44:11 [a]Ps. 44:22;
Rom. 8:36
[b]Lev. 26:33;
Deut. 4:27;
28:64;
Ps. 106:27;
Ezek. 20:23

44:12
[a]Is. 52:3, 4;
Jer. 15:13

44:13
[a]Ps. 79:4; 80:6;
Jer. 24:9

44:14
[a]Deut. 28:37
[b]Job 16:4

44:16 [a]Ps. 8:2

44:17 [a]Dan. 9:13

44:18 [a]Job 23:11

44:19 [a]Is. 34:13
[b][Ps. 23:4]

44:20
[a][Deut. 6:14]

44:21 [a]Job 31:14;
[Ps. 139:1, 2;
Jer. 17:10]

44:22
[a]Rom. 8:36

44:2 [1]*Gentiles, heathen*   **44:4** [1]So with MT, Tg.; LXX, Vg. *and my God*
[2]So with MT, Tg.; LXX, Syr., Vg. *Who commands*   **44:10** [1]*plunder*
44:20 [1]*Worshiped*

23 [a]Awake! Why do You sleep, O Lord?
Arise! Do not cast *us* off forever.
24 [a]Why do You hide Your face,
And forget our affliction and our oppression?
25 For [a]our soul is bowed down to the [1]dust;
Our body clings to the ground.
26 Arise for our help,
And redeem us for Your mercies' sake.

PSALM 45

THE GLORIES OF THE MESSIAH AND HIS BRIDE

To the Chief Musician. [a]Set to [1]"The Lilies."
A [2]Contemplation of the sons of Korah. A Song of Love.

1 MY heart is overflowing with a good theme;
I recite my composition concerning the King;
My tongue *is* the pen of a [1]ready writer.

2 You are fairer than the sons of men;
[a]Grace is poured upon Your lips;
Therefore God has blessed You forever.
3 [1]Gird Your [a]sword upon *Your* thigh, [b]O Mighty One,
With Your [c]glory and Your majesty.
4 [a]And in Your majesty ride prosperously because of truth,
humility, *and* righteousness;
And Your right hand shall teach You awesome things.
5 Your arrows *are* sharp in the heart of the King's enemies;
The peoples fall under You.

6 [a]Your throne, O God, *is* forever and ever;
A [b]scepter of righteousness *is* the scepter of Your
kingdom.
7 You love righteousness and hate wickedness;
Therefore God, Your God, has [a]anointed You
With the oil of [b]gladness more than Your companions.
8 All Your garments *are* [a]scented with myrrh and aloes *and*
cassia,
Out of the ivory palaces, by which they have made You
glad.
9 [a]Kings' daughters *are* among Your honorable women;
[b]At Your right hand stands the queen in gold from Ophir.

10 Listen, O daughter,
Consider and incline your ear;
[a]Forget your own people also, and your father's house;
11 So the King will greatly desire your beauty;
[a]Because He *is* your Lord, worship Him.
12 And the daughter of Tyre *will come* with a gift;
[a]The rich among the people will seek your favor.

13 The royal daughter *is* all glorious within *the palace;*
Her clothing *is* woven with gold.
14 [a]She shall be brought to the King in robes of many
colors;
The virgins, her companions who follow her, shall be
brought to You.

44:23 [a]Ps. 7:6
44:24 [a]Job 13:24
44:25 [a]Ps. 119:25
45:title [a]Ps. 69:title
45:2 [a]Luke 4:22
45:3 [a][Is. 49:2; Heb. 4:12]; Rev. 1:16 [b][Is. 9:6] [c]Jude 25
45:4 [a]Rev. 6:2
45:6 [a][Ps. 93:2]; Heb. 1:8, 9 [b][Num. 24:17]
45:7 [a]Ps. 2:2 [b]Ps. 21:6; Heb. 1:8, 9
45:8 [a]Song 1:12, 13
45:9 [a]Song 6:8 [b]1 Kin. 2:19
45:10 [a]Deut. 21:13; Ruth 1:16, 17
45:11 [a]Ps. 95:6; [Is. 54:5]
45:12 [a]Is. 49:23
45:14 [a]Song 1:4

44:25 [1]Ground, in humiliation 45:title [1]Heb. *Shoshannim* [2]Heb. *Maschil*
45:1 [1]skillful 45:3 [1]Belt on

15 With gladness and rejoicing they shall be brought;
They shall enter the King's palace.

16 Instead of Your fathers shall be Your sons,
ᵃWhom You shall make princes in all the earth.
17 ᵃI will make Your name to be remembered in all
generations;
Therefore the people shall praise You forever and ever.

PSALM 46

GOD THE REFUGE OF HIS PEOPLE AND CONQUEROR OF THE NATIONS

To the Chief Musician. *A Psalm* of the sons
of Korah. A Song ᵃfor Alamoth.

1 GOD *is* our ᵃrefuge and strength,
ᵇA¹ very present help in trouble.
2 Therefore we will not fear,
Even though the earth be removed,
And though the mountains be carried into the ¹midst of
the sea;
3 ᵃ*Though* its waters roar *and* be troubled,
Though the mountains shake with its swelling.   *Selah*

4 *There is* a ᵃriver whose streams shall make glad the ᵇcity
of God,
The holy *place* of the ¹tabernacle of the Most High.
5 God *is* ᵃin the midst of her, she shall not be ¹moved;
God shall help her, just ²at the break of dawn.
6 ᵃThe nations raged, the kingdoms were moved;
He uttered His voice, the earth melted.

7 The ᵃLORD of hosts *is* with us;
The God of Jacob *is* our refuge.   *Selah*

8 Come, behold the works of the LORD,
Who has made desolations in the earth.
9 ᵃHe makes wars cease to the end of the earth;
ᵇHe breaks the bow and cuts the spear in two;
ᶜHe burns the chariot in the fire.

10 Be still, and know that I *am* God;
ᵃI will be exalted among the nations,
I will be exalted in the earth!

11 The LORD of hosts *is* with us;
The God of Jacob *is* our refuge.   *Selah*

PSALM 47

PRAISE TO GOD, THE RULER OF THE EARTH

To the Chief Musician. A Psalm of the sons of Korah.

1 OH, clap your hands, all you peoples!
Shout to God with the voice of triumph!
2 For the LORD Most High *is* awesome;
He is a great ᵃKing over all the earth.

45:16
ᵃ[1 Pet. 2:9;
Rev. 1:6; 20:6]

45:17 ᵃMal. 1:11

46:title
ᵃ1 Chr. 15:20

46:1
ᵃPs. 62:7, 8
ᵇ[Deut. 4:7;
Ps. 145:18]

46:3
ᵃ[Ps. 93:3, 4]

46:4
ᵃ[Ezek. 47:1–12]
ᵇPs. 48:1, 8;
Is. 60:14

46:5
ᵃ[Deut. 23:14;
Is. 12:6];
Ezek. 43:7;
Hos. 11:9;
[Joel 2:27;
Zeph. 3:15;
Zech. 2:5, 10, 11;
8:3]

46:6 ᵃPs. 2:1, 2

46:7
ᵃNum. 14:9;
2 Chr. 13:12

46:9 ᵃIs. 2:4
ᵇPs. 76:3
ᶜEzek. 39:9

46:10
ᵃ[Is. 2:11, 17]

47:2 ᵃDeut. 7:21;
Neh. 1:5;
Ps. 76:12

46:1 ¹*An abundantly available help*   46:2 ¹Lit. *heart*   46:4 ¹*dwelling places*
46:5 ¹*shaken*   ²Lit. *at the turning of the morning*

3 [a]He will subdue the peoples under us,
And the nations under our feet.
4 He will choose our [a]inheritance for us,
The excellence of Jacob whom He loves. *Selah*

5 [a]God has gone up with a shout,
The LORD with the sound of a trumpet.
6 Sing praises to God, sing praises!
Sing praises to our King, sing praises!
7 [a]For God *is* the King of all the earth;
[b]Sing praises with understanding.

8 [a]God reigns over the nations;
God [b]sits on His [c]holy throne.
9 The princes of the people have gathered together,
[a]The people of the God of Abraham.
[b]For the shields of the earth *belong* to God;
He is greatly exalted.

PSALM 48

THE GLORY OF GOD IN ZION

A Song. A Psalm of the sons of Korah.

1 GREAT *is* the LORD, and greatly to be praised
In the [a]city of our God,
In His holy mountain.
2 [a]Beautiful in [1]elevation,
The joy of the whole earth,
Is Mount Zion *on* the sides of the north,
The city of the great King.
3 God *is* in her palaces;
He is known as her refuge.

4 For behold, [a]the kings assembled,
They passed by together.
5 They saw *it, and* so they marveled;
They were troubled, they hastened away.
6 Fear [a]took hold of them there,
And pain, as of a woman in birth pangs,
7 As *when* You break the [a]ships of Tarshish
With an east wind.

8 As we have heard,
So we have seen
In the city of the LORD of hosts,
In the city of our God:
God will [a]establish it forever. *Selah*

9 We have thought, O God, on [a]Your
lovingkindness,
In the midst of Your temple.
10 According to [a]Your name, O God,
So *is* Your praise to the ends of the earth;
Your right hand is full of righteousness.
11 Let Mount Zion rejoice,
Let the daughters of Judah be glad,
Because of Your judgments.

48:2 [1]height

47:3 [a]Ps. 18:47
47:4 [a][1 Pet. 1:4]
47:5
[a]Ps. 68:24, 25
47:7 [a]Zech. 14:9
[b]1 Cor. 14:15
47:8 [a]1 Chr. 16:31
[b]Ps. 97:2
[c]Ps. 48:1
47:9
[a][Rom. 4:11, 12]
[b][Ps. 89:18]
48:1 [a]Ps. 46:4;
87:3; Matt. 5:35
48:2 [a]Ps. 50:2
48:4
[a]2 Sam. 10:6, 14
48:6 [a]Ex. 15:15
48:7
[a]1 Kin. 10:22;
Ezek. 27:25
48:8 [a][Ps. 87:5;
Is. 2:2]; Mic. 4:1
48:9 [a]Ps. 26:3
48:10
[a][Deut. 28:58];
Josh. 7:9;
Mal. 1:11

12 Walk about Zion,
    And go all around her.
    Count her towers;
13 Mark well her bulwarks;
    Consider her palaces;
    That you may ªtell *it* to the generation following.
14 For this *is* God,
    Our God forever and ever;
    ªHe will be our guide
    ¹*Even* to death.

PSALM 49

THE CONFIDENCE OF THE FOOLISH

To the Chief Musician. A Psalm of the sons of Korah.

1 HEAR this, all peoples;
    Give ear, all inhabitants of the world,
2 Both low and high,
    Rich and poor together.
3 My mouth shall speak wisdom,
    And the meditation of my heart *shall give* understanding.
4 I will incline my ear to a proverb;
    I will disclose my ¹dark saying on the harp.
5 Why should I fear in the days of evil,
    When the iniquity at my heels surrounds me?
6 Those who ªtrust in their wealth
    And boast in the multitude of their riches,
7 None *of them* can by any means redeem *his* brother,
    Nor ªgive to God a ransom for him—
8 For ªthe redemption of their souls *is* costly,
    And it shall cease forever—
9 That he should continue to live eternally,
    And ªnot ¹see the Pit.
10 For he sees wise men die;
    Likewise the fool and the senseless person perish,
    And leave their wealth to others.
11 ¹Their inner thought *is that* their houses *will last* forever,
    Their dwelling places to all generations;
    They ªcall *their* lands after their own names.
12 Nevertheless man, *though* in honor, does not ¹remain;
    He is like the beasts *that* perish.
13 This is the way of those who *are* ªfoolish,
    And of their posterity who approve their sayings.   *Selah*
14 Like sheep they are laid in the grave;
    Death shall feed on them;
    ªThe upright shall have dominion over them in the morning;
    ᵇAnd their beauty shall be consumed in ¹the grave, far from their dwelling.
15 But God ªwill redeem my soul from the power of ¹the grave,
    For He shall ᵇreceive me.   *Selah*

48:13
ª[Ps. 78:5–7]
48:14 ªIs. 58:11
49:6 ªJob 31:24;
Ps. 52:7;
[Prov. 11:28;
Mark 10:23, 24]
49:7
ªJob 36:18, 19
49:8
ª[Matt. 16:26]
49:9 ªPs. 89:48
49:11 ªGen. 4:17;
Deut. 3:14
49:13
ª[Luke 12:20]
49:14 ªPs. 47:3;
[Dan. 7:18;
1 Cor. 6:2;
Rev. 2:26]
ᵇJob 4:21
49:15
ª[Hos. 13:4];
Mark 16:6, 7;
Acts 2:31, 32
ᵇPs. 73:24

48:14 ¹So with MT, Syr.; LXX, Vg. *Forever*   49:4 ¹*riddle*   49:9 ¹*experience corruption*   49:11 ¹LXX, Syr., Tg., Vg. *Their graves shall be their houses forever*   49:12 ¹So with MT, Tg.; LXX, Syr., Vg. *understand* (cf. v. 20)
49:14 ¹Or *Sheol*   49:15 ¹Or *Sheol*

16 Do not be afraid when one becomes rich,
 When the glory of his house is increased;
17 For when he dies he shall carry nothing away;
 His glory shall not descend after him.
18 Though while he lives ªhe blesses himself
 (For *men* will praise you when you do well for yourself),
19 He shall go to the generation of his fathers;
 They shall never see ªlight.¹
20 A man *who is* in honor, yet does not understand,
 ªIs like the beasts *that* perish.

PSALM 50

GOD THE RIGHTEOUS JUDGE

A Psalm of Asaph.

1 THE ªMighty One, God the LORD,
 Has spoken and called the earth
 From the rising of the sun to its going down.
2 Out of Zion, the perfection of beauty,
 ªGod will shine forth.
3 Our God shall come, and shall not keep silent;
 ªA fire shall devour before Him,
 And it shall be very tempestuous all around Him.

4 ªHe shall call to the heavens from above,
 And to the earth, that He may judge His people:
5 "Gather ªMy saints together to Me,
 ᵇThose who have ¹made a covenant with Me by
  sacrifice."
6 Let the ªheavens declare His righteousness,
 For ᵇGod Himself *is* Judge.   *Selah*

7 "Hear, O My people, and I will speak,
 O Israel, and I will testify against you;
 ªI *am* God, your God!
8 ªI will not ¹rebuke you ᵇfor your sacrifices
 Or your burnt offerings,
 Which are continually before Me.
9 ªI will not take a bull from your house,
 Nor goats out of your folds.
10 For every beast of the forest *is* Mine,
 And the cattle on a thousand hills.
11 I know all the birds of the mountains,
 And the wild beasts of the field *are* Mine.

12 "If I were hungry, I would not tell you;
 ªFor the world *is* Mine, and all its fullness.
13 ªWill I eat the flesh of bulls,
 Or drink the blood of goats?
14 ªOffer to God thanksgiving,
 And ᵇpay your vows to the Most High.
15 ªCall upon Me in the day of trouble;
 I will deliver you, and you shall glorify Me."

16 But to the wicked God says:
 "What *right* have you to declare My statutes,
 Or take My covenant in your mouth,

49:18
ªDeut. 29:19;
Luke 12:19

49:19
ªJob 33:30

49:20
ªEccl. 3:19

50:1 ªIs. 9:6

50:2
ªDeut. 33:2;
Ps. 80:1

50:3 ªLev. 10:2;
Num. 16:35;
[Ps. 97:3]

50:4
ªDeut. 4:26;
31:28; 32:1;
Is. 1:2

50:5
ªDeut. 33:3
ᵇEx. 24:7

50:6 ª[Ps. 97:6]
ᵇPs. 75:7

50:7 ªEx. 20:2

50:8 ªJer. 7:22
ᵇIs. 1:11;
[Hos. 6:6]

50:9 ªPs. 69:31

50:12 ªEx. 19:5;
[Deut. 10:14;
Job 41:11];
1 Cor. 10:26

50:13
ª[Ps. 51:15–17]

50:14 ªHos. 14:2;
Heb. 13:15
ᵇNum. 30:2;
Deut. 23:21

50:15
ªJob 22:27;
[Zech. 13:9]

49:19 ¹The light of life   50:5 ¹Lit. *cut*   50:8 ¹*reprove*

17 ^aSeeing you hate instruction
  And cast My words behind you?
18 When you saw a thief, you ^aconsented¹ with him,
  And have been a ^bpartaker with adulterers.
19 You give your mouth to evil,
  And ^ayour tongue frames deceit.
20 You sit *and* speak against your brother;
  You slander your own mother's son.
21 These *things* you have done, and I kept silent;
  ^aYou thought that I was altogether like you;
  But I will rebuke you,
  And ^bset *them* in order before your eyes.

22 "Now consider this, you who ^aforget God,
  Lest I tear *you* in pieces,
  And *there be* none to deliver:
23 Whoever offers praise glorifies Me;
  And ^ato him who orders *his* conduct *aright*
  I will show the salvation of God."

PSALM 51

A PRAYER OF REPENTANCE

To the Chief Musician. A Psalm of David ^awhen Nathan the prophet went to him, after he had gone in to Bathsheba.

1 HAVE mercy upon me, O God,
  According to Your lovingkindness;
  According to the multitude of Your tender
    mercies,
  ^aBlot out my transgressions.
2 ^aWash me thoroughly from my iniquity,
  And cleanse me from my sin.

3 For I acknowledge my transgressions,
  And my sin *is* always before me.
4 ^aAgainst You, You only, have I sinned,
  And done *this* evil ^bin Your sight—
  ^cThat You may be found just ¹when You speak,
  And blameless when You judge.

5 ^aBehold, I was brought forth in iniquity,
  And in sin my mother conceived me.
6 Behold, You desire truth in the inward parts,
  And in the hidden *part* You will make me to know
    wisdom.

7 ^aPurge me with hyssop, and I shall be clean;
  Wash me, and I shall be ^bwhiter than snow.
8 Make me hear joy and gladness,
  That the bones You have broken ^amay rejoice.
9 Hide Your face from my sins,
  And blot out all my iniquities.

10 ^aCreate in me a clean heart, O God,
  And renew a steadfast spirit within me.
11 Do not cast me away from Your presence,
  And do not take Your ^aHoly Spirit from me.

50:17 ^aNeh. 9:26; Rom. 2:21
50:18 ^a[Rom. 1:32]; ^b1 Tim. 5:22
50:19 ^aPs. 52:2
50:21 ^a[Rom. 2:4]; ^b[Ps. 90:8]
50:22 ^a[Job 8:13]
50:23 ^aGal. 6:16
51:title ^a2 Sam. 12:1
51:1 ^a[Is. 43:25; 44:22; Acts 3:19; Col. 2:14]
51:2 ^aJer. 33:8; Ezek. 36:33; [Heb. 9:14]; 1 John 1:7, 9]
51:4 ^a2 Sam. 12:13; ^b[Luke 5:21]; ^cRom. 3:4
51:5 ^a[Job 14:4; Ps. 58:3; John 3:6; Rom. 5:12]
51:7 ^aEx. 12:22; Lev. 14:4; Num. 19:18; Heb. 9:19; ^b[Is. 1:18]
51:8 ^a[Matt. 5:4]
51:10 ^a[Ezek. 18:31; Eph. 2:10]
51:11 ^a[Luke 11:13]

50:18 ¹LXX, Syr., Tg., Vg. *ran* 51:4 ¹LXX, Tg., Vg. *in Your words*

12 Restore to me the joy of Your salvation,
And uphold me *by Your* [a]generous Spirit.
13 *Then* I will teach transgressors Your ways,
And sinners shall be converted to You.

14 Deliver me from the guilt of bloodshed, O God,
The God of my salvation,
And my tongue shall sing aloud of Your
righteousness.
15 O Lord, open my lips,
And my mouth shall show forth Your praise.
16 For [a]You do not desire sacrifice, or else I would give *it;*
You do not delight in burnt offering.
17 [a]The sacrifices of God *are* a broken spirit,
A broken and a contrite heart—
These, O God, You will not despise.

18 Do good in Your good pleasure to Zion;
Build the walls of Jerusalem.
19 Then You shall be pleased with [a]the sacrifices of
righteousness,
With burnt offering and whole burnt offering;
Then they shall offer bulls on Your altar.

PSALM 52

THE END OF THE WICKED AND THE PEACE OF THE GODLY

To the Chief Musician. A [1]Contemplation of David
[a]when Doeg the Edomite went and [b]told Saul, and said
to him, "David has gone to the house of Ahimelech."

1 WHY do you boast in evil, O mighty man?
The goodness of God *endures* continually.
2 Your tongue devises destruction,
Like a sharp razor, working deceitfully.
3 You love evil more than good,
Lying rather than speaking righteousness. *Selah*
4 You love all devouring words,
You deceitful tongue.

5 God shall likewise destroy you forever;
He shall take you away, and pluck you out of *your*
dwelling place,
And uproot you from the land of the living. *Selah*
6 The righteous also shall see and fear,
And shall laugh at him, *saying,*
7 "Here is the man *who* did not make God his strength,
But trusted in the abundance of his riches,
And strengthened himself in his [1]wickedness."

8 But I *am* [a]like a green olive tree in the house of God;
I trust in the mercy of God forever and ever.
9 I will praise You forever,
Because You have done *it;*
And in the presence of Your saints
I will wait on Your name, for *it* [1]*is* good.

51:12
[a][2 Cor. 3:17]

51:16
[a][1 Sam. 15:22];
Ps. 50:8–14;
[Mic. 6:6–8]

51:17 [a]Ps. 34:18;
[Is. 57:15]; 66:2

51:19 [a]Ps. 4:5

52:title
[a]1 Sam. 22:9
[b]Ezek. 22:9

52:8 [a]Jer. 11:16

52:title [1]Heb. *Maschil*   52:7 [1]Lit. *desire,* in evil sense   52:9 [1]Or *has a good
reputation*

PSALM 53

FOLLY OF THE GODLESS, AND THE RESTORATION OF ISRAEL

(Ps. 14:1–7)

To the Chief Musician. Set to "Mahalath."
A [1]Contemplation of David.

1   THE [a]fool has said in his heart,
"There is no God."
They are corrupt, and have done abominable iniquity;
[b]*There is* none who does good.

2   God looks down from heaven upon the children of
men,
To see if there are *any* who understand, who [a]seek God.
3   Every one of them has turned aside;
They have together become corrupt;
There is none who does good,
No, not one.

4   Have the workers of iniquity [a]no knowledge,
Who eat up my people *as* they eat bread,
And do not call upon God?
5   [a]There they are in great fear
Where no fear was,
For God has scattered the bones of him who encamps
against you;
You have put *them* to shame,
Because God has despised them.

6   [a]Oh, that the salvation of Israel would come out of Zion!
When God brings back [1]the captivity of His people,
Let Jacob rejoice *and* Israel be glad.

PSALM 54

ANSWERED PRAYER FOR DELIVERANCE FROM ADVERSARIES

To the Chief Musician. With [1]stringed instruments.
A [2]Contemplation of David [a]when the Ziphites went
and said to Saul, "Is David not hiding with us?"

1   SAVE me, O God, by Your name,
And vindicate me by Your strength.
2   Hear my prayer, O God;
Give ear to the words of my mouth.
3   For strangers have risen up against me,
And oppressors have sought after my life;
They have not set God before them.   *Selah*

4   Behold, God *is* my helper;
The Lord *is* with those who [1]uphold my life.
5   He will repay my enemies for their evil.
[1]Cut them off in Your [2]truth.

6   I will freely sacrifice to You;
I will praise Your name, O LORD, for *it is* good.
7   For He has delivered me out of all trouble;
[a]And my eye has seen *its desire* upon my enemies.

53:1 [a]Ps. 10:4
[b]Rom. 3:10–12

53:2
[a][2 Chr. 15:2]

53:4 [a]Jer. 4:22

53:5
[a]Lev. 26:17, 36;
Prov. 28:1

53:6 [a]Ps. 14:7

54:title
[a]1 Sam. 23:19

54:7 [a]Ps. 59:10

53:title [1]Heb. *Maschil*   53:6 [1]Or *His captive people*   54:title [1]Heb. *neginoth*
[2]Heb. *Maschil*   54:4 [1]*sustain my soul*   54:5 [1]*Destroy them*   [2]Or *faithfulness*

PSALM 55

TRUST IN GOD CONCERNING THE TREACHERY OF FRIENDS

To the Chief Musician. With [1]stringed
instruments. A [2]Contemplation of David.

1   GIVE ear to my prayer, O God,
    And do not hide Yourself from my supplication.
2   Attend to me, and hear me;
    I [a]am[1] restless in my complaint, and moan noisily,
3   Because of the voice of the enemy,
    Because of the oppression of the wicked;
    [a]For they bring down trouble upon me,
    And in wrath they hate me.

4   [a]My heart is severely pained within me,
    And the terrors of death have fallen upon me.
5   Fearfulness and trembling have come upon me,
    And horror has overwhelmed me.
6   So I said, "Oh, that I had wings like a dove!
    I would fly away and be at rest.
7   Indeed, I would wander far off,
    And remain in the wilderness.   *Selah*
8   I would hasten my escape
    From the windy storm *and* tempest."

9   Destroy, O Lord, *and* divide their [1]tongues,
    For I have seen [a]violence and strife in the city.
10   Day and night they go around it on its walls;
    [a]Iniquity and trouble *are* also in the midst of it.
11   Destruction *is* in its midst;
    [a]Oppression and deceit do not depart from its streets.

12   [a]For *it is* not an enemy *who* reproaches me;
    Then I could bear *it.*
    Nor *is it* one *who* hates me who has [b]exalted *himself*
    against me;
    Then I could hide from him.
13   But *it was* you, a man my equal,
    [a]My companion and my acquaintance.
14   We took sweet counsel together,
    And [a]walked to the house of God in the throng.

15   Let death seize them;
    Let them [a]go down alive into [1]hell,
    For wickedness *is* in their dwellings *and* among
      them.

16   As for me, I will call upon God,
    And the LORD shall save me.
17   [a]Evening and morning and at noon
    I will pray, and cry aloud,
    And He shall hear my voice.
18   He has redeemed my soul in peace from the battle *that*
      was against me,
    For [a]there were many against me.
19   God will hear, and afflict them,
    [a]Even He who abides from of old.   *Selah*

55:2 [a]Is. 38:14; 59:11; Ezek. 7:16
55:3 [a]2 Sam. 16:7, 8
55:4 [a]Ps. 116:3
55:9 [a]Jer. 6:7
55:10 [a]Ps. 10:7
55:11 [a]Ps. 10:7
55:12 [a]Ps. 41:9 [b]Ps. 35:26; 38:16
55:13 [a]2 Sam. 15:12
55:14 [a]Ps. 42:4
55:15 [a]Num. 16:30, 33
55:17 [a]Dan. 6:10; Luke 18:1; Acts 3:1; 10:3, 30
55:18 [a]2 Chr. 32:7, 8
55:19 [a][Deut. 33:27]

55:title [1]Heb. *neginoth*   [2]Heb. *Maschil*   55:2 [1]*wander*   55:9 [1]*speech,* their counsel   55:15 [1]Or *Sheol*

Because they do not change,
Therefore they do not fear God.

20 He has ªput forth his hands against those who ᵇwere at
peace with him;
He has broken his ¹covenant.
21 ªThe words of his mouth were smoother than butter,
But war was in his heart;
His words were softer than oil,
Yet they were drawn swords.

22 ªCast your burden on the LORD,
And ᵇHe shall sustain you;
He shall never permit the righteous to be ¹moved.

23 But You, O God, shall bring them down to the pit of
destruction;
ªBloodthirsty and deceitful men ᵇshall not live out half
their days;
But I will trust in You.

PSALM 56

PRAYER FOR RELIEF FROM TORMENTORS

To the Chief Musician. Set to ¹"The Silent Dove
in Distant Lands." A Michtam of David when
the ªPhilistines captured him in Gath.

1 BE ªmerciful to me, O God, for man would swallow me up;
Fighting all day he oppresses me.
2 My enemies would ªhound me all day,
For there are many who fight against me, O Most High.

3 Whenever I am afraid,
I will trust in You.
4 In God (I will praise His word),
In God I have put my trust;
ªI will not fear.
What can flesh do to me?

5 All day they twist my words;
All their thoughts are against me for evil.
6 They gather together,
They hide, they mark my steps,
When they lie in wait for my life.
7 Shall they escape by iniquity?
In anger cast down the peoples, O God!

8 You number my wanderings;
Put my tears into Your bottle;
ªAre they not in Your book?
9 When I cry out to You,
Then my enemies will turn back;
This I know, because ªGod is for me.
10 In God (I will praise His word),
In the LORD (I will praise His word),
11 In God I have put my trust;
I will not be afraid.
What can man do to me?

55:20 ªActs 12:1
ᵇPs. 7:4
55:21
ªPs. 28:3; 57:4;
[Prov. 5:3, 4;
12:18]
55:22 ª[Ps. 37:5;
Matt. 6:25–34;
Luke 12:22–31;
1 Pet. 5:7]
ᵇPs. 37:24
55:23 ªPs. 5:6
ᵇProv. 10:27
56:title
ª1 Sam. 21:11
56:1 ªPs. 57:1
56:2 ªPs. 57:3
56:4 ªPs. 118:6;
Is. 31:3;
[Heb. 13:6]
56:8
ª[Mal. 3:16]
56:9 ª[Ps. 118:6;
Rom. 8:31]

55:20 ¹treaty   55:22 ¹shaken   56:title ¹Heb. Jonath Elem Rechokim

12 Vows *made* to You *are binding* upon me, O God;
I will render praises to You,
13 ªFor You have delivered my soul from death.
Have You not *kept* my feet from falling,
That I may walk before God
In the ᵇlight of the living?

PSALM 57

PRAYER FOR SAFETY FROM ENEMIES

(cf. Ps. 108:1–5)

To the Chief Musician. Set to ¹"Do Not Destroy." A Michtam
of David ªwhen he fled from Saul into the cave.

1 BE merciful to me, O God, be merciful to me!
For my soul trusts in You;
ªAnd in the shadow of Your wings I will make my refuge,
ᵇUntil *these* calamities have passed by.
2 I will cry out to God Most High,
To God ªwho performs *all things* for me.
3 ªHe shall send from heaven and save me;
He reproaches the one who ¹would swallow me up. *Selah*
God ᵇshall send forth His mercy and His truth.
4 My soul *is* among lions;
I lie *among* the sons of men
Who are set on fire,
ªWhose teeth *are* spears and arrows,
And their tongue a sharp sword.
5 ªBe exalted, O God, above the heavens;
Let Your glory *be* above all the earth.
6 ªThey have prepared a net for my steps;
My soul is bowed down;
They have dug a pit before me;
Into the midst of it they *themselves* have fallen. *Selah*
7 ªMy heart is steadfast, O God, my heart is steadfast;
I will sing and give praise.
8 Awake, ªmy glory!
Awake, lute and harp!
I will awaken the dawn.
9 ªI will praise You, O Lord, among the peoples;
I will sing to You among the ¹nations.
10 ªFor Your mercy reaches unto the heavens,
And Your truth unto the clouds.
11 ªBe exalted, O God, above the heavens;
Let Your glory *be* above all the earth.

PSALM 58

THE JUST JUDGMENT OF THE WICKED

To the Chief Musician. Set to ¹"Do Not
Destroy." A Michtam of David.

1 DO you indeed speak righteousness, you silent ones?
Do you judge uprightly, you sons of men?

56:13
ªPs. 116:8, 9
ᵇJob 33:30
57:title
ª1 Sam. 22:1
57:1 ªRuth 2:12;
Ps. 17:8; 63:7
ᵇIs. 26:20
57:2 ª[Ps. 138:8]
57:3 ªPs. 144:5, 7
ᵇPs. 43:3
57:4 ªProv. 30:14
57:5 ªPs. 108:5
57:6 ªPs. 9:15
57:7 ªPs. 108:1–5
57:8 ªPs. 16:9
57:9 ªPs. 108:3
57:10 ªPs. 103:11
57:11 ªPs. 57:5

57:title ¹Heb. Al Tashcheth   57:3 ¹snaps at or hounds me, or crushes me
57:9 ¹Gentiles   58:title ¹Heb. Al Tashcheth

2 No, in heart you work wickedness;
You weigh out the violence of your hands in the earth.

3 ªThe wicked are estranged from the womb;
They go astray as soon as they are born, speaking lies.

4 ªTheir poison *is* like the poison of a serpent;
They are like the deaf cobra *that* stops its ear,

5 Which will not ªheed the voice of charmers,
Charming ever so skillfully.

6 ªBreak[1] their teeth in their mouth, O God!
Break out the fangs of the young lions, O LORD!

7 ªLet them flow away as waters *which* run continually;
When he bends *his bow,*
Let his arrows be as if cut in pieces.

8 *Let them be* like a snail which melts away as it goes,
ªLike a stillborn child of a woman, that they may not see
the sun.

9 Before your ªpots can feel *the burning* thorns,
He shall take them away ᵇas with a whirlwind,
As in His living and burning wrath.

10 The righteous shall rejoice when he sees the
ªvengeance;
ᵇHe shall wash his feet in the blood of the wicked,

11 ªSo that men will say,
"Surely *there is* a reward for the righteous;
Surely He is God who ᵇjudges in the earth."

PSALM 59

THE ASSURED JUDGMENT OF THE WICKED

To the Chief Musician. Set to ¹"Do Not Destroy."
A Michtam of David ªwhen Saul sent men, and
they watched the house in order to kill him.

1 DELIVER me from my enemies, O my God;
¹Defend me from those who rise up against me.

2 Deliver me from the workers of iniquity,
And save me from bloodthirsty men.

3 For look, they lie in wait for my life;
ªThe mighty gather against me,
Not *for* my transgression nor *for* my sin, O LORD.

4 They run and prepare themselves through no fault *of*
mine.

ªAwake to help me, and behold!

5 You therefore, O LORD God of hosts, the God of Israel,
Awake to punish all the ¹nations;
Do not be merciful to any wicked transgressors.   *Selah*

6 ªAt evening they return,
They growl like a dog,
And go all around the city.

7 Indeed, they belch with their mouth;
ªSwords *are* in their lips;
For *they say,* ᵇ"Who hears?"

58:3 ª[Ps. 53:3; Is. 48:8]

58:4 ªEccl. 10:11

58:5 ªJer. 8:17

58:6 ªJob 4:10

58:7 ªJosh. 2:11; 7:5; Ps. 112:10; Is. 13:7; Ezek. 21:7

58:8 ªJob 3:16

58:9 ªPs. 118:12; Eccl. 7:6; ᵇJob 27:21; Prov. 10:25

58:10 ª[Deut. 32:43]; Jer. 11:20; ᵇPs. 68:23

58:11 ªPs. 92:15; Prov. 11:18; [2 Cor. 5:10]; ᵇPs. 50:6; 75:7

59:title ª1 Sam. 19:11

59:3 ªPs. 56:6

59:4 ªPs. 35:23

59:6 ªPs. 59:14

59:7 ªPs. 57:4; Prov. 12:18; ᵇJob 22:13; Ps. 10:11

8 But [a]You, O LORD, shall laugh at them;
   You shall have all the [1]nations in derision.
9 I will wait for You, O You [1]his Strength;
   [a]For God *is* my [2]defense.
10 [1]My God of mercy shall [a]come to meet me;
   God shall let [b]me see *my desire* on my enemies.

11 Do not slay them, lest my people forget;
   Scatter them by Your power,
   And bring them down,
   O Lord our shield.
12 [a]*For* the sin of their mouth *and* the words of their lips,
   Let them even be taken in their pride,
   And for the cursing and lying *which* they speak.
13 [a]Consume *them* in wrath, consume *them,*
   That they *may* not *be;*
   And [b]let them know that God rules in Jacob
   To the ends of the earth.   *Selah*

14 And [a]at evening they return,
   They growl like a dog,
   And go all around the city.
15 They [a]wander up and down for food,
   And [1]howl if they are not satisfied.

16 But I will sing of Your power;
   Yes, I will sing aloud of Your mercy in the morning;
   For You have been my defense
   And refuge in the day of my trouble.
17 To You, [a]O my Strength, I will sing praises;
   For God *is* my defense,
   My God of mercy.

PSALM 60

URGENT PRAYER FOR THE RESTORED FAVOR OF GOD

(cf. Ps. 108:6–13)

To the Chief Musician. [a]Set to [1]"Lily of the Testimony."
A Michtam of David. For teaching. [b]When he fought against
Mesopotamia and Syria of Zobah, and Joab returned and
killed twelve thousand Edomites in the Valley of Salt.

1 O GOD, [a]You have cast us off;
   You have broken us down;
   You have been displeased;
   Oh, restore us again!
2 You have made the earth tremble;
   You have broken it;
   [a]Heal its breaches, for it is shaking.
3 [a]You have shown Your people hard things;
   [b]You have made us drink the wine of [1]confusion.

4 [a]You have given a banner to those who fear You,
   That it may be displayed because of the truth.   *Selah*

59:8 [a]Prov. 1:26
59:9 [a][Ps. 62:2]
59:10 [a]Ps. 21:3
[b]Ps. 54:7
59:12
[a]Prov. 12:13
59:13
[a]Ps. 104:35
[b]Ps. 83:18
59:14 [a]Ps. 59:6
59:15 [a]Job 15:23
59:17 [a]Ps. 18:1
60:title [a]Ps. 80
[b]2 Sam. 8:3, 13;
1 Chr. 18:3
60:1 [a]Ps. 44:9
60:2
[a][2 Chr. 7:14];
Is. 30:26
60:3 [a]Ps. 71:20
[b]Is. 51:17, 22;
Jer. 25:15
60:4 [a]Ps. 20:5;
Is. 5:26; 11:12;
13:2

59:8 [1]Gentiles   59:9 [1]So with MT, Syr.; some Heb. mss., LXX, Tg., Vg. *my
Strength*   [2]Lit. *fortress*   59:10 [1]So with Qr.; some Heb. mss., LXX, Vg. *My
God, His mercy;* Kt.; some Heb. mss., Tg. *O God, my mercy;* Syr. *O God, Your
mercy*   59:15 [1]So with LXX, Vg.; MT, Syr., Tg. *spend the night*
60:title [1]Heb. *Shushan Eduth*   60:3 [1]*staggering*

5 ^aThat Your beloved may be delivered,
Save *with* Your right hand, and hear me.

6 God has ^aspoken in His holiness:
"I will rejoice;
I will ^bdivide ^cShechem
And measure out ^dthe Valley of Succoth.

7 Gilead *is* Mine, and Manasseh *is* Mine;
^aEphraim also *is* the ¹helmet for My head;
^bJudah *is* My lawgiver.

8 ^aMoab *is* My washpot;
^bOver Edom I will cast My shoe;
^cPhilistia, shout in triumph because of Me."

9 Who will bring me *to* the strong city?
Who will lead me to Edom?

10 *Is it* not You, O God, ^a*who* cast us off?
And You, O God, *who* did ^bnot go out with our armies?

11 Give us help from trouble,
^aFor the help of man *is* useless.

12 Through God ^awe will do valiantly,
For *it is* He *who* shall tread down our enemies.

PSALM 61

ASSURANCE OF GOD'S ETERNAL PROTECTION

*To the Chief Musician. On ¹a stringed
instrument. A Psalm of David.*

1 HEAR my cry, O God;
Attend to my prayer.

2 From the end of the earth I will cry to You,
When my heart is overwhelmed;
Lead me to the rock that is higher than I.

3 For You have been a shelter for me,
^aA strong tower from the enemy.

4 I will abide in Your ¹tabernacle forever;
^aI will trust in the shelter of Your wings.   *Selah*

5 For You, O God, have heard my vows;
You have given *me* the heritage of those who fear Your
name.

6 You will prolong the king's life,
His years as many generations.

7 He shall abide before God forever.
Oh, prepare mercy ^aand truth, *which* may ¹preserve him!

8 So I will sing praise to Your name forever,
That I may daily perform my vows.

PSALM 62

A CALM RESOLVE TO WAIT FOR THE SALVATION OF GOD

To the Chief Musician. To ^aJeduthun. A Psalm of David.

1 TRULY ^amy soul silently *waits* for God;
From Him *comes* my salvation.

60:5 ^aPs. 108:6–13
60:6 ^aPs. 89:35 ^bJosh. 1:6 ^cGen. 12:6 ^dJosh. 13:27
60:7 ^aDeut. 33:17 ^b[Gen. 49:10]
60:8 ^a2 Sam. 8:2 ^b2 Sam. 8:14; Ps. 108:9 ^c2 Sam. 8:1
60:10 ^aPs. 108:11 ^bJosh. 7:12
60:11 ^aPs. 118:8; 146:3
60:12 ^aNum. 24:18
61:3 ^aProv. 18:10
61:4 ^aPs. 91:4
61:7 ^aPs. 40:11
62:title ^a1 Chr. 25:1
62:1 ^aPs. 33:20

60:7 ¹Lit. *protection* 61:title ¹Heb. *neginah* 61:4 ¹*tent* 61:7 ¹Lit. *guard* or *keep*

2 He only *is* my rock and my salvation;
   He is my ¹defense;
   I shall not be greatly ªmoved.²

3 How long will you attack a man?
   You shall be slain, all of you,
   ªLike a leaning wall and a tottering fence.

4 They only consult to cast *him* down from his high
      position;
   They ªdelight in lies;
   They bless with their mouth,
   But they curse inwardly.   *Selah*

5 My soul, wait silently for God alone,
   For my ¹expectation *is* from Him.

6 He only *is* my rock and my salvation;
   He is my defense;
   I shall not be ¹moved.

7 ªIn God *is* my salvation and my glory;
   The rock of my strength,
   And my refuge, *is* in God.

8 Trust in Him at all times, you people;
   ªPour out your heart before Him;
   God *is* a refuge for us.   *Selah*

9 ªSurely men of low degree *are* ¹a vapor,
   Men of high degree *are* a lie;
   If they are weighed on the scales,
   They *are* altogether *lighter* than vapor.

10 Do not trust in oppression,
   Nor vainly hope in robbery;
   ªIf riches increase,
   Do not set *your* heart *on them.*

11 God has spoken once,
   Twice I have heard this:
   That power *belongs* to God.

12 Also to You, O Lord, *belongs* mercy;
   For ªYou ¹render to each one according to his work.

PSALM 63

JOY IN THE FELLOWSHIP OF GOD

A Psalm of David ªwhen he was in the wilderness of Judah.

1 O GOD, You *are* my God;
   Early will I seek You;
   ªMy soul thirsts for You;
   My flesh longs for You
   In a dry and thirsty land
   Where there is no water.

2 So I have looked for You in the sanctuary,
   To see ªYour power and Your glory.

3 ªBecause Your lovingkindness *is* better than life,
   My lips shall praise You.

4 Thus I will bless You while I live;
   I will ªlift up my hands in Your name.

62:2 ªPs. 55:22
62:3 ªIs. 30:13
62:4 ªPs. 28:3
62:7 ª[Jer. 3:23]
62:8
ª1 Sam. 1:15;
Ps. 42:4;
Lam. 2:19
62:9 ªJob 7:16;
Ps. 39:5;
Is. 40:17
62:10
ªJob 31:25;
[Mark 10:24;
Luke 12:15;
1 Tim. 6:10]
62:12
ª[Matt. 16:27];
Rom. 2:6;
1 Cor. 3:8
63:title
ª1 Sam. 22:5
63:1 ªPs. 42:2;
[Matt. 5:6]
63:2 ªPs. 27:4
63:3 ªPs. 138:2
63:4
ªPs. 28:2; 143:6

62:2 ¹strong tower   ²shaken   62:5 ¹hope   62:6 ¹shaken   62:9 ¹vanity
62:12 ¹reward

5 My soul shall be satisfied as with ¹marrow and ²fatness,
And my mouth shall praise *You* with joyful lips.

6 When ᵃI remember You on my bed,
I meditate on You in the *night* watches.

7 Because You have been my help,
Therefore in the shadow of Your wings I will rejoice.

8 My soul follows close behind You;
Your right hand upholds me.

9 But those *who* seek my life, to destroy *it*,
Shall go into the lower parts of the earth.

10 They shall ¹fall by the sword;
They shall be ²a portion for jackals.

11 But the king shall rejoice in God;
ᵃEveryone who swears by Him shall glory;
But the mouth of those who speak lies shall be stopped.

PSALM 64

OPPRESSED BY THE WICKED BUT REJOICING IN THE LORD

To the Chief Musician. A Psalm of David.

1 HEAR my voice, O God, in my ¹meditation;
Preserve my life from fear of the enemy.

2 Hide me from the secret plots of the wicked,
From the rebellion of the workers of iniquity,

3 Who sharpen their tongue like a sword,
ᵃAnd bend *their bows to shoot* their arrows—bitter words,

4 That they may shoot in secret at the blameless;
Suddenly they shoot at him and do not fear.

5 They encourage themselves *in* an evil matter;
They talk of laying snares secretly;
ᵃThey say, "Who will see them?"

6 They devise iniquities:
"We have perfected a shrewd scheme."
Both the inward thought and the heart of man are deep.

7 But God shall shoot at them *with* an arrow;
Suddenly they shall be wounded.

8 So He will make them stumble over their own tongue;
ᵃAll who see them shall flee away.

9 All men shall fear,
And shall ᵃdeclare the work of God;
For they shall wisely consider His doing.

10 ᵃThe righteous shall be glad in the LORD, and trust in
Him.
And all the upright in heart shall glory.

PSALM 65

PRAISE TO GOD FOR HIS SALVATION AND PROVIDENCE

To the Chief Musician. A Psalm of David. A Song.

1 PRAISE is awaiting You, O God, in Zion;
And to You the ¹vow shall be performed.

63:6 ᵃPs. 42:8
63:11
ᵃDeut. 6:13;
[Is. 45:23; 65:16]
64:3 ᵃPs. 58:7
64:5
ᵃPs. 10:11; 59:7
64:8 ᵃPs. 31:11
64:9
ᵃJer. 50:28; 51:10
64:10
ᵃJob 22:19;
Ps. 32:11

63:5 ¹Lit. *fat*   ²Abundance   **63:10** ¹Lit. *pour him out by the hand of the sword*   ²Prey   **64:1** ¹*complaint*   **65:1** ¹A promised deed

2 O You who hear prayer,
   ^aTo You all flesh will come.
3 Iniquities prevail against me;
   As for our transgressions,
   You will ^aprovide atonement for them.

4 ^aBlessed *is the man* You ^bchoose,
   And cause to approach *You,*
   That he may dwell in Your courts.
   ^cWe shall be satisfied with the goodness of Your house,
   Of Your holy temple.

5 *By* awesome deeds in righteousness You will answer us,
   O God of our salvation,
   You who are the confidence of all the ends of the earth,
   And of the far-off seas;
6 Who established the mountains by His strength,
   ^a*Being* clothed with power;
7 ^aYou who still the noise of the seas,
   The noise of their waves,
   ^bAnd the tumult of the peoples.
8 They also who dwell in the farthest parts are afraid of
      Your signs;
   You make the outgoings of the morning and evening
      ¹rejoice.
9 You ¹visit the earth and ^awater it,
   You greatly enrich it;
   ^bThe river of God is full of water;
   You provide their grain,
   For so You have prepared it.
10 You water its ridges abundantly,
   You settle its furrows;
   You make it soft with showers,
   You bless its growth.

11 You crown the year with Your goodness,
   And Your paths drip *with* abundance.
12 They drop *on* the pastures of the wilderness,
   And the little hills rejoice on every side.
13 The pastures are clothed with flocks;
   ^aThe valleys also are covered with grain;
   They shout for joy, they also sing.

PSALM 66

PRAISE TO GOD FOR HIS AWESOME WORKS

To the Chief Musician. A Song. A Psalm.

1 MAKE ^aa joyful shout to God, all the earth!
2 Sing out the honor of His name;
   Make His praise glorious.
3 Say to God,
   "How ^aawesome are Your works!
   ^bThrough the greatness of Your power
   Your enemies shall submit themselves to You.
4 ^aAll the earth shall worship You
   And sing praises to You;
   They shall sing praises *to* Your name." *Selah*

65:2 ^a[Is. 66:23]

65:3 ^aPs. 51:2;
79:9; Is. 6:7;
[Heb. 9:14;
1 John 1:7, 9]

65:4 ^aPs. 33:12
^bPs. 4:3
^cPs. 36:8

65:6 ^aPs. 93:1

65:7 ^aMatt. 8:26
^bIs. 17:12, 13

65:9
^a[Deut. 11:12];
Jer. 5:24
^bPs. 46:4;
104:13; 147:8

65:13
^aIs. 44:23; 55:12

66:1 ^aPs. 100:1

66:3 ^aPs. 65:5
^bPs. 18:44

66:4 ^aPs. 117:1;
Zech. 14:16

65:8 ¹*shout for joy*   65:9 ¹*give attention to*

5 Come and see the works of God;
He is awesome *in His* doing toward the sons of men.
6 ªHe turned the sea into dry *land;*
ᵇThey went through the river on foot.
There we will rejoice in Him.
7 He rules by His power forever;
His eyes observe the nations;
Do not let the rebellious exalt themselves.   *Selah*

8 Oh, bless our God, you peoples!
And make the voice of His praise to be heard,
9 Who keeps our soul among the living,
And does not allow our feet to ¹be moved.
10 For ªYou, O God, have tested us;
ᵇYou have refined us as silver is refined.
11 ªYou brought us into the net;
You laid affliction on our backs.
12 ªYou have caused men to ride over our heads;
ᵇWe went through fire and through water;
But You brought us out to ¹rich *fulfillment.*
13 ªI will go into Your house with burnt offerings;
ᵇI will pay You my ¹vows,
14 Which my lips have uttered
And my mouth has spoken when I was in trouble.
15 I will offer You burnt sacrifices of fat animals,
With the sweet aroma of rams;
I will offer bulls with goats.   *Selah*

16 Come *and* hear, all you who fear God,
And I will declare what He has done for my soul.
17 I cried to Him with my mouth,
And He was ¹extolled with my tongue.
18 ªIf I regard iniquity in my heart,
The Lord will not hear.
19 *But* certainly God ªhas heard *me;*
He has attended to the voice of my prayer.
20 Blessed *be* God,
Who has not turned away my prayer,
Nor His mercy from me!

PSALM 67

AN INVOCATION AND A DOXOLOGY

To the Chief Musician. On ¹stringed
instruments. A Psalm. A Song.

1 GOD be merciful to us and bless us,
And ªcause His face to shine upon us,   *Selah*
2 That ªYour way may be known on earth,
ᵇYour salvation among all nations.

3 Let the peoples praise You, O God;
Let all the peoples praise You.
4 Oh, let the nations be glad and sing for joy!
For ªYou shall judge the people righteously,
And govern the nations on earth.   *Selah*

66:6 ªEx. 14:21
ᵇJosh. 3:14–16
66:10
ªJob 23:10;
Ps. 17:3
ᵇ[Is. 48:10];
Zech. 13:9;
Mal. 3:3;
1 Pet. 1:7]
66:11 ªLam. 1:13;
Ezek. 12:13
66:12 ªIs. 51:23
ᵇIs. 43:2
66:13 ªPs. 100:4;
116:14, 17–19
ᵇ[Eccl. 5:4]
66:18 ªJob 27:9;
[Prov. 15:29;
28:9]; Is. 1:15;
[John 9:31;
James 4:3]
66:19
ªPs. 116:1, 2
67:1 ªNum. 6:25
67:2 ªActs 18:25
ᵇIs. 52:10;
Titus 2:11
67:4
ª[Ps. 96:10, 13;
98:9]

66:9 ¹*slip*   66:12 ¹*abundance*   66:13 ¹*Promised deeds*   66:17 ¹*praised*
67:title ¹Heb. *neginoth*

5 Let the peoples praise You, O God;
   Let all the peoples praise You.
6 ªThen the earth shall ¹yield her increase;
   God, our own God, shall bless us.
7 God shall bless us,
   And all the ends of the earth shall fear Him.

PSALM 68

THE GLORY OF GOD IN HIS GOODNESS TO ISRAEL

To the Chief Musician. A Psalm of David. A Song.

1 LET ªGod arise,
   Let His enemies be scattered;
   Let those also who hate Him flee before Him.
2 ªAs smoke is driven away,
   So drive *them* away;
   ᵇAs wax melts before the fire,
   So let the wicked perish at the presence of God.
3 But ªlet the righteous be glad;
   Let them rejoice before God;
   Yes, let them rejoice exceedingly.

4 Sing to God, sing praises to His name;
   ªExtol¹ Him who rides on the ²clouds,
   ᵇBy His name ³YAH,
   And rejoice before Him.

5 ªA father of the fatherless, a defender of widows,
   Is God in His holy habitation.
6 ªGod sets the solitary in families;
   ᵇHe brings out those who are bound into prosperity;
   But ᶜthe rebellious dwell in a dry *land*.

7 O God, ªwhen You went out before Your people,
   When You marched through the wilderness,   *Selah*
8 The earth shook;
   The heavens also dropped *rain* at the presence of God;
   Sinai itself *was moved* at the presence of God, the God of
      Israel.
9 ªYou, O God, sent a plentiful rain,
   Whereby You confirmed Your inheritance,
   When it was weary.
10 Your congregation dwelt in it;
   ªYou, O God, provided from Your goodness for the
      poor.

11 The Lord gave the word;
   Great *was* the ¹companyª of those who proclaimed *it*:
12 "Kingsª of armies flee, they flee,
   And she who remains at home divides the ¹spoil.
13 ªThough you lie down among the ¹sheepfolds,
   ᵇ*You will be* like the wings of a dove covered with
      silver,
   And her feathers with yellow gold."
14 ªWhen the Almighty scattered kings in it,
   It was *white* as snow in Zalmon.

67:6 ªLev. 26:4;
Ps. 85:12;
[Ezek. 34:27];
Zech. 8:12

68:1
ªNum. 10:35

68:2 ª[Is. 9:18];
Hos. 13:3
ᵇPs. 97:5;
Mic. 1:4

68:3 ªPs. 32:11

68:4
ªDeut. 33:26
ᵇ[Ex. 6:3]

68:5
ª[Ps. 10:14, 18;
146:9]

68:6
ªPs. 107:4–7
ᵇActs 12:6–11
ᶜPs. 107:34

68:7 ªEx. 13:21;
[Hab. 3:13]

68:9 ªLev. 26:4;
Deut. 11:11;
Job 5:10;
Ezek. 34:26

68:10
ªDeut. 26:5;
Ps. 74:19

68:12
ªNum. 31:8;
Josh. 10:16;
Judg. 5:19

68:13 ªPs. 81:6
ᵇPs. 105:37

68:14
ªJosh. 10:10

67:6 ¹*give her produce*   68:4 ¹*Praise*   ²MT *deserts*; Tg. *heavens* (cf. v. 34 and
Is. 19:1)   ³Lit. LORD, a shortened Heb. form   68:11 ¹*host*   68:12 ¹*plunder*
68:13 ¹Or *saddlebags*

68:16
a[Deut. 12:5];
1 Kin. 9:3

68:17
aDeut. 33:2;
Dan. 7:10

68:18
aMark 16:19;
Acts 1:9;
Eph. 4:8;
Phil. 2:9;
Col. 3:1; Heb. 1:3
bJudg. 5:12
cActs 2:4, 33;
10:44–46;
[1 Cor. 12:4–11;
Eph. 4:7–12]
d[1 Tim. 1:13]
ePs. 78:60

68:20
a[Deut. 32:39]

68:21 aHab. 3:13
bPs. 55:23

68:22
aNum. 21:33;
Deut. 30:1–9;
Amos 9:1–3
bEx. 14:22

68:23 aPs. 58:10
b1 Kin. 21:19;
Jer. 15:3

68:25
a1 Chr. 13:8

68:26
aDeut. 33:28;
Is. 48:1

68:27
aJudg. 5:14;
1 Sam. 9:21

68:28 aPs. 42:8;
Is. 26:12

68:29
a1 Kin. 10:10, 25;
2 Chr. 32:23;
Ps. 45:12; 72:10;
Is. 18:7

68:30 aPs. 22:12
b2 Sam. 8:2

68:31
aIs. 19:19–23
bIs. 45:14;
Zeph. 3:10
cPs. 44:20

68:32
a[Ps. 67:3, 4]

68:33
aDeut. 33:26;
Ps. 18:10
bPs. 46:6;
Is. 30:30

15 A mountain of God *is* the mountain of Bashan;
A mountain *of many* peaks *is* the mountain of Bashan.
16 Why do you ¹fume with envy, you mountains of *many*
peaks?
ªThis *is* the mountain *which* God desires to dwell in;
Yes, the LORD will dwell *in it* forever.

17 ªThe chariots of God *are* twenty thousand,
Even thousands of thousands;
The Lord is among them *as in* Sinai, in the Holy *Place*.
18 ªYou have ascended on high,
bYou have led captivity captive;
cYou have received gifts among men,
Even *from* dthe rebellious,
eThat the LORD God might dwell *there*.

19 Blessed *be* the Lord,
Who daily loads us *with benefits*,
The God of our salvation!   *Selah*
20 Our God *is* the God of salvation;
And ªto GOD the Lord *belong* escapes from death.

21 But ªGod will wound the head of His enemies,
bThe hairy scalp of the one who still goes on in his
trespasses.
22 The Lord said, "I will bring ªback from Bashan,
I will bring *them* back bfrom the depths of the sea,
23 ªThat ¹your foot may crush *them* in blood,
bAnd the tongues of your dogs *may have* their portion
from *your* enemies."

24 They have seen Your ¹procession, O God,
The procession of my God, my King, into the sanctuary.
25 ªThe singers went before, the players on instruments
followed after;
Among *them were* the maidens playing timbrels.
26 Bless God in the congregations,
The Lord, from ªthe fountain of Israel.
27 ªThere *is* little Benjamin, their leader,
The princes of Judah *and* their ¹company,
The princes of Zebulun *and* the princes of Naphtali.

28 ¹Your God has ªcommanded your strength;
Strengthen, O God, what You have done for us.
29 Because of Your temple at Jerusalem,
ªKings will bring presents to You.
30 Rebuke the beasts of the reeds,
ªThe herd of bulls with the calves of the peoples,
Till everyone bsubmits himself with pieces of silver.
Scatter the peoples *who* delight in war.
31 ªEnvoys will come out of Egypt;
bEthiopia will quickly cstretch out her hands to God.

32 Sing to God, you ªkingdoms of the earth;
Oh, sing praises to the Lord,   *Selah*
33 To Him ªwho rides on the heaven of heavens, *which were*
of old!
Indeed, He sends out His voice, a bmighty voice.

68:16 ¹Lit. *stare*   **68:23** ¹LXX, Syr., Tg., Vg. *you may dip your foot*   **68:24** ¹Lit.
goings   **68:27** ¹*throng*   **68:28** ¹LXX, Syr., Tg., Vg. *Command, O God*

34 [a]Ascribe strength to God;
His excellence *is* over Israel,
And His strength *is* in the clouds.
35 O God, [a]*You are* more awesome than Your holy places.
The God of Israel *is* He who gives strength and power to
His people.

Blessed *be* God!

PSALM 69

AN URGENT PLEA FOR HELP IN TROUBLE

To the Chief Musician. Set to [1]"The Lilies." *A Psalm* of David.

1 SAVE me, O God!
For [a]the waters have come up to *my* [1]neck.
2 [a]I sink in deep mire,
Where *there is* no standing;
I have come into deep waters,
Where the floods overflow me.
3 [a]I am weary with my crying;
My throat is dry;
[b]My eyes fail while I wait for my God.

4 Those who [a]hate me without a cause
Are more than the hairs of my head;
They are mighty who would destroy me,
Being my enemies wrongfully;
Though I have stolen nothing,
I *still* must restore *it.*

5 O God, You know my foolishness;
And my sins are not hidden from You.
6 Let not those who [1]wait for You, O Lord GOD of hosts, be
ashamed because of me;
Let not those who seek You be [2]confounded because of
me, O God of Israel.
7 Because for Your sake I have borne reproach;
Shame has covered my face.
8 [a]I have become a stranger to my brothers,
And an alien to my mother's children;
9 [a]Because zeal for Your house has eaten me up,
[b]And the reproaches of those who reproach You have
fallen on me.
10 When I wept *and chastened* my soul with fasting,
That became my reproach.
11 I also [1]made sackcloth my garment;
I became a byword to them.
12 Those who [1]sit in the gate speak against me,
And I *am* the song of the [a]drunkards.

13 But as for me, my prayer *is* to You,
O LORD, *in* the acceptable time;
O God, in the multitude of Your mercy,
Hear me in the truth of Your salvation.
14 Deliver me out of the mire,
And let me not sink;

68:34 [a]Ps. 29:1
68:35 [a]Ps. 76:12
69:1 [a]Job 22:11;
Jon. 2:5
69:2 [a]Ps. 40:2
69:3 [a]Ps. 6:6
[b]Deut. 28:32;
Ps. 119:82, 123;
Is. 38:14
69:4 [a]Ps. 35:19;
John 15:25
69:8 [a]Is. 53:3;
Mark 3:21;
Luke 8:19;
John 7:3–5
69:9 [a]John 2:17
[b]Rom. 15:3
69:12 [a]Job 30:9

69:title [1]Heb. *Shoshannim*   69:1 [1]Lit. *soul*   69:6 [1]Wait in faith
[2]*dishonored*   69:11 [1]Symbolic of sorrow   69:12 [1]Sit as judges

Let me be delivered from those who hate me,
And out of the deep waters.
15 Let not the floodwater overflow me,
Nor let the deep swallow me up;
And let not the pit shut its mouth on me.

16 Hear me, O LORD, for Your lovingkindness *is* good;
Turn to me according to the multitude of Your tender
    mercies.
17 And do not hide Your face from Your servant,
For I am in trouble;
Hear me speedily.
18 Draw near to my soul, *and* redeem it;
Deliver me because of my enemies.

19 You know ªmy reproach, my shame, and my dishonor;
My adversaries *are* all before You.
20 Reproach has broken my heart,
And I am full of ¹heaviness;
ªI looked *for someone* to take pity, but *there was* none;
And for ᵇcomforters, but I found none.
21 They also gave me gall for my food,
ªAnd for my thirst they gave me vinegar to drink.

22 ªLet their table become a snare before them,
And their well-being a trap.
23 ªLet their eyes be darkened, so that they do not see;
And make their loins shake continually.
24 ªPour out Your indignation upon them,
And let Your wrathful anger take hold of them.
25 ªLet their dwelling place be desolate;
Let no one live in their tents.
26 For they persecute the *ones* ªYou have struck,
And talk of the grief of those You have wounded.
27 ªAdd iniquity to their iniquity,
ᵇAnd let them not come into Your righteousness.
28 Let them ªbe blotted out of the book of the living,
ᵇAnd not be written with the righteous.

29 But I *am* poor and sorrowful;
Let Your salvation, O God, set me up on high.
30 ªI will praise the name of God with a song,
And will magnify Him with thanksgiving.
31 ªThis also shall please the LORD better than an ox *or*
    bull,
Which has horns and hooves.
32 ªThe humble shall see *this and* be glad;
And you who seek God, ᵇyour hearts shall live.
33 For the LORD hears the poor,
And does not despise ªHis prisoners.
34 ªLet heaven and earth praise Him,
The seas ᵇand everything that moves in them.
35 ªFor God will save Zion
And build the cities of Judah,
That they may dwell there and possess it.
36 Also, ªthe ¹descendants of His servants shall inherit it,
And those who love His name shall dwell in it.

69:19
ªPs. 22:6, 7;
Heb. 12:2

69:20 ªIs. 63:5
ᵇJob 16:2

69:21
ªMatt. 27:34, 48;
Mark 15:23, 36;
Luke 23:36;
John 19:28–30

69:22
ªRom. 11:9, 10

69:23
ªIs. 6:9, 10

69:24
ª[Jer. 10:25;
1 Thess. 2:16]

69:25
ªMatt. 23:38;
Luke 13:35;
Acts 1:20

69:26 ª[Is. 53:4;
1 Pet. 2:24]

69:27 ªNeh. 4:5;
[Rom. 1:28]
ᵇ[Is. 26:10]

69:28
ª[Ex. 32:32];
Phil. 4:3;
[Rev. 3:5; 13:8]
ᵇEzek. 13:9;
Luke 10:20;
Heb. 12:23

69:30
ª[Ps. 28:7]

69:31
ªPs. 50:13, 14,
23; 51:16

69:32 ªPs. 34:2
ᵇPs. 22:26

69:33
ª[Ps. 68:6];
Eph. 3:1

69:34 ªPs. 96:11;
Is. 44:23; 49:13
ᵇIs. 55:12

69:35 ªPs. 51:18;
Is. 44:26

69:36
ªPs. 102:28

69:20 ¹Lit. *sickness* **69:36** ¹Lit. *seed*

PSALM 70

PRAYER FOR RELIEF FROM ADVERSARIES

(Ps. 40:13–17)

To the Chief Musician. *A Psalm* of David.
[a]To bring to remembrance.

1 *MAKE haste,* [a]O God, to deliver me!
Make haste to help me, O LORD!

2 [a]Let them be ashamed and confounded
Who seek my life;
Let them be [1]turned back and confused
Who desire my hurt.

3 [a]Let them be turned back because of their shame,
Who say, [1]"Aha, aha!"

4 Let all those who seek You rejoice and be glad in You;
And let those who love Your salvation say continually,
"Let God be magnified!"

5 [a]But I *am* poor and needy;
[b]Make haste to me, O God!
You *are* my help and my deliverer;
O LORD, do not delay.

PSALM 71

GOD THE ROCK OF SALVATION

1 IN [a]You, O LORD, I put my trust;
Let me never be put to shame.

2 [a]Deliver me in Your righteousness, and cause me to
escape;
[b]Incline Your ear to me, and save me.

3 [a]Be my [1]strong refuge,
To which I may resort continually;
You have given the [b]commandment to save me,
For You *are* my rock and my fortress.

4 [a]Deliver me, O my God, out of the hand of the wicked,
Out of the hand of the unrighteous and cruel man.

5 For You are [a]my hope, O Lord GOD;
You are my trust from my youth.

6 [a]By You I have been [1]upheld from birth;
You are He who took me out of my mother's womb.
My praise *shall be* continually of You.

7 [a]I have become as a wonder to many,
But You *are* my strong refuge.

8 Let [a]my mouth be filled *with* Your praise
And *with* Your glory all the day.

9 Do not cast me off in the time of old age;
Do not forsake me when my strength fails.

10 For my enemies speak against me;
And those who lie in wait for my life [a]take counsel
together,

70:title
[a]Ps. 38:title

70:1
[a]Ps. 40:13–17

70:2
[a]Ps. 35:4, 26

70:3 [a]Ps. 40:15

70:5
[a]Ps. 72:12, 13
[b]Ps. 141:1

71:1 [a]Ps. 25:2, 3

71:2 [a]Ps. 31:1
[b]Ps. 17:6

71:3 [a]Ps. 31:2, 3
[b]Ps. 44:4

71:4 [a]Ps. 140:1, 3

71:5 [a]Jer. 14:8;
17:7, 13, 17; 50:7

71:6
[a]Ps. 22:9, 10;
Is. 46:3

71:7 [a]Is. 8:18;
Zech. 3:8;
1 Cor. 4:9

71:8 [a]Ps. 35:28

71:10
[a]2 Sam. 17:1

70:2 [1]So with MT, LXX, Tg., Vg.; some Heb. mss., Syr. *appalled* (cf. 40:15)
70:3 [1]An expression of scorn   71:3 [1]Lit. *rock of refuge* or *rock of habitation*
71:6 [1]*sustained from the womb*

11 Saying, "God has forsaken him;
   Pursue and take him, for *there is* none to deliver
      him."

12 ⁿO God, do not be far from me;
   O my God, ᵇmake haste to help me!
13 Let them be ¹confounded *and* consumed
   Who are adversaries of my life;
   Let them be covered *with* reproach and dishonor
   Who seek my hurt.

14 But I will hope continually,
   And will praise You yet more and more.
15 My mouth shall tell of Your righteousness
   And Your salvation all the day,
   For I do not know *their* limits.
16 I will go in the strength of the Lord GOD;
   I will make mention of Your righteousness, of Yours
      only.

17 O God, You have taught me from my ⁿyouth;
   And to this *day* I declare Your wondrous works.
18 Now also ⁿwhen *I am* old and grayheaded,
   O God, do not forsake me,
   Until I declare Your strength to *this* generation,
   Your power to everyone *who* is to come.

19 Also ⁿYour righteousness, O God, *is* ¹very high,
   You who have done great things;
   ᵇO God, who *is* like You?
20 ⁿ*You,* who have shown me great and severe troubles,
   ᵇShall revive me again,
   And bring me up again from the depths of the
      earth.
21 You shall increase my greatness,
   And comfort me on every side.

22 Also ⁿwith the lute I will praise You—
   And Your faithfulness, O my God!
   To You I will sing with the harp,
   O ᵇHoly One of Israel.
23 My lips shall greatly rejoice when I sing to You,
   And ⁿmy soul, which You have redeemed.
24 My tongue also shall talk of Your righteousness all the
      day long;
   For they are confounded,
   For they are brought to shame
   Who seek my hurt.

PSALM 72

GLORY AND UNIVERSALITY OF THE MESSIAH'S REIGN

A Psalm ⁿof Solomon.

1 GIVE the king Your judgments, O God,
   And Your righteousness to the king's Son.
2 ⁿHe will judge Your people with righteousness,
   And Your poor with justice.

71:12 ⁿPs. 35:22
   ᵇPs. 70:1
71:17
ⁿDeut. 4:5; 6:7
71:18 ⁿ[Is. 46:4]
71:19
ⁿDeut. 3:24;
   Ps. 57:10
ᵇPs. 35:10
71:20 ⁿPs. 60:3
   ᵇHos. 6:1, 2
71:22
ⁿPs. 92:1–3
ᵇ2 Kin. 19:22;
   Is. 1:4
71:23 ⁿPs. 103:4
72:title
ⁿPs. 127:title
72:2 ⁿ[Is. 9:7;
   11:2–5; 32:1]

71:13 ¹*ashamed*   71:19 ¹*great,* lit. *to the height* of heaven

3 ᵃThe mountains will bring peace to the people,
  And the little hills, by righteousness.
4 ᵃHe will bring justice to the poor of the people;
  He will save the children of the needy,
  And will ¹break in pieces the oppressor.
5 ¹They shall fear You
  ᵃAs long as the sun and moon endure,
  Throughout all generations.
6 ᵃHe shall come down like rain upon the grass before
    mowing,
  Like showers *that* water the earth.
7 In His days the righteous shall flourish,
  ᵃAnd abundance of peace,
  Until the moon is no more.
8 ᵃHe shall have dominion also from sea to sea,
  And from the River to the ends of the earth.
9 ᵃThose who dwell in the wilderness will bow before
    Him,
  ᵇAnd His enemies will lick the dust.
10 ᵃThe kings of Tarshish and of the isles
   Will bring presents;
   The kings of Sheba and Seba
   Will offer gifts.
11 ᵃYes, all kings shall fall down before Him;
   All nations shall serve Him.
12 For He ᵃwill deliver the needy when he cries,
   The poor also, and *him* who has no helper.
13 He will spare the poor and needy,
   And will save the souls of the needy.
14 He will redeem their life from oppression and
     violence;
   And ᵃprecious shall be their blood in His sight.
15 And He shall live;
   And the gold of ᵃSheba will be given to Him;
   Prayer also will be made for Him continually,
   And daily He shall be praised.

16 There will be an abundance of grain in the earth,
   On the top of the mountains;
   Its fruit shall wave like Lebanon;
   ᵃAnd *those* of the city shall flourish like grass of
     the earth.
17 ᵃHis name shall endure forever;
   His name shall continue as long as the sun.
   And ᵇ*men* shall be blessed in Him;
   ᶜAll nations shall call Him blessed.

18 ᵃBlessed *be* the LORD God, the God of Israel,
   ᵇWho only does wondrous things!
19 And ᵃblessed *be* His glorious name forever!
   ᵇAnd let the whole earth be filled *with* His glory.
   Amen and Amen.

20 The prayers of David the son of Jesse are ended.

72:3 ᵃPs. 85:10

72:4 ᵃIs. 11:4

72:5
ᵃPs. 72:7, 17;
89:36

72:6
ᵃDeut. 32:2;
2 Sam. 23:4;
Hos. 6:3

72:7 ᵃIs. 2:4

72:8 ᵃEx. 23:31;
[Is. 9:6;
Zech. 9:10]

72:9 ᵃPs. 74:14;
Is. 23:13
ᵇIs. 49:23;
Mic. 7:17

72:10
ᵃ1 Kin. 10:2;
2 Chr. 9:21

72:11 ᵃIs. 49:23

72:12 ᵃJob 29:12

72:14
ᵃ1 Sam. 26:21;
[Ps. 116:15]

72:15 ᵃIs. 60:6

72:16
ᵃ1 Kin. 4:20

72:17
ᵃ[Ps. 89:36]
ᵇ[Gen. 12:3]
ᶜLuke 1:48

72:18
ᵃ1 Chr. 29:10
ᵇEx. 15:11;
Job 5:9

72:19
ᵃ[Neh. 9:5]
ᵇNum. 14:21;
Hab. 2:14

72:4 ¹crush   72:5 ¹So with MT, Tg.; LXX, Vg. *They shall continue*

BOOK THREE
Psalms 73–89

PSALM 73
THE TRAGEDY OF THE WICKED, AND THE BLESSEDNESS OF TRUST IN GOD

A Psalm of ᵃAsaph.

1 TRULY God *is* good to Israel,
  To such as are pure in heart.
2 But as for me, my feet had almost stumbled;
  My steps had nearly ᵃslipped.
3 ᵃFor I *was* envious of the boastful,
  When I saw the prosperity of the ᵇwicked.

4 For *there are* no ¹pangs in their death,
  But their strength *is* firm.
5 ᵃThey *are* not in trouble *as other* men,
  Nor are they plagued like *other* men.
6 Therefore pride serves as their necklace;
  Violence covers them ᵃ*like* a garment.
7 ᵃTheir ¹eyes bulge with abundance;
  They have more than heart could wish.
8 ᵃThey scoff and speak wickedly *concerning* oppression;
  They ᵇspeak ¹loftily.
9 They set their mouth ᵃagainst the heavens,
  And their tongue walks through the earth.
10 Therefore his people return here,
  ᵃAnd waters of a full *cup* are drained by them.
11 And they say, ᵃ"How does God know?
  And is there knowledge in the Most High?"
12 Behold, these *are* the ungodly,
  Who are always at ease;
  They increase *in* riches.
13 Surely I have ¹cleansed my heart *in* ᵃvain,
  And washed my hands in innocence.
14 For all day long I have been plagued,
  And chastened every morning.

15 If I had said, "I will speak thus,"
  Behold, I would have been untrue to the generation of
    Your children.
16 When I thought *how* to understand this,
  It *was* ¹too painful for me—
17 Until I went into the sanctuary of God;
  Then I understood their ᵃend.

18 Surely ᵃYou set them in slippery places;
  You cast them down to destruction.
19 Oh, how they are *brought* to desolation, as in a moment!
  They are utterly consumed with terrors.
20 As a dream when *one* awakes,
  So, Lord, when You awake,
  You shall despise their image.

73:title
ᵃPs. 50:title

73:2 ᵃJob 12:5

73:3
ᵃPs. 37:1, 7;
[Prov. 23:17]
ᵇJob 21:5–16;
Jer. 12:1

73:5 ᵃJob 21:9

73:6 ᵃPs. 109:18

73:7 ᵃJob 15:27;
Jer. 5:28

73:8 ᵃPs. 53:1
ᵇ2 Pet. 2:18;
Jude 16

73:9 ᵃRev. 13:6

73:10 ᵃ[Ps. 75:8]

73:11 ᵃJob 22:13

73:13 ᵃJob 21:15;
35:3; Mal. 3:14

73:17
ᵃ[Ps. 37:38;
55:23]

73:18 ᵃPs. 35:6

73:4 ¹pains 73:7 ¹Tg. *face bulges*; LXX, Syr., Vg. *iniquity bulges*
73:8 ¹Proudly 73:13 ¹*kept my heart pure in vain* 73:16 ¹*troublesome in my eyes*

21 Thus my heart was grieved,
And I was [1]vexed in my mind.
22 [a]I *was* so foolish and ignorant;
I was *like* a beast before You.
23 Nevertheless I *am* continually with You;
You hold *me* by my right hand.
24 [a]You will guide me with Your counsel,
And afterward receive me *to* glory.
25 [a]Whom have I in heaven *but You?*
And *there is* none upon earth *that* I desire besides
You.
26 [a]My flesh and my heart fail;
But God *is* the [1]strength of my heart and my [b]portion
forever.

27 For indeed, [a]those who are far from You shall perish;
You have destroyed all those who [1]desert You for
harlotry.
28 But *it is* good for me to [a]draw near to God;
I have put my trust in the Lord GOD,
That I may [b]declare all Your works.

PSALM 74

A PLEA FOR RELIEF FROM OPPRESSORS

A [1]Contemplation of Asaph.

1 O GOD, why have You cast *us* off forever?
Why does Your anger smoke against the sheep of Your
pasture?
2 Remember Your congregation, *which* You have
purchased of old,
The tribe of Your inheritance, *which* You have
redeemed—
This Mount Zion where You have dwelt.
3 Lift up Your feet to the perpetual desolations.
The enemy has damaged everything in the sanctuary.
4 [a]Your enemies roar in the midst of Your meeting place;
[b]They set up their banners *for* signs.
5 They seem like men who lift up
Axes among the thick trees.
6 And now they break down its carved work, all at once,
With axes and hammers.
7 They have set fire to Your sanctuary;
They have defiled the dwelling place of Your name to the
ground.
8 [a]They said in their hearts,
"Let us [1]destroy them altogether."
They have burned up all the meeting places of God in the
land.
9 We do not see our signs;
[a]*There is* no longer any prophet;
Nor *is there* any among us who knows how long.
10 O God, how long will the adversary [1]reproach?
Will the enemy blaspheme Your name forever?

73:22 [a]Ps. 92:6

73:24 [a]Ps. 32:8;
48:14; Is. 58:11

73:25
[a][Phil. 3:8]

73:26 [a]Ps. 84:2
[b]Ps. 16:5

73:27
[a][Ps. 119:155]

73:28
[a][Heb. 10:22;
James 4:8]
[b]Ps. 116:10;
2 Cor. 4:13

74:4 [a]Lam. 2:7
[b]Num. 2:2

74:8 [a]Ps. 83:4

74:9 [a]1 Sam. 3:1;
Lam. 2:9;
Ezek. 7:26;
Amos 8:11

73:21 [1]Lit. *pierced in my kidneys*   73:26 [1]Lit. *rock*   73:27 [1]Are unfaithful to
You   74:title [1]Heb. *Maschil*   74:8 [1]*oppress*   74:10 [1]*revile*

11 ^aWhy do You withdraw Your hand, even Your right hand?
   Take it out of Your bosom and destroy *them.*
12 For ^aGod *is* my King from of old,
   Working salvation in the midst of the earth.
13 ^aYou divided the sea by Your strength;
   You broke the heads of the ¹sea serpents in the waters.
14 You broke the heads of ¹Leviathan in pieces,
   And gave him *as* food to the people inhabiting the
       wilderness.
15 ^aYou broke open the fountain and the flood;
   ^bYou dried up mighty rivers.
16 The day *is* Yours, the night also *is* ^aYours;
   ^bYou have prepared the light and the sun.
17 You have ^aset all the borders of the earth;
   ^bYou have made summer and winter.

18 Remember this, *that* the enemy has reproached, O LORD,
   And *that* a foolish people has blasphemed Your name.
19 Oh, do not deliver the life of Your turtledove to the wild
       beast!
   Do not forget the life of Your poor forever.
20 ^aHave respect to the covenant;
   For the ¹dark places of the earth are full of the ²haunts of
       ³cruelty.
21 Oh, do not let the oppressed return ashamed!
   Let the poor and needy praise Your name.

22 Arise, O God, plead Your own cause;
   Remember how the foolish man ¹reproaches You daily.
23 Do not forget the voice of Your enemies;
   The tumult of those who rise up against You increases
       continually.

PSALM 75

THANKSGIVING FOR GOD'S RIGHTEOUS JUDGMENT

To the Chief Musician. Set to ^a"Do¹ Not
Destroy." A Psalm of Asaph. A Song.

1 WE give thanks to You, O God, we give thanks!
   For Your wondrous works declare *that* Your name is near.

2 "When I choose the ¹proper time,
   I will judge uprightly.
3 The earth and all its inhabitants are dissolved;
   I set up its pillars firmly.   *Selah*

4 "I said to the boastful, 'Do not deal boastfully,'
   And to the wicked, ^a'Do not ¹lift up the horn.
5 Do not lift up your horn on high;
   Do *not* speak with ¹a stiff neck.'"

6 For exaltation *comes* neither from the east
   Nor from the west nor from the south.
7 But ^aGod *is* the Judge:
   ^bHe puts down one,
   And exalts another.

Cross references (margin)

74:11 ^aLam. 2:3

74:12 ^aPs. 44:4

74:13 ^aEx. 14:21

74:15
^aEx. 17:5, 6;
Num. 20:11;
Ps. 105:41;
Is. 48:21
^bEx. 14:21, 22;
Josh. 2:10; 3:13

74:16 ^aJob 38:12
^bGen. 1:14–18

74:17
^aDeut. 32:8;
Acts 17:26
^bGen. 8:22

74:20
^aGen. 17:7, 8;
Lev. 26:44, 45

75:title
^aPs. 57:title

75:4
^a[1 Sam. 2:3];
Ps. 94:4

75:7 ^aPs. 50:6
^b1 Sam. 2:7;
Ps. 147:6;
Dan. 2:21

Footnotes

74:13 ¹*sea monsters*   74:14 ¹A large sea creature of unknown identity
74:20 ¹*hiding places*   ²*homes*   ³*violence*   74:22 ¹*reviles* or *taunts*
75:title ¹Heb. *Al Tashcheth*   75:2 ¹*appointed*   75:4 ¹Raise the head proudly
like a horned animal   75:5 ¹*Insolent pride*

8 For [a]in the hand of the LORD *there is* a cup,
   And the wine is red;
   It is fully mixed, and He pours it out;
   Surely its dregs shall all the wicked of the earth
   Drain *and* drink down.

9 But I will declare forever,
   I will sing praises to the God of Jacob.

10 "All[a] the [1]horns of the wicked I will also cut off,
   But [b]the horns of the righteous shall be [c]exalted."

PSALM 76

THE MAJESTY OF GOD IN JUDGMENT

*To the Chief Musician. On [1]stringed
instruments. A Psalm of Asaph. A Song.*

1 IN [a]Judah God *is* known;
   His name *is* great in Israel.
2 In [1]Salem also is His tabernacle,
   And His dwelling place in Zion.
3 There He broke the arrows of the bow,
   The shield and sword of battle.   *Selah*

4 You *are* more glorious and excellent
   [a]*Than* the mountains of prey.
5 [a]The stouthearted were plundered;
   [b]They [1]have sunk into their sleep;
   And none of the mighty men have found the use of their
      hands.
6 [a]At Your rebuke, O God of Jacob,
   Both the chariot and horse were cast into a dead sleep.

7 You, Yourself, *are* to be feared;
   And [a]who may stand in Your presence
   When once You are angry?
8 [a]You caused judgment to be heard from heaven;
   [b]The earth feared and was still,
9 When God [a]arose to judgment,
   To deliver all the oppressed of the earth.   *Selah*

10 [a]Surely the wrath of man shall praise You;
   With the remainder of wrath You shall gird Yourself.

11 [a]Make vows to the LORD your God, and pay *them*;
   [b]Let all who are around Him bring presents to Him who
      ought to be feared.
12 He shall cut off the spirit of princes;
   [a]*He is* awesome to the kings of the earth.

PSALM 77

THE CONSOLING MEMORY OF GOD'S REDEMPTIVE WORKS

To the Chief Musician. [a]To Jeduthun. A Psalm of Asaph.

1 I CRIED out to God with my voice—
   To God with my voice;
   And He gave ear to me.

75:8 [a]Job 21:20;
Ps. 60:3;
Jer. 25:15;
Rev. 14:10; 16:19

75:10 [a]Ps. 101:8;
Jer. 48:25
[b]Ps. 89:17; 148:14
[c]1 Sam. 2:1

76:1 [a]Ps. 48:1, 3

76:4
[a]Ezek. 38:12

76:5
[a]Is. 10:12; 46:12
[b]Ps. 13:3

76:6
[a]Ex. 15:1–21;
Ezek. 39:20;
Nah. 2:13;
Zech. 12:4

76:7 [a][Ezra 9:15;
Nah. 1:6;
Mal. 3:2;
Rev. 6:17]

76:8 [a]Ex. 19:9
[b]1 Chr. 16:30;
2 Chr. 20:29

76:9
[a][Ps. 9:7–9]

76:10 [a]Ex. 9:16;
Rom. 9:17

76:11
[a][Eccl. 5:4–6]
[b]2 Chr. 32:22, 23

76:12 [a]Ps. 68:35

77:title
[a]Ps. 39:title

75:10 [1]Strength 76:title [1]Heb. *neginoth* 76:2 [1]Jerusalem 76:5 [1]Lit. *have
slumbered their sleep*

2 In the day of my trouble I sought the Lord;
My hand was stretched out in the night without ceasing;
My soul refused to be comforted.
3 I remembered God, and was troubled;
I complained, and my spirit was overwhelmed.   *Selah*

4 You hold my eyelids *open*;
I am so troubled that I cannot speak.
5 I have considered the days of old,
The years of ancient times.
6 I call to remembrance my song in the night;
I meditate within my heart,
And my spirit ¹makes diligent search.

7 Will the Lord cast off forever?
And will He be favorable no more?
8 Has His mercy ceased forever?
Has *His* ªpromise failed ¹forevermore?
9 Has God forgotten to be gracious?
Has He in anger shut up His tender mercies?   *Selah*

10 And I said, "This *is* my ¹anguish;
But I will remember the years of the right hand of the
    Most High."
11 I will remember the works of the LORD;
Surely I will remember Your wonders of old.
12 I will also meditate on all Your work,
And talk of Your deeds.
13 Your way, O God, *is* in ¹the ªsanctuary;
Who *is* so great a God as *our* God?
14 You *are* the God who does wonders;
You have declared Your strength among the peoples.
15 You have with *Your* arm redeemed Your people,
The sons of Jacob and Joseph.   *Selah*

16 The waters saw You, O God;
The waters saw You, they were ªafraid;
The depths also trembled.
17 The clouds poured out water;
The skies sent out a sound;
Your arrows also flashed about.
18 The voice of Your thunder *was* in the whirlwind;
The lightnings lit up the world;
The earth trembled and shook.
19 Your way *was* in the sea,
Your path in the great waters,
And Your footsteps were not known.
20 You led Your people like a flock
By the hand of Moses and Aaron.

PSALM 78

GOD'S KINDNESS TO REBELLIOUS ISRAEL

A ªContemplation¹ of Asaph.

1 GIVE ear, O my people, *to* my law;
Incline your ears to the words of my mouth.

77:8
ª[2 Pet. 3:8, 9]
77:13 ªPs. 73:17
77:16 ªEx. 14:21;
Hab. 3:8, 10
78:title
ªPs. 74:title

77:6 ¹*ponders diligently*   77:8 ¹Lit. *unto generation and generation*
77:10 ¹Lit. *infirmity*   77:13 ¹Or *holiness*   78:title ¹Heb. *Maschil*

2   I will open my mouth in a ªparable;
     I will utter ¹dark sayings of old,
3   Which we have heard and known,
     And our fathers have told us.
4   ªWe will not hide *them* from their children,
       ᵇTelling to the generation to come the praises of the
           LORD,
     And His strength and His wonderful works that He has
           done.

5   For ªHe established a testimony in Jacob,
     And appointed a law in Israel,
     Which He commanded our fathers,
     That ᵇthey should make them known to their children;
6   ªThat the generation to come might know *them,*
     The children *who* would be born,
     That they may arise and declare *them* to their children,
7   That they may set their hope in God,
     And not forget the works of God,
     But keep His commandments;
8   And ªmay not be like their fathers,
       ᵇA stubborn and rebellious generation,
     A generation ᶜ*that* did not ¹set its heart aright,
     And whose spirit was not faithful to God.

9   The children of Ephraim, *being* armed *and* ¹carrying bows,
     Turned back in the day of battle.
10   ªThey did not keep the covenant of God;
     They refused to walk in His law,
11   And ªforgot His works
     And His wonders that He had shown them.

12   ªMarvelous things He did in the sight of their fathers,
     In the land of Egypt, ᵇ*in* the field of Zoan.
13   ªHe divided the sea and caused them to pass through;
     And ᵇHe made the waters stand up like a heap.
14   ªIn the daytime also He led them with the cloud,
     And all the night with a light of fire.
15   ªHe split the rocks in the wilderness,
     And gave *them* drink in abundance like the depths.
16   He also brought ªstreams out of the rock,
     And caused waters to run down like rivers.

17   But they sinned even more against Him
     By ªrebelling against the Most High in the wilderness.
18   And ªthey tested God in their heart
     By asking for the food of their fancy.
19   ªYes, they spoke against God:
     They said, "Can God prepare a table in the wilderness?
20   ªBehold, He struck the rock,
     So that the waters gushed out,
     And the streams overflowed.
     Can He give bread also?
     Can He provide meat for His people?"

21   Therefore the LORD heard *this* and ªwas furious;
     So a fire was kindled against Jacob,
     And anger also came up against Israel,

78:2
ªMatt. 13:34, 35

78:4
ªEx. 12:26, 27;
Deut. 4:9; 6:7;
Job 15:18;
Is. 38:19; Joel 1:3
ᵇEx. 13:8, 14

78:5 ªPs. 147:19
ᵇDeut. 4:9; 11:19

78:6 ªPs. 102:18

78:8
ª2 Kin. 17:14;
2 Chr. 30:7;
Ezek. 20:18
ᵇEx. 32:9;
Deut. 9:7, 24;
31:27; Judg. 2:19;
Is. 30:9
ᶜJob 11:13;
Ps. 78:37

78:10
ª2 Kin. 17:15

78:11 ªPs. 106:13

78:12 ªEx. 7—12
ᵇNum. 13:22;
Is. 19:11; 30:4;
Ezek. 30:14

78:13 ªEx. 14:21
ᵇEx. 15:8

78:14 ªEx. 13:21

78:15 ªEx. 17:6;
Num. 20:11;
Is. 48:21;
[1 Cor. 10:4]

78:16
ªNum. 20:8,
10, 11

78:17
ªDeut. 9:22;
Is. 63:10;
Heb. 3:16

78:18 ªEx. 16:2

78:19 ªEx. 16:3;
Num. 11:4; 20:3;
21:5

78:20
ªNum. 20:11

78:21 ªNum. 11:1

78:2 ¹*obscure sayings* or *riddles*   **78:8** ¹Lit. *prepare its heart*   **78:9** ¹Lit. *bow shooters*

22 Because they ^adid not believe in God,
   And did not trust in His salvation.
23 Yet He had commanded the clouds above,
   ^aAnd opened the doors of heaven,
24 ^aHad rained down manna on them to eat,
   And given them of the ¹bread of ^bheaven.
25 Men ate angels' food;
   He sent them food to ¹the full.

26 ^aHe caused an east wind to blow in the heavens;
   And by His power He brought in the south wind.
27 He also rained meat on them like the dust,
   Feathered fowl like the sand of the seas;
28 And He let *them* fall in the midst of their camp,
   All around their dwellings.
29 ^aSo they ate and were well filled,
   For He gave them their own desire.
30 They were not ¹deprived of their craving;
   But ^awhile their food *was* still in their mouths,
31 The wrath of God came against them,
   And slew the stoutest of them,
   And struck down the choice *men* of Israel.

32 In spite of this ^athey still sinned,
   And ^bdid not believe in His wondrous works.
33 ^aTherefore their days He consumed in futility,
   And their years in fear.

34 ^aWhen He slew them, then they sought Him;
   And they returned and sought earnestly for God.
35 Then they remembered that ^aGod *was* their rock,
   And the Most High God ^btheir Redeemer.
36 Nevertheless they ^aflattered Him with their mouth,
   And they lied to Him with their tongue;
37 For their heart was not steadfast with Him,
   Nor were they faithful in His covenant.
38 ^aBut He, *being* full of ^bcompassion, forgave *their*
     iniquity,
   And did not destroy *them.*
   Yes, many a time ^cHe turned His anger away,
   And ^ddid not stir up all His wrath;
39 For ^aHe remembered ^bthat they *were but* flesh,
   ^cA breath that passes away and does not come again.

40 How often they ^aprovoked¹ Him in the wilderness,
   And grieved Him in the desert!
41 Yes, ^aagain and again they tempted God,
   And limited the Holy One of Israel.
42 They did not remember His ¹power:
   The day when He redeemed them from the enemy,
43 When He worked His signs in Egypt,
   And His wonders in the field of Zoan;
44 ^aTurned their rivers into blood,
   And their streams, that they could not drink.
45 ^aHe sent swarms of flies among them, which devoured
     them,
   And ^bfrogs, which destroyed them.

Cross references (margin):

78:22 ^aDeut. 1:32; 9:23; [Heb. 3:18]
78:23 ^aGen. 7:11; [Mal. 3:10]
78:24 ^aEx. 16:4 ^bJohn 6:31
78:26 ^aNum. 11:31
78:29 ^aNum. 11:19, 20
78:30 ^aNum. 11:33
78:32 ^aNum. 14:16, 17 ^bNum. 14:11; Ps. 78:11, 22
78:33 ^aNum. 14:29, 35
78:34 ^aNum. 21:7; [Hos. 5:15]
78:35 ^a[Deut. 32:4, 15] ^b[Ex. 15:13]; Deut. 7:8; Is. 41:14; 44:6; 63:9
78:36 ^aEx. 24:7, 8; Ezek. 33:31
78:38 ^a[Num. 14:18–20] ^bEx. 34:6 ^c[Is. 48:9] ^d1 Kin. 21:29
78:39 ^aJob 10:9; Ps. 103:14–16 ^bJohn 3:6 ^c[Job 7:7, 16; James 4:14]
78:40 ^aPs. 95:8–10; [Eph. 4:30]; Heb. 3:16
78:41 ^aNum. 14:22; Deut. 6:16
78:44 ^aEx. 7:20
78:45 ^aEx. 8:24 ^bEx. 8:6

78:24 ¹Lit. *grain*   **78:25** ¹*satiation*   **78:30** ¹Lit. *separated*   **78:40** ¹*rebelled against Him*   **78:42** ¹Lit. *hand*

46 He also gave their crops to the caterpillar,
And their labor to the [a]locust.
47 [a]He destroyed their vines with hail,
And their sycamore trees with frost.
48 He also gave up their [a]cattle to the hail,
And their flocks to fiery [1]lightning.
49 He cast on them the fierceness of His anger,
Wrath, indignation, and trouble,
By sending angels of destruction *among them.*
50 He made a path for His anger;
He did not spare their soul from death,
But gave [1]their life over to the plague,
51 And destroyed all the [a]firstborn in Egypt,
The first of *their* strength in the tents of Ham.
52 But He [a]made His own people go forth like sheep,
And guided them in the wilderness like a flock;
53 And He [a]led them on safely, so that they did not fear;
But the sea [b]overwhelmed their enemies.
54 And He brought them to His [a]holy border,
This mountain [b]*which* His right hand had acquired.
55 [a]He also drove out the nations before them,
[b]Allotted them an inheritance by [1]survey,
And made the tribes of Israel dwell in their tents.

56 [a]Yet they tested and provoked the Most High God,
And did not keep His testimonies,
57 But [a]turned back and acted unfaithfully like their
fathers;
They were turned aside [b]like a deceitful bow.
58 [a]For they provoked Him to anger with their [b]high places,
And moved Him to jealousy with their carved images.
59 When God heard *this,* He was furious,
And greatly abhorred Israel,
60 [a]So that He forsook the tabernacle of Shiloh,
The tent He had placed among men,
61 [a]And delivered His strength into captivity,
And His glory into the enemy's hand.
62 [a]He also gave His people over to the sword,
And was furious with His inheritance.
63 The fire consumed their young men,
And [a]their maidens were not given in marriage.
64 [a]Their priests fell by the sword,
And [b]their widows made no lamentation.
65 Then the Lord awoke as *from* sleep,
[a]Like a mighty man who shouts because of wine.
66 And [a]He beat back His enemies;
He put them to a perpetual reproach.
67 Moreover He rejected the tent of Joseph,
And did not choose the tribe of Ephraim,
68 But chose the tribe of Judah,
Mount Zion [a]which He loved.
69 And He built His [a]sanctuary like the heights,
Like the earth which He has established forever.
70 [a]He also chose David His servant,
And took him from the sheepfolds;

78:46 [a]Ex. 10:14
78:47
[a]Ex. 9:23–25
78:48 [a]Ex. 9:19
78:51
[a]Ex. 12:29, 30
78:52 [a]Ps. 77:20
78:53
[a]Ex. 14:19, 20
[b]Ex. 14:27, 28
78:54 [a]Ex. 15:17
[b]Ps. 44:3
78:55
[a]Josh. 11:16–23;
Ps. 44:2
[b]Josh. 13:7;
19:51; 23:4
78:56
[a]Judg. 2:11–13
78:57
[a]Ezek. 20:27, 28
[b]Hos. 7:16
78:58
[a]Deut. 32:16, 21;
Judg. 2:12;
1 Kin. 14:9;
Is. 65:3
[b]Deut. 12:2
78:60
[a]1 Sam. 4:11;
Jer. 7:12–14;
26:6–9
78:61
[a]Judg. 18:30
78:62
[a]Judg. 20:21;
1 Sam. 4:10
78:63 [a]Jer. 7:34;
16:9; 25:10
78:64
[a]1 Sam. 4:17;
22:18 [b]Job 27:15;
Ezek. 24:23
78:65 [a]Is. 42:13
78:66
[a]1 Sam. 5:6
78:68
[a][Ps. 87:2]
78:69
[a]1 Kin. 6:1–38
78:70
[a]1 Sam. 16:11, 12;
2 Sam. 7:8

78:48 [1]*lightning bolts*   78:50 [1]Or *their beasts*   78:55 [1]*surveyed
measurement,* lit. *measuring cord*

71 From following ᵃthe ewes that had young He brought him,
ᵇTo shepherd Jacob His people,
And Israel His inheritance.
72 So he shepherded them according to the ᵃintegrity of his heart,
And guided them by the skillfulness of his hands.

PSALM 79

A DIRGE AND A PRAYER FOR ISRAEL, DESTROYED BY ENEMIES

A Psalm of Asaph.

1 O GOD, the ¹nations have come into ᵃYour inheritance;
Your holy temple they have defiled;
ᵇThey have laid Jerusalem ²in heaps.
2 ᵃThe dead bodies of Your servants
They have given as food for the birds of the heavens,
The flesh of Your saints to the beasts of the earth.
3 Their blood they have shed like water all around Jerusalem,
And there was no one to bury them.
4 We have become a reproach to our ᵃneighbors,
A scorn and derision to those who are around us.

5 ᵃHow long, LORD?
Will You be angry forever?
Will Your ᵇjealousy burn like fire?
6 ᵃPour out Your wrath on the ¹nations that ᵇdo not know You,
And on the kingdoms that ᶜdo not call on Your name.
7 For they have devoured Jacob,
And laid waste his dwelling place.

8 ᵃOh, do not remember ¹former iniquities against us!
Let Your tender mercies come speedily to meet us,
For we have been brought very low.
9 Help us, O God of our salvation,
For the glory of Your name;
And deliver us, and provide atonement for our sins,
ᵃFor Your name's sake!
10 ᵃWhy should the ¹nations say,
"Where is their God?"
Let there be known among the nations in our sight
The avenging of the blood of Your servants which has been shed.

11 Let ᵃthe groaning of the prisoner come before You;
According to the greatness of Your ¹power
Preserve those who are appointed to die;
12 And return to our neighbors ᵃsevenfold into their bosom
ᵇTheir reproach with which they have reproached You,
O Lord.

13 So ᵃwe, Your people and sheep of Your pasture,
Will give You thanks forever;
ᵇWe will show forth Your praise to all generations.

78:71
ᵃ2 Sam. 7:8;
[Is. 40:11]
ᵇ2 Sam. 5:2;
1 Chr. 11:2

78:72 ᵃ1 Kin. 9:4

79:1 ᵃPs. 74:2
ᵇ2 Kin. 25:9, 10;
2 Chr. 36:17–19;
Jer. 26:18;
52:12–14;
Mic. 3:12

79:2
ᵃDeut. 28:26;
Jer. 7:33; 19:7;
34:20

79:4 ᵃPs. 44:13;
[Dan. 9:16]

79:5 ᵃPs. 74:1, 9
ᵇ[Zeph. 3:8]

79:6 ᵃJer. 10:25;
[Zeph. 3:8]
ᵇIs. 45:4, 5;
1 Thess. 4:5;
[2 Thess. 1:8]
ᶜPs. 53:4

79:8 ᵃIs. 64:9

79:9 ᵃJer. 14:7, 21

79:10 ᵃPs. 42:10

79:11 ᵃPs. 102:20

79:12 ᵃGen. 4:15;
Lev. 26:21;
Prov. 6:31;
Is. 30:26
ᵇPs. 74:10, 18, 22

79:13
ᵃPs. 74:1; 95:7
ᵇIs. 43:21

79:1 ¹Gentiles   ²in ruins   79:6 ¹Gentiles   79:8 ¹Or against us the iniquities of those who were before us   79:10 ¹Gentiles   79:11 ¹Lit. arm

PSALM 80

PRAYER FOR ISRAEL'S RESTORATION

To the Chief Musician. ªSet to ¹"The Lilies."
A ²Testimony of Asaph. A Psalm.

1   GIVE ear, O Shepherd of Israel,
     ªYou who lead Joseph ᵇlike a flock;
     You who dwell *between* the cherubim, ᶜshine forth!
2   Before ªEphraim, Benjamin, and Manasseh,
     Stir up Your strength,
     And come *and* save us!

3   ªRestore us, O God;
     ᵇCause Your face to shine,
     And we shall be saved!

4   O LORD God of hosts,
     ªHow long will You be angry
     Against the prayer of Your people?
5   ªYou have fed them with the bread of tears,
     And given them tears to drink in great measure.
6   You have made us a strife to our neighbors,
     And our enemies laugh among themselves.

7   Restore us, O God of hosts;
     Cause Your face to shine,
     And we shall be saved!

8   You have brought ªa vine out of Egypt;
     ᵇYou have cast out the ¹nations, and planted it.
9   You prepared *room* for it,
     And caused it to take deep root,
     And it filled the land.
10   The hills were covered with its shadow,
     And the ¹mighty cedars with its ªboughs.
11   She sent out her boughs to ¹the Sea,
     And her branches to ²the River.

12   Why have You ªbroken down her ¹hedges,
     So that all who pass by the way pluck her *fruit?*
13   The boar out of the woods uproots it,
     And the wild beast of the field devours it.

14   Return, we beseech You, O God of hosts;
     ªLook down from heaven and see,
     And visit this vine
15   And the vineyard which Your right hand has planted,
     And the branch *that* You made strong ªfor Yourself.
16   *It is* burned with fire, *it is* cut down;
     ªThey perish at the rebuke of Your countenance.
17   ªLet Your hand be upon the man of Your right hand,
     Upon the son of man *whom* You made strong for Yourself.
18   Then we will not turn back from You;
     Revive us, and we will call upon Your name.

19   Restore us, O LORD God of hosts;
     Cause Your face to shine,
     And we shall be saved!

80:title
ªPs. 45:title

80:1
ª[Ex. 25:20–22];
1 Sam. 4:4;
2 Sam. 6:2
ᵇPs. 77:20
ᶜDeut. 33:2

80:2
ªPs. 78:9, 67

80:3 ªLam. 5:21
ᵇNum. 6:25;
Ps. 4:6

80:4 ªPs. 79:5

80:5 ªPs. 42:3;
Is. 30:20

80:8 ª[Is. 5:1, 7];
Jer. 2:21;
Ezek. 15:6; 17:6;
19:10 ᵇPs. 44:2;
Acts 7:45

80:10
ªLev. 23:40

80:12 ªIs. 5:5;
Nah. 2:2

80:14 ªIs. 63:15

80:15 ª[Is. 49:5]

80:16
ª[Ps. 39:11]

80:17 ªPs. 89:21

80:title ¹Heb. *Shoshannim*   ²Heb. *Eduth*   80:8 ¹*Gentiles*   80:10 ¹Lit. *cedars of God*   80:11 ¹The Mediterranean   ²The Euphrates   80:12 ¹*walls* or *fences*

PSALM 81

AN APPEAL FOR ISRAEL'S REPENTANCE

To the Chief Musician. [a]On[1] an instrument
of Gath. *A Psalm* of Asaph.

1 SING aloud to God our strength;
   Make a joyful shout to the God of Jacob.
2 Raise a song and strike the timbrel,
   The pleasant harp with the lute.
3 Blow the trumpet at the time of the New Moon,
   At the full moon, on our solemn feast day.
4 For [a]this *is* a statute for Israel,
   A law of the God of Jacob.
5 This He established in Joseph *as* a testimony,
   When He went throughout the land of Egypt,
   [a]*Where* I heard a language I did not understand.

6 "I removed his shoulder from the burden;
   His hands were freed from the baskets.
7 [a]You called in trouble, and I delivered you;
   [b]I answered you in the secret place of thunder;
   I [c]tested you at the waters of [1]Meribah.   *Selah*

8 "Hear,[a] O My people, and I will admonish you!
   O Israel, if you will listen to Me!
9 There shall be no [a]foreign god among you;
   Nor shall you worship any foreign god.
10 [a]I *am* the LORD your God,
   Who brought you out of the land of Egypt;
   [b]Open your mouth wide, and I will fill it.

11 "But My people would not heed My voice,
   And Israel would *have* [a]none of Me.
12 [a]So I gave them over to [1]their own stubborn heart,
   To walk in their own counsels.

13 "Oh,[a] that My people would listen to Me,
   That Israel would walk in My ways!
14 I would soon subdue their enemies,
   And turn My hand against their adversaries.
15 [a]The haters of the LORD would pretend submission to
   Him,
   But their [1]fate would endure forever.
16 He would [a]have fed them also with [1]the finest of wheat;
   And with honey [b]from the rock I would have satisfied
   you."

PSALM 82

A PLEA FOR JUSTICE

A Psalm of Asaph.

1 GOD [a]stands in the congregation of [1]the mighty;
   He judges among [b]the [2]gods.
2 How long will you judge unjustly,
   And [a]show partiality to the wicked?   *Selah*

81:title
[a]Ps. 8:title

81:4 [a]Lev. 23:24;
Num. 10:10

81:5
[a]Deut. 28:49;
Ps. 114:1; Jer. 5:15

81:7 [a]Ex. 2:23;
14:10; Ps. 50:15
[b]Ex. 19:19; 20:18
[c]Ex. 17:6, 7;
Num. 20:13

81:8 [a][Ps. 50:7]

81:9 [a][Ex. 20:3;
Deut. 5:7;
32:12];
Ps. 44:20;
[Is. 43:12]

81:10 [a]Ex. 20:2;
Deut. 5:6
[b]Ps. 103:5

81:11 [a]Ex. 32:1;
Deut. 32:15

81:12 [a][Job 8:4;
Acts 7:42;
Rom. 1:24, 26]

81:13
[a][Deut. 5:29;
Is. 48:18]

81:15 [a]Rom. 1:30

81:16
[a]Deut. 32:14
[b]Job 29:6

82:1
[a][2 Chr. 19:6;
Eccl. 5:8]
[b]Ps. 82:6

82:2
[a][Deut. 1:17];
Prov. 18:5

81:title [1]Heb. *Al Gittith*   81:7 [1]Lit. *Strife* or *Contention*   81:12 [1]*the dictates of
their heart*   81:15 [1]Lit. *time*   81:16 [1]Lit. *fat of wheat*   82:1 [1]Heb. *El*, lit. *God*
[2]Judges; Heb. *elohim*, lit. *mighty ones* or *gods*

3 ¹Defend the poor and fatherless;
Do justice to the afflicted and ªneedy.
4 Deliver the poor and needy;
Free *them* from the hand of the wicked.

5 They do not know, nor do they understand;
They walk about in darkness;
All the ªfoundations of the earth are ¹unstable.

6 I said, ª"You *are* ¹gods,
And all of you *are* children of the Most High.
7 But you shall die like men,
And fall like one of the princes."

8 Arise, O God, judge the earth;
ªFor You shall inherit all nations.

PSALM 83

PRAYER TO FRUSTRATE CONSPIRACY AGAINST ISRAEL

A Song. A Psalm of Asaph.

1 DOª not keep silent, O God!
Do not hold Your peace,
And do not be still, O God!
2 For behold, ªYour enemies make a ¹tumult;
And those who hate You have ²lifted up their head.
3 They have taken crafty counsel against Your
people,
And consulted together ªagainst Your sheltered
ones.
4 They have said, "Come, and ªlet us cut them off from
being a nation,
That the name of Israel may be remembered no
more."

5 For they have consulted together with one
¹consent;
They ²form a confederacy against You:
6 ªThe tents of Edom and the Ishmaelites;
Moab and the Hagrites;
7 Gebal, Ammon, and Amalek;
Philistia with the inhabitants of Tyre;
8 Assyria also has joined with them;
They have helped the children of Lot.   *Selah*

9 Deal with them as *with* ªMidian,
As *with* ᵇSisera,
As *with* Jabin at the Brook Kishon,
10 Who perished at En Dor,
ªWho became *as* refuse on the earth.
11 Make their nobles like ªOreb and like Zeeb,
Yes, all their princes like ᵇZebah and Zalmunna,
12 Who said, "Let us take for ourselves
The pastures of God for a possession."

13 ªO my God, make them like the whirling dust,
ᵇLike the chaff before the wind!

82:3
ª[Deut. 24:17;
Is. 11:4;
Jer. 22:16]

82:5 ªPs. 11:3

82:6
ªJohn 10:34

82:8 ªPs. 2:8;
[Rev. 11:15]

83:1 ªPs. 28:1

83:2 ªPs. 81:15;
Is. 17:12;
Acts 4:25

83:3 ª[Ps. 27:5]

83:4
ªEsth. 3:6, 9;
Jer. 11:19; 31:36

83:6
ª2 Chr. 20:1,
10, 11

83:9
ªNum. 31:7;
Judg. 7:22
ᵇJudg. 4:15–24;
5:20, 21

83:10 ªZeph. 1:17

83:11
ªJudg. 7:25
ᵇJudg. 8:12–21

83:13 ªIs. 17:13
ᵇJob 21:18;
Ps. 35:5;
Is. 40:24;
Jer. 13:24

82:3 ¹*Vindicate*   82:5 ¹*moved*   82:6 ¹Judges; Heb. *elohim*, lit. *mighty ones*
or *gods*   83:2 ¹*uproar*   ²Exalted themselves   83:5 ¹Lit. *heart*   ²Lit. *cut a*
covenant

14 As the fire burns the woods,
   And as the flame [a]sets the mountains on fire,
15 So pursue them with Your tempest,
   And frighten them with Your storm.
16 Fill their faces with shame,
   That they may seek Your name, O LORD.
17 Let them be [1]confounded and dismayed forever;
   Yes, let them be put to shame and perish,
18 [a]That they may know that You, whose [b]name alone *is* the
      LORD,
   Are [c]the Most High over all the earth.

PSALM 84

THE BLESSEDNESS OF DWELLING IN THE HOUSE OF GOD

To the Chief Musician. [a]On[1] an instrument
of Gath. A Psalm of the sons of Korah.

1 HOW [a]lovely [1]*is* Your tabernacle,
   O LORD of hosts!
2 [a]My soul longs, yes, even faints
   For the courts of the LORD;
   My heart and my flesh cry out for the living God.

3 Even the sparrow has found a home,
   And the swallow a nest for herself,
   Where she may lay her young—
   Even Your altars, O LORD of hosts,
   My King and my God.
4 Blessed *are* those who dwell in Your [a]house;
   They will still be praising You. **Selah**

5 Blessed *is* the man whose strength *is* in You,
   Whose heart *is* set on pilgrimage.
6 *As they* pass through the Valley [a]of [1]Baca,
   They make it a spring;
   The rain also covers it with [2]pools.
7 They go [a]from strength to strength;
   [1]*Each one* [b]appears before God in Zion.

8 O LORD God of hosts, hear my prayer;
   Give ear, O God of Jacob! **Selah**
9 [a]O God, behold our shield,
   And look upon the face of Your [1]anointed.

10 For a day in Your courts *is* better than a thousand.
   I would rather [1]be a doorkeeper in the house of my
      God
   Than dwell in the tents of wickedness.
11 For the LORD God *is* [a]a sun and [b]shield;
   The LORD will give grace and glory;
   [c]No good *thing* will He withhold
   From those who walk uprightly.

12 O LORD of hosts,
   [a]Blessed *is* the man who trusts in You!

83:14 [a]Ex. 19:18;
Deut. 32:22
83:18 [a]Ps. 59:13
[b]Ex. 6:3
[c][Ps. 92:8]
84:title
[a]Ps. 8:title
84:1 [a]Ps. 27:4;
46:4, 5
84:2 [a]Ps. 42:1, 2
84:4 [a][Ps. 65:4]
84:6
[a]2 Sam. 5:22–25
84:7 [a]Prov. 4:18;
Is. 40:31;
John 1:16;
2 Cor. 3:18
[b]Ex. 34:23;
Deut. 16:16
84:9 [a]Gen. 15:1
84:11 [a]Is. 60:19,
20; Mal. 4:2;
Rev. 21:23
[b]Gen. 15:1
[c]Ps. 34:9, 10
84:12
[a][Ps. 2:12; 40:4]

83:17 [1]*ashamed*   84:title [1]Heb. *Al Gittith*   84:1 [1]*are Your dwellings*
84:6 [1]Lit. *Weeping*   [2]Or *blessings*   84:7 [1]LXX, Syr., Vg. *The God of gods shall
be seen*   84:9 [1]Commissioned one, Heb. *messiah*   84:10 [1]*stand at the
threshold*

PSALM 85

PRAYER THAT THE LORD WILL RESTORE FAVOR TO THE LAND

To the Chief Musician. A Psalm [a]of the sons of Korah.

1 LORD, You have been favorable to Your land;
   You have [a]brought back the captivity of Jacob.
2 You have forgiven the iniquity of Your people;
   You have covered all their sin.   Selah
3 You have taken away all Your wrath;
   You have turned from the fierceness of Your anger.

4 [a]Restore us, O God of our salvation,
   And cause Your anger toward us to cease.
5 [a]Will You be angry with us forever?
   Will You prolong Your anger to all generations?
6 Will You not [a]revive us again,
   That Your people may rejoice in You?
7 Show us Your mercy, LORD,
   And grant us Your salvation.

8 I will hear what God the LORD will speak,
   For He will speak peace
   To His people and to His saints;
   But let them not turn back to [1]folly.
9 Surely [a]His salvation *is* near to those who fear Him,
   [b]That glory may dwell in our land.

10 Mercy and truth have met together;
   [a]Righteousness and peace have kissed.
11 Truth shall spring out of the earth,
   And righteousness shall look down from heaven.
12 [a]Yes, the LORD will give *what is* good;
   And our land will yield its increase.
13 Righteousness will go before Him,
   And shall make His footsteps *our* pathway.

PSALM 86

PRAYER FOR MERCY, WITH MEDITATION ON
THE EXCELLENCIES OF THE LORD

A Prayer of David.

1 BOW down Your ear, O LORD, hear me;
   For I *am* poor and needy.
2 Preserve my [1]life, for I *am* holy;
   You are my God;
   Save Your servant who trusts in You!
3 Be merciful to me, O Lord,
   For I cry to You all day long.
4 [1]Rejoice the soul of Your servant,
   [a]For to You, O Lord, I lift up my soul.
5 For [a]You, Lord, *are* good, and ready to forgive,
   And abundant in mercy to all those who call upon
      You.

6 Give ear, O LORD, to my prayer;
   And attend to the voice of my supplications.

85:title
[a]Ps. 42:title

85:1
[a]Ezra 1:11—2:1;
Ps. 14:7;
Jer. 30:18; 31:23;
Ezek. 39:25;
Hos. 6:11;
Joel 3:1

85:4 [a]Ps. 80:3, 7
85:5 [a]Ps. 79:5
85:6 [a]Hab. 3:2
85:9 [a]Is. 46:13
[b]Hag. 2:7;
Zech. 2:5;
[John 1:14]

85:10 [a]Ps. 72:3;
[Is. 32:17];
Luke 2:14

85:12 [a][Ps. 84:11;
James 1:17]

86:4
[a]Ps. 25:1; 143:8

86:5 [a]Ps. 130:7;
145:9; [Joel 2:13]

85:8 [1]foolishness   86:2 [1]Lit. soul   86:4 [1]Make glad

7 In the day of my trouble I will call upon You,
For You will answer me.

8 ªAmong the gods *there is* none like You, O Lord;
Nor *are there any works* like Your works.
9 All nations whom You have made
Shall come and worship before You, O Lord,
And shall glorify Your name.
10 For You *are* great, and ªdo wondrous things;
ᵇYou alone *are* God.

11 ªTeach me Your way, O LORD;
I will walk in Your truth;
¹Unite my heart to fear Your name.
12 I will praise You, O Lord my God, with all my heart,
And I will glorify Your name forevermore.
13 For great *is* Your mercy toward me,
And You have delivered my soul from the depths of
¹Sheol.

14 O God, the proud have risen against me,
And a mob of violent *men* have sought my life,
And have not set You before them.
15 But ªYou, O Lord, *are* a God full of compassion, and
gracious,
Longsuffering and abundant in mercy and truth.

16 Oh, turn to me, and have mercy on me!
Give Your strength to Your servant,
And save the son of Your maidservant.
17 Show me a sign for good,
That those who hate me may see *it* and be
ashamed,
Because You, LORD, have helped me and
comforted me.

PSALM 87

THE GLORIES OF THE CITY OF GOD

A Psalm of the sons of Korah. A Song.

1 HIS foundation *is* in the holy mountains.
2 ªThe LORD loves the gates of Zion
More than all the dwellings of Jacob.
3 ªGlorious things are spoken of you,
O city of God! *Selah*

4 "I will make mention of ¹Rahab and Babylon to those who
know Me;
Behold, O Philistia and Tyre, with Ethiopia:
'This *one* was born there.'"

5 And of Zion it will be said,
"This *one* and that *one* were born in her;
And the Most High Himself shall establish her."
6 The LORD will record,
When He ªregisters the peoples:
"This *one* was born there." *Selah*

86:8 ª[Ex. 15:11];
2 Sam. 7:22;
1 Kin. 8:23;
Ps. 89:6;
Jer. 10:6
86:10 ª[Ex. 15:11]
ᵇDeut. 6:4;
Is. 37:16;
Mark 12:29;
1 Cor. 8:4
86:11 ªPs. 27:11;
143:8
86:15 ªEx. 34:6;
[Ps. 86:5]
87:2
ªPs. 78:67, 68
87:3 ªIs. 60:1
87:6 ªIs. 4:3

86:11 ¹Give me singleness of heart   86:13 ¹The abode of the dead
87:4 ¹Egypt

7 Both the singers and the players on instruments *say,*
"All my springs *are* in you."

PSALM 88

A PRAYER FOR HELP IN DESPONDENCY

A Song. A Psalm of the sons of Korah. To the
Chief Musician. Set to "Mahalath Leannoth."
A [1]Contemplation of [a]Heman the Ezrahite.

1 O LORD, [a]God of my salvation,
I have cried out day and night before You.
2 Let my prayer come before You;
[1]Incline Your ear to my cry.

3 For my soul is full of troubles,
And my life [a]draws near to the grave.
4 I am counted with those who [a]go[1] down to the pit;
[b]I am like a man *who has* no strength,
5 [1]Adrift among the dead,
Like the slain who lie in the grave,
Whom You remember no more,
And who are cut off from Your hand.

6 You have laid me in the lowest pit,
In darkness, in the depths.
7 Your wrath lies heavy upon me,
And You have afflicted *me* with all [a]Your waves. *Selah*
8 [a]You have [1]put away my acquaintances far from me;
You have made me an abomination to them;
[b]*I am* shut up, and I cannot get out;
9 My eye wastes away because of affliction.

[a]LORD, I have called daily upon You;
I have stretched out my hands to You.
10 Will You work wonders for the dead?
Shall [1]the dead arise *and* praise You? *Selah*
11 Shall Your lovingkindness be declared in the grave?
Or Your faithfulness in the place of destruction?
12 Shall Your wonders be known in the dark?
And Your righteousness in the land of
forgetfulness?

13 But to You I have cried out, O LORD,
And in the morning my prayer comes before You.
14 LORD, why do You cast off my soul?
Why do You hide Your face from me?
15 I *have been* afflicted and ready to die from *my*
youth;
I suffer Your terrors;
I am distraught.
16 Your fierce wrath has gone over me;
Your terrors have [1]cut me off.
17 They came around me all day long like water;
They engulfed me altogether.
18 [a]Loved one and friend You have put far from me,
And my acquaintances into darkness.

88:title
[a]1 Kin. 4:31;
1 Chr. 2:6

88:1 [a]Ps. 27:9;
[Luke 18:7]

88:3 [a]Ps. 107:18

88:4 [a][Ps. 28:1]
[b]Ps. 31:12

88:7 [a]Ps. 42:7

88:8
[a]Job 19:13, 19;
Ps. 31:11; 142:4
[b]Lam. 3:7

88:9 [a]Ps. 86:3

88:18 [a]Job 19:13;
Ps. 31:11; 38:11

88:title [1]Heb. *Maschil*　88:2 [1]Listen to　88:4 [1]Die　88:5 [1]Lit. *Free*
88:8 [1]*taken away my friends*　88:10 [1]*shades, ghosts*　88:16 [1]*destroyed me*

PSALM 89

REMEMBERING THE COVENANT WITH DAVID,
AND SORROW FOR LOST BLESSINGS

A [1]Contemplation of [a]Ethan the Ezrahite.

1 I WILL sing of the mercies of the LORD forever;
With my mouth will I make known Your faithfulness to
all generations.

2 For I have said, "Mercy shall be built up forever;
[a]Your faithfulness You shall establish in the very
heavens."

3 "I[a] have made a covenant with My chosen,
I have [b]sworn to My servant David:

4 'Your seed I will establish forever,
And build up your throne [a]to all generations.'"   *Selah*

5 And [a]the heavens will praise Your wonders, O LORD;
Your faithfulness also in the assembly of the saints.

6 [a]For who in the heavens can be compared to the LORD?
Who among the sons of the mighty can be likened to the
LORD?

7 [a]God is greatly to be feared in the assembly of the saints,
And to be held in reverence by all *those* around Him.

8 O LORD God of hosts,
Who *is* mighty like You, O LORD?
Your faithfulness also surrounds You.

9 [a]You rule the raging of the sea;
When its waves rise, You still them.

10 [a]You have broken [1]Rahab in pieces, as one who is slain;
You have scattered Your enemies with Your mighty
arm.

11 [a]The heavens *are* Yours, the earth also *is* Yours;
The world and all its fullness, You have founded them.

12 The north and the south, You have created them;
[a]Tabor and [b]Hermon rejoice in Your name.

13 You have a mighty arm;
Strong is Your hand, *and* high is Your right hand.

14 Righteousness and justice *are* the foundation of Your
throne;
Mercy and truth go before Your face.

15 Blessed *are* the people who know the [a]joyful sound!
They walk, O LORD, in the light of Your countenance.

16 In Your name they rejoice all day long,
And in Your righteousness they are exalted.

17 For You *are* the glory of their strength,
And in Your favor our [1]horn is [a]exalted.

18 For our shield *belongs* to the LORD,
And our king to the Holy One of Israel.

19 Then You spoke in a vision to Your [1]holy one,
And said: "I have given help to *one who is* mighty;
I have exalted one [a]chosen from the people.

20 [a]I have found My servant David;
With My holy oil I have anointed him,

89:title
[a]1 Kin. 4:31

89:2
[a][Ps. 119:89, 90]

89:3 [a]1 Kin. 8:16
[b]2 Sam. 7:11;
1 Chr. 17:10–12

89:4
[a][2 Sam. 7:13;
Is. 9:7;
Luke 1:33]

89:5 [a][Ps. 19:1]

89:6
[a]Ps. 86:8; 113:5

89:7 [a]Ps. 76:7, 11

89:9
[a]Ps. 65:7; 93:3,
4; 107:29

89:10
[a]Ex. 14:26–28;
Ps. 87:4;
Is. 30:7; 51:9

89:11 [a][Gen. 1:1;
1 Chr. 29:11]

89:12
[a]Josh. 19:22;
Judg. 4:6;
Jer. 46:18
[b]Deut. 3:8;
Josh. 11:17; 12:1;
Song 4:8

89:15
[a]Lev. 23:24;
Num. 10:10;
Ps. 98:6

89:17
[a]Ps. 75:10; 92:10;
132:17

89:19
[a]1 Kin. 11:34

89:20
[a]1 Sam. 13:14;
16:1–12;
Acts 13:22

89:title [1]Heb. *Maschil*   89:10 [1]Egypt   89:17 [1]Strength   89:19 [1]So with
many Heb. mss.; MT, LXX, Tg., Vg. *holy ones*

21 ^aWith whom My hand shall be established;
Also My arm shall strengthen him.
22 The enemy shall not ¹outwit him,
Nor the son of wickedness afflict him.
23 I will beat down his foes before his face,
And plague those who hate him.

24 "But My faithfulness and My mercy *shall be* with him,
And in My name his horn shall be exalted.
25 Also I will ^aset his hand over the sea,
And his right hand over the rivers.
26 He shall cry to Me, 'You *are* ^amy Father,
My God, and ^bthe rock of my salvation.'
27 Also I will make him ^a*My* firstborn,
^bThe highest of the kings of the earth.
28 ^aMy mercy I will keep for him forever,
And My covenant shall stand firm with him.
29 His seed also I will make *to endure* forever,
^aAnd his throne ^bas the days of heaven.

30 "If^a his sons ^bforsake My law
And do not walk in My judgments,
31 If they ¹break My statutes
And do not keep My commandments,
32 Then I will punish their transgression with the rod,
And their iniquity with stripes.
33 ^aNevertheless My lovingkindness I will not ¹utterly take
from him,
Nor ²allow My faithfulness to fail.
34 My covenant I will not break,
Nor ^aalter the word that has gone out of My lips.
35 Once I have sworn ^aby My holiness;
I will not lie to David:
36 ^aHis seed shall endure forever,
And his throne ^bas the sun before Me;
37 It shall be established forever like the moon,
Even *like* the faithful witness in the sky."   Selah

38 But You have ^acast off and ^babhorred,¹
You have been furious with Your ²anointed.
39 You have renounced the covenant of Your servant;
^aYou have ¹profaned his crown *by casting it* to the
ground.
40 You have broken down all his hedges;
You have brought his ¹strongholds to ruin.
41 All who pass by the way ^aplunder him;
He is a reproach to his neighbors.
42 You have exalted the right hand of his adversaries;
You have made all his enemies rejoice.
43 You have also turned back the edge of his sword,
And have not sustained him in the battle.
44 You have made his ¹glory cease,
And cast his throne down to the ground.
45 The days of his youth You have shortened;
You have covered him with shame.   Selah

89:21 ^aPs. 80:17

89:25 ^aPs. 72:8

89:26
^a2 Sam. 7:14;
[1 Chr. 22:10];
Jer. 3:19
^b2 Sam. 22:47

89:27 ^aEx. 4:22;
Ps. 2:7; Jer. 31:9;
[Col. 1:15, 18]
^bNum. 24:7;
[Ps. 72:11];
Rev. 19:16

89:28 ^aIs. 55:3

89:29
^a[1 Kin. 2:4;
Is. 9:7];
Jer. 33:17
^bDeut. 11:21

89:30
^a[2 Sam. 7:14]
^bPs. 119:53

89:33
^a2 Sam. 7:14, 15

89:34
^a[Num. 23:19];
Jer. 33:20–22

89:35
^a[1 Sam. 15:29];
Amos 4:2;
[Titus 1:2]

89:36
^a[Luke 1:33]
^bPs. 72:17

89:38
^a[1 Chr. 28:9]
^bDeut. 32:19

89:39 ^aPs. 74:7;
Lam. 5:16

89:41 ^aPs. 80:12

89:22 ¹Or *exact usury from him*   89:31 ¹*profane*   89:33 ¹Lit. *break off*
²Lit. *deal falsely with My faithfulness*   89:38 ¹*rejected*   ²Commissioned
one, Heb. *messiah*   89:39 ¹*defiled*   89:40 ¹*fortresses*   89:44 ¹*splendor* or
brightness

46 How long, LORD?
Will You hide Yourself forever?
Will Your wrath burn like fire?
47 Remember how short my time [a]is;
For what [b]futility have You created all the children of men?
48 What man can live and not [1]see [a]death?
Can he deliver his life from the power of [2]the grave?

Selah

49 Lord, where *are* Your former lovingkindnesses,
Which You [a]swore to David [b]in Your truth?
50 Remember, Lord, the reproach of Your servants—
[a]*How* I bear in my bosom *the reproach of* all the many
peoples,
51 [a]With which Your enemies have reproached, O LORD,
With which they have reproached the footsteps of Your
[1]anointed.

52 [a]Blessed *be* the LORD forevermore!
Amen and Amen.

BOOK FOUR
Psalms 90–106

PSALM 90

THE ETERNITY OF GOD, AND MAN'S FRAILTY

A Prayer [a]of Moses the man of God.

1 LORD, [a]You have been our [1]dwelling place in all
generations.
2 [a]Before the mountains were brought forth,
Or ever You [1]had formed the earth and the world,
Even from everlasting to everlasting, You *are* God.

3 You turn man to destruction,
And say, [a]"Return, O children of men."
4 [a]For a thousand years in Your sight
Are like yesterday when it is past,
And *like* a watch in the night.
5 You carry them away *like* a flood;
[a]*They are* like a sleep.
In the morning [b]they are like grass *which* grows up:
6 In the morning it flourishes and grows up;
In the evening it is cut down and withers.

7 For we have been consumed by Your anger,
And by Your wrath we are terrified.
8 [a]You have set our iniquities before You,
Our [b]secret *sins* in the light of Your countenance.
9 For all our days have passed away in Your wrath;
We finish our years like a sigh.
10 The days of our lives *are* seventy years;
And if by reason of strength *they are* eighty years,
Yet their boast *is* only labor and sorrow;
For it is soon cut off, and we fly away.

89:47 [a]Ps. 90:9
[b]Ps. 62:9

89:48
[a][Eccl. 3:19]

89:49
[a][2 Sam. 7:15];
Jer. 30:9;
Ezek. 34:23
[b]Ps. 54:5

89:50
[a]Ps. 69:9, 19

89:51
[a]Ps. 74:10, 18, 22

89:52 [a]Ps. 41:13

90:title
[a]Deut. 33:1

90:1
[a][Deut. 33:27;
Ezek. 11:16]

90:2 [a]Job 15:7;
[Prov. 8:25, 26]

90:3 [a]Gen. 3:19;
Job 34:14, 15

90:4 [a]2 Pet. 3:8

90:5 [a]Ps. 73:20
[b]Is. 40:6

90:8 [a]Ps. 50:21;
[Jer. 16:17];
[b]Ps. 19:12;
[Eccl. 12:14]

89:48 [1]*experience death* [2]Or *Sheol* 89:51 [1]Commissioned one, Heb.
messiah 90:1 [1]LXX, Tg., Vg. *refuge* 90:2 [1]Lit. *gave birth to*

11 Who knows the power of Your anger?
For as the fear of You, *so is* Your wrath.
12 [a]So teach *us* to number our days,
That we may gain a heart of wisdom.

13 Return, O LORD!
How long?
And [a]have compassion on Your servants.
14 Oh, satisfy us early with Your mercy,
[a]That we may rejoice and be glad all our days!
15 Make us glad according to the days *in which* You have
afflicted us,
The years *in which* we have seen evil.
16 Let [a]Your work appear to Your servants,
And Your glory to their children.
17 [a]And let the beauty of the LORD our God be upon us,
And [b]establish the work of our hands for us;
Yes, establish the work of our hands.

PSALM 91

SAFETY OF ABIDING IN THE PRESENCE OF GOD

1 HE [a]who dwells in the secret place of the Most High
Shall abide [b]under the shadow of the Almighty.
2 [a]I will say of the LORD, "*He is* my refuge and my fortress;
My God, in Him I will trust."

3 Surely [a]He shall deliver you from the snare of the [1]fowler
And from the perilous pestilence.
4 [a]He shall cover you with His feathers,
And under His wings you shall take refuge;
His truth *shall be your* shield and [1]buckler.
5 [a]You shall not be afraid of the terror by night,
Nor of the arrow *that* flies by day,
6 *Nor* of the pestilence *that* walks in darkness,
Nor of the destruction *that* lays waste at noonday.

7 A thousand may fall at your side,
And ten thousand at your right hand;
But it shall not come near you.
8 Only [a]with your eyes shall you look,
And see the reward of the wicked.

9 Because you have made the LORD, *who is* [a]my refuge,
Even the Most High, [b]your dwelling place,
10 [a]No evil shall befall you,
Nor shall any plague come near your dwelling;
11 [a]For He shall give His angels charge over you,
To keep you in all your ways.
12 In *their* hands they shall [1]bear you up,
[a]Lest you [2]dash your foot against a stone.
13 You shall tread upon the lion and the cobra,
The young lion and the serpent you shall trample
underfoot.

14 "Because he has set his love upon Me, therefore I will
deliver him;
I will [1]set him on high, because he has [a]known My name.

90:12
[a]Deut. 32:29;
Ps. 39:4

90:13 [a]Ex. 32:12;
Deut. 32:36

90:14 [a]Ps. 85:6

90:16
[a][Deut. 32:4];
Hab. 3:2

90:17 [a]Ps. 27:4
[b]Is. 26:12

91:1 [a]Ps. 27:5;
31:20; 32:7
[b]Ps. 17:8;
Is. 25:4; 32:2

91:2 [a]Ps. 142:5

91:3 [a]Ps. 124:7;
Prov. 6:5

91:4 [a]Ps. 17:8

91:5 [a][Job 5:19;
Ps. 112:7;
Is. 43:2]

91:8 [a]Ps. 37:34;
Mal. 1:5

91:9 [a]Ps. 91:2
[b]Ps. 90:1

91:10
[a][Prov. 12:21]

91:11 [a]Ps. 34:7;
Matt. 4:6;
Luke 4:10;
[Heb. 1:14]

91:12 [a]Matt. 4:6;
Luke 4:11

91:14 [a][Ps. 9:10]

91:3 [1]One who catches birds in a trap or snare   91:4 [1]A small shield
91:12 [1]lift   [2]strike   91:14 [1]exalt him

15 He shall ᵃcall upon Me, and I will answer him;
I *will be* ᵇwith him in trouble;
I will deliver him and honor him.
16 With ¹long life I will satisfy him,
And show him My salvation."

PSALM 92

PRAISE TO THE LORD FOR HIS LOVE AND FAITHFULNESS

A Psalm. A Song for the Sabbath day.

1 IT *is* ᵃgood to give thanks to the LORD,
And to sing praises to Your name, O Most High;
2 To ᵃdeclare Your lovingkindness in the morning,
And Your faithfulness every night,
3 ᵃOn an instrument of ten strings,
On the lute,
And on the harp,
With harmonious sound.
4 For You, LORD, have made me glad through Your
work;
I will triumph in the works of Your hands.
5 ᵃO LORD, how great are Your works!
ᵇYour thoughts are very deep.
6 ᵃA senseless man does not know,
Nor does a fool understand this.
7 When ᵃthe wicked ¹spring up like grass,
And when all the workers of iniquity flourish,
It is that they may be destroyed forever.
8 ᵃBut You, LORD, *are* on high forevermore.
9 For behold, Your enemies, O LORD,
For behold, Your enemies shall perish;
All the workers of iniquity shall ᵃbe scattered.
10 But ᵃmy ¹horn You have exalted like a wild ox;
I have been ᵇanointed with fresh oil.
11 ᵃMy eye also has seen *my desire* on my enemies;
My ears hear *my desire* on the wicked
Who rise up against me.
12 ᵃThe righteous shall flourish like a palm tree,
He shall grow like a cedar in Lebanon.
13 Those who are planted in the house of the LORD
Shall flourish in the courts of our God.
14 They shall still bear fruit in old age;
They shall be ¹fresh and ²flourishing,
15 To declare that the LORD is upright;
ᵃ*He is* my rock, and ᵇ*there is* no unrighteousness in Him.

PSALM 93

THE ETERNAL REIGN OF THE LORD

1 THE ᵃLORD reigns, He is clothed with majesty;
The LORD is clothed,
ᵇHe has girded Himself with strength.

91:15 ᵃJob 12:4;
Ps. 50:15
ᵇIs. 43:2

92:1 ᵃPs. 147:1

92:2 ᵃPs. 89:1

92:3 ᵃ1 Chr. 23:5

92:5 ᵃPs. 40:5;
[Rev. 15:3]
ᵇPs. 139:17, 18;
[Is. 28:29;
Rom. 11:33, 34]

92:6 ᵃPs. 73:22

92:7 ᵃJob 12:6;
Ps. 37:1, 2;
Jer. 12:1, 2;
[Mal. 3:15]

92:8
ᵃ[Ps. 83:18]

92:9 ᵃPs. 68:1

92:10 ᵃPs. 89:17
ᵇPs. 23:5

92:11 ᵃPs. 54:7

92:12
ᵃNum. 24:6;
Ps. 52:8;
Jer. 17:8;
Hos. 14:5, 6

92:15
ᵃ[Deut. 32:4]
ᵇ[Rom. 9:14]

93:1 ᵃPs. 96:10
ᵇPs. 65:6

91:16 ¹Lit. *length of days*   92:7 ¹*sprout*   92:10 ¹Strength   92:14 ¹Full of oil
or sap, lit. *fat*   ²*green*

Surely the world is established, so that it cannot be
[1]moved.

2 [a]Your throne *is* established from of old;
You *are* from everlasting.

3 The floods have [1]lifted up, O LORD,
The floods have lifted up their voice;
The floods lift up their waves.

4 [a]The LORD on high *is* mightier
Than the noise of many waters,
Than the mighty waves of the sea.

5 Your testimonies are very sure;
Holiness adorns Your house,
O LORD, [1]forever.

PSALM 94

GOD THE REFUGE OF THE RIGHTEOUS

1 O LORD God, [a]to whom vengeance belongs—
O God, to whom vengeance belongs, shine forth!

2 Rise up, O [a]Judge of the earth;
[1]Render punishment to the proud.

3 LORD, [a]how long will the wicked,
How long will the wicked triumph?

4 They [a]utter speech, *and* speak insolent things;
All the workers of iniquity boast in themselves.

5 They break in pieces Your people, O LORD,
And afflict Your heritage.

6 They slay the widow and the stranger,
And murder the fatherless.

7 [a]Yet they say, "The LORD does not see,
Nor does the God of Jacob [1]understand."

8 Understand, you senseless among the people;
And *you* fools, when will you be wise?

9 [a]He who planted the ear, shall He not hear?
He who formed the eye, shall He not see?

10 He who [1]instructs the [2]nations, shall He not correct,
He who teaches man knowledge?

11 The LORD [a]knows the thoughts of man,
That they *are* futile.

12 Blessed *is* the man whom You [a]instruct, O LORD,
And teach out of Your law,

13 That You may give him [1]rest from the days of adversity,
Until the pit is dug for the wicked.

14 For the LORD will not [1]cast off His people,
Nor will He forsake His inheritance.

15 But judgment will return to righteousness,
And all the upright in heart will follow it.

16 Who will rise up for me against the evildoers?
Who will stand up for me against the workers of iniquity?

17 Unless the LORD *had been* my help,
My soul would soon have settled in silence.

93:2 [a]Ps. 45:6;
[Lam. 5:19]

93:4 [a]Ps. 65:7

94:1
[a]Deut. 32:35;
[Is. 35:4;
Nah. 1:2;
Rom. 12:19]

94:2
[a][Gen. 18:25]

94:3 [a][Job 20:5]

94:4 [a]Ps. 31:18;
Jude 15

94:7 [a]Job 22:13;
Ps. 10:11

94:9 [a][Ex. 4:11;
Prov. 20:12]

94:11 [a]Job 11:11;
1 Cor. 3:20

94:12
[a][Deut. 8:5;
Job 5:17;
Ps. 119:71;
Prov. 3:11, 12;
Heb. 12:5, 6]

93:1 [1]shaken   **93:3** [1]raised up   **93:5** [1]Lit. *for length of days*   **94:2** [1]Repay
with   **94:7** [1]pay attention   **94:10** [1]disciplines   [2]Gentiles   **94:13** [1]relief
94:14 [1]abandon

18 If I say, "My foot slips,"
   Your mercy, O LORD, will hold me up.
19 In the multitude of my anxieties within me,
   Your comforts delight my soul.

20 Shall ᵃthe throne of iniquity, which devises evil by law,
   Have fellowship with You?
21 They gather together against the life of the righteous,
   And condemn ᵃinnocent blood.
22 But the LORD has been my defense,
   And my God the rock of my refuge.
23 He has brought on them their own iniquity,
   And shall ¹cut them off in their own wickedness;
   The LORD our God shall cut them off.

PSALM 95

A CALL TO WORSHIP AND OBEDIENCE

1 OH come, let us sing to the LORD!
   Let us shout joyfully to the Rock of our salvation.
2 Let us come before His presence with thanksgiving;
   Let us shout joyfully to Him with ᵃpsalms.
3 For ᵃthe LORD *is* the great God,
   And the great King above all gods.
4 ¹In His hand *are* the deep places of the earth;
   The heights of the hills *are* His also.
5 ᵃThe sea *is* His, for He made it;
   And His hands formed the dry *land*.

6 Oh come, let us worship and bow down;
   Let ᵃus kneel before the LORD our Maker.
7 For He *is* our God,
   And ᵃwe *are* the people of His pasture,
   And the sheep ¹of His hand.

   ᵇToday, if you will hear His voice:
8 "Do not harden your hearts, as in the ¹rebellion,
   ᵃAs *in* the day of ²trial in the wilderness,
9 When ᵃyour fathers tested Me;
   They tried Me, though they ᵇsaw My work.
10 For ᵃforty years I was ¹grieved with *that* generation,
   And said, 'It *is* a people who go astray in their hearts,
   And they do not know My ways.'
11 So ᵃI swore in My wrath,
   'They shall not enter My rest.'"

PSALM 96

A SONG OF PRAISE TO GOD COMING IN JUDGMENT

(1 Chr. 16:23–33)

1 OH, ᵃsing to the LORD a new song!
   Sing to the LORD, all the earth.
2 Sing to the LORD, bless His name;
   Proclaim the good news of His salvation from day to day.

Cross references (side column)

94:20
ᵃAmos 6:3

94:21
ᵃ[Ex. 23:7];
Ps. 106:38;
[Prov. 17:15];
Matt. 27:4

95:2 ᵃEph. 5:19;
James 5:13

95:3 ᵃ[Ps. 96:4;
1 Cor. 8:5, 6]

95:5
ᵃGen. 1:9, 10;
Jon. 1:9

95:6
ᵃ2 Chr. 6:13;
Dan. 6:10;
[Phil. 2:10]

95:7 ᵃPs. 79:13
ᵇHeb. 3:7–11,
15; 4:7

95:8 ᵃEx. 17:2–7;
Num. 20:13

95:9 ᵃPs. 78:18;
[1 Cor. 10:9]
ᵇNum. 14:22

95:10
ᵃActs 7:36;
13:18;
Heb. 3:10, 17

95:11
ᵃNum. 14:23,
28–30;
Deut. 1:35;
Heb. 4:3, 5

96:1
ᵃ1 Chr. 16:23–33

Footnotes

94:23 ¹*destroy them*   95:4 ¹In His possession   95:7 ¹Under His care
95:8 ¹Or *Meribah*, lit. *Strife, Contention*   ²Or *Massah*, lit. *Trial, Testing*
95:10 ¹*disgusted*

3 Declare His glory among the ¹nations,
His wonders among all peoples.
4 For ªthe Lord *is* great and ᵇgreatly to be praised;
ᶜHe *is* to be feared above all gods.
5 For ªall the gods of the peoples *are* idols,
ᵇBut the Lord made the heavens.
6 Honor and majesty *are* before Him;
Strength and ªbeauty *are* in His sanctuary.

7 ªGive¹ to the Lord, O families of the peoples,
Give to the Lord glory and strength.
8 ¹Give to the Lord the glory *due* His name;
Bring an offering, and come into His courts.
9 Oh, worship the Lord ªin the beauty of holiness!
Tremble before Him, all the earth.

10 Say among the ¹nations, ª"The Lord reigns;
The world also is firmly established,
It shall not be ²moved;
ᵇHe shall judge the peoples righteously."

11 ªLet the heavens rejoice, and let the earth be glad;
ᵇLet the sea roar, and ¹all its fullness;
12 Let the field be joyful, and all that *is* in it.
Then all the trees of the woods will rejoice
13 before the Lord.
For He is coming, for He is coming to judge the
earth.
ªHe shall judge the world with righteousness,
And the peoples with His truth.

PSALM 97

A SONG OF PRAISE TO THE SOVEREIGN LORD

1 THE Lord ªreigns;
Let the earth rejoice;
Let the multitude of ¹isles be glad!
2 ªClouds and darkness surround Him;
ᵇRighteousness and justice *are* the foundation of His
throne.
3 ªA fire goes before Him,
And burns up His enemies round about.
4 ªHis lightnings light the world;
The earth sees and trembles.
5 ªThe mountains melt like wax at the presence of the
Lord,
At the presence of the Lord of the whole earth.
6 ªThe heavens declare His righteousness,
And all the peoples see His glory.

7 ªLet all be put to shame who serve carved images,
Who boast of idols.
ᵇWorship Him, all *you* gods.
8 Zion hears and is glad,
And the daughters of Judah rejoice
Because of Your judgments, O Lord.

96:4 ªPs. 145:3
ᵇPs. 18:3
ᶜPs. 95:3

96:5
ª1 Chr. 16:26;
[Jer. 10:11]
ᵇPs. 115:15;
Is. 42:5

96:6 ªPs. 29:2

96:7
ª1 Chr. 16:28, 29;
Ps. 29:1, 2

96:9
ª1 Chr. 16:29;
2 Chr. 20:21;
Ps. 29:2

96:10
ªPs. 93:1; 97:1;
[Rev. 11:15; 19:6]
ᵇPs. 67:4

96:11 ªPs. 69:34;
Is. 49:13
ᵇPs. 98:7

96:13
ª[Rev. 19:11]

97:1 ª[Ps. 96:10]

97:2 ªEx. 19:9;
Deut. 4:11;
1 Kin. 8:12;
Ps. 18:11
ᵇ[Ps. 89:14]

97:3 ªPs. 18:8;
Dan. 7:10;
Hab. 3:5

97:4 ªEx. 19:18

97:5 ªPs. 46:6;
Amos 9:5;
Mic. 1:4; Nah. 1:5

97:6 ªPs. 19:1

97:7 ª[Ex. 20:4]
ᵇ[Heb. 1:6]

96:3 ¹*Gentiles*   96:7 ¹*Ascribe*   96:8 ¹*Ascribe*   96:10 ¹*Gentiles*   ²*shaken*
96:11 ¹*all that is in it*   97:1 ¹Or *coastlands*

9 For You, LORD, *are* [a]most high above all the earth;
[b]You are exalted far above all gods.

10 You who love the LORD, [a]hate evil!
[b]He preserves the souls of His saints;
[c]He delivers them out of the hand of the wicked.

11 [a]Light is sown for the righteous,
And gladness for the upright in heart.

12 [a]Rejoice in the LORD, you righteous,
[b]And give thanks [1]at the remembrance of [2]His holy name.

PSALM 98

A SONG OF PRAISE TO THE LORD FOR
HIS SALVATION AND JUDGMENT

A Psalm.

1 OH, [a]sing to the LORD a new song!
For He has [b]done marvelous things;
His right hand and His holy arm have gained Him the
victory.

2 [a]The LORD has made known His salvation;
[b]His righteousness He has revealed in the sight of the
[1]nations.

3 He has remembered His mercy and His faithfulness to
the house of Israel;
[a]All the ends of the earth have seen the salvation of our
God.

4 Shout joyfully to the LORD, all the earth;
Break forth in song, rejoice, and sing praises.

5 Sing to the LORD with the harp,
With the harp and the sound of a psalm,

6 With trumpets and the sound of a horn;
Shout joyfully before the LORD, the King.

7 Let the sea roar, and all its fullness,
The world and those who dwell in it;

8 Let the rivers clap *their* hands;
Let the hills be joyful together

9 before the LORD,
[a]For He is coming to judge the earth.
With righteousness He shall judge the world,
And the peoples with [1]equity.

PSALM 99

PRAISE TO THE LORD FOR HIS HOLINESS

1 THE LORD reigns;
Let the peoples tremble!
[a]He dwells *between* the cherubim;
Let the earth be [1]moved!

2 The LORD *is* great in Zion,
And He *is* high above all the peoples.

3 Let them praise Your great and awesome name—
[1]He *is* holy.

97:9 [a]Ps. 83:18
[b]Ex. 18:11;
Ps. 95:3; 96:4
97:10
[a][Ps. 34:14;
Prov. 8:13;
Amos 5:15;
Rom. 12:9]
[b]Ps. 31:23;
145:20; Prov. 2:8
[c]Ps. 37:40;
Jer. 15:21;
Dan. 3:28
97:11
[a]Job 22:28;
Ps. 112:4;
Prov. 4:18
97:12 [a]Ps. 33:1
[b]Ps. 30:4
98:1 [a]Ps. 33:3;
Is. 42:10
[b]Ex. 15:11;
Ps. 77:14
98:2 [a]Is. 52:10;
[Luke 1:77;
2:30, 31]
[b]Is. 62:2;
Rom. 3:25
98:3 [a][Is. 49:6];
Luke 3:6;
[Acts 13:47;
28:28]
98:9
[a][Ps. 96:10, 13]
99:1 [a]Ex. 25:22;
1 Sam. 4:4;
Ps. 80:1

97:12 [1]Or *for the memory* [2]Or *His holiness* **98:2** [1]*Gentiles*
98:9 [1]*uprightness* **99:1** [1]*shaken* **99:3** [1]Or *It*

4 The King's strength also loves justice;
  You have established equity;
  You have executed justice and righteousness in
    Jacob.
5 Exalt the LORD our God,
  And worship at His footstool—
  He *is* holy.

6 Moses and Aaron were among His priests,
  And Samuel was among those who ªcalled upon His
    name;
  They called upon the LORD, and He answered them.
7 He spoke to them in the cloudy pillar;
  They kept His testimonies and the ¹ordinance He gave
    them.

8 You answered them, O LORD our God;
  You were to them God-Who-Forgives,
  Though You took vengeance on their deeds.
9 Exalt the LORD our God,
  And worship at His holy hill;
  For the LORD our God *is* holy.

PSALM 100

A SONG OF PRAISE FOR THE LORD'S
FAITHFULNESS TO HIS PEOPLE

ªA Psalm of Thanksgiving.

1 MAKE ªa joyful shout to the LORD, ¹all you lands!
2 Serve the LORD with gladness;
  Come before His presence with singing.
3 Know that the LORD, He *is* God;
  ª*It is* He *who* has made us, and ¹not we ourselves;
  ᵇ*We are* His people and the sheep of His pasture.

4 ªEnter into His gates with thanksgiving,
  And into His courts with praise.
  Be thankful to Him, *and* bless His name.
5 For the LORD *is* good;
  ªHis mercy *is* everlasting,
  And His truth *endures* to all generations.

PSALM 101

PROMISED FAITHFULNESS TO THE LORD

A Psalm of David.

1 I WILL sing of mercy and justice;
  To You, O LORD, I will sing praises.

2 I will behave wisely in a ¹perfect way.
  Oh, when will You come to me?
  I will ªwalk within my house with a perfect heart.

3 I will set nothing ¹wicked before my eyes;
  ªI hate the work of those ᵇwho fall away;
  It shall not cling to me.

99:6
ª1 Sam. 7:9;
12:18

100:title
ªPs. 145:title

100:1 ªPs. 95:1

100:3
ªJob 10:3, 8;
Ps. 119:73;
139:13, 14;
[Eph. 2:10]
ᵇPs. 95:7;
[Is. 40:11];
Ezek. 34:30, 31

100:4 ªPs. 66:13;
116:17–19

100:5 ªPs. 136:1

101:2 ª1 Kin. 11:4

101:3 ªPs. 97:10
ᵇJosh. 23:6

99:7 ¹*statute*   100:1 ¹Lit. *all the earth*   100:3 ¹So with Kt., LXX, Vg.; Qr.,
many Heb. mss., Tg. *we are His*   101:2 ¹*blameless*   101:3 ¹*worthless*

4 A perverse heart shall depart from me;
   I will not ^aknow wickedness.

5 Whoever secretly slanders his neighbor,
   Him I will destroy;
   ^aThe one who has a haughty look and a proud heart,
   Him I will not endure.

6 My eyes *shall be* on the faithful of the land,
   That they may dwell with me;
   He who walks in a ¹perfect way,
   He shall serve me.

7 He who works deceit shall not dwell within my house;
   He who tells lies shall not ¹continue in my presence.

8 ^aEarly I will destroy all the wicked of the land,
   That I may cut off all the evildoers ^bfrom the city of the
   LORD.

PSALM 102

THE LORD'S ETERNAL LOVE

A Prayer of the afflicted, ^awhen he is overwhelmed
and pours out his complaint before the LORD.

1 HEAR my prayer, O LORD,
   And let my cry come to You.

2 ^aDo not hide Your face from me in the day of my
       trouble;
   Incline Your ear to me;
   In the day that I call, answer me speedily.

3 For my days ¹are ^aconsumed like smoke,
   And my bones are burned like a hearth.

4 My heart is stricken and withered like grass,
   So that I forget to eat my bread.

5 Because of the sound of my groaning
   My bones cling to my ¹skin.

6 I am like a pelican of the wilderness;
   I am like an owl of the desert.

7 I lie awake,
   And am like a sparrow alone on the housetop.

8 My enemies reproach me all day long;
   Those who deride me swear an oath against me.

9 For I have eaten ashes like bread,
   And mingled my drink with weeping,

10 Because of Your indignation and Your wrath;
   For You have lifted me up and cast me away.

11 My days *are* like a shadow that lengthens,
   And I wither away like grass.

12 But You, O LORD, shall endure forever,
   And the remembrance of Your name to all
       generations.

13 You will arise *and* have mercy on Zion;
   For the time to favor her,
   Yes, the set time, has come.

14 For Your servants take pleasure in her stones,
   And show favor to her dust.

Marginal references: 101:4 ^a[Ps. 119:115]; 101:5 ^aProv. 6:17; 101:8 ^a[Ps. 75:10]; Jer. 21:12; ^bPs. 48:2, 8; 102:title ^aPs. 61:2; 102:2 ^aPs. 27:9; 69:17; 102:3 ^aJames 4:14

15 So the ¹nations shall ªfear the name of the LORD,
And all the kings of the earth Your glory.
16 For the LORD shall build up Zion;
ªHe shall appear in His glory.
17 ªHe shall regard the prayer of the destitute,
And shall not despise their prayer.

18 This will be ªwritten for the generation to come,
That ᵇa people yet to be created may praise the LORD.
19 For He ªlooked down from the height of His sanctuary;
From heaven the LORD viewed the earth,
20 ªTo hear the groaning of the prisoner,
To release those appointed to death,
21 To ªdeclare the name of the LORD in Zion,
And His praise in Jerusalem,
22 ªWhen the peoples are gathered together,
And the kingdoms, to serve the LORD.

23 He weakened my strength in the way;
He ªshortened my days.
24 ªI said, "O my God,
Do not take me away in the midst of my days;
ᵇYour years *are* throughout all generations.
25 ªOf old You laid the foundation of the earth,
And the heavens *are* the work of Your hands.
26 ªThey will perish, but You will ¹endure;
Yes, they will all grow old like a garment;
Like a cloak You will change them,
And they will be changed.
27 But ªYou *are* the same,
And Your years will have no end.
28 ªThe children of Your servants will continue,
And their descendants will be established before You."

PSALM 103

PRAISE FOR THE LORD'S MERCIES

A *Psalm* of David.

1 BLESS ªthe LORD, O my soul;
And all that is within me, *bless* His holy name!
2 Bless the LORD, O my soul,
And forget not all His benefits:
3 ªWho forgives all your iniquities,
Who ᵇheals all your diseases,
4 Who redeems your life from destruction,
ªWho crowns you with lovingkindness and tender
mercies,
5 Who satisfies your mouth with good *things*,
So that ªyour youth is renewed like the eagle's.

6 The LORD executes righteousness
And justice for all who are oppressed.
7 ªHe made known His ways to Moses,
His acts to the children of Israel.
8 ªThe LORD *is* merciful and gracious,
Slow to anger, and abounding in mercy.

102:15
ª1 Kin. 8:43

102:16
ª[Is. 60:1, 2]

102:17 ªNeh. 1:6;
Ps. 22:24

102:18
ªDeut. 31:19;
[Rom. 15:4;
1 Cor. 10:11]
ᵇPs. 22:31

102:19
ªDeut. 26:15;
Ps. 14:2

102:20 ªPs. 79:11

102:21
ªPs. 22:22

102:22
ª[Is. 2:2, 3;
49:22, 23; 60:3];
Zech. 8:20–23

102:23
ªJob 21:21

102:24
ª[Ps. 39:13];
Is. 38:10
ᵇJob 36:26;
[Ps. 90:2];
Hab. 1:12

102:25
ª[Gen. 1:1;
Neh. 9:6;
Heb. 1:10–12]

102:26
ªIs. 34:4; 51:6;
Matt. 24:35;
[2 Pet. 3:7,
10–12];
Rev. 20:11

102:27 ª[Is. 41:4;
43:10; Mal. 3:6;
Heb. 13:8];
James 1:17

102:28
ªPs. 69:36

103:1
ªPs. 104:1, 35

103:3 ªPs. 130:8;
Is. 33:24
ᵇ[Ex. 15:26];
Ps. 147:3;
[Is. 53:5];
Jer. 17:14

103:4 ª[Ps. 5:12]

103:5
ª[Is. 40:31]

103:7
ªEx. 33:12–17;
Ps. 147:19

103:8 ª[Ex. 34:6,
7; Num. 14:18];
Deut. 5:10;
Neh. 9:17;
Ps. 86:15;
Jer. 32:18;
Jon. 4:2;
James 5:11

102:15 ¹*Gentiles* 102:26 ¹*continue*

9 ^aHe will not always strive *with us,*
   Nor will He keep *His anger* forever.
10 ^aHe has not dealt with us according to our sins,
   Nor punished us according to our iniquities.

11 For as the heavens are high above the earth,
   So great is His mercy toward those who fear Him;
12 As far as the east is from the west,
   So far has He ^aremoved our transgressions from us.
13 ^aAs a father pities *his* children,
   So the LORD pities those who fear Him.
14 For He ¹knows our frame;
   He remembers that we *are* dust.

15 *As for* man, ^ahis days *are* like grass;
   As a flower of the field, so he flourishes.
16 ^aFor the wind passes over it, and it is ¹gone,
   And ^bits place remembers it no more.
17 But the mercy of the LORD *is* from everlasting to
      everlasting
   On those who fear Him,
   And His righteousness to children's children,
18 ^aTo such as keep His covenant,
   And to those who remember His commandments to do
      them.

19 The LORD has established His throne in heaven,
   And ^aHis kingdom rules over all.
20 ^aBless the LORD, you His angels,
   Who excel in strength, who ^bdo His word,
   Heeding the voice of His word.
21 Bless the LORD, all *you* His hosts,
   ^a*You* ¹ministers of His, who do His pleasure.
22 Bless the LORD, all His works,
   In all places of His dominion.

   Bless the LORD, O my soul!

PSALM 104

PRAISE TO THE SOVEREIGN LORD FOR
HIS CREATION AND PROVIDENCE

(cf. Gen. 1:1–31)

1 BLESS ^athe LORD, O my soul!

   O LORD my God, You are very great:
   You are clothed with honor and majesty,
2 Who cover *Yourself* with light as *with* a garment,
   Who stretch out the heavens like a curtain.

3 ^aHe lays the beams of His upper chambers in the waters,
   Who makes the clouds His chariot,
   Who walks on the wings of the wind,
4 Who makes His angels spirits,
   His ¹ministers a flame of fire.

5 *You who* ¹laid the foundations of the earth,
   So *that* it should not be moved forever,

103:9
^a[Ps. 30:5;
Is. 57:16];
Jer. 3:5;
[Mic. 7:18]

103:10
^a[Ezra 9:13;
Lam. 3:22]

103:12
^a[2 Sam. 12:13;
Is. 38:17; 43:25;
Zech. 3:9;
Heb. 9:26]

103:13 ^aMal. 3:17

103:15
^aIs. 40:6–8;
James 1:10, 11;
1 Pet. 1:24

103:16
^a[Is. 40:7]
^bJob 7:10

103:18
^a[Deut. 7:9];
Ps. 25:10

103:19
^a[Ps. 47:2;
Dan. 4:17, 25]

103:20
^aPs. 148:2
^b[Matt. 6:10]

103:21
^a[Heb. 1:14]

104:1 ^aPs. 103:1

104:3
^a[Amos 9:6]

103:14 ¹Understands our constitution   103:16 ¹*not*   103:21 ¹*servants*
104:4 ¹*servants*   104:5 ¹Lit. *founded the earth upon her bases*

6 You ^acovered it with the deep as *with* a garment;
The waters stood above the mountains.
7 At Your rebuke they fled;
At the voice of Your thunder they hastened away.
8 ¹They went up over the mountains;
They went down into the valleys,
To the place which You founded for them.
9 You have ^aset a boundary that they may not pass over,
^bThat they may not return to cover the earth.

10 He sends the springs into the valleys;
They flow among the hills.
11 They give drink to every beast of the field;
The wild donkeys quench their thirst.
12 By them the birds of the heavens have their home;
They sing among the branches.
13 ^aHe waters the hills from His upper chambers;
The earth is satisfied with ^bthe fruit of Your works.

14 ^aHe causes the grass to grow for the cattle,
And vegetation for the service of man,
That he may bring forth ^bfood from the earth,
15 And ^awine *that* makes glad the heart of man,
Oil to make *his* face shine,
And bread *which* strengthens man's heart.
16 The trees of the LORD are full *of sap,*
The cedars of Lebanon which He planted,
17 Where the birds make their nests;
The stork has her home in the fir trees.
18 The high hills *are* for the wild goats;
The cliffs are a refuge for the ^arock¹ badgers.

19 ^aHe appointed the moon for seasons;
The ^bsun knows its going down.
20 ^aYou make darkness, and it is night,
In which all the beasts of the forest creep about.
21 ^aThe young lions roar after their prey,
And seek their food from God.
22 *When* the sun rises, they gather together
And lie down in their dens.
23 Man goes out to ^ahis work
And to his labor until the evening.

24 ^aO LORD, how manifold are Your works!
In wisdom You have made them all.
The earth is full of Your ^bpossessions—
25 This great and wide sea,
In which *are* innumerable teeming things,
Living things both small and great.
26 There the ships sail about;
There is that ^aLeviathan¹
Which You have ²made to play there.

27 ^aThese all wait for You,
That You may give *them* their food in due season.
28 *What* You give them they gather in;
You open Your hand, they are filled with good.

104:6 ^aGen. 1:6

104:9
^aJob 26:10;
Ps. 33:7;
[Jer. 5:22]
^bGen. 9:11–15

104:13 ^aPs. 147:8
^bJer. 10:13

104:14
^aGen. 1:29
^bJob 28:5

104:15
^aJudg. 9:13;
Ps. 23:5;
Prov. 31:6;
Eccl. 10:19

104:18 ^aLev. 11:5

104:19 ^aGen. 1:14
^bJob 38:12;
Ps. 19:6

104:20
^a[Ps. 74:16;
Is. 45:7]

104:21
^aJob 38:39

104:23
^aGen. 3:19

104:24
^aPs. 40:5;
Prov. 3:19;
[Jer. 10:12]; 51:15
^bPs. 65:9

104:26 ^aJob 41:1;
Is. 27:1

104:27
^aJob 36:31;
Ps. 136:25

104:8 ¹Or *The mountains rose up; The valleys sank down* 104:18 ¹rock
hyraxes 104:26 ¹A large sea creature of unknown identity ²Lit. *formed*

29 You hide Your face, they are troubled;
　ᵃYou take away their breath, they die and return to their
　　dust.
30 ᵃYou send forth Your Spirit, they are created;
　And You renew the face of the earth.

31 May the glory of the Lord endure forever;
　May the Lord ᵃrejoice in His works.
32 He looks on the earth, and it ᵃtrembles;
　ᵇHe touches the hills, and they smoke.

33 ᵃI will sing to the Lord as long as I live;
　I will sing praise to my God while I have my being.
34 May my ᵃmeditation be sweet to Him;
　I will be glad in the Lord.
35 May ᵃsinners be consumed from the earth,
　And the wicked be no more.

　Bless the Lord, O my soul!
　¹Praise the Lord!

PSALM 105

THE ETERNAL FAITHFULNESS OF THE LORD

(Ex. 7:8—11:10; 1 Chr. 16:8–22)

1 OH, ᵃgive thanks to the Lord!
　Call upon His name;
　ᵇMake known His deeds among the peoples!
2 Sing to Him, sing psalms to Him;
　ᵃTalk of all His wondrous works!
3 Glory in His holy name;
　Let the hearts of those rejoice who seek the Lord!
4 Seek the Lord and His strength;
　ᵃSeek His face evermore!
5 ᵃRemember His marvelous works which He has
　　done,
　His wonders, and the judgments of His mouth,
6 O seed of Abraham His servant,
　You children of Jacob, His chosen ones!

7 He *is* the Lord our God;
　ᵃHis judgments *are* in all the earth.
8 He ᵃremembers His covenant forever,
　The word *which* He commanded, for a thousand
　　generations,
9 ᵃ*The covenant* which He made with Abraham,
　And His oath to Isaac,
10 And confirmed it to Jacob for a statute,
　To Israel *as* an everlasting covenant,
11 Saying, ᵃ"To you I will give the land of Canaan
　As the allotment of your inheritance,"
12 ᵃWhen they were few in number,
　Indeed very few, ᵇand strangers in it.

13 When they went from one nation to another,
　From *one* kingdom to another people,
14 ᵃHe permitted no one to do them wrong;
　Yes, ᵇHe rebuked kings for their sakes,

104:29
ᵃJob 34:15;
[Eccl. 12:7]

104:30 ᵃIs. 32:15

104:31
ᵃGen. 1:31;
Prov. 8:31

104:32
ᵃHab. 3:10
ᵇEx. 19:18;
Ps. 144:5

104:33 ᵃPs. 63:4

104:34 ᵃPs. 19:14

104:35
ᵃPs. 37:38

105:1
ᵃ1 Chr. 16:8–22,
34; Ps. 106:1;
Is. 12:4
ᵇPs. 145:12

105:2 ᵃPs. 119:27

105:4 ᵃPs. 27:8

105:5 ᵃPs. 77:11

105:7 ᵃ[Is. 26:9]

105:8 ᵃLuke 1:72

105:9
ᵃGen. 17:2;
Luke 1:73;
[Gal. 3:17];
Heb. 6:17

105:11
ᵃGen. 13:15;
15:18

105:12
ᵃGen. 34:30;
[Deut. 7:7]
ᵇGen. 23:4;
Heb. 11:9

105:14
ᵃGen. 35:5
ᵇGen. 12:17

104:35 ¹Heb. *Hallelujah*

15 *Saying,* "Do not touch My anointed ones,
And do My prophets no harm."

16 Moreover ªHe called for a famine in the land;
He destroyed all the ᵇprovision of bread.

17 ªHe sent a man before them—
Joseph—*who* ᵇwas sold as a slave.

18 ªThey hurt his feet with fetters,
¹He was laid in irons.

19 Until the time that his word came to pass,
ªThe word of the LORD tested him.

20 ªThe king sent and released him,
The ruler of the people let him go free.

21 ªHe made him lord of his house,
And ruler of all his possessions,

22 To ¹bind his princes at his pleasure,
And teach his elders wisdom.

23 ªIsrael also came into Egypt,
And Jacob dwelt ᵇin the land of Ham.

24 ªHe increased His people greatly,
And made them stronger than their enemies.

25 ªHe turned their heart to hate His people,
To deal craftily with His servants.

26 ªHe sent Moses His servant,
And Aaron whom He had chosen.

27 They ªperformed His signs among them,
And wonders in the land of Ham.

28 He sent darkness, and made *it* dark;
And they did not rebel against His word.

29 ªHe turned their waters into blood,
And killed their fish.

30 ªTheir land abounded with frogs,
Even in the chambers of their kings.

31 ªHe spoke, and there came swarms of flies,
And lice in all their territory.

32 ªHe gave them hail for rain,
And flaming fire in their land.

33 ªHe struck their vines also, and their fig trees,
And splintered the trees of their territory.

34 ªHe spoke, and locusts came,
Young locusts without number,

35 And ate up all the vegetation in their land,
And devoured the fruit of their ground.

36 ªHe also ¹destroyed all the firstborn in their land,
ᵇThe first of all their strength.

37 ªHe also brought them out with silver and gold,
And *there was* none feeble among His tribes.

38 ªEgypt was glad when they departed,
For the fear of them had fallen upon them.

39 ªHe spread a cloud for a covering,
And fire to give light in the night.

40 ª*The people* asked, and He brought quail,
And ᵇsatisfied them with the bread of heaven.

41 ªHe opened the rock, and water gushed out;
It ran in the dry places *like* a river.

105:16
ªGen. 41:54
ᵇLev. 26:26;
Is. 3:1; Ezek. 4:16
105:17
ª[Gen. 45:5]
ᵇGen. 37:28, 36;
Acts 7:9
105:18
ªGen. 40:15
105:19
ªGen. 39:11–21;
41:25, 42, 43
105:20
ªGen. 41:14
105:21
ªGen. 41:40–44
105:23
ªGen. 46:6;
Acts 7:15
ᵇPs. 78:51
105:24 ªEx. 1:7, 9
105:25
ªEx. 1:8–10; 4:21
105:26
ªEx. 3:10;
4:12–15
105:27
ªEx. 7—12;
Ps. 78:43
105:29
ªEx. 7:20, 21;
Ps. 78:44
105:30 ªEx. 8:6
105:31
ªEx. 8:16, 17
105:32
ªEx. 9:23–25
105:33
ªPs. 78:47
105:34 ªEx. 10:4
105:36
ªEx. 12:29; 13:15;
Ps. 135:8; 136:10
ᵇGen. 49:3
105:37
ªEx. 12:35, 36
105:38
ªEx. 12:33
105:39
ªEx. 13:21;
Neh. 9:12;
Ps. 78:14; Is. 4:5
105:40
ªEx. 16:12
ᵇPs. 78:24
105:41 ªEx. 17:6;
Num. 20:11;
Ps. 78:15;
114:8; Is. 48:21;
[1 Cor. 10:4]

105:18 ¹*His soul came into iron*   105:22 ¹*Bind as prisoners*   105:36 ¹Lit.
struck down

⁴² For He remembered ªHis holy promise,
　　And Abraham His servant.
⁴³ He brought out His people with joy,
　　His chosen ones with ¹gladness.
⁴⁴ ªHe gave them the lands of the ¹Gentiles,
　　And they inherited the labor of the nations,
⁴⁵ ªThat they might observe His statutes
　　And keep His laws.

¹Praise the Lord!

PSALM 106

JOY IN FORGIVENESS OF ISRAEL'S SINS

1　PRAISE¹ the Lord!

ªOh, give thanks to the Lord, for *He is* good!
　For His mercy *endures* forever.

2　Who can ¹utter the mighty acts of the Lord?
　　Who can declare all His praise?
3　Blessed *are* those who keep justice,
　　And ¹he who ªdoes righteousness at ᵇall times!

4　ªRemember me, O Lord, with the favor *You have toward*
　　　Your people.
　　Oh, visit me with Your salvation,
5　That I may see the benefit of Your chosen ones,
　　That I may rejoice in the gladness of Your nation,
　　That I may glory with ¹Your inheritance.

6　ªWe have sinned with our fathers,
　　We have committed iniquity,
　　We have done wickedly.
7　Our fathers in Egypt did not understand Your wonders;
　　They did not remember the multitude of Your mercies,
　　ªBut rebelled by the sea—the Red Sea.

8　Nevertheless He saved them for His name's sake,
　　ªThat He might make His mighty power known.
9　ªHe rebuked the Red Sea also, and it dried up;
　　So ᵇHe led them through the depths,
　　As through the wilderness.
10　He ªsaved them from the hand of him who hated *them,*
　　And redeemed them from the hand of the enemy.
11　ªThe waters covered their enemies;
　　There was not one of them left.
12　ªThen they believed His words;
　　They sang His praise.

13　ªThey soon forgot His works;
　　They did not wait for His counsel,
14　ªBut lusted exceedingly in the wilderness,
　　And tested God in the desert.
15　ªAnd He gave them their request,
　　But ᵇsent leanness into their soul.

16　When ªthey envied Moses in the camp,
　　And Aaron the saint of the Lord,

105:42
ªGen. 15:13, 14;
Ps. 105:8

105:44
ªJosh. 11:16–23;
13:7; Ps. 78:55

105:45
ª[Deut. 4:1, 40]

106:1
ª1 Chr. 16:34, 41

106:3 ªPs. 15:2
ᵇ[Gal. 6:9]

106:4
ªPs. 119:132

106:6
ª1 Kin. 8:47;
[Ezra 9:7;
Neh. 1:7;
Jer. 3:25;
Dan. 9:5]

106:7
ªEx. 14:11, 12

106:8 ªEx. 9:16

106:9 ªEx. 14:21;
Ps. 18:15;
Is. 51:10; Nah. 1:4
ᵇIs. 63:11–13

106:10
ªEx. 14:30

106:11 ªEx. 14:27,
28; 15:5

106:12
ªEx. 15:1–21

106:13
ªEx. 15:24; 16:2;
17:2

106:14
ªNum. 11:4;
1 Cor. 10:6

106:15
ªNum. 11:31
ᵇIs. 10:16

106:16
ªNum. 16:1–3

---

17 ^aThe earth opened up and swallowed Dathan,
And covered the faction of Abiram.
18 ^aA fire was kindled in their company;
The flame burned up the wicked.
19 ^aThey made a calf in Horeb,
And worshiped the molded image.
20 Thus ^athey changed their glory
Into the image of an ox that eats grass.
21 They forgot God their Savior,
Who had done great things in Egypt,
22 Wondrous works in the land of Ham,
Awesome things by the Red Sea.
23 ^aTherefore He said that He would destroy them,
Had not Moses His chosen one ^bstood before Him in the
breach,
To turn away His wrath, lest He destroy *them.*
24 Then they despised ^athe pleasant land;
They ^bdid not believe His word,
25 ^aBut complained in their tents,
And did not heed the voice of the LORD.
26 ^aTherefore He raised His hand *in an oath* against them,
^bTo ¹overthrow them in the wilderness,
27 ^aTo ¹overthrow their descendants among the ²nations,
And to scatter them in the lands.
28 ^aThey joined themselves also to Baal of Peor,
And ate sacrifices ¹made to the dead.
29 Thus they provoked *Him* to anger with their deeds,
And the plague broke out among them.
30 ^aThen Phinehas stood up and intervened,
And the plague was stopped.
31 And that was accounted to him ^afor righteousness
To all generations forevermore.
32 ^aThey angered *Him* also at the waters of ¹strife,
^bSo that it went ill with Moses on account of them;
33 ^aBecause they rebelled against His Spirit,
So that he spoke rashly with his lips.
34 ^aThey did not destroy the peoples,
^bConcerning whom the LORD had commanded them,
35 ^aBut they mingled with the Gentiles
And learned their works;
36 ^aThey served their idols,
^bWhich became a snare to them.
37 ^aThey even sacrificed their sons
And their daughters to ^bdemons,
38 And shed innocent blood,
The blood of their sons and daughters,
Whom they sacrificed to the idols of Canaan;
And ^athe land was polluted with blood.
39 Thus they ¹were ^adefiled by their own works,
And ^bplayed² the harlot by their own deeds.

106:38 ^a[Num. 35:33; Is. 24:5; Jer. 3:1, 2]   106:39 ^a[Lev. 18:24]; Ezek. 20:18 ^b[Lev. 17:7;
Num. 15:39]; Judg. 2:17; Hos. 4:12

106:26 ¹*make them fall*   106:27 ¹*make their descendants fall also*   ²*Gentiles*
106:28 ¹*offered*   106:32 ¹Or *Meribah*   106:39 ¹*became unclean*   ²*Were
unfaithful*

106:17
^aNum. 16:31, 32;
Deut. 11:6

106:18
^aNum. 16:35, 46

106:19
^aEx. 32:1–4;
Deut. 9:8;
Acts 7:41

106:20
^aJer. 2:11;
Rom. 1:23

106:23
^aEx. 32:10;
Deut. 9:19
^bEzek. 22:30

106:24
^aDeut. 8:7;
Jer. 3:19;
Ezek. 20:6
^bDeut. 1:32;
9:23;
[Heb. 3:18, 19]

106:25
^aNum. 14:2, 27;
Deut. 1:27

106:26
^aEzek. 20:15, 16;
[Heb. 3:11, 18]
^bNum. 14:28–30

106:27
^aLev. 26:33;
Ezek. 20:23

106:28
^aNum. 25:3;
Deut. 4:3;
Hos. 9:10

106:30
^aNum. 25:7, 8

106:31
^aGen. 15:6;
Num. 25:11–13

106:32
^aNum. 20:3–13;
Ps. 81:7
^bDeut. 1:37;
3:26

106:33
^aNum. 20:3, 10

106:34
^aJudg. 1:21
^b[Deut. 7:2, 16];
Judg. 2:2

106:35
^aJudg. 3:5, 6

106:36
^aJudg. 2:12
^bDeut. 7:16

106:37
^a[Deut. 12:31;
32:17, 18];
2 Kin. 16:3;
17:17;
Ezek. 16:20, 21;
[1 Cor. 10:20]
^b[Lev. 17:7]

40 Therefore [a]the wrath of the LORD was kindled against His
   people,
   So that He abhorred [b]His own inheritance.
41 And [a]He gave them into the hand of the Gentiles,
   And those who hated them ruled over them.
42 Their enemies also oppressed them,
   And they were brought into subjection under their hand.
43 [a]Many times He delivered them;
   But they rebelled in their counsel,
   And were brought low for their iniquity.
44 Nevertheless He regarded their affliction,
   When [a]He heard their cry;
45 [a]And for their sake He remembered His covenant,
   And [b]relented [c]according to the multitude of His
   mercies.
46 [a]He also made them to be pitied
   By all those who carried them away captive.

47 [a]Save us, O LORD our God,
   And gather us from among the Gentiles,
   To give thanks to Your holy name,
   To triumph in Your praise.

48 [a]Blessed *be* the LORD God of Israel
   From everlasting to everlasting!
   And let all the people say, "Amen!"

   [1]Praise the LORD!

BOOK FIVE

Psalms 107–150

PSALM 107

THANKSGIVING TO THE LORD FOR HIS
GREAT WORKS OF DELIVERANCE

1 OH, [a]give thanks to the LORD, for *He is* good!
   For His [1]mercy *endures* forever.
2 Let the redeemed of the LORD say *so,*
   Whom He has redeemed from the hand of the enemy,
3 And [a]gathered out of the lands,
   From the east and from the west,
   From the north and from the south.

4 They wandered in [a]the wilderness in a desolate way;
   They found no city to dwell in.
5 Hungry and thirsty,
   Their soul fainted in them.
6 [a]Then they cried out to the LORD in their trouble,
   And He delivered them out of their distresses.
7 And He led them forth by the [a]right way,
   That they might go to a city for a dwelling place.
8 [a]Oh, that *men* would give thanks to the LORD *for* His
   goodness,
   And *for* His wonderful works to the children of men!

Cross-reference column:

106:40
[a]Judg. 2:14;
Ps. 78:59
[b][Deut. 9:29;
32:9]

106:41
[a]Judg. 2:14;
[Neh. 9:27]

106:43
[a]Judg. 2:16;
[Neh. 9:27]

106:44
[a]Judg. 3:9; 6:7;
10:10

106:45
[a][Lev. 26:41, 42]
[b]Judg. 2:18
[c]Ps. 69:16

106:46
[a]1 Kin. 8:50;
[2 Chr. 30:9];
Ezra 9:9;
Neh. 1:11;
Jer. 42:12

106:47
[a]1 Chr. 16:35, 36

106:48 [a]Ps. 41:13

107:1
[a]1 Chr. 16:34;
Ps. 106:1;
Jer. 33:11

107:3
[a]Is. 43:5, 6;
Jer. 29:14;
31:8–10;
[Ezek. 39:27, 28]

107:4
[a]Num. 14:33;
32:13;
[Deut. 2:7;
32:10];
Josh. 5:6; 14:10

107:6 [a]Ps. 50:15;
[Hos. 5:15]

107:7 [a]Ezra 8:21;
Ps. 5:8; Jer. 31:9

107:8
[a]Ps. 107:15, 21

9   For [a]He satisfies the longing soul,
    And fills the hungry soul with goodness.

10 Those who [a]sat in darkness and in the shadow of death,
    [b]Bound[1] in affliction and irons—
11 Because they [a]rebelled against the words of God,
    And [1]despised [b]the counsel of the Most High,
12 Therefore He brought down their heart with labor;
    They fell down, and *there was* [a]none to help.
13 Then they cried out to the LORD in their trouble,
    And He saved them out of their distresses.
14 [a]He brought them out of darkness and the shadow of
      death,
    And broke their chains in pieces.
15 Oh, that *men* would give thanks to the LORD *for* His
      goodness,
    And *for* His wonderful works to the children of men!
16 For He has [a]broken the gates of bronze,
    And cut the bars of iron in two.

17 Fools, [a]because of their transgression,
    And because of their iniquities, were afflicted.
18 [a]Their soul abhorred all manner of food,
    And they [b]drew near to the gates of death.
19 Then they cried out to the LORD in their trouble,
    And He saved them out of their distresses.
20 [a]He sent His word and [b]healed them,
    And [c]delivered *them* from their destructions.
21 Oh, that *men* would give thanks to the LORD *for* His
      goodness,
    And *for* His wonderful works to the children of men!
22 [a]Let them sacrifice the sacrifices of thanksgiving,
    And [b]declare His works with [1]rejoicing.

23 Those who go down to the sea in ships,
    Who do business on great waters,
24 They see the works of the LORD,
    And His wonders in the deep.
25 For He commands and [a]raises the stormy wind,
    Which lifts up the waves of the sea.
26 They mount up to the heavens,
    They go down again to the depths;
    [a]Their soul melts because of trouble.
27 They reel to and fro, and stagger like a drunken man,
    And [1]are at their wits' end.
28 Then they cry out to the LORD in their trouble,
    And He brings them out of their distresses.
29 [a]He calms the storm,
    So that its waves are still.
30 Then they are glad because they are quiet;
    So He guides them to their desired haven.
31 [a]Oh, that *men* would give thanks to the LORD *for* His
      goodness,
    And *for* His wonderful works to the children of men!
32 Let them exalt Him also [a]in the assembly of the people,
    And praise Him in the company of the elders.

107:9
[a][Ps. 34:10;
Luke 1:53]

107:10 [a][Is. 42:7;
Mic. 7:8;
Luke 1:79]
[b]Job 36:8

107:11
[a]Lam. 3:42
[b][Ps. 73:24]

107:12 [a]Ps. 22:11

107:14 [a]Ps. 68:6

107:16
[a]Is. 45:1, 2

107:17
[a][Is. 65:6, 7;
Jer. 30:14, 15];
Lam. 3:39;
Ezek. 24:23

107:18
[a]Job 33:20
[b]Job 33:22

107:20
[a]Matt. 8:8
[b]2 Kin. 20:5;
Ps. 30:2
[c]Job 33:28, 30

107:22
[a]Lev. 7:12;
Ps. 50:14;
Heb. 13:15
[b]Ps. 9:11

107:25 [a]Jon. 1:4

107:26
[a]Ps. 22:14

107:29
[a]Ps. 89:9;
Matt. 8:26;
Luke 8:24

107:31
[a]Ps. 107:8, 15, 21

107:32
[a]Ps. 22:22, 25

107:10 [1]*Prisoners*   107:11 [1]*scorned*   107:22 [1]*joyful singing*   107:27 [1]Lit. *all their wisdom is swallowed up*

33 He ^aturns rivers into a wilderness,
And the watersprings into dry ground;

34 A ^afruitful land into ¹barrenness,
For the wickedness of those who dwell in it.

35 ^aHe turns a wilderness into pools of water,
And dry land into watersprings.

36 There He makes the hungry dwell,
That they may establish a city for a dwelling place,

37 And sow fields and plant vineyards,
That they may yield a fruitful harvest.

38 ^aHe also blesses them, and they multiply greatly;
And He does not let their cattle ^bdecrease.

39 When they are ^adiminished and brought low
Through oppression, affliction, and sorrow,

40 ^aHe pours contempt on princes,
And causes them to wander in the wilderness *where there is* no way;

41 ^aYet He sets the poor on high, far from affliction,
And ^bmakes *their* families like a flock.

42 ^aThe righteous see *it* and rejoice,
And all ^biniquity stops its mouth.

43 ^aWhoever *is* wise will observe these *things,*
And they will understand the lovingkindness of the
Lord.

PSALM 108

ASSURANCE OF GOD'S VICTORY OVER ENEMIES

(Ps. 57:7–11; 60:5–12)

A Song. A Psalm of David.

1 O ^aGOD, my heart is steadfast;
I will sing and give praise, even with my glory.

2 ^aAwake, lute and harp!
I will awaken the dawn.

3 I will praise You, O Lord, among the peoples,
And I will sing praises to You among the nations.

4 For Your mercy *is* great above the ¹heavens,
And Your truth *reaches* to the clouds.

5 ^aBe exalted, O God, above the heavens,
And Your glory above all the earth;

6 ^aThat Your beloved may be delivered,
Save *with* Your right hand, and ¹hear me.

7 God has spoken in His holiness:
"I will rejoice;
I will divide Shechem
And measure out the Valley of Succoth.

8 Gilead *is* Mine; Manasseh *is* Mine;
Ephraim also *is* the ¹helmet for My head;
^aJudah *is* My lawgiver.

9 Moab *is* My washpot;
Over Edom I will cast My shoe;
Over Philistia I will triumph."

107:33 ^a1 Kin. 17:1, 7; Is. 50:2
107:34 ^aGen. 13:10; Deut. 29:23
107:35 ^aPs. 114:8; [Is. 41:17, 18]
107:38 ^aGen. 12:2; 17:16, 20 ^bEx. 1:7; [Deut. 7:14]
107:39 ^a2 Kin. 10:32
107:40 ^aJob 12:21, 24
107:41 ^a1 Sam. 2:8; [Ps. 113:7, 8] ^bPs. 78:52
107:42 ^aJob 5:15, 16 ^bJob 5:16; Ps. 63:11; [Rom. 3:19]
107:43 ^aPs. 64:9; Jer. 9:12; [Hos. 14:9]
108:1 ^aPs. 57:7–11
108:2 ^aPs. 57:8–11
108:5 ^aPs. 57:5, 11
108:6 ^aPs. 60:5–12
108:8 ^a[Gen. 49:10]

107:34 ¹Lit. *a salty waste* **108:4** ¹*skies* **108:6** ¹Lit. *answer* **108:8** ¹Lit. *protection*

10 aWho will bring me *into* the strong city?
Who will lead me to Edom?
11 *Is it* not *You,* O God, *who* cast us off?
And *You,* O God, *who* did not go out with our armies?
12 Give us help from trouble,
For the help of man is useless.
13 aThrough God we will do valiantly,
For *it is* He *who* shall tread down our enemies.

PSALM 109

PLEA FOR JUDGMENT OF FALSE ACCUSERS

To the Chief Musician. A Psalm of David.

1 DOa not keep silent,
O God of my praise!
2 For the mouth of the wicked and the mouth of the deceitful
Have opened against me;
They have spoken against me with a alying tongue.
3 They have also surrounded me with words of hatred,
And fought against me awithout a cause.
4 In return for my love they are my accusers,
But I *give myself to* prayer.
5 Thus athey have rewarded me evil for good,
And hatred for my love.

6 Set a wicked man over him,
And let aan 1accuser stand at his right hand.
7 When he is judged, let him be found guilty,
And alet his prayer become sin.
8 Let his days be afew,
And blet another take his office.
9 aLet his children be fatherless,
And his wife a widow.
10 Let his children 1continually be vagabonds, and beg;
Let them 2seek *their bread* also from their desolate places.
11 aLet the creditor seize all that he has,
And let strangers plunder his labor.
12 Let there be none to extend mercy to him,
Nor let there be any to favor his fatherless children.
13 aLet his 1posterity be cut off,
And in the generation following let their bname be blotted out.

14 aLet the iniquity of his fathers be remembered before the LORD,
And let not the sin of his mother bbe blotted out.
15 Let them be continually before the LORD,
That He may acut off the memory of them from the earth;
16 Because he did not remember to show mercy,
But persecuted the poor and needy man,
That he might even slay the abroken in heart.
17 aAs he loved cursing, so let it come to him;
As he did not delight in blessing, so let it be far from him.

108:10 aPs. 60:9
108:13 aPs. 60:12
109:1 aPs. 83:1
109:2 aPs. 27:12
109:3 aPs. 35:7; 69:4; John 15:25
109:5 aPs. 35:7, 12; 38:20; Prov. 17:13
109:6 aZech. 3:1
109:7 a[Prov. 28:9]
109:8 a[Ps. 55:23]; John 17:12 bPs. 69:25; Acts 1:20
109:9 aEx. 22:24
109:11 aNeh. 5:7; Job 5:5; 18:9
109:13 aJob 18:19; Ps. 37:28 bProv. 10:7
109:14 a[Ex. 20:5; Num. 14:18]; Is. 65:6; [Jer. 32:18] bNeh. 4:5; Jer. 18:23
109:15 aJob 18:17; [Ps. 34:16]
109:16 a[Ps. 34:18]
109:17 aProv. 14:14; [Matt. 7:2]

109:6 1Heb. *satan*   109:10 1*wander continuously*   2So with MT, Tg.; LXX, Vg. *be cast out*   109:13 1*descendants be destroyed*

18 As he clothed himself with cursing as with his garment,
So let it ᵃenter his body like water,
And like oil into his bones.
19 Let it be to him like the garment which covers him,
And for a belt with which he girds himself continually.
20 *Let* this *be* the LORD's reward to my accusers,
And to those who speak evil against my person.

21 But You, O GOD the Lord,
Deal with me for Your name's sake;
Because Your mercy *is* good, deliver me.
22 For I *am* poor and needy,
And my heart is wounded within me.
23 I am gone ᵃlike a shadow when it lengthens;
I am shaken off like a locust.
24 My ᵃknees are weak through fasting,
And my flesh is feeble from lack of fatness.
25 I also have become ᵃa reproach to them;
When they look at me, ᵇthey shake their heads.

26 Help me, O LORD my God!
Oh, save me according to Your mercy,
27 ᵃThat they may know that this *is* Your hand—
That You, LORD, have done it!
28 ᵃLet them curse, but You bless;
When they arise, let them be ashamed,
But let ᵇYour servant rejoice.
29 ᵃLet my accusers be clothed with shame,
And let them cover themselves with their own disgrace
as with a mantle.

30 I will greatly praise the LORD with my mouth;
Yes, ᵃI will praise Him among the multitude.
31 For ᵃHe shall stand at the right hand of the poor,
To save *him* from those ¹who condemn him.

PSALM 110

ANNOUNCEMENT OF THE MESSIAH'S REIGN

(Matt. 22:44; Acts 2:34, 35)

A Psalm of David.

1 THE ᵃLORD said to my Lord,
"Sit at My right hand,
Till I make Your enemies Your ᵇfootstool."
2 The LORD shall send the rod of Your strength ᵃout of
Zion.
ᵇRule in the midst of Your enemies!
3 ᵃYour people *shall be* volunteers
In the day of Your power;
ᵇIn the beauties of holiness, from the womb of the
morning,
You have the dew of Your youth.
4 The LORD has sworn
And ᵃwill not relent,
"You *are* a ᵇpriest forever
According to the order of ᶜMelchizedek."

Marginal references:
109:18 ᵃNum. 5:22
109:23 ᵃPs. 102:11
109:24 ᵃHeb. 12:12
109:25 ᵃPs. 22:7; Jer. 18:16; Lam. 2:15; ᵇMatt. 27:39; Mark 15:29
109:27 ᵃJob 37:7
109:28 ᵃ2 Sam. 6:11, 12; ᵇIs. 65:14
109:29 ᵃJob 8:22; Ps. 35:26
109:30 ᵃPs. 35:18; 111:1
109:31 ᵃ[Ps. 16:8]
110:1 ᵃMatt. 22:44; Mark 12:36; 16:19; Luke 20:42, 43; Acts 2:34, 35; Col. 3:1; Heb. 1:13; ᵇ[1 Cor. 15:25]; Eph. 1:22]
110:2 ᵃ[Rom. 11:26, 27]; ᵇ[Ps. 2:9; Dan. 7:13, 14]
110:3 ᵃJudg. 5:2; Neh. 11:2; ᵇ1 Chr. 16:29; Ps. 96:9
110:4 ᵃ[Num. 23:19]; ᵇ[Zech. 6:13]; ᶜ[Heb. 5:6, 10; 6:20]

109:31 ¹Lit. *judging his soul*

5 The Lord *is* ^aat Your right hand;
He shall ¹execute kings ^bin the day of His wrath.
6 He shall judge among the nations,
He shall fill *the places* with dead bodies,
^aHe shall ¹execute the heads of many countries.
7 He shall drink of the brook by the wayside;
^aTherefore He shall lift up the head.

PSALM 111

PRAISE TO GOD FOR HIS FAITHFULNESS AND JUSTICE

1 PRAISE¹ the LORD!

^aI will praise the LORD with *my* whole heart,
In the assembly of the upright and *in the*
congregation.
2 ^aThe works of the LORD *are* great,
^bStudied by all who have pleasure in them.
3 His work *is* ^ahonorable and glorious,
And His righteousness endures forever.
4 He has made His wonderful works to be remembered;
^aThe LORD *is* gracious and full of compassion.
5 He has given food to those who fear Him;
He will ever be mindful of His covenant.
6 He has declared to His people the power of His works,
In giving them the ¹heritage of the nations.
7 The works of His hands *are* ^averity¹ and justice;
All His precepts *are* sure.
8 ^aThey stand fast forever and ever,
And are ^bdone in truth and uprightness.
9 ^aHe has sent redemption to His people;
He has commanded His covenant forever:
^bHoly and awesome *is* His name.
10 ^aThe fear of the LORD *is* the beginning of wisdom;
A good understanding have all those who do *His*
commandments.
His praise endures forever.

PSALM 112

THE BLESSED STATE OF THE RIGHTEOUS

1 PRAISE¹ the LORD!

Blessed *is* the man *who* fears the LORD,
Who ^adelights greatly in His commandments.
2 ^aHis descendants will be mighty on earth;
The generation of the upright will be blessed.
3 ^aWealth and riches *will be* in his house,
And his righteousness ¹endures forever.
4 ^aUnto the upright there arises light in the darkness;
He is gracious, and full of compassion, and righteous.
5 ^aA good man deals graciously and lends;
He will guide his affairs ^bwith discretion.

110:5 ^a[Ps. 16:8]
^bPs. 2:5, 12;
[Rom. 2:5;
Rev. 6:17]

110:6 ^aPs. 68:21

110:7 ^a[Is. 53:12]

111:1 ^aPs. 35:18

111:2 ^aPs. 92:5
^bPs. 143:5

111:3
^aPs. 145:4, 5

111:4 ^a[Ps. 86:5]

111:7 ^a[Rev. 15:3]

111:8 ^aIs. 40:8;
Matt. 5:18
^b[Rev. 15:3]

111:9 ^aLuke 1:68
^bLuke 1:49

111:10
^aJob 28:28;
[Prov. 1:7; 9:10];
Eccl. 12:13

112:1 ^aPs. 128:1

112:2
^a[Ps. 102:28]

112:3
^aProv. 3:16; 8:18;
[Matt. 6:33]

112:4 ^aJob 11:17;
Ps. 97:11

112:5 ^aPs. 37:26;
[Luke 6:35]
^b[Eph. 5:15;
Col. 4:5]

110:5 ¹Lit. *break kings in pieces*   110:6 ¹Lit. *break in pieces*   111:1 ¹Heb.
Hallelujah   111:6 ¹*inheritance*   111:7 ¹*truth*   112:1 ¹Heb. *Hallelujah*
112:3 ¹*stands*

6 Surely he will never be shaken;
ᵃThe righteous will be in everlasting remembrance.
7 ᵃHe will not be afraid of evil tidings;
His heart is steadfast, trusting in the LORD.
8 His ᵃheart *is* established;
ᵇHe will not be afraid,
Until he ᶜsees *his desire* upon his enemies.

9 He has dispersed abroad,
He has given to the poor;
His righteousness endures forever;
His ¹horn will be exalted with honor.
10 The wicked will see *it* and be grieved;
He will gnash his teeth and melt away;
The desire of the wicked shall perish.

PSALM 113

THE MAJESTY AND CONDESCENSION OF GOD

1 PRAISE¹ the LORD!

ᵃPraise, O servants of the LORD,
Praise the name of the LORD!
2 ᵃBlessed be the name of the LORD
From this time forth and forevermore!
3 ᵃFrom the rising of the sun to its going down
The LORD's name *is* to be praised.

4 The LORD *is* ᵃhigh above all nations,
ᵇHis glory above the heavens.
5 ᵃWho *is* like the LORD our God,
Who dwells on high,
6 ᵃWho humbles Himself to behold
The things that are in the heavens and in the
earth?

7 ᵃHe raises the poor out of the dust,
And lifts the ᵇneedy out of the ash heap,
8 That He may ᵃseat *him* with princes—
With the princes of His people.
9 ᵃHe grants the ¹barren woman a home,
Like a joyful mother of children.

Praise the LORD!

PSALM 114

THE POWER OF GOD IN HIS DELIVERANCE OF ISRAEL

(cf. Ex. 14:1–31)

1 WHEN ᵃIsrael went out of Egypt,
The house of Jacob ᵇfrom a people ¹of strange
language,
2 ᵃJudah became His sanctuary,
And Israel His dominion.

3 ᵃThe sea saw *it* and fled;
ᵇJordan turned back.

Cross-references (margin):

112:6 ᵃProv. 10:7
112:7 ᵃ[Prov. 1:33]
112:8 ᵃHeb. 13:9 ᵇ[Ps. 27:1; 56:11]; Prov. 1:33; 3:24; [Is. 12:2] ᶜPs. 59:10
113:1 ᵃPs. 135:1
113:2 ᵃ[Dan. 2:20]
113:3 ᵃIs. 59:19; Mal. 1:11
113:4 ᵃPs. 97:9; 99:2 ᵇ[Ps. 8:1]
113:5 ᵃPs. 89:6; [Is. 57:15]
113:6 ᵃ[Ps. 11:4; Is. 57:15]
113:7 ᵃ1 Sam. 2:8; Ps. 107:41 ᵇPs. 72:12
113:8 ᵃ[Job 36:7]
113:9 ᵃ1 Sam. 2:5; Is. 54:1
114:1 ᵃEx. 12:51; 13:3 ᵇPs. 81:5
114:2 ᵃEx. 6:7; 19:6; 25:8; 29:45, 46; Deut. 27:9
114:3 ᵃEx. 14:21; Ps. 77:16 ᵇJosh. 3:13–16

112:9 ¹Strength 113:1 ¹Heb. *Hallelujah* 113:9 ¹childless 114:1 ¹*who spoke unintelligibly*

4 [a]The mountains skipped like rams,
The little hills like lambs.

5 [a]What ails you, O sea, that you fled?
O Jordan, *that* you turned back?

6 O mountains, *that* you skipped like rams?
O little hills, like lambs?

7 Tremble, O earth, at the presence of the Lord,
At the presence of the God of Jacob,

8 [a]Who turned the rock *into* a pool of water,
The flint into a fountain of waters.

PSALM 115

THE FUTILITY OF IDOLS AND THE
TRUSTWORTHINESS OF GOD

1 NOT [a]unto us, O LORD, not unto us,
But to Your name give glory,
Because of Your mercy,
Because of Your truth.

2 Why should the [1]Gentiles say,
[a]"So where *is* their God?"

3 [a]But our God *is* in heaven;
He does whatever He pleases.

4 [a]Their idols *are* silver and gold,
The work of men's hands.

5 They have mouths, but they do not speak;
Eyes they have, but they do not see;

6 They have ears, but they do not hear;
Noses they have, but they do not smell;

7 They have hands, but they do not handle;
Feet they have, but they do not walk;
Nor do they mutter through their throat.

8 [a]Those who make them are like them;
So is everyone who trusts in them.

9 [a]O Israel, trust in the LORD;
[b]He *is* their help and their shield.

10 O house of Aaron, trust in the LORD;
He *is* their help and their shield.

11 You who fear the LORD, trust in the LORD;
He *is* their help and their shield.

12 The LORD [1]has been mindful of *us*;
He will bless us;
He will bless the house of Israel;
He will bless the house of Aaron.

13 [a]He will bless those who fear the LORD,
Both small and great.

14 May the LORD give you increase more and more,
You and your children.

15 *May* you *be* [a]blessed by the LORD,
[b]Who made heaven and earth.

16 The heaven, *even* the heavens, *are* the LORD's;
But the earth He has given to the children of men.

114:4 [a]Ex. 19:18;
Judg. 5:5;
Ps. 29:6;
Hab. 3:6

114:5 [a]Hab. 3:8

114:8 [a]Ex. 17:6;
Num. 20:11;
Ps. 107:35

115:1 [a][Is. 48:11];
Ezek. 36:32

115:2
[a]Ps. 42:3, 10

115:3
[a][1 Chr. 16:26]

115:4
[a]Deut. 4:28;
2 Kin. 19:18;
Is. 37:19; 44:10,
20; Jer. 10:3

115:8 [a]Ps. 135:18;
Is. 44:9–11

115:9
[a]Ps. 118:2, 3
[b]Ps. 33:20

115:13
[a]Ps. 128:1, 4

115:15
[a][Gen. 14:19]
[b]Gen. 1:1;
Acts 14:15;
Rev. 14:7

115:2 [1]nations   115:12 [1]has remembered us

17 aThe dead do not praise the LORD,
Nor any who go down into silence.
18 aBut we will bless the LORD
From this time forth and forevermore.

Praise the LORD!

PSALM 116

THANKSGIVING FOR DELIVERANCE FROM DEATH

1 I aLOVE the LORD, because He has heard
My voice *and* my supplications.
2 Because He has inclined His ear to me,
Therefore I will call *upon Him* as long as I live.

3 aThe ¹pains of death surrounded me,
And the ²pangs of Sheol ³laid hold of me;
I found trouble and sorrow.
4 Then I called upon the name of the LORD:
"O LORD, I implore You, deliver my soul!"

5 aGracious *is* the LORD, and brighteous;
Yes, our God *is* merciful.
6 The LORD preserves the simple;
I was brought low, and He saved me.
7 Return to your arest, O my soul,
For bthe LORD has dealt bountifully with you.

8 aFor You have delivered my soul from death,
My eyes from tears,
And my feet from falling.
9 I will walk before the LORD
aIn the land of the living.
10 aI believed, therefore I spoke,
"I am greatly afflicted."
11 aI said in my haste,
b"All men *are* liars."

12 What shall I render to the LORD
For all His benefits toward me?
13 I will take up the cup of salvation,
And call upon the name of the LORD.
14 aI will pay my vows to the LORD
Now in the presence of all His people.

15 aPrecious in the sight of the LORD
Is the death of His saints.

16 O LORD, truly aI *am* Your servant;
I *am* Your servant, bthe son of Your maidservant;
You have loosed my bonds.
17 I will offer to You athe sacrifice of thanksgiving,
And will call upon the name of the LORD.

18 I will pay my vows to the LORD
Now in the presence of all His people,
19 In the acourts of the LORD's house,
In the midst of you, O Jerusalem.

¹Praise the LORD!

Cross References

115:17 aPs. 6:5; 88:10–12; [Is. 38:18]
115:18 aPs. 113:2; Dan. 2:20
116:1 aPs. 18:1
116:3 aPs. 18:4–6
116:5 a[Ps. 103:8]; b[Ezra 9:15]; Neh. 9:8; [Ps. 119:137; 145:17; Jer. 12:1; Dan. 9:14]
116:7 a[Jer. 6:16; Matt. 11:29]; bPs. 13:6
116:8 aPs. 56:13
116:9 aPs. 27:13
116:10 a2 Cor. 4:13
116:11 aPs. 31:22; bRom. 3:4
116:14 aPs. 116:18
116:15 aPs. 72:14; [Rev. 14:13]
116:16 aPs. 119:125; 143:12 bPs. 86:16
116:17 aLev. 7:12; Ps. 50:14; 107:22
116:19 aPs. 96:8

116:3 ¹Lit. *cords* ²*distresses* ³Lit. *found me* 116:19 ¹Heb. *Hallelujah*

PSALM 117

LET ALL PEOPLES PRAISE THE LORD

1 PRAISE [a]the LORD, all you Gentiles!
[1]Laud Him, all you peoples!
2 For His merciful kindness is great toward us,
And [a]the truth of the LORD *endures* forever.

Praise the LORD!

PSALM 118

PRAISE TO GOD FOR HIS EVERLASTING MERCY

1 OH, [a]give thanks to the LORD, for *He is* good!
[b]For His mercy *endures* forever.

2 [a]Let Israel now say,
"His mercy *endures* forever."
3 Let the house of Aaron now say,
"His mercy *endures* forever."
4 Let those who fear the LORD now say,
"His mercy *endures* forever."

5 [a]I called on the LORD in distress;
The LORD answered me *and* [b]*set me* in a broad place.
6 [a]The LORD *is* on my side;
I will not fear.
What can man do to me?
7 [a]The LORD is for me among those who help me;
Therefore [b]I shall see *my desire* on those who
hate me.
8 [a]*It is* better to trust in the LORD
Than to put confidence in man.
9 [a]*It is* better to trust in the LORD
Than to put confidence in princes.

10 All nations surrounded me,
But in the name of the LORD I will destroy them.
11 They [a]surrounded me,
Yes, they surrounded me;
But in the name of the LORD I will destroy them.
12 They surrounded me [a]like bees;
They were quenched [b]like a fire of thorns;
For in the name of the LORD I will [1]destroy them.
13 You pushed me violently, that I might fall,
But the LORD helped me.
14 [a]The LORD *is* my strength and song,
And He has become my salvation.
15 The voice of rejoicing and salvation
Is in the tents of the righteous;
The right hand of the LORD does valiantly.
16 [a]The right hand of the LORD is exalted;
The right hand of the LORD does valiantly.
17 [a]I shall not die, but live,
And [b]declare the works of the LORD.
18 The LORD has [a]chastened[1] me severely,
But He has not given me over to death.

117:1 [a]Rom. 15:11
117:2
[a][Ps. 100:5]
118:1
[a]1 Chr. 16:8, 34;
Jer. 33:11
[b]2 Chr. 5:13; 7:3;
Ezra 3:11;
[Ps. 136:1–26]
118:2 [a][Ps. 115:9]
118:5 [a]Ps. 120:1
[b]Ps. 18:19
118:6 [a]Ps. 27:1;
56:9;
[Rom. 8:31];
Heb. 13:6]
118:7 [a]Ps. 54:4
[b]Ps. 59:10
118:8
[a]2 Chr. 32:7, 8;
Ps. 40:4;
Is. 31:1, 3; 57:13;
Jer. 17:5
118:9 [a]Ps. 146:3
118:11 [a]Ps. 88:17
118:12
[a]Deut. 1:44
[b]Eccl. 7:6;
Nah. 1:10
118:14 [a]Ex. 15:2;
Is. 12:2
118:16 [a]Ex. 15:6
118:17 [a][Ps. 6:5];
Hab. 1:12
[b]Ps. 73:28
118:18 [a]Ps. 73:14;
Jer. 31:18;
[1 Cor. 11:32];
2 Cor. 6:9

117:1 [1]*Praise*   118:12 [1]*cut them off*   118:18 [1]*disciplined*

19 ^aOpen to me the gates of righteousness;
    I will go through them,
    And I will praise the LORD.

20 ^aThis is the gate of the LORD,
    ^bThrough which the righteous shall enter.

21 I will praise You,
    For You have ^aanswered me,
    And have become my salvation.

22 ^aThe stone *which* the builders rejected
    Has become the chief cornerstone.

23 ¹This was the LORD's doing;
    It *is* marvelous in our eyes.

24 This *is* the day the LORD has made;
    We will rejoice and be glad in it.

25 Save now, I pray, O LORD;
    O LORD, I pray, send now prosperity.

26 ^aBlessed *is* he who comes in the name of the LORD!
    We have blessed you from the house of the LORD.

27 God *is* the LORD,
    And He has given us ^alight;
    Bind the sacrifice with cords to the horns of the altar.

28 You *are* my God, and I will praise You;
    ^a*You are* my God, I will exalt You.

29 Oh, give thanks to the LORD, for *He is* good!
    For His mercy *endures* forever.

PSALM 119

MEDITATIONS ON THE EXCELLENCIES OF THE WORD OF GOD

א ALEPH

1 BLESSED *are* the ¹undefiled in the way,
    ^aWho walk in the law of the LORD!

2 Blessed *are* those who keep His testimonies,
    Who seek Him with the ^awhole heart!

3 ^aThey also do no iniquity;
    They walk in His ways.

4 You have commanded *us*
    To keep Your precepts diligently.

5 Oh, that my ways were directed
    To keep Your statutes!

6 ^aThen I would not be ashamed,
    When I look into all Your commandments.

7 I will praise You with uprightness of heart,
    When I learn Your righteous judgments.

8 I will keep Your statutes;
    Oh, do not forsake me utterly!

ב BETH

9 How can a young man cleanse his way?
    By taking heed according to Your word.

10 With my whole heart I have ^asought You;
    Oh, let me not wander from Your commandments!

118:19 ^aIs. 26:2
118:20 ^aPs. 24:7
^bIs. 35:8;
[Rev. 21:27;
22:14, 15]
118:21 ^aPs. 116:1
118:22
^aMatt. 21:42;
Mark 12:10, 11;
Luke 20:17;
Acts 4:11;
[Eph. 2:20;
1 Pet. 2:7, 8]
118:26
^aMatt. 21:9;
23:39; Mark 11:9;
Luke 13:35;
19:38
118:27
^aEsth. 8:16;
[1 Pet. 2:9]
118:28
^aEx. 15:2; Is. 25:1
119:1 ^aPs. 128:1;
[Ezek. 11:20;
18:17]; Mic. 4:2
119:2 ^aDeut. 6:5;
10:12; 11:13; 13:3
119:3
^a[1 John 3:9;
5:18]
119:6 ^aJob 22:26
119:10
^a2 Chr. 15:15

118:23 ¹Lit. *This is from the LORD*   119:1 ¹*blameless*

11 ^aYour word I have hidden in my heart,
That I might not sin against You.
12 Blessed *are* You, O LORD!
Teach me Your statutes.
13 With my lips I have ^adeclared
All the judgments of Your mouth.
14 I have rejoiced in the way of Your testimonies,
As *much as* in all riches.
15 I will meditate on Your precepts,
And ¹contemplate Your ways.
16 I will ^adelight myself in Your statutes;
I will not forget Your word.

‎ג GIMEL

17 ^aDeal bountifully with Your servant,
That I may live and keep Your word.
18 Open my eyes, that I may see
Wondrous things from Your law.
19 ^aI *am* a stranger in the earth;
Do not hide Your commandments from me.
20 ^aMy soul ¹breaks with longing
For Your judgments at all times.
21 You rebuke the proud—the cursed,
Who stray from Your commandments.
22 ^aRemove from me reproach and contempt,
For I have kept Your testimonies.
23 Princes also sit *and* speak against me,
But Your servant meditates on Your statutes.
24 Your testimonies also *are* my delight
And my counselors.

‎ד DALETH

25 ^aMy soul clings to the dust;
^bRevive me according to Your word.
26 I have declared my ways, and You answered me;
^aTeach me Your statutes.
27 Make me understand the way of Your precepts;
So ^ashall I meditate on Your wonderful works.
28 ^aMy soul ¹melts from ²heaviness;
Strengthen me according to Your word.
29 Remove from me the way of lying,
And grant me Your law graciously.
30 I have chosen the way of truth;
Your judgments I have laid *before me.*
31 I cling to Your testimonies;
O LORD, do not put me to shame!
32 I will run the course of Your commandments,
For You shall ^aenlarge my heart.

‎ה HE

33 ^aTeach me, O LORD, the way of Your statutes,
And I shall keep it *to* the end.
34 ^aGive me understanding, and I shall keep Your law;
Indeed, I shall observe it with *my* whole heart.

119:11 ^aPs. 37:31;
Luke 2:19
119:13 ^aPs. 34:11
119:16 ^aPs. 1:2
119:17 ^aPs. 116:7
119:19
^aGen. 47:9;
Lev. 25:23;
1 Chr. 29:15;
Ps. 39:12;
Heb. 11:13
119:20
^aPs. 42:1, 2; 63:1;
84:2
119:22 ^aPs. 39:8
119:25
^aPs. 44:25
^bPs. 143:11
119:26 ^aPs. 25:4;
27:11; 86:11
119:27
^aPs. 145:5, 6
119:28
^aPs. 107:26
119:32
^a1 Kin. 4:29;
Is. 60:5;
2 Cor. 6:11, 13
119:33
^a[Matt. 10:22;
Rev. 2:26]
119:34
^a[Prov. 2:6;
James 1:5]

119:15 ¹*look into*   119:20 ¹*is crushed*   119:28 ¹Lit. *drops*   ²*grief*

35 Make me walk in the path of Your commandments,
  For I delight in it.
36 ¹Incline my heart to Your testimonies,
  And not to ᵃcovetousness.
37 ᵃTurn¹ away my eyes from ᵇlooking at worthless things,
  And revive me in ²Your way.
38 ᵃEstablish Your word to Your servant,
  Who *is devoted* to fearing You.
39 Turn away my reproach which I dread,
  For Your judgments *are* good.
40 Behold, I long for Your precepts;
  Revive me in Your righteousness.

ו WAW

41 Let Your mercies come also to me, O LORD—
  Your salvation according to Your word.
42 So shall I have an answer for him who ¹reproaches me,
  For I trust in Your word.
43 And take not the word of truth utterly out of my mouth,
  For I have hoped in Your ordinances.
44 So shall I keep Your law continually,
  Forever and ever.
45 And I will walk ¹at ᵃliberty,
  For I seek Your precepts.
46 ᵃI will speak of Your testimonies also before kings,
  And will not be ashamed.
47 And I will delight myself in Your commandments,
  Which I love.
48 My hands also I will lift up to Your commandments,
  Which I love,
  And I will meditate on Your statutes.

ז ZAYIN

49 Remember the word to Your servant,
  Upon which You have caused me to hope.
50 This *is* my ᵃcomfort in my affliction,
  For Your word has given me life.
51 The proud have me in great derision,
  Yet I do not turn aside from Your law.
52 I remembered Your judgments of old, O LORD,
  And have comforted myself.
53 ᵃIndignation has taken hold of me
  Because of the wicked, who forsake Your law.
54 Your statutes have been my songs
  In the house of my pilgrimage.
55 ᵃI remember Your name in the night, O LORD,
  And I keep Your law.
56 This has become mine,
  Because I kept Your precepts.

ח HETH

57 ᵃ*You are* my portion, O LORD;
  I have said that I would keep Your words.

119:36 ᵃEzek. 33:31;
[Mark 7:20–23];
Luke 12:15;
[Heb. 13:5]

119:37 ᵃIs. 33:15
ᵇProv. 23:5

119:38
ᵃ2 Sam. 7:25

119:45
ᵃProv. 4:12

119:46 ᵃPs. 138:1;
Matt. 10:18;
Acts 26

119:50
ᵃJob 6:10;
[Rom. 15:4]

119:53
ᵃEx. 32:19;
Ezra 9:3;
Neh. 13:25

119:55 ᵃPs. 63:6

119:57
ᵃNum. 18:20;
Ps. 16:5;
Jer. 10:16;
Lam. 3:24

119:36 ¹Cause me to long for   **119:37** ¹Lit. *Cause my eyes to pass away from*
²So with MT, LXX, Vg.; Tg. *Your words*   **119:42** ¹*taunts*   **119:45** ¹Lit. *in a wide place*

58 I entreated Your favor with *my* whole heart;
Be merciful to me according to Your word.
59 I ᵃthought about my ways,
And turned my feet to Your testimonies.
60 I made haste, and did not delay
To keep Your commandments.
61 The cords of the wicked have bound me,
But I have not forgotten Your law.
62 ᵃAt midnight I will rise to give thanks to You,
Because of Your righteous judgments.
63 I *am* a companion of all who fear You,
And of those who keep Your precepts.
64 ᵃThe earth, O LORD, is full of Your mercy;
Teach me Your statutes.

ט TETH

65 You have dealt well with Your servant,
O LORD, according to Your word.
66 Teach me good judgment and ᵃknowledge,
For I believe Your commandments.
67 Before I was ᵃafflicted I went astray,
But now I keep Your word.
68 You *are* ᵃgood, and do good;
Teach me Your statutes.
69 The proud have ᵃforged¹ a lie against me,
But I will keep Your precepts with *my* whole heart.
70 ᵃTheir heart is ¹as fat as grease,
But I delight in Your law.
71 *It is* good for me that I have been afflicted,
That I may learn Your statutes.
72 ᵃThe law of Your mouth *is* better to me
Than thousands of *coins of* gold and silver.

י YOD

73 ᵃYour hands have made me and fashioned me;
Give me understanding, that I may learn Your
commandments.
74 ᵃThose who fear You will be glad when they see me,
Because I have hoped in Your word.
75 I know, O LORD, ᵃthat Your judgments *are* ¹right,
And *that* in faithfulness You have afflicted me.
76 Let, I pray, Your merciful kindness be for my
comfort,
According to Your word to Your servant.
77 Let Your tender mercies come to me, that I may
live;
For Your law *is* my delight.
78 Let the proud ᵃbe ashamed,
For they treated me wrongfully with falsehood;
But I will meditate on Your precepts.
79 Let those who fear You turn to me,
Those who know Your testimonies.
80 Let my heart be blameless regarding Your statutes,
That I may not be ashamed.

119:59
ᵃMark 14:72;
Luke 15:17

119:62
ᵃActs 16:25

119:64 ᵃPs. 33:5

119:66 ᵃPhil. 1:9

119:67
ᵃProv. 3:11;
Jer. 31:18, 19;
[Heb. 12:5–11]

119:68
ᵃPs. 106:1; 107:1;
[Matt. 19:17]

119:69 ᵃJob 13:4;
Ps. 109:2

119:70
ᵃDeut. 32:15;
Job 15:27;
Ps. 17:10;
Is. 6:10;
Jer. 5:28;
Acts 28:27

119:72 ᵃPs. 19:10;
Prov. 8:10, 11, 19

119:73
ᵃJob 10:8; 31:15;
[Ps. 139:15, 16]

119:74 ᵃPs. 34:2

119:75
ᵃ[Heb. 12:10]

119:78 ᵃPs. 25:3

119:69 ¹Lit. *smeared me with a lie*   119:70 ¹Insensible   119:75 ¹Lit. *righteous*

‫כ‬ KAPH

81 [a]My soul faints for Your salvation,
   But I hope in Your word.
82 My eyes fail *from searching* Your word,
   Saying, "When will You comfort me?"
83 For [a]I have become like a wineskin in smoke,
   Yet I do not forget Your statutes.
84 [a]How many *are* the days of Your servant?
   [b]When will You execute judgment on those who persecute
      me?
85 [a]The proud have dug pits for me,
   Which *is* not according to Your law.
86 All Your commandments *are* faithful;
   They persecute me [a]wrongfully;
   Help me!
87 They almost made an end of me on earth,
   But I did not forsake Your precepts.
88 Revive me according to Your lovingkindness,
   So that I may keep the testimony of Your mouth.

‫ל‬ LAMED

89 [a]Forever, O LORD,
   Your word [1]is settled in heaven.
90 Your faithfulness *endures* to all generations;
   You established the earth, and it [1]abides.
91 They continue this day according to [a]Your ordinances,
   For all *are* Your servants.
92 Unless Your law *had been* my delight,
   I would then have perished in my affliction.
93 I will never forget Your precepts,
   For by them You have given me life.
94 I *am* Yours, save me;
   For I have sought Your precepts.
95 The wicked wait for me to destroy me,
   But I will [1]consider Your testimonies.
96 [a]I have seen the consummation of all perfection,
   But Your commandment *is* exceedingly broad.

‫מ‬ MEM

97 Oh, how I love Your law!
   [a]It *is* my meditation all the day.
98 You, through Your commandments, make me [a]wiser
      than my enemies;
   For they *are* ever with me.
99 I have more understanding than all my teachers,
   [a]For Your testimonies *are* my meditation.
100 [a]I understand more than the [1]ancients,
   Because I keep Your precepts.
101 I have restrained my feet from every evil way,
   That I may keep Your word.
102 I have not departed from Your judgments,
   For You Yourself have taught me.
103 [a]How sweet are Your words to my taste,
   Sweeter than honey to my mouth!

119:81
[a]Ps. 73:26; 84:2
119:83
[a]Job 30:30
119:84 [a]Ps. 39:4
[b]Rev. 6:10
119:85 [a]Ps. 35:7;
Prov. 16:27;
Jer. 18:22
119:86 [a]Ps. 35:19
119:89 [a]Ps. 89:2;
Is. 40:8;
Matt. 24:35;
[1 Pet. 1:25]
119:91
[a]Jer. 33:25
119:96
[a]Matt. 5:18
119:97 [a]Ps. 1:2
119:98
[a]Deut. 4:6
119:99
[a][2 Tim. 3:15]
119:100
[a][Job 32:7–9]
119:103
[a]Ps. 19:10;
Prov. 8:11

119:89 [1]Lit. *stands firm*   119:90 [1]Lit. *stands*   119:95 [1]*give attention to*
119:100 [1]*aged*

104 Through Your precepts I get understanding;
Therefore I hate every false way.

ן NUN

105 [a]Your word *is* a lamp to my feet
And a light to my path.
106 [a]I have sworn and confirmed
That I will keep Your righteous judgments.
107 I am afflicted very much;
Revive me, O LORD, according to Your word.
108 Accept, I pray, [a]the freewill offerings of my mouth, O LORD,
And teach me Your judgments.
109 [a]My life *is* continually [1]in my hand,
Yet I do not forget Your law.
110 [a]The wicked have laid a snare for me,
Yet I have not strayed from Your precepts.
111 [a]Your testimonies I have taken as a [1]heritage forever,
For they *are* the rejoicing of my heart.
112 I have inclined my heart to perform Your statutes
Forever, to the very end.

ס SAMEK

113 I hate the [1]double-minded,
But I love Your law.
114 [a]You *are* my hiding place and my shield;
I hope in Your word.
115 [a]Depart from me, you evildoers,
For I will keep the commandments of my God!
116 Uphold me according to Your word, that I may live;
And do not let me [a]be ashamed of my hope.
117 [1]Hold me up, and I shall be safe,
And I shall observe Your statutes continually.
118 You reject all those who stray from Your statutes,
For their deceit *is* falsehood.
119 You [1]put away all the wicked of the earth [a]*like* [2]dross;
Therefore I love Your testimonies.
120 [a]My flesh trembles for fear of You,
And I am afraid of Your judgments.

ע AYIN

121 I have done justice and righteousness;
Do not leave me to my oppressors.
122 Be [a]surety[1] for Your servant for good;
Do not let the proud oppress me.
123 My eyes fail *from seeking* Your salvation
And Your righteous word.
124 Deal with Your servant according to Your mercy,
And teach me Your statutes.
125 [a]I *am* Your servant;
Give me understanding,
That I may know Your testimonies.
126 *It is* time for *You* to act, O LORD,
For they have [1]regarded Your law as void.

119:105
[a]Prov. 6:23
119:106
[a]Neh. 10:29
119:108
[a]Hos. 14:2;
Heb. 13:15
119:109
[a]Judg. 12:3;
Job 13:14
119:110
[a]Ps. 140:5
119:111
[a]Deut. 33:4
119:114
[a][Ps. 32:7]
119:115 [a]Ps. 6:8;
Matt. 7:23
119:116 [a]Ps. 25:2;
[Rom. 5:5; 9:33;
10:11; Phil. 1:20]
119:119
[a]Is. 1:22, 25;
Ezek. 22:18, 19
119:120
[a]Job 4:14;
Hab. 3:16
119:122
[a]Job 17:3;
Heb. 7:22
119:125
[a]Ps. 116:16

119:109 [1]In danger   119:111 [1]*inheritance*   119:113 [1]Lit. *divided* in heart or mind   119:117 [1]*Uphold me*   119:119 [1]*destroy*, lit. *cause to cease*   [2]*slag* or *refuse*   119:122 [1]*guaranty*   119:126 [1]*broken Your law*

127 ^aTherefore I love Your commandments
  More than gold, yes, than fine gold!
128 Therefore all *Your* precepts *concerning* all *things*
  I consider *to be* right;
  I hate every false way.

ם PE

129 Your testimonies are wonderful;
  Therefore my soul keeps them.
130 The entrance of Your words gives light;
  ^aIt gives understanding to the ^bsimple.
131 I opened my mouth and ^apanted,
  For I longed for Your commandments.
132 ^aLook upon me and be merciful to me,
  ^bAs Your custom *is* toward those who love Your
    name.
133 ^aDirect my steps by Your word,
  And ^blet no iniquity have dominion over me.
134 ^aRedeem me from the oppression of man,
  That I may keep Your precepts.
135 ^aMake Your face shine upon Your servant,
  And teach me Your statutes.
136 ^aRivers of water run down from my eyes,
  Because *men* do not keep Your law.

צ TSADDE

137 ^aRighteous *are* You, O LORD,
  And upright *are* Your judgments.
138 ^aYour testimonies, *which* You have commanded,
  Are righteous and very faithful.
139 ^aMy zeal has ¹consumed me,
  Because my enemies have forgotten Your words.
140 ^aYour word *is* very ¹pure;
  Therefore Your servant loves it.
141 I *am* small and despised,
  Yet I do not forget Your precepts.
142 Your righteousness *is* an everlasting righteousness,
  And Your law *is* ^atruth.
143 Trouble and anguish have ¹overtaken me,
  Yet Your commandments *are* my delights.
144 The righteousness of Your testimonies *is*
    everlasting;
  Give me understanding, and I shall live.

ק QOPH

145 I cry out with *my* whole heart;
  Hear me, O LORD!
  I will keep Your statutes.
146 I cry out to You;
  Save me, and I will keep Your testimonies.
147 ^aI rise before the dawning of the morning,
  And cry for help;
  I hope in Your word.
148 ^aMy eyes are awake through the *night* watches,
  That I may meditate on Your word.

119:127
^aPs. 19:10
119:130
^aProv. 6:23
^b[Ps. 19:7];
Prov. 1:4
119:131 ^aPs. 42:1
119:132
^aPs. 106:4
^bPs. 51:1;
[2 Thess. 1:6]
119:133 ^aPs. 17:5
^b[Ps. 19:13;
Rom. 6:12]
119:134
^aLuke 1:74
119:135
^aNum. 6:25;
Ps. 4:6
119:136
^aJer. 9:1, 18;
14:17; Lam. 3:48;
Ezek. 9:4
119:137
^aEzra 9:15;
Neh. 9:33;
Jer. 12:1;
Lam. 1:18;
Dan. 9:7, 14
119:138
^a[Ps. 19:7–9]
119:139
^aPs. 69:9;
John 2:17
119:140 ^aPs. 12:6
119:142
^a[Ps. 19:9;
John 17:17]
119:147 ^aPs. 5:3
119:148
^aPs. 63:1, 6

119:139 ¹*put an end to* 119:140 ¹Lit. *refined* or *tried* 119:143 ¹Lit. *found*

149 Hear my voice according to Your lovingkindness;
O LORD, revive me according to Your justice.
150 They draw near who follow after wickedness;
They are far from Your law.
151 You *are* ^anear, O LORD,
And all Your commandments *are* truth.
152 Concerning Your testimonies,
I have known of old that You have founded them
^aforever.

ר RESH

153 ^aConsider my affliction and deliver me,
For I do not forget Your law.
154 ^aPlead my cause and redeem me;
Revive me according to Your word.
155 Salvation *is* far from the wicked,
For they do not seek Your statutes.
156 ¹Great *are* Your tender mercies, O LORD;
Revive me according to Your judgments.
157 Many *are* my persecutors and my enemies,
Yet I do not ^aturn from Your testimonies.
158 I see the treacherous, and ^aam disgusted,
Because they do not keep Your word.
159 Consider how I love Your precepts;
Revive me, O LORD, according to Your lovingkindness.
160 The entirety of Your word *is* truth,
And every one of Your righteous judgments *endures*
forever.

ש SHIN

161 ^aPrinces persecute me without a cause,
But my heart stands in awe of Your word.
162 I rejoice at Your word
As one who finds great treasure.
163 I hate and abhor lying,
But I love Your law.
164 Seven times a day I praise You,
Because of Your righteous judgments.
165 ^aGreat peace have those who love Your law,
And ¹nothing causes them to stumble.
166 ^aLORD, I hope for Your salvation,
And I do Your commandments.
167 My soul keeps Your testimonies,
And I love them exceedingly.
168 I keep Your precepts and Your testimonies,
^aFor all my ways *are* before You.

ת TAU

169 Let my cry come before You, O LORD;
^aGive me understanding according to Your word.
170 Let my ¹supplication come before You;
Deliver me according to Your word.
171 ^aMy lips shall utter praise,
For You teach me Your statutes.

119:151
^a[Ps. 145:18];
Is. 50:8
119:152
^aLuke 21:33
119:153
^aLam. 5:1
119:154
^a1 Sam. 24:15;
Mic. 7:9
119:157
^aPs. 44:18
119:158
^aEzek. 9:4
119:161
^a1 Sam. 24:11;
26:18
119:165
^aProv. 3:2;
[Is. 26:3; 32:17]
119:166
^aGen. 49:18
119:168
^aJob 24:23;
Prov. 5:21
119:169
^aPs. 119:27, 144
119:171 ^aPs. 119:7

119:156 ¹Or *Many*   119:165 ¹Lit. *they have no stumbling block*
119:170 ¹*Prayer of supplication*

172 My tongue shall speak of Your word,
For all Your commandments *are* righteousness.
173 Let Your hand become my help,
For [a]I have chosen Your precepts.
174 [a]I long for Your salvation, O LORD,
And [b]Your law *is* my delight.
175 Let my soul live, and it shall praise You;
And let Your judgments help me.
176 [a]I have gone astray like a lost sheep;
Seek Your servant,
For I do not forget Your commandments.

PSALM 120

PLEA FOR RELIEF FROM BITTER FOES

A Song of Ascents.

1 IN [a]my distress I cried to the LORD,
And He heard me.
2 Deliver my soul, O LORD, from lying lips
And from a deceitful tongue.
3 What shall be given to you,
Or what shall be done to you,
You false tongue?
4 Sharp arrows of the [1]warrior,
With coals of the broom tree!
5 Woe is me, that I dwell in [a]Meshech,
[b]*That* I dwell among the tents of Kedar!
6 My soul has dwelt too long
With one who hates peace.
7 I *am for* peace;
But when I speak, they *are* for war.

PSALM 121

GOD THE HELP OF THOSE WHO SEEK HIM

A Song of Ascents.

1 I [a]WILL lift up my eyes to the hills—
From whence comes my help?
2 [a]My help *comes* from the LORD,
Who made heaven and earth.
3 [a]He will not allow your foot to [1]be moved;
[b]He who keeps you will not slumber.
4 Behold, He who keeps Israel
Shall neither slumber nor sleep.
5 The LORD *is* your [1]keeper;
The LORD *is* [a]your shade [b]at your right hand.
6 [a]The sun shall not strike you by day,
Nor the moon by night.
7 The LORD shall [1]preserve you from all evil;
He shall [a]preserve your soul.
8 The LORD shall [a]preserve[1] your going out and your
coming in
From this time forth, and even forevermore.

119:173
[a]Josh. 24:22;
Luke 10:42

119:174
[a]Ps. 119:166
[b]Ps. 119:16, 24

119:176
[a][Is. 53:6];
Jer. 50:6;
Matt. 18:12;
Luke 15:4;
[1 Pet. 2:25]

120:1 [a]Jon. 2:2

120:5
[a]Gen. 10:2;
1 Chr. 1:5;
Ezek. 27:13;
38:2, 3; 39:1
[b]Gen. 25:13;
Is. 21:16; 60:7;
Jer. 2:10; 49:28;
Ezek. 27:21

121:1 [a][Jer. 3:23]

121:2
[a][Ps. 124:8]

121:3
[a]1 Sam. 2:9;
Prov. 3:23, 26
[b][Ps. 127:1;
Prov. 24:12];
Is. 27:3

121:5 [a]Is. 25:4
[b]Ps. 16:8

121:6 [a]Ps. 91:5;
Is. 49:10;
Jon. 4:8;
Rev. 7:16

121:7 [a]Ps. 41:2

121:8
[a]Deut. 28:6;
[Prov. 2:8; 3:6]

120:4 [1]*mighty one*   121:3 [1]*slip*   121:5 [1]*protector*   121:7 [1]*keep*   121:8 [1]*keep*

PSALM 122

THE JOY OF GOING TO THE HOUSE OF THE LORD

A Song of Ascents. Of David.

1 I WAS glad when they said to me,
a"Let us go into the house of the LORD."
2 Our feet have been standing
Within your gates, O Jerusalem!

3 Jerusalem is built
As a city that is acompact together,
4 aWhere the tribes go up,
The tribes of the LORD,
1To bthe Testimony of Israel,
To give thanks to the name of the LORD.
5 aFor thrones are set there for judgment,
The thrones of the house of David.

6 aPray for the peace of Jerusalem:
"May they prosper who love you.
7 Peace be within your walls,
Prosperity within your palaces."
8 For the sake of my brethren and companions,
I will now say, "Peace be within you."
9 Because of the house of the LORD our God
I will aseek your good.

PSALM 123

PRAYER FOR RELIEF FROM CONTEMPT

A Song of Ascents.

1 UNTO You aI lift up my eyes,
O You bwho dwell in the heavens.
2 Behold, as the eyes of servants look to the hand of their masters,
As the eyes of a maid to the hand of her mistress,
aSo our eyes look to the LORD our God,
Until He has mercy on us.

3 Have mercy on us, O LORD, have mercy on us!
For we are exceedingly filled with contempt.
4 Our soul is exceedingly filled
With the scorn of those who are at ease,
With the contempt of the proud.

PSALM 124

THE LORD THE DEFENSE OF HIS PEOPLE

A Song of Ascents. Of David.

1 "IF it had not been the LORD who was on our aside,"
bLet Israel now say—
2 "If it had not been the LORD who was on our side,
When men rose up against us,
3 Then they would have aswallowed us alive,
When their wrath was kindled against us;

122:1 a[Is. 2:3;
Mic. 4:2];
Zech. 8:21

122:3
a2 Sam. 5:9

122:4 aEx. 23:17;
Deut. 16:16
bEx. 16:34

122:5
aDeut. 17:8;
2 Chr. 19:8

122:6 aPs. 51:18

122:9
aNeh. 2:10;
Esth. 10:3

123:1 aPs. 121:1;
141:8 bPs. 2:4;
11:4; 115:3

123:2 aPs. 25:15

124:1 aPs. 118:6;
[Rom. 8:31]
bPs. 129:1

124:3
aNum. 16:30;
Ps. 56:1, 2; 57:3;
Prov. 1:12

122:4 1Or As a testimony to

4 Then the waters would have overwhelmed us,
The stream would have ¹gone over our soul;

5 Then the swollen waters
Would have ¹gone over our soul."

6 Blessed *be* the LORD,
Who has not given us *as* prey to their teeth.

7 ᵃOur soul has escaped ᵇas a bird from the snare of the
¹fowlers;
The snare is broken, and we have escaped.

8 ᵃOur help *is* in the name of the LORD,
ᵇWho made heaven and earth.

PSALM 125

THE LORD THE STRENGTH OF HIS PEOPLE

A Song of Ascents.

1 THOSE who trust in the LORD
Are like Mount Zion,
Which cannot be moved, *but* abides forever.

2 As the mountains surround Jerusalem,
So the LORD surrounds His people
From this time forth and forever.

3 For ᵃthe scepter of wickedness shall not rest
On the land allotted to the righteous,
Lest the righteous reach out their hands to iniquity.

4 Do good, O LORD, to *those who are* good,
And to *those who are* upright in their hearts.

5 As for such as turn aside to their ᵃcrooked ways,
The LORD shall lead them away
With the workers of iniquity.

ᵇPeace *be* upon Israel!

PSALM 126

A JOYFUL RETURN TO ZION

A Song of Ascents.

1 WHEN ᵃthe LORD brought back ¹the captivity of Zion,
ᵇWe were like those who dream.

2 Then ᵃour mouth was filled with laughter,
And our tongue with singing.
Then they said among the ¹nations,
"The LORD has done great things for them."

3 The LORD has done great things for us,
And we are glad.

4 Bring back our captivity, O LORD,
As the streams in the South.

5 ᵃThose who sow in tears
Shall reap in joy.

6 He who continually goes ¹forth weeping,
Bearing ²seed for sowing,

124:7 ᵃPs. 91:3
ᵇProv. 6:5;
Hos. 9:8

124:8
ᵃ[Ps. 121:2]
ᵇGen. 1:1;
Ps. 134:3

125:3
ᵃProv. 22:8;
Is. 14:5

125:5
ᵃProv. 2:15;
Is. 59:8
ᵇPs. 128:6;
[Gal. 6:16]

126:1 ᵃPs. 85:1;
Jer. 29:14;
Hos. 6:11;
Joel 3:1
ᵇActs 12:9

126:2 ᵃJob 8:21

126:5 ᵃIs. 35:10;
51:11; 61:7;
Jer. 31:9;
[Gal. 6:9]

124:4 ¹*swept over*   124:5 ¹*swept over*   124:7 ¹Persons who catch birds in a trap or snare   126:1 ¹Those of the captivity   126:2 ¹*Gentiles*   126:6 ¹*to and fro*   ²Lit. *a bag of seed for sowing*

Shall doubtless come again ³with ªrejoicing,
Bringing his sheaves *with him.*

PSALM 127

LABORING AND PROSPERING WITH THE LORD

A Song of Ascents. Of Solomon.

1 UNLESS the LORD builds the house,
They labor in vain who build it;
Unless ªthe LORD guards the city,
The watchman stays awake in vain.
2 *It is* vain for you to rise up early,
To sit up late,
To ªeat the bread of sorrows;
For so He gives His beloved sleep.
3 Behold, ªchildren *are* a heritage from the LORD,
ᵇThe fruit of the womb *is* a ᶜreward.
4 Like arrows in the hand of a warrior,
So *are* the children of one's youth.
5 ªHappy *is* the man who has his quiver full of them;
ᵇThey shall not be ashamed,
But shall speak with their enemies in the gate.

PSALM 128

BLESSINGS OF THOSE WHO FEAR THE LORD

A Song of Ascents.

1 BLESSED ªis every one who fears the LORD,
Who walks in His ways.
2 ªWhen you eat the ¹labor of your hands,
You *shall be* happy, and *it shall be* ᵇwell with you.
3 Your wife *shall be* ªlike a fruitful vine
In the very heart of your house,
Your ᵇchildren ᶜlike olive plants
All around your table.
4 Behold, thus shall the man be blessed
Who fears the LORD.
5 ªThe LORD bless you out of Zion,
And may you see the good of Jerusalem
All the days of your life.
6 Yes, may you ªsee your children's children.

ᵇPeace *be* upon Israel!

PSALM 129

SONG OF VICTORY OVER ZION'S ENEMIES

A Song of Ascents.

1 "MANY a time they have ªafflicted¹ me from ᵇmy
youth,"
ᶜLet Israel now say—
2 "Many a time they have afflicted me from my youth;
Yet they have not prevailed against me.

126:6 ªIs. 61:3
127:1
ª[Ps. 121:3–5]
127:2
ª[Gen. 3:17, 19]
127:3
ª[Gen. 33:5;
Josh. 24:3, 4;
Ps. 113:9]
ᵇDeut. 7:13;
28:4; Is. 13:18
ᶜ[Ps. 113:9]
127:5
ªPs. 128:2, 3
ᵇJob 5:4;
Prov. 27:11
128:1 ªPs. 119:1
128:2 ªIs. 3:10
ᵇDeut. 4:40
128:3
ªEzek. 19:10
ᵇPs. 127:3–5
ᶜPs. 52:8; 144:12
128:5 ªPs. 134:3
128:6
ªGen. 48:11;
50:23;
Job 42:16;
Ps. 103:17;
[Prov. 17:6]
ᵇPs. 125:5
129:1
ª[Jer. 1:19; 15:20];
Matt. 16:18;
2 Cor. 4:8, 9
ᵇEzek. 23:3;
Hos. 2:15
ᶜPs. 124:1

126:6 ³*with shouts of joy*   128:2 ¹*Fruit of the labor*   129:1 ¹*persecuted*

3   The plowers plowed on my back;
    They made their furrows long."
4   The LORD *is* righteous;
    He has cut in pieces the cords of the wicked.

5   Let all those who hate Zion
    Be put to shame and turned back.
6   Let them be as the [a]grass *on* the housetops,
    Which withers before it grows up,
7   With which the reaper does not fill his hand,
    Nor he who binds sheaves, his [1]arms.
8   Neither let those who pass by them say,
  [a]"The blessing of the LORD *be* upon you;
    We bless you in the name of the LORD!"

PSALM 130

WAITING FOR THE REDEMPTION OF THE LORD

A Song of Ascents.

1   OUT [a]of the depths I have cried to You, O LORD;
2   Lord, hear my voice!
    Let Your ears be attentive
    To the voice of my supplications.

3   [a]If You, LORD, should [1]mark iniquities,
    O Lord, who could [b]stand?
4   But *there is* [a]forgiveness with You,
    That [b]You may be feared.

5   [a]I wait for the LORD, my soul waits,
    And [b]in His word I do hope.
6   [a]My soul *waits* for the Lord
    More than those who watch for the morning—
    Yes, more than those who watch for the morning.

7   [a]O Israel, hope in the LORD;
    For [b]with the LORD *there is* mercy,
    And with Him *is* abundant redemption.
8   And [a]He shall redeem Israel
    From all his iniquities.

PSALM 131

SIMPLE TRUST IN THE LORD

A Song of Ascents. Of David.

1   LORD, my heart is not [1]haughty,
    Nor my eyes [2]lofty.
    [a]Neither do I [3]concern myself with great matters,
    Nor with things too [4]profound for me.

2   Surely I have calmed and quieted my soul,
    [a]Like a weaned child with his mother;
    Like a weaned child *is* my soul within me.

3   [a]O Israel, hope in the LORD
    From this time forth and forever.

129:6 [a]Ps. 37:2
129:8 [a]Ruth 2:4
130:1 [a]Lam. 3:55
130:3
[a][Ps. 143:2]
[b][Nah. 1:6;
Mal. 3:2];
Rev. 6:17
130:4 [a][Ex. 34:7;
Neh. 9:17;
Ps. 86:5; Is. 55:7;
Dan. 9:9]
[b][1 Kin. 8:39, 40;
Jer. 33:8, 9]
130:5
[a][Ps. 27:14]
[b]Ps. 119:81
130:6
[a]Ps. 119:147
130:7 [a]Ps. 131:3
[b][Ps. 86:5, 15;
Is. 55:7]
130:8
[a][Ps. 103:3, 4];
Luke 1:68;
Titus 2:14
131:1 [a]Jer. 45:5;
[Rom. 12:16]
131:2
[a][Matt. 18:3;
1 Cor. 14:20]
131:3
[a][Ps. 130:7]

129:7 [1]*armsful,* lit. *bosom*   130:3 [1]*take note of*   131:1 [1]*Proud*   [2]*Arrogant*
[3]Lit. *walk in*   [4]*difficult*

PSALM 132

THE ETERNAL DWELLING OF GOD IN ZION

A Song of Ascents.

1   LORD, remember David
    And all his afflictions;

2   How he swore to the LORD,
    [a]*And* vowed to [b]the Mighty One of Jacob:

3   "Surely I will not go into the chamber of my house,
    Or go up to the comfort of my bed;

4   I will [a]not give sleep to my eyes
    Or slumber to my eyelids,

5   Until I [a]find a place for the LORD,
    A dwelling place for the Mighty One of Jacob."

6   Behold, we heard of it [a]in Ephrathah;
    [b]We found it [c]in the fields of [1]the woods.

7   Let us go into His tabernacle;
    [a]Let us worship at His footstool.

8   [a]Arise, O LORD, to Your resting place,
    You and [b]the ark of Your strength.

9   Let Your priests [a]be clothed with righteousness,
    And let Your saints shout for joy.

10 For Your servant David's sake,
    Do not turn away the face of Your [1]Anointed.

11 [a]The LORD has sworn *in* truth to David;
    He will not turn from it:
    "I will set upon your throne [b]the [1]fruit of your body.

12 If your sons will keep My covenant
    And My testimony which I shall teach them,
    Their sons also shall sit upon your throne forevermore."

13 [a]For the LORD has chosen Zion;
    He has desired *it* for His [1]dwelling place:

14 "This[a] *is* My resting place forever;
    Here I will dwell, for I have desired it.

15 [a]I will abundantly bless her [1]provision;
    I will satisfy her poor with bread.

16 [a]I will also clothe her priests with salvation,
    [b]And her saints shall shout aloud for joy.

17 [a]There I will make the [1]horn of David grow;
    [b]I will prepare a lamp for My [2]Anointed.

18 His enemies I will [a]clothe with shame,
    But upon Himself His crown shall flourish."

PSALM 133

BLESSED UNITY OF THE PEOPLE OF GOD

A Song of Ascents. Of David.

1   BEHOLD, how good and how pleasant *it is*
    For [a]brethren to dwell together in unity!

2   *It is* like the precious oil upon the head,
    Running down on the beard,

132:2 [a]Ps. 65:1
[b]Gen. 49:24;
Is. 49:26; 60:16

132:4 [a]Prov. 6:4

132:5
[a]1 Kin. 8:17;
1 Chr. 22:7;
Ps. 26:8;
Acts 7:46

132:6
[a]1 Sam. 17:12
[b]1 Sam. 7:1
[c]1 Chr. 13:5

132:7
[a]Ps. 5:7; 99:5

132:8
[a]Num. 10:35
[b]Ps. 78:61

132:9 [a]Job 29:14

132:11
[a][Ps. 89:3, 4,
33; 110:4]
[b]2 Sam. 7:12;
[1 Kin. 8:25;
2 Chr. 6:16;
Luke 1:69;
Acts 2:30]

132:13
[a][Ps. 48:1, 2]

132:14
[a]Ps. 68:16;
Matt. 23:21

132:15
[a]Ps. 147:14

132:16
[a]2 Chr. 6:41;
Ps. 132:9; 149:4
[b]1 Sam. 4:5;
Hos. 11:12

132:17
[a]Ezek. 29:21;
Luke 1:69
[b]1 Kin. 11:36;
15:4; 2 Kin. 8:19;
2 Chr. 21:7;
Ps. 18:28

132:18
[a]Job 8:22;
Ps. 35:26

133:1 [a]Gen. 13:8;
Heb. 13:1

132:6 [1]Heb. *Jaar,* lit. *Woods*   132:10 [1]Commissioned One, Heb. *Messiah*
132:11 [1]*offspring*   132:13 [1]*home*   132:15 [1]*supply of food*
132:17 [1]Government   [2]Heb. *Messiah*

The beard of Aaron,
Running down on the edge of his garments.
3 *It is* like the dew of [a]Hermon,
Descending upon the mountains of Zion;
For [b]there the LORD commanded the blessing—
Life forevermore.

PSALM 134

PRAISING THE LORD IN HIS HOUSE AT NIGHT

A Song of Ascents.

1 BEHOLD, bless the LORD,
All *you* servants of the LORD,
Who by night stand in the house of the LORD!
2 [a]Lift up your hands *in* the sanctuary,
And bless the LORD.

3 The LORD who made heaven and earth
Bless you from Zion!

PSALM 135

PRAISE TO GOD IN CREATION AND REDEMPTION

1 PRAISE the LORD!

Praise the name of the LORD;
[a]Praise *Him*, O you servants of the LORD!
2 [a]You who stand in the house of the LORD,
In [b]the courts of the house of our God,
3 Praise the LORD, for [a]the LORD *is* good;
Sing praises to His name, [b]for *it is* pleasant.
4 For [a]the LORD has chosen Jacob for Himself,
Israel for His [1]special treasure.

5 For I know that [a]the LORD *is* great,
And our Lord *is* above all gods.
6 [a]Whatever the LORD pleases He does,
In heaven and in earth,
In the seas and in all deep places.
7 [a]He causes the [1]vapors to ascend from the ends of the
earth;
[b]He makes lightning for the rain;
He brings the wind out of His [c]treasuries.

8 [a]He [1]destroyed the firstborn of Egypt,
[2]Both of man and beast.
9 [a]He sent signs and wonders into the midst of you,
O Egypt,
[b]Upon Pharaoh and all his servants.
10 [a]He defeated many nations
And slew mighty kings—
11 Sihon king of the Amorites,
Og king of Bashan,
And [a]all the kingdoms of Canaan—
12 [a]And gave their land *as* a [1]heritage,
A heritage to Israel His people.

133:3
[a]Deut. 4:48
[b]Lev. 25:21;
Deut. 28:8;
Ps. 42:8
134:2
[a][1 Tim. 2:8]
135:1 [a]Ps. 113:1
135:2 [a]Luke 2:37
[b]Ps. 116:19
135:3
[a][Ps. 119:68]
[b]Ps. 147:1
135:4
[a][Ex. 19:5];
Mal. 3:17;
[Titus 2:14;
1 Pet. 2:9]
135:5
[a]Ps. 95:3; 97:9
135:6 [a]Ps. 115:3
135:7 [a]Jer. 10:13
[b]Job 28:25, 26;
38:24–28
[c]Jer. 51:16
135:8 [a]Ex. 12:12;
Ps. 78:51
135:9 [a]Ex. 7:10;
Deut. 6:22;
Ps. 78:43
[b]Ps. 136:15
135:10
[a]Num. 21:24;
Ps. 136:17
135:11
[a]Josh. 12:7–24
135:12
[a]Ps. 78:55;
136:21, 22

135:4 [1]*precious possession*   135:7 [1]Water vapor   135:8 [1]Lit. *struck down*
[2]Lit. *From man to beast*   135:12 [1]*inheritance*

13 ^aYour name, O LORD, *endures* forever,
   Your fame, O LORD, throughout all generations.
14 ^aFor the LORD will judge His people,
   And He will have compassion on His servants.

15 ^aThe idols of the nations *are* silver and gold,
   The work of men's hands.
16 They have mouths, but they do not speak;
   Eyes they have, but they do not see;
17 They have ears, but they do not hear;
   Nor is there *any* breath in their mouths.
18 Those who make them are like them;
   So is everyone who trusts in them.

19 ^aBless the LORD, O house of Israel!
   Bless the LORD, O house of Aaron!
20 Bless the LORD, O house of Levi!
   You who fear the LORD, bless the LORD!
21 Blessed be the LORD ^aout of Zion,
   Who dwells in Jerusalem!

   Praise the LORD!

PSALM 136

THANKSGIVING TO GOD FOR HIS ENDURING MERCY

1   OH, ^agive thanks to the LORD, for *He is* good!
    ^bFor His mercy *endures* forever.
2   Oh, give thanks to ^athe God of gods!
    For His mercy *endures* forever.
3   Oh, give thanks to the Lord of lords!
    For His mercy *endures* forever:

4   To Him ^awho alone does great wonders,
    For His mercy *endures* forever;
5   ^aTo Him who by wisdom made the heavens,
    For His mercy *endures* forever;
6   ^aTo Him who laid out the earth above the waters,
    For His mercy *endures* forever;
7   ^aTo Him who made great lights,
    For His mercy *endures* forever—
8   ^aThe sun to rule by day,
    For His mercy *endures* forever;
9   The moon and stars to rule by night,
    For His mercy *endures* forever.

10 ^aTo Him who struck Egypt in their firstborn,
    For His mercy *endures* forever;
11 ^aAnd brought out Israel from among them,
    For His mercy *endures* forever;
12 ^aWith a strong hand, and with ¹an outstretched arm,
    For His mercy *endures* forever;
13 ^aTo Him who divided the Red Sea in two,
    For His mercy *endures* forever;
14 And made Israel pass through the midst of it,
    For His mercy *endures* forever;
15 ^aBut overthrew Pharaoh and his army in the Red Sea,
    For His mercy *endures* forever;

135:13 ^a[Ex. 3:15;
Ps. 102:12]
135:14
^aDeut. 32:36
135:15
^a[Ps. 115:4–8]
135:19
^a[Ps. 115:9]
135:21 ^aPs. 134:3
136:1 ^aPs. 106:1
^b1 Chr. 16:34;
Jer. 33:11
136:2
^a[Deut. 10:17]
136:4
^aDeut. 6:22;
Job 9:10;
Ps. 72:18
136:5
^aGen. 1:1, 6–8;
Prov. 3:19;
Jer. 51:15
136:6 ^aGen. 1:9;
Ps. 24:2;
[Is. 42:5];
Jer. 10:12
136:7
^aGen. 1:14–18
136:8 ^aGen. 1:16
136:10
^aEx. 12:29;
Ps. 135:8
136:11 ^aEx. 12:51;
13:3, 16
136:12 ^aEx. 6:6;
Deut. 4:34; 5:15;
7:19; 9:29; 11:2;
2 Kin. 17:36;
2 Chr. 6:32;
Jer. 32:17
136:13 ^aEx. 14:21
136:15 ^aEx. 14:27

136:12 ¹Mighty power

16 ªTo Him who led His people through the wilderness,
For His mercy *endures* forever;

17 ªTo Him who struck down great kings,
For His mercy *endures* forever;

18 ªAnd slew famous kings,
For His mercy *endures* forever—

19 ªSihon king of the Amorites,
For His mercy *endures* forever;

20 ªAnd Og king of Bashan,
For His mercy *endures* forever—

21 ªAnd gave their land as a ¹heritage,
For His mercy *endures* forever;

22 A heritage to Israel His servant,
For His mercy *endures* forever.

23 Who ªremembered us in our lowly state,
For His mercy *endures* forever;

24 And ªrescued us from our enemies,
For His mercy *endures* forever;

25 ªWho gives food to all flesh,
For His mercy *endures* forever.

26 Oh, give thanks to the God of heaven!
For His mercy *endures* forever.

PSALM 137

LONGING FOR ZION IN A FOREIGN LAND

1 BY the rivers of Babylon,
There we sat down, yea, we wept
When we remembered Zion.

2 We hung our harps
Upon the willows in the midst of it.

3 For there those who carried us away captive asked of us a
song,
And those who ªplundered us *requested* mirth,
Saying, "Sing us *one* of the songs of Zion!"

4 How shall we sing the LORD's song
In a foreign land?

5 If I forget you, O Jerusalem,
Let my right hand forget *its skill!*

6 If I do not remember you,
Let my ªtongue cling to the roof of my mouth—
If I do not exalt Jerusalem
Above my chief joy.

7 Remember, O LORD, against ªthe sons of Edom
The day of Jerusalem,
Who said, ¹"Raze *it*, raze *it*,
To its very foundation!"

8 O daughter of Babylon, ªwho are to be destroyed,
Happy the one ᵇwho repays you as you have
served us!

9 Happy the one who takes and ªdashes
Your little ones against the rock!

136:16
ªEx. 13:18; 15:22;
Deut. 8:15

136:17
ªPs. 135:10–12

136:18
ªDeut. 29:7

136:19
ªNum. 21:21

136:20
ªNum. 21:33

136:21
ªJosh. 12:1

136:23
ªGen. 8:1;
Deut. 32:36;
Ps. 113:7

136:24 ªPs. 44:7

136:25
ªPs. 104:27;
145:15

137:3 ªPs. 79:1

137:6
ªJob 29:10;
Ps. 22:15;
Ezek. 3:26

137:7
ªJer. 49:7–22;
Lam. 4:21;
Ezek. 25:12–14;
35:2; Amos 1:11;
Obad. 10–14

137:8
ªIs. 13:1–6; 47:1
ᵇJer. 50:15;
Rev. 18:6

137:9
ª2 Kin. 8:12;
Is. 13:16;
Hos. 13:16;
Nah. 3:10

136:21 ¹*inheritance*   137:7 ¹Lit. *Make bare*

PSALM 138

THE LORD'S GOODNESS TO THE FAITHFUL

A Psalm of David.

1 I WILL praise You with my whole heart;
   ^aBefore the gods I will sing praises to You.
2 ^aI will worship ^btoward Your holy temple,
   And praise Your name
   For Your lovingkindness and Your truth;
   For You have ^cmagnified Your word above all Your name.
3 In the day when I cried out, You answered me,
   And made me bold *with* strength in my soul.

4 ^aAll the kings of the earth shall praise You, O Lord,
   When they hear the words of Your mouth.
5 Yes, they shall sing of the ways of the Lord,
   For great *is* the glory of the Lord.
6 ^aThough the Lord *is* on high,
   Yet ^bHe regards the lowly;
   But the proud He knows from afar.

7 ^aThough I walk in the midst of trouble, You will revive me;
   You will stretch out Your hand
   Against the wrath of my enemies,
   And Your right hand will save me.
8 ^aThe Lord will ¹perfect *that which* concerns me;
   Your mercy, O Lord, *endures* forever;
   ^bDo not forsake the works of Your hands.

PSALM 139

GOD'S PERFECT KNOWLEDGE OF MAN

For the Chief Musician. A Psalm of David.

1 O Lord, ^aYou have searched me and known *me.*
2 ^aYou know my sitting down and my rising up;
   You ^bunderstand my thought afar off.
3 ^aYou ¹comprehend my path and my lying down,
   And are acquainted with all my ways.
4 For *there is* not a word on my tongue,
   But behold, O Lord, ^aYou know it altogether.
5 You have ¹hedged me behind and before,
   And laid Your hand upon me.
6 ^a*Such* knowledge *is* too wonderful for me;
   It is high, I cannot *attain* it.

7 ^aWhere can I go from Your Spirit?
   Or where can I flee from Your presence?
8 ^aIf I ascend into heaven, You *are* there;
   ^bIf I make my bed in ¹hell, behold, You *are there.*
9 *If* I take the wings of the morning,
   And dwell in the uttermost parts of the sea,
10 Even there Your hand shall lead me,
   And Your right hand shall hold me.
11 If I say, "Surely the darkness shall ¹fall on me,"
   Even the night shall be light about me;

138:1 ^aPs. 119:46
138:2 ^aPs. 28:2
^b1 Kin. 8:29
^cIs. 42:21
138:4 ^aPs. 102:15
138:6
^a[Ps. 113:4–7]
^bProv. 3:34;
[Is. 57:15];
Luke 1:48;
[James 4:6;
1 Pet. 5:5]
138:7
^a[Ps. 23:3, 4]
138:8 ^aPs. 57:2;
[Phil. 1:6]
^bJob 10:3, 8
139:1 ^aPs. 17:3;
Jer. 12:3
139:2
^a2 Kin. 19:27
^bIs. 66:18;
Matt. 9:4
139:3
^aJob 14:16; 31:4
139:4
^a[Heb. 4:13]
139:6 ^aJob 42:3;
Ps. 40:5
139:7
^a[Jer. 23:24;
Amos 9:2–4]
139:8
^a[Amos 9:2–4]
^b[Job 26:6;
Prov. 15:11]

138:8 ¹*complete*   139:3 ¹Lit. *winnow*   139:5 ¹*enclosed*   139:8 ¹Or *Sheol*
139:11 ¹Vg., Symmachus *cover*

12 Indeed, [a]the darkness [1]shall not hide from You,
But the night shines as the day;
The darkness and the light *are* both alike *to You.*

13 For You formed my inward parts;
You [1]covered me in my mother's womb.

14 I will praise You, for [1]I am fearfully *and* wonderfully
made;
Marvelous are Your works,
And *that* my soul knows very well.

15 [a]My [1]frame was not hidden from You,
When I was made in secret,
And skillfully wrought in the lowest parts of the earth.

16 Your eyes saw my substance, being yet unformed.
And in Your book they all were written,
The days fashioned for me,
When *as yet there were* none of them.

17 [a]How precious also are Your thoughts to me, O God!
How great is the sum of them!

18 *If* I should count them, they would be more in number
than the sand;
When I awake, I am still with You.

19 Oh, that You would [a]slay the wicked, O God!
[b]Depart from me, therefore, you [1]bloodthirsty men.

20 For they [a]speak against You wickedly;
[1]Your enemies take *Your name* in vain.

21 [a]Do I not hate them, O LORD, who hate You?
And do I not loathe those who rise up against You?

22 I hate them with [1]perfect hatred;
I count them my enemies.

23 [a]Search me, O God, and know my heart;
Try me, and know my anxieties;

24 And see if *there is any* wicked way in me,
And [a]lead me in the way everlasting.

PSALM 140

PRAYER FOR DELIVERANCE FROM EVIL MEN

To the Chief Musician. A Psalm of David.

1 DELIVER me, O LORD, from evil men;
Preserve me from violent men,

2 Who plan evil things in *their* hearts;
[a]They continually gather together *for* war.

3 They sharpen their tongues like a serpent;
The [a]poison of asps *is* under their lips.   *Selah*

4 [a]Keep me, O LORD, from the hands of the wicked;
Preserve me from violent men,
Who have purposed to make my steps stumble.

5 The proud have hidden a [a]snare for me, and cords;
They have spread a net by the wayside;
They have set traps for me.   *Selah*

139:12
[a] Job 26:6;
34:22;
[Dan. 2:22;
Heb. 4:13]

139:15
[a] Job 10:8, 9;
Eccl. 11:5

139:17
[a] [Ps. 40:5;
Rom. 11:33]

139:19 [a] [Is. 11:4]
[b] Ps. 119:115

139:20 [a] Jude 15

139:21
[a] 2 Chr. 19:2

139:23
[a] Job 31:6;
Ps. 26:2

139:24
[a] Ps. 5:8; 143:10

140:2 [a] Ps. 56:6

140:3 [a] Ps. 58:4;
Rom. 3:13;
James 3:8

140:4 [a] Ps. 71:4

140:5 [a] Ps. 35:7;
Jer. 18:22

139:12 [1]Lit. *is not dark*   139:13 [1]*wove*   139:14 [1]So with MT, Tg.; LXX, Syr.,
Vg. *You are fearfully wonderful*   139:15 [1]Lit. *bones were*   139:19 [1]Lit. *men of
bloodshed*   139:20 [1]LXX, Vg. *They take Your cities in vain*
139:22 [1]*complete*

6 I said to the LORD: "You *are* my God;
Hear the voice of my supplications, O LORD.
7 O GOD the Lord, the strength of my salvation,
You have ¹covered my head in the day of battle.
8 Do not grant, O LORD, the desires of the wicked;
Do not further his *wicked* scheme,
ᵃ*Lest* they be exalted.   *Selah*

9 "*As for* the head of those who surround me,
Let the evil of their lips cover them;
10 ᵃLet burning coals fall upon them;
Let them be cast into the fire,
Into deep pits, that they rise not up again.
11 Let not a slanderer be established in the earth;
Let evil hunt the violent man to overthrow *him*."

12 I know that the LORD will ᵃmaintain
The cause of the afflicted,
And justice for the poor.
13 Surely the righteous shall give thanks to Your name;
The upright shall dwell in Your presence.

PSALM 141

PRAYER FOR SAFEKEEPING FROM WICKEDNESS

A Psalm of David.

1 LORD, I cry out to You;
Make haste to me!
Give ear to my voice when I cry out to You.
2 Let my prayer be set before You ᵃ*as* incense,
ᵇThe lifting up of my hands *as* ᶜthe evening sacrifice.

3 Set a guard, O LORD, over my ᵃmouth;
Keep watch over the door of my lips.
4 Do not incline my heart to any evil thing,
To practice wicked works
With men who work iniquity;
ᵃAnd do not let me eat of their delicacies.

5 ᵃLet the righteous strike me;
It shall be a kindness.
And let him rebuke me;
It shall be as excellent oil;
Let my head not refuse it.

For still my prayer *is* against the deeds of the wicked.
6 Their judges are overthrown by the sides of the ¹cliff,
And they hear my words, for they are sweet.
7 Our bones are scattered at the mouth of the grave,
As when one plows and breaks up the earth.

8 But ᵃmy eyes *are* upon You, O GOD the Lord;
In You I take refuge;
¹Do not leave my soul destitute.
9 Keep me from ᵃthe snares they have laid for me,
And from the traps of the workers of iniquity.
10 ᵃLet the wicked fall into their own nets,
While I escape safely.

140:8
ᵃDeut. 32:27
140:10 ᵃPs. 11:6
140:12
ᵃ1 Kin. 8:45;
Ps. 9:4
141:2
ᵃ[Ex. 30:8];
Luke 1:10;
[Rev. 5:8; 8:3, 4]
ᵇPs. 134:2;
[1 Tim. 2:8]
ᶜEx. 29:39, 41;
1 Kin. 18:29, 36;
Dan. 9:21
141:3
ᵃ[Prov. 13:3;
21:23]
141:4 ᵃProv. 23:6
141:5
ᵃ[Prov. 9:8;
Eccl. 7:5;
Gal. 6:1]
141:8
ᵃ2 Chr. 20:12;
Ps. 25:15
141:9 ᵃPs. 119:110
141:10 ᵃPs. 35:8

140:7 ¹*sheltered*   141:6 ¹*rock*   141:8 ¹Lit. *Do not make my soul bare*

PSALM 142

A PLEA FOR RELIEF FROM PERSECUTORS

A ªContemplation¹ of David. A Prayer
ᵇwhen he was in the cave.

1 I CRY out to the LORD with my voice;
   With my voice to the LORD I make my supplication.
2 I pour out my complaint before Him;
   I declare before Him my trouble.

3 When my spirit ¹was ªoverwhelmed within me,
   Then You knew my path.
   In the way in which I walk
   They have secretly ᵇset a snare for me.
4 Look on *my* right hand and see,
   For *there is* no one who acknowledges me;
   Refuge has failed me;
   No one cares for my soul.

5 I cried out to You, O LORD:
   I said, "You *are* my refuge,
   My portion in the land of the living.
6 ¹Attend to my cry,
   For I am brought very low;
   Deliver me from my persecutors,
   For they are stronger than I.
7 Bring my soul out of prison,
   That I may ªpraise Your name;
   The righteous shall surround me,
   For You shall deal bountifully with me."

PSALM 143

AN EARNEST APPEAL FOR GUIDANCE AND DELIVERANCE

A Psalm of David.

1 HEAR my prayer, O LORD,
   Give ear to my supplications!
   In Your faithfulness answer me,
   And in Your righteousness.
2 Do not enter into judgment with Your servant,
   ªFor in Your sight no one living is righteous.

3 For the enemy has persecuted my soul;
   He has crushed my life to the ground;
   He has made me dwell in ¹darkness,
   Like those who have long been dead.
4 ªTherefore my spirit is overwhelmed within me;
   My heart within me is distressed.

5 ªI remember the days of old;
   I meditate on all Your works;
   I ¹muse on the work of Your hands.
6 I spread out my hands to You;
   ªMy soul *longs* for You like a thirsty land.   *Selah*

7 Answer me speedily, O LORD;
   My spirit fails!

142:title
ªPs. 32:title
ᵇ1 Sam. 22:1;
Ps. 57:title
142:3 ªPs. 77:3
ᵇPs. 141:9
142:7 ªPs. 34:1, 2
143:2
ª[Ex. 34:7];
Job 4:17; 9:2;
25:4; Ps. 130:3;
Eccl. 7:20;
[Rom. 3:20–23];
Gal. 2:16]
143:4 ªPs. 77:3
143:5
ªPs. 77:5, 10, 11
143:6 ªPs. 63:1

142:title ¹Heb. *Maschil*   142:3 ¹Lit. *fainted*   142:6 ¹*Give heed*   143:3 ¹*dark places*   143:5 ¹*ponder*

Do not hide Your face from me,
^aLest I ¹be like those who ²go down into the pit.
8   Cause me to hear Your lovingkindness ^ain the morning,
For in You do I trust;
^bCause me to know the way in which I should walk,
For ^cI lift up my soul to You.

9   Deliver me, O LORD, from my enemies;
¹In You I take shelter.
10 ^aTeach me to do Your will,
For You *are* my God;
^bYour Spirit *is* good.
Lead me in ^cthe land of uprightness.

11 ^aRevive me, O LORD, for Your name's sake!
For Your righteousness' sake bring my soul out of
trouble.
12 In Your mercy ^acut¹ off my enemies,
And destroy all those who afflict my soul;
For I *am* Your servant.

PSALM 144

A SONG TO THE LORD WHO PRESERVES
AND PROSPERS HIS PEOPLE

A Psalm of David.

1   BLESSED *be* the LORD my Rock,
^aWho trains my hands for war,
And my fingers for battle—
2   My lovingkindness and my fortress,
My high tower and my deliverer,
My shield and *the One* in whom I take refuge,
Who subdues ¹my people under me.

3   ^aLORD, what *is* man, that You take knowledge of him?
Or the son of man, that You are mindful of him?
4   ^aMan is like a breath;
^bHis days *are* like a passing shadow.

5   ^aBow down Your heavens, O LORD, and come down;
^bTouch the mountains, and they shall smoke.
6   ^aFlash forth lightning and scatter them;
Shoot out Your arrows and destroy them.
7   Stretch out Your hand from above;
Rescue me and deliver me out of great waters,
From the hand of foreigners,
8   Whose mouth ^aspeaks ¹lying words,
And whose right hand *is* a right hand of falsehood.

9   I will ^asing a new song to You, O God;
On a harp of ten strings I will sing praises to You,
10 *The One* who gives ¹salvation to kings,
^aWho delivers David His servant
From the deadly sword.

11 Rescue me and deliver me from the hand of foreigners,
Whose mouth speaks lying words,

143:7 ^aPs. 28:1
143:8 ^aPs. 46:5
^bPs. 5:8 ^cPs. 25:1

143:10
^aPs. 25:4, 5
^bNeh. 9:20
^cIs. 26:10

143:11 ^aPs. 119:25

143:12 ^aPs. 54:5

144:1
^a2 Sam. 22:35;
Ps. 18:34

144:3 ^aJob 7:17;
Ps. 8:4; Heb. 2:6

144:4 ^aPs. 39:11
^bJob 8:9; 14:2;
Ps. 102:11

144:5 ^aPs. 18:9;
Is. 64:1
^bPs. 104:32

144:6
^aPs. 18:13, 14

144:8 ^aPs. 12:2

144:9
^aPs. 33:2, 3;
40:3

144:10 ^aPs. 18:50

143:7 ¹become   ²Die   143:9 ¹LXX, Vg. *To You I flee*   143:12 ¹*put an end to*
144:2 ¹So with MT, LXX, Vg.; Syr., Tg. *the peoples* (cf. 18:47)   144:8 ¹*empty* or
worthless   144:10 ¹*deliverance*

And whose right hand *is* a right hand of falsehood—
12 That our sons *may be* [a]as plants grown up in their
youth;
That our daughters *may be* as [1]pillars,
Sculptured in palace style;
13 *That* our barns *may be* full,
Supplying all kinds of produce;
That our sheep may bring forth thousands
And ten thousands in our fields;
14 *That* our oxen *may be* well laden;
That there be no [1]breaking in or going out;
That there be no outcry in our streets.
15 [a]Happy *are* the people who are in such a state;
Happy *are* the people whose God *is* the LORD!

PSALM 145

A SONG OF GOD'S MAJESTY AND LOVE

[a]A Praise of David.

1 I WILL [1]extol You, my God, O King;
And I will bless Your name forever and ever.
2 Every day I will bless You,
And I will praise Your name forever and ever.
3 [a]Great *is* the LORD, and greatly to be praised;
And [b]His greatness *is* [1]unsearchable.

4 [a]One generation shall praise Your works to another,
And shall declare Your mighty acts.
5 [1]I will meditate on the glorious splendor of Your majesty,
And [2]on Your wondrous works.
6 *Men* shall speak of the might of Your awesome acts,
And I will declare Your greatness.
7 They shall [1]utter the memory of Your great goodness,
And shall sing of Your righteousness.

8 [a]The LORD *is* gracious and full of compassion,
Slow to anger and great in mercy.
9 [a]The LORD *is* good to all,
And His tender mercies *are* over all His works.

10 [a]All Your works shall praise You, O LORD,
And Your saints shall bless You.
11 They shall speak of the glory of Your kingdom,
And talk of Your power,
12 To make known to the sons of men His mighty acts,
And the glorious majesty of His kingdom.
13 [a]Your kingdom *is* an everlasting kingdom,
And Your dominion *endures* throughout all
[1]generations.

14 The LORD upholds all who fall,
And [a]raises up all *who are* bowed down.
15 [a]The eyes of all look expectantly to You,
And [b]You give them their food in due season.

144:12 [a]Ps. 128:3

144:15
[a]Deut. 33:29;
[Ps. 33:12;
Jer. 17:7]

145:title
[a]Ps. 100:title

145:3
[a][Ps. 147:5]
[b]Job 5:9; 9:10;
11:7; Is. 40:28;
[Rom. 11:33]

145:4 [a]Is. 38:19

145:8
[a][Ex. 34:6, 7;
Num. 14:18];
Ps. 86:5, 15

145:9
[a][Ps. 100:5];
Jer. 33:11;
Nah. 1:7;
[Matt. 19:17;
Mark 10:18]

145:10 [a]Ps. 19:1

145:13
[a]Dan. 2:44; 4:3;
[1 Tim. 1:17;
2 Pet. 1:11]

145:14 [a]Ps. 146:8

145:15
[a]Ps. 104:27
[b]Ps. 136:25

144:12 [1]*corner pillars* 144:14 [1]Lit. *breach* 145:1 [1]*praise* 145:3 [1]Beyond
our understanding 145:5 [1]So with MT, Tg.; DSS, LXX, Syr., Vg. *They* [2]Lit.
on the words of Your wondrous works 145:7 [1]*eagerly utter*, lit. *bubble forth*
145:13 [1]So with MT, Tg.; DSS, LXX, Syr., Vg. add *The LORD is faithful in all His
words, And holy in all His works*

16 You open Your hand
aAnd satisfy the desire of every living thing.

17 The LORD *is* righteous in all His ways,
Gracious in all His works.

18 aThe LORD *is* near to all who call upon Him,
To all who call upon Him bin truth.

19 He will fulfill the desire of those who fear Him;
He also will hear their cry and save them.

20 aThe LORD preserves all who love Him,
But all the wicked He will destroy.

21 My mouth shall speak the praise of the LORD,
And all flesh shall bless His holy name
Forever and ever.

PSALM 146

THE HAPPINESS OF THOSE WHOSE HELP IS THE LORD

1 PRAISE[1] the LORD!

aPraise the LORD, O my soul!

2 aWhile I live I will praise the LORD;
I will sing praises to my God while I have my being.

3 aDo not put your trust in princes,
Nor in [1]a son of man, in whom *there is* no [2]help.

4 aHis spirit departs, he returns to his earth;
In that very day bhis plans perish.

5 aHappy *is he* who *has* the God of Jacob for his help,
Whose hope *is* in the LORD his God,

6 aWho made heaven and earth,
The sea, and all that *is* in them;
Who keeps truth forever,

7 aWho executes justice for the oppressed,
bWho gives food to the hungry.
cThe LORD gives freedom to the prisoners.

8 aThe LORD opens *the eyes of* the blind;
bThe LORD raises those who are bowed down;
The LORD loves the righteous.

9 aThe LORD watches over the strangers;
He relieves the fatherless and widow;
bBut the way of the wicked He [1]turns upside down.

10 aThe LORD shall reign forever—
Your God, O Zion, to all generations.

Praise the LORD!

PSALM 147

PRAISE TO GOD FOR HIS WORD AND PROVIDENCE

1 PRAISE[1] the LORD!
For ait is good to sing praises to our God;
bFor it is pleasant, *and* cpraise is beautiful.

2 The LORD abuilds up Jerusalem;
bHe gathers together the outcasts of Israel.

145:16 aPs. 104:21, 28
145:18 a[Deut. 4:7] b[John 4:24]
145:20 a[Ps. 31:23]
146:1 aPs. 103:1
146:2 aPs. 104:33
146:3 a[Is. 2:22]
146:4 a[Eccl. 12:7] b[Ps. 33:10; 1 Cor. 2:6]
146:5 aJer. 17:7
146:6 aGen. 1:1; Ex. 20:11; Acts 4:24; Rev. 14:7
146:7 aPs. 103:6 bPs. 107:9 cPs. 107:10; Is. 61:1
146:8 aMatt. 9:30; [John 9:7, 32, 33] bLuke 13:13
146:9 aDeut. 10:18; Ps. 68:5 bPs. 147:6
146:10 aEx. 15:18; Ps. 10:16; [Rev. 11:15]
147:1 aPs. 92:1 bPs. 135:3 cPs. 33:1
147:2 aPs. 102:16 bDeut. 30:3; Is. 11:12; 56:8; Ezek. 39:28

146:1 [1]Heb. *Hallelujah*   146:3 [1]A human being   [2]*salvation*   146:9 [1]Lit. *makes crooked*   147:1 [1]Heb. *Hallelujah*

3 ^aHe heals the brokenhearted
And binds up their ¹wounds.
4 ^aHe counts the number of the stars;
He calls them all by name.
5 ^aGreat *is* our Lord, and ^bmighty in power;
^cHis understanding *is* infinite.
6 ^aThe LORD lifts up the humble;
He casts the wicked down to the ground.

7 Sing to the LORD with thanksgiving;
Sing praises on the harp to our God,
8 ^aWho covers the heavens with clouds,
Who prepares rain for the earth,
Who makes grass to grow on the mountains.
9 ^aHe gives to the beast its food,
And ^bto the young ravens that cry.
10 ^aHe does not delight in the strength of the horse;
He takes no pleasure in the legs of a man.
11 The LORD takes pleasure in those who fear Him,
In those who hope in His mercy.

12 Praise the LORD, O Jerusalem!
Praise your God, O Zion!
13 For He has strengthened the bars of your gates;
He has blessed your children within you.
14 ^aHe makes peace *in* your borders,
And ^bfills you with ¹the finest wheat.

15 ^aHe sends out His command *to the* earth;
His word runs very swiftly.
16 ^aHe gives snow like wool;
He scatters the frost like ashes;
17 He casts out His hail like ¹morsels;
Who can stand before His cold?
18 ^aHe sends out His word and melts them;
He causes His wind to blow, *and* the waters flow.

19 ^aHe declares His word to Jacob,
^bHis statutes and His judgments to Israel.
20 ^aHe has not dealt thus with any nation;
And *as for His* judgments, they have not known them.

¹Praise the LORD!

PSALM 148

PRAISE TO THE LORD FROM CREATION

1 PRAISE¹ the LORD!

Praise the LORD from the heavens;
Praise Him in the heights!
2 Praise Him, all His angels;
Praise Him, all His hosts!
3 Praise Him, sun and moon;
Praise Him, all you stars of light!
4 Praise Him, ^ayou heavens of heavens,
And ^byou waters above the heavens!

147:3
^a[Ps. 51:17];
Is. 61:1;
Luke 4:18

147:4 ^aIs. 40:26

147:5 ^aPs. 48:1
^bNah. 1:3
^cIs. 40:28

147:6
^aPs. 146:8, 9

147:8
^aJob 38:26;
Ps. 104:13

147:9 ^aJob 38:41
^b[Matt. 6:26]

147:10
^aPs. 33:16, 17

147:14 ^aIs. 54:13;
60:17, 18
^bPs. 132:15

147:15
^a[Ps. 107:20]

147:16 ^aJob 37:6

147:18
^aJob 37:10

147:19
^aDeut. 33:4;
Ps. 103:7
^bMal. 4:4

147:20
^aDeut. 4:32–34;
[Rom. 3:1, 2]

148:4
^aDeut. 10:14;
1 Kin. 8:27;
[Neh. 9:6]
^bGen. 1:7

147:3 ¹Lit. *sorrows*   147:14 ¹Lit. *fat of wheat*   147:17 ¹*fragments* of food
147:20 ¹Heb. *Hallelujah*   148:1 ¹Heb. *Hallelujah*

5 Let them praise the name of the LORD,
   For ªHe commanded and they were created.
6 ªHe also established them forever and ever;
   He made a decree which shall not pass away.

7 Praise the LORD from the earth,
   ªYou great sea creatures and all the depths;
8 Fire and hail, snow and clouds;
   Stormy wind, fulfilling His word;
9 ªMountains and all hills;
   Fruitful trees and all cedars;
10 Beasts and all cattle;
   Creeping things and flying fowl;
11 Kings of the earth and all peoples;
   Princes and all judges of the earth;
12 Both young men and maidens;
   Old men and children.

13 Let them praise the name of the LORD,
   For His ªname alone is exalted;
   His glory *is* above the earth and heaven.
14 And He ªhas exalted the ¹horn of His people,
   The praise of ᵇall His saints—
   Of the children of Israel,
   ᶜA people near to Him.

   ²Praise the LORD!

PSALM 149

PRAISE TO GOD FOR HIS SALVATION AND JUDGMENT

1 PRAISE¹ the LORD!

   ªSing to the LORD a new song,
   And His praise in the assembly of saints.

2 Let Israel rejoice in their Maker;
   Let the children of Zion be joyful in their ªKing.
3 ªLet them praise His name with the dance;
   Let them sing praises to Him with the timbrel and
      harp.
4 For ªthe LORD takes pleasure in His people;
   ᵇHe will beautify the ¹humble with salvation.

5 Let the saints be joyful in glory;
   Let them ªsing aloud on their beds.
6 *Let* the high praises of God *be* in their mouth,
   And ªa two-edged sword in their hand,
7 To execute vengeance on the nations,
   And punishments on the peoples;
8 To bind their kings with chains,
   And their nobles with fetters of iron;
9 ªTo execute on them the written judgment—
   ᵇThis honor have all His saints!

   ¹Praise the LORD!

148:5
ªGen. 1:1, 6
148:6
ªPs. 89:37;
[Jer. 31:35, 36;
33:20, 25]
148:7 ªIs. 43:20
148:9
ªIs. 44:23; 49:13
148:13 ªPs. 8:1
148:14
ª1 Sam. 2:1;
Ps. 75:10
ᵇPs. 149:9
ᶜLev. 10:3;
Eph. 2:17
149:1 ªPs. 33:3
149:2
ªJudg. 8:23;
Zech. 9:9;
Matt. 21:5
149:3 ªEx. 15:20;
Ps. 81:2
149:4 ªPs. 35:27
ᵇPs. 132:16;
Is. 61:3
149:5 ªJob 35:10
149:6
ªHeb. 4:12;
Rev. 1:16
149:9
ªDeut. 7:1, 2;
Ezek. 28:26
ᵇPs. 148:14;
1 Cor. 6:2

148:14 ¹Strength or dominion   ²Heb. *Hallelujah*   149:1 ¹Heb. *Hallelujah*
149:4 ¹*meek*   149:9 ¹Heb. *Hallelujah*

PSALM 150

LET ALL THINGS PRAISE THE LORD

1 PRAISE[a1] the LORD!

Praise God in His sanctuary;
Praise Him in His mighty [2]firmament!

2 Praise Him for His mighty acts;
Praise Him according to His excellent [a]greatness!

3 Praise Him with the sound of the [1]trumpet;
Praise Him with the lute and harp!
4 Praise Him with the timbrel and dance;
Praise Him with stringed instruments and flutes!
5 Praise Him with loud cymbals;
Praise Him with clashing cymbals!

6 Let everything that has breath praise the LORD.

[1]Praise the LORD!

150:1
[a]Ps. 145:5, 6
150:2
[a]Deut. 3:24

150:1 [1]Heb. *Hallelujah*   [2]*expanse* of heaven   150:3 [1]*cornet*   150:6 [1]Heb. *Hallelujah*

THE BOOK OF
PROVERBS

THE BEGINNING OF KNOWLEDGE

1 The ᵃproverbs of Solomon the son of David, king of Israel:

2   To know wisdom and instruction,
    To ¹perceive the words of understanding,
3   To receive the instruction of wisdom,
    Justice, judgment, and equity;
4   To give prudence to the ᵃsimple,
    To the young man knowledge and discretion—
5   ᵃA wise *man* will hear and increase learning,
    And a man of understanding will ¹attain wise counsel,
6   To understand a proverb and an enigma,
    The words of the wise and their ᵃriddles.

7   ᵃThe fear of the Lᴏʀᴅ *is* the beginning of knowledge,
    But fools despise wisdom and instruction.

SHUN EVIL COUNSEL

8   ᵃMy son, hear the instruction of your father,
    And do not forsake the law of your mother;
9   For they *will be* a ᵃgraceful ornament on your head,
    And chains about your neck.

10 My son, if sinners entice you,
    ᵃDo not consent.
11 If they say, "Come with us,
    Let us ᵃlie in wait to *shed* blood;
    Let us lurk secretly for the innocent without cause;
12 Let us swallow them alive like ¹Sheol,
    And whole, ᵃlike those who go down to the Pit;
13 We shall find all *kinds* of precious ¹possessions,
    We shall fill our houses with ²spoil;
14 Cast in your lot among us,
    Let us all have one purse"—
15 My son, ᵃdo not walk in the way with them,
    ᵇKeep your foot from their path;
16 ᵃFor their feet run to evil,
    And they make haste to shed blood.
17 Surely, in ¹vain the net is spread
    In the sight of any ²bird;
18 But they lie in wait for their *own* blood,
    They lurk secretly for their *own* lives.
19 ᵃSo *are* the ways of everyone who is greedy for gain;
    It takes away the life of its owners.

THE CALL OF WISDOM

20 ᵃWisdom calls aloud ¹outside;
    She raises her voice in the open squares.

1:1 ᵃ1 Kin. 4:32;
Prov. 10:1; 25:1;
Eccl. 12:9

1:4 ᵃProv. 9:4

1:5 ᵃProv. 9:9

1:6 ᵃNum. 12:8;
Ps. 78:2;
Dan. 8:23

1:7 ᵃJob 28:28;
Ps. 111:10;
Prov. 9:10; 15:33;
[Eccl. 12:13]

1:8 ᵃProv. 4:1

1:9 ᵃProv. 3:22

1:10
ᵃGen. 39:7–10;
Deut. 13:8;
Ps. 50:18;
[Eph. 5:11]

1:11 ᵃProv. 12:6;
Jer. 5:26

1:12 ᵃPs. 28:1

1:15 ᵃPs. 1:1;
Prov. 4:14
ᵇPs. 119:101

1:16
ᵃProv. 6:17, 18;
[Is. 59:7];
Rom. 3:15

1:19 ᵃProv. 15:27;
[1 Tim. 6:10]

1:20 ᵃProv. 8:1;
9:3; [John 7:37]

1:2 ¹*understand* or *discern*   1:5 ¹*acquire*   1:12 ¹*Or the grave*   1:13 ¹Lit.
wealth ²*plunder*   1:17 ¹*futility* ²Lit. *lord of the wing*   1:20 ¹*in the street*

21 She cries out in the ¹chief concourses,
   At the openings of the gates in the city
   She speaks her words:
22 "How long, you ¹simple ones, will you love ²simplicity?
   For scorners delight in their scorning,
   And fools hate knowledge.
23 Turn at my rebuke;
   Surely [a]I will pour out my spirit on you;
   I will make my words known to you.
24 [a]Because I have called and you refused,
   I have stretched out my hand and no one regarded,
25 Because you [a]disdained all my counsel,
   And would have none of my rebuke,
26 [a]I also will laugh at your calamity;
   I will mock when your terror comes,
27 When [a]your terror comes like a storm,
   And your destruction comes like a whirlwind,
   When distress and anguish come upon you.

28 "Then[a] they will call on me, but I will not answer;
   They will seek me diligently, but they will not find me.
29 Because they [a]hated knowledge
   And did not [b]choose the fear of the LORD,
30 [a]They would have none of my counsel
   And despised my every rebuke.
31 Therefore [a]they shall eat the fruit of their own way,
   And be filled to the full with their own fancies.
32 For the ¹turning away of the simple will slay them,
   And the complacency of fools will destroy them;
33 But whoever listens to me will dwell [a]safely,
   And [b]will be ¹secure, without fear of evil."

THE VALUE OF WISDOM

2 My son, if you receive my words,
   And [a]treasure my commands within you,
2 So that you incline your ear to wisdom,
   And apply your heart to understanding;
3 Yes, if you cry out for discernment,
   And lift up your voice for understanding,
4 [a]If you seek her as silver,
   And search for her as *for* hidden treasures;
5 [a]Then you will understand the fear of the LORD,
   And find the knowledge of God.
6 [a]For the LORD gives wisdom;
   From His mouth *come* knowledge and understanding;
7 He stores up sound wisdom for the upright;
   [a]*He is* a shield to those who walk uprightly;
8 He guards the paths of justice,
   And [a]preserves the way of His saints.
9 Then you will understand righteousness and justice,
   Equity *and* every good path.

10 When wisdom enters your heart,
   And knowledge is pleasant to your soul,
11 Discretion will preserve you;
   [a]Understanding will keep you,

1:23 [a]Is. 32:15;
Joel 2:28;
[John 7:39]

1:24 [a]Is. 65:12;
66:4; Jer. 7:13;
Zech. 7:11

1:25 [a]Ps. 107:11;
Luke 7:30

1:26 [a]Ps. 2:4

1:27
[a][Prov. 10:24,
25]

1:28
[a]1 Sam. 8:18;
Job 27:9; 35:12;
Ps. 18:41; Is. 1:15;
Jer. 11:11; 14:12;
Ezek. 8:18;
Mic. 3:4;
Zech. 7:13;
[James 4:3]

1:29 [a]Job 21:14;
Prov. 1:22
[b]Ps. 119:173

1:30 [a]Ps. 81:11;
Prov. 1:25

1:31 [a]Job 4:8;
Prov. 5:22, 23;
22:8; Is. 3:11;
Jer. 6:19

1:33
[a]Prov. 3:24–26
[b]Ps. 112:7

2:1 [a][Prov. 4:21]

2:4 [a][Prov. 3:14]

2:5
[a][James 1:5, 6]

2:6
[a]1 Kin. 3:9, 12;
[Job 32:8];
James 1:5

2:7 [a][Ps. 84:11];
Prov. 30:5

2:8
[a][1 Sam. 2:9];
Ps. 66:9

2:11
[a]Prov. 4:6; 6:22

1:21 ¹LXX, Syr., Tg. *top of the walls;* Vg. *the head of multitudes*   1:22 ¹*naive*
²*naivete*   1:32 ¹*waywardness*   1:33 ¹*at ease*

12 To deliver you from the way of evil,
From the man who speaks perverse things,
13 From those who leave the paths of uprightness
To [a]walk in the ways of darkness;
14 [a]Who rejoice in doing evil,
And delight in the perversity of the wicked;
15 [a]Whose ways *are* crooked,
And *who are* devious in their paths;
16 To deliver you from [a]the immoral woman,
[b]From the seductress *who* flatters with her words,
17 Who forsakes the companion of her youth,
And forgets the covenant of her God.
18 For [a]her house [1]leads down to death,
And her paths to the dead;
19 None who go to her return,
Nor do they [1]regain the paths of life—
20 So you may walk in the way of goodness,
And keep *to* the paths of righteousness.
21 For the upright will dwell in the [a]land,
And the blameless will remain in it;
22 But the wicked will be [1]cut off from the [2]earth,
And the unfaithful will be uprooted from it.

GUIDANCE FOR THE YOUNG

3 My son, do not forget my law,
[a]But let your heart keep my commands;
2 For length of days and long life
And [a]peace they will add to you.

3 Let not mercy and truth forsake you;
[a]Bind them around your neck,
[b]Write them on the tablet of your heart,
4 [a]*And* so find favor and [1]high esteem
In the sight of God and man.

5 [a]Trust in the LORD with all your heart,
[b]And lean not on your own understanding;
6 [a]In all your ways acknowledge Him,
And He shall [1]direct your paths.

7 Do not be wise in your own [a]eyes;
Fear the LORD and depart from evil.
8 It will be health to your [1]flesh,
And [a]strength[2] to your bones.

9 [a]Honor the LORD with your possessions,
And with the firstfruits of all your increase;
10 [a]So your barns will be filled with plenty,
And your vats will overflow with new wine.

11 [a]My son, do not despise the chastening of the LORD,
Nor detest His correction;
12 For whom the LORD loves He corrects,
[a]Just as a father the son *in whom* he delights.

13 [a]Happy *is* the man *who* finds wisdom,
And the man *who* gains understanding;

2:13 [a]Ps. 82:5;
Prov. 4:19;
[John 3:19, 20]

2:14
[a]Prov. 10:23;
Jer. 11:15;
[Rom. 1:32]

2:15 [a]Ps. 125:5;
[Prov. 21:8]

2:16 [a]Prov. 5:20;
6:24; 7:5
[b]Prov. 5:3

2:18 [a]Prov. 7:27

2:21 [a]Ps. 37:3

3:1 [a]Deut. 8:1

3:2 [a]Ps. 119:165;
Prov. 4:10

3:3 [a]Ex. 13:9;
Deut. 6:8;
Prov. 6:21
[b]Prov. 7:3;
Jer. 17:1;
[2 Cor. 3:3]

3:4
[a]1 Sam. 2:26;
Luke 2:52;
Rom. 14:18

3:5
[a][Ps. 37:3, 5];
Prov. 22:19
[b]Prov. 23:4;
[Jer. 9:23, 24]

3:6
[a][1 Chr. 28:9];
Prov. 16:3;
[Phil. 4:6;
James 1:5]

3:7 [a]Rom. 12:16

3:8 [a]Job 21:24

3:9 [a]Ex. 22:29;
Deut. 26:2;
[Mal. 3:10]

3:10 [a]Deut. 28:8

3:11 [a]Job 5:17;
Ps. 94:12;
Heb. 12:5, 6;
Rev. 3:19

3:12 [a]Deut. 8:5;
Prov. 13:24

3:13 [a]Prov. 8:32,
34, 35

2:18 [1]sinks   2:19 [1]Lit. *reach*   2:22 [1]*destroyed*   [2]*land*   3:4 [1]Lit. *good understanding*   3:6 [1]Or *make smooth* or *straight*   3:8 [1]Body, lit. *navel* [2]Lit. *drink*

14 ^aFor her proceeds *are* better than the profits of silver,
  And her gain than fine gold.
15 She *is* more precious than rubies,
  And ^aall the things you may desire cannot compare with
    her.
16 ^aLength of days *is* in her right hand,
  In her left hand riches and honor.
17 ^aHer ways *are* ways of pleasantness,
  And all her paths *are* peace.
18 She *is* ^aa tree of life to those who take hold of her,
  And happy *are all* who ¹retain her.

19 ^aThe LORD by wisdom founded the earth;
  By understanding He established the heavens;
20 By His knowledge the depths were ^abroken up,
  And clouds drop down the dew.

21 My son, let them not depart from your eyes—
  Keep sound wisdom and discretion;
22 So they will be life to your soul
  And grace to your neck.
23 ^aThen you will walk safely in your way,
  And your foot will not stumble.
24 When you lie down, you will not be afraid;
  Yes, you will lie down and your sleep will be sweet.
25 ^aDo not be afraid of sudden terror,
  Nor of trouble from the wicked when it comes;
26 For the LORD will be your confidence,
  And will keep your foot from being caught.

27 ^aDo not withhold good from ¹those to whom it is due,
  When it is in the power of your hand to do *so.*
28 ^aDo not say to your neighbor,
  "Go, and come back,
  And tomorrow I will give *it,*"
  When you have it with you.
29 Do not devise evil against your neighbor,
  For he dwells by you for safety's sake.
30 ^aDo not strive with a man without cause,
  If he has done you no harm.

31 ^aDo not envy the oppressor,
  And choose none of his ways;
32 For the perverse *person is* an abomination to the
    LORD,
  ^aBut His secret counsel *is* with the upright.
33 ^aThe curse of the LORD *is* on the house of the wicked,
  But ^bHe blesses the home of the just.
34 ^aSurely He scorns the scornful,
  But gives grace to the humble.
35 The wise shall inherit glory,
  But shame shall be the legacy of fools.

SECURITY IN WISDOM

4 Hear, ^a*my* children, the instruction of a father,
  And give attention to know understanding;
2 For I give you good doctrine:
  Do not forsake my law.

3:14 ^aJob 28:13
3:15 ^aMatt. 13:44
3:16 ^aProv. 8:18;
  [1 Tim. 4:8]
3:17
  ^a[Matt. 11:29]
3:18 ^aGen. 2:9;
Prov. 11:30; 13:12;
  15:4; Rev. 2:7
3:19 ^aPs. 104:24;
  Prov. 8:27
3:20 ^aGen. 7:11
3:23 ^a[Ps. 37:24;
  91:11, 12];
  Prov. 10:9
3:25 ^aPs. 91:5;
  1 Pet. 3:14
3:27 ^aRom. 13:7;
  [Gal. 6:10]
3:28 ^aLev. 19:13;
  Deut. 24:15
3:30
^aProv. 26:17;
  [Rom. 12:18]
3:31 ^aPs. 37:1;
  Prov. 24:1
3:32 ^aPs. 25:14
3:33
^aLev. 26:14, 16;
  Deut. 11:28;
  Zech. 5:3, 4;
  Mal. 2:2
^bJob 8:6; Ps. 1:3
3:34
^aJames 4:6;
  1 Pet. 5:5
4:1 ^aPs. 34:11;
  Prov. 1:8

3:18 ¹*hold her fast*   3:27 ¹Lit. *its owners*

3 When I was my father's son,
  ^aTender and the only one in the sight of my mother,
4 ^aHe also taught me, and said to me:
  "Let your heart retain my words;
  ^bKeep my commands, and live.
5 ^aGet wisdom! Get understanding!
  Do not forget, nor turn away from the words of my
    mouth.
6 Do not forsake her, and she will preserve you;
  ^aLove her, and she will keep you.
7 ^aWisdom *is* the principal thing;
  Therefore get wisdom.
  And in all your getting, get understanding.
8 ^aExalt her, and she will promote you;
  She will bring you honor, when you embrace her.
9 She will place on your head ^aan ornament of grace;
  A crown of glory she will deliver to you."

10 Hear, my son, and receive my sayings,
   ^aAnd the years of your life will be many.
11 I have ^ataught you in the way of wisdom;
   I have led you in right paths.
12 When you walk, ^ayour steps will not be hindered,
   ^bAnd when you run, you will not stumble.
13 Take firm hold of instruction, do not let go;
   Keep her, for she *is* your life.

14 ^aDo not enter the path of the wicked,
   And do not walk in the way of evil.
15 Avoid it, do not travel on it;
   Turn away from it and pass on.
16 ^aFor they do not sleep unless they have done evil;
   And their sleep is ¹taken away unless they make *someone*
     fall.
17 For they eat the bread of wickedness,
   And drink the wine of violence.

18 ^aBut the path of the just ^b*is* like the shining ¹sun,
   That shines ever brighter unto the perfect day.
19 ^aThe way of the wicked *is* like darkness;
   They do not know what makes them stumble.

20 My son, give attention to my words;
   Incline your ear to my sayings.
21 Do not let them depart from your eyes;
   Keep them in the midst of your heart;
22 For they *are* life to those who find them,
   And health to all their flesh.
23 Keep your heart with all diligence,
   For out of it *spring* the issues of ^alife.
24 Put away from you a ¹deceitful mouth,
   And put perverse lips far from you.
25 Let your eyes look straight ahead,
   And your eyelids look right before you.
26 Ponder the path of your ^afeet,
   And let all your ways be established.
27 Do not turn to the right or the left;
   Remove your foot from evil.

4:3 ^a1 Chr. 29:1
4:4 ^a1 Chr. 28:9;
Eph. 6:4
^bProv. 7:2
4:5 ^aProv. 2:2, 3
4:6
^a2 Thess. 2:10
4:7 ^aProv. 3:13,
14; Matt. 13:44
4:8 ^a1 Sam. 2:30
4:9 ^aProv. 3:22
4:10 ^aProv. 3:2
4:11
^a1 Sam. 12:23
4:12 ^aJob 18:7;
Ps. 18:36
^b[Ps. 91:11];
Prov. 3:23
4:14 ^aPs. 1:1;
Prov. 1:15
4:16 ^aPs. 36:4;
Mic. 2:1
4:18 ^aIs. 26:7;
Matt. 5:14, 45;
Phil. 2:15
^b2 Sam. 23:4
4:19 ^a1 Sam. 2:9;
[Job 18:5, 6];
Prov. 2:13;
[Is. 59:9, 10;
Jer. 23:12];
John 12:35
4:23
^a[Matt. 12:34;
15:18, 19;
Mark 7:21;
Luke 6:45]
4:26 ^aProv. 5:21;
Heb. 12:13

4:16 ¹Lit. *robbed*   4:18 ¹Lit. *light*   4:24 ¹*devious*

THE PERIL OF ADULTERY

5 My son, pay attention to my wisdom;
¹Lend your ear to my understanding,

2 That you may ¹preserve discretion,
And your lips ᵃmay keep knowledge.

3 ᵃFor the lips of ¹an immoral woman drip honey,
And her mouth *is* ᵇsmoother than oil;

4 But in the end she is bitter as wormwood,
Sharp as a two-edged sword.

5 Her feet go down to death,
ᵃHer steps lay hold of ¹hell.

6 Lest you ponder *her* path of life—
Her ways are unstable;
You do not know *them*.

7 Therefore hear me now, *my* children,
And do not depart from the words of my mouth.

8 Remove your way far from her,
And do not go near the door of her house,

9 Lest you give your ¹honor to others,
And your years to the cruel *one*;

10 Lest aliens be filled with your ¹wealth,
And your labors *go* to the house of a foreigner;

11 And you mourn at last,
When your flesh and your body are consumed,

12 And say:
"How I have hated instruction,
And my heart despised correction!

13 I have not obeyed the voice of my teachers,
Nor inclined my ear to those who instructed me!

14 I was on the verge of total ruin,
In the midst of the assembly and congregation."

15 Drink water from your own cistern,
And running water from your own well.

16 Should your fountains be dispersed abroad,
¹Streams of water in the streets?

17 Let them be only your own,
And not for strangers with you.

18 Let your fountain be blessed,
And rejoice with ᵃthe wife of your youth.

19 ᵃAs *a* loving deer and a graceful doe,
Let her breasts satisfy you at all times;
And always be ¹enraptured with her love.

20 For why should you, my son, be enraptured by ᵃan
immoral woman,
And be embraced in the arms of a seductress?

21 ᵃFor the ways of man *are* before the eyes of the
LORD,
And He ¹ponders all his paths.

22 ᵃHis own iniquities entrap the wicked *man*,
And he is caught in the cords of his sin.

23 ᵃHe shall die for lack of instruction,
And in the greatness of his folly he shall go astray.

5:2 ᵃMal. 2:7
5:3 ᵃProv. 2:16
ᵇPs. 55:21
5:5 ᵃProv. 7:27
5:18
ᵃDeut. 24:5;
Eccl. 9:9;
Mal. 2:14
5:19 ᵃSong 2:9
5:20 ᵃProv. 2:16
5:21 ᵃ2 Chr. 16:9;
Job 31:4; 34:21;
Prov. 15:3;
Jer. 16:17;
32:19; Hos. 7:2;
Heb. 4:13
5:22
ᵃNum. 32:23;
Ps. 9:5;
Prov. 1:31; Is. 3:11
5:23 ᵃJob 4:21

5:1 ¹Lit. *Bow*   5:2 ¹*appreciate good judgment*   5:3 ¹Lit. *a strange*   5:5 ¹Or *Sheol*   5:9 ¹*vigor*   5:10 ¹Lit. *strength*   5:16 ¹*Channels*   5:19 ¹Lit. *intoxicated*   5:21 ¹*observes*, lit. *weighs*

DANGEROUS PROMISES

6 My son, [a]if you become [1]surety for your friend,
If you have [2]shaken hands in pledge for a stranger,

2 You are snared by the words of your mouth;
You are taken by the words of your mouth.

3 So do this, my son, and deliver yourself;
For you have come into the hand of your friend:
Go and humble yourself;
Plead with your friend.

4 [a]Give no sleep to your eyes,
Nor slumber to your eyelids.

5 Deliver yourself like a gazelle from the hand *of the hunter,*
And like a bird from the hand of the [1]fowler.

THE FOLLY OF INDOLENCE

6 [a]Go to the ant, you sluggard!
Consider her ways and be wise,

7 Which, having no [1]captain,
Overseer or ruler,

8 Provides her [1]supplies in the summer,
And gathers her food in the harvest.

9 [a]How long will you [1]slumber, O sluggard?
When will you rise from your sleep?

10 A little sleep, a little slumber,
A little folding of the hands to sleep—

11 [a]So shall your poverty come on you like a prowler,
And your need like an armed man.

THE WICKED MAN

12 A worthless person, a wicked man,
Walks with a perverse mouth;

13 [a]He winks with his eyes,
He [1]shuffles his feet,
He points with his fingers;

14 Perversity *is* in his heart,
[a]He devises evil continually,
[b]He sows discord.

15 Therefore his calamity shall come [a]suddenly;
Suddenly he shall [b]be broken [c]without remedy.

16 These six *things* the LORD hates,
Yes, seven *are* an abomination to [1]Him:

17 [a][1]A proud look,
[b]A lying tongue,
[c]Hands that shed innocent blood,

18 [a]A heart that devises wicked plans,
[b]Feet that are swift in running to evil,

19 [a]A false witness *who* speaks lies,
And one who [b]sows discord among brethren.

BEWARE OF ADULTERY

20 [a]My son, keep your father's command,
And do not forsake the law of your mother.

21 [a]Bind them continually upon your heart;
Tie them around your neck.

6:1 [a]Prov. 11:15
6:4 [a]Ps. 132:4
6:6 [a]Job 12:7
6:9
[a]Prov. 24:33, 34
6:11 [a]Prov. 10:4
6:13 [a]Job 15:12;
Ps. 35:19;
Prov. 10:10
6:14 [a]Prov. 3:29;
Mic. 2:1
[b]Prov. 6:19
6:15
[a]Prov. 24:22;
Is. 30:13;
1 Thess. 5:3
[b]Jer. 19:11
[c]2 Chr. 36:16
6:17 [a]Ps. 101:5;
Prov. 21:4
[b]Ps. 120:2;
Prov. 12:22
[c]Deut. 19:10;
Prov. 28:17;
Is. 1:15
6:18 [a]Gen. 6:5;
Ps. 36:4;
Prov. 24:2;
Jer. 18:18;
Mark 14:1, 43–46
[b]2 Kin. 5:20–27;
Is. 59:7;
Rom. 3:15
6:19 [a]Ps. 27:12;
Prov. 19:5, 9;
Matt. 26:59–66
[b]Prov. 6:14;
1 Cor. 1:11–13;
[Jude 3, 4,
16–19]
6:20 [a]Eph. 6:1
6:21 [a]Prov. 3:3

6:1 [1]*guaranty* or *collateral* [2]Lit. *struck*   6:5 [1]One who catches birds in a trap or snare   6:7 [1]Lit. *leader*   6:8 [1]Lit. *bread*   6:9 [1]Lit. *lie down*
6:13 [1]*gives signals*, lit. *scrapes*   6:16 [1]Lit. *His soul*   6:17 [1]Lit. *Haughty eyes*

22 [a]When you roam, [1]they will lead you;
  When you sleep, [b]they will keep you;
  And *when* you awake, they will speak with you.
23 [a]For the commandment *is* a lamp,
  And the law a light;
  Reproofs of instruction *are* the way of life,
24 [a]To keep you from the evil woman,
  From the flattering tongue of a seductress.
25 [a]Do not lust after her beauty in your heart,
  Nor let her allure you with her eyelids.
26 For [a]by means of a harlot
  A man is reduced to a crust of bread;
  [b]And [1]an adulteress will [c]prey upon his precious life.
27 Can a man take fire to his bosom,
  And his clothes not be burned?
28 Can one walk on hot coals,
  And his feet not be seared?
29 So *is* he who goes in to his neighbor's wife;
  Whoever touches her shall not be innocent.

30 *People* do not despise a thief
  If he steals to satisfy himself when he is starving.
31 Yet *when* he is found, [a]he must restore sevenfold;
  He may have to give up all the substance of his
    house.
32 Whoever commits adultery with a woman [a]lacks
    understanding;
  He *who* does so destroys his own soul.
33 Wounds and dishonor he will get,
  And his reproach will not be wiped away.
34 For [a]jealousy *is* a husband's fury;
  Therefore he will not spare in the day of vengeance.
35 He will [1]accept no recompense,
  Nor will he be appeased though you give many gifts.

7 My son, keep my words,
  And [a]treasure my commands within you.
2 [a]Keep my commands and live,
  [b]And my law as the apple of your eye.
3 [a]Bind them on your fingers;
  Write them on the tablet of your heart.
4 Say to wisdom, "You *are* my sister,"
  And call understanding *your* nearest kin,
5 [a]That they may keep you from the immoral woman,
  From the seductress *who* flatters with her words.

THE CRAFTY HARLOT

6 For at the window of my house
  I looked through my lattice,
7 And saw among the simple,
  I perceived among the [1]youths,
  A young man [a]devoid[2] of understanding,
8 Passing along the street near her corner;
  And he took the path to her house
9 [a]In the twilight, in the evening,
  In the black and dark night.

6:22
[a][Prov. 3:23]
[b]Prov. 2:11

6:23 [a]Ps. 19:8;
2 Pet. 1:19

6:24 [a]Prov. 2:16

6:25 [a]Matt. 5:28

6:26 [a]Prov. 29:3
[b]Gen. 39:14
[c]Ezek. 13:18

6:31 [a]Ex. 22:1–4

6:32 [a]Prov. 7:7

6:34 [a]Prov. 27:4;
Song 8:6

7:1 [a]Prov. 2:1

7:2 [a]Lev. 18:5;
Prov. 4:4;
[Is. 55:3]
[b]Deut. 32:10;
Ps. 17:8;
Zech. 2:8

7:3 [a]Deut. 6:8;
Prov. 6:21

7:5
[a]Prov. 2:16; 5:3

7:7 [a][Prov. 6:32;
9:4, 16]

7:9 [a]Job 24:15

6:22 [1]Lit. *it*   6:26 [1]Wife of another, lit. *a man's wife*   6:35 [1]Lit. *lift up the face of any*   7:7 [1]Lit. *sons*   [2]*lacking*

10 And there a woman met him,
   With the attire of a harlot, and a crafty heart.
11 ᵃShe *was* loud and rebellious,
   ᵇHer feet would not stay at home.
12 At times *she was* outside, at times in the open
      square,
   Lurking at every corner.
13 So she caught him and kissed him;
   With an ¹impudent face she said to him:
14 "*I have* peace offerings with me;
   Today I have paid my vows.
15 So I came out to meet you,
   Diligently to seek your face,
   And I have found you.
16 I have spread my bed with tapestry,
   Colored coverings of ᵃEgyptian linen.
17 I have perfumed my bed
   With myrrh, aloes, and cinnamon.
18 Come, let us take our fill of love until morning;
   Let us delight ourselves with love.
19 For ¹my husband *is* not at home;
   He has gone on a long journey;
20 He has taken a bag of money ¹with him,
   And will come home ²on the appointed day."

21 ¹With ᵃher enticing speech she caused him to yield,
   ᵇWith her flattering lips she ²seduced him.
22 Immediately he went after her, as an ox goes to the
      slaughter,
   Or ¹as a fool to the correction of the ²stocks,
23 Till an arrow struck his liver.
   ᵃAs a bird hastens to the snare,
   He did not know it ¹would *cost* his life.

24 Now therefore, listen to me, *my* children;
   Pay attention to the words of my mouth:
25 Do not let your heart turn aside to her ways,
   Do not stray into her paths;
26 For she has cast down many wounded,
   And ᵃall who were slain by her were strong *men*.
27 ᵃHer house *is* the way to ¹hell,
   Descending to the chambers of death.

THE EXCELLENCE OF WISDOM

8 Does not ᵃwisdom cry out,
   And understanding lift up her voice?
2 She takes her stand on the top of the ¹high hill,
   Beside the way, where the paths meet.
3 She cries out by the gates, at the entry of the city,
   At the entrance of the doors:
4 "To you, O men, I call,
   And my voice *is* to the sons of men.
5 O you ¹simple ones, understand prudence,
   And you fools, be of an understanding heart.

7:11 ᵃProv. 9:13;
1 Tim. 5:13
ᵇTitus 2:5

7:16 ᵃIs. 19:9;
Ezek. 27:7

7:21 ᵃProv. 5:3
ᵇPs. 12:2

7:23 ᵃEccl. 9:12

7:26 ᵃNeh. 13:26

7:27 ᵃProv. 2:18;
5:5; 9:18;
[1 Cor. 6:9, 10;
Rev. 22:15]

8:1 ᵃProv. 1:20,
21; 9:3;
[1 Cor. 1:24]

7:13 ¹shameless   7:19 ¹Lit. the man   7:20 ¹Lit. in his hand   ²at the full
moon   7:21 ¹By the greatness of her words   ²compelled   7:22 ¹LXX, Syr.,
Tg. *as a dog to bonds*; Vg. *as a lamb . . . to bonds*   ²shackles   7:23 ¹Lit. is for
7:27 ¹Or Sheol   8:2 ¹Lit. heights   8:5 ¹naive

6 Listen, for I will speak of ᵃexcellent things,
   And from the opening of my lips *will come* right things;
7 For my mouth will speak truth;
   Wickedness *is* an abomination to my lips.
8 All the words of my mouth *are* with righteousness;
   Nothing crooked or perverse *is* in them.
9 They *are* all plain to him who understands,
   And right to those who find knowledge.
10 Receive my instruction, and not silver,
   And knowledge rather than choice gold;
11 ᵃFor wisdom *is* better than rubies,
   And all the things one may desire cannot be compared
      with her.

12 "I, wisdom, dwell with prudence,
   And find out knowledge *and* discretion.
13 ᵃThe fear of the LORD *is* to hate evil;
   ᵇPride and arrogance and the evil way
   And ᶜthe perverse mouth I hate.
14 Counsel *is* mine, and sound wisdom;
   I *am* understanding, ᵃI have strength.
15 ᵃBy me kings reign,
   And rulers decree justice.
16 By me princes rule, and nobles,
   All the judges of ¹the earth.
17 ᵃI love those who love me,
   And ᵇthose who seek me diligently will find me.
18 ᵃRiches and honor *are* with me,
   Enduring riches and righteousness.
19 My fruit *is* better than gold, yes, than fine gold,
   And my revenue than choice silver.
20 I ¹traverse the way of righteousness,
   In the midst of the paths of justice,
21 That I may cause those who love me to inherit wealth,
   That I may fill their treasuries.

22 "Theᵃ LORD possessed me at the beginning of His way,
   Before His works of old.
23 ᵃI have been established from everlasting,
   From the beginning, before there was ever an earth.
24 When *there were* no depths I was brought forth,
   When *there were* no fountains abounding with water.
25 ᵃBefore the mountains were settled,
   Before the hills, I was brought forth;
26 While as yet He had not made the earth or the ¹fields,
   Or the ²primal dust of the world.
27 When He prepared the heavens, I *was* there,
   When He drew a circle on the face of the deep,
28 When He established the clouds above,
   When He strengthened the fountains of the deep,
29 ᵃWhen He assigned to the sea its limit,
   So that the waters would not transgress His command,
   When ᵇHe marked out the foundations of the earth,
30 ᵃThen I was beside Him *as* ¹a master craftsman;
   ᵇAnd I was daily *His* delight,
   Rejoicing always before Him,

8:6 ᵃProv. 22:20

8:11 ᵃJob 28:15;
Ps. 19:10; 119:127;
Prov. 3:14, 15;
4:5, 7; 16:16

8:13
ᵃProv. 3:7; 16:6
ᵇ1 Sam. 2:3;
[Prov. 16:17,
18; Is. 13:11];
ᶜProv. 4:24

8:14
ᵃEccl. 7:19; 9:16

8:15 ᵃ2 Chr. 1:10;
Prov. 29:4;
Dan. 2:21;
[Matt. 28:18];
Rom. 13:1

8:17
ᵃ1 Sam. 2:30;
[Ps. 91:14];
Prov. 4:6;
[John 14:21]
ᵇProv. 2:4, 5;
John 7:37;
James 1:5

8:18 ᵃProv. 3:16;
[Matt. 6:33]

8:22
ᵃJob 28:26–28;
Ps. 104:24;
Prov. 3:19;
[John 1:1]

8:23 ᵃ[Ps. 2:6]

8:25 ᵃJob 15:7, 8

8:29
ᵃGen. 1:9, 10;
Job 38:8–11;
Ps. 33:7; 104:9;
Jer. 5:22
ᵇJob 28:4, 6;
Ps. 104:5

8:30
ᵃ[John 1:1–3, 18]
ᵇ[Matt. 3:17]

8:16 ¹MT, Syr., Tg., Vg. *righteousness;* LXX, Bg., some mss. and editions *earth*
8:20 ¹*walk about on*   8:26 ¹*outer places*   ²Lit. *beginning of the dust*
8:30 ¹A Jewish tradition *one brought up*

31   Rejoicing in His inhabited world,
And [a]my delight *was* with the sons of men.

32   "Now therefore, listen to me, *my* children,
For [a]blessed *are those who* keep my ways.
33   Hear instruction and be wise,
And do not disdain *it.*
34   [a]Blessed is the man who listens to me,
Watching daily at my gates,
Waiting at the posts of my doors.
35   For whoever finds me finds life,
And [a]obtains favor from the LORD;
36   But he who sins against me [a]wrongs his own soul;
All those who hate me love death."

THE WAY OF WISDOM

9 Wisdom has [a]built her house,
   She has hewn out her seven pillars;
2   [a]She has slaughtered her meat,
   [b]She has mixed her wine,
   She has also [1]furnished her table.
3   She has sent out her maidens,
   She cries out from the highest places of the city,
4   "Whoever[a] *is* simple, let him turn in here!"
   As for him who lacks understanding, she says to him,
5   "Come,[a] eat of my bread
   And drink of the wine I have mixed.
6   Forsake foolishness and live,
   And go in the way of understanding.

7   "He who corrects a scoffer gets shame for himself,
   And he who rebukes a wicked *man only* harms himself.
8   [a]Do not correct a scoffer, lest he hate you;
   [b]Rebuke a wise *man,* and he will love you.
9   Give *instruction* to a wise *man,* and he will be still wiser;
   Teach a just *man,* [a]and he will increase in learning.

10   "The[a] fear of the LORD *is* the beginning of wisdom,
   And the knowledge of the Holy One *is* understanding.
11   [a]For by me your days will be multiplied,
   And years of life will be added to you.
12   [a]If you are wise, you are wise for yourself,
   And *if* you scoff, you will bear *it* alone."

THE WAY OF FOLLY

13   [a]A foolish woman is [1]clamorous;
   She is simple, and knows nothing.
14   For she sits at the door of her house,
   On a seat [a]*by* the highest places of the city,
15   To call to those who pass by,
   Who go straight on their way:
16   "Whoever[a] *is* [1]simple, let him turn in here";
   And *as for* him who lacks understanding, she says to him,
17   "Stolen[a] water is sweet,
   And bread *eaten* in secret is pleasant."
18   But he does not know that [a]the dead *are* there,
   That her guests *are* in the depths of [1]hell.

8:31 [a]Ps. 16:3;
John 13:1

8:32
[a]Ps. 119:1, 2;
128:1;
Prov. 29:18;
Luke 11:28

8:34
[a]Prov. 3:13, 18

8:35 [a]Prov. 3:4;
12:2; [John 17:3]

8:36 [a]Prov. 20:2

9:1 [a][Matt. 16:18;
1 Cor. 3:9, 10;
Eph. 2:20–22;
1 Pet. 2:5]

9:2 [a]Matt. 22:4
[b]Prov. 23:30

9:4 [a]Ps. 19:7

9:5 [a]Song 5:1;
Is. 55:1;
[John 6:27]

9:8 [a]Prov. 15:12;
Matt. 7:6
[b]Ps. 141:5;
Prov. 10:8

9:9
[a][Matt. 13:12]

9:10 [a]Job 28:28;
Ps. 111:10;
Prov. 1:7

9:11
[a]Prov. 3:2, 16

9:12
[a]Job 35:6, 7;
Prov. 16:26

9:13 [a]Prov. 7:11

9:14 [a]Prov. 9:3

9:16 [a]Prov. 7:7, 8

9:17 [a]Prov. 20:17

9:18
[a]Prov. 2:18; 7:27

9:2 [1]arranged   9:13 [1]boisterous   9:16 [1]naive   9:18 [1]Or *Sheol*

WISE SAYINGS OF SOLOMON

10
The proverbs of [a]Solomon:

[b]A wise son makes a glad father,
But a foolish son *is* the grief of his mother.

2 [a]Treasures of wickedness profit nothing,
[b]But righteousness delivers from death.

3 [a]The LORD will not allow the righteous soul to famish,
But He casts away the desire of the wicked.

4 [a]He who has a slack hand becomes poor,
But [b]the hand of the diligent makes rich.

5 He who gathers in [a]summer *is* a wise son;
He who sleeps in harvest *is* [b]a son who causes shame.

6 Blessings *are* on the head of the righteous,
But violence covers the mouth of the wicked.

7 [a]The memory of the righteous *is* blessed,
But the name of the wicked will rot.

8 The wise in heart will receive commands,
[a]But [1]a prating fool will [2]fall.

9 [a]He who walks with integrity walks securely,
But he who perverts his ways will become known.

10 He who winks with the eye causes trouble,
But a prating fool will fall.

11 The mouth of the righteous *is* a well of life,
But violence covers the mouth of the wicked.

12 Hatred stirs up strife,
But [a]love covers all sins.

13 Wisdom is found on the lips of him who has understanding,
But [a]a rod *is* for the back of him who [1]is devoid of understanding.

14 Wise *people* store up knowledge,
But [a]the mouth of the foolish *is* near destruction.

15 The [a]rich man's wealth *is* his strong city;
The destruction of the poor *is* their poverty.

16 The labor of the righteous *leads* to [a]life,
The wages of the wicked to sin.

17 He who keeps instruction *is in* the way of life,
But he who refuses correction [1]goes astray.

18 Whoever [a]hides hatred *has* lying lips,
And [b]whoever spreads slander *is* a fool.

19 [a]In the multitude of words sin is not lacking,
But [b]he who restrains his lips *is* wise.

20 The tongue of the righteous *is* choice silver;
The heart of the wicked *is worth* little.

21 The lips of the righteous feed many,
But fools die for lack of [1]wisdom.

10:1
[a]Prov. 1:1; 25:1
[b]Prov. 15:20;
17:21, 25; 19:13;
29:3, 15

10:2 [a]Ps. 49:7;
Prov. 11:4; 21:6;
Ezek. 7:19;
[Luke 12:19, 20]
[b]Dan. 4:27

10:3 [a]Ps. 34:9,
10; 37:25;
Prov. 28:25;
[Matt. 6:33]

10:4 [a]Prov. 19:15
[b]Prov. 12:24;
13:4; 21:5

10:5 [a]Prov. 6:8
[b]Prov. 19:26

10:7 [a]Ps. 112:6;
Eccl. 8:10

10:8 [a]Prov. 10:10

10:9 [a][Ps. 23:4;
Prov. 3:23; 28:18;
Is. 33:15, 16]

10:12 [a]Prov. 17:9;
[1 Cor. 13:4–7;
James 5:20];
1 Pet. 4:8

10:13 [a]Prov. 26:3

10:14 [a]Prov. 18:7

10:15 [a]Job 31:24;
Ps. 52:7;
Prov. 18:11;
[1 Tim. 6:17]

10:16 [a]Prov. 6:23

10:18
[a]Prov. 26:24
[b]Ps. 15:3; 101:5

10:19 [a]Job 11:2;
[Prov. 18:21];
Eccl. 5:3
[b]Prov. 17:27;
[James 1:19; 3:2]

10:8 [1]Lit. *the foolish of lips*   [2]*be thrust down* or *ruined*   10:13 [1]Lit. *lacks heart*   10:17 [1]*leads*   10:21 [1]Lit. *heart*

22 aThe blessing of the LORD makes *one* rich,
And He adds no sorrow with it.

23 aTo do evil *is* like sport to a fool,
But a man of understanding has wisdom.

24 aThe fear of the wicked will come upon him,
And bthe desire of the righteous will be granted.

25 When the whirlwind passes by, athe wicked *is* no *more,*
But bthe righteous *has* an everlasting foundation.

26 As vinegar to the teeth and smoke to the eyes,
So *is* the lazy *man* to those who send him.

27 aThe fear of the LORD prolongs days,
But bthe years of the wicked will be shortened.

28 The hope of the righteous *will be* gladness,
But the aexpectation of the wicked will perish.

29 The way of the LORD *is* strength for the upright,
But adestruction *will come* to the workers of iniquity.

30 aThe righteous will never be removed,
But the wicked will not inhabit the 1earth.

31 aThe mouth of the righteous brings forth wisdom,
But the perverse tongue will be cut out.

32 The lips of the righteous know what is acceptable,
But the mouth of the wicked *what is* perverse.

11 aDishonest1 scales *are* an abomination to the LORD,
But a 2just weight *is* His delight.

2 When pride comes, then comes ashame;
But with the humble *is* wisdom.

3 The integrity of the upright will guide athem,
But the perversity of the unfaithful will destroy them.

4 aRiches do not profit in the day of wrath,
But brighteousness delivers from death.

5 The righteousness of the blameless will 1direct his way aright,
But the wicked will fall by his own awickedness.

6 The righteousness of the upright will deliver them,
But the unfaithful will be caught by *their* lust.

7 When a wicked man dies, *his* expectation will aperish,
And the hope of the unjust perishes.

8 aThe righteous is delivered from trouble,
And it comes to the wicked instead.

9 The hypocrite with *his* mouth destroys his neighbor,
But through knowledge the righteous will be delivered.

10 aWhen it goes well with the righteous, the city rejoices;
And when the wicked perish, *there is* jubilation.

11 By the blessing of the upright the city is aexalted,
But it is overthrown by the mouth of the wicked.

12 He who 1is devoid of wisdom despises his neighbor,
But a man of understanding holds his peace.

13 aA talebearer reveals secrets,
But he who is of a faithful spirit bconceals a matter.

10:22
aGen. 24:35;
26:12;
Deut. 8:18;
Ps. 37:22;
Prov. 8:21

10:23
aProv. 2:14; 15:21

10:24 aJob 15:21;
Prov. 1:27;
Is. 66:4
bPs. 145:19;
Prov. 15:8;
Matt. 5:6;
[1 John 5:14, 15]

10:25
aPs. 37:9, 10
bPs. 15:5;
Prov. 12:3;
Matt. 7:24, 25

10:27 aProv. 9:11
b Job 15:32

10:28 a Job 8:13

10:29 aPs. 1:6

10:30
aPs. 37:22;
Prov. 2:21

10:31 aPs. 37:30;
Prov. 10:13

11:1
aLev. 19:35, 36;
Deut. 25:13–16;
Prov. 20:10, 23;
Mic. 6:11

11:2 aProv. 16:18;
18:12; 29:23

11:3 aProv. 13:6

11:4 aProv. 10:2;
Ezek. 7:19;
Zeph. 1:18
bGen. 7:1

11:5 aProv. 5:22

11:7 aProv. 10:28

11:8 aProv. 21:18

11:10
aProv. 28:12

11:11 aProv. 14:34

11:13 aLev. 19:16;
Prov. 20:19;
1 Tim. 5:13
bProv. 19:11

10:30 1*land*   11:1 1*deceptive*   2Lit. *perfect stone*   11:5 1Or *make smooth* or *straight*   11:12 1Lit. *lacks heart*

14 ᵃWhere *there is* no counsel, the people fall;
But in the multitude of counselors *there is* safety.

15 He who is ᵃsurety¹ for a stranger will suffer,
But one who hates ²being surety is secure.

16 A gracious woman retains honor,
But ruthless *men* retain riches.

17 ᵃThe merciful man does good for his own soul,
But *he who is* cruel troubles his own flesh.

18 The wicked *man* does deceptive work,
But ᵃhe who sows righteousness *will have* a sure reward.

19 As righteousness *leads* to ᵃlife,
So he who pursues evil *pursues it* to his own ᵇdeath.

20 Those who are of a perverse heart *are* an abomination to
the LORD,
But *the* blameless in their ways *are* His delight.

21 ᵃ*Though they join* ¹forces, the wicked will not go
unpunished;
But ᵇthe posterity of the righteous will be delivered.

22 *As* a ring of gold in a swine's snout,
So is a lovely woman who lacks ¹discretion.

23 The desire of the righteous *is* only good,
But the expectation of the wicked ᵃ*is* wrath.

24 There is *one* who ᵃscatters, yet increases more;
And there is *one* who withholds more than is right,
But it *leads* to poverty.

25 ᵃThe generous soul will be made rich,
ᵇAnd he who waters will also be watered himself.

26 The people will curse ᵃhim who withholds grain,
But ᵇblessing *will be* on the head of him who sells *it.*

27 He who earnestly seeks good ¹finds favor,
ᵃBut trouble will come to him who seeks *evil.*

28 ᵃHe who trusts in his riches will fall,
But ᵇthe righteous will flourish like foliage.

29 He who troubles his own house ᵃwill inherit the wind,
And the fool *will be* ᵇservant to the wise of heart.

30 The fruit of the righteous *is a* tree of life,
And ᵃhe who ¹wins souls *is* wise.

31 ᵃIf the righteous will be ¹recompensed on the earth,
How much more the ungodly and the sinner.

12 Whoever loves instruction loves knowledge,
But he who hates correction *is* stupid.

2 A good *man* obtains favor from the LORD,
But a man of wicked intentions He will condemn.

3 A man is not established by wickedness,
But the ᵃroot of the righteous cannot be moved.

4 ᵃAn¹ excellent wife *is* the crown of her husband,
But she who causes shame *is* ᵇlike rottenness in his
bones.

11:14 ᵃ1 Kin. 12:1
11:15 ᵃProv. 6:1, 2
11:17 ᵃ[Matt. 5:7; 25:34–36]
11:18 ᵃHos. 10:12; [Gal. 6:8, 9]; James 3:18
11:19 ᵃProv. 10:16; 12:28 ᵇProv. 21:16; [Rom. 6:23; James 1:15]
11:21 ᵃProv. 16:5 ᵇPs. 112:2; Prov. 14:26
11:23 ᵃProv. 10:28; Rom. 2:8, 9
11:24 ᵃPs. 112:9; Prov. 13:7; 19:17
11:25 ᵃProv. 3:9, 10; [2 Cor. 9:6, 7] ᵇ[Matt. 5:7]
11:26 ᵃAmos 8:5, 6 ᵇJob 29:13
11:27 ᵃEsth. 7:10; Ps. 7:15, 16; 57:6
11:28 ᵃJob 31:24 ᵇPs. 1:3; Jer. 17:8
11:29 ᵃEccl. 5:16 ᵇProv. 14:19
11:30 ᵃProv. 14:25; [Dan. 12:3]; 1 Cor. 9:19–22; James 5:20
11:31 ᵃJer. 25:29
12:3 ᵃ[Prov. 10:25]
12:4 ᵃProv. 31:23; 1 Cor. 11:7 ᵇProv. 14:30; Hab. 3:16

11:15 ¹*guaranty* ²*those pledging guaranty,* lit. *those who strike hands*
11:21 ¹Lit. *hand to hand* 11:22 ¹*taste* 11:27 ¹Lit. *seeks* 11:30 ¹Lit. *takes,*
in the sense of *brings,* cf. 1 Sam. 16:11 11:31 ¹*rewarded* 12:4 ¹Lit. *A wife*
of valor

5 The thoughts of the righteous *are* right,
But the counsels of the wicked *are* deceitful.
6 ªThe words of the wicked *are*, "Lie in wait for blood,"
ᵇBut the mouth of the upright will deliver them.

7 ªThe wicked are overthrown and *are* no more,
But the house of the righteous will stand.

8 A man will be commended according to his wisdom,
ªBut he who is of a perverse heart will be despised.

9 ªBetter *is the one* who is ¹slighted but has a servant,
Than he who honors himself but lacks bread.

10 ªA righteous *man* regards the life of his animal,
But the tender mercies of the wicked *are* cruel.

11 ªHe who ¹tills his land will be satisfied with ᵇbread,
But he who follows ²frivolity ᶜ*is* devoid of
³understanding.

12 The wicked covet the catch of evil *men*,
But the root of the righteous yields *fruit*.
13 ªThe wicked is ensnared by the transgression of *his* lips,
ᵇBut the righteous will come through trouble.
14 ªA man will be satisfied with good by the fruit of *his*
mouth,
ᵇAnd the recompense of a man's hands will be rendered
to him.
15 ªThe way of a fool *is* right in his own eyes,
But he who heeds counsel *is* wise.
16 ªA fool's wrath is known at once,
But a prudent *man* covers shame.

17 ªHe *who* speaks truth declares righteousness,
But a false witness, deceit.
18 ªThere is one who speaks like the piercings of a
sword,
But the tongue of the wise *promotes* health.
19 The truthful lip shall be established forever,
ªBut a lying tongue *is* but for a moment.
20 Deceit is in the heart of those who devise evil,
But counselors of peace have joy.
21 ªNo grave ¹trouble will overtake the righteous,
But the wicked shall be filled with evil.
22 ªLying lips *are* an abomination to the LORD,
But those who deal truthfully *are* His delight.

23 ªA prudent man conceals knowledge,
But the heart of fools proclaims foolishness.

24 ªThe hand of the diligent will rule,
But the lazy *man* will be put to forced labor.

25 ªAnxiety in the heart of man causes depression,
But ᵇa good word makes it glad.

26 The righteous should choose his friends carefully,
For the way of the wicked leads them astray.

27 The lazy *man* does not roast what he took in hunting,
But diligence *is* man's precious possession.

12:6
ªProv. 1:11, 18
ᵇProv. 14:3

12:7
ªPs. 37:35–37;
Prov. 11:21;
Matt. 7:24–27

12:8
ª1 Sam. 25:17;
Prov. 18:3

12:9 ªProv. 13:7

12:10
ªDeut. 25:4

12:11 ªGen. 3:19
ᵇProv. 28:19
ᶜProv. 6:32

12:13 ªProv. 18:7
ᵇ[2 Pet. 2:9]

12:14 ªProv. 13:2;
15:23; 18:20
ᵇJob 34:11;
Prov. 1:31; 24:12;
[Is. 3:10, 11];
Hos. 4:9

12:15 ªProv. 3:7;
Luke 18:11

12:16
ªProv. 11:13;
29:11

12:17 ªProv. 14:5

12:18 ªPs. 57:4;
Prov. 4:22; 15:4

12:19
ª[Ps. 52:4, 5];
Prov. 19:9

12:21 ªPs. 91:10;
Prov. 1:33;
1 Pet. 3:13

12:22
ªProv. 6:17;
11:20; Rev. 22:15

12:23
ªProv. 13:16

12:24 ªProv. 10:4

12:25
ªProv. 15:13
ᵇIs. 50:4

12:9 ¹lightly esteemed   12:11 ¹works or *cultivates*   ²Lit. *vain things*   ³Lit.
heart   12:21 ¹harm

28 In the way of righteousness *is* life,
And in *its* pathway *there is* no death.

13
A wise son *heeds* his father's instruction,
ªBut a scoffer does not listen to rebuke.

2 ªA man shall eat well by the fruit of *his* mouth,
But the soul of the unfaithful feeds on violence.

3 ªHe who guards his mouth preserves his life,
But he who opens wide his lips shall have destruction.

4 ªThe soul of a lazy *man* desires, and *has* nothing;
But the soul of the diligent shall be made rich.

5 A righteous *man* hates lying,
But a wicked *man* is loathsome and comes to shame.

6 ªRighteousness guards *him whose* way is blameless,
But wickedness overthrows the sinner.

7 ªThere is one who makes himself rich, yet *has* nothing;
And one who makes himself poor, yet *has* great riches.

8 The ransom of a man's life *is* his riches,
But the poor does not hear rebuke.

9 The light of the righteous rejoices,
ªBut the lamp of the wicked will be put out.

10 By pride comes nothing but ªstrife,
But with the well-advised *is* wisdom.

11 ªWealth *gained by* dishonesty will be diminished,
But he who gathers by labor will increase.

12 Hope deferred makes the heart sick,
But ª*when* the desire comes, *it is* a tree of life.

13 He who ªdespises the word will be destroyed,
But he who fears the commandment will be rewarded.

14 ªThe law of the wise *is* a fountain of life,
To turn *one* away from ᵇthe snares of death.

15 Good understanding ¹gains ªfavor,
But the way of the unfaithful *is* hard.

16 ªEvery prudent *man* acts with knowledge,
But a fool lays open *his* folly.

17 A wicked messenger falls into trouble,
But ªa faithful ambassador *brings* health.

18 Poverty and shame *will come* to him who ¹disdains
correction,
But ªhe who regards a rebuke will be honored.

19 A desire accomplished is sweet to the soul,
But *it is* an abomination to fools to depart from evil.

20 He who walks with wise *men* will be wise,
But the companion of fools will be destroyed.

21 ªEvil pursues sinners,
But to the righteous, good shall be repaid.

22 A good *man* leaves an inheritance to his children's
children,
But ªthe wealth of the sinner is stored up for the
righteous.

13:1 ªIs. 28:14, 15
13:2 ªProv. 12:14
13:3 ªPs. 39:1;
Prov. 21:23;
[James 3:2]
13:4 ªProv. 10:4
13:6
ªProv. 11:3, 5, 6
13:7
ª[Prov. 11:24;
12:9; Luke 12:20,
21]
13:9
ªJob 18:5, 6;
21:17; Prov. 24:20
13:10
ªProv. 10:12
13:11 ªProv. 10:2;
20:21
13:12 ªProv. 13:19
13:13
ªNum. 15:31;
2 Chr. 36:16;
Is. 5:24
13:14
ªProv. 6:22;
10:11; 14:27
ᵇ2 Sam. 22:6
13:15 ªPs. 111:10;
Prov. 3:4
13:16
ªProv. 12:23
13:17
ªProv. 25:13
13:18 ªProv. 15:5,
31, 32
13:21 ªPs. 32:10;
Is. 47:11
13:22
ªJob 27:16, 17;
Prov. 28:8;
[Eccl. 2:26]

13:15 ¹*gives*   **13:18** ¹Lit. *ignores*

23 aMuch food *is in* the 1fallow *ground* of the poor,
And for lack of justice there is 2waste.

24 aHe who spares his rod hates his son,
But he who loves him disciplines him 1promptly.

25 aThe righteous eats to the satisfying of his soul,
But the stomach of the wicked shall be in want.

14 The wise woman builds her house,
But the foolish pulls it down with her hands.

2 He who walks in his uprightness fears the LORD,
aBut *he who is* perverse in his ways despises Him.

3 In the mouth of a fool *is* a rod of pride,
aBut the lips of the wise will preserve them.

4 Where no oxen *are*, the 1trough *is* clean;
But much increase *comes* by the strength of an ox.

5 A afaithful witness does not lie,
But a false witness will utter blies.

6 A scoffer seeks wisdom and does not *find it*,
But aknowledge *is* easy to him who understands.

7 Go from the presence of a foolish man,
When you do not perceive *in him* the lips of aknowledge.

8 The wisdom of the prudent *is* to understand his way,
But the folly of fools *is* deceit.

9 aFools mock at 1sin,
But among the upright *there is* favor.

10 The heart knows its own bitterness,
And a stranger does not share its joy.

11 aThe house of the wicked will be overthrown,
But the tent of the upright will flourish.

12 aThere is a way *that seems* right to a man,
But bits end *is* the way of cdeath.

13 Even in laughter the heart may sorrow,
And athe end of mirth *may be* grief.

14 The backslider in heart will be afilled with his own ways,
But a good man *will be satisfied* 1from babove.

15 The simple believes every word,
But the prudent considers well his steps.

16 aA wise man fears and departs from evil,
But a fool rages and is self-confident.

17 A quick-tempered *man* acts foolishly,
And a man of wicked intentions is hated.

18 The simple inherit folly,
But the prudent are crowned with knowledge.

19 The evil will bow before the good,
And the wicked at the gates of the righteous.

20 aThe poor *man* is hated even by his own neighbor,
But 1the rich *has* many bfriends.

21 He who despises his neighbor sins;
aBut he who has mercy on the poor, happy *is* he.

13:23 aProv. 12:11

13:24
aProv. 19:18

13:25 aPs. 34:10;
Prov. 10:3

14:2 a[Rom. 2:4]

14:3 aProv. 12:6

14:5
aRev. 1:5; 3:14
bEx. 23:1;
Deut. 19:16;
Prov. 6:19; 12:17

14:6 aProv. 8:9;
17:24

14:7 aProv. 23:9

14:9 aProv. 10:23

14:11 aJob 8:15

14:12
aProv. 16:25
bRom. 6:21
cProv. 12:15

14:13 aProv. 5:4;
Eccl. 2:1, 2

14:14 aProv. 1:31;
12:15 bProv. 13:2;
18:20

14:16
aJob 28:28;
Ps. 34:14;
Prov. 22:3

14:20 aProv. 19:7
bProv. 19:4

14:21 aPs. 112:9;
[Prov. 19:17]

13:23 1uncultivated   2Lit. *what is swept away*   13:24 1early   14:4 1manger
or *feed trough*   14:9 1Lit. *guilt*   14:14 1Lit. *from above himself*   14:20 1Lit.
many are the lovers of the rich

22 Do they not go astray who devise evil?
    But mercy and truth *belong* to those who devise good.

23 In all labor there is profit,
    But [1]idle chatter *leads* only to poverty.

24 The crown of the wise is their riches,
    But the foolishness of fools *is* folly.

25 A true witness [1]delivers [a]souls,
    But a deceitful *witness* speaks lies.

26 In the fear of the LORD *there is* strong confidence,
    And His children will have a place of refuge.

27 [a]The fear of the LORD *is* a fountain of life,
    To turn *one* away from the snares of death.

28 In a multitude of people *is* a king's honor,
    But in the lack of people *is* the downfall of a prince.

29 [a]*He who is* slow to wrath has great understanding,
    But *he who is* [1]impulsive exalts folly.

30 A sound heart *is* life to the body,
    But [a]envy *is* [b]rottenness to the bones.

31 [a]He who oppresses the poor reproaches [b]his Maker,
    But he who honors Him has mercy on the needy.

32 The wicked is banished in his wickedness,
    But [a]the righteous has a refuge in his death.

33 Wisdom rests in the heart of him who has
        understanding,
    But [a]*what is* in the heart of fools is made known.

34 Righteousness exalts a [a]nation,
    But sin *is* a [1]reproach to *any* people.

35 [a]The king's favor *is* toward a wise servant,
    But his wrath *is against* him who causes shame.

15 A [a]soft answer turns away wrath,
       But [b]a harsh word stirs up anger.

2 The tongue of the wise uses knowledge rightly,
    [a]But the mouth of fools pours forth foolishness.

3 [a]The eyes of the LORD *are* in every place,
    Keeping watch on the evil and the good.

4 A [1]wholesome tongue *is* a tree of life,
    But perverseness in it breaks the spirit.

5 [a]A fool despises his father's instruction,
    [b]But he who [1]receives correction is prudent.

6 *In* the house of the righteous *there is* much treasure,
    But in the revenue of the wicked is trouble.

7 The lips of the wise [1]disperse knowledge,
    But the heart of the fool *does* not *do* so.

8 [a]The sacrifice of the wicked *is* an abomination to the
        LORD,
    But the prayer of the upright *is* His delight.

14:25
[a][Ezek. 3:18–21]

14:27
[a]Prov. 13:14

14:29
[a]Prov. 16:32;
19:11; Eccl. 7:9;
James 1:19

14:30 [a]Ps. 112:10
[b]Prov. 12:4;
Hab. 3:16

14:31 [a]Prov. 17:5;
Matt. 25:40;
1 John 3:17
[b][Job 31:15;
Prov. 22:2]

14:32
[a]Gen. 49:18;
Job 13:15;
[Ps. 16:11; 73:24];
2 Cor. 1:9; 5:8;
[2 Tim. 4:18]

14:33
[a]Prov. 12:16

14:34 [a]Prov. 11:11

14:35
[a]Matt. 24:45–47

15:1 [a]Prov. 25:15
[b]1 Sam. 25:10

15:2 [a]Prov. 12:23

15:3 [a]2 Chr. 16:9;
Job 34:21;
Prov. 5:21;
Jer. 16:17; 32:19;
Zech. 4:10;
Heb. 4:13

15:5 [a]Prov. 10:1
[b]Prov. 13:18

15:8
[a]Prov. 21:27;
Eccl. 5:1; Is. 1:11;
Jer. 6:20;
Mic. 6:7

14:23 [1]Lit. *talk of the lips*   14:25 [1]*saves lives*   14:29 [1]Lit. *short of spirit*
14:34 [1]*shame* or *disgrace*   15:4 [1]Lit. *healing*   15:5 [1]Lit. *keeps*   15:7 [1]*spread*

9 The way of the wicked *is* an abomination to the LORD,
   But He loves him who [a]follows righteousness.

10 [a]Harsh discipline *is* for him who forsakes the way,
   And [b]he who hates correction will die.

11 [a]Hell[1] and [2]Destruction *are* before the LORD;
   So how much more [b]the hearts of the sons of men.

12 [a]A scoffer does not love one who corrects him,
   Nor will he go to the wise.

13 [a]A merry heart makes a cheerful [1]countenance,
   But [b]by sorrow of the heart the spirit is broken.

14 The heart of him who has understanding seeks
      knowledge,
   But the mouth of fools feeds on foolishness.

15 All the days of the afflicted *are* evil,
   [a]But he who is of a merry heart *has* a continual feast.

16 [a]Better *is* a little with the fear of the LORD,
   Than great treasure with trouble.

17 [a]Better *is* a dinner of [1]herbs where love is,
   Than a fatted calf with hatred.

18 [a]A wrathful man stirs up strife,
   But *he who is* slow to anger allays contention.

19 [a]The way of the lazy *man is* like a hedge of thorns,
   But the way of the upright *is* a highway.

20 [a]A wise son makes a father glad,
   But a foolish man despises his mother.

21 [a]Folly *is* joy *to him who is* destitute of [1]discernment,
   [b]But a man of understanding walks uprightly.

22 [a]Without counsel, plans go awry,
   But in the multitude of counselors they are established.

23 A man has joy by the answer of his mouth,
   And [a]a word *spoken* [1]in due season, how good *it is!*

24 [a]The way of life *winds* upward for the wise,
   That he may [b]turn away from [1]hell below.

25 [a]The LORD will destroy the house of the proud,
   But [b]He will establish the boundary of the widow.

26 [a]The thoughts of the wicked *are* an abomination to the
      LORD,
   [b]But the words of the pure *are* pleasant.

27 [a]He who is greedy for gain troubles his own house,
   But he who hates bribes will live.

28 The heart of the righteous [a]studies how to answer,
   But the mouth of the wicked pours forth evil.

29 [a]The LORD *is* far from the wicked,
   But [b]He hears the prayer of the righteous.

30 The light of the eyes rejoices the heart,
   And a good report makes the bones [1]healthy.

15:9 [a]Prov. 21:21

15:10
[a]1 Kin. 22:8
[b]Prov. 5:12

15:11 [a]Job 26:6;
Ps. 139:8
[b]1 Sam. 16:7;
2 Chr. 6:30;
Ps. 44:21;
Acts 1:24

15:12 [a]Prov. 13:1;
Amos 5:10;
2 Tim. 4:3

15:13
[a]Prov. 12:25
[b]Prov. 17:22

15:15
[a]Prov. 17:22

15:16 [a]Ps. 37:16;
Prov. 16:8;
Eccl. 4:6;
1 Tim. 6:6

15:17 [a]Prov. 17:1

15:18
[a]Prov. 26:21

15:19 [a]Prov. 22:5

15:20 [a]Prov. 10:1

15:21
[a]Prov. 10:23
[b]Eph. 5:15

15:22 [a]Prov. 11:14

15:23
[a]Prov. 25:11;
Is. 50:4

15:24
[a]Phil. 3:20;
[Col. 3:1, 2]
[b]Prov. 14:16

15:25
[a]Prov. 12:7;
Is. 2:11
[b]Ps. 68:5, 6

15:26
[a]Prov. 6:16, 18
[b]Ps. 37:30

15:27 [a]Is. 5:8;
[Jer. 17:11]

15:28 [a]1 Pet. 3:15

15:29
[a]Ps. 10:1; 34:16
[b]Ps. 145:18;
[James 5:16]

15:11 [1]Or *Sheol* [2]Heb. *Abaddon* 15:13 [1]*face* 15:17 [1]Or *vegetables*
15:21 [1]Lit. *heart* 15:23 [1]Lit. *in its time* 15:24 [1]Or *Sheol* 15:30 [1]Lit. *fat*

31 The ear that hears the rebukes of life
   Will abide among the wise.
32 He who disdains instruction despises his own soul,
   But he who heeds rebuke gets understanding.
33 ªThe fear of the LORD *is* the instruction of wisdom,
   And ᵇbefore honor *is* humility.

16 The ªpreparations¹ of the heart *belong* to man,
   ᵇBut the answer of the tongue *is* from the LORD.

2 All the ways of a man *are* pure in his own ªeyes,
   But the LORD weighs the spirits.

3 ªCommit¹ your works to the LORD,
   And your thoughts will be established.

4 The ªLORD has made all for Himself,
   ᵇYes, even the wicked for the day of ¹doom.

5 ªEveryone proud in heart *is* an abomination to the
      LORD;
   Though they join ¹forces, none will go unpunished.

6 ªIn mercy and truth
   Atonement is provided for iniquity;
   And ᵇby the fear of the LORD *one* departs from evil.

7 When a man's ways please the LORD,
   He makes even his enemies to be at peace with him.

8 ªBetter *is* a little with righteousness,
   Than vast revenues without justice.

9 ªA man's heart plans his way,
   ᵇBut the LORD directs his steps.

10 Divination *is* on the lips of the king;
   His mouth must not transgress in judgment.

11 ªHonest weights and scales *are* the LORD's;
   All the weights in the bag *are* His ¹work.

12 *It is* an abomination for kings to commit wickedness,
   For ªa throne is established by righteousness.

13 ªRighteous lips *are* the delight of kings,
   And they love him who speaks *what is* right.

14 As messengers of death *is* the king's wrath,
   But a wise man will ªappease it.

15 In the light of the king's face *is* life,
   And his favor *is* like a ªcloud of the latter rain.

16 ªHow much better to get wisdom than gold!
   And to get understanding is to be chosen rather than
      silver.

17 The highway of the upright *is* to depart from evil;
   He who keeps his way preserves his soul.

18 Pride *goes* before destruction,
   And a haughty spirit before ¹a fall.

19 Better *to be* of a humble spirit with the lowly,
   Than to divide the ¹spoil with the proud.

20 He who heeds the word wisely will find good,
   And whoever ªtrusts in the LORD, happy *is* he.

15:33 ªProv. 1:7
   ᵇProv. 18:12
16:1 ªJer. 10:23
   ᵇMatt. 10:19
16:2 ªProv. 21:2
16:3 ªPs. 37:5;
   Prov. 3:6;
   [1 Pet. 5:7]
16:4 ªIs. 43:7;
   Rom. 11:36
   ᵇJob 21:30;
   [Rom. 9:22]
16:5
ªProv. 6:17; 8:13
16:6 ªDan. 4:27;
   Luke 11:41
   ᵇProv. 8:13;
   14:16
16:8 ªPs. 37:16;
   Prov. 15:16
16:9 ªProv. 19:21
   ᵇPs. 37:23;
   Prov. 20:24;
   Jer. 10:23
16:11 ªLev. 19:36
16:12 ªProv. 25:5
16:13
ªProv. 14:35
16:14
ªProv. 25:15
16:15 ªZech. 10:1
16:16
ªProv. 8:10,
   11, 19
16:20 ªPs. 34:8;
   Jer. 17:7

16:1 ¹*plans*   16:3 ¹Lit. *Roll*   16:4 ¹Lit. *evil*   16:5 ¹Lit. *hand to hand*
16:11 ¹*concern*   16:18 ¹*stumbling*   16:19 ¹*plunder*

21 The wise in heart will be called prudent,
And sweetness of the lips increases learning.

22 Understanding *is* a wellspring of life to him who has it.
But the correction of fools *is* folly.

23 The heart of the wise teaches his mouth,
And adds learning to his lips.

24 Pleasant words *are like* a honeycomb,
Sweetness to the soul and health to the bones.

25 There is a way *that seems* right to a man,
But its end *is* the way of ªdeath.

26 The person who labors, labors for himself,
For his *hungry* mouth drives ªhim *on.*

27 ¹An ungodly man digs up evil,
And *it is* on his lips like a burning ªfire.

28 A perverse man sows strife,
And ªa whisperer separates the best of friends.

29 A violent man entices his neighbor,
And leads him in a way *that is* not good.

30 He winks his eye to devise perverse things;
He ¹purses his lips *and* brings about evil.

31 ªThe silver-haired head *is* a crown of glory,
If it is found in the way of righteousness.

32 ªHe who is slow to anger is better than the mighty,
And he who rules his spirit than he who takes a city.

33 The lot is cast into the lap,
But its every decision *is* from the LORD.

17 Better *is* ªa dry morsel with quietness,
Than a house full of ¹feasting *with* strife.

2 A wise servant will rule over ªa son who causes shame,
And will share an inheritance among the brothers.

3 The refining pot *is* for silver and the furnace for gold,
ªBut the LORD tests the hearts.

4 An evildoer gives heed to false lips;
A liar listens eagerly to a ¹spiteful tongue.

5 ªHe who mocks the poor reproaches his Maker;
ᵇHe who is glad at calamity will not go unpunished.

6 ªChildren's children *are* the crown of old men,
And the glory of children *is* their father.

7 Excellent speech is not becoming to a fool,
Much less lying lips to a prince.

8 A present *is* a precious stone in the eyes of its possessor;
Wherever he turns, he prospers.

9 ªHe who covers a transgression seeks love,
But ᵇhe who repeats a matter separates friends.

10 ªRebuke is more effective for a wise *man*
Than a hundred blows on a fool.

16:25
ªProv. 14:12

16:26
ª[Eccl. 6:7;
John 6:35]

16:27
ª[James 3:6]

16:28 ªProv. 17:9

16:31
ªProv. 20:29

16:32
ªProv. 14:29;
19:11

17:1 ªProv. 15:17

17:2 ªProv. 10:5

17:3
ª1 Chr. 29:17;
Ps. 26:2;
Prov. 15:11;
Jer. 17:10;
[Mal. 3:3]

17:5 ªProv. 14:31
ᵇ Job 31:29;
Prov. 24:17;
Obad. 12;
1 Cor. 13:6

17:6 ª[Ps. 127:3;
128:3]

17:9
ª[Prov. 10:12;
1 Cor. 13:5–7;
James 5:20]
ᵇProv. 16:28

17:10
ªProv. 10:17;
[Mic. 7:9]

16:27 ¹Lit. *A man of Belial*   16:30 ¹Lit. *compresses*   17:1 ¹Or *sacrificial meals*
17:4 ¹Lit. *destructive*

11 An evil *man* seeks only rebellion;
    Therefore a cruel messenger will be sent against him.

12 Let a man meet ªa bear robbed of her cubs,
    Rather than a fool in his folly.

13 Whoever ªrewards evil for good,
    Evil will not depart from his house.

14 The beginning of strife *is like* releasing water;
    Therefore ªstop contention before a quarrel starts.

15 ªHe who justifies the wicked, and he who condemns the
        just,
    Both of them alike *are* an abomination to the Lord.

16 Why *is there* in the hand of a fool the purchase price of
        wisdom,
    Since *he has* no heart *for it?*

17 ªA friend loves at all times,
    And a brother is born for adversity.

18 ªA man devoid of ¹understanding ²shakes hands in a
        pledge,
    And becomes ³surety for his friend.

19 He who loves transgression loves strife,
    And ªhe who exalts his gate seeks destruction.

20 He who has a ¹deceitful heart finds no good,
    And he who has ªa perverse tongue falls into evil.

21 He who begets a scoffer *does so* to his sorrow,
    And the father of a fool has no joy.

22 A ªmerry heart ¹does good, *like* medicine,
    But a broken spirit dries the bones.

23 A wicked *man* accepts a bribe ¹behind the back
    To pervert the ways of justice.

24 ªWisdom *is* in the sight of him who has understanding,
    But the eyes of a fool *are* on the ends of the earth.

25 A ªfoolish son *is* a grief to his father,
    And bitterness to her who bore him.

26 Also, to punish the righteous *is* not good,
    Nor to strike princes for *their* uprightness.

27 ªHe who has knowledge spares his words,
    And a man of understanding is of a calm spirit.

28 ªEven a fool is counted wise when he holds his peace;
    When he shuts his lips, *he is considered* perceptive.

18

A man who isolates himself seeks his own desire;
    He rages against all ¹wise judgment.

2 A fool has no delight in understanding,
    But in expressing his ªown heart.

3 When the wicked comes, contempt comes also;
    And with dishonor *comes* reproach.

17:12
ª2 Sam. 17:8;
Hos. 13:8

17:13
ªPs. 109:4, 5;
Jer. 18:20;
Rom. 12:17;
1 Thess. 5:15;
[1 Pet. 3:9]

17:14
ª[Prov. 20:3;
1 Thess. 4:11]

17:15 ªEx. 23:7;
Prov. 24:24;
Is. 5:23

17:17 ªRuth 1:16;
Prov. 18:24

17:18 ªProv. 6:1

17:19 ªProv. 16:18

17:20
ªJames 3:8

17:22
ªProv. 12:25;
15:13, 15

17:24 ªEccl. 2:14

17:25 ªProv. 10:1;
15:20; 19:13

17:27
ªProv. 10:19;
James 1:19

17:28 ªJob 13:5

18:2 ªEccl. 10:3

17:18 ¹Lit. *heart*   ²Lit. *strikes the hands*   ³*guaranty* or *collateral*
17:20 ¹*crooked*   **17:22** ¹Or *makes medicine even better*   **17:23** ¹*Under cover,*
lit. *from the bosom*   **18:1** ¹*sound wisdom*

4 ᵃThe words of a man's mouth *are* deep waters;
ᵇThe wellspring of wisdom *is* a flowing brook.

5 *It is* not good to show partiality to the wicked,
Or to overthrow the righteous in ᵃjudgment.

6 A fool's lips enter into contention,
And his mouth calls for blows.

7 ᵃA fool's mouth *is* his destruction,
And his lips *are* the snare of his ᵇsoul.

8 ᵃThe words of a ¹talebearer *are* like ²tasty trifles,
And they go down into the ³inmost body.

9 He who is slothful in his work
Is a brother to him who is a great destroyer.

10 The name of the LORD *is* a strong ᵃtower;
The righteous run to it and are ¹safe.

11 The rich man's wealth *is* his strong city,
And like a high wall in his own esteem.

12 ᵃBefore destruction the heart of a man is haughty,
And before honor *is* humility.

13 He who answers a matter before he hears *it,*
It *is* folly and shame to him.

14 The spirit of a man will sustain him in sickness,
But who can bear a broken spirit?

15 The heart of the prudent acquires knowledge,
And the ear of the wise seeks knowledge.

16 ᵃA man's gift makes room for him,
And brings him before great men.

17 The first *one* to plead his cause *seems* right,
Until his neighbor comes and examines him.

18 Casting ᵃlots causes contentions to cease,
And keeps the mighty apart.

19 A brother offended *is harder to win* than a strong city,
And contentions *are* like the bars of a castle.

20 ᵃA man's stomach shall be satisfied from the fruit of his mouth;
From the produce of his lips he shall be filled.

21 ᵃDeath and life *are* in the power of the tongue,
And those who love it will eat its fruit.

22 ᵃ*He who* finds a wife finds a good *thing,*
And obtains favor from the LORD.

23 The poor *man* uses entreaties,
But the rich answers ᵃroughly.

24 A man *who has* friends ¹must himself be friendly,
ᵃBut there is a friend *who* sticks closer than a brother.

19 Better ᵃ*is* the poor who walks in his integrity
Than *one who is* perverse in his lips, and is a fool.

18:4 ᵃProv. 10:11
ᵇ[James 3:17]

18:5 ᵃLev. 19:15;
Deut. 1:17;
16:19; Ps. 82:2;
Prov. 17:15

18:7 ᵃPs. 64:8;
140:9; Prov. 10:14
ᵇEccl. 10:12

18:8 ᵃProv. 12:18

18:10
ᵃ2 Sam. 22:2, 3,
33; Ps. 18:2;
61:3; 91:2; 144:2

18:12
ᵃProv. 15:33;
16:18

18:16
ᵃGen. 32:20, 21;
1 Sam. 25:27;
Prov. 17:8; 21:14

18:18
ᵃ[Prov. 16:33]

18:20
ᵃProv. 12:14;
14:14

18:21
ᵃProv. 12:13;
13:3; Matt. 12:37

18:22
ᵃGen. 2:18;
[Prov. 12:4;
19:14]

18:23
ᵃJames 2:3, 6

18:24
ᵃProv. 17:17;
[John 15:14, 15]

19:1 ᵃProv. 28:6

18:8 ¹*gossip* or *slanderer*   ²A Jewish tradition *wounds*   ³Lit. *rooms of the belly*   18:10 ¹*secure,* lit. *set on high*   18:24 ¹So with Gr. mss., Syr., Tg., Vg.; MT *may come to ruin*

2 Also it is not good *for* a soul *to be* without knowledge,
And he sins who hastens with *his* feet.

3 The foolishness of a man twists his way,
And his heart frets against the LORD.

4 ^aWealth makes many friends,
But the poor is separated from his friend.

5 A ^afalse witness will not go unpunished,
And *he who* speaks lies will not escape.

6 Many entreat the favor of the nobility,
And every man *is* a friend to one who gives gifts.

7 ^aAll the brothers of the poor hate him;
How much more do his friends go ^bfar from him!
He may pursue *them with* words, *yet* they ¹abandon
him.

8 He who gets ¹wisdom loves his own soul;
He who keeps understanding ^awill find good.

9 A false witness will not go unpunished,
And *he who* speaks lies shall perish.

10 Luxury is not fitting for a fool,
Much less ^afor a servant to rule over princes.

11 ^aThe discretion of a man makes him slow to anger,
^bAnd his glory *is* to overlook a transgression.

12 ^aThe king's wrath *is* like the roaring of a lion,
But his favor *is* ^blike dew on the grass.

13 ^aA foolish son *is* the ruin of his father,
^bAnd the contentions of a wife *are* a continual
¹dripping.

14 ^aHouses and riches *are* an inheritance from fathers,
But ^ba prudent wife *is* from the LORD.

15 ^aLaziness casts *one* into a deep sleep,
And an idle person will ^bsuffer hunger.

16 ^aHe who keeps the commandment keeps his soul,
But he who ¹is careless of his ways will die.

17 ^aHe who has pity on the poor lends to the LORD,
And He will pay back what he has given.

18 ^aChasten your son while there is hope,
And do not set your heart ¹on his destruction.

19 *A man of* great wrath will suffer punishment;
For if you rescue *him,* you will have to do it again.

20 Listen to counsel and receive instruction,
That you may be wise ^ain your latter days.

21 There are many plans in a man's heart,
^aNevertheless the LORD's counsel—that will stand.

22 What is desired in a man is ¹kindness,
And a poor man is better than a liar.

19:4 ^aProv. 14:20
19:5 ^aEx. 23:1;
Deut. 19:16–19;
Prov. 6:19; 21:28
19:7 ^aProv. 14:20
^bPs. 38:11
19:8 ^aProv. 16:20
19:10
^aProv. 30:21, 22
19:11 ^aJames 1:19
^bProv. 16:32;
[Matt. 5:44];
Eph. 4:32;
Col. 3:13
19:12
^aProv. 16:14
^bGen. 27:28;
Deut. 33:28;
Ps. 133:3;
Hos. 14:5;
Mic. 5:7
19:13 ^aProv. 10:1
^bProv. 21:9, 19
19:14
^a2 Cor. 12:14
^bProv. 18:22
19:15 ^aProv. 6:9
^bProv. 10:4
19:16
^aProv. 13:13;
16:17;
Luke 10:28;
11:28
19:17
^aDeut. 15:7, 8;
Job 23:12, 13;
Prov. 28:27;
Eccl. 11:1;
Matt. 10:42;
25:40;
[2 Cor. 9:6–8];
Heb. 6:10
19:18
^aProv. 13:24
19:20 ^aPs. 37:37
19:21
^aPs. 33:10, 11;
Prov. 16:9;
Is. 46:10;
Heb. 6:17

19:7 ¹Lit. *are not*   **19:8** ¹Lit. *heart*   **19:13** ¹Irritation   **19:16** ¹Is reckless, lit.
despises   **19:18** ¹Lit. *to put him to death;* a Jewish tradition *on his crying*
19:22 ¹Lit. *lovingkindness*

23 ᵃThe fear of the LORD *leads* to life,
And *he who has it* will abide in satisfaction;
He will not be visited with evil.

24 ᵃA lazy *man* buries his hand in the ¹bowl,
And will not so much as bring it to his mouth again.

25 Strike a scoffer, and the simple ᵃwill become wary;
ᵇRebuke one who has understanding, *and* he will discern knowledge.

26 He who mistreats *his* father *and* chases away *his* mother
Is ᵃa son who causes shame and brings reproach.

27 Cease listening to instruction, my son,
And you will stray from the words of knowledge.

28 A ¹disreputable witness scorns justice,
And ᵃthe mouth of the wicked devours iniquity.

29 Judgments are prepared for scoffers,
ᵃAnd beatings for the backs of fools.

20 Wine ᵃ*is* a mocker,
Strong drink *is* a brawler,
And whoever is led astray by it is not wise.

2 The ¹wrath of a king *is* like the roaring of a lion;
Whoever provokes him to anger sins *against* his own life.

3 ᵃ*It is* honorable for a man to stop striving,
Since any fool can start a quarrel.

4 ᵃThe lazy *man* will not plow because of winter;
ᵇHe will beg during harvest and *have* nothing.

5 Counsel in the heart of man *is like* deep water,
But a man of understanding will draw it out.

6 Most men will proclaim each his own ¹goodness,
But who can find a faithful man?

7 ᵃThe righteous *man* walks in his integrity;
ᵇHis children *are* blessed after him.

8 A king who sits on the throne of judgment
Scatters all evil with his eyes.

9 ᵃWho can say, "I have made my heart clean,
I am pure from my sin"?

10 ᵃDiverse weights *and* diverse measures,
They *are* both alike, an abomination to the LORD.

11 Even a child is ᵃknown by his deeds,
Whether what he does *is* pure and right.

12 ᵃThe hearing ear and the seeing eye,
The LORD has made them both.

13 ᵃDo not love sleep, lest you come to poverty;
Open your eyes, *and* you will be satisfied with bread.

14 "*It is* ¹good for nothing," cries the buyer;
But when he has gone his way, then he boasts.

19:23
ᵃProv. 14:27;
[1 Tim. 4:8]

19:24
ᵃProv. 15:19

19:25
ᵃDeut. 13:11
ᵇProv. 9:8

19:26 ᵃProv. 17:2

19:28 ᵃJob 15:16

19:29
ᵃProv. 26:3

20:1 ᵃGen. 9:21;
Prov. 23:29–35;
Is. 28:7; Hos. 4:11

20:3 ᵃProv. 17:14

20:4 ᵃProv. 10:4
ᵇProv. 19:15

20:7 ᵃ2 Cor. 1:12
ᵇPs. 37:26

20:9
ᵃ[1 Kin. 8:46;
2 Chr. 6:36];
Job 9:30, 31;
14:4; [Ps. 51:5;
Eccl. 7:20;
Rom. 3:9;
1 John 1:8]

20:10
ᵃDeut. 25:13

20:11 ᵃMatt. 7:16

20:12 ᵃEx. 4:11;
Ps. 94:9

20:13
ᵃRom. 12:11

19:24 ¹LXX, Syr. *bosom;* Tg., Vg. *armpit*   19:28 ¹Lit. *witness of Belial,*
worthless witness   20:2 ¹Lit. *fear* or *terror,* produced by the king's wrath
20:6 ¹Lit. *mercy*   20:14 ¹Lit. *evil, evil*

15 There is gold and a multitude of rubies,
But [a]the lips of knowledge *are* a precious jewel.

16 [a]Take the garment of one who is surety *for* a stranger,
And hold it as a pledge *when it* is for a seductress.

17 [a]Bread gained by deceit *is* sweet to a man,
But afterward his mouth will be filled with gravel.

18 [a]Plans are established by counsel;
[b]By wise counsel wage war.

19 [a]He who goes about *as* a talebearer reveals secrets;
Therefore do not associate with one [b]who flatters with
his lips.

20 [a]Whoever curses his father or his mother,
[b]His lamp will be put out in deep darkness.

21 [a]An inheritance gained hastily at the beginning
[b]Will not be blessed at the end.

22 [a]Do not say, "I will [1]recompense evil";
[b]Wait for the LORD, and He will save you.

23 Diverse weights *are* an abomination to the LORD,
And dishonest scales *are* not good.

24 A man's steps *are* of the LORD;
How then can a man understand his own way?

25 *It is* a snare for a man to devote rashly *something as*
holy,
And afterward to reconsider *his* vows.

26 [a]A wise king sifts out the wicked,
And brings the threshing wheel over them.

27 [a]The spirit of a man *is* the lamp of the LORD,
Searching all the [1]inner depths of his heart.

28 [a]Mercy and truth preserve the king,
And by [1]lovingkindness he upholds his throne.

29 The glory of young men *is* their strength,
And [a]the splendor of old men *is* their gray head.

30 Blows that hurt cleanse away evil,
As *do* stripes the [1]inner depths of the heart.

21

The king's heart *is* in the hand of the LORD,
Like the [1]rivers of water;
He turns it wherever He wishes.

2 [a]Every way of a man *is* right in his own eyes,
[b]But the LORD weighs the hearts.

3 [a]To do righteousness and justice
Is more acceptable to the LORD than sacrifice.

4 [a]A haughty look, a proud heart,
And the [1]plowing of the wicked *are* sin.

5 [a]The plans of the diligent *lead* surely to plenty,
But *those of* everyone *who is* hasty, surely to poverty.

20:15
[a][Job 28:12–19;
Prov. 3:13–15]

20:16
[a]Prov. 22:26

20:17 [a]Prov. 9:17

20:18
[a]Prov. 24:6
[b]Luke 14:31

20:19
[a]Prov. 11:13
[b]Rom. 16:18

20:20 [a]Ex. 21:17;
Lev. 20:9;
Prov. 30:11;
Matt. 15:4
[b]Job 18:5, 6;
Prov. 24:20

20:21
[a]Prov. 28:20
[b]Hab. 2:6

20:22
[a][Deut. 32:35];
Prov. 17:13;
24:29;
[Rom. 12:17–19];
1 Thess. 5:15;
[1 Pet. 3:9]
[b]2 Sam. 16:12

20:26 [a]Ps. 101:8

20:27 [a]1 Cor. 2:11

20:28 [a]Ps. 101:1;
Prov. 21:21

20:29
[a]Prov. 16:31

21:2 [a]Prov. 16:2
[b]Prov. 24:12;
Luke 16:15

21:3
[a]1 Sam. 15:22;
Prov. 15:8;
Is. 1:11, 16, 17;
Hos. 6:6;
[Mic. 6:7, 8]

21:4 [a]Prov. 6:17

21:5 [a]Prov. 10:4

20:22 [1]repay 20:27 [1]Lit. *rooms of the belly* 20:28 [1]*mercy* 20:30 [1]Lit.
rooms of the belly 21:1 [1]*channels* 21:4 [1]Or *lamp*

6 aGetting treasures by a lying tongue
  1Is the fleeting fantasy of those who seek death.

7 The violence of the wicked will 1destroy them,
  Because they refuse to do justice.

8 The way of 1a guilty man *is* perverse;
  But *as for* the pure, his work *is* right.

9 Better to dwell in a corner of a housetop,
  Than in a house shared with aa contentious woman.

10 aThe soul of the wicked desires evil;
   His neighbor finds no favor in his eyes.

11 When the scoffer is punished, the simple is made wise;
   But when the awise is instructed, he receives knowledge.

12 The righteous *God* wisely considers the house of the
     wicked,
   Overthrowing the wicked for *their* wickedness.

13 aWhoever shuts his ears to the cry of the poor
   Will also cry himself and not be heard.

14 A gift in secret pacifies anger,
   And a bribe 1behind the back, strong wrath.

15 *It is* a joy for the just to do justice,
   But destruction *will come* to the workers of iniquity.

16 A man who wanders from the way of understanding
   Will rest in the assembly of the adead.

17 He who loves pleasure *will be* a poor man;
   He who loves wine and oil will not be rich.

18 The wicked *shall be* a ransom for the righteous,
   And the unfaithful for the upright.

19 Better to dwell 1in the wilderness,
   Than with a contentious and angry woman.

20 aThere is desirable treasure,
   And oil in the dwelling of the wise,
   But a foolish man squanders it.

21 aHe who follows righteousness and mercy
   Finds life, righteousness, and honor.

22 A awise *man* 1scales the city of the mighty,
   And brings down the trusted stronghold.

23 aWhoever guards his mouth and tongue
   Keeps his soul from troubles.

24 A proud *and* haughty *man*—"Scoffer" *is* his name;
   He acts with arrogant pride.

25 The adesire of the lazy *man* kills him,
   For his hands refuse to labor.

26 He covets greedily all day long,
   But the righteous agives and does not spare.

21:6 a2 Pet. 2:3
21:9 aProv. 19:13
21:10
aJames 4:5
21:11 aProv. 19:25
21:13
a[Matt. 7:2;
18:30–34];
James 2:13;
1 John 3:17
21:16 aPs. 49:14
21:20 aPs. 112:3;
Prov. 8:21
21:21 aProv. 15:9;
Matt. 5:6;
[Rom. 2:7];
1 Cor. 15:58
21:22
a2 Sam. 5:6–9;
Prov. 24:5;
Eccl. 7:19;
9:15, 16
21:23
aProv. 12:13;
13:3; 18:21;
[James 3:2]
21:25 aProv. 13:4
21:26
a[Prov. 22:9;
Eph. 4:28]

21:6 1LXX *Pursue vanity on the snares of death;* Vg. *Is vain and foolish, and shall stumble on the snares of death;* Tg. *They shall be destroyed, and they shall fall who seek death*   21:7 1Lit. *drag them away*   21:8 1Or *The way of a man is perverse and strange;*   21:14 1Under cover, lit. *in the bosom*   21:19 1Lit. *in the land of the desert*   21:22 1Climbs over the walls of

27 ^aThe sacrifice of the wicked *is* an abomination;
How much more *when* he brings it with wicked
intent!

28 A false witness shall perish,
But the man who hears *him* will speak endlessly.

29 A wicked man hardens his face,
But *as for* the upright, he ¹establishes his way.

30 ^a*There is* no wisdom or understanding
Or counsel against the LORD.

31 The horse *is* prepared for the day of battle,
But ^adeliverance *is* of the LORD.

22 A ^a*good* name is to be chosen rather than great
riches,
Loving favor rather than silver and gold.

2 The ^arich and the poor have this in common,
The ^bLORD *is* the maker of them all.

3 A prudent *man* foresees evil and hides himself,
But the simple pass on and are ^apunished.

4 By humility *and* the fear of the LORD
Are riches and honor and life.

5 Thorns *and* snares *are* in the way of the perverse;
He who guards his soul will be far from them.

6 ^aTrain up a child in the way he should go,
¹And when he is old he will not depart from it.

7 The ^arich rules over the poor,
And the borrower *is* servant to the lender.

8 He who sows iniquity will reap ^asorrow,¹
And the rod of his anger will fail.

9 ^aHe who has a ¹generous eye will be ^bblessed,
For he gives of his bread to the poor.

10 ^aCast out the scoffer, and contention will leave;
Yes, strife and reproach will cease.

11 ^aHe who loves purity of heart
And has grace on his lips,
The king *will be* his friend.

12 The eyes of the LORD preserve knowledge,
But He overthrows the words of the faithless.

13 ^aThe lazy *man* says, "*There is* a lion outside!
I shall be slain in the streets!"

14 ^aThe mouth of an immoral woman *is* a deep pit;
^bHe who is abhorred by the LORD will fall there.

15 Foolishness *is* bound up in the heart of a child;
^aThe rod of correction will drive it far from him.

16 He who oppresses the poor to increase his *riches,*
And he who gives to the rich, *will* surely *come* to
poverty.

21:27
^aProv. 15:8;
Is. 66:3;
Jer. 6:20;
Amos 5:22

21:30
^aIs. 8:9, 10;
[Jer. 9:23, 24];
Acts 5:39;
1 Cor. 3:19, 20

21:31 ^aPs. 3:8;
Jer. 3:23;
[1 Cor. 15:57]

22:1
^a[Prov. 10:7];
Eccl. 7:1

22:2
^aProv. 29:13
^bJob 31:15;
[Prov. 14:31]

22:3
^aProv. 27:12;
Is. 26:20

22:6 ^aEph. 6:4;
2 Tim. 3:15

22:7
^aProv. 18:23;
James 2:6

22:8 ^aJob 4:8

22:9 ^a2 Cor. 9:6
^b[Prov. 19:17]

22:10 ^aPs. 101:5

22:11 ^aPs. 101:6

22:13
^aProv. 26:13

22:14
^aProv. 2:16; 5:3;
7:5 ^bEccl. 7:26

22:15
^aProv. 13:24;
23:13, 14

21:29 ¹Qr., LXX *understands*   22:6 ¹*Even*   22:8 ¹*trouble*   22:9 ¹Lit. *good*

SAYINGS OF THE WISE

17 Incline your ear and hear the words of the wise,
And apply your heart to my knowledge;
18 For *it is* a pleasant thing if you keep them within you;
Let them all be fixed upon your lips,
19 So that your trust may be in the LORD;
I have instructed you today, even you.
20 Have I not written to you excellent things
Of counsels and knowledge,
21 ^aThat I may make you know the certainty of the words of
truth,
^bThat you may answer words of truth
To those who ¹send to you?

22 Do not rob the ^apoor because he *is* poor,
Nor oppress the afflicted at the gate;
23 ^aFor the LORD will plead their cause,
And plunder the soul of those who plunder them.

24 Make no friendship with an angry man,
And with a ^afurious man do not go,
25 Lest you learn his ways
And set a snare for your soul.

26 ^aDo not be one of those who ¹shakes hands in a pledge,
One of those who is ²surety for debts;
27 If you have nothing *with which* to pay,
Why should he take away your bed from under you?

28 ^aDo not remove the ancient ¹landmark
Which your fathers have set.

29 Do you see a man *who* ¹excels in his work?
He will stand before kings;
He will not stand before ²unknown *men.*

23 When you sit down to eat with a ruler,
Consider carefully what *is* before you;
2 And put a knife to your throat
If you *are* a man given to appetite.
3 Do not desire his delicacies,
For they *are* deceptive food.

4 ^aDo not overwork to be rich;
^bBecause of your own understanding, cease!
5 ¹Will you set your eyes on that which is not?
For *riches* certainly make themselves wings;
They fly away like an eagle *toward* heaven.

6 Do not eat the bread of ^aa¹ miser,
Nor desire his delicacies;
7 For as he thinks in his heart, so *is* he.
"Eat and drink!" ^ahe says to you,
But his heart is not with you.
8 The morsel you have eaten, you will vomit up,
And waste your pleasant words.

9 ^aDo not speak in the hearing of a fool,
For he will despise the wisdom of your words.

22:21
^aLuke 1:3, 4
^bProv. 25:13;
1 Pet. 3:15

22:22 ^aEx. 23:6;
Job 31:16–21;
Zech. 7:10

22:23
^a1 Sam. 24:12;
Ps. 12:5; 140:12

22:24
^aProv. 29:22

22:26
^aProv. 11:15

22:28
^aDeut. 19:14;
27:17; Job 24:2;
Prov. 23:10

23:4
^a[Prov. 28:20;
Matt. 6:19;
1 Tim. 6:9,
10; Heb. 13:5]
^bRom. 12:16

23:6
^aDeut. 15:9;
Prov. 28:22

23:7 ^aProv. 12:2

23:9 ^aProv. 9:8;
Matt. 7:6

22:21 ¹Or *send you*   22:26 ¹Lit. *strikes*   ²*guaranty*   22:28 ¹*boundary*
22:29 ¹*is prompt in his business*   ²*obscure*   23:5 ¹Lit. *Will you cause your
eyes to fly upon it and it is not?*   23:6 ¹Lit. *one who has an evil eye*

10 Do not remove the ancient ¹landmark,
Nor enter the fields of the fatherless;
11 ᵃFor their Redeemer *is* mighty;
He will plead their cause against you.

12 Apply your heart to instruction,
And your ears to words of knowledge.

13 ᵃDo not withhold correction from a child,
For *if* you beat him with a rod, he will not die.
14 You shall beat him with a rod,
And deliver his soul from ¹hell.

15 My son, if your heart is wise,
My heart will rejoice—indeed, I myself;
16 Yes, my ¹inmost being will rejoice
When your lips speak right things.

17 ᵃDo not let your heart envy sinners,
But ᵇ*be zealous* for the fear of the LORD all the day;
18 ᵃFor surely there is a ¹hereafter,
And your hope will not be cut off.

19 Hear, my son, and be wise;
And guide your heart in the way.
20 ᵃDo not mix with winebibbers,
Or with gluttonous eaters of meat;
21 For the drunkard and the glutton will come to
poverty,
And drowsiness will clothe *a man* with rags.

22 ᵃListen to your father who begot you,
And do not despise your mother when she is old.

23 ᵃBuy the truth, and do not sell *it,*
Also wisdom and instruction and understanding.

24 ᵃThe father of the righteous will greatly rejoice,
And he who begets a wise *child* will delight in him.
25 Let your father and your mother be glad,
And let her who bore you rejoice.

26 My son, give me your heart,
And let your eyes observe my ways.
27 ᵃFor a harlot *is* a deep pit,
And a seductress *is* a narrow well.
28 ᵃShe also lies in wait as *for* a victim,
And increases the unfaithful among men.

29 ᵃWho has woe?
Who has sorrow?
Who has contentions?
Who has complaints?
Who has wounds without cause?
Who ᵇhas redness of eyes?
30 ᵃThose who linger long at the wine,
Those who go in search of ᵇmixed wine.
31 Do not look on the wine when it is red,
When it sparkles in the cup,
When it ¹swirls around smoothly;

23:11 ᵃProv. 22:23
23:13 ᵃProv. 13:24
23:17 ᵃPs. 37:1; Prov. 24:1, 19 ᵇProv. 28:14
23:18 ᵃ[Ps. 37:37]
23:20 ᵃProv. 20:1; 23:29, 30; Is. 5:22; Matt. 24:49; [Luke 21:34]; Rom. 13:13; [Eph. 5:18]
23:22 ᵃProv. 1:8; Eph. 6:1
23:23 ᵃProv. 4:7; 18:15; [Matt. 13:44]
23:24 ᵃProv. 10:1
23:27 ᵃProv. 22:14
23:28 ᵃProv. 7:12; Eccl. 7:26
23:29 ᵃIs. 5:11, 22 ᵇGen. 49:12
23:30 ᵃ1 Sam. 25:36; Prov. 20:1; 21:17; Is. 5:11; 28:7; [Eph. 5:18] ᵇPs. 75:8

23:10 ¹*boundary* **23:14** ¹Or *Sheol* **23:16** ¹Lit. *kidneys* **23:18** ¹*Future,* lit. *latter end* **23:31** ¹*goes around*

32 At the last it bites like a serpent,
   And stings like a viper.
33 Your eyes will see strange things,
   And your heart will utter perverse things.
34 Yes, you will be like one who lies down in the ¹midst of
   the sea,
   Or like one who lies at the top of the mast, *saying:*
35 "They ᵃ have struck me, *but* I was not hurt;
   They have beaten me, but I did not feel *it.*
   When shall ᵇI awake, that I may seek another
   drink?"

24 Do not be ᵃenvious of evil men,
   Nor desire to be with them;
2 For their heart devises violence,
   And their lips talk of troublemaking.

3 Through wisdom a house is built,
   And by understanding it is established;
4 By knowledge the rooms are filled
   With all precious and pleasant riches.

5 ᵃA wise man *is* strong,
   Yes, a man of knowledge increases strength;
6 ᵃFor by wise counsel you will wage your own war,
   And in a multitude of counselors *there is* safety.

7 ᵃWisdom *is* too lofty for a fool;
   He does not open his mouth in the gate.

8 He who ᵃplots to do evil
   Will be called a ¹schemer.
9 The devising of foolishness *is* sin,
   And the scoffer *is* an abomination to men.

10 *If* you ᵃfaint in the day of adversity,
   Your strength *is* small.

11 ᵃDeliver *those who* are drawn toward death,
   And hold back *those* stumbling to the slaughter.
12 If you say, "Surely we did not know this,"
   Does not ᵃHe who weighs the hearts consider *it?*
   He who keeps your soul, does He *not* know *it?*
   And will He *not* render to *each* man ᵇaccording to his
   deeds?

13 My son, ᵃeat honey because *it is* good,
   And the honeycomb *which is* sweet to your taste;
14 ᵃSo *shall* the knowledge of wisdom *be* to your soul;
   If you have found *it,* there is a ¹prospect,
   And your hope will not be cut off.

15 Do not lie in wait, O wicked *man,* against the dwelling of
   the righteous;
   Do not plunder his resting place;
16 ᵃFor a righteous *man* may fall seven times
   And rise again,
   ᵇBut the wicked shall fall by calamity.

17 ᵃDo not rejoice when your enemy falls,
   And do not let your heart be glad when he stumbles;

23:35 ᵃProv. 27:22; Jer. 5:3; ᵇEph. 4:19
24:1 ᵃPs. 1:1; 37:1; Prov. 23:17
24:5 ᵃProv. 21:22; Eccl. 9:16
24:6 ᵃLuke 14:31
24:7 ᵃPs. 10:5; Prov. 14:6
24:8 ᵃProv. 6:14; 14:22; Rom. 1:30
24:10 ᵃDeut. 20:8; Job 4:5; Jer. 51:46; Heb. 12:3
24:11 ᵃPs. 82:4; Is. 58:6, 7; 1 John 3:16
24:12 ᵃ1 Sam. 16:7; Prov. 21:2; ᵇJob 34:11; Ps. 62:12; Rev. 2:23; 22:12
24:13 ᵃPs. 19:10; 119:103; Prov. 25:16; Song 5:1
24:14 ᵃPs. 19:10; 58:11; Prov. 23:18
24:16 ᵃJob 5:19; [Ps. 34:19; 37:24; Mic. 7:8]; ᵇEsth. 7:10; Amos 5:2
24:17 ᵃJob 31:29; Ps. 35:15, 19; [Prov. 17:5]; Obad. 12

18 Lest the LORD see *it,* and [1]it displease Him,
And He turn away His wrath from him.

19 [a]Do not fret because of evildoers,
Nor be envious of the wicked;

20 For there will be no prospect for the evil *man;*
The lamp of the wicked will be put out.

21 My son, [a]fear the LORD and the king;
Do not associate with those given to change;

22 For their calamity will rise suddenly,
And who knows the ruin those two can bring?

FURTHER SAYINGS OF THE WISE

23These *things* also *belong* to the wise:

[a]*It is* not good to [1]show partiality in judgment.

24 [a]He who says to the wicked, "You *are* righteous,"
Him the people will curse;
Nations will abhor him.

25 But those who rebuke *the wicked* will have [a]delight,
And a good blessing will come upon them.

26 He who gives a right answer kisses the lips.

27 [a]Prepare your outside work,
Make it fit for yourself in the field;
And afterward build your house.

28 [a]Do not be a witness against your neighbor without
cause,
[1]For would you deceive with your lips?

29 [a]Do not say, "I will do to him just as he has done to me;
I will render to the man according to his work."

30 I went by the field of the lazy *man,*
And by the vineyard of the man devoid of
understanding;

31 And there it was, [a]all overgrown with thorns;
Its surface was covered with nettles;
Its stone wall was broken down.

32 When I saw *it,* I considered *it* well;
I looked on *it and* received instruction:

33 [a]A little sleep, a little slumber,
A little folding of the hands to rest;

34 [a]So shall your poverty come *like* [1]a prowler,
And your need like [2]an armed man.

FURTHER WISE SAYINGS OF SOLOMON

25 These[a] also *are* proverbs of Solomon which the men of
Hezekiah king of Judah copied:

2 [a]*It is* the glory of God to conceal a matter,
But the glory of kings *is* to search out a matter.

3 *As* the heavens for height and the earth for depth,
So the heart of kings *is* unsearchable.

4 [a]Take away the dross from silver,
And it will go to the silversmith *for* jewelry.

24:19 [a]Ps. 37:1
24:21 [a][Rom. 13:7; 1 Pet. 2:17]
24:23 [a]Lev. 19:15; Deut. 1:17; 16:19; [John 7:24]
24:24 [a]Prov. 17:15; Is. 5:23
24:25 [a]Prov. 28:23
24:27 [a]1 Kin. 5:17; Prov. 27:23–27
24:28 [a]Lev. 6:2, 3; 19:11; Eph. 4:25
24:29 [a][Prov. 20:22; Matt. 5:39–44; Rom. 12:17–19]
24:31 [a]Gen. 3:18
24:33 [a]Prov. 6:9, 10
24:34 [a]Prov. 6:9–11
25:1 [a]1 Kin. 4:32
25:2 [a]Deut. 29:29; Rom. 11:33
25:4 [a]2 Tim. 2:21

24:18 [1]Lit. *it be evil in His eyes*   24:23 [1]Lit. *recognize faces*   24:28 [1]LXX, Vg.
Do not deceive   24:34 [1]Lit. *one who walks about*   [2]Lit. *a man with a shield*

5 Take away the wicked from before the king,
And his throne will be established in ^arighteousness.

6 Do not exalt yourself in the presence of the king,
And do not stand in the place of the great;
7 ^aFor *it is* better that he say to you,
"Come up here,"
Than that you should be put lower in the presence of the
prince,
Whom your eyes have seen.

8 ^aDo not go hastily to ¹court;
For what will you do in the end,
When your neighbor has put you to shame?
9 ^aDebate your case with your neighbor,
And do not disclose the secret to another;
10 Lest he who hears *it* expose your shame,
And ¹your reputation be ruined.

11 A word fitly ^aspoken *is like* apples of gold
In settings of silver.
12 *Like* an earring of gold and an ornament of fine gold
Is a wise rebuker to an obedient ear.

13 ^aLike the cold of snow in time of harvest
Is a faithful messenger to those who send him,
For he refreshes the soul of his masters.

14 ^aWhoever falsely boasts of giving
Is like ^bclouds and wind without rain.

15 ^aBy long forbearance a ruler is persuaded,
And a gentle tongue breaks a bone.

16 Have you found honey?
Eat only as much as you need,
Lest you be filled with it and vomit.

17 Seldom set foot in your neighbor's house,
Lest he become weary of you and hate you.

18 ^aA man who bears false witness against his
neighbor
Is like a club, a sword, and a sharp arrow.

19 Confidence in an unfaithful *man* in time of trouble
Is like a bad tooth and a foot out of joint.

20 *Like* one who takes away a garment in cold weather,
And like vinegar on soda,
Is one who ^asings songs to a heavy heart.

21 ^aIf your enemy is hungry, give him bread to eat;
And if he is thirsty, give him water to drink;
22 For *so* you will heap coals of fire on his head,
^aAnd the LORD will reward you.

23 The north wind brings forth rain,
And ^aa backbiting tongue an angry countenance.

24 ^a*It is* better to dwell in a corner of a housetop,
Than in a house shared with a contentious woman.

25:5
^aProv. 16:12;
20:8

25:7
^aLuke 14:7–11

25:8
^aProv. 17:14;
Matt. 5:25

25:9
^a[Matt. 18:15]

25:11
^aProv. 15:23;
Is. 50:4

25:13
^aProv. 13:17

25:14
^aProv. 20:6
^bJude 12

25:15 ^aProv. 15:1

25:18 ^aPs. 57:4;
Prov. 12:18

25:20
^aDan. 6:18

25:21
^aEx. 23:4, 5;
2 Kin. 6:22;
2 Chr. 28:15;
Matt. 5:44;
Rom. 12:20

25:22
^a2 Sam. 16:12;
[Matt. 6:4, 6]

25:23 ^aPs. 101:5

25:24
^aProv. 19:13

25:8 ¹Lit. *contend* or *bring a lawsuit*   25:10 ¹*the evil report concerning you
not pass away*

25 *As* cold water to a weary soul,
So *is* ᵃgood news from a far country.

26 A righteous *man* who falters before the wicked
Is like a murky spring and a ¹polluted well.

27 *It is* not good to eat much honey;
So ᵃto seek one's own glory *is not* glory.

28 ᵃWhoever *has* no rule over his own spirit
Is like a city broken down, without walls.

26

As snow in summer ᵃand rain in harvest,
So honor is not fitting for a fool.

2 Like a flitting sparrow, like a flying swallow,
So ᵃa curse without cause shall not alight.

3 ᵃA whip for the horse,
A bridle for the donkey,
And a rod for the fool's back.

4 Do not answer a fool according to his folly,
Lest you also be like him.

5 ᵃAnswer a fool according to his folly,
Lest he be wise in his own eyes.

6 He who sends a message by the hand of a fool
Cuts off *his own* feet *and* drinks violence.

7 *Like* the legs of the lame that hang limp
Is a proverb in the mouth of fools.

8 Like one who binds a stone in a sling
Is he who gives honor to a fool.

9 *Like* a thorn *that* goes into the hand of a drunkard
Is a proverb in the mouth of fools.

10 ¹The great *God* who formed everything
Gives the fool *his* hire and the transgressor *his* wages.

11 ᵃAs a dog returns to his own vomit,
ᵇ*So* a fool repeats his folly.

12 ᵃDo you see a man wise in his own eyes?
There is more hope for a fool than for him.

13 The lazy *man* says, "*There is* a lion in the road!
A fierce lion *is* in the ¹streets!"

14 *As* a door turns on its hinges,
So *does* the lazy *man* on his bed.

15 The ᵃlazy *man* buries his hand in the ¹bowl;
It wearies him to bring it back to his mouth.

16 The lazy *man is* wiser in his own eyes
Than seven men who can answer sensibly.

17 He who passes by *and* meddles in a quarrel not his own
Is like one who takes a dog by the ears.

18 Like a madman who throws firebrands, arrows, and death,

19 *Is* the man *who* deceives his neighbor,
And says, ᵃ"I was only joking!"

20 Where *there is* no wood, the fire goes out;
And where *there is* no ¹talebearer, strife ceases.

25:25
ᵃProv. 15:30

25:27
ᵃProv. 27:2;
[Luke 14:11]

25:28
ᵃProv. 16:32

26:1
ᵃ1 Sam. 12:17

26:2
ᵃNum. 23:8;
Deut. 23:5;
2 Sam. 16:12

26:3 ᵃPs. 32:9;
Prov. 19:29

26:5
ᵃMatt. 16:1–4;
Rom. 12:16

26:11
ᵃ2 Pet. 2:22
ᵇEx. 8:15

26:12
ᵃProv. 29:20;
Luke 18:11, 12;
[Rev. 3:17]

26:15
ᵃProv. 19:24

26:19 ᵃEph. 5:4

25:26 ¹ruined   26:10 ¹Heb. difficult in v. 10; ancient and modern translators differ greatly   26:13 ¹Or *plazas, squares*   26:15 ¹LXX, Syr. *bosom;* Tg., Vg. *armpit*   26:20 ¹*gossip* or *slanderer,* lit. *whisperer*

21 ᵃAs charcoal *is* to burning coals, and wood to fire,
So *is* a contentious man to kindle strife.
22 The words of a ¹talebearer *are* like ²tasty trifles,
And they go down into the ³inmost body.

23 Fervent lips with a wicked heart
Are like earthenware covered with silver dross.

24 He who hates, disguises *it* with his lips,
And lays up deceit within himself;
25 ᵃWhen ¹he speaks kindly, do not believe him,
For *there are* seven abominations in his heart;
26 *Though his* hatred is covered by deceit,
His wickedness will be revealed before the assembly.

27 ᵃWhoever digs a pit will fall into it,
And he who rolls a stone will have it roll back on him.

28 A lying tongue hates *those who are* crushed by it,
And a flattering mouth works ᵃruin.

27 Doᵃ not boast about tomorrow,
For you do not know what a day may bring forth.

2 ᵃLet another man praise you, and not your own
mouth;
A stranger, and not your own lips.

3 A stone *is* heavy and sand *is* weighty,
But a fool's wrath *is* heavier than both of them.

4 Wrath *is* cruel and anger a torrent,
But ᵃwho *is* able to stand before jealousy?

5 ᵃOpen rebuke *is* better
Than love carefully concealed.

6 Faithful *are* the wounds of a friend,
But the kisses of an enemy *are* ᵃdeceitful.

7 A satisfied soul ¹loathes the honeycomb,
But to a hungry soul every bitter thing *is* sweet.

8 Like a bird that wanders from its nest
Is a man who wanders from his place.

9 Ointment and perfume delight the heart,
And the sweetness of a man's friend *gives delight* by
¹hearty counsel.

10 Do not forsake your own friend or your father's friend,
Nor go to your brother's house in the day of your
calamity;
ᵃBetter *is* a neighbor nearby than a brother far away.

11 My son, be wise, and make my heart glad,
ᵃThat I may answer him who reproaches me.

12 A prudent *man* foresees evil *and* hides himself;
The simple pass on *and* are ᵃpunished.

13 Take the garment of him who is surety for a stranger,
And hold it in pledge *when* he is surety for a seductress.

26:21
ᵃProv. 15:18

26:25 ᵃPs. 28:3;
Prov. 26:23;
Jer. 9:8

26:27
ᵃEsth. 7:10;
Ps. 7:15;
Prov. 28:10;
Eccl. 10:8

26:28
ᵃProv. 29:5

27:1
ᵃLuke 12:19–21;
James 4:13–16

27:2
ᵃProv. 25:27;
2 Cor. 10:12, 18;
12:11

27:4 ᵃProv. 6:34;
1 John 3:12

27:5
ᵃ[Prov. 28:23];
Gal. 2:14

27:6
ᵃMatt. 26:49

27:10
ᵃProv. 17:17;
18:24

27:11 ᵃProv. 10:1;
23:15–26

27:12 ᵃProv. 22:3

26:22 ¹*gossip* or *slanderer* ²A Jewish tradition *wounds* ³Lit. *rooms of the belly* 26:25 ¹Lit. *his voice is gracious* 27:7 ¹*tramples on* 27:9 ¹Lit. counsel of the soul*

14 He who blesses his friend with a loud voice, rising early
   in the morning,
   It will be counted a curse to him.

15 A ᵃcontinual dripping on a very rainy day
   And a contentious woman are alike;
16 Whoever ¹restrains her restrains the wind,
   And grasps oil with his right hand.

17 *As* iron sharpens iron,
   So a man sharpens the countenance of his friend.

18 ᵃWhoever ¹keeps the fig tree will eat its fruit;
   So he who waits on his master will be honored.

19 As in water face *reflects* face,
   So a man's heart *reveals* the man.

20 ᵃHell¹ and ²Destruction are never full;
   So ᵇthe eyes of man are never satisfied.

21 ᵃThe refining pot *is* for silver and the furnace for gold,
   And a man *is valued* by what others say of him.

22 ᵃThough you grind a fool in a mortar with a pestle along
   with crushed grain,
   Yet his foolishness will not depart from him.

23 Be diligent to know the state of your ᵃflocks,
   And attend to your herds;
24 For riches *are* not forever,
   Nor does a crown *endure* to all generations.
25 ᵃ*When* the hay is removed, and the tender grass shows
   itself,
   And the herbs of the mountains are gathered in,
26 The lambs *will provide* your clothing,
   And the goats the price of a field;
27 *You shall have* enough goats' milk for your food,
   For the food of your household,
   And the nourishment of your maidservants.

28

The ᵃwicked flee when no one pursues,
But the righteous are bold as a lion.

2 Because of the transgression of a land, many *are* its
   princes;
   But by a man of understanding *and* knowledge
   Right will be prolonged.

3 ᵃA poor man who oppresses the poor
   Is like a driving rain ¹which leaves no food.

4 ᵃThose who forsake the law praise the wicked,
   ᵇBut such as keep the law contend with them.

5 ᵃEvil men do not understand justice,
   But ᵇthose who seek the LORD understand all.

6 Better *is* the poor who walks in his integrity
   Than one perverse *in his* ways, though he *be* rich.

7 Whoever keeps the law *is* a discerning son,
   But a companion of gluttons shames his father.

27:15
ᵃProv. 19:13

27:18
ᵃ2 Kin. 18:31;
Song 8:12;
Is. 36:16;
[1 Cor. 3:8;
9:7–13];
2 Tim. 2:6

27:20
ᵃProv. 30:15,
16; Hab. 2:5
ᵇEccl. 1:8; 4:8

27:21 ᵃProv. 17:3

27:22
ᵃProv. 23:35;
26:11; Jer. 5:3

27:23
ᵃProv. 24:27

27:25 ᵃPs. 104:14

28:1
ᵃLev. 26:17, 36;
Ps. 53:5

28:3
ᵃMatt. 18:28

28:4 ᵃPs. 49:18;
Rom. 1:32
ᵇ1 Kin. 18:18;
Neh. 13:11, 15;
Matt. 3:7; 14:4;
Eph. 5:11

28:5 ᵃPs. 92:6;
Is. 6:9; 44:18
ᵇPs. 119:100;
Prov. 2:9;
John 17:17;
1 Cor. 2:15;
[1 John 2:20, 27]

27:16 ¹Lit. *hides* 27:18 ¹*protects* or *tends* 27:20 ¹Or *Sheol* ²Heb.
Abaddon 28:3 ¹Lit. *and there is no bread*

8 One who increases his possessions by usury and extortion
Gathers it for him who will pity the poor.

9 One who turns away his ear from hearing the law,
ᵃEven his prayer *is* an abomination.

10 ᵃWhoever causes the upright to go astray in an evil way,
He himself will fall into his own pit;
ᵇBut the blameless will inherit good.

11 The rich man *is* wise in his own eyes,
But the poor who has understanding searches him out.

12 When the righteous rejoice, *there is* great ᵃglory;
But when the wicked arise, men ¹hide themselves.

13 ᵃHe who covers his sins will not prosper,
But whoever confesses and forsakes *them* will have mercy.

14 Happy *is* the man who is always reverent,
But he who hardens his heart will fall into calamity.

15 ᵃ*Like* a roaring lion and a charging bear
ᵇ*Is* a wicked ruler over poor people.

16 A ruler who lacks understanding *is* a great ᵃoppressor,
But he who hates covetousness will prolong *his* days.

17 ᵃA man burdened with bloodshed will flee into a pit;
Let no one help him.

18 Whoever walks blamelessly will be ¹saved,
But *he who is* perverse *in his* ways will suddenly fall.

19 ᵃHe who tills his land will have plenty of bread,
But he who follows frivolity will have poverty enough!

20 A faithful man will abound with blessings,
ᵃBut he who hastens to be rich will not go unpunished.

21 ᵃTo ¹show partiality *is* not good,
ᵇBecause for a piece of bread a man will transgress.

22 A man with an evil eye hastens after riches,
And does not consider that ᵃpoverty will come upon him.

23 ᵃHe who rebukes a man will find more favor afterward
Than he who flatters with the tongue.

24 Whoever robs his father or his mother,
And says, "*It is* no transgression,"
The same ᵃis companion to a destroyer.

25 ᵃHe who is of a proud heart stirs up strife,
ᵇBut he who trusts in the LORD will be prospered.

26 He who ᵃtrusts in his own heart is a fool,
But whoever walks wisely will be delivered.

27 ᵃHe who gives to the poor will not lack,
But he who hides his eyes will have many curses.

28 When the wicked arise, ᵃmen hide themselves;
But when they perish, the righteous increase.

28:9 ᵃPs. 66:18; 109:7; Prov. 15:8

28:10 ᵃPs. 7:15; Prov. 26:27
ᵇ[Matt. 6:33; Heb. 6:12; 1 Pet. 3:9]

28:12 ᵃProv. 11:10; 29:2

28:13 ᵃPs. 32:3–5; 1 John 1:8–10

28:15 ᵃProv. 19:12; 1 Pet. 5:8 ᵇEx. 1:14; Prov. 29:2; Matt. 2:16

28:16 ᵃEccl. 10:16; Is. 3:12

28:17 ᵃGen. 9:6

28:19 ᵃProv. 12:11; 20:13

28:20 ᵃProv. 13:11; 20:21; 23:4; 1 Tim. 6:9

28:21 ᵃProv. 18:5 ᵇEzek. 13:19

28:22 ᵃProv. 21:5

28:23 ᵃProv. 27:5, 6

28:24 ᵃProv. 18:9

28:25 ᵃProv. 13:10 ᵇProv. 29:25; 1 Tim. 6:6

28:26 ᵃProv. 3:5

28:27 ᵃDeut. 15:7; Prov. 19:17; 22:9

28:28 ᵃJob 24:4

28:12 ¹Lit. *will be searched for*   28:18 ¹*delivered*   28:21 ¹Lit. *recognize faces*

29

He[a] who is often rebuked, *and* hardens *his* neck,
Will suddenly be destroyed, and that without remedy.

2 When the righteous [1]are in authority, the [a]people rejoice;
But when a wicked *man* rules, [b]the people groan.

3 Whoever loves wisdom makes his father rejoice,
But a companion of harlots wastes *his* wealth.

4 The king establishes the land by justice,
But he who receives bribes overthrows it.

5 A man who [a]flatters his neighbor
Spreads a net for his feet.

6 By transgression an evil man is snared,
But the righteous sings and rejoices.

7 The righteous [a]considers the cause of the poor,
But the wicked does not understand *such* knowledge.

8 Scoffers [a]set a city aflame,
But wise *men* turn away wrath.

9 *If* a wise man contends with a foolish man,
[a]Whether *the fool* rages or laughs, *there is* no peace.

10 [a]The bloodthirsty hate the blameless,
But the upright seek his [1]well-being.

11 A fool vents all his [a]feelings,[1]
But a wise *man* holds them back.

12 If a ruler pays attention to lies,
All his servants *become* wicked.

13 The poor *man* and the oppressor have this in common:
[a]The LORD gives light to the eyes of both.

14 The king who judges the [a]poor with truth,
His throne will be established forever.

15 The rod and rebuke give [a]wisdom,
But a child left *to himself* brings shame to his mother.

16 When the wicked are multiplied, transgression increases;
But the righteous will see their [a]fall.

17 Correct your son, and he will give you rest;
Yes, he will give delight to your soul.

18 [a]Where *there is* no [1]revelation, the people cast off restraint;
But [b]happy *is* he who keeps the law.

19 A servant will not be corrected by mere words;
For though he understands, he will not respond.

20 Do you see a man hasty in his words?
[a]*There is* more hope for a fool than for him.

21 He who pampers his servant from childhood
Will have him as a son in the end.

29:1
[a]2 Chr. 36:16;
Prov. 6:15
29:2 [a]Esth. 8:15;
Prov. 28:12
[b]Esth. 4:3
29:5
[a]Prov. 26:28
29:7 [a]Job 29:16;
Ps. 41:1;
Prov. 31:8, 9
29:8 [a]Prov. 11:11
29:9 [a]Matt. 11:17
29:10
[a]Gen. 4:5–8;
1 John 3:12
29:11
[a]Prov. 14:33
29:13
[a][Matt. 5:45]
29:14 [a]Ps. 72:4;
Is. 11:4
29:15
[a]Prov. 22:15
29:16 [a]Ps. 37:34;
Prov. 21:12
29:18
[a]1 Sam. 3:1;
Ps. 74:9;
Amos 8:11, 12
[b]Prov. 8:32;
John 13:17
29:20
[a]Prov. 26:12

29:2 [1]*become great*   29:10 [1]Lit. *soul* or *life*   29:11 [1]Lit. *spirit*
29:18 [1]*prophetic vision*

22 ᵃAn angry man stirs up strife,
And a furious man abounds in transgression.

23 ᵃA man's pride will bring him low,
But the humble in spirit will retain honor.

24 Whoever is a partner with a thief hates his own life;
ᵃHe ¹swears to tell the truth, but reveals nothing.

25 ᵃThe fear of man brings a snare,
But whoever trusts in the LORD shall be ¹safe.

26 ᵃMany seek the ruler's ¹favor,
But justice for man *comes* from the LORD.

27 An unjust man *is* an abomination to the righteous,
And *he who is* upright in the way *is* an abomination to
the wicked.

THE WISDOM OF AGUR

30 The words of Agur the son of Jakeh, *his* utterance. This
man declared to Ithiel—to Ithiel and Ucal:

2 ᵃSurely I *am* more stupid than *any* man,
And do not have the understanding of a man.

3 I neither learned wisdom
Nor have ᵃknowledge of the Holy One.

4 ᵃWho has ascended into heaven, or descended?
ᵇWho has gathered the wind in His fists?
Who has bound the waters in a garment?
Who has established all the ends of the earth?
What *is* His name, and what *is* His Son's name,
If you know?

5 ᵃEvery word of God *is* ¹pure;
ᵇHe *is* a shield to those who put their trust in Him.

6 ᵃDo not add to His words,
Lest He rebuke you, and you be found a liar.

7 Two *things* I request of You
(Deprive me not before I die):

8 Remove falsehood and lies far from me;
Give me neither poverty nor riches—
ᵃFeed me with the food allotted to me;

9 ᵃLest I be full and deny *You,*
And say, "Who *is* the LORD?"
Or lest I be poor and steal,
And profane the name of my God.

10 Do not malign a servant to his master,
Lest he curse you, and you be found guilty.

11 *There is* a generation *that* curses its ᵃfather,
And does not bless its mother.

12 *There is* a generation ᵃ*that is* pure in its own eyes,
Yet *is* not washed from its filthiness.

13 *There is* a generation—oh, how ᵃlofty are their eyes!
And their eyelids are ¹lifted up.

14 ᵃ*There is* a generation whose teeth *are like* swords,
And whose fangs *are like* knives,

29:22
ᵃProv. 26:21

29:23
ᵃJob 22:29;
Prov. 15:33;
18:12; Is. 66:2;
Dan. 4:30;
Matt. 23:12;
Luke 14:11; 18:14;
Acts 12:23;
[James 4:6–10;
1 Pet. 5:5, 6]

29:24 ᵃLev. 5:1

29:25
ᵃGen. 12:12; 20:2;
Luke 12:4;
John 12:42, 43

29:26 ᵃPs. 20:9

30:2 ᵃPs. 73:22;
Prov. 12:1

30:3
ᵃ[Prov. 9:10]

30:4 ᵃ[Ps. 68:18;
John 3:13]
ᵇJob 38:4;
Ps. 104:3;
Is. 40:12

30:5 ᵃPs. 12:6;
19:8; 119:140
ᵇPs. 18:30; 84:11;
115:9–11

30:6 ᵃDeut. 4:2;
12:32; Rev. 22:18

30:8 ᵃJob 23:12;
Matt. 6:11;
[Phil. 4:19]

30:9
ᵃDeut. 8:12–14;
Neh. 9:25, 26;
Hos. 13:6

30:11 ᵃEx. 21:17;
Prov. 20:20

30:12
ᵃ[Prov. 16:2];
Is. 65:5;
Luke 18:11;
[Titus 1:15, 16]

30:13 ᵃPs. 131:1;
Prov. 6:17;
Is. 2:11; 5:15

30:14
ᵃJob 29:17;
Ps. 52:2

29:24 ¹Lit. *hears the adjuration* or *oath*   29:25 ¹*secure,* lit. *set on high*
29:26 ¹Lit. *face*   30:5 ¹*tested, refined, found pure*   30:13 ¹In arrogance

bTo devour the poor from off the earth,
And the needy from *among* men.

15 The leech has two daughters—
Give *and* Give!

There are three *things that* are never satisfied,
Four never say, "Enough!":
16 aThe¹ grave,
The barren womb,
The earth *that* is not satisfied with water—
And the fire never says, "Enough!"

17 aThe eye *that* mocks *his* father,
And scorns obedience to *his* mother,
The ravens of the valley will pick it out,
And the young eagles will eat it.

18 There are three *things which* are too wonderful
for me,
Yes, four *which* I do not understand:
19 The way of an eagle in the air,
The way of a serpent on a rock,
The way of a ship in the ¹midst of the sea,
And the way of a man with a virgin.

20 This *is* the way of an adulterous woman:
She eats and wipes her mouth,
And says, "I have done no wickedness."

21 For three *things* the earth is perturbed,
Yes, for four it cannot bear up:
22 aFor a servant when he reigns,
A fool when he is filled with food,
23 A ¹hateful *woman* when she is married,
And a maidservant who succeeds her mistress.

24 There are four *things which* are little on the earth,
But they *are* exceedingly wise:
25 aThe ants *are* a people not strong,
Yet they prepare their food in the summer;
26 aThe ¹rock badgers are a feeble folk,
Yet they make their homes in the crags;
27 The locusts have no king,
Yet they all advance in ranks;
28 The ¹spider skillfully grasps with its hands,
And it is in kings' palaces.

29 There are three *things which* are majestic in pace,
Yes, four *which* are stately in walk:
30 A lion, *which is* mighty among beasts
And does not turn away from any;
31 A ¹greyhound,
A male goat also,
And ²a king *whose* troops *are* with him.

32 If you have been foolish in exalting yourself,
Or if you have devised evil, a*put your* hand on *your*
mouth.

30:14 bPs. 14:4;
Amos 8:4

30:16
aProv. 27:20;
Hab. 2:5

30:17
aGen. 9:22;
Lev. 20:9;
Prov. 20:20

30:22
aProv. 19:10;
Eccl. 10:7

30:25 aProv. 6:6

30:26 aLev. 11:5;
Ps. 104:18

30:32
aJob 21:5; 40:4;
Mic. 7:16

30:16 ¹Or *Sheol*   30:19 ¹Lit. *heart*   30:23 ¹Or *hated*   30:26 ¹*rock hyraxes*
30:28 ¹Or *lizard*   30:31 ¹Or perhaps *strutting rooster*, lit. *girded of waist*
²A Jewish tradition *a king against whom there is no uprising*

33 For *as* the churning of milk produces butter,
And wringing the nose produces blood,
So the forcing of wrath produces strife.

THE WORDS OF KING LEMUEL'S MOTHER

31 The words of King Lemuel, the utterance which his mother taught him:

2 What, my son?
And what, son of my womb?
And what, [a]son of my vows?
3 [a]Do not give your strength to women,
Nor your ways [b]to that which destroys kings.

4 [a]*It is* not for kings, O Lemuel,
It is not for kings to drink wine,
Nor for princes intoxicating drink;
5 [a]Lest they drink and forget the law,
And pervert the justice of all [1]the afflicted.
6 [a]Give strong drink to him who is perishing,
And wine to those who are bitter of heart.
7 Let him drink and forget his poverty,
And remember his misery no more.

8 [a]Open your mouth for the speechless,
In the cause of all *who are* [1]appointed to die.
9 Open your mouth, [a]judge righteously,
And [b]plead the cause of the poor and needy.

THE VIRTUOUS WIFE

10 [a]Who[1] can find a [2]virtuous wife?
For her worth *is* far above rubies.
11 The heart of her husband safely trusts her;
So he will have no lack of gain.
12 She does him good and not evil
All the days of her life.
13 She seeks wool and flax,
And willingly works with her hands.
14 She is like the merchant ships,
She brings her food from afar.
15 [a]She also rises while it is yet night,
And [b]provides food for her household,
And a portion for her maidservants.
16 She considers a field and buys it;
From [1]her profits she plants a vineyard.
17 She girds herself with strength,
And strengthens her arms.
18 She perceives that her merchandise *is* good,
And her lamp does not go out by night.
19 She stretches out her hands to the distaff,
And her hand holds the spindle.
20 [a]She extends her hand to the poor,
Yes, she reaches out her hands to the needy.
21 She is not afraid of snow for her household,
For all her household *is* clothed with scarlet.

31:2 [a]Is. 49:15
31:3 [a]Prov. 5:9
[b]Deut. 17:17;
1 Kin. 11:1;
Neh. 13:26;
Prov. 7:26;
Hos. 4:11
31:4 [a]Eccl. 10:17
31:5 [a]Hos. 4:11
31:6 [a]Ps. 104:15
31:8
[a]Job 29:15, 16;
Ps. 82
31:9 [a]Lev. 19:15;
Deut. 1:16
[b]Job 29:12;
Is. 1:17; Jer. 22:16
31:10 [a]Ruth 3:11;
Prov. 12:4; 19:14
31:15
[a]Prov. 20:13;
Rom. 12:11
[b]Luke 12:42
31:20
[a]Deut. 15:11;
Job 31:16–20;
Prov. 22:9;
Rom. 12:13;
Eph. 4:28;
Heb. 13:16

31:5 [1]Lit. *sons of affliction*   31:8 [1]Lit. *sons of passing away*   31:10 [1]Vv. 10–31 are an alphabetic acrostic in Hebrew; cf. Ps. 119   [2]Lit. *a wife of valor*, in the sense of all forms of excellence   31:16 [1]Lit. *the fruit of her hands*

22 She makes tapestry for herself;
    Her clothing *is* fine linen and purple.
23 aHer husband is known in the gates,
    When he sits among the elders of the land.
24 She makes linen garments and sells *them*,
    And supplies sashes for the merchants.
25 Strength and honor *are* her clothing;
    She shall rejoice in time to come.
26 She opens her mouth with wisdom,
    And on her tongue *is* the law of kindness.
27 She watches over the ways of her household,
    And does not eat the bread of idleness.
28 Her children rise up and call her blessed;
    Her husband *also*, and he praises her:
29 "Many daughters have done well,
    But you excel them all."
30 Charm *is* deceitful and beauty *is* passing,
    But a woman *who* fears the Lord, she shall be praised.
31 Give her of the fruit of her hands,
    And let her own works praise her in the gates.

31:23 aProv. 12:4

THE BOOK OF
ECCLESIASTES

THE VANITY OF LIFE

1 The words of the Preacher, the son of David, ᵃking in Jerusalem.

2 "Vanityᵃ¹ of vanities," says the Preacher;
   "Vanity of vanities, ᵇall *is* vanity."

3 ᵃWhat profit has a man from all his labor
   In which he ¹toils under the sun?
4 *One* generation passes away, and *another* generation comes;
   ᵃBut the earth abides forever.
5 ᵃThe sun also rises, and the sun goes down,
   And ¹hastens to the place where it arose.
6 ᵃThe wind goes toward the south,
   And turns around to the north;
   The wind whirls about continually,
   And comes again on its circuit.
7 ᵃAll the rivers run into the sea,
   Yet the sea *is* not full;
   To the place from which the rivers come,
   There they return again.
8 All things *are* ¹full of labor;
   Man cannot express *it.*
   ᵃThe eye is not satisfied with seeing,
   Nor the ear filled with hearing.

9 ᵃThat which has been *is* what will be,
   That which *is* done is what will be done,
   And *there is* nothing new under the sun.
10 Is there anything of which it may be said,
   "See, this *is* new"?
   It has already been in ancient times before us.
11 *There is* ᵃno remembrance of former *things,*
   Nor will there be any remembrance of *things* that are to come
   By *those* who will come after.

THE GRIEF OF WISDOM

12I, the Preacher, was king over Israel in Jerusalem. 13And I set my heart to seek and ᵃsearch out by wisdom concerning all that is done under heaven; ᵇthis burdensome task God has given to the sons of man, by which they may be ¹exercised. 14I have seen all the works that are done under the sun; and indeed, all *is* vanity and grasping for the wind.

15 ᵃ*What is* crooked cannot be made straight,
   And what is lacking cannot be numbered.

1:1 ᵃProv. 1:1
1:2
ᵃPs. 39:5, 6;
62:9; 144:4;
Eccl. 12:8
ᵇ[Rom. 8:20, 21]
1:3
ᵃEccl. 2:22; 3:9
1:4 ᵃPs. 104:5;
119:90
1:5 ᵃPs. 19:4–6
1:6 ᵃEccl. 11:5;
John 3:8
1:7
ᵃ[Ps. 104:8, 9;
Jer. 5:22]
1:8 ᵃProv. 27:20;
Eccl. 4:8
1:9 ᵃEccl. 3:15
1:11 ᵃEccl. 2:16
1:13 ᵃ[Eccl. 7:25;
8:16, 17]
ᵇGen. 3:19;
Eccl. 3:10
1:15 ᵃEccl. 7:13

1:2 ¹Or *Absurdity, Frustration, Futility, Nonsense;* and so throughout the book
1:3 ¹labors   1:5 ¹Is eager for, lit. *panting*   1:8 ¹*wearisome*   1:13 ¹Or *afflicted*

16I communed with my heart, saying, "Look, I have attained greatness, and have gained amore wisdom than all who were before me in Jerusalem. My heart has 1understood great wisdom and knowledge." 17aAnd I set my heart to know wisdom and to know madness and folly. I perceived that this also is grasping for the wind.

18 For ain much wisdom *is* much grief,
And he who increases knowledge increases sorrow.

THE VANITY OF PLEASURE
(cf. 1 Kin. 4:20–28)

2 I said ain my heart, "Come now, I will test you with bmirth; 1therefore enjoy pleasure"; but surely, cthis also *was* vanity. 2I said of laughter—"Madness!"; and of mirth, "What does it accomplish?" 3aI searched in my heart *how* 1to gratify my flesh with wine, while guiding my heart with wisdom, and how to lay hold on folly, till I might see what *was* bgood for the sons of men to do under heaven all the days of their lives.

4I made my works great, I built myself ahouses, and planted myself vineyards. 5I made myself gardens and orchards, and I planted all *kinds* of fruit trees in them. 6I made myself water pools from which to 1water the growing trees of the grove. 7I acquired male and female servants, and had 1servants born in my house. Yes, I had greater possessions of herds and flocks than all who were in Jerusalem before me. 8aI also gathered for myself silver and gold and the special treasures of kings and of the provinces. I acquired male and female singers, the delights of the sons of men, *and* 1musical instruments of all kinds.

9aSo I became great and 1excelled bmore than all who were before me in Jerusalem. Also my wisdom remained with me.

10 Whatever my eyes desired I did not keep from them.
I did not withhold my heart from any pleasure,
For my heart rejoiced in all my labor;
And athis was my 1reward from all my labor.
11 Then I looked on all the works that my hands had done
And on the labor in which I had toiled;
And indeed all *was* avanity and grasping for the wind.
There was no profit under the sun.

THE END OF THE WISE AND THE FOOL

12 Then I turned myself to consider wisdom aand madness
and folly;
For what *can* the man *do* who succeeds the king?—
Only what he has already bdone.
13 Then I saw that wisdom aexcels folly
As light excels darkness.
14 aThe wise man's eyes *are* in his head,
But the fool walks in darkness.
Yet I myself perceived
That bthe same event happens to them all.

1:16
a1 Kin. 3:12, 13;
Eccl. 2:9
1:17 aEccl. 2:3,
12; 7:23, 25;
[1 Thess. 5:21]
1:18 aEccl. 12:12
2:1 aLuke 12:19
bProv. 14:13;
[Eccl. 7:4; 8:15]
cEccl. 1:2
2:3 aEccl. 1:17
b[Eccl. 3:12, 13;
5:18; 6:12]
2:4 a1 Kin. 7:1–12
2:8 a1 Kin. 9:28;
10:10, 14, 21
2:9 aEccl. 1:16
b2 Chr. 9:22
2:10 aEccl. 3:22;
5:18; 9:9
2:11 aEccl. 1:3, 14
2:12 aEccl. 1:17;
7:25 bEccl. 1:9
2:13 aEccl. 7:11,
14, 19; 9:18;
10:10
2:14
aProv. 17:24;
Eccl. 8:1
bPs. 49:10;
Eccl. 9:2, 3, 11

1:16 1Lit. *seen*   2:1 1*gladness*   2:3 1Lit. *to draw my flesh*   2:6 1*irrigate*
2:7 1Lit. *sons of my house*   2:8 1Exact meaning unknown   2:9 1Lit.
increased   2:10 1Lit. *portion*

15 So I said in my heart,
"As it happens to the fool,
It also happens to me,
And why was I then more wise?"
Then I said in my heart,
"This also *is* vanity."
16 For *there is* [a]no more remembrance of the wise than of
the fool forever,
Since all that now *is* will be forgotten in the days to come.
And how does a wise *man* die?
As the fool!

17Therefore I hated life because the work that was done under
the sun *was* distressing to me, for all *is* vanity and grasping
for the wind.

18Then I hated all my labor in which I had toiled under the
sun, because [a]I must leave it to the man who will come after
me. 19And who knows whether he will be wise or a fool? Yet
he will rule over all my labor in which I toiled and in which
I have shown myself wise under the sun. This also *is* vanity.
20Therefore I turned my heart and despaired of all the labor in which I had toiled under the sun. 21For there is a man
whose labor *is* with wisdom, knowledge, and skill; yet he must
leave his [1]heritage to a man who has not labored for it. This
also *is* vanity and a great evil. 22[a]For what has man for all his
labor, and for the striving of his heart with which he has toiled
under the sun? 23For all his days *are* [a]sorrowful, and his work
burdensome; even in the night his heart takes no rest. This
also is vanity.

24[a]Nothing *is* better for a man *than* that he should eat
and drink, and *that* his soul should enjoy good in his labor.
This also, I saw, was from the hand of God. 25For who can eat,
or who can have enjoyment, [1]more than I? 26For *God* gives
[a]wisdom and knowledge and joy to a man who *is* good in His
sight; but to the sinner He gives the work of gathering and
collecting, that [b]he may give to *him who is* good before God.
This also *is* vanity and grasping for the wind.

EVERYTHING HAS ITS TIME

3 To everything *there is* a season,
A [a]time for every purpose under heaven:

2 A time [1]to be born,
And [a]a time to die;
A time to plant,
And a time to pluck *what is* planted;
3 A time to kill,
And a time to heal;
A time to break down,
And a time to build up;
4 A time to [a]weep,
And a time to laugh;
A time to mourn,
And a time to dance;
5 A time to cast away stones,
And a time to gather stones;

2:16
[a]Eccl. 1:11; 4:16
2:18 [a]Ps. 49:10
2:22
[a]Eccl. 1:3; 3:9
2:23
[a]Job 5:7; 14:1
2:24
[a]Eccl. 3:12, 13,
22; Is. 56:12;
Luke 12:19;
1 Cor. 15:32;
[1 Tim. 6:17]
2:26 [a]Job 32:8;
Prov. 2:6;
James 1:5
[b]Job 27:16, 17;
Prov. 28:8
3:1
[a]Eccl. 3:17; 8:6
3:2 [a]Job 14:5;
Heb. 9:27
3:4 [a]Rom. 12:15

2:21 [1]Lit. *portion*   2:25 [1]So with MT, Tg., Vg.; some Heb. mss., LXX, Syr.
without Him   3:2 [1]Lit. *to bear*

^aA time to embrace,
  And a time to refrain from embracing;
6 A time to gain,
  And a time to lose;
  A time to keep,
  And a time to throw away;
7 A time to tear,
  And a time to sew;
  ^aA time to keep silence,
  And a time to ^bspeak;
8 A time to love,
  And a time to ^ahate;
  A time of war,
  And a time of peace.

THE GOD-GIVEN TASK

^{9a}What profit has the worker from that in which he labors? ^{10a}I have seen the God-given task with which the sons of men are to be occupied. ¹¹He has made everything beautiful in its time. Also He has put eternity in their hearts, except that ^ano one can find out the work that God does from beginning to end.

¹²I know that nothing *is* ^abetter for them than to rejoice, and to do good in their lives, ¹³and also that ^aevery man should eat and drink and enjoy the good of all his labor—it *is* the gift of God.

14 I know that whatever God does,
  It shall be forever.
  ^aNothing can be added to it,
  And nothing taken from it.
  God does *it,* that men should fear before Him.
15 ^aThat which is has already been;
  And what is to be has already been;
  And God ¹requires an account of ²what is past.

INJUSTICE SEEMS TO PREVAIL

¹⁶Moreover ^aI saw under the sun:

In the place of ¹judgment,
  Wickedness *was* there;
  And *in* the place of righteousness,
  ²Iniquity *was* there.

¹⁷I said in my heart,

^a"God shall judge the righteous and the wicked,
  For *there is* a time there for every ¹purpose and for every
    work."

¹⁸I said in my heart, "Concerning the condition of the sons of men, God tests them, that they may see that they themselves are *like* animals." ^{19a}For what happens to the sons of men also happens to animals; one thing befalls them: as one dies, so dies the other. Surely, they all have one breath; man has no advantage over animals, for all *is* vanity. ²⁰All go to one place: ^aall are from the dust, and all return to dust. ^{21a}Who¹ knows the spirit of the sons of men, which goes upward, and

---

3:5 ^aJoel 2:16;
1 Cor. 7:5

3:7 ^aAmos 5:13
^bProv. 25:11

3:8 ^aProv. 13:5;
Luke 14:26

3:9 ^aEccl. 1:3

3:10 ^aEccl. 1:13

3:11 ^aJob 5:9;
Eccl. 7:23; 8:17;
Rom. 11:33

3:12
^aEccl. 2:3, 24

3:13 ^aEccl. 2:24

3:14 ^aJames 1:17

3:15 ^aEccl. 1:9

3:16 ^aEccl. 5:8

3:17 ^aGen. 18:25;
Ps. 96:13;
Eccl. 11:9;
[Matt. 16:27;
Rom. 2:6–10;
2 Cor. 5:10;
2 Thess. 1:6–9]

3:19
^aPs. 49:12, 20;
73:22;
[Eccl. 2:16]

3:20 ^aGen. 3:19;
Ps. 103:14

3:21 ^aEccl. 12:7

3:15 ¹Lit. *seeks*   ²*what is pursued*   3:16 ¹*justice*   ²*Wickedness*
3:17 ¹*desire*   3:21 ¹LXX, Syr., Tg., Vg. *Who knows whether the spirit . . . goes upward, and whether . . . goes downward to the earth?*

the spirit of the animal, which goes down to the earth? ^{22a}So
I perceived that nothing *is* better than that a man should re-
joice in his own works, for ^bthat *is* his ¹heritage. ^cFor who can
bring him to see what will happen after him?

4 Then I returned and considered all the ^aoppression that
is done under the sun:

> And look! The tears of the oppressed,
> But they have no comforter—
> ¹On the side of their oppressors *there is* power,
> But they have no comforter.

2 ^aTherefore I praised the dead who were already dead,
More than the living who are still alive.

3 ^aYet, better than both *is he* who has never existed,
Who has not seen the evil work that is done under the sun.

THE VANITY OF SELFISH TOIL

⁴Again, I saw that for all toil and every skillful work a man
is envied by his neighbor. This also *is* vanity and grasping for
the wind.

5 ^aThe fool folds his hands
And consumes his own flesh.

6 ^aBetter a handful *with* quietness
Than both hands full, *together with* toil and grasping for
the wind.

⁷Then I returned, and I saw vanity under the sun:

8 There is one alone, without ¹companion:
He has neither son nor brother.
Yet *there is* no end to all his labors,
Nor is his ^aeye satisfied with riches.
But ^b*he never asks,*
"For whom do I toil and deprive myself of ^cgood?"
This also *is* vanity and a ²grave misfortune.

THE VALUE OF A FRIEND

9 Two *are* better than one,
Because they have a good reward for their labor.

10 For if they fall, one will lift up his companion.
But woe to him *who is* alone when he falls,
For *he has* no one to help him up.

11 Again, if two lie down together, they will keep warm;
But how can one be warm *alone?*

12 Though one may be overpowered by another, two can
withstand him.
And a threefold cord is not quickly broken.

POPULARITY PASSES AWAY

13 Better a poor and wise youth
Than an old and foolish king who will be admonished no
more.

14 For he comes out of prison to be king,
Although ¹he was born poor in his kingdom.

15 I saw all the living who walk under the sun;
They were with the second youth who stands in his place.

3:22 ^aEccl. 2:24;
5:18 ^bEccl. 2:10
^cEccl. 6:12; 8:7

4:1 ^aJob 35:9;
Ps. 12:5;
Eccl. 3:16; 5:8;
Is. 5:7

4:2 ^aJob 3:17, 18

4:3
^aJob 3:11–22;
Eccl. 6:3;
Luke 23:29

4:5 ^aProv. 6:10;
24:33

4:6 ^aProv. 15:16,
17; 16:8

4:8 ^aProv. 27:20;
Eccl. 5:10;
[1 John 2:16]
^bPs. 39:6
^cEccl. 2:18–21

3:22 ¹*portion* or *lot* 4:1 ¹Lit. *At the hand* 4:8 ¹Lit. *a second* ²Lit. *evil task*
4:14 ¹*The youth*

16 *There was* no end of all the people [1]over whom he was
    made king;
  Yet those who come afterward will not rejoice in him.
  Surely this also *is* vanity and grasping for the wind.

FEAR GOD, KEEP YOUR VOWS

5 Walk [a]prudently when you go to the house of God; and
draw near to hear rather [b]than to give the sacrifice of
fools, for they do not know that they do evil.

2   Do not be [a]rash with your mouth,
  And let not your heart utter anything hastily before God.
  For God *is* in heaven, and you on earth;
  Therefore let your words [b]be few.
3   For a dream comes through much activity,
  And [a]a fool's voice *is known* by *his* many words.

4   [a]When you make a vow to God, do not delay to [b]pay it;
  For *He has* no pleasure in fools.
  Pay what you have vowed—
5   [a]Better not to vow than to vow and not pay.

6Do not let your [a]mouth cause your flesh to sin, [b]nor say before the messenger *of God* that it *was* an error. Why should
God be angry at your [1]excuse and destroy the work of your
hands? 7For in the multitude of dreams and many words *there
is* also vanity. But [a]fear God.

THE VANITY OF GAIN AND HONOR

8If you [a]see the oppression of the poor, and the violent
[1]perversion of justice and righteousness in a province, do not
marvel at the matter; for [b]high official watches over high official, and higher officials are over them.
9Moreover the profit of the land is for all; *even* the king is
served from the field.

10   He who loves silver will not be satisfied with silver;
  Nor he who loves abundance, with increase.
  This also *is* vanity.

11   When goods increase,
  They increase who eat them;
  So what profit have the owners
  Except to see *them* with their eyes?

12   The sleep of a laboring man *is* sweet,
  Whether he eats little or much;
  But the abundance of the rich will not permit him to
    sleep.

13   [a]There is a severe evil *which* I have seen under the sun:
  Riches kept for their owner to his hurt.
14   But those riches perish through [1]misfortune;
  When he begets a son, *there is* nothing in his hand.
15   [a]As he came from his mother's womb, naked shall he
    return,
  To go as he came;
  And he shall take nothing from his labor
  Which he may carry away in his hand.

5:1 [a]Ex. 3:5;
Is. 1:12
[b][1 Sam. 15:22];
Ps. 50:8;
Prov. 15:8; 21:27;
[Hos. 6:6]

5:2 [a]Prov. 20:25
[b]Prov. 10:19;
Matt. 6:7

5:3 [a]Prov. 10:19

5:4 [a]Num. 30:2;
Deut. 23:21–23;
Ps. 50:14; 76:11
[b]Ps. 66:13, 14

5:5 [a]Prov. 20:25;
Acts 5:4

5:6 [a]Prov. 6:2
[b]1 Cor. 11:10

5:7 [a][Eccl. 12:13]

5:8 [a]Eccl. 3:16
[b][Ps. 12:5; 58:11;
82:1]

5:13 [a]Eccl. 6:1, 2

5:15 [a]Job 1:21;
Ps. 49:17;
1 Tim. 6:7

4:16 [1]Lit. *to all before whom he was to be*   5:6 [1]Lit. *voice*   5:8 [1]*wresting*
5:14 [1]Lit. *bad business*

16 And this also *is* a severe evil—
   Just exactly as he came, so shall he go.
   And [a]what profit has he [b]who has labored for the wind?
17 All his days [a]he also eats in darkness,
   And *he has* much sorrow and sickness and anger.

18Here is what I have seen: [a]*It is* good and fitting *for one* to eat and drink, and to enjoy the good of all his labor in which he toils under the sun all the days of his life which God gives him; [b]for it *is* his [1]heritage. 19As for [a]every man to whom God has given riches and wealth, and given him power to eat of it, to receive his [1]heritage and rejoice in his labor—this *is* the [b]gift of God. 20For he will not dwell unduly on the days of his life, because God keeps *him* busy with the joy of his heart.

6 There[a] is an evil which I have seen under the sun, and it *is* common among men: 2A man to whom God has given riches and wealth and honor, [a]so that he lacks nothing for himself of all he desires; [b]yet God does not give him power to eat of it, but a foreigner consumes it. This *is* vanity, and it *is* an evil [1]affliction.

3If a man begets a hundred *children* and lives many years, so that the days of his years are many, but his soul is not satisfied with goodness, or [a]indeed he has no burial, I say *that* [b]a [1]stillborn child *is* better than he— 4for it comes in vanity and departs in darkness, and its name is covered with darkness. 5Though it has not seen the sun or known *anything,* this has more rest than that man, 6even if he lives a thousand years twice—but has not seen goodness. Do not all go to one [a]place?

7 [a]All the labor of man *is* for his mouth,
   And yet the soul is not satisfied.
8 For what more has the wise *man* than the fool?
   What does the poor man have,
   Who knows *how* to walk before the living?
9 Better *is* [1]the [a]sight of the eyes than the wandering of
      [2]desire.
   This also *is* vanity and grasping for the wind.

10 Whatever one is, he has been named [a]already,
   For it is known that he *is* man;
   [b]And he cannot contend with Him who is mightier
      than he.
11 Since there are many things that increase vanity,
   How *is* man the better?

12For who knows what *is* good for man in life, [1]all the days of his [2]vain life which he passes like [a]a shadow? [b]Who can tell a man what will happen after him under the sun?

THE VALUE OF PRACTICAL WISDOM

7 A [a]good name *is* better than precious ointment,
   And the day of death than the day of one's [b]birth;
2 Better to go to the house of mourning
   Than to go to the house of feasting,
   For that *is* the end of all men;
   And the living will take *it* to [a]heart.

5:16 [a]Eccl. 1:3
[b]Prov. 11:29

5:17 [a]Ps. 127:2

5:18 [a]Eccl. 2:24;
3:12, 13;
[1 Tim. 6:17]
[b]Eccl. 2:10; 3:22

5:19 [a][Eccl. 6:2]
[b]Eccl. 2:24; 3:13

6:1 [a]Eccl. 5:13

6:2 [a]Job 21:10;
Ps. 17:14; 73:7
[b]Luke 12:20

6:3 [a]2 Kin. 9:35;
Is. 14:19, 20;
Jer. 22:19
[b]Job 3:16;
Ps. 58:8;
Eccl. 4:3

6:6
[a]Eccl. 2:14, 15

6:7 [a]Prov. 16:26

6:9 [a]Eccl. 11:9

6:10 [a]Eccl. 1:9;
3:15 [b]Job 9:32;
Is. 45:9;
Jer. 49:19

6:12 [a]Ps. 102:11;
James 4:14
[b]Ps. 39:6;
Eccl. 3:22

7:1 [a]Prov. 22:1
[b]Eccl. 4:2

7:2 [a][Ps. 90:12]

5:18 [1]Lit. *portion*   5:19 [1]Lit. *portion*   6:2 [1]*disease*   6:3 [1]Or *miscarriage*
6:9 [1]What the eyes see   [2]Lit. *soul*   6:12 [1]Lit. *the number of the days*
[2]*futile*

3 ¹Sorrow *is* better than laughter,
　ᵃFor by a sad countenance the heart is made ²better.
4 　The heart of the wise *is* in the house of mourning,
　　But the heart of fools *is* in the house of mirth.
5 　ᵃ*It is* better to ¹hear the rebuke of the wise
　　Than for a man to hear the song of fools.
6 　ᵃFor like the ¹crackling of thorns under a pot,
　　So *is* the laughter of the fool.
　　This also is vanity.
7 　Surely oppression destroys a wise *man's* reason,
　　ᵃAnd a bribe ¹debases the heart.

8 　The end of a thing *is* better than its beginning;
　　ᵃThe patient in spirit *is* better than the proud in spirit.
9 　ᵃDo not hasten in your spirit to be angry,
　　For anger rests in the bosom of fools.
10 　Do not say,
　　"Why were the former days better than these?"
　　For you do not inquire wisely concerning this.

11 　Wisdom *is* good with an inheritance,
　　And profitable ᵃto those who see the sun.
12 　For wisdom *is* ¹a ᵃdefense *as* money *is* a defense,
　　But the ²excellence of knowledge *is that* wisdom gives
　　ᵇlife to those who have it.

13 　Consider the work of God;
　　For ᵃwho can make straight what He has made
　　crooked?
14 　ᵃIn the day of prosperity be joyful,
　　But in the day of adversity consider:
　　Surely God has appointed the one ¹as well as the other,
　　So that man can find out nothing *that will come* after
　　him.

15 I have seen everything in my days of vanity:

　　ᵃThere is a just *man* who perishes in his righteousness,
　　And there is a wicked *man* who prolongs *life* in his
　　wickedness.

16 　ᵃDo not be overly righteous,
　　ᵇNor be overly wise:
　　Why should you destroy yourself?
17 　Do not be overly wicked,
　　Nor be foolish:
　　ᵃWhy should you die before your time?
18 　*It is* good that you grasp this,
　　And also not remove your hand from the other;
　　For he who ᵃfears God will ¹escape them all.

19 　ᵃWisdom strengthens the wise
　　More than ten rulers of the city.

20 　ᵃFor *there is* not a just man on earth who does good
　　And does not sin.

21 　Also do not take to heart everything people say,
　　Lest you hear your servant cursing you.

7:3 ᵃ[2 Cor. 7:10]
7:5 ᵃPs. 141:5;
[Prov. 13:18;
15:31, 32]
7:6 ᵃEccl. 2:2
7:7 ᵃEx. 23:8;
Deut. 16:19;
[Prov. 17:8, 23]
7:8 ᵃProv. 14:29;
Gal. 5:22;
Eph. 4:2
7:9 ᵃProv. 14:17;
James 1:19
7:11 ᵃEccl. 11:7
7:12 ᵃEccl. 9:18
ᵇProv. 3:18
7:13 ᵃJob 12:14
7:14
ᵃDeut. 28:47
7:15
ᵃEccl. 8:12–14
7:16
ᵃProv. 25:16;
Phil. 3:6
ᵇRom. 12:3
7:17 ᵃJob 15:32;
Ps. 55:23
7:18 ᵃEccl. 3:14;
5:7; 8:12, 13
7:19
ᵃProv. 21:22;
Eccl. 9:13–18
7:20
ᵃ1 Kin. 8:46;
2 Chr. 6:36;
Prov. 20:9;
Rom. 3:23;
1 John 1:8

7:3 ¹*Vexation* or *Grief* ²*well* or *pleasing*　7:5 ¹*listen to*　7:6 ¹Lit. *sound*
7:7 ¹*destroys*　7:12 ¹A protective shade, lit. *shadow* ²*advantage* or *profit*
7:14 ¹*alongside*　7:18 ¹Lit. *come forth from all of them*

22 For many times, also, your own heart has known
   That even you have cursed others.
23 All this I have ¹proved by wisdom.
   ªI said, "I will be wise";
   But it *was* far from me.
24 ªAs for that which is far off and ᵇexceedingly deep,
   Who can find it out?
25 ªI applied my heart to know,
   To search and seek out wisdom and the reason *of
      things,*
   To know the wickedness of folly,
   Even of foolishness *and* madness.
26 ªAnd I find more bitter than death
   The woman whose heart *is* snares and nets,
   Whose hands *are* fetters.
   ¹He who pleases God shall escape from her,
   But the sinner shall be trapped by her.
27 "Here is what I have found," says ªthe Preacher,
   "*Adding* one thing to the other to find out the reason,
28 Which my soul still seeks but I cannot find:
   ªOne man among a thousand I have found,
   But a woman among all these I have not found.
29 Truly, this only I have found:
   ªThat God made man upright,
   But ᵇthey have sought out many schemes."

8 Who *is* like a wise *man?*
   And who knows the interpretation of a thing?
   ªA man's wisdom makes his face shine,
   And ᵇthe ¹sternness of his face is changed.

OBEY AUTHORITIES FOR GOD'S SAKE

2I *say,* "Keep the king's commandment ªfor the sake of your oath to God. 3ªDo not be hasty to go from his presence. Do not take your stand for an evil thing, for he does whatever pleases him."

4 Where the word of a king *is, there is* power;
   And ªwho may say to him, "What are you doing?"
5 He who keeps his command will experience nothing
      harmful;
   And a wise man's heart ¹discerns both time and
      judgment,
6 Because ªfor every matter there is a time and
      judgment,
   Though the misery of man ¹increases greatly.
7 ªFor he does not know what will happen;
   So who can tell him when it will occur?
8 ªNo one has power over the spirit to retain the spirit,
   And no one has power in the day of death.
   There is ᵇno release from that war,
   And wickedness will not deliver those who are given to it.

9All this I have seen, and applied my heart to every work that is done under the sun: *There is* a time in which one man rules over another to his own hurt.

7:23 ªRom. 1:22

7:24 ªJob 28:12;
1 Tim. 6:16
ᵇRom. 11:33

7:25 ªEccl. 1:17

7:26
ªProv. 5:3, 4

7:27 ªEccl. 1:1, 2

7:28 ªJob 33:23

7:29 ªGen. 1:27
ᵇGen. 3:6, 7

8:1
ªProv. 4:8, 9;
Acts 6:15
ᵇDeut. 28:50

8:2 ªEx. 22:11;
2 Sam. 21:7;
1 Chr. 29:24;
Ezek. 17:18;
[Rom. 13:5]

8:3 ªEccl. 10:4

8:4
ª1 Sam. 13:11, 13;
Job 34:18

8:6 ªEccl. 3:1, 17

8:7 ªProv. 24:22;
Eccl. 6:12

8:8
ªPs. 49:6, 7;
Job 14:5
ᵇDeut. 20:5–8

7:23 ¹tested   7:26 ¹Lit. *He who is good before God*   8:1 ¹Lit. *strength*
8:5 ¹Lit. *knows*   8:6 ¹*is great upon him*

DEATH COMES TO ALL

¹⁰Then I saw the wicked buried, who had come and gone from the place of holiness, and they were ᵃforgotten¹ in the city where they had so done. This also *is* vanity. ¹¹ᵃBecause the sentence against an evil work is not executed speedily, therefore the heart of the sons of men is fully set in them to do evil. ¹²ᵃThough a sinner does evil a hundred *times,* and his *days* are prolonged, yet I surely know that ᵇit will be well with those who fear God, who fear before Him. ¹³But it will not be well with the wicked; nor will he prolong *his* days, *which are* as a shadow, because he does not fear before God.

¹⁴There is a vanity which occurs on earth, that there are just *men* to whom it ᵃhappens according to the work of the wicked; again, there are wicked *men* to whom it happens according to the work of the ᵇrighteous. I said that this also *is* vanity.

¹⁵ᵃSo I commended enjoyment, because a man has nothing better under the sun than to eat, drink, and be merry; for this will remain with him in his labor *all* the days of his life which God gives him under the sun.

¹⁶When I applied my heart to know wisdom and to see the business that is done on earth, even though one sees no sleep day or night, ¹⁷then I saw all the work of God, that ᵃa man cannot find out the work that is done under the sun. For though a man labors to discover *it,* yet he will not find *it;* moreover, though a wise *man* attempts to know *it,* he will not be able to find *it.*

9 For I ¹considered all this in my heart, so that I could declare it all: ᵃthat the righteous and the wise and their works *are* in the hand of God. People know neither love nor hatred *by* anything *they see* before them. ²ᵃAll things *come* alike to all:

One event *happens* to the righteous and the wicked;
To the ¹good, the clean, and the unclean;
To him who sacrifices and him who does not sacrifice.
As is the good, so *is* the sinner;
He who takes an oath as *he* who fears an oath.

³This *is* an evil in all that is done under the sun: that one thing *happens* to all. Truly the hearts of the sons of men are full of evil; madness *is* in their hearts while they live, and after that *they go* to the dead. ⁴But for him who is joined to all the living there is hope, for a living dog is better than a dead lion.

5   For the living know that they will die;
     But ᵃthe dead know nothing,
     And they have no more reward,
     For ᵇthe memory of them is forgotten.
6   Also their love, their hatred, and their envy have now
          perished;
     Nevermore will they have a share
     In anything done under the sun.

7   Go, ᵃeat your bread with joy,
     And drink your wine with a merry heart;
     For God has already accepted your works.

8:10
ᵃEccl. 2:16; 9:5

8:11 ᵃPs. 10:6;
50:21; Is. 26:10

8:12 ᵃIs. 65:20;
[Rom. 2:5–7]
ᵇ[Deut. 4:40;
Ps. 37:11, 18, 19;
Prov. 1:32, 33;
Is. 3:10;
Matt. 25:34, 41]

8:14 ᵃPs. 73:14
ᵇEccl. 2:14; 7:15;
9:1–3

8:15 ᵃEccl. 2:24

8:17 ᵃJob 5:9;
Ps. 73:16;
Eccl. 3:11;
Rom. 11:33

9:1 ᵃDeut. 33:3;
Job 12:10;
Eccl. 8:14

9:2
ᵃGen. 3:17–19;
Job 21:7;
Ps. 73:3, 12, 13;
Mal. 3:15

9:5 ᵃJob 14:21;
Is. 63:16
ᵇJob 7:8–10;
Eccl. 1:11; 2:16;
8:10; Is. 26:14

9:7 ᵃEccl. 8:15

8:10 ¹Some Heb. mss., LXX, Vg. *praised*   **9:1** ¹Lit. *put*   **9:2** ¹LXX, Syr., Vg. *good and bad,*

8 Let your garments always be white,
And let your head lack no oil.

9 [1]Live joyfully with the wife whom you love all the days of your vain life which He has given you under the sun, all your days of vanity; [a]for that *is* your portion in life, and in the labor which you perform under the sun.

10 [a]Whatever your hand finds to do, do *it* with your [b]might; for *there is* no work or device or knowledge or wisdom in the grave where you are going.

11 I returned [a]and saw under the sun that—

The race *is* not to the swift,
Nor the battle to the strong,
Nor bread to the wise,
Nor riches to men of understanding,
Nor favor to men of skill;
But time and [b]chance happen to them all.

12 For [a]man also does not know his time:
Like fish taken in a cruel net,
Like birds caught in a snare,
So the sons of men *are* [b]snared in an evil time,
When it falls suddenly upon them.

WISDOM SUPERIOR TO FOLLY

13 This wisdom I have also seen under the sun, and it *seemed* great to me: 14[a]*There was* a little city with few men in it; and a great king came against it, besieged it, and built great [1]snares around it. 15 Now there was found in it a poor wise man, and he by his wisdom delivered the city. Yet no one remembered that same poor man.

16 Then I said:

"Wisdom *is* better than [a]strength.
Nevertheless [b]the poor man's wisdom *is*
despised,
And his words are not heard.
17 Words of the wise, *spoken* quietly, *should be* heard
Rather than the shout of a ruler of fools.
18 Wisdom *is* better than weapons of war;
But [a]one sinner destroys much good."

10 Dead[1] flies [2]putrefy the perfumer's ointment,
And cause it to give off a foul odor;
So does a little folly to one respected for wisdom *and*
honor.
2 A wise man's heart *is* at his right hand,
But a fool's heart at his left.
3 Even when a fool walks along the way,
He lacks wisdom,
[a]And he shows everyone *that* he *is* a fool.
4 If the spirit of the ruler rises against you,
[a]Do not leave your post;
For [b]conciliation[1] pacifies great offenses.

5 There is an evil I have seen under the sun,
As an error proceeding from the ruler:

9:9 [a]Eccl. 2:10

9:10 [a][Col. 3:17]
[b]Rom. 12:11;
Col. 3:23

9:11 [a]Jer. 9:23;
Amos 2:14, 15
[b]1 Sam. 6:9

9:12 [a]Eccl. 8:7
[b]Prov. 29:6;
Luke 12:20, 39;
17:26;
1 Thess. 5:3

9:14
[a]2 Sam. 20:16–22

9:16
[a]Eccl. 7:12, 19
[b]Mark 6:2, 3

9:18
[a]Josh. 7:1–26;
2 Kin. 21:2–17

10:3
[a]Prov. 13:16; 18:2

10:4 [a]Eccl. 8:3
[b]1 Sam. 25:24–
33; Prov. 25:15

9:9 [1]Lit. *See life*   9:14 [1]LXX, Syr., Vg. *bulwarks*   10:1 [1]Lit. *Flies of death*
[2]Tg., Vg. omit *putrefy*   10:4 [1]Lit. *healing, health*

6 ^aFolly is set in ¹great dignity,
    While the rich sit in a lowly place.
7 I have seen servants ^aon horses,
    While princes walk on the ground like servants.

8 ^aHe who digs a pit will fall into it,
    And whoever breaks through a wall will be bitten by a
        serpent.
9 He who quarries stones may be hurt by them,
    And he who splits wood may be endangered by it.
10 If the ax is dull,
    And one does not sharpen the edge,
    Then he must use more strength;
    But wisdom ¹brings success.

11 A serpent may bite ^awhen *it is* not charmed;
    The ¹babbler is no different.
12 ^aThe words of a wise man's mouth *are* gracious,
    But ^bthe lips of a fool shall swallow him up;
13 The words of his mouth begin with foolishness,
    And the end of his talk *is* raving madness.
14 ^aA fool also multiplies words.
    No man knows what is to be;
    Who can tell him ^bwhat will be after him?
15 The labor of fools wearies them,
    For they do not even know how to go to the city!

16 ^aWoe to you, O land, when your king *is* a child,
    And your princes feast in the morning!
17 Blessed *are* you, O land, when your king *is* the son of
        nobles,
    And your ^aprinces feast at the proper time—
    For strength and not for drunkenness!
18 Because of laziness the ¹building decays,
    And ^athrough idleness of hands the house leaks.
19 A feast is made for laughter,
    And ^awine makes merry;
    But money answers everything.

20 ^aDo not curse the king, even in your thought;
    Do not curse the rich, even in your bedroom;
    For a bird of the air may carry your voice,
    And a bird in flight may tell the matter.

THE VALUE OF DILIGENCE

11 Cast your bread ^aupon the waters,
    ^bFor you will find it after many days.
2 ^aGive a serving ^bto seven, and also to eight,
    ^cFor you do not know what evil will be on the
        earth.

3 If the clouds are full of rain,
    They empty *themselves* upon the earth;
    And if a tree falls to the south or the north,
    In the place where the tree falls, there it shall lie.
4 He who observes the wind will not sow,
    And he who regards the clouds will not reap.

10:6 ^aEsth. 3:1
10:7 ^aProv. 19:10;
    30:22
10:8 ^aPs. 7:15;
    Prov. 26:27
10:11
^aPs. 58:4, 5;
    Jer. 8:17
10:12
^aProv. 10:32;
    Luke 4:22
^bProv. 10:14;
    Eccl. 4:5
10:14
^a[Prov. 15:2];
    Eccl. 5:3
^bEccl. 3:22; 8:7
10:16
^aIs. 3:4, 5; 5:11
10:17 ^aProv. 31:4;
    Is. 5:11
10:18
^aProv. 24:30–34
10:19
^aJudg. 9:13;
    Ps. 104:15;
    Eccl. 2:3
10:20
^aEx. 22:28;
    Acts 23:5
11:1 ^aIs. 32:20
^b[Deut. 15:10];
    Prov. 19:17;
    Matt. 10:42;
    2 Cor. 9:8;
    Gal. 6:9, 10;
    Heb. 6:10]
11:2 ^aPs. 112:9;
    Matt. 5:42;
    Luke 6:30;
    [1 Tim. 6:18, 19]
^bMic. 5:5
^cEph. 5:16

10:6 ¹*exalted positions*   10:10 ¹Lit. *is a successful advantage*   10:11 ¹Lit.
master of the tongue   10:18 ¹Lit. *rafters sink*

5   As ᵃyou do not know what *is* the way of the ¹wind,
      ᵇ*Or* how the bones *grow* in the womb of her who is with
           child,
      So you do not know the works of God who makes
           everything.
6   In the morning sow your seed,
      And in the evening do not withhold your hand;
      For you do not know which will prosper,
      Either this or that,
      Or whether both alike *will be* good.

7   Truly the light is sweet,
      And *it is* pleasant for the eyes ᵃto behold the sun;
8   But if a man lives many years
      And ᵃrejoices in them all,
      Yet let him ᵇremember the days of darkness,
      For they will be many.
      All that is coming *is* vanity.

SEEK GOD IN EARLY LIFE

9   Rejoice, O young man, in your youth,
      And let your heart cheer you in the days of your
           youth;
      ᵃWalk in the ¹ways of your heart,
      And ²in the sight of your eyes;
      But know that for all these
      ᵇGod will bring you into judgment.
10   Therefore remove ¹sorrow from your heart,
      And ᵃput away evil from your flesh,
      ᵇFor childhood and ²youth *are* vanity.

12 Remember ᵃ now your Creator in the days of your
           youth,
      Before the ¹difficult days come,
      And the years draw near ᵇwhen you say,
      "I have no pleasure in them":
2   While the sun and the light,
      The moon and the stars,
      Are not darkened,
      And the clouds do not return after the rain;
3   In the day when the keepers of the house tremble,
      And the strong men bow down;
      When the grinders cease because they are few,
      And those that look through the windows grow
           dim;
4   When the doors are shut in the streets,
      And the sound of grinding is low;
      When one rises up at the sound of a bird,
      And all ᵃthe daughters of music are brought low.
5   Also they are afraid of height,
      And of terrors in the way;
      When the almond tree blossoms,
      The grasshopper is a burden,
      And desire fails.
      For man goes to ᵃhis eternal home,
      And ᵇthe mourners go about the streets.

11:5 ᵃJohn 3:8
ᵇPs. 139:14

11:7 ᵃEccl. 7:11

11:8 ᵃEccl. 9:7
ᵇEccl. 12:1

11:9
ᵃNum. 15:39;
Job 31:7;
Eccl. 2:10
ᵇEccl. 3:17; 12:14;
[Rom. 14:10]

11:10 ᵃ2 Cor. 7:1;
2 Tim. 2:22
ᵇPs. 39:5

12:1 ᵃ2 Chr. 34:3;
Prov. 22:6;
Lam. 3:27
ᵇ2 Sam. 19:35

12:4
ᵃ2 Sam. 19:35

12:5 ᵃJob 17:13
ᵇGen. 50:10;
Jer. 9:17

11:5 ¹Or *spirit*   11:9 ¹Impulses   ²As you see to be best   11:10 ¹*vexation*
²Prime of life   12:1 ¹Lit. *evil*

6 *Remember your Creator* before the silver cord is [1]loosed,
  Or the golden bowl is broken,
  Or the pitcher shattered at the fountain,
  Or the wheel broken at the well.
7 [a]Then the dust will return to the earth as it was,
  [b]And the spirit will return to God [c]who gave it.

8 "Vanity[a] of vanities," says the Preacher,
  "All *is* vanity."

THE WHOLE DUTY OF MAN

9And moreover, because the Preacher was wise, he still taught the people knowledge; yes, he pondered and sought out *and* [a]set[1] in order many proverbs. 10The Preacher sought to find [1]acceptable words; and *what was* written *was* upright— words of truth. 11The words of the wise are like goads, and the words of [1]scholars are like well-driven nails, given by one Shepherd. 12And further, my son, be admonished by these. Of making many books *there is* no end, and [a]much study *is* wearisome to the flesh.

13Let us hear the conclusion of the whole matter:

[a]Fear God and keep His commandments,
  For this is man's all.
14 For [a]God will bring every work into judgment,
  Including every secret thing,
  Whether good or evil.

12:7 [a]Gen. 3:19;
Job 34:15;
Ps. 90:3
[b]Eccl. 3:21
[c]Num. 16:22;
27:16; Job 34:14;
Is. 57:16;
Zech. 12:1

12:8 [a]Ps. 62:9

12:9 [a]1 Kin. 4:32

12:12 [a]Eccl. 1:18

12:13
[a][Deut. 6:2;
10:12]; Mic. 6:8

12:14 [a]Eccl. 11:9;
Matt. 12:36;
[Acts 17:30, 31;
Rom. 2:16;
1 Cor. 4:5;
2 Cor. 5:10]

12:6 [1]So with Qr., Tg.; Kt. *removed;* LXX, Vg. *broken*   12:9 [1]*arranged*
12:10 [1]Lit. *delightful*   12:11 [1]Lit. *masters of assemblies*

THE
SONG OF SOLOMON

1 The [a]song of songs, which *is* Solomon's.

THE BANQUET

The [1]Shulamite

2 Let him kiss me with the kisses of his mouth—
[a]For [2]your love *is* better than wine.
3 Because of the fragrance of your good ointments,
Your name *is* ointment poured forth;
Therefore the virgins love you.
4 [a]Draw me away!

The Daughters of Jerusalem

[b]We will run after [1]you.

The Shulamite

The king [c]has brought me into his chambers.

The Daughters of Jerusalem

We will be glad and rejoice in [2]you.

We will remember your love more than wine.

The Shulamite

Rightly do they love you.

5 I *am* dark, but lovely,
O daughters of Jerusalem,
Like the tents of Kedar,
Like the curtains of Solomon.
6 Do not look upon me, because I *am* dark,
Because the sun has [1]tanned me.
My mother's sons were angry with me;
They made me the keeper of the vineyards,
But my own [a]vineyard I have not kept.

(To Her Beloved)

7 Tell me, O you whom I love,
Where you feed *your flock,*
Where you make *it* rest at noon.
For why should I be as one who [1]veils herself
By the flocks of your companions?

The Beloved

8 If you do not know, [a]O fairest among women,
[1]Follow in the footsteps of the flock,

1:1 [a]1 Kin. 4:32

1:2 [a]Song 4:10

1:4 [a]Hos. 11:4;
John 6:44; 12:32
[b]Phil. 3:12–14
[c]Ps. 45:14, 15;
John 14:2;
Eph. 2:6

1:6 [a]Song 8:11, 12

1:8 [a]Song 5:9

1:2 [1]A young woman from the town of Shulam or Shunem, Song 6:13. The speaker and audience are identified according to the number, gender, and person of the Hebrew words. Occasionally the identity is not certain. [2]Masc. sing.: the Beloved 1:4 [1]Masc. sing.: the Beloved [2]Fem. sing.: the Shulamite 1:6 [1]Lit. *looked upon me* 1:7 [1]LXX, Syr., Vg. *wanders* 1:8 [1]Lit. *Go out*

And feed your little goats
Beside the shepherds' tents.
9 I have compared you, [a]my love,
[b]To my filly among Pharaoh's chariots.
10 [a]Your cheeks are lovely with ornaments,
Your neck with chains *of gold.*

The Daughters of Jerusalem

11 We will make [1]you ornaments of gold
With studs of silver.

The Shulamite

12 While the king *is* at his table,
My [1]spikenard sends forth its fragrance.
13 A bundle of myrrh *is* my beloved to me,
That lies all night between my breasts.
14 My beloved *is* to me a cluster of henna *blooms*
In the vineyards of En Gedi.

The Beloved

15 [a]Behold, you *are* fair, [1]my love!
Behold, you *are* fair!
You *have* dove's eyes.

The Shulamite

16 Behold, you *are* [a]handsome, my beloved!
Yes, pleasant!
Also our [1]bed *is* green.
17 The beams of our houses *are* cedar,
And our rafters of fir.

2 I *am* the rose of Sharon,
And the lily of the valleys.

The Beloved

2 Like a lily among thorns,
So is my love among the daughters.

The Shulamite

3 Like an apple tree among the trees of the woods,
So *is* my beloved among the sons.
I sat down in his shade with great delight,
And [a]his fruit *was* sweet to my taste.

The Shulamite to the Daughters of Jerusalem

4 He brought me to the [1]banqueting house,
And his banner over me *was* love.
5 Sustain me with cakes of raisins,
Refresh me with apples,
For I *am* lovesick.
6 [a]His left hand *is* under my head,
And his right hand embraces me.
7 [a]I [1]charge you, O daughters of Jerusalem,
By the gazelles or by the does of the field,

1:9 [a]Song 2:2,
10, 13; 4:1, 7;
John 15:14
[b]2 Chr. 1:16
1:10 [a]Ezek. 16:11
1:15
[a]Song 4:1; 5:12
1:16
[a]Song 5:10–16
2:3 [a]Song 4:16;
Rev. 22:1, 2
2:6 [a]Song 8:3
2:7
[a]Song 3:5; 8:4

1:11 [1]Fem. sing.: the Shulamite   1:12 [1]*perfume*   1:15 [1]*my companion, friend*
1:16 [1]*couch*   2:4 [1]Lit. *house of wine*   2:7 [1]*adjure*

Do not stir up nor awaken love
Until it pleases.

THE BELOVED'S REQUEST

The Shulamite

8 The voice of my beloved!
Behold, he comes
Leaping upon the mountains,
Skipping upon the hills.
9 aMy beloved is like a gazelle or a young stag.
Behold, he stands behind our wall;
He is looking through the windows,
Gazing through the lattice.
10 My beloved spoke, and said to me:
"Rise up, my love, my fair one,
And come away.
11 For lo, the winter is past,
The rain is over and gone.
12 The flowers appear on the earth;
The time of singing has come,
And the voice of the turtledove
Is heard in our land.
13 The fig tree puts forth her green figs,
And the vines with the tender grapes
Give a good smell.
Rise up, my love, my fair one,
And come away!

14 "O my adove, in the clefts of the rock,
In the secret places of the cliff,
Let me see your 1face,
bLet me hear your voice;
For your voice is sweet,
And your face is lovely."

Her Brothers

15 Catch us athe foxes,
The little foxes that spoil the vines,
For our vines have tender grapes.

The Shulamite

16 aMy beloved is mine, and I am his.
He feeds his flock among the lilies.

(To Her Beloved)

17 aUntil the day breaks
And the shadows flee away,
Turn, my beloved,
And be blike a gazelle
Or a young stag
Upon the mountains of 1Bether.

A TROUBLED NIGHT

The Shulamite

3 By anight on my bed I sought the one I love;
I sought him, but I did not find him.

2:9 aProv. 6:5;
Song 2:17
2:14 aSong 5:2
bSong 8:13
2:15 aPs. 80:13;
Ezek. 13:4;
Luke 13:32
2:16 aSong 6:3
2:17 aSong 4:6
bSong 8:14
3:1 aIs. 26:9

2:14 1Lit. appearance   2:17 1Lit. Separation

2 "I will rise now," *I said,*
"And go about the city;
In the streets and in the squares
I will seek the one I love."
I sought him, but I did not find him.
3 ªThe watchmen who go about the city found me;
I said,
"Have you seen the one I love?"

4 Scarcely had I passed by them,
When I found the one I love.
I held him and would not let him go,
Until I had brought him to the ªhouse of my
mother,
And into the ¹chamber of her who conceived me.

5 ªI ¹charge you, O daughters of Jerusalem,
By the gazelles or by the does of the field,
Do not stir up nor awaken love
Until it pleases.

THE COMING OF SOLOMON

The Shulamite

6 ªWho *is* this coming out of the wilderness
Like pillars of smoke,
Perfumed with myrrh and frankincense,
With all the merchant's fragrant powders?
7 Behold, it *is* Solomon's couch,
With sixty valiant men around it,
Of the valiant of Israel.
8 They all hold swords,
Being expert in war.
Every man *has* his sword on his thigh
Because of fear in the night.

9 Of the wood of Lebanon
Solomon the King
Made himself a ¹palanquin:
10 He made its pillars *of* silver,
Its support *of* gold,
Its seat *of* purple,
Its interior paved *with* love
By the daughters of Jerusalem.
11 Go forth, O daughters of Zion,
And see King Solomon with the crown
With which his mother crowned him
On the day of his wedding,
The day of the gladness of his heart.

THE BRIDEGROOM PRAISES THE BRIDE

The Beloved

4 Behold, ªyou *are* fair, my love!
Behold, you *are* fair!
You *have* dove's eyes behind your veil.
Your hair *is* like a ᵇflock of goats,
Going down from Mount Gilead.

3:4 ¹room   3:5 ¹adjure   3:9 ¹A portable enclosed chair

2 [a]Your teeth *are* like a flock of shorn *sheep*
   Which have come up from the washing,
   Every one of which bears twins,
   And none *is* [1]barren among them.
3 Your lips *are* like a strand of scarlet,
   And your mouth is lovely.
   [a]Your temples behind your veil
   Are like a piece of pomegranate.
4 [a]Your neck *is* like the tower of David,
   Built [b]for an armory,
   On which hang a thousand [1]bucklers,
   All shields of mighty men.
5 [a]Your two breasts *are* like two fawns,
   Twins of a gazelle,
   Which feed among the lilies.

6 [a]Until the day breaks
   And the shadows flee away,
   I will go my way to the mountain of myrrh
   And to the hill of frankincense.

7 [a]You *are* all fair, my love,
   And *there is* no spot in you.
8 Come with me from Lebanon, *my* spouse,
   With me from Lebanon.
   Look from the top of Amana,
   From the top of Senir [a]and Hermon,
   From the lions' dens,
   From the mountains of the leopards.
9 You have ravished my heart,
   My sister, *my* spouse;
   You have ravished my heart
   With one *look* of your eyes,
   With one link of your necklace.
10 How fair is your love,
   My sister, *my* spouse!
   [a]How much better than wine is your love,
   And the [1]scent of your perfumes
   Than all spices!
11 Your lips, O *my* spouse,
   Drip as the honeycomb;
   [a]Honey and milk *are* under your tongue;
   And the fragrance of your garments
   Is [b]like the fragrance of Lebanon.
12 A garden [1]enclosed
   Is my sister, *my* spouse,
   A spring shut up,
   A fountain sealed.
13 Your plants *are* an orchard of pomegranates
   With pleasant fruits,
   Fragrant henna with spikenard,
14 Spikenard and saffron,
   Calamus and cinnamon,
   With all trees of frankincense,
   Myrrh and aloes,
   With all the chief spices—

4:2 [a]Song 6:6

4:3 [a]Song 6:7

4:4 [a]Song 7:4
[b]Neh. 3:19

4:5 [a]Prov. 5:19;
Song 7:3

4:6 [a]Song 2:17

4:7 [a]Song 1:15;
Eph. 5:27

4:8 [a]Deut. 3:9;
1 Chr. 5:23;
Ezek. 27:5

4:10 [a]Song 1:2, 4

4:11
[a]Prov. 24:13, 14;
Song 5:1
[b]Gen. 27:27;
Hos. 14:6, 7

4:2 [1]*bereaved*   4:4 [1]*Small shields*   4:10 [1]*fragrance*   4:12 [1]*locked* or *barred*

15 A fountain of gardens,
    A well of ^aliving waters,
    And streams from Lebanon.

The Shulamite

16 Awake, O north *wind,*
    And come, O south!
    Blow upon my garden,
    That its spices may flow out.
    ^aLet my beloved come to his garden
    And eat its pleasant ^bfruits.

The Beloved

5 I ^ahave come to my garden, my ^bsister, *my*
    spouse;
    I have gathered my myrrh with my spice;
    ^cI have eaten my honeycomb with my honey;
    I have drunk my wine with my milk.

(To His Friends)

Eat, O ^dfriends!
Drink, yes, drink deeply,
O beloved ones!

THE SHULAMITE'S TROUBLED EVENING

The Shulamite

2 I sleep, but my heart is awake;
    It is the voice of my beloved!
    ^aHe knocks, *saying,*
    "Open for me, my sister, ¹my love,
    My dove, my perfect one;
    For my head is covered with dew,
    My ²locks with the drops of the night."

3 I have taken off my robe;
    How can I put it on *again?*
    I have washed my feet;
    How can I ¹defile them?

4 My beloved put his hand
    By the ¹latch *of the door,*
    And my heart yearned for him.

5 I arose to open for my beloved,
    And my hands dripped *with* myrrh,
    My fingers with liquid myrrh,
    On the handles of the lock.

6 I opened for my beloved,
    But my beloved had turned away *and* was gone.
    My ¹heart leaped up when he spoke.
    ^aI sought him, but I could not find him;
    I called him, but he gave me no answer.

7 ^aThe watchmen who went about the city found me.
    They struck me, they wounded me;
    The keepers of the walls
    Took my veil away from me.

4:15 ^aZech. 14:8;
John 4:10; 7:38
4:16 ^aSong 5:1
^bSong 7:13
5:1 ^aSong 4:16
^bSong 4:9
^cSong 4:11
^dLuke 15:7, 10;
John 3:29
5:2 ^aRev. 3:20
5:6 ^aSong 3:1
5:7 ^aSong 3:3

5:2 ¹*my companion, friend*   ²*curls* or *hair*   5:3 ¹*dirty*   5:4 ¹*opening*
5:6 ¹Lit. *soul*

8   I charge you, O daughters of Jerusalem,
If you find my beloved,
That you tell him I *am* lovesick!

The Daughters of Jerusalem

9   What *is* your beloved
More than *another* beloved,
[a]O fairest among women?
What *is* your beloved
More than *another* beloved,
That you so [1]charge us?

The Shulamite

10   My beloved *is* white and ruddy,
[1]Chief among ten thousand.
11   His head *is like* the finest gold;
His locks *are* wavy,
And black as a raven.
12   [a]His eyes *are* like doves
By the rivers of waters,
Washed with milk,
And [1]fitly set.
13   His cheeks *are* like a bed of spices,
Banks of scented herbs.
His lips *are* lilies,
Dripping liquid myrrh.
14   His hands *are* rods of gold
Set with beryl.
His body *is* carved ivory
Inlaid *with* sapphires.
15   His legs *are* pillars of marble
Set on bases of fine gold.
His countenance *is* like Lebanon,
Excellent as the cedars.
16   His mouth *is* most sweet,
Yes, he *is* altogether lovely.
This *is* my beloved,
And this *is* my friend,
O daughters of Jerusalem!

The Daughters of Jerusalem

6 Where has your beloved gone,
[a]O fairest among women?
Where has your beloved turned aside,
That we may seek him with you?

The Shulamite

2   My beloved has gone to his [a]garden,
To the beds of spices,
To feed *his flock* in the gardens,
And to gather lilies.
3   [a]I *am* my beloved's,
And my beloved *is* mine.
He feeds *his flock* among the lilies.

5:9
[a]Song 1:8; 6:1
5:12
[a]Song 1:15; 4:1
6:1
[a]Song 1:8; 5:9
6:2
[a]Song 4:16; 5:1
6:3
[a]Song 2:16; 7:10

5:9 [1]*adjure*   5:10 [1]*Distinguished*   5:12 [1]*sitting in a setting*

PRAISE OF THE SHULAMITE'S BEAUTY

The Beloved

4 O my love, you *are as* beautiful as Tirzah,
 Lovely as Jerusalem,
 Awesome as *an army* with banners!
5 Turn your eyes away from me,
 For they have ¹overcome me.
 Your hair *is* ªlike a flock of goats
 Going down from Gilead.
6 ªYour teeth *are* like a flock of sheep
 Which have come up from the washing;
 Every one bears twins,
 And none *is* ¹barren among them.
7 ªLike a piece of pomegranate
 Are your temples behind your veil.

8 There are sixty queens
 And eighty concubines,
 And ªvirgins without number.
9 My dove, my ªperfect one,
 Is the only one,
 The only one of her mother,
 The favorite of the one who bore her.
 The daughters saw her
 And called her blessed,
 The queens and the concubines,
 And they praised her.

10 Who is she who looks forth as the morning,
 Fair as the moon,
 Clear as the sun,
 ªAwesome as *an army* with banners?

The Shulamite

11 I went down to the garden of nuts
 To see the verdure of the valley,
 ªTo see whether the vine had budded
 And the pomegranates had bloomed.
12 Before I was even aware,
 My soul had made me
 As the chariots of ¹my noble people.

The Beloved and His Friends

13 Return, return, O Shulamite;
 Return, return, that we may look upon you!

The Shulamite

What would you see in the Shulamite—
 As it were, the dance of ¹the two camps?

EXPRESSIONS OF PRAISE

The Beloved

7 How beautiful are your feet in sandals,
 ªO prince's daughter!

6:5 ªSong 4:1
6:6 ªSong 4:2
6:7 ªSong 4:3
6:8 ªSong 1:3
6:9
ªSong 2:14; 5:2
6:10 ªSong 6:4
6:11 ªSong 7:12
7:1 ªPs. 45:13

6:5 ¹overwhelmed 6:6 ¹bereaved 6:12 ¹Heb. *Ammi Nadib* 6:13 ¹Heb.
Mahanaim

The curves of your thighs *are* like jewels,
The work of the hands of a skillful workman.
2 Your navel *is* a rounded goblet;
It lacks no [1]blended beverage.
Your waist *is* a heap of wheat
Set about with lilies.
3 [a]Your two breasts *are* like two fawns,
Twins of a gazelle.
4 [a]Your neck *is* like an ivory tower,
Your eyes *like* the pools in Heshbon
By the gate of Bath Rabbim.
Your nose *is* like the tower of Lebanon
Which looks toward Damascus.
5 Your head *crowns* you like *Mount* Carmel,
And the hair of your head *is* like purple;
A king *is* held captive by *your* tresses.

6 How fair and how pleasant you are,
O love, with your delights!
7 This stature of yours is like a palm tree,
And your breasts *like* its clusters.
8 I said, "I will go up to the palm tree,
I will take hold of its branches."
Let now your breasts be like clusters of the vine,
The fragrance of your [1]breath like apples,
9 And the roof of your mouth like the best wine.

The Shulamite

The wine goes *down* smoothly for my beloved,
[1]Moving gently the [2]lips of sleepers.
10 [a]I *am* my beloved's,
And [b]his desire *is* toward me.

11 Come, my beloved,
Let us go forth to the field;
Let us lodge in the villages.
12 Let us get up early to the vineyards;
Let us [a]see if the vine has budded,
Whether the grape blossoms are open,
And the pomegranates are in bloom.
There I will give you my love.
13 The [a]mandrakes give off a fragrance,
And at our gates [b]*are* pleasant *fruits,*
All manner, new and old,
Which I have laid up for you, my beloved.

8 Oh, that you were like my brother,
Who nursed at my mother's breasts!
If I should find you outside,
I would kiss you;
I would not be despised.
2 I would lead you *and* bring you
Into the [a]house of my mother,
She *who* used to instruct me.
I would cause you to drink of [b]spiced wine,
Of the juice of my pomegranate.

7:3 [a]Song 4:5
7:4 [a]Song 4:4
7:10
[a]Song 2:16; 6:3
[b]Ps. 45:11
7:12 [a]Song 6:11
7:13
[a]Gen. 30:14
[b]Song 2:3;
4:13, 16;
Matt. 13:52
8:2 [a]Song 3:4
[b]Prov. 9:2

7:2 [1]Lit. *mixed* or *spiced drink*   7:8 [1]Lit. *nose*   7:9 [1]*Gliding over*   [2]LXX,
Syr., Vg. *lips and teeth.*

(To the Daughters of Jerusalem)

3 ᵃHis left hand *is* under my head,
  And his right hand embraces me.
4 ᵃI charge you, O daughters of Jerusalem,
  Do not stir up nor awaken love
  Until it pleases.

LOVE RENEWED IN LEBANON

A Relative

5 ᵃWho *is* this coming up from the wilderness,
  Leaning upon her beloved?

  I awakened you under the apple tree.
  There your mother brought you forth;
  There she *who* bore you brought *you* forth.

The Shulamite to Her Beloved

6 ᵃSet me as a seal upon your heart,
  As a seal upon your arm;
  For love *is as* strong as death,
  ᵇJealousy *as* ¹cruel as ²the grave;
  Its flames *are* flames of fire,
  ³A most vehement flame.
7 Many waters cannot quench love,
  Nor can the floods drown it.
  ᵃIf a man would give for love
  All the wealth of his house,
  It would be utterly despised.

The Shulamite's Brothers

8 ᵃWe have a little sister,
  And she has no breasts.
  What shall we do for our sister
  In the day when she is spoken for?
9 If she *is* a wall,
  We will build upon her
  A battlement of silver;
  And if she *is* a door,
  We will enclose her
  With boards of cedar.

The Shulamite

10 I *am* a wall,
  And my breasts like towers;
  Then I became in his eyes
  As one who found peace.
11 Solomon had a vineyard at Baal Hamon;
  ᵃHe leased the vineyard to keepers;
  Everyone was to bring for its fruit
  A thousand silver *coins.*

(To Solomon)

12 My own vineyard *is* before me.
  You, O Solomon, *may have* a thousand,
  And those who tend its fruit two hundred.

8:3 ᵃSong 2:6
8:4
ᵃSong 2:7; 3:5
8:5 ᵃSong 3:6
8:6 ᵃIs. 49:16;
Jer. 22:24;
Hag. 2:23
ᵇProv. 6:34, 35
8:7 ᵃProv. 6:35
8:8 ᵃEzek. 23:33
8:11 ᵃMatt. 21:33

8:6 ¹*severe,* lit. *hard* ²Or *Sheol* ³Lit. *A flame of YAH,* poetic form of YHWH, *the* LORD

The Beloved

13 You who dwell in the gardens,
The companions listen for your voice—
^aLet me hear it!

The Shulamite

14 ^aMake¹ haste, my beloved,
And ^bbe like a gazelle
Or a young stag
On the mountains of spices.

8:13 ^aSong 2:14
8:14
^aRev. 22:17, 20
^bSong 2:7, 9, 17

8:14 ¹*Hurry*, lit. *Flee*

THE BOOK OF
ISAIAH

1 The ᵃvision of Isaiah the son of Amoz, which he saw concerning Judah and Jerusalem in the ᵇdays of Uzziah, Jotham, Ahaz, *and* Hezekiah, kings of Judah.

THE WICKEDNESS OF JUDAH

2 ᵃHear, O heavens, and give ear, O earth!
   For the Lᴏʀᴅ has spoken:
   "I have nourished and brought up children,
   And they have rebelled against Me;
3 ᵃThe ox knows its owner
   And the donkey its master's ¹crib;
   But Israel ᵇdoes not know,
   My people do not ²consider."

4 Alas, sinful nation,
   A people ¹laden with iniquity,
   ᵃA ²brood of evildoers,
   Children who are corrupters!
   They have forsaken the Lᴏʀᴅ,
   They have provoked to anger
   The Holy One of Israel,
   They have turned away backward.

5 ᵃWhy should you be stricken again?
   You will revolt more and more.
   The whole head is sick,
   And the whole heart faints.
6 From the sole of the foot even to the head,
   There is no soundness in it,
   But wounds and bruises and putrefying sores;
   They have not been closed or bound up,
   Or soothed with ointment.

7 ᵃYour country *is* desolate,
   Your cities *are* burned with fire;
   Strangers devour your land in your presence;
   And *it is* desolate, as overthrown by strangers.
8 So the daughter of Zion is left ᵃas a ¹booth in a
      vineyard,
   As a hut in a garden of cucumbers,
   ᵇAs a besieged city.
9 ᵃUnless the Lᴏʀᴅ of hosts
   Had left to us a very small remnant,
   We would have become like ᵇSodom,
   We would have been made like Gomorrah.

10 Hear the word of the Lᴏʀᴅ,
   You rulers ᵃof Sodom;

1:1 ᵃNum. 12:6
ᵇ2 Chr. 26—32

1:2 ᵃJer. 2:12

1:3 ᵃJer. 8:7
ᵇJer. 9:3, 6

1:4 ᵃIs. 57:3, 4;
Matt. 3:7

1:5 ᵃJer. 5:3

1:7
ᵃDeut. 28:51, 52;
2 Chr. 36:19

1:8 ᵃJob 27:18
ᵇJer. 4:17

1:9
ᵃ2 Kin. 25:11, 22;
Lam. 3:22
ᵇGen. 19:24;
Rom. 9:29

1:10
ᵃDeut. 32:32

1:3 ¹*manger* or *feed trough* ²*understand* **1:4** ¹Lit. *heavy, weighed down*
²*offspring, seed* **1:8** ¹*shelter*

Give ear to the law of our God,
You people of Gomorrah:

11 "To what purpose *is* the multitude of your [a]sacrifices to
Me?"
Says the LORD.
"I have had enough of burnt offerings of rams
And the fat of fed cattle.
I do not delight in the blood of bulls,
Or of lambs or goats.

12 "When you come [a]to appear before Me,
Who has required this from your hand,
To trample My courts?

13 Bring no more [a]futile[1] sacrifices;
Incense is an abomination to Me.
The New Moons, the Sabbaths, and [b]the calling of
assemblies—
I cannot endure iniquity and the sacred meeting.

14 Your [a]New Moons and your [b]appointed feasts
My soul hates;
They are a trouble to Me,
I am weary of bearing *them*.

15 [a]When you [1]spread out your hands,
I will hide My eyes from you;
[b]Even though you make many prayers,
I will not hear.
Your hands are full of [2]blood.

16 "Wash[a] yourselves, make yourselves clean;
Put away the evil of your doings from before My eyes.
[b]Cease to do evil,

17 Learn to do good;
Seek justice,
Rebuke [1]the oppressor;
[2]Defend the fatherless,
Plead for the widow.

18 "Come now, and let us [a]reason together,"
Says the LORD,
"Though your sins are like scarlet,
[b]They shall be as white as snow;
Though they are red like crimson,
They shall be as wool.

19 If you are willing and obedient,
You shall eat the good of the land;

20 But if you refuse and rebel,
You shall be devoured by the sword";
[a]For the mouth of the LORD has spoken.

THE DEGENERATE CITY

21 [a]How the faithful city has become a [1]harlot!
It was full of justice;
Righteousness lodged in it,
But now [b]murderers.

22 [a]Your silver has become dross,
Your wine mixed with water.

1:11
[a][1 Sam. 15:22]

1:12 [a]Ex. 23:17

1:13 [a]Matt. 15:9
[b]Joel 1:14

1:14 [a]Num. 28:11
[b]Lam. 2:6

1:15 [a]Prov. 1:28
[b]Ps. 66:18;
Is. 59:1–3;
Mic. 3:4

1:16 [a]Jer. 4:14
[b]Rom. 12:9

1:18 [a]Is. 43:26;
Mic. 6:2
[b]Ps. 51:7;
[Is. 43:25];
Rev. 7:14

1:20 [a]Is. 40:5;
58:14; Mic. 4:4;
[Titus 1:2]

1:21
[a]Is. 57:3–9;
Jer. 2:20
[b]Mic. 3:1–3

1:22 [a]Jer. 6:28

1:13 [1]worthless   1:15 [1]Pray   [2]bloodshed   1:17 [1]Some ancient vss. *the
oppressed*   [2]Vindicate   1:21 [1]Unfaithful

23 ^aYour princes *are* rebellious,
 And ^bcompanions of thieves;
 ^cEveryone loves bribes,
 And follows after rewards.
 They ^ddo not defend the fatherless,
 Nor does the cause of the widow come before them.

24 Therefore the Lord says,
 The Lord of hosts, the Mighty One of Israel,
 "Ah, ^aI will ¹rid Myself of My adversaries,
 And ²take vengeance on My enemies.
25 I will turn My hand against you,
 And ^athoroughly¹ purge away your dross,
 And take away all your alloy.
26 I will restore your judges ^aas at the first,
 And your counselors as at the beginning.
 Afterward ^byou shall be called the city of righteousness,
 the faithful city."

27 Zion shall be redeemed with justice,
 And her ¹penitents with righteousness.
28 The ^adestruction of transgressors and of sinners *shall be* together,
 And those who forsake the Lord shall be consumed.
29 For ¹they shall be ashamed of the ²terebinth trees
 Which you have desired;
 And you shall be embarrassed because of the gardens
 Which you have chosen.
30 For you shall be as a terebinth whose leaf fades,
 And as a garden that has no water.
31 ^aThe strong shall be as tinder,
 And the work of it as a spark;
 Both will burn together,
 And no one shall ^bquench *them*.

THE FUTURE HOUSE OF GOD
(Mic. 4:1–5)

2 The word that Isaiah the son of Amoz saw concerning Judah and Jerusalem.

2 Now ^ait shall come to pass ^bin the latter days
 ^c*That* the mountain of the Lord's house
 Shall be established on the top of the mountains,
 And shall be exalted above the hills;
 And all nations shall flow to it.
3 Many people shall come and say,
 ^a"Come, and let us go up to the mountain of the Lord,
 To the house of the God of Jacob;
 He will teach us His ways,
 And we shall walk in His paths."
 ^bFor out of Zion shall go forth the law,
 And the word of the Lord from Jerusalem.
4 He shall judge between the nations,
 And rebuke many people;
 They shall beat their swords into plowshares,
 And their spears into pruning ¹hooks;

Footnotes:
1:23 ^aHos. 9:15 ^bProv. 29:24 ^cJer. 22:17 ^dIs. 10:2; Jer. 5:28; Ezek. 22:7; Zech. 7:10
1:24 ^aDeut. 28:63
1:25 ^aIs. 48:10; Ezek. 22:19–22; Mal. 3:3
1:26 ^aJer. 33:7–11 ^bIs. 33:5; Zech. 8:3
1:28 ^aJob 31:3; Ps. 9:5; [Is. 66:24; 2 Thess. 1:8, 9]
1:31 ^aEzek. 32:21 ^bIs. 66:24; Matt. 3:12; Mark 9:43
2:2 ^aMic. 4:1 ^bGen. 49:1 ^cPs. 68:15
2:3 ^aJer. 50:5; [Zech. 8:21–23; 14:16–21] ^bLuke 24:47

1:24 ¹be relieved of ²avenge Myself 1:25 ¹refine with lye 1:27 ¹Lit. returners 1:29 ¹So with MT, LXX, Vg.; some Heb. mss., Tg. you ²Sites of pagan worship 2:4 ¹knives

Nation shall not lift up sword against nation,
Neither shall they learn war anymore.

THE DAY OF THE LORD

5   O house of Jacob, come and let us ^awalk
    In the light of the LORD.

6   For You have forsaken Your people, the house of Jacob,
    Because they are filled ^awith eastern ways;
    They *are* ^bsoothsayers like the Philistines,
    ^cAnd they ¹are pleased with the children of foreigners.

7   ^aTheir land is also full of silver and gold,
    And there is no end to their treasures;
    Their land is also full of horses,
    And there is no end to their chariots.

8   ^aTheir land is also full of idols;
    They worship the work of their own hands,
    That which their own fingers have made.

9   People bow down,
    And each man humbles himself;
    Therefore do not forgive them.

10   ^aEnter into the rock, and hide in the dust,
    From the terror of the LORD
    And the glory of His majesty.

11   The ¹lofty looks of man shall be ^ahumbled,
    The haughtiness of men shall be bowed down,
    And the LORD alone shall be exalted ^bin that day.

12   For the day of the LORD of hosts
    Shall come upon everything proud and lofty,
    Upon everything lifted up—
    And it shall be brought low—

13   Upon all ^athe cedars of Lebanon *that are* high and lifted
    up,
    And upon all the oaks of Bashan;

14   ^aUpon all the high mountains,
    And upon all the hills *that are* lifted up;

15   Upon every high tower,
    And upon every fortified wall;

16   ^aUpon all the ships of Tarshish,
    And upon all the beautiful sloops.

17   The ¹loftiness of man shall be bowed down,
    And the haughtiness of men shall be brought low;
    The LORD alone will be exalted in that day,

18   But the idols ¹He shall utterly abolish.

19   They shall go into the ^aholes of the rocks,
    And into the caves of the ¹earth,
    ^bFrom the terror of the LORD
    And the glory of His majesty,
    When He arises ^cto shake the earth mightily.

20   In that day a man will cast away his idols of silver
    And his idols of gold,
    Which they made, *each* for himself to worship,
    To the moles and bats,

2:5 ^aEph. 5:8

2:6 ^aNum. 23:7
^bDeut. 18:14
^cPs. 106:35

2:7 ^aDeut. 17:16;
Is. 30:16; 31:1;
Mic. 5:10

2:8
^aIs. 40:19, 20;
Jer. 2:28

2:10 ^aIs. 2:19, 21;
Rev. 6:15, 16

2:11 ^aProv. 16:5;
Is. 5:15
^bHos. 2:16

2:13 ^aIs. 14:8;
Zech. 11:1, 2

2:14 ^aIs. 30:25

2:16
^a1 Kin. 10:22;
Is. 23:1, 14; 60:9

2:19 ^aHos. 10:8;
[Rev. 9:6]
^b[2 Thess. 1:9]
^cPs. 18:7; Is. 2:21;
13:13; 24:1, 19, 20;
Hag. 2:6, 7;
Heb. 12:26

2:6 ¹Or *clap, shake hands to make bargains with the children*   2:11 ¹*proud*
2:17 ¹*pride*   2:18 ¹Or *shall utterly vanish*   2:19 ¹Lit. *dust*

21 To go into the clefts of the rocks,
   And into the crags of the rugged rocks,
   From the terror of the LORD
   And the glory of His majesty,
   When He arises to shake the earth mightily.

22 [a]Sever[1] yourselves from such a man,
   Whose [b]breath *is* in his nostrils;
   For [2]of what account is he?

JUDGMENT ON JUDAH AND JERUSALEM

3 For behold, the Lord, the LORD of hosts,
   [a]Takes away from Jerusalem and from Judah
   [b]The[1] stock and the store,
   The whole supply of bread and the whole supply of
      water;
2 [a]The mighty man and the man of war,
   The judge and the prophet,
   And the diviner and the elder;
3 The captain of fifty and the [1]honorable man,
   The counselor and the skillful artisan,
   And the expert enchanter.
4 "I will give [a]children[1] *to be* their princes,
   And [2]babes shall rule over them.
5 The people will be oppressed,
   Every one by another and every one by his neighbor;
   The child will be insolent toward the [1]elder,
   And the [2]base toward the honorable."

6 When a man takes hold of his brother
   In the house of his father, *saying,*
   "You have clothing;
   You be our ruler,
   And *let* these ruins *be* under your [1]power,"
7 In that day he will protest, saying,
   "I cannot cure *your* ills,
   For in my house *is* neither food nor clothing;
   Do not make me a ruler of the people."

8 For [a]Jerusalem stumbled,
   And Judah is fallen,
   Because their tongue and their doings
   Are against the LORD,
   To provoke the eyes of His glory.
9 The look on their countenance witnesses against
      them,
   And they declare their sin as [a]Sodom;
   They do not hide *it.*
   Woe to their soul!
   For they have brought evil upon themselves.

10 "Say to the righteous [a]that *it shall be* well *with them,*
   [b]For they shall eat the fruit of their doings.
11 Woe to the wicked! [a]*It shall be* ill *with him,*
   For the reward of his hands shall be [1]given him.

2:22 [a]Ps. 146:3;
Jer. 17:5
[b]Job 27:3

3:1 [a]2 Kin. 25:3;
Is. 5:13; Jer. 37:21
[b]Lev. 26:26

3:2
[a]2 Kin. 24:14;
Is. 9:14, 15;
Ezek. 17:12, 13

3:4 [a]Eccl. 10:16

3:8
[a]2 Chr. 36:16, 17;
Mic. 3:12

3:9 [a]Gen. 13:13;
Is. 1:10–15

3:10
[a][Deut. 28:1–14;
Eccl. 8:12;
Is. 54:17]
[b]Ps. 128:2

3:11 [a][Ps. 11:6;
Eccl. 8:12, 13]

2:22 [1]Lit. *Cease yourselves from the man*   [2]Lit. *in what is he to be esteemed*
3:1 [1]Every support   **3:3** [1]Eminent looking men   **3:4** [1]*boys*   [2]Or
capricious ones   **3:5** [1]*aged*   [2]*despised, lightly esteemed*   **3:6** [1]Lit. *hand*
3:11 [1]*done to him*

12 *As for* My people, children *are* their oppressors,
And women rule over them.
O My people! [a]Those who lead you [1]cause *you* to err,
And destroy the way of your paths."

OPPRESSION AND LUXURY CONDEMNED

13 The LORD stands up [a]to [1]plead,
And stands to judge the people.
14 The LORD will enter into judgment
With the elders of His people
And His princes:
"For you have [1]eaten up [a]the vineyard;
The plunder of the poor *is* in your houses.
15 What do you mean by [a]crushing My people
And grinding the faces of the poor?"
Says the Lord GOD of hosts.

16Moreover the LORD says:

"Because the daughters of Zion are haughty,
And walk with [1]outstretched necks
And [2]wanton eyes,
Walking and [3]mincing *as* they go,
Making a jingling with their feet,
17 Therefore the Lord will strike with [a]a scab
The crown of the head of the daughters of Zion,
And the LORD will [b]uncover their secret parts."

18 In that day the Lord will take away the finery:
The jingling anklets, the [1]scarves, and the [a]crescents;
19 The pendants, the bracelets, and the veils;
20 The headdresses, the leg ornaments, and the headbands;
The perfume boxes, the charms,
21 and the rings;
The nose jewels,
22 the festal apparel, and the mantles;
The outer garments, the purses,
23 and the mirrors;
The fine linen, the turbans, and the robes.

24And so it shall be:

Instead of a sweet smell there will be a stench;
Instead of a sash, a rope;
Instead of well-set hair, [a]baldness;
Instead of a rich robe, a girding of sackcloth;
And [1]branding instead of beauty.
25 Your men shall fall by the sword,
And your [1]mighty in the war.

26 [a]Her gates shall lament and mourn,
And she *being* desolate [b]shall sit on the ground.

4 And [a]in that day seven women shall take hold of one
man, saying,
"We will [b]eat our own food and wear our own apparel;
Only let us be called by your name,
To take away [c]our reproach."

3:12 [a]Is. 9:16
3:13 [a]Is. 66:16;
Hos. 4:1;
Mic. 6:2
3:14 [a]Matt. 21:33
3:15 [a]Mic. 3:2, 3
3:17
[a]Deut. 28:27
[b]Jer. 13:22
3:18
[a]Judg. 8:21, 26
3:24 [a]Is. 22:12;
Ezek. 27:31;
Amos 8:10
3:26 [a]Jer. 14:2;
Lam. 1:4
[b]Lam. 2:10
4:1 [a]Is. 2:11, 17
[b]2 Thess. 3:12
[c]Luke 1:25

3:12 [1]lead you astray   3:13 [1]contend, plead His case   3:14 [1]burned
3:16 [1]Head held high   [2]seductive, ogling   [3]tripping or skipping
3:18 [1]headbands   3:24 [1]burning scar   3:25 [1]Lit. strength

THE RENEWAL OF ZION

2 In that day [a]the Branch of the LORD shall be beautiful
and glorious;
And the fruit of the earth *shall be* excellent and appealing
For those of Israel who have escaped.

3And it shall come to pass that *he who is* left in Zion and remains in Jerusalem [a]will be called holy—everyone who is [b]recorded among the living in Jerusalem. 4When [a]the Lord has washed away the filth of the daughters of Zion, and purged the [1]blood of Jerusalem from her midst, by the spirit of judgment and by the spirit of burning, 5then the LORD will create above every dwelling place of Mount Zion, and above her assemblies, [a]a cloud and smoke by day and [b]the shining of a flaming fire by night. For over all the glory there *will be* a [1]covering. 6And there will be a tabernacle for shade in the daytime from the heat, [a]for a place of refuge, and for a shelter from storm and rain.

GOD'S DISAPPOINTING VINEYARD

5 Now let me sing to my Well-beloved
A song of my Beloved [a]regarding His vineyard:

My Well-beloved has a vineyard
[1]On a very fruitful hill.
2 He dug it up and cleared out its stones,
And planted it with the choicest vine.
He built a tower in its midst,
And also [1]made a winepress in it;
[a]So He expected *it* to bring forth *good* grapes,
But it brought forth wild grapes.

3 "And now, O inhabitants of Jerusalem and men of Judah,
[a]Judge, please, between Me and My vineyard.
4 What more could have been done to My vineyard
That I have not done in [a]it?
Why then, when I expected *it* to bring forth *good* grapes,
Did it bring forth wild grapes?
5 And now, please let Me tell you what I will do to My
vineyard:
[a]I will take away its hedge, and it shall be burned;
And break down its wall, and it shall be trampled down.
6 I will lay it [a]waste;
It shall not be pruned or [1]dug,
But there shall come up briers and [b]thorns.
I will also command the clouds
That they rain no rain on it."

7 For the vineyard of the LORD of hosts *is* the house of
Israel,
And the men of Judah are His pleasant plant.
He looked for justice, but behold, oppression;
For righteousness, but behold, [1]a cry *for help.*

IMPENDING JUDGMENT ON EXCESSES

8 Woe to those who [1]join [a]house to house;
They add field to field,

4:2 [a]Is. 12:1–6;
[Jer. 23:5];
Zech. 3:8

4:3 [a]Is. 60:21
[b]Phil. 4:3

4:4 [a]Mal. 3:2, 3

4:5
[a]Ex. 13:21, 22;
Num. 9:15–23
[b]Zech. 2:5

4:6 [a]Ps. 27:5;
Is. 25:4

5:1 [a]Ps. 80:8;
Jer. 2:21;
Matt. 21:33;
Mark 12:1;
Luke 20:9

5:2 [a]Deut. 32:6

5:3 [a][Rom. 3:4]

5:4
[a]2 Chr. 36:15, 16;
Jer. 2:5; 7:25, 26;
Mic. 6:3;
Matt. 23:37

5:5
[a]2 Chr. 36:19;
Ps. 80:12;
89:40, 41

5:6
[a]2 Chr. 36:19–21
[b]Is. 7:19–25;
Jer. 25:11

5:8
[a]Jer. 22:13–17;
Mic. 2:2;
Hab. 2:9–12

4:4 [1]bloodshed   4:5 [1]canopy   5:1 [1]Lit. *In a horn, the son of fatness*   5:2 [1]Lit.
hewed out   5:6 [1]hoed   5:7 [1]wailing   5:8 [1]Accumulate houses

Till *there is* no place
Where they may dwell alone in the midst of the land!

9 ᵃIn my hearing the LORD of hosts *said,*
"Truly, many houses shall be desolate,
Great and beautiful ones, without inhabitant.

10 For ten acres of vineyard shall yield one ᵃbath,¹
And a homer of seed shall yield one ²ephah."

11 ᵃWoe to those who rise early in the morning,
That they may ¹follow intoxicating drink;
Who continue until night, *till* wine inflames them!

12 ᵃThe harp and the strings,
The tambourine and flute,
And wine are in their feasts;
But ᵇthey do not regard the work of the LORD,
Nor consider the operation of His hands.

13 ᵃTherefore my people have gone into captivity,
Because *they have* no ᵇknowledge;
Their honorable men *are* famished,
And their multitude dried up with thirst.

14 Therefore Sheol has enlarged itself
And opened its mouth beyond measure;
Their glory and their multitude and their pomp,
And he who is jubilant, shall descend into it.

15 People shall be brought down,
ᵃEach man shall be humbled,
And the eyes of the lofty shall be humbled.

16 But the LORD of hosts shall be ᵃexalted in judgment,
And God who is holy shall be hallowed in righteousness.

17 Then the lambs shall feed in their pasture,
And in the waste places of ᵃthe ¹fat ones strangers shall eat.

18 Woe to those who ¹draw iniquity with cords of ²vanity,
And sin as if with a cart rope;

19 ᵃThat say, "Let Him make speed *and* hasten His work,
That we may see *it;*
And let the counsel of the Holy One of Israel draw near and come,
That we may know *it.*"

20 Woe to those who call evil good, and good evil;
Who put darkness for light, and light for darkness;
Who put bitter for sweet, and sweet for bitter!

21 Woe to *those who are* ᵃwise in their own eyes,
And prudent in their own sight!

22 Woe to men mighty at drinking wine,
Woe to men valiant for mixing intoxicating drink,

23 Who ᵃjustify the wicked for a bribe,
And take away justice from the righteous man!

24 Therefore, ᵃas the ¹fire devours the stubble,
And the flame consumes the chaff,
So ᵇtheir root will be as rottenness,
And their blossom will ascend like dust;

5:9 ᵃIs. 22:14
5:10 ᵃEzek. 45:11
5:11
ᵃProv. 23:29, 30;
Eccl. 10:16, 17;
Is. 5:22
5:12 ᵃAmos 6:5
ᵇJob 34:27;
Ps. 28:5
5:13
ᵃ2 Kin. 24:14–16
ᵇIs. 1:3; 27:11;
Hos. 4:6
5:15 ᵃIs. 2:9, 11
5:16 ᵃIs. 2:11
5:17 ᵃIs. 10:16
5:19 ᵃJer. 17:15;
Amos 5:18
5:21 ᵃProv. 3:7;
Rom. 1:22; 12:16;
[1 Cor. 3:18–20]
5:23 ᵃEx. 23:8;
Prov. 17:15;
Is. 1:23;
Mic. 3:11; 7:3
5:24 ᵃEx. 15:7
ᵇJob 18:16

5:10 ¹bath=1/10 homer   ²1 ephah=1/10 homer   5:11 ¹*pursue*   5:17 ¹Lit.
fatlings, rich ones   5:18 ¹*drag*   ²*emptiness* or *falsehood*   5:24 ¹Lit. *tongue of fire*

Because they have rejected the law of the LORD of hosts,
And despised the word of the Holy One of Israel.

25 ^aTherefore the anger of the LORD is aroused against His
people;
He has stretched out His hand against them
And stricken them,
And ^bthe hills trembled.
Their carcasses *were* as refuse in the midst of the streets.

^cFor all this His anger is not turned away,
But His hand *is* stretched out still.

26 ^aHe will lift up a banner to the nations from afar,
And will ^bwhistle to them from ^cthe end of the earth;
Surely ^dthey shall come with speed, swiftly.

27 No one will be weary or stumble among them,
No one will slumber or sleep;
Nor ^awill the belt on their loins be loosed,
Nor the strap of their sandals be broken;

28 ^aWhose arrows *are* sharp,
And all their bows bent;
Their horses' hooves will ¹seem like flint,
And their wheels like a whirlwind.

29 Their roaring *will be* like a lion,
They will roar like young lions;
Yes, they will roar
And lay hold of the prey;
They will carry *it* away safely,
And no one will deliver.

30 In that day they will roar against them
Like the roaring of the sea.
And if *one* ^alooks to the land,
Behold, darkness *and* ¹sorrow;
And the light is darkened by the clouds.

ISAIAH CALLED TO BE A PROPHET
(cf. Ezek. 1:4–28)

6 In the year that ^aKing Uzziah died, I ^bsaw the Lord sitting on a throne, high and lifted up, and the train of His *robe* filled the temple. ²Above it stood seraphim; each one had six wings: with two he covered his face, ^awith two he covered his feet, and with two he flew. ³And one cried to another and said:

^a"Holy, holy, holy *is* the LORD of hosts;
^bThe whole earth *is* full of His glory!"

⁴And the posts of the door were shaken by the voice of him who cried out, and the house was filled with smoke.

⁵So I said:

"Woe *is* me, for I am ¹undone!
Because I *am* a man of ^aunclean lips,
And I dwell in the midst of a people of unclean lips;
For my eyes have seen the King,
The LORD of hosts."

⁶Then one of the seraphim flew to me, having in his hand a live coal *which* he had taken with the tongs from ^athe altar. ⁷And he ^atouched my mouth *with it,* and said:

5:25
^a2 Kin. 22:13, 17;
Is. 66:15
^bPs. 18:7;
Is. 64:3;
Jer. 4:24;
Nah. 1:5
^cIs. 9:12, 17;
Jer. 4:8;
Dan. 9:16

5:26
^aIs. 11:10, 12
^bIs. 7:18;
Zech. 10:8
^cMal. 1:11
^dJoel 2:7

5:27 ^aDan. 5:6

5:28 ^aJer. 5:16

5:30 ^aIs. 8:22;
Jer. 4:23–28;
Joel 2:10;
Luke 21:25, 26

6:1 ^a2 Kin. 15:7;
2 Chr. 26:23;
Is. 1:1
^bJohn 12:41;
Rev. 4:2, 3; 20:11

6:2 ^aEzek. 1:11

6:3 ^aRev. 4:8
^bNum. 14:21;
Ps. 72:19

6:5 ^aEx. 6:12, 30

6:6 ^aRev. 8:3

6:7 ^aJer. 1:9;
Dan. 10:16

5:28 ¹Lit. *be regarded as*   **5:30** ¹*distress*   **6:5** ¹*destroyed, cut off*

"Behold, this has touched your lips;
Your iniquity is taken away,
And your sin ¹purged."

⁸Also I heard the voice of the Lord, saying:

"Whom shall I send,
And who will go for ªUs?"

Then I said, "Here *am* I! Send me."
⁹And He said, "Go, and ªtell this people:

'Keep on hearing, but do not understand;
Keep on seeing, but do not perceive.'

10 "Make ªthe heart of this people dull,
And their ears heavy,
And shut their eyes;
ᵇLest they see with their eyes,
And hear with their ears,
And understand with their heart,
And return and be healed."

¹¹Then I said, "Lord, how long?"
And He answered:

ª"Until the cities are laid waste and without inhabitant,
The houses are without a man,
The land is utterly desolate,
12 ªThe LORD has removed men far away,
And the forsaken places *are* many in the midst of the
land.
13 But yet a tenth *will be* in it,
And will return and be for consuming,
As a terebinth tree or as an oak,
Whose stump *remains* when it is cut down.
So ªthe holy seed *shall be* its stump."

ISAIAH SENT TO KING AHAZ
(2 Kin. 16:5; 2 Chr. 28:5–15)

7 Now it came to pass in the days of ªAhaz the son of Jotham, the son of Uzziah, king of Judah, *that* Rezin king
of Syria and Pekah the son of Remaliah, king of Israel, went
up to Jerusalem to *make* war against ᵇit, but could not ¹pre-
vail against it. ²And it was told to the house of David, saying,
"Syria's forces are ¹deployed in Ephraim." So his heart and the
heart of his people were moved as the trees of the woods are
moved with the wind. ³Then the LORD said to Isaiah, "Go out now to meet Ahaz,
you and ¹Shear-Jashub your son, at the end of the aqueduct
from the upper pool, on the highway to the Fuller's Field, ⁴and
say to him: ¹'Take heed, and ²be ªquiet; do not fear or be fainthearted for these two stubs of smoking firebrands, for the
fierce anger of Rezin and Syria, and the son of Remaliah. ⁵Because Syria, Ephraim, and the son of Remaliah have plotted
evil against you, saying, ⁶"Let us go up against Judah and ¹trouble it, and let us make a gap in its wall for ourselves, and set a
king over them, the son of Tabel"— ⁷thus says the Lord GOD:

6:8 ªGen. 1:26

6:9 ªIs. 43:8;
Matt. 13:14;
Mark 4:12;
Luke 8:10;
John 12:40;
Acts 28:26;
Rom. 11:8

6:10 ªPs. 119:70;
Mark 6:1–6;
Acts 7:51;
Rom. 10:1–4
ᵇJer. 5:21

6:11 ªMic. 3:12

6:12
ª2 Kin. 25:21;
Is. 5:9

6:13 ªDeut. 7:6;
Ezra 9:2

7:1 ª2 Chr. 28
ᵇ2 Kin. 16:5, 9

7:4 ªEx. 14:13;
Is. 30:15;
Lam. 3:26

6:7 ¹*atoned for*   7:1 ¹*conquer it*   7:2 ¹Lit. *settled upon*   7:3 ¹Lit. *A Remnant
Shall Return*   7:4 ¹*Be careful*   ²*be calm*   7:6 ¹*cause a sickening dread*

a"It shall not stand,
　Nor shall it come to pass.
8 　aFor the head of Syria *is* Damascus,
　And the head of Damascus *is* Rezin.
　Within sixty-five years Ephraim will be ¹broken,
　So that it will not *be* a people.
9 　The head of Ephraim *is* Samaria,
　And the head of Samaria *is* Remaliah's son.
　aIf you will not believe,
　Surely you shall not be established."'"

THE IMMANUEL PROPHECY

10Moreover the Lᴏʀᴅ spoke again to Ahaz, saying, 11a"Ask a sign for yourself from the Lᴏʀᴅ your God; ¹ask it either in the depth or in the height above."

12But Ahaz said, "I will not ask, nor will I test the Lᴏʀᴅ!"

13Then he said, "Hear now, O house of David! *Is it* a small thing for you to weary men, but will you weary my God also? 14Therefore the Lord Himself will give you a sign: aBehold, the virgin shall conceive and bear ba Son, and shall call His name cImmanuel.¹ 15Curds and honey He shall eat, that He may know to refuse the evil and choose the good. 16aFor before the Child shall know to refuse the evil and choose the good, the land that you dread will be forsaken by bboth her kings. 17aThe Lᴏʀᴅ will bring the king of Assyria upon you and your people and your father's house—days that have not come since the day that bEphraim departed from Judah."

18 And it shall come to pass in that day
　That the Lᴏʀᴅ awill whistle for the fly
　That *is* in the farthest part of the rivers of Egypt,
　And for the bee that *is* in the land of Assyria.
19 They will come, and all of them will rest
　In the desolate valleys and in athe clefts of the rocks,
　And on all thorns and in all pastures.
20 In the same day the Lord will shave with a ahired
　　brazor,
　With those from beyond ¹the River, with the king of
　　Assyria,
　The head and the hair of the legs,
　And will also remove the beard.
21 It shall be in that day
　That a man will keep alive a young cow and two
　　sheep;
22 So it shall be, from the abundance of milk they give,
　That he will eat curds;
　For curds and honey everyone will eat who is left in the
　　land.
23 It shall happen in that day,
　That wherever there could be a thousand vines
　Worth a thousand *shekels* of silver,
　aIt will be for briers and thorns.
24 With arrows and bows *men* will come there,
　Because all the land will become briers and thorns.

7:7 a2 Kin. 16:5; Is. 8:10; Acts 4:25, 26
7:8 a2 Sam. 8:6; 2 Kin. 17:6
7:9 a2 Chr. 20:20; Is. 5:24
7:11 aMatt. 12:38
7:14 aMatt. 1:23; Luke 1:31; John 1:45; Rev. 12:5 b[Is. 9:6] cIs. 8:8, 10
7:16 aIs. 8:4 b2 Kin. 15:30
7:17 a2 Chr. 28:19, 20; Is. 8:7, 8; 10:5, 6 b1 Kin. 12:16
7:18 aIs. 5:26
7:19 aIs. 2:19; Jer. 16:16
7:20 aIs. 10:5, 15 b2 Kin. 16:7; 2 Chr. 28:20
7:23 aIs. 5:6

7:8 ¹Lit. *shattered*　7:11 ¹Lit. *make the request deep or make it high above*
7:14 ¹Lit. *God-With-Us*　7:20 ¹The Euphrates

25 And to any hill which could be dug with the hoe,
You will not go there for fear of briers and thorns;
But it will become a range for oxen
And a place for sheep to roam.

ASSYRIA WILL INVADE THE LAND

8 Moreover the LORD said to me, "Take a large scroll, and [a]write on it with a man's pen concerning [1]Maher-Shalal-Hash-Baz. [2]And I will take for Myself faithful witnesses to record, [a]Uriah the priest and Zechariah the son of Jeberechiah."

[3]Then I went to the prophetess, and she conceived and bore a son. Then the LORD said to me, "Call his name Maher-Shalal-Hash-Baz; [4a]for before the child [1]shall have knowledge to cry 'My father' and 'My mother,' [b]the riches of Damascus and the [2]spoil of Samaria will be taken away before the king of Assyria."

[5]The LORD also spoke to me again, saying:

6 "Inasmuch as these people refused
The waters of [a]Shiloah that flow softly,
And rejoice [b]in Rezin and in Remaliah's son;
7 Now therefore, behold, the Lord brings up over them
The waters of [1]the River, strong and mighty—
The king of Assyria and all his glory;
He will [2]go up over all his channels
And go over all his banks.
8 He will pass through Judah,
He will overflow and pass over,
[a]He will reach up to the neck;
And the stretching out of his wings
Will [1]fill the breadth of Your land, O [b]Immanuel.[2]

9 "Be[a] shattered, O you peoples, and be broken in pieces!
Give ear, all you from far countries.
Gird yourselves, but be broken in pieces;
Gird yourselves, but be broken in pieces.
10 [a]Take counsel together, but it will come to nothing;
Speak the word, [b]but it will not stand,
[c]For [1]God is with us."

FEAR GOD, HEED HIS WORD

[11]For the LORD spoke thus to me with [1]a strong hand, and instructed me that I should not walk in the way of this people, saying:

12 "Do not say, 'A conspiracy,'
Concerning all that this people call a conspiracy,
Nor be afraid of their [1]threats, nor be [2]troubled.
13 The LORD of hosts, Him you shall hallow;
Let Him be your fear,
And let Him be your dread.
14 [a]He will be as a [1]sanctuary,
But [b]a stone of stumbling and a rock of [2]offense
To both the houses of Israel,
As a trap and a snare to the inhabitants of Jerusalem.

8:1 [a]Is. 30:8; Hab. 2:2

8:2 [a]2 Kin. 16:10

8:4 [a]2 Kin. 17:6; Is. 7:16
[b]2 Kin. 15:29

8:6 [a]John 9:7
[b]Is. 7:1, 2

8:8 [a]Is. 30:28
[b]Is. 7:14; Matt. 1:23

8:9 [a]Joel 3:9

8:10 [a]Is. 7:7; Acts 5:38
[b]Is. 7:14
[c]Rom. 8:31

8:14 [a]Is. 4:6; 25:4; Ezek. 11:16
[b]Luke 2:34; 20:17; Rom. 9:33; 1 Pet. 2:8

8:1 [1]Lit. *Speed the Spoil, Hasten the Booty*   8:4 [1]*knows how*   [2]*plunder*
8:7 [1]*The Euphrates*   [2]*Overflow*   8:8 [1]Lit. *be the fullness of*   [2]Lit. *God-With-Us*   8:10 [1]Heb. *Immanuel*   8:11 [1]*Mighty power*   8:12 [1]Lit. *fear* or *terror*
[2]Lit. *in dread*   8:14 [1]*holy abode*   [2]*stumbling over*

15 And many among them shall [a]stumble;
 They shall fall and be broken,
 Be snared and [1]taken."

16 Bind up the testimony,
 Seal the law among my disciples.
17 And I will wait on the LORD,
 Who [a]hides His face from the house of Jacob;
 And I [b]will hope in Him.
18 [a]Here am I and the children whom the LORD has given
  me!
 We [b]are for signs and wonders in Israel
 From the LORD of hosts,
 Who dwells in Mount Zion.

19And when they say to you, [a]"Seek those who are mediums and wizards, [b]who whisper and mutter," should not a people seek their God? *Should they* [c]*seek* the dead on behalf of the living? 20[a]To the law and to the testimony! If they do not speak according to this word, *it is* because [b]*there*[1] *is* no light in them.

21They will pass through it hard-pressed and hungry; and it shall happen, when they are hungry, that they will be enraged and [a]curse [1]their king and their God, and look upward. 22Then they will look to the earth, and see trouble and darkness, gloom of anguish; and *they will be* driven into darkness.

THE GOVERNMENT OF THE PROMISED SON
(Is. 11:1–9)

9 Nevertheless [a]the gloom *will* not *be* upon her who *is* distressed,
 As when at [b]first He lightly esteemed
 The land of Zebulun and the land of Naphtali,
 And [c]afterward more heavily oppressed *her,*
 By the way of the sea, beyond the Jordan,
 In Galilee of the Gentiles.

2 [a]The people who walked in darkness
 Have seen a great light;
 Those who dwelt in the land of the shadow of death,
 Upon them a light has shined.

3 You have multiplied the nation
 And [1]increased its joy;
 They rejoice before You
 According to the joy of harvest,
 As *men* rejoice [a]when they divide the spoil.

4 For You have broken the yoke of his burden
 And the staff of his shoulder,
 The rod of his oppressor,
 As in the day of [a]Midian.

5 For every warrior's [1]sandal from the noisy battle,
 And garments rolled in blood,
 [a]Will be used for burning *and* fuel [2]of fire.

6 [a]For unto us a Child is born,
 Unto us a [b]Son is given;

8:15 [a]Matt. 21:44
8:17
[a]Deut. 31:17;
Is. 54:8
[b]Hab. 2:3
8:18 [a]Heb. 2:13
[b]Ps. 71:7
8:19
[a]1 Sam. 28:8
[b]Is. 29:4
[c]Ps. 106:28
8:20
[a]Is. 1:10; 8:16;
Luke 16:29
[b]Is. 8:22;
Mic. 3:6
8:21 [a]Rev. 16:11
9:1 [a]Is. 8:22
[b]2 Kin. 15:29;
2 Chr. 16:4
[c]Matt. 4:13–16
9:2 [a]Matt. 4:16;
Luke 1:79;
2 Cor. 4:6;
Eph. 5:8
9:3 [a]Judg. 5:30
9:4 [a]Judg. 7:22
9:5 [a]Is. 66:15
9:6 [a][Is. 7:14;
Luke 2:11];
John 1:45
[b]Luke 2:7;
[John 3:16;
1 John 4:9]

And ᶜthe government will be upon His shoulder.
And His name will be called
ᵈWonderful, Counselor, ᵉMighty God,
Everlasting Father, ᶠPrince of Peace.

7 Of the increase of *His* government and peace
ᵃ*There will be* no end,
Upon the throne of David and over His kingdom,
To order it and establish it with judgment and justice
From that time forward, even forever.
The ᵇzeal of the LORD of hosts will perform this.

THE PUNISHMENT OF SAMARIA

8 The Lord sent a word against ᵃJacob,
And it has fallen on Israel.
9 All the people will know—
Ephraim and the inhabitant of Samaria—
Who say in pride and arrogance of heart:
10 "The bricks have fallen down,
But we will rebuild with hewn stones;
The sycamores are cut down,
But we will replace *them* with cedars."
11 Therefore the LORD shall set up
The adversaries of Rezin against him,
And spur his enemies on,
12 The Syrians before and the Philistines behind;
And they shall devour Israel with an open mouth.

For all this His anger is not turned away,
But His hand *is* ¹stretched out still.

13 For the people do not turn to Him who strikes them,
Nor do they seek the LORD of hosts.
14 Therefore the LORD will cut off head and tail from Israel,
Palm branch and bulrush ᵃin one day.
15 The elder and honorable, he *is* the head;
The prophet who teaches lies, he *is* the tail.
16 For ᵃthe leaders of this people cause *them* to err,
And *those who are* led by them are destroyed.
17 Therefore the Lord ᵃwill have no joy in their young men,
Nor have mercy on their fatherless and widows;
For everyone *is* a hypocrite and an evildoer,
And every mouth speaks ¹folly.

ᵇFor all this His anger is not turned away,
But His hand *is* stretched out still.

18 For wickedness ᵃburns as the fire;
It shall devour the briers and thorns,
And kindle in the thickets of the forest;
They shall mount up *like* rising smoke.
19 Through the wrath of the LORD of hosts
ᵃThe land is burned up,
And the people shall be as fuel for the fire;
ᵇNo man shall spare his brother.
20 And he shall ¹snatch on the right hand
And be hungry;
He shall devour on the left hand
ᵃAnd not be satisfied;

9:6
ᶜ[Matt. 28:18;
1 Cor. 15:25];
Rev. 12:5
ᵈJudg. 13:18
ᵉTitus 2:13
ᶠEph. 2:14

9:7 ᵃDan. 2:44;
Matt. 1:1, 6;
Luke 1:32, 33;
John 7:42
ᵇIs. 37:32

9:8 ᵃGen. 32:28

9:14 ᵃRev. 18:8

9:16 ᵃIs. 3:12;
Mic. 3:1, 5, 9;
Matt. 15:14

9:17 ᵃPs. 147:10
ᵇIs. 5:25

9:18 ᵃPs. 83:14;
[Is. 1:7; 10:17];
Nah. 1:10;
Mal. 4:1

9:19 ᵃIs. 8:22
ᵇMic. 7:2, 6

9:20 ᵃLev. 26:26

9:12 ¹In judgment   9:17 ¹foolishness   9:20 ¹slice off or tear

ᵇEvery man shall eat the flesh of his own arm.
21 Manasseh *shall devour* Ephraim, and Ephraim Manasseh;
Together they *shall be* ᵃagainst Judah.

ᵇFor all this His anger is not turned away,
But His hand *is* stretched out still.

10

"Woe to those who ᵃdecree unrighteous decrees,
Who write misfortune,
Which they have prescribed
2 To rob the needy of justice,
And to take what is right from the poor of My people,
That widows may be their prey,
And *that* they may rob the fatherless.
3 ᵃWhat will you do in ᵇthe day of punishment,
And in the desolation *which* will come from ᶜafar?
To whom will you flee for help?
And where will you leave your glory?
4 Without Me they shall bow down among the ᵃprisoners,
And they shall fall ¹among the slain."

ᵇFor all this His anger is not turned away,
But His hand *is* stretched out still.

ARROGANT ASSYRIA ALSO JUDGED

5 "Woe to Assyria, ᵃthe rod of My anger
And the staff in whose hand is My indignation.
6 I will send him against ᵃan ungodly nation,
And against the people of My wrath
I will ᵇgive him charge,
To seize the spoil, to take the prey,
And to tread them down like the mire of the streets.
7 ᵃYet he does not mean so,
Nor does his heart think so;
But *it is* in his heart to destroy,
And cut off not a few nations.
8 ᵃFor he says,
'*Are* not my princes altogether kings?
9 *Is* not ᵃCalno ᵇlike Carchemish?
Is not Hamath like Arpad?
Is not Samaria ᶜlike Damascus?
10 As my hand has found the kingdoms of the idols,
Whose carved images excelled those of Jerusalem and Samaria,
11 As I have done to Samaria and her idols,
Shall I not do also to Jerusalem and her idols?'"

12Therefore it shall come to pass, when the Lord has ¹performed all His work ᵃon Mount Zion and on Jerusalem, *that He will say*, ᵇ"I will punish the fruit of the arrogant heart of the king of Assyria, and the glory of his haughty looks." 13ᵃFor he says:

"By the strength of my hand I have done *it*,
And by my wisdom, for I am prudent;
Also I have removed the boundaries of the people,
And have robbed their treasuries;
So I have put down the inhabitants like a ¹valiant *man*.

9:20 ᵇJer. 19:9
9:21
ᵃ2 Chr. 28:6, 8; Is. 11:13
ᵇIs. 9:12, 17
10:1 ᵃPs. 58:2
10:3 ᵃJob 31:14
ᵇIs. 13:6; Jer. 9:9; Hos. 9:7; Luke 19:44
ᶜIs. 5:26
10:4 ᵃIs. 24:22
ᵇIs. 5:25
10:5 ᵃJer. 51:20
10:6 ᵃIs. 9:17
ᵇ2 Kin. 17:6; Jer. 34:22
10:7
ᵃGen. 50:20; Mic. 4:11, 12; Acts 2:23, 24
10:8
ᵃ2 Kin. 19:10
10:9
ᵃGen. 10:10; Amos 6:2
ᵇ2 Chr. 35:20
ᶜ2 Kin. 16:9
10:12
ᵃ2 Kin. 19:31; Is. 28:21
ᵇ2 Kin. 19:35; 2 Chr. 32:21; Jer. 50:18
10:13
ᵃ[2 Kin. 19:22–24]; Is. 37:24–27; Ezek. 28:4; Dan. 4:30

10:4 ¹Lit. *under*   10:12 ¹*completed*   10:13 ¹*mighty*

14 ªMy hand has found like a nest the riches of the people,
And as one gathers eggs *that are* left,
I have gathered all the earth;
And there was no one who moved *his* wing,
Nor opened *his* mouth with even a peep."

15 Shall ªthe ax boast itself against him who chops with it?
Or shall the saw exalt itself against him who saws with it?
As if a rod could wield *itself* against those who lift it up,
Or as if a staff could lift up, *as if it were* not wood!

16 Therefore the Lord, the ¹Lord of hosts,
Will send leanness among his fat ones;
And under his glory
He will kindle a burning
Like the burning of a fire.

17 So the Light of Israel will be for a fire,
And his Holy One for a flame;
ªIt will burn and devour
His thorns and his briers in one day.

18 And it will consume the glory of his forest and of ªhis
fruitful field,
Both soul and body;
And they will be as when a sick man wastes away.

19 Then the rest of the trees of his forest
Will be so few in number
That a child may write them.

THE RETURNING REMNANT OF ISRAEL

20 And it shall come to pass in that day
That the remnant of Israel,
And such as have escaped of the house of Jacob,
ªWill never again depend on him who ¹defeated them,
But will depend on the LORD, the Holy One of Israel, in
truth.

21 The remnant will return, the remnant of Jacob,
To the ªMighty God.

22 ªFor though your people, O Israel, be as the sand of the
sea,
ᵇA remnant of them will return;
The destruction decreed shall overflow with
righteousness.

23 ªFor the Lord GOD of hosts
Will make a determined end
In the midst of all the land.

24Therefore thus says the Lord GOD of hosts: "O My people, who dwell in Zion, ªdo not be afraid of the Assyrian. He shall strike you with a rod and lift up his staff against you, in the manner of ᵇEgypt. 25For yet a very little while ªand the indignation will cease, as will My anger in their destruction." 26And the LORD of hosts will ¹stir up ªa scourge for him like the slaughter of ᵇMidian at the rock of Oreb; ᶜ*as* His rod was on the sea, so will He lift it up in the manner of Egypt.

27 It shall come to pass in that day
That his burden will be taken away from your shoulder,

10:14 ªJob 31:25
10:15 ªJer. 51:20
10:17 ªIs. 9:18
10:18
ª2 Kin. 19:23
10:20
ª2 Kin. 16:7
10:21 ª[Is. 9:6]
10:22
ªRom. 9:27, 28
ᵇIs. 6:13
10:23 ªIs. 28:22;
Dan. 9:27;
Rom. 9:28
10:24
ªIs. 7:4; 12:2
ᵇEx. 14
10:25 ªIs. 10:5;
26:20;
Dan. 11:36
10:26
ª2 Kin. 19:35
ᵇJudg. 7:25;
Is. 9:4
ᶜEx. 14:26, 27

10:16 ¹So with Bg.; MT, DSS *YHWH* (the LORD)   10:20 ¹Lit. *struck*
10:26 ¹*arouse*

And his yoke from your neck,
And the yoke will be destroyed because of [a]the anointing
oil.

28 He has come to Aiath,
He has passed Migron;
At Michmash he has attended to his equipment.
29 They have gone [1]along [a]the ridge,
They have taken up lodging at Geba.
Ramah is afraid,
[b]Gibeah of Saul has fled.
30 [1]Lift up your voice,
O daughter [a]of Gallim!
Cause it to be heard as far as [b]Laish—
[2]O poor Anathoth!
31 [a]Madmenah has fled,
The inhabitants of Gebim seek refuge.
32 As yet he will remain [a]at Nob that day;
He will [b]shake his fist at the mount of [c]the daughter of
Zion,
The hill of Jerusalem.

33 Behold, the Lord,
The LORD of hosts,
Will lop off the bough with terror;
[a]Those of high stature *will be* hewn down,
And the haughty will be humbled.
34 He will cut down the thickets of the forest with iron,
And Lebanon will fall by the Mighty One.

THE REIGN OF JESSE'S OFFSPRING
(*Is. 9:1–7*)

11 There [a]shall come forth a [1]Rod from the [2]stem
of [b]Jesse,
And [c]a Branch shall [3]grow out of his roots.
2 [a]The Spirit of the LORD shall rest upon Him,
The Spirit of wisdom and understanding,
The Spirit of counsel and might,
The Spirit of knowledge and of the fear of the LORD.

3 His delight *is* in the fear of the LORD,
And He shall not judge by the sight of His eyes,
Nor decide by the hearing of His ears;
4 But [a]with righteousness He shall judge the poor,
And decide with equity for the meek of the earth;
He shall [b]strike the earth with the rod of His mouth,
And with the breath of His lips He shall slay the wicked.
5 Righteousness shall be the belt of His loins,
And faithfulness the belt of His waist.

6 "The[a] wolf also shall dwell with the lamb,
The leopard shall lie down with the young goat,
The calf and the young lion and the fatling together;
And a little child shall lead them.
7 The cow and the bear shall graze;
Their young ones shall lie down together;
And the lion shall eat straw like the ox.

Cross references:
10:27 [a]Ps. 105:15; [1 John 2:20]
10:29 [a]1 Sam. 13:23 [b]1 Sam. 11:4
10:30 [a]1 Sam. 25:44 [b]Judg. 18:7
10:31 [a]Josh. 15:31
10:32 [a]1 Sam. 21:1; Neh. 11:32 [b]Is. 13:2 [c]Is. 37:22
10:33 [a]Is. 37:24, 36–38; Ezek. 31:3; Amos 2:9
11:1 [a][Zech. 6:12]; Rev. 5:5 [b][Is. 9:7; 11:10]; Matt. 1:5; [Acts 13:23] [c]Is. 4:2
11:2 [a][Is. 42:1; 48:16; 61:1; Matt. 3:16]; Mark 1:10; Luke 3:22; [John 1:32]
11:4 [a]Rev. 19:11 [b]Job 4:9; Is. 30:28, 33; Mal. 4:6; 2 Thess. 2:8
11:6 [a]Hos. 2:18

10:29 [1]Or *over the pass*   10:30 [1]Or *Cry shrilly*   [2]So with MT, Tg., Vg.; LXX, Syr. *Listen to her, O Anathoth*   11:1 [1]*Shoot*   [2]*stock* or *trunk*   [3]*be fruitful*

8 The nursing child shall play by the cobra's hole,
And the weaned child shall put his hand in the viper's den.

9 ᵃThey shall not hurt nor destroy in all My holy mountain,
For ᵇthe earth shall be full of the knowledge of the LORD
As the waters cover the sea.

10 "Andᵃ in that day ᵇthere shall be a Root of Jesse,
Who shall stand as a ᶜbanner to the people;
For the ᵈGentiles shall seek Him,
And His resting place shall be glorious."

11 It shall come to pass in that day
That the Lord shall set His hand again the second time
To recover the remnant of His people who are left,
ᵃFrom Assyria and Egypt,
From Pathros and Cush,
From Elam and Shinar,
From Hamath and the ¹islands of the sea.

12 He will set up a banner for the nations,
And will ¹assemble the outcasts of Israel,
And gather together ᵃthe dispersed of Judah
From the four ²corners of the earth.

13 Also ᵃthe envy of Ephraim shall depart,
And the adversaries of Judah shall be cut off;
Ephraim shall not envy Judah,
And Judah shall not harass Ephraim.

14 But they shall fly down upon the shoulder of the
Philistines toward the west;
Together they shall plunder the ¹people of the East;
ᵃThey shall lay their hand on Edom and Moab;
And the people of Ammon shall obey them.

15 The LORD ᵃwill utterly ¹destroy the tongue of the Sea of
Egypt;
With His mighty wind He will shake His fist over ²the
River,
And strike it in the seven streams,
And make *men* cross over ³dry-shod.

16 ᵃThere will be a highway for the remnant of His people
Who will be left from Assyria,
ᵇAs it was for Israel
In the day that he came up from the land of Egypt.

A HYMN OF PRAISE

12 And ᵃin that day you will say:

"O LORD, I will praise You;
Though You were angry with me,
Your anger is turned away, and You comfort me.

2 Behold, God *is* my salvation,
I will trust and not be afraid;
ᵃ'For ᵇYAH, the LORD, *is* my strength and song;
He also has become my salvation.'"

3 Therefore with joy you will draw ᵃwater
From the wells of salvation.

11:9 ᵃJob 5:23;
Is. 65:25;
Ezek. 34:25;
Hos. 2:18
ᵇPs. 98:2, 3;
Is. 45:6;
Hab. 2:14

11:10 ᵃIs. 2:11
ᵇIs. 11:1;
Rom. 15:12
ᶜIs. 27:12, 13
ᵈRom. 15:10

11:11
ᵃIs. 19:23–25;
Hos. 11:11;
Zech. 10:10

11:12 ᵃJohn 7:35

11:13 ᵃIs. 9:21;
Jer. 3:18;
Ezek. 37:16,
17, 22;
Hos. 1:11

11:14 ᵃIs. 63:1;
Dan. 11:41;
Joel 3:19;
Amos 9:12

11:15 ᵃIs. 50:2;
51:10, 11;
Zech. 10:10, 11

11:16 ᵃIs. 19:23
ᵇEx. 14:29

12:1 ᵃIs. 2:11

12:2 ᵃPs. 83:18
ᵇEx. 15:2;
Ps. 118:14

12:3
ᵃ[John 4:10, 14;
7:37, 38]

11:11 ¹Or *coastlands*   11:12 ¹*gather*   ²Lit. *wings*   11:14 ¹Lit. *sons*   11:15 ¹So
with MT, Vg.; LXX, Syr., Tg. *dry up*   ²The Euphrates   ³Lit. *in sandals*

⁴And in that day you will say:

ᵃ"Praise the LORD, call upon His name;
ᵇDeclare His deeds among the peoples,
Make mention that His ᶜname is exalted.
5   ᵃSing to the LORD,
For He has done excellent things;
This *is* known in all the earth.
6   ᵃCry out and shout, O inhabitant of Zion,
For great *is* ᵇthe Holy One of Israel in your
midst!"

PROCLAMATION AGAINST BABYLON

13 The ᵃburden¹ against Babylon which Isaiah the son of
Amoz saw.

2   "Liftᵃ up a banner ᵇon the high mountain,
Raise your voice to them;
ᶜWave your hand, that they may enter the gates of the
nobles.
3   I have commanded My ¹sanctified ones;
I have also called ᵃMy mighty ones for My anger—
Those who ᵇrejoice in My exaltation."

4   The ᵃnoise of a multitude in the mountains,
Like that of many people!
A tumultuous noise of the kingdoms of nations gathered
together!
The LORD of hosts musters
The army for battle.
5   They come from a far country,
From the end of heaven—
The ᵃLORD and His ¹weapons of indignation,
To destroy the whole ᵇland.

6   Wail, ᵃfor the day of the LORD *is* at hand!
ᵇIt will come as destruction from the Almighty.
7   Therefore all hands will be limp,
Every man's heart will melt,
8   And they will be afraid.
ᵃPangs¹ and sorrows will take hold of *them;*
They will be in pain as a woman in childbirth;
They will be amazed at one another;
Their faces *will be like* flames.

9   Behold, ᵃthe day of the LORD comes,
Cruel, with both wrath and fierce anger,
To lay the land desolate;
And He will destroy ᵇits sinners from it.
10   For the stars of heaven and their constellations
Will not give their light;
The sun will be ᵃdarkened in its going forth,
And the moon will not cause its light to shine.

11   "I will ᵃpunish the world for *its* evil,
And the wicked for their iniquity;
ᵇI will halt the arrogance of the proud,
And will lay low the haughtiness of the ¹terrible.

12:4 ᵃ1 Chr. 16:8;
Ps. 105:1
ᵇPs. 145:4–6
ᶜPs. 34:3

12:5 ᵃEx. 15:1;
Ps. 98:1;
Is. 24:14; 42:10,
11; 44:23

12:6
ᵃIs. 52:9; 54:1;
Zeph. 3:14, 15
ᵇPs. 89:18

13:1
ᵃJer. 50; 51;
Matt. 1:11;
Rev. 14:8

13:2 ᵃIs. 18:3
ᵇJer. 51:25
ᶜIs. 10:32

13:3 ᵃJoel 3:11
ᵇPs. 149:2

13:4 ᵃIs. 17:12;
Joel 3:14

13:5 ᵃIs. 42:13
ᵇIs. 24:1; 34:2

13:6 ᵃIs. 2:12;
Ezek. 30:3;
Amos 5:18;
Zeph. 1:7;
Rev. 6:17
ᵇIs. 10:25;
Job 31:23;
Joel 1:15

13:8 ᵃPs. 48:6

13:9 ᵃMal. 4:1
ᵇPs. 104:35;
Prov. 2:22

13:10
ᵃIs. 24:21–23;
Ezek. 32:7;
Joel 2:31;
Matt. 24:29;
Mark 13:24;
Luke 21:25

13:11 ᵃIs. 26:21
ᵇ[Is. 2:17]

13:1 ¹*oracle, prophecy*   **13:3** ¹*consecrated* or *set apart*   **13:5** ¹Or *instruments*
13:8 ¹*Sharp pains*   **13:11** ¹Or *tyrants*

12 I will make a mortal more rare than fine gold,
    A man more than the golden wedge of Ophir.
13 ᵃTherefore I will shake the heavens,
    And the earth will move out of her place,
    In the wrath of the LORD of hosts
    And in ᵇthe day of His fierce anger.
14 It shall be as the hunted gazelle,
    And as a sheep that no man ¹takes up;
    ᵃEvery man will turn to his own people,
    And everyone will flee to his own land.
15 Everyone who is found will be thrust through,
    And everyone who is captured will fall by the sword.
16 Their children also will be ᵃdashed to pieces before their
        eyes;
    Their houses will be plundered
    And their wives ᵇravished.

17 "Behold,ᵃ I will stir up the Medes against them,
    Who will not ¹regard silver;
    And as for gold, they will not delight in it.
18 Also their bows will dash the young men to pieces,
    And they will have no pity on the fruit of the womb;
    Their eye will not spare children.
19 ᵃAnd Babylon, the glory of kingdoms,
    The beauty of the Chaldeans' pride,
    Will be as when God overthrew ᵇSodom and
        Gomorrah.
20 ᵃIt will never be inhabited,
    Nor will it be settled from generation to
        generation;
    Nor will the Arabian pitch tents there,
    Nor will the shepherds make their sheepfolds there.
21 ᵃBut wild beasts of the desert will lie there,
    And their houses will be full of ¹owls;
    Ostriches will dwell there,
    And wild goats will caper there.
22 The hyenas will howl in their citadels,
    And jackals in their pleasant palaces.
    ᵃHer time is near to come,
    And her days will not be prolonged."

MERCY ON JACOB

14 For the LORD ᵃwill have mercy on Jacob, and ᵇwill still choose Israel, and settle them in their own land. ᶜThe strangers will be joined with them, and they will cling to the house of Jacob. ²Then people will take them ᵃand bring them to their place, and the house of Israel will possess them for servants and maids in the land of the LORD; they will take them captive whose captives they were, ᵇand rule over their oppressors.

FALL OF THE KING OF BABYLON

³It shall come to pass in the day the LORD gives you rest from your sorrow, and from your fear and the hard bondage in which you were made to serve, ⁴that you ᵃwill take up this proverb against the king of Babylon, and say:

13:13 ᵃIs. 34:4; 51:6; Hag. 2:6
ᵇPs. 110:5; Lam. 1:12

13:14 ᵃJer. 50:16; 51:9

13:16 ᵃPs. 137:8, 9; Is. 13:18; 14:21; Hos. 10:14; Nah. 3:10
ᵇZech. 14:2

13:17 ᵃIs. 21:2; Jer. 51:11, 28; Dan. 5:28, 31

13:19 ᵃIs. 14:4; Dan. 4:30; Rev. 18:11–16, 19, 21
ᵇGen. 19:24; Deut. 29:23; Jer. 50:40; Amos 4:11

13:20 ᵃJer. 50:3

13:21 ᵃIs. 34:11–15; Zeph. 2:14; Rev. 18:2

13:22 ᵃJer. 51:33

14:1 ᵃPs. 102:13; Is. 49:13, 15; 54:7, 8
ᵇIs. 41:8, 9; Zech. 1:17; 2:12
ᶜIs. 60:4, 5, 10

14:2 ᵃIs. 49:22; 60:9; 66:20
ᵇIs. 60:14

14:4 ᵃIs. 13:19; Hab. 2:6

13:14 ¹gathers   13:17 ¹esteem   13:21 ¹Or howling creatures

"How the oppressor has ceased,
The [b]golden[1] city ceased!
5 The LORD has broken [a]the staff of the wicked,
The scepter of the rulers;
6 He who struck the people in wrath with a continual stroke,
He who ruled the nations in anger,
Is persecuted *and* no one hinders.
7 The whole earth is at rest *and* quiet;
They break forth into singing.
8 [a]Indeed the cypress trees rejoice over you,
And the cedars of Lebanon,
Saying, 'Since you [1]were cut down,
No woodsman has come up against us.'

9 "Hell[a1] from beneath is excited about you,
To meet *you* at your coming;
It stirs up the dead for you,
All the chief ones of the earth;
It has raised up from their thrones
All the kings of the nations.
10 They all shall [a]speak and say to you:
'Have you also become as weak as we?
Have you become like us?
11 Your pomp is brought down to Sheol,
And the sound of your stringed instruments;
The maggot is spread under you,
And worms cover you.'

THE FALL OF LUCIFER

12 "How[a] you are fallen from heaven,
O [1]Lucifer, son of the morning!
How you are cut down to the ground,
You who weakened the nations!
13 For you have said in your heart:
[a]'I will ascend into heaven,
[b]I will exalt my throne above the stars of God;
I will also sit on the [c]mount of the congregation
[d]On the farthest sides of the north;
14 I will ascend above the heights of the clouds,
[a]I will be like the Most High.'
15 Yet you [a]shall be brought down to Sheol,
To the [1]lowest depths of the Pit.

16 "Those who see you will gaze at you,
And consider you, *saying:*
'*Is* this the man who made the earth tremble,
Who shook kingdoms,
17 Who made the world as a wilderness
And destroyed its cities,
Who [1]did not open the house of his prisoners?'

18 "All the kings of the nations,
All of them, sleep in glory,
Everyone in his own house;
19 But you are cast out of your grave
Like an [1]abominable branch,

14:4 [b]Rev. 18:16
14:5 [a]Ps. 125:3
14:8 [a]Is. 55:12;
Ezek. 31:16
14:9 [a]Ezek. 32:21
14:10
[a]Ezek. 32:21
14:12 [a]Is. 34:4;
Luke 10:18;
[Rev. 12:7–9]
14:13
[a]Ezek. 28:2;
Matt. 11:23;
[b]Dan. 8:10;
2 Thess. 2:4
[c]Ezek. 28:14
[d]Ps. 48:2
14:14 [a]Is. 47:8;
2 Thess. 2:4
14:15
[a]Ezek. 28:8;
Matt. 11:23;
Luke 10:15

14:4 [1]Or *insolent*   14:8 [1]*have lain down*   14:9 [1]Or *Sheol*   14:12 [1]Lit. *Day Star*   14:15 [1]Lit. *recesses*   14:17 [1]*Would not release*   14:19 [1]*despised*

Like the garment of those who are slain,
²Thrust through with a sword,
Who go down to the stones of the pit,
Like a corpse trodden underfoot.
20　You will not be joined with them in burial,
Because you have destroyed your land
And slain your people.
ᵃThe brood of evildoers shall never be named.
21　Prepare slaughter for his children
ᵃBecause of the iniquity of their fathers,
Lest they rise up and possess the land,
And fill the face of the world with cities."

BABYLON DESTROYED

22　"For I will rise up against them," says the LORD of
hosts,
"And cut off from Babylon ᵃthe name and ᵇremnant,
ᶜAnd offspring and posterity," says the LORD.
23　"I will also make it a possession for the ᵃporcupine,
And marshes of muddy water;
I will sweep it with the broom of destruction," says the
LORD of hosts.

ASSYRIA DESTROYED

24　The LORD of hosts has sworn, saying,
"Surely, as I have thought, so it shall come to pass,
And as I have purposed, *so* it shall ᵃstand:
25　That I will break the ᵃAssyrian in My land,
And on My mountains tread him underfoot.
Then ᵇhis yoke shall be removed from them,
And his burden removed from their shoulders.
26　This *is* the ᵃpurpose that is purposed against the whole
earth,
And this *is* the hand that is stretched out over all the
nations.
27　For the LORD of hosts has ᵃpurposed,
And who will annul *it*?
His hand *is* stretched out,
And who will turn it back?"

PHILISTIA DESTROYED

28This is the ¹burden which came in the year that ᵃKing
Ahaz died.

29　"Do not rejoice, all you of Philistia,
ᵃBecause the rod that struck you is broken;
For out of the serpent's roots will come forth a viper,
ᵇAnd its offspring *will be* a fiery flying serpent.
30　The firstborn of the poor will feed,
And the needy will lie down in safety;
I will kill your roots with famine,
And it will slay your remnant.
31　Wail, O gate! Cry, O city!
All you of Philistia *are* dissolved;
For smoke will come from the north,
And no one *will be* alone in his ¹appointed times."

14:20
ᵃJob 18:19;
Ps. 21:10; 109:13;
Is. 1:4; 31:2
14:21 ᵃEx. 20:5;
Lev. 26:39;
Is. 13:16;
Matt. 23:35
14:22
ᵃProv. 10:7;
Is. 26:14;
Jer. 51:62
ᵇ1 Kin. 14:10
ᶜJob 18:19;
Is. 47:9
14:23 ᵃIs. 34:11;
Zeph. 2:14
14:24 ᵃIs. 43:13
14:25
ᵃMic. 5:5, 6;
Zeph. 2:13
ᵇIs. 10:27;
Nah. 1:13
14:26 ᵃIs. 23:9;
Zeph. 3:6, 8
14:27
ᵃ2 Chr. 20:6;
Job 9:12;
23:13; Ps. 33:11;
Prov. 19:21;
21:30; Is. 43:13;
Dan. 4:31, 35
14:28
ᵃ2 Kin. 16:20;
2 Chr. 28:27
14:29
ᵃ2 Chr. 26:6
ᵇ2 Kin. 18:8

14:19 ²*Pierced*　14:28 ¹*oracle, prophecy*　14:31 ¹Or *ranks*

32 What will they answer the messengers of the nation?
That ^athe LORD has founded Zion,
And ^bthe poor of His people shall take refuge in it.

PROCLAMATION AGAINST MOAB

15 The ^aburden[1] against Moab.

Because in the night ^bAr of ^cMoab is laid waste
And destroyed,
Because in the night Kir of Moab is laid waste
And destroyed,
2 He has gone up to the [1]temple and Dibon,
To the high places to weep.
Moab will wail over Nebo and over Medeba;
^aOn all their heads *will be* baldness,
And every beard cut off.
3 In their streets they will clothe themselves with
sackcloth;
On the tops of their houses
And in their streets
Everyone will wail, ^aweeping bitterly.
4 Heshbon and Elealeh will cry out,
Their voice shall be heard as far as ^aJahaz;
Therefore the [1]armed soldiers of Moab will cry out;
His life will be burdensome to him.

5 "My^a heart will cry out for Moab;
His fugitives *shall flee* to Zoar,
Like [1]a three-year-old heifer.
For ^bby the Ascent of Luhith
They will go up with weeping;
For in the way of Horonaim
They will raise up a cry of destruction,
6 For the waters ^aof Nimrim will be desolate,
For the green grass has withered away;
The grass fails, there is nothing green.
7 Therefore the abundance they have gained,
And what they have laid up,
They will carry away to the Brook of the Willows.
8 For the cry has gone all around the borders of Moab,
Its wailing to Eglaim
And its wailing to Beer Elim.
9 For the waters of [1]Dimon will be full of blood;
Because I will bring more upon Dimon,
^aLions upon him who escapes from Moab,
And on the remnant of the land."

MOAB DESTROYED

16 Send ^athe lamb to the ruler of the land,
^bFrom [1]Sela to the wilderness,
To the mount of the daughter of Zion.
2 For it shall be as a ^awandering bird thrown out of the
nest;
So shall be the daughters of Moab at the fords of the
^bArnon.

14:32 ^aPs. 87:1, 5
^bZech. 11:11

15:1 ^a2 Kin. 3:4
^bDeut. 2:9;
Num. 21:28
^cIs. 15:1—16:14;
Jer. 25:21;
48:1–47;
Amos 2:1–3;
Zeph. 2:8–11

15:2 ^aLev. 21:5;
Jer. 48:37

15:3 ^aJer. 48:38

15:4
^aNum. 21:28;
32:3; Jer. 48:34

15:5 ^aIs. 16:11;
Jer. 48:31
^bJer. 48:5

15:6
^aNum. 32:36

15:9
^a2 Kin. 17:25;
Jer. 50:17

16:1 ^a2 Kin. 3:4;
Ezra 7:17
^b2 Kin. 14:7;
Is. 42:11

16:2 ^aProv. 27:8
^bNum. 21:13

15:1 [1]*oracle, prophecy*   15:2 [1]Heb. *bayith*, lit. *house*   15:4 [1]So with MT, Tg.,
Vg.; LXX, Syr. *loins*   15:5 [1]Or *The Third Eglath*, an unknown city, Jer. 48:34
15:9 [1]So with MT, Tg.; DSS, Vg. *Dibon*; LXX *Rimon*   16:1 [1]Lit. *Rock*

3 "Take counsel, execute judgment;
  Make your shadow like the night in the middle of the
      day;
  Hide the outcasts,
  Do not betray him who escapes.
4 Let My outcasts dwell with you, O Moab;
  Be a shelter to them from the face of the [1]spoiler.
  For the extortioner is at an end,
  Devastation ceases,
  The oppressors are consumed out of the land.
5 In mercy [a]the throne will be established;
  And One will sit on it in truth, in the tabernacle of
      David,
  [b]Judging and seeking justice and hastening
      [c]righteousness."

6 We have heard of the [a]pride of Moab—
  He is very proud—
  Of his haughtiness and his pride and his wrath;
  [b]*But* his [1]lies *shall* not *be* so.
7 Therefore Moab shall [a]wail for Moab;
  Everyone shall wail.
  For the foundations [b]of Kir Hareseth you shall mourn;
  Surely *they are* stricken.

8 For [a]the fields of Heshbon languish,
  And [b]the vine of Sibmah;
  The lords of the nations have broken down its choice
      plants,
  Which have reached to Jazer
  And wandered through the wilderness.
  Her branches are stretched out,
  They are gone over the [c]sea.
9 Therefore I will bewail the vine of Sibmah,
  With the weeping of Jazer;
  I will drench you with my tears,
  [a]O Heshbon and Elealeh;
  For [1]battle cries have fallen
  Over your summer fruits and your harvest.

10 [a]Gladness is taken away,
  And joy from the plentiful field;
  In the vineyards there will be no singing,
  Nor will there be shouting;
  No treaders will tread out wine in the presses;
  I have made their shouting cease.
11 Therefore [a]my [1]heart shall resound like a harp for Moab,
  And my inner being for [2]Kir Heres.

12 And it shall come to pass,
  When it is seen that Moab is weary on [a]the high place,
  That he will come to his sanctuary to pray;
  But he will not prevail.

13This *is* the word which the LORD has spoken concerning
Moab since that time. 14But now the LORD has spoken, saying,
"Within three years, [a]as the years of a hired man, the glory of

16:5
[a][Is. 9:6, 7; 32:1;
55:4; Dan. 7:14;
Mic. 4:7;
Luke 1:33;
Rev. 11:15]
[b]Ps. 72:2 [c]Is. 9:7

16:6 [a]Jer. 48:29;
Amos 2:1;
Obad. 3, 4;
Zeph. 2:8, 10
[b]Is. 28:15

16:7 [a]Jer. 48:20
[b]2 Kin. 3:25;
Jer. 48:31

16:8 [a]Is. 24:7
[b]Is. 16:9
[c]Jer. 48:32

16:9 [a]Is. 15:4

16:10 [a]Is. 24:8;
Jer. 48:33

16:11 [a]Is. 15:5;
63:15; Jer. 48:36;
Hos. 11:8;
Phil. 2:1

16:12 [a]Is. 15:2

16:14 [a]Job 7:1;
14:6; Is. 21:16

16:4 [1]*devastator*   16:6 [1]Lit. *vain talk*   16:9 [1]Or *shouting has*   16:11 [1]Lit.
belly   [2]*Kir Hareseth, v. 7*

Moab will be despised with all that great multitude, and the remnant *will be* very small *and* feeble."

PROCLAMATION AGAINST SYRIA AND ISRAEL

17 The ᵃburden[1] against Damascus.

"Behold, Damascus will cease from *being* a city,
And it will be a ruinous heap.
2 [1]The cities of ᵃAroer *are* forsaken;
They will be for flocks
Which lie down, and ᵇno one will make *them* afraid.
3 ᵃThe fortress also will cease from Ephraim,
The kingdom from Damascus,
And the remnant of Syria;
They will be as the glory of the children of Israel,"
Says the LORD of hosts.

4 "In that day it shall come to pass
That the glory of Jacob will [1]wane,
And ᵃthe fatness of his flesh grow lean.
5 ᵃIt shall be as when the harvester gathers the grain,
And reaps the heads with his arm;
It shall be as he who gathers heads of grain
In the Valley of Rephaim.
6 ᵃYet gleaning grapes will be left in it,
Like the shaking of an olive tree,
Two *or* three olives at the top of the uppermost bough,
Four *or* five in its most fruitful branches,"
Says the LORD God of Israel.

7 In that day a man will ᵃlook to his Maker,
And his eyes will have respect for the Holy One of Israel.
8 He will not look to the altars,
The work of his hands;
He will not respect what his ᵃfingers have made,
Nor the [1]wooden images nor the incense altars.

9 In that day his strong cities will be as a forsaken [1]bough
And [2]an uppermost branch,
Which they left because of the children of Israel;
And there will be desolation.

10 Because you have forgotten ᵃthe God of your salvation,
And have not been mindful of the Rock of your
[1]stronghold,
Therefore you will plant pleasant plants
And set out foreign seedlings;
11 In the day you will make your plant to grow,
And in the morning you will make your seed to flourish;
But the harvest *will be* a heap of ruins
In the day of grief and desperate sorrow.

12 Woe to the multitude of many people
Who make a noise ᵃlike the roar of the seas,
And to the rushing of nations
That make a rushing like the rushing of mighty waters!

17:1
ᵃGen. 14:15; 15:2;
2 Kin. 16:9;
Jer. 49:23;
Amos 1:3–5;
Zech. 9:1;
Acts 9:2

17:2
ᵃNum. 32:34
ᵇJer. 7:33
17:3 ᵃIs. 7:16; 8:4
17:4 ᵃIs. 10:16
17:5 ᵃIs. 17:11;
Jer. 51:33;
Joel 3:13;
Matt. 13:30
17:6 ᵃDeut. 4:27;
Is. 24:13;
Obad. 5
17:7 ᵃIs. 10:20;
Hos. 3:5;
Mic. 7:7
17:8 ᵃIs. 2:8; 31:7
17:10 ᵃPs. 68:19;
Is. 51:13
17:12 ᵃIs. 5:30;
Jer. 6:23;
Ezek. 43:2;
Luke 21:25

17:1 [1]*oracle, prophecy* 17:2 [1]So with MT, Vg.; LXX *It shall be forsaken forever;* Tg. *Its cities shall be forsaken and desolate* 17:4 [1]*fade* 17:8 [1]Heb. *Asherim,* Canaanite deities 17:9 [1]LXX *Hivites;* Tg. *laid waste;* Vg. *as the plows* [2]LXX *Amorites;* Tg. *in ruins;* Vg. *corn* 17:10 [1]*refuge*

13 The nations will rush like the rushing of many waters;
But *God* will ^arebuke them and they will flee far away,
And ^bbe chased like the chaff of the mountains before
the wind,
Like a rolling thing before the whirlwind.
14 Then behold, at eventide, trouble!
And before the morning, he *is* no more.
This *is* the portion of those who plunder us,
And the lot of those who rob us.

PROCLAMATION AGAINST ETHIOPIA

18 Woe ^ato the land shadowed with buzzing wings,
Which *is* beyond the rivers of ¹Ethiopia,
2 Which sends ambassadors by sea,
Even in vessels of reed on the waters, *saying,*
"Go, swift messengers, to a nation tall and smooth *of skin,*
To a people terrible from their beginning onward,
A nation powerful and treading down,
Whose land the rivers divide."

3 All inhabitants of the world and dwellers on the earth:
^aWhen he lifts up a banner on the mountains, you see *it;*
And when he blows a trumpet, you hear *it.*
4 For so the LORD said to me,
"I will take My rest,
And I will ¹look from My dwelling place
Like clear heat in sunshine,
Like a cloud of dew in the heat of harvest."
5 For before the harvest, when the bud is perfect
And the sour grape is ripening in the flower,
He will both cut off the sprigs with pruning hooks
And take away *and* cut down the branches.
6 They will be left together for the mountain birds of prey
And for the beasts of the earth;
The birds of prey will summer on them,
And all the beasts of the earth will winter on them.

7 In that time ^aa present will be brought to the LORD of
hosts
¹From a people tall and smooth *of skin,*
And from a people terrible from their beginning
onward,
A nation powerful and treading down,
Whose land the rivers divide—
To the place of the name of the LORD of hosts,
To Mount Zion.

PROCLAMATION AGAINST EGYPT

19 The ^aburden¹ against Egypt.

Behold, the LORD ^brides on a swift cloud,
And will come into Egypt;
^cThe idols of Egypt will ²totter at His presence,
And the heart of Egypt will melt in its midst.

2 "I will ^aset Egyptians against Egyptians;
Everyone will fight against his brother,

17:13 ^aPs. 9:5;
Is. 41:11
^bPs. 83:13;
Hos. 13:3

18:1 ^a2 Kin. 19:9;
Is. 20:4, 5;
Ezek. 30:4, 5, 9;
Zeph. 2:12; 3:10

18:3 ^aIs. 5:26

18:7 ^aPs. 68:31;
72:10; Is. 16:1;
Zeph. 3:10;
Mal. 1:11;
Acts 8:27–38

19:1
^aJer. 9:25, 26;
Ezek. 29:1—
30:19; Joel 3:19
^bPs. 18:10; 104:3;
Matt. 26:64;
Rev. 1:7
^cEx. 12:12;
Jer. 43:12

19:2 ^aJudg. 7:22;
1 Sam. 14:16, 20;
2 Chr. 20:23;
Matt. 10:21, 36

18:1 ¹Heb. *Cush*   18:4 ¹*watch*   18:7 ¹So with DSS, LXX, Vg.; MT omits *From;*
Tg. *To*   19:1 ¹*oracle, prophecy*   ²Lit. *shake*

And everyone against his neighbor,
City against city, kingdom against kingdom.

3 The spirit of Egypt will fail in its midst;
I will destroy their counsel,
And they will [a]consult the idols and the charmers,
The mediums and the sorcerers.

4 And the Egyptians I will give
[a]Into the hand of a cruel master,
And a fierce king will rule over them,"
Says the Lord, the LORD of hosts.

5 [a]The waters will fail from the sea,
And the river will be wasted and dried up.

6 The rivers will turn foul;
The brooks [a]of defense will be emptied and dried up;
The reeds and rushes will wither.

7 The papyrus reeds by [1]the River, by the mouth of the
River,
And everything sown by the River,
Will wither, be driven away, and be no more.

8 The fishermen also will mourn;
All those will lament who cast hooks into the River,
And they will languish who spread nets on the
waters.

9 Moreover those who work in [a]fine flax
And those who weave fine fabric will be ashamed;

10 And its foundations will be broken.
All who make wages *will be* troubled of soul.

11 Surely the princes of [a]Zoan *are* fools;
Pharaoh's wise counselors give foolish counsel.
[b]How do you say to Pharaoh, "I *am* the son of the
wise,
The son of ancient kings?"

12 [a]Where *are* they?
Where are your wise men?
Let them tell you now,
And let them know what the LORD of hosts has
[b]purposed against Egypt.

13 The princes of Zoan have become fools;
[a]The princes of [1]Noph are deceived;
They have also [2]deluded Egypt,
Those who are the [3]mainstay of its tribes.

14 The LORD has mingled [a]a perverse spirit in her midst;
And they have caused Egypt to err in all her work,
As a drunken man staggers in his vomit.

15 Neither will there be *any* work for Egypt,
Which [a]the head or tail,
Palm branch or bulrush, may do.

16In that day Egypt will [a]be like women, and will be afraid
and fear because of the waving of the hand of the LORD of
hosts, [b]which He waves over it. 17And the land of Judah will be
a terror to Egypt; everyone who makes mention of it will be
afraid in himself, because of the counsel of the LORD of hosts
which He has [a]determined against it.

19:7 [1]The Nile   **19:13** [1]Ancient Memphis   [2]Lit. *caused to stagger*
[3]*cornerstone*

19:3
[a]1 Chr. 10:13;
Is. 8:19; 47:12;
Dan. 2:2

19:4 [a]Is. 20:4;
Jer. 46:26;
Ezek. 29:19

19:5 [a]Is. 50:2;
Jer. 51:36;
Ezek. 30:12

19:6
[a]2 Kin. 19:24

19:9
[a]1 Kin. 10:28;
Prov. 7:16;
Ezek. 27:7

19:11
[a]Num. 13:22;
Ps. 78:12, 43;
Is. 30:4
[b]Gen. 41:38, 39;
1 Kin. 4:29, 30;
Acts 7:22

19:12 [a]1 Cor. 1:20
[b]Ps. 33:11

19:13 [a]Jer. 2:16;
Ezek. 30:13

19:14
[a]1 Kin. 22:22;
Is. 29:10

19:15 [a]Is. 9:14–16

19:16 [a]Jer. 51:30;
Nah. 3:13
[b]Is. 11:15

19:17 [a]Is. 14:24;
Dan. 4:35

EGYPT, ASSYRIA, AND ISRAEL BLESSED

18In that day five cities in the land of Egypt will ªspeak the language of Canaan and ᵇswear by the LORD of hosts; one will be called the City of ¹Destruction.

19In that day ªthere will be an altar to the LORD in the midst of the land of Egypt, and a pillar to the ᵇLORD at its border. 20And ªit will be for a sign and for a witness to the LORD of hosts in the land of Egypt; for they will cry to the LORD because of the oppressors, and He will send them a ᵇSavior and a Mighty One, and He will deliver them. 21Then the LORD will be known to Egypt, and the Egyptians will ªknow the LORD in that day, and ᵇwill make sacrifice and offering; yes, they will make a vow to the LORD and perform *it.* 22And the LORD will strike Egypt, He will strike and ªheal *it;* they will return to the LORD, and He will be entreated by them and heal them.

23In that day ªthere will be a highway from Egypt to Assyria, and the Assyrian will come into Egypt and the Egyptian into Assyria, and the Egyptians will ᵇserve with the Assyrians.

24In that day Israel will be one of three with Egypt and Assyria—a blessing in the midst of the land, 25whom the LORD of hosts shall bless, saying, "Blessed *is* Egypt My people, and Assyria ªthe work of My hands, and Israel My inheritance."

THE SIGN AGAINST EGYPT AND ETHIOPIA

20 In the year that ªTartan¹ came to Ashdod, when Sargon the king of Assyria sent him, and he fought against Ashdod and took it, 2at the same time the LORD spoke by Isaiah the son of Amoz, saying, "Go, and remove ªthe sackcloth from your ¹body, and take your sandals off your feet." And he did so, ᵇwalking naked and barefoot.

3Then the LORD said, "Just as My servant Isaiah has walked naked and barefoot three years ªfor a sign and a wonder against Egypt and Ethiopia, 4so shall the ªking of Assyria lead away the Egyptians as prisoners and the Ethiopians as captives, young and old, naked and barefoot, ᵇwith their buttocks uncovered, to the shame of Egypt. 5aThen they shall be afraid and ashamed of Ethiopia their expectation and Egypt their glory. 6And the inhabitant of this territory will say in that day, 'Surely such *is* our expectation, wherever we flee for ªhelp to be delivered from the king of Assyria; and how shall we escape?'"

THE FALL OF BABYLON PROCLAIMED

21 The ¹burden against the Wilderness of the Sea.

As ªwhirlwinds in the South pass through,
So it comes from the desert, from a terrible
    land.
2   A distressing vision is declared to me;
    ªThe treacherous dealer deals treacherously,
    And the plunderer plunders.
    ᵇGo up, O Elam!
    Besiege, O Media!
    All its sighing I have made to cease.

19:18 ¹Some Heb. mss., Arab., DSS, Tg., Vg. *Sun;* LXX *Asedek,* lit. *Righteousness*   **20:1** ¹Or *the Commander in Chief*   **20:2** ¹Lit. *loins*   **21:1** ¹*oracle, prophecy*

19:18 ªZeph. 3:9
ᵇIs. 45:23

19:19
ªGen. 28:18;
Ex. 24:4;
Josh. 22:10,
26, 27;
Is. 56:7; 60:7
ᵇPs. 68:31

19:20
ªJosh. 4:20;
22:27 ᵇIs. 43:11

19:21
ª[Is. 2:3, 4; 11:9]
ᵇIs. 56:7; 60:7;
Zech. 14:16–18;
Mal. 1:11

19:22
ªDeut. 32:39;
Is. 30:26; 57:18;
[Heb. 12:11]

19:23
ªIs. 11:16; 35:8;
49:11; 62:10
ᵇIs. 27:13

19:25
ªDeut. 14:2;
Ps. 100:3;
Is. 29:23;
Hos. 2:23;
[Eph. 2:10]

20:1 ª2 Kin. 18:17

20:2
ªZech. 13:4;
Matt. 3:4
ᵇ1 Sam. 19:24;
Mic. 1:8

20:3 ªIs. 8:18

20:4 ªIs. 19:4
ᵇ2 Sam. 10:4;
Is. 3:17;
Jer. 13:22;
Mic. 1:11

20:5
ª2 Kin. 18:21;
Is. 30:3–5; 31:1;
Ezek. 29:6, 7

20:6 ªIs. 30:5, 7

21:1 ªZech. 9:14

21:2 ªIs. 33:1
ᵇIs. 13:17; 22:6;
Jer. 49:34

3 Therefore [a]my loins are filled with pain;
[b]Pangs have taken hold of me, like the pangs of a woman
    in labor.
I was [1]distressed when *I* heard *it;*
I was dismayed when *I* saw *it.*

4 My heart wavered, fearfulness frightened me;
[a]The night for which I longed He turned into fear
    for me.

5 [a]Prepare the table,
Set a watchman in the tower,
Eat and drink.
Arise, you princes,
Anoint the shield!

6 For thus has the Lord said to me:
"Go, set a watchman,
Let him declare what he sees."

7 And he saw a chariot *with* a pair of horsemen,
A chariot of donkeys, *and* a chariot of camels,
And he listened earnestly with great care.

8 [1]Then he cried, "A lion, my Lord!
I stand continually on the [a]watchtower in the
    daytime;
I have sat at my post every night.

9 And look, here comes a chariot of men *with* a pair of
    horsemen!"
Then he answered and said,
[a]"Babylon is fallen, is fallen!
And [b]all the carved images of her gods
He has broken to the ground."

10 [a]Oh, my threshing and the grain of my floor!
That which I have heard from the LORD of hosts,
The God of Israel,
I have declared to you.

PROCLAMATION AGAINST EDOM

11[a]The [1]burden against Dumah.

He calls to me out of [b]Seir,
"Watchman, what of the night?
Watchman, what of the night?"

12 The watchman said,
"The morning comes, and also the night.
If you will inquire, inquire;
Return! Come back!"

PROCLAMATION AGAINST ARABIA

13[a]The [1]burden against Arabia.

In the forest in Arabia you will lodge,
O you traveling companies [b]of Dedanites.

14 O inhabitants of the land of Tema,
Bring water to him who is thirsty;
With their bread they met him who fled.

15 For they fled from the swords, from the drawn sword,
From the bent bow, and from the distress of war.

21:3
[a]Is. 15:5; 16:11
[b]Is. 13:8

21:4
[a]Deut. 28:67

21:5 [a]Jer. 51:39;
Dan. 5:5

21:8 [a]Hab. 2:1

21:9 [a]Is. 13:19;
47:5, 9; 48:14;
Jer. 51:8;
Dan. 5:28, 31;
Rev. 14:8; 18:2
[b]Is. 46:1;
Jer. 50:2; 51:44

21:10
[a]Jer. 51:33;
Mic. 4:13

21:11
[a]Gen. 25:14;
1 Chr. 1:30;
Josh. 15:52
[b]Gen. 32:3;
Jer. 49:7;
Ezek. 35:2;
Obad. 1

21:13 [a]Jer. 25:24;
49:28
[b]Gen. 10:7;
1 Chr. 1:9, 32;
Jer. 25:23;
Ezek. 27:15

21:3 [1]Lit. *bowed*   21:8 [1]DSS *Then the observer cried, "My Lord!*
21:11 [1]*oracle, prophecy*   21:13 [1]*oracle, prophecy*

[16]For thus the LORD has said to me: "Within a year, [a]according to the year of a hired man, all the glory of [b]Kedar will fail; [17]and the remainder of the number of archers, the mighty men of the people of Kedar, will be diminished; for the LORD God of Israel has spoken *it*."

PROCLAMATION AGAINST JERUSALEM

22
The [1]burden against the Valley of Vision.

What ails you now, that you have all gone up to the
    housetops,
2 You who are full of noise,
    A [1]tumultuous city, [a]a joyous city?
    Your slain *men are* not slain with the sword,
    Nor dead in battle.
3 All your rulers have fled together;
    They are captured by the archers.
    All who are found in you are bound together;
    They have fled from afar.
4 Therefore I said, "Look away from me,
    [a]I will weep bitterly;
    Do not labor to comfort me
    Because of the plundering of the daughter of my people."

5 [a]For *it is* a day of trouble and treading down and
    perplexity
    [b]By the Lord GOD of hosts
    In the Valley of Vision—
    Breaking down the walls
    And of crying to the mountain.
6 [a]Elam bore the quiver
    With chariots of men *and* horsemen,
    And [b]Kir uncovered the shield.
7 It shall come to pass *that* your choicest valleys
    Shall be full of chariots,
    And the horsemen shall set themselves in array at the
    gate.

8 [a]He removed the [1]protection of Judah.
    You looked in that day to the armor [b]of the House of the
    Forest;
9 [a]You also saw the [1]damage to the city of David,
    That it was great;
    And you gathered together the waters of the lower pool.
10 You numbered the houses of Jerusalem,
    And the houses you broke down
    To fortify the wall.
11 [a]You also made a reservoir between the two walls
    For the water of the old [b]pool.
    But you did not look to its Maker,
    Nor did you have respect for Him who fashioned it long
    ago.

12 And in that day the Lord GOD of hosts
    [a]Called for weeping and for mourning,
    [b]For baldness and for girding with sackcloth.

21:16 [a]Is. 16:14
[b]Ps. 120:5;
Song 1:5;
Is. 42:11; 60:7;
Ezek. 27:21

22:2 [a]Is. 32:13

22:4 [a]Jer. 4:19

22:5 [a]Is. 37:3
[b]Lam. 1:5; 2:2

22:6 [a]Jer. 49:35
[b]Is. 15:1

22:8
[a]2 Kin. 18:15, 16
[b]1 Kin. 7:2; 10:17

22:9
[a]2 Kin. 20:20;
2 Chr. 32:4;
Neh. 3:16

22:11 [a]Neh. 3:16
[b]2 Kin. 20:20;
2 Chr. 32:3, 4

22:12 [a]Is. 32:11;
Joel 1:13; 2:17
[b]Ezra 9:3;
Is. 15:2; Mic. 1:16

22:1 [1]oracle, prophecy   22:2 [1]boisterous   22:8 [1]Lit. *covering*   22:9 [1]Lit.
breaches in the city walls

13 But instead, joy and gladness,
   Slaying oxen and killing sheep,
   Eating meat and ᵃdrinking wine:
ᵇ"Let us eat and drink, for tomorrow we die!"

14 ᵃThen it was revealed in my hearing by the LORD of hosts,
   "Surely for this iniquity there ᵇwill be no atonement for
      you,
   Even to your death," says the Lord GOD of hosts.

THE JUDGMENT ON SHEBNA

¹⁵Thus says the Lord GOD of hosts:

"Go, proceed to this steward,
   To ᵃShebna, who *is* over the house, *and say:*
16 'What have you here, and whom have you here,
   That you have hewn a sepulcher here,
   As he ᵃwho hews himself a sepulcher on high,
   Who carves a tomb for himself in a rock?
17 Indeed, the LORD will throw you away violently,
   O mighty man,
   ᵃAnd will surely seize you.
18 He will surely turn violently and toss you like a ball
   Into a large country;
   There you shall die, and there ᵃyour glorious chariots
   Shall be the shame of your master's house.
19 So I will drive you out of your office,
   And from your position ¹he will pull you down.
20 'Then it shall be in that day,
   That I will call My servant ᵃEliakim the son of Hilkiah;
21 I will clothe him with your robe
   And strengthen him with your belt;
   I will commit your responsibility into his hand.
   He shall be a father to the inhabitants of Jerusalem
   And to the house of Judah.
22 The key of the house of David
   I will lay on his ᵃshoulder;
   So he shall ᵇopen, and no one shall shut;
   And he shall shut, and no one shall open.
23 I will fasten him *as* ᵃa peg in a secure place,
   And he will become a glorious throne to his father's house.

²⁴"They will hang on him all the glory of his father's house,
the offspring and the posterity, all vessels of small quantity,
from the cups to all the pitchers. ²⁵In that day,' says the LORD
of hosts, 'the peg that is fastened in the secure place will be
removed and be cut down and fall, and the burden that *was*
on it will be cut off; for the LORD has spoken.'"

PROCLAMATION AGAINST TYRE

23

The ᵃburden¹ against Tyre.

Wail, you ships of Tarshish!
For it is laid waste,
So that there is no house, no harbor;
From the land of ²Cyprus it is revealed to them.

22:13
ᵃIs. 5:11, 22;
28:7, 8;
Luke 17:26–29
ᵇIs. 56:12;
1 Cor. 15:32

22:14 ᵃIs. 5:9
ᵇ1 Sam. 3:14;
Ezek. 24:13

22:15
ᵃ2 Kin. 18:37;
Is. 36:3

22:16
ᵃ2 Sam. 18:18;
2 Chr. 16:14;
Matt. 27:60

22:17 ᵃEsth. 7:8

22:18 ᵃIs. 2:7

22:20
ᵃ2 Kin. 18:18;
Is. 36:3, 22; 37:2

22:22 ᵃIs. 9:6
ᵇJob 12:14;
Rev. 3:7

22:23 ᵃEzra 9:8;
Zech. 10:4

23:1
ᵃJer. 25:22; 47:4;
Ezek. 26—28;
Amos 1:9;
Zech. 9:2, 4

22:19 ¹LXX omits *he will pull you down;* Syr., Tg., Vg. *I will pull you down*
23:1 ¹*oracle, prophecy*   ²Heb. *Kittim,* western lands, especially Cyprus

2 Be still, you inhabitants of the coastland,
    You merchants of Sidon,
    ¹Whom those who cross the sea have filled.
3 And on great waters the grain of Shihor,
    The harvest of ¹the River, *is* her revenue;
    And ªshe is a marketplace for the nations.

4 Be ashamed, O Sidon;
    For the sea has spoken,
    The strength of the sea, saying,
    "I do not labor, nor bring forth children;
    Neither do I rear young men,
    Nor bring up virgins."
5 ªWhen the report *reaches* Egypt,
    They also will be in agony at the report of Tyre.

6 Cross over to Tarshish;
    Wail, you inhabitants of the coastland!
7 *Is* this your ªjoyous *city*,
    Whose antiquity *is* from ancient days,
    Whose feet carried her far off to dwell?
8 Who has taken this counsel against Tyre, ªthe crowning
        city,
    Whose merchants *are* princes,
    Whose traders *are* the honorable of the earth?
9 The LORD of hosts has ªpurposed it,
    To ¹bring to dishonor the ᵇpride of all glory,
    To bring into contempt all the honorable of the earth.

10 Overflow through your land like ¹the River,
    O daughter of Tarshish;
    There is no more ²strength.
11 He stretched out His hand over the sea,
    He shook the kingdoms;
    The LORD has given a commandment ªagainst Canaan
    To destroy its strongholds.
12 And He said, "You will rejoice no more,
    O you oppressed virgin daughter of Sidon.
    Arise, ªcross over to Cyprus;
    There also you will have no rest."

13 Behold, the land of the ªChaldeans,
    This people *which* was not;
    Assyria founded it for ᵇwild beasts of the desert.
    They set up its towers,
    They raised up its palaces,
    And brought it to ruin.

14 ªWail, you ships of Tarshish!
    For your strength is laid waste.

¹⁵Now it shall come to pass in that day that Tyre will be forgotten seventy years, according to the days of one king. At the end of seventy years it will happen to Tyre as *in* the song of the harlot:

16 "Take a harp, go about the city,
    You forgotten harlot;

23:3
ªEzek. 27:3–23
23:5 ªIs. 19:16
23:7
ªIs. 22:2; 32:13
23:8
ªEzek. 28:2, 12
23:9 ªIs. 14:26
ᵇJob 40:11, 12;
Is. 13:11; 24:4;
Dan. 4:37
23:11
ªZech. 9:2–4
23:12
ªEzek. 26:13, 14;
Rev. 18:22
23:13 ªIs. 47:1
ᵇPs. 72:9
23:14
ªEzek. 27:25–30

23:2 ¹So with MT, Vg.; LXX, Tg. *Passing over the water;* DSS *Your messengers passing over the sea*   23:3 ¹The Nile   23:9 ¹*pollute*   23:10 ¹The Nile
²*restraint,* lit. *belt*

Make sweet melody, sing many songs,
That you may be remembered."

¹⁷And it shall be, at the end of seventy years, that the LORD will deal with Tyre. She will return to her hire, and ᵃcommit fornication with all the kingdoms of the world on the face of the earth. ¹⁸Her gain and her pay ᵃwill be set apart for the LORD; it will not be treasured nor laid up, for her gain will be for those who dwell before the LORD, to eat sufficiently, and for ¹fine clothing.

IMPENDING JUDGMENT ON THE EARTH

24 Behold, the LORD makes the earth empty and makes
it waste,
Distorts its surface
And scatters abroad its inhabitants.
2 And it shall be:
As with the people, so with the ᵃpriest;
As with the servant, so with his master;
As with the maid, so with her mistress;
ᵇAs with the buyer, so with the seller;
As with the lender, so with the borrower;
As with the creditor, so with the debtor.
3 The land shall be entirely emptied and utterly
plundered,
For the LORD has spoken this word.

4 The earth mourns *and* fades away,
The world languishes *and* fades away;
The ᵃhaughty¹ people of the earth languish.
5 ᵃThe earth is also defiled under its inhabitants,
Because they have ᵇtransgressed the laws,
Changed the ordinance,
Broken the ᶜeverlasting covenant.
6 Therefore ᵃthe curse has devoured the earth,
And those who dwell in it are ¹desolate.
Therefore the inhabitants of the earth are ᵇburned,
And few men *are* left.

7 ᵃThe new wine fails, the vine languishes,
All the merry-hearted sigh.
8 The mirth ᵃof the tambourine ceases,
The noise of the jubilant ends,
The joy of the harp ceases.
9 They shall not drink wine with a song;
Strong drink is bitter to those who drink it.
10 The city of confusion is broken down;
Every house is shut up, so that none may go in.
11 *There is* a cry for wine in the streets,
All joy is darkened,
The mirth of the land is gone.
12 In the city desolation is left,
And the gate is stricken with destruction.
13 When it shall be thus in the midst of the land among the
people,
ᵃ*It shall be* like the shaking of an olive tree,
Like the gleaning of grapes when the vintage is done.

23:17 ᵃRev. 17:2

23:18
ᵃEx. 28:36;
Zech. 14:20, 21

24:2 ᵃHos. 4:9
ᵇEzek. 7:12, 13

24:4 ᵃIs. 25:11

24:5 ᵃGen. 3:17;
Num. 35:33;
Is. 9:17; 10:6
ᵇIs. 59:12
ᶜ1 Chr. 16:14–19;
Ps. 105:7–12

24:6 ᵃMal. 4:6
ᵇIs. 9:19

24:7
ᵃIs. 16:8–10;
Joel 1:10, 12

24:8
ᵃIs. 5:12, 14;
Jer. 7:34;
16:9; 25:10;
Ezek. 26:13;
Hos. 2:11;
Rev. 18:22

24:13
ᵃ[Is. 17:5, 6;
27:12]

23:18 ¹choice   24:4 ¹proud   24:6 ¹Or *held guilty*

14 They shall lift up their voice, they shall sing;
For the majesty of the LORD
They shall cry aloud from the sea.
15 Therefore aglorify the LORD in the dawning light,
bThe name of the LORD God of Israel in the coastlands of
the sea.
16 From the ends of the earth we have heard songs:
"Glory to the righteous!"
But I said, 1"I am ruined, ruined!
Woe to me!
aThe treacherous dealers have dealt treacherously,
Indeed, the treacherous dealers have dealt very
treacherously."

17 aFear and the pit and the snare
Are upon you, O inhabitant of the earth.
18 And it shall be
That he who flees from the noise of the fear
Shall fall into the pit,
And he who comes up from the midst of the pit
Shall be 1caught in the snare;
For athe windows from on high are open,
And bthe foundations of the earth are shaken.

19 aThe earth is violently broken,
The earth is split open,
The earth is shaken exceedingly.
20 The earth shall areel1 to and fro like a drunkard,
And shall totter like a hut;
Its transgression shall be heavy upon it,
And it will fall, and not rise again.

21 It shall come to pass in that day
That the LORD will punish on high the host of exalted
ones,
And on the earth athe kings of the earth.
22 They will be gathered together,
As prisoners are gathered in the 1pit,
And will be shut up in the prison;
After many days they will be punished.
23 Then the amoon will be disgraced
And the sun ashamed;
For the LORD of hosts will breign
On cMount Zion and in Jerusalem
And before His elders, gloriously.

PRAISE TO GOD

25

O LORD, You are my God.
aI will exalt You,
I will praise Your name,
bFor You have done wonderful things;
cYour counsels of old are faithfulness and truth.
2 For You have made aa city a ruin,
A fortified city a ruin,
A palace of foreigners to be a city no more;
It will never be rebuilt.

24:15 aIs. 25:3
bMal. 1:11

24:16
aIs. 21:2; 33:1;
Jer. 3:20; 5:11

24:17
aJer. 48:43;
Amos 5:19

24:18 aGen. 7:11
bPs. 18:7; 46:2;
Is. 2:19, 21; 13:13

24:19 aJer. 4:23

24:20 aIs. 19:14;
24:1; 28:7

24:21 aPs. 76:12

24:23 aIs. 13:10;
60:19;
Ezek. 32:7;
Joel 2:31; 3:15
bRev. 19:4, 6
c[Heb. 12:22]

25:1 aEx. 15:2
bPs. 98:1
cNum. 23:19

25:2 aIs. 21:9;
23:13; Jer. 51:37

24:16 1Lit. Leanness to me, leanness to me   24:18 1Lit. taken
24:20 1stagger   24:22 1dungeon

3 Therefore the strong people will [a]glorify You;
  The city of the [1]terrible nations will fear You.
4 For You have been a strength to the poor,
  A strength to the needy in his distress,
  [a]A refuge from the storm,
  A shade from the heat;
  For the blast of the terrible ones *is* as a storm *against* the
    wall.
5 You will reduce the noise of aliens,
  As heat in a dry place;
  As heat in the shadow of a cloud,
  The song of the terrible ones will be [1]diminished.

6 And in [a]this mountain
  [b]The LORD of hosts will make for [c]all people
  A feast of [1]choice pieces,
  A feast of [2]wines on the lees,
  Of fat things full of marrow,
  Of well-refined wines on the lees.
7 And He will destroy on this mountain
  The surface of the covering cast over all people,
  And [a]the veil that is spread over all nations.
8 He will [a]swallow up death forever,
  And the Lord GOD will [b]wipe away tears from all faces;
  The rebuke of His people
  He will take away from all the earth;
  For the LORD has spoken.

9 And it will be said in that day:
  "Behold, this *is* our God;
  [a]We have waited for Him, and He will save us.
  This *is* the LORD;
  We have waited for Him;
  [b]We will be glad and rejoice in His salvation."

10 For on this mountain the hand of the LORD will rest,
   And [a]Moab shall be trampled down under Him,
   As straw is trampled down for the refuse heap.
11 And He will spread out His hands in their midst
   As a swimmer reaches out to swim,
   And He will bring down their [a]pride
   Together with the trickery of their hands.
12 The [a]fortress of the high fort of your walls
   He will bring down, lay low,
   And bring to the ground, down to the dust.

A SONG OF SALVATION

26 In [a]that day this song will be sung in the land of Judah:

   "We have a strong city;
   [b]God will appoint salvation *for* walls and bulwarks.
2 [a]Open the gates,
   That the righteous nation which [1]keeps the truth may
     enter in.
3 You will keep *him* in perfect [a]peace,
   Whose mind *is* stayed *on You,*
   Because he trusts in You.

25:3 [a]Is. 24:15;
Rev. 11:13
25:4 [a]Is. 4:6
25:6
[a][Is. 2:2–4; 56:7]
[b]Prov. 9:2;
Matt. 22:4
[c][Dan. 7:14;
Matt. 8:11]
25:7 [a]2 Cor. 3:15;
[Eph. 4:18]
25:8
[a][Hos. 13:14;
1 Cor. 15:54;
Rev. 20:14]
[b]Is. 30:19;
Rev. 7:17; 21:4
25:9
[a]Gen. 49:18;
Is. 8:17; 26:8;
[Titus 2:13]
[b]Ps. 20:5
25:10 [a]Is. 16:14;
Jer. 48:1–47;
Ezek. 25:8–11;
Amos 2:1–3;
Zeph. 2:9
25:11
[a]Is. 24:4; 26:5
25:12 [a]Is. 26:5
26:1 [a]Is. 2:11; 12:1
[b]Is. 60:18
26:2
[a]Ps. 118:19, 20
26:3 [a]Is. 57:19;
[Phil. 4:6, 7]

25:3 [1]terrifying **25:5** [1]humbled **25:6** [1]Lit. *fat things* [2]*wines matured on the sediment* **26:2** [1]Or *remains faithful*

4 Trust in the LORD forever,
^aFor in YAH, the LORD, *is* ¹everlasting strength.
5 For He brings ¹down those who dwell on high,
^aThe lofty city;
He lays it low,
He lays it low to the ground,
He brings it down to the dust.
6 The foot shall ¹tread it down—
The feet of the poor
And the steps of the needy."

7 The way of the just *is* uprightness;
^aO Most Upright,
You ¹weigh the path of the just.
8 Yes, ^ain the way of Your judgments,
O LORD, we have ^bwaited for You;
The desire of *our* soul *is* for Your name
And for the remembrance of You.
9 ^aWith my soul I have desired You in the night,
Yes, by my spirit within me I will seek You early;
For when Your judgments *are* in the earth,
The inhabitants of the world will learn righteousness.

10 ^aLet grace be shown to the wicked,
Yet he will not learn righteousness;
In ^bthe land of uprightness he will deal unjustly,
And will not behold the majesty of the LORD.
11 LORD, *when* Your hand is lifted up, ^athey will not see.
But they will see and be ashamed
For ¹*their* envy of people;
Yes, the fire of Your enemies shall devour them.
12 LORD, You will establish peace for us,
For You have also done all our works ¹in us.
13 O LORD our God, ^amasters besides You
Have had dominion over us;
But by You only we make mention of Your name.
14 *They are* dead, they will not live;
They are deceased, they will not rise.
Therefore You have punished and destroyed them,
And made all their memory to ^aperish.
15 You have increased the nation, O LORD,
You have ^aincreased the nation;
You are glorified;
You have expanded all the ¹borders of the land.

16 LORD, ^ain trouble they have visited You,
They poured out a prayer *when* Your chastening *was*
upon them.
17 As ^aa woman with child
Is in pain and cries out in her ¹pangs,
When she draws near the time of her delivery,
So have we been in Your sight, O LORD.
18 We have been with child, we have been in pain;
We have, as it were, ¹brought forth wind;
We have not accomplished any deliverance in the earth,
Nor have ^athe inhabitants of the world fallen.

26:4
^aIs. 12:2; 45:17

26:5 ^aIs. 25:11, 12

26:7 ^aPs. 37:23

26:8 ^aIs. 64:5
^bIs. 25:9; 33:2

26:9 ^aPs. 63:6;
Song 3:1;
Is. 50:10;
Luke 6:12

26:10
^aEccl. 8:12;
[Rom. 2:4]
^bPs. 143:10

26:11
^aJob 34:27;
Ps. 28:5; Is. 5:12

26:13
^a2 Chr. 12:8

26:14 ^aEccl. 9:5;
Is. 14:22

26:15 ^aIs. 9:3

26:16 ^aIs. 37:3;
Hos. 5:15

26:17 ^aIs. 13:8;
[John 16:21]

26:18 ^aPs. 17:14

26:4 ¹Or *Rock of Ages*   26:5 ¹*low*   26:6 ¹*trample*   26:7 ¹Or *make level*
26:11 ¹Or *Your zeal for the people*   26:12 ¹Or *for us*   26:15 ¹Or *ends*
26:17 ¹*sharp pains*   26:18 ¹*given birth to*

19 aYour dead shall live;
Together with ¹my dead body they shall arise.
bAwake and sing, you who dwell in dust;
For your dew *is like* the dew of herbs,
And the earth shall cast out the dead.

TAKE REFUGE FROM THE COMING JUDGMENT

20 Come, my people, aenter your chambers,
And shut your doors behind you;
Hide yourself, as it were, bfor a little moment,
Until the indignation is past.
21 For behold, the LORD acomes out of His place
To punish the inhabitants of the earth for their iniquity;
The earth will also disclose her ¹blood,
And will no more cover her slain.

27 In that day the LORD with His severe sword, great and strong,
Will punish Leviathan the fleeing serpent,
aLeviathan that twisted serpent;
And He will slay bthe reptile that *is* in the sea.

THE RESTORATION OF ISRAEL

2 In that day asing to her,
b"A vineyard of ¹red wine!
3 aI, the LORD, keep it,
I water it every moment;
Lest any hurt it,
I keep it night and day.
4 Fury *is* not in Me.
Who would set abriers *and* thorns
Against Me in battle?
I would go through them,
I would burn them together.
5 Or let him take hold aof My strength,
That he may bmake peace with Me;
And he shall make peace with Me."
6 Those who come He shall cause ato take root in Jacob;
Israel shall blossom and bud,
And fill the face of the world with fruit.
7 aHas He struck ¹Israel as He struck those who struck
him?
Or has He been slain according to the slaughter of those
who were slain by Him?
8 aIn measure, by sending it away,
You contended with it.
bHe removes *it* by His rough wind
In the day of the east wind.
9 Therefore by this the iniquity of Jacob will be covered;
And this *is* all the fruit of taking away his sin:
When he makes all the stones of the altar
Like chalkstones that are beaten to dust,
¹Wooden images and incense altars shall not stand.

26:19 aIs. 25:8;
[Ezek. 37:1–14];
b[Dan. 12:2];
Hos. 13:14
26:20
aEx. 12:22, 23;
[Ps. 91:1, 4];
b[Ps. 30:5;
Is. 54:7, 8;
2 Cor. 4:17]
26:21 aMic. 1:3;
[Jude 14]
27:1 aGen. 3:1;
Ps. 74:13, 14;
Rev. 12:9, 15
bIs. 51:9;
Ezek. 29:3; 32:2
27:2 aIs. 5:1
bPs. 80:8;
Is. 5:7; Jer. 2:21
27:3
a1 Sam. 2:9;
Ps. 121:4, 5;
Is. 31:5;
[John 10:28]
27:4
a2 Sam. 23:6;
Is. 9:18
27:5 aIs. 25:4
bJob 22:21;
Is. 26:3, 12;
[Rom. 5:1;
2 Cor. 5:20]
27:6 aIs. 37:31;
Hos. 14:5, 6
27:7
aIs. 10:12, 17;
30:30–33
27:8 aJob 23:6;
Ps. 6:1;
Jer. 10:24;
30:11; 46:28;
[1 Cor. 10:13]
b[Ps. 78:38]

26:19 ¹So with MT, Vg.; Syr., Tg. *their dead bodies;* LXX *those in the tombs*
26:21 ¹Or *bloodshed*   27:2 ¹So with MT (Kittel's *Biblia Hebraica*), Bg., Vg.;
MT (*Biblia Hebraica Stuttgartensia*), some Heb. mss., LXX *delight;* Tg. *choice vineyard*   27:7 ¹Lit. *him*   27:9 ¹Heb. *Asherim,* Canaanite deities

10 Yet the fortified city *will be* ^adesolate,
The habitation forsaken and left like a wilderness;
There the calf will feed, and there it will lie down
And consume its branches.

11 When its boughs are withered, they will be broken off;
The women come *and* set them on fire.
For ^ait *is* a people of no understanding;
Therefore He who made them will ^bnot have mercy on
them,
And ^cHe who formed them will show them no favor.

12 And it shall come to pass in that day
That the LORD will thresh,
From the channel of ¹the River to the Brook of Egypt;
And you will be ^agathered one by one,
O you children of Israel.

13 ^aSo it shall be in that day:
^bThe great trumpet will be blown;
They will come, who are about to perish in the land of
Assyria,
And they who are outcasts in the land of ^cEgypt,
And shall ^dworship the LORD in the holy mount at
Jerusalem.

WOE TO EPHRAIM AND JERUSALEM

28 Woe to the crown of pride, to the drunkards of
Ephraim,
Whose glorious beauty *is* a fading flower
Which *is* at the head of the ¹verdant valleys,
To those who are overcome with wine!

2 Behold, the Lord has a mighty and strong one,
^aLike a tempest of hail and a destroying storm,
Like a flood of mighty waters overflowing,
Who will bring *them* down to the earth with *His* hand.

3 The crown of pride, the drunkards of Ephraim,
Will be trampled underfoot;

4 And the glorious beauty is a fading flower
Which *is* at the head of the ¹verdant valley,
Like the first fruit before the summer,
Which an observer sees;
He eats it up while it is still in his hand.

5 In that day the LORD of hosts will be
For a crown of glory and a diadem of beauty
To the remnant of His people,

6 For a spirit of justice to him who sits in judgment,
And for strength to those who turn back the battle at the
gate.

7 But they also ^ahave erred through wine,
And through intoxicating drink are out of the way;
^bThe priest and the prophet have erred through
intoxicating drink,
They are swallowed up by wine,
They are out of the way through intoxicating drink;
They err in vision, they stumble *in* judgment.

27:10 ^aIs. 5:6, 17;
32:14; Jer. 26:18

27:11
^aDeut. 32:28;
Is. 1:3 ^bIs. 9:17
^cDeut. 32:18;
Is. 43:1, 7; 44:2,
21, 24

27:12
^a[Is. 11:11; 56:8]

27:13 ^aIs. 2:11
^bLev. 25:9;
1 Chr. 15:24;
Matt. 24:31;
Rev. 11:15
^cIs. 19:21, 22
^d[Is. 2:3];
Zech. 14:16;
[Heb. 12:22]

28:2 ^aIs. 30:30;
Ezek. 13:11

28:7 ^aProv. 20:1;
Is. 5:11, 22;
Hos. 4:11
^bIs. 56:10, 12

27:12 ¹The Euphrates   28:1 ¹Lit. *valleys of fatness*   28:4 ¹Lit. *valley of
fatness*

8 For all tables are full of vomit *and* filth;
   No place *is clean.*

9 "Whom[a] will he teach knowledge?
   And whom will he make to understand the message?
   Those *just* weaned from milk?
   Those *just* drawn from the breasts?

10 [a]For precept *must be* upon precept, precept upon precept,
   Line upon line, line upon line,
   Here a little, there a little."

11 For with [a]stammering lips and another tongue
   He will speak to this people,

12 To whom He said, "This *is* the [a]rest *with which*
   You may cause the weary to rest,"
   And, "This *is* the refreshing";
   Yet they would not hear.

13 But the word of the LORD was to them,
   "Precept upon precept, precept upon precept,
   Line upon line, line upon line,
   Here a little, there a little,"
   That they might go and fall backward, and be broken
   And snared and caught.

14 Therefore hear the word of the LORD, you scornful men,
   Who rule this people who *are* in Jerusalem,

15 Because you have said, "We have made a covenant with
         death,
   And with Sheol we are in agreement.
   When the overflowing scourge passes through,
   It will not come to us,
   [a]For we have made lies our refuge,
   And under falsehood we have hidden ourselves."

A CORNERSTONE IN ZION

16 Therefore thus says the Lord GOD:

   "Behold, I lay in Zion [a]a stone for a foundation,
   A tried stone, a precious cornerstone, a sure foundation;
   Whoever believes will not act hastily.

17 Also I will make justice the measuring line,
   And righteousness the plummet;
   The hail will sweep away the refuge of lies,
   And the waters will overflow the hiding place.

18 Your covenant with death will be annulled,
   And your agreement with Sheol will not stand;
   When the overflowing scourge passes through,
   Then you will be trampled down by it.

19 As often as it goes out it will take you;
   For morning by morning it will pass over,
   And by day and by night;
   It will be a terror just to understand the report."

20 For the bed is too short to stretch out *on,*
   And the covering so narrow that one cannot wrap
         himself *in it.*

21 For the LORD will rise up as *at* Mount [a]Perazim,
   He will be angry as in the Valley of [b]Gibeon—
   That He may do His work, [c]His awesome work,
   And bring to pass His act, His [1]unusual act.

28:9 [a]Jer. 6:10

28:10
[a][2 Chr. 36:15;
Neh. 9:30;
Jer. 25:3, 4;
35:15; 44:4]

28:11 [a]Is. 33:19;
1 Cor. 14:21

28:12 [a]Is. 30:15;
Jer. 6:16;
[Matt. 11:28, 29]

28:15 [a]Is. 9:15;
Ezek. 13:22;
Amos 2:4

28:16
[a]Gen. 49:24;
Ps. 118:22;
Is. 8:14, 15;
Matt. 21:42;
Mark 12:10;
Luke 20:17;
Acts 4:11;
Rom. 9:33; 10:11;
Eph. 2:20;
1 Pet. 2:6–8

28:21
[a]2 Sam. 5:20;
1 Chr. 14:11
[b]Josh. 10:10, 12;
2 Sam. 5:25;
1 Chr. 14:16
[c][Lam. 3:33;
Luke 19:41–44]

28:21 [1]Lit. *foreign*

22 Now therefore, do not be mockers,
Lest your bonds be made strong;
For I have heard from the Lord GOD of hosts,
[a]A [1]destruction determined even upon the whole earth.

LISTEN TO THE TEACHING OF GOD

23 Give ear and hear my voice,
Listen and hear my speech.
24 Does the plowman keep plowing all day to sow?
Does he keep turning his soil and breaking the clods?
25 When he has leveled its surface,
Does he not sow the black cummin
And scatter the cummin,
Plant the wheat in rows,
The barley in the appointed place,
And the [1]spelt in its place?
26 For He instructs him in right judgment,
His God teaches him.

27 For the black cummin is not threshed with a threshing
sledge,
Nor is a cartwheel rolled over the cummin;
But the black cummin is beaten out with a stick,
And the cummin with a rod.
28 Bread *flour* must be ground;
Therefore he does not thresh it forever,
Break *it with* his cartwheel,
Or crush *it with* his horsemen.
29 This also comes from the LORD of hosts,
[a]*Who* is wonderful in counsel *and* excellent in [1]guidance.

WOE TO JERUSALEM

29 "Woe [a]to [1]Ariel, to Ariel, the city [b]*where* David dwelt!
Add year to year;
Let feasts come around.
2 Yet I will distress Ariel;
There shall be heaviness and sorrow,
And it shall be to Me as Ariel.
3 I will encamp against you all around,
I will lay siege against you with a mound,
And I will raise siegeworks against you.
4 You shall be brought down,
You shall speak out of the ground;
Your speech shall be low, out of the dust;
Your voice shall be like a medium's, [a]out of the ground;
And your speech shall whisper out of the dust.

5 "Moreover the multitude of your [a]foes
Shall be like fine dust,
And the multitude of the terrible ones
Like [b]chaff that passes away;
Yes, it shall be [c]in an instant, suddenly.
6 [a]You will be punished by the LORD of hosts
With thunder and [b]earthquake and great noise,
With storm and tempest
And the flame of devouring fire.

28:22 [a]Is. 10:22;
Dan. 9:27

28:29 [a]Ps. 92:5;
Is. 9:6; Jer. 32:19

29:1
[a]Ezek. 24:6, 9
[b]2 Sam. 5:9

29:4 [a]Is. 8:19

29:5 [a]Is. 25:5
[b]Job 21:18;
Is. 17:13
[c]Is. 30:13; 47:11;
1 Thess. 5:3

29:6
[a]Is. 28:2; 30:30
[b]1 Sam. 2:10;
Zech. 14:4;
Matt. 24:7;
Mark 13:8;
Luke 21:11;
Rev. 16:18, 19

28:22 [1]Lit. *complete end*   28:25 [1]*rye*   28:29 [1]*sound wisdom*
29:1 [1]Jerusalem, lit. *Lion of God*

7 ᵃThe multitude of all the nations who fight against
    ¹Ariel,
Even all who fight against her and her fortress,
And distress her,
Shall be ᵇas a dream of a night vision.
8 ᵃIt shall even be as when a hungry man dreams,
And look—he eats;
But he awakes, and his soul is still empty;
Or as when a thirsty man dreams,
And look—he drinks;
But he awakes, and indeed *he is* faint,
And his soul still craves:
So the multitude of all the nations shall be,
Who fight against Mount Zion."

THE BLINDNESS OF DISOBEDIENCE

9   Pause and wonder!
Blind yourselves and be blind!
ᵃThey are drunk, ᵇbut not with wine;
They stagger, but not with intoxicating drink.
10 For ᵃthe Lᴏʀᴅ has poured out on you
The spirit of deep sleep,
And has ᵇclosed your eyes, namely, the prophets;
And He has covered your heads, *namely,* ᶜthe seers.

¹¹The whole vision has become to you like the words of a
¹book ᵃthat is sealed, which *men* deliver to one who is literate,
saying, "Read this, please."
    ᵇAnd he says, "I cannot, for it *is* sealed."
    ¹²Then the book is delivered to one who ¹is illiterate, say-
ing, "Read this, please."
    And he says, "I am not literate."
    ¹³Therefore the Lord said:

ᵃ"Inasmuch as these people draw near with their
        mouths
And honor Me ᵇwith their lips,
But have removed their hearts far from Me,
And their fear toward Me is taught by the commandment
        of men,
14 ᵃTherefore, behold, I will again do a marvelous work
        Among this people,
A marvelous work and a wonder;
ᵇFor the wisdom of their wise *men* shall perish,
And the understanding of their prudent *men* shall be
        hidden."

15 ᵃWoe to those who seek deep to hide their counsel far
        from the Lᴏʀᴅ,
And their works are in the dark;
ᵇThey say, "Who sees us?" and, "Who knows us?"
16 Surely you have things turned around!
Shall the potter be esteemed as the clay;
For shall the ᵃthing made say of him who made it,
"He did not make me"?
Or shall the thing formed say of him who formed it,
"He has no understanding"?

29:7 ᵃIs. 37:36;
Mic. 4:11, 12;
Zech. 12:9
ᵇJob 20:8

29:8 ᵃPs. 73:20

29:9 ᵃIs. 28:7, 8
ᵇIs. 51:21

29:10
ᵃPs. 69:23;
Is. 6:9, 10;
Mic. 3:6;
Rom. 11:8
ᵇPs. 69:23;
Is. 6:10
ᶜ1 Sam. 9:9;
Is. 44:18;
Mic. 3:6;
[2 Thess. 2:9–12]

29:11 ᵃIs. 8:16
ᵇDan. 12:4, 9;
[Matt. 13:11–16];
Rev. 5:1–5, 9

29:13
ᵃPs. 78:36;
Ezek. 33:31;
Matt. 15:8, 9;
Mark 7:6, 7
ᵇCol. 2:22

29:14
ᵃIs. 6:9, 10;
28:21; Hab. 1:5
ᵇIs. 44:25;
Jer. 49:7;
Obad. 8;
1 Cor. 1:19

29:15 ᵃIs. 30:1
ᵇPs. 10:11; 94:7;
Is. 47:10;
Ezek. 8:12;
Mal. 2:17

29:16 ᵃIs. 45:9;
Jer. 18:1–6;
[Rom. 9:19–21]

29:7 ¹Jerusalem   29:11 ¹scroll   29:12 ¹Lit. *does not know books*

FUTURE RECOVERY OF WISDOM

17 *Is* it not yet a very little while
Till ªLebanon shall be turned into a fruitful field,
And the fruitful field be esteemed as a forest?
18 ªIn that day the deaf shall hear the words of the book,
And the eyes of the blind shall see out of obscurity and
out of darkness.
19 ªThe humble also shall increase *their* joy in the LORD,
And ᵇthe poor among men shall rejoice
In the Holy One of Israel.
20 For the ¹terrible one is brought to nothing,
ªThe scornful one is consumed,
And all who ᵇwatch for iniquity are cut off—
21 Who make a man an offender by a word,
And ªlay a snare for him who reproves in the gate,
And turn aside the just ᵇby empty words.

22Therefore thus says the LORD, ªwho redeemed Abraham,
concerning the house of Jacob:

"Jacob shall not now be ᵇashamed,
Nor shall his face now grow pale;
23 But when he sees his children,
ªThe work of My hands, in his midst,
They will hallow My name,
And hallow the Holy One of Jacob,
And fear the God of Israel.
24 These also ªwho erred in spirit will come to understanding,
And those who complained will learn doctrine."

FUTILE CONFIDENCE IN EGYPT

30 "Woe to the rebellious children," says the LORD,
ª"Who take counsel, but not of Me,
And who ¹devise plans, but not of My Spirit,
ᵇThat they may add sin to sin;
2 ªWho walk to go down to Egypt,
And ᵇhave not asked My advice,
To strengthen themselves in the strength of Pharaoh,
And to trust in the shadow of Egypt!
3 ªTherefore the strength of Pharaoh
Shall be your shame,
And trust in the shadow of Egypt
Shall be *your* humiliation.
4 For his princes were at ªZoan,
And his ambassadors came to Hanes.
5 ªThey were all ashamed of a people *who* could not benefit
them,
Or be help or benefit,
But a shame and also a reproach."

6ªThe ¹burden against the beasts of the South.

Through a land of trouble and anguish,
From which *came* the lioness and lion,
ᵇThe viper and fiery flying serpent,
They will carry their riches on the backs of young donkeys,
And their treasures on the humps of camels,
To a people *who* shall not profit;

29:17 ªIs. 32:15

29:18 ªIs. 35:5;
Matt. 11:5;
Mark 7:37

29:19 ª[Ps. 25:9;
37:11; Is. 11:4;
61:1; Matt. 5:5;
11:29] ᵇIs. 14:30;
[Matt. 5:3; 11:5;
James 2:5]

29:20 ªIs. 28:14
ᵇIs. 59:4;
Mic. 2:1

29:21
ªAmos 5:10, 12
ᵇProv. 28:21

29:22
ªJosh. 24:3
ᵇIs. 45:17

29:23 ª[Is. 45:11;
49:20–26;
Eph. 2:10]

29:24 ªIs. 28:7

30:1 ªIs. 29:15
ᵇDeut. 29:19

30:2 ªIs. 31:1;
Jer. 43:7
ᵇNum. 27:21;
Josh. 9:14;
1 Kin. 22:7;
Jer. 21:2;
42:2, 20

30:3 ªIs. 20:5;
Jer. 37:5, 7

30:4 ªIs. 19:11

30:5 ªJer. 2:36

30:6 ªIs. 57:9;
Hos. 8:9; 12:1
ᵇDeut. 8:15;
Is. 14:29

29:20 ¹terrifying   30:1 ¹Lit. *weave a web*   30:6 ¹oracle, prophecy

7 ᵃFor the Egyptians shall help in vain and to no purpose.
Therefore I have called her
¹Rahab-Hem-Shebeth.

A REBELLIOUS PEOPLE

8 Now go, ᵃwrite it before them on a tablet,
And note it on a scroll,
That it may be for time to come,
Forever and ever:

9 That ᵃthis *is* a rebellious people,
Lying children,
Children *who* will not hear the law of the LORD;

10 ᵃWho say to the seers, "Do not see,"
And to the prophets, "Do not prophesy to us right things;
ᵇSpeak to us smooth things, prophesy deceits.

11 Get out of the way,
Turn aside from the path,
Cause the Holy One of Israel
To cease from before us."

12 Therefore thus says the Holy One of Israel:

"Because you ᵃdespise this word,
And trust in oppression and perversity,
And rely on them,

13 Therefore this iniquity shall be to you
ᵃLike a breach ready to fall,
A bulge in a high wall,
Whose breaking ᵇcomes suddenly, in an instant.

14 And ᵃHe shall break it like the breaking of the potter's
vessel,
Which is broken in pieces;
He shall not spare.
So there shall not be found among its fragments
¹A shard to take fire from the hearth,
Or to take water from the cistern."

15 For thus says the Lord GOD, the Holy One of Israel:

ᵃ"In returning and rest you shall be saved;
In quietness and confidence shall be your strength."
ᵇBut you would not,

16 And you said, "No, for we will flee on horses"—
Therefore you shall flee!
And, "We will ride on swift *horses*"—
Therefore those who pursue you shall be swift!

17 ᵃOne thousand *shall flee* at the threat of one,
At the threat of five you shall flee,
Till you are left as a ¹pole on top of a mountain
And as a banner on a hill.

GOD WILL BE GRACIOUS

18 Therefore the LORD will wait, that He may be ᵃgracious to
you;
And therefore He will be exalted, that He may have
mercy on you.

Cross references (margin):

30:7 ᵃJer. 37:7

30:8 ᵃHab. 2:2

30:9
ᵃDeut. 32:20;
Is. 1:2, 4; 65:2

30:10 ᵃIs. 5:20;
Jer. 11:21;
Amos 2:12;
Mic. 2:6
ᵇ1 Kin. 22:8, 13;
Jer. 6:14;
23:17, 26;
Ezek. 13:7;
Mic. 2:11;
Rom. 16:18;
2 Tim. 4:3, 4

30:12
ᵃLev. 26:43;
Num. 15:31;
Prov. 1:30; 13:13;
Is. 5:24;
Ezek. 20:13, 16,
24; Amos 2:4

30:13
ᵃ1 Kin. 20:30;
Ps. 62:3, 4;
Is. 58:12 ᵇIs. 29:5

30:14 ᵃPs. 2:9;
Jer. 19:11

30:15 ᵃPs. 116:7;
Is. 7:4; 28:12
ᵇMatt. 23:37

30:17
ᵃLev. 26:36;
Deut. 28:25;
32:30;
Josh. 23:10;
[Prov. 28:1]

30:18 ᵃIs. 33:2

30:7 ¹Lit. *Rahab Sits Idle*   **30:14** ¹A piece of broken pottery   **30:17** ¹A tree
stripped of branches

For the LORD *is* a God of justice;
^bBlessed *are* all those who ^cwait for Him.

19 For the people ^ashall dwell in Zion at Jerusalem;
You shall ^bweep no more.
He will be very gracious to you at the sound of your cry;
When He hears it, He will ^canswer you.

20 And *though* the Lord gives you
^aThe bread of adversity and the water of ¹affliction,
Yet ^byour teachers will not be moved into a corner
anymore,
But your eyes shall see your teachers.

21 Your ears shall hear a word behind you, saying,
"This *is* the way, walk in it,"
Whenever you ^aturn to the right hand
Or whenever you turn to the left.

22 ^aYou will also defile the covering of your images of
silver,
And the ornament of your molded images of gold.
You will throw them away as an unclean thing;
^bYou will say to them, "Get away!"

23 ^aThen He will give the rain for your seed
With which you sow the ground,
And bread of the increase of the earth;
It will be ¹fat and plentiful.
In that day your cattle will feed
In large pastures.

24 Likewise the oxen and the young donkeys that work the
ground
Will eat cured fodder,
Which has been winnowed with the shovel and fan.

25 There will be ^aon every high mountain
And on every high hill
Rivers *and* streams of waters,
In the day of the ^bgreat slaughter,
When the towers fall.

26 Moreover ^athe light of the moon will be as the light of the
sun,
And the light of the sun will be sevenfold,
As the light of seven days,
In the day that the LORD binds up the bruise of His
people
And heals the stroke of their wound.

JUDGMENT ON ASSYRIA

27 Behold, the name of the LORD comes from afar,
Burning *with* His anger,
And *His* burden *is* heavy;
His lips are full of indignation,
And His tongue like a devouring fire.

28 ^aHis breath is like an overflowing stream,
^bWhich reaches up to the neck,
To sift the nations with the sieve of futility;
And *there shall be* ^ca bridle in the jaws of the people,
Causing *them* to err.

30:18
^bPs. 2:12; 34:8;
Prov. 16:20;
Jer. 17:7 ^cIs. 26:8

30:19 ^aIs. 65:9;
[Ezek. 37:25,
28] ^bIs. 25:8
^cPs. 50:15;
Is. 65:24;
[Matt. 7:7–11]

30:20
^a1 Kin. 22:27;
Ps. 127:2
^bPs. 74:9;
Amos 8:11

30:21 ^aJosh. 1:7

30:22
^a2 Chr. 31:1;
Is. 2:20; 31:7
^bHos. 14:8

30:23
^a[Matt. 6:33];
1 Tim. 6:8

30:25
^aIs. 2:14, 15
^bIs. 2:10–21;
34:2

30:26
^a[Is. 60:19, 20;
Rev. 21:23; 22:5]

30:28 ^aIs. 11:4;
2 Thess. 2:8
^bIs. 8:8
^c2 Kin. 19:28;
Is. 37:29

30:20 ¹oppression   30:23 ¹rich

29 You shall have a song
As in the night *when* a holy festival is kept,
And gladness of heart as when one goes with a flute,
To come into [a]the mountain of the LORD,
To [1]the Mighty One of Israel.
30 [a]The LORD will cause His glorious voice to be heard,
And show the descent of His arm,
With the indignation of *His* anger
And the flame of a devouring fire,
With scattering, tempest, [b]and hailstones.
31 For [a]through the voice of the LORD
Assyria will be [1]beaten down,
As He strikes with the [b]rod.
32 And *in* every place where the staff of punishment passes,
Which the LORD lays on him,
It will be with tambourines and harps;
And in battles of [a]brandishing He will fight with it.
33 [a]For Tophet *was* established of old,
Yes, for the king it is prepared.
He has made *it* deep and large;
Its pyre *is* fire with much wood;
The breath of the LORD, like a stream of brimstone,
Kindles it.

THE FOLLY OF NOT TRUSTING GOD

31 Woe to those [a]who go down to Egypt for help,
And [b]rely on horses,
Who trust in chariots because *they are* many,
And in horsemen because they are very strong,
But who do not look to the Holy One of Israel,
[c]Nor seek the LORD!
2 Yet He also *is* wise and will bring disaster,
And [a]will not [1]call back His words,
But will arise against the house of evildoers,
And against the help of those who work iniquity.
3 Now the Egyptians *are* men, and not God;
And their horses are flesh, and not spirit.
When the LORD stretches out His hand,
Both he who helps will fall,
And he who is helped will fall down;
They all will perish [a]together.

GOD WILL DELIVER JERUSALEM

4For thus the LORD has spoken to me:

[a]"As a lion roars,
And a young lion over his prey
(When a multitude of shepherds is summoned against
him,
He will not be afraid of their voice
Nor be disturbed by their noise),
So the LORD of hosts will come down
To fight for Mount Zion and for its hill.
5 [a]Like birds flying about,
So will the LORD of hosts defend Jerusalem.
Defending, He will also deliver *it*;
Passing over, He will preserve *it*."

30:29 [a][Is. 2:3]
30:30 [a]Is. 29:6
[b]Is. 28:2
30:31
[a]Is. 14:25; 37:36
[b]Is. 10:5, 24
30:32 [a]Is. 11:15
30:33
[a]2 Kin. 23:10;
Jer. 7:31
31:1
[a]Is. 30:1, 2
[b]Deut. 17:16;
Ps. 20:7; Is. 2:7;
30:16 [c]Is. 9:13;
Dan. 9:13;
Amos 5:4–8
31:2
[a]Num. 23:19;
Jer. 44:29
31:3 [a]Is. 20:6
31:4
[a]Num. 24:9;
Hos. 11:10;
Amos 3:8
31:5
[a]Deut. 32:11;
Ps. 91:4

30:29 [1]Lit. *the Rock*   30:31 [1]Lit. *shattered*   31:2 [1]*retract*

⁶Return *to Him* against whom the children of Israel have ᵃdeeply revolted. ⁷For in that day every man shall ᵃthrow away his idols of silver and his idols of gold—ᵇsin, which your own hands have made for yourselves.

8 "Then Assyria shall ᵃfall by a sword not of man,
And a sword not of mankind shall ᵇdevour him.
But he shall flee from the sword,
And his young men shall become forced labor.
9 ᵃHe shall cross over to his stronghold for fear,
And his princes shall be afraid of the banner,"
Says the LORD,
Whose fire *is* in Zion
And whose furnace *is* in Jerusalem.

A REIGN OF RIGHTEOUSNESS

32 Behold, ᵃa king will reign in righteousness,
And princes will rule with justice.
2 A man will be as a hiding place from the wind,
And ᵃa ¹cover from the tempest,
As rivers of water in a dry place,
As the shadow of a great rock in a weary land.
3 ᵃThe eyes of those who see will not be dim,
And the ears of those who hear will listen.
4 Also the heart of the ¹rash will ᵃunderstand knowledge,
And the tongue of the stammerers will be ready to speak plainly.
5 The foolish person will no longer be called ¹generous,
Nor the miser said *to be* bountiful;
6 For the foolish person will speak foolishness,
And his heart will work ᵃiniquity:
To practice ungodliness,
To utter error against the LORD,
To keep the hungry unsatisfied,
And he will cause the drink of the thirsty to fail.
7 Also the schemes of the schemer *are* evil;
He devises wicked plans
To destroy the poor with ᵃlying words,
Even when the needy speaks justice.
8 But a ¹generous man devises generous things,
And by generosity he shall stand.

CONSEQUENCES OF COMPLACENCY

9 Rise up, you women ᵃwho are at ease,
Hear my voice;
You complacent daughters,
Give ear to my speech.
10 In a year and *some* days
You will be troubled, you complacent women;
For the vintage will fail,
The gathering will not come.
11 Tremble, you *women* who are at ease;
Be troubled, you complacent ones;
Strip yourselves, make yourselves bare,
And gird *sackcloth* on *your* waists.

31:6 ᵃHos. 9:9
31:7 ᵃIs. 2:20; 30:22
ᵇ1 Kin. 12:30
31:8 ᵃ2 Kin. 19:35, 36
ᵇIs. 37:36
31:9 ᵃIs. 37:37
32:1 ᵃPs. 45:1
32:2 ᵃIs. 4:6
32:3 ᵃIs. 29:18; 35:5
32:4 ᵃIs. 29:24
32:6 ᵃProv. 24:7–9
32:7 ᵃJer. 5:26–28; Mic. 7:3
32:9 ᵃIs. 47:8; Amos 6:1; Zeph. 2:15

32:2 ¹shelter   32:4 ¹hasty   32:5 ¹noble   32:8 ¹noble

12 People shall mourn upon their breasts
For the pleasant fields, for the fruitful vine.
13 ^aOn the land of my people will come up thorns *and*
briers,
Yes, on all the happy homes *in* ^bthe joyous city;
14 ^aBecause the palaces will be forsaken,
The bustling city will be deserted.
The forts and towers will become lairs forever,
A joy of wild donkeys, a pasture of flocks—
15 Until ^athe Spirit is poured upon us from on high,
And ^bthe wilderness becomes a fruitful field,
And the fruitful field is counted as a forest.

THE PEACE OF GOD'S REIGN

16 Then justice will dwell in the wilderness,
And righteousness remain in the fruitful field.
17 ^aThe work of righteousness will be peace,
And the effect of righteousness, quietness and assurance
forever.
18 My people will dwell in a peaceful habitation,
In secure dwellings, and in quiet ^aresting places,
19 ^aThough hail comes down ^bon the forest,
And the city is brought low in humiliation.

20 Blessed *are* you who sow beside all waters,
Who send out freely the feet of ^athe ox and the donkey.

A PRAYER IN DEEP DISTRESS

33 Woe to you ^awho plunder, though you *have* not *been*
plundered;
And you who deal treacherously, though they have not
dealt treacherously with you!
^bWhen you cease plundering,
You will be ^cplundered;
When you make an end of dealing treacherously,
They will deal treacherously with you.

2 O LORD, be gracious to us;
^aWe have waited for You.
Be ¹their arm every morning,
Our salvation also in the time of trouble.
3 At the noise of the tumult the people ^ashall flee;
When You lift Yourself up, the nations shall be
scattered;
4 And Your plunder shall be gathered
Like the gathering of the caterpillar;
As the running to and fro of locusts,
He shall run upon them.

5 ^aThe LORD is exalted, for He dwells on high;
He has filled Zion with justice and righteousness.
6 Wisdom and knowledge will be the stability of your
times,
And the strength of salvation;
The fear of the LORD *is* His treasure.

7 Surely their valiant ones shall cry outside,
^aThe ambassadors of peace shall weep bitterly.

32:13
^aIs. 7:23–25;
Hos. 9:6
^bIs. 22:2

32:14 ^aIs. 27:10

32:15 ^a[Is. 11:2];
Ezek. 39:29;
[Joel 2:28]
^bPs. 107:35;
Is. 29:17

32:17
^aPs. 119:165;
Is. 2:4;
Rom. 14:17;
James 3:18

32:18 ^aIs. 11:10;
14:3; 30:15;
[Hos. 2:18–23;
Zech. 2:5; 3:10]

32:19 ^aIs. 30:30
^bZech. 11:2

32:20
^a[Eccl. 11:1];
Is. 30:23, 24

33:1 ^aIs. 21:2;
Hab. 2:8
^bRev. 13:10
^cIs. 10:12;
14:25; 31:8

33:2
^aIs. 25:9; 26:8

33:3 ^aIs. 17:13

33:5 ^aPs. 97:9

33:7
^a2 Kin. 18:18, 37

33:2 ¹LXX omits *their*; Syr., Tg., Vg. *our*

8 ᵃThe highways lie waste,
   The traveling man ceases.
   ᵇHe has broken the covenant,
   ¹He has despised the ²cities,
   He regards no man.
9 ᵃThe earth mourns *and* languishes,
   Lebanon is shamed *and* shriveled;
   Sharon is like a wilderness,
   And Bashan and Carmel shake off *their fruits.*

IMPENDING JUDGMENT ON ZION

10 "Nowᵃ I will rise," says the LORD;
   "Now I will be exalted,
   Now I will lift Myself up.
11 ᵃYou shall conceive chaff,
   You shall bring forth stubble;
   Your breath, *as* fire, shall devour you.
12 And the people shall be *like* the burnings of lime;
   ᵃ*Like* thorns cut up they shall be burned in the fire.
13 Hear, ᵃyou *who are* afar off, what I have done;
   And you *who are* near, acknowledge My might."
14 The sinners in Zion are afraid;
   Fearfulness has seized the hypocrites:
   "Who among us shall dwell with the devouring ᵃfire?
   Who among us shall dwell with everlasting burnings?"
15 He who ᵃwalks righteously and speaks uprightly,
   He who despises the gain of oppressions,
   Who gestures with his hands, refusing bribes,
   Who stops his ears from hearing of bloodshed,
   And ᵇshuts his eyes from seeing evil:
16 He will dwell on ¹high;
   His place of defense *will be* the fortress of rocks;
   Bread will be given him,
   His water *will be* sure.

THE LAND OF THE MAJESTIC KING

17 Your eyes will see the King in His ᵃbeauty;
   They will see the land that is very far off.
18 Your heart will meditate on terror:
   ᵃ"Where *is* the scribe?
   Where *is* he who weighs?
   Where *is* he who counts the towers?"
19 ᵃYou will not see a fierce people,
   ᵇA people of obscure speech, beyond perception,
   Of a ¹stammering tongue *that you* cannot understand.
20 ᵃLook upon Zion, the city of our appointed feasts;
   Your eyes will see ᵇJerusalem, a quiet home,
   A tabernacle *that* will not be taken down;
   ᶜNot one of ᵈits stakes will ever be removed,
   Nor will any of its cords be broken.
21 But there the majestic LORD *will be* for us
   A place of broad rivers *and* streams,
   In which no ¹galley with oars will sail,
   Nor majestic ships pass by

33:8 ᵃJudg. 5:6
ᵇ2 Kin. 18:13–17

33:9 ᵃIs. 24:4

33:10 ᵃPs. 12:5;
Is. 2:19, 21

33:11 ᵃ[Ps. 7:14;
Is. 26:18; 59:4;
James 1:15]

33:12 ᵃIs. 9:18

33:13 ᵃPs. 48:10;
Is. 49:1

33:14
ᵃIs. 30:27, 30;
Heb. 12:29

33:15
ᵃPs. 15:2;
24:3, 4;
Is. 58:6–11
ᵇPs. 119:37

33:17 ᵃPs. 27:4

33:18
ᵃ1 Cor. 1:20

33:19
ᵃ2 Kin. 19:32
ᵇDeut. 28:49,
50; Is. 28:11;
Jer. 5:15

33:20 ᵃPs. 48:12
ᵇPs. 46:5;
125:1; Is. 32:18
ᶜIs. 37:33
ᵈIs. 54:2

33:8 ¹Tg. *They have been removed from their cities*   ²So with MT, Vg.; DSS
witnesses; LXX omits *cities*   33:16 ¹Lit. *heights*   33:19 ¹Unintelligible
speech   33:21 ¹*ship*

22 (For the LORD *is* our ªJudge,
   The LORD *is* our ᵇLawgiver,
   ᶜThe LORD *is* our King;
   He will save us);
23 Your tackle is loosed,
   They could not strengthen their mast,
   They could not spread the sail.

   Then the prey of great plunder is divided;
   The lame take the prey.
24 And the inhabitant will not say, "I am sick";
   ªThe people who dwell in it *will be* forgiven *their* iniquity.

JUDGMENT ON THE NATIONS

34 Come ªnear, you nations, to hear;
   And heed, you people!
   ᵇLet the earth hear, and all that is in it,
   The world and all things that come forth from it.
2 For the indignation of the LORD *is* against all nations,
   And *His* fury against all their armies;
   He has utterly destroyed them,
   He has given them over to the ªslaughter.
3 Also their slain shall be thrown out;
   ªTheir stench shall rise from their corpses,
   And the mountains shall be melted with their blood.
4 ªAll the host of heaven shall be dissolved,
   And the heavens shall be rolled up like a scroll;
   ᵇAll their host shall fall down
   As the leaf falls from the vine,
   And as ᶜ*fruit* falling from a fig tree.
5 "For ªMy sword shall be bathed in heaven;
   Indeed it ᵇshall come down on Edom,
   And on the people of My curse, for judgment.
6 The ªsword of the LORD is filled with blood,
   It is made ¹overflowing with fatness,
   With the blood of lambs and goats,
   With the fat of the kidneys of rams.
   For ᵇthe LORD has a sacrifice in Bozrah,
   And a great slaughter in the land of Edom.
7 The wild oxen shall come down with them,
   And the young bulls with the mighty bulls;
   Their land shall be soaked with blood,
   And their dust ¹saturated with fatness."

8 For *it is* the day of the LORD's ªvengeance,
   The year of recompense for the cause of Zion.
9 ªIts streams shall be turned into pitch,
   And its dust into brimstone;
   Its land shall become burning pitch.
10 It shall not be quenched night or day;
   ªIts smoke shall ascend forever.
   ᵇFrom generation to generation it shall lie waste;
   No one shall pass through it forever and ever.
11 ªBut the ¹pelican and the ²porcupine shall possess it,
   Also the owl and the raven shall dwell in it.
   And ᵇHe shall stretch out over it
   The line of confusion and the stones of emptiness.

33:22
ª[Acts 10:42]
ᵇIs. 1:10; 51:4, 7;
James 4:12
ᶜPs. 89:18;
Is. 25:9; 35:4;
Zech. 9:9
33:24 ªIs. 40:2;
Jer. 50:20;
Mic. 7:18, 19;
1 John 1:7–9
34:1 ªPs. 49:1;
Is. 41:1; 43:9
ᵇDeut. 32:1;
Is. 1:2
34:2 ªIs. 13:5
34:3 ªJoel 2:20;
Amos 4:10
34:4
ªPs. 102:26;
Is. 13:13;
Ezek. 32:7, 8;
Joel 2:31;
Matt. 24:29;
2 Pet. 3:10
ᵇIs. 14:12
ᶜRev. 6:12–14
34:5
ªDeut. 32:41,
42; Jer. 46:10;
Ezek. 21:3–5
ᵇIs. 63:1;
Jer. 49:7, 8, 20;
Ezek. 25:12–14;
35:1–15;
Amos 1:11, 12;
Obad. 1–14;
Mal. 1:4
34:6 ªIs. 66:16
ᵇZeph. 1:7
34:8 ªIs. 63:4
34:9
ªDeut. 29:23;
Ps. 11:6; Is. 30:33
34:10 ªRev. 14:11;
18:18; 19:3
ᵇIs. 13:20–22;
24:1; 34:10–15;
Mal. 1:3, 4
34:11 ªIs. 14:23;
Zeph. 2:14;
Rev. 18:2
ᵇ2 Kin. 21:13;
Lam. 2:8

34:6 ¹Lit. *fat*   **34:7** ¹Lit. *made fat*   **34:11** ¹Or *owl*   ²Or *hedgehog*

12 They shall call its nobles to the kingdom,
But none *shall be* there, and all its princes shall be nothing.

13 And ᵃthorns shall come up in its palaces,
Nettles and brambles in its fortresses;
ᵇIt shall be a habitation of jackals,
A courtyard for ostriches.

14 The wild beasts of the desert shall also meet with the
¹jackals,
And the wild goat shall bleat to its companion;
Also ²the night creature shall rest there,
And find for herself a place of rest.

15 There the arrow snake shall make her nest and lay *eggs*
And hatch, and gather *them* under her shadow;
There also shall the hawks be gathered,
Every one with her mate.

16 "Search from ᵃthe book of the LORD, and read:
Not one of these shall fail;
Not one shall lack her mate.
For My mouth has commanded it, and His Spirit has
gathered them.

17 He has cast the lot for them,
And His hand has divided it among them with a
measuring line.
They shall possess it forever;
From generation to generation they shall dwell in it."

THE FUTURE GLORY OF ZION

35 The ᵃwilderness and the ¹wasteland shall be glad for
them,
And the ᵇdesert² shall rejoice and blossom as the rose;

2 ᵃIt shall blossom abundantly and rejoice,
Even with joy and singing.
The glory of Lebanon shall be given to it,
The excellence of Carmel and Sharon.
They shall see the ᵇglory of the LORD,
The excellency of our God.

3 ᵃStrengthen the ¹weak hands,
And make firm the ²feeble knees.

4 Say to those *who are* fearful-hearted,
"Be strong, do not fear!
Behold, your God will come *with* ᵃvengeance,
With the recompense of God;
He will come and ᵇsave you."

5 Then the ᵃeyes of the blind shall be opened,
And ᵇthe ears of the deaf shall be unstopped.

6 Then the ᵃlame shall leap like a deer,
And the ᵇtongue of the dumb sing.
For ᶜwaters shall burst forth in the wilderness,
And streams in the desert.

7 The parched ground shall become a pool,
And the thirsty land springs of water;
In ᵃthe habitation of jackals, where each lay,
There shall be grass with reeds and rushes.

34:13 ᵃIs. 32:13;
Hos. 9:6
ᵇIs. 13:21

34:16
ᵃ[Mal. 3:16]

35:1 ᵃIs. 32:15;
55:12 ᵇIs. 41:19;
51:3

35:2 ᵃIs. 32:15
ᵇIs. 40:5

35:3 ᵃJob 4:3, 4;
Heb. 12:12

35:4 ᵃIs. 34:8
ᵇPs. 145:19;
Is. 33:22

35:5 ᵃIs. 29:18;
Matt. 9:27;
John 9:6, 7
ᵇ[Matt. 11:5]

35:6 ᵃMatt. 11:5;
15:30;
John 5:8, 9;
Acts 8:7
ᵇIs. 32:4;
Matt. 9:32;
12:22 ᶜIs. 41:18;
[John 7:38]

35:7 ᵃIs. 34:13

34:14 ¹Lit. *howling creatures*   ²Heb. *lilith*   35:1 ¹*desert*   ²Heb. *arabah*
35:3 ¹Lit. *sinking*   ²*tottering* or *stumbling*

8   A [a]highway shall be there, and a road,
     And it shall be called the Highway of Holiness.
    [b]The unclean shall not pass over it,
     But it *shall be* for others.
     Whoever walks the road, although a fool,
     Shall not go astray.
9   [a]No lion shall be there,
     Nor shall *any* ravenous beast go up on it;
     It shall not be found there.
     But the redeemed shall walk *there,*
10 And the [a]ransomed of the LORD shall return,
     And come to Zion with singing,
     With everlasting joy on their heads.
     They shall obtain joy and gladness,
     And [b]sorrow and sighing shall flee away.

SENNACHERIB BOASTS AGAINST THE LORD
(2 Kin. 18:13–37; 2 Chr. 32:1–19)

36 Now [a]it came to pass in the fourteenth year of King Hezekiah *that* Sennacherib king of Assyria came up against all the fortified cities of Judah and took them. [2]Then the king of Assyria sent *the* [1]Rabshakeh with a great army from Lachish to King Hezekiah at Jerusalem. And he stood by the aqueduct from the upper pool, on the highway to the Fuller's Field. [3]And [a]Eliakim the son of Hilkiah, who was over the household, [b]Shebna the scribe, and Joah the son of Asaph, the recorder, came out to him.

[4][a]Then *the* Rabshakeh said to them, "Say now to Hezekiah, 'Thus says the great king, the king of Assyria: "What confidence is this in which you trust? [5]I say you speak of having plans and power for war; but *they are* [1]mere words. Now in whom do you trust, that you rebel against me? [6]Look! You are trusting in the [a]staff of this broken reed, Egypt, on which if a man leans, it will go into his hand and pierce it. So *is* Pharaoh king of Egypt to all who [b]trust in him.

[7]"But if you say to me, 'We trust in the LORD our God,' *is it* not He whose high places and whose altars Hezekiah has taken away, and said to Judah and Jerusalem, 'You shall worship before this altar'?" ' [8]Now therefore, I urge you, give a pledge to my master the king of Assyria, and I will give you two thousand horses—if you are able on your part to put riders on them! [9]How then will you repel one captain of the least of my master's servants, and put your trust in Egypt for chariots and horsemen? [10]Have I now come up without the LORD against this land to destroy it? The LORD said to me, 'Go up against this land, and destroy it.' "

[11]Then Eliakim, Shebna, and Joah said to *the* Rabshakeh, "Please speak to your servants in Aramaic, for we understand *it;* and do not speak to us in [1]Hebrew in the hearing of the people who *are* on the wall."

[12]But *the* Rabshakeh said, "Has my master sent me to your master and to you to speak these words, and not to the men who sit on the wall, who will eat and drink their own waste with you?"

[13]Then *the* Rabshakeh stood and called out with a loud

35:8 [a]Is. 19:23
  [b]Is. 52:1;
  Joel 3:17;
  [Matt. 7:13, 14];
  1 Pet. 1:15, 16;
  Rev. 21:27
35:9 [a]Lev. 26:6;
  [Is. 11:7, 9];
  Ezek. 34:25
35:10 [a]Is. 51:11
  [b]Is. 25:8; 30:19;
  65:19; [Rev. 7:17;
  21:4]
36:1
[a]2 Kin. 18:13, 17;
  2 Chr. 32:1
36:3 [a]Is. 22:20
  [b]Is. 22:15
36:4
[a]2 Kin. 18:19
36:6 [a]Ezek. 29:6
  [b]Ps. 146:3;
  Is. 30:3, 5, 7

36:2 [1]A title, probably *Chief of Staff* or *Governor*   36:5 [1]Lit. *a word of the lips*
36:11 [1]Lit. *Judean*

voice in Hebrew, and said, "Hear the words of the great king, the king of Assyria! [14]Thus says the king: 'Do not let Hezekiah deceive you, for he will not be able to deliver you; [15]nor let Hezekiah make you trust in the LORD, saying, "The LORD will surely deliver us; this city will not be given into the hand of the king of Assyria." ' [16]Do not listen to Hezekiah; for thus says the king of Assyria: 'Make *peace* with me *by a* present and come out to me; [a]and every one of you eat from his own vine and every one from his own fig tree, and every one of you drink the waters of his own cistern; [17]until I come and take you away to a land like your own land, a land of grain and new wine, a land of bread and vineyards. [18]*Beware* lest Hezekiah persuade you, saying, "The LORD will deliver us." Has any one of the [a]gods of the nations delivered its land from the hand of the king of Assyria? [19]Where *are* the gods of Hamath and Arpad? Where *are* the gods of Sepharvaim? Indeed, have they delivered [a]Samaria from my hand? [20]Who among all the gods of these lands have delivered their countries from my hand, that the LORD should deliver Jerusalem from my hand?' "

[21]But they [1]held their peace and answered him not a word; for the king's commandment was, "Do not answer him." [22]Then Eliakim the son of Hilkiah, who *was* over the household, Shebna the scribe, and Joah the son of Asaph, the recorder, came to Hezekiah with *their* clothes torn, and told him the words of *the* Rabshakeh.

ISAIAH ASSURES DELIVERANCE
(2 Kin. 19:1–7)

37 And [a]so it was, when King Hezekiah heard *it,* that he tore his clothes, covered himself with sackcloth, and went into the house of the LORD. [2]Then he sent Eliakim, who *was* over the household, Shebna the scribe, and the elders of the priests, covered with sackcloth, to Isaiah the prophet, the son of Amoz. [3]And they said to him, "Thus says Hezekiah: 'This day *is* a day of [a]trouble and rebuke and [1]blasphemy; for the children have come to birth, but *there is* no strength to bring them forth. [4]It may be that the LORD your God will hear the words of *the* Rabshakeh, whom his master the king of Assyria has sent to [a]reproach the living God, and will rebuke the words which the LORD your God has heard. Therefore lift up *your* prayer for the remnant that is left.' "

[5]So the servants of King Hezekiah came to Isaiah. [6]And Isaiah said to them, "Thus you shall say to your master, 'Thus says the LORD: "Do not be afraid of the words which you have heard, with which the servants of the king of Assyria have blasphemed Me. [7]Surely I will send a spirit upon him, and he shall hear a rumor and return to his own land; and I will cause him to fall by the sword in his own land." ' "

SENNACHERIB'S THREAT AND HEZEKIAH'S PRAYER
(2 Kin. 19:8–19)

[8]Then *the* Rabshakeh returned, and found the king of Assyria warring against Libnah, for he heard that he had departed from Lachish. [9]And the king heard concerning Tirhakah king of Ethiopia, "He has come out to make war with you." So when

36:16
[a]1 Kin. 4:25;
Mic. 4:4;
Zech. 3:10

36:18
[a]2 Kin. 19:12;
Is. 37:12

36:19
[a]2 Kin. 17:6

37:1
[a]2 Kin. 19:1–37;
Is. 37:1–38

37:3 [a]Is. 22:5;
26:16; 33:2

37:4 [a]Is. 36:15,
18, 20

36:21 [1]*were silent*   37:3 [1]*contempt*

he heard *it,* he sent messengers to Hezekiah, saying, [10]"Thus you shall speak to Hezekiah king of Judah, saying: 'Do not let your God in whom you trust deceive you, saying, "Jerusalem shall not be given into the hand of the king of Assyria." [11]Look! You have heard what the kings of Assyria have done to all lands by utterly destroying them; and shall you be delivered? [12]Have the [a]gods of the nations delivered those whom my fathers have destroyed, Gozan and Haran and Rezeph, and the people of Eden who *were* in Telassar? [13]Where *is* the king of [a]Hamath, the king of Arpad, and the king of the city of Sepharvaim, Hena, and Ivah?'"

[14]And Hezekiah received the letter from the hand of the messengers, and read it; and Hezekiah went up to the house of the LORD, and spread it before the LORD. [15]Then Hezekiah prayed to the LORD, saying: [16]"O LORD of hosts, God of Israel, *the One* who dwells *between* the cherubim, You *are* God, You [a]alone, of all the kingdoms of the earth. You have made heaven and earth. [17][a]Incline Your ear, O LORD, and hear; open Your eyes, O LORD, and see; and [b]hear all the words of Sennacherib, which he has sent to reproach the living God. [18]Truly, LORD, the kings of Assyria have laid waste all the nations and their [a]lands, [19]and have cast their gods into the fire; for they *were* [a]not gods, but the work of men's hands—wood and stone. Therefore they destroyed them. [20]Now therefore, O LORD our God, [a]save us from his hand, that all the kingdoms of the earth may [b]know that You *are* the LORD, You alone."

THE WORD OF THE LORD CONCERNING SENNACHERIB
(2 Kin. 19:20–34)

[21]Then Isaiah the son of Amoz sent to Hezekiah, saying, "Thus says the LORD God of Israel, 'Because you have prayed to Me against Sennacherib king of Assyria, [22]this *is* the word which the LORD has spoken concerning him:

"The virgin, the daughter of Zion,
Has despised you, laughed you to scorn;
The daughter of Jerusalem
Has shaken *her* head behind your back!

[23] "Whom have you reproached and blasphemed?
Against whom have you raised *your* voice,
And lifted up your eyes on high?
Against the Holy One of Israel.
[24] By your servants you have reproached the Lord,
And said, 'By the multitude of my chariots
I have come up to the height of the mountains,
To the limits of Lebanon;
I will cut down its tall cedars
And its choice cypress trees;
I will enter its farthest height,
To its fruitful forest.
[25] I have dug and drunk water,
And with the soles of my feet I have dried up
All the brooks of [1]defense.'

[26] "Did you not hear [a]long ago
How I made it,

37:12
[a]Is. 36:18, 19
37:13 [a]Is. 49:23
37:16
[a]Is. 43:10, 11
37:17
[a]2 Chr. 6:40;
Ps. 17:6;
Dan. 9:18
[b]Ps. 74:22
37:18
[a]2 Kin. 15:29;
16:9; 17:6, 24;
1 Chr. 5:26
37:19
[a]Is. 40:19, 20
37:20 [a]Is. 33:22
[b]Ps. 83:18
37:26 [a]Is. 25:1;
40:21; 45:21

37:25 [1]Or perhaps *Egypt*

From ancient times that I formed it?
Now I have brought it to pass,
That you should be
For crushing fortified cities *into* heaps of ruins.
27 Therefore their inhabitants *had* little power;
They were dismayed and confounded;
They were *as* the grass of the field
And the green herb,
As the grass on the housetops
And *grain* blighted before it is grown.

28 "But I know your dwelling place,
Your going out and your coming in,
And your rage against Me.
29 Because your rage against Me and your tumult
Have come up to My ears,
Therefore ªI will put My hook in your nose
And My bridle in your lips,
And I will ᵇturn you back
By the way which you came." '

30"This *shall be* a sign to you:

You shall eat this year such as grows of itself,
And the second year what springs from the same;
Also in the third year sow and reap,
Plant vineyards and eat the fruit of them.
31 And the remnant who have escaped of the house of Judah
Shall again take root downward,
And bear fruit upward.
32 For out of Jerusalem shall go a remnant,
And those who escape from Mount Zion.
The ªzeal of the LORD of hosts will do this.

33"Therefore thus says the LORD concerning the king of Assyria:

'He shall not come into this city,
Nor shoot an arrow there,
Nor come before it with shield,
Nor build a siege mound against it.
34 By the way that he came,
By the same shall he return;
And he shall not come into this city,'
Says the LORD.
35 'For I will ªdefend this city, to save it
For My own sake and for My servant ᵇDavid's sake.' "

SENNACHERIB'S DEFEAT AND DEATH
(2 *Kin.* 19:35–37)

36Then the ªangel¹ of the LORD went out, and ²killed in the camp of the Assyrians one hundred and eighty-five thousand; and when *people* arose early in the morning, there were the corpses—all dead. 37So Sennacherib king of Assyria departed and went away, returned *home,* and remained at Nineveh. 38Now it came to pass, as he was worshiping in the house of Nisroch his god, that his sons Adrammelech and Sharezer struck him down with the sword; and they escaped into the land of Ararat. Then ªEsarhaddon his son reigned in his place.

37:36 ¹Or *Angel*   ²Lit. *struck*

37:29
ª2 Kin. 19:35–37;
2 Chr. 32:21;
Is. 30:28;
Ezek. 38:4;
ᵇEzek. 38:4;
39:2

37:32
ª2 Kin. 19:31;
Is. 9:7; 59:17;
Joel 2:18;
Zech. 1:14

37:35
ª2 Kin. 20:6;
Is. 31:5; 38:6
ᵇ1 Kin. 11:13

37:36
ª2 Kin. 19:35;
Is. 10:12, 33, 34

37:38 ªEzra 4:2

HEZEKIAH'S LIFE EXTENDED
(2 Kin. 20:1–11; 2 Chr. 32:24–26)

38 In ᵃthose days Hezekiah was sick and near death. And Isaiah the prophet, the son of Amoz, went to him and said to him, "Thus says the LORD: ᵇ'Set your house in order, for you shall die and not live.' "

2 Then Hezekiah turned his face toward the wall, and prayed to the LORD, 3 and said, ᵃ"Remember now, O LORD, I pray, how I have walked before You in truth and with a ¹loyal heart, and have done *what is* good in Your ᵇsight." And Hezekiah wept bitterly.

4 And the word of the LORD came to Isaiah, saying, 5 "Go and tell Hezekiah, 'Thus says the LORD, the God of David your father: "I have heard your prayer, I have seen your tears; surely I will add to your days fifteen years. 6 I will deliver you and this city from the hand of the king of Assyria, and ᵃI will defend this city." ' 7 And this *is* ᵃthe sign to you from the LORD, that the LORD will do this thing which He has spoken: 8 Behold, I will bring the shadow on the sundial, which has gone down with the sun on the sundial of Ahaz, ten degrees backward." So the sun returned ten degrees on the dial by which it had gone down.

9 This is the writing of Hezekiah king of Judah, when he had been sick and had recovered from his sickness:

10 I said,
"In the prime of my life
 I shall go to the gates of Sheol;
I am deprived of the remainder of my years."

11 I said,
"I shall not see ¹YAH,
 The LORD ᵃin the land of the living;
I shall observe man no more ²among the inhabitants of ³the world.

12 ᵃMy life span is gone,
 Taken from me like a shepherd's tent;
I have cut off my life like a weaver.
 He cuts me off from the loom;
From day until night You make an end of me.

13 I have considered until morning—
Like a lion,
 So He breaks all my bones;
From day until night You make an end of me.

14 Like a crane *or* a swallow, so I chattered;
 ᵃI mourned like a dove;
My eyes fail *from looking* upward.
O ¹LORD, I am oppressed;
 ²Undertake for me!

15 "What shall I say?
 ¹He has both spoken to me,
 And He Himself has done *it*.
I shall walk carefully all my years
 ᵃIn the bitterness of my soul.

38:1
ᵃ2 Kin. 20:1–6, 9–11;
2 Chr. 32:24;
Is. 38:1–8
ᵇ2 Sam. 17:23

38:3 ᵃNeh. 13:14
ᵇ2 Kin. 18:5, 6;
Ps. 26:3

38:6
ᵃ2 Kin. 19:35–37;
2 Chr. 32:21;
Is. 31:5; 37:35

38:7
ᵃJudg. 6:17, 21, 36–40;
2 Kin. 20:8;
Is. 7:11

38:11
ᵃPs. 27:13; 116:9

38:12 ᵃJob 7:6

38:14 ᵃIs. 59:11;
Ezek. 7:16;
Nah. 2:7

38:15 ᵃJob 7:11;
10:1; Is. 38:17

38:3 ¹*whole* or *peaceful* 38:11 ¹Heb. *YAH, YAH* ²LXX omits *among the inhabitants of the world* ³So with some Heb. mss.; MT, Vg. *rest;* Tg. *land*
38:14 ¹So with Bg.; MT, DSS *Lord* ²*Be my surety* 38:15 ¹So with MT, Vg.;
DSS, Tg. *And shall I say to Him;* LXX omits first half of this verse

16 O Lord, by these *things men* live;
And in all these *things is* the life of my spirit;
So You will restore me and make me live.
17 Indeed *it was* for *my own* peace
That I had great bitterness;
But You have lovingly *delivered* my soul from the pit of
corruption,
For You have cast all my sins behind Your back.
18 For ªSheol cannot thank You,
Death cannot praise You;
Those who go down to the pit cannot hope for Your
truth.
19 The living, the living man, he shall praise You,
As I *do* this day;
ªThe father shall make known Your truth to the
children.

20 "The LORD *was ready* to save me;
Therefore we will sing my songs with stringed
instruments
All the days of our life, in the house of the LORD."

21Now ªIsaiah had said, "Let them take a lump of figs, and
apply *it* as a poultice on the boil, and he shall recover."
22And ªHezekiah had said, "What *is* the sign that I shall go
up to the house of the LORD?"

THE BABYLONIAN ENVOYS
(2 Kin. 20:12–19)

39 At ªthat time ¹Merodach-Baladan the son of Baladan,
king of Babylon, sent letters and a present to Hezekiah, for he heard that he had been sick and had recovered.
2ªAnd Hezekiah was pleased with them, and showed them the
house of his treasures—the silver and gold, the spices and
precious ointment, and all his armory—all that was found
among his treasures. There was nothing in his house or in all
his dominion that Hezekiah did not show them.

3Then Isaiah the prophet went to King Hezekiah, and said
to him, "What did these men say, and from where did they
come to you?"

So Hezekiah said, "They came to me from a ªfar country,
from Babylon."

4And he said, "What have they seen in your house?"

So Hezekiah answered, "They have seen all that *is* in my
house; there is nothing among my treasures that I have not
shown them."

5Then Isaiah said to Hezekiah, "Hear the word of the LORD
of hosts: 6'Behold, the days are coming ªwhen all that *is* in
your house, and what your fathers have accumulated until
this day, shall be carried to Babylon; nothing shall be left,' says
the LORD. 7'And they shall take away *some* of your ªsons who
will descend from you, whom you will beget; and they shall be
eunuchs in the palace of the king of Babylon.'"

8So Hezekiah said to Isaiah, ª"The word of the LORD which
you have spoken *is* good!" For he said, "At least there will be
peace and truth in my days."

38:18 ªPs. 6:5;
30:9; 88:11;
115:17;
[Eccl. 9:10]

38:19
ªDeut. 4:9; 6:7;
Ps. 78:3, 4

38:21
ª2 Kin. 20:7

38:22
ª2 Kin. 20:8

39:1
ª2 Kin. 20:12–19;
2 Chr. 32:31;
Is. 39:1–8

39:2
ª2 Chr. 32:25, 31;
Job 31:25

39:3
ªDeut. 28:49;
Jer. 5:15

39:6
ª2 Kin. 24:13;
25:13–15;
Jer. 20:5

39:7 ªDan. 1:1–7

39:8
ª1 Sam. 3:18

39:1 ¹*Berodach-Baladan,* 2 Kin. 20:12

GOD'S PEOPLE ARE COMFORTED
(cf. Luke 3:4–6)

40 "Comfort, yes, comfort My people!"
Says your God.

2 "Speak [1]comfort to Jerusalem, and cry out to her,
That her warfare is ended,
That her iniquity is pardoned;
[a]For she has received from the LORD's hand
Double for all her sins."

3 [a]The voice of one crying in the wilderness:
[b]"Prepare the way of the LORD;
[c]Make straight [1]in the desert
A highway for our God.

4 Every valley shall be exalted
And every mountain and hill brought low;
[a]The crooked places shall be made [1]straight
And the rough places smooth;

5 The [a]glory of the LORD shall be revealed,
And all flesh shall see *it* together;
For the mouth of the LORD has spoken."

6 The voice said, "Cry out!"
And [1]he said, "What shall I cry?"

[a]"All flesh *is* grass,
And all its loveliness *is* like the flower of the field.

7 The grass withers, the flower fades,
Because the breath of the LORD blows upon it;
Surely the people *are* grass.

8 The grass withers, the flower fades,
But [a]the word of our God stands forever."

9 O Zion,
You who bring good tidings,
Get up into the high mountain;
O Jerusalem,
You who bring good tidings,
Lift up your voice with strength,
Lift *it* up, be not afraid;
Say to the cities of Judah, "Behold your God!"

10 Behold, the Lord GOD shall come [1]with a strong *hand,*
And [a]His arm shall rule for Him;
Behold, [b]His reward *is* with Him,
And His [2]work before Him.

11 He will [a]feed His flock like a shepherd;
He will gather the lambs with His arm,
And carry *them* in His bosom,
And gently lead those who are with young.

12 [a]Who has measured the [1]waters in the hollow of His hand,
Measured heaven with a [2]span
And calculated the dust of the earth in a measure?
Weighed the mountains in scales
And the hills in a balance?

40:2 [a]Is. 61:7
40:3 [a]Matt. 3:3;
Mark 1:3;
Luke 3:4–6;
John 1:23
[b][Mal. 3:1; 4:5, 6]
[c]Ps. 68:4
40:4 [a]Is. 45:2
40:5 [a]Is. 35:2
40:6 [a]Job 14:2;
James 1:10;
1 Pet. 1:24, 25
40:8
[a][John 12:34]
40:10
[a]Is. 59:16, 18
[b]Is. 62:11;
Rev. 22:12
40:11 [a]Jer. 31:10;
[Ezek. 34:23, 31];
Mic. 5:4;
[John 10:11,
14–16;
Heb. 13:20;
1 Pet. 2:25]
40:12
[a]Prov. 30:4

40:2 [1]Lit. *to the heart of*   40:3 [1]So with MT, Tg., Vg.; LXX omits *in the desert*
40:4 [1]Or *a plain*   40:6 [1]So with MT, Tg.; DSS, LXX, Vg. I   40:10 [1]*in strength*
[2]*recompense*   40:12 [1]So with MT, LXX, Vg.; DSS adds *of the sea;* Tg. adds *of the world*   [2]A span .5 cubit, 9 inches; or the width of His hand

13 ᵃWho has directed the Spirit of the LORD,
   Or *as* His counselor has taught Him?
14 With whom did He take counsel, and *who* instructed Him,
   And ᵃtaught Him in the path of justice?
   Who taught Him knowledge,
   And showed Him the way of understanding?

15 Behold, the nations *are* as a drop in a bucket,
   And are counted as the small dust on the scales;
   Look, He lifts up the isles as a very little thing.
16 And Lebanon *is* not sufficient to burn,
   Nor its beasts sufficient for a burnt offering.
17 All nations before Him *are* as ᵃnothing,
   And ᵇthey are counted by Him less than nothing and
      worthless.

18 To whom then will you ᵃliken God?
   Or what likeness will you compare to Him?
19 ᵃThe workman molds an image,
   The goldsmith overspreads it with gold,
   And the silversmith casts silver chains.
20 Whoever *is* too impoverished for *such* ¹a contribution
   Chooses a tree *that* will not rot;
   He seeks for himself a skillful workman
   ᵃTo prepare a carved image *that* will not totter.

21 ᵃHave you not known?
   Have you not heard?
   Has it not been told you from the beginning?
   Have you not understood from the foundations of the
      earth?
22 *It is* He who sits above the circle of the earth,
   And its inhabitants *are* like grasshoppers,
   Who ᵃstretches out the heavens like a curtain,
   And spreads them out like a ᵇtent to dwell in.
23 He ¹brings the ᵃprinces to nothing;
   He makes the judges of the earth useless.

24 Scarcely shall they be planted,
   Scarcely shall they be sown,
   Scarcely shall their stock take root in the earth,
   When He will also blow on them,
   And they will wither,
   And the whirlwind will take them away like stubble.

25 "Toᵃ whom then will you liken Me,
   Or *to whom* shall I be equal?" says the Holy One.
26 Lift up your eyes on high,
   And see who has created these *things,*
   Who brings out their host by number;
   ᵃHe calls them all by name,
   By the greatness of His might
   And the strength of *His* power;
   Not one is missing.

27 ᵃWhy do you say, O Jacob,
   And speak, O Israel:
   "My way is hidden from the LORD,
   And my just claim is passed over by my God"?

40:13
ᵃJob 21:22;
Rom. 11:34;
[1 Cor. 2:16]

40:14
ᵃJob 36:22, 23

40:17 ᵃDan. 4:35
ᵇPs. 62:9

40:18 ᵃEx. 8:10;
15:11; 1 Sam. 2:2;
Is. 46:5;
[Mic. 7:18];
Acts 17:29

40:19
ᵃPs. 115:4–8;
Is. 41:7; 44:10;
Hab. 2:18, 19

40:20
ᵃ1 Sam. 5:3, 4;
Is. 41:7; 46:7;
Jer. 10:3

40:21 ᵃPs. 19:1;
Is. 37:26;
Acts 14:17;
Rom. 1:19

40:22 ᵃJob 9:8;
Ps. 104:2;
Is. 42:5; 44:24;
Jer. 10:12
ᵇJob 36:29;
Ps. 19:4

40:23
ᵃJob 12:21;
Ps. 107:40;
Is. 34:12;
[1 Cor. 1:26–29]

40:25
ᵃ[Deut. 4:15];
Is. 40:18;
[John 14:9;
Col. 1:15]

40:26 ᵃPs. 147:4

40:27 ᵃIs. 54:7, 8

40:20 ¹*an offering*   40:23 ¹*reduces*

28 Have you not known?
Have you not heard?
The everlasting God, the LORD,
The Creator of the ends of the earth,
Neither faints nor is weary.
ᵃHis understanding is unsearchable.
29 He gives power to the weak,
And to *those who have* no might He increases strength.
30 Even the youths shall faint and be weary,
And the young men shall utterly fall,
31 But those who ᵃwait on the LORD
ᵇShall renew *their* strength;
They shall mount up with wings like eagles,
They shall run and not be weary,
They shall walk and not faint.

ISRAEL ASSURED OF GOD'S HELP

41 "Keep ᵃsilence before Me, O coastlands,
And let the people renew *their* strength!
Let them come near, then let them speak;
Let us ᵇcome near together for judgment.

2 "Who raised up one ᵃfrom the east?
Who in righteousness called him to His feet?
Who ᵇgave the nations before him,
And made *him* rule over kings?
Who gave *them* as the dust *to* his sword,
As driven stubble to his bow?
3 Who pursued them, *and* passed ¹safely
By the way *that* he had not gone with his feet?
4 ᵃWho has performed and done *it*,
Calling the generations from the beginning?
'I, the LORD, am ᵇthe first;
And with the last I *am* ᶜHe.'"

5 The coastlands saw *it* and feared,
The ends of the earth were afraid;
They drew near and came.
6 ᵃEveryone helped his neighbor,
And said to his brother,
¹"Be of good courage!"
7 ᵃSo the craftsman encouraged the ᵇgoldsmith;¹
He who smooths *with* the hammer *inspired* him who
strikes the anvil,
Saying, ²"It *is* ready for the soldering";
Then he fastened it with pegs,
ᶜ*That* it might not totter.

8 "But you, Israel, *are* My servant,
Jacob whom I have ᵃchosen,
The descendants of Abraham My ᵇfriend.
9 *You* whom I have taken from the ends of the earth,
And called from its farthest regions,
And said to you,
'You *are* My servant,
I have chosen you and have not cast you away:

40:28 ᵃPs. 147:5;
Eccl. 11:5;
Rom. 11:33

40:31
ᵃIs. 30:15; 49:23
ᵇ[Job 17:9];
Ps. 103:5;
[2 Cor. 4:8–
10, 16]

41:1 ᵃHab. 2:20;
Zech. 2:13
ᵇIs. 1:18

41:2 ᵃIs. 46:11
ᵇGen. 14:14;
Is. 45:1, 13

41:4 ᵃIs. 41:26
ᵇRev. 1:8, 17;
22:13
ᶜIs. 43:10; 44:6

41:6 ᵃIs. 40:19

41:7 ᵃIs. 44:13
ᵇIs. 40:19
ᶜIs. 40:20

41:8
ᵃDeut. 7:6; 10:15;
Ps. 135:4;
[Is. 43:1]
ᵇ2 Chr. 20:7;
James 2:23

41:3 ¹Lit. *in peace*   41:6 ¹Lit. *Be strong*   41:7 ¹*refiner*   ²Or *The soldering
is good*

10 ªFear not, ᵇfor I *am* with you;
    Be not dismayed, for I *am* your God.
    I will strengthen you,
    Yes, I will help you,
    I will uphold you with My righteous right hand.'

11 "Behold, all those who were incensed against you
    Shall be ªashamed and disgraced;
    They shall be as nothing,
    And those who strive with you shall perish.
12 You shall seek them and not find them—
    ¹Those who contended with you.
    Those who war against you
    Shall be as nothing,
    As a nonexistent thing.
13 For I, the LORD your God, will hold your right hand,
    Saying to you, 'Fear not, I will help you.'

14 "Fear not, you ªworm Jacob,
    You men of Israel!
    I will help you," says the LORD
    And your Redeemer, the Holy One of Israel.
15 "Behold, ªI will make you into a new threshing sledge with
        sharp teeth;
    You shall thresh the mountains and beat *them* small,
    And make the hills like chaff.
16 You shall ªwinnow them, the wind shall carry them away,
    And the whirlwind shall scatter them;
    You shall rejoice in the LORD,
    And ᵇglory in the Holy One of Israel.

17 "The poor and needy seek water, but *there is* none,
    Their tongues fail for thirst.
    I, the LORD, will hear them;
    I, the God of Israel, will not ªforsake them.
18 I will open ªrivers in desolate heights,
    And fountains in the midst of the valleys;
    I will make the ᵇwilderness a pool of water,
    And the dry land springs of water.
19 I will plant in the wilderness the cedar and the acacia
        tree,
    The myrtle and the oil tree;
    I will set in the ªdesert the cypress tree *and* the pine
    And the box tree together,
20 ªThat they may see and know,
    And consider and understand together,
    That the hand of the LORD has done this,
    And the Holy One of Israel has created it.

THE FUTILITY OF IDOLS

21 "Present your case," says the LORD.
    "Bring forth your strong *reasons*," says the ªKing of Jacob.
22 "Letª them bring forth and show us what will happen;
    Let them show the ᵇformer things, what they *were,*
    That we may ¹consider them,
    And know the latter end of them;
    Or declare to us things to come.

41:10
ªIs. 41:13, 14;
43:5
ᵇ[Deut. 31:6]

41:11 ªEx. 23:22;
Is. 45:24; 60:12;
Zech. 12:3

41:14 ªJob 25:6;
Ps. 22:6

41:15 ªMic. 4:13;
Hab. 3:12;
[2 Cor. 10:4]

41:16 ªJer. 51:2
ᵇIs. 45:25

41:17 ªPs. 94:14;
Rom. 11:2

41:18
ªIs. 35:6, 7;
43:19; 44:3
ᵇPs. 107:35

41:19 ªIs. 35:1

41:20 ªJob 12:9;
Is. 66:14

41:21 ªIs. 43:15

41:22 ªIs. 45:21
ᵇIs. 43:9

41:12 ¹Lit. *Men of your strife*   41:22 ¹Lit. *set our heart on them*

23 ᵃShow the things that are to come hereafter,
That we may know that you *are* gods;
Yes, ᵇdo good or do evil,
That we may be dismayed and see *it* together.
24 Indeed ᵃyou *are* nothing,
And your work *is* nothing;
He who chooses you *is* an abomination.

25 "I have raised up one from the north,
And he shall come;
From the ¹rising of the sun ᵃhe shall call on My name;
ᵇAnd he shall come against princes as *though* mortar,
As the potter treads clay.
26 ᵃWho has declared from the beginning, that we may
know?
And former times, that we may say, '*He is* righteous'?
Surely *there is* no one who shows,
Surely *there is* no one who declares,
Surely *there is* no one who hears your words.
27 ᵃThe first time ᵇ*I* said to Zion,
'Look, there they are!'
And I will give to Jerusalem one who brings good tidings.
28 ᵃFor I looked, and *there was* no man;
I looked among them, but *there was* no counselor,
Who, when I asked of them, could answer a word.
29 ᵃIndeed they *are* all ¹worthless;
Their works *are* nothing;
Their molded images *are* wind and confusion.

THE SERVANT OF THE LORD

42 "Behold! ᵃMy Servant whom I uphold,
My ¹Elect One *in whom* My soul ᵇdelights!
ᶜI have put My Spirit upon Him;
He will bring forth justice to the Gentiles.
2 He will not cry out, nor raise *His voice*,
Nor cause His voice to be heard in the street.
3 A bruised reed He will not break,
And ¹smoking flax He will not ²quench;
He will bring forth justice for truth.
4 He will not fail nor be discouraged,
Till He has established justice in the earth;
ᵃAnd the coastlands shall wait for His law."

5 Thus says God the LORD,
ᵃWho created the heavens and stretched them out,
Who spread forth the earth and that which comes from
it,
ᵇWho gives breath to the people on it,
And spirit to those who walk on it:
6 "I,ᵃ the LORD, have called You in righteousness,
And will hold Your hand;
I will keep You ᵇand give You as a covenant to the people,
As ᶜa light to the Gentiles,
7 ᵃTo open blind eyes,
To ᵇbring out prisoners from the prison,
Those who sit in ᶜdarkness from the prison house.

41:23 ᵃIs. 42:9;
44:7, 8; 45:3;
[John 13:19]
ᵇJer. 10:5

41:24 ᵃPs. 115:8;
Is. 44:9;
[Rom. 3:10–20;
1 Cor. 8:4]

41:25 ᵃEzra 1:2
ᵇIs. 41:2;
Jer. 50:3

41:26 ᵃIs. 43:9

41:27 ᵃIs. 41:4
ᵇIs. 40:9;
Nah. 1:15

41:28 ᵃIs. 63:5

41:29 ᵃIs. 41:24

42:1 ᵃIs. 43:10;
49:3, 6;
Matt. 12:18;
[Phil. 2:7]
ᵇMatt. 3:17; 17:5;
Mark 1:11;
Luke 3:22;
Eph. 1:6
ᶜ[Is. 11:2];
Matt. 3:16;
[Luke 4:18,
19, 21];
John 3:34

42:4
ᵃ[Gen. 49:10]

42:5 ᵃIs. 44:24;
Zech. 12:1
ᵇJob 12:10; 33:4;
Is. 57:16;
Dan. 5:23;
Acts 17:25

42:6 ᵃIs. 43:1
ᵇIs. 49:8
ᶜIs. 49:6;
Luke 2:32;
[Acts 10:45;
13:47; Gal. 3:14]

42:7 ᵃIs. 35:5
ᵇIs. 61:1;
Luke 4:18;
[2 Tim. 2:26;
Heb. 2:14]
ᶜIs. 9:2

41:25 ¹East   **41:29** ¹So with MT, Vg.; DSS, Syr., Tg. *nothing;* LXX omits first
line   **42:1** ¹Chosen   **42:3** ¹*dimly burning*   ²*extinguish*

8 I *am* the LORD, that *is* My name;
 And My ^aglory I will not give to another,
 Nor My praise to carved images.
9 Behold, the former things have come to pass,
 And new things I declare;
 Before they spring forth I tell you of them."

PRAISE TO THE LORD

10 ^aSing to the LORD a new song,
 And His praise from the ends of the earth,
 ^bYou who go down to the sea, and ¹all that is in it,
 You coastlands and you inhabitants of them!
11 Let the wilderness and its cities lift up *their voice,*
 The villages *that* Kedar inhabits.
 Let the inhabitants of Sela sing,
 Let them shout from the top of the mountains.
12 Let them give glory to the LORD,
 And declare His praise in the coastlands.
13 The LORD shall go forth like a mighty man;
 He shall stir up *His* zeal like a man of war.
 He shall cry out, ^ayes, shout aloud;
 He shall prevail against His enemies.

PROMISE OF THE LORD'S HELP

14 "I have held My peace a long time,
 I have been still and restrained Myself.
 Now I will cry like a woman in ¹labor,
 I will pant and gasp at once.
15 I will lay waste the mountains and hills,
 And dry up all their vegetation;
 I will make the rivers coastlands,
 And I will dry up the pools.
16 I will bring the blind by a way they did not know;
 I will lead them in paths they have not known.
 I will make darkness light before them,
 And crooked places straight.
 These things I will do for them,
 And not forsake them.
17 They shall be ^aturned back,
 They shall be greatly ashamed,
 Who trust in carved images,
 Who say to the molded images,
 'You *are* our gods.'
18 "Hear, you deaf;
 And look, you blind, that you may see.
19 ^aWho *is* blind but My servant,
 Or deaf as My messenger *whom* I send?
 Who *is* blind as he who is perfect,
 And blind as the LORD's servant?
20 Seeing many things, ^abut you do not observe;
 Opening the ears, but he does not hear."

ISRAEL'S OBSTINATE DISOBEDIENCE

21 The LORD is well pleased for His righteousness' sake;
 He will exalt the law and make *it* honorable.

42:8
^aEx. 20:3–5;
Is. 48:11

42:10 ^aPs. 33:3;
40:3; 98:1
^bPs. 107:23

42:13 ^aIs. 31:4

42:17 ^aPs. 97:7;
Is. 1:29; 44:11;
45:16

42:19 ^aIs. 43:8;
Ezek. 12:2;
[John 9:39, 41]

42:20
^aRom. 2:21

42:10 ¹Lit. *its fullness*   42:14 ¹*childbirth*

22 But this *is* a people robbed and plundered;
All of them are ¹snared in holes,
And they are hidden in prison houses;
They are for prey, and no one delivers;
For plunder, and no one says, "Restore!"

23 Who among you will give ear to this?
Who will listen and hear for the time to come?
24 Who gave Jacob for plunder, and Israel to the robbers?
Was it not the LORD,
He against whom we have sinned?
ᵃFor they would not walk in His ways,
Nor were they obedient to His law.
25 Therefore He has poured on him the fury of His anger
And the strength of battle;
ᵃIt has set him on fire all around,
ᵇYet he did not know;
And it burned him,
Yet he did not take *it* to ᶜheart.

THE REDEEMER OF ISRAEL

43 But now, thus says the LORD, who created you,
O Jacob,
And He who formed you, O Israel:
"Fear not, ᵃfor I have redeemed you;
ᵇI have called *you* by your name;
You *are* Mine.
2 ᵃWhen you pass through the waters, ᵇI *will be* with you;
And through the rivers, they shall not overflow you.
When you ᶜwalk through the fire, you shall not be burned,
Nor shall the flame scorch you.
3 For I *am* the LORD your God,
The Holy One of Israel, your Savior;
ᵃI gave Egypt for your ransom,
Ethiopia and Seba in your place.
4 Since you were precious in My sight,
You have been honored,
And I have ᵃloved you;
Therefore I will give men for you,
And people for your life.
5 ᵃFear not, for I *am* with you;
I will bring your descendants from the east,
And ᵇgather you from the west;
6 I will say to the ᵃnorth, 'Give them up!'
And to the south, 'Do not keep them back!'
Bring My sons from afar,
And My daughters from the ends of the earth—
7 Everyone who is ᵃcalled by My name,
Whom ᵇI have created for My glory;
I have formed him, yes, I have made him."

8 ᵃBring out the blind people who have eyes,
And the ᵇdeaf who have ears.
9 Let all the nations be gathered together,
And let the people be assembled.
ᵃWho among them can declare this,
And show us former things?

42:24 ᵃIs. 65:2
42:25 ᵃ2 Kin. 25:9
ᵇIs. 1:3; 5:13;
Hos. 7:9
ᶜIs. 29:13
43:1 ᵃIs. 43:5; 44:6
ᵇIs. 42:6; 45:4
43:2 ᵃ[Ps. 66:12;
91:3]
ᵇ[Deut. 31:6];
Jer. 30:11
ᶜDan. 3:25
43:3 ᵃ[Prov. 11:8;
21:18]
43:4 ᵃIs. 63:9
43:5 ᵃIs. 41:10; 44:2;
Jer. 30:10;
46:27, 28
ᵇIs. 54:7
43:6 ᵃIs. 49:12
43:7 ᵃIs. 63:19;
James 2:7
ᵇPs. 100:3;
Is. 29:23;
[John 3:2, 3;
2 Cor. 5:17;
Eph. 2:10]
43:8 ᵃIs. 6:9; 42:19;
Ezek. 12:2
ᵇIs. 29:18
43:9 ᵃIs. 41:21,
22, 26

42:22 ¹Or *trapped in caves*

Let them bring out their witnesses, that they may be
  justified;
Or let them hear and say, "*It is* truth."

10 "You[a] *are* My witnesses," says the LORD,
  [b]"And My servant whom I have chosen,
That you may know and [c]believe Me,
And understand that I *am* He.
Before Me there was no God formed,
Nor shall there be after Me.

11 I, *even* I, [a]*am* the LORD,
And besides Me *there is* no savior.

12 I have declared and saved,
I have proclaimed,
And *there was* no [a]foreign *god* among you;
  [b]Therefore you *are* My witnesses,"
Says the LORD, "that I *am* God.

13 [a]Indeed before the day *was,* I *am* He;
And *there is* no one who can deliver out of My hand;
I work, and who will [b]reverse it?"

14 Thus says the LORD, your Redeemer,
The Holy One of Israel:
"For your sake I will send to Babylon,
And bring them all down as fugitives—
The Chaldeans, who rejoice in their ships.

15 I *am* the LORD, your Holy One,
The Creator of Israel, your [a]King."

16 Thus says the LORD, who [a]makes a way in the sea
And a [b]path through the mighty waters,

17 Who [a]brings forth the chariot and horse,
The army and the power
(They shall lie down together, they shall not rise;
They are extinguished, they are quenched like a wick):

18 "Do[a] not remember the former things,
Nor consider the things of old.

19 Behold, I will do a [a]new thing,
Now it shall spring forth;
Shall you not know it?
  [b]I will even make a road in the wilderness
And rivers in the desert.

20 The beast of the field will honor Me,
The jackals and the ostriches,
Because [a]I give waters in the wilderness
And rivers in the desert,
To give drink to My people, My chosen.

21 [a]This people I have formed for Myself;
They shall declare My [b]praise.

PLEADING WITH UNFAITHFUL ISRAEL

22 "But you have not called upon Me, O Jacob;
And you [a]have been weary of Me, O Israel.

23 [a]You have not brought Me the sheep for your burnt
  offerings,
Nor have you honored Me with your sacrifices.
I have not caused you to serve with grain offerings,
Nor wearied you with incense.

24 You have bought Me no sweet cane with money,
Nor have you satisfied Me with the fat of your sacrifices;

43:10 [a]Is. 44:8
[b]Is. 55:4
[c]Is. 41:4; 44:6

43:11 [a]Is. 45:21;
Hos. 13:4

43:12
[a]Deut. 32:16;
Ps. 81:9 [b]Is. 44:8

43:13 [a]Ps. 90:2;
Is. 48:16
[b]Job 9:12;
Is. 14:27

43:15
[a]Is. 41:20, 21

43:16 [a]Ex. 14:16,
21, 22; Ps. 77:19;
Is. 51:10
[b]Josh. 3:13

43:17
[a]Ex. 14:4–9, 25

43:18 [a]Jer. 16:14

43:19
[a]Is. 42:9; 48:6;
[2 Cor. 5:17];
Rev. 21:5]
[b]Ex. 17:6;
Num. 20:11;
Deut. 8:15;
Ps. 78:16;
Is. 35:1, 6

43:20 [a]Is. 48:21

43:21
[a]Ps. 102:18;
Is. 42:12;
[Luke 1:74, 75;
Eph. 1:5, 6;
1 Pet. 2:9]
[b]Jer. 13:11

43:22 [a]Mic. 6:3;
Mal. 1:13; 3:14

43:23
[a]Amos 5:25

But you have burdened Me with your sins,
You have [a]wearied Me with your iniquities.

25 "I, *even* I, *am* He who [a]blots out your transgressions [b]for
My own sake;
[c]And I will not remember your sins.

26 Put Me in remembrance;
Let us contend together;
State your *case,* that you may be [1]acquitted.

27 Your first father sinned,
And your [1]mediators have transgressed against Me.

28 Therefore I will profane the princes of the sanctuary;
[a]I will give Jacob to the curse,
And Israel to reproaches.

GOD'S BLESSING ON ISRAEL

44 "Yet hear now, O Jacob My servant,
And Israel whom I have chosen.

2 Thus says the LORD who made you
And formed you from the womb, *who* will help you:
'Fear not, O Jacob My servant;
And you, Jeshurun, whom I have chosen.

3 For I will pour water on him who is thirsty,
And floods on the dry ground;
I will pour My Spirit on your descendants,
And My blessing on your offspring;

4 They will spring up among the grass
Like willows by the watercourses.'

5 One will say, 'I *am* the LORD's';
Another will call *himself* by the name of Jacob;
Another will write *with* his hand, 'The LORD's,'
And name *himself* by the name of Israel.

THERE IS NO OTHER GOD

6 "Thus says the LORD, the King of Israel,
And his Redeemer, the LORD of hosts:
[a]'I *am* the First and I *am* the Last;
Besides Me *there is* no God.

7 And [a]who can proclaim as I do?
Then let him declare it and set it in order for Me,
Since I appointed the ancient people.
And the things that are coming and shall come,
Let them show these to them.

8 Do not fear, nor be afraid;
[a]Have I not told you from that time, and declared *it?*
[b]You *are* My witnesses.
Is there a God besides Me?
Indeed [c]*there is* no other Rock;
I know not *one.*'"

IDOLATRY IS FOOLISHNESS

9 [a]Those who make an image, all of them *are* useless,
And their precious things shall not profit;
They *are* their own witnesses;
[b]They neither see nor know, that they may be
ashamed.

43:24
[a]Ps. 95:10;
Is. 1:14; 7:13;
Ezek. 6:9;
Mal. 2:17

43:25 [a]Is. 44:22;
Jer. 50:20;
[Acts 3:19]
[b]Ezek. 36:22
[c]Is. 1:18;
Jer. 31:34

43:28 [a]Ps. 79:4;
Jer. 24:9;
Dan. 9:11;
Zech. 8:13

44:6 [a]Is. 41:4;
[Rev. 1:8, 17;
22:13]

44:7
[a]Is. 41:4, 22, 26

44:8 [a]Is. 41:22
[b]Is. 43:10, 12
[c]Deut. 4:35;
32:39;
1 Sam. 2:2;
2 Sam. 22:32;
Is. 45:5;
Joel 2:27

44:9 [a]Is. 41:24
[b]Ps. 115:4

43:26 [1]*justified*   43:27 [1]*interpreters*

10 Who would form a god or mold an image
  ªThat profits him nothing?
11 Surely all his companions would be ªashamed;
  And the workmen, they *are* mere men.
  Let them all be gathered together,
  Let them stand up;
  Yet they shall fear,
  They shall be ashamed together.

12 ªThe blacksmith with the tongs works one in the coals,
  Fashions it with hammers,
  And works it with the strength of his arms.
  Even so, he is hungry, and his strength fails;
  He drinks no water and is faint.

13 The craftsman stretches out *his* rule,
  He marks one out with chalk;
  He fashions it with a plane,
  He marks it out with the compass,
  And makes it like the figure of a man,
  According to the beauty of a man, that it may remain in
      the house.
14 He cuts down cedars for himself,
  And takes the cypress and the oak;
  He ¹secures *it* for himself among the trees of the forest.
  He plants a pine, and the rain nourishes *it*.
15 Then it shall be for a man to burn,
  For he will take some of it and warm himself;
  Yes, he kindles *it* and bakes bread;
  Indeed he makes a god and worships *it*;
  He makes it a carved image, and falls down to it.
16 He burns half of it in the fire;
  With this half he eats meat;
  He roasts a roast, and is satisfied.
  He even warms *himself* and says,
  "Ah! I am warm,
  I have seen the fire."
17 And the rest of it he makes into a god,
  His carved image.
  He falls down before it and worships *it*,
  Prays to it and says,
  "Deliver me, for you *are* my god!"

18 ªThey do not know nor understand;
  For ᵇHe has ¹shut their eyes, so that they cannot see,
  And their hearts, so that they cannot ᶜunderstand.
19 And no one ªconsiders in his heart,
  Nor *is there* knowledge nor understanding to say,
  "I have burned half of it in the fire,
  Yes, I have also baked bread on its coals;
  I have roasted meat and eaten *it*;
  And shall I make the rest of it an abomination?
  Shall I fall down before a block of wood?"
20 He feeds on ashes;
  ªA deceived heart has turned him aside;
  And he cannot deliver his soul,
  Nor say, "*Is there* not a ᵇlie in my right hand?"

44:10 ªIs. 41:29;
Jer. 10:5;
Hab. 2:18;
Acts 19:26
44:11 ªPs. 97:7;
Is. 1:29; 42:17
44:12 ªIs. 40:19;
Jer. 10:3–5
44:18 ªIs. 45:20
ᵇ[Ps. 81:12];
Is. 6:9, 10; 29:10;
2 Thess. 2:11
ᶜJer. 10:14
44:19 ªIs. 46:8
44:20
ªJob 15:31;
Hos. 4:12;
Rom. 1:21, 22;
2 Thess. 2:11;
2 Tim. 3:13
ᵇIs. 57:11;
59:3, 4, 13;
Rom. 1:25

44:14 ¹Lit. *appropriates*   44:18 ¹Lit. *smeared over*

ISRAEL IS NOT FORGOTTEN

21 "Remember these, O Jacob,
　　And Israel, for you *are* My servant;
　　I have formed you, you *are* My servant;
　　O Israel, you will not be [a]forgotten by Me!
22 [a]I have blotted out, like a thick cloud, your transgressions,
　　And like a cloud, your sins.
　　Return to Me, for [b]I have redeemed you."

23 [a]Sing, O heavens, for the LORD has done *it!*
　　Shout, you lower parts of the earth;
　　Break forth into singing, you mountains,
　　O forest, and every tree in it!
　　For the LORD has redeemed Jacob,
　　And [b]glorified Himself in Israel.

JUDAH WILL BE RESTORED

24 Thus says the LORD, [a]your Redeemer,
　　And [b]He who formed you from the womb:
　　"I *am* the LORD, who makes all *things*,
　　[c]Who stretches out the heavens [1]all alone,
　　Who spreads abroad the earth by Myself;
25 Who [a]frustrates the signs [b]of the babblers,
　　And drives diviners mad;
　　Who turns wise men backward,
　　[c]And makes their knowledge foolishness;
26 [a]Who confirms the word of His servant,
　　And performs the counsel of His messengers;
　　Who says to Jerusalem, 'You shall be inhabited,'
　　To the cities of Judah, 'You shall be built,'
　　And I will raise up her waste places;
27 [a]Who says to the deep, 'Be dry!
　　And I will dry up your rivers';
28 Who says of [a]Cyrus, '*He is* My shepherd,
　　And he shall perform all My pleasure,
　　Saying to Jerusalem, [b]"You shall be built,"
　　And to the temple, "Your foundation shall be laid." '

CYRUS, GOD'S INSTRUMENT

45

"Thus says the LORD to His anointed,
To [a]Cyrus, whose [b]right hand I have [1]held—
[c]To subdue nations before him
　　And [d]loose the armor of kings,
　　To open before him the double doors,
　　So that the gates will not be shut:
2 'I will go before you
　　[a]And[1] make the [2]crooked places straight;
　　[b]I will break in pieces the gates of bronze
　　And cut the bars of iron.
3 I will give you the treasures of darkness
　　And hidden riches of secret places,
　　[a]That you may know that I, the LORD,
　　Who [b]call *you* by your name,
　　Am the God of Israel.

44:21 [a]Is. 49:15
44:22 [a]Is. 43:25
　　[b]Is. 43:1;
　　1 Cor. 6:20;
　　[1 Pet. 1:18, 19]
44:23
[a]Ps. 69:34;
Is. 42:10; 49:13;
Jer. 51:48;
Rev. 18:20
[b]Is. 49:3; 60:21
44:24 [a]Is. 43:14
　　[b]Is. 43:1
　　[c]Job 9:8
44:25 [a]Is. 47:13
　　[b]Jer. 50:36
　　[c]2 Sam. 15:31;
　　Job 5:12–14;
　　Ps. 33:10;
　　Is. 29:14;
　　Jer. 51:57;
　　1 Cor. 1:20, 27
44:26
[a]Zech. 1:6;
Matt. 5:18
44:27
[a]Jer. 50:38;
　　51:36
44:28
[a]2 Chr. 36:22;
Ezra 1:1; Is. 45:13
　　[b]Ezra 6:7
45:1 [a]Is. 44:28
　　[b]Ps. 73:23;
　　Is. 41:13
　　[c]Dan. 5:30
　　[d]Job 12:21;
　　Is. 45:5
45:2 [a]Is. 40:4
　　[b]Ps. 107:16
45:3 [a]Is. 41:23
　　[b]Ex. 33:12

44:24 [1]By Himself　45:1 [1]*strengthened* or *sustained*　45:2 [1]Tg. *I will trample down the walls;* Vg. *I will humble the great ones of the earth*　[2]DSS, LXX *mountains*

4 For ^aJacob My servant's sake,
And Israel My elect,
I have even called you by your name;
I have named you, though you have not known Me.
5 I ^a*am* the LORD, and ^b*there is* no other;
There is no God besides Me.
^cI will gird you, though you have not known Me,
6 ^aThat they may ^bknow from the rising of the sun to its
setting
That *there is* none besides Me.
I *am* the LORD, and *there is* no other;
7 I form the light and create darkness,
I make peace and ^acreate calamity;
I, the LORD, do all these *things.*'

8 "Rain^a down, you heavens, from above,
And let the skies pour down righteousness;
Let the earth open, let them bring forth salvation,
And let righteousness spring up together.
I, the LORD, have created it.

9 "Woe to him who strives with ^ahis Maker!
Let the potsherd *strive* with the potsherds of the earth!
^bShall the clay say to him who forms it, 'What are you
making?'
Or shall your handiwork *say*, 'He has no hands'?
10 Woe to him who says to *his* father, 'What are you
begetting?'
Or to the woman, 'What have you brought forth?'"

11 Thus says the LORD,
The Holy One of Israel, and his Maker:
^a"Ask Me of things to come concerning ^bMy sons;
And concerning ^cthe work of My hands, you command Me.
12 ^aI have made the earth,
And ^bcreated man on it.
I—My hands—stretched out the heavens,
And ^call their host I have commanded.
13 ^aI have raised him up in righteousness,
And I will ¹direct all his ways;
He shall ^bbuild My city
And let My exiles go free,
^cNot for price nor reward,"
Says the LORD of hosts.

THE LORD, THE ONLY SAVIOR

14 Thus says the LORD:

^a"The labor of Egypt and merchandise of Cush
And of the Sabeans, men of stature,
Shall come over to you, and they shall be yours;
They shall walk behind you,
They shall come over ^bin chains;
And they shall bow down to you.
They will make supplication to you, *saying*, ^c'Surely God
is in you,
And *there is* no other;
^d*There is* no other God.'"

45:4 ^aIs. 44:1
45:5
^aDeut. 4:35;
32:39; Is. 44:8
^bIs. 45:14, 18
^cPs. 18:32
45:6 ^aPs. 102:15;
Is. 37:20;
Mal. 1:11
^b[Is. 11:9; 52:10]
45:7 ^aIs. 31:2;
47:11; Amos 3:6
45:8 ^aPs. 85:11
45:9 ^aIs. 64:8
^bJer. 18:6;
Rom. 9:20, 21
45:11 ^aIs. 8:19
^bJer. 31:9
^cIs. 29:23; 60:21;
64:8
45:12 ^aIs. 42:5;
Jer. 27:5
^bGen. 1:26
^cGen. 2:1;
Neh. 9:6
45:13 ^aIs. 41:2
^b2 Chr. 36:22;
Is. 44:28
^c[Rom. 3:24]
45:14 ^aPs. 68:31;
72:10, 11;
Is. 14:1; 49:23;
60:9, 10, 14, 16;
Zech. 8:22, 23
^bPs. 149:8
^cJer. 16:19;
Zech. 8:20–23;
1 Cor. 14:25
^dIs. 45:5

45:13 ¹Or *make all his ways straight*

15 Truly You *are* God, ᵃwho hide Yourself,
    O God of Israel, the Savior!
16 They shall be ᵃashamed
    And also disgraced, all of them;
    They shall go in confusion together,
    Who are makers of idols.
17 ᵃ*But* Israel shall be saved by the LORD
    With an ᵇeverlasting salvation;
    You shall not be ashamed or ᶜdisgraced
    Forever and ever.

18 For thus says the LORD,
    ᵃWho created the heavens,
    Who is God,
    Who formed the earth and made it,
    Who has established it,
    Who did not create it ¹in vain,
    Who formed it to be ᵇinhabited:
  ᶜ"I *am* the LORD, and *there is* no other.
19 I have not spoken in ᵃsecret,
    In a dark place of the earth;
    I did not say to the seed of Jacob,
    'Seek Me ¹in vain';
    ᵇI, the LORD, speak righteousness,
    I declare things that are right.

20 "Assemble yourselves and come;
    Draw near together,
    You *who have* escaped from the nations.
    ᵃThey have no knowledge,
    Who carry the wood of their carved image,
    And pray to a god *that* cannot save.
21 Tell and bring forth *your case;*
    Yes, let them take counsel together.
    ᵃWho has declared this from ancient time?
    Who has told it from that time?
    Have not I, the LORD?
    ᵇAnd *there is* no other God besides Me,
    A just God and a Savior;
    There is none besides Me.

22 "Look to Me, and be saved,
    ᵃAll you ends of the earth!
    For I *am* God, and *there is* no other.
23 ᵃI have sworn by Myself;
    The word has gone out of My mouth *in* righteousness,
    And shall not return,
    That to Me every ᵇknee shall bow,
    ᶜEvery tongue shall take an oath.
24 He shall say,
    ¹'Surely in the LORD I have ᵃrighteousness and strength.
    To Him *men* shall come,
    And ᵇall shall be ashamed
    Who are incensed against Him.
25 ᵃIn the LORD all the descendants of Israel
    Shall be justified, and ᵇshall glory.'"

45:15 ᵃPs. 44:24; Is. 57:17
45:16 ᵃIs. 44:11
45:17 ᵃIs. 26:4; [Rom. 11:26]; ᵇIs. 51:6; ᶜIs. 29:22
45:18 ᵃIs. 42:5; ᵇGen. 1:26; Ps. 115:16; Acts 17:26; ᶜIs. 45:5
45:19 ᵃDeut. 30:11; ᵇPs. 19:8; Is. 45:23; 63:1
45:20 ᵃIs. 44:9; 46:7; Jer. 10:5
45:21 ᵃIs. 41:22; 43:9; ᵇIs. 44:8
45:22 ᵃPs. 22:27; 65:5
45:23 ᵃGen. 22:16; Is. 62:8; [Heb. 6:13]; ᵇRom. 14:11; [Phil. 2:10]; ᶜDeut. 6:13; Ps. 63:11; Is. 19:18; 65:16
45:24 ᵃIs. 54:17; [Jer. 23:5]; 1 Cor. 1:30]; ᵇIs. 41:11
45:25 ᵃIs. 45:17; ᵇ1 Cor. 1:31

45:18 ¹Or *empty, a waste*   45:19 ¹Or *in a waste place*   45:24 ¹Or *Only in the LORD are all righteousness and strength*

DEAD IDOLS AND THE LIVING GOD

46 Bel [a]bows down, Nebo stoops;
Their idols were on the beasts and on the cattle.
Your carriages *were* heavily loaded,
[b]A burden to the weary *beast*.

2 They stoop, they bow down together;
They could not deliver the burden,
[a]But have themselves gone into captivity.

3 "Listen to Me, O house of Jacob,
And all the remnant of the house of Israel,
[a]Who have been upheld *by Me* from [1]birth,
Who have been carried from the womb:

4 Even to *your* old age, [a]I *am* He,
And *even* to gray hairs [b]I will carry *you!*
I have made, and I will bear;
Even I will carry, and will deliver *you.*

5 "To[a] whom will you liken Me, and make *Me* equal
And compare Me, that we should be alike?

6 [a]They lavish gold out of the bag,
And weigh silver on the scales;
They hire a [b]goldsmith, and he makes it a god;
They prostrate themselves, yes, they worship.

7 [a]They bear it on the shoulder, they carry it
And set it in its place, and it stands;
From its place it shall not move.
Though [b]*one* cries out to it, yet it cannot answer
Nor save him out of his trouble.

8 "Remember this, and [1]show yourselves men;
[a]Recall to mind, O you transgressors.

9 [a]Remember the former things of old,
For I *am* God, and [b]*there is* no other;
I am God, and *there is* none like Me,

10 [a]Declaring the end from the beginning,
And from ancient times *things* that are not *yet* done,
Saying, [b]'My counsel shall stand,
And I will do all My pleasure,'

11 Calling a bird of prey [a]from the east,
The man [b]who executes My counsel, from a far country.
Indeed [c]I have spoken *it;*
I will also bring it to pass.
I have purposed *it;*
I will also do it.

12 "Listen to Me, you [a]stubborn-hearted,
[b]Who *are* far from righteousness:

13 [a]I bring My righteousness near, it shall not be far off;
My salvation [b]shall not [1]linger.
And I will place [c]salvation in Zion,
For Israel My glory.

THE HUMILIATION OF BABYLON

47 "Come [a]down and [b]sit in the dust,
O virgin daughter of [c]Babylon;
Sit on the ground without a throne,
O daughter of the Chaldeans!

46:1 [a]Is. 21:9;
Jer. 50:2
[b]Jer. 10:5

46:2
[a]Judg. 18:17, 18,
24; 2 Sam. 5:21;
Jer. 48:7;
Hos. 10:5, 6

46:3
[a]Deut. 32:11;
Ps. 71:6; Is. 63:9

46:4 [a]Mal. 3:6
[b]Ps. 48:14

46:5
[a]Is. 40:18, 25

46:6 [a]Is. 40:19;
41:6; Jer. 10:4
[b]Is. 44:12

46:7 [a]Is. 45:20;
46:1; Jer. 10:5
[b]Is. 45:20

46:8 [a]Is. 44:19

46:9
[a]Deut. 32:7;
Is. 42:9; 65:17
[b]Is. 45:5, 21

46:10 [a]Is. 45:21;
48:3 [b]Ps. 33:11;
Prov. 19:21;
21:30; Is. 14:24;
25:1; Acts 5:39;
Heb. 6:17

46:11
[a]Is. 41:2, 25
[b]Is. 44:28
[c]Num. 23:19

46:12 [a]Ps. 76:5;
Is. 48:4;
Zech. 7:11, 12;
Mal. 3:13
[b][Rom. 10:3]

46:13
[a][Rom. 1:17]
[b]Hab. 2:3
[c]Is. 62:11;
Joel 3:17;
[1 Pet. 2:6]

47:1 [a]Jer. 48:18
[b]Is. 3:26
[c]Is. 14:18−23;
Jer. 25:12;
50:1−51:64

46:3 [1]Lit. *the belly*   46:8 [1]*be men*, take courage   46:13 [1]*delay*

For you shall no more be called
Tender and ¹delicate.
2 ᵃTake the millstones and grind meal.
Remove your veil,
Take off the skirt,
Uncover the thigh,
Pass through the rivers.
3 ᵃYour nakedness shall be uncovered,
Yes, your shame will be seen;
ᵇI will take vengeance,
And I will not arbitrate with a man."

4 As for ᵃour Redeemer, the LORD of hosts *is* His name,
The Holy One of Israel.

5 "Sit in ᵃsilence, and go into darkness,
O daughter of the Chaldeans;
ᵇFor you shall no longer be called
The Lady of Kingdoms.
6 ᵃI was angry with My people;
ᵇI have profaned My inheritance,
And given them into your hand.
You showed them no mercy;
ᶜOn the elderly you laid your yoke very heavily.
7 And you said, 'I shall be ᵃa lady forever,'
So that you did not ᵇtake these *things* to heart,
ᶜNor remember the latter end of them.

8 "Therefore hear this now, *you who are* given to pleasures,
Who dwell securely,
Who say in your heart, 'I *am,* and *there is* no one else
besides me;
I shall not sit *as* a widow,
Nor shall I know the loss of children';
9 But these two *things* shall come to you
ᵃIn a moment, in one day:
The loss of children, and widowhood.
They shall come upon you in their fullness
Because of the multitude of your sorceries,
For the great abundance of your enchantments.

10 "For you have trusted in your wickedness;
You have said, 'No one ᵃsees me';
Your wisdom and your knowledge have ¹warped you;
And you have said in your heart,
'I *am,* and *there is* no one else besides me.'
11 Therefore evil shall come upon you;
You shall not know from where it arises.
And trouble shall fall upon you;
You will not be able ¹to put it off.
And ᵃdesolation shall come upon you ᵇsuddenly,
Which you shall not know.

12 "Stand now with your enchantments
And the multitude of your sorceries,
In which you have labored from your youth—
Perhaps you will be able to profit,
Perhaps you will prevail.

47:2 ᵃEx. 11:5;
Jer. 25:10
47:3 ᵃIs. 3:17;
20:4
ᵇ[Rom. 12:19]
47:4 ᵃJer. 50:34
47:5 ᵃ1 Sam. 2:9
ᵇIs. 13:19;
[Dan. 2:37];
Rev. 17:18
47:6
ᵃ2 Sam. 24:14
ᵇIs. 43:28
ᶜDeut. 28:49, 50
47:7 ᵃRev. 18:7
ᵇIs. 42:25; 46:8
ᶜDeut. 32:29;
Jer. 5:31;
Ezek. 7:2, 3
47:9 ᵃPs. 73:19;
1 Thess. 5:3;
Rev. 18:8
47:10 ᵃIs. 29:15;
Ezek. 8:12; 9:9
47:11 ᵃIs. 13:6;
Jer. 51:8, 43;
Luke 17:27;
1 Thess. 5:3
ᵇIs. 29:5

47:1 ¹dainty   47:10 ¹led you astray   47:11 ¹Lit. *to cover it* or *atone for it*

13 ^aYou are wearied in the multitude of your
counsels;
Let now ^bthe¹ astrologers, the stargazers,
And ²the monthly prognosticators
Stand up and save you
From what shall come upon you.
14 Behold, they shall be ^aas stubble,
The fire shall ^bburn them;
They shall not deliver themselves
From the power of the flame;
It shall not *be* a coal to be warmed by,
Nor a fire to sit before!
15 Thus shall they be to you
With whom you have labored,
^aYour merchants from your youth;
They shall wander each one to his ¹quarter.
No one shall save you.

ISRAEL REFINED FOR GOD'S GLORY

48 "Hear this, O house of Jacob,
Who are called by the name of Israel,
And have come forth from the wellsprings of Judah;
Who swear by the name of the LORD,
And make mention of the God of Israel,
But ^anot in truth or in righteousness;
2 For they call themselves ^aafter the holy city,
And ^blean on the God of Israel;
The LORD of hosts *is* His name:

3 "I have ^adeclared the former things from the
beginning;
They went forth from My mouth, and I caused them to
hear it.
Suddenly I did *them,* ^band they came to pass.
4 Because I knew that you *were* ¹obstinate,
And ^ayour neck *was* an iron sinew,
And your brow bronze,
5 Even from the beginning I have declared *it* to you;
Before it came to pass I proclaimed *it* to you,
Lest you should say, 'My idol has done them,
And my carved image and my molded image
Have commanded them.'

6 "You have heard;
See all this.
And will you not declare *it?*
I have made you hear new things from this time,
Even hidden things, and you did not know them.
7 They are created now and not from the beginning;
And before this day you have not heard them,
Lest you should say, 'Of course I knew them.'
8 Surely you did not hear,
Surely you did not know;
Surely from long ago your ear was not opened.
For I knew that you would deal very treacherously,
And were called ^aa transgressor from the womb.

47:13 ^aIs. 57:10
^bIs. 8:19; 44:25;
47:9; Dan. 2:2, 10

47:14 ^aIs. 5:24;
Nah. 1:10;
Mal. 4:1
^b[Is. 10:17];
Jer. 51:58

47:15 ^aRev. 18:11

48:1 ^aIs. 58:2;
Jer. 4:2; 5:2

48:2
^aIs. 52:1; 64:10
^bIs. 10:20;
Jer. 7:4; 21:2;
Mic. 3:11;
Rom. 2:17

48:3
^aIs. 44:7, 8;
46:10
^bJosh. 21:45;
Is. 42:9

48:4 ^aEx. 32:9;
Deut. 31:27;
Ezek. 2:4; 3:7

48:8
^aDeut. 9:7, 24;
Ps. 58:3;
Is. 46:3, 8

47:13 ¹Lit. *viewers of the heavens*   ²Lit. *those giving knowledge for new moons*   47:15 ¹*own side* or *way*   48:4 ¹Heb. *hard*

9 "For[a] My name's sake [b]I will [1]defer My anger,
   And *for* My praise I will restrain it from you,
   So that I do not cut you off.
10 Behold, [a]I have refined you, but not as silver;
   I have tested you in the [b]furnace of affliction.
11 For My own sake, for My own sake, I will do *it*;
   For [a]how should *My name* be profaned?
   And [b]I will not give My glory to another.

GOD'S ANCIENT PLAN TO REDEEM ISRAEL

12 "Listen to Me, O Jacob,
   And Israel, My called:
   I *am* He, [a]I *am* the [b]First,
   I *am* also the Last.
13 Indeed [a]My hand has laid the foundation of the earth,
   And My right hand has stretched out the heavens;
   When [b]I call to them,
   They stand up together.
14 "All of you, assemble yourselves, and hear!
   Who among them has declared these *things?*
   [a]The LORD loves him;
   [b]He shall do His pleasure on Babylon,
   And His arm *shall be against* the Chaldeans.
15 I, *even* I, have spoken;
   Yes, [a]I have called him,
   I have brought him, and his way will prosper.
16 "Come near to Me, hear this:
   [a]I have not spoken in secret from the beginning;
   From the time that it was, I *was* there.
   And now [b]the Lord GOD and His Spirit
   [1]Have sent Me."

17 Thus says [a]the LORD, your Redeemer,
   The Holy One of Israel:
   "I *am* the LORD your God,
   Who teaches you to profit,
   [b]Who leads you by the way you should go.
18 [a]Oh, that you had heeded My commandments!
   [b]Then your peace would have been like a river,
   And your righteousness like the waves of the sea.
19 [a]Your descendants also would have been like the sand,
   And the offspring of your body like the grains of sand;
   His name would not have been cut off
   Nor destroyed from before Me."

20 [a]Go forth from Babylon!
   Flee from the Chaldeans!
   With a voice of singing,
   Declare, proclaim this,
   Utter it to the end of the earth;
   Say, "The LORD has [b]redeemed
   His servant Jacob!"
21 And they [a]did not thirst
   When He led them through the deserts;
   He [b]caused the waters to flow from the rock for them;
   He also split the rock, and the waters gushed out.

22 "There[a] *is* no peace," says the LORD, "for the wicked."

48:9 [a]Ps. 79:9; 106:8;
Is. 43:25;
Ezek. 20:9,
14, 22, 44
[b][Neh. 9:30, 31];
Ps. 78:38;
Is. 30:18; 65:8
48:10 [a]Ps. 66:10;
Jer. 9:7
[b]Deut. 4:20;
1 Kin. 8:51;
Jer. 11:4
48:11 [a]Lev. 22:2, 32;
Deut. 32:26, 27;
Ezek. 20:9
[b]Is. 42:8
48:12 [a]Deut. 32:39
[b]Is. 44:6;
[Rev. 22:13]
48:13 [a]Ex. 20:11;
Ps. 102:25;
Is. 42:5; 45:12, 18;
Heb. 1:10–12
[b]Is. 40:26
48:14 [a]Is. 45:1
[b]Is. 44:28;
47:1–15
48:15 [a]Is. 45:1, 2
48:16 [a]Is. 45:19
[b]Is. 61:1;
Zech. 2:8, 9, 11
48:17 [a]Is. 43:14
[b]Ps. 32:8;
Is. 49:9, 10
48:18 [a]Deut. 5:29;
Ps. 81:13
[b]Deut. 28:1–14;
Ps. 119:165;
Is. 32:16–18;
66:12
48:19 [a]Gen. 22:17;
Is. 10:22; 44:3, 4;
54:3; Jer. 33:22;
Hos. 1:10
48:20 [a]Jer. 50:8;
51:6, 45;
Zech. 2:6, 7;
Rev. 18:4
[b][Ex. 19:4–6]
48:21 [a][Is. 41:17, 18]
[b]Ex. 17:6;
Ps. 105:41
48:22 [a][Is. 57:21]

48:9 [1]*delay*   48:16 [1]Heb. verb is sing.; or *Has sent Me and His Spirit*

THE SERVANT, THE LIGHT TO THE GENTILES

49 "Listen, [a]O coastlands, to Me,
And take heed, you peoples from afar!
[b]The LORD has called Me from the womb;
From the [1]matrix of My mother He has made mention of
My name.

2 And He has made [a]My mouth like a sharp sword;
[b]In the shadow of His hand He has hidden Me,
And made Me [c]a polished shaft;
In His quiver He has hidden Me."

3 "And He said to me,
[a]'You *are* My servant, O Israel,
[b]In whom I will be glorified.'

4 [a]Then I said, 'I have labored in vain,
I have spent my strength for nothing and in vain;
Yet surely my [1]just reward *is* with the LORD,
And my [2]work with my God.'"

5 "And now the LORD says,
Who formed Me from the womb *to be* His Servant,
To bring Jacob back to Him,
So that Israel [a]is [1]gathered to Him
(For I shall be glorious in the eyes of the LORD,
And My God shall be My strength),

6 Indeed He says,
'It is too small a thing that You should be My Servant
To raise up the tribes of Jacob,
And to restore the preserved ones of Israel;
I will also give You as a [a]light to the Gentiles,
That You should be My salvation to the ends of the
earth.'"

7 Thus says the LORD,
The Redeemer of Israel, [1]their Holy One,
[a]To Him [2]whom man despises,
To Him whom the nation abhors,
To the Servant of rulers:
[b]"Kings shall see and arise,
Princes also shall worship,
Because of the LORD who is faithful,
The Holy One of Israel;
And He has chosen You."

8 Thus says the LORD:

"In an [a]acceptable[1] time I have heard You,
And in the day of salvation I have helped You;
I will [2]preserve You [b]and give You
As a covenant to the people,
To restore the earth,
To cause them to inherit the desolate [3]heritages;

9 That You may say [a]to the prisoners, 'Go forth,'
To those who *are* in darkness, 'Show yourselves.'

"They shall feed along the roads,
And their pastures *shall be* on all desolate heights.

49:1 [a]Is. 41:1
[b]Jer. 1:5;
Matt. 1:20;
Luke 1:35;
John 1:14; 10:36

49:2 [a]Is. 11:4;
Hos. 6:5;
[Heb. 4:12];
Rev. 1:16; 2:12
[b]Is. 51:16
[c]Ps. 45:5

49:3 [a][Is. 41:8;
42:1; Zech. 3:8]
[b]Is. 44:23;
Matt. 12:18;
[John 13:31, 32;
14:13; 15:8; 17:4;
Eph. 1:6]

49:4
[a][Ezek. 3:19]

49:5
[a]Matt. 23:37;
[Rom. 11:25–29]

49:6
[a]Is. 42:6; 51:4;
[Luke 2:32];
Acts 13:47;
[Gal. 3:14]

49:7 [a][Ps. 22:6;
Is. 53:3;
Matt. 26:67;
27:41];
Mark 15:29;
Luke 23:35
[b][Is. 52:15]

49:8 [a]Ps. 69:13;
2 Cor. 6:2
[b]Is. 42:6

49:9 [a]Is. 61:1;
Zech. 9:12;
Luke 4:18

49:1 [1]Lit. *inward parts*   49:4 [1]*justice*   [2]*recompense*   49:5 [1]Qr., DSS, LXX
gathered to Him; Kt. *not gathered*   49:7 [1]Lit. *his or its*   [2]Lit. *who is despised
of soul*   49:8 [1]*favorable*   [2]*keep*   [3]*inheritances*

10   They shall neither ªhunger nor thirst,
      ᵇNeither heat nor sun shall strike them;
      For He who has mercy on them ᶜwill lead them,
      Even by the springs of water He will guide them.
11   ªI will make each of My mountains a road,
      And My highways shall be elevated.
12   Surely ªthese shall come from afar;
      Look! Those from the north and the west,
      And these from the land of Sinim."

13   ªSing, O heavens!
      Be joyful, O earth!
      And break out in singing, O mountains!
      For the LORD has comforted His people,
      And will have mercy on His afflicted.

GOD WILL REMEMBER ZION

14   ªBut Zion said, "The LORD has forsaken me,
      And my Lord has forgotten me."
15   "Canª a woman forget her nursing child,
      ¹And not have compassion on the son of her womb?
      Surely they may forget,
      ᵇYet I will not forget you.
16   See, ªI have inscribed you on the palms *of My hands;*
      Your walls *are* continually before Me.
17   Your ¹sons shall make haste;
      Your destroyers and those who laid you waste
      Shall go away from you.
18   ªLift up your eyes, look around and see;
      All these gather together *and* come to you.
      As I live," says the LORD,
      "You shall surely clothe yourselves with them all ᵇas an
            ornament,
      And bind them *on you* as a bride *does.*
19   "For your waste and desolate places,
      And the land of your destruction,
      ªWill even now be too small for the inhabitants;
      And those who swallowed you up will be far away.
20   ªThe children you will have,
      ᵇAfter you have lost the others,
      Will say again in your ears,
      'The place *is* too small for me;
      Give me a place where I may dwell.'
21   Then you will say in your heart,
      'Who has begotten these for me,
      Since I have lost my children and am desolate,
      A captive, and wandering to and fro?
      And who has brought these up?
      There I was, left alone;
      But these, where *were* they?'"

22ªThus says the Lord GOD:

      "Behold, I will lift My hand in an oath to the nations,
      And set up My ¹standard for the peoples;
      They shall bring your sons in *their* ²arms,
      And your daughters shall be carried on *their* shoulders;

49:10
ªIs. 33:16; 48:21;
Rev. 7:16
ᵇPs. 121:6
ᶜPs. 23:2;
Is. 40:11; 48:17
49:11 ªIs. 40:4
49:12 ªIs. 43:5, 6
49:13 ªIs. 44:23
49:14 ªIs. 40:27
49:15
ªPs. 103:13;
Mal. 3:17
ᵇRom. 11:29
49:16 ªEx. 13:9;
Song 8:6;
Hag. 2:23
49:18 ªIs. 60:4;
John 4:35
ᵇProv. 17:6
49:19 ªIs. 54:1, 2;
Zech. 10:10
49:20 ªIs. 60:4
ᵇ[Matt. 3:9;
Rom. 11:11]
49:22 ªIs. 60:4

49:15 ¹Lit. *From having compassion*   49:17 ¹DSS, LXX, Tg., Vg. *builders*
49:22 ¹*banner*   ²Lit. *bosom*

23 ªKings shall be your foster fathers,
  And their queens your nursing mothers;
  They shall bow down to you with *their* faces to the earth,
  And ᵇlick up the dust of your feet.
  Then you will know that I *am* the LORD,
  ᶜFor they shall not be ashamed who wait for Me."

24 ªShall the prey be taken from the mighty,
  Or the captives ¹of the righteous be delivered?

25But thus says the LORD:

"Even the captives of the mighty shall be taken away,
  And the prey of the terrible be delivered;
  For I will contend with him who contends with you,
  And I will save your children.
26 I will ªfeed those who oppress you with their own flesh,
  And they shall be drunk with their own ᵇblood as with
    sweet wine.
  All flesh ᶜshall know
  That I, the LORD, *am* your Savior,
  And your Redeemer, the Mighty One of Jacob."

THE SERVANT, ISRAEL'S HOPE

50 Thus says the LORD:

"Where *is* ªthe certificate of your mother's divorce,
  Whom I have put away?
  Or which of My ᵇcreditors *is it* to whom I have sold
    you?
  For your iniquities ᶜyou have sold yourselves,
  And for your transgressions your mother has been put
    away.
2 Why, when I came, *was there* no man?
  Why, when I called, *was there* none to answer?
  Is My hand shortened at all that it cannot redeem?
  Or have I no power to deliver?
  Indeed with My ªrebuke I dry up the sea,
  I make the rivers a wilderness;
  Their fish stink because *there is* no water,
  And die of thirst.
3 ªI clothe the heavens with blackness,
  ᵇAnd I make sackcloth their covering."

4 "Theª Lord GOD has given Me
  The tongue of the learned,
  That I should know how to speak
  A word in season to *him who is* ᵇweary.
  He awakens Me morning by morning,
  He awakens My ear
  To hear as the learned.
5 The Lord GOD ªhas opened My ear;
  And I was not ᵇrebellious,
  Nor did I turn away.
6 ªI gave My back to those who struck *Me,*
  And ᵇMy cheeks to those who plucked out the
    beard;
  I did not hide My face from shame and ᶜspitting.

49:23 ªPs. 72:11;
Is. 52:15
ᵇPs. 72:9;
Mic. 7:17
ᶜPs. 34:22;
[Rom. 5:5]

49:24
ªMatt. 12:29;
Luke 11:21, 22

49:26 ªIs. 9:20
ᵇRev. 14:20
ᶜPs. 9:16;
Is. 60:16

50:1 ªDeut. 24:1;
Jer. 3:8
ᵇDeut. 32:30;
2 Kin. 4:1;
Neh. 5:5
ᶜIs. 52:3

50:2
ªPs. 106:9;
Nah. 1:4

50:3 ªEx. 10:21
ᵇIs. 13:10;
Rev. 6:12

50:4 ªEx. 4:11
ᵇMatt. 11:28

50:5 ªPs. 40:6;
Is. 35:5
ᵇMatt. 26:39;
Mark 14:36;
Luke 22:42;
John 8:29; 14:31;
15:10; Acts 26:19;
[Phil. 2:8;
Heb. 5:8; 10:7]

50:6
ªMatt. 27:26;
John 18:22
ᵇMatt. 26:67;
27:30;
Mark 14:65; 15:19
ᶜLam. 3:30

49:24 ¹So with MT, Tg.; DSS, Syr., Vg. *of the mighty;* LXX *unjustly*

7 "For the Lord GOD will help Me;
  Therefore I will not be disgraced;
  Therefore [a]I have set My face like a flint,
  And I know that I will not be ashamed.
8 [a]*He is* near who justifies Me;
  Who will contend with Me?
  Let us stand together.
  Who *is* [1]My adversary?
  Let him come near Me.
9 Surely the Lord GOD will help Me;
  Who *is* he *who* will condemn Me?
  [a]Indeed they will all grow old like a garment;
  [b]The moth will eat them up.

10 "Who among you fears the LORD?
  Who obeys the voice of His Servant?
  Who [a]walks in darkness
  And has no light?
  [b]Let him trust in the name of the LORD
  And rely upon his God.
11 Look, all you who kindle a fire,
  Who encircle *yourselves* with sparks:
  Walk in the light of your fire and in the sparks you have
    kindled—
  [a]This you shall have from My hand:
  You shall lie down [b]in torment.

THE LORD COMFORTS ZION
(*cf. Gen. 12:1–3*)

51 "Listen to Me, [a]you who [1]follow after righteousness,
  You who seek the LORD:
  Look to the rock *from which* you were hewn,
  And to the hole of the pit *from which* you were dug.
2 [a]Look to Abraham your father,
  And to Sarah *who* bore you;
  [b]For I called him alone,
  And [c]blessed him and increased him."

3 For the LORD will [a]comfort Zion,
  He will comfort all her waste places;
  He will make her wilderness like Eden,
  And her desert [b]like the garden of the LORD;
  Joy and gladness will be found in it,
  Thanksgiving and the voice of melody.

4 "Listen to Me, My people;
  And give ear to Me, O My nation:
  [a]For law will proceed from Me,
  And I will make My justice rest
  [b]As a light of the peoples.
5 [a]My righteousness *is* near,
  My salvation has gone forth,
  [b]And My arms will judge the peoples;
  [c]The coastlands will wait upon Me,
  And [d]on My arm they will trust.
6 [a]Lift up your eyes to the heavens,
  And look on the earth beneath.

50:7
[a]Ezek. 3:8, 9;
Luke 9:51

50:8 [a]Acts 2:24;
[Rom. 8:32–34]

50:9 [a]Job 13:28;
Ps. 102:26;
Heb. 1:11
[b]Is. 51:6, 8

50:10 [a]Ps. 23:4
[b]2 Chr. 20:20

50:11
[a][John 9:39]
[b]Ps. 16:4

51:1
[a][Rom. 9:30–32]

51:2
[a]Rom. 4:1–3;
Heb. 11:11
[b]Gen. 12:1
[c]Gen. 24:35;
Deut. 1:10;
Ezek. 33:24

51:3
[a]Is. 40:1; 52:9;
Ps. 102:13
[b]Gen. 13:10;
Joel 2:3

51:4 [a]Is. 2:3
[b]Is. 42:6

51:5 [a]Is. 46:13
[b]Ps. 67:4
[c]Is. 60:9
[d][Rom. 1:16]

51:6 [a]Is. 40:26

50:8 [1]Lit. *master of My judgment*   **51:1** [1]*pursue*

For bthe heavens will vanish away like smoke,
cThe earth will grow old like a garment,
And those who dwell in it will die in like manner;
But My salvation will be dforever,
And My righteousness will not be 1abolished.

7 "Listen to Me, you who know righteousness,
You people ain whose heart *is* My law:
bDo not fear the reproach of men,
Nor be afraid of their insults.

8 For athe moth will eat them up like a garment,
And the worm will eat them like wool;
But My righteousness will be forever,
And My salvation from generation to generation."

9 aAwake, awake, bput on strength,
O arm of the LORD!
Awake cas in the ancient days,
In the generations of old.
dAre You not *the arm* that cut eRahab apart,
And wounded the fserpent?

10 *Are* You not *the One* who adried up the sea,
The waters of the great deep;
That made the depths of the sea a road
For the redeemed to cross over?

11 So athe ransomed of the LORD shall return,
And come to Zion with singing,
With everlasting joy on their heads.
They shall obtain joy and gladness;
Sorrow and sighing shall flee away.

12 "I, *even* I, *am* He awho comforts you.
Who *are* you that you should be afraid
bOf a man *who* will die,
And of the son of a man *who* will be made clike grass?

13 And ayou forget the LORD your Maker,
bWho stretched out the heavens
And laid the foundations of the earth;
You have feared continually every day
Because of the fury of the oppressor,
When *he has* prepared to destroy.
cAnd where *is* the fury of the oppressor?

14 The captive exile hastens, that he may be loosed,
aThat he should not die in the pit,
And that his bread should not fail.

15 But I *am* the LORD your God,
Who adivided the sea whose waves roared—
The LORD of hosts *is* His name.

16 And aI have put My words in your mouth;
bI have covered you with the shadow of My hand,
cThat I may 1plant the heavens,
Lay the foundations of the earth,
And say to Zion, 'You *are* My people.'"

GOD'S FURY REMOVED

17 aAwake, awake!
Stand up, O Jerusalem,

51:6 bPs. 102:25, 26;
Is. 13:13; 34:4;
Matt. 24:35;
Heb. 1:10–12;
2 Pet. 3:10
cIs. 24:19, 20;
50:9;
Heb. 1:10–12
dIs. 45:17

51:7 aPs. 37:31;
Jer. 31:33;
[Heb. 10:16]
bIs. 25:8; 54:4;
[Matt. 5:11, 12;
10:28; Acts 5:41]

51:8 aIs. 50:9

51:9 aPs. 44:23
bPs. 93:1
cPs. 44:1
dJob 26:12;
Ps. 89:10;
Is. 30:7 ePs. 87:4
fPs. 74:13;
Is. 27:1

51:10 aEx. 14:21;
Is. 63:11–13

51:11 aIs. 35:10;
Jer. 31:11, 12

51:12 a2 Cor. 1:3
bPs. 118:6;
Is. 2:22
cIs. 40:6, 7;
James 1:10;
1 Pet. 1:24

51:13
aDeut. 6:12;
8:11; Is. 17:10;
Jer. 2:32
bPs. 104:2
cJob 20:7

51:14 aZech. 9:11

51:15 aJob 26:12

51:16
aDeut. 18:18;
Is. 59:21;
John 3:34
bEx. 33:22;
Is. 49:2 cIs. 65:17

51:17 aIs. 52:1

51:6 1broken **51:16** 1establish

You who ᵇhave drunk at the hand of the LORD
The cup of His fury;
You have drunk the dregs of the cup of trembling,
And drained *it* out.
18 *There is* no one to guide her
Among all the sons she has brought forth;
Nor *is there any* who takes her by the hand
Among all the sons she has brought up.
19 ᵃThese two *things* have come to you;
Who will be sorry for you?—
Desolation and destruction, famine and sword—
ᵇBy whom will I comfort you?
20 ᵃYour sons have fainted,
They lie at the head of all the streets,
Like an antelope in a net;
They are full of the fury of the LORD,
The rebuke of your God.
21 Therefore please hear this, you afflicted,
And drunk ᵃbut not with wine.
22 Thus says your Lord,
The LORD and your God,
Who ᵃpleads the cause of His people:
"See, I have taken out of your hand
The cup of trembling,
The dregs of the cup of My fury;
You shall no longer drink it.
23 ᵃBut I will put it into the hand of those who afflict you,
Who have said to ¹you,
'Lie down, that we may walk over you.'
And you have laid your body like the ground,
And as the street, for those who walk over."

GOD REDEEMS JERUSALEM

52 Awake, awake!
Put on your strength, O Zion;
Put on your beautiful garments,
O Jerusalem, the holy city!
For the uncircumcised ᵃand the unclean
Shall no longer come to you.
2 ᵃShake yourself from the dust, arise;
Sit down, O Jerusalem!
ᵇLoose yourself from the bonds of your neck,
O captive daughter of Zion!

³For thus says the LORD:

ᵃ"You have sold yourselves for nothing,
And you shall be redeemed ᵇwithout money."

⁴For thus says the Lord GOD:

"My people went down at first
Into ᵃEgypt to ¹dwell there;
Then the Assyrian oppressed them without cause.
5 Now therefore, what have I here," says the LORD,
"That My people are taken away for nothing?
Those who rule over them

51:17 ᵇ Job 21:20;
Is. 29:9;
Jer. 25:15;
Rev. 14:10; 16:19
51:19 ᵃIs. 47:9
ᵇAmos 7:2
51:20 ᵃLam. 2:11
51:21 ᵃLam. 3:15
51:22
ᵃIs. 3:12, 13;
49:25; Jer. 50:34
51:23 ᵃIs. 14:2;
Jer. 25:17,
26–28;
Zech. 12:2
52:1 ᵃNeh. 11:1;
Is. 48:2; 64:10;
Zech. 14:20, 21;
Matt. 4:5;
[Rev. 21:2–27]
52:2 ᵃIs. 3:26
ᵇIs. 9:4; 10:27;
14:25; Zech. 2:7
52:3 ᵃPs. 44:12;
Jer. 15:13
ᵇIs. 45:13
52:4 ᵃGen. 46:6

51:23 ¹Lit. *your soul*   52:4 ¹As resident aliens

[1]"Make them wail," says the LORD,
"And My name is [a]blasphemed continually every day.
6   Therefore My people shall know My name;
    Therefore *they shall know* in that day
    That I *am* He who speaks:
    'Behold, *it is* I.'"

7   [a]How beautiful upon the mountains
    Are the feet of him who brings good news,
    Who proclaims peace,
    Who brings glad tidings of good *things,*
    Who proclaims salvation,
    Who says to Zion,
    [b]"Your God reigns!"
8   Your watchmen shall lift up *their* voices,
    With their voices they shall sing together;
    For they shall see eye to eye
    When the LORD brings back Zion.
9   Break forth into joy, sing together,
    You waste places of Jerusalem!
    For the LORD has comforted His people,
    He has redeemed Jerusalem.
10 [a]The LORD has [1]made bare His holy arm
    In the eyes of [b]all the nations;
    And all the ends of the earth shall see
    The salvation of our God.

11 [a]Depart! Depart! Go out from there,
    Touch no unclean *thing;*
    Go out from the midst of her,
    [b]Be clean,
    You who bear the vessels of the LORD.
12 For [a]you shall not go out with haste,
    Nor go by flight;
    [b]For the LORD will go before you,
    [c]And the God of Israel *will be* your rear guard.

THE SIN-BEARING SERVANT

13 Behold, [a]My Servant shall [1]deal prudently;
    [b]He shall be exalted and [2]extolled and be very high.
14 Just as many were astonished at you,
    So His [a]visage[1] was marred more than any man,
    And His form more than the sons of men;
15 [a]So shall He [1]sprinkle many nations.
    Kings shall shut their mouths at Him;
    For [b]what had not been told them they shall see,
    And what they had not heard they shall consider.

53 Who [a]has believed our report?
    And to whom has the arm of the LORD been revealed?
2   For He shall grow up before Him as a tender plant,
    And as a root out of dry ground.
    He has no [1]form or [2]comeliness;
    And when we see Him,
    There is no [3]beauty that we should desire Him.

52:5
[a]Ezek. 36:20,
23; Rom. 2:24

52:7 [a]Is. 40:9;
61:1; Nah. 1:15;
Rom. 10:15;
Eph. 6:15
[b]Ps. 93:1;
Is. 24:23

52:10
[a]Ps. 98:1–3
[b]Luke 3:6

52:11 [a]Is. 48:20;
Jer. 50:8;
Zech. 2:6, 7;
2 Cor. 6:17
[b]Lev. 22:2;
[Is. 1:16]

52:12
[a]Ex. 12:11, 33;
Deut. 16:3
[b]Mic. 2:13
[c]Ex. 14:19, 20;
Is. 58:8

52:13 [a]Is. 42:1
[b]Is. 57:15;
Phil. 2:9

52:14
[a]Ps. 22:6, 7;
Matt. 26:67;
27:30; John 19:3

52:15
[a]Num. 19:18–21;
Ezek. 36:25
[b]Rom. 15:21;
[Eph. 3:5, 9];
1 Pet. 1:2

53:1
[a]John 12:38;
Rom. 10:16

52:5 [1]DSS *Mock;* LXX *Marvel and wail;* Tg. *Boast themselves;* Vg. *Treat them
unjustly*   52:10 [1]*Revealed His power*   52:13 [1]*prosper*   [2]Lit. *be lifted up*
52:14 [1]*appearance*   52:15 [1]Or *startle*   53:2 [1]*Stately form*   [2]*splendor*
[3]Lit. *appearance*

3 [a]He is despised and [1]rejected by men,
   A Man of [2]sorrows and [b]acquainted with [3]grief.
   And we hid, as it were, *our* faces from Him;
   He was despised, and [c]we did not esteem Him.

4 Surely [a]He has borne our [1]griefs
   And carried our [2]sorrows;
   Yet we [3]esteemed Him stricken,
   [4]Smitten by God, and afflicted.

5 But He *was* [a]wounded[1] for our transgressions,
   He was [2]bruised for our iniquities;
   The chastisement for our peace *was* upon Him,
   And by His [b]stripes[3] we are healed.

6 All we like sheep have gone astray;
   We have turned, every one, to his own way;
   And the LORD [1]has laid on Him the iniquity of us all.

7 He was oppressed and He was afflicted,
   Yet [a]He opened not His mouth;
   [b]He was led as a lamb to the slaughter,
   And as a sheep before its shearers is silent,
   So He opened not His mouth.

8 He was [a]taken from [1]prison and from judgment,
   And who will declare His generation?
   For [b]He was cut off from the land of the living;
   For the transgressions of My people He was stricken.

9 [a]And [1]they made His grave with the wicked—
   But with the rich at His death,
   Because He had done no violence,
   Nor *was any* [b]deceit in His mouth.

10 Yet it pleased the LORD to [1]bruise Him;
   He has put *Him* to grief.
   When You make His soul [a]an offering for sin,
   He shall see *His* seed, He shall prolong *His* days,
   And the pleasure of the LORD shall prosper in His hand.

11 [1]He shall see the labor of His soul, *and* be satisfied.
   By His knowledge [a]My righteous [b]Servant shall [c]justify
      many,
   For He shall bear their iniquities.

12 [a]Therefore I will divide Him a portion with the great,
   [b]And He shall divide the [1]spoil with the strong,
   Because He [c]poured out His soul unto death,
   And He was [d]numbered with the transgressors,
   And He bore the sin of many,
   And [e]made intercession for the transgressors.

A PERPETUAL COVENANT OF PEACE

54 "Sing, O [a]barren,
   You *who* have not borne!
   Break forth into singing, and cry aloud,
   You *who* have not labored with child!
   For more *are* the children of the desolate
   Than the children of the married woman," says the LORD.

53:3 [a]Ps. 22:6;
[Is. 49:7;
Matt. 27:30, 31;
Luke 18:31–33;
23:18]
[b][Heb. 4:15]
[c][John 1:10, 11]

53:4
[a][Matt. 8:17;
Heb. 9:28;
1 Pet. 2:24]

53:5 [a][Is. 53:10;
Rom. 4:25;
1 Cor. 15:3, 4]
[b][1 Pet. 2:24, 25]

53:7
[a]Matt. 26:63;
27:12–14;
Mark 14:61; 15:5;
Luke 23:9;
John 19:9
[b]Acts 8:32, 33;
Rev. 5:6

53:8
[a]Matt. 27:11–26;
Luke 23:1–25
[b][Dan. 9:26]

53:9
[a]Matt. 27:57–60;
Luke 23:33
[b]1 Pet. 2:22;
1 John 3:5

53:10
[a]John 1:29;
Acts 2:24;
[2 Cor. 5:21]

53:11
[a][1 John 2:1]
[b]Is. 42:1
[c][Acts 13:38, 39;
Rom. 5:15–18]

53:12 [a]Ps. 2:8
[b]Col. 2:15
[c]Is. 50:6;
[Rom. 3:25]
[d]Matt. 27:38;
Mark 15:28;
Luke 22:37;
2 Cor. 5:21
[e]Luke 23:34

54:1 [a]Gal. 4:27

53:3 [1]Or *forsaken* [2]Lit. *pains* [3]Lit. *sickness* **53:4** [1]Lit. *sicknesses* [2]Lit. *pains* [3]*reckoned* [4]*Struck down* **53:5** [1]Or *pierced through* [2]*crushed* [3]Blows that cut in **53:6** [1]Lit. *has caused to land on Him* **53:8** [1]*confinement* **53:9** [1]Lit. *he or He* **53:10** [1]*crush* **53:11** [1]So with MT, Tg., Vg.; DSS, LXX *From the labor of His soul He shall see light* **53:12** [1]*plunder*

2 "Enlarge[a] the place of your tent,
And let them stretch out the curtains of your dwellings;
Do not spare;
Lengthen your cords,
And strengthen your stakes.
3 For you shall expand to the right and to the left,
And your descendants will [a]inherit the nations,
And make the desolate cities inhabited.

4 "Do[a] not fear, for you will not be ashamed;
Neither be disgraced, for you will not be put to shame;
For you will forget the shame of your youth,
And will not remember the reproach of your widowhood
anymore.
5 [a]For your Maker is your husband,
The LORD of hosts is His name;
And your Redeemer is the Holy One of Israel;
He is called [b]the God of the whole earth.
6 For the LORD [a]has called you
Like a woman forsaken and grieved in spirit,
Like a youthful wife when you were refused,"
Says your God.
7 "For[a] a mere moment I have forsaken you,
But with great mercies [b]I will gather you.
8 With a little wrath I hid My face from you for a moment;
[a]But with everlasting kindness I will have mercy on you,"
Says the LORD, your Redeemer.

9 "For this is like the waters of [a]Noah to Me;
For as I have sworn
That the waters of Noah would no longer cover the earth,
So have I sworn
That I would not be angry with [b]you, nor rebuke you.
10 For [a]the mountains shall depart
And the hills be removed,
[b]But My kindness shall not depart from you,
Nor shall My covenant of peace be removed,"
Says the LORD, who has mercy on you.

11 "O you afflicted one,
Tossed with tempest, and not comforted,
Behold, I will lay your stones with [a]colorful gems,
And lay your foundations with sapphires.
12 I will make your pinnacles of rubies,
Your gates of crystal,
And all your walls of precious stones.
13 All your children shall be [a]taught by the LORD,
And [b]great shall be the peace of your children.
14 In righteousness you shall be established;
You shall be far from oppression, for you shall not fear;
And from terror, for it shall not come near you.
15 Indeed they shall surely assemble, but not because of Me.
Whoever assembles against you shall [a]fall for your sake.

16 "Behold, I have created the blacksmith
Who blows the coals in the fire,
Who brings forth an [1]instrument for his work;
And I have created the [2]spoiler to destroy.

54:2
[a]Is. 49:19, 20

54:3 [a]Is. 14:2;
49:22, 23; 60:9

54:4 [a]Is. 41:10

54:5 [a]Jer. 3:14;
Hos. 2:19
[b]Zech. 14:9;
Rom. 3:29

54:6 [a]Is. 62:4

54:7 [a]Ps. 30:5;
Is. 26:20; 60:10;
2 Cor. 4:17
[b][Is. 43:5; 56:8]

54:8 [a]Is. 55:3;
Jer. 31:3

54:9
[a]Gen. 8:21; 9:11;
[2 Pet. 3:6, 7]
[b]Is. 12:1;
Ezek. 39:29

54:10 [a]Ps. 46:2;
Is. 51:6;
Matt. 5:18
[b]2 Sam. 23:5;
Ps. 89:33, 34;
Is. 55:3; 59:21;
61:8

54:11
[a]1 Chr. 29:2;
Job 28:16;
Rev. 21:18, 19

54:13 [a]Jer. 31:34;
[John 6:45;
1 Cor. 2:10];
1 Thess. 4:9;
[1 John 2:20]
[b]Ps. 119:165

54:15
[a]Is. 41:11–16

54:16 [1]Or weapon   [2]destroyer

17 No weapon formed against you shall ^aprosper,
And every tongue *which* rises against you in judgment
You shall condemn.
This *is* the heritage of the servants of the LORD,
^bAnd their righteousness *is* from Me,"
Says the LORD.

AN INVITATION TO ABUNDANT LIFE

55 "Ho! ^aEveryone who thirsts,
Come to the waters;
And you who have no money,
^bCome, buy and eat.
Yes, come, buy wine and milk
Without money and without price.

2 Why do you ¹spend money for *what is* not bread,
And your wages for *what* does not satisfy?
Listen carefully to Me, and eat *what is* good,
And let your soul delight itself in abundance.

3 Incline your ear, and ^acome to Me.
Hear, and your soul shall live;
^bAnd I will make an everlasting covenant with you—
The ^csure mercies of David.

4 Indeed I have given him *as* ^aa witness to the people,
^bA leader and commander for the people.

5 ^aSurely you shall call a nation you do not know,
^bAnd nations *who* do not know you shall run to you,
Because of the LORD your God,
And the Holy One of Israel;
^cFor He has glorified you."

6 ^aSeek the LORD while He may be ^bfound,
Call upon Him while He is near.

7 ^aLet the ¹wicked forsake his way,
And the unrighteous man ^bhis thoughts;
Let him return to the LORD,
^cAnd He will have mercy on him;
And to our God,
For He will abundantly pardon.

8 "For^a My thoughts *are* not your thoughts,
Nor *are* your ways My ways," says the LORD.

9 "For^a *as* the heavens are higher than the earth,
So are My ways higher than your ways,
And My thoughts than your thoughts.

10 "For ^aas the rain comes down, and the snow from
heaven,
And do not return there,
But water the earth,
And make it bring forth and bud,
That it may give seed to the sower
And bread to the eater,

11 ^aSo shall My word be that goes forth from My mouth;
It shall not return to Me ¹void,
But it shall accomplish what I please,
And it shall ^bprosper *in the thing* for which I sent it.

Cross references (margin):
54:17 ^aIs. 17:12–14; 29:8 ^bIs. 45:24, 25; 54:14
55:1 ^a[Matt. 5:6; John 4:14; 7:37; Rev. 21:6; 22:17] ^b[Matt. 13:44; Rev. 3:18]
55:3 ^aMatt. 11:28 ^bIs. 54:8; 61:8; Jer. 32:40 ^c2 Sam. 7:8; Ps. 89:28; [Acts 13:34]
55:4 ^a[John 18:37; Rev. 1:5] ^b[Jer. 30:9; Ezek. 34:23; Dan. 9:25]
55:5 ^aIs. 52:15; Eph. 2:11, 12 ^bIs. 60:5 ^cIs. 60:9
55:6 ^aMatt. 5:25; 25:11; John 7:34; 8:21; 2 Cor. 6:2; [Heb. 3:13] ^bPs. 32:6; Is. 49:8
55:7 ^aIs. 1:16 ^bIs. 59:7; Zech. 8:17 ^cPs. 130:7; Jer. 3:12
55:8 ^a2 Sam. 7:19
55:9 ^aPs. 103:11
55:10 ^aDeut. 32:2
55:11 ^aIs. 45:23; Matt. 24:35 ^bIs. 46:9–11

55:2 ¹Lit. *weigh out silver* 55:7 ¹Lit. *man of iniquity* 55:11 ¹*empty, without fruit*

12 "For[a] you shall go out with joy,
    And be led out with peace;
    The mountains and the hills
    Shall [b]break forth into singing before you,
    And [c]all the trees of the field shall clap *their* hands.
13 [a]Instead of [b]the thorn shall come up the cypress tree,
    And instead of the brier shall come up the myrtle tree;
    And it shall be to the LORD [c]for a name,
    For an everlasting sign *that* shall not be cut off."

SALVATION FOR THE GENTILES

56 Thus says the LORD:

"Keep justice, and do righteousness,
[a]For My salvation *is* about to come,
And My righteousness to be revealed.
2   Blessed *is* the man *who* does this,
    And the son of man *who* lays hold on it;
    [a]Who keeps from defiling the Sabbath,
    And keeps his hand from doing any evil."

3   Do not let [a]the son of the foreigner
    Who has joined himself to the LORD
    Speak, saying,
    "The LORD has utterly separated me from His people";
    Nor let the [b]eunuch say,
    "Here I am, a dry tree."
4   For thus says the LORD:
    "To the eunuchs who keep My Sabbaths,
    And choose what pleases Me,
    And hold fast My covenant,
5   Even to them I will give in [a]My house
    And within My walls a place [b]and a name
    Better than that of sons and daughters;
    I will give [1]them an everlasting name
    That shall not be cut off.

6   "Also the sons of the foreigner
    Who join themselves to the LORD, to serve Him,
    And to love the name of the LORD, to be His servants—
    Everyone who keeps from defiling the Sabbath,
    And holds fast My covenant—
7   Even them I will [a]bring to My holy mountain,
    And make them joyful in My [b]house of prayer.
    [c]Their burnt offerings and their sacrifices
    Will be [d]accepted on My altar;
    For [e]My house shall be called a house of prayer [f]for all
        nations."
8   The Lord GOD, [a]who gathers the outcasts of Israel, says,
    [b]"Yet I will gather to him
    Others besides those who are gathered to him."

ISRAEL'S IRRESPONSIBLE LEADERS

9   [a]All you beasts of the field, come to devour,
    All you beasts in the forest.
10 His watchmen *are* [a]blind,
    They are all ignorant;

55:12 [a]Is. 35:10
[b]Ps. 98:8
[c]1 Chr. 16:33

55:13 [a]Is. 41:19
[b]Mic. 7:4
[c]Jer. 13:11

56:1 [a]Is. 46:13;
Matt. 3:2; 4:17;
Rom. 13:11, 12

56:2
[a]Ex. 20:8–11;
31:13–17;
Is. 58:13;
Jer. 17:21, 22;
Ezek. 20:12, 20

56:3 [a]Is. 14:1;
[Eph. 2:12–19];
[b]Deut. 23:1;
Jer. 38:7;
Acts 8:27

56:5 [a]1 Tim. 3:15
[b][1 John 3:1, 2]

56:7 [a][Is. 2:2, 3;
60:11; Mic. 4:1, 2]
[b]Matt. 21:13;
Mark 11:17;
Luke 19:46
[c][Rom. 12:1;
Heb. 13:15;
1 Pet. 2:5]
[d]Is. 60:7
[e]Matt. 21:13
[f][Mal. 1:11]

56:8 [a]Ps. 147:2;
Is. 11:12; 27:12;
54:7 [b]Is. 60:3–11;
66:18–21;
[John 10:16]

56:9 [a]Jer. 12:9

56:10
[a]Matt. 15:14

56:5 [1]Lit. *him*

[b]They *are* all dumb dogs,
They cannot bark;
[1]Sleeping, lying down, loving to slumber.

11 Yes, *they are* [a]greedy[1] dogs
Which [b]never[2] have enough.
And they *are* shepherds
Who cannot understand;
They all look to their own way,
Every one for his own gain,
From his *own* territory.

12 "Come," *one says*, "I will bring wine,
And we will fill ourselves with intoxicating [a]drink;
[b]Tomorrow will be [c]as today,
And much more abundant."

ISRAEL'S FUTILE IDOLATRY

57 The righteous perishes,
And no man takes *it* to heart;
[a]Merciful men *are* taken away,
[b]While no one considers
That the righteous is taken away from [1]evil.

2 He shall enter into peace;
They shall rest in [a]their beds,
Each one walking *in* his uprightness.

3 "But come here,
[a]You sons of the sorceress,
You offspring of the adulterer and the harlot!

4 Whom do you ridicule?
Against whom do you make a wide mouth
And stick out the tongue?
Are you not children of transgression,
Offspring of falsehood,

5 Inflaming yourselves with gods [a]under every green tree,
[b]Slaying the children in the valleys,
Under the clefts of the rocks?

6 Among the smooth [a]*stones* of the stream
Is your portion;
They, they, *are* your lot!
Even to them you have poured a drink offering,
You have offered a grain offering.
Should I receive comfort in [b]these?

7 "On[a] a lofty and high mountain
You have set [b]your bed;
Even there you went up
To offer sacrifice.

8 Also behind the doors and their posts
You have set up your remembrance;
For you have uncovered yourself *to those other* than Me,
And have gone up to them;
You have enlarged your bed
And [1]made *a covenant* with them;
[a]You have loved their bed,
Where you saw *their* [2]nudity.

Cross references (margin)

56:10 [b]Phil. 3:2

56:11 [a]Is. 28:7;
Ezek. 13:19;
[Mic. 3:5, 11]
[b]Ezek. 34:2–10

56:12 [a]Is. 28:7
[b]Ps. 10:6;
Prov. 23:35;
Is. 22:13;
Luke 12:19;
1 Cor. 15:32
[c]2 Pet. 3:4

57:1 [a]Ps. 12:1
[b]1 Kin. 14:13

57:2 [a]2 Chr. 16:14

57:3 [a]Is. 1:4;
Matt. 16:4

57:5 [a]2 Kin. 16:4
[b]2 Kin. 23:10;
Ps. 106:37, 38;
Jer. 7:31;
Ezek. 16:20

57:6 [a]Jer. 3:9;
Hab. 2:19
[b]Jer. 5:9, 29; 9:9

57:7 [a]Jer. 3:6;
Ezek. 16:16
[b]Ezek. 23:41

57:8 [a]Ezek. 16:26

56:10 [1]Or *Dreaming*   56:11 [1]Lit. *strong of soul*   [2]Lit. *do not know satisfaction*   57:1 [1]Lit. *the face of evil*   57:8 [1]Lit. *cut*   [2]Lit. *hand,* a euphemism

9 ^aYou went to the king with ointment,
And increased your perfumes;
You sent your ^bmessengers far off,
And *even* descended to Sheol.
10 You are wearied in the length of your way;
^a*Yet* you did not say, 'There is no hope.'
You have found the life of your hand;
Therefore you were not grieved.

11 "And ^aof whom have you been afraid, or feared,
That you have lied
And not remembered Me,
Nor taken *it* to your heart?
Is it not because ^bI have ¹held My peace from of old
That you do not fear Me?
12 I will declare your righteousness
And your works,
For they will not profit you.
13 When you cry out,
Let your collection *of idols* deliver you.
But the wind will carry them all away,
A breath will take *them*.
But he who puts his trust in Me shall possess the land,
And shall inherit My holy mountain."

HEALING FOR THE BACKSLIDER

14 And one shall say,
^a"Heap it up! Heap it up!
Prepare the way,
Take the stumbling block out of the way of My people."

15 For thus says the High and Lofty One
Who inhabits eternity, ^awhose name *is* Holy:
^b"I dwell in the high and holy *place*,
^cWith him *who* has a contrite and humble spirit,
^dTo revive the spirit of the humble,
And to revive the heart of the contrite ones.
16 ^aFor I will not contend forever,
Nor will I always be angry;
For the spirit would fail before Me,
And the souls ^b*which* I have made.
17 For the iniquity of ^ahis covetousness
I was angry and struck him;
^bI hid and was angry,
^cAnd he went on ¹backsliding in the way of his heart.
18 I have seen his ways, and ^awill heal him;
I will also lead him,
And restore comforts to him
And to ^bhis mourners.

19 "I create ^athe fruit of the lips:
Peace, peace ^bto *him who is* far off and to *him who is* near,"
Says the LORD,
"And I will heal him."
20 ^aBut the wicked *are* like the troubled sea,
When it cannot rest,
Whose waters cast up mire and dirt.

57:9 ^aHos. 7:11
^bEzek. 23:16, 40
57:10
^aJer. 2:25; 18:12
57:11
^aProv. 29:25;
Is. 51:12, 13
^bPs. 50:21;
Eccl. 8:11;
Is. 42:14
57:14 ^aIs. 40:3;
62:10; Jer. 18:15
57:15 ^aJob 6:10;
Luke 1:49
^bPs. 68:35;
Zech. 2:13
^cPs. 34:18;
51:17; Is. 66:2
^dPs. 147:3;
Is. 61:1–3
57:16
^aPs. 85:5; 103:9;
[Mic. 7:18]
^bNum. 16:22;
Job 34:14;
Heb. 12:9
57:17 ^aIs. 2:7;
56:11; Jer. 6:13
^bIs. 8:17; 45:15;
59:2 ^cIs. 9:13
57:18 ^aJer. 3:22
^bIs. 61:2
57:19 ^aIs. 6:7;
51:16; 59:21;
Heb. 13:15
^bActs 2:39;
Eph. 2:17
57:20
^aJob 15:20;
Prov. 4:16;
Jude 13

57:11 ¹*remained silent*   57:17 ¹Or *turning back*

21 *There*[a] *is* no peace,"
　　Says my God, "for the wicked."

FASTING THAT PLEASES GOD

58 "Cry aloud, [1]spare not;
　　Lift up your voice like a trumpet;
[a]Tell My people their transgression,
And the house of Jacob their sins.

2　Yet they seek Me daily,
And delight to know My ways,
As a nation that did righteousness,
And did not forsake the ordinance of their God.
They ask of Me the ordinances of justice;
They take delight in approaching God.

3　'Why[a] have we fasted,' *they say,* 'and You have not seen?
Why have we [b]afflicted our souls, and You take no
　　notice?'

"In fact, in the day of your fast you find pleasure,
And [1]exploit all your laborers.

4　[a]Indeed you fast for strife and debate,
And to strike with the fist of wickedness.
You will not fast as *you do* this day,
To make your voice heard on high.

5　Is [a]it a fast that I have chosen,
[b]A day for a man to afflict his soul?
Is it to bow down his head like a bulrush,
And [c]to spread out sackcloth and ashes?
Would you call this a fast,
And an acceptable day to the LORD?

6　"*Is* this not the fast that I have chosen:
To [a]loose the bonds of wickedness,
[b]To undo the [1]heavy burdens,
[c]To let the oppressed go free,
And that you break every yoke?

7　*Is it* not [a]to share your bread with the hungry,
And that you bring to your house the poor who are [1]cast
　　out;
[b]When you see the naked, that you cover him,
And not hide yourself from [c]your own flesh?

8　[a]Then your light shall break forth like the morning,
Your healing shall spring forth speedily,
And your righteousness shall go before you;
[b]The glory of the LORD shall be your rear guard.

9　Then you shall call, and the LORD will answer;
You shall cry, and He will say, 'Here I *am.*'

"If you take away the yoke from your midst,
The [1]pointing of the finger, and [a]speaking wickedness,

10　*If* you extend your soul to the hungry
And satisfy the afflicted soul,
Then your light shall dawn in the darkness,
And your [1]darkness shall *be* as the noonday.

11　The LORD will guide you continually,
And satisfy your soul in drought,
And strengthen your bones;

57:21 [a]Is. 48:22
58:1 [a]Mic. 3:8
58:3
[a]Mal. 3:13–18;
Luke 18:12
[b]Lev. 16:29;
23:27
58:4 [a]1 Kin. 21:9
58:5 [a]Zech. 7:5
[b]Lev. 16:29
[c]Esth. 4:3;
Job 2:8;
Dan. 9:3
58:6
[a]Luke 4:18, 19
[b]Neh. 5:10–12
[c]Jer. 34:9
58:7 [a]Ezek. 18:7;
Matt. 25:35
[b]Job 31:19–22;
James 2:14–17
[c]Gen. 29:14;
Neh. 5:5
58:8 [a]Job 11:17
[b]Ex. 14:19;
Is. 52:12
58:9 [a]Ps. 12:2;
Is. 59:13

58:1 [1]*do not hold back*　　58:3 [1]Lit. *drive hard*　　58:6 [1]Lit. *bonds of the yoke*
58:7 [1]*wandering*　　58:9 [1]Lit. *sending out of*　　58:10 [1]Or *gloom*

You shall be like a watered garden,
And like a spring of water, whose waters do not fail.
12 Those from among you
aShall build the old waste places;
You shall raise up the foundations of many generations;
And you shall be called the Repairer of the Breach,
The Restorer of 1Streets to Dwell In.

13 "If ayou turn away your foot from the Sabbath,
From doing your pleasure on My holy day,
And call the Sabbath a delight,
The holy *day* of the LORD honorable,
And shall honor Him, not doing your own ways,
Nor finding your own pleasure,
Nor speaking *your own* words,
14 aThen you shall delight yourself in the LORD;
And I will cause you to bride on the high hills of the
earth,
And feed you with the heritage of Jacob your father.
cThe mouth of the LORD has spoken."

SEPARATED FROM GOD

59 Behold, the LORD's hand is not ashortened,
That it cannot save;
Nor His ear heavy,
That it cannot hear.
2 But your iniquities have separated you from your God;
And your sins have hidden *His* face from you,
So that He will anot hear.
3 For ayour hands are defiled with 1blood,
And your fingers with iniquity;
Your lips have spoken lies,
Your tongue has muttered perversity.

4 No one calls for justice,
Nor does *any* plead for truth.
They trust in aempty words and speak lies;
bThey conceive 1evil and bring forth iniquity.
5 They hatch vipers' eggs and weave the spider's web;
He who eats of their eggs dies,
And *from* that which is crushed a viper breaks out.

6 aTheir webs will not become garments,
Nor will they cover themselves with their works;
Their works *are* works of iniquity,
And the act of violence *is* in their hands.
7 aTheir feet run to evil,
And they make haste to shed binnocent blood;
cTheir thoughts *are* thoughts of iniquity;
Wasting and ddestruction *are* in their paths.
8 The way of apeace they have not known,
And *there is* no justice in their ways;
bThey have made themselves crooked paths;
Whoever takes that way shall not know peace.

SIN CONFESSED

9 Therefore justice is far from us,
Nor does righteousness overtake us;

58:12 aIs. 61:4

58:13
aEx. 31:16, 17;
35:2, 3;
Is. 56:2, 4, 6;
Jer. 17:21–27

58:14
aJob 22:26;
Is. 61:10
bDeut. 32:13;
33:29; Is. 33:16;
Hab. 3:19
cIs. 1:20; 40:5;
Mic. 4:4

59:1
aNum. 11:23;
Is. 50:2;
Jer. 32:17

59:2 aIs. 1:15

59:3 aIs. 1:15, 21;
Jer. 2:30, 34;
Ezek. 7:23;
Hos. 4:2

59:4 aIs. 30:12;
Jer. 7:4
bJob 15:35;
Ps. 7:14; Is. 33:11

59:6 aJob 8:14

59:7 aProv. 1:16;
Rom. 3:15
bProv. 6:17
cIs. 55:7
dRom. 3:16, 17

59:8
aIs. 57:20, 21
bPs. 125:5;
Prov. 2:15

58:12 1Lit. *Paths*   59:3 1*bloodshed*   59:4 1*trouble*

ᵃWe look for light, but there is darkness!
For brightness, *but* we walk in blackness!

10 ᵃWe grope for the wall like the blind,
And we grope as if *we had* no eyes;
We stumble at noonday as at twilight;
We are as dead *men* in desolate places.

11 We all growl like bears,
And ᵃmoan sadly like doves;
We look for justice, but *there is* none;
For salvation, *but* it is far from us.

12 For our ᵃtransgressions are multiplied before You,
And our sins testify against us;
For our transgressions *are* with us,
And *as for* our iniquities, we know them:

13 In transgressing and lying against the LORD,
And departing from our God,
Speaking oppression and revolt,
Conceiving and uttering ᵃfrom the heart words of
falsehood.

14 Justice is turned back,
And righteousness stands afar off;
For truth is fallen in the street,
And equity cannot enter.

15 So truth fails,
And he *who* departs from evil makes himself a ᵃprey.

THE REDEEMER OF ZION

Then the LORD saw *it*, and ¹it displeased Him
That *there was* no justice.

16 ᵃHe saw that *there was* no man,
And ᵇwondered that *there was* no intercessor;
ᶜTherefore His own arm brought salvation for Him;
And His own righteousness, it sustained Him.

17 ᵃFor He put on righteousness as a breastplate,
And a helmet of salvation on His head;
He put on the garments of vengeance for clothing,
And was clad with zeal as a cloak.

18 ᵃAccording to *their* deeds, accordingly He will repay,
Fury to His adversaries,
Recompense to His enemies;
The coastlands He will fully repay.

19 ᵃSo shall they fear
The name of the LORD from the west,
And His glory from the rising of the sun;
When the enemy comes in ᵇlike a flood,
The Spirit of the LORD will lift up a standard against him.

20 "The ᵃRedeemer will come to Zion,
And to those who turn from transgression in Jacob,"
Says the LORD.

21"As ᵃ for Me," says the LORD, "this *is* My covenant with them: My Spirit who *is* upon you, and My words which I have put in your mouth, shall not depart from your mouth, nor from the mouth of your descendants, nor from the mouth of your descendants' descendants," says the LORD, "from this time and forevermore."

59:9 ᵃ Jer. 8:15
59:10 ᵃDeut. 28:29; Job 5:14; Amos 8:9
59:11 ᵃIs. 38:14; Ezek. 7:16
59:12 ᵃIs. 24:5; 58:1
59:13 ᵃMatt. 12:34
59:15 ᵃIs. 5:23; 10:2; 29:21; 32:7
59:16 ᵃIs. 41:28; 63:5; 64:7; Ezek. 22:30 ᵇMark 6:6 ᶜPs. 98:1; Is. 63:5
59:17 ᵃEph. 6:14, 17; 1 Thess. 5:8
59:18 ᵃIs. 63:6; Rom. 2:6
59:19 ᵃPs. 113:3; Mal. 1:11 ᵇRev. 12:15
59:20 ᵃRom. 11:26
59:21 ᵃ[Heb. 8:10; 10:16]

59:15 ¹Lit. *it was evil in His eyes*

THE GENTILES BLESS ZION

60 Arise, [a]shine;
For your light has come!
And [b]the glory of the Lord is risen upon you.
2 For behold, the darkness shall cover the earth,
And deep darkness the people;
But the Lord will arise over you,
And His glory will be seen upon you.
3 The [a]Gentiles shall come to your light,
And kings to the brightness of your rising.

4 "Lift[a] up your eyes all around, and see:
They all gather together, [b]they come to you;
Your sons shall come from afar,
And your daughters shall be nursed at *your* side.
5 Then you shall see and become radiant,
And your heart shall swell with joy;
Because [a]the abundance of the sea shall be turned to you,
The wealth of the Gentiles shall come to you.
6 The multitude of camels shall cover your *land,*
The dromedaries of Midian and [a]Ephah;
All those from [b]Sheba shall come;
They shall bring [c]gold and incense,
And they shall proclaim the praises of the Lord.
7 All the flocks of [a]Kedar shall be gathered together to you,
The rams of Nebaioth shall minister to you;
They shall ascend with [b]acceptance on My altar,
And [c]I will glorify the house of My glory.

8 "Who *are* these *who* fly like a cloud,
And like doves to their roosts?
9 [a]Surely the coastlands shall wait for Me;
And the ships of Tarshish *will come* first,
[b]To bring your sons from afar,
[c]Their silver and their gold with them,
To the name of the Lord your God,
And to the Holy One of Israel,
[d]Because He has glorified you.

10 "The[a] sons of foreigners shall build up your walls,
[b]And their kings shall minister to you;
For [c]in My wrath I struck you,
[d]But in My favor I have had mercy on you.
11 Therefore your gates [a]shall be open continually;
They shall not be shut day or night,
That *men* may bring to you the wealth of the Gentiles,
And their kings in procession.
12 [a]For the nation and kingdom which will not serve you
shall perish,
And *those* nations shall be utterly ruined.

13 "The[a] glory of Lebanon shall come to you,
The cypress, the pine, and the box tree together,
To beautify the place of My sanctuary;
And I will make [b]the place of My feet glorious.
14 Also the sons of those who afflicted you
Shall come [a]bowing to you,
And all those who despised you shall [b]fall prostrate at
the soles of your feet;

60:1 [a]Eph. 5:14
[b]Mal. 4:2

60:3 [a]Is. 49:6,
23; Rev. 21:24

60:4 [a]Is. 49:18
[b]Is. 49:20–22

60:5
[a][Rom. 11:25–27]

60:6 [a]Gen. 25:4
[b]Gen. 25:3;
Ps. 72:10
[c]Is. 61:6;
Matt. 2:11

60:7 [a]Gen. 25:13
[b]Is. 56:7
[c]Is. 60:13;
Hag. 2:7, 9

60:9 [a]Ps. 72:10
[b][Gal. 4:26]
[c]Jer. 3:17
[d]Is. 55:5

60:10 [a]Is. 14:1, 2;
61:5; Zech. 6:15
[b]Is. 49:23;
Rev. 21:24
[c]Is. 57:17
[d]Is. 54:7, 8

60:11 [a]Is. 26:2;
60:18; 62:10;
Rev. 21:25, 26

60:12 [a]Is. 14:2;
Zech. 14:17;
Matt. 21:44

60:13 [a]Is. 35:2
[b]1 Chr. 28:2;
Ps. 132:7

60:14 [a]Is. 45:14
[b]Is. 49:23;
Rev. 3:9

And they shall call you The City of the LORD,
ᶜZion of the Holy One of Israel.

15 "Whereas you have been forsaken and hated,
So that no one went through *you,*
I will make you an eternal excellence,
A joy of many generations.

16 You shall drink the milk of the Gentiles,
ᵃAnd milk the breast of kings;
You shall know that ᵇI, the LORD, *am* your Savior
And your Redeemer, the Mighty One of Jacob.

17 "Instead of bronze I will bring gold,
Instead of iron I will bring silver,
Instead of wood, bronze,
And instead of stones, iron.
I will also make your officers peace,
And your magistrates righteousness.

18 Violence shall no longer be heard in your land,
Neither ¹wasting nor destruction within your borders;
But you shall call ᵃyour walls Salvation,
And your gates Praise.

GOD THE GLORY OF HIS PEOPLE

19 "The ᵃsun shall no longer be your light by day,
Nor for brightness shall the moon give light to you;
But the LORD will be to you an everlasting light,
And ᵇyour God your glory.

20 ᵃYour sun shall no longer go down,
Nor shall your moon withdraw itself;
For the LORD will be your everlasting light,
And the days of your mourning shall be ended.

21 ᵃAlso your people *shall* all *be* righteous;
ᵇThey shall inherit the land forever,
ᶜThe branch of My planting,
ᵈThe work of My hands,
That I may be glorified.

22 ᵃA little one shall become a thousand,
And a small one a strong nation.
I, the LORD, will hasten it in its time."

THE GOOD NEWS OF SALVATION

61 "The ᵃSpirit of the Lord GOD *is* upon Me,
Because the LORD ᵇhas anointed Me
To preach good tidings to the poor;
He has sent Me ᶜto ¹heal the brokenhearted,
To proclaim ᵈliberty to the captives,
And the opening of the prison to *those who are* bound;

2 ᵃTo proclaim the acceptable year of the LORD,
And ᵇthe day of vengeance of our God;
ᶜTo comfort all who mourn,

3 To ¹console those who mourn in Zion,
ᵃTo give them beauty for ashes,
The oil of joy for mourning,
The garment of praise for the spirit of heaviness;
That they may be called trees of righteousness,
ᵇThe planting of the LORD, ᶜthat He may be glorified."

60:14
ᶜ[Heb. 12:22;
Rev. 14:1]

60:16 ᵃIs. 49:23
ᵇIs. 43:3

60:18 ᵃIs. 26:1

60:19
ᵃRev. 21:23; 22:5
ᵇIs. 41:16; 45:25;
Zech. 2:5

60:20
ᵃAmos 8:9

60:21 ᵃIs. 52:1;
Rev. 21:27
ᵇPs. 37:11;
Matt. 5:5
ᶜIs. 61:3;
[Matt. 15:13;
John 15:2]
ᵈIs. 29:23;
[Eph. 2:10]

60:22
ᵃMatt. 13:31, 32

61:1 ᵃIs. 11:2;
Matt. 3:17;
Luke 4:18, 19;
John 1:32; 3:34
ᵇPs. 45:7;
Matt. 11:5;
Luke 7:22
ᶜPs. 147:3
ᵈIs. 42:7;
[Acts 10:43]

61:2 ᵃLev. 25:9
ᵇIs. 34:8;
Mal. 4:1, 3;
[2 Thess. 1:7]
ᶜIs. 57:18;
Jer. 31:13;
Matt. 5:4

61:3 ᵃPs. 30:11
ᵇIs. 60:21;
[Jer. 17:7, 8]
ᶜ[John 15:8]

60:18 ¹*devastation*   **61:1** ¹Lit. *bind up*   **61:3** ¹Lit. *appoint*

4 And they shall ªrebuild the old ruins,
They shall raise up the former desolations,
And they shall repair the ruined cities,
The desolations of many generations.
5 ªStrangers shall stand and feed your flocks,
And the sons of the foreigner
Shall be your plowmen and your vinedressers.
6 ªBut you shall be named the priests of the LORD,
They shall call you the servants of our God.
ᵇYou shall eat the riches of the Gentiles,
And in their glory you shall boast.
7 ªInstead of your shame *you shall have* double *honor,*
And *instead of* confusion they shall rejoice in their
portion.
Therefore in their land they shall possess double;
Everlasting joy shall be theirs.

8 "For ªI, the LORD, love justice;
ᵇI hate robbery ¹for burnt offering;
I will direct their work in truth,
ᶜAnd will make with them an everlasting covenant.
9 Their descendants shall be known among the Gentiles,
And their offspring among the people.
All who see them shall acknowledge them,
ªThat they *are* the posterity *whom* the LORD has blessed."

10 ªI will greatly rejoice in the LORD,
My soul shall be joyful in my God;
For ᵇHe has clothed me with the garments of salvation,
He has covered me with the robe of righteousness,
ᶜAs a bridegroom decks *himself* with ornaments,
And as a bride adorns *herself* with her jewels.
11 For as the earth brings forth its bud,
As the garden causes the things that are sown in it to
spring forth,
So the Lord GOD will cause ªrighteousness and ᵇpraise to
spring forth before all the nations.

ASSURANCE OF ZION'S SALVATION

62 For Zion's sake I will not ¹hold My peace,
And for Jerusalem's sake I will not rest,
Until her righteousness goes forth as brightness,
And her salvation as a lamp *that* burns.
2 ªThe Gentiles shall see your righteousness,
And all ᵇkings your glory.
ᶜYou shall be called by a new name,
Which the mouth of the LORD will name.
3 You shall also be ªa crown of glory
In the hand of the LORD,
And a royal diadem
In the hand of your God.
4 ªYou shall no longer be termed ᵇForsaken,¹
Nor shall your land any more be termed ᶜDesolate;²
But you shall be called ³Hephzibah, and your land ⁴Beulah;
For the LORD delights in you,
And your land shall be married.

61:4 ªIs. 49:8;
58:12;
Ezek. 36:33;
Amos 9:14

61:5 ª[Eph. 2:12]

61:6 ªEx. 19:6
ᵇIs. 60:5, 11

61:7 ªIs. 40:2;
Zech. 9:12

61:8 ªPs. 11:7
ᵇIs. 1:11, 13
ᶜGen. 17:7;
Ps. 105:10;
Is. 55:3;
Jer. 32:40

61:9 ªIs. 65:23

61:10 ªHab. 3:18
ᵇPs. 132:9, 16
ᶜIs. 49:18;
Rev. 21:2

61:11
ªPs. 72:3; 85:11
ᵇIs. 60:18; 62:7

62:2 ªIs. 60:3
ᵇPs. 102:15,
16; 138:4, 5;
148:11, 13
ᶜIs. 62:4, 12;
65:15

62:3 ªIs. 28:5;
Zech. 9:16;
1 Thess. 2:19

62:4 ªHos. 1:10;
1 Pet. 2:10
ᵇIs. 49:14;
54:6, 7
ᶜIs. 54:1

61:8 ¹Or *in* 62:1 ¹*keep silent* 62:4 ¹Heb. *Azubah* ²Heb. *Shemamah*
³Lit. *My Delight Is in Her* ⁴Lit. *Married*

5 For *as* a young man marries a virgin,
  So shall your sons marry you;
  And *as* the bridegroom rejoices over the bride,
  ᵃ*So* shall your God rejoice over you.

6 ᵃI have set watchmen on your walls, O Jerusalem;
  They shall ¹never hold their peace day or night.
  You who ²make mention of the LORD, do not keep silent,
7 And give Him no rest till He establishes
  And till He makes Jerusalem ᵃa praise in the earth.

8 The LORD has sworn by His right hand
  And by the arm of His strength:
  "Surely I will no longer ᵃgive your grain
  As food for your enemies;
  And the sons of the foreigner shall not drink your new
      wine,
  For which you have labored.
9 But those who have gathered it shall eat it,
  And praise the LORD;
  Those who have brought it together shall drink it ᵃin My
      holy courts."

10 Go through,
  Go through the gates!
  ᵃPrepare the way for the people;
  Build up,
  Build up the highway!
  Take out the stones,
  ᵇLift up a banner for the peoples!

11 Indeed the LORD has proclaimed
  To the end of the world:
  ᵃ"Say to the daughter of Zion,
  'Surely your salvation is coming;
  Behold, His ᵇreward *is* with Him,
  And His ¹work before Him.'"
12 And they shall call them The Holy People,
  The Redeemed of the LORD;
  And you shall be called Sought Out,
  A City Not Forsaken.

THE LORD IN JUDGMENT AND SALVATION

63 Who *is* this who comes from Edom,
  With dyed garments from Bozrah,
  This *One who is* ¹glorious in His apparel,
  Traveling in the greatness of His strength?—

  "I who speak in righteousness, mighty to save."

2 Why ᵃ*is* Your apparel red,
  And Your garments like one who treads in the
      winepress?

3 "I have ᵃtrodden the winepress alone,
  And from the peoples no one *was* with Me.
  For I have trodden them in My anger,
  And trampled them in My fury;
  Their blood is sprinkled upon My garments,
  And I have stained all My robes.

Cross references (left margin):

62:5 ᵃIs. 65:19
62:6 ᵃIs. 52:8;
Jer. 6:17;
Ezek. 3:17; 33:7
62:7 ᵃIs. 60:18;
61:11; Jer. 33:9;
Zeph. 3:19, 20
62:8 ᵃLev. 26:16;
Deut. 28:31, 33;
Judg. 6:3–6;
Is. 1:7; Jer. 5:17
62:9
ᵃDeut. 12:12;
14:23, 26
62:10
ᵃIs. 40:3; 57:14
ᵇIs. 11:12
62:11 ᵃZech. 9:9;
Matt. 21:5;
John 12:15
ᵇIs. 40:10;
[Rev. 22:12]
63:2
ᵃ[Rev. 19:13, 15]
63:3 ᵃLam. 1:15;
Rev. 14:19, 20;
19:15

62:6 ¹*not be silent* ²*remember*   62:11 ¹*recompense*   63:1 ¹Or *adorned*

4 For the [a]day of vengeance *is* in My heart,
And the year of My redeemed has come.
5 [a]I looked, but [b]*there was* no one to help,
And I wondered
That *there was* no one to uphold;
Therefore My own [c]arm brought salvation for Me;
And My own fury, it sustained Me.
6 I have trodden down the peoples in My anger,
Made them drunk in My fury,
And brought down their strength to the earth."

GOD'S MERCY REMEMBERED

7 I will mention the lovingkindnesses of the LORD
And the praises of the LORD,
According to all that the LORD has bestowed on us,
And the great goodness toward the house of Israel,
Which He has bestowed on them according to His
mercies,
According to the multitude of His lovingkindnesses.
8 For He said, "Surely they *are* My people,
Children *who* will not lie."
So He became their Savior.
9 [a]In all their affliction He was [1]afflicted,
[b]And the Angel of His Presence saved them;
[c]In His love and in His pity He redeemed them;
And [d]He bore them and carried them
All the days of old.
10 But they [a]rebelled and [b]grieved His Holy Spirit;
[c]So He turned Himself against them as an enemy,
And He fought against them.

11 Then he [a]remembered the days of old,
Moses *and* his people, *saying:*
"Where *is* He who [b]brought them up out of the sea
With the [1]shepherd of His flock?
[c]Where *is* He who put His Holy Spirit within them,
12 Who led *them* by the right hand of Moses,
[a]With His glorious arm,
[b]Dividing the water before them
To make for Himself an everlasting name,
13 [a]Who led them through the deep,
As a horse in the wilderness,
That they might not stumble?"

14 As a beast goes down into the valley,
And the Spirit of the LORD causes him to rest,
So You lead Your people,
[a]To make Yourself a glorious name.

A PRAYER OF PENITENCE

15 [a]Look down from heaven,
And see [b]from Your habitation, holy and glorious.
Where *are* Your zeal and Your strength,
The yearning [c]of Your heart and Your mercies toward me?
Are they restrained?
16 [a]Doubtless You *are* our Father,
Though Abraham [b]was ignorant of us,

63:4 [a]Is. 34:8;
35:4; 61:2;
Jer. 51:6

63:5 [a]Is. 41:28;
59:16
[b][John 16:32]
[c]Ps. 98:1;
Is. 59:16

63:9
[a]Judg. 10:16
[b]Ex. 14:19
[c]Deut. 7:7
[d]Ex. 19:4

63:10 [a]Ex. 15:24
[b]Num. 14:11;
Ps. 78:40;
Acts 7:51;
1 Cor. 10:1–11
[c]Ex. 23:21;
Ps. 106:40

63:11
[a]Ps. 106:44, 45
[b]Ex. 14:30
[c]Num. 11:17, 25,
29; Hag. 2:5

63:12 [a]Ex. 15:6
[b]Ex. 14:21, 22;
Josh. 3:16;
Is. 11:15; 51:10

63:13 [a]Ps. 106:9

63:14
[a]2 Sam. 7:23

63:15
[a]Deut. 26:15;
Ps. 80:14
[b]Ps. 33:14
[c]Jer. 31:20;
Hos. 11:8

63:16
[a]Deut. 32:6
[b]Job 14:21

63:9 [1]Kt., LXX, Syr. *not afflicted* 63:11 [1]MT, Vg. *shepherds*

And Israel does not acknowledge us.
You, O LORD, *are* our Father;
Our Redeemer from Everlasting *is* Your name.

17 O LORD, why have You ᵃmade us stray from Your ways,
And hardened our heart from Your fear?
Return for Your servants' sake,
The tribes of Your inheritance.

18 ᵃYour holy people have possessed *it* but a little while;
ᵇOur adversaries have trodden down Your sanctuary.

19 We have become *like* those of old, over whom You never ruled,
Those who were never called by Your name.

64 Oh, that You would ¹rend the heavens!
That You would come down!
That the mountains might shake at Your ᵃpresence—

2 As fire burns brushwood,
As fire causes water to boil—
To make Your name known to Your adversaries,
That the nations may tremble at Your presence!

3 When ᵃYou did awesome things *for which* we did not look,
You came down,
The mountains shook at Your presence.

4 For since the beginning of the world
ᵃ*Men* have not heard nor perceived by the ear,
Nor has the eye seen any God besides You,
Who acts for the one who waits for Him.

5 You meet him who rejoices and does righteousness,
Who remembers You in Your ways.
You are indeed angry, for we have sinned—
ᵃIn these ways we continue;
And we need to be saved.

6 But we are all like an unclean *thing*,
And all ᵃour righteousnesses *are* like ¹filthy rags;
We all ᵇfade as a leaf,
And our iniquities, like the wind,
Have taken us away.

7 And *there is* no one who calls on Your name,
Who stirs himself up to take hold of You;
For You have hidden Your face from us,
And have ¹consumed us because of our iniquities.

8 But now, O LORD,
You *are* our Father;
We *are* the clay, and You our ᵃpotter;
And all we *are* the work of Your hand.

9 Do not be furious, O LORD,
Nor remember iniquity forever;
Indeed, please look—we all *are* Your people!

10 Your holy cities are a wilderness,
Zion is a wilderness,
Jerusalem a desolation.

11 Our holy and beautiful ¹temple,
Where our fathers praised You,
Is burned up with fire;
And all ᵃour pleasant things ²are laid waste.

63:17 ᵃIs. 6:9, 10;
John 12:40

63:18 ᵃDeut. 7:6
ᵇPs. 74:3–7;
Is. 64:11

64:1 ᵃEx. 19:18;
Ps. 18:9; 144:5;
Mic. 1:3, 4;
[Hab. 3:13]

64:3 ᵃEx. 34:10

64:4 ᵃPs. 31:19

64:5 ᵃMal. 3:6

64:6 ᵃ[Phil. 3:9]
ᵇPs. 90:5, 6;
Is. 1:30

64:8 ᵃIs. 29:16; 45:9;
Jer. 18:6;
[Rom. 9:20, 21]

64:11 ᵃEzek. 24:21

64:1 ¹*tear open*   64:6 ¹Lit. *a filthy garment*   64:7 ¹Lit. *caused us to melt*
64:11 ¹Lit. *house*   ²*have become a ruin*

12 ᵃWill You restrain Yourself because of these *things,*
O LORD?
ᵇWill You ¹hold Your peace, and afflict us very severely?

THE RIGHTEOUSNESS OF GOD'S JUDGMENT

65 "I was ᵃsought by *those who* did not ask *for Me;*
I was found by *those who* did not seek Me.
I said, 'Here I am, here I am,'
To a nation *that* ᵇwas not called by My name.

2 ᵃI have stretched out My hands all day long to a
ᵇrebellious people,
Who ᶜwalk in a way *that is* not good,
According to their own thoughts;

3 A people ᵃwho provoke Me to anger continually to My
face;
ᵇWho sacrifice in gardens,
And burn incense on altars of brick;

4 ᵃWho sit among the graves,
And spend the night in the tombs;
ᵇWho eat swine's flesh,
And the broth of ¹abominable things is *in* their vessels;

5 ᵃWho say, 'Keep to yourself,
Do not come near me,
For I am holier than you!'
These ¹*are* smoke in My nostrils,
A fire that burns all the day.

6 "Behold, ᵃ*it is* written before Me:
ᵇI will not keep silence, ᶜbut will repay—
Even repay into their bosom—

7 Your iniquities and ᵃthe iniquities of your fathers
together,"
Says the LORD,
ᵇ"Who have burned incense on the mountains
ᶜAnd blasphemed Me on the hills;
Therefore I will measure their former work into their
bosom."

8Thus says the LORD:

"As the new wine is found in the cluster,
And *one* says, 'Do not destroy it,
For ᵃa blessing *is* in it,'
So will I do for My servants' sake,
That I may not destroy them ᵇall.

9 I will bring forth descendants from Jacob,
And from Judah an heir of My mountains;
My ᵃelect shall inherit it,
And My servants shall dwell there.

10 ᵃSharon shall be a fold of flocks,
And ᵇthe Valley of Achor a place for herds to lie down,
For My people who have ᶜsought Me.

11 "But you *are* those who forsake the LORD,
Who forget ᵃMy holy mountain,
Who prepare ᵇa table for ¹Gad,
And who furnish a drink offering for ²Meni.

64:12 ᵃIs. 42:14
ᵇPs. 83:1

65:1
ᵃRom. 9:24;
10:20 ᵇIs. 63:19

65:2
ᵃRom. 10:21
ᵇIs. 1:2, 23
ᶜIs. 42:24

65:3
ᵃDeut. 32:21
ᵇIs. 1:29

65:4 ᵃDeut. 18:11
ᵇLev. 11:7;
Is. 66:17

65:5 ᵃMatt. 9:11;
Luke 7:39;
18:9–12

65:6
ᵃDeut. 32:34
ᵇPs. 50:3
ᶜPs. 79:12

65:7 ᵃEx. 20:5
ᵇEzek. 18:6
ᶜIs. 57:7;
Ezek. 20:27, 28

65:8 ᵃJoel 2:14
ᵇIs. 1:9;
Amos 9:8, 9

65:9
ᵃMatt. 24:22

65:10 ᵃIs. 33:9
ᵇJosh. 7:24;
Hos. 2:15
ᶜIs. 55:6

65:11 ᵃIs. 56:7
ᵇEzek. 23:41;
[1 Cor. 10:21]

64:12 ¹*keep silent* 65:4 ¹Unclean meats, Lev. 7:18; 19:7 65:5 ¹*Cause My
wrath to smoke* 65:11 ¹Lit. *Troop* or *Fortune;* a pagan deity ²Lit. *Number*
or *Destiny;* a pagan deity

12 Therefore I will number you for the sword,
  And you shall all bow down to the slaughter;
  ªBecause, when I called, you did not answer;
  When I spoke, you did not hear,
  But did evil before My eyes,
  And chose *that* in which I do not delight."

13Therefore thus says the Lord GOD:

"Behold, My servants shall eat,
  But you shall be hungry;
  Behold, My servants shall drink,
  But you shall be thirsty;
  Behold, My servants shall rejoice,
  But you shall be ashamed;
14 Behold, My servants shall sing for joy of heart,
  But you shall cry for sorrow of heart,
  And ªwail for ¹grief of spirit.
15 You shall leave your name ªas a curse to ᵇMy chosen;
  For the Lord GOD will slay you,
  And ᶜcall His servants by another name;
16 ªSo that he who blesses himself in the earth
  Shall bless himself in the God of truth;
  And ᵇhe who swears in the earth
  Shall swear by the God of truth;
  Because the former troubles are forgotten,
  And because they are hidden from My eyes.

THE GLORIOUS NEW CREATION

17 "For behold, I create ªnew heavens and a new earth;
  And the former shall not be remembered or ¹come to mind.
18 But be glad and rejoice forever in what I create;
  For behold, I create Jerusalem *as* a rejoicing,
  And her people a joy.
19 ªI will rejoice in Jerusalem,
  And joy in My people;
  The ᵇvoice of weeping shall no longer be heard in her,
  Nor the voice of crying.

20 "No more shall an infant from there *live but a few* days,
  Nor an old man who has not fulfilled his days;
  For the child shall die one hundred years old,
  ªBut the sinner *being* one hundred years old shall be accursed.
21 ªThey shall build houses and inhabit *them;*
  They shall plant vineyards and eat their fruit.
22 They shall not build and another inhabit;
  They shall not plant and ªanother eat;
  For ᵇas the days of a tree, *so shall be* the days of My people,
  And ᶜMy elect shall long enjoy the work of their hands.
23 They shall not labor in vain,
  ªNor bring forth children for trouble;
  For ᵇthey *shall be* the descendants of the blessed of the LORD,
  And their offspring with them.

65:12
ª2 Chr. 36:15, 16;
Prov. 1:24;
Is. 41:28; 50:2;
66:4; Jer. 7:13

65:14
ªMatt. 8:12;
Luke 13:28

65:15
ªJer. 29:22;
Zech. 8:13
ᵇIs. 65:9, 22
ᶜ[Acts 11:26]

65:16 ªPs. 72:17;
Jer. 4:2
ᵇDeut. 6:13;
Zeph. 1:5

65:17 ªIs. 51:16;
66:22;
[2 Pet. 3:13];
Rev. 21:1

65:19 ªIs. 62:4, 5
ᵇIs. 35:10; 51:11;
Rev. 7:17; 21:4

65:20
ªEccl. 8:12, 13;
Is. 3:11; 22:14

65:21
ªEzek. 28:26;
45:4; Hos. 11:11;
Amos 9:14

65:22
ªIs. 62:8, 9
ᵇPs. 92:12
ᶜIs. 65:9, 15

65:23 ªHos. 9:12
ᵇIs. 61:9;
[Jer. 32:38, 39;
Acts 2:39]

65:14 ¹Or *a broken spirit*   **65:17** ¹Lit. *come upon the heart*

24 "It shall come to pass
That [a]before they call, I will answer;
And while they are still speaking, I will [b]hear.
25 The [a]wolf and the lamb shall feed together,
The lion shall eat straw like the ox,
[b]And dust *shall be* the serpent's food.
They shall not hurt nor destroy in all My holy mountain,"
Says the LORD.

TRUE WORSHIP AND FALSE

66

Thus says the LORD:

[a]"Heaven *is* My throne,
And earth *is* My footstool.
Where *is* the house that you will build Me?
And where *is* the place of My rest?
2 For all those *things* My hand has made,
And all those *things* exist,"
Says the LORD.
[a]"But on this *one* will I look:
[b]On *him who is* poor and of a contrite spirit,
And who trembles at My word.

3 "He[a] who kills a bull *is as if* he slays a man;
He who sacrifices a lamb, *as if* he [b]breaks a dog's neck;
He who offers a grain offering, *as if he offers* swine's blood;
He who burns incense, *as if* he blesses an idol.
Just as they have chosen their own ways,
And their soul delights in their abominations,
4 So will I choose their delusions,
And bring their fears on them;
[a]Because, when I called, no one answered,
When I spoke they did not hear;
But they did evil before My eyes,
And chose *that* in which I do not delight."

THE LORD VINDICATES ZION

5 Hear the word of the LORD,
You who tremble at His word:
"Your brethren who [a]hated you,
Who cast you out for My name's sake, said,
[b]'Let the LORD be glorified,
That [c]we may see your joy.'
But they shall be ashamed."

6 The sound of noise from the city!
A voice from the temple!
The voice of the LORD,
Who fully repays His enemies!

7 "Before she was in labor, she gave birth;
Before her pain came,
She delivered a male child.
8 Who has heard such a thing?
Who has seen such things?
Shall the earth be made to give birth in one day?
Or shall a nation be born at once?
For as soon as Zion was in labor,
She gave birth to her children.

65:24 [a]Ps. 91:15;
Is. 58:9
[b]Is. 30:19;
Dan. 9:20–23

65:25
[a]Is. 11:6–9
[b]Gen. 3:14;
Mic. 7:17

66:1 [a]1 Kin. 8:27;
2 Chr. 6:18;
Ps. 11:4;
Matt. 5:34;
Acts 17:24

66:2 [a]Ps. 34:18;
[Is. 57:15; 61:1];
Matt. 5:3, 4;
Luke 18:13, 14]
[b]Ps. 34:18; 51:17

66:3
[a][Is. 1:10–17;
58:1–7;
Mic. 6:7, 8]
[b]Deut. 23:18

66:4 [a]Prov. 1:24;
Is. 65:12; Jer. 7:13

66:5 [a]Ps. 38:20;
Is. 60:15;
[Luke 6:22, 23]
[b]Is. 5:19
[c][2 Thess. 1:10;
Titus 2:13]

9   Shall I bring to the time of birth, and not cause delivery?"
     says the LORD.
  "Shall I who cause delivery shut up *the womb?*" says your
     God.

10   "Rejoice with Jerusalem,
     And be glad with her, all you who love her;
     Rejoice for joy with her, all you who mourn for her;
11   That you may feed and be satisfied
     With the consolation of her bosom,
     That you may drink deeply and be delighted
     With the abundance of her glory."

12For thus says the LORD:

  "Behold, ªI will extend peace to her like a river,
     And the glory of the Gentiles like a flowing stream.
     Then you shall bfeed;
     On *her* sides shall you be ccarried,
     And be dandled on *her* knees.
13   As one whom his mother comforts,
     So I will ªcomfort you;
     And you shall be comforted in Jerusalem."

THE REIGN AND INDIGNATION OF GOD

14   When you see *this,* your heart shall rejoice,
     And ªyour bones shall flourish like grass;
     The hand of the LORD shall be known to His servants,
     And *His* indignation to His enemies.
15   ªFor behold, the LORD will come with fire
     And with His chariots, like a whirlwind,
     To render His anger with fury,
     And His rebuke with flames of fire.
16   For by fire and by ªHis sword
     The LORD will judge all flesh;
     And the slain of the LORD shall be bmany.

17   "Thoseª who sanctify themselves and purify themselves,
     To go to the gardens
     ¹After an *idol* in the midst,
     Eating swine's flesh and the abomination and the
       mouse,
     Shall ²be consumed together," says the LORD.

18"For I *know* their works and their ªthoughts. It shall be that I will bgather all nations and tongues; and they shall come and see My glory. 19ªI will set a sign among them; and those among them who escape I will send to the nations: *to* Tarshish and ¹Pul and Lud, who draw the bow, and Tubal and Javan, *to* the coastlands afar off who have not heard My fame nor seen My glory. bAnd they shall declare My glory among the Gentiles. 20Then they shall ªbring all your brethren bfor an offering to the LORD out of all nations, on horses and in chariots and in litters, on mules and on camels, to My holy mountain Jerusalem," says the LORD, "as the children of Israel bring an offering in a clean vessel into the house of the LORD. 21And I will also take some of them for ªpriests *and* Levites," says the LORD.

66:12
ªIs. 48:18; 60:5
bIs. 60:16
cIs. 49:22; 60:4

66:13 ªIs. 51:3;
[2 Cor. 1:3, 4]

66:14 ªEzek. 37:1

66:15 ªIs. 9:5;
[2 Thess. 1:8]

66:16 ªIs. 27:1
bIs. 34:6

66:17
ªIs. 65:3–8

66:18 ªIs. 59:7
bIs. 45:22–25;
Jer. 3:17

66:19
ªLuke 2:34
bMal. 1:11

66:20 ªIs. 49:22
bIs. 18:7;
[Rom. 15:16]

66:21 ªEx. 19:6;
Is. 61:6;
1 Pet. 2:9;
Rev. 1:6

66:17 ¹Lit. *After one*   ²*come to an end*   66:19 ¹So with MT, Tg.; LXX *Put* (cf. Jer. 46:9)

22 "For as ᵃthe new heavens and the new earth
   Which I will make shall remain before Me," says the
      LORD,
   "So shall your descendants and your name remain.
23   And ᵃit shall come to pass
   That from one New Moon to another,
   And from one Sabbath to another,
   ᵇAll flesh shall come to worship before Me," says the
      LORD.

24 "And they shall go forth and look
   Upon the corpses of the men
   Who have transgressed against Me.
   For their ᵃworm does not die,
   And their fire is not quenched.
   They shall be an abhorrence to all flesh."

66:22 ᵃIs. 65:17;
Heb. 12:26, 27;
2 Pet. 3:13;
Rev. 21:1

66:23
ᵃZech. 14:16
ᵇZech. 14:17–21

66:24 ᵃIs. 14:11;
Mark 9:44,
46, 48

THE BOOK OF

JEREMIAH

1 The words of Jeremiah the son of Hilkiah, of the priests who *were* ^ain Anathoth in the land of Benjamin, ²to whom the word of the LORD came in the days of ^aJosiah the son of Amon, king of Judah, ^bin the thirteenth year of his reign. ³It came also in the days of ^aJehoiakim the son of Josiah, king of Judah, ^buntil the end of the eleventh year of Zedekiah the son of Josiah, king of Judah, ^cuntil the carrying away of Jerusalem captive ^din the fifth month.

THE PROPHET IS CALLED

⁴Then the word of the LORD came to me, saying:

5 "Before I ^aformed you in the womb ^bI knew you;
  Before you were born I ^csanctified[1] you;
  I ²ordained you a prophet to the nations."

⁶Then said I:

^a"Ah, Lord GOD!
  Behold, I cannot speak, for I *am* a youth."

⁷But the LORD said to me:

"Do not say, 'I *am* a youth,'
  For you shall go to all to whom I send you,
  And ^awhatever I command you, you shall speak.
8 ^aDo not be afraid of their faces,
  For ^bI *am* with you to deliver you," says the LORD.

⁹Then the LORD put forth His hand and ^atouched my mouth, and the LORD said to me:

"Behold, I have ^bput My words in your mouth.
10 ^aSee, I have this day set you over the nations and over the kingdoms,
  To ^broot out and to pull down,
  To destroy and to throw down,
  To build and to plant."

¹¹Moreover the word of the LORD came to me, saying, "Jeremiah, what do you see?"
  And I said, "I see a [1]branch of an almond tree."
¹²Then the LORD said to me, "You have seen well, for I am [1]ready to perform My word."
¹³And the word of the LORD came to me the second time, saying, "What do you see?"
  And I said, "I see ^aa boiling pot, and it is facing away from the north."
¹⁴Then the LORD said to me:

"Out of the ^anorth calamity shall break forth
  On all the inhabitants of the land.
15 For behold, I am ^acalling

1:1 ^aJosh. 21:18;
1 Kin. 2:26;
1 Chr. 6:60;
Is. 10:30;
Jer. 29:27
1:2 ^a1 Kin. 13:2;
2 Kin. 21:24;
2 Chr. 34:1;
Jer. 3:6; 36:2
^bJer. 25:3
1:3
^a2 Kin. 23:34;
1 Chr. 3:15;
2 Chr. 36:5–8;
Jer. 25:1
^b2 Kin. 24:17;
1 Chr. 3:15;
2 Chr. 36:11–13;
Jer. 39:2
^cJer. 52:12
^d2 Kin. 25:8
1:5 ^aIs. 49:1, 5
^bEx. 33:12
^c[Luke 1:15];
Gal. 1:15
1:6 ^aEx. 4:10;
6:12, 30
1:7
^aNum. 22:20,
38; Jer. 1:17;
Matt. 28:20
1:8
^aEzek. 2:6; 3:9
^bEx. 3:12;
Deut. 31:6;
Josh. 1:5;
Jer. 15:20;
Heb. 13:6
1:9 ^aIs. 6:7;
Mark 7:33–35
^bEx. 4:11–16;
Deut. 18:18;
Is. 51:16
1:10 ^a1 Kin. 19:17
^bJer. 18:7–10;
Ezek. 22:18;
[2 Cor. 10:4, 5]
1:13
^aEzek. 11:3; 24:3
1:14 ^aJer. 6:1
1:15
^aJer. 6:22; 25:9

1:5 ¹*set you apart*   ²*appointed*   1:11 ¹Lit. *rod*   1:12 ¹Lit. *watching*

All the families of the kingdoms of the north," says the
    Lord;
"They shall come and [b]each one set his throne
At the entrance of the gates of Jerusalem,
Against all its walls all around,
And against all the cities of Judah.
16 I will utter My judgments
Against them concerning all their wickedness,
Because [a]they have forsaken Me,
Burned [b]incense to other gods,
And worshiped the works of their own [c]hands.

17 "Therefore [a]prepare yourself and arise,
And speak to them all that I command you.
[b]Do not be dismayed before their faces,
Lest I dismay you before them.
18 For behold, I have made you this day
[a]A fortified city and an iron pillar,
And bronze walls against the whole land—
Against the kings of Judah,
Against its princes,
Against its priests,
And against the people of the land.
19 They will fight against you,
But they shall not prevail against you.
For I *am* with you," says the Lord, "to deliver you."

GOD'S CASE AGAINST ISRAEL

2 Moreover the word of the Lord came to me, saying, [2]"Go
and cry in the hearing of Jerusalem, saying, 'Thus says
the Lord:

"I remember you,
The kindness of your [a]youth,
The love of your betrothal,
[b]When you [1]went after Me in the wilderness,
In a land not sown.
3 [a]Israel *was* holiness to the Lord,
[b]The firstfruits of His increase.
[c]All that devour him will offend;
Disaster will [d]come upon them," says the Lord.'"

[4]Hear the word of the Lord, O house of Jacob and all the
families of the house of Israel. [5]Thus says the Lord:

[a]"What injustice have your fathers found in Me,
That they have gone far from Me,
[b]Have followed [1]idols,
And have become idolaters?
6 Neither did they say, 'Where *is* the Lord,
Who [a]brought us up out of the land of Egypt,
Who led us through [b]the wilderness,
Through a land of deserts and pits,
Through a land of drought and the shadow of death,
Through a land that no one crossed
And where no one dwelt?'
7 I brought you into [a]a bountiful country,
To eat its fruit and its goodness.

1:15 [b]Is. 22:7;
Jer. 39:3

1:16
[a]Deut. 28:20;
Jer. 17:13
[b]Is. 65:3, 4;
Jer. 7:9
[c]Is. 37:19;
Jer. 2:28

1:17 [a]1 Kin. 18:46;
2 Kin. 4:29;
Job 38:3;
Luke 12:35;
[1 Pet. 1:13]
[b]Ezek. 2:6

1:18 [a]Is. 50:7;
Jer. 6:27; 15:20

2:2 [a]Ezek. 16:8;
Hos. 2:15
[b]Deut. 2:7;
Jer. 2:6

2:3 [a][Ex. 19:5, 6;
Deut. 7:6; 14:2]
[b]James 1:18;
Rev. 14:4
[c]Jer. 12:14
[d]Gen. 12:3;
Is. 41:11;
Jer. 30:15, 16;
50:7

2:5 [a]Is. 5:4;
Mic. 6:3
[b]2 Kin. 17:15;
Jer. 8:19;
[Jon. 2:8];
Rom. 1:21

2:6 [a]Ex. 20:2;
Is. 63:11
[b]Deut. 8:15;
32:10

2:7 [a]Num. 13:27

2:2 [1]*followed*   2:5 [1]*vanities* or *futilities*

But when you entered, you [b]defiled My land
And made My heritage an abomination.
8 The priests did not say, 'Where *is* the LORD?'
And those who handle the [a]law did not know Me;
The rulers also transgressed against Me;
[b]The prophets prophesied by Baal,
And walked after *things that* do not profit.

9 "Therefore [a]I will yet [1]bring charges against you," says the LORD,
"And against your children's children I will bring charges.
10 For pass beyond the coasts of [1]Cyprus and see,
Send to [2]Kedar and consider diligently,
And see if there has been such *a* [a]thing.
11 [a]Has a nation changed *its* gods,
Which *are* [b]not gods?
[c]But My people have changed their Glory
For *what* does not profit.
12 Be astonished, O heavens, at this,
And be horribly afraid;
Be very desolate," says the LORD.
13 "For My people have committed two evils:
They have forsaken Me, the [a]fountain of living waters,
And hewn themselves cisterns—broken cisterns that can
hold no water.
14 "*Is* Israel [a]a servant?
Is he a homeborn *slave?*
Why is he plundered?
15 [a]The young lions roared at him, *and* growled;
They made his land waste;
His cities are burned, without inhabitant.
16 Also the people of [1]Noph and [a]Tahpanhes
Have [2]broken the crown of your head.
17 [a]Have you not brought this on yourself,
In that you have forsaken the LORD your God
When [b]He led you in the way?
18 And now why take [a]the road to Egypt,
To drink the waters of [b]Sihor?
Or why take the road to [c]Assyria,
To drink the waters of [1]the River?
19 Your own wickedness will [a]correct you,
And your backslidings will rebuke you.
Know therefore and see that *it is* an evil and bitter *thing*
That you have forsaken the LORD your God,
And the [1]fear of Me *is* not in you,"
Says the Lord GOD of hosts.
20 "For of old I have [a]broken your yoke *and* burst your bonds;
And [b]you said, 'I will not [1]transgress,'
When [c]on every high hill and under every green tree
You lay down, [d]playing the harlot.
21 Yet I had [a]planted you a noble vine, a seed of highest
quality.
How then have you turned before Me
Into [b]the degenerate plant of an alien vine?

2:7
[b]Num. 35:33;
Is. 24:5; Hos. 4:3
2:8 [a]Rom. 2:20
[b]Jer. 23:13
2:9 [a]Jer. 2:35;
Ezek. 20:35, 36;
Mic. 6:2
2:10 [a]Jer. 18:13
2:11 [a]Mic. 4:5
[b]Ps. 115:4;
Is. 37:19
[c]Ps. 106:20;
Rom. 1:23
2:13 [a]Ps. 36:9;
Jer. 17:13;
[John 4:14]
2:14 [a][Ex. 4:22]
2:15 [a]Is. 1:7;
Jer. 50:17
2:16
[a]2 Kin. 23:29–37;
Jer. 43:7–9
2:17 [a]Jer. 4:18
[b]Deut. 32:10
2:18 [a]Is. 30:1–3
[b]Josh. 13:3
[c]Hos. 5:13
2:19 [a]Is. 3:9;
Jer. 4:18;
Hos. 5:5
2:20 [a]Lev. 26:13
[b]Ex. 19:8;
Josh. 24:18;
Judg. 10:16;
1 Sam. 12:10
[c]Deut. 12:2;
Is. 57:5, 7;
Jer. 3:6
[d]Ex. 34:15
2:21 [a]Ex. 15:17;
Ps. 44:2;
80:8; Is. 5:2
[b]Deut. 32:32;
Is. 5:4

2:9 [1]*contend with* **2:10** [1]Heb. *Kittim,* representative of western cultures
[2]In northern Arabian desert, representative of eastern cultures
2:16 [1]Memphis in ancient Egypt [2]Or *grazed* **2:18** [1]The Euphrates
2:19 [1]*dread* **2:20** [1]Kt. *serve*

22 For though you wash yourself with lye, and use much
    soap,
   Yet your iniquity is ^amarked¹ before Me," says the Lord
    God.

23 "How^a can you say, 'I am not ¹polluted,
   I have not gone after the Baals'?
   See your way in the valley;
   Know what you have done:
   You are a swift dromedary breaking loose in her ways,
24 A wild donkey used to the wilderness,
   That sniffs at the wind in her desire;
   In her time of mating, who can turn her away?
   All those who seek her will not weary themselves;
   In her month they will find her.
25 Withhold your foot from being unshod, and your throat
    from thirst.
   But you said, ^a"There is no hope.
   No! For I have loved ^baliens, and after them I will go.'

26 "As the thief is ashamed when he is found out,
   So is the house of Israel ashamed;
   They and their kings and their princes, and their priests
    and their ^aprophets,
27 Saying to a tree, 'You *are* my father,'
   And to a ^astone, 'You gave birth to me.'
   For they have turned *their* back to Me, and not *their* face.
   But in the time of their ^btrouble
   They will say, 'Arise and save us.'
28 But ^awhere *are* your gods that you have made for
    yourselves?
   Let them arise,
   If they ^bcan save you in the time of your ¹trouble;
   For ^c*according to* the number of your cities
   Are your gods, O Judah.

29 "Why will you plead with Me?
   You all have transgressed against Me," says the LORD.
30 "In vain I have ^achastened your children;
   They ^breceived no correction.
   Your sword has ^cdevoured your prophets
   Like a destroying lion.

31 "O generation, see the word of the LORD!
   Have I been a wilderness to Israel,
   Or a land of darkness?
   Why do My people say, 'We ¹are lords;
   ^aWe will come no more to You'?
32 Can a virgin forget her ornaments,
   Or a bride her attire?
   Yet My people ^ahave forgotten Me days without
    number.

33 "Why do you beautify your way to seek love?
   Therefore you have also taught
   The wicked women your ways.
34 Also on your skirts is found
   ^aThe blood of the lives of the poor innocents.

2:22
^aJob 14:16, 17;
Jer. 17:1, 2;
Hos. 13:12

2:23
^aProv. 30:12

2:25 ^aIs. 57:10;
Jer. 18:12
^bJer. 3:13

2:26 ^aIs. 28:7;
Jer. 5:31

2:27 ^aJer. 3:9
^bJudg. 10:10;
Is. 26:16;
Hos. 5:15

2:28
^aDeut. 32:37;
Judg. 10:14
^bIs. 45:20
^c2 Kin. 17:30, 31;
Jer. 11:13

2:30 ^aIs. 9:13
^bIs. 1:5; Jer. 5:3;
7:28 ^cNeh. 9:26;
Jer. 26:20–24;
Acts 7:52;
1 Thess. 2:15

2:31
^aDeut. 32:15;
Jer. 2:20, 25

2:32 ^aPs. 106:21;
Is. 17:10;
Jer. 3:21; 13:25;
Hos. 8:14

2:34
^a2 Kin. 21:16;
24:4; Ps. 106:38;
Jer. 7:6; 19:4

2:22 ¹stained 2:23 ¹defiled 2:28 ¹Or *evil* 2:31 ¹*have dominion*

I have not found it by ¹secret search,
But plainly on all these things.
35 ᵃYet you say, 'Because I am innocent,
Surely His anger shall turn from me.'
Behold, ᵇI will plead My case against you,
ᶜBecause you say, 'I have not sinned.'
36 ᵃWhy do you gad about so much to change your way?
Also ᵇyou shall be ashamed of Egypt ᶜas you were
ashamed of Assyria.
37 Indeed you will go forth from him
With your hands on ᵃyour head;
For the LORD has rejected your trusted allies,
And you will ᵇnot prosper by them.

ISRAEL IS SHAMELESS

3 "They say, 'If a man divorces his wife,
And she goes from him
And becomes another man's,
ᵃMay he return to her again?'
Would not that ᵇland be greatly polluted?
But you have ᶜplayed the harlot with many lovers;
ᵈYet return to Me," says the LORD.

2 "Lift up your eyes to ᵃthe desolate heights and see:
Where have you not ¹lain *with men*?
ᵇBy the road you have sat for them
Like an Arabian in the wilderness;
ᶜAnd you have polluted the land
With your harlotries and your wickedness.
3 Therefore the ᵃshowers have been withheld,
And there has been no latter rain.
You have had a ᵇharlot's forehead;
You refuse to be ashamed.
4 Will you not from this time cry to Me,
'My Father, You *are* ᵃthe guide of ᵇmy youth?
5 ᵃWill He remain angry forever?
Will He keep it to the end?'
Behold, you have spoken and done evil things,
As you were able."

A CALL TO REPENTANCE

6The LORD said also to me in the days of Josiah the king: "Have you seen what ᵃbacksliding Israel has done? She has ᵇgone up on every high mountain and under every green tree, and there played the harlot. 7ᵃAnd I said, after she had done all these *things*, 'Return to Me.' But she did not return. And her treacherous ᵇsister Judah saw it. 8Then I saw that ᵃfor all the causes for which backsliding Israel had committed adultery, I had ᵇput her away and given her a certificate of divorce; ᶜyet her treacherous sister Judah did not fear, but went and played the harlot also. 9So it came to pass, through her casual harlotry, that she ᵃdefiled the land and committed adultery with ᵇstones and trees. 10And yet for all this her treacherous sister Judah has not turned to Me ᵃwith her whole heart, but in pretense," says the LORD.
11Then the LORD said to me, ᵃ"Backsliding Israel has

2:35 ᵃJer. 2:23, 29; Mal. 2:17; 3:8 ᵇJer. 2:9 ᶜ[Prov. 28:13; 1 John 1:8, 10]
2:36 ᵃJer. 31:22; Hos. 5:13; 12:1 ᵇIs. 30:3 ᶜ2 Chr. 28:16
2:37 ᵃ2 Sam. 13:19; Jer. 14:3, 4 ᵇJer. 37:7–10
3:1 ᵃDeut. 24:1–4 ᵇJer. 2:7 ᶜJer. 2:20; Ezek. 16:26 ᵈJer. 4:1; [Zech. 1:3]
3:2 ᵃDeut. 12:2; Jer. 2:20; 3:21; 7:29 ᵇProv. 23:28 ᶜJer. 2:7
3:3 ᵃLev. 26:19; Jer. 14:3–6 ᵇZeph. 3:5
3:4 ᵃPs. 71:17; Prov. 2:17 ᵇJer. 2:2; Hos. 2:15
3:5 ᵃPs. 103:9; [Is. 57:16]; Jer. 3:12
3:6 ᵃJer. 7:24 ᵇJer. 2:20
3:7 ᵃ2 Kin. 17:13 ᵇJer. 3:11; Ezek. 16:47, 48
3:8 ᵃEzek. 23:9 ᵇ2 Kin. 17:6; Is. 50:1 ᶜEzek. 23:11
3:9 ᵃJer. 2:7 ᵇIs. 57:6; Jer. 2:27
3:10 ᵃJer. 12:2; Hos. 7:14
3:11 ᵃEzek. 16:51, 52

shown herself more righteous than treacherous Judah. [12]Go and proclaim these words toward [a]the north, and say:

'Return, backsliding Israel,' says the LORD;
'I will not cause My anger to fall on you.
For I *am* [b]merciful,' says the LORD;
'I will not remain angry forever.
[13] [a]Only acknowledge your iniquity,
That you have transgressed against the LORD your God,
And have [b]scattered your [1]charms
To [c]alien deities [d]under every green tree,
And you have not obeyed My voice,' says the LORD.

[14]"Return, O backsliding children," says the LORD; [a]"for I am married to you. I will take you, [b]one from a city and two from a family, and I will bring you to [c]Zion. [15]And I will give you [a]shepherds according to My heart, who will [b]feed you with knowledge and understanding.

[16]"Then it shall come to pass, when you are multiplied and [a]increased in the land in those days," says the LORD, "that they will say no more, 'The ark of the covenant of the LORD.' [b]It shall not come to mind, nor shall they remember it, nor shall they visit *it,* nor shall it be made anymore.

[17]"At that time Jerusalem shall be called The Throne of the LORD, and all the nations shall be gathered to it, [a]to the name of the LORD, to Jerusalem. No more shall they [b]follow[1] the dictates of their evil hearts.

[18]"In those days [a]the house of Judah shall walk with the house of Israel, and they shall come together out of the land of [b]the north to [c]the land that I have given as an inheritance to your fathers.

[19]"But I said:

'How can I put you among the children
And give you [a]a pleasant land,
A beautiful heritage of the hosts of nations?'

"And I said:

'You shall call Me, [b]"My Father,"
And not turn away from Me.'
[20] Surely, *as* a wife treacherously departs from her
[1]husband,
So [a]have you dealt treacherously with Me,
O house of Israel," says the LORD.

[21] A voice was heard on [a]the desolate heights,
Weeping *and* supplications of the children of Israel.
For they have perverted their way;
They have forgotten the LORD their God.

[22] "Return, you backsliding children,
And I will [a]heal your backslidings."

"Indeed we do come to You,
For You are the LORD our God.
[23] [a]Truly, in vain *is salvation hoped for* from the hills,
And *from* the multitude of mountains;
[b]Truly, in the LORD our God
Is the salvation of Israel.

3:12 [a]2 Kin. 17:6
[b]Ps. 86:15;
Jer. 12:15; 31:20;
33:26

3:13 [a]Lev. 26:40;
Deut. 30:1, 2;
[Prov. 28:13;
1 John 1:9]
[b]Ezek. 16:15
[c]Jer. 2:25
[d]Deut. 12:2

3:14 [a]Jer. 31:32;
Hos. 2:19, 20
[b]Jer. 31:6
[c][Rom. 11:5]

3:15 [a]Jer. 23:4;
31:10;
[Ezek. 34:23];
Eph. 4:11
[b]Acts 20:28

3:16 [a]Is. 49:19;
Jer. 23:3
[b]Is. 65:17

3:17 [a]Is. 60:9
[b]Deut. 29:19;
Jer. 7:24

3:18 [a]Is. 11:13;
Jer. 50:4;
Ezek. 37:16–22;
Hos. 1:11
[b]Jer. 31:8
[c]Amos 9:15

3:19 [a]Ps. 106:24
[b]Is. 63:16;
Jer. 3:4

3:20 [a]Is. 48:8

3:21 [a]Is. 15:2

3:22 [a]Jer. 30:17;
33:6; Hos. 6:1;
14:4

3:23 [a]Ps. 121:1, 2
[b]Ps. 3:8;
Prov. 21:31;
Jer. 17:14; 31:7;
Jon. 2:9

3:13 [1]Lit. *ways*   3:17 [1]*walk after the stubbornness* or *imagination*
3:20 [1]Lit. *companion*

24 aFor shame has devoured
   The labor of our fathers from our youth—
   Their flocks and their herds,
   Their sons and their daughters.
25 We lie down in our shame,
   And our ¹reproach covers us.
   aFor we have sinned against the LORD our God,
   We and our fathers,
   From our youth even to this day,
   And bhave not obeyed the voice of the LORD our God."

4 "If you will return, O Israel," says the LORD,
   a"Return to Me;
   And if you will put away your abominations out of My
      sight,
   Then you shall not be moved.
2 aAnd you shall swear, 'The LORD lives,'
   bIn truth, in ¹judgment, and in righteousness;
   cThe nations shall bless themselves in Him,
   And in Him they shall dglory."

3For thus says the LORD to the men of Judah and Jerusalem:

   a"Break up your ¹fallow ground,
   And bdo not sow among thorns.
4 aCircumcise yourselves to the LORD,
   And take away the foreskins of your hearts,
   You men of Judah and inhabitants of Jerusalem,
   Lest My fury come forth like fire,
   And burn so that no one can quench it,
   Because of the evil of your doings."

AN IMMINENT INVASION

   5Declare in Judah and proclaim in Jerusalem, and say:

   a"Blow the trumpet in the land;
   Cry, 'Gather together,'
   And say, b'Assemble yourselves,
   And let us go into the fortified cities.'
6 Set up the ¹standard toward Zion.
   Take refuge! Do not delay!
   For I will bring disaster from the anorth,
   And great destruction."
7 aThe lion has come up from his thicket,
   And bthe destroyer of nations is on his way.
   He has gone forth from his place
   cTo make your land desolate.
   Your cities will be laid waste,
   Without inhabitant.
8 For this, aclothe yourself with sackcloth,
   Lament and wail.
   For the fierce anger of the LORD
   Has not turned back from us.

9 "And it shall come to pass in that day," says the LORD,
   "That the heart of the king shall perish,
   And the heart of the princes;

3:24 aJer. 11:13;
14:20; Hos. 9:10

3:25
aEzra 9:6, 7
bJer. 22:21

4:1 aJer. 3:1, 22;
15:19; Joel 2:12

4:2
aDeut. 10:20;
Is. 45:23;
65:16; Jer. 12:16
bIs. 48:1;
Zech. 8:8
c[Gen. 22:18];
Ps. 72:18;
Is. 65:16;
Jer. 3:17;
[Gal. 3:8]
dIs. 45:25;
Jer. 9:24;
1 Cor. 1:31;
2 Cor. 10:17

4:3 aHos. 10:12
bMatt. 13:7

4:4
aDeut. 10:16;
30:6;
Jer. 9:25, 26;
[Rom. 2:28, 29;
Col. 2:11]

4:5 aJer. 6:1;
Hos. 8:1
bJosh. 10:20;
Jer. 8:14

4:6 aJer. 1:13–15;
6:1, 22; 50:17

4:7 a2 Kin. 24:1;
Dan. 7:4
bJer. 25:9;
Ezek. 26:7–10
cIs. 1:7; 6:11;
Jer. 2:15

4:8 aIs. 22:12;
Jer. 6:26

3:25 ¹disgrace   4:2 ¹justice   4:3 ¹untilled   4:6 ¹banner

The priests shall be astonished,
And the prophets shall wonder."

10 Then I said, "Ah, Lord GOD!
   aSurely You have greatly deceived this people and
      Jerusalem,
   bSaying, 'You shall have peace,'
   Whereas the sword reaches to the ¹heart."

11 At that time it will be said
   To this people and to Jerusalem,
   a"A dry wind of the desolate heights *blows* in the
      wilderness
   Toward the daughter of My people—
   Not to fan or to cleanse—
12 A wind too strong for these will come for Me;
   Now aI will also speak judgment against them."

13 "Behold, he shall come up like clouds,
   And ahis chariots like a whirlwind.
   bHis horses are swifter than eagles.
   Woe to us, for we are plundered!"

14 O Jerusalem, awash your heart from wickedness,
   That you may be saved.
   How long shall your evil thoughts lodge within you?
15 For a voice declares afrom Dan
   And proclaims ¹affliction from Mount Ephraim:
16 "Make mention to the nations,
   Yes, proclaim against Jerusalem,
   That watchers come from a afar country
   And raise their voice against the cities of Judah.
17 aLike keepers of a field they are against her all around,
   Because she has been rebellious against Me," says the
      LORD.
18 "Youra ways and your doings
   Have procured these *things* for you.
   This *is* your wickedness,
   Because it is bitter,
   Because it reaches to your heart."

SORROW FOR THE DOOMED NATION

19 O my asoul, my soul!
   I am pained in my very heart!
   My heart makes a noise in me;
   I cannot hold my peace,
   Because you have heard, O my soul,
   The sound of the trumpet,
   The alarm of war.
20 aDestruction upon destruction is cried,
   For the whole land is plundered.
   Suddenly bmy tents are plundered,
   And my curtains in a moment.
21 How long will I see the ¹standard,
   And hear the sound of the trumpet?

22 "For My people *are* foolish,
   They have not known Me.

4:10
a 2 Kin. 25:10–12;
Ezek. 14:9;
2 Thess. 2:11
b Jer. 5:12; 14:13

4:11 a Jer. 51:1;
Ezek. 17:10;
Hos. 13:15

4:12 a Jer. 1:16

4:13 a Is. 5:28
b Deut. 28:49;
Lam. 4:19;
Hos. 8:1;
Hab. 1:8

4:14 a Prov. 1:22;
Is. 1:16;
Jer. 13:27;
James 4:8

4:15
a Jer. 8:16; 50:17

4:16 a Is. 39:3;
Jer. 5:15

4:17
a 2 Kin. 25:1, 4

4:18 a Ps. 107:17;
Is. 50:1;
Jer. 2:17, 19

4:19
a 2 Kin. 25:11;
2 Chr. 36:20;
Is. 15:5; 16:11;
21:3; 22:4;
Jer. 9:1, 10; 20:9

4:20 a Ps. 42:7;
Ezek. 7:26
b Jer. 10:20

4:10 ¹Lit. *soul*   4:15 ¹Or *wickedness*   4:21 ¹*banner*

They *are* [1]silly children,
And they have no understanding.
[a]They *are* wise to do evil,
But to do good they have no knowledge."

23 [a]I beheld the earth, and indeed *it was* [b]without form, and void;
And the heavens, they *had* no light.
24 [a]I beheld the mountains, and indeed they trembled,
And all the hills moved back and forth.
25 I beheld, and indeed *there was* no man,
And [a]all the birds of the heavens had fled.
26 I beheld, and indeed the fruitful land *was* a [a]wilderness,
And all its cities were broken down
At the presence of the LORD,
By His fierce anger.

27For thus says the LORD:

"The whole land shall be desolate;
[a]Yet I will not make a full end.
28 For this [a]shall the earth mourn,
And [b]the heavens above be black,
Because I have spoken.
I have [c]purposed and [d]will not relent,
Nor will I turn back from it.
29 The whole city shall flee from the noise of the horsemen and bowmen.
They shall go into thickets and climb up on the rocks.
Every city *shall be* forsaken,
And not a man shall dwell in it.

30 "And *when* you *are* plundered,
What will you do?
Though you clothe yourself with crimson,
Though you adorn *yourself* with ornaments of gold,
[a]Though you enlarge your eyes with paint,
In vain you will make yourself fair;
[b]*Your* lovers will despise you;
They will seek your life.

31 "For I have heard a voice as of a woman in [1]labor,
The anguish as of her who brings forth her first child,
The voice of the daughter of Zion bewailing herself;
She [a]spreads her hands, *saying,*
'Woe *is* me now, for my soul is [2]weary
Because of murderers!'

THE JUSTICE OF GOD'S JUDGMENT

5 "Run to and fro through the streets of Jerusalem;
See now and know;
And seek in her open places
[a]If you can find a man,
[b]If there is *anyone* who executes [1]judgment,
Who seeks the truth,
[c]And I will pardon her.
2 [a]Though they say, 'As [b]the LORD lives,'
Surely they [c]swear falsely."

4:22
[a]Jer. 9:3; 13:23;
Rom. 16:19;
1 Cor. 14:20

4:23 [a]Is. 24:19
[b]Gen. 1:2

4:24 [a]Is. 5:25;
Jer. 10:10;
Ezek. 38:20

4:25 [a]Jer. 9:10;
12:4; Zeph. 1:3

4:26 [a]Jer. 9:10

4:27
[a]Jer. 5:10, 18;
30:11; 46:28

4:28
[a]Jer. 12:4, 11;
14:2; Hos. 4:3
[b]Is. 5:30; 50:3;
Joel 2:30, 31
[c]Is. 46:10, 11;
[Dan. 4:35]
[d][Num. 23:19];
Jer. 7:16; 23:30;
30:24

4:30
[a]2 Kin. 9:30;
Ezek. 23:40
[b]Jer. 22:20, 22;
Lam. 1:2, 19;
Ezek. 23:9,
10, 22

4:31 [a]Is. 1:15;
Lam. 1:17

5:1 [a]Ezek. 22:30
[b]Gen. 18:23–32
[c]Gen. 18:26

5:2 [a]Is. 48:1;
Titus 1:16
[b]Jer. 4:2
[c]Jer. 7:9

4:22 [1]foolish   4:31 [1]childbirth   [2]faint   5:1 [1]justice

3 O Lord, *are* not ᵃYour eyes on the truth?
You have ᵇstricken them,
But they have not grieved;
You have consumed them,
But ᶜthey have refused to receive correction.
They have made their faces harder than rock;
They have refused to return.

4 Therefore I said, "Surely these *are* poor.
They are foolish;
For ᵃthey do not know the way of the Lord,
The judgment of their God.

5 I will go to the great men and speak to them,
For ᵃthey have known the way of the Lord,
The judgment of their God."

But these have altogether ᵇbroken the yoke
And burst the bonds.

6 Therefore ᵃa lion from the forest shall slay them,
ᵇA wolf of the deserts shall destroy them;
ᶜA leopard will watch over their cities.
Everyone who goes out from there shall be torn in
   pieces,
Because their transgressions are many;
Their backslidings have increased.

7 "How shall I pardon you for this?
Your children have forsaken Me
And ᵃsworn by *those* ᵇ*that are* not gods.
ᶜWhen I had fed them to the full,
Then they committed adultery
And assembled themselves by troops in the harlots'
   houses.

8 ᵃThey were *like* well-fed lusty stallions;
Every one neighed after his neighbor's wife.

9 Shall I not punish *them* for these *things*?" says the Lord.
"And shall I not ᵃavenge Myself on such a nation as this?

10 "Go up on her walls and destroy,
But do not ¹make a ᵃcomplete end.
Take away her branches,
For they *are* not the Lord's.

11 For ᵃthe house of Israel and the house of Judah
Have dealt very treacherously with Me," says the Lord.

12 ᵃThey have lied about the Lord,
And said, ᵇ"*It is* not He.
ᶜNeither will ¹evil come upon us,
Nor shall we see sword or famine.

13 And the prophets become wind,
For the word *is* not in them.
Thus shall it be done to them."

¹⁴Therefore thus says the Lord God of hosts:

"Because you speak this word,
ᵃBehold, I will make My words in your mouth fire,
And this people wood,
And it shall devour them.

5:3 ᵃ2 Kin. 25:1;
[2 Chr. 16:9];
Jer. 16:17]
ᵇIs. 1:5; 9:13;
Jer. 2:30
ᶜIs. 9:13;
Jer. 7:28;
Zeph. 3:2

5:4 ᵃIs. 27:11;
Jer. 8:7; Hos. 4:6

5:5 ᵃMic. 3:1
ᵇEx. 32:25;
Ps. 2:3; Jer. 2:20

5:6 ᵃJer. 4:7
ᵇPs. 104:20;
Ezek. 22:27;
Hab. 1:8;
Zeph. 3:3
ᶜHos. 13:7

5:7 ᵃJosh. 23:7;
Jer. 12:16;
Zeph. 1:5
ᵇDeut. 32:21;
Jer. 2:11; Gal. 4:8
ᶜDeut. 32:15

5:8 ᵃJer. 13:27;
29:23;
Ezek. 22:11

5:9 ᵃJer. 9:9

5:10 ᵃJer. 4:27

5:11
ᵃJer. 3:6, 7, 20

5:12
ᵃ2 Chr. 36:16;
Jer. 4:10
ᵇIs. 28:15;
47:8; Jer. 23:17
ᶜJer. 14:13

5:14 ᵃIs. 24:6;
Jer. 1:9; 23:29;
Hos. 6:5;
Zech. 1:6

5:10 ¹*completely destroy*   5:12 ¹*disaster*

15 Behold, I will bring a ªnation against you ᵇfrom afar,
O house of Israel," says the LORD.
"It *is* a mighty nation,
It *is* an ancient nation,
A nation whose language you do not know,
Nor can you understand what they say.
16 Their quiver *is* like an open tomb;
They *are* all mighty men.
17 And they shall eat up your ªharvest and your bread,
Which your sons and daughters should eat.
They shall eat up your flocks and your herds;
They shall eat up your vines and your fig trees;
They shall destroy your fortified cities,
In which you trust, with the sword.

18"Nevertheless in those days," says the LORD, "I ªwill not ¹make a complete end of you. 19And it will be when you say, ª'Why does the LORD our God do all these *things* to us?' then you shall answer them, 'Just as you have ᵇforsaken Me and served foreign gods in your land, so ᶜyou shall serve aliens in a land *that is* not yours.'

20 "Declare this in the house of Jacob
And proclaim it in Judah, saying,
21 'Hear this now, O ªfoolish people,
Without ¹understanding,
Who have eyes and see not,
And who have ears and hear not:
22 ªDo you not fear Me?' says the LORD.
'Will you not tremble at My presence,
Who have placed the sand as the ᵇbound of the sea,
By a perpetual decree, that it cannot pass beyond it?
And though its waves toss to and fro,
Yet they cannot prevail;
Though they roar, yet they cannot pass over it.
23 But this people has a defiant and rebellious heart;
They have revolted and departed.
24 They do not say in their heart,
"Let us now fear the LORD our God,
ªWho gives rain, both the ᵇformer and the latter, in its
season.
ᶜHe reserves for us the appointed weeks of the harvest."
25 ªYour iniquities have turned these *things* away,
And your sins have withheld good from you.
26 'For among My people are found wicked *men*;
They ªlie in wait as one who sets snares;
They set a trap;
They catch men.
27 As a cage is full of birds,
So their houses *are* full of deceit.
Therefore they have become great and grown rich.
28 They have grown ªfat, they are sleek;
Yes, they ¹surpass the deeds of the wicked;
They do not plead ᵇthe cause,
The cause of the fatherless;
ᶜYet they prosper,

5:15
ªDeut. 28:49;
Is. 5:26; Jer. 1:15;
6:22 ᵇIs. 39:3;
Jer. 4:16
5:17 ªLev. 26:16;
Deut. 28:31, 33;
Jer. 8:16; 50:7, 17
5:18 ªJer. 30:11;
Amos 9:8
5:19
ªDeut. 29:24–29;
1 Kin. 9:8, 9;
Jer. 13:22;
16:10–13
ᵇJer. 1:16; 2:13
ᶜDeut. 28:48;
Jer. 16:13
5:21 ªIs. 6:9;
Jer. 6:10;
Ezek. 12:2;
Matt. 13:14;
John 12:40;
Acts 28:26;
Rom. 11:8
5:22
ªDeut. 28:58;
Ps. 119:120;
Jer. 2:19; 10:7;
[Rev. 15:4]
ᵇJob 26:10
5:24 ªPs. 147:8;
Jer. 14:22;
[Matt. 5:45];
Acts 14:17
ᵇDeut. 11:14;
Joel 2:23;
James 5:7
ᶜ[Gen. 8:22]
5:25 ªJer. 3:3
5:26 ªPs. 10:9;
Prov. 1:11;
Jer. 18:22;
Hab. 1:15
5:28
ªDeut. 32:15
ᵇIs. 1:23; Jer. 7:6;
22:3; Zech. 7:10
ᶜJob 12:6;
Ps. 73:12

5:18 ¹*completely destroy* **5:21** ¹Lit. *heart* **5:28** ¹Or *pass over* or *overlook*

And the right of the needy they do not defend.

29 [a]Shall I not punish *them* for these *things?*' says the LORD.
'Shall I not avenge Myself on such a nation as this?'

30 "An astonishing and [a]horrible thing
Has been committed in the land:

31 The prophets prophesy [a]falsely,
And the priests rule by their *own* power;
And My people [b]love *to have it* so.
But what will you do in the end?

IMPENDING DESTRUCTION FROM THE NORTH

6 "O you children of Benjamin,
Gather yourselves to flee from the midst of Jerusalem!
Blow the trumpet in Tekoa,
And set up a signal-fire in [a]Beth Haccerem;
[b]For disaster appears out of the north,
And great destruction.

2 I have likened the daughter of Zion
To a lovely and delicate woman.

3 The [a]shepherds with their flocks shall come to her.
They shall pitch *their* tents against her all around.
Each one shall pasture in his own place."

4 "Prepare[a] war against her;
Arise, and let us go up [b]at noon.
Woe to us, for the day goes away,
For the shadows of the evening are lengthening.

5 Arise, and let us go by night,
And let us destroy her palaces."

6For thus has the LORD of hosts said:

"Cut down trees,
And build a mound against Jerusalem.
This *is* the city to be punished.
She *is* full of oppression in her midst.

7 [a]As a fountain [1]wells up with water,
So she wells up with her wickedness.
[b]Violence and plundering are heard in her.
Before Me continually *are* [2]grief and wounds.

8 Be instructed, O Jerusalem,
Lest [a]My soul depart from you;
Lest I make you desolate,
A land not inhabited."

9Thus says the LORD of hosts:

"They shall thoroughly glean as a vine the remnant of
Israel;
As a grape-gatherer, put your hand back into the
branches."

10 To whom shall I speak and give warning,
That they may hear?
Indeed their [a]ear *is* uncircumcised,
And they cannot give heed.
Behold, [b]the word of the LORD is a reproach to them;
They have no delight in it.

5:29 [a]Jer. 5:9;
Mal. 3:5

5:30 [a]Jer. 23:14;
Hos. 6:10;
2 Tim. 4:3

5:31 [a]Jer. 14:14;
Ezek. 13:6
[b]Mic. 2:11

6:1 [a]Neh. 3:14
[b]Jer. 4:6

6:3
[a]2 Kin. 25:1–4;
Jer. 4:17; 12:10

6:4 [a]Jer. 51:27;
Joel 3:9
[b]Jer. 15:8;
Zeph. 2:4

6:7 [a]Is. 57:20
[b]Ps. 55:9

6:8 [a]Ezek. 23:18;
Hos. 9:12

6:10 [a]Ex. 6:12;
Jer. 5:21; 7:26;
[Acts 7:51]
[b]Jer. 8:9; 20:8

6:7 [1]gushes [2]sickness

11 Therefore I am full of the fury of the LORD.
    [a]I am weary of holding *it* in.
"I will pour it out [b]on the children outside,
And on the assembly of young men together;
For even the husband shall be taken with the wife,
The aged with *him who is* full of days.

12 And [a]their houses shall be turned over to others,
Fields and wives together;
For I will stretch out My hand
Against the inhabitants of the land," says the LORD.

13 "Because from the least of them even to the greatest of
    them,
Everyone *is* given to [a]covetousness;
And from the prophet even to the [b]priest,
Everyone deals falsely.

14 They have also [a]healed the [1]hurt of My people [2]slightly,
[b]Saying, 'Peace, peace!'
When *there is* no peace.

15 Were they [a]ashamed when they had committed
    abomination?
No! They were not at all ashamed;
Nor did they know how to blush.
Therefore they shall fall among those who fall;
At the time I punish them,
They shall be cast down," says the LORD.

16 Thus says the LORD:

"Stand in the ways and see,
And ask for the [a]old paths, where the good way *is*,
And walk in it;
Then you will find [b]rest for your souls.
But they said, 'We will not walk *in it*.'

17 Also, I set [a]watchmen over you, *saying*,
[b]'Listen to the sound of the trumpet!'
But they said, 'We will not listen.'

18 Therefore hear, you nations,
And know, O congregation, what *is* among them.

19 [a]Hear, O earth!
Behold, I will certainly bring [b]calamity on this people—
[c]The fruit of their thoughts,
Because they have not heeded My words
Nor My law, but rejected it.

20 [a]For what purpose to Me
Comes frankincense [b]from Sheba,
And [c]sweet cane from a far country?
[d]Your burnt offerings *are* not acceptable,
Nor your sacrifices sweet to Me."

21 Therefore thus says the LORD:

"Behold, I will lay stumbling blocks before this people,
And the fathers and the sons together shall fall on them.
The neighbor and his friend shall perish."

22 Thus says the LORD:

"Behold, a people comes from the [a]north country,
And a great nation will be raised from the farthest parts
    of the earth.

6:11 [a]Jer. 20:9
    [b]Jer. 9:21
6:12 [a]Deut. 28:30;
Jer. 8:10; 38:22
6:13 [a]Is. 56:11;
Jer. 8:10; 22:17
[b]Jer. 5:31; 23:11;
Mic. 3:5, 11
6:14 [a]Jer. 8:11–15;
Ezek. 13:10
[b]Jer. 4:10; 23:17
6:15 [a]Jer. 3:3; 8:12
6:16 [a]Is. 8:20;
Jer. 18:15;
Mal. 4:4;
Luke 16:29
[b]Matt. 11:29
6:17 [a]Is. 21:11; 58:1;
Jer. 25:4;
Ezek. 3:17;
Hab. 2:1
[b]Deut. 4:1
6:19 [a]Is. 1:2
[b]Jer. 19:3, 15
[c]Prov. 1:31
6:20 [a]Ps. 40:6;
50:7–9; Is. 1:11;
66:3; Amos 5:21;
Mic. 6:6, 7
[b]Is. 60:6
[c]Is. 43:24
[d]Jer. 7:21–23
6:22 [a]Jer. 1:15;
10:22; 50:41–43

6:14 [1]Lit. *crushing* [2]Superficially

23 They will lay hold on bow and spear;
They *are* cruel and have no mercy;
Their voice ^aroars like the sea;
And they ride on horses,
As men of war set in array against you, O daughter of
Zion."

24 We have heard the report of it;
Our hands grow feeble.
^aAnguish has taken hold of us,
Pain as of a woman in ¹labor.

25 Do not go out into the field,
Nor walk by the way.
Because of the sword of the enemy,
Fear *is* on every side.

26 O daughter of my people,
^aDress in sackcloth
^bAnd roll about in ashes!
^cMake mourning *as for* an only son, most bitter
lamentation;
For the plunderer will suddenly come upon us.

27 "I have set you *as* an assayer *and* ^aa fortress among My
people,
That you may know and test their way.

28 ^aThey *are* all stubborn rebels, ^bwalking as slanderers.
They are ^cbronze and iron,
They are all corrupters;

29 The bellows blow fiercely,
The lead is consumed by the fire;
The smelter refines in vain,
For the wicked are not drawn off.

30 *People* will call them ^arejected silver,
Because the LORD has rejected them."

TRUSTING IN LYING WORDS
(cf. Jer. 26:4–6)

7 The word that came to Jeremiah from the LORD, saying,
²ᵃ"Stand in the gate of the LORD's house, and proclaim
there this word, and say, 'Hear the word of the LORD, all *you*
of Judah who enter in at these gates to worship the LORD!'"
³Thus says the LORD of hosts, the God of Israel: ᵃ"Amend your
ways and your doings, and I will cause you to dwell in this
place. ⁴ᵃDo not trust in these lying words, saying, 'The temple
of the LORD, the temple of the LORD, the temple of the LORD
are these.'

⁵"For if you thoroughly amend your ways and your doings,
if you thoroughly ᵃexecute ¹judgment between a man and his
neighbor, ⁶*if* you do not oppress the stranger, the fatherless,
and the widow, and do not shed innocent blood in this place,
ᵃor walk after other gods to your hurt, ⁷ᵃthen I will cause you
to dwell in this place, in ᵇthe land that I gave to your fathers
forever and ever.

⁸"Behold, you trust in ᵃlying words that cannot profit.
⁹ᵃWill you steal, murder, commit adultery, swear falsely, burn
incense to Baal, and ᵇwalk after other gods whom you do not
know, ¹⁰ᵃand *then* come and stand before Me in this house

6:23 ᵃIs. 5:30
6:24 ᵃJer. 4:31;
13:21; 49:24
6:26 ᵃJer. 4:8
ᵇJer. 25:34;
Mic. 1:10
ᶜAmos 8:10;
[Zech. 12:10]
6:27 ᵃJer. 1:18
6:28 ᵃJer. 5:23
ᵇJer. 9:4
ᶜEzek. 22:18
6:30 ᵃIs. 1:22;
Jer. 7:29
7:2
ᵃJer. 17:19; 26:2
7:3 ᵃJer. 4:1;
18:11; 26:13
7:4 ᵃJer. 7:8;
Mic. 3:11
7:5 ᵃ1 Kin. 6:12;
Jer. 21:12; 22:3
7:6
ᵃDeut. 6:14, 15;
Jer. 13:10
7:7 ᵃDeut. 4:40
ᵇJer. 3:18
7:8 ᵃJer. 5:31;
14:13, 14
7:9 ᵃ1 Kin. 18:21;
Hos. 4:1, 2;
Zeph. 1:5
ᵇEx. 20:3;
Jer. 7:6; 19:4
7:10
ᵃEzek. 23:39

7:10 ᵇJer. 7:11, 14;
32:34; 34:15

7:11 ᵃIs. 56:7
ᵇMatt. 21:13;
Mark 11:17;
Luke 19:46

7:12 ᵃJosh. 18:1;
Judg. 18:31
ᵇDeut. 12:11
ᶜ1 Sam. 4:10;
Ps. 78:60;
Jer. 26:6

7:13
ᵃ2 Chr. 36:15;
Jer. 11:7
ᵇProv. 1:24;
Is. 65:12; 66:4

7:14
ᵃ1 Sam. 4:10, 11;
Ps. 78:60;
Jer. 26:6, 9

7:15
ᵃ2 Kin. 17:23
ᵇPs. 78:67;
Hos. 7:13;
9:13; 12:1

7:16 ᵃEx. 32:10;
Deut. 9:14;
Jer. 11:14 ᵇJer. 15:1

7:18
ᵃJer. 44:17
ᵇJer. 19:13

7:19
ᵃDeut. 32:16, 21

7:21 ᵃIs. 1:11;
Jer. 6:20;
Hos. 8:13;
Amos 5:21, 22

7:22
ᵃ1 Sam. 15:22;
Ps. 51:16;
[Hos. 6:6]

7:23
ᵃEx. 15:26;
16:32; Deut. 6:3
ᵇ[Ex. 19:5, 6];
Lev. 26:12;
[Jer. 11:4; 13:11]

7:24
ᵃPs. 81:11;
Jer. 11:8
ᵇDeut. 29:19;
Jer. 9:14
ᶜJer. 32:33

7:25
ᵃ2 Chr. 36:15;
Jer. 25:4; 29:19;
Mark 12:1–10;
Luke 11:47–49

7:26 ᵃJer. 11:8
ᵇNeh. 9:17
ᶜJer. 16:12;
Matt. 23:32

7:27 ᵃJer. 1:7;
26:2; 37:14, 15;
43:1–4; Ezek. 2:7

7:28 ᵃJer. 5:3
ᵇJer. 9:3

ᵇwhich is called by My name, and say, 'We are delivered to do all these abominations'? ¹¹Has ᵃthis house, which is called by My name, become a ᵇden of thieves in your eyes? Behold, I, even I, have seen *it*," says the LORD.

¹²"But go now to ᵃMy place which *was* in Shiloh, ᵇwhere I set My name at the first, and see ᶜwhat I did to it because of the wickedness of My people Israel. ¹³And now, because you have done all these works," says the LORD, "and I spoke to you, ᵃrising up early and speaking, but you did not hear, and I ᵇcalled you, but you did not answer, ¹⁴therefore I will do to the house which is called by My name, in which you trust, and to this place which I gave to you and your fathers, as I have done to ᵃShiloh. ¹⁵And I will cast you out of My sight, ᵃas I have cast out all your brethren—ᵇthe whole posterity of Ephraim.

¹⁶"Therefore ᵃdo not pray for this people, nor lift up a cry or prayer for them, nor make intercession to Me; ᵇfor I will not hear you. ¹⁷Do you not see what they do in the cities of Judah and in the streets of Jerusalem? ¹⁸ᵃThe children gather wood, the fathers kindle the fire, and the women knead dough, to make cakes for the queen of heaven; and *they* ᵇpour out drink offerings to other gods, that they may provoke Me to anger. ¹⁹ᵃDo they provoke Me to anger?" says the LORD. "*Do they* not *provoke* themselves, to the shame of their own faces?"

²⁰Therefore thus says the Lord GOD: "Behold, My anger and My fury will be poured out on this place—on man and on beast, on the trees of the field and on the fruit of the ground. And it will burn and not be quenched."

²¹Thus says the LORD of hosts, the God of Israel: ᵃ"Add your burnt offerings to your sacrifices and eat meat. ²²ᵃFor I did not speak to your fathers, or command them in the day that I brought them out of the land of Egypt, concerning burnt offerings or sacrifices. ²³But this is what I commanded them, saying, ᵃ'Obey My voice, and ᵇI will be your God, and you shall be My people. And walk in all the ways that I have commanded you, that it may be well with you.' ²⁴ᵃYet they did not obey or incline their ear, but ᵇfollowed¹ the counsels *and* the ²dictates of their evil hearts, and ᶜwent³ backward and not forward. ²⁵Since the day that your fathers came out of the land of Egypt until this day, I have even ᵃsent to you all My servants the prophets, daily rising up early and sending *them.* ²⁶ᵃYet they did not obey Me or incline their ear, but ᵇstiffened their neck. ᶜThey did worse than their fathers.

²⁷"Therefore ᵃyou shall speak all these words to them, but they will not obey you. You shall also call to them, but they will not answer you.

JUDGMENT ON OBSCENE RELIGION

²⁸"So you shall say to them, 'This *is* a nation that does not obey the voice of the LORD their God ᵃnor receive correction. ᵇTruth has perished and has been cut off from their mouth. ²⁹ᵃCut off your hair and cast *it* away, and take up a lamentation on the desolate heights; for the LORD has rejected and forsaken the generation of His wrath.' ³⁰For the children of Judah have done evil in My sight," says the LORD. ᵃ"They have

7:29 ᵃJob 1:20; Is. 15:2; Jer. 48:37; Mic. 1:16   7:30 ᵃ2 Kin. 21:4; 2 Chr. 33:3–5, 7;
Jer. 32:34, 35; Ezek. 7:20; Dan. 9:27; 11:31

7:24 ¹*walked in*   ²*stubbornness* or *imagination*   ³Lit. *they were*

set their abominations in the house which is called by My name, to ¹pollute it. ³¹And they have built the ᵃhigh places of Tophet, which *is* in the Valley of the Son of Hinnom, to ᵇburn their sons and their daughters in the fire, ᶜwhich I did not command, nor did it come into My heart.

³²"Therefore behold, ᵃthe days are coming," says the LORD, "when it will no more be called Tophet, or the Valley of the Son of Hinnom, but the Valley of Slaughter; ᵇfor they will bury in Tophet until there is no room. ³³The ᵃcorpses of this people will be food for the birds of the heaven and for the beasts of the earth. And no one will frighten *them away.* ³⁴Then I will cause to ᵃcease from the cities of Judah and from the streets of Jerusalem the voice of mirth and the voice of gladness, the voice of the bridegroom and the voice of the bride. For ᵇthe land shall be desolate.

8 "At that time," says the LORD, "they shall bring out the bones of the kings of Judah, and the bones of its princes, and the bones of the priests, and the bones of the prophets, and the bones of the inhabitants of Jerusalem, out of their graves. ²They shall spread them before the sun and the moon and all the host of heaven, which they have loved and which they have served and after which they have walked, which they have sought and ᵃwhich they have worshiped. They shall not be gathered ᵇnor buried; they shall be like refuse on the face of the earth. ³Then ᵃdeath shall be chosen rather than life by all the ¹residue of those who remain of this evil family, who remain in all the places where I have driven them," says the LORD of hosts.

THE PERIL OF FALSE TEACHING

⁴"Moreover you shall say to them, 'Thus says the LORD:

"Will they fall and not rise?
Will one turn away and not return?
5 Why has this people ᵃslidden back,
   Jerusalem, in a perpetual backsliding?
   ᵇThey hold fast to deceit,
   ᶜThey refuse to return.
6 ᵃI listened and heard,
   But they do not speak aright.
   ᵇNo man repented of his wickedness,
   Saying, 'What have I done?'
   Everyone turned to his own course,
   As the horse rushes into the battle.
7 "Even ᵃthe stork in the heavens
   Knows her appointed times;
   And the turtledove, the swift, and the swallow
   Observe the time of their coming.
   But ᵇMy people do not know the judgment of the LORD.
8 "How can you say, 'We *are* wise,
   ᵃAnd the law of the LORD *is* with us'?
   Look, the false pen of the scribe certainly works falsehood.
9 ᵃThe wise men are ashamed,
   They are dismayed and taken.
   Behold, they have rejected the word of the LORD;
   So ᵇwhat wisdom do they have?

7:31
ᵃ2 Kin. 23:10;
Jer. 19:5; 32:35
ᵇLev. 18:21;
2 Kin. 17:17;
Ps. 106:38
ᶜDeut. 17:3

7:32 ᵃJer. 19:6
ᵇ2 Kin. 23:10;
Jer. 19:11

7:33 ᵃJer. 9:22;
19:11; Ezek. 6:5

7:34 ᵃIs. 24:7, 8;
Jer. 16:9; 25:10;
Ezek. 26:13;
Hos. 2:11;
Rev. 18:23
ᵇLev. 26:33;
Is. 1:7; Jer. 4:27

8:2 ᵃ2 Kin. 23:5;
Jer. 19:13;
Ezek. 8:16;
Zeph. 1:5;
Acts 7:42
ᵇJer. 22:19

8:3
ᵃJob 3:21, 22;
7:15, 16; Jon. 4:3;
Rev. 9:6

8:5 ᵃJer. 7:24
ᵇJer. 9:6
ᶜJer. 5:3

8:6 ᵃPs. 14:2;
[Is. 30:18;
Mal. 3:16;
2 Pet. 3:9]
ᵇEzek. 22:30;
Mic. 7:2;
Rev. 9:20

8:7
ᵃProv. 6:6–8;
Song 2:12; Is. 1:3;
Matt. 16:2, 3
ᵇJer. 5:4; 9:3

8:8 ᵃRom. 2:17

8:9 ᵃIs. 19:11;
Jer. 6:15;
[1 Cor. 1:27]
ᵇIs. 44:25;
Jer. 4:22

7:30 ¹*defile*   8:3 ¹*remnant*

10　Therefore [a]I will give their wives to others,
　　And their fields to those who will inherit *them*;
　　Because from the least even to the greatest
　　Everyone is given to [b]covetousness;
　　From the prophet even to the priest
　　Everyone deals falsely.

11　For they have [a]healed the hurt of the daughter of My
　　　people [1]slightly,
　　Saying, [b]'Peace, peace!'
　　When *there is* no peace.

12　Were they [a]ashamed when they had committed
　　　abomination?
　　No! They were not at all ashamed,
　　Nor did they know how to blush.
　　Therefore they shall fall among those who fall;
　　In the time of their punishment
　　They shall be cast down," says the LORD.

13　"I will surely [1]consume them," says the LORD.
　　"No grapes *shall be* [a]on the vine,
　　Nor figs on the [b]fig tree,
　　And the leaf shall fade;
　　And *the things* I have given them shall [c]pass away from
　　　them."' "

14　"Why do we sit still?
　　[a]Assemble yourselves,
　　And let us enter the fortified cities,
　　And let us be silent there.
　　For the LORD our God has put us to silence
　　And given us [b]water[1] of gall to drink,
　　Because we have sinned against the LORD.

15　"*We* [a]looked for peace, but no good *came;*
　　And for a time of health, and there was trouble!

16　The snorting of His horses was heard from [a]Dan.
　　The whole land trembled at the sound of the neighing of
　　　His [b]strong ones;
　　For they have come and devoured the land and all that
　　　is in it,
　　The city and those who dwell in it."

17　"For behold, I will send serpents among you,
　　Vipers which cannot be [a]charmed,
　　And they shall bite you," says the LORD.

THE PROPHET MOURNS FOR THE PEOPLE

18　I would comfort myself in sorrow;
　　My heart *is* faint in me.

19　Listen! The voice,
　　The cry of the daughter of my people
　　From [a]a far country:
　　"*Is* not the LORD in Zion?
　　Is not her King in her?"

　　"Why have they provoked Me to anger
　　With their carved images—
　　With foreign idols?"

8:10
[a]Deut. 28:30;
Amos 5:11;
Zeph. 1:13
[b]Is. 56:11; 57:17;
Jer. 6:13
8:11 [a]Jer. 6:14
[b]Ezek. 13:10
8:12 [a]Ps. 52:1, 7;
Is. 3:9; Jer. 3:3;
6:15; Zeph. 3:5
8:13
[a]Jer. 5:17; 7:20;
Joel 1:17
[b]Matt. 21:19;
Luke 13:6
[c]Deut. 28:39, 40
8:14 [a]Jer. 4:5
[b]Deut. 29:18;
Ps. 69:21;
Jer. 9:15;
Lam. 3:19;
Matt. 27:34
8:15 [a]Jer. 14:19
8:16
[a]Judg. 18:29;
Jer. 4:15
[b]Jer. 47:3
8:17 [a]Ps. 58:4, 5
8:19 [a]Is. 39:3;
Jer. 5:15

8:11 [1]Superficially　**8:13** [1]Or *take them away*　**8:14** [1]Bitter or poisonous water

20 "The harvest is past,
 The summer is ended,
 And we are not saved!"

21 ^aFor the hurt of the daughter of my people I am hurt.
 I am ^bmourning;
 Astonishment has taken hold of me.
22 *Is there* no ^abalm in Gilead,
 Is there no physician there?
 Why then is there no recovery
 For the health of the daughter of my people?

9 Oh, ^athat my head were waters,
 And my eyes a fountain of tears,
 That I might weep day and night
 For the slain of the daughter of my people!
2 Oh, that I had in the wilderness
 A lodging place for travelers;
 That I might leave my people,
 And go from them!
 For ^athey *are* all adulterers,
 An assembly of treacherous men.

3 "And *like* their bow ^athey have bent their tongues *for* lies.
 They are not valiant for the truth on the earth.
 For they proceed from ^bevil to evil,
 And they ^cdo not know Me," says the LORD.
4 "Everyone^a take heed to his ¹neighbor,
 And do not trust any brother;
 For every brother will utterly supplant,
 And every neighbor will ^bwalk with slanderers.
5 Everyone will ^adeceive his neighbor,
 And will not speak the truth;
 They have taught their tongue to speak lies;
 They weary themselves to commit iniquity.
6 Your dwelling place *is* in the midst of deceit;
 Through deceit they refuse to know Me," says the LORD.

⁷Therefore thus says the LORD of hosts:

"Behold, ^aI will refine them and ¹try them;
 ^bFor how shall I deal with the daughter of My people?
8 Their tongue *is* an arrow shot out;
 It speaks ^adeceit;
 One speaks ^bpeaceably to his neighbor with his mouth,
 But ¹in his heart he ²lies in wait.
9 ^aShall I not punish them for these *things*?" says the
 LORD.
 "Shall I not avenge Myself on such a nation as this?"

10 I will take up a weeping and wailing for the mountains,
 And ^afor the ¹dwelling places of the wilderness a
 lamentation,
 Because they are burned up,
 So that no one can pass through;
 Nor can *men* hear the voice of the cattle.
 ^bBoth the birds of the heavens and the beasts have fled;
 They are gone.

8:21 ^aJer. 9:1
^bJer. 14:2;
Joel 2:6;
Nah. 2:10

8:22
^aGen. 37:25;
Jer. 46:11

9:1 ^aIs. 22:4;
Jer. 10:19;
Lam. 2:18

9:2 ^aJer. 5:7, 8;
23:10; Hos. 4:2

9:3 ^aPs. 64:3;
Is. 59:4; Jer. 9:8;
Hos. 4:1, 2
^bJer. 4:22; 13:23
^cJudg. 2:10;
1 Sam. 2:12;
Jer. 4:22;
Hos. 4:1;
1 Cor. 15:34

9:4 ^aPs. 12:2;
Prov. 26:24, 25;
Jer. 9:8;
Mic. 7:5, 6
^bPs. 15:3;
Prov. 10:18;
Jer. 6:28

9:5 ^aPs. 36:3, 4;
Is. 59:4

9:7 ^aIs. 1:25;
Jer. 6:27;
Mal. 3:3
^bHos. 11:8

9:8 ^aPs. 12:2
^bPs. 55:21

9:9 ^aIs. 1:24;
Jer. 5:9, 29

9:10 ^aJer. 4:26;
Hos. 4:3
^bJer. 4:25;
Hos. 4:3

9:4 ¹friend 9:7 ¹test 9:8 ¹Inwardly he ²sets his ambush 9:10 ¹Or
pastures

11 "I will make Jerusalem ᵃa heap of ruins, ᵇa den of jackals.
   I will make the cities of Judah desolate, without an
   inhabitant."

12ᵃWho *is* the wise man who may understand this? And
who is he to whom the mouth of the LORD has spoken, that he
may declare it? Why does the land perish *and* burn up like a
wilderness, so that no one can pass through?

13And the LORD said, "Because they have forsaken My law
which I set before them, and have ᵃnot obeyed My voice, nor
walked according to it, 14but they have ᵃwalked according to
the ¹dictates of their own hearts and after the Baals, ᵇwhich
their fathers taught them," 15therefore thus says the LORD of
hosts, the God of Israel: "Behold, I will ᵃfeed them, this people, ᵇwith wormwood, and give them ¹water of gall to drink.
16I will ᵃscatter them also among the Gentiles, whom neither
they nor their fathers have known. ᵇAnd I will send a sword
after them until I have consumed them."

THE PEOPLE MOURN IN JUDGMENT

17Thus says the LORD of hosts:

"Consider and call for ᵃthe mourning women,
   That they may come;
And send for skillful *wailing* women,
   That they may come.
18 Let them make haste
   And take up a wailing for us,
   That ᵃour eyes may run with tears,
   And our eyelids gush with water.
19 For a voice of wailing is heard from Zion:
   'How we are plundered!
   We are greatly ashamed,
   Because we have forsaken the land,
   Because we have been cast out of ᵃour dwellings.'"

20 Yet hear the word of the LORD, O women,
   And let your ear receive the word of His mouth;
   Teach your daughters wailing,
   And everyone her neighbor a lamentation.
21 For death has come through our windows,
   Has entered our palaces,
   To kill off ᵃthe children—¹*no longer to be* outside!
   And the young men—²*no longer* on the streets!

22Speak, "Thus says the LORD:

'Even the carcasses of men shall fall ᵃas refuse on the
      open field,
   Like cuttings after the harvester,
   And no one shall gather *them*.'"

23Thus says the LORD:

ᵃ"Let not the wise *man* glory in his wisdom,
   Let not the mighty *man* glory in his ᵇmight,
   Nor let the rich *man* glory in his riches;
24 But ᵃlet him who glories glory in this,
   That he understands and knows Me,

Cross references (left margin):

9:11 ᵃIs. 25:2;
Jer. 19:3, 8; 26:9
ᵇIs. 13:22; 34:13
9:12 ᵃPs. 107:43;
Is. 42:23;
Hos. 14:9
9:13
ᵃJer. 3:25; 7:24
9:14
ᵃJer. 7:24; 11:8;
Rom. 1:21–24
ᵇGal. 1:14;
1 Pet. 1:18
9:15 ᵃPs. 80:5
ᵇDeut. 29:18;
Jer. 8:14; 23:15;
Lam. 3:15
9:16 ᵃLev. 26:33;
Deut. 28:64;
Jer. 15:2–4
ᵇLev. 26:33;
Jer. 44:27;
Ezek. 5:2
9:17
ᵃ2 Chr. 35:25;
Job 3:8;
Eccl. 12:5;
Amos 5:16;
Matt. 9:23
9:18 ᵃIs. 22:4;
Jer. 9:1; 14:17
9:19 ᵃLev. 18:28
9:21
ᵃ2 Chr. 36:17;
Jer. 6:11; 18:21;
Ezek. 9:5, 6
9:22 ᵃPs. 83:10;
Is. 5:25;
Jer. 8:1, 2
9:23 ᵃ[Eccl. 9:11;
Is. 47:10];
Ezek. 28:3–7
ᵇPs. 33:16–18
9:24 ᵃPs. 20:7;
44:8; Is. 41:16;
Jer. 4:2;
1 Cor. 1:31;
2 Cor. 10:17;
[Gal. 6:14]

9:14 ¹*stubbornness* or *imagination*   **9:15** ¹*Bitter or poisonous water*
9:21 ¹Lit. *from outside*   ²Lit. *from the square*

That I *am* the LORD, exercising lovingkindness,
¹judgment, and righteousness in the earth.
ᵇFor in these I delight," says the LORD.

²⁵"Behold, the days are coming," says the LORD, "that ᵃI will punish all *who are* circumcised with the uncircumcised— ²⁶Egypt, Judah, Edom, the people of Ammon, Moab, and all *who are* in the ᵃfarthest corners, who dwell in the wilderness. For all *these* nations *are* uncircumcised, and all the house of Israel *are* ᵇuncircumcised in the heart."

IDOLS AND THE TRUE GOD

10 Hear the word which the LORD speaks to you, O house of Israel.

²Thus says the LORD:

ᵃ"Do not learn the way of the Gentiles;
Do not be dismayed at the signs of heaven,
For the Gentiles are dismayed at them.
3   For the customs of the peoples *are* ¹futile;
For ᵃ*one* cuts a tree from the forest,
The work of the hands of the workman, with the ax.
4   They decorate it with silver and gold;
They ᵃfasten it with nails and hammers
So that it will not topple.
5   They *are* upright, like a palm tree,
And ᵃthey cannot speak;
They must be ᵇcarried,
Because they cannot go *by themselves*.
Do not be afraid of them,
For ᶜthey cannot do evil,
Nor can they do any good."

6   Inasmuch as *there is* none ᵃlike You, O LORD
(You *are* great, and Your name *is* great in might),
7   ᵃWho would not fear You, O King of the nations?
For this is Your rightful due.
For ᵇamong all the wise *men* of the nations,
And in all their kingdoms,
There is none like You.
8   But they are altogether ᵃdull-hearted and foolish;
A wooden idol *is* a ¹worthless doctrine.
9   Silver is beaten into plates;
It is brought from Tarshish,
And ᵃgold from Uphaz,
The work of the craftsman
And of the hands of the metalsmith;
Blue and purple *are* their clothing;
They *are* all ᵇthe work of skillful *men*.
10   But the LORD *is* the true God;
He *is* ᵃthe living God and the ᵇeverlasting King.
At His wrath the earth will tremble,
And the nations will not be able to endure His
indignation.

¹¹Thus you shall say to them: ᵃ"The gods that have not made the heavens and the earth ᵇshall perish from the earth and from under these heavens."

9:24 ᵇIs. 61:8;
Mic. 7:18

9:25 ᵃ[Jer. 4:4;
Rom. 2:28, 29]

9:26 ᵃJer. 25:23
ᵇLev. 26:41;
Jer. 4:4; 6:10;
Ezek. 44:7;
[Rom. 2:28]

10:2
ᵃ[Lev. 18:3;
20:23;
Deut. 12:30]

10:3 ᵃIs. 40:19;
45:20

10:4 ᵃIs. 41:7

10:5 ᵃPs. 115:5;
Is. 46:7;
Jer. 10:5;
1 Cor. 12:2
ᵇPs. 115:7;
Is. 46:1, 7
ᶜIs. 41:23, 24

10:6 ᵃEx. 15:11;
Deut. 33:26;
Ps. 86:8, 10;
Is. 46:5–9;
Jer. 10:16

10:7 ᵃJer. 5:22;
Rev. 15:4
ᵇPs. 89:6

10:8 ᵃPs. 115:8;
Hab. 2:18

10:9 ᵃDan. 10:5
ᵇPs. 115:4

10:10
ᵃ1 Tim. 6:17
ᵇPs. 10:16

10:11 ᵃPs. 96:5
ᵇIs. 2:18;
Zeph. 2:11

9:24 ¹*justice*   10:3 ¹Lit. *vanity*   10:8 ¹*vain teaching*

12 He ᵃhas made the earth by His power,
   He has ᵇestablished the world by His wisdom,
   And ᶜhas stretched out the heavens at His discretion.
13 ᵃWhen He utters His voice,
   There is a ¹multitude of waters in the heavens:
   ᵇ"And He causes the vapors to ascend from the ends of the
      earth.
   He makes lightning for the rain,
   He brings the wind out of His treasuries."
14 ᵃEveryone is ᵇdull-hearted, without knowledge;
   ᶜEvery metalsmith is put to shame by an image;
   ᵈFor his molded image *is* falsehood,
   And *there is* no breath in them.
15 They *are* futile, a work of errors;
   In the time of their punishment they shall perish.
16 ᵃThe Portion of Jacob *is* not like them,
   For He *is* the Maker of all *things,*
   And ᵇIsrael *is* the tribe of His inheritance;
   ᶜThe LORD of hosts *is* His name.

THE COMING CAPTIVITY OF JUDAH

17 ᵃGather up your wares from the land,
   O ¹inhabitant of the fortress!

   18For thus says the LORD:

   "Behold, I will ᵃthrow out at this time
   The inhabitants of the land,
   And will distress them,
   ᵇThat they may find *it so."*

19 ᵃWoe is me for my hurt!
   My wound is severe.
   But I say, ᵇ"Truly this *is* an infirmity,
   And ᶜI must bear it."
20 ᵃMy tent is plundered,
   And all my cords are broken;
   My children have gone from me,
   And they *are* ᵇno more.
   There is no one to pitch my tent anymore,
   Or set up my curtains.
21 For the shepherds have become dull-hearted,
   And have not sought the LORD;
   Therefore they shall not prosper,
   And all their flocks shall be ᵃscattered.
22 Behold, the noise of the report has come,
   And a great commotion out of the ᵃnorth country,
   To make the cities of Judah desolate, a ᵇden of jackals.
23 O LORD, I know the ᵃway of man *is* not in himself;
   It is not in man who walks to direct his own steps.
24 O LORD, ᵃcorrect me, but with justice;
   Not in Your anger, lest You bring me to nothing.
25 ᵃPour out Your fury on the Gentiles, ᵇwho do not know You,
   And on the families who do not call on Your name;
   For they have eaten up Jacob,
   ᶜDevoured him and consumed him,
   And made his dwelling place desolate.

Cross-references

10:12
ᵃGen. 1:1, 6, 7;
Jer. 51:15
ᵇPs. 93:1
ᶜJob 9:8;
Ps. 104:2;
Is. 40:22

10:13 ᵃJob 38:34
ᵇPs. 135:7

10:14 ᵃJer. 51:17
ᵇProv. 30:2
ᶜIs. 42:17; 44:11
ᵈHab. 2:18

10:16 ᵃPs. 16:5;
Jer. 51:19;
Lam. 3:24
ᵇDeut. 32:9;
Ps. 74:2 ᶜIs. 47:4

10:17 ᵃJer. 6:1

10:18
ᵃ1 Sam. 25:29;
2 Chr. 36:20
ᵇEzek. 6:10

10:19 ᵃJer. 8:21
ᵇPs. 77:10
ᶜMic. 7:9

10:20 ᵃJer. 4:20;
Lam. 2:4
ᵇJer. 31:15;
Lam. 1:5

10:21 ᵃJer. 23:2

10:22 ᵃJer. 5:15
ᵇJer. 9:11

10:23
ᵃProv. 16:1;
20:24

10:24
ᵃPs. 6:1; 38:1;
Jer. 30:11

10:25
ᵃPs. 79:6, 7;
Zeph. 3:8
ᵇJob 18:21;
1 Thess. 4:5;
[2 Thess. 1:8]
ᶜJer. 8:16

10:13 ¹Or *noise*   10:17 ¹Or *you who dwell under siege*

THE BROKEN COVENANT

11 The word that came to Jeremiah from the LORD, saying, ²"Hear the words of this covenant, and speak to the men of Judah and to the inhabitants of Jerusalem; ³and say to them, 'Thus says the LORD God of Israel: ᵃ"Cursed *is* the man who does not obey the words of this covenant ⁴which I commanded your fathers in the day I brought them out of the land of Egypt, ᵃfrom the iron furnace, saying, ᵇ'Obey My voice, and do according to all that I command you; so shall you be My people, and I will be your God,' ⁵that I may establish the ᵃoath which I have sworn to your fathers, to give them ᵇ'a land flowing with milk and honey,' as *it is* this day."'"

And I answered and said, ¹"So be it, LORD."

⁶Then the LORD said to me, "Proclaim all these words in the cities of Judah and in the streets of Jerusalem, saying: 'Hear the words of this covenant ᵃand do them. ⁷For I earnestly exhorted your fathers in the day I brought them up out of the land of Egypt, until this day, ᵃrising early and exhorting, saying, "Obey My voice." ⁸ᵃYet they did not obey or incline their ear, but ᵇeveryone ¹followed the dictates of his evil heart; therefore I will bring upon them all the words of this covenant, which I commanded *them* to do, but *which* they have not done.'"

⁹And the LORD said to me, ᵃ"A conspiracy has been found among the men of Judah and among the inhabitants of Jerusalem. ¹⁰They have turned back to ᵃthe iniquities of their forefathers who refused to hear My words, and they have gone after other gods to serve them; the house of Israel and the house of Judah have broken My covenant which I made with their fathers."

¹¹Therefore thus says the LORD: "Behold, I will surely bring calamity on them which they will not be able to ¹escape; and ᵃthough they cry out to Me, I will not listen to them. ¹²Then the cities of Judah and the inhabitants of Jerusalem will go and ᵃcry out to the gods to whom they offer incense, but they will not save them at all in the time of their trouble. ¹³For *according to* the number of your ᵃcities were your gods, O Judah; and *according to* the number of the streets of Jerusalem you have set up altars to *that* shameful thing, altars to burn incense to Baal.

¹⁴"So ᵃdo not pray for this people, or lift up a cry or prayer for them; for I will not hear *them* in the time that they cry out to Me because of their trouble.

15 "Whatᵃ has My beloved to do in My house,
　Having ᵇdone lewd deeds with many?
　And ᶜthe holy flesh has passed from you.
　When you do evil, then you ᵈrejoice.
16 The LORD called your name,
　ᵃGreen Olive Tree, Lovely *and* of Good Fruit.
　With the noise of a great tumult
　He has kindled fire on it,
　And its branches are broken.

¹⁷"For the LORD of hosts, ᵃwho planted you, has pronounced doom against you for the evil of the house of Israel and of the

11:3
ᵃDeut. 27:26;
[Jer. 17:5];
Gal. 3:10

11:4 ᵃDeut. 4:20;
1 Kin. 8:51
ᵇLev. 26:3;
Deut. 11:27;
Jer. 7:23

11:5 ᵃEx. 13:5;
Deut. 7:12;
Ps. 105:9;
Jer. 32:22
ᵇEx. 3:8

11:6 ᵃDeut. 17:19;
[Rom. 2:13];
James 1:22

11:7 ᵃJer. 35:15

11:8 ᵃJer. 7:26
ᵇJer. 13:10

11:9
ᵃEzek. 22:25;
Hos. 6:9

11:10
ᵃ1 Sam. 15:11;
Jer. 3:10, 11;
Ezek. 20:18

11:11 ᵃPs. 18:41;
Prov. 1:28;
Is. 1:15; Jer. 14:12;
Ezek. 8:18;
Mic. 3:4;
Zech. 7:13

11:12
ᵃDeut. 32:37;
Jer. 44:17

11:13
ᵃ2 Kin. 23:13;
Jer. 2:28

11:14 ᵃEx. 32:10;
Jer. 7:16; 14:11;
[1 John 5:16]

11:15 ᵃPs. 50:16
ᵇEzek. 16:25
ᶜ[Titus 1:15]
ᵈProv. 2:14

11:16 ᵃPs. 52:8;
[Rom. 11:17]

11:17 ᵃIs. 5:2;
Jer. 2:21; 12:2

11:5 ¹Heb. Amen　11:8 ¹*walked in the stubbornness* or *imagination*
11:11 ¹Lit. *go out*

house of Judah, which they have done against themselves to provoke Me to anger in offering incense to Baal."

JEREMIAH'S LIFE THREATENED

18Now the LORD gave me knowledge *of it,* and I know *it;* for You showed me their doings. 19But I *was* like a docile lamb brought to the slaughter; and I did not know that they had devised schemes against me, *saying,* "Let us destroy the tree with its fruit, ªand let us cut him off from ᵇthe land of the living, that his name may be remembered no more."

20 But, O LORD of hosts,
     You who judge righteously,
   ªTesting the ¹mind and the heart,
     Let me see Your ᵇvengeance on them,
     For to You I have revealed my cause.

21"Therefore thus says the LORD concerning the men of ªAnathoth who seek your life, saying, ᵇ'Do not prophesy in the name of the LORD, lest you die by our hand'— 22therefore thus says the LORD of hosts: 'Behold, I will punish them. The young men shall die by the sword, their sons and their daughters shall ªdie by famine; 23and there shall be no remnant of them, for I will bring catastrophe on the men of Anathoth, *even* ªthe year of their punishment.'"

JEREMIAH'S QUESTION

12 Righteous ªare You, O LORD, when I plead with You;
     Yet let me talk with You about *Your* judgments.
   ᵇWhy does the way of the wicked prosper?
     Why are those happy who deal so treacherously?
2   You have planted them, yes, they have taken root;
     They grow, yes, they bear fruit.
   ªYou *are* near in their mouth
     But far from their ¹mind.
3   But You, O LORD, ªknow me;
     You have seen me,
     And You have ᵇtested my heart toward You.
     Pull them out like sheep for the slaughter,
     And prepare them for ᶜthe day of slaughter.
4   How long will ªthe land mourn,
     And the herbs of every field wither?
   ᵇThe beasts and birds are consumed,
   ᶜFor the wickedness of those who dwell there,
     Because they said, "He will not see our final end."

THE LORD ANSWERS JEREMIAH

5   "If you have run with the footmen, and they have wearied you,
     Then how can you contend with horses?
     And *if* in the land of peace,
     In which you trusted, *they wearied you,*
     Then how will you do in ªthe ¹floodplain of the Jordan?
6   For even ªyour brothers, the house of your father,
     Even they have dealt treacherously with you;
     Yes, they have called ¹a multitude after you.

11:19 ªPs. 83:4;
Jer. 18:18
ᵇPs. 27:13

11:20
ª1 Sam. 16:7;
1 Chr. 28:9;
Ps. 7:9 ᵇJer. 15:15

11:21
ªJer. 1:1; 12:5, 6
ᵇIs. 30:10;
Amos 2:12;
Mic. 2:6

11:22 ªJer. 9:21

11:23 ªJer. 23:12;
Hos. 9:7;
Mic. 7:4

12:1 ªEzra 9:15;
Ps. 51:4;
Jer. 11:20
ᵇJob 12:6;
Jer. 5:27, 28;
Hab. 1:4;
Mal. 3:15

12:2 ªIs. 29:13;
Ezek. 33:31;
Matt. 15:8;
Mark 7:6

12:3 ªPs. 17:3
ᵇPs. 7:9; 11:5;
Jer. 11:20
ᶜJer. 17:18;
50:27;
James 5:5

12:4 ªJer. 23:10;
Hos. 4:3
ᵇJer. 9:10;
Hos. 4:3;
Hab. 3:17
ᶜPs. 107:34

12:5 ªJosh. 3:15;
1 Chr. 12:15

12:6
ªGen. 37:4–11;
Job 6:15;
Ps. 69:8;
Jer. 9:4, 5

11:20 ¹Most secret parts, lit. *kidneys*   12:2 ¹Most secret parts, lit. *kidneys*
12:5 ¹Or *thicket*   12:6 ¹Or *abundantly*

> ᵇDo not believe them,
> Even though they speak ²smooth words to you.

7 "I have forsaken My house, I have left My
> heritage;
> I have given the dearly beloved of My soul into the hand
> of her enemies.
8 My heritage is to Me like a lion in the forest;
> It cries out against Me;
> Therefore I have ᵃhated it.
9 My ¹heritage *is* to Me *like* a speckled vulture;
> The vultures all around *are* against her.
> Come, assemble all the beasts of the field,
> ᵃBring them to devour!

10 "Many ᵃrulers¹ have destroyed ᵇMy vineyard,
> They have ᶜtrodden My portion underfoot;
> They have made My ²pleasant portion a desolate
> wilderness.
11 They have made it ᵃdesolate;
> Desolate, it mourns to Me;
> The whole land is made desolate,
> Because ᵇno one takes *it* to heart.
12 The plunderers have come
> On all the desolate heights in the wilderness,
> For the sword of the LORD shall devour
> From *one* end of the land to the *other* end of the land;
> No flesh shall have peace.
13 ᵃThey have sown wheat but reaped thorns;
> They have ¹put themselves to pain *but* do not profit.
> But be ashamed of your harvest
> Because of the fierce anger of the LORD."

¹⁴Thus says the LORD: "Against all My evil neighbors who
ᵃtouch the inheritance which I have caused My people Israel
to inherit—behold, I will ᵇpluck them out of their land and
pluck out the house of Judah from among them. ¹⁵ᵃThen it
shall be, after I have plucked them out, that I will return and
have compassion on them ᵇand bring them back, everyone to
his heritage and everyone to his land. ¹⁶And it shall be, if they
will learn carefully the ways of My people, ᵃto swear by My
name, 'As the LORD lives,' as they taught My people to swear
by Baal, then they shall be ᵇestablished in the midst of My
people. ¹⁷But if they do not ᵃobey, I will utterly pluck up and
destroy that nation," says the LORD.

SYMBOL OF THE LINEN SASH

13 Thus the LORD said to me: "Go and get yourself a linen
sash, and put it ¹around your waist, but do not put it in
water." ²So I got a ¹sash according to the word of the LORD,
and put *it* around my waist.

³And the word of the LORD came to me the second time,
saying, ⁴"Take the ¹sash that you acquired, which *is* ²around
your waist, and arise, go to the ³Euphrates, and hide it there
in a hole in the rock." ⁵So I went and hid it by the Euphrates,
as the LORD commanded me.

12:6 ᵇPs. 12:2;
Prov. 26:25

12:8 ᵃHos. 9:15;
Amos 6:8

12:9 ᵃLev. 26:22

12:10
ᵃJer. 6:3; 23:1
ᵇPs. 80:8–16;
Is. 5:1–7
ᶜIs. 63:18

12:11
ᵃJer. 10:22; 22:6
ᵇIs. 42:25

12:13
ᵃLev. 26:16;
Deut. 28:38;
Mic. 6:15;
Hag. 1:6

12:14 ᵃJer. 2:3;
50:11, 12;
Zech. 2:8
ᵇDeut. 30:3;
Ps. 106:47;
Is. 11:11–16;
Jer. 32:37

12:15 ᵃJer. 31:20;
Lam. 3:32;
Ezek. 28:25
ᵇAmos 9:14

12:16 ᵃ[Jer. 4:2];
Zeph. 1:5
ᵇ[Eph. 2:20, 21;
1 Pet. 2:5]

12:17
ᵃPs. 2:8–12;
Is. 60:12

12:6 ²Lit. *good*   12:9 ¹*inheritance*   12:10 ¹Lit. *shepherds* or *pastors*
²*desired portion* of land   12:13 ¹Or *strained*   13:1 ¹Lit. *upon your loins*
13:2 ¹*waistband*   13:4 ¹*waistband*   ²Lit. *upon your loins*   ³Heb. *Perath*

6Now it came to pass after many days that the LORD said to me, "Arise, go to the Euphrates, and take from there the sash which I commanded you to hide there." 7Then I went to the Euphrates and dug, and I took the ¹sash from the place where I had hidden it; and there was the sash, ruined. It was profitable for nothing.

8Then the word of the LORD came to me, saying, 9"Thus says the LORD: 'In this manner ªI will ruin the pride of Judah and the great ᵇpride of Jerusalem. 10This evil people, who ªrefuse to hear My words, who ᵇfollow¹ the dictates of their hearts, and walk after other gods to serve them and worship them, shall be just like this sash which is profitable for nothing. 11For as the sash clings to the waist of a man, so I have caused the whole house of Israel and the whole house of Judah to cling to Me,' says the LORD, 'that ªthey may become My people, ᵇfor renown, for praise, and for ᶜglory; but they would ᵈnot hear.'

SYMBOL OF THE WINE BOTTLES

12"Therefore you shall speak to them this word: 'Thus says the LORD God of Israel: "Every bottle shall be filled with wine."'

"And they will say to you, 'Do we not certainly know that every bottle will be filled with wine?'

13"Then you shall say to them, 'Thus says the LORD: "Behold, I will fill all the inhabitants of this land—even the kings who sit on David's throne, the priests, the prophets, and all the inhabitants of Jerusalem—ªwith drunkenness! 14And ªI will dash them ¹one against another, even the fathers and the sons together," says the LORD. "I will not pity nor spare nor have mercy, but will destroy them."'"

PRIDE PRECEDES CAPTIVITY

15 Hear and give ear:
    Do not be proud,
    For the LORD has spoken.
16 ªGive glory to the LORD your God
    Before He causes ᵇdarkness,
    And before your feet stumble
    On the dark mountains,
    And while you are ᶜlooking for light,
    He turns it into ᵈthe shadow of death
    And makes it dense darkness.
17 But if you will not hear it,
    My soul will ªweep in secret for your pride;
    My eyes will weep bitterly
    And run down with tears,
    Because the LORD's flock has been taken captive.

18 Say to ªthe king and to the queen mother,
    "Humble yourselves;
    Sit down,
    For your rule shall collapse, the crown of your glory."
19 The cities of the South shall be shut up,
    And no one shall open them;
    Judah shall be carried away captive, all of it;
    It shall be wholly carried away captive.

13:9 ªLev. 26:19
ᵇ[Is. 2:10–17; 23:9]; Zeph. 3:11
13:10 ªJer. 16:12
ᵇJer. 7:24; 16:12

13:11
ª[Ex. 19:5, 6; Deut. 32:10, 11]
ᵇJer. 33:9
ᶜIs. 43:21
ᵈPs. 81:11; Jer. 7:13, 24, 26

13:13
ªPs. 60:3; 75:8; Is. 51:17; 63:6; Jer. 25:27; 51:7, 57

13:14
ª2 Chr. 36:17; Ps. 2:9; Is. 9:20, 21; Jer. 19:9–11

13:16
ªJosh. 7:19; Ps. 96:8; Mal. 2:2
ᵇIs. 5:30; 8:22; Amos 8:9
ᶜIs. 59:9
ᵈPs. 44:19; Jer. 2:6

13:17
ªPs. 119:136; Jer. 9:1; 14:17; Luke 19:41, 42

13:18
ª2 Kin. 24:12; Jer. 22:26

13:7 ¹waistband   13:10 ¹walk in the stubbornness or imagination
13:14 ¹Lit. a man against his brother

20 Lift up your eyes and see
Those who come from the ªnorth.
Where *is* the flock *that* was given to you,
Your beautiful sheep?
21 What will you say when He punishes you?
For you have taught them
To be chieftains, to be head over you.
Will not ªpangs seize you,
Like a woman in ¹labor?
22 And if you say in your heart,
ª"Why have these things come upon me?"
For the greatness of your iniquity
ᵇYour skirts have been uncovered,
Your heels ¹made bare.
23 Can the Ethiopian change his skin or the leopard its
spots?
Then may you also do good who are accustomed to do
evil.
24 "Therefore I will ªscatter them ᵇlike stubble
That passes away by the wind of the wilderness.
25 ªThis is your lot,
The portion of your measures from Me," says the
LORD,
"Because you have forgotten Me
And trusted in ᵇfalsehood.
26 Therefore ªI will uncover your skirts over your face,
That your shame may appear.
27 I have seen your adulteries
And your *lustful* ªneighings,
The lewdness of your harlotry,
Your abominations ᵇon the hills in the fields.
Woe to you, O Jerusalem!
Will you still not be made clean?"

SWORD, FAMINE, AND PESTILENCE

14 The word of the LORD that came to Jeremiah concerning the droughts.

2 "Judah mourns,
And ªher gates languish;
They ᵇmourn for the land,
And ᶜthe cry of Jerusalem has gone up.
3 Their nobles have sent their lads for water;
They went to the cisterns *and* found no water.
They returned with their vessels empty;
They were ªashamed and confounded
ᵇAnd covered their heads.
4 Because the ground is parched,
For there was ªno rain in the land,
The plowmen were ashamed;
They covered their heads.
5 Yes, the deer also gave birth in the field,
But ¹left because there was no grass.
6 And ªthe wild donkeys stood in the desolate heights;
They sniffed at the wind like jackals;
Their eyes failed because *there was* no grass."

13:20
ªJer. 10:22;
46:20

13:21 ªJer. 6:24

13:22 ªJer. 16:10
ᵇIs. 47:2;
Ezek. 16:37;
Nah. 3:5

13:24
ªLev. 26:33;
Jer. 9:16;
Ezek. 5:2, 12
ᵇPs. 1:4;
Hos. 13:3

13:25
ªJob 20:29;
Ps. 11:6;
Matt. 24:51
ᵇJer. 10:14

13:26 ªLam. 1:8;
Ezek. 16:37;
Hos. 2:10

13:27 ªJer. 5:7, 8
ᵇIs. 65:7;
Jer. 2:20;
Ezek. 6:13

14:2
ª2 Kin. 25:3;
Is. 3:26
ᵇJer. 8:21
ᶜ1 Sam. 5:12;
Jer. 11:11; 46:12;
Zech. 7:13

14:3 ªJob 6:20;
Ps. 40:14
ᵇ2 Sam. 15:30

14:4 ªJer. 3:3;
Ezek. 22:24

14:6
ªJob 39:5, 6;
Jer. 2:24

7 O Lᴏʀᴅ, though our iniquities testify against us,
Do it ᵃfor Your name's sake;
For our backslidings are many,
We have sinned against You.

8 ᵃO the Hope of Israel, his Savior in time of trouble,
Why should You be like a stranger in the land,
And like a traveler *who* turns aside to tarry for a night?

9 Why should You be like a man astonished,
Like a mighty one ᵃ*who* cannot save?
Yet You, O Lᴏʀᴅ, ᵇ*are* in our midst,
And we are called by Your name;
Do not leave us!

10Thus says the Lᴏʀᴅ to this people:

ᵃ"Thus they have loved to wander;
They have not restrained their feet.
Therefore the Lᴏʀᴅ does not accept them;
ᵇHe will remember their iniquity now,
And punish their sins."

11Then the Lᴏʀᴅ said to me, ᵃ"Do not pray for this people, for *their* good. 12ᵃWhen they fast, I will not hear their cry; and ᵇwhen they offer burnt offering and grain offering, I will not accept them. But ᶜI will consume them by the sword, by the famine, and by the pestilence."

13ᵃThen I said, "Ah, Lord Gᴏᴅ! Behold, the prophets say to them, 'You shall not see the sword, nor shall you have famine, but I will give you ¹assured ᵇpeace in this place.'"

14And the Lᴏʀᴅ said to me, ᵃ"The prophets prophesy lies in My name. ᵇI have not sent them, commanded them, nor spoken to them; they prophesy to you a false vision, ¹divination, a worthless thing, and the ᶜdeceit of their heart. 15Therefore thus says the Lᴏʀᴅ concerning the prophets who prophesy in My name, whom I did not send, ᵃand who say, 'Sword and famine shall not be in this land'—'By sword and famine those prophets shall be consumed! 16And the people to whom they prophesy shall be cast out in the streets of Jerusalem because of the famine and the sword; ᵃthey will have no one to bury them—them nor their wives, their sons nor their daughters—for I will pour their wickedness on them.'

17"Therefore you shall say this word to them:

ᵃ'Let my eyes flow with tears night and day,
And let them not cease;
ᵇFor the virgin daughter of my people
Has been broken with a mighty stroke, with a very severe blow.

18 If I go out to ᵃthe field,
Then behold, those slain with the sword!
And if I enter the city,
Then behold, those sick from famine!
Yes, both prophet and ᵇpriest go about in a land they do not know.'"

THE PEOPLE PLEAD FOR MERCY

19 ᵃHave You utterly rejected Judah?
Has Your soul loathed Zion?

14:7 ᵃPs. 25:11;
Jer. 14:21

14:8 ᵃJer. 17:13

14:9 ᵃIs. 59:1
ᵇEx. 29:45;
Lev. 26:11;
Ps. 46:5;
Jer. 8:19

14:10
ᵃJer. 2:23–25
ᵇ[Jer. 44:21–23];
Hos. 8:13

14:11 ᵃEx. 32:10;
Jer. 7:16; 11:14

14:12 ᵃProv. 1:28;
[Is. 1:15; 58:3–6];
Ezek. 8:18;
Mic. 3:4;
Zech. 7:13
ᵇJer. 6:20
ᶜJer. 9:16

14:13 ᵃJer. 4:10
ᵇJer. 8:11; 23:17

14:14 ᵃJer. 27:10
ᵇJer. 29:8, 9
ᶜJer. 23:16;
Ezek. 12:24

14:15 ᵃJer. 5:12;
Ezek. 14:10

14:16
ᵃPs. 79:2, 3;
Jer. 7:32; 15:2, 3

14:17 ᵃJer. 9:1;
13:17; Lam. 1:16
ᵇIs. 37:22;
Jer. 8:21;
Lam. 1:15; 2:13

14:18 ᵃJer. 6:25;
Lam. 1:20;
Ezek. 7:15
ᵇJer. 23:11

14:19 ᵃJer. 6:30;
7:29; 12:7;
Lam. 5:22

14:13 ¹*true*   14:14 ¹Telling the future by signs and omens

Why have You stricken us so that ᵇthere is no healing for us?
ᶜWe looked for peace, but there was no good;
And for the time of healing, and there was trouble.

20 We acknowledge, O LORD, our wickedness
And the iniquity of our ᵃfathers,
For ᵇwe have sinned against You.

21 Do not abhor us, for Your name's sake;
Do not disgrace the throne of Your glory.
ᵃRemember, do not break Your covenant with us.

22 ᵃAre there any among ᵇthe idols of the nations that can cause ᶜrain?
Or can the heavens give showers?
ᵈAre You not He, O LORD our God?
Therefore we will wait for You,
Since You have made all these.

THE LORD WILL NOT RELENT

15 Then the LORD said to me, ᵃ"Even if ᵇMoses and ᶜSamuel stood before Me, My ¹mind would not be favorable toward this people. Cast them out of My sight, and let them go forth. ²And it shall be, if they say to you, 'Where should we go?' then you shall tell them, 'Thus says the LORD:

ᵃ"Such as are for death, to death;
And such as are for the sword, to the sword;
And such as are for the famine, to the famine;
And such as are for the ᵇcaptivity, to the captivity."'

³"And I will ᵃappoint over them four forms of destruction," says the LORD: "the sword to slay, the dogs to drag, ᵇthe birds of the heavens and the beasts of the earth to devour and destroy. ⁴I will hand them over to ᵃtrouble, to all kingdoms of the earth, because of ᵇManasseh the son of Hezekiah, king of Judah, for what he did in Jerusalem.

5 "For who will have pity on you, O Jerusalem?
Or who will bemoan you?
Or who will turn aside to ask how you are doing?

6 ᵃYou have forsaken Me," says the LORD,
"You have ᵇgone backward.
Therefore I will stretch out My hand against you and destroy you;
ᶜI am ¹weary of relenting!

7 And I will winnow them with a winnowing fan in the gates of the land;
I will ᵃbereave them of children;
I will destroy My people,
Since they ᵇdo not return from their ways.

8 Their widows will be increased to Me more than the sand of the seas;
I will bring against them,
Against the mother of the young men,
A plunderer at noonday;
I will cause anguish and terror to fall on them ᵃsuddenly.

9 "Sheᵃ languishes who has borne seven;
She has breathed her last;

14:19 ᵇJer. 15:18
ᶜJob 30:26;
Jer. 8:15;
1 Thess. 5:3
14:20 ᵃNeh. 9:2;
Ps. 32:5;
Jer. 3:25
ᵇPs. 106:6;
Jer. 8:14; 14:7;
Dan. 9:8
14:21 ᵃPs. 106:45
14:22 ᵃZech. 10:1
ᵇDeut. 32:21
ᶜ1 Kin. 17:1;
Jer. 5:24
ᵈPs. 135:7

15:1 ᵃPs. 99:6;
Ezek. 14:14
ᵇEx. 32:11–14;
Num. 14:13–20;
Ps. 99:6
ᶜ1 Sam. 7:9

15:2 ᵃJer. 43:11;
Ezek. 5:2, 12;
Zech. 11:9;
[Rev. 13:10]
ᵇJer. 9:16; 16:13

15:3 ᵃLev. 26:16,
21, 25; Jer. 12:3;
Ezek. 14:21
ᵇJer. 7:33

15:4
ᵃDeut. 28:25
ᵇ2 Kin. 24:3, 4

15:6 ᵃJer. 2:13
ᵇIs. 1:4; Jer. 7:24
ᶜJer. 20:16;
Zech. 8:14

15:7 ᵃJer. 18:21;
Hos. 9:12–16
ᵇIs. 9:13; Jer. 5:3;
Amos 4:10, 11

15:8 ᵃIs. 29:5

15:9 ᵃ1 Sam. 2:5;
Is. 47:9

15:1 ¹Lit. soul was not toward   15:6 ¹tired

ᵇHer sun has gone down
While *it was* yet day;
She has been ashamed and confounded.
And the remnant of them I will deliver to the sword
Before their enemies," says the LORD.

JEREMIAH'S DEJECTION

10 ᵃWoe is me, my mother,
That you have borne me,
A man of strife and a man of contention to the whole
¹earth!
I have neither lent for interest,
Nor have men lent to me for interest.
Every one of them curses me.

¹¹The LORD said:

"Surely it will be well with your remnant;
Surely I will cause ᵃthe enemy to intercede with you
In the time of adversity and in the time of
affliction.

12 Can anyone break iron,
The northern iron and the bronze?

13 Your wealth and your treasures
I will give as ᵃplunder without price,
Because of all your sins,
Throughout your territories.

14 And I will ¹make *you* cross over with your enemies
ᵃInto a land *which* you do not know;
For a ᵇfire is kindled in My anger,
Which shall burn upon you."

15 O LORD, ᵃYou know;
Remember me and ¹visit me,
And ᵇtake vengeance for me on my persecutors.
In Your enduring patience, do not take me away.
Know that ᶜfor Your sake I have suffered rebuke.

16 Your words were found, and I ᵃate them,
And ᵇYour word was to me the joy and rejoicing of my
heart;
For I am called by Your name,
O LORD God of hosts.

17 ᵃI did not sit in the assembly of the mockers,
Nor did I rejoice;
I sat alone because of Your hand,
For You have filled me with indignation.

18 Why is my ᵃpain perpetual
And my wound incurable,
Which refuses to be healed?
Will You surely be to me ᵇlike an unreliable stream,
As waters *that* ¹fail?

THE LORD REASSURES JEREMIAH

¹⁹Therefore thus says the LORD:

ᵃ"If you return,
Then I will bring you back;

15:9 ᵇJer. 6:4; Amos 8:9
15:10 ᵃJob 3:1; Jer. 20:14
15:11 ᵃJer. 40:4, 5
15:13 ᵃPs. 44:12; Is. 52:3
15:14 ᵃDeut. 28:36, 64; Jer. 16:13 ᵇDeut. 32:22; Ps. 21:9; Jer. 17:4
15:15 ᵃJer. 12:3 ᵇJer. 20:12 ᶜPs. 69:7–9; Jer. 20:8
15:16 ᵃEzek. 3:1, 3; Rev. 10:9 ᵇ[Job 23:12; Ps. 119:72]
15:17 ᵃPs. 26:4, 5
15:18 ᵃJob 34:6; Jer. 10:19; 30:15; Mic. 1:9 ᵇJob 6:15
15:19 ᵃJer. 4:1; Zech. 3:7

15:10 ¹Or *land*   15:14 ¹So with MT, Vg.; LXX, Syr., Tg. *cause you to serve* (cf. 17:4)   15:15 ¹*attend to*   15:18 ¹Or *cannot be trusted*

You shall ^bstand before Me;
If you ^ctake out the precious from the vile,
You shall be as My mouth.
Let them return to you,
But you must not return to them.

20 And I will make you to this people a fortified bronze
    ^awall;
And they will fight against you,
But ^bthey shall not prevail against you;
For I *am* with you to save you
And deliver you," says the LORD.

21 "I will deliver you from the hand of the wicked,
And I will redeem you from the grip of the
    terrible."

JEREMIAH'S LIFESTYLE AND MESSAGE

16 The word of the LORD also came to me, saying, ²"You shall not take a wife, nor shall you have sons or daughters in this place." ³For thus says the LORD concerning the sons and daughters who are born in this place, and concerning their mothers who bore them and their fathers who begot them in this land: ⁴"They shall die ^agruesome deaths; they shall not be ^blamented nor shall they be ^cburied, *but* they shall be ^dlike refuse on the face of the earth. They shall be consumed by the sword and by famine, and their ^ecorpses shall be meat for the birds of heaven and for the beasts of the earth."

⁵For thus says the LORD: ^a"Do not enter the house of mourning, nor go to lament or bemoan them; for I have taken away My peace from this people," says the LORD, "lovingkindness and mercies. ⁶Both the great and the small shall die in this land. They shall not be buried; ^aneither shall men lament for them, ^bcut themselves, nor ^cmake themselves bald for them. ⁷Nor shall *men* break *bread* in mourning for them, to comfort them for the dead; nor shall *men* give them the cup of consolation to ^adrink for their father or their mother. ⁸Also you shall not go into the house of feasting to sit with them, to eat and drink."

⁹For thus says the LORD of hosts, the God of Israel: "Behold, ^aI will cause to cease from this place, before your eyes and in your days, the voice of ¹mirth and the voice of gladness, the voice of the bridegroom and the voice of the bride.

¹⁰"And it shall be, when you show this people all these words, and they say to you, ^a'Why has the LORD pronounced all this great disaster against us? Or what *is* our iniquity? Or what *is* our sin that we have committed against the LORD our God?' ¹¹then you shall say to them, ^a'Because your fathers have forsaken Me,' says the LORD; 'they have walked after other gods and have served them and worshiped them, and have forsaken Me and not kept My law. ¹²And you have done ^aworse than your fathers, for behold, ^beach one ¹follows the dictates of his own evil heart, so that no one listens to Me. ^{13a}Therefore I will cast you out of this land ^binto a land that you do not know, neither you nor your fathers; and there you shall serve other gods day and night, where I will not show you favor.'

15:19 ^b1 Kin. 17:1;
Jer. 15:1
^cJer. 6:29;
Ezek. 22:26;
44:23

15:20
^aJer. 1:18; 6:27;
Ezek. 3:9
^bPs. 46:7;
Is. 41:10;
Jer. 1:8, 19; 20:11;
37:21; 38:13;
39:11, 12

16:4 ^aJer. 15:2
^bJer. 22:18; 25:33
^cJer. 14:16; 19:11
^dPs. 83:10;
Jer. 8:2; 9:22
^ePs. 79:2;
Is. 18:6;
Jer. 7:33; 34:20

16:5
^aEzek. 24:17,
22, 23

16:6 ^aJer. 22:18
^bLev. 19:28;
Deut. 14:1;
Jer. 41:5; 47:5
^cIs. 22:12;
Jer. 7:29

16:7 ^aProv. 31:6

16:9 ^aIs. 24:7, 8;
Jer. 7:34; 25:10;
Ezek. 26:13;
Hos. 2:11;
Rev. 18:23

16:10
^aDeut. 29:24;
1 Kin. 9:8;
Jer. 5:19

16:11
^aDeut. 29:25;
1 Kin. 9:9;
2 Chr. 7:22;
Neh. 9:26-29;
Jer. 22:9

16:12 ^aJer. 7:26
^bJer. 3:17; 18:12

16:13
^aDeut. 4:26;
28:36, 63
^bJer. 15:14

16:9 ¹rejoicing   16:12 ¹walks after the stubbornness or imagination

GOD WILL RESTORE ISRAEL

(cf. Jer. 23:7, 8)

[14]"Therefore behold, the [a]days are coming," says the LORD, "that it shall no more be said, 'The LORD lives who brought up the children of Israel from the land of Egypt,' [15]but, 'The LORD lives who brought up the children of Israel from the land of the [a]north and from all the lands where He had driven them.' For [b]I will bring them back into their land which I gave to their fathers.

[16]"Behold, I will send for many [a]fishermen," says the LORD, "and they shall fish them; and afterward I will send for many hunters, and they shall hunt them from every mountain and every hill, and out of the holes of the rocks. [17]For My [a]eyes *are* on all their ways; they are not hidden from My face, nor is their iniquity hidden from My eyes. [18]And first I will repay [a]double for their iniquity and their sin, because [b]they have defiled My land; they have filled My inheritance with the carcasses of their detestable and abominable idols."

19 O LORD, [a]my strength and my fortress,
　　[b]My refuge in the day of affliction,
　　The Gentiles shall come to You
　　From the ends of the earth and say,
　　"Surely our fathers have inherited lies,
　　Worthlessness and [c]unprofitable *things.*"
20 Will a man make gods for himself,
　　[a]Which *are* not gods?

21 "Therefore behold, I will this once cause them to
　　　know,
　　I will cause them to know
　　My hand and My might;
　　And they shall know that [a]My name *is* the LORD.

JUDAH'S SIN AND PUNISHMENT

17 "The sin of Judah *is* [a]written with a [b]pen of iron;
　　With the point of a diamond *it is* [c]engraved
　　On the tablet of their heart,
　　And on the horns of your altars,
2　While their children remember
　　Their altars and their [a]wooden[1] images
　　By the green trees on the high hills.
3　O My mountain in the field,
　　I will give as plunder your wealth, all your treasures,
　　And your high places of sin within all your borders.
4　And you, even yourself,
　　Shall let go of your heritage which I gave you;
　　And I will cause you to serve your enemies
　　In [a]the land which you do not know;
　　For [b]you have kindled a fire in My anger *which* shall burn
　　　forever."

[5]Thus says the LORD:

[a]"Cursed *is* the man who trusts in man
　　And makes [b]flesh his [1]strength,
　　Whose heart departs from the LORD.

16:14 [a]Is. 43:18;
Jer. 23:7, 8;
[Ezek. 37:21–25]

16:15 [a]Jer. 3:18
[b]Jer. 24:6; 30:3;
32:37

16:16
[a]Amos 4:2;
Hab. 1:15

16:17
[a]2 Chr. 16:9;
Job 34:21;
Ps. 90:8;
Prov. 5:21;
Jer. 23:24; 32:19;
Zech. 4:10;
[Luke 12:2;
1 Cor. 4:5];
Heb. 4:13

16:18 [a]Is. 40:2;
Jer. 17:18;
Rev. 18:6
[b][Ezek. 43:7]

16:19 [a]Ps. 18:1, 2;
Is. 25:4
[b]Jer. 17:17
[c]Is. 44:10

16:20
[a]Ps. 115:4–8;
Is. 37:19;
Jer. 2:11; 5:7;
Hos. 8:4–6;
Gal. 4:8

16:21 [a]Ex. 15:3;
Ps. 83:18;
Is. 43:3;
Jer. 33:2;
Amos 5:8

17:1 [a]Jer. 2:22
[b]Job 19:24
[c]Prov. 3:3; 7:3;
Is. 49:16;
2 Cor. 3:3

17:2 [a]Judg. 3:7

17:4 [a]Jer. 16:13
[b]Is. 5:25;
Jer. 15:14

17:5 [a]Ps. 146:3;
Is. 30:1, 2; 31:1
[b]Is. 31:3

17:2 [1]Heb. *Asherim,* Canaanite deities　**17:5** [1]Lit. *arm*

6   For he shall be ᵃlike a shrub in the desert,
And ᵇshall not see when good comes,
But shall inhabit the parched places in the wilderness,
ᶜ*In a salt land which is* not inhabited.

7   "Blessedᵃ *is* the man who trusts in the LORD,
And whose hope is the LORD.
8   For he shall be ᵃlike a tree planted by the waters,
Which spreads out its roots by the river,
And will not ¹fear when heat comes;
But its leaf will be green,
And will not be anxious in the year of drought,
Nor will cease from yielding fruit.

9   "The ᵃheart *is* deceitful above all *things,*
And ¹desperately wicked;
Who can know it?
10   I, the LORD, ᵃsearch the heart,
I test the ¹mind,
ᵇEven to give every man according to his ways,
According to the fruit of his doings.

11   "*As* a partridge that ¹broods but does not hatch,
So is he who gets riches, but not by right;
It ᵃwill leave him in the midst of his days,
And at his end he will be ᵇa fool."

12   A glorious high throne from the beginning
Is the place of our sanctuary.
13   O LORD, ᵃthe hope of Israel,
ᵇAll who forsake You shall be ashamed.

"Those who depart from Me
Shall be ᶜwritten in the earth,
Because they have forsaken the LORD,
The ᵈfountain of living waters."

JEREMIAH PRAYS FOR DELIVERANCE

14   Heal me, O LORD, and I shall be healed;
Save me, and I shall be saved,
For ᵃYou *are* my praise.
15   Indeed they say to me,
ᵃ"Where *is* the word of the LORD?
Let it come now!"
16   As for me, ᵃI have not hurried away from *being* a
shepherd *who* follows You,
Nor have I desired the woeful day;
You know what came out of my lips;
It was right there before You.
17   Do not be a terror to me;
ᵃYou *are* my hope in the day of doom.
18   ᵃLet them be ashamed who persecute me,
But ᵇdo not let me be put to shame;
Let them be dismayed,
But do not let me be dismayed.
Bring on them the day of doom,
And ᶜdestroy¹ them with double destruction!

17:6 ᵃJer. 48:6
ᵇJob 20:17
ᶜDeut. 29:23;
Job 39:6

17:7 ᵃPs. 2:12;
34:8; 125:1;
146:5;
Prov. 16:20;
[Is. 30:18];
Jer. 39:18

17:8 ᵃJob 8:16;
[Ps. 1:3;
Ezek. 31:3–9]

17:9 ᵃ[Eccl. 9:3];
Matt. 15:19;
[Mark 7:21, 22]

17:10
ᵃ1 Sam. 16:7;
1 Chr. 28:9;
Ps. 7:9; 139:23,
24; Prov. 17:3;
Jer. 11:20; 20:12;
Rom. 8:27;
Rev. 2:23
ᵇPs. 62:12;
Jer. 32:19;
Rom. 2:6

17:11 ᵃPs. 55:23
ᵇLuke 12:20

17:13 ᵃJer. 14:8
ᵇ[Ps. 73:27;
Is. 1:28]
ᶜLuke 10:20
ᵈJer. 2:13

17:14
ᵃDeut. 10:21;
Ps. 109:1

17:15 ᵃIs. 5:19;
Ezek. 12:22;
2 Pet. 3:4

17:16 ᵃJer. 1:4–12

17:17 ᵃJer. 16:19;
Nah. 1:7

17:18 ᵃPs. 35:4;
70:2; Jer. 15:10;
18:18 ᵇPs. 25:2
ᶜJer. 11:20

17:8 ¹Qr., Tg. *see*   17:9 ¹Or *incurably sick*   17:10 ¹Most secret parts, lit.
kidneys   17:11 ¹Sits on eggs   17:18 ¹Lit. *crush*

HALLOW THE SABBATH DAY

¹⁹Thus the LORD said to me: "Go and stand in the gate of the children of the people, by which the kings of Judah come in and by which they go out, and in all the gates of Jerusalem; ²⁰and say to them, ᵃ'Hear the word of the LORD, you kings of Judah, and all Judah, and all the inhabitants of Jerusalem, who enter by these gates. ²¹Thus says the LORD: ᵃ"Take heed to yourselves, and bear no burden on the Sabbath day, nor bring *it* in by the gates of Jerusalem; ²²nor carry a burden out of your houses on the Sabbath day, nor do any work, but hallow the Sabbath day, as I ᵃcommanded your fathers. ²³ᵃBut they did not obey nor incline their ear, but ¹made their neck stiff, that they might not hear nor receive instruction.

²⁴"And it shall be, ᵃif you heed Me carefully," says the LORD, "to bring no burden through the gates of this city on the ᵇSabbath day, but hallow the Sabbath day, to do no work in it, ²⁵ᵃthen shall enter the gates of this city kings and princes sitting on the throne of David, riding in chariots and on horses, they and their princes, accompanied by the men of Judah and the inhabitants of Jerusalem; and this city shall remain forever. ²⁶And they shall come from the cities of Judah and from ᵃthe places around Jerusalem, from the land of Benjamin and from ᵇthe ¹lowland, from the mountains and from ᶜthe ²South, bringing burnt offerings and sacrifices, grain offerings and incense, bringing ᵈsacrifices of praise to the house of the LORD.

²⁷"But if you will not heed Me to hallow the Sabbath day, such as not carrying a burden when entering the gates of Jerusalem on the Sabbath day, then ᵃI will kindle a fire in its gates, ᵇand it shall devour the palaces of Jerusalem, and it shall not be ᶜquenched."'"

THE POTTER AND THE CLAY

18 The word which came to Jeremiah from the LORD, saying: ²"Arise and go down to the potter's house, and there I will cause you to hear My words." ³Then I went down to the potter's house, and there he was, making something at the ¹wheel. ⁴And the vessel that he ¹made of clay was ²marred in the hand of the potter; so he made it again into another vessel, as it seemed good to the potter to make.

⁵Then the word of the LORD came to me, saying: ⁶"O house of Israel, ᵃcan I not do with you as this potter?" says the LORD. "Look, ᵇas the clay *is* in the potter's hand, so *are* you in My hand, O house of Israel! ⁷The instant I speak concerning a nation and concerning a kingdom, to ᵃpluck up, to pull down, and to destroy *it*, ⁸ᵃif that nation against whom I have spoken turns from its evil, ᵇI will relent of the disaster that I thought to bring upon it. ⁹And the instant I speak concerning a nation and concerning a kingdom, to build and to plant *it*, ¹⁰if it does evil in My sight so that it does not obey My voice, then I will relent concerning the good with which I said I would benefit it.

¹¹"Now therefore, speak to the men of Judah and to the inhabitants of Jerusalem, saying, 'Thus says the LORD: "Behold, I am fashioning a disaster and devising a plan against you.

17:20
ᵃPs. 49:1, 2;
Jer. 19:3, 4

17:21
ᵃNum. 15:32;
Neh. 13:19;
[John 5:9–12, 17;
7:22–24]

17:22 ᵃEx. 20:8;
31:13; Ezek. 20:12

17:23
ᵃJer. 7:24, 26

17:24
ᵃJer. 11:4; 26:3
ᵇEx. 16:23–30;
20:8–10;
Num. 15:32–36;
Deut. 5:12–14;
Neh. 13:15;
[Is. 58:13]

17:25 ᵃJer. 22:4

17:26 ᵃJer. 33:13
ᵇZech. 7:7
ᶜJudg. 1:9
ᵈPs. 107:22;
116:17; Jer. 33:11

17:27 ᵃJer. 21:14;
Lam. 4:11;
Amos 1:4, 7, 10, 12
ᵇ2 Kin. 25:9;
2 Chr. 36:19;
Jer. 39:8; 52:13;
Amos 2:5
ᶜJer. 7:20;
Ezek. 20:47

18:6 ᵃIs. 45:9;
Rom. 9:20, 21
ᵇIs. 64:8

18:7 ᵃJer. 1:10

18:8
ᵃJer. 7:3–7;
12:16;
[Ezek. 18:21;
33:11]
ᵇ[Ps. 106:45];
Jer. 26:3;
[Hos. 11:8;
Joel 2:13];
Jon. 3:10

17:23 ¹Were stubborn   **17:26** ¹Heb. *shephelah*   ²Heb. *Negev*
18:3 ¹Potter's wheel   **18:4** ¹*was making*   ²*ruined*

ᵃReturn now every one from his evil way, and make your ways and your doings ᵇgood."'"

GOD'S WARNING REJECTED

¹²And they said, ᵃ"That is hopeless! So we will walk according to our own plans, and we will every one ¹obey the ᵇdictates² of his evil heart."

¹³Therefore thus says the LORD:

ᵃ"Ask now among the Gentiles,
Who has heard such things?
The virgin of Israel has done ᵇa very horrible thing.
14 Will *a man* ¹leave the snow water of Lebanon,
Which comes from the rock of the field?
Will the cold flowing waters be forsaken for strange
waters?
15 "Because My people have forgotten ᵃMe,
They have burned incense to worthless idols.
And they have caused themselves to stumble in their
ways,
From the ᵇancient paths,
To walk in pathways and not on a highway,
16 To make their land ᵃdesolate *and* a perpetual ᵇhissing;
Everyone who passes by it will be astonished
And shake his head.
17 ᵃI will scatter them ᵇas with an east wind before the
enemy;
ᶜI will ¹show them the back and not the face
In the day of their calamity."

JEREMIAH PERSECUTED

¹⁸Then they said, ᵃ"Come and let us devise plans against Jeremiah; ᵇfor the law shall not perish from the priest, nor counsel from the wise, nor the word from the prophet. Come and let us attack him with the tongue, and let us not give heed to any of his words."

19 Give heed to me, O LORD,
And listen to the voice of those who contend with me!
20 ᵃShall evil be repaid for good?
For they have ᵇdug a pit for my life.
Remember that I ᶜstood before You
To speak good ¹for them,
To turn away Your wrath from them.
21 Therefore ᵃdeliver up their children to the famine,
And pour out their *blood*
By the force of the sword;
Let their wives *become* widows
And ᵇbereaved of their children.
Let their men be put to death,
Their young men *be* slain
By the sword in battle.
22 Let a cry be heard from their houses,
When You bring a troop suddenly upon them;
For they have dug a pit to take me,
And hidden snares for my feet.

18:11
ᵃ2 Kin. 17:13;
Is. 1:16–19;
Jer. 4:1;
Acts 26:20
ᵇJer. 7:3–7

18:12 ᵃIs. 57:10;
Jer. 2:25
ᵇJer. 3:17; 23:17

18:13 ᵃIs. 66:8;
Jer. 2:10, 11;
1 Cor. 5:1
ᵇJer. 5:30;
Hos. 6:10

18:15
ᵃJer. 2:13, 32
ᵇJer. 6:16

18:16 ᵃJer. 19:8
ᵇ1 Kin. 9:8;
Lam. 2:15;
Mic. 6:16

18:17 ᵃJer. 13:24
ᵇPs. 48:7
ᶜJer. 2:27

18:18 ᵃJer. 11:19
ᵇLev. 10:11;
Mal. 2:7;
[John 7:48]

18:20 ᵃPs. 109:4
ᵇPs. 35:7;
57:6; Jer. 5:26
ᶜJer. 14:7—15:1

18:21
ᵃPs. 109:9–20;
Jer. 11:22; 14:16
ᵇJer. 15:7, 8;
Ezek. 22:25

18:12 ¹Lit. *do*   ²*stubbornness* or *imagination*   18:14 ¹*forsake*   18:17 ¹So
with LXX, Syr., Tg., Vg.; MT *look them in*   18:20 ¹*concerning*

23 Yet, LORD, You know all their counsel
Which is against me, to slay *me*.
ªProvide no atonement for their iniquity,
Nor blot out their sin from Your sight;
But let them be overthrown before You.
Deal *thus* with them
In the time of Your ᵇanger.

THE SIGN OF THE BROKEN FLASK

19 Thus says the LORD: "Go and get a potter's earthen flask, and *take* some of the elders of the people and some of the elders of the priests. 2And go out to ªthe Valley of the Son of Hinnom, which *is* by the entry of the Potsherd Gate; and proclaim there the words that I will tell you, 3ªand say, 'Hear the word of the LORD, O kings of Judah and inhabitants of Jerusalem. Thus says the LORD of hosts, the God of Israel: "Behold, I will bring such a catastrophe on this place, that whoever hears of it, his ears will ᵇtingle.

4"Because they ªhave forsaken Me and made this an alien place, because they have burned incense in it to other gods whom neither they, their fathers, nor the kings of Judah have known, and have filled this place with ᵇthe blood of the innocents 5ª(they have also built the high places of Baal, to burn their sons with fire *for* burnt offerings to Baal, ᵇwhich I did not command or speak, nor did it come into My mind), 6therefore behold, the days are coming," says the LORD, "that this place shall no more be called Tophet or ªthe Valley of the Son of Hinnom, but the Valley of Slaughter. 7And I will make void the counsel of Judah and Jerusalem in this place, ªand I will cause them to fall by the sword before their enemies and by the hands of those who seek their lives; their ᵇcorpses I will give as meat for the birds of the heaven and for the beasts of the earth. 8I will make this city ªdesolate and a hissing; everyone who passes by it will be astonished and hiss because of all its plagues. 9And I will cause them to eat the ªflesh of their sons and the flesh of their daughters, and everyone shall eat the flesh of his friend in the siege and in the desperation with which their enemies and those who seek their lives shall drive them to despair."'

10ª"Then you shall break the flask in the sight of the men who go with you, 11and say to them, 'Thus says the LORD of hosts: ª"Even so I will break this people and this city, as *one* breaks a potter's vessel, which cannot be ¹made whole again; and they shall ᵇbury *them* in Tophet till *there is* no place to bury. 12Thus I will do to this place," says the LORD, "and to its inhabitants, and make this city like Tophet. 13And the houses of Jerusalem and the houses of the kings of Judah shall be defiled ªlike the place of Tophet, because of all the houses on whose ᵇroofs they have burned incense to all the host of heaven, and ᶜpoured out drink offerings to other gods."'"

14Then Jeremiah came from Tophet, where the LORD had sent him to prophesy; and he stood in ªthe court of the Lord's house and said to all the people, 15"Thus says the LORD of hosts, the God of Israel: 'Behold, I will bring on this city and on all her towns all the doom that I have pronounced against

19:11 ¹*restored*

it, because ^athey have stiffened their necks that they might not hear My words.'"

THE WORD OF GOD TO PASHHUR

20 Now ^aPashhur the son of ^bImmer, the priest who *was* also chief governor in the house of the LORD, heard that Jeremiah prophesied these things. ²Then Pashhur struck Jeremiah the prophet, and put him in the stocks that *were* in the high ^agate of Benjamin, which *was* by the house of the LORD.

³And it happened on the next day that Pashhur brought Jeremiah out of the stocks. Then Jeremiah said to him, "The LORD has not called your name Pashhur, but ¹Magor-Missabib. ⁴For thus says the LORD: 'Behold, I will make you a terror to yourself and to all your friends; and they shall fall by the sword of their enemies, and your eyes shall see *it*. I will ^agive all Judah into the hand of the king of Babylon, and he shall carry them captive to Babylon and slay them with the sword. ⁵Moreover I ^awill deliver all the wealth of this city, all its produce, and all its precious things; all the treasures of the kings of Judah I will give into the hand of their enemies, who will plunder them, seize them, and ^bcarry them to Babylon. ⁶And you, Pashhur, and all who dwell in your house, shall go into captivity. You shall go to Babylon, and there you shall die, and be buried there, you and all your friends, to whom you have ^aprophesied lies.'"

JEREMIAH'S UNPOPULAR MINISTRY

7 O LORD, You ¹induced me, and I was persuaded;
   ^aYou are stronger than I, and have prevailed.
   ^bI am ²in derision daily;
   Everyone mocks me.
8 For when I spoke, I cried out;
   ^aI shouted, "Violence and plunder!"
   Because the word of the LORD was made to me
   A reproach and a derision daily.
9 Then I said, "I will not make mention of Him,
   Nor speak anymore in His name."
   But *His word* was in my heart like a ^aburning fire
   Shut up in my bones;
   I was weary of holding *it* back,
   And ^bI could not.
10 ^aFor I heard many ¹mocking:
   "Fear on every side!"
   "Report," *they say*, "and we will report it!"
   ^bAll my acquaintances watched for my stumbling, *saying*,
   "Perhaps he can be induced;
   Then we will prevail against him,
   And we will take our revenge on him."

11 But the LORD *is* ^awith me as a mighty, awesome One.
   Therefore my persecutors will stumble, and will not
      ^bprevail.
   They will be greatly ashamed, for they will not prosper.
   Their ^ceverlasting confusion will never be forgotten.
12 But, O LORD of hosts,
   You who ^atest the righteous,

19:15
^aNeh. 9:17, 29;
Jer. 7:26; 17:23

20:1
^aEzra 2:37, 38
^b1 Chr. 24:14

20:2 ^aJer. 37:13;
Zech. 14:10

20:4
^aJer. 21:4–10

20:5
^a2 Kin. 20:17;
2 Chr. 36:10;
Jer. 3:24;
27:21, 22
^bIs. 39:6

20:6
^aJer. 14:13–15;
Lam. 2:14

20:7 ^aJer. 1:6, 7
^bJob 12:4;
Lam. 3:14

20:8 ^aJer. 6:7

20:9
^aJob 32:18–20;
Ps. 39:3;
Jer. 4:19; 23:9;
[Ezek. 3:14];
Acts 4:20
^bJob 32:18;
Jer. 6:11;
Acts 18:5

20:10 ^aPs. 31:13
^bJob 19:19;
Ps. 41:9; 55:13, 14;
Luke 11:53, 54

20:11
^aJer. 1:18, 19
^bJer. 15:20; 17:18
^cJer. 23:40

20:12 ^aPs. 7:9;
11:5; 17:3; 139:23;
[Jer. 11:20; 17:10]

And see the [1]mind and heart,
   [b]Let me see Your vengeance on them;
   For I have pleaded my cause before You.

13 Sing to the LORD! Praise the LORD!
   For [a]He has delivered the life of the poor
   From the hand of evildoers.

14 [a]Cursed *be* the day in which I was born!
   Let the day not be blessed in which my mother bore me!

15 Let the man *be* cursed
   Who brought news to my father, saying,
   "A male child has been born to you!"
   Making him very glad.

16 And let that man be like the cities
   Which the LORD [a]overthrew, and did not relent;
   Let him [b]hear the cry in the morning
   And the shouting at noon,

17 [a]Because he did not kill me from the womb,
   That my mother might have been my grave,
   And her womb always enlarged *with me.*

18 [a]Why did I come forth from the womb to [b]see [1]labor and
    sorrow,
   That my days should be consumed with shame?

JERUSALEM'S DOOM IS SEALED

21 The word which came to Jeremiah from the LORD when
[a]King Zedekiah sent to him [b]Pashhur the son of Melchi-
ah, and [c]Zephaniah the son of Maaseiah, the priest, saying,
2 [a]"Please inquire of the LORD for us, for [1]Nebuchadnezzar
king of Babylon makes war against us. Perhaps the LORD will
deal with us according to all His wonderful works, that *the
king* may go away from us."

3 Then Jeremiah said to them, "Thus you shall say to Zedekiah, 4 Thus says the LORD God of Israel: "Behold, I will turn
back the weapons of war that *are* in your hands, with which
you fight against the king of Babylon and the [1]Chaldeans who
besiege you outside the walls; and [a]I will assemble them in
the midst of this city. 5 I [a]Myself will fight against you with an
[b]outstretched hand and with a strong arm, even in anger and
fury and great wrath. 6 I will strike the inhabitants of this city,
both man and beast; they shall die of a great pestilence. 7 And
afterward," says the LORD, [a]"I will deliver Zedekiah king of Judah, his servants and the people, and such as are left in this
city from the pestilence and the sword and the famine, into
the hand of Nebuchadnezzar king of Babylon, into the hand
of their enemies, and into the hand of those who seek their
life; and he shall strike them with the edge of the sword. [b]He
shall not spare them, or have pity or mercy."'

8 "Now you shall say to this people, 'Thus says the LORD:
"Behold, [a]I set before you the way of life and the way of death.
9 He who [a]remains in this city shall die by the sword, by famine, and by pestilence; but he who goes out and [1]defects to the
Chaldeans who besiege you, he shall [b]live, and his life shall
be as a prize to him. 10 For I have [a]set My face against this city

20:12 [b]Ps. 54:7;
59:10; Jer. 15:15

20:13
[a]Ps. 35:9, 10;
109:30, 31

20:14 [a]Job 3:3;
Jer. 15:10

20:16
[a]Gen. 19:25
[b]Jer. 18:22

20:17
[a]Job 3:10, 11

20:18 [a]Job 3:20;
Jer. 15:10
[b]Lam. 3:1

21:1
[a]2 Kin. 24:17, 18;
Jer. 32:1–3;
37:1; 52:1–3
[b]1 Chr. 9:12;
Jer. 38:1
[c]2 Kin. 25:18;
Jer. 29:25; 37:3

21:2 [a]Ex. 9:28;
1 Sam. 9:9;
Jer. 37:3, 7;
Ezek. 14:7;
20:1–3

21:4 [a]Is. 13:4;
Jer. 39:3;
Lam. 2:5, 7;
Zech. 14:2

21:5
[a]Jer. 32:24; 33:5;
Is. 63:10
[b]Ex. 6:6;
Deut. 4:34;
Jer. 6:12

21:7
[a]2 Kin. 25:5–7,
18–21; Jer. 37:17;
39:5; 52:9
[b]Deut. 28:50;
2 Chr. 36:17;
Jer. 13:14;
Ezek. 7:9;
Hab. 1:6–10

21:8
[a]Deut. 30:15, 19;
Is. 1:19, 20

21:9 [a]Jer. 38:2
[b]Jer. 39:18

21:10 [a]Lev. 17:10;
Jer. 44:11, 27;
Amos 9:4

20:12 [1]Most secret parts, lit. *kidneys* **20:18** [1]*toil* **21:2** [1]Heb.
Nebuchadrezzar, and so elsewhere in the book **21:4** [1]Or *Babylonians,* and
so elsewhere in the book **21:9** [1]Lit. *falls away to*

for adversity and not for good," says the LORD. ᵇ"It shall be given into the hand of the king of Babylon, and he shall ᶜburn it with fire."'

MESSAGE TO THE HOUSE OF DAVID

¹¹"And concerning the house of the king of Judah, *say,* 'Hear the word of the LORD, ¹²O house of David! Thus says the LORD:

ᵃ"Execute¹ judgment ᵇin the morning;
And deliver *him who is* plundered
Out of the hand of the oppressor,
Lest My fury go forth like fire
And burn so that no one can quench *it,*
Because of the evil of your doings.

¹³ "Behold, ᵃI *am* against you, O ¹inhabitant of the valley,
And rock of the plain," says the LORD,
"Who say, ᵇ'Who shall come down against us?
Or who shall enter our dwellings?'
¹⁴ But I will punish you according to the ᵃfruit of your
¹doings," says the LORD;
"I will kindle a fire in its forest,
And ᵇit shall devour all things around it."'"

22 Thus says the LORD: "Go down to the house of the king of Judah, and there speak this word, ²and say, ᵃ'Hear the word of the LORD, O king of Judah, you who sit on the throne of David, you and your servants and your people who enter these gates! ³Thus says the LORD: ᵃ"Execute¹ judgment and righteousness, and deliver the plundered out of the hand of the oppressor. Do no wrong and do no violence to the stranger, the ᵇfatherless, or the widow, nor shed innocent blood in this place. ⁴For if you indeed do this thing, ᵃthen shall enter the gates of this house, riding on horses and in chariots, accompanied by servants and people, kings who sit on the throne of David. ⁵But if you will not ¹hear these words, ᵃI swear by Myself," says the LORD, "that this house shall become a desolation."'"

⁶For thus says the LORD to the house of the king of Judah:

"You *are* ᵃGilead to Me,
The head of Lebanon;
Yet I surely will make you a wilderness,
Cities *which* are not inhabited.
⁷ I will prepare destroyers against you,
Everyone with his weapons;
They shall cut down ᵃyour choice cedars
ᵇAnd cast *them* into the fire.

⁸And many nations will pass by this city; and everyone will say to his neighbor, ᵃ'Why has the LORD done so to this great city?' ⁹Then they will answer, ᵃ'Because they have forsaken the covenant of the LORD their God, and worshiped other gods and served them.'"

¹⁰ Weep not for ᵃthe dead, nor bemoan him;
Weep bitterly for him ᵇwho goes away,
For he shall return no more,
Nor see his native country.

21:10 ᵇJer. 38:3
ᶜ2 Kin. 25:9;
2 Chr. 36:19;
Jer. 34:2, 22;
37:10

21:12 ᵃPs. 72:1;
Is. 1:17; Jer. 22:3;
Zech. 7:9
ᵇPs. 101:8;
Zeph. 3:5

21:13
ᵃ[Jer. 23:30–32;
Ezek. 13:8]
ᵇ2 Sam. 5:6, 7;
Jer. 49:4;
Lam. 4:12;
Obad. 3, 4

21:14 ᵃProv. 1:31;
Is. 3:10, 11;
Jer. 17:10; 32:19
ᵇ2 Chr. 36:19;
Is. 10:16, 18;
Jer. 11:16;
17:27; 52:13;
Ezek. 20:47, 48

22:2 ᵃJer. 17:20

22:3 ᵃIs. 58:6;
Jer. 21:12;
[Mic. 6:8];
Zech. 7:9; 8:16;
Matt. 23:23
ᵇJer. 7:6;
Zech. 7:10

22:4 ᵃJer. 17:25

22:5
ᵃMatt. 23:38;
Heb. 6:13, 17

22:6
ᵃGen. 37:25;
Num. 32:1;
Song 4:1

22:7 ᵃIs. 37:24
ᵇJer. 21:14

22:8
ᵃDeut. 29:24–26;
1 Kin. 9:8, 9;
2 Chr. 7:20–22;
Jer. 16:10

22:9
ᵃ2 Kin. 22:17;
2 Chr. 34:25;
Jer. 11:3

22:10
ᵃ2 Kin. 22:20
ᵇJer. 14:17; 22:11;
Lam. 3:48

21:12 ¹*Dispense justice* 21:13 ¹*dweller* 21:14 ¹*deeds* 22:3 ¹*Dispense justice* 22:5 ¹Obey

MESSAGE TO THE SONS OF JOSIAH

11For thus says the LORD concerning ªShallum¹ the son of Josiah, king of Judah, who reigned instead of Josiah his father, ᵇwho went from this place: "He shall not return here anymore, 12but he shall die in the place where they have led him captive, and shall see this land no more.

13 "Woeª to him who builds his house by unrighteousness
        And his ¹chambers by injustice,
      ᵇWho uses his neighbor's service without wages
        And gives him nothing for his work,
14 Who says, 'I will build myself a wide house with spacious
            ¹chambers,
        And cut out windows for it,
        Paneling *it* with cedar
        And painting *it* with vermilion.'

15 "Shall you reign because you enclose *yourself* in cedar?
        Did not your father eat and drink,
        And do justice and righteousness?
        Then ªit *was* well with him.
16 He ¹judged the cause of the poor and needy;
        Then *it was* well.
        Was not this knowing Me?" says the LORD.
17 "Yetª your eyes and your heart *are* for nothing but your
            covetousness,
        For shedding innocent blood,
        And practicing oppression and violence."

18Therefore thus says the LORD concerning Jehoiakim the son of Josiah, king of Judah:

    ª"They shall not lament for him,
        Saying, ᵇ'Alas, my brother!' or 'Alas, my sister!'
        They shall not lament for him,
        Saying, 'Alas, master!' or 'Alas, his glory!'
19 ªHe shall be buried with the burial of a donkey,
        Dragged and cast out beyond the gates of Jerusalem.

20 "Go up to Lebanon, and cry out,
        And lift up your voice in Bashan;
        Cry from Abarim,
        For all your lovers are destroyed.
21 I spoke to you in your prosperity,
        But you said, 'I will not hear.'
        ªThis *has been* your manner from your youth,
        That you did not obey My voice.
22 The wind shall eat up all ªyour ¹rulers,
        And your lovers shall go into captivity;
        Surely then you will be ashamed and humiliated
        For all your wickedness.
23 O inhabitant of Lebanon,
        Making your nest in the cedars,
        How gracious will you be when pangs come upon
            you,
        Like ªthe pain of a woman in ¹labor?

22:11 ª1 Chr. 3:15
ᵇ2 Kin. 23:34;
2 Chr. 36:4;
Ezek. 19:4

22:13
ª2 Kin. 23:35;
Jer. 17:11;
Ezek. 22:13
ᵇLev. 19:13;
Deut. 24:14, 15;
Mic. 3:10;
Hab. 2:9;
James 5:4

22:15
ª2 Kin. 23:25;
Ps. 128:2;
Is. 3:10;
Jer. 7:23; 42:6

22:17 ªJer. 6:13;
8:10; Ezek. 19:6;
[Luke 12:15–20]

22:18
ªJer. 16:4, 6
ᵇ1 Kin. 13:30

22:19
ª1 Kin. 21:23, 24;
2 Chr. 36:6;
Jer. 36:30;
Dan. 1:2

22:21 ªJer. 3:24,
25; 32:30

22:22 ªJer. 23:1

22:23 ªJer. 6:24

22:11 ¹Or *Jehoahaz*   **22:13** ¹Lit. *roof chambers, upper chambers*   **22:14** ¹Lit. *roof chambers, upper chambers*   **22:16** ¹*Defended*   **22:22** ¹Lit. *shepherds*
22:23 ¹*childbirth*

MESSAGE TO CONIAH

24"As I live," says the LORD, a"though 1Coniah the son of Jehoiakim, king of Judah, bwere the 2signet on My right hand, yet I would pluck you off; 25aand I will give you into the hand of those who seek your life, and into the hand *of those* whose face you fear—the hand of Nebuchadnezzar king of Babylon and the hand of the 1Chaldeans. 26aSo I will cast you out, and your mother who bore you, into another country where you were not born; and there you shall die. 27But to the land to which they desire to return, there they shall not return.

28 "Is this man 1Coniah a despised, broken idol—
aA vessel in which *is* no pleasure?
Why are they cast out, he and his descendants,
And cast into a land which they do not know?
29 aO earth, earth, earth,
Hear the word of the LORD!
30 Thus says the LORD:
'Write this man down as achildless,
A man *who* shall not prosper in his days;
For bnone of his descendants shall prosper,
Sitting on the throne of David,
And ruling anymore in Judah.'"

THE BRANCH OF RIGHTEOUSNESS

23 "Woe ato the shepherds who destroy and scatter the sheep of My pasture!" says the LORD. 2Therefore thus says the LORD God of Israel against the shepherds who feed My people: "You have scattered My flock, driven them away, and not attended to them. aBehold, I will attend to you for the evil of your doings," says the LORD. 3"But aI will gather the remnant of My flock out of all countries where I have driven them, and bring them back to their folds; and they shall be fruitful and increase. 4I will set up ashepherds over them who will feed them; and they shall fear no more, nor be dismayed, nor shall they be lacking," says the LORD.

5 "Behold, athe days are coming," says the LORD,
"That I will raise to David a Branch of righteousness;
A King shall reign and 1prosper,
bAnd execute 2judgment and righteousness in the 3earth.
6 aIn His days Judah will be saved,
And Israel bwill dwell safely;
Now cthis *is* His name by which He will be called:

1THE LORD OUR RIGHTEOUSNESS.

7"Therefore, behold, athe days are coming," says the LORD, "that they shall no longer say, 'As the LORD lives who brought up the children of Israel from the land of Egypt,' 8but, 'As the LORD lives who brought up and led the descendants of the house of Israel from the north country aand from all the countries where I had driven them.' And they shall dwell in their own bland."

22:24
a2 Kin. 24:6, 8;
1 Chr. 3:16;
2 Chr. 36:9;
Jer. 37:1
bSong 8:6;
Is. 49:16;
Hag. 2:23

22:25
a2 Kin. 24:15, 16;
Jer. 34:20

22:26
a2 Kin. 24:15;
Jer. 10:18; 16:13

22:28 aPs. 31:12;
Jer. 48:38;
Hos. 8:8

22:29
aDeut. 32:1;
Is. 1:2; 34:1;
Mic. 1:2

22:30
a1 Chr. 3:16, 17;
Matt. 1:12
bPs. 94:20;
Jer. 36:30

23:1
aIs. 56:9–12;
Jer. 10:21

23:2 aEx. 32:34

23:3
aIs. 11:11, 12, 16;
Jer. 32:37

23:4 aJer. 3:15;
[Ezek. 34:23]

23:5
aIs. 4:2; 11:1;
40:10, 11;
Jer. 33:14;
[Dan. 9:24;
Zech. 6:12];
Matt. 1:1, 6;
Luke 3:31;
[John 1:45; 7:42]
bPs. 72:2;
Is. 9:7; 32:1, 18;
[Dan. 9:24]

23:6
aDeut. 33:28;
Jer. 30:10;
Zech. 14:11
bJer. 32:37
cIs. 45:24;
Jer. 33:16;
[Dan. 9:24];
Rom. 3:22;
1 Cor. 1:30]

23:7
aIs. 43:18, 19;
Jer. 16:14

23:8 aIs. 43:5, 6;
Ezek. 34:13;
Amos 9:14, 15
bGen. 12:7;
Jer. 16:14, 15; 31:8

FALSE PROPHETS AND EMPTY ORACLES

9 My heart within me is broken
Because of the prophets;
^aAll my bones shake.
I am like a drunken man,
And like a man whom wine has overcome,
Because of the LORD,
And because of His holy words.

10 For ^athe land is full of adulterers;
For ^bbecause of a curse the land mourns.
^cThe pleasant places of the wilderness are dried up.
Their course of life is evil,
And their might *is* not right.

11 "For ^aboth prophet and priest are profane;
Yes, ^bin My house I have found their wickedness," says
the LORD.

12 "Therefore^a their way shall be to them
Like slippery *ways;*
In the darkness they shall be driven on
And fall in them;
For I ^bwill bring disaster on them,
The year of their punishment," says the LORD.

13 "And I have seen ¹folly in the prophets of Samaria:
^aThey prophesied by Baal
And ^bcaused My people Israel to err.

14 Also I have seen a horrible thing in the prophets of
Jerusalem:
^aThey commit adultery and walk in lies;
They also ^bstrengthen the hands of evildoers,
So that no one turns back from his wickedness.
All of them are like ^cSodom to Me,
And her inhabitants like Gomorrah.

15"Therefore thus says the LORD of hosts concerning the
prophets:

'Behold, I will feed them with ^awormwood,
And make them drink the water of gall;
For from the prophets of Jerusalem
¹Profaneness has gone out into all the land.'"

16Thus says the LORD of hosts:

"Do not listen to the words of the prophets who prophesy
to you.
They make you worthless;
^aThey speak a vision of their own heart,
Not from the mouth of the LORD.

17 They continually say to those who despise Me,
'The LORD has said, ^a"You shall have peace"';
And *to* everyone who ^bwalks according to the ¹dictates of
his own heart, they say,
^c'No evil shall come upon you.'"

18 For ^awho has stood in the counsel of the LORD,
And has perceived and heard His word?
Who has marked His word and heard *it?*

23:9 ^aJer. 8:18; Hab. 3:16
23:10 ^aJer. 9:2 ^bHos. 4:2; Mal. 3:5 ^cPs. 107:34; Jer. 9:10
23:11 ^aJer. 6:13; Zeph. 3:4 ^bJer. 7:30; 32:34; Ezek. 8:11; 23:39
23:12 ^aPs. 35:6; [Prov. 4:19]; Jer. 13:16 ^bJer. 11:23
23:13 ^a1 Kin. 18:18–21; Jer. 2:8 ^bIs. 9:16
23:14 ^aJer. 29:23 ^bJer. 23:22; Ezek. 13:22, 23 ^cGen. 18:20; Deut. 32:32; Is. 1:9, 10
23:15 ^aDeut. 29:18; Jer. 9:15
23:16 ^aJer. 14:14; Ezek. 13:3, 6
23:17 ^aJer. 8:11; Ezek. 13:10; Zech. 10:2 ^bDeut. 29:19; Jer. 3:17 ^cJer. 5:12; Amos 9:10; Mic. 3:11
23:18 ^aJob 15:8, 9; [Jer. 23:22; 1 Cor. 2:16]

23:13 ¹Lit. *distastefulness* **23:15** ¹Or *Pollution* **23:17** ¹*stubbornness* or *imagination*

19 Behold, a ªwhirlwind of the LORD has gone forth in
fury—
A violent whirlwind!
It will fall violently on the head of the wicked.
20 The ªanger of the LORD will not turn back
Until He has executed and performed the thoughts of
His heart.
ᵇIn the latter days you will understand it perfectly.

21 "Iª have not sent these prophets, yet they ran.
I have not spoken to them, yet they prophesied.
22 But if they had stood in My counsel,
And had caused My people to hear My words,
Then they would have ªturned them from their evil way
And from the evil of their doings.

23 "*Am* I a God near at hand," says the LORD,
"And not a God afar off?
24 Can anyone ªhide himself in secret places,
So I shall not see him?" says the LORD;
ᵇ"Do I not fill heaven and earth?" says the LORD.

25"I have heard what the prophets have said who prophesy
lies in My name, saying, 'I have dreamed, I have dreamed!'
26How long will *this* be in the heart of the prophets who
prophesy lies? Indeed *they are* prophets of the deceit of their
own heart, 27who try to make My people forget My name by
their dreams which everyone tells his neighbor, ªas their fathers forgot My name for Baal.

28 "The prophet who has a dream, let him tell a dream;
And he who has My word, let him speak My word
faithfully.
What *is* the chaff to the wheat?" says the LORD.
29 "*Is* not My word like a ªfire?" says the LORD,
"And like a hammer *that* breaks the rock in pieces?

30"Therefore behold, ªI *am* against the prophets," says the
LORD, "who steal My words every one from his neighbor. 31Be-
hold, I *am* ªagainst the prophets," says the LORD, "who use
their tongues and say, 'He says.' 32Behold, I *am* against those
who prophesy false dreams," says the LORD, "and tell them,
and cause My people to err by their ªlies and by ᵇtheir reck-
lessness. Yet I did not send them or command them; therefore they shall not ᶜprofit this people at all," says the LORD.

33"So when these people or the prophet or the priest ask
you, saying, 'What is ªthe ¹oracle of the LORD?' you shall then
say to them, ²'What oracle?' I will even forsake you," says the
LORD. 34"And *as for* the prophet and the priest and the people
who say, 'The ¹oracle of the LORD!' I will even punish that
man and his house. 35Thus every one of you shall say to his
neighbor, and every one to his brother, 'What has the LORD
answered?' and, 'What has the LORD spoken?' 36And the ¹oracle of the LORD you shall mention no more. For every man's
word will be his oracle, for you have ªperverted the words of
the living God, the LORD of hosts, our God. 37Thus you shall
say to the prophet, 'What has the LORD answered you?' and,

23:19
ªJer. 25:32;
30:23; Amos 1:14
23:20
ª2 Kin. 23:26, 27;
Jer. 30:24
ᵇGen. 49:1

23:21 ªJer. 14:14;
23:32; 27:15
23:22 ªJer. 25:5
23:24
ª[Ps. 139:7];
Amos 9:2, 3
ᵇ[1 Kin. 8:27];
Ps. 139:7
23:27 ªJudg. 3:7
23:29 ªJer. 5:14
23:30
ªDeut. 18:20;
Ps. 34:16;
Jer. 14:14, 15;
Ezek. 13:8, 9
23:31
ªEzek. 13:9
23:32
ªJer. 20:6; 27:10;
Lam. 2:14; 3:37
ᵇZeph. 3:4
ᶜJer. 7:8;
Lam. 2:14
23:33 ªIs. 13:1;
Nah. 1:1; Hab. 1:1;
Zech. 9:1;
Mal. 1:1
23:36
ªDeut. 4:2

23:33 ¹*burden, prophecy*   ²LXX, Tg., Vg. *'You are the burden.'*
23:34 ¹*burden, prophecy*   23:36 ¹*burden, prophecy*

'What has the LORD spoken?' ³⁸But since you say, 'The ¹oracle of the LORD!' therefore thus says the LORD: 'Because you say this word, "The oracle of the LORD!" and I have sent to you, saying, "Do not say, 'The oracle of the LORD!'"' ³⁹therefore behold, I, even I, ªwill utterly forget you and forsake you, and the city that I gave you and your fathers, and *will cast you* out of My presence. ⁴⁰And I will bring ªan everlasting reproach upon you, and a perpetual ᵇshame, which shall not be forgotten.'"

THE SIGN OF TWO BASKETS OF FIGS

24 The ªLORD showed me, and there were two baskets of figs set before the temple of the LORD, after Nebuchadnezzar ᵇking of Babylon had carried away captive ᶜJeconiah the son of Jehoiakim, king of Judah, and the princes of Judah with the craftsmen and smiths, from Jerusalem, and had brought them to Babylon. ²One basket *had* very good figs, like the figs *that are* first ripe; and the other basket *had* very bad figs which could not be eaten, they were so ªbad. ³Then the LORD said to me, "What do you see, Jeremiah?"

And I said, "Figs, the good figs, very good; and the bad, very bad, which cannot be eaten, they are so bad."

⁴Again the word of the LORD came to me, saying, ⁵"Thus says the LORD, the God of Israel: 'Like these good figs, so will I ¹acknowledge those who are carried away captive from Judah, whom I have sent out of this place for *their own* good, into the land of the Chaldeans. ⁶For I will set My eyes on them for good, and ªI will bring them back to this land; ᵇI will build them and not pull *them* down, and I will plant them and not pluck *them* up. ⁷Then I will give them ªa heart to know Me, that I *am* the LORD; and they shall be ᵇMy people, and I will be their God, for they shall return to Me ᶜwith their whole heart.

⁸'And as the bad ªfigs which cannot be eaten, they are so bad'—surely thus says the LORD—'so will I give up Zedekiah the king of Judah, his princes, the ᵇresidue of Jerusalem who remain in this land, and ᶜthose who dwell in the land of Egypt. ⁹I will deliver them to ªtrouble into all the kingdoms of the earth, for *their* harm, ᵇ*to be* a reproach and a byword, a taunt and a curse, in all places where I shall drive them. ¹⁰And I will send the sword, the famine, and the pestilence among them, till they are ¹consumed from the land that I gave to them and their fathers.'"

SEVENTY YEARS OF DESOLATION

25 The word that came to Jeremiah concerning all the people of Judah, ªin the fourth year of ᵇJehoiakim the son of Josiah, king of Judah (which *was* the first year of Nebuchadnezzar king of Babylon), ²which Jeremiah the prophet spoke to all the people of Judah and to all the inhabitants of Jerusalem, saying: ³ª"From the thirteenth year of Josiah the son of Amon, king of Judah, even to this day, this *is* the twenty-third year in which the word of the LORD has come to me; and I have spoken to you, rising early and speaking, ᵇbut you have not listened. ⁴And the LORD has sent to you all His servants the prophets, ªrising early and sending *them*, but you have not listened nor inclined your ear to hear. ⁵They said, ª'Repent now everyone of his evil way and his evil doings, and dwell

Cross-references (margin)

23:39 ªHos. 4:6

23:40
ªJer. 20:11;
Ezek. 5:14, 15
ᵇMic. 3:5–7

24:1
ªAmos 7:1, 4; 8:1
ᵇ2 Kin. 24:12–16;
2 Chr. 36:10
ᶜJer. 22:24–28;
29:2

24:2 ªIs. 5:4, 7;
Jer. 29:17

24:6
ªJer. 12:15; 29:10;
Ezek. 11:17
ᵇJer. 32:41;
33:7; 42:10

24:7
ª[Deut. 30:6;
Jer. 32:39;
Ezek. 11:19;
36:26, 27]
ᵇIs. 51:16;
Jer. 30:22;
31:33; 32:38;
Ezek. 14:11;
Zech. 8:8;
[Heb. 8:10]
ᶜ1 Sam. 7:3;
Ps. 119:2;
Jer. 29:13

24:8 ªJer. 29:17
ᵇJer. 39:9
ᶜJer. 44:1, 26–30

24:9
ªDeut. 28:25, 37;
1 Kin. 9:7;
2 Chr. 7:20;
Jer. 15:4;
29:18; 34:17
ᵇPs. 44:13, 14

25:1 ªJer. 36:1
ᵇ2 Kin. 24:1, 2;
2 Chr. 36:4–6;
Dan. 1:1, 2

25:3 ªJer. 1:2
ᵇJer. 7:13;
11:7, 8, 10

25:4
ªJer. 7:13, 25

25:5
ª2 Kin. 17:13;
[Is. 55:6, 7];
Jer. 18:11;
Ezek. 18:30;
[Jon. 3:8–10]

23:38 ¹burden, prophecy   24:5 ¹regard   24:10 ¹destroyed

in the land that the LORD has given to you and your fathers forever and ever. 6Do not go after other gods to serve them and worship them, and do not provoke Me to anger with the works of your hands; and I will not harm you.' 7Yet you have not listened to Me," says the LORD, "that you might aprovoke Me to anger with the works of your hands to your own hurt.

8"Therefore thus says the LORD of hosts: 'Because you have not heard My words, 9behold, I will send and take aall the families of the north,' says the LORD, 'and Nebuchadnezzar the king of Babylon, bMy servant, and will bring them against this land, against its inhabitants, and against these nations all around, and will utterly destroy them, and cmake them an astonishment, a hissing, and perpetual desolations. 10Moreover I will 1take from them the avoice of mirth and the voice of gladness, the voice of the bridegroom and the voice of the bride, bthe sound of the millstones and the light of the lamp. 11And this whole land shall be a desolation and an astonishment, and these nations shall serve the king of Babylon seventy ayears.

12'Then it will come to pass, awhen 1seventy years are completed, that I will punish the king of Babylon and that nation, the land of the Chaldeans, for their iniquity,' says the LORD; b'and I will make it a perpetual desolation. 13So I will bring on that land all My words which I have pronounced against it, all that is written in this book, which Jeremiah has prophesied concerning all the nations. 14a(For many nations band great kings shall cbe served by them also; dand I will repay them according to their deeds and according to the works of their own hands.)'"

JUDGMENT ON THE NATIONS

15For thus says the LORD God of Israel to me: "Take this awine cup of 1fury from My hand, and cause all the nations, to whom I send you, to drink it. 16And athey will drink and stagger and go mad because of the sword that I will send among them."

17Then I took the cup from the LORD's hand, and made all the nations drink, to whom the LORD had sent me: 18Jerusalem and the cities of Judah, its kings and its princes, to make them aa desolation, an astonishment, a hissing, and ba curse, as it is this day; 19Pharaoh king of Egypt, his servants, his princes, and all his people; 20all the mixed multitude, all the kings of athe land of Uz, all the kings of the land of the bPhilistines (namely, Ashkelon, Gaza, Ekron, and cthe remnant of Ashdod); 21aEdom, Moab, and the people of Ammon; 22all the kings of aTyre, all the kings of Sidon, and the kings of the coastlands which are across the bsea; 23aDedan, Tema, Buz, and all who are in the farthest corners; 24all the kings of Arabia and all the kings of the amixed multitude who dwell in the desert; 25all the kings of Zimri, all the kings of aElam, and all the kings of the bMedes; 26aall the kings of the north, far and near, one with another; and all the kingdoms of the world which are on the face of the earth. Also the king of 1Sheshach shall drink after them.

27"Therefore you shall say to them, 'Thus says the LORD of hosts, the God of Israel: a"Drink, bbe drunk, and vomit!

25:7
aDeut. 32:21;
Jer. 7:19; 32:30

25:9 aJer. 1:15
bIs. 45:1;
Jer. 27:6
cJer. 18:16

25:10
aIs. 24:7–11;
Jer. 7:34; 16:9;
Ezek. 26:13;
Hos. 2:11;
Rev. 18:23
bEccl. 12:4;
Is. 47:2

25:11
a2 Chr. 36:21;
Jer. 29:10;
Dan. 9:2;
Zech. 7:5

25:12
a2 Chr. 36:21, 22;
Ezra 1:1;
Jer. 29:10;
Dan. 9:2
bIs. 13:20;
Jer. 50:3

25:14 aJer. 50:9;
51:27, 28
bJer. 51:27
cJer. 27:7
dJer. 50:29;
51:6, 24

25:15
aJob 21:20;
Ps. 75:8; Is. 51:17;
Rev. 14:10

25:16 aJer. 51:7;
Ezek. 23:34;
Nah. 3:11

25:18
aJer. 25:9, 11
bJer. 24:9

25:20 aJob 1:1;
Lam. 4:21
bJer. 47:1–7;
Ezek. 25:16, 17
cIs. 20:1

25:21 aJer. 49:7

25:22 aJer. 47:4;
Zech. 9:2–4
bJer. 49:23

25:23 aIs. 21:13;
Jer. 49:7, 8

25:24
aJer. 25:20;
50:37;
Ezek. 30:5

25:25
aGen. 10:22;
Is. 11:11;
Jer. 49:34
bIs. 13:17;
Jer. 51:11, 28

25:26 aJer. 50:9

25:27
aJer. 25:16;
Hab. 2:16
bIs. 63:6

25:10 1Lit. cause to perish from them   25:12 1Beginning circa 605 B.C. (2 Kin. 24:1) and ending circa 536 B.C. (Ezra 1:1)   25:15 1wrath
25:26 1A code word for Babylon, Jer. 51:41

Fall and rise no more, because of the sword which I will send among you."' ²⁸And it shall be, if they refuse to take the cup from your hand to drink, then you shall say to them, 'Thus says the LORD of hosts: "You shall certainly drink! ²⁹For behold, ᵃI begin to bring calamity on the city ᵇwhich is called by My name, and should you be utterly unpunished? You shall not be unpunished, for ᶜI will call for a sword on all the inhabitants of the earth," says the LORD of hosts.'

³⁰"Therefore prophesy against them all these words, and say to them:

'The LORD will ᵃroar from on high,
And utter His voice from ᵇHis holy habitation;
He will roar mightily against ᶜHis fold.
He will give ᵈa shout, as those who tread *the grapes*,
Against all the inhabitants of the earth.
31 A noise will come to the ends of the earth—
For the LORD has ᵃa controversy with the nations;
ᵇHe will plead His case with all flesh.
He will give those *who are* wicked to the sword,' says the
LORD."

³²Thus says the LORD of hosts:

"Behold, disaster shall go forth
From nation to nation,
And ᵃa great whirlwind shall be raised up
From the farthest parts of the earth.
33ᵃAnd at that day the slain of the LORD shall be from *one* end of the earth even to the *other* end of the earth. They shall not be ᵇlamented, ᶜor gathered, or buried; they shall become refuse on the ground.

34 "Wail,ᵃ shepherds, and cry!
Roll about *in the ashes*,
You leaders of the flock!
For the days of your slaughter and your dispersions are
fulfilled;
You shall fall like a precious vessel.
35 And the shepherds will have no ¹way to flee,
Nor the leaders of the flock to escape.
36 A voice of the cry of the shepherds,
And a wailing of the leaders to the flock *will be heard*.
For the LORD has plundered their pasture,
37 And the peaceful dwellings are cut down
Because of the fierce anger of the LORD.
38 He has left His lair like the lion;
For their land is desolate
Because of the fierceness of the Oppressor,
And because of His fierce anger."

JEREMIAH SAVED FROM DEATH
(cf. Jer. 7:1–15)

26 In the beginning of the reign of Jehoiakim the son of Josiah, king of Judah, this word came from the LORD, saying, ²"Thus says the LORD: 'Stand in ᵃthe court of the LORD's house, and speak to all the cities of Judah, which

25:29
ᵃ[Prov. 11:31];
Is. 10:12;
Jer. 13:13;
Ezek. 9:6;
[Luke 23:31];
1 Pet. 4:17]
ᵇDan. 9:18
ᶜEzek. 38:21

25:30 ᵃIs. 42:13;
Joel 3:16;
Amos 1:2
ᵇPs. 11:4
ᶜ1 Kin. 9:3;
Ps. 132:14
ᵈIs. 16:9;
Jer. 48:33

25:31 ᵃHos. 4:1;
Mic. 6:2
ᵇIs. 66:16;
Joel 3:2

25:32
ᵃJer. 23:19;
30:23

25:33
ᵃIs. 34:2, 3;
66:16
ᵇJer. 16:4, 6;
Ezek. 39:4, 17
ᶜPs. 79:3;
Jer. 8:2; Rev. 11:9

25:34
ᵃJer. 4:8; 6:26;
Ezek. 27:30

26:2
ᵃ2 Chr. 24:20, 21;
Jer. 19:14

25:35 ¹Or *refuge*

come to worship *in* the LORD's house, ᵇall the words that I command you to speak to them. ᶜDo not diminish a word. ³ᵃPerhaps everyone will listen and turn from his evil way, that I may ᵇrelent concerning the calamity which I purpose to bring on them because of the evil of their doings.' ⁴And you shall say to them, 'Thus says the LORD: ᵃ"If you will not listen to Me, to walk in My law which I have set before you, ⁵to heed the words of My servants the prophets ᵃwhom I sent to you, both rising up early and sending *them* (but you have not heeded), ⁶then I will make this house like ᵃShiloh, and will make this city ᵇa curse to all the nations of the earth."'"

⁷So the priests and the prophets and all the people heard Jeremiah speaking these words in the house of the LORD. ⁸Now it happened, when Jeremiah had made an end of speaking all that the LORD had commanded *him* to speak to all the people, that the priests and the prophets and all the people seized him, saying, "You will surely die! ⁹Why have you prophesied in the name of the LORD, saying, 'This house shall be like Shiloh, and this city shall be ᵃdesolate, without an inhabitant'?" And all the people were gathered against Jeremiah in the house of the LORD.

¹⁰When the princes of Judah heard these things, they came up from the king's house to the house of the LORD and sat down in the entry of the New Gate of the LORD's *house.* ¹¹And the priests and the prophets spoke to the princes and all the people, saying, ¹"This man deserves to ᵃdie! For he has prophesied against this city, as you have heard with your ears."

¹²Then Jeremiah spoke to all the princes and all the people, saying: "The LORD sent me to prophesy against this house and against this city with all the words that you have heard. ¹³Now therefore, ᵃamend your ways and your doings, and obey the voice of the LORD your God; then the LORD will relent concerning the doom that He has pronounced against you. ¹⁴As for me, here ᵃI am, in your hand; do with me as seems good and ¹proper to you. ¹⁵But know for certain that if you put me to death, you will surely bring innocent blood on yourselves, on this city, and on its inhabitants; for truly the LORD has sent me to you to speak all these words in your hearing."

¹⁶So the princes and all the people said to the priests and the prophets, "This man does not deserve to die. For he has spoken to us in the name of the LORD our God."

¹⁷ᵃThen certain of the elders of the land rose up and spoke to all the assembly of the people, saying: ¹⁸ᵃ"Micah of Moresheth prophesied in the days of Hezekiah king of Judah, and spoke to all the people of Judah, saying, 'Thus says the LORD of hosts:

ᵇ"Zion shall be plowed *like* a field,
Jerusalem shall become ᶜheaps of ruins,
And the mountain of the ¹temple
Like the ²bare hills of the forest."'

¹⁹Did Hezekiah king of Judah and all Judah ever put him to death? ᵃDid he not fear the LORD and ᵇseek the LORD's favor?

26:2 ᵇDeut. 4:2;
Jer. 43:1;
Ezek. 3:10;
Matt. 28:20;
[Rev. 22:19]
ᶜActs 20:27

26:3 ᵃIs. 1:16–19;
Jer. 36:3–7
ᵇJer. 18:8;
Jon. 3:9

26:4
ᵃLev. 26:14, 15;
Deut. 28:15;
1 Kin. 9:6;
Is. 1:20;
Jer. 17:27; 22:5

26:5
ᵃJer. 25:4; 29:19

26:6
ᵃ1 Sam. 4:10, 11;
Ps. 78:60;
Jer. 7:12, 14
ᵇ2 Kin. 22:19;
Is. 65:15;
Jer. 24:9

26:9 ᵃJer. 9:11

26:11 ᵃJer. 38:4

26:13 ᵃJer. 7:3;
[Joel 2:13];
Jon. 3:8

26:14 ᵃJer. 38:5

26:17 ᵃActs 5:34

26:18 ᵃMic. 1:1
ᵇMic. 3:12
ᶜNeh. 4:2;
Ps. 79:1; Jer. 9:11

26:19
ᵃ2 Chr. 32:26;
Is. 37:1, 4, 15–20
ᵇ2 Kin. 20:1–19

26:11 ¹Lit. *A judgment of death to this man*   26:14 ¹*right*   26:18 ¹Lit. *house*
²Lit. *high places*

And the LORD [c]relented concerning the doom which He had pronounced against them. [d]But we are doing great evil against ourselves."

20Now there was also a man who prophesied in the name of the LORD, Urijah the son of Shemaiah of Kirjath Jearim, who prophesied against this city and against this land according to all the words of Jeremiah. 21And when Jehoiakim the king, with all his mighty men and all the princes, heard his words, the king sought to put him to death; but when Urijah heard *it*, he was afraid and fled, and went to Egypt. 22Then Jehoiakim the king sent men to Egypt: Elnathan the son of Achbor, and *other* men *who went* with him to Egypt. 23And they brought Urijah from Egypt and brought him to Jehoiakim the king, who killed him with the sword and cast his dead body into the graves of the [1]common people.

24Nevertheless [a]the hand of Ahikam the son of Shaphan was with Jeremiah, so that they should not give him into the hand of the people to put him to death.

SYMBOL OF THE BONDS AND YOKES

27 In[1] the beginning of the reign of [2]Jehoiakim the son of Josiah, [a]king of Judah, this word came to Jeremiah from the LORD, saying, 2"Thus says the LORD to me: 'Make for yourselves bonds and yokes, [a]and put them on your neck, 3and send them to the king of Edom, the king of Moab, the king of the Ammonites, the king of Tyre, and the king of Sidon, by the hand of the messengers who come to Jerusalem to Zedekiah king of Judah. 4And command them to say to their masters, "Thus says the LORD of hosts, the God of Israel—thus you shall say to your masters: 5a'I have made the earth, the man and the beast that *are* on the ground, by My great power and by My outstretched arm, and [b]have given it to whom it seemed proper to Me. 6aAnd now I have given all these lands into the hand of Nebuchadnezzar the king of Babylon, [b]My servant; and [c]the beasts of the field I have also given him to serve him. 7aSo all nations shall serve him and his son and his son's son, [b]until the time of his land comes; [c]and then many nations and great kings shall make him serve them. 8And it shall be, *that* the nation and kingdom which will not serve Nebuchadnezzar the king of Babylon, and which will not put its neck under the yoke of the king of Babylon, that nation I will punish,' says the LORD, 'with the sword, the famine, and the pestilence, until I have consumed them by his hand. 9Therefore do not listen to your prophets, your diviners, your [1]dreamers, your soothsayers, or your sorcerers, who speak to you, saying, "You shall not serve the king of Babylon." 10For they prophesy a [a]lie to you, to remove you far from your land; and I will drive you out, and you will perish. 11But the nations that bring their necks under the yoke of the king of Babylon and serve him, I will let them remain in their own land,' says the LORD, 'and they shall till it and dwell in it.'"'"

12I also spoke to [a]Zedekiah king of Judah according to all these words, saying, "Bring your necks under the yoke of the king of Babylon, and serve him and his people, and live! 13aWhy will you die, you and your people, by the sword, by the

---

26:19 [c]Ex. 32:14;
2 Sam. 24:16;
Jer. 18:8
[d][Acts 5:39]

26:24
[a]2 Kin. 22:12–14;
Jer. 39:14;
40:5–7

27:1 [a]Jer. 27:3,
12, 20; 28:1

27:2
[a]Jer. 28:10, 12;
Ezek. 4:1;
12:3; 24:3

27:5 [a]Ps. 115:15;
146:6; Is. 45:12
[b]Deut. 9:29;
Ps. 115:16;
Jer. 32:17;
Dan. 4:17, 25, 32

27:6 [a]Jer. 28:14
[b]Jer. 25:9; 43:10;
Ezek. 29:18, 20
[c]Jer. 28:14;
Dan. 2:38

27:7
[a]2 Chr. 36:20
[b]Jer. 25:12;
50:27;
[Dan. 5:26];
Zech. 2:8, 9
[c]Jer. 25:14

27:10
[a]Jer. 23:16, 32;
28:15

27:12
[a]Jer. 28:1; 38:17

27:13
[a][Prov. 8:36];
Jer. 27:8; 38:23;
[Ezek. 18:31]

---

famine, and by the pestilence, as the Lord has spoken against the nation that will not serve the king of Babylon? ¹⁴Therefore ᵃdo not listen to the words of the prophets who speak to you, saying, 'You shall not serve the king of Babylon,' for they prophesy ᵇa lie to you; ¹⁵for I have ᵃnot sent them," says the Lord, "yet they prophesy a lie in My name, that I may drive you out, and that you may perish, you and the prophets who prophesy to you."

¹⁶Also I spoke to the priests and to all this people, saying, "Thus says the Lord: 'Do not listen to the words of your prophets who prophesy to you, saying, "Behold, ᵃthe vessels of the Lord's house will now shortly be brought back from Babylon"; for they prophesy a lie to you. ¹⁷Do not listen to them; serve the king of Babylon, and live! Why should this city be laid waste? ¹⁸But if they *are* prophets, and if the word of the Lord is with them, let them now make intercession to the Lord of hosts, that the vessels which are left in the house of the Lord, *in* the house of the king of Judah, and at Jerusalem, do not go to Babylon.'

¹⁹"For thus says the Lord of hosts ᵃconcerning the pillars, concerning the Sea, concerning the carts, and concerning the remainder of the vessels that remain in this city, ²⁰which Nebuchadnezzar king of Babylon did not take, when he carried away ᵃcaptive Jeconiah the son of Jehoiakim, king of Judah, from Jerusalem to Babylon, and all the nobles of Judah and Jerusalem— ²¹yes, thus says the Lord of hosts, the God of Israel, concerning the ᵃvessels that remain in the house of the Lord, and in the house of the king of Judah and of Jerusalem: ²²'They shall be ᵃcarried to Babylon, and there they shall be until the day that I ᵇvisit them,' says the Lord. 'Then ᶜI will bring them up and restore them to this place.'"

HANANIAH'S FALSEHOOD AND DOOM

28 And ᵃit happened in the same year, at the beginning of the reign of Zedekiah king of Judah, in the ᵇfourth year *and* in the fifth month, *that* Hananiah the son of ᶜAzur the prophet, who *was* from Gibeon, spoke to me in the house of the Lord in the presence of the priests and of all the people, saying, ²"Thus speaks the Lord of hosts, the God of Israel, saying: 'I have broken ᵃthe yoke of the king of Babylon. ³ᵃWithin two full years I will bring back to this place all the vessels of the Lord's house, that Nebuchadnezzar king of Babylon ᵇtook away from this place and carried to Babylon. ⁴And I will bring back to this place ¹Jeconiah the son of Jehoiakim, king of Judah, with all the captives of Judah who went to Babylon,' says the Lord, 'for I will break the yoke of the king of Babylon.'"

⁵Then the prophet Jeremiah spoke to the prophet Hananiah in the presence of the priests and in the presence of all the people who stood in the house of the Lord, ⁶and the prophet Jeremiah said, ᵃ"Amen! The Lord do so; the Lord perform your words which you have prophesied, to bring back the vessels of the Lord's house and all who were carried away captive, from Babylon to this place. ⁷Nevertheless hear now this word that I speak in your hearing and in the hearing of all the people: ⁸The prophets who have been before

27:14 ᵃJer. 23:16
ᵇJer. 14:14;
23:21; 29:8, 9;
Ezek. 13:22

27:15 ᵃJer. 23:21;
29:9

27:16
ᵃ2 Kin. 24:13;
2 Chr. 36:7, 10;
Jer. 28:3;
Dan. 1:2

27:19
ᵃ1 Kin. 7:15;
2 Kin. 25:13–17;
Jer. 52:17, 20, 21

27:20
ᵃ2 Kin. 24:14, 15;
2 Chr. 36:10, 18;
Jer. 24:1

27:21 ᵃJer. 20:5

27:22
ᵃ2 Kin. 25:13;
2 Chr. 36:18
ᵇ2 Chr. 36:21;
Jer. 29:10; 32:5
ᶜEzra 1:7; 7:19

28:1 ᵃJer. 27:1
ᵇJer. 51:59
ᶜEzek. 11:1

28:2 ᵃJer. 27:12

28:3 ᵃJer. 27:16
ᵇ2 Kin. 24:13;
Dan. 1:2

28:6 ᵃ1 Kin. 1:36;
Ps. 41:13; Jer. 11:5

28:4 ¹*Jehoiachin,* 2 Kin. 24:12

me and before you of old prophesied against many countries and great kingdoms—of war and disaster and pestilence. 9As for ᵃthe prophet who prophesies of ᵇpeace, when the word of the prophet comes to pass, the prophet will be known *as* one whom the LORD has truly sent."

10Then Hananiah the prophet took the ᵃyoke off the prophet Jeremiah's neck and broke it. 11And Hananiah spoke in the presence of all the people, saying, "Thus says the LORD: 'Even so I will break the yoke of Nebuchadnezzar king of Babylon ᵃfrom the neck of all nations within the space of two full years.'" And the prophet Jeremiah went his way.

12Now the word of the LORD came to Jeremiah, after Hananiah the prophet had broken the yoke from the neck of the prophet Jeremiah, saying, 13"Go and tell Hananiah, saying, 'Thus says the LORD: "You have broken the yokes of wood, but you have made in their place yokes of iron." 14For thus says the LORD of hosts, the God of Israel: ᵃ"I have put a yoke of iron on the neck of all these nations, that they may serve Nebuchadnezzar king of Babylon; and they shall serve him. ᵇI have given him the beasts of the field also."'"

15Then the prophet Jeremiah said to Hananiah the prophet, "Hear now, Hananiah, the LORD has not sent you, but ᵃyou make this people trust in a ᵇlie. 16Therefore thus says the LORD: 'Behold, I will cast you from the face of the earth. This year you shall ᵃdie, because you have taught ᵇrebellion against the LORD.'"

17So Hananiah the prophet died the same year in the seventh month.

JEREMIAH'S LETTER TO THE CAPTIVES

29 Now these *are* the words of the letter that Jeremiah the prophet sent from Jerusalem to the remainder of the elders who were ᵃcarried away captive—to the priests, the prophets, and all the people whom Nebuchadnezzar had carried away captive from Jerusalem to Babylon. 2(This happened after ᵃJeconiah[1] the king, the ᵇqueen mother, the ²eunuchs, the princes of Judah and Jerusalem, the craftsmen, and the smiths had departed from Jerusalem.) 3*The letter was sent* by the hand of Elasah the son of ᵃShaphan, and Gemariah the son of Hilkiah, whom Zedekiah king of Judah sent to Babylon, to Nebuchadnezzar king of Babylon, saying,

4 Thus says the LORD of hosts, the God of Israel, to all who were carried away captive, whom I have caused to be carried away from Jerusalem to Babylon:

5 Build houses and dwell *in them;* plant gardens and eat their fruit. 6Take wives and beget sons and daughters; and take wives for your sons and give your daughters to husbands, so that they may bear sons and daughters— that you may be increased there, and not diminished. 7And seek the peace of the city where I have caused you to be carried away captive, ᵃand pray to the LORD for it; for in its peace you will have peace. 8For thus says the LORD of hosts, the God of Israel: Do not let your prophets and your diviners who are in your midst ᵃdeceive you, nor listen to your dreams which you cause to be

---

28:9
ᵃDeut. 18:22
ᵇJer. 23:17;
Ezek. 13:10, 16

28:10 ᵃJer. 27:2

28:11 ᵃJer. 27:7

28:14
ᵃDeut. 28:48;
Jer. 27:7, 8
ᵇJer. 27:6

28:15
ᵃJer. 20:6; 29:31;
Lam. 2:14;
Ezek. 13:22;
Zech. 13:3
ᵇJer. 27:10; 29:9

28:16 ᵃJer. 20:6
ᵇDeut. 13:5;
Jer. 29:32

29:1 ᵃJer. 27:20

29:2
ᵃ2 Kin. 24:12–16;
2 Chr. 36:9, 10;
Jer. 22:24–28
ᵇ2 Kin. 24:12, 15;
Jer. 13:18

29:3
ᵃ2 Chr. 34:8

29:7 ᵃEzra 6:10;
Neh. 1:4–11;
Dan. 9:16;
1 Tim. 2:2

29:8 ᵃJer. 14:14;
23:21; 27:14, 15;
Eph. 5:6

29:2 ¹*Jehoiachin,* 2 Kin. 24:12; 2 Chr. 36:10 ²Or *officers*

dreamed. 9For they prophesy ᵃfalsely to you in My name; I have not sent them, says the LORD.

10 For thus says the LORD: After ᵃseventy years are completed at Babylon, I will visit you and perform My good word toward you, and cause you to ᵇreturn to this place. 11For I know the thoughts that I think toward you, says the LORD, thoughts of peace and not of evil, to give you a future and a hope. 12Then you will ᵃcall upon Me and go and pray to Me, and I will ᵇlisten to you. 13And ᵃyou will seek Me and find *Me*, when you search for Me ᵇwith all your heart. 14ᵃI will be found by you, says the LORD, and I will bring you back from your captivity; ᵇI will gather you from all the nations and from all the places where I have driven you, says the LORD, and I will bring you to the place from which I cause you to be carried away captive.

15 Because you have said, "The LORD has raised up prophets for us in Babylon"— 16ᵃtherefore thus says the LORD concerning the king who sits on the throne of David, concerning all the people who dwell in this city, and concerning your brethren who have not gone out with you into captivity— 17thus says the LORD of hosts: Behold, I will send on them the sword, the famine, and the pestilence, and will make them like ᵃrotten figs that cannot be eaten, they are so bad. 18And I will pursue them with the sword, with famine, and with pestilence; and I ᵃwill deliver them to trouble among all the kingdoms of the earth—to be ᵇa curse, an astonishment, a hissing, and a reproach among all the nations where I have driven them, 19because they have not heeded My words, says the LORD, which ᵃI sent to them by My servants the prophets, rising up early and sending *them;* neither would you heed, says the LORD. 20Therefore hear the word of the LORD, all you of the captivity, whom I have sent from Jerusalem to Babylon.

21 Thus says the LORD of hosts, the God of Israel, concerning Ahab the son of Kolaiah, and Zedekiah the son of Maaseiah, who prophesy a ᵃlie to you in My name: Behold, I will deliver them into the hand of Nebuchadnezzar king of Babylon, and he shall slay them before your eyes. 22ᵃAnd because of them a curse shall be taken up by all the captivity of Judah who *are* in Babylon, saying, "The LORD make you like Zedekiah and Ahab, ᵇwhom the king of Babylon roasted in the fire"; 23because ᵃthey have done disgraceful things in Israel, have committed adultery with their neighbors' wives, and have spoken lying words in My name, which I have not commanded them. Indeed I ᵇknow, and *am* a witness, says the LORD.

24 You shall also speak to Shemaiah the Nehelamite, saying, 25Thus speaks the LORD of hosts, the God of Israel, saying: You have sent letters in your name to all the people who *are* at Jerusalem, ᵃto Zephaniah the son of Maaseiah the priest, and to all the priests, saying, 26"The LORD has made you priest instead of Jehoiada the priest, so that there should be ᵃofficers *in* the house of the LORD

29:9
ᵃJer. 28:15; 37:19

29:10
ᵃ2 Chr. 36:21–23;
Ezra 1:1–4;
Jer. 25:12;
27:22; Dan. 9:2;
Zech. 7:5
ᵇ[Jer. 24:6, 7];
Zeph. 2:7

29:12 ᵃPs. 50:15;
Jer. 33:3;
Dan. 9:3
ᵇPs. 145:19

29:13
ᵃLev. 26:39–42;
Deut. 30:1–3
ᵇ1 Chr. 22:19;
2 Chr. 22:9;
Jer. 24:7

29:14
ᵃ[Deut. 4:7];
Ps. 32:6; 46:1;
[Is. 55:6, 7];
Jer. 24:7
ᵇIs. 43:5, 6;
Jer. 23:8; 32:37

29:16
ᵃJer. 38:2, 3,
17–23

29:17 ᵃJer. 24:3,
8–10

29:18
ᵃDeut. 28:25;
2 Chr. 29:8;
Jer. 15:4; 24:9;
34:17; Ezek. 12:15
ᵇJer. 26:6; 42:18

29:19 ᵃJer. 25:4;
26:5; 35:15

29:21
ᵃJer. 14:14, 15;
Lam. 2:14;
2 Pet. 2:1

29:22
ᵃGen. 48:20;
Is. 65:15
ᵇDan. 3:6, 21

29:23 ᵃJer. 23:14
ᵇ[Prov. 5:21;
Jer. 16:17];
Mal. 3:5;
[Heb. 4:13]

29:25
ᵃ2 Kin. 25:18;
Jer. 21:1

29:26 ᵃJer. 20:1

over every man *who* is [b]demented and considers himself a prophet, that you should [c]put him in prison and in the stocks. [27]Now therefore, why have you not rebuked Jeremiah of Anathoth who makes himself a prophet to you? [28]For he has sent to us *in* Babylon, saying, 'This *captivity is* long; build houses and dwell *in them,* and plant gardens and eat their fruit.'"

[29] Now Zephaniah the priest read this letter in the hearing of Jeremiah the prophet. [30]Then the word of the LORD came to Jeremiah, saying: [31]Send to all those in captivity, saying, Thus says the LORD concerning Shemaiah the Nehelamite: Because Shemaiah has prophesied to you, [a]and I have not sent him, and he has caused you to trust in a [b]lie— [32]therefore thus says the LORD: Behold, I will punish Shemaiah the Nehelamite and his [1]family: he shall not have anyone to dwell among this people, nor shall he see the good that I will do for My people, says the LORD, [a]because he has taught rebellion against the LORD.

RESTORATION OF ISRAEL AND JUDAH

30 The word that came to Jeremiah from the LORD, saying, [2]"Thus speaks the LORD God of Israel, saying: 'Write in a book for yourself all the words that I have spoken to you. [3]For behold, the days are coming,' says the LORD, 'that [a]I will bring back from captivity My people Israel and Judah,' says the LORD. [b]'And I will cause them to return to the land that I gave to their fathers, and they shall possess it.'"

[4]Now these *are* the words that the LORD spoke concerning Israel and Judah.

[5]"For thus says the LORD:

'We have heard a voice of trembling,
Of [1]fear, and not of peace.
[6] Ask now, and see,
Whether a [1]man is ever in [2]labor with child?
So why do I see every man *with* his hands on his loins
[a]Like a woman in labor,
And all faces turned pale?
[7] [a]Alas! For that day *is* great,
[b]So that none *is* like it;
And it *is* the time of Jacob's trouble,
But he shall be saved out of it.
[8] 'For it shall come to pass in that day,'
Says the LORD of hosts,
'*That* I will break his yoke from your neck,
And will burst your bonds;
Foreigners shall no more enslave them.
[9] But they shall serve the LORD their God,
And [a]David their king,
Whom I will [b]raise up for them.

[10] 'Therefore [a]do not fear, O My servant Jacob,' says the
LORD,
'Nor be dismayed, O Israel;

29:26
[b]2 Kin. 9:11;
Hos. 9:7;
Mark 3:21;
John 10:20;
Acts 26:24;
[2 Cor. 5:13]
[c]Jer. 20:1, 2;
Acts 16:24

29:31 [a]Jer. 28:15
[b]Ezek. 13:8–16,
22, 23

29:32
[a]Jer. 28:16

30:3 [a]Ps. 53:6;
Jer. 29:14;
30:18; 32:44;
Ezek. 39:25;
Amos 9:14;
Zeph. 3:20
[b]Jer. 16:15;
Ezek. 20:42;
36:24

30:6
[a]Jer. 4:31; 6:24

30:7 [a][Is. 2:12];
Hos. 1:11;
Joel 2:11;
Amos 5:18;
Zeph. 1:14
[b]Lam. 1:12;
Dan. 9:12; 12:1

30:9 [a]Is. 55:3;
Ezek. 34:23;
37:24; Hos. 3:5
[b][Luke 1:69;
Acts 2:30;
13:23]

30:10 [a]Is. 41:13;
43:5; 44:2;
Jer. 46:27, 28

29:32 [1]*descendants,* lit. *seed*　　**30:5** [1]*dread*　　**30:6** [1]Lit. *male can give birth*
[2]*childbirth*

For behold, I will save you from afar,
And your seed ᵇfrom the land of their captivity.
Jacob shall return, have rest and be quiet,
And no one shall make *him* afraid.
11 For I *am* with ᵃyou,' says the LORD, 'to save you;
ᵇThough I make a full end of all nations where I have
scattered you,
ᶜYet I will not make a complete end of you.
But I will correct you ᵈin justice,
And will not let you go altogether unpunished.'

12"For thus says the LORD:

ᵃ'Your affliction *is* incurable,
Your wound *is* severe.
13 *There is* no one to plead your cause,
That you may be bound up;
ᵃYou have no healing medicines.
14 ᵃAll your lovers have forgotten you;
They do not seek you;
For I have wounded you with the wound ᵇof an enemy,
With the chastisement ᶜof a cruel one,
For the multitude of your iniquities,
ᵈ*Because* your sins have increased.
15 Why ᵃdo you cry about your affliction?
Your sorrow *is* incurable.
Because of the multitude of your iniquities,
Because your sins have increased,
I have done these things to you.

16 'Therefore all those who devour you ᵃshall be devoured;
And all your adversaries, every one of them, shall go into
ᵇcaptivity;
Those who plunder you shall become ᶜplunder,
And all who prey upon you I will make a ᵈprey.
17 ᵃFor I will restore health to you
And heal you of your wounds,' says the LORD,
'Because they called you an outcast *saying:*
"This *is* Zion;
No one seeks her."'

18"Thus says the LORD:

'Behold, I will bring back the captivity of Jacob's tents,
And ᵃhave mercy on his dwelling places;
The city shall be built upon its own ¹mound,
And the palace shall remain according to its own plan.
19 Then ᵃout of them shall proceed thanksgiving
And the voice of those who make merry;
ᵇI will multiply them, and they shall not diminish;
I will also glorify them, and they shall not be small.
20 Their children also shall be ᵃas before,
And their congregation shall be established before Me;
And I will punish all who oppress them.
21 Their nobles shall be from among them,
ᵃAnd their governor shall come from their midst;
Then I will ᵇcause him to draw near,
And he shall approach Me;

30:10 ᵇJer. 3:18

30:11
ᵃ[Is. 43:2–5]
ᵇAmos 9:8
ᶜJer. 4:27;
46:27, 28
ᵈPs. 6:1; Is. 27:8;
Jer. 10:24; 46:28

30:12
ᵃ2 Chr. 36:16;
Jer. 15:18

30:13 ᵃJer. 8:22

30:14
ᵃJer. 22:20, 22;
Lam. 1:2
ᵇJob 13:24; 16:9;
19:11 ᶜJob 30:21
ᵈJer. 5:6

30:15 ᵃJer. 15:18

30:16
ᵃEx. 23:22;
Is. 41:11;
Jer. 10:25
ᵇIs. 14:2;
Joel 3:8 ᶜIs. 33:1;
Ezek. 39:10
ᵈJer. 2:3

30:17 ᵃEx. 15:26;
Ps. 107:20;
Is. 30:26;
Jer. 33:6

30:18 ᵃPs. 102:13

30:19
ᵃPs. 126:1, 2;
Is. 51:11; Jer. 31:4;
Zeph. 3:14
ᵇIs. 49:19–21;
Jer. 23:3; 33:22;
Zech. 10:8

30:20 ᵃIs. 1:26

30:21
ᵃGen. 49:10
ᵇNum. 16:5;
Ps. 65:4

30:18 ¹*ruins*

For who *is* this who pledged his heart to approach Me?'
says the LORD.

22 'You shall be ªMy people,
And I will be your God.'"

23 Behold, the ªwhirlwind of the LORD
Goes forth with fury,
A ¹continuing whirlwind;
It will fall violently on the head of the wicked.

24 The fierce anger of the LORD will not return until He has
done it,
And until He has performed the intents of His heart.

ªIn the latter days you will consider it.

THE REMNANT OF ISRAEL SAVED

31 "At ªthe same time," says the LORD, ᵇ"I will be the God of all the families of Israel, and they shall be My people." ²Thus says the LORD:

"The people who survived the sword
Found grace in the wilderness—
Israel, when ªI went to give him rest."

3 The LORD has appeared ¹of old to me, *saying:*
"Yes, ªI have loved you with ᵇan everlasting love;
Therefore with lovingkindness I have ᶜdrawn you.

4 Again ªI will build you, and you shall be rebuilt,
O virgin of Israel!
You shall again be adorned with your ᵇtambourines,
And shall go forth in the dances of those who rejoice.

5 ªYou shall yet plant vines on the mountains of Samaria;
The planters shall plant and ¹eat *them* as ordinary
food.

6 For there shall be a day
When the watchmen will cry on Mount Ephraim,
ª'Arise, and let us go up *to* Zion,
To the LORD our God.'"

⁷For thus says the LORD:

ª"Sing with gladness for Jacob,
And shout among the chief of the nations;
Proclaim, give praise, and say,
'O LORD, save Your people,
The remnant of Israel!'

8 Behold, I will bring them ªfrom the north country,
And ᵇgather them from the ends of the earth,
Among them the blind and the lame,
The woman with child
And the one who labors with child, together;
A great throng shall return there.

9 ªThey shall come with weeping,
And with supplications I will lead them.
I will cause them to walk ᵇby the rivers of waters,
In a straight way in which they shall not stumble;
For I am a Father to Israel,
And Ephraim *is* My ᶜfirstborn.

30:22 ªEx. 6:7;
Jer. 32:38;
Ezek. 36:28;
Hos. 2:23;
Zech. 13:9

30:23
ªJer. 23:19, 20;
25:32

30:24
ªGen. 49:1

31:1 ªJer. 30:24
ᵇJer. 30:22

31:2 ªEx. 33:14;
Num. 10:33;
Deut. 1:33;
Josh. 1:13;
Ps. 95:11;
Is. 63:14

31:3
ªDeut. 4:37; 7:8;
Mal. 1:2
ᵇIs. 43:4;
Rom. 11:28
ᶜHos. 11:4

31:4 ªJer. 33:7
ᵇEx. 15:20;
Judg. 11:34;
Ps. 149:3

31:5 ªPs. 107:37;
Is. 65:21;
Ezek. 28:26;
Amos 9:14

31:6
ª[Is. 2:3;
Jer. 31:12;
50:4, 5;
Mic. 4:2]

31:7 ªIs. 12:5, 6

31:8 ªJer. 3:12,
18; 23:8
ᵇDeut. 30:4;
Is. 43:6;
Ezek. 20:34, 41;
34:13

31:9 ª[Ps. 126:5;
Jer. 50:4]
ᵇIs. 35:8; 43:19;
49:10, 11
ᶜEx. 4:22

30:23 ¹Or *sweeping*   31:3 ¹Lit. *from afar*   31:5 ¹Lit. *treat them as common*

10 "Hear the word of the LORD, O nations,
And declare *it* in the [1]isles afar off, and say,
'He who scattered Israel [a]will gather him,
And keep him as a shepherd *does* his flock.'
11 For [a]the LORD has redeemed Jacob,
And ransomed him [b]from the hand of one stronger
than he.
12 Therefore they shall come and sing in [a]the height of
Zion,
Streaming to [b]the goodness of the LORD—
For wheat and new wine and oil,
For the young of the flock and the herd;
Their souls shall be like a [c]well-watered garden,
[d]And they shall sorrow no more at all.

13 "Then shall the virgin rejoice in the dance,
And the young men and the old, together;
For I will turn their mourning to joy,
Will comfort them,
And make them rejoice rather than sorrow.
14 I will [1]satiate the soul of the priests with abundance,
And My people shall be satisfied with My goodness, says
the LORD."

MERCY ON EPHRAIM

15 Thus says the LORD:

[a]"A voice was heard in [b]Ramah,
Lamentation *and* bitter [c]weeping,
Rachel weeping for her children,
Refusing to be comforted for her children,
Because [d]they *are* no more."

16 Thus says the LORD:

"Refrain your voice from [a]weeping,
And your eyes from tears;
For your work shall be rewarded, says the LORD,
And they shall come back from the land of the enemy.
17 There is [a]hope in your future, says the LORD,
That *your* children shall come back to their own border.

18 "I have surely heard Ephraim bemoaning himself:
'You have [a]chastised me, and I was chastised,
Like an untrained bull;
[b]Restore me, and I will return,
For You *are* the LORD my God.
19 Surely, [a]after my turning, I repented;
And after I was instructed, I struck myself on the
thigh;
I was [b]ashamed, yes, even humiliated,
Because I bore the reproach of my youth.'
20 *Is* Ephraim My dear son?
Is he a pleasant child?
For though I spoke against him,
I earnestly remember him still;
[a]Therefore My [1]heart yearns for him;
[b]I will surely have mercy on him, says the LORD.

31:10 [a]Is. 40:11;
Ezek. 34:12–14

31:11 [a]Is. 44:23;
48:20; Jer. 15:21;
50:19 [b]Is. 49:24

31:12
[a]Ezek. 17:23
[b]Hos. 3:5
[c]Is. 58:11
[d]Is. 35:10; 65:19;
[John 16:22;
Rev. 21:4]

31:15
[a]Matt. 2:17, 18
[b]Josh. 18:25;
Judg. 4:5;
Is. 10:29;
Jer. 40:1
[c]Gen. 37:35
[d]Jer. 10:20

31:16 [a][Is. 25:8;
30:19]

31:17 [a]Jer. 29:11

31:18 [a]Job 5:17;
Ps. 94:12
[b]Ps. 80:3, 7, 19;
Jer. 17:4;
Lam. 5:21;
[Acts 3:26]

31:19
[a]Deut. 30:2
[b]Ezek. 36:31;
[Zech. 12:10]

31:20
[a]Gen. 43:30;
Deut. 32:36;
Judg. 10:16;
Is. 63:15;
Hos. 11:8
[b]Is. 57:18;
Jer. 3:12; 12:15;
[Hos. 14:4];
Mic. 7:18

31:10 [1]Or *coastlands*   31:14 [1]Fill to the full   31:20 [1]Lit. *inward parts*

21 "Set up signposts,
    Make landmarks;
    ᵃSet your heart toward the highway,
    The way in *which* you went.
    ¹Turn back, O virgin of Israel,
    Turn back to these your cities.
22 How long will you ᵃgad about,
    O you ᵇbacksliding daughter?
    For the LORD has created a new thing in the earth—
    A woman shall encompass a man."

FUTURE PROSPERITY OF JUDAH

23Thus says the LORD of hosts, the God of Israel: "They shall again use this speech in the land of Judah and in its cities, when I bring back their captivity: ᵃ'The LORD bless you, O home of justice, *and* ᵇmountain of holiness!' 24And there shall dwell in Judah itself, and ᵃin all its cities together, farmers and those going out with flocks. 25For I have ¹satiated the weary soul, and I have replenished every sorrowful soul."

26After this I awoke and looked around, and my sleep was ᵃsweet to me.

27"Behold, the days are coming, says the LORD, that ᵃI will sow the house of Israel and the house of Judah with the seed of man and the seed of beast. 28And it shall come to pass, *that* as I have ᵃwatched over them ᵇto pluck up, to break down, to throw down, to destroy, and to afflict, so I will watch over them ᶜto build and to plant, says the LORD. 29ᵃIn those days they shall say no more:

'The fathers have eaten sour grapes,
    And the children's teeth are set on edge.'

30ᵃBut every one shall die for his own iniquity; every man who eats the sour grapes, his teeth shall be set on edge.

A NEW COVENANT

31"Behold, the ᵃdays are coming, says the LORD, when I will make a new covenant with the house of Israel and with the house of Judah— 32not according to the covenant that I made with their fathers in the day *that* ᵃI took them by the hand to lead them out of the land of Egypt, My covenant which they broke, ¹though I was a husband to them, says the LORD. 33ᵃBut this *is* the covenant that I will make with the house of Israel after those days, says the LORD: ᵇI will put My law in their minds, and write it on their ¹hearts; ᶜand I will be their God, and they shall be My people. 34No more shall every man teach his neighbor, and every man his brother, saying, 'Know the LORD,' for ᵃthey all shall know Me, from the least of them to the greatest of them, says the LORD. For ᵇI will forgive their iniquity, and their sin I will remember no more."

35 Thus says the LORD,
    ᵃWho gives the sun for a light by day,
    The ordinances of the moon and the stars for a light by
        night,
    Who disturbs ᵇthe sea,

31:21 ᵃJer. 50:5

31:22 ᵃJer. 2:18, 23, 36 ᵇJer. 3:6, 8, 11, 12, 14, 22

31:23 ᵃPs. 122:5–8; Is. 1:26 ᵇ[Zech. 8:3]

31:24 ᵃJer. 33:12

31:26 ᵃProv. 3:24

31:27 ᵃEzek. 36:9–11; Hos. 2:23

31:28 ᵃJer. 44:27; Dan. 9:14 ᵇJer. 1:10; 18:7 ᶜJer. 24:6

31:29 ᵃLam. 5:7; Ezek. 18:2, 3

31:30 ᵃDeut. 24:16; 2 Chr. 25:4; Is. 3:11; [Ezek. 18:4, 20; Gal. 6:5, 7]

31:31 ᵃJer. 32:40; 33:14; Ezek. 37:26; Heb. 8:8–12; 10:16, 17

31:32 ᵃDeut. 1:31; Is. 63:12

31:33 ᵃJer. 32:40; Heb. 10:16; ᵇPs. 40:8; [Ezek. 11:19; 36:26, 27; 2 Cor. 3:3] ᶜJer. 24:7; 30:22; 32:38

31:34 ᵃIs. 11:9; 54:13; Jer. 24:7; Hab. 2:14; [John 6:45; 1 Cor. 2:10; 1 John 2:20] ᵇJer. 33:8; 50:20; Mic. 7:18; [Acts 10:43; 13:39; Rom. 11:27]

31:35 ᵃGen. 1:14–18; Deut. 4:19; Ps. 72:5, 17; 89:2, 36; 119:91 ᵇIs. 51:15

31:21 ¹Or *Return*   31:25 ¹*fully satisfied*   31:32 ¹So with MT, Tg., Vg.; LXX, Syr. *and I turned away from them*   31:33 ¹Lit. *inward parts*

And its waves roar
c(The LORD of hosts *is* His name):

36 "If athose ordinances depart
From before Me, says the LORD,
Then the seed of Israel shall also cease
From being a nation before Me forever."

37Thus says the LORD:

a"If heaven above can be measured,
And the foundations of the earth searched out beneath,
I will also bcast off all the seed of Israel
For all that they have done, says the LORD.

38"Behold, the days are coming, says the LORD, that the city shall be built for the LORD afrom the Tower of Hananel to the Corner Gate. 39aThe surveyor's line shall again extend straight forward over the hill Gareb; then it shall turn toward Goath. 40And the whole valley of the dead bodies and of the ashes, and all the fields as far as the Brook Kidron, ato the corner of the Horse Gate toward the east, bshall *be* holy to the LORD. It shall not be plucked up or thrown down anymore forever."

JEREMIAH BUYS A FIELD

32 The word that came to Jeremiah from the LORD ain the tenth year of Zedekiah king of Judah, which was the eighteenth year of Nebuchadnezzar. 2For then the king of Babylon's army besieged Jerusalem, and Jeremiah the prophet was shut up ain the court of the prison, which *was in* the king of Judah's house. 3For Zedekiah king of Judah had shut him up, saying, "Why do you aprophesy and say, 'Thus says the LORD: b"Behold, I will give this city into the hand of the king of Babylon, and he shall take it; 4and Zedekiah king of Judah ashall not escape from the hand of the Chaldeans, but shall surely be delivered into the hand of the king of Babylon, and shall speak with him 1face to face, and see him beye to eye; 5then he shall alead Zedekiah to Babylon, and there he shall be buntil I visit him," says the LORD; c"though you fight with the Chaldeans, you shall not succeed" '?"

6And Jeremiah said, "The word of the LORD came to me, saying, 7'Behold, Hanamel the son of Shallum your uncle will come to you, saying, "Buy my field which *is* in Anathoth, for the aright of redemption *is* yours to buy *it.*" ' 8Then Hanamel my uncle's son came to me in the court of the prison according to the word of the LORD, and said to me, 'Please buy my field that *is* in Anathoth, which *is* in the country of Benjamin; for the right of inheritance *is* yours, and the redemption yours; buy *it* for yourself.' Then I knew that this was the word of the LORD. 9So I bought the field from Hanamel, the son of my uncle who *was* in Anathoth, and aweighed *out to* him the money—seventeen shekels of silver. 10And I signed the 1deed and sealed *it,* took witnesses, and weighed the money on the scales. 11So I took the purchase deed, *both* that which was sealed *according* to the law and custom, and that which was open; 12and I gave the purchase deed to aBaruch the son of Neriah, son of Mahseiah, in the presence of Hanamel my uncle's *son,* and in the presence of the bwitnesses who signed

31:35 cJer. 10:16

31:36 aPs. 148:6;
Is. 54:9, 10;
Jer. 33:20

31:37 aIs. 40:12;
Jer. 33:22
bJer. 33:24–26;
[Rom. 11:2–5,
26, 27]

31:38
aNeh. 3:1; 12:39;
Zech. 14:10

31:39
aEzek. 40:8;
Zech. 2:1, 2

31:40
a2 Kin. 11:16;
2 Chr. 23:15;
Neh. 3:28
b[Joel 3:17];
Zech. 14:20

32:1
a2 Kin. 25:1, 2;
Jer. 39:1, 2

32:2 aNeh. 3:25;
Jer. 33:1; 37:21;
39:14

32:3
aJer. 26:8, 9
bJer. 21:3–7;
34:2

32:4
a2 Kin. 25:4–7;
Jer. 34:3; 38:18,
23; 39:5; 52:9
bJer. 39:5

32:5
aJer. 27:22; 39:7;
Ezek. 12:12, 13
bJer. 27:22
cJer. 21:4; 33:5

32:7 aLev. 25:24,
25, 32; Ruth 4:4

32:9
aGen. 23:16;
Zech. 11:12

32:12 aJer. 36:4
bIs. 8:2

32:4 1Lit. *mouth to mouth* 32:10 1Lit. *book*

the purchase deed, before all the Jews who sat in the court of the prison.

13"Then I charged aBaruch before them, saying, 14'Thus says the LORD of hosts, the God of Israel: "Take these deeds, both this purchase deed which is sealed and this deed which is open, and put them in an earthen vessel, that they may last many days." 15For thus says the LORD of hosts, the God of Israel: "Houses and fields and vineyards shall be apossessed again in this land."'

JEREMIAH PRAYS FOR UNDERSTANDING

16"Now when I had delivered the purchase deed to Baruch the son of Neriah, I prayed to the LORD, saying: 17'Ah, Lord GOD! Behold, aYou have made the heavens and the earth by Your great power and outstretched arm. bThere is nothing too 1hard for You. 18You show alovingkindness to thousands, and repay the iniquity of the fathers into the bosom of their children after them—the Great, bthe Mighty God, whose name is cthe LORD of hosts. 19You are agreat in counsel and mighty in 1work, for Your beyes are open to all the ways of the sons of men, cto give everyone according to his ways and according to the fruit of his doings. 20You have set signs and wonders in the land of Egypt, to this day, and in Israel and among other men; and You have made Yourself aa name, as it is this day. 21You ahave brought Your people Israel out of the land of Egypt with signs and wonders, with a strong hand and an outstretched arm, and with great terror; 22You have given them this land, of which You swore to their fathers to give them—a"a land flowing with milk and honey." 23And they came in and took possession of it, but athey have not obeyed Your voice or walked in Your law. They have done nothing of all that You commanded them to do; therefore You have caused all this calamity to come upon them.

24'Look, the siege mounds! They have come to the city to take it; and the city has been given into the hand of the Chaldeans who fight against it, because of athe sword and famine and pestilence. What You have spoken has happened; there You see it! 25And You have said to me, O Lord GOD, "Buy the field for money, and take witnesses"!—yet the city has been given into the hand of the Chaldeans.'"

GOD'S ASSURANCE OF THE PEOPLE'S RETURN

26Then the word of the LORD came to Jeremiah, saying, 27"Behold, I am the LORD, the aGod of all flesh. Is there anything too hard for Me? 28Therefore thus says the LORD: 'Behold, I will give this city into the hand of the Chaldeans, into the hand of Nebuchadnezzar king of Babylon, and he shall take it. 29And the Chaldeans who fight against this city shall come and aset fire to this city and burn it, with the houses bon whose roofs they have offered incense to Baal and poured out drink offerings to other gods, to provoke Me to anger; 30because the children of Israel and the children of Judah ahave done only evil before Me from their youth. For the children of Israel have provoked Me only to anger with the work of their hands,' says the LORD. 31'For this city has been to Me a provocation of My anger and My fury from the day that they

32:13 aJer. 36:4
32:15 aEzra 2:1;
[Jer. 31:5, 12, 14];
Amos 9:14, 15;
Zech. 3:10
32:17
a2 Kin. 19:15;
Ps. 102:25;
Is. 40:26–29;
Jer. 27:5
bGen. 18:14;
Jer. 32:27;
Zech. 8:6;
Matt. 19:26;
Mark 10:27;
Luke 18:27
32:18
aEx. 20:6; 34:7;
Deut. 5:9, 10
bPs. 50:1;
[Is. 9:6];
Jer. 20:11
cJer. 10:16
32:19 aIs. 28:29
bJob 34:21;
Ps. 33:13;
Prov. 5:21;
Jer. 16:17
cPs. 62:12;
Jer. 17:10;
[Matt. 16:27];
John 5:29]
32:20 aEx. 9:16;
1 Chr. 17:21;
Is. 63:12;
Jer. 13:11;
Dan. 9:15
32:21 aEx. 6:6;
2 Sam. 7:23;
1 Chr. 17:21;
Ps. 136:11, 12
32:22
aEx. 3:8, 17;
Deut. 1:8;
Ps. 105:9–11;
Jer. 11:5
32:23
a[Neh. 9:26];
Jer. 11:8;
[Dan. 9:10–14]
32:24 aJer. 14:12;
Ezek. 14:21
32:27
a[Num. 16:22]
32:29
a2 Chr. 36:19;
Jer. 21:10;
37:8, 10; 52:13
bJer. 19:13
32:30
aDeut. 9:7–12;
Is. 63:10;
Jer. 2:7; 3:25;
7:22–26;
Ezek. 20:28

32:17 1difficult   32:19 1deed

built it, even to this day; ^aso I will remove it from before My face ³²because of all the evil of the children of Israel and the children of Judah, which they have done to provoke Me to anger—^athey, their kings, their princes, their priests, ^btheir prophets, the men of Judah, and the inhabitants of Jerusalem. ³³And they have turned to Me the ^aback, and not the face; though I taught them, ^brising up early and teaching *them,* yet they have not listened to receive instruction. ³⁴But they ^aset their abominations in ¹the house which is called by My name, to defile it. ³⁵And they built the high places of Baal which *are* in the Valley of the Son of Hinnom, to ^acause their sons and their daughters to pass through *the fire* to ^bMolech, ^cwhich I did not command them, nor did it come into My mind that they should do this abomination, to cause Judah to sin.'

³⁶"Now therefore, thus says the LORD, the God of Israel, concerning this city of which you say, 'It shall be delivered into the hand of the king of Babylon by the sword, by the famine, and by the pestilence: ³⁷Behold, I will ^agather them out of all countries where I have driven them in My anger, in My fury, and in great wrath; I will bring them back to this place, and I will cause them ^bto dwell safely. ³⁸They shall be ^aMy people, and I will be their God; ³⁹then I will ^agive them one heart and one way, that they may fear Me forever, for the good of them and their children after them. ⁴⁰And ^aI will make an everlasting covenant with them, that I will not turn away from doing them good; but ^bI will put My fear in their hearts so that they will not depart from Me. ⁴¹Yes, ^aI will rejoice over them to do them good, and ^bI will ¹assuredly plant them in this land, with all My heart and with all My soul.'

⁴²"For thus says the LORD: ^a'Just as I have brought all this great calamity on this people, so I will bring on them all the good that I have promised them. ⁴³And fields will be bought in this land ^aof which you say, "*It is* desolate, without man or beast; it has been given into the hand of the Chaldeans." ⁴⁴Men will buy fields for money, sign deeds and seal *them,* and take witnesses, in ^athe land of Benjamin, in the places around Jerusalem, in the cities of Judah, in the cities of the mountains, in the cities of the ¹lowland, and in the cities of the ²South; for ^bI will cause their captives to return,' says the LORD."

EXCELLENCE OF THE RESTORED NATION

33 Moreover the word of the LORD came to Jeremiah a second time, while he was still ^ashut up in the court of the prison, saying, ²"Thus says the LORD ^awho made it, the LORD who formed it to establish it ^b(the¹ LORD *is* His name): ^{3a}'Call to Me, and I will answer you, and show you great and ¹mighty things, which you do not know.'

⁴"For thus says the LORD, the God of Israel, concerning the houses of this city and the houses of the kings of Judah, which have been pulled down *to fortify* against ^athe siege mounds and the sword: ⁵They come to fight with the Chaldeans, but *only* to ^afill their places with the dead bodies of men whom I will slay in My anger and My fury, all for whose wickedness I have hidden My face from this city. ⁶Behold, ^aI will bring it

32:31
^a2 Kin. 23:27; 24:3; Jer. 27:10

32:32 ^aEzra 9:7; Is. 1:4, 6; Dan. 9:8
^bJer. 23:14

32:33 ^aJer. 2:27; 7:24 ^bJer. 7:13

32:34
^a2 Kin. 21:1–7; Jer. 7:10–12, 30; 23:11; Ezek. 8:5, 6

32:35
^a2 Chr. 28:2, 3; 33:6; Jer. 7:31; 19:5 ^bLev. 18:21; 1 Kin. 11:33; 2 Kin. 23:10; Acts 7:43
^cJer. 7:31

32:37
^aDeut. 30:3; Jer. 23:3; 29:14; 31:10; 50:19; Ezek. 37:21
^bJer. 33:16

32:38 ^a[Jer. 24:7; 30:22; 31:33]

32:39
^a[Jer. 24:7; Ezek. 11:19]

32:40 ^aIs. 55:3; Jer. 31:31; Ezek. 37:26
^bDeut. 31:6, 8; [Ezek. 39:29; Jer. 31:33]

32:41
^aDeut. 30:9; Is. 62:5; 65:19; Zeph. 3:17
^bJer. 24:6; 31:28; Amos 9:15

32:42
^aJer. 31:28; Zech. 8:14, 15

32:43 ^aJer. 33:10

32:44 ^aJer. 17:26
^bJer. 33:7, 11

33:1 ^aJer. 32:2, 3

33:2 ^aIs. 37:26
^bEx. 15:3; [Jer. 10:16]; Amos 5:8; 9:6

33:3 ^aPs. 91:15; [Is. 55:6, 7]; Jer. 29:12

33:4 ^aIs. 22:10; Jer. 32:24; Ezek. 4:2; 21:22; Hab. 1:10

33:5
^a2 Kin. 23:14; Jer. 21:4–7; 32:5

33:6 ^aJer. 30:17; Hos. 6:1

health and healing; I will heal them and reveal to them the abundance of peace and truth. 7And aI will cause the captives of Judah and the captives of Israel to return, and will rebuild those places bas at the first. 8I will acleanse them from all their iniquity by which they have sinned against Me, and I will pardon all their iniquities by which they have sinned and by which they have transgressed against Me. 9aThen it shall be to Me a name of joy, a praise, and an honor before all nations of the earth, who shall hear all the good that I do to them; they shall bfear and tremble for all the goodness and all the prosperity that I provide for it.'

10"Thus says the LORD: 'Again there shall be heard in this place—aof which you say, "It is desolate, without man and without beast"—in the cities of Judah, in the streets of Jerusalem that are desolate, without man and without inhabitant and without beast, 11the avoice of joy and the voice of gladness, the voice of the bridegroom and the voice of the bride, the voice of those who will say:

b"Praise the LORD of hosts,
For the LORD is good,
For His mercy endures forever"—

and of those who will bring cthe sacrifice of praise into the house of the LORD. For I will cause the captives of the land to return as at the first,' says the LORD.

12"Thus says the LORD of hosts: a'In this place which is desolate, without man and without beast, and in all its cities, there shall again be a dwelling place of shepherds causing their flocks to lie down. 13aIn the cities of the mountains, in the cities of the lowland, in the cities of the South, in the land of Benjamin, in the places around Jerusalem, and in the cities of Judah, the flocks shall again bpass under the hands of him who counts them,' says the LORD.

14a'Behold, the days are coming,' says the LORD, 'that bI will perform that good thing which I have promised to the house of Israel and to the house of Judah:

15   'In those days and at that time
    I will cause to grow up to David
    A aBranch of righteousness;
    He shall execute judgment and righteousness in the
        earth.
16   In those days Judah will be saved,
    And Jerusalem will dwell safely.
    And this is the name by which she will be called:

        1'THE LORD OUR RIGHTEOUSNESS.'

17"For thus says the LORD: 'David shall never alack a man to sit on the throne of the house of Israel; 18nor shall the apriests, the Levites, lack a man to boffer burnt offerings before Me, to 1kindle grain offerings, and to sacrifice continually.'"

THE PERMANENCE OF GOD'S COVENANT

19And the word of the LORD came to Jeremiah, saying, 20"Thus says the LORD: 'If you can break My covenant with the day and My covenant with the night, so that there will not be

---

33:7 aPs. 85:1;
Jer. 30:3; 32:44;
Amos 9:14
bIs. 1:26;
Jer. 24:6; 30:20;
31:4, 28; 42:10;
Amos 9:14, 15

33:8 aPs. 51:2;
Is. 44:22;
Jer. 50:20;
Ezek. 36:25, 33;
Mic. 7:18, 19;
Zech. 13:1;
[Heb. 9:11–14]

33:9 aIs. 62:7;
Jer. 13:11
bIs. 60:5

33:10 aJer. 32:43

33:11 aJer. 7:34;
16:9; 25:10;
Rev. 18:23
b1 Chr. 16:8;
2 Chr. 5:13;
Ezra 3:11;
Ps. 136:1; Is. 12:4
cLev. 7:12;
Ps. 107:22;
116:17; Heb. 13:15

33:12 aIs. 65:10;
[Jer. 31:24;
50:19;
Ezek. 34:12–15;
Zeph. 2:6, 7]

33:13 aJer. 17:26;
32:44
bLev. 27:32;
[Luke 15:4]

33:14 aJer. 23:5;
31:27, 31 bIs. 32:1;
Jer. 29:10; 32:42;
Ezek. 34:23–25;
Hag. 2:6–9

33:15
aIs. 4:2; 11:1;
Jer. 23:5;
Zech. 3:8;
6:12, 13

33:17
a2 Sam. 7:16;
1 Kin. 2:4;
Ps. 89:29;
[Luke 1:32]

33:18
aNum. 3:5–10;
Deut. 18:1; 24:8;
Josh. 3:3;
Ezek. 44:15
b[Rom. 12:1;
15:16;
1 Pet. 2:5, 9;
Rev. 1:6]

33:16 1Heb. YHWH Tsidkenu; cf. Jer. 23:5, 6   33:18 1burn

day and night in their season, ²¹then ^aMy covenant may also be broken with David My servant, so that he shall not have a son to reign on his throne, and with the Levites, the priests, My ministers. ²²As ^athe host of heaven cannot be numbered, nor the sand of the sea measured, so will I ^bmultiply the descendants of David My servant and the ^cLevites who minister to Me.'"

²³Moreover the word of the LORD came to Jeremiah, saying, ²⁴"Have you not considered what these people have spoken, saying, 'The two families which the LORD has chosen, He has also cast them off'? Thus they have ^adespised My people, as if they should no more be a nation before them.

²⁵"Thus says the LORD: 'If ^aMy covenant *is* not with day and night, *and if* I have not ^bappointed the ordinances of heaven and earth, ^{26a}then I will ^bcast away the descendants of Jacob and David My servant, *so* that I will not take *any* of his descendants *to be* rulers over the descendants of Abraham, Isaac, and Jacob. For I will cause their captives to return, and will have mercy on them.'"

ZEDEKIAH WARNED BY GOD

34 The word which came to Jeremiah from the LORD, ^awhen Nebuchadnezzar king of Babylon and all his army, ^ball the kingdoms of the earth under his dominion, and all the people, fought against Jerusalem and all its cities, saying, ²"Thus says the LORD, the God of Israel: 'Go and ^aspeak to Zedekiah king of Judah and tell him, "Thus says the LORD: 'Behold, ^bI will give this city into the hand of the king of Babylon, and he shall burn it with fire. ³And ^ayou shall not escape from his hand, but shall surely be taken and delivered into his hand; your eyes shall see the eyes of the king of Babylon, he shall speak with you ^bface[1] to face, and you shall go to Babylon.'"' ⁴Yet hear the word of the LORD, O Zedekiah king of Judah! Thus says the LORD concerning you: 'You shall not die by the sword. ⁵You shall die in peace; as in ^athe ceremonies of your fathers, the former kings who were before you, ^bso they shall burn *incense* for you and ^clament for you, *saying*, "Alas, lord!" For I have pronounced the word, says the LORD.'"

⁶Then Jeremiah the prophet spoke all these words to Zedekiah king of Judah in Jerusalem, ⁷when the king of Babylon's army fought against Jerusalem and all the cities of Judah that were left, against Lachish and Azekah; for *only* ^athese fortified cities remained of the cities of Judah.

TREACHEROUS TREATMENT OF SLAVES

⁸*This is* the word that came to Jeremiah from the LORD, after King Zedekiah had made a covenant with all the people who *were* at Jerusalem to proclaim ^aliberty to them: ^{9a}that every man should set free his male and female slave—a Hebrew man or woman—^bthat no one should keep a Jewish brother in bondage. ¹⁰Now when all the princes and all the people, who had entered into the covenant, heard that everyone should set free his male and female slaves, that no one should keep them in bondage anymore, they obeyed and let *them* go. ¹¹But afterward they changed their minds and made the male and female slaves return, whom they

33:21
^a2 Sam. 23:5;
2 Chr. 7:18; 21:7;
Ps. 89:34

33:22
^aGen. 15:5;
22:17; Jer. 31:37
^bJer. 30:19;
Ezek. 36:10, 11
^cIs. 66:21;
Jer. 33:18

33:24
^aNeh. 4:2–4;
Esth. 3:6–8;
Ps. 44:13, 14;
83:4; Ezek. 36:2

33:25
^aGen. 8:22;
Jer. 33:20
^bPs. 74:16; 104:19

33:26 ^aJer. 31:37
^bRom. 11:1, 2

34:1 ^a2 Kin. 25:1;
Jer. 32:1, 2;
39:1; 52:4
^bJer. 1:15; 25:9;
Dan. 2:37, 38

34:2
^a2 Chr. 36:11, 12;
Jer. 22:1, 2; 37:1, 2
^b2 Kin. 25:9;
Jer. 21:10;
32:3, 28

34:3
^a2 Kin. 25:4, 5;
Jer. 21:7; 52:7–11
^b2 Kin. 25:6, 7;
Jer. 32:4; 39:5, 6

34:5
^a2 Chr. 16:14;
21:19 ^bDan. 2:46
^cJer. 22:18

34:7
^a2 Kin. 18:13;
19:8; 2 Chr. 11:5, 9

34:8 ^aEx. 21:2;
Lev. 25:10;
Neh. 5:1–13;
Is. 58:6;
Jer. 34:14, 17

34:9 ^aNeh. 5:11
^bLev. 25:39–46

34:3 [1]Lit. *mouth to mouth*

had set free, and brought them into subjection as male and female slaves.

12Therefore the word of the LORD came to Jeremiah from the LORD, saying, 13"Thus says the LORD, the God of Israel: 'I made a ᵃcovenant with your fathers in the day that I brought them out of the land of Egypt, out of the house of bondage, saying, 14"At the end of ᵃseven years let every man set free his Hebrew brother, who ¹has been sold to him; and when he has served you six years, you shall let him go free from you." But your fathers did not obey Me nor incline their ear. 15Then you ¹recently turned and did what was right in My sight—every man proclaiming liberty to his neighbor; and you ᵃmade a covenant before Me ᵇin the house which is called by My name. 16Then you turned around and ᵃprofaned My name, and every one of you brought back his male and female slaves, whom you had set at liberty, at their pleasure, and brought them back into subjection, to be your male and female slaves.'

17"Therefore thus says the LORD: 'You have not obeyed Me in proclaiming liberty, every one to his brother and every one to his neighbor. ᵃBehold, I proclaim liberty to you,' says the LORD—ᵇ'to the sword, to pestilence, and to famine! And I will deliver you to ᶜtrouble among all the kingdoms of the earth. 18And I will give the men who have transgressed My covenant, who have not performed the words of the covenant which they made before Me, when ᵃthey cut the calf in two and passed between the parts of it— 19the princes of Judah, the princes of Jerusalem, the ¹eunuchs, the priests, and all the people of the land who passed between the parts of the calf— 20I will ᵃgive them into the hand of their enemies and into the hand of those who seek their life. Their ᵇdead bodies shall be for meat for the birds of the heaven and the beasts of the earth. 21And I will give Zedekiah king of Judah and his princes into the hand of their enemies, into the hand of those who seek their life, and into the hand of the king of Babylon's army ᵃwhich has gone back from you. 22ᵃBehold, I will command,' says the LORD, 'and cause them to return to this city. They will fight against it ᵇand take it and burn it with fire; and ᶜI will make the cities of Judah a desolation without inhabitant.'"

THE OBEDIENT RECHABITES

35 The word which came to Jeremiah from the LORD in the days of Jehoiakim the son of Josiah, king of Judah, saying, 2"Go to the house of the ᵃRechabites, speak to them, and bring them into the house of the LORD, into one of ᵇthe chambers, and give them wine to drink."

3Then I took Jaazaniah the son of Jeremiah, the son of Habazziniah, his brothers and all his sons, and the whole house of the Rechabites, 4and I brought them into the house of the LORD, into the chamber of the sons of Hanan the son of Igdaliah, a man of God, which *was* by the chamber of the princes, above the chamber of Maaseiah the son of Shallum, ᵃthe keeper of the ¹door. 5Then I set before the sons of the house of the Rechabites bowls full of wine, and cups; and I said to them, "Drink wine."

34:13 ᵃEx. 24:3, 7, 8; Deut. 5:2, 3, 27; Jer. 31:32

34:14 ᵃEx. 21:2; 23:10; Deut. 15:12; 1 Kin. 9:22

34:15 ᵃ2 Kin. 23:3; Neh. 10:29 ᵇJer. 7:10

34:16 ᵃEx. 20:7; Lev. 19:12

34:17 ᵃLev. 26:34, 35; Esth. 7:10; Dan. 6:24; [Matt. 7:2; Gal. 6:7]; James 2:13 ᵇJer. 32:24, 36 ᶜDeut. 28:25, 64; Jer. 29:18

34:18 ᵃGen. 15:10, 17

34:20 ᵃ2 Kin. 25:19–21; Jer. 22:25 ᵇDeut. 28:26; 1 Sam. 17:44, 46; 1 Kin. 14:11; 16:4; Ps. 79:2; Jer. 7:33; 16:4; 19:7

34:21 ᵃJer. 37:5–11; 39:4–7

34:22 ᵃJer. 37:8, 10 ᵇJer. 38:3; 39:1, 2, 8; 52:7, 13 ᶜJer. 9:11; 44:2, 6

35:2 ᵃ2 Sam. 4:2; 2 Kin. 10:15; 1 Chr. 2:55 ᵇ1 Kin. 6:5, 8; 1 Chr. 9:26, 33

35:4 ᵃ2 Kin. 12:9; 25:18; 1 Chr. 9:18, 19

34:14 ¹Or *sold himself* **34:15** ¹Lit. *today* **34:19** ¹Or *officers* **35:4** ¹Lit. *threshold*

⁶But they said, "We will drink no wine, for ᵃJonadab the son of Rechab, our father, commanded us, saying, 'You shall drink ᵇno wine, you nor your sons, forever. ⁷You shall not build a house, sow seed, plant a vineyard, nor have *any of these;* but all your days you shall dwell in tents, ᵃthat you may live many days in the land where you are sojourners.' ⁸Thus we have ᵃobeyed the voice of Jonadab the son of Rechab, our father, in all that he charged us, to drink no wine all our days, we, our wives, our sons, or our daughters, ⁹nor to build ourselves houses to dwell in; nor do we have vineyard, field, or seed. ¹⁰But we have dwelt in tents, and have obeyed and done according to all that Jonadab our father commanded us. ¹¹But it came to pass, when Nebuchadnezzar king of Babylon came up into the land, that we said, 'Come, let us ᵃgo to Jerusalem for fear of the army of the Chaldeans and for fear of the army of the Syrians.' So we dwell at Jerusalem."

¹²Then came the word of the LORD to Jeremiah, saying, ¹³"Thus says the LORD of hosts, the God of Israel: 'Go and tell the men of Judah and the inhabitants of Jerusalem, "Will you not ᵃreceive instruction to ¹obey My words?" says the LORD. ¹⁴"The words of Jonadab the son of Rechab, which he commanded his sons, not to drink wine, are performed; for to this day they drink none, and obey their father's commandment. ᵃBut although I have spoken to you, ᵇrising early and speaking, you did not ¹obey Me. ¹⁵I have also sent to you all My ᵃservants the prophets, rising up early and sending *them,* saying, ᵇ'Turn now everyone from his evil way, amend your doings, and do not go after other gods to serve them; then you will ᶜdwell in the land which I have given you and your fathers.' But you have not inclined your ear, nor obeyed Me. ¹⁶Surely the sons of Jonadab the son of Rechab have performed the commandment of their ᵃfather, which he commanded them, but this people has not obeyed Me."'

¹⁷"Therefore thus says the LORD God of hosts, the God of Israel: 'Behold, I will bring on Judah and on all the inhabitants of Jerusalem all the doom that I have pronounced against them; ᵃbecause I have spoken to them but they have not heard, and I have called to them but they have not answered.'"

¹⁸And Jeremiah said to the house of the Rechabites, "Thus says the LORD of hosts, the God of Israel: 'Because you have obeyed the commandment of Jonadab your father, and kept all his precepts and done according to all that he commanded you, ¹⁹therefore thus says the LORD of hosts, the God of Israel: "Jonadab the son of Rechab shall not lack a man to ᵃstand before Me forever."'"

THE SCROLL READ IN THE TEMPLE

36 Now it came to pass in the ᵃfourth year of Jehoiakim the son of Josiah, king of Judah, *that* this word came to Jeremiah from the LORD, saying: ²"Take a ᵃscroll of a book and ᵇwrite on it all the words that I have spoken to you against Israel, against Judah, and against ᶜall the nations, from the day I spoke to you, from the days of ᵈJosiah even to this day. ³It ᵃmay be that the house of Judah will hear all the adversities which I purpose to bring upon them, that everyone may

---

35:6
ᵃ2 Kin. 10:15, 23
ᵇLev. 10:9;
Num. 6:2–4;
Judg. 13:7, 14;
Prov. 31:4;
Ezek. 44:21;
Luke 1:15

35:7 ᵃEx. 20:12;
Eph. 6:2, 3

35:8
ᵃ[Prov. 1:8, 9;
4:1, 2, 10;
6:20; Eph. 6:1;
Col. 3:20]

35:11
ᵃJer. 4:5–7;
8:14

35:13
ᵃ[Is. 28:9–12];
Jer. 6:10; 17:23;
32:33

35:14
ᵃ2 Chr. 36:15
ᵇJer. 7:13; 25:3

35:15
ᵃJer. 26:4, 5;
29:19
ᵇ[Is. 1:16, 17];
Jer. 18:11; 25:5, 6;
[Ezek. 18:30–32];
Acts 26:20
ᶜJer. 7:7; 25:5, 6

35:16
ᵃ[Heb. 12:9]

35:17
ᵃProv. 1:24;
Is. 65:12; 66:4;
Jer. 7:13

35:19
ᵃ[Ex. 20:12;
Jer. 15:19;
[Luke 21:36;
Eph. 6:2, 3]

36:1 ᵃ2 Kin. 24:1;
2 Chr. 36:5–7;
Jer. 25:1, 3; 45:1;
Dan. 1:1

36:2 ᵃIs. 8:1;
Ezek. 2:9;
Zech. 5:1
ᵇJer. 30:2;
Hab. 2:2
ᶜJer. 25:15
ᵈJer. 25:3

36:3 ᵃJer. 26:3;
Ezek. 12:3

35:13 ¹listen to   35:14 ¹listen to

ᵇturn from his evil way, that I may forgive their iniquity and their sin."

⁴Then Jeremiah ᵃcalled Baruch the son of Neriah; and ᵇBaruch wrote on a scroll of a book, ¹at the instruction of Jeremiah, all the words of the LORD which He had spoken to him. ⁵And Jeremiah commanded Baruch, saying, "I *am* confined, I cannot go into the house of the LORD. ⁶You go, therefore, and read from the scroll which you have written ¹at my instruction, the words of the LORD, in the hearing of the people in the LORD's house on ᵃthe day of fasting. And you shall also read them in the hearing of all Judah who come from their cities. ⁷It may be that they will present their supplication before the LORD, and everyone will turn from his evil way. For great *is* the anger and the fury that the LORD has pronounced against this people." ⁸And Baruch the son of Neriah did according to all that Jeremiah the prophet commanded him, reading from the book the words of the LORD in the LORD's house.

⁹Now it came to pass in the fifth year of Jehoiakim the son of Josiah, king of Judah, in the ninth month, *that* they proclaimed a fast before the LORD to all the people in Jerusalem, and to all the people who came from the cities of Judah to Jerusalem. ¹⁰Then Baruch read from the book the words of Jeremiah in the house of the LORD, in the chamber of Gemariah the son of Shaphan the scribe, in the upper court at the ᵃentry of the New Gate of the LORD's house, in the ¹hearing of all the people.

THE SCROLL READ IN THE PALACE

¹¹When Michaiah the son of Gemariah, the son of Shaphan, heard all the words of the LORD from the book, ¹²he then went down to the king's house, into the scribe's chamber; and there all the princes were sitting—ᵃElishama the scribe, Delaiah the son of Shemaiah, ᵇElnathan the son of Achbor, Gemariah the son of Shaphan, Zedekiah the son of Hananiah, and all the princes. ¹³Then Michaiah declared to them all the words that he had heard when Baruch read the book in the hearing of the people. ¹⁴Therefore all the princes sent Jehudi the son of Nethaniah, the son of Shelemiah, the son of Cushi, to Baruch, saying, "Take in your hand the scroll from which you have read in the hearing of the people, and come." So Baruch the son of Neriah took the scroll in his hand and came to them. ¹⁵And they said to him, "Sit down now, and read it in our hearing." So Baruch read *it* in their hearing.

¹⁶Now it happened, when they had heard all the words, that they looked in fear from one to another, and said to Baruch, "We will surely tell the king of all these words." ¹⁷And they asked Baruch, saying, "Tell us now, how did you write all these words—¹at his instruction?"

¹⁸So Baruch answered them, "He proclaimed with his mouth all these words to me, and I wrote *them* with ink in the book."

¹⁹Then the princes said to Baruch, "Go and hide, you and Jeremiah; and let no one know where you are."

36:3
ᵇ[Deut. 30:2, 8;
1 Sam. 7:3];
Is. 55:7; Jer. 18:8;
Jon. 3:8

36:4 ᵃJer. 32:12
ᵇJer. 45:1

36:6 ᵃLev. 16:29;
23:27–32;
Acts 27:9

36:10 ᵃJer. 26:10

36:12 ᵃJer. 41:1
ᵇJer. 26:22

36:4 ¹Lit. *from Jeremiah's mouth*   36:6 ¹Lit. *from my mouth*   36:10 ¹Lit. *ears*   36:17 ¹Lit. *with his mouth*

THE KING DESTROYS JEREMIAH'S SCROLL

20And they went to the king, into the court; but they stored the scroll in the chamber of Elishama the scribe, and told all the words in the hearing of the king. 21So the king sent Jehudi to bring the scroll, and he took it from Elishama the scribe's chamber. And Jehudi read it in the hearing of the king and in the hearing of all the princes who stood beside the king. 22Now the king was sitting in ᵃthe winter house in the ninth month, with *a fire* burning on the hearth before him. 23And it happened, when Jehudi had read three or four columns, *that the king* cut it with the scribe's knife and cast *it* into the fire that *was* on the hearth, until all the scroll was consumed in the fire that *was* on the hearth. 24Yet they were ᵃnot afraid, nor did they ᵇtear their garments, the king nor any of his servants who heard all these words. 25Nevertheless Elnathan, Delaiah, and Gemariah implored the king not to burn the scroll; but he would not listen to them. 26And the king commanded Jerahmeel ¹the king's son, Seraiah the son of Azriel, and Shelemiah the son of Abdeel, to seize Baruch the scribe and Jeremiah the prophet, but the LORD hid them.

JEREMIAH REWRITES THE SCROLL

27Now after the king had burned the scroll with the words which Baruch had written ¹at the instruction of Jeremiah, the word of the LORD came to Jeremiah, saying: 28"Take yet another scroll, and write on it all the former words that were in the first scroll which Jehoiakim the king of Judah has burned. 29And you shall say to Jehoiakim king of Judah, 'Thus says the LORD: "You have burned this scroll, saying, ᵃ'Why have you written in it that the king of Babylon will certainly come and destroy this land, and cause man and beast to ᵇcease from here?'" 30Therefore thus says the LORD concerning Jehoiakim king of Judah: ᵃ"He shall have no one to sit on the throne of David, and his dead body shall be ᵇcast out to the heat of the day and the frost of the night. 31I will punish him, his ¹family, and his servants for their iniquity; and I will bring on them, on the inhabitants of Jerusalem, and on the men of Judah all the doom that I have pronounced against them; but they did not heed."'"

32Then Jeremiah took another scroll and gave it to Baruch the scribe, the son of Neriah, who wrote on it ¹at the instruction of Jeremiah all the words of the book which Jehoiakim king of Judah had burned in the fire. And besides, there were added to them many similar words.

ZEDEKIAH'S VAIN HOPE
(2 Kin. 24:17; 2 Chr. 36:10)

37 Now King ᵃZedekiah the son of Josiah reigned instead of Coniah the son of Jehoiakim, whom Nebuchadnezzar king of Babylon made king in the land of Judah. 2ᵃBut neither he nor his servants nor the people of the land gave heed to the words of the LORD which He spoke by the prophet Jeremiah.

3And Zedekiah the king sent Jehucal the son of Shelemiah,

36:22
ᵃJudg. 3:20;
Amos 3:15

36:24
ᵃ[Ps. 36:1];
Jer. 36:16
ᵇGen. 37:29, 34;
2 Sam. 1:11;
1 Kin. 21:27;
2 Kin. 19:1, 2;
22:11; Is. 36:22;
37:1; Jon. 3:6

36:29 ᵃJer. 32:3
ᵇJer. 25:9–11;
26:9

36:30
ᵃJer. 22:30
ᵇJer. 22:19

37:1
ᵃ2 Kin. 24:17;
1 Chr. 3:15;
2 Chr. 36:10;
Jer. 22:24

37:2
ᵃ2 Kin. 24:19, 20;
2 Chr. 36:12–16;
[Prov. 29:12]

36:26 ¹Or *son of Hammelech* 36:27 ¹Lit. *from Jeremiah's mouth*
36:31 ¹Lit. *seed* 36:32 ¹Lit. *from Jeremiah's mouth*

and [a]Zephaniah the son of Maaseiah, the priest, to the prophet Jeremiah, saying, [b]"Pray now to the LORD our God for us." [4]Now Jeremiah was coming and going among the people, for they had not *yet* put him in prison. [5]Then [a]Pharaoh's army came up from Egypt; and when the Chaldeans who were besieging Jerusalem heard news of them, they departed from Jerusalem.

[6]Then the word of the LORD came to the prophet Jeremiah, saying, [7]"Thus says the LORD, the God of Israel, 'Thus you shall say to the king of Judah, [a]who sent you to Me to inquire of Me: "Behold, Pharaoh's army which has come up to help you will return to Egypt, to their own land. [8a]And the Chaldeans shall come back and fight against this city, and take it and burn it with fire."' [9]Thus says the LORD: 'Do not deceive yourselves, saying, "The Chaldeans will surely depart from us," for they will not depart. [10a]For though you had defeated the whole army of the Chaldeans who fight against you, and there remained *only* wounded men among them, they would rise up, every man in his tent, and burn the city with fire.'"

JEREMIAH IMPRISONED

[11]And it happened, when the army of the Chaldeans left *the siege* of Jerusalem for fear of Pharaoh's army, [12]that Jeremiah went out of Jerusalem to go into the land of Benjamin to claim his property there among the people. [13]And when he was in the Gate of Benjamin, a captain of the guard *was* there whose name *was* Irijah the son of Shelemiah, the son of Hananiah; and he seized Jeremiah the prophet, saying, "You are defecting to the Chaldeans!"

[14]Then Jeremiah said, [1]"False! I am not defecting to the Chaldeans." But he did not listen to him.

So Irijah seized Jeremiah and brought him to the princes. [15]Therefore the princes were angry with Jeremiah, and they struck him [a]and put him in prison in the [b]house of Jonathan the scribe. For they had made that the prison.

[16]When Jeremiah entered [a]the dungeon and the cells, and Jeremiah had remained there many days, [17]then Zedekiah the king sent and took him *out*. The king asked him secretly in his house, and said, "Is there *any* word from the LORD?"

And Jeremiah said, "There is." Then he said, "You shall be [a]delivered into the hand of the king of Babylon!"

[18]Moreover Jeremiah said to King Zedekiah, "What offense have I committed against you, against your servants, or against this people, that you have put me in prison? [19]Where now *are* your prophets who prophesied to you, saying, 'The king of Babylon will not come against you or against this land'? [20]Therefore please hear now, O my lord the king. Please, let my petition be accepted before you, and do not make me return to the house of Jonathan the scribe, lest I die there."

[21]Then Zedekiah the king commanded that they should commit Jeremiah [a]to the court of the prison, and that they should give him daily a piece of bread from the bakers' street, [b]until all the bread in the city was gone. Thus Jeremiah remained in the court of the prison.

37:3
[a]Jer. 21:1, 2; 29:25; 52:24
[b]1 Kin. 13:6; Jer. 42:2; Acts 8:24

37:5
[a]2 Kin. 24:7; Jer. 37:7; Ezek. 17:15

37:7 [a]Is. 36:6; Jer. 21:2; Ezek. 17:17

37:8
[a]2 Chr. 36:19; Jer. 34:22

37:10
[a]Lev. 26:36–38; Is. 30:17; Jer. 21:4, 5

37:15 [a]Jer. 20:2; [Matt. 21:35]
[b]Gen. 39:20; 2 Chr. 16:10; 18:26; Jer. 38:26; Acts 5:18

37:16 [a]Jer. 38:6

37:17
[a]2 Kin. 25:4–7; Jer. 21:7; Ezek. 12:12, 13; 17:19–21

37:21 [a]Jer. 32:2; 38:13, 28
[b]2 Kin. 25:3; Jer. 38:9; 52:6

37:14 [1]a lie

JEREMIAH IN THE DUNGEON

38 Now Shephatiah the son of Mattan, Gedaliah the son of Pashhur, ªJucal[1] the son of Shelemiah, and ᵇPashhur the son of Malchiah ᶜheard the words that Jeremiah had spoken to all the people, saying, 2"Thus says the LORD: ª'He who remains in this city shall die by the sword, by famine, and by pestilence; but he who goes over to the Chaldeans shall live; his life shall be as a prize to him, and he shall live.' 3Thus says the LORD: ª'This city shall surely be ᵇgiven into the hand of the king of Babylon's army, which shall take it.'"

4Therefore the princes said to the king, "Please, ªlet this man be put to death, for thus he [1]weakens the hands of the men of war who remain in this city, and the hands of all the people, by speaking such words to them. For this man does not seek the [2]welfare of this people, but their harm."

5Then Zedekiah the king said, "Look, he *is* in your hand. For the king can *do* nothing against you." 6ªSo they took Jeremiah and cast him into the dungeon of Malchiah [1]the king's son, which *was* in the court of the prison, and they let Jeremiah down with ropes. And in the dungeon *there was* no water, but mire. So Jeremiah sank in the mire.

7ªNow Ebed-Melech the Ethiopian, one of the [1]eunuchs, who was in the king's house, heard that they had put Jeremiah in the dungeon. When the king was sitting at the Gate of Benjamin, 8Ebed-Melech went out of the king's house and spoke to the king, saying: 9"My lord the king, these men have done evil in all that they have done to Jeremiah the prophet, whom they have cast into the dungeon, and he is likely to die from hunger in the place where he is. For *there is* ªno more bread in the city." 10Then the king commanded Ebed-Melech the Ethiopian, saying, "Take from here thirty men with you, and lift Jeremiah the prophet out of the dungeon before he dies." 11So Ebed-Melech took the men with him and went into the house of the king under the treasury, and took from there old clothes and old rags, and let them down by ropes into the dungeon to Jeremiah. 12Then Ebed-Melech the Ethiopian said to Jeremiah, "Please put these old clothes and rags under your armpits, under the ropes." And Jeremiah did so. 13So they pulled Jeremiah up with ropes and lifted him out of the dungeon. And Jeremiah remained ªin the court of the prison.

ZEDEKIAH'S FEARS AND JEREMIAH'S ADVICE

14Then Zedekiah the king sent and had Jeremiah the prophet brought to him at the third entrance of the house of the LORD. And the king said to Jeremiah, "I will ªask you something. Hide nothing from me."

15Jeremiah said to Zedekiah, "If I declare *it* to you, will you not surely put me to death? And if I give you advice, you will not listen to me."

16So Zedekiah the king swore secretly to Jeremiah, saying, "As the LORD lives, ªwho made our very souls, I will not put you to death, nor will I give you into the hand of these men who seek your life."

17Then Jeremiah said to Zedekiah, "Thus says the LORD,

38:1 ªJer. 37:3
ᵇJer. 21:1
ᶜJer. 21:8

38:2 ªJer. 21:9

38:3 ªJer. 21:10;
32:3 ᵇJer. 34:2

38:4 ªJer. 26:11

38:6 ªJer. 37:21;
Lam. 3:55

38:7 ªJer. 39:16

38:9 ªJer. 37:21

38:13
ªNeh. 3:25;
Jer. 37:21;
Acts 23:35;
24:27; 28:16, 30

38:14
ªJer. 21:1, 2;
37:17

38:16
ªNum. 16:22;
Is. 57:16;
Zech. 12:1;
[Acts 17:25, 28]

38:1 [1]*Jehucal*, Jer. 37:3   38:4 [1]Is discouraging   [2]Well-being; lit. *peace*
38:6 [1]Or *son of Hammelech*   38:7 [1]Or *officers*

the God of hosts, the God of Israel: 'If you surely ªsurrender¹ ᵇto the king of Babylon's princes, then your soul shall live; this city shall not be burned with fire, and you and your house shall live. ¹⁸But if you do not ¹surrender to the king of Babylon's princes, then this city shall be given into the hand of the Chaldeans; they shall burn it with fire, and ªyou shall not escape from their hand.'"

¹⁹And Zedekiah the king said to Jeremiah, "I am afraid of the Jews who have ªdefected to the Chaldeans, lest they deliver me into their hand, and they ᵇabuse me."

²⁰But Jeremiah said, "They shall not deliver *you*. Please, obey the voice of the LORD which I speak to you. So it shall be ªwell with you, and your soul shall live. ²¹But if you refuse to ¹surrender, this *is* the word that the LORD has shown me: ²²'Now behold, all the ªwomen who are left in the king of Judah's house *shall be* surrendered to the king of Babylon's princes, and those *women* shall say:

> "Your close friends have ¹set upon you
> And prevailed against you;
> Your feet have sunk in the mire,
> *And* they have ²turned away again."

²³'So they shall surrender all your wives and ªchildren to the Chaldeans. ᵇYou shall not escape from their hand, but shall be taken by the hand of the king of Babylon. And you shall cause this city to be burned with fire.'"

²⁴Then Zedekiah said to Jeremiah, "Let no one know of these words, and you shall not die. ²⁵But if the princes hear that I have talked with you, and they come to you and say to you, 'Declare to us now what you have said to the king, and also what the king said to you; do not hide *it* from us, and we will not put you to death,' ²⁶then you shall say to them, ª'I presented my request before the king, that he would not make me return ᵇto Jonathan's house to die there.'"

²⁷Then all the princes came to Jeremiah and asked him. And he told them according to all these words that the king had commanded. So they stopped speaking with him, for the conversation had not been heard. ²⁸Now ªJeremiah remained in the court of the prison until the day that Jerusalem was taken. And he was *there* when Jerusalem was taken.

THE FALL OF JERUSALEM
(2 Kin. 25:1–12; Jer. 52:4–16)

39 In the ªninth year of Zedekiah king of Judah, in the tenth month, Nebuchadnezzar king of Babylon and all his army came against Jerusalem, and besieged it. ²In the ªeleventh year of Zedekiah, in the fourth month, on the ninth *day* of the month, the ¹city was penetrated.

³ªThen all the princes of the king of Babylon came in and sat in the Middle Gate: Nergal-Sharezer, Samgar-Nebo, Sarsechim, ¹Rabsaris, Nergal-Sarezer, ²Rabmag, with the rest of the princes of the king of Babylon.

⁴ªSo it was, when Zedekiah the king of Judah and all the

Cross references (margin)

38:17
ª2 Kin. 24:12
ᵇJer. 39:3

38:18
ªJer. 32:4; 34:3

38:19 ªJer. 39:9
ᵇ1 Sam. 31:4

38:20 ªJer. 40:9

38:22 ªJer. 8:10

38:23
ªJer. 39:6; 41:10
ᵇJer. 39:5

38:26
ªJer. 37:20
ᵇJer. 37:15

38:28
ª[Ps. 23:4];
Jer. 37:21; 39:14

39:1
ª2 Kin. 25:1–12;
Jer. 52:4;
Ezek. 24:1, 2

39:2 ªJer. 1:3

39:3
ªJer. 1:15; 38:17

39:4
ª2 Kin. 25:4;
Is. 30:16;
Jer. 52:7;
Amos 2:14

38:17 ¹Lit. *go out*   38:18 ¹Lit. *go out*   38:21 ¹Lit. *go out*   38:22 ¹Or *misled*   ²Deserted you   39:2 ¹*city wall was breached*   39:3 ¹A title, probably *Chief Officer;* also v. 13   ²A title, probably *Troop Commander;* also v. 13

men of war saw them, that they fled and went out of the city by night, by way of the king's garden, by the gate between the two walls. And he went out by way of the ¹plain. ⁵But the Chaldean army pursued them and ᵃovertook Zedekiah in the plains of Jericho. And when they had captured him, they brought him up to Nebuchadnezzar king of Babylon, to ᵇRiblah in the land of Hamath, where he pronounced judgment on him. ⁶Then the king of Babylon killed the sons of Zedekiah before his ᵃeyes in Riblah; the king of Babylon also killed all the ᵇnobles of Judah. ⁷Moreover ᵃhe put out Zedekiah's eyes, and bound him with bronze ¹fetters to carry him off to Babylon. ⁸ᵃAnd the Chaldeans burned the king's house and the houses of the people with ᵇfire, and broke down the ᶜwalls of Jerusalem. ⁹ᵃThen Nebuzaradan the captain of the guard carried away captive to Babylon the remnant of the people who remained in the city and those who ᵇdefected to him, with the rest of the people who remained. ¹⁰But Nebuzaradan the captain of the guard left in the land of Judah the ᵃpoor people, who had nothing, and gave them vineyards and fields ¹at the same time.

JEREMIAH GOES FREE

¹¹Now Nebuchadnezzar king of Babylon gave charge concerning Jeremiah to Nebuzaradan the captain of the guard, saying, ¹²"Take him and look after him, and do him no ᵃharm; but do to him just as he says to you." ¹³So Nebuzaradan the captain of the guard sent Nebushasban, Rabsaris, Nergal-Sharezer, Rabmag, and all the king of Babylon's chief officers; ¹⁴then they sent *someone* ᵃto take Jeremiah from the court of the prison, and committed him ᵇto Gedaliah the son of ᶜAhikam, the son of Shaphan, that he should take him home. So he dwelt among the people.

¹⁵Meanwhile the word of the LORD had come to Jeremiah while he was shut up in the court of the prison, saying, ¹⁶"Go and speak to ᵃEbed-Melech the Ethiopian, saying, 'Thus says the LORD of hosts, the God of Israel: "Behold, ᵇI will bring My words upon this city for adversity and not for good, and they shall be *performed* in that day before you. ¹⁷But I will deliver you in that day," says the LORD, "and you shall not be given into the hand of the men of whom you *are* afraid. ¹⁸For I will surely deliver you, and you shall not fall by the sword; but ᵃyour life shall be as a prize to you, ᵇbecause you have put your trust in Me," says the LORD.'"

JEREMIAH WITH GEDALIAH THE GOVERNOR
(2 Kin. 25:22–26)

40 The word that came to Jeremiah from the LORD ᵃafter Nebuzaradan the captain of the guard had let him go from Ramah, when he had taken him bound in chains among all who were carried away captive from Jerusalem and Judah, who were carried away captive to Babylon.

²And the captain of the guard took Jeremiah and ᵃsaid to him: "The LORD your God has pronounced this doom on this place. ³Now the LORD has brought *it,* and has done just as He said. ᵃBecause you *people* have sinned against the LORD, and

39:5 ᵃJer. 21:7; 32:4; 38:18, 23
ᵇ2 Kin. 23:33; Jer. 52:9, 26, 27

39:6 ᵃDeut. 28:34
ᵇJer. 34:19–21

39:7 ᵃ2 Kin. 25:7; Jer. 52:11; Ezek. 12:13

39:8 ᵃ2 Kin. 25:9; Jer. 38:18; 52:13
ᵇJer. 21:10
ᶜ2 Kin. 25:10; Neh. 1:3; Jer. 52:14

39:9 ᵃ2 Kin. 25:8, 11, 12, 20 ᵇJer. 38:19

39:10 ᵃJer. 40:7

39:12 ᵃJer. 1:18, 19; 15:20, 21

39:14 ᵃJer. 38:28
ᵇJer. 40:5
ᶜ2 Kin. 22:12, 14; 2 Chr. 34:20; Jer. 26:24

39:16 ᵃJer. 38:7, 12
ᵇJer. 21:10; [Dan. 9:12; Zech. 1:6]

39:18 ᵃJer. 21:9; 45:5
ᵇ1 Chr. 5:20; Ps. 37:40; [Jer. 17:7, 8]

40:1 ᵃJer. 39:9, 11

40:2 ᵃJer. 50:7

40:3 ᵃDeut. 29:24, 25; Jer. 50:7; Dan. 9:11; [Rom. 2:5]

39:4 ¹Or *Arabah;* the Jordan Valley   39:7 ¹*chains*   39:10 ¹Lit. *on that day*

not obeyed His voice, therefore this thing has come upon you. [4]And now look, I free you this day from the chains that [1]*were* on your hand. [a]If it seems good to you to come with me to Babylon, come, and I will look after you. But if it seems wrong for you to come with me to Babylon, remain here. See, [b]all the land *is* before you; wherever it seems good and convenient for you to go, go there."

[5]Now while Jeremiah had not yet gone back, *Nebuzaradan said,* "Go back to [a]Gedaliah the son of Ahikam, the son of Shaphan, [b]whom the king of Babylon has made governor over the cities of Judah, and dwell with him among the people. Or go wherever it seems convenient for you to go." So the captain of the guard gave him rations and a gift and let him go. [6][a]Then Jeremiah went to Gedaliah the son of Ahikam, to [b]Mizpah, and dwelt with him among the people who were left in the land.

[7][a]And when all the captains of the armies who *were* in the fields, they and their men, heard that the king of Babylon had made Gedaliah the son of Ahikam governor in the land, and had committed to him men, women, children, and [b]the poorest of the land who had not been carried away captive to Babylon, [8]then they came to Gedaliah at Mizpah—[a]Ishmael the son of Nethaniah, [b]Johanan and Jonathan the sons of Kareah, Seraiah the son of Tanhumeth, the sons of Ephai the Netophathite, and [c]Jezaniah[1] the son of a [d]Maachathite, they and their men. [9]And Gedaliah the son of Ahikam, the son of Shaphan, took an oath before them and their men, saying, "Do not be afraid to serve the Chaldeans. Dwell in the land and serve the king of Babylon, and it shall be [a]well with you. [10]As for me, I will indeed dwell at Mizpah and serve the Chaldeans who come to us. But you, gather wine and summer fruit and oil, put *them* in your vessels, and dwell in your cities that you have taken." [11]Likewise, when all the Jews who *were* in Moab, among the Ammonites, in Edom, and who *were* in all the countries, heard that the king of Babylon had left a remnant of Judah, and that he had set over them Gedaliah the son of Ahikam, the son of Shaphan, [12]then all the Jews [a]returned out of all places where they had been driven, and came to the land of Judah, to Gedaliah at Mizpah, and gathered wine and summer fruit in abundance.

[13]Moreover Johanan the son of Kareah and all the captains of the forces that *were* in the fields came to Gedaliah at Mizpah, [14]and said to him, [1]"Do you certainly know that [a]Baalis the king of the Ammonites has sent Ishmael the son of Nethaniah to murder you?" But Gedaliah the son of Ahikam did not believe them.

[15]Then Johanan the son of Kareah spoke secretly to Gedaliah in Mizpah, saying, "Let me go, please, and I will kill Ishmael the son of Nethaniah, and no one will know *it*. Why should he murder you, so that all the Jews who are gathered to you would be scattered, and the [a]remnant in Judah perish?"

[16]But Gedaliah the son of Ahikam said to Johanan the son of Kareah, "You shall not do this thing, for you speak falsely concerning Ishmael."

40:4 [a]Jer. 39:12
[b]Gen. 20:15

40:5 [a]Jer. 39:14
[b]2 Kin. 25:22;
Jer. 41:10

40:6 [a]Jer. 39:14
[b]Judg. 20:1;
1 Sam. 7:5;
2 Chr. 16:6

40:7
[a]2 Kin. 25:23, 24
[b]Jer. 39:10

40:8
[a]Jer. 41:1–10
[b]Jer. 41:11; 43:2
[c]Jer. 42:1
[d]Deut. 3:14;
Josh. 12:5;
2 Sam. 10:6

40:9 [a]Jer. 27:11;
38:17–20

40:12 [a]Jer. 43:5

40:14 [a]Jer. 41:10

40:15 [a]Jer. 42:2

40:4 [1]Or *are*   40:8 [1]*Jaazaniah*, 2 Kin. 25:23   40:14 [1]Or *Certainly you know that*

INSURRECTION AGAINST GEDALIAH

41 Now it came to pass in the seventh month [a]*that* Ishmael the son of Nethaniah, the son of Elishama, of the royal [1]family and of the officers of the king, came with ten men to Gedaliah the son of Ahikam, at [b]Mizpah. And there they ate bread together in Mizpah. [2]Then Ishmael the son of Nethaniah, and the ten men who were with him, arose and [a]struck Gedaliah the son of [b]Ahikam, the son of Shaphan, with the sword, and killed him whom the king of Babylon had made [c]governor over the land. [3]Ishmael also struck down all the Jews who were with him, *that is*, with Gedaliah at Mizpah, and the Chaldeans who were found there, the men of war.

[4]And it happened, on the second day after he had killed Gedaliah, when as yet no one knew *it*, [5]that certain men came from Shechem, from Shiloh, and from Samaria, eighty men [a]with their beards shaved and their clothes torn, having cut themselves, with offerings and incense in their hand, to bring *them* to [b]the house of the LORD. [6]Now Ishmael the son of Nethaniah went out from Mizpah to meet them, weeping as he went along; and it happened as he met them that he said to them, "Come to Gedaliah the son of Ahikam!" [7]So it was, when they came into the midst of the city, that Ishmael the son of Nethaniah [a]killed them *and cast them* into the midst of a [1]pit, he and the men who were with him. [8]But ten men were found among them who said to Ishmael, "Do not kill us, for we have treasures of wheat, barley, oil, and honey in the field." So he desisted and did not kill them among their brethren. [9]Now the [1]pit into which Ishmael had cast all the dead bodies of the men whom he had slain, because of Gedaliah, *was* [a]the same one Asa the king had made for fear of Baasha king of Israel. Ishmael the son of Nethaniah filled it with *the* slain. [10]Then Ishmael carried away captive all the [a]rest of the people who *were* in Mizpah, [b]the king's daughters and all the people who remained in Mizpah, [c]whom Nebuzaradan the captain of the guard had committed to Gedaliah the son of Ahikam. And Ishmael the son of Nethaniah carried them away captive and departed to go over to [d]the Ammonites.

[11]But when [a]Johanan the son of Kareah and all the captains of the forces that *were* with him heard of all the evil that Ishmael the son of Nethaniah had done, [12]they took all the men and went to fight with Ishmael the son of Nethaniah; and they found him by [a]the great pool that *is* in Gibeon. [13]So it was, when all the people who *were* with Ishmael saw Johanan the son of Kareah, and all the captains of the forces who *were* with him, that they were glad. [14]Then all the people whom Ishmael had carried away captive from Mizpah turned around and came back, and went to Johanan the son of Kareah. [15]But Ishmael the son of Nethaniah escaped from Johanan with eight men and went to the Ammonites.

[16]Then Johanan the son of Kareah, and all the captains of the forces that were with him, took from Mizpah all the [a]rest of the people whom he had recovered from Ishmael the son of Nethaniah after he had murdered Gedaliah the son

41:1
[a]2 Kin. 25:25
[b]Jer. 40:6, 10

41:2
[a]2 Sam. 3:27;
20:9, 10;
2 Kin. 25:25;
Ps. 41:9; 109:5;
John 13:18
[b]Jer. 26:24
[c]Jer. 40:5

41:5
[a]Lev. 19:27, 28;
Deut. 14:1;
Is. 15:2
[b]1 Sam. 1:7;
2 Kin. 25:9;
Neh. 10:34, 35

41:7 [a]Ps. 55:23;
Is. 59:7;
Ezek. 22:27;
33:24, 26

41:9
[a]1 Kin. 15:22;
2 Chr. 16:6

41:10
[a]Jer. 40:11, 12
[b]Jer. 43:6
[c]Jer. 40:7
[d]Jer. 40:14

41:11
[a]Jer. 40:7, 8,
13–16

41:12
[a]2 Sam. 2:13

41:16
[a]Jer. 40:11, 12;
43:4–7

41:1 [1]Lit. *seed*   41:7 [1]Or *cistern*   41:9 [1]Or *cistern*

of Ahikam—the mighty men of war and the women and the children and the eunuchs, whom he had brought back from Gibeon. [17]And they departed and dwelt in the habitation of [a]Chimham, which is near Bethlehem, as they went on their way to [b]Egypt, [18]because of the Chaldeans; for they were afraid of them, because Ishmael the son of Nethaniah had murdered Gedaliah the son of Ahikam, [a]whom the king of Babylon had made governor in the land.

THE FLIGHT TO EGYPT FORBIDDEN

42 Now all the captains of the forces, [a]Johanan the son of Kareah, Jezaniah the son of Hoshaiah, and all the people, from the least to the greatest, came near [2]and said to Jeremiah the prophet, [a]"Please, let our petition be acceptable to you, and [b]pray for us to the LORD your God, for all this remnant (since we are left but [c]a few of many, as you can see), [3]that the LORD your God may show us [a]the way in which we should walk and the thing we should do."

[4]Then Jeremiah the prophet said to them, "I have heard. Indeed, I will pray to the LORD your God according to your words, and it shall be, that [a]whatever the LORD answers you, I will declare it to you. I will [b]keep nothing back from you."

[5]So they said to Jeremiah, [a]"Let the LORD be a true and faithful witness between us, if we do not do according to everything which the LORD your God sends us by you. [6]Whether it is [1]pleasing or [2]displeasing, we will [a]obey the voice of the LORD our God to whom we send you, [b]that it may be well with us when we obey the voice of the LORD our God."

[7]And it happened after ten days that the word of the LORD came to Jeremiah. [8]Then he called Johanan the son of Kareah, all the captains of the forces which were with him, and all the people from the least even to the greatest, [9]and said to them, "Thus says the LORD, the God of Israel, to whom you sent me to present your petition before Him: [10]'If you will still remain in this land, then [a]I will build you and not pull you down, and I will plant you and not pluck you up. For I [b]relent concerning the disaster that I have brought upon you. [11]Do not be afraid of the king of Babylon, of whom you are afraid; do not be afraid of him,' says the LORD, [a]'for I am with you, to save you and deliver you from his hand. [12]And [a]I will show you mercy, that he may have mercy on you and cause you to return to your own land.'

[13]"But if [a]you say, 'We will not dwell in this land,' disobeying the voice of the LORD your God, [14]saying, 'No, but we will go to the land of [a]Egypt where we shall see no war, nor hear the sound of the trumpet, nor be hungry for bread, and there we will dwell'— [15]Then hear now the word of the LORD, O remnant of Judah! Thus says the LORD of hosts, the God of Israel: 'If you [a]wholly[1] set [b]your faces to enter Egypt, and go to dwell there, [16]then it shall be that the [a]sword which you feared shall overtake you there in the land of Egypt; the famine of which you were afraid shall follow close after you there in Egypt; and there you shall die. [17]So shall it be with all the men who set their faces to go to Egypt to dwell there. They shall die by the sword, by famine, and by pestilence. And [a]none of them

41:17
[a]2 Sam. 19:37, 38
[b]Jer. 43:7

41:18 [a]Jer. 40:5

42:1
[a]Jer. 40:8, 13;
41:11

42:2 [a]Jer. 15:11
[b]Ex. 8:28;
1 Sam. 7:8;
12:19; 1 Kin. 13:6;
Is. 37:4;
Jer. 37:3;
Acts 8:24;
[James 5:16]
[c]Lev. 26:22;
Deut. 28:62;
Is. 1:9; Lam. 1:1

42:3 [a]Ezra 8:21

42:4
[a]1 Kin. 22:14;
Jer. 23:28
[b]1 Sam. 3:17, 18;
Ps. 40:10;
Acts 20:20

42:5
[a]Gen. 31:50;
Judg. 11:10;
Jer. 43:2;
Mic. 1:2;
Mal. 2:14; 3:5

42:6 [a]Ex. 24:7;
Deut. 5:27;
Josh. 24:24
[b]Deut. 5:29, 33;
6:3; Jer. 7:23

42:10 [a]Jer. 24:6;
31:28; 33:7;
Ezek. 36:36
[b]Deut. 32:36;
[Jer. 18:8]

42:11
[a]Num. 14:9;
2 Chr. 32:7, 8;
Is. 8:9, 10;
43:2, 5; Jer. 1:19;
15:20; Rom. 8:31

42:12 [a]Neh. 1:11;
Ps. 106:46;
Prov. 16:7

42:13 [a]Jer. 44:16

42:14 [a]Is. 31:1;
Jer. 41:17; 43:7

42:15
[a]Deut. 17:16;
Jer. 44:12–14
[b]Luke 9:51

42:16
[a]Jer. 44:13, 27;
Ezek. 11:8;
Amos 9:1–4

42:17
[a]Jer. 44:14, 28

42:6 [1]Lit. good   [2]Lit. evil   42:15 [1]Or surely

shall remain or escape from the disaster that I will bring upon them.'

18"For thus says the LORD of hosts, the God of Israel: 'As My anger and My fury have been ªpoured out on the inhabitants of Jerusalem, so will My fury be poured out on you when you enter Egypt. And ᵇyou shall be an oath, an astonishment, a curse, and a reproach; and you shall see this place no more.'

19"The LORD has said concerning you, O remnant of Judah, ª'Do not go to Egypt!' Know certainly that I have ¹admonished you this day. 20For you ¹were hypocrites in your hearts when you sent me to the LORD your God, saying, 'Pray for us to the LORD our God, and according to all that the LORD your God says, so declare to us and we will do it.' 21And I have this day declared it to you, but you have ªnot obeyed the voice of the LORD your God, or anything which He has sent you by me. 22Now therefore, know certainly that you ªshall die by the sword, by famine, and by pestilence in the place where you desire to go to dwell."

JEREMIAH TAKEN TO EGYPT

43 Now it happened, when Jeremiah had stopped speaking to all the people all the ªwords of the LORD their God, for which the LORD their God had sent him to them, all these words, 2ªthat Azariah the son of Hoshaiah, Johanan the son of Kareah, and all the proud men spoke, saying to Jeremiah, "You speak falsely! The LORD our God has not sent you to say, 'Do not go to Egypt to dwell there.' 3But ªBaruch the son of Neriah has ¹set you against us, to deliver us into the hand of the Chaldeans, that they may put us to death or carry us away captive to Babylon." 4So Johanan the son of Kareah, all the captains of the forces, and all the people would ªnot obey the voice of the LORD, to remain in the land of Judah. 5But Johanan the son of Kareah and all the captains of the forces took ªall the remnant of Judah who had returned to dwell in the land of Judah, from all nations where they had been driven— 6men, women, children, ªthe king's daughters, ᵇand every person whom Nebuzaradan the captain of the guard had left with Gedaliah the son of Ahikam, the son of Shaphan, and Jeremiah the prophet and Baruch the son of Neriah. 7ªSo they went to the land of Egypt, for they did not obey the voice of the LORD. And they went as far as ᵇTahpanhes.

8Then the ªword of the LORD came to Jeremiah in Tahpanhes, saying, 9"Take large stones in your hand, and hide them in the sight of the men of Judah, in the ¹clay in the brick courtyard which is at the entrance to Pharaoh's house in Tahpanhes; 10and say to them, 'Thus says the LORD of hosts, the God of Israel: "Behold, I will send and bring Nebuchadnezzar the king of Babylon, ªMy servant, and will set his throne above these stones that I have hidden. And he will spread his royal pavilion over them. 11ªWhen he comes, he shall strike the land of Egypt and deliver to death ᵇthose appointed for death, and to captivity those appointed for captivity, and to the sword those appointed for the sword. 12¹I will kindle a fire in the houses of ªthe gods of Egypt, and he shall burn them

42:18
ª2 Chr. 36:16–19;
Jer. 7:20
ᵇDeut. 29:21;
Is. 65:15;
Jer. 18:16; 24:9;
26:6; 29:18, 22;
44:12

42:19
ªDeut. 17:16;
Is. 30:1–7

42:21 ªIs. 30:1–7

42:22
ªJer. 42:17;
Ezek. 6:11

43:1
ªJer. 42:9–18

43:2 ªJer. 42:1

43:3
ªJer. 36:4; 45:1

43:4
ª2 Kin. 25:26

43:5
ªJer. 40:11, 12

43:6 ªJer. 41:10
ᵇJer. 39:10; 40:7

43:7 ªJer. 42:19
ᵇJer. 2:16; 44:1

43:8
ªJer. 44:1–30

43:10
ªJer. 25:9; 27:6;
Ezek. 29:18, 20
ᵇJer. 15:2;
Zech. 11:9

43:11
ªIs. 19:1–25;
Jer. 25:15–19;
44:13; 46:1, 2,
13–26;
Ezek. 29:19, 20

43:12 ªEx. 12:12;
Is. 19:1;
Jer. 46:25;
Ezek. 30:13

42:19 ¹warned   42:20 ¹Lit. used deceit against your souls   43:3 ¹Or incited
43:9 ¹Or mortar   43:12 ¹So with MT, Tg.; LXX, Syr., Vg. He

and carry them away captive. And he shall array himself with the land of Egypt, as a shepherd puts on his garment, and he shall go out from there in peace. ¹³He shall also break the *sacred* pillars of ¹Beth Shemesh that *are* in the land of Egypt; and the houses of the gods of the Egyptians he shall burn with fire."'"

ISRAELITES WILL BE PUNISHED IN EGYPT

44 The word that came to Jeremiah concerning all the Jews who dwell in the land of Egypt, who dwell at ᵃMigdol, at ᵇTahpanhes, at ᶜNoph,¹ and in the country of ᵈPathros, saying, ²"Thus says the LORD of hosts, the God of Israel: 'You have seen all the calamity that I have brought on Jerusalem and on all the cities of Judah; and behold, this day they *are* ᵃa desolation, and no one dwells in them, ³because of their wickedness which they have committed to provoke Me to anger, in that they went ᵃto burn incense *and* to ᵇserve other gods whom they did not know, they nor you nor your fathers. ⁴However ᵃI have sent to you all My servants the prophets, rising early and sending *them,* saying, "Oh, do not do this abominable thing that I hate!" ⁵But they did not listen or incline their ear to turn from their wickedness, to burn no incense to other gods. ⁶So My fury and My anger were poured out and kindled in the cities of Judah and in the streets of Jerusalem; and they ¹are wasted *and* desolate, as it is this day.'

⁷"Now therefore, thus says the LORD, the God of hosts, the God of Israel: 'Why do you commit *this* great evil ᵃagainst yourselves, to cut off from you man and woman, child and infant, out of Judah, leaving none to remain, ⁸in that you ᵃprovoke Me to wrath with the works of your hands, burning incense to other gods in the land of Egypt where you have gone to dwell, that you may cut yourselves off and be ᵇa curse and a reproach among all the nations of the earth? ⁹Have you forgotten the wickedness of your fathers, the wickedness of the kings of Judah, the wickedness of their wives, your own wickedness, and the wickedness of your wives, which they committed in the land of Judah and in the streets of Jerusalem? ¹⁰They have not been ᵃhumbled,¹ to this day, nor have they ᵇfeared; they have not walked in My law or in My statutes that I set before you and your fathers.'

¹¹"Therefore thus says the LORD of hosts, the God of Israel: 'Behold, ᵃI will set My face against you for catastrophe and for ¹cutting off all Judah. ¹²And I will take the remnant of Judah who have set their faces to go into the land of Egypt to dwell there, and ᵃthey shall all be consumed *and* fall in the land of Egypt. They shall be consumed by the sword *and* by famine. They shall die, from the least to the greatest, by the sword and by famine; and ᵇthey shall be an oath, an astonishment, a curse and a reproach! ¹³ᵃFor I will punish those who dwell in the land of Egypt, as I have punished Jerusalem, by the sword, by famine, and by pestilence, ¹⁴so that none of the remnant of Judah who have gone into the land of Egypt to dwell there shall escape or survive, lest they return to the land of Judah,

44:1 ᵃEx. 14:2;
Jer. 46:14
ᵇJer. 43:7;
Ezek. 30:18
ᶜIs. 19:13;
Jer. 2:16; 46:14;
Ezek. 30:13, 16;
Hos. 9:6
ᵈIs. 11:11;
Ezek. 29:14;
30:14
44:2 ᵃIs. 6:11;
Jer. 4:7; 9:11;
34:22; Mic. 3:12
44:3 ᵃJer. 19:4
ᵇDeut. 13:6;
32:17
44:4
ᵃ2 Chr. 36:15;
Jer. 7:25; 25:4;
26:5; 29:19;
Zech. 7:7
44:7
ᵃNum. 16:38;
Jer. 7:19;
[Ezek. 33:11];
Hab. 2:10
44:8
ᵃ2 Kin. 17:15–17;
Jer. 25:6, 7;
44:3;
1 Cor. 10:21, 22
ᵇ1 Kin. 9:7, 8;
2 Chr. 7:20;
Jer. 42:18
44:10
ᵃ2 Chr. 36:12;
Jer. 6:15; 8:12;
Dan. 5:22
ᵇ[Prov. 28:14]
44:11 ᵃLev. 17:10;
20:5, 6;
Jer. 21:10;
Amos 9:4
44:12
ᵃJer. 42:15–17, 22
ᵇIs. 65:15;
Jer. 42:18
44:13 ᵃJer. 43:11

43:13 ¹Lit. *House of the Sun,* ancient On, later called Heliopolis
44:1 ¹Ancient Memphis   44:6 ¹Or *became a ruin*   44:10 ¹Lit. *crushed*
44:11 ¹*destroying*

to which they ^adesire¹ to return and dwell. For ^bnone shall return except those who escape.' "

¹⁵Then all the men who knew that their wives had burned incense to other gods, with all the women who stood by, a great multitude, and all the people who dwelt in the land of Egypt, in Pathros, answered Jeremiah, saying: ¹⁶"*As for* the word that you have spoken to us in the name of the LORD, ^awe will not listen to you! ¹⁷But we will certainly do ^awhatever has gone out of our own mouth, to burn incense to the ^bqueen of heaven and pour out drink offerings to her, as we have done, we and our fathers, our kings and our princes, in the cities of Judah and in the streets of Jerusalem. For *then* we had plenty of ¹food, were well-off, and saw no trouble. ¹⁸But since we stopped burning incense to the queen of heaven and pouring out drink offerings to her, we have lacked everything and have been consumed by the sword and by famine."

¹⁹*The women also said,* ^a"And when we burned incense to the queen of heaven and poured out drink offerings to her, did we make cakes for her, to worship her, and pour out drink offerings to her without our husbands' *permission?*"

²⁰Then Jeremiah spoke to all the people—the men, the women, and all the people who had given him *that* answer—saying: ²¹"The incense that you burned in the cities of Judah and in the streets of Jerusalem, you and your fathers, your kings and your princes, and the people of the land, did not the LORD remember them, and did it *not* come into His mind? ²²So the LORD could no longer bear *it,* because of the evil of your doings *and* because of the abominations which you committed. Therefore your land is a desolation, an astonishment, a curse, and without an inhabitant, ^aas *it is* this day. ²³Because you have burned incense and because you have sinned against the LORD, and have not obeyed the voice of the LORD or walked in His law, in His statutes or in His testimonies, ^atherefore this calamity has happened to you, as *at* this day."

²⁴Moreover Jeremiah said to all the people and to all the women, "Hear the word of the LORD, all Judah who *are* in the land of Egypt! ²⁵Thus says the LORD of hosts, the God of Israel, saying: 'You and your wives have spoken with your mouths and fulfilled with your hands, saying, "We will surely keep our vows that we have made, to burn incense to the queen of heaven and pour out drink offerings to her." You will surely keep your vows and perform your vows!' ²⁶Therefore hear the word of the LORD, all Judah who dwell in the land of Egypt: 'Behold, ^aI have sworn by My ^bgreat name,' says the LORD, 'that ^cMy name shall no more be named in the mouth of any man of Judah in all the land of Egypt, saying, "The Lord GOD lives." ²⁷Behold, I will watch over them for adversity and not for good. And all the men of Judah who *are* in the land of Egypt ^ashall be consumed by the sword and by famine, until there is an end to them. ²⁸Yet ^aa small number who escape the sword shall return from the land of Egypt to the land of Judah; and all the remnant of Judah, who have gone to the land of Egypt to dwell there, shall know whose words will stand, Mine or theirs. ²⁹And this *shall be* a sign to

44:14 ^aJer. 22:26, 27
^b[Is. 4:2; 10:20];
Jer. 44:28;
[Rom. 9:27]

44:16 ^aJer. 6:16

44:17
^aNum. 30:12;
Deut. 23:23;
Judg. 11:36
^b2 Kin. 17:16;
Jer. 7:18

44:19 ^aJer. 7:18

44:22
^aJer. 25:11, 18, 38

44:23
^a1 Kin. 9:9;
Neh. 13:18;
Jer. 44:2;
Dan. 9:11, 12

44:26
^aGen. 22:16;
Deut. 32:40, 41;
Jer. 22:5;
Amos 6:8;
Heb. 6:13
^bJer. 10:6
^cNeh. 9:5;
Ps. 50:16;
Ezek. 20:39

44:27 ^aJer. 1:10;
31:28; Ezek. 7:6

44:28 ^aIs. 10:19;
27:12, 13

44:14 ¹Lit. *lift up their soul*   **44:17** ¹Lit. *bread*

you,' says the LORD, 'that I will punish you in this place, that you may know that My words will surely ᵃstand against you for adversity.'

30"Thus says the LORD: 'Behold, ᵃI will give Pharaoh Hophra king of Egypt into the hand of his enemies and into the hand of those who seek his life, as I gave ᵇZedekiah king of Judah into the hand of Nebuchadnezzar king of Babylon, his enemy who sought his life.'"

ASSURANCE TO BARUCH

45 The ᵃword that Jeremiah the prophet spoke to ᵇBaruch the son of Neriah, when he had written these words in a book ¹at the instruction of Jeremiah, in the ᶜfourth year of Jehoiakim the son of Josiah, king of Judah, saying, 2"Thus says the LORD, the God of Israel, to you, O Baruch: 3'You said, "Woe is me now! For the LORD has added grief to my sorrow. I ᵃfainted in my sighing, and I find no rest."'

4"Thus you shall say to him, 'Thus says the LORD: "Behold, ᵃwhat I have built I will break down, and what I have planted I will pluck up, that is, this whole land. 5And do you seek great things for yourself? Do not seek *them;* for behold, ᵃI will bring adversity on all flesh," says the LORD. "But I will give your ᵇlife to you as a prize in all places, wherever you go."'"

JUDGMENT ON EGYPT

46 The word of the LORD which came to Jeremiah the prophet against ᵃthe nations. 2Against ᵃEgypt.
ᵇConcerning the army of Pharaoh Necho, king of Egypt, which was by the River Euphrates in Carchemish, and which Nebuchadnezzar king of Babylon ᶜdefeated in the ᵈfourth year of Jehoiakim the son of Josiah, king of Judah:

3 "Order¹ the ²buckler and shield,
 And draw near to battle!
4 Harness the horses,
 And mount up, you horsemen!
 Stand forth with *your* helmets,
 Polish the spears,
 ᵃPut on the armor!
5 Why have I seen them dismayed *and* turned
  back?
 Their mighty ones are beaten down;
 They have speedily fled,
 And did not look back,
 For ᵃfear *was* all around," says the LORD.
6 "Do not let the swift flee away,
 Nor the mighty man escape;
 They will ᵃstumble and fall
 Toward the north, by the River Euphrates.

7 "Who *is* this coming up ᵃlike a flood,
 Whose waters move like the rivers?
8 Egypt rises up like a flood,
 And *its* waters move like the rivers;
 And he says, 'I will go up *and* cover the earth,
 I will destroy the city and its inhabitants.'

44:29
ᵃ[Ps. 33:11]

44:30
ᵃJer. 46:25, 26;
Ezek. 29:3; 30:21
ᵇ2 Kin. 25:4-7;
Jer. 39:5

45:1
ᵃJer. 36:1, 4, 32
ᵇJer. 32:12, 16;
43:3 ᶜJer. 25:1;
36:1; 46:2

45:3
ᵃPs. 6:6; 69:3;
[2 Cor. 4:1, 16;
Gal. 6:9]

45:4 ᵃIs. 5:5;
Jer. 1:10; 11:17;
18:7-10; 31:28

45:5
ᵃJer. 25:17-26
ᵇJer. 21:9; 38:2;
39:18

46:1 ᵃJer. 25:15

46:2
ᵃJer. 25:17-19;
Ezek. 29:2-
32:32
ᵇ2 Kin. 23:33-35
ᶜ2 Kin. 23:29;
24:7;
2 Chr. 35:20
ᵈJer. 45:1

46:4 ᵃIs. 21:5;
Jer. 51:11, 12;
Joel 3:9;
Nah. 2:1; 3:14

46:5 ᵃJer. 49:29

46:6
ᵃJer. 46:12, 16;
Dan. 11:19

46:7
ᵃIs. 8:7, 8;
Jer. 47:2;
Dan. 11:22

45:1 ¹Lit. *from Jeremiah's mouth* 46:3 ¹*Set in order* ²A small shield

9   Come up, O horses, and rage, O chariots!
    And let the mighty men come forth:
    ¹The Ethiopians and ²the Libyans who handle the
      shield,
    And the Lydians ªwho handle *and* bend the bow.
10 For this *is* ªthe day of the Lord GOD of hosts,
    A day of vengeance,
    That He may avenge Himself on His adversaries.
    ᵇThe sword shall devour;
    It shall be ¹satiated and made drunk with their blood;
    For the Lord GOD of hosts ᶜhas a sacrifice
    In the north country by the River Euphrates.

11 "Goª up to Gilead and take balm,
    ᵇO virgin, the daughter of Egypt;
    In vain you will use many medicines;
    ᶜYou shall not be cured.
12 The nations have heard of your ªshame,
    And your cry has filled the land;
    For the mighty man has stumbled against the mighty;
    They both have fallen together."

BABYLONIA WILL STRIKE EGYPT

13The word that the LORD spoke to Jeremiah the prophet, how Nebuchadnezzar king of Babylon would come *and* ªstrike the land of Egypt.

14 "Declare in Egypt, and proclaim in ªMigdol;
    Proclaim in ¹Noph and in ᵇTahpanhes;
    Say, 'Stand fast and prepare yourselves,
    For the sword devours all around you.'
15 Why are your valiant *men* swept away?
    They did not stand
    Because the LORD drove them away.
16 He made many fall;
    Yes, ªone fell upon another.
    And they said, 'Arise!
    ᵇLet us go back to our own people
    And to the land of our nativity
    From the oppressing sword.'
17 They cried there,
    'Pharaoh, king of Egypt, *is but* a noise.
    He has passed by the appointed time!'

18 "*As* I live," says the King,
    ªWhose name *is* the LORD of hosts,
    "Surely as Tabor *is* among the mountains
    And as Carmel by the sea, *so* he shall come.
19 O ªyou daughter dwelling in Egypt,
    Prepare yourself ᵇto go into captivity!
    For ¹Noph shall be waste and desolate, without
      inhabitant.

20 "Egypt *is* a very pretty ªheifer,
    But destruction comes, it comes ᵇfrom the north.
21 Also her mercenaries are in her midst like ¹fat bulls,
    For they also are turned back,

46:9 ªIs. 66:19

46:10 ªIs. 13:6;
Joel 1:15
ᵇDeut. 32:42;
Is. 31:8; Jer. 12:12
ᶜIs. 34:6;
Zeph. 1:7;
Ezek. 39:17

46:11 ªJer. 8:22
ᵇIs. 47:1;
Jer. 31:4, 21
ᶜEzek. 30:21

46:12 ªJer. 2:36;
Nah. 3:8–10

46:13 ªIs. 19:1;
Jer. 43:10, 11;
Ezek. 29:1–21

46:14 ªJer. 44:1
ᵇEzek. 30:18

46:16
ªLev. 26:36, 37;
Jer. 46:6
ᵇJer. 51:9

46:18 ªIs. 47:4;
Jer. 48:15;
Mal. 1:14

46:19 ªJer. 48:18
ᵇIs. 20:4

46:20
ªHos. 10:11
ᵇJer. 1:14

46:9 ¹Heb. *Cush* ²Heb. *Put* 46:10 ¹Filled to the full 46:14 ¹Ancient Memphis 46:19 ¹Ancient Memphis 46:21 ¹Lit. *calves of the stall*

They have fled away together.
They did not stand,
For ᵃthe day of their calamity had come upon
    them,
The time of their punishment.

22 ᵃHer noise shall go like a serpent,
    For they shall march with an army
    And come against her with axes,
    Like those who chop wood.

23 "They shall ᵃcut down her forest," says the LORD,
    "Though it cannot be searched,
    Because they *are* innumerable,
    And more numerous than ᵇgrasshoppers.
24   The daughter of Egypt shall be ashamed;
    She shall be delivered into the hand
    Of ᵃthe people of the north."

25 The LORD of hosts, the God of Israel, says: "Behold, I will bring punishment on ¹Amon of ᵃNo,² and Pharaoh and Egypt, ᵇwith their gods and their kings—Pharaoh and those who ᶜtrust in him. 26ᵃAnd I will deliver them into the hand of those who seek their lives, into the hand of Nebuchadnezzar king of Babylon and the hand of his servants. ᵇAfterward it shall be inhabited as in the days of old," says the LORD.

GOD WILL PRESERVE ISRAEL
(cf. Jer. 30:10, 11)

27 "Butᵃ do not fear, O My servant Jacob,
    And do not be dismayed, O Israel!
    For behold, I will ᵇsave you from afar,
    And your offspring from the land of their captivity;
    Jacob shall return, have rest and be at ease;
    No one shall make *him* afraid.
28   Do not fear, O Jacob My servant," says the LORD,
    "For I *am* with you;
    For I will make a complete end of all the nations
    To which I have driven you,
    But I will not make ᵃa complete end of you.
    I will rightly ᵇcorrect you,
    For I will not leave you wholly unpunished."

JUDGMENT ON PHILISTIA

47 The word of the LORD that came to Jeremiah the prophet ᵃagainst the Philistines, ᵇbefore Pharaoh attacked Gaza.

2 Thus says the LORD:

"Behold, ᵃwaters rise ᵇout of the north,
    And shall be an overflowing flood;
    They shall overflow the land and all that is in it,
    The city and those who dwell within;
    Then the men shall cry,
    And all the inhabitants of the land shall wail.
3   At the ᵃnoise of the stamping hooves of his strong
    horses,
    At the rushing of his chariots,

46:21 ᵃ[Ps. 37:13]; Jer. 50:27
46:22 ᵃ[Is. 29:4]
46:23 ᵃIs. 10:34 ᵇJudg. 6:5; 7:12; Joel 2:25
46:24 ᵃJer. 1:15
46:25 ᵃEzek. 30:14–16; Nah. 3:8 ᵇEx. 12:12; Jer. 43:12, 13; Ezek. 30:13; Zeph. 2:11 ᶜIs. 30:1–5; 31:1–3
46:26 ᵃJer. 44:30; Ezek. 32:11 ᵇEzek. 29:8–14
46:27 ᵃIs. 41:13, 14; 43:5; 44:2; Jer. 30:10, 11 ᵇIs. 11:11; Jer. 23:3, 4; Mic. 7:12
46:28 ᵃJer. 10:24; Amos 9:8, 9 ᵇJer. 30:11
47:1 ᵃIs. 14:29–31; Ezek. 25:15–17; Zeph. 2:4, 5; Zech. 9:6 ᵇAmos 1:6
47:2 ᵃIs. 8:7, 8; Jer. 46:7, 8 ᵇJer. 1:14
47:3 ᵃJudg. 5:22; Jer. 8:16; Nah. 3:2

46:25 ¹A sun god   ²Ancient Thebes

At the rumbling of his wheels,
The fathers will not look back for *their* children,
[1]Lacking courage,

4 Because of the day that comes to plunder all the
[a]Philistines,
To cut off from [b]Tyre and Sidon every helper who
remains;
For the LORD shall plunder the Philistines,
[c]The remnant of the country of [d]Caphtor.[1]

5 [a]Baldness has come upon Gaza,
[b]Ashkelon is cut off
With the remnant of their valley.
How long will you cut yourself?

6 "O you [a]sword of the LORD,
How long until you are quiet?
Put yourself up into your scabbard,
Rest and be still!

7 How can [1]it be quiet,
Seeing the LORD has [a]given it a charge
Against Ashkelon and against the seashore?
There He has [b]appointed it."

JUDGMENT ON MOAB

48 Against [a]Moab.
Thus says the LORD of hosts, the God of Israel:

"Woe to [b]Nebo!
For it is plundered,
[c]Kirjathaim is shamed *and* taken;
[1]The high stronghold is shamed and dismayed—

2 [a]No more praise of Moab.
In [b]Heshbon they have devised evil against her:
'Come, and let us cut her off as a nation.'
You also shall be cut down, O [c]Madmen![1]
The sword shall pursue you;

3 A voice of crying *shall be* from [a]Horonaim:
'Plundering and great destruction!'

4 "Moab is destroyed;
[1]Her little ones have caused a cry to be heard;

5 [a]For in the Ascent of Luhith they ascend with continual
weeping;
For in the descent of Horonaim the enemies have heard
a cry of destruction.

6 "Flee, save your lives!
And be like [1]the [a]juniper in the wilderness.

7 For because you have trusted in your works and your
[a]treasures,
You also shall be taken.
And [b]Chemosh shall go forth into captivity,
His [c]priests and his princes together.

8 And [a]the plunderer shall come against every city;
No one shall escape.
The valley also shall perish,

Cross references

47:4
[a]Is. 14:29–31
[b]Is. 23:1–18;
Jer. 25:22;
Ezek. 26:1–21;
28:20–24;
Amos 1:9, 10;
Zech. 9:2–4
[c]Ezek. 25:16;
Amos 1:8
[d]Gen. 10:14;
Deut. 2:23;
Amos 9:7

47:5 [a]Jer. 48:37;
Mic. 1:16;
Zeph. 2:4
[b]Judg. 1:18;
Jer. 25:20;
Amos 1:7, 8;
Zech. 9:5

47:6
[a]Deut. 32:41;
Judg. 7:20;
Jer. 12:12;
Ezek. 21:3–5

47:7 [a]Is. 10:6;
Ezek. 14:17
[b]Mic. 6:9

48:1
[a]Is. 15:1—16:14;
25:10;
Ezek. 25:8–11;
Amos 2:1–3;
Zeph. 2:8–11
[b]Is. 15:2
[c]Num. 32:37;
Jer. 48:23;
Ezek. 25:9

48:2 [a]Is. 16:14
[b]Is. 15:4;
Jer. 49:3
[c]Is. 10:31

48:3 [a]Is. 15:5;
Jer. 48:5, 34

48:5 [a]Is. 15:5

48:6 [a]Jer. 17:6

48:7 [a]Ps. 52:7;
Is. 59:4;
Jer. 9:23;
[1 Tim. 6:17]
[b]Num. 21:29;
Judg. 11:24;
Jer. 48:13
[c]Jer. 49:3

48:8 [a]Jer. 6:26

47:3 [1]Lit. *From sinking hands*   47:4 [1]Crete   47:7 [1]Lit. *you*   48:1 [1]Heb.
Misgab   48:2 [1]A city of Moab   48:4 [1]So with MT, Tg., Vg.; LXX *Proclaim it
in Zoar*   48:6 [1]Or *Aroer,* a city of Moab

And the plain shall be destroyed,
As the LORD has spoken.

9 "Give[a] wings to Moab,
That she may flee and get away;
For her cities shall be desolate,
Without any to dwell in them.

10 [a]Cursed *is* he who does the work of the LORD
deceitfully,
And cursed *is* he who keeps back his sword from
blood.

11 "Moab has been at ease from [1]his youth;
He [a]has settled on his dregs,
And has not been emptied from vessel to vessel,
Nor has he gone into captivity.
Therefore his taste remained in him,
And his scent has not changed.

12 "Therefore behold, the days are coming," says the LORD,
"That I shall send him [1]wine-workers
Who will tip him over
And empty his vessels
And break the bottles.

13 Moab shall be ashamed of [a]Chemosh,
As the house of Israel [b]was ashamed of [c]Bethel, their
confidence.

14 "How can you say, [a]'We *are* mighty
And strong men for the war'?

15 Moab is plundered and gone up *from* her cities;
Her chosen young men have [a]gone down to the
slaughter," says [b]the King,
Whose name *is* the LORD of hosts.

16 "The calamity of Moab *is* near at hand,
And his affliction comes quickly.

17 Bemoan him, all you who are around him;
And all you who know his name,
Say, [a]'How the strong staff is broken,
The beautiful rod!'

18 "O [a]daughter inhabiting [b]Dibon,
Come down from *your* glory,
And sit in thirst;
For the plunderer of Moab has come against you,
He has destroyed your strongholds.

19 O inhabitant of [a]Aroer,
[b]Stand by the way and watch;
Ask him who flees
And her who escapes;
Say, 'What has happened?'

20 Moab is shamed, for he is broken down.
[a]Wail and cry!
Tell it in [b]Arnon, that Moab is plundered.

21 "And judgment has come on the plain country:
On Holon and Jahzah and Mephaath,

22 On Dibon and Nebo and Beth Diblathaim,

48:9 [a]Ps. 55:6
48:10
[a]Judg. 5:23;
1 Sam. 15:3, 9;
1 Kin. 20:42
48:11 [a]Zeph. 1:12
48:13 [a]1 Kin. 11:7
[b]Hos. 10:6
[c]1 Kin. 12:29;
13:32–34;
Hos. 8:5, 6
48:14 [a]Is. 16:6
48:15
[a][Is. 40:30, 31];
Jer. 50:27
[b]Jer. 46:18;
51:57; Mal. 1:14
48:17
[a]Is. 9:4; 14:4, 5
48:18 [a]Is. 47:1
[b]Num. 21:30;
Josh. 13:9, 17;
Is. 15:2;
Jer. 48:22
48:19
[a]Deut. 2:36;
Josh. 12:2;
Is. 17:2
[b]1 Sam. 4:13,
14, 16
48:20 [a]Is. 16:7
[b]Num. 21:13

48:11 [1]Heb. uses masc. and fem. pronouns interchangeably in this chapter.
48:12 [1]Lit. *tippers* of wine bottles

23 On Kirjathaim and Beth Gamul and Beth Meon,
24 On [a]Kerioth and Bozrah,
   On all the cities of the land of Moab,
   Far or near.
25 [a]The [1]horn of Moab is cut off,
   And his [b]arm is broken," says the LORD.

26 "Make[a] him drunk,
   Because he exalted *himself* against the LORD.
   Moab shall wallow in his vomit,
   And he shall also be in derision.
27 For [a]was not Israel a derision to you?
   [b]Was he found among thieves?
   For whenever you speak of him,
   You shake *your head in* [c]scorn.
28 You who dwell in Moab,
   Leave the cities and [a]dwell in the rock,
   And be like [b]the dove *which* makes her nest
   In the sides of the cave's mouth.

29 "We have heard the [a]pride of Moab
   (He *is* exceedingly proud),
   Of his loftiness and arrogance and [b]pride,
   And of the haughtiness of his heart."
30 "I know his wrath," says the LORD,
   "But it *is* not right;
   [a]His [1]lies have made nothing right.
31 Therefore [a]I will wail for Moab,
   And I will cry out for all Moab;
   [1]I will mourn for the men of Kir Heres.
32 [a]O vine of Sibmah! I will weep for you with the weeping of
      [b]Jazer.
   Your plants have gone over the sea,
   They reach to the sea of Jazer.
   The plunderer has fallen on your summer fruit and your
      vintage.
33 [a]Joy and gladness are taken
   From the plentiful field
   And from the land of Moab;
   I have caused wine to [1]fail from the winepresses;
   No one will tread with joyous shouting—
   Not joyous shouting!

34 "From[a] the cry of Heshbon to [b]Elealeh and to Jahaz
   They have uttered their voice,
   [c]From Zoar to Horonaim,
   Like [1]a three-year-old heifer;
   For the waters of Nimrim also shall be desolate.

35 "Moreover," says the LORD,
   "I will cause to cease in Moab
   [a]The one who offers *sacrifices* in the [1]high places
   And burns incense to his gods.
36 Therefore [a]My heart shall wail like flutes for
      Moab,
   And like flutes My heart shall wail

48:24
[a]Jer. 48:41;
Amos 2:2

48:25 [a]Ps. 75:10;
Zech. 1:19–21
[b]Ezek. 30:21

48:26 [a]Jer. 25:15

48:27
[a]Zeph. 2:8
[b]Jer. 2:26
[c]Lam. 2:15;
[Mic. 7:8–10]

48:28
[a]Ps. 55:6, 7
[b]Song 2:14

48:29 [a]Is. 16:6;
Zeph. 2:8, 10
[b]Jer. 49:16

48:30 [a]Is. 16:6;
Jer. 50:36

48:31
[a]Is. 15:5; 16:7, 11

48:32
[a]Is. 16:8, 9
[b]Num. 21:32;
Is. 16:10

48:33 [a]Is. 16:10;
Jer. 25:10;
Joel 1:12

48:34
[a]Is. 15:4–6
[b]Num. 32:3, 37
[c]Is. 15:5, 6

48:35
[a]Is. 15:2; 16:12

48:36
[a]Is. 15:5; 16:11

48:25 [1]Strength   48:30 [1]*idle talk*   48:31 [1]So with DSS, LXX, Vg.; MT *He*
48:33 [1]*cease*   48:34 [1]Or *The Third Eglath*, an unknown city, Is. 15:5
48:35 [1]Places for pagan worship

For the men of Kir Heres.
Therefore [b]the riches they have acquired have perished.

37 "For [a]every head *shall be* bald, and every beard clipped;
On all the hands *shall be* cuts, and [b]on the loins
  sackcloth—

38 A general lamentation
On all the [a]housetops of Moab,
And in its streets;
For I have [b]broken Moab like a vessel in which *is* no
  pleasure," says the LORD.

39 "They shall wail:
'How she is broken down!
How Moab has turned her back with shame!'
So Moab shall be a derision
And a dismay to all those about her."

40 For thus says the LORD:

"Behold, [a]one shall fly like an eagle,
And [b]spread his wings over Moab.

41 Kerioth is taken,
And the strongholds are surprised;
[a]The mighty men's hearts in Moab on that day shall be
Like the heart of a woman in birth pangs.

42 And Moab shall be destroyed [a]as a people,
Because he exalted *himself* against the LORD.

43 [a]Fear and the pit and the snare *shall be* upon you,
O inhabitant of Moab," says the LORD.

44 "He who flees from the fear shall fall into the pit,
And he who gets out of the pit shall be caught in the
  [a]snare.
For upon Moab, upon it [b]I will bring
The year of their punishment," says the LORD.

45 "Those who fled stood under the shadow of Heshbon
Because of exhaustion.
But [a]a fire shall come out of Heshbon,
A flame from the midst of [b]Sihon,
And [c]shall devour the brow of Moab,
The crown of the head of the sons of tumult.

46 [a]Woe to you, O Moab!
The people of Chemosh perish;
For your sons have been taken captive,
And your daughters captive.

47 "Yet I will bring back the captives of Moab
[a]In the latter days," says the LORD.

Thus far *is* the judgment of Moab.

JUDGMENT ON AMMON

49 Against the [a]Ammonites.
Thus says the LORD:

"Has Israel no sons?
Has he no heir?
Why *then* does [1]Milcom inherit [b]Gad,
And his people dwell in its cities?

Cross references (margin):

48:36 [b]Is. 15:7
48:37 [a]Is. 15:2, 3; Jer. 16:6; 41:5; 47:5 [b]Gen. 37:34; Is. 15:3; 20:2
48:38 [a]Is. 15:3 [b]Jer. 22:28
48:40 [a]Deut. 28:49; Jer. 49:22; Hos. 8:1; Hab. 1:8 [b]Is. 8:8
48:41 [a]Is. 13:8; 21:3; Jer. 30:6; Mic. 4:9, 10
48:42 [a]Ps. 83:4; Jer. 48:2
48:43 [a]Is. 24:17, 18; Lam. 3:47
48:44 [a]1 Kin. 19:17; Is. 24:18; Amos 5:19 [b]Jer. 11:23
48:45 [a]Num. 21:28, 29 [b]Num. 21:21, 26; Ps. 135:11 [c]Num. 24:17
48:46 [a]Num. 21:29
48:47 [a]Jer. 49:6, 39
49:1 [a]Deut. 23:3, 4; 2 Chr. 20:1; Jer. 25:21; Ezek. 21:28–32; 25:1–7 [b]Amos 1:13–15; Zeph. 2:8–11

49:1 [1]Heb. *Malcam*, lit. *their king;* an Ammonite god, 1 Kin. 11:5; *Molech,* Lev. 18:21

2 ^aTherefore behold, the days are coming," says the LORD,
"That I will cause to be heard an alarm of war
In ^bRabbah of the Ammonites;
It shall be a desolate mound,
And her ¹villages shall be burned with fire.
Then Israel shall take possession of his inheritance," says
the LORD.

3 "Wail, O ^aHeshbon, for Ai is plundered!
Cry, you daughters of Rabbah,
^bGird yourselves with sackcloth!
Lament and run to and fro by the walls;
For ¹Milcom shall go into captivity
With his ^cpriests and his princes together.
4 Why ^ado you boast in the valleys,
¹Your flowing valley, O ^bbacksliding daughter?
Who trusted in her ^ctreasures, ^d*saying,*
'Who will come against me?'
5 Behold, I will bring fear upon you,"
Says the Lord GOD of hosts,
"From all those who are around you;
You shall be driven out, everyone headlong,
And no one will gather those who wander off.
6 But ^aafterward I will bring back
The captives of the people of Ammon," says the
LORD.

JUDGMENT ON EDOM

7^aAgainst Edom.
Thus says the LORD of hosts:

^b*"Is* wisdom no more in Teman?
^cHas counsel perished from the prudent?
Has their wisdom ^dvanished?
8 Flee, turn back, dwell in the depths, O inhabitants of
^aDedan!
For I will bring the calamity of Esau upon him,
The time *that* I will punish him.
9 ^aIf grape-gatherers came to you,
Would they not leave *some* gleaning grapes?
If thieves by night,
Would they not destroy until they have enough?
10 ^aBut I have made Esau bare;
I have uncovered his secret places,
And he shall not be able to hide himself.
His descendants are plundered,
His brethren and his neighbors,
And ^bhe *is* no more.
11 Leave your fatherless children,
I will preserve *them* alive;
And let your widows trust in Me."

12For thus says the LORD: "Behold, ^athose whose judgment
was not to drink of the cup have assuredly drunk. And *are*
you the one who will altogether go unpunished? You shall not
go unpunished, but you shall surely drink *of it.* 13For ^aI have
sworn by Myself," says the LORD, "that ^bBozrah shall become a

Cross references

49:2 ^aAmos 1:13–15 ^bEzek. 25:5

49:3 ^aJer. 48:2 ^bIs. 32:11; Jer. 48:37 ^cJer. 48:7

49:4 ^aJer. 9:23 ^bJer. 3:14 ^cJer. 48:7 ^dJer. 21:13

49:6 ^aJer. 48:47

49:7 ^aGen. 25:30; 32:3; Is. 34:5, 6; Jer. 25:21; Ezek. 25:12–14; 35:1–15; Joel 3:19; Amos 1:11, 12; Obad. 1–9, 15, 16 ^bGen. 36:11; Job 2:11 ^cIs. 19:11 ^dJer. 8:9

49:8 ^aIs. 21:13; Jer. 25:23

49:9 ^aObad. 5, 6

49:10 ^aObad. 5, 6; Mal. 1:3 ^bIs. 17:14

49:12 ^aJer. 25:29; Obad. 16

49:13 ^aGen. 22:16; Is. 45:23; Jer. 44:26; Amos 6:8 ^bGen. 36:33; 1 Chr. 1:44; Is. 34:6; 63:1; Amos 1:12

desolation, a reproach, a ¹waste, and a curse. And all its cities shall be perpetual ²wastes."

14 ᵃI have heard a message from the LORD,
   And an ambassador has been sent to the nations:
   "Gather together, come against her,
   And rise up to battle!

15 "For indeed, I will make you small among nations,
   Despised among men.

16 Your fierceness has deceived you,
   The ᵃpride of your heart,
   O you who dwell in the clefts of the rock,
   Who hold the height of the hill!
   ᵇThough you make your ᶜnest as high as the eagle,
   ᵈI will bring you down from there," says the LORD.

17 "Edom also shall be an astonishment;
   ᵃEveryone who goes by it will be astonished
   And will hiss at all its plagues.

18 ᵃAs in the overthrow of Sodom and Gomorrah
   And their neighbors," says the LORD,
   "No one shall remain there,
   Nor shall a son of man dwell in it.

19 "Behold,ᵃ he shall come up like a lion from ᵇthe
      ¹floodplain of the Jordan
   Against the dwelling place of the strong;
   But I will suddenly make him run away from her.
   And who is a chosen man that I may appoint over her?
   For ᶜwho is like Me?
   Who will arraign Me?
   And ᵈwho is that shepherd
   Who will withstand Me?"

20 ᵃTherefore hear the counsel of the LORD that He has
      taken against Edom,
   And His purposes that He has proposed against the
      inhabitants of Teman:
   Surely the least of the flock shall ¹draw them out;
   Surely He shall make their dwelling places desolate with
      them.

21 ᵃThe earth shakes at the noise of their fall;
   At the cry its noise is heard at the Red Sea.

22 Behold, ᵃHe shall come up and fly like the eagle,
   And spread His wings over Bozrah;
   The heart of the mighty men of Edom in that day
      shall be
   Like the heart of a woman in birth pangs.

JUDGMENT ON DAMASCUS

23ᵃAgainst Damascus.

ᵇ"Hamath and Arpad are shamed,
   For they have heard bad news.
   They are fainthearted;
   ᶜThere is ¹trouble on the sea;
   It cannot be quiet.

49:14
ᵃObad. 1–4

49:16
ᵃJer. 48:29
ᵇObad. 3, 4
ᶜJob 39:27;
Is. 14:13–15
ᵈAmos 9:2

49:17 ᵃJer. 18:16;
49:13; 50:13;
Ezek. 35:7

49:18
ᵃGen. 19:24, 25;
Deut. 29:23;
Jer. 50:40;
Amos 4:11;
Zeph. 2:9

49:19
ᵃJer. 50:44
ᵇJosh. 3:15;
Jer. 12:5
ᶜEx. 15:11;
Is. 46:9
ᵈJob 41:10

49:20
ᵃIs. 14:24, 27;
Jer. 50:45

49:21
ᵃJer. 50:46;
Ezek. 26:15, 18

49:22
ᵃJer. 48:40, 41

49:23
ᵃIs. 17:1–3;
Amos 1:3, 5;
Zech. 9:1, 2
ᵇJer. 39:5;
Zech. 9:2
ᶜ[Is. 57:20]

49:13 ¹ruin   ²ruins   49:19 ¹Or thicket   49:20 ¹Or drag them away
49:23 ¹anxiety

24 Damascus has grown feeble;
　　She turns to flee,
　　And fear has seized *her.*
　　^aAnguish and sorrows have taken her like a woman in
　　　¹labor.
25 Why is ^athe city of praise not deserted, the city of My joy?
26 ^aTherefore her young men shall fall in her streets,
　　And all the men of war shall be cut off in that day," says
　　　the Lord of hosts.
27 "I^a will kindle a fire in the wall of Damascus,
　　And it shall consume the palaces of Ben-Hadad."

JUDGMENT ON KEDAR AND HAZOR

28^aAgainst Kedar and against the kingdoms of Hazor,
which Nebuchadnezzar king of Babylon shall strike.
　　Thus says the Lord:

　　"Arise, go up to Kedar,
　　And devastate ^bthe men of the East!
29 Their ^atents and their flocks they shall take away.
　　They shall take for themselves their curtains,
　　All their vessels and their camels;
　　And they shall cry out to them,
　　^b'Fear *is* on every side!'

30 "Flee, get far away! Dwell in the depths,
　　O inhabitants of Hazor!" says the Lord.
　　"For Nebuchadnezzar king of Babylon has taken counsel
　　　against you,
　　And has conceived a plan against you.

31 "Arise, go up to ^athe wealthy nation that dwells securely,"
　　　says the Lord,
　　"Which has neither gates nor bars,
　　^bDwelling alone.
32 Their camels shall be for booty,
　　And the multitude of their cattle for plunder.
　　I will ^ascatter to all winds those ¹in the farthest corners,
　　And I will bring their calamity from all its sides," says the
　　　Lord.
33 "Hazor ^ashall be a dwelling for jackals, a desolation
　　　forever;
　　No one shall reside there,
　　Nor son of man dwell in it."

JUDGMENT ON ELAM

34The word of the Lord that came to Jeremiah the proph-
et against ^aElam, in the ^bbeginning of the reign of Zedekiah
king of Judah, saying, 35"Thus says the Lord of hosts:

　　'Behold, I will break ^athe ¹bow of Elam,
　　The foremost of their might.
36 Against Elam I will bring the four winds
　　From the four quarters of heaven,
　　And scatter them toward all those winds;
　　There shall be no nations where the outcasts of Elam will
　　　not go.

49:24 ^aIs. 13:8;
Jer. 4:31; 6:24;
48:21
49:25 ^aJer. 33:9
49:26
^aJer. 50:30;
Amos 4:10
49:27 ^aAmos 1:4
49:28
^aGen. 25:13;
Ps. 120:5;
Is. 21:16, 17;
Jer. 2:10;
Ezek. 27:21
^bJudg. 6:3;
Job 1:3
49:29 ^aPs. 120:5
^bJer. 46:5
49:31
^aEzek. 38:11
^bNum. 23:9;
Deut. 33:28;
Mic. 7:16
49:32
^aEzek. 5:10
49:33 ^aJer. 9:11;
10:22; Zeph. 2:9,
12–15; Mal. 1:3
49:34
^aGen. 10:22;
Jer. 25:25;
Ezek. 32:24;
Dan. 8:2
^b2 Kin. 24:17, 18;
Jer. 28:1
49:35 ^aPs. 46:9;
Is. 22:6

49:24 ¹*childbirth*　49:32 ¹Lit. *cut off at the corner,* Jer. 9:26; 25:23
49:35 ¹Power

37 For I will cause Elam to be dismayed before their
enemies
And before those who seek their life.
[a]I will bring disaster upon them,
My fierce anger,' says the LORD;
'And I will send the sword after them
Until I have consumed them.

38 I will [a]set My throne in Elam,
And will destroy from there the king and the princes,'
says the LORD.

39 'But it shall come to pass [a]in the latter days:
I will bring back the captives of Elam,' says the LORD."

JUDGMENT ON BABYLON AND BABYLONIA

50 The word that the LORD spoke [a]against Babylon *and* against the land of the Chaldeans by Jeremiah the prophet.

2 "Declare among the nations,
Proclaim, and [1]set up a standard;
Proclaim—do not conceal *it*—
Say, 'Babylon is [a]taken, [b]Bel is shamed.
[2]Merodach is broken in pieces;
[c]Her idols are humiliated,
Her images are broken in pieces.'

3 [a]For out of the north [b]a nation comes up against her,
Which shall make her land desolate,
And no one shall dwell therein.
They shall [1]move, they shall depart,
Both man and beast.

4 "In those days and in that time," says the LORD,
"The children of Israel shall come,
[a]They and the children of Judah together;
[b]With continual weeping they shall come,
[c]And seek the LORD their God.

5 They shall ask the way to Zion,
With their faces toward it, *saying,*
'Come and let us join ourselves to the LORD
In [a]a perpetual covenant
That will not be forgotten.'

6 "My people have been [a]lost sheep.
Their shepherds have led them [b]astray;
They have turned them away *on* [c]the mountains.
They have gone from mountain to hill;
They have forgotten their resting place.

7 All who found them have [a]devoured them;
And [b]their adversaries said, [c]'We have not offended,
Because they have sinned against the LORD, [d]the
habitation of justice,
The LORD, [e]the hope of their fathers.'

8 "Move[a] from the midst of Babylon,
Go out of the land of the Chaldeans;
And be like the [1]rams before the flocks.

49:37 [a] Jer. 9:16
49:38
[a] Jer. 43:10
49:39
[a] Jer. 48:47
50:1
[a] Gen. 10:10; 11:9;
2 Kin. 17:24;
Is. 13:1; 47:1;
Dan. 1:1;
Rev. 14:8
50:2 [a] Is. 21:9
[b] Is. 46:1;
Jer. 51:44
[c] Jer. 43:12, 13
50:3 [a] Jer. 51:48;
Dan. 5:30, 31
[b] Is. 13:17, 18, 20
50:4 [a] Ezra 2:1;
Is. 11:12, 13;
Jer. 3:18; 31:31;
33:7; Hos. 1:11
[b] Ezra 3:12, 13;
[Ps. 126:5];
Jer. 31:9;
[Zech. 12:10]
[c] Hos. 3:5
50:5 [a] Jer. 31:31
50:6 [a] Is. 53:6;
[Ezek. 34:15, 16];
Matt. 9:36; 10:6;
1 Pet. 2:25
[b] Jer. 23:1;
Ezek. 34:2
[c] [Jer. 2:20;
3:6, 23]
50:7 [a] Ps. 79:7
[b] Jer. 40:2, 3;
Zech. 11:5
[c] Jer. 2:3;
Dan. 9:16
[d] [Ps. 90:1; 91:1]
[e] Ps. 22:4;
Jer. 14:8; 17:13
50:8 [a] Is. 48:20;
Jer. 51:6, 45;
Zech. 2:6, 7;
[Rev. 18:4]

50:2 [1]lift   [2]Or *Marduk;* a Babylonian god   50:3 [1]Or *wander*   50:8 [1]*male goats*

9 ^aFor behold, I will raise and cause to come up against Babylon
An assembly of great nations from the north country,
And they shall array themselves against her;
From there she shall be captured.
Their arrows *shall be* like *those* of ¹an expert warrior;
^bNone shall return in vain.

10 And Chaldea shall become plunder;
^aAll who plunder her shall be satisfied," says the LORD.

11 "Because^a you were glad, because you rejoiced,
You destroyers of My heritage,
Because you have grown fat ^blike a heifer threshing grain,
And you ¹bellow like bulls,

12 Your mother shall be deeply ashamed;
She who bore you shall be ashamed.
Behold, the least of the nations *shall be* a ^awilderness,
A dry land and a desert.

13 Because of the wrath of the LORD
She shall not be inhabited,
^aBut she shall be wholly desolate.
^bEveryone who goes by Babylon shall be horrified
And hiss at all her plagues.

14 "Put^a yourselves in array against Babylon all around,
All you who bend the bow;
Shoot at her, spare no arrows,
For she has sinned against the LORD.

15 Shout against her all around;
She has ^agiven her hand,
Her foundations have fallen,
^bHer walls are thrown down;
For ^cit *is* the vengeance of the LORD.
Take vengeance on her.
As she has done, so do to her.

16 Cut off the sower from Babylon,
And him who handles the sickle at harvest time.
For fear of the oppressing sword
^aEveryone shall turn to his own people,
And everyone shall flee to his own land.

17 "Israel *is* like ^ascattered sheep;
^bThe lions have driven *him* away.
First ^cthe king of Assyria devoured him;
Now at last this ^dNebuchadnezzar king of Babylon has broken his bones."

18Therefore thus says the LORD of hosts, the God of Israel:

"Behold, I will punish the king of Babylon and his land,
As I have punished the king of ^aAssyria.

19 ^aBut I will bring back Israel to his home,
And he shall feed on Carmel and Bashan;
His soul shall be satisfied on Mount Ephraim and Gilead.

20 In those days and in that time," says the LORD,
^a"The iniquity of Israel shall be sought, but *there shall be* none;

50:9
^aJer. 15:14; 51:27
^b2 Sam. 1:22

50:10
^a[Rev. 17:16]

50:11 ^aIs. 47:6
^bHos. 10:11

50:12 ^aJer. 51:43

50:13 ^aJer. 25:12
^bJer. 49:17

50:14 ^aJer. 51:2

50:15
^a1 Chr. 29:24;
2 Chr. 30:8;
Lam. 5:6;
Ezek. 17:18
^bJer. 51:58
^cJer. 51:6, 11

50:16 ^aIs. 13:14;
Jer. 51:9

50:17
^a2 Kin. 24:10, 14
^bJer. 2:15
^c2 Kin. 15:29;
17:6; 18:9–13
^d2 Kin. 24:10–14;
25:1–7

50:18 ^aIs. 10:12;
Ezek. 31:3, 11, 12;
Nah. 3:7, 18, 19

50:19 ^aIs. 65:10;
Jer. 33:12;
Ezek. 34:13

50:20
^aNum. 23:21;
Is. 43:25;
[Jer. 31:34;
Mic. 7:19]

50:9 ¹So with some Heb. mss., LXX, Syr.; MT, Tg., Vg. *a warrior who makes childless* **50:11** ¹Or *neigh like steeds*

And the sins of Judah, but they shall not be found;
For I will pardon those ᵇwhom I preserve.

21 "Go up against the land of Merathaim, against it,
And against the inhabitants of ᵃPekod.
¹Waste and utterly destroy them," says the LORD,
"And do ᵇaccording to all that I have commanded you.

22 ᵃA sound of battle *is* in the land,
And of great destruction.

23 How ᵃthe hammer of the whole earth has been cut apart
and broken!
How Babylon has become a desolation among the
nations!

24 I have laid a snare for you;
You have indeed been ᵃtrapped, O Babylon,
And you were not aware;
You have been found and also caught,
Because you have ᵇcontended against the LORD.

25 The LORD has opened His armory,
And has brought out ᵃthe weapons of His indignation;
For this *is* the work of the Lord GOD of hosts
In the land of the Chaldeans.

26 Come against her from the farthest border;
Open her storehouses;
Cast her up as heaps of ruins,
And destroy her utterly;
Let nothing of her be left.

27 Slay all her ᵃbulls,
Let them go down to the slaughter.
Woe to them!
For their day has come, the time of ᵇtheir punishment.

28 The voice of those who flee and escape from the land of
Babylon
ᵃDeclares in Zion the vengeance of the LORD our God,
The vengeance of His temple.

29 "Call together the archers against Babylon.
All you who bend the bow, encamp against it all around;
Let none of them ¹escape.
ᵃRepay her according to her work;
According to all she has done, do to her;
ᵇFor she has been proud against the LORD,
Against the Holy One of Israel.

30 ᵃTherefore her young men shall fall in the streets,
And all her men of war shall be cut off in that day," says
the LORD.

31 "Behold, I *am* against you,
O most haughty one!" says the Lord GOD of hosts;
"For your day has come,
¹The time *that* I will punish you.

32 The most ᵃproud shall stumble and fall,
And no one will raise him up;
ᵇI will kindle a fire in his cities,
And it will devour all around him."

³³Thus says the LORD of hosts:

50:20 ᵇIs. 1:9
50:21
ᵃEzek. 23:23
ᵇ2 Sam. 16:11;
2 Kin. 18:25;
2 Chr. 36:23;
Is. 10:6; 44:28;
48:14
50:22 ᵃJer. 51:54
50:23 ᵃIs. 14:6;
Jer. 51:20–24
50:24
ᵃJer. 51:8, 31;
Dan. 5:30
ᵇ[Is. 45:9]
50:25 ᵃIs. 13:5
50:27 ᵃPs. 22:12;
Is. 34:7;
Jer. 46:21
ᵇPs. 37:13;
Jer. 48:44;
Ezek. 7:7
50:28
ᵃPs. 149:6–9;
Jer. 51:10
50:29
ᵃPs. 137:8;
Jer. 51:56;
[2 Thess. 1:6];
Rev. 18:6
ᵇ[Is. 47:10]
50:30 ᵃIs. 13:18;
Jer. 49:26; 51:4
50:32 ᵃIs. 26:5;
Mal. 4:1
ᵇJer. 21:14

50:21 ¹Or *Attack* with the sword   50:29 ¹Qr., some Heb. mss., LXX, Tg. add *to her*   50:31 ¹So with MT, Tg.; LXX, Vg. *The time of your punishment*

"The children of Israel *were* oppressed,
Along with the children of Judah;
All who took them captive have held them fast;
They have refused to let them go.
34 ᵃTheir Redeemer *is* strong;
ᵇThe Lᴏʀᴅ of hosts *is* His name.
He will thoroughly plead their ᶜcase,
That He may give rest to the land,
And disquiet the inhabitants of Babylon.

35 "A sword *is* against the Chaldeans," says the Lᴏʀᴅ,
"Against the inhabitants of Babylon,
And ᵃagainst her princes and ᵇher wise men.
36 A sword *is* ᵃagainst the soothsayers, and they will be
fools.
A sword *is* against her mighty men, and they will be
dismayed.
37 A sword *is* against their horses,
Against their chariots,
And against all ᵃthe mixed peoples who *are* in her midst;
And ᵇthey will become like women.
A sword *is* against her treasures, and they will be robbed.
38 ᵃA ¹drought *is* against her waters, and they will be dried
up.
For it *is* the land of carved images,
And they are insane with *their* idols.

39 "Thereforeᵃ the wild desert beasts shall dwell *there* with
the jackals,
And the ostriches shall dwell in it.
ᵇIt shall be inhabited no more forever,
Nor shall it be dwelt in from generation to generation.
40 ᵃAs God overthrew Sodom and Gomorrah
And their neighbors," says the Lᴏʀᴅ,
"*So* no one shall reside there,
Nor son of man ᵇdwell in it.

41 "Behold,ᵃ a people shall come from the north,
And a great nation and many kings
Shall be raised up from the ends of the earth.
42 ᵃThey shall hold the bow and the lance;
ᵇThey *are* cruel and shall not show mercy.
ᶜTheir voice shall roar like the sea;
They shall ride on horses,
Set in array, like a man for the battle,
Against you, O daughter of Babylon.

43 "The king of Babylon has ᵃheard the report about them,
And his hands grow feeble;
Anguish has taken hold of him,
Pangs as of a woman in ᵇchildbirth.

44 "Behold,ᵃ he shall come up like a lion from the ¹floodplain
of the Jordan
Against the dwelling place of the strong;
But I will make them suddenly run away from her.
And who *is* a chosen *man that* I may appoint over her?

50:34
ᵃProv. 23:11;
Is. 43:14;
Jer. 15:21;
31:11; Rev. 18:8
ᵇIs. 47:4
ᶜJer. 51:36;
Mic. 7:9

50:35
ᵃDan. 5:30
ᵇIs. 47:13;
Jer. 51:57

50:36 ᵃIs. 44:25;
Jer. 48:30

50:37
ᵃJer. 25:20;
Ezek. 30:5
ᵇJer. 51:30;
Nah. 3:13

50:38 ᵃIs. 44:27;
Jer. 51:36;
Rev. 16:12

50:39
ᵃIs. 13:21, 22;
34:14; Jer. 51:37;
Rev. 18:2
ᵇIs. 13:20;
Jer. 25:12

50:40
ᵃGen. 19:24, 25;
Is. 13:19;
Jer. 49:18;
[Luke 17:28–30];
2 Pet. 2:6;
Jude 7 ᵇIs. 13:20

50:41
ᵃIs. 13:2–5;
Jer. 6:22; 25:14;
51:27

50:42 ᵃJer. 6:23
ᵇIs. 13:18
ᶜIs. 5:30

50:43 ᵃJer. 51:31
ᵇJer. 6:24

50:44
ᵃJer. 49:19–21

50:38 ¹So with MT, Tg., Vg.; Syr. *sword*; LXX omits *A drought is*   50:44 ¹Or
thicket

For who *is* like Me?
Who will arraign Me?
And ^bwho *is* that shepherd
Who will withstand Me?"

45 Therefore hear ^athe counsel of the LORD that He has
    taken against Babylon,
And His ^bpurposes that He has proposed against the
    land of the Chaldeans:
    ^cSurely the least of the flock shall draw them out;
    Surely He will make their dwelling place desolate with
    them.
46 ^aAt the noise of the taking of Babylon
    The earth trembles,
    And the cry is heard among the nations.

THE UTTER DESTRUCTION OF BABYLON

51 Thus says the LORD:

"Behold, I will raise up against ^aBabylon,
    Against those who dwell in ¹Leb Kamai,
    ^bA destroying wind.
2 And I will send ^awinnowers to Babylon,
    Who shall winnow her and empty her land.
    ^bFor in the day of doom
    They shall be against her all around.
3 Against *her* ^alet the archer bend his bow,
    And lift himself up against *her* in his armor.
    Do not spare her young men;
    ^bUtterly destroy all her army.
4 Thus the slain shall fall in the land of the Chaldeans,
    ^aAnd *those* thrust through in her streets.
5 For Israel is ^anot forsaken, nor Judah,
    By his God, the LORD of hosts,
    Though their land was filled with sin against the Holy
    One of Israel."

6 ^aFlee from the midst of Babylon,
    And every one save his life!
    Do not be cut off in her iniquity,
    For ^bthis *is* the time of the LORD's vengeance;
    ^cHe shall recompense her.
7 ^aBabylon *was* a golden cup in the LORD's hand,
    That made all the earth drunk.
    ^bThe nations drank her wine;
    Therefore the nations ^care deranged.
8 Babylon has suddenly ^afallen and been destroyed.
    ^bWail for her!
    ^cTake balm for her pain;
    Perhaps she may be healed.

9 We would have healed Babylon,
    But she is not healed.
    Forsake her, and ^alet us go everyone to his own country;
    ^bFor her judgment reaches to heaven and is lifted up to
    the skies.

Cross references (left column):

50:44
^bJob 41:10;
Jer. 49:19

50:45
^a[Ps. 33:11;
Is. 14:24];
Jer. 51:10, 11
^bJer. 51:29
^cJer. 49:19, 20

50:46 ^aRev. 18:9

51:1 ^aIs. 47:1;
Jer. 50:1
^b2 Kin. 19:7;
Jer. 4:11;
Hos. 13:15

51:2 ^aIs. 41:16;
Jer. 15:7;
Matt. 3:12
^bJer. 50:14

51:3
^aJer. 50:14, 29
^bJer. 50:21

51:4 ^aJer. 49:26;
50:30, 37

51:5 ^a[Is. 54:7, 8;
Jer. 33:24–26;
46:28]

51:6 ^aJer. 50:8;
Rev. 18:4
^bJer. 50:15
^cJer. 25:14

51:7 ^aJer. 25:15;
Hab. 2:16;
Rev. 17:4
^bRev. 14:8
^cJer. 25:16

51:8 ^aIs. 21:9;
Jer. 50:2;
Rev. 14:8; 18:2
^b[Is. 48:20];
Rev. 18:9, 11, 19
^cJer. 46:11

51:9 ^aIs. 13:14;
Jer. 46:16; 50:16
^bEzra 9:6;
Rev. 18:5

51:1 ¹Lit. *The Midst of Those Who Rise Up Against Me*; a code word for
Chaldea, Babylonia

10 The LORD has ^arevealed our righteousness.
Come and let us ^bdeclare in Zion the work of the LORD
   our God.

11 ^aMake¹ the arrows bright!
Gather the shields!
^bThe LORD has raised up the spirit of the kings of the
   Medes.
^cFor His plan *is* against Babylon to destroy it,
Because it *is* ^dthe vengeance of the LORD,
The vengeance for His temple.

12 ^aSet up the standard on the walls of Babylon;
Make the guard strong,
Set up the watchmen,
Prepare the ambushes.
For the LORD has both devised and done
What He spoke against the inhabitants of Babylon.

13 ^aO you who dwell by many waters,
Abundant in treasures,
Your end has come,
The measure of your covetousness.

14 ^aThe LORD of hosts has sworn by Himself:
"Surely I will fill you with men, ^bas with locusts,
And they shall lift ^cup a shout against you."

15 ^aHe has made the earth by His power;
He has established the world by His wisdom,
And ^bstretched out the heaven by His understanding.

16 When He utters *His* voice—
There is a multitude of waters in the heavens:
^a"He causes the vapors to ascend from the ends of the
   earth;
He makes lightnings for the rain;
He brings the wind out of His treasuries."

17 ^aEveryone is dull-hearted, without knowledge;
Every metalsmith is put to shame by the carved image;
^bFor his molded image *is* falsehood,
And *there is* no breath in them.

18 They *are* futile, a work of errors;
In the time of their punishment they shall perish.

19 The Portion of Jacob *is* not like them,
For He *is* the Maker of all things;
And *Israel is* the tribe of His inheritance.
The LORD of hosts *is* His name.

20 "You^a *are* My battle-ax *and* weapons of war:
For with you I will break the nation in pieces;
With you I will destroy kingdoms;

21 With you I will break in pieces the horse and its rider;
With you I will break in pieces the chariot and its
   rider;

22 With you also I will break in pieces man and woman;
With you I will break in pieces ^aold and young;
With you I will break in pieces the young man and the
   maiden;

23 With you also I will break in pieces the shepherd and his
   flock;

51:10 ^aPs. 37:6;
Mic. 7:9
^b[Is. 40:2];
Jer. 50:28

51:11
^aJer. 46:4, 9;
Joel 3:9, 10
^bIs. 13:17
^cJer. 50:45
^dJer. 50:28

51:12
^aNah. 2:1; 3:14

51:13
^aRev. 17:1, 15

51:14 ^aJer. 49:13;
Amos 6:8
^bJer. 51:27;
Nah. 3:15
^cJer. 50:15

51:15
^aGen. 1:1, 6;
Jer. 10:12–16
^bJob 9:8;
Ps. 104:2;
Is. 40:22

51:16 ^aPs. 135:7;
Jer. 10:13

51:17
^a[Is. 44:18–20];
Jer. 10:14
^bJer. 50:2

51:20
^aIs. 10:5, 15;
Jer. 50:23

51:22
^a2 Chr. 36:17;
Is. 13:15, 16

51:11 ¹*Polish the arrows!*

With you I will break in pieces the farmer and his yoke
of oxen;
And with you I will break in pieces governors and rulers.

24 "And[a] I will repay Babylon
And all the inhabitants of Chaldea
For all the evil they have done
In Zion in your sight," says the LORD.

25 "Behold, I *am* against you, [a]O destroying mountain,
Who destroys all the earth," says the LORD.
"And I will stretch out My hand against you,
Roll you down from the rocks,
[b]And make you a burnt mountain.

26 They shall not take from you a stone for a corner
Nor a stone for a foundation,
[a]But you shall be desolate forever," says the LORD.

27 [a]Set up a banner in the land,
Blow the trumpet among the nations!
[b]Prepare the nations against her,
Call [c]the kingdoms together against her:
Ararat, Minni, and Ashkenaz.
Appoint a general against her;
Cause the horses to come up like the bristling locusts.

28 Prepare against her the nations,
With the kings of the Medes,
Its governors and all its rulers,
All the land of his dominion.

29 And the land will tremble and sorrow;
For every [a]purpose of the LORD shall be performed
against Babylon,
[b]To make the land of Babylon a desolation without
inhabitant.

30 The mighty men of Babylon have ceased fighting,
They have remained in their strongholds;
Their might has failed,
[a]They became *like* women;
They have burned her dwelling places,
[b]The bars of her *gate* are broken.

31 [a]One runner will run to meet another,
And one messenger to meet another,
To show the king of Babylon that his city is taken on *all*
sides;

32 [a]The passages are blocked,
The reeds they have burned with fire,
And the men of war are terrified.

33 For thus says the LORD of hosts, the God of Israel:

"The daughter of Babylon *is* [a]like a threshing floor
When [b]*it is* time to thresh her;
Yet a little while
[c]And the time of her harvest will come."

34 "Nebuchadnezzar the king of Babylon
Has [a]devoured me, he has crushed me;
He has made me an [b]empty vessel,
He has swallowed me up like a monster;
He has filled his stomach with my delicacies,
He has spit me out.

51:24
[a]Jer. 50:15, 29

51:25 [a]Is. 13:2;
Zech. 4:7
[b]Rev. 8:8

51:26
[a]Jer. 50:26, 40

51:27 [a]Is. 13:2;
Jer. 50:2; 51:12
[b]Jer. 25:14
[c]Jer. 50:41, 42

51:29 [a]Jer. 50:45
[b]Is. 13:19, 20;
47:11; Jer. 50:13;
51:26, 43

51:30 [a]Is. 19:16;
Jer. 48:41
[b]Is. 45:1, 2;
Lam. 2:9;
Amos 1:5;
Nah. 3:13

51:31 [a]Jer. 50:24

51:32
[a]Jer. 50:38

51:33 [a]Is. 21:10;
Dan. 2:35;
Amos 1:3;
Mic. 4:13
[b]Is. 41:15;
Hab. 3:12
[c]Is. 17:5;
Hos. 6:11;
Joel 3:13;
Rev. 14:15

51:34 [a]Jer. 50:17
[b]Is. 24:1-3

35 Let the violence *done* to me and my flesh *be* upon
　　　Babylon,"
　The inhabitant of Zion will say;
　"And my blood *be* upon the inhabitants of Chaldea!"
　Jerusalem will say.

36Therefore thus says the LORD:

　"Behold, ªI will plead your case and take vengeance for
　　　you.
　ᵇI will dry up her sea and make her springs dry.
37 ªBabylon shall become a heap,
　　A dwelling place for jackals,
　ᵇAn astonishment and a hissing,
　　Without an inhabitant.
38 They shall roar together like lions,
　　They shall growl like lions' whelps.
39 In their excitement I will prepare their feasts;
　ªI will make them drunk,
　　That they may rejoice,
　　And sleep a perpetual sleep
　　And not awake," says the LORD.
40 "I will bring them down
　　Like lambs to the slaughter,
　　Like rams with male goats.
41 "Oh, how ªSheshach¹ is taken!
　　Oh, how ᵇthe praise of the whole earth is seized!
　　How Babylon has become desolate among the nations!
42 ªThe sea has come up over Babylon;
　　She is covered with the multitude of its waves.
43 ªHer cities are a desolation,
　　A dry land and a wilderness,
　　A land where ᵇno one dwells,
　　Through which no son of man passes.
44 I will punish ªBel¹ in Babylon,
　　And I will bring out of his mouth what he has
　　　swallowed;
　　And the nations shall not stream to him anymore.
　　Yes, ᵇthe wall of Babylon shall fall.

45 "Myª people, go out of the midst of her!
　　And let everyone deliver ¹himself from the fierce anger
　　　of the LORD.
46 And lest your heart faint,
　　And you fear ªfor the rumor that *will be* heard in the
　　　land
　　(A rumor will come *one* year,
　　And after that, in *another* year
　　A rumor *will come*,
　　And violence in the land,
　　Ruler against ruler),
47 Therefore behold, the days are coming
　　That I will bring judgment on the carved images of
　　　Babylon;
　　Her whole land shall be ashamed,
　　And all her slain shall fall in her midst.

51:36
ª[Ps. 140:12];
Jer. 50:34
ᵇJer. 50:38

51:37 ªIs. 13:22;
Jer. 50:39;
[Rev. 18:2]
ᵇJer. 25:9, 11

51:39 ªJer. 51:57

51:41 ªJer. 25:26
ᵇIs. 13:19;
Jer. 49:25;
[Dan. 4:30]

51:42 ªIs. 8:7, 8;
Jer. 51:55;
Dan. 9:26

51:43
ªJer. 50:39, 40
ᵇIs. 13:20

51:44 ªJer. 50:2;
Is. 46:1
ᵇJer. 50:15

51:45 ªIs. 48:20;
[Jer. 50:8, 28;
51:6; Rev. 18:4]

51:46
ª2 Kin. 19:7;
Is. 13:3–5

51:41 ¹A code word for Babylon, Jer. 25:26　51:44 ¹A Babylonian god
51:45 ¹Lit. *his soul*

48 Then ᵃthe heavens and the earth and all that *is* in them
    Shall sing joyously over Babylon;
    ᵇFor the plunderers shall come to her from the north,"
      says the LORD.

49 As Babylon *has caused* the slain of Israel to fall,
    So at Babylon the slain of all the earth shall fall.
50 ᵃYou who have escaped the sword,
    Get away! Do not stand still!
    ᵇRemember the LORD afar off,
    And let Jerusalem come to your mind.

51 ᵃWe are ashamed because we have heard reproach.
    Shame has covered our faces,
    For strangers ᵇhave come into the ¹sanctuaries of the
      LORD's house.

52 "Therefore behold, the days are coming," says the LORD,
    "That I will bring judgment on her carved images,
    And throughout all her land the wounded shall groan.
53 ᵃThough Babylon were to ¹mount up to heaven,
    And though she were to fortify the height of her strength,
    Yet from Me plunderers would come to her," says the
      LORD.

54 ᵃThe sound of a cry *comes* from Babylon,
    And great destruction from the land of the Chaldeans,
55 Because the LORD is plundering Babylon
    And silencing her loud voice,
    Though her waves roar like great waters,
    And the noise of their voice is uttered,
56 Because the plunderer comes against her, against
      Babylon,
    And her mighty men are taken.
    Every one of their bows is broken;
    ᵃFor the LORD *is* the God of recompense,
    He will surely repay.

57 "And I will make drunk
    Her princes and ᵃwise men,
    Her governors, her deputies, and her mighty men.
    And they shall sleep a perpetual sleep
    And not awake," says ᵇthe King,
    Whose name *is* the LORD of hosts.

58Thus says the LORD of hosts:

"The broad walls of Babylon shall be utterly ᵃbroken,¹
    And her high gates shall be burned with fire;
    ᵇThe people will labor in vain,
    And the nations, because of the fire;
    And they shall be weary."

JEREMIAH'S COMMAND TO SERAIAH

59The word which Jeremiah the prophet commanded Seraiah the son of ᵃNeriah, the son of Mahseiah, when he went with Zedekiah the king of Judah to Babylon in the fourth year of his reign. And Seraiah *was* the quartermaster. 60So Jeremiah ᵃwrote in a book all the evil that would come upon Babylon, all these words that are written against Babylon. 61And

---

51:48 ᵃIs. 44:23;
48:20; 49:13;
Rev. 18:20
ᵇJer. 50:3, 41

51:50 ᵃJer. 44:28
ᵇ[Deut. 4:29–31];
Ezek. 6:9

51:51
ᵃPs. 44:15; 79:4
ᵇPs. 74:3–8;
Jer. 52:13;
Lam. 1:10

51:53 ᵃGen. 11:4;
Job 20:6;
[Ps. 139:8–10;
Is. 14:12–14];
Jer. 49:16;
Amos 9:2;
Obad. 4

51:54 ᵃJer. 50:22

51:56 ᵃPs. 94:1;
Jer. 50:29

51:57 ᵃJer. 50:35
ᵇJer. 46:18;
48:15

51:58 ᵃJer. 50:15
ᵇHab. 2:13

51:59 ᵃJer. 32:12

51:60 ᵃIs. 30:8;
Jer. 36:2

51:51 ¹holy places   51:53 ¹ascend   51:58 ¹Lit. *laid utterly bare*

Jeremiah said to Seraiah, "When you arrive in Babylon and see it, and read all these words, [62]then you shall say, 'O LORD, You have spoken against this place to cut it off, so that [a]none shall remain in it, neither man nor beast, but it shall be desolate forever.' [63]Now it shall be, when you have finished reading this book, [a]*that* you shall tie a stone to it and throw it out into the Euphrates. [64]Then you shall say, 'Thus Babylon shall sink and not rise from the catastrophe that I will bring upon her. And they shall be weary.'"

Thus far *are* the words of Jeremiah.

THE FALL OF JERUSALEM REVIEWED
(2 Kin. 24:18—25:26; 2 Chr. 36:11–20; Jer. 39:1–10)

52 Zedekiah *was* [a]twenty-one years old when he became king, and he reigned eleven years in Jerusalem. His mother's name *was* Hamutal the daughter of Jeremiah of [b]Libnah. [2]He also did evil in the sight of the LORD, according to all that Jehoiakim had done. [3]For because of the anger of the LORD *this* happened in Jerusalem and Judah, till He finally cast them out from His presence. Then Zedekiah [a]rebelled against the king of Babylon.

[4]Now it came to pass in the [a]ninth year of his reign, in the tenth month, on the tenth *day* of the month, *that* Nebuchadnezzar king of Babylon and all his army came against Jerusalem and encamped against it; and *they* built a siege wall against it all around. [5]So the city was besieged until the eleventh year of King Zedekiah. [6]By the fourth month, on the ninth day of the month, the famine had become so severe in the city that there was no food for the people of the land. [7]Then the city *wall* was broken through, and all the men of war fled and went out of the city at night by way of the gate between the two walls, which *was* by the king's garden, even though the Chaldeans *were* near the city all around. And they went by way of the [1]plain.

[8]But the army of the Chaldeans pursued the king, and they overtook Zedekiah in the plains of Jericho. All his army was scattered from him. [9a]So they took the king and brought him up to the king of Babylon at Riblah in the land of Hamath, and he pronounced judgment on him. [10a]Then the king of Babylon killed the sons of Zedekiah before his eyes. And he killed all the princes of Judah in Riblah. [11]He also [a]put out the eyes of Zedekiah; and the king of Babylon bound him in [1]bronze fetters, took him to Babylon, and put him in prison till the day of his death.

THE TEMPLE AND CITY PLUNDERED AND BURNED

[12a]Now in the fifth month, on the tenth *day* of the month ([b]which *was* the nineteenth year of King Nebuchadnezzar king of Babylon), [c]Nebuzaradan, the captain of the guard, *who* served the king of Babylon, came to Jerusalem. [13]He burned the house of the LORD and the king's house; all the houses of Jerusalem, that is, all the houses of the great, he burned with fire. [14]And all the army of the Chaldeans who *were* with the captain of the guard broke down all the walls of Jerusalem all around. [15a]Then Nebuzaradan the captain of the guard carried

51:62 [a]Is. 13:20;
14:22, 23;
Jer. 50:3, 39

51:63
[a]Jer. 19:10, 11;
Rev. 18:21

52:1
[a]2 Kin. 24:18;
2 Chr. 36:11
[b]Josh. 10:29;
2 Kin. 8:22;
Is. 37:8

52:3
[a]2 Chr. 36:13

52:4
[a]2 Kin. 25:1;
Jer. 39:1;
Ezek. 24:1, 2;
Zech. 8:19

52:9
[a]2 Kin. 25:6;
Jer. 32:4; 39:5

52:10
[a]Ezek. 12:13

52:11
[a]Ezek. 12:13

52:12
[a]2 Kin. 25:8–21
[b]Jer. 52:29
[c]Jer. 39:9

52:15 [a]Jer. 39:9

52:7 [1]Or *Arabah;* the Jordan Valley   52:11 [1]*shackles*

away captive *some* of the poor people, the rest of the people who remained in the city, the defectors who had deserted to the king of Babylon, and the rest of the craftsmen. [16]But Nebuzaradan the captain of the guard left *some* of the poor of the land as vinedressers and farmers.

[17a]The [b]bronze pillars that *were* in the house of the LORD, and the carts and the bronze Sea that *were* in the house of the LORD, the Chaldeans broke in pieces, and carried all their bronze to Babylon. [18]They also took away [a]the pots, the shovels, the trimmers, the [1]bowls, the spoons, and all the bronze utensils with which the *priests* ministered. [19]The basins, the firepans, the bowls, the pots, the lampstands, the spoons, and the cups, whatever *was* solid gold and whatever *was* solid silver, the captain of the guard took away. [20]The two pillars, one Sea, the twelve bronze bulls which *were* under *it, and* the carts, which King Solomon had made for the house of the LORD—[a]the bronze of all these articles was beyond measure. [21]Now *concerning* the [a]pillars: the height of one pillar *was* eighteen [1]cubits, a measuring line of twelve cubits could measure its circumference, and its thickness *was* [2]four fingers; *it was* hollow. [22]A capital of bronze *was* on it; and the height of one capital *was* five cubits, with a network and pomegranates all around the capital, all of bronze. The second pillar, with pomegranates was the same. [23]There were ninety-six pomegranates on the sides; [a]all the pomegranates, all around on the network, *were* one hundred.

THE PEOPLE TAKEN CAPTIVE TO BABYLONIA

[24a]The captain of the guard took Seraiah the chief priest, [b]Zephaniah the second priest, and the three doorkeepers. [25]He also took out of the city an [1]officer who had charge of the men of war, seven men of the king's close associates who were found in the city, the principal scribe of the army who mustered the people of the land, and sixty men of the people of the land who were found in the midst of the city. [26]And Nebuzaradan the captain of the guard took these and brought them to the king of Babylon at Riblah. [27]Then the king of Babylon struck them and put them to death at Riblah in the land of Hamath. Thus Judah was carried away captive from its own land.

[28a]These *are* the people whom Nebuchadnezzar carried away captive: [b]in the seventh year, [c]three thousand and twenty-three Jews; [29a]in the eighteenth year of Nebuchadnezzar he carried away captive from Jerusalem eight hundred and thirty-two persons; [30]in the twenty-third year of Nebuchadnezzar, Nebuzaradan the captain of the guard carried away captive of the Jews seven hundred and forty-five persons. All the persons *were* four thousand six hundred.

JEHOIACHIN RELEASED FROM PRISON
(2 Kin. 25:27–30)

[31a]Now it came to pass in the thirty-seventh year of the captivity of Jehoiachin king of Judah, in the twelfth month, on the twenty-fifth *day* of the month, *that* [1]Evil-Merodach

---

52:17 [a]Jer. 27:19
[b]1 Kin. 7:15, 23, 27, 50

52:18 [a]Ex. 27:3; 1 Kin. 7:40, 45; 2 Kin. 25:14

52:20 [a]1 Kin. 7:47; 2 Kin. 25:16

52:21 [a]1 Kin. 7:15; 2 Kin. 25:17; 2 Chr. 3:15

52:23 [a]1 Kin. 7:20

52:24 [a]2 Kin. 25:18; 1 Chr. 6:14; Ezra 7:1
[b]Jer. 21:1; 29:25

52:28 [a]2 Kin. 24:2
[b]2 Kin. 24:12
[c]2 Kin. 24:14

52:29 [a]2 Kin. 25:11; Jer. 39:9

52:31 [a]2 Kin. 25:27–30

52:18 [1]basins   52:21 [1]18 inches each   [2]3 inches   52:25 [1]Lit. *eunuch*
52:31 [1]Or *Awil-Marduk*; lit. *The Man of Marduk*

king of Babylon, in the *first* year of his reign, [b]lifted[2] up the head of Jehoiachin king of Judah and brought him out of prison. 32And he spoke kindly to him and gave him a more prominent seat than those of the kings who *were* with him in Babylon. 33So [1]Jehoiachin changed from his prison garments, [a]and he ate bread regularly before the *king* all the days of his life. 34And as for his provisions, there was a regular ration given him by the king of Babylon, a portion for each day until the day of his death, all the days of his life.

52:31
[b]Gen. 40:13, 20;
Ps. 3:3; 27:6

52:33
[a]2 Sam. 9:7, 13;
1 Kin. 2:7

52:31 [2]Showed favor to   52:33 [1]Lit. *he*

THE BOOK OF
LAMENTATIONS

JERUSALEM IN AFFLICTION

1 How lonely sits the city
That was full of people!
[a]*How* like a widow is she,
Who *was* great among the nations!
The [b]princess among the provinces
Has become a [1]slave!

2 She [a]weeps bitterly in the [b]night,
Her tears *are* on her cheeks;
Among all her lovers
She has none to comfort *her.*
All her friends have dealt treacherously with her;
They have become her enemies.

3 [a]Judah has gone into captivity,
Under affliction and hard servitude;
[b]She dwells among the [1]nations,
She finds no [c]rest;
All her persecutors overtake her in dire straits.

4 The roads to Zion mourn
Because no one comes to the [1]set feasts.
All her gates are [a]desolate;
Her priests sigh,
Her virgins are afflicted,
And she *is* in bitterness.

5 Her adversaries [a]have become [1]the master,
Her enemies prosper;
For the LORD has afflicted her
[b]Because of the multitude of her transgressions.
Her [c]children have gone into captivity before the
enemy.

6 And from the daughter of Zion
All her splendor has departed.
Her princes have become like deer
That find no pasture,
That [1]flee without strength
Before the pursuer.

7 In the days of her affliction and roaming,
Jerusalem [a]remembers all her pleasant things
That she had in the days of old.
When her people fell into the hand of the enemy,
With no one to help her,
The adversaries saw her
And mocked at her [1]downfall.

1:1 [a]Is. 47:7–9
[b]1 Kin. 4:21;
Ezra 4:20;
Jer. 31:7
1:2 [a]Jer. 13:17
[b]Job 7:3
1:3 [a]Jer. 52:27
[b]Lam. 2:9
[c]Deut. 28:65
1:4 [a]Is. 27:10
1:5 [a]Deut. 28:43
[b]Jer. 30:14, 15;
Dan. 9:7, 16
[c]Jer. 52:28
1:7 [a]Ps. 137:1

1:1 [1]Lit. *forced laborer*   1:3 [1]*Gentiles*   1:4 [1]*appointed*   1:5 [1]Lit. *her head*
1:6 [1]Lit. *are gone*   1:7 [1]Vg. *Sabbaths*

8 ᵃJerusalem has sinned gravely,
  Therefore she has become ¹vile.
  All who honored her despise her
  Because ᵇthey have seen her nakedness;
  Yes, she sighs and turns away.

9 Her uncleanness *is* in her skirts;
  She ᵃdid not consider her destiny;
  Therefore her collapse was awesome;
  She had no comforter.
  "O Lᴏʀᴅ, behold my affliction,
  For *the* enemy is exalted!"

10 The adversary has spread his hand
   Over all her ¹pleasant things;
   For she has seen ᵃthe nations enter her ²sanctuary,
   Those whom You commanded
   ᵇNot to enter Your assembly.

11 All her people sigh,
   ᵃThey ¹seek bread;
   They have given their ²valuables for food to restore life.
   "See, O Lᴏʀᴅ, and consider,
   For I am scorned."

12 "*Is it* nothing to you, all you who ¹pass by?
   Behold and see
   ᵃIf there is any sorrow like my sorrow,
   Which has been brought on me,
   Which the Lᴏʀᴅ has inflicted
   In the day of His fierce anger.

13 "From above He has sent fire into my bones,
   And it overpowered them;
   He has ᵃspread a net for my feet
   And turned me back;
   He has made me desolate
   And faint all the day.

14 "Theᵃ yoke of my transgressions was ¹bound;
   They were woven together by His hands,
   And thrust upon my neck.
   He made my strength fail;
   The Lord delivered me into the hands of *those whom* I
      am not able to withstand.

15 "The Lord has trampled underfoot all my mighty *men* in
      my midst;
   He has called an assembly against me
   To crush my young men;
   ᵃThe Lord trampled *as* in a winepress
   The virgin daughter of Judah.

16 "For these *things* I weep;
   My eye, ᵃmy eye overflows with water;
   Because the comforter, who should restore my life,
   Is far from me.
   My children are desolate

1:8 ᵃ[1 Kin. 8:46]
ᵇJer. 13:22;
Ezek. 16:37;
Hos. 2:10

1:9
ᵃDeut. 32:29;
Is. 47:7; Jer. 5:31

1:10 ᵃPs. 74:4–8;
Is. 64:10, 11;
Jer. 51:51
ᵇDeut. 23:3;
Neh. 13:1

1:11 ᵃJer. 38:9;
52:6

1:12 ᵃDan. 9:12

1:13 ᵃEzek. 12:13;
17:20

1:14
ᵃDeut. 28:48

1:15 ᵃIs. 63:3;
[Rev. 14:19]

1:16 ᵃPs. 69:20;
Eccl. 4:1;
Jer. 13:17;
Lam. 2:18

1:8 ¹LXX, Vg. *moved* or *removed*   1:10 ¹*desirable*   ²*holy place*, the temple
1:11 ¹*hunt food*   ²*desirable things*   1:12 ¹Lit. *pass by this way*   1:14 ¹So with
MT, Tg.; LXX, Syr., Vg. *watched over*

Because the enemy prevailed."

17 aZion 1spreads out her hands,
But no one comforts her;
The LORD has commanded concerning Jacob
That those baround him *become* his adversaries;
Jerusalem has become an unclean thing among them.

18 "The LORD is arighteous,
For I brebelled against His 1commandment.
Hear now, all peoples,
And behold my sorrow;
My virgins and my young men
Have gone into captivity.

19 "I called for my lovers,
But they deceived me;
My priests and my elders
Breathed their last in the city,
While they sought food
To restore their life.

20 "See, O LORD, that I *am* in distress;
My asoul1 is troubled;
My heart is overturned within me,
For I have been very rebellious.
bOutside the sword bereaves,
At home *it is* like death.

21 "They have heard that I sigh,
But no one comforts me.
All my enemies have heard of my trouble;
They are aglad that You have done *it*.
Bring on bthe day You have 1announced,
That they may become like me.

22 "Leta all their wickedness come before You,
And do to them as You have done to me
For all my transgressions;
For my sighs *are* many,
And my heart *is* faint."

GOD'S ANGER WITH JERUSALEM

2 How the Lord has covered the daughter of Zion
With a acloud in His anger!
bHe cast down from heaven to the earth
cThe beauty of Israel,
And did not remember dHis footstool
In the day of His anger.

2 The Lord has swallowed up and has anot pitied
All the dwelling places of Jacob.
He has thrown down in His wrath
The strongholds of the daughter of Judah;
He has brought *them* down to the ground;
bHe has profaned the kingdom and its princes.

3 He has cut off in fierce anger
Every 1horn of Israel;

1:17 a[Is. 1:15];
Jer. 4:31
b2 Kin. 24:2–4;
Jer. 12:9
1:18 aNeh. 9:33;
Ps. 119:75;
Dan. 9:7, 14
b1 Sam. 12:14, 15;
Jer. 4:17
1:20 aJob 30:27;
Is. 16:11; Jer. 4:19;
Lam. 2:11;
Hos. 11:8
bDeut. 32:25;
Ezek. 7:15
1:21 aPs. 35:15;
Jer. 48:27; 50:11;
Lam. 2:15;
Obad. 12
bIs. 13; [Jer. 46]
1:22
aNeh. 4:4, 5;
Ps. 109:15;
137:7, 8;
Jer. 30:16
2:1 a[Lam. 3:44]
bMatt. 11:23
c2 Sam. 1:19
d1 Chr. 28:2;
Ps. 99:5;
Ezek. 43:7
2:2 aPs. 21:9;
Lam. 3:43
bPs. 89:39, 40;
Is. 43:28

1:17 1Prays 1:18 1Lit. *mouth* 1:20 1Lit. *inward parts* 1:21 1proclaimed
2:3 1Strength

ᵃHe has drawn back His right hand
From before the enemy.
ᵇHe has blazed against Jacob like a flaming fire
Devouring all around.

4 ᵃStanding like an enemy, He has bent His bow;
With His right hand, like an adversary,
He has slain ᵇall *who were* pleasing to His eye;
On the tent of the daughter of Zion,
He has poured out His fury like fire.

5 ᵃThe Lord was like an enemy.
He has swallowed up Israel,
He has swallowed up all her palaces;
ᵇHe has destroyed her strongholds,
And has increased mourning and lamentation
In the daughter of Judah.

6 He has done violence ᵃto His ¹tabernacle,
ᵇ*As if it were* a garden;
He has destroyed His place of assembly;
The LORD has caused
The appointed feasts and Sabbaths to be forgotten in
Zion.
In His burning indignation He has ᶜspurned the king
and the priest.

7 The Lord has spurned His altar,
He has ᵃabandoned His sanctuary;
He has ¹given up the walls of her palaces
Into the hand of the enemy.
ᵇThey have made a noise in the house of the LORD
As on the day of a set feast.

8 The LORD has ¹purposed to destroy
The ᵃwall of the daughter of Zion.
ᵇHe has stretched out a line;
He has not withdrawn His hand from destroying;
Therefore He has caused the rampart and wall to lament;
They languished together.

9 Her gates have sunk into the ground;
He has destroyed and ᵃbroken her bars.
ᵇHer king and her princes *are* among the ¹nations;
ᶜThe Law *is* no *more*,
And her ᵈprophets find no ²vision from the LORD.

10 The elders of the daughter of Zion
ᵃSit on the ground *and* keep silence;
¹They ᵇthrow dust on their heads
And ᶜgird themselves with sackcloth.
The virgins of Jerusalem
Bow their heads to the ground.

11 ᵃMy eyes fail with tears,
My ¹heart is troubled;
ᵇMy ²bile is poured on the ground
Because of the destruction of the daughter of my people,
Because ᶜthe children and the infants
Faint in the streets of the city.

2:3 ᵃPs. 74:11;
Jer. 21:4, 5
ᵇPs. 89:46

2:4 ᵃIs. 63:10
ᵇEzek. 24:25

2:5 ᵃJer. 30:14
ᵇ2 Kin. 25:9;
Jer. 52:13;
Lam. 2:2

2:6 ᵃPs. 80:12;
89:40; Is. 5:5;
Jer. 7:14 ᵇIs. 1:8;
Jer. 52:13
ᶜIs. 43:28

2:7 ᵃEzek. 24:21
ᵇPs. 74:3–8

2:8 ᵃJer. 52:14
ᵇ[2 Kin. 21:13;
Is. 34:11;
Amos 7:7–9]

2:9 ᵃJer. 51:30
ᵇDeut. 28:36;
2 Kin. 24:15;
25:7; Lam. 1:3;
4:20 ᶜ2 Chr. 15:3
ᵈPs. 74:9;
Mic. 3:6

2:10 ᵃJob 2:13;
Is. 3:26
ᵇJob 2:12;
Ezek. 27:30
ᶜIs. 15:3;
Jon. 3:6–8

2:11 ᵃPs. 6:7;
Lam. 3:48
ᵇJob 16:13;
Ps. 22:14
ᶜLam. 4:4

2:6 ¹Lit. *booth* 2:7 ¹*delivered* 2:8 ¹*determined* 2:9 ¹*Gentiles* ²Prophetic
revelation 2:10 ¹A sign of mourning 2:11 ¹Lit. *inward parts* ²Lit. *liver*

12 They say to their mothers,
　"Where *is* grain and wine?"
　As they swoon like the wounded
　In the streets of the city,
　As their life is poured out
　In their mothers' bosom.

13 How shall I ªconsole¹ you?
　To what shall I liken you,
　O daughter of Jerusalem?
　What shall I compare with you, that I may comfort you,
　O virgin daughter of Zion?
　For your ruin *is* spread wide as the sea;
　Who can heal you?

14 Your ªprophets have seen for you
　False and deceptive visions;
　They have not ᵇuncovered your iniquity,
　To bring back your captives,
　But have envisioned for you false ᶜprophecies and
　　delusions.

15 All who ¹pass by ªclap *their* hands at you;
　They hiss ᵇand shake their heads
　At the daughter of Jerusalem:
　"*Is* this the city that is called
　ᶜ'The perfection of beauty,
　The joy of the whole earth'?"

16 ªAll your enemies have opened their mouth against you;
　They hiss and gnash *their* teeth.
　They say, ᵇ"We have swallowed *her* up!
　Surely this *is* the ᶜday we have waited for;
　We have found *it,* ᵈwe have seen *it!*"

17 The LORD has done what He ªpurposed;
　He has fulfilled His word
　Which He commanded in days of old.
　He has thrown down and has not pitied,
　And He has caused an enemy to ᵇrejoice over you;
　He has exalted the ¹horn of your adversaries.

18 Their heart cried out to the Lord,
　"O wall of the daughter of Zion,
　ªLet tears run down like a river day and night;
　Give yourself no relief;
　Give ¹your eyes no rest.

19 "Arise, ªcry out in the night,
　At the beginning of the watches;
　ᵇPour out your heart like water before the face of the
　　Lord.
　Lift your hands toward Him
　For the life of your young children,
　Who faint from hunger ᶜat the head of every street."

20 "See, O LORD, and consider!
　To whom have You done this?
　ªShould the women eat their offspring,
　The children ¹they have cuddled?

2:13 ªLam. 1:12;
Dan. 9:12

2:14 ªJer. 2:8;
23:25–29;
29:8, 9; 37:19;
Ezek. 13:2
ᵇIs. 58:1;
Ezek. 23:36;
Mic. 3:8
ᶜJer. 23:33–36;
Ezek. 22:25, 28

2:15 ª1 Kin. 9:8;
Job 27:23;
Jer. 18:16;
Ezek. 25:6;
Nah. 3:19
ᵇ2 Kin. 19:21;
Ps. 44:14
ᶜ[Ps. 48:2;
50:2];
Ezek. 16:14

2:16
ªJob 16:9, 10;
Ps. 22:13;
Lam. 3:46
ᵇPs. 56:2;
124:3; Jer. 51:34
ᶜLam. 1:21;
[Obad. 12–15]
ᵈPs. 35:21

2:17 ªLev. 26:16
ᵇPs. 38:16

2:18 ªJer. 14:17;
Lam. 1:16

2:19 ªPs. 119:147
ᵇ1 Sam. 1:15;
Ps. 42:4; 62:8
ᶜIs. 51:20

2:20
ªLev. 26:29;
Deut. 28:53;
Jer. 19:9;
Lam. 4:10;
Ezek. 5:10

2:13 ¹Or *bear witness to*　　2:15 ¹Lit. *pass by this way*　　2:17 ¹Strength
2:18 ¹Lit. *the daughter of your eye*　　2:20 ¹Vg. *a span long*

Should the priest and prophet be slain
In the sanctuary of the Lord?

21 "Young[a] and old lie
On the ground in the streets;
My virgins and my young men
Have fallen by the [b]sword;
You have slain *them* in the day of Your anger,
You have slaughtered *and* not pitied.

22 "You have invited as to a feast day
[a]The terrors that surround me.
In the day of the LORD's anger
There was no refugee or survivor.
[b]Those whom I have borne and brought up
My enemies have [c]destroyed."

THE PROPHET'S ANGUISH AND HOPE

3 I *am* the man *who* has seen affliction by the rod of His wrath.
2 He has led me and made *me* walk
In darkness and not *in* light.
3 Surely He has turned His hand against me
Time and time again throughout the day.

4 He has aged [a]my flesh and my skin,
And [b]broken my bones.
5 He has besieged me
And surrounded *me* with bitterness and [1]woe.
6 [a]He has set me in dark places
Like the dead of long ago.

7 [a]He has hedged me in so that I cannot get out;
He has made my chain heavy.
8 Even [a]when I cry and shout,
He shuts out my prayer.
9 He has blocked my ways with hewn stone;
He has made my paths crooked.

10 [a]He *has been* to me a bear lying in wait,
Like a lion in [1]ambush.
11 He has turned aside my ways and [a]torn me in pieces;
He has made me desolate.
12 He has bent His bow
And [a]set me up as a target for the arrow.

13 He has caused [a]the [1]arrows of His quiver
To pierce my [2]loins.
14 I have become the [a]ridicule of all my people—
[b]Their taunting song all the day.
15 [a]He has filled me with bitterness,
He has made me drink wormwood.

16 He has also broken my teeth [a]with gravel,
And [1]covered me with ashes.
17 You have moved my soul far from peace;
I have forgotten [1]prosperity.
18 [a]And I said, "My strength and my hope
Have perished from the LORD."

2:21
[a]2 Chr. 36:17;
Jer. 6:11
[b]Jer. 18:21

2:22 [a]Ps. 31:13;
Is. 24:17;
Jer. 6:25
[b]Hos. 9:12
[c]Jer. 16:2–4;
44:7

3:4 [a]Job 16:8
[b]Ps. 51:8;
Is. 38:13

3:6
[a][Ps. 88:5, 6;
143:3]

3:7 [a]Job 3:23;
19:8; Hos. 2:6

3:8 [a]Job 30:20;
Ps. 22:2

3:10 [a]Is. 38:13

3:11
[a]Job 16:12, 13;
Jer. 15:3;
Hos. 6:1

3:12 [a]Job 7:20;
16:12; Ps. 38:2

3:13 [a]Job 6:4

3:14 [a]Ps. 22:6, 7;
123:4; Jer. 20:7
[b]Job 30:9;
Ps. 69:12;
Lam. 3:63

3:15 [a]Jer. 9:15

3:16
[a][Prov. 20:17]

3:18 [a]Ps. 31:22

3:5 [1]hardship or *weariness*   3:10 [1]Lit. *secret places*   3:13 [1]Lit. *sons of*
[2]Lit. *kidneys*   3:16 [1]Lit. *bent me down in*   3:17 [1]Lit. *good*

19 Remember my affliction and roaming,
  aThe wormwood and the 1gall.
20 My soul still remembers
  And 1sinks within me.
21 This I recall to my mind,
  Therefore I have ahope.

22 aThrough the LORD's mercies we are not consumed,
  Because His compassions bfail not.
23 They are new aevery morning;
  Great is Your faithfulness.
24 "The LORD is my aportion," says my soul,
  "Therefore I bhope in Him!"

25 The LORD is good to those who await for Him,
  To the soul who seeks Him.
26 It is good that one should ahope band wait quietly
  For the salvation of the LORD.
27 aIt is good for a man to bear
  The yoke in his youth.

28 aLet him sit alone and keep silent,
  Because God has laid it on him;
29 aLet him put his mouth in the dust—
  There may yet be hope.
30 aLet him give his cheek to the one who strikes him,
  And be full of reproach.

31 aFor the Lord will not cast off forever.
32 Though He causes grief,
  Yet He will show compassion
  According to the multitude of His mercies.
33 For aHe does not afflict 1willingly,
  Nor grieve the children of men.

34 To crush under one's feet
  All the prisoners of the earth,
35 To turn aside the justice due a man
  Before the face of the Most High,
36 Or subvert a man in his cause—
  aThe Lord does not approve.

37 Who is he awho speaks and it comes to pass,
  When the Lord has not commanded it?
38 Is it not from the mouth of the Most High
  That awoe and well-being proceed?
39 aWhy should a living man 1complain,
  bA man for the punishment of his sins?

40 Let us search out and examine our ways,
  And turn back to the LORD;
41 aLet us lift our hearts and hands
  To God in heaven.
42 aWe have transgressed and rebelled;
  You have not pardoned.

43 You have covered Yourself with anger
  And pursued us;
  You have slain and not pitied.

3:19 aJer. 9:15;
Lam. 3:5, 15
3:21 aPs. 130:7
3:22 a[Mal. 3:6]
bPs. 78:38;
[Jer. 3:12; 30:11]
3:23 aIs. 33:2;
Zeph. 3:5
3:24 aPs. 16:5;
73:26; 119:57;
Jer. 10:16
bJer. 17:17;
Mic. 7:7
3:25 aPs. 130:6;
Is. 30:18
3:26
a[Rom. 4:16–18]
bEx. 14:13;
Ps. 37:7; Is. 7:4
3:27 aPs. 94:12
3:28 aJer. 15:17
3:29 aJob 42:6
3:30 aJob 16:10;
Is. 50:6;
[Matt. 5:39;
26:67];
Mark 14:65;
Luke 22:63
3:31
aPs. 77:7; 94:14;
[Is. 54:7–10]
3:33 a[Ps. 119:67,
71, 75; Is. 28:21;
Ezek. 33:11;
Heb. 12:10]
3:36 a[Jer. 22:3;
Hab. 1:13]
3:37
a[Ps. 33:9–11]
3:38 aJob 2:10;
[Is. 45:7];
Jer. 32:42;
Amos 3:6;
[James 3:10, 11]
3:39 aProv. 19:3
bJer. 30:15;
Mic. 7:9;
[Heb. 12:5, 6]
3:41 aPs. 86:4
3:42 aNeh. 9:26;
Jer. 14:20;
Dan. 9:5

3:19 1bitterness 3:20 1Lit. bowed down 3:33 1Lit. from His heart
3:39 1Or murmur

44 You have covered Yourself with a cloud,
That prayer should not pass through.
45 You have made us an [a]offscouring and refuse
In the midst of the peoples.

46 [a]All our enemies
Have opened their mouths against us.
47 [a]Fear and a snare have come upon us,
[b]Desolation and destruction.
48 [a]My eyes overflow with rivers of water
For the destruction of the daughter of my people.

49 [a]My eyes flow and do not cease,
Without interruption,
50 Till the LORD from heaven
[a]Looks down and sees.
51 My eyes bring suffering to my soul
Because of all the daughters of my city.

52 My enemies [a]without cause
Hunted me down like a bird.
53 They [1]silenced my life [a]in the pit
And [b]threw [2]stones at me.
54 [a]The waters flowed over my head;
[b]I said, "I am cut off!"

55 [a]I called on Your name, O LORD,
From the lowest [b]pit.
56 [a]You have heard my voice:
"Do not hide Your ear
From my sighing, from my cry for help."
57 You [a]drew near on the day I called on You,
And said, [b]"Do not fear!"

58 O Lord, You have [a]pleaded the case for my soul;
[b]You have redeemed my life.
59 O LORD, You have seen [1]how I am wronged;
[a]Judge my case.
60 You have seen all their vengeance,
All their [a]schemes against me.

61 You have heard their reproach, O LORD,
All their schemes against me,
62 The lips of my enemies
And their whispering against me all the day.
63 Look at their [a]sitting down and their rising up;
I am their taunting song.

64 [a]Repay them, O LORD,
According to the work of their hands.
65 Give them [1]a veiled heart;
Your curse be upon them!
66 In Your anger,
Pursue and destroy them
[a]From under the heavens of the [b]LORD.

THE DEGRADATION OF ZION

4 How the gold has become dim!
How changed the fine gold!

3:53 [1]LXX put to death   [2]Lit. a stone on   3:59 [1]Lit. my wrong
3:65 [1]A Jewish tradition sorrow of

3:45 [a]1 Cor. 4:13
3:46
[a]Job 30:9, 10;
Ps. 22:6–8;
Lam. 2:16
3:47
[a]Is. 24:17, 18;
Jer. 48:43, 44
[b]Is. 51:19
3:48 [a]Jer. 4:19;
14:17; Lam. 2:11
3:49 [a]Ps. 77:2;
Jer. 14:17
3:50 [a]Ps. 80:14;
Is. 63:15;
Lam. 5:1
3:52 [a]Ps. 35:7, 19
3:53 [a]Jer. 37:16
[b]Dan. 6:17
3:54 [a]Ps. 69:2;
Jon. 2:3–5
[b]Is. 38:10
3:55 [a]Ps. 130:1;
Jon. 2:2
[b]Jer. 38:6–13
3:56 [a]Ps. 3:4
3:57 [a]James 4:8
[b]Is. 41:10, 14;
Dan. 10:12
3:58 [a]Ps. 35:1;
Jer. 51:36
[b]Ps. 71:23
3:59 [a]Ps. 9:4
3:60 [a]Jer. 11:19
3:63 [a]Ps. 139:2
3:64 [a]Ps. 28:4;
Jer. 11:20;
2 Tim. 4:14
3:66
[a]Deut. 25:19;
Jer. 10:11 [b]Ps. 8:3

The stones of the sanctuary are [1]scattered
At the head of every street.

2 The precious sons of Zion,
[1]Valuable as fine gold,
How they are [2]regarded [a]as clay pots,
The work of the hands of the potter!

3 Even the jackals present their breasts
To nurse their young;
But the daughter of my people *is* cruel,
[a]Like ostriches in the wilderness.

4 The tongue of the infant clings
To the roof of its mouth for thirst;
[a]The young children ask for bread,
But no one breaks *it* for them.

5 Those who ate delicacies
Are desolate in the streets;
Those who were brought up in scarlet
[a]Embrace ash heaps.

6 The punishment of the iniquity of the daughter of my
people
Is greater than the punishment of the [a]sin of Sodom,
Which was [b]overthrown in a moment,
With no hand to help her!

7 Her [1]Nazirites were [2]brighter than snow
And whiter than milk;
They were more ruddy in body than rubies,
Like sapphire in their [3]appearance.

8 *Now* their appearance is blacker than soot;
They go unrecognized in the streets;
[a]Their skin clings to their bones,
It has become as dry as wood.

9 *Those* slain by the sword are better off
Than *those* who die of hunger;
For these [a]pine away,
Stricken *for lack* of the fruits of the [b]field.

10 The hands of the [a]compassionate women
Have [1]cooked their [b]own children;
They became [c]food for them
In the destruction of the daughter of my people.

11 The LORD has fulfilled His fury,
[a]He has poured out His fierce anger.
[b]He kindled a fire in Zion,
And it has devoured its foundations.

12 The kings of the earth,
And all inhabitants of the world,
Would not have believed
That the adversary and the enemy
Could [a]enter the gates of Jerusalem—

13 [a]Because of the sins of her prophets
And the iniquities of her priests,

4:2 [a]Is. 30:14;
Jer. 19:11;
[2 Cor. 4:7]

4:3
[a]Job 39:14–17

4:4 [a]Ps. 22:15

4:5 [a]Job 24:8

4:6 [a]Ezek. 16:48
[b]Gen. 19:25;
Jer. 20:16

4:8 [a]Job 19:20;
Ps. 102:5

4:9 [a]Lev. 26:39;
Ezek. 24:23
[b]Jer. 16:4

4:10 [a]Lev. 26:29;
Deut. 28:57;
2 Kin. 6:29;
Jer. 19:9;
Lam. 2:20;
Ezek. 5:10
[b]Is. 49:15
[c]Deut. 28:57

4:11 [a]Jer. 7:20;
Lam. 2:17;
Ezek. 22:31
[b]Deut. 32:22;
Jer. 21:14

4:12 [a]Jer. 21:13

4:13 [a]Jer. 5:31;
Ezek. 22:26, 28;
Zeph. 3:4

4:1 [1]Lit. *poured out*   4:2 [1]Lit. *Weighed against*   [2]*reckoned*   4:7 [1]Or *nobles*
[2]Or *purer*   [3]Lit. *polishing*   4:10 [1]*boiled*

ᵇWho shed in her midst
The blood of the just.

14 They wandered blind in the streets;
ᵃThey have defiled themselves with blood,
ᵇSo that no one would touch their garments.

15 They cried out to them,
"Go away, ᵃunclean!
Go away, go away,
Do not touch us!"
When they fled and wandered,
Those among the nations said,
"They shall no longer dwell *here*."

16 The ¹face of the LORD scattered them;
He no longer regards them.
ᵃ*The people* do not respect the priests
Nor show favor to the elders.

17 Still ᵃour eyes failed us,
Watching vainly for our help;
In our watching we watched
For a nation *that* could not save *us*.

18 ᵃThey ¹tracked our steps
So that we could not walk in our streets.
ᵇOur end was near;
Our days were over,
For our end had come.

19 Our pursuers were ᵃswifter
Than the eagles of the heavens.
They pursued us on the mountains
And lay in wait for us in the wilderness.

20 The ᵃbreath of our nostrils, the anointed of the LORD,
ᵇWas caught in their pits,
Of whom we said, "Under his shadow
We shall live among the nations."

21 Rejoice and be glad, O daughter of ᵃEdom,
You who dwell in the land of Uz!
ᵇThe cup shall also pass over to you
And you shall become drunk and make yourself naked.

22 ᵃ*The punishment of* your iniquity ¹is accomplished,
O daughter of Zion;
He will no longer send you into captivity.
ᵇHe will punish your iniquity,
O daughter of Edom;
He will uncover your sins!

PRAYER FOR RESTORATION

5 Remember, ᵃO LORD, what has come upon us;
Look, and behold ᵇour reproach!
2 ᵃOur inheritance has been turned over to aliens,
And our houses to foreigners.
3 We have become orphans and waifs,
Our mothers *are* like ᵃwidows.

4:13 ᵇJer. 2:30;
26:8, 9;
Matt. 23:31

4:14 ᵃJer. 2:34
ᵇNum. 19:16

4:15
ᵃLev. 13:45, 46

4:16 ᵃLam. 5:12

4:17 ᵃ2 Kin. 24:7

4:18 ᵃ2 Kin. 25:4
ᵇEzek. 7:2, 3, 6;
Amos 8:2

4:19
ᵃDeut. 28:49

4:20 ᵃGen. 2:7
ᵇJer. 52:9;
Ezek. 12:13

4:21
ᵃPs. 83:3–6
ᵇJer. 25:15;
Obad. 10

4:22 ᵃ[Is. 40:2;
Jer. 33:7, 8]
ᵇPs. 137:7

5:1 ᵃPs. 89:50
ᵇPs. 79:4;
Lam. 2:15

5:2 ᵃPs. 79:1

5:3 ᵃEx. 22:24;
Jer. 15:8; 18:21

4:16 ¹Tg. *anger*   4:18 ¹Lit. *hunted*   4:22 ¹*has been completed*

4   We pay for the water we drink,
    And our wood comes at a price.

5   ᵃ*They* pursue at our ¹heels;
    We labor *and* have no rest.

6   ᵃWe have given our hand ᵇ*to* the Egyptians
    And the ᶜAssyrians, to be satisfied with bread.

7   ᵃOur fathers sinned *and are* no more,
    But we bear their iniquities.

8   Servants rule over us;
    There is none to deliver *us* from their hand.

9   We get our bread *at the risk* of our lives,
    Because of the sword in the wilderness.

10   Our skin is hot as an oven,
    Because of the fever of famine.

11   They ᵃravished the women in Zion,
    The maidens in the cities of Judah.

12   Princes were hung up by their hands,
    And elders were not respected.

13   Young men ᵃground at the millstones;
    Boys staggered under *loads of* wood.

14   The elders have ceased *gathering* at the gate,
    And the young men from their ᵃmusic.

15   The joy of our heart has ceased;
    Our dance has turned into ᵃmourning.

16   ᵃThe crown has fallen *from* our head.
    Woe to us, for we have sinned!

17   Because of this our heart is faint;
    ᵃBecause of these *things* our eyes grow dim;

18   Because of Mount Zion which is ᵃdesolate,
    With foxes walking about on it.

19   You, O LORD, ᵃremain forever;
    ᵇYour throne from generation to generation.

20   ᵃWhy do You forget us forever,
    And forsake us for so long a time?

21   ᵃTurn us back to You, O LORD, and we will be ¹restored;
    Renew our days as of old,

22   Unless You have utterly rejected us,
    And are very angry with us!

5:5
ᵃDeut. 28:48;
Jer. 28:14

5:6 ᵃGen. 24:2
ᵇHos. 9:3; 12:1
ᶜJer. 2:18;
Hos. 5:13

5:7 ᵃJer. 31:29

5:11 ᵃIs. 13:16;
Zech. 14:2

5:13 ᵃJudg. 16:21

5:14 ᵃIs. 24:8;
Jer. 7:34

5:15 ᵃJer. 25:10;
Amos 8:10

5:16 ᵃJob 19:9;
Ps. 89:39;
Jer. 13:18

5:17 ᵃPs. 6:7

5:18 ᵃIs. 27:10

5:19 ᵃPs. 9:7;
Hab. 1:12
ᵇPs. 45:6

5:20
ᵃPs. 13:1; 44:24

5:21
ᵃPs. 80:3, 7, 19;
Jer. 31:18

5:5 ¹Lit. *necks*   5:21 ¹*returned*

THE BOOK OF
EZEKIEL

EZEKIEL'S VISION OF GOD

1 Now it came to pass in the thirtieth year, in the fourth *month,* on the fifth *day* of the month, as I *was* among the captives by ᵃthe River Chebar, *that* ᵇthe heavens were opened and I saw ᶜvisions¹ of God. ²On the fifth *day* of the month, which *was* in the fifth year of King Jehoiachin's captivity, ³the word of the LORD came expressly to Ezekiel the priest, the son of Buzi, in the land of the ¹Chaldeans by the River Chebar; and ᵃthe hand of the LORD was upon him there.

⁴Then I looked, and behold, ᵃa whirlwind was coming ᵇout of the north, a great cloud with raging fire engulfing itself; and brightness *was* all around it and radiating out of its midst like the color of amber, out of the midst of the fire. ⁵ᵃAlso from within it *came* the likeness of four living creatures. And ᵇthis *was* their appearance: they had ᶜthe likeness of a man. ⁶Each one had four faces, and each one had four wings. ⁷Their ¹legs *were* straight, and the soles of their feet *were* like the soles of calves' feet. They sparkled ᵃlike the color of burnished bronze. ⁸ᵃThe hands of a man *were* under their wings on their four sides; and each of the four had faces and wings. ⁹Their wings touched one another. *The creatures* did not turn when they went, but each one went straight ᵃforward.

¹⁰As for ᵃthe likeness of their faces, *each* ᵇhad the face of a man; each of the four had ᶜthe face of a lion on the right side, ᵈeach of the four had the face of an ox on the left side, ᵉand each of the four had the face of an eagle. ¹¹Thus *were* their faces. Their wings stretched upward; two *wings* of each one touched one another, and ᵃtwo covered their bodies. ¹²And ᵃeach one went straight forward; they went wherever the spirit wanted to go, and they did not turn when they went.

¹³As for the likeness of the living creatures, their appearance *was* like burning coals of fire, ᵃlike the appearance of torches going back and forth among the living creatures. The fire was bright, and out of the fire went lightning. ¹⁴And the living creatures ran back and forth, ᵃin appearance like a flash of lightning.

¹⁵Now as I looked at the living creatures, behold, ᵃa wheel *was* on the earth beside each living creature with its four faces. ¹⁶ᵃThe appearance of the wheels and their workings *was* ᵇlike the color of beryl, and all four had the same likeness. The appearance of their workings *was,* as it were, a wheel in the middle of a wheel. ¹⁷When they moved, they went toward any one of four directions; they did not turn aside when they went. ¹⁸As for their rims, they were so high they were awesome; and their rims *were* ᵃfull of eyes, all around the four of

1:1
ᵃEzek. 3:15, 23; 10:15
ᵇMatt. 3:16; Mark 1:10; Luke 3:21; Acts 7:56; 10:11; Rev. 4:1; 19:11
ᶜEx. 24:10; Num. 12:6; Is. 1:1; 6:1; Ezek. 8:3; Dan. 8:1, 2

1:3 ᵃ1 Kin. 18:46; 2 Kin. 3:15; Ezek. 3:14, 22

1:4 ᵃIs. 21:1; Jer. 23:19; 25:32; Ezek. 13:11, 13
ᵇJer. 1:14

1:5
ᵃEzek. 10:15, 17, 20; Rev. 4:6–8
ᵇEzek. 10:8
ᶜEzek. 10:14

1:7 ᵃDan. 10:6; Rev. 1:15

1:8
ᵃEzek. 10:8, 21

1:9 ᵃEzek. 1:12; 10:20–22

1:10 ᵃEzek. 10:14; Rev. 4:7
ᵇNum. 2:10
ᶜNum. 2:3
ᵈNum. 2:18
ᵉNum. 2:25

1:11 ᵃIs. 6:2; Ezek. 1:23

1:12
ᵃEzek. 10:11, 22

1:13 ᵃPs. 104:4; Rev. 4:5

1:14 ᵃZech. 4:10; [Matt. 24:27; Luke 17:24]

1:15 ᵃEzek. 10:9

1:16
ᵃEzek. 10:9, 10
ᵇDan. 10:6

1:18 ᵃEzek. 10:12; [Zech. 4:10]; Rev. 4:6, 8

1:1 ¹So with MT, LXX, Vg.; Syr., Tg. *a vision* **1:3** ¹Or *Babylonians,* and so elsewhere in the book **1:7** ¹Lit. *feet*

1:19
a Ezek. 10:16, 17

1:20 a Ezek. 10:17

1:22 a Ezek. 10:1
b Rev. 4:6
c Ezek. 10:1

1:24
a Ezek. 3:13; 10:5
b Ezek. 43:2;
Dan. 10:6;
Rev. 1:15
c Job 37:4, 5;
Ps. 29:3, 4;
68:33

1:26 a Ezek. 10:1
b Ex. 24:10, 16;
Ezek. 8:4;
11:22, 23; 43:4, 5
c Ezek. 8:2

1:27 a Ezek. 8:2

1:28
a [Gen. 9:13];
Rev. 4:3; 10:1
b Ezek. 3:23;
8:4 c Gen. 17:3;
Ezek. 3:23;
Dan. 8:17;
Acts 9:4;
Rev. 1:17

2:1 a Dan. 10:11;
Acts 9:6

2:2 a Ezek. 3:24;
Dan. 8:18

2:3 a Ezek. 5:6;
20:8, 13, 18
b 1 Sam. 8:7, 8;
Jer. 3:25;
Ezek. 20:18,
21, 30

2:4 a Ps. 95:8;
Is. 48:4; Jer. 5:3;
6:15; Ezek. 3:7

2:5 a Is. 6:9, 10;
Ezek. 3:11, 26, 27;
[Matt. 10:12–15;
Acts 13:46]
b Ezek. 3:26
c Ezek. 33:33;
[Luke 10:10, 11;
John 15:22]

2:6 a Is. 51:12;
Jer. 1:8, 17;
Ezek. 3:9;
Luke 12:4
b [2 Sam. 23:6, 7;
Is. 9:18];
Jer. 6:28;
Ezek. 28:24;
Mic. 7:4
c Ezek. 3:9;
[1 Pet. 3:14]
d Ezek. 3:9,
26, 27

2:7 a Jer. 1:7, 17;
[Ezek. 3:10, 17]

them. [19a]When the living creatures went, the wheels went beside them; and when the living creatures were lifted up from the earth, the wheels were lifted up. [20]Wherever the spirit wanted to go, they went, *because* there the spirit went; and the wheels were lifted together with them, [a]for the spirit of the [1]living creatures *was* in the wheels. [21]When those went, *these* went; when those stood, *these* stood; and when those were lifted up from the earth, the wheels were lifted up together with them, for the spirit of the [1]living creatures *was* in the wheels.

[22a]The likeness of the [1]firmament above the heads of the [2]living creatures *was* like the color of an awesome [b]crystal, stretched out [c]over their heads. [23]And under the firmament their wings *spread out* straight, one toward another. Each one had two which covered one side, and each one had two which covered the other side of the body. [24a]When they went, I heard the noise of their wings, [b]like the noise of many waters, like [c]the voice of the Almighty, a tumult like the noise of an army; and when they stood still, they let down their wings. [25]A voice came from above the firmament that *was* over their heads; whenever they stood, they let down their wings.

[26a]And above the firmament over their heads *was* the likeness of a throne, [b]in appearance like a sapphire stone; on the likeness of the throne *was* a likeness with the appearance of a man high above [c]it. [27]Also from the appearance of His waist and upward [a]I saw, as it were, the color of amber with the appearance of fire all around within it; and from the appearance of His waist and downward I saw, as it were, the appearance of fire with brightness all around. [28a]Like the appearance of a rainbow in a cloud on a rainy day, so *was* the appearance of the brightness all around it. [b]This *was* the appearance of the likeness of the glory of the LORD.

EZEKIEL SENT TO REBELLIOUS ISRAEL

So when I saw *it*, [c]I fell on my face, and I heard a voice of One speaking.

2 And He said to me, "Son of man, [a]stand on your feet, and I will speak to you." [2]Then [a]the Spirit entered me when He spoke to me, and set me on my feet; and I heard Him who spoke to me. [3]And He said to me: "Son of man, I am sending you to the children of Israel, to a rebellious nation that has [a]rebelled against Me; [b]they and their fathers have transgressed against Me to this very day. [4a]For *they are* [1]impudent and stubborn children. I am sending you to them, and you shall say to them, 'Thus says the Lord GOD.' [5a]As for them, whether they hear or whether they refuse—for they *are* a [b]rebellious house—yet they [c]will know that a prophet has been among them.

[6]"And you, son of man, [a]do not be afraid of them nor be afraid of their words, though [b]briers and thorns *are* with you and you dwell among scorpions; [c]do not be afraid of their words or dismayed by their looks, [d]though they *are* a rebellious house. [7a]You shall speak My words to them, whether they hear or whether they refuse, for they *are* rebellious. [8]But

1:20 [1]Lit. *living creature*; LXX, Vg. *spirit of life*; Tg. *creatures*   1:21 [1]See note at v. 20   1:22 [1]Or *expanse*   [2]So with LXX, Tg., Vg.; MT *living creature*
2:4 [1]Lit. *stiff-faced and hard-hearted sons*

you, son of man, hear what I say to you. Do not be rebellious like that rebellious house; open your mouth and [a]eat what I give you."

9Now when I looked, there was [a]a hand stretched out to me; and behold, [b]a scroll of a book *was* in it. 10Then He spread it before me; and *there was* writing on the inside and on the outside, and written on it *were* lamentations and mourning and woe.

3 Moreover He said to me, "Son of man, eat what you find; [a]eat this scroll, and go, speak to the house of Israel." 2So I opened my mouth, and He caused me to eat that scroll.

3And He said to me, "Son of man, feed your belly, and fill your stomach with this scroll that I give you." So I [a]ate, and it was in my mouth [b]like honey in sweetness.

4Then He said to me: "Son of man, go to the house of Israel and speak with My words to them. 5For you *are* not sent to a people of unfamiliar speech and of hard language, *but* to the house of Israel, 6not to many people of unfamiliar speech and of hard language, whose words you cannot understand. Surely, [a]had I sent you to them, they would have listened to you. 7But the house of Israel will not listen to you, [a]because they will not listen to Me; [b]for all the house of Israel *are* [1]impudent and hard-hearted. 8Behold, I have made your face strong against their faces, and your forehead strong against their foreheads. 9[a]Like adamant stone, harder than flint, I have made your forehead; [b]do not be afraid of them, nor be dismayed at their looks, though they *are* a rebellious house."

10Moreover He said to me: "Son of man, receive into your heart all My words that I speak to you, and hear with your ears. 11And go, get to the captives, to the children of your people, and speak to them and tell them, [a]'Thus says the Lord GOD,' whether they hear, or whether they refuse."

12Then [a]the Spirit lifted me up, and I heard behind me a great thunderous voice: "Blessed *is* the [b]glory of the LORD from His place!" 13I also *heard* the [a]noise of the wings of the living creatures that touched one another, and the noise of the wheels beside them, and a great thunderous noise. 14So the Spirit lifted me up and took me away, and I went in bitterness, in the [1]heat of my spirit; but [a]the hand of the LORD was strong upon me. 15Then I came to the captives at Tel Abib, who dwelt by the River Chebar; and [a]I sat where they sat, and remained there astonished among them seven days.

EZEKIEL IS A WATCHMAN

16Now it [a]came to pass at the end of seven days that the word of the LORD came to me, saying, 17[a]"Son of man, I have made you [b]a watchman for the house of Israel; therefore hear a word from My mouth, and give them [c]warning from Me: 18When I say to the wicked, 'You shall surely die,' and you give him no warning, nor speak to warn the wicked from his wicked way, to save his life, that same wicked *man* [a]shall die in his iniquity; but his blood I will require at your hand. 19Yet, if you warn the wicked, and he does not turn from his wickedness, nor from his wicked way, he shall die in his iniquity; [a]but you have delivered your soul.

3:7 [1]Lit. *strong of forehead*   3:14 [1]Or *anger*

2:8
[a]Ezek. 3:1–3;
Rev. 10:9

2:9 [a]Jer. 1:9;
[Ezek. 8:3]
[b]Jer. 36:2;
Ezek. 3:1;
Rev. 5:1–5;
10:8–11

3:1 [a]Ezek. 2:8, 9

3:3 [a]Jer. 15:16;
Rev. 10:9
[b]Ps. 19:10;
119:103

3:6
[a]Jon. 3:5–10;
Matt. 11:21

3:7
[a]John 15:20, 21
[b]Ezek. 2:4

3:9 [a]Is. 50:7;
Jer. 1:18; Mic. 3:8
[b]Jer. 1:8, 17;
Ezek. 2:6

3:11 [a]Ezek. 2:5, 7

3:12 [a]1 Kin. 18:12;
Ezek. 8:3;
Acts 8:39
[b]Ezek. 1:28; 8:4

3:13
[a]Ezek. 1:24; 10:5

3:14 [a]2 Kin. 3:15;
Ezek. 1:3; 8:1

3:15 [a]Job 2:13;
Ps. 137:1

3:16 [a]Jer. 42:7

3:17
[a]Ezek. 33:7–9
[b]Is. 52:8;
56:10; Jer. 6:17
[c][Lev. 19:17;
Prov. 14:25];
Is. 58:1

3:18 [a]Ezek. 33:6;
[John 8:21, 24]

3:19 [a]Is. 49:4, 5;
Ezek. 14:14, 20;
Acts 18:6; 20:26;
1 Tim. 4:16

20"Again, when a ªrighteous *man* turns from his righteousness and commits iniquity, and I lay a stumbling block before him, he shall die; because you did not give him warning, he shall die in his sin, and his righteousness which he has done shall not be remembered; but his blood I will require at your hand. 21Nevertheless if you warn the righteous *man* that the righteous should not sin, and he does not sin, he shall surely live because he took warning; also you will have delivered your soul."

22ªThen the hand of the LORD was upon me there, and He said to me, "Arise, go out ᵇinto the plain, and there I shall talk with you."

23So I arose and went out into the plain, and behold, ªthe glory of the LORD stood there, like the glory which I ᵇsaw by the River Chebar; ᶜand I fell on my face. 24Then ªthe Spirit entered me and set me on my feet, and spoke with me and said to me: "Go, shut yourself inside your house. 25And you, O son of man, surely ªthey will put ropes on you and bind you with them, so that you cannot go out among them. 26ªI will make your tongue cling to the roof of your mouth, so that you shall be mute and ᵇnot be ¹one to rebuke them, ᶜfor they *are* a rebellious house. 27ªBut when I speak with you, I will open your mouth, and you shall say to them, ᵇ'Thus says the Lord GOD.' He who hears, let him hear; and he who refuses, let him refuse; for they *are* a rebellious house.

THE SIEGE OF JERUSALEM PORTRAYED

4 "You also, son of man, take a clay tablet and lay it before you, and portray on it a city, Jerusalem. 2ªLay siege against it, build a ᵇsiege wall against it, and heap up a mound against it; set camps against it also, and place battering rams against it all around. 3Moreover take for yourself an iron plate, and set it *as* an iron wall between you and the city. Set your face against it, and it shall be ªbesieged, and you shall lay siege against it. ᵇThis *will be* a sign to the house of Israel.

4"Lie also on your left side, and lay the iniquity of the house of Israel upon it. *According* to the number of the days that you lie on it, you shall bear their iniquity. 5For I have laid on you the years of their iniquity, according to the number of the days, three hundred and ninety days; ªso you shall bear the iniquity of the house of Israel. 6And when you have completed them, lie again on your right side; then you shall bear the iniquity of the house of Judah forty days. I have laid on you a day for each year.

7"Therefore you shall set your face toward the siege of Jerusalem; your arm *shall be* uncovered, and you shall prophesy against it. 8ªAnd surely I will ¹restrain you so that you cannot turn from one side to another till you have ended the days of your siege.

9"Also take for yourself wheat, barley, beans, lentils, millet, and spelt; put them into one vessel, and make bread of them for yourself. *During* the number of days that you lie on your side, three hundred and ninety days, you shall eat it. 10And your food which you eat *shall be* by weight, twenty shekels a day; from time to time you shall eat it. 11You shall also drink water by measure, one-sixth of a hin; from time to time you

3:20 ªPs. 125:5;
Ezek. 18:24;
33:18; Zeph. 1:6
3:22 ªEzek. 1:3
ᵇEzek. 8:4
3:23 ªEzek. 1:28;
Acts 7:55
ᵇEzek. 1:1
ᶜEzek. 1:28
3:24 ªEzek. 2:2
3:25 ªEzek. 4:8
3:26
ªEzek. 24:27;
Luke 1:20, 22
ᵇHos. 4:17;
Amos 8:11
ᶜEzek. 2:5–7
3:27
ªEx. 4:11, 12;
Ezek. 24:27;
33:22
ᵇEzek. 3:11
4:2 ªJer. 6:6;
Ezek. 21:22
ᵇ2 Kin. 25:1
4:3
ªJer. 39:1, 2;
Ezek. 5:2
ᵇEzek. 12:6, 11;
24:24, 27
4:5 ªNum. 14:34
4:8 ªEzek. 3:25

3:26 ¹Lit. *one who rebukes*   4:8 ¹Lit. *put ropes on*

shall drink. 12And you shall eat it *as* barley cakes; and bake it using fuel of human waste in their sight."

13Then the LORD said, "So ªshall the children of Israel eat their defiled bread among the Gentiles, where I will drive them."

14So I said, ª"Ah, Lord GOD! Indeed I have never defiled myself from my youth till now; I have never eaten bwhat died of itself or was torn by beasts, nor has cabominable¹ flesh ever come into my mouth."

15Then He said to me, "See, I am giving you cow dung instead of human waste, and you shall prepare your bread over it."

16Moreover He said to me, "Son of man, surely I will cut off the ªsupply of bread in Jerusalem; they shall beat bread by weight and with anxiety, and shall cdrink water by measure and with dread, 17that they may lack bread and water, and be dismayed with one another, and ªwaste away because of their iniquity.

A SWORD AGAINST JERUSALEM

5 "And you, son of man, take a sharp sword, take it as a barber's razor, ªand pass *it* over your head and your beard; then take scales to weigh and divide the *hair*. 2aYou shall burn with fire one-third in the midst of bthe city, when cthe days of the siege are finished; then you shall take one-third and strike around *it* with the sword, and one-third you shall scatter in the wind: I will draw out a sword after dthem. 3aYou shall also take a small number of them and bind them in the edge of your *garment*. 4Then take some of them again and ªthrow them into the midst of the fire, and burn them in the fire. From there a fire will go out into all the house of Israel.

5"Thus says the Lord GOD: 'This *is* Jerusalem; I have set her in the midst of the nations and the countries all around her. 6She has rebelled against My judgments by doing wickedness more than the nations, and against My statutes more than the countries that *are* all around her; for they have refused My judgments, and they have not walked in My statutes.' 7Therefore thus says the Lord GOD: 'Because you have ¹multiplied *disobedience* more than the nations that *are* all around you, have not walked in My statutes ªnor kept My judgments, ²nor even done according to the judgments of the nations that *are* all around you'— 8therefore thus says the Lord GOD: 'Indeed I, even I, *am* against you and will execute judgments in your midst in the sight of the nations. 9aAnd I will do among you what I have never done, and the like of which I will never do again, because of all your abominations. 10Therefore fathers ªshall eat *their* sons in your midst, and sons shall eat their fathers; and I will execute judgments among you, and all of you who remain I will bscatter to all the winds.

11"Therefore, *as* I live,' says the Lord GOD, 'surely, because you have ªdefiled My sanctuary with all your bdetestable things and with all your abominations, therefore I will also diminish *you;* cMy eye will not spare, nor will I have any pity. 12aOne-third of you shall die of the pestilence, and be consumed with famine in your midst; and one-third shall fall by

4:13 ªDan. 1:8; Hos. 9:3

4:14 ªActs 10:14
bEx. 22:31;
Lev. 17:15; 22:8;
Ezek. 44:31
cDeut. 14:3;
Is. 65:4; 66:17

4:16 ªLev. 26:26;
Ps. 105:16; Is. 3:1;
Ezek. 5:16; 14:13
bEzek. 4:10, 11;
12:19 cEzek. 4:11

4:17 ªLev. 26:39;
Ezek. 24:23

5:1 ªLev. 21:5;
Is. 7:20;
Ezek. 44:20

5:2 ªEzek. 5:12
bEzek. 4:1
cEzek. 4:8, 9
dLev. 26:25;
Lam. 1:20

5:3 ªJer. 40:6;
52:16

5:4 ªJer. 41:1, 2;
44:14

5:7
ª2 Kin. 21:9–11;
2 Chr. 33:9;
Jer. 2:10, 11;
Ezek. 16:47

5:9 ªLam. 4:6;
Dan. 9:12;
[Amos 3:2];
Matt. 24:21

5:10 ªLev. 26:29;
Deut. 28:53;
2 Kin. 6:29;
Jer. 19:9;
Lam. 2:20; 4:10
bLev. 26:33;
Deut. 28:64;
Ps. 44:11;
Ezek. 5:2, 12;
6:8; 12:14;
Amos 9:9;
Zech. 2:6; 7:14

5:11
ª2 Chr. 36:14;
[Jer. 7:9–11];
Ezek. 8:5, 6, 16
bEzek. 11:21
cEzek. 7:4, 9;
8:18; 9:10

5:12 ªJer. 15:2;
21:9; Ezek. 6:12

the sword all around you; and [b]I will scatter another third to all the winds, and I will draw out a sword after [c]them.

13Thus shall My anger [a]be spent, and I will [b]cause My fury to rest upon them, [c]and I will be avenged; [d]and they shall know that I, the LORD, have spoken *it* in My zeal, when I have spent My fury upon them. 14Moreover [a]I will make you a waste and a reproach among the nations that *are* all around you, in the sight of all who pass by.

15'So [1]it shall be a [a]reproach, a taunt, a [b]lesson, and an astonishment to the nations that *are* all around you, when I execute judgments among you in anger and in fury and in [c]furious rebukes. I, the LORD, have spoken. 16When I [a]send against them the terrible arrows of famine which shall be for destruction, which I will send to destroy you, I will increase the famine upon you and cut off your [b]supply of bread. 17So I will send against you famine and [a]wild beasts, and they will bereave you. [b]Pestilence and blood shall pass through you, and I will bring the sword against you. I, the LORD, have spoken.'"

JUDGMENT ON IDOLATROUS ISRAEL

6 Now the word of the LORD came to me, saying: 2"Son of man, [a]set your face toward the [b]mountains of Israel, and prophesy against them, 3and say, 'O mountains of Israel, hear the word of the Lord GOD! Thus says the Lord GOD to the mountains, to the hills, to the ravines, and to the valleys: "Indeed I, *even* I, will bring a sword against you, and [a]I will destroy your [1]high places. 4Then your altars shall be desolate, your incense altars shall be broken, and [a]I will cast down your slain *men* before your idols. 5And I will lay the corpses of the children of Israel before their idols, and I will scatter your bones all around your altars. 6In all your dwelling places the cities shall be laid waste, and the [1]high places shall be desolate, so that your altars may be laid waste and made desolate, your idols may be broken and made to cease, your incense altars may be cut down, and your works may be abolished. 7The slain shall fall in your midst, and [a]you shall know that I *am* the LORD.

8[a]"Yet I will leave a remnant, so that you may have *some* who escape the sword among the nations, when you are [b]scattered through the countries. 9Then those of you who escape will [a]remember Me among the nations where they are carried captive, because [b]I was crushed by their adulterous heart which has departed from Me, and [c]by their eyes which play the harlot after their idols; [d]they will loathe themselves for the evils which they committed in all their abominations. 10And they shall know that I *am* the LORD; I have not said in vain that I would bring this calamity upon them."

11"Thus says the Lord GOD: [a]"Pound[1] your fists and stamp your feet, and say, 'Alas, for all the evil abominations of the house of Israel! [b]For they shall fall by the sword, by famine, and by pestilence. 12He who is far off shall die by the pestilence, he who is near shall fall by the sword, and he who remains and is besieged shall die by the famine. [a]Thus will I spend My fury upon them. 13Then you shall know that I *am*

Cross References

5:12 [b]Jer. 9:16; [Ezek. 6:8]
[c]Jer. 43:10, 11; 44:27; Ezek. 5:2; 12:14

5:13 [a]Lam. 4:11; Ezek. 6:12; 7:8
[b]Ezek. 21:17
[c][Deut. 32:36]; Is. 1:24 [d]Is. 59:17; Ezek. 36:6; 38:19

5:14 [a]Lev. 26:31; Neh. 2:17

5:15
[a]Deut. 28:37; 1 Kin. 9:7; Ps. 79:4; Jer. 24:9; Lam. 2:15
[b][Is. 26:9]; Jer. 22:8, 9; 1 Cor. 10:11
[c]Is. 66:15, 16; Ezek. 5:8; 25:17

5:16
[a]Deut. 32:23
[b]Lev. 26:26; Ezek. 4:16; 14:13

5:17 [a]Lev. 26:22; Deut. 32:24; Ezek. 14:21; 33:27; 34:25; Rev. 6:8
[b]Ezek. 38:22

6:2
[a]Ezek. 20:46; 21:2; 25:2
[b]Ezek. 36:1

6:3 [a]Lev. 26:30

6:4 [a]Lev. 26:30

6:7 [a]Ezek. 7:4, 9

6:8 [a]Jer. 44:28; Ezek. 5:2, 12; 12:16; 14:22
[b]Ezek. 5:12

6:9
[a][Deut. 4:29]; Ps. 137; Jer. 51:50
[b]Ps. 78:40; Is. 7:13; 43:24; Hos. 11:8
[c]Num. 15:39; Ezek. 20:7, 24
[d]Lev. 26:39; Job 42:6; Ezek. 20:43; 36:31

6:11 [a]Ezek. 21:14
[b]Ezek. 5:12

6:12
[a]Lam. 4:11, 22; Ezek. 5:13

5:15 [1]LXX, Syr., Tg., Vg. *you*   6:3 [1]Places for pagan worship   6:6 [1]Places for pagan worship   6:11 [1]Lit. *Strike your hands*

the LORD, when their slain are among their idols all around their altars, ^aon every high hill, ^bon all the mountaintops, ^cunder every green tree, and under every thick oak, wherever they offered sweet incense to all their idols. ¹⁴So I will ^astretch out My hand against them and make the land desolate, yes, more desolate than the wilderness toward ^bDiblah, in all their dwelling places. Then they shall know that I *am* the LORD.'"'

JUDGMENT ON ISRAEL IS NEAR

7 Moreover the word of the LORD came to me, saying, ²"And you, son of man, thus says the Lord GOD to the land of Israel:

^a'An end! The end has come upon the four corners of the
    land.
³ Now the end *has come* upon you,
    And I will send My anger against you;
    I will judge you ^aaccording to your ways,
    And I will repay you for all your abominations.
⁴ ^aMy eye will not spare you,
    Nor will I have pity;
    But I will repay your ways,
    And your abominations will be in your midst;
    ^bThen you shall know that I *am* the LORD!'

⁵"Thus says the Lord GOD:

'A disaster, a singular ^adisaster;
    Behold, it has come!
⁶ An end has come,
    The end has come;
    It has dawned for you;
    Behold, it has come!
⁷ ^aDoom has come to you, you who dwell in the land;
    ^bThe time has come,
    A day of trouble *is* near,
    And not of rejoicing in the mountains.
⁸ Now upon you I will soon ^apour out My fury,
    And spend My anger upon you;
    I will judge you according to your ways,
    And I will repay you for all your abominations.

⁹ 'My eye will not spare,
    Nor will I have pity;
    I will ¹repay you according to your ways,
    And your abominations will be in your midst.
    Then you shall know that I *am* the LORD who strikes.
¹⁰ 'Behold, the day!
    Behold, it has come!
  ^aDoom has gone out;
    The rod has blossomed,
    Pride has budded.
¹¹ ^aViolence has risen up into a rod of wickedness;
    None of them *shall remain*,
    None of their multitude,
    None of ¹them;
    ^bNor *shall there be* wailing for them.

6:13
^aJer. 2:20; 3:6
^b1 Kin. 14:23;
2 Kin. 16:4;
Ezek. 20:28;
Hos. 4:13
^cIs. 57:5

6:14 ^aIs. 5:25;
Ezek. 14:13;
20:33, 34
^bNum. 33:46

7:2 ^aEzek. 7:3,
5, 6; 11:13;
Amos 8:2, 10;
[Matt. 24:6,
13, 14]

7:3 ^a[Rom. 2:6]

7:4 ^aEzek. 5:11
^bEzek. 12:20

7:5
^a2 Kin. 21:12, 13;
Nah. 1:9

7:7 ^aEzek. 7:10
^bZeph. 1:14, 15

7:8
^aEzek. 20:8, 21

7:10 ^aEzek. 7:7

7:11 ^aJer. 6:7
^bJer. 16:5, 6;
Ezek. 24:16, 22

7:9 ¹Lit. *give*   7:11 ¹Or *their wealth*

12 The time has come,
  The day draws near.

  'Let not the buyer ᵃrejoice,
  Nor the seller ᵇmourn,
  For wrath *is* on their whole multitude.
13 For the seller shall not return to what has been sold,
  Though he may still be alive;
  For the vision concerns the whole multitude,
  And it shall not turn back;
  No one will strengthen himself
  Who lives in iniquity.

14 'They have blown the trumpet and made everyone ready,
  But no one goes to battle;
  For My wrath *is* on all their multitude.
15 ᵃThe sword *is* outside,
  And the pestilence and famine within.
  Whoever *is* in the field
  Will die by the sword;
  And whoever *is* in the city,
  Famine and pestilence will devour him.

16 'Those who ᵃsurvive will escape and be on the mountains
  Like doves of the valleys,
  All of them mourning,
  Each for his iniquity.
17 Every ᵃhand will be feeble,
  And every knee will be *as* weak *as* water.
18 They will also ᵃbe girded with sackcloth;
  Horror will cover them;
  Shame *will be* on every face,
  Baldness on all their heads.

19 'They will throw their silver into the streets,
  And their gold will be like refuse;
  Their ᵃsilver and their gold will not be able to deliver
    them
  In the day of the wrath of the LORD;
  They will not satisfy their souls,
  Nor fill their stomachs,
  Because it became their stumbling block of iniquity.

20 'As for the beauty of his ornaments,
  He set it in majesty;
  ᵃBut they made from it
  The images of their abominations—
  Their detestable things;
  Therefore I have made it
  Like refuse to them.
21 I will give it as ᵃplunder
  Into the hands of strangers,
  And to the wicked of the earth as spoil;
  And they shall defile it.
22 I will turn My face from them,
  And they will defile My secret place;
  For robbers shall enter it and defile it.

23 'Make a chain,
  For ᵃthe land is filled with crimes of blood,
  And the city is full of violence.

7:12
ᵃProv. 20:14;
1 Cor. 7:30
ᵇIs. 24:2

7:15
ᵃDeut. 32:25;
Jer. 14:18;
Lam. 1:20;
Ezek. 5:12

7:16 ᵃEzra 9:15;
Is. 37:31;
Ezek. 6:8; 14:22

7:17 ᵃIs. 13:7;
Jer. 6:24;
Ezek. 21:7;
Heb. 12:12

7:18 ᵃIs. 3:24;
15:2, 3;
Jer. 48:37;
Ezek. 27:31;
Amos 8:10

7:19 ᵃProv. 11:4;
Jer. 15:13;
Zeph. 1:18

7:20 ᵃJer. 7:30

7:21
ᵃ2 Kin. 24:13;
Jer. 20:5

7:23
ᵃ2 Kin. 21:16

24 Therefore I will bring the ªworst of the Gentiles,
And they will possess their houses;
I will cause the pomp of the strong to cease,
And their holy places shall be ᵇdefiled.
25 ¹Destruction comes;
They will seek peace, but *there shall be* none.
26 ªDisaster will come upon disaster,
And rumor will be upon rumor.
ᵇThen they will seek a vision from a prophet;
But the law will perish from the priest,
And counsel from the elders.
27 'The king will mourn,
The prince will be clothed with desolation,
And the hands of the common people will tremble.
I will do to them according to their way,
And according to what they deserve I will judge
    them;
Then they shall know that I *am* the LORD!' "

ABOMINATIONS IN THE TEMPLE

8 And it came to pass in the sixth year, in the sixth *month,* on the fifth *day* of the month, as I sat in my house with ªthe elders of Judah sitting before me, that ᵇthe hand of the Lord GOD fell upon me there. 2ªThen I looked, and there was a likeness, like the appearance of fire—from the appearance of His waist and downward, fire; and from His waist and upward, like the appearance of brightness, ᵇlike the color of amber. 3He ªstretched out the form of a hand, and took me by a lock of my hair; and ᵇthe Spirit lifted me up between earth and heaven, and ᶜbrought me in visions of God to Jerusalem, to the door of the north gate of the inner *court,* ᵈwhere the seat of the image of jealousy *was,* which ᵉprovokes¹ to jealousy. 4And behold, the ªglory of the God of Israel *was* there, like the vision that I ᵇsaw in the plain.

5Then He said to me, "Son of man, lift your eyes now toward the north." So I lifted my eyes toward the north, and there, north of the altar gate, was this image of jealousy in the entrance.

6Furthermore He said to me, "Son of man, do you see what they are doing, the great ªabominations that the house of Israel commits here, to make Me go far away from My sanctuary? Now turn again, you will see greater abominations." 7So He brought me to the door of the court; and when I looked, there was a hole in the wall. 8Then He said to me, "Son of man, dig into the wall"; and when I dug into the wall, there was a door.

9And He said to me, "Go in, and see the wicked abominations which they are doing there." 10So I went in and saw, and there—every ªsort of ᵇcreeping thing, abominable beasts, and all the idols of the house of Israel, ¹portrayed all around on the walls. 11And there stood before them ªseventy men of the elders of the house of Israel, and in their midst stood Jaazaniah the son of Shaphan. Each man had a censer in his hand, and a thick cloud of incense went up. 12Then He said to me, "Son of man, have you seen what the elders of the house of

7:24
ªEzek. 21:31;
28:7
ᵇ2 Chr. 7:20;
Ezek. 24:21

7:26
ªDeut. 32:23;
Is. 47:11;
Jer. 4:20
ᵇPs. 74:9;
Lam. 2:9;
Ezek. 20:1, 3;
Mic. 3:6

8:1 ªEzek. 14:1;
20:1; 33:31
ᵇEzek. 1:3; 3:22

8:2
ªEzek. 1:26, 27
ᵇEzek. 1:4, 27

8:3 ªDan. 5:5
ᵇEzek. 3:14;
Acts 8:39
ᶜEzek. 11:1, 24;
40:2 ᵈJer. 7:30;
32:34; Ezek. 5:11
ᵉEx. 20:4;
Deut. 32:16, 21

8:4
ªEzek. 3:12; 9:3
ᵇEzek. 1:28;
3:22, 23

8:6
ª2 Kin. 23:4, 5;
Ezek. 5:11;
8:9, 17

8:10 ªEx. 20:4;
Deut. 4:16–18
ᵇRom. 1:23

8:11
ªNum. 11:16, 25;
Luke 10:1

7:25 ¹Lit. *Shuddering*　　8:3 ¹Arouses the LORD's jealousy　　8:10 ¹Or *carved*

Israel do in the dark, every man in the room of his idols? For they say, [a]"The LORD does not see us, the LORD has forsaken the land.'"

13And He said to me, "Turn again, *and* you will see greater abominations that they are doing." 14So He brought me to the door of the north gate of the LORD's house; and to my dismay, women were sitting there weeping for [1]Tammuz.

15Then He said to me, "Have you seen *this,* O son of man? Turn again, you will see greater abominations than these." 16So He brought me into the inner court of the LORD's house; and there, at the door of the temple of the LORD, [a]between the porch and the altar, [b]*were* about twenty-five men [c]with their backs toward the temple of the LORD and their faces toward the east, and they were worshiping [d]the sun toward the east.

17And He said to me, "Have you seen *this,* O son of man? Is it a trivial thing to the house of Judah to commit the abominations which they commit here? For they have [a]filled the land with violence; then they have returned to provoke Me to anger. Indeed they put the branch to their nose. 18[a]Therefore I also will act in fury. My [b]eye will not spare nor will I have pity; and though they [c]cry in My ears with a loud voice, I will not hear them."

THE WICKED ARE SLAIN

9 Then He called out in my hearing with a loud voice, saying, "Let those who have charge over the city draw near, each *with* a [1]deadly weapon in his hand." 2And suddenly six men came from the direction of the upper gate, which faces north, each with his [1]battle-ax in his hand. [a]One man among them *was* clothed with linen and had a writer's inkhorn [2]at his side. They went in and stood beside the bronze altar.

3Now [a]the glory of the God of Israel had gone up from the cherub, where it had been, to the threshold of the [1]temple. And He called to the man clothed with linen, who *had* the writer's inkhorn at his side; 4and the LORD said to him, "Go through the midst of the city, through the midst of Jerusalem, and put [a]a mark on the foreheads of the men [b]who sigh and cry over all the abominations that are done within it."

5To the others He said in my [1]hearing, "Go after him through the city and [a]kill;[2] [b]do not let your eye spare, nor have any pity. 6[a]Utterly[1] slay old *and* young men, maidens and little children and women; but [b]do not come near anyone on whom *is* the mark; and [c]begin at My sanctuary." [d]So they began with the elders who *were* before the [2]temple. 7Then He said to them, "Defile the [1]temple, and fill the courts with the slain. Go out!" And they went out and killed in the city.

8So it was, that while they were killing them, I was left *alone;* and I [a]fell on my face and cried out, and said, [b]"Ah, Lord GOD! Will You destroy all the remnant of Israel in pouring out Your fury on Jerusalem?"

9Then He said to me, "The iniquity of the house of Israel and Judah *is* exceedingly great, and [a]the land is full of bloodshed,

8:12 [a]Ps. 14:1; Is. 29:15; Ezek. 9:9

8:16 [a]Joel 2:17 [b]Ezek. 11:1 [c]2 Chr. 29:6; Jer. 2:27; 32:33; Ezek. 23:39 [d]Deut. 4:19; 2 Kin. 23:5, 11; Job 31:26; Jer. 44:17

8:17 [a]Ezek. 9:9; Amos 3:10; Mic. 2:2

8:18 [a]Ezek. 5:13; 16:42; 24:13 [b]Ezek. 5:11; 7:4, 9; 9:5, 10 [c]Prov. 1:28; Is. 1:15; Jer. 11:11; 14:12; Mic. 3:4; Zech. 7:13

9:2 [a]Lev. 16:4; Ezek. 10:2; Rev. 15:6

9:3 [a]Ezek. 3:23; 8:4; 10:4, 18; 11:22, 23

9:4 [a]Ex. 12:7, 13; Ezek. 9:6; [2 Cor. 1:22; 2 Tim. 2:19]; Rev. 7:2, 3; 9:4; 14:1 [b]Ps. 119:53, 136; Jer. 13:17; Ezek. 6:11; 21:6; 2 Cor. 12:21; 2 Pet. 2:8

9:5 [a]Ezek. 7:9 [b]Ezek. 5:11

9:6 [a]2 Chr. 36:17 [b]Ex. 12:23; Rev. 9:4 [c]Jer. 25:29; Amos 3:2; [Luke 12:42; 1 Pet. 4:17] [d]Ezek. 8:11, 12, 16

9:8 [a]Num. 14:5; 16:4, 22, 45; Josh. 7:6 [b]Ezek. 11:13; Amos 7:2–6

9:9 [a]2 Kin. 21:16; Jer. 2:34; Ezek. 8:17

8:14 [1]A Sumerian fertility god similar to the Gr. god Adonis   9:1 [1]Or *destroying*   9:2 [1]Lit. *shattering weapon*   [2]Lit. *upon his loins*   9:3 [1]Lit. *house*   9:5 [1]Lit. *ears*   [2]Lit. *strike*   9:6 [1]Lit. *Slay to destruction*   [2]Lit. *house*   9:7 [1]Lit. *house*

and the city full of perversity; for they say, [b]"The LORD has forsaken the land, and [c]the LORD does not see!' [10]And as for Me also, My [a]eye will neither spare, nor will I have pity, *but* [b]I will recompense their deeds on their own head."

[11]Just then, the man clothed with linen, who *had* the inkhorn at his side, reported back and said, "I have done as You commanded me."

THE GLORY DEPARTS FROM THE TEMPLE

10 And I looked, and there in the [a]firmament[1] that was above the head of the cherubim, there appeared something like a sapphire stone, having the appearance of the likeness of a throne. [2a]Then He spoke to the man clothed with linen, and said, "Go in among the wheels, under the cherub, fill your hands with [b]coals of fire from among the cherubim, and [c]scatter *them* over the city." And he went in as I watched.

[3]Now the cherubim were standing on the [1]south side of the [2]temple when the man went in, and the [a]cloud filled the inner court. [4a]Then the glory of the LORD went up from the cherub, *and paused* over the threshold of the [1]temple; and [b]the house was filled with the cloud, and the court was full of the brightness of the LORD's [c]glory. [5]And the [a]sound of the wings of the cherubim was heard *even* in the outer court, like [b]the voice of Almighty God when He speaks.

[6]Then it happened, when He commanded the man clothed in linen, saying, "Take fire from among the wheels, from among the cherubim," that he went in and stood beside the wheels. [7]And the cherub stretched out his hand from among the cherubim to the fire that *was* among the cherubim, and took *some of it* and put *it* into the hands of the *man* clothed with linen, who took *it* and went out. [8a]The cherubim appeared to have the form of a man's hand under their wings.

[9a]And when I looked, there were four wheels by the cherubim, one wheel by one cherub and another wheel by each other cherub; the wheels appeared *to have* the color of a [b]beryl stone. [10]As *for* their appearance, all four looked alike—as it were, a wheel in the middle of a wheel. [11a]When they went, they went toward *any of* their four directions; they did not turn aside when they went, but followed in the direction the head was facing. They did not turn aside when they went. [12]And their whole body, with their back, their hands, their wings, and the wheels that the four had, *were* [a]full of eyes all around. [13]As for the wheels, they were called in my [1]hearing, "Wheel."

[14a]Each one had four faces: the first face *was* the face of a cherub, the second face the face of a man, the third the face of a lion, and the fourth the face of an eagle. [15]And the cherubim were lifted up. This *was* [a]the living creature I saw by the River Chebar. [16a]When the cherubim went, the wheels went beside them; and when the cherubim lifted their wings to mount up from the earth, the same wheels also did not turn from beside them. [17a]When [1]*the cherubim* stood still, *the wheels* stood still, and when [2]*one* was lifted up, [3]*the other* lifted itself up, for the spirit of the living creature *was* in them.

9:9 [b]Job 22:13; Ezek. 8:12
[c]Ps. 10:11; Is. 29:15

9:10 [a]Is. 65:6; Ezek. 5:11; 7:4; 8:18 [b]Ezek. 11:21; Hos. 9:7

10:1 [a]Ezek. 1:22, 26

10:2 [a]Ezek. 9:2, 3; Dan. 10:5 [b]Ps. 18:10–13; Is. 6:6; Ezek. 1:13 [c]Rev. 8:5

10:3 [a]1 Kin. 8:10, 11

10:4 [a]Ezek. 1:28 [b]1 Kin. 8:10; Ezek. 43:5 [c]Ezek. 11:22, 23

10:5 [a][Job 40:9]; Ezek. 1:24; [Rev. 10:3] [b][Ps. 29:3]

10:8 [a]Ezek. 1:8; 10:21

10:9 [a]Ezek. 1:15 [b]Ezek. 1:16

10:11 [a]Ezek. 1:17

10:12 [a]Rev. 4:6, 8

10:14 [a]1 Kin. 7:29, 36; Ezek. 1:6, 10, 11; Rev. 4:7

10:15 [a]Ezek. 1:3, 5

10:16 [a]Ezek. 1:19

10:17 [a]Ezek. 1:12, 20, 21

10:1 [1]*expanse* 10:3 [1]Lit. *right* [2]Lit. *house* 10:4 [1]Lit. *house* 10:13 [1]Lit. *ears* 10:17 [1]Lit. *they* [2]Lit. *they were* [3]Lit. *they lifted them*

18Then ªthe glory of the LORD ᵇdeparted from the threshold of the ¹temple and stood over the cherubim. 19And ªthe cherubim lifted their wings and mounted up from the earth in my sight. When they went out, the wheels *were* beside them; and they stood at the door of the ᵇeast gate of the LORD's house, and the glory of the God of Israel *was* above them.

20ªThis *is* the living creature I saw under the God of Israel ᵇby the River Chebar, and I knew they *were* cherubim. 21ªEach one had four faces and each one four wings, and the likeness of the hands of a man *was* under their wings. 22And ªthe likeness of their faces *was* the same *as* the faces which I had seen by the River Chebar, their appearance and their persons. ᵇThey each went straight forward.

JUDGMENT ON WICKED COUNSELORS

11 Then ªthe Spirit lifted me up and brought me to ᵇthe East Gate of the LORD's house, which faces eastward; and there ᶜat the door of the gate were twenty-five men, among whom I saw Jaazaniah the son of Azzur, and Pelatiah the son of Benaiah, princes of the people. 2And He said to me: "Son of man, these *are* the men who devise iniquity and give wicked ¹counsel in this city, 3who say, '*The time is* not ªnear to build houses; ᵇthis *city is* the ¹caldron, and we *are* the meat.' 4Therefore prophesy against them, prophesy, O son of man!"

5Then ªthe Spirit of the LORD fell upon me, and said to me, "Speak! 'Thus says the LORD: "Thus you have said, O house of Israel; for ᵇI know the things that come into your mind. 6ªYou have multiplied your slain in this city, and you have filled its streets with the slain." 7Therefore thus says the Lord GOD: ª"Your slain whom you have laid in its midst, they *are* the meat, and this *city is* the caldron; ᵇbut I shall bring you out of the midst of it. 8You have ªfeared the sword; and I will bring a sword upon you," says the Lord GOD. 9"And I will bring you out of its midst, and deliver you into the hands of strangers, and ªexecute judgments on you. 10ªYou shall fall by the sword. I will judge you at ᵇthe border of Israel. ᶜThen you shall know that I *am* the LORD. 11ªThis *city* shall not be your ¹caldron, nor shall you be the meat in its midst. I will judge you at the border of Israel. 12And you shall know that I *am* the LORD; for you have not walked in My statutes nor executed My judgments, but ªhave done according to the customs of the Gentiles which *are* all around you."'"

13Now it happened, while I was prophesying, that ªPelatiah the son of Benaiah died. Then ᵇI fell on my face and cried with a loud voice, and said, "Ah, Lord GOD! Will You make a complete end of the remnant of Israel?"

GOD WILL RESTORE ISRAEL

14Again the word of the LORD came to me, saying, 15"Son of man, your brethren, your relatives, your countrymen, and all the house of Israel in its entirety, *are* those about whom the inhabitants of Jerusalem have said, 'Get far away from the LORD; this land has been given to us as a possession.' 16Therefore say, 'Thus says the Lord GOD: "Although I have

---

10:18 ªEzek. 10:4
ᵇHos. 9:12

10:19
ªEzek. 11:22
ᵇEzek. 11:1

10:20
ªEzek. 1:22
ᵇEzek. 1:1

10:21
ªEzek. 1:6, 8;
10:14; 41:18, 19

10:22 ªEzek. 1:10
ᵇEzek. 1:9, 12

11:1
ªEzek. 3:12, 14
ᵇEzek. 10:19
ᶜEzek. 8:16

11:3
ªEzek. 12:22, 27;
2 Pet. 3:4
ᵇJer. 1:13;
Ezek. 11:7, 11;
24:3, 6

11:5
ªEzek. 2:2; 3:24
ᵇ[Jer. 16:17;
17:10]

11:6 ªIs. 1:15;
Ezek. 7:23;
22:2–6, 9, 12, 27

11:7
ªEzek. 24:3, 6;
Mic. 3:2, 3
ᵇ2 Kin. 25:18–22;
Jer. 52:24–27;
Ezek. 11:9

11:8 ªJer. 42:16

11:9 ªEzek. 5:8

11:10
ª2 Kin. 25:19–21;
Jer. 39:6; 52:10
ᵇ1 Kin. 8:65;
2 Kin. 14:25
ᶜPs. 9:16;
Ezek. 6:7; 13:9,
14, 21, 23

11:11
ªEzek. 11:3, 7

11:12
ªLev. 18:3, 24;
Deut. 12:30, 31;
Ezek. 8:10, 14, 16

11:13 ªActs 5:5
ᵇEzek. 9:8

10:18 ¹Lit. *house* 11:2 ¹Advice 11:3 ¹Pot 11:11 ¹Pot

cast them far off among the Gentiles, and although I have scattered them among the countries, ᵃyet I shall be a little ¹sanctuary for them in the countries where they have gone." ' ¹⁷Therefore say, 'Thus says the Lord GOD: ᵃ"I will gather you from the peoples, assemble you from the countries where you have been scattered, and I will give you the land of Israel." ' ¹⁸And they will go there, and they will take away all its ᵃdetestable things and all its abominations from there. ¹⁹Then ᵃI will give them one heart, and I will put ᵇa new spirit within ¹them, and take ᶜthe stony heart out of their flesh, and give them a heart of flesh, ²⁰ᵃthat they may walk in My statutes and keep My judgments and do them; ᵇand they shall be My people, and I will be their God. ²¹But *as for those* whose hearts follow the desire for their detestable things and their abominations, ᵃI will recompense their deeds on their own heads," says the Lord GOD.

²²So the cherubim ᵃlifted up their wings, with the wheels beside them, and the glory of the God of Israel *was* high above them. ²³And ᵃthe glory of the LORD went up from the midst of the city and stood ᵇon the mountain, ᶜwhich *is* on the east side of the city.

²⁴Then ᵃthe Spirit took me up and brought me in a vision by the Spirit of God into ¹Chaldea, to those in captivity. And the vision that I had seen went up from me. ²⁵So I spoke to those in captivity of all the things the LORD had shown me.

JUDAH'S CAPTIVITY PORTRAYED

12 Now the word of the LORD came to me, saying: ²"Son of man, you dwell in the midst of ᵃa rebellious house, which ᵇhas eyes to see but does not see, and ears to hear but does not hear; ᶜfor they *are* a rebellious house.

³"Therefore, son of man, prepare your belongings for captivity, and go into captivity by day in their sight. You shall go from your place into captivity to another place in their sight. It may be that they will consider, though they *are* a rebellious house. ⁴By day you shall bring out your belongings in their sight, as though going into captivity; and at evening you shall go in their sight, like those who go into captivity. ⁵Dig through the wall in their sight, and carry *your belongings* out through it. ⁶In their sight you shall bear *them* on *your* shoulders *and* carry *them* out at twilight; you shall cover your face, so that you cannot see the ground, ᵃfor I have made you a sign to the house of Israel."

⁷So I did as I was commanded. I brought out my belongings by day, as though going into captivity, and at evening I dug through the wall with my hand. I brought *them* out at twilight, *and* I bore *them* on *my* shoulder in their sight.

⁸And in the morning the word of the LORD came to me, saying, ⁹"Son of man, has not the house of Israel, ᵃthe rebellious house, said to you, ᵇ'What are you doing?' ¹⁰Say to them, 'Thus says the Lord GOD: "This ᵃburden¹ *concerns* the prince in Jerusalem and all the house of Israel who are among them." ' ¹¹Say, ᵃ'I *am* a sign to you. As I have done, so shall it be done to them; ᵇthey shall be carried away into captivity.' ¹²And ᵃthe prince who *is* among them shall bear *his belongings* on

11:16 ᵃPs. 90:1; 91:9; Is. 8:14; Jer. 29:7, 11

11:17 ᵃIs. 11:11–16; Jer. 3:12, 18; 24:5; Ezek. 20:41, 42; 28:5

11:18 ᵃEzek. 37:23

11:19 ᵃJer. 32:39; Ezek. 36:26; Zeph. 3:9 ᵇPs. 51:10; [Jer. 31:33]; Ezek. 18:31 ᶜZech. 7:12; [Rom. 2:4, 5]

11:20 ᵃPs. 105:45 ᵇJer. 24:7; Ezek. 14:11; 36:28; 37:27

11:21 ᵃEzek. 9:10

11:22 ᵃEzek. 1:19

11:23 ᵃEzek. 8:4; 9:3 ᵇZech. 14:4 ᶜEzek. 43:2

11:24 ᵃEzek. 8:3; 2 Cor. 12:2–4

12:2 ᵃIs. 1:23; Ezek. 2:3, 6–8 ᵇIs. 6:9; 42:20; Jer. 5:21; Matt. 13:13, 14; Mark 4:12; 8:18; [Luke 8:10; John 9:39–41; 12:40]; Acts 28:26; Rom. 11:8 ᶜEzek. 2:5

12:6 ᵃIs. 8:18; Ezek. 4:3; 24:24

12:9 ᵃEzek. 2:5 ᵇEzek. 17:12; 24:19

12:10 ᵃMal. 1:1

12:11 ᵃEzek. 12:6 ᵇ2 Kin. 25:4, 5, 7

12:12 ᵃ2 Kin. 25:4; Jer. 39:4; 52:7; Ezek. 12:6

11:16 ¹*holy place*   **11:19** ¹Lit. *you* (pl.)   **11:24** ¹Or *Babylon*, and so elsewhere in the book   **12:10** ¹*oracle, prophecy*

his shoulder at twilight and go out. They shall dig through the wall to carry *them* out through it. He shall cover his face, so that he cannot see the ground with *his* eyes. [13]I will also spread My [a]net over him, and he shall be caught in My snare. [b]I will bring him to Babylon, *to* the land of the Chaldeans; yet he shall not see it, though he shall die there. [14a]I will scatter to every wind all who *are* around him to help him, and all his troops; and [b]I will draw out the sword after them.

[15a]"Then they shall know that I *am* the LORD, when I scatter them among the nations and disperse them throughout the countries. [16a]But I will spare a few of their men from the sword, from famine, and from pestilence, that they may declare all their abominations among the Gentiles wherever they go. Then they shall know that I *am* the LORD."

JUDGMENT NOT POSTPONED

[17]Moreover the word of the LORD came to me, saying, [18]"Son of man, [a]eat your bread with [1]quaking, and drink your water with trembling and anxiety. [19]And say to the people of the land, 'Thus says the Lord GOD to the inhabitants of Jerusalem *and* to the land of Israel: "They shall eat their bread with anxiety, and drink their water with dread, so that her land may [a]be emptied of all who are in it, [b]because of the violence of all those who dwell in it. [20]Then the cities that are inhabited shall be laid waste, and the land shall become desolate; and you shall know that I *am* the LORD."'"

[21]And the word of the LORD came to me, saying, [22]"Son of man, what *is* this proverb *that* you *people* have about the land of Israel, which says, [a]'The days are prolonged, and every vision fails'? [23]Tell them therefore, 'Thus says the Lord GOD: "I will lay this proverb to rest, and they shall no more use it as a proverb in Israel."' But say to them, '[a]"The days are at hand, and the [1]fulfillment of every vision. [24]For [a]no more shall there be any [b]false[1] vision or flattering divination within the house of Israel. [25]For I *am* the LORD. I speak, and [a]the word which I speak will come to pass; it will no more be postponed; for in your days, O rebellious house, I will say the word and [b]perform it," says the Lord GOD.'"

[26]Again the word of the LORD came to me, saying, [27a]"Son of man, look, the house of Israel is saying, 'The vision that he sees *is* [b]for many days *from now,* and he prophesies of times far off.' [28a]Therefore say to them, 'Thus says the Lord GOD: "None of My words will be postponed any more, but the word which I speak [b]will be done," says the Lord GOD.'"

WOE TO FOOLISH PROPHETS

13 And the word of the LORD came to me, saying, [2]"Son of man, prophesy [a]against the prophets of Israel who prophesy, and say to [b]those who prophesy out of their own [c]heart,[1] 'Hear the word of the LORD!'"

[3]Thus says the Lord GOD: "Woe to the foolish prophets, who follow their own spirit and have seen [1]nothing! [4]O Israel, your prophets are [a]like foxes in the deserts. [5]You [a]have not gone up into the [1]gaps to build a wall for the house of Israel to stand in battle on the day of the LORD. [6a]They have envisioned

---

12:13 [a]Job 19:6;
Jer. 52:9;
Lam. 1:13;
Ezek. 17:20
[b]2 Kin. 25:7;
Jer. 52:11;
Ezek. 17:16

12:14
[a]2 Kin. 25:4;
Ezek. 5:10
[b]Ezek. 5:2, 12

12:15 [a][Ps. 9:16];
Ezek. 6:7, 14;
12:16, 20

12:16
[a]2 Kin. 25:11, 22;
Ezek. 6:8–10

12:18 [a]Lam. 5:9;
Ezek. 4:16

12:19 [a]Jer. 10:22;
Ezek. 6:6, 7, 14;
Mic. 7:13;
Zech. 7:14
[b]Ps. 107:34

12:22 [a]Jer. 5:12;
Ezek. 11:3; 12:27;
Amos 6:3;
2 Pet. 3:4

12:23 [a]Ps. 37:13;
Joel 2:1;
Zeph. 1:14

12:24
[a]Jer. 14:13–16;
Ezek. 13:6;
Zech. 13:2–4
[b]Lam. 2:14

12:25
[a][Is. 55:11];
Dan. 9:12;
[Luke 21:33]
[b]Num. 23:19;
[Is. 14:24]

12:27
[a]Ezek. 12:22
[b]Dan. 10:14

12:28
[a]Ezek. 12:23, 25
[b]Jer. 4:7

13:2 [a]Is. 28:7;
Jer. 23:1–40;
Lam. 2:14;
Ezek. 22:25–28
[b]Ezek. 13:17
[c]Jer. 14:14;
23:16, 26

13:4 [a]Song 2:15

13:5 [a]Ps. 106:23;
[Jer. 23:22];
Ezek. 22:30

13:6 [a]Jer. 29:8;
Ezek. 22:28

12:18 [1]*shaking*   12:23 [1]Lit. *word*   12:24 [1]Lit. *vain*   13:2 [1]*Inspiration*
13:3 [1]*No vision*   13:5 [1]*breaches*

futility and false divination, saying, 'Thus says the LORD!' But the LORD has [b]not sent them; yet they hope that the word may [1]be confirmed. [7]Have you not seen a futile vision, and have you not spoken false divination? You say, 'The LORD says,' but I have not spoken."

[8]Therefore thus says the Lord GOD: "Because you have spoken nonsense and envisioned lies, therefore I *am* indeed against you," says the Lord GOD. [9]"My hand will be [a]against the prophets who envision futility and who [b]divine lies; they shall not be in the assembly of My people, [c]nor be written in the record of the house of Israel, [d]nor shall they enter into the land of Israel. [e]Then you shall know that I *am* the Lord GOD.

[10]"Because, indeed, because they have seduced My people, saying, [a]'Peace!' when *there is* no peace—and one builds a wall, and they [b]plaster[1] it with untempered *mortar*— [11]say to those who plaster *it* with untempered *mortar,* that it will fall. [a]There will be flooding rain, and you, O great hailstones, shall fall; and a stormy wind shall tear *it* down. [12]Surely, when the wall has fallen, will it not be said to you, 'Where *is* the mortar with which you plastered *it?'"

[13]Therefore thus says the Lord GOD: "I will cause a stormy wind to break forth in My fury; and there shall be a flooding rain in My anger, and great hailstones in fury to consume *it.* [14]So I will break down the wall you have plastered with untempered *mortar,* and bring it down to the ground, so that its foundation will be uncovered; it will fall, and you shall be consumed in the midst of it. [a]Then you shall know that I *am* the LORD.

[15]"Thus will I accomplish My wrath on the wall and on those who have plastered it with untempered *mortar;* and I will say to you, 'The wall *is* no *more,* nor those who plastered it, [16]*that is,* the prophets of Israel who prophesy concerning Jerusalem, and who [a]see visions of peace for her when *there is* no peace,'" says the Lord GOD.

[17]"Likewise, son of man, [a]set your face against the daughters of your people, [b]who prophesy out of their own [1]heart; prophesy against them, [18]and say, 'Thus says the Lord GOD: "Woe to the *women* who sew *magic* charms [1]on their sleeves and make veils for the heads of people of every height to hunt souls! Will you [a]hunt the souls of My people, and keep yourselves alive? [19]And will you profane Me among My people [a]for handfuls of barley and for pieces of bread, killing people who should not die, and keeping people alive who should not live, by your lying to My people who listen to lies?"

[20]'Therefore thus says the Lord GOD: "Behold, I *am* against your *magic* charms by which you hunt souls there like [1]birds. I will tear them from your arms, and let the souls go, the souls you hunt like birds. [21]I will also tear off your veils and deliver My people out of your hand, and they shall no longer be as prey in your hand. [a]Then you shall know that I *am* the LORD.

[22]"Because with [a]lies you have made the heart of the righteous sad, whom I have not made sad; and you have

---

13:6
[b]Jer. 27:8–15

13:9 [a]Jer. 23:30
[b]Jer. 20:3–6
[c]Ezra 2:59, 62;
Neh. 7:5;
[Ps. 69:28]
[d]Jer. 20:3–6
[e]Ezek. 11:10, 12

13:10
[a]Jer. 6:14; 8:11
[b]Ezek. 22:28

13:11
[a]Ezek. 38:22

13:14
[a]Ezek. 13:9, 21,
23; 14:8

13:16 [a]Jer. 6:14;
8:11; 28:9;
Ezek. 13:10

13:17
[a]Ezek. 20:46;
21:2 [b]Ezek. 13:2;
Rev. 2:20

13:18
[a][2 Pet. 2:14]

13:19
[a]1 Sam. 2:15–17;
Prov. 28:21;
Mic. 3:5;
Rom. 16:18;
1 Pet. 5:2

13:21 [a]Ezek. 13:9

13:22 [a]Jer. 28:15

13:6 [1]Come true　13:10 [1]Or *whitewash*　13:17 [1]Inspiration　13:18 [1]Lit. *over all the joints of My hands;* Vg. *under every elbow;* LXX, Tg. *on all elbows of the hands*　13:20 [1]Lit. *flying ones*

13:22 ^bJer. 23:14
13:23
^aEzek. 12:24;
13:6; Mic. 3:5, 6;
Zech. 13:3
14:1 ^a2 Kin. 6:32;
Ezek. 8:1; 20:1;
33:31
14:3 ^aEzek. 7:19;
Zeph. 1:3
^b2 Kin. 3:13;
Is. 1:15; Jer. 11:11;
Ezek. 20:3, 31
14:6 ^a1 Sam. 7:3;
Neh. 1:9;
Is. 2:20;
30:22; 55:6, 7;
Ezek. 18:30
14:8 ^aLev. 17:10;
20:3, 5, 6;
Jer. 44:11;
Ezek. 15:7
^bNum. 26:10;
Deut. 28:37;
Ezek. 5:15
^cEzek. 6:7; 13:14
14:9
^a1 Kin. 22:23;
Job 12:16;
Is. 66:4;
Jer. 4:10;
2 Thess. 2:11
14:11
^aPs. 119:67, 71;
Jer. 31:18, 19;
[Heb. 12:11];
2 Pet. 2:15
^bEzek. 11:20;
37:27
14:13
^aLev. 26:26;
2 Kin. 25:3;
Is. 3:1; Jer. 52:6;
Ezek. 4:16; 5:16
14:14 ^aJer. 15:1
^b[Prov. 11:4]
14:15
^aLev. 26:22;
Num. 21:6;
Ezek. 5:17; 14:21
14:16
^aEzek. 14:14,
18, 20
^bEzek. 15:8;
33:28, 29

^bstrengthened the hands of the wicked, so that he does not turn from his wicked way to save his life. ²³Therefore ^ayou shall no longer envision futility nor practice divination; for I will deliver My people out of your hand, and you shall know that I *am* the LORD."'"

IDOLATRY WILL BE PUNISHED

14 Now ^asome of the elders of Israel came to me and sat before me. ²And the word of the LORD came to me, saying, ³"Son of man, these men have set up their idols in their hearts, and put before them ^athat which causes them to stumble into iniquity. ^bShould I let Myself be inquired of at all by them?

⁴"Therefore speak to them, and say to them, 'Thus says the Lord GOD: "Everyone of the house of Israel who sets up his idols in his heart, and puts before him what causes him to stumble into iniquity, and then comes to the prophet, I the LORD will answer him who comes, according to the multitude of his idols, ⁵that I may seize the house of Israel by their heart, because they are all estranged from Me by their idols."'

⁶"Therefore say to the house of Israel, 'Thus says the Lord GOD: "Repent, turn away from your idols, and ^aturn your faces away from all your abominations. ⁷For anyone of the house of Israel, or of the strangers who dwell in Israel, who separates himself from Me and sets up his idols in his heart and puts before him what causes him to stumble into iniquity, then comes to a prophet to inquire of him concerning Me, I the LORD will answer him by Myself. ^{8a}I will set My face against that man and make him a ^bsign and a proverb, and I will cut him off from the midst of My people. ^cThen you shall know that I *am* the LORD.

⁹"And if the prophet is induced to speak anything, I the LORD ^ahave induced that prophet, and I will stretch out My hand against him and destroy him from among My people Israel. ¹⁰And they shall bear their iniquity; the punishment of the prophet shall be the same as the punishment of the one who inquired, ¹¹that the house of Israel may ^ano longer stray from Me, nor be profaned anymore with all their transgressions, ^bbut that they may be My people and I may be their God," says the Lord GOD.'"

JUDGMENT ON PERSISTENT UNFAITHFULNESS

¹²The word of the LORD came again to me, saying: ¹³"Son of man, when a land sins against Me by persistent unfaithfulness, I will stretch out My hand against it; I will cut off its ^asupply of bread, send famine on it, and cut off man and beast from it. ^{14a}Even *if* these three men, Noah, Daniel, and Job, were in it, they would deliver *only* themselves ^bby their righteousness," says the Lord GOD.

¹⁵"If I cause ^awild beasts to pass through the land, and they ¹empty it, and make it so desolate that no man may pass through because of the beasts, ¹⁶*even* ^a*though* these three men *were* ¹in it, *as* I live," says the Lord GOD, "they would deliver neither sons nor daughters; only they would be delivered, and the land would be ^bdesolate.

14:15 ¹Lit. *bereave it* of children   14:16 ¹Lit. *in the midst of it*

¹⁷"Or *if* ᵃI bring a sword on that land, and say, 'Sword, go through the land,' and I ᵇcut off man and beast from it, ¹⁸even ᵃ*though* these three men *were* in it, *as* I live," says the Lord GOD, "they would deliver neither sons nor daughters, but only they themselves would be delivered.

¹⁹"Or *if* I send ᵃa pestilence into that land and ᵇpour out My fury on it in blood, and cut off from it man and beast, ²⁰even ᵃ*though* Noah, Daniel, and Job *were* in it, *as* I live," says the Lord GOD, "they would deliver neither son nor daughter; they would deliver *only* themselves by their righteousness."

²¹For thus says the Lord GOD: "How much more it shall be when ᵃI send My four ¹severe judgments on Jerusalem—the sword and famine and wild beasts and pestilence—to cut off man and beast from it? ²²ᵃYet behold, there shall be left in it a remnant who will be ᵇbrought out, *both* sons and daughters; surely they will come out to you, and ᶜyou will see their ways and their doings. Then you will be comforted concerning the disaster that I have brought upon Jerusalem, all that I have brought upon it. ²³And they will comfort you, when you see their ways and their doings; and you shall know that I have done nothing ᵃwithout cause that I have done in it," says the Lord GOD.

THE OUTCAST VINE

15 Then the word of the LORD came to me, saying: ²"Son of man, how is the wood of the vine *better* than any other wood, the vine branch which is among the trees of the forest? ³Is wood taken from it to make any object? Or can *men* make a peg from it to hang any vessel on? ⁴Instead, ᵃit is thrown into the fire for fuel; the fire devours both ends of it, and its middle is burned. Is it useful for *any* work? ⁵Indeed, when it was whole, no object could be made from it. How much less will it be useful for *any* work when the fire has devoured it, and it is burned?

⁶"Therefore thus says the Lord GOD: 'Like the wood of the vine among the trees of the forest, which I have given to the fire for fuel, so I will give up the inhabitants of Jerusalem; ⁷and ᵃI will set My face against them. ᵇThey will go out from *one* fire, but *another* fire shall devour them. ᶜThen you shall know that I *am* the LORD, when I set My face against them. ⁸Thus I will make the land desolate, because they have persisted in unfaithfulness,' says the Lord GOD."

GOD'S LOVE FOR JERUSALEM

16 Again the word of the LORD came to me, saying, ²"Son of man, ᵃcause Jerusalem to know her abominations, ³and say, 'Thus says the Lord GOD to Jerusalem: "Your ¹birth ᵃand your nativity *are* from the land of Canaan; ᵇyour father *was* an Amorite and your mother a Hittite. ⁴*As for* your nativity, ᵃon the day you were born your navel cord was not cut, nor were you washed in water to cleanse *you;* you were not rubbed with salt nor wrapped in swaddling cloths. ⁵No eye pitied you, to do any of these things for you, to have compassion on you; but you were thrown out into the open field, when you yourself were ¹loathed on the day you were born.

14:17
ᵃLev. 26:25;
Ezek. 5:12;
21:3, 4;
29:8; 38:21
ᵇEzek. 25:13;
Zeph. 1:3

14:18
ᵃEzek. 14:14

14:19
ᵃ2 Sam. 24:15;
Ezek. 38:22
ᵇEzek. 7:8

14:20
ᵃEzek. 14:14

14:21 ᵃEzek. 5:17;
33:27;
Amos 4:6–10;
Rev. 6:8

14:22
ᵃ2 Kin. 25:11, 12;
Ezra 2:1;
Ezek. 12:16;
36:20 ᵇEzek. 6:8
ᶜEzek. 20:43

14:23
ᵃJer. 22:8, 9

15:4 ᵃ[John 15:6]

15:7 ᵃLev. 26:17;
[Ps. 34:16];
Jer. 21:10;
Ezek. 14:8
ᵇIs. 24:18
ᶜEzek. 7:4

16:2 ᵃIs. 58:1;
Ezek. 20:4; 22:2

16:3
ᵃEzek. 21:30
ᵇGen. 15:16;
Deut. 7:1;
Josh. 24:15;
Ezek. 16:45

16:4 ᵃHos. 2:3

14:21 ¹Lit. *evil*   16:3 ¹*origin and your birth*   16:5 ¹*abhorred*

6"And when I passed by you and saw you struggling in your own blood, I said to you in your blood, 'Live!' Yes, I said to you in your blood, 'Live!' 7aI made you ¹thrive like a plant in the field; and you grew, matured, and became very beautiful. *Your* breasts were formed, your hair grew, but you *were* naked and bare.

8"When I passed by you again and looked upon you, indeed your time *was* the time of love; ªso I spread ¹My wing over you and covered your nakedness. Yes, I ᵇswore an oath to you and entered into a ᶜcovenant with you, and ᵈyou became Mine," says the Lord GOD.

9"Then I washed you in water; yes, I thoroughly washed off your blood, and I anointed you with oil. ¹⁰I clothed you in embroidered cloth and gave you sandals of ¹badger skin; I clothed you with fine linen and covered you with silk. ¹¹I adorned you with ornaments, ªput bracelets on your wrists, ᵇand a chain on your neck. ¹²And I put a ¹jewel in your nose, earrings in your ears, and a beautiful crown on your head. ¹³Thus you were adorned with gold and silver, and your clothing *was* of fine linen, silk, and embroidered cloth. ªYou ate *pastry of* fine flour, honey, and oil. You were exceedingly ᵇbeautiful, and succeeded to royalty. ¹⁴ªYour fame went out among the nations because of your beauty, for it *was* perfect through My splendor which I had bestowed on you," says the Lord GOD.

JERUSALEM'S HARLOTRY

15ª"But you trusted in your own beauty, ᵇplayed the harlot because of your fame, and poured out your harlotry on everyone passing by who *would have* it. ¹⁶ªYou took some of your garments and adorned multicolored ¹high places for yourself, and played the harlot on them. *Such* things should not happen, nor be. ¹⁷You have also taken your beautiful jewelry from My gold and My silver, which I had given you, and made for yourself male images and played the harlot with them. ¹⁸You took your embroidered garments and covered them, and you set My oil and My incense before them. ¹⁹Also ªMy food which I gave you—the pastry of fine flour, oil, and honey *which* I fed you—you set it before them as ¹sweet incense; and *so* it was," says the Lord GOD.

20ª"Moreover you took your sons and your daughters, whom you bore to Me, and these you sacrificed to them to be devoured. *Were* your *acts* of harlotry a small matter, ²¹that you have slain My children and offered them up to them by causing them to pass through the ªfire? ²²And in all your abominations and acts of harlotry you did not remember the days of your ªyouth, ᵇwhen you were naked and bare, struggling in your blood.

23"Then it was so, after all your wickedness—'Woe, woe to you!' says the Lord GOD— ²⁴that ªyou also built for yourself a shrine, and ᵇmade a ¹high place for yourself in every street. ²⁵You built your high places ªat the head of every road, and made your beauty to be abhorred. You offered yourself to everyone who passed by, and multiplied your acts of harlotry.

16:7 ªEx. 1:7;
Deut. 1:10

16:8 ªRuth 3:9;
Jer. 2:2
ᵇGen. 22:16–18
ᶜEx. 24:6–8
ᵈ[Ex. 19:5];
Jer. 2:2;
Ezek. 20:5;
[Hos. 2:19, 20]

16:11
ªGen. 24:22, 47;
Is. 3:19;
Ezek. 23:42
ᵇGen. 41:42;
Prov. 1:9

16:13
ªDeut. 32:13, 14
ᵇPs. 48:2

16:14 ªPs. 50:2;
Lam. 2:15

16:15
ªDeut. 32:15;
Jer. 7:4; Mic. 3:11
ᵇIs. 1:21; 57:8;
Jer. 2:20; 3:2,
6, 20;
Ezek. 23:11–20;
Hos. 1:2

16:16
ª2 Kin. 23:7;
Ezek. 7:20;
Hos. 2:8

16:19 ªHos. 2:8

16:20
ª2 Kin. 16:3;
Ps. 106:37;
Is. 57:5; Jer. 7:31;
Ezek. 20:26

16:21
ª2 Kin. 17:17;
Jer. 19:5;
Ezek. 20:31;
23:37

16:22 ªJer. 2:2;
Hos. 11:1
ᵇEzek. 16:4–6

16:24 ªJer. 11:13;
Ezek. 16:31, 39;
20:28, 29
ᵇPs. 78:58;
Is. 57:7;
Jer. 2:20; 3:2

16:25 ªProv. 9:14

16:7 ¹Lit. *a myriad*   16:8 ¹Or *the corner of My garment*   16:10 ¹Or *dolphin or dugong*   16:12 ¹Lit. *ring*   16:16 ¹Places for pagan worship   16:19 ¹Or *a sweet aroma*   16:24 ¹Place for pagan worship

26You also committed harlotry with ᵃthe Egyptians, your very fleshly neighbors, and increased your acts of harlotry to ᵇprovoke Me to anger.

27"Behold, therefore, I stretched out My hand against you, diminished your ¹allotment, and gave you up to the will of those who hate you, ᵃthe daughters of the Philistines, who were ashamed of your lewd behavior. 28You also played the harlot with the ᵃAssyrians, because you were insatiable; indeed you played the harlot with them and still were not satisfied. 29Moreover you multiplied your acts of harlotry as far as the land of the trader, ᵃChaldea; and even then you were not satisfied.

30"How degenerate is your heart!" says the Lord GOD, "seeing you do all these *things,* the deeds of a brazen harlot.

JERUSALEM'S ADULTERY

31ᵃ"You erected your shrine at the head of every road, and built your ¹high place in every street. Yet you were not like a harlot, because you scorned ᵇpayment. 32*You are* an adulterous wife, *who* takes strangers instead of her husband. 33Men make payment to all harlots, but ᵃyou made your payments to all your lovers, and ¹hired them to come to you from all around for your harlotry. 34You are the opposite of *other* women in your harlotry, because no one solicited you to be a harlot. In that you gave payment but no payment was given you, therefore you are the opposite."

JERUSALEM'S LOVERS WILL ABUSE HER

35'Now then, O harlot, hear the word of the LORD! 36Thus says the Lord GOD: "Because your filthiness was poured out and your nakedness uncovered in your harlotry with your lovers, and with all your abominable idols, and because of ᵃthe blood of your children which you gave to them, 37surely, therefore, ᵃI will gather all your lovers with whom you took pleasure, all those you loved, *and* all those you hated; I will gather them from all around against you and will uncover your nakedness to them, that they may see all your nakedness. 38And I will judge you as ᵃwomen who break wedlock or ᵇshed blood are judged; I will bring blood upon you in fury and jealousy. 39I will also give you into their hand, and they shall throw down your shrines and break down ᵃyour ¹high places. ᵇThey shall also strip you of your clothes, take your beautiful jewelry, and leave you naked and bare.

40ᵃ"They shall also bring up an assembly against you, ᵇand they shall stone you with stones and thrust you through with their swords. 41They shall ᵃburn your houses with fire, and ᵇexecute judgments on you in the sight of many women; and I will make you ᶜcease playing the harlot, and you shall no longer hire lovers. 42So ᵃI will lay to rest My fury toward you, and My jealousy shall depart from you. I will be quiet, and be angry no more. 43Because ᵃyou did not remember the days of your youth, but ¹agitated Me with all these *things,* surely ᵇI will also recompense your ²deeds on *your own* head," says the Lord GOD. "And you shall not commit lewdness in addition to all your abominations.

16:26
ᵃEzek. 16:26;
20:7, 8
ᵇDeut. 31:20

16:27
ᵃ2 Chr. 28:18;
Is. 9:12;
Ezek. 16:57

16:28
ᵃ2 Kin. 16:7,
10–18;
2 Chr. 28:16,
20–23;
Jer. 2:18, 36;
Ezek. 23:12;
Hos. 10:6

16:29
ᵃEzek. 23:14–17

16:31
ᵃEzek. 16:24, 39
ᵇIs. 52:3

16:33
ᵃIs. 30:6; 57:9;
Ezek. 16:41;
Hos. 8:9, 10

16:36 ᵃJer. 2:34;
Ezek. 16:20

16:37
ᵃJer. 13:22, 26;
Lam. 1:8;
Ezek. 23:9,
10, 22, 29;
Hos. 2:10; 8:10;
Nah. 3:5

16:38
ᵃLev. 20:10;
Deut. 22:22;
Ezek. 23:45
ᵇGen. 9:6;
Ex. 21:12;
Ezek. 16:20, 36

16:39
ᵃEzek. 16:24, 31
ᵇEzek. 23:26;
Hos. 2:3

16:40
ᵃEzek. 23:45–47;
Hab. 1:6–10
ᵇJohn 8:5, 7

16:41
ᵃDeut. 13:16;
2 Kin. 25:9;
Jer. 39:8; 52:13
ᵇEzek. 5:8;
23:10, 48
ᶜEzek. 23:27

16:42
ᵃ2 Sam. 24:25;
Ezek. 5:13; 21:17;
Zech. 6:8

16:43 ᵃPs. 78:42;
Ezek. 16:22
ᵇEzek. 9:10;
11:21; 22:31

16:27 ¹Allowance of food　16:31 ¹Place for pagan worship　16:33 ¹Or *bribed*　16:39 ¹Places for pagan worship　16:43 ¹So with LXX, Syr., Tg., Vg.; MT *were agitated with Me*　²Lit. *way*

MORE WICKED THAN SAMARIA AND SODOM

44"Indeed everyone who quotes proverbs will use *this* proverb against you: 'Like mother, like daughter!' 45You *are* your mother's daughter, ¹loathing husband and children; and you *are* the ªsister of your sisters, who loathed their husbands and children; ᵇyour mother *was* a Hittite and your father an Amorite.

46"Your elder sister *is* Samaria, who dwells with her daughters to the north of you; and ªyour younger sister, who dwells to the south of you, *is* Sodom and her daughters. 47You did not walk in their ways nor act according to their abominations; but, as *if that were* too little, ªyou became more corrupt than they in all your ways.

48"As I live," says the Lord GOD, "neither ªyour sister Sodom nor her daughters have done as you and your daughters have done. 49Look, this was the iniquity of your sister Sodom: She and her daughter had pride, ªfullness of food, and abundance of idleness; neither did she strengthen the hand of the poor and needy. 50And they were haughty and ªcommitted abomination before Me; therefore ᵇI took them away as ¹I saw *fit.*

51"Samaria did not commit ªhalf of your sins; but you have multiplied your abominations more than they, and ᵇhave justified your sisters by all the abominations which you have done. 52You who judged your sisters, bear your own shame also, because the sins which you committed were more abominable than theirs; they are more righteous than you. Yes, be disgraced also, and bear your own shame, because you justified your sisters.

53ª"When I bring back their captives, the captives of Sodom and her daughters, and the captives of Samaria and her daughters, then *I will also bring back* ᵇthe captives of your captivity among them, 54that you may bear your own shame and be disgraced by all that you did when ªyou comforted them. 55When your sisters, Sodom and her daughters, return to their former state, and Samaria and her daughters return to their former state, then you and your daughters will return to your former state. 56For your sister Sodom was not a byword in your mouth in the days of your pride, 57before your wickedness was uncovered. It was like the time of the ªreproach of the daughters of ¹Syria and all *those* around her, and of ᵇthe daughters of the Philistines, who despise you everywhere. 58ªYou have paid for your lewdness and your abominations," says the LORD. 59For thus says the Lord GOD: "I will deal with you as you have done, who ªdespised ᵇthe oath by breaking the covenant.

AN EVERLASTING COVENANT

60"Nevertheless I will ªremember My covenant with you in the days of your youth, and I will establish ᵇan everlasting covenant with you. 61Then ªyou will remember your ways and be ashamed, when you receive your older and your younger sisters; for I will give them to you for ᵇdaughters, ᶜbut not because of My covenant with you. 62ªAnd I will establish My

---

16:45
ªEzek. 23:2–4
ᵇEzek. 16:3

16:46
ªDeut. 32:32;
Is. 1:10

16:47
ª2 Kin. 21:9;
Ezek. 5:6, 7

16:48 ªIs. 3:9;
Lam. 4:6;
Matt. 10:15;
11:24; Rev. 11:8

16:49
ªGen. 13:10;
Is. 22:13;
Amos 6:4–6

16:50
ªGen. 13:13;
18:20; 19:5
ᵇGen. 19:24

16:51
ªEzek. 23:11
ᵇJer. 3:8–11;
Matt. 12:41

16:53 ªIs. 1:9;
[Ezek. 16:60]
ᵇJer. 20:16

16:54
ªEzek. 14:22

16:57
ª2 Kin. 16:5;
2 Chr. 28:18;
Is. 7:1;
Ezek. 5:14, 15;
22:4
ᵇEzek. 16:27

16:58
ªEzek. 23:49

16:59
ªEzek. 17:13
ᵇDeut. 29:12

16:60
ªLev. 26:42–45;
Ps. 106:45
ᵇIs. 55:3;
Jer. 32:40; 50:5;
Ezek. 37:26

16:61
ªJer. 50:4, 5;
Ezek. 20:43;
36:31 ᵇIs. 54:1;
60:4; [Gal. 4:26]
ᶜJer. 31:31

16:62
ªHos. 2:19, 20

16:45 ¹Or *despising* 16:50 ¹Vg. *you saw*; LXX *he saw*; Tg. *as was revealed to Me* 16:57 ¹Heb. *Aram*; so with MT, LXX, Tg., Vg.; many Heb. mss., Syr. *Edom*

covenant with you. Then you shall know that I *am* the LORD, [63]that you may [a]remember and be ashamed, [b]and never open your mouth anymore because of your shame, when I provide you an atonement for all you have done," says the Lord GOD.'"

THE EAGLES AND THE VINE

17 And the word of the LORD came to me, saying, [2]"Son of man, pose a riddle, and speak a [a]parable to the house of Israel, [3]and say, 'Thus says the Lord GOD:

[a]"A great eagle with large wings and long pinions,
Full of feathers of various colors,
Came to Lebanon
And [b]took from the cedar the highest branch.
[4] He cropped off its topmost young twig
And carried it to a land of trade;
He set it in a city of merchants.
[5] Then he took some of the seed of the land
And planted it in [a]a fertile field;
He placed *it* by abundant waters
And set it [b]like a willow tree.
[6] And it grew and became a spreading vine [a]of low stature;
Its branches turned toward him,
But its roots were under it.
So it became a vine,
Brought forth branches,
And put forth shoots.
[7] "But there was [1]another great eagle with large wings and many feathers;
And behold, [a]this vine bent its roots toward him,
And stretched its branches toward him,
From the garden terrace where it had been planted,
That he might water it.
[8] It was planted in [1]good soil by many waters,
To bring forth branches, bear fruit,
And become a majestic vine.'"

[9]"Say, 'Thus says the Lord GOD:

"Will it thrive?
[a]Will he not pull up its roots,
Cut off its fruit,
And leave it to wither?
All of its spring leaves will wither,
And no great power or many people
Will be needed to pluck it up by its roots.
[10] Behold, *it is* planted,
Will it thrive?
[a]Will it not utterly wither when the east wind touches it?
It will wither in the garden terrace where it grew."'"

[11]Moreover the word of the LORD came to me, saying, [12]"Say now to [a]the rebellious house: 'Do you not know what these *things mean?*' Tell *them,* 'Indeed [b]the king of Babylon went to Jerusalem and took its king and princes, and led them with him to Babylon. [13a]And he took the king's offspring, made a covenant with him, [b]and put him under oath. He also

---

16:63
[a]Ezek. 36:31, 32;
Dan. 9:7, 8
[b]Ps. 39:9;
[Rom. 3:19]

17:2
[a]Ezek. 20:49;
24:3

17:3 [a]Jer. 48:40;
Ezek. 17:12;
Hos. 8:1
[b]2 Kin. 24:12

17:5
[a]Deut. 8:7–9
[b]Is. 44:4

17:6 [a]Ezek. 17:14

17:7 [a]Ezek. 17:15

17:9 [a]2 Kin. 25:7

17:10
[a]Ezek. 19:12;
Hos. 13:15

17:12
[a]Ezek. 2:3–5;
12:9
[b]2 Kin. 24:11–16;
Ezek. 1:2; 17:3

17:13
[a]2 Kin. 24:17;
Jer. 37:1;
Ezek. 17:5
[b]2 Chr. 36:13

17:7 [1]So with LXX, Syr., Vg.; MT, Tg. *one*   17:8 [1]Lit. *a good field*

took away the mighty of the land, [14]that the kingdom might be [a]brought low and not lift itself up, *but* that by keeping his covenant it might stand. [15]But [a]he rebelled against him by sending his ambassadors to Egypt, [b]that they might give him horses and many people. [c]Will he prosper? Will he who does such *things* escape? Can he break a covenant and still be delivered?

[16]'As I live,' says the Lord GOD, 'surely [a]in the place *where* the king *dwells* who made him king, whose oath he despised and whose covenant he broke—with him in the midst of Babylon he shall die. [17a]Nor will Pharaoh with *his* mighty army and great company do anything in the war, [b]when they heap up a siege mound and build a [1]wall to cut off many persons. [18]Since he despised the oath by breaking the covenant, and in fact [a]gave[1] his hand and still did all these *things,* he shall not escape.'"

[19]Therefore thus says the Lord GOD: "As I live, surely My oath which he despised, and My covenant which he broke, I will recompense on his own head. [20]I will [a]spread My net over him, and he shall be taken in My snare. I will bring him to Babylon and [b]try him there for the [1]treason which he committed against Me. [21a]All his [1]fugitives with all his troops shall fall by the sword, and those who remain shall be [b]scattered to every wind; and you shall know that I, the LORD, have spoken."

ISRAEL EXALTED AT LAST
(cf. Ezek. 31:1–9)

[22]Thus says the Lord GOD: "I will take also *one* of the highest [a]branches of the high cedar and set *it* out. I will crop off from the topmost of its young twigs [b]a tender one, and will [c]plant *it* on a high and prominent mountain. [23a]On the mountain height of Israel I will plant it; and it will bring forth boughs, and bear fruit, and be a majestic cedar. [b]Under it will dwell birds of every sort; in the shadow of its branches they will dwell. [24]And all the trees of the field shall know that I, the LORD, [a]have brought down the high tree and exalted the low tree, dried up the green tree and made the dry tree flourish; [b]I, the LORD, have spoken and have done *it.*"

A FALSE PROVERB REFUTED

18 The word of the LORD came to me again, saying, [2]"What do you mean when you use this proverb concerning the land of Israel, saying:

'The [a]fathers have eaten sour grapes,
And the children's teeth are set on edge'?

[3]"As I live," says the Lord GOD, "you shall no longer use this proverb in Israel.

4 "Behold, all souls are [a]Mine;
The soul of the father
As well as the soul of the son is Mine;
[b]The soul who sins shall die.
5 But if a man is just
And does what is lawful and right;

17:14 [a]Ezek. 29:14

17:15 [a]2 Kin. 24:20; 2 Chr. 36:13; Jer. 52:3; Ezek. 17:7 [b]Deut. 17:16; Is. 31:1, 3; 36:6, 9 [c]Ezek. 17:9

17:16 [a]Jer. 52:11; Ezek. 12:13

17:17 [a]Jer. 37:7; Ezek. 29:6 [b]Jer. 52:4; Ezek. 4:2

17:18 [a]1 Chr. 29:24; Lam. 5:6

17:20 [a]Ezek. 12:13 [b]Jer. 2:35; Ezek. 20:36

17:21 [a]Ezek. 12:14 [b]Ezek. 12:15; 22:15

17:22 [a][Is. 11:1; Jer. 23:5; Zech. 3:8] [b]Is. 53:2 [c][Ps. 2:6]

17:23 [a][Is. 2:2, 3]; Ezek. 20:40; [Mic. 4:1] [b]Ezek. 31:6; Dan. 4:12

17:24 [a]Ezek. 37:3; Amos 9:11; Luke 1:52; [Rom. 11:23, 24] [b]Ezek. 22:14

18:2 [a]Jer. 31:29; Lam. 5:7

18:4 [a]Num. 16:22; 27:16; Is. 42:5; 57:16 [b]Ezek. 18:20; [Rom. 6:23]

17:17 [1]Or *siege wall*   **17:18** [1]Took an oath   **17:20** [1]Lit. *unfaithful act*
17:21 [1]So with MT, Vg.; many Heb. mss., Syr. *choice men;* Tg. *mighty men;* LXX omits *All his fugitives*

6 ᵃIf he has not eaten ¹on the mountains,
  Nor lifted up his eyes to the idols of the house of Israel,
  Nor ᵇdefiled his neighbor's wife,
  Nor approached ᶜa woman during her impurity;
7 If he has not ᵃoppressed anyone,
  But has restored to the debtor his ᵇpledge;
  Has robbed no one by violence,
  But has ᶜgiven his bread to the hungry
  And covered the naked with ᵈclothing;
8 If he has not ¹exacted ᵃusury
  Nor taken any increase,
  But has withdrawn his hand from iniquity
  And ᵇexecuted true ²judgment between man and man;
9 *If* he has walked in My statutes
  And kept My judgments faithfully—
  He *is* just;
  He shall surely ᵃlive!"
  Says the Lord GOD.

10 "If he begets a son *who is* a robber
   Or ᵃa shedder of blood,
   Who does any of these *things*
11 And does none of those *duties*,
   But has eaten ¹on the mountains
   Or defiled his neighbor's wife;
12 If he has oppressed the poor and needy,
   Robbed by violence,
   Not restored the pledge,
   Lifted his eyes to the idols,
   Or ᵃcommitted abomination;
13 If he has exacted usury
   Or taken increase—
   Shall he then live?
   He shall not live!
   If he has done any of these abominations,
   He shall surely die;
   ᵃHis blood shall be upon him.

14 "If, however, he begets a son
   Who sees all the sins which his father has done,
   And considers but does not do likewise;
15 ᵃWho has not eaten ¹on the mountains,
   Nor lifted his eyes to the idols of the house of Israel,
   Nor defiled his neighbor's wife;
16 Has not oppressed anyone,
   Nor withheld a pledge,
   Nor robbed by violence,
   But has given his bread to the hungry
   And covered the naked with clothing;
17 Who has withdrawn his hand from ¹the poor
   And not received usury or increase,
   But has executed My judgments
   And walked in My statutes—
   He shall not die for the iniquity of his father;
   He shall surely live!

18:6 ᵃEzek. 22:9
ᵇLev. 18:20;
20:10 ᶜLev. 18:19;
20:18

18:7 ᵃEx. 22:21;
Lev. 19:15; 25:14
ᵇEx. 22:26;
Deut. 24:12
ᶜDeut. 15:7, 11;
Ezek. 18:16;
[Matt. 25:35–
40]; Luke 3:11
ᵈIs. 58:7

18:8 ᵃEx. 22:25;
Lev. 25:36;
Deut. 23:19;
Neh. 5:7; Ps. 15:5
ᵇDeut. 1:16;
Zech. 8:16

18:9
ᵃEzek. 20:11;
Amos 5:4;
[Hab. 2:4;
Rom. 1:17]

18:10 ᵃGen. 9:6;
Ex. 21:12;
Num. 35:31

18:12
ᵃ2 Kin. 21:11;
Ezek. 8:6, 17

18:13 ᵃLev. 20:9,
11–13, 16, 27;
Ezek. 3:18;
Acts 18:6

18:15 ᵃEzek. 18:6

18:6 ¹At the mountain shrines   18:8 ¹Lent money at interest   ²*justice*
18:11 ¹At the mountain shrines   18:15 ¹At the mountain shrines
18:17 ¹So with MT, Tg., Vg.; LXX *iniquity* (cf. v. 8)

18:18 ªEzek. 3:18

18:19 ªEx. 20:5;
Deut. 5:9;
2 Kin. 23:26;
24:3, 4

18:20
ª2 Kin. 14:6;
22:18–20;
Ezek. 18:4
ᵇDeut. 24:16;
2 Kin. 14:6;
2 Chr. 25:4;
Jer. 31:29, 30
ᶜ1 Kin. 8:32;
Is. 3:10, 11;
[Matt. 16:27]
ᵈRom. 2:6–9

18:21
ªEzek. 18:27;
33:12, 19

18:22 ªIs. 43:25;
Jer. 50:20;
Ezek. 18:24;
33:16; Mic. 7:19
ᵇ[Ps. 18:20–24]

18:23
ªLam. 3:33;
[Ezek. 18:32;
33:11; 1 Tim. 2:4;
2 Pet. 3:9]

18:24
ª1 Sam. 15:11;
2 Chr. 24:2, 17–
22; Ezek. 3:20;
18:26; 33:18
ᵇ[2 Pet. 2:20]

18:25
ªEzek. 18:29;
33:17, 20;
Mal. 2:17;
3:13–15

18:26
ªEzek. 18:24

18:27
ªEzek. 18:21

18:28
ªEzek. 18:14

18:29
ªEzek. 18:25

18:30 ªEzek. 7:3;
33:20
ᵇMatt. 3:2;
Rev. 2:5

18:31
ªIs. 1:16; 55:7;
Eph. 4:22, 23
ᵇPs. 51:10;
Jer. 32:39;
Ezek. 11:19;
36:26

18:32
ªLam. 3:33;
Ezek. 33:11;
[2 Pet. 3:9]
ᵇ[Prov. 4:2, 5, 6]

19:1 ªEzek. 26:17;
27:2

19:3 ªEzek. 19:2;
2 Kin. 23:31, 32

18 "As for his father,
Because he cruelly oppressed,
Robbed his brother by violence,
And did what is not good among his people,
Behold, ªhe shall die for his iniquity.

TURN AND LIVE

19"Yet you say, 'Why ªshould the son not bear the guilt of the father?' Because the son has done what is lawful and right, and has kept all My statutes and observed them, he shall surely live. 20ªThe soul who sins shall die. ᵇThe son shall not bear the guilt of the father, nor the father bear the guilt of the son. ᶜThe righteousness of the righteous shall be upon himself, ᵈand the wickedness of the wicked shall be upon himself.

21"But ªif a wicked man turns from all his sins which he has committed, keeps all My statutes, and does what is lawful and right, he shall surely live; he shall not die. 22ªNone of the transgressions which he has committed shall be remembered against him; because of the righteousness which he has done, he shall ᵇlive. 23ªDo I have any pleasure at all that the wicked should die?" says the Lord GOD, "and not that he should turn from his ways and live?

24"But ªwhen a righteous man turns away from his righteousness and commits iniquity, and does according to all the abominations that the wicked man does, shall he live? ᵇAll the righteousness which he has done shall not be remembered; because of the unfaithfulness of which he is guilty and the sin which he has committed, because of them he shall die.

25"Yet you say, ª'The way of the Lord is not fair.' Hear now, O house of Israel, is it not My way which is fair, and your ways which are not fair? 26ªWhen a righteous man turns away from his righteousness, commits iniquity, and dies in it, it is because of the iniquity which he has done that he dies. 27Again, ªwhen a wicked man turns away from the wickedness which he committed, and does what is lawful and right, he preserves himself alive. 28Because he ªconsiders and turns away from all the transgressions which he committed, he shall surely live; he shall not die. 29ªYet the house of Israel says, 'The way of the Lord is not fair.' O house of Israel, is it not My ways which are fair, and your ways which are not fair?

30ª"Therefore I will judge you, O house of Israel, every one according to his ways," says the Lord GOD. ᵇ"Repent, and turn from all your transgressions, so that iniquity will not be your ruin. 31ªCast away from you all the transgressions which you have committed, and get yourselves a ᵇnew heart and a new spirit. For why should you die, O house of Israel? 32For ªI have no pleasure in the death of one who dies," says the Lord GOD. "Therefore turn and ᵇlive!"

ISRAEL DEGRADED

19 "Moreover ªtake up a lamentation for the princes of Israel, 2and say:

'What is your mother? A lioness:
She lay down among the lions;
Among the young lions she nourished her cubs.
3 She brought up one of her cubs,
And ªhe became a young lion;

He learned to catch prey,
And he devoured men.
4 The nations also heard of him;
He was trapped in their pit,
And they brought him with chains to the land of ᵃEgypt.

5 'When she saw that she waited, *that* her hope was lost,
She took ᵃanother of her cubs *and* made him a young
lion.
6 ᵃHe roved among the lions,
And ᵇbecame a young lion;
He learned to catch prey;
He devoured men.
7 ¹He knew their desolate places,
And laid waste their cities;
The land with its fullness was desolated
By the noise of his roaring.
8 ᵃThen the nations set against him from the provinces on
every side,
And spread their net over him;
ᵇHe was trapped in their pit.
9 ᵃThey put him in a cage with ¹chains,
And brought him to the king of Babylon;
They brought him in nets,
That his voice should no longer be heard on ᵇthe
mountains of Israel.

10 'Your mother *was* ᵃlike a vine in your ¹bloodline,
Planted by the waters,
ᵇFruitful and full of branches
Because of many waters.
11 She had strong branches for scepters of rulers.
ᵃShe towered in stature above the thick branches,
And was seen in her height amid the ¹dense foliage.
12 But she was ᵃplucked up in fury,
She was cast down to the ground,
And the ᵇeast wind dried her fruit.
Her strong branches were broken and withered;
The fire consumed them.
13 And now she *is* planted in the wilderness,
In a dry and thirsty land.
14 ᵃFire has come out from a rod of her branches
And devoured her fruit,
So that she has no strong branch—a scepter for ruling.'"

ᵇThis *is* a lamentation, and has become a lamentation.

THE REBELLIONS OF ISRAEL

20 It came to pass in the seventh year, in the fifth *month,* on the tenth *day* of the month, *that* ᵃcertain of the elders of Israel came to inquire of the LORD, and sat before me. ²Then the word of the LORD came to me, saying, ³"Son of man, speak to the elders of Israel, and say to them, 'Thus says the Lord GOD: "Have you come to inquire of Me? *As* I live," says the Lord GOD, ᵃ"I will not be inquired of by you."' ⁴Will

---

19:4
ᵃ2 Kin. 23:33, 34;
2 Chr. 36:4

19:5
ᵃ2 Kin. 23:34

19:6
ᵃ2 Kin. 24:8, 9
ᵇEzek. 19:3

19:8
ᵃ2 Kin. 24:2, 11
ᵇEzek. 19:4

19:9
ᵃ2 Chr. 36:6;
Jer. 22:18
ᵇEzek. 6:2

19:10 ᵃEzek. 17:6
ᵇDeut. 8:7–9

19:11 ᵃEzek. 31:3;
Dan. 4:11

19:12
ᵃJer. 31:27, 28
ᵇEzek. 17:10;
Hos. 13:5

19:14
ᵃJudg. 9:15;
2 Kin. 24:20;
Ezek. 17:18
ᵇLam. 2:5

20:1 ᵃEzek. 8:1,
11, 12; 14:1

20:3
ᵃEzek. 7:26; 14:3

19:7 ¹LXX *He stood in insolence;* Tg. *He destroyed its palaces;* Vg. *He learned to make widows* **19:9** ¹Or *hooks* **19:10** ¹Lit. *blood,* so with MT, Syr., Vg.; LXX *like a flower on a pomegranate tree;* Tg. *in your likeness* **19:11** ¹Or *many branches*

20:4
[a]Ezek. 16:2;
22:2; Matt. 23:32

20:5
[a]Ex. 6:6–8;
Deut. 7:6
[b]Ex. 3:8; 4:31;
Deut. 4:34
[c]Ex. 20:2

20:6 [a]Ex. 3:8, 17;
Deut. 8:7–9;
Jer. 32:22
[b]Ex. 3:8
[c]Ex. 3:8, 17; 13:5;
33:3; Ps. 48:2;
Jer. 11:5; 32:22;
Ezek. 20:15;
Dan. 8:9;
Zech. 7:14

20:7 [a]Ezek. 18:31
[b]2 Chr. 15:8
[c]Lev. 18:3;
Deut. 29:16;
Josh. 24:14

20:8 [a]Ezek. 7:8

20:9
[a]Num. 14:13
[b]Josh. 2:10;
9:9, 10

20:10 [a]Ex. 13:18

20:11 [a]Deut. 4:8;
Neh. 9:13;
Ps. 147:19
[b]Lev. 18:5;
Ezek. 20:13;
Rom. 10:5;
[Gal. 3:12]

20:12 [a]Ex. 20:8;
Deut. 5:12;
Neh. 9:14

20:13
[a]Num. 14:22;
Ps. 78:40;
Ezek. 20:8
[b]Prov. 1:25
[c]Lev. 18:5
[d]Ex. 16:27
[e]Num. 14:29;
Ps. 106:23

20:14
[a]Ezek. 20:9, 20

20:15
[a]Num. 14:28;
Ps. 95:11; 106:26
[b]Ex. 3:8
[c]Ezek. 20:6

20:16
[a]Ezek. 20:13, 24
[b]Num. 15:39;
Ps. 78:37;
Amos 5:25;
Acts 7:42

20:17
[a][Ps. 78:38]

20:19
[a]Deut. 5:32

20:20
[a]Is. 58:13, 14;
Jer. 17:22

you judge them, son of man, will you judge *them?* Then [a]make known to them the abominations of their fathers.

5 "Say to them, 'Thus says the Lord GOD: "On the day when [a]I chose Israel and raised My hand in an oath to the descendants of the house of Jacob, and made Myself [b]known to them in the land of Egypt, I raised My hand in an oath to them, saying, [c]'I *am* the LORD your God.' 6 On that day I raised My hand in an oath to them, [a]to bring them out of the land of Egypt into a land that I had searched out for them, [b]'flowing with milk and honey,' [c]the glory of all lands. 7 Then I said to them, 'Each of you, [a]throw away [b]the abominations which are before his eyes, and do not defile yourselves with [c]the idols of Egypt. I *am* the LORD your God.' 8 But they rebelled against Me and would not [1]obey Me. They did not all cast away the abominations which were before their eyes, nor did they forsake the idols of Egypt. Then I said, 'I will [a]pour out My fury on them and fulfill My anger against them in the midst of the land of Egypt.' 9 [a]But I acted for My name's sake, that it should not be profaned before the Gentiles among whom they *were,* in whose sight I had made Myself [b]known to them, to bring them out of the land of Egypt.

10 "Therefore I [a]made them go out of the land of Egypt and brought them into the wilderness. 11 And I gave them My statutes and [1]showed them My judgments, [b]'which, *if* a man does, he shall live by them.' 12 Moreover I also gave them My [a]Sabbaths, to be a sign between them and Me, that they might know that I *am* the LORD who sanctifies them. 13 Yet the house of Israel [a]rebelled against Me in the wilderness; they did not walk in My statutes; they [b]despised My judgments, [c]'which, *if* a man does, he shall live by them'; and they greatly [d]defiled My Sabbaths. Then I said I would pour out My fury on them in the [e]wilderness, to consume them. 14 [a]But I acted for My name's sake, that it should not be profaned before the Gentiles, in whose sight I had brought them out. 15 So [a]I also raised My hand in an oath to them in the wilderness, that I would not bring them into the land which I had given *them,* [b]'flowing with milk and honey,' [c]the glory of all lands, 16 [a]because they despised My judgments and did not walk in My statutes, but profaned My Sabbaths; for [b]their heart went after their idols. 17 [a]Nevertheless My eye spared them from destruction. I did not make an end of them in the wilderness.

18 "But I said to their children in the wilderness, 'Do not walk in the statutes of your fathers, nor observe their judgments, nor defile yourselves with their idols. 19 I *am* the LORD your God: [a]Walk in My statutes, keep My judgments, and do them; 20 [a]hallow My Sabbaths, and they will be a sign between Me and you, that you may know that I *am* the LORD your God.'

21 "Notwithstanding, [a]the children rebelled against Me; they did not walk in My statutes, and were not careful to observe My judgments, [b]'which, *if* a man does, he shall live by them'; but they profaned My Sabbaths. Then I said I would pour out My fury on them and fulfill My anger against them in the wilderness. 22 Nevertheless I [1]withdrew My hand and acted for My name's sake, that it should not be profaned in the sight of the Gentiles, in whose sight I had brought them

20:21 [a]Num. 25:1; Deut. 9:23 [b]Lev. 18:5

20:8 [1]Lit. *listen to*   20:11 [1]Lit. *made known to*   20:22 [1]Refrained from judgment

out. 23Also I raised My hand in an oath to those in the wilderness, that aI would scatter them among the Gentiles and disperse them throughout the countries, 24abecause they had not executed My judgments, but had despised My statutes, profaned My Sabbaths, and btheir eyes were fixed on their fathers' idols.

25"Therefore aI also gave them up to statutes *that were* not good, and judgments by which they could not live; 26and I pronounced them unclean because of their ritual gifts, in that they caused all 1their firstborn to pass athrough *the fire,* that I might make them desolate and that they bmight know that I am the LORD."'

27"Therefore, son of man, speak to the house of Israel, and say to them, 'Thus says the Lord GOD: "In this too your fathers have ablasphemed Me, by being unfaithful to Me. 28When I brought them into the land *concerning* which I had raised My hand in an oath to give them, and athey saw all the high hills and all the thick trees, there they offered their sacrifices and provoked Me with their offerings. There they also sent up their bsweet aroma and poured out their drink offerings. 29Then I said to them, 'What *is* this 1high place to which you go?' So its name is called 2Bamah to this day."' 30Therefore say to the house of Israel, 'Thus says the Lord GOD: "Are you defiling yourselves in the manner of your afathers, and committing harlotry according to their babominations? 31For when you offer ayour gifts and make your sons pass through the fire, you defile yourselves with all your idols, even to this day. So shall I be inquired of by you, O house of Israel? *As* I live," says the Lord GOD, "I will bnot be inquired of by you. 32aWhat you have in your mind shall never be, when you say, 'We will be like the Gentiles, like the families in other countries, serving wood and stone.'

GOD WILL RESTORE ISRAEL

33"*As* I live," says the Lord GOD, "surely with a mighty hand, awith an outstretched arm, and with fury poured out, I will rule over you. 34I will bring you out from the peoples and gather you out of the countries where you are scattered, with a mighty hand, with an outstretched arm, and with fury poured out. 35And I will bring you into the wilderness of the peoples, and there aI will plead My case with you face to face. 36aJust as I pleaded My case with your fathers in the wilderness of the land of Egypt, so I will plead My case with you," says the Lord GOD.

37"I will make you apass under the rod, and I will bring you into the bond of the bcovenant; 38aI will purge the rebels from among you, and those who transgress against Me; I will bring them out of the country where they dwell, but bthey shall not enter the land of Israel. Then you will know that I *am* the LORD.

39"As for you, O house of Israel," thus says the Lord GOD: a"Go, serve every one of you his idols—and hereafter—if you will not obey Me; bbut profane My holy name no more with your gifts and your idols. 40For aon My holy mountain, on the mountain height of Israel," says the Lord GOD, "there ball

---

20:26 1Lit. *that open the womb* 20:29 1Place for pagan worship
2Lit. *High Place*

20:23
aLev. 26:33;
Deut. 28:64;
Ps. 106:27;
Jer. 15:4

20:24
aEzek. 20:13, 16
bEzek. 6:9

20:25 aPs. 81:12;
Rom. 1:24;
2 Thess. 2:11

20:26
a2 Kin. 17:17;
2 Chr. 28:3;
Jer. 32:35;
Ezek. 16:20
bEzek. 6:7;
20:12, 20

20:27
aNum. 15:30;
Is. 65:7;
Rom. 2:24

20:28
a1 Kin. 14:23;
Ps. 78:58;
Is. 57:5–7;
Jer. 3:6;
Ezek. 6:13
bEzek. 16:19

20:30
aJudg. 2:19
bJer. 7:26; 16:12

20:31
aPs. 106:37–39;
Jer. 7:31;
Ezek. 16:20;
20:26
bEzek. 20:3

20:32
aEzek. 11:5

20:33 aJer. 21:5

20:35 aJer. 2:9,
35; Ezek. 17:20

20:36
aNum. 14:21–
23, 28

20:37
aLev. 27:32;
Jer. 33:13
bPs. 89:30–34;
Ezek. 16:60, 62

20:38
aEzek. 34:17;
Amos 9:9, 10;
Zech. 13:8, 9;
[Mal. 3:3; 4:1–3;
Matt. 25:32]
bJer. 44:14

20:39
aJudg. 10:14;
Ps. 81:12;
Amos 4:4
bIs. 1:13–15;
Ezek. 23:38

20:40 aIs. 2:2, 3;
Ezek. 17:23;
Mic. 4:1
bEzek. 37:22

the house of Israel, all of them in the land, shall serve Me; there ^cI will accept them, and there I will require your offerings and the firstfruits of your ¹sacrifices, together with all your holy things. ⁴¹I will accept you as a ^asweet aroma when I bring you out from the peoples and gather you out of the countries where you have been scattered; and I will be hallowed in you before the Gentiles. ^{42a}Then you shall know that I *am* the LORD, ^bwhen I bring you into the land of Israel, into the country *for* which I raised My hand in an oath to give to your fathers. ⁴³And ^athere you shall remember your ways and all your doings with which you were defiled; and ^byou shall ¹loathe yourselves in your own sight because of all the evils that you have committed. ^{44a}Then you shall know that I *am* the LORD, when I have dealt with you ^bfor My name's sake, not according to your wicked ways nor according to your corrupt doings, O house of Israel," says the Lord GOD.'"

FIRE IN THE FOREST

⁴⁵Furthermore the word of the LORD came to me, saying, ^{46a}"Son of man, set your face toward the south; ¹preach against the south and prophesy against the forest land, the ²South, ⁴⁷and say to the forest of the South, 'Hear the word of the LORD! Thus says the Lord GOD: "Behold, ^aI will kindle a fire in you, and it shall devour ^bevery green tree and every dry tree in you; the blazing flame shall not be quenched, and all faces ^cfrom the south to the north shall be scorched by it. ⁴⁸All flesh shall see that I, the LORD, have kindled it; it shall not be quenched."'"

⁴⁹Then I said, "Ah, Lord GOD! They say of me, 'Does he not speak ^aparables?'"

BABYLON, THE SWORD OF GOD

21 And the word of the LORD came to me, saying, ^{2a}"Son of man, set your face toward Jerusalem, ^bpreach¹ against the holy places, and prophesy against the land of Israel; ³and say to the land of Israel, 'Thus says the LORD: "Behold, I *am* ^aagainst you, and I will draw My sword out of its sheath and cut off both ^brighteous and wicked from you. ⁴Because I will cut off both righteous and wicked from you, therefore My sword shall go out of its sheath against all flesh ^afrom south *to* north, ⁵that all flesh may know that I, the LORD, have drawn My sword out of its sheath; it ^ashall not return anymore."' ^{6a}Sigh therefore, son of man, with ¹a breaking heart, and sigh with bitterness before their eyes. ⁷And it shall be when they say to you, 'Why are you sighing?' that you shall answer, 'Because of the news; when it comes, every heart will melt, ^aall hands will be feeble, every spirit will faint, and all knees will be weak *as* water. Behold, it is coming and shall be brought to pass,' says the Lord GOD."

⁸Again the word of the LORD came to me, saying, ⁹"Son of man, prophesy and say, 'Thus says the LORD!' Say:

^a'A sword, a sword is sharpened
And also polished!

20:40 ¹*offerings*   **20:43** ¹Or *despise*   **20:46** ¹*proclaim*, lit. *drop*   ²Heb. *Negev*   **21:2** ¹*proclaim*, lit. *drop*   **21:6** ¹Emotional distress, lit. *the breaking of your loins*

20:40
^cIs. 56:7; 60:7;
Ezek. 43:27;
Zech. 8:20–22;
Mal. 3:4;
[Rom. 12:1]

20:41 ^aEph. 5:2;
Phil. 4:18

20:42
^aEzek. 36:23;
38:23
^bEzek. 11:17;
34:13; 36:24

20:43
^aEzek. 16:61
^bLev. 26:39;
Ezek. 6:9;
Hos. 5:15

20:44
^aEzek. 24:24
^bEzek. 36:22

20:46
^aEzek. 21:2;
Amos 7:16

20:47
^aIs. 9:18, 19;
Jer. 21:14
^bLuke 23:31
^cEzek. 21:4

20:49
^aEzek. 12:9;
17:2; Matt. 13:13;
John 16:25

21:2
^aEzek. 20:46
^bAmos 7:16

21:3 ^aJer. 21:13;
Ezek. 5:8;
Nah. 2:13; 3:5
^bJob 9:22

21:4 ^aJer. 12:12;
Ezek. 20:47

21:5 ^a[Is. 45:23;
55:11]

21:6 ^aIs. 22:4;
Jer. 4:19;
Luke 19:41

21:7 ^aEzek. 7:17

21:9
^aDeut. 32:41;
Ezek. 5:1;
21:15, 28

10 Sharpened to make a dreadful slaughter,
Polished to flash like lightning!
Should we then make mirth?
It despises the scepter of My son,
As it does all wood.

11 And He has given it to be polished,
That it may be handled;
This sword is sharpened, and it is polished
To be given into the hand of ªthe slayer.'

12 "Cry and wail, son of man;
For it will be against My people,
Against all the princes of Israel.
Terrors including the sword will be against My people;
Therefore ªstrike *your* thigh.

13 "Because *it is* ªa testing,
And what if *the sword* despises even the scepter?
ᵇ*The scepter* shall be no *more,*"

says the Lord GOD.

14 "You therefore, son of man, prophesy,
And ªstrike *your* hands together.
The third time let the sword do double *damage.*
It *is* the sword *that* slays,
The sword that slays the great *men,*
That enters their ᵇprivate chambers.

15 I have set the point of the sword against all their gates,
That the heart may melt and many may stumble.
Ah! ª*It is* made bright;
It is grasped for slaughter:

16 "Swordsª¹ at the ready!
Thrust right!
Set your blade!
Thrust left—
Wherever your ²edge is ordered!

17 "I also will ªbeat My fists together,
And ᵇI will cause My fury to rest;
I, the LORD, have spoken."

18The word of the LORD came to me again, saying: 19"And son of man, appoint for yourself two ways for the sword of the king of Babylon to go; both of them shall go from the same land. Make a sign; put *it* at the head of the road to the city. 20Appoint a road for the sword to go to ªRabbah of the Ammonites, and to Judah, into fortified Jerusalem. 21For the king of Babylon stands at the parting of the road, at the fork of the two roads, to use divination: he shakes the arrows, he consults the ¹images, he looks at the liver. 22In his right hand is the divination for Jerusalem: to set up battering rams, to call for a slaughter, to ªlift the voice with shouting, ᵇto set battering rams against the gates, to heap up a *siege* mound, and to build a wall. 23And it will be to them like a false divination in the eyes of those who ªhave sworn oaths with them; but he will bring their iniquity to remembrance, that they may be taken.

24"Therefore thus says the Lord GOD: 'Because you have

21:11 ªEzek. 21:19
21:12 ªJer. 31:19
21:13 ªJob 9:23;
2 Cor. 8:2
ᵇEzek. 21:27
21:14
ªNum. 24:10;
Ezek. 6:11
ᵇ1 Kin. 20:30
21:15
ªEzek. 21:10, 28
21:16
ªEzek. 14:17
21:17
ªEzek. 22:13
ᵇEzek. 5:13;
16:42; 24:13
21:20
ªDeut. 3:11;
Jer. 49:2;
Ezek. 25:5;
Amos 1:14
21:22 ªJer. 51:14
ᵇEzek. 4:2
21:23
ªEzek. 17:16, 18

21:16 ¹Lit. *Sharpen yourself!* or *Unite yourself!*   ²Lit. *face*   21:21 ¹Heb. *teraphim*

made your iniquity to be remembered, in that your transgressions are uncovered, so that in all your doings your sins appear—because you have come to remembrance, you shall be taken in hand.

25'Now to you, O ªprofane, wicked prince of Israel, ᵇwhose day has come, whose iniquity *shall* end, 26thus says the Lord GOD:

"Remove the turban, and take off the crown;
Nothing *shall remain* the same.
ªExalt the humble, and humble the exalted.
27 ¹Overthrown, overthrown,
I will make it overthrown!
ªIt shall be no *longer*,
Until He comes whose right it is,
And I will give it *to* ᵇ*Him*."'

A SWORD AGAINST THE AMMONITES

28"And you, son of man, prophesy and say, 'Thus says the Lord GOD ªconcerning the Ammonites and concerning their reproach,' and say:

'A sword, a sword *is* drawn,
Polished for slaughter,
For consuming, for flashing—
29 While they ªsee false visions for you,
While they divine a lie to you,
To bring you on the necks of the wicked, the slain
ᵇWhose day has come,
Whose iniquity *shall* end.

30 'Return ª *it* to its sheath.
ᵇI will judge you
In the place where you were created,
ᶜIn the land of your ¹nativity.
31 I will ªpour out My indignation on you;
I will ᵇblow against you with the fire of My wrath,
And deliver you into the hands of brutal men *who are*
skillful to ᶜdestroy.
32 You shall be fuel for the fire;
Your blood shall be in the midst of the land.
ªYou shall not be remembered,
For I the LORD have spoken.'"

SINS OF JERUSALEM

22 Moreover the word of the LORD came to me, saying, 2"Now, son of man, ªwill you judge, will you judge ᵇthe bloody city? Yes, show her all her abominations! 3Then say, 'Thus says the Lord GOD: "The city sheds ªblood in her own midst, that her time may come; and she makes idols within herself to defile herself. 4You have become guilty by the blood which you have ªshed, and have defiled yourself with the idols which you have made. You have caused your days to draw near, and have come to *the end of* your years; ᵇtherefore I have made you a reproach to the nations, and a mockery to all countries. 5*Those* near and *those* far from you will mock you as ¹infamous *and* full of tumult.

6"Look, ᵃthe princes of Israel: each one has used his ¹power to shed blood in you. 7In you they have ᵃmade light of father and mother; in your midst they have ᵇoppressed the stranger; in you they have mistreated the ¹fatherless and the widow. 8You have despised My holy things and ᵃprofaned My Sabbaths. 9In you are ᵃmen who slander to cause bloodshed; ᵇin you are those who eat on the mountains; in your midst they commit lewdness. 10In you men ᵃuncover their fathers' nakedness; in you they violate women who are ᵇset apart during their impurity. 11One commits abomination ᵃwith his neighbor's wife; ᵇanother lewdly defiles his daughter-in-law; and another in you violates his sister, his father's ᶜdaughter. 12In you ᵃthey take bribes to shed blood; ᵇyou take usury and increase; you have made profit from your neighbors by extortion, and ᶜhave forgotten Me," says the Lord GOD.

13"Behold, therefore, I ᵃbeat My fists at the dishonest profit which you have made, and at the bloodshed which has been in your midst. 14ᵃCan your heart endure, or can your hands remain strong, in the days when I shall deal with you? ᵇI, the LORD, have spoken, and will do it. 15ᵃI will scatter you among the nations, disperse you throughout the countries, and ᵇremove your filthiness completely from you. 16You shall defile yourself in the sight of the nations; then ᵃyou shall know that I am the LORD."'"

ISRAEL IN THE FURNACE

17The word of the LORD came to me, saying, 18"Son of man, ᵃthe house of Israel has become dross to Me; they are all bronze, tin, iron, and lead, in the midst of a ᵇfurnace; they have become dross from silver. 19Therefore thus says the Lord GOD: 'Because you have all become dross, therefore behold, I will gather you into the midst of Jerusalem. 20As men gather silver, bronze, iron, lead, and tin into the midst of a furnace, to blow fire on it, to ᵃmelt it; so I will gather you in My anger and in My fury, and I will leave you there and melt you. 21Yes, I will gather you and blow on you with the fire of My wrath, and you shall be melted in its midst. 22As silver is melted in the midst of a furnace, so shall you be melted in its midst; then you shall know that I, the LORD, have ᵃpoured out My fury on you.'"

ISRAEL'S WICKED LEADERS

23And the word of the LORD came to me, saying, 24"Son of man, say to her: 'You are a land that is ᵃnot ¹cleansed or rained on in the day of indignation.' 25ᵃThe conspiracy of her ¹prophets in her midst is like a roaring lion tearing the prey; they ᵇhave devoured ²people; ᶜthey have taken treasure and precious things; they have made many widows in her midst. 26ᵃHer priests have ¹violated My law and ᵇprofaned My holy things; they have not ᶜdistinguished between the holy and unholy, nor have they made known the difference between the unclean and the clean; and they have hidden their eyes from My Sabbaths, so that I am profaned among them. 27Her ᵃprinces in her midst are like wolves tearing the prey, to shed blood, to destroy ¹people, and to get dishonest gain. 28ᵃHer

22:27 ᵃIs. 1:23; Ezek. 22:6; Mic. 3:1–3, 9–11; Zeph. 3:3   22:28 ᵃEzek. 13:10

22:6 ¹Lit. arm   22:7 ¹Lit. orphan   22:24 ¹So with MT, Syr., Vg.; LXX showered upon   22:25 ¹So with MT, Vg.; LXX princes; Tg. scribes   ²Lit. souls   22:26 ¹Lit. done violence to   22:27 ¹Lit. souls

22:6 ᵃIs. 1:23; Ezek. 22:27; Mic. 3:1–3; Zeph. 3:3

22:7 ᵃEx. 20:12; Lev. 20:9; Deut. 5:16; 27:16 ᵇEx. 22:22; Jer. 5:28; Ezek. 22:25; Mal. 3:5

22:8 ᵃLev. 19:30

22:9 ᵃLev. 19:16; Jer. 9:4 ᵇEzek. 18:6, 11

22:10 ᵃLev. 18:7, 8 ᵇLev. 18:19; 20:18; Ezek. 18:6

22:11 ᵃLev. 18:20; Jer. 5:8; Ezek. 18:11 ᵇLev. 18:15 ᶜLev. 18:9

22:12 ᵃEx. 23:8; Deut. 16:19; 27:25; Mic. 7:2, 3 ᵇEx. 22:25 ᶜDeut. 32:18; Ps. 106:21; Jer. 3:21; Ezek. 23:35

22:13 ᵃEzek. 21:17

22:14 ᵃEzek. 21:7 ᵇEzek. 17:24

22:15 ᵃDeut. 4:27; Neh. 1:8; Ezek. 20:23; Zech. 7:14 ᵇEzek. 23:27, 48

22:16 ᵃPs. 9:16

22:18 ᵃPs. 119:119; Is. 1:22; Jer. 6:28; Lam. 4:1 ᵇProv. 17:3; Is. 48:10

22:20 ᵃIs. 1:25; Jer. 9:7

22:22 ᵃEzek. 20:8, 33; Hos. 5:10

22:24 ᵃIs. 9:13; Jer. 2:30; Ezek. 24:13; Zeph. 3:2

22:25 ᵃJer. 11:9; Hos. 6:9 ᵇMatt. 23:14 ᶜMic. 3:11; Zeph. 3:3, 4

22:26 ᵃJer. 32:32; Lam. 4:3; Mal. 2:8 ᵇ1 Sam. 2:29 ᶜLev. 10:10

prophets plastered them with untempered *mortar,* ᵇseeing false visions, and divining ᶜlies for them, saying, 'Thus says the Lord GOD,' when the LORD had not spoken. ²⁹The people of the land have used oppressions, committed robbery, and mistreated the poor and needy; and they wrongfully ᵃoppress the stranger. ³⁰ᵃSo I sought for a man among them who would ᵇmake a wall, and ᶜstand in the gap before Me on behalf of the land, that I should not destroy it; but I found no one. ³¹Therefore I have ᵃpoured out My indignation on them; I have consumed them with the fire of My wrath; and I have recompensed ᵇtheir deeds on their own heads," says the Lord GOD.

TWO HARLOT SISTERS

23 The word of the LORD came again to me, saying:

2 "Son of man, there were ᵃtwo women,
    The daughters of one mother.
3 ᵃThey committed harlotry in Egypt,
    They committed harlotry in ᵇtheir youth;
    Their breasts were there embraced,
    Their virgin bosom was there pressed.
4 Their names: ¹Oholah the elder and ²Oholibah ᵃher
        sister;
    ᵇThey were Mine,
    And they bore sons and daughters.
    As for their names,
    Samaria *is* Oholah, and Jerusalem *is* Oholibah.

THE OLDER SISTER, SAMARIA

5 "Oholah played the harlot even though she was Mine;
    And she lusted for her lovers, the neighboring
        ᵃAssyrians,
6 *Who were* clothed in purple,
    Captains and rulers,
    All of them desirable young men,
    Horsemen riding on horses.
7 Thus she committed her harlotry with them,
    All of them choice men of Assyria;
    And with all for whom she lusted,
    With all their idols, she defiled herself.
8 She has never given up her harlotry *brought* ᵃfrom
        Egypt,
    For in her youth they had lain with her,
    Pressed her virgin bosom,
    And poured out their immorality upon her.

9 "Therefore I have delivered her
    Into the hand of her lovers,
    Into the hand of the ᵃAssyrians,
    For whom she lusted.
10 They uncovered her nakedness,
    Took away her sons and daughters,
    And slew her with the sword;
    She became a byword among women,
    For they had executed judgment on her.

23:4 ¹Lit. *Her Own Tabernacle*   ²Lit. *My Tabernacle Is in Her*

THE YOUNGER SISTER, JERUSALEM

11"Now ªalthough her sister Oholibah saw *this,* ᵇshe became more corrupt in her lust than she, and in her harlotry more corrupt than her sister's harlotry.

12 "She lusted for the neighboring ªAssyrians,
ᵇCaptains and rulers,
Clothed most gorgeously,
Horsemen riding on horses,
All of them desirable young men.
13 Then I saw that she was defiled;
Both *took* the same way.
14 But she increased her harlotry;
She looked at men portrayed on the wall,
Images of ªChaldeans portrayed in vermilion,
15 Girded with belts around their waists,
Flowing turbans on their heads,
All of them looking like captains,
In the manner of the Babylonians of Chaldea,
The land of their nativity.
16 ªAs soon as her eyes saw them,
She lusted for them
And sent ᵇmessengers to them in Chaldea.

17 "Then the ¹Babylonians came to her, into the bed of love,
And they defiled her with their immorality;
So she was defiled by them, ªand alienated herself from
them.
18 She revealed her harlotry and uncovered her nakedness.
Then ªI ᵇalienated Myself from her,
As I had alienated Myself from her sister.

19 "Yet she multiplied her harlotry
In calling to remembrance the days of her youth,
ªWhen she had played the harlot in the land of Egypt.
20 For she lusted for her ¹paramours,
Whose flesh *is like* the flesh of donkeys,
And whose issue *is like* the issue of horses.
21 Thus you called to remembrance the lewdness of your
youth,
When the ªEgyptians pressed your bosom
Because of your youthful breasts.

JUDGMENT ON JERUSALEM

22"Therefore, Oholibah, thus says the Lord GOD:

ª'Behold, I will stir up your lovers against you,
From whom you have alienated yourself,
And I will bring them against you from every side:
23 The Babylonians,
All the Chaldeans,
ªPekod, Shoa, Koa,
ᵇAll the Assyrians with them,
All of them desirable young men,
Governors and rulers,
Captains and men of renown,
All of them riding on horses.

23:11 ªJer. 3:8
ᵇJer. 3:8–11;
Ezek. 16:51, 52

23:12
ª2 Kin. 16:7, 8;
Ezek. 16:28
ᵇEzek. 23:6, 23

23:14 ªJer. 50:2;
Ezek. 8:10;
16:29

23:16
ª2 Kin. 24:1
ᵇIs. 57:9

23:17
ªEzek. 23:22, 28

23:18 ªJer. 6:8
ᵇPs. 78:59;
106:40; Jer. 12:8

23:19 ªLev. 18:3;
Ezek. 23:2

23:21
ªEzek. 16:26

23:22
ªEzek. 16:37–41;
23:28

23:23 ªJer. 50:21
ᵇEzek. 23:12

23:17 ¹Lit. *sons of Babel*   23:20 ¹Illicit lovers

24 And they shall come against you
With chariots, wagons, and war-horses,
With a horde of people.
They shall array against you
Buckler, shield, and helmet all around.

'I will delegate judgment to them,
And they shall judge you according to their judgments.
25 I will set My ᵃjealousy against you,
And they shall deal furiously with you;
They shall remove your nose and your ears,
And your remnant shall fall by the sword;
They shall take your sons and your daughters,
And your remnant shall be devoured by fire.
26 ᵃThey shall also strip you of your clothes
And take away your beautiful jewelry.
27 'Thus ᵃI will make you cease your lewdness and your
ᵇharlotry
Brought from the land of Egypt,
So that you will not lift your eyes to them,
Nor remember Egypt anymore.'

28"For thus says the Lord GOD: 'Surely I will deliver you into
the hand of ᵃthose you hate, into the hand *of those* ᵇfrom whom
you alienated yourself. 29ᵃThey will deal hatefully with you, take
away all you have worked for, and ᵇleave you naked and bare.
The nakedness of your harlotry shall be uncovered, both your
lewdness and your harlotry. 30I will do these *things* to you because you have ᵃgone as a harlot after the Gentiles, because you
have become defiled by their idols. 31You have walked in the
way of your sister; therefore I will put her ᵃcup in your hand.'
32"Thus says the Lord GOD:

'You shall drink of your sister's cup,
The deep and wide one;
ᵃYou shall be laughed to scorn
And held in derision;
It contains much.
33 You will be filled with drunkenness and sorrow,
The cup of horror and desolation,
The cup of your sister Samaria.
34 You shall ᵃdrink and drain it,
You shall break its ¹shards,
And tear at your own breasts;
For I have spoken,'
Says the Lord GOD.

35"Therefore thus says the Lord GOD:

'Because you ᵃhave forgotten Me and ᵇcast Me behind
your back,
Therefore you shall bear the *penalty*
Of your lewdness and your harlotry.'"

BOTH SISTERS JUDGED

36The LORD also said to me: "Son of man, will you ᵃjudge
Oholah and Oholibah? Then ᵇdeclare to them their abominations. 37For they have committed adultery, and ᵃblood *is* on

23:25 ᵃEx. 34:14;
Ezek. 5:13; 8:17,
18; Zeph. 1:18

23:26
ᵃIs. 3:18–23;
Ezek. 16:39

23:27
ᵃEzek. 16:41;
22:15
ᵇEzek. 23:3, 19

23:28
ᵃJer. 21:7–10;
Ezek. 16:37–41
ᵇEzek. 23:17

23:29
ᵃDeut. 28:48;
Ezek. 23:25,
26, 45–47
ᵇEzek. 16:39

23:30
ᵃEzek. 6:9

23:31
ᵃ2 Kin. 21:13;
Jer. 7:14, 15;
25:15;
Ezek. 23:33

23:32
ᵃEzek. 22:4, 5

23:34 ᵃPs. 75:8;
Is. 51:17

23:35 ᵃIs. 17:10;
Jer. 3:21;
Ezek. 22:12;
Hos. 8:14; 13:6
ᵇ1 Kin. 14:9;
Jer. 2:27; 32:33;
Neh. 9:26

23:36 ᵃJer. 1:10;
Ezek. 20:4; 22:2
ᵇIs. 58:1;
Ezek. 16:2;
Mic. 3:8

23:37
ᵃEzek. 16:38

23:34 ¹Earthenware fragments

their hands. They have committed adultery with their idols, and even *sacrificed* their sons [b]whom they bore to Me, passing them through *the fire,* to devour *them.* [38]Moreover they have done this to Me: They have [a]defiled My sanctuary on the same day and [b]profaned My Sabbaths. [39]For after they had slain their children for their idols, on the same day they came into My sanctuary to profane it; and indeed [a]thus they have done in the midst of My house.

[40]"Furthermore you sent for men to come from afar, [a]to whom a messenger *was* sent; and there they came. And you [b]washed yourself for them, [c]painted your eyes, and adorned yourself with ornaments. [41]You sat on a stately [a]couch, with a table prepared before it, [b]on which you had set My incense and My oil. [42]The sound of a carefree multitude *was* with her, and [1]Sabeans *were* brought from the wilderness with men of the common sort, who put bracelets on their [2]wrists and beautiful crowns on their heads. [43]Then I said concerning *her who had grown* old in adulteries, 'Will they commit harlotry with her now, and she *with them?*' [44]Yet they went in to her, as men go in to a woman who plays the harlot; thus they went in to Oholah and Oholibah, the lewd women. [45]But righteous men will [a]judge them after the manner of adulteresses, and after the manner of women who shed blood, because they *are* adulteresses, and [b]blood *is* on their hands.

[46]"For thus says the Lord GOD: [a]'Bring up an assembly against them, give them up to trouble and plunder. [47a]The assembly shall stone them with stones and [1]execute them with their swords; [b]they shall slay their sons and their daughters, and burn their houses with fire. [48]Thus [a]I will cause lewdness to cease from the land, [b]that all women may be taught not to practice your lewdness. [49]They shall repay you for your lewdness, and you shall [a]pay for your idolatrous sins. [b]Then you shall know that I *am* the Lord GOD.'"

SYMBOL OF THE COOKING POT
(*cf. Jer.* 1:13–19)

24 Again, in the ninth year, in the tenth month, on the tenth *day* of the month, the word of the LORD came to me, saying, [2]"Son of man, write down the name of the day, this very day—the king of Babylon started his siege against Jerusalem [a]this very day. [3a]And utter a parable to the rebellious house, and say to them, 'Thus says the Lord GOD:

[b]"Put on a pot, set *it* on,
    And also pour water into it.
[4]   Gather pieces *of meat* in it,
    Every good piece,
    The thigh and the shoulder.
    Fill *it* with choice [1]cuts.
[5]   Take the choice of the flock.
    Also pile *fuel* bones under it,
    Make it boil well,
    And let the cuts simmer in it."

[6]"Therefore thus says the Lord GOD:

"Woe to [a]the bloody city,
    To the pot whose scum *is* in it,

23:37
[b]Ezek. 16:20, 21, 36, 45; 20:26, 31

23:38
[a]2 Kin. 21:4, 7; Ezek. 5:11; 7:20
[b]Ezek. 22:8

23:39
[a]2 Kin. 21:2–8

23:40 [a]Is. 57:9
[b]Ruth 3:3
[c]2 Kin. 9:30; Jer. 4:30

23:41 [a]Esth. 1:6; Is. 57:7; Amos 2:8; 6:4
[b]Prov. 7:17; Ezek. 16:18, 19; Hos. 2:8

23:45
[a]Ezek. 16:38
[b]Ezek. 23:37

23:46
[a]Ezek. 16:40

23:47
[a]Lev. 20:10; Ezek. 16:40
[b]2 Chr. 36:17, 19; Ezek. 24:21

23:48
[a]Ezek. 22:15
[b]Deut. 13:11; Ezek. 22:15; 2 Pet. 2:6

23:49 [a]Is. 59:18; Ezek. 23:35
[b]Ezek. 20:38, 42, 44; 25:5

24:2
[a]2 Kin. 25:1; Jer. 39:1; 52:4

24:3 [a]Ezek. 17:12
[b]Jer. 1:13; Ezek. 11:3

24:6
[a]2 Kin. 24:3, 4; Ezek. 22:2, 3, 27; Mic. 7:2; Nah. 3:1

And whose scum is not gone from it!
Bring it out piece by piece,
On which no [b]lot has fallen.
7 For her blood is in her midst;
She set it on top of a rock;
[a]She did not pour it on the ground,
To cover it with dust.
8 That it may raise up fury and take vengeance,
[a]I have set her blood on top of a rock,
That it may not be covered."

9"Therefore thus says the Lord GOD:

[a]"Woe to the bloody city!
I too will make the pyre great.
10 Heap on the wood,
Kindle the fire;
Cook the meat well,
Mix in the spices,
And let the [1]cuts be burned up.

11 "Then set the pot empty on the coals,
That it may become hot and its bronze may burn,
That [a]its filthiness may be melted in it,
That its scum may be consumed.
12 She has [1]grown weary with [2]lies,
And her great scum has not gone from her.
Let her scum be in the fire!
13 In your [a]filthiness is lewdness.
Because I have cleansed you, and you were not cleansed,
You will [b]not be cleansed of your filthiness anymore,
[c]Till I have caused My fury to rest upon you.
14 [a]I, the LORD, have spoken it;
[b]It shall come to pass, and I will do it;
I will not hold back,
[c]Nor will I spare,
Nor will I relent;
According to your ways
And according to your deeds
[1]They will judge you,"
Says the Lord GOD.' "

THE PROPHET'S WIFE DIES

15Also the word of the LORD came to me, saying, 16"Son of man, behold, I take away from you the desire of your eyes with one stroke; yet you shall [a]neither mourn nor weep, nor shall your tears run down. 17Sigh in silence, [a]make no mourning for the dead; [b]bind your turban on your head, and [c]put your sandals on your feet; [d]do not cover your [1]lips, and do not eat man's bread of sorrow."

18So I spoke to the people in the morning, and at evening my wife died; and the next morning I did as I was commanded.

19And the people said to me, [a]"Will you not tell us what these things signify to us, that you behave so?"

20Then I answered them, "The word of the LORD came to me, saying, 21Speak to the house of Israel, "Thus says the Lord

24:6
[b]2 Sam. 8:2;
Joel 3:3;
Obad. 11;
Nah. 3:10
24:7 [a]Lev. 17:13;
Deut. 12:16
24:8
[a][Matt. 7:2]
24:9
[a]Ezek. 24:6;
Nah. 3:1;
Hab. 2:12
24:11
[a]Ezek. 22:15
24:13
[a]Ezek. 23:36–48
[b]Jer. 6:28–30;
Ezek. 22:24
[c]Ezek. 5:13;
8:18; 16:42
24:14
[a][1 Sam. 15:29]
[b]Num. 23:19;
Ps. 33:9; Is. 55:11
[c]Ezek. 5:11
24:16 [a]Jer. 16:5
24:17 [a]Jer. 16:5
[b]Lev. 10:6; 21:10
[c]2 Sam. 15:30
[d]Mic. 3:7
24:19
[a]Ezek. 12:9;
37:18

24:10 [1]Lit. bones   24:12 [1]Or wearied Me   [2]Or toil   24:14 [1]LXX, Syr., Tg.,
Vg. I   24:17 [1]Lit. moustache

GOD: 'Behold, [a]I will profane My sanctuary, [1]your arrogant boast, the desire of your eyes, the [2]delight of your soul; [b]and your sons and daughters whom you left behind shall fall by the sword. [22]And you shall do as I have done; [a]you shall not cover *your* [1]lips nor eat man's bread *of sorrow*. [23]Your turbans shall be on your heads and your sandals on your feet; [a]you shall neither mourn nor weep, but [b]you shall pine away in your iniquities and mourn with one another. [24]Thus [a]Ezekiel is a sign to you; according to all that he has done you shall do; [b]and when this comes, [c]you shall know that I *am* the Lord GOD.'"

[25]'And you, son of man—*will it* not *be* in the day when I take from them [a]their stronghold, their joy and their glory, the desire of their eyes, and [1]that on which they set their minds, their sons and their daughters: [26]*that* on that day [a]one who escapes will come to you to let *you* hear *it* with *your* ears? [27][a]On that day your mouth will be opened to him who has escaped; you shall speak and no longer be mute. Thus you will be a sign to them, and they shall know that I *am* the LORD.'"

PROCLAMATION AGAINST AMMON

25 The word of the LORD came to me, saying, [2]"Son of man, [a]set your face [b]against the Ammonites, and prophesy against them. [3]Say to the Ammonites, 'Hear the word of the Lord GOD! Thus says the Lord GOD: [a]"Because you said, 'Aha!' against My sanctuary when it was profaned, and against the land of Israel when it was desolate, and against the house of Judah when they went into captivity, [4]indeed, therefore, I will deliver you as a possession to the [1]men of the East, and they shall set their encampments among you and make their dwellings among you; they shall eat your fruit, and they shall drink your milk. [5]And I will make [a]Rabbah [b]a stable for camels and Ammon a resting place for flocks. [c]Then you shall know that I *am* the LORD."

[6]'For thus says the Lord GOD: "Because you [a]clapped *your* hands, stamped your feet, and [b]rejoiced in heart with all your disdain for the land of Israel, [7]indeed, therefore, I will [a]stretch out My hand against you, and give you as plunder to the nations; I will cut you off from the peoples, and I will cause you to perish from the countries; I will destroy you, and you shall know that I *am* the LORD."

PROCLAMATION AGAINST MOAB

[8]'Thus says the Lord GOD: "Because [a]Moab and [b]Seir say, 'Look! The house of Judah *is* like all the nations,' [9]therefore, behold, I will clear the territory of Moab of cities, of the cities on its frontier, the glory of the country, Beth Jeshimoth, Baal Meon, and [a]Kirjathaim. [10][a]To the men of the East I will give it as a possession, together with the Ammonites, that the Ammonites [b]may not be remembered among the nations. [11]And I will execute judgments upon Moab, and they shall know that I *am* the LORD."

PROCLAMATION AGAINST EDOM

[12]'Thus says the Lord GOD: [a]"Because of what Edom did against the house of Judah by taking vengeance, and has

24:21 [a]Jer. 7:14; Lam. 2:7; Ezek. 7:20, 24
[b]Jer. 6:11; 16:3, 4; Ezek. 23:25, 47

24:22
[a]Jer. 16:6, 7

24:23
[a]Job 27:15; Ps. 78:64
[b]Lev. 26:39; Ezek. 33:10

24:24
[a]Is. 20:3; Ezek. 4:3; 12:6, 11; Luke 11:29, 30
[b]Jer. 17:15; John 13:19; 14:29
[c]Ezek. 6:7; 25:5

24:25 [a]Ps. 48:2; 50:2; Ezek. 24:21

24:26
[a]Ezek. 33:21

24:27
[a]Ezek. 3:26; 33:22

25:2 [a]Ezek. 35:2
[b]Jer. 49:1; Ezek. 21:28; Amos 1:13–15; Zeph. 2:9

25:3
[a]Ps. 70:2, 3; [Prov. 17:5]; Ezek. 26:2

25:5 [a]Deut. 3:11; 2 Sam. 12:26; Jer. 49:2; Ezek. 21:20
[b]Is. 17:2
[c]Ezek. 24:24

25:6 [a]Job 27:23; Lam. 2:15; Nah. 3:19; Zeph. 2:15
[b]Ezek. 36:5

25:7 [a]Ezek. 35:3

25:8 [a]Is. 15:6; Jer. 48:1; Amos 2:1, 2
[b]Ezek. 35:2, 5

25:9
[a]Num. 32:3, 38; Josh. 13:17; 1 Chr. 5:8; Jer. 48:23

25:10
[a]Ezek. 25:4
[b]Ezek. 21:32

25:12
[a]2 Chr. 28:17; Ps. 137:7; Jer. 49:7, 8; Amos 1:11; Obad. 10–14

24:21 [1]Lit. *the pride of your strength* [2]Lit. *compassion* 24:22 [1]Lit. *moustache* 24:25 [1]Lit. *the lifting up of their soul* 25:4 [1]Lit. *sons*

greatly offended by avenging itself on them," [13]therefore thus says the Lord GOD: "I will also stretch out My hand against Edom, cut off man and beast from it, and make it desolate from Teman; [1]Dedan shall fall by the sword. [14a]I will lay My vengeance on Edom by the hand of My people Israel, that they may do in Edom according to My anger and according to My fury; and they shall know My vengeance," says the Lord GOD.

PROCLAMATION AGAINST PHILISTIA

[15]"Thus says the Lord GOD: [a]"Because [b]the Philistines dealt vengefully and took vengeance with [1]a spiteful heart, to destroy because of the [2]old hatred," [16]therefore thus says the Lord GOD: [a]"I will stretch out My hand against the Philistines, and I will cut off the [b]Cherethites [c]and destroy the remnant of the seacoast. [17]I will [a]execute great vengeance on them with furious rebukes; [b]and they shall know that I *am* the LORD, when I lay My vengeance upon them."'"

PROCLAMATION AGAINST TYRE

26 And it came to pass in the eleventh year, on the first *day* of the month, *that* the word of the LORD came to me, saying, [2]"Son of man, [a]because Tyre has said against Jerusalem, [b]'Aha! She is broken who *was* the gateway of the peoples; now she is turned over to me; I shall be filled; she is laid waste.'

[3]"Therefore thus says the Lord GOD: 'Behold, I *am* against you, O Tyre, and will cause many nations to come up against you, as the sea causes its waves to come up. [4]And they shall destroy the walls of Tyre and break down her towers; I will also scrape her dust from her, and [a]make her like the top of a rock. [5]It shall be *a place for* spreading nets [a]in the midst of the sea, for I have spoken,' says the Lord GOD; 'it shall become plunder for the nations. [6]Also her daughter *villages* which *are* in the fields shall be slain by the sword. [a]Then they shall know that I am the LORD.'

[7]"For thus says the Lord GOD: 'Behold, I will bring against Tyre from the north [a]Nebuchadnezzar[1] king of Babylon, [b]king of kings, with horses, with chariots, and with horsemen, and an army with many people. [8]He will slay with the sword your daughter *villages* in the fields; he will [a]heap up a siege mound against you, build a wall against you, and raise a [1]defense against you. [9]He will direct his battering rams against your walls, and with his axes he will break down your towers. [10]Because of the abundance of his horses, their dust will cover you; your walls will shake at the noise of the horsemen, the wagons, and the chariots, when he enters your gates, as men enter a city that has been breached. [11]With the hooves of his [a]horses he will trample all your streets; he will slay your people by the sword, and your strong pillars will fall to the ground. [12]They will plunder your riches and pillage your merchandise; they will break down your walls and destroy your pleasant houses; they will lay your stones, your timber, and your soil in the [a]midst of the water. [13a]I will put an end to the

25:14 [a]Is. 11:14

25:15
[a]Jer. 25:20;
Amos 1—6
[b]2 Chr. 28:18

25:16 [a]Zeph. 2:4
[b]1 Sam. 30:14
[c]Jer. 47:4

25:17 [a]Ezek. 5:15
[b]Ps. 9:16

26:2
[a]2 Sam. 5:11;
Is. 23:1;
Jer. 25:22;
Amos 1:9;
Zech. 9:2
[b]Ezek. 25:3

26:4
[a]Ezek. 26:14

26:5
[a]Ezek. 27:32

26:6 [a]Ezek. 25:5

26:7
[a]Jer. 27:3–6;
Ezek. 29:18
[b]Ezra 7:12;
Is. 10:8;
Jer. 52:32;
Dan. 2:37, 47

26:8 [a]Jer. 52:4;
Ezek. 21:22

26:11 [a]Hab. 1:8

26:12
[a]Ezek. 27:27, 32

26:13
[a]Is. 14:11; 24:8;
Jer. 7:34; 25:10;
Amos 6:5

25:13 [1]Or *even to Dedan they shall fall*   25:15 [1]Lit. *spite in soul*   [2]Or *perpetual*   26:7 [1]Heb. *Nebuchadrezzar,* and so elsewhere in the book 26:8 [1]Lit. *a large shield*

sound of ᵇyour songs, and the sound of your harps shall be heard no more. ¹⁴ᵃI will make you like the top of a rock; you shall be *a place for* spreading nets, and you shall never be rebuilt, for I the LORD have spoken,' says the Lord GOD.

¹⁵"Thus says the Lord GOD to Tyre: 'Will the coastlands not ᵃshake at the sound of your fall, when the wounded cry, when slaughter is made in the midst of you? ¹⁶Then all the ᵃprinces of the sea will ᵇcome down from their thrones, lay aside their robes, and take off their embroidered garments; they will clothe themselves with trembling; ᶜthey will sit on the ground, ᵈtremble *every* moment, and ᵉbe astonished at you. ¹⁷And they will take up a ᵃlamentation for you, and say to you:

"How you have perished,
　O one inhabited by seafaring men,
O renowned city,
Who was ᵇstrong at sea,
She and her inhabitants,
Who caused their terror *to be* on all her inhabitants!
¹⁸ Now ᵃthe coastlands tremble on the day of your fall;
Yes, the coastlands by the sea are troubled at your
　　departure."'

¹⁹"For thus says the Lord GOD: 'When I make you a desolate city, like cities that are not inhabited, when I bring the deep upon you, and great waters cover you, ²⁰then I will bring you down ᵃwith those who descend into the Pit, to the people of old, and I will make you dwell in the lowest part of the earth, in places desolate from antiquity, with those who go down to the Pit, so that you may never be inhabited; and I shall establish glory ᵇin the land of the living. ²¹ᵃI will make you a terror, and you *shall be* no *more;* ᵇthough you are sought for, you will never be found again,' says the Lord GOD."

LAMENTATION FOR TYRE

27 The word of the LORD came again to me, saying, ²"Now, son of man, ᵃtake up a lamentation for Tyre, ³and say to Tyre, ᵃ'You who ¹are situated at the entrance of the sea, ᵇmerchant of the peoples on many coastlands, thus says the Lord GOD:

"O Tyre, you have said,
ᶜ'I *am* perfect in beauty.'
⁴　Your borders *are* in the midst of the seas.
　Your builders have perfected your beauty.
⁵　They ¹made all *your* planks of fir trees from ᵃSenir;
　They took a cedar from Lebanon to make you a mast.
⁶　*Of* ᵃoaks from Bashan they made your oars;
　The company of Ashurites have inlaid your planks
　With ivory from ᵇthe coasts of ¹Cyprus.
⁷　Fine embroidered linen from Egypt was what you spread
　　for your sail;
　Blue and purple from the coasts of Elishah was what
　　covered you.

26:13 ᵇIs. 23:16;
Ezek. 28:13;
Rev. 18:22

26:14
ᵃEzek. 26:4, 5

26:15
ᵃJer. 49:21;
Ezek. 27:28

26:16 ᵃIs. 23:8
ᵇJon. 3:6
ᶜJob 2:13
ᵈEzek. 32:10;
Hos. 11:10
ᵉEzek. 27:35

26:17
ᵃEzek. 27:2–36;
Rev. 18:9
ᵇJosh. 19:29;
Is. 23:4

26:18
ᵃEzek. 26:15

26:20
ᵃEzek. 32:18
ᵇEzek. 32:23

26:21
ᵃEzek. 27:36;
28:19
ᵇPs. 37:10, 36;
Ezek. 28:19

27:2
ᵃEzek. 26:17

27:3
ᵃEzek. 26:17;
28:2 ᵇIs. 23:3
ᶜEzek. 28:12

27:5 ᵃDeut. 3:9;
1 Chr. 5:23;
Song 4:8

27:6 ᵃIs. 2:12, 13;
Zech. 11:2
ᵇGen. 10:4;
Is. 23:1, 12;
Jer. 2:10

27:3 ¹Lit. *sit* or *dwell*　27:5 ¹built　27:6 ¹Heb. *Kittim,* western lands, especially Cyprus

8 "Inhabitants of Sidon and Arvad were your oarsmen;
  Your wise men, O Tyre, were in you;
  They became your pilots.
9 Elders of ªGebal and its wise men
  Were in you to caulk your seams;
  All the ships of the sea
  And their oarsmen were in you
  To market your merchandise.

10 "Those from Persia, ¹Lydia, and ²Libya
  Were in your army as men of war;
  They hung shield and helmet in you;
  They gave splendor to you.
11 Men of Arvad with your army *were* on your walls *all*
    around,
  And the men of Gammad were in your towers;
  They hung their shields on your walls *all* around;
  They made ªyour beauty perfect.

12ª"Tarshish *was* your merchant because of your many luxury goods. They gave you silver, iron, tin, and lead for your goods. 13ªJavan, Tubal, and Meshech *were* your traders. They bartered ᵇhuman lives and vessels of bronze for your merchandise. 14Those from the house of ªTogarmah traded for your wares with horses, steeds, and mules. 15The men of ªDedan *were* your traders; many isles *were* the market of your hand. They brought you ivory tusks and ebony as payment. 16Syria *was* your merchant because of the abundance of goods you made. They gave you for your wares emeralds, purple, embroidery, fine linen, corals, and rubies. 17Judah and the land of Israel *were* your traders. They traded for your merchandise wheat of ªMinnith, millet, honey, oil, and ᵇbalm. 18Damascus *was* your merchant because of the abundance of goods you made, because of your many luxury items, with the wine of Helbon and with white wool. 19Dan and Javan paid for your wares, ¹traversing back and forth. Wrought iron, cassia, and cane were among your merchandise. 20ªDedan *was* your merchant in saddlecloths for riding. 21Arabia and all the princes of ªKedar *were* your regular merchants. They traded with you in lambs, rams, and goats. 22The merchants of ªSheba and Raamah *were* your merchants. They traded for your wares the choicest spices, all kinds of precious stones, and gold. 23ªHaran, Canneh, Eden, the merchants of ᵇSheba, Assyria, *and* Chilmad *were* your merchants. 24These *were* your merchants in choice items—in purple clothes, in embroidered garments, in chests of multicolored apparel, in sturdy woven cords, which were in your marketplace.

25 "The ªships of Tarshish were carriers of your
    merchandise.
  You were filled and very glorious ᵇin the midst of the
    seas.
26 Your oarsmen brought you into many waters,
  But ªthe east wind broke you in the midst of the seas.

27 "Your ªriches, wares, and merchandise,
  Your mariners and pilots,
  Your caulkers and merchandisers,

27:9 ªJosh. 13:5;
1 Kin. 5:18;
Ps. 83:7

27:11 ªEzek. 27:3

27:12
ªGen. 10:4;
2 Chr. 20:36;
Ezek. 38:13

27:13
ªGen. 10:2;
Is. 66:19;
Ezek. 27:19
ᵇJoel 3:3–6;
Rev. 18:13

27:14
ªGen. 10:3;
Ezek. 38:6

27:15 ªGen. 10:7;
Is. 21:13

27:17
ªJudg. 11:33;
1 Kin. 5:9, 11;
Ezra 3:7;
Acts 12:20
ᵇJer. 8:22

27:20
ªGen. 25:3

27:21
ªGen. 25:13;
Is. 60:7;
Jer. 49:28

27:22
ªGen. 10:7;
1 Kin. 10:1, 2;
Ps. 72:10;
Is. 60:6;
Ezek. 38:13

27:23
ªGen. 11:31;
2 Kin. 19:12;
Is. 37:12
ᵇGen. 25:3

27:25 ªPs. 48:7;
Is. 2:16
ᵇEzek. 27:4

27:26 ªPs. 48:7;
Jer. 18:17;
Acts 27:14

27:27
ª[Prov. 11:4]

27:10 ¹Heb. *Lud* ²Heb. *Put* 27:19 ¹LXX, Syr. *from Uzal*

All your men of war who *are* in you,
And the entire company which *is* in your midst,
Will fall into the midst of the seas on the day of your
ruin.
28 The ªcommon-land[1] will shake at the sound of the cry of
your pilots.

29 "All ªwho handle the oar,
The mariners,
All the pilots of the sea
Will come down from their ships *and* stand on the
[1]shore.
30 They will make their voice heard because of you;
They will cry bitterly and ªcast dust on their heads;
They [b]will roll about in ashes;
31 They ªshave themselves completely bald because of
you,
Gird themselves with sackcloth,
And weep for you
With bitterness of heart *and* bitter wailing.
32 In their wailing for you
They will ªtake up a lamentation,
And lament for you:
[b]'What *city is* like Tyre,
Destroyed in the midst of the sea?

33 'When[a] your wares went out by sea,
You satisfied many people;
You enriched the kings of the earth
With your many luxury goods and your merchandise.
34 But ªyou are broken by the seas in the depths of the
waters;
[b]Your merchandise and the entire company will fall in
your midst.
35 ªAll the inhabitants of the isles will be astonished at
you;
Their kings will be greatly afraid,
And *their* countenance will be troubled.
36 The merchants among the peoples ªwill hiss at you;
[b]You will become a horror, and *be* no [c]more forever.' " '"

PROCLAMATION AGAINST THE KING OF TYRE

28 The word of the LORD came to me again, saying, 2"Son
of man, say to the prince of Tyre, 'Thus says the Lord
GOD:

"Because your heart *is* ªlifted[1] up,
And [b]you say, 'I *am* a god,
I sit *in* the seat of gods,
[c]In the midst of the seas,'
[d]Yet you *are* a man, and not a god,
Though you set your heart as the heart of a god
3 (Behold, ªyou *are* wiser than Daniel!
There is no secret that can be hidden from you!
4 With your wisdom and your understanding
You have gained ªriches for yourself,
And gathered gold and silver into your treasuries;

27:28
ªEzek. 26:15

27:29 ªRev. 18:17

27:30
ª1 Sam. 4:12;
2 Sam. 1:2;
Job 2:12;
Lam. 2:10;
Rev. 18:19
[b]Esth. 4:1, 3;
Jer. 6:26;
Jon. 3:6

27:31 ªIs. 15:2;
Jer. 16:6;
Ezek. 29:18

27:32
ªEzek. 26:17
[b]Ezek. 26:4, 5;
Rev. 18:18

27:33 ªRev. 18:19

27:34
ªEzek. 26:19
[b]Ezek. 27:27

27:35 ªIs. 23:6;
Ezek. 26:15, 16

27:36
ªJer. 18:16;
Zeph. 2:15
[b]Ezek. 26:2
[c]Ps. 37:10, 36;
Ezek. 28:19

28:2 ªJer. 49:16;
Ezek. 31:10
[b]Is. 14:14; 47:8;
Ezek. 28:9;
2 Thess. 2:4
[c]Ezek. 27:3, 4
[d]Is. 31:3;
Ezek. 28:9

28:3
ªEzek. 14:14;
Dan. 1:20;
2:20–23, 28;
5:11, 12; Zech. 9:3

28:4
ªEzek. 27:33;
Zech. 9:1–3

27:28 [1]*open lands* or *pasturelands*   27:29 [1]Lit. *land*   28:2 [1]Proud

⁵ ^aBy your great wisdom in trade you have increased your
    riches,
And your heart is lifted up because of your riches),"

⁶'Therefore thus says the Lord GOD:

"Because you have set your heart as the heart of a god,
⁷   Behold, therefore, I will bring ^astrangers against you,
^bThe most terrible of the nations;
And they shall draw their swords against the beauty of
    your wisdom,
And defile your splendor.
⁸   They shall throw you down into the ^aPit,
And you shall die the death of the slain
In the midst of the seas.

⁹   "Will you still ^asay before him who slays you,
'I *am* a god'?
But you *shall be* a man, and not a god,
In the hand of him who slays you.
¹⁰ You shall die the death of ^athe uncircumcised
By the hand of aliens;
For I have spoken," says the Lord GOD.'"

LAMENTATION FOR THE KING OF TYRE

¹¹Moreover the word of the LORD came to me, saying,
¹²"Son of man, ^atake up a lamentation for the king of Tyre,
and say to him, 'Thus says the Lord GOD:

^b"You *were* the seal of perfection,
Full of wisdom and perfect in beauty.
¹³ You were in ^aEden, the garden of God;
Every precious stone *was* your covering:
The sardius, topaz, and diamond,
Beryl, onyx, and jasper,
Sapphire, turquoise, and emerald with gold.
The workmanship of ^byour timbrels and pipes
Was prepared for you on the day you were created.

¹⁴ "You *were* the anointed ^acherub who covers;
I established you;
You were on ^bthe holy mountain of God;
You walked back and forth in the midst of fiery stones.
¹⁵ You *were* perfect in your ways from the day you were
    created,
Till ^ainiquity was found in you.

¹⁶ "By the abundance of your trading
You became filled with violence within,
And you sinned;
Therefore I cast you as a profane thing
Out of the mountain of God;
And I destroyed you, ^aO covering cherub,
From the midst of the fiery stones.

¹⁷ "Your ^aheart was ¹lifted up because of your beauty;
You corrupted your wisdom for the sake of your
    splendor;
I cast you to the ground,

28:5 ^aPs. 62:10;
Zech. 9:3

28:7 ^aEzek. 26:7
^bEzek. 7:24;
21:31; 30:11;
Hab. 1:6–8

28:8 ^aIs. 14:15

28:9 ^aEzek. 28:2

28:10
^a1 Sam. 17:26,
36; Ezek. 31:18;
32:19, 21, 25, 27

28:12
^aEzek. 27:2
^bEzek. 27:3;
28:3

28:13 ^aGen. 2:8;
Is. 51:3;
Ezek. 31:8, 9;
36:35
^bEzek. 26:13

28:14
^aEx. 25:20;
Ezek. 28:16
^bIs. 14:13;
Ezek. 20:40

28:15 ^a[Is. 14:12]

28:16
^aEzek. 28:14

28:17
^aEzek. 28:2, 5

28:17 ¹Proud

I laid you before kings,
That they might gaze at you.
18 "You defiled your sanctuaries
By the multitude of your iniquities,
By the iniquity of your trading;
Therefore I brought fire from your midst;
It devoured you,
And I turned you to ashes upon the earth
In the sight of all who saw you.
19 All who knew you among the peoples are astonished at
you;
^aYou have become a horror,
And *shall be* no ^bmore forever."'"

PROCLAMATION AGAINST SIDON

²⁰Then the word of the LORD came to me, saying, ²¹"Son of
man, ^aset your face ^btoward Sidon, and prophesy against her,
²²and say, 'Thus says the Lord GOD:

^a"Behold, I *am* against you, O Sidon;
I will be glorified in your midst;
And ^bthey shall know that I *am* the LORD,
When I execute judgments in her and am ^challowed in
her.
23 ^aFor I will send pestilence upon her,
And blood in her streets;
The wounded shall be judged in her midst
By the sword against her on every side;
Then they shall know that I *am* the LORD.

²⁴"And there shall no longer be a pricking brier or ^aa pain-
ful thorn for the house of Israel from among all *who are*
around them, who ^bdespise them. Then they shall know that
I *am* the Lord GOD."

ISRAEL'S FUTURE BLESSING

²⁵'Thus says the Lord GOD: "When I have ^agathered the
house of Israel from the peoples among whom they are scattered, and am ^bhallowed in them in the sight of the Gentiles,
then they will dwell in their own land which I gave to My ser-
vant Jacob. ²⁶And they will ^adwell ¹safely there, ^bbuild houses,
and ^cplant vineyards; yes, they will dwell securely, when I ex-
ecute judgments on all those around them who despise them.
Then they shall know that I *am* the LORD their God."'"

PROCLAMATION AGAINST EGYPT

29 In the tenth year, in the tenth *month,* on the twelfth
day of the month, the word of the LORD came to me,
saying, ²"Son of man, ^aset your face against Pharaoh king
of Egypt, and prophesy against him, and ^bagainst all Egypt.
³Speak, and say, 'Thus says the Lord GOD:

^a"Behold, I *am* against you,
O Pharaoh king of Egypt,
O great ^bmonster who lies in the midst of his rivers,
^cWho has said, 'My ¹River *is* my own;
I have made *it* for myself.'

28:19
^aEzek. 26:21
^bEzek. 27:36

28:21
^aEzek. 6:2;
25:2; 29:2
^bGen. 10:15, 19;
Is. 23:2, 4, 12;
Ezek. 27:8;
32:30

28:22
^aEx. 14:4, 17;
Ezek. 39:13
^bPs. 9:16
^cEzek. 28:25

28:23
^aEzek. 38:22

28:24
^aNum. 33:55;
Josh. 23:13;
Is. 55:13;
Ezek. 2:6
^bEzek. 16:57;
25:6, 7

28:25
^aPs. 106:47;
Is. 11:12, 13;
Jer. 32:37;
Ezek. 11:17; 20:41;
34:13; 37:21
^bEzek. 28:22

28:26
^aJer. 23:6;
Ezek. 36:28
^bIs. 65:21;
Jer. 32:15, 43, 44;
Amos 9:13, 14
^cJer. 31:5;
Amos 9:14

29:2
^aEzek. 28:21
^bIs. 19:1;
Jer. 25:19; 46:2,
25; Ezek. 30:1—
32:32; Joel 3:19

29:3
^aJer. 44:30;
Ezek. 28:22;
29:10
^bPs. 74:13, 14;
Is. 37:1; 51:9;
Ezek. 32:2
^cEzek. 28:2

28:26 ¹securely   29:3 ¹The Nile

4 But ^aI will put hooks in your jaws,
And cause the fish of your rivers to stick to your
   scales;
I will bring you up out of the midst of your rivers,
And all the fish in your rivers will stick to your scales.
5 I will leave you in the wilderness,
You and all the fish of your rivers;
You shall fall on the ¹open ^afield;
^bYou shall not be picked up or ²gathered.
^cI have given you as food
To the beasts of the field
And to the birds of the heavens.

6 "Then all the inhabitants of Egypt
Shall know that I *am* the LORD,
Because they have been a ^astaff of reed to the house of
   Israel.
7 ^aWhen they took hold of you with the hand,
You broke and tore all their ¹shoulders;
When they leaned on you,
You broke and made all their backs quiver."

8"Therefore thus says the Lord GOD: "Surely I will bring ^aa sword upon you and cut off from you man and beast. 9And the land of Egypt shall become ^adesolate and waste; then they will know that I *am* the LORD, because he said, 'The River *is* mine, and I have made *it*.' 10Indeed, therefore, I *am* against you and against your rivers, ^aand I will make the land of Egypt utterly waste and desolate, ^bfrom ¹Migdol *to* Syene, as far as the border of Ethiopia. 11^aNeither foot of man shall pass through it nor foot of beast pass through it, and it shall be uninhabited forty years. 12^aI will make the land of Egypt desolate in the midst of the countries *that are* desolate; and among the cities *that are* laid waste, her cities shall be desolate forty years; and I will ^bscatter the Egyptians among the nations and disperse them throughout the countries."

13"Yet, thus says the Lord GOD: "At the ^aend of forty years I will gather the Egyptians from the peoples among whom they were scattered. 14I will bring back the captives of Egypt and cause them to return to the land of Pathros, to the land of their origin, and there they shall be a ^alowly kingdom. 15It shall be the lowliest of kingdoms; it shall never again exalt itself above the nations, for I will diminish them so that they will not rule over the nations anymore. 16No longer shall it be ^athe confidence of the house of Israel, but will remind them of *their* iniquity when they turned to follow them. Then they shall know that I *am* the Lord GOD." "

BABYLONIA WILL PLUNDER EGYPT

17And it came to pass in the twenty-seventh year, in the first *month*, on the first *day* of the month, *that* the word of the LORD came to me, saying, 18"Son of man, ^aNebuchadnezzar king of Babylon caused his army to labor strenuously against Tyre; every head *was* made ^bbald, and every shoulder rubbed raw; yet neither he nor his army received wages from Tyre, for the labor which they expended on it. 19Therefore

Cross references (left margin)

29:4
^a2 Kin. 19:28;
Is. 37:29;
Ezek. 38:4

29:5
^aEzek. 32:4–6
^bJer. 8:2;
16:4; 25:33
^cJer. 7:33; 34:20;
Ezek. 39:4

29:6
^a2 Kin. 18:21;
Is. 36:6;
Ezek. 17:15

29:7
^aJer. 37:5, 7, 11;
Ezek. 17:17

29:8 ^aJer. 46:13;
Ezek. 14:17;
32:11–13

29:9
^aEzek. 30:7, 8

29:10
^aEzek. 30:12
^bEzek. 30:6

29:11
^aJer. 43:11, 12;
46:19;
Ezek. 32:13

29:12
^aJer. 25:15–19;
27:6–11;
Ezek. 30:7, 26
^bJer. 46:19;
Ezek. 30:23, 26

29:13 ^aIs. 19:23;
Jer. 46:26

29:14
^aEzek. 17:6, 14

29:16
^aIs. 30:2, 3;
36:4, 6;
Lam. 4:17;
Ezek. 17:15; 29:6

29:18
^aJer. 25:9; 27:6;
Ezek. 26:7–12
^bJer. 48:37;
Ezek. 27:31

29:5 ¹Lit. *face of the field*   ²So with MT, LXX, Vg.; some Heb. mss., Tg. *buried*
29:7 ¹So with MT, Vg.; LXX, Syr. *hand*   29:10 ¹Or *the tower*

thus says the Lord GOD: 'Surely I will give the land of Egypt to ªNebuchadnezzar king of Babylon; he shall take away her wealth, carry off her spoil, and remove her pillage; and that will be the wages for his army. ²⁰I have given him the land of Egypt *for* his labor, because they ªworked for Me,' says the Lord GOD.

²¹'In that day ªI will cause the ¹horn of the house of Israel to spring forth, and I will ᵇopen your mouth to speak in their midst. Then they shall know that I *am* the LORD.' "

EGYPT AND HER ALLIES WILL FALL

30 The word of the LORD came to me again, saying, ²"Son of man, prophesy and say, 'Thus says the Lord GOD:

ª"Wail, 'Woe to the day!'

3 For ªthe day *is* near,
   Even the day of the LORD *is* near;
   It will be a day of clouds, the time of the Gentiles.
4 The sword shall come upon Egypt,
   And great anguish shall be in ¹Ethiopia,
   When the slain fall in Egypt,
   And they ªtake away her wealth,
   And ᵇher foundations are broken down.

⁵"Ethiopia, ¹Libya, ²Lydia, ªall the mingled people, Chub, and the men of the lands who are allied, shall fall with them by the sword."

⁶'Thus says the LORD:

"Those who uphold Egypt shall fall,
And the pride of her power shall come down.
ªFrom ¹Migdol *to* Syene
Those within her shall fall by the sword,"
Says the Lord GOD.

7 "Theyª shall be desolate in the midst of the desolate
      countries,
   And her cities shall be in the midst of the cities *that are*
      laid waste.
8 Then they will know that I *am* the LORD,
   When I have set a fire in Egypt
   And all her helpers are destroyed.
9 On that day ªmessengers shall go forth from Me in
      ships
   To make the ¹careless Ethiopians afraid,
   And great anguish shall come upon them,
   As on the day of Egypt;
   For indeed it is coming!"

¹⁰'Thus says the Lord GOD:

ª"I will also make a multitude of Egypt to cease
By the hand of Nebuchadnezzar king of Babylon.
11 He and his people with him, ªthe most terrible of the
      nations,
   Shall be brought to destroy the land;
   They shall draw their swords against Egypt,
   And fill the land with the slain.

29:19
ª Jer. 43:10–13;
Ezek. 30:10

29:20
ª Is. 10:6, 7;
45:1–3; Jer. 25:9

29:21
ª 1 Sam. 2:10;
Ps. 92:10; 132:17
ᵇ Ezek. 24:27;
Amos 3:7, 8;
[Luke 21:15]

30:2 ª Is. 13:6;
15:2; Ezek. 21:12;
Joel 1:5, 11, 13

30:3
ª Ezek. 7:7, 12;
Joel 2:1;
Obad. 15;
Zeph. 1:7

30:4
ª Ezek. 29:19
ᵇ Jer. 50:15

30:5
ª Jer. 25:20, 24

30:6
ª Ezek. 29:10

30:7
ª Jer. 25:18–26;
Ezek. 29:12

30:9 ª Is. 18:1, 2

30:10
ª Ezek. 29:19

30:11
ª Ezek. 28:7;
31:12

29:21 ¹Strength   30:4 ¹Heb. *Cush*   30:5 ¹Heb. *Put*   ²Heb. *Lud*   30:6 ¹Or *the tower*   30:9 ¹Or *secure*

12 ^aI will make the rivers dry,
And ^bsell the land into the hand of the wicked;
I will make the land waste, and all that is in it,
By the hand of aliens.
I, the LORD, have spoken."

13"Thus says the Lord GOD:

"I will also ^adestroy the idols,
And cause the images to cease from ¹Noph;
^bThere shall no longer be princes from the land of
Egypt;
^cI will put fear in the land of Egypt.
14 I will make ^aPathros desolate,
Set fire to ^bZoan,
^cAnd execute judgments in ¹No.
15 I will pour My fury on ¹Sin, the strength of Egypt;
^aI will cut off the multitude of ²No,
16 And ^aset a fire in Egypt;
Sin shall have great pain,
No shall be split open,
And Noph *shall be in* distress daily.
17 The young men of ¹Aven and Pi Beseth shall fall by the
sword,
And these *cities* shall go into captivity.
18 ^aAt ¹Tehaphnehes the day shall also be ²darkened,
When I break the yokes of Egypt there.
And her arrogant strength shall cease in her;
As for her, a cloud shall cover her,
And her daughters shall go into captivity.
19 Thus I will ^aexecute judgments on Egypt,
Then they shall know that I *am* the LORD."'"

PROCLAMATION AGAINST PHARAOH

20And it came to pass in the eleventh year, in the first *month*, on the seventh *day* of the month, *that* the word of the LORD came to me, saying, 21"Son of man, I have ^abroken the arm of Pharaoh king of Egypt; and see, ^bit has not been bandaged for healing, nor a ¹splint put on to bind it, to make it strong enough to hold a sword. 22Therefore thus says the Lord GOD: 'Surely I *am* ^aagainst Pharaoh king of Egypt, and will ^bbreak his arms, both the strong one and the one that was broken; and I will make the sword fall out of his hand. 23^aI will scatter the Egyptians among the nations, and disperse them throughout the countries. 24I will strengthen the arms of the king of Babylon and put My sword in his hand; but I will break Pharaoh's arms, and he will groan before him with the groanings of a mortally wounded *man*. 25Thus I will strengthen the arms of the king of Babylon, but the arms of Pharaoh shall fall down; ^athey shall know that I *am* the LORD, when I put My sword into the hand of the king of Babylon and he stretches it out against the land of Egypt. 26^aI will scatter the Egyptians among the nations and disperse them throughout the countries. Then they shall know that I *am* the LORD.'"

30:12 ^aIs. 19:5, 6
^bIs. 19:4

30:13 ^aIs. 19:1;
Jer. 43:12; 46:25;
Zech. 13:2
^bZech. 10:11
^cIs. 19:16

30:14 ^aIs. 11:11;
Jer. 44:1, 15;
Ezek. 29:14
^bPs. 78:12, 43;
Is. 19:11, 13
^cJer. 46:25;
Ezek. 30:15, 16;
Nah. 3:8–10

30:15 ^aJer. 46:25

30:16
^aEzek. 30:8

30:18 ^aJer. 2:16

30:19
^a[Ps. 9:16];
Ezek. 5:8; 25:11

30:21
^aJer. 48:25
^bJer. 46:11

30:22
^aJer. 46:25;
Ezek. 29:3
^bPs. 37:17

30:23
^aEzek. 29:12;
30:17, 18, 26

30:25 ^aPs. 9:16

30:26
^aEzek. 29:12

30:13 ¹Ancient Memphis   30:14 ¹Ancient Thebes   30:15 ¹Ancient Pelusium   ²Ancient Thebes   30:17 ¹Ancient On, Heliopolis
30:18 ¹*Tahpanhes,* Jer. 43:7   ²So with many Heb. mss., Bg., LXX, Syr., Tg., Vg.; MT *refrained*   30:21 ¹Lit. *bandage*

EGYPT CUT DOWN LIKE A GREAT TREE
(cf. Ezek. 17:22–24)

31 Now it came to pass in the [a]eleventh year, in the third *month,* on the first *day* of the month, *that* the word of the LORD came to me, saying, 2"Son of man, say to Pharaoh king of Egypt and to his multitude:

[a]'Whom are you like in your greatness?
3   [a]Indeed Assyria *was* a cedar in Lebanon,
       With fine branches that shaded the forest,
       And of high stature;
       And its top was among the thick boughs.
4   [a]The waters made it grow;
       Underground waters gave it height,
       With their rivers running around the place where it was
           planted,
       And sent out [1]rivulets to all the trees of the field.
5   'Therefore [a]its height was exalted above all the trees of
           the field;
       Its boughs were multiplied,
       And its branches became long because of the abundance
           of water,
       As it sent them out.
6   All the [a]birds of the heavens made their nests in its
           boughs;
       Under its branches all the beasts of the field brought
           forth their young;
       And in its shadow all great nations [1]made their home.
7   'Thus it was beautiful in greatness and in the length of its
           branches,
       Because its roots reached to abundant waters.
8   The cedars in the [a]garden of God could not hide it;
       The fir trees were not like its boughs,
       And the [1]chestnut trees were not like its branches;
       No tree in the garden of God was like it in beauty.
9   I made it beautiful with a multitude of branches,
       So that all the trees of Eden envied it,
       That *were* in the garden of God.'

10"Therefore thus says the Lord GOD: 'Because you have increased in height, and it set its top among the thick boughs, and [a]its heart was [1]lifted up in its height, 11therefore I will deliver it into the hand of the [a]mighty one of the nations, and he shall surely deal with it; I have driven it out for its wickedness. 12And aliens, [a]the most terrible of the nations, have cut it down and left it; its branches have fallen [b]on the mountains and in all the valleys; its boughs lie [c]broken by all the rivers of the land; and all the peoples of the earth have gone from under its shadow and left it.

13   'On [a]its ruin will remain all the birds of the heavens,
        And all the beasts of the field will come to its
            branches—

14So that no trees by the waters may ever again exalt themselves for their height, nor set their tops among the thick

Cross references

31:1 [a]Jer. 52:5, 6;
Ezek. 30:20;
32:1
31:2 [a]Ezek. 31:18
31:3
[a]Is. 10:33, 34;
Ezek. 17:3, 4, 22;
31:16; Dan. 4:10,
20–23
31:4 [a]Jer. 51:36;
Ezek. 29:3–9
31:5 [a]Dan. 4:11
31:6
[a]Ezek. 17:23;
31:13; Dan. 4:12,
21; Matt. 13:32
31:8
[a]Gen. 2:8, 9;
13:10; Is. 51:3;
Ezek. 28:13;
31:16, 18
31:10
[a]2 Chr. 32:25;
Is. 10:12; 14:13, 14;
Ezek. 28:17;
Dan. 5:20
31:11
[a]Ezek. 30:10;
Dan. 5:18, 19
31:12
[a]Ezek. 28:7;
30:11; 32:12
[b]Ezek. 32:5;
35:8
[c]Ezek. 30:24, 25
31:13 [a]Is. 18:6;
Ezek. 32:4

31:4 [1]Or *channels*   31:6 [1]Lit. *dwelled*   31:8 [1]Or *plane,* Heb. *armon*
31:10 [1]Proud

boughs, that no tree which drinks water may ever be high enough to reach up to them.

'For ᵃthey have all been delivered to death,
ᵇTo the depths of the earth,
Among the children of men who go down to the Pit.'

¹⁵"Thus says the Lord GOD: 'In the day when it ᵃwent down to ¹hell, I caused mourning. I covered the deep because of it. I restrained its rivers, and the great waters were held back. I caused Lebanon to ²mourn for it, and all the trees of the field wilted because of it. ¹⁶I made the nations ᵃshake at the sound of its fall, when I ᵇcast it down to ¹hell together with those who descend into the Pit; and ᶜall the trees of Eden, the choice and best of Lebanon, all that drink water, ᵈwere comforted in the depths of the earth. ¹⁷They also went down to hell with it, with those slain by the sword; and *those who were* its *strong* arm ᵃdwelt in its shadows among the nations.

¹⁸ᵃ'To which of the trees in Eden will you then be likened in glory and greatness? Yet you shall be brought down with the trees of Eden to the depths of the earth; ᵇyou shall lie in the midst of the uncircumcised, with *those* slain by the sword. This *is* Pharaoh and all his multitude,' says the Lord GOD."

LAMENTATION FOR PHARAOH AND EGYPT

32 And it came to pass in the twelfth year, in the ᵃtwelfth *month,* on the first *day* of the month, *that* the word of the LORD came to me, saying, ²"Son of man, ᵃtake up a lamentation for Pharaoh king of Egypt, and say to him:

ᵇ'You are like a young lion among the nations,
And ᶜyou *are* like a monster in the seas,
ᵈBursting forth in your rivers,
Troubling the waters with your feet,
And ᵉfouling their rivers.

³'Thus says the Lord GOD:

"I will therefore ᵃspread My net over you with a company of many people,
And they will draw you up in My net.
4   Then ᵃI will leave you on the land;
I will cast you out on the open fields,
ᵇAnd cause to ¹settle on you all the birds of the heavens.
And with you I will fill the beasts of the whole earth.
5   I will lay your flesh ᵃon the mountains,
And fill the valleys with your carcass.

6   "I will also water the land with the flow of your blood,
Even to the mountains;
And the riverbeds will be full of you.
7   When *I* put out your light,
ᵃI will cover the heavens, and make its stars dark;
I will cover the sun with a cloud,
And the moon shall not give her light.
8   All the ¹bright lights of the heavens I will make dark over you,

---

31:14 ᵃPs. 82:7
ᵇEzek. 32:18

31:15
ᵃEzek. 32:22, 23

31:16
ᵃEzek. 26:15;
Hag. 2:7
ᵇIs. 14:15;
Ezek. 32:18
ᶜIs. 14:8;
Hab. 2:17
ᵈEzek. 32:31

31:17 ᵃLam. 4:20

31:18
ᵃEzek. 32:19
ᵇJer. 9:25, 26;
Ezek. 28:10;
32:19, 21

32:1 ᵃEzek. 31:1;
33:21

32:2 ᵃEzek. 27:2
ᵇJer. 4:7;
Ezek. 19:2–6;
Nah. 2:11–13
ᶜIs. 27:1;
Ezek. 29:3
ᵈJer. 46:7, 8
ᵉEzek. 34:18

32:3
ᵃEzek. 12:13;
17:20

32:4 ᵃEzek. 29:5
ᵇIs. 18:6;
Ezek. 31:13

32:5 ᵃEzek. 31:12

32:7 ᵃIs. 13:10;
Joel 2:31; 3:15;
Amos 8:9;
Matt. 24:29;
Mark 13:24;
Luke 21:25;
Rev. 6:12, 13;
8:12

31:15 ¹Or *Sheol*   ²Lit. *be darkened*   **31:16** ¹Or *Sheol*   **32:4** ¹Lit. *sit* or *dwell*
32:8 ¹Or *shining*

And bring darkness upon your land,"
Says the Lord GOD.

9'I will also trouble the hearts of many peoples, when I bring your destruction among the nations, into the countries which you have not known. 10Yes, I will make many peoples astonished at you, and their kings shall be horribly afraid of you when I brandish My sword before them; and ªthey shall tremble *every* moment, every man for his own life, in the day of your fall.

11ª'For thus says the Lord GOD: "The sword of the king of Babylon shall come upon you. 12By the swords of the mighty warriors, all of them ªthe most terrible of the nations, I will cause your multitude to fall.

ᵇ"They shall plunder the pomp of Egypt,
And all its multitude shall be destroyed.
13 Also I will destroy all its animals
From beside its great waters;
ªThe foot of man shall muddy them no more,
Nor shall the hooves of animals muddy them.
14 Then I will make their waters ¹clear,
And make their rivers run like oil,"
Says the Lord GOD.

15 "When I make the land of Egypt desolate,
And the country is destitute of all that once filled it,
When I strike all who dwell in it,
ªThen they shall know that I *am* the LORD.

16 "This *is* the ªlamentation
With which they shall lament her;
The daughters of the nations shall lament her;
They shall lament for her, for Egypt,
And for all her multitude,"
Says the Lord GOD.' "

EGYPT AND OTHERS CONSIGNED TO THE PIT

17It came to pass also in the twelfth year, on the fifteenth *day* of the month, ªthat the word of the LORD came to me, saying:

18 "Son of man, wail over the multitude of Egypt,
And ªcast them down to the depths of the earth,
Her and the daughters of the famous nations,
With those who go down to the Pit:
19 'Whom ªdo you surpass in beauty?
ᵇGo down, be placed with the uncircumcised.'
20 "They shall fall in the midst of *those* slain by the
sword;
She is delivered to the sword,
ªDrawing her and all her multitudes.
21 ªThe strong among the mighty
Shall speak to him out of the midst of hell
With those who help him:
'They have ᵇgone down,
They lie with the uncircumcised, slain by the sword.'

32:10
ªEzek. 26:16

32:11
ªJer. 46:26;
Ezek. 30:4

32:12
ªEzek. 28:7;
30:11; 31:12
ᵇEzek. 29:19

32:13
ªEzek. 29:11

32:15 ªEx. 7:5;
14:4, 18; Ps. 9:16;
Ezek. 6:7

32:16
ª2 Sam. 1:17;
2 Chr. 35:25;
Jer. 9:17;
Ezek. 26:17

32:17
ªEzek. 32:1;
33:21

32:18
ªEzek. 26:20;
31:14

32:19
ªJer. 9:25, 26;
Ezek. 31:2, 18
ᵇEzek. 28:10

32:20 ªPs. 28:3

32:21 ªIs. 1:31;
14:9, 10;
Ezek. 32:27
ᵇEzek. 32:19, 25

32:14 ¹Lit. *sink;* settle, grow clear

22 "Assyria[a] *is* there, and all her company,
　　With their graves all around her,
　　All of them slain, fallen by the sword.
23 [a]Her graves are set in the recesses of the Pit,
　　And her company is all around her grave,
　　All of them slain, fallen by the sword,
　　Who [b]caused terror in the land of the living.

24 "There *is* [a]Elam and all her multitude,
　　All around her grave,
　　All of them slain, fallen by the sword,
　　Who have [b]gone down uncircumcised to the lower parts
　　　　of the earth,
　　[c]Who caused their terror in the land of the living;
　　Now they bear their shame with those who go down to
　　　　the Pit.
25 They have set her [a]bed in the midst of the slain,
　　With all her multitude,
　　With her graves all around it,
　　All of them uncircumcised, slain by the sword;
　　Though their terror was caused
　　In the land of the living,
　　Yet they bear their shame
　　With those who go down to the Pit;
　　It was put in the midst of the slain.

26 "There *are* [a]Meshech and Tubal and all their multitudes,
　　With all their graves around it,
　　All of them [b]uncircumcised, slain by the sword,
　　Though they caused their terror in the land of the living.
27 [a]They do not lie with the mighty
　　Who are fallen of the uncircumcised,
　　Who have gone down to hell with their weapons of war;
　　They have laid their swords under their heads,
　　But their iniquities will be on their bones,
　　Because of the terror of the mighty in the land of the
　　　　living.
28 Yes, you shall be broken in the midst of the
　　　　uncircumcised,
　　And lie with *those* slain by the sword.

29 "There *is* [a]Edom,
　　Her kings and all her princes,
　　Who despite their might
　　Are laid beside *those* slain by the sword;
　　They shall lie with the uncircumcised,
　　And with those who go down to the Pit.
30 [a]There *are* the princes of the north,
　　All of them, and all the [b]Sidonians,
　　Who have gone down with the slain
　　In shame at the terror which they caused by their might;
　　They lie uncircumcised with *those* slain by the sword,
　　And bear their shame with those who go down to the Pit.

31 "Pharaoh will see them
　　And be [a]comforted over all his multitude,
　　Pharaoh and all his army,
　　Slain by the sword,"
　　Says the Lord GOD.

32:22
[a]Ezek. 31:3, 16

32:23 [a]Is. 14:15
[b]Ezek. 32:24–
27, 32

32:24
[a]Gen. 10:22;
14:1; Is. 11:11;
Jer. 25:25;
49:34–39
[b]Ezek. 32:21
[c]Ezek. 32:23

32:25 [a]Ps. 139:8

32:26
[a]Gen. 10:2;
Ezek. 27:13;
38:2, 3; 39:1
[b]Ezek. 32:19

32:27
[a]Is. 14:18, 19

32:29
[a]Is. 9:5, 6;
34:5, 6;
Jer. 49:7–22;
Ezek. 25:12–14

32:30 [a]Jer. 1:15;
25:26;
Ezek. 38:6, 15;
39:2 [b]Jer. 25:22;
Ezek. 28:21–23

32:31
[a]Ezek. 14:22;
31:16

32 "For I have caused My terror in the land of the living;
And he shall be placed in the midst of the uncircumcised
With *those* slain by the sword,
Pharaoh and all his multitude,"
Says the Lord GOD.

THE WATCHMAN AND HIS MESSAGE

33 Again the word of the LORD came to me, saying, 2"Son of man, speak to ªthe children of your people, and say to them: ᵇ'When I bring the sword upon a land, and the people of the land take a man from their territory and make him their ᶜwatchman, 3when he sees the sword coming upon the land, if he blows the trumpet and warns the people, 4then whoever hears the sound of the trumpet and does ªnot take warning, if the sword comes and takes him away, ᵇhis blood shall be on his *own* head. 5He heard the sound of the trumpet, but did not take warning; his blood shall be upon himself. But he who takes warning will ¹save his life. 6But if the watchman sees the sword coming and does not blow the trumpet, and the people are not warned, and the sword comes and takes *any* person from among them, ªhe is taken away in his iniquity; but his blood I will require at the watchman's hand.'

7ª"So you, son of man: I have made you a watchman for the house of Israel; therefore you shall hear a word from My mouth and warn them for Me. 8When I say to the wicked, 'O wicked *man,* you shall surely die!' and you do not speak to warn the wicked from his way, that wicked *man* shall die in his iniquity; but his blood I will require at your hand. 9Nevertheless if you warn the wicked to turn from his way, and he does not turn from his way, he shall die in his iniquity; but you have ¹delivered your soul.

10"Therefore you, O son of man, say to the house of Israel: 'Thus you say, "If our transgressions and our sins *lie* upon us, and we ªpine¹ away in them, ᵇhow can we then live?"' 11Say to them: 'As I live,' says the Lord GOD, ª'I have no pleasure in the death of the wicked, but that the wicked ᵇturn from his way and live. Turn, turn from your evil ways! For ᶜwhy should you die, O house of Israel?'

THE FAIRNESS OF GOD'S JUDGMENT

12"Therefore you, O son of man, say to the children of your people: 'The ªrighteousness of the righteous man shall not deliver him in the day of his transgression; as for the wickedness of the wicked, ᵇhe shall not fall because of it in the day that he turns from his wickedness; nor shall the righteous be able to live because of *his righteousness* in the day that he sins.' 13When I say to the righteous *that* he shall surely live, ªbut he trusts in his own righteousness and commits iniquity, none of his righteous works shall be remembered; but because of the iniquity that he has committed, he shall die. 14Again, ªwhen I say to the wicked, 'You shall surely die,' if he turns from his sin and does ¹what is lawful and ²right, 15if the wicked ªrestores the pledge, ᵇgives back what he has stolen, and walks in ᶜthe statutes of life without committing iniquity, he shall surely live; he shall not die. 16ªNone of his sins which

33:2 ªEzek. 3:11
ᵇEzek. 14:17
ᶜ2 Sam. 18:24, 25; 2 Kin. 9:17; Hos. 9:8

33:4 ª2 Chr. 25:16; Jer. 6:17; Zech. 1:4
ᵇEzek. 18:13; 35:9; [Acts 18:6]

33:6 ªEzek. 33:8

33:7 ªIs. 62:6; Ezek. 3:17–21

33:10 ªLev. 26:39; Ezek. 24:23
ᵇIs. 49:14; Ezek. 37:11

33:11 ª[2 Sam. 14:14; Lam. 3:33]; Ezek. 18:23, 32; Hos. 11:8; [2 Pet. 3:9]
ᵇ[Hos. 14:1, 4; Acts 3:19]
ᶜ[Is. 55:6, 7]; Jer. 3:22; Ezek. 18:30, 31; Hos. 14:1; [Acts 3:19]

33:12 ªEzek. 3:20; 18:24, 26
ᵇ[2 Chr. 7:14]; Ezek. 18:21; 33:19

33:13 ªEzek. 3:20; 18:24

33:14 ª[Is. 55:7]; Jer. 18:7, 8; Ezek. 3:18, 19; 18:27; Hos. 14:1, 4

33:15 ªEzek. 18:7
ᵇEx. 22:1–4; Lev. 6:2, 4, 5; Num. 5:6, 7; Luke 19:8
ᶜLev. 18:5; Ps. 119:59; 143:8; Ezek. 20:11, 13, 21

33:16 ª[Is. 1:18; 43:25]; Ezek. 18:22

33:5 ¹Or *deliver his soul*   **33:9** ¹Or *saved your life*   **33:10** ¹Or *waste away*
33:14 ¹*justice*   ²*righteousness*

he has committed shall be remembered against him; he has done what is lawful and right; he shall surely live.

17a"Yet the children of your people say, 'The way of the Lord is not ¹fair.' But it is their way which is not fair! 18aWhen the righteous turns from his righteousness and commits iniquity, he shall die because of it. 19But when the wicked turns from his wickedness and does what is lawful and right, he shall live because of it. 20Yet you say, a"The way of the Lord is not ¹fair.' O house of Israel, I will judge every one of you according to his own ways."

THE FALL OF JERUSALEM

21And it came to pass in the twelfth year aof our captivity, in the tenth *month*, on the fifth *day* of the month, b*that* one who had escaped from Jerusalem came to me and said, c"The city has been ¹captured!"

22Now athe hand of the LORD had been upon me the evening before the man came who had escaped. And He had bopened my mouth; so when he came to me in the morning, my mouth was opened, and I was no longer mute.

THE CAUSE OF JUDAH'S RUIN

23Then the word of the LORD came to me, saying: 24"Son of man, athey who inhabit those bruins in the land of Israel are saying, c'Abraham was only one, and he inherited the land. dBut we *are* many; the land has been given to us as a epossession.'

25"Therefore say to them, 'Thus says the Lord GOD: a"You eat *meat* with blood, you blift up your eyes toward your idols, and cshed blood. Should you then possess the dland? 26You rely on your sword, you commit abominations, and you adefile one another's wives. Should you then possess the land?" '

27"Say thus to them, 'Thus says the Lord GOD: "*As* I live, surely athose who *are* in the ruins shall fall by the sword, and the one who *is* in the open field bI will give to the beasts to be devoured, and those who *are* in the strongholds and ccaves shall die of the pestilence. 28aFor I will make the land most desolate, ¹her barrogant strength shall cease, and cthe mountains of Israel shall be so desolate that no one will pass through. 29Then they shall know that I *am* the LORD, when I have made the land most desolate because of all their abominations which they have committed."'

HEARING AND NOT DOING

30"As for you, son of man, the children of your people are talking about you beside the walls and in the doors of the houses; and they aspeak to one another, everyone saying to his brother, 'Please come and hear what the word is that comes from the LORD.' 31So athey come to you as people do, they bsit before you *as* My people, and they chear your words, but they do not do them; dfor with their mouth they show much love, *but* etheir hearts pursue their *own* gain. 32Indeed you *are* to them as a very lovely song of one who has a pleasant voice and can play well on an instrument; for they hear your words, but they do anot do them. 33aAnd when this

Cross references (left margin)

33:17
aEzek. 18:25, 29

33:18
aEzek. 18:26

33:20
aEzek. 18:25, 29

33:21 aEzek. 1:2
bEzek. 24:26
c2 Kin. 25:4

33:22
aEzek. 1:3;
8:1; 37:1
bEzek. 24:27

33:24
aEzek. 34:2
bEzek. 36:4
cIs. 51:2;
[Acts 7:5;
Rom. 4:12]
dMic. 3:11;
[Matt. 3:9;
John 8:39]
eEzek. 11:15

33:25 aGen. 9:4;
Lev. 3:17; 7:26;
17:10–14; 19:26;
Deut. 12:16, 23;
15:23 bEzek. 18:6
cEzek. 22:6, 9
dDeut. 29:28

33:26
aEzek. 18:6;
22:11

33:27
aEzek. 33:24
bEzek. 39:4
cJudg. 6:2;
1 Sam. 13:6;
Is. 2:19

33:28
aJer. 44:2, 6, 22;
Ezek. 36:34, 35
bEzek. 7:24;
24:21
cEzek. 6:2, 3, 6

33:30 aIs. 29:13;
Ezek. 14:3;
20:3, 31

33:31 aEzek. 14:1
bEzek. 8:1
cIs. 58:2
dPs. 78:36, 37;
Is. 29:13;
Jer. 12:2;
1 John 3:18
e[Matt. 13:22]

33:32
a[Matt. 7:21–28;
James 1:22–25]

33:33
a1 Sam. 3:20

33:17 ¹Or *equitable*   **33:20** ¹Or *equitable*   **33:21** ¹Lit. *struck down*
33:28 ¹Lit. *pride of her strength*

comes to pass—surely it will come—then [b]they will know that a prophet has been among them."

IRRESPONSIBLE SHEPHERDS

34 And the word of the LORD came to me, saying, 2"Son of man, prophesy against the shepherds of Israel, prophesy and say to them, 'Thus says the Lord GOD to the shepherds: [a]"Woe to the shepherds of Israel who feed themselves! Should not the shepherds feed the flocks? 3[a]You eat the fat and clothe yourselves with the wool; you [b]slaughter the fatlings, *but* you do not feed the flock. 4[a]The weak you have not strengthened, nor have you healed those who were sick, nor bound up the broken, nor brought back what was driven away, nor [b]sought what was lost; but with [c]force and [1]cruelty you have ruled them. 5[a]So they were [b]scattered because *there was* no shepherd; [c]and they became food for all the beasts of the field when they were scattered. 6My sheep [a]wandered through all the mountains, and on every high hill; yes, My flock was scattered over the whole face of the earth, and no one was seeking or searching *for them*."

7"Therefore, you shepherds, hear the word of the LORD: 8"*As* I live," says the Lord GOD, "surely because My flock became a prey, and My flock [a]became food for every beast of the field, because *there was* no shepherd, nor did My shepherds search for My flock, [b]but the shepherds fed themselves and did not feed My flock"— 9therefore, O shepherds, hear the word of the LORD! 10Thus says the Lord GOD: "Behold, I *am* [a]against the shepherds, and [b]I will require My flock at their hand; I will cause them to cease feeding the sheep, and the shepherds shall [c]feed themselves no more; for I will [d]deliver My flock from their mouths, that they may no longer be food for them."

GOD, THE TRUE SHEPHERD

11"For thus says the Lord GOD: "Indeed I Myself will search for My sheep and seek them out. 12As a [a]shepherd seeks out his flock on the day he is among his scattered sheep, so will I seek out My sheep and deliver them from all the places where they were scattered on [b]a cloudy and dark day. 13And [a]I will bring them out from the peoples and gather them from the countries, and will bring them to their own land; I will feed them on the mountains of Israel, [1]in the valleys and in all the inhabited places of the country. 14[a]I will feed them in good pasture, and their fold shall be on the high mountains of Israel. [b]There they shall lie down in a good fold and feed in rich pasture on the mountains of Israel. 15I will feed My flock, and I will make them lie down," says the Lord GOD. 16[a]"I will seek what was lost and bring back what was driven away, bind up the broken and strengthen what was sick; but I will destroy [b]the fat and the strong, and feed them [c]in judgment."

17"And *as for* you, O My flock, thus says the Lord GOD: [a]"Behold, I shall judge between sheep and sheep, between rams and goats. 18*Is it* too little for you to have eaten up the good pasture, that you must tread down with your feet the [1]residue

33:33 [b]Ezek. 2:5

34:2 [a]Jer. 23:1; Ezek. 22:25; Mic. 3:1–3, 11; Zech. 11:17

34:3 [a]Is. 56:11; Zech. 11:16 [b]Ezek. 33:25, 26; Mic. 3:1–3; Zech. 11:5

34:4 [a]Zech. 11:16 [b]Matt. 9:36; 10:16; 18:12, 13; Luke 15:4 [c][1 Pet. 5:3]

34:5 [a]Ezek. 33:21 [b]Num. 27:17; 1 Kin. 22:17; Jer. 10:21; Matt. 9:36; Mark 6:34 [c]Is. 56:9; Jer. 12:9

34:6 [a]Jer. 40:11, 12; 50:6; Ezek. 7:16; 1 Pet. 2:25

34:8 [a]Ezek. 34:5, 6 [b]Ezek. 34:2, 10

34:10 [a]Jer. 21:13; 52:24–27; Ezek. 5:8; 13:8; Zech. 10:3 [b]Ezek. 3:18; Heb. 13:17 [c]Ezek. 34:2, 8 [d]Ps. 72:12–14; Ezek. 13:23

34:12 [a]Jer. 31:10 [b]Jer. 13:16; Ezek. 30:3; Joel 2:2

34:13 [a]Is. 65:9, 10; Jer. 23:3; Ezek. 11:17; 20:41; 28:25; 36:24; 37:21, 22

34:14 [a]Ps. 23:2; Jer. 3:15; [John 10:9] [b]Jer. 33:12

34:16 [a]Is. 40:11; Mic. 4:6; [Matt. 18:11]; Mark 2:17; Luke 5:32] [b]Is. 10:16; Amos 4:1 [c]Jer. 10:24

34:17 [a]Ezek. 20:37; Mal. 4:1; [Matt. 25:32]

34:4 [1]*harshness* or *rigor*   34:13 [1]Or *by the streams*   34:18 [1]*remainder*

34:20
a Ezek. 34:17

34:23 a [Is. 40:11;
Jer. 23:4, 5];
Hos. 1:11;
[John 10:11;
Heb. 13:20;
1 Pet. 2:25; 5:4]
b Jer. 30:9;
Ezek. 37:24;
Hos. 3:5

34:24 a Ex. 29:45;
Ezek. 37:25
b Is. 55:3;
Jer. 30:9;
Ezek. 37:24, 25;
Hos. 3:5

34:25
a Ezek. 37:26
b Lev. 26:6;
Job 5:22, 23;
Is. 11:6–9;
Hos. 2:18
c Jer. 23:6

34:26 a Is. 56:7
b Gen. 12:2;
Is. 19:24;
Zech. 8:13
c Lev. 26:4
d Ps. 68:9

34:27 a Lev. 26:4;
Ps. 85:12; Is. 4:2
b Lev. 26:13;
Is. 52:2, 3;
Jer. 2:20
c Jer. 25:14

34:28
a Jer. 30:10;
Ezek. 39:26

34:29 a [Is. 11:1]
b Ezek. 36:29
c Ezek. 36:3, 6, 15

34:30
a Ezek. 34:24
b Ps. 46:7, 11;
Ezek. 14:11;
36:28

34:31 a Ps. 100:3;
Jer. 23:1;
[John 10:11]

35:2 a Gen. 36:8;
Deut. 2:5;
Jer. 25:21;
49:7–22;
Ezek. 25:12–14;
Joel 3:19;
Amos 1:11, 12;
Obad. 1–9, 15, 16
b Amos 1:11

35:3 a Ezek. 6:14

35:5
a Ezek. 25:12
b Ps. 137:7;
Dan. 9:24;
Amos 1:11;
Obad. 10

35:6 a Is. 63:1–6;
Ezek. 16:38; 32:6
b Ps. 109:17

35:7 a Judg. 5:6

of your pasture—and to have drunk of the clear waters, that you must foul the residue with your feet? [19]And *as for* My flock, they eat what you have trampled with your feet, and they drink what you have fouled with your feet."

[20]"Therefore thus says the Lord GOD to them: a "Behold, I Myself will judge between the fat and the lean sheep. [21]Because you have pushed with side and shoulder, butted all the weak ones with your horns, and scattered them abroad, [22]therefore I will save My flock, and they shall no longer be a prey; and I will judge between sheep and sheep. [23]I will establish one a shepherd over them, and he shall feed them—b My servant David. He shall feed them and be their shepherd. [24]And a I, the LORD, will be their God, and My servant David b a prince among them; I, the LORD, have spoken.

[25]a "I will make a covenant of peace with them, and b cause wild beasts to cease from the land; and they c will dwell safely in the wilderness and sleep in the woods. [26]I will make them and the places all around a My hill b a blessing; and I will c cause showers to come down in their season; there shall be d showers of blessing. [27]Then a the trees of the field shall yield their fruit, and the earth shall yield her increase. They shall be safe in their land; and they shall know that I *am* the LORD, when I have b broken the bands of their yoke and delivered them from the hand of those who c enslaved them. [28]And they shall no longer be a prey for the nations, nor shall beasts of the land devour them; but a they shall dwell safely, and no one shall make *them* afraid. [29]I will raise up for them a a garden[1] of renown, and they shall b no longer be consumed with hunger in the land, c nor bear the shame of the Gentiles anymore. [30]Thus they shall know that a I, the LORD their God, *am* with them, and they, the house of Israel, *are* b My people," says the Lord GOD.'

[31]"You are My a flock, the flock of My pasture; you *are* men, *and* I *am* your God," says the Lord GOD.

JUDGMENT ON MOUNT SEIR

35 Moreover the word of the LORD came to me, saying, [2]"Son of man, set your face against a Mount Seir and b prophesy against it, [3]and say to it, 'Thus says the Lord GOD:

"Behold, O Mount Seir, I *am* against you;
a I will stretch out My hand against you,
And make you [1]most desolate;
[4] I shall lay your cities waste,
And you shall be desolate.
Then you shall know that I *am* the LORD.

[5]a "Because you have had an [1]ancient hatred, and have shed *the blood of* the children of Israel by the power of the sword at the time of their calamity, b when their iniquity *came to an* end, [6]therefore, *as* I live," says the Lord GOD, "I will prepare you for a blood, and blood shall pursue you; b since you have not hated [1]blood, therefore blood shall pursue you. [7]Thus I will make Mount Seir [1]most desolate, and cut off from it the a one who leaves and the one who returns. [8]And I will fill its mountains with the slain; on your hills and

---

34:29 [1]Lit. *planting place* **35:3** [1]Lit. *a desolation and a waste* **35:5** [1]Or *everlasting* **35:6** [1]Or *bloodshed* **35:7** [1]Lit. *a waste and a desolation*

in your valleys and in all your ravines those who are slain by the sword shall fall. ⁹ªI will make you ¹perpetually desolate, and your cities shall be uninhabited; ᵇthen you shall know that I *am* the LORD.

¹⁰"Because you have said, 'These two nations and these two countries shall be mine, and we will ªpossess them,' although ᵇthe LORD was there, ¹¹therefore, *as* I live," says the Lord GOD, "I will do ªaccording to your anger and according to the envy which you showed in your hatred against them; and I will make Myself known among them when I judge you. ¹²ªThen you shall know that I *am* the LORD. I have ᵇheard all your ᶜblasphemies which you have spoken against the mountains of Israel, saying, 'They are desolate; they are given to us to consume.' ¹³Thus ªwith your mouth you have ¹boasted against Me and multiplied your ᵇwords against Me; I have heard *them*."

¹⁴Thus says the Lord GOD: ª"The whole earth will rejoice when I make you desolate. ¹⁵ªAs you rejoiced because the inheritance of the house of Israel was desolate, ᵇso I will do to you; you shall be desolate, O Mount Seir, as well as all of Edom—all of it! Then they shall know that I *am* the LORD."'

BLESSING ON ISRAEL

36 "And you, son of man, prophesy to the ªmountains of Israel, and say, 'O mountains of Israel, hear the word of the LORD! ²Thus says the Lord GOD: "Because ªthe enemy has said of you, 'Aha! ᵇThe ¹ancient heights ᶜhave become our possession,'"' ³therefore prophesy, and say, 'Thus says the Lord GOD: "Because they made *you* desolate and swallowed you up on every side, so that you became the possession of the rest of the nations, ªand you are taken up by the lips of ᵇtalkers and slandered by the people"— ⁴therefore, O mountains of Israel, hear the word of the Lord GOD! Thus says the Lord GOD to the mountains, the hills, the ¹rivers, the valleys, the desolate wastes, and the cities that have been forsaken, which ªbecame plunder and ᵇmockery to the rest of the nations all around— ⁵therefore thus says the Lord GOD: ª"Surely I have spoken in My burning jealousy against the rest of the nations and against all Edom, ᵇwho gave My land to themselves as a possession, with wholehearted joy *and* ¹spiteful minds, in order to plunder its open country."'

⁶"Therefore prophesy concerning the land of Israel, and say to the mountains, the hills, the rivers, and the valleys, 'Thus says the Lord GOD: "Behold, I have spoken in My jealousy and My fury, because you have ªborne the shame of the nations." ⁷Therefore thus says the Lord GOD: "I have ªraised My hand in an oath that surely the nations that *are* around you shall ᵇbear their own shame. ⁸But you, O mountains of Israel, you shall shoot forth your branches and yield your fruit to My people Israel, for they are about to come. ⁹For indeed I *am* for you, and I will turn to you, and you shall be tilled and sown. ¹⁰I will multiply men upon you, all the house of Israel, all of it; and the cities shall be inhabited and ªthe ruins rebuilt. ¹¹ªI will multiply upon you man and beast; and they shall increase and ¹bear young; I will make you inhabited as in

---

35:9 ª Jer. 49:13; Ezek. 25:13
ᵇ Ezek. 36:11

35:10
ª Ps. 83:4–12; Ezek. 36:2, 5
ᵇ [Ps. 48:1–3; 132:13, 14]; Is. 12:6; Ezek. 48:35; Zeph. 3:15

35:11
ª [Matt. 7:2; James 2:13]

35:12 ª Ps. 9:16
ᵇ Zeph. 2:8
ᶜ Is. 52:5

35:13
ª [1 Sam. 2:3]
ᵇ Ezek. 36:3

35:14
ª Is. 65:13, 14

35:15
ª Obad. 12, 15
ᵇ Jer. 50:11; Lam. 4:21

36:1
ª Ezek. 6:2, 3

36:2 ª Jer. 33:24; Ezek. 25:3; 26:2
ᵇ Deut. 32:13; Ps. 78:69; Is. 58:14; Hab. 3:19
ᶜ Ezek. 35:10

36:3
ª Deut. 28:37; 1 Kin. 9:7; Lam. 2:15; Dan. 9:16
ᵇ Ps. 44:13, 14; Jer. 18:16; Ezek. 35:13

36:4
ª Ezek. 34:8, 28 ᵇ Ps. 79:4; Jer. 48:27

36:5
ª Deut. 4:24; Ezek. 38:19
ᵇ Ezek. 35:10, 12

36:6 ª Ps. 74:10; 123:3, 4; Ezek. 34:29

36:7 ª Ezek. 20:5
ᵇ Jer. 25:9, 15, 29

36:10 ª Is. 58:12; 61:4; Amos 9:14

36:11 ª Jer. 31:27; 33:12

35:9 ¹Lit. *desolated forever*   35:13 ¹Lit. *made yourself great*   36:2 ¹Or *everlasting*   36:4 ¹Or *ravines*   36:5 ¹Lit. *scorning souls*   36:11 ¹Lit. *be fruitful*

36:11
b Job 42:12;
Is. 51:3
c Ezek. 35:9;
37:6, 13

36:12 a Obad. 17
b Jer. 15:7;
Ezek. 22:12, 27

36:13
a Num. 13:32

36:15 a Is. 60:14;
Ezek. 34:29

36:17
a Lev. 18:25,
27, 28; Jer. 2:7
b Lev. 15:19

36:18
a Ezek. 16:36, 38;
23:37

36:19
a Deut. 28:64;
Ezek. 5:12;
22:15; Amos 9:9
b Ezek. 7:3;
18:30; 39:24;
[Rom. 2:6]

36:20 a Is. 52:5;
Ezek. 12:16;
Rom. 2:24

36:21
a Ezek. 20:9, 14

36:22 a Ps. 106:8;
Ezek. 20:44

36:23 a Is. 5:16;
Ezek. 20:41;
28:22

36:24
a Is. 43:5, 6;
Ezek. 34:13;
37:21

36:25
a Num. 19:17–19;
Ps. 51:7; Is. 52:15;
Heb. 9:13, 19;
10:22 b Jer. 33:8

36:26 a Ps. 51:10;
Jer. 32:39;
Ezek. 11:19;
[John 3:3]

36:27
a Is. 44:3; 59:21;
Ezek. 11:19; 37:14;
[Joel 2:28, 29]

36:28
a Ezek. 28:25;
37:25
b Jer. 30:22;
Ezek. 11:20;
37:27

36:29
a Zech. 13:1;
[Matt. 1:21;
Rom. 11:26]
b Ps. 105:16
c Ezek. 34:27, 29;
Hos. 2:21–23

36:30 a Lev. 26:4;
Ezek. 34:27

former times, and do ᵇbetter *for you* than at your beginnings. ᶜThen you shall know that I *am* the Lᴏʀᴅ. ¹²Yes, I will cause men to walk on you, My people Israel; ᵃthey shall take possession of you, and you shall be their inheritance; no more shall you ᵇbereave them *of children.*"

¹³"Thus says the Lord Gᴏᴅ: "Because they say to you, ᵃ'You devour men and bereave your nation *of children,*' ¹⁴therefore you shall devour men no more, nor bereave your nation anymore," says the Lord Gᴏᴅ. ¹⁵ᵃ"Nor will I let you hear the taunts of the nations anymore, nor bear the reproach of the peoples anymore, nor shall you cause your nation to stumble anymore," says the Lord Gᴏᴅ.'"

THE RENEWAL OF ISRAEL

¹⁶Moreover the word of the Lᴏʀᴅ came to me, saying: ¹⁷"Son of man, when the house of Israel dwelt in their own land, ᵃthey defiled it by their own ways and deeds; to Me their way was like ᵇthe uncleanness of a woman in her customary impurity. ¹⁸Therefore I poured out My fury on them ᵃfor the blood they had shed on the land, and for their idols *with which* they had defiled it. ¹⁹So I ᵃscattered them among the nations, and they were dispersed throughout the countries; I judged them ᵇaccording to their ways and their deeds. ²⁰When they came to the nations, wherever they went, they ᵃprofaned My holy name—when they said of them, 'These *are* the people of the Lᴏʀᴅ, *and* yet they have gone out of His land.' ²¹But I had concern ᵃfor My holy name, which the house of Israel had profaned among the nations wherever they went.

²²"Therefore say to the house of Israel, 'Thus says the Lord Gᴏᴅ: "I do not do *this* for your sake, O house of Israel, ᵃbut for My holy name's sake, which you have profaned among the nations wherever you went. ²³And I will sanctify My great name, which has been profaned among the nations, which you have profaned in their midst; and the nations shall know that I *am* the Lᴏʀᴅ," says the Lord Gᴏᴅ, "when I am ᵃhallowed in you before their eyes. ²⁴For ᵃI will take you from among the nations, gather you out of all countries, and bring you into your own land. ²⁵ᵃThen I will sprinkle clean water on you, and you shall be clean; I will cleanse you ᵇfrom all your filthiness and from all your idols. ²⁶I will give you a ᵃnew heart and put a new spirit within you; I will take the heart of stone out of your flesh and give you a heart of flesh. ²⁷I will put My ᵃSpirit within you and cause you to walk in My statutes, and you will keep My judgments and do *them.* ²⁸ᵃThen you shall dwell in the land that I gave to your fathers; ᵇyou shall be My people, and I will be your God. ²⁹I will ᵃdeliver you from all your uncleannesses. ᵇI will call for the grain and multiply it, and ᶜbring no famine upon you. ³⁰ᵃAnd I will multiply the fruit of your trees and the increase of your fields, so that you need never again bear the reproach of famine among the nations. ³¹Then ᵃyou will remember your evil ways and your deeds that *were* not good; and you ᵇwill ¹loathe yourselves in your own sight, for your iniquities and your abominations. ³²ᵃNot for your sake do I do *this,*" says the Lord Gᴏᴅ, "let it be known to you. Be ashamed and confounded for your own ways, O house of Israel!"

36:31 ᵃEzek. 16:61, 63 ᵇLev. 26:39; Ezek. 6:9; 20:43   36:32 ᵃDeut. 9:5

36:31 ¹despise

[33]"Thus says the Lord GOD: "On the day that I cleanse you from all your iniquities, I will also enable *you* to dwell in the cities, [a]and the ruins shall be rebuilt. [34]The desolate land shall be tilled instead of lying desolate in the sight of all who pass by. [35]So they will say, 'This land that was desolate has become like the garden of [a]Eden; and the wasted, desolate, and ruined cities *are now* fortified *and* inhabited.' [36]Then the nations which are left all around you shall know that I, the LORD, have rebuilt the ruined places *and* planted what was desolate. [a]I, the LORD, have spoken *it,* and I will do *it.*"

[37]"Thus says the Lord GOD: [a]"I will also let the house of Israel inquire of Me to do this for them: I will [b]increase their men like a flock. [38]Like a [1]flock *offered as* holy *sacrifices,* like the flock at Jerusalem on its [2]feast days, so shall the ruined cities be filled with flocks of men. Then they shall know that I *am* the LORD." '"

THE DRY BONES LIVE

37 The [a]hand of the LORD came upon me and brought me out [b]in the Spirit of the LORD, and set me down in the midst of the valley; and it *was* full of bones. [2]Then He caused me to pass by them all around, and behold, *there were* very many in the open valley; and indeed *they were* very dry. [3]And He said to me, "Son of man, can these bones live?"

So I answered, "O Lord GOD, [a]You know."

[4]Again He said to me, "Prophesy to these bones, and say to them, 'O dry bones, hear the word of the LORD! [5]Thus says the Lord GOD to these bones: "Surely I will [a]cause breath to enter into you, and you shall live. [6]I will put sinews on you and bring flesh upon you, cover you with skin and put breath in you; and you shall live. [a]Then you shall know that I *am* the LORD." '"

[7]So I prophesied as I was commanded; and as I prophesied, there was a noise, and suddenly a rattling; and the bones came together, bone to bone. [8]Indeed, as I looked, the sinews and the flesh came upon them, and the skin covered them over; but *there was* no breath in them.

[9]Also He said to me, "Prophesy to the breath, prophesy, son of man, and say to the [1]breath, 'Thus says the Lord GOD: [a]"Come from the four winds, O breath, and breathe on these slain, that they may live." '" [10]So I prophesied as He commanded me, [a]and [1]breath came into them, and they lived, and stood upon their feet, an exceedingly great army.

[11]Then He said to me, "Son of man, these bones are the [a]whole house of Israel. They indeed say, [b]'Our bones are dry, our hope is lost, and we ourselves are cut off!' [12]Therefore prophesy and say to them, 'Thus says the Lord GOD: "Behold, [a]O My people, I will open your graves and cause you to come up from your graves, and [b]bring you into the land of Israel. [13]Then you shall know that I *am* the LORD, when I have opened your graves, O My people, and brought you up from your graves. [14]I [a]will put My Spirit in you, and you shall live, and I will place you in your own land. Then you shall know that I, the LORD, have spoken *it* and performed *it,*" says the LORD.' "

36:33
[a]Ezek. 36:10

36:35 [a]Is. 51:3;
Ezek. 28:13;
Joel 2:3

36:36
[a]Ezek. 17:24;
22:14; 37:14;
Hos. 14:4–9

36:37
[a]Ezek. 14:3;
20:3, 31
[b]Ezek. 36:10

37:1 [a]Ezek. 1:3
[b]Ezek. 3:14; 8:3;
11:24; Acts 8:39

37:3
[a][Deut. 32:39];
1 Sam. 2:6;
John 5:21;
Rom. 4:17;
2 Cor. 1:9]

37:5 [a]Gen. 2:7;
Ps. 104:29, 30;
Ezek. 37:9,
10, 14

37:6 [a]Is. 49:23;
Ezek. 6:7; 35:12;
Joel 2:27; 3:17

37:9
[a][Ps. 104:30]

37:10 [a]Rev. 11:11

37:11 [a]Jer. 33:24;
Ezek. 36:10
[b]Ps. 141:7;
Is. 49:14

37:12
[a]Deut. 32:39;
1 Sam. 2:6;
Is. 26:19; 66:14;
[Dan. 12:2];
Hos. 13:14
[b]Ezek. 36:24

37:14 [a]Is. 32:15;
Ezek. 36:27;
[Joel 2:28, 29];
Zech. 12:10

36:38 [1]Lit. *holy flock*   [2]*appointed feasts*   **37:9** [1]Breath of life
37:10 [1]Breath of life

37:16
ªNum. 17:2, 3
ᵇ2 Chr. 11:12, 13,
16; 15:9; 30:11, 18

37:17 ªIs. 11:13;
Jer. 50:4;
Ezek. 37:22–24;
Hos. 1:11;
Zeph. 3:9

37:18
ªEzek. 12:9; 24:19

37:19 ªZech. 10:6
ᵇEzek. 37:16, 17

37:20
ªEzek. 12:3

37:21 ªIs. 43:5, 6;
Jer. 32:37;
Ezek. 36:24;
Amos 9:14, 15

37:22 ªIs. 11:13;
Jer. 3:18;
Hos. 1:11
ᵇEzek. 34:23;
John 10:16

37:23
ªEzek. 36:25
ᵇEzek. 36:28, 29

37:24 ªIs. 40:11;
[Jer. 23:5; 30:9];
Ezek. 34:23, 24;
Hos. 3:5;
[Luke 1:32]
ᵇ[John 10:16]
ᶜEzek. 36:27

37:25
ªEzek. 36:28
ᵇIs. 60:21;
Joel 3:20;
Amos 9:15
ᶜPs. 89:3, 4;
John 12:34

37:26 ªPs. 89:3;
Is. 55:3;
[Jer. 32:40];
ᵇJer. 30:19;
Ezek. 36:10
ᶜ[2 Cor. 6:16]

37:27
ªLev. 26:11;
[John 1:14];
Rev. 21:3
ᵇEzek. 11:20

37:28
ªEzek. 36:23
ᵇEx. 31:13;
Ezek. 20:12

38:2 ªEzek. 39:1
ᵇEzek. 35:2, 3
ᶜEzek. 38:1–
39:24; Rev. 20:8
ᵈGen. 10:2;
Ezek. 39:6;
Rev. 20:8
ᵉEzek. 32:26

38:4
ª2 Kin. 19:28;
Ezek. 29:4
ᵇIs. 43:17
ᶜEzek. 23:12

ONE KINGDOM, ONE KING

¹⁵Again the word of the LORD came to me, saying, ¹⁶"As for you, son of man, ªtake a stick for yourself and write on it: 'For Judah and for ᵇthe children of Israel, his companions.' Then take another stick and write on it, 'For Joseph, the stick of Ephraim, and *for* all the house of Israel, his companions.' ¹⁷Then ªjoin them one to another for yourself into one stick, and they will become one in your hand.

¹⁸"And when the children of your people speak to you, saying, ª'Will you not show us what you *mean* by these?'— ¹⁹ªsay to them, 'Thus says the Lord GOD: "Surely I will take ᵇthe stick of Joseph, which *is* in the hand of Ephraim, and the tribes of Israel, his companions; and I will join them with it, with the stick of Judah, and make them one stick, and they will be one in My hand."' ²⁰And the sticks on which you write will be in your hand ªbefore their eyes.

²¹"Then say to them, 'Thus says the Lord GOD: "Surely ªI will take the children of Israel from among the nations, wherever they have gone, and will gather them from every side and bring them into their own land; ²²and ªI will make them one nation in the land, on the mountains of Israel; and ᵇone king shall be king over them all; they shall no longer be two nations, nor shall they ever be divided into two kingdoms again. ²³ªThey shall not defile themselves anymore with their idols, nor with their detestable things, nor with any of their transgressions; but ᵇI will deliver them from all their dwelling places in which they have sinned, and will cleanse them. Then they shall be My people, and I will be their God.

²⁴ª"David My servant *shall be* king over them, and ᵇthey shall all have one shepherd; ᶜthey shall also walk in My judgments and observe My statutes, and do them. ²⁵ªThen they shall dwell in the land that I have given to Jacob My servant, where your fathers dwelt; and they shall dwell there, they, their children, and their children's children, ᵇforever; and ᶜMy servant David *shall be* their prince forever. ²⁶Moreover I will ¹make ªa covenant of peace with them, and it shall be an everlasting covenant with them; I will establish them and ᵇmultiply them, and I will set My ᶜsanctuary in their midst forevermore. ²⁷ªMy tabernacle also shall be with them; indeed I will be ᵇtheir God, and they shall be My people. ²⁸ªThe nations also will know that I, the LORD, ᵇsanctify Israel, when My sanctuary is in their midst forevermore."'"

GOG AND ALLIES ATTACK ISRAEL

38 Now the word of the LORD came to me, saying, ²ª"Son of man, ᵇset your face against ᶜGog, of the land of ᵈMagog, ¹the prince of Rosh, ᵉMeshech, and Tubal, and prophesy against him, ³and say, 'Thus says the Lord GOD: "Behold, I *am* against you, O Gog, the prince of Rosh, Meshech, and Tubal. ⁴ªI will turn you around, put hooks into your jaws, and ᵇlead you out, with all your army, horses, and horsemen, ᶜall splendidly clothed, a great company *with* bucklers and shields, all of them handling swords. ⁵Persia, ¹Ethiopia, and ²Libya are with them, all of them *with* shield and helmet;

37:26 ¹Lit. *cut* 38:2 ¹Tg., Vg., Aquila *the chief prince of Meshech*, also v. 3 38:5 ¹Heb. *Cush* ²Heb. *Put*

6aGomer and all its troops; the house of bTogarmah *from* the far north and all its troops—many people *are* with you.

7a"Prepare yourself and be ready, you and all your companies that are gathered about you; and be a guard for them. 8aAfter many days byou will be visited. In the latter years you will come into the land of those brought back from the sword c*and* gathered from many people on dthe mountains of Israel, which had long been desolate; they were brought out of the nations, and now all of them edwell safely. 9You will ascend, coming alike a storm, covering the bland like a cloud, you and all your troops and many peoples with you."

10Thus says the Lord GOD: "On that day it shall come to pass *that* thoughts will arise in your mind, and you will make an evil plan: 11You will say, 'I will go up against a land of aunwalled villages; I will bgo to a peaceful people, cwho dwell 1safely, all of them dwelling without walls, and having neither bars nor gates'— 12to take plunder and to take booty, to stretch out your hand against the waste places *that are again* inhabited, aand against a people gathered from the nations, who have acquired livestock and goods, who dwell in the midst of the land. 13aSheba, bDedan, the merchants cof Tarshish, and all dtheir young lions will say to you, 'Have you come to take plunder? Have you gathered your army to take booty, to carry away silver and gold, to take away livestock and goods, to take great plunder?'"'

14"Therefore, son of man, prophesy and say to Gog, 'Thus says the Lord GOD: a"On that day when My people Israel bdwell safely, will you not know *it*? 15aThen you will come from your place out of the far north, you and many peoples with you, all of them riding on horses, a great company and a mighty army. 16You will come up against My people Israel like a cloud, to cover the land. It will be in the latter days that I will bring you against My land, so that the nations may aknow Me, when I am bhallowed in you, O Gog, before their eyes."

17Thus says the Lord GOD: "Are *you* he of whom I have spoken in former days by My servants the prophets of Israel, who prophesied for years in those days that I would bring you against them?

JUDGMENT ON GOG

18"And it will come to pass at the same time, when Gog comes against the land of Israel," says the Lord GOD, "*that* My fury will show in My face. 19For ain My jealousy b*and* in the fire of My wrath I have spoken: c'Surely in that day there shall be a great 1earthquake in the land of Israel, 20so that athe fish of the sea, the birds of the heavens, the beasts of the field, all creeping things that creep on the earth, and all men who *are* on the face of the earth shall shake at My presence. bThe mountains shall be thrown down, the steep places shall fall, and every wall shall fall to the ground.' 21I will acall for ba sword against Gog throughout all My mountains," says the Lord GOD. c"Every man's sword will be against his brother. 22And I will abring him to judgment with bpestilence and bloodshed; cI will rain down on him, on his troops, and on the many peoples who *are* with him, flooding rain, dgreat hailstones, fire, and brimstone. 23Thus I will magnify Myself

38:6 aGen. 10:2
bGen. 10:3;
Ezek. 27:14

38:7 aIs. 8:9, 10;
Jer. 46:3, 4

38:8
aDeut. 4:30;
Is. 24:22
bIs. 29:6
cEzek. 34:13
dEzek. 36:1, 4
eJer. 23:6;
Ezek. 34:25;
39:26

38:9 aIs. 28:2
bJer. 4:13

38:11 aZech. 2:4
bJer. 49:31
cEzek. 38:8

38:12
aEzek. 38:8

38:13
aEzek. 27:22
bEzek. 27:15, 20
cEzek. 27:12
dEzek. 19:3, 5

38:14 aIs. 4:1
bJer. 23:6;
Ezek. 38:8, 11;
[Zech. 2:5, 8]

38:15
aEzek. 39:2

38:16
aEzek. 35:11
bIs. 5:16;
8:13; 29:23;
Ezek. 28:22

38:19
aDeut. 32:21, 22;
Ps. 18:7, 8;
Ezek. 36:5, 6;
[Nah. 1:2];
Heb. 12:29
bPs. 89:46
cJoel 3:16;
Hag. 2:6, 7;
Rev. 16:18

38:20 aHos. 4:3
bJer. 4:24;
Nah. 1:5, 6

38:21 aPs. 105:16
bEzek. 14:17
cJudg. 7:22;
1 Sam. 14:20;
2 Chr. 20:23;
Hag. 2:22

38:22 aIs. 66:16;
Jer. 25:31
bEzek. 5:17
cPs. 11:6;
Is. 30:30;
Ezek. 13:11
dRev. 16:21

38:11 1*securely*   38:19 1Lit. *shaking*

and [a]sanctify Myself, [b]and I will be known in the eyes of many nations. Then they shall know that I *am* the LORD."'

GOG'S ARMIES DESTROYED

39 "And [a]you, son of man, prophesy against Gog, and say, 'Thus says the Lord GOD: "Behold, I *am* against you, O Gog, [1]the prince of Rosh, Meshech, and Tubal; [2]and I will [a]turn you around and lead you on, [b]bringing you up from the far north, and bring you against the mountains of Israel. [3]Then I will knock the bow out of your left hand, and cause the arrows to fall out of your right hand. [4a]You shall [1]fall upon the mountains of Israel, you and all your troops and the peoples who *are* with you; [b]I will give you to birds of prey of every sort and *to* the beasts of the field to be devoured. [5]You shall [1]fall on [2]the open field; for I have spoken," says the Lord GOD. [6a]"And I will send fire on Magog and on those who live [1]in security in [b]the coastlands. Then they shall know that I *am* the LORD. [7a]So I will make My holy name known in the midst of My people Israel, and I will not *let them* [b]profane My holy name anymore. [c]Then the nations shall know that *I am* the LORD, the Holy One in Israel. [8a]Surely it is coming, and it shall be done," says the Lord GOD. "This *is* the day [b]of which I have spoken.

[9]"Then those who dwell in the cities of Israel will go out and set on fire and burn the weapons, both the shields and bucklers, the bows and arrows, the [1]javelins and spears; and they will make fires with them for seven years. [10]They will not take wood from the field nor cut down *any* from the forests, because they will make fires with the weapons; [a]and they will plunder those who plundered them, and pillage those who pillaged them," says the Lord GOD.

THE BURIAL OF GOG

[11]"It will come to pass in that day *that* I will give Gog a burial place there in Israel, the valley of those who pass by east of the sea; and it will obstruct travelers, because there they will bury Gog and all his multitude. Therefore they will call *it* the Valley of [1]Hamon Gog. [12]For seven months the house of Israel will be burying them, [a]in order to cleanse the land. [13]Indeed all the people of the land will be burying, and they will gain [a]renown for it on the day that [b]I am glorified," says the Lord GOD. [14]"They will set apart men regularly employed, with the help of [1]a search party, to pass through the land and bury those bodies remaining on the ground, in order [a]to cleanse it. At the end of seven months they will make a search. [15]The search party will pass through the land; and *when anyone* sees a man's bone, he shall [1]set up a marker by it, till the buriers have buried it in the Valley of Hamon Gog. [16]*The* name of *the* city *will* also *be* [1]Hamonah. Thus they shall [a]cleanse the land."'

A TRIUMPHANT FESTIVAL

[17]"And as for you, son of man, thus says the Lord GOD, [a]'Speak to every sort of bird and to every beast of the field:

Cross references (margin)

38:23
[a]Ezek. 36:23
[b]Ps. 9:16;
Ezek. 37:28;
38:16

39:1
[a]Ezek. 38:2, 3

39:2 [a]Ezek. 38:8
[b]Ezek. 38:15

39:4
[a]Ezek. 38:4, 21
[b]Ezek. 33:27

39:6
[a]Ezek. 38:22;
Amos 1:4, 7, 10;
Nah. 1:6
[b]Ps. 72:10;
Is. 66:19;
Jer. 25:22

39:7
[a]Ezek. 39:25
[b]Lev. 18:21;
Ezek. 36:23
[c]Ezek. 38:16

39:8
[a]Rev. 16:17; 21:6
[b]Ezek. 38:17

39:10
[a]Is. 14:2; 33:1;
Mic. 5:8;
Hab. 2:8

39:12
[a]Deut. 21:23;
Ezek. 39:14, 16

39:13 [a]Jer. 33:9;
Zeph. 3:19, 20
[b]Ezek. 28:22

39:14
[a]Ezek. 39:12

39:16
[a]Ezek. 39:12

39:17 [a]Is. 56:9;
[Jer. 12:9];
Ezek. 39:4;
Rev. 19:17, 18

39:1 [1]Tg., Vg., Aquila *the chief prince of Meshech* **39:4** [1]*Be slain* **39:5** [1]*Be slain* [2]Lit. *the face of the field* **39:6** [1]*securely* or *confidently* **39:9** [1]Lit. *hand staffs* **39:11** [1]Lit. *The Multitude of Gog* **39:14** [1]Lit. *those who pass through* **39:15** [1]*build* **39:16** [1]Lit. *Multitude*

^b"Assemble yourselves and come;
Gather together from all sides to My ^csacrificial meal
Which I am sacrificing for you,
A great sacrificial meal ^don the mountains of Israel,
That you may eat flesh and drink blood.
18 ^aYou shall eat the flesh of the mighty,
Drink the blood of the princes of the earth,
Of rams and lambs,
Of goats and bulls,
All of them ^bfatlings of Bashan.
19 You shall eat fat till you are full,
And drink blood till you are drunk,
At My sacrificial meal
Which I am sacrificing for you.
20 ^aYou shall be filled at My table
With horses and riders,
^bWith mighty men
And with all the men of war," says the Lord GOD.

ISRAEL RESTORED TO THE LAND

21^a"I will set My glory among the nations; all the nations shall see My judgment which I have executed, and ^bMy hand which I have laid on them. ^{22a}So the house of Israel shall know that I *am* the LORD their God from that day forward. ^{23a}The Gentiles shall know that the house of Israel went into captivity for their iniquity; because they were unfaithful to Me, therefore ^bI hid My face from them. I ^cgave them into the hand of their enemies, and they all fell by the sword. ^{24a}According to their uncleanness and according to their transgressions I have dealt with them, and hidden My face from them."'

²⁵"Therefore thus says the Lord GOD: ^a'Now I will bring back the captives of Jacob, and have mercy on the ^bwhole house of Israel; and I will be jealous for My holy name— ^{26a}after they have borne their shame, and all their unfaithfulness in which they were unfaithful to Me, when they ^bdwelt safely in their *own* land and no one made *them* afraid. ^{27a}When I have brought them back from the peoples and gathered them out of their enemies' lands, and I ^bam hallowed in them in the sight of many nations, ^{28a}then they shall know that I *am* the LORD their God, who sent them into captivity among the nations, but also brought them back to their land, and left none of them ¹captive any longer. ^{29a}And I will not hide My face from them anymore; for I shall have ^bpoured out My Spirit on the house of Israel,' says the Lord GOD."

A NEW CITY, A NEW TEMPLE

40 In the twenty-fifth year of our captivity, at the beginning of the year, on the tenth *day* of the month, in the fourteenth year after ^athe city was ¹captured, on the very same day ^bthe hand of the LORD was upon me; and He took me there. ^{2a}In the visions of God He took me into the land of Israel and ^bset me on a very high mountain; on it toward the south *was* something like the structure of a city. ³He took me there, and behold, *there was* a man whose appearance *was*

39:17 ^bIs. 18:6
^cIs. 34:6, 7;
Jer. 46:10;
Zeph. 1:7
^dEzek. 39:4
39:18
^aEzek. 29:5;
Rev. 19:18
^bDeut. 32:14;
Ps. 22:12
39:20
^aPs. 76:5, 6;
Ezek. 38:4;
Hag. 2:22
^bRev. 19:18
39:21 ^aEx. 9:16;
Is. 37:20;
Ezek. 36:23;
38:23 ^bEx. 7:4
39:22
^aEx. 39:7, 28
39:23
^aJer. 22:8, 9;
44:22;
Ezek. 36:18–20,
23 ^bDeut. 31:17;
Is. 1:15; 59:2;
Ezek. 39:29
^cLev. 26:25
39:24
^a2 Kin. 17:7;
Jer. 2:17, 19; 4:18;
Ezek. 36:19
39:25
^aIs. 27:12, 13;
Jer. 30:3, 18;
Ezek. 34:13;
36:24 ^bJer. 31:1;
Ezek. 20:40;
Hos. 1:11
39:26
^aDan. 9:16
^bLev. 26:5, 6
39:27
^aEzek. 28:25, 26
^bEzek. 36:23,
24; 38:16
39:28
^aEzek. 34:30
39:29
^aIs. 54:8, 9
^bIs. 32:15;
Ezek. 36:27;
37:14; [Joel 2:28;
Zech. 12:10];
Acts 2:17
40:1
^a2 Kin. 25:1–4;
Jer. 39:2, 3;
52:4–7;
Ezek. 33:21
^bEzek. 1:3; 3:14,
22; 37:1
40:2 ^aEzek. 1:1;
3:14; 8:3; 37:1;
Dan. 7:1, 7
^b[Is. 2:2, 3];
Ezek. 17:23;
20:40; 37:22;
[Mic. 4:1];
Rev. 21:10

[a]like the appearance of bronze. [b]He had a line of flax [c]and a measuring rod in his hand, and he stood in the gateway.

[4]And the man said to me, [a]"Son of man, look with your eyes and hear with your ears, and [1]fix your mind on everything I show you; for you *were* brought here so that I might show *them* to you. [b]Declare to the house of Israel everything you see." [5]Now there was [a]a wall all around the outside of the [1]temple. In the man's hand was a measuring rod six [2]cubits *long, each being a* cubit and a handbreadth; and he measured the width of the wall structure, one rod; and the height, one rod.

THE EASTERN GATEWAY OF THE TEMPLE

[6]Then he went to the gateway which faced [a]east; and he went up its stairs and measured the threshold of the gateway, *which was* one rod wide, and the other threshold *was* one rod wide. [7]Each gate chamber *was* one rod long and one rod wide; between the gate chambers *was a space of* five cubits; and the threshold of the gateway by the vestibule of the inside gate *was* one rod. [8]He also measured the vestibule of the inside gate, one rod. [9]Then he measured the vestibule of the gateway, eight cubits; and the gateposts, two cubits. The vestibule of the gate *was* on the inside. [10]In the eastern gateway *were* three gate chambers on one side and three on the other; the three *were* all the same size; also the gateposts were of the same size on this side and that side.

[11]He measured the width of the entrance to the gateway, ten cubits; *and* the length of the gate, thirteen cubits. [12]*There was* a [1]space in front of the gate chambers, one cubit *on this side* and one cubit on that side; the gate chambers *were* six cubits on this side and six cubits on that side. [13]Then he measured the gateway from the roof of *one* gate chamber to the roof of the other; the width *was* twenty-five cubits, as door faces door. [14]He measured the gateposts, sixty cubits high, and the court all around the gateway *extended* to the gatepost. [15]*From* the front of the entrance gate to the front of the vestibule of the inner gate *was* fifty cubits. [16]There *were* [a]beveled window *frames* in the gate chambers and in their intervening archways on the inside of the gateway all around, and likewise in the vestibules. *There were* windows all around on the inside. And on each gatepost *were* [b]palm trees.

THE OUTER COURT

[17]Then he brought me into [a]the outer court; and *there were* [b]chambers and a pavement made all around the court; [c]thirty chambers faced the pavement. [18]The pavement was by the side of the gateways, corresponding to the length of the gateways; *this was* the lower pavement. [19]Then he measured the width from the front of the lower gateway to the front of the inner court exterior, one hundred cubits toward the east and the north.

THE NORTHERN GATEWAY

[20]On the outer court was also a gateway facing north, and he measured its length and its width. [21]Its gate chambers,

40:3 [a]Ezek. 1:7; Dan. 10:6; Rev. 1:15
[b]Ezek. 47:3; Zech. 2:1, 2
[c]Rev. 11:1; 21:15

40:4 [a]Ezek. 44:5
[b]Ezek. 43:10

40:5 [a][Is. 26:1]; Ezek. 42:20

40:6 [a]Ezek. 43:1

40:16 [a]1 Kin. 6:4; Ezek. 41:16, 26
[b]1 Kin. 6:29, 32, 35; 2 Chr. 3:5; Ezek. 40:22, 26, 31, 34, 37; 41:18–20, 25, 26

40:17 [a]Ezek. 10:5; 42:1; 46:21; Rev. 11:2
[b]1 Kin. 6:5; 2 Chr. 31:11; Ezek. 40:38
[c]Ezek. 45:5

40:4 [1]Lit. *set your heart*   **40:5** [1]Lit. *house*   [2]A royal cubit of about 21 inches
40:12 [1]Lit. *border*

three on this side and three on that side, its gateposts and its archways, had the same measurements as the first gate; its length *was* fifty cubits and its width twenty-five cubits. 22Its windows and those of its archways, and also its palm trees, *had* the same measurements as the gateway facing east; it was ascended by seven steps, and its archway *was* in front of it. 23A gate of the inner court was opposite the northern gateway, just as the eastern *gateway;* and he measured from gateway to gateway, one hundred cubits.

THE SOUTHERN GATEWAY

24After that he brought me toward the south, and there a gateway was facing south; and he measured its gateposts and archways according to these same measurements. 25*There were* windows in it and in its archways all around like those windows; its length *was* fifty cubits and its width twenty-five cubits. 26Seven steps led up to it, and its archway *was* in front of them; and it had palm trees on its gateposts, one on this side and one on that side. 27*There was* also a gateway on the inner court, facing south; and he measured from gateway to gateway toward the south, one hundred cubits.

GATEWAYS OF THE INNER COURT

28Then he brought me to the inner court through the southern gateway; he measured the southern gateway according to these same measurements. 29Also its gate chambers, its gateposts, and its archways *were* according to these same measurements; *there were* windows in it and in its archways all around; *it was* fifty cubits long and twenty-five cubits wide. 30*There were* archways all around, [a]twenty-five cubits long and five cubits wide. 31Its archways faced the outer court, palm trees *were* on its gateposts, and going up to it *were* eight steps.

32And he brought me into the inner court facing east; he measured the gateway according to these same measurements. 33Also its gate chambers, its gateposts, and its archways *were* according to these same measurements; and *there were* windows in it and in its archways all around; *it was* fifty cubits long and twenty-five cubits wide. 34Its archways faced the outer court, and palm trees *were* on its gateposts on this side and on that side; and going up to it *were* eight steps.

35Then he brought me to the north gateway and measured *it* according to these same measurements— 36also its gate chambers, its gateposts, and its archways. It had windows all around; its length *was* fifty cubits and its width twenty-five cubits. 37Its gateposts faced the outer court, palm trees *were* on its gateposts on this side and on that side, and going up to it *were* eight steps.

WHERE SACRIFICES WERE PREPARED

38*There was* a chamber and its entrance by the gateposts of the gateway, where they [a]washed the burnt offering. 39In the vestibule of the gateway *were* two tables on this side and two tables on that side, on which to slay the burnt offering, [a]the sin offering, and [b]the trespass offering. 40At the outer side of the *vestibule,* as one goes up to the entrance of the northern gateway, *were* two tables; and on the other side of

40:30
[a]Ezek. 40:21, 25, 33, 36

40:38
[a]2 Chr. 4:6

40:39
[a]Lev. 4:2, 3
[b]Lev. 5:6; 6:6; 7:1

the vestibule of the gateway *were* two tables. ⁴¹Four tables *were* on this side and four tables on that side, by the side of the gateway, eight tables on which they slaughtered *the sacrifices.* ⁴²There *were* also four tables of hewn stone for the burnt offering, one cubit and a half long, one cubit and a half wide, and one cubit high; on these they laid the instruments with which they slaughtered the burnt offering and the sacrifice. ⁴³Inside *were* hooks, a handbreadth wide, fastened all around; and the flesh of the sacrifices *was* on the tables.

CHAMBERS FOR SINGERS AND PRIESTS

⁴⁴Outside the inner gate *were* the chambers for ᵃthe singers in the inner court, one facing south at the side of the northern gateway, and the other facing north at the side of the ¹southern gateway. ⁴⁵Then he said to me, "This chamber which faces south *is* for ᵃthe priests who have charge of the temple. ⁴⁶The chamber which faces north *is* for the priests ᵃwho have charge of the altar; these *are* the sons of ᵇZadok, from the sons of Levi, who come near the LORD to minister to Him."

DIMENSIONS OF THE INNER COURT AND VESTIBULE
(cf. 1 Kin. 7:14–22)

⁴⁷And he measured the court, one hundred cubits long and one hundred cubits wide, foursquare. The altar *was* in front of the temple. ⁴⁸Then he brought me to the ᵃvestibule of the temple and measured the doorposts of the vestibule, five cubits on this side and five cubits on that side; and the width of the gateway was three cubits on this side and three cubits on that side. ⁴⁹ᵃThe length of the vestibule *was* twenty cubits, and the width eleven cubits; and by the steps which led up to it *there were* ᵇpillars by the doorposts, one on this side and another on that side.

DIMENSIONS OF THE SANCTUARY

41 Then he ᵃbrought me into the ¹sanctuary and measured the doorposts, six cubits wide on one side and six cubits wide on the other side—the width of the tabernacle. ²The width of the entryway *was* ten cubits, and the side walls of the entrance *were* five cubits on this side and five cubits on the other side; and he measured its length, forty cubits, and its width, twenty cubits.

³Also he went inside and measured the doorposts, two cubits; and the entrance, six cubits *high;* and the width of the entrance, seven cubits. ⁴ᵃHe measured the length, twenty cubits; and the width, twenty cubits, beyond the sanctuary; and he said to me, "This *is* the Most Holy *Place.*"

THE SIDE CHAMBERS ON THE WALL

⁵Next, he measured the wall of the ¹temple, six cubits. The width of each side chamber all around the temple *was* four cubits on every side. ⁶ᵃThe side chambers *were* in three stories, one above the other, thirty chambers in each story; they rested on ¹ledges which *were* for the side chambers all

40:44
ᵃ1 Chr. 6:31, 32;
16:41–43; 25:1–7

40:45
ᵃLev. 8:35;
Num. 3:27, 28,
32, 38; 18:5;
1 Chr. 9:23;
2 Chr. 13:11;
Ps. 134:1

40:46
ᵃLev. 6:12, 13;
Num. 18:5;
Ezek. 44:15
ᵇ1 Kin. 2:35;
Ezek. 43:19;
44:15, 16

40:48
ᵃ1 Kin. 6:3;
2 Chr. 3:4

40:49 ᵃ1 Kin. 6:3
ᵇ1 Kin. 7:15–22;
2 Chr. 3:17;
Jer. 52:17–23;
[Rev. 3:12]

41:1
ᵃEzek. 40:2, 3, 17

41:4 ᵃ1 Kin. 6:20;
2 Chr. 3:8

41:6
ᵃ1 Kin. 6:5–10

40:44 ¹So with LXX; MT, Vg. *eastern*   41:1 ¹Heb. *heykal;* the main room in the temple, the holy place, Ex. 26:33   41:5 ¹Lit. *house*   41:6 ¹Lit. *the wall*

around, that they might be supported, but ^bnot fastened to the wall of the temple. ⁷As one went up from story to story, the side chambers ^abecame wider all around, because their supporting ledges in the wall of the temple ascended like steps; therefore the width of the structure increased as one went up *from* the lowest *story* to the highest by way of the middle one. ⁸I also saw an elevation all around the temple; it was the foundation of the side chambers, ^aa full rod, *that is,* six cubits *high.* ⁹The thickness of the outer wall of the side chambers *was* five cubits, and so also the remaining terrace by the place of the side chambers of the ¹temple. ¹⁰And between *it and* the *wall* chambers was a width of twenty cubits all around the temple on every side. ¹¹The doors of the side chambers opened on the terrace, one door toward the north and another toward the south; and the width of the terrace *was* five cubits all around.

THE BUILDING AT THE WESTERN END

¹²The building that faced the separating courtyard at its western end *was* seventy cubits wide; the wall of the building *was* five cubits thick all around, and its length ninety cubits.

DIMENSIONS AND DESIGN OF THE TEMPLE AREA

¹³So he measured the temple, one ^ahundred cubits long; and the separating courtyard with the building and its walls *was* one hundred cubits long; ¹⁴also the width of the eastern face of the temple, including the separating courtyard, *was* one hundred cubits. ¹⁵He measured the length of the building behind it, facing the separating courtyard, with its ^agalleries on the one side and on the other side, one hundred cubits, as well as the inner ¹temple and the porches of the court, ¹⁶their doorposts and ^athe beveled window frames. And the galleries all around their three stories opposite the threshold were paneled with ^bwood from the ground to the windows—the windows were covered— ¹⁷from the space above the door, even to the inner ¹room, as well as outside, and on every wall all around, inside and outside, by measure.

¹⁸And *it was* made ^awith cherubim and ^bpalm trees, a palm tree between cherub and cherub. *Each* cherub had two faces, ^{19a}so that the face of a man *was* toward a palm tree on one side, and the face of a young lion toward a palm tree on the other side; thus *it was* made throughout the temple all around. ²⁰From the floor to the space above the door, and on the wall of the sanctuary, cherubim and palm trees *were* carved.

²¹The ^adoorposts of the temple *were* square, *as was* the front of the sanctuary; their appearance was similar. ^{22a}The altar *was* of wood, three cubits high, and its length two cubits. Its corners, its length, and its sides *were* of wood; and he said to me, "This *is* ^bthe table that *is* ^cbefore the LORD."

^{23a}The temple and the sanctuary had two doors. ²⁴The doors had two ^apanels *apiece,* two folding panels: two *panels* for one door and two panels for the other *door.* ²⁵Cherubim and palm trees *were* carved on the doors of the temple just as they *were* carved on the walls. A wooden canopy *was* on the front of the vestibule outside. ²⁶*There were* ^abeveled window

41:6
^b1 Kin. 6:6, 10

41:7 ^a1 Kin. 6:8

41:8 ^aEzek. 40:5

41:13
^aEzek. 40:47

41:15
^aEzek. 42:3, 5

41:16 ^a1 Kin. 6:4;
Ezek. 40:16, 25
^b1 Kin. 6:15

41:18
^a1 Kin. 6:29;
2 Chr. 3:7
^b2 Chr. 3:5;
Ezek. 40:16

41:19 ^aEzek. 1:10;
10:14

41:21
^a1 Kin. 6:33;
Ezek. 40:9, 14,
16; 41:1

41:22
^aEx. 30:1–3;
1 Kin. 6:20;
Rev. 8:3
^bEx. 25:23, 30;
Lev. 24:6;
Ezek. 23:41;
44:16; Mal. 1:7, 12
^cEx. 30:8

41:23
^a1 Kin. 6:31–35

41:24
^a1 Kin. 6:34

41:26
^aEzek. 40:16

41:9 ¹Lit. *house*   41:15 ¹Or *sanctuary*   41:17 ¹Lit. *house;* the Most Holy Place

frames and palm trees on one side and on the other, on the sides of the vestibule—also on the side chambers of the temple and on the canopies.

THE CHAMBERS FOR THE PRIESTS

42 Then he ªbrought me out into the outer court, by the way toward the ᵇnorth; and he brought me into ᶜthe chamber which *was* opposite the separating courtyard, and which *was* opposite the building toward the north. ²Facing the length, *which was* one hundred cubits (the width was fifty cubits), was the north door. ³Opposite the inner court of twenty *cubits,* and opposite the ªpavement of the outer court, *was* ᵇgallery against gallery in three *stories.* ⁴In front of the chambers, toward the inside, *was* a walk ten cubits wide, at a distance of one cubit; and their doors faced north. ⁵Now the upper chambers *were* shorter, because the galleries took away *space* from them more than from the lower and middle stories of the building. ⁶For they *were* in three *stories* and did not have pillars like the pillars of the courts; therefore *the upper level* was ¹shortened more than the lower and middle levels from the ground up. ⁷And a wall which *was* outside ran parallel to the chambers, at the front of the chambers, toward the outer court; its length *was* fifty cubits. ⁸The length of the chambers toward the outer court *was* fifty cubits, whereas that facing the temple *was* one ªhundred cubits. ⁹At the lower chambers *was* the entrance on the east side, as one goes into them from the outer court.

¹⁰Also *there were* chambers in the thickness of the wall of the court toward the east, opposite the separating courtyard and opposite the building. ¹¹ªThere was* a walk in front of them also, and their appearance *was* like the chambers which *were* toward the north; they *were* as long and as wide as the others, and all their exits and entrances *were* according to plan. ¹²And corresponding to the doors of the chambers that *were* facing south, as one enters them, *there was* a door in front of the walk, the way directly in front of the wall toward the east.

¹³Then he said to me, "The north chambers *and* the south chambers, which *are* opposite the separating courtyard, *are* the holy chambers where the priests who approach the LORD ªshall eat the most holy offerings. There they shall lay the most holy offerings—ᵇthe grain offering, the sin offering, and the trespass offering—for the place *is* holy. ¹⁴ªWhen the priests enter them, they shall not go out of the holy *chamber* into the outer court; but there they shall leave their garments in which they minister, for they *are* holy. They shall put on other garments; then they may approach *that* which *is* for the people."

OUTER DIMENSIONS OF THE TEMPLE

¹⁵Now when he had finished measuring the inner ¹temple, he brought me out through the gateway that faces toward the ªeast, and measured it all around. ¹⁶He measured the east side with the ¹measuring rod, five hundred rods by the measuring rod all around. ¹⁷He measured the north side, five hundred rods by the measuring rod all around. ¹⁸He measured the south side, five hundred rods by the measuring rod. ¹⁹He

---

42:1 ªEzek. 41:1
ᵇEzek. 40:20
ᶜEzek. 41:12, 15
42:3
ªEzek. 40:17
ᵇEzek. 41:15, 16;
42:5
42:8
ªEzek. 41:13, 14
42:11 ªEzek. 42:4
42:13
ªLev. 6:16, 26;
24:9; Ezek. 43:19
ᵇLev. 2:3, 10;
6:14, 17, 25
42:14
ªEzek. 44:19
42:15
ªEzek. 40:6;
43:1

42:6 ¹Or *narrowed*   42:15 ¹Lit. *house*   42:16 ¹About 10.5 feet, Ezek. 40:5

came around to the west side *and* measured five hundred rods by the measuring rod. [20]He measured it on the four sides; [a]it had a wall all around, [b]five hundred *cubits* long and five hundred wide, to separate the holy areas from the [1]common.

THE TEMPLE, THE LORD'S DWELLING PLACE

43 Afterward he brought me to the gate, the gate [a]that faces toward the east. [2a]And behold, the glory of the God of Israel came from the way of the east. [b]His voice *was* like the sound of many waters; [c]and the earth shone with His glory. [3]*It was* [a]like the appearance of the vision which I saw—like the vision which I saw when [1]I came [b]to destroy the city. The visions *were* like the vision which I saw [c]by the River Chebar; and I fell on my face. [4a]And the glory of the LORD came into the [1]temple by way of the gate which faces toward the east. [5a]The Spirit lifted me up and brought me into the inner court; and behold, [b]the glory of the LORD filled the [1]temple.

[6]Then I heard *Him* speaking to me from the temple, while [a]a man stood beside me. [7]And He said to me, "Son of man, *this is* [a]the place of My throne and [b]the place of the soles of My feet, [c]where I will dwell in the midst of the children of Israel forever. [d]No more shall the house of Israel defile My holy name, they nor their kings, by their [1]harlotry or with [e]the carcasses of their kings on their high places. [8a]When they set their threshold by My threshold, and their doorpost by My doorpost, with a wall between them and Me, they defiled My holy name by the abominations which they committed; therefore I have consumed them in My anger. [9]Now let them put their harlotry and the carcasses of their kings far away from Me, and I will dwell in their midst forever.

[10]"Son of man, [a]describe the [1]temple to the house of Israel, that they may be ashamed of their iniquities; and let them measure the pattern. [11]And if they are ashamed of all that they have done, make known to them the design of the [1]temple and its arrangement, its exits and its entrances, its entire design and all its [a]ordinances, all its forms and all its laws. Write *it* down in their sight, so that they may keep its whole design and all its ordinances, and [b]perform them. [12]This *is* the law of the [1]temple: The whole area surrounding [a]the mountaintop *is* most holy. Behold, this *is* the law of the temple.

DIMENSIONS OF THE ALTAR

[13]"These are the measurements of the [a]altar in cubits [b](the [1]cubit *is* one cubit and a handbreadth): the base one cubit high and one cubit wide, with a rim all around its edge of one span. This *is* the height of the altar: [14]from the base on the ground to the lower ledge, two cubits; the width of the ledge, one cubit; from the smaller ledge to the larger ledge, four cubits; and the width of the ledge, *one* cubit. [15]The altar hearth *is* four cubits high, with four [a]horns extending upward from the [1]hearth. [16]The altar hearth *is* twelve *cubits* long, twelve wide,

42:20 [1]Or *profane*   43:3 [1]Some Heb. mss., Vg. *He*   43:4 [1]Lit. *house*
43:5 [1]Lit. *house*   43:7 [1]Unfaithful idolatry   43:10 [1]Lit. *house*   43:11 [1]Lit.
house   43:12 [1]Lit. *house*   43:13 [1]A royal cubit of about 21 inches
43:15 [1]Heb. *ariel*

42:20
[a][Is. 60:18];
Ezek. 40:5;
Zech. 2:5
[b]Ezek. 45:2;
Rev. 21:16

43:1
[a]Ezek. 10:19;
46:1

43:2 [a]Ezek. 11:23
[b]Ezek. 1:24;
Rev. 1:15; 14:2
[c]Ezek. 10:4;
Rev. 18:1

43:3
[a]Ezek. 1:4–28
[b]Jer. 1:10;
Ezek. 9:1, 5;
32:18
[c]Ezek. 1:28;
3:23

43:4
[a]Ezek. 10:19;
11:23

43:5 [a]Ezek. 3:12,
14; 8:3;
2 Cor. 12:2–4
[b]Ezek. 40:34;
1 Kin. 8:10, 11

43:6 [a]Ezek. 1:26;
40:3

43:7 [a]Ps. 99:1;
Is. 60:13
[b]1 Chr. 28:2;
Ps. 99:5
[c]Ex. 29:45;
Ps. 68:16; 132:14;
Ezek. 37:26–28;
Joel 3:17;
[John 1:14;
2 Cor. 6:16]
[d]Ezek. 39:7
[e]Lev. 26:30;
Jer. 16:18;
Ezek. 6:5, 13

43:8
[a]2 Kin. 16:14;
21:4, 5, 7;
Ezek. 8:3; 23:39;
44:7

43:10
[a]Ezek. 40:4

43:11 [a]Ezek. 44:5
[b]Ezek. 11:20

43:12
[a]Ezek. 40:2

43:13
[a]Ex. 27:1–8;
2 Chr. 4:1
[b]Ezek. 41:8

43:15 [a]Ex. 27:2;
Lev. 9:9;
1 Kin. 1:50

ᵃsquare at its four corners; ¹⁷the ledge, fourteen *cubits* long and fourteen wide on its four sides, with a rim of half a cubit around it; its base, one cubit all around; and ᵃits steps face toward the east."

CONSECRATING THE ALTAR

¹⁸And He said to me, "Son of man, thus says the Lord GOD: 'These *are* the ordinances for the altar on the day when it is made, for sacrificing ᵃburnt offerings on it, and for ᵇsprinkling blood on it. ¹⁹You shall give ᵃa young bull for a sin offering to ᵇthe priests, the Levites, who are of the seed of ᶜZadok, who approach Me to minister to Me,' says the Lord GOD. ²⁰'You shall take some of its blood and put *it* on the four horns of the altar, on the four corners of the ledge, and on the rim around it; thus you shall cleanse it and make atonement for it. ²¹Then you shall also take the bull of the sin offering, and ᵃburn it in the appointed place of the ¹temple, ᵇoutside the sanctuary. ²²On the second day you shall offer a kid of the goats without blemish for a sin offering; and they shall cleanse the altar, as they cleansed *it* with the bull. ²³When you have finished cleansing *it,* you shall offer a young bull without blemish, and a ram from the flock without blemish. ²⁴When you offer them before the LORD, ᵃthe priests shall throw salt on them, and they will offer them up *as* a burnt offering to the LORD. ²⁵Every day for ᵃseven days you shall prepare a goat *for* a sin offering; they shall also prepare a young bull and a ram from the flock, both without blemish. ²⁶Seven days they shall make atonement for the altar and purify it, and so ¹consecrate ²it. ²⁷ᵃWhen these days are over it shall be, on the eighth day and thereafter, that the priests shall offer your burnt offerings and your peace offerings on the altar; and I will ᵇaccept you,' says the Lord GOD."

THE EAST GATE AND THE PRINCE

44 Then He brought me back to the outer gate of the sanctuary ᵃwhich faces toward the east, but it *was* shut. ²And the LORD said to me, "This gate shall be shut; it shall not be opened, and no man shall enter by it, ᵃbecause the LORD God of Israel has entered by it; therefore it shall be shut. ³*As* for the ᵃprince, *because* he *is* the prince, he may sit in it to ᵇeat bread before the LORD; he shall enter by way of the vestibule of the gateway, and go out the same way."

THOSE ADMITTED TO THE TEMPLE

⁴Also He brought me by way of the north gate to the front of the ¹temple; so I looked, and ᵃbehold, the glory of the LORD filled the house of the LORD; ᵇand I fell on my face. ⁵And the LORD said to me, ᵃ"Son of man, ¹mark well, see with your eyes and hear with your ears, all that I say to you concerning all the ᵇordinances of the house of the LORD and all its laws. Mark well who may enter the house and all who go out from the sanctuary.

⁶"Now say to the ᵃrebellious, to the house of Israel, 'Thus says the Lord GOD: "O house of Israel, ᵇlet Us have no more of all your abominations. ⁷ᵃWhen you brought in ᵇforeigners, ᶜuncircumcised in heart and uncircumcised in flesh, to be in

43:16 ᵃEx. 27:1

43:17 ᵃEx. 20:26

43:18 ᵃEx. 40:29
ᵇLev. 1:5, 11;
[Heb. 9:21, 22]

43:19 ᵃEx. 29:10;
Lev. 8:14;
Ezek. 45:18, 19
ᵇEzek. 44:15, 16
ᶜ1 Kin. 2:35;
Ezek. 40:46

43:21 ᵃEx. 29:14;
Lev. 4:12
ᵇHeb. 13:11

43:24 ᵃLev. 2:13;
Num. 18:19;
[Mark 9:49, 50;
Col. 4:6]

43:25
ᵃEx. 29:35;
Lev. 8:33

43:27
ᵃLev. 9:1–4
ᵇEzek. 20:40, 41;
[Rom. 12:1;
1 Pet. 2:5]

44:1 ᵃEzek. 43:1

44:2
ᵃEzek. 43:2–4

44:3
ᵃGen. 31:54;
Ex. 24:9–11;
[1 Cor. 10:18]
ᵇEzek. 46:2, 8

44:4 ᵃIs. 6:3;
Ezek. 3:23; 43:5
ᵇEzek. 1:28;
43:3

44:5
ᵃDeut. 32:46;
Ezek. 40:4
ᵇDeut. 12:32;
Ezek. 43:10, 11

44:6 ᵃEzek. 2:5
ᵇEzek. 45:9;
1 Pet. 4:3

44:7
ᵃEzek. 43:8;
Acts 21:28
ᵇLev. 22:25
ᶜLev. 26:41;
Deut. 10:16;
Jer. 4:4; 9:26;
[Acts 7:51]

43:21 ¹Lit. *house*   43:26 ¹Lit. *fill its hands*   ²LXX, Syr. *themselves*   44:4 ¹Lit. *house*   44:5 ¹Lit. *set your heart*

My sanctuary to defile it—My house—and when you offered ᵈMy food, ᵉthe fat and the blood, then they broke My covenant because of all your abominations. ⁸And you have not ᵃkept charge of My holy things, but you have set *others* to keep charge of My sanctuary for you." ⁹Thus says the Lord GOD: ᵃ"No foreigner, uncircumcised in heart or uncircumcised in flesh, shall enter My sanctuary, including any foreigner who *is* among the children of Israel.

LAWS GOVERNING PRIESTS

¹⁰ᵃ"And the Levites who went far from Me, when Israel went astray, who strayed away from Me after their idols, they shall bear their iniquity. ¹¹Yet they shall be ministers in My sanctuary, ᵃ*as* gatekeepers of the house and ministers of the house; ᵇthey shall slay the burnt offering and the sacrifice for the people, and ᶜthey shall stand before them to minister to them. ¹²Because they ministered to them before their idols and ᵃcaused¹ the house of Israel to fall into iniquity, therefore I have ᵇraised My hand in an oath against them," says the Lord GOD, "that they shall bear their iniquity. ¹³ᵃAnd they shall not come near Me to minister to Me as priest, nor come near any of My holy things, nor into the Most Holy *Place;* but they shall ᵇbear their shame and their abominations which they have committed. ¹⁴Nevertheless I will make them ᵃkeep charge of the temple, for all its work, and for all that has to be done in it.

¹⁵ᵃ"But the priests, the Levites, ᵇthe sons of Zadok, who kept charge of My sanctuary ᶜwhen the children of Israel went astray from Me, they shall come near Me to minister to Me; and they ᵈshall stand before Me to offer to Me the ᵉfat and the blood," says the Lord GOD. ¹⁶"They shall ᵃenter My sanctuary, and they shall come near ᵇMy table to minister to Me, and they shall keep My charge. ¹⁷And it shall be, whenever they enter the gates of the inner court, that ᵃthey shall put on linen garments; no wool shall come upon them while they minister within the gates of the inner court or within the house. ¹⁸ᵃThey shall have linen turbans on their heads and linen trousers on their bodies; they shall not clothe themselves with *anything that causes* sweat. ¹⁹When they go out to the outer court, to the outer court to the people, ᵃthey shall take off their garments in which they have ministered, leave them in the holy chambers, and put on other garments; and in their holy garments they shall ᵇnot sanctify the people.

²⁰ᵃ"They shall neither shave their heads nor let their hair grow ᵇlong, but they shall keep their hair well trimmed. ²¹ᵃNo priest shall drink wine when he enters the inner court. ²²They shall not take as wife a ᵃwidow or a divorced woman, but take virgins of the descendants of the house of Israel, or widows of priests.

²³"And ᵃthey shall teach My people *the difference* between the holy and the unholy, and cause them to ᵇdiscern between the unclean and the clean. ²⁴ᵃIn controversy they shall stand as judges, *and* judge it according to My judgments. They shall keep My laws and My statutes in all My appointed meetings, ᵇand they shall hallow My Sabbaths.

44:23 ᵃLev. 10:10, 11; Ezek. 22:26; Hos. 4:6; Mic. 3:9–11; Zeph. 3:4; Hag. 2:11–13; Mal. 2:6–8 ᵇLev. 20:25 44:24 ᵃDeut. 17:8, 9; 1 Chr. 23:4; 2 Chr. 19:8–10 ᵇEzek. 22:26

44:12 ¹Lit. *became a stumbling block of iniquity to the house of Israel*

44:7
ᵈLev. 21:17
ᵉLev. 3:16

44:8
ᵃLev. 22:2;
Num. 18:7

44:9
ᵃEzek. 44:7;
Joel 3:17;
Zech. 14:21

44:10
ᵃ2 Kin. 23:8;
Ezek. 48:11

44:11
ᵃ1 Chr. 26:1–19
ᵇ2 Chr. 29:34;
30:17
ᶜNum. 16:9

44:12
ᵃIs. 9:16;
Mal. 2:8
ᵇPs. 106:26

44:13
ᵃNum. 18:3;
2 Kin. 23:9
ᵇEzek. 32:30

44:14
ᵃNum. 18:4;
1 Chr. 23:28–32;
Ezek. 44:11

44:15
ᵃEzek. 40:46
ᵇ[1 Sam. 2:35];
2 Sam. 15:27;
Ezek. 43:19; 48:11
ᶜEzek. 44:10
ᵈDeut. 10:8
ᵉLev. 3:16,
17; 17:5, 6;
Ezek. 44:7

44:16
ᵃNum. 18:5,
7, 8 ᵇEzek. 41:22;
Mal. 1:7, 12

44:17
ᵃEx. 28:39–43;
39:27–29;
Rev. 19:8

44:18
ᵃEx. 28:40;
39:28; Is. 3:20;
Ezek. 24:17, 23

44:19
ᵃLev. 6:10;
16:4, 23, 24;
Ezek. 42:14
ᵇEx. 30:29;
Lev. 6:27;
Ezek. 46:20;
[Matt. 23:17]

44:20
ᵃLev. 21:5
ᵇNum. 6:5

44:21
ᵃLev. 10:9

44:22
ᵃLev. 21:7, 13, 14

25"They shall not defile *themselves* by coming near a dead person. Only for father or mother, for son or daughter, for brother or unmarried sister may they defile themselves. 26aAfter he is cleansed, they shall count seven days for him. 27And on the day that he goes to the sanctuary to minister in the sanctuary, ahe must offer his sin offering bin the inner court," says the Lord GOD.

28"It shall be, in regard to their inheritance, *that* I aam their inheritance. You shall give them no bpossession in Israel, for I *am* their possession. 29aThey shall eat the grain offering, the sin offering, and the trespass offering; bevery dedicated thing in Israel shall be theirs. 30The abest[1] of all firstfruits of any kind, and every sacrifice of any kind from all your sacrifices, shall be the priest's; also you bshall give to the priest the first of your ground meal, cto cause a blessing to rest on your house. 31The priests shall not eat anything, bird or beast, that adied naturally or was torn *by wild beasts.*

THE HOLY DISTRICT

45 "Moreover, when you adivide the land by lot into inheritance, you shall bset apart a district for the LORD, a holy section of the land; its length *shall be* twenty-five thousand *cubits,* and the width ten thousand. It *shall be* holy throughout its territory all around. 2Of this there shall be a square plot for the sanctuary, afive hundred by five hundred *rods,* with fifty cubits around it for an open space. 3So this is the district you shall measure: twenty-five thousand *cubits* long and ten thousand wide; ain it shall be the sanctuary, the Most Holy *Place.* 4It shall be aa holy *section* of the land, belonging to the priests, the ministers of the sanctuary, who come near to minister to the LORD; it shall be a place for their houses and a holy place for the sanctuary. 5aAn *area* twenty-five thousand *cubits* long and ten thousand wide shall belong to the Levites, the ministers of the [1]temple; they shall have btwenty[2] chambers as a possession.

PROPERTIES OF THE CITY AND THE PRINCE

6a"You shall appoint as the property of the city *an area* five thousand *cubits* wide and twenty-five thousand long, adjacent to the district of the holy *section;* it shall belong to the whole house of Israel.

7a"The prince shall have *a section* on one side and the other of the holy district and the city's property; and bordering on the holy district and the city's property, extending westward on the west side and eastward on the east side, the length *shall be* side by side with one of the *tribal* portions, from the west border to the east border. 8The land shall be his possession in Israel; and aMy princes shall no more oppress My people, but they shall give *the rest of* the land to the house of Israel, according to their tribes."

LAWS GOVERNING THE PRINCE

9"Thus says the Lord GOD: a"Enough, O princes of Israel! bRemove violence and plundering, execute justice and righteousness, and stop dispossessing My people," says the Lord

---

44:30 [1]Lit. *first*   **45:5** [1]Lit. *house*   [2]So with MT, Tg., Vg.; LXX *a possession, cities of dwelling*

GOD. [10]"You shall have [a]honest scales, an honest ephah, and an honest bath. [11]The ephah and the bath shall be of the same measure, so that the bath contains one-tenth of a homer, and the ephah one-tenth of a homer; their measure shall be according to the homer. [12]The [a]shekel *shall be* twenty gerahs; twenty shekels, twenty-five shekels, *and* fifteen shekels shall be your mina.

[13]"This *is* the offering which you shall offer: you shall give one-sixth of an ephah from a homer of wheat, and one-sixth of an ephah from a homer of barley. [14]The ordinance concerning oil, the bath of oil, *is* one-tenth of a bath from a kor. *A kor is* a homer or ten baths, for ten baths *are* a homer. [15]And one lamb shall be given from a flock of two hundred, from the rich pastures of Israel. These shall be for grain offerings, burnt offerings, and peace offerings, [a]to make atonement for them," says the Lord GOD. [16]"All the people of the land shall give this offering for the prince in Israel. [17]Then it shall be the [a]prince's part *to give* burnt offerings, grain offerings, and drink offerings, at the feasts, the New Moons, the Sabbaths, and at all the appointed seasons of the house of Israel. He shall prepare the sin offering, the grain offering, the burnt offering, and the peace offerings to make atonement for the house of Israel."

KEEPING THE FEASTS
(Ex. 12:1–20; Lev. 23:33–43)

[18]Thus says the Lord GOD: "In the first *month,* on the first *day* of the month, you shall take a young bull without blemish and [a]cleanse the sanctuary. [19a]The priest shall take some of the blood of the sin offering and put *it* on the doorposts of the [1]temple, on the four corners of the ledge of the altar, and on the gateposts of the gate of the inner court. [20]And so you shall do on the seventh *day* of the month [a]for everyone who has sinned unintentionally or in ignorance. Thus you shall make atonement for the temple.

[21a]"In the first *month,* on the fourteenth day of the month, you shall observe the Passover, a feast of seven days; unleavened bread shall be eaten. [22]And on that day the prince shall prepare for himself and for all the people of the land [a]a bull *for* a sin offering. [23]On the [a]seven days of the feast he shall prepare a burnt offering to the LORD, seven bulls and seven rams without blemish, daily for seven days, [b]and a kid of the goats daily *for* a sin offering. [24a]And he shall prepare a grain offering of one ephah for each bull and one ephah for each ram, together with a hin of oil for each ephah.

[25]"In the seventh *month,* on the fifteenth day of the month, at the [a]feast, he shall do likewise for seven days, according to the sin offering, the burnt offering, the grain offering, and the oil."

THE MANNER OF WORSHIP

46 [1]Thus says the Lord GOD: "The gateway of the inner court that faces toward the east shall be shut the six [a]working days; but on the Sabbath it shall be opened, and on the day of the New Moon it shall be opened. [2a]The prince shall enter by way of the vestibule of the gateway from the

---

45:10
[a]Lev. 19:36;
Deut. 25:15;
Prov. 16:11;
Amos 8:4–6;
Mic. 6:10, 11

45:12 [a]Ex. 30:13;
Lev. 27:25;
Num. 3:47

45:15
[a]Lev. 1:4; 6:30

45:17
[a]Ezek. 46:4–12

45:18
[a]Lev. 16:16, 33;
Ezek. 43:22, 26

45:19
[a]Lev. 16:18–20;
Ezek. 43:20

45:20
[a]Lev. 4:27;
Ps. 19:12

45:21 [a]Ex. 12:18;
Lev. 23:5, 6;
Num. 9:2, 3;
28:16, 17;
Deut. 16:1

45:22 [a]Lev. 4:14

45:23 [a]Lev. 23:8
[b]Num. 28:15,
22, 30; 29:5, 11,
16, 19

45:24
[a]Num. 28:12–15;
Ezek. 46:5, 7

45:25
[a]Lev. 23:34;
Num. 29:12;
Deut. 16:13;
2 Chr. 5:3;
7:8, 10

46:1 [a]Ex. 20:9

46:2 [a]Ezek. 44:3

45:19 [1]Lit. *house*

outside, and stand by the gatepost. The priests shall prepare his burnt offering and his peace offerings. He shall worship at the threshold of the gate. Then he shall go out, but the gate shall not be shut until evening. ³Likewise the people of the land shall worship at the entrance to this gateway before the LORD on the Sabbaths and the New Moons. ⁴The burnt offering that ªthe prince offers to the LORD on the ᵇSabbath day *shall be* six lambs without blemish, and a ram without blemish; ⁵ªand the grain offering *shall be one* ephah for a ram, and the grain offering for the lambs, ¹as much as he wants to give, as well as a hin of oil with every ephah. ⁶On the day of the New Moon *it shall be* a young bull without blemish, six lambs, and a ram; they shall be without blemish. ⁷He shall prepare a grain offering of an ephah for a bull, an ephah for a ram, ¹as much as he wants to give for the lambs, and a hin of oil with every ephah. ⁸ªWhen the prince enters, he shall go in by way of the vestibule of the gateway, and go out the same way.

⁹"But when the people of the land ªcome before the LORD on the appointed feast days, whoever enters by way of the north ᵇgate to worship shall go out by way of the south gate; and whoever enters by way of the south gate shall go out by way of the north gate. He shall not return by way of the gate through which he came, but shall go out through the opposite gate. ¹⁰The prince shall then be in their midst. When they go in, he shall go in; and when they go out, he shall go out. ¹¹At the festivals and the appointed feast days ªthe grain offering shall be an ephah for a bull, an ephah for a ram, as much as he wants to give for the lambs, and a hin of oil with every ephah.

¹²"Now when the prince makes a voluntary burnt offering or voluntary peace offering to the LORD, the gate that faces toward the east ªshall then be opened for him; and he shall prepare his burnt offering and his peace offerings as he did on the Sabbath day. Then he shall go out, and after he goes out the gate shall be shut.

¹³ª"You shall daily make a burnt offering to the LORD *of* a lamb of the first year without blemish; you shall prepare it ¹every morning. ¹⁴And you shall prepare a grain offering with it every morning, a sixth of an ephah, and a third of a hin of oil to moisten the fine flour. This grain offering is a perpetual ordinance, to be made regularly to the LORD. ¹⁵Thus they shall prepare the lamb, the grain offering, and the oil, *as* a ªregular burnt offering every morning."

THE PRINCE AND INHERITANCE LAWS

¹⁶"Thus says the Lord GOD: "If the prince gives a gift *of* some of his inheritance to any of his sons, it shall belong to his sons; it is their possession by inheritance. ¹⁷But if he gives a gift of some of his inheritance to one of his servants, it shall be his until ªthe year of liberty, after which it shall return to the prince. But his inheritance shall belong to his sons; it shall become theirs. ¹⁸Moreover ªthe prince shall not take any of the people's inheritance by evicting them from their property; he shall provide an inheritance for his sons from his own property, so that none of My people may be scattered from his property."'"

46:4
ªEzek. 45:17
ᵇNum. 28:9, 10

46:5
ªNum. 28:12;
Ezek. 45:24;
46:7, 11

46:8
ªEzek. 44:3;
46:2

46:9
ªEx. 23:14–17;
34:23;
Deut. 16:16, 17;
Ps. 84:7;
Mic. 6:6
ᵇEzek. 48:31, 33

46:11
ªEzek. 46:5, 7

46:12
ªEzek. 44:3;
46:1, 2, 8

46:13
ªEx. 29:38;
Num. 28:3–5

46:15
ªEx. 29:42;
Num. 28:6

46:17 ªLev. 25:10

46:18
ªEzek. 45:8

46:5 ¹Lit. *the gift of his hand*   46:7 ¹Lit. *as much as his hand can reach*
46:13 ¹Lit. *morning by morning*

HOW THE OFFERINGS WERE PREPARED

[19]Now he brought me through the entrance, which *was* at the side of the gate, into the holy [a]chambers of the priests which face toward the north; and there a place *was* situated at their extreme western end. [20]And he said to me, "This *is* the place where the priests shall [a]boil the trespass offering and the sin offering, *and* where they shall [b]bake the grain offering, so that they do not bring *them* out into the outer court [c]to sanctify the people."

[21]Then he brought me out into the outer court and caused me to pass by the four corners of the court; and in fact, in every corner of the court *there was another* court. [22]In the four corners of the court *were* enclosed courts, forty *cubits* long and thirty wide; all four corners *were* the same size. [23]*There was* a row *of building stones* all around in them, all around the four of them; and [1]cooking hearths were made under the rows of stones all around. [24]And he said to me, "These *are* the [1]kitchens where the ministers of the [2]temple shall [a]boil the sacrifices of the people."

THE HEALING WATERS AND TREES

47 Then he brought me back to the door of the [1]temple; and there was [a]water, flowing from under the threshold of the temple toward the east, for the front of the temple faced east; the water was flowing from under the right side of the temple, south of the altar. [2]He brought me out by way of the north gate, and led me around on the outside to the outer gateway that faces [a]east; and there was water, running out on the right side.

[3]And when [a]the man went out to the east with the line in his hand, he measured one thousand cubits, and he brought me through the waters; the water *came up to my* ankles. [4]Again he measured one thousand and brought me through the waters; the water *came up to my* knees. Again he measured one thousand and brought me through; the water *came up to my* waist. [5]Again he measured one thousand, *and it was* a river that I could not cross; for the water was too deep, water in which one must swim, a river that could not be crossed. [6]He said to me, "Son of man, have you seen *this?*" Then he brought me and returned me to the bank of the river.

[7]When I returned, there, along the bank of the river, *were* very many [a]trees on one side and the other. [8]Then he said to me: "This water flows toward the eastern region, goes down into the [1]valley, and enters the sea. *When it* reaches the sea, *its* waters are healed. [9]And it shall be *that* every living thing that moves, wherever [1]the rivers go, will live. There will be a very great multitude of fish, because these waters go there; for they will be healed, and everything will live wherever the river goes. [10]It shall be *that* fishermen will stand by it from En Gedi to En Eglaim; they will be *places* for spreading their nets. Their fish will be of the same kinds as the fish [a]of the Great Sea, exceedingly many. [11]But its swamps and marshes will not be healed; they will be given over to salt. [12][a]Along the bank of the river, on this side and that, will grow all *kinds of* trees

46:19
[a]Ezek. 42:13

46:20
[a]2 Chr. 35:13
[b]Lev. 2:4, 5, 7
[c]Ezek. 44:19

46:24
[a]Ezek. 46:20

47:1 [a]Ps. 46:4;
Is. 30:25; 55:1;
[Jer. 2:13];
Joel 3:18;
Zech. 13:1; 14:8;
[Rev. 22:1, 17]

47:2
[a]Ezek. 44:1, 2

47:3 [a]Ezek. 40:3

47:7
[a][Is. 60:13, 21;
61:3; Ezek. 47:12;
Rev. 22:2]

47:10
[a]Num. 34:3;
Josh. 23:4;
Ezek. 48:28

47:12
[a]Ezek. 47:7;
[Rev. 22:2]

46:23 [1]Lit. *boiling places*   46:24 [1]Lit. *house of those who boil*   [2]Lit. *house*
47:1 [1]Lit. *house*   47:8 [1]Or *Arabah*, the Jordan Valley   47:9 [1]Lit. *two rivers*

used for food; [b]their leaves will not wither, and their fruit will not fail. They will bear fruit every month, because their water flows from the sanctuary. Their fruit will be for food, and their leaves for [c]medicine."[1]

BORDERS OF THE LAND

(cf. Num. 34:1–12)

[13]Thus says the Lord GOD: "These *are* the [a]borders by which you shall divide the land as an inheritance among the twelve tribes of Israel. [b]Joseph *shall have two* portions. [14]You shall inherit it equally with one another; for I [a]raised My hand in an oath to give it to your fathers, and this land shall [b]fall to you as your inheritance.

[15]"This *shall be* the border of the land on the north: from the Great Sea, *by* [a]the road to Hethlon, as one goes to [b]Zedad, [16a]Hamath, [b]Berothah, Sibraim (which *is* between the border of Damascus and the border of Hamath), to Hazar Hatticon (which *is* on the border of Hauran). [17]Thus the boundary shall be from the Sea to [a]Hazar Enan, the border of Damascus; and as for the north, northward, it is the border of Hamath. *This is* the north side.

[18]"On the east side you shall mark out the border from between Hauran and Damascus, and between Gilead and the land of Israel, along the Jordan, and along the eastern side of the sea. *This is* the east side.

[19]"The south side, toward the [1]South, *shall be* from Tamar to [a]the waters of [2]Meribah by Kadesh, along the brook to the Great Sea. *This is* the south side, toward the South.

[20]"The west side *shall be* the Great Sea, from the *southern* boundary until one comes to a point opposite Hamath. This *is* the west side.

[21]"Thus you shall [a]divide this land among yourselves according to the tribes of Israel. [22]It shall be that you will divide it by [a]lot as an inheritance for yourselves, [b]and for the strangers who dwell among you and who bear children among you. [c]They shall be to you as native-born among the children of Israel; they shall have an inheritance with you among the tribes of Israel. [23]And it shall be *that* in whatever tribe the stranger dwells, there you shall give *him* his inheritance," says the Lord GOD.

DIVISION OF THE LAND

48 "Now these *are* the names of the tribes: [a]From the northern border along the road to Hethlon at the entrance of Hamath, to Hazar Enan, the border of Damascus northward, in the direction of Hamath, *there shall be* one *section for* [b]Dan from its east to its west side; [2]by the border of Dan, from the east side to the west, one *section for* [a]Asher; [3]by the border of Asher, from the east side to the west, one *section for* [a]Naphtali; [4]by the border of Naphtali, from the east side to the west, one *section for* [a]Manasseh; [5]by the border of Manasseh, from the east side to the west, one *section for* [a]Ephraim; [6]by the border of Ephraim, from the east side to the west, one *section for* [a]Reuben; [7]by the border of Reuben, from the east side to the west, one *section for* [a]Judah; [8]by the border of

47:12 [b]Job 18:16; [Ps. 1:3; Jer. 17:8]; [c][Rev. 22:2]

47:13 [a]Num. 34:1–29 [b]Gen. 48:5; 1 Chr. 5:1; Ezek. 48:4, 5

47:14 [a]Gen. 12:7; 13:15; 15:7; 17:8; 26:3; 28:13; Deut. 1:8; Ezek. 20:5, 6, 28, 42 [b]Ezek. 48:29

47:15 [a]Ezek. 48:1 [b]Num. 34:7, 8

47:16 [a]Num. 34:8 [b]2 Sam. 8:8

47:17 [a]Num. 34:9; Ezek. 48:1

47:19 [a]Num. 20:13; Deut. 32:51; Ps. 81:7; Ezek. 48:28

47:21 [a]Ezek. 45:1

47:22 [a]Num. 26:55, 56 [b][Eph. 3:6; Rev. 7:9, 10] [c][Acts 11:18; 15:9; Gal. 3:28; Eph. 2:12–14; Col. 3:11]

48:1 [a]Ezek. 47:15 [b]Josh. 19:40–48

48:2 [a]Josh. 19:24–31

48:3 [a]Josh. 19:32–39

48:4 [a]Josh. 13:29–31; 17:1–11, 17, 18

48:5 [a]Josh. 16:5–10; 17:8–10, 14–18

48:6 [a]Josh. 13:15–23

48:7 [a]Josh. 15:1–63; 19:9

47:12 [1]Or *healing*   **47:19** [1]Heb. *Negev*   [2]Lit. *Strife*

Judah, from the east side to the west, shall be [a]the district which you shall set apart, twenty-five thousand *cubits* in width, and *in* length the same as one of the *other* portions, from the east side to the west, with the [b]sanctuary in the center.

9"The district that you shall set apart for the LORD *shall be* twenty-five thousand *cubits* in length and ten thousand in width. 10To these—to the priests—the holy district shall belong: on the north twenty-five thousand *cubits in length,* on the west ten thousand in width, on the east ten thousand in width, and on the south twenty-five thousand in length. The sanctuary of the LORD shall be in the center. 11a*It shall be* for the priests of the sons of Zadok, who are sanctified, who have kept My charge, who did not go astray when the children of Israel went astray, [b]as the Levites went astray. 12And *this* district of land that is set apart shall be to them a thing most [a]holy by the border of the Levites.

13"Opposite the border of the priests, the [a]Levites *shall have an area* twenty-five thousand *cubits* in length and ten thousand in width; its entire length *shall be* twenty-five thousand and its width ten thousand. 14a And they shall not sell or exchange any of it; they may not alienate this best *part* of the land, for *it is* holy to the LORD.

15a"The five thousand *cubits* in width that remain, along the edge of the twenty-five thousand, shall be [b]for general use by the city, for dwellings and common-land; and the city shall be in the center. 16These *shall be* its measurements: the north side four thousand five hundred *cubits,* the south side four thousand five hundred, the east side four thousand five hundred, and the west side four thousand five hundred. 17The common-land of the city shall be: to the north two hundred and fifty *cubits,* to the south two hundred and fifty, to the east two hundred and fifty, and to the west two hundred and fifty. 18The rest of the length, alongside the district of the holy *section, shall be* ten thousand *cubits* to the east and ten thousand to the west. It shall be adjacent to the district of the holy *section,* and its produce shall be food for the workers of the city. 19aThe workers of the city, from all the tribes of Israel, shall cultivate it. 20The entire district *shall be* twenty-five thousand *cubits* by twenty-five thousand *cubits,* foursquare. You shall set apart the holy district with the property of the city.

21a"The rest *shall belong* to the prince, on one side and on the other of the holy district and of the city's property, next to the twenty-five thousand *cubits* of the *holy* district as far as the eastern border, and westward next to the twenty-five thousand as far as the western border, adjacent to the *tribal* portions; *it shall belong* to the prince. It shall be the holy district, [b]and the sanctuary of the [1]temple *shall be* in the center. 22Moreover, apart from the possession of the Levites and the possession of the city *which are* in the midst of what *belongs* to the prince, *the area* between the border of Judah and the border of [a]Benjamin shall belong to the prince.

23"As for the rest of the tribes, from the east side to the west, Benjamin *shall have* one *section;* 24by the border of Benjamin, from the east side to the west, [a]Simeon *shall have* one *section;* 25by the border of Simeon, from the east side to the west, [a]Issachar *shall have* one *section;* 26by the border of

---

48:8
[a]Ezek. 45:1–6
[b][Is. 12:6;
33:20–22];
Ezek. 45:3, 4

48:11
[a]Ezek. 40:46;
44:15
[b]Ezek. 44:10, 12

48:12
[a]Ezek. 45:4

48:13
[a]Ezek. 45:5

48:14
[a]Ex. 22:29;
Lev. 27:10, 28, 33;
Ezek. 44:30

48:15
[a]Ezek. 45:6
[b]Ezek. 42:20

48:19
[a]Ezek. 45:6

48:21
[a]Ezek. 34:24;
45:7; 48:22
[b]Ezek. 48:8, 10

48:22
[a]Josh. 18:21–28

48:24
[a]Josh. 19:1–9

48:25
[a]Josh. 19:17–23

48:21 [1]Lit. *house*

Issachar, from the east side to the west, ªZebulun *shall have* one *section;* ²⁷by the border of Zebulun, from the east side to the west, ªGad *shall have* one *section;* ²⁸by the border of Gad, on the south side, toward the ¹South, the border shall be from Tamar *to* ªthe waters of ²Meribah *by* Kadesh, along the brook to the ᵇGreat Sea. ²⁹ªThis *is* the land which you shall divide by lot as an inheritance among the tribes of Israel, and these *are* their portions," says the Lord GOD.

THE GATES OF THE CITY AND ITS NAME

³⁰"These *are* the exits of the city. On the north side, measuring four thousand five hundred *cubits* ³¹ª(the gates of the city *shall be* named after the tribes of Israel), the three gates northward: one gate for Reuben, one gate for Judah, and one gate for Levi; ³²on the east side, four thousand five hundred *cubits,* three gates: one gate for Joseph, one gate for Benjamin, and one gate for Dan; ³³on the south side, measuring four thousand five hundred *cubits,* three gates: one gate for Simeon, one gate for Issachar, and one gate for Zebulun; ³⁴on the west side, four thousand five hundred *cubits* with their three gates: one gate for Gad, one gate for Asher, and one gate for Naphtali. ³⁵All the way around *shall be* eighteen thousand *cubits;* ªand the name of the city from *that* day *shall be:* ᵇTHE¹ LORD *IS* THERE."

48:26
ªJosh. 19:10–16

48:27
ªJosh. 13:24–28

48:28
ªGen. 14:7;
2 Chr. 20:2;
Ezek. 47:19
ᵇEzek. 47:10, 15,
19, 20

48:29
ªEzek. 47:14,
21, 22

48:31
ª[Rev. 21:10–14]

48:35
ªJer. 23:6; 33:16
ᵇIs. 12:6; 14:32;
24:23; Jer. 3:17;
8:19; 14:9;
Ezek. 35:10;
Joel 3:21;
Zech. 2:10;
Rev. 21:3; 22:3

48:28 ¹Heb. *Negev*   ²Lit. *Strife*   48:35 ¹Heb. *YHWH Shammah*

THE BOOK OF
DANIEL

DANIEL AND HIS FRIENDS OBEY GOD
(cf. 2 Kin. 24:10–17)

1 In the third year of the reign of ᵃJehoiakim king of Judah, Nebuchadnezzar king of Babylon came to Jerusalem and besieged it. ²And the Lord gave Jehoiakim king of Judah into his hand, with ᵃsome of the articles of ¹the house of God, which he carried ᵇinto the land of Shinar to the house of his god; ᶜand he brought the articles into the treasure house of his god.

³Then the king instructed Ashpenaz, the master of his eunuchs, to bring ᵃsome of the children of Israel and some of the king's descendants and some of the nobles, ⁴young men ᵃin whom *there was* no blemish, but good-looking, gifted in all wisdom, possessing knowledge and quick to understand, who *had* ability to serve in the king's palace, and ᵇwhom they might teach the language and ¹literature of the Chaldeans. ⁵And the king appointed for them a daily provision of the king's delicacies and of the wine which he drank, and three years of training for them, so that at the end of *that time* they might ᵃserve before the king. ⁶Now from among those of the sons of Judah were Daniel, Hananiah, Mishael, and Azariah. ⁷ᵃTo them the chief of the eunuchs gave names: ᵇhe gave Daniel *the name* Belteshazzar; to Hananiah, Shadrach; to Mishael, Meshach; and to Azariah, Abed-Nego.

⁸But Daniel purposed in his heart that he would not defile himself ᵃwith the portion of the king's delicacies, nor with the wine which he drank; therefore he requested of the chief of the eunuchs that he might not defile himself. ⁹Now ᵃGod had brought Daniel into the favor and ¹goodwill of the chief of the eunuchs. ¹⁰And the chief of the eunuchs said to Daniel, "I fear my lord the king, who has appointed your food and drink. For why should he see your faces looking worse than the young men who *are* your age? Then you would endanger my head before the king."

¹¹So Daniel said to ¹the steward whom the chief of the eunuchs had set over Daniel, Hananiah, Mishael, and Azariah, ¹²"Please test your servants for ten days, and let them give us vegetables to eat and water to drink. ¹³Then let our appearance be examined before you, and the appearance of the young men who eat the portion of the king's delicacies; and as you see fit, *so* deal with your servants." ¹⁴So he consented with them in this matter, and tested them ten days.

¹⁵And at the end of ten days their features appeared better and fatter in flesh than all the young men who ate the portion of the king's delicacies. ¹⁶Thus ¹the steward took away their portion of delicacies and the wine that they were to drink, and gave them vegetables.

1:1
ᵃ2 Kin. 24:1, 2;
2 Chr. 36:5–7;
Jer. 25:1;
52:12–30

1:2 ᵃ2 Chr. 36:7;
Jer. 27:19, 20;
Dan. 5:2
ᵇGen. 10:10;
11:2; Is. 11:11;
Zech. 5:11
ᶜ2 Chr. 36:7

1:3 ᵃ2 Kin. 20:17,
18; Is. 39:7

1:4
ᵃLev. 24:19, 20
ᵇActs 7:22

1:5 ᵃGen. 41:46;
1 Sam. 16:22;
1 Kin. 10:8;
Dan. 1:19

1:7 ᵃGen. 41:45;
2 Kin. 24:17
ᵇDan. 2:26;
4:8; 5:12

1:8 ᵃLev. 11:47;
Deut. 32:38;
Ezek. 4:13;
Hos. 9:3

1:9 ᵃGen. 39:21;
1 Kin. 8:50;
[Job 5:15, 16];
Ps. 106:46;
[Prov. 16:7];
Acts 7:10; 27:3

1:2 ¹The temple   1:4 ¹Lit. *writing* or *book*   1:9 ¹kindness   1:11 ¹Or *Melzar*
1:16 ¹Or *Melzar*

[17]As for these four young men, [a]God gave them [b]knowledge and skill in all literature and wisdom; and Daniel had [c]understanding in all visions and dreams.

[18]Now at the end of the days, when the king had said that they should be brought in, the chief of the eunuchs brought them in before Nebuchadnezzar. [19]Then the king [1]interviewed them, and among them all none was found like Daniel, Hananiah, Mishael, and Azariah; therefore [a]they served before the king. [20][a]And in all matters of wisdom *and* understanding about which the king examined them, he found them ten times better than all the magicians *and* astrologers who *were* in all his realm. [21][a]Thus Daniel continued until the first year of King Cyrus.

NEBUCHADNEZZAR'S DREAM

2 Now in the second year of Nebuchadnezzar's reign, Nebuchadnezzar had dreams; [a]and his spirit was *so* troubled that [b]his sleep left him. [2][a]Then the king gave the command to call the magicians, the astrologers, the sorcerers, and the Chaldeans to tell the king his dreams. So they came and stood before the king. [3]And the king said to them, "I have had a dream, and my spirit is anxious to [1]know the dream."

[4]Then the Chaldeans spoke to the king in Aramaic, [a]"O[1] king, live forever! Tell your servants the dream, and we will give the interpretation."

[5]The king answered and said to the Chaldeans, "My [1]decision is firm: if you do not make known the dream to me, and its interpretation, you shall be [a]cut in pieces, and your houses shall be made an ash heap. [6][a]However, if you tell the dream and its interpretation, you shall receive from me gifts, rewards, and great honor. Therefore tell me the dream and its interpretation."

[7]They answered again and said, "Let the king tell his servants the dream, and we will give its interpretation."

[8]The king answered and said, "I know for certain that you would gain time, because you see that my decision is firm: [9]if you do not make known the dream to me, *there is only* one decree for you! For you have agreed to speak lying and corrupt words before me till the [1]time has changed. Therefore tell me the dream, and I shall know that you can [2]give me its interpretation."

[10]The Chaldeans answered the king, and said, "There is not a man on earth who can tell the king's matter; therefore no king, lord, or ruler has *ever* asked such things of any magician, astrologer, or Chaldean. [11]*It is* a [1]difficult thing that the king requests, and there is no other who can tell it to the king [a]except the gods, whose dwelling is not with flesh."

[12]For this reason the king was angry and very furious, and gave the command to destroy all the wise *men* of Babylon. [13]So the decree went out, and they began killing the wise *men*; and they sought [a]Daniel and his companions, to kill *them.*

GOD REVEALS NEBUCHADNEZZAR'S DREAM

[14]Then with counsel and wisdom Daniel answered Arioch, the captain of the king's guard, who had gone out to kill the

1:17
[a]1 Kin. 3:12, 28;
2 Chr. 1:10–12;
[Luke 21:15;
James 1:5–7]
[b]Acts 7:22
[c]Num. 12:6;
2 Chr. 26:5;
Dan. 5:11, 12,
14; 10:1

1:19 [a]Gen. 41:46;
[Prov. 22:29];
Dan. 1:5

1:20 [a]1 Kin. 10:1

1:21
[a]Dan. 6:28; 10:1

2:1
[a]Gen. 40:5–8;
41:1, 8;
Job 33:15–17;
Dan. 2:3; 4:5
[b]Esth. 6:1;
Dan. 6:18

2:2 [a]Gen. 41:8;
Ex. 7:11;
Is. 47:12, 13;
Dan. 1:20; 2:10,
27; 4:6; 5:7

2:4 [a]1 Kin. 1:31;
Dan. 3:9; 5:10;
6:6, 21

2:5
[a]2 Kin. 10:27;
Ezra 6:11;
Dan. 3:29

2:6 [a]Dan. 5:16

2:11 [a]Gen. 41:39;
Dan. 5:11

2:13
[a]Dan. 1:19, 20

1:19 [1]Lit. *talked with them*   **2:3** [1]Or *understand*   **2:4** [1]The original language of Daniel 2:4b through 7:28 is Aramaic.   **2:5** [1]The command
2:9 [1]Situation   [2]Or *declare to me*   **2:11** [1]Or *rare*

wise *men* of Babylon; ¹⁵he answered and said to Arioch the king's captain, "Why is the decree from the king so ¹urgent?" Then Arioch made the decision known to Daniel.

¹⁶So Daniel went in and asked the king to give him time, that he might tell the king the interpretation. ¹⁷Then Daniel went to his house, and made the decision known to Hananiah, Mishael, and Azariah, his companions, ¹⁸ᵃthat they might seek mercies from the God of heaven concerning this secret, so that Daniel and his companions might not perish with the rest of the wise *men* of Babylon. ¹⁹Then the secret was revealed to Daniel ᵃin a night vision. So Daniel blessed the God of heaven.

²⁰Daniel answered and said:

ᵃ"Blessed be the name of God forever and ever,
ᵇFor wisdom and might are His.
21   And He changes ᵃthe times and the seasons;
ᵇHe removes kings and raises up kings;
ᶜHe gives wisdom to the wise
And knowledge to those who have understanding.
22 ᵃHe reveals deep and secret things;
ᵇHe knows what *is* in the darkness,
And ᶜlight dwells with Him.

23 "I thank You and praise You,
O God of my fathers;
You have given me wisdom and might,
And have now made known to me what we ᵃasked of You,
For You have made known to us the king's ¹demand."

DANIEL EXPLAINS THE DREAM

²⁴Therefore Daniel went to Arioch, whom the king had appointed to destroy the wise *men* of Babylon. He went and said thus to him: "Do not destroy the wise *men* of Babylon; take me before the king, and I will tell the king the interpretation."

²⁵Then Arioch quickly brought Daniel before the king, and said thus to him, "I have found a man of the ¹captives of Judah, who will make known to the king the interpretation."

²⁶The king answered and said to Daniel, whose name *was* Belteshazzar, "Are you able to make known to me the dream which I have seen, and its interpretation?"

²⁷Daniel answered in the presence of the king, and said, "The secret which the king has demanded, the wise *men*, the astrologers, the magicians, and the soothsayers cannot declare to the king. ²⁸ᵃBut there is a God in heaven who reveals secrets, and He has made known to King Nebuchadnezzar ᵇwhat will be in the latter days. Your dream, and the visions of your head upon your bed, were these: ²⁹As for you, O king, thoughts came *to* your *mind while* on your bed, *about* what would come to pass after this; ᵃand He who reveals secrets has made known to you what will be. ³⁰ᵃBut as for me, this secret has not been revealed to me because I have more wisdom than anyone living, but for *our* sakes who make known the interpretation to the king, ᵇand that you may ¹know the thoughts of your heart.

2:18 ᵃ[Dan. 9:9; Matt. 18:19]

2:19 ᵃNum. 12:6; Job 33:15; [Prov. 3:32]; Amos 3:7

2:20 ᵃPs. 113:2; ᵇ[1 Chr. 29:11, 12; Job 12:13; Ps. 147:5; Jer. 32:19; Matt. 6:13; Rom. 11:33]

2:21 ᵃPs. 31:15; Esth. 1:13; Dan. 2:9; 7:25; ᵇJob 12:18; [Ps. 75:6, 7; Jer. 27:5; Dan. 4:35]; ᶜ1 Kin. 3:9, 10; 4:29; [James 1:5]

2:22 ᵃJob 12:22; Ps. 25:14; [Prov. 3:22]; ᵇJob 26:6; Ps. 139:12; [Is. 45:7; Jer. 23:24; Heb. 4:13]; ᶜ[Ps. 36:9]; Dan. 5:11, 14; [1 Tim. 6:16; James 1:17; 1 John 1:5]

2:23 ᵃPs. 21:2, 4; Dan. 2:18, 29, 30

2:28 ᵃGen. 40:8; Amos 4:13; ᵇGen. 49:1; Is. 2:2; Dan. 10:14; Mic. 4:1

2:29 ᵃ[Dan. 2:22, 28]

2:30 ᵃActs 3:12; ᵇDan. 2:47

2:15 ¹Or *harsh*   2:23 ¹Lit. *word*   2:25 ¹Lit. *sons of the captivity*
2:30 ¹Understand

2:32
aDan. 2:38, 45

2:34 aDan. 8:25;
[Zech. 4:6];
2 Cor. 5:1;
Heb. 9:24

2:35
aDan. 7:23–27;
[Rev. 16:14]
bPs. 1:4;
Is. 17:13; 41:15, 16;
Hos. 13:3
cPs. 37:10, 36
d[Is. 2:2, 3];
Mic. 4:1
ePs. 80:9

2:37 aEzra 7:12;
Is. 47:5;
Jer. 27:6, 7;
Ezek. 26:7;
Hos. 8:10
bEzra 1:2

2:38
aPs. 50:10, 11;
Jer. 27:6;
Dan. 4:21, 22
bDan. 2:32

2:39
aDan. 5:28, 31
bDan. 2:32

2:40
aDan. 7:7, 23

2:42 aDan. 7:24

2:44
aDan. 2:28, 37
bIs. 9:6, 7;
Ezek. 37:25;
Dan. 4:3, 34;
6:26; 7:14, 27;
Mic. 4:7;
[Luke 1:32, 33]
cPs. 2:9;
Is. 60:12;
Dan. 2:34, 35;
[1 Cor. 15:24]

2:45 aDan. 2:35;
Is. 28:16

2:46
aDan. 3:5, 7;
Acts 10:25; 14:13;
Rev. 19:10; 22:8
bLev. 26:31;
Ezra 6:10

2:47
aDan. 3:28, 29;
4:34–37
b[Deut. 10:17]

2:48
a[Prov. 14:35;
21:1] bDan. 2:6
cDan. 4:9; 5:11

2:49
aDan. 1:7; 3:12
bEsth. 2:19, 21;
3:2; Amos 5:15

31"You, O king, were watching; and behold, a great image! This great image, whose splendor *was* excellent, stood before you; and its form *was* awesome. 32aThis image's head *was* of fine gold, its chest and arms of silver, its belly and 1thighs of bronze, 33its legs of iron, its feet partly of iron and partly of 1clay. 34You watched while a stone was cut out awithout hands, which struck the image on its feet of iron and clay, and broke them in pieces. 35aThen the iron, the clay, the bronze, the silver, and the gold were crushed together, and became blike chaff from the summer threshing floors; the wind carried them away so that cno trace of them was found. And the stone that struck the image dbecame a great mountain eand filled the whole earth.

36"This *is* the dream. Now we will tell the interpretation of it before the king. 37aYou, O king, *are* a king of kings. bFor the God of heaven has given you a kingdom, power, strength, and glory; 38aand wherever the children of men dwell, or the beasts of the field and the birds of the heaven, He has given *them* into your hand, and has made you ruler over them all—byou *are* this head of gold. 39But after you shall arise aanother kingdom binferior to yours; then another, a third kingdom of bronze, which shall rule over all the earth. 40And athe fourth kingdom shall be as strong as iron, inasmuch as iron breaks in pieces and shatters everything; and like iron that crushes, *that kingdom* will break in pieces and crush all the others. 41Whereas you saw the feet and toes, partly of potter's clay and partly of iron, the kingdom shall be divided; yet the strength of the iron shall be in it, just as you saw the iron mixed with ceramic clay. 42And *as* the toes of the feet *were* partly of iron and partly of clay, aso the kingdom shall be partly strong and partly 1fragile. 43As you saw iron mixed with ceramic clay, they will mingle with the seed of men; but they will not adhere to one another, just as iron does not mix with clay. 44And in the days of these kings athe God of heaven will set up a kingdom bwhich shall never be destroyed; and the kingdom shall not be left to other people; cit shall 1break in pieces and 2consume all these kingdoms, and it shall stand forever. 45aInasmuch as you saw that the stone was cut out of the mountain without hands, and that it broke in pieces the iron, the bronze, the clay, the silver, and the gold—the great God has made known to the king what will come to pass after this. The dream is certain, and its interpretation is sure."

DANIEL AND HIS FRIENDS PROMOTED

46aThen King Nebuchadnezzar fell on his face, prostrate before Daniel, and commanded that they should present an offering band incense to him. 47The king answered Daniel, and said, "Truly ayour God *is* the God of bgods, the Lord of kings, and a revealer of secrets, since you could reveal this secret." 48aThen the king promoted Daniel band gave him many great gifts; and he made him ruler over the whole province of Babylon, and cchief administrator over all the wise *men* of Babylon. 49Also Daniel petitioned the king, aand he set Shadrach, Meshach, and Abed-Nego over the affairs of the province of Babylon; but Daniel bsat in 1the gate of the king.

2:32 1Or *sides*   2:33 1Or *baked clay*, also vv. 34, 35, 42   2:42 1Or *brittle*
2:44 1Or *crush*   2Lit. *put an end to*   2:49 1The king's court

THE IMAGE OF GOLD

3 Nebuchadnezzar the king made an image of gold, whose height *was* [1]sixty cubits *and* its width six cubits. He set it up in the plain of Dura, in the province of Babylon. [2]And King Nebuchadnezzar sent *word* to gather together the satraps, the administrators, the governors, the counselors, the treasurers, the judges, the magistrates, and all the officials of the provinces, to come to the dedication of the image which King Nebuchadnezzar had set up. [3]So the satraps, the administrators, the governors, the counselors, the treasurers, the judges, the magistrates, and all the officials of the provinces gathered together for the dedication of the image that King Nebuchadnezzar had set up; and they stood before the image that Nebuchadnezzar had set up. [4]Then a herald cried [1]aloud: "To you it is commanded, [a]O peoples, nations, and languages, [5]*that* at the time you hear the sound of the horn, flute, harp, lyre, *and* psaltery, in symphony with all kinds of music, you shall fall down and worship the gold image that King Nebuchadnezzar has set up; [6]and whoever does not fall down and worship shall [a]be cast immediately into the midst of a burning fiery furnace."

[7]So at that time, when all the people heard the sound of the horn, flute, harp, *and* lyre, in symphony with all kinds of music, all the people, nations, and languages fell down *and* worshiped the gold image which King Nebuchadnezzar had set up.

DANIEL'S FRIENDS DISOBEY THE KING

[8]Therefore at that time certain Chaldeans [a]came forward and accused the Jews. [9]They spoke and said to King Nebuchadnezzar, [a]"O king, live forever! [10]You, O king, have made a decree that everyone who hears the sound of the horn, flute, harp, lyre, *and* psaltery, in symphony with all kinds of music, shall fall down and worship the gold image; [11]and whoever does not fall down and worship shall be cast into the midst of a burning fiery furnace. [12a]There are certain Jews whom you have set over the affairs of the province of Babylon: Shadrach, Meshach, and Abed-Nego; these men, O king, have [b]not paid due regard to you. They do not serve your gods or worship the gold image which you have set up."

[13]Then Nebuchadnezzar, in [a]rage and fury, gave the command to bring Shadrach, Meshach, and Abed-Nego. So they brought these men before the king. [14]Nebuchadnezzar spoke, saying to them, "*Is it* true, Shadrach, Meshach, and Abed-Nego, *that* you do not serve my gods or worship the gold image which I have set up? [15]Now if you are ready at the time you hear the sound of the horn, flute, harp, lyre, *and* psaltery, in symphony with all kinds of music, and you fall down and worship the image which I have made, [a]*good!* But if you do not worship, you shall be cast immediately into the midst of a burning fiery furnace. [b]And who *is* the god who will deliver you from my hands?"

[16]Shadrach, Meshach, and Abed-Nego answered and said to the king, "O Nebuchadnezzar, [a]we have no need to answer you in this matter. [17]If that *is the case,* our [a]God whom we serve is able to [b]deliver us from the burning fiery furnace, and

3:4
[a]Dan. 4:1; 6:25

3:6 [a]Jer. 29:22;
Ezek. 22:18–22;
Matt. 13:42, 50;
Rev. 9:2; 13:15;
14:11

3:8
[a]Ezra 4:12–16;
Esth. 3:8, 9;
Dan. 6:12, 13

3:9 [a]Dan. 2:4;
5:10; 6:6, 21

3:12 [a]Dan. 2:49
[b]Dan. 1:8;
6:12, 13

3:13
[a]Dan. 2:12; 3:19

3:15 [a]Ex. 32:32;
Luke 13:9
[b]Ex. 5:2;
2 Kin. 18:35;
Is. 36:18–20;
Dan. 2:47

3:16
[a][Matt. 10:19]

3:17 [a]Job 5:19;
[Ps. 27:1, 2;
Is. 26:3, 4];
Jer. 1:8; 15:20, 21;
Dan. 6:19–22
[b]1 Sam. 17:37;
Jer. 1:8; 15:20, 21;
42:11; Dan. 6:16,
19–22; Mic. 7:7;
2 Cor. 1:10

3:1 [1]About 90 feet   3:4 [1]Lit. *with strength*

He will deliver *us* from your hand, O king. ¹⁸But if not, let it be known to you, O king, that we do not serve your gods, nor will we ªworship the gold image which you have set up."

SAVED IN FIERY TRIAL

¹⁹Then Nebuchadnezzar was full of fury, and the expression on his face changed toward Shadrach, Meshach, and Abed-Nego. He spoke and commanded that they heat the furnace seven times more than it was usually heated. ²⁰And he commanded certain mighty men of valor who *were* in his army to bind Shadrach, Meshach, and Abed-Nego, *and* cast *them* into the burning fiery furnace. ²¹Then these men were bound in their coats, their trousers, their turbans, and their *other* garments, and were cast into the midst of the burning fiery furnace. ²²Therefore, because the king's command was ¹urgent, and the furnace exceedingly hot, the flame of the fire killed those men who took up Shadrach, Meshach, and Abed-Nego. ²³And these three men, Shadrach, Meshach, and Abed-Nego, fell down bound into the midst of the burning fiery furnace.

²⁴Then King Nebuchadnezzar was astonished; and he rose in haste *and* spoke, saying to his ¹counselors, "Did we not cast three men bound into the midst of the fire?"

They answered and said to the king, "True, O king."

²⁵"Look!" he answered, "I see four men loose, ªwalking in the midst of the fire; and they are not hurt, and the form of the fourth is like ᵇthe¹ Son of God."

NEBUCHADNEZZAR PRAISES GOD

²⁶Then Nebuchadnezzar went near the ¹mouth of the burning fiery furnace *and* spoke, saying, "Shadrach, Meshach, and Abed-Nego, servants of the ªMost High God, come out, and come *here*." Then Shadrach, Meshach, and Abed-Nego came from the midst of the fire. ²⁷And the satraps, administrators, governors, and the king's counselors gathered together, and they saw these men ªon whose bodies the fire had no power; the hair of their head was not singed nor were their garments affected, and the smell of fire was not on them.

²⁸Nebuchadnezzar spoke, saying, "Blessed be the God of Shadrach, Meshach, and Abed-Nego, who sent His ªAngel¹ and delivered His servants who trusted in Him, and they have frustrated the king's word, and yielded their bodies, that they should not serve nor worship any god except their own God! ²⁹ªTherefore I make a decree that any people, nation, or language which speaks anything amiss against the ᵇGod of Shadrach, Meshach, and Abed-Nego shall be ᶜcut in pieces, and their houses shall be made an ash heap; ᵈbecause there is no other God who can deliver like this."

³⁰Then the king ¹promoted Shadrach, Meshach, and Abed-Nego in the province of Babylon.

NEBUCHADNEZZAR'S SECOND DREAM

4 Nebuchadnezzar the king,

ªTo all peoples, nations, and languages that dwell in all the earth:

3:18 ªJob 13:15

3:25
ª[Ps. 91:3–9];
Is. 43:2 ᵇJob 1:6;
38:7; [Ps. 34:7];
Dan. 3:28

3:26
ª[Dan. 4:2, 3,
17, 34, 35]

3:27 ª[Is. 43:2];
Heb. 11:34

3:28
ª[Ps. 34:7, 8];
Is. 37:36;
[Jer. 17:7];
Dan. 6:22, 23;
Acts 5:19; 12:7

3:29 ªDan. 6:26
ᵇDan. 2:46, 47;
4:34–37
ᶜEzra 6:11;
Dan. 2:5
ᵈDan. 6:27

4:1 ªEzra 4:17;
Dan. 3:4; 6:25

3:22 ¹Or *harsh*   3:24 ¹High officials   3:25 ¹Or *a son of the gods*   3:26 ¹Lit.
door   3:28 ¹Or *angel*   3:30 ¹Lit. *caused to prosper*

Peace be multiplied to you.

2 I thought it good to declare the signs and wonders ᵃthat the Most High God has worked for me.

3 ᵃHow great *are* His signs,
And how mighty His wonders!
His kingdom *is* ᵇan everlasting kingdom,
And His dominion *is* from generation to generation.

4 I, Nebuchadnezzar, was at rest in my house, and flourishing in my palace. ⁵I saw a dream which made me afraid, ᵃand the thoughts on my bed and the visions of my head ᵇtroubled me. ⁶Therefore I issued a decree to bring in all the wise *men* of Babylon before me, that they might make known to me the interpretation of the dream. ⁷ᵃThen the magicians, the astrologers, the Chaldeans, and the soothsayers came in, and I told them the dream; but they did not make known to me its interpretation. ⁸But at last Daniel came before me ᵃ(his name *is* Belteshazzar, according to the name of my god; ᵇin him *is* the Spirit of the Holy God), and I told the dream before him, *saying:* ⁹"Belteshazzar, ᵃchief of the magicians, because I know that the Spirit of the Holy God *is* in you, and no secret troubles you, explain to me the visions of my dream that I have seen, and its interpretation.

10 "These *were* the visions of my head *while* on my bed:

I was looking, and behold,
ᵃA tree in the midst of the earth,
And its height was great.
11 The tree grew and became strong;
Its height reached to the heavens,
And it could be seen to the ends of all the earth.
12 Its leaves *were* lovely,
Its fruit abundant,
And in it *was* food for all.
ᵃThe beasts of the field found shade under it,
The birds of the heavens dwelt in its branches,
And all flesh was fed from it.

13 "I saw in the visions of my head *while* on my bed, and there was ᵃa watcher, ᵇa holy one, coming down from heaven. ¹⁴He cried ¹aloud and said thus:

ᵃ'Chop down the tree and cut off its branches,
Strip off its leaves and scatter its fruit.
ᵇLet the beasts get out from under it,
And the birds from its branches.
15 Nevertheless leave the stump and roots in the earth,
Bound with a band of iron and bronze,
In the tender grass of the field.
Let it be wet with the dew of heaven,
And *let* him graze with the beasts
On the grass of the earth.
16 Let his heart be changed from *that of* a man,
Let him be given the heart of a beast,
And let seven ᵃtimes¹ pass over him.

4:2 ᵃDan. 3:26

4:3 ᵃ2 Sam. 7:16;
Ps. 89:35–37;
Dan. 6:27;
7:13, 14;
[Luke 1:31–33]
ᵇ[Dan. 2:44;
4:34; 6:26]

4:5
ᵃDan. 2:28, 29
ᵇDan. 2:1

4:7 ᵃDan. 2:2

4:8 ᵃDan. 1:7
ᵇIs. 63:11;
Dan. 2:11; 4:18;
5:11, 14

4:9
ᵃDan. 2:48; 5:11

4:10 ᵃEzek. 31:3;
Dan. 4:20

4:12 ᵃJer. 27:6;
Ezek. 17:23; 31:6;
Lam. 4:20

4:13
ᵃ[Dan. 4:17, 23]
ᵇDeut. 33:2;
Ps. 89:7;
Dan. 8:13;
Zech. 14:5;
Jude 14

4:14
ᵃEzek. 31:10–14;
Dan. 4:23;
[Matt. 3:10; 7:19;
Luke 13:7–9]
ᵇEzek. 31:12, 13;
Dan. 4:12

4:16
ᵃDan. 11:13; 12:7

4:14 ¹Lit. *with strength*   4:16 ¹Possibly *years*

17 'This decision *is* by the decree of the watchers,
And the sentence by the word of the holy ones,
In order ᵃthat the living may know
ᵇThat the Most High rules in the kingdom of men,
ᶜGives it to whomever He will,
And sets over it the ᵈlowest of men.'

18 "This dream I, King Nebuchadnezzar, have seen. Now you, Belteshazzar, declare its interpretation, ᵃsince all the wise *men* of my kingdom are not able to make known to me the interpretation; but you *are* able, ᵇfor the Spirit of the Holy God *is* in you."

DANIEL EXPLAINS THE SECOND DREAM

19 Then Daniel, ᵃwhose name *was* Belteshazzar, was astonished for a time, and his thoughts ᵇtroubled him. *So* the king spoke, and said, "Belteshazzar, do not let the dream or its interpretation trouble you."

Belteshazzar answered and said, "My lord, *may* ᶜthe dream ¹concern those who hate you, and its interpretation ²concern your enemies!

20 ᵃ"The tree that you saw, which grew and became strong, whose height reached to the heavens and which *could be* seen by all the earth, ²¹whose leaves *were* lovely and its fruit abundant, in which *was* food for all, under which the beasts of the field dwelt, and in whose branches the birds of the heaven had their home— ²²ᵃit *is* you, O king, who have grown and become strong; for your greatness has grown and reaches to the heavens, ᵇand your dominion to the end of the earth.

23 ᵃ"And inasmuch as the king saw a watcher, a holy one, coming down from heaven and saying, 'Chop down the tree and destroy it, but leave its stump and roots in the earth, *bound* with a band of iron and bronze in the tender grass of the field; let it be wet with the dew of heaven, ᵇand let him graze with the beasts of the field, till seven ¹times pass over him'; ²⁴this is the interpretation, O king, and this is the decree of the Most High, which has come upon my lord the king: ²⁵They shall ᵃdrive you from men, your dwelling shall be with the beasts of the field, and they shall make you ᵇeat grass like oxen. They shall wet you with the dew of heaven, and seven ¹times shall pass over you, ᶜtill you know that the Most High rules in the kingdom of men, and ᵈgives it to whomever He chooses.

26 "And inasmuch as they gave the command to leave the stump *and* roots of the tree, your kingdom shall be assured to you, after you come to know that ᵃHeaven¹ rules. ²⁷Therefore, O king, let my advice be acceptable to you; ᵃbreak off your sins by *being* righteous, and your iniquities by showing mercy to *the* poor. ᵇPerhaps there may be ᶜa ¹lengthening of your prosperity."

NEBUCHADNEZZAR'S HUMILIATION

28 All *this* came upon King Nebuchadnezzar. ²⁹At the end of the twelve months he was walking ¹about the royal

---

4:17
ᵃPs. 9:16; 83:18
ᵇDan. 2:21;
4:25, 32; 5:21
ᶜJer. 27:5–7;
Ezek. 29:18–20;
Dan. 2:37; 5:18
ᵈ1 Sam. 2:8;
Dan. 11:21

4:18
ᵃGen. 41:8, 15;
Dan. 5:8, 15
ᵇDan. 4:8, 9;
5:11, 14

4:19 ᵃDan. 4:8
ᵇJer. 4:19;
Dan. 7:15,
28; 8:27
ᶜ2 Sam. 18:32;
Jer. 29:7;
Dan. 4:24; 10:16

4:20
ᵃDan. 4:10–12

4:22
ᵃDan. 2:37, 38
ᵇJer. 27:6–8

4:23
ᵃDan. 4:13–15
ᵇDan. 5:21

4:25
ᵃDan. 4:32; 5:21
ᵇPs. 106:20
ᶜPs. 83:18;
Dan. 4:2, 17, 32
ᵈJer. 27:5

4:26
ᵃMatt. 21:25;
Luke 15:18

4:27
ᵃ[Prov. 28:13];
Is. 55:7;
Ezek. 18:21, 22;
[Rom. 2:9–11;
1 Pet. 4:8]
ᵇ[Ps. 41:1–3];
Is. 58:6, 7, 10
ᶜ1 Kin. 21:29

4:19 ¹*be for*   ²*for*   4:23 ¹Possibly *years*   4:25 ¹Possibly *years*   4:26 ¹God
4:27 ¹*prolonging*   4:29 ¹Or *upon*

palace of Babylon. [30]The king [a]spoke, saying, "Is not this great Babylon, that I have built for a royal dwelling by my mighty power and for the honor of my majesty?"

31 [a]While the word *was still* in the king's mouth, [b]a voice fell from heaven: "King Nebuchadnezzar, to you it is spoken: the kingdom has departed from you! [32]And [a]they shall drive you from men, and your dwelling *shall be* with the beasts of the field. They shall make you eat grass like oxen; and seven [1]times shall pass over you, until you know that the Most High rules in the kingdom of men, and gives it to whomever He chooses."

33 That very hour the word was fulfilled concerning Nebuchadnezzar; he was driven from men and ate grass like oxen; his body was wet with the dew of heaven till his hair had grown like eagles' *feathers* and his nails like birds' *claws*.

NEBUCHADNEZZAR PRAISES GOD

34 And [a]at the end of the [1]time I, Nebuchadnezzar, lifted my eyes to heaven, and my understanding returned to me; and I blessed the Most High and praised and honored Him [b]who lives forever:

For His dominion *is* [c]an everlasting dominion,
And His kingdom *is* from generation to generation.

35 [a]All the inhabitants of the earth *are* reputed as nothing;
[b]He does according to His will in the army of heaven
And *among* the inhabitants of the earth.
[c]No one can restrain His hand
Or say to Him, [d]"What have You done?"

36 At the same time my reason returned to me, [a]and for the glory of my kingdom, my honor and splendor returned to me. My counselors and nobles resorted to me, I was [b]restored to my kingdom, and excellent majesty was [c]added to me. [37]Now I, Nebuchadnezzar, [a]praise and extol and honor the King of heaven, [b]all of whose works *are* truth, and His ways justice. [c]And those who walk in pride He is able to put down.

BELSHAZZAR'S FEAST

5 Belshazzar the king [a]made a great feast for a thousand of his lords, and drank wine in the presence of the thousand. [2]While he tasted the wine, Belshazzar gave the command to bring the gold and silver vessels [a]which his [1]father Nebuchadnezzar had taken from the temple which *had been* in Jerusalem, that the king and his lords, his wives, and his concubines might drink from them. [3]Then they brought the gold [a]vessels that had been taken from the temple of the house of God which *had been* in Jerusalem; and the king and his lords, his wives, and his concubines drank from them. [4]They drank wine, [a]and praised the gods of gold and silver, bronze and iron, wood and stone.

[5a]In the same hour the fingers of a man's hand appeared and wrote opposite the lampstand on the plaster of the wall of the king's palace; and the king saw the part of the hand that wrote. [6]Then the king's countenance changed, and his

4:30
[a]Prov. 16:18;
Is. 13:19;
Dan. 5:20

4:31 [a]Dan. 5:5;
Luke 12:20
[b]Dan. 4:24

4:32
[a][Dan. 4:25]

4:34 [a]Dan. 4:26
[b]Ps. 102:24–27;
Dan. 6:26;
12:7; [Rev. 4:10]
[c][Ps. 10:16];
Dan. 2:44;
7:14; Mic. 4:7;
[Luke 1:33]

4:35 [a]Ps. 39:5;
Is. 40:15, 17
[b]Ps. 115:3;
135:6; Dan. 6:27
[c]Job 34:29;
Is. 43:13
[d]Job 9:12;
Is. 45:9;
Jer. 18:6;
Rom. 9:20;
[1 Cor. 2:16]

4:36 [a]Dan. 4:26
[b]2 Chr. 20:20
[c]Job 42:12;
[Prov. 22:4];
Matt. 6:33]

4:37
[a]Dan. 2:46, 47;
3:28, 29
[b]Deut. 32:4;
[Ps. 33:4];
Is. 5:16;
[Rev. 15:3]
[c]Ex. 18:11;
Job 40:11, 12;
Dan. 5:20

5:1 [a]Esth. 1:3;
Is. 22:12–14

5:2
[a]2 Kin. 24:13;
25:15; Ezra 1:7–11;
Jer. 52:19;
Dan. 1:2

5:3 [a]2 Chr. 36:10

5:4 [a]Is. 42:8;
Dan. 5:23;
Rev. 9:20

5:5 [a]Dan. 4:31

thoughts troubled him, so that the joints of his hips were loosened and his ᵃknees knocked against each other. ⁷ᵃThe king cried ¹aloud to bring in ᵇthe astrologers, the Chaldeans, and the soothsayers. The king spoke, saying to the wise *men* of Babylon, "Whoever reads this writing, and tells me its interpretation, shall be clothed with purple and *have* a chain of gold around his neck; ᶜand he shall be the third ruler in the kingdom." ⁸Now all the king's wise *men* came, ᵃbut they could not read the writing, or make known to the king its interpretation. ⁹Then King Belshazzar was greatly ᵃtroubled, his countenance was changed, and his lords were ¹astonished.

¹⁰The queen, because of the words of the king and his lords, came to the banquet hall. The queen spoke, saying, "O king, live forever! Do not let your thoughts trouble you, nor let your countenance change. ¹¹ᵃThere is a man in your kingdom in whom *is* the Spirit of the Holy God. And in the days of your ¹father, light and understanding and wisdom, like the wisdom of the gods, were found in him; and King Nebuchadnezzar your ¹father—your father the king—made him chief of the magicians, astrologers, Chaldeans, *and* soothsayers. ¹²Inasmuch as an excellent spirit, knowledge, understanding, interpreting dreams, solving riddles, and ¹explaining enigmas were found in this Daniel, ᵃwhom the king named Belteshazzar, now let Daniel be called, and he will give the interpretation."

THE WRITING ON THE WALL EXPLAINED

¹³Then Daniel was brought in before the king. The king spoke, and said to Daniel, "*Are* you that Daniel ¹who is one of the captives from Judah, whom my ²father the king brought from Judah? ¹⁴I have heard of you, that ᵃthe ¹Spirit of God *is* in you, and *that* light and understanding and excellent wisdom are found in you. ¹⁵Now ᵃthe wise *men,* the astrologers, have been brought in before me, that they should read this writing and make known to me its interpretation, but they could not give the interpretation of the thing. ¹⁶And I have heard of you, that you can give interpretations and ¹explain enigmas. ᵃNow if you can read the writing and make known to me its interpretation, you shall be clothed with purple and *have* a chain of gold around your neck, and shall be the third ruler in the kingdom."

¹⁷Then Daniel answered, and said before the king, "Let your gifts be for yourself, and give your rewards to another; yet I will read the writing to the king, and make known to him the interpretation. ¹⁸O king, ᵃthe Most High God gave Nebuchadnezzar your ¹father a kingdom and majesty, glory and honor. ¹⁹And because of the majesty that He gave him, ᵃall peoples, nations, and languages trembled and feared before him. Whomever he wished, he ᵇexecuted; whomever he wished, he kept alive; whomever he wished, he set up; and whomever he wished, he put down. ²⁰ᵃBut when his heart was lifted up, and his spirit was hardened in pride, he was deposed from his kingly throne, and they took his glory from

5:6 ᵃEzek. 7:17; 21:7
5:7 ᵃDan. 4:6, 7; 5:11, 15 ᵇIs. 47:13 ᶜDan. 6:2, 3
5:8 ᵃGen. 41:8; Dan. 2:27; 4:7; 5:15
5:9 ᵃJob 18:11; Is. 21:2–4; Jer. 6:24; Dan. 2:1; 5:6
5:11 ᵃDan. 2:48; 4:8, 9, 18
5:12 ᵃDan. 1:7; 4:8
5:14 ᵃDan. 4:8, 9, 18; 5:11, 12
5:15 ᵃDan. 5:7, 8
5:16 ᵃDan. 5:7, 29
5:18 ᵃJer. 27:5–7; Dan. 2:37, 38; 4:17, 22, 25
5:19 ᵃJer. 27:7 ᵇDan. 2:12, 13; 3:6
5:20 ᵃEx. 9:17; Job 15:25; Is. 14:13–15; Dan. 4:30, 37

5:7 ¹Lit. *with strength*   5:9 ¹*perplexed*   5:11 ¹Or *ancestor*
5:12 ¹Lit. *untying knots*   5:13 ¹Lit. *who is of the sons of the captivity*
²Or *ancestor*   5:14 ¹Or *spirit of the gods*   5:16 ¹Lit. *untie knots*
5:18 ¹Or *ancestor*

him. [21]Then he was [a]driven from the sons of men, his heart was made like the beasts, and his dwelling *was* with the wild donkeys. They fed him with grass like oxen, and his body was wet with the dew of heaven, [b]till he [1]knew that the Most High God rules in the kingdom of men, and appoints over it whomever He chooses.

[22]"But you his son, Belshazzar, [a]have not humbled your heart, although you knew all this. [23a]And you have [1]lifted yourself up against the Lord of heaven. They have brought the [b]vessels of [2]His house before you, and you and your lords, your wives and your concubines, have drunk wine from them. And you have praised the gods of silver and gold, bronze and iron, wood and stone, [c]which do not see or hear or know; and the God who *holds* your breath in His hand [d]and owns all your ways, you have not glorified. [24]Then the [1]fingers of the hand were sent from Him, and this writing was written.

[25]"And this is the inscription that was written:

[1]MENE, MENE, [2]TEKEL, [3]UPHARSIN.

[26]This *is* the interpretation of *each* word. MENE: God has numbered your kingdom, and finished it; [27]TEKEL: [a]You have been weighed in the balances, and found wanting; [28]PERES: Your kingdom has been divided, and given to the [a]Medes and [b]Persians."[1] [29]Then Belshazzar gave the command, and they clothed Daniel with purple and *put* a chain of gold around his neck, and made a proclamation concerning him [a]that he should be the third ruler in the kingdom.

BELSHAZZAR'S FALL

[30a]That very night Belshazzar, king of the Chaldeans, was slain. [31a]And Darius the Mede received the kingdom, *being* about sixty-two years old.

THE PLOT AGAINST DANIEL

6 It pleased Darius to set over the kingdom one hundred and twenty satraps, to be over the whole kingdom; [2]and over these, three governors, of whom Daniel *was* one, that the satraps might give account to them, so that the king would suffer no loss. [3]Then this Daniel distinguished himself above the governors and satraps, [a]because an excellent spirit *was* in him; and the king gave thought to setting him over the whole realm. [4a]So the governors and satraps sought to find *some* charge against Daniel concerning the kingdom; but they could find no charge or fault, because he *was* faithful; nor was there any error or fault found in him. [5]Then these men said, "We shall not find any charge against this Daniel unless we find *it* against him concerning the law of his God."

[6]So these governors and satraps thronged before the king, and said thus to him: [a]"King Darius, live forever! [7]All the governors of the kingdom, the administrators and satraps, the counselors and advisors, have [a]consulted together to establish a royal statute and to make a firm decree, that whoever

---

5:21
[a]Job 30:3–7;
Dan. 4:32, 33
[b]Ex. 9:14–16;
Ps. 83:17, 18;
Ezek. 17:24;
[Dan. 4:17, 34, 35]

5:22 [a]Ex. 10:3;
2 Chr. 33:23;
36:12

5:23
[a]Dan. 5:3, 4
[b]Ex. 40:9;
Num. 18:3;
Is. 52:11;
Heb. 9:21
[c]Ps. 115:5, 6;
Is. 37:19;
Hab. 2:18, 19;
Acts 17:24–26;
Rom. 1:21
[d]Ps. 139:3;
Prov. 20:24;
[Jer. 10:23]

5:27 [a]Job 31:6;
Ps. 62:9;
Jer. 6:30

5:28 [a]Is. 21:2;
Dan. 5:31; 9:1
[b]Dan. 6:28;
Acts 2:9

5:29
[a]Dan. 5:7, 16

5:30 [a]Jer. 51:31, 39, 57

5:31
[a]Dan. 2:39; 9:1

6:3 [a]Dan. 5:12

6:4 [a]Eccl. 4:4

6:6 [a]Neh. 2:3;
Dan. 2:4; 6:21

6:7 [a]Ps. 59:3;
62:4; 64:2–6

5:21 [1]Recognized   **5:23** [1]Exalted   [2]The temple   **5:24** [1]Lit. *palm*
5:25 [1]Lit. *a mina* (50 shekels) from the verb "to number"   [2]Lit. *a shekel*
from the verb "to weigh"   [3]Lit. *and half-shekels* from the verb "to divide";
pl. of *Peres*, v. 28   **5:28** [1]Aram. *Paras*, consonant with *Peres*

petitions any god or man for thirty days, except you, O king, shall be cast into the den of lions. [8]Now, O king, establish the decree and sign the writing, so that it cannot be changed, according to the [a]law of the Medes and Persians, which [1]does not alter." [9]Therefore King Darius signed the written decree.

DANIEL IN THE LIONS' DEN

[10]Now when Daniel knew that the writing was signed, he went home. And in his upper room, with his windows open [a]toward Jerusalem, he knelt down on his knees [b]three times that day, and prayed and gave thanks before his God, as was his custom since early days.

[11]Then these men assembled and found Daniel praying and making supplication before his God. [12a]And they went before the king, and spoke concerning the king's decree: "Have you not signed a decree that every man who petitions any god or man within thirty days, except you, O king, shall be cast into the den of lions?"

The king answered and said, "The thing *is* true, [b]according to the law of the Medes and Persians, which [1]does not alter."

[13]So they answered and said before the king, "That Daniel, [a]who is [1]one of the captives from Judah, [b]does not show due regard for you, O king, or for the decree that you have signed, but makes his petition three times a day."

[14]And the king, when he heard *these* words, [a]was greatly displeased with himself, and set *his* heart on Daniel to deliver him; and he [1]labored till the going down of the sun to deliver him. [15]Then these men [1]approached the king, and said to the king, "Know, O king, that *it is* [a]the law of the Medes and Persians that no decree or statute which the king establishes may be changed."

[16]So the king gave the command, and they brought Daniel and cast *him* into the den of lions. *But* the king spoke, saying to Daniel, "Your God, whom you serve continually, He will deliver you." [17a]Then a stone was brought and laid on the mouth of the den, [b]and the king sealed it with his own signet ring and with the signets of his lords, that the purpose concerning Daniel might not be changed.

DANIEL SAVED FROM THE LIONS

[18]Now the king went to his palace and spent the night fasting; and no [1]musicians were brought before him. [a]Also his sleep [2]went from him. [19]Then the [a]king arose very early in the morning and went in haste to the den of lions. [20]And when he came to the den, he cried out with a [1]lamenting voice to Daniel. The king spoke, saying to Daniel, "Daniel, servant of the living God, [a]has your God, whom you serve continually, been able to deliver you from the lions?"

[21]Then Daniel said to the king, [a]"O king, live forever! [22a]My God sent His angel and [b]shut the lions' mouths, so that they have not hurt me, because I was found innocent before Him; and also, O king, I have done no wrong before you."

[23]Now the king was exceedingly glad for him, and commanded that they should take Daniel up out of the den. So

---

6:8 [a]Esth. 1:19; 8:8; Dan. 6:12, 15

6:10 [a]1 Kin. 8:29, 30, 46–48; Ps. 5:7; Jon. 2:4 [b]Ps. 55:17; Acts 2:1, 2, 15; [Phil. 4:6]; 1 Thess. 5:17, 18

6:12 [a]Dan. 3:8–12; Acts 16:19–21 [b]Esth. 1:19; Dan. 6:8, 15

6:13 [a]Dan. 1:6; 5:13 [b]Esth. 3:8; Dan. 3:12; Acts 5:29

6:14 [a]Mark 6:26

6:15 [a]Esth. 8:8; Ps. 94:20, 21; Dan. 6:8, 12

6:17 [a]Lam. 3:53 [b]Matt. 27:66

6:18 [a]Esth. 6:1; Ps. 77:4; Dan. 2:1

6:19 [a]Dan. 3:24

6:20 [a]Gen. 18:14; Num. 11:23; Jer. 32:17; Dan. 3:17; [Luke 1:37]

6:21 [a]Dan. 2:4; 6:6

6:22 [a]Num. 20:16; Is. 63:9; Dan. 3:28; Acts 12:11; [Heb. 1:14] [b]Ps. 91:11–13; 2 Tim. 4:17; Heb. 11:33

6:8 [1]Lit. *does not pass away*   6:12 [1]Lit. *does not pass away*   6:13 [1]Lit. *of the sons of the captivity*   6:14 [1]*strove*   6:15 [1]Lit. *thronged before*   6:18 [1]Exact meaning unknown   [2]Or *fled*   6:20 [1]Or *grieved*

Daniel was taken up out of the den, and no injury whatever was found on him, [a]because he believed in his God.

DARIUS HONORS GOD

[24]And the king gave the command, [a]and they brought those men who had accused Daniel, and they cast *them* into the den of lions—them, [b]their children, and their wives; and the lions overpowered them, and broke all their bones in pieces before they ever came to the bottom of the den.

[25a]Then King Darius wrote:

To all peoples, nations, and languages that dwell in all the earth:

Peace be multiplied to you.

[26] [a]I make a decree that in every dominion of my kingdom *men must* [b]tremble and fear before the God of Daniel.

[c]For He *is* the living God,
And steadfast forever;
His kingdom *is the one* which shall not be [d]destroyed,
And His dominion *shall endure* to the end.
[27] He delivers and rescues,
[a]And He works signs and wonders
In heaven and on earth,
Who has delivered Daniel from the [1]power of the lions.

[28]So this Daniel prospered in the reign of Darius [a]and in the reign of [b]Cyrus the Persian.

VISION OF THE FOUR BEASTS

7 In the first year of Belshazzar king of Babylon, [a]Daniel [1]had a dream and [b]visions of his head *while* on his bed. Then he wrote down the dream, telling [2]the main facts.

[2]Daniel spoke, saying, "I saw in my vision by night, and behold, the four winds of heaven were stirring up the Great Sea. [3]And four great beasts [a]came up from the sea, each different from the other. [4]The first *was* [a]like a lion, and had eagle's wings. I watched till its wings were plucked off; and it was lifted up from the earth and made to stand on two feet like a man, and a [b]man's heart was given to it.

[5a]"And suddenly another beast, a second, like a bear. It was raised up on one side, and *had* three ribs in its mouth between its teeth. And they said thus to it: 'Arise, devour much flesh!'

[6]"After this I looked, and there was another, like a leopard, which had on its back four wings of a bird. The beast also had [a]four heads, and dominion was given to it.

[7]"After this I saw in the night visions, and behold, [a]a fourth beast, dreadful and terrible, exceedingly strong. It had huge iron teeth; it was devouring, breaking in pieces, and trampling the residue with its feet. It *was* different from all the beasts that *were* before it, [b]and it had ten horns. [8]I was considering the horns, and [a]there was another horn, a little one, coming up among them, before whom three of the first horns were plucked out by the roots. And there, in this horn, *were* eyes like the eyes [b]of a man, [c]and a mouth speaking [1]pompous words.

6:23 [a]Heb. 11:33

6:24
[a]Deut. 19:18, 19;
Esth. 7:10
[b]Deut. 24:16;
2 Kin. 14:6;
Esth. 9:10

6:25 [a]Ezra 1:1, 2;
Esth. 3:12; 8:9;
Dan. 4:1

6:26
[a]Ezra 6:8–12;
7:13; Dan. 3:29
[b]Ps. 99:1
[c]Dan. 4:34;
6:20; Hos. 1:10;
Rom. 9:26
[d]Dan. 2:44;
4:3; 7:14, 27;
[Luke 1:33]

6:27
[a]Dan. 4:2, 3

6:28 [a]Dan. 1:21
[b]Ezra 1:1, 2

7:1 [a]Num. 12:6;
[Amos 3:7]
[b][Dan. 2:28]

7:3 [a]Dan. 7:17;
Rev. 13:1; 17:8

7:4
[a]Deut. 28:49;
2 Sam. 1:23;
Jer. 48:40;
Ezek. 17:3;
Hab. 1:8
[b]Dan. 4:16, 34

7:5 [a]Dan. 2:39

7:6
[a]Dan. 8:8, 22

7:7 [a]Dan. 2:40
[b]Dan. 2:41;
Rev. 12:3; 13:1

7:8 [a]Dan. 8:9
[b]Rev. 9:7
[c]Ps. 12:3;
Rev. 13:5, 6

6:27 [1]Lit. *hand* 7:1 [1]Lit. *saw* [2]Lit. *the head* or *chief of the words* 7:8 [1]Lit. *great things*

VISION OF THE ANCIENT OF DAYS

9 "I[a] watched till thrones were [1]put in place,
And [b]the Ancient of Days was seated;
[c]His garment *was* white as snow,
And the hair of His head *was* like pure wool.
His throne *was* a fiery flame,
[d]Its wheels a burning fire;

10 [a]A fiery stream issued
And came forth from before Him.
[b]A thousand thousands ministered to Him;
Ten thousand times ten thousand stood before Him.
[c]The [1]court was seated,
And the books were opened.

11"I watched then because of the sound of the [1]pompous words which the horn was speaking; [a]I watched till the beast was slain, and its body destroyed and given to the burning flame. 12As for the rest of the beasts, they had their dominion taken away, yet their lives were prolonged for a season and a time.

13 "I was watching in the night visions,
And behold, [a]*One* like the Son of Man,
Coming with the clouds of heaven!
He came to the Ancient of Days,
And they brought Him near before Him.

14 [a]Then to Him was given dominion and glory and a kingdom,
That all [b]peoples, nations, and languages should serve Him.
His dominion *is* [c]an everlasting dominion,
Which shall not pass away,
And His kingdom *the one*
Which shall not be destroyed.

DANIEL'S VISIONS INTERPRETED

15"I, Daniel, was grieved in my spirit [1]within *my* body, and the visions of my head troubled me. 16I came near to one of those who stood by, and asked him the truth of all this. So he told me and made known to me the interpretation of these things: 17"Those great beasts, which are four, *are* four [1]kings *which* arise out of the earth. 18But [a]the saints of the Most High shall receive the kingdom, and possess the kingdom forever, even forever and ever.'

19"Then I wished to know the truth about the fourth beast, which was different from all the others, exceedingly dreadful, *with* its teeth of iron and its nails of bronze, *which* devoured, broke in pieces, and trampled the residue with its feet; 20and the ten horns that *were* on its head, and the other *horn* which came up, before which three fell, namely, that horn which had eyes and a mouth which spoke [1]pompous words, whose appearance *was* greater than his fellows.

21"I was watching; [a]and the same horn was making war against the saints, and prevailing against them, 22until the Ancient of Days came, [a]and a judgment was made *in favor* of

7:9 a[Rev. 20:4]
bPs. 90:2
cPs. 104:2;
Rev. 1:14
dEzek. 1:15

7:10 aPs. 50:3;
Is. 30:33; 66:15
bDeut. 33:2;
1 Kin. 22:19;
Ps. 68:17;
Rev. 5:11
cDan. 12:1;
[Rev. 20:11–15]

7:11 a[Rev. 19:20;
20:10]

7:13 aEzek. 1:26;
[Matt. 24:30;
26:64;
Mark 13:26;
14:62;
Luke 21:27;
Rev. 1:7, 13;
14:14]

7:14 aPs. 2:6–8;
Dan. 7:27;
[Matt. 28:18;
John 3:35, 36;
1 Cor. 15:27;
Eph. 1:22;
Phil. 2:9–11;
Rev. 1:6; 11:15]
bDan. 3:4
cPs. 145:13;
Mic. 4:7;
[Luke 1:33];
John 12:34;
Heb. 12:28

7:18
aPs. 149:5–9;
Is. 60:12–14;
Dan. 7:14;
[2 Tim. 2:11;
Rev. 2:26, 27;
20:4; 22:5]

7:21 aRev. 11:7;
13:7; 17:14

7:22 a[Rev. 1:6]

7:9 [1]Or *set up*   7:10 [1]Or *judgment*   7:11 [1]Lit. *great*   7:15 [1]Lit. *in the midst of its sheath*   7:17 [1]Representing their kingdoms, v. 23   7:20 [1]Lit. *great things*

the saints of the Most High, and the time came for the saints to possess the kingdom.

23"Thus he said:

'The fourth beast shall be
ª A fourth kingdom on earth,
Which shall be different from all *other* kingdoms,
And shall devour the whole earth,
Trample it and break it in pieces.
24 ª The ten horns *are* ten kings
Who shall arise from this kingdom.
And another shall rise after them;
He shall be different from the first *ones,*
And shall subdue three kings.
25 ª He shall speak *pompous* words against the Most High,
Shall ᵇpersecute¹ the saints of the Most High,
And shall ᶜintend to change times and law.
Then ᵈ*the saints* shall be given into his hand
ᵉFor a time and times and half a time.

26 'Butª the court shall be seated,
And they shall ᵇtake away his dominion,
To consume and destroy *it* forever.
27 Then the ªkingdom and dominion,
And the greatness of the kingdoms under the whole
heaven,
Shall be given to the people, the saints of the Most High.
ᵇHis kingdom *is* an everlasting kingdom,
ᶜAnd all dominions shall serve and obey Him.'

28"This *is* the end of the ¹account. As for me, Daniel, ªmy thoughts greatly troubled me, and my countenance changed; but I ᵇkept the matter in my heart."

VISION OF A RAM AND A GOAT

8 In¹ the third year of the reign of King Belshazzar a vision appeared *to* me—to me, Daniel—after the one that appeared to me ªthe first time. 2I saw in the vision, and it so happened while I was looking, that I *was* in ªShushan,¹ the ²citadel, which *is* in the province of Elam; and I saw in the vision that I was by the River Ulai. 3Then I lifted my eyes and saw, and there, standing beside the river, was a ram which had two horns, and the two horns *were* high; but one *was* ªhigher than the other, and the higher *one* came up last. 4I saw the ram pushing westward, northward, and southward, so that no animal could ¹withstand him; nor *was there any* that could deliver from his hand, ªbut he did according to his will and became great.

5And as I was considering, suddenly a male goat came from the west, across the surface of the whole earth, without touching the ground; and the goat *had* a notable ªhorn between his eyes. 6Then he came to the ram that had two horns, which I had seen standing beside the river, and ran at him with furious power. 7And I saw him confronting the ram; he was moved with rage against him, ¹attacked the ram, and broke his two horns. There was no power in the ram to

7:23 ªDan. 2:40

7:24 ªDan. 7:7;
Rev. 13:1; 17:12

7:25 ªIs. 37:23;
Dan. 11:36;
Rev. 13:1–6
ᵇRev. 17:6
ᶜDan. 2:21
ᵈRev. 13:7; 18:24
ᵉDan. 12:7;
Rev. 12:14

7:26
ª[Dan. 2:35;
7:10, 22]
ᵇRev. 19:20

7:27 ªIs. 54:3;
Dan. 7:14, 18, 22;
Rev. 20:4
ᵇ2 Sam. 7:16;
Ps. 89:35–37;
Is. 9:7;
Dan. 2:44; 4:34;
7:14; [Luke 1:33,
34]; John 12:34;
[Rev. 11:15; 22:5]
ᶜPs. 2:6–12;
22:27; 72:11;
86:9; Is. 60:12;
Rev. 11:1

7:28 ªDan. 8:27
ᵇLuke 2:19, 51

8:1 ªDan. 7:1

8:2 ªNeh. 1:1;
Esth. 1:2, 2:8

8:3 ªDan. 7:5

8:4 ªDan. 5:19

8:5 ªDan. 8:8,
21; 11:3

7:25 ¹Lit. *wear out*   7:28 ¹Lit. *word*   8:1 ¹The Hebrew language resumes in Dan. 8:1.   8:2 ¹Or *Susa*   ²Or *fortified palace*   8:4 ¹Lit. *stand before him*
8:7 ¹Lit. *struck*

withstand him, but he cast him down to the ground and trampled him; and there was no one that could deliver the ram from his hand.

8Therefore the male goat grew very great; but when he became strong, the large horn was broken, and in place of it ᵃfour notable ones came up toward the four winds of heaven. 9ᵃAnd out of one of them came a little horn which grew exceedingly great toward the south, ᵇtoward the east, and toward the ᶜGlorious *Land.* 10ᵃAnd it grew up to ᵇthe host of heaven; and ᶜit cast down *some* of the host and *some* of the stars to the ground, and trampled them. 11ᵃHe even exalted *himself* as high as ᵇthe Prince of the host; ᶜand by him ᵈthe daily *sacrifices* were taken away, and the place of ¹His sanctuary was cast down. 12Because of transgression, ᵃan army was given over *to the horn* to oppose the daily *sacrifices;* and he cast ᵇtruth down to the ground. He ᶜdid *all this* and prospered.

13Then I heard ᵃa holy one speaking; and *another* holy one said to that certain *one* who was speaking, "How long *will* the vision *be, concerning* the daily *sacrifices* and the transgression ¹of desolation, the giving of both the sanctuary and the host to be trampled underfoot?"

14And he said to me, "For two thousand three hundred ¹days; then the sanctuary shall be cleansed."

GABRIEL INTERPRETS THE VISION

15Then it happened, when I, Daniel, had seen the vision and ᵃwas seeking the meaning, that suddenly there stood before me ᵇone having the appearance of a man. 16And I heard a man's voice ᵃbetween *the banks of* the Ulai, who called, and said, ᵇ"Gabriel, make this *man* understand the vision." 17So he came near where I stood, and when he came I was afraid and ᵃfell on my face; but he said to me, "Understand, son of man, that the vision *refers* to the time of the end."

18ᵃNow, as he was speaking with me, I was in a deep sleep with my face to the ground; ᵇbut he touched me, and stood me upright. 19And he said, "Look, I am making known to you what shall happen in the latter time of the indignation; ᵃfor at the appointed time the end *shall be.* 20The ram which you saw, having the two horns—*they are* the kings of Media and Persia. 21And the ¹male goat *is* the ²kingdom of Greece. The large horn that *is* between its eyes ᵃ*is* the first king. 22ᵃAs for the broken *horn* and the four that stood up in its place, four kingdoms shall arise out of that nation, but not with its power.

23 "And in the latter time of their kingdom,
　　When the transgressors have reached their fullness,
　　A king shall arise,
　ᵃHaving fierce ¹features,
　　Who understands sinister schemes.
24 His power shall be mighty, ᵃbut not by his own power;
　　He shall destroy ¹fearfully,
　ᵇAnd shall prosper and thrive;
　ᶜHe shall destroy the mighty, and *also* the holy people.

8:8 ᵃDan. 7:6;
8:22; 11:4
8:9 ᵃDan. 11:21
ᵇDan. 11:25
ᶜPs. 48:2
8:10 ᵃDan. 11:28
ᵇIs. 14:13;
Jer. 48:26
ᶜRev. 12:4
8:11
ᵃ2 Kin. 19:22, 23;
2 Chr. 32:15–17;
Is. 37:23;
Dan. 8:25;
11:36, 37
ᵇJosh. 5:14
ᶜEzek. 46:14;
Dan. 11:31; 12:11
ᵈEx. 29:38
8:12 ᵃDan. 11:31
ᵇPs. 119:43;
Is. 59:14
ᶜDan. 8:4; 11:36
8:13
ᵃDan. 4:13, 23;
1 Pet. 1:12
8:15 ᵃ1 Pet. 1:10
ᵇEzek. 1:26
8:16
ᵃDan. 12:6, 7
ᵇDan. 9:21;
Luke 1:19, 26
8:17 ᵃEzek. 1:28;
44:4; Dan. 2:46;
Rev. 1:17
8:18 ᵃDan. 10:9;
Luke 9:32
ᵇEzek. 2:2;
Dan. 10:10,
16, 18
8:19 ᵃHab. 2:3
8:21 ᵃDan. 11:3
8:22 ᵃDan. 11:4
8:23
ᵃDeut. 28:50
8:24 ᵃRev. 17:13
ᵇDan. 11:36
ᶜDan. 7:25

8:11 ¹The temple　8:13 ¹Or *making desolate*　8:14 ¹Lit. *evening-mornings*
8:21 ¹*shaggy male*　²Lit. *king,* representing his kingdom, Dan. 7:17, 23
8:23 ¹Lit. *countenance*　8:24 ¹Or *extraordinarily*

25 "Through[a] his cunning
    He shall cause deceit to prosper under his [1]rule;
    [b]And he shall exalt *himself* in his heart.
    He shall destroy many in *their* prosperity.
    [c]He shall even rise against the Prince of princes;
    But he shall be [d]broken without *human* [2]means.

26 "And the vision of the evenings and mornings
    Which was told is true;
    [a]Therefore seal up the vision,
    For *it refers* to many days *in the future.*"

27[a]And I, Daniel, fainted and was sick for days; afterward I arose and went about the king's business. I was [1]astonished by the vision, but no one understood it.

DANIEL'S PRAYER FOR THE PEOPLE

9 In the first year [a]of Darius the son of Ahasuerus, of the lineage of the Medes, who was made king over the realm of the Chaldeans— [2]in the first year of his reign I, Daniel, understood by the books the number of the years *specified* by the word of the LORD through [a]Jeremiah the prophet, that He would accomplish seventy years in the desolations of Jerusalem.

3[a]Then I set my face toward the Lord God to make request by prayer and supplications, with fasting, sackcloth, and ashes. 4And I prayed to the LORD my God, and made confession, and said, "O [a]Lord, great and awesome God, who keeps His covenant and mercy with those who love Him, and with those who keep His commandments, 5[a]we have sinned and committed iniquity, we have done wickedly and rebelled, even by departing from Your precepts and Your judgments. 6[a]Neither have we heeded Your servants the prophets, who spoke in Your name to our kings and our princes, to our fathers and all the people of the land. 7O Lord, [a]righteousness *belongs* to You, but to us shame of face, as *it is* this day—to the men of Judah, to the inhabitants of Jerusalem and all Israel, those near and those far off in all the countries to which You have driven them, because of the unfaithfulness which they have committed against You.

8"O Lord, to us *belongs* shame of face, to our kings, our princes, and our fathers, because we have sinned against You. 9[a]To the Lord our God *belong* mercy and forgiveness, though we have rebelled against Him. 10We have not obeyed the voice of the LORD our God, to walk in His laws, which He set before us by His servants the prophets. 11Yes, [a]all Israel has transgressed Your law, and has departed so as not to obey Your voice; therefore the curse and the oath written in the [b]Law of Moses the servant of God have been poured out on us, because we have sinned against Him. 12And He has [a]confirmed His words, which He spoke against us and against our judges who judged us, by bringing upon us a great disaster; [b]for under the whole heaven such has never been done as what has been done to Jerusalem.

13[a]"As *it is* written in the Law of Moses, all this disaster has come upon us; [b]yet we have not made our prayer before the LORD our God, that we might turn from our iniquities and

Cross references

8:25 [a]Dan. 11:21
[b]Dan. 8:11–13;
11:36; 12:7
[c]Dan. 11:36;
Rev. 19:19, 20
[d]Job 34:20;
Lam. 4:6

8:26
[a]Ezek. 12:27;
Dan. 12:4, 9;
Rev. 22:10

8:27 [a]Dan. 7:28;
8:17; Hab. 3:16

9:1 [a]Dan. 1:21

9:2
[a]2 Chr. 36:21;
Ezra 1:1;
Jer. 25:11, 12;
29:10; Zech. 7:5

9:3 [a]Neh. 1:4;
Dan. 6:10; 10:15

9:4 [a]Ex. 20:6

9:5
[a]1 Kin. 8:47, 48;
Neh. 9:33;
Ps. 106:6;
Is. 64:5–7;
Jer. 14:7

9:6
[a]2 Chr. 36:15;
Jer. 44:4, 5

9:7 [a]Neh. 9:33

9:9 [a][Neh. 9:17;
Ps. 130:4, 7]

9:11 [a]Is. 1:3–6;
Jer. 8:5–10
[b]Lev. 26:14;
Neh. 1:6;
Ps. 106:6

9:12 [a]Is. 44:26;
Jer. 44:2–6;
Lam. 2:17;
Zech. 1:6
[b]Lam. 1:12;
2:13; Ezek. 5:9;
[Amos 3:2]

9:13
[a]Lev. 26:14–45;
Deut. 28:15–68;
Lam. 2:17
[b]Job 36:13;
Is. 9:13;
Jer. 2:30;
Hos. 7:7

8:25 [1]Lit. *hand*   [2]Lit. *hand*   8:27 [1]*amazed*

understand Your truth. [14]Therefore the LORD has [a]kept the disaster in mind, and brought it upon us; for [b]the LORD our God *is* righteous in all the works which He does, though we have not obeyed His voice. [15]And now, O Lord our God, [a]who brought Your people out of the land of Egypt with a mighty hand, and made Yourself [b]a name, as *it is* this day—we have sinned, we have done wickedly!

[16]"O Lord, [a]according to all Your righteousness, I pray, let Your anger and Your fury be turned away from Your city Jerusalem, [b]Your holy mountain; because for our sins, [c]and for the iniquities of our fathers, [d]Jerusalem and Your people [e]*are* a reproach to all *those* around us. [17]Now therefore, our God, hear the prayer of Your servant, and his supplications, [a]and [b]for the Lord's sake [1]cause Your face to shine on [2]Your sanctuary, [c]which is desolate. [18][a]O my God, incline Your ear and hear; open Your eyes [b]and see our desolations, and the city [c]which is called by Your name; for we do not present our supplications before You because of our righteous deeds, but because of Your great mercies. [19]O Lord, hear! O Lord, forgive! O Lord, listen and act! Do not delay for Your own sake, my God, for Your city and Your people are called by Your name."

THE SEVENTY-WEEKS PROPHECY

[20]Now while I *was* speaking, praying, and confessing my sin and the sin of my people Israel, and presenting my supplication before the LORD my God for the holy mountain of my God, [21]yes, while I *was* speaking in prayer, the man [a]Gabriel, whom I had seen in the vision at the beginning, [1]being caused to fly swiftly, reached me about the time of the evening offering. [22]And he informed *me,* and talked with me, and said, "O Daniel, I have now come forth to give you skill to understand. [23]At the beginning of your supplications the [1]command went out, and I have come to tell *you,* for you *are* greatly [a]beloved; therefore [b]consider the matter, and understand the vision:

[24] "Seventy [1]weeks are determined
    For your people and for your holy city,
      To finish the transgression,
    [2]To make an end of sins,
    [a]To make reconciliation for iniquity,
    [b]To bring in everlasting righteousness,
      To seal up vision and prophecy,
    [c]And to anoint [3]the Most Holy.

[25] "Know therefore and understand,
    That from the going forth of the command
      To restore and build Jerusalem
    Until [a]Messiah [b]the Prince,
    There shall be seven weeks and sixty-two weeks;
    The [1]street shall be built again, and the [2]wall,
      Even in troublesome times.

[26] "And after the sixty-two weeks
    [a]Messiah shall [1]be cut off, [b]but not for Himself;

Cross references

9:14 [a]Jer. 31:28; 44:27 [b]Neh. 9:33
9:15 [a]Ex. 32:11; 1 Kin. 8:51; Neh. 1:10 [b]Ex. 14:18; Neh. 9:10; Jer. 32:20
9:16 [a]1 Sam. 12:7; Ps. 31:1; Mic. 6:4, 5 [b]Ps. 87:1–3; Dan. 9:20; Joel 3:17; Zech. 8:3 [c]Ex. 20:5 [d]Ps. 122:6; Jer. 29:7; Lam. 2:16 [e]Ps. 79:4
9:17 [a]Num. 6:24–26; Ps. 80:3, 7, 19 [b]Lam. 5:18 [c][John 16:24]
9:18 [a]Is. 37:17 [b]Ex. 3:7 [c]Jer. 25:29
9:21 [a]Dan. 8:16; Luke 1:19, 26
9:23 [a]Dan. 10:11, 19 [b]Matt. 24:15
9:24 [a]2 Chr. 29:24; [Is. 53:10]; Acts 10:43; [Rom. 5:10]; Heb. 9:12, 14 [b]Rev. 14:6 [c]Ps. 45:7
9:25 [a]Luke 2:1, 2; John 1:41; 4:25 [b]Is. 55:4
9:26 [a][Is. 53:8]; Matt. 27:50; Mark 9:12; 15:37; [Luke 23:46; 24:26]; John 19:30; Acts 8:32 [b][1 Pet. 2:21]

9:17 [1]Be gracious   [2]The temple   9:21 [1]Or *being weary with weariness*
9:23 [1]Lit. *word*   9:24 [1]Lit. *sevens,* and so throughout the chapter   [2]So with Qr., LXX, Syr., Vg.; Kt., Theodotion *To seal up*   [3]The Most Holy Place
9:25 [1]Or *open square*   [2]Or *moat*   9:26 [1]Suffer the death penalty

And ^cthe people of the prince who is to come
^dShall destroy the city and the sanctuary.
The end of it *shall be* with a flood,
And till the end of the war desolations are determined.
27 Then he shall confirm ^aa ¹covenant with ^bmany for one
week;
But in the middle of the week
He shall bring an end to sacrifice and offering.
And on the wing of abominations shall be one who
makes desolate,
^cEven until the consummation, which is determined,
Is poured out on the ²desolate."

VISION OF THE GLORIOUS MAN

10 In the third year of Cyrus king of Persia a message was revealed to Daniel, whose ^aname was called Belteshazzar. The message *was* true, ¹but the appointed time *was* long; and he understood the message, and had understanding of the vision. ²In those days I, Daniel, was mourning three full weeks. ³I ate no ¹pleasant food, no meat or wine came into my mouth, nor did I anoint myself at all, till three whole weeks were fulfilled.

⁴Now on the twenty-fourth day of the first month, as I was by the side of the great river, that *is*, the ¹Tigris, ⁵I lifted my eyes and looked, and behold, a certain man clothed in ^alinen, whose waist *was* ^bgirded with gold of Uphaz! ⁶His body *was* like beryl, his face like the appearance of lightning, his eyes like torches of fire, his arms and feet like burnished bronze in color, ^aand the sound of his words like the voice of a multitude.

⁷And I, Daniel, alone saw the vision, for the men who were with me did not see the vision; but a great terror fell upon them, so that they fled to hide themselves. ⁸Therefore I was left alone when I saw this great vision, and no strength remained in me; for my ¹vigor was turned to ²frailty in me, and I retained no strength. ⁹Yet I heard the sound of his words; and while I heard the sound of his words I was in a deep sleep on my face, with my face to the ground.

PROPHECIES CONCERNING PERSIA AND GREECE

^{10a}Suddenly, a hand touched me, which made me tremble on my knees and *on* the palms of my hands. ¹¹And he said to me, "O Daniel, ^aman greatly beloved, understand the words that I speak to you, and stand upright, for I have now been sent to you." While he was speaking this word to me, I stood trembling.

¹²Then he said to me, ^a"Do not fear, Daniel, for from the first day that you set your heart to understand, and to humble yourself before your God, ^byour words were heard; and I have come because of your words. ^{13a}But the prince of the kingdom of Persia withstood me twenty-one days; and behold, ^bMichael, one of the chief princes, came to help me, for I had been left alone there with the kings of Persia. ¹⁴Now I have come to make you understand what will happen to your people ^ain the latter days, ^bfor the vision *refers* to *many* days yet *to come.*"

9:26 ^cMatt. 22:7
^dMatt. 24:2;
Mark 13:2;
Luke 19:43, 44
9:27 ^aIs. 42:6
^b[Matt. 26:28]
^cDan. 11:36

10:1 ^aDan. 1:7

10:5
^aEzek. 9:2; 10:2
^bRev. 1:13; 15:6

10:6 ^a[Rev. 1:15]

10:10 ^aDan. 9:21

10:11 ^aDan. 9:23

10:12 ^aRev. 1:17
^bDan. 9:3, 4, 22,
23; Acts 10:4

10:13
^aDan. 10:20
^bDan. 10:21;
12:1; Jude 9;
[Rev. 12:7]

10:14 ^aGen. 49:1;
Deut. 31:29;
Dan. 2:28
^bDan. 8:26; 10:1

9:27 ¹Or *treaty*   ²Or *desolator*   10:1 ¹Or *and of great conflict;*
10:3 ¹*desirable*   10:4 ¹Heb. *Hiddekel*   10:8 ¹Lit. *splendor*   ²Lit. *ruin*

¹⁵When he had spoken such words to me, ᵃI ¹turned my face toward the ground and became speechless. ¹⁶And suddenly, ᵃone having the likeness of the ¹sons of men ᵇtouched my lips; then I opened my mouth and spoke, saying to him who stood before me, "My lord, because of the vision ᶜmy sorrows have ²overwhelmed me, and I have retained no strength. ¹⁷For how can this servant of my lord talk with you, my lord? As for me, no strength remains in me now, nor is any breath left in me."

¹⁸Then again, *the one* having the likeness of a man touched me and strengthened me. ¹⁹ᵃAnd he said, "O man greatly beloved, ᵇfear not! Peace *be* to you; be strong, yes, be strong!"

So when he spoke to me I was strengthened, and said, "Let my lord speak, for you have strengthened me."

²⁰Then he said, "Do you know why I have come to you? And now I must return to fight ᵃwith the prince of Persia; and when I have gone forth, indeed the prince of Greece will come. ²¹But I will tell you what is noted in the Scripture of Truth. (No one upholds me against these, ᵃexcept Michael your prince.

11 "Also ᵃin the first year of ᵇDarius the Mede, I, *even* I, stood up to confirm and strengthen him.) ²And now I will tell you the truth: Behold, three more kings will arise in Persia, and the fourth shall be far richer than *them* all; by his strength, through his riches, he shall stir up all against the realm of Greece. ³Then ᵃa mighty king shall arise, who shall rule with great dominion, and ᵇdo according to his will. ⁴And when he has arisen, ᵃhis kingdom shall be broken up and divided toward the four winds of heaven, but not among his posterity ᵇnor according to his dominion with which he ruled; for his kingdom shall be uprooted, even for others besides these.

WARRING KINGS OF NORTH AND SOUTH

⁵"Also the king of the South shall become strong, as well as *one* of his princes; and he shall gain power over him and have dominion. His dominion *shall be* a great dominion. ⁶And at the end of *some* years they shall join forces, for the daughter of the king of the South shall go to the king of the North to make an agreement; but she shall not retain the power of her ¹authority, and neither he nor his ¹authority shall stand; but she shall be given up, with those who brought her, and with him who begot her, and with him who strengthened her in *those* times. ⁷But from a branch of her roots *one* shall arise in his place, who shall come with an army, enter the fortress of the king of the North, and deal with them and prevail. ⁸And he shall also carry their gods captive to Egypt, with their ¹princes *and* their precious articles of silver and gold; and he shall continue *more* years than the king of the North.

⁹"Also *the king of the North* shall come to the kingdom of the king of the South, but shall return to his own land. ¹⁰However his sons shall stir up strife, and assemble a multitude of great forces; and *one* shall certainly come ᵃand overwhelm and pass through; then he shall return ᵇto his fortress and stir up strife.

10:15
ᵃDan. 8:18; 10:9

10:16 ᵃDan. 8:15
ᵇJer. 1:9;
Dan. 10:10
ᶜDan. 10:8, 9

10:19 ᵃDan. 10:11
ᵇJudg. 6:23;
Is. 43:1;
Dan. 10:12

10:20
ᵃDan. 10:13

10:21
ᵃDan. 10:13;
Jude 9;
[Rev. 12:7]

11:1 ᵃDan. 9:1
ᵇDan. 5:31

11:3
ᵃDan. 7:6; 8:5
ᵇDan. 8:4;
11:16, 36

11:4 ᵃJer. 49:36;
Ezek. 37:9;
Dan. 7:2; 8:8;
Zech. 2:6;
Rev. 7:1
ᵇDan. 8:22

11:10 ᵃIs. 8:8;
Jer. 46:7, 8;
51:42;
Dan. 9:26;
11:26, 40
ᵇDan. 11:7

10:15 ¹Lit. *set*   10:16 ¹Theodotion, Vg. *the son;* LXX *a hand*   ²Or *turned upon*   11:6 ¹Lit. *arm*   11:8 ¹Or *molded images*

[11]"And the king of the South shall be [a]moved with rage, and go out and fight with him, with the king of the North, who shall muster a great multitude; but the [b]multitude shall be given into the hand of his *enemy.* [12]When he has taken away the multitude, his heart will be [1]lifted up; and he will cast down tens of thousands, but he will not prevail. [13]For the king of the North will return and muster a multitude greater than the former, and shall certainly come at the end of some years with a great army and much equipment.

[14]"Now in those times many shall rise up against the king of the South. Also, [1]violent men of your people shall exalt themselves [2]in fulfillment of the vision, but they shall [a]fall. [15]So the king of the North shall come and [a]build a siege mound, and take a fortified city; and the [1]forces of the South shall not withstand *him.* Even his choice troops *shall have* no strength to resist. [16]But he who comes against him [a]shall do according to his own will, and [b]no one shall stand against him. He shall stand in the Glorious Land with destruction in his [1]power.

[17]"He shall also [a]set his face to enter with the strength of his whole kingdom, and [1]upright ones with him; thus shall he do. And he shall give him the daughter of women to destroy it; but she shall not stand *with him,* [b]or be for him. [18]After this he shall turn his face to the coastlands, and shall take many. But a ruler shall bring the reproach against them to an end; and with the reproach removed, he shall turn back on him. [19]Then he shall turn his face toward the fortress of his own land; but he shall [a]stumble and fall, [b]and not be found.

[20]"There shall arise in his place one who imposes taxes *on* the glorious kingdom; but within a few days he shall be destroyed, but not in anger or in battle. [21]And in his place [a]shall arise a vile person, to whom they will not give the honor of royalty; but he shall come in peaceably, and seize the kingdom by intrigue. [22]With the [1]force of a [a]flood they shall be swept away from before him and be broken, [b]and also the prince of the covenant. [23]And after the league *is made* with him [a]he shall act deceitfully, for he shall come up and become strong with a small *number of* people. [24]He shall enter peaceably, even into the richest places of the province; and he shall do *what* his fathers have not done, nor his forefathers: he shall disperse among them the plunder, [1]spoil, and riches; and he shall devise his plans against the strongholds, but *only* for a time.

[25]"He shall stir up his power and his courage against the king of the South with a great army. And the king of the South shall be stirred up to battle with a very great and mighty army; but he shall not stand, for they shall devise plans against him. [26]Yes, those who eat of the portion of his delicacies shall destroy him; his army shall [1]be swept away, and many shall fall down slain. [27]Both these kings' hearts *shall be* bent on evil, and they shall speak lies at the same table; but it shall not prosper, for the end *will* still *be* at the [a]appointed time. [28]While returning to his land with great riches, his heart shall

11:11 [a]Prov. 16:14
[b][Ps. 33:10, 16]

11:14 [a]Job 9:13

11:15 [a]Jer. 6:6; Ezek. 4:2; 17:17

11:16
[a]Dan. 8:4, 7
[b]Josh. 1:5

11:17
[a]2 Kin. 12:17; 2 Chr. 20:3; Ezek. 4:3, 7
[b]Dan. 9:26

11:19 [a]Ps. 27:2; Jer. 46:6
[b]Job 20:8; Ps. 37:36; Ezek. 26:21

11:21 [a]Dan. 7:8

11:22 [a]Dan. 9:26
[b]Dan. 8:10, 11

11:23 [a]Dan. 8:25

11:27 [a]Dan. 8:19; Hab. 2:3

11:12 [1]Proud   11:14 [1]Or *robbers,* lit. *sons of breakage*   [2]Lit. *to establish*
11:15 [1]Lit. *arms*   11:16 [1]Lit. *hand*   11:17 [1]Or *bring equitable terms*
11:22 [1]Lit. *arms*   11:24 [1]*booty*   11:26 [1]Or *overflow*

be *moved* against the holy covenant; so he shall do *damage* and return to his own land.

THE NORTHERN KING'S BLASPHEMIES

29"At the appointed time he shall return and go toward the south; but it shall not be like the former or the latter. 30aFor ships from ¹Cyprus shall come against him; therefore he shall be grieved, and return in rage against the holy covenant, and do *damage.*

"So he shall return and show regard for those who forsake the holy covenant. 31And ¹forces shall be mustered by him, aand they shall defile the sanctuary fortress; then they shall take away the daily *sacrifices,* and place *there* the abomination of desolation. 32Those who do wickedly against the covenant he shall ¹corrupt with flattery; but the people who know their God shall be strong, and carry out *great exploits.* 33And those of the people who understand shall instruct many; yet *for many* days they shall fall by sword and flame, by captivity and plundering. 34Now when they fall, they shall be aided with a little help; but many shall join with them by ¹intrigue. 35And *some* of those of understanding shall fall, ato refine them, purify *them,* and make *them* white, *until* the time of the end; because *it is* still for the appointed time.

36"Then the king shall do according to his own will: he shall aexalt and magnify himself above every god, shall speak blasphemies against the God of gods, and shall prosper till the wrath has been accomplished; for what has been determined shall be done. 37He shall regard neither the ¹God of his fathers nor the desire of women, anor regard any god; for he shall exalt himself above *them* all. 38But in their place he shall honor a god of fortresses; and a god which his fathers did not know he shall honor with gold and silver, with precious stones and pleasant things. 39Thus he shall act against the strongest fortresses with a foreign god, which he shall acknowledge, *and* advance *its* glory; and he shall cause them to rule over many, and divide the land for ¹gain.

THE NORTHERN KING'S CONQUESTS

40"At the atime of the end the king of the South shall attack him; and the king of the North shall come against him blike a whirlwind, with chariots, chorsemen, and with many ships; and he shall enter the countries, overwhelm *them,* and pass through. 41He shall also enter the Glorious Land, and many *countries* shall be overthrown; but these shall escape from his hand: aEdom, Moab, and the ¹prominent people of Ammon. 42He shall stretch out his hand against the countries, and the land of aEgypt shall not escape. 43He shall have power over the treasures of gold and silver, and over all the precious things of Egypt; also the Libyans and Ethiopians *shall follow* aat his heels. 44But news from the east and the north shall trouble him; therefore he shall go out with great fury to destroy and annihilate many. 45And he shall plant the tents of his palace between the seas and athe glorious holy mountain; byet he shall come to his end, and no one will help him.

11:30 aGen. 10:4; Num. 24:24; Is. 23:1, 12; Jer. 2:10

11:31 aDan. 8:11–13; 12:11

11:35 a[Deut. 8:16; Prov. 17:3]; Dan. 12:10; Zech. 13:9; Mal. 3:2, 3

11:36 aDan. 7:8, 25

11:37 aIs. 14:13; 2 Thess. 2:4

11:40 aDan. 11:27, 35; 12:4, 9 bIs. 21:1 cEzek. 38:4; Rev. 9:16

11:41 aIs. 11:14

11:42 aJoel 3:19

11:43 aEx. 11:8

11:45 aPs. 48:2 bRev. 19:20

11:30 ¹Heb. *Kittim,* western lands, especially Cyprus   11:31 ¹Lit. *arms*
11:32 ¹*pollute*   11:34 ¹Or *slipperiness, flattery*   11:37 ¹Or *gods*   11:39 ¹*profit*
11:41 ¹Lit. *chief of the sons of Ammon*

PROPHECY OF THE END TIME

12 "At that time Michael shall stand up,
The great prince who stands *watch* over the sons of
your people;
ᵃAnd there shall be a time of trouble,
Such as never was since there was a nation,
Even to that time.
And at that time your people ᵇshall be delivered,
Every one who is found ᶜwritten in the book.
2   And many of those who sleep in the dust of the earth
shall awake,
ᵃSome to everlasting life,
Some to shame ᵇ*and* everlasting ¹contempt.
3   Those who are wise shall ᵃshine
Like the brightness of the firmament,
ᵇAnd those who turn many to righteousness
ᶜLike the stars forever and ever.

⁴"But you, Daniel, ᵃshut up the words, and seal the book until the time of the end; many shall ᵇrun to and fro, and knowledge shall increase."

⁵Then I, Daniel, looked; and there stood two others, one on this riverbank and the other on that ᵃriverbank. ⁶And *one* said to the man clothed in ᵃlinen, who *was* above the waters of the river, ᵇ"How long shall the fulfillment of these wonders *be?*"

⁷Then I heard the man clothed in linen, who *was* above the waters of the river, when he ᵃheld up his right hand and his left hand to heaven, and swore by Him ᵇwho lives forever, ᶜthat *it shall be* for a time, times, and half *a time;* ᵈand when the power of ᵉthe holy people has been completely shattered, all these *things* shall be finished.

⁸Although I heard, I did not understand. Then I said, "My lord, what *shall be* the end of these *things?*"

⁹And he said, "Go *your way,* Daniel, for the words *are* closed up and sealed till the time of the end. ¹⁰ᵃMany shall be purified, made white, and refined, ᵇbut the wicked shall do wickedly; and none of the wicked shall understand, but ᶜthe wise shall understand.

¹¹"And from the time *that* the daily *sacrifice* is taken away, and the abomination of desolation is set up, *there shall be* one thousand two hundred and ninety days. ¹²Blessed *is* he who waits, and comes to the one thousand three hundred and thirty-five days.

¹³"But you, go *your way* till the end; ᵃfor you shall rest, ᵇand will arise to your inheritance at the end of the days."

12:1 ᵃIs. 26:20;
Jer. 30:7;
Ezek. 5:9;
Dan. 9:12;
Matt. 24:21;
Mark 13:19
ᵇRom. 11:26
ᶜEx. 32:32;
Ps. 56:8

12:2
ᵃ[Matt. 25:46;
John 5:28, 29;
Acts 24:15]
ᵇ[Is. 66:24;
Rom. 9:21]

12:3 ᵃProv. 3:35;
Dan. 11:33, 35;
Matt. 13:43
ᵇProv. 11:30;
[James 5:19, 20]
ᶜ1 Cor. 15:41

12:4 ᵃIs. 8:16;
Dan. 12:9;
Rev. 22:10
ᵇAmos 8:12

12:5 ᵃDan. 10:4

12:6 ᵃEzek. 9:2;
Dan. 10:5
ᵇDan. 8:13; 12:8;
Matt. 24:3;
Mark 13:4

12:7
ᵃDeut. 32:40
ᵇDan. 4:34
ᶜDan. 7:25;
Rev. 12:14
ᵈLuke 21:24
ᵉDan. 8:24

12:10 ᵃZech. 13:9
ᵇIs. 32:6, 7;
Rev. 22:11
ᶜDan. 12:3;
Hos. 14:9;
John 7:17; 8:47

12:13 ᵃIs. 57:2;
Rev. 14:13
ᵇPs. 1:5

12:2 ¹Lit. *abhorrence*

THE BOOK OF
HOSEA

1 The word of the LORD that came to Hosea the son of Beeri, in the days of ᵃUzziah, ᵇJotham, ᶜAhaz, *and* ᵈHezekiah, kings of Judah, and in the days of ᵉJeroboam the son of Joash, king of Israel.

THE FAMILY OF HOSEA

2When the LORD began to speak by Hosea, the LORD said to Hosea:

ᵃ"Go, take yourself a wife of harlotry
    And children of harlotry,
    For ᵇthe land has committed great ¹harlotry
    By departing from the LORD."

3So he went and took Gomer the daughter of Diblaim, and she conceived and bore him a son. 4Then the LORD said to him:

"Call his name Jezreel,
    For in a little *while*
ᵃI will avenge the bloodshed of Jezreel on the house of
        Jehu,
ᵇAnd bring an end to the kingdom of the house of Israel.
5 ᵃIt shall come to pass in that day
    That I will break the bow of Israel in the Valley of
        Jezreel."

6And she conceived again and bore a daughter. Then *God* said to him:

"Call her name ¹Lo-Ruhamah,
ᵃFor I will no longer have mercy on the house of Israel,
²But I will utterly take them away.
7 ᵃYet I will have mercy on the house of Judah,
    Will save them by the LORD their God,
    And ᵇwill not save them by bow,
    Nor by sword or battle,
    By horses or horsemen."

8Now when she had weaned Lo-Ruhamah, she conceived and bore a son. 9Then *God* said:

"Call his name ¹Lo-Ammi,
    For you *are* not My people,
    And I will not be your *God*.

THE RESTORATION OF ISRAEL

10 "Yet ᵃthe number of the children of Israel
    Shall be as the sand of the sea,
    Which cannot be measured or numbered.
ᵇAnd it shall come to pass

1:1 ᵃ2 Chr. 26;
Is. 1:1; Amos 1:1
ᵇ2 Kin. 15:5, 7,
32–38;
2 Chr. 27; Mic. 1:1
ᶜ2 Kin. 16:1–20;
2 Chr. 28
ᵈ2 Kin. 18—20;
2 Chr. 29:1—
32:33; Mic. 1:1
ᵉ2 Kin. 13:13;
14:23–29;
Amos 1:1

1:2 ᵃHos. 3:1
ᵇDeut. 31:16;
Judg. 2:17;
Ps. 73:27;
Jer. 2:13;
Ezek. 16:1–59;
23:1–49

1:4 ᵃ2 Kin. 10:11
ᵇ2 Kin. 15:8–10;
17:6, 23; 18:11

1:5 ᵃ2 Kin. 15:29

1:6 ᵃ2 Kin. 17:6

1:7
ᵃ2 Kin. 19:29–35;
Is. 30:18;
37:36, 37
ᵇPs. 44:3–7;
[Zech. 4:6]

1:10 ᵃGen. 22:17;
32:12; Jer. 33:22
ᵇ1 Pet. 2:10

1:2 ¹Spiritual adultery   1:6 ¹Lit. *No-Mercy*   ²Or *That I may forgive them at all*   1:9 ¹Lit. *Not-My-People*

In the place where it was said to them,
'You *are* [1]not My [c]people,'
There it shall be said to them,
'You *are* [d]sons of the living God.'

11 [a]Then the children of Judah and the children of Israel
Shall be gathered together,
And appoint for themselves one head;
And they shall come up out of the land,
For great *will be* the day of Jezreel!

2 Say to your brethren, [1]'My people,'
And to your sisters, [2]'Mercy *is shown.*'

GOD'S UNFAITHFUL PEOPLE

2 "Bring[1] charges against your mother, [2]bring
charges;
For [a]she *is* not My wife, nor *am* I her Husband!
Let her put away her [b]harlotries from her sight,
And her adulteries from between her breasts;
3 Lest [a]I strip her naked
And expose her, as in the day she was [b]born,
And make her like a wilderness,
And set her like a dry land,
And slay her with [c]thirst.
4 "I will not have mercy on her children,
For they *are* the [a]children of harlotry.
5 For their mother has played the harlot;
She who conceived them has behaved shamefully.
For she said, 'I will go after my lovers,
[a]Who give *me* my bread and my water,
My wool and my linen,
My oil and my drink.'
6 "Therefore, behold,
[a]I will hedge up your way with thorns,
And [1]wall her in,
So that she cannot find her paths.
7 She will [1]chase her lovers,
But not overtake them;
Yes, she will seek them, but not find *them.*
Then she will say,
[a]'I will go and return to my [b]first husband,
For then *it was* better for me than now.'
8 For she did not [a]know
That I gave her grain, new wine, and oil,
And multiplied her silver and gold—
Which they prepared for Baal.
9 "Therefore I will return and take away
My grain in its time
And My new wine in its season,
And will take back My wool and My linen,
Given to cover her nakedness.
10 Now [a]I will uncover her lewdness in the sight of her
lovers,
And no one shall deliver her from My hand.

1:10 [c]Rom. 9:26
[d]Is. 63:16; 64:8;
[John 1:12]

1:11 [a]Is. 11:11–13;
Jer. 3:18; 50:4;
[Ezek. 34:23;
37:15–28]

2:2 [a]Is. 50:1
[b]Ezek. 16:25

2:3
[a]Jer. 13:22, 26;
Ezek. 16:37–39
[b]Ezek. 16:4–7, 22
[c]Jer. 14:3;
Amos 8:11–13

2:4 [a]John 8:41

2:5 [a]Ezek. 23:5;
Hos. 2:8, 12

2:6 [a]Job 19:8;
Lam. 3:7, 9

2:7
[a]Luke 15:17, 18
[b]Is. 54:5–8;
Jer. 2:2; 3:1;
Ezek. 16:8; 23:4

2:8 [a]Is. 1:3;
Ezek. 16:19

2:10
[a]Ezek. 16:37

1:10 [1]Heb. *lo-ammi*, v. 9   2:1 [1]Heb. *Ammi*, Hos. 1:9, 10   [2]Heb. *Ruhamah*,
Hos. 1:6   2:2 [1]Or *Contend with*   [2]Or *contend*   2:6 [1]Lit. *wall up her wall*
2:7 [1]Or *pursue*

11 ᵃI will also cause all her mirth to cease,
Her feast days,
Her New Moons,
Her Sabbaths—
All her appointed feasts.

12 "And I will destroy her vines and her fig trees,
Of which she has said,
'These *are* my wages that my lovers have given me.'
So I will make them a forest,
And the beasts of the field shall eat them.

13 I will punish her
For the days of the Baals to which she burned incense.
She decked herself with her earrings and jewelry,
And went after her lovers;
But Me she forgot," says the LORD.

GOD'S MERCY ON HIS PEOPLE

14 "Therefore, behold, I will allure her,
Will bring her into the wilderness,
And speak ¹comfort to her.

15 I will give her her vineyards from there,
And ᵃthe Valley of Achor as a door of hope;
She shall sing there,
As in ᵇthe days of her youth,
ᶜAs in the day when she came up from the land of
Egypt.

16 "And it shall be, in that day,"
Says the LORD,
"*That* you will call Me ¹'My Husband,'
And no longer call Me ²'My Master,'

17 For ᵃI will take from her mouth the names of the Baals,
And they shall be remembered by their name no more.

18 In that day I will make a ᵃcovenant for them
With the beasts of the field,
With the birds of the air,
And *with* the creeping things of the ground.
Bow and sword of battle ᵇI will shatter from the earth,
To make them ᶜlie down safely.

19 "I will betroth you to Me forever;
Yes, I will betroth you to Me
In righteousness and justice,
In lovingkindness and mercy;

20 I will betroth you to Me in faithfulness,
And ᵃyou shall know the LORD.

21 "It shall come to pass in that day
That ᵃI will answer," says the LORD;
"I will answer the heavens,
And they shall answer the earth.

22 The earth shall answer
With grain,
With new wine,
And with oil;
They shall answer ¹Jezreel.

2:11
ᵃJer. 7:34; 16:9;
Hos. 3:4;
Amos 5:21; 8:10

2:15 ᵃJosh. 7:26
ᵇJer. 2:1–3;
Ezek. 16:8–14
ᶜEx. 15:1

2:17 ᵃEx. 23:13;
Josh. 23:7;
Ps. 16:4

2:18 ᵃJob 5:23;
Is. 11:6–9;
Ezek. 34:25
ᵇIs. 2:4;
Ezek. 39:1–10
ᶜLev. 26:5;
Is. 32:18;
Jer. 23:6;
Ezek. 34:25

2:20
ᵃ[Jer. 31:33, 34];
Hos. 6:6; 13:4;
[John 17:3]

2:21 ᵃIs. 55:10;
Zech. 8:12;
[Mal. 3:10, 11]

2:14 ¹Lit. *to her heart*   **2:16** ¹Heb. *Ishi*   ²Heb. *Baali*   **2:22** ¹Lit. *God Will Sow*

23 Then ᵃI will sow her for Myself in the earth,
ᵇAnd I will have mercy on *her who had* ¹not obtained
mercy;
Then ᶜI will say to *those who were* ²not My people,
'You *are* ³My people!'
And they shall say, '*You are* my God!'"

ISRAEL WILL RETURN TO GOD

3 Then the LORD said to me, "Go again, love a woman *who is* loved by a ᵃlover¹ and is committing adultery, just like the love of the LORD for the children of Israel, who look to other gods and love *the* raisin cakes *of the pagans.*"

²So I bought her for myself for fifteen *shekels* of silver, and one and one-half homers of barley. ³And I said to her, "You shall ᵃstay with me many days; you shall not play the harlot, nor shall you have a man—so, too, *will* I *be* toward you."

⁴For the children of Israel shall abide many days ᵃwithout king or prince, without sacrifice or *sacred* pillar, without ᵇephod or ᶜteraphim. ⁵Afterward the children of Israel shall return and ᵃseek the LORD their God and ᵇDavid their king. They shall fear the LORD and His goodness in the ᶜlatter days.

GOD'S CHARGE AGAINST ISRAEL

4 Hear the word of the LORD,
You children of Israel,
For the LORD *brings* a ᵃcharge¹ against the inhabitants of
the land:

"There is no truth or mercy
Or ᵇknowledge of God in the land.
2 *By* swearing and lying,
Killing and stealing and committing adultery,
They break all restraint,
With bloodshed ¹upon bloodshed.
3 Therefore ᵃthe land will mourn;
And ᵇeveryone who dwells there will waste away
With the beasts of the field
And the birds of the air;
Even the fish of the sea will be taken away.

4 "Now let no man contend, or rebuke another;
For your people *are* like those ᵃwho contend with the
priest.
5 Therefore you shall stumble ᵃin the day;
The prophet also shall stumble with you in the night;
And I will destroy your mother.
6 ᵃMy people are destroyed for lack of knowledge.
Because you have rejected knowledge,
I also will reject you from being priest for Me;
ᵇBecause you have forgotten the law of your God,
I also will forget your children.

7 "The more they increased,
The more they sinned against Me;
ᵃI¹ will change ²their glory into shame.

2:23 ᵃJer. 31:27;
Amos 9:15
ᵇHos. 1:6
ᶜHos. 1:10;
Zech. 13:9;
Rom. 9:25, 26;
[Eph. 2:11–22];
1 Pet. 2:10

3:1 ᵃJer. 3:20

3:3 ᵃDeut. 21:13

3:4 ᵃHos. 10:3
ᵇEx. 28:4–12;
1 Sam. 23:9–12
ᶜGen. 31:19, 34;
Judg. 17:5;
18:14, 17;
[1 Sam. 15:23]

3:5 ᵃJer. 50:4
ᵇJer. 30:9;
Ezek. 34:24
ᶜ[Is. 2:2, 3];
Jer. 31:9

4:1 ᵃIs. 1:18;
Hos. 12:2;
Mic. 6:2
ᵇJer. 4:22

4:3
ᵃIs. 24:4; 33:9;
Jer. 4:28; 12:4;
Amos 5:16; 8:8
ᵇZeph. 1:3

4:4 ᵃDeut. 17:12

4:5 ᵃJer. 15:8;
Hos. 2:2, 5

4:6 ᵃIs. 5:13
ᵇEzek. 22:26

4:7 ᵃ1 Sam. 2:30;
Mal. 2:9

2:23 ¹Heb. *lo-ruhamah* ²Heb. *lo-ammi* ³Heb. *ammi* 3:1 ¹Lit. *friend* or *husband* 4:1 ¹A legal complaint 4:2 ¹Lit. *touching* 4:7 ¹So with MT, LXX, Vg.; scribal tradition, Syr., Tg. *They will change* ²So with MT, LXX, Syr., Tg., Vg.; scribal tradition *My glory*

8 They eat up the sin of My people;
And they set their ¹heart on their iniquity.
9 And it shall be: ªlike people, like priest.
So I will punish them for their ways,
And ¹reward them for their deeds.
10 For ªthey shall eat, but not have enough;
They shall commit harlotry, but not increase;
Because they have ceased obeying the LORD.

THE IDOLATRY OF ISRAEL

11 "Harlotry, wine, and new wine ªenslave the heart.
12 My people ask counsel from their ªwooden *idols,*
And their ¹staff informs them.
For ᵇthe spirit of harlotry has caused *them* to stray,
And they have played the harlot against their God.
13 ªThey offer sacrifices on the mountaintops,
And burn incense on the hills,
Under oaks, poplars, and terebinths,
Because their shade *is* good.
ᵇTherefore your daughters commit harlotry,
And your brides commit adultery.
14 "I will not punish your daughters when they commit
harlotry,
Nor your brides when they commit adultery;
For *the men* themselves go apart with harlots,
And offer sacrifices with a ªritual harlot.
Therefore people *who* do not understand will be
trampled.
15 "Though you, Israel, play the harlot,
Let not Judah offend.
ªDo not come up to Gilgal,
Nor go up to ᵇBeth¹ Aven,
ᶜNor swear an oath, *saying,* 'As the LORD lives'—
16 "For Israel ªis stubborn
Like a stubborn calf;
Now the LORD will let them forage
Like a lamb in ¹open country.
17 "Ephraim *is* joined to idols,
ªLet him alone.
18 Their drink ¹is rebellion,
They commit harlotry continually.
ªHer ²rulers ³dearly love dishonor.
19 ªThe wind has wrapped her up in its wings,
And ᵇthey shall be ashamed because of their sacrifices.

IMPENDING JUDGMENT ON ISRAEL AND JUDAH

5 "Hear this, O priests!
Take heed, O house of Israel!
Give ear, O house of the king!
For ¹yours *is* the judgment,
Because ªyou have been a snare to Mizpah
And a net spread on Tabor.

4:9 ªIs. 24:2;
Jer. 5:30, 31;
2 Tim. 4:3, 4
4:10 ªLev. 26:26;
Is. 65:13;
Mic. 6:14;
Hag. 1:6
4:11 ªProv. 20:1;
Is. 5:12; 28:7
4:12 ªJer. 2:27
ᵇIs. 44:19, 20
4:13
ªIs. 1:29; 57:5, 7;
Jer. 2:20;
Ezek. 6:13;
20:28
ᵇAmos 7:17;
[Rom. 1:28–32]
4:14
ªDeut. 23:18
4:15
ªHos. 9:15; 12:11
ᵇ1 Kin. 12:29;
Josh. 7:2;
Hos. 10:8
ᶜJer. 5:2; 44:26;
Amos 8:14
4:16 ªJer. 3:6;
7:24; 8:5;
Zech. 7:11
4:17 ªMatt. 15:14
4:18 ªMic. 3:11
4:19 ªJer. 51:1
ᵇIs. 1:29
5:1 ªHos. 6:9

4:8 ¹Desires   **4:9** ¹*repay*   **4:12** ¹Diviner's rod   **4:15** ¹Lit. *House of Idolatry*
or *Wickedness*   **4:16** ¹Lit. *a large place*   **4:18** ¹Or *has turned aside*   ²Lit.
shields   ³Heb. difficult; a Jewish tradition *shamefully love, 'Give!'*   **5:1** ¹Or
to you

2 The revolters are ^adeeply involved in slaughter,
Though I rebuke them all.
3 ^aI know Ephraim,
And Israel is not hidden from Me;
For now, O Ephraim, ^byou commit harlotry;
Israel is defiled.

4 "They[1] do not direct their deeds
Toward turning to their God,
For ^athe spirit of harlotry is in their midst,
And they do not know the LORD.
5 The ^apride of Israel testifies to his face;
Therefore Israel and Ephraim stumble in their iniquity;
Judah also stumbles with them.

6 "With their flocks and herds
^aThey shall go to seek the LORD,
But they will not find *Him;*
He has withdrawn Himself from them.
7 They have ^adealt treacherously with the LORD,
For they have begotten [1]pagan children.
Now a New Moon shall devour them and their heritage.

8 "Blow^a the ram's horn in Gibeah,
The trumpet in Ramah!
^bCry aloud *at* ^cBeth Aven,
'*Look* behind you, O Benjamin!'
9 Ephraim shall be desolate in the day of rebuke;
Among the tribes of Israel I make known what is sure.

10 "The princes of Judah are like those who ^aremove a landmark;
I will pour out My wrath on them like water.
11 Ephraim is ^aoppressed *and* broken in judgment,
Because he willingly walked by ^b*human* precept.
12 Therefore I *will be* to Ephraim like a moth,
And to the house of Judah ^alike rottenness.

13 "When Ephraim saw his sickness,
And Judah *saw* his ^awound,
Then Ephraim went ^bto Assyria
And sent to King Jareb;
Yet he cannot cure you,
Nor heal you of your wound.
14 For ^aI *will be* like a lion to Ephraim,
And like a young lion to the house of Judah.
^bI, *even* I, will tear *them* and go away;
I will take *them* away, and no one shall rescue.
15 I will return again to My place
Till they [1]acknowledge their offense.
Then they will seek My face;
In their affliction they will earnestly seek Me."

A CALL TO REPENTANCE

6 Come,^a and let us return to the LORD;
For ^bHe has torn, but ^cHe will heal us;
He has stricken, but He will [1]bind us up.

5:4 [1]Or *Their deeds will not allow them to turn*   5:7 [1]Lit. *strange*   5:15 [1]Lit. *become guilty* or *bear punishment*   6:1 [1]Bandage

5:2 ^aIs. 29:15; Hos. 4:2; 6:9

5:3 ^aAmos 3:2; 5:12 ^bHos. 4:17

5:4 ^aHos. 4:12

5:5 ^aHos. 7:10

5:6 ^aProv. 1:28; Is. 1:15; Jer. 11:11; Ezek. 8:18; Mic. 3:4; John 7:34

5:7 ^aIs. 48:8; Jer. 3:20; Hos. 6:7

5:8 ^aHos. 8:1; Joel 2:1 ^bIs. 10:30 ^cJosh. 7:2

5:10 ^aDeut. 19:14; 27:17

5:11 ^aDeut. 28:33 ^bMic. 6:16

5:12 ^aProv. 12:4

5:13 ^aJer. 30:12–15 ^b2 Kin. 15:19; Hos. 7:11; 10:6

5:14 ^aPs. 7:2; Lam. 3:10; Hos. 13:7, 8 ^bPs. 50:22

6:1 ^aIs. 1:18; Acts 10:43 ^bDeut. 32:39; Hos. 5:14 ^cJer. 30:17; Hos. 14:4

2 [a]After two days He will revive us;
    On the third day He will raise us up,
    That we may live in His sight.
3 [a]Let us know,
    Let us pursue the knowledge of the LORD.
    His going forth is established [b]as the morning;
    [c]He will come to us [d]like the rain,
    Like the latter and former rain to the earth.

IMPENITENCE OF ISRAEL AND JUDAH

4 "O Ephraim, what shall I do to you?
    O Judah, what shall I do to you?
    For your faithfulness is like a morning cloud,
    And like the early dew it goes away.
5 Therefore I have hewn them by the prophets,
    I have slain them by [a]the words of My mouth;
    And [1]your judgments are like light that goes forth.
6 For I desire [a]mercy[1] and [b]not sacrifice,
    And the [c]knowledge of God more than burnt offerings.
7 "But like [1]men they transgressed the covenant;
    There they dealt treacherously with Me.
8 [a]Gilead is a city of evildoers
    And [1]defiled with blood.
9 As bands of robbers lie in wait for a man,
    So the company of [a]priests [b]murder on the way to
        Shechem;
    Surely they commit [c]lewdness.
10 I have seen a horrible thing in the house of Israel:
    There is the [1]harlotry of Ephraim;
    Israel is defiled.
11 Also, O Judah, a harvest is appointed for you,
    When I return the captives of My people.

7 "When I would have healed Israel,
    Then the iniquity of Ephraim was uncovered,
    And the wickedness of Samaria.
    For [a]they have committed fraud;
    A thief comes in;
    A band of robbers [1]takes spoil outside.
2 They [1]do not consider in their hearts
    That [a]I remember all their wickedness;
    Now their own deeds have surrounded them;
    They are before My face.
3 They make a [a]king glad with their wickedness,
    And princes [b]with their lies.

4 "They[a] are all adulterers.
    Like an oven heated by a baker—
    He ceases stirring the fire after kneading the dough,
    Until it is leavened.
5 In the day of our king
    Princes have made him sick, [1]inflamed with [a]wine;
    He stretched out his hand with scoffers.
6 They prepare their heart like an oven,
    While they lie in wait;

6:2 [a]Luke 24:46;
Acts 10:40;
[1 Cor. 15:4]

6:3 [a]Is. 54:13
[b]2 Sam. 23:4
[c]Ps. 72:6;
Joel 2:23
[d]Job 29:23

6:5 [a][Jer. 23:29]

6:6
[a]Matt. 9:13; 12:7
[b]Is. 1:12, 13;
[Mic. 6:6–8]
[c][John 17:3]

6:8 [a]Hos. 12:11

6:9 [a]Hos. 5:1
[b]Jer. 7:9, 10;
Hos. 4:2
[c]Ezek. 22:9;
23:27; Hos. 2:10

7:1
[a]Ezek. 23:4–8;
Hos. 5:1

7:2 [a]Ps. 25:7;
Jer. 14:10; 17:1;
Hos. 8:13; 9:9;
Amos 8:7

7:3 [a]Hos. 7:1
[b]Mic. 7:3;
[Rom. 1:32]

7:4 [a]Jer. 9:2;
23:10

7:5 [a]Is. 28:1, 7

6:5 [1]Or the judgments on you   6:6 [1]Or faithfulness or loyalty   6:7 [1]Or Adam
6:8 [1]Lit. foot-tracked   6:10 [1]Spiritual adultery   7:1 [1]plunders   7:2 [1]Lit. do
not say to   7:5 [1]Lit. with the heat of

¹Their baker sleeps all night;
In the morning it burns like a flaming fire.
7 They are all hot, like an oven,
And have devoured their judges;
All their kings have fallen.
^aNone among them calls upon Me.

8 "Ephraim ^ahas mixed himself among the peoples;
Ephraim is a cake unturned.
9 ^aAliens have devoured his strength,
But he does not know *it;*
Yes, gray hairs are here and there on him,
Yet he does not know *it.*
10 And the ^apride of Israel testifies to his face,
But ^bthey do not return to the LORD their God,
Nor seek Him for all this.

FUTILE RELIANCE ON THE NATIONS

11 "Ephraim^a also is like a silly dove, without ¹sense—
^bThey call to Egypt,
They go to ^cAssyria.
12 Wherever they go, I will ^aspread My net on them;
I will bring them down like birds of the air;
I will chastise them
^bAccording to what their congregation has heard.

13 "Woe to them, for they have fled from Me!
Destruction to them,
Because they have transgressed against Me!
Though ^aI redeemed them,
Yet they have spoken lies against Me.
14 ^aThey did not cry out to Me with their heart
When they wailed upon their beds.

"They ¹assemble together for grain and new ^bwine,
²They rebel against Me;
15 Though I disciplined *and* strengthened their
arms,
Yet they devise evil against Me;
16 They return, *but* not ¹to the Most High;
^aThey are like a treacherous bow.
Their princes shall fall by the sword
For the ^bcursings of their tongue.
This *shall be* their derision ^cin the land of Egypt.

THE APOSTASY OF ISRAEL

8 "*Set* the ¹trumpet to your mouth!
He shall come ^alike an eagle against the house of the
LORD,
Because they have transgressed My covenant
And rebelled against My law.
2 ^aIsrael will cry to Me,
'My God, ^bwe know You!'
3 Israel has rejected the good;
The enemy will pursue him.

7:7 ^aIs. 64:7

7:8 ^aPs. 106:35

7:9 ^aIs. 1:7;
42:25; Hos. 8:7

7:10 ^aHos. 5:5
^bIs. 9:13

7:11 ^aHos. 11:11
^bIs. 30:3
^cHos. 5:13; 8:9

7:12 ^aEzek. 12:13
^bLev. 26:14;
Deut. 28:15;
2 Kin. 17:13

7:13 ^aEx. 18:8;
Mic. 6:4

7:14
^aJob 35:9, 10;
Ps. 78:36;
Jer. 3:10;
Zech. 7:5
^bJudg. 9:27;
Amos 2:8

7:16 ^aPs. 78:57
^bPs. 73:9;
Dan. 7:25;
Mal. 3:13, 14
^cDeut. 28:68;
Ezek. 23:32;
Hos. 8:13; 9:3

8:1
^aDeut. 28:49;
Jer. 4:13

8:2 ^aPs. 78:34;
Hos. 5:15; 7:14
^bTitus 1:16

7:6 ¹So with MT, Vg.; Syr., Tg. *Their anger;* LXX *Ephraim*   7:11 ¹Lit. *heart*
7:14 ¹So with MT, Tg.; Vg. *thought upon;* LXX *slashed themselves for* (cf. 1 Kin.
18:28)   ²So with MT, Syr., Tg.; LXX omits *They rebel against Me;* Vg. *They
departed from Me*   7:16 ¹Or *upward*   8:1 ¹*ram's horn,* Heb. *shophar*

4 "They[a] set up kings, but not by Me;
   They made princes, but I did not acknowledge *them*.
   From their silver and gold
   They made idols for themselves—
   That they might be cut off.
5 Your [1]calf [2]is rejected, O Samaria!
   My anger is aroused against them—
   [a]How long until they attain to innocence?
6 For from Israel *is* even this:
   A [a]workman made it, and it *is* not God;
   But the calf of Samaria shall be broken to pieces.

7 "They[a] sow the wind,
   And reap the whirlwind.
   The stalk has no bud;
   It shall never produce meal.
   If it should produce,
   [b]Aliens would swallow it up.
8 [a]Israel is swallowed up;
   Now they are among the Gentiles
   [b]Like a vessel in which *is* no pleasure.
9 For they have gone up to Assyria,
   Like [a]a wild donkey alone by itself;
   Ephraim [b]has hired lovers.
10 Yes, though they have hired among the nations,
   Now [a]I will gather them;
   And they shall [1]sorrow a little,
   Because of the [2]burden of [b]the king of princes.

11 "Because Ephraim has made many altars for sin,
   They have become for him altars for sinning.
12 I have written for him [a]the great things of My law,
   But they were considered a strange thing.
13 *For* the sacrifices of My offerings [a]they sacrifice flesh and
       eat *it,*
   [b]*But* the LORD does not accept them.
   [c]Now He will remember their iniquity and punish their
       sins.
   They shall return to Egypt.

14 "For[a] Israel has forgotten [b]his Maker,
   And has built [1]temples;
   Judah also has multiplied [c]fortified cities;
   But [d]I will send fire upon his cities,
   And it shall devour his [2]palaces."

JUDGMENT OF ISRAEL'S SIN

9 Do[a] not rejoice, O Israel, with joy like *other* peoples,
   For you have played the harlot against your God.
   You have made love *for* [b]hire on every threshing floor.
2 The threshing floor and the winepress
   Shall not feed them,
   And the new wine shall fail in her.

3 They shall not dwell in [a]the LORD's land,
   [b]But Ephraim shall return to Egypt,
   And [c]shall eat unclean *things* in Assyria.

8:4 [a]1 Kin. 12:20;
2 Kin. 15:23, 25;
Hos. 13:10, 11

8:5 [a]Ps. 19:13;
Jer. 13:27

8:6 [a]Is. 40:19

8:7 [a]Prov. 22:8
[b]Hos. 7:9

8:8 [a]2 Kin. 17:6;
Jer. 51:34
[b]Jer. 22:28;
25:34

8:9
[a]Hos. 7:11; 12:1;
Jer. 2:24
[b]Ezek. 16:33, 34

8:10
[a]Ezek. 16:37;
22:20 [b]Is. 10:8;
Ezek. 26:7;
Dan. 2:37

8:12
[a][Deut. 4:6–8];
Ps. 119:18;
147:19, 20

8:13 [a]Zech. 7:6
[b]Jer. 14:10;
Hos. 6:6; 9:4;
1 Cor. 4:5
[c]Hos. 9:9;
Amos 8:7;
Luke 12:2

8:14
[a]Deut. 32:18;
[Hos. 2:13; 4:6;
13:6] [b]Is. 29:23
[c]Num. 32:17;
2 Kin. 18:13
[d]Jer. 17:27

9:1 [a]Is. 22:12, 13;
Hos. 10:5
[b]Jer. 44:17

9:3
[a][Lev. 25:23];
Jer. 2:7
[b]Hos. 7:16; 8:13
[c]Ezek. 4:13

4 They shall not offer wine *offerings* to the Lord,
Nor ªshall their ᵇsacrifices be pleasing to Him.
It shall be like bread of mourners to them;
All who eat it shall be defiled.
For their bread *shall be* for their *own* life;
It shall not come into the house of the Lord.

5 What will you do in the appointed day,
And in the day of the feast of the Lord?
6 For indeed they are gone because of destruction.
Egypt shall gather them up;
Memphis shall bury them.
ªNettles shall possess their valuables of silver;
Thorns *shall be* in their tents.

7 The ªdays of punishment have come;
The days of recompense have come.
Israel knows!
The prophet *is* a ᵇfool,
ᶜThe spiritual man *is* insane,
Because of the greatness of your iniquity and great
enmity.
8 The ªwatchman of Ephraim *is* with my God;
But the prophet *is* a ¹fowler's snare in all his ways—
Enmity in the house of his God.
9 ªThey are deeply corrupted,
As in the days of ᵇGibeah.
He will remember their iniquity;
He will punish their sins.

10 "I found Israel
Like grapes in the ªwilderness;
I saw your fathers
As the ᵇfirstfruits on the fig tree in its first season.
But they went to ᶜBaal Peor,
And ¹separated themselves *to that* shame;
ᵈThey became an abomination like the thing they loved.
11 *As for* Ephraim, their glory shall fly away like a bird—
No birth, no pregnancy, and no conception!
12 Though they bring up their children,
Yet I will bereave them to the last man.
Yes, ªwoe to them when I depart from them!
13 Just ªas I saw Ephraim like Tyre, planted in a pleasant
place,
So Ephraim will bring out his children to the
murderer."

14 Give them, O Lord—
What will You give?
Give them ªa miscarrying womb
And dry breasts!

15 "All their wickedness *is* in ªGilgal,
For there I hated them.
Because of the evil of their deeds
I will drive them from My house;
I will love them no more.
ᵇAll their princes *are* rebellious.

9:4 ªJer. 6:20
ᵇHos. 8:13;
Amos 5:22

9:6
ªIs. 5:6; 7:23;
Hos. 10:8

9:7 ªIs. 10:3;
Jer. 10:15;
Mic. 7:4;
Luke 21:22
ᵇLam. 2:14;
[Ezek. 13:3, 10]
ᶜMic. 2:11

9:8
ªJer. 6:17; 31:6;
Ezek. 3:17; 33:7

9:9 ªHos. 10:9
ᵇJudg. 19:22

9:10 ªJer. 2:2
ᵇIs. 28:4;
Mic. 7:1
ᶜNum. 25:3;
Ps. 106:28
ᵈPs. 81:12

9:12
ªDeut. 31:17;
Hos. 7:13

9:13
ªEzek. 26—28

9:14
ªLuke 23:29

9:15
ªHos. 4:15; 12:11
ᵇIs. 1:23;
Hos. 5:2

9:8 ¹One who catches birds in a trap or snare   9:10 ¹Or *dedicated*

16 Ephraim is ^astricken,
  Their root is dried up;
  They shall bear no fruit.
  Yes, were they to bear children,
  I would kill the darlings of their womb."

17 My God will ^acast them away,
  Because they did not obey Him;
  And they shall be ^bwanderers among the nations.

ISRAEL'S SIN AND CAPTIVITY

10 Israel ^aempties *his* vine;
  He brings forth fruit for himself.
  According to the multitude of his fruit
  ^bHe has increased the altars;
  According to the bounty of his land
  They have embellished *his sacred* pillars.

2 Their heart is ^adivided;¹
  Now they are held guilty.
  He will break down their altars;
  He will ruin their *sacred* pillars.

3 For now they say,
  "We have no king,
  Because we did not fear the LORD.
  And as for a king, what would he do for us?"
4 They have spoken words,
  Swearing falsely in making a covenant.
  Thus judgment springs up ^alike hemlock in the furrows
    of the field.

5 The inhabitants of Samaria fear
  Because of the ^acalf¹ of Beth Aven.
  For its people mourn for it,
  And ²its priests shriek for it—
  Because its ^bglory has departed from it.
6 *The idol* also shall be carried to Assyria
  As a present for King ^aJareb.
  Ephraim shall receive shame,
  And Israel shall be ashamed of his own counsel.

7 *As for* Samaria, her king is cut off
  Like a twig on the water.
8 Also the ^ahigh places of ¹Aven, ^bthe sin of Israel,
  Shall be destroyed.
  The thorn and thistle shall grow on their altars;
  ^cThey shall say to the mountains, "Cover us!"
  And to the hills, "Fall on us!"

9 "O Israel, you have sinned from the days of ^aGibeah;
  There they stood.
  The ^bbattle in Gibeah against the children of
    ¹iniquity
  Did not ²overtake them.
10 When *it is* My desire, I will chasten them.
  ^aPeoples shall be gathered against them
  When I bind them ¹for their two transgressions.

9:16 ^aHos. 5:11
9:17
^a2 Kin. 17:20;
[Zech. 10:6]
^bLev. 26:33
10:1 ^aNah. 2:2
^bJer. 2:28;
Hos. 8:11; 12:11
10:2
^a1 Kin. 18:21;
Zeph. 1:5;
[Matt. 6:24]
10:4
^aDeut. 31:16, 17;
2 Kin. 17:3, 4;
Amos 5:7
10:5
^a1 Kin. 12:28, 29;
Hos. 8:5, 6; 13:2
^bHos. 9:11
10:6 ^aHos. 5:13
10:8 ^aHos. 4:15
^bDeut. 9:21;
1 Kin. 13:34
^cIs. 2:19;
Luke 23:30;
Rev. 6:16
10:9 ^aHos. 9:9
^bJudg. 20
10:10 ^aJer. 16:16

10:2 ¹Divided in loyalty **10:5** ¹Lit. *calves,* images ²idolatrous priests
10:8 ¹Lit. *Idolatry* or *Wickedness* **10:9** ¹So with many Heb. mss., LXX, Vg.;
MT *unruliness* ²Or *overcome* **10:10** ¹Or *in their two habitations*

11 Ephraim *is* ᵃa trained heifer
   That loves to thresh *grain;*
   But I harnessed her fair neck,
   I will make Ephraim ¹pull *a plow.*
   Judah shall plow;
   Jacob shall break his clods."

12 Sow for yourselves righteousness;
   Reap in mercy;
   ᵃBreak up your fallow ground,
   For *it is* time to seek the LORD,
   Till He ᵇcomes and rains righteousness on you.

13 ᵃYou have plowed wickedness;
   You have reaped iniquity.
   You have eaten the fruit of lies,
   Because you trusted in your own way,
   In the multitude of your mighty men.

14 Therefore tumult shall arise among your people,
   And all your fortresses shall be plundered
   As Shalman plundered Beth Arbel in the day of
      battle—
   A mother dashed in pieces upon *her* children.

15 Thus it shall be done to you, O Bethel,
   Because of your great wickedness.
   At dawn the king of Israel
   Shall be cut off utterly.

GOD'S CONTINUING LOVE FOR ISRAEL

11 "When Israel *was* a ¹child, I loved him,
   And out of Egypt ᵃI called My ᵇson.

2 ¹*As* they called them,
   So they ᵃwent ²from them;
   They sacrificed to the Baals,
   And burned incense to carved images.

3 "Iᵃ taught Ephraim to walk,
   Taking them by ¹their arms;
   But they did not know that ᵇI healed them.

4 I drew them with ¹gentle cords,
   With bands of love,
   And ᵃI was to them as those who take the yoke from their
      ²neck.
   ᵇI stooped *and* fed them.

5 "He shall not return to the land of Egypt;
   But the Assyrian shall be his king,
   Because they refused to repent.

6 And the sword shall slash in his cities,
   Devour his districts,
   And consume *them,*
   Because of their own counsels.

7 My people are bent on ᵃbacksliding from Me.
   Though ¹they call ²to the Most High,
   None at all exalt *Him.*

10:11 ᵃ[Jer. 50:11;
Hos. 4:16;
Mic. 4:13]

10:12 ᵃJer. 4:3
ᵇHos. 6:3

10:13 ᵃ[Job 4:8;
Prov. 22:8;
Gal. 6:7, 8]

11:1 ᵃMatt. 2:15
ᵇEx. 4:22, 23

11:2
ᵃ2 Kin. 17:13–15

11:3 ᵃDeut. 1:31;
32:10, 11
ᵇEx. 15:26

11:4 ᵃLev. 26:13
ᵇEx. 16:32;
Ps. 78:25

11:7
ᵃJer. 3:6, 7; 8:5

10:11 ¹Lit. *to ride*   11:1 ¹Or *youth*   11:2 ¹So with MT, Vg.; LXX *Just as I called them;* Tg. interprets as *I sent prophets to a thousand of them.*   ²So with MT, Tg., Vg.; LXX *from My face*   11:3 ¹Some Heb. mss., LXX, Syr., Vg. *My arms*   11:4 ¹Lit. *cords of a man*   ²Lit. *jaws*   11:7 ¹The prophets   ²Or *upward*

8 "How[a] can I give you up, Ephraim?
How can I hand you over, Israel?
How can I make you like [b]Admah?
How can I set you like Zeboiim?
My heart [1]churns within Me;
My sympathy is stirred.
9 I will not execute the fierceness of My anger;
I will not again destroy Ephraim.
[a]For I *am* God, and not man,
The Holy One in your midst;
And I will not [1]come with terror.

10 "They shall walk after the LORD.
[a]He will roar like a lion.
When He roars,
Then *His* sons shall come trembling from the
west;
11 They shall come trembling like a bird from Egypt,
[a]Like a dove from the land of Assyria.
[b]And I will let them dwell in their houses,"
Says the LORD.

GOD'S CHARGE AGAINST EPHRAIM

12 "Ephraim has encircled Me with lies,
And the house of Israel with deceit;
But Judah still walks with God,
Even with the [1]Holy One *who is* faithful.

12 "Ephraim [a]feeds on the wind,
And pursues the east wind;
He daily increases lies and [1]desolation.
[b]Also they make a [2]covenant with the Assyrians,
And [c]oil is carried to Egypt.

2 "The[a] LORD also *brings* a [1]charge against Judah,
And will punish Jacob according to his ways;
According to his deeds He will recompense him.
3 He took his brother [a]by the heel in the womb,
And in his strength he [b]struggled with God.
4 Yes, he struggled with the Angel and prevailed;
He wept, and sought favor from Him.
He found Him *in* [a]Bethel,
And there He spoke to us—
5 That is, the LORD God of hosts.
The LORD *is* His [a]memorable name.
6 [a]So you, by *the help of* your God, return;
Observe mercy and justice,
And wait on your God continually.

7 "A cunning [1]Canaanite!
[a]Deceitful scales *are* in his hand;
He loves to oppress.
8 And Ephraim said,
[a]'Surely I have become rich,
I have found wealth for myself;
In all my labors
They shall find in me no iniquity that *is* sin.'

11:8 [a]Jer. 9:7
[b]Gen. 14:8;
19:24, 25;
Deut. 29:23
11:9 [a]Num. 23:19
11:10 [a]Is. 31:4;
[Joel 3:16];
Amos 1:2
11:11
[a]Is. 11:11; 60:8;
Hos. 7:11
[b]Ezek. 28:25, 26;
34:27, 28
12:1 [a]Job 15:2, 3;
Hos. 8:7
[b]2 Kin. 17:4;
Hos. 8:9
[c]Is. 30:6
12:2 [a]Hos. 4:1;
Mic. 6:2
12:3 [a]Gen. 25:26
[b]Gen. 32:24–28
12:4
[a][Gen. 28:12–19;
35:9–15]
12:5 [a]Ex. 3:15
12:6 [a]Hos. 14:1;
Mic. 6:8
12:7 [a]Prov. 11:1;
Amos 8:5;
Mic. 6:11
12:8 [a]Ps. 62:10;
Hos. 13:6;
Rev. 3:17

11:8 [1]Lit. *turns over*   11:9 [1]Or *enter a city*   11:12 [1]Or *holy ones*   12:1 [1]*ruin*
[2]Or *treaty*   12:2 [1]A legal complaint   12:7 [1]Or *merchant*

9 "But I *am* the LORD your God,
Ever since the land of Egypt;
ªI will again make you dwell in tents,
As in the days of the appointed feast.

10 ªI have also spoken by the prophets,
And have multiplied visions;
I have given ¹symbols ²through the witness of the
prophets."

11 Though ªGilead *has* idols—
Surely they are ¹vanity—
Though they sacrifice bulls in ᵇGilgal,
Indeed their altars *shall be* heaps in the furrows of the
field.

12 Jacob ªfled to the country of Syria;
ᵇIsrael served for a spouse,
And for a wife he tended *sheep.*

13 ªBy a prophet the LORD brought Israel out of Egypt,
And by a prophet he was preserved.

14 Ephraim ªprovoked *Him* to anger most bitterly;
Therefore his Lord will leave the guilt of his bloodshed
upon him,
ᵇAnd return his reproach upon him.

RELENTLESS JUDGMENT ON ISRAEL

13 When Ephraim spoke, trembling,
He exalted *himself* in Israel;
But when he offended through Baal *worship,* he died.

2 Now they sin more and more,
And have made for themselves molded images,
Idols of their silver, according to their skill;
All of it *is* the work of craftsmen.
They say of them,
"Let ¹the men who sacrifice ²kiss the calves!"

3 Therefore they shall be like the morning cloud
And like the early dew that passes away,
ªLike chaff blown off from a threshing floor
And like smoke from a chimney.

4 "Yet ªI *am* the LORD your God
Ever since the land of Egypt,
And you shall know no God but Me;
For ᵇ*there is* no savior besides Me.

5 ªI ¹knew you in the wilderness,
ᵇIn the land of ²great drought.

6 ªWhen they had pasture, they were filled;
They were filled and their heart was exalted;
Therefore they forgot Me.

7 "So ªI will be to them like a lion;
Like ᵇa leopard by the road I will lurk;

8 I will meet them ªlike a bear deprived *of her cubs;*
I will tear open their rib cage,
And there I will devour them like a lion.
The ¹wild beast shall tear them.

12:9 ªLev. 23:42

12:10
ª2 Kin. 17:13;
Jer. 7:25

12:11 ªHos. 6:8
ᵇHos. 9:15

12:12
ªGen. 28:5;
Deut. 26:5
ᵇGen. 29:20, 28

12:13
ªEx. 12:50, 51;
13:3; Ps. 77:20;
Is. 63:11, 12;
Mic. 6:4

12:14
ªEzek. 18:10–13
ᵇDan. 11:18;
Mic. 6:16

13:3 ªPs. 1:4;
Is. 17:13;
Dan. 2:35

13:4 ªIs. 43:11
ᵇIs. 43:11;
45:21, 22;
[1 Tim. 2:5]

13:5
ªDeut. 2:7; 32:10
ᵇDeut. 8:15

13:6
ªDeut. 8:12, 14;
32:13–15; Jer. 5:7

13:7 ªLam. 3:10;
Hos. 5:14
ᵇJer. 5:6

13:8
ª2 Sam. 17:8;
Prov. 17:12

12:10 ¹Or *parables*   ²Lit. *by the hand*   12:11 ¹*worthless*   13:2 ¹Or *those who offer human sacrifice*   ²Worship with kisses   13:5 ¹Cared for you   ²Lit. *droughts*   13:8 ¹Lit. *beast of the field*

9 "O Israel, ¹you are destroyed,
But ²your help *is* from Me.
10 ¹I will be your King;
ᵃWhere *is any other*,
That he may save you in all your cities?
And your judges to whom ᵇyou said,
'Give me a king and princes'?
11 ᵃI gave you a king in My anger,
And took *him* away in My wrath.

12 "Theᵃ iniquity of Ephraim *is* bound up;
His sin *is* stored up.
13 ᵃThe sorrows of a woman in childbirth shall come upon
him.
He *is* an unwise son,
For he should not stay long where children are born.

14 "I will ransom them from the ¹power of ²the grave;
I will redeem them from death.
ᵃO Death, ³I will be your plagues!
O ⁴Grave, ⁵I will be your destruction!
ᵇPity is hidden from My eyes."

15 Though he is fruitful among *his* brethren,
ᵃAn east wind shall come;
The wind of the LORD shall come up from the
wilderness.
Then his spring shall become dry,
And his fountain shall be dried up.
He shall plunder the treasury of every desirable
prize.
16 Samaria ¹is held guilty,
For she has ᵃrebelled against her God.
They shall fall by the sword,
Their infants shall be dashed in pieces,
And their women with child ᵇripped open.

ISRAEL RESTORED AT LAST

14 O Israel, ᵃreturn to the LORD your God,
For you have stumbled because of your iniquity;
2 Take words with you,
And return to the LORD.
Say to Him,
"Take away all iniquity;
Receive *us* graciously,
For we will offer the ᵃsacrifices¹ of our lips.
3 Assyria shall ᵃnot save us,
ᵇWe will not ride on horses,
Nor will we say anymore to the work of our hands, '*You
are* our gods.'
ᶜFor in You the fatherless finds mercy."

4 "I will heal their ᵃbacksliding,
I will ᵇlove them freely,
For My anger has turned away from him.

Cross references (left margin)

13:10
ᵃDeut. 32:38
ᵇ1 Sam. 8:5, 6

13:11 ᵃ1 Sam. 8:7;
10:17–24

13:12
ᵃDeut. 32:34, 35;
Job 14:17;
[Rom. 2:5]

13:13 ᵃIs. 13:8;
Mic. 4:9, 10

13:14
ᵃ[1 Cor. 15:54, 55]
ᵇJer. 15:6

13:15 ᵃGen. 41:6;
Jer. 4:11, 12;
Ezek. 17:10; 19:12

13:16
ᵃ2 Kin. 18:12
ᵇ2 Kin. 15:16

14:1 ᵃHos. 12:6;
[Joel 2:13]

14:2
ᵃ[Ps. 51:16, 17;
Hos. 6:6;
Heb. 13:15]

14:3 ᵃHos. 7:11;
10:13; 12:1
ᵇ[Ps. 33:17];
Is. 31:1
ᶜPs. 10:14; 68:5

14:4 ᵃJer. 14:7
ᵇ[Eph. 1:6]

13:9 ¹Lit. *it* or *he destroyed you*   ²Lit. *in your help*   **13:10** ¹LXX, Syr., Tg., Vg.
Where is your king?   **13:14** ¹Lit. *hand*   ²Or *Sheol*   ³LXX *where is your
punishment?*   ⁴Or *Sheol*   ⁵LXX *where is your sting?*   **13:16** ¹LXX *shall be
disfigured*   **14:2** ¹Lit. *bull calves*; LXX *fruit*

5 I will be like the ªdew to Israel;
   He shall ¹grow like the lily,
   And ²lengthen his roots like Lebanon.
6 His branches shall ¹spread;
   ªHis beauty shall be like an olive tree,
   And ᵇhis fragrance like Lebanon.
7 ªThose who dwell under his shadow shall return;
   They shall be revived *like* grain,
   And ¹grow like a vine.
   Their ²scent *shall be* like the wine of Lebanon.

8 "Ephraim *shall say*, 'What have I to do anymore with
       idols?'
   I have heard and observed him.
   I *am* like a green cypress tree;
   ªYour fruit is found in Me."

9 Who *is* wise?
   Let him understand these things.
   Who is prudent?
   Let him know them.
   For ªthe ways of the LORD *are* right;
   The righteous walk in them,
   But transgressors stumble in them.

14:5 ªJob 29:19;
Prov. 19:12;
Is. 26:19

14:6
ªPs. 52:8; 128:3
ᵇGen. 27:27

14:7 ªDan. 4:12

14:8
ª[John 15:4]

14:9
ª[Ps. 111:7, 8;
Prov. 10:29];
Zeph. 3:5

14:5 ¹Lit. *bud* or *sprout*   ²Lit. *strike*   14:6 ¹Lit. *go*   14:7 ¹Lit. *bud* or *sprout*
²Lit. *remembrance*

THE BOOK OF
JOEL

1

The word of the Lord that came to ªJoel the son of Pethuel.

THE LAND LAID WASTE
(Ex. 10:1–20)

2 Hear this, you elders,
  And give ear, all you inhabitants of the land!
  ªHas *anything like* this happened in your days,
  Or even in the days of your fathers?
3 ªTell your children about it,
  Let your children *tell* their children,
  And their children another generation.

4 ªWhat the chewing ¹locust left, the ᵇswarming locust has
      eaten;
  What the swarming locust left, the crawling locust has
      eaten;
  And what the crawling locust left, the consuming locust
      has eaten.

5 Awake, you ªdrunkards, and weep;
  And wail, all you drinkers of wine,
  Because of the new wine,
  ᵇFor it has been cut off from your mouth.
6 For ªa nation has come up against My land,
  Strong, and without number;
  ᵇHis teeth *are* the teeth of a lion,
  And he has the fangs of a ¹fierce lion.
7 He has ªlaid waste My vine,
  And ¹ruined My fig tree;
  He has stripped it bare and thrown *it* away;
  Its branches are made white.

8 ªLament like a virgin girded with sackcloth
  For ᵇthe husband of her youth.
9 ªThe grain offering and the drink offering
  Have been cut off from the house of the Lord;
  The priests ᵇmourn, who minister to the Lord.
10 The field is wasted,
  ªThe land mourns;
  For the grain is ruined,
  ᵇThe new wine is dried up,
  The oil fails.

11 ªBe ashamed, you farmers,
  Wail, you vinedressers,
  For the wheat and the barley;
  Because the harvest of the field has perished.

1:1 ªActs 2:16
1:2 ªJer. 30:7;
  Joel 2:2
1:3 ªEx. 10:2;
  Ps. 78:4;
  Is. 38:19
1:4
ªDeut. 28:38;
  Joel 2:25;
  Amos 4:9
ᵇIs. 33:4
1:5 ªIs. 5:11; 28:1;
  Hos. 7:5
ᵇIs. 32:10
1:6 ªProv. 30:25;
  Joel 2:2, 11, 25
ᵇRev. 9:8
1:7 ªIs. 5:6;
  Amos 4:9
1:8 ªIs. 22:12
ᵇProv. 2:17;
  Jer. 3:4
1:9 ªHos. 9:4;
  Joel 1:13; 2:14
ᵇJoel 2:17
1:10 ªJer. 12:11;
  Hos. 3:4
ᵇIs. 24:7
1:11 ªJer. 14:3, 4;
  Amos 5:16

1:4 ¹Exact identity of these locusts unknown 1:6 ¹Or *lioness*
1:7 ¹Or *splintered*

12 [a]The vine has dried up,
  And the fig tree has withered;
  The pomegranate tree,
  The palm tree also,
  And the apple tree—
  All the trees of the field are withered;
  Surely [b]joy has withered away from the sons of men.

MOURNING FOR THE LAND

13 [a]Gird yourselves and lament, you priests;
  Wail, you who minister before the altar;
  Come, lie all night in sackcloth,
  You who minister to my God;
  For the grain offering and the drink offering
  Are withheld from the house of your God.
14 [a]Consecrate a fast,
  Call [b]a sacred assembly;
  Gather the elders
  And [c]all the inhabitants of the land
  Into the house of the LORD your God,
  And cry out to the LORD.

15 [a]Alas for the day!
  For [b]the day of the LORD is at hand;
  It shall come as destruction from the Almighty.
16 Is not the food [a]cut off before our eyes,
  [b]Joy and gladness from the house of our God?
17 The seed shrivels under the clods,
  Storehouses are in shambles;
  Barns are broken down,
  For the grain has withered.
18 How [a]the animals groan!
  The herds of cattle are restless,
  Because they have no pasture;
  Even the flocks of sheep [1]suffer punishment.

19 O LORD, [a]to You I cry out;
  For [b]fire has devoured the [1]open pastures,
  And a flame has burned all the trees of the field.
20 The beasts of the field also [a]cry out to You,
  For [b]the water brooks are dried up,
  And fire has devoured the [1]open pastures.

THE DAY OF THE LORD

2 Blow [a]the [1]trumpet in Zion,
  And [b]sound an alarm in My holy mountain!
  Let all the inhabitants of the land tremble;
  For [c]the day of the LORD is coming,
  For it is at hand:
2 [a]A day of darkness and gloominess,
  A day of clouds and thick darkness,
  Like the morning clouds spread over the mountains.
  [b]A people come, great and strong,
  [c]The like of whom has never been;
  Nor will there ever be any such after them,
  Even for many successive generations.

1:12 [a]Joel 1:10;
Hab. 3:17
[b]Is. 16:10; 24:11;
Jer. 48:33

1:13 [a]Jer. 4:8;
Ezek. 7:18

1:14 [a]2 Chr. 20:3;
Joel 2:15, 16
[b]Lev. 23:36
[c]2 Chr. 20:13

1:15 [a][Is. 13:9;
Jer. 30:7];
Amos 5:16
[b]Is. 13:6;
Ezek. 7:2–12

1:16 [a]Is. 3:1;
Amos 4:6
[b]Deut. 12:7;
Ps. 43:4

1:18 [a]1 Kin. 8:5;
Jer. 12:4; 14:5, 6;
Hos. 4:3

1:19 [a][Ps. 50:15];
Mic. 7:7
[b]Jer. 9:10;
Amos 7:4

1:20 [a]Job 38:41;
Ps. 104:21;
147:9; Joel 1:18
[b]1 Kin. 17:7; 18:5

2:1 [a]Jer. 4:5;
Joel 2:15;
Zeph. 1:16
[b]Num. 10:5
[c]Joel 1:15;
2:11, 31; 3:14;
[Obad. 15];
Zeph. 1:14

2:2
[a]Joel 2:10, 31;
Amos 5:18;
Zeph. 1:15
[b]Joel 1:6; 2:11, 25
[c]Ex. 10:14;
Lam. 1:12;
Dan. 9:12; 12:1;
Joel 1:2

1:18 [1]LXX, Vg. are made desolate   1:19 [1]Lit. pastures of the wilderness
1:20 [1]Lit. pastures of the wilderness   2:1 [1]ram's horn

3 A fire devours before them,
  And behind them a flame burns;
  The land *is* like [a]the Garden of Eden before them,
  [b]And behind them a desolate wilderness;
  Surely nothing shall escape them.
4 [a]Their appearance is like the appearance of horses;
  And like [1]swift steeds, so they run.
5 [a]With a noise like chariots
  Over mountaintops they leap,
  Like the noise of a flaming fire that devours the stubble,
  Like a strong people set in battle array.

6 Before them the people writhe in pain;
  [a]All faces [1]are drained of color.
7 They run like mighty men,
  They climb the wall like men of war;
  Every one marches in formation,
  And they do not break [a]ranks.
8 They do not push one another;
  Every one marches in his own [1]column.
  Though they lunge between the weapons,
  They are not [2]cut down.
9 They run to and fro in the city,
  They run on the wall;
  They climb into the houses,
  They [a]enter at the windows [b]like a thief.

10 [a]The earth quakes before them,
  The heavens tremble;
  [b]The sun and moon grow dark,
  And the stars diminish their brightness.
11 [a]The LORD gives voice before His army,
  For His camp is very great;
  [b]For strong *is the* One who executes His word.
  For the [c]day of the LORD *is* great and very terrible;
  [d]Who can endure it?

A CALL TO REPENTANCE

12 "Now, therefore," says the LORD,
  [a]"Turn to Me with all your heart,
  With fasting, with weeping, and with mourning."
13 So [a]rend your heart, and not [b]your garments;
  Return to the LORD your God,
  For He *is* [c]gracious and merciful,
  Slow to anger, and of great kindness;
  And He relents from doing harm.
14 [a]Who knows *if* He will turn and relent,
  And leave [b]a blessing behind Him—
  [c]A grain offering and a drink offering
  For the LORD your God?

15 [a]Blow the [1]trumpet in Zion,
  [b]Consecrate a fast,
  Call a sacred assembly;
16 Gather the people,
  [a]Sanctify the congregation,

2:3 [a]Gen. 2:8;
  Is. 51:3;
  Ezek. 36:35
  [b]Ex. 10:5, 15;
  Ps. 105:34, 35;
  Zech. 7:14
2:4 [a]Rev. 9:7
2:5 [a]Rev. 9:9
2:6 [a]Is. 13:8;
  Jer. 8:21;
  Lam. 4:8;
  Nah. 2:10
2:7 [a]Prov. 30:27
2:9 [a]Jer. 9:21
  [b]John 10:1
2:10 [a]Ps. 18:7;
  Joel 3:16;
  Nah. 1:5
  [b]Is. 13:10; 34:4;
  Jer. 4:23;
  Ezek. 32:7, 8;
  Joel 2:31; 3:15;
  Matt. 24:29;
  Rev. 8:12
2:11 [a]Jer. 25:30;
  Joel 3:16;
  Amos 1:2
  [b]Jer. 50:34;
  Rev. 18:8
  [c]Jer. 30:7;
  Amos 5:18;
  Zeph. 1:15
  [d][Mal. 3:2]
2:12
[a][Deut. 4:29];
  Jer. 4:1;
  Ezek. 33:11;
  Hos. 12:6; 14:1
2:13
[a][Ps. 34:18; 51:17];
  Is. 57:15]
  [b]Gen. 37:34;
  2 Sam. 1:11;
  Job 1:20;
  Jer. 41:5
  [c][Ex. 34:6]
2:14 [a]Josh. 14:12;
  2 Sam. 12:22;
  2 Kin. 19:4;
  Jer. 26:3;
  Jon. 3:9
  [b]Hag. 2:19
  [c]Joel 1:9, 13
2:15 [a]Num. 10:3;
  2 Kin. 10:20
  [b]Joel 1:14
2:16 [a]Ex. 19:10

2:4 [1]Or *horsemen*   2:6 [1]LXX, Tg., Vg. *gather blackness*   2:8 [1]Lit. *highway*
[2]Halted by losses   2:15 [1]*ram's horn*

    Assemble the elders,
    Gather the children and nursing babes;
    ᵇLet the bridegroom go out from his chamber,
    And the bride from her dressing room.
17   Let the priests, who minister to the LORD,
    Weep ᵃbetween the porch and the altar;
    Let them say, ᵇ"Spare Your people, O LORD,
    And do not give Your heritage to reproach,
    That the nations should ¹rule over them.
    ᶜWhy should they say among the peoples,
    'Where *is* their God?'"

THE LAND REFRESHED

(Acts 2:17)

18   Then the LORD will ᵃbe zealous for His land,
    And pity His people.
19   The LORD will answer and say to His people,
    "Behold, I will send you ᵃgrain and new wine and oil,
    And you will be satisfied by them;
    I will no longer make you a reproach among the nations.

20   "But ᵃI will remove far from you ᵇthe northern *army*,
    And will drive him away into a barren and desolate land,
    With his face toward the eastern sea
    And his back ᶜtoward the western sea;
    His stench will come up,
    And his foul odor will rise,
    Because he has done ¹monstrous things."

21   Fear not, O land;
    Be glad and rejoice,
    For the LORD has done ¹marvelous things!
22   Do not be afraid, you beasts of the field;
    For ᵃthe open pastures are springing up,
    And the tree bears its fruit;
    The fig tree and the vine yield their strength.
23   Be glad then, you children of Zion,
    And ᵃrejoice in the LORD your God;
    For He has given you the ¹former rain faithfully,
    And He ᵇwill cause the rain to come down for you—
    The former rain,
    And the latter rain in the first *month*.
24   The threshing floors shall be full of wheat,
    And the vats shall overflow with new wine and oil.

25   "So I will restore to you the years ᵃthat the swarming
      ¹locust has eaten,
    The crawling locust,
    The consuming locust,
    And the chewing locust,
    My great army which I sent among you.
26   You shall ᵃeat in plenty and be satisfied,
    And praise the name of the LORD your God,
    Who has dealt wondrously with you;
    And My people shall never be put to ᵇshame.

2:16 ᵇPs. 19:5

2:17
ᵃMatt. 23:35
ᵇEx. 32:11, 12;
[Is. 37:20];
Amos 7:2, 5
ᶜPs. 42:10

2:18
ᵃ[Is. 60:10;
63:9, 15]

2:19 ᵃJer. 31:12;
Hos. 2:21, 22;
Joel 1:10;
[Mal. 3:10]

2:20 ᵃEx. 10:19
ᵇJer. 1:14, 15
ᶜDeut. 11:24

2:22 ᵃJoel 1:19

2:23
ᵃDeut. 11:14;
Is. 41:16;
Jer. 5:24;
Hab. 3:18;
Zech. 10:7
ᵇLev. 26:4;
Hos. 6:3;
Zech. 10:1;
James 5:7

2:25
ᵃJoel 1:4–7;
2:2–11

2:26 ᵃLev. 26:5;
Deut. 11:15;
Is. 62:9 ᵇIs. 45:17

2:17 ¹Or *speak a proverb against them*   2:20 ¹Lit. *great*   2:21 ¹Lit. *great*
2:23 ¹Or *teacher of righteousness*   2:25 ¹Exact identity of these locusts
unknown

27 Then you shall know that I *am* ^ain the midst of Israel:
^bI *am* the LORD your God
And there is no other.
My people shall never be put to shame.

GOD'S SPIRIT POURED OUT

28 "And^a it shall come to pass afterward
That ^bI will pour out My Spirit on all flesh;
^cYour sons and your ^ddaughters shall prophesy,
Your old men shall dream dreams,
Your young men shall see visions.

29 And also on *My* ^amenservants and on *My* maidservants
I will pour out My Spirit in those days.

30 "And ^aI will show wonders in the heavens and in the earth:
Blood and fire and pillars of smoke.

31 ^aThe sun shall be turned into darkness,
And the moon into blood,
^bBefore the coming of the great and awesome day of the
LORD.

32 And it shall come to pass
That ^awhoever calls on the name of the LORD
Shall be ¹saved.
For ^bin Mount Zion and in Jerusalem there shall be
²deliverance,
As the LORD has said,
Among ^cthe remnant whom the LORD calls.

GOD JUDGES THE NATIONS

3 "For behold, ^ain those days and at that time,
When I bring back the captives of Judah and Jerusalem,

2 ^aI will also gather all nations,
And bring them down to the Valley of Jehoshaphat;
And I ^bwill enter into judgment with them there
On account of My people, My heritage Israel,
Whom they have scattered among the nations;
They have also divided up My land.

3 They have ^acast lots for My people,
Have given a boy *as payment* for a harlot,
And sold a girl for wine, that they may drink.

4 "Indeed, what have you to do with Me,
^aO Tyre and Sidon, and all the coasts of Philistia?
Will you ¹retaliate against Me?
But if you ²retaliate against Me,
Swiftly and speedily I will return your ³retaliation upon
your own head;

5 Because you have taken My silver and My gold,
And have carried into your temples My ¹prized
possessions.

6 Also the people of Judah and the people of Jerusalem
You have sold to the Greeks,
That you may remove them far from their borders.

7 "Behold, ^aI will raise them
Out of the place to which you have sold them,
And will return your ¹retaliation upon your own head.

2:27
^aLev. 26:11, 12;
[Joel 3:17, 21]
^b[Is. 45:5, 6]

2:28
^aEzek. 39:29;
Acts 2:17–21
^bZech. 12:10
^cIs. 54:13
^dActs 21:9

2:29
^a[1 Cor. 12:13;
Gal. 3:28]

2:30
^aMatt. 24:29;
Mark 13:24, 25;
Luke 21:11, 25, 26;
Acts 2:19

2:31
^aIs. 13:9, 10;
34:4;
Joel 2:10; 3:15;
Matt. 24:29;
Mark 13:24;
Luke 21:25;
Acts 2:20;
Rev. 6:12, 13
^bIs. 13:9;
Zeph. 1:14–16;
[Mal. 4:1, 5, 6]

2:32 ^aJer. 33:3;
Acts 2:21;
Rom. 10:13
^bIs. 46:13;
[Rom. 11:26]
^cIs. 11:11; Jer. 31:7;
[Mic. 4:7];
Rom. 9:27

3:1 ^aJer. 30:3;
Ezek. 38:14

3:2 ^aIs. 66:18;
Mic. 4:12;
Zech. 14:2
^bIs. 66:16;
Jer. 25:31;
Ezek. 38:22

3:3 ^aObad. 11;
Nah. 3:10

3:4
^aIs. 14:29–31;
Jer. 47:1–7;
Ezek. 25:15–17;
Amos 1:6–8;
Zech. 9:5–7

3:7 ^aIs. 43:5, 6;
Jer. 23:8;
Zech. 9:13

2:32 ¹Or *delivered*   ²Or *salvation*   **3:4** ¹Or *render Me repayment*
²Or *repay Me*   ³Or *repayment*   **3:5** ¹Lit. *precious good things*   **3:7** ¹Or
repayment

8 I will sell your sons and your daughters
Into the hand of the people of Judah,
And they will sell them to the ᵃSabeans,¹
To a people ᵇfar off;
For the LORD has spoken."

9 ᵃProclaim this among the nations:
"Prepare for war!
Wake up the mighty men,
Let all the men of war draw near,
Let them come up.

10 ᵃBeat your plowshares into swords
And your ¹pruning hooks into spears;
ᵇLet the weak say, 'I *am* strong.'"

11 Assemble and come, all you nations,
And gather together all around.
Cause ᵃYour mighty ones to go down there, O LORD.

12 "Let the nations be wakened, and come up to the Valley of
Jehoshaphat;
For there I will sit to ᵃjudge all the surrounding nations.

13 ᵃPut in the sickle, for ᵇthe harvest is ripe.
Come, go down;
For the ᶜwinepress is full,
The vats overflow—
For their wickedness *is* great."

14 Multitudes, multitudes in the valley of decision!
For ᵃthe day of the LORD *is* near in the valley of decision.

15 The sun and moon will grow dark,
And the stars will diminish their brightness.

16 The LORD also will roar from Zion,
And utter His voice from Jerusalem;
The heavens and earth will shake;
ᵃBut the LORD will be a shelter for His people,
And the strength of the children of Israel.

17 "So you shall know that I *am* the LORD your God,
Dwelling in Zion My ᵃholy mountain.
Then Jerusalem shall be holy,
And no aliens shall ever pass through her again."

GOD BLESSES HIS PEOPLE

18 And it will come to pass in that day
That the mountains shall drip with new wine,
The hills shall flow with milk,
And all the brooks of Judah shall be flooded with water;
A ᵃfountain shall flow from the house of the LORD
And water the Valley of ¹Acacias.

19 "Egypt shall be a desolation,
And Edom a desolate wilderness,
Because of violence *against* the people of Judah,
For they have shed innocent blood in their land.

20 But Judah shall abide forever,
And Jerusalem from generation to generation.

21 For I will ᵃacquit them of the guilt of bloodshed, whom I
had not acquitted;
For the LORD dwells in Zion."

3:8 ᵃEzek. 23:42
ᵇJer. 6:20

3:9 ᵃJer. 6:4;
Ezek. 38:7;
Mic. 3:5

3:10
ᵃ[Is. 2:4;
Mic. 4:3]
ᵇZech. 12:8

3:11 ᵃPs. 103:20;
Is. 13:3

3:12
ᵃ[Ps. 96:13];
Is. 2:4

3:13
ᵃ[Matt. 13:39];
Rev. 14:15
ᵇJer. 51:33;
Hos. 6:11
ᶜ[Is. 63:3];
Lam. 1:5;
Rev. 14:19

3:14 ᵃJoel 2:1

3:16 ᵃ[Is. 51:5, 6]

3:17 ᵃObad. 16;
Zech. 8:3

3:18 ᵃPs. 46:4;
Ezek. 47:1;
Zech. 14:8;
[Rev. 22:1]

3:21 ᵃIs. 4:4

3:8 ¹Lit. *Shebaites*, Is. 60:6; Ezek. 27:22   3:10 ¹*pruning knives*   3:18 ¹Heb. *Shittim*

THE BOOK OF
AMOS

1 The words of Amos, who was among the ᵃsheepbreeders of ᵇTekoa, which he saw concerning Israel in the days of ᶜUzziah king of Judah, and in the days of ᵈJeroboam the son of Joash, king of Israel, two years before the ᵉearthquake. ²And he said:

> "The LORD ᵃroars from Zion,
> And utters His voice from Jerusalem;
> The pastures of the shepherds mourn,
> And the top of ᵇCarmel withers."

JUDGMENT ON THE NATIONS

³Thus says the LORD:

> "For three transgressions of ᵃDamascus, and for four,
> I will not turn away its *punishment,*
> Because they have ᵇthreshed Gilead with implements of
> iron.
4 ᵃBut I will send a fire into the house of Hazael,
> Which shall devour the palaces of ᵇBen-Hadad.
5 I will also break the *gate* ᵃbar of Damascus,
> And cut off the inhabitant from the Valley of Aven,
> And the one who ¹holds the scepter from ²Beth Eden.
> The people of Syria shall go captive to Kir,"
> Says the LORD.

⁶Thus says the LORD:

> "For three transgressions of ᵃGaza, and for four,
> I will not turn away its *punishment,*
> Because they took captive the whole captivity
> To deliver *them* up to Edom.
7 ᵃBut I will send a fire upon the wall of Gaza,
> Which shall devour its palaces.
8 I will cut off the inhabitant ᵃfrom Ashdod,
> And the one who holds the scepter from Ashkelon;
> I will ᵇturn My hand against Ekron,
> And ᶜthe remnant of the Philistines shall perish,"
> Says the Lord GOD.

⁹Thus says the LORD:

> "For three transgressions of ᵃTyre, and for four,
> I will not turn away its *punishment,*
> Because they delivered up the whole captivity to Edom,
> And did not remember the covenant of brotherhood.
10 But I will send a fire upon the wall of Tyre,
> Which shall devour its palaces."

¹¹Thus says the LORD:

1:1 ᵃ2 Kin. 3:4;
Amos 7:14
ᵇ2 Sam. 14:2;
Jer. 6:1
ᶜ2 Kin. 15:1–7;
2 Chr. 26:1–23;
Is. 1:1; Hos. 1:1
ᵈ2 Kin. 14:23–29;
Amos 7:10
ᵉZech. 14:5

1:2 ᵃIs. 42:13;
Jer. 25:30;
Joel 3:16
ᵇ1 Sam. 25:2;
Is. 33:9

1:3
ᵃIs. 8:4; 17:1–3;
Jer. 49:23–27;
Zech. 9:1
ᵇ2 Kin. 10:32, 33

1:4 ᵃJer. 49:27;
51:30
ᵇ1 Kin. 20:1;
2 Kin. 6:24

1:5 ᵃ2 Kin. 14:28;
Is. 8:4;
Jer. 51:30;
Lam. 2:9

1:6 ᵃ1 Sam. 6:17;
Jer. 47:1, 5;
Zeph. 2:4

1:7 ᵃJer. 47:1

1:8 ᵃJer. 47:5;
Zeph. 2:4
ᵇPs. 81:14
ᶜIs. 14:29–31;
Jer. 47:1–7;
Ezek. 25:16;
Joel 3:4–8;
Zeph. 2:4–7;
Zech. 9:5–7

1:9
ᵃIs. 23:1–18;
Jer. 25:22;
Ezek. 26:2–4;
Joel 3:4–8

1:5 ¹Rules   ²Lit. *House of Eden*

"For three transgressions of ªEdom, and for four,
I will not turn away its *punishment,*
Because he pursued his ᵇbrother with the sword,
And cast off all pity;
His anger tore perpetually,
And he kept his wrath forever.
12 But ªI will send a fire upon Teman,
Which shall devour the palaces of Bozrah."

13Thus says the LORD:

"For three transgressions of ªthe people of Ammon, and
for four,
I will not turn away its *punishment,*
Because they ripped open the women with child in Gilead,
That they might enlarge their territory.
14 But I will kindle a fire in the wall of ªRabbah,
And it shall devour its palaces,
ᵇAmid shouting in the day of battle,
And a tempest in the day of the whirlwind.
15 ªTheir king shall go into captivity,
He and his princes together,"
Says the LORD.

2 Thus says the LORD:

ª"For three transgressions of Moab, and for four,
I will not turn away its *punishment,*
Because he ᵇburned the bones of the king of Edom to lime.
2 But I will send a fire upon Moab,
And it shall devour the palaces of ªKerioth;
Moab shall die with tumult,
With shouting *and* trumpet sound.
3 And I will cut off ªthe judge from its midst,
And slay all its princes with him,"
Says the LORD.

JUDGMENT ON JUDAH

4Thus says the LORD:

"For three transgressions of ªJudah, and for four,
I will not turn away its *punishment,*
ᵇBecause they have despised the law of the LORD,
And have not kept His commandments.
ᶜTheir lies lead them astray,
Lies ᵈwhich their fathers followed.
5 ªBut I will send a fire upon Judah,
And it shall devour the palaces of Jerusalem."

JUDGMENT ON ISRAEL

6Thus says the LORD:

"For three transgressions of ªIsrael, and for four,
I will not turn away its *punishment,*
Because ᵇthey sell the righteous for silver,
And the ᶜpoor for a pair of sandals.
7 They ¹pant after the dust of the earth *which is* on the
head of the poor,
And ªpervert the way of the humble."

2:7 ¹Or *trample on*

1:11 ªIs. 21:11;
Jer. 49:8;
Ezek. 25:12–14;
Mal. 1:2–5
ᵇNum. 20:14–21;
2 Chr. 28:17;
Obad. 10–12

1:12
ªJer. 49:7, 20;
Obad. 9, 10

1:13 ªJer. 49:1;
Ezek. 25:2;
Zeph. 2:8, 9

1:14 ªDeut. 3:11;
1 Chr. 20:1;
Jer. 49:2
ᵇEzek. 21:22;
Amos 2:2

1:15 ªJer. 49:3

2:1 ªIs. 16:1–6;
Jer. 25:21;
Ezek. 25:8–11;
Zeph. 2:8–11
ᵇ2 Kin. 3:26, 27

2:2
ªJer. 48:24, 41

2:3 ªNum. 24:17;
Jer. 48:7

2:4 ª2 Kin. 17:19;
Hos. 12:2;
Amos 3:2
ᵇLev. 26:14
ᶜIs. 9:15, 16;
28:15; Jer. 16:19;
Hab. 2:18
ᵈJer. 9:14;
16:11, 12;
Ezek. 20:13,
16, 18

2:5 ªJer. 17:27;
Hos. 8:14

2:6
ªJudg. 2:17–20;
2 Kin. 17:7–18;
18:12;
Ezek. 22:1–13,
23–29 ᵇIs. 29:21
ᶜJoel 3:3;
Amos 4:1; 5:11;
8:6; Mic. 2:2; 3:3

2:7 ªAmos 5:12

ᵇA man and his father go in to the *same* girl,
ᶜTo defile My holy name.

8 They lie down ᵃby every altar on clothes ᵇtaken in pledge,
And drink the wine of ¹the condemned *in* the house of
their god.

9 "Yet *it was* I *who* destroyed the ᵃAmorite before them,
Whose height *was* like the ᵇheight of the cedars,
And he *was as* strong as the oaks;
Yet I ᶜdestroyed his fruit above
And his roots beneath.

10 Also *it was* ᵃI *who* brought you up from the land of Egypt,
And ᵇled you forty years through the wilderness,
To possess the land of the Amorite.

11 I raised up some of your sons as ᵃprophets,
And some of your young men as ᵇNazirites.
Is it not so, O you children of Israel?"
Says the LORD.

12 "But you gave the Nazirites wine to drink,
And commanded the prophets ᵃsaying,
'Do not prophesy!'

13 "Behold,ᵃ I am ¹weighed down by you,
As a cart full of sheaves ²is weighed down.

14 ᵃTherefore ¹flight shall perish from the swift,
The strong shall not strengthen his power,
ᵇNor shall the mighty ²deliver himself;

15 He shall not stand who handles the bow,
The swift of foot shall not ¹escape,
Nor shall he who rides a horse deliver himself.

16 The most ¹courageous men of might
Shall flee naked in that day,"
Says the LORD.

AUTHORITY OF THE PROPHET'S MESSAGE

3 Hear this word that the LORD has spoken against you,
O children of Israel, against the whole family which I
brought up from the land of Egypt, saying:

2 "Youᵃ only have I known of all the families of the earth;
ᵇTherefore I will punish you for all your iniquities."

3 Can two walk together, unless they are agreed?

4 Will a lion roar in the forest, when he has no prey?
Will a young lion ¹cry out of his den, if he has caught
nothing?

5 Will a bird fall into a snare on the earth, where there is
no ¹trap for it?
Will a snare spring up from the earth, if it has caught
nothing at all?

6 If a ¹trumpet is blown in a city, will not the people be
afraid?
ᵃIf there is calamity in a city, will not the LORD have done *it*?

7 Surely the Lord GOD does nothing,
Unless ᵃHe reveals His secret to His servants the prophets.

2:7
ᵇLev. 18:6–8;
Ezek. 22:11
ᶜLev. 20:3;
Ezek. 36:20–22

2:8 ᵃ1 Cor. 8:10
ᵇEx. 22:26

2:9 ᵃGen. 15:16;
Num. 21:25;
Deut. 2:31;
Josh. 10:12
ᵇEzek. 31:3
ᶜIs. 5:24;
Ezek. 17:9;
[Mal. 4:1]

2:10 ᵃEx. 12:51;
Amos 3:1; 9:7
ᵇDeut. 2:7

2:11 ᵃNum. 12:6
ᵇNum. 6:2, 3;
Judg. 13:5

2:12 ᵃIs. 30:10;
Jer. 11:21;
Amos 7:13, 16;
Mic. 2:6

2:13 ᵃIs. 1:14

2:14 ᵃJer. 46:6
ᵇPs. 33:16;
Jer. 9:23

3:2 ᵃ[Gen. 18:19;
Ex. 19:5, 6;
Deut. 7:6;
Ps. 147:19]
ᵇJer. 14:10;
Ezek. 20:36;
Dan. 9:12;
Matt. 11:22;
[Rom. 2:9]

3:6 ᵃIs. 45:7

3:7
ᵃGen. 6:13; 18:17;
[Jer. 23:22];
Dan. 9:22;
[John 15:15]

2:8 ¹Or *those punished by fines*   **2:13** ¹Or *tottering under*   ²Or *totters*
2:14 ¹Or *the place of refuge*   ²Lit. *save his soul* or *life*   **2:15** ¹Or *save*
2:16 ¹Lit. *strong of his heart among the mighty*   **3:4** ¹Lit. *give his voice*
3:5 ¹Or *bait* or *lure*   **3:6** ¹*ram's horn*

8 A lion has roared!
   Who will not fear?
   The Lord GOD has spoken!
   [a]Who can but prophesy?

PUNISHMENT OF ISRAEL'S SINS

9 "Proclaim in the palaces at [1]Ashdod,
   And in the palaces in the land of Egypt, and say:
   'Assemble on the mountains of Samaria;
   See great tumults in her midst,
   And the [2]oppressed within her.
10 For they [a]do not know to do right,'
   Says the LORD,
   'Who store up violence and [1]robbery in their palaces.'"

[11]Therefore thus says the Lord GOD:

   "An adversary *shall be* all around the land;
   He shall sap your strength from you,
   And your palaces shall be plundered."

[12]Thus says the LORD:

   "As a shepherd [1]takes from the mouth of a lion
   Two legs or a piece of an ear,
   So shall the children of Israel be taken out
   Who dwell in Samaria—
   In the corner of a bed and [2]on the edge of a couch!
13 Hear and testify against the house of Jacob,"
   Says the Lord GOD, the God of hosts,
14 "That in the day I punish Israel for their transgressions,
   I will also visit *destruction* on the altars of [a]Bethel;
   And the horns of the altar shall be cut off
   And fall to the ground.
15 I will [1]destroy [a]the winter house along with [b]the summer
      house;
   The [c]houses of ivory shall perish,
   And the great houses shall have an end,"
   Says the LORD.

4 Hear this word, you [a]cows of Bashan, who *are* on the
      mountain of Samaria,
   Who oppress the [b]poor,
   Who crush the needy,
   Who say to [1]your husbands, "Bring *wine,* let us [c]drink!"
2 [a]The Lord GOD has sworn by His holiness:
   "Behold, the days shall come upon you
   When He will take you away [b]with fishhooks,
   And your posterity with fishhooks.
3 [a]You will go out *through* broken *walls,*
   Each one straight ahead of her,
   And you will [1]be cast into Harmon,"
   Says the LORD.

4 "Come[a] to Bethel and transgress,
   At [b]Gilgal multiply transgression;
   [c]Bring your sacrifices every morning,
   [d]Your tithes every three [1]days.

3:8 [a]Jer. 20:9;
[Mic. 3:8];
Acts 4:20;
1 Cor. 9:16

3:10 [a]Ps. 14:4;
Jer. 4:22;
Amos 5:7; 6:12

3:14
[a]2 Kin. 23:15;
Hos. 10:5–8,
14, 15;
Amos 4:4

3:15 [a]Jer. 36:22
[b]Judg. 3:20
[c]1 Kin. 22:39;
Ps. 45:8

4:1 [a]Ps. 22:12;
Ezek. 39:18
[b]Amos 2:6
[c]Prov. 23:20

4:2 [a]Ps. 89:35
[b]Jer. 16:16;
Ezek. 29:4;
Hab. 1:15

4:3 [a]Ezek. 12:5

4:4
[a]Ezek. 20:39;
Amos 3:14
[b]Hos. 4:15
[c]Num. 28:3;
Amos 5:21, 22
[d]Deut. 14:28

3:9 [1]So with MT; LXX *Assyria*   [2]Or *oppression*   3:10 [1]Or *devastation*
3:12 [1]Or *snatches*   [2]Heb. uncertain, possibly *on the cover*   3:15 [1]Lit. *strike*
4:1 [1]Lit. *their masters* or *lords*   4:3 [1]Or *cast them*   4:4 [1]Or *years,* Deut. 14:28

5 ªOffer a sacrifice of thanksgiving with leaven,
   Proclaim *and* announce ᵇthe freewill offerings;
   For this you love,
   You children of Israel!"
   Says the Lord GOD.

ISRAEL DID NOT ACCEPT CORRECTION

6 "Also I gave you ¹cleanness of teeth in all your cities,
   And lack of bread in all your places;
   ªYet you have not returned to Me,"
   Says the LORD.

7 "I also withheld rain from you,
   When *there were* still three months to the harvest.
   I made it rain on one city,
   I withheld rain from another city.
   One part was rained upon,
   And where it did not rain the part withered.

8 So two *or* three cities wandered to another city to drink
         water,
   But they were not satisfied;
   Yet you have not returned to Me,"
   Says the LORD.

9 "Iª blasted you with blight and mildew.
   When your gardens increased,
   Your vineyards,
   Your fig trees,
   And your olive trees,
   ᵇThe locust devoured *them;*
   Yet you have not returned to Me,"
   Says the LORD.

10 "I sent among you a plague ªafter the manner of Egypt;
    Your young men I killed with a sword,
    Along with your captive horses;
    I made the stench of your camps come up into your
          nostrils;
    Yet you have not returned to Me,"
    Says the LORD.

11 "I overthrew *some* of you,
    As God overthrew ªSodom and Gomorrah,
    And you were like a firebrand plucked from the
          burning;
    Yet you have not returned to Me,"
    Says the LORD.

12 "Therefore thus will I do to you, O Israel;
    Because I will do this to you,
    ªPrepare to meet your God, O Israel!"

13 For behold,
    He who forms mountains,
    And creates the ¹wind,
    ªWho declares to man what ²his thought *is,*
    And makes the morning darkness,
    ᵇWho treads the high places of the earth—
    ᶜThe LORD God of hosts *is* His name.

4:5 ªLev. 7:13
ᵇLev. 22:18;
Deut. 12:6

4:6
ª2 Chr. 28:22;
Is. 26:11; Jer. 5:3;
Hag. 2:17

4:9
ªDeut. 28:22;
Hag. 2:17
ᵇJoel 1:4, 7;
Amos 7:1, 2

4:10 ªEx. 9:3, 6;
Lev. 26:25;
Deut. 28:27, 60;
Ps. 78:50

4:11
ªGen. 19:24, 25;
Deut. 29:23;
Is. 13:19;
Jer. 49:18;
Lam. 4:6

4:12 ªJer. 5:22

4:13 ªPs. 139:2;
Dan. 2:28
ᵇMic. 1:3
ᶜIs. 47:4;
Jer. 10:16

4:6 ¹Hunger   4:13 ¹Or *spirit*   ²Or *His*

A LAMENT FOR ISRAEL

5 Hear this word which I ᵃtake up against you, a lamentation, O house of Israel:

2 The virgin of Israel has fallen;
She will rise no more.
She lies forsaken on her land;
There is no one to raise her up.

³For thus says the Lord GOD:

"The city that goes out by a thousand
Shall have a hundred left,
And that which goes out by a hundred
Shall have ten left to the house of Israel."

A CALL TO REPENTANCE

⁴For thus says the LORD to the house of Israel:

ᵃ"Seek Me ᵇand live;

5 But do not seek ᵃBethel,
Nor enter Gilgal,
Nor pass over to ᵇBeersheba;
For Gilgal shall surely go into captivity,
And ᶜBethel shall come to nothing.

6 ᵃSeek the LORD and live,
Lest He break out like fire *in* the house of Joseph,
And devour *it*,
With no one to quench *it* in Bethel—

7 You who ᵃturn justice to wormwood,
And lay righteousness to rest in the earth!"

8 He made the ᵃPleiades and Orion;
He turns the shadow of death into morning
ᵇAnd makes the day dark as night;
He ᶜcalls for the waters of the sea
And pours them out on the face of the earth;
ᵈThe LORD *is* His name.

9 He ¹rains ruin upon the strong,
So that fury comes upon the fortress.

10 ᵃThey hate the one who rebukes in the gate,
And they ᵇabhor the one who speaks uprightly.

11 ᵃTherefore, because you ¹tread down the poor
And take grain ²taxes from him,
Though ᵇyou have built houses of hewn stone,
Yet you shall not dwell in them;
You have planted ³pleasant vineyards,
But you shall not drink wine from them.

12 For I ᵃknow your manifold transgressions
And your mighty sins:
ᵇAfflicting the just *and* taking bribes;
ᶜDiverting the poor *from justice* at the gate.

13 Therefore ᵃthe prudent keep silent at that time,
For it *is* an evil time.

14 Seek good and not evil,
That you may live;
So the LORD God of hosts will be with you,
ᵃAs you have spoken.

5:1 ᵃJer. 7:29;
9:10, 17;
Ezek. 19:1

5:4
ᵃ[Deut. 4:29;
2 Chr. 15:2;
Jer. 29:13]
ᵇ[Is. 55:3]

5:5
ᵃ1 Kin. 12:28, 29;
Amos 4:4
ᵇGen. 21:31–33;
Amos 8:14
ᶜHos. 4:15

5:6
ᵃ[Is. 55:3, 6, 7;
Amos 5:14]

5:7 ᵃAmos 6:12

5:8
ᵃJob 9:9; 38:31
ᵇPs. 104:20
ᶜJob 38:34
ᵈ[Amos 4:13]

5:10
ᵃIs. 29:21; 66:5;
Amos 5:15
ᵇ1 Kin. 22:8;
Is. 59:15;
Jer. 17:16–18

5:11 ᵃAmos 2:6
ᵇDeut. 28:30,
38, 39;
Mic. 6:15;
Zeph. 1:13;
Hag. 1:6

5:12 ᵃHos. 5:3
ᵇIs. 1:23; 5:23;
Amos 2:6
ᶜIs. 29:21

5:13 ᵃAmos 6:10

5:14 ᵃMic. 3:11

5:9 ¹Or *flashes forth destruction*   5:11 ¹*trample*   ²Or *tribute*   ³*desirable*

15 ^aHate evil, love good;
   Establish justice in the gate.
   ^bIt may be that the LORD God of hosts
   Will be gracious to the remnant of Joseph.

THE DAY OF THE LORD

¹⁶Therefore the LORD God of hosts, the Lord, says this:

"*There shall be* wailing in all streets,
   And they shall say in all the highways,
   'Alas! Alas!'
   They shall call the farmer to mourning,
   ^aAnd skillful lamenters to wailing.
17   In all vineyards *there shall be* wailing,
   For ^aI will pass through you,"
   Says the LORD.

18   ^aWoe to you who desire the day of the LORD!
   For what good *is* ^bthe day of the LORD to you?
   It *will be* darkness, and not light.
19   It *will be* ^aas though a man fled from a lion,
   And a bear met him!
   Or *as though* he went into the house,
   Leaned his hand on the wall,
   And a serpent bit him!
20   *Is* not the day of the LORD darkness, and not light?
   Is it not very dark, with no brightness in it?

21   "I^a hate, I despise your feast days,
   And ^bI do not savor your sacred assemblies.
22   ^aThough you offer Me burnt offerings and your grain
      offerings,
   I will not accept *them,*
   Nor will I regard your fattened peace offerings.
23   Take away from Me the noise of your songs,
   For I will not hear the melody of your stringed
      instruments.
24   ^aBut let justice run down like water,
   And righteousness like a mighty stream.

25   "Did^a you offer Me sacrifices and offerings
   In the wilderness forty years, O house of Israel?
26   You also carried ¹Sikkuth² ^ayour king
   And Chiun, your idols,
   The star of your gods,
   Which you made for yourselves.
27   Therefore I will send you into captivity ^abeyond
      Damascus,"
   Says the LORD, ^bwhose name *is* the God of hosts.

WARNINGS TO ZION AND SAMARIA

6 Woe ^ato you *who are* at ^bease in Zion,
   And ^ctrust in Mount Samaria,
   Notable persons in the ^dchief nation,
   To whom the house of Israel comes!
2   ^aGo over to ^bCalneh and see;
   And from there go to ^cHamath the great;
   Then go down to Gath of the Philistines.

Cross references (left margin):
5:15 ^aPs. 97:10;
Rom. 12:9
^bJoel 2:14
5:16
^a2 Chr. 35:25;
Jer. 9:17
5:17 ^aEx. 12:12
5:18 ^aIs. 5:19;
Jer. 17:15;
Joel 1:15;
2:1, 11, 31
^bIs. 5:30;
Joel 2:2
5:19 ^aJob 20:24;
Is. 24:17, 18;
Jer. 48:44
5:21 ^aIs. 1:11–16;
Amos 4:4, 5; 8:10
^bLev. 26:31;
Jer. 14:12;
Hos. 5:6
5:22 ^aIs. 66:3;
Mic. 6:6, 7
5:24 ^aJer. 22:3;
Ezek. 45:9;
Hos. 6:6;
Mic. 6:8
5:25
^aDeut. 32:17;
Josh. 24:14;
Neh. 9:18–21;
Acts 7:42, 43
5:26 ^a1 Kin. 11:33
5:27 ^a2 Kin. 17:6;
Amos 7:11, 17;
Mic. 4:10
^bAmos 4:13
6:1 ^aLuke 6:24
^bPs. 123:4;
Is. 32:9–11;
Zeph. 1:12
^cIs. 31:1; Jer. 49:4
^dEx. 19:5;
Amos 3:2
6:2 ^aJer. 2:10
^bGen. 10:10;
Is. 10:9
^c1 Kin. 8:65;
2 Kin. 18:34

5:26 ¹LXX, Vg. *tabernacle of Moloch*   ²A pagan deity

ᵈ*Are you* better than these kingdoms?
Or is their territory greater than your territory?

3 *Woe to* you who ᵃput far off the day of ᵇdoom,
ᶜWho cause ᵈthe seat of violence to come near;
4 Who lie on beds of ivory,
Stretch out on your couches,
Eat lambs from the flock
And calves from the midst of the stall;
5 ᵃWho sing idly to the sound of stringed instruments,
And invent for yourselves ᵇmusical instruments ᶜlike
David;
6 Who ᵃdrink wine from bowls,
And anoint yourselves with the best ointments,
ᵇBut are not grieved for the affliction of Joseph.
7 Therefore they shall now go ᵃcaptive as the first of the
captives,
And those who recline at banquets shall be removed.

8 ᵃThe Lord GOD has sworn by Himself,
The LORD God of hosts says:
"I abhor ᵇthe pride of Jacob,
And hate his palaces;
Therefore I will deliver up *the* city
And all that is in it."

⁹Then it shall come to pass, that if ten men remain in one house, they shall die. ¹⁰And when ¹a relative *of the dead,* with one who will burn *the bodies,* picks up the ²bodies to take them out of the house, he will say to one inside the house, "*Are there* any more with you?"

Then someone will say, "None."

And he will say, ᵃ"Hold your tongue! ᵇFor we dare not mention the name of the LORD."

11 For behold, ᵃthe LORD gives a command:
ᵇHe will break the great house into bits,
And the little house into pieces.

12 Do horses run on rocks?
Does *one* plow *there* with oxen?
Yet ᵃyou have turned justice into gall,
And the fruit of righteousness into wormwood,
13 You who rejoice over ¹Lo Debar,
Who say, "Have we not taken ²Karnaim for ourselves
By our own strength?"

14 "But, behold, ᵃI will raise up a nation against you,
O house of Israel,"
Says the LORD God of hosts;
"And they will afflict you from the ᵇentrance of Hamath
To the Valley of the Arabah."

VISION OF THE LOCUSTS

7 Thus the Lord GOD showed me: Behold, He formed locust swarms at the ¹beginning of the late crop; indeed *it was* the late crop after the king's mowings. ²And so it was, when they had finished eating the grass of the land, that I said:

6:2 ᵈNah. 3:8

6:3 ᵃIs. 56:12;
Ezek. 12:27;
Amos 9:10;
Matt. 24:37–39
ᵇAmos 5:18
ᶜAmos 5:12
ᵈPs. 94:20

6:5 ᵃIs. 5:12;
Amos 5:23
ᵇ1 Chr. 15:16; 16:42
ᶜ1 Chr. 23:5

6:6
ᵃAmos 2:8; 4:1
ᵇGen. 37:25

6:7 ᵃAmos 5:27

6:8 ᵃGen. 22:16;
Jer. 51:14;
Amos 4:2; 8:7;
Heb. 6:13–17
ᵇPs. 47:4;
Ezek. 24:21;
Amos 8:7

6:10 ᵃAmos 5:13
ᵇAmos 8:3

6:11 ᵃIs. 55:11
ᵇ2 Kin. 25:9;
Amos 3:15

6:12
ᵃ1 Kin. 21:7–13;
Is. 59:13, 14;
Hos. 10:4;
Amos 5:7, 11, 12

6:14 ᵃJer. 5:15
ᵇNum. 34:7, 8;
1 Kin. 8:65;
2 Kin. 14:25

6:10 ¹Lit. *his loved one* or *uncle*   ²Lit. *bones*   6:13 ¹Lit. *Nothing*
²Lit. *Horns,* a symbol of strength   7:1 ¹Lit. *beginning of the sprouting of*

"O Lord GOD, forgive, I pray!
aOh,[1] that Jacob may stand,
    For he *is* small!"
3   *So* athe LORD relented concerning this.
"It shall not be," said the LORD.

VISION OF THE FIRE

4Thus the Lord GOD showed me: Behold, the Lord GOD called [1]for conflict by fire, and it consumed the great deep and devoured the [2]territory. 5Then I said:

"O Lord GOD, cease, I pray!
aOh, that Jacob may stand,
    For he *is* small!"
6   *So* the LORD relented concerning this.
"This also shall not be," said the Lord GOD.

VISION OF THE PLUMB LINE

7Thus He showed me: Behold, the Lord stood on a wall *made* with a plumb line, with a plumb line in His hand. 8And the LORD said to me, "Amos, what do you see?"
And I said, "A plumb line."
Then the Lord said:

"Behold, aI am setting a plumb line
In the midst of My people Israel;
bI will not pass by them anymore.
9   aThe [1]high places of Isaac shall be desolate,
    And the [2]sanctuaries of Israel shall be laid waste.
bI will rise with the sword against the house of
    Jeroboam."

AMAZIAH'S COMPLAINT

10Then Amaziah the apriest of bBethel sent to cJeroboam king of Israel, saying, "Amos has conspired against you in the midst of the house of Israel. The land is not able to [1]bear all his words. 11For thus Amos has said:

'Jeroboam shall die by the sword,
And Israel shall surely be led away acaptive
From their own land.'"

12Then Amaziah said to Amos:

"Go, you seer!
Flee to the land of Judah.
There eat bread,
And there prophesy.
13   But anever again prophesy at Bethel,
bFor it *is* the king's [1]sanctuary,
    And it *is* the royal [2]residence."

14Then Amos answered, and said to Amaziah:

"I *was* no prophet,
Nor *was* I aa son of a prophet,
But I *was* a bsheepbreeder
And a tender of sycamore fruit.

7:2 aIs. 51:19

7:3
aDeut. 32:36;
Jer. 26:19;
Hos. 11:8;
Amos 5:15;
Jon. 3:10;
[James 5:16]

7:5 aAmos 7:2, 3

7:8 a2 Kin. 21:13;
Is. 28:17; 34:11;
Lam. 2:8
bMic. 7:18

7:9 aGen. 46:1;
Hos. 10:8;
Mic. 1:5
b2 Kin. 15:8–10;
Amos 7:11

7:10 a1 Kin. 12:31,
32; 13:33
b1 Kin. 13:32;
Amos 4:4
c2 Kin. 14:23

7:11
aAmos 5:27; 6:7

7:13 aAmos 2:12;
Acts 4:18
b1 Kin. 12:29, 32;
Amos 7:9

7:14
a1 Kin. 20:35;
2 Kin. 2:5;
2 Chr. 19:2
b2 Kin. 3:4;
Amos 1:1;
Zech. 13:5

7:2 [1]Or *How shall Jacob stand*   7:4 [1]*to contend*   [2]Lit. *portion*   7:9 [1]*Places of pagan worship*   [2]Or *holy places*   7:10 [1]Or *endure*   7:13 [1]Or *holy place*   [2]Lit. *house*

15 Then the LORD took me [1]as I followed the flock,
And the LORD said to me,
'Go, [a]prophesy to My people Israel.'
16 Now therefore, hear the word of the LORD:
You say, 'Do not prophesy against Israel,
And [a]do not [1]spout against the house of Isaac.'

17"Therefore[a] thus says the LORD:

[b]'Your wife shall be a harlot in the city;
Your sons and daughters shall fall by the sword;
Your land shall be divided by *survey* line;
You shall die in a [c]defiled land;
And Israel shall surely be led away captive
From his own land.'"

VISION OF THE SUMMER FRUIT

8 Thus the Lord GOD showed me: Behold, a basket of summer fruit. [2]And He said, "Amos, what do you see?"
So I said, "A basket of summer fruit."
Then the LORD said to me:

[a]"The end has come upon My people Israel;
[b]I will not pass by them anymore.
3 And [a]the songs of the temple
Shall be wailing in that day,"
Says the Lord GOD—
"Many dead bodies everywhere,
[b]They shall be thrown out in silence."

4 Hear this, you who [1]swallow up the needy,
And make the poor of the land fail,

[5]Saying:

"When will the New Moon be past,
That we may sell grain?
And [a]the Sabbath,
That we may [1]trade wheat?
[b]Making the ephah small and the shekel large,
Falsifying the scales by [c]deceit,
6 That we may buy the poor for [a]silver,
And the needy for a pair of sandals—
Even sell the bad wheat?"

7 The LORD has sworn by [a]the pride of Jacob:
"Surely [b]I will never forget any of their works.
8 [a]Shall the land not tremble for this,
And everyone mourn who dwells in it?
All of it shall swell like [1]the River,
Heave and subside
[b]Like the River of Egypt.

9 "And it shall come to pass in that day," says the Lord GOD,
[a]"That I will make the sun go down at noon,
And I will darken the earth in [1]broad daylight;
10 I will turn your feasts into [a]mourning,
[b]And all your songs into lamentation;

Cross-references

7:15 [a]Amos 3:8
7:16 [a]Deut. 32:2; Ezek. 21:2; Mic. 2:6
7:17 [a]Jer. 28:12; 29:21, 32 [b]Is. 13:16; Lam. 5:11; Hos. 4:13; Zech. 14:2 [c]2 Kin. 17:6; Ezek. 4:13; Hos. 9:3
8:2 [a]Ezek. 7:2 [b]Amos 7:8
8:3 [a]Amos 5:23 [b]Amos 6:9, 10
8:5 [a]Ex. 31:13–17; Neh. 13:15 [b]Mic. 6:10, 11 [c]Lev. 19:35, 36; Deut. 25:13–15
8:6 [a]Amos 2:6
8:7 [a]Deut. 33:26, 29; Ps. 68:34; Amos 6:8 [b]Ps. 10:11; Hos. 7:2; 8:13
8:8 [a]Hos. 4:3 [b]Jer. 46:7, 8; Amos 9:5
8:9 [a]Job 5:14; Is. 13:10; 59:9, 10; Jer. 15:9; [Mic. 3:6]; Matt. 27:45; Mark 15:33; Luke 23:44
8:10 [a]Lam. 5:15; Ezek. 7:18 [b]Is. 15:2, 3; Jer. 48:37; Ezek. 27:31

7:15 [1]Lit. *from behind* 7:16 [1]Lit. *drip* 8:4 [1]Or *trample on*, Amos 2:7 8:5 [1]Lit. *open* 8:8 [1]The Nile; some Heb. mss., LXX, Tg., Syr., Vg. *River* (cf. 9:5); MT *the light* 8:9 [1]Lit. *a day of light*

cI will bring sackcloth on every waist,
And baldness on every head;
I will make it like mourning for an only *son*,
And its end like a bitter day.

11 "Behold, the days are coming," says the Lord GOD,
"That I will send a famine on the land,
Not a famine of bread,
Nor a thirst for water,
But aof hearing the words of the LORD.
12 They shall wander from sea to sea,
And from north to east;
They shall run to and fro, seeking the word of the LORD,
But shall anot find *it*.
13 "In that day the fair virgins
And strong young men
Shall faint from thirst.
14 Those who aswear by bthe 1sin of Samaria,
Who say,
'As your god lives, O Dan!'
And, 'As the way of cBeersheba lives!'
They shall fall and never rise again."

THE DESTRUCTION OF ISRAEL

9 I saw the Lord standing by the altar, and He said:

"Strike the 1doorposts, that the thresholds may shake,
And abreak them on the heads of them all.
I will slay the last of them with the sword.
bHe who flees from them shall not get away,
And he who escapes from them shall not be delivered.
2 "Thougha they dig into 1hell,
From there My hand shall take them;
bThough they climb up to heaven,
From there I will bring them down;
3 And though they ahide themselves on top of Carmel,
From there I will search and take them;
Though they hide from My sight at the bottom of the sea,
From there I will command the serpent, and it shall bite them;
4 Though they go into captivity before their enemies,
From there aI will command the sword,
And it shall slay them.
bI will set My eyes on them for harm and not for good."

5 The Lord GOD of hosts,
He who touches the earth and it amelts,
bAnd all who dwell there mourn;
All of it shall swell like 1the River,
And subside like the River of Egypt.
6 He who builds His alayers1 in the sky,
And has founded His strata in the earth;
Who bcalls for the waters of the sea,
And pours them out on the face of the earth—
cThe LORD *is* His name.

8:10 cJer. 6:26;
[Zech. 12:10]

8:11 a1 Sam. 3:1;
2 Chr. 15:3;
Ps. 74:9;
Ezek. 7:26;
Mic. 3:6

8:12 aHos. 5:6

8:14 aHos. 4:15
bDeut. 9:21
cAmos 5:5

9:1 aPs. 68:21;
Hab. 3:13
bAmos 2:14

9:2 aPs. 139:8;
Jer. 23:24
bJob 20:6;
Jer. 51:53;
Obad. 4;
Matt. 11:23

9:3 aJer. 23:24

9:4 aLev. 26:33
bLev. 17:10;
Jer. 21:10;
39:16; 44:11

9:5 aPs. 104:32;
144:5; Is. 64:1;
Mic. 1:4
bAmos 8:8

9:6
aPs. 104:3, 13
bAmos 5:8
cAmos 4:13; 5:27

8:14 1Or *Ashima*, a Syrian goddess   9:1 1Capitals of the pillars   9:2 1Or *Sheol*   9:5 1The Nile   9:6 1Or *stairs*

7 "*Are* you not like the ¹people of Ethiopia to Me,
O children of Israel?" says the LORD.
"Did I not bring up Israel from the land of Egypt,
The ªPhilistines from ᵇCaphtor,²
And the Syrians from ᶜKir?

8 "Behold, ªthe eyes of the Lord GOD *are* on the sinful
kingdom,
And I ᵇwill destroy it from the face of the earth;
Yet I will not utterly destroy the house of Jacob,"
Says the LORD.

9 "For surely I will command,
And will ¹sift the house of Israel among all nations,
As *grain* is sifted in a sieve;
ªYet not the smallest ²grain shall fall to the ground.

10 All the sinners of My people shall die by the sword,
ªWho say, 'The calamity shall not overtake nor
confront us.'

ISRAEL WILL BE RESTORED

11 "Onª that day I will raise up
The ¹tabernacle of David, which has fallen down,
And ²repair its damages;
I will raise up its ruins,
And rebuild it as in the days of old;

12 ªThat they may possess the remnant of ᵇEdom,¹
And all the Gentiles who are called by My name,"
Says the LORD who does this thing.

13 "Behold, ªthe days are coming," says the LORD,
"When the plowman shall overtake the reaper,
And the treader of grapes him who sows seed;
ᵇThe mountains shall drip with sweet wine,
And all the hills shall flow *with it*.

14 ªI will bring back the captives of My people Israel;
ᵇThey shall build the waste cities and inhabit *them;*
They shall plant vineyards and drink wine from them;
They shall also make gardens and eat fruit from them.

15 I will plant them in their land,
ªAnd no longer shall they be pulled up
From the land I have given them,"
Says the LORD your God.

9:7 ªJer. 47:4
ᵇDeut. 2:23
ᶜAmos 1:5

9:8 ªJer. 44:27;
Amos 9:4
ᵇJer. 5:10; 30:11;
[Joel 2:32];
Amos 3:12;
[Obad. 16, 17]

9:9
ª[Is. 65:8–16]

9:10 ª[Is. 28:15];
Jer. 5:12;
Amos 6:3

9:11
ªActs 15:16–18

9:12 ªObad. 19
ᵇNum. 24:18;
Is. 11:14

9:13 ªLev. 26:5
ᵇJoel 3:18

9:14 ªPs. 53:6;
Is. 60:4;
Jer. 30:3, 18
ᵇIs. 61:4

9:15 ªIs. 60:21;
Ezek. 34:28;
37:25

9:7 ¹Lit. *sons of the Ethiopians*   ²Crete   9:9 ¹*shake*   ²Lit. *pebble*   9:11 ¹Lit.
booth; a figure of a deposed dynasty   ²Lit. *wall up its breaches*   9:12 ¹LXX
mankind

THE BOOK OF
OBADIAH

THE COMING JUDGMENT ON EDOM

The vision of Obadiah.

Thus says the Lord GOD ᵃconcerning Edom
ᵇ(We have heard a report from the LORD,
And a messenger has been sent among the nations,
saying,
"Arise, and let us rise up against her for battle"):

2 "Behold, I will make you small among the nations;
You shall be greatly despised.
3 The ᵃpride of your heart has deceived you,
You who dwell in the clefts of the rock,
Whose habitation is high;
ᵇYou who say in your heart, 'Who will bring me down to
the ground?'
4 ᵃThough you ascend as high as the eagle,
And though you ᵇset your nest among the stars,
From there I will bring you down," says the LORD.

5 "If ᵃthieves had come to you,
If robbers by night—
Oh, how you will be cut off!—
Would they not have stolen till they had enough?
If grape-gatherers had come to you,
ᵇWould they not have left some gleanings?

6 "Oh, how Esau shall be searched out!
How his hidden treasures shall be sought after!
7 All the men in your confederacy
Shall force you to the border;
ᵃThe men at peace with you
Shall deceive you and prevail against you.
Those who eat your bread shall lay a ¹trap for you.
ᵇNo² one is aware of it.

8 "Will ᵃI not in that day," says the LORD,
"Even destroy the wise men from Edom,
And understanding from the mountains of Esau?
9 Then your ᵃmighty men, O ᵇTeman, shall be dismayed,
To the end that everyone from the mountains of Esau
May be cut off by slaughter.

EDOM MISTREATED HIS BROTHER

10 "For ᵃviolence against your brother Jacob,
Shame shall cover you,
And ᵇyou shall be cut off forever.
11 In the day that you ᵃstood on the other side—
In the day that strangers carried captive his forces,

1 ᵃIs. 21:11;
Ezek. 25:12;
Joel 3:19;
Mal. 1:3
ᵇJer. 49:14–16;
Obad. 1–4

3 ᵃIs. 16:6;
Jer. 49:16
ᵇIs. 14:13–15;
Rev. 18:7

4 ᵃJob 20:6
ᵇHab. 2:9;
Mal. 1:4

5 ᵃJer. 49:9
ᵇDeut. 24:21

7 ᵃJer. 38:22
ᵇIs. 19:11;
Jer. 49:7

8
ᵃ[Job 5:12–14];
Is. 29:14

9 ᵃPs. 76:5
ᵇGen. 36:11;
1 Chr. 1:45;
Job 2:11;
Jer. 49:7

10 ᵃGen. 27:41;
Ezek. 25:12;
Amos 1:11
ᵇEzek. 35:9;
Joel 3:19

11 ᵃPs. 83:5–8;
Amos 1:6, 9

---

7 ¹Or wound or plot   ²Or There is no understanding in him

When foreigners entered his gates
And ᵇcast lots for Jerusalem—
Even you *were* as one of them.

12 "But you should not have ᵃgazed¹ on the day of your
        brother
    ²In the day of his captivity;
    Nor should you have ᵇrejoiced over the children of Judah
    In the day of their destruction;
    Nor should you have spoken proudly
    In the day of distress.
13 You should not have entered the gate of My people
    In the day of their calamity.
    Indeed, you should not have ¹gazed on their affliction
    In the day of their calamity,
    Nor laid *hands* on their substance
    In the day of their calamity.
14 You should not have stood at the crossroads
    To cut off those among them who escaped;
    Nor should you have ¹delivered up those among them
        who remained
    In the day of distress.

15 "Forᵃ the day of the LORD upon all the nations *is* near;
    ᵇAs you have done, it shall be done to you;
    Your ¹reprisal shall return upon your own head.
16 ᵃFor as you drank on My holy mountain,
    So shall all the nations drink continually;
    Yes, they shall drink, and swallow,
    And they shall be as though they had never been.

ISRAEL'S FINAL TRIUMPH

17 "But on Mount Zion there ᵃshall be ¹deliverance,
    And there shall be holiness;
    The house of Jacob shall possess their possessions.
18 The house of Jacob shall be a fire,
    And the house of Joseph ᵃa flame;
    But the house of Esau *shall be* stubble;
    They shall kindle them and devour them,
    And no survivor shall *remain* of the house of Esau,"
    For the LORD has spoken.

19 The ¹South ᵃshall possess the mountains of Esau,
    ᵇAnd the Lowland shall possess Philistia.
    They shall possess the fields of Ephraim
    And the fields of Samaria.
    Benjamin *shall possess* Gilead.
20 And the captives of this host of the children of Israel
    Shall possess the land of the Canaanites
    As ᵃfar as Zarephath.
    The captives of Jerusalem who are in Sepharad
    ᵇShall possess the cities of the ¹South.
21 Then ᵃsaviors¹ shall come to Mount Zion
    To judge the mountains of Esau,
    And the ᵇkingdom shall be the LORD's.

11 ᵇJoel 3:3;
Nah. 3:10

12
ᵃMic. 4:11; 7:10
ᵇ[Prov. 17:5];
Ezek. 35:15;
36:5

15 ᵃEzek. 30:3;
[Joel 1:15;
2:1, 11, 31;
Amos 5:18, 20]
ᵇJer. 50:29;
51:56; Hab. 2:8

16 ᵃJoel 3:17

17 ᵃIs. 14:1, 2;
Joel 2:32;
Amos 9:8

18
ᵃIs. 5:24; 9:18, 19;
Zech. 12:6

19 ᵃIs. 11:14;
Amos 9:12
ᵇZeph. 2:7

20 ᵃ1 Kin. 17:9;
Luke 4:26
ᵇJer. 32:44

21
ᵃ[James 5:20]
ᵇPs. 22:28;
[Dan. 2:44;
7:14; Zech. 14:9;
Rev. 11:15]

---

12 ¹Gloated over   ²Lit. *On the day he became a foreigner*   13 ¹Gloated over
14 ¹Handed over to the enemy   15 ¹Or *reward*   17 ¹Or *salvation*   19 ¹Heb.
Negev   20 ¹Heb. *Negev*   21 ¹*deliverers*

THE BOOK OF
JONAH

JONAH'S DISOBEDIENCE

1 Now the word of the LORD came to ªJonah the son of Amittai, saying, ²"Arise, go to ªNineveh, that ᵇgreat city, and cry out against it; for ᶜtheir wickedness has come up before Me." ³But Jonah arose to flee to Tarshish from the presence of the LORD. He went down to ªJoppa, and found a ship going to Tarshish; so he paid the fare, and went down into it, to go with them to ᵇTarshish ᶜfrom the presence of the LORD.

THE STORM AT SEA

⁴But ªthe LORD ¹sent out a great wind on the sea, and there was a mighty tempest on the sea, so that the ship was about to be broken up.

⁵Then the mariners were afraid; and every man cried out to his god, and threw the cargo that *was* in the ship into the sea, to lighten ¹the load. But Jonah had gone down ªinto the lowest parts of the ship, had lain down, and was fast asleep.

⁶So the captain came to him, and said to him, "What do you mean, sleeper? Arise, ªcall on your God; ᵇperhaps your God will consider us, so that we may not perish."

⁷And they said to one another, "Come, let us ªcast lots, that we may know for whose cause this trouble *has come* upon us." So they cast lots, and the lot fell on Jonah. ⁸Then they said to him, ª"Please tell us! For whose cause *is* this trouble upon us? What is your occupation? And where do you come from? What is your country? And of what people are you?"

⁹So he said to them, "I *am* a Hebrew; and I fear ¹the LORD, the God of heaven, ªwho made the sea and the dry *land*."

JONAH THROWN INTO THE SEA

¹⁰Then the men were exceedingly afraid, and said to him, "Why have you done this?" For the men knew that he fled from the presence of the LORD, because he had told them. ¹¹Then they said to him, "What shall we do to you that the sea may be calm for us?"—for the sea was growing more tempestuous.

¹²And he said to them, ª"Pick me up and ¹throw me into the sea; then the sea will become calm for you. For I know that this great tempest *is* because of me."

¹³Nevertheless the men rowed hard to return to land, ªbut they could not, for the sea continued to grow more tempestuous against them. ¹⁴Therefore they cried out to the LORD and said, "We pray, O LORD, please do not let us perish for this man's life, and ªdo not charge us with innocent blood; for You, O LORD, ᵇhave done as it pleased You." ¹⁵So they picked up Jonah and threw him into the sea, ªand the sea ceased from its raging. ¹⁶Then the men ªfeared the LORD exceedingly, and offered a sacrifice to the LORD and took vows.

1:1 ª2 Kin. 14:25; Matt. 12:39–41; 16:4; Luke 11:29, 30, 32

1:2 ªIs. 37:37 ᵇGen. 10:11, 12; 2 Kin. 19:36; Jon. 4:11; Nah. 1:1; Zeph. 2:13 ᶜGen. 18:20; Hos. 7:2

1:3 ªJosh. 19:46; 2 Chr. 2:16; Ezra 3:7; Acts 9:36, 43 ᵇIs. 23:1 ᶜGen. 4:16; Job 1:12; 2:7

1:4 ªPs. 107:25

1:5 ª1 Sam. 24:3

1:6 ªPs. 107:28 ᵇJoel 2:14

1:7 ªJosh. 7:14; 1 Sam. 14:41, 42; Prov. 16:33

1:8 ªJosh. 7:19; 1 Sam. 14:43

1:9 ª[Neh. 9:6]; Ps. 146:6; Acts 17:24

1:12 ªJohn 11:50

1:13 ª[Prov. 21:30]

1:14 ªDeut. 21:8 ᵇPs. 115:3; [Dan. 4:35]

1:15 ª[Ps. 89:9; 107:29]; Luke 8:24

1:16 ªMark 4:41; Acts 5:11

JONAH'S PRAYER AND DELIVERANCE

[17]Now the LORD had prepared a great fish to swallow Jonah. And [a]Jonah was in the belly of the fish three days and three nights.

2 Then Jonah prayed to the LORD his God from the fish's belly. [2]And he said:

"I [a]cried out to the LORD because of my affliction,
[b]And He answered me.

"Out of the belly of Sheol I cried,
And You heard my voice.
3 [a]For You cast me into the deep,
Into the heart of the seas,
And the floods surrounded me;
[b]All Your billows and Your waves passed over me.
4 [a]Then I said, 'I have been cast out of Your sight;
Yet I will look again [b]toward Your holy temple.'
5 The [a]waters surrounded me, *even* to my soul;
The deep closed around me;
Weeds were wrapped around my head.
6 I went down to the [1]moorings of the mountains;
The earth with its bars *closed* behind me forever;
Yet You have brought up my [a]life from the pit,
O LORD, my God.

7 "When my soul fainted within me,
I remembered the LORD;
[a]And my prayer went *up* to You,
Into Your holy temple.
8 "Those who regard [a]worthless idols
Forsake their own [1]Mercy.
9 But I will [a]sacrifice to You
With the voice of thanksgiving;
I will pay what I have [b]vowed.
[c]Salvation *is* of the [d]LORD."

[10]So the LORD spoke to the fish, and it vomited Jonah onto dry *land.*

JONAH PREACHES AT NINEVEH

3 Now the word of the LORD came to Jonah the second time, saying, [2]"Arise, go to Nineveh, that great city, and preach to it the message that I tell you." [3]So Jonah arose and went to Nineveh, according to the word of the LORD. Now Nineveh was an exceedingly great city, [1]a three-day journey *in extent.* [4]And Jonah began to enter the city on the first day's walk. Then [a]he cried out and said, "Yet forty days, and Nineveh shall be overthrown!"

THE PEOPLE OF NINEVEH BELIEVE

[5]So the [a]people of Nineveh believed God, proclaimed a fast, and put on sackcloth, from the greatest to the least of them. [6]Then word came to the king of Nineveh; and he arose from his throne and laid aside his robe, covered *himself* with sackcloth [a]and sat in ashes. [7a]And he caused *it* to be proclaimed

1:17
[a][Matt. 12:40;
Luke 11:30]

2:2
[a]1 Sam. 30:6;
Ps. 120:1;
Lam. 3:55
[b]Ps. 65:2

2:3 [a]Ps. 88:6
[b]Ps. 42:7

2:4 [a]Ps. 31:22;
Jer. 7:15
[b]1 Kin. 8:38;
2 Chr. 6:38;
Ps. 5:7

2:5 [a]Ps. 69:1;
Lam. 3:54

2:6 [a]Job 33:28;
[Ps. 16:10;
Is. 38:17]

2:7
[a]2 Chr. 30:27;
Ps. 18:6

2:8 [a]2 Kin. 17:15;
Ps. 31:6; Jer. 10:8

2:9
[a]Ps. 50:14, 23;
Jer. 33:11;
Hos. 14:2
[b]Job 22:27;
[Eccl. 5:4, 5]
[c]Ps. 3:8;
[Is. 45:17]
[d][Jer. 3:23]

3:4
[a][Deut. 18:22]

3:5
[a][Matt. 12:41;
Luke 11:32]

3:6 [a]Job 2:8

3:7 [a]2 Chr. 20:3;
Dan. 3:29;
Joel 2:15

2:6 [1]*foundations* or *bases*   2:8 [1]Or *Lovingkindness*   3:3 [1]Exact meaning unknown

and published throughout Nineveh by the decree of the king and his ¹nobles, saying,

> Let neither man nor beast, herd nor flock, taste anything; do not let them eat, or drink water. ⁸But let man and beast be covered with sackcloth, and cry mightily to God; yes, ªlet every one turn from his evil way and from ᵇthe violence that is in his hands. ⁹ªWho can tell *if* God will turn and relent, and turn away from His fierce anger, so that we may not perish?

¹⁰ªThen God saw their works, that they turned from their evil way; and God relented from the disaster that He had said He would bring upon them, and He did not do it.

JONAH'S ANGER AND GOD'S KINDNESS

4 But it displeased Jonah exceedingly, and he became angry. ²So he prayed to the Lᴏʀᴅ, and said, "Ah, Lᴏʀᴅ, was not this what I said when I was still in my country? Therefore I ªfled previously to Tarshish; for I know that You *are* a ᵇgracious and merciful God, slow to anger and abundant in lovingkindness, One who relents from doing harm. ³ªTherefore now, O Lᴏʀᴅ, please take my life from me, for ᵇ*it is* better for me to die than to live!"

⁴Then the Lᴏʀᴅ said, "*Is it* right for you to be angry?"

⁵So Jonah went out of the city and sat on the east side of the city. There he made himself a shelter and sat under it in the shade, till he might see what would become of the city. ⁶And the Lᴏʀᴅ God prepared a ¹plant and made it come up over Jonah, that it might be shade for his head to deliver him from his misery. So Jonah ²was very grateful for the plant. ⁷But as morning dawned the next day God prepared a worm, and it *so* damaged the plant that it withered. ⁸And it happened, when the sun arose, that God prepared a vehement east wind; and the sun beat on Jonah's head, so that he grew faint. Then he wished death for himself, and said, ª"*It is* better for me to die than to live."

⁹Then God said to Jonah, "*Is it* right for you to be angry about the plant?"

And he said, "*It is* right for me to be angry, even to death!"

¹⁰But the Lᴏʀᴅ said, "You have had pity on the plant for which you have not labored, nor made it grow, which ¹came up in a night and perished in a night. ¹¹And should I not pity Nineveh, ªthat great city, in which are more than one hundred and twenty thousand persons ᵇwho cannot discern between their right hand and their left—and much livestock?"

3:8 ªIs. 58:6
ᵇIs. 59:6
3:9
ª2 Sam. 12:22;
Joel 2:14;
Amos 5:15
3:10 ªEx. 32:14;
Jer. 18:8;
Amos 7:3, 6
4:2 ªJon. 1:3
ᵇEx. 34:6;
Num. 14:18;
Ps. 86:5, 15;
Joel 2:13
4:3 ª1 Kin. 19:4;
Job 6:8, 9
ᵇJon. 4:8
4:8 ªJon. 4:3
4:11 ªJon. 1:2;
3:2, 3
ᵇDeut. 1:39;
Is. 7:16

3:7 ¹Lit. *great ones* **4:6** ¹Heb. *kikayon,* exact identity unknown ²Lit. *rejoiced with great joy* **4:10** ¹Lit. *was a son of a night*

THE BOOK OF
MICAH

1 The word of the LORD that came to ªMicah of Moresheth in the days of ᵇJotham, Ahaz, *and* Hezekiah, kings of Judah, which he saw concerning Samaria and Jerusalem.

THE COMING JUDGMENT ON ISRAEL

2 Hear, all you peoples!
   Listen, O earth, and all that is in it!
   Let the Lord GOD be a witness against you,
   The Lord from ªHis holy temple.

3 For behold, the LORD is coming out of His place;
   He will come down
   And tread on the high places of the earth.
4 ªThe mountains will melt under Him,
   And the valleys will split
   Like wax before the fire,
   Like waters poured down a steep place.
5 All this is for the transgression of Jacob
   And for the sins of the house of Israel.
   What *is* the transgression of Jacob?
   Is it not Samaria?
   And what *are* the ªhigh places of Judah?
   Are they not Jerusalem?

6 "Therefore I will make Samaria ªa heap of ruins in the field,
   Places for planting a vineyard;
   I will pour down her stones into the valley,
   And I will ᵇuncover her foundations.
7 All her carved images shall be beaten to pieces,
   And all her ªpay as a harlot shall be burned with the fire;
   All her idols I will lay desolate,
   For she gathered *it* from the pay of a harlot,
   And they shall return to the ᵇpay of a harlot."

MOURNING FOR ISRAEL AND JUDAH

8 Therefore I will wail and howl,
   I will go stripped and naked;
   ªI will make a wailing like the jackals
   And a mourning like the ostriches,
9 For her wounds *are* incurable.
   For ªit has come to Judah;
   It has come to the gate of My people—
   To Jerusalem.

10 ªTell *it* not in Gath,
    Weep not at all;
    In ¹Beth Aphrah
    Roll yourself in the dust.

1:1 ª[2 Pet. 1:21];
Jer. 26:18
ᵇ2 Kin. 15:5,
7, 32–38;
2 Chr. 27:1–9;
Is. 1:1; Hos. 1:1

1:2 ª[Ps. 11:4]

1:4 ªAmos 9:5

1:5 ªDeut. 32:13;
33:29;
Amos 4:13

1:6 ª2 Kin. 19:25;
Mic. 3:12
ᵇEzek. 13:14

1:7 ªHos. 2:5
ᵇDeut. 23:18;
Is. 23:17

1:8 ªPs. 102:6

1:9 ª2 Kin. 18:13;
Is. 8:7, 8

1:10 ª2 Sam. 1:20

1:10 ¹Lit. *House of Dust*

11 Pass by in naked shame, you inhabitant of [1]Shaphir;
The inhabitant of [2]Zaanan does not go out.
Beth Ezel mourns;
Its place to stand is taken away from you.

12 For the inhabitant of [1]Maroth [2]pined for good,
But [a]disaster came down from the LORD
To the gate of Jerusalem.

13 O inhabitant of [a]Lachish,
Harness the chariot to the swift steeds
(She *was* the beginning of sin to the daughter of Zion),
For the transgressions of Israel were [b]found in you.

14 Therefore you shall [a]give presents to [1]Moresheth Gath;
The houses of [b]Achzib[2] *shall be* a lie to the kings of
Israel.

15 I will yet bring an heir to you, O inhabitant of
[a]Mareshah;[1]
The glory of Israel shall come to [b]Adullam.[2]

16 Make yourself [a]bald and cut off your hair,
Because of your [b]precious children;
Enlarge your baldness like an eagle,
For they shall go from you into [c]captivity.

WOE TO EVILDOERS

2 Woe to those who devise iniquity,
And [1]work out evil on their beds!
At [a]morning light they practice it,
Because it is in the power of their hand.

2 They [a]covet fields and take *them* by violence,
Also houses, and seize *them*.
So they oppress a man and his house,
A man and his inheritance.

3 Therefore thus says the LORD:

"Behold, against this [a]family I am devising [b]disaster,
From which you cannot remove your necks;
Nor shall you walk haughtily,
For this *is* an evil time.

4 In that day *one* shall take up a proverb against you,
And [a]lament with a bitter lamentation, saying:
'We are utterly destroyed!
He has changed the [1]heritage of my people;
How He has removed *it* from me!
To [2]a turncoat He has divided our fields.'"

5 Therefore you will have no [1]one to determine boundaries
by lot
In the assembly of the LORD.

LYING PROPHETS

6 "Do not prattle," *you say to those* who [1]prophesy.
So they shall not prophesy [2]to you;
[3]They shall not return insult for insult.

Cross-references (side column)

1:12
[a]Is. 59:9–11;
Jer. 14:19;
Amos 3:6

1:13 [a]Josh. 10:3;
2 Kin. 14:19;
18:14; Is. 36:2
[b]Ezek. 23:11

1:14 [a]2 Sam. 8:2
[b]Josh. 15:44

1:15 [a]Josh. 15:44
[b]2 Chr. 11:7

1:16 [a]Job 1:20
[b]Lam. 4:5
[c]2 Kin. 17:6;
Amos 7:11, 17;
[Mic. 4:10]

2:1 [a]Hos. 7:6, 7

2:2 [a]Is. 5:8

2:3 [a]Ex. 20:5;
Jer. 8:3;
Amos 3:1, 2
[b]Amos 5:13

2:4 [a]2 Sam. 1:17

1:11 [1]Lit. *Beautiful*   [2]Lit. *Going Out*   1:12 [1]Lit. *Bitterness*   [2]Lit. *was sick*
1:14 [1]Lit. *Possession of Gath*   [2]Lit. *Lie*   1:15 [1]Lit. *Inheritance*   [2]Lit. *Refuge*
2:1 [1]*Plan*   2:4 [1]Lit. *portion*   [2]Lit. *one turning back,* an apostate   2:5 [1]Lit.
one casting a surveyor's line   2:6 [1]Or *preach,* lit. *drip* words   [2]Lit. *to these*
[3]Vg. *He shall not take shame*

7 *You who are* named the house of Jacob:
"Is the Spirit of the LORD restricted?
Are these His doings?
Do not My words do good
To him who walks uprightly?

8 "Lately My people have risen up as an enemy—
You pull off the robe with the garment
From those who trust *you,* as they pass by,
Like men returned from war.

9 The women of My people you cast out
From their pleasant houses;
From their children
You have taken away My glory forever.

10 "Arise and depart,
For this *is* not *your* ªrest;
Because it is ᵇdefiled, it shall destroy,
Yes, with utter destruction.

11 If a man should walk in a false spirit
And speak a lie, *saying,*
'I will ¹prophesy to you ²of wine and drink,'
Even he would be the ªprattler of this people.

ISRAEL RESTORED

12 "Iª will surely assemble all of you, O Jacob,
I will surely gather the remnant of Israel;
I will put them together ᵇlike sheep of ¹the fold,
Like a flock in the midst of their pasture;
ᶜThey shall make a loud noise because of *so many* people.

13 The one who breaks open will come up before them;
They will break out,
Pass through the gate,
And go out by it;
ªTheir king will pass before them,
ᵇWith the LORD at their head."

WICKED RULERS AND PROPHETS

3 And I said:

"Hear now, O heads of Jacob,
And you ªrulers of the house of Israel:
ᵇ*Is it* not for you to know justice?

2 You who hate good and love evil;
Who strip the skin from ¹My people,
And the flesh from their bones;

3 Who also ªeat the flesh of My people,
Flay their skin from them,
Break their bones,
And chop *them* in pieces
Like *meat* for the pot,
ᵇLike flesh in the caldron."

4 Then ªthey will cry to the LORD,
But He will not hear them;
He will even hide His face from them at that time,
Because they have been evil in their deeds.

2:10 ªDeut. 12:9
ᵇLev. 18:25

2:11 ªIs. 30:10;
Jer. 5:30, 31;
2 Tim. 4:3, 4

2:12
ª[Mic. 4:6, 7]
ᵇJer. 31:10
ᶜEzek. 33:22;
36:37

2:13 ª[Hos. 3:5]
ᵇIs. 52:12

3:1 ªEzek. 22:27
ᵇPs. 82:1–5;
Jer. 5:4, 5

3:3 ªPs. 14:4;
27:2; Zeph. 3:3
ᵇEzek. 11:3, 6, 7

3:4 ªPs. 18:41;
Prov. 1:28;
Is. 1:15; Jer. 11:11

2:11 ¹Or *preach,* lit. *drip*   ²*concerning*   2:12 ¹Heb. *Bozrah*   3:2 ¹Lit. *them*

5 Thus says the LORD [a]concerning the prophets
 Who make my people stray;
 Who chant [1]"Peace"
 [2]While they [b]chew with their teeth,
 But who prepare war against him
 [c]Who puts nothing into their mouths:

6 "Therefore[a] you shall have night without [1]vision,
 And you shall have darkness without divination;
 The sun shall go down on the prophets,
 And the day shall be dark for [b]them.

7 So the seers shall be ashamed,
 And the diviners abashed;
 Indeed they shall all cover their lips;
 [a]For *there is* no answer from God."

8 But truly I am full of power by the Spirit of the LORD,
 And of justice and might,
 [a]To declare to Jacob his transgression
 And to Israel his sin.

9 Now hear this,
 You heads of the house of Jacob
 And rulers of the house of Israel,
 Who abhor justice
 And [1]pervert all equity,

10 [a]Who build up Zion with [b]bloodshed
 And Jerusalem with iniquity:

11 [a]Her heads judge for a bribe,
 [b]Her priests teach for pay,
 And her prophets divine for [1]money.
 [c]Yet they lean on the LORD, and say,
 "Is not the LORD among us?
 No harm can come upon us."

12 Therefore because of you
 Zion shall be [a]plowed *like* a field,
 [b]Jerusalem shall become heaps of ruins,
 And [c]the mountain of the [1]temple
 Like the bare hills of the forest.

THE LORD'S REIGN IN ZION
(*cf.* Is. 2:2–4)

4 Now [a]it shall come to pass in the latter days
 That the mountain of the LORD's house
 Shall be established on the top of the mountains,
 And shall be exalted above the hills;
 And peoples shall flow to it.

2 Many nations shall come and say,
 "Come, and let us go up to the mountain of the LORD,
 To the house of the God of Jacob;
 He will teach us His ways,
 And we shall walk in His paths."
 For out of Zion the law shall go forth,
 And the word of the LORD from Jerusalem.

3 He shall judge between many peoples,
 And rebuke strong nations afar off;
 They shall beat their swords into [a]plowshares,

3:5
[a]Is. 56:10, 11;
 Jer. 6:13;
Ezek. 13:10, 19
 [b]Matt. 7:15
 [c]Ezek. 13:18
3:6
[a]Is. 8:20–22;
 29:10–12
 [b]Is. 29:10;
[Jer. 23:33–40];
 Ezek. 13:23
3:7 [a]Amos 8:11
3:8 [a]Is. 58:1
3:10
[a]Jer. 22:13, 17
 [b]Ezek. 22:27;
 Hab. 2:12
3:11 [a]Is. 1:23;
 Mic. 7:3
 [b]Jer. 6:13
[c]Is. 48:2; Jer. 7:4
3:12 [a]Jer. 26:18
 [b]Ps. 79:1;
 Jer. 9:11
 [c]Mic. 4:1, 2
4:1 [a]Is. 2:2–4;
 Ezek. 17:22;
Dan. 2:28; 10:14;
 Hos. 3:5
4:3 [a]Is. 2:4;
 Joel 3:10

3:5 [1]All is well   [2]For those who feed them   3:6 [1]Prophetic revelation
3:9 [1]Lit. *twist*   3:11 [1]Lit. *silver*   3:12 [1]Lit. *house*

And their spears into ¹pruning hooks;
Nation shall not lift up sword against nation,
ᵇNeither shall they learn war anymore.

4 ᵃBut everyone shall sit under his vine and under his fig tree,
And no one shall make *them* afraid;
For the mouth of the LORD of hosts has spoken.

5 For all people walk each in the name of his god,
But ᵃwe will walk in the name of the LORD our God
Forever and ever.

ZION'S FUTURE TRIUMPH

6 "In that day," says the LORD,
ᵃ"I will assemble the lame,
ᵇI will gather the outcast
And those whom I have afflicted;

7 I will make the lame ᵃa remnant,
And the outcast a strong nation;
So the LORD ᵇwill reign over them in Mount Zion
From now on, even forever.

8 And you, O tower of the flock,
The stronghold of the daughter of Zion,
To you shall it come,
Even the former dominion shall come,
The kingdom of the daughter of Jerusalem."

9 Now why do you cry aloud?
ᵃ*Is there* no king in your midst?
Has your counselor perished?
For ᵇpangs have seized you like a woman in ¹labor.

10 Be in pain, and labor to bring forth,
O daughter of Zion,
Like a woman in birth pangs.
For now you shall go forth from the city,
You shall dwell in the field,
And to ᵃBabylon you shall go.
There you shall be delivered;
There the ᵇLORD will ᶜredeem you
From the hand of your enemies.

11 ᵃNow also many nations have gathered against you,
Who say, "Let her be defiled,
And let our eye ᵇlook upon Zion."

12 But they do not know ᵃthe thoughts of the LORD,
Nor do they understand His counsel;
For He will gather them ᵇlike sheaves to the threshing
floor.

13 "Ariseᵃ and ᵇthresh, O daughter of Zion;
For I will make your horn iron,
And I will make your hooves bronze;
You shall ᶜbeat in pieces many peoples;
ᵈI will consecrate their gain to the LORD,
And their substance to ᵉthe Lord of the whole earth."

5 Now gather yourself in troops,
O daughter of troops;
He has laid siege against us;
They will ᵃstrike the judge of Israel with a rod on the cheek.

Cross references

4:3 ᵇPs. 72:7
4:4 ᵃ1 Kin. 4:25; Zech. 3:10
4:5 ᵃZech. 10:12
4:6 ᵃEzek. 34:16; ᵇPs. 147:2
4:7 ᵃMic. 2:12; ᵇ[Is. 9:6; 24:23; Luke 1:33; Rev. 11:15]
4:9 ᵃJer. 8:19; ᵇIs. 13:8; Jer. 30:6
4:10 ᵃ2 Chr. 36:20; Amos 5:27; ᵇ[Is. 45:13; Mic. 7:8–12]; ᶜEzra 1:1–3; 2:1; Ps. 18:17
4:11 ᵃLam. 2:16; ᵇObad. 12
4:12 ᵃ[Is. 55:8, 9]; ᵇIs. 21:10
4:13 ᵃJer. 51:33; [Zech. 12:1–8; 14:14]; ᵇIs. 41:15; ᶜDan. 2:44; ᵈIs. 18:7; ᵉZech. 4:14
5:1 ᵃ1 Kin. 22:24; Job 16:10; Lam. 3:30; Matt. 27:30; Mark 15:19

4:3 ¹*pruning knives*   4:9 ¹*childbirth*

THE COMING MESSIAH

2 "But you, [a]Bethlehem [b]Ephrathah,
Though you are little [c]among the [d]thousands of Judah,
Yet out of you shall come forth to Me
The One to be [e]Ruler in Israel,
[f]Whose goings forth *are* from of old,
From [1]everlasting."

3 Therefore He shall give them up,
Until the time *that* [a]she who is in labor has given birth;
Then [b]the remnant of His brethren
Shall return to the children of Israel.
4 And He shall stand and [a]feed[1] *His flock*
In the strength of the LORD,
In the majesty of the name of the LORD His God;
And they shall abide,
For now He [b]shall be great
To the ends of the earth;
5 And this *One* [a]shall be peace.

JUDGMENT ON ISRAEL'S ENEMIES

When the Assyrian comes into our land,
And when he treads in our palaces,
Then we will raise against him
Seven shepherds and eight princely men.
6 They shall [1]waste with the sword the land of Assyria,
And the land of [a]Nimrod at its entrances;
Thus He shall [b]deliver *us* from the Assyrian,
When he comes into our land
And when he treads within our borders.

7 Then [a]the remnant of Jacob
Shall be in the midst of many peoples,
[b]Like dew from the LORD,
Like showers on the grass,
That [1]tarry for no man
Nor [2]wait for the sons of men.
8 And the remnant of Jacob
Shall be among the Gentiles,
In the midst of many peoples,
Like a [a]lion among the beasts of the forest,
Like a young lion among flocks of sheep,
Who, if he passes through,
Both treads down and tears in pieces,
And none can deliver.
9 Your hand shall be lifted against your adversaries,
And all your enemies shall be [1]cut off.

10 "And it shall be in that day," says the LORD,
"That I will [a]cut[1] off your [b]horses from your midst
And destroy your [c]chariots.
11 I will cut off the cities of your land
And throw down all your strongholds.
12 I will cut off sorceries from your hand,
And you shall have no [a]soothsayers.
13 [a]Your carved images I will also cut off,
And your *sacred* pillars from your midst;
You shall [b]no more worship the work of your hands;

5:2 [a]Is. 11:1; Matt. 2:6; Luke 2:4, 11; John 7:42 [b]Gen. 35:19; 48:7; Ruth 4:11 [c]1 Sam. 23:23 [d]Ex. 18:25 [e][Gen. 49:10]; Is. 9:6] [f]Ps. 90:2; [John 1:1]
5:3 [a]Hos. 11:8; Mic. 4:10 [b]Mic. 4:7; 7:18
5:4 [a][Is. 40:11; 49:9]; Ezek. 34:13–15, 23, 24]; Mic. 7:14 [b]Ps. 72:8; Is. 52:13; Zech. 9:10; [Luke 1:32]
5:5 [a][Is. 9:6]; Luke 2:14; [Eph. 2:14]; Col. 1:20]
5:6 [a]Gen. 10:8–11 [b]Is. 14:25; Luke 1:71
5:7 [a]Mic. 5:3 [b]Gen. 27:28; Deut. 32:2; Ps. 72:6; Hos. 14:5
5:8 [a]Gen. 49:9; Num. 24:9
5:10 [a]Zech. 9:10 [b]Deut. 17:16 [c]Is. 2:7; 22:18; Hos. 14:3
5:12 [a]Deut. 18:10–12; Is. 2:6
5:13 [a]Zech. 13:2 [b]Is. 2:8

5:2 [1]Lit. *the days of eternity* 5:4 [1]*shepherd* 5:6 [1]*devastate* 5:7 [1]*wait* [2]*delay* 5:9 [1]*destroyed* 5:10 [1]*destroy*

14 I will pluck your [1]wooden images from your midst;
    Thus I will destroy your cities.
15 And I will [a]execute vengeance in anger and fury
    On the nations that have not [1]heard."

GOD PLEADS WITH ISRAEL

6 Hear now what the LORD says:

"Arise, plead your case before the mountains,
    And let the hills hear your voice.
2 [a]Hear, O you mountains, [b]the LORD's complaint,
    And you strong foundations of the earth;
    For [c]the LORD has a complaint against His people,
    And He will [1]contend with Israel.

3 "O My people, what [a]have I done to you?
    And how have I [b]wearied you?
    Testify against Me.
4 [a]For I brought you up from the land of Egypt,
    I redeemed you from the house of bondage;
    And I sent before you Moses, Aaron, and Miriam.
5 O My people, remember now
    What [a]Balak king of Moab counseled,
    And what Balaam the son of Beor answered him,
    From [1]Acacia Grove to Gilgal,
    That you may know [b]the righteousness of the LORD."

6 With what shall I come before the LORD,
    And bow myself before the High God?
    Shall I come before Him with burnt offerings,
    With calves a year old?
7 [a]Will the LORD be pleased with thousands of rams,
    Ten thousand [b]rivers of oil?
    [c]Shall I give my firstborn *for* my transgression,
    [1]The fruit of my body *for* the sin of my soul?

8 He has [a]shown you, O man, what *is* good;
    And what does the LORD require of you
    But [b]to do justly,
    To love [1]mercy,
    And to walk humbly with your God?

PUNISHMENT OF ISRAEL'S INJUSTICE

9 The LORD's voice cries to the city—
    Wisdom shall see Your name:

"Hear the rod!
    Who has appointed it?
10 Are there yet the treasures of wickedness
    In the house of the wicked,
    And the short measure *that is* an abomination?
11 Shall I count pure *those* with [a]the wicked scales,
    And with the bag of deceitful weights?
12 For her rich men are full of [a]violence,
    Her inhabitants have spoken lies,
    And [b]their tongue is deceitful in their mouth.

13 "Therefore I will also [a]make *you* sick by striking you,
    By making *you* desolate because of your sins.

5:15
[a][2 Thess. 1:8]

6:2 [a]Ps. 50:1, 4
[b][Is. 1:18];
Hos. 12:2
[c][Is. 1:18]

6:3 [a]Is. 5:4;
Jer. 2:5, 31
[b]Is. 43:22, 23;
Mal. 1:13

6:4
[a][Deut. 4:20]

6:5
[a]Num. 22:5, 6;
Josh. 24:9
[b]Judg. 5:11

6:7
[a]Ps. 50:9; Is. 1:11
[b]Job 29:6
[c]Lev. 18:21;
20:1–5;
2 Kin. 16:3;
Jer. 7:31;
Ezek. 23:37

6:8
[a][Deut. 10:12;
1 Sam. 15:22];
Hos. 6:6; 12:6
[b]Gen. 18:19;
Is. 1:17

6:11 [a]Lev. 19:36;
Hos. 12:7

6:12
[a]Is. 1:23; 5:7;
Amos 6:3, 4;
Mic. 2:1, 2
[b]Jer. 9:2–6, 8;
Hos. 7:13;
Amos 2:4

6:13 [a]Lev. 26:16;
Ps. 107:17

5:14 [1]Heb. *Asherim,* Canaanite deities   5:15 [1]*obeyed*   6:2 [1]*bring charges against*   6:5 [1]Heb. *Shittim,* Num. 25:1; Josh. 2:1; 3:1   6:7 [1]*My own child* 6:8 [1]Or *lovingkindness*

14 ªYou shall eat, but not be satisfied;
 ¹Hunger *shall be* in your midst.
 You may carry *some* away,² but shall not save *them;*
 And what you do rescue I will give over to the sword.
15 "You shall ªsow, but not reap;
 You shall tread the olives, but not anoint yourselves with oil;
 And *make* sweet wine, but not drink wine.
16 For the statutes of ªOmri are ᵇkept;
 All the works of Ahab's house *are done;*
 And you walk in their counsels,
 That I may make you a ¹desolation,
 And your inhabitants a hissing.
 Therefore you shall bear the ᶜreproach of ²My people."

SORROW FOR ISRAEL'S SINS

7 Woe is me!
 For I am like those who gather summer fruits,
 Like those who ªglean vintage grapes;
 There is no cluster to eat
 Of the first-ripe fruit *which* ᵇmy soul desires.
2 The ªfaithful¹ *man* has perished from the earth,
 And *there is* no one upright among men.
 They all lie in wait for blood;
 ᵇEvery man hunts his brother with a net.
3 That they may successfully do evil with both hands—
 The prince asks *for gifts,*
 The judge *seeks* a ªbribe,
 And the great *man* utters his evil desire;
 So they scheme together.
4 The best of them *is* ªlike a brier;
 The most upright *is sharper* than a thorn hedge;
 The day of your watchman and your punishment comes;
 Now shall be their perplexity.
5 ªDo not trust in a friend;
 Do not put your confidence in a companion;
 Guard the doors of your mouth
 From her who lies in your ᵇbosom.
6 For ªson dishonors father,
 Daughter rises against her mother,
 Daughter-in-law against her mother-in-law;
 A man's enemies *are* the men of his own household.
7 Therefore I will look to the LORD;
 I will ªwait for the God of my salvation;
 My God will hear me.

ISRAEL'S CONFESSION AND COMFORT

8 ªDo not rejoice over me, my enemy;
 ᵇWhen I fall, I will arise;
 When I sit in darkness,
 The LORD *will be* a light to me.
9 ªI will bear the indignation of the LORD,
 Because I have sinned against Him,
 Until He pleads my ᵇcase

6:14 ªLev. 26:26
6:15
ªDeut. 28:38–40;
Amos 5:11;
Zeph. 1:13;
Hag. 1:6
6:16
ª1 Kin. 16:25, 26
ᵇ1 Kin. 16:30;
21:25, 26;
2 Kin. 21:3;
Hos. 5:11
ᶜIs. 25:8
7:1 ªIs. 17:6
ᵇIs. 28:4;
Hos. 9:10
7:2
ªPs. 12:1; Is. 57:1
ᵇHab. 1:15
7:3 ªAmos 5:12;
Mic. 3:11
7:4 ªIs. 55:13;
Ezek. 2:6
7:5 ªJer. 9:4
ᵇDeut. 28:56
7:6
ªMatt. 10:36;
Mark 3:21;
Luke 8:19;
John 7:5
7:7 ªPs. 130:5;
Is. 25:9;
Lam. 3:24, 25
7:8 ªProv. 24:17;
Obad. 12;
[Acts 10:43]
ᵇPs. 37:24;
[Prov. 24:16];
2 Cor. 4:9
7:9
ªLam. 3:39, 40;
[2 Cor. 5:21]
ᵇJer. 50:34

6:14 ¹Or *Emptiness* or *Humiliation* ²Tg., Vg. *You shall take hold* 6:16 ¹Or *object of horror* ²So with MT, Tg., Vg.; LXX *nations* 7:2 ¹Or *loyal*

And executes justice for me.
He will bring me forth to the light;
I will see His righteousness.
10 Then *she who is* my enemy will see,
And [a]shame will cover her who said to me,
[b]"Where is the LORD your God?"
My eyes will see her;
Now she will be trampled down
Like mud in the streets.

11 *In* the day when your [a]walls are to be built,
In that day [1]the decree shall go far and wide.
12 *In* that day [a]they[1] shall come to you
From Assyria and the [2]fortified cities,
From the [3]fortress to [4]the River,
From sea to sea,
And mountain *to* mountain.
13 Yet the land shall be desolate
Because of those who dwell in it,
And [a]for the fruit of their deeds.

GOD WILL FORGIVE ISRAEL

14 Shepherd Your people with Your staff,
The flock of Your heritage,
Who dwell [1]solitarily *in* a [a]woodland,
In the midst of Carmel;
Let them feed *in* Bashan and Gilead,
As in days of old.

15 "As[a] in the days when you came out of the land of Egypt,
I will show [1]them [b]wonders."

16 The nations [a]shall see and be ashamed of all their might;
[b]They shall put *their* hand over *their* mouth;
Their ears shall be deaf.
17 They shall lick the [a]dust like a serpent;
[b]They shall crawl from their holes like [1]snakes of the earth.
[c]They shall be afraid of the LORD our God,
And shall fear because of You.
18 [a]Who *is* a God like You,
[b]Pardoning iniquity
And passing over the transgression of [c]the remnant of
His heritage?

[d]He does not retain His anger forever,
Because He delights *in* [e]mercy.[1]
19 He will again have compassion on us,
And will subdue our iniquities.

You will cast all [1]our sins
Into the depths of the sea.
20 [a]You will give truth to Jacob
And [1]mercy to Abraham,
[b]Which You have sworn to our fathers
From days of old.

7:10 [a]Ps. 35:26
[b]Ps. 42:3

7:11 [a]Is. 54:11;
[Amos 9:11]

7:12 [a][Is. 11:16;
19:23–25]

7:13 [a]Jer. 21:14

7:14 [a]Is. 37:24

7:15
[a]Ps. 68:22; 78:12
[b]Ex. 34:10

7:16 [a]Is. 26:11
[b]Job 21:5

7:17 [a]Ps. 72:9;
[Is. 49:23]
[b]Ps. 18:45
[c]Jer. 33:9

7:18 [a]Ex. 15:11
[b]Ex. 34:6, 7, 9;
Is. 43:25;
Jer. 50:20
[c]Mic. 4:7
[d]Ps. 103:8, 9, 13;
[Is. 57:16]
[e][Ezek. 33:11]

7:20
[a]Luke 1:72, 73
[b]Ps. 105:9

7:11 [1]Or *the boundary shall be extended* 7:12 [1]Lit. *he,* collective of the
captives [2]Heb. *arey mazor,* possibly *cities of Egypt* [3]Heb. *mazor,* possibly
Egypt [4]The Euphrates 7:14 [1]Alone 7:15 [1]Lit. *him,* collective for the
captives 7:17 [1]Lit. *crawlers* 7:18 [1]Or *lovingkindness* 7:19 [1]Lit. *their*
7:20 [1]Or *lovingkindness*

THE BOOK OF
NAHUM

1 The ¹burden ªagainst Nineveh. The book of the vision of Nahum the Elkoshite.

GOD'S WRATH ON HIS ENEMIES

2 God *is* ªjealous, and the LORD avenges;
  The LORD avenges and *is* furious.
  The LORD will take vengeance on His adversaries,
  And He reserves *wrath* for His enemies;

3 The LORD *is* ªslow to anger and ᵇgreat in power,
  And will not at all acquit *the wicked.*

  ᶜThe LORD has His way
  In the whirlwind and in the storm,
  And the clouds *are* the dust of His feet.

4 ªHe rebukes the sea and makes it dry,
  And dries up all the rivers.
  ᵇBashan and Carmel wither,
  And the flower of Lebanon wilts.

5 The mountains quake before Him,
  The hills melt,
  And the earth ¹heaves at His presence,
  Yes, the world and all who dwell in it.

6 Who can stand before His indignation?
  And ªwho can endure the fierceness of His anger?
  His fury is poured out like fire,
  And the rocks are thrown down by Him.

7 ªThe LORD *is* good,
  A stronghold in the day of trouble;
  And ᵇHe knows those who trust in Him.

8 But with an overflowing flood
  He will make an utter end of its place,
  And darkness will pursue His enemies.

9 ªWhat do you ¹conspire against the LORD?
  ᵇHe will make an utter end *of it.*
  Affliction will not rise up a second time.

10 For while tangled ªlike thorns,
  ᵇAnd while drunken *like* drunkards,
  ᶜThey shall be devoured like stubble fully dried.

11 From you comes forth *one*
  Who plots evil against the LORD,
  A ¹wicked counselor.

12 Thus says the LORD:

  "Though *they are* ¹safe, and likewise many,
  Yet in this manner they will be ªcut down
  When he passes through.

1:1 ª2 Kin. 19:36;
Jon. 1:2;
Nah. 2:8;
Zeph. 2:13

1:2 ªEx. 20:5;
Josh. 24:19

1:3 ªEx. 34:6, 7;
Neh. 9:17;
Ps. 103:8
ᵇ[Job 9:4]
ᶜPs. 18:17

1:4
ªJosh. 3:15, 16;
Ps. 106:9;
Is. 50:2;
Matt. 8:26
ᵇIs. 33:9

1:6 ªJer. 10:10;
[Mal. 3:2]

1:7 ªPs. 25:8;
37:39, 40; 100:5;
[Jer. 33:11];
Lam. 3:25
ᵇPs. 1:6;
John 10:14;
2 Tim. 2:19

1:9 ªPs. 2:1;
Nah. 1:11
ᵇ1 Sam. 3:12

1:10
ª2 Sam. 23:6;
Mic. 7:4
ᵇIs. 56:12;
Nah. 3:11
ᶜIs. 5:24; 10:17;
Mal. 4:1

1:12
ª[Is. 10:16–19,
33, 34]

1:1 ¹*oracle, prophecy*   1:5 ¹Tg. *burns*   1:9 ¹Or *devise*   1:11 ¹Lit. *counselor of Belial*   1:12 ¹Or *at peace* or *complete*

Though I have afflicted you,
I will afflict you no more;
13 For now I will break off his yoke from you,
And burst your bonds apart."

14 The LORD has given a command concerning you:
[1]"Your name shall be perpetuated no longer.
Out of the house of your gods
I will cut off the carved image and the molded image.
I will dig your [a]grave,
For you are [b]vile."[2]

15 Behold, on the mountains
The [a]feet of him who brings good tidings,
Who proclaims peace!
O Judah, keep your appointed feasts,
Perform your vows.
For the [1]wicked one shall no more pass through you;
He is [b]utterly cut off.

THE DESTRUCTION OF NINEVEH

2 He[1] who scatters has come up before your face.
Man the fort!
Watch the road!
Strengthen *your* flanks!
Fortify *your* power mightily.

2 For the LORD will restore the excellence of Jacob
Like the excellence of Israel,
For the emptiers have emptied them out
And ruined their vine branches.

3 The shields of his mighty men *are* made red,
The valiant men *are* in scarlet.
The chariots *come* with flaming torches
In the day of his preparation,
And [1]the spears are brandished.
4 The chariots rage in the streets,
They jostle one another in the broad roads;
They seem like torches,
They run like lightning.

5 He remembers his nobles;
They stumble in their walk;
They make haste to her walls,
And the defense is prepared.
6 The gates of the rivers are opened,
And the palace is dissolved.
7 [1]It is decreed:
She shall be led away captive,
She shall be brought up;
And her maidservants shall lead *her* as with the voice of
doves,
Beating their breasts.

8 Though Nineveh of old *was* like a pool of water,
Now they flee away.

1:14
[a] Ezek. 32:22, 23
[b] Nah. 3:6
1:15
[a] Is. 40:9; 52:7;
Rom. 10:15
[b] Is. 29:7, 8

1:14 [1]Lit. *No more of your name shall be fruitful*   [2]Or *contemptible*
1:15 [1]Lit. *one of Belial*   2:1 [1]Vg. *He who destroys*   2:3 [1]Lit. *the cypresses are
shaken;* LXX, Syr. *the horses rush about;* Vg. *the drivers are stupefied*
2:7 [1]Heb. *Huzzab*

[1]"Halt! Halt!" *they cry;*
But no one turns back.
9 ¹Take spoil of silver!
Take spoil of ᵃgold!
There is no end of treasure,
Or wealth of every desirable prize.
10 She is empty, desolate, and waste!
The heart melts, and the knees shake;
Much pain *is* in every side,
And all their faces ¹are drained of color.

11 Where *is* the dwelling of the ᵃlions,
And the feeding place of the young lions,
Where the lion walked, the lioness *and* lion's cub,
And no one made *them* afraid?
12 The lion tore in pieces enough for his cubs,
¹Killed for his lionesses,
ᵃFilled his caves with prey,
And his dens with ²flesh.

13"Behold, ᵃI *am* against you," says the LORD of hosts, "I will burn ¹your chariots in smoke, and the sword shall devour your young lions; I will cut off your prey from the earth, and the voice of your ᵇmessengers shall be heard no more."

THE WOE OF NINEVEH

3 Woe to the ᵃbloody city!
It *is* all full of lies *and* robbery.
Its ¹victim never departs.
2 The noise of a whip
And the noise of rattling wheels,
Of galloping horses,
Of ¹clattering chariots!
3 Horsemen charge with bright sword and glittering spear.
There is a multitude of slain,
A great number of bodies,
Countless corpses—
They stumble over the corpses—
4 Because of the multitude of ¹harlotries of the ²seductive harlot,
ᵃThe mistress of sorceries,
Who sells nations through her harlotries,
And families through her sorceries.

5 "Behold, I *am* ᵃagainst you," says the LORD of hosts;
ᵇ"I will lift your skirts over your face,
I will show the nations your nakedness,
And the kingdoms your shame.
6 I will cast abominable filth upon you,
Make you ᵃvile,¹
And make you ᵇa spectacle.
7 It shall come to pass *that* all who look upon you
ᵃWill flee from you, and say,
ᵇ'Nineveh is laid waste!

2:9 ᵃEzek. 7:19;
Zeph. 1:18
2:11 ᵃJob 4:10, 11;
Ezek. 19:2–7
2:12 ᵃIs. 10:6;
Jer. 51:34
2:13 ᵃJer. 21:13;
Ezek. 5:8;
Nah. 3:5
ᵇ2 Kin. 18:17–25;
19:9–13, 23
3:1
ᵃEzek. 22:2, 3;
24:6–9;
Hab. 2:12
3:4 ᵃIs. 47:9–12;
Rev. 18:2, 3
3:5 ᵃJer. 50:31;
Ezek. 26:3;
Nah. 2:13
ᵇIs. 47:2, 3;
Jer. 13:26
3:6 ᵃNah. 1:14
ᵇHeb. 10:33
3:7 ᵃRev. 18:10
ᵇJon. 3:3; 4:11

2:8 ¹Lit. *Stand*   **2:9** ¹*Plunder*   **2:10** ¹LXX, Tg., Vg. *gather blackness*; Joel 2:6
2:12 ¹Lit. *Strangled*   ²Torn flesh   **2:13** ¹Lit. *her*   **3:1** ¹Lit. *prey*
3:2 ¹*bounding* or *jolting*   **3:4** ¹Spiritual unfaithfulness   ²Lit. *goodly charm,*
in a bad sense   **3:6** ¹*despicable*

^cWho will bemoan her?'
Where shall I seek comforters for you?"

8 ^aAre you better than ^bNo¹ Amon
That was situated by the ²River,
That had the waters around her,
Whose rampart *was* the sea,
Whose wall *was* the sea?

9 Ethiopia and Egypt *were* her strength,
And *it was* boundless;
^aPut and Lubim were ¹your helpers.

10 Yet she *was* carried away,
She went into captivity;
^aHer young children also were dashed to pieces
^bAt the head of every street;
They ^ccast lots for her honorable men,
And all her great men were bound in chains.

11 You also will be ^adrunk;
You will be hidden;
You also will seek refuge from the enemy.

12 All your strongholds *are* ^afig trees with ripened figs:
If they are shaken,
They fall into the mouth of the eater.

13 Surely, ^ayour people in your midst *are* women!
The gates of your land are wide open for your enemies;
Fire shall devour the ^bbars of your *gates.*

14 Draw your water for the siege!
^aFortify your strongholds!
Go into the clay and tread the mortar!
Make strong the brick kiln!

15 There the fire will devour you,
The sword will cut you off;
It will eat you up like a ^alocust.

Make yourself many—like the locust!
Make yourself many—like the *swarming* locusts!

16 You have multiplied your ^amerchants more than the
stars of heaven.
The locust plunders and flies away.

17 ^aYour commanders *are* like *swarming* locusts,
And your generals like great grasshoppers,
Which camp in the hedges on a cold day;
When the sun rises they flee away,
And the place where they *are* is not known.

18 ^aYour shepherds slumber, O ^bking of Assyria;
Your nobles rest *in the dust.*
Your people are ^cscattered on the mountains,
And no one gathers them.

19 Your injury *has* no healing,
^aYour wound is severe.
^bAll who hear news of you
Will clap *their* hands over you,
For upon whom has not your wickedness passed
continually?

3:7 ^cIs. 51:19;
Jer. 15:5
3:8 ^aAmos 6:2
^bJer. 46:25;
Ezek. 30:14–16
3:9 ^aGen. 10:6;
Jer. 46:9;
Ezek. 27:10
3:10 ^aPs. 137:9;
Is. 13:16;
Hos. 13:16
^bLam. 2:19
^cJoel 3:3;
Obad. 11
3:11 ^aIs. 49:26;
Jer. 25:27;
Nah. 1:10
3:12
^aRev. 6:12, 13
3:13 ^aIs. 19:16;
Jer. 50:37; 51:30
^bPs. 147:13;
Jer. 51:30
3:14 ^aNah. 2:1
3:15 ^aJoel 1:4
3:16
^aRev. 18:3, 11–19
3:17 ^aRev. 9:7
3:18 ^aEx. 15:16;
Ps. 76:5, 6;
Is. 56:10;
Jer. 51:57
^bJer. 50:18;
Ezek. 31:3
^c1 Kin. 22:17;
Is. 13:14
3:19 ^aJer. 46:11;
Mic. 1:9
^bJob 27:23;
Lam. 2:15;
Zeph. 2:15

3:8 ¹Ancient Thebes; Tg., Vg. *populous Alexandria*   ²Lit. *rivers,* the Nile and
the surrounding canals   3:9 ¹LXX *her*

THE BOOK OF
HABAKKUK

1 The ¹burden which the prophet Habakkuk saw.

THE PROPHET'S QUESTION

2 O LORD, how long shall I cry,
   ᵃAnd You will not hear?
   Even cry out to You, ᵇ"Violence!"
   And You will ᶜnot save.
3 Why do You show me iniquity,
   And cause *me* to see ¹trouble?
   For plundering and violence *are* before me;
   There is strife, and contention arises.
4 Therefore the law is powerless,
   And justice never goes forth.
   For the ᵃwicked surround the righteous;
   Therefore perverse judgment proceeds.

THE LORD'S REPLY

5 "Lookᵃ among the nations and watch—
   Be utterly astounded!
   For *I will* work a work in your days
   Which you would not believe, though it were told *you.*
6 For indeed I am ᵃraising up the Chaldeans,
   A bitter and hasty ᵇnation
   Which marches through the breadth of the earth,
   To possess dwelling places *that are* not theirs.
7 They are terrible and dreadful;
   Their judgment and their dignity proceed from themselves.
8 Their horses also are ᵃswifter than leopards,
   And more fierce than evening wolves.
   Their ¹chargers ²charge ahead;
   Their cavalry comes from afar;
   They fly as the ᵇeagle *that* hastens to eat.
9 "They all come for violence;
   Their faces are set *like* the east wind.
   They gather captives like sand.
10 They scoff at kings,
   And princes are scorned by them.
   They deride every stronghold,
   For they heap up earthen *mounds* and seize it.
11 Then *his* ¹mind changes, and he transgresses;
   He commits offense,
   ᵃAscribing this power to his god."

THE PROPHET'S SECOND QUESTION

12 Are You not ᵃfrom everlasting,
   O LORD my God, my Holy One?

1:2 ᵃLam. 3:8
ᵇMic. 2:1, 2;
3:1–3
ᶜ[Job 21:5–16]

1:4 ᵃJer. 12:1

1:5 ᵃIs. 29:14;
Ezek. 12:22–28

1:6
ᵃDeut. 28:49, 50;
2 Kin. 24:2;
2 Chr. 36:17;
Jer. 4:11–13;
Mic. 4:10
ᵇEzek. 7:24;
21:31

1:8 ᵃJer. 4:13
ᵇJob 9:26;
39:29, 30;
Lam. 4:19;
Ezek. 17:3;
Hos. 8:1;
Matt. 24:28;
Luke 17:37

1:11 ᵃDan. 5:4

1:12
ᵃDeut. 33:27;
Ps. 90:2; 93:2;
Mal. 3:6

1:1 ¹*oracle, prophecy* 1:3 ¹Or *toil* 1:8 ¹Lit. *horsemen* ²Lit. *spring about*
1:11 ¹Lit. *spirit* or *wind*

We shall not die.
O LORD, [b]You have appointed them for judgment;
O Rock, You have marked them for [c]correction.
13 *You are* of purer eyes than to behold evil,
And cannot look on wickedness.
Why do You look on those who deal treacherously,
And hold Your tongue when the wicked devours
A *person* more righteous than he?
14 *Why* do You make men like fish of the sea,
Like creeping things *that have* no ruler over them?

15 They take up all of them with a hook,
They catch them in their net,
And gather them in their dragnet.
Therefore they rejoice and are glad.
16 Therefore [a]they sacrifice to their net,
And burn incense to their dragnet;
Because by them their share *is* [1]sumptuous
And their food plentiful.
17 Shall they therefore empty their net,
And continue to slay nations without pity?

2 I will [a]stand my watch
And set myself on the rampart,
And watch to see what He will say to me,
And what I will answer when I am corrected.

THE JUST LIVE BY FAITH

2 Then the LORD answered me and said:

[a]"Write the vision
And make *it* plain on tablets,
That he may run who reads it.
3 For [a]the vision *is* yet for an appointed time;
But at the end it will speak, and it will [b]not lie.
Though it tarries, [c]wait for it;
Because it will [d]surely come,
It will not tarry.

4 "Behold the proud,
His soul is not upright in him;
But the [a]just shall live by his faith.

WOE TO THE WICKED

5 "Indeed, because he transgresses by wine,
He is a proud man,
And he does not stay at home.
Because he [a]enlarges his desire as [1]hell,
And he *is* like death, and cannot be satisfied,
He gathers to himself all nations
And heaps up for himself all peoples.

6 "Will not all these [a]take up a proverb against him,
And a taunting riddle against him, and say,
'Woe to him who increases
What is not his—how long?
And to him who loads himself with [1]many
    pledges'?

1:12
[b]Is. 10:5–7;
Mal. 3:5
[c]Jer. 25:9

1:16 [a]Deut. 8:17

2:1 [a]Is. 21:8, 11

2:2 [a]Is. 8:1

2:3
[a]Dan. 8:17, 19;
10:14
[b]Ezek. 12:24, 25
[c][Heb. 10:37, 38]
[d]Ps. 27:13, 14;
[James 5:7, 8;
2 Pet. 3:9]

2:4
[a][John 3:36];
Rom. 1:17;
Heb. 10:38

2:5 [a]Prov. 27:20;
30:16; Is. 5:11–15

2:6 [a]Mic. 2:4

1:16 [1]Lit. *fat* 2:5 [1]Or *Sheol* 2:6 [1]Syr., Vg. *thick clay*

7 Will not [1]your creditors rise up suddenly?
Will they not awaken who oppress you?
And you will become their booty.

8 [a]Because you have plundered many nations,
All the remnant of the people shall plunder you,
Because of men's [1]blood
And the violence of the land *and* the city,
And of all who dwell in it.

9 "Woe to him who covets evil gain for his house,
That he may [a]set his nest on high,
That he may be delivered from the [1]power of
disaster!

10 You give shameful counsel to your house,
Cutting off many peoples,
And sin *against* your soul.

11 For the stone will cry out from the wall,
And the beam from the timbers will answer it.

12 "Woe to him who builds a town with bloodshed,
Who establishes a city by iniquity!

13 Behold, *is it* not of the LORD of hosts
That the peoples labor [1]to feed the fire,
And nations weary themselves in vain?

14 For the earth will be filled
With the knowledge of the glory of the LORD,
As the waters cover the sea.

15 "Woe to him who gives drink to his neighbor,
[1]Pressing *him to* your [a]bottle,
Even to make *him* drunk,
That you may look on [2]his nakedness!

16 You are filled with shame instead of glory.
You also—drink!
And [1]be exposed as uncircumcised!
The cup of the LORD's right hand *will be* turned against
you,
And utter shame will be on your glory.

17 For the violence *done to* Lebanon will cover you,
And the plunder of beasts *which* made them afraid,
Because of men's blood
And the violence of the land *and* the city,
And of all who dwell in it.

18 "What profit is the image, that its maker should
carve it,
The molded image, a teacher of lies,
That the maker of its mold should trust in it,
To make mute idols?

19 Woe to him who says to wood, 'Awake!'
To silent stone, 'Arise! It shall teach!'
Behold, it is overlaid with gold and silver,
Yet in it there is no breath at all.

20 "But[a] the LORD is in His holy temple.
Let all the earth keep silence before Him."

2:8 [a]Is. 33:1;
Jer. 27:7;
Ezek. 39:10;
Zech. 2:8
2:9 [a]Jer. 49:16;
Obad. 4
2:15 [a]Hos. 7:5
2:20 [a]Zeph. 1:7;
Zech. 2:13

2:7 [1]Lit. *those who bite you*   2:8 [1]Or *bloodshed*   2:9 [1]Lit. *hand of evil*
2:13 [1]Lit. *for what satisfies fire,* for what is of no lasting value   2:15 [1]Lit.
Attaching or *Joining*   [2]Lit. *their*   2:16 [1]DSS, LXX *reel;* Syr., Vg. *fall fast
asleep!*

THE PROPHET'S PRAYER

3 A prayer of Habakkuk the prophet, on [1]Shigionoth.

2 O Lord, I have heard Your speech *and* was afraid;
O Lord, revive Your work in the midst of the years!
In the midst of the years make *it* known;
In wrath remember mercy.

3 God came from Teman,
The Holy One from Mount Paran.   **Selah**

His glory covered the heavens,
And the earth was full of His praise.
4 *His* brightness was like the light;
He had rays *flashing* from His hand,
And there His power *was* hidden.
5 Before Him went pestilence,
And fever followed at His feet.

6 He stood and measured the earth;
He looked and startled the nations.
[a]And the everlasting mountains were scattered,
The perpetual hills bowed.
His ways *are* everlasting.
7 I saw the tents of Cushan in affliction;
The curtains of the land of Midian trembled.

8 O Lord, were *You* displeased with the rivers,
Was Your anger against the rivers,
Was Your wrath against the sea,
That You rode on Your horses,
Your chariots of salvation?
9 Your bow was made quite ready;
Oaths were sworn over *Your* [1]arrows.   **Selah**

You divided the earth with rivers.
10 The mountains saw You *and* trembled;
The overflowing of the water passed by.
The deep uttered its voice,
And [a]lifted its hands on high.
11 The [a]sun and moon stood still in their habitation;
At the light of Your arrows they went,
At the shining of Your glittering spear.

12 You marched through the land in indignation;
You [1]trampled the nations in anger.
13 You went forth for the salvation of Your people,
For salvation with Your Anointed.
You struck the head from the house of the wicked,
By laying bare from foundation to neck.   **Selah**

14 You thrust through with his own arrows
The head of his villages.
They came out like a whirlwind to scatter me;
Their rejoicing was like feasting on the poor in secret.
15 [a]You walked through the sea with Your horses,
Through the heap of great waters.

16 When I heard, [a]my body trembled;
My lips quivered at *the* voice;

3:6 [a]Nah. 1:5
3:10 [a]Ex. 14:22
3:11
[a]Josh. 10:12–14
3:15 [a]Ps. 77:19;
Hab. 3:8
3:16 [a]Ps. 119:120

3:1 [1]Exact meaning unknown   3:9 [1]Lit. *tribes* or *rods*, cf. v. 14
3:12 [1]Or *threshed*

Rottenness entered my bones;
And I trembled in myself,
That I might rest in the day of trouble.
When he comes up to the people,
He will invade them with his troops.

A HYMN OF FAITH

17 Though the fig tree may not blossom,
Nor fruit be on the vines;
Though the labor of the olive may fail,
And the fields yield no food;
Though the flock may be cut off from the fold,
And there be no herd in the stalls—
18 Yet I will ^arejoice in the LORD,
I will joy in the God of my salvation.

19 ¹The LORD God is my strength;
He will make my feet like ^adeer's *feet*,
And He will make me ^bwalk on my high hills.

To the Chief Musician. With my stringed instruments.

3:18
^aIs. 41:16; 61:10
3:19
^a2 Sam. 22:34;
Ps. 18:33
^bDeut. 32:13;
33:29

3:19 ¹Heb. *YHWH Adonai*

THE BOOK OF

ZEPHANIAH

1 The word of the LORD which came to Zephaniah the son of Cushi, the son of Gedaliah, the son of Amariah, the son of Hezekiah, in the days of ᵃJosiah the son of Amon, king of Judah.

THE GREAT DAY OF THE LORD

2 "I will ¹utterly consume everything
  From the face of the land,"
  Says the LORD;
3 "Iᵃ will consume man and beast;
  I will consume the birds of the heavens,
  The fish of the sea,
  And the ¹stumbling blocks along with the wicked.
  I will cut off man from the face of the ²land,"
  Says the LORD.

4 "I will stretch out My hand against Judah,
  And against all the inhabitants of Jerusalem.
  ¹I will cut off every trace of Baal from this place,
  The names of the ᵃidolatrous² priests with the *pagan* priests—
5 Those ᵃwho worship the host of heaven on the housetops;
  Those who worship and swear *oaths* by the LORD,
  But who *also* swear ᵇby ¹Milcom;
6 ᵃThose who have turned back from *following* the LORD,
  And ᵇhave not sought the LORD, nor inquired of Him."

7 ᵃBe silent in the presence of the Lord GOD;
  ᵇFor the day of the LORD *is* at hand,
  For ᶜthe LORD has prepared a sacrifice;
  He has ¹invited His guests.

8 "And it shall be,
  In the day of the LORD's sacrifice,
  That I will punish ᵃthe princes and the king's children,
  And all such as are clothed with foreign apparel.
9 In the same day I will punish
  All those who ᵃleap over the threshold,
  Who fill their masters' houses with violence and deceit.

10 "And there shall be on that day," says the LORD,
  "The sound of a mournful cry from ᵃthe Fish Gate,
  A wailing from the Second Quarter,
  And a loud crashing from the hills.

1:1
ᵃ2 Kin. 22:1, 2;
2 Chr. 34:1–33;
Jer. 1:2; 22:11

1:3 ᵃHos. 4:3

1:4 ᵃ2 Kin. 23:5;
Hos. 10:5

1:5 ᵃ2 Kin. 23:12;
Jer. 19:13
ᵇJosh. 23:7

1:6 ᵃIs. 1:4;
Jer. 2:13
ᵇHos. 7:7

1:7 ᵃHab. 2:20;
Zech. 2:13
ᵇIs. 13:6
ᶜDeut. 28:26;
Is. 34:6;
Jer. 46:10;
Ezek. 39:17–19

1:8 ᵃJer. 39:6

1:9 ᵃ1 Sam. 5:5

1:10
ᵃ2 Chr. 33:14;
Neh. 3:3; 12:39

1:2 ¹Lit. *make a complete end of,* Jer. 8:13   1:3 ¹Idols   ²*ground*
1:4 ¹Fulfilled in 2 Kin. 23:4, 5   ²Heb. *chemarim*   1:5 ¹Or *Malcam,* an
Ammonite god, 1 Kin. 11:5; Jer. 49:1; *Molech,* Lev. 18:21   1:7 ¹Lit. *set apart,*
consecrated

11 ᵃWail, you inhabitants of ¹Maktesh!
　　For all the merchant people are cut down;
　　All those who handle money are cut off.

12 "And it shall come to pass at that time
　　That I will search Jerusalem with lamps,
　　And punish the men
　　Who are ᵃsettled¹ in complacency,
　　ᵇWho say in their heart,
　　'The LORD will not do good,
　　Nor will He do evil.'
13 　Therefore their goods shall become booty,
　　And their houses a desolation;
　　They shall build houses, but not inhabit *them*;
　　They shall plant vineyards, but ᵃnot drink their
　　　wine."

14 ᵃThe great day of the LORD *is* near;
　　It is near and hastens quickly.
　　The noise of the day of the LORD is bitter;
　　There the mighty men shall cry out.
15 ᵃThat day *is* a day of wrath,
　　A day of trouble and distress,
　　A day of devastation and desolation,
　　A day of darkness and gloominess,
　　A day of clouds and thick darkness,
16 　A day of ᵃtrumpet and alarm
　　Against the fortified cities
　　And against the high towers.

17 "I will bring distress upon men,
　　And they shall ᵃwalk like blind men,
　　Because they have sinned against the LORD;
　　Their blood shall be poured out like dust,
　　And their flesh like refuse."

18 ᵃNeither their silver nor their gold
　　Shall be able to deliver them
　　In the day of the LORD's wrath;
　　But the whole land shall be devoured
　　By the fire of His jealousy,
　　For He will make speedy riddance
　　Of all those who dwell in the land.

A CALL TO REPENTANCE

2 Gatherᵃ yourselves together, yes, gather together,
　　O ¹undesirable nation,
2 　Before the decree is issued,
　　Or the day passes like chaff,
　　Before the LORD's fierce anger comes upon you,
　　Before the day of the LORD's anger comes upon
　　　you!
3 　ᵃSeek the LORD, ᵇall you meek of the earth,
　　Who have upheld His justice.
　　Seek righteousness, seek humility.
　　ᶜIt may be that you will be hidden
　　In the day of the LORD's anger.

1:11 ᵃJames 5:1
1:12 ᵃJer. 48:11;
Amos 6:1
ᵇPs. 94:7
1:13
ᵃDeut. 28:39
1:14 ᵃJer. 30:7;
Joel 2:1, 11
1:15 ᵃIs. 22:5
1:16 ᵃIs. 27:13;
Jer. 4:19
1:17
ᵃDeut. 28:29
1:18 ᵃEzek. 7:19
2:1 ᵃ2 Chr. 20:4;
Joel 1:14; 2:16
2:3 ᵃPs. 105:4;
Amos 5:6
ᵇPs. 76:9
ᶜJoel 2:14;
Amos 5:14, 15

1:11 ¹A market district of Jerusalem, lit. *Mortar*　　1:12 ¹Lit. *on their lees;* like the dregs of wine　　2:1 ¹Or *shameless*

JUDGMENT ON NATIONS

4 For [a]Gaza shall be forsaken,
  And Ashkelon desolate;
  They shall drive out Ashdod [b]at noonday,
  And Ekron shall be uprooted.
5 Woe to the inhabitants of [a]the seacoast,
  The nation of the Cherethites!
  The word of the LORD *is* against you,
  O [b]Canaan, land of the Philistines:
  "I will destroy you;
  So there shall be no inhabitant."
6 The seacoast shall be pastures,
  With [1]shelters for shepherds [a]and folds for flocks.
7 The coast shall be for [a]the remnant of the house of
    Judah;
  They shall feed *their* flocks there;
  In the houses of Ashkelon they shall lie down at evening.
  For the LORD their God will [b]intervene[1] for them,
  And [c]return their captives.
8 "I[a] have heard the reproach of Moab,
  And [b]the insults of the people of Ammon,
  With which they have reproached My people,
  And [c]made arrogant threats against their borders.
9 Therefore, as I live,"
  Says the LORD of hosts, the God of Israel,
  "Surely [a]Moab shall be like Sodom,
  And [b]the people of Ammon like Gomorrah—
  [c]Overrun[1] with weeds and saltpits,
  And a [2]perpetual desolation.
  The residue of My people shall plunder them,
  And the remnant of My people shall possess them."
10 This they shall have [a]for their pride,
  Because they have reproached and made arrogant
    threats
  Against the people of the LORD of hosts.
11 The LORD *will be* awesome to them,
  For He will reduce to nothing all the gods of the earth;
  [a]*People* shall worship Him,
  Each one from his place,
  Indeed all [b]the shores of the nations.
12 "You[a] Ethiopians also,
  You shall be slain by [b]My sword."
13 And He will stretch out His hand against the north,
  [a]Destroy Assyria,
  And make Nineveh a desolation,
  As dry as the wilderness.
14 The herds shall lie down in her midst,
  [a]Every beast of the nation.
  Both the [b]pelican and the bittern
  Shall lodge on the capitals *of* her *pillars;*
  Their voice shall sing in the windows;
  Desolation *shall be* at the threshold;
  For He will lay bare the [c]cedar work.

2:4
[a]Jer. 47:1, 5;
Amos 1:7, 8;
Zech. 9:5
[b]Jer. 6:4

2:5
[a]Ezek. 25:15–17
[b]Josh. 13:3

2:6 [a]Is. 17:2

2:7 [a][Mic. 5:7, 8]
[b]Luke 1:68
[c]Jer. 29:14

2:8 [a]Jer. 48:27;
Amos 2:1–3
[b]Ezek. 25:3;
Amos 1:13
[c]Jer. 49:1

2:9 [a]Is. 15:1–9;
Jer. 48:1–47
[b]Amos 1:13
[c]Deut. 29:23

2:10 [a]Is. 16:6

2:11 [a]Mal. 1:11
[b]Gen. 10:5

2:12 [a]Is. 18:1–7;
Ezek. 30:4, 5
[b]Ps. 17:13

2:13
[a]Is. 10:5–27;
14:24–27;
Mic. 5:5, 6

2:14 [a]Is. 13:21
[b]Is. 14:23; 34:11
[c]Jer. 22:14

2:6 [1]Underground huts or cisterns, lit. *excavations*   2:7 [1]Lit. *visit them*
2:9 [1]Lit. *Possessed by nettles*   [2]Or *permanent ruin*

15   This is the rejoicing city
    ᵃThat dwelt securely,
    ᵇThat said in her heart,
  "I *am it,* and *there is* none besides me."
  How has she become a desolation,
  A place for beasts to lie down!
  Everyone who passes by her
    ᶜShall hiss and ᵈshake his fist.

THE WICKEDNESS OF JERUSALEM

3 Woe to her who is rebellious and polluted,
  To the oppressing city!
2   She has not obeyed *His* voice,
  She has not received correction;
  She has not trusted in the LORD,
  She has not drawn near to her God.

3   ᵃHer princes in her midst *are* roaring lions;
  Her judges *are* ᵇevening wolves
  That leave not a bone till morning.
4   Her ᵃprophets are insolent, treacherous people;
  Her priests have ¹polluted the sanctuary,
  They have done ᵇviolence to the law.
5   The LORD *is* righteous in her midst,
  He will do no unrighteousness.
  ¹Every morning He brings His justice to light;
  He never fails,
  But ᵃthe unjust knows no shame.

6   "I have cut off nations,
  Their fortresses are devastated;
  I have made their streets desolate,
  With none passing by.
  Their cities are destroyed;
  There is no one, no inhabitant.
7   ᵃI said, 'Surely you will fear Me,
  You will receive instruction'—
  So that her dwelling would not be cut off,
  Despite everything for which I punished her.
  But ¹they rose early and ᵇcorrupted all their deeds.

A FAITHFUL REMNANT
(cf. Gen. 11:1–9; Acts 2:1–11)

8   "Therefore ᵃwait for Me," says the LORD,
  "Until the day I rise up ¹for plunder;
  My determination *is* to ᵇgather the nations
  To My assembly of kingdoms,
  To pour on them My indignation,
  All My fierce anger;
  All the earth ᶜshall be devoured
  With the fire of My jealousy.

9   "For then I will restore to the peoples ᵃa pure ¹language,
  That they all may call on the name of the LORD,
  To serve Him with one accord.

2:15 ᵃIs. 47:8
  ᵇRev. 18:7
  ᶜLam. 2:15
  ᵈNah. 3:19

3:3 ᵃEzek. 22:27
  ᵇJer. 5:6;
  Hab. 1:8

3:4 ᵃHos. 9:7
  ᵇEzek. 22:26;
  Mal. 2:7, 8

3:5 ᵃJer. 3:3

3:7 ᵃJer. 8:6
  ᵇGen. 6:12

3:8
ᵃProv. 20:22;
  Mic. 7:7;
  Hab. 2:3
  ᵇIs. 66:18;
Ezek. 38:14–23;
  Joel 3:2;
  Mic. 4:12;
  Matt. 25:32
  ᶜZeph. 1:18

3:9
ᵃIs. 19:18; 57:19

3:4 ¹Or *profaned*   3:5 ¹Lit. *Morning by morning*   3:7 ¹They were eager
3:8 ¹LXX, Syr. *for witness;* Tg. *for the day of My revelation for judgment;* Vg.
for the day of My resurrection that is to come   3:9 ¹Lit. *lip*

10 ^aFrom beyond the rivers of Ethiopia
   My worshipers,
   The daughter of My dispersed ones,
   Shall bring My offering.
11 In that day you shall not be shamed for any of your
         deeds
   In which you transgress against Me;
   For then I will take away from your midst
   Those who ^arejoice in your pride,
   And you shall no longer be haughty
   In My holy mountain.
12 I will leave in your midst
   ^aA meek and humble people,
   And they shall trust in the name of the LORD.
13 ^aThe remnant of Israel ^bshall do no unrighteousness
   ^cAnd speak no lies,
   Nor shall a deceitful tongue be found in their mouth;
   For ^dthey shall feed *their* flocks and lie down,
   And no one shall make *them* afraid."

JOY IN GOD'S FAITHFULNESS

14 ^aSing, O daughter of Zion!
   Shout, O Israel!
   Be glad and rejoice with all *your* heart,
   O daughter of Jerusalem!
15 The LORD has taken away your judgments,
   He has cast out your enemy.
   ^aThe King of Israel, the LORD, ^b*is* in your midst;
   You shall ¹see disaster no more.
16 In that day ^ait shall be said to Jerusalem:
   "Do not fear;
   Zion, ^blet not your hands be weak.
17 The LORD your God ^ain your midst,
   The Mighty One, will save;
   ^bHe will rejoice over you with gladness,
   He will quiet *you* with His love,
   He will rejoice over you with singing."
18 "I will gather those who ^asorrow over the appointed
         assembly,
   Who are among you,
   To whom its reproach *is* a burden.
19 Behold, at that time
   I will deal with all who afflict you;
   I will save the ^alame,
   And gather those who were driven out;
   I will appoint them for praise and fame
   In every land where they were put to shame.
20 At that time ^aI will bring you back,
   Even at the time I gather you;
   For I will give you ¹fame and praise
   Among all the peoples of the earth,
   When I return your captives before your eyes,"
   Says the LORD.

3:10 ^aPs. 68:31;
Is. 18:1; Acts 8:27

3:11
^aIs. 2:12; 5:15;
Matt. 3:9

3:12 ^aIs. 14:32;
Zech. 13:8, 9

3:13
^aIs. 10:20–22;
[Mic. 4:7]
^bIs. 60:21
^cZech. 8:3, 16;
Rev. 14:5
^dEzek. 34:13–
15, 28

3:14 ^aIs. 12:6

3:15
^a[John 1:49]
^bEzek. 48:35;
[Rev. 7:15]

3:16 ^aIs. 35:3, 4
^bJob 4:3;
Heb. 12:12

3:17
^aZeph. 3:5, 15
^bDeut. 30:9;
Is. 62:5; 65:19;
Jer. 32:41

3:18 ^aLam. 2:6

3:19
^a[Ezek. 34:16;
Mic. 4:6, 7]

3:20 ^aIs. 11:12;
Ezek. 28:25;
Amos 9:14

3:15 ¹So with Heb. mss., LXX, Bg.; MT, Vg. *fear*   3:20 ¹Lit. *a name*

THE BOOK OF
HAGGAI

THE COMMAND TO BUILD GOD'S HOUSE
(Ezra 5:1)

1 In ᵃthe second year of King Darius, in the sixth month, on the first day of the month, the word of the LORD came by ᵇHaggai the prophet to ᶜZerubbabel the son of Shealtiel, governor of Judah, and to ᵈJoshua the son of ᵉJehozadak, the high priest, saying, 2"Thus speaks the LORD of hosts, saying: 'This people says, "The time has not come, the time that the LORD's house should be built."'"

3Then the word of the LORD ᵃcame by Haggai the prophet, saying, 4"*Is it* ᵃtime for you yourselves to dwell in your paneled houses, and this ¹temple *to lie* in ruins?" 5Now therefore, thus says the LORD of hosts: ᵃ"Consider your ways!

6 "You have ᵃsown much, and bring in little;
  You eat, but do not have enough;
  You drink, but you are not filled with drink;
  You clothe yourselves, but no one is warm;
  And ᵇhe who earns wages,
  Earns wages *to put* into a bag with holes."

7Thus says the LORD of hosts: "Consider your ways! 8Go up to the ᵃmountains and bring wood and build the ¹temple, that I may take pleasure in it and be glorified," says the LORD. 9ᵃ"*You* looked for much, but indeed *it came to* little; and when you brought it home, ᵇI blew it away. Why?" says the LORD of hosts. "Because of My house that *is in* ruins, while every one of you runs to his own house. 10Therefore ᵃthe heavens above you withhold the dew, and the earth withholds its fruit. 11For I ᵃcalled for a drought on the land and the mountains, on the grain and the new wine and the oil, on whatever the ground brings forth, on men and livestock, and on ᵇall the labor of *your* hands."

THE PEOPLE'S OBEDIENCE

12ᵃThen Zerubbabel the son of Shealtiel, and Joshua the son of Jehozadak, the high priest, with all the remnant of the people, obeyed the voice of the LORD their God, and the words of Haggai the prophet, as the LORD their God had sent him; and the people feared the presence of the LORD. 13Then Haggai, the LORD's messenger, spoke the LORD's message to the people, saying, ᵃ"I *am* with you, says the LORD." 14So ᵃthe LORD stirred up the spirit of Zerubbabel the son of Shealtiel, ᵇgovernor of Judah, and the spirit of Joshua the son of Jehozadak, the high priest, and the spirit of all the remnant of the people; ᶜand they came and worked on the house of the LORD of hosts, their God, 15on the twenty-fourth day of the sixth month, in the second year of King Darius.

1:1 ᵃEzra 4:24;
Hag. 2:10;
Zech. 1:1, 7
ᵇEzra 5:1; 6:14
ᶜ1 Chr. 3:19;
Ezra 2:2;
Neh. 7:7;
Zech. 4:6;
Matt. 1:12, 13
ᵈEzra 5:2, 3;
Zech. 6:11
ᵉ1 Chr. 6:15

1:3 ᵃEzra 5:1

1:4 ᵃ2 Sam. 7:2

1:5 ᵃLam. 3:40

1:6
ᵃDeut. 28:38–
40; Hos. 8:7;
Hag. 1:9, 10;
   2:16, 17
ᵇZech. 8:10

1:8 ᵃEzra 3:7

1:9 ᵃHag. 2:16
ᵇHag. 2:17

1:10 ᵃLev. 26:19;
Deut. 28:23;
1 Kin. 8:35;
Joel 1:18–20

1:11 ᵃ1 Kin. 17:1;
2 Kin. 8:1
ᵇHag. 2:17

1:12 ᵃEzra 5:2

1:13
ᵃ[Matt. 28:20;
Rom. 8:31]

1:14
ᵃ2 Chr. 36:22;
Ezra 1:1
ᵇHag. 2:21
ᶜEzra 5:2, 8;
Neh. 4:6

THE COMING GLORY OF GOD'S HOUSE

2 In the seventh *month,* on the twenty-first of the month, the word of the LORD came ¹by Haggai the prophet, saying: ²"Speak now to Zerubbabel the son of Shealtiel, governor of Judah, and to Joshua the son of Jehozadak, the high priest, and to the remnant of the people, saying: ³ᵃ'Who is left among you who saw this ¹temple in its former glory? And how do you see it now? In comparison with it, ᵇ*is this* not in your eyes as nothing? ⁴Yet now ᵃbe strong, Zerubbabel,' says the LORD; 'and be strong, Joshua, son of Jehozadak, the high priest; and be strong, all you people of the land,' says the LORD, 'and work; for I *am* with you,' says the LORD of hosts. ⁵ᵃ*According to* the word that I covenanted with you when you came out of Egypt, so ᵇMy Spirit remains among you; do not fear!'

⁶"For thus says the LORD of hosts: ᵃ'Once more (it *is* a little while) ᵇI will shake heaven and earth, the sea and dry land; ⁷and I will shake all nations, and they shall come to ᵃthe ¹Desire of All Nations, and I will fill this ²temple with ᵇglory,' says the LORD of hosts. ⁸'The silver *is* Mine, and the gold *is* Mine,' says the LORD of hosts. ⁹ᵃ'The glory of this latter ¹temple shall be greater than the former,' says the LORD of hosts. 'And in this place I will give ᵇpeace,' says the LORD of hosts."

THE PEOPLE ARE DEFILED

¹⁰On the twenty-fourth *day* of the ninth *month,* in the second year of Darius, the word of the LORD came by Haggai the prophet, saying, ¹¹"Thus says the LORD of hosts: 'Now, ᵃask the priests *concerning the* law, saying, ¹²"If one carries holy meat in the fold of his garment, and with the edge he touches bread or stew, wine or oil, or any food, will it become holy?"'"

Then the priests answered and said, "No."

¹³And Haggai said, "If *one who is* ᵃunclean *because* of a dead body touches any of these, will it be unclean?"

So the priests answered and said, "It shall be unclean."

¹⁴Then Haggai answered and said, ᵃ"'So is this people, and so is this nation before Me,' says the LORD, 'and so is every work of their hands; and what they offer there is unclean.

PROMISED BLESSING

¹⁵'And now, carefully ᵃconsider from this day forward: from before stone was laid upon stone in the temple of the LORD— ¹⁶since those *days,* ᵃwhen *one* came to a heap of twenty ephahs, there were *but* ten; when *one* came to the wine vat to draw out fifty baths from the press, there were *but* twenty. ¹⁷ᵃI struck you with blight and mildew and hail ᵇin all the labors of your hands; ᶜyet you did not *turn* to Me,' says the LORD. ¹⁸'Consider now from this day forward, from the twenty-fourth day of the ninth month, from ᵃthe day that the foundation of the LORD's temple was laid—consider it: ¹⁹ᵃIs the seed still in the barn? As yet the vine, the fig tree, the pomegranate, and the olive tree have not yielded *fruit. But* from this day I will ᵇbless *you.'"*

2:3
ᵃEzra 3:12, 13
ᵇZech. 4:10

2:4 ᵃDeut. 31:23;
1 Chr. 22:13;
28:20;
Zech. 8:9;
Eph. 6:10

2:5
ᵃEx. 29:45, 46
ᵇ[Neh. 9:20];
Is. 63:11, 14

2:6 ᵃHeb. 12:26
ᵇ[Joel 3:16]

2:7 ᵃGen. 49:10;
Mal. 3:1
ᵇ1 Kin. 8:11;
Is. 60:7;
Zech. 2:5

2:9 ᵃ[John 1:14]
ᵇPs. 85:8, 9;
Luke 2:14;
[Eph. 2:14]

2:11
ᵃLev. 10:10, 11;
Deut. 33:10;
Mal. 2:7

2:13
ᵃLev. 22:4–6;
Num. 19:11, 22

2:14 ᵃ[Titus 1:15]

2:15
ᵃHag. 1:5, 7;
2:18

2:16
ᵃHag. 1:6, 9;
Zech. 8:10

2:17
ᵃDeut. 28:22;
1 Kin. 8:37;
Amos 4:9
ᵇHag. 1:11
ᶜJer. 5:3;
Amos 4:6–11

2:18
ᵃEzra 5:1, 2, 16;
Zech. 8:9

2:19 ᵃZech. 8:12
ᵇPs. 128:1–6;
Jer. 31:12, 14;
[Mal. 3:10]

2:1 ¹Lit. *by the hand of*   2:3 ¹Lit. *house*   2:7 ¹Or *desire of all nations*
²Lit. *house*   2:9 ¹Lit. *house*

ZERUBBABEL CHOSEN AS A SIGNET

20And again the word of the LORD came to Haggai on the twenty-fourth day of the month, saying, 21"Speak to Zerubbabel, ªgovernor of Judah, saying:

ᵇ'I will shake heaven and earth.
22 ªI will overthrow the throne of kingdoms;
I will destroy the strength of the Gentile kingdoms.
ᵇI will overthrow the chariots
And those who ride in them;
The horses and their riders shall come down,
Every one by the sword of his brother.

23'In that day,' says the LORD of hosts, 'I will take you, Zerubbabel My servant, the son of Shealtiel,' says the LORD, ª'and will make you like a signet *ring*; for ᵇI have chosen you,' says the LORD of hosts."

2:21 ªEzra 5:2;
Hag. 1:1, 14;
Zech. 4:6–10
ᵇHag. 2:6, 7;
[Heb. 12:26, 27]

2:22
ª[Dan. 2:44;
Rev. 19:11–21]
ᵇPs. 46:9;
Ezek. 39:20;
Mic. 5:10;
Zech. 9:10

2:23 ªSong 8:6;
Jer. 22:24
ᵇIs. 42:1; 43:10

THE BOOK OF
ZECHARIAH

A CALL TO REPENTANCE
(Ezra 5:1)

1 In the eighth month ᵃof the second year of Darius, the word of the LORD came ᵇto Zechariah the son of Berechiah, the son of ᶜIddo the prophet, saying, 2"The LORD has been very angry with your fathers. 3Therefore say to them, 'Thus says the LORD of hosts: "Return ᵃto Me," says the LORD of hosts, "and I will return to you," says the LORD of hosts. 4"Do not be like your fathers, ᵃto whom the former prophets preached, saying, 'Thus says the LORD of hosts: ᵇ"Turn now from your evil ways and your evil deeds."' But they did not hear nor heed Me," says the LORD.

5 "Your fathers, where *are* they?
   And the prophets, do they live forever?
6 Yet surely ᵃMy words and My statutes,
   Which I commanded My servants the prophets,
   Did they not overtake your fathers?

   "So they returned and said:

   ᵇ'Just as the LORD of hosts determined to do to us,
   According to our ways and according to our deeds,
   So He has dealt with us.'"'"

VISION OF THE HORSES

7On the twenty-fourth day of the eleventh month, which is the month Shebat, in the second year of Darius, the word of the LORD came to Zechariah the son of Berechiah, the son of Iddo the prophet: 8I saw by night, and behold, ᵃa man riding on a red horse, and it stood among the myrtle trees in the hollow; and behind him *were* ᵇhorses: red, sorrel, and white. 9Then I said, ᵃ"My lord, what *are* these?" So the angel who talked with me said to me, "I will show you what they *are.*"

10And the man who stood among the myrtle trees answered and said, ᵃ"These *are the ones* whom the LORD has sent to walk to and fro throughout the earth."

11ᵃSo they answered the Angel of the LORD, who stood among the myrtle trees, and said, "We have walked to and fro throughout the earth, and behold, all the earth is ¹resting quietly."

THE LORD WILL COMFORT ZION

12Then the Angel of the LORD answered and said, "O LORD of hosts, ᵃhow long will You not have mercy on Jerusalem and on the cities of Judah, against which You were angry ᵇthese seventy years?"

1:11 ¹Lit. *sitting and quiet*

[13]And the LORD answered the angel who talked to me, *with* [a]good *and* comforting words. [14]So the angel who spoke with me said to me, [1]"Proclaim, saying, 'Thus says the LORD of hosts:

"I am [a]zealous[2] for Jerusalem
And for Zion with great [3]zeal.
[15] I am exceedingly angry with the nations at ease;
For [a]I was a little angry,
And they helped—*but* with evil *intent.*

[16]Therefore thus says the LORD:

[a]"I am returning to Jerusalem with mercy;
My [b]house [c]shall be built in it," says the LORD of hosts,
"And [d]a *surveyor's* line shall be stretched out over Jerusalem."'

[17]"Again proclaim, saying, 'Thus says the LORD of hosts:

"My cities shall again [1]spread out through prosperity;
[a]The LORD will again comfort Zion,
And [b]will again choose Jerusalem."'"

VISION OF THE HORNS

[18]Then I raised my eyes and looked, and there *were* four [a]horns. [19]And I said to the angel who talked with me, "What *are* these?"

So he answered me, [a]"These *are* the [1]horns that have scattered Judah, Israel, and Jerusalem."

[20]Then the LORD showed me four craftsmen. [21]And I said, "What are these coming to do?"

So he said, "These *are* the [a]horns that scattered Judah, so that no one could lift up his head; but [1]the craftsmen are coming to terrify them, to cast out the horns of the nations that [b]lifted up *their* horn against the land of Judah to scatter it."

VISION OF THE MEASURING LINE

2 Then I raised my eyes and looked, and behold, [a]a man with a measuring line in his hand. [2]So I said, "Where are you going?"

And he said to me, [a]"To measure Jerusalem, to see what *is* its width and what *is* its length."

[3]And there *was* the angel who talked with me, going out; and another angel was coming out to meet him, [4]who said to him, "Run, speak to this young man, saying: [a]'Jerusalem shall be inhabited *as* towns without walls, because of the multitude of men and livestock in it. [5]For I,' says the LORD, 'will be [a]a wall of fire all around her, [b]and I will be the glory in her midst.'"

FUTURE JOY OF ZION AND MANY NATIONS

[6]"Up, up! Flee [a]from the land of the north," says the LORD; "for I have [b]spread you abroad like the four winds of heaven," says the LORD. [7]"Up, Zion! [a]Escape, you who dwell with the daughter of Babylon."

[8]For thus says the LORD of hosts: "He sent Me after glory, to the nations which plunder you; for he who [a]touches you

1:13 [a]Jer. 29:10
1:14 [a]Joel 2:18; Zech. 8:2
1:15 [a]Is. 47:6
1:16 [a][Is. 12:1; 54:8; Zech. 2:10; 8:3]
[b]Ezra 6:14, 15; Hag. 1:4; Zech. 4:9
[c]2 Chr. 36:23; Ezra 1:2, 3; Is. 44:28
[d]Zech. 2:1–3
1:17 [a][Is. 40:1, 2; 51:3]
[b]Is. 14:1; Zech. 2:12
1:18 [a][Lam. 2:17]
1:19 [a]Ezra 4:1, 4, 7
1:21 [a][Ps. 75:10]
[b]Ps. 75:4, 5
2:1 [a]Jer. 31:39; Ezek. 40:3; 47:3; Zech. 1:16
2:2 [a]Rev. 11:1
2:4 [a]Jer. 31:27
2:5 [a][Is. 26:1]
[b][Is. 60:19]
2:6 [a]Is. 48:20
[b]Deut. 28:64
2:7 [a]Is. 48:20; Jer. 51:6; [Rev. 18:4]
2:8 [a]Deut. 32:10; Ps. 17:8

1:14 [1]Lit. *Cry out*   [2]Or *jealous*   [3]Or *jealousy*   1:17 [1]Or *overflow with good*
1:19 [1]*Kingdoms or powers*   1:21 [1]Lit. *these*

touches the ¹apple of His eye. ⁹For surely I will ªshake My hand against them, and they shall become ¹spoil for their servants. Then ᵇyou will know that the LORD of hosts has sent Me.

¹⁰ª"Sing and rejoice, O daughter of Zion! For behold, I am coming and I ᵇwill dwell in your midst," says the LORD. ¹¹ª"Many nations shall be joined to the LORD ᵇin that day, and they shall become ᶜMy people. And I will dwell in your midst. Then ᵈyou will know that the LORD of hosts has sent Me to you. ¹²And the LORD will ªtake possession of Judah as His inheritance in the Holy Land, and will again choose Jerusalem. ¹³ªBe silent, all flesh, before the LORD, for He is aroused ᵇfrom His holy habitation!"

VISION OF THE HIGH PRIEST

3 Then he showed me ªJoshua the high priest standing before the Angel of the LORD, and ᵇSatan¹ standing at his right hand to oppose him. ²And the LORD said to Satan, ª"The LORD rebuke you, Satan! The LORD who ᵇhas chosen Jerusalem rebuke you! ᶜ*Is* this not a brand plucked from the fire?"

³Now Joshua was clothed with ªfilthy garments, and was standing before the Angel.

⁴Then He answered and spoke to those who stood before Him, saying, "Take away the filthy garments from him." And to him He said, "See, I have removed your iniquity from you, ªand I will clothe you with rich robes."

⁵And I said, "Let them put a clean ªturban on his head."

So they put a clean turban on his head, and they put the clothes on him. And the Angel of the LORD stood by.

THE COMING BRANCH

⁶Then the Angel of the LORD admonished Joshua, saying, ⁷"Thus says the LORD of hosts:

'If you will walk in My ways,
And if you will ªkeep My command,
Then you shall also ᵇjudge My house,
And likewise have charge of My courts;
I will give you places to walk
Among these who ᶜstand here.

8   'Hear, O Joshua, the high priest,
You and your companions who sit before you,
For they are ªª¹ wondrous sign;
For behold, I am bringing forth ᵇMy Servant the
    ᶜBRANCH.
9   For behold, the stone
That I have laid before Joshua:
ªUpon the stone *are* ᵇseven eyes.
Behold, I will engrave its inscription,'
Says the LORD of hosts,
'And ᶜI will remove the iniquity of that land in one
    day.
10   ªIn that day,' says the LORD of hosts,
'Everyone will invite his neighbor
ᵇUnder his vine and under his fig tree.'"

2:9 ªIs. 19:16
ᵇZech. 4:9
2:10 ªIs. 12:6
ᵇ[Lev. 26:12]
2:11 ª[Is. 2:2, 3]
ᵇZech. 3:10
ᶜEx. 12:49
ᵈEzek. 33:33
2:12
ª[Deut. 32:9];
Ps. 33:12;
Jer. 10:16
2:13 ªHab. 2:20;
Zeph. 1:7
ᵇPs. 68:5
3:1 ªEzra 5:2;
Hag. 1:1;
Zech. 6:11
ᵇ1 Chr. 21:1;
Job 1:6;
Ps. 109:6;
[Rev. 12:9, 10]
3:2 ªMark 9:25;
[Jude 9]
ᵇ[Rom. 8:33]
ᶜAmos 4:11;
Jude 23
3:3 ªEzra 9:15;
Is. 64:6
3:4 ªGen. 3:21;
Is. 61:10
3:5 ªEx. 29:6
3:7 ªLev. 8:35;
Ezek. 44:16
ᵇDeut. 17:9, 12
ᶜZech. 3:4
3:8 ªPs. 71:7
ᵇIs. 42:1 ᶜIs. 11:1;
53:2; Jer. 23:5;
33:15; Zech. 6:12
3:9
ª[Zech. 4:10;
Rev. 5:6]
ᵇPs. 118:22
ᶜJer. 31:34;
50:20; Zech. 3:4
3:10 ªZech. 2:11
ᵇ1 Kin. 4:25;
Is. 36:16;
Mic. 4:4

2:8 ¹Lit. *pupil*   2:9 ¹*booty* or *plunder*   3:1 ¹Lit. *the Adversary*   3:8 ¹Lit. *men of a sign* or *wonder*

VISION OF THE LAMPSTAND AND OLIVE TREES

4 Now [a]the angel who talked with me came back and wakened me, [b]as a man who is wakened out of his sleep. [2]And he said to me, "What do you see?"

So I said, "I am looking, and there *is* [a]a lampstand of solid gold with a bowl on top of it, [b]and on the *stand* seven lamps with seven pipes to the seven lamps. [3a]Two olive trees *are* by it, one at the right of the bowl and the other at its left." [4]So I answered and spoke to the angel who talked with me, saying, "What *are* these, my lord?"

[5]Then the angel who talked with me answered and said to me, "Do you not know what these are?"

And I said, "No, my lord."

[6]So he answered and said to me:

"This *is* the word of the LORD to [a]Zerubbabel:
[b]'Not by might nor by power, but by My Spirit,'
Says the LORD of hosts.
[7] 'Who *are* you, [a]O great mountain?
Before Zerubbabel *you shall become* a plain!
And he shall bring forth [b]the capstone
[c]With shouts of "Grace, grace to it!"'"

[8]Moreover the word of the LORD came to me, saying:

[9] "The hands of Zerubbabel
[a]Have laid the foundation of this [1]temple;
His hands [b]shall also finish *it.*
Then [c]you will know
That the [d]LORD of hosts has sent Me to you.
[10] For who has despised the day of [a]small things?
For these seven rejoice to see
The [1]plumb line in the hand of Zerubbabel.
[b]They are the eyes of the LORD,
Which scan to and fro throughout the whole earth."

[11]Then I answered and said to him, "What *are* these [a]two olive trees—at the right of the lampstand and at its left?" [12]And I further answered and said to him, "What *are these* two olive branches that *drip* [1]into the receptacles of the two gold pipes from which the golden *oil* drains?"

[13]Then he answered me and said, "Do you not know what these *are?*"

And I said, "No, my lord."

[14]So he said, [a]"These *are* the two [1]anointed ones, [b]who stand beside the Lord of the whole earth."

VISION OF THE FLYING SCROLL

5 Then I turned and raised my eyes, and saw there a flying [a]scroll.

[2]And he said to me, "What do you see?"

So I answered, "I see a flying scroll. Its length *is* twenty cubits and its width ten cubits."

[3]Then he said to me, "This *is* the [a]curse that goes out over the face of the whole earth: 'Every thief shall be expelled,' according *to* this side of *the scroll;* and, 'Every perjurer shall be expelled,' according *to* that side of it."

4:1 [a]Zech. 1:9; 2:3 [b]Dan. 8:18
4:2 [a]Rev. 1:12 [b]Ex. 25:37; [Rev. 4:5]
4:3 [a]Rev. 11:3, 4
4:6 [a]Hag. 1:1 [b]Is. 30:1; Hos. 1:7; Hag. 2:4, 5
4:7 [a]Ps. 114:4, 6; Is. 40:4; Jer. 51:25; Nah. 1:5; Zech. 14:4, 5; [Matt. 21:21] [b]Ps. 118:22 [c]Ezra 3:10, 11, 13; Ps. 84:11
4:9 [a]Ezra 3:8–10; 5:16; Hag. 2:18 [b]Ezra 6:14, 15; Zech. 6:12, 13 [c]Zech. 2:9, 11; 6:15 [d][Is. 43:16]; Zech. 2:8
4:10 [a]Neh. 4:2–4; Amos 7:2, 5; Hag. 2:3 [b]2 Chr. 16:9; Prov. 15:3; Zech. 3:9
4:11 [a]Zech. 4:3; Rev. 11:4
4:14 [a]Rev. 11:4 [b]Zech. 3:1–7
5:1 [a]Jer. 36:2; Ezek. 2:9; Rev. 5:1
5:3 [a]Mal. 4:6

4:9 [1]Lit. *house*   4:10 [1]Lit. *plummet stone*   4:12 [1]Lit. *into the hands of*
4:14 [1]Lit. *sons of fresh oil*

4 "I will send out *the curse*," says the Lord of hosts;
"It shall enter the house of the ªthief
And the house of ᵇthe one who swears falsely by My
    name.
It shall remain in the midst of his house
And consume ᶜit, with its timber and stones."

VISION OF THE WOMAN IN A BASKET

5Then the angel who talked with me came out and said to me, "Lift your eyes now, and see what this *is* that goes forth."

6So I asked, "What *is* it?" And he said, "It *is* a ¹basket that is going forth."

He also said, "This *is* their resemblance throughout the earth: 7Here *is* a lead disc lifted up, and this *is* a woman sitting inside the basket"; 8then he said, "This *is* Wickedness!" And he thrust her down into the basket, and threw the lead ¹cover over its mouth. 9Then I raised my eyes and looked, and there *were* two women, coming with the wind in their wings; for they had wings like the wings of a ªstork, and they lifted up the basket between earth and heaven.

10So I said to the ªangel who talked with me, "Where are they carrying the basket?"

11And he said to me, "To ªbuild a house for it in ᵇthe land of ¹Shinar; when it is ready, *the basket* will be set there on its base."

VISION OF THE FOUR CHARIOTS

6 Then I turned and raised my eyes and looked, and behold, four chariots *were* coming from between two mountains, and the mountains *were* mountains of bronze. 2With the first chariot *were* ªred horses, with the second chariot ᵇblack horses, 3with the third chariot white horses, and with the fourth chariot dappled horses—strong *steeds*. 4Then I answered ªand said to the angel who talked with me, "What *are* these, my lord?"

5And the angel answered and said to me, ª"These *are* four spirits of heaven, who go out from *their* ᵇstation before the Lord of all the earth. 6¹The one with the black horses is going to ªthe north country, the white are going after them, and the dappled are going toward the south country." 7Then the strong *steeds* went out, eager to go, that they might ªwalk to and fro throughout the earth. And He said, "Go, walk to and fro throughout the earth." So they walked to and fro throughout the earth. 8And He called to me, and spoke to me, saying, "See, those who go toward the north country have given rest to My ªSpirit in the north country."

THE COMMAND TO CROWN JOSHUA

9Then the word of the Lord came to me, saying: 10"Receive *the gift* from the captives—from Heldai, Tobijah, and Jedaiah, who have come from Babylon—and go the same day and enter the house of Josiah the son of Zephaniah. 11Take the silver and gold, make ªan¹ elaborate crown, and set *it* on the head of ᵇJoshua the son of Jehozadak, the high priest. 12Then speak to him, saying, 'Thus says the Lord of hosts, saying:

5:4 ªEx. 20:15;
Lev. 19:11
ᵇEx. 20:7;
Lev. 19:12;
Is. 48:1; Jer. 5:2;
Zech. 8:17;
Mal. 3:5
ᶜLev. 14:34, 35;
Job 18:15

5:9
ªLev. 11:13, 19;
Ps. 104:17;
Jer. 8:7

5:10 ªZech. 5:5

5:11
ªJer. 29:5, 28
ᵇGen. 10:10;
Is. 11:11; Dan. 1:2

6:2 ªZech. 1:8;
Rev. 6:4
ᵇRev. 6:5

6:4 ªZech. 5:10

6:5 ª[Ps. 104:4;
Heb. 1:7, 14]
ᵇ1 Kin. 22:19;
Dan. 7:10;
Zech. 4:14;
Luke 1:19

6:6 ªJer. 1:14;
Ezek. 1:4

6:7 ªGen. 13:17;
Zech. 1:10

6:8 ªEccl. 10:4

6:11 ªEx. 29:6
ᵇEzra 3:2;
Hag. 1:1;
Zech. 3:1

5:6 ¹Heb. *ephah,* a measuring container, and so elsewhere   5:8 ¹Lit. *stone*
5:11 ¹Babylon   6:6 ¹The chariot   6:11 ¹Lit. *crowns*

"Behold, ᵃthe Man whose name *is* the ᵇBRANCH!
From His place He shall ¹branch out,
ᶜAnd He shall build the temple of the LORD;
13 Yes, He shall build the temple of the LORD.
He ᵃshall bear the glory,
And shall sit and rule on His throne;
So ᵇHe shall be a priest on His throne,
And the counsel of peace shall be between ¹them both."'

¹⁴"Now the ¹elaborate crown shall be ᵃfor a memorial in the temple of the LORD ²for Helem, Tobijah, Jedaiah, and Hen the son of Zephaniah. ¹⁵Even ᵃthose from afar shall come and build the temple of the LORD. Then you shall know that the LORD of hosts has sent Me to you. And *this* shall come to pass if you diligently obey the voice of the LORD your God."

OBEDIENCE BETTER THAN FASTING

7 Now in the fourth year of King Darius it came to pass *that* the word of the LORD came to Zechariah, on the fourth *day* of the ninth month, Chislev, ²when ¹*the people* sent ²Sherezer, with Regem-Melech and his men, *to* ³the house of God, ⁴to pray before the LORD, ³*and* to ᵃask the priests who *were* in the house of the LORD of hosts, and the prophets, saying, "Should I weep in ᵇthe fifth month and ¹fast as I have done for so many years?"

⁴Then the word of the LORD of hosts came to me, saying, ⁵"Say to all the people of the land, and to the priests: 'When you ᵃfasted and mourned in the fifth ᵇand seventh *months* ᶜduring those seventy years, did you really fast ᵈfor Me—for Me? ⁶ᵃWhen you eat and when you drink, do you not eat and drink *for yourselves*? ⁷*Should you* not *have obeyed* the words which the LORD proclaimed through the ᵃformer prophets when Jerusalem and the cities around it were inhabited and prosperous, and ᵇthe ¹South and the Lowland were inhabited?'"

DISOBEDIENCE RESULTED IN CAPTIVITY

⁸Then the word of the LORD came to Zechariah, saying, ⁹"Thus says the LORD of hosts:

ᵃ'Execute true justice,
Show ¹mercy and compassion
Everyone to his brother.
10 ᵃDo not oppress the widow or the fatherless,
The alien or the poor.
ᵇLet none of you plan evil in his heart
Against his brother.'

¹¹"But they refused to heed, ᵃshrugged¹ their shoulders, and ᵇstopped² their ears so that they could not hear. ¹²Yes, they made their ᵃhearts like flint, ᵇrefusing to hear the law and the words which the LORD of hosts had sent by His Spirit through the former prophets. ᶜThus great wrath came from the LORD of hosts. ¹³Therefore it happened, *that* just as He proclaimed and they would not hear, so ᵃthey called out and

---

6:12 ᵃJohn 1:45
ᵇIs. 4:2; 11:1;
Jer. 23:5; 33:15;
Zech. 3:8
ᶜ[Matt. 16:18;
Eph. 2:20;
Heb. 3:3]

6:13 ᵃIs. 22:24
ᵇPs. 110:4;
[Heb. 3:1]

6:14 ᵃEx. 12:14;
Mark 14:9

6:15 ᵃIs. 57:19;
[Eph. 2:13]

7:3 ᵃDeut. 17:9;
Mal. 2:7
ᵇZech. 8:19

7:5
ᵃ[Is. 58:1–9]
ᵇJer. 41:1
ᶜZech. 1:12
ᵈ[Rom. 14:6]

7:6
ᵃDeut. 12:7;
14:26;
1 Chr. 29:22

7:7 ᵃIs. 1:16–20;
Jer. 7:5, 23;
Zech. 1:4
ᵇJer. 17:26

7:9 ᵃIs. 58:6, 7;
Jer. 7:28

7:10 ᵃEx. 22:22;
Ps. 72:4; Is. 1:17;
Jer. 5:28
ᵇPs. 36:4;
Ezek. 38:10; 45:9;
Mic. 2:1;
Zech. 8:16, 17

7:11 ᵃNeh. 9:29
ᵇJer. 17:23;
Acts 7:57

7:12 ᵃEzek. 11:19
ᵇNeh. 9:29, 30
ᶜ2 Chr. 36:16;
Dan. 9:11, 12

7:13
ᵃProv. 1:24–28;
Is. 1:15; Jer. 11:11;
Mic. 3:4

6:12 ¹Lit. *sprout up*   6:13 ¹Both offices   6:14 ¹Lit. *crowns*   ²So with MT, Tg., Vg.; Syr. *for Heldai* (cf. v. 10); LXX *for the patient ones*   7:2 ¹Lit. *they,* cf. v. 5   ²Or *Sar-Ezer*   ³Heb. *Bethel*   ⁴Or *to entreat the favor of*   7:3 ¹Lit. *consecrate myself*   7:7 ¹Heb. *Negev*   7:9 ¹Or *lovingkindness*   7:11 ¹Lit. *gave a stubborn* or *rebellious shoulder*   ²Lit. *made their ears heavy*

I would not listen," says the LORD of hosts. 14"But ªI scattered them with a whirlwind among all the nations which they had not known. Thus the land became desolate after them, so that no one passed through or returned; for they made the pleasant land desolate."

JERUSALEM, HOLY CITY OF THE FUTURE

8 Again the word of the LORD of hosts came, saying, 2"Thus says the LORD of hosts:

ª'I am ¹zealous for Zion with great ²zeal;
With great ³fervor I am zealous for her.'

3"Thus says the LORD:

ª'I will return to Zion,
And ᵇdwell in the midst of Jerusalem.
Jerusalem ᶜshall be called the City of Truth,
ᵈThe Mountain of the LORD of hosts,
ᵉThe Holy Mountain.'

4"Thus says the LORD of hosts:

ª'Old men and old women shall again sit
In the streets of Jerusalem,
Each one with his staff in his hand
Because of ¹great age.
5   The streets of the city
Shall be ªfull of boys and girls
Playing in its streets.'

6"Thus says the LORD of hosts:

'If it is ¹marvelous in the eyes of the remnant of this
     people in these days,
ªWill it also be marvelous in My eyes?'
Says the LORD of hosts.

7"Thus says the LORD of hosts:

'Behold, ªI will save My people from the land of the ¹east
And from the land of the ²west;
8   I will ªbring them *back,*
And they shall dwell in the midst of Jerusalem.
ᵇThey shall be My people
And I will be their God,
ᶜIn truth and righteousness.'

9"Thus says the LORD of hosts:

ª'Let your hands be strong,
You who have been hearing in these days
These words by the mouth of ᵇthe prophets,
Who *spoke* in ᶜthe day the foundation was laid
For the house of the LORD of hosts,
That the temple might be built.
10   For before these days
There were no ªwages for man nor any hire for beast;
There was no peace from the enemy for whoever went
     out or came in;
For I set all men, everyone, against his neighbor.

7:14 ªLev. 26:33;
Deut. 4:27;
28:64; Neh. 1:8

8:2 ªJoel 2:18;
Nah. 1:2;
Zech. 1:14

8:3 ªZech. 1:16
ᵇZech. 2:10, 11
ᶜIs. 1:21
ᵈ[Is. 2:2, 3]
ᵉJer. 31:23

8:4 ª1 Sam. 2:31;
Is. 65:20

8:5
ªJer. 30:19, 20

8:6 ª[Gen. 18:14;
Luke 1:37]

8:7 ªPs. 107:3;
Is. 11:11;
Ezek. 37:21

8:8 ªZeph. 3:20;
Zech. 10:10
ᵇ[Jer. 30:22;
31:1, 33;
Zech. 13:9]
ᶜJer. 4:2

8:9 ª1 Chr. 22:13;
Is. 35:4; Hag. 2:4
ᵇEzra 5:1, 2; 6:14;
Zech. 4:9
ᶜHag. 2:18

8:10 ªHag. 1:6, 9

8:2 ¹Or *jealous*   ²Or *jealousy*   ³Lit. *heat or rage*   8:4 ¹Lit. *many days*
8:6 ¹Or *wonderful*   8:7 ¹Lit. *rising sun*   ²Lit. *setting sun*

¹¹ᵃBut now I *will* not *treat* the remnant of this people as in the former days,' says the LORD of hosts.

12 'Forᵃ the ¹seed *shall be* prosperous,
    The vine shall give its fruit,
    ᵇThe ground shall give her increase,
    And ᶜthe heavens shall give their dew—
    I will cause the remnant of this people
    To possess all these.
13 And it shall come to pass
    That just as you were ᵃa curse among the nations,
    O house of Judah and house of Israel,
    So I will save you, and ᵇyou shall be a blessing.
    Do not fear,
    Let your hands be strong.'

¹⁴"For thus says the LORD of hosts:

ᵃ'Just as I determined to ¹punish you
    When your fathers provoked Me to wrath,'
    Says the LORD of hosts,
    ᵇ'And I would not relent,
15 So again in these days
    I am determined to do good
    To Jerusalem and to the house of Judah.
    Do not fear.
16 These *are* the things you shall ᵃdo:
    ᵇSpeak each man the truth to his neighbor;
    Give judgment in your gates for truth, justice, and peace;
17 ᵃLet none of you think evil in ¹your heart against your
        neighbor;
    And do not love a false oath.
    For all these *are things* that I hate,'
    Says the LORD."

¹⁸Then the word of the LORD of hosts came to me, saying,
¹⁹"Thus says the LORD of hosts:

ᵃ'The fast of the fourth *month,*
    ᵇThe fast of the fifth,
    ᶜThe fast of the seventh,
    ᵈAnd the fast of the tenth,
    Shall be ᵉjoy and gladness and cheerful feasts
    For the house of Judah.
    ᶠTherefore love truth and peace.'

²⁰"Thus says the LORD of hosts:

'Peoples shall yet come,
    Inhabitants of many cities;
21 The inhabitants of one *city* shall go to another, saying,
    ᵃ"Let us continue to go and pray before the LORD,
    And seek the LORD of hosts.
    I myself will go also."
22 Yes, ᵃmany peoples and strong nations
    Shall come to seek the LORD of hosts in Jerusalem,
    And to pray before the LORD.'

²³"Thus says the LORD of hosts: 'In those days ten men
ᵃfrom every language of the nations shall ᵇgrasp the ¹sleeve of

---

8:11 ᵃ[Ps. 103:9];
  Is. 12:1;
  Hag. 2:15–19

8:12 ᵃJoel 2:22
  ᵇPs. 67:6
  ᶜHag. 1:10

8:13 ᵃJer. 42:18
  ᵇGen. 12:2;
  Ruth 4:11, 12;
  Is. 19:24, 25;
  Ezek. 34:26;
  [Zeph. 3:20]

8:14 ᵃJer. 31:28
  ᵇ[2 Chr. 36:16]

8:16
  ᵃZech. 7:9, 10
  ᵇPs. 15:2;
  [Prov. 12:17–19];
  Zech. 8:3;
  [Eph. 4:25]

8:17 ᵃProv. 3:29;
  Jer. 4:14;
  Zech. 7:10

8:19 ᵃJer. 52:6
  ᵇJer. 52:12
  ᶜ2 Kin. 25:25;
  Jer. 41:1, 2
  ᵈJer. 52:4
  ᵉEsth. 8:17
  ᶠZech. 8:16;
  Luke 1:74, 75

8:21 ᵃ[Is. 2:2, 3;
  Mic. 4:1, 2]

8:22 ᵃIs. 60:3;
  66:23;
  [Zech. 14:16–21]

8:23 ᵃIs. 3:6
  ᵇ[Is. 45:14]

8:12 ¹Lit. *seed of peace*   8:14 ¹Lit. *bring calamity to you*   8:17 ¹Lit. *his*
8:23 ¹Lit. *wing,* corner of a garment

a Jewish man, saying, "Let us go with you, for we have heard ᶜ*that* God *is* with you."'"

ISRAEL DEFENDED AGAINST ENEMIES

9 The ¹burden of the word of the LORD
Against the land of Hadrach,
And ᵃDamascus its resting place
(For ᵇthe eyes of men
And all the tribes of Israel
Are on the LORD);

2 Also *against* ᵃHamath, *which* borders on it,
And *against* ᵇTyre and ᶜSidon, though they are very ᵈwise.

3 For Tyre built herself a tower,
Heaped up silver like the dust,
And gold like the mire of the streets.

4 Behold, ᵃthe Lord will cast her out;
He will destroy ᵇher power in the sea,
And she will be devoured by fire.

5 Ashkelon shall see *it* and fear;
Gaza also shall be very sorrowful;
And ᵃEkron, for He dried up her expectation.
The king shall perish from Gaza,
And Ashkelon shall not be inhabited.

6 "A¹ mixed race shall settle ᵃin Ashdod,
And I will cut off the pride of the ᵇPhilistines.

7 I will take away the blood from his mouth,
And the abominations from between his teeth.
But he who remains, even he *shall be* for our God,
And shall be like a leader in Judah,
And Ekron like a Jebusite.

8 ᵃI will camp around My house
Because of the army,
Because of him who passes by and him who returns.
No more shall an oppressor pass through them,
For now I have seen with My eyes.

THE COMING KING

(Matt. 21:5; John 12:14, 15)

9 "Rejoice ᵃgreatly, O daughter of Zion!
Shout, O daughter of Jerusalem!
Behold, ᵇyour King is coming to you;
He *is* just and having salvation,
Lowly and riding on a donkey,
A colt, the foal of a donkey.

10 I ᵃwill cut off the chariot from Ephraim
And the horse from Jerusalem;
The ᵇbattle bow shall be cut off.
He shall speak peace to the nations;
His dominion *shall be* ᶜ'from sea to sea,
And from the River to the ends of the earth.'

GOD WILL SAVE HIS PEOPLE

11 "As for you also,
Because of the blood of your covenant,
I will set your ᵃprisoners free from the waterless pit.

8:23
ᶜ1 Cor. 14:25

9:1 ᵃIs. 17:1;
Jer. 23:33
ᵇAmos 1:3–5

9:2 ᵃJer. 49:23
ᵇIs. 23;
Jer. 25:22; 47:4;
Ezek. 26;
Amos 1:9, 10
ᶜ1 Kin. 17:9
ᵈEzek. 28:3

9:4 ᵃIs. 23:1
ᵇEzek. 26:17

9:5 ᵃZeph. 2:4, 5

9:6 ᵃAmos 1:8;
Zeph. 2:4
ᵇEzek. 25:15–17

9:8 ᵃ[Ps. 34:7]

9:9
ᵃZeph. 3:14, 15;
Zech. 2:10
ᵇ[Ps. 110:1];
Is. 9:6, 7;
Jer. 23:5, 6];
Matt. 21:5;
Mark 11:7, 9;
Luke 19:38;
John 12:15

9:10 ᵃHos. 1:7;
Mic. 5:10
ᵇPs. 46:9;
Is. 2:4;
Hos. 2:18;
Mic. 4:3
ᶜPs. 72:8

9:11 ᵃIs. 42:7

9:1 ¹oracle, prophecy   9:6 ¹Lit. An illegitimate one

12 Return to the stronghold,
  ^aYou prisoners of hope.
  Even today I declare
  That I will restore ^bdouble to you.
13 For I have bent Judah, My *bow,*
  Fitted the bow with Ephraim,
  And raised up your sons, O Zion,
  Against your sons, O Greece,
  And made you like the sword of a mighty man."

14 Then the LORD will be seen over them,
  And ^aHis arrow will go forth like lightning.
  The Lord GOD will blow the trumpet,
  And go ^bwith whirlwinds from the south.
15 The LORD of hosts will ^adefend them;
  They shall devour and subdue with slingstones.
  They shall drink *and* roar as if with wine;
  They shall be filled *with blood* like ¹basins,
  Like the corners of the altar.
16 The LORD their God will ^asave them in that day,
  As the flock of His people.
  For ^bthey *shall be like* the ¹jewels of a crown,
  ^cLifted like a banner over His land—
17 For ^ahow great is ¹its goodness
  And how great its ^bbeauty!
  ^cGrain shall make the young men thrive,
  And new wine the young women.

RESTORATION OF JUDAH AND ISRAEL

10 Ask ^athe LORD for ^brain
  In ^cthe time of the ¹latter rain.
  The LORD will make ²flashing clouds;
  He will give them showers of rain,
  Grass in the field for everyone.
2 For the ^aidols¹ speak delusion;
  The diviners envision ^blies,
  And tell false dreams;
  They ^ccomfort in vain.
  Therefore *the people* wend their way like ^dsheep;
  They are ²in trouble ^ebecause *there is* no shepherd.
3 "My anger is kindled against the ^ashepherds,
  ^bAnd I will punish the ¹goatherds.
  For the LORD of hosts ^cwill visit His flock,
  The house of Judah,
  And ^dwill make them as His royal horse in the battle.
4 From him comes ^athe cornerstone,
  From him ^bthe tent peg,
  From him the battle bow,
  From him every ¹ruler together.
5 They shall be like mighty men,
  Who ^atread down *their enemies*
  In the mire of the streets in the battle.
  They shall fight because the LORD is with them,
  And the riders on horses shall be put to shame.

9:12 ^aIs. 49:9;
Jer. 17:13;
Heb. 6:18–20
^bIs. 61:7
9:14
^aPs. 18:14;
Hab. 3:11
^bIs. 21:1
9:15 ^aIs. 37:35;
Zech. 12:8
9:16
^aJer. 31:10, 11
^bIs. 62:3;
Mal. 3:17
^cIs. 11:12
9:17 ^a[Ps. 31:19]
^b[Ps. 45:1–16]
^cJoel 3:18
10:1 ^a[Jer. 14:22]
^b[Deut. 11:13, 14]
^c[Joel 2:23]
10:2 ^aJer. 10:8
^bJer. 27:9;
[Ezek. 13]
^cJob 13:4
^dJer. 50:6, 17
^eEzek. 34:5–8;
Matt. 9:36;
Mark 6:34
10:3
^aJer. 25:34–36;
Ezek. 34:2;
Zech. 11:17
^bEzek. 34:17
^cLuke 1:68
^dSong 1:9
10:4 ^aIs. 28:16
^bIs. 22:23
10:5 ^aPs. 18:42

9:15 ¹Sacrificial basins   **9:16** ¹Lit. *stones*   **9:17** ¹Lit. *His*   **10:1** ¹Spring rain
²Or *lightning flashes*   **10:2** ¹Heb. *teraphim*   ²*afflicted*   **10:3** ¹Leaders
10:4 ¹Or *despot*

6 "I will strengthen the house of Judah,
And I will save the house of Joseph.
ᵃI will bring them back,
Because I ᵇhave mercy on them.
They shall be as though I had not cast them aside;
For I *am* the LORD their God,
And I ᶜwill hear them.
7 *Those of* Ephraim shall be like a mighty man,
And their ᵃheart shall rejoice as if with wine.
Yes, their children shall see *it* and be glad;
Their heart shall rejoice in the LORD.
8 I will ᵃwhistle for them and gather them,
For I will redeem them;
ᵇAnd they shall increase as they once increased.

9 "Iᵃ will ¹sow them among the peoples,
And they shall ᵇremember Me in far countries;
They shall live, together with their children,
And they shall return.
10 ᵃI will also bring them back from the land of Egypt,
And gather them from Assyria.
I will bring them into the land of Gilead and Lebanon,
ᵇUntil no *more room* is found for them.
11 ᵃHe shall pass through the sea with affliction,
And strike the waves of the sea:
All the depths of ¹the River shall dry up.
Then ᵇthe pride of Assyria shall be brought down,
And ᶜthe scepter of Egypt shall depart.
12 "So I will strengthen them in the LORD,
And ᵃthey shall walk up and down in His name,"
Says the LORD.

DESOLATION OF ISRAEL

11 Open ᵃyour doors, O Lebanon,
That fire may devour your cedars.
2 Wail, O cypress, for the ᵃcedar has fallen,
Because the mighty *trees* are ruined.
Wail, O oaks of Bashan,
ᵇFor the thick forest has come down.
3 *There is* the sound of wailing ᵃshepherds!
For their glory is in ruins.
There is the sound of roaring lions!
For the ¹pride of the Jordan is in ruins.

PROPHECY OF THE SHEPHERDS

⁴Thus says the LORD my God, "Feed the flock for slaughter, ⁵whose owners slaughter them and ᵃfeel no guilt; those who sell them ᵇsay, 'Blessed be the LORD, for I am rich'; and their shepherds do ᶜnot pity them. ⁶For I will no longer pity the inhabitants of the land," says the LORD. "But indeed I will give everyone into his neighbor's hand and into the hand of his king. They shall ¹attack the land, and I will not deliver *them* from their hand."

⁷So I fed the flock for slaughter, ¹in particular ᵃthe poor of the flock. I took for myself two staffs: the one I called ²Beau-

10:6 ᵃJer. 3:18;
Ezek. 37:21
ᵇHos. 1:7;
Zech. 1:16
ᶜZech. 13:9

10:7 ᵃPs. 104:15

10:8 ᵃIs. 5:26
ᵇIs. 49:19;
Ezek. 36:37;
Zech. 2:4

10:9 ᵃHos. 2:23
ᵇDeut. 30:1

10:10 ᵃIs. 11:11;
Hos. 11:11
ᵇIs. 49:19, 20

10:11 ᵃIs. 11:15
ᵇIs. 14:25;
Zeph. 2:13
ᶜEzek. 30:13

10:12 ᵃMic. 4:5

11:1 ᵃZech. 10:10

11:2 ᵃEzek. 31:3
ᵇIs. 32:19

11:3
ᵃJer. 25:34–36

11:5
ᵃ[Jer. 2:3]; 50:7
ᵇDeut. 29:19;
Hos. 12:8;
1 Tim. 6:9
ᶜEzek. 34:2, 3

11:7 ᵃJer. 39:10;
Zeph. 3:12;
Matt. 11:5

10:9 ¹Or *scatter*   10:11 ¹The Nile   11:3 ¹Or *floodplain, thicket*   11:6 ¹Lit. *strike*   11:7 ¹So with MT, Tg., Vg.; LXX *for the Canaanites*   ²Or *Grace*

ty, and the other I called [3]Bonds; and I fed the flock. [8]I [1]dismissed the three shepherds [a]in one month. My soul loathed them, and their soul also abhorred me. [9]Then I said, "I will not feed you. [a]Let what is dying die, and what is perishing perish. Let those that are left eat each other's flesh." [10]And I took my staff, [1]Beauty, and cut it in two, that I might break the covenant which I had made with all the peoples. [11]So it was broken on that day. Thus [a]the[1] poor of the flock, who were watching me, knew that it *was* the word of the LORD. [12]Then I said to them, "If it is [1]agreeable to you, give *me* my wages; and if not, refrain." So they [a]weighed out for my wages thirty *pieces* of silver.

[13]And the LORD said to me, "Throw it to the [a]potter"—that princely price they set on me. So I took the thirty *pieces* of silver and threw them into the house of the LORD for the potter. [14]Then I cut in two my other staff, [1]Bonds, that I might break the brotherhood between Judah and Israel.

[15]And the LORD said to me, [a]"Next, take for yourself the implements of a foolish shepherd. [16]For indeed I will raise up a shepherd in the land *who* will not care for those who are cut off, nor seek the young, nor heal those that are broken, nor feed those that still stand. But he will eat the flesh of the fat and tear their hooves in [a]pieces.

[17] "Woe[a] to the worthless shepherd,
Who leaves the flock!
A sword *shall be* against his arm
And against his right eye;
His arm shall completely wither,
And his right eye shall be totally blinded."

THE COMING DELIVERANCE OF JUDAH

12 The [1]burden of the word of the LORD against Israel. Thus says the LORD, [a]who stretches out the heavens, lays the foundation of the earth, and [b]forms the spirit of man within him: [2]"Behold, I will make Jerusalem [a]a cup of [1]drunkenness to all the surrounding peoples, when they lay siege against Judah and Jerusalem. [3a]And it shall happen in that day that I will make Jerusalem [b]a very heavy stone for all peoples; all who would heave it away will surely be cut in pieces, though all nations of the earth are gathered against it. [4]In that day," says the LORD, [a]"I will strike every horse with confusion, and its rider with madness; I will open My eyes on the house of Judah, and will strike every horse of the peoples with blindness. [5]And the governors of Judah shall say in their heart, 'The inhabitants of Jerusalem *are* my strength in the LORD of hosts, their God.' [6]In that day I will make the governors of Judah [a]like a firepan in the woodpile, and like a fiery torch in the sheaves; they shall devour all the surrounding peoples on the right hand and on the left, but Jerusalem shall be inhabited again in her own place—Jerusalem.

[7]"The LORD will save the tents of Judah first, so that the glory of the house of David and the glory of the inhabitants of Jerusalem shall not become greater than that of Judah. [8]In that day the LORD will defend the inhabitants of Jerusalem;

11:8 [a]Hos. 5:7

11:9 [a]Jer. 15:2

11:11 [a]Zeph. 3:12; Matt. 27:50; Mark 15:37; Luke 23:46; Acts 8:32

11:12 [a]Gen. 37:28; Ex. 21:32; Matt. 26:15; 27:9, 10

11:13 [a]Matt. 27:3–10; Acts 1:18, 19

11:15 [a]Is. 56:11; Ezek. 34:2

11:16 [a]Ezek. 34:1–10; Mic. 3:1–3

11:17 [a]Jer. 23:1; Ezek. 34:2; Zech. 10:2; 11:15; John 10:12, 13

12:1 [a]Is. 42:5; 44:24 [b]Num. 16:22; [Eccl. 12:7; Is. 57:16]; Heb. 12:9

12:2 [a]Is. 51:17

12:3 [a]Zech. 12:4, 6, 8; 13:1 [b]Matt. 21:44

12:4 [a]Ps. 76:6; Ezek. 38:4

12:6 [a]Is. 10:17, 18; Obad. 18; Zech. 11:1

11:7 [3]Or *Unity*   11:8 [1]Or *destroyed*, lit. *cut off*   11:10 [1]Or *Grace*   11:11 [1]So with MT, Tg., Vg.; LXX *the Canaanites*   11:12 [1]*good in your sight*   11:14 [1]Or *Unity*   12:1 [1]*oracle, prophecy*   12:2 [1]Lit. *reeling*

the one who is feeble among them in that day shall be like David, and the house of David *shall be* like God, like the Angel of the LORD before them. 9It shall be in that day *that* I will seek to ªdestroy all the nations that come against Jerusalem.

MOURNING FOR THE PIERCED ONE

10ª"And I will pour on the house of David and on the inhabitants of Jerusalem the Spirit of grace and supplication; then they will ᵇlook on Me whom they pierced. Yes, they will mourn for Him ᶜas one mourns for *his* only *son,* and grieve for Him as one grieves for a firstborn. 11In that day there shall be a great ªmourning in Jerusalem, ᵇlike the mourning at Hadad Rimmon in the plain of ¹Megiddo. 12ªAnd the land shall mourn, every family by itself: the family of the house of David by itself, and their wives by themselves; the family of the house of ᵇNathan by itself, and their wives by themselves; 13the family of the house of Levi by itself, and their wives by themselves; the family of Shimei by itself, and their wives by themselves; 14all the families that remain, every family by itself, and their wives by themselves.

IDOLATRY CUT OFF

13 "In that ªday ᵇa fountain shall be opened for the house of David and for the inhabitants of Jerusalem, for sin and for ᶜuncleanness.

2"It shall be in that day," says the LORD of hosts, "*that* I will ªcut off the names of the idols from the land, and they shall no longer be remembered. I will also cause ᵇthe prophets and the unclean spirit to depart from the land. 3It shall come to pass *that* if anyone still prophesies, then his father and mother who begot him will say to him, 'You shall ªnot live, because you have spoken lies in the name of the LORD.' And his father and mother who begot him ᵇshall thrust him through when he prophesies.

4"And it shall be in that day *that* ªevery prophet will be ashamed of his vision when he prophesies; they will not wear ᵇa robe of coarse hair to deceive. 5ªBut he will say, 'I *am* no prophet, I *am* a farmer; for a man taught me to keep cattle from my youth.' 6And *one* will say to him, 'What are these wounds between your ¹arms?' Then he will answer, '*Those* with which I was wounded in the house of my friends.'

THE SHEPHERD SAVIOR

7 "Awake, O sword, against ªMy Shepherd,
    Against the Man ᵇwho is My Companion,"
    Says the LORD of hosts.
    ᶜ"Strike the Shepherd,
    And the sheep will be scattered;
    Then I will turn My hand against ᵈthe little ones.
8   And it shall come to pass in all the land,"
    Says the LORD,
    "That ªtwo-thirds in it shall be cut off *and* die,
    ᵇBut *one*-third shall be left in it:
9   I will bring the *one*-third ªthrough the fire,
    Will ᵇrefine them as silver is refined,
    And test them as gold is tested.

12:9 ªHag. 2:22

12:10
ªJer. 31:9; 50:4;
Ezek. 39:29;
[Joel 2:28, 29]
ᵇJohn 19:34, 37;
20:27; [Rev. 1:7]
ᶜJer. 6:26;
Amos 8:10

12:11
ª[Matt. 24:30];
Acts 2:37;
[Rev. 1:7]
ᵇ2 Kin. 23:29

12:12
ª[Matt. 24:30];
Rev. 1:7]
ᵇLuke 3:31

13:1 ªActs 10:43;
[Rev. 21:6, 7]
ᵇPs. 36:9;
[Heb. 9:14;
1 John 1:7]
ᶜNum. 19:17;
Is. 4:4;
Ezek. 36:25

13:2 ªEx. 23:13;
Hos. 2:17
ᵇJer. 23:14, 15;
2 Pet. 2:1

13:3
ªDeut. 18:20;
[Ezek. 14:9]
ᵇDeut. 13:6–11;
[Matt. 10:37]

13:4
ªJer. 6:15; 8:9;
[Mic. 3:6, 7]
ᵇ2 Kin. 1:8;
Is. 20:2;
Matt. 3:4

13:5 ªAmos 7:14

13:7 ªIs. 40:11;
Ezek. 34:23, 24;
37:24;
Mic. 5:2, 4
ᵇ[John 10:30]
ᶜMatt. 26:31,
56, 67;
Mark 14:27;
1 Pet. 5:4;
Rev. 7:16, 17
ᵈLuke 12:32

13:8 ªIs. 6:13;
Ezek. 5:2, 4, 12
ᵇ[Rom. 11:5]

13:9 ªIs. 48:10;
Ezek. 20:38;
Mal. 3:3
ᵇ1 Pet. 1:6, 7

12:11 ¹Heb. *Megiddon*   13:6 ¹Or *hands*

cThey will call on My name,
And I will answer them.
dI will say, 'This *is* My people';
And each one will say, 'The LORD *is* my God.' "

THE DAY OF THE LORD
(cf. Ezek. 38; 39; Mark 13; Rev. 20—22)

14 Behold, athe day of the LORD is coming,
And your 1spoil will be divided in your midst.
2   For aI will gather all the nations to battle against
      Jerusalem;
The city shall be taken,
The houses 1rifled,
And the women ravished.
Half of the city shall go into captivity,
But the remnant of the people shall not be cut off from
      the city.

3   Then the LORD will go forth
And fight against those nations,
As He fights in the day of battle.
4   And in that day His feet will stand aon the Mount of
      Olives,
Which faces Jerusalem on the east.
And the Mount of Olives shall be split in two,
From east to west,
b*Making* a very large valley;
Half of the mountain shall move toward the north
And half of it toward the south.

5   Then you shall flee *through* My mountain valley,
For the mountain valley shall reach to Azal.
Yes, you shall flee
As you fled from the aearthquake
In the days of Uzziah king of Judah.
bThus the LORD my God will come,
And call the saints with 1You.

6   It shall come to pass in that day
That there will be no light;
The 1lights will diminish.
7   It shall be one day
aWhich is known to the LORD—
Neither day nor night.
But at bevening time it shall happen
That it will be light.

8   And in that day it shall be
That living awaters shall flow from Jerusalem,
Half of them toward 1the eastern sea
And half of them toward 2the western sea;
In both summer and winter it shall occur.
9   And the LORD shall be aKing over all the earth.
In that day it shall be—
b"The LORD *is* one,"
And His name one.

13:9 cPs. 50:15;
Zeph. 3:9;
[Zech. 12:10]
dJer. 30:22;
Hos. 2:23

14:1
a[Is. 13:6, 9;
Joel 2:1;
Mal. 4:1]

14:2 aJoel 3:2;
Zech. 12:2, 3

14:4 aEzek. 11:23;
Acts 1:9–12
bJoel 3:12

14:5 aIs. 29:6;
Amos 1:1
b[Ps. 96:13];
Is. 66:15, 16;
Matt. 24:30, 31;
25:31; Jude 14
cJoel 3:11

14:7
aMatt. 24:36
bIs. 30:26

14:8
aEzek. 47:1–12;
Joel 3:18;
[John 7:38;
Rev. 22:1, 2]

14:9
a[Jer. 23:5, 6;
Rev. 11:15]
b[Eph. 4:5, 6];
Deut. 6:4

14:1 1*plunder* or *booty*   14:2 1Or *plundered*   14:5 1Or *you*; LXX, Tg., Vg. *Him*
14:6 1Lit. *glorious ones*   14:8 1The Dead Sea   2The Mediterranean Sea

¹⁰All the land shall be turned into a plain from Geba to Rimmon south of Jerusalem. ¹*Jerusalem* shall be raised up and ᵃinhabited in her place from Benjamin's Gate to the place of the First Gate and the Corner Gate, ᵇand *from* the Tower of Hananel to the king's winepresses.

11   *The people* shall dwell in it;
     And ᵃno longer shall there be utter destruction,
     ᵇBut Jerusalem shall be safely inhabited.

¹²And this shall be the plague with which the LORD will strike all the people who fought against Jerusalem:

     Their flesh shall ¹dissolve while they stand on their feet,
     Their eyes shall dissolve in their sockets,
     And their tongues shall dissolve in their mouths.

13   It shall come to pass in that day
     That ᵃa great panic from the LORD will be among them.
     Everyone will seize the hand of his neighbor,
     And raise ᵇhis hand against his neighbor's hand;
14   Judah also will fight at Jerusalem.
     ᵃAnd the wealth of all the surrounding nations
     Shall be gathered together:
     Gold, silver, and apparel in great abundance.

15   ᵃSuch also shall be the plague
     On the horse *and* the mule,
     On the camel and the donkey,
     And on all the cattle that will be in those camps.
     So *shall* this plague *be.*

THE NATIONS WORSHIP THE KING

¹⁶And it shall come to pass *that* everyone who is left of all the nations which came against Jerusalem shall ᵃgo up from year to year to ᵇworship the King, the LORD of hosts, and to keep ᶜthe Feast of Tabernacles. ¹⁷ᵃAnd it shall be *that* whichever of the families of the earth do not come up to Jerusalem to worship the King, the LORD of hosts, on them there will be no rain. ¹⁸If the family of ᵃEgypt will not come up and enter in, ᵇthey *shall have* no *rain;* they shall receive the plague with which the LORD strikes the nations who do not come up to keep the Feast of Tabernacles. ¹⁹This shall be the ¹punishment of Egypt and the punishment of all the nations that do not come up to keep the Feast of Tabernacles.

²⁰In that day ᵃ"HOLINESS TO THE LORD" shall be *engraved* on the bells of the horses. The ᵇpots in the LORD's house shall be like the bowls before the altar. ²¹Yes, ¹every pot in Jerusalem and Judah shall be holiness to the LORD of hosts. Everyone who sacrifices shall come and take them and cook in them. In that day there shall no longer be a ᵃCanaanite ᵇin the house of the LORD of hosts.

14:10 ᵃJer. 30:18;
Zech. 12:6
ᵇNeh. 3:1;
Jer. 31:38

14:11 ᵃJer. 31:40
ᵇJer. 23:6;
Ezek. 34:25–28;
Hos. 2:18

14:13
ᵃ1 Sam. 14:15, 20
ᵇJudg. 7:22;
2 Chr. 20:23;
Ezek. 38:21

14:14
ᵃEzek. 39:10, 17

14:15
ᵃZech. 14:12

14:16
ᵃ[Is. 2:2, 3;
60:6–9;
66:18–21;
Mic. 4:1, 2]
ᵇIs. 27:13
ᶜLev. 23:34–44;
Neh. 8:14;
Hos. 12:9;
John 7:2

14:17 ᵃIs. 60:12

14:18 ᵃIs. 19:21
ᵇDeut. 11:10

14:20
ᵃEx. 28:36;
39:30; Is. 23:18;
Jer. 2:3
ᵇEzek. 46:20

14:21 ᵃIs. 35:8;
Ezek. 44:9;
Joel 3:17;
Rev. 21:27; 22:15
ᵇ[Eph. 2:19–22]

14:10 ¹Lit. *She*   14:12 ¹Lit. *decay*   14:19 ¹Lit. *sin*   14:21 ¹Or *on every pot . . . shall be engraved "HOLINESS TO THE LORD OF HOSTS"*

THE BOOK OF
MALACHI

1 The ¹burden of the word of the LORD to Israel ²by Malachi.

ISRAEL BELOVED OF GOD

2 "Iᵃ have loved you," says the LORD.
"Yet you say, 'In what way have You loved us?'
Was not Esau Jacob's brother?"
Says the LORD.
"Yet ᵇJacob I have loved;

3 But Esau I have hated,
And ᵃlaid waste his mountains and his heritage
For the jackals of the wilderness."

4 Even though Edom has said,
"We have been impoverished,
But we will return and build the desolate places,"

Thus says the LORD of hosts:

"They may build, but I will ᵃthrow down;
They shall be called the Territory of Wickedness,
And the people against whom the LORD will have
    indignation forever.

5 Your eyes shall see,
And you shall say,
ᵃ'The LORD is magnified beyond the border of Israel.'

POLLUTED OFFERINGS

6 "A son ᵃhonors *his* father,
And a servant *his* master.
ᵇIf then I am the Father,
Where *is* My honor?
And if I *am* a Master,
Where *is* My reverence?
Says the LORD of hosts
To you priests who despise My name.
ᶜYet you say, 'In what way have we despised Your
    name?'

7 "You offer ᵃdefiled food on My altar,
But say,
'In what way have we defiled You?'
By saying,
ᵇ'The table of the LORD is ¹contemptible.'

8 And ᵃwhen you offer the blind as a sacrifice,
Is it not evil?
And when you offer the lame and sick,
Is it not evil?
Offer it then to your governor!
Would he be pleased with you?

1:2 ᵃDeut. 4:37;
7:8; 23:5;
Is. 41:8, 9;
[Jer. 31:3];
John 15:12
ᵇRom. 9:13
1:3 ᵃJer. 49:18;
Ezek. 35:9, 15
1:4
ᵃJer. 49:16–18
1:5 ᵃPs. 35:27;
Mic. 5:4
1:6 ᵃ[Ex. 20:12];
Prov. 30:11, 17;
[Matt. 15:4–8;
Eph. 6:2, 3]
ᵇ[Is. 63:16; 64:8];
Jer. 31:9;
Luke 6:46
ᶜMal. 2:14
1:7 ᵃDeut. 15:21
ᵇEzek. 41:22
1:8 ᵃLev. 22:22;
Deut. 15:19–23

1:1 ¹oracle, prophecy   ²Lit. *by the hand of*   1:7 ¹Or *to be despised*

Would he ᵇaccept¹ you favorably?"
Says the LORD of hosts.

9 "But now entreat God's favor,
That He may be gracious to us.
ᵃWhile this is being *done* by your hands,
Will He accept you favorably?"
Says the LORD of hosts.

10 "Who *is there* even among you who would shut the
doors,
ᵃSo that you would not kindle fire *on* My altar in vain?
I have no pleasure in you,"
Says the LORD of hosts,
ᵇ"Nor will I accept an offering from your hands.

11 For ᵃfrom the rising of the sun, even to its going down,
My name *shall be* great ᵇamong the Gentiles;
ᶜIn every place ᵈincense *shall be* offered to My name,
And a pure offering;
ᵉFor My name shall be great among the nations,"
Says the LORD of hosts.

12 "But you profane it,
In that you say,
ᵃ'The table of the ¹LORD is defiled;
And its fruit, its food, *is* contemptible.'

13 You also say,
'Oh, what a ᵃweariness!'
And you sneer at it,"
Says the LORD of hosts.
"And you bring the stolen, the lame, and the sick;
Thus you bring an offering!
ᵇShould I accept this from your hand?"
Says the LORD.

14 "But cursed *be* ᵃthe deceiver
Who has in his flock a male,
And takes a vow,
But sacrifices to the Lord ᵇwhat is blemished—
For ᶜI *am* a great King,"
Says the LORD of hosts,
"And My name *is to be* feared among the nations.

CORRUPT PRIESTS

2 "And now, O ᵃpriests, this commandment is
for you.
2 ᵃIf you will not hear,
And if you will not take *it* to heart,
To give glory to My name,"
Says the LORD of hosts,
"I will send a curse upon you,
And I will curse your blessings.
Yes, I have cursed them ᵇalready,
Because you do not take *it* to heart.

3 "Behold, I will rebuke your descendants
And spread ᵃrefuse on your faces,
The refuse of your solemn feasts;
And *one* will ᵇtake you away ¹with it.

1:8 ᵇ[Job 42:8]

1:9 ᵃHos. 13:9

1:10 ᵃ1 Cor. 9:13
ᵇIs. 1:11

1:11 ᵃIs. 59:19
ᵇIs. 60:3, 5
ᶜ1 Tim. 2:8
ᵈRev. 8:3
ᵉIs. 66:18, 19

1:12 ᵃMal. 1:7

1:13 ᵃIs. 43:22
ᵇLev. 22:20

1:14 ᵃMal. 1:8
ᵇLev. 22:18–20
ᶜPs. 47:2

2:1 ᵃMal. 1:6

2:2
ᵃ[Lev. 26:14, 15;
Deut. 28:15]
ᵇMal. 3:9

2:3 ᵃEx. 29:14
ᵇ1 Kin. 14:10

1:8 ¹Lit. *lift up your face*   1:12 ¹So with Bg.; MT *Lord*   2:3 ¹Lit. *to it*

4 Then you shall know that I have sent this commandment
    to you,
That My covenant with Levi may continue,"
Says the LORD of hosts.

5 "My[a] covenant was with him, *one* of life and peace,
And I gave them to him [b]*that he might* fear *Me;*
So he feared Me
And was reverent before My name.

6 [a]The[1] law of truth was in his mouth,
And [2]injustice was not found on his lips.
He walked with Me in peace and equity,
And [b]turned many away from iniquity.

7 "For[a] the lips of a priest should keep knowledge,
And *people* should seek the law from his mouth;
[b]For he is the messenger of the LORD of hosts.

8 But you have departed from the way;
You [a]have caused many to stumble at the law.
[b]You have corrupted the covenant of Levi,"
Says the LORD of hosts.

9 "Therefore [a]I also have made you contemptible and base
Before all the people,
Because you have not kept My ways
But have shown [b]partiality in the law."

TREACHERY OF INFIDELITY

10 [a]Have we not all one Father?
[b]Has not one God created us?
Why do we deal treacherously with one another
By profaning the covenant of the fathers?

11 Judah has dealt treacherously,
And an abomination has been committed in Israel and
    in Jerusalem,
For Judah has [a]profaned
The LORD's holy *institution* which He loves:
He has married the daughter of a foreign god.

12 May the LORD cut off from the tents of Jacob
The man who does this, being [1]awake and aware,
Yet [a]who brings an offering to the LORD of hosts!

13 And this is the second thing you do:
You cover the altar of the LORD with tears,
With weeping and crying;
So He does not regard the offering anymore,
Nor receive *it* with goodwill from your hands.

14 Yet you say, "For what reason?"
Because the LORD has been witness
Between you and [a]the wife of your youth,
With whom you have dealt treacherously;
[b]Yet she is your companion
And your wife by covenant.

15 But [a]did He not make *them* one,
Having a remnant of the Spirit?
And why one?
He seeks [b]godly offspring.
Therefore take heed to your spirit,
And let none deal treacherously with the wife of his youth.

2:5
[a]Num. 25:12;
Ezek. 34:25
[b]Deut. 33:9

2:6 [a]Deut. 33:10
[b]Jer. 23:22;
[James 5:20]

2:7 [a]Num. 27:21;
Deut. 17:8–11;
Jer. 18:18
[b][Gal. 4:14]

2:8 [a]Jer. 18:15
[b]Num. 25:12, 13;
Neh. 13:29;
Ezek. 44:10

2:9 [a]1 Sam. 2:30
[b]Deut. 1:17;
Mic. 3:11;
1 Tim. 5:21

2:10 [a]Jer. 31:9;
1 Cor. 8:6;
[Eph. 4:6]
[b]Job 31:15

2:11 [a]Ezra 9:1, 2;
Neh. 13:23

2:12 [a]Neh. 13:29

2:14 [a]Prov. 5:18;
Jer. 9:2; Mal. 3:5
[b]Prov. 2:17

2:15 [a]Gen. 2:24;
Matt. 19:4, 5
[b]Ezra 9:2;
[1 Cor. 7:14]

2:6 [1]Or *True instruction*   [2]Or *unrighteousness*   2:12 [1]Talmud, Vg. *teacher and student*

16 "For ^athe LORD God of Israel says
    That He hates divorce,
    For it covers one's garment with violence,"
    Says the LORD of hosts.
    "Therefore take heed to your spirit,
    That you do not deal treacherously."

17 ^aYou have wearied the LORD with your words;
    Yet you say,
    "In what way have we wearied *Him?*"
    In that you say,
    ^b"Everyone who does evil
    Is good in the sight of the LORD,
    And He delights in them,"
    Or, "Where *is* the God of justice?"

THE COMING MESSENGER

3 "Behold, ^aI send My messenger,
    And he will ^bprepare the way before Me.
    And the Lord, whom you seek,
    Will suddenly come to His temple,
    ^cEven the Messenger of the covenant,
    In whom you delight.
    Behold, ^dHe is coming,"
    Says the LORD of hosts.

2 "But who can endure ^athe day of His coming?
    And ^bwho can stand when He appears?
    For ^cHe *is* like a refiner's fire
    And like launderers' soap.
3 ^aHe will sit as a refiner and a purifier of silver;
    He will purify the sons of Levi,
    And ¹purge them as gold and silver,
    That they may ^boffer to the LORD
    An offering in righteousness.
4 "Then ^athe offering of Judah and Jerusalem
    Will be ¹pleasant to the LORD,
    As in the days of old,
    As in former years.
5 And I will come near you for judgment;
    I will be a swift witness
    Against sorcerers,
    Against adulterers,
    ^aAgainst perjurers,
    Against those who ^bexploit wage earners and ^cwidows
      and orphans,
    And against those who turn away an alien—
    Because they do not fear Me,"
    Says the LORD of hosts.

6 "For I *am* the LORD, ^aI do not change;
    ^bTherefore you are not consumed, O sons of Jacob.
7 Yet from the days of ^ayour fathers
    You have gone away from My ordinances
    And have not kept *them.*
    ^bReturn to Me, and I will return to you,"
    Says the LORD of hosts.

3:3 ¹Or *refine*   3:4 ¹*pleasing*

2:16 ^aDeut. 24:1;
[Matt. 5:31;
19:6–8]

2:17
^aIs. 43:22, 24
^bIs. 5:20;
Zeph. 1:12

3:1 ^aMatt. 11:10;
Mark 1:2;
Luke 1:76; 7:27;
John 1:23;
2:14, 15
^b[Is. 40:3]
^cIs. 63:9
^dHab. 2:7

3:2 ^aJer. 10:10;
Joel 2:11;
Nah. 1:6;
[Mal. 4:1]
^bIs. 33:14;
Ezek. 22:14;
Rev. 6:17 ^cIs. 4:4;
Zech. 13:9;
[Matt. 3:10–12;
1 Cor. 3:13–15]

3:3 ^aIs. 1:25;
Dan. 12:10;
Zech. 13:9
^b[1 Pet. 2:5]

3:4 ^aMal. 1:11

3:5 ^aLev. 19:12;
Zech. 5:4;
[James 5:12]
^bLev. 19:13;
James 5:4
^cEx. 22:22

3:6
^a[Num. 23:19;
Rom. 11:29;
James 1:17]
^b[Lam. 3:22]

3:7 ^aActs 7:51
^bZech. 1:3

c"But you said,
'In what way shall we return?'

DO NOT ROB GOD

8 "Will a man rob God?
Yet you have robbed Me!
But you say,
'In what way have we robbed You?'
aIn tithes and offerings.
9 You are cursed with a curse,
For you have robbed Me,
Even this whole nation.
10 aBring all the tithes into the bstorehouse,
That there may be food in My house,
And try Me now in this,"
Says the LORD of hosts,
"If I will not open for you the cwindows of heaven
And dpour out for you *such* blessing
That *there will* not *be room* enough *to receive it.*

11 "And I will rebuke athe devourer for your sakes,
So that he will not destroy the fruit of your ground,
Nor shall the vine fail to bear fruit for you in the field,"
Says the LORD of hosts;
12 "And all nations will call you blessed,
For you will be aa delightful land,"
Says the LORD of hosts.

THE PEOPLE COMPLAIN HARSHLY

13 "Youra words have been ¹harsh against Me,"
Says the LORD,
"Yet you say,
'What have we spoken against You?'
14 aYou have said,
'It is useless to serve God;
What profit *is it* that we have kept His ordinance,
And that we have walked as mourners
Before the LORD of hosts?
15 So now awe call the proud blessed,
For those who do wickedness are ¹raised up;
They even btempt God and go free.'"

A BOOK OF REMEMBRANCE

16 Then those awho feared the LORD bspoke to one another,
And the LORD listened and heard *them*;
So ca book of remembrance was written before Him
For those who fear the LORD
And who ¹meditate on His name.

17 "Theya shall be Mine," says the LORD of hosts,
"On the day that I make them My bjewels.¹
And cI will spare them
As a man spares his own son who serves him."
18 aThen you shall again discern
Between the righteous and the wicked,
Between one who serves God
And one who does not serve Him.

3:13 ¹Lit. *strong*　**3:15** ¹Lit. *built*　**3:16** ¹Or *esteem*　**3:17** ¹Lit. *special treasure*

3:7 cMal. 1:6
3:8
aNeh. 13:10–12
3:10
aProv. 3:9, 10
b1 Chr. 26:20
cGen. 7:11
d2 Chr. 31:10
3:11 aAmos 4:9
3:12 aDan. 8:9
3:13 aMal. 2:17
3:14 aJob 21:14
3:15 aPs. 73:12
bPs. 95:9
3:16 aPs. 66:16
bHeb. 3:13
cPs. 56:8
3:17 aEx. 19:5;
Deut. 7:6;
Is. 43:21;
[1 Pet. 2:9]
bIs. 62:3
cPs. 103:13
3:18 a[Ps. 58:11]

THE GREAT DAY OF GOD

4 "For behold, [a]the day is coming,
Burning like an oven,
And all [b]the proud, yes, all who do wickedly will be
[c]stubble.
And the day which is coming shall burn them up,"
Says the LORD of hosts,
"That will [d]leave them neither root nor branch.

2 But to you who [a]fear My name
The [b]Sun of Righteousness shall arise
With healing in His wings;
And you shall go out
And grow fat like stall-fed calves.

3 [a]You shall trample the wicked,
For they shall be ashes under the soles of your feet
On the day that I do *this*,"
Says the LORD of hosts.

4 "Remember the [a]Law of Moses, My servant,
Which I commanded him in Horeb for all Israel,
With [b]*the* statutes and judgments.

5 Behold, I will send you [a]Elijah the prophet
[b]Before the coming of the great and dreadful day of the
LORD.

6 And [a]he will turn
The hearts of the fathers to the children,
And the hearts of the children to their fathers,
Lest I come and [b]strike the earth with [c]a curse."

4:1 [a]Ps. 21:9;
[Nah. 1:5, 6;
Mal. 3:2, 3;
2 Pet. 3:7]
[b]Mal. 3:18
[c]Is. 5:24;
Obad. 18
[d]Amos 2:9

4:2 [a]Mal. 3:16
[b]Matt. 4:16;
Luke 1:78;
Acts 10:43;
2 Cor. 4:6;
Eph. 5:14

4:3 [a]Mic. 7:10

4:4 [a]Ex. 20:3
[b]Deut. 4:10

4:5
[a][Matt. 11:14;
17:10–13;
Mark 9:11–13;
Luke 1:17];
John 1:21
[b]Joel 2:31

4:6 [a]Zech. 1:17
[b]Zech. 14:12
[c]Zech. 5:3

NEW TESTAMENT

THE GOSPEL ACCORDING TO
MATTHEW

THE GENEALOGY OF JESUS CHRIST

(Ruth 4:18–22; 1 Chr. 2:1–15; Luke 3:23–38)

1 The book of the ᵃgenealogy[1] of Jesus Christ, ᵇthe Son of David, ᶜthe Son of Abraham:

2 ᵃAbraham begot Isaac, ᵇIsaac begot Jacob, and Jacob begot ᶜJudah and his brothers. 3 ᵃJudah begot Perez and Zerah by Tamar, ᵇPerez begot Hezron, and Hezron begot Ram. 4 Ram begot Amminadab, Amminadab begot Nahshon, and Nahshon begot Salmon. 5 Salmon begot ᵃBoaz by Rahab, Boaz begot Obed by Ruth, Obed begot Jesse, 6 and ᵃJesse begot David the king.

ᵇDavid the king begot Solomon by her ¹*who had been the wife* of Uriah. 7 ᵃSolomon begot Rehoboam, Rehoboam begot ᵇAbijah, and Abijah begot ¹Asa. 8 Asa begot ᵃJehoshaphat, Jehoshaphat begot Joram, and Joram begot ᵇUzziah. 9 Uzziah begot Jotham, Jotham begot ᵃAhaz, and Ahaz begot Hezekiah. 10 ᵃHezekiah begot Manasseh, Manasseh begot ¹Amon, and Amon begot ᵇJosiah. 11 ᵃJosiah begot ¹Jeconiah and his brothers about the time they were ᵇcarried away to Babylon.

12 And after they were brought to Babylon, ᵃJeconiah begot Shealtiel, and Shealtiel begot ᵇZerubbabel. 13 Zerubbabel begot Abiud, Abiud begot Eliakim, and Eliakim begot Azor. 14 Azor begot Zadok, Zadok begot Achim, and Achim begot Eliud. 15 Eliud begot Eleazar, Eleazar begot Matthan, and Matthan begot Jacob. 16 And Jacob begot Joseph the husband of ᵃMary, of whom was born Jesus who is called Christ.

17 So all the generations from Abraham to David *are* fourteen generations, from David until the captivity in Babylon *are* fourteen generations, and from the captivity in Babylon until the Christ *are* fourteen generations.

CHRIST BORN OF MARY

(Luke 2:1–7)

18 Now the ᵃbirth of Jesus Christ was as follows: After His mother Mary was betrothed to Joseph, before they came together, she was found with child ᵇof the Holy Spirit. 19 Then Joseph her husband, being ¹a just *man*, and not wanting ᵃto make her a public example, was minded to put her away secretly. 20 But while he thought about these things, behold, an angel of the Lord appeared to him in a dream, saying, "Joseph, son of David, do not be afraid to take to you Mary your wife, ᵃfor that which is ¹conceived in her is of the Holy Spirit. 21 ᵃAnd she will bring forth a Son, and you shall call

1:1 ¹Lit. *generation*   1:6 ¹Words in italic type have been added for clarity. They are not found in the original Greek.   1:7 ¹NU *Asaph*
1:10 ¹NU *Amos*   1:11 ¹Or *Coniah* or *Jehoiachin*   1:19 ¹*an upright*
1:20 ¹Lit. *begotten*

His name [1]JESUS, [b]for He will save His people from their sins."

[22]So all this was done that it might be fulfilled which was spoken by the Lord through the prophet, saying: [23a]"Behold, the virgin shall be with child, and bear a Son, and they shall call His name Immanuel," which is translated, "God with us."

[24]Then Joseph, being aroused from sleep, did as the angel of the Lord commanded him and took to him his wife, [25]and [1]did not know her till she had brought forth [a]her[2] firstborn Son. And he called His name JESUS.

WISE MEN FROM THE EAST

2 Now after [a]Jesus was born in Bethlehem of Judea in the days of Herod the king, behold, [1]wise men [b]from the East came to Jerusalem, [2]saying, [a]"Where is He who has been born King of the Jews? For we have seen [b]His star in the East and have come to worship Him."

[3]When Herod the king heard *this,* he was troubled, and all Jerusalem with him. [4]And when he had gathered all [a]the chief priests and [b]scribes of the people together, [c]he inquired of them where the Christ was to be born.

[5]So they said to him, "In Bethlehem of Judea, for thus it is written by the prophet:

6 'But[a] you, Bethlehem, *in* the land of Judah,
    Are not the least among the rulers of Judah;
    For out of you shall come a Ruler
    [b]Who will shepherd My people Israel.'"

[7]Then Herod, when he had secretly called the [1]wise men, determined from them what time the [a]star appeared. [8]And he sent them to Bethlehem and said, "Go and search carefully for the young Child, and when you have found *Him,* bring back word to me, that I may come and worship Him also."

[9]When they heard the king, they departed; and behold, the star which they had seen in the East went before them, till it came and stood over where the young Child was. [10]When they saw the star, they rejoiced with exceedingly great joy. [11]And when they had come into the house, they saw the young Child with Mary His mother, and fell down and worshiped Him. And when they had opened their treasures, [a]they presented gifts to Him: gold, frankincense, and myrrh.

[12]Then, being divinely warned [a]in a dream that they should not return to Herod, they departed for their own country another way.

THE FLIGHT INTO EGYPT

[13]Now when they had departed, behold, an angel of the Lord appeared to Joseph in a dream, saying, "Arise, take the young Child and His mother, flee to Egypt, and stay there until I bring you word; for Herod will seek the young Child to destroy Him."

[14]When he arose, he took the young Child and His mother by night and departed for Egypt, [15]and was there until the death of Herod, that it might be fulfilled which was spoken by

1:21 [b]Luke 2:11;
John 1:29;
[Acts 4:12;
5:31; 13:23, 38;
Rom. 5:18, 19;
Col. 1:20–23]

1:23 [a]Is. 7:14

1:25 [a]Ex. 13:2;
Luke 2:7, 21

2:1 [a]Mic. 5:2;
Luke 2:4–7
[b]Gen. 25:6;
1 Kin. 4:30

2:2 [a]Luke 2:11
[b][Num. 24:17;
Is. 60:3]

2:4 [a]2 Chr. 36:14
[b]2 Chr. 34:13
[c]Mal. 2:7

2:6 [a]Mic. 5:2;
John 7:42
[b]Gen. 49:10;
[Rev. 2:27]

2:7 [a]Num. 24:17

2:11 [a]Ps. 72:10;
Is. 60:6

2:12
[a][Job 33:15, 16];
Matt. 1:20

1:21 [1]Lit. *Savior*   1:25 [1]Kept her a virgin   [2]NU *a Son*   2:1 [1]Gr. *magoi*
2:7 [1]Gr. *magoi*

the Lord through the prophet, saying, a"Out of Egypt I called My Son."

MASSACRE OF THE INNOCENTS

16Then Herod, when he saw that he was deceived by the wise men, was exceedingly angry; and he sent forth and put to death all the male children who were in Bethlehem and in all its districts, from two years old and under, according to the time which he had determined from the wise men. 17Then was fulfilled what was spoken by Jeremiah the prophet, saying:

18 "A avoice was heard in Ramah,
    Lamentation, weeping, and great mourning,
    Rachel weeping *for* her children,
    Refusing to be comforted,
    Because they are no more."

THE HOME IN NAZARETH

(Luke 2:39)

19Now when Herod was dead, behold, an angel of the Lord appeared in a dream to Joseph in Egypt, 20asaying, "Arise, take the young Child and His mother, and go to the land of Israel, for those who bsought the young Child's life are dead." 21Then he arose, took the young Child and His mother, and came into the land of Israel.

22But when he heard that Archelaus was reigning over Judea instead of his father Herod, he was afraid to go there. And being warned by God in a adream, he turned aside binto the region of Galilee. 23And he came and dwelt in a city called aNazareth, that it might be fulfilled bwhich was spoken by the prophets, "He shall be called a Nazarene."

JOHN THE BAPTIST PREPARES THE WAY

(Mark 1:2–8; Luke 3:1–20)

3 In those days aJohn the Baptist came preaching bin the wilderness of Judea, 2and saying, "Repent, for athe kingdom of heaven is at hand!" 3For this is he who was spoken of by the prophet Isaiah, saying:

a"The voice of one crying in the wilderness:
    b'Prepare the way of the LORD;
    Make His paths straight.'"

4Now aJohn himself was clothed in camel's hair, with a leather belt around his waist; and his food was blocusts and cwild honey. 5aThen Jerusalem, all Judea, and all the region around the Jordan went out to him 6aand were baptized by him in the Jordan, confessing their sins.

7But when he saw many of the Pharisees and Sadducees coming to his baptism, he said to them, a"Brood of vipers! Who warned you to flee from bthe wrath to come? 8Therefore bear fruits worthy of repentance, 9and do not think to say to yourselves, a'We have Abraham as *our* father.' For I say to you that God is able to raise up children to Abraham from these stones. 10And even now the ax is laid to the root of the trees. aTherefore every tree which does not bear good fruit is cut down and thrown into the fire. 11aI indeed baptize you with water unto repentance, but He who is coming after me is

2:15
aNum. 24:8;
   Hos. 11:1

2:18 aJer. 31:15

2:20 aLuke 2:39
   bMatt. 2:16

2:22
aMatt. 2:12, 13, 19
   bMatt. 3:13;
   Luke 2:39

2:23
aLuke 1:26; 2:39;
   John 1:45, 46
   bJudg. 13:5

3:1
aMatt. 3:1–12;
   Mark 1:3–8;
   Luke 3:2–17;
   John 1:6–8,
     19–28
   bJosh. 14:10

3:2 aDan. 2:44;
   Mal. 4:6;
   Matt. 4:17;
   Mark 1:15;
   Luke 1:17; 10:9;
   11:20; 21:31

3:3 aIs. 40:3;
   Luke 3:4;
   John 1:23
   bLuke 1:76

3:4 a2 Kin. 1:8;
   Zech. 13:4;
   Matt. 11:8;
   Mark 1:6
   bLev. 11:22
   c1 Sam. 14:25, 26

3:5 aMark 1:5

3:6
aActs 19:4, 18

3:7 aMatt. 12:34;
   Luke 3:7–9
   b[Rom. 5:9;
   1 Thess. 1:10]

3:9 aJohn 8:33;
   Acts 13:26;
   [Rom. 4:1, 11, 16;
   Gal. 3:29]

3:10
a[Ps. 92:12–14];
   Matt. 7:19;
   Luke 13:7, 9;
   [John 15:6]

3:11 aMark 1:4, 8;
   Luke 3:16;
   John 1:26;
   Acts 1:5

mightier than I, whose sandals I am not worthy to carry. bHe will baptize you with the Holy Spirit 1and fire. 12aHis winnowing fan *is* in His hand, and He will thoroughly clean out His threshing floor, and gather His wheat into the barn; but He will bburn up the chaff with unquenchable fire."

JOHN BAPTIZES JESUS
(Mark 1:9–11; Luke 3:21, 22; John 1:29–34)

13aThen Jesus came bfrom Galilee to John at the Jordan to be baptized by him. 14And John *tried to* prevent Him, saying, "I need to be baptized by You, and are You coming to me?"

15But Jesus answered and said to him, "Permit *it to be so* now, for thus it is fitting for us to fulfill all righteousness." Then he allowed Him.

16aWhen He had been baptized, Jesus came up immediately from the water; and behold, the heavens were opened to Him, and 1He saw bthe Spirit of God descending like a dove and alighting upon Him. 17aAnd suddenly a voice *came* from heaven, saying, b"This is My beloved Son, in whom I am well pleased."

SATAN TEMPTS JESUS
(Mark 1:12, 13; Luke 4:1–13)

4 Then aJesus was led up by bthe Spirit into the wilderness to be tempted by the devil. 2And when He had fasted forty days and forty nights, afterward He was hungry. 3Now when the tempter came to Him, he said, "If You are the Son of God, command that these stones become bread."

4But He answered and said, "It is written, a'Man shall not live by bread alone, but by every word that proceeds from the mouth of God.'"

5Then the devil took Him up ainto the holy city, set Him on the pinnacle of the temple, 6and said to Him, "If You are the Son of God, throw Yourself down. For it is written:

a'He shall give His angels charge over you,'

and,

b'In *their* hands they shall bear you up,
Lest you dash your foot against a stone.'"

7Jesus said to him, "It is written again, a'You shall not 1tempt the LORD your God.'"

8Again, the devil took Him up on an exceedingly high mountain, and ashowed Him all the kingdoms of the world and their glory. 9And he said to Him, "All these things I will give You if You will fall down and worship me."

10Then Jesus said to him, 1"Away with you, Satan! For it is written, a'You shall worship the LORD your God, and Him only you shall serve.'"

11Then the devil aleft Him, and behold, bangels came and ministered to Him.

JESUS BEGINS HIS GALILEAN MINISTRY
(Mark 1:14, 15; Luke 4:14, 15)

12aNow when Jesus heard that John had been put in prison, He departed to Galilee. 13And leaving Nazareth, He came

3:11 b[Is. 4:4;
John 20:22;
Acts 2:3, 4;
1 Cor. 12:13]

3:12 aMal. 3:3
bMal. 4:1;
Matt. 13:30

3:13
aMatt. 3:13–17;
Mark 1:9–11;
Luke 3:21, 22;
John 1:31–34
bMatt. 2:22

3:16 aMark 1:10
b[Is. 11:2];
Luke 3:22;
John 1:32;
Acts 7:56

3:17 aJohn 12:28
bPs. 2:7; Is. 42:1;
Mark 1:11;
Luke 1:35; 9:35;
Col. 1:13

4:1
aMatt. 4:1–11;
Mark 1:12;
Luke 4:1
bEzek. 3:14;
Acts 8:39

4:4 aDeut. 8:3

4:5
aNeh. 11:1, 18;
Dan. 9:24;
Matt. 27:53

4:6 aPs. 91:11
bPs. 91:12

4:7 aDeut. 6:16

4:8
a[Matt. 16:26;
1 John 2:15–17]

4:10 aDeut. 6:13;
10:20;
Josh. 24:14

4:11
a[James 4:7]
bMatt. 26:53;
Luke 22:43;
[Heb. 1:14]

4:12 aMatt. 14:3;
Mark 1:14;
Luke 3:20;
John 4:43

3:11 1M omits *and fire*   3:16 1Or *he*   4:7 1test   4:10 1M *Get behind Me*

and dwelt in Capernaum, which is by the sea, in the regions of Zebulun and Naphtali, [14]that it might be fulfilled which was spoken by Isaiah the prophet, saying:

15 "The[a] land of Zebulun and the land of Naphtali,
By the way of the sea, beyond the Jordan,
Galilee of the Gentiles:
16 [a]The people who sat in darkness have seen a great light,
And upon those who sat in the region and shadow of
    death
Light has dawned."

17[a]From that time Jesus began to preach and to say, [b]"Repent, for the kingdom of heaven [1]is at hand."

FOUR FISHERMEN CALLED AS DISCIPLES
(Mark 1:16–20; Luke 5:1–11)

18[a]And Jesus, walking by the Sea of Galilee, saw two brothers, Simon [b]called Peter, and Andrew his brother, casting a net into the sea; for they were fishermen. [19]Then He said to them, "Follow Me, and [a]I will make you fishers of men." [20][a]They immediately left *their* nets and followed Him.

21[a]Going on from there, He saw two other brothers, James *the son* of Zebedee, and John his brother, in the boat with Zebedee their father, mending their nets. He called them, [22]and immediately they left the boat and their father, and followed Him.

JESUS HEALS A GREAT MULTITUDE
(Mark 1:35–39; Luke 4:44; 6:17–19)

23And Jesus went about all Galilee, [a]teaching in their synagogues, preaching [b]the gospel of the kingdom, [c]and healing all kinds of sickness and all kinds of disease among the people. [24]Then [1]His fame went throughout all Syria; and they [a]brought to Him all sick people who were afflicted with various diseases and torments, and those who were demon-possessed, epileptics, and paralytics; and He healed them. [25][a]Great multitudes followed Him—from Galilee, and *from* [1]Decapolis, Jerusalem, Judea, and beyond the Jordan.

THE BEATITUDES
(Luke 6:20–26)

5 And seeing the multitudes, [a]He went up on a mountain, and when He was seated His disciples came to Him. [2]Then He opened His mouth and [a]taught them, saying:

3 "Blessed[a] *are* the poor in spirit,
    For theirs is the kingdom of heaven.
4 [a]Blessed *are* those who mourn,
    For they shall be comforted.
5 [a]Blessed *are* the meek,
    For [b]they shall inherit the [1]earth.
6 Blessed *are* those who [a]hunger and thirst for
    righteousness,
    [b]For they shall be filled.
7 Blessed *are* the merciful,
    [a]For they shall obtain mercy.

4:15 [a]Is. 9:1, 2
4:16 [a]Is. 42:7; Luke 2:32
4:17 [a]Mark 1:14, 15 [b]Matt. 3:2; 10:7
4:18 [a]Matt. 4:18–22; Mark 1:16–20; Luke 5:2–11; John 1:40–42 [b]Matt. 10:2; 16:18; John 1:40–42
4:19 [a]Luke 5:10
4:20 [a]Matt. 19:27; Mark 10:28
4:21 [a]Mark 1:19
4:23 [a]Ps. 22:22; Matt. 9:35; Mark 1:21; 6:2; 10:1; Luke 4:15; 6:6; 13:10; John 6:59; 18:20 [b][Matt. 24:14]; Mark 1:14; Luke 4:43; 8:1; 16:16 [c]Mark 1:34; Luke 4:40; 7:21; Acts 10:38
4:24 [a]Mark 1:32, 33; Luke 4:40
4:25 [a]Matt. 5:1; 8:1, 18; Mark 3:7, 8
5:1 [a]Matt. 14:23; 15:29; 17:1; Mark 3:13; Luke 6:17; 9:28; John 6:3, 15
5:2 [a][Matt. 7:29]; Mark 10:1; 12:35; John 8:2
5:3 [a]Prov. 16:19; Is. 66:2; Luke 6:20–23
5:4 [a]Is. 61:2, 3; Luke 6:21; [John 16:20]; Acts 16:34; [2 Cor. 1:7]; Rev. 21:4
5:5 [a]Ps. 37:11; Is. 29:19 [b][Rom. 4:13]
5:6 [a]Luke 1:53; Acts 2:4 [b][Is. 55:1; 65:13; John 4:14; 6:48; 7:37]
5:7 [a]Ps. 41:1; Mark 11:25

4:17 [1]*has drawn near*   4:24 [1]*Lit. the report of Him*   4:25 [1]*Lit. Ten Cities*
5:5 [1]*Or land*

8 ᵃBlessed *are* the pure in heart,
  For ᵇthey shall see God.
9 Blessed *are* the peacemakers,
  For they shall be called sons of God.
10 ᵃBlessed *are* those who are persecuted for righteousness'
  sake,
  For theirs is the kingdom of heaven.

11ᵃBlessed are you when they revile and persecute you, and say all kinds of ᵇevil against you falsely for My sake. 12ᵃRejoice and be exceedingly glad, for great *is* your reward in heaven, for ᵇso they persecuted the prophets who were before you.

BELIEVERS ARE SALT AND LIGHT
(Mark 9:50; Luke 14:34, 35)

13"You are the salt of the earth; ᵃbut if the salt loses its flavor, how shall it be seasoned? It is then good for nothing but to be thrown out and trampled underfoot by men.

14ᵃ"You are the light of the world. A city that is set on a hill cannot be hidden. 15Nor do they ᵃlight a lamp and put it under a basket, but on a lampstand, and it gives light to all *who are* in the house. 16Let your light so shine before men, ᵃthat they may see your good works and ᵇglorify your Father in heaven.

CHRIST FULFILLS THE LAW

17ᵃ"Do not think that I came to destroy the Law or the Prophets. I did not come to destroy but to fulfill. 18For assuredly, I say to you, ᵃtill heaven and earth pass away, one ¹jot or one ²tittle will by no means pass from the law till all is fulfilled. 19ᵃWhoever therefore breaks one of the least of these commandments, and teaches men so, shall be called least in the kingdom of heaven; but whoever does and teaches *them,* he shall be called great in the kingdom of heaven. 20For I say to you, that unless your righteousness exceeds ᵃ*the righteousness* of the scribes and Pharisees, you will by no means enter the kingdom of heaven.

MURDER BEGINS IN THE HEART
(Luke 12:57–59)

21"You have heard that it was said to those ¹of old, ᵃ'You shall not murder, and whoever murders will be in danger of the judgment.' 22But I say to you that ᵃwhoever is angry with his brother ¹without a cause shall be in danger of the judgment. And whoever says to his brother, ᵇ'Raca!'² shall be in danger of the council. But whoever says, ³'You fool!' shall be in danger of ⁴hell fire. 23Therefore ᵃif you bring your gift to the altar, and there remember that your brother has something against you, 24ᵃleave your gift there before the altar, and go your way. First be reconciled to your brother, and then come and offer your gift. 25ᵃAgree with your adversary quickly, ᵇwhile you are on the way with him, lest your adversary deliver you to the judge, the judge hand you over to the officer, and you be thrown into prison. 26Assuredly, I say to you, you will by no means get out of there till you have paid the last penny.

5:8 ᵃPs. 15:2;
24:4; Heb. 12:14
ᵇActs 7:55, 56;
1 Cor. 13:12

5:10
ᵃ[2 Cor. 4:17];
1 Pet. 3:14

5:11 ᵃLuke 6:22
ᵇ1 Pet. 4:14

5:12 ᵃLuke 6:23;
Acts 5:41;
1 Pet. 4:13, 14
ᵇ2 Chr. 36:16;
Neh. 9:26;
Matt. 23:37;
Acts 7:52;
1 Thess. 2:15;
Heb. 11:35–37;
James 5:10

5:13 ᵃMark 9:50;
Luke 14:34

5:14 ᵃ[Prov. 4:18;
John 8:12];
Phil. 2:15

5:15 ᵃMark 4:21;
Luke 8:16;
Phil. 2:15

5:16 ᵃ1 Pet. 2:12
ᵇ[John 15:8];
1 Cor. 14:25

5:17 ᵃRom. 10:4

5:18
ᵃMatt. 24:35;
Luke 16:17

5:19
ᵃ[James 2:10]

5:20
ᵃ[Rom. 10:3]

5:21 ᵃEx. 20:13;
Deut. 5:17

5:22
ᵃ[1 John 3:15];
ᵇ[James 2:20;
3:6]

5:23 ᵃMatt. 8:4

5:24 ᵃ[Job 42:8;
1 Tim. 2:8;
1 Pet. 3:7]

5:25
ᵃ[Prov. 25:8];
Luke 12:58, 59
ᵇ[Ps. 32:6;
Is. 55:6]

5:18 ¹Gr. *iota,* Heb. *yod,* the smallest letter ²The smallest stroke in a Heb. letter 5:21 ¹*in ancient times* 5:22 ¹NU omits *without a cause* ²Lit., in Aram., *Empty head* ³Gr. *More* ⁴Gr. *Gehenna*

5:27 ªEx. 20:14;
Deut. 5:18

5:28
ª2 Sam. 11:2–5;
Job 31:1;
Prov. 6:25;
[Matt. 15:19;
James 1:14, 15]

5:29 ªMark 9:43
ᵇ[Col. 3:5]

5:31 ªDeut. 24:1;
[Jer. 3:1];
Mark 10:2

5:32
ª[Matt. 19:9;
Mark 10:11;
Luke 16:18;
Rom. 7:3];
1 Cor. 7:11

5:33
ªMatt. 23:16
ᵇ[Ex. 20:7];
Lev. 19:12;
Num. 30:2
ᶜDeut. 23:23

5:34
ªMatt. 23:16;
James 5:12
ᵇIs. 66:1

5:35 ªPs. 48:2;
[Matt. 5:2, 19;
6:10]

5:37 ª[Col. 4:6];
James 5:12

5:38 ªEx. 21:24;
Lev. 24:20;
Deut. 19:21

5:39
ª[Prov. 20:22];
Luke 6:29;
[Rom. 12:17;
1 Cor. 6:7;
1 Pet. 3:9]
ᵇIs. 50:6;
Lam. 3:30

5:41
ªMatt. 27:32

5:42
ªDeut. 15:7–11;
Luke 6:30–34;
1 Tim. 6:18

5:43 ªLev. 19:18
ᵇDeut. 23:3–6;
Ps. 41:10

5:44 ªLuke 6:27;
Rom. 12:14
ᵇ[Rom. 12:20]
ᶜLuke 23:34;
Acts 7:60;
1 Cor. 4:12;
1 Pet. 2:23

5:45 ªJob 25:3;
Ps. 65:9–13;
Luke 12:16, 17;
Acts 14:17

5:46 ªLuke 6:32

ADULTERY IN THE HEART

27"You have heard that it was said ¹to those of old, ª'You shall not commit adultery.' 28But I say to you that whoever ªlooks at a woman to lust for her has already committed adultery with her in his heart. 29aIf your right eye causes you to ¹sin, ᵇpluck it out and cast *it* from you; for it is more profitable for you that one of your members perish, than for your whole body to be cast into hell. 30And if your right hand causes you to ¹sin, cut it off and cast *it* from you; for it is more profitable for you that one of your members perish, than for your whole body to be cast into hell.

MARRIAGE IS SACRED AND BINDING
(Matt. 19:9; Mark 10:11, 12; Luke 16:18)

31"Furthermore it has been said, ª'Whoever divorces his wife, let him give her a certificate of divorce.' 32But I say to you that ªwhoever divorces his wife for any reason except ¹sexual immorality causes her to commit adultery; and whoever marries a woman who is divorced commits adultery.

JESUS FORBIDS OATHS

33"Again you have heard that ªit was said to those of ¹old, ᵇ'You shall not swear falsely, but ᶜshall perform your oaths to the Lord.' 34But I say to you, ªdo not swear at all: neither by heaven, for it is ᵇGod's throne; 35nor by the earth, for it is His footstool; nor by Jerusalem, for it is the city of ªthe great King. 36Nor shall you swear by your head, because you cannot make one hair white or black. 37aBut let ¹your 'Yes' be 'Yes,' and your 'No,' 'No.' For whatever is more than these is from the evil one.

GO THE SECOND MILE
(Luke 6:29–31)

38"You have heard that it was said, ª'An eye for an eye and a tooth for a tooth.' 39aBut I tell you not to resist an evil person. ᵇBut whoever slaps you on your right cheek, turn the other to him also. 40If anyone wants to sue you and take away your tunic, let him have *your* cloak also. 41And whoever ªcompels you to go one mile, go with him two. 42Give to him who asks you, and ªfrom him who wants to borrow from you do not turn away.

LOVE YOUR ENEMIES
(Luke 6:27, 28, 32–36)

43"You have heard that it was said, ª'You shall love your neighbor ᵇand hate your enemy.' 44But I say to you, ªlove your enemies, bless those who curse you, ᵇdo good to those who hate you, and pray ᶜfor those who spitefully use you and persecute you, 45that you may be sons of your Father in heaven; for ªHe makes His sun rise on the evil and on the good, and sends rain on the just and on the unjust. 46aFor if you love those who love you, what reward have you? Do not even the tax collectors do the same? 47And if you greet your ¹brethren

5:27 ¹NU, M omit *to those of old*   5:29 ¹Lit. *stumble* or *offend*   5:30 ¹Lit. *stumble* or *offend*   5:32 ¹Or *fornication*   5:33 ¹*ancient times*   5:37 ¹Lit. *your word be yes yes*   5:44 ¹NU *But I say to you, love your enemies and pray for those who persecute you*   5:47 ¹M *friends*

only, what do you do more *than others?* Do not even the [2]tax collectors do so? [48a]Therefore you shall be perfect, just [b]as your Father in heaven is perfect.

DO GOOD TO PLEASE GOD

6 "Take heed that you do not do your charitable deeds before men, to be seen by them. Otherwise you have no reward from your Father in heaven. [2]Therefore, [a]when you do a charitable deed, do not sound a trumpet before you as the hypocrites do in the synagogues and in the streets, that they may have glory from men. Assuredly, I say to you, they have their reward. [3]But when you do a charitable deed, do not let your left hand know what your right hand is doing, [4]that your charitable deed may be in secret; and your Father who sees in secret [a]will Himself reward you [1]openly.

THE MODEL PRAYER

(Luke 11:2–4)

[5]"And when you pray, you shall not be like the [1]hypocrites. For they love to pray standing in the synagogues and on the corners of the streets, that they may be seen by men. Assuredly, I say to you, they have their reward. [6]But you, when you pray, [a]go into your room, and when you have shut your door, pray to your Father who *is* in the secret *place;* and your Father who sees in secret will reward you [1]openly. [7]And when you pray, [a]do not use vain repetitions as the heathen *do.* [b]For they think that they will be heard for their many words.

[8]"Therefore do not be like them. For your Father [a]knows the things you have need of before you ask Him. [9]In this [a]manner, therefore, pray:

[b]Our Father in heaven,
Hallowed be Your [c]name.
10   Your kingdom come.
[a]Your will be done
On earth [b]as *it is* in heaven.
11   Give us this day our [a]daily bread.
12   And [a]forgive us our debts,
As we forgive our debtors.
13   [a]And do not lead us into temptation,
But [b]deliver us from the evil one.
[1]For Yours is the kingdom and the power and the glory
forever. Amen.

[14a]"For if you forgive men their trespasses, your heavenly Father will also forgive you. [15]But [a]if you do not forgive men their trespasses, neither will your Father forgive your trespasses.

FASTING TO BE SEEN ONLY BY GOD

[16]"Moreover, [a]when you fast, do not be like the [1]hypocrites, with a sad countenance. For they disfigure their faces that they may appear to men to be fasting. Assuredly, I say to you, they have their reward. [17]But you, when you fast, [a]anoint your head and wash your face, [18]so that you do not appear to men

5:48 [a]Gen. 17:1;
Lev. 11:44; 19:2;
Luke 6:36;
[Col. 1:28; 4:12];
James 1:4;
1 Pet. 1:15
[b]Eph. 5:1

6:2 [a]Rom. 12:8

6:4
[a]Luke 14:12–14

6:6 [a]2 Kin. 4:33

6:7 [a]Eccl. 5:2
[b]1 Kin. 18:26

6:8
[a][Rom. 8:26, 27]

6:9
[a]Matt. 6:9–13;
Luke 11:2–4;
[John 16:24];
Eph. 6:18;
Jude 20]
[b][Matt. 5:9, 16]
[c]Mal. 1:11

6:10
[a]Matt. 26:42;
Luke 22:42;
Acts 21:14
[b]Ps. 103:20

6:11
[a][Job 23:12];
Prov. 30:8;
Is. 33:16;
Luke 11:3

6:12
[a][Matt. 18:21, 22]

6:13
[a][Matt. 26:41;
1 Cor. 10:31;
2 Pet. 2:9;
Rev. 3:10]
[b]John 17:15;
[2 Thess. 3:3];
2 Tim. 4:18;
[1 John 5:18]

6:14
[a][Matt. 7:2];
Mark 11:25;
[Eph. 4:32;
Col. 3:13]

6:15
[a]Matt. 18:35;
James 2:13

6:16 [a]Is. 58:3–7;
Luke 18:12

6:17 [a]Ruth 3:3;
2 Sam. 12:20;
Dan. 10:3

5:47 [2]NU *Gentiles*   6:4 [1]NU omits *openly*   6:5 [1]*pretenders*   6:6 [1]NU omits *openly*   6:13 [1]NU omits the rest of v. 13.   6:16 [1]*pretenders*

to be fasting, but to your Father who *is* in the secret *place;* and your Father who sees in secret will reward you [1]openly.

LAY UP TREASURES IN HEAVEN
(Luke 12:33, 34)

19[a]"Do not lay up for yourselves treasures on earth, where moth and rust destroy and where thieves break in and steal; 20[a]but lay up for yourselves treasures in heaven, where neither moth nor rust destroys and where thieves do not break in and steal. 21For where your treasure is, there your heart will be also.

THE LAMP OF THE BODY
(Luke 11:34–36)

22[a]"The lamp of the body is the eye. If therefore your eye is [1]good, your whole body will be full of light. 23But if your eye is [1]bad, your whole body will be full of darkness. If therefore the light that is in you is darkness, how great *is* that darkness!

YOU CANNOT SERVE GOD AND RICHES

24[a]"No one can serve two masters; for either he will hate the one and love the other, or else he will be loyal to the one and despise the other. [b]You cannot serve God and [1]mammon.

DO NOT WORRY
(Luke 12:22–31)

25"Therefore I say to you, [a]do not worry about your life, what you will eat or what you will drink; nor about your body, what you will put on. Is not life more than food and the body more than clothing? 26[a]Look at the birds of the air, for they neither sow nor reap nor gather into barns; yet your heavenly Father feeds them. Are you not of more value than they? 27Which of you by worrying can add one [1]cubit to his [2]stature?

28"So why do you worry about clothing? Consider the lilies of the field, how they grow: they neither toil nor spin; 29and yet I say to you that even Solomon in all his glory was not [1]arrayed like one of these. 30Now if God so clothes the grass of the field, which today is, and tomorrow is thrown into the oven, *will He* not much more *clothe* you, O you of little faith?

31"Therefore do not worry, saying, 'What shall we eat?' or 'What shall we drink?' or 'What shall we wear?' 32For after all these things the Gentiles seek. For your heavenly Father knows that you need all these things. 33But [a]seek first the kingdom of God and His righteousness, and all these things shall be added to you. 34Therefore do not worry about tomorrow, for tomorrow will worry about its own things. Sufficient for the day *is* its own trouble.

DO NOT JUDGE
(Luke 6:37–42)

7 "Judge[1] [a]not, that you be not judged. 2For with what [1]judgment you judge, you will be judged; [a]and with the measure you use, it will be measured back to you. 3[a]And why do you

Cross-references (margin)
6:19 [a]Prov. 23:4; [1 Tim. 6:17; Heb. 13:5]; James 5:1
6:20 [a]Matt. 19:21; Luke 12:33; 18:22; 1 Tim. 6:19; 1 Pet. 1:4
6:22 [a]Luke 11:34, 35
6:24 [a]Luke 16:9, 11, 13 [b][Gal. 1:10; 1 Tim. 6:17; James 4:4; 1 John 2:15]
6:25 [a][Ps. 55:22]; Luke 12:22; [Phil. 4:6; 1 Pet. 5:7]
6:26 [a]Job 38:41; Ps. 147:9; Matt. 10:29; Luke 12:24
6:33 [a]1 Kin. 3:13; Luke 12:31; [1 Tim. 4:8]
7:1 [a]Matt. 7:1–5; Luke 6:37; Rom. 14:3; [1 Cor. 4:3, 4]
7:2 [a]Mark 4:24; Luke 6:38
7:3 [a]Luke 6:41

Footnotes
6:18 [1]NU, M omit *openly*   6:22 [1]Clear, or healthy   6:23 [1]Evil, or unhealthy
6:24 [1]Lit., in Aram., *riches*   6:27 [1]About 18 inches   [2]*height*   6:29 [1]*dressed*
7:1 [1]Condemn   7:2 [1]Condemnation

look at the speck in your brother's eye, but do not consider the plank in your own eye? 4Or how can you say to your brother, 'Let me remove the speck from your eye'; and look, a plank *is* in your own eye? 5Hypocrite! First remove the plank from your own eye, and then you will see clearly to remove the speck from your brother's eye.

6a"Do not give what is holy to the dogs; nor cast your pearls before swine, lest they trample them under their feet, and turn and tear you in pieces.

KEEP ASKING, SEEKING, KNOCKING
(Luke 11:9–13)

7a"Ask, and it will be given to you; seek, and you will find; knock, and it will be opened to you. 8For aeveryone who asks receives, and he who seeks finds, and to him who knocks it will be opened. 9aOr what man is there among you who, if his son asks for bread, will give him a stone? 10Or if he asks for a fish, will he give him a serpent? 11If you then, abeing evil, know how to give good gifts to your children, how much more will your Father who is in heaven give good things to those who ask Him! 12Therefore, awhatever you want men to do to you, do also to them, for bthis is the Law and the Prophets.

THE NARROW WAY
(Luke 13:24)

13a"Enter by the narrow gate; for wide *is* the gate and broad *is* the way that leads to destruction, and there are many who go in by it. 14¹Because narrow *is* the gate and ²difficult *is* the way which leads to life, and there are few who find it.

YOU WILL KNOW THEM BY THEIR FRUITS
(Matt. 12:33; Luke 6:43–45)

15a"Beware of false prophets, bwho come to you in sheep's clothing, but inwardly they are ravenous wolves. 16aYou will know them by their fruits. bDo men gather grapes from thornbushes or figs from thistles? 17Even so, aevery good tree bears good fruit, but a bad tree bears bad fruit. 18A good tree cannot bear bad fruit, nor *can* a bad tree bear good fruit. 19aEvery tree that does not bear good fruit is cut down and thrown into the fire. 20Therefore by their fruits you will know them.

I NEVER KNEW YOU
(Luke 6:46; 13:26, 27)

21"Not everyone who says to Me, a'Lord, Lord,' shall enter the kingdom of heaven, but he who bdoes the will of My Father in heaven. 22Many will say to Me in that day, 'Lord, Lord, have we anot prophesied in Your name, cast out demons in Your name, and done many wonders in Your name?' 23And athen I will declare to them, 'I never knew you; bdepart from Me, you who practice lawlessness!'

BUILD ON THE ROCK
(Luke 6:47–49)

24"Therefore awhoever hears these sayings of Mine, and

7:6 aProv. 9:7, 8;
Acts 13:45
7:7
a[Matt. 21:22;
Mark 11:24];
Luke 11:9–13;
18:1–8;
[John 15:7;
James 1:5, 6;
1 John 3:22]
7:8 aProv. 8:17;
Jer. 29:12
7:9 aLuke 11:11
7:11 aGen. 6:5;
8:21; Ps. 84:11;
Is. 63:7;
[Rom. 8:32;
James 1:17];
1 John 3:1
7:12 aLuke 6:31
bMatt. 22:40;
Rom. 13:8;
Gal. 5:14;
[1 Tim. 1:5]
7:13 aLuke 13:24
7:15 aDeut. 13:3;
Jer. 23:16;
Ezek. 22:28;
Mark 13:22;
[Luke 6:26];
Rom. 16:17;
Eph. 5:6;
[Col. 2:8;
2 Pet. 2:1;
1 John 4:1–3]
bMic. 3:5
7:16 aMatt. 7:20;
12:33; Luke 6:44;
James 3:12
bLuke 6:43
7:17 aJer. 11:19;
Matt. 12:33
7:19 aMatt. 3:10;
Luke 3:9;
[John 15:2, 6]
7:21 aHos. 8:2;
Matt. 25:11;
Luke 6:46;
Acts 19:13
bRom. 2:13;
James 1:22
7:22 aNum. 24:4
7:23
aMatt. 25:12;
Luke 13:25;
[2 Tim. 2:19]
bPs. 5:5; 6:8;
[Matt. 25:41];
Luke 13:27
7:24
aMatt. 7:24–27;
Luke 6:47–49

7:14 ¹NU, M *How narrow . . . !*   ²*confined*

does them, I will liken him to a wise man who built his house on the rock: 25and the rain descended, the floods came, and the winds blew and beat on that house; and it did not fall, for it was founded on the rock.

26"But everyone who hears these sayings of Mine, and does not do them, will be like a foolish man who built his house on the sand: 27and the rain descended, the floods came, and the winds blew and beat on that house; and it fell. And great was its fall."

28And so it was, when Jesus had ended these sayings, that athe people were astonished at His teaching, 29afor He taught them as one having authority, and not as the scribes.

JESUS CLEANSES A LEPER
(Mark 1:40–45; Luke 5:12–16)

8 When He had come down from the mountain, great multitudes followed Him. 2aAnd behold, a leper came and bworshiped Him, saying, "Lord, if You are willing, You can make me clean."

3Then Jesus put out *His* hand and touched him, saying, "I am willing; be cleansed." Immediately his leprosy awas cleansed.

4And Jesus said to him, a"See that you tell no one; but go your way, show yourself to the priest, and offer the gift that bMoses ccommanded, as a testimony to them."

JESUS HEALS A CENTURION'S SERVANT
(Luke 7:1–10)

5aNow when Jesus had entered Capernaum, a bcenturion came to Him, pleading with Him, 6saying, "Lord, my servant is lying at home paralyzed, dreadfully tormented."

7And Jesus said to him, "I will come and heal him."

8The centurion answered and said, "Lord, aI am not worthy that You should come under my roof. But only bspeak a word, and my servant will be healed. 9For I also am a man under authority, having soldiers under me. And I say to this *one*, 'Go,' and he goes; and to another, 'Come,' and he comes; and to my servant, 'Do this,' and he does *it*."

10When Jesus heard *it*, He marveled, and said to those who followed, "Assuredly, I say to you, I have not found such great faith, not even in Israel! 11And I say to you that amany will come from east and west, and sit down with Abraham, Isaac, and Jacob in the kingdom of heaven. 12But athe sons of the kingdom bwill be cast out into outer darkness. There will be weeping and gnashing of teeth." 13Then Jesus said to the centurion, "Go your way; and as you have believed, *so* let it be done for you." And his servant was healed that same hour.

PETER'S MOTHER-IN-LAW HEALED
(Mark 1:29–31; Luke 4:38, 39)

14aNow when Jesus had come into Peter's house, He saw bhis wife's mother lying sick with a fever. 15So He touched her hand, and the fever left her. And she arose and served 1them.

7:28
aMatt. 13:54;
Mark 1:22; 6:2;
Luke 4:32;
John 7:46

7:29
a[John 7:46]

8:2
aMatt. 8:2–4;
Mark 1:40–45;
Luke 5:12–14
bMatt. 2:11;
9:18; 15:25;
John 9:38;
Acts 10:25

8:3 aMatt. 11:5;
Luke 4:27

8:4 aMatt. 9:30;
Mark 5:43;
Luke 4:41; 8:56;
9:21 bLev. 14:3,
4, 10; Mark 1:44;
Luke 5:14
cLev. 14:4–32;
Deut. 24:8

8:5 aLuke 7:1–3
bMatt. 27:54;
Acts 10:1

8:8
aLuke 15:19, 21
bPs. 107:20

8:11 a[Gen. 12:3;
Is. 2:2, 3; 11:10];
Mal. 1:11;
Luke 13:29;
[Acts 10:45;
11:18; 14:27];
Rom. 15:9–13;
Eph. 3:6]

8:12
a[Matt. 21:43]
bMatt. 13:42,
50; 22:13;
24:51; 25:30;
Luke 13:28;
2 Pet. 2:17;
Jude 13

8:14
aMatt. 8:14–16;
Mark 1:29–31;
Luke 4:38, 39
b1 Cor. 9:5

8:15 1NU, M *Him*

MANY HEALED IN THE EVENING
(Mark 1:32–34; Luke 4:40, 41)

[16][a]When evening had come, they brought to Him many who were demon-possessed. And He cast out the spirits with a word, and healed all who were sick, [17]that it might be fulfilled which was spoken by Isaiah the prophet, saying:

> [a]"He Himself took our infirmities
> And bore *our* sicknesses."

THE COST OF DISCIPLESHIP
(Luke 9:57–62)

[18]And when Jesus saw great multitudes about Him, He gave a command to depart to the other side. [19][a]Then a certain scribe came and said to Him, "Teacher, I will follow You wherever You go."

[20]And Jesus said to him, "Foxes have holes and birds of the air *have* nests, but the Son of Man has nowhere to lay *His* head."

[21][a]Then another of His disciples said to Him, "Lord, [b]let me first go and bury my father."

[22]But Jesus said to him, "Follow Me, and let the dead bury their own dead."

WIND AND WAVE OBEY JESUS
(Mark 4:35–41; Luke 8:22–25)

[23]Now when He got into a boat, His disciples followed Him. [24][a]And suddenly a great tempest arose on the sea, so that the boat was covered with the waves. But He was asleep. [25]Then His disciples came to *Him* and awoke Him, saying, "Lord, save us! We are perishing!"

[26]But He said to them, "Why are you fearful, O you of little faith?" Then [a]He arose and rebuked the winds and the sea, and there was a great calm. [27]So the men marveled, saying, [1]"Who can this be, that even the winds and the sea obey Him?"

TWO DEMON-POSSESSED MEN HEALED
(Mark 5:1–20; Luke 8:26–39)

[28][a]When He had come to the other side, to the country of the [1]Gergesenes, there met Him two demon-possessed *men,* coming out of the tombs, exceedingly fierce, so that no one could pass that way. [29]And suddenly they cried out, saying, "What have we to do with You, Jesus, You Son of God? Have You come here to torment us before the time?"

[30]Now a good way off from them there was a herd of many swine feeding. [31]So the demons begged Him, saying, "If You cast us out, [1]permit us to go away into the herd of swine."

[32]And He said to them, "Go." So when they had come out, they went into the herd of swine. And suddenly the whole herd of swine ran violently down the steep place into the sea, and perished in the water.

[33]Then those who kept *them* fled; and they went away into the city and told everything, including what *had happened* to the demon-possessed *men.* [34]And behold, the whole city came out to meet Jesus. And when they saw Him, [a]they begged *Him* to depart from their region.

8:16
[a] Mark 1:32–34;
Luke 4:40, 41

8:17 [a] Is. 53:4;
1 Pet. 2:24

8:19
[a] Matt. 8:19–22;
Luke 9:57, 58

8:21
[a] Luke 9:59, 60
[b] 1 Kin. 19:20

8:24
[a] Mark 4:37;
Luke 8:23–25

8:26 [a] Ps. 65:7;
89:9; 107:29

8:28
[a] Mark 5:1–4;
Luke 8:26–33

8:34
[a] Deut. 5:25;
1 Kin. 17:18;
Amos 7:12;
Luke 5:8;
Acts 16:39

8:27 [1]Lit. *What sort of man is this*   8:28 [1]NU *Gadarenes*   8:31 [1]NU *send us into*

JESUS FORGIVES AND HEALS A PARALYTIC
(Mark 2:1–12; Luke 5:17–26)

9 So He got into a boat, crossed over, ᵃand came to His own city. ²ᵃThen behold, they brought to Him a paralytic lying on a bed. ᵇWhen Jesus saw their faith, He said to the paralytic, "Son, be of good cheer; your sins are forgiven you."

³And at once some of the scribes said within themselves, "This Man blasphemes!"

⁴But Jesus, ᵃknowing their thoughts, said, "Why do you think evil in your hearts? ⁵For which is easier, to say, '*Your* sins are forgiven you,' or to say, 'Arise and walk'? ⁶But that you may know that the Son of Man has power on earth to forgive sins"—then He said to the paralytic, "Arise, take up your bed, and go to your house." ⁷And he arose and departed to his house.

⁸Now when the multitudes saw *it,* they ᵃmarveled¹ and glorified God, who had given such power to men.

MATTHEW THE TAX COLLECTOR
(Mark 2:13–17; Luke 5:27–32)

⁹ᵃAs Jesus passed on from there, He saw a man named Matthew sitting at the tax office. And He said to him, "Follow Me." So he arose and followed Him.

¹⁰ᵃNow it happened, as Jesus sat at the table in the house, *that* behold, many tax collectors and sinners came and sat down with Him and His disciples. ¹¹And when the Pharisees saw *it,* they said to His disciples, "Why does your Teacher eat with ᵃtax collectors and ᵇsinners?"

¹²When Jesus heard *that,* He said to them, "Those who are well have no need of a physician, but those who are sick. ¹³But go and learn what *this* means: ᵃ'I desire mercy and not sacrifice.' For I did not come to call the righteous, ᵇbut sinners, ¹to repentance."

JESUS IS QUESTIONED ABOUT FASTING
(Mark 2:18–22; Luke 5:33–39)

¹⁴Then the disciples of John came to Him, saying, ᵃ"Why do we and the Pharisees fast ¹often, but Your disciples do not fast?"

¹⁵And Jesus said to them, "Can ᵃthe ¹friends of the bridegroom mourn as long as the bridegroom is with them? But the days will come when the bridegroom will be taken away from them, and ᵇthen they will fast. ¹⁶No one puts a piece of unshrunk cloth on an old garment; for ¹the patch pulls away from the garment, and the tear is made worse. ¹⁷Nor do they put new wine into old wineskins, or else the wineskins ¹break, the wine is spilled, and the wineskins are ruined. But they put new wine into new wineskins, and both are preserved."

A GIRL RESTORED TO LIFE AND A WOMAN HEALED
(Mark 5:21–43; Luke 8:40–56)

¹⁸ᵃWhile He spoke these things to them, behold, a ruler came and worshiped Him, saying, "My daughter has just died,

9:1 ᵃMatt. 4:13; 11:23; Mark 5:21

9:2 ᵃMark 2:3–12; Luke 5:18–26 ᵇMatt. 8:10

9:4 ᵃPs. 139:2; Matt. 12:25; Mark 12:15; Luke 5:22; 6:8; 9:47; 11:17

9:8 ᵃMatt. 8:27; John 7:15

9:9 ᵃMark 2:14; Luke 5:27

9:10 ᵃMark 2:15; Luke 5:29

9:11 ᵃMatt. 11:19; Mark 2:16; Luke 5:30; 15:2 ᵇ[Gal. 2:15]

9:13 ᵃHos. 6:6; [Mic. 6:6–8]; Matt. 12:7 ᵇMark 2:17; Luke 5:32; 1 Tim. 1:15

9:14 ᵃMark 2:18; Luke 5:33–35; 18:12

9:15 ᵃJohn 3:29 ᵇActs 13:2, 3; 14:23

9:18 ᵃMark 5:22–43; Luke 8:41–56

but come and lay Your hand on her and she will live." [19]So Jesus arose and followed him, and so *did* His [a]disciples.

[20a]And suddenly, a woman who had a flow of blood for twelve years came from behind and [b]touched the hem of His garment. [21]For she said to herself, "If only I may touch His garment, I shall be made well." [22]But Jesus turned around, and when He saw her He said, "Be of good cheer, daughter; [a]your faith has made you well." And the woman was made well from that hour.

[23a]When Jesus came into the ruler's house, and saw [b]the flute players and the noisy crowd wailing, [24]He said to them, [a]"Make room, for the girl is not dead, but sleeping." And they ridiculed Him. [25]But when the crowd was put outside, He went in and [a]took her by the hand, and the girl arose. [26]And the [a]report of this went out into all that land.

TWO BLIND MEN HEALED

[27]When Jesus departed from there, [a]two blind men followed Him, crying out and saying, [b]"Son of David, have mercy on us!"

[28]And when He had come into the house, the blind men came to Him. And Jesus said to them, "Do you believe that I am able to do this?"

They said to Him, "Yes, Lord."

[29]Then He touched their eyes, saying, "According to your faith let it be to you." [30]And their eyes were opened. And Jesus sternly warned them, saying, [a]"See *that* no one knows *it.*" [31a]But when they had departed, they [1]spread the news about Him in all that [2]country.

A MUTE MAN SPEAKS

[32a]As they went out, behold, they brought to Him a man, mute and demon-possessed. [33]And when the demon was cast out, the mute spoke. And the multitudes marveled, saying, "It was never seen like this in Israel!"

[34]But the Pharisees said, [a]"He casts out demons by the ruler of the demons."

THE COMPASSION OF JESUS
(Luke 10:2, 3)

[35]Then Jesus went about all the cities and villages, [a]teaching in their synagogues, preaching the gospel of the kingdom, and healing every sickness and every disease [1]among the people. [36a]But when He saw the multitudes, He was moved with compassion for them, because they were [1]weary and scattered, [b]like sheep having no shepherd. [37]Then He said to His disciples, [a]"The harvest truly *is* plentiful, but the laborers *are* few. [38a]Therefore pray the Lord of the harvest to send out laborers into His harvest."

THE TWELVE APOSTLES
(Mark 3:13–19; Luke 6:12–16)

10 And [a]when He had called His twelve disciples to *Him,* He gave them power *over* unclean spirits, to cast them out, and to heal all kinds of sickness and all kinds of disease.

9:19
[a]Matt. 10:2–4

9:20
[a]Mark 5:25;
Luke 8:43
[b]Num. 15:38;
Deut. 22:12;
Matt. 14:36;
23:5; Mark 6:56

9:22
[a]Matt. 9:29;
15:28;
Mark 5:34;
10:52;
Luke 7:50; 8:48;
17:19; 18:42

9:23
[a]Mark 5:38;
Luke 8:51
[b]2 Chr. 35:25;
Jer. 9:17; 16:6;
Ezek. 24:17

9:24 [a]John 11:3;
Acts 20:10

9:25
[a]Matt. 8:3, 15;
Mark 1:31

9:26
[a]Matt. 4:24;
Mark 1:28, 45;
Luke 4:14, 37;
5:15; 7:17

9:27
[a]Matt. 20:29–34
[b]Matt. 15:22;
Mark 10:47;
Luke 18:38, 39

9:30 [a]Matt. 8:4;
Luke 5:14

9:31 [a]Mark 7:36

9:32
[a]Matt. 12:22, 24;
Luke 11:14

9:34
[a]Matt. 12:24;
Mark 3:22;
Luke 11:15;
John 7:20

9:35 [a]Matt. 4:23

9:36 [a]Mark 6:34
[b]Num. 27:17;
1 Kin. 22:17;
Ezek. 34:5;
Zech. 10:2;
Mark 6:34

9:37 [a]Luke 10:2;
John 4:35

9:38
[a][Matt. 28:19, 20;
Eph. 4:11, 12];
2 Thess. 3:1

10:1 [a]Mark 3:13;
Luke 6:13

9:31 [1]Lit. *made Him known*   [2]Lit. *land*   9:35 [1]NU omits *among the people*
9:36 [1]NU, M *harassed*

10:2 ªJohn 1:42

10:4 ªLuke 6:15;
Acts 1:13
ᵇMatt. 26:14;
Luke 22:3;
John 13:2, 26

10:5 ªMatt. 4:15
ᵇ2 Kin. 17:24;
Luke 9:52;
10:33; 17:16;
John 4:9

10:6
ªMatt. 15:24;
Acts 13:46
ᵇIs. 53:6;
Jer. 50:6

10:7 ªLuke 9:2
ᵇMatt. 3:2;
Luke 10:9

10:8 ª[Acts 8:18]

10:9 ª1 Sam. 9:7;
Mark 6:8
ᵇMark 6:8

10:10
ªLuke 10:7;
[1 Cor. 9:4–14];
1 Tim. 5:18

10:11 ªLuke 10:8

10:13 ªLuke 10:5
ᵇPs. 35:13

10:14 ªMark 6:11;
Luke 9:5
ᵇNeh. 5:13;
Luke 10:10, 11;
Acts 13:51

10:15
ªMatt. 11:22, 24

10:16 ªLuke 10:3
ᵇ2 Cor. 12:16;
Eph. 5:15;
Col. 4:5
ᶜ[Phil. 2:14–16]

10:17
ªMatt. 23:34;
Mark 13:9;
Luke 12:11
ᵇActs 5:40;
22:19; 26:11

10:18 ªActs 12:1;
2 Tim. 4:16

10:19
ªMark 13:11;
Luke 12:11, 12;
21:14, 15
ᵇEx. 4:12; Jer. 1:7

10:20
ª2 Sam. 23:2;
[2 Tim. 4:17]

10:21 ªMic. 7:6;
Luke 21:16

10:22
ªMatt. 24:9;
Luke 21:17;
John 15:18
ᵇ[Dan. 12:12];
Matt. 24:13;
Mark 13:13

2Now the names of the twelve apostles are these: first, Simon, ªwho is called Peter, and Andrew his brother; James the *son* of Zebedee, and John his brother; 3Philip and Bartholomew; Thomas and Matthew the tax collector; James the *son* of Alphaeus, and ¹Lebbaeus, whose surname was Thaddaeus; 4ªSimon the ¹Cananite, and Judas ᵇIscariot, who also betrayed Him.

SENDING OUT THE TWELVE
(Mark 6:7–13; Luke 9:1–6)

5These twelve Jesus sent out and commanded them, saying: ª"Do not go into the way of the Gentiles, and do not enter a city of ᵇthe Samaritans. 6ªBut go rather to the ᵇlost sheep of the house of Israel. 7ªAnd as you go, preach, saying, ᵇ'The kingdom of heaven ¹is at hand.' 8Heal the sick, ¹cleanse the lepers, ²raise the dead, cast out demons. ªFreely you have received, freely give. 9ªProvide neither gold nor silver nor ᵇcopper in your money belts, 10nor bag for *your* journey, nor two tunics, nor sandals, nor staffs; ªfor a worker is worthy of his food.

11ª"Now whatever city or town you enter, inquire who in it is worthy, and stay there till you go out. 12And when you go into a household, greet it. 13ªIf the household is worthy, let your peace come upon it. ᵇBut if it is not worthy, let your peace return to you. 14ªAnd whoever will not receive you nor hear your words, when you depart from that house or city, ᵇshake off the dust from your feet. 15Assuredly, I say to you, ªit will be more tolerable for the land of Sodom and Gomorrah in the day of judgment than for that city!

PERSECUTIONS ARE COMING
(Mark 13:9–13; Luke 21:12–17)

16ª"Behold, I send you out as sheep in the midst of wolves. ᵇTherefore be wise as serpents and ᶜharmless¹ as doves. 17But beware of men, for ªthey will deliver you up to councils and ᵇscourge you in their synagogues. 18ªYou will be brought before governors and kings for My sake, as a testimony to them and to the Gentiles. 19ªBut when they deliver you up, do not worry about how or what you should speak. For ᵇit will be given to you in that hour what you should speak; 20ªfor it is not you who speak, but the Spirit of your Father who speaks in you.

21ª"Now brother will deliver up brother to death, and a father *his* child; and children will rise up against parents and cause them to be put to death. 22And ªyou will be hated by all for My name's sake. ᵇBut he who endures to the end will be saved. 23ªWhen they persecute you in this city, flee to another. For assuredly, I say to you, you will not have ᵇgone through the cities of Israel ᶜbefore the Son of Man comes.

24ª"A disciple is not above *his* teacher, nor a servant above his master. 25It is enough for a disciple that he be like his teacher, and a servant like his master. If ªthey have called the

10:23 ªMatt. 2:13; Acts 8:1 ᵇ[Matt. 24:14; Mark 13:10] ᶜMatt. 16:28 10:24 ªLuke 6:40; John 15:20 10:25 ªMark 3:22; Luke 11:15, 18, 19; John 8:48, 52

10:3 ¹NU omits *Lebbaeus, whose surname was* 10:4 ¹NU *Cananaean*
10:7 ¹*has drawn near* 10:8 ¹NU *raise the dead, cleanse the lepers*
²M omits *raise the dead* 10:16 ¹*innocent*

master of the house ¹Beelzebub, how much more *will they call* those of his household! **26**Therefore do not fear them. ªFor there is nothing covered that will not be revealed, and hidden that will not be known.

JESUS TEACHES THE FEAR OF GOD
(Luke 12:3–7)

27"Whatever I tell you in the dark, ªspeak in the light; and what you hear in the ear, preach on the housetops. **28**ªAnd do not fear those who kill the body but cannot kill the soul. But rather ᵇfear Him who is able to destroy both soul and body in ¹hell. **29**Are not two ªsparrows sold for a ¹copper coin? And not one of them falls to the ground apart from your Father's will. **30**ªBut the very hairs of your head are all numbered. **31**Do not fear therefore; you are of more value than many sparrows.

CONFESS CHRIST BEFORE MEN
(Luke 12:8, 9)

32ª"Therefore whoever confesses Me before men, ᵇhim I will also confess before My Father who is in heaven. **33**ªBut whoever denies Me before men, him I will also deny before My Father who is in heaven.

CHRIST BRINGS DIVISION
(Luke 12:51–53; 14:26, 27)

34ª"Do not think that I came to bring peace on earth. I did not come to bring peace but a sword. **35**For I have come to ª'set¹ a man against his father, a daughter against her mother, and a daughter-in-law against her mother-in-law'; **36**and ª'a man's enemies *will be* those of his *own* household.' **37**ªHe who loves father or mother more than Me is not worthy of Me. And he who loves son or daughter more than Me is not worthy of Me. **38**ªAnd he who does not take his cross and follow after Me is not worthy of Me. **39**ªHe who finds his life will lose it, and he who loses his life for My sake will find it.

A CUP OF COLD WATER
(Mark 9:41)

40ª"He who receives you receives Me, and he who receives Me receives Him who sent Me. **41**ªHe who receives a prophet in the name of a prophet shall receive a prophet's reward. And he who receives a righteous man in the name of a righteous man shall receive a righteous man's reward. **42**ªAnd whoever gives one of these little ones only a cup of cold *water* in the name of a disciple, assuredly, I say to you, he shall by no means lose his reward."

JOHN THE BAPTIST SENDS MESSENGERS TO JESUS
(Luke 7:18–35)

11 Now it came to pass, when Jesus finished commanding His twelve disciples, that He departed from there to ªteach and to preach in their cities.

10:25 ¹NU, M *Beelzebul*; a Philistine deity, 2 Kin. 1:2, 3   **10:28** ¹Gr. *Gehenna*
10:29 ¹Gr. *assarion*, a coin worth about 1/16 of a denarius   **10:35** ¹alienate
a man from

10:26
ªMark 4:22;
Luke 8:17; 12:2, 3;
[1 Cor. 4:5]

10:27
ªLuke 12:3;
Acts 5:20

10:28
ªLuke 12:4;
[1 Pet. 3:14]
ᵇIs. 8:13;
Matt. 5:22;
Luke 12:5

10:29
ªLuke 12:6, 7

10:30
ª1 Sam. 14:45;
2 Sam. 14:11;
1 Kin. 1:52;
Luke 21:18;
Acts 27:34

10:32
ªPs. 119:46;
Luke 12:8;
[Rom. 10:9]
ᵇ[Rev. 3:5]

10:33
ª[Mark 8:38;
Luke 9:26];
2 Tim. 2:12

10:34
ª[Luke 12:49]

10:35 ªMic. 7:6;
Matt. 10:21;
Luke 12:53

10:36
ªPs. 41:9; 55:13;
John 13:18

10:37
ªDeut. 33:9;
Luke 14:26

10:38
ª[Matt. 16:24;
Mark 8:34;
Luke 9:23;
14:27]

10:39
ªMatt. 16:25;
Mark 8:35;
Luke 9:24; 17:33;
John 12:25

10:40
ªMark 9:37;
Luke 9:48;
John 12:44;
Gal. 4:14

10:41
ª1 Kin. 17:10;
2 Kin. 4:8

10:42
ª[Matt. 25:40];
Mark 9:41;
Heb. 6:10

11:1 ªMatt. 9:35;
Luke 23:5

2a And when John had heard b in prison about the works of Christ, he [1] sent two of his disciples [3] and said to Him, "Are You a the Coming One, or do we look for another?"

4 Jesus answered and said to them, "Go and tell John the things which you hear and see: 5a *The* blind see and *the* lame walk; *the* lepers are cleansed and *the* deaf hear; *the* dead are raised up and b *the* poor have the gospel preached to them. 6 And blessed is he who is not a offended because of Me."

7a As they departed, Jesus began to say to the multitudes concerning John: "What did you go out into the wilderness to see? b A reed shaken by the wind? 8 But what did you go out to see? A man clothed in soft garments? Indeed, those who wear soft *clothing* are in kings' houses. 9 But what did you go out to see? A prophet? Yes, I say to you, a and more than a prophet. 10 For this is *he* of whom it is written:

a 'Behold, I send My messenger before Your face,
Who will prepare Your way before You.'

11 "Assuredly, I say to you, among those born of women there has not risen one greater than John the Baptist; but he who is least in the kingdom of heaven is greater than he. 12a And from the days of John the Baptist until now the kingdom of heaven suffers violence, and the violent take it by force. 13a For all the prophets and the law prophesied until John. 14 And if you are willing to receive *it,* he is a Elijah who is to come. 15a He who has ears to hear, let him hear!

16a "But to what shall I liken this generation? It is like children sitting in the marketplaces and calling to their companions, 17 and saying:

'We played the flute for you,
And you did not dance;
We mourned to you,
And you did not [1] lament.'

18 For John came neither eating nor drinking, and they say, 'He has a demon.' 19 The Son of Man came eating and drinking, and they say, 'Look, a glutton and a [1] winebibber, a a friend of tax collectors and sinners!' b But wisdom is justified by her [2] children."

WOE TO THE IMPENITENT CITIES
(Gen. 19:12–14; Luke 10:13–15)

20a Then He began to rebuke the cities in which most of His mighty works had been done, because they did not repent: 21 "Woe to you, Chorazin! Woe to you, Bethsaida! For if the mighty works which were done in you had been done in Tyre and Sidon, they would have repented long ago a in sackcloth and ashes. 22 But I say to you, a it will be more tolerable for Tyre and Sidon in the day of judgment than for you. 23 And you, Capernaum, a who[1] are exalted to heaven, will be brought down to Hades; for if the mighty works which were done in you had been done in Sodom, it would have remained until this day. 24 But I say to you a that it shall be more tolerable for the land of Sodom in the day of judgment than for you."

11:2
a Luke 7:18–35
b Matt. 4:12; 14:3;
Mark 6:17;
Luke 9:7

11:3 a Gen. 49:10;
Num. 24:17;
Deut. 18:15, 18;
Dan. 9:24;
John 6:14

11:5 a Is. 29:18;
35:4–6;
John 2:23
b Ps. 22:26;
Is. 61:1;
Luke 4:18;
James 2:5

11:6 a Is. 8:14, 15;
[Rom. 9:32];
1 Pet. 2:8

11:7 a Luke 7:24
b [Eph. 4:14]

11:9
a Matt. 14:5;
21:26;
Luke 1:76; 20:6

11:10 a Mal. 3:1;
Mark 1:2;
Luke 1:76

11:12 a Luke 16:16

11:13
a Mal. 4:4–6

11:14 a Mal. 4:5;
Matt. 17:10–13;
Mark 9:11–13;
Luke 1:17;
John 1:21

11:15 a Matt. 13:9;
Luke 8:8;
Rev. 2:7, 11, 17,
29; 3:6, 13

11:16 a Luke 7:31

11:19 a Matt. 9:10
b Luke 7:35;
John 2:1–11

11:20
a Luke 10:13–
15, 18

11:21
a Jon. 3:6–8

11:22
a Matt. 10:15;
11:24

11:23 a Is. 14:13;
Lam. 2:1;
Ezek. 26:20;
31:14; 32:18, 24

11:24
a Matt. 10:15

11:2 [1] NU *sent by his*   11:17 [1] Lit. *beat your breast*   11:19 [1] *wine drinker*
[2] NU *works*   11:23 [1] NU *will you be exalted to heaven? No, you will be*

JESUS GIVES TRUE REST
(Luke 10:21, 22)

25a At that time Jesus answered and said, "I thank You, Father, Lord of heaven and earth, that bYou have hidden these things from *the* wise and prudent cand have revealed them to babes. 26Even so, Father, for so it seemed good in Your sight. 27aAll things have been delivered to Me by My Father, and no one knows the Son except the Father. bNor does anyone know the Father except the Son, and *the one* to whom the Son wills to reveal *Him.* 28Come to aMe, all *you* who labor and are heavy laden, and I will give you rest. 29Take My yoke upon you aand learn from Me, for I am 1gentle and blowly in heart, cand you will find rest for your souls. 30aFor My yoke *is* easy and My burden is light."

JESUS IS LORD OF THE SABBATH
(Mark 2:23–28; Luke 6:1–5)

12 At that time aJesus went through the grainfields on the Sabbath. And His disciples were hungry, and began to bpluck heads of grain and to eat. 2And when the Pharisees saw *it,* they said to Him, "Look, Your disciples are doing what is not lawful to do on the Sabbath!"

3But He said to them, "Have you not read awhat David did when he was hungry, he and those who were with him: 4how he entered the house of God and ate athe showbread which was not lawful for him to eat, nor for those who were with him, bbut only for the priests? 5Or have you not read in the alaw that on the Sabbath the priests in the temple 1profane the Sabbath, and are blameless? 6Yet I say to you that in this place there is aOne greater than the temple. 7But if you had known what *this* means, a'I desire mercy and not sacrifice,' you would not have condemned the guiltless. 8For the Son of Man is Lord 1even of the Sabbath."

HEALING ON THE SABBATH
(Mark 3:1–6; Luke 6:6–11)

9aNow when He had departed from there, He went into their synagogue. 10And behold, there was a man who had a withered hand. And they asked Him, saying, a"Is it lawful to heal on the Sabbath?"—that they might accuse Him.

11Then He said to them, "What man is there among you who has one sheep, and if it falls into a pit on the Sabbath, will not lay hold of it and lift *it* out? 12Of how much more value then is a man than a sheep? Therefore it is lawful to do good on the Sabbath." 13Then He said to the man, "Stretch out your hand." And he stretched *it* out, and it was restored as whole as the other. 14Then athe Pharisees went out and plotted against Him, how they might destroy Him.

BEHOLD, MY SERVANT

15But when Jesus knew *it,* aHe withdrew from there. bAnd great 1multitudes followed Him, and He healed them all. 16Yet He awarned them not to make Him known, 17that it might be fulfilled which was spoken by Isaiah the prophet, saying:

11:25
aLuke 10:21, 22
bPs. 8:2;
1 Cor. 1:19;
[2 Cor. 3:14]
cMatt. 16:17

11:27
aMatt. 28:18;
Luke 10:22;
John 3:35; 13:3;
1 Cor. 15:27
bJohn 1:18; 6:46;
10:15

11:28
a[John 6:35–37]

11:29
a[John 13:15];
Eph. 4:2;
[Phil. 2:5;
1 Pet. 2:21;
1 John 2:6]
bZech. 9:9;
[Phil. 2:7, 8]
cJer. 6:16

11:30
a[1 John 5:3]

12:1 aMark 2:23;
Luke 6:1–5
bDeut. 23:25

12:3
aEx. 31:15; 35:2;
1 Sam. 21:6

12:4 aEx. 25:30;
Lev. 24:5
bEx. 29:32;
Lev. 8:31; 24:9

12:5
aNum. 28:9;
[John 7:22]

12:6
a[2 Chr. 6:18;
Is. 66:1, 2;
Mal. 3:1];
Matt. 12:41, 42

12:7
a[1 Sam. 15:22;
Hos. 6:6;
Mic. 6:6–8];
Matt. 9:13

12:9
aMark 3:1–6;
Luke 6:6–11

12:10
aLuke 13:14; 14:3;
John 9:16

12:14 aPs. 2:2;
Matt. 27:1;
Mark 3:6;
[Luke 6:11];
John 5:18; 10:39;
11:53

12:15
aMatt. 10:23;
Mark 3:7
bMatt. 19:2

12:16 aMatt. 8:4;
9:30; 17:9

11:29 1meek   12:5 1desecrate   12:8 1NU, M omit *even*   12:15 1NU brackets *multitudes* as disputed.

18 "Behold!ᵃ My Servant whom I have chosen,
My Beloved ᵇin whom My soul is well pleased!
I will put My Spirit upon Him,
And He will declare justice to the Gentiles.

19 He will not quarrel nor cry out,
Nor will anyone hear His voice in the streets.

20 A bruised reed He will not break,
And smoking flax He will not quench,
Till He sends forth justice to victory;

21 And in His name Gentiles will trust."

A HOUSE DIVIDED CANNOT STAND
(Mark 3:22–27; Luke 11:14–23)

22ᵃThen one was brought to Him who was demon-possessed, blind and mute; and He healed him, so that the ¹blind and mute man both spoke and saw. 23And all the multitudes were amazed and said, "Could this be the ᵃSon of David?" 24ᵃNow when the Pharisees heard *it* they said, "This *fellow* does not cast out demons except by ¹Beelzebub, the ruler of the demons."

25But Jesus ᵃknew their thoughts, and said to them: "Every kingdom divided against itself is brought to desolation, and every city or house divided against itself will not stand. 26If Satan casts out Satan, he is divided against himself. How then will his kingdom stand? 27And if I cast out demons by Beelzebub, by whom do your sons cast *them* out? Therefore they shall be your judges. 28But if I cast out demons by the Spirit of God, ᵃsurely the kingdom of God has come upon you. 29ᵃOr how can one enter a strong man's house and plunder his goods, unless he first binds the strong man? And then he will plunder his house. 30He who is not with Me is against Me, and he who does not gather with Me scatters abroad.

THE UNPARDONABLE SIN
(Mark 3:28–30)

31"Therefore I say to you, ᵃevery sin and blasphemy will be forgiven men, ᵇbut the blasphemy *against* the Spirit will not be forgiven men. 32Anyone who ᵃspeaks a word against the Son of Man, ᵇit will be forgiven him; but whoever speaks against the Holy Spirit, it will not be forgiven him, either in this age or in the *age* to come.

A TREE KNOWN BY ITS FRUIT
(Matt. 7:15–20)

33"Either make the tree good and ᵃits fruit good, or else make the tree bad and its fruit bad; for a tree is known by *its* fruit. 34ᵃBrood¹ of vipers! How can you, being evil, speak good things? ᵇFor out of the abundance of the heart the mouth speaks. 35A good man out of the good treasure ¹of his heart brings forth good things, and an evil man out of the evil treasure brings forth evil things. 36But I say to you that for every idle word men may speak, they will give account of it in the day of judgment. 37For by your words you will be justified, and by your words you will be condemned."

12:18
ᵃIs. 42:1–4; 49:3
ᵇMatt. 3:17; 17:5

12:22
ᵃMatt. 9:32;
[Mark 3:11];
Luke 11:14, 15

12:23
ᵃMatt. 9:27; 21:9

12:24
ᵃMatt. 9:34;
Mark 3:22;
Luke 11:15

12:25
ᵃMatt. 9:4;
John 2:25;
Rev. 2:23

12:28
ᵃ[Dan. 2:44; 7:14;
Luke 1:33]; 11:20;
[17:20, 21;
1 John 3:8]

12:29 ᵃIs. 49:24;
[Luke 11:21–23]

12:31
ᵃMark 3:28–30;
Luke 12:10;
[Heb. 6:4–6;
10:26, 29;
1 John 5:16]
ᵇActs 7:51

12:32
ᵃMatt. 11:19;
13:55;
John 7:12, 52
ᵇ1 Tim. 1:13

12:33
ᵃMatt. 7:16–18;
Luke 6:43, 44;
[John 15:4–7]

12:34
ᵃMatt. 3:7; 23:33;
Luke 3:7
ᵇ1 Sam. 24:13;
Is. 32:6;
[Matt. 15:18];
Luke 6:45;
Eph. 4:29;
[James 3:2–12]

12:22 ¹NU omits *blind and*   12:24 ¹NU, M *Beelzebul*, a Philistine deity
12:34 ¹*Offspring*   12:35 ¹NU, M omit *of his heart*

THE SCRIBES AND PHARISEES ASK FOR A SIGN
(Luke 11:29–32)

38aThen some of the scribes and Pharisees answered, saying, "Teacher, we want to see a sign from You."

39But He answered and said to them, "An evil and aadulterous generation seeks after a sign, and no sign will be given to it except the sign of the prophet Jonah. 40aFor as Jonah was three days and three nights in the belly of the great fish, so will the Son of Man be three days and three nights in the heart of the earth. 41aThe men of Nineveh will rise up in the judgment with this generation and bcondemn it, cbecause they repented at the preaching of Jonah; and indeed a greater than Jonah *is* here. 42aThe queen of the South will rise up in the judgment with this generation and condemn it, for she came from the ends of the earth to hear the wisdom of Solomon; and indeed a greater than Solomon *is* here.

AN UNCLEAN SPIRIT RETURNS
(Luke 11:24–26)

43a"When an unclean spirit goes out of a man, bhe goes through dry places, seeking rest, and finds none. 44Then he says, 'I will return to my house from which I came.' And when he comes, he finds *it* empty, swept, and put in order. 45Then he goes and takes with him seven other spirits more wicked than himself, and they enter and dwell there; aand the last *state* of that man is worse than the first. So shall it also be with this wicked generation."

JESUS' MOTHER AND BROTHERS SEND FOR HIM
(Mark 3:31–35; Luke 8:19–21)

46While He was still talking to the multitudes, abehold, His mother and bbrothers stood outside, seeking to speak with Him. 47Then one said to Him, "Look, aYour mother and Your brothers are standing outside, seeking to speak with You."

48But He answered and said to the one who told Him, "Who is My mother and who are My brothers?" 49And He stretched out His hand toward His disciples and said, "Here are My mother and My abrothers! 50For awhoever does the will of My Father in heaven is My brother and sister and mother."

THE PARABLE OF THE SOWER
(Mark 4:1–9; Luke 8:4–8)

13 On the same day Jesus went out of the house aand sat by the sea. 2aAnd great multitudes were gathered together to Him, so that bHe got into a boat and sat; and the whole multitude stood on the shore.

3Then He spoke many things to them in parables, saying: a"Behold, a sower went out to sow. 4And as he sowed, some *seed* fell by the wayside; and the birds came and devoured them. 5Some fell on stony places, where they did not have much earth; and they immediately sprang up because they had no depth of earth. 6But when the sun was up they were scorched, and because they had no root they withered away. 7And some fell among thorns, and the thorns sprang up and choked them. 8But others fell on good ground and yielded a crop: some aa hundredfold, some sixty, some thirty. 9aHe who has ears to hear, let him hear!"

Cross References

12:38
aMatt. 16:1;
Mark 8:11;
Luke 11:16;
John 2:18;
1 Cor. 1:22

12:39 aIs. 57:3;
Matt. 16:4;
Mark 8:38;
[Luke 11:29–32];
John 4:48

12:40 aJon. 1:17;
Luke 24:46;
Acts 10:40;
1 Cor. 15:4

12:41 aJon. 3:5;
Luke 11:32
bJer. 3:11;
Ezek. 16:51;
[Rom. 2:27]
cJon. 3:5

12:42
a1 Kin. 10:1–13;
2 Chr. 9:1;
Luke 11:31

12:43
aLuke 11:24–26
b[Job 1:7;
1 Pet. 5:8]

12:45 aMark 5:9;
Luke 11:26;
[Heb. 6:4–8;
10:26];
2 Pet. 2:20–22]

12:46
aMark 3:31–35;
Luke 8:19–21
bMatt. 13:55;
Mark 6:3;
John 2:12; 7:3, 5;
Acts 1:14;
1 Cor. 9:5;
Gal. 1:19

12:47
aMatt. 13:55, 56;
John 2:12;
Acts 1:14

12:49
aJohn 20:17;
[Rom. 8:29]

12:50
aJohn 15:14;
[Gal. 5:6; 6:15;
Col. 3:11;
Heb. 2:11]

13:1
aMatt. 13:1–15;
Mark 4:1–12;
Luke 8:4–10

13:2 aLuke 8:4
bLuke 5:3

13:3 aLuke 8:5

13:8
aGen. 26:12;
Matt. 13:23

13:9 aMatt. 11:15;
Mark 4:9;
Rev. 2:7, 11, 17,
29; 3:6, 13, 22

THE PURPOSE OF PARABLES
(Mark 4:10–12; Luke 8:9, 10)

¹⁰And the disciples came and said to Him, "Why do You speak to them in parables?"

¹¹He answered and said to them, "Because ªit has been given to you to know the ¹mysteries of the kingdom of heaven, but to them it has not been given. ¹²ªFor whoever has, to him more will be given, and he will have abundance; but whoever does not have, even what he has will be taken away from him. ¹³Therefore I speak to them in parables, because seeing they do not see, and hearing they do not hear, nor do they understand. ¹⁴And in them the prophecy of Isaiah is fulfilled, which says:

ª'Hearing you will hear and shall not understand,
And seeing you will see and not ᵇperceive;
15 For the hearts of this people have grown dull.
Their ears ªare hard of hearing,
And their eyes they have ᵇclosed,
Lest they should see with *their* eyes and hear with *their* ears,
Lest they should understand with *their* hearts and turn,
So that I ¹should ᶜheal them.'

¹⁶But ªblessed *are* your eyes for they see, and your ears for they hear; ¹⁷for assuredly, I say to you ªthat many prophets and righteous *men* desired to see what you see, and did not see *it,* and to hear what you hear, and did not hear *it.*

THE PARABLE OF THE SOWER EXPLAINED
(Mark 4:13–20; Luke 8:11–15)

¹⁸ª"Therefore hear the parable of the sower: ¹⁹When anyone hears the word ªof the kingdom, and does not understand *it,* then the wicked *one* comes and snatches away what was sown in his heart. This is he who received seed by the wayside. ²⁰But he who received the seed on stony places, this is he who hears the word and immediately ªreceives it with joy; ²¹yet he has no root in himself, but endures only for a while. For when ªtribulation or persecution arises because of the word, immediately ᵇhe stumbles. ²²Now ªhe who received seed ᵇamong the thorns is he who hears the word, and the cares of this world and the deceitfulness of riches choke the word, and he becomes unfruitful. ²³But he who received seed on the good ground is he who hears the word and understands *it,* who indeed bears ªfruit and produces: some a hundredfold, some sixty, some thirty."

THE PARABLE OF THE WHEAT AND THE TARES

²⁴Another parable He put forth to them, saying: "The kingdom of heaven is like a man who sowed good seed in his field; ²⁵but while men slept, his enemy came and sowed tares among the wheat and went his way. ²⁶But when the grain had sprouted and produced a crop, then the tares also appeared. ²⁷So the servants of the owner came and said to him, 'Sir, did you not sow good seed in your field? How then does it have tares?' ²⁸He said to them, 'An enemy has done this.' The servants said to him, 'Do you want us then to go and gather

---

13:11
ª[Matt. 11:25; 16:17];
Mark 4:10, 11;
[John 6:65;
1 Cor. 2:10;
Col. 1:27;
1 John 2:20, 27]

13:12
ªMatt. 25:29;
Mark 4:25;
Luke 8:18; 19:26

13:14 ªIs. 6:9, 10;
Ezek. 12:2;
Mark 4:12;
Luke 8:10;
John 12:40;
Acts 28:26, 27;
Rom. 11:8;
[2 Cor. 3:14, 15]
ᵇ[John 3:36]

13:15 ªPs. 119:70;
Zech. 7:11;
2 Tim. 4:4;
Heb. 5:11
ᵇLuke 19:42
ᶜActs 28:26, 27

13:16
ª[Prov. 20:12;
Matt. 16:17];
Luke 10:23, 24;
[John 20:29]

13:17
ªJohn 8:56;
Heb. 11:13;
1 Pet. 1:10, 11

13:18
ªMark 4:13–20;
Luke 8:11–15

13:19
ªMatt. 4:23

13:20 ªIs. 58:2;
Ezek. 33:31, 32;
John 5:35

13:21
ª[Acts 14:22]
ᵇMatt. 11:6;
2 Tim. 1:15

13:22
ªMatt. 19:23;
Mark 10:23;
Luke 18:24;
1 Tim. 6:9;
2 Tim. 4:10
ᵇJer. 4:3

13:23
ª[John 15:5];
Phil. 1:11; Col. 1:6

13:11 ¹*secret* or *hidden truths*   13:15 ¹NU, M *would*

them up?' 29But he said, 'No, lest while you gather up the tares you also uproot the wheat with them. 30Let both grow together until the harvest, and at the time of harvest I will say to the reapers, "First gather together the tares and bind them in bundles to burn them, but ªgather the wheat into my barn."'"

THE PARABLE OF THE MUSTARD SEED
(Mark 4:30–32; Luke 13:18, 19)

31Another parable He put forth to them, saying: ª"The kingdom of heaven is like a mustard seed, which a man took and sowed in his field, 32which indeed is the least of all the seeds; but when it is grown it is greater than the herbs and becomes a ªtree, so that the birds of the air come and nest in its branches."

THE PARABLE OF THE LEAVEN
(Luke 13:20, 21)

33ªAnother parable He spoke to them: "The kingdom of heaven is like leaven, which a woman took and hid in three ¹measures of meal till ᵇit was all leavened."

PROPHECY AND THE PARABLES

34ªAll these things Jesus spoke to the multitude in parables; and without a parable He did not speak to them, 35that it might be fulfilled which was spoken by the prophet, saying:

ª"I will open My mouth in parables;
ᵇI will utter things kept secret from the foundation of the world."

THE PARABLE OF THE TARES EXPLAINED

36Then Jesus sent the multitude away and went into the house. And His disciples came to Him, saying, "Explain to us the parable of the tares of the field."

37He answered and said to them: "He who sows the good seed is the Son of Man. 38ªThe field is the world, the good seeds are the sons of the kingdom, but the tares are ᵇthe sons of the wicked *one*. 39The enemy who sowed them is the devil, ªthe harvest is the end of the age, and the reapers are the angels. 40Therefore as the tares are gathered and burned in the fire, so it will be at the end of this age. 41The Son of Man will send out His angels, ªand they will gather out of His kingdom all things that offend, and those who practice lawlessness, 42ªand will cast them into the furnace of fire. ᵇThere will be wailing and gnashing of teeth. 43ªThen the righteous will shine forth as the sun in the kingdom of their Father. ᵇHe who has ears to hear, let him hear!

THE PARABLE OF THE HIDDEN TREASURE

44"Again, the kingdom of heaven is like treasure hidden in a field, which a man found and hid; and for joy over it he goes and ªsells all that he has and ᵇbuys that field.

THE PARABLE OF THE PEARL OF GREAT PRICE

45"Again, the kingdom of heaven is like a merchant seeking beautiful pearls, 46who, when he had found ªone pearl of great price, went and sold all that he had and bought it.

13:30
ªMatt. 3:12

13:31 ª[Is. 2:2, 3;
Mic. 4:1];
Mark 4:30;
Luke 13:18, 19

13:32
ªPs. 104:12;
Ezek. 17:22–24;
31:3–9; Dan. 4:12

13:33
ªLuke 13:20, 21
ᵇ[1 Cor. 5:6;
Gal. 5:9]

13:34
ªMark 4:33, 34;
John 10:6; 16:25

13:35 ªPs. 78:2
ᵇRom. 16:25, 26;
1 Cor. 2:7;
Eph. 3:9;
Col. 1:26

13:38
ªMatt. 24:14;
28:19;
Mark 16:15;
Luke 24:47;
Rom. 10:18;
Col. 1:6
ᵇGen. 3:15;
John 8:44;
Acts 13:10

13:39 ªJoel 3:13;
Rev. 14:15

13:41
ªMatt. 18:7;
2 Pet. 2:1, 2

13:42
ªMatt. 3:12;
Rev. 19:20; 20:10
ᵇMatt. 8:12;
13:50

13:43
ª[Dan. 12:3;
1 Cor. 15:42, 43,
58] ᵇMatt. 13:9

13:44
ªPhil. 3:7, 8
ᵇ[Is. 55:1;
Rev. 3:18]

13:46 ªProv. 2:4;
3:14, 15; 8:10, 19

13:33 ¹Gr. *sata*, same as a Heb. *seah*; approximately 2 pecks in all

THE PARABLE OF THE DRAGNET

47"Again, the kingdom of heaven is like a dragnet that was cast into the sea and ªgathered some of every kind, 48which, when it was full, they drew to shore; and they sat down and gathered the good into vessels, but threw the bad away. 49So it will be at the end of the age. The angels will come forth, ªseparate the wicked from among the just, 50and cast them into the furnace of fire. There will be wailing and gnashing of teeth."

51Jesus said to them, "Have you understood all these things?"

They said to Him, "Yes, 2Lord."

52Then He said to them, "Therefore every 1scribe instructed 2concerning the kingdom of heaven is like a householder who brings out of his treasure ªthings new and old."

JESUS REJECTED AT NAZARETH
(Mark 6:1–6; Luke 4:16–30)

53Now it came to pass, when Jesus had finished these parables, that He departed from there. 54ªWhen He had come to His own country, He taught them in their synagogue, so that they were astonished and said, "Where did this *Man* get this wisdom and *these* mighty works? 55ªIs this not the carpenter's son? Is not His mother called Mary? And ᵇHis brothers ᶜJames, 1Joses, Simon, and Judas? 56And His sisters, are they not all with us? Where then did this *Man* get all these things?" 57So they ªwere offended at Him.

But Jesus said to them, ᵇ"A prophet is not without honor except in his own country and in his own house." 58Now ªHe did not do many mighty works there because of their unbelief.

JOHN THE BAPTIST BEHEADED
(Mark 6:14–29; Luke 9:7–9)

14 At that time ªHerod the tetrarch heard the report about Jesus 2and said to his servants, "This is John the Baptist; he is risen from the dead, and therefore these powers are at work in him." 3ªFor Herod had laid hold of John and bound him, and put *him* in prison for the sake of Herodias, his brother Philip's wife. 4Because John had said to him, ª"It is not lawful for you to have her." 5And although he wanted to put him to death, he feared the multitude, ªbecause they counted him as a prophet.

6But when Herod's birthday was celebrated, the daughter of Herodias danced before them and pleased Herod. 7Therefore he promised with an oath to give her whatever she might ask.

8So she, having been prompted by her mother, said, "Give me John the Baptist's head here on a platter." 9And the king was sorry; nevertheless, because of the oaths and because of those who sat with him, he commanded *it* to be given *to her.* 10So he sent and had John beheaded in prison. 11And his head was brought on a platter and given to the girl, and she brought *it* to her mother. 12Then his disciples

Cross-references (margin)

13:47
ªMatt. 22:9, 10

13:49
ªMatt. 25:32

13:52 ªSong 7:13

13:54 ªPs. 22:22;
Matt. 2:23;
Mark 6:1;
Luke 4:16;
John 7:15

13:55 ªIs. 49:7;
Mark 6:3;
[Luke 3:23];
John 6:42
ᵇMatt. 12:46
ᶜMark 15:40

13:57
ªMatt. 11:6;
Mark 6:3, 4
ᵇLuke 4:24;
John 4:44

13:58
ªMark 6:5, 6;
John 5:44,
46, 47

14:1
ªMark 6:14–29;
Luke 9:7–9

14:3 ªMatt. 4:12;
Mark 6:17;
Luke 3:19, 20

14:4
ªLev. 18:16;
20:21

14:5
ªMatt. 21:26;
Luke 20:6

13:51 1NU omits *Jesus said to them*   2NU omits *Lord*   13:52 1A scholar of the Old Testament   2Or *for*   13:55 1NU *Joseph*

came and took away the body and buried it, and went and told Jesus.

FEEDING THE FIVE THOUSAND
(Mark 6:30–44; Luke 9:10–17; John 6:1–14)

13aWhen Jesus heard *it,* He departed from there by boat to a deserted place by Himself. But when the multitudes heard it, they followed Him on foot from the cities. 14And when Jesus went out He saw a great multitude; and He awas moved with compassion for them, and healed their sick. 15aWhen it was evening, His disciples came to Him, saying, "This is a deserted place, and the hour is already late. Send the multitudes away, that they may go into the villages and buy themselves food."

16But Jesus said to them, "They do not need to go away. You give them something to eat."

17And they said to Him, "We have here only five loaves and two fish."

18He said, "Bring them here to Me." 19Then He commanded the multitudes to sit down on the grass. And He took the five loaves and the two fish, and looking up to heaven, aHe blessed and broke and gave the loaves to the disciples; and the disciples gave to the multitudes. 20So they all ate and were filled, and they took up twelve baskets full of the fragments that remained. 21Now those who had eaten were about five thousand men, besides women and children.

JESUS WALKS ON THE SEA
(Mark 6:45–52; John 6:15–21)

22Immediately Jesus 1made His disciples get into the boat and go before Him to the other side, while He sent the multitudes away. 23aAnd when He had sent the multitudes away, He went up on the mountain by Himself to pray. bNow when evening came, He was alone there. 24But the boat was now 1in the middle of the sea, tossed by the waves, for the wind was contrary.

25Now in the fourth watch of the night Jesus went to them, walking on the sea. 26And when the disciples saw Him awalking on the sea, they were troubled, saying, "It is a ghost!" And they cried out for fear.

27But immediately Jesus spoke to them, saying, 1"Be of good acheer! 2It is I; do not be afraid."

28And Peter answered Him and said, "Lord, if it is You, command me to come to You on the water."

29So He said, "Come." And when Peter had come down out of the boat, he walked on the water to go to Jesus. 30But when he saw 1that the wind *was* boisterous, he was afraid; and beginning to sink he cried out, saying, "Lord, save me!"

31And immediately Jesus stretched out *His* hand and caught him, and said to him, "O you of alittle faith, why did you doubt?" 32And when they got into the boat, the wind ceased.

33Then those who were in the boat 1came and worshiped Him, saying, "Truly aYou are the Son of God."

14:13
aMatt. 10:23;
12:15;
Mark 6:32–44;
Luke 9:10–17;
John 6:1, 2

14:14
aMatt. 9:36;
Mark 6:34

14:15
aMark 6:35;
Luke 9:12

14:19
a1 Sam. 9:13;
Matt. 15:36;
26:26;
Mark 6:41;
8:7; 14:22;
Luke 24:30;
Acts 27:35;
[Rom. 14:6]

14:23
aMark 6:46;
Luke 9:28;
John 6:15
bJohn 6:16

14:26 aJob 9:8

14:27
aActs 23:11;
27:22, 25, 36

14:31
aMatt. 6:30;
8:26

14:33 aPs. 2:7;
Matt. 16:16;
26:63; Mark 1:1;
Luke 4:41;
John 1:49; 6:69;
11:27; Acts 8:37;
Rom. 1:4

14:22 1invited, strongly urged   14:24 1NU many furlongs away from the land
14:27 1Take courage   2Lit. I am   14:30 1NU brackets that and boisterous as
disputed.   14:33 1NU omits came and

MANY TOUCH HIM AND ARE MADE WELL

(Mark 6:53–56)

34aWhen they had crossed over, they came ¹to the land of Gennesaret. 35And when the men of that place recognized Him, they sent out into all that surrounding region, brought to Him all who were sick, 36and begged Him that they might only atouch the hem of His garment. And bas many as touched *it* were made perfectly well.

DEFILEMENT COMES FROM WITHIN

(Mark 7:1–23)

15 Then athe scribes and Pharisees who were from Jerusalem came to Jesus, saying, 2a"Why do Your disciples transgress the tradition of the elders? For they do not wash their hands when they eat bread."

3He answered and said to them, "Why do you also transgress the commandment of God because of your tradition? 4For God commanded, saying, a'Honor your father and your mother'; and, b'He who curses father or mother, let him be put to death.' 5But you say, 'Whoever says to his father or mother, a"Whatever profit you might have received from me *is* a gift *to God"*— 6then he need not honor his father ¹or mother.' Thus you have made the ²commandment of God of no effect by your tradition. 7aHypocrites! Well did Isaiah prophesy about you, saying:

8 'Thesea people ¹draw near to Me with their mouth,
   And honor Me with *their* lips,
   But their heart is far from Me.
9 And in vain they worship Me,
   aTeaching *as* doctrines the commandments
      of men.'"

10aWhen He had called the multitude to *Himself,* He said to them, "Hear and understand: 11aNot what goes into the mouth defiles a man; but what comes out of the mouth, this defiles a man."

12Then His disciples came and said to Him, "Do You know that the Pharisees were offended when they heard this saying?"

13But He answered and said, a"Every plant which My heavenly Father has not planted will be uprooted. 14Let them alone. aThey are blind leaders of the blind. And if the blind leads the blind, both will fall into a ditch."

15aThen Peter answered and said to Him, "Explain this parable to us."

16So Jesus said, a"Are you also still without understanding? 17Do you not yet understand that awhatever enters the mouth goes into the stomach and is eliminated? 18But athose things which proceed out of the mouth come from the heart, and they defile a man. 19aFor out of the heart proceed evil thoughts, murders, adulteries, fornications, thefts, false witness, blasphemies. 20These are *the things* which defile a man, but to eat with unwashed hands does not defile a man."

14:34
aMark 6:53;
Luke 5:1

14:36
a[Mark 5:24–34]
bMatt. 9:20;
Mark 3:10;
[Luke 6:19];
Acts 19:12

15:1 aMark 7:1;
John 1:19;
Acts 25:7

15:2 aMark 7:5

15:4
aEx. 20:1, 12;
Lev. 19:3;
[Deut. 5:16];
Prov. 23:22;
[Eph. 6:2, 3]
bEx. 21:17;
Lev. 20:9;
Deut. 27:16;
Prov. 20:20;
30:17

15:5
aMark 7:11, 12

15:7 aMark 7:6

15:8 aPs. 78:36;
Is. 29:13;
Ezek. 33:31

15:9 aIs. 29:13;
[Col. 2:18–22];
Titus 1:14

15:10 aMark 7:14

15:11
a[Acts 10:15;
Rom. 14:14,
17, 20;
1 Tim. 4:4;
Titus 1:15]

15:13
a[Is. 60:21; 61:3;
John 15:2;
1 Cor. 3:12, 13]

15:14 aIs. 9:16;
Mal. 2:8;
Matt. 23:16, 24;
Luke 6:39;
Rom. 2:19

15:15 aMark 7:17

15:16
aMatt. 16:9;
Mark 7:18

15:17
a[1 Cor. 6:13]

15:18
a[Matt. 12:34];
Mark 7:20;
[James 3:6]

15:19
aGen. 6:5; 8:21;
Prov. 6:14;
Jer. 17:9;
Mark 7:21;
[Rom. 1:29–32;
Gal. 5:19–21]

14:34 ¹NU *to land at*   15:6 ¹NU omits *or mother*   ²NU *word*
15:8 ¹NU omits *draw near to Me with their mouth, And*

A GENTILE SHOWS HER FAITH
(Mark 7:24–30)

[21a]Then Jesus went out from there and departed to the region of Tyre and Sidon. [22]And behold, a woman of Canaan came from that region and cried out to Him, saying, "Have mercy on me, O Lord, [a]Son of David! My daughter is severely demon-possessed."

[23]But He answered her not a word.

And His disciples came and urged Him, saying, "Send her away, for she cries out after us."

[24]But He answered and said, [a]"I was not sent except to the lost sheep of the house of Israel."

[25]Then she came and worshiped Him, saying, "Lord, help me!"

[26]But He answered and said, "It is not good to take the children's bread and throw *it* to the little [a]dogs."

[27]And she said, "Yes, Lord, yet even the little dogs eat the crumbs which fall from their masters' table."

[28]Then Jesus answered and said to her, "O woman, [a]great *is* your faith! Let it be to you as you desire." And her daughter was healed from that very hour.

JESUS HEALS GREAT MULTITUDES
(Mark 7:31–37)

[29a]Jesus departed from there, [b]skirted the Sea of Galilee, and went up on the mountain and sat down there. [30a]Then great multitudes came to Him, having with them *the* lame, blind, mute, [1]maimed, and many others; and they laid them down at Jesus' [b]feet, and He healed them. [31]So the multitude marveled when they saw *the* mute speaking, *the* [1]maimed made whole, *the* lame walking, and *the* blind seeing; and they [a]glorified the God of Israel.

FEEDING THE FOUR THOUSAND
(Mark 8:1–10)

[32a]Now Jesus called His disciples to *Himself* and said, "I have compassion on the multitude, because they have now continued with Me three days and have nothing to eat. And I do not want to send them away hungry, lest they faint on the way."

[33a]Then His disciples said to Him, "Where could we get enough bread in the wilderness to fill such a great multitude?"

[34]Jesus said to them, "How many loaves do you have?"

And they said, "Seven, and a few little fish."

[35]So He commanded the multitude to sit down on the ground. [36]And [a]He took the seven loaves and the fish and [b]gave thanks, broke *them* and gave *them* to His disciples; and the disciples *gave* to the multitude. [37]So they all ate and were filled, and they took up seven large baskets full of the fragments that were left. [38]Now those who ate were four thousand men, besides women and children. [39a]And He sent away the multitude, got into the boat, and came to the region of [1]Magdala.

15:21
[a]Mark 7:24–30

15:22 [a]Matt. 1:1; 22:41, 42

15:24
[a]Matt. 10:5, 6; [Rom. 15:8]

15:26
[a]Matt. 7:6; Phil. 3:2

15:28 [a]Luke 7:9

15:29
[a]Matt. 15:29–31; Mark 7:31–37
[b]Matt. 4:18

15:30
[a]Is. 35:5, 6; Matt. 11:5; Luke 7:22
[b]Mark 7:25; Luke 7:38; 8:41; 10:39

15:31
[a]Luke 5:25, 26; 19:37, 38

15:32
[a]Mark 8:1–10

15:33
[a]2 Kin. 4:43

15:36
[a]Matt. 14:19; 26:27; Luke 22:17, 19; John 6:11, 23; Acts 27:35; [Rom. 14:6]
[b]1 Sam. 9:13; Luke 22:19

15:39
[a]Mark 8:10

15:30 [1]crippled   15:31 [1]crippled   15:39 [1]NU *Magadan*

THE PHARISEES AND SADDUCEES SEEK A SIGN
(Mark 8:11–13; Luke 12:54–56)

16 Then the [a]Pharisees and Sadducees came, and testing Him asked that He would show them a sign from heaven. [2]He answered and said to them, "When it is evening you say, '*It will be* fair weather, for the sky is red'; [3]and in the morning, '*It will be* foul weather today, for the sky is red and threatening.' [1]Hypocrites! You know how to discern the face of the sky, but you cannot *discern* the signs of the times. [4a]A wicked and adulterous generation seeks after a sign, and no sign shall be given to it except the sign of [1]the prophet Jonah." And He left them and departed.

THE LEAVEN OF THE PHARISEES AND SADDUCEES
(Mark 8:14–21)

[5]Now [a]when His disciples had come to the other side, they had forgotten to take bread. [6]Then Jesus said to them, [a]"Take heed and beware of the [1]leaven of the Pharisees and the Sadducees."

[7]And they reasoned among themselves, saying, "*It is* because we have taken no bread."

[8]But Jesus, being aware of *it,* said to them, "O you of little faith, why do you reason among yourselves because you [1]have brought no bread? [9a]Do you not yet understand, or remember the five loaves of the five thousand and how many baskets you took up? [10a]Nor the seven loaves of the four thousand and how many large baskets you took up? [11]How is it you do not understand that I did not speak to you concerning bread?—*but* to beware of the [1]leaven of the Pharisees and Sadducees." [12]Then they understood that He did not tell *them* to beware of the leaven of bread, but of the [1]doctrine of the Pharisees and Sadducees.

PETER CONFESSES JESUS AS THE CHRIST
(Mark 8:27–30; Luke 9:18–20)

[13]When Jesus came into the region of Caesarea Philippi, He asked His disciples, saying, [a]"Who do men say that I, the Son of Man, am?"

[14]So they said, [a]"Some *say* John the Baptist, some Elijah, and others Jeremiah or [b]one of the prophets."

[15]He said to them, "But who do [a]you say that I am?"

[16]Simon Peter answered and said, [a]"You are the Christ, the Son of the living God."

[17]Jesus answered and said to him, "Blessed are you, Simon Bar-Jonah, [a]for flesh and blood has not revealed *this* to you, but [b]My Father who is in heaven. [18]And I also say to you that [a]you are Peter, and [b]on this rock I will build My church, and [c]the gates of Hades shall not [1]prevail against it. [19a]And I will give you the keys of the kingdom of heaven, and whatever you bind on earth [1]will be bound in heaven, and whatever you loose on earth will be loosed in heaven."

[20a]Then He commanded His disciples that they should tell no one that He was Jesus the Christ.

16:1 [a]Matt. 12:38; Mark 8:11; Luke 11:16; 12:54–56; 1 Cor. 1:22
16:4 [a]Prov. 30:12; Matt. 12:39; Luke 11:29; 24:46
16:5 [a]Mark 8:14
16:6 [a]Mark 8:15; Luke 12:1
16:9 [a]Matt. 14:15–21; Mark 6:30–44; Luke 9:10–17; John 6:1–14
16:10 [a]Matt. 15:32–38; Mark 8:1–9
16:13 [a]Mark 8:27; Luke 9:18
16:14 [a]Matt. 14:2; Luke 9:7–9; [b]Matt. 21:11
16:15 [a]John 6:67
16:16 [a]Matt. 14:33; Mark 8:29; Luke 9:20; John 6:69; 11:27; Acts 8:37; 9:20; Heb. 1:2, 5; 1 John 4:15
16:17 [a][Eph. 2:8]; [b][Matt. 11:27]; 1 Cor. 2:10]; Gal. 1:16
16:18 [a]John 1:42; [b]Acts 2:41; [Eph. 2:20]; Rev. 21:14]; [c]Job 33:17; Ps. 9:13; 107:18; Is. 38:10
16:19 [a]Matt. 18:18; John 20:23
16:20 [a]Matt. 17:9; Mark 8:30; Luke 9:21

16:3 [1]NU omits *Hypocrites* 16:4 [1]NU omits *the prophet* 16:6 [1]*yeast* 16:8 [1]NU *have no bread* 16:11 [1]*yeast* 16:12 [1]*teaching* 16:18 [1]*be victorious* 16:19 [1]Or *will have been bound . . . will have been loosed*

JESUS PREDICTS HIS DEATH AND RESURRECTION
(Mark 8:31–33; Luke 9:21, 22)

21From that time Jesus began ato show to His disciples that He must go to Jerusalem, and suffer many things from the elders and chief priests and scribes, and be killed, and be raised the third day.

22Then Peter took Him aside and began to rebuke Him, saying, 1"Far be it from You, Lord; this shall not happen to You!"

23But He turned and said to Peter, "Get behind Me, aSatan! bYou are 1an offense to Me, for you are not mindful of the things of God, but the things of men."

TAKE UP THE CROSS AND FOLLOW HIM
(Mark 8:34–38; Luke 9:23–26)

24aThen Jesus said to His disciples, "If anyone desires to come after Me, let him deny himself, and take up his cross, and bfollow Me. 25For awhoever desires to save his life will lose it, but whoever loses his life for My sake will find it. 26For what aprofit is it to a man if he gains the whole world, and loses his own soul? Or bwhat will a man give in exchange for his soul? 27For athe Son of Man will come in the glory of His Father bwith His angels, cand then He will reward each according to his works. 28Assuredly, I say to you, athere are some standing here who shall not taste death till they see the Son of Man coming in His kingdom."

JESUS TRANSFIGURED ON THE MOUNT
(Mark 9:1–13; Luke 9:27–36; 2 Pet. 1:16–18)

17 Now aafter six days Jesus took Peter, James, and John his brother, led them up on a high mountain by themselves; 2and He was transfigured before them. His face shone like the sun, and His clothes became as white as the light. 3And behold, Moses and Elijah appeared to them, talking with Him. 4Then Peter answered and said to Jesus, "Lord, it is good for us to be here; if You wish, 1let us make here three tabernacles: one for You, one for Moses, and one for Elijah."

5aWhile he was still speaking, behold, a bright cloud overshadowed them; and suddenly a voice came out of the cloud, saying, b"This is My beloved Son, cin whom I am well pleased. dHear Him!" 6aAnd when the disciples heard *it*, they fell on their faces and were greatly afraid. 7But Jesus came and atouched them and said, "Arise, and do not be afraid." 8When they had lifted up their eyes, they saw no one but Jesus only.

9Now as they came down from the mountain, Jesus commanded them, saying, "Tell the vision to no one until the Son of Man is risen from the dead."

10And His disciples asked Him, saying, a"Why then do the scribes say that Elijah must come first?"

11Jesus answered and said to them, "Indeed, Elijah is coming 1first and will arestore all things. 12aBut I say to you that Elijah has come already, and they bdid not know him but did to him whatever they wished. Likewise cthe Son of Man is also

---

16:21
a Matt. 20:17;
Mark 8:31; 9:31;
Luke 9:22; 18:31;
24:46; John 2:19

16:23
a Matt. 4:10
b [Rom. 8:7]

16:24
a Mark 8:34;
Luke 9:23;
[Acts 14:22;
2 Cor. 4:10, 11;
1 Thess. 3:3;
2 Tim. 3:12]
b [1 Pet. 2:21]

16:25
a Luke 17:33;
John 12:25

16:26
a Luke 12:20, 21
b Ps. 49:7, 8

16:27
a Matt. 26:64;
Mark 8:38;
Luke 9:26
b [Dan. 7:10];
Zech. 14:5
c Job 34:11;
Ps. 62:12;
Prov. 24:12;
Rom. 2:6;
2 Cor. 5:10;
1 Pet. 1:17;
Rev. 2:23

16:28 a Mark 9:1;
Luke 9:27;
Acts 7:55, 56;
Rev. 19:11

17:1
a Matt. 17:1–8;
Mark 9:2–8;
Luke 9:28–36

17:5 a 2 Pet. 1:17
b Ps. 2:7;
Matt. 3:17;
Mark 1:11;
Luke 1:35; 3:22;
[John 12:28–30]
c Is. 42:1;
Matt. 3:17; 12:18;
2 Pet. 1:17
d [Deut. 18:15, 19;
Acts 3:22, 23]

17:6 a 2 Pet. 1:18

17:7 a Dan. 8:18

17:10 a Mal. 4:5;
Matt. 11:14; 16:14;
Mark 9:11

17:11 a [Mal. 4:6];
Luke 1:17

17:12
a Matt. 11:14;
Mark 9:12, 13
b Matt. 14:3, 10
c Matt. 16:21

16:22 1Lit. *Merciful to You* (May God be merciful)   16:23 1*a stumbling block*
17:4 1NU *I will make*   17:11 1NU omits *first*

about to suffer at their hands." [13a]Then the disciples understood that He spoke to them of John the Baptist.

A BOY IS HEALED
(Mark 9:14–29; Luke 9:37–42)

[14a]And when they had come to the multitude, a man came to Him, kneeling down to Him and saying, [15]"Lord, have mercy on my son, for he is [1]an epileptic and suffers severely; for he often falls into the fire and often into the water. [16]So I brought him to Your disciples, but they could not cure him."

[17]Then Jesus answered and said, "O [1]faithless and [a]perverse generation, how long shall I be with you? How long shall I bear with you? Bring him here to Me." [18]And Jesus [a]rebuked the demon, and it came out of him; and the child was cured from that very hour.

[19]Then the disciples came to Jesus privately and said, "Why could we not cast it out?"

[20]So Jesus said to them, "Because of your [1]unbelief; for assuredly, I say to you, [a]if you have faith as a mustard seed, you will say to this mountain, 'Move from here to there,' and it will move; and nothing will be impossible for you. [21]However, this kind does not go out except by prayer and fasting."

JESUS AGAIN PREDICTS HIS DEATH AND RESURRECTION
(Mark 9:30–32; Luke 9:43–45)

[22a]Now while they were [1]staying in Galilee, Jesus said to them, "The Son of Man is about to be betrayed into the hands of men, [23]and they will kill Him, and the third day He will be raised up." And they were exceedingly [a]sorrowful.

PETER AND HIS MASTER PAY THEIR TAXES

[24a]When they had come to [1]Capernaum, those who received the [2]*temple* tax came to Peter and said, "Does your Teacher not pay the *temple* tax?"

[25]He said, "Yes."

And when he had come into the house, Jesus anticipated him, saying, "What do you think, Simon? From whom do the kings of the earth take customs or taxes, from their sons or from [a]strangers?"

[26]Peter said to Him, "From strangers."

Jesus said to him, "Then the sons are free. [27]Nevertheless, lest we offend them, go to the sea, cast in a hook, and take the fish that comes up first. And when you have opened its mouth, you will find a [1]piece of money; take that and give it to them for Me and you."

WHO IS THE GREATEST?
(Mark 9:33–37; Luke 9:46–48)

18 At [a]that time the disciples came to Jesus, saying, "Who then is greatest in the kingdom of heaven?" [2]Then Jesus called a little [a]child to Him, set him in the midst of them, [3]and said, "Assuredly, I say to you, [a]unless you

---

17:13 [a]Matt. 11:14

17:14
[a]Matt. 17:14–19;
Mark 9:14–28;
Luke 9:37–42

17:17
[a]Deut. 32:5;
Phil. 2:15

17:18 [a]Luke 4:41

17:20
[a]Matt. 21:21;
Mark 11:23;
Luke 17:6;
[1 Cor. 12:9]

17:22
[a]Matt. 16:21;
26:57;
Mark 8:31;
Luke 9:22, 44;
John 18:12

17:23
[a]Matt. 26:22;
27:50;
Luke 23:46;
24:46;
John 16:6;
19:30;
Acts 10:40

17:24
[a]Mark 9:33

17:25
[a][Is. 60:10–17]

18:1
[a]Mark 9:33–37;
Luke 9:46–48;
22:24–27

18:2
[a]Matt. 19:14;
Mark 10:14;
Luke 18:14–17

18:3 [a]Ps. 131:2;
Matt. 19:14;
Mark 10:15;
Luke 18:16;
[1 Cor. 14:20;
1 Pet. 2:2]

17:15 [1]Lit. *moonstruck*   17:17 [1]*unbelieving*   17:20 [1]NU *little faith*
17:21 [1]NU omits v. 21.   17:22 [1]NU *gathering together*   17:24 [1]NU
Capharnaum, here and elsewhere   [2]Lit. *double drachma*   17:27 [1]Gr.
stater, the exact temple tax for two

are converted and become as little children, you will by no means enter the kingdom of heaven. [4a]Therefore whoever humbles himself as this little child is the greatest in the kingdom of heaven. [5a]Whoever receives one little child like this in My name receives Me.

JESUS WARNS OF OFFENSES
(Mark 9:42–48; Luke 17:1, 2)

[6a]"But whoever causes one of these little ones who believe in Me to sin, it would be better for him if a millstone were hung around his neck, and he were drowned in the depth of the sea. [7]Woe to the world because of [1]offenses! For [a]offenses must come, but [b]woe to that man by whom the offense comes!

[8a]"If your hand or foot causes you to sin, cut it off and cast it from you. It is better for you to enter into life lame or maimed, rather than having two hands or two feet, to be cast into the everlasting fire. [9]And if your eye causes you to sin, pluck it out and cast it from you. It is better for you to enter into life with one eye, rather than having two eyes, to be cast into [1]hell fire.

THE PARABLE OF THE LOST SHEEP
(Luke 15:1–7)

[10]"Take heed that you do not despise one of these little ones, for I say to you that in heaven [a]their angels always [b]see the face of My Father who is in heaven. [11a]For[1] the Son of Man has come to save that which was lost.

[12a]"What do you think? If a man has a hundred sheep, and one of them goes astray, does he not leave the ninety-nine and go to the mountains to seek the one that is straying? [13]And if he should find it, assuredly, I say to you, he rejoices more over that sheep than over the ninety-nine that did not go astray. [14]Even so it is not the [a]will of your Father who is in heaven that one of these little ones should perish.

DEALING WITH A SINNING BROTHER

[15]"Moreover [a]if your brother sins against you, go and tell him his fault between you and him alone. If he hears you, [b]you have gained your brother. [16]But if he will not hear, take with you one or two more, that [a]'by the mouth of two or three witnesses every word may be established.' [17]And if he refuses to hear them, tell it to the church. But if he refuses even to hear the church, let him be to you like a [a]heathen and a tax collector. [18]"Assuredly, I say to you, [a]whatever you bind on earth will be bound in heaven, and whatever you loose on earth will be loosed in heaven.

[19a]"Again[1] I say to you that if two of you agree on earth concerning anything that they ask, [b]it will be done for them by My Father in heaven. [20]For where two or three are gathered [a]together in My name, I am there in the midst of them."

THE PARABLE OF THE UNFORGIVING SERVANT

[21]Then Peter came to Him and said, "Lord, how often shall my brother sin against me, and I forgive him? [a]Up to seven times?"

18:4
[a][Matt. 20:27; 23:11]

18:5
[a][Matt. 10:42]; Luke 9:48

18:6 [a]Mark 9:42; Luke 17:2; [1 Cor. 8:12]

18:7 [a]Luke 17:1; [1 Cor. 11:19]; 1 Tim. 4:1
[b]Matt. 26:24; 27:4, 5

18:8
[a]Matt. 5:29, 30; Mark 9:43, 45

18:10
[a][Ps. 34:7]; Zech. 13:7; [Heb. 1:14]
[b]Esth. 1:14; Luke 1:19; Acts 12:15; [Rev. 8:2]

18:11 [a]Luke 9:56; John 3:17

18:12
[a]Matt. 18:12–14; Luke 15:4–7

18:14
[a][1 Tim. 2:4]

18:15 [a]Lev. 19:17; [Luke 17:3, 4; Gal. 6:1]; 2 Thess. 3:15; [James 5:19]
[b][James 5:20]; 1 Pet. 3:1

18:16
[a]Deut. 17:6; 19:15; John 8:17; 2 Cor. 13:1; 1 Tim. 5:19; Heb. 10:28

18:17
[a]Rom. 16:17; 1 Cor. 5:9; [2 Thess. 3:6, 14; 2 John 10]

18:18
[a]Matt. 16:19; [John 20:22, 23; 1 Cor. 5:4]

18:19
[a][1 Cor. 1:10]
[b][1 John 3:22; 5:14]

18:20
[a]Acts 20:7; 1 Cor. 14:26

18:21 [a]Luke 17:4

18:7 [1]enticements to sin   18:9 [1]Gr. Gehenna   18:11 [1]NU omits v. 11.
18:19 [1]NU, M Again, assuredly, I say

²²Jesus said to him, "I do not say to you, ªup to seven times, but up to seventy times seven. ²³Therefore the kingdom of heaven is like a certain king who wanted to settle accounts with his servants. ²⁴And when he had begun to settle accounts, one was brought to him who owed him ten thousand talents. ²⁵But as he was not able to pay, his master commanded ªthat he be sold, with his wife and children and all that he had, and that payment be made. ²⁶The servant therefore fell down before him, saying, 'Master, have patience with me, and I will pay you all.' ²⁷Then the master of that servant was moved with compassion, released him, and forgave him the debt.

²⁸"But that servant went out and found one of his fellow servants who owed him a hundred denarii; and he laid hands on him and took *him* by the throat, saying, 'Pay me what you owe!' ²⁹So his fellow servant fell down ¹at his feet and begged him, saying, 'Have patience with me, and I will pay you ²all.' ³⁰And he would not, but went and threw him into prison till he should pay the debt. ³¹So when his fellow servants saw what had been done, they were very grieved, and came and told their master all that had been done. ³²Then his master, after he had called him, said to him, 'You wicked servant! I forgave you ªall that debt because you begged me. ³³Should you not also have had compassion on your fellow servant, just as I had pity on you?' ³⁴And his master was angry, and delivered him to the torturers until he should pay all that was due to him.

³⁵ª"So My heavenly Father also will do to you if each of you, from his heart, does not forgive his brother ¹his trespasses."

MARRIAGE AND DIVORCE
(Mark 10:1–12)

19 Now it came to pass, ªwhen Jesus had finished these sayings, *that* He departed from Galilee and came to the region of Judea beyond the Jordan. ²ªAnd great multitudes followed Him, and He healed them there.

³The Pharisees also came to Him, testing Him, and saying to Him, "Is it lawful for a man to divorce his wife for *just* any reason?"

⁴And He answered and said to them, "Have you not read that He who ¹made *them* at the beginning ª'made them male and female,' ⁵and said, ª'For this reason a man shall leave his father and mother and be joined to his wife, and ᵇthe two shall become one flesh'? ⁶So then, they are no longer two but one flesh. Therefore what God has joined together, let not man separate."

⁷They said to Him, ª"Why then did Moses command to give a certificate of divorce, and to put her away?"

⁸He said to them, "Moses, because of the ªhardness of your hearts, permitted you to divorce your ᵇwives, but from the beginning it was not so. ⁹ªAnd I say to you, whoever divorces his wife, except for ¹sexual immorality, and marries another, commits adultery; and whoever marries her who is divorced commits adultery."

18:22
ª[Matt. 6:14; Mark 11:25]; Col. 3:13

18:25 ªEx. 21:2; Lev. 25:39; 2 Kin. 4:1; Neh. 5:5, 8

18:32
ªLuke 7:41–43

18:35
ªProv. 21:13; Matt. 6:12; Mark 11:26; James 2:13

19:1
ªMatt. 19:1–9; Mark 10:1–12; John 10:40

19:2 ªMatt. 12:15

19:4
ªGen. 1:27; 5:2; [Mal. 2:15]

19:5 ªGen. 2:24; Mark 10:5–9; Eph. 5:31
ᵇ[1 Cor. 6:16; 7:2]

19:7
ªDeut. 24:1–4; Matt. 5:31

19:8 ªHeb. 3:15
ᵇMal. 2:16

19:9
ª[Matt. 5:32]; Mark 10:11; Luke 16:18; 1 Cor. 7:10

18:29 ¹NU omits *at his feet*   ²NU, M omit *all*   18:35 ¹NU omits *his trespasses*   19:4 ¹NU *created*   19:9 ¹Or *fornication*

[10]His disciples said to Him, [a]"If such is the case of the man with *his* wife, it is better not to marry."

JESUS TEACHES ON CELIBACY

[11]But He said to them, [a]"All cannot accept this saying, but only *those* to whom it has been given: [12]For there are [1]eunuchs who were born thus from *their* mother's womb, and [a]there are eunuchs who were made eunuchs by men, and there are eunuchs who have made themselves eunuchs for the kingdom of heaven's sake. He who is able to accept *it,* let him accept *it.*"

JESUS BLESSES LITTLE CHILDREN
(Mark 10:13–16; Luke 18:15–17)

[13a]Then little children were brought to Him that He might put *His* hands on them and pray, but the disciples rebuked them. [14]But Jesus said, "Let the little children come to Me, and do not forbid them; for [a]of such is the kingdom of heaven." [15]And He laid *His* hands on them and departed from there.

JESUS COUNSELS THE RICH YOUNG RULER
(Mark 10:17–22; Luke 18:18–23)

[16a]Now behold, one came and said to Him, [b]"Good[1] Teacher, what good thing shall I do that I may have eternal life?"

[17]So He said to him, [1]"Why do you call Me good? [2]No one *is* [a]good but One, *that is,* God. But if you want to enter into life, [b]keep the commandments."

[18]He said to Him, "Which ones?"

Jesus said, [a]"'You shall not murder,' 'You shall not commit adultery,' 'You shall not steal,' 'You shall not bear false witness,' [19a]'Honor your father and *your* mother,' and, [b]'You shall love your neighbor as yourself.'"

[20]The young man said to Him, "All these things I have [a]kept [1]from my youth. What do I still lack?"

[21]Jesus said to him, "If you want to be perfect, [a]go, sell what you have and give to the poor, and you will have treasure in heaven; and come, follow Me."

[22]But when the young man heard that saying, he went away sorrowful, for he had great possessions.

WITH GOD ALL THINGS ARE POSSIBLE
(Mark 10:23–31; Luke 18:24–30)

[23]Then Jesus said to His disciples, "Assuredly, I say to you that [a]it is hard for a rich man to enter the kingdom of heaven. [24]And again I say to you, it is easier for a camel to go through the eye of a needle than for a rich man to enter the kingdom of God."

[25]When His disciples heard *it,* they were greatly astonished, saying, "Who then can be saved?"

[26]But Jesus looked at *them* and said to them, "With men this is impossible, but [a]with God all things are possible."

[27]Then Peter answered and said to Him, "See, [a]we have left all and followed You. Therefore what shall we have?"

[28]So Jesus said to them, "Assuredly I say to you, that in

19:10
[a][Prov. 21:19]

19:11 [a][1 Cor. 7:2, 7, 9, 17]

19:12
[a][1 Cor. 7:32]

19:13
[a]Matt. 20:31;
Mark 10:13;
Luke 18:15

19:14
[a]Matt. 18:3, 4;
Mark 10:15;
Luke 18:17;
[1 Cor. 14:20;
1 Pet. 2:2]

19:16
[a]Matt. 19:16–29;
Mark 10:17–30;
Luke 18:18–30
[b]Luke 10:25

19:17 [a]Ps. 25:8;
34:8; Nah. 1:7;
[Rom. 2:4]
[b]Lev. 18:5;
Deut. 4:40;
6:17; 7:11; 11:22;
28:9; Neh. 9:29;
Ezek. 20:21;
[Gal. 3:10]

19:18
[a]Ex. 20:13–16;
Deut. 5:17–20

19:19
[a]Ex. 20:12–16;
Deut. 5:16–20;
Matt. 15:4
[b]Lev. 19:18;
Matt. 22:39;
[Rom. 13:9;
Gal. 5:14;
James 2:8]

19:20
[a][Phil. 3:6, 7]

19:21
[a]Matt. 6:20;
Luke 12:33;
Acts 2:45;
4:34, 35;
1 Tim. 6:18, 19

19:23
[a][Matt. 13:22];
Mark 10:24;
1 Cor. 1:26;
[1 Tim. 6:9]

19:26
[a]Gen. 18:14;
Num. 11:23;
Job 42:2;
Is. 59:1;
Jer. 32:17;
Zech. 8:6;
Luke 1:37

19:27
[a]Deut. 33:9;
Matt. 4:20;
Luke 5:11

19:12 [1]Emasculated men   19:16 [1]NU omits *Good*   19:17 [1]NU *Why do you ask Me about what is good?*   [2]NU *There is One who is good. But*
19:20 [1]NU omits *from my youth*

the regeneration, when the Son of Man sits on the throne of His glory, [a]you who have followed Me will also sit on twelve thrones, judging the twelve tribes of Israel. 29[a]And everyone who has left houses or brothers or sisters or father or mother [1]or wife or children or [2]lands, for My name's sake, shall receive a hundredfold, and inherit eternal life. 30[a]But many *who are* first will be last, and the last first.

THE PARABLE OF THE WORKERS IN THE VINEYARD

20 "For the kingdom of heaven is like a landowner who went out early in the morning to hire laborers for his vineyard. 2Now when he had agreed with the laborers for a denarius a day, he sent them into his vineyard. 3And he went out about the third hour and saw others standing idle in the marketplace, 4and said to them, 'You also go into the vineyard, and whatever is right I will give you.' So they went. 5Again he went out about the sixth and the ninth hour, and did likewise. 6And about the eleventh hour he went out and found others standing [1]idle, and said to them, 'Why have you been standing here idle all day?' 7They said to him, 'Because no one hired us.' He said to them, 'You also go into the vineyard, [1]and whatever is right you will receive.'

8"So when evening had come, the owner of the vineyard said to his steward, 'Call the laborers and give them *their* wages, beginning with the last to the first.' 9And when those came who *were hired* about the eleventh hour, they each received a denarius. 10But when the first came, they supposed that they would receive more; and they likewise received each a denarius. 11And when they had received *it*, they [1]complained against the landowner, 12saying, 'These last *men* have worked *only* one hour, and you made them equal to us who have borne the burden and the heat of the day.' 13But he answered one of them and said, 'Friend, I am doing you no wrong. Did you not agree with me for a denarius? 14Take *what is* yours and go your way. I wish to give to this last man *the same* as to you. 15[a]Is it not lawful for me to do what I wish with my own things? Or [b]is your eye evil because I am good?' 16[a]So the last will be first, and the first last. [b]For[1] many are called, but few chosen."

JESUS A THIRD TIME PREDICTS HIS DEATH AND RESURRECTION
(Mark 10:32–34; Luke 18:31–34)

17[a]Now Jesus, going up to Jerusalem, took the twelve disciples aside on the road and said to them, 18[a]"Behold, we are going up to Jerusalem, and the Son of Man will be betrayed to the chief priests and to the scribes; and they will condemn Him to death, 19[a]and deliver Him to the Gentiles to [b]mock and to [c]scourge and to [d]crucify. And the third day He will [e]rise again."

GREATNESS IS SERVING
(Mark 10:35–45)

20[a]Then the mother of [b]Zebedee's sons came to Him with her sons, kneeling down and asking something from Him.

19:28
[a]Matt. 20:21;
Luke 22:28–30;
[1 Cor. 6:2;
Rev. 2:26]

19:29
[a][Matt. 6:33];
Mark 10:29, 30;
Luke 18:29, 30

19:30
[a][Matt. 20:16;
21:31, 32];
Mark 10:31;
Luke 13:30

20:15
[a][Rom. 9:20, 21]
[b]Deut. 15:9;
Prov. 23:6;
[Matt. 6:23];
Mark 7:22

20:16
[a]Matt. 19:30;
Mark 10:31;
Luke 13:30
[b]Matt. 22:14

20:17
[a]Matt. 20:17–19;
Mark 10:32–34;
Luke 18:31–33;
John 12:12

20:18
[a]Matt. 16:21;
26:47–57;
Mark 14:42, 64;
John 18:5; 19:7

20:19
[a]Matt. 27:2;
Mark 15:1, 16;
Luke 23:1;
John 18:28;
Acts 3:13
[b]Matt. 26:67,
68; 27:29, 41;
Mark 15:20, 31
[c]Matt. 27:26;
Mark 15:15;
John 19:1
[d]Matt. 27:35;
Luke 23:33;
Acts 3:13–15
[e]Matt. 28:5, 6;
Mark 16:6, 9;
Luke 24:5–8, 46;
Acts 10:40;
1 Cor. 15:4

20:20
[a]Mark 10:35–45
[b]Matt. 4:21; 10:2

19:29 [1]NU omits *or wife*   [2]Lit. *fields*   **20:6** [1]NU omits *idle*
20:7 [1]NU omits the rest of v. 7.   **20:11** [1]*grumbled*   **20:16** [1]NU omits the rest of v. 16.

²¹And He said to her, "What do you wish?"

She said to Him, "Grant that these two sons of mine ᵃmay sit, one on Your right hand and the other on the left, in Your kingdom."

²²But Jesus answered and said, "You do not know what you ask. Are you able to drink ᵃthe cup that I am about to drink, ¹and be baptized with ᵇthe baptism that I am baptized with?"

They said to Him, "We are able."

²³So He said to them, ᵃ"You will indeed drink My cup, ¹and be baptized with the baptism that I am baptized with; but to sit on My right hand and on My left is not Mine to give, but *it is for those* for whom it is prepared by My Father."

²⁴ᵃAnd when the ten heard *it,* they were greatly displeased with the two brothers. ²⁵But Jesus called them to *Himself* and said, "You know that the rulers of the Gentiles lord it over them, and those who are great exercise authority over them. ²⁶Yet ᵃit shall not be so among you; but ᵇwhoever desires to become great among you, let him be your servant. ²⁷ᵃAnd whoever desires to be first among you, let him be your slave— ²⁸ᵃjust as the ᵇSon of Man did not come to be served, ᶜbut to serve, and ᵈto give His life a ransom ᵉfor many."

TWO BLIND MEN RECEIVE THEIR SIGHT
(Mark 10:46–52; Luke 18:35–43)

²⁹ᵃNow as they went out of Jericho, a great multitude followed Him. ³⁰And behold, ᵃtwo blind men sitting by the road, when they heard that Jesus was passing by, cried out, saying, "Have mercy on us, O Lord, ᵇSon of David!"

³¹Then the multitude ᵃwarned them that they should be quiet; but they cried out all the more, saying, "Have mercy on us, O Lord, Son of David!"

³²So Jesus stood still and called them, and said, "What do you want Me to do for you?"

³³They said to Him, "Lord, that our eyes may be opened." ³⁴So Jesus had ᵃcompassion and touched their eyes. And immediately their eyes received sight, and they followed Him.

THE TRIUMPHAL ENTRY
(Mark 11:1–10; Luke 19:28–40; John 12:12–19)

21 Now ᵃwhen they drew near Jerusalem, and came to ¹Bethphage, at ᵇthe Mount of Olives, then Jesus sent two disciples, ²saying to them, "Go into the village opposite you, and immediately you will find a donkey tied, and a colt with her. Loose *them* and bring *them* to Me. ³And if anyone says anything to you, you shall say, 'The Lord has need of them,' and immediately he will send them."

⁴¹All this was done that it might be fulfilled which was spoken by the prophet, saying:

⁵ "Tellᵃ the daughter of Zion,
　'Behold, your King is coming to you,
　Lowly, and sitting on a donkey,
　A colt, the foal of a donkey.'"

20:22 ¹NU omits *and be baptized with the baptism that I am baptized with*
20:23 ¹NU omits *and be baptized with the baptism that I am baptized with*
21:1 ¹M *Bethsphage*　21:4 ¹NU omits *All*

20:21
ᵃ[Matt. 19:28]

20:22
ᵃIs. 51:17, 22;
Jer. 49:12;
Matt. 26:39, 42;
Mark 14:36;
Luke 22:42;
John 18:11
ᵇLuke 12:50

20:23
ᵃ[Acts 12:2;
Rom. 8:17;
2 Cor. 1:7;
Rev. 1:9]

20:24
ᵃMark 10:41;
Luke 22:24, 25

20:26
ᵃ[1 Pet. 5:3]
ᵇMatt. 23:11;
Mark 9:35;
10:43;
Luke 22:26

20:27
ᵃ[Matt. 18:4]

20:28
ᵃJohn 13:4
ᵇ[Matt. 26:28;
John 13:13;
2 Cor. 8:9;
Phil. 2:6, 7;
1 Tim. 2:5, 6;
Titus 2:14;
Heb. 9:28;
Rev. 1:5]
ᶜLuke 22:27;
John 13:14
ᵈ[Is. 53:10, 11;
Dan. 9:24, 26;
John 11:51, 52;
1 Pet. 1:18, 19]
ᵉ[Rom. 5:15, 19;
Heb. 9:28]

20:29
ᵃMark 10:46–52;
Luke 18:35–43

20:30
ᵃMatt. 9:27
ᵇ[2 Sam. 7:14–17;
Ps. 89:3–5,
19–37;
Is. 11:10–12;
Ezek. 37:21–25];
Matt. 1:1;
Luke 1:31, 32;
[Acts 15:14–17]

20:31
ᵃMatt. 19:13

20:34
ᵃMatt. 9:36;
14:14; 15:32;
18:27

21:1
ᵃMark 11:1–10;
Luke 19:29–38
ᵇZech. 14:4

21:5 ᵃIs. 62:11;
Zech. 9:9;
John 12:15

6aSo the disciples went and did as Jesus commanded them. 7They brought the donkey and the colt, alaid their clothes on them, 1and set *Him* on them. 8And a very great multitude spread their clothes on the road; aothers cut down branches from the trees and spread *them* on the road. 9Then the multitudes who went before and those who followed cried out, saying:

"Hosanna to the Son of David!
a'Blessed *is* He who comes in the name of the LORD!'
Hosanna in the highest!"

10aAnd when He had come into Jerusalem, all the city was moved, saying, "Who is this?"

11So the multitudes said, "This is Jesus, athe prophet from Nazareth of Galilee."

JESUS CLEANSES THE TEMPLE
(Mark 11:15–19; Luke 19:45–48; John 2:13–22)

12aThen Jesus went into the temple 1of God and drove out all those who bought and sold in the temple, and overturned the tables of the bmoney changers and the seats of those who sold doves. 13And He said to them, "It is written, a'My house shall be called a house of prayer,' but you have made it a b'den of thieves.'"

14Then *the* blind and *the* lame came to Him in the temple, and He healed them. 15But when the chief priests and scribes saw the wonderful things that He did, and the children crying out in the temple and saying, "Hosanna to the aSon of David!" they were 1indignant 16and said to Him, "Do You hear what these are saying?"

And Jesus said to them, "Yes. Have you never read,

a'Out of the mouth of babes and nursing infants
You have perfected praise'?"

17Then He left them and awent out of the city to Bethany, and He lodged there.

THE FIG TREE WITHERED
(Mark 11:12–14)

18aNow in the morning, as He returned to the city, He was hungry. 19aAnd seeing a fig tree by the road, He came to it and found nothing on it but leaves, and said to it, "Let no fruit grow on you ever again." Immediately the fig tree withered away.

THE LESSON OF THE WITHERED FIG TREE
(Mark 11:20–24)

20aAnd when the disciples saw *it,* they marveled, saying, "How did the fig tree wither away so soon?"

21So Jesus answered and said to them, "Assuredly, I say to you, aif you have faith and bdo not doubt, you will not only do what was done to the fig tree, cbut also if you say to this mountain, 'Be removed and be cast into the sea,' it will be done. 22And awhatever things you ask in prayer, believing, you will receive."

21:6 aMark 11:4
21:7 a2 Kin. 9:13
21:8 aLev. 23:40; John 12:13
21:9 aPs. 118:26; Matt. 23:39
21:10 aJohn 2:13, 15
21:11 a[Deut. 18:15, 18]; Matt. 2:23; 16:14; Luke 4:16–29; John 6:14; 7:40; 9:17; [Acts 3:22, 23]
21:12 aMal. 3:1; Mark 11:15–18; Luke 19:45–47; John 2:13–16 bDeut. 14:25
21:13 aIs. 56:7 bJer. 7:11
21:15 aMatt. 1:1; John 7:42
21:16 aPs. 8:2; Matt. 11:25
21:17 aMatt. 26:6; Mark 11:1, 11, 12; 14:3; Luke 19:29; 24:50; John 11:1, 18; 12:1
21:18 aMark 11:12–14, 20–24
21:19 aMark 11:13
21:20 aMark 11:20
21:21 aMatt. 17:20 bJames 1:6 c1 Cor. 13:2
21:22 aMatt. 7:7–11; Mark 11:24; Luke 11:9; [John 15:7; James 5:16; 1 John 3:22; 5:14]

21:7 1NU *and He sat* 21:12 1NU omits *of God* 21:15 1angry

JESUS' AUTHORITY QUESTIONED
(Mark 11:27–33; Luke 20:1–8)

23ªNow when He came into the temple, the chief priests and the elders of the people confronted Him as He was teaching, and ᵇsaid, "By what authority are You doing these things? And who gave You this authority?"

24But Jesus answered and said to them, "I also will ask you one thing, which if you tell Me, I likewise will tell you by what authority I do these things: 25The ªbaptism of ᵇJohn—where was it from? From heaven or from men?"

And they reasoned among themselves, saying, "If we say, 'From heaven,' He will say to us, 'Why then did you not believe him?' 26But if we say, 'From men,' we ªfear the multitude, ᵇfor all count John as a prophet." 27So they answered Jesus and said, "We do not know."

And He said to them, "Neither will I tell you by what authority I do these things.

THE PARABLE OF THE TWO SONS

28"But what do you think? A man had two sons, and he came to the first and said, 'Son, go, work today in my ªvineyard.' 29He answered and said, 'I will not,' but afterward he regretted it and went. 30Then he came to the second and said likewise. And he answered and said, 'I *go*, sir,' but he did not go. 31Which of the two did the will of *his* father?"

They said to Him, "The first."

Jesus said to them, ª"Assuredly, I say to you that tax collectors and harlots enter the kingdom of God before you. 32For ªJohn came to you in the way of righteousness, and you did not believe him; ᵇbut tax collectors and harlots believed him; and when you saw *it*, you did not afterward ¹relent and believe him.

THE PARABLE OF THE WICKED VINEDRESSERS
(Mark 12:1–12; Luke 20:9–19)

33"Hear another parable: There was a certain landowner ªwho planted a vineyard and set a hedge around it, dug a winepress in it and built a tower. And he leased it to vinedressers and ᵇwent into a far country. 34Now when vintage-time drew near, he sent his servants to the vinedressers, that they might receive its fruit. 35ªAnd the vinedressers took his servants, beat one, killed one, and stoned another. 36Again he sent other servants, more than the first, and they did likewise to them. 37Then last of all he sent his ªson to them, saying, 'They will respect my son.' 38But when the vinedressers saw the son, they said among themselves, ª'This is the heir. ᵇCome, let us kill him and seize his inheritance.' 39ªSo they took him and cast *him* out of the vineyard and killed *him*.

40"Therefore, when the owner of the vineyard comes, what will he do to those vinedressers?"

41ªThey said to Him, ᵇ"He will destroy those wicked men miserably, ᶜand lease *his* vineyard to other vinedressers who will ¹render to him the fruits in their seasons."

42Jesus said to them, "Have you never read in the Scriptures:

21:23
ªMark 11:27–33;
Luke 20:1–8
ᵇEx. 2:14;
Acts 4:7; 7:27

21:25
ª[John 1:29–34]
ᵇJohn 1:15–28

21:26
ªMatt. 14:5;
21:46; Luke 20:6
ᵇMatt. 14:5;
Mark 6:20

21:28
ªMatt. 20:1;

21:33

21:31
ªLuke 7:29,
37–50

21:32
ªLuke 3:1–12;
7:29
ᵇLuke 3:12, 13

21:33 ªPs. 80:9;
Mark 12:1–12;
Luke 20:9–19
ᵇMatt. 25:14

21:35
ª2 Chr. 24:21;
36:16;
[Matt. 23:34, 37;
Acts 7:52;
1 Thess. 2:15];
Heb. 11:36, 37

21:37
ª[John 3:16]

21:38 ª[Ps. 2:8;
Heb. 1:2]
ᵇ[Ps. 2:2];
John 11:53;
Acts 4:27

21:39
ª[Matt. 26:50];
Mark 14:46;
Luke 22:54;
John 18:12;
[Acts 2:23]

21:41
ªLuke 20:16
ᵇ[Luke 21:24]
ᶜ[Matt. 8:11;
Acts 13:46;
Rom. 9; 10]

21:32 ¹*regret it* 21:41 ¹*give*

a"The stone which the builders rejected
Has become the chief cornerstone.
This was the LORD's doing,
And it is marvelous in our eyes'?

⁴³"Therefore I say to you, ^athe kingdom of God will be taken from you and given to a nation bearing the fruits of it. ⁴⁴And ^awhoever falls on this stone will be broken; but on whomever it falls, ^bit will grind him to powder."

⁴⁵Now when the chief priests and Pharisees heard His parables, they ¹perceived that He was speaking of them. ⁴⁶But when they sought to lay hands on Him, they ^afeared the multitudes, because ^bthey took Him for a prophet.

THE PARABLE OF THE WEDDING FEAST
(Luke 14:15–24)

22 And Jesus answered ^aand spoke to them again by parables and said: ²"The kingdom of heaven is like a certain king who arranged a marriage for his son, ³and sent out his servants to call those who were invited to the wedding; and they were not willing to come. ⁴Again, he sent out other servants, saying, 'Tell those who are invited, "See, I have prepared my dinner; ^amy oxen and fatted cattle *are* killed, and all things *are* ready. Come to the wedding."' ⁵But they made light of it and went their ways, one to his own farm, another to his business. ⁶And the rest seized his servants, treated *them* ¹spitefully, and killed *them*. ⁷But when the king heard *about it*, he was furious. And he sent out ^ahis armies, destroyed those murderers, and burned up their city. ⁸Then he said to his servants, 'The wedding is ready, but those who were invited were not ^aworthy. ⁹Therefore go into the highways, and as many as you find, invite to the wedding.' ¹⁰So those servants went out into the highways and ^agathered together all whom they found, both bad and good. And the wedding *hall* was filled with guests.

¹¹"But when the king came in to see the guests, he saw a man there ^awho did not have on a wedding garment. ¹²So he said to him, 'Friend, how did you come in here without a wedding garment?' And he was ^aspeechless. ¹³Then the king said to the servants, 'Bind him hand and foot, ¹take him away, and cast *him* ^ainto outer darkness; there will be weeping and gnashing of teeth.'

^{14a}"For many are called, but few *are* chosen."

THE PHARISEES: IS IT LAWFUL TO PAY TAXES TO CAESAR?
(Mark 12:13–17; Luke 20:20–26)

^{15a}Then the Pharisees went and plotted how they might entangle Him in *His* talk. ¹⁶And they sent to Him their disciples with the ^aHerodians, saying, "Teacher, we know that You are true, and teach the way of God in truth; nor do You care about anyone, for You do not ¹regard the person of men. ¹⁷Tell us, therefore, what do You think? Is it lawful to pay taxes to Caesar, or not?"

¹⁸But Jesus ¹perceived their wickedness, and said, "Why do you test Me, *you* hypocrites? ¹⁹Show Me the tax money."

So they brought Him a denarius.

21:42
^aPs. 118:22, 23;
Is. 28:16;
Mark 12:10;
Luke 20:17;
Acts 4:11;
[Rom. 9:33];
Eph. 2:20;
[1 Pet. 2:6, 7]

21:43
^a[Matt. 8:12];
Acts 13:46

21:44
^aIs. 8:14, 15;
Zech. 12:3;
Luke 20:18;
[Rom. 9:33];
1 Pet. 2:8
^b[Is. 60:12;
Dan. 2:44]

21:46
^aMatt. 21:26;
Mark 11:18, 32
^bMatt. 21:11;
Luke 7:16;
John 7:40

22:1 ^aLuke 14:16;
[Rev. 19:7–9]

22:4 ^aProv. 9:2

22:7
^a[Dan. 9:26]

22:8 ^aMatt. 10:11

22:10
^aMatt. 13:38, 47,
48; [Acts 28:28]

22:11
^a[2 Cor. 5:3;
Eph. 4:24;
Col. 3:10, 12;
Rev. 3:4; 16:15;
19:8]

22:12
^a[Rom. 3:19]

22:13
^aMatt. 8:12;
25:30;
Luke 13:28

22:14
^aMatt. 20:16

22:15
^aMark 12:13–17;
Luke 20:20–26

22:16
^aMark 3:6;
8:15; 12:13

21:45 ¹knew   22:6 ¹insolently   22:13 ¹NU omits *take him away, and*
22:16 ¹Lit. *look at the face of*   22:18 ¹knew

²⁰And He said to them, "Whose image and inscription *is* this?"

²¹They said to Him, "Caesar's."

And He said to them, ^a"Render¹ therefore to Caesar the things that are ^bCaesar's, and to God the things that are ^cGod's." ²²When they had heard *these words,* they marveled, and left Him and went their way.

THE SADDUCEES: WHAT ABOUT THE RESURRECTION?
(Mark 12:18–27; Luke 20:27–40)

^{23a}The same day the Sadducees, ^bwho say there is no resurrection, came to Him and asked Him, ²⁴saying: "Teacher, ^aMoses said that if a man dies, having no children, his brother shall marry his wife and raise up offspring for his brother. ²⁵Now there were with us seven brothers. The first died after he had married, and having no offspring, left his wife to his brother. ²⁶Likewise the second also, and the third, even to the seventh. ²⁷Last of all the woman died also. ²⁸Therefore, in the resurrection, whose wife of the seven will she be? For they all had her."

²⁹Jesus answered and said to them, "You are ¹mistaken, ^anot knowing the Scriptures nor the power of God. ³⁰For in the resurrection they neither marry nor are given in marriage, but ^aare like angels ¹of God in heaven. ³¹But concerning the resurrection of the dead, have you not read what was spoken to you by God, saying, ^{32a}'I am the God of Abraham, the God of Isaac, and the God of Jacob'? God is not the God of the dead, but of the living." ³³And when the multitudes heard *this,* ^athey were astonished at His teaching.

THE SCRIBES: WHICH IS THE FIRST COMMANDMENT OF ALL?
(Mark 12:28–34; Luke 10:25–28)

^{34a}But when the Pharisees heard that He had silenced the Sadducees, they gathered together. ³⁵Then one of them, ^aa lawyer, asked *Him a question,* testing Him, and saying, ³⁶"Teacher, which *is* the great commandment in the law?"

³⁷Jesus said to him, ^a"'You shall love the Lord your God with all your heart, with all your soul, and with all your mind.' ³⁸This is *the* first and great commandment. ³⁹And *the* second *is* like it: ^a'You shall love your neighbor as yourself.' ^{40a}On these two commandments hang all the Law and the Prophets."

JESUS: HOW CAN DAVID CALL HIS DESCENDANT LORD?
(Mark 12:35–37; Luke 20:41–44)

^{41a}While the Pharisees were gathered together, Jesus asked them, ⁴²saying, "What do you think about the Christ? Whose Son is He?"

They said to Him, "The ^aSon of David."

⁴³He said to them, "How then does David in the Spirit call Him 'Lord,' saying:

⁴⁴ 'The^a Lord said to my Lord,
  "Sit at My right hand,
  Till I make Your enemies Your footstool" '?

22:21
^aMatt. 17:25
^b[Rom. 13:1–7;
1 Pet. 2:13–15]
^c[1 Cor. 3:23;
6:19, 20; 12:27]

22:23
^aMark 12:18–27;
Luke 20:27–40
^bActs 23:8

22:24
^aDeut. 25:5

22:29
^aJohn 20:9

22:30
^a[1 John 3:2]

22:32
^aGen. 17:7;
26:24; 28:21;
Ex. 3:6, 15;
Mark 12:26;
Luke 20:37;
Acts 7:32;
[Heb. 11:16]

22:33
^aMatt. 7:28

22:34
^aMark 12:28–31;
Luke 10:25–37

22:35
^aLuke 7:30;
10:25; 11:45,
46, 52; 14:3;
Titus 3:13

22:37
^aDeut. 6:5;
10:12; 30:6

22:39
^aLev. 19:18;
Matt. 19:19;
Mark 12:31;
Luke 10:27;
[Rom. 13:9;
Gal. 5:14;
James 2:8]

22:40
^a[Matt. 7:12;
Rom. 13:10;
1 Tim. 1:5]

22:41
^aMark 12:35–37;
Luke 20:41–44

22:42
^aMatt. 1:1; 21:9

22:44 ^aPs. 110:1;
[Matt. 26:64];
Mark 16:19;
Acts 2:34;
1 Cor. 15:25;
Heb. 1:13; 10:13

22:21 ¹*Pay*   22:29 ¹*deceived*   22:30 ¹NU omits *of God*

22:46
[a] Luke 14:6
[b] Mark 12:34;
Luke 20:40

23:2
[a] Deut. 33:3;
Ezra 7:6, 25;
Neh. 8:4, 8;
[Mal. 2:7];
Mark 12:38;
Luke 20:45

23:3
[a] [Rom. 2:19]

23:4
[a] [Matt. 11:29,
30]; Luke 11:46;
Acts 15:10;
Rom. 2:17–24;
[Gal. 5:1; 6:13;
Col. 2:16, 17]

23:5
[a] [Matt. 6:1–6,
16–18]

23:6
[a] Mark 12:38, 39;
Luke 11:43;
20:46;
3 John 9

23:8
[a] [2 Cor. 1:24;
James 3:1;
1 Pet. 5:3]

23:9
[a] [Mal. 1:6];
Matt. 5:16, 48;
6:1, 9, 14, 26,
32; 7:11

23:11
[a] Matt. 20:26, 27

23:12
[a] Job 22:29;
Prov. 15:33;
29:23;
Luke 14:11; 18:14;
James 4:6;
1 Pet. 5:5

23:13
[a] Luke 11:52

23:14
[a] Mark 12:40;
Luke 20:47;
[2 Tim. 3:6;
Titus 1:10, 11]

23:16
[a] Matt. 15:14;
23:24
[b] [Matt. 5:33,
34]

23:17 [a] Ex. 30:29

23:19 [a] Ex. 29:37

23:21
[a] 1 Kin. 8:13;
2 Chr. 6:2;
Ps. 26:8;
132:14

23:22
[a] Ps. 11:4; Is. 66:1;
Matt. 5:34;
Acts 7:49

[45]If David then calls Him 'Lord,' how is He his Son?" [46a]And no one was able to answer Him a word, [b]nor from that day on did anyone dare question Him anymore.

WOE TO THE SCRIBES AND PHARISEES
(Mark 12:38–40; Luke 20:45–47)

23 Then Jesus spoke to the multitudes and to His disciples, [2]saying: [a]"The scribes and the Pharisees sit in Moses' seat. [3]Therefore whatever they tell you [1]to observe, *that* observe and do, but do not do according to their works; for [a]they say, and do not do. [4a]For they bind heavy burdens, hard to bear, and lay *them* on men's shoulders; but they *themselves* will not move them with one of their fingers. [5]But all their works they do to [a]be seen by men. They make their phylacteries broad and enlarge the borders of their garments. [6a]They love the [1]best places at feasts, the best seats in the synagogues, [7]greetings in the marketplaces, and to be called by men, 'Rabbi, Rabbi.' [8a]But you, do not be called 'Rabbi'; for One is your [1]Teacher, [2]the Christ, and you are all brethren. [9]Do not call anyone on earth your father; [a]for One is your Father, He who is in heaven. [10]And do not be called teachers; for One is your Teacher, the Christ. [11]But [a]he who is greatest among you shall be your servant. [12a]And whoever exalts himself will be [1]humbled, and he who humbles himself will be [2]exalted.

[13]"But [a]woe to you, scribes and Pharisees, hypocrites! For you shut up the kingdom of heaven against men; for you neither go in *yourselves,* nor do you allow those who are entering to go in. [14][1]Woe to you, scribes and Pharisees, hypocrites! [a]For you devour widows' houses, and for a pretense make long prayers. Therefore you will receive greater condemnation.

[15]"Woe to you, scribes and Pharisees, hypocrites! For you travel land and sea to win one proselyte, and when he is won, you make him twice as much a son of [1]hell as yourselves.

[16]"Woe to you, [a]blind guides, who say, [b]'Whoever swears by the temple, it is nothing; but whoever swears by the gold of the temple, he is obliged *to perform it.*' [17]Fools and blind! For which is greater, the gold [a]or the temple that [1]sanctifies the gold? [18]And, 'Whoever swears by the altar, it is nothing; but whoever swears by the gift that is on it, he is obliged *to perform it.*' [19]Fools and blind! For which is greater, the gift [a]or the altar that sanctifies the gift? [20]Therefore he who [1]swears by the altar, swears by it and by all things on it. [21]He who swears by the temple, swears by it and by [a]Him who [1]dwells in it. [22]And he who swears by heaven, swears by [a]the throne of God and by Him who sits on it.

[23]"Woe to you, scribes and Pharisees, hypocrites! [a]For you pay tithe of mint and anise and cummin, and [b]have neglected the weightier *matters* of the law: justice and mercy and faith. These you ought to have done, without leaving the others undone. [24]Blind guides, who strain out a gnat and swallow a camel!

[25]"Woe to you, scribes and Pharisees, hypocrites! [a]For you

23:23 [a] Matt. 23:13; Luke 11:42; 18:12 [b] [1 Sam. 15:22; Hos. 6:6; Mic. 6:8]; Matt. 9:13; 12:7
23:25 [a] Mark 7:4; Luke 11:39

23:3 [1] NU omits *to observe*   23:6 [1] Or *place of honor*   23:8 [1] *Leader*
[2] NU omits *the Christ*   23:12 [1] *put down*   [2] *lifted up*   23:14 [1] NU omits v. 14.
23:15 [1] Gr. *Gehenna*   23:17 [1] NU *sanctified*   23:20 [1] *Swears an oath*
23:21 [1] M *dwelt*

cleanse the outside of the cup and dish, but inside they are full of extortion and ¹self-indulgence. ²⁶Blind Pharisee, first cleanse the inside of the cup and dish, that the outside of them may be clean also.

²⁷"Woe to you, scribes and Pharisees, hypocrites! ᵃFor you are like whitewashed tombs which indeed appear beautiful outwardly, but inside are full of dead *men's* bones and all uncleanness. ²⁸Even so you also outwardly appear righteous to men, but inside you are full of hypocrisy and lawlessness.

²⁹ᵃ"Woe to you, scribes and Pharisees, hypocrites! Because you build the tombs of the prophets and ¹adorn the monuments of the righteous, ³⁰and say, 'If we had lived in the days of our fathers, we would not have been partakers with them in the blood of the prophets.'

³¹"Therefore you are witnesses against yourselves that ᵃyou are sons of those who murdered the prophets. ³²ᵃFill up, then, the measure of your fathers' *guilt.* ³³Serpents, ᵃbrood¹ of vipers! How can you escape the condemnation of hell? ³⁴ᵃTherefore, indeed, I send you prophets, wise men, and scribes: ᵇ*some* of them you will kill and crucify, and ᶜ*some* of them you will scourge in your synagogues and persecute from city to city, ³⁵ᵃthat on you may come all the righteous blood shed on the earth, ᵇfrom the blood of righteous Abel to ᶜthe blood of Zechariah, son of Berechiah, whom you murdered between the temple and the altar. ³⁶Assuredly, I say to you, all these things will come upon this generation.

JESUS LAMENTS OVER JERUSALEM
(Luke 13:34, 35)

³⁷ᵃ"O Jerusalem, Jerusalem, the one who kills the prophets ᵇand stones those who are sent to her! How often ᶜI wanted to gather your children together, as a hen gathers her chicks ᵈunder *her* wings, but you were not willing! ³⁸See! Your house is left to you desolate; ³⁹for I say to you, you shall see Me no more till you say, ᵃ'Blessed *is* He who comes in the name of the LORD!'"

JESUS PREDICTS THE DESTRUCTION OF THE TEMPLE
(Mark 13:1, 2; Luke 21:5, 6)

24 Then ᵃJesus went out and departed from the temple, and His disciples came up to show Him the buildings of the temple. ²And Jesus said to them, "Do you not see all these things? Assuredly, I say to you, ᵃnot *one* stone shall be left here upon another, that shall not be thrown down."

THE SIGNS OF THE TIMES AND THE END OF THE AGE
(Mark 13:3–13; Luke 21:7–19)

³Now as He sat on the Mount of Olives, ᵃthe disciples came to Him privately, saying, ᵇ"Tell us, when will these things be? And what *will be* the sign of Your coming, and of the end of the age?"

⁴And Jesus answered and said to them: ᵃ"Take heed that no one deceives you. ⁵For ᵃmany will come in My name, saying, 'I am the Christ,' ᵇand will deceive many. ⁶And you will hear of ᵃwars and rumors of wars. See that you are not

23:27 ᵃLuke 11:44; Acts 23:3
23:29 ᵃLuke 11:47, 48
23:31 ᵃMatt. 23:34, 37; [Acts 7:51, 52]; 1 Thess. 2:15
23:32 ᵃGen. 15:16; [1 Thess. 2:16]
23:33 ᵃMatt. 3:7; 12:34; Luke 3:7
23:34 ᵃMatt. 21:34, 35; Luke 11:49 ᵇJohn 16:2; Acts 7:54–60; 22:19 ᶜMatt. 10:17; Acts 5:40; 2 Cor. 11:24, 25
23:35 ᵃRev. 18:24 ᵇGen. 4:8; Heb. 11:4; 1 John 3:12 ᶜ2 Chr. 24:20, 21
23:37 ᵃLuke 13:34, 35 ᵇ2 Chr. 24:20, 21; 36:15, 16; Neh. 9:26; Matt. 21:35, 36 ᶜDeut. 32:11, 12; Matt. 11:28–30 ᵈPs. 17:8; 91:4; Is. 49:5
23:39 ᵃPs. 118:26; Matt. 21:9
24:1 ᵃMark 13:1; Luke 21:5–36
24:2 ᵃ1 Kin. 9:7; Mic. 3:12; Luke 19:44
24:3 ᵃMark 13:3 ᵇ[Matt. 24:27, 37, 39; Luke 17:20–37; 1 Thess. 5:1–3]
24:4 ᵃEph. 5:6; [Col. 2:8, 18; 2 Thess. 2:3; 1 John 4:1–3]
24:5 ᵃJer. 14:14; John 5:43; Acts 5:36; [1 John 2:18; 4:3] ᵇMatt. 24:11
24:6 ᵃ[Rev. 6:2–4]

24:7
a 2 Chr. 15:6;
Is. 19:2;
Hag. 2:22;
Zech. 14:13
b Acts 11:28;
Rev. 6:5, 6

24:9
a Matt. 10:17;
Luke 21:12;
[John 16:2];
Acts 4:2, 3;
Rev. 2:10

24:11
a Acts 20:29;
2 Pet. 2:1;
Rev. 13:11; 19:20
b [1 Tim. 4:1]

24:12
a [2 Thess. 2:3;
2 Tim. 3:1–3]

24:13
a Matt. 10:22;
Mark 13:13

24:14
a Matt. 4:23
b Rom. 10:18;
Col. 1:6, 23

24:15
a Mark 13:14;
Luke 21:20;
[John 11:48];
Acts 6:13; 21:28
b Dan. 9:27; 11:31;
12:11 c Dan. 9:23

24:19
a Luke 23:29

24:21
a Dan. 9:26

24:22
a Is. 65:8, 9;
[Zech. 14:2]

24:23
a Mark 13:21;
Luke 17:23

24:24
a Deut. 13:1;
John 4:48;
[2 Thess. 2:9];
Rev. 13:13
b [John 6:37;
Rom. 8:28;
2 Tim. 2:19]

24:27
a Luke 17:24

24:28
a Job 39:30;
Ezek. 39:17;
Hab. 1:8;
Luke 17:37

24:29
a [Dan. 7:11]
b Is. 13:10; 24:23;
Ezek. 32:7;
Joel 2:10, 31;
3:15; Amos 5:20;
8:9; Zeph. 1:15;
Matt. 24:29–35;
Acts 2:20;
Rev. 6:12–17;
8:12

troubled; for ¹all *these things* must come to pass, but the end is not yet. 7For a nation will rise against nation, and kingdom against kingdom. And there will be b famines, ¹pestilences, and earthquakes in various places. 8All these *are* the beginning of sorrows.

9a "Then they will deliver you up to tribulation and kill you, and you will be hated by all nations for My name's sake. 10And then many will be offended, will betray one another, and will hate one another. 11Then a many false prophets will rise up and b deceive many. 12And because lawlessness will abound, the love of many will grow a cold. 13aBut he who endures to the end shall be saved. 14And this a gospel of the kingdom b will be preached in all the world as a witness to all the nations, and then the end will come.

THE GREAT TRIBULATION
(Mark 13:14–23; Luke 17:23, 24, 37; 21:20–24)

15a "Therefore when you see the b 'abomination of desolation,' spoken of by Daniel the prophet, standing in the holy place" c (whoever reads, let him understand), 16"then let those who are in Judea flee to the mountains. 17Let him who is on the housetop not go down to take anything out of his house. 18And let him who is in the field not go back to get his clothes. 19But a woe to those who are pregnant and to those who are nursing babies in those days! 20And pray that your flight may not be in winter or on the Sabbath. 21For a then there will be great tribulation, such as has not been since the beginning of the world until this time, no, nor ever shall be. 22And unless those days were shortened, no flesh would be saved; a but for the ¹elect's sake those days will be shortened.

23a "Then if anyone says to you, 'Look, here *is* the Christ!' or 'There!' do not believe *it*. 24For a false christs and false prophets will rise and show great signs and wonders to deceive, b if possible, even the elect. 25See, I have told you beforehand.

26"Therefore if they say to you, 'Look, He is in the desert!' do not go out; *or* 'Look, *He is* in the inner rooms!' do not believe *it*. 27aFor as the lightning comes from the east and flashes to the west, so also will the coming of the Son of Man be. 28aFor wherever the carcass is, there the eagles will be gathered together.

THE COMING OF THE SON OF MAN
(Mark 13:24–27; Luke 21:25–28)

29a "Immediately after the tribulation of those days b the sun will be darkened, and the moon will not give its light; the stars will fall from heaven, and the powers of the heavens will be shaken. 30aThen the sign of the Son of Man will appear in heaven, b and then all the tribes of the earth will mourn, and they will see the Son of Man coming on the clouds of heaven with power and great glory. 31aAnd He will send His angels with a great sound of a trumpet, and they will gather together His ¹elect from the four winds, from one end of heaven to the other.

24:30 a [Dan. 7:13, 14; Matt. 16:27; 24:3, 37, 39] b Zech. 12:12   24:31 a Ex. 19:16;
Deut. 30:4; Is. 27:13; Zech. 9:14; [1 Cor. 15:52; 1 Thess. 4:16]; Heb. 12:19; Rev. 8:2; 11:15

24:6 ¹NU omits *all*   24:7 ¹NU omits *pestilences*   24:22 ¹*chosen ones*
24:31 ¹*chosen ones*

THE PARABLE OF THE FIG TREE
(*Mark 13:28–31; Luke 21:29–33*)

[32]"Now learn [a]this parable from the fig tree: When its branch has already become tender and puts forth leaves, you know that summer *is* near. [33]So you also, when you see all these things, know [a]that [1]it is near—at the doors! [34]Assuredly, I say to you, [a]this generation will by no means pass away till all these things take place. [35][a]Heaven and earth will pass away, but My words will by no means pass away.

NO ONE KNOWS THE DAY OR HOUR
(*Mark 13:32–37; Luke 17:26, 27, 34, 35; 21:34–36*)

[36][a]"But of that day and hour no one knows, not even the angels of [1]heaven, [b]but My Father only. [37]But as the days of Noah *were,* so also will the coming of the Son of Man be. [38][a]For as in the days before the flood, they were eating and drinking, marrying and giving in marriage, until the day that Noah entered the ark, [39]and did not know until the flood came and took them all away, so also will the coming of the Son of Man be. [40][a]Then two *men* will be in the field: one will be taken and the other left. [41]Two *women will be* grinding at the mill: one will be taken and the other left. [42][a]Watch therefore, for you do not know what [1]hour your Lord is coming. [43][a]But know this, that if the master of the house had known what [1]hour the thief would come, he would have watched and not allowed his house to be broken into. [44][a]Therefore you also be ready, for the Son of Man is coming at an hour you do not expect.

THE FAITHFUL SERVANT AND THE EVIL SERVANT
(*Luke 12:41–48*)

[45][a]"Who then is a faithful and wise servant, whom his master made ruler over his household, to give them food [1]in due season? [46][a]Blessed *is* that servant whom his master, when he comes, will find so doing. [47]Assuredly, I say to you that [a]he will make him ruler over all his goods. [48]But if that evil servant says in his heart, 'My master [a]is delaying [1]his coming,' [49]and begins to beat *his* fellow servants, and to eat and drink with the drunkards, [50]the master of that servant will come on a day when he is not looking for *him* and at an hour that he is [a]not aware of, [51]and will cut him in two and appoint *him* his portion with the hypocrites. [a]There shall be weeping and gnashing of teeth.

THE PARABLE OF THE WISE AND FOOLISH VIRGINS

25 "Then the kingdom of heaven shall be likened to ten virgins who took their lamps and went out to meet [a]the bridegroom. [2][a]Now five of them were wise, and five *were* foolish. [3]Those who *were* foolish took their lamps and took no oil with them, [4]but the wise took oil in their vessels with their lamps. [5]But while the bridegroom was delayed, [a]they all slumbered and slept.

[6]"And at midnight [a]a cry was *heard:* 'Behold, the bridegroom [1]is coming; go out to meet him!' [7]Then all those virgins

---

24:32
[a]Luke 21:29

24:33
[a][James 5:9;
Rev. 3:20]

24:34
[a][Matt. 10:23;
16:28; 23:36]

24:35
[a]Ps. 102:25, 26;
Is. 51:6;
Mark 13:31;
Luke 21:33;
[1 Pet. 1:23–25;
2 Pet. 3:10]

24:36
[a]Mark 13:32;
Acts 1:7;
1 Thess. 5:2;
2 Pet. 3:10
[b]Zech. 14:7

24:38
[a][Gen. 6:3–5];
Luke 17:26;
[1 Pet. 3:20]

24:40
[a]Luke 17:34

24:42
[a]Matt. 25:13;
Luke 21:36;
1 Thess. 5:6

24:43
[a]Luke 12:39;
1 Thess. 5:2;
Rev. 3:3

24:44
[a]Luke 12:35–40;
[1 Thess. 5:6]

24:45
[a]Luke 12:42–46;
[Acts 20:28]

24:46
[a]Rev. 16:15

24:47
[a]Matt. 25:21, 23;
Luke 22:29

24:48
[a][2 Pet. 3:4–9]

24:50
[a]Mark 13:32

24:51
[a]Matt. 8:12;
25:30

25:1
[a][Eph. 5:29, 30;
Rev. 19:7; 21:2, 9]

25:2
[a]Matt. 13:47;
22:10

25:5
[a]1 Thess. 5:6

25:6
[a][Matt. 24:31;
1 Thess. 4:16]

24:33 [1]Or *He*   24:36 [1]NU adds *nor the Son*   24:42 [1]NU *day*   24:43 [1]Lit. *watch of the night*   24:45 [1]*at the right time*   24:48 [1]NU omits *his coming*
25:6 [1]NU omits *is coming*

arose and [a]trimmed their lamps. [8]And the foolish said to the wise, 'Give us *some* of your oil, for our lamps are going out.' [9]But the wise answered, saying, '*No,* lest there should not be enough for us and you; but go rather to those who sell, and buy for yourselves.' [10]And while they went to buy, the bridegroom came, and those who were ready went in with him to the wedding; and [a]the door was shut.

[11]"Afterward the other virgins came also, saying, [a]'Lord, Lord, open to us!' [12]But he answered and said, 'Assuredly, I say to you, [a]I do not know you.'

[13a]"Watch therefore, for you [b]know neither the day nor the hour [1]in which the Son of Man is coming.

THE PARABLE OF THE TALENTS
(Luke 19:11–27)

[14a]"For *the kingdom of heaven is* [b]like a man traveling to a far country, *who* called his own servants and delivered his goods to them. [15]And to one he gave five talents, to another two, and to another one, [a]to each according to his own ability; and immediately he went on a journey. [16]Then he who had received the five talents went and traded with them, and made another five talents. [17]And likewise he who *had received* two gained two more also. [18]But he who had received one went and dug in the ground, and hid his lord's money. [19]After a long time the lord of those servants came and settled accounts with them.

[20]"So he who had received five talents came and brought five other talents, saying, 'Lord, you delivered to me five talents; look, I have gained five more talents besides them.' [21]His lord said to him, 'Well *done,* good and faithful servant; you were [a]faithful over a few things, [b]I will make you ruler over many things. Enter into [c]the joy of your lord.' [22]He also who had received two talents came and said, 'Lord, you delivered to me two talents; look, I have gained two more talents besides them.' [23]His lord said to him, [a]'Well *done,* good and faithful servant; you have been faithful over a few things, I will make you ruler over many things. Enter into [b]the joy of your lord.'

[24]"Then he who had received the one talent came and said, 'Lord, I knew you to be a hard man, reaping where you have not sown, and gathering where you have not scattered seed. [25]And I was afraid, and went and hid your talent in the ground. Look, *there* you have *what is* yours.'

[26]"But his lord answered and said to him, 'You [a]wicked and lazy servant, you knew that I reap where I have not sown, and gather where I have not scattered seed. [27]So you ought to have deposited my money with the bankers, and at my coming I would have received back my own with interest. [28]So take the talent from him, and give *it* to him who has ten talents.

[29a]'For to everyone who has, more will be given, and he will have abundance; but from him who does not have, even what he has will be taken away. [30]And cast the unprofitable servant [a]into the outer darkness. [b]There will be weeping and [c]gnashing of teeth.'

25:7 [a]Luke 12:35

25:10 [a][Matt. 7:21]; Luke 13:25

25:11 [a][Matt. 7:21–23; Luke 13:25–30]

25:12 [a][Ps. 5:5; Hab. 1:13; John 9:31]

25:13 [a]Mark 13:35; [Luke 21:36]; 1 Thess. 5:6 [b]Matt. 24:36, 42

25:14 [a]Luke 19:12–27 [b]Matt. 21:33

25:15 [a][Rom. 12:6; 1 Cor. 12:7, 11, 29; Eph. 4:11]

25:21 [a][Luke 16:10; 1 Cor. 4:2; 2 Tim. 4:7, 8] [b][Matt. 24:47; 25:34, 46; Luke 12:44; 22:29, 30; Rev. 3:21; 21:7] [c][2 Tim. 2:12; Heb. 12:2; 1 Pet. 1:8]

25:23 [a]Matt. 24:45, 47; 25:21 [b][Ps. 16:11; John 15:10, 11]

25:26 [a]Matt. 18:32; Luke 19:22

25:29 [a]Matt. 13:12; Mark 4:25; Luke 8:18; [John 15:2]

25:30 [a]Matt. 8:12; 22:13; [Luke 13:28] [b]Matt. 7:23; 8:12; 24:51 [c]Ps. 112:10

25:13 [1]NU omits the rest of v. 13.

THE SON OF MAN WILL JUDGE THE NATIONS

31a"When the Son of Man comes in His glory, and all the ¹holy angels with Him, then He will sit on the throne of His glory. 32aAll the nations will be gathered before Him, and bHe will separate them one from another, as a shepherd divides *his* sheep from the goats. 33And He will set the asheep on His right hand, but the goats on the left. 34Then the King will say to those on His right hand, 'Come, you blessed of My Father, ainherit the kingdom bprepared for you from the foundation of the world: 35afor I was hungry and you gave Me food; I was thirsty and you gave Me drink; bI was a stranger and you took Me in; 36I *was* anaked and you clothed Me; I was sick and you visited Me; bI was in prison and you came to Me.'

37"Then the righteous will answer Him, saying, 'Lord, when did we see You hungry and feed *You*, or thirsty and give *You* drink? 38When did we see You a stranger and take *You* in, or naked and clothe *You*? 39Or when did we see You sick, or in prison, and come to You?' 40And the King will answer and say to them, 'Assuredly, I say to you, ainasmuch as you did *it* to one of the least of these My brethren, you did *it* to Me.'

41"Then He will also say to those on the left hand, a'Depart from Me, you cursed, binto the everlasting fire prepared for cthe devil and his angels: 42for I was hungry and you gave Me no food; I was thirsty and you gave Me no drink; 43I was a stranger and you did not take Me in, naked and you did not clothe Me, sick and in prison and you did not visit Me.'

44"Then they also will answer ¹Him, saying, 'Lord, when did we see You hungry or thirsty or a stranger or naked or sick or in prison, and did not minister to You?' 45Then He will answer them, saying, 'Assuredly, I say to you, ainasmuch as you did not do *it* to one of the least of these, you did not do *it* to Me.' 46And athese will go away into everlasting punishment, but the righteous into eternal life."

THE PLOT TO KILL JESUS
(Mark 14:1, 2; Luke 22:1, 2; John 11:45–53)

26 Now it came to pass, when Jesus had finished all these sayings, *that* He said to His disciples, 2a"You know that after two days is the Passover, and the Son of Man will be delivered up to be crucified."

3aThen the chief priests, ¹the scribes, and the elders of the people assembled at the palace of the high priest, who was called Caiaphas, 4and aplotted to take Jesus by ¹trickery and kill *Him*. 5But they said, "Not during the feast, lest there be an uproar among the apeople."

THE ANOINTING AT BETHANY
(Mark 14:3–9; John 12:1–8)

6And when Jesus was in aBethany at the house of Simon the leper, 7a woman came to Him having an alabaster flask of very costly fragrant oil, and she poured *it* on His head as He sat *at the table*. 8aBut when His disciples saw *it*, they were

26:5 aMatt. 21:26   26:6 aMatt. 8:2; Mark 14:3–9; Luke 7:37–39; John 11:1, 2; 12:1–8
26:8 aJohn 12:4

25:31 ¹NU omits *holy*   25:44 ¹NU, M omit *Him*   26:3 ¹NU omits *the scribes*
26:4 ¹*deception*

Cross references

25:31
a[Zech. 14:5];
Matt. 16:27;
Mark 8:38;
Acts 1:11;
[1 Thess. 4:16];
2 Thess. 1:7;
[Jude 14];
Rev. 1:7

25:32
a[Rom. 14:10;
2 Cor. 5:10;
Rev. 20:12]
bEzek. 20:38

25:33 aPs. 79:13;
100:3;
[John 10:11,
27, 28]

25:34
a[Rom. 8:17;
1 Pet. 1:4, 9;
Rev. 21:7]
bMatt. 20:23;
Mark 10:40;
1 Cor. 2:9;
Heb. 11:16

25:35
aIs. 58:7;
Ezek. 18:7, 16;
[James 1:27;
2:15, 16]
b Job 31:32;
[Heb. 13:2];
3 John 5

25:36 aIs. 58:7;
Ezek. 18:7, 16;
[James 2:15, 16]
b2 Tim. 1:16

25:40
aProv. 14:31;
Matt. 10:42;
Mark 9:41;
Heb. 6:10

25:41 aPs. 6:8;
Matt. 7:23;
Luke 13:27
bMatt. 13:40, 42
c[2 Pet. 2:4];
Jude 6

25:45
aProv. 14:31;
Zech. 2:8;
Acts 9:5

25:46
a[Dan. 12:2;
John 5:29;
Acts 24:15;
Rom. 2:7]

26:2
aMatt. 27:35;
Mark 14:1, 2;
Luke 22:1, 2;
John 13:1; 19:18

26:3 aPs. 2:2;
John 11:47;
Acts 4:25

26:4
aJohn 11:47;
Acts 4:25–28

26:11
a[Deut. 15:11;
Mark 14:7];
John 12:8
b[Matt. 18:20;
28:20;
John 13:33;
14:19; 16:5, 28;
17:11]

26:12
aMatt. 27:60;
Luke 23:53;
John 19:38–42

26:14
aMark 14:10, 11;
Luke 22:3–6;
John 13:2, 30
bMatt. 10:4

26:15
aEx. 21:32;
Zech. 11:12;
Matt. 27:3

26:17
aEx. 12:6, 18–20

26:18
aLuke 9:51;
John 12:23;
13:1; 17:1

26:20
aMark 14:17–21;
Luke 22:14;
John 13:21

26:21
aMatt. 26:46;
Mark 14:42;
Luke 22:21–23;
John 6:70, 71;
13:21

26:23 aPs. 41:9;
Luke 22:21;
John 13:18

26:24 aPs. 22;
Dan. 9:26;
Mark 9:12;
Luke 24:25, 26,
46; Acts 17:2, 3;
26:22, 23;
1 Cor. 15:3
bMatt. 27:3–5;
Luke 17:1;
Acts 1:16–20
cJohn 17:12;
Acts 1:25

26:26
aMark 14:22–25;
Luke 22:17–20
b1 Cor. 11:23–25
c[1 Pet. 2:24]

26:27
aMark 14:23

26:28
a[Ex. 24:8;
Lev. 17:11;
Heb. 9:20]
bJer. 31:31
cMatt. 20:28;
[Rom. 5:15;
Heb. 9:22]

indignant, saying, "Why this waste? [9]For this fragrant oil might have been sold for much and given to *the* poor."

[10]But when Jesus was aware of *it,* He said to them, "Why do you trouble the woman? For she has done a good work for Me. [11]aFor you have the poor with you always, but bMe you do not have always. [12]For in pouring this fragrant oil on My body, she did *it* for My aburial. [13]Assuredly, I say to you, wherever this gospel is preached in the whole world, what this woman has done will also be told as a memorial to her."

JUDAS AGREES TO BETRAY JESUS
(Mark 14:10, 11; Luke 22:3–6)

[14]aThen one of the twelve, called bJudas Iscariot, went to the chief priests [15]and said, a"What are you willing to give me if I deliver Him to you?" And they counted out to him thirty pieces of silver. [16]So from that time he sought opportunity to betray Him.

JESUS CELEBRATES PASSOVER WITH HIS DISCIPLES
(Mark 14:12–21; Luke 22:7–13)

[17]aNow on the first *day of the Feast* of the Unleavened Bread the disciples came to Jesus, saying to Him, "Where do You want us to prepare for You to eat the Passover?"

[18]And He said, "Go into the city to a certain man, and say to him, 'The Teacher says, a"My time is at hand; I will keep the Passover at your house with My disciples."'"

[19]So the disciples did as Jesus had directed them; and they prepared the Passover.

[20]aWhen evening had come, He sat down with the twelve. [21]Now as they were eating, He said, "Assuredly, I say to you, one of you will abetray Me."

[22]And they were exceedingly sorrowful, and each of them began to say to Him, "Lord, is it I?"

[23]He answered and said, a"He who dipped *his* hand with Me in the dish will betray Me. [24]The Son of Man indeed goes just aas it is written of Him, but bwoe to that man by whom the Son of Man is betrayed! cIt would have been good for that man if he had not been born."

[25]Then Judas, who was betraying Him, answered and said, "Rabbi, is it I?"

He said to him, "You have said it."

JESUS INSTITUTES THE LORD'S SUPPER
(Mark 14:22–26; Luke 22:14–23; 1 Cor. 11:23–26)

[26]aAnd as they were eating, bJesus took bread, [1]blessed and broke *it,* and gave *it* to the disciples and said, "Take, eat; cthis is My body."

[27]Then He took the cup, and gave thanks, and gave *it* to them, saying, a"Drink from it, all of you. [28]For athis is My blood bof the [1]new covenant, which is shed cfor many for the [2]remission of sins. [29]But aI say to you, I will not drink of this fruit of the vine from now on buntil that day when I drink it new with you in My Father's kingdom."

[30]aAnd when they had sung a hymn, they went out to the Mount of Olives.

26:29 aMark 14:25; Luke 22:18 bActs 10:41   26:30 aMark 14:26–31; Luke 22:31–34

26:26 [1]M *gave thanks for*   26:28 [1]NU omits *new*   [2]*forgiveness*

JESUS PREDICTS PETER'S DENIAL
(Mark 14:27–31; Luke 22:31–34; John 13:36–38)

31Then Jesus said to them, ᵃ"All of you will ᵇbe ¹made to stumble because of Me this night, for it is written:

ᶜ'I will strike the Shepherd,
And the sheep of the flock will be scattered.'

32But after I have been raised, ᵃI will go before you to Galilee." **33**Peter answered and said to Him, "Even if all are ¹made to stumble because of You, I will never be made to stumble." **34**Jesus said to him, ᵃ"Assuredly, I say to you that this night, before the rooster crows, you will deny Me three times." **35**Peter said to Him, "Even if I have to die with You, I will not deny You!"

And so said all the disciples.

THE PRAYER IN THE GARDEN
(Mark 14:32–42; Luke 22:39–46)

36ᵃThen Jesus came with them to a place called Gethsemane, and said to the disciples, "Sit here while I go and pray over there." **37**And He took with Him Peter and ᵃthe two sons of Zebedee, and He began to be sorrowful and deeply distressed. **38**Then He said to them, ᵃ"My soul is exceedingly sorrowful, even to death. Stay here and watch with Me."

39He went a little farther and fell on His face, and ᵃprayed, saying, ᵇ"O My Father, if it is possible, ᶜlet this cup pass from Me; nevertheless, ᵈnot as I will, but as You *will*." **40**Then He came to the disciples and found them sleeping, and said to Peter, "What! Could you not watch with Me one hour? **41**ᵃWatch and pray, lest you enter into temptation. ᵇThe spirit indeed *is* willing, but the flesh *is* weak." **42**Again, a second time, He went away and prayed, saying, "O My Father, ¹if this cup cannot pass away from Me unless I drink it, Your will be done." **43**And He came and found them asleep again, for their eyes were heavy.

44So He left them, went away again, and prayed the third time, saying the same words. **45**Then He came to His disciples and said to them, "Are *you* still sleeping and resting? Behold, the hour ¹is at hand, and the Son of Man is being ᵃbetrayed into the hands of sinners. **46**Rise, let us be going. See, My betrayer is at hand."

BETRAYAL AND ARREST IN GETHSEMANE
(Mark 14:43–52; Luke 22:47–53; John 18:1–11)

47And ᵃwhile He was still speaking, behold, Judas, one of the twelve, with a great multitude with swords and clubs, came from the chief priests and elders of the people. **48**Now His betrayer had given them a sign, saying, "Whomever I kiss, He is the One; seize Him." **49**Immediately he went up to Jesus and said, "Greetings, Rabbi!" ᵃand kissed Him. **50**But Jesus said to him, ᵃ"Friend, why have you come?"

Then they came and laid hands on Jesus and took Him. **51**And suddenly, ᵃone of those *who were* with Jesus stretched out *his* hand and drew his sword, struck the servant of the high priest, and cut off his ear.

26:31 ᵃMatt. 26:56; Mark 14:27; John 16:32 ᵇ[Matt. 11:6] ᶜZech. 13:7
26:32 ᵃMatt. 28:7, 10, 16; Mark 14:28; 16:7; John 21:1
26:34 ᵃMatt. 26:74, 75; Mark 14:30; Luke 22:34; John 13:38
26:36 ᵃMark 14:32–35; Luke 22:39, 40; John 18:1
26:37 ᵃMatt. 4:21; 17:1; Mark 5:37
26:38 ᵃJohn 12:27
26:39 ᵃMark 14:36; Luke 22:42; [Heb. 5:7–9] ᵇJohn 12:27 ᶜMatt. 20:22 ᵈPs. 40:8; Is. 50:5; John 5:30; 6:38; Phil. 2:8
26:41 ᵃMark 13:33; 14:38; Luke 22:40, 46; [Eph. 6:18] ᵇPs. 103:14–16; [Rom. 7:15; 8:23; Gal. 5:17]
26:45 ᵃMatt. 17:22, 23; 20:18, 19
26:47 ᵃMark 14:43–50; Luke 22:47–53; John 18:3–11; Acts 1:16
26:49 ᵃ2 Sam. 20:9; [Prov. 27:6]
26:50 ᵃPs. 41:9; 55:13
26:51 ᵃMark 14:47; Luke 22:50; John 18:10

26:31 ¹caused to take offense at Me 26:33 ¹caused to take offense at You 26:42 ¹NU if this may not pass away unless 26:45 ¹has drawn near

26:52
ªGen. 9:6;
Rev. 13:10

26:53
ª2 Kin. 6:17;
Dan. 7:10

26:54 ªIs. 50:6;
53:2–11;
Luke 24:25–27,
44–46;
John 19:28;
Acts 13:29; 17:3;
26:23

26:56
ªLam. 4:20
ᵇZech. 13:7;
Matt. 26:31;
Mark 14:27;
John 18:15

26:57
ªMatt. 17:22;
Mark 14:53–65;
Luke 22:54;
John 18:12,
19–24

26:58
ªJohn 18:15, 16

26:59
ªEx. 20:16;
Ps. 35:11

26:60
ªPs. 27:12; 35:11;
Mark 14:55;
Acts 6:13
ᵇDeut. 19:15

26:61
ªMatt. 27:40;
Mark 14:58;
15:29; John 2:19;
Acts 6:14

26:62
ªMark 14:60

26:63
ªPs. 38:13, 14;
Is. 53:7;
Matt. 27:12, 14;
Acts 8:32
ᵇLev. 5:1;
1 Sam. 14:24, 26;
Luke 22:67–71

26:64
ªDan. 7:13;
Matt. 16:27;
24:30; 25:31;
Luke 21:27;
[John 1:51];
Rom. 14:10;
1 Thess. 4:16];
Rev. 1:7
ᵇPs. 110:1;
[Acts 7:55]

26:65
ª2 Kin. 18:37
ᵇJohn 10:30–36

26:66
ªLev. 24:16;
Matt. 20:18;
John 19:7

⁵²But Jesus said to him, "Put your sword in its place, ªfor all who take the sword will ¹perish by the sword. ⁵³Or do you think that I cannot now pray to My Father, and He will provide Me with ªmore than twelve legions of angels? ⁵⁴How then could the Scriptures be fulfilled, ªthat it must happen thus?"

⁵⁵In that hour Jesus said to the multitudes, "Have you come out, as against a robber, with swords and clubs to take Me? I sat daily with you, teaching in the temple, and you did not seize Me. ⁵⁶But all this was done that the ªScriptures of the prophets might be fulfilled."

Then ᵇall the disciples forsook Him and fled.

JESUS FACES THE SANHEDRIN
(Mark 14:53–65; Luke 22:66–71; John 18:12–14, 19–24)

⁵⁷ªAnd those who had laid hold of Jesus led *Him* away to Caiaphas the high priest, where the scribes and the elders were assembled. ⁵⁸But ªPeter followed Him at a distance to the high priest's courtyard. And he went in and sat with the servants to see the end.

⁵⁹Now the chief priests, ¹the elders, and all the council sought ªfalse testimony against Jesus to put Him to death, ⁶⁰¹but found none. Even though ªmany false witnesses came forward, they found none. But at last ᵇtwo ²false witnesses came forward ⁶¹and said, "This *fellow* said, ª'I am able to destroy the temple of God and to build it in three days.'"

⁶²ªAnd the high priest arose and said to Him, "Do You answer nothing? What *is it* these men testify against You?" ⁶³But ªJesus kept silent. And the high priest answered and said to Him, ᵇ"I put You under oath by the living God: Tell us if You are the Christ, the Son of God!"

⁶⁴Jesus said to him, "*It is as* you said. Nevertheless, I say to you, ªhereafter you will see the Son of Man ᵇsitting at the right hand of the Power, and coming on the clouds of heaven."

⁶⁵ªThen the high priest tore his clothes, saying, "He has spoken blasphemy! What further need do we have of witnesses? Look, now you have heard His ᵇblasphemy! ⁶⁶What do you think?"

They answered and said, ª"He is deserving of death."

⁶⁷ªThen they spat in His face and beat Him; and ᵇothers struck *Him* with ¹the palms of their hands, ⁶⁸saying, ª"Prophesy to us, Christ! Who is the one who struck You?"

PETER DENIES JESUS, AND WEEPS BITTERLY
(Mark 14:66–72; Luke 22:54–62; John 18:15–18, 25–27)

⁶⁹ªNow Peter sat outside in the courtyard. And a servant girl came to him, saying, "You also were with Jesus of Galilee."

⁷⁰But he denied it before *them* all, saying, "I do not know what you are saying."

⁷¹And when he had gone out to the gateway, another *girl* saw him and said to those *who were* there, "This *fellow* also was with Jesus of Nazareth."

26:67 ªJob 16:10; Is. 50:6; 53:3; Lam. 3:30; Matt. 27:30 ᵇMic. 5:1; Luke 22:63–65; John 19:3   26:68 ªMark 14:65; Luke 22:64   26:69 ªMark 14:66–72; Luke 22:55–62; John 18:16–18, 25–27

26:52 ¹M die   26:59 ¹NU omits *the elders*   26:60 ¹NU *but found none, even though many false witnesses came forward.*   ²NU omits *false witnesses*   26:67 ¹Or *rods,*

⁷²But again he denied with an oath, "I do not know the Man!"

⁷³And a little later those who stood by came up and said to Peter, "Surely you also are *one* of them, for your ᵃspeech betrays you."

⁷⁴Then ᵃhe began to ¹curse and ²swear, *saying*, "I do not know the Man!"

Immediately a rooster crowed. ⁷⁵And Peter remembered the word of Jesus who had said to him, ᵃ"Before the rooster crows, you will deny Me three times." So he went out and wept bitterly.

JESUS HANDED OVER TO PONTIUS PILATE
(Mark 15:1; Luke 23:1; John 18:28)

27 When morning came, ᵃall the chief priests and elders of the people plotted against Jesus to put Him to death. ²And when they had bound Him, they led Him away and ᵃdelivered Him to ¹Pontius Pilate the governor.

JUDAS HANGS HIMSELF
(Acts 1:18, 19)

³ᵃThen Judas, His betrayer, seeing that He had been condemned, was remorseful and brought back the thirty ᵇpieces of silver to the chief priests and elders, ⁴saying, "I have sinned by betraying innocent blood."

And they said, "What *is that* to us? You see *to it!*"

⁵Then he threw down the pieces of silver in the temple and ᵃdeparted, and went and hanged himself.

⁶But the chief priests took the silver pieces and said, "It is not lawful to put them into the treasury, because they are the price of blood." ⁷And they consulted together and bought with them the potter's field, to bury strangers in. ⁸Therefore that field has been called ᵃthe Field of Blood to this day.

⁹Then was fulfilled what was spoken by Jeremiah the prophet, saying, ᵃ"And they took the thirty pieces of silver, the value of Him who was priced, whom they of the children of Israel priced, ¹⁰and ᵃgave them for the potter's field, as the LORD directed me."

JESUS FACES PILATE
(Mark 15:2–5; Luke 23:2–5; John 18:29–38)

¹¹Now Jesus stood before the governor. ᵃAnd the governor asked Him, saying, "Are You the King of the Jews?"

Jesus said to him, ᵇ"*It is as* you say." ¹²And while He was being accused by the chief priests and elders, ᵃHe answered nothing.

¹³Then Pilate said to Him, ᵃ"Do You not hear how many things they testify against You?" ¹⁴But He answered him not one word, so that the governor marveled greatly.

TAKING THE PLACE OF BARABBAS
(Mark 15:6–15; Luke 23:13–25; John 18:39, 40)

¹⁵ᵃNow at the feast the governor was accustomed to releasing to the multitude one prisoner whom they wished. ¹⁶And

---

26:73
ᵃMark 14:70;
Luke 22:59;
John 18:26

26:74
ᵃMatt. 26:34;
Mark 14:71;
Luke 22:34;
John 13:38

26:75
ᵃMatt. 26:34;
Luke 22:61;
John 13:38

27:1 ᵃPs. 2:2;
Mark 15:1;
Luke 22:66; 23:1;
John 18:28

27:2
ᵃMatt. 20:19;
Luke 18:32;
Acts 3:13

27:3
ᵃMatt. 26:14
ᵇMatt. 26:15

27:5
ᵃ2 Sam. 17:23;
Matt. 18:7;
26:24;
John 17:12;
Acts 1:18

27:8 ᵃActs 1:19

27:9 ᵃZech. 11:12

27:10
ᵃJer. 32:6–9;
Zech. 11:12, 13

27:11
ᵃMark 15:2–5;
Luke 23:2, 3;
John 18:29–38;
ᵇJohn 18:37;
1 Tim. 6:13

27:12
ᵃPs. 38:13, 14;
Matt. 26:63;
John 19:9

27:13
ᵃMatt. 26:62;
John 19:10

27:15
ᵃMark 15:6–15;
Luke 23:17–25;
John 18:39—
19:16

26:74 ¹call down curses   ²Swear oaths   27:2 ¹NU omits *Pontius*

at that time they had a notorious prisoner called [1]Barabbas. [17]Therefore, when they had gathered together, Pilate said to them, "Whom do you want me to release to you? Barabbas, or Jesus who is called Christ?" [18]For he knew that they had handed Him over because of [a]envy.

[19]While he was sitting on the judgment seat, his wife sent to him, saying, "Have nothing to do with that just Man, for I have suffered many things today in a dream because of Him."

[20a]But the chief priests and elders persuaded the multitudes that they should ask for Barabbas and destroy Jesus. [21]The governor answered and said to them, "Which of the two do you want me to release to you?"

They said, [a]"Barabbas!"

[22]Pilate said to them, "What then shall I do with Jesus who is called Christ?"

They all said to him, "Let Him be crucified!"

[23]Then the governor said, [a]"Why, what evil has He done?"

But they cried out all the more, saying, "Let Him be crucified!"

[24]When Pilate saw that he could not prevail at all, but rather *that* a [1]tumult was rising, he [a]took water and washed *his* hands before the multitude, saying, "I am innocent of the blood of this [2]just Person. You see *to it.*"

[25]And all the people answered and said, [a]"His blood *be* on us and on our children."

[26]Then he released Barabbas to them; and when [a]he had [1]scourged Jesus, he delivered *Him* to be crucified.

THE SOLDIERS MOCK JESUS
(Mark 15:16–20)

[27a]Then the soldiers of the governor took Jesus into the [1]Praetorium and gathered the whole [2]garrison around Him. [28]And they [a]stripped Him and [b]put a scarlet robe on Him. [29a]When they had [1]twisted a crown of thorns, they put *it* on His head, and a reed in His right hand. And they bowed the knee before Him and mocked Him, saying, "Hail, King of the Jews!" [30]Then [a]they spat on Him, and took the reed and struck Him on the head. [31]And when they had mocked Him, they took the robe off Him, put His *own* clothes on Him, [a]and led Him away to be crucified.

THE KING ON A CROSS
(Mark 15:21–32; Luke 23:26–43; John 19:17–27)

[32a]Now as they came out, [b]they found a man of Cyrene, Simon by name. Him they compelled to bear His cross. [33a]And when they had come to a place called Golgotha, that is to say, Place of a Skull, [34a]they gave Him [1]sour wine mingled with gall to drink. But when He had tasted *it,* He would not drink.

[35a]Then they crucified Him, and divided His garments, casting lots, [1]that it might be fulfilled which was spoken by the prophet:

[b]"They divided My garments among them,
And for My clothing they cast lots."

27:18
[a]Matt. 21:38;
[John 15:22–25]

27:20
[a]Mark 15:11;
Luke 23:18;
John 18:40;
Acts 3:14

27:21 [a]Acts 3:14

27:23 [a]Acts 3:13

27:24
[a]Deut. 21:6–8

27:25
[a]Deut. 19:10;
Josh. 2:19;
2 Sam. 1:16;
1 Kin. 2:32;
Acts 5:28

27:26
[a][Is. 50:6; 53:5];
Matt. 20:19;
Mark 15:15;
Luke 23:16, 24,
25; John 19:1, 16

27:27
[a]Mark 15:16–20;
John 19:2

27:28
[a]Mark 15:17;
John 19:2
[b]Luke 23:11

27:29
[a]Ps. 69:19;
Is. 53:3;
Matt. 20:19;
Mark 10:34;
Luke 18:32

27:30
[a]Is. 50:6; 52:14;
Mic. 5:1;
Matt. 26:67;
Mark 10:34;
14:65; 15:19

27:31 [a]Is. 53:7;
Matt. 20:19

27:32
[a]1 Kin. 21:13;
Acts 7:58;
Heb. 13:12
[b]Mark 15:21;
Luke 23:26;
John 19:17

27:33
[a]Mark 15:22–32;
Luke 23:33–43;
John 19:17

27:34 [a]Ps. 69:21;
Matt. 27:48

27:35
[a]Mark 15:24;
Luke 23:34;
John 19:24
[b]Ps. 22:18

27:16 [1]NU *Jesus Barabbas*   27:24 [1]*an uproar*   [2]NU omits *just*
27:26 [1]*flogged* with a Roman scourge   27:27 [1]The governor's headquarters
[2]*cohort*   27:29 [1]Lit. *woven*   27:34 [1]NU omits *sour*   27:35 [1]NU, M omit the rest of v. 35.

[36a]Sitting down, they kept watch over Him there. [37]And they [a]put up over His head the accusation written against Him:

THIS IS JESUS THE KING OF THE JEWS.

[38a]Then two robbers were crucified with Him, one on the right and another on the left.

[39]And [a]those who passed by blasphemed Him, wagging their heads [40]and saying, [a]"You who destroy the temple and build *it* in three days, save Yourself! [b]If You are the Son of God, come down from the cross."

[41]Likewise the chief priests also, mocking with the [1]scribes and elders, said, [42]"He [a]saved others; Himself He cannot save. [1]If He is the King of Israel, let Him now come down from the cross, and we will believe [2]Him. [43a]He trusted in God; let Him deliver Him now if He will have Him; for He said, 'I am the Son of God.'"

[44a]Even the robbers who were crucified with Him reviled Him with the same thing.

JESUS DIES ON THE CROSS
(Mark 15:33–41; Luke 23:44–49; John 19:28–30)

[45a]Now from the sixth hour until the ninth hour there was darkness over all the land. [46]And about the ninth hour [a]Jesus cried out with a loud voice, saying, "Eli, Eli, lama sabachthani?" that is, [b]"My God, My God, why have You forsaken Me?"

[47]Some of those who stood there, when they heard *that,* said, "This Man is calling for Elijah!" [48]Immediately one of them ran and took a sponge, [a]filled *it* with sour wine and put *it* on a reed, and offered it to Him to drink.

[49]The rest said, "Let Him alone; let us see if Elijah will come to save Him."

[50]And Jesus [a]cried out again with a loud voice, and [b]yielded up His spirit.

[51]Then, behold, [a]the veil of the temple was torn in two from top to bottom; and the earth quaked, and the rocks were split, [52]and the graves were opened; and many bodies of the saints who had fallen asleep were raised; [53]and coming out of the graves after His resurrection, they went into the holy city and appeared to many.

[54a]So when the centurion and those with him, who were guarding Jesus, saw the earthquake and the things that had happened, they feared greatly, saying, [b]"Truly this was the Son of God!"

[55]And many women [a]who followed Jesus from Galilee, ministering to Him, were there looking on from afar, [56a]among whom were Mary Magdalene, Mary the mother of James and [1]Joses, and the mother of Zebedee's sons.

JESUS BURIED IN JOSEPH'S TOMB
(Mark 15:42–47; Luke 23:50–56; John 19:38–42)

[57]Now [a]when evening had come, there came a rich man from Arimathea, named Joseph, who himself had also become a disciple of Jesus. [58]This man went to Pilate and asked for the body of Jesus. Then Pilate commanded the body to be

---

27:36 [a]Ps. 22:17; Matt. 27:54

27:37 [a]Mark 15:26; Luke 23:38; John 19:19

27:38 [a]Is. 53:9, 12; Mark 15:27; Luke 23:32, 33; John 19:18

27:39 [a]Job 16:4; Ps. 22:7; 109:25; Lam. 2:15; Mark 15:29; Luke 23:35

27:40 [a]Matt. 26:61; John 2:19 [b]Matt. 26:63

27:42 [a][Matt. 18:11]; John 3:14, 15]

27:43 [a]Ps. 22:8

27:44 [a]Mark 15:32; Luke 23:39–43

27:45 [a]Amos 8:9; Mark 15:33–41; Luke 23:44–49

27:46 [a][Heb. 5:7] [b]Ps. 22:1

27:48 [a]Ps. 69:21; Mark 15:36; Luke 23:36; John 19:29

27:50 [a]Mark 15:37; Luke 23:46; John 19:30 [b]Dan. 9:26; Zech. 11:10, 11; Matt. 17:23; [John 10:18; 1 Cor. 15:3]

27:51 [a]Ex. 26:31; 2 Chr. 3:14; Zech. 11:10; Mark 15:38; Luke 23:45; Heb. 9:3

27:54 [a]Mark 15:39; Luke 23:47 [b]Matt. 14:33

27:55 [a]Mark 15:41; Luke 8:2, 3

27:56 [a]Matt. 28:1; Mark 15:40, 47; 16:9; Luke 8:2; John 19:25; 20:1, 18

27:57 [a]Mark 15:42–47; Luke 23:50–56; John 19:38–42

27:41 [1]M *scribes, the Pharisees, and the elders*   27:42 [1]NU omits *If* [2]NU, M *in Him*   27:56 [1]NU *Joseph*

given to him. [59]When Joseph had taken the body, he wrapped it in a clean linen cloth, [60]and [a]laid it in his new tomb which he had hewn out of the rock; and he rolled a large stone against the door of the tomb, and departed. [61]And Mary Magdalene was there, and the other Mary, sitting [1]opposite the tomb.

PILATE SETS A GUARD

[62]On the next day, which followed the Day of Preparation, the chief priests and Pharisees gathered together to Pilate, [63]saying, "Sir, we remember, while He was still alive, how that deceiver said, [a]'After three days I will rise.' [64]Therefore command that the tomb be made secure until the third day, lest His disciples come [1]by night and steal Him *away,* and say to the people, 'He has risen from the dead.' So the last deception will be worse than the first."

[65]Pilate said to them, "You have a guard; go your way, make *it* as secure as you know how." [66]So they went and made the tomb secure, [a]sealing the stone and setting the guard.

HE IS RISEN

(Mark 16:1–8; Luke 24:1–12; John 20:1–10)

28 Now [a]after the Sabbath, as the first *day* of the week began to dawn, Mary Magdalene [b]and the other Mary came to see the tomb. [2]And behold, there was a great earthquake; for [a]an angel of the Lord descended from heaven, and came and rolled back the stone [1]from the door, and sat on it. [3a]His countenance was like lightning, and his clothing as white as snow. [4]And the guards shook for fear of him, and became like [a]dead *men.*

[5]But the angel answered and said to the women, "Do not be afraid, for I know that you seek Jesus who was crucified. [6]He is not here; for He is risen, [a]as He said. Come, see the place where the Lord lay. [7]And go quickly and tell His disciples that He is risen from the dead, and indeed [a]He is going before you into Galilee; there you will see Him. Behold, I have told you."

[8]So they went out quickly from the tomb with fear and great joy, and ran to bring His disciples word.

THE WOMEN WORSHIP THE RISEN LORD

[9]And [1]as they went to tell His disciples, behold, [a]Jesus met them, saying, "Rejoice!" So they came and held Him by the feet and worshiped Him. [10]Then Jesus said to them, "Do not be afraid. Go *and* tell [a]My brethren to go to Galilee, and there they will see Me."

THE SOLDIERS ARE BRIBED

[11]Now while they were going, behold, some of the guard came into the city and reported to the chief priests all the things that had happened. [12]When they had assembled with the elders and consulted together, they gave a large sum of money to the soldiers, [13]saying, "Tell them, 'His disciples came at night and stole Him *away* while we slept.' [14]And if this comes to the governor's ears, we will appease him and make

---

27:60 [a]Is. 53:9; Matt. 26:12

27:63 [a]Matt. 16:21; 17:23; 20:19; 26:61; Mark 8:31; 10:34; Luke 9:22; 13:33; 24:6, 7; John 2:19

27:66 [a]Dan. 6:17

28:1 [a]Mark 16:1–8; Luke 24:1–10; John 20:1–8 [b]Matt. 27:56, 61

28:2 [a]Mark 16:5; Luke 24:4; John 20:12

28:3 [a]Dan. 7:9; 10:6; Mark 9:3; John 20:12; Acts 1:10

28:4 [a]Rev. 1:17

28:6 [a]Hos. 6:2; Ps. 16:10; 49:15; Matt. 12:40; 16:21; 17:23; 20:19

28:7 [a]Matt. 26:32; 28:10, 16; Mark 16:7

28:9 [a]Mark 16:9; John 20:14

28:10 [a]Ps. 22:22; John 20:17; Rom. 8:29; [Heb. 2:11]

27:61 [1]*in front of*   **27:64** [1]NU omits *by night*   **28:2** [1]NU omits *from the door*
28:9 [1]NU omits *as they went to tell His disciples*

you secure." ¹⁵So they took the money and did as they were instructed; and this saying is commonly reported among the Jews until this day.

THE GREAT COMMISSION
(Mark 16:14–18; Luke 24:36–49; John 20:19–23; Acts 1:6–8)

¹⁶Then the eleven disciples went away into Galilee, to the mountain ^awhich Jesus had appointed for them. ¹⁷When they saw Him, they worshiped Him; but some ^adoubted.

¹⁸And Jesus came and spoke to them, saying, ^a"All authority has been given to Me in heaven and on earth. ^{19a}Go ¹therefore and ^bmake disciples of all the nations, baptizing them in the name of the Father and of the Son and of the Holy Spirit, ^{20a}teaching them to observe all things that I have commanded you; and lo, I am ^bwith you always, *even* to the end of the age." ¹Amen.

28:16
^aMatt. 26:32;
28:7, 10;
Mark 14:28;
15:41; 16:7

28:17
^aJohn 20:24–29

28:18
^a[Dan. 7:13, 14];
Matt. 11:27;
Luke 1:32; 10:22;
John 3:35;
Acts 2:36;
Rom. 14:9;
1 Cor. 15:27;
[Eph. 1:10, 21];
Phil. 2:9, 10;
[Heb. 1:2];
1 Pet. 3:22

28:19
^aMark 16:15
^bIs. 52:10;
Luke 24:47;
[Acts 2:38, 39];
Rom. 10:18;
Col. 1:23

28:20
^a[Acts 2:42]
^b[Acts 4:31;
18:10; 23:11]

28:19 ¹M omits *therefore*   28:20 ¹NU omits *Amen.*

THE GOSPEL ACCORDING TO
MARK

JOHN THE BAPTIST PREPARES THE WAY
(Matt. 3:1–12; Luke 3:1–20; John 1:19–28)

1 The ᵃbeginning of the gospel of Jesus Christ, ᵇthe Son of God. ²As it is written in ¹the Prophets:

ᵃ"Behold, I send My messenger before Your face,
Who will prepare Your way before You."
3 "Theᵃ voice of one crying in the wilderness:
'Prepare the way of the LORD;
Make His paths straight.'"

⁴ᵃJohn came baptizing in the wilderness and preaching a baptism of repentance ¹for the remission of sins. ⁵ᵃThen all the land of Judea, and those from Jerusalem, went out to him and were all baptized by him in the Jordan River, confessing their sins.

⁶Now John was ᵃclothed with camel's hair and with a leather belt around his waist, and he ate locusts and wild honey. ⁷And he preached, saying, ᵃ"There comes One after me who is mightier than I, whose sandal strap I am not worthy to stoop down and loose. ⁸ᵃI indeed baptized you with water, but He will baptize you ᵇwith the Holy Spirit."

JOHN BAPTIZES JESUS
(Matt. 3:13–17; Luke 3:21, 22; John 1:29–34)

⁹ᵃIt came to pass in those days *that* Jesus came from Nazareth of Galilee, and was baptized by John in the Jordan. ¹⁰ᵃAnd immediately, coming up ¹from the water, He saw the heavens ²parting and the Spirit ᵇdescending upon Him like a dove. ¹¹Then a voice came from heaven, ᵃ"You are My beloved Son, in whom I am well pleased."

SATAN TEMPTS JESUS
(Matt. 4:1–11; Luke 4:1–13)

¹²ᵃImmediately the Spirit ¹drove Him into the wilderness. ¹³And He was there in the wilderness forty days, tempted by Satan, and was with the wild beasts; ᵃand the angels ministered to Him.

JESUS BEGINS HIS GALILEAN MINISTRY
(Matt. 4:12–17; Luke 4:14, 15)

¹⁴ᵃNow after John was put in prison, Jesus came to Galilee, ᵇpreaching the gospel ¹of the kingdom of God, ¹⁵and saying, ᵃ"The time is fulfilled, and ᵇthe kingdom of God ¹is at hand. Repent, and believe in the gospel."

1:2 ¹NU *Isaiah the prophet* **1:4** ¹Or *because of forgiveness* **1:10** ¹NU *out of* ²*torn open* **1:12** ¹*sent Him out* **1:14** ¹NU omits *of the kingdom* **1:15** ¹*has drawn near*

FOUR FISHERMEN CALLED AS DISCIPLES
(Matt. 4:18–22; Luke 5:1–11)

16ªAnd as He walked by the Sea of Galilee, He saw Simon and Andrew his brother casting a net into the sea; for they were fishermen. 17Then Jesus said to them, "Follow Me, and I will make you become ªfishers of men." 18ªThey immediately left their nets and followed Him.

19When He had gone a little farther from there, He saw James the *son* of Zebedee, and John his brother, who also *were* in the boat mending their nets. 20And immediately He called them, and they left their father Zebedee in the boat with the hired servants, and went after Him.

JESUS CASTS OUT AN UNCLEAN SPIRIT
(Luke 4:31–37)

21ªThen they went into Capernaum, and immediately on the Sabbath He entered the ᵇsynagogue and taught. 22ªAnd they were astonished at His teaching, for He taught them as one having authority, and not as the scribes.

23Now there was a man in their synagogue with an ªunclean spirit. And he cried out, 24saying, "Let *us* alone! ªWhat have we to do with You, Jesus of Nazareth? Did You come to destroy us? I ᵇknow who You are—the ᶜHoly One of God!"

25But Jesus ªrebuked him, saying, ¹"Be quiet, and come out of him!" 26And when the unclean spirit ªhad convulsed him and cried out with a loud voice, he came out of him. 27Then they were all amazed, so that they questioned among themselves, saying, ¹"What is this? What new ²doctrine *is* this? For with authority He commands even the unclean spirits, and they obey Him." 28And immediately His ªfame spread throughout all the region around Galilee.

PETER'S MOTHER-IN-LAW HEALED
(Matt. 8:14, 15; Luke 4:38, 39)

29ªNow as soon as they had come out of the synagogue, they entered the house of Simon and Andrew, with James and John. 30But Simon's wife's mother lay sick with a fever, and they told Him about her at once. 31So He came and took her by the hand and lifted her up, and immediately the fever left her. And she served them.

MANY HEALED AFTER SABBATH SUNSET
(Matt. 8:16, 17; Luke 4:40, 41)

32ªAt evening, when the sun had set, they brought to Him all who were sick and those who were demon-possessed. 33And the whole city was gathered together at the door. 34Then He healed many who were sick with various diseases, and ªcast out many demons; and He ᵇdid not allow the demons to speak, because they knew Him.

PREACHING IN GALILEE
(Matt. 4:23–25; Luke 4:42–44)

35Now ªin the morning, having risen a long while before daylight, He went out and departed to a ¹solitary place; and

1:16
ªMatt. 4:18–22;
Luke 5:2–11;
John 1:40–42
1:17
ªMatt. 13:47, 48
1:18
ªMatt. 19:27;
[Luke 14:26]
1:21 ªMatt. 4:13;
Luke 4:31–37
ᵇPs. 22:22;
Matt. 4:23;
Luke 4:16; 13:10
1:22 ªMatt. 7:28,
29; 13:54
1:23
ª[Matt. 12:43];
Mark 5:2; 7:25;
Luke 4:33
1:24
ªMatt. 8:28, 29;
Mark 5:7, 8;
Luke 8:28
ᵇMark 3:11;
Luke 4:41;
James 2:19
ᶜPs. 16:10
1:25
ª[Luke 4:39]
1:26 ªMark 9:20
1:28
ªMatt. 4:24;
9:31
1:29
ªMatt. 8:14, 15;
Luke 4:38, 39
1:32
ªMatt. 8:16, 17;
Luke 4:40, 41
1:34 ªMatt. 9:33;
Luke 13:32
ᵇMark 3:12;
Luke 4:41;
Acts 16:17, 18
1:35
ªLuke 4:42, 43

1:25 ¹Lit. *Be muzzled*   1:27 ¹NU *What is this? A new doctrine with authority! He*   ²*teaching*   1:35 ¹*deserted*

there He [b]prayed. [36]And Simon and those *who were* with Him searched for Him. [37]When they found Him, they said to Him, [a]"Everyone [b]is looking for You."

[38]But He said to them, [a]"Let us go into the next towns, that I may preach there also, because [b]for this purpose I have come forth."

[39a]And He was preaching in their synagogues throughout all Galilee, and [b]casting out demons.

JESUS CLEANSES A LEPER
(Matt. 8:1–4; Luke 5:12–16)

[40a]Now a leper came to Him, imploring Him, kneeling down to Him and saying to Him, "If You are willing, You can make me clean."

[41]Then Jesus, moved with [a]compassion, stretched out *His* hand and touched him, and said to him, "I am willing; be cleansed." [42]As soon as He had spoken, [a]immediately the leprosy left him, and he was cleansed. [43]And He strictly warned him and sent him away at once, [44]and said to him, "See that you say nothing to anyone; but go your way, show yourself to the priest, and offer for your cleansing those things [a]which Moses commanded, as a testimony to them."

[45a]However, he went out and began to proclaim *it* freely, and to spread the matter, so that Jesus could no longer openly enter the city, but was outside in deserted places; [b]and they came to Him from every direction.

JESUS FORGIVES AND HEALS A PARALYTIC
(Matt. 9:2–8; Luke 5:17–26)

2 And again [a]He entered Capernaum after *some* days, and it was heard that He was in the house. [2][1]Immediately many gathered together, so that there was no longer room to receive *them,* not even near the door. And He preached the word to them. [3]Then they came to Him, bringing a [a]paralytic who was carried by four *men.* [4]And when they could not come near Him because of the crowd, they uncovered the roof where He was. So when they had broken through, they let down the bed on which the paralytic was lying.

[5]When Jesus saw their faith, He said to the paralytic, "Son, your sins are forgiven you."

[6]And some of the scribes were sitting there and reasoning in their hearts, [7]"Why does this *Man* speak blasphemies like this? [a]Who can forgive sins but God alone?"

[8]But immediately, when Jesus perceived in His spirit that they reasoned thus within themselves, He said to them, "Why do you reason about these things in your hearts? [9a]Which is easier, to say to the paralytic, '*Your* sins are forgiven you,' or to say, 'Arise, take up your bed and walk'? [10]But that you may know that the Son of Man has [1]power on earth to forgive sins"—He said to the paralytic, [11]"I say to you, arise, take up your bed, and go to your house." [12]Immediately he arose, took up the bed, and went out in the presence of them all, so that all were amazed and [a]glorified God, saying, "We never saw *anything* like this!"

Cross references (margin):

1:35
[b]Matt. 26:39, 44;
Mark 6:46;
Luke 5:16;
6:12; 9:28, 29;
Heb. 5:7

1:37 [a]Matt. 4:25;
John 3:26; 12:19
[b][Heb. 11:6]

1:38 [a]Luke 4:43
[b][Is. 61:1, 2;
Mark 10:45;
John 16:28;
17:4, 8]

1:39 [a]Ps. 22:22;
Matt. 4:23;
9:35;
Mark 1:21; 3:1;
Luke 4:44
[b]Mark 5:8, 13;
7:29, 30

1:40
[a]Matt. 8:2–4;
Luke 5:12–14

1:41 [a]Luke 7:13

1:42
[a]Matt. 15:28;
Mark 5:29

1:44
[a]Lev. 14:1–32

1:45
[a]Matt. 28:15;
Luke 5:15
[b]Mark 2:2, 13;
3:7; Luke 5:17;
John 6:2

2:1 [a]Matt. 9:1

2:3
[a]Matt. 4:24; 8:6;
Acts 8:7; 9:33

2:7 [a]Job 14:4;
Is. 43:25;
Dan. 9:9

2:9 [a]Matt. 9:5

2:12
[a]Matt. 15:31;
[Phil. 2:11]

MATTHEW THE TAX COLLECTOR
(Matt. 9:9–13; Luke 5:27–32)

13aThen He went out again by the sea; and all the multitude came to Him, and He taught them. 14aAs He passed by, He saw Levi the *son* of Alphaeus sitting at the tax office. And He said to him, b"Follow Me." So he arose and cfollowed Him.

15aNow it happened, as He was dining in *Levi's* house, that many tax collectors and sinners also sat together with Jesus and His disciples; for there were many, and they followed Him. 16And when the scribes 1and Pharisees saw Him eating with the tax collectors and sinners, they said to His disciples, "How *is it* that He eats and drinks with tax collectors and sinners?"

17When Jesus heard *it,* He said to them, a"Those who are well have no need of a physician, but those who are sick. I did not come to call *the* righteous, but sinners, 1to repentance."

JESUS IS QUESTIONED ABOUT FASTING
(Matt. 9:14–17; Luke 5:33–39)

18aThe disciples of John and of the Pharisees were fasting. Then they came and said to Him, "Why do the disciples of John and of the Pharisees fast, but Your disciples do not fast?"

19And Jesus said to them, "Can the 1friends of the bridegroom fast while the bridegroom is with them? As long as they have the bridegroom with them they cannot fast. 20But the days will come when the bridegroom will be ataken away from them, and then they will fast in those days. 21No one sews a piece of unshrunk cloth on an old garment; or else the new piece pulls away from the old, and the tear is made worse. 22And no one puts new wine into old wineskins; or else the new wine bursts the wineskins, the wine is spilled, and the wineskins are ruined. But new wine must be put into new wineskins."

JESUS IS LORD OF THE SABBATH
(Matt. 12:1–8; Luke 6:1–5)

23aNow it happened that He went through the grainfields on the Sabbath; and as they went His disciples began bto pluck the heads of grain. 24And the Pharisees said to Him, "Look, why do they do what is anot lawful on the Sabbath?"

25But He said to them, "Have you never read awhat David did when he was in need and hungry, he and those with him: 26how he went into the house of God *in the days* of Abiathar the high priest, and ate the showbread, awhich is not lawful to eat except for the priests, and also gave some to those who were with him?"

27And He said to them, "The Sabbath was made for man, and not man for the aSabbath. 28Therefore athe Son of Man is also Lord of the Sabbath."

HEALING ON THE SABBATH
(Matt. 12:9–14; Luke 6:6–11)

3 And aHe entered the synagogue again, and a man was there who had a withered hand. 2So they awatched Him closely, whether He would bheal him on the Sabbath, so that

2:13 aMatt. 9:9
2:14
aMatt. 9:9–13;
Luke 5:27–32;
bMatt. 4:19;
8:22; 19:21;
John 1:43;
12:26; 21:22
cLuke 18:28

2:15 aMatt. 9:10

2:17
aMatt. 9:12, 13;
18:11; Luke 5:31,
32; 19:10

2:18
aMatt. 9:14–17;
Luke 5:33–38

2:20 aActs 1:9;
13:2, 3; 14:23

2:23
aMatt. 12:1–8;
Luke 6:1–5
bDeut. 23:25

2:24
aEx. 20:10; 31:15

2:25
a1 Sam. 21:1–6

2:26
aEx. 29:32, 33;
Lev. 24:5–9

2:27 aGen. 2:3;
Ex. 23:12;
Deut. 5:14;
Neh. 9:14;
Ezek. 20:12

2:28 aMatt. 12:8

3:1
aMatt. 12:9–14;
Luke 6:6–11

3:2 a[Ps. 37:32];
Luke 14:1; 20:20
bLuke 13:14

they might [1]accuse Him. 3And He said to the man who had the withered hand, [1]"Step forward." 4Then He said to them, "Is it lawful on the Sabbath to do good or to do evil, to save life or to kill?" But they kept silent. 5And when He had looked around at them with anger, being grieved by the [a]hardness of their hearts, He said to the man, "Stretch out your hand." And he stretched *it* out, and his hand was restored [1]as whole as the other. 6[a]Then the Pharisees went out and immediately plotted with [b]the Herodians against Him, how they might destroy Him.

A GREAT MULTITUDE FOLLOWS JESUS

(Matt. 12:15–21)

7But Jesus withdrew with His disciples to the sea. And a great multitude from Galilee followed Him, [a]and from Judea 8and Jerusalem and Idumea and beyond the Jordan; and those from Tyre and Sidon, a great multitude, when they heard how [a]many things He was doing, came to Him. 9So He told His disciples that a small boat should be kept ready for Him because of the multitude, lest they should crush Him. 10For He healed [a]many, so that as many as had afflictions pressed about Him to [b]touch Him. 11[a]And the unclean spirits, whenever they saw Him, fell down before Him and cried out, saying, [b]"You are the Son of God." 12But [a]He sternly warned them that they should not make Him known.

THE TWELVE APOSTLES

(Matt. 10:1–4; Luke 6:12–16)

13[a]And He went up on the mountain and called to *Him* those He Himself wanted. And they came to Him. 14Then He appointed twelve, [1]that they might be with Him and that He might send them out to preach, 15and to have [1]power [2]to heal sicknesses and to cast out demons: 16[1]Simon, [a]to whom He gave the name Peter; 17James the *son* of Zebedee and John the brother of James, to whom He gave the name Boanerges, that is, "Sons of Thunder"; 18Andrew, Philip, Bartholomew, Matthew, Thomas, James the *son* of Alphaeus, Thaddaeus, Simon the Cananite; 19and Judas Iscariot, who also betrayed Him. And they went into a house.

A HOUSE DIVIDED CANNOT STAND

(Matt. 12:22–30; Luke 11:14–23)

20Then the multitude came together again, [a]so that they could not so much as eat bread. 21But when His [a]own people heard *about this,* they went out to lay hold of Him, [b]for they said, "He is out of His mind."

22And the scribes who came down from Jerusalem said, [a]"He has Beelzebub," and, "By the [b]ruler of the demons He casts out demons."

23[a]So He called them to *Himself* and said to them in parables: "How can Satan cast out Satan? 24If a kingdom is divided against itself, that kingdom cannot stand. 25And if a house is

3:5 [a]Zech. 7:12
3:6 [a]Ps. 2:2; Mark 12:13 [b]Matt. 22:16
3:7 [a]Matt. 4:25; Luke 6:17
3:8 [a]Mark 5:19
3:10 [a]Mark 5:29, 34; Luke 7:21 [b]Matt. 9:21; 14:36; Mark 6:56; 8:22
3:11 [a]Mark 1:23, 24; Luke 4:41 [b]Matt. 8:29; 14:33; Mark 1:1; 5:7; Luke 8:28
3:12 [a]Matt. 12:16; Mark 1:25, 34
3:13 [a]Matt. 10:1; Mark 6:7; Luke 9:1
3:16 [a]Matt. 16:18; John 1:42
3:20 [a]Mark 6:31
3:21 [a]Ps. 69:8; Matt. 13:55; Mark 6:3; John 2:12 [b]John 7:5; 10:20; Acts 26:24; [2 Cor. 5:13]
3:22 [a]Matt. 9:34; 10:25; Luke 11:15; John 7:20; 8:48, 52; 10:20 [b][John 12:31; 14:30; 16:11; Eph. 2:2]
3:23 [a]Matt. 12:25–29; Luke 11:17–22

3:2 [1]*bring charges against* 3:3 [1]Lit. *Arise into the midst* 3:5 [1]NU omits *as whole as the other* 3:14 [1]NU adds *whom He also named apostles* 3:15 [1]*authority* [2]NU omits *to heal sicknesses and* 3:16 [1]NU *and He appointed the twelve: Simon . . .*

divided against itself, that house cannot stand. [26]And if Satan has risen up against himself, and is divided, he cannot stand, but has an end. [27a]No one can enter a strong man's house and plunder his goods, unless he first binds the strong man. And then he will plunder his house.

THE UNPARDONABLE SIN
(Matt. 12:31, 32; Luke 12:10)

[28a]"Assuredly, I say to you, all sins will be forgiven the sons of men, and whatever blasphemies they may utter; [29]but he who blasphemes against the Holy Spirit never has forgiveness, but is subject to eternal condemnation"— [30]because they [a]said, "He has an unclean spirit."

JESUS' MOTHER AND BROTHERS SEND FOR HIM
(Matt. 12:46–50; Luke 8:19–21)

[31a]Then His brothers and His mother came, and standing outside they sent to Him, calling Him. [32]And a multitude was sitting around Him; and they said to Him, "Look, Your mother and Your brothers [1]are outside seeking You."

[33]But He answered them, saying, "Who is My mother, or My brothers?" [34]And He looked around in a circle at those who sat about Him, and said, "Here are My mother and My brothers! [35]For whoever does the [a]will of God is My brother and My sister and mother."

THE PARABLE OF THE SOWER
(Matt. 13:1–9; Luke 8:4–8)

4 And [a]again He began to teach by the sea. And a great multitude was gathered to Him, so that He got into a boat and sat *in it* on the sea; and the whole multitude was on the land facing the sea. [2]Then He taught them many things by parables, [a]and said to them in His teaching:

[3]"Listen! Behold, a sower went out to sow. [4]And it happened, as he sowed, *that* some *seed* fell by the wayside; and the birds [1]of the air came and devoured it. [5]Some fell on stony ground, where it did not have much earth; and immediately it sprang up because it had no depth of earth. [6]But when the sun was up it was scorched, and because it had no root it withered away. [7]And some *seed* fell among thorns; and the thorns grew up and choked it, and it yielded no [1]crop. [8]But other *seed* fell on good ground and yielded a crop that sprang up, increased and produced: some thirtyfold, some sixty, and some a hundred."

[9]And He said [1]to them, "He who has ears to hear, let him hear!"

THE PURPOSE OF PARABLES
(Matt. 13:10–17; Luke 8:9, 10)

[10a]But when He was alone, those around Him with the twelve asked Him about the parable. [11]And He said to them, "To you it has been given to [a]know the [1]mystery of the kingdom of God; but to [b]those who are outside, all things come in parables, [12]so that

---

3:27
[a][Is. 49:24, 25];
Matt. 12:29

3:28
[a]Matt. 12:31, 32;
Luke 12:10;
[1 John 5:16]

3:30
[a]Matt. 9:34;
John 7:20; 8:48,
52; 10:20

3:31
[a]Matt. 12:46–50;
Luke 8:19–21

3:35 [a]Eph. 6:6;
Heb. 10:36;
1 Pet. 4:2;
[1 John 2:17]

4:1
[a]Matt. 13:1–15;
Luke 8:4–10

4:2 [a]Mark 12:38

4:10
[a]Matt. 13:10;
Luke 8:9

4:11
[a][Matt. 11:25;
1 Cor. 2:10–16;
2 Cor. 4:6]
[b][1 Cor. 5:12, 13;
Col. 4:5;
1 Thess. 4:12;
1 Tim. 3:7]

3:32 [1]NU, M add *and Your sisters*   4:4 [1]NU, M omit *of the air*   4:7 [1]Lit. *fruit*
4:9 [1]NU, M omit *to them*   4:11 [1]*secret* or *hidden truths*

a'Seeing they may see and not perceive,
And hearing they may hear and not understand;
Lest they should turn,
And *their* sins be forgiven them.'"

THE PARABLE OF THE SOWER EXPLAINED
(Matt. 13:18–23; Luke 8:11–15)

13And He said to them, "Do you not understand this parable? How then will you understand all the parables? 14aThe sower sows the word. 15And these are the ones by the wayside where the word is sown. When they hear, Satan comes immediately and takes away the word that was sown in their hearts. 16These likewise are the ones sown on stony ground who, when they hear the word, immediately receive it with gladness; 17and they have no root in themselves, and so endure only for a time. Afterward, when tribulation or persecution arises for the word's sake, immediately they stumble. 18Now these are the ones sown among thorns; *they are* the ones who hear the word, 19and the acares of this world, bthe deceitfulness of riches, and the desires for other things entering in choke the word, and it becomes unfruitful. 20But these are the ones sown on good ground, those who hear the word, 1accept *it,* and bear afruit: some thirtyfold, some sixty, and some a hundred."

LIGHT UNDER A BASKET
(Luke 8:16–18)

21aAlso He said to them, "Is a lamp brought to be put under a basket or under a bed? Is it not to be set on a lampstand? 22aFor there is nothing hidden which will not be revealed, nor has anything been kept secret but that it should come to light. 23aIf anyone has ears to hear, let him hear."

24Then He said to them, "Take heed what you hear. aWith the same measure you use, it will be measured to you; and to you who hear, more will be given. 25aFor whoever has, to him more will be given; but whoever does not have, even what he has will be taken away from him."

THE PARABLE OF THE GROWING SEED

26And He said, a"The kingdom of God is as if a man should 1scatter seed on the ground, 27and should sleep by night and rise by day, and the seed should sprout and agrow, he himself does not know how. 28For the earth ayields crops by itself: first the blade, then the head, after that the full grain in the head. 29But when the grain ripens, immediately ahe puts in the sickle, because the harvest has come."

THE PARABLE OF THE MUSTARD SEED
(Matt. 13:31, 32; Luke 13:18, 19)

30Then He said, a"To what shall we liken the kingdom of God? Or with what parable shall we picture it? 31*It is* like a mustard seed which, when it is sown on the ground, is smaller than all the seeds on earth; 32but when it is sown, it grows up and becomes greater than all herbs, and shoots out large branches, so that the birds of the air may nest under its shade."

4:12
aIs. 6:9, 10; 43:8;
Jer. 5:21;
Ezek. 12:2;
Matt. 13:14;
Luke 8:10;
John 12:40;
Rom. 11:8

4:14
aMatt. 13:18–23;
Luke 8:11–15

4:19 aLuke 21:34
bProv. 23:5;
Eccl. 5:13;
Luke 18:24;
1 Tim. 6:9, 10, 17

4:20
a[John 15:2, 5;
Rom. 7:4]

4:21 aMatt. 5:15;
Luke 8:16; 11:33

4:22 aEccl. 12:14;
Matt. 10:26, 27;
Luke 12:3;
[1 Cor. 4:5]

4:23
aMatt. 11:15;
13:9, 43;
Mark 4:9;
Luke 8:8; 14:35;
Rev. 3:6, 13,
22; 13:9

4:24 aMatt. 7:2;
Luke 6:38;
2 Cor. 9:6

4:25
aMatt. 13:12;
25:29;
Luke 8:18; 19:26

4:26
a[Matt. 13:24–
30, 36–43];
Luke 8:1

4:27
a[2 Cor. 3:18;
2 Pet. 3:18]

4:28
a[John 12:24]

4:29 a[Matthew
13:30, 39];
Rev. 14:15

4:30
aMatt. 13:31, 32;
Luke 13:18, 19;
[Acts 2:41; 4:4;
5:14; 19:20]

4:20 1*receive*   4:26 1*sow*

JESUS' USE OF PARABLES

[33a]And with many such parables He spoke the word to them as they were able to hear *it*. [34]But without a parable He did not speak to them. And when they were alone, [a]He explained all things to His disciples.

WIND AND WAVE OBEY JESUS
(Matt. 8:23–27; Luke 8:22–25)

[35a]On the same day, when evening had come, He said to them, "Let us cross over to the other side." [36]Now when they had left the multitude, they took Him along in the boat as He was. And other little boats were also with Him. [37]And a great windstorm arose, and the waves beat into the boat, so that it was already filling. [38]But He was in the stern, asleep on a pillow. And they awoke Him and said to Him, [a]"Teacher, [b]do You not care that we are perishing?"

[39]Then He arose and [a]rebuked the wind, and said to the sea, [b]"Peace,[1] be still!" And the wind ceased and there was a great calm. [40]But He said to them, "Why are you so fearful? [a]How[1] *is it* that you have no faith?" [41]And they feared exceedingly, and said to one another, "Who can this be, that even the wind and the sea obey Him!"

A DEMON-POSSESSED MAN HEALED
(Matt. 8:28—9:1; Luke 8:26–39)

5 Then [a]they came to the other side of the sea, to the country of the [1]Gadarenes. [2]And when He had come out of the boat, immediately there met Him out of the tombs a man with an [a]unclean spirit, [3]who had *his* dwelling among the tombs; and no one could bind [1]him, not even with chains, [4]because he had often been bound with shackles and chains. And the chains had been pulled apart by him, and the shackles broken in pieces; neither could anyone tame him. [5]And always, night and day, he was in the mountains and in the tombs, crying out and cutting himself with stones.

[6]When he saw Jesus from afar, he ran and worshiped Him. [7]And he cried out with a loud voice and said, "What have I to do with You, Jesus, Son of the Most High God? I [a]implore[1] You by God that You do not torment me."

[8]For He said to him, [a]"Come out of the man, unclean spirit!" [9]Then He asked him, "What *is* your name?"

And he answered, saying, "My name *is* Legion; for we are many." [10]Also he begged Him earnestly that He would not send them out of the country.

[11]Now a large herd of [a]swine was feeding there near the mountains. [12]So all the demons begged Him, saying, "Send us to the swine, that we may enter them." [13]And [1]at once Jesus gave them permission. Then the unclean spirits went out and entered the swine (there were about two thousand); and the herd ran violently down the steep place into the sea, and drowned in the sea.

[14]So those who fed the swine fled, and they told *it* in the city and in the country. And they went out to see what it was that had happened. [15]Then they came to Jesus, and saw the

4:33
[a]Matt. 13:34, 35;
[John 16:12]

4:34
[a]Luke 24:27, 45

4:35
[a]Matt. 8:18,
23–27;
Luke 8:22, 25

4:38
[a][Matt. 23:8–10]
[b]Ps. 44:23

4:39
[a]Mark 9:25;
Luke 4:39
[b]Ps. 65:7; 89:9;
93:4; 104:6, 7;
Matt. 8:26;
Luke 8:24

4:40
[a]Matt. 14:31, 32;
Luke 8:25

5:1
[a]Matt. 8:28–34;
Luke 8:26–37

5:2
[a]Mark 1:23; 7:25;
[Rev. 16:13, 14]

5:7
[a]Matt. 26:63;
Mark 1:24;
Acts 19:13

5:8 [a]Mark 1:25;
9:25;
[Acts 16:18]

5:11
[a]Lev. 11:7, 8;
Deut. 14:8;
Luke 15:15, 16

4:39 [1]Lit. *Be quiet* 4:40 [1]NU *Have you still no faith?* 5:1 [1]NU *Gerasenes*
5:3 [1]NU adds *anymore* 5:7 [1]*adjure* 5:13 [1]NU *He gave*

one *who had been* [a]demon-possessed and had the legion, [b]sitting and [c]clothed and in his right mind. And they were afraid. [16]And those who saw it told them how it happened to him *who had been* demon-possessed, and about the swine. [17]Then [a]they began to plead with Him to depart from their region.

[18]And when He got into the boat, [a]he who had been demon-possessed begged Him that he might be with Him. [19]However, Jesus did not permit him, but said to him, "Go home to your friends, and tell them what great things the Lord has done for you, and how He has had compassion on you." [20]And he departed and began to [a]proclaim in [1]Decapolis all that Jesus had done for him; and all [b]marveled.

A GIRL RESTORED TO LIFE AND A WOMAN HEALED
(Matt. 9:18–26; Luke 8:40–56)

[21][a]Now when Jesus had crossed over again by boat to the other side, a great multitude gathered to Him; and He was by the sea. [22][a]And behold, one of the rulers of the synagogue came, Jairus by name. And when he saw Him, he fell at His feet [23]and begged Him earnestly, saying, "My little daughter lies at the point of death. Come and [a]lay Your hands on her, that she may be healed, and she will live." [24]So *Jesus* went with him, and a great multitude followed Him and thronged Him.

[25]Now a certain woman [a]had a flow of blood for twelve years, [26]and had suffered many things from many physicians. She had spent all that she had and was no better, but rather grew worse. [27]When she heard about Jesus, she came behind *Him* in the crowd and [a]touched His garment. [28]For she said, "If only I may touch His clothes, I shall be made well."

[29]Immediately the fountain of her blood was dried up, and she felt in *her* body that she was healed of the [1]affliction. [30]And Jesus, immediately knowing in Himself that [a]power had gone out of Him, turned around in the crowd and said, "Who touched My clothes?"

[31]But His disciples said to Him, "You see the multitude thronging You, and You say, 'Who touched Me?'"

[32]And He looked around to see her who had done this thing. [33]But the woman, [a]fearing and trembling, knowing what had happened to her, came and fell down before Him and told Him the whole truth. [34]And He said to her, "Daughter, [a]your faith has made you well. [b]Go in peace, and be healed of your affliction."

[35][a]While He was still speaking, *some* came from the ruler of the synagogue's *house* who said, "Your daughter is dead. Why trouble the Teacher any further?"

[36]As soon as Jesus heard the word that was spoken, He said to the ruler of the synagogue, "Do not be afraid; only [a]believe." [37]And He permitted no one to follow Him except Peter, James, and John the brother of James. [38]Then He came to the house of the ruler of the synagogue, and saw [1]a tumult and those who [a]wept and wailed loudly. [39]When He came in, He said to them, "Why make this commotion and weep? The child is not dead, but [a]sleeping."

[40]And they ridiculed Him. [a]But when He had put them all outside, He took the father and the mother of the child,

5:15 [a]Matt. 4:24; 8:16; Mark 1:32 [b]Luke 10:39 [c][Is. 61:10]
5:17 [a]Matt. 8:34; Acts 16:39
5:18 [a]Luke 8:38, 39
5:20 [a]Ex. 15:2; Ps. 66:16 [b]Matt. 9:8, 33; John 5:20; 7:21; Acts 3:12; 4:13
5:21 [a]Matt. 9:1; Luke 8:40
5:22 [a]Matt. 9:18–26; Luke 8:41–56; Acts 13:15
5:23 [a]Matt. 8:15; Mark 6:5; 7:32; 8:23, 25; 16:18; Luke 4:40; Acts 9:17; 28:8
5:25 [a]Lev. 15:19, 25; Matt. 9:20
5:27 [a]Matt. 14:35, 36; Mark 3:10; 6:56
5:30 [a]Luke 6:19; 8:46
5:33 [a][Ps. 89:7]
5:34 [a]Matt. 9:22; Mark 10:52; Acts 14:9 [b]1 Sam. 1:17; 20:42; 2 Kin. 5:19; Luke 7:50; 8:48; Acts 16:36; [James 2:16]
5:35 [a]Luke 8:49
5:36 [a][Mark 9:23; John 11:40]
5:38 [a]Mark 16:10; Acts 9:39
5:39 [a]John 11:4, 11
5:40 [a]Acts 9:40

5:20 [1]Lit. *Ten Cities*   **5:29** [1]*suffering*   **5:38** [1]*an uproar*

and those *who were* with Him, and entered where the child was lying. [41]Then He took the child by the hand, and said to her, "Talitha, cumi," which is translated, "Little girl, I say to you, arise." [42]Immediately the girl arose and walked, for she was twelve years *of age*. And they were [a]overcome with great amazement. [43]But [a]He commanded them strictly that no one should know it, and said that *something* should be given her to eat.

JESUS REJECTED AT NAZARETH
(Matt. 13:53–58; Luke 4:16–30)

6 Then [a]He went out from there and came to His own country, and His disciples followed Him. [2]And when the Sabbath had come, He began to teach in the synagogue. And many hearing *Him* were [a]astonished, saying, [b]"Where *did* this Man *get* these things? And what wisdom *is* this which is given to Him, that such mighty works are performed by His hands! [3]Is this not the carpenter, the Son of Mary, and [a]brother of James, Joses, Judas, and Simon? And are not His sisters here with us?" So they [b]were offended at Him.

[4]But Jesus said to them, [a]"A prophet is not without honor except in his own country, among his own relatives, and in his own house." [5a]Now He could do no mighty work there, except that He laid His hands on a few sick people and healed *them*. [6]And [a]He marveled because of their unbelief. [b]Then He went about the villages in a circuit, teaching.

SENDING OUT THE TWELVE
(Matt. 10:1, 5–15; Luke 9:1–6)

[7a]And He called the twelve to *Himself*, and began to send them out [b]two *by* two, and gave them power over unclean spirits. [8]He commanded them to take nothing for the journey except a staff—no bag, no bread, no copper in *their* money belts— [9]but [a]to wear sandals, and not to put on two tunics. [10a]Also He said to them, "In whatever place you enter a house, stay there till you depart from that place. [11a]And [1]whoever will not receive you nor hear you, when you depart from there, [b]shake off the dust under your feet as a testimony against them. [2]Assuredly, I say to you, it will be more tolerable for Sodom and Gomorrah in the day of judgment than for that city!"

[12]So they went out and preached that *people* should repent. [13]And they cast out many demons, [a]and anointed with oil many who were sick, and healed *them*.

JOHN THE BAPTIST BEHEADED
(Matt. 14:1–12; Luke 9:7–9)

[14a]Now King Herod heard *of Him*, for His name had become well known. And he said, "John the Baptist is risen from the dead, and therefore [b]these powers are at work in him." [15a]Others said, "It is Elijah."

And others said, "It is [1]the Prophet, [b]or like one of the prophets."

[16a]But when Herod heard, he said, "This is John, whom

5:42
[a]Mark 1:27; 7:37

5:43
[a][Matt. 8:4; 12:16–19; 17:9]; Mark 3:12

6:1 [a]Matt. 13:54; Luke 4:16

6:2 [a]Matt. 7:28; Luke 4:32; Acts 4:13 [b]John 6:42

6:3 [a]Matt. 12:46; Gal. 1:19 [b][Matt. 11:6]

6:4 [a]Matt. 13:57; Luke 4:24; John 4:44

6:5 [a]Gen. 19:22; 32:25; Matt. 13:58; [Mark 9:23]

6:6 [a]Is. 59:16; Matt. 17:17, 20; [Heb. 3:18, 19; 4:2] [b]Matt. 9:35; Luke 13:22; Acts 10:38; Eph. 2:17

6:7 [a]Matt. 10:1; 28:19, 20; Mark 3:13, 14; Luke 9:1 [b][Eccl. 4:9, 10]

6:9 [a][Eph. 6:15]

6:10 [a]Matt. 10:11; Luke 9:4; 10:7, 8

6:11 [a]Matt. 10:14; Luke 10:10 [b]Acts 13:51; 18:6

6:13 [a][James 5:14]

6:14 [a]Matt. 14:1–12; Mark 6:14–16; Luke 9:7–9 [b]Luke 19:37

6:15 [a]Matt. 16:14; Mark 8:28; Luke 9:19 [b]Matt. 21:11

6:16 [a]Matt. 14:2; Luke 3:19

6:11 [1]NU *whatever place* [2]NU omits the rest of v. 11. 6:15 [1]NU, M *a prophet, like one*

I beheaded; he has been raised from the dead!" 17For Herod himself had sent and laid hold of John, and bound him in prison for the sake of Herodias, his brother Philip's wife; for he had married her. 18Because John had said to Herod, a"It is not lawful for you to have your brother's wife."

19Therefore Herodias 1held it against him and wanted to kill him, but she could not; 20for Herod afeared John, knowing that he *was* a just and holy man, and he protected him. And when he heard him, he 1did many things, and heard him gladly.

21aThen an opportune day came when Herod bon his birthday gave a feast for his nobles, the high officers, and the chief *men* of Galilee. 22And when Herodias' daughter herself came in and danced, and pleased Herod and those who sat with him, the king said to the girl, "Ask me whatever you want, and I will give *it* to you." 23He also swore to her, a"Whatever you ask me, I will give you, up to half my kingdom."

24So she went out and said to her mother, "What shall I ask?"

And she said, "The head of John the Baptist!"

25Immediately she came in with haste to the king and asked, saying, "I want you to give me at once the head of John the Baptist on a platter."

26aAnd the king was exceedingly sorry; *yet,* because of the oaths and because of those who sat with him, he did not want to refuse her. 27Immediately the king sent an executioner and commanded his head to be brought. And he went and beheaded him in prison, 28brought his head on a platter, and gave it to the girl; and the girl gave it to her mother. 29When his disciples heard *of it,* they came and atook away his corpse and laid it in a tomb.

FEEDING THE FIVE THOUSAND
(Matt. 14:13–21; Luke 9:10–17; John 6:1–14)

30aThen the apostles gathered to Jesus and told Him all things, both what they had done and what they had taught. 31aAnd He said to them, "Come aside by yourselves to a deserted place and rest a while." For bthere were many coming and going, and they did not even have time to eat. 32aSo they departed to a deserted place in the boat by themselves.

33But 1the multitudes saw them departing, and many aknew Him and ran there on foot from all the cities. They arrived before them and came together to Him. 34aAnd Jesus, when He came out, saw a great multitude and was moved with compassion for them, because they were like bsheep not having a shepherd. So cHe began to teach them many things. 35aWhen the day was now far spent, His disciples came to Him and said, "This is a deserted place, and already the hour *is* late. 36Send them away, that they may go into the surrounding country and villages and buy themselves 1bread; for they have nothing to eat."

37But He answered and said to them, "You give them something to eat."

And they said to Him, a"Shall we go and buy two hundred denarii worth of bread and give them *something* to eat?"

Cross-references (left margin):

6:18 aLev. 18:16; 20:21

6:20 aMatt. 14:5; 21:26

6:21 aMatt. 14:6 bGen. 40:20

6:23 aEsth. 5:3, 6, 7:2

6:26 aMatt. 14:9

6:29 a1 Kin. 13:29, 30; Matt. 27:58–61; Acts 8:2

6:30 aLuke 9:10

6:31 aMatt. 14:13 bMark 3:20

6:32 aMatt. 14:13–21; Luke 9:10–17; John 6:5–13

6:33 a[Col. 1:6]

6:34 aMatt. 9:36; 14:14; [Heb. 5:2] bNum. 27:17; 1 Kin. 22:17; 2 Chr. 18:16; Zech. 10:2 c[Is. 48:17; 61:1–3]; Luke 9:11

6:35 aMatt. 14:15; Luke 9:12

6:37 aNum. 11:13, 22; 2 Kin. 4:43

³⁸But He said to them, "How many loaves do you have? Go and see."

And when they found out they said, ᵃ"Five, and two fish."

³⁹Then He ᵃcommanded them to make them all sit down in groups on the green grass. ⁴⁰So they sat down in ranks, in hundreds and in fifties. ⁴¹And when He had taken the five loaves and the two fish, He ᵃlooked up to heaven, ᵇblessed and broke the loaves, and gave *them* to His disciples to set before them; and the two fish He divided among *them* all. ⁴²So they all ate and were filled. ⁴³And they took up twelve baskets full of fragments and of the fish. ⁴⁴Now those who had eaten the loaves were ¹about five thousand men.

JESUS WALKS ON THE SEA
(Matt. 14:22–33; John 6:15–21)

⁴⁵ᵃImmediately He ¹made His disciples get into the boat and go before Him to the other side, to Bethsaida, while He sent the multitude away. ⁴⁶And when He had sent them away, He ᵃdeparted to the mountain to pray. ⁴⁷Now when evening came, the boat was in the middle of the sea; and He *was* alone on the land. ⁴⁸Then He saw them straining at rowing, for the wind was against them. Now about the fourth watch of the night He came to them, walking on the sea, and ᵃwould have passed them by. ⁴⁹And when they saw Him walking on the sea, they supposed it was a ᵃghost, and cried out; ⁵⁰for they all saw Him and were troubled. But immediately He talked with them and said to them, ᵃ"Be¹ of good cheer! It is I; do not be ᵇafraid." ⁵¹Then He went up into the boat to them, and the wind ᵃceased. And they were greatly ᵇamazed in themselves beyond measure, and marveled. ⁵²For ᵃthey had not understood about the loaves, because their ᵇheart was hardened.

MANY TOUCH HIM AND ARE MADE WELL
(Matt. 14:34–36)

⁵³ᵃWhen they had crossed over, they came to the land of Gennesaret and anchored there. ⁵⁴And when they came out of the boat, immediately ¹the people recognized Him, ⁵⁵ran through that whole surrounding region, and began to carry about on beds those who were sick to wherever they heard He was. ⁵⁶Wherever He entered, into villages, cities, or the country, they laid the sick in the marketplaces, and begged Him that ᵃthey might just touch the ᵇhem of His garment. And as many as touched Him were made well.

DEFILEMENT COMES FROM WITHIN
(Matt. 15:1–20)

7 Then ᵃthe Pharisees and some of the scribes came together to Him, having come from Jerusalem. ²Now ¹when they saw some of His disciples eat bread with defiled, that is, with ᵃunwashed hands, ²they found fault. ³For the Pharisees and all the Jews do not eat unless they wash *their* hands ¹in a special way, holding the ᵃtradition of the elders. ⁴*When they come* from the marketplace, they do not eat unless they wash.

6:38
ᵃMatt. 14:17;
Luke 9:13;
John 6:9

6:39
ᵃMatt. 15:35;
Mark 8:6

6:41
ᵃJohn 11:41, 42
ᵇ1 Sam. 9:13;
Matt. 15:36;
26:26; Mark 8:7;
Luke 24:30

6:45
ᵃMatt. 14:22–32;
John 6:15–21

6:46 ᵃMark 1:35;
Luke 5:16

6:48
ᵃLuke 24:28

6:49
ᵃMatt. 14:26;
Luke 24:37

6:50 ᵃMatt. 9:2;
John 16:33
ᵇIs. 41:10

6:51 ᵃPs. 107:29
ᵇMark 1:27; 2:12;
5:42; 7:37

6:52
ᵃMatt. 16:9–11;
Mark 8:17, 18
ᵇIs. 63:17;
Mark 3:5; 16:14

6:53
ᵃMatt. 14:34–36;
John 6:24, 25

6:56
ᵃMatt. 9:20;
Mark 5:27, 28;
[Acts 19:12]
ᵇNum. 15:38, 39

7:1
ᵃMatt. 15:1–20

7:2 ᵃMatt. 15:20

7:3 ᵃMark 7:5,
8, 9, 13; Gal. 1:14;
1 Pet. 1:18

6:44 ¹NU, M omit *about*   6:45 ¹*invited, strongly urged*   6:50 ¹*Take courage*   6:54 ¹Lit. *they*   7:2 ¹NU omits *when*   ²NU omits *they found fault*   7:3 ¹Lit. *with the fist*

And there are many other things which they have received and hold, *like* the washing of cups, pitchers, copper vessels, and couches.

5aThen the Pharisees and scribes asked Him, "Why do Your disciples not walk according to the tradition of the elders, but eat bread with unwashed hands?"

6He answered and said to them, "Well did Isaiah prophesy of you ahypocrites, as it is written:

b"This people honors Me with *their* lips,
> But their heart is far from Me.
7 And in vain they worship Me,
> Teaching *as* doctrines the commandments of men.'

8For laying aside the commandment of God, you hold the tradition of men—1the washing of pitchers and cups, and many other such things you do."

9He said to them, "*All too* well ayou 1reject the commandment of God, that you may keep your tradition. 10For Moses said, a'Honor your father and your mother'; and, b'He who curses father or mother, let him be put to death.' 11But you say, 'If a man says to his father or mother, a"Whatever profit you might have received from me *is* Corban"—' (that is, a gift *to God*), 12then you no longer let him do anything for his father or his mother, 13making the word of God of no effect through your tradition which you have handed down. And many such things you do."

14aWhen He had called all the multitude to *Himself,* He said to them, "Hear Me, everyone, and bunderstand: 15There is nothing that enters a man from outside which can defile him; but the things which come out of him, those are the things that adefile a man. 16aIf1 anyone has ears to hear, let him hear!"

17aWhen He had entered a house away from the crowd, His disciples asked Him concerning the parable. 18So He said to them, a"Are you thus without understanding also? Do you not perceive that whatever enters a man from outside cannot defile him, 19because it does not enter his heart but his stomach, and is eliminated, 1*thus* purifying all foods?" 20And He said, a"What comes out of a man, that defiles a man. 21aFor from within, out of the heart of men, bproceed evil thoughts, cadulteries, dfornications, murders, 22thefts, acovetousness, wickedness, bdeceit, clewdness, an evil eye, dblasphemy, epride, foolishness. 23All these evil things come from within and defile a man."

A GENTILE SHOWS HER FAITH
(Matt. 15:21–28)

24aFrom there He arose and went to the region of Tyre 1and Sidon. And He entered a house and wanted no one to know *it,* but He could not be bhidden. 25For a woman whose young daughter had an unclean spirit heard about Him, and she came and afell at His feet. 26The woman was a 1Greek, a 2Syro-Phoenician by birth, and she kept 3asking Him to cast

7:5 aMatt. 15:2

7:6 aMatt. 23:13–29 bIs. 29:13

7:9 aProv. 1:25; Is. 24:5; Jer. 7:23, 24

7:10 aEx. 20:12; Deut. 5:16; Matt. 15:4 bEx. 21:17; Lev. 20:9; Prov. 20:20

7:11 aMatt. 15:5; 23:18

7:14 aMatt. 15:10 bMatt. 16:9, 11, 12

7:15 aIs. 59:3; [Heb. 12:15]

7:16 aMatt. 11:15

7:17 aMatt. 15:15

7:18 a[Is. 28:9–11; 1 Cor. 3:2; Heb. 5:11–14]

7:20 aPs. 39:1; [Matt. 12:34–37; James 3:6]

7:21 aGen. 6:5; 8:21; Prov. 6:18; Jer. 17:9; Matt. 15:19 b[Gal. 5:19–21] c2 Pet. 2:14 d1 Thess. 4:3

7:22 aLuke 12:15 bRom. 1:28, 29 c1 Pet. 4:3 dRev. 2:9 e1 John 2:16

7:24 aMatt. 15:21 bMark 2:1, 2

7:25 aMark 5:22; John 11:32; Rev. 1:17

7:8 1NU omits the rest of v. 8.   7:9 1*set aside*   7:16 1NU omits v. 16.
7:19 1NU sets off the final phrase as Mark's comment that Jesus has declared all foods clean.   7:24 1NU omits *and Sidon*   7:26 1*Gentile*
2A Syrian of Phoenicia   3*begging*

the demon out of her daughter. [27]But Jesus said to her, "Let the children be filled first, for it is not good to take the children's bread and throw *it* to the little dogs."

[28]And she answered and said to Him, "Yes, Lord, yet even the little dogs under the table eat from the children's crumbs."

[29]Then He said to her, "For this saying go your way; the demon has gone out of your daughter."

[30]And when she had come to her house, she found the demon gone out, and her daughter lying on the bed.

JESUS HEALS A DEAF-MUTE
(Matt. 15:29–31)

[31a]Again, departing from the region of Tyre and Sidon, He came through the midst of the region of Decapolis to the Sea of Galilee. [32]Then [a]they brought to Him one who was deaf and had an impediment in his speech, and they begged Him to put His hand on him. [33]And He took him aside from the multitude, and put His fingers in his ears, and [a]He spat and touched his tongue. [34]Then, [a]looking up to heaven, [b]He sighed, and said to him, "Ephphatha," that is, "Be opened."

[35a]Immediately his ears were opened, and the [1]impediment of his tongue was loosed, and he spoke plainly. [36]Then [a]He commanded them that they should tell no one; but the more He commanded them, the more widely they proclaimed *it*. [37]And they were [a]astonished beyond measure, saying, "He has done all things well. He [b]makes both the deaf to hear and the mute to speak."

FEEDING THE FOUR THOUSAND
(Matt. 15:32–39)

8 In those days, [a]the multitude being very great and having nothing to eat, Jesus called His disciples *to Him* and said to them, [2]"I have [a]compassion on the multitude, because they have now continued with Me three days and have nothing to eat. [3]And if I send them away hungry to their own houses, they will faint on the way; for some of them have come from afar."

[4]Then His disciples answered Him, "How can one satisfy these people with bread here in the wilderness?"

[5a]He asked them, "How many loaves do you have?"

And they said, "Seven."

[6]So He commanded the multitude to sit down on the ground. And He took the seven loaves and gave thanks, broke *them* and gave *them* to His disciples to set before *them;* and they set *them* before the multitude. [7]They also had a few small fish; and [a]having blessed them, He said to set them also before *them.* [8]So they ate and were filled, and they took up seven large baskets of leftover fragments. [9]Now those who had eaten were about four thousand. And He sent them away, [10a]immediately got into the boat with His disciples, and came to the region of Dalmanutha.

THE PHARISEES SEEK A SIGN
(Matt. 16:1–4)

[11a]Then the Pharisees came out and began to dispute with Him, seeking from Him a sign from heaven, testing Him.

7:31
[a]Matt. 15:29;
Mark 15:37;
Luke 23:46;
24:46;
Acts 10:40;
1 Cor. 15:4

7:32
[a]Matt. 9:32;
Luke 11:14

7:33
[a]Mark 8:23;
John 9:6

7:34 [a]Mark 6:41;
John 11:41; 17:1
[b]John 11:33, 38

7:35 [a]Is. 35:5, 6

7:36 [a]Mark 5:43

7:37 [a]Mark 6:51;
10:26
[b]Matt. 12:22

8:1
[a]Matt. 15:32–39;
Mark 6:34–44;
Luke 9:12

8:2 [a]Matt. 9:36;
14:14; Mark 1:41;
6:34

8:5 [a]Matt. 15:34;
Mark 6:38;
John 6:9

8:7 [a]Matt. 14:19;
Mark 6:41

8:10
[a]Matt. 15:39

8:11
[a]Matt. 12:38;
16:1; Luke 11:16;
John 2:18; 6:30;
1 Cor. 1:22

7:35 [1]Lit. *bond*

12But He [a]sighed deeply in His spirit, and said, "Why does this generation seek a sign? Assuredly, I say to you, [b]no sign shall be given to this generation."

BEWARE OF THE LEAVEN OF THE PHARISEES AND HEROD
(Matt. 16:5–12)

13And He left them, and getting into the boat again, departed to the other side. 14[a]Now [1]the disciples had forgotten to take bread, and they did not have more than one loaf with them in the boat. 15[a]Then He charged them, saying, "Take heed, beware of the [1]leaven of the Pharisees and the leaven of Herod."

16And they reasoned among themselves, saying, "*It is* because we have no bread."

17But Jesus, being aware of *it,* said to them, "Why do you reason because you have no bread? [a]Do you not yet perceive nor understand? Is your heart [1]still hardened? 18Having eyes, do you not see? And having ears, do you not hear? And do you not remember? 19[a]When I broke the five loaves for the five thousand, how many baskets full of fragments did you take up?"

They said to Him, "Twelve."

20"Also, [a]when I broke the seven for the four thousand, how many large baskets full of fragments did you take up?"

And they said, "Seven."

21So He said to them, "How *is it* [a]you do not understand?"

A BLIND MAN HEALED AT BETHSAIDA

22Then He came to Bethsaida; and they brought a [a]blind man to Him, and begged Him to [b]touch him. 23So He took the blind man by the hand and led him out of the town. And when [a]He had spit on his eyes and put His hands on him, He asked him if he saw anything.

24And he looked up and said, "I see men like trees, walking."

25Then He put *His* hands on his eyes again and made him look up. And he was restored and saw everyone clearly. 26Then He sent him away to his house, saying, [1]"Neither go into the town, [a]nor tell anyone in the town."

PETER CONFESSES JESUS AS THE CHRIST
(Matt. 16:13–20; Luke 9:18–20)

27[a]Now Jesus and His disciples went out to the towns of Caesarea Philippi; and on the road He asked His disciples, saying to them, "Who do men say that I am?"

28So they answered, [a]"John the Baptist; but some *say,* [b]Elijah; and others, one of the prophets."

29He said to them, "But who do you say that I am?"

Peter answered and said to Him, [a]"You are the Christ."

30[a]Then He strictly warned them that they should tell no one about Him.

JESUS PREDICTS HIS DEATH AND RESURRECTION
(Matt. 16:21–23; Luke 9:21, 22)

31And [a]He began to teach them that the Son of Man must

8:12 [a]Mark 7:34
[b]Matt. 12:39
8:14 [a]Matt. 16:5
8:15 [a]Matt. 16:6;
Luke 12:1
8:17 [a]Mark 6:52;
16:14
8:19
[a]Matt. 14:20;
Mark 6:43;
Luke 9:17;
John 6:13
8:20
[a]Matt. 15:37
8:21
[a][Mark 6:52]
8:22
[a]Matt. 9:27;
John 9:1
[b]Luke 18:15
8:23 [a]Mark 7:33
8:26 [a]Matt. 8:4;
Mark 5:43; 7:36
8:27
[a]Matt. 16:13–16;
Luke 9:18–20
8:28 [a]Matt. 14:2
[b]Mark 6:14, 15;
Luke 9:7, 8
8:29
[a]John 1:41; 4:42;
6:69; 11:27;
Acts 2:36; 8:37;
9:20
8:30
[a]Matt. 8:4;
16:20;
Luke 9:21
8:31
[a][Is. 53:3–11];
Matt. 16:21;
20:19;
Luke 18:31–33;
1 Pet. 1:11

8:14 [1]NU, M *they*   8:15 [1]*yeast*   8:17 [1]NU omits *still*   8:26 [1]NU *"Do not even go into the town."*

suffer many things, and be ᵇrejected by the elders and chief priests and scribes, and be ᶜkilled, and after three days rise again. ³²He spoke this word openly. Then Peter took Him aside and began to rebuke Him. ³³But when He had turned around and looked at His disciples, He ªrebuked Peter, saying, "Get behind Me, Satan! For you are not ¹mindful of the things of God, but the things of men."

TAKE UP THE CROSS AND FOLLOW HIM
(Matt. 16:24–27; Luke 9:23–26)

³⁴When He had called the people to *Himself,* with His disciples also, He said to them, ª"Whoever desires to come after Me, let him deny himself, and take up his cross, and follow Me. ³⁵For ªwhoever desires to save his life will lose it, but whoever loses his life for My sake and the gospel's will save it. ³⁶For what will it profit a man if he gains the whole world, and loses his own soul? ³⁷Or what will a man give in exchange for his soul? ³⁸ªFor whoever ᵇis ashamed of Me and My words in this adulterous and sinful generation, of him the Son of Man also will be ashamed when He comes in the glory of His Father with the holy angels."

9 And He said to them, ª"Assuredly, I say to you that there are some standing here who will not taste death till they see ᵇthe kingdom of God ¹present with power."

JESUS TRANSFIGURED ON THE MOUNT
(Matt. 16:28—17:13; Luke 9:27–36; 2 Pet. 1:16–18)

²ªNow after six days Jesus took Peter, James, and John, and led them up on a high mountain apart by themselves; and He was transfigured before them. ³His clothes became shining, exceedingly ªwhite, like snow, such as no launderer on earth can whiten them. ⁴And Elijah appeared to them with Moses, and they were talking with Jesus. ⁵Then Peter answered and said to Jesus, "Rabbi, it is good for us to be here; and let us make three tabernacles: one for You, one for Moses, and one for Elijah"— ⁶because he did not know what to say, for they were greatly afraid.

⁷And a ªcloud came and overshadowed them; and a voice came out of the cloud, saying, "This is ᵇMy beloved Son. ᶜHear Him!" ⁸Suddenly, when they had looked around, they saw no one anymore, but only Jesus with themselves.

⁹ªNow as they came down from the mountain, He commanded them that they should tell no one the things they had seen, till the Son of Man had risen from the dead. ¹⁰So they kept this word to themselves, questioning ªwhat the rising from the dead meant.

¹¹And they asked Him, saying, "Why do the scribes say ªthat Elijah must come first?"

¹²Then He answered and told them, "Indeed, Elijah is coming first and restores all things. And ªhow is it written concerning the Son of Man, that He must suffer many things and ᵇbe treated with contempt? ¹³But I say to you that ªElijah has also come, and they did to him whatever they wished, as it is written of him."

8:31
ᵇMark 10:33
ᶜMark 9:31; 10:34

8:33
ªMark 16:14; [Rev. 3:19]

8:34
ª[Matt. 10:38]; Luke 14:27

8:35
ªMatt. 10:39; Luke 17:33; John 12:25

8:38
ªMatt. 10:33; Luke 9:26; 12:9
ᵇRom. 1:16; 2 Tim. 1:8, 9; 2:12

9:1 ªMatt. 16:28; Mark 13:26; Luke 9:27; Acts 7:55, 56; Rev. 20:4
ᵇ[Matt. 24:30]

9:2
ªMatt. 17:1–8; Luke 9:28–36

9:3 ªDan. 7:9; Matt. 28:3

9:7 ªEx. 40:34; 1 Kin. 8:10; Acts 1:9; Rev. 1:7 ᵇPs. 2:7; [Is. 42:1]; Matt. 3:17; Mark 1:11; Luke 1:35; 3:22; 2 Pet. 1:17
ᶜActs 3:22

9:9
ªMatt. 17:9–13; Mark 16:6; Luke 24:6, 7, 46

9:10
ªJohn 2:19–22

9:11 ªMal. 4:5; Matt. 17:10

9:12 ªPs. 22:6; Is. 53:3; Dan. 9:26
ᵇLuke 23:11; Phil. 2:7

9:13 ªMal. 4:5; Matt. 11:14; 17:12; Luke 1:17

8:33 ¹setting your mind on   9:1 ¹having come

A BOY IS HEALED
(Matt. 17:14–21; Luke 9:37–42)

[14a] And when He came to the disciples, He saw a great multitude around them, and scribes disputing with them. [15] Immediately, when they saw Him, all the people were greatly amazed, and running to *Him,* greeted Him. [16] And He asked the scribes, "What are you discussing with them?"

[17] Then [a] one of the crowd answered and said, "Teacher, I brought You my son, who has a mute spirit. [18] And wherever it seizes him, it throws him down; he foams at the mouth, gnashes his teeth, and becomes rigid. So I spoke to Your disciples, that they should cast it out, but they could not."

[19] He answered him and said, "O [a] faithless[1] generation, how long shall I be with you? How long shall I [2] bear with you? Bring him to Me." [20] Then they brought him to Him. And [a] when he saw Him, immediately the spirit convulsed him, and he fell on the ground and wallowed, foaming at the mouth.

[21] So He asked his father, "How long has this been happening to him?"

And he said, "From childhood. [22] And often he has thrown him both into the fire and into the water to destroy him. But if You can do anything, have compassion on us and help us."

[23] Jesus said to him, [a] "If[1] you can believe, all things *are* possible to him who believes."

[24] Immediately the father of the child cried out and said with tears, "Lord, I believe; [a] help my unbelief!"

[25] When Jesus saw that the people came running together, He [a] rebuked the unclean spirit, saying to it, "Deaf and dumb spirit, I command you, come out of him and enter him no more!" [26] Then *the spirit* cried out, convulsed him greatly, and came out of him. And he became as one dead, so that many said, "He is dead." [27] But Jesus took him by the hand and lifted him up, and he arose.

[28a] And when He had come into the house, His disciples asked Him privately, "Why could we not cast it out?"

[29] So He said to them, "This kind can come out by nothing but [a] prayer [1] and fasting."

JESUS AGAIN PREDICTS HIS DEATH AND RESURRECTION

[30] Then they departed from there and passed through Galilee, and He did not want anyone to know *it.* [31a] For He taught His disciples and said to them, "The Son of Man is being betrayed into the hands of men, and they will [b] kill Him. And after He is killed, He will [c] rise the third day." [32] But they [a] did not understand this saying, and were afraid to ask Him.

WHO IS THE GREATEST?
(Matt. 18:1–5; Luke 9:46–48)

[33a] Then He came to Capernaum. And when He was in the house He asked them, "What was it you [1] disputed among yourselves on the road?" [34] But they kept silent, for on the road they had [a] disputed among themselves who *would be the* [b] greatest. [35] And He sat down, called the twelve, and said to them, [a] "If anyone desires to be first, he shall be last of all and

---

9:14
[a] Matt. 17:14–19;
Luke 9:37–42

9:17 [a] Matt. 17:14;
Luke 9:38

9:19 [a] John 4:48

9:20
[a] Mark 1:26;
Luke 9:42

9:23
[a] Matt. 17:20;
Mark 11:23;
Luke 17:6;
John 11:40

9:24 [a] Luke 17:5

9:25 [a] Mark 1:25

9:28
[a] Matt. 17:19

9:29
[a] [James 5:16]

9:31
[a] Matt. 17:22;
Luke 9:44
[b] Matt. 16:21;
27:50;
Luke 18:33;
23:46; Acts 2:23
[c] Matt. 20:19;
Luke 24:46;
Acts 10:40;
1 Cor. 15:4

9:32
[a] Luke 2:50;
18:34;
John 12:16

9:33
[a] Matt. 18:1–5;
Mark 14:53, 64;
Luke 9:46–48;
22:24;
John 18:12; 19:7

9:34
[a] [Prov. 13:10];
Mark 15:20, 31
[b] Matt. 18:4;
[Mark 9:50];
14:65; 15:15, 37;
Luke 22:24;
23:46; 24:46

9:35
[a] Matt. 20:26,
27; 23:11;
Mark 10:43, 44;
Luke 22:26, 27

9:19 [1] *unbelieving*   [2] *put up with*   **9:23** [1] NU *"'If You can!' All things*
9:29 [1] NU omits *and fasting*   **9:33** [1] *discussed*

servant of all." 36Then ªHe took a little child and set him in the midst of them. And when He had taken him in His arms, He said to them, 37"Whoever receives one of these little children in My name receives Me; and ªwhoever receives Me, receives not Me but Him who sent Me."

JESUS FORBIDS SECTARIANISM
(Matt. 10:40–42; Luke 9:49, 50)

38ªNow John answered Him, saying, "Teacher, we saw someone who does not follow us casting out demons in Your name, and we forbade him because he does not follow us."

39But Jesus said, "Do not forbid him, ªfor no one who works a miracle in My name can soon afterward speak evil of Me. 40For ªhe who is not against ¹us is on ²our side. 41ªFor whoever gives you a cup of water to drink in My name, because you belong to Christ, assuredly, I say to you, he will by no means lose his reward.

JESUS WARNS OF OFFENSES
(Matt. 18:6–9; Luke 17:1, 2)

42ª"But whoever causes one of these little ones who believe in Me ¹to stumble, it would be better for him if a millstone were hung around his neck, and he were thrown into the sea. 43ªIf your hand causes you to sin, cut it off. It is better for you to enter into life ¹maimed, rather than having two hands, to go to ²hell, into the fire that shall never be quenched— 44¹where

ª'Their worm does not die
And the fire is not quenched.'

45And if your foot causes you to sin, cut it off. It is better for you to enter life lame, rather than having two feet, to be cast into ¹hell, ²into the fire that shall never be quenched— 46where

ª'Their worm does not die
And the fire is not quenched.'

47And if your eye causes you to sin, pluck it out. It is better for you to enter the kingdom of God with one eye, rather than having two eyes, to be cast into ¹hell fire— 48where

ª'Their worm does not die
And the ᵇfire is not quenched.'

TASTELESS SALT IS WORTHLESS

49"For everyone will be ªseasoned with fire, ᵇand¹ every sacrifice will be seasoned with salt. 50ªSalt *is* good, but if the salt loses its flavor, how will you season it? ᵇHave salt in yourselves, and ᶜhave peace with one another."

MARRIAGE AND DIVORCE
(Matt. 19:1–9)

10 Then ªHe arose from there and came to the region of Judea by the other side of the Jordan. And multitudes

9:36
ªMark 10:13–16

9:37
ªMatt. 10:40;
Luke 10:16;
John 13:20

9:38
ªNum. 11:27–29;
Luke 9:49

9:39 ª1 Cor. 12:3

9:40
ª[Matt. 12:30];
Luke 11:23

9:41
ªMatt. 10:42

9:42
ªMatt. 18:6;
Luke 17:1, 2;
[1 Cor. 8:12]

9:43
ª[Deut. 13:6];
Matt. 5:29, 30;
18:8, 9

9:44 ªIs. 66:24

9:46 ªIs. 66:24

9:48 ªIs. 66:24
ᵇJer. 7:20;
[Rev. 21:8]

9:49
ª[Matt. 3:11]
ᵇLev. 2:13;
Ezek. 43:24

9:50
ªMatt. 5:13;
Luke 14:34
ᵇ[Eph. 4:29];
Col. 4:6
ᶜRom. 12:18;
14:19; 2 Cor. 13:11;
1 Thess. 5:13;
Heb. 12:14

10:1
ªMatt. 19:1–9;
John 10:40; 11:7

9:40 ¹M *you*   ²M *your*   9:42 ¹To fall into sin   9:43 ¹*crippled*
²Gr. *Gehenna*   9:44 ¹NU omits v. 44.   9:45 ¹Gr. *Gehenna*   ²NU omits the rest of v. 45 and all of v. 46.   9:47 ¹Gr. *Gehenna*   9:49 ¹NU omits the rest of v. 49.

gathered to Him again, and as He was accustomed, He taught them again.

2ªThe Pharisees came and asked Him, "Is it lawful for a man to divorce *his* wife?" testing Him.

3And He answered and said to them, "What did Moses command you?"

4They said, ª"Moses permitted *a man* to write a certificate of divorce, and to dismiss *her.*"

5And Jesus answered and said to them, "Because of the hardness of your heart he wrote you this 1precept. 6But from the beginning of the creation, God ª'made them male and female.' 7ª'For this reason a man shall leave his father and mother and be joined to his wife, 8and the two shall become one flesh'; so then they are no longer two, but one flesh. 9Therefore what God has joined together, let not man separate."

10In the house His disciples also asked Him again about the same *matter.* 11So He said to them, ª"Whoever divorces his wife and marries another commits adultery against her. 12And if a woman divorces her husband and marries another, she commits adultery."

JESUS BLESSES LITTLE CHILDREN
(Matt. 19:13–15; Luke 18:15–17)

13ªThen they brought little children to Him, that He might touch them; but the disciples rebuked those who brought *them.* 14But when Jesus saw *it,* He was greatly displeased and said to them, "Let the little children come to Me, and do not forbid them; for ªof such is the kingdom of God. 15Assuredly, I say to you, ªwhoever does not receive the kingdom of God as a little child will bby no means enter it." 16And He took them up in His arms, laid *His* hands on them, and blessed them.

JESUS COUNSELS THE RICH YOUNG RULER
(Matt. 19:16–22; Luke 18:18–23)

17ªNow as He was going out on the road, one came running, knelt before Him, and asked Him, "Good Teacher, what shall I bdo that I may inherit eternal life?"

18So Jesus said to him, "Why do you call Me good? No one *is* good but One, *that is,* ªGod. 19You know the commandments: ª'Do not commit adultery,' 'Do not murder,' 'Do not steal,' 'Do not bear false witness,' 'Do not defraud,' 'Honor your father and your mother.'"

20And he answered and said to Him, "Teacher, all these things I have ªkept from my youth."

21Then Jesus, looking at him, loved him, and said to him, "One thing you lack: Go your way, ªsell whatever you have and give to the poor, and you will have btreasure in heaven; and come, ctake up the cross, and follow Me."

22But he was sad at this word, and went away sorrowful, for he had great possessions.

WITH GOD ALL THINGS ARE POSSIBLE
(Matt. 19:23–30; Luke 18:24–30)

23ªThen Jesus looked around and said to His disciples, "How hard it is for those who have riches to enter the

10:2 ªMatt. 19:3
10:4 ªDeut. 24:1–4; Matt. 5:31; 19:7
10:6 ªGen. 1:27; 5:2
10:7 ªGen. 2:24; [1 Cor. 6:16]; Eph. 5:31
10:11 ªEx. 20:14; [Matt. 5:32; 19:9]; Luke 16:18; [Rom. 7:3]; 1 Cor. 7:10, 11
10:13 ªMatt. 19:13–15; Luke 18:15–17
10:14 ª[1 Cor. 14:20; 1 Pet. 2:2]
10:15 ªMatt. 18:3, 4; 19:14; Luke 18:17 bLuke 13:28
10:17 ªMatt. 19:16–30; Luke 18:18–30 bJohn 6:28; Acts 2:37
10:18 ª1 Sam. 2:2
10:19 ªEx. 20:12–16; Deut. 5:16–20; [Rom. 13:9; James 2:10, 11]
10:20 ªPhil. 3:6
10:21 ª[Luke 12:33; 16:9] bMatt. 6:19, 20; 19:21 c[Mark 8:34]
10:23 ªMatt. 19:23; [Mark 4:19]; Luke 18:24

10:5 1command

kingdom of God!" 24And the disciples were astonished at His words. But Jesus answered again and said to them, "Children, how hard it is ¹for those ªwho trust in riches to enter the kingdom of God! 25It is easier for a camel to go through the eye of a needle than for a ªrich man to enter the kingdom of God."

26And they were greatly astonished, saying among themselves, "Who then can be saved?"

27But Jesus looked at them and said, "With men *it is* impossible, but not ªwith God; for with God all things are possible."

28ªThen Peter began to say to Him, "See, we have left all and followed You."

29So Jesus answered and said, "Assuredly, I say to you, there is no one who has left house or brothers or sisters or father or mother ¹or wife or children or ²lands, for My sake and the gospel's, 30ªwho shall not receive a hundredfold now in this time—houses and brothers and sisters and mothers and children and lands, with ᵇpersecutions—and in the age to come, eternal life. 31ªBut many *who are* first will be last, and the last first."

JESUS A THIRD TIME PREDICTS HIS DEATH AND RESURRECTION
(Matt. 20:17–19; Luke 18:31–34)

32ªNow they were on the road, going up to Jerusalem, and Jesus was going before them; and they were amazed. And as they followed they were afraid. ᵇThen He took the twelve aside again and began to tell them the things that would happen to Him: 33"Behold, we are going up to Jerusalem, and the Son of Man will be betrayed to the chief priests and to the scribes; and they will condemn Him to death and deliver Him to the Gentiles; 34and they will mock Him, and ¹scourge Him, and spit on Him, and kill Him. And the third day He will rise again."

GREATNESS IS SERVING
(Matt. 20:20–28)

35ªThen James and John, the sons of Zebedee, came to Him, saying, "Teacher, we want You to do for us whatever we ask."

36And He said to them, "What do you want Me to do for you?"

37They said to Him, "Grant us that we may sit, one on Your right hand and the other on Your left, in Your glory."

38But Jesus said to them, "You do not know what you ask. Are you able to drink the ªcup that I drink, and be baptized with the ᵇbaptism that I am baptized with?"

39They said to Him, "We are able."

So Jesus said to them, ª"You will indeed drink the cup that I drink, and with the baptism I am baptized with you will be baptized; 40but to sit on My right hand and on My left is not Mine to give, but *it is for those* ªfor whom it is prepared."

41ªAnd when the ten heard *it,* they began to be greatly displeased with James and John. 42But Jesus called them to *Himself* and said to them, ª"You know that those who are

Cross references
10:24
ªJob 31:24;
Ps. 52:7; 62:10;
[Prov. 11:28;
1 Tim. 6:17]

10:25
ª[Matt. 13:22;
19:24]

10:27 ªJob 42:2;
Jer. 32:17;
Matt. 19:26;
Luke 1:37

10:28
ªMatt. 19:27;
Luke 18:28

10:30
ª2 Chr. 25:9;
Luke 18:29, 30
ᵇ1 Thess. 3:3;
2 Tim. 3:12;
[1 Pet. 4:12, 13]

10:31
ªMatt. 19:30;
20:16;
Luke 13:30

10:32
ªMatt. 20:17–19;
Luke 18:31–33
ᵇMark 8:31; 9:31;
Luke 9:22; 18:31

10:35
ª[James 4:3]

10:38
ªMatt. 26:39, 42;
Mark 14:36;
Luke 22:42;
John 18:11
ᵇLuke 12:50

10:39
ªMatt. 10:17,
18, 21, 22; 24:9;
John 16:33;
Acts 12:2;
Rev. 1:9

10:40
ª[Matt. 25:34;
John 17:2, 6, 24;
Rom. 8:30;
Heb. 11:16]

10:41
ªMatt. 20:24

10:42
ªLuke 22:25

10:24 ¹NU omits *for those who trust in riches*   10:29 ¹NU omits *or wife*
²Lit. *fields*   10:34 ¹*flog Him* with a Roman scourge

considered rulers over the Gentiles lord it over them, and their great ones exercise authority over them. ⁴³ªYet it shall not be so among you; but whoever desires to become great among you shall be your servant. ⁴⁴And whoever of you desires to be first shall be slave of all. ⁴⁵For even ªthe Son of Man did not come to be served, but to serve, and ᵇto give His life a ransom for many."

JESUS HEALS BLIND BARTIMAEUS
(Matt. 20:29–34; Luke 18:35–43)

⁴⁶ªNow they came to Jericho. As He went out of Jericho with His disciples and a great multitude, blind Bartimaeus, the son of Timaeus, sat by the road begging. ⁴⁷And when he heard that it was Jesus of Nazareth, he began to cry out and say, "Jesus, ªSon of David, ᵇhave mercy on me!"

⁴⁸Then many warned him to be quiet; but he cried out all the more, "Son of David, have mercy on me!"

⁴⁹So Jesus stood still and commanded him to be called.

Then they called the blind man, saying to him, "Be of good cheer. Rise, He is calling you."

⁵⁰And throwing aside his garment, he rose and came to Jesus.

⁵¹So Jesus answered and said to him, "What do you want Me to do for you?"

The blind man said to Him, ¹"Rabboni, that I may receive my sight."

⁵²Then Jesus said to him, "Go your way; ªyour faith has ¹made you well." And immediately he received his sight and followed Jesus on the road.

THE TRIUMPHAL ENTRY
(Matt. 21:1–11; Luke 19:28–40; John 12:12–19)

11 Now ªwhen they drew near Jerusalem, to ¹Bethphage and Bethany, at the Mount of Olives, He sent two of His disciples; ²and He said to them, "Go into the village opposite you; and as soon as you have entered it you will find a colt tied, on which no one has sat. Loose it and bring *it*. ³And if anyone says to you, 'Why are you doing this?' say, 'The Lord has need of it,' and immediately he will send it here."

⁴So they went their way, and found ¹the colt tied by the door outside on the street, and they loosed it. ⁵But some of those who stood there said to them, "What are you doing, loosing the colt?"

⁶And they spoke to them just as Jesus had commanded. So they let them go. ⁷Then they brought the colt to Jesus and threw their clothes on it, and He sat on it. ⁸ªAnd many spread their clothes on the road, and others cut down leafy branches from the trees and spread *them* on the road. ⁹Then those who went before and those who followed cried out, saying:

"Hosanna!
ª'Blessed *is* He who comes in the name of the LORD!'
10 Blessed *is* the kingdom of our father David
    That comes ¹in the name of the Lord!
ªHosanna in the highest!"

Cross-references (margin):

10:43 ªMatt. 20:26, 28; Mark 9:35; Luke 9:48

10:45 ªLuke 22:27; John 13:14; [Phil. 2:7, 8] ᵇMatt. 20:28; [2 Cor. 5:21]; 1 Tim. 2:5, 6; Titus 2:14]

10:46 ªMatt. 20:29–34; Luke 18:35–43

10:47 ªJer. 23:5; Matt. 22:42; Rom. 1:3, 4; Rev. 22:16 ᵇMatt. 15:22; Luke 17:13

10:52 ªMatt. 9:22; Mark 5:34

11:1 ªMatt. 21:1–9; Luke 19:29; John 2:13

11:8 ªMatt. 21:8

11:9 ªPs. 118:25, 26; Matt. 21:9

11:10 ªPs. 148:1

10:51 ¹Lit. *My Great One*   10:52 ¹Lit. *saved you*   11:1 ¹M *Bethphage*
11:4 ¹NU, M *a*   11:10 ¹NU omits *in the name of the Lord*

^{11a}And Jesus went into Jerusalem and into the temple. So when He had looked around at all things, as the hour was already late, He went out to Bethany with the twelve.

THE FIG TREE WITHERED
(Matt. 21:18, 19)

^{12a}Now the next day, when they had come out from Bethany, He was hungry. ^{13a}And seeing from afar a fig tree having leaves, He went to see if perhaps He would find something on it. When He came to it, He found nothing but leaves, for it was not the season for figs. ¹⁴In response Jesus said to it, "Let no one eat fruit from you ever again."

And His disciples heard *it.*

JESUS CLEANSES THE TEMPLE
(Matt. 21:12–17; Luke 19:45–48; John 2:13–22)

^{15a}So they came to Jerusalem. Then Jesus went into the temple and began to drive out those who bought and sold in the temple, and overturned the tables of the money changers and the seats of those who sold ^bdoves. ¹⁶And He would not allow anyone to carry wares through the temple. ¹⁷Then He taught, saying to them, "Is it not written, ^a'My house shall be called a house of prayer for all nations'? But you have made it a ^b'den of thieves.'"

¹⁸And ^athe scribes and chief priests heard it and sought how they might destroy Him; for they feared Him, because ^ball the people were astonished at His teaching. ¹⁹When evening had come, He went out of the city.

THE LESSON OF THE WITHERED FIG TREE
(Matt. 21:20–22)

^{20a}Now in the morning, as they passed by, they saw the fig tree dried up from the roots. ²¹And Peter, remembering, said to Him, "Rabbi, look! The fig tree which You cursed has withered away."

²²So Jesus answered and said to them, "Have faith in God. ²³For ^aassuredly, I say to you, whoever says to this mountain, 'Be removed and be cast into the sea,' and does not doubt in his heart, but believes that those things he says will be done, he will have whatever he says. ²⁴Therefore I say to you, ^awhatever things you ask when you pray, believe that you receive *them,* and you will have *them.*

FORGIVENESS AND PRAYER
(Matt. 6:14, 15)

²⁵"And whenever you stand praying, ^aif you have anything against anyone, forgive him, that your Father in heaven may also forgive you your trespasses. ²⁶¹But ^aif you do not forgive, neither will your Father in heaven forgive your trespasses."

JESUS' AUTHORITY QUESTIONED
(Matt. 21:23–27; Luke 20:1–8)

²⁷Then they came again to Jerusalem. ^aAnd as He was walking in the temple, the chief priests, the scribes, and the

11:11 ^aMatt. 21:12

11:12
^aMatt. 21:18–22

11:13 ^aMatt. 21:19

11:15 ^aMal. 3:1;
Matt. 21:12–16;
Luke 19:45–47;
John 2:13–16
^bLev. 14:22

11:17 ^aIs. 56:7
^bJer. 7:11

11:18 ^aPs. 2:2;
Matt. 21:45, 46;
Luke 19:47
^bMatt. 7:28;
Mark 1:22; 6:2;
Luke 4:32

11:20
^aMatt. 21:19–22

11:23
^aMatt. 17:20;
21:21; Luke 17:6

11:24 ^aMatt. 7:7;
Luke 11:9;
[John 14:13;
15:7; 16:24];
James 1:5, 6]

11:25
^aMatt. 6:14;
18:23–35;
Eph. 4:32;
[Col. 3:13]

11:26
^aMatt. 6:15;
18:35

11:27
^aMatt. 21:23–27;
Luke 20:1–8

11:26 ¹NU omits v. 26.

elders came to Him. 28And they said to Him, "By what ᵃauthority are You doing these things? And who gave You this authority to do these things?"

29But Jesus answered and said to them, "I also will ask you one question; then answer Me, and I will tell you by what authority I do these things: 30The ᵃbaptism of John—was it from heaven or from men? Answer Me."

31And they reasoned among themselves, saying, "If we say, 'From heaven,' He will say, 'Why then did you not believe him?' 32But if we say, 'From men' "—they feared the people, for ᵃall counted John to have been a prophet indeed. 33So they answered and said to Jesus, "We do not know."

And Jesus answered and said to them, "Neither will I tell you by what authority I do these things."

THE PARABLE OF THE WICKED VINEDRESSERS
(Matt. 21:33–46; Luke 20:9–19)

12 Then ᵃHe began to speak to them in parables: "A man planted a vineyard and set a hedge around *it,* dug *a place for* the wine vat and built a tower. And he leased it to ¹vinedressers and went into a far country. 2Now at vintagetime he sent a servant to the vinedressers, that he might receive some of the fruit of the vineyard from the vinedressers. 3And they took *him* and beat him and sent *him* away emptyhanded. 4Again he sent them another servant, ¹and at him they threw stones, wounded *him* in the head, and sent *him* away shamefully treated. 5And again he sent another, and him they killed; and many others, ᵃbeating some and killing some. 6Therefore still having one son, his beloved, he also sent him to them last, saying, 'They will respect my son.' 7But those ¹vinedressers said among themselves, 'This is the heir. Come, let us kill him, and the inheritance will be ours.' 8So they took him and ᵃkilled *him* and cast *him* out of the vineyard.

9"Therefore what will the owner of the vineyard do? He will come and destroy the vinedressers, and give the vineyard to others. 10Have you not even read this Scripture:

ᵃ"The stone which the builders rejected
   Has become the chief cornerstone.
11 This was the LORD's doing,
   And it is marvelous in our eyes'?"

12ᵃAnd they sought to lay hands on Him, but feared the multitude, for they knew He had spoken the parable against them. So they left Him and went away.

THE PHARISEES: IS IT LAWFUL TO PAY TAXES TO CAESAR?
(Matt. 22:15–22; Luke 20:20–26)

13ᵃThen they sent to Him some of the Pharisees and the Herodians, to catch Him in *His* words. 14When they had come, they said to Him, "Teacher, we know that You are true, and ¹care about no one; for You do not ²regard the person of men, but teach the ᵃway of God in truth. Is it lawful to pay taxes to Caesar, or not? 15Shall we pay, or shall we not pay?"

Cross-references (margin):

11:28 ᵃJohn 5:27
11:30 ᵃ[Mark 1:4, 5, 8]; Luke 7:29, 30
11:32 ᵃMatt. 3:5; 14:5; Mark 6:20
12:1 ᵃMatt. 21:33–46; Luke 20:9–19
12:5 ᵃ2 Chr. 36:16
12:8 ᵃ[Acts 2:23]
12:10 ᵃPs. 118:22, 23
12:12 ᵃMatt. 21:45, 46; Mark 11:18; John 7:25, 30, 44
12:13 ᵃMatt. 22:15–22; Luke 20:20–26
12:14 ᵃActs 18:26

12:1 ¹tenant farmers   12:4 ¹NU omits *and at him they threw stones*
12:7 ¹tenant farmers   12:14 ¹Court no man's favor   ²Lit. *look at the face of men*

But He, knowing their ᵃhypocrisy, said to them, "Why do you test Me? Bring Me a denarius that I may see *it*." ¹⁶So they brought *it*.

And He said to them, "Whose image and inscription *is* this?" They said to Him, "Caesar's."

¹⁷And Jesus answered and said to them, ¹"Render to Caesar the things that are Caesar's, and to ᵃGod the things that are God's."

And they marveled at Him.

THE SADDUCEES: WHAT ABOUT THE RESURRECTION?
(Matt. 22:23–33; Luke 20:27–40)

¹⁸ᵃThen *some* Sadducees, ᵇwho say there is no resurrection, came to Him; and they asked Him, saying: ¹⁹"Teacher, ᵃMoses wrote to us that if a man's brother dies, and leaves *his* wife behind, and leaves no children, his brother should take his wife and raise up offspring for his brother. ²⁰Now there were seven brothers. The first took a wife; and dying, he left no offspring. ²¹And the second took her, and he died; nor did he leave any offspring. And the third likewise. ²²So the seven had her and left no offspring. Last of all the woman died also. ²³Therefore, in the resurrection, when they rise, whose wife will she be? For all seven had her as wife."

²⁴Jesus answered and said to them, "Are you not therefore ¹mistaken, because you do not know the Scriptures nor the power of God? ²⁵For when they rise from the dead, they neither marry nor are given in marriage, but ᵃare like angels in heaven. ²⁶But concerning the dead, that they ᵃrise, have you not read in the book of Moses, in the *burning* bush *passage,* how God spoke to him, saying, ᵇ'I *am* the God of Abraham, the God of Isaac, and the God of Jacob'? ²⁷He is not the God of the dead, but the God of the living. You are therefore greatly ¹mistaken."

THE SCRIBES: WHICH IS THE FIRST COMMANDMENT OF ALL?
(Matt. 22:34–40; Luke 10:25–28)

²⁸ᵃThen one of the scribes came, and having heard them reasoning together, ¹perceiving that He had answered them well, asked Him, "Which is the ²first commandment of all?"

²⁹Jesus answered him, "The ¹first of all the commandments *is:* ᵃ'Hear, O Israel, the LORD our God, the LORD is one. ³⁰And you shall ᵃlove the LORD your God with all your heart, with all your soul, with all your mind, and with all your strength.' ¹This *is* the first commandment. ³¹And the second, like *it, is* this: ᵃ'You shall love your neighbor as yourself.' There is no other commandment greater than ᵇthese."

³²So the scribe said to Him, "Well *said,* Teacher. You have spoken the truth, for there is one God, ᵃand there is no other but He. ³³And to love Him with all the heart, with all the understanding, ¹with all the soul, and with all the strength, and to love one's neighbor as oneself, ᵃis more than all the whole burnt offerings and sacrifices."

³⁴Now when Jesus saw that he answered wisely, He said to him, "You are not far from the kingdom of God." ᵃBut after that no one dared question Him.

Cross references

12:15
ᵃMatt. 23:28;
Luke 12:1

12:17
ᵃ[Eccl. 5:4, 5]

12:18
ᵃMatt. 22:23–33;
Luke 20:27–38
ᵇActs 23:8

12:19
ᵃDeut. 25:5

12:25
ᵃ[1 Cor. 15:42, 49, 52]

12:26
ᵃ[John 5:25, 28, 29];
Acts 26:8;
Rom. 4:17;
[Rev. 20:12, 13]
ᵇEx. 3:6, 15

12:28
ᵃMatt. 22:34–40;
Luke 10:25–28;
20:39

12:29
ᵃDeut. 6:4, 5;
Is. 44:8; 45:22;
46:9; 1 Cor. 8:6

12:30
ᵃ[Deut. 10:12;
30:6];
Luke 10:27

12:31 ᵃLev. 19:18;
Matt. 22:39;
Gal. 5:14;
James 2:8
ᵇ[Rom. 13:9]

12:32
ᵃDeut. 4:39;
Is. 45:6, 14; 46:9;
[John 1:14, 17;
14:6]

12:33
ᵃ[1 Sam. 15:22;
Hos. 6:6;
Mic. 6:6–8;
Matt. 9:13; 12:7]

12:34
ᵃMatt. 22:46

12:17 ¹*Pay* 12:24 ¹Or *deceived* 12:27 ¹Or *deceived* 12:28 ¹NU *seeing* ²*foremost* 12:29 ¹*foremost* 12:30 ¹NU omits the rest of v. 30. 12:33 ¹NU omits *with all the soul*

JESUS: HOW CAN DAVID CALL HIS DESCENDANT LORD?
(Matt. 22:41–46; Luke 20:41–44)

35aThen Jesus answered and said, while He taught in the temple, "How *is it* that the scribes say that the Christ is the Son of David? 36For David himself said ªby the Holy Spirit:

> ᵇ'The LORD said to my Lord,
> "Sit at My right hand,
> Till I make Your enemies Your footstool."'

37Therefore David himself calls Him 'Lord'; how is He *then* his ªSon?"

And the common people heard Him gladly.

BEWARE OF THE SCRIBES
(Matt. 23:1–7; Luke 20:45–47)

38Then ªHe said to them in His teaching, ᵇ"Beware of the scribes, who desire to go around in long robes, ᶜ*love* greetings in the marketplaces, 39the ªbest seats in the synagogues, and the best places at feasts, 40ªwho devour widows' houses, and ¹for a pretense make long prayers. These will receive greater condemnation."

THE WIDOW'S TWO MITES
(Luke 21:1–4)

41aNow Jesus sat opposite the treasury and saw how the people put money ᵇinto the treasury. And many *who were* rich put in much. 42Then one poor widow came and threw in two ¹mites, which make a ²quadrans. 43So He called His disciples to *Himself* and said to them, "Assuredly, I say to you that ªthis poor widow has put in more than all those who have given to the treasury; 44for they all put in out of their abundance, but she out of her poverty put in all that she had, ªher whole livelihood."

JESUS PREDICTS THE DESTRUCTION OF THE TEMPLE
(Matt. 24:1, 2; Luke 21:5, 6)

13 Then ªas He went out of the temple, one of His disciples said to Him, "Teacher, see what manner of stones and what buildings *are here!*"

2And Jesus answered and said to him, "Do you see these great buildings? ªNot *one* stone shall be left upon another, that shall not be thrown down."

THE SIGNS OF THE TIMES AND THE END OF THE AGE
(Matt. 24:3–14; Luke 21:7–19)

3Now as He sat on the Mount of Olives opposite the temple, ªPeter, ᵇJames, ᶜJohn, and ᵈAndrew asked Him privately, 4ª"Tell us, when will these things be? And what *will be* the sign when all these things will be fulfilled?"

5And Jesus, answering them, began to say: ª"Take heed that no one deceives you. 6For many will come in My name, saying, 'I am *He,*' and will deceive many. 7But when you hear of wars and rumors of wars, do not be troubled; for *such things* must happen, but the end *is* not yet. 8For nation

---

12:35
ªMatt. 22:41–46;
Luke 20:41–44

12:36
ª2 Sam. 23:2
ᵇPs. 110:1

12:37
ª[Acts 2:29–31]

12:38 ªMark 4:2
ᵇMatt. 23:1–7;
Luke 20:45–47
ᶜMatt. 23:7;
Luke 11:43

12:39 ªLuke 14:7

12:40
ªMatt. 23:14

12:41
ªLuke 21:1–4
ᵇ2 Kin. 12:9

12:43
ª[2 Cor. 8:12]

12:44
ªDeut. 24:6;
[1 John 3:17]

13:1 ªMatt. 24:1;
Luke 21:5–36

13:2 ªLuke 19:44

13:3
ªMatt. 16:18;
Mark 1:16
ᵇMark 1:19
ᶜMark 1:19
ᵈJohn 1:40

13:4 ªMatt. 24:3;
Luke 21:7

13:5 ªJer. 29:8;
Eph. 5:6;
[Col. 2:8];
1 Thess. 2:3;
2 Thess. 2:3

12:40 ¹*for appearance' sake*   **12:42** ¹Gr. *lepta*, very small copper coins
²A Roman coin

will rise against nation, and [a]kingdom against kingdom. And there will be earthquakes in various places, and there will be famines [1]and troubles. [b]These *are* the beginnings of [2]sorrows.

9"But [a]watch out for yourselves, for they will deliver you up to councils, and you will be beaten in the synagogues. You will [1]be brought before rulers and kings for My sake, for a testimony to them. [10]And [a]the gospel must first be preached to all the nations. [11a]But when they arrest *you* and deliver you up, do not worry beforehand, [1]or premeditate what you will speak. But whatever is given you in that hour, speak that; for it is not you who speak, [b]but the Holy Spirit. [12]Now [a]brother will betray brother to death, and a father *his* child; and children will rise up against parents and cause them to be put to death. [13a]And you will be hated by all for My name's sake. But [b]he who [1]endures to the end shall be saved.

THE GREAT TRIBULATION
(Matt. 24:15–28; Luke 21:20–24)

[14a]"So when you see the [b]'abomination of desolation,' [1]spoken of by Daniel the prophet, standing where it ought not" (let the reader understand), "then [c]let those who are in Judea flee to the mountains. [15]Let him who is on the housetop not go down into the house, nor enter to take anything out of his house. [16]And let him who is in the field not go back to get his clothes. [17a]But woe to those who are pregnant and to those who are nursing babies in those days! [18]And pray that your flight may not be in winter. [19a]For *in* those days there will be tribulation, such as has not been since the beginning of the creation which God created until this time, nor ever shall be. [20]And unless the Lord had shortened those days, no flesh would be saved; but for the elect's sake, whom He chose, He shortened the days.

[21a]"Then if anyone says to you, 'Look, here *is* the Christ!' or, 'Look, *He is* there!' do not believe it. [22]For false christs and false prophets will rise and show signs and [a]wonders to deceive, if possible, even the [1]elect. [23]But [a]take heed; see, I have told you all things beforehand.

THE COMING OF THE SON OF MAN
(Matt. 24:29–31; Luke 21:25–28)

[24a]"But in those days, after that tribulation, the sun will be darkened, and the moon will not give its light; [25]the stars of heaven will fall, and the powers in the heavens will be [a]shaken. [26a]Then they will see the Son of Man coming in the clouds with great power and glory. [27]And then He will send His angels, and gather together His [1]elect from the four winds, from the farthest part of earth to the farthest part of heaven.

THE PARABLE OF THE FIG TREE
(Matt. 24:32–35; Luke 21:29–33)

[28a]"Now learn this parable from the fig tree: When its branch has already become tender, and puts forth leaves,

---

13:8 [a]Hag. 2:22
[b]Matt. 24:8

13:9
[a]Matt. 10:17, 18;
24:9; Acts 12:4;
[Rev. 2:10]

13:10
[a]Matt. 24:14

13:11
[a]Matt. 10:19–22;
Luke 12:11;
21:12–17
[b]Acts 2:4; 4:8, 31

13:12 [a]Mic. 7:6;
Matt. 10:21;
24:10; Luke 21:16

13:13
[a]Matt. 24:9;
Luke 21:17;
John 15:21
[b]Dan. 12:12;
Matt. 10:22;
24:13; [Rev. 2:10]

13:14
[a]Matt. 24:15
[b]Dan. 9:27;
11:31; 12:11
[c]Luke 21:21

13:17
[a]Luke 21:23

13:19
[a]Dan. 9:26; 12:1;
Joel 2:2;
Matt. 24:21;
Mark 10:6

13:21
[a]Matt. 24:23;
Luke 17:23; 21:8

13:22
[a]Deut. 13:1–3;
Rev. 13:13, 14

13:23
[a]John 16:1–4;
[2 Pet. 3:17]

13:24
[a]Zeph. 1:15;
Matt. 24:29

13:25
[a]Is. 13:10; 34:4;
Heb. 12:26;
Rev. 6:13

13:26
[a][Dan. 7:13, 14;
Matt. 16:27;
24:30];
Mark 14:62;
Acts 1:11;
[1 Thess. 4:16;
2 Thess. 1:7, 10];
Rev. 1:7

13:28
[a]Matt. 24:32;
Luke 21:29

13:8 [1]NU omits *and troubles* [2]Lit. *birth pangs* 13:9 [1]NU, M *stand*
13:11 [1]NU omits *or premeditate* 13:13 [1]*bears patiently* 13:14 [1]NU omits
spoken of by Daniel the prophet 13:22 [1]*chosen ones* 13:27 [1]*chosen ones*

you know that summer is near. 29So you also, when you see these things happening, know that 1it is near—at the doors! 30Assuredly, I say to you, this generation will by no means pass away till all these things take place. 31Heaven and earth will pass away, but aMy words will by no means pass away.

NO ONE KNOWS THE DAY OR HOUR
(Matt. 24:36–44; Luke 21:34–36)

32"But of that day and hour ano one knows, not even the angels in heaven, nor the Son, but only the bFather. 33aTake heed, watch and pray; for you do not know when the time is. 34aIt is like a man going to a far country, who left his house and gave bauthority to his servants, and to each his work, and commanded the doorkeeper to watch. 35aWatch therefore, for you do not know when the master of the house is coming—in the evening, at midnight, at the crowing of the rooster, or in the morning— 36lest, coming suddenly, he find you sleeping. 37And what I say to you, I say to all: Watch!"

THE PLOT TO KILL JESUS
(Matt. 26:1–5; Luke 22:1, 2; John 11:45–53)

14 After atwo days it was the Passover and bthe Feast of Unleavened Bread. And the chief priests and the scribes sought how they might take Him by 1trickery and put *Him* to death. 2But they said, "Not during the feast, lest there be an uproar of the people."

THE ANOINTING AT BETHANY
(Matt. 26:6–13; John 12:1–8)

3aAnd being in Bethany at the house of Simon the leper, as He sat at the table, a woman came having an alabaster flask of very costly 1oil of spikenard. Then she broke the flask and poured *it* on His head. 4But there were some who were indignant among themselves, and said, "Why was this fragrant oil wasted? 5For it might have been sold for more than three hundred adenarii and given to the poor." And they bcriticized1 her sharply.

6But Jesus said, "Let her alone. Why do you trouble her? She has done a good work for Me. 7aFor you have the poor with you always, and whenever you wish you may do them good; bbut Me you do not have always. 8She has done what she could. She has come beforehand to anoint My body for burial. 9Assuredly, I say to you, wherever this gospel is apreached in the whole world, what this woman has done will also be told as a memorial to her."

JUDAS AGREES TO BETRAY JESUS
(Matt. 26:14–16; Luke 22:3–6)

10aThen Judas Iscariot, one of the twelve, went to the chief priests to betray Him to them. 11And when they heard *it*, they were glad, and promised to give him money. So he sought how he might conveniently betray Him.

13:29 1Or He   **14:1** 1deception   **14:3** 1Perfume of pure nard
14:5 1scolded

JESUS CELEBRATES THE PASSOVER WITH HIS DISCIPLES
(Matt. 26:17–25; Luke 22:7–13; John 13:21–30)

¹²ᵃNow on the first day of Unleavened Bread, when they ¹killed the Passover *lamb,* His disciples said to Him, "Where do You want us to go and prepare, that You may eat the Passover?"

¹³And He sent out two of His disciples and said to them, "Go into the city, and a man will meet you carrying a pitcher of water; follow him. ¹⁴Wherever he goes in, say to the master of the house, 'The Teacher says, "Where is the guest room in which I may eat the Passover with My disciples?"' ¹⁵Then he will show you a large upper room, furnished *and* prepared; there make ready for us."

¹⁶So His disciples went out, and came into the city, and found it just as He had said to them; and they prepared the Passover.

¹⁷ᵃIn the evening He came with the twelve. ¹⁸Now as they sat and ate, Jesus said, "Assuredly, I say to you, ᵃone of you who eats with Me will betray Me."

¹⁹And they began to be sorrowful, and to say to Him one by one, *"Is it I?"* ¹And another *said, "Is it I?"*

²⁰He answered and said to them, "*It is* one of the twelve, who dips with Me in the dish. ²¹ᵃThe Son of Man indeed goes just as it is written of Him, but woe to that man by whom the Son of Man is betrayed! It would have been good for that man if he had never been born."

JESUS INSTITUTES THE LORD'S SUPPER
(Matt. 26:26–29; Luke 22:14–23; 1 Cor. 11:23–26)

²²ᵃAnd as they were eating, Jesus took bread, blessed and broke *it,* and gave *it* to them and said, "Take, ¹eat; this is My ᵇbody."

²³Then He took the cup, and when He had given thanks He gave *it* to them, and they all drank from it. ²⁴And He said to them, "This is My blood of the ¹new covenant, which is shed for many. ²⁵Assuredly, I say to you, I will no longer drink of the fruit of the vine until that day when I drink it new in the kingdom of God."

²⁶ᵃAnd when they had sung ¹a hymn, they went out to the Mount of Olives.

JESUS PREDICTS PETER'S DENIAL
(Matt. 26:31–35; Luke 22:31–34; John 13:36–38)

²⁷ᵃThen Jesus said to them, "All of you will be made to stumble ¹because of Me this night, for it is written:

ᵇ'I will strike the Shepherd,
And the sheep will be scattered.'

²⁸"But ᵃafter I have been raised, I will go before you to Galilee."

²⁹ᵃPeter said to Him, "Even if all are made to ¹stumble, yet I *will* not *be.*"

³⁰Jesus said to him, "Assuredly, I say to you that today,

14:12 ᵃEx. 12:8; Matt. 26:17–19; Luke 22:7–13

14:17 ᵃMatt. 26:20–24; Luke 22:14, 21–23

14:18 ᵃPs. 41:9; Matt. 26:46; Mark 14:42; John 6:70, 71; 13:18

14:21 ᵃMatt. 26:24; Luke 22:22; Acts 1:16–20

14:22 ᵃMatt. 26:26–29; Luke 22:17–20; 1 Cor. 11:23–25 ᵇ[1 Pet. 2:24]

14:26 ᵃMatt. 26:30

14:27 ᵃMatt. 26:31–35; Mark 14:50; John 16:32 ᵇ[Is. 53:5, 10]; Zech. 13:7

14:28 ᵃMatt. 28:16; Mark 16:7; John 21:1

14:29 ᵃMatt. 26:33, 34; Luke 22:33, 34; John 13:37, 38

14:12 ¹*sacrificed*   14:19 ¹NU omits the rest of v. 19.   14:22 ¹NU omits *eat*
14:24 ¹NU omits *new*   14:26 ¹Or *hymns*   14:27 ¹NU omits *because of Me this night*   14:29 ¹*fall away*

even this night, before the rooster crows twice, you will deny Me three times."

31But he spoke more vehemently, "If I have to die with You, I will not deny You!"

And they all said likewise.

THE PRAYER IN THE GARDEN
(Matt. 26:36–46; Luke 22:39–46)

32aThen they came to a place which was named Gethsemane; and He said to His disciples, "Sit here while I pray." 33And He atook Peter, James, and John with Him, and He began to be troubled and deeply distressed. 34Then He said to them, a"My soul is exceedingly sorrowful, *even* to death. Stay here and watch."

35He went a little farther, and fell on the ground, and prayed that if it were possible, the hour might pass from Him. 36And He said, a"Abba, Father, ball things *are* possible for You. Take this cup away from Me; cnevertheless, not what I will, but what You *will*."

37Then He came and found them sleeping, and said to Peter, "Simon, are you sleeping? Could you not watch one hour? 38aWatch and pray, lest you enter into temptation. bThe spirit indeed *is* willing, but the flesh *is* weak."

39Again He went away and prayed, and spoke the same words. 40And when He returned, He found them asleep again, for their eyes were heavy; and they did not know what to answer Him.

41Then He came the third time and said to them, "Are you still sleeping and resting? It is enough! aThe hour has come; behold, the Son of Man is being betrayed into the hands of sinners. 42aRise, let us be going. See, My betrayer is at hand."

BETRAYAL AND ARREST IN GETHSEMANE
(Matt. 26:47–56; Luke 22:47–53; John 18:1–11)

43aAnd immediately, while He was still speaking, Judas, one of the twelve, with a great multitude with swords and clubs, came from the chief priests and the scribes and the elders. 44Now His betrayer had given them a signal, saying, "Whomever I akiss, He is the One; seize Him and lead *Him* away safely."

45As soon as he had come, immediately he went up to Him and said to Him, "Rabbi, Rabbi!" and kissed Him.

46Then they laid their hands on Him and took Him. 47And one of those who stood by drew his sword and struck the servant of the high priest, and cut off his ear.

48aThen Jesus answered and said to them, "Have you come out, as against a robber, with swords and clubs to take Me? 49I was daily with you in the temple ateaching, and you did not seize Me. But bthe Scriptures must be fulfilled."

50aThen they all forsook Him and fled.

A YOUNG MAN FLEES NAKED

51Now a certain young man followed Him, having a linen cloth thrown around *his* naked *body*. And the young men laid hold of him, 52and he left the linen cloth and fled from them naked.

14:32
aMatt. 26:36–46;
Luke 22:40–46;
John 18:1

14:33
aMark 5:37;
9:2; 13:3

14:34
aIs. 53:3, 4;
Matt. 26:38;
John 12:27

14:36
aRom. 8:15;
Gal. 4:6
b[Heb. 5:7]
cIs. 50:5;
John 5:30; 6:38

14:38
aLuke 21:36
b[Rom. 7:18,
21–24;
Gal. 5:17]

14:41
aJohn 13:1; 17:1

14:42
aMatt. 26:46;
Mark 14:18;
Luke 9:44;
John 13:21;
18:1, 2

14:43 aPs. 3:1;
Matt. 26:47–56;
Luke 22:47–53;
John 18:3–11

14:44
a[Prov. 27:6]

14:48
aMatt. 26:55;
Luke 22:52

14:49
aMatt. 21:23
bPs. 22:6;
Is. 53:7;
Luke 22:37;
24:44

14:50 aPs. 88:8;
Zech. 13:7;
Matt. 26:31;
Mark 14:27

JESUS FACES THE SANHEDRIN
(*Matt. 26:57–68; Luke 22:66–71; John 18:12–14, 19–24*)

53a And they led Jesus away to the high priest; and with him were b assembled all the c chief priests, the elders, and the scribes. 54 But a Peter followed Him at a distance, right into the courtyard of the high priest. And he sat with the servants and warmed himself at the fire.

55a Now the chief priests and all the council sought testimony against Jesus to put Him to death, but found none. 56 For many bore a false witness against Him, but their testimonies 1 did not agree.

57 Then some rose up and bore false witness against Him, saying, 58 "We heard Him say, a 'I will destroy this temple made with hands, and within three days I will build another made without hands.'" 59 But not even then did their testimony agree.

60a And the high priest stood up in the midst and asked Jesus, saying, "Do You answer nothing? What *is it* these men testify against You?" 61 But a He kept silent and answered nothing.

b Again the high priest asked Him, saying to Him, "Are You the Christ, the Son of the Blessed?"

62 Jesus said, "I am. a And you will see the Son of Man sitting at the right hand of the Power, and coming with the clouds of heaven."

63 Then the high priest tore his clothes and said, "What further need do we have of witnesses? 64 You have heard the a blasphemy! What do you think?"

And they all condemned Him to be deserving of b death.

65 Then some began to a spit on Him, and to blindfold Him, and to beat Him, and to say to Him, "Prophesy!" And the officers 1 struck Him with the palms of their hands.

PETER DENIES JESUS, AND WEEPS
(*Matt. 26:69–75; Luke 22:54–62; John 18:15–18, 25–27*)

66a Now as Peter was below in the courtyard, one of the servant girls of the high priest came. 67 And when she saw Peter warming himself, she looked at him and said, "You also were with a Jesus of Nazareth."

68 But he denied it, saying, "I neither know nor understand what you are saying." And he went out on the porch, and a rooster crowed.

69a And the servant girl saw him again, and began to say to those who stood by, "This is *one* of them." 70 But he denied it again.

a And a little later those who stood by said to Peter again, "Surely you are *one* of them; b for you are a Galilean, 1 and your 2 speech shows *it*."

71 Then he began to curse and swear, "I do not know this Man of whom you speak!"

72a A second time *the* rooster crowed. Then Peter called to mind the word that Jesus had said to him, "Before the rooster crows twice, you will deny Me three times." And when he thought about it, he wept.

14:72 a Matt. 26:75; Mark 14:30; Luke 22:34; John 13:38

14:56 1 *were not consistent*   14:65 1 NU *received Him with slaps*
14:70 1 NU *omits the rest of v. 70.*   2 *accent*

Cross-references

14:53
a Matt. 26:57–68;
Mark 10:33;
Luke 22:54;
John 18:12, 13,
19–24
b Mark 15:1
c Matt. 16:21;
27:12; Luke 9:22;
23:23;
John 7:32; 18:3;
19:6

14:54
a John 18:15

14:55
a Matt. 26:59

14:56 a Ex. 20:16;
Ps. 27:12; 35:11;
Prov. 6:16–19;
19:5

14:58
a Matt. 26:61;
Mark 15:29;
John 2:19;
[2 Cor. 5:1]

14:60
a Matt. 26:62;
Mark 15:3–5

14:61 a Is. 53:7;
John 19:9;
Acts 8:32;
[1 Pet. 2:23]
b Matt. 26:63;
Luke 22:67–71

14:62
a Matt. 24:30;
26:64;
Luke 22:69

14:64
a John 10:33, 36
b Matt. 20:18;
Mark 10:33;
John 19:7

14:65 a Job 16:10;
Is. 50:6; 52:14;
Lam. 3:30;
Mark 10:34;
Luke 18:32

14:66
a Matt. 26:58,
69–75;
Luke 22:55–62;
John 18:16–18,
25–27

14:67
a Mark 10:47;
John 1:45;
Acts 10:38

14:69
a Matt. 26:71;
Luke 22:58;
John 18:25

14:70
a Matt. 26:73;
Luke 22:59;
John 18:26
b Acts 2:7

JESUS FACES PILATE
(Matthew 27:1, 2, 11–14; Luke 23:1–5; John 18:28–38)

15 Immediately, [a]in the morning, the chief priests held a consultation with the elders and scribes and the whole council; and they bound Jesus, led *Him* away, and [b]delivered *Him* to Pilate. [2][a]Then Pilate asked Him, "Are You the King of the Jews?"

He answered and said to him, "*It is as* you say."

[3]And the chief priests accused Him of many things, but He [a]answered nothing. [4][a]Then Pilate asked Him again, saying, "Do You answer nothing? See how many things [1]they testify against You!" [5][a]But Jesus still answered nothing, so that Pilate marveled.

TAKING THE PLACE OF BARABBAS
(Matt. 27:15–26; Luke 23:17–25; John 18:39—19:16)

[6]Now [a]at the feast he was accustomed to releasing one prisoner to them, whomever they requested. [7]And there was one named Barabbas, *who was* chained with his fellow rebels; they had committed murder in the rebellion. [8]Then the multitude, [1]crying aloud, began to ask *him to do* just as he had always done for them. [9]But Pilate answered them, saying, "Do you want me to release to you the King of the Jews?" [10]For he knew that the chief priests had handed Him over because of envy.

[11]But [a]the chief priests stirred up the crowd, so that he should rather release Barabbas to them. [12]Pilate answered and said to them again, "What then do you want me to do *with Him* whom you call the [a]King of the Jews?"

[13]So they cried out again, "Crucify Him!"

[14]Then Pilate said to them, "Why, [a]what evil has He done?"

But they cried out all the more, "Crucify Him!"

[15][a]So Pilate, wanting to gratify the crowd, released Barabbas to them; and he delivered Jesus, after he had scourged *Him,* to be [b]crucified.

THE SOLDIERS MOCK JESUS
(Matt. 27:27–31)

[16][a]Then the soldiers led Him away into the hall called [1]Praetorium, and they called together the whole garrison. [17]And they clothed Him with purple; and they twisted a crown of thorns, put it on His *head,* [18]and began to salute Him, "Hail, King of the Jews!" [19]Then they [a]struck Him on the head with a reed and spat on Him; and bowing the knee, they worshiped Him. [20]And when they had [a]mocked Him, they took the purple off Him, put His own clothes on Him, and led Him out to crucify Him.

THE KING ON A CROSS
(Matt. 27:32–44; Luke 23:26–43; John 19:17–27)

[21][a]Then they compelled a certain man, Simon a Cyrenian, the father of Alexander and Rufus, as he was coming out of the country and passing by, to bear His cross. [22][a]And they brought Him to the place Golgotha, which is translated, Place

---

15:1 [a]Ps. 2:2;
Matt. 27:1;
Luke 22:66;
23:1;
John 18:28;
Acts 3:13; 4:26
[b]Luke 18:32;
Acts 3:13

15:2
[a]Matt. 27:11–14;
Luke 23:2, 3;
John 18:29–38

15:3 [a]Is. 53:7;
John 19:9;
Acts 8:32

15:4 [a]Matt. 27:13

15:5
[a]Ps. 38:13, 14;
Is. 53:7;
John 19:9

15:6
[a]Matt. 27:15–26;
Luke 23:18–25;
John 18:39—
19:16

15:11
[a]Matt. 27:20;
Acts 3:14

15:12 [a]Ps. 2:6;
[Is. 9:7];
Jer. 23:5; 33:15;
Mic. 5:2

15:14 [a]Is. 53:9;
John 8:46;
1 Pet. 2:21–23

15:15 [a]Is. 50:6;
Matt. 27:26;
Mark 10:34;
John 19:1, 16
[b][Is. 53:8]

15:16
[a]Matt. 27:27–31

15:19 [a][Is. 50:6;
52:14; 53:5];
Mic. 5:1;
Mark 14:65

15:20 [a]Ps. 35:16;
69:19; Is. 53:3;
Matt. 20:19;
Mark 10:34;
Luke 22:63;
23:11

15:21
[a]Matt. 27:32;
Luke 23:26

15:22
[a]Matt. 27:33–44;
Luke 23:33–43;
John 19:17–24;
Heb. 13:12

15:4 [1]NU *of which they accuse You*   15:8 [1]NU *going up*   15:16 [1]The governor's headquarters

of a Skull. 23aThen they gave Him wine mingled with myrrh to drink, but He did not take *it*. 24And when they crucified Him, athey divided His garments, casting lots for them *to determine* what every man should take.

25Now ait was the third hour, and they crucified Him. 26And athe inscription of His 1accusation was written above:

THE KING OF THE JEWS.

27aWith Him they also crucified two robbers, one on His right and the other on His left. 281So the Scripture was fulfilled which says, a"And He was numbered with the transgressors."

29And athose who passed by blasphemed Him, bwagging their heads and saying, "Aha! cYou who destroy the temple and build *it* in three days, 30save Yourself, and come down from the cross!"

31Likewise the chief priests also, amocking among themselves with the scribes, said, "He saved bothers; Himself He cannot save. 32Let the Christ, the King of Israel, descend now from the cross, that we may see and 1believe."

Even athose who were crucified with Him reviled Him.

JESUS DIES ON THE CROSS
(Matt. 27:45–56; Luke 23:44–49; John 19:28–30)

33Now awhen the sixth hour had come, there was darkness over the whole land until the ninth hour. 34And at the ninth hour Jesus cried out with a loud voice, saying, "Eloi, Eloi, lama sabachthani?" which is translated, a"My God, My God, why have You forsaken Me?"

35Some of those who stood by, when they heard *that*, said, "Look, He is calling for Elijah!" 36Then asomeone ran and filled a sponge full of sour wine, put *it* on a reed, and boffered *it* to Him to drink, saying, "Let Him alone; let us see if Elijah will come to take Him down."

37aAnd Jesus cried out with a loud voice, and breathed His last.

38Then athe veil of the temple was torn in two from top to bottom. 39So awhen the centurion, who stood opposite Him, saw that 1He cried out like this and breathed His last, he said, "Truly this Man was the Son of God!"

40aThere were also women looking on bfrom afar, among whom were Mary Magdalene, Mary the mother of James the Less and of Joses, and Salome, 41who also afollowed Him and ministered to Him when He was in Galilee, and many other women who came up with Him to Jerusalem.

JESUS BURIED IN JOSEPH'S TOMB
(Matt. 27:57–61; Luke 23:50–56; John 19:38–42)

42aNow when evening had come, because it was the Preparation Day, that is, the day before the Sabbath, 43Joseph of Arimathea, a prominent council member, who awas himself waiting for the kingdom of God, coming and taking courage, went in to Pilate and asked for the body of Jesus. 44Pilate marveled that He was already dead; and summoning

15:43 aMatt. 27:57; Luke 2:25, 38; 23:51; John 19:38

15:26 1crime   15:28 1NU omits v. 28.   15:32 1M believe Him   15:39 1NU He thus breathed His last

15:23
aPs. 69:21;
Matt. 27:34

15:24
aPs. 22:18;
Luke 23:34;
John 19:23

15:25
aMatt. 27:45;
Luke 23:44;
John 19:14

15:26
aMatt. 27:37;
John 19:19

15:27
aIs. 53:9, 12;
Matt. 27:38;
Luke 22:37

15:28
aIs. 53:12;
Luke 22:37

15:29
aPs. 22:6, 7;
69:7 bPs. 109:25
cMark 14:58;
John 2:19–21

15:31
aLuke 18:32
bLuke 7:14, 15;
John 11:43, 44

15:32
aMatt. 27:44;
Luke 23:39

15:33
aAmos 8:9;
Matt. 27:45–56;
Luke 23:44–49

15:34 aPs. 22:1;
Matt. 27:46

15:36
aMatt. 27:48;
John 19:29
bPs. 69:21

15:37
aDan. 9:26;
Zech. 11:10, 11;
Matt. 27:50;
Mark 8:31;
Luke 23:46;
John 19:30

15:38
aEx. 26:31–33;
Matt. 27:51;
Luke 23:45

15:39
aMatt. 27:54;
Luke 23:47

15:40
aMatt. 27:55;
Luke 23:49;
John 19:25
bPs. 38:11

15:41
aLuke 8:2, 3

15:42
aMatt. 27:57–61;
Luke 23:50–56;
John 19:38–42

the centurion, he asked him if He had been dead for some time. ⁴⁵So when he found out from the centurion, he granted the body to Joseph. ⁴⁶ᵃThen he bought fine linen, took Him down, and wrapped Him in the linen. And he laid Him in a tomb which had been hewn out of the rock, and rolled a stone against the door of the tomb. ⁴⁷And Mary Magdalene and Mary *the mother* of Joses observed where He was laid.

HE IS RISEN
(Matt. 28:1–8; Luke 24:1–12; John 20:1–10)

16 Now ᵃwhen the Sabbath was past, Mary Magdalene, Mary *the mother* of James, and Salome ᵇbought spices, that they might come and anoint Him. ²ᵃVery early in the morning, on the first *day* of the week, they came to the tomb when the sun had risen. ³And they said among themselves, "Who will roll away the stone from the door of the tomb for us?" ⁴But when they looked up, they saw that the stone had been rolled away—for it was very large. ⁵ᵃAnd entering the tomb, they saw a young man clothed in a long white robe sitting on the right side; and they were alarmed.

⁶ᵃBut he said to them, "Do not be alarmed. You seek Jesus of Nazareth, who was crucified. He is risen! He is not here. See the place where they laid Him. ⁷But go, tell His disciples—and Peter—that He is going ¹before you into Galilee; there you will see Him, ᵃas He said to you."

⁸So they went out ¹quickly and fled from the tomb, for they trembled and were amazed. ᵃAnd they said nothing to anyone, for they were afraid.

MARY MAGDALENE SEES THE RISEN LORD
(Matt. 28:9, 10; John 20:11–18)

⁹¹Now when *He* rose early on the first *day* of the week, He appeared first to Mary Magdalene, ᵃout of whom He had cast seven demons. ¹⁰ᵃShe went and told those who had been with Him, as they mourned and wept. ¹¹ᵃAnd when they heard that He was alive and had been seen by her, they did not believe.

JESUS APPEARS TO TWO DISCIPLES
(Luke 24:13–35)

¹²After that, He appeared in another form ᵃto two of them as they walked and went into the country. ¹³And they went and told *it* to the rest, *but* they did not believe them either.

THE GREAT COMMISSION
(Matt. 28:16–20; Luke 24:44–49; Acts 1:6–8)

¹⁴ᵃLater He appeared to the eleven as they sat at the table; and He rebuked their unbelief and hardness of heart, because they did not believe those who had seen Him after He had risen. ¹⁵ᵃAnd He said to them, "Go into all the world ᵇand preach the gospel to every creature. ¹⁶ᵃHe who believes and is baptized will be saved; ᵇbut he who does not believe will be condemned. ¹⁷And these ᵃsigns will follow those who ¹believe:

15:46 ᵃIs. 53:9;
Matt. 27:59, 60;
Luke 23:53;
John 19:40

16:1
ᵃMatt. 28:1–8;
Luke 24:1–10;
John 20:1–8
ᵇLuke 23:56;
John 19:39

16:2 ᵃLuke 24:1;
John 20:1

16:5 ᵃLuke 24:3;
John 20:11, 12

16:6
ᵃPs. 16:10; 49:15;
Hos. 6:2;
Matt. 28:6;
Mark 9:31;
Luke 24:6

16:7
ᵃMatt. 26:32;
28:16, 17;
Mark 14:28

16:8 ᵃMatt. 28:8

16:9 ᵃLuke 8:2

16:10
ᵃLuke 24:10

16:11
ᵃMatt. 28:17;
Luke 24:11, 41;
John 20:25

16:12
ᵃLuke 24:13–35

16:14
ᵃLuke 24:36;
John 20:19, 26;
1 Cor. 15:5

16:15
ᵃMatt. 28:19;
[John 15:16];
Acts 1:8];
Col. 1:6
ᵇ[Col. 1:23]

16:16
ᵃ[John 3:18, 36];
Acts 2:38;
16:30, 31;
Rom. 10:8–10]
ᵇ[John 12:48]

16:17 ᵃActs 5:12

16:7 ¹*ahead of*   16:8 ¹NU, M omit *quickly*   16:9 ¹Vv. 9–20 are bracketed in NU as not in the original text. They are lacking in Codex Sinaiticus and Codex Vaticanus, although nearly all other mss. of Mark contain them.
16:17 ¹*have believed*

[b]In My name they will cast out demons; [c]they will speak with new tongues; [18a]they[1] will take up serpents; and if they drink anything deadly, it will by no means hurt them; [b]they will lay hands on the sick, and they will recover."

CHRIST ASCENDS TO GOD'S RIGHT HAND
(Luke 24:50–53)

[19]So then, [a]after the Lord had spoken to them, He was [b]received up into heaven, and [c]sat down at the right hand of God. [20]And they went out and preached everywhere, the Lord working with *them* [a]and confirming the word through the accompanying signs. Amen.

16:17
[b]Mark 9:38;
Luke 10:17;
Acts 5:16; 8:7;
16:18; 19:12
[c][Acts 2:4;
1 Cor. 12:10]

16:18
[a][Luke 10:19];
Acts 28:3–6
[b][Acts 5:15];
James 5:14

16:19
[a]Acts 1:2, 3
[b]Ps. 68:18;
Luke 9:51; 24:51;
John 6:62;
20:17;
Acts 1:2, 9–11;
[1 Tim. 3:16];
Rev. 4:2]
[c][Ps. 110:1];
Luke 22:69;
[Acts 7:55];
1 Pet. 3:22

16:20
[a]Acts 5:12;
[1 Cor. 2:4, 5;
Heb. 2:4]

THE GOSPEL ACCORDING TO
LUKE

DEDICATION TO THEOPHILUS

1 Inasmuch as many have taken in hand to set in order a narrative of those ᵃthings which ¹have been fulfilled among us, ²just as those who ᵃfrom the beginning were ᵇeyewitnesses and ministers of the word ᶜdelivered them to us, ³it seemed good to me also, having ¹had perfect understanding of all things from the very first, to write to you an orderly account, ᵃmost excellent Theophilus, ⁴ᵃthat you may know the certainty of those things in which you were instructed.

JOHN'S BIRTH ANNOUNCED TO ZACHARIAS

⁵There was ᵃin the days of Herod, the king of Judea, a certain priest named Zacharias, ᵇof the division of ᶜAbijah. His ᵈwife *was* of the daughters of Aaron, and her name *was* Elizabeth. ⁶And they were both righteous before God, walking in all the commandments and ordinances of the Lord blameless. ⁷But they had no child, because Elizabeth was barren, and they were both well advanced in years.

⁸So it was, that while he was serving as priest before God in the order of his division, ⁹according to the custom of the priesthood, ¹his lot fell ᵃto burn incense when he went into the temple of the Lord. ¹⁰ᵃAnd the whole multitude of the people was praying outside at the hour of incense. ¹¹Then an angel of the Lord appeared to him, standing on the right side of ᵃthe altar of incense. ¹²And when Zacharias saw *him,* ᵃhe was troubled, and fear fell upon him.

¹³But the angel said to him, "Do not be afraid, Zacharias, for your prayer is heard; and your wife Elizabeth will bear you a son, and ᵃyou shall call his name John. ¹⁴And you will have joy and gladness, and ᵃmany will rejoice at his birth. ¹⁵For he will be ᵃgreat in the sight of the Lord, and ᵇshall drink neither wine nor strong drink. He will also be filled with the Holy Spirit, ᶜeven from his mother's womb. ¹⁶And he will turn many of the children of Israel to the Lord their God. ¹⁷ᵃHe will also go before Him in the spirit and power of Elijah, 'to turn the hearts of the fathers to the children,' and the disobedient to the wisdom of the just, to make ready a people prepared for the Lord."

¹⁸And Zacharias said to the angel, ᵃ"How shall I know this? For I am an old man, and my wife is well advanced in years."

¹⁹And the angel answered and said to him, "I am ᵃGabriel, who stands in the presence of God, and was sent to speak to you and bring you ¹these glad ᵇtidings. ²⁰But behold, ᵃyou will be mute and not able to speak until the day these things take place, because you did not believe my words which will be fulfilled in their own time."

1:1 ᵃJohn 20:31

1:2 ᵃMark 1:1; John 15:27; Acts 1:21, 22
ᵇActs 1:2
ᶜActs 1:3; 10:39; Heb. 2:3; 1 Pet. 5:1; 2 Pet. 1:16; 1 John 1:1

1:3 ᵃActs 1:1

1:4
ᵃ[John 20:31]

1:5 ᵃMatt. 2:1
ᵇ1 Chr. 24:1, 10
ᶜNeh. 12:4
ᵈLev. 21:13, 14

1:9 ᵃEx. 30:7, 8; 1 Chr. 23:13; 2 Chr. 29:11

1:10 ᵃLev. 16:17

1:11 ᵃEx. 30:1

1:12 ᵃJudg. 6:22; Dan. 10:8; Luke 2:9; Acts 10:4; Rev. 1:17

1:13 ᵃLuke 1:57, 60, 63

1:14 ᵃLuke 1:58

1:15
ᵃ[Luke 7:24–28]
ᵇNum. 6:3; Judg. 13:4; Matt. 11:18
ᶜJer. 1:5; Gal. 1:15

1:17 ᵃMal. 4:5, 6; Matt. 3:2; 11:14; Mark 1:4; 9:12

1:18 ᵃGen. 17:17

1:19 ᵃDan. 8:16; [Matt. 18:10]; Heb. 1:4
ᵇLuke 2:10

1:20
ᵃEzek. 3:26; 24:27

21And the people waited for Zacharias, and marveled that he lingered so long in the temple. 22But when he came out, he could not speak to them; and they perceived that he had seen a vision in the temple, for he beckoned to them and remained speechless.

23So it was, as soon as ªthe days of his service were completed, that he departed to his own house. 24Now after those days his wife Elizabeth conceived; and she hid herself five months, saying, 25"Thus the Lord has dealt with me, in the days when He looked on *me*, to ªtake away my reproach among people."

CHRIST'S BIRTH ANNOUNCED TO MARY

26Now in the sixth month the angel Gabriel was sent by God to a city of Galilee named Nazareth, 27to a virgin ªbetrothed to a man whose name was Joseph, of the house of David. The virgin's name *was* Mary. 28And having come in, the angel said to her, ª"Rejoice, highly favored *one*, ᵇthe Lord *is* with you; ¹blessed *are* you among women!"

29But ¹when she saw *him*, ªshe was troubled at his saying, and considered what manner of greeting this was. 30Then the angel said to her, "Do not be afraid, Mary, for you have found ªfavor with God. 31ªAnd behold, you will conceive in your womb and bring forth a Son, and ᵇshall call His name JESUS. 32He will be great, ªand will be called the Son of the Highest; and ᵇthe Lord God will give Him the ᶜthrone of His ᵈfather David. 33ªAnd He will reign over the house of Jacob forever, and of His kingdom there will be no end."

34Then Mary said to the angel, "How can this be, since I ¹do not know a man?"

35And the angel answered and said to her, ª"*The* Holy Spirit will come upon you, and the power of the Highest will overshadow you; therefore, also, that Holy One who is to be born will be called ᵇthe Son of God. 36Now indeed, Elizabeth your relative has also conceived a son in her old age; and this is now the sixth month for her who was called barren. 37For ªwith God nothing will be impossible."

38Then Mary said, "Behold the maidservant of the Lord! Let it be to me according to your word." And the angel departed from her.

MARY VISITS ELIZABETH

39Now Mary arose in those days and went into the hill country with haste, ªto a city of Judah, 40and entered the house of Zacharias and greeted Elizabeth. 41And it happened, when Elizabeth heard the greeting of Mary, that the babe leaped in her womb; and Elizabeth was ªfilled with the Holy Spirit. 42Then she spoke out with a loud voice and said, ª"Blessed *are* you among women, and blessed *is* the fruit of your womb! 43But why *is* this *granted* to me, that the mother of my Lord should come to me? 44For indeed, as soon as the voice of your greeting sounded in my ears, the babe leaped in my womb for joy. 45ªBlessed *is* she who ¹believed, for there will be a fulfillment of those things which were told her from the Lord."

1:23 ª2 Kin. 11:5; 1 Chr. 9:25

1:25 ªGen. 30:23; Is. 4:1; 54:1, 4

1:27 ªMatt. 1:18; Luke 2:4, 5

1:28 ªDan. 9:23 ᵇJudg. 6:12

1:29 ªLuke 1:12

1:30 ªLuke 2:52

1:31 ªIs. 7:14; Matt. 1:21, 25; Gal. 4:4 ᵇLuke 2:21; [Phil. 2:9–11]

1:32 ªMatt. 3:17; 17:5; Mark 5:7; Luke 1:35, 76; 6:35; Acts 7:48 ᵇ2 Sam. 7:12, 13, 16; Ps. 132:11; [Is. 9:6, 7; 16:5; Jer. 23:5] ᶜ2 Sam. 7:14–17; Acts 2:33; 7:55 ᵈMatt. 1:1

1:33 ª[Dan. 2:44; Obad. 21; Mic. 4:7]; John 12:34; [Heb. 1:8]; 2 Pet. 1:11

1:35 ªMatt. 1:20 ᵇPs. 2:7; Matt. 3:17; 14:33; 17:5; Mark 1:11; John 1:34; 20:31; Acts 8:37; [Rom. 1:1–4; Heb. 1:2, 8]

1:37 ªGen. 18:14; Jer. 32:17; Matt. 19:26; Mark 10:27; Rom. 4:21

1:39 ªJosh. 21:9

1:41 ªActs 6:3

1:42 ªJudg. 5:24

1:45 ªJohn 20:29

1:28 ¹NU omits *blessed are you among women*   1:29 ¹NU omits *when she saw him*   1:34 ¹Am a virgin   1:45 ¹Or *believed that there*

THE SONG OF MARY

46And Mary said:

a"My soul 1magnifies the Lord,
47 And my spirit has arejoiced in bGod my Savior.
48 For aHe has regarded the lowly state of His
maidservant;
For behold, henceforth ball generations will call
me blessed.
49 For He who is mighty ahas done great things for me,
And bholy is His name.
50 And aHis mercy is on those who fear Him
From generation to generation.
51 aHe has shown strength with His arm;
bHe has scattered the proud in the imagination of their
hearts.
52 aHe has put down the mighty from their thrones,
And exalted the lowly.
53 He has afilled the hungry with good things,
And the rich He has sent away empty.
54 He has helped His aservant Israel,
bIn remembrance of His mercy,
55 aAs He spoke to our bfathers,
To Abraham and to his cseed forever."

56And Mary remained with her about three months, and
returned to her house.

BIRTH OF JOHN THE BAPTIST

57Now Elizabeth's full time came for her to be delivered,
and she brought forth a son. 58When her neighbors and relatives heard how the Lord had shown great mercy to her, they
arejoiced with her.

CIRCUMCISION OF JOHN THE BAPTIST

59So it was, aon the eighth day, that they came to circumcise the child; and they would have called him by the name of
his father, Zacharias. 60His mother answered and said, a"No;
he shall be called John."

61But they said to her, "There is no one among your relatives who is called by this name." 62So they made signs to his
father—what he would have him called.

63And he asked for a writing tablet, and wrote, saying, "His
name is John." So they all marveled. 64Immediately his mouth
was opened and his tongue loosed, and he spoke, praising
God. 65Then fear came on all who dwelt around them; and
all these sayings were discussed throughout all the hill country of Judea. 66And all those who heard them akept them in
their hearts, saying, "What kind of child will this be?" And bthe
hand of the Lord was with him.

ZACHARIAS' PROPHECY

67Now his father Zacharias awas filled with the Holy Spirit,
and prophesied, saying:

68 "Blesseda is the Lord God of Israel,
For bHe has visited and redeemed His people,

1:46 a1 Sam. 2:1–10;
Ps. 34:2, 3;
Hab. 3:18
1:47 aPs. 35:9;
Hab. 3:18
b1 Tim. 1:1; 2:3;
Titus 1:3; 2:10;
3:4; Jude 25
1:48 a1 Sam. 1:11;
Ps. 138:6
bLuke 11:27
1:49 aPs. 71:19;
126:2, 3
bPs. 111:9;
Rev. 4:8
1:50 aGen. 17:7;
Ex. 20:6; 34:6, 7;
Ps. 103:17
1:51
aPs. 98:1; 118:15;
Is. 40:10
bPs. 33:10;
[1 Pet. 5:5]
1:52
a1 Sam. 2:7, 8
1:53 a[Matt. 5:6]
1:54 aIs. 41:8
bPs. 98:3;
[Jer. 31:3]
1:55 aGen. 17:19;
Ps. 132:11;
[Gal. 3:16]
b[Rom. 11:28]
cGen. 17:7
1:58
a[Rom. 12:15]
1:59 aGen. 17:12;
Lev. 12:3;
Luke 2:21;
Phil. 3:5
1:60
aLuke 1:13, 63
1:66 aLuke 2:19
bGen. 39:2;
Acts 11:21
1:67 aJoel 2:28
1:68 a1 Kin. 1:48;
Ps. 106:48
bEx. 3:16

1:46 1Declares the greatness of

69 ^aAnd has raised up a horn of salvation for us
   In the house of His servant David,
70 ^aAs He spoke by the mouth of His holy prophets,
   Who *have been* ^bsince the world began,
71 That we should be saved from our enemies
   And from the hand of all who hate us,
72 ^aTo perform the mercy *promised* to our fathers
   And to remember His holy covenant,
73 ^aThe oath which He swore to our father Abraham:
74 To grant us that we,
   Being delivered from the hand of our enemies,
   Might ^aserve Him without fear,
75 ^aIn holiness and righteousness before Him all the days of
   our life.

76 "And you, child, will be called the ^aprophet of the Highest;
   For ^byou will go before the face of the Lord to prepare
   His ways,
77 To give ^aknowledge of salvation to His people
   By the remission of their sins,
78 Through the tender mercy of our God,
   With which the ¹Dayspring from on high ²has visited us;
79 ^aTo give light to those who sit in darkness and the shadow
   of death,
   To ^bguide our feet into the way of peace."

⁸⁰So ^athe child grew and became strong in spirit, and ^bwas in the deserts till the day of his manifestation to Israel.

CHRIST BORN OF MARY
(Matt. 1:18–25)

2 And it came to pass in those days *that* a decree went out from Caesar Augustus that all the world should be registered. ^{2a}This census first took place while Quirinius was governing Syria. ³So all went to be registered, everyone to his own city.

⁴Joseph also went up from Galilee, out of the city of Nazareth, into Judea, to ^athe city of David, which is called Bethlehem, ^bbecause he was of the house and lineage of David, ⁵to be registered with Mary, ^ahis betrothed ¹wife, who was with child. ⁶So it was, that while they were there, the days were completed for her to be delivered. ⁷And ^ashe brought forth her firstborn Son, and wrapped Him in swaddling cloths, and laid Him in a ¹manger, because there was no room for them in the inn.

GLORY IN THE HIGHEST

⁸Now there were in the same country shepherds living out in the fields, keeping watch over their flock by night. ⁹And ¹behold, an angel of the Lord stood before them, and the glory of the Lord shone around them, ^aand they were greatly afraid. ¹⁰Then the angel said to them, ^a"Do not be afraid, for behold, I bring you good tidings of great joy ^bwhich will be to all people. ^{11a}For there is born to you this day in the city of David ^ba Savior, ^cwho is Christ the Lord. ¹²And this *will be* the sign to you: You will find a Babe wrapped in swaddling cloths, lying in a ¹manger."

1:69
^a2 Sam. 22:3;
Ps. 132:17;
Ezek. 29:21

1:70 ^aJer. 23:5;
Rom. 1:2
^bActs 3:21

1:72 ^aLev. 26:42

1:73 ^aGen. 12:3;
22:16–18;
[Heb. 6:13]

1:74
^a[Rom. 6:18;
Heb. 9:14]

1:75 ^aJer. 32:39;
[Eph. 4:24;
2 Thess. 2:13]

1:76
^aMatt. 3:3; 11:9;
Mark 3:2, 3;
Luke 3:4;
John 1:23
^bIs. 40:3;
Mal. 3:1;
Matt. 11:10

1:77 ^a[Jer. 31:34;
Mark 1:4];
Luke 3:3

1:79 ^aIs. 9:2;
Matt. 4:16;
[Acts 26:18;
2 Cor. 4:6;
Eph. 5:14]
^b[John 10:4;
14:27; 16:33]

1:80 ^aLuke 2:40
^bMatt. 3:1

2:2 ^aDan. 9:25;
Acts 5:37

2:4 ^a1 Sam. 16:1;
Mic. 5:2
^bMatt. 1:16

2:5 ^a[Matt. 1:18]

2:7 ^aMatt. 1:25;
Luke 1:31

2:9 ^aLuke 1:12

2:10
^aLuke 1:13, 30
^bGen. 12:3;
Is. 49:6;
[Matt. 28:19;
Mark 1:15;
Col. 1:23]

2:11 ^aIs. 9:6
^bMatt. 1:21;
John 4:42;
[Acts 5:31]
^cMatt. 1:16;
16:16, 20;
John 11:27;
Acts 2:36;
Phil. 2:11

1:78 ¹Lit. *Dawn;* the Messiah   ²NU *shall visit*   2:5 ¹NU omits *wife*
2:7 ¹*feed trough*   2:9 ¹NU omits *behold*   2:12 ¹*feed trough*

2:13 ᵃGen. 28:12;
Ps. 103:20;
148:2; Dan. 7:10;
[Heb. 1:14];
Rev. 5:11

2:14 ᵃMatt. 21:9;
Luke 19:38;
Eph. 1:6
ᵇIs. 57:19;
[Rom. 5:1];
Eph. 2:17;
[Col. 1:20]
ᶜ[John 3:16;
Eph. 2:4, 7;
2 Thess. 2:16;
1 John 4:9]

2:19 ᵃGen. 37:11;
Luke 1:66

2:20
ᵃLuke 19:37

2:21 ᵃGen. 17:12;
Lev. 12:3
ᵇ[Matt. 1:21]
ᶜLuke 1:31

2:22
ᵃLev. 12:2–8

2:23 ᵃEx. 13:12;
22:29;
Lev. 27:26;
Deut. 18:4;
Neh. 10:36
ᵇEx. 13:2, 12, 15;
Num. 3:13; 8:17

2:24
ᵃLev. 12:2, 8

2:25 ᵃIs. 40:1;
Mark 15:43;
Luke 2:38; 23:51

2:26 ᵃPs. 89:48;
[John 8:51;
Heb. 11:5]

2:27 ᵃMatt. 4:1

2:29
ᵃGen. 46:30;
[Phil. 1:23]

2:30
ᵃPs. 119:166, 174;
[Is. 52:10;
Luke 3:6]

2:32 ᵃIs. 9:2;
42:6; 49:6;
60:1–3;
Matt. 4:16;
Acts 10:45;
13:47; 28:28;
[Rom. 9:24;
Gal. 3:14]

2:34 ᵃIs. 8:14;
Hos. 14:9;
Matt. 21:44;
[Rom. 9:32];
1 Cor. 1:23;
[2 Cor. 2:16;
1 Pet. 2:7, 8]
ᵇMatt. 28:12–15;
Acts 4:2;
17:32; 28:22;
[1 Pet. 2:12;
4:14]

13ᵃAnd suddenly there was with the angel a multitude of the heavenly host praising God and saying:

14 "Glory ᵃto God in the highest,
    And on earth ᵇpeace, ᶜgoodwill[1] toward men!"

15So it was, when the angels had gone away from them into heaven, that the shepherds said to one another, "Let us now go to Bethlehem and see this thing that has come to pass, which the Lord has made known to us." 16And they came with haste and found Mary and Joseph, and the Babe lying in a manger. 17Now when they had seen *Him,* they made [1]widely known the saying which was told them concerning this Child. 18And all those who heard *it* marveled at those things which were told them by the shepherds. 19ᵃBut Mary kept all these things and pondered *them* in her heart. 20Then the shepherds returned, glorifying and ᵃpraising God for all the things that they had heard and seen, as it was told them.

CIRCUMCISION OF JESUS

21ᵃAnd when eight days were completed [1]for the circumcision of the Child, His name was called ᵇJESUS, the name given by the angel ᶜbefore He was conceived in the womb.

JESUS PRESENTED IN THE TEMPLE

22Now when ᵃthe days of her purification according to the law of Moses were completed, they brought Him to Jerusalem to present *Him* to the Lord 23ᵃ(as it is written in the law of the Lord, ᵇ"Every male who opens the womb shall be called holy to the LORD"), 24and to offer a sacrifice according to what is said in the law of the Lord, ᵃ"A pair of turtledoves or two young pigeons."

SIMEON SEES GOD'S SALVATION

25And behold, there was a man in Jerusalem whose name *was* Simeon, and this man *was* just and devout, ᵃwaiting for the Consolation of Israel, and the Holy Spirit was upon him. 26And it had been revealed to him by the Holy Spirit that he would not ᵃsee death before he had seen the Lord's Christ. 27So he came ᵃby the Spirit into the temple. And when the parents brought in the Child Jesus, to do for Him according to the custom of the law, 28he took Him up in his arms and blessed God and said:

29 "Lord, ᵃnow You are letting Your servant depart in peace,
    According to Your word;
30 For my eyes ᵃhave seen Your salvation
31 Which You have prepared before the face of all peoples,
32 ᵃA light to *bring* revelation to the Gentiles,
    And the glory of Your people Israel."

33[1]And Joseph and His mother marveled at those things which were spoken of Him. 34Then Simeon blessed them, and said to Mary His mother, "Behold, this *Child* is destined for the ᵃfall and rising of many in Israel, and for ᵇa sign which will be spoken against 35(yes, ᵃa sword will pierce through your own soul also), that the thoughts of many hearts may be revealed."

2:35 ᵃPs. 42:10; John 19:25

2:14 [1]NU *toward men of goodwill*   **2:17** [1]NU omits *widely*   **2:21** [1]NU *for His circumcision*   **2:33** [1]NU *And His father and mother*

ANNA BEARS WITNESS TO THE REDEEMER

[36]Now there was one, Anna, a prophetess, the daughter of Phanuel, of the tribe of [a]Asher. She was of a great age, and had lived with a husband seven years from her virginity; [37]and this woman *was* a widow [1]of about eighty-four years, who did not depart from the temple, but served *God* with fastings and prayers [a]night and day. [38]And coming in that instant she gave thanks to [1]the Lord, and spoke of Him to all those who [a]looked for redemption in Jerusalem.

THE FAMILY RETURNS TO NAZARETH

[39]So when they had performed all things according to the law of the Lord, they returned to Galilee, to their *own* city, Nazareth. [40][a]And the Child grew and became strong [1]in spirit, filled with wisdom; and the grace of God was upon Him.

THE BOY JESUS AMAZES THE SCHOLARS

[41]His parents went to [a]Jerusalem [b]every year at the Feast of the Passover. [42]And when He was twelve years old, they went up to Jerusalem according to the [a]custom of the feast. [43]When they had finished the [a]days, as they returned, the Boy Jesus lingered behind in Jerusalem. And [1]Joseph and His mother did not know *it;* [44]but supposing Him to have been in the company, they went a day's journey, and sought Him among *their* relatives and acquaintances. [45]So when they did not find Him, they returned to Jerusalem, seeking Him. [46]Now so it was *that* after three days they found Him in the temple, sitting in the midst of the teachers, both listening to them and asking them questions. [47]And [a]all who heard Him were astonished at His understanding and answers. [48]So when they saw Him, they were amazed; and His mother said to Him, "Son, why have You done this to us? Look, Your father and I have sought You anxiously."

[49]And He said to them, "Why did you seek Me? Did you not know that I must be [a]about [b]My Father's business?" [50]But [a]they did not understand the statement which He spoke to them.

JESUS ADVANCES IN WISDOM AND FAVOR

[51]Then He went down with them and came to Nazareth, and was [1]subject to them, but His mother [a]kept all these things in her heart. [52]And Jesus [a]increased in wisdom and stature, [b]and in favor with God and men.

JOHN THE BAPTIST PREPARES THE WAY

(Matt. 3:1–6; Mark 1:2–6; John 1:19–23)

3 Now in the fifteenth year of the reign of Tiberius Caesar, [a]Pontius Pilate being governor of Judea, Herod being tetrarch of Galilee, his brother Philip tetrarch of Iturea and the region of Trachonitis, and Lysanias tetrarch of Abilene, [2][1]while [a]Annas and Caiaphas were high priests, the word of God came to [b]John the son of Zacharias in the wilderness. [3][a]And he went into all the region around the Jordan, preaching a baptism of

2:36
[a]Josh. 19:24

2:37 [a]Acts 26:7;
1 Tim. 5:5

2:38
[a]Lam. 3:25, 26;
Mark 15:43;
Luke 24:21

2:40
[a]Luke 1:80; 2:52;
[1 Cor. 1:24, 30]

2:41 [a]John 4:20
[b]Ex. 23:15,
17; 34:23;
Deut. 16:1, 16;
Luke 22:15

2:42
[a]Ex. 23:14, 15

2:43 [a]Ex. 12:15

2:47
[a]Matt. 7:28;
13:54; 22:33;
Mark 1:22; 6:2;
11:18; Luke 4:32;
John 7:15

2:49 [a]John 9:4
[b][Mark 1:22;
Luke 4:22, 32;
John 4:34;
5:17, 36]

2:50
[a]Mark 9:32;
Luke 9:45;
18:34;
John 7:15, 46

2:51 [a]Dan. 7:28

2:52
[a][Is. 11:2, 3;
Col. 2:2, 3]
[b]1 Sam. 2:26;
[Prov. 3:1–4]

3:1 [a]Matt. 27:2

3:2
[a]John 11:49;
18:13;
Acts 4:6
[b]Luke 1:13

3:3 [a]Matt. 3:1;
Mark 1:4

2:37 [1]NU *until she was eighty-four*   2:38 [1]NU *God*   2:40 [1]NU omits *in spirit*   2:43 [1]NU *His parents*   2:51 [1]*obedient*   3:2 [1]NU, M *in the high priesthood of Annas and Caiaphas*

repentance [b]for the remission of sins, [4]as it is written in the book of the words of Isaiah the prophet, saying:

[a]"The voice of one crying in the wilderness:
'Prepare the way of the LORD;
Make His paths straight.
5 Every valley shall be filled
And every mountain and hill brought low;
The crooked places shall be made straight
And the rough ways smooth;
6 And [a]all flesh shall see the salvation of God.'"

JOHN PREACHES TO THE PEOPLE
(Matt. 3:7–12; Mark 1:7, 8; John 1:24–28)

[7]Then he said to the multitudes that came out to be baptized by him, [a]"Brood[1] of vipers! Who warned you to flee from the wrath to come? [8]Therefore bear fruits [a]worthy of repentance, and do not begin to say to yourselves, 'We have Abraham as *our* father.' For I say to you that God is able to raise up children to Abraham from these stones. [9]And even now the ax is laid to the root of the trees. Therefore [a]every tree which does not bear good fruit is cut down and thrown into the fire."

[10]So the people asked him, saying, [a]"What shall we do then?"

[11]He answered and said to them, [a]"He who has two tunics, let him give to him who has none; and he who has food, [b]let him do likewise."

[12]Then [a]tax collectors also came to be baptized, and said to him, "Teacher, what shall we do?"

[13]And he said to them, [a]"Collect no more than what is appointed for you."

[14]Likewise the soldiers asked him, saying, "And what shall we do?"

So he said to them, "Do not [1]intimidate anyone [a]or accuse falsely, and be content with your wages."

[15]Now as the people were in expectation, and all reasoned in their hearts about John, whether he was the Christ *or not*, [16]John answered, saying to all, [a]"I indeed baptize you with water; but One mightier than I is coming, whose sandal strap I am not worthy to loose. He will [b]baptize you with the Holy Spirit and fire. [17]His winnowing fan *is* in His hand, and He will thoroughly clean out His threshing floor, and [a]gather the wheat into His barn; but the chaff He will burn with unquenchable fire."

[18]And with many other exhortations he preached to the people. [19a]But Herod the tetrarch, being rebuked by him concerning Herodias, his [1]brother Philip's wife, and for all the evils which Herod had done, [20]also added this, above all, that he shut John up in prison.

JOHN BAPTIZES JESUS
(Matt. 3:13–17; Mark 1:9–11; John 1:29–34)

[21]When all the people were baptized, [a]it came to pass that Jesus also was baptized; and while He prayed, the heaven was opened. [22]And the Holy Spirit descended in bodily form like

---

3:3 [b]Luke 1:77

3:4 [a]Is. 40:3–5; Matt. 3:3; Mark 1:3

3:6 [a]Ps. 98:2; Is. 52:10; Luke 2:10; [Rom. 10:8–18]

3:7 [a]Matt. 3:7; 12:34; 23:33

3:8 [a][2 Cor. 7:9–11]

3:9 [a]Matt. 7:19; Luke 13:6–9

3:10 [a]Luke 3:12, 14; [Acts 2:37, 38; 16:30, 31]

3:11 [a]Luke 11:41; 2 Cor. 8:14; James 2:15, 16; [1 John 3:17; 4:20] [b]Is. 58:7; [1 Tim. 6:17, 18]

3:12 [a]Matt. 21:32; Luke 7:29

3:13 [a]Luke 19:8

3:14 [a]Ex. 20:16; 23:1; Lev. 19:11

3:16 [a]Matt. 3:11, 12; Mark 1:7, 8 [b]John 7:39; 20:22; Acts 2:1–4

3:17 [a]Mic. 4:12; Matt. 13:24–30

3:19 [a]Matt. 14:3; Mark 6:17

3:21 [a]Matt. 3:13–17; John 1:32

3:7 [1]Offspring   3:14 [1]Lit. *shake down* for money   3:19 [1]NU *brother's wife*

a dove upon Him, and a voice came from heaven which said, "You are My beloved Son; in You I am ᵃwell pleased."

THE GENEALOGY OF JESUS CHRIST

(Gen. 5:1–32; 11:10–26; Ruth 4:18–22; 1 Chr. 1:1–4, 24–27, 34; 2:1–15; Matt. 1:2–16)

²³Now Jesus Himself began *His ministry at* ᵃabout thirty years of age, being (as was supposed) ᵇ*the* son of Joseph, *the son* of Heli, ²⁴*the son* of Matthat, *the son* of Levi, *the son* of Melchi, *the son* of Janna, *the son* of Joseph, ²⁵*the son* of Mattathiah, *the son* of Amos, *the son* of Nahum, *the son* of Esli, *the son* of Naggai, ²⁶*the son* of Maath, *the son* of Mattathiah, *the son* of Semei, *the son* of Joseph, *the son* of Judah, ²⁷*the son* of Joannas, *the son* of Rhesa, *the son* of ᵃZerubbabel, *the son* of Shealtiel, *the son* of Neri, ²⁸*the son* of Melchi, *the son* of Addi, *the son* of Cosam, *the son* of Elmodam, *the son* of Er, ²⁹*the son* of Jose, *the son* of Eliezer, *the son* of Jorim, *the son* of Matthat, *the son* of Levi, ³⁰*the son* of Simeon, *the son* of Judah, *the son* of Joseph, *the son* of Jonan, *the son* of Eliakim, ³¹*the son* of Melea, *the son* of Menan, *the son* of Mattathah, *the son* of ᵃNathan, ᵇ*the son* of David, ³²ᵃ*the son* of Jesse, *the son* of Obed, *the son* of Boaz, *the son* of Salmon, *the son* of Nahshon, ³³*the son* of Amminadab, *the son* of Ram, *the son* of Hezron, *the son* of Perez, *the son* of Judah, ³⁴*the son* of Jacob, *the son* of Isaac, *the son* of Abraham, ᵃ*the son* of Terah, *the son* of Nahor, ³⁵*the son* of Serug, *the son* of Reu, *the son* of Peleg, *the son* of Eber, *the son* of Shelah, ³⁶ᵃ*the son* of Cainan, *the son* of ᵇArphaxad, ᶜ*the son* of Shem, *the son* of Noah, *the son* of Lamech, ³⁷*the son* of Methuselah, *the son* of Enoch, *the son* of Jared, *the son* of Mahalalel, *the son* of Cainan, ³⁸*the son* of Enosh, *the son* of Seth, *the son* of Adam, ᵃ*the son* of God.

SATAN TEMPTS JESUS

(Matt. 4:1–11; Mark 1:12, 13)

4 Then ᵃJesus, being filled with the Holy Spirit, returned from the Jordan and ᵇwas led by the Spirit ¹into the wilderness, ²being ¹tempted for forty days by the devil. And ᵃin those days He ate nothing, and afterward, when they had ended, He was hungry.

³And the devil said to Him, "If You are ᵃthe Son of God, command this stone to become bread."

⁴But Jesus answered him, saying, "It is written, ᵃ'Man shall not live by bread alone, ¹but by every word of God.'"

⁵¹Then the devil, taking Him up on a high mountain, showed Him all the kingdoms of the world in a moment of time. ⁶And the devil said to Him, "All this authority I will give You, and their glory; for ᵃ*this* has been delivered to me, and I give it to whomever I wish. ⁷Therefore, if You will worship before me, all will be Yours."

⁸And Jesus answered and said to him, ¹"Get behind Me, Satan! ²For it is written, ᵃ'You shall worship the LORD your God, and Him only you shall serve.'"

⁹ᵃThen he brought Him to Jerusalem, set Him on the pinnacle of the temple, and said to Him, "If You are the Son of God, throw Yourself down from here. ¹⁰For it is written:

3:22 ᵃPs. 2:7; [Is. 42:1]; Matt. 3:17; 17:5; Mark 1:11; Luke 1:35; 9:35; 2 Pet. 1:17

3:23 ᵃ[Num. 4:3, 35, 39, 43, 47] ᵇMatt. 13:55; John 6:42

3:27 ᵃEzra 2:2; 3:8

3:31 ᵃZech. 12:12 ᵇ2 Sam. 5:14; 7:12; 1 Chr. 3:5; 17:11; Is. 9:7; Jer. 23:5

3:32 ᵃRuth 4:18–22; 1 Chr. 2:10–12; Is. 11:1, 10

3:34 ᵃGen. 11:24, 26–30; 12:3; Num. 24:17; 1 Chr. 1:24–27

3:36 ᵃGen. 11:12 ᵇGen. 10:22, 24; 11:10–13; 1 Chr. 1:17, 18 ᶜGen. 5:6–32; 9:27; 11:10

3:38 ᵃGen. 5:1, 2

4:1 ᵃ[Is. 11:2; 61:1]; Matt. 4:1–11; Mark 1:12, 13 ᵇEzek. 3:12; Luke 2:27

4:2 ᵃEx. 34:28; 1 Kin. 19:8

4:3 ᵃMark 3:11; John 20:31

4:4 ᵃDeut. 8:3

4:6 ᵃ[John 12:31; 14:30; Rev. 13:2, 7]

4:8 ᵃDeut. 6:13; 10:20; Matt. 4:10

4:9 ᵃMatt. 4:5–7

4:1 ¹NU *in*   4:2 ¹*tested*   4:4 ¹NU omits *but by every word of God*
4:5 ¹NU *And taking Him up, he showed Him*   4:8 ¹NU omits *Get behind Me, Satan*   ²NU, M omit *For*

[a]'He shall give His angels charge over you,
To keep you,'

[11]and,

[a]'In *their* hands they shall bear you up,
Lest you dash your foot against a stone.'"

[12]And Jesus answered and said to him, "It has been said, [a]'You shall not [1]tempt the LORD your God.'"

[13]Now when the devil had ended every [1]temptation, he departed from Him [a]until an opportune time.

JESUS BEGINS HIS GALILEAN MINISTRY
(Matt. 4:12–17; Mark 1:14, 15)

[14a]Then Jesus returned [b]in the power of the Spirit to [c]Galilee, and [d]news of Him went out through all the surrounding region. [15]And He [a]taught in their synagogues, [b]being glorified by all.

JESUS REJECTED AT NAZARETH
(Matt. 13:54–58; Mark 6:1–6)

[16]So He came to [a]Nazareth, where He had been brought up. And as His custom was, [b]He went into the synagogue on the Sabbath day, and stood up to read. [17]And He was handed the book of the prophet Isaiah. And when He had opened the book, He found the place where it was written:

18 "The[a] Spirit of the LORD *is* upon Me,
Because He has anointed Me
To preach the gospel to *the* poor;
He has sent Me [1]to heal the brokenhearted,
To proclaim liberty to *the* captives
And recovery of sight to *the* blind,
To [b]set at liberty those who are [2]oppressed;
19   To proclaim the acceptable year of the LORD."

[20]Then He closed the book, and gave *it* back to the attendant and sat down. And the eyes of all who were in the synagogue were fixed on Him. [21]And He began to say to them, "Today this Scripture is [a]fulfilled in your hearing." [22]So all bore witness to Him, and [a]marveled at the gracious words which proceeded out of His mouth. And they said, [b]"Is this not Joseph's son?"

[23]He said to them, "You will surely say this proverb to Me, 'Physician, heal yourself! Whatever we have heard done in [a]Capernaum,[1] do also here in [b]Your country.'" [24]Then He said, "Assuredly, I say to you, no [a]prophet is accepted in his own country. [25]But I tell you truly, [a]many widows were in Israel in the days of Elijah, when the heaven was shut up three years and six months, and there was a great famine throughout all the land; [26]but to none of them was Elijah sent except to [1]Zarephath, *in the region* of Sidon, to a woman *who was* a widow. [27a]And many lepers were in Israel in the time of Elisha the prophet, and none of them was cleansed except Naaman the Syrian."

[28]So all those in the synagogue, when they heard these things, were [a]filled with [1]wrath, [29a]and rose up and thrust Him out of the city; and they led Him to the brow of the hill on

---

Cross References (margin)

4:10 [a]Ps. 91:11
4:11 [a]Ps. 91:12
4:12 [a]Deut. 6:16
4:13
[a][John 14:30; Heb. 4:15; James 4:7]
4:14 [a]Matt. 4:12
[b]John 4:43
[c]Acts 10:37
[d]Matt. 4:24
4:15 [a]Ps. 22:22; Matt. 4:23
[b]Is. 52:13
4:16 [a]Matt. 2:23; 13:54; Mark 6:1
[b]Mark 1:21; John 18:20; Acts 13:14–16; 17:2
4:18
[a]Is. 49:8, 9; 61:1, 2; Matt. 11:5; 12:18; John 3:34
[b][Dan. 9:24]
4:21
[a]Matt. 1:22, 23; Acts 13:29
4:22 [a][Ps. 45:2]; Matt. 13:54; Mark 6:2; Luke 2:47; [John 1:14, 17]
[b]John 6:42
4:23
[a]Matt. 4:13; 11:23
[b]Matt. 13:54; Mark 6:1
4:24
[a]Matt. 13:57; Mark 6:4; John 4:44
4:25 [a]1 Kin. 17:9; James 5:17
4:27
[a]2 Kin. 5:1–14
4:28 [a]Luke 6:11
4:29
[a]Luke 17:25; John 8:37; 10:31

4:12 [1]test   4:13 [1]testing   4:18 [1]NU omits *to heal the brokenhearted* [2]*downtrodden*   4:23 [1]NU *Capharnaum,* here and elsewhere
4:26 [1]Gr. *Sarepta*   4:28 [1]*rage*

which their city was built, that they might throw Him down over the cliff. 30Then apassing through the midst of them, He went His way.

JESUS CASTS OUT AN UNCLEAN SPIRIT
(Mark 1:21–28)

31Then aHe went down to Capernaum, a city of Galilee, and was teaching them on the Sabbaths. 32And they were aastonished at His teaching, bfor His word was with authority. 33aNow in the synagogue there was a man who had a spirit of an unclean demon. And he cried out with a loud voice, 34saying, "Let us alone! What have we to do with You, Jesus of Nazareth? Did You come to destroy us? aI know who You are—bthe Holy One of God!"

35But Jesus rebuked him, saying, 1"Be quiet, and come out of him!" And when the demon had thrown him in their midst, it came out of him and did not hurt him. 36Then they were all amazed and spoke among themselves, saying, "What a word this is! For with authority and power He commands the unclean spirits, and they come out." 37And the report about Him went out into every place in the surrounding region.

PETER'S MOTHER-IN-LAW HEALED
(Matt. 8:14, 15; Mark 1:29–31)

38aNow He arose from the synagogue and entered Simon's house. But Simon's wife's mother was 1sick with a high fever, and they bmade request of Him concerning her. 39So He stood over her and arebuked the fever, and it left her. And immediately she arose and served them.

MANY HEALED AFTER SABBATH SUNSET
(Matt. 8:16, 17; Mark 1:32–34)

40aWhen the sun was setting, all those who had any that were sick with various diseases brought them to Him; and He laid His hands on every one of them and healed them. 41aAnd demons also came out of many, crying out and saying, b"You are 1the Christ, the Son of God!"

And He, crebuking them, did not allow them to 2speak, for they knew that He was the Christ.

JESUS PREACHES IN GALILEE
(Matt. 4:23–25; Mark 1:35–39)

42aNow when it was day, He departed and went into a deserted place. And the crowd sought Him and came to Him, and tried to keep Him from leaving them; 43but He said to them, "I must apreach the kingdom of God to the other cities also, because for this purpose I have been sent." 44aAnd He was preaching in the synagogues of 1Galilee.

FOUR FISHERMEN CALLED AS DISCIPLES
(Matt. 4:18–22; Mark 1:16–20)

5 So ait was, as the multitude pressed about Him to bhear the word of God, that He stood by the Lake of Gennesaret, 2and saw two boats standing by the lake; but the fishermen

---

4:30
aJohn 8:59;
10:39

4:31 aIs. 9:1;
Matt. 4:13;
Mark 1:21

4:32
aMatt. 7:28, 29
bLuke 4:36;
[John 6:63;
7:46; 8:26, 28,
38, 47; 12:49,
50]

4:33 aMark 1:23

4:34 aLuke 4:41
bPs. 16:10;
Is. 49:7;
Dan. 9:24;
Luke 1:35

4:38
aMatt. 8:14, 15;
Mark 1:29–31
bMark 5:23

4:39 aLuke 8:24

4:40
aMatt. 8:16, 17;
Mark 1:32–34

4:41 aMark 1:34;
3:11; Acts 8:7
bMark 8:29
cMark 1:25, 34;
3:11; Luke 4:34,
35

4:42
aMark 1:35–38;
Luke 9:10

4:43 aMark 1:14;
[John 9:4]

4:44
aMatt. 4:23;
9:35; Mark 1:39

5:1
aMatt. 4:18–22;
Mark 1:16–20;
John 1:40–42
bActs 13:44

4:35 1Lit. Be muzzled   4:38 1afflicted with   4:41 1NU omits the Christ
2Or say that they knew   4:44 1NU Judea

had gone from them and were washing *their* nets. ³Then He got into one of the boats, which was Simon's, and asked him to put out a little from the land. And He ªsat down and taught the multitudes from the boat.

⁴When He had stopped speaking, He said to Simon, ª"Launch out into the deep and let down your nets for a catch."

⁵But Simon answered and said to Him, "Master, we have toiled all night and caught ªnothing; nevertheless ᵇat Your word I will let down the net." ⁶And when they had done this, they caught a great number of fish, and their net was breaking. ⁷So they signaled to *their* partners in the other boat to come and help them. And they came and filled both the boats, so that they began to sink. ⁸When Simon Peter saw *it,* he fell down at Jesus' knees, saying, ª"Depart from me, for I am a sinful man, O Lord!"

⁹For he and all who were with him were ªastonished at the catch of fish which they had taken; ¹⁰and so also *were* James and John, the sons of Zebedee, who were partners with Simon. And Jesus said to Simon, "Do not be afraid. ªFrom now on you will catch men." ¹¹So when they had brought their boats to land, ªthey ¹forsook all and followed Him.

JESUS CLEANSES A LEPER
(Matt. 8:1–4; Mark 1:40–45)

¹²ªAnd it happened when He was in a certain city, that behold, a man who was full of ᵇleprosy saw Jesus; and he fell on *his* face and ¹implored Him, saying, "Lord, if You are willing, You can make me clean."

¹³Then He put out *His* hand and touched him, saying, "I am willing; be cleansed." ªImmediately the leprosy left him. ¹⁴ªAnd He charged him to tell no one, "But go and show yourself to the priest, and make an offering for your cleansing, as a testimony to them, ᵇjust as Moses commanded."

¹⁵However, ªthe report went around concerning Him all the more; and ᵇgreat multitudes came together to hear, and to be healed by Him of their infirmities. ¹⁶ªSo He Himself *often* withdrew into the wilderness and ᵇprayed.

JESUS FORGIVES AND HEALS A PARALYTIC
(Matt. 9:2–8; Mark 2:1–12)

¹⁷Now it happened on a certain day, as He was teaching, that there were Pharisees and teachers of the law sitting by, who had come out of every town of Galilee, Judea, and Jerusalem. And the power of the Lord was *present* ¹to heal them. ¹⁸ªThen behold, men brought on a bed a man who was paralyzed, whom they sought to bring in and lay before Him. ¹⁹And when they could not find how they might bring him in, because of the crowd, they went up on the housetop and let him down with *his* bed through the tiling into the midst ªbefore Jesus.

²⁰When He saw their faith, He said to him, "Man, your sins are forgiven you."

²¹ªAnd the scribes and the Pharisees began to reason, saying, "Who is this who speaks blasphemies? ᵇWho can forgive sins but God alone?"

5:3 ªJohn 8:2
5:4 ªJohn 21:6
5:5 ªJohn 21:3 ᵇPs. 33:9
5:8 ª2 Sam. 6:9; 1 Kin. 17:18
5:9 ªMark 5:42; 10:24, 26
5:10 ªMatt. 4:19; Mark 1:17
5:11 ªMatt. 4:20; 19:27; [Mark 1:18; 8:34, 35; Luke 9:59–62]; John 12:26
5:12 ªMatt. 8:2–4; Mark 1:40–44 ᵇLev. 13:14
5:13 ªMatt. 20:34; Luke 8:44; John 5:9
5:14 ªMatt. 8:4; Luke 17:14 ᵇLev. 13:1–3; 14:2–32
5:15 ªMark 1:45 ᵇMatt. 4:25; Mark 3:7; John 6:2
5:16 ªLuke 9:10 ᵇMatt. 14:23; Mark 1:35; Luke 6:12; 9:18; 11:1
5:18 ªMatt. 9:2–8; Mark 2:3–12
5:19 ªMatt. 15:30
5:21 ªMatt. 9:3; 26:65; Mark 2:6, 7; John 10:33 ᵇPs. 32:5; 130:4; Is. 43:25

[22]But when Jesus [a]perceived their thoughts, He answered and said to them, "Why are you reasoning in your hearts? [23]Which is easier, to say, 'Your sins are forgiven you,' or to say, 'Rise up and walk'? [24]But that you may know that the Son of Man has power on earth to forgive sins"—He said to the man who was paralyzed, [a]"I say to you, arise, take up your bed, and go to your house."

[25]Immediately he rose up before them, took up what he had been lying on, and departed to his own house, [a]glorifying God. [26]And they were all amazed, and they [a]glorified God and were filled with fear, saying, "We have seen strange things today!"

MATTHEW THE TAX COLLECTOR
(Matt. 9:9–13; Mark 2:13–17)

[27a]After these things He went out and saw a tax collector named Levi, sitting at the tax office. And He said to him, [b]"Follow Me." [28]So he left all, rose up, and [a]followed Him.

[29a]Then Levi gave Him a great feast in his own house. And [b]there were a great number of tax collectors and others who sat down with them. [30 1]And their scribes and the Pharisees [2]complained against His disciples, saying, [a]"Why do You eat and drink with tax collectors and sinners?"

[31]Jesus answered and said to them, "Those who are well have no need of a physician, but those who are sick. [32a]I have not come to call *the* righteous, but sinners, to repentance."

JESUS IS QUESTIONED ABOUT FASTING
(Matt. 9:14–17; Mark 2:18–22)

[33]Then they said to Him, [a]"Why[1] do the disciples of John fast often and make prayers, and likewise those of the Pharisees, but Yours eat and drink?"

[34]And He said to them, "Can you make the friends of the bridegroom fast while the [a]bridegroom is with them? [35]But the days will come when the bridegroom will be taken away from them; then they will fast in those days."

[36a]Then He spoke a parable to them: "No one [1]puts a piece from a new garment on an old one; otherwise the new makes a tear, and also the piece that was *taken* out of the new does not match the old. [37]And no one puts new wine into old wineskins; or else the new wine will burst the wineskins and be spilled, and the wineskins will be ruined. [38]But new wine must be put into new wineskins, [1]and both are preserved. [39]And no one, having drunk old *wine*, [1]immediately desires new; for he says, 'The old is [2]better.'"

JESUS IS LORD OF THE SABBATH
(Matt. 12:1–8; Mark 2:23–28)

6 Now [a]it happened [1]on the second Sabbath after the first that He went through the grainfields. And His disciples plucked the heads of grain and ate *them*, rubbing *them* in *their*

5:22 [a]Luke 9:47; John 2:25

5:24 [a]Mark 2:11; 5:41; Luke 7:14

5:25 [a]Luke 17:15, 18; Acts 3:8

5:26 [a]Luke 1:65; 7:16

5:27 [a]Matt. 9:9–17; Mark 2:13–22 [b][Mark 8:34]; Luke 9:59; John 12:26; 21:19, 22

5:28 [a]Matt. 4:22; 19:27; Mark 10:28

5:29 [a]Matt. 9:9, 10; Mark 2:15 [b]Luke 15:1

5:30 [a]Matt. 11:19; Luke 15:2; Acts 23:9

5:32 [a]Matt. 9:13; 1 Tim. 1:15

5:33 [a]Matt. 9:14; Mark 2:18; Luke 7:33

5:34 [a]John 3:29

5:36 [a]Matt. 9:16, 17; Mark 2:21, 22

6:1 [a]Matt. 12:1–8; Mark 2:23–28

5:30 [1]NU *But the Pharisees and their scribes* [2]*grumbled*   5:33 [1]NU omits *Why do,* making the verse a statement   5:36 [1]NU *tears a piece from a new garment and puts it on an old one*   5:38 [1]NU omits *and both are preserved* 5:39 [1]NU omits *immediately* [2]NU *good*   6:1 [1]NU *on a Sabbath that He went*

hands. 2And some of the Pharisees said to them, "Why are you doing ªwhat is not lawful to do on the Sabbath?"

3But Jesus answering them said, "Have you not even read this, ªwhat David did when he was hungry, he and those who were with him: 4how he went into the house of God, took and ate the showbread, and also gave some to those with him, ªwhich is not lawful for any but the priests to eat?" 5And He said to them, "The Son of Man is also Lord of the Sabbath."

HEALING ON THE SABBATH
(Matt. 12:9–14; Mark 3:1–6)

6ªNow it happened on another Sabbath, also, that He entered the synagogue and taught. And a man was there whose right hand was withered. 7So the scribes and Pharisees watched Him closely, whether He would ªheal on the Sabbath, that they might find an ᵇaccusation against Him. 8But He ªknew their thoughts, and said to the man who had the withered hand, "Arise and stand here." And he arose and stood. 9Then Jesus said to them, "I will ask you one thing: ªIs it lawful on the Sabbath to do good or to do evil, to save life or 1to destroy?" 10And when He had looked around at them all, He said to 1the man, "Stretch out your hand." And he did so, and his hand was restored 2as whole as the other. 11But they were filled with rage, and discussed with one another what they might do to Jesus.

THE TWELVE APOSTLES
(Matt. 10:1–4; Mark 3:13–19)

12Now it came to pass in those days that He went out to the mountain to pray, and continued all night in ªprayer to God. 13And when it was day, He called His disciples to *Himself;* ªand from them He chose ᵇtwelve whom He also named apostles: 14Simon, ªwhom He also named Peter, and Andrew his brother; James and John; Philip and Bartholomew; 15Matthew and Thomas; James the *son* of Alphaeus, and Simon called the Zealot; 16Judas ªthe son of James, and ᵇJudas Iscariot who also became a traitor.

JESUS HEALS A GREAT MULTITUDE
(cf. Matt. 4:24, 25; Mark 3:7–12)

17And He came down with them and stood on a level place with a crowd of His disciples ªand a great multitude of people from all Judea and Jerusalem, and from the seacoast of Tyre and Sidon, who came to hear Him and be healed of their diseases, 18as well as those who were tormented with unclean spirits. And they were healed. 19And the whole multitude ªsought to ᵇtouch Him, for ᶜpower went out from Him and healed *them* all.

THE BEATITUDES
(Matt. 5:1–12)

20Then He lifted up His eyes toward His disciples, and said:

ª"Blessed *are you* poor,
For yours is the kingdom of God.

6:2 ªEx. 20:10
6:3 ª1 Sam. 21:6
6:4 ªLev. 24:9
6:6
ªMatt. 12:9–14;
Mark 3:1–6;
Luke 13:14; 14:3;
John 9:16
6:7
ªLuke 13:14;
14:1–6
ᵇLuke 20:20
6:8 ªMatt. 9:4;
John 2:24, 25
6:9 ªJohn 7:23
6:12
ªMatt. 14:23;
Mark 1:35;
Luke 5:16;
9:18; 11:1
6:13 ªJohn 6:70
ᵇMatt. 10:1
6:14 ªJohn 1:42
6:16 ªJude 1
ᵇLuke 22:3–6
6:17 ªMatt. 4:25;
Mark 3:7, 8
6:19
ªMatt. 9:21;
14:36;
Mark 3:10
ᵇMark 5:27, 28;
Luke 8:44–47
ᶜMark 5:30;
Luke 8:46
6:20
ªMatt. 5:3–12;
[11:5];
Luke 6:20–23;
[James 2:5]

6:9 ¹M *to kill*   6:10 ¹NU, M *him*   ²NU omits *as whole as the other*

21 ᵃBlessed *are you* who hunger now,
　　For you shall be ᵇfilled.¹
　ᶜBlessed *are you* who weep now,
　　For you shall ᵈlaugh.
22 ᵃBlessed are you when men hate you,
　　And when they ᵇexclude you,
　　And revile *you*, and cast out your name as evil,
　　For the Son of Man's sake.
23 ᵃRejoice in that day and leap for joy!
　　For indeed your reward *is* great in heaven,
　　For ᵇin like manner their fathers did to the prophets.

JESUS PRONOUNCES WOES

24 "Butᵃ woe to you ᵇwho are rich,
　　For ᶜyou have received your consolation.
25 ᵃWoe to you who are full,
　　For you shall hunger.
　ᵇWoe to you who laugh now,
　　For you shall mourn and ᶜweep.
26 ᵃWoe ¹to you when ²all men speak well of you,
　　For so did their fathers to the false prophets.

LOVE YOUR ENEMIES
(Matt. 5:38–48)

27ᵃ"But I say to you who hear: Love your enemies, do good to those who hate you, 28ᵃbless those who curse you, and ᵇpray for those who spitefully use you. 29ᵃTo him who strikes you on the *one* cheek, offer the other also. ᵇAnd from him who takes away your cloak, do not withhold *your* tunic either. 30ᵃGive to everyone who asks of you. And from him who takes away your goods do not ask *them* back. 31ᵃAnd just as you want men to do to you, you also do to them likewise.

32ᵃ"But if you love those who love you, what credit is that to you? For even sinners love those who love them. 33And if you do good to those who do good to you, what credit is that to you? For even sinners do the same. 34ᵃAnd if you lend *to those* from whom you hope to receive back, what credit is that to you? For even sinners lend to sinners to receive as much back. 35But ᵃlove your enemies, ᵇdo good, and ᶜlend, ¹hoping for nothing in return; and your reward will be great, and ᵈyou will be sons of the Most High. For He is kind to the unthankful and evil. 36ᵃTherefore be merciful, just as your Father also is merciful.

DO NOT JUDGE
(Matt. 7:1–5)

37ᵃ"Judge not, and you shall not be judged. Condemn not, and you shall not be condemned. ᵇForgive, and you will be forgiven. 38ᵃGive, and it will be given to you: good measure, pressed down, shaken together, and running over will be put into your ᵇbosom. For ᶜwith the same measure that you use, it will be measured back to you."

39And He spoke a parable to them: ᵃ"Can the blind lead the blind? Will they not both fall into the ditch? 40ᵃA disciple is not

6:39 ᵃMatt. 15:14; 23:16; Rom. 2:19　6:40 ᵃMatt. 10:24; [John 13:16; 15:20]

6:21 ¹satisfied　6:26 ¹NU, M omit *to you*　²M omits *all*　6:35 ¹expecting

---

6:21
ᵃIs. 55:1; 65:13;
Matt. 5:6
ᵇ[Rev. 7:16]
ᶜ[Is. 61:3;
Rev. 7:17]
ᵈPs. 126:5

6:22
ᵃMatt. 5:11;
1 Pet. 2:19; 3:14;
4:14 ᵇ[John 16:2]

6:23 ᵃMatt. 5:12;
Acts 5:41;
[Col. 1:24];
James 1:2
ᵇActs 7:51

6:24 ᵃAmos 6:1;
Luke 12:21;
James 5:1–6
ᵇLuke 12:21
ᶜMatt. 6:2, 5, 16;
Luke 16:25

6:25 ᵃ[Is. 65:13]
ᵇ[Prov. 14:13]
ᶜJames 4:9

6:26
ᵃ[John 15:19;
1 John 4:5]

6:27 ᵃEx. 23:4;
Prov. 25:21;
Matt. 5:44;
Rom. 12:20

6:28
ᵃRom. 12:14
ᵇLuke 23:24;
Acts 7:60

6:29
ᵃMatt. 5:39–42
ᵇ[1 Cor. 6:7]

6:30
ᵃDeut. 15:7, 8;
Prov. 3:27; 21:26;
Matt. 5:42

6:31 ᵃMatt. 7:12

6:32 ᵃMatt. 5:46

6:34 ᵃMatt. 5:42

6:35
ᵃ[Rom. 13:10]
ᵇHeb. 13:16
ᶜLev. 25:35–37;
Ps. 37:26
ᵈMatt. 5:46

6:36
ᵃMatt. 5:48;
Eph. 4:32

6:37
ᵃMatt. 7:1–5;
Rom. 14:4;
[1 Cor. 4:5]
ᵇMatt. 18:21–35

6:38
ᵃ[Prov. 19:17;
28:27]
ᵇPs. 79:12;
Is. 65:6, 7;
Jer. 32:18
ᶜMatt. 7:2;
Mark 4:24;
James 2:13

above his teacher, but everyone who is perfectly trained will be like his teacher. [41a]And why do you look at the speck in your brother's eye, but do not perceive the plank in your own eye? [42]Or how can you say to your brother, 'Brother, let me remove the speck that *is* in your eye,' when you yourself do not see the plank that *is* in your own eye? Hypocrite! First remove the plank from your own eye, and then you will see clearly to remove the speck that is in your brother's eye.

A TREE IS KNOWN BY ITS FRUIT
(Matt. 7:15–20)

[43a]"For a good tree does not bear bad fruit, nor does a bad tree bear good fruit. [44]For [a]every tree is known by its own fruit. For *men* do not gather figs from thorns, nor do they gather grapes from a bramble bush. [45a]A good man out of the good treasure of his heart brings forth good; and an evil man out of the evil [1]treasure of his heart brings forth evil. For out [b]of the abundance of the heart his mouth speaks.

BUILD ON THE ROCK
(Matt. 7:21–27)

[46a]"But why do you call Me 'Lord, Lord,' and not do the things which I say? [47a]Whoever comes to Me, and hears My sayings and does them, I will show you whom he is like: [48]He is like a man building a house, who dug deep and laid the foundation on the rock. And when the flood arose, the stream beat vehemently against that house, and could not shake it, for it was [1]founded on the rock. [49]But he who heard and did nothing is like a man who built a house on the earth without a foundation, against which the stream beat vehemently; and immediately it [1]fell. And the ruin of that house was great."

JESUS HEALS A CENTURION'S SERVANT
(Matt. 8:5–13)

7 Now when He concluded all His sayings in the hearing of the people, He [a]entered Capernaum. [2]And a certain centurion's servant, who was dear to him, was sick and ready to die. [3]So when he heard about Jesus, he sent elders of the Jews to Him, pleading with Him to come and heal his servant. [4]And when they came to Jesus, they begged Him earnestly, saying that the one for whom He should do this was deserving, [5]"for he loves our nation, and has built us a synagogue."

[6]Then Jesus went with them. And when He was already not far from the house, the centurion sent friends to Him, saying to Him, "Lord, do not trouble Yourself, for I am not worthy that You should enter under my roof. [7]Therefore I did not even think myself worthy to come to You. But [a]say the word, and my servant will be healed. [8]For I also am a man placed under [a]authority, having soldiers under me. And I say to one, 'Go,' and he goes; and to another, 'Come,' and he comes; and to my servant, 'Do this,' and he does *it.*"

[9]When Jesus heard these things, He marveled at him, and

6:41 [a]Matt. 7:3

6:43
[a]Matt. 7:16–
18, 20

6:44
[a]Matt. 12:33

6:45
[a]Matt. 12:35
[b]Prov. 15:2, 28;
16:23; 18:21;
Matt. 12:34

6:46 [a]Mal. 1:6;
Matt. 7:21; 25:11;
Luke 13:25

6:47
[a]Matt. 7:24–27;
[John 14:21];
James 1:22–25

7:1 [a]Matt. 8:5–13

7:7 [a]Ps. 33:9;
107:20

7:8
[a][Mark 13:34]

6:45 [1]NU omits *treasure of his heart*   6:48 [1]NU *well built*
6:49 [1]NU *collapsed*

turned around and said to the crowd that followed Him, "I say to you, I have not found such great faith, not even in Israel!" ¹⁰And those who were sent, returning to the house, found the servant well ¹who had been sick.

JESUS RAISES THE SON OF THE WIDOW OF NAIN

¹¹Now it happened, the day after, *that* He went into a city called Nain; and many of His disciples went with Him, and a large crowd. ¹²And when He came near the gate of the city, behold, a dead man was being carried out, the only son of his mother; and she was a widow. And a large crowd from the city was with her. ¹³When the Lord saw her, He had ªcompassion on her and said to her, ᵇ"Do not weep." ¹⁴Then He came and touched the open coffin, and those who carried *him* stood still. And He said, "Young man, I say to you, ªarise." ¹⁵So he who was dead ªsat up and began to speak. And He ᵇpresented him to his mother.

¹⁶ªThen fear ¹came upon all, and they ᵇglorified God, saying, ᶜ"A great prophet has risen up among us"; and, ᵈ"God has visited His people." ¹⁷And this report about Him went throughout all Judea and all the surrounding region.

JOHN THE BAPTIST SENDS MESSENGERS TO JESUS
(Matt. 11:2–19)

¹⁸ªThen the disciples of John reported to him concerning all these things. ¹⁹And John, calling two of his disciples to *him,* sent *them* to ¹Jesus, saying, "Are You ªthe Coming One, or ²do we look for another?"

²⁰When the men had come to Him, they said, "John the Baptist has sent us to You, saying, 'Are You the Coming One, or do we look for another?'" ²¹And that very hour He cured many of ¹infirmities, afflictions, and evil spirits; and to many blind He gave sight.

²²ªJesus answered and said to them, "Go and tell John the things you have seen and heard: ᵇthat *the* blind ᶜsee, *the* lame ᵈwalk, *the* lepers are ᵉcleansed, *the* deaf ᶠhear, *the* dead are raised, ᵍ*the* poor have the gospel preached to them. ²³And blessed is *he* who is not ¹offended because of Me."

²⁴ªWhen the messengers of John had departed, He began to speak to the multitudes concerning John: "What did you go out into the wilderness to see? A reed shaken by the wind? ²⁵But what did you go out to see? A man clothed in soft garments? Indeed those who are gorgeously appareled and live in luxury are in kings' courts. ²⁶But what did you go out to see? A prophet? Yes, I say to you, and more than a prophet. ²⁷This is *he* of whom it is written:

ª'Behold, I send My messenger before Your face,
Who will prepare Your way before You.'

²⁸For I say to you, among those born of women there is ¹not a ªgreater prophet than John the Baptist; but he who is least in the kingdom of God is greater than he."

²⁹And when all the people heard *Him,* even the tax collectors ¹justified God, ªhaving been baptized with the baptism

---

7:13 ªLam. 3:32;
John 11:35;
[Heb. 4:15]
ᵇLuke 8:52

7:14 ªMark 5:41;
Luke 8:54;
John 11:43;
Acts 9:40;
[Rom. 4:17]

7:15 ªMatt. 11:5;
Luke 8:55;
John 11:44
ᵇ1 Kin. 17:23;
2 Kin. 4:36

7:16 ªLuke 1:65
ᵇLuke 5:26
ᶜLuke 24:19;
John 4:19;
6:14; 9:17
ᵈLuke 1:68

7:18
ªMatt. 11:2–19

7:19
ª[Mic. 5:2;
Zech. 9:9;
Mal. 3:1–3]

7:22 ªMatt. 11:4
ᵇIs. 35:5
ᶜJohn 9:7
ᵈMatt. 15:31
ᵉLuke 17:12–14
ᶠMark 7:37
ᵍ[Is. 61:1–3;
Luke 4:18]

7:24 ªMatt. 11:7

7:27 ªIs. 40:3;
Mal. 3:1;
Matt. 11:10;
Mark 1:2

7:28 ª[Luke 1:15]

7:29 ªMatt. 3:5;
Luke 3:12

7:10 ¹NU omits *who had been sick*   7:16 ¹*seized them all*   7:19 ¹NU *the Lord*
²*should we expect*   7:21 ¹*illnesses*   7:23 ¹*caused to stumble*   7:28 ¹NU *none greater than John;*   7:29 ¹*declared the righteousness of*

of John. ³⁰But the Pharisees and ¹lawyers rejected ^athe will of God for themselves, not having been baptized by him.

³¹¹And the Lord said, ^a"To what then shall I liken the men of this generation, and what are they like? ³²They are like children sitting in the marketplace and calling to one another, saying:

'We played the flute for you,
　And you did not dance;
We mourned to you,
　And you did not weep.'

³³For ^aJohn the Baptist came ^bneither eating bread nor drinking wine, and you say, 'He has a demon.' ³⁴The Son of Man has come ^aeating and drinking, and you say, 'Look, a glutton and a ¹winebibber, a friend of tax collectors and sinners!' ^{35a}But wisdom is justified by all her children."

A SINFUL WOMAN FORGIVEN

^{36a}Then one of the Pharisees asked Him to eat with him. And He went to the Pharisee's house, and sat down to eat. ³⁷And behold, a woman in the city who was a sinner, when she knew that *Jesus* sat at the table in the Pharisee's house, brought an alabaster flask of fragrant oil, ³⁸and stood at His feet behind *Him* weeping; and she began to wash His feet with her tears, and wiped *them* with the hair of her head; and she kissed His feet and anointed *them* with the fragrant oil. ³⁹Now when the Pharisee who had invited Him saw *this,* he spoke to himself, saying, ^a"This Man, if He were a prophet, would know who and what manner of woman *this is* who is touching Him, for she is a sinner."

⁴⁰And Jesus answered and said to him, "Simon, I have something to say to you."

So he said, "Teacher, say it."

⁴¹"There was a certain creditor who had two debtors. One owed five hundred ^adenarii, and the other fifty. ⁴²And when they had nothing with which to repay, he freely forgave them both. Tell Me, therefore, which of them will love him more?"

⁴³Simon answered and said, "I suppose the *one* whom he forgave more."

And He said to him, "You have rightly judged." ⁴⁴Then He turned to the woman and said to Simon, "Do you see this woman? I entered your house; you gave Me no ^awater for My feet, but she has washed My feet with her tears and wiped *them* with the hair of her head. ⁴⁵You gave Me no ^akiss, but this woman has not ceased to kiss My feet since the time I came in. ^{46a}You did not anoint My head with oil, but this woman has anointed My feet with fragrant oil. ^{47a}Therefore I say to you, her sins, which *are* many, are forgiven, for she loved much. But to whom little is forgiven, *the same* loves little."

⁴⁸Then He said to her, ^a"Your sins are forgiven."

⁴⁹And those who sat at the table with Him began to say to themselves, ^a"Who is this who even forgives sins?"

⁵⁰Then He said to the woman, ^a"Your faith has saved you. Go in peace."

Cross-references

7:30 ^aActs 20:27
7:31 ^aMatt. 11:16
7:33 ^aMatt. 3:1 ^b[Matt. 3:4]; Luke 1:15
7:34 ^aLuke 15:2
7:35 ^aMatt. 11:19
7:36 ^aMatt. 26:6; Mark 14:3; John 11:2
7:39 ^aLuke 15:2
7:41 ^aMatt. 18:28; Mark 6:37
7:44 ^aGen. 18:4; 19:2; 43:24; Judg. 19:21; 1 Tim. 5:10
7:45 ^aRom. 16:16
7:46 ^a2 Sam. 12:20; Ps. 23:5; Eccl. 9:8; Dan. 10:3
7:47 ^a[1 Tim. 1:14]
7:48 ^aMatt. 9:2; Mark 2:5
7:49 ^aMatt. 9:3; [Mark 2:7]; Luke 5:21
7:50 ^aMatt. 9:22; Mark 5:34; 10:52; Luke 8:48; 18:42

7:30 ¹the experts in the law　　7:31 ¹NU, M omit *And the Lord said*
7:34 ¹An excessive drinker

MANY WOMEN MINISTER TO JESUS

8 Now it came to pass, afterward, that He went through every city and village, preaching and [1]bringing the glad tidings of the kingdom of God. And the twelve *were* with Him, [2]and [a]certain women who had been healed of evil spirits and [1]infirmities—Mary called Magdalene, [b]out of whom had come seven demons, [3]and Joanna the wife of Chuza, Herod's steward, and Susanna, and many others who provided for [1]Him from their [2]substance.

THE PARABLE OF THE SOWER
(Matt. 13:1–9; Mark 4:1–9)

[4][a]And when a great multitude had gathered, and they had come to Him from every city, He spoke by a parable: [5]"A sower went out to sow his seed. And as he sowed, some fell by the wayside; and it was trampled down, and the birds of the air devoured it. [6]Some fell on rock; and as soon as it sprang up, it withered away because it lacked moisture. [7]And some fell among thorns, and the thorns sprang up with it and choked it. [8]But others fell on good ground, sprang up, and yielded [1]a crop a hundredfold." When He had said these things He cried, [a]"He who has ears to hear, let him hear!"

THE PURPOSE OF PARABLES
(Matt. 13:10–17; Mark 4:10–12)

[9][a]Then His disciples asked Him, saying, "What does this parable mean?"

[10]And He said, "To you it has been given to know the [1]mysteries of the kingdom of God, but to the rest *it is given* in parables, that

[a]'Seeing they may not see,
And hearing they may not understand.'

THE PARABLE OF THE SOWER EXPLAINED
(Matt. 13:18–23; Mark 4:13–20)

[11][a]"Now the parable is this: The seed is the [b]word of God. [12]Those by the wayside are the ones who hear; then the devil comes and takes away the word out of their hearts, lest they should believe and be saved. [13]But the ones on the rock *are* those who, when they hear, receive the word with joy; and these have no root, who believe for a while and in time of [1]temptation fall away. [14]Now the ones *that* fell among thorns are those who, when they have heard, go out and are choked with cares, [a]riches, and pleasures of life, and bring no fruit to maturity. [15]But the ones *that* fell on the good ground are those who, having heard the word with a noble and good heart, keep *it* and bear fruit with [a]patience.[1]

THE PARABLE OF THE REVEALED LIGHT
(Mark 4:21–25)

[16][a]"No one, when he has lit a lamp, covers it with a vessel or puts *it* under a bed, but sets *it* on a lampstand, that those

8:2
[a]Matt. 27:55;
Mark 15:40, 41;
Luke 23:49, 55
[b]Matt. 27:56;
Mark 16:9

8:4
[a]Matt. 13:2–9;
Mark 4:1–9

8:8 [a]Matt. 11:15;
Mark 7:16;
Luke 14:35;
Rev. 2:7, 11, 17,
29; 3:6, 13, 22;
13:9

8:9
[a]Matt. 13:10–23;
Mark 4:10–20

8:10 [a]Is. 6:9;
Matt. 13:14;
Acts 28:26

8:11 [a]Matt. 13:18;
Mark 4:14;
[1 Pet. 1:23]
[b]Luke 5:1; 11:28

8:14
[a]Matt. 19:23;
1 Tim. 6:9, 10

8:15 [a][Rom. 2:7;
Heb. 10:36–39;
James 5:7, 8]

8:16 [a]Matt. 5:15;
Mark 4:21;
Luke 11:33

8:1 [1]*proclaiming the good news* 8:2 [1]*sicknesses* 8:3 [1]NU, M *them*
[2]*possessions* 8:8 [1]Lit. *fruit* 8:10 [1]*secret* or *hidden truths* 8:13 [1]*testing*
8:15 [1]*endurance*

who enter may see the [b]light. [17a]For nothing is secret that will not be [b]revealed, nor *anything* hidden that will not be known and come to light. [18]Therefore take heed how you hear. [a]For whoever has, to him *more* will be given; and whoever does not have, even what he [1]seems to [b]have will be taken from him."

JESUS' MOTHER AND BROTHERS COME TO HIM
(Matt. 12:46–50, Mark 3:31–35)

[19a]Then His mother and brothers came to Him, and could not approach Him because of the crowd. [20]And it was told Him *by some,* who said, "Your mother and Your brothers are standing outside, desiring to see You."

[21]But He answered and said to them, "My mother and My brothers are these who hear the word of God and do it."

WIND AND WAVE OBEY JESUS
(Matt. 8:23–27; Mark 4:35–41)

[22a]Now it happened, on a certain day, that He got into a boat with His disciples. And He said to them, "Let us cross over to the other side of the lake." And they launched out. [23]But as they sailed He fell asleep. And a windstorm came down on the lake, and they were filling *with water,* and were in [1]jeopardy. [24]And they came to Him and awoke Him, saying, "Master, Master, we are perishing!"

Then He arose and rebuked the wind and the raging of the water. And they ceased, and there was a calm. [25]But He said to them, [a]"Where is your faith?"

And they were afraid, and marveled, saying to one another, [b]"Who can this be? For He commands even the winds and water, and they obey Him!"

A DEMON-POSSESSED MAN HEALED
(Matt. 8:28—9:1; Mark 5:1–20)

[26a]Then they sailed to the country of the [1]Gadarenes, which is opposite Galilee. [27]And when He stepped out on the land, there met Him a certain man from the city who had demons [1]for a long time. And he wore no clothes, nor did he live in a house but in the tombs. [28]When he saw Jesus, he [a]cried out, fell down before Him, and with a loud voice said, [b]"What have I to do with [c]You, Jesus, Son of the Most High God? I beg You, do not torment me!" [29]For He had commanded the unclean spirit to come out of the man. For it had often seized him, and he was kept under guard, bound with chains and shackles; and he broke the bonds and was driven by the demon into the wilderness.

[30]Jesus asked him, saying, "What is your name?"

And he said, "Legion," because many demons had entered him. [31]And they begged Him that He would not command them to go out [a]into the abyss.

[32]Now a herd of many [a]swine was feeding there on the mountain. So they begged Him that He would permit them to enter them. And He permitted them. [33]Then the demons went out of the man and entered the swine, and the herd ran violently down the steep place into the lake and drowned.

8:16 [b]Matt. 5:14
8:17 [a]Matt. 10:26; Luke 12:2; [1 Cor. 4:5]; [b][Eccl. 12:14; 2 Cor. 5:10]
8:18 [a]Matt. 25:29 [b]Matt. 13:12
8:19 [a]Ps. 69:8; Matt. 12:46–50; Mark 3:31–35
8:22 [a]Matt. 8:23–27; Mark 4:36–41
8:25 [a]Luke 9:41 [b]Luke 4:36; 5:26
8:26 [a]Matt. 8:28–34; Mark 5:1–17
8:28 [a]Mark 1:26; 9:26 [b]Mark 1:23, 24 [c]Luke 4:41
8:31 [a]Rom. 10:7; [Rev. 20:1, 3]
8:32 [a]Lev. 11:7; Deut. 14:8

8:18 [1]*thinks that he has* **8:23** [1]*danger* **8:26** [1]NU *Gerasenes*
8:27 [1]NU *and for a long time wore no clothes*

34When those who fed *them* saw what had happened, they fled and told *it* in the city and in the country. 35Then they went out to see what had happened, and came to Jesus, and found the man from whom the demons had departed, asitting at the bfeet of Jesus, clothed and in his cright mind. And they were afraid. 36They also who had seen *it* told them by what means he who had been demon-possessed was 1healed. 37aThen the whole multitude of the surrounding region of the 1Gadarenes basked Him to cdepart from them, for they were seized with great dfear. And He got into the boat and returned.

38Now athe man from whom the demons had departed begged Him that he might be with Him. But Jesus sent him away, saying, 39"Return to your own house, and tell what great things God has done for you." And he went his way and proclaimed throughout the whole city what great things Jesus had done for him.

A GIRL RESTORED TO LIFE AND A WOMAN HEALED

40So it was, when Jesus returned, that the multitude welcomed Him, for they were all waiting for Him. 41aAnd behold, there came a man named Jairus, and he was a ruler of the synagogue. And he fell down at Jesus' feet and begged Him to come to his house, 42for he had an only daughter about twelve years of age, and she awas dying.

But as He went, the multitudes thronged Him. 43aNow a woman, having a bflow of blood for twelve years, who had spent all her livelihood on physicians and could not be healed by any, 44came from behind and atouched the border of His garment. And immediately her flow of blood stopped.

45And Jesus said, "Who touched Me?"

When all denied it, Peter 1and those with him said, "Master, the multitudes throng and press You, 2and You say, 'Who touched Me?'"

46But Jesus said, "Somebody touched Me, for I perceived apower going out from Me." 47Now when the woman saw that she was not hidden, she came trembling; and falling down before Him, she declared to Him in the presence of all the people the reason she had touched Him and how she was healed immediately.

48And He said to her, "Daughter, 1be of good cheer; ayour faith has made you well. bGo in peace."

49aWhile He was still speaking, someone came from the ruler of the synagogue's *house,* saying to him, "Your daughter is dead. Do not trouble the 1Teacher."

50But when Jesus heard *it,* He answered him, saying, "Do not be afraid; aonly believe, and she will be made well." 51When He came into the house, He permitted no one to go 1in except 2Peter, James, and John, and the father and mother of the girl. 52Now all wept and mourned for her; but He said, a"Do not weep; she is not dead, bbut sleeping." 53And they ridiculed Him, knowing that she was dead.

54But He 1put them all outside, took her by the hand and called, saying, "Little girl, aarise." 55Then her spirit returned,

8:35
a[Matt. 11:28]
bMatt. 28:9;
Mark 7:25;
Luke 10:39; 17:16;
John 11:32
c[2 Tim. 1:7]

8:37 aMatt. 8:34
bMark 1:24;
Luke 4:34
cJob 21:14;
Acts 16:39
dLuke 5:26

8:38
aMark 5:18–20

8:41
aMatt. 9:18–26;
Mark 5:22–43

8:42 aLuke 7:2

8:43
aMatt. 9:20
bLuke 15:19–22

8:44
aMark 6:56;
Luke 5:13

8:46
aMark 5:30;
Luke 6:19

8:48
aMark 5:34;
Luke 7:50
bJohn 8:11

8:49 aMark 5:35

8:50
a[Mark 11:22–24]

8:52 aLuke 7:13
b[John 11:11, 13]

8:54 aLuke 7:14;
John 11:43

8:36 1delivered   **8:37** 1NU *Gerasenes*   **8:45** 1NU omits *and those with him*   2NU omits the rest of v. 45.   **8:48** 1NU omits *be of good cheer*
8:49 1NU adds *anymore*   **8:51** 1NU adds *with Him*   2NU, M *Peter, John, and James*   **8:54** 1NU omits *put them all outside*

and she arose immediately. And He commanded that she be given *something* to eat. 56And her parents were astonished, but aHe charged them to tell no one what had happened.

SENDING OUT THE TWELVE
(Matt. 10:5–15)

9 Then aHe called His twelve disciples together and bgave them power and authority over all demons, and to cure diseases. 2aHe sent them to preach the kingdom of God and to heal the sick. 3aAnd He said to them, "Take nothing for the journey, neither staffs nor bag nor bread nor money; and do not have two tunics apiece.

4a"Whatever house you enter, stay there, and from there depart. 5aAnd whoever will not receive you, when you go out of that city, bshake off the very dust from your feet as a testimony against them."

6aSo they departed and went through the towns, preaching the gospel and healing everywhere.

HEROD SEEKS TO SEE JESUS
(Matt. 14:1–12; Mark 6:14–29)

7aNow Herod the tetrarch heard of all that was done by Him; and he was perplexed, because it was said by some that John had risen from the dead, 8and by some that Elijah had appeared, and by others that one of the old prophets had risen again. 9Herod said, "John I have beheaded, but who is this of whom I hear such things?" aSo he sought to see Him.

FEEDING THE FIVE THOUSAND
(Matt. 14:13–21; Mark 6:30–44; John 6:1–15)

10aAnd the apostles, when they had returned, told Him all that they had done. bThen He took them and went aside privately into a deserted place belonging to the city called Bethsaida. 11But when the multitudes knew *it*, they followed Him; and He received them and spoke to them about the kingdom of God, and healed those who had need of healing. 12aWhen the day began to wear away, the twelve came and said to Him, "Send the multitude away, that they may go into the surrounding towns and country, and lodge and get provisions; for we are in a deserted place here."

13But He said to them, "You give them something to eat."

And they said, "We have no more than five loaves and two fish, unless we go and buy food for all these people." 14For there were about five thousand men.

Then He said to His disciples, "Make them sit down in groups of fifty." 15And they did so, and made them all sit down.

16Then He took the five loaves and the two fish, and looking up to heaven, He ablessed and broke them, and gave *them* to the disciples to set before the multitude. 17So they all ate and were 1filled, and twelve baskets of the leftover fragments were taken up by them.

PETER CONFESSES JESUS AS THE CHRIST
(Matt. 16:13–20; Mark 8:27–30)

18aAnd it happened, as He was alone praying, *that* His

8:56
aMatt. 8:4; 9:30;
Mark 5:43

9:1
aMatt. 10:1, 2;
Mark 3:13; 6:7
bMark 16:17, 18;
[John 14:12]

9:2
aMatt. 10:7, 8;
Mark 6:12;
Luke 10:1, 9

9:3
aMatt. 10:9–15;
Mark 6:8–11;
Luke 10:4–12;
22:35

9:4 aMatt. 10:11;
Mark 6:10

9:5 aMatt. 10:14
bLuke 10:11;
Acts 13:51

9:6 aMark 6:12;
Luke 8:1

9:7
aMatt. 14:1, 2;
Mark 6:14

9:9 aLuke 23:8

9:10 aMark 6:30
bMatt. 14:13

9:12
aMatt. 14:15;
Mark 6:35;
John 6:1, 5

9:16
aLuke 22:19;
24:30

9:18
aMatt. 16:13–16;
Mark 8:27–29

9:17 1*satisfied*

disciples joined Him, and He asked them, saying, "Who do the crowds say that I am?"

[19]So they answered and said, [a]"John the Baptist, but some *say* Elijah; and others *say* that one of the old prophets has risen again."

[20]He said to them, "But who do you say that I am?"

[a]Peter answered and said, "The Christ of God."

JESUS PREDICTS HIS DEATH AND RESURRECTION
(Matt. 16:20–23; Mark 8:30–33)

[21a]And He strictly warned and commanded them to tell this to no one, [22]saying, [a]"The Son of Man must suffer many things, and be rejected by the elders and chief priests and scribes, and be killed, and be raised the third day."

TAKE UP THE CROSS AND FOLLOW HIM
(Matt. 16:24–27; Mark 8:34–38)

[23a]Then He said to *them* all, "If anyone desires to come after Me, let him deny himself, and take up his cross [1]daily, and follow Me. [24a]For whoever desires to save his life will lose it, but whoever loses his life for My sake will save it. [25a]For what profit is it to a man if he gains the whole world, and is himself destroyed or lost? [26a]For whoever is ashamed of Me and My words, of him the Son of Man will be [b]ashamed when He comes in His *own* glory, and *in His* Father's, and of the holy angels. [27a]But I tell you truly, there are some standing here who shall not taste death till they see the kingdom of God."

JESUS TRANSFIGURED ON THE MOUNT
(Matt. 16:28—17:9; Mark 9:2–10; 2 Pet. 1:16–18)

[28a]Now it came to pass, about eight days after these sayings, that He took Peter, John, and James and went up on the mountain to pray. [29]As He prayed, the appearance of His face was altered, and His robe *became* white *and* glistening. [30]And behold, two men talked with Him, who were [a]Moses and [b]Elijah, [31]who appeared in glory and spoke of His [1]decease which He was about to accomplish at Jerusalem. [32]But Peter and those with him [a]were heavy with sleep; and when they were fully awake, they saw His glory and the two men who stood with Him. [33]Then it happened, as they were parting from Him, *that* Peter said to Jesus, "Master, it is good for us to be here; and let us make three [1]tabernacles: one for You, one for Moses, and one for Elijah"—not knowing what he said.

[34]While he was saying this, a cloud came and overshadowed them; and they were fearful as they entered the [a]cloud. [35]And a voice came out of the cloud, saying, [a]"This is [1]My beloved Son. [b]Hear Him!" [36]When the voice had ceased, Jesus was found alone. [a]But they kept quiet, and told no one in those days any of the things they had seen.

A BOY IS HEALED
(Matt. 17:14–21; Mark 9:14–29)

[37a]Now it happened on the next day, when they had come down from the mountain, that a great multitude met Him.

9:19 [a]Matt. 14:2
9:20 [a]Matt. 16:16; John 6:68, 69
9:21 [a]Matt. 8:4; 16:20; Mark 8:30
9:22 [a]Matt. 16:21; 17:22; Luke 18:31–33; 23:46; 24:46
9:23 [a]Matt. 10:38; 16:24; Mark 8:34; Luke 14:27
9:24 [a]Matt. 10:39; Luke 17:33; [John 12:25]
9:25 [a]Matt. 16:26; Mark 8:36; [Luke 16:19–31]; Acts 1:18, 25
9:26 [a][Rom. 1:16] [b]Matt. 10:33; Mark 8:38; Luke 12:9; 2 Tim. 2:12
9:27 [a]Matt. 16:28; Mark 9:1; Acts 7:55, 56; Rev. 20:4
9:28 [a]Matt. 17:1–8; Mark 9:2–8
9:30 [a]Heb. 11:23–29 [b]2 Kin. 2:1–11
9:32 [a]Dan. 8:18; 10:9; Matt. 26:40, 43; Mark 14:40
9:34 [a]Ex. 13:21; Acts 1:9
9:35 [a]Ps. 2:7; [Is. 42:1; Matt. 3:17; 12:18]; Mark 1:11; Luke 3:22 [b]Acts 3:22
9:36 [a]Matt. 17:9; Mark 9:9
9:37 [a]Matt. 17:14–18; Mark 9:14–27

9:23 [1]M omits *daily*   9:31 [1]Death, lit. *departure*   9:33 [1]tents
9:35 [1]NU *My Son, the Chosen One*

[38]Suddenly a man from the multitude cried out, saying, "Teacher, I implore You, look on my son, for he is my only child. [39]And behold, a spirit seizes him, and he suddenly cries out; it convulses him so that he foams *at the mouth;* and it departs from him with great difficulty, bruising him. [40]So I implored Your disciples to cast it out, but they could not."

[41]Then Jesus answered and said, "O [1]faithless and perverse generation, how long shall I be with you and [2]bear with you? Bring your son here." [42]And as he was still coming, the demon threw him down and convulsed *him.* Then Jesus rebuked the unclean spirit, healed the child, and gave him back to his father.

JESUS AGAIN PREDICTS HIS DEATH

(Matt. 17:22, 23; Mark 9:30–32)

[43]And they were all amazed at the majesty of God.

But while everyone marveled at all the things which Jesus did, He said to His disciples, [44a]"Let these words sink down into your ears, for the Son of Man is about to be betrayed into the hands of men." [45a]But they did not understand this saying, and it was hidden from them so that they did not perceive it; and they were afraid to ask Him about this saying.

WHO IS THE GREATEST?

(Matt. 18:1–5; Mark 9:33–37)

[46a]Then a dispute arose among them as to which of them would be greatest. [47]And Jesus, [a]perceiving the thought of their heart, took a [b]little child and set him by Him, [48]and said to them, [a]"Whoever receives this little child in My name receives Me; and [b]whoever receives Me [c]receives Him who sent Me. [d]For he who is least among you all will be great."

JESUS FORBIDS SECTARIANISM

(Mark 9:38–41)

[49a]Now John answered and said, "Master, we saw someone casting out demons in Your name, and we forbade him because he does not follow with us."

[50]But Jesus said to him, "Do not forbid *him,* for [a]he who is not against [1]us is on [2]our side."

A SAMARITAN VILLAGE REJECTS THE SAVIOR

[51]Now it came to pass, when the time had come for [a]Him to be received up, that He steadfastly set His face to go to Jerusalem, [52]and sent messengers before His face. And as they went, they entered a village of the Samaritans, to prepare for Him. [53]But [a]they did not receive Him, because His face was *set* for the journey to Jerusalem. [54]And when His disciples [a]James and John saw *this,* they said, "Lord, do You want us to command fire to come down from heaven and consume them, [1]just as [b]Elijah did?"

[55]But He turned and rebuked them, [1]and said, "You do not know what manner of [a]spirit you are of. [56][1]For [a]the Son of Man

9:44
[a]Matt. 17:22;
Mark 10:33;
14:53;
Luke 22:54;
John 18:12

9:45
[a]Mark 9:32;
Luke 2:50; 18:34

9:46
[a]Matt. 18:1–5;
Mark 9:33–37;
Luke 22:24

9:47 [a]Matt. 9:4;
John 2:24, 25
[b]Luke 18:17

9:48 [a]Matt. 18:5
[b]Matt. 10:40;
Mark 9:37;
John 12:44
[c]John 13:20
[d][Matt. 23:11, 12];
1 Cor. 15:9;
Eph. 3:8

9:49
[a]Mark 9:38–40

9:50
[a]Matt. 12:30;
Luke 11:23

9:51 [a]Is. 50:7;
Mark 16:19;
Acts 1:2

9:53
[a]John 4:4, 9

9:54 [a]Mark 3:17
[b]2 Kin. 1:10, 12

9:55
[a][Rom. 8:15;
2 Tim. 1:7]

9:56
[a]Luke 19:10;
John 3:17; 12:47

9:41 [1]unbelieving   [2]put up with   9:50 [1]NU you   [2]NU your
9:54 [1]NU omits *just as Elijah did*   9:55 [1]NU omits the rest of v. 55.
9:56 [1]NU omits *For the Son of Man did not come to destroy men's lives but to save them.*

did not come to destroy men's lives but to save *them*." And they went to another village.

THE COST OF DISCIPLESHIP
(Matt. 8:18–22)

57aNow it happened as they journeyed on the road, *that* someone said to Him, "Lord, I will follow You wherever You go."

58And Jesus said to him, "Foxes have holes and birds of the air *have* nests, but the Son of Man ahas nowhere to lay *His* head."

59aThen He said to another, "Follow Me."

But he said, "Lord, let me first go and bury my father."

60Jesus said to him, "Let the dead bury their own dead, but you go and preach the kingdom of God."

61And another also said, "Lord, aI will follow You, but let me first go *and* bid them farewell who are at my house."

62But Jesus said to him, "No one, having put his hand to the plow, and looking back, is afit for the kingdom of God."

THE SEVENTY SENT OUT

10 After these things the Lord appointed 1seventy others also, and asent them two by two before His face into every city and place where He Himself was about to go. 2Then He said to them, a"The harvest truly *is* great, but the laborers *are* few; therefore bpray the Lord of the harvest to send out laborers into His harvest. 3Go your way; abehold, I send you out as lambs among wolves. 4aCarry neither money bag, knapsack, nor sandals; and bgreet no one along the road. 5aBut whatever house you enter, first say, 'Peace to this house.' 6And if a son of peace is there, your peace will rest on it; if not, it will return to you. 7aAnd remain in the same house, beating and drinking such things as they give, for cthe laborer is worthy of his wages. Do not go from house to house. 8Whatever city you enter, and they receive you, eat such things as are set before you. 9aAnd heal the sick there, and say to them, b'The kingdom of God has come near to you.' 10But whatever city you enter, and they do not receive you, go out into its streets and say, 11a'The very dust of your city which clings to 1us we wipe off against you. Nevertheless know this, that the kingdom of God has come near you.' 12'But I say to you that ait will be more tolerable in that Day for Sodom than for that city.

WOE TO THE IMPENITENT CITIES
(Matt. 11:20–24)

13a"Woe to you, Chorazin! Woe to you, Bethsaida! bFor if the mighty works which were done in you had been done in Tyre and Sidon, they would have repented long ago, sitting in sackcloth and ashes. 14But it will be more tolerable for Tyre and Sidon at the judgment than for you. 15aAnd you, Capernaum, 1who are bexalted to heaven, cwill be brought down to Hades. 16aHe who hears you hears Me, bhe who rejects you rejects Me, and che who rejects Me rejects Him who sent Me."

9:57
aMatt. 8:19–22

9:58 aLuke 2:7;
8:23

9:59
aMatt. 8:21, 22

9:61
a1 Kin. 19:20

9:62
a2 Tim. 4:10

10:1 aMatt. 10:1;
Mark 6:7

10:2
aMatt. 9:37, 38;
John 4:35
b[1 Cor. 3:9];
2 Thess. 3:1

10:3 aMatt. 10:16

10:4
aMatt. 10:9–14;
Mark 6:8–11;
Luke 9:3–5
b2 Kin. 4:29

10:5
a1 Sam. 25:6;
Matt. 10:12

10:7 aMatt. 10:11
b1 Cor. 10:27
c[Matt. 10:10];
1 Cor. 9:4–8;
1 Tim. 5:18

10:9 aMark 3:15
bMatt. 3:2; 10:7;
Luke 10:11

10:11
aMatt. 10:14;
Mark 6:11;
Luke 9:5;
Acts 13:51

10:12
aGen. 19:24–28;
Lam. 4:6;
Matt. 10:15;
11:24; Mark 6:11

10:13
aMatt. 11:21–23
bEzek. 3:6

10:15
aMatt. 11:23
bGen. 11:4;
Deut. 1:28;
Is. 14:13–15;
Jer. 51:53
cEzek. 26:20

10:16
aMatt. 10:40;
Mark 9:37;
John 13:20;
Gal. 4:14
b[John 12:48];
1 Thess. 4:8
cJohn 5:23

10:1 1NU *seventy-two others* **10:11** 1NU *our feet* **10:12** 1NU, M omit *But*
10:15 1NU *will you be exalted to heaven? You will be thrust down to Hades!*

THE SEVENTY RETURN WITH JOY

17Then [a]the [1]seventy returned with joy, saying, "Lord, even the demons are subject to us in Your name." 18And He said to them, [a]"I saw Satan fall like lightning from heaven. 19Behold, [a]I give you the authority to trample on serpents and scorpions, and over all the power of the enemy, and nothing shall by any means hurt you. 20Nevertheless do not rejoice in this, that the spirits are subject to you, but [1]rather rejoice because [a]your names are written in heaven."

JESUS REJOICES IN THE SPIRIT
(Matt. 11:25–27)

21[a]In that hour Jesus rejoiced in the Spirit and said, "I thank You, Father, Lord of heaven and earth, that You have hidden these things from *the* wise and prudent and revealed them to babes. Even so, Father, for so it seemed good in Your sight. 22All[1] things have been delivered to Me by My Father, and [b]no one knows who the Son is except the Father, and who the Father is except the Son, and *the one* to whom the Son wills to reveal *Him*."

23Then He turned to *His* disciples and said privately, [a]"Blessed *are* the eyes which see the things you see; 24for I tell you [a]that many prophets and kings have desired to see what you see, and have not seen *it*, and to hear what you hear, and have not heard *it*."

THE PARABLE OF THE GOOD SAMARITAN
(Matt. 22:34–40; Mark 12:28–34)

25And behold, a certain [1]lawyer stood up and tested Him, saying, [a]"Teacher, what shall I do to inherit eternal life?" 26He said to him, "What is written in the law? What is your reading *of it?*" 27So he answered and said, [a]" 'You shall love the LORD your God with all your heart, with all your soul, with all your strength, and with all your mind,' and [b]'your neighbor as yourself.' " 28And He said to him, "You have answered rightly; do this and [a]you will live."

29But he, wanting to [a]justify himself, said to Jesus, "And who is my neighbor?" 30Then Jesus answered and said: "A certain *man* went down from Jerusalem to Jericho, and fell among [1]thieves, who stripped him of his clothing, wounded *him,* and departed, leaving *him* half dead. 31Now by chance a certain priest came down that road. And when he saw him, [a]he passed by on the other side. 32Likewise a Levite, when he arrived at the place, came and looked, and passed by on the other side. 33But a certain [a]Samaritan, as he journeyed, came where he was. And when he saw him, he had [b]compassion. 34So he went to *him* and bandaged his wounds, pouring on oil and wine; and he set him on his own animal, brought him to an inn, and took care of him. 35On the next day, [1]when he departed, he took out two [a]denarii, gave *them* to the innkeeper,

---

10:17 [a]Luke 10:1

10:18
[a]John 12:31;
Rev. 9:1; 12:8, 9

10:19 [a]Ps. 91:13;
Mark 16:18;
Acts 28:5

10:20
[a][Ex. 32:32, 33];
Ps. 69:28;
Is. 4:3; Dan. 12:1;
Phil. 4:3;
Heb. 12:23;
Rev. 13:8

10:21
[a]Matt. 11:25–27

10:22
[a]Matt. 28:18;
John 3:35;
5:27; 17:2
[b][John 1:18;
6:44, 46]

10:23
[a]Matt. 13:16, 17

10:24
[a]1 Pet. 1:10, 11

10:25
[a]Matt. 19:16–19;
22:35

10:27 [a]Deut. 6:5
[b]Lev. 19:18;
Matt. 19:19

10:28 [a]Lev. 18:5;
Neh. 9:29;
Ezek. 20:11,
13, 21;
Matt. 19:17;
Rom. 10:5

10:29
[a]Luke 16:15

10:31 [a]Ps. 38:11

10:33 [a]John 4:9
[b]Luke 15:20

10:35
[a]Matt. 20:2

10:17 [1]NU *seventy-two*   10:20 [1]NU, M omit *rather*   10:22 [1]M *And turning to the disciples He said, "All*   10:25 [1]*expert in the law*   10:30 [1]*robbers*
10:35 [1]NU omits *when he departed*

and said to him, 'Take care of him; and whatever more you spend, when I come again, I will repay you.' 36So which of these three do you think was neighbor to him who fell among the thieves?"

37And he said, "He who showed mercy on him."

Then Jesus said to him, a"Go and do likewise."

MARY AND MARTHA WORSHIP AND SERVE

38Now it happened as they went that He entered a certain village; and a certain woman named aMartha welcomed Him into her house. 39And she had a sister called Mary, awho also bsat at 1Jesus' feet and heard His word. 40But Martha was distracted with much serving, and she approached Him and said, "Lord, do You not care that my sister has left me to serve alone? Therefore tell her to help me."

41And 1Jesus answered and said to her, "Martha, Martha, you are worried and troubled about many things. 42But aone thing is needed, and Mary has chosen that good part, which will not be taken away from her."

THE MODEL PRAYER
(Matt. 6:9–15)

11 Now it came to pass, as He was praying in a certain place, when He ceased, *that* one of His disciples said to Him, "Lord, teach us to pray, as John also taught his disciples."

2So He said to them, "When you pray, say:

aOur1 Father 2in heaven,
Hallowed be Your name.
Your kingdom come.
3Your will be done
On earth as *it is* in heaven.
3   Give us day by day our daily bread.
4   And aforgive us our sins,
For we also forgive everyone who is indebted to us.
And do not lead us into temptation,
1But deliver us from the evil one."

A FRIEND COMES AT MIDNIGHT

5And He said to them, "Which of you shall have a friend, and go to him at midnight and say to him, 'Friend, lend me three loaves; 6for a friend of mine has come to me on his journey, and I have nothing to set before him'; 7and he will answer from within and say, 'Do not trouble me; the door is now shut, and my children are with me in bed; I cannot rise and give to you'? 8I say to you, athough he will not rise and give to him because he is his friend, yet because of his persistence he will rise and give him as many as he needs.

KEEP ASKING, SEEKING, KNOCKING
(Matt. 7:7–11)

9a"So I say to you, ask, and it will be given to you; bseek, and you will find; knock, and it will be opened to you. 10For everyone who asks receives, and he who seeks finds, and to

10:37
aProv. 14:21;
[Matt. 9:13;
12:7]

10:38 aJohn 11:1;
12:2, 3

10:39
a[1 Cor. 7:32–40]
bLuke 8:35;
Acts 22:3

10:42 a[Ps. 27:4;
John 6:27]

11:2
aMatt. 6:9–13

11:4 a[Eph. 4:32]

11:8
a[Luke 18:1–5]

11:9
aPs. 50:14, 15;
Jer. 33:3;
[Matt. 7:7; 21:22;
Mark 11:24;
John 15:7;
James 1:5, 6;
1 John 3:22;
5:14, 15]
bIs. 55:6

10:39 1NU *the Lord's*   10:41 1NU *the Lord*   11:2 1NU omits *Our*
2NU omits *in heaven*   3NU omits the rest of v. 2.   11:4 1NU omits *But deliver us from the evil one*

him who knocks it will be opened. [11a]If a son asks for [1]bread from any father among you, will he give him a stone? Or if *he asks* for a fish, will he give him a serpent instead of a fish? [12]Or if he asks for an egg, will he offer him a scorpion? [13]If you then, being evil, know how to give [a]good gifts to your children, how much more will *your* heavenly Father give the Holy Spirit to those who ask Him!"

A HOUSE DIVIDED CANNOT STAND
(Matt. 12:22–30; Mark 3:22–27)

[14a]And He was casting out a demon, and it was mute. So it was, when the demon had gone out, that the mute spoke; and the multitudes marveled. [15]But some of them said, [a]"He casts out demons by [1]Beelzebub, the ruler of the demons."

[16]Others, testing *Him,* [a]sought from Him a sign from heaven. [17a]But [b]He, knowing their thoughts, said to them: "Every kingdom divided against itself is brought to desolation, and a house *divided* against a house falls. [18]If Satan also is divided against himself, how will his kingdom stand? Because you say I cast out demons by Beelzebub. [19]And if I cast out demons by Beelzebub, by whom do your sons cast *them* out? Therefore they will be your judges. [20]But if I cast out demons [a]with the finger of God, surely the kingdom of God has come upon you. [21a]When a strong man, fully armed, guards his own palace, his goods are in peace. [22]But [a]when a stronger than he comes upon him and overcomes him, he takes from him all his armor in which he trusted, and divides his [1]spoils. [23a]He who is not with Me is against Me, and he who does not gather with Me scatters.

AN UNCLEAN SPIRIT RETURNS
(Matt. 12:43–45)

[24a]"When an unclean spirit goes out of a man, he goes through dry places, seeking rest; and finding none, he says, 'I will return to my house from which I came.' [25]And when he comes, he finds *it* swept and put in order. [26]Then he goes and takes with *him* seven other spirits more wicked than himself, and they enter and dwell there; and [a]the last *state* of that man is worse than the first."

KEEPING THE WORD

[27]And it happened, as He spoke these things, that a certain woman from the crowd raised her voice and said to Him, [a]"Blessed *is* the womb that bore You, and *the* breasts which nursed You!"

[28]But He said, [a]"More than that, blessed *are* those who hear the word of God and keep it!"

SEEKING A SIGN
(Matt. 12:38–42)

[29a]And while the crowds were thickly gathered together, He began to say, "This is an evil generation. It seeks a [b]sign, and no sign will be given to it except the sign of Jonah [1]the prophet. [30]For as [a]Jonah became a sign to the Ninevites, so

11:11 [a]Matt. 7:9

11:13 [a]James 1:17

11:14
[a]Matt. 9:32–34;
12:22, 24

11:15
[a]Matt. 9:34;
12:24

11:16
[a]Matt. 12:38;
16:1; Mark 8:11

11:17
[a]Matt. 12:25–29;
Mark 3:23–27
[b]Matt. 9:4;
John 2:25

11:20 [a]Ex. 8:19

11:21
[a]Matt. 12:29;
Mark 3:27

11:22 [a][Is. 53:12;
Col. 2:15]

11:23
[a]Matt. 12:30;
Mark 9:40

11:24
[a]Matt. 12:43–45;
Mark 1:27; 3:11;
5:13; Acts 5:16;
8:7

11:26 [a]John 5:14;
[Heb. 6:4–6;
10:26];
2 Pet. 2:20]

11:27
[a]Luke 1:28, 48

11:28
[a]Ps. 1:1, 2;
112:1; 119:1, 2;
Is. 48:17, 18;
[Matt. 7:21;
Luke 8:21];
James 1:25

11:29
[a]Matt. 12:38–42
[b]1 Cor. 1:22

11:30 [a]Jon. 1:17;
2:10; 3:3–10;
Luke 24:46;
Acts 10:40;
1 Cor. 15:4

11:11 [1]NU omits *bread from any father among you, will he give him a stone? Or if he asks for*   11:15 [1]NU, M *Beelzebul*   11:22 [1]*plunder*   11:29 [1]NU omits *the prophet*

also the Son of Man will be to this generation. [31a]The queen of the South will rise up in the judgment with the men of this generation and condemn them, for she came from the ends of the earth to hear the wisdom of Solomon; and indeed a [b]greater than Solomon *is* here. [32]The men of Nineveh will rise up in the judgment with this generation and condemn it, for [a]they repented at the preaching of Jonah; and indeed a greater than Jonah *is* here.

THE LAMP OF THE BODY
(Matt. 6:22, 23)

[33a]"No one, when he has lit a lamp, puts *it* in a secret place or under a [b]basket, but on a lampstand, that those who come in may see the light. [34a]The lamp of the body is the eye. Therefore, when your eye is [1]good, your whole body also is full of light. But when *your eye* is [2]bad, your body also *is* full of darkness. [35]Therefore take heed that the light which is in you is not darkness. [36]If then your whole body *is* full of light, having no part dark, *the* whole *body* will be full of light, as when the bright shining of a lamp gives you light."

WOE TO THE PHARISEES AND LAWYERS

[37]And as He spoke, a certain Pharisee asked Him to dine with him. So He went in and sat down to eat. [38a]When the Pharisee saw *it,* he marveled that He had not first washed before dinner.

[39a]Then the Lord said to him, "Now you Pharisees make the outside of the cup and dish clean, but [b]your inward part is full of [1]greed and wickedness. [40]Foolish ones! Did not [a]He who made the outside make the inside also? [41a]But rather give alms of [1]such things as you have; then indeed all things are clean to you.

[42a]"But woe to you Pharisees! For you tithe mint and rue and all manner of herbs, and [b]pass by justice and the [c]love of God. These you ought to have done, without leaving the others undone. [43a]Woe to you Pharisees! For you love the [1]best seats in the synagogues and greetings in the marketplaces. [44a]Woe to you, [1]scribes and Pharisees, hypocrites! [b]For you are like graves which are not seen, and the men who walk over *them* are not aware *of them.*"

[45]Then one of the lawyers answered and said to Him, "Teacher, by saying these things You reproach us also."

[46]And He said, "Woe to you also, lawyers! [a]For you load men with burdens hard to bear, and you yourselves do not touch the burdens with one of your fingers. [47a]Woe to you! For you build the tombs of the prophets, and your fathers killed them. [48]In fact, you bear witness that you approve the deeds of your fathers; for they indeed killed them, and you build their tombs. [49]Therefore the wisdom of God also said, [a]'I will send them prophets and apostles, and *some* of them they will kill and persecute,' [50]that the blood of all the prophets which was shed from the foundation of the world may be required of this generation, [51a]from the blood of Abel to [b]the blood of Zechariah who perished between the altar

11:31
[a]1 Kin. 10:1–9;
2 Chr. 9:1–8
[b][Is. 9:6;
Rom. 9:5]

11:32 [a]Jon. 3:5

11:33
[a]Matt. 5:15;
Mark 4:21;
Luke 8:16
[b]Matt. 5:15

11:34
[a]Matt. 6:22, 23

11:38
[a]Matt. 15:2;
Mark 7:2, 3

11:39
[a]Matt. 23:25
[b]Gen. 6:5;
Titus 1:15

11:40
[a]Gen. 1:26, 27

11:41 [a]Is. 58:7;
Dan. 4:27;
[Luke 12:33;
16:9]

11:42
[a]Matt. 23:23
[b][Mic. 6:7, 8]
[c]John 5:42

11:43
[a]Matt. 23:6;
Mark 12:38, 39;
Luke 14:7; 20:46

11:44
[a]Matt. 23:27
[b]Ps. 5:9

11:46
[a]Matt. 23:4

11:47
[a]Matt. 23:29;
Acts 7:52

11:49
[a]Prov. 1:20;
Matt. 23:34

11:51 [a]Gen. 4:8;
2 Chr. 36:16
[b]2 Chr. 24:20, 21

11:34 [1]Clear, or healthy   [2]Evil, or unhealthy   **11:39** [1]Lit. *eager grasping* or *robbery*   **11:41** [1]Or *what is inside*   **11:43** [1]Or *places of honor*
11:44 [1]NU omits *scribes and Pharisees, hypocrites*

and the temple. Yes, I say to you, it shall be required of this generation.

52 a"Woe to you lawyers! For you have taken away the key of knowledge. You did not enter in yourselves, and those who were entering in you hindered."

53 1And as He said these things to them, the scribes and the Pharisees began to assail *Him* vehemently, and to cross-examine Him about many things, 54lying in wait for Him, 1and a seeking to catch Him in something He might say, 2that they might accuse Him.

BEWARE OF HYPOCRISY
(Matt. 10:26, 27)

12 In a the meantime, when an innumerable multitude of people had gathered together, so that they trampled one another, He began to say to His disciples first *of all,* b"Beware of the 1leaven of the Pharisees, which is hypocrisy. 2a For there is nothing covered that will not be revealed, nor hidden that will not be known. 3Therefore whatever you have spoken in the dark will be heard in the light, and what you have spoken in the ear in inner rooms will be proclaimed on the housetops.

JESUS TEACHES THE FEAR OF GOD
(Matt. 10:8–31)

4a"And I say to you, b My friends, do not be afraid of those who kill the body, and after that have no more that they can do. 5But I will show you whom you should fear: Fear Him who, after He has killed, has power to cast into hell; yes, I say to you, a fear Him! 6"Are not five sparrows sold for two 1copper coins? And a not one of them is forgotten before God. 7But the very hairs of your head are all numbered. Do not fear therefore; you are of more value than many sparrows.

CONFESS CHRIST BEFORE MEN
(Matt. 10:32, 33)

8a"Also I say to you, whoever confesses Me b before men, him the Son of Man also will confess before the angels of God. 9But he who a denies Me before men will be denied before the angels of God.

10"And a anyone who speaks a word against the Son of Man, it will be forgiven him; but to him who blasphemes against the Holy Spirit, it will not be forgiven.

11a"Now when they bring you to the synagogues and magistrates and authorities, do not worry about how or what you should answer, or what you should say. 12For the Holy Spirit will a teach you in that very hour what you ought to say."

THE PARABLE OF THE RICH FOOL

13Then one from the crowd said to Him, "Teacher, tell my brother to divide the inheritance with me."

Cross-references column:
11:52 aMatt. 23:13
11:54 aMark 12:13
12:1 aMatt. 16:6; Mark 8:15; bMatt. 16:12; Luke 11:39
12:2 aMatt. 10:26; Mark 4:22; Luke 8:17; [1 Cor. 4:5]
12:4 aIs. 51:7, 8, 12, 13; Jer. 1:8; Matt. 10:28; b[John 15:13–15]
12:5 aPs. 119:120
12:6 aMatt. 6:26
12:8 a1 Sam. 2:30; Matt. 10:32; [Mark 8:38; Rom. 10:9; 2 Tim. 2:12; 1 John 2:23]; bPs. 119:46
12:9 aMatt. 10:33; [Mark 8:38; 2 Tim. 2:12]
12:10 a[Matt. 12:31, 32; Mark 3:28; 1 John 5:16]
12:11 aMatt. 6:25; 10:19; Mark 13:11
12:12 a[John 14:26]

11:53 1NU *And when He left there* 11:54 1NU omits *and seeking*
2NU omits *that they might accuse Him* 12:1 1yeast 12:6 1Gr. *assarion,* a coin worth about 1/16 of a denarius

¹⁴But He said to him, ᵃ"Man, who made Me a judge or an arbitrator over you?" ¹⁵And He said to them, ᵃ"Take heed and beware of ¹covetousness, for one's life does not consist in the abundance of the things he possesses."

¹⁶Then He spoke a parable to them, saying: "The ground of a certain rich man yielded plentifully. ¹⁷And he thought within himself, saying, 'What shall I do, since I have no room to store my crops?' ¹⁸So he said, 'I will do this: I will pull down my barns and build greater, and there I will store all my crops and my goods. ¹⁹And I will say to my soul, ᵃ"Soul, you have many goods laid up for many years; take your ease; ᵇeat, drink, and be merry."' ²⁰But God said to him, 'Fool! This night ᵃyour soul will be required of you; ᵇthen whose will those things be which you have provided?'

²¹"So is he who lays up treasure for himself, ᵃand is not rich toward God."

DO NOT WORRY
(Matt. 6:19–21, 25–34)

²²Then He said to His disciples, "Therefore I say to you, ᵃdo not worry about your life, what you will eat; nor about the body, what you will put on. ²³Life is more than food, and the body is more than clothing. ²⁴Consider the ravens, for they neither sow nor reap, which have neither storehouse nor barn; and ᵃGod feeds them. Of how much more value are you than the birds? ²⁵And which of you by worrying can add one cubit to his stature? ²⁶If you then are not able to do the least, why ¹are you anxious for the rest? ²⁷Consider the lilies, how they grow: they neither toil nor spin; and yet I say to you, even ᵃSolomon in all his glory was not ¹arrayed like one of these. ²⁸If then God so clothes the grass, which today is in the field and tomorrow is thrown into the oven, how much more will He clothe you, O you of ᵃlittle faith?

²⁹"And do not seek what you should eat or what you should drink, nor have an anxious mind. ³⁰For all these things the nations of the world seek after, and your Father ᵃknows that you need these things. ³¹ᵃBut seek ¹the kingdom of God, and all these things shall be added to you.

³²"Do not fear, little flock, for ᵃit is your Father's good pleasure to give you the kingdom. ³³ᵃSell what you have and give ᵇalms; ᶜprovide yourselves money bags which do not grow old, a treasure in the heavens that does not fail, where no thief approaches nor moth destroys. ³⁴For where your treasure is, there your heart will be also.

THE FAITHFUL SERVANT AND THE EVIL SERVANT
(Matt. 24:42–51)

³⁵ᵃ"Let your waist be girded and ᵇyour lamps burning; ³⁶and you yourselves be like men who wait for their master, when he will return from the wedding, that when he comes and knocks they may open to him immediately. ³⁷ᵃBlessed are those servants whom the master, when he comes, will find watching. Assuredly, I say to you that he will gird himself and have them sit down to eat, and will come and serve them.

12:14
ᵃ[John 18:36]

12:15
ᵃ[1 Tim. 6:6–10]

12:19 ᵃEccl. 11:9;
1 Cor. 15:32;
James 5:5
ᵇ[Eccl. 2:24;
3:13; 5:18; 8:15]

12:20 ᵃJob 27:8;
Ps. 52:7;
[James 4:14]
ᵇPs. 39:6;
Jer. 17:11

12:21
ᵃ[Matt. 6:20;
Luke 12:33;
1 Tim. 6:18, 19;
James 2:5;
5:1–5]

12:22
ᵃMatt. 6:25–33

12:24
ᵃJob 38:41;
Ps. 147:9

12:27
ᵃ1 Kin. 10:4–7;
2 Chr. 9:3–6

12:28
ᵃMatt. 6:30;
8:26; 14:31; 16:8

12:30
ᵃMatt. 6:31, 32

12:31
ᵃMatt. 6:33

12:32
ᵃ[Dan. 7:18, 27];
Zech. 13:7;
[Matt. 11:25, 26;
Luke 22:29, 30]

12:33
ᵃMatt. 19:21;
Acts 2:45; 4:34
ᵇLuke 11:41
ᶜMatt. 6:20;
Luke 16:9;
[1 Tim. 6:19]

12:35
ᵃ[Eph. 6:14;
1 Pet. 1:13]
ᵇ[Matt. 25:1–13]

12:37
ᵃMatt. 24:46

12:15 ¹NU all covetousness   12:26 ¹do you worry   12:27 ¹clothed
12:31 ¹NU His kingdom, and these things

³⁸And if he should come in the second watch, or come in the third watch, and find *them* so, blessed are those servants. ³⁹ᵃBut know this, that if the master of the house had known what hour the thief would come, he would ¹have watched and not allowed his house to be broken into. ⁴⁰ᵃTherefore you also be ready, for the Son of Man is coming at an hour you do not expect."

⁴¹Then Peter said to Him, "Lord, do You speak this parable *only* to us, or to all *people?*"

⁴²And the Lord said, ᵃ"Who then is that faithful and wise steward, whom *his* master will make ruler over his household, to give *them their* portion of food ¹in due season? ⁴³Blessed *is* that servant whom his master will find so doing when he comes. ⁴⁴ᵃTruly, I say to you that he will make him ruler over all that he has. ⁴⁵ᵃBut if that servant says in his heart, 'My master is delaying his coming,' and begins to beat the male and female servants, and to eat and drink and be drunk, ⁴⁶the master of that servant will come on a ᵃday when he is not looking for *him,* and at an hour when he is not aware, and will cut him in two and appoint *him* his portion with the unbelievers. ⁴⁷And ᵃthat servant who ᵇknew his master's will, and did not prepare *himself* or do according to his will, shall be beaten with many *stripes.* ⁴⁸ᵃBut he who did not know, yet committed things deserving of stripes, shall be beaten with few. For everyone to whom much is given, from him much will be required; and to whom much has been committed, of him they will ask the more.

CHRIST BRINGS DIVISION
(Matt. 10:34–39)

⁴⁹ᵃ"I came to send fire on the earth, and how I wish it were already kindled! ⁵⁰But ᵃI have a baptism to be baptized with, and how distressed I am till it is ᵇaccomplished! ⁵¹ᵃDo *you* suppose that I came to give peace on earth? I tell you, not at all, ᵇbut rather division. ⁵²ᵃFor from now on five in one house will be divided: three against two, and two against three. ⁵³ᵃFather will be divided against son and son against father, mother against daughter and daughter against mother, mother-in-law against her daughter-in-law and daughter-in-law against her mother-in-law."

DISCERN THE TIME
(Matt. 16:1–4)

⁵⁴Then He also said to the multitudes, ᵃ"Whenever you see a cloud rising out of the west, immediately you say, 'A shower is coming'; and so it is. ⁵⁵And when *you see* the ᵃsouth wind blow, you say, 'There will be hot weather'; and there is. ⁵⁶Hypocrites! You can discern the face of the sky and of the earth, but how *is it* you do not discern ᵃthis time?

MAKE PEACE WITH YOUR ADVERSARY

⁵⁷"Yes, and why, even of yourselves, do you not judge what is right? ⁵⁸ᵃWhen you go with your adversary to the magistrate, make every effort ᵇalong the way to settle with him, lest he drag you to the judge, the judge deliver you to the officer,

12:39 ¹NU *not have allowed*   **12:42** ¹*at the right time*

12:39
ᵃMatt. 24:43;
1 Thess. 5:2;
[2 Pet. 3:10];
Rev. 3:3; 16:15

12:40
ᵃMatt. 24:44;
25:13;
Mark 13:33;
[Luke 21:34, 36];
1 Thess. 5:6;
[2 Pet. 3:12]

12:42
ᵃMatt. 24:45,
46; 25:21;
[1 Cor. 4:2]

12:44
ᵃMatt. 24:47;
25:21; [Rev. 3:21]

12:45
ᵃMatt. 24:48;
2 Pet. 3:3, 4

12:46
ᵃ1 Thess. 5:3

12:47
ᵃNum. 15:30;
Deut. 25:2;
[John 9:41;
15:22;
Acts 17:30]
ᵇ[James 4:17]

12:48
ᵃ[Lev. 5:17];
Num. 15:29;
[1 Tim. 1:13]

12:49
ᵃLuke 12:51

12:50
ᵃMatt. 20:18,
22, 23;
Mark 10:38
ᵇJohn 12:27;
19:30

12:51
ᵃMatt. 10:34–36
ᵇMic. 7:6;
John 7:43; 9:16;
10:19; Acts 14:4

12:52
ᵃMatt. 10:35;
Mark 13:12

12:53
ᵃMatt. 10:21, 36

12:54
ᵃMatt. 16:2, 3

12:55 ᵃJob 37:17

12:56
ᵃLuke 19:41–44

12:58
ᵃProv. 25:8;
Matt. 5:25, 26
ᵇ[Ps. 32:6;
Is. 55:6]

and the officer throw you into prison. 59I tell you, you shall not depart from there till you have paid the very last mite."

REPENT OR PERISH

13 There were present at that season some who told Him about the Galileans whose blood Pilate had 1mingled with their sacrifices. 2And Jesus answered and said to them, "Do you suppose that these Galileans were worse sinners than all *other* Galileans, because they suffered such things? 3I tell you, no; but unless you repent you will all likewise perish. 4Or those eighteen on whom the tower in Siloam fell and killed them, do you think that they were worse sinners than all *other* men who dwelt in Jerusalem? 5I tell you, no; but unless you repent you will all likewise perish."

THE PARABLE OF THE BARREN FIG TREE

6He also spoke this parable: a"A certain *man* had a fig tree planted in his vineyard, and he came seeking fruit on it and found none. 7Then he said to the keeper of his vineyard, 'Look, for three years I have come seeking fruit on this fig tree and find none. Cut it down; why does it 1use up the ground?' 8But he answered and said to him, 'Sir, let it alone this year also, until I dig around it and fertilize *it*. 9And if it bears fruit, *well*. But if not, after that you can acut it down.'"

A SPIRIT OF INFIRMITY

10Now He was teaching in one of the synagogues on the Sabbath. 11And behold, there was a woman who had a spirit of infirmity eighteen years, and was bent over and could in no way 1raise *herself* up. 12But when Jesus saw her, He called *her* to *Him* and said to her, "Woman, you are loosed from your ainfirmity." 13aAnd He laid *His* hands on her, and immediately she was made straight, and glorified God.

14But the ruler of the synagogue answered with indignation, because Jesus had ahealed on the Sabbath; and he said to the crowd, b"There are six days on which men ought to work; therefore come and be healed on them, and cnot on the Sabbath day."

15The Lord then answered him and said, 1"Hypocrite! aDoes not each one of you on the Sabbath loose his ox or donkey from the stall, and lead *it* away to water it? 16So ought not this woman, abeing a daughter of Abraham, whom Satan has bound—think of it—for eighteen years, be loosed from this bond on the Sabbath?" 17And when He said these things, all His adversaries were put to shame; and all the multitude rejoiced for all the glorious things that were adone by Him.

THE PARABLE OF THE MUSTARD SEED
(Matt. 13:31, 32; Mark 4:30–32)

18aThen He said, "What is the kingdom of God like? And to what shall I compare it? 19It is like a mustard seed, which a man took and put in his garden; and it grew and became a 1large tree, and the birds of the air nested in its branches."

13:6 aIs. 5:2; Matt. 21:19

13:9 a[John 15:2]

13:12 aLuke 7:21; 8:2

13:13 aMark 16:18; Acts 9:17

13:14 a[Luke 6:6–11; 14:1–6]; John 5:16 bEx. 20:9; 23:12 cMatt. 12:10; Mark 3:2; Luke 6:7; 14:3

13:15 a[Matt. 7:5; 23:13]; Luke 14:5

13:16 aLuke 19:9

13:17 aMark 5:19, 20

13:18 aMatt. 13:31, 32; Mark 4:30–32

13:1 1mixed 13:7 1waste 13:9 1NU *And if it bears fruit after that, well. But if not, you can* 13:11 1straighten up 13:15 1NU, M *Hypocrites*
13:19 1NU omits *large*

THE PARABLE OF THE LEAVEN

(Matt. 13:33)

²⁰And again He said, "To what shall I liken the kingdom of God? ²¹It is like ¹leaven, which a woman took and hid in three ᵃmeasures² of meal till it was all leavened."

THE NARROW WAY

(Matt. 7:13, 14)

²²ᵃAnd He went through the cities and villages, teaching, and journeying toward Jerusalem. ²³Then one said to Him, "Lord, are there ᵃfew who are saved?"

And He said to them, ²⁴ᵃ"Strive to enter through the narrow gate, for ᵇmany, I say to you, will seek to enter and will not be able. ²⁵ᵃWhen once the Master of the house has risen up and ᵇshut the door, and you begin to stand outside and knock at the door, saying, ᶜ'Lord, Lord, open for us,' and He will answer and say to you, ᵈ'I do not know you, where you are from,' ²⁶then you will begin to say, 'We ate and drank in Your presence, and You taught in our streets.' ²⁷ᵃBut He will say, 'I tell you I do not know you, where you are from. ᵇDepart from Me, all you workers of iniquity.' ²⁸ᵃThere will be weeping and gnashing of teeth, ᵇwhen you see Abraham and Isaac and Jacob and all the prophets in the kingdom of God, and yourselves thrust out. ²⁹They will come from the east and the west, from the north and the south, and sit down in the kingdom of God. ³⁰ᵃAnd indeed there are last who will be first, and there are first who will be last."

³¹¹On that very day some Pharisees came, saying to Him, "Get out and depart from here, for Herod wants to kill You."

³²And He said to them, "Go, tell that fox, 'Behold, I cast out demons and perform cures today and tomorrow, and the third *day* ᵃI shall be ¹perfected.' ³³Nevertheless I must journey today, tomorrow, and the *day* following; for it cannot be that a prophet should perish outside of Jerusalem.

JESUS LAMENTS OVER JERUSALEM

(Matt. 23:37–39)

³⁴ᵃ"O Jerusalem, Jerusalem, the one who kills the prophets and stones those who are sent to her! How often I wanted to gather your children together, as a hen *gathers* her brood under *her* wings, but you were not willing! ³⁵See! ᵃYour house is left to you desolate; and ¹assuredly, I say to you, you shall not see Me until *the time* comes when you say, ᵇ'Blessed is He who comes in the name of the LORD!' "

A MAN WITH DROPSY HEALED ON THE SABBATH

14 Now it happened, as He went into the house of one of the rulers of the Pharisees to eat bread on the Sabbath, that they watched Him closely. ²And behold, there was a certain man before Him who had dropsy. ³And Jesus, answering, spoke to the lawyers and Pharisees, saying, ᵃ"Is it lawful to heal on the ¹Sabbath?"

⁴But they kept silent. And He took *him* and healed him,

13:21
ᵃMatt. 13:33

13:22
ᵃMatt. 9:35;
Mark 6:6

13:23
ᵃ[Matt. 7:14;
20:16]

13:24
ᵃ[Matt. 7:13]
ᵇ[John 7:34;
8:21; 13:33;
Rom. 9:31]

13:25
ᵃ[Ps. 32:6];
Is. 55:6
ᵇMatt. 25:10;
Rev. 22:11
ᶜLuke 6:46
ᵈMatt. 7:23;
25:12

13:27
ᵃ[Matt. 7:23;
25:41] ᵇPs. 6:8;
[Matt. 25:41];
Titus 1:16

13:28
ᵃMatt. 8:12;
13:42; 24:51
ᵇMatt. 8:11

13:30
ᵃ[Matt. 19:30;
20:16];
Mark 10:31

13:32
ᵃLuke 24:46;
Acts 10:40;
1 Cor. 15:4;
[Heb. 2:10; 5:9;
7:28]

13:34
ᵃMatt. 23:37–39;
2 Chr. 24:20, 21;
36:15, 16

13:35
ᵃLev. 26:31, 32;
Ps. 69:25;
Is. 1:7; Jer. 22:5;
Dan. 9:27;
Mic. 3:12
ᵇPs. 118:26;
Matt. 21:9;
Mark 11:10;
Luke 19:38;
John 12:13

14:3 ᵃMatt. 12:10

13:21 ¹*yeast*   ²Gr. *sata,* same as Heb. *seah;* approximately 2 pecks in all
13:31 ¹NU *In that very hour*   **13:32** ¹*Resurrected*   **13:35** ¹NU, M omit
assuredly   **14:3** ¹NU adds *or not*

and let him go. [5]Then He answered them, saying, [a]"Which of you, having a [1]donkey or an ox that has fallen into a pit, will not immediately pull him out on the Sabbath day?" [6]And they could not answer Him regarding these things.

TAKE THE LOWLY PLACE

[7]So He told a parable to those who were invited, when He noted how they chose the best places, saying to them: [8]"When you are invited by anyone to a wedding feast, do not sit down in the best place, lest one more honorable than you be invited by him; [9]and he who invited you and him come and say to you, 'Give place to this man,' and then you begin with shame to take the lowest place. [10a]But when you are invited, go and sit down in the lowest place, so that when he who invited you comes he may say to you, 'Friend, go up higher.' Then you will have glory in the presence of those who sit at the table with you. [11a]For whoever exalts himself will be [1]humbled, and he who humbles himself will be exalted."

[12]Then He also said to him who invited Him, "When you give a dinner or a supper, do not ask your friends, your brothers, your relatives, nor rich neighbors, lest they also invite you back, and you be repaid. [13]But when you give a feast, invite [a]*the* poor, *the* [1]maimed, *the* lame, *the* blind. [14]And you will be [a]blessed, because they cannot repay you; for you shall be repaid at the resurrection of the just."

THE PARABLE OF THE GREAT SUPPER
(Matt. 22:1–14)

[15]Now when one of those who sat at the table with Him heard these things, he said to Him, [a]"Blessed *is* he who shall eat [1]bread in the kingdom of God!"

[16a]Then He said to him, "A certain man gave a great supper and invited many, [17]and [a]sent his servant at supper time to say to those who were invited, 'Come, for all things are now ready.' [18]But they all with one *accord* began to make excuses. The first said to him, 'I have bought a piece of ground, and I must go and see it. I ask you to have me excused.' [19]And another said, 'I have bought five yoke of oxen, and I am going to test them. I ask you to have me excused.' [20]Still another said, 'I have married a wife, and therefore I cannot come.' [21]So that servant came and reported these things to his master. Then the master of the house, being angry, said to his servant, 'Go out quickly into the streets and lanes of the city, and bring in here *the* poor and *the* [1]maimed and *the* lame and *the* blind.' [22]And the servant said, 'Master, it is done as you commanded, and still there is room.' [23]Then the master said to the servant, 'Go out into the highways and hedges, and compel *them* to come in, that my house may be filled. [24]For I say to you [a]that none of those men who were invited shall taste my supper.'"

LEAVING ALL TO FOLLOW CHRIST
(Matt. 10:34–39)

[25]Now great multitudes went with Him. And He turned and said to them, [26a]"If anyone comes to Me [b]and does not

14:5 [a][Ex. 23:5; Deut. 22:4]; Luke 13:15

14:10 [a]Prov. 25:6, 7

14:11 [a]Job 22:29; Ps. 18:27; Prov. 29:23; Matt. 23:12; Luke 18:14; James 4:6; [1 Pet. 5:5]

14:13 [a]Neh. 8:10, 12

14:14 [a][Matt. 25:34–40]

14:15 [a]Rev. 19:9

14:16 [a]Matt. 22:2–14

14:17 [a]Prov. 9:2, 5

14:24 [a][Matt. 21:43; 22:8; Acts 13:46]

14:26 [a]Deut. 13:6; 33:9; Matt. 10:37 [b]Rom. 9:13

14:5 [1]NU, M son   14:11 [1]*put down*   14:13 [1]*crippled*   14:15 [1]M *dinner*
14:21 [1]*crippled*

hate his father and mother, wife and children, brothers and sisters, ᶜyes, and his own life also, he cannot be My disciple. ²⁷And ᵃwhoever does not bear his cross and come after Me cannot be My disciple. ²⁸For ᵃwhich of you, intending to build a tower, does not sit down first and count the cost, whether he has *enough* to finish *it*— ²⁹lest, after he has laid the foundation, and is not able to finish, all who see *it* begin to mock him, ³⁰saying, 'This man began to build and was not able to finish'? ³¹Or what king, going to make war against another king, does not sit down first and consider whether he is able with ten thousand to meet him who comes against him with twenty thousand? ³²Or else, while the other is still a great way off, he sends a delegation and asks conditions of peace. ³³So likewise, whoever of you ᵃdoes not forsake all that he has cannot be My disciple.

TASTELESS SALT IS WORTHLESS
(Matt. 5:13; Mark 9:50)

³⁴ᵃ"Salt *is* good; but if the salt has lost its flavor, how shall it be seasoned? ³⁵It is neither fit for the land nor for the ¹dunghill, *but* men throw it out. He who has ears to hear, let him hear!"

THE PARABLE OF THE LOST SHEEP
(Matt. 18:10–14)

15 Then ᵃall the tax collectors and the sinners drew near to Him to hear Him. ²And the Pharisees and scribes complained, saying, "This Man ¹receives sinners ᵃand eats with them." ³So He spoke this parable to them, saying:

⁴ᵃ"What man of you, having a hundred sheep, if he loses one of them, does not leave the ninety-nine in the wilderness, and go after the one which is lost until he finds it? ⁵And when he has found *it*, he lays *it* on his shoulders, rejoicing. ⁶And when he comes home, he calls together *his* friends and neighbors, saying to them, ᵃ'Rejoice with me, for I have found my sheep ᵇwhich was lost!' ⁷I say to you that likewise there will be more joy in heaven over one sinner who repents ᵃthan over ninety-nine ¹just persons who ᵇneed no repentance.

THE PARABLE OF THE LOST COIN

⁸"Or what woman, having ten silver ¹coins, if she loses one coin, does not light a lamp, sweep the house, and search carefully until she finds *it*? ⁹And when she has found *it*, she calls *her* friends and neighbors together, saying, 'Rejoice with me, for I have found the piece which I lost!' ¹⁰Likewise, I say to you, there is joy in the presence of the angels of God over one sinner who repents."

THE PARABLE OF THE LOST SON

¹¹Then He said: "A certain man had two sons. ¹²And the younger of them said to *his* father, 'Father, give me the portion of goods that falls *to me*.' So he divided to them ᵃ*his* livelihood. ¹³And not many days after, the younger son gathered all together, journeyed to a far country, and there wasted his

---

14:26 ᶜRev. 12:11
14:27 ᵃMatt. 16:24; Mark 8:34; Luke 9:23; [2 Tim. 3:12]
14:28 ᵃProv. 24:27
14:33 ᵃMatt. 19:27
14:34 ᵃMatt. 5:13; [Mark 9:50]
15:1 ᵃ[Matt. 9:10–13]
15:2 ᵃActs 11:3; Gal. 2:12
15:4 ᵃMatt. 18:12–14; 1 Pet. 2:25
15:6 ᵃ[Rom. 12:15]; ᵇ[Luke 19:10]; 1 Pet. 2:10, 25]
15:7 ᵃ[Luke 5:32]; ᵇ[Mark 2:17]
15:12 ᵃMark 12:44

14:35 ¹rubbish heap   15:2 ¹welcomes   15:7 ¹upright   15:8 ¹Gr. *drachma*, a valuable coin often worn in a ten-piece garland by married women

possessions with ¹prodigal living. ¹⁴But when he had spent all, there arose a severe famine in that land, and he began to be in want. ¹⁵Then he went and joined himself to a citizen of that country, and he sent him into his fields to feed swine. ¹⁶And he would gladly have filled his stomach with the ¹pods that the swine ate, and no one gave him *anything*.

¹⁷"But when he came to himself, he said, 'How many of my father's hired servants have bread enough and to spare, and I perish with hunger! ¹⁸I will arise and go to my father, and will say to him, "Father, ªI have sinned against heaven and before you, ¹⁹and I am no longer worthy to be called your son. Make me like one of your hired servants."'

²⁰"And he arose and came to his father. But ªwhen he was still a great way off, his father saw him and had compassion, and ran and fell on his neck and kissed him. ²¹And the son said to him, 'Father, I have sinned against heaven ªand in your sight, and am no longer worthy to be called your son.'

²²"But the father said to his servants, ¹'Bring out the best robe and put *it* on him, and put a ring on his hand and sandals on *his* feet. ²³And bring the fatted calf here and kill *it*, and let us eat and be merry; ²⁴ªfor this my son was dead and is alive again; he was lost and is found.' And they began to be merry.

²⁵"Now his older son was in the field. And as he came and drew near to the house, he heard music and dancing. ²⁶So he called one of the servants and asked what these things meant. ²⁷And he said to him, 'Your brother has come, and because he has received him safe and sound, your father has killed the fatted calf.'

²⁸"But he was angry and would not go in. Therefore his father came out and pleaded with him. ²⁹So he answered and said to *his* father, 'Lo, these many years I have been serving you; I never transgressed your commandment at any time; and yet you never gave me a young goat, that I might make merry with my friends. ³⁰But as soon as this son of yours came, who has devoured your livelihood with harlots, you killed the fatted calf for him.'

³¹"And he said to him, 'Son, you are always with me, and all that I have is yours. ³²It was right that we should make merry and be glad, ªfor your brother was dead and is alive again, and was lost and is found.'"

THE PARABLE OF THE UNJUST STEWARD

16 He also said to His disciples: "There was a certain rich man who had a steward, and an accusation was brought to him that this man was ¹wasting his goods. ²So he called him and said to him, 'What is this I hear about you? Give an ªaccount of your stewardship, for you can no longer be steward.'

³"Then the steward said within himself, 'What shall I do? For my master is taking the stewardship away from me. I cannot dig; I am ashamed to beg. ⁴I have resolved what to do, that when I am put out of the stewardship, they may receive me into their houses.'

⁵"So he called every one of his master's debtors to *him*, and said to the first, 'How much do you owe my master?' ⁶And

15:18 ªEx. 9:27;
10:16;
Num. 22:34;
Josh. 7:20;
1 Sam. 15:24,
30; 26:21;
2 Sam. 12:13;
24:10, 17;
Ps. 51:4;
Matt. 27:4

15:20
ª[Jer. 3:12];
Matt. 9:36;
[Acts 2:39;
Eph. 2:13, 17]

15:21 ªPs. 51:4

15:24
ªMatt. 8:22;
Luke 9:60;
15:32;
Rom. 11:15;
[Eph. 2:1, 5;
5:14; Col. 2:13;
1 Tim. 5:6]

15:32
ªLuke 15:24

16:2
ª[Rom. 14:12;
2 Cor. 5:10;
1 Pet. 4:5, 6]

15:13 ¹*wasteful*   15:16 ¹*carob pods*   15:22 ¹NU *Quickly bring*
16:1 ¹*squandering*

he said, 'A hundred [1]measures of oil.' So he said to him, 'Take your bill, and sit down quickly and write fifty.' [7]Then he said to another, 'And how much do you owe?' So he said, 'A hundred [1]measures of wheat.' And he said to him, 'Take your bill, and write eighty.' [8]So the master commended the unjust steward because he had dealt shrewdly. For the sons of this world are more shrewd in their generation than [a]the sons of light.

[9]"And I say to you, [a]make friends for yourselves by unrighteous [1]mammon, that when [2]you fail, they may receive you into an everlasting home. [10a]He who *is* faithful in *what is* least is faithful also in much; and he who is unjust in *what is* least is unjust also in much. [11]Therefore if you have not been faithful in the unrighteous mammon, who will commit to your trust the true *riches?* [12]And if you have not been faithful in what is another man's, who will give you what is your [a]own?

[13a]"No servant can serve two masters; for either he will hate the one and love the other, or else he will be loyal to the one and despise the other. You cannot serve God and mammon."

THE LAW, THE PROPHETS, AND THE KINGDOM

[14]Now the Pharisees, [a]who were lovers of money, also heard all these things, and they [1]derided Him. [15]And He said to them, "You are those who [a]justify yourselves [b]before men, but [c]God knows your hearts. For [d]what is highly esteemed among men is an abomination in the sight of God.

[16a]"The law and the prophets *were* until John. Since that time the kingdom of God has been preached, and everyone is pressing into it. [17a]And it is easier for heaven and earth to pass away than for one [1]tittle of the law to fail.

[18a]"Whoever divorces his wife and marries another commits adultery; and whoever marries her who is divorced from *her* husband commits adultery.

THE RICH MAN AND LAZARUS

[19]"There was a certain rich man who was clothed in purple and fine linen and [1]fared sumptuously every day. [20]But there was a certain beggar named Lazarus, full of sores, who was laid at his gate, [21]desiring to be fed with [1]the crumbs which fell from the rich man's table. Moreover the dogs came and licked his sores. [22]So it was that the beggar died, and was carried by the angels to [a]Abraham's bosom. The rich man also died and was buried. [23]And being in torments in Hades, he lifted up his eyes and saw Abraham afar off, and Lazarus in his bosom. [24]"Then he cried and said, 'Father Abraham, have mercy on me, and send Lazarus that he may dip the tip of his finger in water and [a]cool my tongue; for I [b]am tormented in this flame.' [25]But Abraham said, 'Son, [a]remember that in your lifetime you received your good things, and likewise Lazarus evil things; but now he is comforted and you are tormented. [26]And besides all this, between us and you there is a great gulf fixed, so that those who want to pass from here to you cannot, nor can those from there pass to us.'

[27]"Then he said, 'I beg you therefore, father, that you

16:8
[a][John 12:36; Eph. 5:8];
1 Thess. 5:5

16:9 [a]Dan. 4:27;
[Matt. 6:19;
19:21]; Luke 11:41;
[1 Tim. 6:17–19]

16:10
[a]Matt. 25:21;
Luke 19:17

16:12
[a][1 Pet. 1:3, 4]

16:13
[a]Matt. 6:24;
Gal. 1:10

16:14
[a]Matt. 23:14

16:15
[a]Luke 10:29
[b][Matt. 6:2, 5, 16]
[c]1 Chr. 28:9;
2 Chr. 6:30;
Ps. 7:9;
Prov. 15:11;
Jer. 17:10
[d]1 Sam. 16:7;
Ps. 10:3;
Prov. 6:16–19;
16:5

16:16
[a]Matt. 3:1–12;
4:17; 11:12, 13;
Luke 7:29

16:17
[a]Ps. 102:26, 27;
Is. 40:8; 51:6;
Matt. 5:18;
1 Pet. 1:25

16:18
[a]Matt. 5:32;
19:9;
Mark 10:11;
1 Cor. 7:10, 11

16:22 [a]Matt. 8:11

16:24
[a]Zech. 14:12
[b][Is. 66:24;
Mark 9:42–48]

16:25 [a]Job 21:13;
Luke 6:24;
James 5:5

16:6 [1]Gr. *batos,* same as Heb. *bath;* 8 or 9 gallons each   16:7 [1]Gr. *koros,* same as Heb. *kor;* 10 or 12 bushels each   16:9 [1]Lit., in Aram., *wealth*   [2]NU *it fails*   16:14 [1]Lit. *turned up their nose at*   16:17 [1]The smallest stroke in a Heb. letter   16:19 [1]*lived in luxury*   16:21 [1]NU *what fell*

would send him to my father's house, ²⁸for I have five brothers, that he may testify to them, lest they also come to this place of torment.' ²⁹Abraham said to him, ᵃ'They have Moses and the prophets; let them hear them.' ³⁰And he said, 'No, father Abraham; but if one goes to them from the dead, they will repent.' ³¹But he said to him, ᵃ'If they do not hear Moses and the prophets, ᵇneither will they be persuaded though one rise from the dead.'"

JESUS WARNS OF OFFENSES
(Matt. 18:6, 7; Mark 9:42)

17 Then He said to the disciples, ᵃ"It is impossible that no ¹offenses should come, but ᵇwoe *to him* through whom they do come! ²It would be better for him if a millstone were hung around his neck, and he were thrown into the sea, than that he should ¹offend one of these little ones. ³Take heed to yourselves. ᵃIf your brother sins ¹against you, ᵇrebuke him; and if he repents, forgive him. ⁴And if he sins against you seven times in a day, and seven times in a day returns ¹to you, saying, 'I repent,' you shall forgive him."

FAITH AND DUTY
(Matt. 17:19–21; Mark 9:28, 29)

⁵And the apostles said to the Lord, "Increase our faith."

⁶ᵃSo the Lord said, "If you have faith as a mustard seed, you can say to this mulberry tree, 'Be pulled up by the roots and be planted in the sea,' and it would obey you. ⁷And which of you, having a servant plowing or tending sheep, will say to him when he has come in from the field, 'Come at once and sit down to eat'? ⁸But will he not rather say to him, 'Prepare something for my supper, and gird yourself ᵃand serve me till I have eaten and drunk, and afterward you will eat and drink'? ⁹Does he thank that servant because he did the things that were commanded ¹him? I think not. ¹⁰So likewise you, when you have done all those things which you are commanded, say, 'We are ᵃunprofitable servants. We have done what was our duty to do.'"

TEN LEPERS CLEANSED

¹¹Now it happened ᵃas He went to Jerusalem that He passed through the midst of Samaria and Galilee. ¹²Then as He entered a certain village, there met Him ten men who were lepers, ᵃwho stood afar off. ¹³And they lifted up *their* voices and said, "Jesus, Master, have mercy on us!"

¹⁴So when He saw *them,* He said to them, ᵃ"Go, show yourselves to the priests." And so it was that as they went, they were cleansed.

¹⁵And one of them, when he saw that he was healed, returned, and with a loud voice ᵃglorified God, ¹⁶and fell down on *his* face at His feet, giving Him thanks. And he was a ᵃSamaritan.

¹⁷So Jesus answered and said, "Were there not ten cleansed? But where *are* the nine? ¹⁸Were there not any found

---

16:29
ᵃIs. 8:20; 34:16;
[John 5:39, 45];
Acts 15:21; 17:11;
[2 Tim. 3:15]

16:31
ᵃ[John 5:46]
ᵇJohn 12:10, 11

17:1 ᵃ[1 Cor. 11:19]
ᵇMatt. 18:6, 7;
26:24;
Mark 9:42;
[2 Thess. 1:6];
Jude 11

17:3
ᵃ[Matt. 18:15, 21]
ᵇLev. 19:17;
[Prov. 17:10;
Gal. 6:1;
James 5:19, 20]

17:6
ᵃMatt. 17:20;
21:21;
[Mark 9:23;
11:23];
Luke 13:19

17:8
ᵃ[Luke 12:37]

17:10
ᵃJob 22:3; 35:7;
Ps. 16:2;
Matt. 25:30;
Rom. 3:12; 11:35;
[1 Cor. 9:16, 17];
Philem. 11

17:11
ᵃLuke 9:51, 52;
John 4:4

17:12 ᵃLev. 13:46;
Num. 5:2

17:14
ᵃLev. 13:1–59;
14:1–32;
Matt. 8:4;
Luke 5:14

17:15
ᵃLuke 5:25;
18:43

17:16
ᵃ2 Kin. 17:24;
Luke 9:52, 53;
John 4:9

17:1 ¹*stumbling blocks*   17:2 ¹*cause one of these little ones to stumble*
17:3 ¹NU omits *against you*   17:4 ¹M omits *to you*   17:9 ¹NU omits *the rest of v. 9; M omits* him

who returned to give glory to God except this foreigner?" ¹⁹ᵃAnd He said to him, "Arise, go your way. Your faith has made you well."

THE COMING OF THE KINGDOM
(Gen. 6:5—8:22; 19:12–14)

²⁰Now when He was asked by the Pharisees when the kingdom of God would come, He answered them and said, "The kingdom of God does not come with observation; ²¹ᵃnor will they say, ¹'See here!' or 'See there!' For indeed, ᵇthe kingdom of God is ²within you."

²²Then He said to the disciples, ᵃ"The days will come when you will desire to see one of the days of the Son of Man, and you will not see *it.* ²³ᵃAnd they will say to you, ¹'Look here!' or 'Look there!' Do not go after *them* or follow *them.* ²⁴ᵃFor as the lightning that flashes out of one *part* under heaven shines to the other *part* under heaven, so also the Son of Man will be in His day. ²⁵ᵃBut first He must suffer many things and be ᵇrejected by this generation. ²⁶ᵃAnd as it ᵇwas in the ᶜdays of ᵈNoah, so it will be also in the days of the Son of Man: ²⁷They ate, they drank, they married wives, they were given in marriage, until the ᵃday that Noah entered the ark, and the flood came and ᵇdestroyed them all. ²⁸ᵃLikewise as it was also in the days of Lot: They ate, they drank, they bought, they sold, they planted, they built; ²⁹but on ᵃthe day that Lot went out of Sodom it rained fire and brimstone from heaven and destroyed *them* all. ³⁰Even so will it be in the day when the Son of Man ᵃis revealed.

³¹"In that day, he ᵃwho is on the housetop, and his ¹goods *are* in the house, let him not come down to take them away. And likewise the one who is in the field, let him not turn back. ³²ᵃRemember Lot's wife. ³³ᵃWhoever seeks to save his life will lose it, and whoever loses his life will preserve it. ³⁴ᵃI tell you, in that night there will be two ¹men in one bed: the one will be taken and the other will be left. ³⁵ᵃTwo *women* will be grinding together: the one will be taken and the other left. ³⁶¹Two *men* will be in the field: the one will be taken and the other left."

³⁷And they answered and said to Him, ᵃ"Where, Lord?"

So He said to them, "Wherever the body is, there the eagles will be gathered together."

THE PARABLE OF THE PERSISTENT WIDOW

18 Then He spoke a parable to them, that men ᵃalways ought to pray and not lose heart, ²saying: "There was in a certain city a judge who did not fear God nor ¹regard man. ³Now there was a widow in that city; and she came to him, saying, ¹'Get justice for me from my adversary.' ⁴And he would not for a while; but afterward he said within himself, 'Though I do not fear God nor regard man, ⁵ᵃyet because this widow troubles me I will ¹avenge her, lest by her continual coming she weary me.'"

⁶Then the Lord said, "Hear what the unjust judge said. ⁷And ᵃshall God not avenge His own elect who cry out day

18:5 ᵃLuke 11:8   18:7 ᵃRev. 6:10

17:21 ¹NU reverses *here* and *there*   ²*in your midst*   17:23 ¹NU reverses *here* and *there*   17:31 ¹*possessions*   17:34 ¹Or *people*   17:36 ¹NU, M omit v. 36.   18:2 ¹*respect*   18:3 ¹*Avenge me on*   18:5 ¹*vindicate*

and night to Him, though He bears long with them? [8]I tell you [a]that He will avenge them speedily. Nevertheless, when the Son of Man comes, will He really find faith on the earth?"

THE PARABLE OF THE PHARISEE AND THE TAX COLLECTOR

[9]Also He spoke this parable to some [a]who trusted in themselves that they were righteous, and despised others: [10]"Two men went up to the temple to pray, one a Pharisee and the other a tax collector. [11]The Pharisee [a]stood and prayed thus with himself, [b]'God, I thank You that I am not like other men—extortioners, unjust, adulterers, or even as this tax collector. [12]I fast twice a week; I give tithes of all that I possess.' [13]And the tax collector, standing afar off, would not so much as raise *his* eyes to heaven, but beat his breast, saying, 'God, be merciful to me a sinner!' [14]I tell you, this man went down to his house justified *rather* than the other; [a]for everyone who exalts himself will be [1]humbled, and he who humbles himself will be exalted."

JESUS BLESSES LITTLE CHILDREN
(Matt. 19:13–15; Mark 10:13–16)

[15a]Then they also brought infants to Him that He might touch them; but when the disciples saw *it,* they rebuked them. [16]But Jesus called them to *Him* and said, "Let the little children come to Me, and do not forbid them; for [a]of such is the kingdom of God. [17a]Assuredly, I say to you, whoever does not receive the kingdom of God as a little child will by no means enter it."

JESUS COUNSELS THE RICH YOUNG RULER
(Matt. 19:16–22; Mark 10:17–22)

[18a]Now a certain ruler asked Him, saying, "Good Teacher, what shall I do to inherit eternal life?"

[19]So Jesus said to him, "Why do you call Me good? No one *is* good but [a]One, *that is,* God. [20]You know the commandments: [a]'Do not commit adultery,' 'Do not murder,' 'Do not steal,' 'Do not bear false witness,' [b]'Honor your father and your mother.'"

[21]And he said, "All [a]these things I have kept from my youth."

[22]So when Jesus heard these things, He said to him, "You still lack one thing. [a]Sell all that you have and distribute to the poor, and you will have treasure in heaven; and come, follow Me."

[23]But when he heard this, he became very sorrowful, for he was very rich.

WITH GOD ALL THINGS ARE POSSIBLE
(Matt. 19:23–30; Mark 10:23–31)

[24]And when Jesus saw that he became very sorrowful, He said, [a]"How hard it is for those who have riches to enter the kingdom of God! [25]For it is easier for a camel to go through the eye of a needle than for a rich man to enter the kingdom of God."

[26]And those who heard it said, "Who then can be saved?"

18:8
[a]Heb. 10:37;
[2 Pet. 3:8, 9]

18:9
[a]Prov. 30:12;
Luke 10:29;
16:15

18:11 [a]Ps. 135:2
[b]Is. 1:15; 58:2;
Rev. 3:17

18:14
[a]Job 22:29;
Matt. 23:12;
Luke 14:11;
[James 4:6;
1 Pet. 5:5]

18:15
[a]Matt. 19:13–15;
Mark 10:13–16

18:16
[a]Matt. 18:3;
1 Cor. 14:20;
1 Pet. 2:2

18:17
[a]Matt. 18:3;
19:14; Mark 10:15

18:18
[a]Matt. 19:16–29;
Mark 10:17–30

18:19
[a]Ps. 86:5; 119:68

18:20
[a]Ex. 20:12–16;
Deut. 5:16–20;
Mark 10:19;
Rom. 13:9
[b]Eph. 6:2;
Col. 3:20

18:21 [a]Phil. 3:6

18:22
[a]Matt. 6:19,
20; 19:21;
[1 Tim. 6:19]

18:24
[a]Prov. 11:28;
Matt. 19:23;
Mark 10:23

18:14 [1]*put down*

27But He said, a"The things which are impossible with men are possible with God."

28aThen Peter said, "See, we have left 1all and followed You."

29So He said to them, "Assuredly, I say to you, athere is no one who has left house or parents or brothers or wife or children, for the sake of the kingdom of God, 30awho shall not receive many times more in this present time, and in the age to come eternal life."

JESUS A THIRD TIME PREDICTS HIS DEATH AND RESURRECTION
(Matt. 20:17–19; Mark 10:32–34)

31aThen He took the twelve aside and said to them, "Behold, we are going up to Jerusalem, and all things bthat are written by the prophets concerning the Son of Man will be 1accomplished. 32For aHe will be delivered to the Gentiles and will be mocked and insulted and spit upon. 33They will scourge *Him* and kill Him. And the third day He will rise again."

34aBut they understood none of these things; this saying was hidden from them, and they did not know the things which were spoken.

A BLIND MAN RECEIVES HIS SIGHT
(Matt. 20:29–34; Mark 10:46–52)

35aThen it happened, as He was coming near Jericho, that a certain blind man sat by the road begging. 36And hearing a multitude passing by, he asked what it meant. 37So they told him that Jesus of Nazareth was passing by. 38And he cried out, saying, "Jesus, aSon of David, have mercy on me!"

39Then those who went before warned him that he should be quiet; but he cried out all the more, "Son of David, have mercy on me!"

40So Jesus stood still and commanded him to be brought to Him. And when he had come near, He asked him, 41saying, "What do you want Me to do for you?"

He said, "Lord, that I may receive my sight."

42Then Jesus said to him, "Receive your sight; ayour faith has made you well." 43And immediately he received his sight, and followed Him, aglorifying God. And all the people, when they saw *it*, gave praise to God.

JESUS COMES TO ZACCHAEUS' HOUSE

19 Then *Jesus* entered and passed through aJericho. 2Now behold, *there was* a man named Zacchaeus who was a chief tax collector, and he was rich. 3And he sought to asee who Jesus was, but could not because of the crowd, for he was of short stature. 4So he ran ahead and climbed up into a sycamore tree to see Him, for He was going to pass that *way.* 5And when Jesus came to the place, He looked up 1and saw him, and said to him, "Zacchaeus, 2make haste and come down, for today I must stay at your house." 6So he 1made haste and came down, and received Him joyfully. 7But when they saw *it,*

18:27 aJob 42:2;
Jer. 32:17;
Zech. 8:6;
Matt. 19:26;
Luke 1:37
18:28
aMatt. 19:27
18:29
aDeut. 33:9
18:30 aJob 42:10
18:31
aMatt. 16:21;
17:22; 20:17;
Mark 10:32;
Luke 9:51
bPs. 22; [Is. 53]
18:32
aMatt. 26:67;
27:2, 29, 41;
Mark 14:65; 15:1,
19, 20, 31;
Luke 23:1;
John 18:28;
Acts 3:13
18:34
aMark 9:32;
Luke 2:50; 9:45;
[John 10:6;
12:16]
18:35
aMatt. 20:29–34;
Mark 10:46–52
18:38
aMatt. 9:27
18:42
aLuke 17:19
18:43
aLuke 5:26;
Acts 4:21; 11:18
19:1 aJosh. 6:26;
1 Kin. 16:34
19:3 aJohn 12:21

18:28 1NU *our own*   18:31 1*fulfilled*   19:5 1NU omits *and saw him*   2*hurry*
19:6 1*hurried*

they all [1]complained, saying, [a]"He has gone to be a guest with a man who is a sinner."

[8]Then Zacchaeus stood and said to the Lord, "Look, Lord, I give half of my goods to the [a]poor; and if I have taken anything from anyone by [b]false accusation, [c]I restore fourfold."

[9]And Jesus said to him, "Today salvation has come to this house, because [a]he also is [b]a son of Abraham; [10a]for the Son of Man has come to seek and to save that which was lost."

THE PARABLE OF THE MINAS
(Matt. 25:14–30)

[11]Now as they heard these things, He spoke another parable, because He was near Jerusalem and because [a]they thought the kingdom of God would appear immediately. [12a]Therefore He said: "A certain nobleman went into a far country to receive for himself a kingdom and to return. [13]So he called ten of his servants, delivered to them ten [1]minas, and said to them, 'Do business till I come.' [14a]But his citizens hated him, and sent a delegation after him, saying, 'We will not have this *man* to reign over us.'

[15]"And so it was that when he returned, having received the kingdom, he then commanded these servants, to whom he had given the money, to be called to him, that he might know how much every man had gained by trading. [16]Then came the first, saying, 'Master, your mina has earned ten minas.' [17]And he said to him, [a]'Well *done,* good servant; because you were [b]faithful in a very little, have authority over ten cities.' [18]And the second came, saying, 'Master, your mina has earned five minas.' [19]Likewise he said to him, 'You also be over five cities.'

[20]"Then another came, saying, 'Master, here is your mina, which I have kept put away in a handkerchief. [21a]For I feared you, because you are [1]an austere man. You collect what you did not deposit, and reap what you did not sow.' [22]And he said to him, [a]'Out of your own mouth I will judge you, *you* wicked servant. [b]You knew that I was an austere man, collecting what I did not deposit and reaping what I did not sow. [23]Why then did you not put my money in the bank, that at my coming I might have collected it with interest?'

[24]"And he said to those who stood by, 'Take the mina from him, and give *it* to him who has ten minas.' [25](But they said to him, 'Master, he has ten minas.') [26]'For I say to you, [a]that to everyone who has will be given; and from him who does not have, even what he has will be taken away from him. [27]But bring here those enemies of mine, who did not want me to reign over them, and slay *them* before me.'"

THE TRIUMPHAL ENTRY
(Matt. 21:1–11; Mark 11:1–11; John 12:12–19)

[28]When He had said this, [a]He went on ahead, going up to Jerusalem. [29a]And it came to pass, when He drew near to [1]Bethphage and [b]Bethany, at the mountain called [c]Olivet, *that* He sent two of His disciples, [30]saying, "Go into the village opposite *you,* where as you enter you will find a colt tied, on

19:7 [a]Matt. 9:11;
Luke 5:30; 15:2

19:8 [a][Ps. 41:1]
[b]Luke 3:14
[c]Ex. 22:1;
Lev. 6:5;
Num. 5:7;
1 Sam. 12:3;
2 Sam. 12:6

19:9
[a]Luke 3:8; 13:16;
[Rom. 4:16;
Gal. 3:7]
[b][Luke 13:16]

19:10
[a]Matt. 18:11;
[Luke 5:32;
Rom. 5:8]

19:11 [a]Acts 1:6

19:12
[a]Matt. 25:14–30;
Mark 13:34

19:14 [a][John 1:11]

19:17
[a]Matt. 25:21, 23
[b]Luke 16:10

19:21
[a]Matt. 25:24

19:22
[a]2 Sam. 1:16;
Job 15:6;
[Matt. 12:37]
[b]Matt. 25:26

19:26
[a]Matt. 13:12;
25:29;
Mark 4:25;
Luke 8:18

19:28
[a]Mark 10:32

19:29
[a]Matt. 21:1;
Mark 11:1
[b]Matt. 26:6;
John 12:1
[c]John 8:1;
Acts 1:12

19:7 [1]grumbled　19:13 [1]Gr. *mna,* same as Heb. *minah,* each worth about three months' salary　19:21 [1]*a severe*　19:29 [1]M Bethsphage

which no one has ever sat. Loose it and bring *it here.* ³¹And if anyone asks you, 'Why are you loosing *it?*' thus you shall say to him, 'Because the Lord has need of it.'"

³²So those who were sent went their way and found *it* just ᵃas He had said to them. ³³But as they were loosing the colt, the owners of it said to them, "Why are you loosing the colt?"

³⁴And they said, "The Lord has need of him." ³⁵Then they brought him to Jesus. ᵃAnd they threw their own clothes on the colt, and they set Jesus on him. ³⁶And as He went, *many* spread their clothes on the road.

³⁷Then, as He was now drawing near the descent of the Mount of Olives, the whole multitude of the disciples began to ᵃrejoice and praise God with a loud voice for all the mighty works they had seen, ³⁸saying:

ᵃ" 'Blessed *is* the King who comes in the name of the LORD!'
ᵇPeace in heaven and glory in the highest!"

³⁹And some of the Pharisees called to Him from the crowd, "Teacher, rebuke Your disciples."

⁴⁰But He answered and said to them, "I tell you that if these should keep silent, ᵃthe stones would immediately cry out."

JESUS WEEPS OVER JERUSALEM

⁴¹Now as He drew near, He saw the city and ᵃwept over it, ⁴²saying, "If you had known, even you, especially in this ᵃyour day, the things *that* ᵇ*make* for your ᶜpeace! But now they are hidden from your eyes. ⁴³For days will come upon you when your enemies will ᵃbuild an embankment around you, surround you and close you in on every side, ⁴⁴ᵃand level you, and your children within you, to the ground; and ᵇthey will not leave in you one stone upon another, ᶜbecause you did not know the time of your visitation."

JESUS CLEANSES THE TEMPLE
(Matt. 21:12–17; Mark 11:15–19; John 2:12–25)

⁴⁵ᵃThen He went into the temple and began to drive out those who ¹bought and sold in it, ⁴⁶saying to them, "It is written, ᵃ'My house ¹is a house of prayer,' but you have made it a ᵇ'den of thieves.'"

⁴⁷And He ᵃwas teaching daily in the temple. But ᵇthe chief priests, the scribes, and the leaders of the people sought to destroy Him, ⁴⁸and were unable to do anything; for all the people were very attentive to ᵃhear Him.

JESUS' AUTHORITY QUESTIONED
(Matt. 21:23–27; Mark 11:27–33)

20 Now ᵃit happened on one of those days, as He taught the people in the temple and preached the gospel, *that* the chief priests and the scribes, together with the elders, confronted *Him* ²and spoke to Him, saying, "Tell us, ᵃby what authority are You doing these things? Or who is he who gave You this authority?"

³But He answered and said to them, "I also will ask you one thing, and answer Me: ⁴The ᵃbaptism of John—was it from heaven or from men?"

19:32 ᵃLuke 22:13

19:35 ᵃ2 Kin. 9:13; Matt. 21:7; Mark 11:7

19:37 ᵃLuke 13:17; 18:43

19:38 ᵃPs. 118:26; Luke 13:35 ᵇLuke 2:14; [Eph. 2:14]

19:40 ᵃHab. 2:11

19:41 ᵃIs. 53:3; John 11:35

19:42 ᵃPs. 95:7, 8; Heb. 3:13 ᵇ[Luke 1:77–79; Acts 10:36] ᶜ[Rom. 5:1]

19:43 ᵃIs. 29:3, 4; Jer. 6:3, 6; Luke 21:20

19:44 ᵃ1 Kin. 9:7, 8; Mic. 3:12 ᵇMatt. 24:2; Mark 13:2; Luke 21:6 ᶜ[Dan. 9:24; Luke 1:68, 78; 1 Pet. 2:12]

19:45 ᵃMal. 3:1; Matt. 21:12, 13; Mark 11:11, 15–17; John 2:13–16

19:46 ᵃIs. 56:7 ᵇJer. 7:11

19:47 ᵃLuke 21:37; 22:53 ᵇMark 11:18; Luke 20:19; John 7:19; 8:37

19:48 ᵃLuke 21:38

20:1 ᵃMatt. 21:23–27; Mark 11:27–33

20:2 ᵃActs 4:7; 7:27

20:4 ᵃJohn 1:26, 31

19:45 ¹NU *were selling, saying*   **19:46** ¹NU *shall be*

⁵And they reasoned among themselves, saying, "If we say, 'From heaven,' He will say, 'Why ¹then did you not believe him?' ⁶But if we say, 'From men,' all the people will stone us, ªfor they are persuaded that John was a prophet." ⁷So they answered that they did not know where *it was* from.

⁸And Jesus said to them, "Neither will I tell you by what authority I do these things."

THE PARABLE OF THE WICKED VINEDRESSERS
(Matt. 21:33–46; Mark 12:1–12)

⁹Then He began to tell the people this parable: ª"A certain man planted a vineyard, leased it to ¹vinedressers, and went into a far country for a long time. ¹⁰Now at ¹vintage-time he ªsent a servant to the vinedressers, that they might give him some of the fruit of the vineyard. But the vinedressers beat him and sent *him* away empty-handed. ¹¹Again he sent another servant; and they beat him also, treated *him* shamefully, and sent *him* away empty-handed. ¹²And again he sent a third; and they wounded him also and cast *him* out.

¹³"Then the owner of the vineyard said, 'What shall I do? I will send my beloved son. Probably they will respect *him* when they see him.' ¹⁴But when the vinedressers saw him, they reasoned among themselves, saying, 'This is the ªheir. Come, ᵇlet us kill him, that the inheritance may be ᶜours.' ¹⁵So they cast him out of the vineyard and ªkilled *him*. Therefore what will the owner of the vineyard do to them? ¹⁶He will come and destroy those vinedressers and give the vineyard to ªothers."

And when they heard *it* they said, "Certainly not!"

¹⁷Then He looked at them and said, "What then is this that is written:

ª'The stone which the builders rejected
Has become the chief cornerstone'?

¹⁸Whoever falls on that stone will be ªbroken; but ᵇon whomever it falls, it will grind him to powder."

¹⁹And the chief priests and the scribes that very hour sought to lay hands on Him, but they ¹feared the people—for they knew He had spoken this parable against them.

THE PHARISEES: IS IT LAWFUL TO PAY TAXES TO CAESAR?
(Matt. 22:15–22; Mark 12:13–17)

²⁰ªSo they watched *Him,* and sent spies who pretended to be righteous, that they might seize on His words, in order to deliver Him to the power and the authority of the governor. ²¹Then they asked Him, saying, ª"Teacher, we know that You say and teach rightly, and You do not show personal favoritism, but teach the way of God in truth: ²²Is it lawful for us to pay taxes to Caesar or not?"

²³But He perceived their craftiness, and said to them, ¹"Why do you test Me? ²⁴Show Me a denarius. Whose image and inscription does it have?"

They answered and said, "Caesar's."

²⁵And He said to them, ª"Render¹ therefore to Caesar the things that are Caesar's, and to God the things that are God's."

20:6 ªMatt. 14:5; 21:26; Mark 6:20; Luke 7:24–30

20:9 ªPs. 80:8; Matt. 21:33–46; Mark 12:1–12

20:10 ª2 Kin. 17:13, 14; 2 Chr. 36:15, 16; [Acts 7:52; 1 Thess. 2:15]

20:14 ª[Heb. 1:1–3]; ᵇMatt. 27:21–23; ᶜJohn 11:47, 48

20:15 ªLuke 23:33; Acts 2:22, 23; 3:15

20:16 ª[John 1:11–13]; Rom. 11:1, 11; 1 Cor. 6:15; Gal. 2:17; 3:21; 6:14

20:17 ªPs. 118:22; Matt. 21:42; 1 Pet. 2:7, 8

20:18 ªIs. 8:14, 15; ᵇ[Dan. 2:34, 35, 44, 45]; Matt. 21:44

20:20 ªMatt. 22:15

20:21 ªMatt. 22:16; Mark 12:14

20:25 ªMatt. 17:24–27; Rom. 13:7; [1 Pet. 2:13–17]

20:5 ¹NU, M omit *then* 20:9 ¹*tenant farmers* 20:10 ¹Lit. *the season*
20:19 ¹M *were afraid—for* 20:23 ¹NU omits *Why do you test Me?*
20:25 ¹*Pay*

26But they could not catch Him in His words in the presence of the people. And they marveled at His answer and kept silent.

THE SADDUCEES: WHAT ABOUT THE RESURRECTION?
(*Matt. 22:23–33; Mark 12:18–27*)

27aThen some of the Sadducees, bwho deny that there is a resurrection, came to *Him* and asked Him, 28saying: "Teacher, Moses wrote to us *that* if a man's brother dies, having a wife, and he dies without children, his brother should take his wife and raise up offspring for his brother. 29Now there were seven brothers. And the first took a wife, and died without children. 30And the second 1took her as wife, and he died childless. 31Then the third took her, and in like manner the seven 1also; and they left no children, and died. 32Last of all the woman died also. 33Therefore, in the resurrection, whose wife does she become? For all seven had her as wife."

34Jesus answered and said to them, "The sons of this age marry and are given in marriage. 35But those who are acounted worthy to attain that age, and the resurrection from the dead, neither marry nor are given in marriage; 36nor can they die anymore, for athey are equal to the angels and are sons of God, bbeing sons of the resurrection. 37But even Moses showed in the *burning* bush *passage* that the dead are raised, when he called the Lord a'the God of Abraham, the God of Isaac, and the God of Jacob.' 38For He is not the God of the dead but of the living, for aall live to Him."

39Then some of the scribes answered and said, "Teacher, You have spoken well." 40But after that they dared not question Him anymore.

JESUS: HOW CAN DAVID CALL HIS DESCENDANT LORD?
(*Matt. 22:41–46; Mark 12:35–37*)

41And He said to them, a"How can they say that the Christ is the Son of David? 42Now David himself said in the Book of Psalms:

a'The LORD said to my Lord,
   "Sit at My right hand,
43   Till I make Your enemies Your footstool." '

44Therefore David calls Him 'Lord'; ahow is He then his Son?"

BEWARE OF THE SCRIBES
(*Matt. 23:1–7; Mark 12:38–40*)

45aThen, in the hearing of all the people, He said to His disciples, 46a"Beware of the scribes, who desire to go around in long robes, blove greetings in the marketplaces, the best seats in the synagogues, and the best places at feasts, 47awho devour widows' houses, and for a bpretense make long prayers. These will receive greater condemnation."

THE WIDOW'S TWO MITES
(*Mark 12:41–44*)

21 And He looked up aand saw the rich putting their gifts into the treasury, 2and He saw also a certain apoor

---

20:27
aMatt. 22:23–33;
Mark 12:18–27
bActs 23:6, 8

20:35 aPhil. 3:11

20:36
a[1 Cor. 15:42,
49, 52;
1 John 3:2]
bRom. 8:23

20:37
aEx. 3:1–6, 15;
Acts 7:30–32

20:38
a[Rom. 6:10,
11; 14:8, 9;
Heb. 11:16]

20:41
aMatt. 22:41–46;
Mark 12:35–37

20:42 aPs. 110:1;
Acts 2:34, 35

20:44
aActs 13:22, 23;
Rom. 1:3; 9:4, 5

20:45
aMatt. 23:1–7;
Mark 12:38–40

20:46
aMatt. 23:5
bLuke 11:43; 14:7

20:47
aMatt. 23:14
b[Matt. 6:5, 6]

21:1
aMark 12:41–44

21:2
a[2 Cor. 6:10]

20:30 1NU omits the rest of v. 30.   20:31 1NU, M *also left no children*

widow putting in two bmites.[1] 3So He said, "Truly I say to you athat this poor widow has put in more than all; 4for all these out of their abundance have put in offerings [1]for God, but she out of her poverty put in aall the livelihood that she had."

JESUS PREDICTS THE DESTRUCTION OF THE TEMPLE
(Matt. 24:1, 2; Mark 13:1, 2)

5aThen, as some spoke of the temple, how it was [1]adorned with beautiful stones and donations, He said, 6"These things which you see—the days will come in which anot one stone shall be left upon another that shall not be thrown down."

THE SIGNS OF THE TIMES AND THE END OF THE AGE
(Matt. 24:3–14; Mark 13:3–13)

7So they asked Him, saying, "Teacher, but when will these things be? And what sign will there be when these things are about to take place?"

8And He said: a"Take heed that you not be deceived. For many will come in My name, saying, 'I am He,' and, 'The time has drawn near.' [1]Therefore do not [2]go after them. 9But when you hear of awars and commotions, do not be terrified; for these things must come to pass first, but the end will not come immediately."

10aThen He said to them, "Nation will rise against nation, and kingdom against kingdom. 11And there will be great aearthquakes in various places, and famines and pestilences; and there will be fearful sights and great signs from heaven. 12aBut before all these things, they will lay their hands on you and persecute you, delivering you up to the synagogues and bprisons. cYou will be brought before kings and rulers dfor My name's sake. 13But ait will turn out for you as an occasion for testimony. 14aTherefore settle it in your hearts not to meditate beforehand on what you will [1]answer; 15for I will give you a mouth and wisdom awhich all your adversaries will not be able to contradict or [1]resist. 16aYou will be betrayed even by parents and brothers, relatives and friends; and they will put bsome of you to death. 17And ayou will be hated by all for My name's sake. 18aBut not a hair of your head shall be lost. 19By your patience possess your souls.

THE DESTRUCTION OF JERUSALEM
(Matt. 24:15–28; Mark 13:14–23)

20a"But when you see Jerusalem surrounded by armies, then know that its desolation is near. 21Then let those who are in Judea flee to the mountains, let those who are in the midst of her depart, and let not those who are in the country enter her. 22For these are the days of vengeance, that aall things which are written may be fulfilled. 23aBut woe to those who are pregnant and to those who are nursing babies in those days! For there will be great distress in the land and wrath upon this people. 24And they will fall by the edge of the sword, and be led away captive into all nations. And Jerusalem will be trampled by Gentiles auntil the times of the Gentiles are fulfilled.

21:2 bMark 12:42

21:3
a[2 Cor. 8:12]

21:4
a[2 Cor. 8:12]

21:5 aMatt. 24:1;
Mark 13:1

21:6
aIs. 64:10, 11;
Lam. 2:6–9;
Mic. 3:12;
Luke 19:41–44

21:8 aMatt. 24:4;
Mark 13:5;
Eph. 5:6;
2 Thess. 2:3;
[1 John 4:1]

21:9 aRev. 6:4

21:10
aMatt. 24:7

21:11 aRev. 6:12

21:12
aMark 13:9;
John 16:2;
[Rev. 2:10]
bActs 4:3; 5:18;
12:4; 16:24
cActs 25:23
d1 Pet. 2:13

21:13
a[Phil. 1:12–14, 28;
2 Thess. 1:5]

21:14
aMatt. 10:19;
Mark 13:11;
Luke 12:11

21:15 aActs 6:10

21:16 aMic. 7:6;
Mark 13:12
bActs 7:59; 12:2

21:17
aMatt. 10:22

21:18
aMatt. 10:30;
Luke 12:7

21:20
aMatt. 24:15;
Mark 13:14

21:22 aIs. 63:4;
[Dan. 9:24–27];
Hos. 9:7;
[Zech. 11:1]

21:23
aMatt. 24:19

21:24
a[Dan. 9:27;
12:7]

21:2 [1]Gr. lepta, very small copper coins   21:4 [1]NU omits for God
21:5 [1]decorated   21:8 [1]NU omits Therefore   [2]follow   21:14 [1]say in
defense   21:15 [1]withstand

21:25 ᵃIs. 13:9,
10, 13;
Matt. 24:29;
Mark 13:24;
[2 Pet. 3:10–12]

21:26
ᵃMatt. 24:29

21:27 ᵃDan. 7:13;
[Matt. 16:27;
24:30; 26:64];
Mark 13:26;
Rev. 1:7; 14:14

21:28
ᵃ[Rom. 8:19, 23]

21:29
ᵃMatt. 24:32;
Mark 13:28

21:33 ᵃIs. 51:6;
Matt. 24:35;
Heb. 1:10, 11;
[2 Pet. 3:7,
10, 12]
ᵇIs. 40:8;
Luke 16:17;
1 Pet. 1:24, 25

21:34
ᵃMatt. 24:42–44;
Mark 4:19;
Luke 12:40, 45;
Rom. 13:13;
1 Thess. 5:6;
1 Pet. 4:7
ᵇLuke 8:14

21:35
ᵃ1 Thess. 5:2;
[2 Pet. 3:10];
Rev. 3:3; 16:15

21:36
ᵃMatt. 24:42;
25:13;
Mark 13:33;
Luke 12:40
ᵇLuke 18:1;
[Eph. 6:18];
Col. 4:2;
1 Thess. 5:17
ᶜLuke 20:35
ᵈPs. 1:5;
[Eph. 6:13]

21:37
ᵃJohn 8:1, 2
ᵇLuke 22:39

22:1
ᵃMatt. 26:2–5;
Mark 14:1, 2

22:2 ᵃPs. 2:2;
John 11:47;
Acts 4:27

22:3
ᵃMatt. 26:14–16;
Mark 14:10, 11;
John 13:2, 27
ᵇMatt. 10:2–4

22:5 ᵃZech. 11:12

22:6 ᵃPs. 41:9

22:7
ᵃMatt. 26:17–19;
Mark 14:12–16

THE COMING OF THE SON OF MAN
(Matt. 24:29–31; Mark 13:24–27)

25ᵃ"And there will be signs in the sun, in the moon, and in the stars; and on the earth distress of nations, with perplexity, the sea and the waves roaring; 26men's hearts failing them from fear and the expectation of those things which are coming on the earth, ᵃfor the powers of the heavens will be shaken. 27Then they will see the Son of Man ᵃcoming in a cloud with power and great glory. 28Now when these things begin to happen, look up and lift up your heads, because ᵃyour redemption draws near."

THE PARABLE OF THE FIG TREE
(Matt. 24:32–35; Mark 13:28–31)

29ᵃThen He spoke to them a parable: "Look at the fig tree, and all the trees. 30When they are already budding, you see and know for yourselves that summer is now near. 31So you also, when you see these things happening, know that the kingdom of God is near. 32Assuredly, I say to you, this generation will by no means pass away till all things take place. 33ᵃHeaven and earth will pass away, but My ᵇwords will by no means pass away.

THE IMPORTANCE OF WATCHING
(Matt. 24:36–44; Mark 13:32–37)

34"But ᵃtake heed to yourselves, lest your hearts be weighed down with ¹carousing, drunkenness, and ᵇcares of this life, and that Day come on you unexpectedly. 35For ᵃit will come as a snare on all those who dwell on the face of the whole earth. 36ᵃWatch therefore, and ᵇpray always that you may ¹be counted ᶜworthy to escape all these things that will come to pass, and ᵈto stand before the Son of Man."

37ᵃAnd in the daytime He was teaching in the temple, but ᵇat night He went out and stayed on the mountain called Olivet. 38Then early in the morning all the people came to Him in the temple to hear Him.

THE PLOT TO KILL JESUS
(Matt. 26:1–5, 14–16; Mark 14:1, 2, 10, 11; John 11:45–53)

22 Now ᵃthe Feast of Unleavened Bread drew near, which is called Passover. 2And ᵃthe chief priests and the scribes sought how they might kill Him, for they feared the people.

3ᵃThen Satan entered Judas, surnamed Iscariot, who was numbered among the ᵇtwelve. 4So he went his way and conferred with the chief priests and captains, how he might betray Him to them. 5And they were glad, and ᵃagreed to give him money. 6So he promised and sought opportunity to ᵃbetray Him to them in the absence of the multitude.

JESUS AND HIS DISCIPLES PREPARE THE PASSOVER

7ᵃThen came the Day of Unleavened Bread, when the Passover must be ¹killed. 8And He sent Peter and John, saying, "Go and prepare the Passover for us, that we may eat."

21:34 ¹dissipation   21:36 ¹NU have strength to   22:7 ¹Sacrificed

⁹So they said to Him, "Where do You want us to prepare?" ¹⁰And He said to them, "Behold, when you have entered the city, a man will meet you carrying a pitcher of water; follow him into the house which he enters. ¹¹Then you shall say to the master of the house, 'The Teacher says to you, "Where is the guest room where I may eat the Passover with My disciples?"' ¹²Then he will show you a large, furnished upper room; there make ready."

¹³So they went and ᵃfound it just as He had said to them, and they prepared the Passover.

JESUS INSTITUTES THE LORD'S SUPPER

¹⁴ᵃWhen the hour had come, He sat down, and the ¹twelve apostles with Him. ¹⁵Then He said to them, "With *fervent* desire I have desired to eat this Passover with you before I suffer; ¹⁶for I say to you, I will no longer eat of it ᵃuntil it is fulfilled in the kingdom of God."

¹⁷Then He took the cup, and gave thanks, and said, "Take this and divide *it* among yourselves; ¹⁸for ᵃI say to you, ¹I will not drink of the fruit of the vine until the kingdom of God comes."

¹⁹ᵃAnd He took bread, gave thanks and broke *it*, and gave *it* to them, saying, "This is My ᵇbody which is given for you; ᶜdo this in remembrance of Me."

²⁰Likewise He also *took* the cup after supper, saying, ᵃ"This cup *is* the new covenant in My blood, which is shed for you. ²¹ᵃBut behold, the hand of My betrayer *is* with Me on the table. ²²ᵃAnd truly the Son of Man goes ᵇas it has been determined, but woe to that man by whom He is betrayed!"

²³ᵃThen they began to question among themselves, which of them it was who would do this thing.

THE DISCIPLES ARGUE ABOUT GREATNESS

²⁴ᵃNow there was also a dispute among them, as to which of them should be considered the greatest. ²⁵ᵃAnd He said to them, "The kings of the Gentiles exercise lordship over them, and those who exercise authority over them are called 'benefactors.' ²⁶ᵃBut not so *among* you; on the contrary, ᵇhe who is greatest among you, let him be as the younger, and he who governs as he who serves. ²⁷ᵃFor who *is* greater, he who sits at the table, or he who serves? *Is* it not he who sits at the table? Yet ᵇI am among you as the One who serves.

²⁸"But you are those who have continued with Me in ᵃMy trials. ²⁹And ᵃI bestow upon you a kingdom, just as My Father bestowed *one* upon Me, ³⁰that ᵃyou may eat and drink at My table in My kingdom, ᵇand sit on thrones judging the twelve tribes of Israel."

JESUS PREDICTS PETER'S DENIAL
(Matt. 26:31–35; Mark 14:27–31; John 13:36–38)

³¹And the Lord said, "Simon, Simon! Indeed, ᵃSatan has asked for you, that he may ᵇsift *you* as wheat. ³²But ᵃI have prayed for you, that your faith should not fail; and when you have returned to *Me*, ᵇstrengthen your brethren."

22:14 ¹NU omits *twelve*   22:18 ¹NU adds *from now on*   22:31 ¹NU omits *And the Lord said*

22:13
ᵃLuke 19:32

22:14
ᵃMatt. 26:20;
Mark 14:17

22:16
ᵃLuke 14:15;
[Acts 10:41;
Rev. 19:9]

22:18
ᵃMatt. 26:29;
Mark 14:25

22:19
ᵃMatt. 26:26;
Mark 14:22
ᵇ[1 Pet. 2:24]
ᶜ1 Cor. 11:23–26

22:20
ᵃ1 Cor. 10:16

22:21 ᵃPs. 41:9;
Matt. 26:21, 23;
Mark 14:18;
Luke 22:48;
John 13:21,
26, 27

22:22
ᵃMatt. 26:24
ᵇJohn 17:12;
Acts 2:23

22:23
ᵃMatt. 26:22;
John 13:22, 25

22:24
ᵃMark 9:34;
Luke 9:46–48

22:25
ᵃ[Matt. 20:25–28];
Mark 10:42–45

22:26
ᵃMatt. 20:26;
[1 Pet. 5:3]
ᵇLuke 9:48

22:27
ᵃ[Luke 12:37]
ᵇMatt. 20:28;
John 13:13, 14;
Phil. 2:7

22:28
ᵃ[Heb. 2:18;
4:15]

22:29
ᵃMatt. 24:47

22:30
ᵃ[Matt. 8:11;
Rev. 19:9]
ᵇPs. 49:14;
[Matt. 19:28;
1 Cor. 6:2;
Rev. 3:21]

22:31 ᵃ1 Pet. 5:8
ᵇAmos 9:9

22:32
ᵃ[John 17:9,
11, 15]
ᵇJohn 21:15–17;
Acts 1:15; 2:14;
2 Pet. 1:10–15

33But he said to Him, "Lord, I am ready to go with You, both to prison and to death."

34aThen He said, "I tell you, Peter, the rooster shall not crow this day before you will deny three times that you know Me."

SUPPLIES FOR THE ROAD

35aAnd He said to them, "When I sent you without money bag, knapsack, and sandals, did you lack anything?"

So they said, "Nothing."

36Then He said to them, "But now, he who has a money bag, let him take *it,* and likewise a knapsack; and he who has no sword, let him sell his garment and buy one. 37For I say to you that this which is written must still be ¹accomplished in Me: a'And He was numbered with the transgressors.' For the things concerning Me have an end."

38So they said, "Lord, look, here *are* two swords."

And He said to them, "It is enough."

THE PRAYER IN THE GARDEN
(Matt. 26:36–46; Mark 14:32–42; John 18:1)

39aComing out, bHe went to the Mount of Olives, as He was accustomed, and His disciples also followed Him. 40aWhen He came to the place, He said to them, "Pray that you may not enter into temptation."

41aAnd He was withdrawn from them about a stone's throw, and He knelt down and prayed, 42saying, "Father, if it is Your will, take this cup away from Me; nevertheless anot My will, but Yours, be done." 43¹Then aan angel appeared to Him from heaven, strengthening Him. 44aAnd being in agony, He prayed more earnestly. Then His sweat became like great drops of blood falling down to the ground.

45When He rose up from prayer, and had come to His disciples, He found them sleeping from sorrow. 46Then He said to them, "Why ado you sleep? Rise and bpray, lest you enter into temptation."

BETRAYAL AND ARREST IN GETHSEMANE
(Matt. 26:47–56; Mark 14:43–52; John 18:1–11)

47And while He was still speaking, abehold, a multitude; and he who was called bJudas, one of the twelve, went before them and drew near to Jesus to kiss Him. 48But Jesus said to him, "Judas, are you betraying the Son of Man with a akiss?"

49When those around Him saw what was going to happen, they said to Him, "Lord, shall we strike with the sword?" 50And aone of them struck the servant of the high priest and cut off his right ear.

51But Jesus answered and said, "Permit even this." And He touched his ear and healed him.

52aThen Jesus said to the chief priests, captains of the temple, and the elders who had come to Him, "Have you come out, as against a brobber, with swords and clubs? 53When I was with you daily in the atemple, you did not try to seize Me. But this is your bhour, and the power of darkness."

22:37 ¹*fulfilled*   **22:43** ¹NU brackets vv. 43 and 44 as not in the original text.

Cross-references:
22:34 aMatt. 26:33–35; Mark 14:29–31; Luke 22:61; John 13:37, 38
22:35 aMatt. 10:9; Mark 6:8; Luke 9:3; 10:4
22:37 aIs. 53:12; Matt. 27:38; Mark 15:28; Luke 22:32
22:39 aMatt. 26:36; John 18:1; bLuke 21:37
22:40 aMatt. 26:36–46; Mark 14:32–42
22:41 aMatt. 26:39; Mark 14:35; [Luke 18:11–14]
22:42 aIs. 50:5; John 4:34; 5:30; 6:38; 8:29
22:43 aMatt. 4:11
22:44 aJohn 12:27; [Heb. 5:7]
22:46 aLuke 9:32; b1 Chr. 16:11; Luke 22:40; [Eph. 6:18]; 1 Thess. 5:17
22:47 aMatt. 26:47–56; Mark 14:43–50; John 18:3–11; bPs. 41:9; Matt. 20:18; Luke 9:44; 22:21; Acts 1:16, 17
22:48 a[Prov. 27:6]
22:50 aMatt. 26:51
22:52 aMatt. 26:55; bLuke 23:32
22:53 aLuke 19:47, 48; b[John 12:27]

PETER DENIES JESUS, AND WEEPS BITTERLY
(Matt. 26:69–75; Mark 14:66–72; John 18:13–18, 25–27)

⁵⁴ᵃHaving arrested Him, they led *Him* and brought Him into the high priest's house. ᵇBut Peter followed at a distance. ⁵⁵ᵃNow when they had kindled a fire in the midst of the courtyard and sat down together, Peter sat among them. ⁵⁶And a certain servant girl, seeing him as he sat by the fire, looked intently at him and said, "This man was also with Him."

⁵⁷But he denied ¹Him, saying, "Woman, I do not know Him."

⁵⁸ᵃAnd after a little while another saw him and said, "You also are of them."

But Peter said, "Man, I am not!"

⁵⁹ᵃThen after about an hour had passed, another confidently affirmed, saying, "Surely this *fellow* also was with Him, for he is a ᵇGalilean."

⁶⁰But Peter said, "Man, I do not know what you are saying!"

Immediately, while he was still speaking, ¹the rooster crowed. ⁶¹And the Lord turned and looked at Peter. Then ᵃPeter remembered the word of the Lord, how He had said to him, ᵇ"Before the rooster ¹crows, you will deny Me three times." ⁶²So Peter went out and wept bitterly.

JESUS MOCKED AND BEATEN
(Matt. 26:67, 68; Mark 14:65)

⁶³ᵃNow the men who held Jesus mocked Him and ᵇbeat Him. ⁶⁴¹And having blindfolded Him, they ᵃstruck Him on the face and asked Him, saying, "Prophesy! Who is the one who struck You?" ⁶⁵And many other things they blasphemously spoke against Him.

JESUS FACES THE SANHEDRIN
(Matt. 26:57–68; Mark 14:61–64; John 18:12–14, 19–24)

⁶⁶ᵃAs soon as it was day, ᵇthe elders of the people, both chief priests and scribes, came together and led Him into their council, saying, ⁶⁷ᵃ"If You are the Christ, tell us."

But He said to them, "If I tell you, you will ᵇby no means believe. ⁶⁸And if I ¹also ask *you,* you will by no means answer ²Me or let *Me* go. ⁶⁹ᵃHereafter the Son of Man will sit on the right hand of the power of God."

⁷⁰Then they all said, "Are You then the Son of God?"

So He said to them, ᵃ"You *rightly* say that I am."

⁷¹ᵃAnd they said, "What further testimony do we need? For we have heard it ourselves from His own mouth."

JESUS HANDED OVER TO PONTIUS PILATE
(Matt. 27:1, 2, 11–14; Mark 15:1–5; John 18:28–38)

23 Then ᵃthe whole multitude of them arose and led Him to ᵇPilate. ²And they began to ᵃaccuse Him, saying, "We found this *fellow* ᵇperverting ¹the nation, and ᶜforbidding

23:1 ᵃMatt. 27:2; Mark 15:1; Luke 18:32; John 18:28 ᵇLuke 3:1; 13:1 23:2 ᵃActs 24:2 ᵇActs 17:7 ᶜMatt. 17:27; Mark 12:17

22:57 ¹NU *it* 22:60 ¹NU, M *a rooster* 22:61 ¹NU adds *today* 22:64 ¹NU *And having blindfolded Him, they asked Him* 22:68 ¹NU omits *also* ²NU omits the rest of v. 68. 23:2 ¹NU *our*

22:54
ᵃIs. 53:7, 8;
Matt. 26:57;
Mark 14:53;
Luke 9:44;
Acts 8:32
ᵇMatt. 26:58;
Mark 14:54;
John 18:15

22:55
ᵃMatt. 26:69–75;
Mark 14:66–72;
John 18:15, 17, 18

22:58
ᵃMatt. 26:71;
Mark 14:69;
John 18:25

22:59
ᵃMatt. 26:73;
Mark 14:70;
John 18:26
ᵇActs 1:11; 2:7

22:61
ᵃMatt. 26:75;
Mark 14:72
ᵇMatt. 26:34, 75;
Mark 14:30;
Luke 22:34;
John 13:38

22:63
ᵃPs. 69:1, 4, 7–9;
Matt. 26:67, 68;
Mark 14:65;
John 18:22
ᵇJob 16:10;
Is. 50:6;
Lam. 3:30

22:64
ᵃZech. 13:7

22:66
ᵃMatt. 27:1;
Mark 15:1
ᵇPs. 2:2;
Acts 4:26

22:67
ᵃMatt. 26:63–66;
Mark 14:61–63;
Luke 22:67–71;
John 18:19–21
ᵇLuke 20:5–7

22:69
ᵃ[Ps. 110:1];
Matt. 26:64;
Mark 14:62;
16:19];
Acts 2:33;
7:55; Eph. 1:20;
Col. 3:1;
Heb. 1:3; 8:1

22:70
ᵃMatt. 26:64;
27:11;
Mark 14:62;
Luke 1:35

22:71
ᵃMatt. 26:65;
Mark 14:63;
John 19:7

to pay taxes to Caesar, saying ^dthat He Himself is Christ, a King."

^{3a}Then Pilate asked Him, saying, "Are You the King of the Jews?"

He answered him and said, *"It is as* you say."

⁴So Pilate said to the chief priests and the crowd, ^a"I find no fault in this Man."

⁵But they were the more fierce, saying, "He stirs up the people, teaching throughout all Judea, beginning from ^aGalilee to this place."

JESUS FACES HEROD

⁶When Pilate heard ¹of Galilee, he asked if the Man were a Galilean. ⁷And as soon as he knew that He belonged to ^aHerod's jurisdiction, he sent Him to Herod, who was also in Jerusalem at that time. ⁸Now when Herod saw Jesus, ^ahe was exceedingly glad; for he had desired for a long *time* to see Him, because ^bhe had heard many things about Him, and he hoped to see some miracle done by Him. ⁹Then he questioned Him with many words, but He answered him ^anothing. ¹⁰And the chief priests and scribes stood and vehemently accused Him. ^{11a}Then Herod, with his ¹men of war, treated Him with contempt and mocked *Him,* arrayed Him in a gorgeous robe, and sent Him back to Pilate. ¹²That very day ^aPilate and Herod became friends with each other, for previously they had been at enmity with each other.

TAKING THE PLACE OF BARABBAS
(Matt. 27:15–26; Mark 15:6–15; John 18:38—19:16)

^{13a}Then Pilate, when he had called together the chief priests, the rulers, and the people, ¹⁴said to them, ^a"You have brought this Man to me, as one who misleads the people. And indeed, ^bhaving examined *Him* in your presence, I have found no fault in this Man concerning those things of which you accuse Him; ¹⁵no, neither did Herod, for ¹I sent you back to him; and indeed nothing deserving of death has been done by Him. ^{16a}I will therefore chastise Him and release *Him*" ^{17a}(for¹ it was necessary for him to release one to them at the feast).

¹⁸And ^athey all cried out at once, saying, "Away with this *Man,* and release to us Barabbas"— ¹⁹who had been thrown into prison for a certain rebellion made in the city, and for murder.

²⁰Pilate, therefore, wishing to release Jesus, again called out to them. ²¹But they shouted, saying, "Crucify *Him,* crucify Him!"

²²Then he said to them the third time, "Why, what evil has He done? I have found no reason for death in Him. I will therefore chastise Him and let *Him* go."

²³But they were insistent, demanding with loud voices that He be crucified. And the voices of these men ¹and of the chief priests prevailed. ²⁴So ^aPilate gave sentence that it should be as they requested. ^{25a}And he released ¹to them the one they requested, who for rebellion and murder had been thrown into prison; but he delivered Jesus to their will.

Cross references (margin)

23:2 ^dJohn 19:12
23:3 ^aMatt. 27:11; 1 Tim. 6:13
23:4 ^aMatt. 27:19; [1 Pet. 2:22]
23:5 ^aJohn 7:41
23:7 ^aMatt. 14:1; Mark 6:14; Luke 3:1; 9:7; 13:31
23:8 ^aLuke 9:9 ^bMatt. 14:1; Mark 6:14
23:9 ^aIs. 53:7; Matt. 27:12, 14; Mark 15:5; John 19:9
23:11 ^aIs. 53:3
23:12 ^aActs 4:26, 27
23:13 ^aMatt. 27:23; Mark 15:14; John 18:38
23:14 ^aLuke 23:1, 2 ^bLuke 23:4
23:16 ^aMatt. 27:26; Mark 15:15; Luke 23:22; John 19:1; Acts 16:37
23:17 ^aMatt. 27:15; Mark 15:6; John 18:39
23:18 ^aIs. 53:3; Acts 3:13–15
23:24 ^aMatt. 27:26; Mark 15:15; John 19:16
23:25 ^aIs. 53:8

THE KING ON A CROSS
(Matt. 27:32–44; Mark 15:21–32; John 19:17–24)

26aNow as they led Him away, they laid hold of a certain man, Simon a Cyrenian, who was coming from the country, and on him they laid the cross that he might bear *it* after Jesus.

27And a great multitude of the people followed Him, and women who also mourned and lamented Him. 28But Jesus, turning to them, said, "Daughters of Jerusalem, do not weep for Me, but weep for yourselves and for your children. 29aFor indeed the days are coming in which they will say, 'Blessed *are* the barren, wombs that never bore, and breasts which never nursed!' 30Then they will begin a'to say to the mountains, "Fall on us!" and to the hills, "Cover us!" ' 31aFor if they do these things in the green wood, what will be done in the dry?"

32aThere were also two others, criminals, led with Him to be put to death. 33And awhen they had come to the place called Calvary, there they crucified Him, and the criminals, one on the right hand and the other on the left. 341Then Jesus said, "Father, aforgive them, for bthey do not know what they do."

And cthey divided His garments and cast lots. 35And athe people stood looking on. But even the brulers with them sneered, saying, "He saved others; let Him save Himself if He is the Christ, the chosen of God."

36The soldiers also mocked Him, coming and offering Him asour wine, 37and saying, "If You are the King of the Jews, save Yourself."

38aAnd an inscription also was 1written over Him in letters of Greek, Latin, and Hebrew:

THIS IS THE KING OF THE JEWS.

39aThen one of the criminals who were hanged blasphemed Him, saying, 1"If You are the Christ, save Yourself and us."

40But the other, answering, rebuked him, saying, "Do you not even fear God, seeing you are under the same condemnation? 41And we indeed justly, for we receive the due reward of our deeds; but this Man has done anothing wrong." 42Then he said 1to Jesus, "Lord, remember me when You come into Your kingdom."

43And Jesus said to him, "Assuredly, I say to you, today you will be with Me in aParadise."

JESUS DIES ON THE CROSS
(Matt. 27:45–56; Mark 15:33–41; John 19:25–30)

44aNow it 1was about the sixth hour, and there was darkness over all the earth until the ninth hour. 45Then the sun was 1darkened, and athe veil of the temple was torn in 2two. 46And when Jesus had cried out with a loud voice, He said, "Father, a'into Your hands I commit My spirit.' " bHaving said this, He breathed His last.

23:46 aPs. 31:5; 1 Pet. 2:23 bDan. 9:26; Zech. 11:10, 11; Matt. 27:50; Mark 15:37; Luke 9:22; 18:33; John 19:30

23:34 1NU brackets the first sentence as a later addition.   23:38 1NU omits *written* and *in letters of Greek, Latin, and Hebrew*   23:39 1NU *Are You not the Christ? Save*   23:42 1NU *"Jesus, remember me*   23:44 1NU adds *already*   23:45 1NU *obscured*   2*the middle*

Cross references (right column):

23:26
aMatt. 27:32;
Mark 15:21;
John 19:17

23:29
aMatt. 24:19;
Luke 21:23

23:30
aIs. 2:19;
Hos. 10:8;
Rev. 6:16, 17; 9:6

23:31
a[Prov. 11:31;
Jer. 25:29];
Ezek. 20:47;
21:3, 4; 1 Pet. 4:17

23:32
aIs. 53:9, 12;
Matt. 27:38;
Mark 15:27;
John 19:18

23:33
aPs. 22:16–18;
Matt. 27:33–44;
Mark 15:22–32;
John 19:17–24

23:34
aPs. 109:4;
[Matt. 5:44];
Acts 7:60;
1 Cor. 4:12
bActs 3:17
cPs. 22:18;
Matt. 27:35;
Mark 15:24;
John 19:23

23:35
aPs. 22:17;
[Zech. 12:10]
bPs. 22:8;
Matt. 27:39;
Mark 15:29

23:36 aPs. 69:21

23:38
aMatt. 27:37;
Mark 15:26;
John 19:19

23:39
aMatt. 27:44;
Mark 15:32

23:41
a[2 Cor. 5:21;
Heb. 7:26;
1 Pet. 2:21–24]

23:43
a[2 Cor. 12:4;
Eph. 4:8–10;
Rev. 2:7]

23:44
aAmos 8:9;
Matt. 27:45–56;
Mark 15:33–41

23:45
aEx. 26:31–33;
Zech. 11:10;
Matt. 27:51;
Mark 15:38;
[Heb. 9:3;
10:19, 20]

⁴⁷ᵃSo when the centurion saw what had happened, he glorified God, saying, "Certainly this was a righteous Man!"

⁴⁸And the whole crowd who came together to that sight, seeing what had been done, beat their breasts and returned. ⁴⁹ᵃBut all His acquaintances, and the women who followed Him from Galilee, stood at a distance, watching these things.

JESUS BURIED IN JOSEPH'S TOMB
(Matt. 27:57–61; Mark 15:42–47; John 19:38–42)

⁵⁰ᵃNow behold, *there was* a man named Joseph, a council member, a good and just man. ⁵¹He had not consented to their decision and deed. *He was* from Arimathea, a city of the Jews, ᵃwho¹ himself was also waiting for the kingdom of God. ⁵²This man went to Pilate and asked for the body of Jesus. ⁵³ᵃThen he took it down, wrapped it in linen, and laid it in a tomb *that was* hewn out of the rock, where no one had ever lain before. ⁵⁴That day was ᵃthe Preparation, and the Sabbath drew near.

⁵⁵And the women ᵃwho had come with Him from Galilee followed after, and ᵇthey observed the tomb and how His body was laid. ⁵⁶Then they returned and ᵃprepared spices and fragrant oils. And they rested on the Sabbath ᵇaccording to the commandment.

HE IS RISEN
(Matt. 28:1–10; Mark 16:1–8; John 20:1–10)

24 Now ᵃon the first *day* of the week, very early in the morning, they, ¹and certain *other women* with them, came to the tomb ᵇbringing the spices which they had prepared. ²ᵃBut they found the stone rolled away from the tomb. ³ᵃThen they went in and did not find the body of the Lord Jesus. ⁴And it happened, as they were ¹greatly perplexed about this, that ᵃbehold, two men stood by them in shining garments. ⁵Then, as they were afraid and bowed *their* faces to the earth, they said to them, "Why do you seek the living among the dead? ⁶He is not here, but is risen! ᵃRemember how He spoke to you when He was still in Galilee, ⁷saying, 'The Son of Man must be ᵃdelivered into the hands of sinful men, and be crucified, and the third day rise again.'"

⁸And ᵃthey remembered His words. ⁹ᵃThen they returned from the tomb and told all these things to the eleven and to all the rest. ¹⁰It was Mary Magdalene, ᵃJoanna, Mary *the mother* of James, and the other *women* with them, who told these things to the apostles. ¹¹ᵃAnd their words seemed to them like ¹idle tales, and they did not believe them. ¹²ᵃBut Peter arose and ran to the tomb; and stooping down, he saw the linen cloths ¹lying by themselves; and he departed, marveling to himself at what had happened.

THE ROAD TO EMMAUS
(Mark 16:12, 13)

¹³ᵃNow behold, two of them were traveling that same day to a village called Emmaus, which was ¹seven miles from

23:47
ᵃMatt. 27:54;
Mark 15:39

23:49 ᵃPs. 38:11;
Matt. 27:55;
Mark 15:40;
John 16:20–22;
19:25

23:50
ᵃMatt. 27:57–61;
Mark 15:42–47;
John 19:38–42

23:51
ᵃMark 15:43;
Luke 2:25, 38

23:53 ᵃIs. 53:9;
Matt. 27:59;
Mark 15:46

23:54
ᵃMatt. 27:62;
Mark 15:42

23:55 ᵃLuke 8:2
ᵇMark 15:47

23:56
ᵃMark 16:1;
Luke 24:1
ᵇEx. 20:10;
Deut. 5:14

24:1
ᵃMatt. 28:1–8;
Mark 16:1–8;
John 20:1–8
ᵇLuke 23:56

24:2
ᵃMatt. 28:2;
Mark 16:4

24:3 ᵃMark 16:5

24:4
ᵃJohn 20:12;
Acts 1:10

24:6
ᵃMatt. 16:21;
Mark 8:31;
Luke 9:22

24:7
ᵃHos. 6:1, 2;
Luke 9:44; 11:29,
30; 18:31–33

24:8
ᵃLuke 9:22, 44;
John 2:19–22

24:9
ᵃMatt. 28:8;
Mark 16:10

24:10 ᵃLuke 8:3

24:11
ᵃLuke 24:25

24:12
ᵃJohn 20:3–6

24:13
ᵃMark 16:12

23:51 ¹NU *who was waiting* 24:1 ¹NU omits *and certain other women with them* 24:4 ¹NU omits *greatly* 24:11 ¹*nonsense* 24:12 ¹NU omits *lying* 24:13 ¹Lit. *60 stadia*

Jerusalem. ¹⁴And they talked together of all these things which had happened. ¹⁵So it was, while they conversed and reasoned, that ᵃJesus Himself drew near and went with them. ¹⁶But ᵃtheir eyes were restrained, so that they did not know Him.

¹⁷And He said to them, "What kind of conversation *is* this that you have with one another as you ¹walk and are sad?"

¹⁸Then the one ᵃwhose name was Cleopas answered and said to Him, "Are You the only stranger in Jerusalem, and have You not known the things which happened there in these days?"

¹⁹And He said to them, "What things?"

So they said to Him, "The things concerning Jesus of Nazareth, ᵃwho was a Prophet ᵇmighty in deed and word before God and all the people, ²⁰ᵃand how the chief priests and our rulers delivered Him to be condemned to death, and crucified Him. ²¹But we were hoping ᵃthat it was He who was going to redeem Israel. Indeed, besides all this, today is the third day since these things happened. ²²Yes, and ᵃcertain women of our company, who arrived at the tomb early, astonished us. ²³When they did not find His body, they came saying that they had also seen a vision of angels who said He was alive. ²⁴And ᵃcertain of those *who were* with us went to the tomb and found *it* just as the women had said; but Him they did not see."

²⁵Then He said to them, "O foolish ones, and slow of heart to believe in all that the prophets have spoken! ²⁶ᵃOught not the Christ to have suffered these things and to enter into His ᵇglory?" ²⁷And beginning at ᵃMoses and ᵇall the Prophets, He ¹expounded to them in all the Scriptures the things concerning Himself.

THE DISCIPLES' EYES OPENED

²⁸Then they drew near to the village where they were going, and ᵃHe ¹indicated that He would have gone farther. ²⁹But ᵃthey constrained Him, saying, ᵇ"Abide with us, for it is toward evening, and the day is far spent." And He went in to stay with them.

³⁰Now it came to pass, as ᵃHe sat at the table with them, that He took bread, blessed and broke *it*, and gave it to them. ³¹Then their eyes were opened and they knew Him; and He vanished from their sight.

³²And they said to one another, "Did not our heart burn within us while He talked with us on the road, and while He opened the Scriptures to us?" ³³So they rose up that very hour and returned to Jerusalem, and found the eleven and those *who were* with them gathered together, ³⁴saying, "The Lord is risen indeed, and ᵃhas appeared to Simon!" ³⁵And they told about the things *that had happened* on the road, and how He was ¹known to them in the breaking of bread.

JESUS APPEARS TO HIS DISCIPLES

(John 20:19–23; Acts 1:3–5; 1 Cor. 15:5)

³⁶ᵃNow as they said these things, Jesus Himself stood in the midst of them, and said to them, "Peace to you." ³⁷But they

24:15
ᵃ[Matt. 18:20]

24:16
ᵃJohn 20:14;
21:4

24:18
ᵃJohn 19:25

24:19
ᵃMatt. 21:11;
Luke 7:16;
John 3:2;
Acts 2:22
ᵇActs 7:22

24:20
ᵃLuke 23:1;
Acts 13:27, 28

24:21
ᵃLuke 1:68;
2:38; [Acts 1:6]

24:22
ᵃMatt. 28:8;
Mark 16:10;
Luke 24:9, 10

24:24
ᵃLuke 24:12

24:26
ᵃActs 17:2, 3;
[Heb. 2:9, 10]
ᵇ[1 Pet. 1:10–12]

24:27
ᵃ[Gen. 3:15;
12:3; Num. 21:9;
Deut. 18:15];
John 5:46
ᵇ[Ps. 16:9,
10; 22; 132:11;
Is. 7:14; 9:6;
Jer. 23:5;
33:14, 15;
Ezek. 34:23;
37:25;
Dan. 9:24];
Mic. 7:20;
[Mal. 3:1; 4:2];
John 1:45; 5:39;
[Rom. 1:1–6]

24:28
ᵃGen. 32:26;
42:7; Mark 6:48

24:29
ᵃGen. 19:2, 3;
Acts 16:15
ᵇ[John 14:23]

24:30
ᵃMatt. 14:19;
Mark 8:6;
Luke 9:16

24:34
ᵃ1 Cor. 15:5

24:36
ᵃMark 16:14;
John 20:19;
1 Cor. 15:5

24:17 ¹NU *walk? And they stood still, looking sad.*   24:27 ¹*explained*
24:28 ¹*acted as if*   24:35 ¹*recognized*

were terrified and frightened, and supposed they had seen ᵃa spirit. ³⁸And He said to them, "Why are you troubled? And why do doubts arise in your hearts? ³⁹Behold My hands and My feet, that it is I Myself. ᵃHandle Me and see, for a ᵇspirit does not have flesh and bones as you see I have."

⁴⁰¹When He had said this, He showed them His hands and His feet. ⁴¹But while they still did not believe ᵃfor joy, and marveled, He said to them, ᵇ"Have you any food here?" ⁴²So they gave Him a piece of a broiled fish ¹and some honeycomb. ⁴³ᵃAnd He took *it* and ate in their presence.

THE SCRIPTURES OPENED

⁴⁴Then He said to them, ᵃ"These *are* the words which I spoke to you while I was still with you, that all things must be fulfilled which were written in the Law of Moses and *the* Prophets and *the* Psalms concerning Me." ⁴⁵And ᵃHe opened their understanding, that they might comprehend the Scriptures.

⁴⁶Then He said to them, ᵃ"Thus it is written, ¹and thus it was necessary for the Christ to suffer and to rise from the dead the third day, ⁴⁷and that repentance and ᵃremission of sins should be preached in His name ᵇto all nations, beginning at Jerusalem. ⁴⁸And ᵃyou are witnesses of these things. ⁴⁹ᵃBehold, I send the Promise of My Father upon you; but tarry in the city ¹of Jerusalem until you are endued with power from on high."

THE ASCENSION
(Mark 16:19, 20; Acts 1:9)

⁵⁰And He led them out ᵃas far as Bethany, and He lifted up His hands and blessed them. ⁵¹ᵃNow it came to pass, while He blessed them, that He was parted from them and carried up into heaven. ⁵²ᵃAnd they worshiped Him, and returned to Jerusalem with great joy, ⁵³and were continually ᵃin the temple ¹praising and blessing God. ²Amen.

24:37
ᵃMatt. 14:26;
Mark 6:49

24:39
ᵃJohn 20:20, 27;
1 John 1:1
ᵇ[1 Cor. 15:50]

24:41
ᵃGen. 45:26
ᵇJohn 21:5

24:43
ᵃActs 10:39–41

24:44
ᵃMatt. 16:21;
17:22; 20:18;
Mark 8:31;
Luke 9:22; 18:31

24:45
ᵃActs 16:14;
1 John 5:20

24:46 ᵃPs. 22;
Hos. 6:2;
Luke 11:29, 30;
Acts 17:3

24:47
ᵃDan. 9:24;
Acts 5:31; 10:43;
13:38; 26:18
ᵇ[Ps. 22:27;
Jer. 31:34;
Mic. 4:2]

24:48
ᵃ[Acts 1:8];
1 Pet. 5:1

24:49 ᵃIs. 44:3;
Joel 2:28;
Acts 2:4

24:50
ᵃMatt. 21:17;
Acts 1:12

24:51
ᵃPs. 68:18; 110:1;
Mark 16:19;
Acts 1:9–11

24:52
ᵃMatt. 28:9

24:53
ᵃActs 2:46

24:40 ¹Some printed New Testaments omit v. 40. It is found in nearly all Gr. mss.   **24:42** ¹NU omits *and some honeycomb*   **24:46** ¹NU *that the Christ should suffer and rise*   **24:49** ¹NU omits *of Jerusalem*   **24:53** ¹NU omits *praising and*   ²NU omits *Amen.*

THE GOSPEL ACCORDING TO
JOHN

THE ETERNAL WORD
(Gen. 1:1—2:3)

1 In the beginning ªwas the Word, and the ᵇWord was ᶜwith God, and the Word was ᵈGod. ²ªHe was in the beginning with God. ³ªAll things were made through Him, and without Him nothing was made that was made. ⁴ªIn Him was life, and ᵇthe life was the light of men. ⁵And ªthe light shines in the darkness, and the darkness did not ¹comprehend it.

JOHN'S WITNESS: THE TRUE LIGHT

⁶There was a ªman sent from God, whose name *was* John. ⁷This man came for a ªwitness, to bear witness of the Light, that all through him might ᵇbelieve. ⁸He was not that Light, but *was sent* to bear witness of that ªLight. ⁹ªThat¹ was the true Light which gives light to every man coming into the world.

¹⁰He was in the world, and the world was made through Him, and ªthe world did not know Him. ¹¹ªHe came to His ¹own, and His ²own did not receive Him. ¹²But ªas many as received Him, to them He gave the ¹right to become children of God, to those who believe in His name: ¹³ªwho were born, not of blood, nor of the will of the flesh, nor of the will of man, but of God.

THE WORD BECOMES FLESH

¹⁴ªAnd the Word ᵇbecame ᶜflesh and dwelt among us, and ᵈwe beheld His glory, the glory as of the only begotten of the Father, ᵉfull of grace and truth.

¹⁵ªJohn bore witness of Him and cried out, saying, "This was He of whom I said, ᵇ'He who comes after me ¹is preferred before me, ᶜfor He was before me.'"

¹⁶¹And of His ªfullness we have all received, and grace for grace. ¹⁷For ªthe law was given through Moses, *but* ᵇgrace and ᶜtruth came through Jesus Christ. ¹⁸ªNo one has seen God at any time. ᵇThe only begotten ¹Son, who is in the bosom of the Father, He has declared *Him.*

A VOICE IN THE WILDERNESS
(Matt. 3:1–12; Mark 1:1–8; Luke 3:1–20)

¹⁹Now this is ªthe testimony of John, when the Jews sent priests and Levites from Jerusalem to ask him, "Who are you?"

1:15 ªMal. 3:1; John 3:32 ᵇ[Matt. 3:11] ᶜ[Col. 1:17]   1:16 ª[Eph. 1:23; 3:19; 4:13; Col. 1:19; 2:9]   1:17 ª[Ex. 20:1] ᵇJohn 1:14; [Rom. 5:21; 6:14] ᶜ[John 8:32; 14:6; 18:37]   1:18 ªEx. 33:20; Matt. 11:27; 1 Tim. 6:16 ᵇPs. 2:7; John 3:16, 18; 1 John 4:9   1:19 ªJohn 5:33

1:5 ¹Or *overcome*   1:9 ¹Or *That was the true Light which, coming into the world, gives light to every man.*   1:11 ¹His own things or domain   ²His own people   1:12 ¹*authority*   1:15 ¹*ranks higher than I*   1:16 ¹NU *For*   1:18 ¹NU *God*

1:1 ªGen. 1:1; [Col. 1:17]; 1 John 1:1 ᵇ[John 1:14]; Rev. 19:13 ᶜ[John 17:5; 1 John 1:2] ᵈ[1 John 5:20]

1:2 ªGen. 1:1

1:3 ªPs. 33:6; [Eph. 3:9; Col. 1:16, 17; Heb. 1:2]

1:4 ª[1 John 5:11] ᵇJohn 8:12; 9:5; 12:46

1:5 ª[John 3:19]

1:6 ªMal. 3:1; Matt. 3:1–17; Mark 1:1–11; Luke 3:1–22

1:7 ªJohn 3:25–36; 5:33–35 ᵇ[John 3:16]

1:8 ªIs. 9:2; 49:6

1:9 ªIs. 49:6

1:10 ªActs 13:27; 1 Cor. 8:6; Col. 1:16; Heb. 1:2

1:11 ªIs. 53:3; [Luke 19:14]

1:12 ª[John 11:52]; Gal. 3:26

1:13 ª[John 3:5]; James 1:18; [1 Pet. 1:23; 1 John 2:29; 3:9]

1:14 ªMatt. 1:16; Rev. 19:13 ᵇRom. 1:3; Gal. 4:4; Phil. 2:7; 1 Tim. 3:16; Heb. 2:14; 1 John 1:1; 4:2; 2 John 7 ᶜHeb. 2:11 ᵈIs. 40:5; 2 Pet. 1:16–18 ᵉ[John 8:32; 14:6; 18:37]; Col. 1:19

20aHe confessed, and did not deny, but confessed, "I am not the Christ."

21And they asked him, "What then? Are you Elijah?"

He said, "I am not."

"Are you athe Prophet?"

And he answered, "No."

22Then they said to him, "Who are you, that we may give an answer to those who sent us? What do you say about yourself?"

23He said: a"I am

b"The voice of one crying in the wilderness:
"Make straight the way of the LORD,"'

as the prophet Isaiah said."

24Now those who were sent were from the Pharisees. 25And they asked him, saying, "Why then do you baptize if you are not the Christ, nor Elijah, nor the Prophet?"

26John answered them, saying, a"I baptize with water, bbut there stands One among you whom you do not know. 27aIt is He who, coming after me, 1is preferred before me, whose sandal strap I am not worthy to loose."

28These things were done ain 1Bethabara beyond the Jordan, where John was baptizing.

THE LAMB OF GOD
(Matt. 3:13–17; Mark 1:9–11; Luke 3:21, 22)

29The next day John saw Jesus coming toward him, and said, "Behold! aThe Lamb of God bwho takes away the sin of the world! 30This is He of whom I said, 'After me comes a Man who 1is preferred before me, for He was before me.' 31I did not know Him; but that He should be revealed to Israel, atherefore I came baptizing with water."

32aAnd John bore witness, saying, "I saw the Spirit descending from heaven like a dove, and He remained upon Him. 33I did not know Him, but He who sent me to baptize with water said to me, 'Upon whom you see the Spirit descending, and remaining on Him, athis is He who baptizes with the Holy Spirit.' 34And I have seen and testified that this is the aSon of God."

THE FIRST DISCIPLES

35Again, the next day, John stood with two of his disciples. 36And looking at Jesus as He walked, he said, a"Behold the Lamb of God!"

37The two disciples heard him speak, and they afollowed Jesus. 38Then Jesus turned, and seeing them following, said to them, "What do you seek?"

They said to Him, "Rabbi" (which is to say, when translated, Teacher), "where are You staying?"

39He said to them, "Come and see." They came and saw where He was staying, and remained with Him that day (now it was about the tenth hour).

40One of the two who heard John *speak,* and followed Him, was aAndrew, Simon Peter's brother. 41He first found his own brother Simon, and said to him, "We have found the 1Messiah"

1:20 aLuke 3:15; John 3:28; Acts 13:25

1:21 aDeut. 18:15, 18; Matt. 21:11; John 6:14; 7:40

1:23 aMatt. 3:3 bIs. 40:3; Mal. 3:1

1:26 aMatt. 3:11; [Mark 1:8; Luke 3:16; Acts 1:5] bMal. 3:1; John 4:10; 8:19; 9:30; Acts 13:27

1:27 a[John 3:31]; Acts 19:4; [Col. 1:17]

1:28 aJudg. 7:24

1:29 a[Ex. 12:3]; Acts 8:32; [1 Pet. 1:19]; Rev. 5:6–14 b[Is. 53:11; 1 Cor. 15:3; Gal. 1:4; 1 Pet. 2:24; 1 John 2:2; Rev. 1:5]

1:31 aMal. 3:1; Matt. 3:6

1:32 aIs. 42:1; 61:1; Matt. 3:16; Mark 1:10; Luke 3:22

1:33 aMatt. 3:11; Mark 1:8; Luke 3:16; Acts 1:5

1:34 aPs. 2:7; Luke 1:35; John 11:27

1:36 aJohn 1:29

1:37 aMatt. 4:20, 22

1:40 aMatt. 4:18; Mark 1:29; 13:3; John 6:8; 12:22

1:27 1*ranks higher than I* 1:28 1NU, M *Bethany* 1:30 1*ranks higher than I*
1:41 1Lit. *Anointed One*

(which is translated, the Christ). [42]And he brought him to Jesus.

Now when Jesus looked at him, He said, "You are Simon the son of [1]Jonah. [a]You shall be called Cephas" (which is translated, [2]A Stone).

PHILIP AND NATHANAEL

[43]The following day Jesus wanted to go to Galilee, and He found [a]Philip and said to him, "Follow Me." [44]Now [a]Philip was from Bethsaida, the city of Andrew and Peter. [45]Philip found [a]Nathanael and said to him, "We have found Him of whom [b]Moses in the law, and also the [c]prophets, wrote—Jesus [d]of Nazareth, the [e]son of Joseph."

[46]And Nathanael said to him, [a]"Can anything good come out of Nazareth?"

Philip said to him, "Come and see."

[47]Jesus saw Nathanael coming toward Him, and said of him, "Behold, [a]an Israelite indeed, in whom is no deceit!"

[48]Nathanael said to Him, "How do You know me?"

Jesus answered and said to him, "Before Philip called you, when you were under the fig tree, I saw you."

[49]Nathanael answered and said to Him, "Rabbi, [a]You are the Son of God! You are [b]the King of Israel!"

[50]Jesus answered and said to him, "Because I said to you, 'I saw you under the fig tree,' do you believe? You will see greater things than these." [51]And He said to him, "Most assuredly, I say to you, [a]hereafter[1] you shall see heaven open, and the angels of God ascending and descending upon the Son of Man."

WATER TURNED TO WINE

2 On the third day there was a [a]wedding in [b]Cana of Galilee, and the [c]mother of Jesus was there. [2]Now both Jesus and His disciples were invited to the wedding. [3]And when they ran out of wine, the mother of Jesus said to Him, "They have no wine."

[4]Jesus said to her, [a]"Woman, [b]what does your concern have to do with Me? [c]My hour has not yet come."

[5]His mother said to the servants, "Whatever He says to you, do it."

[6]Now there were set there six waterpots of stone, [a]according to the manner of purification of the Jews, containing twenty or thirty gallons apiece. [7]Jesus said to them, "Fill the waterpots with water." And they filled them up to the brim. [8]And He said to them, "Draw some out now, and take it to the master of the feast." And they took it. [9]When the master of the feast had tasted [a]the water that was made wine, and did not know where it came from (but the servants who had drawn the water knew), the master of the feast called the bridegroom. [10]And he said to him, "Every man at the beginning sets out the good wine, and when the guests have well drunk, then the inferior. You have kept the good wine until now!"

[11]This [a]beginning of signs Jesus did in Cana of Galilee, [b]and [1]manifested His glory; and His disciples believed in Him.

[12]After this He went down to [a]Capernaum, He, His mother,

Cross references

1:42 [a]Matt. 16:18

1:43 [a]Matt. 10:3; John 6:5; 12:21, 22; 14:8, 9

1:44 [a]John 12:21

1:45 [a]John 21:2 [b][Gen. 3:15; Deut. 18:18]; Luke 24:27 [c][Is. 4:2; 7:14; 9:6; Mic. 5:2; Zech. 6:12]; Luke 24:27 [d][Matt. 2:23]; Luke 2:4 [e]Luke 3:23

1:46 [a]John 7:41, 42, 52

1:47 [a]Ps. 32:2; 73:1

1:49 [a]Ps. 2:7; Matt. 14:33; Luke 1:35 [b]Matt. 21:5

1:51 [a]Gen. 28:12; [Luke 2:9, 13]; Acts 1:10; 7:55, 56

2:1 [a][Heb. 13:4] [b]John 4:46 [c]John 19:25

2:4 [a]John 19:26 [b]2 Sam. 16:10 [c]John 7:6, 8, 30; 8:20

2:6 [a]Matt. 15:2; [Mark 7:3; Luke 11:39]; John 3:25

2:9 [a]John 4:46

2:11 [a]John 4:54 [b][John 1:14]

2:12 [a]Matt. 4:13; John 4:46

1:42 [1]NU John   [2]Gr. Petros, usually translated Peter   1:51 [1]NU omits hereafter   2:11 [1]revealed

2:12
[b]Matt. 12:46;
13:55

2:13 [a]Ex. 12:14;
Deut. 16:1–6;
John 5:1; 6:4;
11:55

2:14 [a]Mal. 3:1;
Matt. 21:12;
Mark 11:15, 17;
Luke 19:45

2:16 [a]Luke 2:49

2:17 [a]Ps. 69:9

2:18
[a]Matt. 12:38;
John 6:30

2:19
[a]Matt. 26:61;
27:40;
[Mark 14:58;
15:29];
Luke 24:46;
Acts 6:14; 10:40;
1 Cor. 15:4

2:21
[a][1 Cor. 3:16;
6:19; 2 Cor. 6:16;
Col. 2:9;
Heb. 8:2]

2:22
[a]Luke 24:8;
John 2:17; 12:16;
14:26

2:23
[a][John 5:36;
Acts 2:22]

2:24 [a]Matt. 9:4;
John 16:30;
Rev. 2:23

2:25
[a]1 Sam. 16:7;
1 Chr. 28:9;
Matt. 9:4;
[Mark 2:8];
John 6:64;
16:30; Acts 1:24;
Rev. 2:23

3:2 [a]John 7:50;
19:39
[b]John 9:16, 33;
Acts 2:22
[c][Acts 10:38]

3:3 [a][John 1:13];
Gal. 6:15;
Titus 3:5;
James 1:18;
1 Pet. 1:23;
1 John 3:9

3:5 [a]Mark 16:16;
[Acts 2:38]

3:6 [a]John 1:13;
1 Cor. 15:50

3:8 [a]Ps. 135:7;
Eccl. 11:5;
Ezek. 37:9;
1 Cor. 2:11

3:9
[a]John 6:52, 60

[b]His brothers, and His disciples; and they did not stay there many days.

JESUS CLEANSES THE TEMPLE
(Matt. 21:12–17; Mark 11:15–19; Luke 19:45–48)

[13a]Now the Passover of the Jews was at hand, and Jesus went up to Jerusalem. [14a]And He found in the temple those who sold oxen and sheep and doves, and the money changers [1]doing business. [15]When He had made a whip of cords, He drove them all out of the temple, with the sheep and the oxen, and poured out the changers' money and overturned the tables. [16]And He said to those who sold doves, "Take these things away! Do not make [a]My Father's house a house of merchandise!" [17]Then His disciples remembered that it was written, [a]"Zeal for Your house [1]has eaten Me up."

[18]So the Jews answered and said to Him, [a]"What sign do You show to us, since You do these things?"

[19]Jesus answered and said to them, [a]"Destroy this temple, and in three days I will raise it up."

[20]Then the Jews said, "It has taken forty-six years to build this temple, and will You raise it up in three days?"

[21]But He was speaking [a]of the temple of His body. [22]Therefore, when He had risen from the dead, [a]His disciples remembered that He had said this [1]to them; and they believed the Scripture and the word which Jesus had said.

THE DISCERNER OF HEARTS

[23]Now when He was in Jerusalem at the Passover, during the feast, many believed in His name when they saw the [a]signs which He did. [24]But Jesus did not commit Himself to them, because He [a]knew all *men,* [25]and had no need that anyone should testify of man, for [a]He knew what was in man.

THE NEW BIRTH

3 There was a man of the Pharisees named Nicodemus, a ruler of the Jews. [2a]This man came to Jesus by night and said to Him, "Rabbi, we know that You are a teacher come from God; for [b]no one can do these signs that You do unless [c]God is with him."

[3]Jesus answered and said to him, "Most assuredly, I say to you, [a]unless one is born [1]again, he cannot see the kingdom of God."

[4]Nicodemus said to Him, "How can a man be born when he is old? Can he enter a second time into his mother's womb and be born?"

[5]Jesus answered, "Most assuredly, I say to you, [a]unless one is born of water and the Spirit, he cannot enter the kingdom of God. [6]That which is born of the flesh is [a]flesh, and that which is born of the Spirit is spirit. [7]Do not marvel that I said to you, 'You must be born again.' [8a]The wind blows where it wishes, and you hear the sound of it, but cannot tell where it comes from and where it goes. So is everyone who is born of the Spirit."

[9]Nicodemus answered and said to Him, [a]"How can these things be?"

2:14 [1]Lit. *sitting*   2:17 [1]NU, M *will eat*   2:22 [1]NU, M omit *to them*
3:3 [1]Or *from above*

¹⁰Jesus answered and said to him, "Are you the teacher of Israel, and do not know these things? ¹¹ᵃMost assuredly, I say to you, We speak what We know and testify what We have seen, and ᵇyou do not receive Our witness. ¹²If I have told you earthly things and you do not believe, how will you believe if I tell you heavenly things? ¹³ᵃNo one has ascended to heaven but He who came down from heaven, *that is,* the Son of Man ¹who is in heaven. ¹⁴ᵃAnd as Moses lifted up the serpent in the wilderness, even so ᵇmust the Son of Man be lifted up, ¹⁵that whoever ᵃbelieves in Him should ¹not perish but ᵇhave eternal life. ¹⁶ᵃFor God so loved the world that He gave His only begotten ᵇSon, that whoever believes in Him should not perish but have everlasting life. ¹⁷ᵃFor God did not send His Son into the world to condemn the world, but that the world through Him might be saved.

¹⁸ᵃ"He who believes in Him is not condemned; but he who does not believe is condemned already, because he has not believed in the name of the only begotten Son of God. ¹⁹And this is the condemnation, ᵃthat the light has come into the world, and men loved darkness rather than light, because their deeds were evil. ²⁰For ᵃeveryone practicing evil hates the light and does not come to the light, lest his deeds should be exposed. ²¹But he who does the truth comes to the light, that his deeds may be clearly seen, that they have been ᵃdone in God."

JOHN THE BAPTIST EXALTS CHRIST

²²After these things Jesus and His disciples came into the land of Judea, and there He remained with them ᵃand baptized. ²³Now John also was baptizing in Aenon near ᵃSalim, because there was much water there. ᵇAnd they came and were baptized. ²⁴For ᵃJohn had not yet been thrown into prison.

²⁵Then there arose a dispute between *some* of John's disciples and the Jews about purification. ²⁶And they came to John and said to him, "Rabbi, He who was with you beyond the Jordan, ᵃto whom you have testified—behold, He is baptizing, and all ᵇare coming to Him!"

²⁷John answered and said, ᵃ"A man can receive nothing unless it has been given to him from heaven. ²⁸You yourselves bear me witness, that I said, ᵃ'I am not the Christ,' but, ᵇ'I have been sent before Him.' ²⁹ᵃHe who has the bride is the bridegroom; but ᵇthe friend of the bridegroom, who stands and hears him, rejoices greatly because of the bridegroom's voice. Therefore this joy of mine is fulfilled. ³⁰ᵃHe must increase, but I *must* decrease. ³¹ᵃHe who comes from above ᵇis above all; ᶜhe who is of the earth is earthly and speaks of the earth. ᵈHe who comes from heaven is above all. ³²And ᵃwhat He has seen and heard, that He testifies; and no one receives His testimony. ³³He who has received His testimony ᵃhas certified that God is true. ³⁴ᵃFor He whom God has sent speaks the words of God, for God does not give the Spirit ᵇby measure. ³⁵ᵃThe Father loves the Son, and has given all things into

Cross references

3:11
ᵃ[Matt. 11:27]
ᵇJohn 3:32; 8:14

3:13
ᵃDeut. 30:12;
Prov. 30:4;
Acts 2:34;
Rom. 10:6;
1 Cor. 15:47;
Eph. 4:9

3:14 ᵃNum. 21:9
ᵇMatt. 27:35;
Mark 15:24;
Luke 23:33;
John 8:28;
12:34; 19:18

3:15 ᵃJohn 6:47
ᵇJohn 3:36

3:16 ᵃRom. 5:8;
Eph. 2:4;
2 Thess. 2:16;
[1 John 4:9, 10;
Rev. 1:5]
ᵇ[Is. 9:6]

3:17 ᵃMatt. 1:21;
Luke 9:56;
1 John 4:14

3:18 ᵃJohn 5:24;
6:40, 47; 20:31;
Rom. 8:1

3:19
ᵃ[John 1:4, 9–11]

3:20
ᵃJob 24:13;
Eph. 5:11, 13

3:21
ᵃ[John 15:4, 5];
1 Cor. 15:10

3:22
ᵃJohn 4:1, 2

3:23 ᵃ1 Sam. 9:4
ᵇMatt. 3:5, 6

3:24 ᵃMatt. 4:12;
14:3; Mark 6:17;
Luke 3:20

3:26 ᵃJohn 1:7,
15, 27, 34
ᵇMark 2:2; 3:10;
5:24; Luke 8:19

3:27
ᵃ[Rom. 12:5–8];
1 Cor. 3:5, 6;
4:7; Heb. 5:4;
[James 1:17;
1 Pet. 4:10, 11]

3:28
ᵃJohn 1:19–27
ᵇMal. 3:1;
Mark 1:2;
[Luke 1:17]

3:29
ᵃMatt. 22:2;
[2 Cor. 11:2;
Eph. 5:25, 27];
Rev. 21:9
ᵇSong 5:1

3:30 ᵃ[Is. 9:7]

3:31 ᵃJohn 3:13; 8:23 ᵇMatt. 28:18; John 1:15, 27; 13:13; Rom. 9:5; [Col. 1:17, 18]
ᶜ1 Cor. 15:47 ᵈJohn 6:33; 1 Cor. 15:47; Eph. 1:21; Phil. 2:9   3:32 ᵃIs. 53:1, 3;
John 3:11; 15:15   3:33 ᵃRom. 3:4; 1 John 5:10   3:34 ᵃDeut. 18:18; John 7:16 ᵇJohn 1:16
3:35 ᵃMatt. 11:27; Luke 10:22; John 5:20; [Heb. 2:8]

3:13 ¹NU omits *who is in heaven*   3:15 ¹NU omits *not perish but*

His hand. ³⁶ᵃHe who believes in the Son has everlasting life; and he who does not believe the Son shall not see life, but the ᵇwrath of God abides on him."

A SAMARITAN WOMAN MEETS HER MESSIAH

4 Therefore, when the Lord knew that the Pharisees had heard that Jesus made and ᵃbaptized more disciples than John ²(though Jesus Himself did not baptize, but His disciples), ³He left Judea and departed again to Galilee. ⁴But He needed to go through Samaria.

⁵So He came to a city of Samaria which is called Sychar, near the plot of ground that ᵃJacob ᵇgave to his son Joseph. ⁶Now Jacob's well was there. Jesus therefore, being wearied from *His* journey, sat thus by the well. It was about the sixth hour.

⁷A woman of Samaria came to draw water. Jesus said to her, "Give Me a drink." ⁸For His disciples had gone away into the city to buy food.

⁹Then the woman of Samaria said to Him, "How is it that You, being a Jew, ask a drink from me, a Samaritan woman?" For ᵃJews have no dealings with ᵇSamaritans.

¹⁰Jesus answered and said to her, "If you knew the ᵃgift of God, and who it is who says to you, 'Give Me a drink,' you would have asked Him, and He would have given you ᵇliving water."

¹¹The woman said to Him, "Sir, You have nothing to draw with, and the well is deep. Where then do You get that living water? ¹²Are You greater than our father Jacob, who gave us the well, and drank from it himself, as well as his sons and his livestock?"

¹³Jesus answered and said to her, "Whoever drinks of this water will thirst again, ¹⁴but ᵃwhoever drinks of the water that I shall give him will never thirst. But the water that I shall give him ᵇwill become in him a fountain of water springing up into everlasting life."

¹⁵ᵃThe woman said to Him, "Sir, give me this water, that I may not thirst, nor come here to draw."

¹⁶Jesus said to her, "Go, call your husband, and come here."

¹⁷The woman answered and said, "I have no husband."

Jesus said to her, "You have well said, 'I have no husband,' ¹⁸for you have had five husbands, and the one whom you now have is not your husband; in that you spoke truly."

¹⁹The woman said to Him, "Sir, ᵃI perceive that You are a prophet. ²⁰Our fathers worshiped on ᵃthis mountain, and you *Jews* say that in ᵇJerusalem is the place where one ought to worship."

²¹Jesus said to her, "Woman, believe Me, the hour is coming ᵃwhen you will neither on this mountain, nor in Jerusalem, worship the Father. ²²You worship ᵃwhat you do not know; we know what we worship, for ᵇsalvation is of the Jews. ²³But the hour is coming, and now is, when the true worshipers will ᵃworship the Father in ᵇspirit ᶜand truth; for the Father is seeking such to worship Him. ²⁴ᵃGod *is* Spirit, and those who worship Him must worship in spirit and truth."

²⁵The woman said to Him, "I know that Messiah ᵃis coming" (who is called Christ). "When He comes, ᵇHe will tell us all things."

²⁶Jesus said to her, ᵃ"I who speak to you am *He.*"

3:36 ªJohn 3:16, 17; 6:47; Rom. 1:17; 1 John 5:10 ᵇRom. 1:18; Eph. 5:6; 1 Thess. 1:10

4:1 ªJohn 3:22, 26; 1 Cor. 1:17

4:5 ªGen. 33:19; Josh. 24:32 ᵇGen. 48:22; Josh. 4:12

4:9 ªActs 10:28 ᵇ2 Kin. 17:24; Matt. 10:5, 6; Luke 9:52; 10:33; 17:16; John 8:48

4:10 ª[Rom. 5:15] ᵇIs. 12:3; 44:3; Jer. 2:13; Zech. 13:1; 14:8; John 7:38

4:14 ª[John 6:35, 58] ᵇJohn 7:37, 38

4:15 ªJohn 6:34, 35; 17:2, 3; [Rom. 6:23]; 1 John 5:20]

4:19 ªMatt. 21:11; Luke 7:16, 39; 24:19; John 6:14; 7:40; 9:17

4:20 ªGen. 12:6–8; 33:18, 20; Judg. 9:7 ᵇDeut. 12:5, 11; 1 Kin. 9:3; 2 Chr. 7:12; Ps. 122:1–9

4:21 ª[Mal. 1:11]; 1 Tim. 2:8

4:22 ª[2 Kin. 17:28–41] ᵇ[Is. 2:3; Luke 24:47; Rom. 3:1; 9:4, 5]

4:23 ªMatt. 18:20; [Heb. 13:10–14] ᵇPhil. 3:3 ᶜ[John 1:17]

4:24 ª2 Cor. 3:17

4:25 ªDeut. 18:15 ᵇJohn 4:29, 39

4:26 ªDan. 9:25; Matt. 26:63, 64; Mark 14:61, 62

THE WHITENED HARVEST

27And at this *point* His disciples came, and they marveled that He talked with a woman; yet no one said, "What do You seek?" or, "Why are You talking with her?"

28The woman then left her waterpot, went her way into the city, and said to the men, 29"Come, see a Man ᵃwho told me all things that I ever did. Could this be the Christ?" 30Then they went out of the city and came to Him.

31In the meantime His disciples urged Him, saying, "Rabbi, eat."

32But He said to them, "I have food to eat of which you do not know."

33Therefore the disciples said to one another, "Has anyone brought Him *anything* to eat?"

34Jesus said to them, ᵃ"My food is to do the will of Him who sent Me, and to ᵇfinish His work. 35Do you not say, 'There are still four months and *then* comes ᵃthe harvest'? Behold, I say to you, lift up your eyes and look at the fields, ᵇfor they are already white for harvest! 36ᵃAnd he who reaps receives wages, and gathers fruit for eternal life, that ᵇboth he who sows and he who reaps may rejoice together. 37For in this the saying is true: ᵃ'One sows and another reaps.' 38I sent you to reap that for which you have not labored; ᵃothers have labored, and you have entered into their labors."

THE SAVIOR OF THE WORLD

39And many of the Samaritans of that city believed in Him ᵃbecause of the word of the woman who testified, "He told me all that I *ever* did." 40So when the Samaritans had come to Him, they urged Him to stay with them; and He stayed there two days. 41And many more believed because of His own ᵃword.

42Then they said to the woman, "Now we believe, not because of what you said, for ᵃwe ourselves have heard *Him* and we know that this is indeed ¹the Christ, the Savior of the world."

WELCOME AT GALILEE

43Now after the two days He departed from there and went to Galilee. 44For ᵃJesus Himself testified that a prophet has no honor in his own country. 45So when He came to Galilee, the Galileans received Him, ᵃhaving seen all the things He did in Jerusalem at the feast; ᵇfor they also had gone to the feast.

A NOBLEMAN'S SON HEALED

46So Jesus came again to Cana of Galilee ᵃwhere He had made the water wine. And there was a certain ¹nobleman whose son was sick at Capernaum. 47When he heard that Jesus had come out of Judea into Galilee, he went to Him and implored Him to come down and heal his son, for he was at the point of death. 48Then Jesus said to him, ᵃ"Unless you *people* see signs and wonders, you will by no means believe."

49The nobleman said to Him, "Sir, come down before my child dies!"

50Jesus said to him, "Go your way; your son lives." So the

4:29 ᵃJohn 4:25

4:34
ᵃPs. 40:7, 8;
Heb. 10:9
ᵇJob 23:12;
[John 6:38; 17:4;
19:30]

4:35 ᵃGen. 8:22
ᵇMatt. 9:37;
Luke 10:2

4:36 ᵃDan. 12:3;
Rom. 6:22
ᵇ1 Thess. 2:19

4:37
ᵃ1 Cor. 3:5–9

4:38 ᵃJer. 44:4;
[1 Pet. 1:12]

4:39 ᵃJohn 4:29

4:41 ᵃLuke 4:32;
[John 6:63]

4:42 ᵃJohn 17:8;
1 John 4:14

4:44
ᵃMatt. 13:57;
Mark 6:4;
Luke 4:24

4:45
ᵃJohn 2:13, 23;
3:2 ᵇDeut. 16:16

4:46
ᵃJohn 2:1, 11

4:48
ᵃJohn 6:30;
Rom. 15:19;
1 Cor. 1:22;
2 Cor. 12:12;
[2 Thess. 2:9];
Heb. 2:4

4:42 ¹NU omits *the Christ* 4:46 ¹royal official

man believed the word that Jesus spoke to him, and he went his way. 51And as he was now going down, his servants met him and told *him,* saying, "Your son lives!"

52Then he inquired of them the hour when he got better. And they said to him, "Yesterday at the seventh hour the fever left him." 53So the father knew that *it was* at the same hour in which Jesus said to him, "Your son lives." And he himself believed, and his whole household.

54This again *is* the second sign Jesus did when He had come out of Judea into Galilee.

A MAN HEALED AT THE POOL OF BETHESDA

5 After ªthis there was a feast of the Jews, and Jesus ᵇwent up to Jerusalem. 2Now there is in Jerusalem ªby the Sheep *Gate* a pool, which is called in Hebrew, ¹Bethesda, having five porches. 3In these lay a great multitude of sick people, blind, lame, ¹paralyzed, ²waiting for the moving of the water. 4For an angel went down at a certain time into the pool and stirred up the water; then whoever stepped in first, after the stirring of the water, was made well of whatever disease he had. 5Now a certain man was there who had an infirmity thirty-eight years. 6When Jesus saw him lying there, and knew that he already had been *in that condition* a long time, He said to him, "Do you want to be made well?"

7The sick man answered Him, "Sir, I have no man to put me into the pool when the water is stirred up; but while I am coming, another steps down before me."

8Jesus said to him, ª"Rise, take up your bed and walk." 9And immediately the man was made well, took up his bed, and walked.

And ªthat day was the Sabbath. 10The Jews therefore said to him who was cured, "It is the Sabbath; ªit is not lawful for you to carry your bed."

11He answered them, "He who made me well said to me, 'Take up your bed and walk.'"

12Then they asked him, "Who is the Man who said to you, 'Take up your bed and walk'?" 13But the one who was ªhealed did not know who it was, for Jesus had withdrawn, a multitude being in *that* place. 14Afterward Jesus found him in the temple, and said to him, "See, you have been made well. ªSin no more, lest a worse thing come upon you."

15The man departed and told the Jews that it was Jesus who had made him well.

HONOR THE FATHER AND THE SON

16For this reason the Jews ªpersecuted Jesus, ¹and sought to kill Him, because He had done these things on the Sabbath. 17But Jesus answered them, ª"My Father has been working until now, and I have been working."

18Therefore the Jews ªsought all the more to kill Him, because He not only broke the Sabbath, but also said that God was His Father, ᵇmaking Himself equal with God. 19Then Jesus answered and said to them, "Most assuredly, I say to you, ªthe Son can do nothing of Himself, but what He sees the Father do; for whatever He does, the Son also does in like

5:1 ªLev. 23:2;
Deut. 16:16
ᵇJohn 2:13

5:2
ªNeh. 3:1, 32;
12:39

5:8 ªMatt. 9:6;
Mark 2:11;
Luke 5:24

5:9 ªJohn 9:14

5:10 ªEx. 20:10;
Neh. 13:19;
Jer. 17:21, 22;
Matt. 12:2;
Mark 2:24;
Luke 6:2

5:13 ªLuke 13:14;
22:51

5:14
ªMatt. 12:45;
[Mark 2:5];
John 8:11

5:16 ªLuke 4:29;
John 8:37;
10:39

5:17 ª[John 9:4;
17:4]

5:18
ªJohn 7:1, 19
ᵇJohn 10:30;
Phil. 2:6

5:19
ªMatt. 26:39;
John 5:30; 6:38;
8:28; 12:49;
14:10

5:2 ¹NU *Bethzatha* 5:3 ¹*withered* ²NU omits the rest of v. 3 and all of v. 4.
5:16 ¹NU omits *and sought to kill Him*

manner. 20For athe Father loves the Son, and bshows Him all things that He Himself does; and He will show Him greater works than these, that you may marvel. 21For as the Father raises the dead and gives life to *them,* aeven so the Son gives life to whom He will. 22For the Father judges no one, but ahas committed all judgment to the Son, 23that all should honor the Son just as they honor the Father. aHe who does not honor the Son does not honor the Father who sent Him.

LIFE AND JUDGMENT ARE THROUGH THE SON

24"Most assuredly, I say to you, ahe who hears My word and believes in Him who sent Me has everlasting life, and shall not come into judgment, bbut has passed from death into life. 25Most assuredly, I say to you, the hour is coming, and now is, when athe dead will hear the voice of the Son of God; and those who hear will live. 26For aas the Father has life in Himself, so He has granted the Son to have blife in Himself, 27and ahas given Him authority to execute judgment also, bbecause He is the Son of Man. 28Do not marvel at this; for the hour is coming in which all who are in the graves will ahear His voice 29aand come forth—bthose who have done good, to the resurrection of life, and those who have done evil, to the resurrection of condemnation. 30aI can of Myself do nothing. As I hear, I judge; and My judgment is righteous, because bI do not seek My own will but the will of the Father who sent Me.

THE FOURFOLD WITNESS

31a"If I bear witness of Myself, My witness is not 1true. 32aThere is another who bears witness of Me, and I know that the witness which He witnesses of Me is true. 33You have sent to John, aand he has borne witness to the truth. 34Yet I do not receive testimony from man, but I say these things that you may be saved. 35He was the burning and ashining lamp, and byou were willing for a time to rejoice in his light. 36But aI have a greater witness than John's; for bthe works which the Father has given Me to finish—the very cworks that I do—bear witness of Me, that the Father has sent Me. 37And the Father Himself, who sent Me, ahas testified of Me. You have neither heard His voice at any time, bnor seen His form. 38But you do not have His word abiding in you, because whom He sent, Him you do not believe. 39aYou search the Scriptures, for in them you think you have eternal life; and bthese are they which testify of Me. 40aBut you are not willing to come to Me that you may have life.

41a"I do not receive honor from men. 42But I know you, that you do not have the love of God in you. 43I have come in My Father's name, and you do not receive Me; if another comes in his own name, him you will receive. 44aHow can you believe, who receive honor from one another, and do not seek bthe honor that *comes* from the only God? 45Do not think that I shall accuse you to the Father; athere is *one* who accuses you—Moses, in whom you trust. 46For if you believed Moses, you would believe Me; afor he wrote about Me. 47But if you ado not believe his writings, how will you believe My words?"

5:40 a[John 1:11; 3:19]   5:41 aJohn 5:44; 7:18; 1 Thess. 2:6   5:44 aJohn 12:43 [Rom. 2:29]   5:45 aRom. 2:12   5:46 a[Gen. 3:15]; Deut. 18:15, 18; John 1:45; Acts 26:22 5:47 aLuke 16:29, 31

5:31 1*valid* as testimony

5:20 aMatt. 3:17; John 3:35; 2 Pet. 1:17
b[Matt. 11:27]

5:21 aLuke 7:14; 8:54; [John 11:25]

5:22 aMatt. 11:27; 28:18; [John 3:35; 17:2; Acts 17:31; 1 Pet. 4:5]

5:23 aLuke 10:16; 1 John 2:23

5:24 aJohn 3:16, 18; 6:47
b[1 John 3:14]

5:25 a[Eph. 2:1, 5; Col. 2:13]

5:26 aPs. 36:9
b[John 1:4; 14:6]; 1 Cor. 15:45

5:27 aJohn 9:39; [Acts 10:42; 17:31]
bDan. 7:13

5:28 a[1 Thess. 4:15–17]

5:29 aIs. 26:19; [1 Cor. 15:52]
bDan. 12:2; Matt. 25:46; Acts 24:15

5:30 aJohn 5:19
bMatt. 26:39; John 4:34; 6:38

5:31 aJohn 8:14; Rev. 3:14

5:32 a[Matt. 3:17; John 8:18; 1 John 5:6]

5:33 a[John 1:15, 19, 27, 32]

5:35 a2 Sam. 21:17; 2 Pet. 1:19
bMatt. 13:20; Mark 6:20

5:36 a1 John 5:9
bJohn 3:2; 10:25; 17:4
cJohn 9:16; 10:38

5:37 aMatt. 3:17; John 6:27; 8:18
bDeut. 4:12; John 1:18; 1 Tim. 1:17; 1 John 4:12

5:39 aIs. 8:20; 34:16; Luke 16:29; Acts 17:11
bDeut. 18:15, 18; Luke 24:27

FEEDING THE FIVE THOUSAND
(Matt. 14:13–21; Mark 6:30–44; Luke 9:10–17)

6 After [a]these things Jesus went over the Sea of Galilee, which is *the Sea* of [b]Tiberias. [2]Then a great multitude followed Him, because they saw His signs which He performed on those who were [a]diseased.[1] [3]And Jesus went up on the mountain, and there He sat with His disciples.

[4a]Now the Passover, a feast of the Jews, was near. [5a]Then Jesus lifted up *His* eyes, and seeing a great multitude coming toward Him, He said to [b]Philip, "Where shall we buy bread, that these may eat?" [6]But this He said to test him, for He Himself knew what He would do.

[7]Philip answered Him, [a]"Two hundred denarii worth of bread is not sufficient for them, that every one of them may have a little."

[8]One of His disciples, [a]Andrew, Simon Peter's brother, said to Him, [9]"There is a lad here who has five barley loaves and two small fish, [a]but what are they among so many?"

[10]Then Jesus said, "Make the people sit down." Now there was much grass in the place. So the men sat down, in number about five thousand. [11]And Jesus took the loaves, and when He had given thanks He distributed *them* [1]to the disciples, and the disciples to those sitting down; and likewise of the fish, as much as they wanted. [12]So when they were filled, He said to His disciples, "Gather up the fragments that remain, so that nothing is lost." [13]Therefore they gathered *them* up, and filled twelve baskets with the fragments of the five barley loaves which were left over by those who had eaten. [14]Then those men, when they had seen the sign that Jesus did, said, "This is truly [a]the Prophet who is to come into the world."

JESUS WALKS ON THE SEA
(Matt. 14:22–33; Mark 6:45–52)

[15]Therefore when Jesus perceived that they were about to come and take Him by force to make Him [a]king, He departed again to the mountain by Himself alone.

[16a]Now when evening came, His disciples went down to the sea, [17]got into the boat, and went over the sea toward Capernaum. And it was already dark, and Jesus had not come to them. [18]Then the sea arose because a great wind was blowing. [19]So when they had rowed about [1]three or four miles, they saw Jesus walking on the sea and drawing near the boat; and they were [a]afraid. [20]But He said to them, [a]"It is I; do not be afraid." [21]Then they willingly received Him into the boat, and immediately the boat was at the land where they were going.

THE BREAD FROM HEAVEN

[22]On the following day, when the people who were standing on the other side of the sea saw that there was no other boat there, except [1]that one [2]which His disciples had entered, and that Jesus had not entered the boat with His disciples, but His disciples had gone away alone— [23]however, other boats came from Tiberias, near the place where they ate bread after

6:1 [a]Matt. 14:13; Mark 6:32; Luke 9:10, 12 [b]John 6:23; 21:1
6:2 [a]Matt. 4:23; 8:16; 9:35; 14:36; 15:30; 19:2
6:4 [a]Lev. 23:5, 7; Deut. 16:1; John 2:13
6:5 [a]Matt. 14:14; Mark 6:35; Luke 9:12 [b]John 1:43
6:7 [a]Num. 11:21, 22
6:8 [a]John 1:40
6:9 [a]2 Kin. 4:43
6:14 [a]Gen. 49:10; Deut. 18:15, 18; John 1:21; 7:40; Acts 3:22; 7:37
6:15 [a][John 18:36]
6:16 [a]Matt. 14:23; Mark 6:47
6:19 [a]Matt. 17:6
6:20 [a]Is. 43:1, 2

6:2 [1]sick 6:11 [1]NU omits *to the disciples, and the disciples* 6:19 [1]Lit. 25 or 30 stadia 6:22 [1]NU omits *that* [2]NU omits *which His disciples had entered*

the Lord had given thanks— [24]when the people therefore saw that Jesus was not there, nor His disciples, they also got into boats and came to Capernaum, [a]seeking Jesus. [25]And when they found Him on the other side of the sea, they said to Him, "Rabbi, when did You come here?"

[26]Jesus answered them and said, "Most assuredly, I say to you, you seek Me, not because you saw the signs, but because you ate of the loaves and were filled. [27a]Do not labor for the food which perishes, but [b]for the food which endures to everlasting life, which the Son of Man will give you, [c]because God the Father has set His seal on Him."

[28]Then they said to Him, "What shall we do, that we may work the works of God?"

[29]Jesus answered and said to them, [a]"This is the work of God, that you believe in Him whom He sent."

[30]Therefore they said to Him, [a]"What sign will You perform then, that we may see it and believe You? What work will You do? [31a]Our fathers ate the manna in the desert; as it is written, [b]'He gave them bread from heaven to eat.'"

[32]Then Jesus said to them, "Most assuredly, I say to you, Moses did not give you the bread from heaven, but [a]My Father gives you the true bread from heaven. [33]For the bread of God is He who comes down from heaven and gives life to the world."

[34a]Then they said to Him, "Lord, give us this bread always."

[35]And Jesus said to them, [a]"I am the bread of life. [b]He who comes to Me shall never hunger, and he who believes in Me shall never [c]thirst. [36]But I said to you that you have seen Me and yet [b]do not believe. [37a]All that the Father gives Me will come to Me, and [b]the one who comes to Me I will [1]by no means cast out. [38]For I have come down from heaven, [a]not to do My own will, [b]but the will of Him who sent Me. [39]This is the will of the Father who sent Me, [a]that of all He has given Me I should lose nothing, but should raise it up at the last day. [40]And this is the will of Him who sent Me, [a]that everyone who sees the Son and believes in Him may have everlasting life; and I will raise him up at the last day."

REJECTED BY HIS OWN

[41]The Jews then [1]complained about Him, because He said, "I am the bread which came down from heaven." [42]And they said, [a]"Is not this Jesus, the son of Joseph, whose father and mother we know? How is it then that He says, 'I have come down from heaven'?"

[43]Jesus therefore answered and said to them, [1]"Do not murmur among yourselves. [44a]No one can come to Me unless the Father who sent Me [b]draws him; and I will raise him up at the last day. [45]It is written in the prophets, [a]'And they shall all be taught by God.' [b]Therefore everyone who [1]has heard and learned from the Father comes to Me. [46a]Not that anyone has seen the Father, [b]except He who is from God; He has seen the Father. [47]Most assuredly, I say to you, [a]he who believes [1]in Me has everlasting life. [48a]I am the bread of life. [49a]Your fathers

6:46 [a]John 1:18 [b]Matt. 11:27; [Luke 10:22]; John 7:29   6:47 [a][John 3:16, 18]   6:48 [a]John 6:33, 35; [Gal. 2:20; Col. 3:3, 4]   6:49 [a]John 6:31, 58

6:37 [1]certainly not   6:41 [1]grumbled   6:43 [1]Stop grumbling   6:45 [1]M hears and has learned   6:47 [1]NU omits in Me

---

6:24 [a]Mark 1:37; Luke 4:42

6:27 [a]Matt. 6:19 [b]John 4:14; [Eph. 2:8, 9] [c]Ps. 2:7; Is. 42:1; Matt. 3:17; 17:5; Mark 1:11; 9:7; Luke 3:22; 9:35; John 5:37; Acts 2:22; 2 Pet. 1:17

6:29 [a]1 Thess. 1:3; James 2:22; [1 John 3:23]; Rev. 2:26

6:30 [a]Matt. 12:38; 16:1; Mark 8:11; 1 Cor. 1:22

6:31 [a]Ex. 16:15; Num. 11:7; 1 Cor. 10:3 [b]Ex. 16:4, 15; Neh. 9:15; Ps. 78:24

6:32 [a]John 3:13, 16

6:34 [a]John 4:15

6:35 [a]John 6:48, 58 [b]John 4:14; 7:37; Rev. 7:16 [c]Is. 55:1, 2

6:36 [a]John 6:26, 64; 15:24 [b]John 10:26

6:37 [a]John 6:45 [b][Matt. 24:24; John 10:28, 29]; 2 Tim. 2:19; 1 John 2:19

6:38 [a]Matt. 26:39; John 5:30 [b]John 4:34

6:39 [a]John 10:28; 17:12; 18:9

6:40 [a]John 3:15, 16; 4:14; 6:27, 47, 54

6:42 [a]Matt. 13:55; Mark 6:3; Luke 4:22

6:44 [a]Song 1:4 [b][Eph. 2:8, 9; Phil. 1:29; 2:12, 13]

6:45 [a]Is. 54:13; Jer. 31:34; Mic. 4:2; [Heb. 8:10] [b]John 6:37

ate the manna in the wilderness, and are dead. [50a]This is the bread which comes down from heaven, that one may eat of it and not die. [51]I am the living bread [a]which came down from heaven. If anyone eats of this bread, he will live forever; and [b]the bread that I shall give is My flesh, which I shall give for the life of the world."

[52]The Jews therefore [a]quarreled among themselves, saying, "How can this Man give us *His* flesh to eat?"

[53]Then Jesus said to them, "Most assuredly, I say to you, unless [a]you eat the flesh of the Son of Man and drink His blood, you have no life in you. [54a]Whoever eats My flesh and drinks My blood has eternal life, and I will raise him up at the last day. [55]For My flesh is [1]food indeed, and My blood is [2]drink indeed. [56]He who eats My flesh and drinks My blood [a]abides in Me, and I in him. [57]As the living Father sent Me, and I live because of the Father, so he who feeds on Me will live because of Me. [58a]This is the bread which came down from heaven— not [b]as your fathers ate the manna, and are dead. He who eats this bread will live forever."

[59]These things He said in the synagogue as He taught in Capernaum.

MANY DISCIPLES TURN AWAY

[60a]Therefore many of His disciples, when they heard *this,* said, "This is a [1]hard saying; who can understand it?"

[61]When Jesus knew in Himself that His disciples [1]complained about this, He said to them, "Does this [2]offend you? [62a]*What* then if you should see the Son of Man ascend where He was before? [63a]It is the Spirit who gives life; the [b]flesh profits nothing. The [c]words that I speak to you are spirit, and *they* are life. [64]But [a]there are some of you who do not believe." For [b]Jesus knew from the beginning who they were who did not believe, and who would betray Him. [65]And He said, "Therefore [a]I have said to you that no one can come to Me unless it has been granted to him by My Father."

[66a]From that *time* many of His disciples went [1]back and walked with Him no more. [67]Then Jesus said to the twelve, "Do you also want to go away?"

[68]But Simon Peter answered Him, "Lord, to whom shall we go? You have [a]the words of eternal life. [69a]Also we have come to believe and know that You are the [1]Christ, the Son of the living God."

[70]Jesus answered them, [a]"Did I not choose you, the twelve, [b]and one of you is a devil?" [71]He spoke of [a]Judas Iscariot, *the son* of Simon, for it was he who would [b]betray Him, being one of the twelve.

JESUS' BROTHERS DISBELIEVE

7 After these things Jesus walked in Galilee; for He did not want to walk in Judea, [a]because the [1]Jews sought to kill Him. [2a]Now the Jews' Feast of Tabernacles was at hand. [3a]His brothers therefore said to Him, "Depart from here and go into Judea, that Your disciples also may see the works that You are doing. [4]For no one does anything in secret while he himself

6:50
[a]John 6:51, 58

6:51 [a]John 3:13
[b]Heb. 10:5

6:52 [a]John 7:43;
9:16; 10:19

6:53
[a]Matt. 26:26

6:54 [a]John 4:14;
6:27, 40

6:56
[a][1 John 3:24;
4:15, 16]

6:58
[a]John 6:49–51
[b]Ex. 16:14–35

6:60 [a]Matt. 11:6;
John 6:66

6:62
[a]Mark 16:19;
John 3:13;
Acts 1:9;
2:32, 33;
Eph. 4:8

6:63 [a]Gen. 2:7;
2 Cor. 3:6
[b]John 3:6
[c][John 6:68;
14:24]

6:64 [a]John 6:36
[b]John 2:24, 25;
13:11

6:65 [a]John 6:37,
44, 45

6:66
[a]Luke 9:62;
John 6:60

6:68 [a]Acts 5:20

6:69
[a]Matt. 16:16;
Mark 8:29;
Luke 9:20;
John 1:49; 11:27

6:70 [a]Luke 6:13
[b][John 13:27]

6:71 [a]John 12:4;
13:2, 26
[b]Matt. 26:14–16

7:1 [a]Matt. 21:38;
26:4; John 5:18;
7:19, 25; 8:37, 40

7:2 [a]Lev. 23:34;
Deut. 16:13–15;
Neh. 8:14, 18;
Zech. 14:16–19

7:3 [a]Matt. 12:46;
Mark 3:21;
John 7:5, 10;
Acts 1:14

6:55 [1]NU *true food*   [2]NU *true drink*   6:60 [1]*difficult*   6:61 [1]*grumbled*
[2]*make you stumble*   6:66 [1]Or *away;* lit. *to the back*   6:69 [1]NU *Holy One of God.*   7:1 [1]The ruling authorities

seeks to be known openly. If You do these things, show Yourself to the world." [5]For [a]even His [b]brothers did not believe in Him.

[6]Then Jesus said to them, [a]"My time has not yet come, but your time is always ready. [7a]The world cannot hate you, but it hates Me [b]because I testify of it that its works are evil. [8]You go up to this feast. I am not [1]yet going up to this feast, [a]for My time has not yet fully come." [9]When He had said these things to them, He remained in Galilee.

THE HEAVENLY SCHOLAR

[10]But when His brothers had gone up, then He also went up to the feast, not openly, but as it were in secret. [11]Then [a]the Jews sought Him at the feast, and said, "Where is He?" [12]And [a]there was much complaining among the people concerning Him. [b]Some said, "He is good"; others said, "No, on the contrary, He deceives the people." [13]However, no one spoke openly of Him [a]for fear of the Jews.

[14]Now about the middle of the feast Jesus went up into the temple and [a]taught. [15a]And the Jews marveled, saying, "How does this Man know letters, having never studied?"

[16l]Jesus answered them and said, [a]"My doctrine is not Mine, but His who sent Me. [17a]If anyone wills to do His will, he shall know concerning the doctrine, whether it is from God or *whether* I speak on My own *authority*. [18a]He who speaks from himself seeks his own glory; but He who [b]seeks the glory of the One who sent Him is true, and [c]no unrighteousness is in Him. [19a]Did not Moses give you the law, yet none of you keeps the law? [b]Why do you seek to kill Me?"

[20]The people answered and said, [a]"You have a demon. Who is seeking to kill You?"

[21]Jesus answered and said to them, "I did one work, and you all marvel. [22a]Moses therefore gave you circumcision (not that it is from Moses, [b]but from the fathers), and you circumcise a man on the Sabbath. [23]If a man receives circumcision on the Sabbath, so that the law of Moses should not be broken, are you angry with Me because [a]I made a man completely well on the Sabbath? [24a]Do not judge according to appearance, but judge with righteous judgment."

COULD THIS BE THE CHRIST?

[25]Now some of them from Jerusalem said, "Is this not He whom they seek to [a]kill? [26]But look! He speaks boldly, and they say nothing to Him. [a]Do the rulers know indeed that this is [1]truly the Christ? [27a]However, we know where this Man is from; but when the Christ comes, no one knows where He is from."

[28]Then Jesus cried out, as He taught in the temple, saying, [a]"You both know Me, and you know where I am from; and [b]I have not come of Myself, but He who sent Me [c]is true, [d]whom you do not know. [29l]But [a]I know Him, for I am from Him, and He sent Me."

[30]Therefore [a]they sought to take Him; but [b]no one laid a hand on Him, because His hour had not yet come. [31]And

7:28 [a]John 8:14 [b]John 5:43 [c]Rom. 3:4 [d]John 1:18; 8:55   7:29 [a]Matt. 11:27; John 8:55; 17:25   7:30 [a]Mark 11:18 [b]Matt. 21:46; John 7:32, 44; 8:20; 10:39

7:8 [1]NU omits *yet*   7:16 [1]NU, M *So Jesus*   7:26 [1]NU omits *truly*
7:29 [1]NU, M omit *But*

7:5 [a]Ps. 69:8; Mic. 7:6
[b]Matt. 12:46; 13:55; Mark 3:21; John 7:3, 10

7:6
[a]John 2:4; 8:20

7:7 [a][John 15:19]
[b]John 3:19

7:8 [a]John 8:20

7:11 [a]John 11:56

7:12
[a]John 9:16; 10:19
[b]Matt. 21:46;
Luke 7:16;
John 6:14; 7:40

7:13
[a][John 9:22;
12:42; 19:38]

7:14 [a]Ps. 22:22;
Matt. 4:23; 5:2;
7:29; Mark 6:34;
Luke 4:15; 5:3;
John 8:2

7:15
[a]Matt. 13:54;
Mark 6:2;
[Luke 4:22];
Acts 2:7

7:16
[a]Deut. 18:15, 18,
19; John 3:11

7:17
[a]Ps. 25:9, 14;
Prov. 3:32;
Dan. 12:10;
John 3:21; 8:43

7:18 [a]John 5:41
[b]John 8:50
[c]John 8:46;
[2 Cor. 5:21;
Heb. 4:15; 7:26;
1 Pet. 1:19; 2:22]

7:19 [a]Ex. 24:3;
Deut. 33:4;
Acts 7:38
[b]Matt. 12:14

7:20
[a]John 8:48, 52

7:22 [a]Lev. 12:3
[b]Gen. 17:9–14;
Acts 7:8

7:23
[a]John 5:8, 9, 16

7:24 [a]Deut. 1:16;
Prov. 24:23;
John 8:15;
James 2:1

7:25
[a]Matt. 21:38;
26:4; Luke 22:2;
John 5:18;
8:37, 40

7:26 [a]John 7:48

7:27
[a]Matt. 13:55;
Mark 6:3;
Luke 4:22

ᵃmany of the people believed in Him, and said, "When the Christ comes, will He do more signs than these which this *Man* has done?"

JESUS AND THE RELIGIOUS LEADERS

³²The Pharisees heard the crowd murmuring these things concerning Him, and the Pharisees and the chief priests sent officers to take Him. ³³Then Jesus said ¹to them, ᵃ"I shall be with you a little while longer, and *then* I ᵇgo to Him who sent Me. ³⁴You ᵃwill seek Me and not find *Me,* and where I am you ᵇcannot come."

³⁵Then the Jews said among themselves, "Where does He intend to go that we shall not find Him? Does He intend to go to ᵃthe Dispersion among the Greeks and teach the Greeks? ³⁶What is this thing that He said, 'You will seek Me and not find Me, and where I am you cannot come'?"

THE PROMISE OF THE HOLY SPIRIT

³⁷ᵃOn the last day, that great *day* of the feast, Jesus stood and cried out, saying, ᵇ"If anyone thirsts, let him come to Me and drink. ³⁸ᵃHe who believes in Me, as the Scripture has said, ᵇout of his heart will flow rivers of living water." ³⁹ᵃBut this He spoke concerning the Spirit, whom those ¹believing in Him would receive; for the ²Holy Spirit was not yet *given,* because Jesus was not yet ᵇglorified.

WHO IS HE?

⁴⁰Therefore ¹many from the crowd, when they heard this saying, said, "Truly this is ᵃthe Prophet." ⁴¹Others said, "This is ᵃthe Christ."

But some said, "Will the Christ come out of Galilee? ⁴²ᵃHas not the Scripture said that the Christ comes from the seed of David and from the town of Bethlehem, ᵇwhere David was?" ⁴³So ᵃthere was a division among the people because of Him. ⁴⁴Now ᵃsome of them wanted to take Him, but no one laid hands on Him.

REJECTED BY THE AUTHORITIES

⁴⁵Then the officers came to the chief priests and Pharisees, who said to them, "Why have you not brought Him?" ⁴⁶The officers answered, ᵃ"No man ever spoke like this Man!"

⁴⁷Then the Pharisees answered them, "Are you also deceived? ⁴⁸Have any of the rulers or the Pharisees believed in Him? ⁴⁹But this crowd that does not know the law is accursed." ⁵⁰Nicodemus ᵃ(he who came to ¹Jesus ²by night, being one of them) said to them, ⁵¹ᵃ"Does our law judge a man before it hears him and knows what he is doing?"

⁵²They answered and said to him, "Are you also from Galilee? Search and look, for ᵃno prophet ¹has arisen out of Galilee."

AN ADULTERESS FACES THE LIGHT OF THE WORLD

⁵³¹And everyone went to his *own* house.

7:31 ᵃMatt. 12:23
7:33 ᵃJohn 13:33
ᵇ[Mark 16:19;
Luke 24:51;
Acts 1:9;
Heb. 9:24;
1 Pet. 3:22]
7:34 ᵃHos. 5:6
ᵇ[Matt. 5:20;
1 Cor. 6:9; 15:50;
Rev. 21:27]
7:35 ᵃPs. 147:2;
[Is. 11:12; 56:8;
Zeph. 3:10];
James 1:1;
1 Pet. 1:1
7:37 ᵃLev. 23:36;
Num. 29:35;
Neh. 8:18
ᵇ[Is. 55:1]
7:38
ᵃDeut. 18:15
ᵇIs. 12:3; 43:20;
44:3; 55:1;
[John 6:35];
Rev. 21:6; 22:17
7:39 ᵃIs. 44:3;
[Joel 2:28];
John 1:33
ᵇJohn 12:16;
13:31; 17:5
7:40
ᵃDeut. 18:15, 18
7:41 ᵃJohn 4:42;
6:69
7:42 ᵃPs. 132:11;
Jer. 23:5;
Mic. 5:2;
Matt. 2:5;
[Luke 2:4]
ᵇ1 Sam. 16:1, 4
7:43 ᵃJohn 7:12
7:44 ᵃJohn 7:30
7:46
ᵃMatt. 13:54, 56;
Luke 4:22
7:50
ᵃJohn 3:1, 2;
19:39
7:51
ᵃDeut. 1:16, 17;
19:15
7:52 ᵃ[Is. 9:1, 2];
Matt. 4:15

7:33 ¹NU, M omit *to them*   7:39 ¹NU *who believed*   ²NU omits *Holy*
7:40 ¹NU *some*   7:50 ¹Lit. *Him*   ²NU *before*   7:52 ¹NU *is to rise*
7:53 ¹NU brackets 7:53 through 8:11 as not in the original text. They are present in over 900 mss. of John.

8 But Jesus went to the Mount of Olives. [2]Now [1]early in the morning He came again into the temple, and all the people came to Him; and He sat down and [a]taught them. [3]Then the scribes and Pharisees brought to Him a woman caught in adultery. And when they had set her in the midst, [4]they said to Him, "Teacher, [1]this woman was caught in [a]adultery, in the very act. [5a]Now [1]Moses, in the law, commanded us [2]that such should be stoned. But what do You [3]say?" [6]This they said, testing Him, that they [a]might have *something* of which to accuse Him. But Jesus stooped down and wrote on the ground with *His* finger, [1]as though He did not hear.

[7]So when they continued asking Him, He [1]raised Himself up and said to them, [a]"He who is without sin among you, let him throw a stone at her first." [8]And again He stooped down and wrote on the ground. [9]Then those who heard *it*, [a]being[1] convicted by *their* conscience, went out one by one, beginning with the oldest *even* to the last. And Jesus was left alone, and the woman standing in the midst. [10]When Jesus had raised Himself up [1]and saw no one but the woman, He said to her, "Woman, where are those accusers [2]of yours? Has no one condemned you?"

[11]She said, "No one, Lord."

And Jesus said to her, [a]"Neither do I condemn you; go [1]and [b]sin no more."

[12]Then Jesus spoke to them again, saying, [a]"I am the light of the world. He who [b]follows Me shall not walk in darkness, but have the light of life."

JESUS DEFENDS HIS SELF-WITNESS

[13]The Pharisees therefore said to Him, [a]"You bear witness of Yourself; Your witness is not [1]true."

[14]Jesus answered and said to them, "Even if I bear witness of Myself, My witness is true, for I know where I came from and where I am going; but [a]you do not know where I come from and where I am going. [15a]You judge according to the flesh; [b]I judge no one. [16]And yet if I do judge, My judgment is true; for [a]I am not alone, but I *am* with the Father who sent Me. [17a]It is also written in your law that the testimony of two men is true. [18]I am One who bears witness of Myself, and [a]the Father who sent Me bears witness of Me."

[19]Then they said to Him, "Where is Your Father?"

Jesus answered, [a]"You know neither Me nor My Father. [b]If you had known Me, you would have known My Father also."

[20]These words Jesus spoke in [a]the treasury, as He taught in the temple; and [b]no one laid hands on Him, for [c]His hour had not yet come.

JESUS PREDICTS HIS DEPARTURE

[21]Then Jesus said to them again, "I am going away, and [a]you will seek Me, and [b]will die in your sin. Where I go you cannot come."

8:2 [a]John 8:20; 18:20

8:4 [a]Ex. 20:14; [Matt. 5:27; 19:9; Rom. 7:3]

8:5 [a]Lev. 20:10; Deut. 22:22–24

8:6 [a]Matt. 22:15

8:7 [a]Deut. 17:7; [Rom. 2:1]

8:9 [a]Rom. 2:22

8:11 [a][Luke 9:56; 12:14; John 3:17] [b][John 5:14]

8:12 [a]Is. 9:2; Mal. 4:2; John 1:4; 9:5; 12:35; [2 Tim. 1:10] [b]1 Thess. 5:5

8:13 [a]John 5:31

8:14 [a]John 7:28; 9:29

8:15 [a]1 Sam. 16:7; John 7:24 [b][John 3:17; 12:47; 18:36]

8:16 [a]John 16:32

8:17 [a]Deut. 17:6; 19:15; Matt. 18:16; 2 Cor. 13:1; Heb. 10:28

8:18 [a]John 5:37; 1 John 5:9

8:19 [a]John 16:3 [b]John 14:7

8:20 [a]Mark 12:41, 43; Luke 21:1 [b]John 2:4; 7:30 [c]John 7:8

8:21 [a]John 7:34; 13:33 [b]John 8:24

8:2 [1]M *very early* 8:4 [1]M *we found this woman* 8:5 [1]M *in our law Moses commanded* [2]NU, M *to stone such* [3]M adds *about her* 8:6 [1]NU, M omit *as though He did not hear* 8:7 [1]M *He looked up* 8:9 [1]NU, M omit *being convicted by their conscience* 8:10 [1]NU omits *and saw no one but the woman*; M *He saw her and said*, [2]NU, M omit *of yours* 8:11 [1]NU, M add *from now on* 8:13 [1]*valid* as testimony

8:23 ªJohn 3:31
ᵇJohn 15:19;
17:16; 1 John 4:5

8:24 ªJohn 8:21
ᵇ[Mark 16:16]

8:25 ªJohn 4:26

8:26 ªJohn 7:28
ᵇJohn 3:32; 15:15

8:28
ªMatt. 27:35;
Mark 15:24;
Luke 23:33;
John 3:14;
12:32; 19:18
ᵇ[Rom. 1:4]
ᶜJohn 5:19, 30
ᵈDeut. 18:15,
18, 19; John 3:11

8:29 ªJohn 14:10
ᵇJohn 8:16;
16:32
ᶜJohn 4:34;
5:30; 6:38

8:30 ªJohn 7:31;
10:42; 11:45

8:31
ª[John 14:15, 23]

8:32 ª[John 1:14,
17; 14:6]
ᵇ[Rom. 6:14,
18, 22;
James 1:25;
2:12]

8:33
ªLev. 25:42;
[Matt. 3:9];
Luke 3:8

8:34 ªProv. 5:22;
Rom. 6:16;
2 Pet. 2:19

8:35
ªGen. 21:10;
Gal. 4:30

8:36
ª[Rom. 8:2;
2 Cor. 3:17];
Gal. 5:1

8:37 ªJohn 7:19

8:38
ª[John 3:32;
5:19, 30; 14:10,
24]

8:39 ªMatt. 3:9;
John 8:37
ᵇ[Rom. 2:28;
Gal. 3:7, 29]

8:40 ªJohn 8:37
ᵇJohn 8:26

8:41
ªDeut. 32:6;
Is. 63:16;
Mal. 1:6

8:42 ª1 John 5:1
ᵇJohn 16:27;
17:8, 25
ᶜJohn 5:43;
Gal. 4:4

²²So the Jews said, "Will He kill Himself, because He says, 'Where I go you cannot come'?"

²³And He said to them, ª"You are from beneath; I am from above. ᵇYou are of this world; I am not of this world. ²⁴ªTherefore I said to you that you will die in your sins; ᵇfor if you do not believe that I am *He,* you will die in your sins."

²⁵Then they said to Him, "Who are You?"

And Jesus said to them, "Just what I ªhave been saying to you from the beginning. ²⁶I have many things to say and to judge concerning you, but ªHe who sent Me is true; and ᵇI speak to the world those things which I heard from Him."

²⁷They did not understand that He spoke to them of the Father. ²⁸Then Jesus said to them, "When you ªlift¹ up the Son of Man, ᵇthen you will know that I am *He,* and ᶜ*that* I do nothing of Myself; but ᵈas My Father taught Me, I speak these things. ²⁹And ªHe who sent Me is with Me. ᵇThe Father has not left Me alone, ᶜfor I always do those things that please Him." ³⁰As He spoke these words, ªmany believed in Him.

THE TRUTH SHALL MAKE YOU FREE

³¹Then Jesus said to those Jews who believed Him, "If you ªabide in My word, you are My disciples indeed. ³²And you shall know the ªtruth, and ᵇthe truth shall make you free."

³³They answered Him, ª"We are Abraham's descendants, and have never been in bondage to anyone. How *can* You say, 'You will be made free'?"

³⁴Jesus answered them, "Most assuredly, I say to you, ªwhoever commits sin is a slave of sin. ³⁵And ªa slave does not abide in the house forever, *but* a son abides forever. ³⁶ªTherefore if the Son makes you free, you shall be free indeed.

ABRAHAM'S SEED AND SATAN'S

³⁷"I know that you are Abraham's descendants, but ªyou seek to kill Me, because My word has no place in you. ³⁸ªI speak what I have seen with My Father, and you do what you have ¹seen with your father."

³⁹They answered and said to Him, ª"Abraham is our father."

Jesus said to them, ᵇ"If you were Abraham's children, you would do the works of Abraham. ⁴⁰ªBut now you seek to kill Me, a Man who has told you the truth ᵇwhich I heard from God. Abraham did not do this. ⁴¹You do the deeds of your father."

Then they said to Him, "We were not born of fornication; ªwe have one Father—God."

⁴²Jesus said to them, ª"If God were your Father, you would love Me, for ᵇI proceeded forth and came from God; ᶜnor have I come of Myself, but He sent Me. ⁴³ªWhy do you not understand My speech? Because you are not able to listen to My word. ⁴⁴ªYou are of *your* father the devil, and the ᵇdesires of your father you want to ᶜdo. He was a murderer from the beginning, and ᵈdoes not stand in the truth, because there is no truth in him. When he speaks a lie, he speaks from his own *resources,* for he is a liar and the father of it. ⁴⁵But because

8:43 ª[John 7:17]   8:44 ªMatt. 13:38; 1 John 3:8 ᵇ1 John 2:16, 17 ᶜ[1 John 3:8–10, 15]
ᵈ[Jude 6]

8:28 ¹Crucify   8:38 ¹NU *heard from*

I tell the truth, you do not believe Me. ⁴⁶Which of you convicts Me of sin? And if I tell the truth, why do you not believe Me? ⁴⁷ᵃHe who is of God hears God's words; therefore you do not hear, because you are not of God."

BEFORE ABRAHAM WAS, I AM

⁴⁸Then the Jews answered and said to Him, "Do we not say rightly that You are a Samaritan and ᵃhave a demon?"

⁴⁹Jesus answered, "I do not have a demon; but I honor My Father, and ᵃyou dishonor Me. ⁵⁰And ᵃI do not seek My *own* glory; there is One who seeks and judges. ⁵¹Most assuredly, I say to you, ᵃif anyone keeps My word he shall never see death."

⁵²Then the Jews said to Him, "Now we know that You ᵃhave a demon! ᵇAbraham is dead, and the prophets; and You say, 'If anyone keeps My word he shall never taste death.' ⁵³Are You greater than our father Abraham, who is dead? And the prophets are dead. ᵃWho do You make Yourself out to be?"

⁵⁴Jesus answered, ᵃ"If I honor Myself, My honor is nothing. ᵇIt is My Father who honors Me, of whom you say that He is ¹your God. ⁵⁵Yet ᵃyou have not known Him, but I know Him. And if I say, 'I do not know Him,' I shall be a liar like you; but I do know Him and ᵇkeep His word. ⁵⁶Your father Abraham ᵃrejoiced to see My day, ᵇand he saw *it* and was glad."

⁵⁷Then the Jews said to Him, "You are not yet fifty years old, and have You seen Abraham?"

⁵⁸Jesus said to them, "Most assuredly, I say to you, ᵃbefore Abraham was, ᵇI AM."

⁵⁹Then ᵃthey took up stones to throw at Him; but Jesus hid Himself and went out of the temple, ᵇgoing¹ through the midst of them, and so passed by.

A MAN BORN BLIND RECEIVES SIGHT

9 Now as *Jesus* passed by, He saw a man who was blind from birth. ²And His disciples asked Him, saying, "Rabbi, ᵃwho sinned, this man or his parents, that he was born blind?"

³Jesus answered, "Neither this man nor his parents sinned, ᵇbut that the works of God should be revealed in him. ⁴ᵃI¹ must work the works of Him who sent Me while it is ᵇday; *the* night is coming when no one can work. ⁵As long as I am in the world, ᵃI am the light of the world."

⁶When He had said these things, ᵃHe spat on the ground and made clay with the saliva; and He anointed the eyes of the blind man with the clay. ⁷And He said to him, "Go, wash ᵃin the pool of Siloam" (which is translated, Sent). So ᵇhe went and washed, and came back seeing.

⁸Therefore the neighbors and those who previously had seen that he was ¹blind said, "Is not this he who sat and begged?"

⁹Some said, "This is he." Others *said*, ¹"He is like him."

He said, "I am *he*."

¹⁰Therefore they said to him, "How were your eyes opened?"

¹¹He answered and said, ᵃ"A Man called Jesus made clay and anointed my eyes and said to me, 'Go to ¹the pool of Siloam and wash.' So I went and washed, and I received sight."

8:54 ¹NU, M *our*   8:59 ¹NU omits the rest of v. 59.   9:4 ¹NU *We*
9:8 ¹NU *a beggar*   9:9 ¹NU *"No, but he is like him."*   9:11 ¹NU omits
the pool of

8:47 ᵃLuke 8:15;
John 10:26;
1 John 4:6

8:48
ᵃJohn 7:20;
10:20

8:49 ᵃJohn 5:41

8:50
ᵃJohn 5:41; 7:18;
[Phil. 2:6–8]

8:51
ᵃJohn 5:24; 11:26

8:52
ᵃJohn 7:20;
10:20
ᵇZech. 1:5;
Heb. 11:13

8:53
ᵃJohn 10:33;
19:7

8:54
ᵃJohn 5:31, 32
ᵇJohn 5:41;
Acts 3:13

8:55
ᵃJohn 7:28, 29
ᵇ[John 15:10]

8:56
ᵃLuke 10:24
ᵇMatt. 13:17;
Heb. 11:13

8:58 ᵃMic. 5:2;
John 17:5;
Heb. 7:3;
Rev. 22:13
ᵇEx. 3:14;
Is. 43:13;
John 17:5, 24;
Col. 1:17; Rev. 1:8

8:59
ᵃJohn 10:31; 11:8
ᵇLuke 4:30;
John 10:39

9:2 ᵃLuke 13:2;
John 9:34;
Acts 28:4

9:3 ᵃJohn 11:4

9:4 ᵃ[John 4:34;
5:19, 36; 17:4]
ᵇJohn 11:9, 10;
12:35; Gal. 6:10

9:5
ᵃ[John 1:5, 9;
3:19; 8:12;
12:35, 46]

9:6 ᵃMark 7:33;
8:23

9:7 ᵃNeh. 3:15;
Is. 8:6;
Luke 13:4;
John 9:11
ᵇ2 Kin. 5:14

9:11 ᵃJohn 9:6, 7

¹²Then they said to him, "Where is He?"

He said, "I do not know."

THE PHARISEES EXCOMMUNICATE THE HEALED MAN

¹³They brought him who formerly was blind to the Pharisees. ¹⁴Now it was a Sabbath when Jesus made the clay and opened his eyes. ¹⁵Then the Pharisees also asked him again how he had received his sight. He said to them, "He put clay on my eyes, and I washed, and I see."

¹⁶Therefore some of the Pharisees said, "This Man is not from God, because He does not [1]keep the Sabbath."

Others said, ^a"How can a man who is a sinner do such signs?" And ^bthere was a division among them.

¹⁷They said to the blind man again, "What do you say about Him because He opened your eyes?"

He said, ^a"He is a prophet."

¹⁸But the Jews did not believe concerning him, that he had been blind and received his sight, until they called the parents of him who had received his sight. ¹⁹And they asked them, saying, "Is this your son, who you say was born blind? How then does he now see?"

²⁰His parents answered them and said, "We know that this is our son, and that he was born blind; ²¹but by what means he now sees we do not know, or who opened his eyes we do not know. He is of age; ask him. He will speak for himself." ²²His parents said these *things* because ^athey feared the Jews, for the Jews had agreed already that if anyone confessed *that* He *was* Christ, he ^bwould be put out of the synagogue. ²³Therefore his parents said, "He is of age; ask him."

²⁴So they again called the man who was blind, and said to him, ^a"Give God the glory! ^bWe know that this Man is a sinner."

²⁵He answered and said, "Whether He is a sinner *or not* I do not know. One thing I know: that though I was blind, now I see."

²⁶Then they said to him again, "What did He do to you? How did He open your eyes?"

²⁷He answered them, "I told you already, and you did not listen. Why do you want to hear *it* again? Do you also want to become His disciples?"

²⁸Then they reviled him and said, "You are His disciple, but we are Moses' disciples. ²⁹We know that God ^aspoke to ^bMoses; *as for* this *fellow*, ^cwe do not know where He is from."

³⁰The man answered and said to them, ^a"Why, this is a marvelous thing, that you do not know where He is from; yet He has opened my eyes! ³¹Now we know that ^aGod does not hear sinners; but if anyone is a worshiper of God and does His will, He hears him. ³²Since the world began it has been unheard of that anyone opened the eyes of one who was born blind. ^{33a}If this Man were not from God, He could do nothing."

³⁴They answered and said to him, ^a"You were completely born in sins, and are you teaching us?" And they [1]cast him out.

TRUE VISION AND TRUE BLINDNESS

³⁵Jesus heard that they had cast him out; and when He had ^afound him, He said to him, "Do you ^bbelieve in ^cthe Son of [1]God?"

Cross references

9:16
^aJohn 3:2; 9:33
^bJohn 7:12, 43; 10:19

9:17 ^a[John 4:19; 6:14]

9:22 ^aJohn 7:13; 12:42; 19:38; Acts 5:13
^bJohn 16:2

9:24 ^aJosh. 7:19; 1 Sam. 6:5; Ezra 10:11; Rev. 11:13
^bJohn 9:16

9:29
^aEx. 19:19, 20; 33:11; 34:29; Num. 12:6–8
^b[John 5:45–47]
^cJohn 7:27, 28; 8:14

9:30 ^aJohn 3:10

9:31
^aJob 27:9; 35:12; Ps. 18:41; Prov. 1:28; 15:29; 28:9; Is. 1:15; Jer. 11:11; 14:12; Ezek. 8:18; Mic. 3:4; Zech. 7:13; [James 5:16]

9:33
^aJohn 3:2; 9:16

9:34 ^aPs. 51:5; John 9:2

9:35 ^aJohn 5:14
^bJohn 1:7; 16:31
^cMatt. 14:33; 16:16; Mark 1:1; John 10:36; 1 John 5:13

9:16 [1]*observe*   **9:34** [1]Excommunicated him   **9:35** [1]NU *Man*

[36]He answered and said, "Who is He, Lord, that I may believe in Him?"

[37]And Jesus said to him, "You have both seen Him and [a]it is He who is talking with you."

[38]Then he said, "Lord, I believe!" And he [a]worshiped Him.

[39]And Jesus said, [a]"For judgment I have come into this world, [b]that those who do not see may see, and that those who see may be made blind."

[40]Then *some* of the Pharisees who were with Him heard these words, [a]and said to Him, "Are we blind also?"

[41]Jesus said to them, [a]"If you were blind, you would have no sin; but now you say, 'We see.' Therefore your sin remains.

JESUS THE TRUE SHEPHERD

10 "Most assuredly, I say to you, he who does not enter the sheepfold by the door, but climbs up some other way, the same is a thief and a robber. [2]But he who enters by the door is the shepherd of the sheep. [3]To him the doorkeeper opens, and the sheep hear his voice; and he calls his own sheep by [a]name and leads them out. [4]And when he brings out his own sheep, he goes before them; and the sheep follow him, for they know his voice. [5]Yet they will by no means follow a [a]stranger, but will flee from him, for they do not know the voice of strangers." [6]Jesus used this illustration, but they did not understand the things which He spoke to them.

JESUS THE GOOD SHEPHERD

[7]Then Jesus said to them again, "Most assuredly, I say to you, I am the door of the sheep. [8]All who *ever* came [1]before Me are thieves and robbers, but the sheep did not hear them. [9a]I am the door. If anyone enters by Me, he will be saved, and will go in and out and find pasture. [10]The thief does not come except to steal, and to kill, and to destroy. I have come that they may have life, and that they may have *it* more abundantly.

[11a]"I am the good shepherd. The good shepherd gives His life for the sheep. [12]But a [1]hireling, *he who is* not the shepherd, one who does not own the sheep, sees the wolf coming and [a]leaves the sheep and flees; and the wolf catches the sheep and scatters them. [13]The hireling flees because he is a hireling and does not care about the sheep. [14]I am the good shepherd; and [a]I know My *sheep,* and [b]am known by My own. [15a]As the Father knows Me, even so I know the Father; [b]and I lay down My life for the sheep. [16]And [a]other sheep I have which are not of this fold; them also I must bring, and they will hear My voice; [b]and there will be one flock *and* one shepherd.

[17]"Therefore My Father [a]loves Me, [b]because I lay down My life that I may take it again. [18]No one takes it from Me, but I lay it down of Myself. I [a]have power to lay it down, and I have power to take it again. [b]This command I have received from My Father."

[19]Therefore [a]there was a division again among the Jews because of these sayings. [20]And many of them said, [a]"He has a demon and is [1]mad. Why do you listen to Him?"

[21]Others said, "These are not the words of one who has a demon. [a]Can a demon [b]open the eyes of the blind?"

9:37 [a]John 4:26
9:38 [a]Matt. 8:2
9:39
[a][John 3:17; 5:22, 27; 12:47]
[b]Matt. 13:13; 15:14
9:40
[a][Rom. 2:19]
9:41
[a]John 15:22, 24
10:3
[a]John 20:16
10:5
[a][2 Cor. 11:13–15]
10:9
[a][John 14:6; Eph. 2:18]
10:11
[a]Gen. 49:24; Is. 40:11; Ezek. 34:23; [Heb. 13:20]; 1 Pet. 2:25; 5:4; Rev. 7:17
10:12
[a]Zech. 11:16, 17
10:14 [a]Is. 40:11; Nah. 1:7; Zech. 13:7; John 6:64; 2 Tim. 2:19
[b]2 Tim. 1:12
10:15
[a]Matt. 11:27
[b]Matt. 27:50; Mark 15:37; Luke 23:46; [John 15:13; 19:30]; 1 John 3:16
10:16 [a]Is. 42:6; 56:8; Acts 10:45; 11:18; 13:46
[b]Ezek. 37:22; John 11:52; 17:20; Eph. 2:13–18; 1 Pet. 2:25
10:17 [a]John 5:20
[b][Is. 53:7, 8, 12; Heb. 2:9]
10:18
[a]Matt. 26:53; [John 2:19; 5:26]
[b][John 6:38; 14:31; 17:4; Acts 2:24, 32]
10:19
[a]John 7:43; 9:16
10:20
[a]John 7:20
10:21 [a][Ex. 4:11]
[b]John 9:6, 7, 32, 33

10:8 [1]M omits *before Me*   10:12 [1]*hired man*   10:20 [1]*insane*

THE SHEPHERD KNOWS HIS SHEEP

²²Now it was the Feast of Dedication in Jerusalem, and it was winter. ²³And Jesus walked in the temple, ᵃin Solomon's porch. ²⁴Then the Jews surrounded Him and said to Him, "How long do You keep us in ¹doubt? If You are the Christ, tell us plainly."

²⁵Jesus answered them, "I told you, and you do not believe. ᵃThe works that I do in My Father's name, they ᵇbear witness of Me. ²⁶But ᵃyou do not believe, because you are not of My sheep, ¹as I said to you. ²⁷ᵃMy sheep hear My voice, and I know them, and they follow Me. ²⁸And I give them eternal life, and they shall never perish; neither shall anyone snatch them out of My hand. ²⁹ᵃMy Father, ᵇwho has given *them* to Me, is greater than all; and no one is able to snatch *them* out of My Father's hand. ³⁰ᵃI and *My* Father are one."

RENEWED EFFORTS TO STONE JESUS

³¹Then ᵃthe Jews took up stones again to stone Him. ³²Jesus answered them, "Many good works I have shown you from My Father. For which of those works do you stone Me?"

³³The Jews answered Him, saying, "For a good work we do not stone You, but for ᵃblasphemy, and because You, being a Man, ᵇmake Yourself God."

³⁴Jesus answered them, "Is it not written in your law, ᵃ'I said, "You are gods" '? ³⁵If He called them gods, ᵃto whom the word of God came (and the Scripture ᵇcannot be broken), ³⁶do you say of Him ᵃwhom the Father sanctified and ᵇsent into the world, 'You are blaspheming,' ᶜbecause I said, 'I am ᵈthe Son of God'? ³⁷ᵃIf I do not do the works of My Father, do not believe Me; ³⁸but if I do, though you do not believe Me, ᵃbelieve the works, that you may know and ¹believe ᵇthat the Father *is* in Me, and I in Him." ³⁹ᵃTherefore they sought again to seize Him, but He escaped out of their hand.

THE BELIEVERS BEYOND JORDAN

⁴⁰And He went away again beyond the Jordan to the place ᵃwhere John was baptizing at first, and there He stayed. ⁴¹Then many came to Him and said, "John performed no sign, ᵃbut all the things that John spoke about this Man were true." ⁴²And many believed in Him there.

THE DEATH OF LAZARUS

11 Now a certain *man* was sick, Lazarus of Bethany, the town of ᵃMary and her sister Martha. ²ᵃIt was *that* Mary who anointed the Lord with fragrant oil and wiped His feet with her hair, whose brother Lazarus was sick. ³Therefore the sisters sent to Him, saying, "Lord, behold, he whom You love is sick."

⁴When Jesus heard *that,* He said, "This sickness is not unto death, but for the glory of God, that the Son of God may be glorified through it."

⁵Now Jesus loved Martha and her sister and Lazarus. ⁶So, when He heard that he was sick, ᵃHe stayed two more days in the place where He was. ⁷Then after this He said to *the* disciples, "Let us go to Judea again."

10:23
ᵃActs 3:11; 5:12

10:25
ᵃJohn 5:36;
10:38
ᵇMatt. 11:4;
John 2:11; 20:30

10:26
ᵃ[John 8:47]

10:27
ᵃJohn 10:4, 14

10:29
ᵃJohn 14:28
ᵇ[John 17:2, 6,
12, 24]

10:30
ᵃJohn 17:11,
21–24

10:31
ᵃJohn 8:59

10:33 ᵃMatt. 9:3
ᵇJohn 5:18

10:34 ᵃPs. 82:6

10:35
ᵃMatt. 5:17, 18
ᵇ1 Pet. 1:25

10:36
ᵃJohn 6:27
ᵇJohn 3:17
ᶜJohn 5:17, 18
ᵈLuke 1:35

10:37
ᵃJohn 10:25;
15:24

10:38
ᵃJohn 5:36
ᵇJohn 14:10, 11

10:39
ᵃJohn 7:30, 44

10:40
ᵃJohn 1:28

10:41
ᵃ[John 1:29, 36;
3:28–36; 5:33]

11:1 ᵃLuke 10:38,
39; John 11:5, 19

11:2 ᵃMatt. 26:7

11:6 ᵃJohn 10:40

10:24 ¹Suspense   10:26 ¹NU omits *as I said to you*   10:38 ¹NU *understand*

[8]*The* disciples said to Him, "Rabbi, lately the Jews sought to [a]stone You, and are You going there again?"

[9]Jesus answered, "Are there not twelve hours in the day? [a]If anyone [b]walks in the day, he does not stumble, because he sees the [b]light of this world. [10]But [a]if one walks in the night, he stumbles, because the light is not in him." [11]These things He said, and after that He said to them, "Our friend Lazarus [a]sleeps, but I go that I may wake him up."

[12]Then His disciples said, "Lord, if he sleeps he will get well." [13]However, Jesus spoke of his death, but they thought that He was speaking about taking rest in sleep.

[14]Then Jesus said to them plainly, "Lazarus is dead. [15]And I am glad for your sakes that I was not there, that you may believe. Nevertheless let us go to him."

[16]Then [a]Thomas, who is called the Twin, said to his fellow disciples, "Let us also go, that we may die with Him."

I AM THE RESURRECTION AND THE LIFE

[17]So when Jesus came, He found that he had already been in the tomb four days. [18]Now Bethany was near Jerusalem, about [1]two miles away. [19]And many of the Jews had joined the women around Martha and Mary, to comfort them concerning their brother.

[20]Then Martha, as soon as she heard that Jesus was coming, went and met Him, but Mary was sitting in the house. [21]Now Martha said to Jesus, "Lord, if You had been here, my brother would not have died. [22]But even now I know that [a]whatever You ask of God, God will give You."

[23]Jesus said to her, "Your brother will rise again."

[24]Martha said to Him, [a]"I know that he will rise again in the resurrection at the last day."

[25]Jesus said to her, "I am [a]the resurrection and the life. [b]He who believes in Me, though he may [c]die, he shall live. [26]And whoever lives and believes in Me shall never die. Do you believe this?"

[27]She said to Him, "Yes, Lord, [a]I believe that You are the Christ, the Son of God, who is to come into the world."

JESUS AND DEATH, THE LAST ENEMY

[28]And when she had said these things, she went her way and secretly called Mary her sister, saying, "The Teacher has come and is calling for you." [29]As soon as she heard *that*, she arose quickly and came to Him. [30]Now Jesus had not yet come into the town, but [1]was in the place where Martha met Him. [31][a]Then the Jews who were with her in the house, and comforting her, when they saw that Mary rose up quickly and went out, followed her, [1]saying, "She is going to the tomb to weep there."

[32]Then, when Mary came where Jesus was, and saw Him, she [a]fell down at His feet, saying to Him, [b]"Lord, if You had been here, my brother would not have died."

[33]Therefore, when Jesus saw her weeping, and the Jews who came with her weeping, He groaned in the spirit and was troubled. [34]And He said, "Where have you laid him?"

They said to Him, "Lord, come and see."

11:8 [a]John 8:59; 10:31

11:9 [a]Luke 13:33; John 9:4; 12:35 [b]Is. 9:2

11:10 [a]John 12:35

11:11 [a]Deut. 31:16; [Dan. 12:2]; Matt. 9:24; Acts 7:60; [1 Cor. 15:18, 51]

11:16 [a]Matt. 10:3; Mark 3:18; Luke 6:15; John 14:5; 20:26–28; Acts 1:13

11:22 [a][John 9:31; 11:41]

11:24 [a][Luke 14:14; John 5:29]

11:25 [a]John 5:21; 6:39, 40, 44; [Rev. 1:18] [b]John 3:16, 36; 1 John 5:10 [c]1 Cor. 15:22; [Heb. 9:27]

11:27 [a]Matt. 16:16; Luke 2:11; John 4:42; 6:14, 69

11:31 [a]John 11:19, 33

11:32 [a]Mark 5:22; 7:25; Rev. 1:17 [b]John 11:21

11:18 [1]Lit. *15 stadia*   11:30 [1]NU *was still*   11:31 [1]NU *supposing that she was going*

11:35 ᵃLuke 19:41

11:37
ᵃJohn 9:6, 7

11:38
ᵃMatt. 27:60, 66;
Mark 15:46;
Luke 24:2;
John 20:1

11:40
ᵃ[John 11:4, 23]

11:42
ᵃJohn 12:30;
17:21

11:44
ᵃJohn 19:40
ᵇJohn 20:7

11:45
ᵃJohn 2:23;
10:42; 12:11, 18

11:46 ᵃJohn 5:15

11:47 ᵃPs. 2:2;
Matt. 26:3;
Mark 14:1;
Luke 22:2
ᵇJohn 12:19;
Acts 4:16

11:49
ᵃMatt. 26:3;
Luke 3:2;
John 18:14;
Acts 4:6

11:50
ᵃJohn 18:14

11:52 ᵃIs. 49:6;
Acts 10:45;
11:18; 13:46;
[1 John 2:2]
ᵇPs. 22:27;
John 10:16;
[Eph. 2:14–17]

11:53
ᵃMatt. 26:4;
Luke 6:11;
19:47; 22:2;
John 5:16

11:54
ᵃJohn 4:1, 3; 7:1
ᵇ2 Chr. 13:19

11:55
ᵃMatt. 26:1;
Mark 14:1;
Luke 22:1;
John 2:13;
5:1; 6:4
ᵇNum. 9:10, 13;
31:19, 20;
2 Chr. 30:17;
Luke 2:22

11:56 ᵃJohn 7:11

11:57
ᵃMatt. 26:14–16

³⁵ᵃJesus wept. ³⁶Then the Jews said, "See how He loved him!"

³⁷And some of them said, "Could not this Man, ᵃwho opened the eyes of the blind, also have kept this man from dying?"

LAZARUS RAISED FROM THE DEAD

³⁸Then Jesus, again groaning in Himself, came to the tomb. It was a cave, and a ᵃstone lay against it. ³⁹Jesus said, "Take away the stone."

Martha, the sister of him who was dead, said to Him, "Lord, by this time there is a stench, for he has been *dead* four days."

⁴⁰Jesus said to her, "Did I not say to you that if you would believe you would ᵃsee the glory of God?" ⁴¹Then they took away the stone ¹*from the place* where the dead man was lying. And Jesus lifted up *His* eyes and said, "Father, I thank You that You have heard Me. ⁴²And I know that You always hear Me, but ᵃbecause of the people who are standing by I said *this*, that they may believe that You sent Me." ⁴³Now when He had said these things, He cried with a loud voice, "Lazarus, come forth!" ⁴⁴And he who had died came out bound hand and foot with ᵃgraveclothes, and ᵇhis face was wrapped with a cloth. Jesus said to them, "Loose him, and let him go."

THE PLOT TO KILL JESUS
(Matt. 26:1–5; Mark 14:1, 2; Luke 22:1, 2)

⁴⁵Then many of the Jews who had come to Mary, ᵃand had seen the things Jesus did, believed in Him. ⁴⁶But some of them went away to the Pharisees and ᵃtold them the things Jesus did. ⁴⁷ᵃThen the chief priests and the Pharisees gathered a council and said, ᵇ"What shall we do? For this Man works many signs. ⁴⁸If we let Him alone like this, everyone will believe in Him, and the Romans will come and take away both our place and nation."

⁴⁹And one of them, ᵃCaiaphas, being high priest that year, said to them, "You know nothing at all, ⁵⁰ᵃnor do you consider that it is expedient for ¹us that one man should die for the people, and not that the whole nation should perish." ⁵¹Now this he did not say on his own *authority;* but being high priest that year he prophesied that Jesus would die for the nation, ⁵²and ᵃnot for that nation only, but ᵇalso that He would gather together in one the children of God who were scattered abroad.

⁵³Then, from that day on, they plotted to ᵃput Him to death. ⁵⁴ᵃTherefore Jesus no longer walked openly among the Jews, but went from there into the country near the wilderness, to a city called ᵇEphraim, and there remained with His disciples.

⁵⁵ᵃAnd the Passover of the Jews was near, and many went from the country up to Jerusalem before the Passover, to ᵇpurify themselves. ⁵⁶ᵃThen they sought Jesus, and spoke among themselves as they stood in the temple, "What do you think—that He will not come to the feast?" ⁵⁷Now both the chief priests and the Pharisees had given a command, that if anyone knew where He was, he should report *it*, that they might ᵃseize Him.

11:41 ¹NU omits *from the place where the dead man was lying*
11:50 ¹NU *you*

THE ANOINTING AT BETHANY
(Matt. 26:6–13; Mark 14:3–9)

12 Then, six days before the Passover, Jesus came to Bethany, [a]where Lazarus was [1]who had been dead, whom He had raised from the dead. [2a]There they made Him a supper; and Martha served, but Lazarus was one of those who sat at the table with Him. [3]Then [a]Mary took a pound of very costly oil of [b]spikenard, anointed the feet of Jesus, and wiped His feet with her hair. And the house was filled with the fragrance of the oil.

[4]But one of His disciples, [a]Judas Iscariot, Simon's *son*, who would betray Him, said, [5]"Why was this fragrant oil not sold for [1]three hundred denarii and given to the poor?" [6]This he said, not that he cared for the poor, but because he was a thief, and [a]had the money box; and he used to take what was put in it.

[7]But Jesus said, "Let her alone; [1]she has kept this for the day of My burial. [8]For [a]the poor you have with you always, but Me you do not have always."

THE PLOT TO KILL LAZARUS

[9]Now a great many of the Jews knew that He was there; and they came, not for Jesus' sake only, but that they might also see Lazarus, [a]whom He had raised from the dead. [10a]But the chief priests plotted to put Lazarus to death also, [11a]because on account of him many of the Jews went away and believed in Jesus.

THE TRIUMPHAL ENTRY
(Matt. 21:1–11; Mark 11:1–11; Luke 19:28–40)

[12a]The next day a great multitude that had come to the feast, when they heard that Jesus was coming to Jerusalem, [13]took branches of palm trees and went out to meet Him, and cried out:

"Hosanna!
[a]'Blessed *is* He who comes in the name of the LORD!'
The King of Israel!"

[14a]Then Jesus, when He had found a young donkey, sat on it; as it is written:

15 "Fear[a] not, daughter of Zion;
Behold, your King is coming,
Sitting on a donkey's colt."

[16a]His disciples did not understand these things at first; [b]but when Jesus was glorified, [c]then they remembered that these things were written about Him and *that* they had done these things to Him.

[17]Therefore the people, who were with Him when He called Lazarus out of his tomb and raised him from the dead, bore witness. [18a]For this reason the people also met Him, because they heard that He had done this sign. [19]The Pharisees therefore said among themselves, [a]"You see that you are accomplishing nothing. Look, the world has gone after Him!"

12:1 [a]Matt. 21:17; John 11:1, 43
12:2 [a]Matt. 26:6; Mark 14:3; Luke 10:38–41
12:3 [a]Luke 10:38, 39; John 11:2; [b]Song 1:12
12:4 [a]John 13:26
12:6 [a]John 13:29
12:8 [a]Deut. 15:11; Matt. 26:11; Mark 14:7; John 17:11
12:9 [a]John 11:43, 44
12:10 [a]Luke 16:31
12:11 [a]John 11:45; 12:18
12:12 [a]Matt. 21:4–9; Mark 11:7–10; Luke 19:35–38
12:13 [a]Ps. 118:25, 26
12:14 [a]Matt. 21:7
12:15 [a]Is. 40:9; Zech. 9:9
12:16 [a]Luke 18:34; [b]John 7:39; 12:23; [c][John 14:26]
12:18 [a]John 12:11
12:19 [a]John 11:47, 48

12:1 [1]NU omits *who had been dead*   12:5 [1]About one year's wages for a worker   12:7 [1]NU *that she may keep*

12:20
a Mark 7:26;
Acts 17:4
b 1 Kin. 8:41, 42;
Acts 8:27

12:21 a John 1:43,
44; 14:8–11

12:23
a Matt. 26:18, 45;
John 13:32;
Acts 3:13

12:24
a [Rom. 14:9];
1 Cor. 15:36

12:25
a Matt. 10:39;
Mark 8:35;
Luke 9:24

12:26
a [Matt. 16:24];
b John 14:3;
17:24;
[1 Thess. 4:17]

12:27
a [Matt. 26:38,
39]; Mark 14:34;
Luke 12:50;
John 11:33
b Luke 22:53;
John 18:37

12:28
a Matt. 3:17; 17:5;
Mark 1:11; 9:7;
Luke 3:22; 9:35

12:30
a John 11:42

12:31
a Matt. 12:29;
Luke 10:18;
[Acts 26:18;
2 Cor. 4:4]

12:32
a John 3:14; 8:28
b [Rom. 5:18;
Heb. 2:9]

12:33
a John 18:32;
21:19

12:34
a Ps. 89:36, 37;
Is. 9:6, 7;
Mic. 4:7

12:35
a [John 1:9; 7:33;
8:12] b Jer. 13:16;
[Gal. 6:10];
Eph. 5:8
c John 11:10;
[1 John 2:9–11]

12:36
a Luke 16:8;
John 8:12
b John 8:59

12:37
a John 11:47

12:38 a Is. 53:1;
Rom. 10:16

THE FRUITFUL GRAIN OF WHEAT

20 Now there a were certain Greeks among those b who came up to worship at the feast. 21 Then they came to Philip, a who was from Bethsaida of Galilee, and asked him, saying, "Sir, we wish to see Jesus."

22 Philip came and told Andrew, and in turn Andrew and Philip told Jesus.

23 But Jesus answered them, saying, a "The hour has come that the Son of Man should be glorified. 24 Most assuredly, I say to you, a unless a grain of wheat falls into the ground and dies, it remains alone; but if it dies, it produces much 1 grain. 25a He who loves his life will lose it, and he who hates his life in this world will keep it for eternal life. 26 If anyone serves Me, let him a follow Me; and b where I am, there My servant will be also. If anyone serves Me, him *My* Father will honor.

JESUS PREDICTS HIS DEATH ON THE CROSS

27a "Now My soul is troubled, and what shall I say? 'Father, save Me from this hour'? b But for this purpose I came to this hour. 28 Father, glorify Your name."

a Then a voice came from heaven, *saying,* "I have both glorified *it* and will glorify *it* again."

29 Therefore the people who stood by and heard *it* said that it had thundered. Others said, "An angel has spoken to Him."

30 Jesus answered and said, a "This voice did not come because of Me, but for your sake. 31 Now is the judgment of this world; now a the ruler of this world will be cast out. 32 And I, a if I am 1 lifted up from the earth, will draw b all *peoples* to Myself." 33a This He said, signifying by what death He would die.

34 The people answered Him, a "We have heard from the law that the Christ remains forever; and how *can* You say, 'The Son of Man must be lifted up'? Who is this Son of Man?"

35 Then Jesus said to them, "A little while longer a the light is with you. b Walk while you have the light, lest darkness overtake you; c he who walks in darkness does not know where he is going. 36 While you have the light, believe in the light, that you may become a sons of light." These things Jesus spoke, and departed, and b was hidden from them.

WHO HAS BELIEVED OUR REPORT?

37 But although He had done so many a signs before them, they did not believe in Him, 38 that the word of Isaiah the prophet might be fulfilled, which he spoke:

a "Lord, who has believed our report?
And to whom has the arm of the LORD been revealed?"

39 Therefore they could not believe, because Isaiah said again:

40 "He a has blinded their eyes and hardened their hearts,
b Lest they should see with *their* eyes,
Lest they should understand with *their* hearts and turn,
So that I should heal them."

41a These things Isaiah said 1 when he saw His glory and spoke of Him.

12:40 a Is. 6:9, 10 b Matt. 13:14   12:41 a Is. 6:1

12:24 1 Lit. *fruit*   12:32 1 Crucified   12:41 1 NU *because*

WALK IN THE LIGHT

42Nevertheless even among the rulers many believed in Him, but ªbecause of the Pharisees they did not confess *Him,* lest they should be put out of the synagogue; 43ªfor they loved the praise of men more than the praise of God.

44Then Jesus cried out and said, ª"He who believes in Me, ᵇbelieves not in Me ᶜbut in Him who sent Me. 45And ªhe who sees Me sees Him who sent Me. 46ªI have come *as* a light into the world, that whoever believes in Me should not abide in darkness. 47And if anyone hears My words and does not ¹believe, ªI do not judge him; for ᵇI did not come to judge the world but to save the world. 48ªHe who rejects Me, and does not receive My words, has that which judges him—ᵇthe word that I have spoken will judge him in the last day. 49For ªI have not spoken on My own *authority;* but the Father who sent Me gave Me a command, ᵇwhat I should say and what I should speak. 50And I know that His command is everlasting life. Therefore, whatever I speak, just as the Father has told Me, so I ªspeak."

JESUS WASHES THE DISCIPLES' FEET

13 Now ªbefore the Feast of the Passover, when Jesus knew that ᵇHis hour had come that He should depart from this world to the Father, having loved His own who were in the world, He ᶜloved them to the end.

2And ¹supper being ended, ªthe devil having already put it into the heart of Judas Iscariot, Simon's *son,* to betray Him, 3Jesus, knowing ªthat the Father had given all things into His hands, and that He ᵇhad come from God and ᶜwas going to God, 4ªrose from supper and laid aside His garments, took a towel and girded Himself. 5After that, He poured water into a basin and began to wash the disciples' feet, and to wipe *them* with the towel with which He was girded. 6Then He came to Simon Peter. And *Peter* said to Him, ª"Lord, are You washing my feet?"

7Jesus answered and said to him, "What I am doing you ªdo not understand now, ᵇbut you will know after this."

8Peter said to Him, "You shall never wash my feet!"

Jesus answered him, ª"If I do not wash you, you have no part with Me."

9Simon Peter said to Him, "Lord, not my feet only, but also *my* hands and *my* head!"

10Jesus said to him, "He who is bathed needs only to wash *his* feet, but is completely clean; and ªyou are clean, but not all of you." 11For ªHe knew who would betray Him; therefore He said, "You are not all clean."

12So when He had washed their feet, taken His garments, and sat down again, He said to them, "Do you ¹know what I have done to you? 13ªYou call Me Teacher and Lord, and you say well, for *so* I am. 14ªIf I then, *your* Lord and Teacher, have washed your feet, ᵇyou also ought to wash one another's feet. 15For ªI have given you an example, that you should do as I have done to you. 16ªMost assuredly, I say to you, a servant is not greater than his master; nor is he who is sent greater than

12:42
ªJohn 7:13; 9:22

12:43
ªJohn 5:41, 44

12:44
ªMark 9:37
ᵇ[John 3:16, 18, 36; 11:25, 26]
ᶜ[John 5:24]

12:45
ª[John 14:9]

12:46 ªJohn 1:4, 5; 8:12; 12:35, 36

12:47 ªJohn 5:45
ᵇJohn 3:17

12:48
ª[Luke 10:16]
ᵇDeut. 18:18, 19; [John 5:45; 8:47]

12:49
ªJohn 8:38
ᵇDeut. 18:18

12:50
ªJohn 5:19; 8:28

13:1 ªMatt. 26:2
ᵇJohn 12:23; 17:1
ᶜJohn 15:9

13:2 ªLuke 22:3

13:3 ªMatt. 11:27; [John 5:20–23; 17:2]; Acts 2:36; 1 Cor. 15:27; [Heb. 2:8]
ᵇJohn 8:42; 16:28
ᶜJohn 17:11; 20:17

13:4
ª[Luke 22:27; Phil. 2:7, 8]

13:6 ªMatt. 3:14

13:7 ªJohn 12:16; 16:12 ᵇJohn 13:19

13:8
ª[Ps. 51:2, 7; Ezek. 36:25; Acts 22:16; 1 Cor. 6:11; Eph. 5:26; Titus 3:5; Heb. 10:22]

13:10
ª[John 15:3; Eph. 5:26]

13:11
ªJohn 6:64; 18:4

13:13
ªMatt. 23:8, 10; Luke 6:46; [1 Cor. 8:6; 12:3]; Eph. 6:9; [Phil. 2:11]

13:14
ªLuke 22:27
ᵇ[Rom. 12:10; Gal. 6:1, 2; 1 Pet. 5:5]

13:15 ªMatt. 11:29; Phil. 2:5; [1 Pet. 2:21–24]; 1 John 2:6   13:16 ªMatt. 10:24; [Luke 6:40]; John 15:20

12:47 ¹NU *keep them*   13:2 ¹NU *during supper*   13:12 ¹understand

13:17
ᵃMatt. 7:24;
Luke 11:28;
[James 1:25]

13:18
ᵃJohn 15:25;
17:12 ᵇPs. 41:9;
Matt. 26:23

13:19
ᵃJohn 14:29;
16:4

13:20
ᵃMatt. 10:40;
Mark 9:37;
Luke 9:48; 10:16;
Gal. 4:14

13:21
ᵃMatt. 26:21;
Mark 14:18;
Luke 22:21
ᵇJohn 12:27
ᶜPs. 41:9;
Matt. 26:46;
Mark 14:42;
Luke 22:48;
John 6:64; 18:5;
Acts 1:17;
1 John 2:19

13:23
ᵃJohn 19:26;
20:2; 21:7, 20

13:26
ᵃMatt. 10:4;
John 6:70, 71;
12:4; Acts 1:16

13:27 ᵃLuke 22:3

13:29 ᵃJohn 12:6

13:31
ᵃJohn 12:23;
Acts 3:13
ᵇ[John 14:13;
17:4; 1 Pet. 4:11]

13:32
ᵃJohn 12:23

13:33
ᵃJohn 12:35;
14:19; 16:16–19
ᵇMark 16:19;
[John 7:34;
8:21]; Acts 1:9

13:34
ᵃLev. 19:18;
Eph. 5:2;
1 Thess. 4:9;
James 2:8;
1 Pet. 1:22;
1 John 2:7

13:35
ᵃ1 John 2:5

13:36
ᵃJohn 13:33;
14:2; 16:5
ᵇJohn 21:17;
2 Pet. 1:14

13:37
ᵃMatt. 26:33–35;
Mark 14:29–31;
Luke 22:33, 34

he who sent him. 17ᵃIf you know these things, blessed are you if you do them.

JESUS IDENTIFIES HIS BETRAYER
(Matt. 26:21–25; Mark 14:18, 19; Luke 22:21–23)

18"I do not speak concerning all of you. I know whom I have chosen; but that the ᵃScripture may be fulfilled, ᵇ'He who eats ¹bread with Me has lifted up his heel against Me.' 19ᵃNow I tell you before it comes, that when it does come to pass, you may believe that I am *He*. 20ᵃMost assuredly, I say to you, he who receives whomever I send receives Me; and he who receives Me receives Him who sent Me."

21ᵃWhen Jesus had said these things, ᵇHe was troubled in spirit, and testified and said, "Most assuredly, I say to you, ᶜone of you will betray Me." 22Then the disciples looked at one another, perplexed about whom He spoke.

23Now ᵃthere was ¹leaning on Jesus' bosom one of His disciples, whom Jesus loved. 24Simon Peter therefore motioned to him to ask who it was of whom He spoke.

25Then, leaning ¹back on Jesus' breast, he said to Him, "Lord, who is it?"

26Jesus answered, "It is he to whom I shall give a piece of bread when I have dipped *it*." And having dipped the bread, He gave *it* to ᵃJudas Iscariot, *the son* of Simon. 27ᵃNow after the piece of bread, Satan entered him. Then Jesus said to him, "What you do, do quickly." 28But no one at the table knew for what reason He said this to him. 29For some thought, because ᵃJudas had the money box, that Jesus had said to him, "Buy *those things* we need for the feast," or that he should give something to the poor.

30Having received the piece of bread, he then went out immediately. And it was night.

THE NEW COMMANDMENT

31So, when he had gone out, Jesus said, ᵃ"Now the Son of Man is glorified, and ᵇGod is glorified in Him. 32If God is glorified in Him, God will also glorify Him in Himself, and ᵃglorify Him immediately. 33Little children, I shall be with you a ᵃlittle while longer. You will seek Me; ᵇand as I said to the Jews, 'Where I am going, you cannot come,' so now I say to you. 34ᵃA new commandment I give to you, that you love one another; as I have loved you, that you also love one another. 35ᵃBy this all will know that you are My disciples, if you have love for one another."

JESUS PREDICTS PETER'S DENIAL

36Simon Peter said to Him, "Lord, where are You going?"

Jesus answered him, "Where I ᵃam going you cannot follow Me now, but ᵇyou shall follow Me afterward."

37Peter said to Him, "Lord, why can I not follow You now? I will ᵃlay down my life for Your sake."

38Jesus answered him, "Will you lay down your life for My sake? Most assuredly, I say to you, the rooster shall not ᵃcrow till you have denied Me three times.

13:38 ᵃMatt. 26:74; Mark 14:30; Luke 22:61; John 18:25–27

13:18 ¹NU *My bread has*   13:23 ¹*reclining*   13:25 ¹NU, M add *thus*

THE WAY, THE TRUTH, AND THE LIFE

14 "Let [a]not your heart be troubled; you believe in God, believe also in Me. [2]In My Father's house are many [1]mansions; if *it were* not *so,* [2]I would have told you. [a]I go to prepare a place for you. [3]And if I go and prepare a place for you, [a]I will come again and receive you to Myself; that [b]where I am, *there* you may be also. [4]And where I go you know, and the way you know."

[5a]Thomas said to Him, "Lord, we do not know where You are going, and how can we know the way?"

[6]Jesus said to him, "I am [a]the way, [b]the truth, and [c]the life. [d]No one comes to the Father [e]except through Me.

THE FATHER REVEALED

[7a]"If you had known Me, you would have known My Father also; and from now on you know Him and have seen Him."

[8]Philip said to Him, "Lord, show us the Father, and it is sufficient for us."

[9]Jesus said to him, "Have I been with you so long, and yet you have not known Me, Philip? [a]He who has seen Me has seen the Father; so how can you say, 'Show us the Father'? [10]Do you not believe that [a]I am in the Father, and the Father in Me? The words that I speak to you [b]I do not speak on My own *authority;* but the Father who dwells in Me does the works. [11]Believe Me that I *am* in the Father and the Father in Me, [a]or else believe Me for the sake of the works themselves.

THE ANSWERED PRAYER

[12a]"Most assuredly, I say to you, he who believes in Me, the works that I do he will do also; and greater *works* than these he will do, because I go to My Father. [13a]And whatever you ask in My name, that I will do, that the Father may be [b]glorified in the Son. [14]If you [1]ask anything in My name, I will do *it.*

JESUS PROMISES ANOTHER HELPER

[15a]"If you love Me, [1]keep My commandments. [16]And I will pray the Father, and [a]He will give you another [1]Helper, that He may abide with you forever— [17a]the Spirit of truth, [b]whom the world cannot receive, because it neither sees Him nor knows Him; but you know Him, for He dwells with you [c]and will be in you. [18a]I will not leave you orphans; [b]I will come to you.

INDWELLING OF THE FATHER AND THE SON

[19]"A little while longer and the world will see Me no more, but [a]you will see Me. [b]Because I live, you will live also. [20]At that day you will know that [a]I *am* in My Father, and you in Me, and I in you. [21a]He who has My commandments and keeps them, it is he who loves Me. And he who loves Me will be loved by My Father, and I will love him and [1]manifest Myself to him."

[22a]Judas (not Iscariot) said to Him, "Lord, how is it that You will manifest Yourself to us, and not to the world?"

[23]Jesus answered and said to him, "If anyone loves Me, he will keep My word; and My Father will love him, [a]and We will

14:20 [a]John 10:38; 14:11   14:21 [a]1 John 2:5   14:22 [a]Luke 6:16; Acts 1:13   14:23 [a]2 Cor. 6:16; Eph. 3:17; [1 John 2:24]; Rev. 3:20; 21:3

14:2 [1]Lit. *dwellings*   [2]NU *would I have told you that I go* or *I would have told you; for I go*   14:14 [1]NU *ask Me*   14:15 [1]NU *you will keep*   14:16 [1]*Comforter,* Gr. *Parakletos*   14:21 [1]*reveal*

14:1
[a][John 14:27; 16:22, 24]

14:2
[a]Matt. 25:34; John 13:33, 36; Heb. 11:16

14:3 [a][Acts 1:11]
[b][John 12:26]; 1 Thess. 4:17]

14:5
[a]Matt. 10:3; John 11:16; 20:24–29; 21:2

14:6
[a][John 10:9; Rom. 5:2; Eph. 2:18; Heb. 9:8; 10:19, 20] [b][John 1:14, 17; 8:32; 18:37]
[c][John 11:25]
[d]1 Tim. 2:5
[e][John 10:7–9; Acts 4:12]

14:7 [a]John 8:19

14:9
[a]John 12:45; Col. 1:15; Heb. 1:3

14:10
[a]John 10:38; 14:11, 20 [b]Deut. 18:18; John 5:19; 14:24

14:11 [a]John 5:36; 10:38

14:12
[a]Matt. 21:21; Mark 16:17; Luke 10:17

14:13 [a]Matt. 7:7; [Mark 11:24]; Luke 11:9; John 15:16; 16:23, 24; [James 1:5–7]; 1 John 3:22]
[b]John 13:31

14:15 [a]1 John 5:3

14:16
[a][John 15:26; 20:22]; Acts 2:4, 33; Rom. 8:15

14:17
[a][John 15:26; 16:13]; 1 John 4:6; 5:7] [b][1 Cor. 2:14]
[c][1 John 2:27]

14:18
[a][Matt. 28:20]
[b][John 14:3, 28]

14:19
[a]John 16:16, 22
[b][Rom. 5:10]; 1 Cor. 15:20; 2 Cor. 4:10]

14:24 ªJohn 5:19

14:26
ªLuke 24:49;
ᵇJohn 15:26
ᶜ1 Cor. 2:13
ᵈJohn 2:22;
12:16;
1 John 2:20

14:27 ªLuke 1:79;
[John 16:33;
20:19; Phil. 4:7];
Col. 3:15

14:28
ªJohn 14:3, 18
ᵇJohn 16:16
ᶜ[John 5:18;
Phil. 2:6]

14:29
ªJohn 13:19

14:30
ª[John 12:31]
ᵇ[John 8:46;
2 Cor. 5:21;
Heb. 4:15;
1 Pet. 1:19; 2:22]

14:31 ªIs. 50:5;
John 10:18;
Phil. 2:8

15:2 ªMatt. 15:13
ᵇ[Matt. 13:12]

15:3
ª[John 13:10;
17:17]; Eph. 5:26

15:4 ªJohn 17:23;
Eph. 3:17;
[Col. 1:23]

15:5 ªHos. 14:8;
[Gal. 5:22, 23]
ᵇ2 Cor. 3:5

15:6 ªMatt. 3:10

15:7 ª1 John 2:14
ᵇJohn 14:13;
16:23

15:8 ªPs. 22:23;
[Matt. 5:16];
John 13:31;
17:4; [Phil. 1:11];
1 Pet. 4:11
ᵇJohn 8:31

15:9 ªJohn 5:20;
17:26

15:10 ªJohn 14:15

15:11
ª[John 16:24];
1 John 1:4

15:12
ªJohn 13:34;
1 John 3:11
ᵇRom. 12:9

15:13 ªEph. 5:2;
1 John 3:16

15:14
ª[Matt. 12:50;
28:20];
John 14:15, 21;
Acts 10:42;
1 John 3:23, 24

come to him and make Our home with him. ²⁴He who does not love Me does not keep My words; and ªthe word which you hear is not Mine but the Father's who sent Me.

THE GIFT OF HIS PEACE

²⁵"These things I have spoken to you while being present with you. ²⁶But ªthe ¹Helper, the Holy Spirit, whom the Father will ᵇsend in My name, ᶜHe will teach you all things, and bring to your ᵈremembrance all things that I said to you. ²⁷ªPeace I leave with you, My peace I give to you; not as the world gives do I give to you. Let not your heart be troubled, neither let it be afraid. ²⁸You have heard Me ªsay to you, 'I am going away and coming *back* to you.' If you loved Me, you would rejoice because ¹I said, ᵇ'I am going to the Father,' for ᶜMy Father is greater than I.

²⁹"And ªnow I have told you before it comes, that when it does come to pass, you may believe. ³⁰I will no longer talk much with you, ªfor the ruler of this world is coming, and he has ᵇnothing in Me. ³¹But that the world may know that I love the Father, and ªas the Father gave Me commandment, so I do. Arise, let us go from here.

THE TRUE VINE

15 "I am the true vine, and My Father is the vinedresser. ²ªEvery branch in Me that does not bear fruit He ¹takes away; and every *branch* that bears fruit He prunes, that it may bear ᵇmore fruit. ³ªYou are already clean because of the word which I have spoken to you. ⁴ªAbide in Me, and I in you. As the branch cannot bear fruit of itself, unless it abides in the vine, neither can you, unless you abide in Me.

⁵"I am the vine, you *are* the branches. He who abides in Me, and I in him, bears much ªfruit; for without Me you can do ᵇnothing. ⁶If anyone does not abide in Me, ªhe is cast out as a branch and is withered; and they gather them and throw *them* into the fire, and they are burned. ⁷If you abide in Me, and My words ªabide in you, ᵇyou¹ will ask what you desire, and it shall be done for you. ⁸ªBy this My Father is glorified, that you bear much fruit; ᵇso you will be My disciples.

LOVE AND JOY PERFECTED

⁹"As the Father ªloved Me, I also have loved you; abide in My love. ¹⁰ªIf you keep My commandments, you will abide in My love, just as I have kept My Father's commandments and abide in His love.

¹¹"These things I have spoken to you, that My joy may remain in you, and ªthat your joy may be full. ¹²ªThis is My ᵇcommandment, that you love one another as I have loved you. ¹³ªGreater love has no one than this, than to lay down one's life for his friends. ¹⁴ªYou are My friends if you do whatever I command you. ¹⁵No longer do I call you servants, for a servant does not know what his master is doing; but I have called you friends, ªfor all things that I heard from My Father I have made known to you. ¹⁶ªYou did not choose Me, but I chose you and ᵇappointed you that you should go and bear

15:15 ªGen. 18:17   15:16 ªJohn 6:70; 13:18; 15:19; 1 John 4:10 ᵇ[Matt. 28:19; Mark 16:15; Col. 1:6]

14:26 ¹*Comforter*, Gr. *Parakletos*   14:28 ¹NU omits *I said*   15:2 ¹Or *lifts up*
15:7 ¹NU omits *you will*

fruit, and *that* your fruit should remain, that whatever you ask the Father ^cin My name He may give you. ¹⁷These things I command you, that you love one another.

THE WORLD'S HATRED

^{18a}"If the world hates you, you know that it hated Me before *it hated* you. ^{19a}If you were of the world, the world would love its own. Yet ^bbecause you are not of the world, but I chose you out of the world, therefore the world hates you. ²⁰Remember the word that I said to you, ^a'A servant is not greater than his master.' If they persecuted Me, they will also persecute you. ^bIf they kept My word, they will keep yours also. ²¹But ^aall these things they will do to you for My name's sake, because they do not know Him who sent Me. ^{22a}If I had not come and spoken to them, they would have no sin, ^bbut now they have no excuse for their sin. ^{23a}He who hates Me hates My Father also. ²⁴If I had not done among them ^athe works which no one else did, they would have no sin; but now they have ^bseen and also hated both Me and My Father. ²⁵But *this happened* that the word might be fulfilled which is written in their law, ^a'They hated Me without a cause.'

THE COMING REJECTION

^{26a}"But when the ¹Helper comes, whom I shall send to you from the Father, the Spirit of truth who proceeds from the Father, ^bHe will testify of Me. ²⁷And ^ayou also will bear witness, because ^byou have been with Me from the beginning.

16 "These things I have spoken to you, that you ^ashould not be made to stumble. ^{2a}They will put you out of the synagogues; yes, the time is coming ^bthat whoever kills you will think that he offers God service. ³And ^athese things they will do ¹to you because they have not known the Father nor Me. ⁴But these things I have told you, that when ¹the time comes, you may remember that I told you of them.

"And these things I did not say to you at the beginning, because I was with you.

THE WORK OF THE HOLY SPIRIT

⁵"But now I ^ago away to Him who sent Me, and none of you asks Me, 'Where are You going?' ⁶But because I have said these things to you, ^asorrow has filled your heart. ⁷Nevertheless I tell you the truth. It is to your advantage that I go away; for if I do not go away, the Helper will not come to you; but ^aif I depart, I will send Him to you. ⁸And when He has ^acome, He will convict the world of sin, and of righteousness, and of judgment: ^{9a}of sin, because they do not believe in Me; ^{10a}of righteousness, ^bbecause I go to My Father and you see Me no more; ^{11a}of judgment, because ^bthe ruler of this world is judged.

¹²"I still have many things to say to you, ^abut you cannot bear *them* now. ¹³However, when He, ^athe Spirit of truth, has come, ^bHe will guide you into all truth; for He will not speak on His own *authority*, but whatever He hears He will speak; and He will tell you things to come. ^{14a}He will glorify Me, for He will take of what is Mine and declare *it* to you. ^{15a}All things

16:15 ^aMatt. 11:27; John 3:35

15:26 ¹Comforter, Gr. *Parakletos* 16:3 ¹NU, M omit *to you* 16:4 ¹NU *their*

Cross references

15:16
^cJohn 14:13; 16:23, 24

15:18 ^aJohn 7:7; 1 John 3:13

15:19 ^a1 John 4:5
^bJohn 17:14

15:20
^aMatt. 10:24; John 13:16
^bEzek. 3:7

15:21
^aMatt. 10:22; 24:9;
[1 Pet. 4:14];
Rev. 2:3

15:22
^aJohn 9:41; 15:24
^b[Rom. 1:20; James 4:17]

15:23
^a1 John 2:23

15:24 ^aJohn 3:2
^bJohn 14:9

15:25 ^aPs. 35:19; 69:4; 109:3–5

15:26
^aLuke 24:49;
[John 14:17];
Acts 2:4, 33
^b1 John 5:6

15:27
^aLuke 24:48;
1 Pet. 5:1;
2 Pet. 1:16
^bMatt. 3:14;
Luke 1:2;
1 John 1:1

16:1 ^aMatt. 11:6

16:2 ^aJohn 9:22
^bActs 8:1

16:3 ^aJohn 8:19; 15:21; Acts 13:27; Rom. 10:2

16:5 ^aJohn 7:33; 13:33; 14:28; 17:11

16:6
^aMatt. 17:23;
[John 16:20, 22]

16:7 ^aActs 2:33

16:8 ^aActs 1:8; 2:1–4, 37

16:9 ^aActs 2:22

16:10 ^aActs 2:32
^bJohn 5:32

16:11 ^aActs 26:18
^b[Luke 10:18]

16:12 ^aMark 4:33

16:13
^a[John 14:17]
^bJohn 14:26;
Acts 11:28;
Rev. 1:19

16:14
^aJohn 15:26

that the Father has are Mine. Therefore I said that He [1]will take of Mine and declare *it* to you.

SORROW WILL TURN TO JOY

[16]"A [a]little while, and you will not see Me; and again a little while, and you will see Me, [b]because I go to the Father."

[17]Then *some* of His disciples said among themselves, "What is this that He says to us, 'A little while, and you will not see Me; and again a little while, and you will see Me'; and, 'because I go to the Father'?" [18]They said therefore, "What is this that He says, 'A little while'? We do not [1]know what He is saying."

[19]Now Jesus knew that they desired to ask Him, and He said to them, "Are you inquiring among yourselves about what I said, 'A little while, and you will not see Me; and again a little while, and you will see Me'? [20]Most assuredly, I say to you that you will weep and [a]lament, but the world will rejoice; and you will be sorrowful, but your sorrow will be turned into [b]joy. [21a]A woman, when she is in labor, has sorrow because her hour has come; but as soon as she has given birth to the child, she no longer remembers the anguish, for joy that a human being has been born into the world. [22]Therefore you now have sorrow; but I will see you again and [a]your heart will rejoice, and your joy no one will take from you.

[23]"And in that day you will ask Me nothing. [a]Most assuredly, I say to you, whatever you ask the Father in My name He will give you. [24]Until now you have asked nothing in My name. Ask, and you will receive, [a]that your joy may be [b]full.

JESUS CHRIST HAS OVERCOME THE WORLD

[25]"These things I have spoken to you in figurative language; but the time is coming when I will no longer speak to you in figurative language, but I will tell you [a]plainly about the Father. [26]In that day you will ask in My name, and I do not say to you that I shall pray the Father for you; [27a]for the Father Himself loves you, because you have loved Me, and [b]have believed that I came forth from God. [28a]I came forth from the Father and have come into the world. Again, I leave the world and go to the Father."

[29]His disciples said to Him, "See, now You are speaking plainly, and using no figure of speech! [30]Now we are sure that [a]You know all things, and have no need that anyone should question You. By this [b]we believe that You came forth from God."

[31]Jesus answered them, "Do you now believe? [32a]Indeed the hour is coming, yes, has now come, that you will be scattered, [b]each to his [1]own, and will leave Me alone. And [c]yet I am not alone, because the Father is with Me. [33]These things I have spoken to you, that [a]in Me you may have peace. [b]In the world you [1]will have tribulation; but be of good cheer, [c]I have overcome the world."

JESUS PRAYS FOR HIMSELF

17 Jesus spoke these words, lifted up His eyes to heaven, and said: "Father, [a]the hour has come. Glorify Your Son, that Your Son also may glorify You, [2a]as You have given Him

Cross-references (margin)

16:16
[a]John 7:33;
12:35; 13:33;
14:19; 19:40–42;
20:19 [b]John 13:3

16:20
[a]Mark 16:10;
Luke 23:48;
24:17
[b]Luke 24:32, 41

16:21 [a]Gen. 3:16;
Is. 13:8;
26:17; 42:14;
1 Thess. 5:3

16:22
[a]Luke 24:41;
John 14:1, 27;
20:20;
Acts 2:46;
13:52;
1 Pet. 1:8

16:23 [a]Matt. 7:7;
[John 14:13;
15:16]

16:24
[a]John 17:13
[b]John 15:11

16:25 [a]John 7:13

16:27
[a][John 14:21, 23]
[b]John 3:13

16:28
[a]John 13:1, 3;
16:5, 10, 17

16:30
[a]John 21:17
[b]John 17:8

16:32
[a]Zech. 13:7;
Matt. 26:31, 56;
Mark 14:27, 50;
Acts 8:1
[b]John 20:10
[c]John 8:29

16:33 [a][Is. 9:6;
Rom. 5:1;
Eph. 2:14]
[b]2 Tim. 3:12
[c]Rom. 8:37;
[1 John 4:4]

17:1 [a]John 12:23

17:2 [a]Dan. 7:14;
Matt. 11:27;
John 3:35;
[Phil. 2:10;
Heb. 2:8]

16:15 [1]NU, M *takes of Mine and will declare*   **16:18** [1]*understand*   **16:32** [1]*own things* or *place*   **16:33** [1]NU, M omit *will*

authority over all flesh, that He [1]should give eternal life to as many [b]as You have given Him. [3]And [a]this is eternal life, that they may know You, [b]the only true God, and Jesus Christ [c]whom You have sent. [4a]I have glorified You on the earth. [b]I have finished the work [c]which You have given Me to do. [5]And now, O Father, glorify Me together [1]with Yourself, with the glory [a]which I had with You before the world was.

JESUS PRAYS FOR HIS DISCIPLES

[6a]"I have [1]manifested Your name to the men [b]whom You have given Me out of the world. [c]They were Yours, You gave them to Me, and they have kept Your word. [7]Now they have known that all things which You have given Me are from You. [8]For I have given to them the words [a]which You have given Me; and they have received *them*, [b]and have known surely that I came forth from You; and they have believed that [c]You sent Me.

[9]"I pray for them. [a]I do not pray for the world but for those whom You have given Me, for they are Yours. [10]And all Mine are Yours, and [a]Yours are Mine, and I am glorified in them. [11a]Now I am no longer in the world, but these are in the world, and I come to You. Holy Father, [b]keep[1] through Your name those whom You have given Me, that they may be one [c]as We *are*. [12]While I was with them [1]in the world, [a]I kept them in [2]Your name. Those whom You gave Me I have kept; and [b]none of them is [3]lost [c]except the son of [4]perdition, [d]that the Scripture might be fulfilled. [13]But now I come to You, and these things I speak in the world, that they may have My joy fulfilled in themselves. [14]I have given them Your word; [a]and the world has hated them because they are not of the world, [b]just as I am not of the world. [15]I do not pray that You should take them out of the world, but [a]that You should keep them from the evil one. [16]They are not of the world, just as I am not of the world. [17a]Sanctify[1] them by Your truth. [b]Your word is truth. [18a]As You sent Me into the world, I also have sent them into the world. [19]And [a]for their sakes I sanctify Myself, that they also may be sanctified by the truth.

JESUS PRAYS FOR ALL BELIEVERS

[20]"I do not pray for these alone, but also for those who [1]will believe in Me through their word; [21a]that they all may be one, as [b]You, Father, *are* in Me, and I in You; that they also may be one in Us, that the world may believe that You sent Me. [22]And the [a]glory which You gave Me I have given them, [b]that they may be one just as We are one: [23]I in them, and You in Me; [a]that they may be made perfect in one, and that the world may know that You have sent Me, and have loved them as You have loved Me.

[24a]"Father, I desire that they also whom You gave Me may be with Me where I am, that they may behold My glory which You have given Me; [b]for You loved Me before the foundation

---

17:19 [a]1 Cor. 1:2; 1 Thess. 4:7; [Heb. 10:10]   17:21 [a][John 10:16; Rom. 12:5; Gal. 3:28]; Eph. 4:4, 6 [b]John 10:38; 17:11, 23   17:22 [a]John 14:20; 1 John 1:3 [b][2 Cor. 3:18]   17:23 [a][Col. 3:14]   17:24 [a][John 12:26; 14:3; 1 Thess. 4:17] [b]Matt. 25:34; John 17:5

17:2 [1]M *shall*   17:5 [1]Lit. *alongside*   17:6 [1]*revealed*   17:11 [1]NU, M *keep them through Your name which You have given Me*   17:12 [1]NU omits *in the world* [2]NU *Your name which You gave Me. And I guarded them;* (or *it;*)   [3]*destroyed* [4]*destruction*   17:17 [1]*Set them apart*   17:20 [1]NU, M omit *will*

17:2 [b]John 6:37, 39; 17:6, 9, 24

17:3 [a][Is. 53:11]; Jer. 9:23, 24 [b]1 Cor. 8:4; 1 Thess. 1:9 [c]John 3:34

17:4 [a]John 13:31 [b][Dan. 9:24]; John 4:34; 19:30 [c]Is. 49:3; 50:5; John 14:31

17:5 [a]Prov. 8:22–30; John 1:1, 2; Phil. 2:6; Col. 1:15; Heb. 1:3

17:6 [a]Ps. 22:22 [b]John 6:37 [c]Ezek. 18:4; Rom. 14:8

17:8 [a]John 8:28 [b]John 8:42; 16:27, 30 [c]Deut. 18:15, 18

17:9 [a][1 John 5:19]

17:10 [a]John 16:15

17:11 [a][Mark 16:19; Luke 24:51]; John 13:1; [Acts 1:9; Heb. 4:14; 9:24; 1 Pet. 3:22] [b][1 Pet. 1:5]; Jude 1 [c]John 10:30

17:12 [a]Heb. 2:13 [b][John 6:39; 18:9]; 1 John 2:19 [c]Matt. 27:4, 5; John 6:70; Acts 1:16–20 [d]Ps. 41:9; 109:8; John 13:18; Acts 1:20

17:14 [a]Matt. 24:9; Luke 6:22; 21:17; John 15:19; 1 John 3:13 [b]John 8:23

17:15 [a]Matt. 6:13; Gal. 1:4; 2 Thess. 3:3; [2 Tim. 4:18]; 2 Pet. 2:9; 1 John 5:18

17:17 [a][Acts 15:9; Eph. 5:26; 1 Pet. 1:22] [b]Ps. 119:9, 142, 151

17:18 [a]John 4:38; 20:21

17:25
a John 15:21
b John 7:29;
8:55; 10:15
c John 3:17; 17:3,
8, 18, 21, 23

17:26
a Ex. 34:5–7;
John 17:6
b John 15:9;
[Eph. 3:17–19]

18:1
a Matt. 26:30, 36;
Mark 14:26, 32;
Luke 22:39
b 2 Sam. 15:23;
1 Kin. 2:37; 15:13;
2 Kin. 23:4, 6, 12;
2 Chr. 15:16;
29:16; 30:14;
Jer. 31:40

18:2
a Luke 21:37;
22:39

18:3
a Matt. 26:47–56;
Mark 14:43–50;
Luke 22:47–53;
Acts 1:16

18:4 a John 6:64;
13:1, 3; 19:28

18:5 a Matt. 21:11;
Mark 1:24; 14:67;
16:6; Luke 18:37;
24:19 b Ps. 41:9;
Matt. 20:18;
26:21; John 13:21

18:9
a [John 6:39;
17:12]

18:10
a Matt. 26:51;
Mark 14:47;
Luke 22:49, 50

18:11
a Matt. 20:22;
26:39;
Mark 14:36;
Luke 22:42

18:13
a Matt. 26:57
b Luke 3:2;
John 18:24;
Acts 4:6
c Matt. 26:3;
John 11:49, 51

18:14
a John 11:50

18:15
a Matt. 26:58;
Mark 14:54;
Luke 22:54
b John 20:2–5

18:16
a Matt. 26:69;
Mark 14:66–68;
Luke 22:55–57

18:17
a Matt. 26:34

of the world. 25O righteous Father! aThe world has not known You, but bI have known You; and cthese have known that You sent Me. 26aAnd I have declared to them Your name, and will declare *it,* that the love bwith which You loved Me may be in them, and I in them."

BETRAYAL AND ARREST IN GETHSEMANE
(Matt. 26:47–56; Mark 14:43–52; Luke 22:47–53)

18 When Jesus had spoken these words, aHe went out with His disciples over bthe Brook Kidron, where there was a garden, which He and His disciples entered. 2And Judas, who betrayed Him, also knew the place; afor Jesus often met there with His disciples. 3aThen Judas, having received a detachment *of troops,* and officers from the chief priests and Pharisees, came there with lanterns, torches, and weapons. 4Jesus therefore, aknowing all things that would come upon Him, went forward and said to them, "Whom are you seeking?"

5They answered Him, a"Jesus 1of Nazareth."

Jesus said to them, "I am *He.*" And Judas, who bbetrayed Him, also stood with them. 6Now when He said to them, "I am *He,*" they drew back and fell to the ground.

7Then He asked them again, "Whom are you seeking?"

And they said, "Jesus of Nazareth."

8Jesus answered, "I have told you that I am *He.* Therefore, if you seek Me, let these go their way," 9that the saying might be fulfilled which He spoke, a"Of those whom You gave Me I have lost none."

10aThen Simon Peter, having a sword, drew it and struck the high priest's servant, and cut off his right ear. The servant's name was Malchus.

11So Jesus said to Peter, "Put your sword into the sheath. Shall I not drink athe cup which My Father has given Me?"

BEFORE THE HIGH PRIEST

12Then the detachment *of troops* and the captain and the officers of the Jews arrested Jesus and bound Him. 13And athey led Him away to bAnnas first, for he was the father-in-law of cCaiaphas who was high priest that year. 14aNow it was Caiaphas who advised the Jews that it was 1expedient that one man should die for the people.

PETER DENIES JESUS
(Matt. 26:69–75; Mark 14:66–72; Luke 22:54–62)

15aAnd Simon Peter followed Jesus, and so *did* banother1 disciple. Now that disciple was known to the high priest, and went with Jesus into the courtyard of the high priest. 16aBut Peter stood at the door outside. Then the other disciple, who was known to the high priest, went out and spoke to her who kept the door, and brought Peter in. 17Then the servant girl who kept the door said to Peter, "You are not also *one* of this Man's disciples, are you?"

He said, "I am anot."

18Now the servants and officers who had made a fire of coals stood there, for it was cold, and they warmed themselves. And Peter stood with them and warmed himself.

18:5 1Lit. *the Nazarene*   18:14 1advantageous   18:15 1M *the other*

JESUS QUESTIONED BY THE HIGH PRIEST

¹⁹The high priest then asked Jesus about His disciples and His doctrine.

²⁰Jesus answered him, ᵃ"I spoke openly to the world. I always taught ᵇin synagogues and ᶜin the temple, where ¹the Jews always meet, and in secret I have said nothing. ²¹Why do you ask Me? Ask ᵃthose who have heard Me what I said to them. Indeed they know what I said."

²²And when He had said these things, one of the officers who stood by ᵃstruck¹ Jesus with the palm of his hand, saying, "Do You answer the high priest like that?"

²³Jesus answered him, "If I have spoken evil, bear witness of the evil; but if well, why do you strike Me?"

²⁴ᵃThen Annas sent Him bound to ᵇCaiaphas the high priest.

PETER DENIES TWICE MORE

²⁵Now Simon Peter stood and warmed himself. ᵃTherefore they said to him, "You are not also *one* of His disciples, are you?"

He denied *it* and said, "I am not!"

²⁶One of the servants of the high priest, a relative *of him* whose ear Peter cut off, said, "Did I not see you in the garden with Him?" ²⁷Peter then denied again; and ᵃimmediately a rooster crowed.

IN PILATE'S COURT
(Matt. 27:1, 2, 11–14; Mark 15:1–5; Luke 23:1–5)

²⁸ᵃThen they led Jesus from Caiaphas to the Praetorium, and it was early morning. ᵇBut they themselves did not go into the ¹Praetorium, lest they should be defiled, but that they might eat the Passover. ²⁹ᵃPilate then went out to them and said, "What accusation do you bring against this Man?"

³⁰They answered and said to him, "If He were not ¹an evildoer, we would not have delivered Him up to you."

³¹Then Pilate said to them, "You take Him and judge Him according to your law."

Therefore the Jews said to him, "It is not lawful for us to put anyone to death," ³²ᵃthat the saying of Jesus might be fulfilled which He spoke, ᵇsignifying by what death He would die.

³³ᵃThen Pilate entered the ¹Praetorium again, called Jesus, and said to Him, "Are You the King of the Jews?"

³⁴Jesus answered him, "Are you speaking for yourself about this, or did others tell you this concerning Me?"

³⁵Pilate answered, "Am I a Jew? Your own nation and the chief priests have delivered You to me. What have You done?"

³⁶ᵃJesus answered, ᵇ"My kingdom is not of this world. If My kingdom were of this world, My servants would fight, so that I should not be delivered to the Jews; but now My kingdom is not from here."

³⁷Pilate therefore said to Him, "Are You a king then?"

Jesus answered, "You say *rightly* that I am a king. For this cause I was born, and for this cause I have come into the

18:20
ᵃMatt. 26:55;
Luke 4:15;
John 8:26
ᵇJohn 6:59
ᶜMark 14:49;
John 7:14, 28

18:21
ᵃMark 12:37

18:22
ᵃJob 16:10;
Is. 50:6;
Jer. 20:2;
Lam. 3:30;
Acts 23:2

18:24
ᵃMatt. 26:57;
Luke 3:2;
Acts 4:6
ᵇJohn 11:49

18:25
ᵃMatt. 26:71–75;
Mark 14:69–72;
Luke 22:58–62

18:27
ᵃMatt. 26:74;
Mark 14:72;
Luke 22:60;
John 13:38

18:28
ᵃMatt. 27:2;
Mark 15:1;
Luke 23:1;
Acts 3:13
ᵇJohn 11:55;
Acts 10:28; 11:3

18:29
ᵃMatt. 27:11–14;
Mark 15:2–5;
Luke 23:2, 3

18:32
ᵃMatt. 20:17–19;
26:2;
Mark 10:33;
Luke 18:32
ᵇJohn 3:14;
8:28; 12:32, 33

18:33
ᵃMatt. 27:11

18:36
ᵃ1 Tim. 6:13
ᵇ[Dan. 2:44;
7:14]; Luke 12:14;
John 6:15; 8:15

18:20 ¹NU *all the Jews meet*   **18:22** ¹Lit. *gave Jesus a slap*,   **18:28** ¹The governor's headquarters   **18:30** ¹*a criminal*   **18:33** ¹The governor's headquarters

world, ^athat I should bear ^bwitness to the truth. Everyone who ^cis of the truth ^dhears My voice."

³⁸Pilate said to Him, "What is truth?" And when he had said this, he went out again to the Jews, and said to them, ^a"I find no fault in Him at all.

TAKING THE PLACE OF BARABBAS
(Matt. 27:15–23; Mark 15:6–14; Luke 23:13–23)

³⁹"But you have a custom that I should release someone to you at the Passover. Do you therefore want me to release to you the King of the Jews?"

⁴⁰^aThen they all cried again, saying, "Not this Man, but Barabbas!" ^bNow Barabbas was a robber.

THE SOLDIERS MOCK JESUS
(Matt. 27:27–31; Mark 15:16–20)

19 So then ^aPilate took Jesus and scourged *Him.* ²And the soldiers twisted a crown of thorns and put *it* on His head, and they put on Him a purple robe. ³¹Then they said, "Hail, King of the Jews!" And they ^astruck Him with their hands.

⁴Pilate then went out again, and said to them, "Behold, I am bringing Him out to you, ^athat you may know that I find no fault in Him."

PILATE'S DECISION

⁵Then Jesus came out, wearing the crown of thorns and the purple robe. And *Pilate* said to them, "Behold the Man!"

⁶^aTherefore, when the chief priests and officers saw Him, they cried out, saying, "Crucify *Him,* crucify *Him!*"

Pilate said to them, "You take Him and crucify *Him,* for I find no fault in Him."

⁷The Jews answered him, ^a"We have a law, and according to ¹our law He ought to die, because ^bHe made Himself the Son of God."

⁸Therefore, when Pilate heard that saying, he was the more afraid, ⁹and went again into the Praetorium, and said to Jesus, "Where are You from?" ^aBut Jesus gave him no answer.

¹⁰Then Pilate said to Him, "Are You not speaking to me? Do You not know that I have ¹power to crucify You, and power to release You?"

¹¹Jesus answered, ^a"You could have no power at all against Me unless it had been given you from above. Therefore ^bthe one who delivered Me to you has the greater sin."

¹²From then on Pilate sought to release Him, but the Jews cried out, saying, "If you let this Man go, you are not Caesar's friend. ^aWhoever makes himself a king speaks against Caesar."

¹³^aWhen Pilate therefore heard that saying, he brought Jesus out and sat down in the judgment seat in a place that is called *The* Pavement, but in Hebrew, Gabbatha. ¹⁴Now ^ait was the Preparation Day of the Passover, and about the sixth hour. And he said to the Jews, "Behold your King!"

¹⁵But they cried out, "Away with *Him,* away with *Him!* Crucify Him!"

18:37
^a[Matt. 5:17;
20:28;
Luke 4:43;
12:49; 19:10;
John 3:17; 9:39;
10:10; 12:47]
^bIs. 55:4; Rev. 1:5
^c[John 14:6]
^dJohn 8:47;
10:27;
[1 John 3:19;
4:6]

18:38 ^aIs. 53:9;
Matt. 27:24;
Luke 23:4;
John 19:4, 6;
1 Pet. 2:22–24

18:39
^aMatt. 27:15–26;
Mark 15:6–15;
Luke 23:17–25

18:40 ^aIs. 53:3;
Acts 3:14
^bLuke 23:19

19:1
^aMatt. 20:19;
27:26;
Mark 15:15;
Luke 18:33

19:3 ^aIs. 50:6

19:4 ^aIs. 53:9;
John 18:33, 38;
1 Pet. 2:22–24

19:6 ^aActs 3:13

19:7 ^aLev. 24:16
^bMatt. 26:63–
66; John 5:18;
10:33

19:9 ^aIs. 53:7;
Matt. 27:12, 14;
Luke 23:9

19:11
^a[Luke 22:53];
John 7:30
^bJohn 3:27;
Rom. 13:1

19:12
^aLuke 23:2;
John 18:33;
Acts 17:7

19:13 ^aDeut. 1:17;
1 Sam. 15:24;
Prov. 29:25;
Is. 51:12;
Acts 4:19

19:14
^aMatt. 27:62;
John 19:31, 42

19:3 ¹NU *And they came up to Him and said*   **19:7** ¹NU *the law*
19:10 ¹*authority*

Pilate said to them, "Shall I crucify your King?"

The chief priests answered, a"We have no king but Caesar!" 16aThen he delivered Him to them to be crucified. Then they took Jesus 1and led *Him* away.

THE KING ON A CROSS
(Matt. 27:32–56; Mark 15:21–41; Luke 23:26–49)

17aAnd He, bearing His cross, bwent out to a place called *the Place* of a Skull, which is called in Hebrew, Golgotha, 18where they crucified Him, and atwo others with Him, one on either side, and Jesus in the center. 19aNow Pilate wrote a title and put *it* on the cross. And the writing was:

JESUS OF NAZARETH, THE KING OF THE JEWS.

20Then many of the Jews read this title, for the place where Jesus was crucified was near the city; and it was written in Hebrew, Greek, *and* Latin. 21Therefore the chief priests of the Jews said to Pilate, "Do not write, 'The King of the Jews,' but, 'He said, "I am the King of the Jews."'" 22Pilate answered, "What I have written, I have written."

23aThen the soldiers, when they had crucified Jesus, took His garments and made four parts, to each soldier a part, and also the tunic. Now the tunic was without seam, woven from the top in one piece. 24They said therefore among themselves, "Let us not tear it, but cast lots for it, whose it shall be," that the Scripture might be fulfilled which says:

a"They divided My garments among them,
And for My clothing they cast lots."

Therefore the soldiers did these things.

BEHOLD YOUR MOTHER

25aNow there stood by the cross of Jesus His mother, and His mother's sister, Mary the *wife* of bClopas, and Mary Magdalene. 26When Jesus therefore saw His mother, and athe disciple whom He loved standing by, He said to His mother, b"Woman, behold your son!" 27Then He said to the disciple, "Behold your mother!" And from that hour that disciple took her ato his own *home*.

IT IS FINISHED

28After this, Jesus, 1knowing that all things were now accomplished, athat the Scripture might be fulfilled, said, "I thirst!" 29Now a vessel full of sour wine was sitting there; and athey filled a sponge with sour wine, put *it* on hyssop, and put *it* to His mouth. 30So when Jesus had received the sour wine, He said, a"It is finished!" And bowing His head, He gave up His spirit.

JESUS' SIDE IS PIERCED

31aTherefore, because it was the Preparation *Day,* bthat the bodies should not remain on the cross on the Sabbath (for that Sabbath was a chigh day), the Jews asked Pilate that their legs might be broken, and *that* they might be taken away. 32Then the soldiers came and broke the legs of the first and

19:15
a[Gen. 49:10]

19:16
aMatt. 27:26, 31;
Mark 15:15;
Luke 23:24

19:17
aMatt. 27:31, 33;
Mark 15:21, 22;
Luke 23:26, 33
bNum. 15:36;
Heb. 13:12

19:18
aPs. 22:16–18;
Is. 53:12;
Matt. 20:19;
26:2

19:19
aMatt. 27:37;
Mark 15:26;
Luke 23:38

19:23
aMatt. 27:35;
Mark 15:24;
Luke 23:34

19:24 aPs. 22:18

19:25
aMatt. 27:55;
Mark 15:40;
Luke 2:35; 23:49
bLuke 24:18

19:26
aJohn 13:23;
20:2; 21:7, 20, 24
bJohn 2:4

19:27
aLuke 18:28;
John 1:11; 16:32;
Acts 21:6

19:28 aPs. 22:15

19:29 aPs. 69:21;
Matt. 27:48, 50;
Mark 15:36;
Luke 23:36

19:30
aDan. 9:26;
Zech. 11:10, 11;
John 17:4

19:31
aMatt. 27:62;
Mark 15:42;
Luke 23:54
bDeut. 21:23;
Josh. 8:29;
10:26 cEx. 12:16;
Lev. 23:6, 7

of the other who was crucified with Him. ³³But when they came to Jesus and saw that He was already dead, they did not break His legs. ³⁴But one of the soldiers pierced His side with a spear, and immediately ᵃblood and water came out. ³⁵And he who has seen has testified, and his testimony is ᵃtrue; and he knows that he is telling the truth, so that you may ᵇbelieve. ³⁶For these things were done that the Scripture should be fulfilled, ᵃ"Not *one* of His bones shall be broken." ³⁷And again another Scripture says, ᵃ"They shall look on Him whom they pierced."

JESUS BURIED IN JOSEPH'S TOMB
(Matt. 27:57–61; Mark 15:42–47; Luke 23:50–56)

³⁸ᵃAfter this, Joseph of Arimathea, being a disciple of Jesus, but secretly, ᵇfor fear of the Jews, asked Pilate that he might take away the body of Jesus; and Pilate gave *him* permission. So he came and took the body of Jesus. ³⁹And ᵃNicodemus, who at first came to Jesus by night, also came, bringing a mixture of ᵇmyrrh and aloes, about a hundred pounds. ⁴⁰Then they took the body of Jesus, and ᵃbound it in strips of linen with the spices, as the custom of the Jews is to bury. ⁴¹Now in the place where He was crucified there was a garden, and in the garden a new tomb in which no one had yet been laid. ⁴²So ᵃthere they laid Jesus, ᵇbecause of the Jews' Preparation *Day,* for the tomb was nearby.

THE EMPTY TOMB
(Matt. 28:1–10; Mark 16:1–8; Luke 24:1–12)

20 Now the ᵃfirst *day* of the week Mary Magdalene went to the tomb early, while it was still dark, and saw *that* the ᵇstone had been taken away from the tomb. ²Then she ran and came to Simon Peter, and to the ᵃother disciple, ᵇwhom Jesus loved, and said to them, "They have taken away the Lord out of the tomb, and we do not know where they have laid Him."

³ᵃPeter therefore went out, and the other disciple, and were going to the tomb. ⁴So they both ran together, and the other disciple outran Peter and came to the tomb first. ⁵And he, stooping down and looking in, saw ᵃthe linen cloths lying *there;* yet he did not go in. ⁶Then Simon Peter came, following him, and went into the tomb; and he saw the linen cloths lying *there,* ⁷and ᵃthe ¹handkerchief that had been around His head, not lying with the linen cloths, but folded together in a place by itself. ⁸Then the ᵃother disciple, who came to the tomb first, went in also; and he saw and believed. ⁹For as yet they did not ¹know the ᵃScripture, that He must rise again from the dead. ¹⁰Then the disciples went away again to their own homes.

MARY MAGDALENE SEES THE RISEN LORD

¹¹ᵃBut Mary stood outside by the tomb weeping, and as she wept she stooped down *and looked* into the tomb. ¹²And she saw two angels in white sitting, one at the head and the other at the feet, where the body of Jesus had lain. ¹³Then they said to her, "Woman, why are you weeping?"

19:34
ᵃ[1 John 5:6, 8]

19:35
ᵃJohn 21:24
ᵇ[John 20:31]

19:36
ᵃ[Ex. 12:46;
Num. 9:12];
Ps. 34:20

19:37
ᵃPs. 22:16, 17;
Zech. 12:10; 13:6;
Rev. 1:7

19:38
ᵃMatt. 27:57–61;
Mark 15:42–47;
Luke 23:50–56
ᵇ[John 7:13;
9:22; 12:42]

19:39
ᵃJohn 3:1, 2; 7:50
ᵇPs. 45:8;
Prov. 7:17;
Song 4:14;
Matt. 2:11

19:40
ᵃLuke 24:12;
John 20:5, 7;
Acts 5:6

19:42 ᵃIs. 53:9;
Matt. 26:12;
Mark 14:8
ᵇJohn 19:14, 31

20:1
ᵃMatt. 28:1–8;
Mark 16:1–8;
Luke 24:1–10;
Acts 20:7;
1 Cor. 16:2
ᵇMatt. 27:60,
66; 28:2;
Mark 15:46; 16:4;
Luke 24:2;
John 11:38

20:2
ᵃJohn 21:23, 24
ᵇJohn 13:23;
19:26; 21:7,
20, 24

20:3
ᵃLuke 24:12

20:5
ᵃJohn 19:40

20:7 ᵃJohn 11:44

20:8
ᵃJohn 21:23, 24

20:9 ᵃPs. 16:10;
Acts 2:25, 31;
13:34, 35

20:11 ᵃMark 16:5

She said to them, "Because they have taken away my Lord, and I do not know where they have laid Him."

[14a]Now when she had said this, she turned around and saw Jesus standing *there,* and [b]did not know that it was Jesus. [15]Jesus said to her, "Woman, why are you weeping? Whom are you seeking?"

She, supposing Him to be the gardener, said to Him, "Sir, if You have carried Him away, tell me where You have laid Him, and I will take Him away."

[16]Jesus said to her, [a]"Mary!"

She turned and said to [1]Him, "Rabboni!" (which is to say, Teacher).

[17]Jesus said to her, "Do not cling to Me, for I have not yet [a]ascended to My Father; but go to [b]My brethren and say to them, [c]'I am ascending to My Father and your Father, and *to* [d]My God and your God.'"

[18a]Mary Magdalene came and told the [1]disciples that she had seen the Lord, and *that* He had spoken these things to her.

THE APOSTLES COMMISSIONED
(Luke 24:36–43; 1 Cor. 15:5)

[19a]Then, the same day at evening, being the first *day* of the week, when the doors were shut where the disciples were [1]assembled, for [b]fear of the Jews, Jesus came and stood in the midst, and said to them, [c]"Peace *be* with you." [20]When He had said this, He [a]showed them *His* hands and His side. [b]Then the disciples were glad when they saw the Lord.

[21]So Jesus said to them again, "Peace to you! [a]As the Father has sent Me, I also send you." [22]And when He had said this, He breathed on *them,* and said to them, "Receive the Holy Spirit. [23a]If you forgive the sins of any, they are forgiven them; if you retain the *sins* of any, they are retained."

SEEING AND BELIEVING

[24]Now Thomas, [a]called the Twin, one of the twelve, was not with them when Jesus came. [25]The other disciples therefore said to him, "We have seen the Lord."

So he said to them, "Unless I see in His hands the print of the nails, and put my finger into the print of the nails, and put my hand into His side, I will not believe."

[26]And after eight days His disciples were again inside, and Thomas with them. Jesus came, the doors being shut, and stood in the midst, and said, "Peace to you!" [27]Then He said to Thomas, "Reach your finger here, and look at My hands; and [a]reach your hand *here,* and put *it* into My side. Do not be [b]unbelieving, but believing."

[28]And Thomas answered and said to Him, "My Lord and my God!"

[29]Jesus said to him, [1]"Thomas, because you have seen Me, you have believed. [a]Blessed *are* those who have not seen and *yet* have believed."

THAT YOU MAY BELIEVE

[30]And [a]truly Jesus did many other signs in the presence of His disciples, which are not written in this book; [31a]but these

20:14
[a]Matt. 28:9;
Mark 16:9
[b][Luke 24:16, 31];
John 21:4

20:16
[a]John 10:3

20:17
[a]Mark 16:19;
Luke 24:5;
Acts 1:9;
2:34–36;
Eph. 4:8–10;
Heb. 4:14
[b]Ps. 22:22;
Matt. 18:10;
Rom. 8:29;
Heb. 2:11
[c]John 16:28;
17:11 [d]Eph. 1:17

20:18
[a]Matt. 28:10;
Luke 24:10, 23

20:19
[a]Mark 16:14;
Luke 24:36;
John 14:27;
1 Cor. 15:5
[b]John 9:22;
19:38
[c]John 14:27;
16:33; Eph. 2:17

20:20 [a]Acts 1:3
[b]John 16:20, 22

20:21
[a][Matt. 28:18–20]; John 17:18,
19; [2 Tim. 2:2];
Heb. 3:1

20:23
[a]Matt. 16:19;
18:18

20:24
[a]John 11:16

20:27
[a]Ps. 22:16;
Zech. 12:10; 13:6;
1 John 1:1
[b]Mark 16:14

20:29
[a]2 Cor. 5:7;
1 Pet. 1:8

20:30
[a]John 21:25

20:31
[a]Luke 1:4

20:16 [1]NU adds *in Hebrew*   **20:18** [1]NU *disciples, "I have seen the Lord,"*
20:19 [1]NU omits *assembled*   **20:29** [1]NU, M omit *Thomas*

are written that [b]you may believe that Jesus [c]is the Christ, the Son of God, [d]and that believing you may have life in His name.

BREAKFAST BY THE SEA

21 After these things Jesus showed Himself again to the disciples at the [a]Sea of Tiberias, and in this way He showed Himself: 2[a]Simon Peter, [a]Thomas called the Twin, [b]Na-thanael of [c]Cana in Galilee, [d]the [a]sons of Zebedee, and two others of His disciples were together. 3Simon Peter said to them, "I am going fishing."

They said to him, "We are going with you also." They went out and [a]immediately got into the boat, and that night they caught nothing. 4[a]But when the morning had now come, Jesus stood on the shore; yet the disciples [a]did not know that it was Jesus. 5Then Jesus [a]said to them, "Children, have you any food?"

They answered Him, "No."

6And He said to them, [a]"Cast the net on the right side of the boat, and you will find some." So they cast, and now they were not able to draw it in because of the multitude of fish.

7Therefore [a]that disciple whom Jesus loved said to Peter, "It is the Lord!" Now when Simon Peter heard that it was the Lord, he put on [a]his outer garment (for he had removed it), and plunged into the sea. 8But the other disciples came in the little boat (for they were not far from land, but about two hundred cubits), dragging the net with fish. 9Then, as soon as they had come to land, they saw a fire of coals there, and fish laid on it, and bread. 10Jesus said to them, "Bring some of the fish which you have just caught."

11Simon Peter went up and dragged the net to land, full of large fish, one hundred and fifty-three; and although there were so many, the net was not broken. 12Jesus said to them, [a]"Come and eat breakfast." Yet none of the disciples dared ask Him, "Who are You?"—knowing that it was the Lord. 13Jesus then came and took the bread and gave it to them, and like-wise the fish.

14This is now [a]the third time Jesus showed Himself to His disciples after He was raised from the dead.

JESUS RESTORES PETER

15So when they had eaten breakfast, Jesus said to Simon Peter, "Simon, [1]son of [1]Jonah, do you love Me more than these?"

He said to Him, "Yes, Lord; You know that I [2]love You."

He said to him, [a]"Feed My lambs."

16He said to him again a second time, "Simon, [1]son of [1]Jo-nah, do you love Me?"

He said to Him, "Yes, Lord; You know that I [2]love You."

He said to him, [a]"Tend My [b]sheep."

17He said to him the third time, "Simon, [1]son of [1]Jonah, do you [2]love Me?" Peter was grieved because He said to him the third time, "Do you love Me?"

And he said to Him, "Lord, [a]You know all things; You know that I love You."

Jesus said to him, "Feed My sheep. 18aMost assuredly, I

20:31
[b]John 19:35;
[c]Luke 2:11;
1 John 5:13
[d]1 John 3:15, 16;
5:24;
[1 Pet. 1:8, 9]
21:1
[a]Matt. 26:32;
Mark 14:28;
John 6:1
21:2
[a]John 20:24
[b]John 1:45–51
[c]John 2:1
[d]Matt. 4:21;
Mark 1:19;
Luke 5:10
21:4
[a]Luke 24:16;
John 20:14
21:5
[a]Luke 24:41
21:6
[a]Luke 5:4, 6, 7
21:7
[a]John 13:23;
20:2
21:12
[a]Acts 10:41
21:14
[a]John 20:19, 26
21:15
[a]Acts 20:28;
1 Tim. 4:6;
1 Pet. 5:2
21:16
[a]Matt. 2:6;
Heb. 13:20;
Acts 20:28;
1 Pet. 2:25;
[b]Ps. 79:13;
5:2, 4
Matt. 10:16;
15:24; 25:33;
26:31
21:17
[a]John 2:24, 25;
16:30
21:18
[a]Acts 13:36;
Acts 2:3, 4

21:3 [1]NU omits *immediately* 21:15 [1]NU *John* [2]*have affection for* 21:16 [1]NU *John* [2]*have affection for* 21:17 [1]NU *John* [2]*have affection for*

say to you, when you were younger, you girded yourself and walked where you wished; but when you are old, you will stretch out your hands, and another will gird you and carry *you* where you do not wish." [19]This He spoke, signifying [a]by what death he would glorify God. And when He had spoken this, He said to him, [b]"Follow Me."

THE BELOVED DISCIPLE AND HIS BOOK

[20]Then Peter, turning around, saw the disciple [a]whom Jesus loved following, [b]who also had leaned on His breast at the supper, and said, "Lord, who is the one who betrays You?" [21]Peter, seeing him, said to Jesus, "But Lord, what *about* this man?"

[22]Jesus said to him, "If I [1]will that he remain [a]till I come, what *is that* to you? You follow Me."

[23]Then this saying went out among the brethren that this disciple would not die. Yet Jesus did not say to him that he would not die, but, "If I will that he remain till I come, what *is that* to you?"

[24]This is the disciple who [a]testifies of these things, and wrote these things; and we know that his testimony is true.

[25a]And there are also many other things that Jesus did, which if they were written one by one, [b]I suppose that even the world itself could not contain the books that would be written. Amen.

21:19
[a]2 Pet. 1:13, 14
[b][Matt. 4:19; 16:24];
John 21:22

21:20
[a]John 13:23;
20:2
[b]John 13:25

21:22
[a][Matt. 16:27, 28; 25:31;
1 Cor. 4:5; 11:26;
Rev. 2:25; 3:11;
22:7, 20]

21:24
[a]John 19:35;
3 John 12

21:25
[a]John 20:30
[b]Amos 7:10

21:22 [1]desire

THE ACTS
OF THE APOSTLES

1:1 ªLuke 1:3

1:2 ªMark 16:19;
Acts 1:9, 11, 22
ᵇMatt. 28:19;
Mark 16:15;
John 20:21;
Acts 10:42

1:3 ªMatt. 28:17;
Mark 16:12, 14;
Luke 24:34, 36;
John 20:19,
26; 21:1, 14;
1 Cor. 15:5–7

1:4 ªLuke 24:49
ᵇ[John 14:16,
17, 26; 15:26];
Acts 2:33

1:5 ªMatt. 3:11;
Mark 1:8;
Luke 3:16;
John 1:33;
Acts 11:16
ᵇ[Joel 2:28]

1:7 ª1 Thess. 5:1
ᵇMatt. 24:36;
Mark 13:32

1:8
ª[Acts 2:1, 4]
ᵇLuke 24:49
ᶜLuke 24:48;
John 15:27
ᵈActs 8:1, 5, 14
ᵉMatt. 28:19;
Mark 16:15;
Rom. 10:18;
Col. 1:23;
[Rev. 14:6]

1:9
ªLuke 24:50, 51
ᵇPs. 68:18; 110:1;
Mark 16:19;
Luke 23:43;
John 20:17;
Acts 1:2;
[Heb. 4:14; 9:24;
1 Pet. 3:22]

1:10
ªMatt. 28:3;
Mark 16:5;
Luke 24:4;
John 20:12;
Acts 10:3, 30

1:11 ªDan. 7:13;
Mark 13:26;
Luke 21:27;
[John 14:3];
2 Thess. 1:10;
Rev. 1:7

1:12 ªLuke 24:52

PROLOGUE

1 The former account I made, O ªTheophilus, of all that Jesus began both to do and teach, ²ªuntil the day in which ¹He was taken up, after He through the Holy Spirit ᵇhad given commandments to the apostles whom He had chosen, ³ªto whom He also presented Himself alive after His suffering by many ¹infallible proofs, being seen by them during forty days and speaking of the things pertaining to the kingdom of God.

THE HOLY SPIRIT PROMISED

⁴ªAnd being assembled together with *them,* He commanded them not to depart from Jerusalem, but to wait for the Promise of the Father, "which," *He said,* "you have ᵇheard from Me; ⁵ªfor John truly baptized with water, ᵇbut you shall be baptized with the Holy Spirit not many days from now." ⁶Therefore, when they had come together, they asked Him, saying, "Lord, will You at this time restore the kingdom to Israel?" ⁷And He said to them, ª"It is not for you to ᵇknow times or seasons which the Father has put in His own authority. ⁸ªBut you shall receive power ᵇwhen the Holy Spirit has come upon you; and ᶜyou shall be ¹witnesses to Me in Jerusalem, and in all Judea and ᵈSamaria, and to the ᵉend of the earth."

JESUS ASCENDS TO HEAVEN
(Mark 16:19, 20; Luke 24:50–53)

⁹ªNow when He had spoken these things, while they watched, ᵇHe was taken up, and a cloud received Him out of their sight. ¹⁰And while they looked steadfastly toward heaven as He went up, behold, two men stood by them ªin white apparel, ¹¹who also said, "Men of Galilee, why do you stand gazing up into heaven? This *same* Jesus, who was taken up from you into heaven, ªwill so come in like manner as you saw Him go into heaven."

THE UPPER ROOM PRAYER MEETING

¹²ªThen they returned to Jerusalem from the mount called Olivet, which is near Jerusalem, a Sabbath day's journey. ¹³And when they had entered, they went up ªinto the upper room where they were staying: ᵇPeter, James, John, and Andrew; Philip and Thomas; Bartholomew and Matthew; James *the son* of Alphaeus and ᶜSimon the Zealot; and ᵈJudas *the son* of James. ¹⁴ªThese all continued with one ¹accord in prayer ²and supplication, with ᵇthe women and Mary the mother of Jesus, and with ᶜHis brothers.

1:13 ªMark 14:15; Luke 22:12; Acts 9:37, 39; 20:8 ᵇMatt. 10:2–4 ᶜLuke 6:15 ᵈJude 1
1:14 ªActs 2:1, 46 ᵇLuke 23:49, 55 ᶜMatt. 13:55

1:2 ¹He ascended into heaven. 1:3 ¹*unmistakable* 1:8 ¹NU *My witnesses*
1:14 ¹*purpose* or *mind* ²NU omits *and supplication*

MATTHIAS CHOSEN
(cf. Ps. 109:8; Matt. 27:7, 8)

[15]And in those days Peter stood up in the midst of the [1]disciples (altogether the number [a]of names was about a hundred and twenty), and said, [16]"Men *and* brethren, this Scripture had to be fulfilled, [a]which the Holy Spirit spoke before by the mouth of David concerning Judas, [b]who became a guide to those who arrested Jesus; [17]for [a]he was numbered with us and obtained a part in [b]this ministry."

[18a](Now this man purchased a field with [b]the [1]wages of iniquity; and falling headlong, he burst open in the middle and all his [2]entrails gushed out. [19]And it became known to all those dwelling in Jerusalem; so that field is called in their own language, Akel Dama, that is, Field of Blood.)

[20]"For it is written in the Book of Psalms:

[a]'Let his dwelling place be [1]desolate,
And let no one live in it';

and,

[b]'Let another take his [2]office.'

[21]"Therefore, of these men who have accompanied us all the time that the Lord Jesus went in and out among us, [22]beginning from the baptism of John to that day when [a]He was taken up from us, one of these must [b]become a witness with us of His resurrection."

[23]And they proposed two: Joseph called [a]Barsabas, who was surnamed Justus, and Matthias. [24]And they prayed and said, "You, O Lord, [a]who know the hearts of all, show which of these two You have chosen [25a]to take part in this ministry and apostleship from which Judas by transgression fell, that he might go to his own place." [26]And they cast their lots, and the lot fell on Matthias. And he was numbered with the eleven apostles.

COMING OF THE HOLY SPIRIT

2 When [a]the Day of Pentecost had fully come, [b]they were all [1]with one accord in one place. [2]And suddenly there came a sound from heaven, as of a rushing mighty wind, and [a]it filled the whole house where they were sitting. [3]Then there appeared to them [1]divided tongues, as of fire, and *one* sat upon each of them. [4]And [a]they were all filled with the Holy Spirit and began [b]to speak with other tongues, as the Spirit gave them utterance.

THE CROWD'S RESPONSE

[5]And there were dwelling in Jerusalem Jews, [a]devout men, from every nation under heaven. [6]And when this sound occurred, the [a]multitude came together, and were confused, because everyone heard them speak in his own language. [7]Then they were all amazed and marveled, saying to one another, "Look, are not all these who speak [a]Galileans? [8]And how *is it that* we hear, each in our own [1]language in which we were born? [9]Parthians and Medes and Elamites, those

---

1:15 [a]Luke 22:32; Rev. 3:4

1:16 [a]Ps. 41:9
[b]Matt. 26:47; Mark 14:43; Luke 22:47; John 18:3

1:17 [a]Matt. 10:4
[b]Acts 1:25

1:18
[a]Matt. 27:3–10
[b]Matt. 18:7; 26:14, 15, 24; Mark 14:21; Luke 22:22; John 17:12

1:20 [a]Ps. 69:25
[b]Ps. 109:8

1:22 [a]Acts 1:9
[b]Acts 1:8; 2:32

1:23 [a]Acts 15:22

1:24
[a]1 Sam. 16:7; Jer. 17:10; Acts 1:2

1:25 [a]Acts 1:17

2:1 [a]Lev. 23:15; Deut. 16:9; Acts 20:16; 1 Cor. 16:8
[b]Acts 1:14

2:2 [a]Acts 4:31

2:4 [a]Matt. 3:11; 5:6; 10:20; Luke 3:16; John 14:16; 16:7–15; Acts 1:5
[b]Mark 16:17; Acts 10:46; 19:6; [1 Cor. 12:10, 28, 30; 13:1]

2:5 [a]Luke 2:25; Acts 8:2

2:6 [a]Acts 4:32

2:7
[a]Matt. 26:73; Acts 1:11

1:15 [1]NU brethren   1:18 [1]reward of unrighteousness   [2]intestines
1:20 [1]deserted   [2]Gr. episkopen, position of overseer   2:1 [1]NU together
2:3 [1]Or tongues as of fire, distributed and resting on each   2:8 [1]dialect

dwelling in Mesopotamia, Judea and ªCappadocia, Pontus and Asia, ¹⁰Phrygia and Pamphylia, Egypt and the parts of Libya adjoining Cyrene, visitors from Rome, both Jews and proselytes, ¹¹Cretans and ¹Arabs—we hear them speaking in our own tongues the wonderful works of God." ¹²So they were all amazed and perplexed, saying to one another, "Whatever could this mean?"

¹³Others mocking said, "They are full of new wine."

PETER'S SERMON
(Joel 2:28–32)

¹⁴But Peter, standing up with the eleven, raised his voice and said to them, "Men of Judea and all who dwell in Jerusalem, let this be known to you, and heed my words. ¹⁵For these are not drunk, as you suppose, ªsince it is *only* ¹the third hour of the day. ¹⁶But this is what was spoken by the prophet Joel:

17 'Andª it shall come to pass in the last days, says God,
     ᵇThat I will pour out of My Spirit on all flesh;
     Your sons and ᶜyour daughters shall prophesy,
     Your young men shall see visions,
     Your old men shall dream dreams.
18 And on My menservants and on My maidservants
     I will pour out My Spirit in those days;
     ªAnd they shall prophesy.
19 ªI will show wonders in heaven above
     And signs in the earth beneath:
     Blood and fire and vapor of smoke.
20 ªThe sun shall be turned into darkness,
     And the moon into blood,
     Before the coming of the great and awesome day
          of the LORD.
21 And it shall come to pass
     That ªwhoever calls on the name of the LORD
     Shall be saved.'

²²"Men of Israel, hear these words: Jesus of Nazareth, a Man attested by God to you ªby miracles, wonders, and signs which God did through Him in your midst, as you yourselves also know— ²³Him, ªbeing delivered by the determined purpose and foreknowledge of God, ᵇyou ¹have taken by lawless hands, have crucified, and put to death; ²⁴ªwhom God raised up, having ¹loosed the ²pains of death, because it was not possible that He should be held by it. ²⁵For David says concerning Him:

ª'I foresaw the LORD always before my face,
     For He is at my right hand, that I may not be shaken.
26 Therefore my heart rejoiced, and my tongue was glad;
     Moreover my flesh also will rest in hope.
27 For You will not leave my soul in Hades,
     Nor will You allow Your Holy One to see ªcorruption.
28 You have made known to me the ways of life;
     You will make me full of joy in Your presence.'

²⁹"Men *and* brethren, let *me* speak freely to you ªof the patriarch David, that he is both dead and buried, and his tomb is

---

2:9 ª1 Pet. 1:1
2:15 ª1 Thess. 5:7
2:17 ªIs. 44:3;
Ezek. 11:19;
Joel 2:28–32;
[Zech. 12:10;
John 7:38]
ᵇActs 10:45
ᶜActs 21:9
2:18 ªActs 21:4, 9;
1 Cor. 12:10
2:19 ªJoel 2:30
2:20 ªIs. 13:10;
Ezek. 32:7;
Matt. 24:29;
Mark 13:24, 25;
Luke 21:25;
Rev. 6:12
2:21 ªRom. 10:13
2:22 ªIs. 50:5;
John 3:2; 5:6;
Acts 10:38
2:23 ªMatt. 26:4;
Luke 22:22;
Acts 3:18; 4:28;
[1 Pet. 1:20]
ᵇActs 5:30
2:24 ª[Rom. 8:11;
1 Cor. 6:14;
2 Cor. 4:14;
Eph. 1:20;
Col. 2:12];
1 Thess. 1:10;
Heb. 13:20
2:25 ªPs. 16:8–11
2:27 ªActs 13:30–37
2:29 ªActs 13:36

2:11 ¹*Arabians*   2:15 ¹9 A.M.   2:23 ¹NU omits *have taken*   2:24 ¹*destroyed* or *abolished*   ²Lit. *birth pangs*

with us to this day. ³⁰Therefore, being a prophet, ªand knowing that God had sworn with an oath to him that of the fruit of his body, ¹according to the flesh, He would raise up the Christ to sit on his throne, ³¹he, foreseeing this, spoke concerning the resurrection of the Christ, ªthat His soul was not left in Hades, nor did His flesh see corruption. ³²ªThis Jesus God has raised up, ᵇof which we are all witnesses. ³³Therefore ªbeing exalted ¹to ᵇthe right hand of God, and ᶜhaving received from the Father the promise of the Holy Spirit, He ᵈpoured out this which you now see and hear.

³⁴"For David did not ascend into the heavens, but he says himself:

ª"The LORD said to my Lord,
    "Sit at My right hand,
³⁵   Till I make Your enemies Your footstool." '

³⁶"Therefore let all the house of Israel know assuredly that God has made this Jesus, whom you crucified, both Lord and Christ."

³⁷Now when they heard *this,* ªthey were cut to the heart, and said to Peter and the rest of the apostles, "Men *and* brethren, what shall we do?"

³⁸Then Peter said to them, ª"Repent, and let every one of you be baptized in the name of Jesus Christ for the ¹remission of sins; and you shall receive the gift of the Holy Spirit. ³⁹For the promise is to you and ªto your children, and ᵇto all who are afar off, as many as the Lord our God will call."

A VITAL CHURCH GROWS

⁴⁰And with many other words he testified and exhorted them, saying, "Be saved from this ¹perverse generation." ⁴¹Then those who ¹gladly received his word were baptized; and that day about three thousand souls were added *to them.* ⁴²ªAnd they continued steadfastly in the apostles' ¹doctrine and fellowship, in the breaking of bread, and in prayers. ⁴³Then fear came upon every soul, and ªmany wonders and signs were done through the apostles. ⁴⁴Now all who believed were together, and ªhad all things in common, ⁴⁵and ¹sold their possessions and goods, and ªdivided² them among all, as anyone had need.

⁴⁶ªSo continuing daily with one accord ᵇin the temple, and ᶜbreaking bread from house to house, they ate their food with gladness and simplicity of heart, ⁴⁷praising God and having favor with all the people. And ªthe Lord added ¹to the church daily those who were being saved.

A LAME MAN HEALED

3 Now Peter and John went up together ªto the temple at the hour of prayer, ᵇthe ninth *hour.* ²And ªa certain man lame from his mother's womb was carried, whom they laid daily at the gate of the temple which is called Beautiful, ᵇto ¹ask alms from those who entered the temple; ³who, seeing Peter and John about to go into the temple, asked for alms. ⁴And fixing his eyes on him, with John, Peter said, "Look at us." ⁵So he

2:30
ª2 Sam. 7:12;
Ps. 132:11;
Luke 1:32;
Rom. 1:3;
2 Tim. 2:8

2:31 ªPs. 16:10;
Is. 50:8; 53:10

2:32 ªActs 2:24
ᵇActs 1:8; 3:15

2:33 ªPs. 68:18;
[Acts 5:31];
Phil. 2:9
ᵇPs. 110:1;
Mark 16:19;
[Heb. 10:12]
ᶜLuke 24:49;
[John 14:26]
ᵈMatt. 3:11; 5:6;
Luke 3:16;
22:69;
John 14:16;
16:7–15;
Acts 2:1–11, 17;
10:45; Eph. 4:8

2:34
ªPs. 68:18; 110:1;
Matt. 22:44;
Luke 23:43;
John 20:17;
1 Cor. 15:25;
Eph. 1:20;
Heb. 1:13

2:37
ª[Zech. 12:10];
Luke 3:10, 12, 14;
John 16:8

2:38
ªLuke 24:47

2:39
ªJoel 2:28, 32
ᵇActs 11:15, 18;
Eph. 2:13

2:42 ªActs 1:14;
Rom. 12:12;
Eph. 6:18;
Col. 4:2;
Heb. 10:25

2:43
ªMark 16:17;
Acts 2:22

2:44 ªActs 4:32,
34, 37; 5:2

2:45 ªIs. 58:7

2:46 ªActs 1:14
ᵇLuke 24:53
ᶜLuke 24:30;
Acts 2:42; 20:7;
[1 Cor. 10:16]

2:47 ªActs 5:14

3:1 ªActs 2:46
ᵇPs. 55:17;
Matt. 27:45;
Acts 10:30

3:2 ªActs 14:8
ᵇJohn 9:8;
Acts 3:10

2:30 ¹NU *He would seat one on his throne,*   **2:33** ¹Possibly *by*
2:38 ¹*forgiveness*   **2:40** ¹*crooked*   **2:41** ¹NU omits *gladly*   **2:42** ¹*teaching*
2:45 ¹*would sell*   ²*distributed*   **2:47** ¹NU omits *to the church*   **3:2** ¹Beg

3:6 ªActs 4:10

3:8 ªIs. 35:6

3:9
ªActs 4:16, 21

3:10 ªJohn 9:8;
Acts 3:2

3:11 ªJohn 10:23;
Acts 5:12

3:13 ªJohn 5:30
ᵇIs. 49:3;
John 7:39; 12:23;
13:31 ᶜMatt. 27:2
ᵈMatt. 27:20;
Mark 15:11;
Luke 23:18;
John 18:40;
Acts 13:28

3:14 ªPs. 16:10;
Mark 1:24;
Luke 1:35
ᵇActs 7:52;
2 Cor. 5:21
ᶜJohn 18:40

3:15 ªActs 2:24
ᵇActs 2:32

3:16
ªMatt. 9:22;
Acts 4:10; 14:9

3:17
ªLuke 23:34;
John 16:3;
[Acts 13:27;
17:30]; 1 Cor. 2:8;
1 Tim. 1:13

3:18
ªLuke 24:44;
Acts 26:22
ᵇPs. 22; Is. 50:6;
53:5; Dan. 9:26;
Hos. 6:1;
Zech. 13:6;
1 Pet. 1:10

3:19 ª[Acts 2:38;
26:20]

3:21 ªActs 1:11
ᵇMatt. 17:11;
[Rom. 8:21]
ᶜLuke 1:70

3:22
ªDeut. 18:15, 18,
19; Acts 7:37

3:24
ª2 Sam. 7:12;
Luke 24:25

3:25 ªActs 2:39;
[Rom. 9:4, 8;
Gal. 3:26]
ᵇGen. 12:3;
18:18; 22:18;
26:4; 28:14

3:26
ªMatt. 15:24;
John 4:22;
Acts 13:46;
[Rom. 1:16; 2:9]
ᵇIs. 42:1;
Matt. 1:21

4:1 ªMatt. 22:23

gave them his attention, expecting to receive something from them. ⁶Then Peter said, "Silver and gold I do not have, but what I do have I give you: ªIn the name of Jesus Christ of Nazareth, rise up and walk." ⁷And he took him by the right hand and lifted *him* up, and immediately his feet and ankle bones received strength. ⁸So he, ªleaping up, stood and walked and entered the temple with them—walking, leaping, and praising God. ⁹ªAnd all the people saw him walking and praising God. ¹⁰Then they knew that it was he who ªsat begging alms at the Beautiful Gate of the temple; and they were filled with wonder and amazement at what had happened to him.

PREACHING IN SOLOMON'S PORTICO

¹¹Now as the lame man who was healed held on to Peter and John, all the people ran together to them in the porch ªwhich is called Solomon's, greatly amazed. ¹²So when Peter saw *it*, he responded to the people: "Men of Israel, why do you marvel at this? Or why look so intently at us, as though by our own power or godliness we had made this man walk? ¹³ªThe God of Abraham, Isaac, and Jacob, the God of our fathers, ᵇglorified His Servant Jesus, whom you ᶜdelivered up and ᵈdenied in the presence of Pilate, when he was determined to let *Him* go. ¹⁴But you denied ªthe Holy One ᵇand the Just, and ᶜasked for a murderer to be granted to you, ¹⁵and killed the ¹Prince of life, ªwhom God raised from the dead, ᵇof which we are witnesses. ¹⁶ªAnd His name, through faith in His name, has made this man strong, whom you see and know. Yes, the faith which *comes* through Him has given him this perfect soundness in the presence of you all.

¹⁷"Yet now, brethren, I know that ªyou did *it* in ignorance, as *did* also your rulers. ¹⁸But ªthose things which God foretold ᵇby the mouth of all His prophets, that the Christ would suffer, He has thus fulfilled. ¹⁹ªRepent therefore and be converted, that your sins may be blotted out, so that times of refreshing may come from the presence of the Lord, ²⁰and that He may send ¹Jesus Christ, who was ²preached to you before, ²¹ªwhom heaven must receive until the times of ᵇrestoration of all things, ᶜwhich God has spoken by the mouth of all His holy prophets since ¹the world began. ²²For Moses truly said to the fathers, ª"The Lᴏʀᴅ your God will raise up for you a Prophet like me from your brethren. Him you shall hear in all things, whatever He says to you. ²³And it shall be *that* every soul who will not hear that Prophet shall be utterly destroyed from among the people.' ²⁴Yes, and ªall the prophets, from Samuel and those who follow, as many as have spoken, have also ¹foretold these days. ²⁵ªYou are sons of the prophets, and of the covenant which God made with our fathers, saying to Abraham, ᵇ'And in your seed all the families of the earth shall be blessed.' ²⁶To you ªfirst, God, having raised up His Servant Jesus, sent Him to bless you, ᵇin turning away every one *of you* from your iniquities."

PETER AND JOHN ARRESTED

4 Now as they spoke to the people, the priests, the captain of the temple, and the ªSadducees came upon them, ²being

3:15 ¹Or *Originator*   3:20 ¹NU, M *Christ Jesus*   ²NU, M *ordained for you before*   3:21 ¹Or *time*   3:24 ¹NU, M *proclaimed*

greatly disturbed that they taught the people and preached in Jesus the resurrection from the dead. ³And they laid hands on them, and put *them* in custody until the next day, for it was already evening. ⁴However, many of those who heard the word believed; and the number of the men came to be about five thousand.

ADDRESSING THE SANHEDRIN

⁵And it came to pass, on the next day, that their rulers, elders, and scribes, ⁶as well as ᵃAnnas the high priest, Caiaphas, John, and Alexander, and as many as were of the family of the high priest, were gathered together at Jerusalem. ⁷And when they had set them in the midst, they asked, ᵃ"By what power or by what name have you done this?"

⁸ᵃThen Peter, filled with the Holy Spirit, said to them, "Rulers of the people and elders of Israel: ⁹If we this day are judged for a good deed *done* to a helpless man, by what means he has been made well, ¹⁰let it be known to you all, and to all the people of Israel, ᵃthat by the name of Jesus Christ of Nazareth, whom you crucified, ᵇwhom God raised from the dead, by Him this man stands here before you whole. ¹¹This is the ᵃ'stone which was rejected by you builders, which has become the chief cornerstone.' ¹²ᵃNor is there salvation in any other, for there is no other name under heaven given among men by which we must be saved."

THE NAME OF JESUS FORBIDDEN

¹³Now when they saw the boldness of Peter and John, ᵃand perceived that they were uneducated and untrained men, they marveled. And they realized that they had been with Jesus. ¹⁴And seeing the man who had been healed ᵃstanding with them, they could say nothing against it. ¹⁵But when they had commanded them to go aside out of the council, they conferred among themselves, ¹⁶saying, ᵃ"What shall we do to these men? For, indeed, that a ¹notable miracle has been done through them *is* ᵇevident² to all who dwell in Jerusalem, and we cannot deny *it.* ¹⁷But so that it spreads no further among the people, let us severely threaten them, that from now on they speak to no man in this name."

¹⁸ᵃSo they called them and commanded them not to speak at all nor teach in the name of Jesus. ¹⁹But Peter and John answered and said to them, ᵃ"Whether it is right in the sight of God to listen to you more than to God, you judge. ²⁰ᵃFor we cannot but speak the things which ᵇwe have seen and heard." ²¹So when they had further threatened them, they let them go, finding no way of punishing them, ᵃbecause of the people, since they all ᵇglorified God for ᶜwhat had been done. ²²For the man was over forty years old on whom this miracle of healing had been performed.

PRAYER FOR BOLDNESS
(cf. Ps. 2:1, 2)

²³And being let go, ᵃthey went to their own *companions* and reported all that the chief priests and elders had said to them. ²⁴So when they heard that, they raised their voice to God with one accord and said: "Lord, ᵃYou *are* God, who made

4:6 ᵃLuke 3:2; John 11:49; 18:13

4:7 ᵃEx. 2:14; Matt. 21:23; Acts 7:27

4:8 ᵃLuke 12:11, 12

4:10 ᵃActs 2:22; 3:6, 16 ᵇActs 2:24

4:11 ᵃPs. 118:22; Is. 28:16; Matt. 21:42

4:12 ᵃIs. 42:1, 6, 7; 53:11; Dan. 9:24; [Matt. 1:21; John 14:6; Acts 10:43; 1 Tim. 2:5, 6]

4:13 ᵃMatt. 11:25; [1 Cor. 1:27]

4:14 ᵃActs 3:11

4:16 ᵃJohn 11:47 ᵇActs 3:7–10

4:18 ᵃActs 5:28, 40

4:19 ᵃActs 5:29

4:20 ᵃActs 1:8; 2:32 ᵇActs 22:15; [1 John 1:1, 3]

4:21 ᵃMatt. 21:26; Luke 20:6, 19; 22:2; Acts 5:26 ᵇMatt. 15:31 ᶜActs 3:7, 8

4:23 ᵃActs 2:44–46; 12:12

4:24 ᵃEx. 20:11; 2 Kin. 19:15; Neh. 9:6; Ps. 146:6

heaven and earth and the sea, and all that is in them, 25who [1]by the mouth of Your servant David have said:

> [a]'Why did the nations rage,
>   And the people plot vain things?
> 26 The kings of the earth took their stand,
>   And the rulers were gathered together
>   Against the LORD and against His Christ.'

27"For [a]truly against [b]Your holy Servant Jesus, [c]whom You anointed, both Herod and Pontius Pilate, with the Gentiles and the people of Israel, were gathered together 28[a]to do whatever Your hand and Your purpose determined before to be done. 29Now, Lord, look on their threats, and grant to Your servants [a]that with all boldness they may speak Your word, 30by stretching out Your hand to heal, [a]and that signs and wonders may be done [b]through the name of [c]Your holy Servant Jesus."

31And when they had prayed, [a]the place where they were assembled together was shaken; and they were all filled with the Holy Spirit, [b]and they spoke the word of God with boldness.

SHARING IN ALL THINGS

32Now the multitude of those who believed [a]were of one heart and one soul; [b]neither did anyone say that any of the things he possessed was his own, but they had all things in common. 33And with [a]great power the apostles gave [b]witness to the resurrection of the Lord Jesus. And [c]great grace was upon them all. 34Nor was there anyone among them who lacked; [a]for all who were possessors of lands or houses sold them, and brought the proceeds of the things that were sold, 35[a]and laid *them* at the apostles' feet; [b]and they distributed to each as anyone had need.

36And [1]Joses, who was also named Barnabas by the apostles (which is translated Son of [2]Encouragement), a Levite of the country of Cyprus, 37[a]having land, sold *it*, and brought the money and laid *it* at the apostles' feet.

LYING TO THE HOLY SPIRIT

5 But a certain man named Ananias, with Sapphira his wife, sold a possession. 2And he kept back *part* of the proceeds, his wife also being aware *of it*, and brought a certain part and laid *it* at the apostles' feet. 3[a]But Peter said, "Ananias, why has [b]Satan filled your heart to lie to the Holy Spirit and keep back *part* of the price of the land for yourself? 4While it remained, was it not your own? And after it was sold, was it not in your own control? Why have you conceived this thing in your heart? You have not lied to men but to God."

5Then Ananias, hearing these words, [a]fell down and breathed his last. So great fear came upon all those who heard these things. 6And the young men arose and [a]wrapped him up, carried *him* out, and buried *him*.

7Now it was about three hours later when his wife came in, not knowing what had happened. 8And Peter answered her, "Tell me whether you sold the land for so much?"

She said, "Yes, for so much."

4:25 [a]Ps. 2:1, 2

4:27
[a]Matt. 26:3;
Luke 22:2;
23:1, 8
[b][Luke 1:35]
[c]Luke 4:18;
John 10:36

4:28
[a]Acts 2:23; 3:18

4:29
[a]Acts 4:13, 31;
9:27; 13:46; 14:3;
19:8; 26:26;
Eph. 6:19

4:30
[a]Acts 2:43; 5:12
[b]Acts 3:6, 16
[c]Acts 4:27

4:31 [a]Matt. 5:6;
Acts 2:2, 4; 16:26
[b]Acts 4:29

4:32 [a]Acts 5:12;
Rom. 15:5, 6;
2 Cor. 13:11;
Phil. 1:27; 2:2;
1 Pet. 3:8
[b]Acts 2:44

4:33 [a][Acts 1:8]
[b]Acts 1:22
[c]Rom. 6:15

4:34
[a][Matt. 19:21];
Acts 2:45

4:35
[a]Acts 4:37; 5:2
[b]Acts 2:45; 6:1

4:37 [a]Acts 4:34,
35; 5:1, 2

5:3 [a]Num. 30:2;
Deut. 23:21;
Eccl. 5:4
[b]Matt. 4:10;
Luke 22:3;
John 13:2, 27

5:5 [a]Ezek. 11:13;
Acts 5:10, 11

5:6 [a]John 19:40

4:25 [1]NU *through the Holy Spirit, by the mouth of our father, Your servant David,* 4:36 [1]NU *Joseph* [2]Or *Consolation*

9Then Peter said to her, "How is it that you have agreed together ato test the Spirit of the Lord? Look, the feet of those who have buried your husband *are* at the door, and they will carry you out." 10aThen immediately she fell down at his feet and breathed her last. And the young men came in and found her dead, and carrying *her* out, buried *her* by her husband. 11aSo great fear came upon all the church and upon all who heard these things.

CONTINUING POWER IN THE CHURCH

12And athrough the hands of the apostles many signs and wonders were done among the people. bAnd they were all with one accord in Solomon's Porch. 13Yet anone of the rest dared join them, bbut the people esteemed them highly. 14And believers were increasingly added to the Lord, multitudes of both men and women, 15so that they brought the sick out into the streets and laid *them* on beds and couches, athat at least the shadow of Peter passing by might fall on some of them. 16Also a multitude gathered from the surrounding cities to Jerusalem, bringing asick people and those who were tormented by unclean spirits, and they were all healed.

IMPRISONED APOSTLES FREED

17aThen the high priest rose up, and all those who *were* with him (which is the sect of the Sadducees), and they were filled with [1]indignation, 18aand laid their hands on the apostles and put them in the common prison. 19But at night aan angel of the Lord opened the prison doors and brought them out, and said, 20"Go, stand in the temple and speak to the people aall the words of this life."

21And when they heard *that,* they entered the temple early in the morning and taught. aBut the high priest and those with him came and called the [1]council together, with all the [2]elders of the children of Israel, and sent to the prison to have them brought.

APOSTLES ON TRIAL AGAIN

22But when the officers came and did not find them in the prison, they returned and reported, 23saying, "Indeed we found the prison shut securely, and the guards standing [1]outside before the doors; but when we opened them, we found no one inside!" 24Now when [1]the high priest, athe captain of the temple, and the chief priests heard these things, they wondered what the outcome would be. 25So one came and told them, [1]saying, "Look, the men whom you put in prison are standing in the temple and teaching the people!"

26Then the captain went with the officers and brought them without violence, afor they feared the people, lest they should be stoned. 27And when they had brought them, they set *them* before the council. And the high priest asked them, 28saying, a"Did we not strictly command you not to teach in this name? And look, you have filled Jerusalem with your doctrine, band intend to bring this Man's cblood on us!"

29But Peter and the *other* apostles answered and said: a"We

5:9 aMatt. 4:7; Acts 5:3, 4

5:10 aEzek. 11:13; Acts 5:5

5:11 aActs 2:43; 5:5; 19:17

5:12 aActs 2:43; 4:30; 6:8; 14:3; 15:12; [Rom. 15:19]; 2 Cor. 12:12; Heb. 2:4 bActs 3:11; 4:32

5:13 aJohn 9:22 bActs 2:47; 4:21

5:15 aMatt. 9:21; 14:36; Acts 19:12

5:16 aMark 16:17, 18; [John 14:12]

5:17 aMatt. 3:7; Acts 4:1, 2, 6

5:18 aLuke 21:12; Acts 4:3; 16:37

5:19 aMatt. 1:20, 24; 2:13, 19; 28:2; Luke 1:11; 2:9; Acts 12:7; 16:26

5:20 a[John 6:63, 68; 17:3; 1 John 5:11]

5:21 aActs 4:5, 6

5:24 aLuke 22:4; Acts 4:1; 5:26

5:26 aMatt. 21:26

5:28 aActs 4:17, 18 bActs 2:23, 36 cMatt. 23:35

5:29 aActs 4:19

5:17 [1]*jealousy*   5:21 [1]*Sanhedrin*   [2]*council of elders* or *senate*
5:23 [1]NU, M omit *outside*   5:24 [1]NU omits *the high priest*
5:25 [1]NU, M omit *saying*

5:30
a Acts 3:13, 15
b Acts 10:39;
13:29; [Gal. 3:13;
1 Pet. 2:24]

5:31
a Mark 16:19;
[Acts 2:33, 36;
Phil. 2:9–11]
b Acts 3:15;
Rev. 1:5
c Matt. 1:21
d Luke 24:47;
[Eph. 1:7;
Col. 1:14]

5:32
a John 15:26, 27;
Acts 15:28;
Rom. 8:16;
Heb. 2:4
b Acts 2:4; 10:44

5:33
a Acts 2:37; 7:54

5:34
a Acts 22:3

5:39
a Luke 21:15;
1 Cor. 1:25
b Acts 7:51; 9:5

5:40 a Acts 4:18
b Matt. 10:17;
Mark 13:9;
Acts 16:22,
23; 21:32;
2 Cor. 11:25

5:41
a Matt. 5:10–12;
Rom. 5:3;
2 Cor. 12:10;
Heb. 10:34;
[James 1:2;
1 Pet. 4:13–16]

5:42 a Acts 2:46
b Acts 4:20, 29

6:1
a Acts 2:41; 4:4
b Acts 9:29; 11:20
c Acts 4:35; 11:29

6:2 a Ex. 18:17

6:3 a Deut. 1:13;
1 Tim. 3:7
b Phil. 1:1;
1 Tim. 3:8–13

6:4
a Acts 2:42

6:5
a Acts 6:3; 11:24
b Acts 8:5, 26;
21:8 c Rev. 2:6, 15

6:6
a Acts 1:24
b Num. 8:10;
27:18;
Deut. 34:9;
[Mark 5:23;
Acts 8:17; 9:17;
13:3; 19:6;
1 Tim. 4:14;
2 Tim. 1:6];
Heb. 6:2

ought to obey God rather than men. [30a]The God of our fathers raised up Jesus whom you murdered by [b]hanging on a tree. [31a]Him God has exalted to His right hand *to be* [b]Prince and [c]Savior, [d]to give repentance to Israel and forgiveness of sins. [32]And [a]we are His witnesses to these things, and *so* also *is the* Holy Spirit [b]whom God has given to those who obey Him."

GAMALIEL'S ADVICE

[33]When they heard *this,* they were [a]furious[1] and plotted to kill them. [34]Then one in the council stood up, a Pharisee named [a]Gamaliel, a teacher of the law held in respect by all the people, and commanded them to put the apostles outside for a little while. [35]And he said to them: "Men of Israel, [1]take heed to yourselves what you intend to do regarding these men. [36]For some time ago Theudas rose up, claiming to be somebody. A number of men, about four hundred, [1]joined him. He was slain, and all who obeyed him were scattered and came to nothing. [37]After this man, Judas of Galilee rose up in the days of the census, and drew away many people after him. He also perished, and all who obeyed him were dispersed. [38]And now I say to you, keep away from these men and let them alone; for if this plan or this work is of men, it will come to nothing; [39a]but if it is of God, you cannot overthrow it—lest you even be found [b]to fight against God."

[40]And they agreed with him, and when they had [a]called for the apostles [b]and beaten *them,* they commanded that they should not speak in the name of Jesus, and let them go. [41]So they departed from the presence of the council, [a]rejoicing that they were counted worthy to suffer shame for [1]His name. [42]And daily [a]in the temple, and in every house, [b]they did not cease teaching and preaching Jesus *as* the Christ.

SEVEN CHOSEN TO SERVE

6 Now in those days, [a]when *the number of* the disciples was multiplying, there arose a complaint against the Hebrews by the [b]Hellenists,[1] because their widows were neglected [c]in the daily distribution. [2]Then the twelve summoned the multitude of the disciples and said, [a]"It is not desirable that we should leave the word of God and serve tables. [3]Therefore, brethren, [a]seek out from among you seven men of *good* reputation, full of the Holy Spirit and wisdom, whom we may appoint over this [b]business; [4]but we [a]will give ourselves continually to prayer and to the ministry of the word."

[5]And the saying pleased the whole multitude. And they chose Stephen, [a]a man full of faith and the Holy Spirit, and [b]Philip, Prochorus, Nicanor, Timon, Parmenas, and [c]Nicolas, a proselyte from Antioch, [6]whom they set before the apostles; and [a]when they had prayed, [b]they laid hands on them.

[7]Then [a]the word of God spread, and the number of the disciples multiplied greatly in Jerusalem, and a great many [b]of the priests were obedient to the faith.

STEPHEN ACCUSED OF BLASPHEMY

[8]And Stephen, full of [1]faith and power, did great [a]wonders and signs among the people. [9]Then there arose some

---

6:7 a Acts 12:24; Col. 1:6 b John 12:42   **6:8** a Acts 2:43; 5:12; 8:15; 14:3

5:33 [1]*cut to the quick*   **5:35** [1]*be careful*   **5:36** [1]*followed*   **5:41** [1]NU *the name;* M *the name of Jesus*   **6:1** [1]*Greek-speaking Jews*   **6:8** [1]NU *grace*

from what is called the Synagogue of the Freedmen (Cyrenians, Alexandrians, and those from Cilicia and Asia), disputing with Stephen. ¹⁰And ᵃthey were not able to resist the wisdom and the Spirit by which he spoke. ¹¹ᵃThen they secretly induced men to say, "We have heard him speak blasphemous words against Moses and God." ¹²And they stirred up the people, the elders, and the scribes; and they came upon *him,* seized him, and brought *him* to the council. ¹³They also set up false witnesses who said, "This man does not cease to speak ¹blasphemous words against this holy place and the law; ¹⁴ᵃfor we have heard him say that this Jesus of Nazareth will destroy this place and change the customs which Moses delivered to us." ¹⁵And all who sat in the council, looking steadfastly at him, saw his face as the face of an angel.

STEPHEN'S ADDRESS: THE CALL OF ABRAHAM

7 Then the high priest said, "Are these things so?" ²And he said, ᵃ"Brethren and fathers, listen: The ᵇGod of glory appeared to our father Abraham when he was in Mesopotamia, before he dwelt in ᶜHaran, ³and said to him, ᵃ'Get out of your country and from your relatives, and come to a land that I will show you.' ⁴Then ᵃhe came out of the land of the Chaldeans and dwelt in Haran. And from there, when his father was ᵇdead, He moved him to this land in which you now dwell. ⁵And *God* gave him no inheritance in it, not even *enough* to set his foot on. But even when *Abraham* had no child, ᵃHe promised to give it to him for a possession, and to his descendants after him. ⁶But God spoke in this way: ᵃthat his descendants would dwell in a foreign land, and that they would bring them into ᵇbondage and oppress *them* four hundred years. ⁷ᵃ'And the nation to whom they will be in bondage I will ᵇjudge,' said God, ᶜ'and after that they shall come out and serve Me in this place.' ⁸ᵃThen He gave him the covenant of circumcision; ᵇand so *Abraham* begot Isaac and circumcised him on the eighth day; ᶜand Isaac *begot* Jacob, and ᵈJacob *begot* the twelve patriarchs.

THE PATRIARCHS IN EGYPT

⁹ᵃ"And the patriarchs, becoming envious, ᵇsold Joseph into Egypt. ᶜBut God was with him ¹⁰and delivered him out of all his troubles, ᵃand gave him favor and wisdom in the presence of Pharaoh, king of Egypt; and he made him governor over Egypt and all his house. ¹¹ᵃNow a famine and great ¹trouble came over all the land of Egypt and Canaan, and our fathers found no sustenance. ¹²ᵃBut when Jacob heard that there was grain in Egypt, he sent out our fathers first. ¹³And the ᵃsecond *time* Joseph was made known to his brothers, and Joseph's family became known to the Pharaoh. ¹⁴ᵃThen Joseph sent and called his father Jacob and ᵇall his relatives to *him,* ¹seventy-five people. ¹⁵ᵃSo Jacob went down to Egypt; ᵇand he died, he and our fathers. ¹⁶And ᵃthey were carried back to Shechem and laid in ᵇthe tomb that Abraham bought for a sum of money from the sons of Hamor, *the father* of Shechem.

6:10 ᵃEx. 4:12; Is. 54:17; Luke 21:15
6:11 ᵃ1 Kin. 21:10, 13; Matt. 26:59, 60
6:14 ᵃActs 10:38; 25:8
7:2 ᵃActs 22:1 ᵇPs. 29:3; 1 Cor. 2:8 ᶜGen. 11:31, 32
7:3 ᵃGen. 12:1
7:4 ᵃGen. 11:31; 15:7; Heb. 11:8–10 ᵇGen. 11:32
7:5 ᵃGen. 12:7; 13:15; 15:3, 18; 17:8; 26:3
7:6 ᵃGen. 15:13, 14, 16; 47:11, 12 ᵇEx. 1:8–14; 12:40, 41; Gal. 3:17
7:7 ᵃGen. 15:14 ᵇEx. 14:13–31 ᶜEx. 3:12; Josh. 3:1–17
7:8 ᵃGen. 17:9–14 ᵇGen. 21:1–5 ᶜGen. 25:21–26 ᵈGen. 29:31—30:24; 35:18, 22–26
7:9 ᵃGen. 37:4, 11, 28; Ps. 105:17 ᵇGen. 37:28 ᶜGen. 39:2, 21, 23
7:10 ᵃGen. 41:38–44
7:11 ᵃGen. 41:54; 42:5
7:12 ᵃGen. 42:1, 2
7:13 ᵃGen. 45:4, 16
7:14 ᵃGen. 45:9, 27 ᵇGen. 46:26, 27; Deut. 10:22
7:15 ᵃGen. 46:1–7 ᵇGen. 49:33; Ex. 1:6
7:16 ᵃGen. 50:13; Ex. 13:19; Josh. 24:32 ᵇGen. 23:16

6:13 ¹NU omits *blasphemous*   7:11 ¹*affliction*   7:14 ¹Or *seventy,* Ex. 1:5

GOD DELIVERS ISRAEL BY MOSES

17"But when [a]the time of the promise drew near which God had sworn to Abraham, [b]the people grew and multiplied in Egypt 18till another king [a]arose who did not know Joseph. 19This man dealt treacherously with our people, and oppressed our forefathers, [a]making them expose their babies, so that they might not live. 20[a]At this time Moses was born, and [b]was well pleasing to God; and he was brought up in his father's house for three months. 21But [a]when he was set out, [b]Pharaoh's daughter took him away and brought him up as her own son. 22And Moses was learned in all the wisdom of the Egyptians, and was [a]mighty in words and deeds.

23[a]"Now when he was forty years old, it came into his heart to visit his brethren, the children of Israel. 24And seeing one of *them* suffer wrong, he defended and avenged him who was oppressed, and struck down the Egyptian. 25For he supposed that his brethren would have understood that God would deliver them by his hand, but they did not understand. 26And the next day he appeared to *two of* them as they were fighting, and *tried to* reconcile them, saying, 'Men, you are brethren; why do you wrong one another?' 27But he who did his neighbor wrong pushed him away, saying, [a]'Who made you a ruler and a judge over us? 28Do you want to kill me as you did the Egyptian yesterday?' 29[a]Then, at this saying, Moses fled and became a dweller in the land of Midian, where he [b]had two sons.

30[a]"And when forty years had passed, an Angel [1]of the Lord appeared to him in a flame of fire in a bush, in the wilderness of Mount Sinai. 31When Moses saw *it*, he marveled at the sight; and as he drew near to observe, the voice of the Lord came to him, 32*saying*, [a]'I *am* the God of your fathers—the God of Abraham, the God of Isaac, and the God of Jacob.' And Moses trembled and dared not look. 33[a]'Then the LORD said to him, "Take your sandals off your feet, for the place where you stand is holy ground. 34I have surely [a]seen the oppression of My people who are in Egypt; I have heard their groaning and have come down to deliver them. And now come, I will [b]send you to Egypt."'

35"This Moses whom they rejected, saying, [a]'Who made you a ruler and a judge?' is the one God sent *to be* a ruler and a deliverer [b]by the hand of the Angel who appeared to him in the bush. 36[a]He brought them out, after he had [b]shown wonders and signs in the land of Egypt, [c]and in the Red Sea, [d]and in the wilderness forty years.

ISRAEL REBELS AGAINST GOD

37"This is that Moses who said to the children of Israel, [a]'The LORD your God will raise up for you a Prophet like me from your brethren. [b]Him[1] you shall hear.'

38[a]"This is he who was in the [1]congregation in the wilderness with [b]the Angel who spoke to him on Mount Sinai, and *with* our fathers, [c]the one who received the living [d]oracles[2] to give to us, 39whom our fathers [a]would not obey, but rejected. And in their hearts they turned back to Egypt, 40[a]saying to Aaron, 'Make us gods to go before us; *as for* this Moses who

7:17 [a]Gen. 15:13; Ex. 2:23–25; Acts 7:6, 7 [b]Ex. 1:7–9; Ps. 105:24, 25
7:18 [a]Ex. 1:8
7:19 [a]Ex. 1:22
7:20 [a]Ex. 2:1, 2 [b]Heb. 11:23
7:21 [a]Ex. 2:3, 4 [b]Ex. 2:5–10
7:22 [a]Luke 24:19
7:23 [a]Ex. 2:11, 12; Heb. 11:24–26
7:27 [a]Ex. 2:14; Luke 12:14; Acts 7:35
7:29 [a]Heb. 11:27 [b]Ex. 2:15, 21, 22; 4:20; 18:3
7:30 [a]Ex. 3:1–10; Is. 63:9
7:32 [a]Ex. 3:6, 15; [Matt. 22:32]; Heb. 11:16
7:33 [a]Ex. 3:5, 7, 8, 10
7:34 [a]Ex. 2:24, 25 [b]Ps. 105:26
7:35 [a]Ex. 2:14; Acts 7:27 [b]Ex. 14:21
7:36 [a]Ex. 12:41; 33:1; Deut. 6:21, 23; Heb. 8:9 [b]Ex. 7:8, 9; Deut. 6:22; Ps. 105:27; John 4:48 [c]Ex. 14:21 [d]Ex. 16:1, 35; Num. 14:33; Ps. 95:8–10; Acts 7:42; 13:18; Heb. 3:8
7:37 [a]Deut. 18:15, 18, 19; Acts 3:22 [b]Matt. 17:5
7:38 [a]Ex. 19:3 [b]Is. 63:9; Gal. 3:19; Heb. 2:2 [c]Ex. 21:1; Deut. 5:27; John 1:17 [d]Rom. 3:2; Heb. 5:12; 1 Pet. 4:11
7:39 [a]Ps. 95:8–11
7:40 [a]Ex. 32:1, 23

7:30 [1]NU omits *of the Lord*   7:37 [1]NU, M omit *Him you shall hear*
7:38 [1]Gr. *ekklesia, assembly* or *church*   [2]*sayings*

brought us out of the land of Egypt, we do not know what has become of him.' [41a]And they made a calf in those days, offered sacrifices to the idol, and [b]rejoiced in the works of their own hands. [42]Then [a]God turned and gave them up to worship [b]the host of heaven, as it is written in the book of the Prophets:

[c]'Did you offer Me slaughtered animals and sacrifices
  during forty years in the wilderness,
  O house of Israel?
[43] You also took up the tabernacle of Moloch,
  And the star of your god Remphan,
  Images which you made to worship;
  And [a]I will carry you away beyond Babylon.'

GOD'S TRUE TABERNACLE

[44]"Our fathers had the tabernacle of witness in the wilderness, as He appointed, instructing Moses [a]to make it according to the pattern that he had seen, [45a]which our fathers, having received it in turn, also brought with Joshua into the land possessed by the Gentiles, [b]whom God drove out before the face of our fathers until the [c]days of David, [46a]who found favor before God and [b]asked to find a dwelling for the God of Jacob. [47a]But Solomon built Him a house.

[48]"However, [a]the Most High does not dwell in temples made with hands, as the prophet says:

[49] 'Heaven[a] *is* My throne,
  And earth *is* My footstool.
  What house will you build for Me? says the LORD,
  Or what *is* the place of My rest?
[50] Has My hand not [a]made all these things?'

ISRAEL RESISTS THE HOLY SPIRIT

[51]"*You* [a]stiff-necked[1] and [b]uncircumcised in heart and ears! You always resist the Holy Spirit; as your fathers *did,* so *do* you. [52a]Which of the prophets did your fathers not persecute? And they killed those who foretold the coming of [b]the Just One, of whom you now have become the betrayers and murderers, [53a]who have received the law by the direction of angels and have not kept *it.*"

STEPHEN THE MARTYR

[54a]When they heard these things they were [1]cut to the heart, and they gnashed at him with *their* teeth. [55]But he, [a]being full of the Holy Spirit, gazed into heaven and saw the [b]glory of God, and Jesus standing at the right hand of God, [56]and said, "Look! [a]I see the heavens opened and the [b]Son of Man standing at the right hand of God!"

[57]Then they cried out with a loud voice, stopped their ears, and ran at him with one accord; [58]and they cast *him* out of the city and stoned *him.* And [a]the witnesses laid down their clothes at the feet of a young man named Saul. [59]And they stoned Stephen as he was calling on *God* and saying, "Lord Jesus, [a]receive my spirit." [60]Then he knelt down and cried out with a loud voice, [a]"Lord, do not charge them with this sin." And when he had said this, he fell asleep.

7:51 [1]stubborn   7:54 [1]furious

7:41
[a]Ex. 32:2–4;
Deut. 9:16;
Ps. 106:19
[b]Ex. 32:6, 18, 19

7:42 [a]Ps. 81:12;
[2 Thess. 2:11]
[b]Deut. 4:19;
2 Kin. 21:3
[c]Amos 5:25–27

7:43
[a]2 Chr. 36:11–21;
Jer. 25:9–12

7:44 [a]Ex. 25:40;
[Heb. 8:5]

7:45
[a]Deut. 32:49;
Josh. 3:14; 18:1;
23:9 [b]Neh. 9:24;
Ps. 44:2
[c]2 Sam. 6:2–15

7:46
[a]2 Sam. 7:1–13;
1 Kin. 8:17
[b]1 Chr. 22:7;
Ps. 132:4, 5

7:47
[a]1 Kin. 6:1–38;
8:20, 21;
2 Chr. 3:1–17

7:48 [a]1 Kin. 8:27;
2 Chr. 2:6;
Acts 17:24

7:49 [a]Is. 66:1, 2;
Matt. 5:34

7:50 [a]Ps. 102:25

7:51 [a]Ex. 32:9;
Is. 6:10
[b]Lev. 26:41

7:52
[a]2 Chr. 36:16;
Matt. 21:35;
23:35;
1 Thess. 2:15
[b]Acts 3:14;
22:14; 1 John 2:1

7:53 [a]Ex. 20:1;
Deut. 33:2;
Acts 7:38;
Gal. 3:19;
Heb. 2:2

7:54 [a]Acts 5:33

7:55 [a]Matt. 5:8;
16:28; Mark 9:1;
Luke 9:27;
Acts 6:5
[b][Ex. 24:17]

7:56 [a]Matt. 3:16
[b]Dan. 7:13

7:58
[a]Acts 22:20

7:59 [a]Ps. 31:5

7:60
[a]Matt. 5:44;
Luke 23:34

SAUL PERSECUTES THE CHURCH

8 Now Saul was consenting to his death.

At that time a great persecution arose against the church which was at Jerusalem; and ᵃthey were all scattered throughout the regions of Judea and Samaria, except the apostles. ²And devout men carried Stephen *to his burial,* and ᵃmade great lamentation over him.

³As for Saul, ᵃhe made havoc of the church, entering every house, and dragging off men and women, committing *them* to prison.

CHRIST IS PREACHED IN SAMARIA

⁴Therefore ᵃthose who were scattered went everywhere preaching the word. ⁵Then ᵃPhilip went down to ¹the city of Samaria and preached Christ to them. ⁶And the multitudes with one accord heeded the things spoken by Philip, hearing and seeing the miracles which he did. ⁷For ᵃunclean spirits, crying with a loud voice, came out of many who were possessed; and many who were paralyzed and lame were healed. ⁸And there was great joy in that city.

THE SORCERER'S PROFESSION OF FAITH

⁹But there was a certain man called Simon, who previously ᵃpracticed ¹sorcery in the city and ᵇastonished the ²people of Samaria, claiming that he was someone great, ¹⁰to whom they all gave heed, from the least to the greatest, saying, "This man is the great power of God." ¹¹And they heeded him because he had astonished them with his ¹sorceries for a long time. ¹²But when they believed Philip as he preached the things ᵃconcerning the kingdom of God and the name of Jesus Christ, both men and women were baptized. ¹³Then Simon himself also believed; and when he was baptized he continued with Philip, and was amazed, seeing the miracles and signs which were done.

THE SORCERER'S SIN

¹⁴Now when the ᵃapostles who were at Jerusalem heard that Samaria had received the word of God, they sent Peter and John to them, ¹⁵who, when they had come down, prayed for them ᵃthat they might receive the Holy Spirit. ¹⁶For ᵃas yet He had fallen upon none of them. ᵇThey had only been baptized in ᶜthe name of the Lord Jesus. ¹⁷Then ᵃthey laid hands on them, and they received the Holy Spirit.

¹⁸And when Simon saw that through the laying on of the apostles' hands the Holy Spirit was given, he offered them money, ¹⁹saying, "Give me this power also, that anyone on whom I lay hands may receive the Holy Spirit."

²⁰But Peter said to him, "Your money perish with you, because ᵃyou thought that ᵇthe gift of God could be purchased with money! ²¹You have neither part nor portion in this matter, for your ᵃheart is not right in the sight of God. ²²Repent therefore of this your wickedness, and pray God ᵃif perhaps the thought of your heart may be forgiven you. ²³For I see that you are ᵃpoisoned by bitterness and bound by iniquity."

²⁴Then Simon answered and said, ᵃ"Pray to the Lord for

8:1 ᵃJohn 16:2; Acts 8:4; 11:19

8:2 ᵃGen. 23:2

8:3 ᵃActs 7:58; 1 Cor. 15:9; Gal. 1:13; Phil. 3:6; 1 Tim. 1:13

8:4 ᵃMatt. 10:23

8:5 ᵃActs 6:5; 8:26, 30

8:7 ᵃMark 16:17

8:9 ᵃActs 8:11; 13:6; ᵇActs 5:36

8:12 ᵃActs 1:3; 8:4

8:14 ᵃActs 5:12, 29, 40

8:15 ᵃActs 2:38; 19:2

8:16 ᵃActs 19:2; ᵇMatt. 28:19; Acts 2:38; ᶜActs 10:48; 19:5

8:17 ᵃActs 6:6; 19:6; Heb. 6:2

8:20 ᵃ2 Kin. 5:16; Is. 55:1; Dan. 5:17; [Matt. 10:8]; ᵇ[Acts 2:38; 10:45; 11:17]

8:21 ᵃJer. 17:9

8:22 ᵃDan. 4:27; 2 Tim. 2:25

8:23 ᵃHeb. 12:15

8:24 ᵃGen. 20:7, 17; Ex. 8:8; Num. 21:7; 1 Kin. 13:6; Job 42:8; James 5:16

8:5 ¹Or *a*   **8:9** ¹*magic*   ²Or *nation*   **8:11** ¹*magic arts*

me, that none of the things which you have spoken may come upon me."

[25]So when they had testified and preached the word of the Lord, they returned to Jerusalem, preaching the gospel in many villages of the Samaritans.

CHRIST IS PREACHED TO AN ETHIOPIAN
(cf. Is. 53:7, 8)

[26]Now an angel of the Lord spoke to [a]Philip, saying, "Arise and go toward the south along the road which goes down from Jerusalem to Gaza." This is [1]desert. [27]So he arose and went. And behold, [a]a man of Ethiopia, a eunuch of great authority under Candace the queen of the Ethiopians, who had charge of all her treasury, and [b]had come to Jerusalem to worship, [28]was returning. And sitting in his chariot, he was reading Isaiah the prophet. [29]Then the Spirit said to Philip, "Go near and overtake this chariot."

[30]So Philip ran to him, and heard him reading the prophet Isaiah, and said, "Do you understand what you are reading?"

[31]And he said, "How can I, unless someone guides me?" And he asked Philip to come up and sit with him. [32]The place in the Scripture which he read was this:

[a]"He was led as a sheep to the slaughter;
And as a lamb before its shearer *is* silent,
[b]So He opened not His mouth.
[33]   In His humiliation His [a]justice was taken away,
And who will declare His generation?
For His life is [b]taken from the earth."

[34]So the eunuch answered Philip and said, "I ask you, of whom does the prophet say this, of himself or of some other man?" [35]Then Philip opened his mouth, [a]and beginning at this Scripture, preached Jesus to him. [36]Now as they went down the road, they came to some water. And the eunuch said, "See, *here is* water. [a]What hinders me from being baptized?"

[37][1]Then Philip said, [a]"If you believe with all your heart, you may."

And he answered and said, [b]"I believe that Jesus Christ is the Son of God."

[38]So he commanded the chariot to stand still. And both Philip and the eunuch went down into the water, and he baptized him. [39]Now when they came up out of the water, [a]the Spirit of the Lord caught Philip away, so that the eunuch saw him no more; and he went on his way rejoicing. [40]But Philip was found at [1]Azotus. And passing through, he preached in all the cities till he came to [a]Caesarea.

THE DAMASCUS ROAD: SAUL CONVERTED
(Acts 22:6–16; 26:12–18)

9 Then [a]Saul, still breathing threats and murder against the disciples of the Lord, went to the high priest [2]and asked [a]letters from him to the synagogues of Damascus, so that if he found any who were of the Way, whether men or women, he might bring them bound to Jerusalem.

8:26 [a]Acts 6:5

8:27 [a]Ps. 68:31; 87:4; Is. 56:3; Zeph. 3:10 [b]1 Kin. 8:41, 42; John 12:20

8:32 [a]Is. 53:7, 8 [b]Matt. 26:62, 63; 27:12, 14; John 19:9

8:33 [a]Luke 23:1–25 [b]Luke 23:33–46

8:35 [a]Luke 24:27; Acts 17:2; 18:28; 28:23

8:36 [a]Acts 10:47; 16:33

8:37 [a]Matt. 28:19; [Mark 16:16; Rom. 10:9, 10] [b]Matt. 16:16; John 6:69; 9:35, 38; 11:27

8:39 [a]1 Kin. 18:12; 2 Kin. 2:16; Ezek. 3:12, 14; 2 Cor. 12:2

8:40 [a]Acts 21:8

9:1 [a]Acts 7:57; 8:1, 3; 26:10, 11; Gal. 1:13; 1 Tim. 1:13

9:2 [a]Acts 22:5

^{3a}As he journeyed he came near Damascus, and suddenly a light shone around him from heaven. ⁴Then he fell to the ground, and heard a voice saying to him, "Saul, Saul, ^awhy are you persecuting Me?"

⁵And he said, "Who are You, Lord?"

Then the Lord said, "I am Jesus, whom you are persecuting. ¹It *is* hard for you to kick against the goads."

⁶So he, trembling and astonished, said, "Lord, what do You want me to do?"

Then the Lord *said* to him, "Arise and go into the city, and you will be told what you must do."

⁷And ^athe men who journeyed with him stood speechless, hearing a voice but seeing no one. ⁸Then Saul arose from the ground, and when his eyes were opened he saw no one. But they led him by the hand and brought *him* into Damascus. ⁹And he was three days without sight, and neither ate nor drank.

ANANIAS BAPTIZES SAUL

¹⁰Now there was a certain disciple at Damascus ^anamed Ananias; and to him the Lord said in a vision, "Ananias."

And he said, "Here I am, Lord."

¹¹So the Lord *said* to him, "Arise and go to the street called Straight, and inquire at the house of Judas for *one* called Saul ^aof Tarsus, for behold, he is praying. ¹²And in a vision he has seen a man named Ananias coming in and putting *his* hand on him, so that he might receive his sight."

¹³Then Ananias answered, "Lord, I have heard from many about this man, ^ahow much ¹harm he has done to Your saints in Jerusalem. ¹⁴And here he has authority from the chief priests to bind all ^awho call on Your name."

¹⁵But the Lord said to him, "Go, for ^ahe is a chosen vessel of Mine to bear My name before ^bGentiles, ^ckings, and the ^dchildren¹ of Israel. ¹⁶For ^aI will show him how many things he must suffer for My ^bname's sake."

^{17a}And Ananias went his way and entered the house; and ^blaying his hands on him he said, "Brother Saul, the Lord ¹Jesus, who appeared to you on the road as you came, has sent me that you may receive your sight and ^cbe filled with the Holy Spirit." ¹⁸Immediately there fell from his eyes *something* like scales, and he received his sight at once; and he arose and was baptized.

¹⁹So when he had received food, he was strengthened. ^aThen Saul spent some days with the disciples at Damascus.

SAUL PREACHES CHRIST

²⁰Immediately he preached ¹the Christ in the synagogues, that He is the Son of God.

²¹Then all who heard were amazed, and said, ^a"Is this not he who destroyed those who called on this name in Jerusalem, and has come here for that purpose, so that he might bring them bound to the chief priests?"

²²But Saul increased all the more in strength, ^aand confounded the Jews who dwelt in Damascus, proving that this *Jesus* is the Christ.

9:3 ^aActs 22:6; 26:12, 13; 1 Cor. 15:8

9:4 ^a[Matt. 25:40]

9:7 ^aDan. 10:7; John 12:29; [Acts 22:9; 26:13]

9:10 ^aActs 22:12

9:11 ^aActs 21:39; 22:3

9:13 ^aActs 9:1

9:14 ^aActs 7:59; 9:2, 21; 1 Cor. 1:2; 2 Tim. 2:22

9:15 ^aActs 13:2; 22:21; Rom. 1:1; 1 Cor. 15:10; Gal. 1:15; Eph. 3:7, 8; 1 Tim. 2:7; 2 Tim. 1:11 ^bRom. 1:5; 11:13; Gal. 2:7, 8 ^cActs 25:22, 23; 26:1 ^dActs 21:40; Rom. 1:16; 9:1–5

9:16 ^aActs 20:23; 2 Cor. 11:23–28; 12:7–10; Gal. 6:17; Phil. 1:29, 30 ^b2 Cor. 4:11

9:17 ^aActs 22:12, 13 ^bActs 8:17 ^cActs 2:4; 4:31; 8:17; 13:52

9:19 ^aActs 26:20

9:21 ^aActs 8:3; 9:13; Gal. 1:13, 23

9:22 ^aActs 18:28

9:5 ¹NU, M omit the rest of v. 5 and begin v. 6 with *But arise and go* 9:13 ¹*bad things* 9:15 ¹Lit. *sons* 9:17 ¹M omits *Jesus* 9:20 ¹NU *Jesus*

SAUL ESCAPES DEATH

23Now after many days were past, ªthe Jews plotted to kill him. 24ªBut their plot became known to Saul. And they watched the gates day and night, to kill him. 25Then the disciples took him by night and ªlet *him* down through the wall in a large basket.

SAUL AT JERUSALEM

26And ªwhen Saul had come to Jerusalem, he tried to join the disciples; but they were all afraid of him, and did not believe that he was a disciple. 27ªBut Barnabas took him and brought *him* to the apostles. And he declared to them how he had seen the Lord on the road, and that He had spoken to him, band how he had preached boldly at Damascus in the name of Jesus. 28So ªhe was with them at Jerusalem, coming in and going out. 29And he spoke boldly in the name of the Lord Jesus and disputed against the ªHellenists,[1] bbut they attempted to kill him. 30When the brethren found out, they brought him down to Caesarea and sent him out to Tarsus.

THE CHURCH PROSPERS

31ªThen the [1]churches throughout all Judea, Galilee, and Samaria had peace and were bedified.[2] And walking in the cfear of the Lord and in the dcomfort of the Holy Spirit, they were emultiplied.

AENEAS HEALED

32Now it came to pass, as Peter went ªthrough all *parts of the country,* that he also came down to the saints who dwelt in Lydda. 33There he found a certain man named Aeneas, who had been bedridden eight years and was paralyzed. 34And Peter said to him, "Aeneas, ªJesus the Christ heals you. Arise and make your bed." Then he arose immediately. 35So all who dwelt at Lydda and ªSharon saw him and bturned to the Lord.

DORCAS RESTORED TO LIFE

36At Joppa there was a certain disciple named [1]Tabitha, which is translated [2]Dorcas. This woman was full ªof good works and charitable deeds which she did. 37But it happened in those days that she became sick and died. When they had washed her, they laid *her* in ªan upper room. 38And since Lydda was near Joppa, and the disciples had heard that Peter was there, they sent two men to him, imploring *him* not to delay in coming to them. 39Then Peter arose and went with them. When he had come, they brought *him* to the upper room. And all the widows stood by him weeping, showing the tunics and garments which Dorcas had made while she was with them. 40But Peter ªput them all out, and bknelt down and prayed. And turning to the body he csaid, "Tabitha, arise." And she opened her eyes, and when she saw Peter she sat up. 41Then he gave her *his* hand and lifted her up; and when he had called the saints and widows, he presented her alive. 42And it became known throughout all Joppa, ªand many believed on the Lord. 43So it was that he stayed many days in Joppa with ªSimon, a tanner.

9:23
ªActs 23:12;
2 Cor. 11:26

9:24
ª2 Cor. 11:32

9:25 ªJosh. 2:15;
1 Sam. 19:12

9:26
ªActs 22:17–20;
26:20;
Gal. 1:17, 18

9:27
ªActs 4:36; 13:2
bActs 9:20, 22

9:28 ªGal. 1:18

9:29 ªActs 6:1;
11:20 bActs 9:23;
2 Cor. 11:26

9:31 ªActs 5:11;
8:1; 16:5
b[Eph. 4:16, 29]
cPs. 34:9
dJohn 14:16
eActs 16:5

9:32 ªActs 8:14

9:34 ª[Acts 3:6,
16; 4:10]

9:35 ª1 Chr. 5:16;
27:29; Is. 33:9;
35:2; 65:10
bActs 11:21; 15:19

9:36
ª1 Tim. 2:10;
Titus 3:8

9:37
ªActs 1:13; 9:39

9:40
ªMatt. 9:25
bLuke 22:41;
Acts 7:60
cMark 5:41, 42;
John 11:43

9:42 ªJohn 11:45

9:43 ªActs 10:6

CORNELIUS SENDS A DELEGATION

10 There was a certain man in ªCaesarea called Cornelius, a centurion of what was called the Italian ¹Regiment, 2ªa devout *man* and one who ªfeared God with all his household, who gave ¹alms generously to the people, and prayed to God always. ³About ¹the ninth hour of the day ªhe saw clearly in a vision an angel of God coming in and saying to him, "Cornelius!"

⁴And when he observed him, he was afraid, and said, "What is it, lord?"

So he said to him, "Your prayers and your alms have come up for a memorial before God. ⁵Now ªsend men to Joppa, and send for Simon whose surname is Peter. ⁶He is lodging with ªSimon, a tanner, whose house is by the sea. ªHe¹ will tell you what you must do." ⁷And when the angel who spoke to him had departed, Cornelius called two of his household servants and a devout soldier from among those who waited on him continually. ⁸So when he had explained all *these* things to them, he sent them to Joppa.

PETER'S VISION

⁹The next day, as they went on their journey and drew near the city, ªPeter went up on the housetop to pray, about ¹the sixth hour. ¹⁰Then he became very hungry and wanted to eat; but while they made ready, he fell into a trance ¹¹and ªsaw heaven opened and an object like a great sheet bound at the four corners, descending to him and let down to the earth. ¹²In it were all kinds of four-footed animals of the earth, wild beasts, creeping things, and birds of the air. ¹³And a voice came to him, "Rise, Peter; kill and eat."

¹⁴But Peter said, "Not so, Lord! ªFor I have never eaten anything common or unclean."

¹⁵And a voice *spoke* to him again the second time, ª"What God has ¹cleansed you must not call common." ¹⁶This was done three times. And the object was taken up into heaven again.

SUMMONED TO CAESAREA

¹⁷Now while Peter ¹wondered within himself what this vision which he had seen meant, behold, the men who had been sent from Cornelius had made inquiry for Simon's house, and stood before the gate. ¹⁸And they called and asked whether Simon, whose surname was Peter, was lodging there.

¹⁹While Peter thought about the vision, ªthe Spirit said to him, "Behold, three men are seeking you. 20ªArise therefore, go down and go with them, doubting nothing; for I have sent them."

²¹Then Peter went down to the men ¹who had been sent to him from Cornelius, and said, "Yes, I am he whom you seek. For what reason have you come?"

²²And they said, "Cornelius *the* centurion, a just man, one who fears God and ªhas a good reputation among all the nation of the Jews, was divinely instructed by a holy angel to summon you to his house, and to hear words from you." ²³Then he invited them in and lodged *them*.

On the next day Peter went away with them, ªand some brethren from Joppa accompanied him.

10:1 ªActs 8:40; 23:23
10:2 ªActs 8:2; 9:22; 22:12 ª[Acts 10:22, 35; 13:16, 26]
10:3 ªActs 10:30; 11:13
10:5 ªActs 11:13, 14
10:6 ªActs 9:43 ªActs 11:14
10:9 ªActs 10:9–32; 11:5–14
10:11 ªEzek. 1:1; Matt. 3:16; Acts 7:56; Rev. 4:1; 19:11
10:14 ªLev. 11:4; 20:25; Deut. 14:3, 7; Ezek. 4:14
10:15 ª[Matt. 15:11; Mark 7:19]; Acts 10:28; [Rom. 14:14]; 1 Cor. 10:25; [1 Tim. 4:4; Titus 1:15]
10:19 ªActs 11:12
10:20 ªActs 15:7–9
10:22 ªActs 22:12
10:23 ªActs 10:45; 11:12

10:1 ¹*Cohort*   10:2 ¹*charitable gifts*   10:3 ¹3 P.M.   10:6 ¹NU, M omit the rest of v. 6.   10:9 ¹Noon   10:15 ¹*Declared clean*   10:17 ¹*was perplexed* 10:21 ¹NU, M omit *who had been sent to him from Cornelius*

PETER MEETS CORNELIUS

24And the following day they entered Caesarea. Now Cornelius was waiting for them, and had called together his relatives and close friends. 25As Peter was coming in, Cornelius met him and fell down at his feet and worshiped *him.* 26But Peter lifted him up, saying, a"Stand up; I myself am also a man." 27And as he talked with him, he went in and found many who had come together. 28Then he said to them, "You know how aunlawful it is for a Jewish man to keep company with or go to one of another nation. But bGod has shown me that I should not call any man common or unclean. 29Therefore I came without objection as soon as I was sent for. I ask, then, for what reason have you sent for me?"

30So Cornelius said, 1"Four days ago I was fasting until this hour; and at the ninth hour I prayed in my house, and behold, aa man stood before me bin bright clothing, 31and said, 'Cornelius, ayour prayer has been heard, and byour 1alms are remembered in the sight of God. 32Send therefore to Joppa and call Simon here, whose surname is Peter. He is lodging in the house of Simon, a tanner, by the sea. 1When he comes, he will speak to you.' 33So I sent to you immediately, and you have done well to come. Now therefore, we are all present before God, to hear all the things commanded you by God."

PREACHING TO CORNELIUS' HOUSEHOLD

34Then Peter opened *his* mouth and said: a"In truth I perceive that God shows no partiality. 35But ain every nation whoever fears Him and works righteousness is baccepted by Him. 36The word which *God* sent to the 1children of Israel, apreaching peace through Jesus Christ—bHe is Lord of all— 37that word you know, which was proclaimed throughout all Judea, and abegan from Galilee after the baptism which John preached: 38how aGod anointed Jesus of Nazareth with the Holy Spirit and with power, who bwent about doing good and healing all who were oppressed by the devil, cfor God was with Him. 39And we are awitnesses of all things which He did both in the land of the Jews and in Jerusalem, whom 1they bkilled by hanging on a tree. 40Him aGod raised up on the third day, and showed Him openly, 41anot to all the people, but to witnesses chosen before by God, *even* to us bwho ate and drank with Him after He arose from the dead. 42And aHe commanded us to preach to the people, and to testify bthat it is He who was ordained by God *to be* Judge cof the living and the dead. 43aTo Him all the prophets witness that, through His name, bwhoever believes in Him will receive cremission1 of sins."

THE HOLY SPIRIT FALLS ON THE GENTILES

44While Peter was still speaking these words, athe Holy Spirit fell upon all those who heard the word. 45aAnd 1those of the circumcision who believed were astonished, as many as came with Peter, bbecause the gift of the Holy Spirit had been poured out on the Gentiles also. 46For they heard them speak with tongues and magnify God.

10:45 aActs 10:23 bIs. 42:1, 6; 49:6; Luke 2:32; John 11:52; Acts 11:18

10:30 1NU *Four days ago to this hour, at the ninth hour* 10:31 1*charitable gifts* 10:32 1NU omits the rest of v. 32. 10:36 1Lit. *sons*
10:39 1NU, M *they also* 10:43 1*forgiveness* 10:45 1The Jews

10:26
aActs 14:14, 15;
Rev. 19:10; 22:8

10:28 aJohn 4:9;
18:28; Acts 11:3;
Gal. 2:12
b[Acts 10:14, 35;
15:8, 9]

10:30 aActs 1:10
bMatt. 28:3;
Mark 16:5

10:31 aDan. 10:12
bHeb. 6:10

10:34
aDeut. 10:17;
2 Chr. 19:7;
Rom. 2:11;
Gal. 2:6;
Eph. 6:9

10:35
aActs 15:9;
[1 Cor. 12; 13];
Eph. 2:13]
bPs. 15:1, 2

10:36 aIs. 57:19;
Eph. 2:14;
[Col. 1:20]
bMatt. 28:18;
Acts 2:36;
Rom. 10:12;
1 Cor. 15:27

10:37 aLuke 4:14

10:38
aIs. 61:1–3;
Luke 4:18
bMatt. 4:23
cJohn 3:2; 8:29

10:39 aActs 1:8
bActs 2:23

10:40 aHos. 6:2;
Matt. 12:39, 40;
16:4; 20:19;
John 2:19–21;
Acts 2:24

10:41
a[John 14:17,
19, 22; 15:27]
bLuke 24:30,
41–43

10:42
aMatt. 28:19
bJohn 5:22,
27; Acts 17:31
cRom. 14:9;
2 Tim. 4:1;
1 Pet. 4:5

10:43 a[Is. 42:1;
53:11; 61:1];
Jer. 31:34;
Dan. 9:24;
Hos. 6:1–3;
Mic. 7:18;
Zech. 13:1;
Mal. 4:2
b[John 3:16, 18;
Acts 26:18];
Rom. 10:11;
Gal. 3:22
cActs 13:38, 39

10:44 aActs 4:31

Then Peter answered, [47]"Can anyone forbid water, that these should not be baptized who have received the Holy Spirit [a]just as we *have?*" [48a]And he commanded them to be baptized [b]in the name of the Lord. Then they asked him to stay a few days.

PETER DEFENDS GOD'S GRACE

11 Now the apostles and brethren who were in Judea heard that the Gentiles had also received the word of God. [2]And when Peter came up to Jerusalem, [a]those of the circumcision contended with him, [3]saying, [a]"You went in to uncircumcised men [b]and ate with them!"

[4]But Peter explained *it* to them [a]in order from the beginning, saying: [5a]"I was in the city of Joppa praying; and in a trance I saw a vision, an object descending like a great sheet, let down from heaven by four corners; and it came to me. [6]When I observed it intently and considered, I saw four-footed animals of the earth, wild beasts, creeping things, and birds of the air. [7]And I heard a voice saying to me, 'Rise, Peter; kill and eat.' [8]But I said, 'Not so, Lord! For nothing common or unclean has at any time entered my mouth.' [9]But the voice answered me again from heaven, 'What God has cleansed you must not call common.' [10]Now this was done three times, and all were drawn up again into heaven. [11]At that very moment, three men stood before the house where I was, having been sent to me from Caesarea. [12]Then [a]the Spirit told me to go with them, doubting nothing. Moreover [b]these six brethren accompanied me, and we entered the man's house. [13a]And he told us how he had seen an angel standing in his house, who said to him, 'Send men to Joppa, and call for Simon whose surname is Peter, [14]who will tell you words by which you and all your household will be saved.' [15]And as I began to speak, the Holy Spirit fell upon them, [a]as upon us at the beginning. [16]Then I remembered the word of the Lord, how He said, [a]'John indeed baptized with water, but [b]you shall be baptized with the Holy Spirit.' [17a]If therefore God gave them the same gift as *He gave* us when we believed on the Lord Jesus Christ, [b]who was I that I could withstand God?"

[18]When they heard these things they became silent; and they glorified God, saying, [a]"Then God has also granted to the Gentiles repentance to life."

BARNABAS AND SAUL AT ANTIOCH

[19a]Now those who were scattered after the persecution that arose over Stephen traveled as far as Phoenicia, Cyprus, and Antioch, preaching the word to no one but the Jews only. [20]But some of them were men from Cyprus and Cyrene, who, when they had come to Antioch, spoke to [a]the Hellenists, preaching the Lord Jesus. [21]And [a]the hand of the Lord was with them, and a great number believed and [b]turned to the Lord.

[22]Then news of these things came to the ears of the church in Jerusalem, and they sent out [a]Barnabas to go as far as Antioch. [23]When he came and had seen the grace of God, he was glad, and [a]encouraged them all that with purpose of heart they should continue with the Lord. [24]For he was a good man, [a]full of the Holy Spirit and of faith. [b]And a great many people were added to the Lord.

10:47 [a]Acts 2:4;
10:44; 11:17; 15:8

10:48
[a]1 Cor. 1:14–17
[b]Acts 2:38; 8:16;
19:5

11:2 [a]Acts 10:45

11:3 [a]Matt. 9:11;
Acts 10:28
[b]Gal. 2:12

11:4 [a]Luke 1:3

11:5 [a]Acts 10:9

11:12
[a][John 16:13];
Acts 10:19; 15:7
[b]Acts 10:23

11:13 [a]Acts 10:30

11:15
[a]Acts 2:1–4;
15:7–9

11:16 [a]Matt. 3:11;
Mark 1:8;
John 1:26, 33;
Acts 1:5; 19:4
[b]Is. 44:3

11:17
[a][Acts 15:8, 9]
[b]Acts 10:47

11:18 [a]Is. 42:1, 6;
49:6; Luke 2:32;
John 11:52;
Rom. 10:12, 13;
15:9, 16

11:19 [a]Acts 8:1, 4

11:20
[a]Acts 6:1; 9:29

11:21 [a]Luke 1:66;
Acts 2:47
[b]Acts 9:35; 14:1

11:22
[a]Acts 4:36; 9:27

11:23
[a]Acts 13:43;
14:22

11:24 [a]Acts 6:5
[b]Acts 5:14; 11:21

25Then Barnabas departed for aTarsus to seek Saul. 26And when he had found him, he brought him to Antioch. So it was that for a whole year they assembled with the church and taught a great many people. And the disciples were first called Christians in Antioch.

RELIEF TO JUDEA

27And in these days aprophets came from Jerusalem to Antioch. 28Then one of them, named aAgabus, stood up and showed by the Spirit that there was going to be a great famine throughout all the world, which also happened in the days of bClaudius Caesar. 29Then the disciples, each according to his ability, determined to send arelief to the brethren dwelling in Judea. 30aThis they also did, and sent it to the elders by the hands of Barnabas and Saul.

HEROD'S VIOLENCE TO THE CHURCH

12 Now about that time Herod the king stretched out *his* hand to harass some from the church. 2Then he killed James athe brother of John with the sword. 3And because he saw that it pleased the Jews, he proceeded further to seize Peter also. Now it was *during* athe Days of Unleavened Bread. 4So awhen he had arrested him, he put *him* in prison, and delivered *him* to four 1squads of soldiers to keep him, intending to bring him before the people after Passover.

PETER FREED FROM PRISON

5Peter was therefore kept in prison, but 1constant prayer was offered to God for him by the church. 6And when Herod was about to bring him out, that night Peter was sleeping, bound with two chains between two soldiers; and the guards before the door were 1keeping the prison. 7Now behold, aan angel of the Lord stood by *him,* and a light shone in the prison; and he struck Peter on the side and raised him up, saying, "Arise quickly!" And his chains fell off *his* hands. 8Then the angel said to him, "Gird yourself and tie on your sandals"; and so he did. And he said to him, "Put on your garment and follow me." 9So he went out and followed him, and adid not know that what was done by the angel was real, but thought bhe was seeing a vision. 10When they were past the first and the second guard posts, they came to the iron gate that leads to the city, awhich opened to them of its own accord; and they went out and went down one street, and immediately the angel departed from him.

11And when Peter had come to himself, he said, "Now I know for certain that athe Lord has sent His angel, and bhas delivered me from the hand of Herod and *from* all the expectation of the Jewish people."

12So, when he had considered *this,* ahe came to the house of Mary, the mother of bJohn whose surname was Mark, where many were gathered together cpraying. 13And as Peter knocked at the door of the gate, a girl named Rhoda came to answer. 14When she recognized Peter's voice, because of *her* gladness she did not open the gate, but ran in and announced that Peter stood before the gate. 15But they said to her, "You

11:25
aActs 9:11, 30

11:27 aActs 2:17;
13:1; 15:32; 21:9;
1 Cor. 12:28;
Eph. 4:11

11:28
aJohn 16:13;
Acts 21:10
bActs 18:2

11:29
aRom. 15:26;
1 Cor. 16:1;
2 Cor. 9:1

11:30 aActs 12:25

12:2 aMatt. 4:21;
20:23

12:3 aEx. 12:15;
23:15; Acts 20:6

12:4 aJohn 21:18

12:7 aActs 5:19

12:9 aPs. 126:1
bActs 10:3,
17; 11:5

12:10 aActs 5:19;
16:26

12:11 a[Ps. 34:7];
Dan. 3:28; 6:22;
[Heb. 1:14]
bJob 5:19;
[Ps. 33:18, 19;
34:22; 41:2];
2 Cor. 1:10;
[2 Pet. 2:9]

12:12 aActs 4:23
bActs 13:5, 13;
15:37;
2 Tim. 4:11;
Philem. 24;
1 Pet. 5:13
cActs 12:5

12:4 1Gr. *tetrads,* squads of four   12:5 1NU *constantly* or *earnestly*
12:6 1*guarding*

are beside yourself!" Yet she kept insisting that it was so. So they said, [a]"It is his angel."

[16]Now Peter continued knocking; and when they opened *the door* and saw him, they were astonished. [17]But [a]motioning to them with his hand to keep silent, he declared to them how the Lord had brought him out of the prison. And he said, "Go, tell these things to James and to the brethren." And he departed and went to another place.

[18]Then, as soon as it was day, there was no small [1]stir among the soldiers about what had become of Peter. [19]But when Herod had searched for him and not found him, he examined the guards and commanded that *they* should be put to death.

And he went down from Judea to Caesarea, and stayed *there.*

HEROD'S VIOLENT DEATH

[20]Now Herod had been very angry with the people of [a]Tyre and Sidon; but they came to him with one accord, and having made Blastus [1]the king's personal aide their friend, they asked for peace, because [b]their country was [2]supplied with food by the king's *country.*

[21]So on a set day Herod, arrayed in royal apparel, sat on his throne and gave an oration to them. [22]And the people kept shouting, "The voice of a god and not of a man!" [23]Then immediately an angel of the Lord [a]struck him, because [b]he did not give glory to God. And he was eaten by worms and [1]died. [24]But [a]the word of God grew and multiplied.

BARNABAS AND SAUL APPOINTED

[25]And [a]Barnabas and Saul returned [1]from Jerusalem when they had [b]fulfilled *their* ministry, and they also [c]took with them [d]John whose surname was Mark.

13 Now [a]in the church that was at Antioch there were certain prophets and teachers: [b]Barnabas, Simeon who was called Niger, [c]Lucius of Cyrene, Manaen who had been brought up with Herod the tetrarch, and Saul. [2]As they ministered to the Lord and fasted, the Holy Spirit said, [a]"Now separate to Me Barnabas and Saul for the work [b]to which I have called them." [3]Then, [a]having fasted and prayed, and laid hands on them, they sent *them* away.

PREACHING IN CYPRUS

[4]So, being sent out by the Holy Spirit, they went down to Seleucia, and from there they sailed to [a]Cyprus. [5]And when they arrived in Salamis, [a]they preached the word of God in the synagogues of the Jews. They also had [b]John as *their* assistant.

[6]Now when they had gone through [1]the island to Paphos, they found [a]a certain sorcerer, a false prophet, a Jew whose name *was* Bar-Jesus, [7]who was with the proconsul, Sergius Paulus, an intelligent man. This man called for Barnabas and Saul and sought to hear the word of God. [8]But [a]Elymas the sorcerer (for so his name is translated) [1]withstood them, seeking

12:15 [a]Gen. 48:16; [Matt. 18:10]

12:17 [a]Acts 13:16; 19:33; 21:40

12:20 [a]Matt. 11:21 [b]1 Kin. 5:11; Ezra 3:7; Ezek. 27:17

12:23 [a]1 Sam. 25:38; 2 Sam. 24:16, 17; 2 Kin. 19:35; Acts 5:19 [b]Ps. 115:1

12:24 [a]Is. 55:11; Acts 6:7; 19:20

12:25 [a]Acts 11:30 [b]Acts 11:30 [c]Acts 13:5, 13 [d]Acts 12:12; 15:37

13:1 [a]Acts 14:26 [b]Acts 11:22 [c]Rom. 16:21

13:2 [a]Num. 8:14; Acts 9:15; 22:21; Rom. 1:1; Gal. 1:15; 2:9 [b]Matt. 9:38; Acts 14:26; Rom. 10:15; Eph. 3:7, 8; 1 Tim. 2:7; 2 Tim. 1:11; Heb. 5:4

13:3 [a]Matt. 9:15; Mark 2:20; Luke 5:35; Acts 6:6

13:4 [a]Acts 4:36

13:5 [a][Acts 13:46] [b]Acts 12:25; 15:37

13:6 [a]Acts 8:9

13:8 [a]Ex. 7:11; 2 Tim. 3:8

12:18 [1]*disturbance* **12:20** [1]*who was in charge of the king's bedchamber* [2]Lit. *nourished* **12:23** [1]*breathed his last* **12:25** [1]NU, M *to* **13:6** [1]NU *the whole island* **13:8** [1]*opposed*

to turn the proconsul away from the faith. 9Then Saul, who also *is called* Paul, ªfilled with the Holy Spirit, looked intently at him 10and said, "O full of all deceit and all fraud, ªyou son of the devil, *you* enemy of all righteousness, will you not cease perverting the straight ways of the Lord? 11And now, indeed, ªthe hand of the Lord *is* upon you, and you shall be blind, not seeing the sun for a time."

And immediately a dark mist fell on him, and he went around seeking someone to lead him by the hand. 12Then the proconsul believed, when he saw what had been done, being astonished at the teaching of the Lord.

AT ANTIOCH IN PISIDIA

13Now when Paul and his party set sail from Paphos, they came to Perga in Pamphylia; and ªJohn, departing from them, returned to Jerusalem. 14But when they departed from Perga, they came to Antioch in Pisidia, and ªwent into the synagogue on the Sabbath day and sat down. 15And ªafter the reading of the Law and the Prophets, the rulers of the synagogue sent to them, saying, "Men *and* brethren, if you have ᵇany word of ¹exhortation for the people, say on."

16Then Paul stood up, and motioning with *his* hand said, "Men of Israel, and ªyou who fear God, listen: 17The God of this people ¹Israel ªchose our fathers, and exalted the people ᵇwhen they dwelt as strangers in the land of Egypt, and with ²an uplifted arm He ᶜbrought them out of it. 18Now ªfor a time of about forty years He put up with their ways in the wilderness. 19And when He had destroyed ªseven nations in the land of Canaan, ᵇHe distributed their land to them by allotment.

20"After that ªHe gave *them* judges for about four hundred and fifty years, ᵇuntil Samuel the prophet. 21ªAnd afterward they asked for a king; so God gave them ᵇSaul the son of Kish, a man of the tribe of Benjamin, for forty years. 22And ªwhen He had removed him, ᵇHe raised up for them David as king, to whom also He gave testimony and said, ᶜ'I have found David the *son* of Jesse, ᵈa man after My *own* heart, who will do all My will.' 23ªFrom this man's seed, according ᵇto *the* promise, God raised up for Israel ᶜa¹ Savior—Jesus— 24ªafter John had first preached, before His coming, the baptism of repentance to all the people of Israel. 25And as John was finishing his course, he said, ª'Who do you think I am? I am not *He*. But behold, ᵇthere comes One after me, the sandals of whose feet I am not worthy to loose.'

26"Men *and* brethren, sons of the ¹family of Abraham, and ªthose among you who fear God, ᵇto you the ²word of this salvation has been sent. 27For those who dwell in Jerusalem, and their rulers, ªbecause they did not know Him, nor even the voices of the Prophets which are read every Sabbath, have fulfilled *them* in condemning *Him*. 28ªAnd though they found no cause for death *in Him,* they asked Pilate that He should be put to death. 29ªNow when they had fulfilled all that was written concerning Him, ᵇthey took *Him* down from the tree and laid *Him* in a tomb. 30ªBut God raised Him from the dead.

13:29 ªLuke 18:31 ᵇMatt. 27:57–61; Mark 15:42–47; Luke 23:50–56; John 19:38–42
13:30 ªPs. 16:10, 11; Hos. 6:2; Matt. 12:39, 40; 28:6

13:15 ¹*encouragement* 13:17 ¹M omits *Israel* ²Mighty power
13:23 ¹M *salvation, after* 13:26 ¹*stock* ²*message*

13:9 ªActs 2:4; 4:8
13:10 ªMatt. 13:38; John 8:44; [1 John 3:8]
13:11 ªEx. 9:3; 1 Sam. 5:6; Job 19:21; Ps. 32:4; Heb. 10:31
13:13 ªActs 15:38
13:14 ªActs 16:13
13:15 ªLuke 4:16 ᵇHeb. 13:22
13:16 ªActs 10:35
13:17 ªEx. 6:1, 6; 13:14, 16; Deut. 7:6–8 ᵇActs 7:17 ᶜEx. 14:8
13:18 ªEx. 16:35; Num. 14:34; Acts 7:36
13:19 ªDeut. 7:1 ᵇJosh. 14:1, 2; 19:51; Ps. 78:55
13:20 ªJudg. 2:16; 1 Sam. 4:18; 7:15 ᵇ1 Sam. 3:20; Acts 3:24
13:21 ª1 Sam. 8:5 ᵇ1 Sam. 10:20–24
13:22 ª1 Sam. 15:23, 26, 28 ᵇ1 Sam. 16:1, 12, 13 ᶜPs. 89:20 ᵈ1 Sam. 13:14
13:23 ªIs. 11:1 ᵇPs. 132:11 ᶜ[Matt. 1:21]
13:24 ªMatt. 3:1; [Luke 3:3]
13:25 ªMatt. 3:11; Mark 1:7; Luke 3:16 ᵇJohn 1:20, 27
13:26 ªPs. 66:16 ᵇMatt. 10:6
13:27 ªLuke 23:34
13:28 ªMatt. 27:22, 23; Mark 15:13, 14; Luke 23:21–23; John 19:15; Acts 3:14; [2 Cor. 5:21; Heb. 4:15]; 1 Pet. 2:22

³¹ᵃHe was seen for many days by those who came up with Him from Galilee to Jerusalem, who are His witnesses to the people. ³²And we declare to you glad tidings—ᵃthat promise which was made to the fathers. ³³God has fulfilled this for us their children, in that He has raised up Jesus. As it is also written in the second Psalm:

ᵃ'You are My Son,
Today I have begotten You.'

³⁴And that He raised Him from the dead, no more to return to ¹corruption, He has spoken thus:

ᵃ'I will give you the sure ²mercies of David.'

³⁵Therefore He also says in another *Psalm*:

ᵃ'You will not allow Your Holy One to see corruption.'

³⁶"For David, after he had served ¹his own generation by the will of God, ᵃfell asleep, was buried with his fathers, and ²saw corruption; ³⁷but He whom God raised up ¹saw no corruption. ³⁸Therefore let it be known to you, brethren, that ᵃthrough this Man is preached to you the forgiveness of sins; ³⁹and ᵃby Him everyone who believes is justified from all things from which you could not be justified by the law of Moses. ⁴⁰Beware therefore, lest what has been spoken in the prophets come upon you:

⁴¹ 'Behold,ᵃ you despisers,
Marvel and perish!
For I work a work in your days,
A work which you will by no means believe,
Though one were to declare it to you.'"

BLESSING AND CONFLICT AT ANTIOCH

⁴²¹So when the Jews went out of the synagogue, the Gentiles begged that these words might be preached to them the next Sabbath. ⁴³Now when the congregation had broken up, many of the Jews and devout proselytes followed Paul and Barnabas, who, speaking to them, ᵃpersuaded them to continue in ᵇthe grace of God.

⁴⁴On the next Sabbath almost the whole city came together to hear the word of God. ⁴⁵But when the Jews saw the multitudes, they were filled with envy; and contradicting and blaspheming, they ᵃopposed the things spoken by Paul. ⁴⁶Then Paul and Barnabas grew bold and said, ᵃ"It was necessary that the word of God should be spoken to you first; but ᵇsince you reject it, and judge yourselves unworthy of everlasting life, behold, ᶜwe turn to the Gentiles. ⁴⁷For so the Lord has commanded us:

ᵃ'I have set you as a light to the Gentiles,
That you should be for salvation to the ends of the earth.'"

⁴⁸Now when the Gentiles heard this, they were glad and glorified the word of the Lord. ᵃAnd as many as had been appointed to eternal life believed.

13:31
ᵃMatt. 28:16;
Acts 1:3, 11;
1 Cor. 15:5–8

13:32
ᵃ[Gen. 3:15]

13:33 ᵃPs. 2:7;
Heb. 1:5

13:34 ᵃIs. 55:3

13:35 ᵃPs. 16:10;
Acts 2:27

13:36 ᵃActs 2:29

13:38 ᵃJer. 31:34

13:39 ᵃ[Is. 53:11;
John 3:16]

13:41 ᵃHab. 1:5

13:43 ᵃActs 11:23
ᵇTitus 2:11;
Heb. 12:15;
1 Pet. 5:12

13:45 ᵃActs 18:6;
1 Pet. 4:4;
Jude 10

13:46
ᵃMatt. 10:6;
Acts 3:26;
Rom. 1:16
ᵇEx. 32:10;
Deut. 32:21;
Is. 55:5;
Matt. 21:43;
Rom. 10:19
ᶜActs 18:6

13:47
ᵃIs. 42:6; 49:6;
Luke 2:32

13:48
ᵃ[Acts 2:47]

13:34 ¹the state of decay ²blessings 13:36 ¹in his ²underwent decay
13:37 ¹underwent no decay 13:42 ¹Or And when they went out of the
synagogue of the Jews; NU And when they went out, they begged

⁴⁹And the word of the Lord was being spread throughout all the region. ⁵⁰But the Jews stirred up the devout and prominent women and the chief men of the city, ᵃraised up persecution against Paul and Barnabas, and expelled them from their region. ⁵¹ᵃBut they shook off the dust from their feet against them, and came to Iconium. ⁵²And the disciples ᵃwere filled with joy and ᵇwith the Holy Spirit.

AT ICONIUM

14 Now it happened in Iconium that they went together to the synagogue of the Jews, and so spoke that a great multitude both of the Jews and of the ᵃGreeks believed. ²But the unbelieving Jews stirred up the Gentiles and ¹poisoned their ²minds against the brethren. ³Therefore they stayed there a long time, speaking boldly in the Lord, ᵃwho was bearing witness to the word of His grace, granting signs and ᵇwonders to be done by their hands. ⁴But the multitude of the city was ᵃdivided: part sided with the Jews, and part with the ᵇapostles. ⁵And when a violent attempt was made by both the Gentiles and Jews, with their rulers, ᵃto abuse and stone them, ⁶they became aware of it and ᵃfled to Lystra and Derbe, cities of Lycaonia, and to the surrounding region. ⁷And they were preaching the gospel there.

IDOLATRY AT LYSTRA

⁸ᵃAnd in Lystra a certain man without strength in his feet was sitting, a cripple from his mother's womb, who had never walked. ⁹*This* man heard Paul speaking. ¹Paul, observing him intently and seeing that he had faith to be healed, ¹⁰said with a loud voice, ᵃ"Stand up straight on your feet!" And he leaped and walked. ¹¹Now when the people saw what Paul had done, they raised their voices, saying in the Lycaonian *language*, ᵃ"The gods have come down to us in the likeness of men!" ¹²And Barnabas they called ¹Zeus, and Paul, ²Hermes, because he was the chief speaker. ¹³Then the priest of Zeus, whose temple was in front of their city, brought oxen and garlands to the gates, ᵃintending to sacrifice with the multitudes.

¹⁴But when the apostles Barnabas and Paul heard this, ᵃthey tore their clothes and ran in among the multitude, crying out ¹⁵and saying, "Men, ᵃwhy are you doing these things? ᵇWe also are men with the same nature as you, and preach to you that you should turn from ᶜthese useless things ᵈto the living God, ᵉwho made the heaven, the earth, the sea, and all things that are in them, ¹⁶ᵃwho in bygone generations allowed all nations to walk in their own ways. ¹⁷ᵃNevertheless He did not leave Himself without witness, in that He did good, ᵇgave us rain from heaven and fruitful seasons, filling our hearts with ᶜfood and gladness." ¹⁸And with these sayings they could scarcely restrain the multitudes from sacrificing to them.

STONING, ESCAPE TO DERBE

¹⁹ᵃThen Jews from Antioch and Iconium came there; and having persuaded the multitudes, ᵇthey stoned Paul *and* dragged *him* out of the city, supposing him to be ᶜdead. ²⁰However, when the disciples gathered around him, he rose up and went into the city. And the next day he departed with Barnabas to Derbe.

14:2 ¹embittered   ²Lit. *souls*   14:9 ¹Lit. *Who*   14:12 ¹Jupiter   ²Mercury

13:50
ᵃActs 7:52;
2 Tim. 3:11

13:51
ᵃMatt. 10:14;
Mark 6:11;
[Luke 9:5]

13:52
ᵃMatt. 5:12;
John 16:22
ᵇActs 2:4; 4:8,
31; 13:9

14:1 ᵃJohn 7:35;
Acts 18:4;
Rom. 1:14, 16;
1 Cor. 1:22

14:3
ᵃMark 16:20;
Acts 4:29;
20:32; Heb. 2:4
ᵇActs 5:12

14:4 ᵃLuke 12:51
ᵇActs 13:2, 3

14:5 ᵃ2 Tim. 3:11

14:6
ᵃMatt. 10:23

14:8 ᵃActs 3:2

14:10 ᵃ[Is. 35:6]

14:11
ᵃActs 8:10; 28:6

14:13 ᵃDan. 2:46

14:14
ᵃNum. 14:6;
Matt. 26:65;
Mark 14:63

14:15
ᵃActs 10:26
ᵇJames 5:17
ᶜ1 Sam. 12:21;
Jer. 8:19; 14:22;
Amos 2:4;
1 Cor. 8:4
ᵈ1 Thess. 1:9
ᵉGen. 1:1;
Ex. 20:11;
Ps. 146:6;
Acts 4:24; 17:24;
Rev. 14:7

14:16 ᵃPs. 81:12;
Mic. 4:5;
1 Pet. 4:3

14:17
ᵃActs 17:24–27;
Rom. 1:19, 20
ᵇLev. 26:4;
Deut. 11:14;
[Matt. 5:45]
ᶜPs. 145:16

14:19
ᵃActs 13:45, 50;
14:2–5;
1 Thess. 2:14
ᵇActs 14:5;
2 Cor. 11:25;
2 Tim. 3:11
ᶜ[2 Cor. 12:1–4]

STRENGTHENING THE CONVERTS

14:21
a Matt. 28:19

14:22 a Acts 11:23
b Matt. 10:38;
Luke 22:28;
[Rom. 8:17;
2 Tim. 2:12;
3:12]

14:23
a Matt. 9:15;
Mark 2:20;
Luke 5:35;
2 Cor. 8:19;
Titus 1:5

14:27
a Acts 15:4, 12
b 1 Cor. 16:9;
2 Cor. 2:12;
Col. 4:3; Rev. 3:8

15:1 a Gal. 2:12
b John 7:22;
Acts 15:5;
Gal. 5:2;
Phil. 3:2;
[Col. 2:8, 11, 16]

15:2 a Gal. 2:1

15:3
a Acts 20:38;
21:5; Rom. 15:24;
1 Cor. 16:6, 11;
2 Cor. 1:16;
Titus 3:13;
3 John 6
b Acts 14:27;
15:4, 12

15:7 a Acts 10:20

15:8 a 1 Chr. 28:9;
Acts 1:24
b Acts 2:4;
10:44, 47

15:9 a Rom. 10:12
b Acts 10:15, 28

15:10
a Matt. 23:4;
Gal. 5:1

15:11
a Rom. 3:4; 5:15;
2 Cor. 13:14;
[Eph. 2:5–8;
Titus 2:11]

15:12
a Acts 14:27;
15:3, 4

15:13 a Acts 12:17

15:14 a Acts 15:7;
2 Pet. 1:1

21And when they had preached the gospel to that city a and made many disciples, they returned to Lystra, Iconium, and Antioch, 22strengthening the souls of the disciples, a exhorting *them* to continue in the faith, and *saying*, b "We must through many tribulations enter the kingdom of God." 23So when they had a appointed elders in every church, and prayed with fasting, they commended them to the Lord in whom they had believed. 24And after they had passed through Pisidia, they came to Pamphylia. 25Now when they had preached the word in Perga, they went down to Attalia. 26From there they sailed to Antioch, where they had been commended to the grace of God for the work which they had completed.

27Now when they had come and gathered the church together, a they reported all that God had done with them, and that He had b opened the door of faith to the Gentiles. 28So they stayed there a long time with the disciples.

CONFLICT OVER CIRCUMCISION

15 And a certain *men* came down from Judea and taught the brethren, b "Unless you are circumcised according to the custom of Moses, you cannot be saved." 2Therefore, when Paul and Barnabas had no small dissension and dispute with them, they determined that a Paul and Barnabas and certain others of them should go up to Jerusalem, to the apostles and elders, about this question.

3So, a being sent on their way by the church, they passed through Phoenicia and Samaria, b describing the conversion of the Gentiles; and they caused great joy to all the brethren. 4And when they had come to Jerusalem, they were received by the church and the apostles and the elders; and they reported all things that God had done with them. 5But some of the sect of the Pharisees who believed rose up, saying, "It is necessary to circumcise them, and to command *them* to keep the law of Moses."

THE JERUSALEM COUNCIL

6Now the apostles and elders came together to consider this matter. 7And when there had been much dispute, Peter rose up *and* said to them: a "Men *and* brethren, you know that a good while ago God chose among us, that by my mouth the Gentiles should hear the word of the gospel and believe. 8So God, a who knows the heart, 1acknowledged them by b giving them the Holy Spirit, just as *He did* to us, 9a and made no distinction between us and them, b purifying their hearts by faith. 10Now therefore, why do you test God a by putting a yoke on the neck of the disciples which neither our fathers nor we were able to bear? 11But a we believe that through the grace of the Lord Jesus 1Christ we shall be saved in the same manner as they."

12Then all the multitude kept silent and listened to Barnabas and Paul declaring how many miracles and wonders God had a worked through them among the Gentiles. 13And after they had 1become silent, a James answered, saying, "Men *and* brethren, listen to me: 14a Simon has declared how God at the first visited the Gentiles to take out of them a people for

---

15:8 1bore witness to   15:11 1NU, M omit *Christ*   15:13 1stopped speaking

His name. ¹⁵And with this the words of the prophets agree, just as it is written:

16 'After[a] this I will return
   And will rebuild the tabernacle of David, which has fallen down;
   I will rebuild its ruins,
   And I will set it up;
17 So that the rest of mankind may seek the LORD,
   Even all the Gentiles who are called by My name,
   Says the ¹LORD who does all these things.'

¹⁸¹"Known to God from eternity are all His works. ¹⁹Therefore [a]I judge that we should not trouble those from among the Gentiles who [b]are turning to God, ²⁰but that we [a]write to them to abstain [b]from things polluted by idols, [c]from ¹sexual immorality, [d]from things strangled, and from blood. ²¹For Moses has had throughout many generations those who preach him in every city, [a]being read in the synagogues every Sabbath."

THE JERUSALEM DECREE

²²Then it pleased the apostles and elders, with the whole church, to send chosen men of their own company to Antioch with Paul and Barnabas, namely, Judas who was also named [a]Barsabas,¹ and Silas, leading men among the brethren. ²³They wrote this letter by them:

The apostles, the elders, and the brethren,

To the brethren who are of the Gentiles in Antioch, Syria, and Cilicia:

Greetings.

24 Since we have heard that [a]some who went out from us have troubled you with words, [b]unsettling your souls, ¹saying, "You must be circumcised and keep the law"—to whom we gave no such commandment— ²⁵it seemed good to us, being assembled with one ¹accord, to send chosen men to you with our beloved Barnabas and Paul, ²⁶[a]men who have risked their lives for the name of our Lord Jesus Christ. ²⁷We have therefore sent Judas and Silas, who will also report the same things by word of mouth. ²⁸For it seemed good to the Holy Spirit, and to us, to lay upon you no greater burden than these necessary things: ²⁹[a]that you abstain from things offered to idols, [b]from blood, from things strangled, and from [c]sexual¹ immorality. If you keep yourselves from these, you will do well.

Farewell.

CONTINUING MINISTRY IN SYRIA

³⁰So when they were sent off, they came to Antioch; and when they had gathered the multitude together, they delivered the letter. ³¹When they had read it, they rejoiced over

15:16
[a]Amos 9:11, 12

15:19
[a]Acts 15:28;
21:25
[b]1 Thess. 1:9

15:20
[a]Acts 21:25
[b]Gen. 35:2;
Ex. 20:3, 23;
Ezek. 20:30;
[1 Cor. 8:1;
10:20, 28];
Rev. 2:14
[c][1 Cor. 6:9];
Gal. 5:19;
Eph. 5:3;
Col. 3:5;
1 Thess. 4:3;
1 Pet. 4:3
[d]Gen. 9:4;
Lev. 3:17;
Deut. 12:16;
1 Sam. 14:33

15:21
[a]Acts 13:15, 27;
2 Cor. 3:14

15:22 [a]Acts 1:23

15:24 [a]Acts 15:1;
Gal. 2:4; 5:12;
Titus 1:10, 11
[b]Gal. 1:7; 5:10

15:26
[a]Acts 13:50;
14:19;
1 Cor. 15:30;
2 Cor. 11:23–26

15:29
[a]Acts 15:20;
21:25;
Rev. 2:14, 20
[b]Lev. 17:14
[c]1 Cor. 5:11; 6:18;
7:2; Col. 3:5;
1 Thess. 4:3

15:17 ¹NU LORD, who makes these things   15:18 ¹NU (continuing v. 17) known from eternity (of old).'   15:20 ¹Or fornication   15:22 ¹NU, M Barsabbas
15:24 ¹NU omits saying, "You must be circumcised and keep the law"
15:25 ¹purpose or mind   15:29 ¹Or fornication

its encouragement. [32]Now Judas and Silas, themselves being [a]prophets also, [b]exhorted and strengthened the brethren with many words. [33]And after they had stayed *there* for a time, they were [a]sent back with greetings from the brethren to [1]the apostles.

[34][1]However, it seemed good to Silas to remain there. [35a]Paul and Barnabas also remained in Antioch, teaching and preaching the word of the Lord, with many others also.

DIVISION OVER JOHN MARK

[36]Then after some days Paul said to Barnabas, "Let us now go back and visit our brethren in every city where we have preached the word of the Lord, *and see* how they are doing." [37]Now Barnabas [1]was determined to take with them [a]John called Mark. [38]But Paul insisted that they should not take with them [a]the one who had departed from them in Pamphylia, and had not gone with them to the work. [39]Then the contention became so sharp that they parted from one another. And so Barnabas took Mark and sailed to [a]Cyprus; [40]but Paul chose Silas and departed, [a]being [1]commended by the brethren to the grace of God. [41]And he went through Syria and Cilicia, [a]strengthening the churches.

TIMOTHY JOINS PAUL AND SILAS

16 Then he came to [a]Derbe and Lystra. And behold, a certain disciple was there, [b]named Timothy, [c]*the* son of a certain Jewish woman who believed, but his father *was* Greek. [2]He was well spoken of by the brethren who were at Lystra and Iconium. [3]Paul wanted to have him go on with him. And he [a]took *him* and circumcised him because of the Jews who were in that region, for they all knew that his father was Greek. [4]And as they went through the cities, they delivered to them the [a]decrees to keep, [b]which were determined by the apostles and elders at Jerusalem. [5a]So the churches were strengthened in the faith, and increased in number daily.

THE MACEDONIAN CALL

[6]Now when they had gone through Phrygia and the region of [a]Galatia, they were forbidden by the Holy Spirit to preach the word in [1]Asia. [7]After they had come to Mysia, they tried to go into Bithynia, but the [1]Spirit did not permit them. [8]So passing by Mysia, they [a]came down to Troas. [9]And a vision appeared to Paul in the night. A [a]man of Macedonia stood and pleaded with him, saying, "Come over to Macedonia and help us." [10]Now after he had seen the vision, immediately we sought to go [a]to Macedonia, concluding that the Lord had called us to preach the gospel to them.

LYDIA BAPTIZED AT PHILIPPI

[11]Therefore, sailing from Troas, we ran a straight course to Samothrace, and the next *day* came to Neapolis, [12]and from there to [a]Philippi, which is the [1]foremost city of that part of Macedonia, a colony. And we were staying in that city for some days. [13]And on the Sabbath day we went out of the city to the riverside, where prayer was customarily made; and we

Cross references (margin)

15:32 [a]Acts 11:27; 1 Cor. 12:28; Eph. 4:11; Rev. 18:20 [b]Acts 14:22; 18:23

15:33 [a]Mark 5:34; Acts 16:36; 1 Cor. 16:11; Heb. 11:31

15:35 [a]Acts 13:1

15:37 [a]Acts 12:12, 25; Col. 4:10; 2 Tim. 4:11; Philem. 24

15:38 [a]Acts 13:13

15:39 [a]Acts 4:36; 13:4

15:40 [a]Acts 11:23; 14:26

15:41 [a]Acts 15:5

16:1 [a]Acts 14:6 [b]Acts 19:22; Rom. 16:21; 1 Cor. 4:17; 16:10; Phil. 1:1; 2:19; 1 Thess. 3:2; 2 Tim. 1:2 [c]2 Tim. 1:5; 3:15

16:3 [a][1 Cor. 9:20; Gal. 2:3; 5:2]

16:4 [a]Acts 15:19–21 [b]Acts 15:28, 29

16:5 [a]Acts 2:47; 15:41

16:6 [a]Acts 18:23; Gal. 1:1, 2

16:8 [a]Acts 16:11; 20:5; 2 Cor. 2:12; 2 Tim. 4:13

16:9 [a]Acts 10:30

16:10 [a]2 Cor. 2:13

16:12 [a]Acts 20:6; Phil. 1:1; 1 Thess. 2:2

15:33 [1]NU *those who had sent them*   15:34 [1]NU, M omit v. 34.
15:37 [1]*resolved*   15:40 [1]*committed*   16:6 [1]The Roman province of Asia
16:7 [1]NU adds *of Jesus*   16:12 [1]Lit. *first*

sat down and spoke to the women who met *there*. [14]Now a certain woman named Lydia heard *us*. She was a seller of purple from the city of [a]Thyatira, who worshiped God. [b]The Lord opened her heart to heed the things spoken by Paul. [15]And when she and her household were baptized, she begged *us*, saying, "If you have judged me to be faithful to the Lord, come to my house and stay." So [a]she persuaded us.

PAUL AND SILAS IMPRISONED

[16]Now it happened, as we went to prayer, that a certain slave girl [a]possessed with a spirit of divination met us, who brought her masters [b]much profit by fortune-telling. [17]This girl followed Paul and us, and cried out, saying, "These men are the servants of the Most High God, who proclaim to us the way of salvation." [18]And this she did for many days.

But Paul, [a]greatly [1]annoyed, turned and said to the spirit, "I command you in the name of Jesus Christ to come out of her." [b]And he came out that very hour. [19]But [a]when her masters saw that their hope of profit was gone, they seized Paul and Silas and [b]dragged *them* into the marketplace to the authorities.

[20]And they brought them to the magistrates, and said, "These men, being Jews, [a]exceedingly trouble our city; [21]and they teach customs which are not lawful for us, being Romans, to receive or observe." [22]Then the multitude rose up together against them; and the magistrates tore off their clothes [a]and commanded *them* to be beaten with rods. [23]And when they had laid many stripes on them, they threw *them* into prison, commanding the jailer to keep them securely. [24]Having received such a charge, he put them into the inner prison and fastened their feet in the stocks.

THE PHILIPPIAN JAILER SAVED

[25]But at midnight Paul and Silas were praying and singing hymns to God, and the prisoners were listening to them. [26a]Suddenly there was a great earthquake, so that the foundations of the prison were shaken; and immediately [b]all the doors were opened and everyone's chains were loosed. [27]And the keeper of the prison, awaking from sleep and seeing the prison doors open, supposing the prisoners had fled, drew his sword and was about to kill himself. [28]But Paul called with a loud voice, saying, "Do yourself no harm, for we are all here."

[29]Then he called for a light, ran in, and fell down trembling before Paul and Silas. [30]And he brought them out and said, [a]"Sirs, what must I do to be saved?"

[31]So they said, [a]"Believe on the Lord Jesus Christ, and you will be saved, you and your household." [32]Then they spoke the word of the Lord to him and to all who were in his house. [33]And he took them the same hour of the night and washed *their* stripes. And immediately he and all his *family* were baptized. [34]Now when he had brought them into his house, [a]he set food before them; and he rejoiced, having believed in God with all his household.

PAUL REFUSES TO DEPART SECRETLY

[35]And when it was day, the magistrates sent the [1]officers, saying, "Let those men go."

16:14 [a]Rev. 1:11; 2:18, 24 [b]Luke 24:45

16:15 [a]Gen. 19:3; 33:11; Judg. 19:21; Luke 24:29; [Heb. 13:2]

16:16 [a]Lev. 19:31; 20:6, 27; Deut. 18:11; 1 Sam. 28:3, 7; 2 Kin. 21:6; 1 Chr. 10:13; Is. 8:19 [b]Acts 19:24

16:18 [a]Mark 1:25, 34 [b]Mark 16:17

16:19 [a]Acts 16:16; 19:25, 26 [b]Matt. 10:18

16:20 [a]1 Kin. 18:17; Acts 17:8

16:22 [a]2 Cor. 6:5; 11:23, 25; 1 Thess. 2:2

16:26 [a]Acts 4:31 [b]Acts 5:19; 12:7, 10

16:30 [a]Luke 3:10; Acts 2:37; 9:6; 22:10

16:31 [a][John 3:16, 36; 6:47; Acts 13:38, 39; Rom. 10:9–11; 1 John 5:10]

16:34 [a]Matt. 5:4; Luke 5:29; 19:6

16:18 [1]distressed   16:35 [1]lictors, lit. *rod bearers*

36So the keeper of the prison reported these words to Paul, saying, "The magistrates have sent to let you go. Now therefore depart, and go in peace."

37But Paul said to them, "They have beaten us openly, uncondemned aRomans, *and* have thrown *us* into prison. And now do they put us out secretly? No indeed! Let them come themselves and get us out."

38And the officers told these words to the magistrates, and they were afraid when they heard that they were Romans. 39Then they came and pleaded with them and brought *them* out, and aasked *them* to depart from the city. 40So they went out of the prison aand entered *the house of* Lydia; and when they had seen the brethren, they encouraged them and departed.

PREACHING CHRIST AT THESSALONICA

17 Now when they had passed through Amphipolis and Apollonia, they came to aThessalonica, where there was a synagogue of the Jews. 2Then Paul, as his custom was, awent in to them, and for three Sabbaths breasoned with them from the Scriptures, 3explaining and demonstrating athat the Christ had to suffer and rise again from the dead, and *saying,* "This Jesus whom I preach to you is the Christ." 4aAnd some of them were persuaded; and a great multitude of the devout Greeks, and not a few of the leading women, joined Paul and bSilas.

ASSAULT ON JASON'S HOUSE

5But the Jews 1who were not persuaded, 2becoming aenvious, took some of the evil men from the marketplace, and gathering a mob, set all the city in an uproar and attacked the house of bJason, and sought to bring them out to the people. 6But when they did not find them, they dragged Jason and some brethren to the rulers of the city, crying out, a"These who have turned the world upside down have come here too. 7Jason has 1harbored them, and these are all acting contrary to the decrees of Caesar, asaying there is another king— Jesus." 8And they troubled the crowd and the rulers of the city when they heard these things. 9So when they had taken security from Jason and the rest, they let them go.

MINISTERING AT BEREA

10Then athe brethren immediately sent Paul and Silas away by night to Berea. When they arrived, they went into the synagogue of the Jews. 11These were more 1fair-minded than those in Thessalonica, in that they received the word with all readiness, and asearched the Scriptures daily *to find out* whether these things were so. 12Therefore many of them believed, and also not a few of the Greeks, prominent women as well as men. 13But when the Jews from Thessalonica learned that the word of God was preached by Paul at Berea, they came there also and stirred up the crowds. 14aThen immediately the brethren sent Paul away, to go to the sea; but both Silas and Timothy remained there. 15So those who conducted Paul brought him to Athens; and areceiving a command for Silas and Timothy to come to him with all speed, they departed.

16:37
aActs 22:25–29

16:39
aMatt. 8:34

16:40
aActs 16:14

17:1
aActs 17:11, 13;
20:4; 27:2;
Phil. 4:16;
1 Thess. 1:1;
2 Thess. 1:1;
2 Tim. 4:10

17:2 aLuke 4:16;
Acts 9:20;
13:5, 14; 14:1;
16:13; 19:8
b1 Thess. 2:1–16

17:3
aLuke 24:26, 46;
Acts 18:5, 28;
Gal. 3:1

17:4 aActs 28:24
bActs 15:22, 27,
32, 40

17:5 aActs 13:45
bActs 17:6, 7, 9;
Rom. 16:21

17:6
a[Acts 16:20]

17:7 aLuke 23:2;
John 19:12;
1 Pet. 2:13

17:10 aActs 9:25;
17:14

17:11 aIs. 34:16;
Luke 16:29;
John 5:39

17:14
aMatt. 10:23

17:15 aActs 18:5

17:5 1NU omits *who were not persuaded*   2M omits *becoming envious*
17:7 1*welcomed*   17:11 1Lit. *noble*

THE PHILOSOPHERS AT ATHENS

16Now while Paul waited for them at Athens, [a]his spirit was provoked within him when he saw that the city was [1]given over to idols. 17Therefore he reasoned in the synagogue with the Jews and with the *Gentile* worshipers, and in the marketplace daily with those who happened to be there. 18[1]Then certain Epicurean and Stoic philosophers encountered him. And some said, "What does this [2]babbler want to say?"

Others said, "He seems to be a proclaimer of foreign gods," because he preached to them [a]Jesus and the resurrection.

19And they took him and brought him to the [1]Areopagus, saying, "May we know what this new doctrine *is* of which you speak? 20For you are bringing some strange things to our ears. Therefore we want to know what these things mean." 21For all the Athenians and the foreigners who were there spent their time in nothing else but either to tell or to hear some new thing.

ADDRESSING THE AREOPAGUS

22Then Paul stood in the midst of the [1]Areopagus and said, "Men of Athens, I perceive that in all things you are very religious; 23for as I was passing through and considering the objects of your worship, I even found an altar with this inscription:

TO THE UNKNOWN GOD.

Therefore, the One whom you worship without knowing, Him I proclaim to you: 24[a]God, who made the world and everything in it, since He is [b]Lord of heaven and earth, [c]does not dwell in temples made with hands. 25Nor is He worshiped with men's hands, as though He needed anything, since He [a]gives to all life, breath, and all things. 26And He has made from one [1]blood every nation of men to dwell on all the face of the earth, and has determined their preappointed times and [a]the boundaries of their dwellings, 27[a]so that they should seek the Lord, in the hope that they might grope for Him and find Him, [b]though He is not far from each one of us; 28for [a]in Him we live and move and have our being, [b]as also some of your own poets have said, 'For we are also His offspring.' 29Therefore, since we are the offspring of God, [a]we ought not to think that the Divine Nature is like gold or silver or stone, something shaped by art and man's devising. 30Truly, [a]these times of ignorance God overlooked, but [b]now commands all men everywhere to repent, 31because He has appointed a day on which [a]He will judge the world in righteousness by the Man whom He has ordained. He has given assurance of this to all by [b]raising Him from the dead."

32And when they heard of the resurrection of the dead, some mocked, while others said, "We will hear you again on this *matter.*" 33So Paul departed from among them. 34However, some men joined him and believed, among them Dionysius the Areopagite, a woman named Damaris, and others with them.

17:16 [a]2 Pet. 2:8

17:18 [a]1 Cor. 15:12

17:24 [a]Is. 42:5;
Acts 14:15
[b]Deut. 10:14;
Ps. 115:16;
Matt. 11:25
[c]1 Kin. 8:27;
Acts 7:48–50

17:25 [a]Gen. 2:7;
Is. 42:5;
Dan. 5:23

17:26
[a]Deut. 32:8;
Job 12:23;
Dan. 4:35

17:27
[a][Rom. 1:20]
[b]Deut. 4:7;
Ps. 139:7, 10;
Jer. 23:23, 24;
[Acts 14:17]

17:28 [a][Col. 1:17;
Heb. 1:3]
[b]Titus 1:12

17:29
[a]Ps. 115:4–7;
Is. 40:18, 19;
Rom. 1:23

17:30
[a]Acts 14:16;
[Rom. 3:25]
[b]Luke 24:47;
Acts 26:20;
[Titus 2:11, 12];
1 Pet. 1:14; 4:3

17:31 [a]Ps. 9:8;
96:13; 98:9;
John 5:22, 27;
Acts 10:42;
Rom. 2:16
[b]Acts 2:24

17:16 [1]*full of idols*   17:18 [1]NU, M add *also*   [2]Lit. *seed picker,* an idler who makes a living picking up scraps   17:19 [1]Lit. *Hill of Ares,* or *Mars' Hill*   17:22 [1]Lit. *Hill of Ares,* or *Mars' Hill*   17:26 [1]NU omits *blood*

MINISTERING AT CORINTH

18 After these things Paul departed from Athens and went to Corinth. ²And he found a certain Jew named ᵃAquila, born in Pontus, who had recently come from Italy with his wife Priscilla (because Claudius had commanded all the Jews to depart from Rome); and he came to them. ³So, because he was of the same trade, he stayed with them ᵃand worked; for by occupation they were tentmakers. ⁴ᵃAnd he reasoned in the synagogue every Sabbath, and persuaded both Jews and Greeks.

⁵ᵃWhen Silas and Timothy had come from Macedonia, Paul was ᵇcompelled ¹by the Spirit, and testified to the Jews *that* Jesus *is* the Christ. ⁶But ᵃwhen they opposed him and blasphemed, ᵇhe shook *his* garments and said to them, ᶜ"Your blood *be* upon your *own* heads; ᵈI *am* clean. ᵉFrom now on I will go to the Gentiles." ⁷And he departed from there and entered the house of a certain *man* named ¹Justus, *one* who worshiped God, whose house was next door to the synagogue. ⁸ᵃThen Crispus, the ruler of the synagogue, believed on the Lord with all his household. And many of the Corinthians, hearing, believed and were baptized.

⁹Now ᵃthe Lord spoke to Paul in the night by a vision, "Do not be afraid, but speak, and do not keep silent; ¹⁰ᵃfor I am with you, and no one will attack you to hurt you; for I have many people in this city." ¹¹And he continued *there* a year and six months, teaching the word of God among them.

¹²When Gallio was proconsul of Achaia, the Jews with one accord rose up against Paul and brought him to the ¹judgment seat, ¹³saying, "This *fellow* persuades men to worship God contrary to the law."

¹⁴And when Paul was about to open *his* mouth, Gallio said to the Jews, "If it were a matter of wrongdoing or wicked crimes, O Jews, there would be reason why I should bear with you. ¹⁵But if it is a ᵃquestion of words and names and your own law, look *to it* yourselves; for I do not want to be a judge of such *matters*." ¹⁶And he drove them from the judgment seat. ¹⁷Then ¹all the Greeks took ᵃSosthenes, the ruler of the synagogue, and beat *him* before the judgment seat. But Gallio took no notice of these things.

PAUL RETURNS TO ANTIOCH

¹⁸So Paul still remained ¹a good while. Then he took leave of the brethren and sailed for Syria, and Priscilla and Aquila *were* with him. ᵃHe had *his* hair cut off at ᵇCenchrea, for he had taken a vow. ¹⁹And he came to Ephesus, and left them there; but he himself entered the synagogue and reasoned with the Jews. ²⁰When they asked *him* to stay a longer time with them, he did not consent, ²¹but took leave of them, saying, ᵃ"I¹ must by all means keep this coming feast in Jerusalem; but I will return again to you, ᵇGod willing." And he sailed from Ephesus.

²²And when he had landed at ᵃCaesarea, and ¹gone up and greeted the church, he went down to Antioch. ²³After he had spent some time *there*, he departed and went over the region of ᵃGalatia and Phrygia ¹in order, ᵇstrengthening all the disciples.

18:2 ᵃRom. 16:3;
1 Cor. 16:19;
2 Tim. 4:19

18:3
ᵃActs 20:34;
1 Cor. 4:12; 9:14;
2 Cor. 11:7; 12:13;
1 Thess. 2:9; 4:11;
2 Thess. 3:8

18:4 ᵃActs 17:2

18:5
ᵃActs 17:14, 15
ᵇActs 18:28

18:6 ᵃActs 13:45;
ᵇNeh. 5:13;
Matt. 10:14;
Acts 13:51
ᶜLev. 20:9, 11, 12;
2 Sam. 1:16;
1 Kin. 2:33;
Ezek. 18:13;
33:4, 6, 8;
Matt. 27:25;
Acts 20:26
ᵈ[Ezek. 3:18, 19]
ᵉActs 13:46–48;
28:28

18:8 ᵃ1 Cor. 1:14

18:9 ᵃActs 23:11

18:10
ᵃJer. 1:18, 19

18:15
ᵃActs 23:29;
25:19

18:17 ᵃ1 Cor. 1:1

18:18
ᵃNum. 6:2, 5,
9, 18;
Acts 21:24
ᵇRom. 16:1

18:21
ᵃActs 19:21;
20:16
ᵇ1 Cor. 4:19;
Heb. 6:3;
James 4:15

18:22
ᵃActs 8:40

18:23 ᵃGal. 1:2
ᵇActs 14:22;
15:32, 41

18:5 ¹Or *in his spirit* or *in the Spirit*   **18:7** ¹NU *Titius Justus*   **18:12** ¹Gr. *bema*
18:17 ¹NU *they all*   **18:18** ¹Lit. *many days*   **18:21** ¹NU omits *I must by all means keep this coming feast in Jerusalem*   **18:22** ¹To Jerusalem
18:23 ¹*successively*

MINISTRY OF APOLLOS

24aNow a certain Jew named Apollos, born at Alexandria, an eloquent man *and* mighty in the Scriptures, came to Ephesus. 25This man had been instructed in the way of the Lord; and being afervent in spirit, he spoke and taught accurately the things of the Lord, bthough he knew only the baptism of John. 26So he began to speak boldly in the synagogue. When Aquila and Priscilla heard him, they took him aside and explained to him the way of God more accurately. 27And when he desired to cross to Achaia, the brethren wrote, exhorting the disciples to receive him; and when he arrived, ahe greatly helped those who had believed through grace; 28for he vigorously refuted the Jews publicly, ashowing from the Scriptures that Jesus is the Christ.

PAUL AT EPHESUS

19 And it happened, while aApollos was at Corinth, that Paul, having passed through bthe upper regions, came to Ephesus. And finding some disciples 2he said to them, "Did you receive the Holy Spirit when you believed?"

So they said to him, a"We have not so much as heard whether there is a Holy Spirit."

3And he said to them, "Into what then were you baptized?"

So they said, a"Into John's baptism."

4Then Paul said, a"John indeed baptized with a baptism of repentance, saying to the people that they should believe on Him who would come after him, that is, on Christ Jesus."

5When they heard *this,* they were baptized ain the name of the Lord Jesus. 6And when Paul had alaid hands on them, the Holy Spirit came upon them, and bthey spoke with tongues and prophesied. 7Now the men were about twelve in all.

8aAnd he went into the synagogue and spoke boldly for three months, reasoning and persuading bconcerning the things of the kingdom of God. 9But awhen some were hardened and did not believe, but spoke evil bof the Way before the multitude, he departed from them and withdrew the disciples, reasoning daily in the school of Tyrannus. 10And athis continued for two years, so that all who dwelt in Asia heard the word of the Lord Jesus, both Jews and Greeks.

MIRACLES GLORIFY CHRIST

11Now aGod worked unusual miracles by the hands of Paul, 12aso that even handkerchiefs or aprons were brought from his body to the sick, and the diseases left them and the evil spirits went out of them. 13aThen some of the itinerant Jewish exorcists btook it upon themselves to call the name of the Lord Jesus over those who had evil spirits, saying, 1"We 2exorcise you by the Jesus whom Paul cpreaches." 14Also there were seven sons of Sceva, a Jewish chief priest, who did so.

15And the evil spirit answered and said, "Jesus I know, and Paul I know; but who are you?"

16Then the man in whom the evil spirit was leaped on them, 1overpowered them, and prevailed against 2them, so that they fled out of that house naked and wounded. 17This became known both to all Jews and Greeks dwelling in Ephesus;

18:24
aActs 19:1;
1 Cor. 1:12; 3:4;
16:12; Titus 3:13

18:25
aRom. 12:11
b[Matt. 3:1–11;
Mark 1:7, 8;
Luke 3:16, 17;
7:29; John 1:26,
33]; Acts 19:3

18:27 a1 Cor. 3:6

18:28
aActs 9:22; 17:3;
18:5

19:1
a1 Cor. 1:12;
3:5, 6;
Titus 3:13
bActs 18:23

19:2 a1 Sam. 3:7;
Acts 8:16

19:3 aLuke 7:29;
Acts 18:25

19:4 aMatt. 3:11;
Mark 1:4, 7, 8;
Luke 3:16;
[John 1:15, 26,
27]; Acts 13:24

19:5
aMatt. 28:19;
Acts 8:12, 16;
10:48

19:6
aActs 6:6; 8:17
bMark 16:17;
Acts 2:4; 10:46

19:8
aActs 17:2; 18:4
bActs 1:3; 28:23

19:9 a2 Tim. 1:15;
2 Pet. 2:2;
Jude 10
bActs 9:2; 19:23;
22:4; 24:14

19:10
aActs 19:8;
20:31

19:11
aMark 16:20;
Acts 14:3

19:12
a2 Kin. 4:29;
Acts 5:15

19:13
aMatt. 12:27;
Luke 11:19
bMark 9:38;
Luke 9:49
c1 Cor. 1:23; 2:2

19:13 1NU I 2*adjure,* solemnly command 19:16 1M *and they overpowered them* 2NU *both of them*

and [a]fear fell on them all, and the name of the Lord Jesus was magnified. [18]And many who had believed came [a]confessing and telling their deeds. [19]Also, many of those who had practiced magic brought their books together and burned *them* in the sight of all. And they counted up the value of them, and *it* totaled fifty thousand *pieces* of silver. [20a]So the word of the Lord grew mightily and prevailed.

THE RIOT AT EPHESUS

[21a]When these things were accomplished, Paul [b]purposed in the Spirit, when he had passed through [c]Macedonia and Achaia, to go to Jerusalem, saying, "After I have been there, [d]I must also see Rome." [22]So he sent into Macedonia two of those who ministered to him, [a]Timothy and [b]Erastus, but he himself stayed in Asia for a time.

[23]And [a]about that time there arose a great commotion about [b]the Way. [24]For a certain man named Demetrius, a silversmith, who made silver shrines of [1]Diana, brought [a]no small profit to the craftsmen. [25]He called them together with the workers of similar occupation, and said: "Men, you know that we have our prosperity by this trade. [26]Moreover you see and hear that not only at Ephesus, but throughout almost all Asia, this Paul has persuaded and turned away many people, saying that [a]they are not gods which are made with hands. [27]So not only is this trade of ours in danger of falling into disrepute, but also the temple of the great goddess Diana may be despised and [1]her magnificence destroyed, whom all Asia and the world worship."

[28]Now when they heard *this,* they were full of wrath and cried out, saying, "Great *is* Diana of the Ephesians!" [29]So the whole city was filled with confusion, and rushed into the theater with one accord, having seized [a]Gaius and [b]Aristarchus, Macedonians, Paul's travel companions. [30]And when Paul wanted to go in to the people, the disciples would not allow him. [31]Then some of the [1]officials of Asia, who were his friends, sent to him pleading that he would not venture into the theater. [32]Some therefore cried one thing and some another, for the assembly was confused, and most of them did not know why they had come together. [33]And they drew Alexander out of the multitude, the Jews putting him forward. And [a]Alexander [b]motioned with his hand, and wanted to make his defense to the people. [34]But when they found out that he was a Jew, all with one voice cried out for about two hours, "Great *is* Diana of the Ephesians!"

[35]And when the city clerk had quieted the crowd, he said: "Men of Ephesus, what man is there who does not know that the city of the Ephesians is temple guardian of the great goddess [1]Diana, and of the *image* which fell down from [2]Zeus? [36]Therefore, since these things cannot be denied, you ought to be quiet and do nothing rashly. [37]For you have brought these men here who are neither robbers of temples nor blasphemers of [1]your goddess. [38]Therefore, if Demetrius and his fellow craftsmen have a [1]case against anyone, the courts are open and there are proconsuls. Let them bring charges

Cross-references (margin)

19:17
[a]Luke 1:65; 7:16;
Acts 2:43; 5:5, 11

19:18 [a]Matt. 3:6

19:20
[a]Acts 6:7; 12:24

19:21
[a]Rom. 15:25;
Gal. 2:1
[b]Acts 20:22;
2 Cor. 1:16
[c]Acts 20:1;
1 Cor. 16:5
[d]Acts 18:21; 23:11;
Rom. 1:13;
15:22–29

19:22 [a]1 Tim. 1:2
[b]Rom. 16:23;
2 Tim. 4:20

19:23 [a]2 Cor. 1:8
[b]Acts 9:2

19:24
[a]Acts 16:16, 19

19:26
[a]Deut. 4:28;
Ps. 115:4;
Is. 44:10–20;
Jer. 10:3;
Acts 17:29;
1 Cor. 8:4; 10:19;
Rev. 9:20

19:29
[a]Acts 20:4;
Rom. 16:23;
1 Cor. 1:14;
3 John 1
[b]Acts 20:4; 27:2;
Col. 4:10;
Philem. 24

19:33
[a]1 Tim. 1:20;
2 Tim. 4:14
[b]Acts 12:17

Footnotes

19:24 [1]Gr. Artemis   19:27 [1]NU *she be deposed from her magnificence*
19:31 [1]*Asiarchs, rulers of Asia,* the province   19:35 [1]Gr. *Artemis*   [2]*heaven*
19:37 [1]NU *our*   19:38 [1]Lit. *matter*

against one another. ³⁹But if you have any other inquiry to make, it shall be determined in the lawful assembly. ⁴⁰For we are in danger of being ¹called in question for today's uproar, there being no reason which we may give to account for this disorderly gathering." ⁴¹And when he had said these things, he dismissed the assembly.

JOURNEYS IN GREECE

20 After the uproar had ceased, Paul called the disciples to *himself,* embraced *them,* and ªdeparted to go to Macedonia. ²Now when he had gone over that region and encouraged them with many words, he came to ªGreece ³and stayed three months. And ªwhen the Jews plotted against him as he was about to sail to Syria, he decided to return through Macedonia. ⁴And Sopater of Berea accompanied him to Asia—also ªAristarchus and Secundus of the Thessalonians, and ᵇGaius of Derbe, and ᶜTimothy, and ᵈTychicus and ᵉTrophimus of Asia. ⁵These men, going ahead, waited for us at ªTroas. ⁶But we sailed away from Philippi after ªthe Days of Unleavened Bread, and in five days joined them ᵇat Troas, where we stayed seven days.

MINISTERING AT TROAS

⁷Now on ªthe first *day* of the week, when the disciples came together ᵇto break bread, Paul, ready to depart the next day, spoke to them and continued his message until midnight. ⁸There were many lamps ªin the upper room where ¹they were gathered together. ⁹And in a window sat a certain young man named Eutychus, who was sinking into a deep sleep. He was overcome by sleep; and as Paul continued speaking, he fell down from the third story and was taken up dead. ¹⁰But Paul went down, ªfell on him, and embracing *him* said, ᵇ"Do not trouble yourselves, for his life is in him." ¹¹Now when he had come up, had broken bread and eaten, and talked a long while, even till daybreak, he departed. ¹²And they brought the young man in alive, and they were not a little comforted.

FROM TROAS TO MILETUS

¹³Then we went ahead to the ship and sailed to Assos, there intending to take Paul on board; for so he had ¹given orders, intending himself to go on foot. ¹⁴And when he met us at Assos, we took him on board and came to Mitylene. ¹⁵We sailed from there, and the next *day* came opposite Chios. The following *day* we arrived at Samos and stayed at Trogyllium. The next *day* we came to Miletus. ¹⁶For Paul had decided to sail past Ephesus, so that he would not have to spend time in Asia; for ªhe was hurrying ᵇto be at Jerusalem, if possible, on ᶜthe Day of Pentecost.

THE EPHESIAN ELDERS EXHORTED

¹⁷From Miletus he sent to Ephesus and called for the elders of the church. ¹⁸And when they had come to him, he said to them: "You know, ªfrom the first day that I came to Asia, in what manner I always lived among you, ¹⁹serving the Lord

20:1 ª1 Cor. 16:5; 1 Tim. 1:3

20:2 ªActs 17:15; 18:1

20:3 ªActs 9:23; 23:12; 25:3; 2 Cor. 11:26

20:4 ªActs 19:29; Col. 4:10 ᵇActs 19:29 ᶜActs 16:1 ᵈEph. 6:21; Col. 4:7; 2 Tim. 4:12; Titus 3:12 ᵉActs 21:29; 2 Tim. 4:20

20:5 ª2 Cor. 2:12; 2 Tim. 4:13

20:6 ªEx. 12:14, 15 ᵇActs 16:8; 2 Cor. 2:12; 2 Tim. 4:13

20:7 ª1 Cor. 16:2; Rev. 1:10 ᵇActs 2:42, 46; 20:11; 1 Cor. 10:16

20:8 ªActs 1:13

20:10 ª1 Kin. 17:21; 2 Kin. 4:34 ᵇMatt. 9:23, 24; Mark 5:39

20:16 ªActs 18:21; 19:21; 21:4 ᵇActs 24:17 ᶜActs 2:1; 1 Cor. 16:8

20:18 ªActs 18:19; 19:1, 10; 20:4, 16

19:40 ¹Or *charged with rebellion concerning today*   20:8 ¹NU, M *we*
20:13 ¹*arranged it*

20:19
a Acts 20:3

20:20
a Acts 20:27

20:21
a Acts 18:5; 19:10
b Mark 1:15

20:22
a Acts 19:21

20:23
a Acts 21:4, 11

20:24
a Acts 21:13
b Acts 13:25;
2 Tim. 4:7
c Acts 1:17
d Gal. 1:1

20:26
a Acts 18:6;
2 Cor. 7:2

20:27
a Luke 7:30;
John 15:15;
Eph. 1:11

20:28
a Luke 12:32;
John 21:15–17;
Acts 20:29;
[1 Tim. 4:16];
1 Pet. 5:2
b 1 Cor. 12:28
c Eph. 1:7, 14;
Col. 1:14;
Titus 2:14;
Heb. 9:12;
[1 Pet. 1:19];
Rev. 5:9
d Heb. 9:14

20:29
a Ezek. 22:27;
Matt. 7:15

20:30
a 1 Tim. 1:20;
2 Tim. 1:15

20:31
a Acts 19:8, 10;
24:17

20:32
a Heb. 13:9
b Acts 9:31
c Acts 26:18;
Eph. 1:14, 18; 5:5;
Col. 1:12; 3:24;
[Heb. 9:15;
1 Pet. 1:4]

20:34
a Acts 18:3;
1 Cor. 4:12;
1 Thess. 2:9;
2 Thess. 3:8

20:35
a Rom. 15:1;
1 Cor. 9:12;
2 Cor. 11:9, 12;
Eph. 4:28;
1 Thess. 4:11;
2 Thess. 3:8

with all humility, with many tears and trials which happened to me ^aby the plotting of the Jews; ²⁰how ^aI kept back nothing that was helpful, but proclaimed it to you, and taught you publicly and from house to house, ^{21a}testifying to Jews, and also to Greeks, ^brepentance toward God and faith toward our Lord Jesus Christ. ²²And see, now ^aI go bound in the spirit to Jerusalem, not knowing the things that will happen to me there, ²³except that ^athe Holy Spirit testifies in every city, saying that chains and tribulations await me. ²⁴[1]But ^anone of these things move me; nor do I count my life dear to myself, ^bso that I may finish my [2]race with joy, ^cand the ministry ^dwhich I received from the Lord Jesus, to testify to the gospel of the grace of God.

²⁵"And indeed, now I know that you all, among whom I have gone preaching the kingdom of God, will see my face no more. ²⁶Therefore I testify to you this day that I *am* ^ainnocent[1] of the blood of all *men*. ²⁷For I have not [1]shunned to declare to you ^athe whole counsel of God. ^{28a}Therefore take heed to yourselves and to all the flock, among which the Holy Spirit ^bhas made you overseers, to shepherd the church [1]of God ^cwhich He purchased ^dwith His own blood. ²⁹For I know this, that after my departure ^asavage wolves will come in among you, not sparing the flock. ³⁰Also ^afrom among yourselves men will rise up, speaking [1]perverse things, to draw away the disciples after themselves. ³¹Therefore watch, and remember that ^afor three years I did not cease to warn everyone night and day with tears.

³²"So now, brethren, I commend you to God and ^ato the word of His grace, which is able ^bto build you up and give you ^can inheritance among all those who are sanctified. ³³I have coveted no one's silver or gold or apparel. ³⁴[1]Yes, you yourselves know ^athat these hands have provided for my necessities, and for those who were with me. ³⁵I have shown you in every way, ^aby laboring like this, that you must support the weak. And remember the words of the Lord Jesus, that He said, 'It is more blessed to give than to receive.'"

³⁶And when he had said these things, he knelt down and prayed with them all. ³⁷Then they all ^awept [1]freely, and ^bfell on Paul's neck and kissed him, ³⁸sorrowing most of all for the words which he spoke, that they would see his face no more. And they accompanied him to the ship.

WARNINGS ON THE JOURNEY TO JERUSALEM

21 Now it came to pass, that when we had departed from them and set sail, running a straight course we came to Cos, the following *day* to Rhodes, and from there to Patara. ²And finding a ship sailing over to Phoenicia, we went aboard and set sail. ³When we had sighted Cyprus, we passed it on the left, sailed to Syria, and landed at Tyre; for there the ship was to unload her cargo. ⁴And finding [1]disciples, we stayed there seven days. ^aThey told Paul through the Spirit not to go up to Jerusalem. ⁵When we had come to the end of those days, we

20:37 ^aActs 21:13 ^bGen. 45:14   21:4 ^a[Acts 20:23; 21:12]

20:24 [1]NU *But I do not count my life of any value or dear to myself*   [2]*course*
20:26 [1]Lit. *clean*   20:27 [1]*avoided declaring*   20:28 [1]M *of the Lord and God*   20:30 [1]*misleading*   20:34 [1]NU, M omit *Yes*   20:37 [1]Lit. *much*
21:4 [1]NU *the disciples*

departed and went on our way; and they all accompanied us, with wives and children, till *we were* out of the city. And [a]we knelt down on the shore and prayed. [6]When we had taken our leave of one another, we boarded the ship, and they returned [a]home.

[7]And when we had finished *our* voyage from Tyre, we came to Ptolemais, greeted the brethren, and stayed with them one day. [8]On the next *day* we [1]who were Paul's companions departed and came to [a]Caesarea, and entered the house of Philip [b]the evangelist, [c]who was *one* of the seven, and stayed with him. [9]Now this man had four virgin daughters [a]who prophesied. [10]And as we stayed many days, a certain prophet named [a]Agabus came down from Judea. [11]When he had come to us, he took Paul's belt, bound his *own* hands and feet, and said, "Thus says the Holy Spirit, [a]'So shall the Jews at Jerusalem bind the man who owns this belt, and deliver *him* into the hands of the Gentiles.'"

[12]Now when we heard these things, both we and those from that place pleaded with him not to go up to Jerusalem. [13]Then Paul answered, [a]"What do you mean by weeping and breaking my heart? For I am ready not only to be bound, but also to die at Jerusalem for the name of the Lord Jesus."

[14]So when he would not be persuaded, we ceased, saying, [a]"The will of the Lord be done."

PAUL URGED TO MAKE PEACE

[15]And after those days we [1]packed and went up to Jerusalem. [16]Also some of the disciples from Caesarea went with us and brought with them a certain Mnason of Cyprus, an early disciple, with whom we were to lodge.

[17a]And when we had come to Jerusalem, the brethren received us gladly. [18]On the following *day* Paul went in with us to [a]James, and all the elders were present. [19]When he had greeted them, [a]he told in detail those things which God had done among the Gentiles [b]through his ministry. [20]And when they heard *it,* they glorified the Lord. And they said to him, "You see, brother, how many myriads of Jews there are who have believed, and they are all [a]zealous for the law; [21]but they have been informed about you that you teach all the Jews who are among the Gentiles to forsake Moses, saying that they ought not to circumcise *their* children nor to walk according to the customs. [22][1]What then? The assembly must certainly meet, for they will hear that you have come. [23]Therefore do what we tell you: We have four men who have taken a vow. [24]Take them and be purified with them, and pay their expenses so that they may [a]shave *their* heads, and that all may know that those things of which they were informed concerning you are nothing, but *that* you yourself also walk orderly and keep the law. [25]But concerning the Gentiles who believe, [a]we have written *and* decided [1]that they should observe no such thing, except that they should keep themselves from *things* offered to idols, from blood, from things strangled, and from [2]sexual immorality."

21:5 [a]Luke 22:41; Acts 9:40; 20:36

21:6 [a]John 1:11

21:8 [a]Acts 8:40; 21:16 [b]Acts 8:5, 26, 40; Eph. 4:11; 2 Tim. 4:5 [c]Acts 6:5

21:9 [a]Joel 2:28; Acts 2:17

21:10 [a]Acts 11:28

21:11 [a]Acts 20:23; 21:33; 22:25

21:13 [a]Acts 20:24, 37

21:14 [a]Matt. 6:10; 26:42; Luke 11:2; 22:42

21:17 [a]Acts 15:4

21:18 [a]Acts 15:13; Gal. 1:19; 2:9

21:19 [a]Acts 15:4, 12; Rom. 15:18, 19 [b]Acts 1:17; 20:24; 1 Tim. 2:7

21:20 [a]Acts 15:1; 22:3; [Rom. 10:2]; Gal. 1:14

21:24 [a]Num. 6:2, 13, 18; Acts 18:18

21:25 [a]Acts 15:19, 20, 29

21:8 [1]NU omits *who were Paul's companions* 21:15 [1]made preparations 21:22 [1]NU *What then is to be done? They will certainly hear* 21:25 [1]NU omits *that they should observe no such thing, except* [2]fornication

ARRESTED IN THE TEMPLE

26Then Paul took the men, and the next day, having been purified with them, [a]entered the temple [b]to announce the [1]expiration of the days of purification, at which time an offering should be made for each one of them.

27Now when the seven days were almost ended, [a]the Jews from Asia, seeing him in the temple, stirred up the whole crowd and [b]laid hands on him, 28crying out, "Men of Israel, help! This is the man [a]who teaches all *men* everywhere against the people, the law, and this place; and furthermore he also brought Greeks into the temple and has defiled this holy place." 29(For they had [1]previously seen [a]Trophimus the Ephesian with him in the city, whom they supposed that Paul had brought into the temple.)

30And [a]all the city was disturbed; and the people ran together, seized Paul, and dragged him out of the temple; and immediately the doors were shut. 31Now as they were [a]seeking to kill him, news came to the commander of the [1]garrison that all Jerusalem was in an uproar. 32[a]He immediately took soldiers and centurions, and ran down to them. And when they saw the commander and the soldiers, they stopped beating Paul. 33Then the [a]commander came near and took him, and [b]commanded *him* to be bound with two chains; and he asked who he was and what he had done. 34And some among the multitude cried one thing and some another.

So when he could not ascertain the truth because of the tumult, he commanded him to be taken into the barracks. 35When he reached the stairs, he had to be carried by the soldiers because of the violence of the mob. 36For the multitude of the people followed after, crying out, [a]"Away with him!"

ADDRESSING THE JERUSALEM MOB

(Acts 9:1–19; 26:12–18)

37Then as Paul was about to be led into the barracks, he said to the commander, "May I speak to you?"

He replied, "Can you speak Greek? 38[a]Are you not the Egyptian who some time ago stirred up a rebellion and led the four thousand assassins out into the wilderness?"

39But Paul said, [a]"I am a Jew from Tarsus, in Cilicia, a citizen of no [1]mean city; and I implore you, permit me to speak to the people."

40So when he had given him permission, Paul stood on the stairs and [a]motioned with his hand to the people. And when there was a great silence, he spoke to *them* in the [b]Hebrew language, saying,

22 "Brethren[a] and fathers, hear my defense before you now." 2And when they heard that he spoke to them in the [a]Hebrew language, they kept all the more silent.

Then he said: 3[a]"I am indeed a Jew, born in Tarsus of Cilicia, but brought up in this city [b]at the feet of [c]Gamaliel, taught [d]according to the strictness of our fathers' law, and [e]was zealous toward God [f]as you all are today. 4[a]I persecuted this Way to the death, binding and delivering into prisons both men and women, 5as also the high priest bears me witness, and [a]all the

---

21:26
[a]John 11:55;
Acts 21:24; 24:18
[b]Num. 6:13;
Acts 24:18

21:27
[a]Acts 20:19;
24:18
[b]Acts 26:21

21:28
[a][Matt. 24:15];
Acts 6:13; 24:6

21:29 [a]Acts 20:4

21:30
[a]2 Kin. 11:15;
Acts 16:19; 26:21

21:31
[a]2 Cor. 11:23

21:32
[a]Acts 23:27;
24:7

21:33 [a]Acts 24:7
[b]Acts 20:23;
21:11;
Eph. 6:20;
2 Tim. 1:16; 2:9

21:36
[a]Luke 23:18;
John 19:15;
Acts 22:22

21:38 [a]Acts 5:36

21:39
[a]Acts 9:11; 22:3;
2 Cor. 11:22;
Phil. 3:4–6

21:40 [a]Acts 12:17
[b]John 5:2;
Acts 22:2

22:1 [a]Acts 7:2

22:2 [a]Acts 21:40

22:3
[a]Acts 21:39;
2 Cor. 11:22
[b]Deut. 33:3
[c]Acts 5:34
[d]Acts 23:6; 26:5;
Phil. 3:6
[e]Acts 21:20;
Gal. 1:14
[f][Rom. 10:2]

22:4 [a]Acts 8:3;
26:9–11;
Phil. 3:6;
1 Tim. 1:13

22:5
[a]Acts 23:14;
24:1; 25:15

21:26 [1]completion   21:29 [1]M omits *previously*   21:31 [1]cohort
21:39 [1]insignificant

council of the elders, ^bfrom whom I also received letters to the brethren, and went to Damascus ^cto bring in chains even those who were there to Jerusalem to be punished.

6"Now ^ait happened, as I journeyed and came near Damascus at about noon, suddenly a great light from heaven shone around me. 7And I fell to the ground and heard a voice saying to me, 'Saul, Saul, why are you persecuting Me?' 8So I answered, 'Who are You, Lord?' And He said to me, 'I am Jesus of Nazareth, whom you are persecuting.'

9"And ^athose who were with me indeed saw the light ¹and were afraid, but they did not hear the voice of Him who spoke to me. 10So I said, 'What shall I do, Lord?' And the Lord said to me, 'Arise and go into Damascus, and there you will be told all things which are appointed for you to do.' 11And since I could not see for the glory of that light, being led by the hand of those who were with me, I came into Damascus.

12"Then ^aa certain Ananias, a devout man according to the law, ^bhaving a good testimony with all the ^cJews who dwelt *there,* 13came to me; and he stood and said to me, 'Brother Saul, receive your sight.' And at that same hour I looked up at him. 14Then he said, ^a'The God of our fathers ^bhas chosen you that you should ^cknow His will, and ^dsee the Just One, ^eand hear the voice of His mouth. 15aFor you will be His witness to all men of ^bwhat you have seen and heard. 16And now why are you waiting? Arise and be baptized, ^aand wash away your sins, ^bcalling on the name of the Lord.'

17"Now ^ait happened, when I returned to Jerusalem and was praying in the temple, that I was in a trance 18and ^asaw Him saying to me, ^b'Make haste and get out of Jerusalem quickly, for they will not receive your testimony concerning Me.' 19So I said, 'Lord, ^athey know that in every synagogue I imprisoned and ^bbeat those who believe on You. 20aAnd when the blood of Your martyr Stephen was shed, I also was standing by ^bconsenting ¹to his death, and guarding the clothes of those who were killing him.' 21Then He said to me, 'Depart, ^afor I will send you far from here to the Gentiles.'"

PAUL'S ROMAN CITIZENSHIP

22And they listened to him until this word, and *then* they raised their voices and said, ^a"Away with such a *fellow* from the earth, for ^bhe is not fit to live!" 23Then, as they cried out and ¹tore off *their* clothes and threw dust into the air, 24the commander ordered him to be brought into the barracks, and said that he should be examined under scourging, so that he might know why they shouted so against him. 25And as they bound him with thongs, Paul said to the centurion who stood by, ^a"Is it lawful for you to scourge a man who is a Roman, and uncondemned?"

26When the centurion heard *that,* he went and told the commander, saying, "Take care what you do, for this man is a Roman."

27Then the commander came and said to him, "Tell me, are you a Roman?"

He said, "Yes."

28The commander answered, "With a large sum I obtained this citizenship."

And Paul said, "But I was born *a citizen.*"

22:5
^bLuke 22:66;
Acts 4:5;
1 Tim. 4:14
^cActs 9:2

22:6 ^aActs 9:3;
26:12, 13

22:9 ^aDan. 10:7;
Acts 9:7

22:12 ^aActs 9:17
^bActs 10:22
^c1 Tim. 3:7

22:14
^aActs 3:13; 5:30
^bActs 9:15;
26:16;
Gal. 1:15
^cActs 3:14; 7:52
^dActs 9:17; 26:16;
1 Cor. 9:1; 15:8
^e1 Cor. 11:23;
Gal. 1:12

22:15
^aActs 23:11
^bActs 4:20;
26:16

22:16
^aActs 2:38;
1 Cor. 6:11;
[Eph. 5:26];
Heb. 10:22
^bActs 9:14;
Rom. 10:13

22:17
^aActs 9:26;
26:20;
2 Cor. 12:2

22:18
^aActs 22:14
^bMatt. 10:14

22:19
^aActs 8:3; 22:4
^bMatt. 10:17;
Acts 26:11

22:20
^aActs 7:54—8:1
^bLuke 11:48

22:21 ^aActs 9:15;
Rom. 1:5; 11:13;
Gal. 2:7, 8;
Eph. 3:7, 8;
1 Tim. 2:7;
2 Tim. 1:11

22:22
^aActs 21:36;
1 Thess. 2:16
^bActs 25:24

22:25
^aActs 16:37

22:9 ¹NU omits *and were afraid*   22:20 ¹NU omits *to his death*
22:23 ¹Lit. *threw*

²⁹Then immediately those who were about to examine him withdrew from him; and the commander was also afraid after he found out that he was a Roman, and because he had bound him.

THE SANHEDRIN DIVIDED

³⁰The next day, because he wanted to know for certain why he was accused by the Jews, he released him from *his* bonds, and commanded the chief priests and all their council to appear, and brought Paul down and set him before them.

23 Then Paul, looking earnestly at the council, said, "Men *and* brethren, ᵃI have lived in all good conscience before God until this day." ²And the high priest Ananias commanded those who stood by him ᵃto strike him on the mouth. ³Then Paul said to him, "God will strike you, *you* whitewashed wall! For you sit to judge me according to the law, and ᵃdo you command me to be struck contrary to the law?"

⁴And those who stood by said, "Do you revile God's high priest?"

⁵Then Paul said, ᵃ"I did not know, brethren, that he was the high priest; for it is written, ᵇ'You shall not speak evil of a ruler of your people.'"

⁶But when Paul perceived that one part were Sadducees and the other Pharisees, he cried out in the council, "Men *and* brethren, ᵃI am a Pharisee, the son of a Pharisee; ᵇconcerning the hope and resurrection of the dead I am being judged!"

⁷And when he had said this, a dissension arose between the Pharisees and the Sadducees; and the assembly was divided. ⁸ᵃFor Sadducees say that there is no resurrection—and no angel or spirit; but the Pharisees confess both. ⁹Then there arose a loud outcry. And the scribes of the Pharisees' party arose and protested, saying, ᵃ"We find no evil in this man; ¹but ᵇif a spirit or an angel has spoken to him, ᶜlet us not fight against God."

¹⁰Now when there arose a great dissension, the commander, fearing lest Paul might be pulled to pieces by them, commanded the soldiers to go down and take him by force from among them, and bring *him* into the barracks.

THE PLOT AGAINST PAUL

¹¹But ᵃthe following night the Lord stood by him and said, ¹"Be of good cheer, Paul; for as you have testified for Me in ᵇJerusalem, so you must also bear witness at ᶜRome."

¹²And when it was day, ᵃsome of the Jews banded together and bound themselves under an oath, saying that they would neither eat nor drink till they had ᵇkilled Paul. ¹³Now there were more than forty who had formed this conspiracy. ¹⁴They came to the chief priests and ᵃelders, and said, "We have bound ourselves under a great oath that we will eat nothing until we have killed Paul. ¹⁵Now you, therefore, together with the council, suggest to the commander that he be brought down to you ¹tomorrow, as though you were going to make further inquiries concerning him; but we are ready to kill him before he comes near."

¹⁶So when Paul's sister's son heard of their ambush, he went and entered the barracks and told Paul. ¹⁷Then Paul

---

23:1 ᵃActs 24:16;
1 Cor. 4:4;
2 Cor. 1:12; 4:2;
2 Tim. 1:3;
Heb. 13:18
23:2
ᵃ1 Kin. 22:24;
Jer. 20:2;
John 18:22
23:3 ᵃLev. 19:35;
Deut. 25:1, 2;
John 7:51
23:5
ᵃLev. 5:17, 18
ᵇEx. 22:28;
Eccl. 10:20;
2 Pet. 2:10
23:6 ᵃActs 26:5;
Phil. 3:5
ᵇActs 24:15, 21;
26:6; 28:20
23:8
ᵃMatt. 22:23;
Mark 12:18;
Luke 20:27
23:9
ᵃActs 25:25;
26:31
ᵇJohn 12:29;
Acts 22:6, 7,
17, 18
ᶜActs 5:39
23:11 ᵃActs 18:9;
27:23, 24
ᵇActs 21:18,
19; 22:1–21
ᶜActs 28:16,
17, 23
23:12
ᵃActs 23:21,
30; 25:3
ᵇActs 9:23, 24;
25:3; 26:21;
27:42;
1 Thess. 2:15
23:14
ᵃActs 4:5, 23;
6:12; 22:5;
24:1; 25:15

23:9 ¹NU *what if a spirit or an angel has spoken to him?* omitting the last clause   23:11 ¹*Take courage*   23:15 ¹NU omits *tomorrow*

called one of the centurions to *him* and said, "Take this young man to the commander, for he has something to tell him." ¹⁸So he took him and brought *him* to the commander and said, "Paul the prisoner called me to *him* and asked *me* to bring this young man to you. He has something to say to you."

¹⁹Then the commander took him by the hand, went aside, and asked privately, "What is it that you have to tell me?"

²⁰And he said, ᵃ"The Jews have agreed to ask that you bring Paul down to the council tomorrow, as though they were going to inquire more fully about him. ²¹But do not yield to them, for more than forty of them lie in wait for him, men who have bound themselves by an oath that they will neither eat nor drink till they have killed him; and now they are ready, waiting for the promise from you."

²²So the commander let the young man depart, and commanded *him,* "Tell no one that you have revealed these things to me."

SENT TO FELIX

²³And he called for two centurions, saying, "Prepare two hundred soldiers, seventy horsemen, and two hundred spearmen to go to ᵃCaesarea at the third hour of the night; ²⁴and provide mounts to set Paul on, and bring *him* safely to Felix the governor." ²⁵He wrote a letter in the following manner:

²⁶ Claudius Lysias,

To the most excellent governor Felix:

Greetings.

²⁷ ᵃThis man was seized by the Jews and was about to be killed by them. Coming with the troops I rescued him, having learned that he was a Roman. ²⁸ᵃAnd when I wanted to know the reason they accused him, I brought him before their council. ²⁹I found out that he was accused ᵃconcerning questions of their law, ᵇbut had nothing charged against him deserving of death or chains. ³⁰And ᵃwhen it was told me that ¹the Jews lay in wait for the man, I sent him immediately to you, and ᵇalso commanded his accusers to state before you the charges against him.

Farewell.

³¹Then the soldiers, as they were commanded, took Paul and brought *him* by night to Antipatris. ³²The next day they left the horsemen to go on with him, and returned to the barracks. ³³When they came to ᵃCaesarea and had delivered the ᵇletter to the governor, they also presented Paul to him. ³⁴And when the governor had read *it,* he asked what province he was from. And when he understood that *he was* from ᵃCilicia, ³⁵he said, ᵃ"I will hear you when your accusers also have come." And he commanded him to be kept in ᵇHerod's ¹Praetorium.

ACCUSED OF SEDITION

24 Now after ᵃfive days ᵇAnanias the high priest came down with the elders and a certain orator *named* Tertullus. These gave evidence to the governor against Paul.

23:20
ᵃActs 23:12

23:23
ᵃActs 8:40;
23:33

23:27
ᵃActs 21:30, 33;
24:7

23:28
ᵃActs 22:30

23:29
ᵃActs 18:15;
25:19
ᵇActs 25:25;
26:31

23:30
ᵃActs 23:20
ᵇActs 24:8; 25:6

23:33
ᵃActs 8:40
ᵇActs 23:26–30

23:34
ᵃActs 6:9; 21:39

23:35
ᵃActs 24:1, 10;
25:16
ᵇMatt. 27:27

24:1 ᵃActs 21:27
ᵇActs 23:2, 30,
35; 25:2

23:30 ¹NU *there would be a plot against the man*   23:35 ¹Headquarters

²And when he was called upon, Tertullus began his accusation, saying: "Seeing that through you we enjoy great peace, and ¹prosperity is being brought to this nation by your foresight, ³we accept *it* always and in all places, most noble Felix, with all thankfulness. ⁴Nevertheless, not to be tedious to you any further, I beg you to hear, by your ¹courtesy, a few words from us. ⁵ᵃFor we have found this man a plague, a creator of dissension among all the Jews throughout the world, and a ringleader of the sect of the Nazarenes. ⁶ᵃHe even tried to profane the temple, and we seized him, ¹and wanted ᵇto judge him according to our law. ⁷ᵃBut the commander Lysias came by and with great violence took *him* out of our hands, ⁸ᵃcommanding his accusers to come to you. By examining him yourself you may ascertain all these things of which we accuse him." ⁹And the Jews also ¹assented, maintaining that these things were so.

THE DEFENSE BEFORE FELIX

¹⁰Then Paul, after the governor had nodded to him to speak, answered: "Inasmuch as I know that you have been for many years a judge of this nation, I do the more cheerfully answer for myself, ¹¹because you may ascertain that it is no more than twelve days since I went up to Jerusalem ᵃto worship. ¹²ᵃAnd they neither found me in the temple disputing with anyone nor inciting the crowd, either in the synagogues or in the city. ¹³Nor can they prove the things of which they now accuse me. ¹⁴But this I confess to you, that according to ᵃthe Way which they call a sect, so I worship the ᵇGod of my fathers, believing all things which are written in ᶜthe Law and in the Prophets. ¹⁵ᵃI have hope in God, which they themselves also accept, ᵇthat there will be a resurrection ¹of *the* dead, both of *the* just and *the* unjust. ¹⁶ᵃThis *being* so, I myself always strive to have a conscience without offense toward God and men.

¹⁷"Now after many years ᵃI came to bring alms and offerings to my nation, ¹⁸ᵃin the midst of which some Jews from Asia found me ᵇpurified in the temple, neither with a mob nor with tumult. ¹⁹ᵃThey ought to have been here before you to object if they had anything against me. ²⁰Or else let those who are *here* themselves say ¹if they found any wrongdoing in me while I stood before the council, ²¹unless *it is* for this one statement which I cried out, standing among them, ᵃ'Concerning the resurrection of the dead I am being judged by you this day.'"

FELIX PROCRASTINATES

²²But when Felix heard these things, having more accurate knowledge of *the* ᵃWay, he adjourned the proceedings and said, "When ᵇLysias the commander comes down, I will make a decision on your case." ²³So he commanded the centurion to keep Paul and to let *him* have liberty, and ᵃtold him not to forbid any of his friends to provide for or visit him.

²⁴And after some days, when Felix came with his wife

Cross references (left margin)

24:5 ᵃLuke 23:2; Acts 6:13; 16:20; 17:6; 21:28; 1 Pet. 2:12, 15

24:6 ᵃActs 21:28 ᵇJohn 18:31

24:7 ᵃActs 21:33; 23:10

24:8 ᵃActs 23:30

24:11 ᵃActs 21:15, 18, 26, 27; 24:17

24:12 ᵃActs 25:8; 28:17

24:14 ᵃAmos 8:14; Acts 9:2; 24:22 ᵇ2 Tim. 1:3 ᶜActs 26:22; 28:23

24:15 ᵃActs 23:6; 26:6, 7; 28:20 ᵇ[Dan. 12:2; John 5:28, 29; 11:24]

24:16 ᵃActs 23:1

24:17 ᵃActs 11:29, 30; Rom. 15:25–28; 1 Cor. 16:1–4; 2 Cor. 8:1–4; 9:1, 2, 12; Gal. 2:10

24:18 ᵃActs 21:27; 26:21 ᵇActs 21:26

24:19 ᵃ[Acts 23:30; 25:16]

24:21 ᵃ[Acts 23:6; 24:15; 28:20]

24:22 ᵃActs 9:2; 18:26; 19:9, 23; 22:4 ᵇActs 23:26; 24:7

24:23 ᵃActs 23:16; 27:3; 28:16

24:2 ¹Or *reforms are*   24:4 ¹*graciousness*   24:6 ¹NU ends the sentence here and omits the rest of v. 6, all of v. 7, and the first clause of v. 8.
24:9 ¹NU, M *joined the attack*   24:15 ¹NU omits *of the dead*
24:20 ¹NU, M *what wrongdoing they found*

Drusilla, who was Jewish, he sent for Paul and heard him concerning the ªfaith in Christ. ²⁵Now as he reasoned about righteousness, self-control, and the judgment to come, Felix was afraid and answered, "Go away for now; when I have a convenient time I will call for you." ²⁶Meanwhile he also hoped that ªmoney would be given him by Paul, ¹that he might release him. Therefore he sent for him more often and conversed with him.

²⁷But after two years Porcius Festus succeeded Felix; and Felix, ªwanting to do the Jews a favor, left Paul bound.

PAUL APPEALS TO CAESAR

25 Now when Festus had come to the province, after three days he went up from ªCaesarea to Jerusalem. ²ªThen the ¹high priest and the chief men of the Jews informed him against Paul; and they petitioned him, ³asking a favor against him, that he would summon him to Jerusalem—ªwhile *they* lay in ambush along the road to kill him. ⁴But Festus answered that Paul should be kept at Caesarea, and that he himself was going *there* shortly. ⁵"Therefore," he said, "let those who have authority among you go down with *me* and accuse this man, to see ªif there is any fault in him."

⁶And when he had remained among them more than ten days, he went down to Caesarea. And the next day, sitting on the judgment seat, he commanded Paul to be brought. ⁷When he had come, the Jews who had come down from Jerusalem stood about ªand laid many serious complaints against Paul, which they could not prove, ⁸while he answered for himself, ª"Neither against the law of the Jews, nor against the temple, nor against Caesar have I offended in anything at all."

⁹But Festus, ªwanting to do the Jews a favor, answered Paul and said, ᵇ"Are you willing to go up to Jerusalem and there be judged before me concerning these things?"

¹⁰So Paul said, "I stand at Caesar's judgment seat, where I ought to be judged. To the Jews I have done no wrong, as you very well know. ¹¹ªFor if I am an offender, or have committed anything deserving of death, I do not object to dying; but if there is nothing in these things of which these men accuse me, no one can deliver me to them. ᵇI appeal to Caesar."

¹²Then Festus, when he had conferred with the council, answered, "You have appealed to Caesar? To Caesar you shall go!"

PAUL BEFORE AGRIPPA

¹³And after some days King Agrippa and Bernice came to Caesarea to greet Festus. ¹⁴When they had been there many days, Festus laid Paul's case before the king, saying: ª"There is a certain man left a prisoner by Felix, ¹⁵ªabout whom the chief priests and the elders of the Jews informed *me*, when I was in Jerusalem, asking for a judgment against him. ¹⁶ªTo them I answered, 'It is not the custom of the Romans to deliver any man ¹to destruction before the accused meets the accusers face to face, and has opportunity to answer for himself concerning the charge against him.' ¹⁷Therefore when they had come together, ªwithout any delay, the next day I sat on the judgment seat and commanded the man to be

24:24
ª[John 3:15;
5:24; 11:25;
12:46; 20:31;
Rom. 10:9]

24:26 ªEx. 23:8

24:27 ªEx. 23:2;
Acts 12:3; 23:35;
25:9, 14

25:1
ªActs 8:40;
25:4, 6, 13

25:2
ªActs 24:1; 25:15

25:3
ªActs 23:12, 15

25:5 ªActs 18:14;
25:18

25:7 ªMark 15:3;
Luke 23:2, 10;
Acts 24:5, 13

25:8 ªActs 6:13;
24:12; 28:17

25:9 ªActs 12:2;
24:27
ᵇActs 25:20

25:11
ªActs 18:14;
23:29;
25:25; 26:31
ᵇActs 26:32;
28:19

25:14
ªActs 24:27

25:15 ªActs 24:1;
25:2, 3

25:16
ªActs 25:4, 5

25:17
ªMatt. 27:19;
Acts 25:6, 10

24:26 ¹NU omits *that he might release him*   25:2 ¹NU *chief priests*
25:16 ¹NU omits *to destruction*, although it is implied

brought in. 18When the accusers stood up, they brought no accusation against him of such things as I 1supposed, 19abut had some questions against him about their own religion and about a certain Jesus, who had died, whom Paul affirmed to be alive. 20And because I was uncertain of such questions, I asked whether he was willing to go to Jerusalem and there be judged concerning these matters. 21But when Paul aappealed to be reserved for the decision of Augustus, I commanded him to be kept till I could send him to Caesar."

22Then aAgrippa said to Festus, "I also would like to hear the man myself."

"Tomorrow," he said, "you shall hear him."

23So the next day, when Agrippa and Bernice had come with great 1pomp, and had entered the auditorium with the commanders and the prominent men of the city, at Festus' command aPaul was brought in. 24And Festus said: "King Agrippa and all the men who are here present with us, you see this man about whom athe whole assembly of the Jews petitioned me, both at Jerusalem and here, crying out that he was bnot fit to live any longer. 25But when I found that ahe had committed nothing deserving of death, band that he himself had appealed to Augustus, I decided to send him. 26I have nothing certain to write to my lord concerning him. Therefore I have brought him out before you, and especially before you, King Agrippa, so that after the examination has taken place I may have something to write. 27For it seems to me unreasonable to send a prisoner and not to specify the charges against him."

PAUL'S EARLY LIFE

26 Then Agrippa said to Paul, "You are permitted to speak for yourself."

So Paul stretched out his hand and answered for himself: 2"I think myself ahappy, King Agrippa, because today I shall answer bfor myself before you concerning all the things of which I am caccused by the Jews, 3especially because you are expert in all customs and questions which have to do with the Jews. Therefore I beg you to hear me patiently.

4"My manner of life from my youth, which was spent from the beginning among my own nation at Jerusalem, all the Jews know. 5They knew me from the first, if they were willing to testify, that according to athe strictest sect of our religion I lived a Pharisee. 6aAnd now I stand and am judged for the hope of bthe promise made by God to our fathers. 7To this promise aour twelve tribes, earnestly serving God bnight and day, chope to attain. For this hope's sake, King Agrippa, I am accused by the Jews. 8Why should it be thought incredible by you that God raises the dead?

9a"Indeed, I myself thought I must do many things 1contrary to the name of bJesus of Nazareth. 10aThis I also did in Jerusalem, and many of the saints I shut up in prison, having received authority bfrom the chief priests; and when they were put to death, I cast my vote against them. 11aAnd I punished them often in every synagogue and compelled them to blaspheme; and being exceedingly enraged against them, I persecuted them even to foreign cities.

25:19
aActs 18:14, 15;
23:29

25:21
aActs 25:11, 12

25:22 aActs 9:15

25:23 aActs 9:15

25:24
aActs 25:2, 3, 7
bActs 21:36;
22:22

25:25
aActs 23:9,
29; 26:31
bActs 25:11, 12

26:2
a[1 Pet. 3:14;
4:14]
b[1 Pet. 3:15, 16]
cActs 21:28;
24:5, 6

26:5
a[Acts 22:3;
23:6; 24:15, 21];
Phil. 3:5

26:6 aActs 23:6
b[Gen. 3:15;
22:18; 26:4;
49:10;
Deut. 18:15;
2 Sam. 7:12;
Ps. 132:11;
Is. 4:2; 7:14;
9:6; 40:10;
Jer. 23:5;
33:14–16;
Ezek. 34:23;
37:24;
Dan. 9:24];
Acts 13:32;
Rom. 15:8;
[Titus 2:13]

26:7 aJames 1:1
bLuke 2:37;
1 Thess. 3:10;
1 Tim. 5:5
cPhil. 3:11

26:9 aJohn 16:2;
1 Cor. 15:9;
1 Tim. 1:12, 13
bActs 2:22;
10:38

26:10
aActs 8:1–3;
9:13;
Gal. 1:13
bActs 9:14

26:11
aMatt. 10:17;
Acts 22:19

25:18 1suspected   25:23 1pageantry   26:9 1against

PAUL RECOUNTS HIS CONVERSION
(Acts 9:1–19; 22:6–16)

12a"While thus occupied, as I journeyed to Damascus with authority and commission from the chief priests, 13at midday, O king, along the road I saw a light from heaven, brighter than the sun, shining around me and those who journeyed with me. 14And when we all had fallen to the ground, I heard a voice speaking to me and saying in the Hebrew language, 'Saul, Saul, why are you persecuting Me? *It is* hard for you to kick against the goads.' 15So I said, 'Who are You, Lord?' And He said, 'I am Jesus, whom you are persecuting. 16But rise and stand on your feet; for I have appeared to you for this purpose, ato make you a minister and a witness both of the things which you have seen and of the things which I will yet reveal to you. 17I will 1deliver you from the *Jewish* people, as well as *from* the Gentiles, ato whom I 2now send you, 18ato open their eyes, *in order* bto turn *them* from darkness to light, and *from* the power of Satan to God, cthat they may receive forgiveness of sins and dan inheritance among those who are esanctified1 by faith in Me.'

PAUL'S POST-CONVERSION LIFE

19"Therefore, King Agrippa, I was not disobedient to the heavenly vision, 20but adeclared first to those in Damascus and in Jerusalem, and throughout all the region of Judea, and *then* to the Gentiles, that they should repent, turn to God, and do bworks befitting repentance. 21For these reasons the Jews seized me in the temple and tried to kill *me.* 22Therefore, having obtained help from God, to this day I stand, witnessing both to small and great, saying no other things than those awhich the prophets and bMoses said would come— 23athat the Christ would suffer, bthat He would be the first to rise from the dead, and cwould proclaim light to the *Jewish* people and to the Gentiles."

AGRIPPA PARRIES PAUL'S CHALLENGE

24Now as he thus made his defense, Festus said with a loud voice, "Paul, ayou are beside yourself! Much learning is driving you mad!"

25But he said, "I am not 1mad, most noble Festus, but speak the words of truth and reason. 26For the king, before whom I also speak freely, aknows these things; for I am convinced that none of these things escapes his attention, since this thing was not done in a corner. 27King Agrippa, do you believe the prophets? I know that you do believe."

28Then Agrippa said to Paul, "You almost persuade me to become a Christian."

29And Paul said, a"I would to God that not only you, but also all who hear me today, might become both almost and altogether such as I am, except for these chains."

30When he had said these things, the king stood up, as well as the governor and Bernice and those who sat with them; 31and when they had gone aside, they talked among themselves, saying, a"This man is doing nothing deserving of death or chains."

26:12
a Acts 9:3–8;
22:6–11;
26:12–18

26:16
a Acts 22:15;
Eph. 3:6–8

26:17
a Acts 22:21

26:18
a Is. 35:5; 42:7, 16;
Luke 1:79;
[John 8:12;
2 Cor. 4:4];
Eph. 1:18;
1 Thess. 5:5
b 2 Cor. 6:14;
Eph. 4:18; 5:8;
[Col. 1:13];
1 Pet. 2:9
c Luke 1:77
d Eph. 1:11;
Col. 1:12
e Acts 20:32

26:20
a Acts 9:19,
20, 22; 11:26
b Matt. 3:8;
Luke 3:8

26:22
a Luke 24:27;
Acts 24:14;
28:23; Rom. 3:21
b John 5:46

26:23
a Luke 24:26
b 1 Cor. 15:20, 23;
Col. 1:18; Rev. 1:5
c Is. 42:6; 49:6;
Luke 2:32;
2 Cor. 4:4

26:24
a 2 Kin. 9:11;
John 10:20;
[1 Cor. 1:23; 2:13,
14; 4:10]

26:26
a Acts 26:3

26:29 a 1 Cor. 7:7

26:31
a Acts 23:9, 29;
25:25

26:17 1rescue   2NU, M omit *now*   26:18 1set apart   26:25 1out of my mind

[32]Then Agrippa said to Festus, "This man might have been set [a]free [b]if he had not appealed to Caesar."

THE VOYAGE TO ROME BEGINS

27 And when [a]it was decided that we should sail to Italy, they delivered Paul and some other prisoners to *one* named Julius, a centurion of the Augustan Regiment. [2]So, entering a ship of Adramyttium, we put to sea, meaning to sail along the coasts of Asia. [a]Aristarchus, a Macedonian of Thessalonica, was with us. [3]And the next *day* we landed at Sidon. And Julius [a]treated Paul kindly and gave *him* liberty to go to his friends and receive care. [4]When we had put to sea from there, we sailed under *the shelter of* Cyprus, because the winds were contrary. [5]And when we had sailed over the sea which is off Cilicia and Pamphylia, we came to Myra, *a city* of Lycia. [6]There the centurion found [a]an Alexandrian ship sailing to Italy, and he put us on board.

[7]When we had sailed slowly many days, and arrived with difficulty off Cnidus, the wind not permitting us to proceed, we sailed under *the shelter of* [a]Crete off Salmone. [8]Passing it with difficulty, we came to a place called Fair Havens, near the city *of* Lasea.

PAUL'S WARNING IGNORED

[9]Now when much time had been spent, and sailing was now dangerous [a]because [1]the Fast was already over, Paul advised them, [10]saying, "Men, I perceive that this voyage will end with disaster and much loss, not only of the cargo and ship, but also our lives." [11]Nevertheless the centurion was more persuaded by the helmsman and the owner of the ship than by the things spoken by Paul. [12]And because the harbor was not suitable to winter in, the majority advised to set sail from there also, if by any means they could reach Phoenix, a harbor of Crete opening toward the southwest and northwest, *and* winter *there.*

IN THE TEMPEST

[13]When the south wind blew softly, supposing that they had obtained *their* desire, putting out to sea, they sailed close by Crete. [14]But not long after, a tempestuous head wind arose, called [1]Euroclydon. [15]So when the ship was caught, and could not head into the wind, we let *her* [1]drive. [16]And running under *the shelter of* an island called [1]Clauda, we secured the skiff with difficulty. [17]When they had taken it on board, they used cables to undergird the ship; and fearing lest they should run aground on the [1]Syrtis *Sands,* they struck sail and so were driven. [18]And because we were exceedingly tempest-tossed, the next *day* they lightened the ship. [19]On the third *day* [a]we threw the ship's tackle overboard with our own hands. [20]Now when neither sun nor stars appeared for many days, and no small tempest beat on *us,* all hope that we would be saved was finally given up.

[21]But after long abstinence from food, then Paul stood in the midst of them and said, "Men, you should have listened to

---

26:32
[a]Acts 28:18
[b]Acts 25:11

27:1
[a]Acts 25:12, 25

27:2 [a]Acts 19:29

27:3
[a]Acts 24:23;
28:16

27:6 [a]Acts 28:11

27:7 [a]Acts 2:11;
27:12, 21;
Titus 1:5, 12

27:9
[a]Lev. 16:29–31;
23:27–29;
Num. 29:7

27:19 [a]Jon. 1:5

27:9 [1]The Day of Atonement, late September or early October
27:14 [1]A southeast wind that stirs up broad waves; NU *Euraquilon,* a northeaster   27:15 [1]*be driven*   27:16 [1]NU *Cauda*   27:17 [1]M *Syrtes*

me, and not have sailed from Crete and incurred this disaster and loss. ²²And now I urge you to take [1]heart, for there will be no loss of life among you, but only of the ship. ^{23a}For there stood by me this night an angel of the God to whom I belong and ^bwhom I serve, ²⁴saying, 'Do not be afraid, Paul; you must be brought before Caesar; and indeed God has granted you all those who sail with you.' ²⁵Therefore take heart, men, ^afor I believe God that it will be just as it was told me. ²⁶However, ^awe must run aground on a certain island."

²⁷Now when the fourteenth night had come, as we were driven up and down in the Adriatic *Sea*, about midnight the sailors sensed that they were drawing near some land. ²⁸And they took soundings and found *it* to be twenty fathoms; and when they had gone a little farther, they took soundings again and found *it* to be fifteen fathoms. ²⁹Then, fearing lest we should run aground on the rocks, they dropped four anchors from the stern, and [1]prayed for day to come. ³⁰And as the sailors were seeking to escape from the ship, when they had let down the skiff into the sea, under pretense of putting out anchors from the prow, ³¹Paul said to the centurion and the soldiers, "Unless these men stay in the ship, you cannot be saved." ³²Then the soldiers cut away the ropes of the skiff and let it fall off.

³³And as day was about to dawn, Paul implored *them* all to take food, saying, "Today is the fourteenth day you have waited and continued without food, and eaten nothing. ³⁴Therefore I urge you to take nourishment, for this is for your survival, ^asince not a hair will fall from the head of any of you." ³⁵And when he had said these things, he took bread and ^agave thanks to God in the presence of them all; and when he had broken *it* he began to eat. ³⁶Then they were all encouraged, and also took food themselves. ³⁷And in all we were two hundred and seventy-six ^apersons on the ship. ³⁸So when they had eaten enough, they lightened the ship and threw out the wheat into the sea.

SHIPWRECKED ON MALTA

³⁹When it was day, they did not recognize the land; but they observed a bay with a beach, onto which they planned to run the ship if possible. ⁴⁰And they [1]let go the anchors and left *them* in the sea, meanwhile loosing the rudder ropes; and they hoisted the mainsail to the wind and made for shore. ⁴¹But striking [1]a place where two seas met, ^athey ran the ship aground; and the prow stuck fast and remained immovable, but the stern was being broken up by the violence of the waves.

⁴²And the soldiers' plan was to kill the prisoners, lest any of them should swim away and escape. ⁴³But the centurion, wanting to save Paul, kept them from *their* purpose, and commanded that those who could swim should jump *overboard* first and get to land, ⁴⁴and the rest, some on boards and some on *parts* of the ship. And so it was ^athat they all escaped safely to land.

PAUL'S MINISTRY ON MALTA

28 Now when they had escaped, they then found out that ^athe island was called Malta. ²And the ^anatives[1] showed us unusual kindness; for they kindled a fire and made

Cross references

27:23
^aActs 18:9;
23:11; 2 Tim. 4:17
^bDan. 6:16;
Rom. 1:9;
2 Tim. 1:3

27:25
^aLuke 1:45;
Rom. 4:20, 21;
2 Tim. 1:12

27:26 ^aActs 28:1

27:34
^a1 Kin. 1:52;
[Matt. 10:30;
Luke 12:7; 21:18]

27:35
^a1 Sam. 9:13;
Matt. 15:36;
Mark 8:6;
John 6:11;
[1 Tim. 4:3, 4]

27:37
^aActs 2:41; 7:14;
Rom. 13:1;
1 Pet. 3:20

27:41
^a2 Cor. 11:25

27:44
^aActs 27:22, 31

28:1 ^aActs 27:26

28:2 ^aActs 28:4;
Rom. 1:14;
1 Cor. 14:11;
Col. 3:11

27:22 [1]courage   27:29 [1]Or *wished*   27:40 [1]*cast off*   27:41 [1]A reef
28:2 [1]Lit. *barbarians*

us all welcome, because of the rain that was falling and because of the cold. ³But when Paul had gathered a bundle of sticks and laid *them* on the fire, a viper came out because of the heat, and fastened on his hand. ⁴So when the natives saw the creature hanging from his hand, they said to one another, "No doubt this man is a murderer, whom, though he has escaped the sea, yet justice does not allow to live." ⁵But he shook off the creature into the fire and ᵃsuffered no harm. ⁶However, they were expecting that he would swell up or suddenly fall down dead. But after they had looked for a long time and saw no harm come to him, they changed their minds and ᵃsaid that he was a god.

⁷In that region there was an estate of the ¹leading citizen of the island, whose name was Publius, who received us and entertained us courteously for three days. ⁸And it happened that the father of Publius lay sick of a fever and dysentery. Paul went in to him and ᵃprayed, and ᵇhe laid his hands on him and healed him. ⁹So when this was done, the rest of those on the island who had diseases also came and were healed. ¹⁰They also honored us in many ᵃways; and when we departed, they provided such things as were ᵇnecessary.

ARRIVAL AT ROME

¹¹After three months we sailed in ᵃan Alexandrian ship whose figurehead was the ¹Twin Brothers, which had wintered at the island. ¹²And landing at Syracuse, we stayed three days. ¹³From there we circled round and reached Rhegium. And after one day the south wind blew; and the next day we came to Puteoli, ¹⁴where we found ᵃbrethren, and were invited to stay with them seven days. And so we went toward Rome. ¹⁵And from there, when the brethren heard about us, they came to meet us as far as Appii Forum and Three Inns. When Paul saw them, he thanked God and took courage.

¹⁶Now when we came to Rome, the centurion delivered the prisoners to the captain of the guard; but ᵃPaul was permitted to dwell by himself with the soldier who guarded him.

PAUL'S MINISTRY AT ROME

¹⁷And it came to pass after three days that Paul called the leaders of the Jews together. So when they had come together, he said to them: "Men *and* brethren, ᵃthough I have done nothing against our people or the customs of our fathers, yet ᵇI was delivered as a prisoner from Jerusalem into the hands of the Romans, ¹⁸who, ᵃwhen they had examined me, wanted to let *me* go, because there was no cause for putting me to death. ¹⁹But when the ¹Jews spoke against *it,* ᵃI was compelled to appeal to Caesar, not that I had anything of which to accuse my nation. ²⁰For this reason therefore I have called for you, to see *you* and speak with *you,* because ᵃfor the hope of Israel I am bound with ᵇthis chain."

²¹Then they said to him, "We neither received letters from Judea concerning you, nor have any of the brethren who came reported or spoken any evil of you. ²²But we desire to hear from you what you think; for concerning this sect, we know that ᵃit is spoken against everywhere."

28:5
ᵃMark 16:18;
Luke 10:19

28:6
ᵃActs 12:22; 14:11

28:8 ᵃActs 9:40;
[James 5:14, 15]
ᵇMatt. 9:18;
Mark 5:23; 6:5;
7:32; 16:18;
Luke 4:40;
Acts 19:11, 12;
[1 Cor. 12:9, 28]

28:10
ᵃMatt. 15:6;
1 Tim. 5:17
ᵇ[Phil. 4:19]

28:11 ᵃActs 27:6

28:14 ᵃRom. 1:8

28:16
ᵃActs 23:11;
24:25; 27:3

28:17
ᵃActs 23:29;
24:12, 13; 26:31
ᵇActs 21:33

28:18
ᵃActs 22:24;
24:10; 25:8;
26:32

28:19
ᵃActs 25:11,
21, 25

28:20
ᵃActs 26:6, 7
ᵇActs 26:29;
Eph. 3:1; 4:1;
6:20;
2 Tim. 1:8, 16;
Philem. 10, 13

28:22
ᵃLuke 2:34;
Acts 24:5, 14;
[1 Pet. 2:12; 3:16;
4:14, 16]

28:7 ¹Magistrate   **28:11** ¹Gr. *Dioskouroi,* Zeus's sons Castor and Pollux
28:19 ¹The ruling authorities

²³So when they had appointed him a day, many came to him at *his* lodging, ªto whom he explained and solemnly testified of the kingdom of God, persuading them concerning Jesus ᵇfrom both the Law of Moses and the Prophets, from morning till evening. ²⁴And ªsome were persuaded by the things which were spoken, and some disbelieved. ²⁵So when they did not agree among themselves, they departed after Paul had said one word: "The Holy Spirit spoke rightly through Isaiah the prophet to ¹our fathers, ²⁶saying,

ª'Go to this people and say:
"Hearing you will hear, and shall not understand;
And seeing you will see, and not perceive;
²⁷   For the hearts of this people have grown dull.
Their ears are hard of hearing,
And their eyes they have closed,
Lest they should see with *their* eyes and hear with
     their ears,
Lest they should understand with *their* hearts and turn,
So that I should heal them."'

²⁸"Therefore let it be known to you that the salvation of God has been ªto the Gentiles, and they will hear it!" ²⁹¹And when he had said these words, the Jews departed and had a great dispute among themselves.

³⁰Then Paul dwelt two whole years in his own rented house, and received all who came to him, ³¹ªpreaching the kingdom of God and teaching the things which concern the Lord Jesus Christ with all confidence, no one forbidding him.

28:23
ªLuke 24:27;
[Acts 17:3; 19:8]
ᵇActs 26:6, 22

28:24
ªActs 14:4; 19:9

28:26
ªIs. 6:9, 10;
Jer. 5:21;
Ezek. 12:2;
Matt. 13:14, 15;
Mark 4:12;
Luke 8:10;
John 12:40, 41;
Rom. 11:8

28:28
ªIs. 42:1, 6; 49:6;
Matt. 21:41;
Luke 2:32;
Rom. 11:11

28:31 ªActs 4:31;
Eph. 6:19

THE EPISTLE OF PAUL THE APOSTLE TO THE
ROMANS

GREETING

1 Paul, a bondservant of Jesus Christ, ᵃcalled *to be* an apostle, ᵇseparated to the gospel of God 2ᵃwhich He promised before ᵇthrough His prophets in the Holy Scriptures, 3concerning His Son Jesus Christ our Lord, who ¹was ᵃborn of the seed of David according to the flesh, 4*and* ᵃdeclared *to be* the Son of God with power according ᵇto the Spirit of holiness, by the resurrection from the dead. 5Through Him ᵃwe have received grace and apostleship for ᵇobedience to the faith among all nations ᶜfor His name, 6among whom you also are the called of Jesus Christ;

7To all who are in Rome, beloved of God, ᵃcalled *to be* saints:

ᵇGrace to you and peace from God our Father and the Lord Jesus Christ.

DESIRE TO VISIT ROME

8First, ᵃI thank my God through Jesus Christ for you all, that ᵇyour faith is spoken of throughout the whole world. 9For ᵃGod is my witness, ᵇwhom I serve ¹with my spirit in the gospel of His Son, that ᶜwithout ceasing I make mention of you always in my prayers, 10making request if, by some means, now at last I may find a way in the will of God to come to you. 11For I long to see you, that ᵃI may impart to you some spiritual gift, so that you may be established— 12that is, that I may be encouraged together with you by ᵃthe mutual faith both of you and me.

13Now I do not want you to be unaware, brethren, that I often planned to come to you (but ᵃwas hindered until now), that I might have some ᵇfruit among you also, just as among the other Gentiles. 14I am a debtor both to Greeks and to barbarians, both to wise and to unwise. 15So, as much as is in me, *I am* ready to preach the gospel to you who are in Rome also.

THE JUST LIVE BY FAITH

16For ᵃI am not ashamed of the gospel ¹of Christ, for ᵇit is the power of God to salvation for everyone who believes, ᶜfor the Jew first and also for the Greek. 17For ᵃin it the righteousness of God is revealed from faith to faith; as it is written, ᵇ"The just shall live by faith."

GOD'S WRATH ON UNRIGHTEOUSNESS

18ᵃFor the wrath of God is revealed from heaven against all ungodliness and ᵇunrighteousness of men, who ¹suppress

1:3 ¹came   **1:9** ¹Or *in*   **1:16** ¹NU omits *of Christ*   **1:18** ¹hold down

the truth in unrighteousness, [19]because [a]what may be known of God is [1]manifest [2]in them, for [b]God has shown *it* to them. [20]For since the creation of the world [a]His invisible *attributes* are clearly seen, being understood by the things that are made, *even* His eternal power and [1]Godhead, so that they are without excuse, [21]because, although they knew God, they did not glorify *Him* as God, nor were thankful, but [a]became futile in their thoughts, and their foolish hearts were darkened. [22a]Professing to be wise, they became fools, [23]and changed the glory of the [a]incorruptible [b]God into an image made like [1]corruptible man—and birds and four-footed animals and creeping things.

[24a]Therefore God also gave them up to uncleanness, in the lusts of their hearts, [b]to dishonor their bodies [c]among themselves, [25]who exchanged [a]the truth of God [b]for the lie, and worshiped and served the creature rather than the Creator, who is blessed forever. Amen.

[26]For this reason God gave them up to [a]vile passions. For even their [1]women exchanged the natural use for what is against nature. [27]Likewise also the [1]men, leaving the natural use of the [2]woman, burned in their lust for one another, men with men committing what is shameful, and receiving in themselves the penalty of their error which was due.

[28]And even as they did not like to retain God in *their* knowledge, God gave them over to a debased mind, to do those things [a]which are not fitting; [29]being filled with all unrighteousness, [1]sexual immorality, wickedness, [2]covetousness, [3]maliciousness; full of envy, murder, strife, deceit, evilmindedness; *they are* whisperers, [30]backbiters, haters of God, violent, proud, boasters, inventors of evil things, disobedient to parents, [31]undiscerning, untrustworthy, unloving, [2]unforgiving, unmerciful; [32]who, [a]knowing the righteous judgment of God, that those who practice such things [b]are deserving of death, not only do the same but also [c]approve of those who practice them.

GOD'S RIGHTEOUS JUDGMENT

2 Therefore you are [a]inexcusable, O man, whoever you are who judge, [b]for in whatever you judge another you condemn yourself; for you who judge practice the same things. [2]But we know that the judgment of God is according to truth against those who practice such things. [3]And do you think this, O man, you who judge those practicing such things, and doing the same, that you will escape the judgment of God? [4]Or do you despise [a]the riches of His goodness, [b]forbearance, and [c]longsuffering, [d]not knowing that the goodness of God leads you to repentance? [5]But in accordance with your hardness and your [1]impenitent heart [a]you are [2]treasuring up for yourself wrath in the day of wrath and revelation of the righteous judgment of God, [6]who [a]"will render to each one according to his deeds": [7]eternal life to those who by patient continuance in doing good seek for glory, honor, and immortality; [8]but to those who are self-seeking and [a]do not obey the truth, but

1:19 [a][Acts 14:17; 17:24]
[b][John 1:9]

1:20 [a]Job 12:7–9; Ps. 19:1–6; Jer. 5:22

1:21 [a]2 Kin. 17:15; Jer. 2:5; Eph. 4:17

1:22 [a]Jer. 10:14; [1 Cor. 1:20]

1:23 [a]1 Tim. 1:17; 6:15, 16
[b]Deut. 4:16–18; Ps. 106:20; Jer. 2:11; Acts 17:29

1:24 [a]Ps. 81:12; Acts 7:42; Eph. 4:18, 19
[b]1 Cor. 6:18
[c]Lev. 18:22

1:25 [a]1 Thess. 1:9
[b]Is. 44:20; Jer. 10:14; 13:25; 16:19

1:26 [a]Lev. 18:22; Eph. 5:12

1:28 [a]Eph. 5:4

1:32 [a][Rom. 2:2]
[b][Rom. 6:21]
[c][Ps. 50:18]; Hos. 7:3

2:1 [a][Rom. 1:20]
[b]2 Sam. 12:5–7; [Matt. 7:1–5; Luke 6:37]; John 8:9; Rom. 14:22

2:4 [a]Rom. 9:23; 11:33; [2 Cor. 8:2; Eph. 1:7, 18; 2:7; Phil. 4:19; Col. 1:27; 2:2; Titus 3:6]
[b][Rom. 3:25]
[c]Ex. 34:6; [Rom. 9:22; 1 Tim. 1:16]; 1 Pet. 3:20
[d]Is. 30:18; [2 Pet. 3:9, 15]

2:5 [a][Deut. 32:34]; Prov. 1:18; James 5:3

2:6 [a][Job 34:11]; Ps. 62:12; Prov. 24:12; Jer. 17:10; [2 Cor. 5:10; Rev. 20:12, 13]

2:8 [a]Job 24:13; [2 Thess. 1:8]

1:19 [1]*evident* [2]*among* 1:20 [1]*divine nature, deity* 1:23 [1]*perishable* 1:26 [1]Lit. *females* 1:27 [1]Lit. *males* [2]Lit. *female* 1:29 [1]NU omits *sexual immorality* [2]*greed* [3]*malice* 1:31 [1]*without understanding* [2]NU omits *unforgiving* 2:5 [1]*unrepentant* [2]*storing*

2:9 ªAmos 3:2;
Luke 12:47;
Acts 3:26;
Rom. 1:16;
1 Pet. 4:17

2:10 ªRom. 2:7;
Heb. 2:7;
[1 Pet. 1:7]

2:11
ªDeut. 10:17;
[Job 34:19];
Acts 10:34;
[Eph. 6:9]

2:13
ªMatt. 7:21, 22;
John 13:17;
[James 1:22, 25;
1 John 3:7]

2:15 ª1 Cor. 5:1
ᵇActs 24:25

2:16
ªEccl. 12:14;
[Matt. 25:31];
Rev. 20:12
ᵇJohn 5:22;
Acts 10:42; 17:31;
Rom. 3:6; 14:10
ᶜ1 Tim. 1:11

2:17
ª[Matt. 3:9];
John 8:33
ᵇMic. 3:11;
John 5:45;
Rom. 2:23; 9:4
ᶜIs. 48:1, 2

2:18
ªDeut. 4:8
ᵇPhil. 1:10

2:19
ªMatt. 15:14;
John 9:34

2:20
ª[2 Tim. 3:5]

2:21 ªPs. 50:16;
Matt. 23:3

2:22 ªMal. 3:8

2:23
ªMic. 3:11;
John 5:45;
Rom. 2:17; 9:4

2:24
ªEzek. 16:27
ᵇ2 Sam. 12:14;
Is. 52:5;
Ezek. 36:22

2:25
ªGen. 17:10–14;
[Gal. 5:3]

2:26
ª[Acts 10:34]

2:27
ªMatt. 12:41

2:28
ª[Matt. 3:9];
John 8:39;
Rom. 2:17; 9:6;
[Gal. 6:15]

obey unrighteousness—indignation and wrath, ⁹tribulation and anguish, on every soul of man who does evil, of the Jew ªfirst and also of the ¹Greek; ¹⁰ªbut glory, honor, and peace to everyone who works what is good, to the Jew first and also to the Greek. ¹¹For ªthere is no partiality with God.

¹²For as many as have sinned without law will also perish without law, and as many as have sinned in the law will be judged by the law ¹³(for ªnot the hearers of the law *are* just in the sight of God, but the doers of the law will be justified; ¹⁴for when Gentiles, who do not have the law, by nature do the things in the law, these, although not having the law, are a law to themselves, ¹⁵who show the ªwork of the law written in their hearts, their ᵇconscience also bearing witness, and between themselves *their* thoughts accusing or else excusing *them*) ¹⁶ªin the day when God will judge the secrets of men ᵇby Jesus Christ, ᶜaccording to my gospel.

THE JEWS GUILTY AS THE GENTILES

¹⁷¹Indeed ªyou are called a Jew, and ᵇrest² on the law, ᶜand make your boast in God, ¹⁸and ªknow *His* will, and ᵇapprove the things that are excellent, being instructed out of the law, ¹⁹and ªare confident that you yourself are a guide to the blind, a light to those who are in darkness, ²⁰an instructor of the foolish, a teacher of babes, ªhaving the form of knowledge and truth in the law. ²¹ªYou, therefore, who teach another, do you not teach yourself? You who preach that a man should not steal, do you steal? ²²You who say, "Do not commit adultery," do you commit adultery? You who abhor idols, ªdo you rob temples? ²³You who ªmake your boast in the law, do you dishonor God through breaking the law? ²⁴For ª"the name of God is ᵇblasphemed among the Gentiles because of you," as it is written.

CIRCUMCISION OF NO AVAIL

²⁵ªFor circumcision is indeed profitable if you keep the law; but if you are a breaker of the law, your circumcision has become uncircumcision. ²⁶Therefore, ªif an uncircumcised man keeps the righteous requirements of the law, will not his uncircumcision be counted as circumcision? ²⁷And will not the physically uncircumcised, if he fulfills the law, ªjudge you who, *even* with *your* ¹written *code* and circumcision, *are* a transgressor of the law? ²⁸For ªhe is not a Jew who *is one* outwardly, nor *is* circumcision that which *is* outward in the flesh; ²⁹but *he is* a Jew ªwho *is one* inwardly; and ᵇcircumcision *is that* of the heart, ᶜin the Spirit, not in the letter; ᵈwhose ¹praise *is* not from men but from God.

GOD'S JUDGMENT DEFENDED

3 What advantage then has the Jew, or what *is* the profit of circumcision? ²Much in every way! Chiefly because ªto them were committed the ¹oracles of God. ³For what if ªsome did not believe? ᵇWill their unbelief make the faithfulness of

2:29 ª[1 Pet. 3:4] ᵇPhil. 3:3; Col. 2:11 ᶜDeut. 30:6; Rom. 2:27; 7:6; [2 Cor. 3:6]
ᵈJohn 5:44; 12:43; [1 Cor. 4:5; 2 Cor. 10:18]; 1 Thess. 2:4   3:2 ªDeut. 4:5–8; Ps. 147:19;
Rom. 9:4   3:3 ªRom. 10:16; Heb. 4:2 ᵇNum. 23:19; [2 Tim. 2:13]

2:9 ¹Gentile   2:17 ¹NU *But if*   ²*rely*   2:27 ¹Lit. *letter*   2:29 ¹A play on words—*Jew* is literally *praise*.   3:2 ¹*sayings*, Scriptures

God without effect? ⁴ªCertainly not! Indeed, let ᵇGod be ¹true but ᶜevery man a liar. As it is written:

> ᵈ"That You may be justified in Your words,
>   And may overcome when You are judged."

⁵But if our unrighteousness demonstrates the righteousness of God, what shall we say? *Is* God unjust who inflicts wrath? ª(I speak as a man.) ⁶Certainly not! For then ªhow will God judge the world?

⁷For if the truth of God has increased through my lie to His glory, why am I also still judged as a sinner? ⁸And *why* not *say*, ª"Let us do evil that good may come"?—as we are slanderously reported and as some affirm that we say. Their ¹condemnation is just.

ALL HAVE SINNED
(Ps. 14:1–3; 53:1–4)

⁹What then? Are we better *than they?* Not at all. For we have previously charged both Jews and Greeks that ªthey are all under sin.

¹⁰As it is written:

> ª"There is none righteous, no, not one;
> 11 There is none who understands;
>   There is none who seeks after God.
> 12 They have all turned aside;
>   They have together become unprofitable;
>   There is none who does good, no, not one."
> 13 "Theirª throat *is* an open ¹tomb;
>   With their tongues they have practiced deceit";
>   ᵇ"The poison of asps *is* under their lips";
> 14 "Whoseª mouth *is* full of cursing and bitterness."
> 15 "Theirª feet *are* swift to shed blood;
> 16 Destruction and misery *are* in their ways;
> 17 And the way of peace they have not known."
> 18 "Thereª is no fear of God before their eyes."

¹⁹Now we know that whatever ªthe law says, it says to those who are under the law, that ᵇevery mouth may be stopped, and all the world may become ¹guilty before God. ²⁰Therefore ªby the deeds of the law no flesh will be justified in His sight, for by the law *is* the knowledge of sin.

GOD'S RIGHTEOUSNESS THROUGH FAITH

²¹But now ªthe righteousness of God apart from the law is revealed, ᵇbeing witnessed by the Law ᶜand the Prophets, ²²even the righteousness of God, through faith in Jesus Christ, to all ¹and on all who believe. For ªthere is no difference; ²³for ªall have sinned and fall short of the glory of God, ²⁴being justified ¹freely ªby His grace ᵇthrough the redemption that is in Christ Jesus, ²⁵whom God set forth ªas a ¹propitiation ᵇby His blood, through faith, to demonstrate His righteousness, because in His forbearance God had passed over ᶜthe sins that were previously committed, ²⁶to demonstrate at the present time His righteousness, that He might be just and the justifier of the one who has faith in Jesus.

3:4 ªJob 40:8
ᵇ[John 3:33]
ᶜPs. 62:9
ᵈPs. 51:4

3:5 ªRom. 6:19;
1 Cor. 9:8; 15:32;
Gal. 3:15

3:6
ª[Gen. 18:25]

3:8 ªRom. 5:20

3:9
ªRom. 3:19, 23;
11:32; Gal. 3:22

3:10
ªPs. 14:1–3;
53:1–3;
Eccl. 7:20

3:13 ªPs. 5:9
ᵇPs. 140:3

3:14 ªPs. 10:7

3:15 ªProv. 1:16;
Is. 59:7, 8

3:18 ªPs. 36:1

3:19 ªJohn 10:34
ᵇJob 5:16;
Ps. 107:42

3:20 ªPs. 143:2;
[Acts 13:39;
Gal. 2:16]

3:21 ªActs 15:11
ᵇJohn 5:46
ᶜ1 Pet. 1:10

3:22
ªRom. 10:12;
[Gal. 3:28;
Col. 3:11]

3:23 ªGal. 3:22

3:24
ªRom. 4:4, 16;
[Eph. 2:8;
Titus 3:5, 7]
ᵇ[Matt. 20:28;
Eph. 1:7;
Col. 1:14;
1 Tim. 2:6;
Heb. 9:12, 15;
1 Pet. 1:18, 19]

3:25 ªLev. 16:15
ᵇCol. 1:20
ᶜActs 14:16;
17:30;
[Rom. 2:4]

3:4 ¹Found true 3:8 ¹Lit. *judgment* 3:13 ¹*grave* 3:19 ¹*accountable*
3:22 ¹NU omits *and on all* 3:24 ¹*without any cost* 3:25 ¹*mercy seat*

BOASTING EXCLUDED

^{27a}Where *is* boasting then? It is excluded. By what law? Of works? No, but by the law of faith. ²⁸Therefore we conclude ^athat a man is ¹justified by faith apart from the deeds of the law. ²⁹Or *is He* the God of the Jews only? *Is He* not also the God of the Gentiles? Yes, of the Gentiles also, ³⁰since ^a*there is* one God who will justify the circumcised by faith and the uncircumcised through faith. ³¹Do we then make void the law through faith? Certainly not! On the contrary, we establish the law.

ABRAHAM JUSTIFIED BY FAITH
(Gen. 17:10)

4 What then shall we say that ^aAbraham our ^bfather¹ has found according to the flesh? ²For if Abraham was ^ajustified by works, he has *something* to boast about, but not before God. ³For what does the Scripture say? ^a"Abraham believed God, and it was ¹accounted to him for righteousness." ⁴Now ^ato him who works, the wages are not counted ¹as grace but as debt.

DAVID CELEBRATES THE SAME TRUTH

⁵But to him who ^adoes not work but believes on Him who justifies ^bthe ungodly, his faith is accounted for righteousness, ⁶just as David also ^adescribes the blessedness of the man to whom God imputes righteousness apart from works:

⁷ "Blessed^a *are those* whose lawless deeds are forgiven,
  And whose sins are covered;
⁸ Blessed *is the* man to whom the LORD shall not impute
  sin."

ABRAHAM JUSTIFIED BEFORE CIRCUMCISION

⁹*Does* this blessedness then *come* upon the circumcised *only*, or upon the uncircumcised also? For we say that faith was accounted to Abraham for righteousness. ¹⁰How then was it accounted? While he was circumcised, or uncircumcised? Not while circumcised, but while uncircumcised. ¹¹And ^ahe received the sign of circumcision, a seal of the righteousness of the faith which *he had while still* uncircumcised, that ^bhe might be the father of all those who believe, though they are uncircumcised, that righteousness might be imputed to them also, ¹²and the father of circumcision to those who not only *are* of the circumcision, but who also walk in the steps of the faith which our father ^aAbraham *had while still* uncircumcised.

THE PROMISE GRANTED THROUGH FAITH

¹³For the promise that he would be the ^aheir of the world *was* not to Abraham or to his seed through the law, but through the righteousness of faith. ¹⁴For ^aif those who are of the law *are* heirs, faith is made void and the promise made of no effect, ¹⁵because ^athe law brings about wrath; for where there is no law *there is* no transgression.

¹⁶Therefore *it is* of faith that *it might be* ^aaccording to

---

3:27
^aRom. 2:17, 23;
[1 Cor. 1:29];
Eph. 2:9
3:28 ^aGal. 2:16
3:30
^aRom. 10:12;
[Gal. 3:8, 20]
4:1
^aGen. 11:27—
25:9; Is. 51:2;
[Matt. 3:9];
John 8:33
^b[Luke 3:8];
John 8:53;
James 2:21
4:2
^aRom. 3:20, 27
4:3 ^aGen. 15:6;
Rom. 4:9, 22;
Gal. 3:6;
James 2:23
4:4 ^aRom. 11:6
4:5 ^a[Gal. 2:16;
Eph. 2:8, 9]
^bJosh. 24:2
4:6 ^aPs. 32:1, 2
4:7 ^aPs. 32:1, 2
4:11 ^aGen. 17:10
^bLuke 19:9;
Rom. 4:16
4:12
^aRom. 4:18–22
4:13
^aGen. 17:4–6;
22:17
4:14 ^aGal. 3:18
4:15 ^aRom. 3:20
4:16
^a[Rom. 3:24]

3:28 ¹*declared righteous* **4:1** ¹Or *(fore)father according to the flesh has found?* **4:3** ¹*imputed, credited, reckoned, counted* **4:4** ¹*according to*

grace, [b]so that the promise might be [1]sure to all the seed, not only to those who are of the law, but also to those who are of the faith of Abraham, [c]who is the father of us all [17](as it is written, [a]"I have made you a father of many nations") in the presence of Him whom he believed—God, [b]who gives life to the dead and calls those [c]things which do not exist as though they did; [18]who, contrary to hope, in hope believed, so that he became the father of many nations, according to what was spoken, [a]"So shall your descendants be." [19]And not being weak in faith, [a]he did not consider his own body, already dead (since he was about a hundred years old), [b]and the deadness of Sarah's womb. [20]He did not waver at the promise of God through unbelief, but was strengthened in faith, giving glory to God, [21]and being fully convinced that what He had promised [a]He was also able to perform. [22]And therefore [a]"it was accounted to him for righteousness."

[23]Now [a]it was not written for his sake alone that it was imputed to him, [24]but also for us. It shall be imputed to us who believe [a]in Him who raised up Jesus our Lord from the dead, [25a]who was delivered up because of our offenses, and [b]was raised because of our justification.

FAITH TRIUMPHS IN TROUBLE

5 Therefore, [a]having been justified by faith, [1]we have [b]peace with God through our Lord Jesus Christ, [2a]through whom also we have access by faith into this grace [b]in which we stand, and [c]rejoice in hope of the glory of God. [3]And not only *that,* but [a]we also glory in tribulations, [b]knowing that tribulation produces [1]perseverance; [4a]and perseverance, [1]character; and character, hope. [5a]Now hope does not disappoint, [b]because the love of God has been poured out in our hearts by the Holy Spirit who was given to us.

CHRIST IN OUR PLACE

[6]For when we were still without strength, [1]in due time [a]Christ died for the ungodly. [7]For scarcely for a righteous man will one die; yet perhaps for a good man someone would even dare to die. [8]But [a]God demonstrates His own love toward us, in that while we were still sinners, Christ died for us. [9]Much more then, having now been justified [a]by His blood, we shall be saved [b]from wrath through Him. [10]For [a]if when we were enemies [b]we were reconciled to God through the death of His Son, much more, having been reconciled, we shall be saved [c]by His life. [11]And not only *that,* but we also [a]rejoice in God through our Lord Jesus Christ, through whom we have now received the reconciliation.

DEATH IN ADAM, LIFE IN CHRIST
(Gen. 3:1–19)

[12]Therefore, just as [a]through one man sin entered the world, and [b]death through sin, and thus death spread to all men, because all sinned— [13](For until the law sin was in the world, but [a]sin is not imputed when there is no law. [14]Nevertheless death reigned from Adam to Moses, even over those

4:16 [b][Gal. 3:22]
[c]Is. 51:2

4:17 [a]Gen. 17:5
[b][Rom. 8:11]
[c]Rom. 9:26

4:18 [a]Gen. 15:5

4:19 [a]Gen. 17:17
[b]Heb. 11:11

4:21 [a]Gen. 18:14;
[Ps. 115:3;
Luke 1:37;
Heb. 11:19]

4:22 [a]Gen. 15:6

4:23
[a]Rom. 15:4;
1 Cor. 10:6

4:24 [a]Acts 2:24

4:25 [a]Is. 53:4, 5;
[Rom. 5:6, 8;
8:32; Gal. 2:20;
Eph. 5:2;
Heb. 9:28]
[b][Rom. 5:18;
1 Cor. 15:17;
2 Cor. 5:15]

5:1 [a]Is. 32:17;
John 16:33
[b][Is. 53:5];
Acts 10:36;
[Eph. 2:14]

5:2
[a][John 10:9;
Eph. 2:18; 3:12;
Heb. 10:19;
1 Pet. 3:18]
[b]1 Cor. 15:1
[c]Heb. 3:6

5:3
[a]Matt. 5:11, 12;
[John 16:33;
Acts 5:41;
2 Cor. 12:9];
James 1:2
[b]James 1:3

5:4 [a]Phil. 2:22;
[James 1:12]

5:5 [a]Phil. 1:20
[b]2 Cor. 1:22;
Eph. 1:13

5:6 [a]Is. 53:5;
[Rom. 4:25; 5:8;
8:32; Gal. 2:20;
Eph. 5:2]

5:8 [a][John 3:16;
15:13;
Rom. 8:39]

5:9 [a]Eph. 2:13;
[1 John 1:7]
[b]Rom. 1:18;
1 Thess. 1:10

5:10
[a][Rom. 8:32]
[b]Rom. 11:28;
2 Cor. 5:18;
[Eph. 2:5, 6];
Col. 1:21
[c]John 14:19

5:11 [a][Gal. 4:9]

5:12 [a]Gen. 2:17; 3:6, 19; [Rom. 5:15–17; 1 Cor. 15:21] [b]Gen. 2:17   5:13 [a]1 John 3:4

4:16 [1]certain   5:1 [1]Some ancient mss. *let us have*   5:3 [1]endurance
5:4 [1]approved character   5:6 [1]at the right time

5:14
a[1 Cor. 15:21, 22]

5:15 a[Is. 53:11]

5:18
a[1 Cor. 15:21, 45]
b Matt. 1:21;
[John 12:32]

5:19
a Is. 53:11, 12;
[Phil. 2:8]

5:20
a John 15:22
b Luke 7:47;
Rom. 6:1;
1 Tim. 1:14

6:1
a Rom. 3:8; 6:15

6:2
a[Rom. 6:11;
7:4, 6;
Gal. 2:19;
Col. 2:20; 3:3];
1 Pet. 2:24

6:3 a Acts 2:38;
8:16; 19:5;
[Gal. 3:27];
Col. 2:12
b[1 Cor. 15:29]

6:4 a Col. 2:12
b 1 Cor. 6:14
c John 2:11
d Rom. 7:6;
[2 Cor. 5:17;
Gal. 6:15;
Eph. 4:23;
Col. 3:10]

6:5 a 2 Cor. 4:10;
Phil. 3:10;
Col. 2:12; 3:1

6:6 a Gal. 2:20;
5:24; 6:14
b Col. 2:11

6:7 a 1 Pet. 4:1

6:8 a Rom. 6:4;
2 Cor. 4:10;
2 Tim. 2:11

6:9 a Rev. 1:18

6:10 a Heb. 9:27
b Luke 20:38

6:11 a[Rom. 6:2;
7:4, 6]
b[Gal. 2:19;
Col. 2:20; 3:3];
1 Pet. 2:24

6:12 a Ps. 19:13

6:13
a Rom. 6:16, 19;
7:5; Col. 3:5;
James 4:1
b Rom. 12:1;
2 Cor. 5:14;
1 Pet. 2:24; 4:2

6:14
a[Rom. 7:4, 6;
8:2; Gal. 5:18]

who had not sinned according to the likeness of the transgression of Adam, [a]who is a type of Him who was to come. [15]But the free gift *is* not like the [1]offense. For if by the one man's offense many died, much more the grace of God and the gift by the grace of the one Man, Jesus Christ, abounded [a]to many. [16]And the gift *is* not like *that which came* through the one who sinned. For the judgment *which came* from one *offense resulted* in condemnation, but the free gift *which came* from many [1]offenses *resulted* in justification. [17]For if by the one man's [1]offense death reigned through the one, much more those who receive abundance of grace and of the gift of righteousness will reign in life through the One, Jesus Christ.)

[18]Therefore, as through [1]one man's offense *judgment came* to all men, resulting in condemnation, even so through [a]one[2] Man's righteous act *the free gift came* [b]to all men, resulting in justification of life. [19]For as by one man's disobedience many were made sinners, so also by [a]one Man's obedience many will be made righteous.

[20]Moreover [a]the law entered that the offense might abound. But where sin abounded, grace [b]abounded much more, [21]so that as sin reigned in death, even so grace might reign through righteousness to eternal life through Jesus Christ our Lord.

DEAD TO SIN, ALIVE TO GOD

6 What shall we say then? [a]Shall we continue in sin that grace may abound? [2]Certainly not! How shall we who [a]died to sin live any longer in it? [3]Or do you not know that [a]as many of us as were baptized into Christ Jesus [b]were baptized into His death? [4]Therefore we were [a]buried with Him through baptism into death, that [b]just as Christ was raised from the dead by [c]the glory of the Father, [d]even so we also should walk in newness of life.

[5a]For if we have been united together in the likeness of His death, certainly we also shall be *in the likeness* of His resurrection, [6]knowing this, that [a]our old man was crucified with *Him,* that [b]the body of sin might be [1]done away with, that we should no longer be slaves of sin. [7]For [a]he who has died has been [1]freed from sin. [8]Now [a]if we died with Christ, we believe that we shall also live with Him, [9]knowing that [a]Christ, having been raised from the dead, dies no more. Death no longer has dominion over Him. [10]For *the death* that He died, [a]He died to sin once for all; but *the life* that He lives, [b]He lives to God. [11]Likewise you also, [1]reckon yourselves to be [a]dead indeed to sin, but [b]alive to God in Christ Jesus our Lord.

[12a]Therefore do not let sin reign in your mortal body, that you should obey it in its lusts. [13]And do not present your [a]members *as* [1]instruments of unrighteousness to sin, but [b]present yourselves to God as being alive from the dead, and your members *as* instruments of righteousness to God. [14]For [a]sin shall not have dominion over you, for you are not under law but under grace.

5:15 [1]*trespass* or *false step*   5:16 [1]*trespasses*   5:17 [1]*trespass*   5:18 [1]Or *one trespass*   [2]Or *one righteous act*   6:6 [1]*rendered inoperative*   6:7 [1]*cleared*   6:11 [1]*consider*   6:13 [1]Or *weapons*

FROM SLAVES OF SIN TO SLAVES OF GOD

15What then? Shall we sin ªbecause we are not under law but under grace? Certainly not! 16Do you not know that ªto whom you present yourselves slaves to obey, you are that one's slaves whom you obey, whether of sin *leading* to death, or of obedience *leading* to righteousness? 17But God be thanked that *though* you were slaves of sin, yet you obeyed from the heart ªthat form of doctrine to which you were 1delivered. 18And ªhaving been set free from sin, you became slaves of righteousness. 19I speak in human *terms* because of the weakness of your flesh. For just as you presented your members *as* slaves of uncleanness, and of lawlessness *leading* to *more* lawlessness, so now present your members *as* slaves *of* righteousness 1for holiness.

20For when you were ªslaves of sin, you were free in regard to righteousness. 21ªWhat fruit did you have then in the things of which you are now ashamed? For ᵇthe end of those things *is* death. 22But now ªhaving been set free from sin, and having become slaves of God, you have your fruit 1to holiness, and the end, everlasting life. 23For ªthe wages of sin *is* death, but ᵇthe 1gift of God *is* eternal life in Christ Jesus our Lord.

FREED FROM THE LAW

7 Or do you not know, brethren (for I speak to those who know the law), that the law 1has dominion over a man as long as he lives? 2For ªthe woman who has a husband is bound by the law to *her* husband as long as he lives. But if the husband dies, she is released from the law of *her* husband. 3So then ªif, while *her* husband lives, she marries another man, she will be called an adulteress; but if her husband dies, she is free from that law, so that she is no adulteress, though she has married another man. 4Therefore, my brethren, you also have become ªdead to the law through the body of Christ, that you may be married to another—to Him who was raised from the dead, that we should ᵇbear fruit to God. 5For when we were in the flesh, the sinful passions which were aroused by the law ªwere at work in our members ᵇto bear fruit to death. 6But now we have been delivered from the law, having died to what we were held by, so that we should serve ªin the newness of the Spirit and not *in* the oldness of the letter.

SIN'S ADVANTAGE IN THE LAW

7What shall we say then? *Is* the law sin? Certainly not! On the contrary, ªI would not have known sin except through the law. For I would not have known covetousness unless the law had said, ᵇ"You shall not covet." 8But ªsin, taking opportunity by the commandment, produced in me all *manner of evil* desire. For ᵇapart from the law sin *was* dead. 9I was alive once without the law, but when the commandment came, sin revived and I died. 10And the commandment, ªwhich *was* to *bring* life, I found to *bring* death. 11For sin, taking occasion by the commandment, deceived me, and by it killed *me*. 12Therefore ªthe law *is* holy, and the commandment holy and just and good.

6:17 1entrusted   6:19 1unto sanctification   6:22 1unto sanctification
6:23 1free gift   7:1 1rules

6:15 ª1 Cor. 9:21

6:16 ªProv. 5:22;
[Matt. 6:24];
John 8:34;
2 Pet. 2:19

6:17 ª2 Tim. 1:13

6:18 ªJohn 8:32;
Rom. 6:22; 8:2;
1 Cor. 7:22;
Gal. 5:1;
1 Pet. 2:16

6:20 ªJohn 8:34

6:21 ªJer. 12:13;
Ezek. 16:63;
Rom. 7:5
ᵇRom. 1:32;
Gal. 6:8

6:22
ª[John 8:32];
Rom. 6:18; 8:2

6:23 ªGen. 2:17
ᵇRom. 2:7;
1 Pet. 1:4

7:2 ª1 Cor. 7:39

7:3
ª[Matt. 5:32]

7:4 ªRom. 8:2;
Gal. 2:19; 5:18;
[Col. 2:14]
ᵇGal. 5:22

7:5 ªRom. 6:13
ᵇRom. 6:21;
Gal. 5:19;
James 1:15

7:6 ªRom. 2:29;
2 Cor. 3:6

7:7 ªRom. 3:20
ᵇEx. 20:17;
Deut. 5:21;
Acts 20:33

7:8 ªRom. 4:15
ᵇ1 Cor. 15:56

7:10 ªLev. 18:5;
Ezek. 20:11,
13, 21;
Luke 10:28;
Rom. 10:5;
2 Cor. 3:7;
Gal. 3:12

7:12 ªPs. 19:8

LAW CANNOT SAVE FROM SIN

¹³Has then what is good become death to me? Certainly not! But sin, that it might appear sin, was producing death in me through what is good, so that sin through the commandment might become exceedingly sinful. ¹⁴For we know that the law is spiritual, but I am carnal, ªsold under sin. ¹⁵For what I am doing, I do not understand. ªFor what I will to do, that I do not practice; but what I hate, that I do. ¹⁶If, then, I do what I will not to do, I agree with the law that *it is* good. ¹⁷But now, *it is* no longer I who do it, but sin that dwells in me. ¹⁸For I know that ªin me (that is, in my flesh) nothing good dwells; for to will is present with me, but *how* to perform what is good I do not find. ¹⁹For the good that I will *to do,* I do not do; but the evil I will not *to do,* that I practice. ²⁰Now if I do what I will not *to do,* it is no longer I who do it, but sin that dwells in me.

²¹I find then a law, that evil is present with me, the one who wills to do good. ²²For I ªdelight in the law of God according to ᵇthe inward man. ²³But ªI see another law in ᵇmy members, warring against the law of my mind, and bringing me into captivity to the law of sin which is in my members. ²⁴O wretched man that I am! Who will deliver me ªfrom this body of death? ²⁵ªI thank God—through Jesus Christ our Lord! So then, with the mind I myself serve the law of God, but with the flesh the law of sin.

FREE FROM INDWELLING SIN

8 *There is* therefore now no condemnation to those who are in Christ Jesus, ªwho¹ do not walk according to the flesh, but according to the Spirit. ²For ªthe law of ᵇthe Spirit of life in Christ Jesus has made me free from ᶜthe law of sin and death. ³For ªwhat the law could not do in that it was weak through the flesh, ᵇGod *did* by sending His own Son in the likeness of sinful flesh, on account of sin: He condemned sin in the flesh, ⁴that the righteous requirement of the law might be fulfilled in us who ªdo not walk according to the flesh but according to the Spirit. ⁵For ªthose who live according to the flesh set their minds on the things of the flesh, but those *who live* according to the Spirit, ᵇthe things of the Spirit. ⁶For ªto be ¹carnally minded *is* death, but to be spiritually minded *is* life and peace. ⁷Because ªthe ¹carnal mind *is* enmity against God; for it is not subject to the law of God, ᵇnor indeed can be. ⁸So then, those who are in the flesh cannot please God.

⁹But you are not in the flesh but in the Spirit, if indeed the Spirit of God dwells in you. Now if anyone does not have the Spirit of Christ, he is not His. ¹⁰And if Christ *is* in you, the body *is* dead because of sin, but the Spirit *is* life because of righteousness. ¹¹But if the Spirit of ªHim who raised Jesus from the dead dwells in you, ᵇHe who raised Christ from the dead will also give life to your mortal bodies ¹through His Spirit who dwells in you.

SONSHIP THROUGH THE SPIRIT

¹²ªTherefore, brethren, we are debtors—not to the flesh, to live according to the flesh. ¹³For ªif you live according to the flesh you will die; but if by the Spirit you ᵇput to death

7:14
ª1 Kin. 21:20, 25;
2 Kin. 17:17;
Rom. 6:16
7:15 ªRom. 7:19;
[Gal. 5:17]
7:18 ª[Gen. 6:5;
8:21]
7:22 ªPs. 1:2
ᵇ[2 Cor. 4:16;
Eph. 3:16;
1 Pet. 3:4]
7:23 ªRom. 6:19;
[Gal. 5:17];
James 4:1;
1 Pet. 2:11
ᵇRom. 6:13, 19
7:24
ª[Rom. 8:11;
1 Cor. 15:51, 52;
1 Thess. 4:14–17]
7:25 ª1 Cor. 15:57
8:1 ªGal. 5:16
8:2
ªRom. 6:18, 22
ᵇ[1 Cor. 15:45]
ᶜRom. 7:24, 25
8:3 ªActs 13:39;
[Heb. 7:18]
ᵇ[2 Cor. 5:21;
Gal. 3:13]
8:4 ª[Rom. 6:4;
2 Cor. 5:7];
Gal. 5:16, 25;
Eph. 4:1; 5:2, 15;
[1 John 1:7; 2:6]
8:5 ªJohn 3:6
ᵇ[Gal. 5:22–25]
8:6 ªGal. 6:8
8:7 ªJames 4:4
ᵇ1 Cor. 2:14
8:11 ªActs 2:24;
Rom. 6:4
ᵇ1 Cor. 6:14
8:12
ª[Rom. 6:7, 14]
8:13 ªGal. 6:8
ᵇEph. 4:22;
[Col. 3:5–10]

8:1 ¹NU omits the rest of v. 1.   **8:6** ¹*fleshly*   **8:7** ¹*fleshly*
8:11 ¹Or *because of*

the deeds of the body, you will live. [14]For [a]as many as are led by the Spirit of God, these are sons of God. [15]For [a]you did not receive the spirit of bondage again [b]to fear, but you received the [c]Spirit of adoption by whom we cry out, [d]"Abba,[1] Father." [16][a]The Spirit Himself bears witness with our spirit that we are children of God, [17]and if children, then [a]heirs—heirs of God and joint heirs with Christ, [b]if indeed we suffer with *Him,* that we may also be glorified together.

FROM SUFFERING TO GLORY

[18]For I consider that [a]the sufferings of this present time are not worthy *to be compared* with the glory which shall be revealed in us. [19]For [a]the earnest expectation of the creation eagerly waits for the revealing of the sons of God. [20]For [a]the creation was subjected to futility, not willingly, but because of Him who subjected *it* in hope; [21]because the creation itself also will be delivered from the bondage of [1]corruption into the glorious [a]liberty of the children of God. [22]For we know that the whole creation [a]groans and labors with birth pangs together until now. [23]Not only *that,* but we also who have [a]the firstfruits of the Spirit, [b]even we ourselves groan [c]within ourselves, eagerly waiting for the adoption, the [d]redemption of our body. [24]For we were saved in this hope, but [a]hope that is seen is not hope; for why does one still hope for what he sees? [25]But if we hope for what we do not see, we eagerly wait for *it* with perseverance.

[26]Likewise the Spirit also helps in our weaknesses. For [a]we do not know what we should pray for as we ought, but [b]the Spirit Himself makes intercession [1]for us with groanings which cannot be uttered. [27]Now [a]He who searches the hearts knows what the mind of the Spirit *is,* because He makes intercession for the saints [b]according to *the will of* God.

[28]And we know that all things work together for good to those who love God, to those [a]who are the called according to *His* purpose. [29]For whom [a]He foreknew, [b]He also predestined [c]*to be* conformed to the image of His Son, [d]that He might be the firstborn among many brethren. [30]Moreover whom He predestined, these He also [a]called; whom He called, these He also [b]justified; and whom He justified, these He also [c]glorified.

GOD'S EVERLASTING LOVE

[31]What then shall we say to these things? [a]If God *is* for us, who *can be* against us? [32a]He who did not spare His own Son, but [b]delivered Him up for us all, how shall He not with Him also freely give us all things? [33]Who shall bring a charge against God's elect? [a]*It is* God who justifies. [34a]Who *is* he who condemns? *It is* Christ who died, and furthermore is also risen, [b]who is even at the right hand of God, [c]who also makes intercession for us. [35]Who shall separate us from the love of Christ? *Shall* tribulation, or distress, or persecution, or famine, or nakedness, or peril, or sword? [36]As it is written:

[a]"For Your sake we are killed all day long;
We are accounted as sheep for the slaughter."

8:34 [a]John 3:18 [b]Mark 16:19; Col. 3:1; Heb. 1:3 [c]Heb. 7:25; 9:24   8:36 [a]Ps. 44:22; Acts 20:24; 1 Cor. 4:9; 15:30; [2 Cor. 1:9; 4:10; 6:9; 11:23]

8:15 [1]Lit., in Aram., *Father*   8:21 [1]*decay*   8:26 [1]NU omits *for us*

8:14 [a][Gal. 5:18]

8:15
[a][1 Cor. 2:12];
Heb. 2:15
[b]2 Tim. 1:7
[c][Is. 56:5]
[d]Mark 14:36;
Gal. 4:6

8:16 [a]Eph. 1:13

8:17 [a]Acts 26:18
[b]Phil. 1:29

8:18 [a]2 Cor. 4:17;
[1 Pet. 1:6; 4:13]

8:19
[a][2 Pet. 3:13]

8:20
[a]Gen. 3:17–19

8:21
[a][2 Cor. 3:17];
Gal. 5:1, 13

8:22 [a]Jer. 12:4, 11

8:23 [a]2 Cor. 5:5;
Eph. 1:14
[b]2 Cor. 5:2, 4
[c][Luke 20:36]
[d]Luke 21:28;
Eph. 1:14; 4:30;
[Phil. 3:20, 21]

8:24
[a]Rom. 4:18;
2 Cor. 5:7;
Heb. 11:1

8:26
[a]Matt. 20:22;
2 Cor. 12:8
[b]John 14:16;
Rom. 8:15;
Eph. 6:18

8:27 [a]1 Chr. 28:9
[b]1 John 5:14

8:28 [a]2 Tim. 1:9

8:29
[a]2 Tim. 2:19
[b]Rom. 9:23;
1 Cor. 2:7;
Eph. 1:5, 11
[c][2 Cor. 3:18]
[d][Col. 1:15, 18];
Heb. 1:6

8:30
[a]Rom. 8:28;
9:24; 1 Cor. 1:9;
Gal. 1:6, 15; 5:8;
Eph. 1:11; 3:11;
2 Thess. 2:14;
[Heb. 9:15;
1 Pet. 2:9; 3:9]
[b]1 Cor. 6:11;
[Gal. 2:16]
[c]John 17:22;
Rom. 8:21

8:31 [a]Num. 14:9

8:32
[a]Rom. 5:6, 10
[b][Rom. 4:25]

8:33
[a]Is. 50:8, 9;
Rev. 12:10

8:37
a John 16:33;
1 Cor. 15:57;
2 Cor. 2:14;
1 John 5:4

8:38
a [1 Cor. 15:24;
Eph. 1:21;
1 Pet. 3:22]

9:1 a 2 Cor. 1:23

9:2 a Rom. 10:1

9:3 a Ex. 32:32

9:4 a Ex. 4:22;
[Rom. 8:15]
b 1 Sam. 4:21
c Gen. 17:2;
Deut. 29:14;
Luke 1:72;
Acts 3:25
d Deut. 4:13;
Ps. 147:19
e Heb. 9:1, 6
f [Acts 2:39;
13:32;
Eph. 2:12]

9:5 a Deut. 10:15
b [Luke 1:34, 35;
3:23] c Jer. 23:6

9:6 a Num. 23:19
b [John 8:39;
Gal. 6:16]

9:7
a [John 8:33, 39;
Gal. 4:23]
b Gen. 21:12;
Heb. 11:18

9:8 a Gal. 4:28

9:9
a Gen. 18:10, 14;
Heb. 11:11

9:10 a Gen. 25:21

9:11 a [Rom. 4:17;
8:28]

9:12 a Gen. 25:23

9:13 a Mal. 1:2, 3

9:14 a Deut. 32:4

9:15 a Ex. 33:19

9:17 a Gal. 3:8
b Ex. 9:16

9:18 a Ex. 4:21;
Deut. 2:30;
Josh. 11:20;
John 12:40;
Rom. 11:7, 25

9:19
a 2 Chr. 20:6;
Job 9:12;
Dan. 4:35

9:20 a Is. 29:16;
Jer. 18:6;
Rom. 9:22;
2 Tim. 2:20

9:21 a Prov. 16:4
b 2 Tim. 2:20

[37a]Yet in all these things we are more than conquerors through Him who loved us. [38]For I am persuaded that neither death nor life, nor angels nor [a]principalities nor powers, nor things present nor things to come, [39]nor height nor depth, nor any other created thing, shall be able to separate us from the love of God which is in Christ Jesus our Lord.

ISRAEL'S REJECTION OF CHRIST

9 I [a]tell the truth in Christ, I am not lying, my conscience also bearing me witness in the Holy Spirit, [2a]that I have great sorrow and continual grief in my heart. [3]For [a]I could wish that I myself were accursed from Christ for my brethren, my [1]countrymen according to the flesh, [4]who are Israelites, [a]to whom *pertain* the adoption, [b]the glory, [c]the covenants, [d]the giving of the law, [e]the service *of God,* and [f]the promises; [5a]of whom *are* the fathers and from [b]whom, according to the flesh, Christ *came,* [c]who is over all, *the* eternally blessed God. Amen.

ISRAEL'S REJECTION AND GOD'S PURPOSE
(Gen. 25:19–23)

[6a]But it is not that the word of God has taken no effect. For [b]they *are* not all Israel who *are* of Israel, [7a]nor *are they* all children because they are the seed of Abraham; but, [b]"In Isaac your seed shall be called." [8]That is, those who *are* the children of the flesh, these *are* not the children of God; but [a]the children of the promise are counted as the seed. [9]For this *is* the word of promise: [a]"At this time I will come and Sarah shall have a son."

[10]And not only *this,* but when [a]Rebecca also had conceived by one man, *even* by our father Isaac [11](for *the children* not yet being born, nor having done any good or evil, that the purpose of God according to election might stand, not of works but of [a]Him who calls), [12]it was said to her, [a]"The older shall serve the younger." [13]As it is written, [a]"Jacob I have loved, but Esau I have hated."

ISRAEL'S REJECTION AND GOD'S JUSTICE

[14]What shall we say then? [a]Is there unrighteousness with God? Certainly not! [15]For He says to Moses, [a]"I will have mercy on whomever I will have mercy, and I will have compassion on whomever I will have compassion." [16]So then *it is* not of him who wills, nor of him who runs, but of God who shows mercy. [17]For [a]the Scripture says to the Pharaoh, [b]"For this very purpose I have raised you up, that I may show My power in you, and that My name may be declared in all the earth." [18]Therefore He has mercy on whom He wills, and whom He wills He [a]hardens.

[19]You will say to me then, "Why does He still find fault? For [a]who has resisted His will?" [20]But indeed, O man, who are you to reply against God? [a]Will the thing formed say to him who formed *it,* "Why have you made me like this?" [21]Does not the [a]potter have power over the clay, from the same lump to make [b]one vessel for honor and another for dishonor?

[22]*What* if God, wanting to show *His* wrath and to make His

---

9:3 [1]Or *relatives*

power known, endured with much longsuffering [a]the vessels of wrath [b]prepared for destruction, 23and that He might make known [a]the riches of His glory on the vessels of mercy, which He had [b]prepared beforehand for glory, 24even us whom He [a]called, [b]not of the Jews only, but also of the Gentiles?

25As He says also in Hosea:

[a]"I will call them My people, who were not My people,
And her beloved, who was not beloved."
26 "And[a] it shall come to pass in the place where it was said to them,
'You *are* not My people,'
There they shall be called sons of the living God."

27Isaiah also cries out concerning Israel:

[a]"Though the number of the children of Israel be as the sand of the sea,
[b]The remnant will be saved.
28 For [1]He will finish the work and cut *it* short in righteousness,
[a]Because the LORD will make a short work upon the earth."

29And as Isaiah said before:

[a]"Unless the LORD of [1]Sabaoth had left us a seed,
[b]We would have become like Sodom,
And we would have been made like Gomorrah."

PRESENT CONDITION OF ISRAEL

30What shall we say then? [a]That Gentiles, who did not pursue righteousness, have attained to righteousness, [b]even the righteousness of faith; 31but Israel, [a]pursuing the law of righteousness, [b]has not attained to the law [1]of righteousness. 32Why? Because *they did* not *seek it* by faith, but as it were, [1]by the works of the law. For [a]they stumbled at that stumbling stone. 33As it is written:

[a]"Behold, I lay in Zion a stumbling stone and rock of offense,
And [b]whoever believes on Him will not be put to shame."

ISRAEL NEEDS THE GOSPEL

10 Brethren, my heart's desire and prayer to God for [1]Israel is that they may be saved. 2For I bear them witness [a]that they have a zeal for God, but not according to knowledge. 3For they being ignorant of [a]God's righteousness, and seeking to establish their own [b]righteousness, have not submitted to the righteousness of God. 4For [a]Christ *is* the end of the law for righteousness to everyone who believes.

5For Moses writes about the righteousness which is of the law, [a]"The man who does those things shall live by them." 6But the righteousness of faith speaks in this way, [a]"Do not say in your heart, 'Who will ascend into heaven?'" (that is, to bring Christ down *from above*) 7or, [a]"'Who will descend into the abyss?'" (that is, to bring Christ up from the dead). 8But what does it say? [a]"The word is near you, in your mouth and in

9:22
[a][1 Thess. 5:9]
[b]Prov. 16:4;
[1 Pet. 2:8]

9:23
[a][Col. 1:27]
[b][Rom. 8:28–30]

9:24
[a][Rom. 8:28]
[b]Is. 42:6, 7; 49:6;
Luke 2:32;
Rom. 3:29

9:25 [a]Hos. 2:23;
1 Pet. 2:10

9:26 [a]Hos. 1:10

9:27
[a]Is. 10:22, 23
[b]Rom. 11:5

9:28
[a]Is. 10:23; 28:22

9:29 [a]Is. 1:9
[b]Deut. 29:23;
Is. 13:19;
Jer. 49:18;
50:40;
Amos 4:11

9:30 [a]Rom. 4:11
[b]Rom. 1:17; 3:21;
10:6; [Gal. 2:16;
3:24; Phil. 3:9];
Heb. 11:7

9:31
[a][Rom. 10:2–4]
[b][Gal. 5:4]

9:32
[a][Luke 2:34;
1 Cor. 1:23]

9:33
[a][Ps. 118:22];
Is. 8:14; 28:16;
[Matt. 21:42;
1 Pet. 2:6–8]
[b]Rom. 5:5; 10:11

10:2
[a]Acts 21:20;
Gal. 1:14

10:3
[a][Rom. 1:17]
[b][Phil. 3:9]

10:4 [a]Matt. 5:17;
[Rom. 7:1–4;
Gal. 3:24; 4:5]

10:5 [a]Lev. 18:5;
Neh. 9:29;
Ezek. 20:11, 13, 21;
Rom. 7:10;
Gal. 3:12

10:6
[a]Deut. 30:12–14

10:7
[a]Deut. 30:13

10:8
[a]Deut. 30:14

9:28 [1]NU *the* LORD *will finish the work and cut it short upon the earth*   9:29 [1]Lit., in Heb., *Hosts*   9:31 [1]NU omits *of righteousness*   9:32 [1]NU *by works*, omitting *of the law*   10:1 [1]NU *them*

your heart" (that is, the word of faith which we preach): 9that aif you confess with your mouth the Lord Jesus and believe in your heart that God has raised Him from the dead, you will be saved. 10For with the heart one believes unto righteousness, and with the mouth confession is made unto salvation. 11For the Scripture says, a"Whoever believes on Him will not be put to shame." 12For athere is no distinction between Jew and Greek, for bthe same Lord over all cis rich to all who call upon Him. 13For a"whoever calls bon the name of the LORD shall be saved."

ISRAEL REJECTS THE GOSPEL

14How then shall they call on Him in whom they have not believed? And how shall they believe in Him of whom they have not heard? And how shall they hear awithout a preacher? 15And how shall they preach unless they are sent? As it is written:

a"How beautiful are the feet of those who 1preach the
     gospel of peace,
Who bring glad tidings of good things!"

16But they have not all obeyed the gospel. For Isaiah says, a"LORD, who has believed our report?" 17So then faith *comes* by hearing, and hearing by the word of God.

18But I say, have they not heard? Yes indeed:

a"Their sound has gone out to all the earth,
And their words to the ends of the world."

19But I say, did Israel not know? First Moses says:

a"I will provoke you to jealousy by *those who are* not a
     nation,
I will move you to anger by a bfoolish nation."

20But Isaiah is very bold and says:

a"I was found by those who did not seek Me;
I was made manifest to those who did not ask for Me."

21But to Israel he says:

a"All day long I have stretched out My hands
To a disobedient and contrary people."

ISRAEL'S REJECTION NOT TOTAL

11 I say then, ahas God cast away His people? bCertainly not! For cI also am an Israelite, of the seed of Abraham, *of* the tribe of Benjamin. 2God has not cast away His people whom aHe foreknew. Or do you not know what the Scripture says of Elijah, how he pleads with God against Israel, saying, 3a"LORD, they have killed Your prophets and torn down Your altars, and I alone am left, and they seek my life"? 4But what does the divine response say to him? a"I have reserved for Myself seven thousand men who have not bowed the knee to Baal." 5aEven so then, at this present time there is a remnant according to the election of grace. 6And aif by grace, then *it is* no longer of works; otherwise grace is no longer grace. 1But if *it is* of works, it is no longer grace; otherwise work is no longer work.

10:9 aMatt. 10:32; Luke 12:8; Acts 8:37; Rom. 14:9; [1 Cor. 12:3]; Phil. 2:11
10:11 aIs. 28:16; Jer. 17:7; Rom. 9:33
10:12 aActs 15:9; Rom. 3:22, 29; Gal. 3:28; bActs 10:36; 1 Tim. 2:5; cEph. 1:7
10:13 aJoel 2:32; Acts 2:21; bActs 9:14
10:14 aActs 8:31; Titus 1:3
10:15 aIs. 52:7; Nah. 1:15
10:16 aIs. 53:1; John 12:38
10:18 aPs. 19:4; Matt. 24:14; Mark 16:15; Rom. 1:8; Col. 1:6, 23; 1 Thess. 1:8
10:19 aDeut. 32:21; Rom. 11:11; bTitus 3:3
10:20 aIs. 65:1; Rom. 9:30
10:21 aIs. 65:2
11:1 aPs. 94:14; Jer. 46:28; b1 Sam. 12:22; Jer. 31:37; c2 Cor. 11:22; Phil. 3:5
11:2 a[Rom. 8:29]
11:3 a1 Kin. 19:10, 14
11:4 a1 Kin. 19:18
11:5 a2 Kin. 19:4; Rom. 9:27
11:6 aRom. 4:4

10:15 1NU omits *preach the gospel of peace, Who*   11:6 1NU omits the rest of v. 6.

⁷What then? ªIsrael has not obtained what it seeks; but the elect have obtained it, and the rest were ᵇblinded. ⁸Just as it is written:

ª"God has given them a spirit of stupor,
ᵇEyes that they should not see
And ears that they should not hear,
To this very day."

⁹And David says:

ª"Let their table become a snare and a trap,
A stumbling block and a recompense to them.
10   Let their eyes be darkened, so that they do not see,
And bow down their back always."

ISRAEL'S REJECTION NOT FINAL

¹¹I say then, have they stumbled that they should fall? Certainly not! But ªthrough their ¹fall, to provoke them to ᵇjealousy, salvation *has come* to the Gentiles. ¹²Now if their ¹fall *is* riches for the world, and their failure riches for the Gentiles, how much more their fullness!

¹³For I speak to you Gentiles; inasmuch as ªI am an apostle to the Gentiles, I magnify my ministry, ¹⁴if by any means I may provoke to jealousy *those who are* my flesh and ªsave some of them. ¹⁵For if their being cast away *is* the reconciling of the world, what *will* their acceptance *be* ªbut life from the dead?

¹⁶For if ªthe firstfruit *is* holy, the lump *is* also *holy;* and if the root *is* holy, so *are* the branches. ¹⁷And if ªsome of the branches were broken off, ᵇand you, being a wild olive tree, were grafted in among them, and with them became a partaker of the root and ¹fatness of the olive tree, ¹⁸ªdo not boast against the branches. But if you do boast, *remember that* you do not support the root, but the root *supports* you.

¹⁹You will say then, "Branches were broken off that I might be grafted in." ²⁰Well *said.* Because of ªunbelief they were broken off, and you stand by faith. Do not be haughty, but fear. ²¹For if God did not spare the natural branches, He may not spare you either. ²²Therefore consider the goodness and severity of God: on those who fell, severity; but toward you, ¹goodness, ªif you continue in *His* goodness. Otherwise ᵇyou also will be cut off. ²³And they also, ªif they do not continue in unbelief, will be grafted in, for God is able to graft them in again. ²⁴For if you were cut out of the olive tree which is wild by nature, and were grafted contrary to nature into a cultivated olive tree, how much more will these, who *are* natural *branches,* be grafted into their own olive tree?

²⁵For I do not desire, brethren, that you should be ignorant of this mystery, lest you should be ªwise in your own ¹opinion, that ᵇblindness in part has happened to Israel ᶜuntil the fullness of the Gentiles has come in. ²⁶And so all Israel will be ¹saved, as it is written:

ª"The Deliverer will come out of Zion,
And He will turn away ungodliness from Jacob;
27   For ªthis *is* My covenant with them,
When I take away their sins."

11:7 ªRom. 9:31
ᵇMark 6:52;
Rom. 9:18; 11:25;
2 Cor. 3:14

11:8
ªIs. 29:10, 13
ᵇDeut. 29:3, 4;
Is. 6:9;
Matt. 13:13, 14;
John 12:40;
Acts 28:26, 27

11:9
ªPs. 69:22, 23

11:11
ªIs. 42:6, 7;
Acts 28:28
ᵇDeut. 32:21;
Acts 13:46;
Rom. 10:19

11:13 ªActs 9:15;
22:21; Gal. 1:16;
2:7–9; Eph. 3:8

11:14
ª1 Cor. 9:22;
1 Tim. 4:16;
James 5:20

11:15
ª[Is. 26:16–19]

11:16 ªLev. 23:10;
[James 1:18]

11:17 ªJer. 11:16;
[John 15:2]
ᵇActs 2:39;
[Eph. 2:12]

11:18
ª[1 Cor. 10:12]

11:20 ªHeb. 3:19

11:22
ª1 Cor. 15:2;
Heb. 3:6, 14
ᵇ[John 15:2]

11:23
ª[2 Cor. 3:16]

11:25
ªRom. 12:16
ᵇ2 Cor. 3:14
ᶜLuke 21:24;
John 10:16;
Rom. 11:12

11:26 ªPs. 14:7;
Is. 59:20, 21

11:27 ªIs. 27:9;
Heb. 8:12

11:11 ¹trespass   11:12 ¹trespass   11:17 ¹richness   11:22 ¹NU adds *of God*
11:25 ¹estimation   11:26 ¹Or *delivered*

11:28
aDeut. 7:8; 10:15;
Rom. 9:5

11:29
aNum. 23:19

11:30 a[Eph. 2:2]

11:32 aRom. 3:9;
[Gal. 3:22]

11:34 aIs. 40:13;
Jer. 23:18;
1 Cor. 2:16
bJob 36:22

11:35 aJob 41:11

11:36
a[1 Cor. 8:6;
11:12];
Col. 1:16;
Heb. 2:10
bHeb. 13:21

12:1 a1 Cor. 1:10;
2 Cor. 10:1–4
bPhil. 4:18;
Heb. 10:18, 20

12:2
aMatt. 13:22;
Gal. 1:4;
1 John 2:15
bEph. 4:23;
[Titus 3:5]
c[1 Thess. 4:3]

12:3
aRom. 1:5; 15:15;
1 Cor. 3:10; 15:10;
Gal. 2:9;
Eph. 3:7
bProv. 25:27
c[Eph. 4:7]

12:4
a1 Cor. 12:12–14;
[Eph. 4:4, 16]

12:5
a[1 Cor. 10:17];
Gal. 3:28

12:6
a[John 3:27]
bActs 11:27

12:7 aEph. 4:11

12:8
aActs 15:32
b[Matt. 6:1–3]
c[Acts 20:28]
d2 Cor. 9:7

12:9
a2 Cor. 6:6;
1 Tim. 1:5
bPs. 34:14

12:10
aJohn 13:34;
1 Thess. 4:9;
Heb. 13:1;
2 Pet. 1:7
bRom. 13:7;
Phil. 2:3;
[1 Pet. 2:17]

12:12
aLuke 10:20
bLuke 21:19
cLuke 18:1

28Concerning the gospel *they are* enemies for your sake, but concerning the election *they are* abeloved for the sake of the fathers. 29For the gifts and the calling of God *are* airrevocable. 30For as you awere once disobedient to God, yet have now obtained mercy through their disobedience, 31even so these also have now been disobedient, that through the mercy shown you they also may obtain mercy. 32For God has 1committed them aall to disobedience, that He might have mercy on all.

33Oh, the depth of the riches both of the wisdom and knowledge of God! How unsearchable *are* His judgments and His ways past finding out!

34 "For who has known the amind of the LORD?
Or bwho has become His counselor?"
35 "Ora who has first given to Him
And it shall be repaid to him?"

36For aof Him and through Him and to Him *are* all things, bto whom *be* glory forever. Amen.

LIVING SACRIFICES TO GOD

12 I abeseech1 you therefore, brethren, by the mercies of God, that you present your bodies ba living sacrifice, holy, acceptable to God, *which is* your 2reasonable service. 2And ado not be conformed to this world, but bbe transformed by the renewing of your mind, that you may cprove what *is* that good and acceptable and perfect will of God.

SERVE GOD WITH SPIRITUAL GIFTS

3For I say, athrough the grace given to me, to everyone who is among you, bnot to think *of himself* more highly than he ought to think, but to think soberly, as God has dealt cto each one a measure of faith. 4For aas we have many members in one body, but all the members do not have the same function, 5so awe, *being* many, are one body in Christ, and individually members of one another. 6Having then gifts differing according to the grace that is agiven to us, *let us use them:* if prophecy, *let us* bprophesy in proportion to our faith; 7or ministry, *let us use it* in *our* ministering; ahe who teaches, in teaching; 8ahe who exhorts, in exhortation; bhe who gives, with liberality; che who leads, with diligence; he who shows mercy, dwith cheerfulness.

BEHAVE LIKE A CHRISTIAN

9a*Let* love *be* without hypocrisy. bAbhor what is evil. Cling to what is good. 10a*Be* kindly affectionate to one another with brotherly love, bin honor giving preference to one another; 11not lagging in diligence, fervent in spirit, serving the Lord; 12arejoicing in hope, bpatient1 in tribulation, ccontinuing steadfastly in prayer; 13adistributing to the needs of the saints, bgiven1 to hospitality.

14aBless those who persecute you; bless and do not curse. 15aRejoice with those who rejoice, and weep with those who

12:13 a1 Cor. 16:1; Heb. 13:16; 1 Pet. 4:9 bMatt. 25:35; 1 Tim. 3:2 12:14 a[Matt. 5:44]; Luke 6:28; 1 Cor. 4:12 12:15 a[1 Cor. 12:26]

11:32 1shut them all up in 12:1 1urge 2rational 12:12 1persevering
12:13 1Lit. pursuing

weep. [16a]Be of the same mind toward one another. [b]Do not set your mind on high things, but associate with the humble. Do not be wise in your own opinion.

[17a]Repay no one evil for evil. [b]Have[1] regard for good things in the sight of all men. [18]If it is possible, as much as depends on you, [a]live peaceably with all men. [19]Beloved, [a]do not avenge yourselves, but *rather* give place to wrath; for it is written, [b]"Vengeance *is* Mine, I will repay," says the Lord. [20]Therefore

[a]"If your enemy is hungry, feed him;
   If he is thirsty, give him a drink;
   For in so doing you will heap coals of fire on his head."

[21]Do not be overcome by evil, but [a]overcome evil with good.

SUBMIT TO GOVERNMENT

13 Let every soul be [a]subject to the governing authorities. For there is no authority except from God, and the authorities that exist are appointed by God. [2]Therefore whoever resists [a]the authority resists the ordinance of God, and those who resist will [1]bring judgment on themselves. [3]For rulers are not a terror to good works, but to evil. Do you want to be unafraid of the authority? [a]Do what is good, and you will have praise from the same. [4]For he is God's minister to you for good. But if you do evil, be afraid; for he does not bear the sword in vain; for he is God's minister, an avenger to *execute* wrath on him who practices evil. [5]Therefore [a]*you* must be subject, not only because of wrath [b]but also for conscience' sake. [6]For because of this you also pay taxes, for they are God's ministers attending continually to this very thing. [7a]Render therefore to all their due: taxes to whom taxes *are due,* customs to whom customs, fear to whom fear, honor to whom honor.

LOVE YOUR NEIGHBOR
(cf. Mark 12:31; James 2:8)

[8]Owe no one anything except to love one another, for [a]he who loves another has fulfilled the law. [9]For the commandments, [a]"You shall not commit adultery," "You shall not murder," "You shall not steal," [1]"You shall not bear false witness," "You shall not covet," and if *there is* any other commandment, are *all* summed up in this saying, namely, [b]"You shall love your neighbor as yourself." [10]Love does no harm to a neighbor; therefore [a]love *is* the fulfillment of the law.

PUT ON CHRIST

[11]And *do* this, knowing the time, that now *it is* high time [a]to awake out of sleep; for now our salvation *is* nearer than when we *first* believed. [12]The night is far spent, the day is at hand. [a]Therefore let us cast off the works of darkness, and [b]let us put on the armor of light. [13a]Let us walk [1]properly, as in the day, [b]not in revelry and drunkenness, [c]not in lewdness and lust, [d]not in strife and envy. [14]But [a]put on the Lord Jesus Christ, and [b]make no provision for the flesh, to *fulfill its* lusts.

13:13 [a]Phil. 4:8 [b]Prov. 23:20 [c][1 Cor. 6:9] [d]James 3:14 13:14 [a]Job 29:14; Gal. 3:27; [Eph. 4:24; Col. 3:10, 12] [b][Gal. 5:16]; 1 Pet. 2:11

12:17 [1]Or *Provide good* 13:2 [1]Lit. *receive* 13:9 [1]NU omits *"You shall not bear false witness,"* 13:13 [1]*decently*

12:16
[a]Rom. 15:5;
2 Cor. 13:11;
[Phil. 2:2; 4:2];
1 Pet. 3:8
[b]Jer. 45:5

12:17
[a][Matt. 5:39];
1 Pet. 3:9
[b]2 Cor. 8:21

12:18
[a]Heb. 12:14

12:19
[a]Lev. 19:18
[b]Deut. 32:35;
Ps. 94:1;
1 Thess. 4:6;
Heb. 10:30

12:20
[a]2 Kin. 6:22;
Prov. 25:21, 22;
[Matt. 5:44];
Luke 6:27

12:21
[a][Rom. 12:1, 2]

13:1 [a]Titus 3:1;
1 Pet. 2:13

13:2 [a][Titus 3:1]

13:3 [a]1 Pet. 2:14

13:5 [a]Eccl. 8:2
[b]Acts 24:16;
[1 Pet. 2:13, 19]

13:7
[a]Matt. 22:21;
Mark 12:17;
Luke 20:25

13:8
[a][Matt. 7:12;
22:39;
John 13:34;
Rom. 13:10;
Gal. 5:13, 14;
1 Tim. 1:5;
James 2:8]

13:9
[a]Ex. 20:13–17;
Deut. 5:17–21;
Matt. 19:18
[b]Lev. 19:18;
Mark 12:31;
James 2:8

13:10
[a][Matt. 7:12;
22:39, 40;
John 13:34];
Rom. 13:8;
Gal. 5:14;
James 2:8

13:11
[a]Mark 13:37;
[1 Cor. 15:34;
Eph. 5:14];
1 Thess. 5:6

13:12
[a]Eph. 5:11
[b][2 Cor. 6:7; 10:4;
Eph. 6:11, 13;
1 Thess. 5:8]

14:1
a[Rom. 14:2; 15:1;
1 Cor. 8:9; 9:22]

14:2
a1 Cor. 10:25;
[Titus 1:15]

14:3
a[Rom. 14:10, 13;
Col. 2:16]

14:4
aRom. 9:20;
James 4:11, 12

14:5 aGal. 4:10

14:6 aGal. 4:10
bMatt. 14:19;
15:36;
[1 Cor. 10:31;
1 Tim. 4:3]

14:7
a[1 Cor. 6:19;
Gal. 2:20];
1 Thess. 5:10;
[1 Pet. 4:2]

14:8
a2 Cor. 5:14, 15

14:9 a2 Cor. 5:15
bActs 10:36

14:10
aRom. 2:16;
2 Cor. 5:10

14:11 aIs. 45:23;
[Phil. 2:10, 11]

14:12
aMatt. 12:36;
16:27; [Gal. 6:5];
1 Pet. 4:5

14:13 a1 Cor. 8:9

14:14
a1 Cor. 10:25

14:15
aRom. 14:20;
1 Cor. 8:11

14:16
a[Rom. 12:17]

14:17 a1 Cor. 8:8
b[Rom. 8:6]

14:18
a2 Cor. 8:21;
Phil. 4:8;
1 Pet. 2:12

14:19 aPs. 34:14;
Rom. 12:18;
1 Cor. 7:15;
2 Tim. 2:22;
Heb. 12:14
b1 Cor. 14:12;
1 Thess. 5:11

14:20
aRom. 14:15
bActs 10:15
c1 Cor. 8:9–12

14:21 a1 Cor. 8:13

14:22
a[1 John 3:21]

14:23 aTitus 1:15

THE LAW OF LIBERTY

14 Receive[a] one who is weak in the faith, *but* not to disputes over doubtful things. [2]For one believes he [a]may eat all things, but he who is weak eats *only* vegetables. [3]Let not him who eats despise him who does not eat, and [a]let not him who does not eat judge him who eats; for God has received him. [4][a]Who are you to judge another's servant? To his own master he stands or falls. Indeed, he will be made to stand, for God is able to make him stand.

[5][a]One person esteems *one* day above another; another esteems every day *alike*. Let each be fully convinced in his own mind. [6]He who [a]observes the day, observes *it* to the Lord; [1]and he who does not observe the day, to the Lord he does not observe *it*. He who eats, eats to the Lord, for [b]he gives God thanks; and he who does not eat, to the Lord he does not eat, and gives God thanks. [7]For [a]none of us lives to himself, and no one dies to himself. [8]For if we [a]live, we live to the Lord; and if we die, we die to the Lord. Therefore, whether we live or die, we are the Lord's. [9]For [a]to this end Christ died [1]and rose and lived again, that He might be [b]Lord of both the dead and the living. [10]But why do you judge your brother? Or why do you show contempt for your brother? For [a]we shall all stand before the judgment seat of [1]Christ. [11]For it is written:

[a]"*As* I live, says the LORD,
　Every knee shall bow to Me,
　And every tongue shall confess to God."

[12]So then [a]each of us shall give account of himself to God. [13]Therefore let us not judge one another [1]anymore, but rather resolve this, [a]not to put a stumbling block or a cause to fall in *our* brother's way.

THE LAW OF LOVE

[14]I know and am convinced by the Lord Jesus [a]that *there is* nothing unclean of itself; but to him who considers anything to be unclean, to him *it is* unclean. [15]Yet if your brother is grieved because of *your* food, you are no longer walking in love. [a]Do not destroy with your food the one for whom Christ died. [16][a]Therefore do not let your good be spoken of as evil; [17][a]for the kingdom of God is not eating and drinking, but righteousness and [b]peace and joy in the Holy Spirit. [18]For he who serves Christ in [1]these things [a]is acceptable to God and approved by men.

[19][a]Therefore let us pursue the things *which make* for peace and the things by which [b]one may [1]edify another. [20][a]Do not destroy the work of God for the sake of food. [b]All things indeed *are* pure, [c]but *it is* evil for the man who eats with [1]offense. [21]*It is* good neither to eat [a]meat nor drink wine nor *do anything* by which your brother stumbles [1]or is offended or is made weak. [22][1]Do you have faith? Have *it* to yourself before God. [a]Happy *is* he who does not condemn himself in what he approves. [23]But he who doubts is condemned if he eats, because *he does* not *eat* from faith; for [a]whatever *is* not from faith is [1]sin.

BEARING OTHERS' BURDENS

15 We [a]then who are strong ought to bear with the [1]scruples of the weak, and not to please ourselves. [2][a]Let each of us please *his* neighbor for *his* good, leading to [1]edification. [3][a]For even Christ did not please Himself; but as it is written, [b]"The reproaches of those who reproached You fell on Me." [4]For [a]whatever things were written before were written for our learning, that we through the [1]patience and comfort of the Scriptures might have hope. [5][a]Now may the God of patience and comfort grant you to be like-minded toward one another, according to Christ Jesus, [6]that you may [a]with one mind *and* one mouth glorify the God and Father of our Lord Jesus Christ.

GLORIFY GOD TOGETHER

[7]Therefore [a]receive one another, just [b]as Christ also received [1]us, to the glory of God. [8]Now I say that [a]Jesus Christ has become a [1]servant to the circumcision for the truth of God, [b]to confirm the promises *made* to the fathers, [9]and [a]that the Gentiles might glorify God for *His* mercy, as it is written:

[b]"For this reason I will confess to You among the Gentiles,
And sing to Your name."

[10]And again he says:

[a]"Rejoice, O Gentiles, with His people!"

[11]And again:

[a]"Praise the LORD, all you Gentiles!
Laud Him, all you peoples!"

[12]And again, Isaiah says:

[a]"There shall be a root of Jesse;
And He who shall rise to reign over the Gentiles,
In Him the Gentiles shall hope."

[13]Now may the God of hope fill you with all [a]joy and peace in believing, that you may abound in hope by the power of the Holy Spirit.

FROM JERUSALEM TO ILLYRICUM

[14]Now [a]I myself am confident concerning you, my brethren, that you also are full of goodness, [b]filled with all knowledge, able also to admonish [1]one another. [15]Nevertheless, brethren, I have written more boldly to you on *some* points, as reminding you, [a]because of the grace given to me by God, [16]that [a]I might be a minister of Jesus Christ to the Gentiles, ministering the gospel of God, that the [b]offering [1]of the Gentiles might be acceptable, sanctified by the Holy Spirit. [17]Therefore I have reason to glory in Christ Jesus [a]in the things *which pertain* to God. [18]For I will not dare to speak of any of those things [a]which Christ has not accomplished through me, in word and deed, [b]to make the Gentiles obedient— [19][a]in mighty signs and wonders, by the power of the Spirit of God, so that from Jerusalem and round about to Illyricum I have fully preached the gospel of Christ. [20]And so

15:1 [a]Rom. 14:1;
[Gal. 6:1, 2];
1 Thess. 5:14

15:2
[a]1 Cor. 9:22;
10:24, 33;
2 Cor. 13:9

15:3
[a]Matt. 26:39;
[Phil. 2:5–8]
[b]Ps. 69:9

15:4
[a]Rom. 4:23, 24;
1 Cor. 10:11;
2 Tim. 3:16, 17

15:5 [a]1 Cor. 1:10;
Phil. 1:27

15:6 [a]Acts 4:24

15:7
[a]Rom. 14:1, 3
[b]Rom. 5:2

15:8
[a]Matt. 15:24;
Acts 3:26
[b][Rom. 4:16];
2 Cor. 1:20

15:9 [a]John 10:16
[b]2 Sam. 22:50;
Ps. 18:49

15:10
[a]Deut. 32:43

15:11 [a]Ps. 117:1

15:12 [a]Is. 11:1, 10

15:13
[a]Rom. 12:12;
14:17

15:14 [a]2 Pet. 1:12
[b]1 Cor. 1:5; 8:1,
7, 10

15:15
[a]Rom. 1:5; 12:3

15:16 [a]Acts 9:15;
Rom. 11:13
[b][Is. 66:20]

15:17
[a]Heb. 2:17; 5:1

15:18 [a]Acts 15:12;
21:19; 2 Cor. 3:5;
Gal. 2:8
[b]Rom. 1:5

15:19 [a]Acts 19:11

15:1 [1]weaknesses   15:2 [1]building up   15:4 [1]perseverance   15:7 [1]NU, M you
15:8 [1]minister   15:14 [1]M others   15:16 [1]Consisting of

I have made it my aim to preach the gospel, not where Christ was named, [a]lest I should build on another man's foundation, 21but as it is written:

[a]"To whom He was not announced, they shall see;
And those who have not heard shall understand."

PLAN TO VISIT ROME

22For this reason [a]I also have been much hindered from coming to you. 23But now no longer having a place in these parts, and [a]having a great desire these many years to come to you, 24whenever I journey to Spain, [1]I shall come to you. For I hope to see you on my journey, [a]and to be helped on my way there by you, if first I may [b]enjoy your *company* for a while. 25But now [a]I am going to Jerusalem to [1]minister to the saints. 26For [a]it pleased those from Macedonia and Achaia to make a certain contribution for the poor among the saints who are in Jerusalem. 27It pleased them indeed, and they are their debtors. For [a]if the Gentiles have been partakers of their spiritual things, [b]their duty is also to minister to them in material things. 28Therefore, when I have performed this and have sealed to them [a]this fruit, I shall go by way of you to Spain. 29[a]But I know that when I come to you, I shall come in the fullness of the blessing [1]of the gospel of Christ.

30Now I beg you, brethren, through the Lord Jesus Christ, and [a]through the love of the Spirit, [b]that you strive together with me in prayers to God for me, 31[a]that I may be delivered from those in Judea who [1]do not believe, and that [b]my service for Jerusalem may be acceptable to the saints, 32[a]that I may come to you with joy [b]by the will of God, and may [c]be refreshed together with you. 33Now [a]the God of peace *be* with you all. Amen.

SISTER PHOEBE COMMENDED

16 I commend to you Phoebe our sister, who is a servant of the church in [a]Cenchrea, 2[a]that you may receive her in the Lord [b]in a manner worthy of the saints, and assist her in whatever business she has need of you; for indeed she has been a helper of many and of myself also.

GREETING ROMAN SAINTS

3Greet [a]Priscilla and Aquila, my fellow workers in Christ Jesus, 4who risked their own necks for my life, to whom not only I give thanks, but also all the churches of the Gentiles. 5Likewise *greet* [a]the church that is in their house.

Greet my beloved Epaenetus, who is [b]the firstfruits of [1]Achaia to Christ. 6Greet Mary, who labored much for us. 7Greet Andronicus and Junia, my countrymen and my fellow prisoners, who are of note among the [a]apostles, who also [b]were in Christ before me.

8Greet Amplias, my beloved in the Lord. 9Greet Urbanus, our fellow worker in Christ, and Stachys, my beloved. 10Greet Apelles, approved in Christ. Greet those who are of the *household* of Aristobulus. 11Greet Herodion, my [1]countryman. Greet those who are of the *household* of Narcissus who are in the Lord.

15:20 [a]1 Cor. 3:10; [2 Cor. 10:13, 15, 16]
15:21 [a]Is. 52:15
15:22 [a]Rom. 1:13; 1 Thess. 2:17, 18
15:23 [a]Acts 19:21; 23:11; Rom. 1:10, 11
15:24 [a]Acts 15:3 [b]Rom. 1:12
15:25 [a]Acts 19:21
15:26 [a]1 Cor. 16:1; 2 Cor. 8:1–15
15:27 [a]Rom. 11:17 [b]1 Cor. 9:11
15:28 [a]Phil. 4:17
15:29 [a][Rom. 1:11]
15:30 [a]Phil. 2:1 [b]2 Cor. 1:11; Col. 4:12
15:31 [a]2 Tim. 3:11; 4:17 [b]2 Cor. 8:4
15:32 [a]Rom. 1:10 [b]Acts 18:21 [c]1 Cor. 16:18
15:33 [a]Rom. 16:20; 1 Cor. 14:33; 2 Cor. 13:11; Phil. 4:9; [1 Thess. 5:23]; 2 Thess. 3:16; Heb. 13:20
16:1 [a]Acts 18:18
16:2 [a]Phil. 2:29 [b]Phil. 1:27
16:3 [a]Acts 18:2, 18, 26; 1 Cor. 16:19; 2 Tim. 4:19
16:5 [a]1 Cor. 16:19; Col. 4:15; Philem. 2 [b]1 Cor. 16:15
16:7 [a]Acts 1:13, 26 [b]Rom. 8:11; 16:3, 9, 10; 2 Cor. 5:17; 12:2; Gal. 1:22

15:24 [1]NU omits *I shall come to you* and joins *Spain* with the next sentence.
15:25 [1]*serve*   **15:29** [1]NU omits *of the gospel*   **15:31** [1]*are disobedient*
16:5 [1]NU *Asia*   **16:11** [1]Or *relative*

¹²Greet Tryphena and Tryphosa, who have labored in the Lord. Greet the beloved Persis, who labored much in the Lord. ¹³Greet Rufus, ᵃchosen in the Lord, and his mother and mine. ¹⁴Greet Asyncritus, Phlegon, Hermas, Patrobas, Hermes, and the brethren who are with them. ¹⁵Greet Philologus and Julia, Nereus and his sister, and Olympas, and all the saints who are with them.

¹⁶ᵃGreet one another with a holy kiss. ¹The churches of Christ greet you.

AVOID DIVISIVE PERSONS

¹⁷Now I urge you, brethren, note those ᵃwho cause divisions and offenses, contrary to the doctrine which you learned, and ᵇavoid them. ¹⁸For those who are such do not serve our Lord ¹Jesus Christ, but ᵃtheir own belly, and ᵇby smooth words and flattering speech deceive the hearts of the simple. ¹⁹For ᵃyour obedience has become known to all. Therefore I am glad on your behalf; but I want you to be ᵇwise in what is good, and ¹simple concerning evil. ²⁰And ᵃthe God of peace ᵇwill crush Satan under your feet shortly. ᶜThe grace of our Lord Jesus Christ *be* with you. Amen.

GREETINGS FROM PAUL'S FRIENDS

²¹ᵃTimothy, my fellow worker, and ᵇLucius, ᶜJason, and ᵈSosipater, my countrymen, greet you.

²²I, Tertius, who wrote *this* epistle, greet you in the Lord.

²³ᵃGaius, my host and *the host* of the whole church, greets you. ᵇErastus, the treasurer of the city, greets you, and Quartus, a brother. ²⁴ᵃThe¹ grace of our Lord Jesus Christ *be* with you all. Amen.

BENEDICTION

²⁵¹Now ᵃto Him who is able to establish you ᵇaccording to my gospel and the preaching of Jesus Christ, ᶜaccording to the revelation of the mystery ᵈkept secret since the world began ²⁶but ᵃnow made manifest, and by the prophetic Scriptures made known to all nations, according to the commandment of the everlasting God, for ᵇobedience to the faith— ²⁷to ᵃGod, alone wise, *be* glory through Jesus Christ forever. Amen.

16:13 ᵃ2 John 1

16:16
ᵃ1 Cor. 16:20;
2 Cor. 13:12;
1 Thess. 5:26;
1 Pet. 5:14

16:17 ᵃ[Acts 15:1]
ᵇ[1 Cor. 5:9]

16:18 ᵃPhil. 3:19
ᵇCol. 2:4;
2 Pet. 2:3

16:19 ᵃRom. 1:8
ᵇJer. 4:22;
Matt. 10:16;
1 Cor. 14:20

16:20
ᵃRom. 15:33
ᵇGen. 3:15
ᶜ1 Cor. 16:23;
2 Cor. 13:14;
Gal. 6:18;
Phil. 4:23;
1 Thess. 5:28;
2 Thess. 3:18;
Rev. 22:21

16:21 ᵃActs 16:1;
Heb. 13:23
ᵇActs 13:1
ᶜActs 17:5
ᵈActs 20:4

16:23 ᵃ1 Cor. 1:14
ᵇActs 19:22;
2 Tim. 4:20

16:24
ᵃ1 Thess. 5:28

16:25
ᵃ[Eph. 3:20;
Jude 24]
ᵇRom. 2:16
ᶜMatt. 13:35;
Rom. 11:25;
1 Cor. 2:1, 7; 4:1;
Eph. 1:9
ᵈCol. 1:26; 2:2;
4:3; [1 Tim. 3:16]

16:26 ᵃEph. 1:9
ᵇ[Acts 6:7];
Rom. 1:5

16:27 ᵃJude 25

16:16 ¹NU *All the churches*   16:18 ¹NU, M omit *Jesus*   16:19 ¹*innocent*
16:24 ¹NU omits v. 24.   16:25 ¹M puts Rom. 16:25–27 after Rom. 14:23.

THE FIRST EPISTLE OF PAUL
THE APOSTLE TO THE
CORINTHIANS

GREETING

1 Paul, ᵃcalled *to be* an apostle of Jesus Christ ᵇthrough the will of God, and ᶜSosthenes *our* brother,

²To the church of God which is at Corinth, to those who ᵃare ¹sanctified in Christ Jesus, ᵇcalled *to be* saints, with all who in every place call on the name of Jesus Christ ᶜour Lord, ᵈboth theirs and ours:

³ᵃGrace to you and peace from God our Father and the Lord Jesus Christ.

SPIRITUAL GIFTS AT CORINTH

⁴ᵃI thank my God always concerning you for the grace of God which was given to you by Christ Jesus, ⁵that you were enriched in everything by Him ᵃin all ¹utterance and all knowledge, ⁶even as ᵃthe testimony of Christ was confirmed ¹in you, ⁷so that you come short in no gift, eagerly ᵃwaiting for the revelation of our Lord Jesus Christ, ⁸ᵃwho will also confirm you to the end, ᵇ*that you may be* blameless in the day of our Lord Jesus Christ. ⁹ᵃGod *is* faithful, by whom you were called into ᵇthe fellowship of His Son, Jesus Christ our Lord.

SECTARIANISM IS SIN

¹⁰Now I plead with you, brethren, by the name of our Lord Jesus Christ, ᵃthat you all ¹speak the same thing, and *that* there be no ²divisions among you, but *that* you be perfectly joined together in the same mind and in the same judgment. ¹¹For it has been declared to me concerning you, my brethren, by those of Chloe's *household,* that there are ¹contentions among you. ¹²Now I say this, that ᵃeach of you says, "I am of Paul," or "I am of ᵇApollos," or "I am of ᶜCephas," or "I am of Christ." ¹³ᵃIs Christ divided? Was Paul crucified for you? Or were you baptized in the name of Paul?

¹⁴I thank God that I baptized ᵃnone of you except ᵇCrispus and ᶜGaius, ¹⁵lest anyone should say that I had baptized in my own name. ¹⁶Yes, I also baptized the household of ᵃStephanas. Besides, I do not know whether I baptized any other. ¹⁷For Christ did not send me to baptize, but to preach the gospel, ᵃnot with wisdom of words, lest the cross of Christ should be made of no effect.

CHRIST THE POWER AND WISDOM OF GOD
(cf. Is. 29:14)

¹⁸For the ¹message of the cross is ᵃfoolishness to ᵇthose who are perishing, but to us ᶜwho are being saved it is the ᵈpower of God. ¹⁹For it is written:

1:2 ¹*set apart*   1:5 ¹*speech*   1:6 ¹Or *among*   1:10 ¹Have a uniform testimony   ²*schisms* or *dissensions*   1:11 ¹*quarrels*   1:18 ¹Lit. *word*

a"I will destroy the wisdom of the wise,
And bring to nothing the understanding of the prudent."

20aWhere *is* the wise? Where *is* the scribe? Where *is* the ¹disputer of this age? bHas not God made foolish the wisdom of this world? 21For since, in the awisdom of God, the world through wisdom did not know God, it pleased God through the foolishness of the message preached to save those who believe. 22For aJews request a sign, and Greeks seek after wisdom; 23but we preach Christ crucified, ato the Jews a ¹stumbling block and to the ²Greeks bfoolishness, 24but to those who are called, both Jews and Greeks, Christ athe power of God and bthe wisdom of God. 25Because the foolishness of God is wiser than men, and the weakness of God is stronger than men.

GLORY ONLY IN THE LORD

26For ¹you see your calling, brethren, athat not many wise according to the flesh, not many mighty, not many ²noble, *are called.* 27But aGod has chosen the foolish things of the world to put to shame the wise, and God has chosen the weak things of the world to put to shame the things which are mighty; 28and the ¹base things of the world and the things which are despised God has chosen, and the things which are not, to bring to nothing the things that are, 29that no flesh should glory in His presence. 30But of Him you are in Christ Jesus, who became for us wisdom from God—and arighteousness and sanctification and redemption— 31that, as it is written, a"He who glories, let him glory in the LORD."

CHRIST CRUCIFIED

2 And I, brethren, when I came to you, did not come with excellence of speech or of wisdom declaring to you the ¹testimony of God. 2For I determined not to know anything among you aexcept Jesus Christ and Him crucified. 3aI was with you bin weakness, in fear, and in much trembling. 4And my speech and my preaching awere not with persuasive words of ¹human wisdom, bbut in demonstration of the Spirit and of power, 5that your faith should not be in the wisdom of men but in the apower of God.

SPIRITUAL WISDOM

6However, we speak wisdom among those who are mature, yet not the wisdom of this age, nor of the rulers of this age, who are coming to nothing. 7But we speak the wisdom of God in a mystery, the hidden *wisdom* which God ¹ordained before the ages for our glory, 8which none of the rulers of this age knew; for ahad they known, they would not have bcrucified the Lord of glory.

9But as it is written:

a"Eye has not seen, nor ear heard,
Nor have entered into the heart of man
The things which God has prepared for those who love Him."

1:19 aIs. 29:14

1:20
aIs. 19:12; 33:18
bJob 12:17;
Matt. 13:22;
1 Cor. 2:6, 8;
3:18, 19

1:21 aDan. 2:20;
[Rom. 11:33]

1:22
aMatt. 12:38;
Mark 8:11;
John 2:18; 4:48

1:23 aIs. 8:14;
Luke 2:34;
John 6:60;
Gal. 5:11;
[1 Pet. 2:8]
b[1 Cor. 2:14]

1:24 a[Rom. 1:4]
bCol. 2:3

1:26 aJohn 7:48

1:27 aPs. 8:2;
Matt. 11:25

1:30
aJer. 23:5; 33:16;
[2 Cor. 5:21;
Phil. 3:9]

1:31
aJer. 9:23, 24;
2 Cor. 10:17

2:2 a1 Cor. 1:23;
Gal. 6:14

2:3 aActs 18:1
b[2 Cor. 4:7]

2:4 a2 Pet. 1:16
bRom. 15:19;
1 Cor. 4:20

2:5 aRom. 1:16;
1 Thess. 1:5

2:8 aLuke 23:34
bMatt. 27:33–50

2:9
a[Is. 64:4; 65:17]

1:20 ¹debater   1:23 ¹Gr. skandalon, offense   ²NU Gentiles   1:26 ¹consider
²well-born   1:28 ¹insignificant or lowly   2:1 ¹NU mystery   2:4 ¹NU omits
human   2:7 ¹predetermined

2:10
ᵃMatt. 11:25;
13:11; 16:17;
[Gal. 1:12;
Eph. 3:3, 5]

2:11 ᵃJob 32:8;
Eccl. 12:7;
[1 Cor. 6:20];
James 2:26]
ᵇRom. 11:33

2:12
ᵃ[Rom. 8:15]

2:14
ᵃMatt. 16:23

2:16 ᵃJob 15:8;
Is. 40:13;
Rom. 11:34
ᵇ[John 15:15]

3:1 ᵃ1 Cor. 2:6;
Eph. 4:14;
Heb. 5:13

3:2 ᵃHeb. 5:12;
1 Pet. 2:2
ᵇJohn 16:12

3:5 ᵃRom. 15:16;
2 Cor. 3:3, 6;
4:1; 5:18; 6:4;
Eph. 3:7;
Col. 1:25;
1 Tim. 1:12

3:6 ᵃActs 18:4;
1 Cor. 4:15; 9:1;
15:1; 2 Cor. 10:14
ᵇActs 18:24–27;
1 Cor. 1:12
ᶜ[2 Cor. 3:5]

3:7 ᵃ2 Cor. 12:11;
[Gal. 6:3]

3:8 ᵃPs. 62:12;
Rom. 2:6

3:9 ᵃMark 16:20;
Acts 15:4;
2 Cor. 6:1
ᵇ[1 Cor. 3:16];
Eph. 2:20–22];
Col. 2:7;
Heb. 3:3, 4;
[1 Pet. 2:5]

3:10 ᵃRom. 1:5
ᵇ1 Cor. 4:15

3:11 ᵃIs. 28:16;
Matt. 16:18;
2 Cor. 11:4
ᵇEph. 2:20;
1 Pet. 2:4

3:13 ᵃ1 Pet. 1:7
ᵇMal. 3:1–3;
Luke 2:35

3:16 ᵃRom. 8:9;
1 Cor. 6:19;
2 Cor. 6:16;
Eph. 2:21

3:18 ᵃProv. 3:7

¹⁰But ᵃGod has revealed *them* to us through His Spirit. For the Spirit searches all things, yes, the deep things of God. ¹¹For what man knows the things of a man except the ᵃspirit of the man which is in him? ᵇEven so no one knows the things of God except the Spirit of God. ¹²Now we have received, not the spirit of the world, but ᵃthe Spirit who is from God, that we might know the things that have been freely given to us by God.

¹³These things we also speak, not in words which man's wisdom teaches but which the ¹Holy Spirit teaches, comparing spiritual things with spiritual. ¹⁴ᵃBut the natural man does not receive the things of the Spirit of God, for they are foolishness to him; nor can he know *them,* because they are spiritually discerned. ¹⁵But he who is spiritual judges all things, yet he himself is *rightly* judged by no one. ¹⁶For ᵃ"who has known the mind of the LORD that he may instruct Him?" ᵇBut we have the mind of Christ.

SECTARIANISM IS CARNAL

3 And I, brethren, could not speak to you as to spiritual *people* but as to carnal, as to ᵃbabes in Christ. ²I fed you with ᵃmilk and not with solid food; ᵇfor until now you were not able *to receive it,* and even now you are still not able; ³for you are still carnal. For where *there are* envy, strife, and divisions among you, are you not carnal and ¹behaving like *mere* men? ⁴For when one says, "I am of Paul," and another, "I *am* of Apollos," are you not carnal?

WATERING, WORKING, WARNING

⁵Who then is Paul, and who *is* Apollos, but ᵃministers through whom you believed, as the Lord gave to each one? ⁶ᵃI planted, ᵇApollos watered, ᶜbut God gave the increase. ⁷So then ᵃneither he who plants is anything, nor he who waters, but God who gives the increase. ⁸Now he who plants and he who waters are one, ᵃand each one will receive his own reward according to his own labor. ⁹For ᵃwe are God's fellow workers; you are God's field, *you are* ᵇGod's building. ¹⁰ᵃAccording to the grace of God which was given to me, as a wise master builder I have laid ᵇthe foundation, and another builds on it. But let each one take heed how he builds on it. ¹¹For no other foundation can anyone lay than ᵃthat which is laid, ᵇwhich is Jesus Christ. ¹²Now if anyone builds on this foundation *with* gold, silver, precious stones, wood, hay, straw, ¹³each one's work will become clear; for the Day ᵃwill declare it, because ᵇit will be revealed by fire; and the fire will test each one's work, of what sort it is. ¹⁴If anyone's work which he has built on *it* endures, he will receive a reward. ¹⁵If anyone's work is burned, he will suffer loss; but he himself will be saved, yet so as through fire.

¹⁶ᵃDo you not know that you are the temple of God and *that* the Spirit of God dwells in you? ¹⁷If anyone ¹defiles the temple of God, God will destroy him. For the temple of God is holy, which *temple* you are.

AVOID WORLDLY WISDOM

¹⁸ᵃLet no one deceive himself. If anyone among you seems to be wise in this age, let him become a fool that he

---

2:13 ¹NU omits *Holy*   3:3 ¹Lit. *walking according to man*   3:17 ¹*destroys*

may become wise. ¹⁹For the wisdom of this world is foolishness with God. For it is written, ᵃ"He catches the wise in their *own* craftiness"; ²⁰and again, ᵃ"The LORD knows the thoughts of the wise, that they are futile." ²¹Therefore let no one boast in men. For ᵃall things are yours: ²²whether Paul or Apollos or Cephas, or the world or life or death, or things present or things to come—all are yours. ²³And ᵃyou *are* Christ's, and Christ *is* God's.

STEWARDS OF THE MYSTERIES OF GOD

4 Let a man so consider us, as ᵃservants of Christ ᵇand stewards of the mysteries of God. ²Moreover it is required in stewards that one be found faithful. ³But with me it is a very small thing that I should be judged by you or by a human ¹court. In fact, I do not even judge myself. ⁴For I know of nothing against myself, yet I am not justified by this; but He who judges me is the Lord. ⁵ᵃTherefore judge nothing before the time, until the Lord comes, who will both bring to ᵇlight the hidden things of darkness and ᶜreveal the ¹counsels of the hearts. ᵈThen each one's praise will come from God.

FOOLS FOR CHRIST'S SAKE

⁶Now these things, brethren, I have figuratively transferred to myself and Apollos for your sakes, that you may learn in us not to think beyond what is written, that none of you may be ¹puffed up on behalf of one against the other. ⁷For who ¹makes you differ *from another?* And ᵃwhat do you have that you did not receive? Now if you did indeed receive *it*, why do you boast as if you had not received *it?*

⁸You are already full! ᵃYou are already rich! You have reigned as kings without us—and indeed I could wish you did reign, that we also might reign with you! ⁹For I think that God has displayed us, the apostles, last, as men condemned to death; for we have been made a ᵃspectacle ¹to the world, both to angels and to men. ¹⁰We *are* ᵃfools for Christ's sake, but you *are* wise in Christ! ᵇWe *are* weak, but you *are* strong! You *are* distinguished, but we *are* dishonored! ¹¹To the present hour we both hunger and thirst, and we are poorly clothed, and beaten, and homeless. ¹²ᵃAnd we labor, working with our own hands. ᵇBeing reviled, we bless; being persecuted, we endure; ¹³being defamed, we ¹entreat. ᵃWe have been made as the filth of the world, the offscouring of all things until now.

PAUL'S PATERNAL CARE

¹⁴I do not write these things to shame you, but ᵃas my beloved children I warn *you.* ¹⁵For though you might have ten thousand instructors in Christ, yet *you do* not *have* many fathers; for ᵃin Christ Jesus I have begotten you through the gospel. ¹⁶Therefore I urge you, ᵃimitate me. ¹⁷For this reason I have sent ᵃTimothy to you, ᵇwho is my beloved and faithful son in the Lord, who will ᶜremind you of my ways in Christ, as I ᵈteach everywhere ᵉin every church.

¹⁸ᵃNow some are ¹puffed up, as though I were not coming to you. ¹⁹ᵃBut I will come to you shortly, ᵇif the Lord wills, and

4:19 ᵃActs 19:21; 20:2; 1 Cor. 11:34; 16:5, 7–9; 2 Cor. 1:15 ᵇActs 18:21; Heb. 6:3; James 4:15

4:3 ¹Lit. *day* 4:5 ¹*motives* 4:6 ¹*arrogant* 4:7 ¹*distinguishes you*
4:9 ¹Lit. *theater* 4:13 ¹*exhort, encourage* 4:18 ¹*arrogant*

3:19 ᵃJob 5:13
3:20 ᵃPs. 94:11
3:21
ᵃ[2 Cor. 4:5]
3:23
ᵃ[Rom. 14:8];
1 Cor. 15:23;
2 Cor. 10:7;
[Gal. 3:29]
4:1
ᵃMatt. 24:45;
Rom. 13:6;
2 Cor. 3:6;
Col. 1:25
ᵇLuke 12:42;
1 Cor. 9:17;
Titus 1:7;
1 Pet. 4:10
4:5 ᵃMatt. 7:1;
Rom. 2:1;
[Rev. 20:12]
ᵇMatt. 10:26
ᶜ1 Cor. 3:13
ᵈRom. 2:29;
1 Cor. 3:8;
[2 Cor. 5:10]
4:7
ᵃJohn 3:27;
Rom. 12:3, 6;
1 Pet. 4:10
4:8 ᵃRev. 3:17
4:9 ᵃHeb. 10:33
4:10 ᵃActs 17:18;
26:24; 1 Cor. 1:18
ᵇ1 Cor. 2:3;
2 Cor. 13:9
4:12
ᵃActs 18:3; 20:34
ᵇMatt. 5:44
4:13 ᵃLam. 3:45
4:14
ᵃ2 Cor. 6:13; 12:14;
1 Thess. 2:11;
1 John 2:1;
3 John 4
4:15
ᵃNum. 11:12;
Acts 18:11;
1 Cor. 3:8;
Gal. 4:19;
Philem. 10
4:16
ᵃ[1 Cor. 11:1];
Phil. 3:17; 4:9;
[1 Thess. 1:6];
2 Thess. 3:9
4:17
ᵃActs 19:22;
Phil. 2:19
ᵇ1 Cor. 4:14;
1 Tim. 1:2, 18;
2 Tim. 1:2
ᶜ1 Cor. 11:2
ᵈ1 Cor. 7:17;
Titus 1:5
ᵉ1 Cor. 14:33
4:18 ᵃ1 Cor. 5:2

I will know, not the word of those who are puffed up, but the power. 20For athe kingdom of God *is* not in word but in bpower. 21What do you want? aShall I come to you with a rod, or in love and a spirit of gentleness?

IMMORALITY DEFILES THE CHURCH

5 It is actually reported *that there is* sexual immorality among you, and such sexual immorality as is not even 1named among the Gentiles—that a man has his father's awife! 2aAnd you are 1puffed up, and have not rather bmourned, that he who has done this deed might be taken away from among you. 3aFor I indeed, as absent in body but present in spirit, have already judged (as though I were present) him who has so done this deed. 4In the aname of our Lord Jesus Christ, when you are gathered together, along with my spirit, bwith the power of our Lord Jesus Christ, 5adeliver such a one to bSatan for the destruction of the flesh, that his spirit may be saved in the day of the Lord 1Jesus.

6aYour glorying *is* not good. Do you not know that ba little leaven leavens the whole lump? 7Therefore 1purge out the old leaven, that you may be a new lump, since you truly are unleavened. For indeed aChrist, our bPassover, was sacrificed 2for us. 8Therefore alet us keep the feast, bnot with old leaven, nor cwith the leaven of malice and wickedness, but with the unleavened *bread* of sincerity and truth.

IMMORALITY MUST BE JUDGED

9I wrote to you in my epistle anot to 1keep company with sexually immoral people. 10Yet *I* certainly *did* not *mean* with the sexually immoral people of this world, or with the covetous, or extortioners, or idolaters, since then you would need to go aout of the world. 11But now I have written to you not to keep company awith anyone named a brother, who is sexually immoral, or covetous, or an idolater, or a reviler, or a drunkard, or an extortioner—bnot even to eat with such a person.

12For what *have* I *to do* with judging those also who are outside? Do you not judge those who are inside? 13But those who are outside God judges. Therefore a"put away from yourselves the evil person."

DO NOT SUE THE BRETHREN

6 Dare any of you, having a matter against another, go to law before the unrighteous, and not before the asaints? 2Do you not know that athe saints will judge the world? And if the world will be judged by you, are you unworthy to judge the smallest matters? 3Do you not know that we shall ajudge angels? How much more, things that pertain to this life? 4If then you have 1judgments concerning things pertaining to this life, do you appoint those who are least esteemed by the church to judge? 5I say this to your shame. Is it so, that there is not a wise man among you, not even one, who will be able to judge between his brethren? 6But brother goes to law against brother, and that before unbelievers!

7Now therefore, it is already an utter failure for you that you go to law against one another. aWhy do you not rath-

4:20
a1 Thess. 1:5
b1 Cor. 2:4
4:21 a2 Cor. 10:2
5:1 aLev. 18:6–8;
Deut. 22:30;
27:20
5:2 a1 Cor. 4:18
b2 Cor. 7:7–10
5:3 aCol. 2:5;
1 Thess. 2:17
5:4
a[Matt. 18:20]
b[Matt. 16:19;
John 20:23];
2 Cor. 12:9
5:5 aPs. 109:6;
Prov. 23:14;
Luke 22:31;
1 Tim. 1:20
b[Acts 26:18]
5:6 a1 Cor. 3:21
bHos. 7:4;
Matt. 16:6, 12;
Gal. 5:9;
2 Tim. 2:17
5:7 aIs. 53:7
bJohn 19:14
5:8 aEx. 12:15
bDeut. 16:3
cMatt. 16:6
5:9 a2 Cor. 6:14;
Eph. 5:11;
2 Thess. 3:6
5:10 aJohn 17:15
5:11 aMatt. 18:17
bGal. 2:12
5:13
aDeut. 13:5; 17:7,
12; 19:19; 21:21;
22:21, 24; 24:7;
1 Cor. 5:2
6:1 aDan. 7:22;
Matt. 19:28
6:2 aPs. 49:14
6:3 a2 Pet. 2:4
6:7
a[Prov. 20:22]

er accept wrong? Why do you not rather *let yourselves* be cheated? [8]No, you yourselves do wrong and cheat, and *you do* these things *to your* brethren! [9]Do you not know that the unrighteous will not inherit the kingdom of God? Do not be deceived. [a]Neither fornicators, nor idolaters, nor adulterers, nor [1]homosexuals, nor [2]sodomites, [10]nor thieves, nor covetous, nor drunkards, nor revilers, nor extortioners will inherit the kingdom of God. [11]And such were [a]some of you. [b]But you were washed, but you were [1]sanctified, but you were justified in the name of the Lord Jesus and by the Spirit of our God.

GLORIFY GOD IN BODY AND SPIRIT

[12a]All things are lawful for me, but all things are not [1]helpful. All things are lawful for me, but I will not be brought under the power of [2]any. [13a]Foods for the stomach and the stomach for foods, but God will destroy both it and them. Now the body *is* not for [b]sexual immorality but [c]for the Lord, [d]and the Lord for the body. [14]And [a]God both raised up the Lord and will also raise us up [b]by His power.

[15]Do you not know that [a]your bodies are members of Christ? Shall I then take the members of Christ and make *them* members of a harlot? Certainly not! [16]Or do you not know that he who is joined to a harlot is one body *with her*? For [a]"the two," He says, "shall become one flesh." [17a]But he who is joined to the Lord is one spirit *with Him*.

[18a]Flee sexual immorality. Every sin that a man does is outside the body, but he who commits sexual immorality sins [b]against his own body. [19]Or [a]do you not know that your body is the temple of the Holy Spirit *who is* in you, whom you have from God, [b]and you are not your own? [20]For [a]you were bought at a price; therefore glorify God in your body [1]and in your spirit, which are God's.

PRINCIPLES OF MARRIAGE

7 Now concerning the things of which you wrote to me: [a]*It is* good for a man not to touch a woman. [2]Nevertheless, because of sexual immorality, let each man have his own wife, and let each woman have her own husband. [3a]Let the husband render to his wife the affection due her, and likewise also the wife to her husband. [4]The wife does not have authority over her own body, but the husband *does*. And likewise the husband does not have authority over his own body, but the wife *does*. [5a]Do not deprive one another except with consent for a time, that you may give yourselves to fasting and prayer; and come together again so that [b]Satan does not tempt you because of your lack of self-control. [6]But I say this as a concession, [a]not as a commandment. [7]For [a]I wish that all men were even as I myself. But each one has his own gift from God, one in this manner and another in that.

[8]But I say to the unmarried and to the widows: [a]It is good for them if they remain even as I am; [9]but [a]if they cannot exercise self-control, let them marry. For it is better to marry than to burn *with passion*.

6:9
[a]Acts 20:32;
[1 Cor. 15:50];
Gal. 5:21;
Eph. 5:5;
1 Tim. 1:9

6:11 [a][1 Cor. 12:2;
Col. 3:5–7;
Titus 3:3–7]
[b]Heb. 10:22

6:12
[a]1 Cor. 10:23

6:13
[a]Matt. 15:17;
[Rom. 14:17];
Col. 2:22
[b]1 Cor. 5:1;
Gal. 5:19;
Eph. 5:3;
Col. 3:5;
1 Thess. 4:3
[c]1 Thess. 4:3
[d][Eph. 5:23]

6:14
[a]Rom. 6:5, 8;
2 Cor. 4:14
[b]Eph. 1:19

6:15 [a]Rom. 12:5;
1 Cor. 6:13; 12:27;
Eph. 5:30

6:16 [a]Gen. 2:24;
Matt. 19:5;
Mark 10:8;
Eph. 5:31

6:17
[a][John 17:21–23;
Rom. 8:9–11];
1 Cor. 6:15;
[Gal. 2:20];
Eph. 4:4

6:18 [a]Rom. 6:12;
1 Cor. 6:9;
2 Cor. 12:21;
Eph. 5:3;
Col. 3:5;
Heb. 13:4
[b]Rom. 1:24;
1 Thess. 4:4

6:19 [a]John 2:21;
1 Cor. 3:16;
2 Cor. 6:16
[b]Rom. 14:7

6:20
[a]Acts 20:28;
1 Cor. 7:23;
Gal. 3:13;
1 Pet. 1:18;
2 Pet. 2:1;
Rev. 5:9

7:1 [a]1 Cor. 7:8, 26

7:3 [a]Ex. 21:10

7:5
[a]Joel 2:16
[b]1 Thess. 3:5

7:6 [a]2 Cor. 8:8

7:7 [a]Acts 26:29

7:8 [a]1 Cor. 7:1, 26

7:9 [a]1 Tim. 5:14

6:9 [1]*catamites,* those submitting to homosexuals   [2]*male homosexuals*
6:11 [1]*set apart*   6:12 [1]*profitable*   [2]Or *anything*   6:20 [1]NU omits the rest of v. 20.

KEEP YOUR MARRIAGE VOWS

[10]Now to the married I command, *yet* not I but the [a]Lord: [b]A wife is not to depart from *her* husband. [11]But even if she does depart, let her remain unmarried or be reconciled to *her* husband. And a husband is not to divorce *his* wife.

[12]But to the rest I, not the Lord, say: If any brother has a wife who does not believe, and she is willing to live with him, let him not divorce her. [13]And a woman who has a husband who does not believe, if he is willing to live with her, let her not divorce him. [14]For the unbelieving husband is sanctified by the wife, and the unbelieving wife is sanctified by the husband; otherwise [a]your children would be unclean, but now they are holy. [15]But if the unbeliever departs, let him depart; a brother or a sister is not under bondage in such *cases*. But God has called us [a]to peace. [16]For how do you know, O wife, whether you will [a]save *your* husband? Or how do you know, O husband, whether you will save *your* wife?

LIVE AS YOU ARE CALLED

[17]But as God has distributed to each one, as the Lord has called each one, so let him walk. And [a]so I [1]ordain in all the churches. [18]Was anyone called while circumcised? Let him not become uncircumcised. Was anyone called while uncircumcised? [a]Let him not be circumcised. [19a]Circumcision is nothing and uncircumcision is nothing, but [b]keeping the commandments of God *is what matters*. [20]Let each one remain in the same calling in which he was called. [21]Were you called *while* a slave? Do not be concerned about it; but if you can be made free, rather use *it*. [22]For he who is called in the Lord *while* a slave is [a]the Lord's freedman. Likewise he who is called *while* free is [b]Christ's slave. [23a]You were bought at a price; do not become slaves of men. [24]Brethren, let each one remain with [a]God in that *state* in which he was called.

TO THE UNMARRIED AND WIDOWS

[25]Now concerning virgins: [a]I have no commandment from the Lord; yet I give judgment as one [b]whom the Lord in His mercy has made [c]trustworthy. [26]I suppose therefore that this is good because of the present distress—[a]that *it is* good for a man to remain as he is: [27]Are you bound to a wife? Do not seek to be loosed. Are you loosed from a wife? Do not seek a wife. [28]But even if you do marry, you have not sinned; and if a virgin marries, she has not sinned. Nevertheless such will have trouble in the flesh, but I would spare you.

[29]But [a]this I say, brethren, the time *is* short, so that from now on even those who have wives should be as though they had none, [30]those who weep as though they did not weep, those who rejoice as though they did not rejoice, those who buy as though they did not possess, [31]and those who use this world as not [a]misusing *it*. For [b]the form of this world is passing away.

[32]But I want you to be without [1]care. [a]He who is unmarried [2]cares for the things of the Lord—how he may please the Lord. [33]But he who is married cares about the things of the world—how he may please *his* wife. [34]There is a difference between a wife and a virgin. The unmarried woman [a]cares

7:10 [a]Mark 10:6–10 [b]Mal. 2:14; [Matt. 5:32]
7:14 [a]Ezra 9:2; Mal. 2:15
7:15 [a]Rom. 12:18
7:16 [a]Rom. 11:14; 1 Pet. 3:1
7:17 [a]1 Cor. 4:17
7:18 [a]Acts 15:1
7:19 [a][Rom. 2:27, 29; Gal. 3:28; 5:6; 6:15; Col. 3:11] [b][John 15:14]
7:22 [a][John 8:36]; Rom. 6:18; Philem. 16 [b][1 Cor. 9:21]; Gal. 5:13]; Eph. 6:6; Col. 3:24; 1 Pet. 2:16
7:23 [a]Lev. 25:42; 1 Cor. 6:20; 1 Pet. 1:18, 19; Rev. 5:9
7:24 [a][Eph. 6:5–8; Col. 3:22–24]
7:25 [a]2 Cor. 8:8 [b]2 Cor. 4:1; 1 Tim. 1:13, 16 [c]1 Tim. 1:12
7:26 [a]1 Cor. 7:1, 8
7:29 [a][Rom. 13:11]; 1 Cor. 7:31; 1 Pet. 4:7; [2 Pet. 3:8, 9]
7:31 [a]1 Cor. 9:18 [b]Ps. 39:6; 1 Cor. 7:29; James 1:10; 4:14; 1 Pet. 1:24; 4:7; [1 John 2:17]
7:32 [a]1 Tim. 5:5
7:34 [a]Luke 10:40

7:17 [1]direct   **7:32** [1]concern   [2]is concerned about

about the things of the Lord, that she may be holy both in body and in spirit. But she who is married cares about the things of the world—how she may please *her* husband. [35]And this I say for your own profit, not that I may put a leash on you, but for what is proper, and that you may serve the Lord without distraction.

[36]But if any man thinks he is behaving improperly toward his [1]virgin, if she is past the flower of youth, and thus it must be, let him do what he wishes. He does not sin; let them marry. [37]Nevertheless he who stands steadfast in his heart, having no necessity, but has power over his own will, and has so determined in his heart that he will keep his [1]virgin, does well. [38a]So then he who gives [1]*her* in marriage does well, but he who does not give *her* in marriage does better.

[39a]A wife is bound by law as long as her husband lives; but if her husband dies, she is at liberty to be married to whom she wishes, [b]only in the Lord. [40]But she is happier if she remains as she is, [a]according to my judgment—and [b]I think I also have the Spirit of God.

BE SENSITIVE TO CONSCIENCE

8 Now [a]concerning things offered to idols: We know that we all have [b]knowledge. [c]Knowledge [1]puffs up, but love [2]edifies. [2]And [a]if anyone thinks that he knows anything, he knows nothing yet as he ought to know. [3]But if anyone loves God, this one is known by Him.

[4]Therefore concerning the eating of things offered to idols, we know that [a]an idol *is* nothing in the world, [b]and that *there is* no other God but one. [5]For even if there are [a]so-called gods, whether in heaven or on earth (as there are many gods and many lords), [6]yet [a]for us *there is* one God, the Father, [b]of whom *are* all things, and we for Him; and [c]one Lord Jesus Christ, [d]through whom *are* all things, and [e]through whom we *live*.

[7]However, *there is* not in everyone that knowledge; for some, [a]with consciousness of the idol, until now eat *it* as a thing offered to an idol; and their conscience, being weak, is [b]defiled. [8]But [a]food does not commend us to God; for neither if we eat are we the better, nor if we do not eat are we the worse.

[9]But [a]beware lest somehow this liberty of yours become [b]a [1]stumbling block to those who are weak. [10]For if anyone sees you who have knowledge eating in an idol's temple, will not [a]the conscience of him who is weak be emboldened to eat those things offered to idols? [11]And [a]because of your knowledge shall the weak brother perish, for whom Christ died? [12]But [a]when you thus sin against the brethren, and wound their weak conscience, you sin against Christ. [13]Therefore, [a]if food makes my brother stumble, I will never again eat meat, lest I make my brother stumble.

A PATTERN OF SELF-DENIAL

9 Am [a]I not an apostle? Am I not free? [b]Have I not seen Jesus Christ our Lord? [c]Are you not my work in the Lord? [2]If I am not an apostle to others, yet doubtless I am to you. For you are [a]the [1]seal of my apostleship in the Lord.

7:38 [a]Heb. 13:4

7:39 [a]Rom. 7:2
[b]2 Cor. 6:14

7:40
[a]1 Cor. 7:6, 25
[b]1 Thess. 4:8

8:1 [a]Acts 15:20;
1 Cor. 8:4, 7, 10
[b]Rom. 14:14
[c]Rom. 14:3

8:2
[a][1 Cor. 13:8–12];
Gal. 6:3;
[1 Tim. 6:4]

8:4 [a]Is. 41:24
[b]Deut. 4:35, 39;
6:4; 1 Cor. 8:6

8:5
[a][John 10:34]

8:6 [a]Mal. 2:10;
Eph. 4:6
[b]Acts 17:28
[c]John 13:13;
1 Cor. 1:2;
Eph. 4:5;
[1 Tim. 2:5]
[d]John 1:3;
[Col. 1:16, 17];
Heb. 1:2
[e]Rom. 5:11;
Rev. 4:11; 5:9, 10

8:7
[a][1 Cor. 10:28]
[b]Rom. 14:14, 22

8:8
[a][Rom. 14:17]

8:9 [a]Gal. 5:13
[b]Rom. 14:13, 21;
1 Cor. 10:28

8:10
[a]1 Cor. 10:28

8:11
[a]Rom. 14:15, 20

8:12
[a]Matt. 25:40

8:13
[a]Rom. 14:21;
1 Cor. 10:32;
2 Cor. 6:3; 11:29

9:1 [a]Acts 9:15;
2 Cor. 12:12
[b]Acts 9:3, 17;
18:9; 22:14, 18;
23:11; 1 Cor. 15:8
[c]1 Cor. 3:6; 4:15

9:2 [a]2 Cor. 12:12

7:36 [1]Or *virgin daughter*   7:37 [1]Or *virgin daughter*   7:38 [1]NU *his own virgin*
8:1 [1]*makes arrogant*   [2]*builds up*   8:9 [1]*cause of offense*   9:2 [1]*certification*

9:4
[a]1 Cor. 9:14;
[1 Thess. 2:6, 9];
2 Thess. 3:8

9:5 [a]Matt. 13:55
[b]Matt. 8:14;
John 1:42

9:6 [a]Acts 4:36;
[2 Thess. 3:8]

9:7 [a]2 Cor. 10:4;
1 Tim. 1:18;
2 Tim. 2:3
[b]Deut. 20:6;
Prov. 27:18;
1 Cor. 3:6, 8
[c]John 21:15

9:9 [a]Deut. 25:4;
1 Tim. 5:18

9:10 [a]2 Tim. 2:6

9:11 [a]Rom. 15:27;
1 Cor. 9:14

9:12 [a][Acts 18:3;
20:33];
1 Cor. 9:15, 18
[b]2 Cor. 11:12

9:13 [a]Lev. 6:16,
26; 7:6, 31
[b]Num. 18:8–31;
Deut. 18:1

9:14
[a]Matt. 10:10;
Luke 10:7, 8;
1 Tim. 5:18
[b]Rom. 10:15

9:15 [a]Acts 18:3;
20:33;
1 Cor. 9:12, 18
[b]2 Cor. 11:10

9:16 [a]Acts 9:15;
[Rom. 1:14]

9:17
[a]John 4:36;
1 Cor. 3:8, 14; 9:18
[b]1 Cor. 4:1;
Gal. 2:7;
Eph. 3:2;
Col. 1:25

9:18
[a]1 Cor. 10:33
[b]1 Cor. 7:31; 9:12

9:19 [a]1 Cor. 9:1
[b]2 Cor. 4:5;
Gal. 5:13
[c]Matt. 18:15;
1 Pet. 3:1

9:20 [a]Acts 16:3;
21:23–26;
Rom. 11:14

9:21
[a][Gal. 2:3; 3:2]
[b][Rom. 2:12, 14]
[c][1 Cor. 7:22;
Gal. 6:2]

9:22
[a]Rom. 14:1; 15:1;
2 Cor. 11:29
[b]1 Cor. 10:33
[c]Rom. 11:14

³My defense to those who examine me is this: ⁴[a]Do we have no ¹right to eat and drink? ⁵Do we have no right to take along ¹a believing wife, as *do* also the other apostles, [a]the brothers of the Lord, and [b]Cephas? ⁶Or *is it* only Barnabas and I [a]*who* have no right to refrain from working? ⁷Who ever [a]goes to war at his own expense? Who [b]plants a vineyard and does not eat of its fruit? Or who [c]tends a flock and does not drink of the milk of the flock?

⁸Do I say these things as a *mere* man? Or does not the law say the same also? ⁹For it is written in the law of Moses, [a]"You shall not muzzle an ox while it treads out the grain." Is it oxen God is concerned about? ¹⁰Or does He say *it* altogether for our sakes? For our sakes, no doubt, *this* is written, that [a]he who plows should plow in hope, and he who threshes in hope should be partaker of his hope. ¹¹[a]If we have sown spiritual things for you, *is it* a great thing if we reap your material things? ¹²If others are partakers of *this* right over you, *are* we not even more?

[a]Nevertheless we have not used this right, but endure all things [b]lest we hinder the gospel of Christ. ¹³[a]Do you not know that those who minister the holy things eat *of the things* of the [b]temple, and those who serve at the altar partake of *the offerings of* the altar? ¹⁴Even so [a]the Lord has commanded [b]that those who preach the gospel should live from the gospel.

¹⁵But [a]I have used none of these things, nor have I written these things that it should be done so to me; for [b]it *would be* better for me to die than that anyone should make my boasting void. ¹⁶For if I preach the gospel, I have nothing to boast of, for [a]necessity is laid upon me; yes, woe is me if I do not preach the gospel! ¹⁷For if I do this willingly, [a]I have a reward; but if against my will, [b]I have been entrusted with a stewardship. ¹⁸What is my reward then? That [a]when I preach the gospel, I may present the gospel ¹of Christ without charge, that I [b]may not abuse my authority in the gospel.

SERVING ALL MEN

¹⁹For though I am [a]free from all *men,* [b]I have made myself a servant to all, [c]that I might win the more; ²⁰and [a]to the Jews I became as a Jew, that I might win Jews; to those *who are* under the law, as under the ¹law, that I might win those *who are* under the law; ²¹[a]to [b]those *who are* without law, as without law [c](not being without ¹law toward God, but under ²law toward Christ), that I might win those *who are* without law; ²²[a]to the weak I became ¹as weak, that I might win the weak. [b]I have become all things to all *men,* [c]that I might by all means save some. ²³Now this I do for the gospel's sake, that I may be partaker of it with *you.*

STRIVING FOR A CROWN

²⁴Do you not know that those who run in a race all run, but one receives the prize? [a]Run in such a way that you may ¹obtain *it.* ²⁵And everyone who competes *for the prize* ¹is temperate

9:24 [a]Gal. 2:2; 2 Tim. 4:7; Heb. 12:1

9:4 ¹*authority* 9:5 ¹Lit. *a sister, a wife* 9:18 ¹NU omits *of Christ*
9:20 ¹NU adds *though not being myself under the law* 9:21 ¹NU *God's law* ²NU *Christ's law* 9:22 ¹NU omits *as* 9:24 ¹*win* 9:25 ¹*exercises self-control*

in all things. Now they *do it* to obtain a perishable crown, but we *for* [a]an imperishable *crown*. [26]Therefore I run thus: [a]not with uncertainty. Thus I fight: not as *one who* beats the air. [27a]But I discipline my body and [b]bring *it* into subjection, lest, when I have preached to others, I myself should become [c]disqualified.

OLD TESTAMENT EXAMPLES

10 Moreover, brethren, I do not want you to be unaware that all our fathers were under [a]the cloud, all passed through [b]the sea, [2]all were baptized into Moses in the cloud and in the sea, [3]all ate the same [a]spiritual food, [4]and all drank the same [a]spiritual drink. For they drank of that spiritual Rock that followed them, and that Rock was Christ. [5]But with most of them God was not well pleased, for *their bodies* [a]were scattered in the wilderness.

[6]Now these things became our examples, to the intent that we should not lust after evil things as [a]they also lusted. [7a]And do not become idolaters as *were* some of them. As it is written, [b]"The people sat down to eat and drink, and rose up to play." [8a]Nor let us commit sexual immorality, as [b]some of them did, and [c]in one day twenty-three thousand fell; [9]nor let us [1]tempt Christ, as [a]some of them also tempted, and [b]were destroyed by serpents; [10]nor complain, as [a]some of them also complained, and [b]were destroyed by [c]the destroyer. [11]Now [1]all these things happened to them as examples, and [a]they were written for our [2]admonition, [b]upon whom the ends of the ages have come.

[12]Therefore [a]let him who thinks he stands take heed lest he fall. [13]No temptation has overtaken you except such as is common to man; but [a]God *is* faithful, [b]who will not allow you to be tempted beyond what you are able, but with the temptation will also make the way of escape, that you may be able to [1]bear *it*.

FLEE FROM IDOLATRY

[14]Therefore, my beloved, [a]flee from idolatry. [15]I speak as to [a]wise men; judge for yourselves what I say. [16a]The cup of blessing which we bless, is it not the [1]communion of the blood of Christ? [b]The bread which we break, is it not the communion of the body of Christ? [17]For [a]we, *though* many, are one bread *and* one body; for we all partake of that one bread.

[18]Observe [a]Israel [b]after the flesh: [c]Are not those who eat of the sacrifices [1]partakers of the altar? [19]What am I saying then? [a]That an idol is anything, or what is offered to idols is anything? [20]Rather, that the things which the Gentiles [a]sacrifice [b]they sacrifice to demons and not to God, and I do not want you to have fellowship with demons. [21a]You cannot drink the cup of the Lord and [b]the cup of demons; you cannot partake of the [c]Lord's table and of the table of demons. [22]Or do we [a]provoke the Lord to jealousy? [b]Are we stronger than He?

10:18 [a]Rom. 4:12 [b]Rom. 4:1 [c]Lev. 3:3; 7:6, 14; Deut. 12:17   10:19 [a]1 Cor. 8:4
10:20 [a]Lev. 17:7 [b]Deut. 32:17; Ps. 106:37; Gal. 4:8; Rev. 9:20   10:21 [a]2 Cor. 6:15, 16
[b]Deut. 32:38 [c][1 Cor. 11:23–29]   10:22 [a]Deut. 32:21 [b]Ezek. 22:14

10:9 [1]*test*   10:11 [1]NU omits *all*   [2]*instruction*   10:13 [1]*endure*
10:16 [1]*fellowship* or *sharing*   10:18 [1]*fellowshippers* or *sharers*

9:25
[a]2 Tim. 4:8;
James 1:12;
[1 Pet. 5:4;
Rev. 2:10; 3:11]
9:26 [a]2 Tim. 2:5
9:27
[a][Rom. 8:13]
[b][Rom. 6:18]
[c]Jer. 6:30;
2 Cor. 13:5

10:1 [a]Ex. 13:21, 22;
Ps. 105:39
[b]Ex. 14:21, 22, 29;
Neh. 9:11;
Ps. 66:6

10:3 [a]Ex. 16:4,
15, 35; Deut. 8:3;
Neh. 9:15, 20;
Ps. 78:24;
John 6:31

10:4 [a]Ex. 17:5–7;
Num. 20:11;
Ps. 78:15

10:5
[a]Num. 14:29, 37;
26:65; Heb. 3:17;
Jude 5

10:6
[a]Num. 11:4, 34;
Ps. 106:14

10:7 [a]Ex. 32:4;
1 Cor. 5:11; 10:14
[b]Ex. 32:6;
1 Cor. 15:32

10:8 [a]Rev. 2:14
[b]Num. 25:1–9
[c]Ps. 106:29

10:9 [a]Ex. 17:2, 7
[b]Num. 21:6–9

10:10 [a]Ex. 16:2
[b]Num. 14:37
[c]Ex. 12:23;
2 Sam. 24:16;
1 Chr. 21:15;
Heb. 11:28

10:11 [a]Rom. 15:4
[b]Phil. 4:5

10:12
[a]Rom. 11:20

10:13 [a]1 Cor. 1:9
[b]Ps. 125:3

10:14 [a]2 Cor. 6:17

10:15 [a]1 Cor. 8:1

10:16
[a]Matt. 26:26–28;
Mark 14:23;
Luke 22:20;
1 Cor. 11:25
[b]Matt. 26:26;
Luke 22:19;
Acts 2:42;
1 Cor. 11:23

10:17
[a]Rom. 12:5;
1 Cor. 12:12, 27;
Eph. 4:4, 16;
Col. 3:15

ALL TO THE GLORY OF GOD

(cf. Ps. 24:1)

²³All things are lawful ¹for me, but not all things are ᵃhelpful; all things are lawful for me, but not all things ²edify. ²⁴Let no one seek his own, but each one ᵃthe other's *well-being.*

²⁵ᵃEat whatever is sold in the meat market, asking no questions for conscience' sake; ²⁶for ᵃ"the earth *is* the Lᴏʀᴅ's, and all its fullness."

²⁷If any of those who do not believe invites you *to dinner,* and you desire to go, ᵃeat whatever is set before you, asking no question for conscience' sake. ²⁸But if anyone says to you, "This was offered to idols," do not eat it ᵃfor the sake of the one who told you, and for conscience' sake; ¹for ᵇ"the earth *is* the Lᴏʀᴅ's, and all its fullness." ²⁹"Conscience," I say, not your own, but that of the other. For ᵃwhy is my liberty judged by another *man's* conscience? ³⁰But if I partake with thanks, why am I evil spoken of for *the food* ᵃover which I give thanks?

³¹ᵃTherefore, whether you eat or drink, or whatever you do, do all to the glory of God. ³²ᵃGive no offense, either to the Jews or to the Greeks or to the church of God, ³³just ᵃas I also please all *men* in all *things,* not seeking my own profit, but the *profit* of many, that they may be saved.

11 Imitateᵃ me, just as I also *imitate* Christ.

HEAD COVERINGS

²Now I praise you, brethren, that you remember me in all things and keep the traditions just as I delivered *them* to you. ³But I want you to know that ᵃthe head of every man is Christ, ᵇthe head of woman *is* man, and ᶜthe head of Christ *is* God. ⁴Every man praying or ᵃprophesying, having *his* head covered, dishonors his head. ⁵But every woman who prays or prophesies with *her* head uncovered dishonors her head, for that is one and the same as if her head were ᵃshaved. ⁶For if a woman is not covered, let her also be shorn. But if it is ᵃshameful for a woman to be shorn or shaved, let her be covered. ⁷For a man indeed ought not to cover *his* head, since ᵃhe is the image and glory of God; but woman is the glory of man. ⁸For man is not from woman, but woman ᵃfrom man. ⁹Nor was man created for the woman, but woman ᵃfor the man. ¹⁰For this reason the woman ought to have *a symbol of* authority on *her* head, because of the angels. ¹¹Nevertheless, ᵃneither *is* man independent of woman, nor woman independent of man, in the Lord. ¹²For as woman *came* from man, even so man also *comes* through woman; but all things are from God.

¹³Judge among yourselves. Is it proper for a woman to pray to God with her head uncovered? ¹⁴Does not even nature itself teach you that if a man has long hair, it is a dishonor to him? ¹⁵But if a woman has long hair, it is a glory to her; for *her* hair is given ¹to her for a covering. ¹⁶But ᵃif anyone seems to be contentious, we have no such custom, ᵇnor *do* the churches of God.

CONDUCT AT THE LORD'S SUPPER

¹⁷Now in giving these instructions I do not praise *you,* since you come together not for the better but for the worse.

10:23 ᵃ1 Cor. 6:12
10:24 ᵃPhil. 2:4
10:25 ᵃ[1 Tim. 4:4]
10:26 ᵃEx. 19:5; Ps. 24:1; 50:12; 1 Tim. 4:4
10:27 ᵃLuke 10:7, 8
10:28 ᵃ[1 Cor. 8:7, 10, 12]; ᵇDeut. 10:14; Ps. 24:1
10:29 ᵃRom. 14:16; [1 Cor. 9:19]
10:30 ᵃRom. 14:6
10:31 ᵃCol. 3:17; 1 Pet. 4:11
10:32 ᵃRom. 14:13
10:33 ᵃRom. 15:2; 1 Cor. 9:22; [Gal. 1:10]
11:1 ᵃEph. 5:1
11:3 ᵃEph. 1:22; 4:15; 5:23; Col. 1:18; 2:19; ᵇGen. 3:16; [Eph. 5:23]; ᶜJohn 14:28
11:4 ᵃ1 Cor. 12:10
11:5 ᵃDeut. 21:12
11:6 ᵃNum. 5:18
11:7 ᵃGen. 1:26, 27; 5:1; 9:6; James 3:9
11:8 ᵃGen. 2:21–23; 1 Tim. 2:13
11:9 ᵃGen. 2:18
11:11 ᵃ[Gal. 3:28]
11:16 ᵃ1 Tim. 6:4; ᵇ1 Cor. 7:17

10:23 ¹NU omits *for me*   ²*build up*   **10:28** ¹NU omits the rest of v. 28.
11:15 ¹M omits *to her*

[18]For first of all, when you come together as a church, [a]I hear that there are divisions among you, and in part I believe it. [19]For [a]there must also be factions among you, [b]that those who are approved may be [1]recognized among you. [20]Therefore when you come together in one place, it is not to eat the Lord's Supper. [21]For in eating, each one takes his own supper ahead of *others;* and one is hungry and [a]another is drunk. [22]What! Do you not have houses to eat and drink in? Or do you despise [a]the church of God and [b]shame [1]those who have nothing? What shall I say to you? Shall I praise you in this? I do not praise *you.*

INSTITUTION OF THE LORD'S SUPPER
(Matt. 26:26–29; Mark 14:22–25; Luke 22:14–23)

[23]For [a]I received from the Lord that which I also delivered to you: [b]that the Lord Jesus on the *same* night in which He was betrayed took bread; [24]and when He had given thanks, He broke *it* and said, [1]"Take, eat; this is My body which is [2]broken for you; do this in remembrance of Me." [25]In the same manner *He* also *took* the cup after supper, saying, "This cup is the new covenant in My blood. This do, as often as you drink *it,* in remembrance of Me."

[26]For as often as you eat this bread and drink this cup, you proclaim the Lord's death [a]till He comes.

EXAMINE YOURSELF

[27]Therefore whoever eats [a]this bread or drinks *this* cup of the Lord in an unworthy manner will be guilty of the body and [1]blood of the Lord. [28]But [a]let a man examine himself, and so let him eat of the bread and drink of the cup. [29]For he who eats and drinks [1]in an unworthy manner eats and drinks judgment to himself, not discerning the [2]Lord's body. [30]For this reason many *are* weak and sick among you, and many [1]sleep. [31]For [a]if we would judge ourselves, we would not be judged. [32]But when we are judged, [a]we are chastened by the Lord, that we may not be condemned with the world.

[33]Therefore, my brethren, when you [a]come together to eat, wait for one another. [34]But if anyone is hungry, let him eat at home, lest you come together for judgment. And the rest I will set in order when I come.

SPIRITUAL GIFTS: UNITY IN DIVERSITY

12 Now [a]concerning spiritual *gifts,* brethren, I do not want you to be ignorant: [2]You know [a]that[1] you were Gentiles, carried away to these [b]dumb[2] idols, however you were led. [3]Therefore I make known to you that no one speaking by the Spirit of God calls Jesus [1]accursed, and [a]no one can say that Jesus is Lord except by the Holy Spirit.

[4a]There are [1]diversities of gifts, but [b]the same Spirit. [5a]There are differences of ministries, but the same Lord. [6]And there are diversities of activities, but it is the same God [a]who works [1]all in all. [7]But the manifestation of the Spirit is

11:18
[a]1 Cor. 1:10–12; 3:3

11:19
[a]Matt. 18:7; Luke 17:1; 1 Tim. 4:1; 2 Pet. 2:1
[b][Deut. 13:3]; Luke 2:35; 1 John 2:19

11:21
[a]2 Pet. 2:13; Jude 12

11:22
[a]1 Cor. 10:32
[b]James 2:6

11:23 [a]1 Cor. 15:3; Gal. 1:12; Col. 3:24
[b]Matt. 26:26–28; Mark 14:22–24; Luke 22:17–20; 1 Cor. 10:16

11:26 [a]John 14:3; [Acts 1:11]

11:27
[a][John 6:51]

11:28
[a]Matt. 26:22; 2 Cor. 13:5; Gal. 6:4

11:31 [a][Ps. 32:5; 1 John 1:9]

11:32
[a]2 Sam. 7:14; Ps. 94:12; [Heb. 12:5–10]; Rev. 3:19]

11:33
[a]1 Cor. 14:26

12:1 [a]1 Cor. 12:4; 14:1, 37

12:2 [a]1 Cor. 6:11; Eph. 2:11; 1 Pet. 4:3
[b]Ps. 115:5; Is. 46:7; Jer. 10:5; Hab. 2:18

12:3 [a]Matt. 16:17

12:4
[a]Rom. 12:3–8; 1 Cor. 12:11; Eph. 4:4, 11; Heb. 2:4
[b]Eph. 4:4

12:5 [a]Rom. 12:6

12:6
[a]1 Cor. 15:28; Eph. 1:23; 4:6

11:19 [1]Lit. *manifest, evident* **11:22** [1]The poor **11:24** [1]NU omits *Take, eat* [2]NU omits *broken* **11:27** [1]NU, M *the blood* **11:29** [1]NU omits *in an unworthy manner* [2]NU omits *Lord's* **11:30** [1]Are dead **12:2** [1]NU, M *that when* [2]*mute, silent* **12:3** [1]Gr. *anathema* **12:4** [1]*allotments* or *various kinds* **12:6** [1]*all things in*

given to each one for the profit *of all:* [8]for to one is given [a]the word of wisdom through the Spirit, to another [b]the word of knowledge through the same Spirit, [9a]to another faith by the same Spirit, to another [b]gifts of healings by [1]the same Spirit, [10a]to another the working of miracles, to another [b]prophecy, to another [c]discerning of spirits, to another [d]*different* kinds of tongues, to another the interpretation of tongues. [11]But one and the same Spirit works all these things, [a]distributing to each one individually [b]as He wills.

UNITY AND DIVERSITY IN ONE BODY
(cf. Eph. 4:1–16)

[12]For [a]as the body is one and has many members, but all the members of that one body, being many, are one body, [b]so also *is* Christ. [13]For [a]by one Spirit we were all baptized into one body—[b]whether Jews or Greeks, whether slaves or free—and [c]have all been made to drink [1]into one Spirit. [14]For in fact the body is not one member but many.

[15]If the foot should say, "Because I am not a hand, I am not of the body," is it therefore not of the body? [16]And if the ear should say, "Because I am not an eye, I am not of the body," is it therefore not of the body? [17]If the whole body *were* an eye, where *would be* the hearing? If the whole *were* hearing, where *would be* the smelling? [18]But now [a]God has set the members, each one of them, in the body [b]just as He pleased. [19]And if they were all one member, where *would* the body *be?*

[20]But now indeed *there are* many members, yet one body. [21]And the eye cannot say to the hand, "I have no need of you"; nor again the head to the feet, "I have no need of you." [22]No, much rather, those members of the body which seem to be weaker are necessary. [23]And those *members* of the body which we think to be less honorable, on these we bestow greater honor; and our unpresentable *parts* have greater modesty, [24]but our presentable *parts* have no need. But God composed the body, having given greater honor to that *part* which lacks it, [25]that there should be no [1]schism in the body, but *that* the members should have the same care for one another. [26]And if one member suffers, all the members suffer with *it;* or if one member is honored, all the members rejoice with *it.*

[27]Now [a]you are the body of Christ, and [b]members individually. [28]And [a]God has appointed these in the church: first [b]apostles, second [c]prophets, third teachers, after that [d]miracles, then [e]gifts of healings, [f]helps, [g]administrations, varieties of tongues. [29]*Are* all apostles? *Are* all prophets? *Are* all teachers? *Are* all workers of miracles? [30]Do all have gifts of healings? Do all speak with tongues? Do all interpret? [31]But [a]earnestly desire the [1]best gifts. And yet I show you a more excellent way.

THE GREATEST GIFT

13 Though I speak with the tongues of men and of angels, but have not love, I have become sounding brass or a clanging cymbal. [2]And though I have *the gift of* [a]prophecy, and understand all mysteries and all knowledge, and though I have all faith, [b]so that I could remove mountains, but have

---

12:8
[a]1 Cor. 2:6, 7;
2 Cor. 1:12
[b]Rom. 15:14;
[1 Cor. 2:11, 16];
2 Cor. 8:7

12:9
[a]Matt. 17:19;
[1 Cor. 13:2];
2 Cor. 4:13
[b]Matt. 10:1;
Mark 3:15; 16:18;
James 5:14

12:10
[a]Mark 16:17
[b]Rom. 12:6
[c]1 John 4:1
[d]Acts 2:4–11

12:11 [a]Rom. 12:6;
2 Cor. 10:13
[b][John 3:8]

12:12
[a]Rom. 12:4, 5;
1 Cor. 10:17;
Eph. 4:4
[b][Gal. 3:16]

12:13
[a][Rom. 6:5]
[b]Rom. 3:22;
Gal. 3:28;
[Eph. 2:13–18];
Col. 3:11
[c][John 7:37–39]

12:18
[a]1 Cor. 12:28
[b]Rom. 12:3

12:27
[a]Rom. 12:5;
Eph. 1:23; 4:12;
5:23, 30;
Col. 1:24
[b]Eph. 5:30

12:28 [a]Eph. 4:11
[b][Eph. 2:20; 3:5]
[c]Acts 13:1;
Rom. 12:6
[d]1 Cor. 12:10, 29;
Gal. 3:5
[e]Mark 16:18;
1 Cor. 12:9, 30
[f]Num. 11:17
[g]Rom. 12:8;
1 Tim. 5:17;
Heb. 13:17, 24

12:31
[a]1 Cor. 14:1, 39

13:2 [a]Matt. 7:22;
1 Cor. 12:8–10,
28; 14:1
[b]Matt. 17:20;
21:21;
Mark 11:23;
Luke 17:6

12:9 [1]NU *one*   **12:13** [1]NU omits *into*   **12:25** [1]division   **12:31** [1]NU *greater*

not love, I am nothing. ³And ªthough I bestow all my goods to feed *the poor,* and though I give my body ¹to be burned, but have not love, it profits me nothing.

⁴ªLove suffers long *and* is ᵇkind; love ᶜdoes not envy; love does not parade itself, is not ¹puffed up; ⁵does not behave rudely, ªdoes not seek its own, is not provoked, ¹thinks no evil; ⁶ªdoes not rejoice in iniquity, but ᵇrejoices in the truth; ⁷ªbears all things, believes all things, hopes all things, endures all things.

⁸Love never fails. But whether *there are* prophecies, they will fail; whether *there are* tongues, they will cease; whether *there is* knowledge, it will vanish away. ⁹ªFor we know in part and we prophesy in part. ¹⁰But when that which is ¹perfect has come, then that which is in part will be done away.

¹¹When I was a child, I spoke as a child, I understood as a child, I thought as a child; but when I became a man, I put away childish things. ¹²For ªnow we see in a mirror, dimly, but then ᵇface to face. Now I know in part, but then I shall know just as I also am known.

¹³And now abide faith, hope, love, these three; but the greatest of these *is* love.

PROPHECY AND TONGUES

14 Pursue love, and ªdesire spiritual *gifts,* ᵇbut especially that you may prophesy. ²For he who ªspeaks in a tongue does not speak to men but to God, for no one understands *him;* however, in the spirit he speaks mysteries. ³But he who prophesies speaks ªedification and ᵇexhortation and comfort to men. ⁴He who speaks in a tongue edifies himself, but he who prophesies edifies the church. ⁵I wish you all spoke with tongues, but even more that you prophesied; ¹for he who prophesies *is* greater than he who speaks with tongues, unless indeed he interprets, that the church may receive edification.

TONGUES MUST BE INTERPRETED

⁶But now, brethren, if I come to you speaking with tongues, what shall I profit you unless I speak to you either by ªrevelation, by knowledge, by prophesying, or by teaching? ⁷Even things without life, whether flute or harp, when they make a sound, unless they make a distinction in the sounds, how will it be known what is piped or played? ⁸For if the trumpet makes an uncertain sound, who will prepare for battle? ⁹So likewise you, unless you utter by the tongue words easy to understand, how will it be known what is spoken? For you will be speaking into the air. ¹⁰There are, it may be, so many kinds of languages in the world, and none of them *is* without ¹significance. ¹¹Therefore, if I do not know the meaning of the language, I shall be a ¹foreigner to him who speaks, and he who speaks *will be* a foreigner to me. ¹²Even so you, since you are ¹zealous for spiritual *gifts, let it be* for the ²edification of the church *that* you seek to excel.

¹³Therefore let him who speaks in a tongue pray that he may ªinterpret. ¹⁴For if I pray in a tongue, my spirit prays, but my understanding is unfruitful. ¹⁵What is *the conclusion* then?

13:3 ªMatt. 6:1, 2

13:4
ªProv. 10:12; 17:9;
1 Thess. 5:14;
[1 Pet. 4:8]
ᵇEph. 4:32
ᶜGal. 5:26

13:5
ª1 Cor. 10:24;
Phil. 2:4

13:6 ªPs. 10:3;
Rom. 1:32
ᵇ2 John 4;
3 John 3

13:7 ªRom. 15:1;
Gal. 6:2;
2 Tim. 2:24

13:9
ª1 Cor. 8:2; 13:12

13:12
ª[2 Cor. 3:18; 5:7];
Phil. 3:12;
James 1:23
ᵇGen. 32:30;
Num. 12:8;
Matt. 18:10;
[1 John 3:2]

14:1
ª1 Cor. 12:31;
14:39
ᵇNum. 11:25, 29

14:2
ªActs 2:4; 10:46

14:3
ªRom. 14:19; 15:2;
2 Cor. 10:8; 12:19;
Eph. 4:12, 29
ᵇ1 Tim. 4:13;
2 Tim. 4:2;
Titus 1:9; 2:15;
Heb. 3:13; 10:25

14:6
ª1 Cor. 14:26;
Eph. 1:17

14:13
ª1 Cor. 12:10

13:3 ¹NU *so I may boast*   13:4 ¹*arrogant*   13:5 ¹*keeps no accounts of evil*
13:10 ¹*complete*   14:5 ¹NU *and*   14:10 ¹*meaning*   14:11 ¹Lit. *barbarian*
14:12 ¹*eager*   ²*building up*

I will pray with the spirit, and I will also pray with the understanding. [a]I will sing with the spirit, and I will also sing [b]with the understanding. 16Otherwise, if you bless with the spirit, how will he who occupies the place of the uninformed say "Amen" [a]at your giving of thanks, since he does not understand what you say? 17For you indeed give thanks well, but the other is not edified.

18I thank my God I speak with tongues more than you all; 19yet in the church I would rather speak five words with my understanding, that I may teach others also, than ten thousand words in a tongue.

TONGUES A SIGN TO UNBELIEVERS

20Brethren, [a]do not be children in understanding; however, in malice [b]be babes, but in understanding be mature. 21[a]In the law it is written:

[b]"With *men of* other tongues and other lips
I will speak to this people;
And yet, for all that, they will not hear Me,"

says the Lord.

22Therefore tongues are for a [a]sign, not to those who believe but to unbelievers; but prophesying is not for unbelievers but for those who believe. 23Therefore if the whole church comes together in one place, and all speak with tongues, and there come in *those who are* uninformed or unbelievers, [a]will they not say that you are [1]out of your mind? 24But if all prophesy, and an unbeliever or an uninformed person comes in, he is convinced by all, he is convicted by all. 25[1]And thus the secrets of his heart are revealed; and so, falling down on *his* face, he will worship God and report [a]that God is truly among you.

ORDER IN CHURCH MEETINGS

26How is it then, brethren? Whenever you come together, each of you has a psalm, [a]has a teaching, has a tongue, has a revelation, has an interpretation. [b]Let all things be done for [1]edification. 27If anyone speaks in a tongue, *let there be* two or at the most three, *each* in turn, and let one interpret. 28But if there is no interpreter, let him keep silent in church, and let him speak to himself and to God. 29Let two or three prophets speak, and [a]let the others judge. 30But if *anything* is revealed to another who sits by, [a]let the first keep silent. 31For you can all prophesy one by one, that all may learn and all may be encouraged. 32And [a]the spirits of the prophets are subject to the prophets. 33For God is not *the author* of [1]confusion but of peace, [a]as in all the churches of the saints.

34[a]Let [1]your women keep silent in the churches, for they are not permitted to speak; but *they are* to be submissive, as the [b]law also says. 35And if they want to learn something, let them ask their own husbands at home; for it is shameful for women to speak in church.

36Or did the word of God come *originally* from you? Or *was it* you only that it reached? 37[a]If anyone thinks himself to be a prophet or spiritual, let him acknowledge that the things

14:15 [a]Eph. 5:19;
Col. 3:16
[b]Ps. 47:7

14:16
[a]Deut. 27:15–26;
1 Chr. 16:36;
Neh. 5:13; 8:6;
Ps. 106:48;
Jer. 11:5; 28:6;
1 Cor. 11:24;
Rev. 5:14; 7:12

14:20 [a]Ps. 131:2;
[Matt. 11:25;
18:3; 19:14];
Rom. 16:19;
1 Cor. 3:1;
Eph. 4:14;
Heb. 5:12, 13
[b][Matt. 18:3;
1 Pet. 2:2]

14:21
[a]John 10:34;
1 Cor. 14:34
[b]Is. 28:11, 12

14:22
[a]Mark 16:17

14:23 [a]Acts 2:13

14:25 [a]Is. 45:14;
Dan. 2:47;
Zech. 8:23;
Acts 4:13

14:26
[a]1 Cor. 12:8–10;
14:6
[b]1 Cor. 12:7;
[2 Cor. 12:19]

14:29
[a]1 Cor. 12:10

14:30
[a][1 Thess. 5:19,
20]

14:32 [a]1 John 4:1

14:33
[a]1 Cor. 11:16

14:34
[a]1 Tim. 2:11;
1 Pet. 3:1
[b]Gen. 3:16

14:37
[a]2 Cor. 10:7;
[1 John 4:6]

14:23 [1]insane   14:25 [1]NU omits *And thus*   14:26 [1]*building up*
14:33 [1]*disorder*   14:34 [1]NU omits *your*

which I write to you are the commandments of the Lord. 38But 1if anyone is ignorant, let him be ignorant.

39Therefore, brethren, adesire earnestly to prophesy, and do not forbid to speak with tongues. 40aLet all things be done decently and in order.

THE RISEN CHRIST, FAITH'S REALITY
(cf. Mark 16:9–20)

15 Moreover, brethren, I declare to you the gospel awhich I preached to you, which also you received and bin which you stand, 2aby which also you are saved, if you hold fast that word which I preached to you—unless byou believed in vain.

3For aI delivered to you first of all that bwhich I also received: that Christ died for our sins caccording to the Scriptures, 4and that He was buried, and that He rose again the third day aaccording to the Scriptures, 5aand that He was seen by 1Cephas, then bby the twelve. 6After that He was seen by over five hundred brethren at once, of whom the greater part remain to the present, but some have 1fallen asleep. 7After that He was seen by James, then aby all the apostles. 8aThen last of all He was seen by me also, as by one born out of due time.

9For I am athe least of the apostles, who am not worthy to be called an apostle, because bI persecuted the church of God. 10But aby the grace of God I am what I am, and His grace toward me was not in vain; but I labored more abundantly than they all, byet not I, but the grace of God *which was* with me. 11Therefore, whether *it was* I or they, so we preach and so you believed.

THE RISEN CHRIST, OUR HOPE
(cf. 1 Thess. 4:13–18)

12Now if Christ is preached that He has been raised from the dead, how do some among you say that there is no resurrection of the dead? 13But if there is no resurrection of the dead, athen Christ is not risen. 14And if Christ is not risen, then our preaching *is* empty and your faith *is* also empty. 15Yes, and we are found false witnesses of God, because awe have testified of God that He raised up Christ, whom He did not raise up—if in fact the dead do not rise. 16For if *the* dead do not rise, then Christ is not risen. 17And if Christ is not risen, your faith *is* futile; ayou are still in your sins! 18Then also those who have 1fallen aasleep in Christ have perished. 19aIf in this life only we have hope in Christ, we are of all men the most pitiable.

THE LAST ENEMY DESTROYED

20But now aChrist is risen from the dead, *and* has become bthe firstfruits of those who have 1fallen asleep. 21For asince by man *came* death, bby Man also *came* the resurrection of the dead. 22For as in Adam all die, even so in Christ all shall abe made alive. 23But aeach one in his own order: Christ the

14:39
a1 Cor. 12:31;
1 Thess. 5:20

14:40
a1 Cor. 14:33

15:1 aRom. 2:16;
[Gal. 1:11]
b[Rom. 5:2;
11:20;
2 Cor. 1:24]

15:2 aRom. 1:16;
1 Cor. 1:21
bGal. 3:4

15:3
a1 Cor. 11:2, 23
b[Gal. 1:12]
cPs. 22:15;
Is. 53:5–12;
Acts 3:18;
1 Pet. 1:11

15:4
aGen. 1:9–13;
2 Kin. 20:8;
Ps. 16:9–11;
68:18; 110:1;
Is. 53:10;
Hos. 6:2;
Jon. 1:17; 2:10;
Matt. 12:39, 40;
Mark 8:31;
Luke 11:29, 30;
24:26;
John 2:19–21;
Acts 2:25

15:5 aLuke 24:34
bMatt. 28:17

15:7
aLuke 24:50;
Acts 1:3, 4

15:8
a[Acts 9:3–8;
22:6–11;
26:12–18];
1 Cor. 9:1

15:9 a2 Cor. 12:11;
Eph. 3:8;
1 Tim. 1:15
bActs 8:3

15:10
aEph. 3:7, 8
bMatt. 10:20;
Rom. 15:18;
Gal. 2:8;
Phil. 2:13

15:13
a[1 Thess. 4:14]

15:15 aActs 2:24

15:17
a[Rom. 4:25]

15:18 aJob 14:12;
Ps. 13:3

15:19 a1 Cor. 4:9;
2 Tim. 3:12

15:20
aActs 2:24;
1 Pet. 1:3
bActs 26:23;
1 Cor. 15:23;
Rev. 1:5

15:21 aGen. 3:19; Ezek. 18:4; Rom. 5:12; 6:23; Heb. 9:27 bJohn 11:25
15:22 a[John 5:28, 29]　15:23 a[1 Thess. 4:15–17]

14:38 1NU *if anyone does not recognize this, he is not recognized.*
15:5 1Peter　15:6 1Died　15:18 1Died　15:20 1Died

firstfruits, afterward those *who are* Christ's at His coming. ²⁴Then *comes* the end, when He delivers ªthe kingdom to God the Father, when He puts an end to all rule and all authority and power. ²⁵For He must reign ªtill He has put all enemies under His feet. ²⁶ªThe last enemy *that* will be destroyed *is* death. ²⁷For ª"He has put all things under His feet." But when He says "all things are put under *Him*," *it is* evident that He who put all things under Him is excepted. ²⁸ªNow when all things are made subject to Him, then ᵇthe Son Himself will also be subject to Him who put all things under Him, that God may be all in all.

EFFECTS OF DENYING THE RESURRECTION

²⁹Otherwise, what will they do who are baptized for the dead, if the dead do not rise at all? Why then are they baptized for the dead? ³⁰And ªwhy do we stand in ¹jeopardy every hour? ³¹I affirm, by ªthe boasting in you which I have in Christ Jesus our Lord, ᵇI die daily. ³²If, in the manner of men, ªI have fought with beasts at Ephesus, what advantage *is it* to me? If *the* dead do not rise, ᵇ"Let us eat and drink, for tomorrow we die!"

³³Do not be deceived: ª"Evil company corrupts good habits." ³⁴ªAwake to righteousness, and do not sin; ᵇfor some do not have the knowledge of God. ᶜI speak *this* to your shame.

A GLORIOUS BODY

³⁵But someone will say, ª"How are the dead raised up? And with what body do they come?" ³⁶Foolish one, ªwhat you sow is not made alive unless it dies. ³⁷And what you sow, you do not sow that body that shall be, but mere grain—perhaps wheat or some other *grain*. ³⁸But God gives it a body as He pleases, and to each seed its own body.

³⁹All flesh *is* not the same flesh, but *there is* one kind ¹of flesh of men, another flesh of animals, another of fish, *and* another of birds.

⁴⁰*There are* also ¹celestial bodies and ²terrestrial bodies; but the glory of the celestial *is* one, and the *glory* of the terrestrial *is* another. ⁴¹*There is* one glory of the sun, another glory of the moon, and another glory of the stars; for *one* star differs from *another* star in glory.

⁴²ªSo also *is* the resurrection of the dead. *The body* is sown in corruption, it is raised in incorruption. ⁴³ªIt is sown in dishonor, it is raised in glory. It is sown in weakness, it is raised in power. ⁴⁴It is sown a natural body, it is raised a spiritual body. There is a natural body, and there is a spiritual body. ⁴⁵And so it is written, ª"The first man Adam became a living being." ᵇThe last Adam *became* ᶜa life-giving spirit.

⁴⁶However, the spiritual is not first, but the natural, and afterward the spiritual. ⁴⁷ªThe first man *was* of the earth, ᵇmade¹ of dust; the second Man *is* ²the Lord ᶜfrom heaven. ⁴⁸As *was* the ¹man of dust, so also *are* those *who are made* of dust; ªand as *is* the heavenly *Man*, so also *are* those *who are* heavenly. ⁴⁹And ªas we have borne the image of the *man* of dust, ᵇwe¹ shall also bear the image of the heavenly *Man*.

15:24 ª[Dan. 2:44; 7:14, 27; 2 Pet. 1:11]
15:25 ªPs. 110:1; Matt. 22:44
15:26 ª[2 Tim. 1:10; Rev. 20:14; 21:4]
15:27 ªPs. 8:6
15:28 ª[Phil. 3:21]; ᵇ1 Cor. 3:23; 11:3; 12:6
15:30 ª2 Cor. 11:26
15:31 ª1 Thess. 2:19; ᵇRom. 8:36
15:32 ª2 Cor. 1:8; ᵇEccl. 2:24; Is. 22:13; 56:12; Luke 12:19
15:33 ª[1 Cor. 5:6]
15:34 ªRom. 13:11; Eph. 5:14; ᵇ[1 Thess. 4:5]; ᶜ1 Cor. 6:5
15:35 ªEzek. 37:3
15:36 ªJohn 12:24
15:42 ª[Dan. 12:3; Matt. 13:43]
15:43 ª[Phil. 3:21; Col. 3:4]
15:45 ªGen. 2:7; ᵇ[Rom. 5:14]; ᶜJohn 5:21; 6:57; [Rom. 8:2; Phil. 3:21; Col. 3:4]
15:47 ªJohn 3:31; ᵇGen. 2:7; 3:19; ᶜJohn 3:13
15:48 ªPhil. 3:20
15:49 ªGen. 5:3; ᵇRom. 8:29; [2 Cor. 3:18; Phil. 3:21; 1 John 3:2]

15:30 ¹danger 15:39 ¹NU, M omit *of flesh* 15:40 ¹heavenly ²earthly 15:47 ¹earthy ²NU omits *the Lord* 15:48 ¹earthy 15:49 ¹M *let us also bear*

OUR FINAL VICTORY

[50]Now this I say, brethren, that [a]flesh and blood cannot inherit the kingdom of God; nor does corruption inherit incorruption. [51]Behold, I tell you a [1]mystery: [a]We shall not all sleep, [b]but we shall all be changed— [52]in a moment, in the twinkling of an eye, at the last trumpet. [a]For the trumpet will sound, and the dead will be raised incorruptible, and we shall be changed. [53]For this corruptible must put on incorruption, and [a]this mortal *must* put on immortality. [54]So when this corruptible has put on incorruption, and this mortal has put on immortality, then shall be brought to pass the saying that is written: [a]"Death is swallowed up in victory."

[55] "O[a1] Death, where *is* your sting?
O Hades, where *is* your victory?"

[56]The sting of death *is* sin, and [a]the strength of sin *is* the law. [57a]But thanks *be* to God, who gives us [b]the victory through our Lord Jesus Christ. [58a]Therefore, my beloved brethren, be steadfast, immovable, always abounding in the work of the Lord, knowing [b]that your labor is not in vain in the Lord.

COLLECTION FOR THE SAINTS

16 Now concerning [a]the collection for the saints, as I have given orders to the churches of Galatia, so you must do also: [2a]On the first *day* of the week let each one of you lay something aside, storing up as he may prosper, that there be no collections when I come. [3]And when I come, [a]whomever you approve by *your* letters I will send to bear your gift to Jerusalem. [4a]But if it is fitting that I go also, they will go with me.

PERSONAL PLANS
(cf. Acts 19:21)

[5]Now I will come to you [a]when I pass through Macedonia (for I am passing through Macedonia). [6]And it may be that I will remain, or even spend the winter with you, that you may [a]send me on my journey, wherever I go. [7]For I do not wish to see you now on the way; but I hope to stay a while with you, [a]if the Lord permits.

[8]But I will tarry in Ephesus until [a]Pentecost. [9]For [a]a great and effective door has opened to me, and [b]*there are* many adversaries.

[10]And [a]if Timothy comes, see that he may be with you without fear; for [b]he does the work of the Lord, as I also *do*. [11a]Therefore let no one despise him. But send him on his journey [b]in peace, that he may come to me; for I am waiting for him with the brethren.

[12]Now concerning *our* brother [a]Apollos, I strongly urged him to come to you with the brethren, but he was quite unwilling to come at this time; however, he will come when he has a convenient time.

FINAL EXHORTATIONS

[13a]Watch, [b]stand fast in the faith, be brave, [c]be strong. [14a]Let all *that* you *do* be done with love.

16:14 [a][1 Pet. 4:8]

15:51 [1]*hidden truth*   15:55 [1]NU *O Death, where is your victory? O Death, where is your sting?*

15:50
[a]Matt. 16:17;
[John 3:3, 5]

15:51
[a][1 Thess. 4:15]
[b][Phil. 3:21]

15:52
[a]Zech. 9:14;
Matt. 24:31;
John 5:25

15:53 [a]2 Cor. 5:4

15:54 [a]Is. 25:8;
[Rev. 20:14]

15:55 [a]Hos. 13:14

15:56
[a][Rom. 3:20;
4:15; 7:8]

15:57
[a][Rom. 7:25];
2 Cor. 2:14
[b]Rom. 8:37;
[Heb. 2:14;
1 John 5:4];
Rev. 21:4

15:58
[a]2 Pet. 3:14
[b][1 Cor. 3:8]

16:1 [a]Acts 11:29;
Gal. 2:10

16:2 [a]Acts 20:7

16:3
[a]2 Cor. 3:1; 8:18

16:4
[a]2 Cor. 8:4, 19

16:5 [a]Acts 19:21;
2 Cor. 1:15, 16

16:6 [a]Acts 15:3;
Rom. 15:24;
1 Cor. 16:11

16:7 [a]Acts 18:21;
James 4:15

16:8
[a]Lev. 23:15–22

16:9 [a]Acts 14:27;
2 Cor. 2:12;
Col. 4:3
[b]Acts 19:9

16:10
[a]Acts 19:22;
2 Tim. 1:2
[b]Phil. 2:20;
1 Thess. 3:2

16:11
[a]1 Tim. 4:12;
Titus 2:15
[b]Acts 15:33

16:12
[a]Acts 18:24;
1 Cor. 1:12; 3:5

16:13
[a]Matt. 24:42
[b]1 Cor. 15:1;
Gal. 5:1;
Phil. 1:27; 4:1;
1 Thess. 3:8;
2 Thess. 2:15
[c][Ps. 31:24];
Eph. 3:16; 6:10;
Col. 1:11]

[15]I urge you, brethren—you know [a]the household of Stephanas, that it is [b]the firstfruits of Achaia, and *that* they have devoted themselves to [c]the ministry of the saints— [16a]that you also submit to such, and to everyone who works and [b]labors with *us*.

[17]I am glad about the coming of Stephanas, Fortunatus, and Achaicus, [a]for what was lacking on your part they supplied. [18a]For they refreshed my spirit and yours. Therefore [b]acknowledge such men.

GREETINGS AND A SOLEMN FAREWELL

[19]The churches of Asia greet you. Aquila and Priscilla greet you heartily in the Lord, [a]with the church that is in their house. [20]All the brethren greet you.

[a]Greet one another with a holy kiss.

[21a]The salutation with my own hand—Paul's.

[22]If anyone [a]does not love the Lord Jesus Christ, [b]let him be [1]accursed. [c]O[2] Lord, come!

[23a]The grace of our Lord Jesus Christ *be* with you. [24]My love *be* with you all in Christ Jesus. Amen.

16:15 [a]1 Cor. 1:16
[b]Rom. 16:5
[c]2 Cor. 8:4

16:16 [a]Eph. 5:21;
1 Thess. 5:12;
Heb. 13:17
[b][Heb. 6:10]

16:17 [a]2 Cor. 11:9;
Phil. 2:30

16:18 [a]Col. 4:8
[b]Phil. 2:29

16:19 [a]Rom. 16:5

16:20
[a]Rom. 16:16

16:21
[a]Rom. 16:22;
Gal. 6:11;
Col. 4:18;
2 Thess. 3:17;
Philem. 19

16:22 [a]Eph. 6:24
[b]Gal. 1:8, 9
[c]Jude 14, 15

16:23
[a]Rom. 16:20

16:22 [1]Gr. *anathema*   [2]Aram. *Marana tha;* possibly *Maran atha, Our Lord has come*

THE SECOND EPISTLE OF PAUL
THE APOSTLE TO THE
CORINTHIANS

GREETING

1 Paul, ᵃan apostle of Jesus Christ by the will of God, and ᵇTimothy *our* brother,

To the church of God which is at Corinth, ᶜwith all the saints who are in all Achaia:

²ᵃGrace to you and peace from God our Father and the Lord Jesus Christ.

COMFORT IN SUFFERING

³ᵃBlessed *be* the God and Father of our Lord Jesus Christ, the Father of mercies and God of all comfort, ⁴who ᵃcomforts us in all our tribulation, that we may be able to comfort those who are in any ¹trouble, with the comfort with which we ourselves are comforted by God. ⁵For as ᵃthe sufferings of Christ abound in us, so our ¹consolation also abounds through Christ. ⁶Now if we are afflicted, ᵃ*it is* for your consolation and salvation, which is effective for enduring the same sufferings which we also suffer. Or if we are comforted, *it is* for your consolation and salvation. ⁷And our hope for you *is* steadfast, because we know that ᵃas you are partakers of the sufferings, so also *you will partake* of the consolation.

DELIVERED FROM SUFFERING

⁸For we do not want you to be ignorant, brethren, of ᵃour ¹trouble which came to us in Asia: that we were burdened beyond measure, above strength, so that we despaired even of life. ⁹Yes, we had the sentence of death in ourselves, that we should ᵃnot trust in ourselves but in God who raises the dead, ¹⁰ᵃwho delivered us from so great a death, and ¹does deliver us; in whom we trust that He will still deliver *us,* ¹¹you also ᵃhelping together in prayer for us, that thanks may be given by many persons on ¹our behalf ᵇfor the gift *granted* to us through many.

PAUL'S SINCERITY

¹²For our boasting is this: the testimony of our conscience that we conducted ourselves in the world in ¹simplicity and ᵃgodly sincerity, ᵇnot with fleshly wisdom but by the grace of God, and more abundantly toward you. ¹³For we are not writing any other things to you than what you read or understand. Now I trust you will understand, even to the end ¹⁴(as also you have understood us in part), ᵃthat we are your boast as ᵇyou also *are* ours, in the day of the Lord Jesus.

1:1 ᵃ1 Cor. 1:1;
Eph. 1:1; Col. 1:1;
1 Tim. 1:1;
2 Tim. 1:1
ᵇActs 16:1;
1 Cor. 16:10
ᶜPhil. 1:1; Col. 1:2

1:2 ᵃRom. 1:7

1:3 ᵃEph. 1:3;
1 Pet. 1:3

1:4
ᵃIs. 51:12; 66:13;
2 Cor. 7:6, 7, 13

1:5 ᵃ[Acts 9:4];
2 Cor. 4:10;
Phil. 3:10;
Col. 1:24

1:6
ᵃ2 Cor. 4:15; 12:15;
Eph. 3:1, 13;
2 Tim. 2:10

1:7 ᵃ[Rom. 8:17;
2 Tim. 2:12]

1:8 ᵃActs 19:23;
1 Cor. 15:32; 16:9

1:9 ᵃJer. 17:5, 7

1:10 ᵃ[2 Pet. 2:9]

1:11 ᵃRom. 15:30;
Phil. 1:19;
Philem. 22
ᵇ2 Cor. 4:15; 9:11

1:12 ᵃ2 Cor. 2:17
ᵇ[1 Cor. 2:4]

1:14 ᵃ2 Cor. 5:12
ᵇPhil. 2:16;
1 Thess. 2:19

1:4 ¹*tribulation*   1:5 ¹*comfort*   1:8 ¹*tribulation*   1:10 ¹NU *shall*
1:11 ¹M *your behalf*   1:12 ¹The opposite of duplicity

1:15 ᵃ1 Cor. 4:19
ᵇRom. 1:11; 15:29

1:16 ᵃActs 19:21;
1 Cor. 16:3–6

1:17 ᵃ2 Cor. 10:2;
11:18

1:18 ᵃ1 John 5:20

1:19 ᵃMark 1:1;
Luke 1:35;
John 1:34; 20:31;
1 John 5:5, 20
ᵇ1 Thess. 1:1;
2 Thess. 1:1;
1 Pet. 5:12
ᶜActs 18:5;
2 Cor. 1:1
ᵈ[Heb. 13:8]

1:20
ᵃ[Rom. 15:8, 9]

1:21
ᵃ[1 John 2:20,
27]

1:22
ᵃ[Eph. 4:30]
ᵇRom. 8:16;
2 Cor. 5:5;
[Eph. 1:14]

1:23 ᵃRom. 1:9;
Gal. 1:20;
Phil. 1:8
ᵇ1 Cor. 4:21;
2 Cor. 2:3; 12:20

1:24 ᵃ1 Cor. 3:5;
2 Cor. 4:5; 11:20;
[1 Pet. 5:3]
ᵇRom. 11:20;
1 Cor. 15:1

2:1 ᵃ2 Cor. 1:23

2:2 ᵃ2 Cor. 7:8

2:3 ᵃ1 Cor. 4:21;
2 Cor. 12:21
ᵇ2 Cor. 8:22;
Gal. 5:10;
2 Thess. 3:4;
Philem. 21

2:4 ᵃ[2 Cor. 2:9;
7:8, 12]

2:5 ᵃ[1 Cor. 5:1]
ᵇGal. 4:12

2:6
ᵃ1 Cor. 5:4, 5;
2 Cor. 7:11;
1 Tim. 5:20

2:7 ᵃGal. 6:1;
Eph. 4:32

2:9
ᵃ2 Cor. 7:15; 10:6

2:12 ᵃActs 16:8
ᵇ1 Cor. 16:9

2:13
ᵃ2 Cor. 7:6, 13;
8:6; Gal. 2:1, 3;
2 Tim. 4:10;
Titus 1:4

2:15 ᵃ[1 Cor. 1:18]
ᵇ[2 Cor. 4:3]

SPARING THE CHURCH

15And in this confidence ᵃI intended to come to you before, that you might have ᵇa second benefit— 16to pass by way of you to Macedonia, ᵃto come again from Macedonia to you, and be helped by you on my way to Judea. 17Therefore, when I was planning this, did I do it lightly? Or the things I plan, do I plan ᵃaccording to the flesh, that with me there should be Yes, Yes, and No, No? 18But *as* God *is* ᵃfaithful, our ¹word to you was not Yes and No. 19For ᵃthe Son of God, Jesus Christ, who was preached among you by us—by me, ᵇSilvanus, and ᶜTimothy—was not Yes and No, ᵈbut in Him was Yes. 20ᵃFor all the promises of God in Him *are* Yes, and in Him Amen, to the glory of God through us. 21Now He who establishes us with you in Christ and ᵃhas anointed us *is* God, 22who ᵃalso has sealed us and ᵇgiven us the Spirit in our hearts as a guarantee.

23Moreover ᵃI call God as witness against my soul, ᵇthat to spare you I came no more to Corinth. 24Not ᵃthat we ¹have dominion over your faith, but are fellow workers for your joy; for ᵇby faith you stand.

2 But I determined this within myself, ᵃthat I would not come again to you in sorrow. 2For if I make you ᵃsorrowful, then who is he who makes me glad but the one who is made sorrowful by me?

FORGIVE THE OFFENDER

3And I wrote this very thing to you, lest, when I came, ᵃI should have sorrow over those from whom I ought to have joy, ᵇhaving confidence in you all that my joy is *the joy* of you all. 4For out of much ¹affliction and anguish of heart I wrote to you, with many tears, ᵃnot that you should be grieved, but that you might know the love which I have so abundantly for you.

5But ᵃif anyone has caused grief, he has not ᵇgrieved me, but all of you to some extent—not to be too severe. 6This punishment which *was inflicted* ᵃby the majority *is* sufficient for such a man, 7ᵃso that, on the contrary, you *ought* rather to forgive and comfort *him*, lest perhaps such a one be swallowed up with too much sorrow. 8Therefore I urge you to reaffirm *your* love to him. 9For to this end I also wrote, that I might put you to the test, whether you are ᵃobedient in all things. 10Now whom you forgive anything, I also *forgive*. For ¹if indeed I have forgiven anything, I have forgiven that one for your sakes in the presence of Christ, 11lest Satan should take advantage of us; for we are not ignorant of his devices.

TRIUMPH IN CHRIST

12Furthermore, ᵃwhen I came to Troas to *preach* Christ's gospel, and ᵇa ¹door was opened to me by the Lord, 13ᵃI had no rest in my spirit, because I did not find Titus my brother; but taking my leave of them, I departed for Macedonia.

14Now thanks *be* to God who always leads us in triumph in Christ, and through us ¹diffuses the fragrance of His knowledge in every place. 15For we are to God the fragrance of Christ ᵃamong those who are being saved and ᵇamong those who

1:18 ¹message   1:24 ¹rule   2:4 ¹tribulation   2:10 ¹NU *indeed, what I have forgiven, if I have forgiven anything, I did it for your sakes*
2:12 ¹Opportunity   2:14 ¹manifests

are perishing. 16aTo the one *we are* the aroma of death *leading* to death, and to the other the aroma of life *leading* to life. And bwho *is* sufficient for these things? 17For we are not, as 1so many, apeddling2 the word of God; but as bof sincerity, but as from God, we speak in the sight of God in Christ.

CHRIST'S EPISTLE
(cf. Jer. 31:31–34)

3 Do awe begin again to commend ourselves? Or do we need, as some *others,* bepistles of commendation to you or *letters* of commendation from you? 2aYou are our epistle written in our hearts, known and read by all men; 3clearly you are an epistle of Christ, aministered by us, written not with ink but by the Spirit of the living God, not bon tablets of stone but con tablets of flesh, *that is,* of the heart.

THE SPIRIT, NOT THE LETTER

4And we have such trust through Christ toward God. 5aNot that we are sufficient of ourselves to think of anything as *being* from ourselves, but bour sufficiency *is* from God, 6who also made us sufficient as aministers of bthe new covenant, not cof the letter but of the 1Spirit; for dthe letter kills, ebut the Spirit gives life.

GLORY OF THE NEW COVENANT

7But if athe ministry of death, bwritten *and* engraved on stones, was glorious, cso that the children of Israel could not look steadily at the face of Moses because of the glory of his countenance, which *glory* was passing away, 8how will athe ministry of the Spirit not be more glorious? 9For if the ministry of condemnation *had* glory, the ministry aof righteousness exceeds much more in glory. 10For even what was made glorious had no glory in this respect, because of the glory that excels. 11For if what is passing away *was* glorious, what remains *is* much more glorious.

12Therefore, since we have such hope, awe use great boldness of speech— 13unlike Moses, awho put a veil over his face so that the children of Israel could not look steadily at bthe end of what was passing away. 14But atheir minds were blinded. For until this day the same veil remains unlifted in the reading of the Old Testament, because the *veil* is taken away in Christ. 15But even to this day, when Moses is read, a veil lies on their heart. 16Nevertheless awhen one turns to the Lord, bthe veil is taken away. 17Now athe Lord is the Spirit; and where the Spirit of the Lord *is,* there *is* bliberty. 18But we all, with unveiled face, beholding aas in a mirror bthe glory of the Lord, care being transformed into the same image from glory to glory, just as 1by the Spirit of the Lord.

THE LIGHT OF CHRIST'S GOSPEL

4 Therefore, since we have this ministry, aas we have received mercy, we bdo not lose heart. 2But we have renounced the hidden things of shame, not walking in craftiness nor 1handling the word of God deceitfully, but by manifesta-

2:16 aLuke 2:34;
[John 9:39];
1 Pet. 2:7]
b[1 Cor. 15:10]

2:17 a2 Pet. 2:3
b1 Cor. 5:8;
2 Cor. 1:12;
1 Thess. 2:4;
1 Pet. 4:11

3:1 a2 Cor. 5:12;
10:12, 18; 12:11
bActs 18:27

3:2 a1 Cor. 9:2

3:3 a1 Cor. 3:5
bEx. 24:12; 31:18;
32:15; 2 Cor. 3:7
cPs. 40:8

3:5 a[John 15:5]
b1 Cor. 15:10

3:6 a1 Cor. 3:5;
Eph. 3:7
bJer. 31:31;
Matt. 26:28;
Luke 22:20
cRom. 2:27
d[Rom. 3:20];
Gal. 3:10
eJohn 6:63;
Rom. 8:2

3:7 aRom. 7:10
bEx. 34:1;
Deut. 10:1
cEx. 34:29

3:8 a[Gal. 3:5]

3:9
a[Rom. 1:17; 3:21]

3:12
aActs 4:13, 29;
2 Cor. 7:4;
Eph. 6:19

3:13
aEx. 34:33–35;
2 Cor. 3:7
bRom. 10:4;
[Gal. 3:23]

3:14 aIs. 6:10;
29:10;
Acts 28:26;
Rom. 11:7, 8;
2 Cor. 4:4

3:16 aEx. 34:34;
Rom. 11:23
bIs. 25:7

3:17
a[1 Cor. 15:45]
bJohn 8:32;
Gal. 5:1, 13

3:18 a1 Cor. 13:12
b[2 Cor. 4:4, 6]
c[Rom. 8:29, 30]

4:1 a1 Cor. 7:25
bLuke 18:1;
2 Cor. 4:16;
Gal. 6:9;
Eph. 3:13;
2 Thess. 3:13

2:17 1M the rest   2adulterating for gain   3:6 1Or *spirit*   3:18 1Or *from the Lord, the Spirit*   4:2 1adulterating the word of God

tion of the truth [a]commending ourselves to every man's conscience in the sight of God. [3]But even if our gospel is veiled, [a]it is veiled to those who are perishing, [4]whose minds [a]the god of this age [b]has blinded, who do not believe, lest [c]the light of the gospel of the glory of Christ, [d]who is the image of God, should shine on them. [5a]For we do not preach ourselves, but Christ Jesus the Lord, and [b]ourselves your bondservants for Jesus' sake. [6]For it is the God [a]who commanded light to shine out of darkness, who has [b]shone in our hearts to *give* the light of the knowledge of the glory of God in the face of Jesus Christ.

CAST DOWN BUT UNCONQUERED

[7]But we have this treasure in earthen vessels, [a]that the excellence of the power may be of God and not of us. [8]*We are* [a]hard-pressed on every side, yet not crushed; *we are* perplexed, but not in despair; [9]persecuted, but not [a]forsaken; [b]struck down, but not destroyed— [10a]always carrying about in the body the dying of the Lord Jesus, [b]that the life of Jesus also may be manifested in our body. [11]For we who live [a]are always delivered to death for Jesus' sake, that the life of Jesus also may be manifested in our mortal flesh. [12]So then death is working in us, but life in you.

[13]And since we have [a]the same spirit of faith, according to what is written, [b]"I believed and therefore I spoke," we also believe and therefore speak, [14]knowing that [a]He who raised up the Lord Jesus will also raise us up with Jesus, and will present *us* with you. [15]For [a]all things *are* for your sakes, that [b]grace, having spread through the many, may cause thanksgiving to abound to the glory of God.

SEEING THE INVISIBLE

[16]Therefore we [a]do not lose heart. Even though our outward man is perishing, yet the inward *man* is [b]being renewed day by day. [17]For [a]our light affliction, which is but for a moment, is working for us a far more exceeding *and* eternal weight of glory, [18a]while we do not look at the things which are seen, but at the things which are not seen. For the things which are seen *are* temporary, but the things which are not seen *are* eternal.

ASSURANCE OF THE RESURRECTION

5 For we know that if [a]our earthly [1]house, *this* tent, is destroyed, we have a building from God, a house [b]not made with hands, eternal in the heavens. [2]For in this [a]we groan, earnestly desiring to be clothed with our [1]habitation which is from heaven, [3]if indeed, [a]having been clothed, we shall not be found naked. [4]For we who are in *this* tent groan, being burdened, not because we want to be unclothed, [a]but further clothed, that mortality may be swallowed up by life. [5]Now He who has prepared us for this very thing *is* God, who also [a]has given us the Spirit as [1]a guarantee.

[6]So *we are* always confident, knowing that while we are at home in the body we are absent from the Lord. [7]For [a]we walk by faith, not by sight. [8]We are confident, yes, [a]well pleased rather to be absent from the body and to be present with the Lord.

4:2 [a]2 Cor. 5:11
4:3 [a][1 Cor. 1:18];
2 Cor. 2:15
4:4 [a]John 12:31;
[Eph. 6:12]
[b]John 12:40
[c][2 Cor. 3:8, 9]
[d][John 1:18];
Phil. 2:6;
Col. 1:15;
Heb. 1:3
4:5 [a]1 Cor. 1:13
[b]1 Cor. 9:19
4:6 [a]Gen. 1:3
[b]Is. 9:2;
Mal. 4:2;
Luke 1:78;
2 Pet. 1:19
4:7 [a]Judg. 7:2;
1 Cor. 2:5
4:8 [a]2 Cor. 1:8; 7:5
4:9 [a]Ps. 129:2;
[Heb. 13:5]
[b]Ps. 37:24
4:10 [a]Phil. 3:10
[b]Rom. 8:17
4:11 [a]Rom. 8:36
4:13 [a]2 Pet. 1:1
[b]Ps. 116:10
4:14 [a][Rom. 8:11]
4:15 [a]Col. 1:24
[b]1 Cor. 9:19;
2 Cor. 1:11
4:16 [a]2 Cor. 4:1;
Gal. 6:9
[b][Is. 40:29, 31;
Col. 3:10]
4:17 [a]Matt. 5:12;
Rom. 8:18;
1 Pet. 1:6
4:18 [a]Rom. 8:24;
[2 Cor. 5:7;
Heb. 11:1, 13]
5:1 [a]Job 4:19;
1 Cor. 15:47;
2 Cor. 4:7
[b]Mark 14:58;
Acts 7:48;
Heb. 9:11, 24
5:2 [a]Rom. 8:23;
2 Cor. 5:4
5:3 [a]Rev. 3:18
5:4 [a]1 Cor. 15:53
5:5 [a]Rom. 8:23;
[2 Cor. 1:22];
Eph. 1:14
5:7 [a]Rom. 8:24;
Heb. 11:1
5:8 [a]Phil. 1:23

5:1 [1]Physical body   5:2 [1]dwelling   5:5 [1]down payment, earnest

THE JUDGMENT SEAT OF CHRIST

9Therefore we make it our aim, whether present or absent, to be well pleasing to Him. 10aFor we must all appear before the judgment seat of Christ, bthat each one may receive the things *done* in the body, according to what he has done, whether good or bad. 11Knowing, therefore, athe terror of the Lord, we persuade men; but we are well known to God, and I also trust are well known in your consciences.

BE RECONCILED TO GOD

12For awe do not commend ourselves again to you, but give you opportunity bto boast on our behalf, that you may have *an answer* for those who boast in appearance and not in heart. 13For aif we are beside ourselves, *it is* for God; or if we are of sound mind, *it is* for you. 14For the love of Christ compels us, because we judge thus: that aif One died for all, then all died; 15and He died for all, athat those who live should live no longer for themselves, but for Him who died for them and rose again.

16aTherefore, from now on, we regard no one according to the flesh. Even though we have known Christ according to the flesh, byet now we know *Him thus* no longer. 17Therefore, if anyone ais in Christ, *he is* ba new creation; cold things have passed away; behold, all things have become dnew. 18Now all things *are* of God, awho has reconciled us to Himself through Jesus Christ, and has given us the ministry of reconciliation, 19that is, that aGod was in Christ reconciling the world to Himself, not 1imputing their trespasses to them, and has committed to us the word of reconciliation.

20Now then, we are aambassadors for Christ, as though God were pleading through us: we implore *you* on Christ's behalf, be reconciled to God. 21For aHe made Him who knew no sin *to be* sin for us, that we might become bthe righteousness of God in Him.

MARKS OF THE MINISTRY

6 We then, *as* aworkers together *with Him* also bplead with *you* not to receive the grace of God in vain. 2For He says:

a"In an acceptable time I have heard you,
And in the day of salvation I have helped you."

Behold, now *is* the accepted time; behold, now *is* the day of salvation.

3aWe give no offense in anything, that our ministry may not be blamed. 4But in all *things* we commend ourselves aas ministers of God: in much 1patience, in tribulations, in needs, in distresses, 5ain stripes, in imprisonments, in tumults, in labors, in sleeplessness, in fastings; 6by purity, by knowledge, by longsuffering, by kindness, by the Holy Spirit, by 1sincere love, 7aby the word of truth, by bthe power of God, by cthe armor of righteousness on the right hand and on the left, 8by honor and dishonor, by evil report and good report; as deceivers, and *yet* true; 9as unknown, and ayet well known; bas dying, and behold we live; cas chastened, and *yet* not killed; 10as sorrowful, yet always rejoicing; as poor, yet making many arich; as having nothing, and *yet* possessing all things.

5:10
aMatt. 16:27;
Acts 10:42;
Rom. 2:16;
14:10, 12
bGal. 6:7;
Eph. 6:8

5:11
a[Heb. 10:31;
12:29; Jude 23]

5:12 a2 Cor. 3:1
b2 Cor. 1:14;
Phil. 1:26

5:13 aMark 3:21;
2 Cor. 11:1, 16;
12:11

5:14
a[Rom. 5:15; 6:6;
Gal. 2:20;
Col. 3:3]

5:15
a[Rom. 6:11]

5:16 a2 Cor. 10:3
b[Matt. 12:50]

5:17
a[John 6:63]
b[Rom. 8:9]
cIs. 43:18; 65:17;
[Eph. 4:24];
Rev. 21:4
d[Rom. 6:3–10;
Col. 3:3]

5:18 aRom. 5:10;
[Eph. 2:16];
Col. 1:20]

5:19
a[Rom. 3:24]

5:20 aMal. 2:7;
Eph. 6:20

5:21
aIs. 53:6, 9
b[Rom. 1:17;
3:21];
1 Cor. 1:30

6:1 a1 Cor. 3:9
b2 Cor. 5:20

6:2 aIs. 49:8

6:3 aRom. 14:13

6:4 a1 Cor. 4:1

6:5 a2 Cor. 11:23

6:7 a2 Cor. 7:14
b1 Cor. 2:4
cRom. 13:12;
2 Cor. 10:4

6:9
a2 Cor. 4:2; 5:11
b1 Cor. 4:9, 11
cPs. 118:18

6:10 a1 Cor. 1:5;
[2 Cor. 8:9]

5:19 1reckoning 6:4 1endurance 6:6 1Lit. *unhypocritical*

BE HOLY

¹¹O Corinthians! ⁷We have spoken openly to you, ªour heart is wide open. ¹²You are not restricted by us, but ªyou are restricted by your *own* affections. ¹³Now in return for the same ª(I speak as to children), you also be open.

¹⁴ªDo not be unequally yoked together with unbelievers. For ᵇwhat ¹fellowship has righteousness with lawlessness? And what ²communion has light with darkness? ¹⁵And what accord has Christ with Belial? Or what part has a believer with an unbeliever? ¹⁶And what agreement has the temple of God with idols? For ªyou¹ are the temple of the living God. As God has said:

ᵇ"I will dwell in them
And walk among *them*.
I will be their God,
And they shall be My people."

¹⁷Therefore

ª"Come out from among them
And be separate, says the Lord.
Do not touch what is unclean,
And I will receive you."
¹⁸ "I ªwill be a Father to you,
And you shall be My ᵇsons and daughters,
Says the LORD Almighty."

7 Therefore,ª having these promises, beloved, let us cleanse ourselves from all filthiness of the flesh and spirit, perfecting holiness in the fear of God.

THE CORINTHIANS' REPENTANCE

²Open *your hearts* to us. We have wronged no one, we have corrupted no one, ªwe have cheated no one. ³I do not say *this* to condemn; for ªI have said before that you are in our hearts, to die together and to live together. ⁴ªGreat *is* my boldness of speech toward you, ᵇgreat *is* my boasting on your behalf. ᶜI am filled with comfort. I am exceedingly joyful in all our tribulation.

⁵For indeed, ªwhen we came to Macedonia, our bodies had no rest, but ᵇwe were troubled on every side. ᶜOutside *were* conflicts, inside *were* fears. ⁶Nevertheless ªGod, who comforts the downcast, comforted us by ᵇthe coming of Titus, ⁷and not only by his coming, but also by the ¹consolation with which he was comforted in you, when he told us of your earnest desire, your mourning, your zeal for me, so that I rejoiced even more.

⁸For even if I made you ªsorry with my letter, I do not regret it; ᵇthough I did regret it. For I perceive that the same epistle made you sorry, though only for a while. ⁹Now I rejoice, not that you were made sorry, but that your sorrow led to repentance. For you were made sorry in a godly manner, that you might suffer loss from us in nothing. ¹⁰For ªgodly sorrow produces repentance *leading* to salvation, not to be regretted; ᵇbut the sorrow of the world produces death. ¹¹For observe this very thing, that you sorrowed in a godly

---

6:11 ªIs. 60:5;
2 Cor. 7:3

6:12 ª2 Cor. 12:15

6:13 ª1 Cor. 4:14

6:14
ªDeut. 7:2, 3;
22:10; 1 Cor. 5:9
ᵇ1 Sam. 5:2, 3;
1 Kin. 18:21;
Eph. 5:6, 7, 11;
1 John 1:6

6:16
ª[1 Cor. 3:16, 17;
6:19]; Eph. 2:21;
[Heb. 3:6]
ᵇEx. 29:45;
Lev. 26:12;
Jer. 31:33; 32:38;
Ezek. 37:26, 27;
Zech. 8:8

6:17
ªNum. 33:51–56;
Is. 52:11;
Rev. 18:4

6:18
ª2 Sam. 7:14;
Jer. 31:1, 9;
[Rev. 21:7]
ᵇ[John 1:12;
Rom. 8:14;
Gal. 4:5–7];
Phil. 2:15;
1 John 3:1

7:1 ª[1 John 3:3]

7:2 ªActs 20:33

7:3
ª2 Cor. 6:11, 12

7:4 ª2 Cor. 3:12
ᵇ1 Cor. 1:4
ᶜPhil. 2:17;
Col. 1:24

7:5 ªRom. 15:26;
2 Cor. 2:13
ᵇ2 Cor. 4:8
ᶜDeut. 32:25

7:6 ªIs. 49:13;
2 Cor. 1:3, 4
ᵇ2 Cor. 2:13; 7:13

7:8 ª2 Cor. 2:2
ᵇ2 Cor. 2:4

7:10
ª2 Sam. 12:13;
Ps. 32:10;
Matt. 26:75
ᵇProv. 17:22

6:11 ¹Lit. *Our mouth is open*   6:14 ¹*in common*   ²*fellowship*   6:16 ¹NU *we*
7:7 ¹*comfort*

manner: What diligence it produced in you, *what* [a]clearing *of yourselves, what* indignation, *what* fear, *what* vehement desire, *what* zeal, *what* vindication! In all *things* you proved yourselves to be [b]clear in this matter. [12]Therefore, although I wrote to you, *I did* not *do it* for the sake of him who had done the wrong, nor for the sake of him who suffered wrong, [a]but that our care for you in the sight of God might appear to you.

THE JOY OF TITUS

[13]Therefore we have been comforted in your comfort. And we rejoiced exceedingly more for the joy of Titus, because his spirit [a]has been refreshed by you all. [14]For if in anything I have boasted to him about you, I am not ashamed. But as we spoke all things to you in truth, even so our boasting to Titus was found true. [15]And his affections are greater for you as he remembers [a]the obedience of you all, how with fear and trembling you received him. [16]Therefore I rejoice that [a]I have confidence in you in everything.

EXCEL IN GIVING

8 Moreover, brethren, we make known to you the grace of God bestowed on the churches of Macedonia: [2]that in a great trial of affliction the abundance of their joy and [a]their deep poverty abounded in the riches of their liberality. [3]For I bear witness that according to *their* ability, yes, and beyond *their* ability, *they were* freely willing, [4]imploring us with much urgency [1]that we would receive the gift and [a]the fellowship of the ministering to the saints. [5]And not *only* as we had hoped, but they first [a]gave themselves to the Lord, and *then* to us by the [b]will of God. [6]So [a]we urged Titus, that as he had begun, so he would also complete this grace in you as well. [7]But as [a]you abound in everything—in faith, in speech, in knowledge, in all diligence, and in your love for us—*see* [b]that you abound in this grace also.

CHRIST OUR PATTERN

[8][a]I speak not by commandment, but I am testing the sincerity of your love by the diligence of others. [9]For you know the grace of our Lord Jesus Christ, [a]that though He was rich, yet for your sakes He became poor, that you through His poverty might become [b]rich.

[10]And in this [a]I give advice: [b]It is to your advantage not only to be doing what you began and [c]were desiring to do a year ago; [11]but now you also must complete the doing *of it;* that as *there was* a readiness to desire *it,* so *there* also *may be* a completion out of what *you* have. [12]For [a]if there is first a willing mind, *it is* accepted according to what one has, *and* not according to what he does not have.

[13]For *I do* not *mean* that others should be eased and you burdened; [14]but by an equality, *that* now at this time your abundance *may supply* their lack, that their abundance also may *supply* your lack—that there may be equality. [15]As it is written, [a]"He who *gathered* much had nothing left over, and he who *gathered* little had no lack."

Cross References

7:11 [a]Eph. 5:11
[b]2 Cor. 2:5–11

7:12 [a]2 Cor. 2:4

7:13 [a]Rom. 15:32

7:15 [a]2 Cor. 2:9;
Phil. 2:12

7:16
[a]2 Cor. 2:3; 8:22;
2 Thess. 3:4;
Philem. 8, 21

8:2 [a]Mark 12:44

8:4
[a]Acts 11:29;
24:17;
Rom. 15:25, 26;
1 Cor. 16:1, 3, 4;
2 Cor. 9:1

8:5
[a][Rom. 12:1, 2]
[b][Eph. 6:6]

8:6
[a]2 Cor. 8:17;
12:18

8:7
[a][1 Cor. 1:5; 12:13]
[b]2 Cor. 9:8

8:8 [a]1 Cor. 7:6

8:9 [a]Matt. 8:20;
Luke 9:58;
Phil. 2:6, 7
[b]Rom. 9:23;
[Eph. 1:7;
Rev. 3:18]

8:10
[a]1 Cor. 7:25, 40
[b][Prov. 19:17;
Matt. 10:42;
1 Tim. 6:18, 19;
Heb. 13:16]
[c]1 Cor. 16:2;
2 Cor. 9:2

8:12
[a]Mark 12:43, 44;
Luke 21:3, 4;
2 Cor. 9:7

8:15 [a]Ex. 16:18

8:4 [1]NU, M omit *that we would receive,* thus changing text to *urgency for the favor and fellowship*

COLLECTION FOR THE JUDEAN SAINTS

16But thanks *be* to God who [1]puts the same earnest care for you into the heart of Titus. 17For he not only accepted the exhortation, but being more diligent, he went to you of his own accord. 18And we have sent with him [a]the brother whose praise *is* in the gospel throughout all the churches, 19and not only *that,* but who was also [a]chosen by the churches to travel with us with this gift, which is administered by us [b]to the glory of the Lord Himself and *to show* your ready mind, 20avoiding this: that anyone should blame us in this lavish gift which is administered by us— 21[a]providing honorable things, not only in the sight of the Lord, but also in the sight of men.

22And we have sent with them our brother whom we have often proved diligent in many things, but now much more diligent, because of the great confidence which *we have* in you. 23If *anyone inquires* about [a]Titus, *he is* my partner and fellow worker concerning you. Or if our brethren *are inquired about, they are* [b]messengers[1] of the churches, the glory of Christ. 24Therefore show to them, [1]and before the churches, the proof of your love and of our [a]boasting on your behalf.

ADMINISTERING THE GIFT

9 Now concerning [a]the ministering to the saints, it is superfluous for me to write to you; 2for I know your willingness, about which I boast of you to the Macedonians, that Achaia was ready a [a]year ago; and your zeal has stirred up the majority. 3[a]Yet I have sent the brethren, lest our boasting of you should be in vain in this respect, that, as I said, you may be ready; 4lest if *some* Macedonians come with me and find you unprepared, we (not to mention you!) should be ashamed of this [1]confident boasting. 5Therefore I thought it necessary to [1]exhort the brethren to go to you ahead of time, and prepare your generous gift beforehand, which *you had* previously promised, that it may be ready as *a matter of* generosity and not as a [2]grudging obligation.

THE CHEERFUL GIVER

6[a]But this *I say:* He who sows sparingly will also reap sparingly, and he who sows [1]bountifully will also reap bountifully. 7*So let* each one *give* as he purposes in his heart, [a]not grudgingly or of [1]necessity; for [b]God loves a cheerful giver. 8[a]And God *is* able to make all grace abound toward you, that you, always having all sufficiency in all *things,* may have an abundance for every good work. 9As it is written:

[a]"He has dispersed abroad,
He has given to the poor;
His righteousness endures forever."

10Now [1]may He who [a]supplies seed to the sower, and bread for food, [2]supply and multiply the seed you have *sown* and increase the fruits of your [b]righteousness, 11while *you are* enriched in everything for all liberality, [a]which causes thanksgiving through us to God. 12For the administration of this service not only [a]supplies the needs of the saints, but also is abound-

Cross references (margin)

8:18 [a]1 Cor. 16:3; 2 Cor. 12:18

8:19 [a]Acts 14:23; 1 Cor. 16:3, 4 [b]2 Cor. 4:15

8:21 [a]Rom. 12:17; Phil. 4:8; 1 Pet. 2:12

8:23 [a]2 Cor. 7:13, 14 [b][John 13:16]; Phil. 2:25

8:24 [a]2 Cor. 7:4, 14; 9:2

9:1 [a]Acts 11:29; Rom. 15:26; 1 Cor. 16:1; 2 Cor. 8:4; Gal. 2:10

9:2 [a]2 Cor. 8:10

9:3 [a]2 Cor. 8:6, 17

9:6 [a]Prov. 11:24; 22:9; Gal. 6:7, 9

9:7 [a]Deut. 15:7 [b]Deut. 15:10; 1 Chr. 29:17; [Prov. 11:25]; Rom. 12:8; [2 Cor. 8:12]

9:8 [a][Prov. 11:24]

9:9 [a]Ps. 112:9

9:10 [a]Is. 55:10 [b]Hos. 10:12

9:11 [a]2 Cor. 1:11

9:12 [a]2 Cor. 8:14

8:16 [1]NU *has put*   8:23 [1]Lit. *apostles,* "sent ones"   8:24 [1]NU, M omit *and*   9:4 [1]NU *confidence.*   9:5 [1]*encourage*   [2]Lit. *covetousness*   9:6 [1]*with blessings*   9:7 [1]*compulsion*   9:10 [1]NU omits *may*   [2]NU *will supply*

ing through many thanksgivings to God, [13]while, through the proof of this ministry, they [a]glorify God for the obedience of your confession to the gospel of Christ, and for *your* liberal [b]sharing with them and all *men,* [14]and by their prayer for you, who long for you because of the exceeding [a]grace of God in you. [15]Thanks *be* to God [a]for His indescribable gift!

THE SPIRITUAL WAR

10 Now [a]I, Paul, myself am pleading with you by the meekness and gentleness of Christ—[b]who in presence *am* lowly among you, but being absent am bold toward you. [2]But I beg *you* [a]that when I am present I may not be bold with that confidence by which I intend to be bold against some, who think of us as if we walked according to the flesh. [3]For though we walk in the flesh, we do not war according to the flesh. [4a]For the weapons [b]of our warfare *are* not [1]carnal but [c]mighty in God [d]for pulling down strongholds, [5a]casting down arguments and every high thing that exalts itself against the knowledge of God, bringing every thought into captivity to the obedience of Christ, [6a]and being ready to punish all disobedience when [b]your obedience is fulfilled.

REALITY OF PAUL'S AUTHORITY

[7a]Do you look at things according to the outward appearance? [b]If anyone is convinced in himself that he is Christ's, let him again consider this in himself, that just as he *is* Christ's, even [1]so [c]we *are* Christ's. [8]For even if I should boast somewhat more [a]about our authority, which the Lord gave [1]us for [2]edification and not for your destruction, [b]I shall not be ashamed—[9]lest I seem to terrify you by letters. [10]"For *his* letters," they say, "*are* weighty and powerful, but [a]*his* bodily presence *is* weak, and *his* [b]speech contemptible." [11]Let such a person consider this, that what we are in word by letters when we are absent, such *we will* also *be* in deed when we are present.

LIMITS OF PAUL'S AUTHORITY

[12a]For we dare not class ourselves or compare ourselves with those who commend themselves. But they, measuring themselves by themselves, and comparing themselves among themselves, are not wise. [13a]We, however, will not boast beyond measure, but within the limits of the sphere which God appointed us—a sphere which especially includes you. [14]For we are not overextending ourselves (as though *our authority* did not extend to you), [a]for it was to you that we came with the gospel of Christ; [15]not boasting of things beyond measure, *that is,* [a]in other men's labors, but having hope, *that* as your faith is increased, we shall be greatly enlarged by you in our sphere, [16]to preach the gospel in the *regions* beyond you, *and* not to boast in another man's sphere of accomplishment.

[17]But [a]"he who glories, let him glory in the LORD." [18]For [a]not he who commends himself is approved, but [b]whom the Lord commends.

CONCERN FOR THEIR FAITHFULNESS

11 Oh, that you would bear with me in a little [a]folly—and indeed you do bear with me. [2]For I am [a]jealous for you

---

9:13
[a][Matt. 5:16]
[b][Heb. 13:16]

9:14 [a]2 Cor. 8:1

9:15
[a][John 3:16;
4:10;
Rom. 6:23;
8:32; Eph. 2:8;
James 1:17]

10:1 [a]Rom. 12:1
[b]1 Thess. 2:7

10:2 [a]1 Cor. 4:21;
2 Cor. 13:2, 10

10:4 [a]Eph. 6:13
[b]1 Cor. 9:7;
[2 Cor. 6:7];
1 Tim. 1:18
[c]Acts 7:22
[d]Jer. 1:10;
[2 Cor. 10:8;
13:10]

10:5 [a]1 Cor. 1:19

10:6
[a]2 Cor. 13:2, 10
[b]2 Cor. 7:15

10:7
[a][John 7:24];
2 Cor. 5:12
[b]1 Cor. 1:12; 14:37
[c][Rom. 14:8];
1 Cor. 3:23

10:8
[a]2 Cor. 13:10
[b]2 Cor. 7:14

10:10
[a]1 Cor. 2:3, 4;
2 Cor. 12:7;
Gal. 4:13
[b][1 Cor. 1:17];
2 Cor. 11:6

10:12 [a]2 Cor. 5:12

10:13
[a]2 Cor. 10:15

10:14
[a]1 Cor. 3:5, 6

10:15
[a]Rom. 15:20

10:17 [a]Is. 65:16;
Jer. 9:24;
1 Cor. 1:31

10:18 [a]Prov. 27:2
[b]Rom. 2:29;
[1 Cor. 4:5]

11:1 [a]Matt. 17:17;
2 Cor. 11:4, 16, 19

11:2 [a]Gal. 4:17

10:4 [1]*of the flesh*   10:7 [1]NU *as we are.*   10:8 [1]NU omits *us*   [2]*building up*

11:2 ᵇHos. 2:19;
[Eph. 5:26]
ᶜCol. 1:28
ᵈLev. 21:13

11:3
ᵃGen. 3:4, 13;
John 8:44;
1 Thess. 3:5;
1 Tim. 2:14;
[Rev. 12:9, 15]
ᵇEph. 6:24

11:4 ᵃGal. 1:6–8

11:5
ᵃ[1 Cor. 15:10];
2 Cor. 12:11;
Gal. 2:6

11:6 ᵃ[1 Cor. 1:17]
ᵇ[1 Cor. 12:8;
Eph. 3:4]
ᶜ[2 Cor. 12:12]

11:7 ᵃActs 18:3;
1 Cor. 9:18;
2 Cor. 12:13

11:9 ᵃActs 20:33
ᵇPhil. 4:10

11:10
ᵃRom. 1:9; 9:1;
2 Cor. 1:23;
[Gal. 2:20]
ᵇ1 Cor. 9:15

11:11 ᵃ2 Cor. 6:11;
12:15

11:12 ᵃ1 Cor. 9:12

11:13 ᵃActs 15:24;
Rom. 16:18;
Gal. 1:7;
Phil. 1:15;
2 Pet. 2:1;
Rev. 2:2
ᵇPhil. 3:2;
Titus 1:10

11:14 ᵃGal. 1:8

11:15 ᵃ[Phil. 3:19]

11:17 ᵃ1 Cor. 7:6

11:19 ᵃ1 Cor. 4:10

11:20
ᵃ2 Cor. 1:24;
[Gal. 2:4; 4:3,
9; 5:1]

11:21
ᵃ2 Cor. 10:10
ᵇPhil. 3:4

11:22 ᵃActs 22:3;
Rom. 11:1;
Phil. 3:4–6

11:23
ᵃ1 Cor. 15:10
ᵇActs 9:16
ᶜ1 Cor. 15:30

11:24
ᵃDeut. 25:3
ᵇ2 Cor. 6:5

11:25
ᵃActs 16:22, 23;
21:32

with godly jealousy. For ᵇI have betrothed you to one husband, ᶜthat I may present *you* ᵈ*as* a chaste virgin to Christ. ³But I fear, lest somehow, as ᵃthe serpent deceived Eve by his craftiness, so your minds ᵇmay be corrupted from the ¹simplicity that is in Christ. ⁴For if he who comes preaches another Jesus whom we have not preached, or *if* you receive a different spirit which you have not received, or a ᵃdifferent gospel which you have not accepted—you may well put up with it!

PAUL AND FALSE APOSTLES

⁵For I consider that ᵃI am not at all inferior to the most eminent apostles. ⁶Even though ᵃ*I am* untrained in speech, yet *I am* not ᵇin knowledge. But ᶜwe have ¹been thoroughly manifested among you in all things.

⁷Did I commit sin in ¹humbling myself that you might be exalted, because I preached the gospel of God to you ᵃfree of charge? ⁸I robbed other churches, taking wages *from them* to minister to you. ⁹And when I was present with you, and in need, ᵃI was a burden to no one, for what I lacked ᵇthe brethren who came from Macedonia supplied. And in everything I kept myself from being burdensome to you, and so I will keep *myself*. ¹⁰ᵃAs the truth of Christ is in me, ᵇno one shall stop me from this boasting in the regions of Achaia. ¹¹Why? ᵃBecause I do not love you? God knows!

¹²But what I do, I will also continue to do, ᵃthat I may cut off the opportunity from those who desire an opportunity to be regarded just as we are in the things of which they boast. ¹³For such ᵃ*are* false apostles, ᵇdeceitful workers, transforming themselves into apostles of Christ. ¹⁴And no wonder! For Satan himself transforms himself into ᵃan angel of light. ¹⁵Therefore *it is* no great thing if his ministers also transform themselves into ministers of righteousness, ᵃwhose end will be according to their works.

RELUCTANT BOASTING

¹⁶I say again, let no one think me a fool. If otherwise, at least receive me as a fool, that I also may boast a little. ¹⁷What I speak, ᵃI speak not according to the Lord, but as it were, foolishly, in this confidence of boasting. ¹⁸Seeing that many boast according to the flesh, I also will boast. ¹⁹For you put up with fools gladly, ᵃsince you *yourselves* are wise! ²⁰For you put up with it ᵃif one brings you into bondage, if one devours *you*, if one takes *from you*, if one exalts himself, if one strikes you on the face. ²¹To *our* shame ᵃI say that we were too weak for that! But ᵇin whatever anyone is bold—I speak foolishly—I am bold also.

SUFFERING FOR CHRIST

²²Are they ᵃHebrews? So *am* I. Are they Israelites? So *am* I. Are they the seed of Abraham? So *am* I. ²³Are they ministers of Christ?—I speak as a fool—I *am* more: ᵃin labors more abundant, ᵇin stripes above measure, in prisons more frequently, ᶜin deaths often. ²⁴From the Jews five times I received ᵃforty ᵇ*stripes* minus one. ²⁵Three times I was ᵃbeaten

---

11:3 ¹NU adds *and purity*   11:6 ¹NU omits *been*   11:7 ¹*putting myself down*

with rods; [b]once I was stoned; three times I [c]was shipwrecked; a night and a day I have been in the deep; [26]*in* journeys often, *in* perils of waters, *in* perils of robbers, [a]*in* perils of *my own* countrymen, [b]*in* perils of the Gentiles, *in* perils in the city, *in* perils in the wilderness, *in* perils in the sea, *in* perils among false brethren; [27]in weariness and toil, [a]in sleeplessness often, [b]in hunger and thirst, in [c]fastings often, in cold and nakedness— [28]besides the other things, what comes upon me daily: [a]my deep concern for all the churches. [29a]Who is weak, and I am not weak? Who is made to stumble, and I do not burn *with indignation?*

[30]If I must boast, [a]I will boast in the things which concern my [1]infirmity. [31a]The God and Father of our Lord Jesus Christ, [b]who is blessed forever, knows that I am not lying. [32a]In Damascus the governor, under Aretas the king, was guarding the city of the Damascenes with a garrison, desiring to arrest me; [33]but I was let down in a basket through a window in the wall, and escaped from his hands.

THE VISION OF PARADISE

12 It is [1]doubtless not profitable for me to boast. I will come to [a]visions and [b]revelations of the Lord: [2]I know a man [a]in Christ who fourteen years ago—whether in the body I do not know, or whether out of the body I do not know, God knows—such a one [b]was caught up to the third heaven. [3]And I know such a man—whether in the body or out of the body I do not know, God knows— [4]how he was caught up into [a]Paradise and heard inexpressible words, which it is not lawful for a man to utter. [5]Of such a one I will boast; yet of myself I will not [a]boast, except in my infirmities. [6]For though I might desire to boast, I will not be a fool; for I will speak the truth. But I refrain, lest anyone should think of me above what he sees me *to be* or hears from me.

THE THORN IN THE FLESH

[7]And lest I should be exalted above measure by the abundance of the revelations, a [a]thorn in the flesh was given to me, [b]a messenger of Satan to [1]buffet me, lest I be exalted above measure. [8a]Concerning this thing I pleaded with the Lord three times that it might depart from me. [9]And He said to me, "My grace is sufficient for you, for My strength is made perfect in weakness." Therefore most gladly [a]I will rather boast in my infirmities, [b]that the power of Christ may rest upon me. [10]Therefore [a]I take pleasure in infirmities, in reproaches, in needs, in persecutions, in distresses, for Christ's sake. [b]For when I am weak, then I am strong.

SIGNS OF AN APOSTLE

[11]I have become [a]a fool [1]in boasting; you have compelled me. For I ought to have been commended by you; for [b]in nothing was I behind the most eminent apostles, though [c]I am nothing. [12a]Truly the signs of an apostle were accomplished among you with all perseverance, in signs and [b]wonders and

11:25
[b]Acts 14:5, 19
[c]Acts 27:1–44

11:26
[a]Acts 9:23, 24;
13:45, 50; 17:5, 13;
1 Thess. 2:15
[b]Acts 14:5, 19;
19:23; 27:42

11:27
[a]Acts 20:31
[b]1 Cor. 4:11;
Phil. 4:12
[c]Acts 9:9;
13:2, 3; 14:23

11:28
[a]Acts 20:18;
[Rom. 1:14];
2 Cor. 7:12;
12:20; Gal. 4:11;
1 Thess. 3:10

11:29
[a][1 Cor. 8:9, 13;
9:22]

11:30
[a][2 Cor. 12:5,
9, 10]

11:31 [a]Rom. 1:9;
Gal. 1:20;
1 Thess. 2:5
[b]Rom. 9:5

11:32
[a]Acts 9:19–25

12:1
[a]Acts 16:9; 18:9;
22:17, 18; 23:11;
26:13–15; 27:23
[b]Acts 9:3–6;
1 Cor. 14:6;
2 Cor. 12:7;
[Gal. 1:12; 2:2;
Eph. 3:3–6]

12:2 [a]Rom. 16:7;
Gal. 1:22
[b]Acts 22:17

12:4
[a]Luke 23:43;
[Rev. 2:7]

12:5 [a]2 Cor. 11:30

12:7
[a]Num. 33:55;
Ezek. 28:24;
Hos. 2:6;
Gal. 4:13, 14
[b]Job 2:7;
Matt. 4:10;
Luke 13:16;
[1 Cor. 5:5]

12:8
[a]Deut. 3:23;
Matt. 26:44

12:9
[a]2 Cor. 11:30
[b][1 Pet. 4:14]

12:10
[a][Rom. 5:3;
8:35]
[b]2 Cor. 13:4

12:11 [a]2 Cor. 5:13; 11:1, 16; 12:6 [b]1 Cor. 15:10; 2 Cor. 11:5 [c]1 Cor. 3:7; 13:2; 15:9
12:12 [a]Acts 14:3; Rom. 15:18 [b]Acts 15:12

11:30 [1]*weakness*   12:1 [1]NU *necessary, though not profitable, to boast*
12:7 [1]*beat*   12:11 [1]NU omits *in boasting*

12:12
c Acts 14:8–10;
16:16–18;
19:11, 12;
20:6–12; 28:1–10

12:14
a 2 Cor. 1:15;
13:1, 2
b Acts 20:33;
[1 Cor. 10:24–33]
c 1 Cor. 4:14;
Gal. 4:19

12:15
a John 10:11;
Rom. 9:3;
2 Cor. 1:6;
Phil. 2:17;
Col. 1:24;
1 Thess. 2:8;
[2 Tim. 2:10]
b 2 Cor. 6:12, 13

12:16 a 2 Cor. 11:9

12:18
a 2 Cor. 8:18

12:19 a 2 Cor. 5:12
b [Rom. 9:1, 2];
2 Cor. 11:31
c 1 Cor. 10:33

12:20
a 1 Cor. 4:21;
2 Cor. 13:2, 10

12:21
a 2 Cor. 2:1, 4
b 2 Cor. 13:2
c 1 Cor. 5:1

13:1 a 2 Cor. 12:14
b Num. 35:30;
Deut. 17:6; 19:15;
Matt. 18:16;
John 8:17;
Heb. 10:28

13:2 a 2 Cor. 10:2
b 2 Cor. 12:21
c 2 Cor. 1:23;
10:11

13:3
a Matt. 10:20;
[1 Cor. 5:4; 7:40]
b [1 Cor. 9:2]

13:4
a Phil. 2:7, 8;
[1 Pet. 3:18]
b [Rom. 1:4; 6:4];
1 Cor. 6:14]
c [2 Cor. 10:3, 4]

13:5 a Rom. 8:10;
[Gal. 4:19]
b 1 Cor. 9:27

13:7 a 2 Cor. 6:9

13:9 a 1 Cor. 4:10
b 1 Cor. 1:10;
2 Cor. 13:11;
Eph. 4:12;
[1 Thess. 3:10]

13:10 a 1 Cor. 4:21
b 1 Cor. 5:4;
2 Cor. 10:8

mighty c deeds. 13 For what is it in which you were inferior to other churches, except that I myself was not burdensome to you? Forgive me this wrong!

LOVE FOR THE CHURCH

14a Now *for* the third time I am ready to come to you. And I will not be burdensome to you; for b I do not seek yours, but you. c For the children ought not to lay up for the parents, but the parents for the children. 15 And I will very gladly spend and be spent a for your souls; though b the more abundantly I love you, the less I am loved.

16 But be that *as it may,* a I did not burden you. Nevertheless, being crafty, I caught you by cunning! 17 Did I take advantage of you by any of those whom I sent to you? 18 I urged Titus, and sent our a brother with *him.* Did Titus take advantage of you? Did we not walk in the same spirit? Did *we* not *walk* in the same steps?

19a Again,[1] do you think that we excuse ourselves to you? b We speak before God in Christ. c But *we do* all things, beloved, for your edification. 20 For I fear lest, when I come, I shall not find you such as I wish, and *that* a I shall be found by you such as you do not wish; lest *there be* contentions, jealousies, outbursts of wrath, selfish ambitions, backbitings, whisperings, conceits, tumults; 21 lest, when I come again, my God a will humble me among you, and I shall mourn for many b who have sinned before and have not repented of the uncleanness, c fornication, and lewdness which they have practiced.

COMING WITH AUTHORITY

13 This *will be* a the third *time* I am coming to you. b "By the mouth of two or three witnesses every word shall be established." 2a I have told you before, and foretell as if I were present the second time, and now being absent[1] I write to those b who have sinned before, and to all the rest, that if I come again c I will not spare— 3 since you seek a proof of Christ a speaking in me, who is not weak toward you, but mighty b in you. 4a For though He was crucified in weakness, yet b He lives by the power of God. For c we also are weak in Him, but we shall live with Him by the power of God toward you.

5 Examine yourselves *as to* whether you are in the faith. Test yourselves. Do you not know yourselves, a that Jesus Christ is in you?—unless indeed you[1] are b disqualified. 6 But I trust that you will know that we are not disqualified.

PAUL PREFERS GENTLENESS

7 Now[1] I pray to God that you do no evil, not that we should appear approved, but that you should do what is honorable, though a we may seem disqualified. 8 For we can do nothing against the truth, but for the truth. 9 For we are glad a when we are weak and you are strong. And this also we pray, b that you may be made complete. 10a Therefore I write these things being absent, lest being present I should use sharpness, according to the b authority which the Lord has given me for edification and not for destruction.

12:19 [1] NU *You have been thinking for a long time that we*   **13:2** [1] NU omits *I write*   **13:5** [1] *do not stand the test*   **13:7** [1] NU *we*

GREETINGS AND BENEDICTION

[11]Finally, brethren, farewell. Become complete. [a]Be of good comfort, be of one mind, live in peace; and the God of love [b]and peace will be with you.

[12][a]Greet one another with a holy kiss.

[13]All the saints greet you.

[14][a]The grace of the Lord Jesus Christ, and the love of God, and [b]the [1]communion of the Holy Spirit *be* with you all. Amen.

13:11
[a]Rom. 12:16, 18
[b]Rom. 15:33;
Eph. 6:23

13:12
[a]Rom. 16:16

13:14
[a]Rom. 16:24
[b]Phil. 2:1

13:14 [1]*fellowship*

GALATIANS

GREETING

1 Paul, an apostle (not from men nor through man, but ᵃthrough Jesus Christ and God the Father ᵇwho raised Him from the dead), ²and all the brethren who are with me,

To the churches of Galatia:

³Grace to you and peace from God the Father and our Lord Jesus Christ, ⁴ᵃwho gave Himself for our sins, that He might deliver us ᵇfrom this present evil age, according to the will of our God and Father, ⁵to whom *be* glory forever and ever. Amen.

ONLY ONE GOSPEL

⁶I marvel that you are turning away so soon ᵃfrom Him who called you in the grace of Christ, to a different gospel, ⁷ᵃwhich is not another; but there are some ᵇwho trouble you and want to ᶜpervert¹ the gospel of Christ. ⁸But even if ᵃwe, or an angel from heaven, preach any other gospel to you than what we have preached to you, let him be ¹accursed. ⁹As we have said before, so now I say again, if anyone preaches any other gospel to you ᵃthan what you have received, let him be accursed.

¹⁰For ᵃdo I now ᵇpersuade men, or God? Or ᶜdo I seek to please men? For if I still pleased men, I would not be a bondservant of Christ.

CALL TO APOSTLESHIP
(cf. Acts 9:1–25)

¹¹ᵃBut I make known to you, brethren, that the gospel which was preached by me is not according to man. ¹²For ᵃI neither received it from man, nor was I taught *it,* but *it came* ᵇthrough the revelation of Jesus Christ.

¹³For you have heard of my former conduct in Judaism, how ᵃI persecuted the church of God beyond measure and ᵇ*tried to* destroy it. ¹⁴And I advanced in Judaism beyond many of my contemporaries in my own nation, ᵃbeing more exceedingly zealous ᵇfor the traditions of my fathers.

¹⁵But when it pleased God, ᵃwho separated me from my mother's womb and called *me* through His grace, ¹⁶ᵃto reveal His Son in me, that ᵇI might preach Him among the Gentiles, I did not immediately confer with ᶜflesh and blood, ¹⁷nor did I go up to Jerusalem to those *who were* apostles before me; but I went to Arabia, and returned again to Damascus.

CONTACTS AT JERUSALEM
(cf. Acts 9:26–31)

¹⁸Then after three years ᵃI went up to Jerusalem to see ¹Peter, and remained with him fifteen days. ¹⁹But ᵃI saw

1:1 ᵃActs 9:6
ᵇActs 2:24

1:4
ᵃ[Matt. 20:28];
ᵇHeb. 2:5

1:6
ᵃ[Rom. 8:28];
Gal. 1:15; 5:8

1:7 ᵃ2 Cor. 11:4
ᵇActs 15:1;
Gal. 5:10, 12
ᶜ2 Cor. 2:17

1:8 ᵃ1 Cor. 16:22

1:9 ᵃDeut. 4:2

1:10
ᵃ[1 Cor. 10:33];
1 Thess. 2:4
ᵇ1 Sam. 24:7
ᶜ1 Thess. 2:4

1:11
ᵃ[Rom. 2:16];
1 Cor. 15:1

1:12 ᵃ1 Cor. 15:1
ᵇ[Eph. 3:3–5]

1:13 ᵃActs 9:1
ᵇActs 8:3;
22:4, 5

1:14 ᵃActs 26:9;
Phil. 3:6
ᵇJer. 9:14;
Matt. 15:2;
Mark 7:3;
[Col. 2:8]

1:15 ᵃIs. 49:1, 5;
Jer. 1:5;
Acts 9:15;
Rom. 1:1; Gal. 1:6

1:16
ᵃ[2 Cor. 4:5–7]
ᵇActs 9:15;
Gal. 2:9
ᶜMatt. 16:17

1:18 ᵃActs 9:26

1:19 ᵃ1 Cor. 9:5

none of the other apostles except [b]James, the Lord's brother. [20](Now *concerning* the things which I write to you, indeed, before God, I do not lie.)

[21a]Afterward I went into the regions of Syria and Cilicia. [22]And I was unknown by face to the churches of Judea which [a]*were* in Christ. [23]But they were [a]hearing only, "He who formerly [b]persecuted us now preaches the faith which he once *tried to* destroy." [24]And they [a]glorified God in me.

DEFENDING THE GOSPEL
(cf. Acts 15:1–21)

2 Then after fourteen years [a]I went up again to Jerusalem with Barnabas, and also took Titus with *me.* [2]And I went up [1]by revelation, and communicated to them that gospel which I preach among the Gentiles, but [a]privately to those who were of reputation, lest by any means [b]I might run, or had run, in vain. [3]Yet not even Titus who *was* with me, being a Greek, was compelled to be circumcised. [4]And *this occurred* because of [a]false brethren secretly brought in (who came in by stealth to spy out our [b]liberty which we have in Christ Jesus, [c]that they might bring us into bondage), [5]to whom we did not yield submission even for an hour, that [a]the truth of the gospel might continue with you.

[6]But from those [a]who seemed to be something—whatever they were, it makes no difference to me; [b]God [1]shows personal favoritism to no man—for those who seemed *to be something* [c]added nothing to me. [7]But on the contrary, [a]when they saw that the gospel for the uncircumcised [b]had been committed to me, as *the gospel* for the circumcised *was* to Peter [8](for He who worked effectively in Peter for the apostleship to the [a]circumcised [b]also [c]worked effectively in me toward the Gentiles), [9]and when James, [1]Cephas, and John, who seemed to be [a]pillars, perceived [b]the grace that had been given to me, they gave me and Barnabas the right hand of fellowship, [c]that we *should go* to the Gentiles and they to the circumcised. [10]*They desired* only that we should remember the poor, [a]the very thing which I also was eager to do.

NO RETURN TO THE LAW

[11a]Now when [1]Peter had come to Antioch, I [2]withstood him to his face, because he was to be blamed; [12]for before certain men came from James, [a]he would eat with the Gentiles; but when they came, he withdrew and separated himself, fearing [1]those who were of the circumcision. [13]And the rest of the Jews also played the hypocrite with him, so that even Barnabas was carried away with their hypocrisy.

[14]But when I saw that they were not straightforward about [a]the truth of the gospel, I said to Peter [b]before *them* all, [c]"If you, being a Jew, live in the manner of Gentiles and not as the Jews, [1]why do you compel Gentiles to live as [2]Jews? [15a]We *who are* Jews by nature, and not [b]sinners of the Gentiles, [16a]knowing that a man is not [1]justified by the works of the law but [b]by faith in Jesus Christ, even we have believed in Christ Jesus,

---

1:19 [b]Matt. 13:55

1:21 [a]Acts 9:30

1:22 [a]Rom. 16:7

1:23
[a]Acts 9:20, 21
[b]Acts 8:3

1:24 [a]Acts 11:18

2:1 [a]Acts 15:2

2:2 [a]Acts 15:1–4
[b][Rom. 9:16;
1 Cor. 9:24];
Gal. 5:7;
Phil. 2:16;
1 Thess. 3:5;
2 Tim. 4:7;
Heb. 12:1

2:4
[a]Acts 15:1, 24;
2 Cor. 11:13, 26;
Gal. 1:7
[b]Gal. 3:25;
5:1, 13;
[James 1:25]
[c]Gal. 4:3, 9

2:5 [a][Gal. 1:6;
2:14; 3:1]; Col. 1:5

2:6 [a]Gal. 2:9;
6:3 [b]Acts 10:34;
Rom. 2:11
[c]2 Cor. 11:5; 12:11

2:7 [a]Acts 9:15;
13:46; 22:21;
Rom. 11:13
[b]1 Cor. 9:17;
1 Thess. 2:4;
1 Tim. 1:11

2:8 [a]1 Pet. 1:1
[b]Acts 9:15
[c][Gal. 3:5]

2:9 [a]Matt. 16:18
[b]Rom. 1:5
[c]Acts 13:3

2:10 [a]Acts 11:30

2:11 [a]Acts 15:35

2:12
[a][Acts 10:28;
11:2, 3]

2:14
[a]Gal. 1:6; 2:5;
Col. 1:5
[b]1 Tim. 5:20
[c][Acts 10:28];
Gal. 2:12

2:15
[a][Acts 15:10]
[b]Matt. 9:11

2:16
[a]Acts 13:38, 39;
Gal. 3:11
[b]Rom. 1:17

2:2 [1]*because of*   2:6 [1]Lit. *does not receive the face of a man*   2:9 [1]Peter
2:11 [1]NU *Cephas*   [2]*opposed*   2:12 [1]Jewish Christians   2:14 [1]NU *how can you*   [2]Some interpreters stop the quotation here.   2:16 [1]*declared righteous*

that we might be justified by faith in Christ and not ^cby the works of the law; for by the works of the law no flesh shall be justified.

¹⁷"But if, while we seek to be justified by Christ, we ourselves also are found ^asinners, *is* Christ therefore a minister of sin? Certainly not! ¹⁸For if I build again those things which I destroyed, I make myself a transgressor. ¹⁹For I ^athrough the law ^bdied to the law that I might ^clive to God. ²⁰I have been ^acrucified with Christ; it is no longer I who live, but Christ lives in me; and the *life* which I now live in the flesh ^bI live by faith in the Son of God, ^cwho loved me and gave Himself for me. ²¹I do not set aside the grace of God; for ^aif righteousness *comes* through the law, then Christ died [1]in vain."

JUSTIFICATION BY FAITH
(cf. Rom. 4:1–25)

3 O foolish Galatians! Who has bewitched you [1]that you should not obey the truth, before whose eyes Jesus Christ was clearly portrayed [2]among you as crucified? ²This only I want to learn from you: Did you receive the Spirit by the works of the law, ^aor by the hearing of faith? ³Are you so foolish? ^aHaving begun in the Spirit, are you now being made perfect by ^bthe flesh? ^{4a}Have you suffered so [1]many things in vain—if indeed *it was* in vain?

⁵Therefore He who supplies the Spirit to you and works miracles among you, *does He do it* by the works of the law, or by the hearing of faith?— ⁶just as Abraham ^a"believed God, and it was accounted to him for righteousness." ⁷Therefore know that *only* ^athose who are of faith are sons of Abraham. ⁸And ^athe Scripture, foreseeing that God would justify the Gentiles by faith, preached the gospel to Abraham beforehand, *saying,* ^b"In you all the nations shall be blessed." ⁹So then those who *are* of faith are blessed with believing Abraham.

THE LAW BRINGS A CURSE

¹⁰For as many as are of the works of the law are under the curse; for it is written, ^a"Cursed *is* everyone who does not continue in all things which are written in the book of the law, to do them." ¹¹But that no one is [1]justified by the law in the sight of God *is* evident, for ^a"the just shall live by faith." ¹²Yet ^athe law is not of faith, but ^b"the man who does them shall live by them."

^{13a}Christ has redeemed us from the curse of the law, having become a curse for us (for it is written, ^b"Cursed *is* everyone who hangs on a tree"), ^{14a}that the blessing of Abraham might come upon the ^bGentiles in Christ Jesus, that we might receive ^cthe promise of the Spirit through faith.

THE CHANGELESS PROMISE
(cf. Gen. 12:1–3)

¹⁵Brethren, I speak in the manner of men: ^aThough *it is* only a man's covenant, yet *if it is* confirmed, no one annuls or adds to it. ¹⁶Now to Abraham and his Seed were the promises

---

2:16 ^cPs. 143:2; Rom. 3:20

2:17 ^a[1 John 3:8]

2:19 ^aRom. 8:2 ^b[Rom. 6:2, 14; 7:4]; 1 Cor. 9:20 ^c[Rom. 6:11]

2:20 ^a[Rom. 6:6; Gal. 5:24; 6:14] ^bRom. 6:8–11; 2 Cor. 5:15; [Eph. 2:4–6; Col. 3:1–4] ^cIs. 53:12; Eph. 5:2

2:21 ^aHeb. 7:11

3:2 ^aRom. 10:16, 17

3:3 ^a[Gal. 4:9] ^bHeb. 7:16

3:4 ^aHeb. 10:35

3:6 ^aGen. 15:6

3:7 ^aJohn 8:39

3:8 ^aRom. 9:17 ^bGen. 12:3; 18:18; 22:18; 26:4; 28:14

3:10 ^aDeut. 27:26

3:11 ^aHab. 2:4; Rom. 1:17; Heb. 10:38

3:12 ^aRom. 4:4, 5 ^bLev. 18:5; Rom. 10:5

3:13 ^a[Rom. 8:3] ^bDeut. 21:23

3:14 ^a[Rom. 4:1–5, 9, 16; Gal. 3:28] ^bIs. 42:1, 6; 49:6; Luke 2:32; Rom. 3:29, 30 ^cIs. 32:15

3:15 ^aHeb. 9:17

2:21 [1]*for nothing*   **3:1** [1]NU omits *that you should not obey the truth* [2]NU omits *among you*   **3:4** [1]Or *great*   **3:11** [1]*declared righteous*

made. He does not say, "And to seeds," as of many, but as of [a]one, [b]"And to your Seed," who is [c]Christ. [17]And this I say, *that* the law, [a]which was four hundred and thirty years later, cannot annul the covenant that was confirmed before by God [1]in Christ, [b]that it should make the promise of no effect. [18]For if [a]the inheritance *is* of the law, [b]*it is* no longer of promise; but God gave *it* to Abraham by promise.

PURPOSE OF THE LAW

[19]What purpose then *does* the law *serve?* [a]It was added because of transgressions, till the [b]Seed should come to whom the promise was made; *and it was* [c]appointed through angels by the hand [d]of a mediator. [20]Now a mediator does not *mediate* for one *only,* [a]but God is one.

[21]*Is* the law then against the promises of God? Certainly not! For if there had been a law given which could have given life, truly righteousness would have been by the law. [22]But the Scripture has confined [a]all under sin, [b]that the promise by faith in Jesus Christ might be given to those who believe. [23]But before faith came, we were kept under guard by the law, [1]kept for the faith which would afterward be revealed. [24]Therefore [a]the law was our [1]tutor *to bring us* to Christ, [b]that we might be justified by faith. [25]But after faith has come, we are no longer under a tutor.

SONS AND HEIRS

[26]For you [a]are all sons of God through faith in Christ Jesus. [27]For [a]as many of you as were baptized into Christ [b]have put on Christ. [28][a]There is neither Jew nor Greek, [b]there is neither slave nor free, there is neither male nor female; for you are all [c]one in Christ Jesus. [29]And [a]if you *are* Christ's, then you are Abraham's [b]seed, and [c]heirs according to the promise.

4 Now I say *that* the heir, as long as he is a child, does not differ at all from a slave, though he is master of all, [2]but is under guardians and stewards until the time appointed by the father. [3]Even so we, when we were children, [a]were in bondage under the elements of the world. [4]But [a]when the fullness of the time had come, God sent forth His Son, [b]born[1] [c]of a woman, [d]born under the law, [5][a]to redeem those who were under the law, [b]that we might receive the adoption as sons.

[6]And because you are sons, God has sent forth [a]the Spirit of His Son into your hearts, crying out, [1]"Abba, Father!" [7]Therefore you are no longer a slave but a son, [a]and if a son, then an heir [1]of God [2]through Christ.

FEARS FOR THE CHURCH

[8]But then, indeed, [a]when you did not know God, [b]you served those which by nature are not gods. [9]But now [a]after you have known God, or rather are known by God, [b]how *is it that* you turn again to [c]the weak and beggarly elements, to which you desire again to be in bondage? [10][a]You observe days

---

3:16
[a]Gen. 22:18
[b]Gen. 12:3, 7;
13:15; 24:7
[c][1 Cor. 12:12]

3:17 [a]Gen. 15:13;
Ex. 12:40;
Acts 7:6
[b][Rom. 4:13]

3:18
[a][Rom. 8:17]
[b]Rom. 4:14

3:19 [a]John 15:22
[b]Gal. 4:4
[c]Acts 7:53
[d]Ex. 20:19;
Deut. 5:5

3:20
[a][Rom. 3:29]

3:22 [a]Rom. 11:32
[b]Rom. 4:11

3:24 [a]Rom. 10:4
[b]Acts 13:39

3:26 [a]John 1:12

3:27
[a]Matt. 28:19;
[Rom. 6:3];
1 Cor. 10:2
[b]Rom. 10:12;
13:14

3:28
[a][John 10:16];
Rom. 3:22;
10:12;
[Eph. 2:14];
Col. 3:11
[b][1 Cor. 12:13]
[c]John 17:11;
[1 Cor. 12:13];
Eph. 2:15, 16]

3:29
[a]Gen. 21:10;
Heb. 11:18
[b]Rom. 4:11;
Gal. 3:7
[c]Gen. 12:3; 18:18;
Rom. 8:17

4:3 [a]Gal. 4:9;
Col. 2:8, 20;
Heb. 5:12; 9:10

4:4
[a][Gen. 49:10]
[b][John 1:14];
Rom. 1:3; 8:3;
[Phil. 2:7]
[c]Gen. 3:15;
[Is. 7:14;
Matt. 1:25]
[d][Matt. 5:17];
Luke 2:21, 27

4:5
[a][Matt. 20:28;
Gal. 3:13]
[b][John 1:12]

4:6 [a][Acts 16:7;
Rom. 5:5;
8:9, 15, 16;
2 Cor. 3:17]

4:7 [a][Rom. 8:16, 17]   4:8 [a]1 Cor. 1:21; Eph. 2:12; 1 Thess. 4:5; 2 Thess. 1:8 [b]Rom. 1:25
4:9 [a][1 Cor. 8:3] [b]Gal. 3:1-3; Col. 2:20 [c]Heb. 7:18   4:10 [a]Rom. 14:5; Col. 2:16

3:17 [1]NU omits *in Christ*   3:23 [1]Lit. *confined*   3:24 [1]In a household, the guardian responsible for the care and discipline of the children
4:4 [1]Or *made*   4:6 [1]Lit., in Aram., *Father*   4:7 [1]NU *through God*
[2]NU omits *through Christ*

and months and seasons and years. [11]I am afraid for you, [a]lest I have labored for you in vain.

[12]Brethren, I urge you to become like me, for I *became* like you. [a]You have not injured me at all. [13]You know that [a]because of physical infirmity I preached the gospel to you at the first. [14]And my trial which was in my flesh you did not despise or reject, but you received me [a]as an [1]angel of God, [b]*even* as Christ Jesus. [15][1]What then was the blessing you *enjoyed?* For I bear you witness that, if possible, you would have plucked out your own eyes and given them to me. [16]Have I therefore become your enemy because I tell you the truth?

[17]They [a]zealously court you, *but* for no good; yes, they want to exclude you, that you may be zealous for them. [18]But it is good to be zealous in a good thing always, and not only when I am present with you. [19][a]My little children, for whom I labor in birth again until Christ is formed in you, [20]I would like to be present with you now and to change my tone; for I have doubts about you.

TWO COVENANTS
(Gen. 21:8–21; Is. 54:1)

[21]Tell me, you who desire to be under the law, do you not hear the law? [22]For it is written that Abraham had two sons: [a]the one by a bondwoman, [b]the other by a freewoman. [23]But he *who was* of the bondwoman [a]was born according to the flesh, [b]and he of the freewoman through promise, [24]which things are symbolic. For these are [1]the two covenants: the one from Mount [a]Sinai which gives birth to bondage, which is Hagar— [25]for this Hagar is Mount Sinai in Arabia, and corresponds to Jerusalem which now is, and is in bondage with her children— [26]but the [a]Jerusalem above is free, which is the mother of us all. [27]For it is written:

[a]"Rejoice, O barren,
You who do not bear!
Break forth and shout,
You who are not in labor!
For the desolate has many more children
Than she who has a husband."

[28]Now [a]we, brethren, as Isaac *was,* are [b]children of promise. [29]But, as [a]he who was born according to the flesh then persecuted him *who was born* according to the Spirit, [b]even so *it is* now. [30]Nevertheless what does [a]the Scripture say? [b]"Cast out the bondwoman and her son, for [c]the son of the bondwoman shall not be heir with the son of the freewoman." [31]So then, brethren, we are not children of the bondwoman but of the free.

CHRISTIAN LIBERTY

5 [a]Stand[1] fast therefore in the liberty by which Christ has made us free, and do not be entangled again with a [b]yoke of bondage. [2]Indeed I, Paul, say to you that [a]if you become circumcised, Christ will profit you nothing. [3]And I testify again to every man who becomes circumcised [a]that he is [1]a debtor to keep the whole law. [4][a]You have become estranged from

---

4:11 [a]1 Thess. 3:5
4:12 [a]2 Cor. 2:5
4:13 [a]1 Cor. 2:3
4:14 [a]Mal. 2:7
[b][Luke 10:16]
4:17 [a]Rom. 10:2
4:19 [a]1 Cor. 4:15
4:22 [a]Gen. 16:15
[b]Gen. 21:2
4:23
[a]Rom. 9:7, 8;
Gal. 4:29
[b]Gen. 16:15;
17:15–19; 18:10;
21:1; Gal. 4:28;
Heb. 11:11
4:24
[a]Ex. 24:6–8;
Deut. 33:2
4:26 [a][Is. 2:2]
4:27 [a]Is. 54:1
4:28
[a]Rom. 9:7, 8;
Gal. 3:29
[b]Acts 3:25
4:29 [a]Gen. 21:9
[b]Gal. 5:11
4:30
[a][Gal. 3:8, 22]
[b]Gen. 21:10, 12
[c][John 8:35]
5:1 [a]Phil. 4:1
[b]Acts 15:10;
Gal. 2:4
5:2 [a]Acts 15:1;
Gal. 5:3, 6, 11
5:3
[a][Deut. 27:26;
Rom. 2:25;
Gal. 3:10]
5:4 [a][Rom. 9:31]

4:14 [1]Or *messenger*   4:15 [1]NU *Where*   4:24 [1]NU, M omit *the*   5:1 [1]NU *For freedom Christ has made us free; stand fast therefore, and*   5:3 [1]*obligated*

Christ, you who *attempt to* be justified by law; [b]you have fallen from grace. [5]For we through the Spirit eagerly [a]wait for the hope of righteousness by faith. [6]For [a]in Christ Jesus neither circumcision nor uncircumcision avails anything, but [b]faith working through love.

LOVE FULFILLS THE LAW

[7]You [a]ran well. Who hindered you from obeying the truth? [8]This persuasion does not *come* from Him who calls you. [9a]A little leaven leavens the whole lump. [10]I have confidence in you, in the Lord, that you will have no other mind; but he who troubles you shall bear his judgment, whoever he is.

[11]And I, brethren, if I still preach circumcision, [a]why do I still suffer persecution? Then [b]the offense of the cross has ceased. [12a]I could wish that those [b]who trouble you would even [1]cut themselves off!

[13]For you, brethren, have been called to liberty; only [a]do not *use* liberty as an [b]opportunity for the flesh, but [c]through love serve one another. [14]For [a]all the law is fulfilled in one word, *even* in this: [b]"You shall love your neighbor as yourself." [15]But if you bite and devour one another, beware lest you be consumed by one another!

WALKING IN THE SPIRIT

[16]I say then: [a]Walk in the Spirit, and you shall not fulfill the lust of the flesh. [17]For [a]the flesh lusts against the Spirit, and the Spirit against the flesh; and these are contrary to one another, [b]so that you do not do the things that you wish. [18]But [a]if you are led by the Spirit, you are not under the law.

[19]Now [a]the works of the flesh are evident, which are: [1]adultery, [2]fornication, uncleanness, lewdness, [20]idolatry, sorcery, hatred, contentions, jealousies, outbursts of wrath, selfish ambitions, dissensions, heresies, [21]envy, [1]murders, drunkenness, revelries, and the like; of which I tell you beforehand, just as I also told *you* in time past, that [a]those who practice such things will not inherit the kingdom of God.

[22]But [a]the fruit of the Spirit is [b]love, joy, peace, longsuffering, kindness, [c]goodness, [d]faithfulness, [23][1]gentleness, self-control. [a]Against such there is no law. [24]And those *who are* Christ's [a]have crucified the flesh with its passions and desires. [25a]If we live in the Spirit, let us also walk in the Spirit. [26a]Let us not become conceited, provoking one another, envying one another.

BEAR AND SHARE BURDENS

6 Brethren, if a man is [1]overtaken in any trespass, you who *are* spiritual restore such a one in a spirit of [a]gentleness, considering yourself lest you also be tempted. [2a]Bear one another's burdens, and so fulfill [b]the law of Christ. [3]For [a]if anyone thinks himself to be something, when [b]he is nothing, he deceives himself. [4]But [a]let each one examine his own work, and then he will have rejoicing in himself alone, and [b]not in another. [5]For [a]each one shall bear his own load.

Cross-references (right margin)

5:4 [b]Heb. 12:15; 2 Pet. 3:17

5:5 [a]Rom. 8:24

5:6 [a][1 Cor. 7:19; Gal. 6:15; Col. 3:11] [b]Col. 1:4; 1 Thess. 1:3; [James 2:18, 20, 22]

5:7 [a]1 Cor. 9:24

5:9 [a]1 Cor. 5:6

5:11 [a]1 Cor. 15:30 [b]Rom. 9:33; [1 Cor. 1:23]

5:12 [a]Josh. 7:25 [b]Acts 15:1, 2

5:13 [a][Rom. 8:2]; 1 Cor. 8:9; Gal. 5:1 [b]Rom. 6:1; 1 Pet. 2:16 [c]1 Cor. 9:19; Eph. 5:21

5:14 [a]Matt. 7:12; 22:40; Rom. 13:8, 10; Gal. 6:2 [b]Lev. 19:18; Matt. 22:39; Rom. 13:9

5:16 [a]Rom. 6:12

5:17 [a]Rom. 7:18, 22, 23; 8:5 [b]Rom. 7:15

5:18 [a][Rom. 6:14; 7:4; 8:14; 1 Tim. 1:9]

5:19 [a]Rom. 1:26–31; Eph. 5:3, 11; 2 Tim. 3:2–4

5:21 [a]1 Cor. 6:9, 10

5:22 [a][John 15:2] [b][Rom. 5:1–5; 1 Cor. 13:4; Col. 3:12–15] [c]Rom. 15:14 [d]1 Cor. 13:7

5:23 [a]1 Tim. 1:9

5:24 [a]Rom. 6:6; [Gal. 2:20; 6:14]

5:25 [a][Rom. 8:4, 5]

5:26 [a]Phil. 2:3

6:1 [a]Eph. 4:2

6:2 [a]Acts 20:35; Rom. 15:1; 1 Thess. 5:14 [b][James 2:8]

6:3 [a]Rom. 12:3 [b][2 Cor. 3:5; James 1:22]

6:4 [a]1 Cor. 11:28 [b]Luke 18:11   6:5 [a][Rom. 2:6]

5:12 [1]*mutilate themselves*   5:19 [1]NU omits *adultery*   [2]*sexual immorality*
5:21 [1]NU omits *murders*   5:23 [1]*meekness*   6:1 [1]*caught*

BE GENEROUS AND DO GOOD

6 [a]Let him who is taught the word share in all good things with him who teaches.

7 Do not be deceived, God is not mocked; for [a]whatever a man sows, that he will also reap. 8 For he who sows to his flesh will of the flesh reap corruption, but he who sows to the Spirit will of the Spirit reap [a]everlasting life. 9 And [a]let us not grow weary while doing good, for in due season we shall reap [b]if we do not lose heart. 10 [a]Therefore, as we have opportunity, [b]let us do good to all, [c]especially to those who are of the household of faith.

GLORY ONLY IN THE CROSS

11 See with what large letters I have written to you with my own hand! 12 As many as desire to make a good showing in the flesh, these *would* compel you to be circumcised, [a]only that they may not suffer persecution for the cross of Christ. 13 For not even those who are circumcised keep the law, but they desire to have you circumcised that they may boast in your flesh. 14 But God forbid that I should boast except in the [a]cross of our Lord Jesus Christ, by [1]whom the world has been crucified to me, and [b]I to the world. 15 For [a]in Christ Jesus neither circumcision nor uncircumcision avails anything, but a new creation.

BLESSING AND A PLEA

16 And as many as walk according to this rule, peace and mercy *be* upon them, and upon the Israel of God.

17 From now on let no one trouble me, for I bear in my body the marks of the Lord Jesus.

18 Brethren, the grace of our Lord Jesus Christ *be* with your spirit. Amen.

6:6
[a]1 Cor. 9:11, 14

6:7 [a][Rom. 2:6]

6:8 [a][Rom. 6:8]

6:9 [a]1 Cor. 15:58;
2 Cor. 4:1;
2 Thess. 3:13
[b][Matt. 24:13];
Heb. 12:3, 5;
[James 5:7, 8]

6:10 [a]Prov. 3:27;
[John 9:4; 12:35]
[b]Titus 3:8
[c]Rom. 12:13

6:12 [a]Gal. 5:11;
Phil. 3:8

6:14 [a][1 Cor. 1:18]
[b][Gal. 2:20];
Col. 2:20

6:15
[a][Rom. 2:26, 28];
1 Cor. 7:19;
[Gal. 5:6]

6:14 [1]Or *which*, the cross

EPHESIANS

GREETING

1 Paul, an apostle of Jesus Christ by the will of God,

To the saints who are in Ephesus, and faithful in Christ Jesus:

²Grace to you and peace from God our Father and the Lord Jesus Christ.

REDEMPTION IN CHRIST

³ᵃBlessed *be* the God and Father of our Lord Jesus Christ, who has blessed us with every spiritual blessing in the heavenly *places* in Christ, ⁴just as ᵃHe chose us in Him ᵇbefore the foundation of the world, that we should ᶜbe holy and without blame before Him in love, ⁵ᵃhaving predestined us to ᵇadoption as sons by Jesus Christ to Himself, ᶜaccording to the good pleasure of His will, ⁶to the praise of the glory of His grace, ᵃby which He ¹made us accepted in ᵇthe Beloved.

⁷ᵃIn Him we have redemption through His blood, the forgiveness of sins, according to ᵇthe riches of His grace ⁸which He made to abound toward us in all wisdom and ¹prudence, ⁹ᵃhaving made known to us the mystery of His will, according to His good pleasure ᵇwhich He purposed in Himself, ¹⁰that in the dispensation of ᵃthe fullness of the times ᵇHe might gather together in one ᶜall things in Christ, ¹both which are in heaven and which are on earth—in Him. ¹¹ᵃIn Him also we have obtained an inheritance, being predestined according to ᵇthe purpose of Him who works all things according to the counsel of His will, ¹²ᵃthat we ᵇwho first trusted in Christ should be to the praise of His glory.

¹³In Him you also *trusted,* after you heard ᵃthe word of truth, the gospel of your salvation; in whom also, having believed, ᵇyou were sealed with the Holy Spirit of promise, ¹⁴ᵃwho¹ is the ²guarantee of our inheritance ᵇuntil the redemption of ᶜthe purchased possession, ᵈto the praise of His glory.

PRAYER FOR SPIRITUAL WISDOM

¹⁵Therefore I also, ᵃafter I heard of your faith in the Lord Jesus and your love for all the saints, ¹⁶ᵃdo not cease to give thanks for you, making mention of you in my prayers: ¹⁷that ᵃthe God of our Lord Jesus Christ, the Father of glory, ᵇmay give to you the spirit of wisdom and revelation in the knowledge of Him, ¹⁸ᵃthe eyes of your ¹understanding being enlightened; that you may know what is ᵇthe hope of His

1:3 ᵃ2 Cor. 1:3
1:4 ᵃRom. 8:28
ᵇ1 Pet. 1:2
ᶜLuke 1:75
1:5 ᵃActs 13:48; [Rom. 8:29]
ᵇJohn 1:12
ᶜ[1 Cor. 1:21]
1:6 ᵃ[Rom. 3:24]
ᵇMatt. 3:17
1:7 ᵃ[Heb. 9:12]
ᵇ[Rom. 3:24, 25]
1:9 ᵃ[Rom. 16:25]
ᵇ[2 Tim. 1:9]
1:10 ᵃGal. 4:4
ᵇ1 Cor. 3:22
ᶜEph. 3:15; [Phil. 2:9; Col. 1:16, 20]
1:11 ᵃRom. 8:17
ᵇIs. 46:10
1:12 ᵃ2 Thess. 2:13
ᵇJames 1:18
1:13 ᵃ1 John 1:17
ᵇ[2 Cor. 1:22]
1:14 ᵃ2 Cor. 5:5
ᵇRom. 8:23
ᶜ[Acts 20:28]
ᵈ1 Pet. 2:9
1:15 ᵃCol. 1:4; Philem. 5
1:16 ᵃRom. 1:9
1:17 ᵃJohn 20:17; Rom. 15:6
ᵇIs. 11:2; Col. 1:9
1:18 ᵃActs 26:18; 2 Cor. 4:6; Heb. 6:4
ᵇEph. 2:12

1:6 ¹Lit. *bestowed grace (favor) upon us*   1:8 ¹*understanding*
1:10 ¹NU, M omit *both*   1:14 ¹NU *which*   ²*down payment, earnest*
1:18 ¹NU, M *hearts*

calling, what are the riches of the glory of His inheritance in the saints, [19]and what *is* the exceeding greatness of His power toward us who believe, [a]according to the working of His mighty power [20]which He worked in Christ when [a]He raised Him from the dead and [b]seated *Him* at His right hand in the heavenly *places,* [21a]far above all [b]principality[1] and [2]power and [3]might and dominion, and every name that is named, not only in this age but also in that which is to come.

[22]And [a]He put all *things* under His feet, and gave Him [b]*to be* head over all *things* to the church, [23a]which is His body, [b]the fullness of Him [c]who fills all in all.

BY GRACE THROUGH FAITH

2 And [a]you He made alive, [b]who were dead in trespasses and sins, [2a]in which you once walked according to the [1]course of this world, according to [b]the prince of the power of the air, the spirit who now works in [c]the sons of disobedience, [3a]among whom also we all once conducted ourselves in [b]the lusts of our flesh, fulfilling the desires of the flesh and of the mind, and [c]were by nature children of wrath, just as the others.

[4]But God, [a]who is rich in mercy, because of His [b]great love with which He loved us, [5a]even when we were dead in trespasses, [b]made us alive together with Christ (by grace you have been saved), [6]and raised *us* up together, and made *us* sit together [a]in the heavenly *places* in Christ Jesus, [7]that in the ages to come He might show the exceeding riches of His grace in [a]*His* kindness toward us in Christ Jesus. [8a]For by grace you have been saved [b]through faith, and that not of yourselves; [c]*it is* the gift of God, [9]not of [a]works, lest anyone should [b]boast. [10]For we are [a]His workmanship, created in Christ Jesus for good works, which God prepared beforehand that we should walk in them.

BROUGHT NEAR BY HIS BLOOD

[11]Therefore remember that you, once Gentiles in the flesh—who are called Uncircumcision by what is called [a]the Circumcision made in the flesh by hands— [12]that at that time you were without Christ, being aliens from the commonwealth of Israel and strangers from the covenants of promise, having no hope and without God in the world. [13]But now in Christ Jesus you who once were far off have been brought near by the blood of Christ.

CHRIST OUR PEACE

[14]For He Himself is our peace, who has made both one, and has broken down the middle wall of separation, [15]having abolished in His flesh the enmity, *that is,* the law of commandments *contained* in ordinances, so as to create in Himself one [a]new man *from* the two, *thus* making peace, [16]and that He might [a]reconcile them both to God in one body through the cross, thereby [b]putting to death the enmity. [17]And He came and preached peace to you who were afar off and to those who were near. [18]For [a]through Him we both have access [b]by one Spirit to the Father.

1:19 [a]Col. 2:12
1:20 [a]Acts 2:24
[b]Ps. 110:1
1:21 [a]Is. 9:6, 7;
Luke 1:32, 33;
Phil. 2:9, 10;
Rev. 19:12
[b][Rom. 8:38, 39]
1:22 [a]Ps. 8:6;
110:1;
Matt. 28:18;
1 Cor. 15:27
[b]Heb. 2:7
1:23 [a]Rom. 12:5
[b]Col. 2:9
[c][1 Cor. 12:6]
2:1 [a]Eph. 2:5;
Col. 2:13
[b]Eph. 4:18
2:2 [a]Col. 1:21
[b][John 12:31];
Eph. 6:12
[c]Col. 3:6
2:3 [a]1 Pet. 4:3
[b]Gal. 5:16
[c][Ps. 51:5]
2:4 [a]Ps. 103:8–11;
Rom. 10:12
[b]John 3:16;
1 John 4:9, 10
2:5 [a]Rom. 5:6, 8
[b][Rom. 6:4, 5]
2:6 [a]Eph. 1:20
2:7 [a]Titus 3:4
2:8 [a][2 Tim. 1:9]
[b]Rom. 4:16
[c][John 1:12, 13]
2:9 [a]Rom. 4:4, 5; 11:6
[b]Rom. 3:27
2:10 [a]Is. 19:25
2:11 [a][Rom. 2:28;
Col. 2:11]
2:15 [a]Gal. 6:15
2:16 [a]2 Cor. 5:18;
[Col. 1:20–22]
[b][Rom. 6:6]
2:18 [a]John 10:9
[b]1 Cor. 12:13;
Eph. 4:4

1:21 [1]*rule* [2]*authority* [3]*power* 2:2 [1]Gr. *aion,* aeon

CHRIST OUR CORNERSTONE

19Now, therefore, you are no longer strangers and foreigners, but fellow citizens with the saints and members of the household of God, 20having been ªbuilt ᵇon the foundation of the ᶜapostles and prophets, Jesus Christ Himself being ᵈthe chief cornerstone, 21in whom the whole building, being fitted together, grows into ªa holy temple in the Lord, 22ªin whom you also are being built together for a ᵇdwelling place of God in the Spirit.

THE MYSTERY REVEALED

3 For this reason I, Paul, the prisoner of Christ Jesus for you Gentiles— 2if indeed you have heard of the ¹dispensation of the grace of God ªwhich was given to me for you, 3ªhow that by revelation ᵇHe made known to me the mystery (as I have briefly written already, 4by which, when you read, you may understand my knowledge in the mystery of Christ), 5which in other ages was not made known to the sons of men, as it has now been revealed by the Spirit to His holy apostles and prophets: 6that the Gentiles ªshould be fellow heirs, of the same body, and partakers of His promise in Christ through the gospel, 7ªof which I became a minister ᵇaccording to the gift of the grace of God given to me by ᶜthe effective working of His power.

PURPOSE OF THE MYSTERY

8To me, ªwho am less than the least of all the saints, this grace was given, that I should preach among the Gentiles ᵇthe unsearchable riches of Christ, 9and to make all see what *is* the ¹fellowship of the mystery, which from the beginning of the ages has been hidden in God who ªcreated all things ²through Jesus Christ; 10ªto the intent that now ᵇthe ¹manifold wisdom of God might be made known by the church ᶜto the ²principalities and powers in the heavenly *places,* 11ªaccording to the eternal purpose which He accomplished in Christ Jesus our Lord, 12in whom we have boldness and access ªwith confidence through faith in Him. 13ªTherefore I ask that you do not lose heart at my tribulations for you, ᵇwhich is your glory.

APPRECIATION OF THE MYSTERY

14For this reason I bow my knees to the ªFather ¹of our Lord Jesus Christ, 15from whom the whole family in heaven and earth is named, 16that He would grant you, ªaccording to the riches of His glory, ᵇto be strengthened with might through His Spirit in ᶜthe inner man, 17ªthat Christ may dwell in your hearts through faith; that you, ᵇbeing rooted and grounded in love, 18ªmay be able to comprehend with all the saints ᵇwhat *is* the width and length and depth and height— 19to know the love of Christ which passes knowledge; that you may be filled ªwith all the fullness of God.

20Now ªto Him who is able to do exceedingly abundantly ᵇabove all that we ask or think, ᶜaccording to the power that works in us, 21ªto Him *be* glory in the church by Christ Jesus to all generations, forever and ever. Amen.

2:20 ª1 Pet. 2:4
ᵇMatt. 16:18;
1 Cor. 3:10,
11; Rev. 21:14
ᶜ1 Cor. 12:28;
Eph. 3:5
ᵈPs. 118:22;
Luke 20:17

2:21
ª1 Cor. 3:16, 17

2:22 ª1 Pet. 2:5
ᵇJohn 17:23

3:2 ªActs 9:15

3:3
ªActs 22:17, 21;
26:16
ᵇ[Rom. 11:25;
16:25;
Eph. 3:4, 9;
6:19]; Col. 1:26;
4:3

3:6
ªGal. 3:28, 29

3:7 ªRom. 15:16
ᵇRom. 1:5
ᶜRom. 15:18

3:8 ª[1 Cor. 15:9]
ᵇ[Col. 1:27;
2:2, 3]

3:9 ªJohn 1:3;
Col. 1:16;
Heb. 1:2

3:10 ª1 Pet. 1:12
ᵇ[1 Tim. 3:16]
ᶜEph. 1:21; 6:12;
Col. 1:16; 2:10, 15

3:11
ª[Eph. 1:4, 11]

3:12
ª2 Cor. 3:4;
Heb. 4:16;
10:19, 35;
[1 John 2:28;
3:21]

3:13 ªPhil. 1:14
ᵇ2 Cor. 1:6

3:14 ªEph. 1:3

3:16
ª[Eph. 1:7; 2:4;
Phil. 4:19]
ᵇ1 Cor. 16:13;
Phil. 4:13;
Col. 1:11
ᶜRom. 7:22

3:17
ªJohn 14:23;
Rom. 8:9;
2 Cor. 13:5;
[Eph. 2:22]
ᵇCol. 1:23

3:18 ªEph. 1:18
ᵇRom. 8:39

3:19 ªEph. 1:23

3:20
ªRom. 16:25
ᵇ1 Cor. 2:9
ᶜCol. 1:29

3:21 ªRom. 11:36

3:2 ¹*stewardship*   3:9 ¹NU, M *stewardship* (dispensation)   ²NU omits *through Jesus Christ*   3:10 ¹*variegated* or *many-sided*   ²*rulers*
3:14 ¹NU omits *of our Lord Jesus Christ*

WALK IN UNITY

4 I, therefore, the prisoner [1]of the Lord, [2]beseech you to [a]walk worthy of the calling with which you were called, [2]with all lowliness and gentleness, with longsuffering, bearing with one another in love, [3]endeavoring to keep the unity of the Spirit [a]in the bond of peace. [4a]There is one body and one Spirit, just as you were called in one hope of your calling; [5a]one Lord, [b]one faith, [c]one baptism; [6a]one God and Father of all, who is above all, and [b]through all, and in [1]you all.

SPIRITUAL GIFTS

[7]But [a]to each one of us grace was given according to the measure of Christ's gift. [8]Therefore He says:

[a]"When He ascended on high,
He led captivity captive,
And gave gifts to men."

[9a](Now this, "He ascended"—what does it mean but that He also [1]first descended into the lower parts of the earth? [10]He who descended is also the One [a]who ascended far above all the heavens, [b]that He might fill all things.)

[11]And He Himself gave some to be apostles, some prophets, some evangelists, and some pastors and teachers, [12]for the equipping of the saints for the work of ministry, [a]for the [1]edifying of [b]the body of Christ, [13]till we all come to the unity of the faith [a]and of the knowledge of the Son of God, to [b]a perfect man, to the measure of the stature of the fullness of Christ; [14]that we should no longer be [a]children, tossed to and fro and carried about with every wind of doctrine, by the trickery of men, in the cunning craftiness of [b]deceitful plotting, [15]but, speaking the truth in love, may grow up in all things into Him who is the [a]head—Christ— [16a]from whom the whole body, joined and knit together by what every joint supplies, according to the effective working by which every part does its share, causes growth of the body for the edifying of itself in love.

THE NEW MAN

[17]This I say, therefore, and testify in the Lord, that you should [a]no longer walk as [1]the rest of the Gentiles walk, in the futility of their mind, [18]having their understanding darkened, being alienated from the life of God, because of the ignorance that is in them, because of the [a]blindness of their heart; [19a]who, being past feeling, [b]have given themselves over to lewdness, to work all uncleanness with greediness.

[20]But you have not so learned Christ, [21]if indeed you have heard Him and have been taught by Him, as the truth is in Jesus: [22]that you [a]put off, concerning your former conduct, the old man which grows corrupt according to the deceitful lusts, [23]and [a]be renewed in the spirit of your mind, [24]and that you [a]put on the new man which was created according to God, in true righteousness and holiness.

DO NOT GRIEVE THE SPIRIT

[25]Therefore, putting away lying, [a]"Let each one of you speak truth with his neighbor," for [b]we are members of one

---

4:1 [a]Eph. 2:10;
[Col. 1:10; 2:6];
1 Thess. 2:12

4:3 [a]Col. 3:14

4:4 [a]Rom. 12:5

4:5 [a]1 Cor. 1:13;
[b][1 Cor. 15:1–8];
Jude 3
[c]1 Cor. 12:12, 13;
[Heb. 6:6]

4:6 [a]Mal. 2:10;
1 Cor. 8:6; 12:6
[b]Rom. 11:36

4:7
[a][1 Cor. 12:7, 11]

4:8 [a]Ps. 68:18;
[Col. 2:15]

4:9 [a]Luke 23:43;
John 3:13; 20:17;
[1 Pet. 3:19, 20]

4:10 [a]Acts 1:9
[b][Acts 2:33;
Eph. 1:23]

4:12 [a]1 Cor. 14:26
[b]Col. 1:24

4:13 [a]Col. 2:2
[b]1 Cor. 14:20;
Col. 1:28;
Heb. 5:14

4:14 [a]1 Cor. 14:20
[b]Rom. 16:18

4:15 [a]Eph. 1:22

4:16
[a][Rom. 12:4];
Col. 2:19

4:17
[a]Eph. 2:2; 4:22

4:18 [a]Rom. 1:21

4:19 [a]1 Tim. 4:2
[b]1 Pet. 4:3

4:22 [a]Col. 3:8

4:23
[a][Rom. 12:2;
Col. 3:10]

4:24
[a][Rom. 6:4; 7:6;
12:2; 2 Cor. 5:17;
Col. 3:10]

4:25
[a]Zech. 8:16;
Eph. 4:15;
Col. 3:9
[b]Rom. 12:5

4:1 [1]Lit. in [2]exhort, encourage 4:6 [1]NU omits you; M us 4:9 [1]NU omits first 4:12 [1]building up 4:17 [1]NU omits the rest of

another. [26a]"Be angry, and do not sin": do not let the sun go down on your wrath, [27a]nor give [1]place to the devil. [28]Let him who stole steal no longer, but rather [a]let him labor, working with *his* hands what is good, that he may have something [b]to give him who has need. [29a]Let no corrupt word proceed out of your mouth, but [b]what is good for necessary [1]edification, [c]that it may impart grace to the hearers. [30]And [a]do not grieve the Holy Spirit of God, by whom you were sealed for the day of redemption. [31a]Let all bitterness, wrath, anger, [1]clamor, and [b]evil speaking be put away from you, [c]with all malice. [32]And [a]be kind to one another, tenderhearted, [b]forgiving one another, even as God in Christ forgave you.

WALK IN LOVE

5 Therefore[a] be imitators of God as dear [b]children. [2]And [a]walk in love, [b]as Christ also has loved us and given Himself for us, an offering and a sacrifice to God [c]for a sweet-smelling aroma.

[3]But fornication and all [a]uncleanness or [b]covetousness, let it not even be named among you, as is fitting for saints; [4a]neither filthiness, nor [b]foolish talking, nor coarse jesting, [c]which are not fitting, but rather [d]giving of thanks. [5]For [1]this you know, that no fornicator, unclean person, nor covetous man, who is an idolater, has any [a]inheritance in the kingdom of Christ and God. [6]Let no one deceive you with empty words, for because of these things the wrath of God comes upon the sons of disobedience. [7]Therefore do not be [a]partakers with them.

WALK IN LIGHT

[8]For you were once darkness, but now *you are* [a]light in the Lord. Walk as children of light [9](for [a]the fruit of the [1]Spirit *is* in all goodness, righteousness, and truth), [10a]finding out what is acceptable to the Lord. [11]And have [a]no fellowship with the unfruitful works of darkness, but rather [1]expose *them*. [12a]For it is shameful even to speak of those things which are done by them in secret. [13]But [a]all things that are [1]exposed are made manifest by the light, for whatever makes manifest is light. [14]Therefore He says:

> [a]"Awake, you who sleep,
> Arise from the dead,
> And Christ will give you light."

WALK IN WISDOM

[15a]See then that you walk [1]circumspectly, not as fools but as wise, [16a]redeeming the time, [b]because the days are evil. [17a]Therefore do not be unwise, but [b]understand [c]what the will of the Lord *is*. [18]And [a]do not be drunk with wine, in which is dissipation; but be filled with the Spirit, [19]speaking to one another [a]in psalms and hymns and spiritual songs, singing and making [b]melody in your heart to the Lord, [20a]giving

5:16 [a]Col. 4:5 [b]Eccl. 11:2   5:17 [a]Col. 4:5 [b][Rom. 12:2]; Col. 1:9 [c]1 Thess. 4:3
5:18 [a]Prov. 20:1; 23:31; Rom. 13:13; 1 Cor. 5:11; 1 Thess. 5:7   5:19 [a]Acts 16:25
[b]James 5:13   5:20 [a]Ps. 34:1

4:27 [1]*an opportunity*   4:29 [1]*building up*   4:31 [1]*loud quarreling*
5:5 [1]*NU know this*   5:9 [1]*NU light*   5:11 [1]*reprove*   5:13 [1]*reproved*
5:15 [1]*carefully*

4:26
[a]Ps. 4:4; 37:8

4:27
[a][Rom. 12:19;
James 4:7];
1 Pet. 5:9

4:28
[a]Acts 20:35;
1 Cor. 4:12;
Gal. 6:10
[b]Luke 3:11;
1 Thess. 4:12

4:29
[a]Matt. 12:34;
Eph. 5:4;
Col. 3:8
[b]1 Thess. 5:11
[c]Col. 3:16

4:30 [a]Is. 7:13

4:31 [a]Rom. 3:14;
Col. 3:8, 19
[b]James 4:11
[c]Titus 3:3

4:32
[a][Matt. 6:14];
2 Cor. 6:10
[b][Mark 11:25;
Luke 6:37]

5:1
[a][Matt. 5:48];
Luke 6:36;
Eph. 4:32
[b]1 Pet. 1:14–16

5:2 [a]1 Thess. 4:9
[b]John 15:9;
Gal. 1:4;
1 John 3:16
[c]Ex. 29:18, 25;
2 Cor. 2:14, 15

5:3 [a]Col. 3:5–7
[b][Luke 12:15]

5:4
[a]Matt. 12:34, 35;
Eph. 4:29;
Col. 3:8;
James 1:21
[b]Titus 3:9
[c]Rom. 1:28
[d]Phil. 4:6;
Col. 3:17;
[1 Thess. 5:18]

5:5
[a]1 Cor. 6:9, 10;
Col. 3:5

5:7 [a]1 Tim. 5:22

5:8 [a]1 Thess. 5:5

5:9 [a]Gal. 5:22

5:10
[a][Rom. 12:1, 2]

5:11 [a]1 Cor. 5:9;
2 Cor. 6:14

5:12 [a]Rom. 1:24

5:13
[a][John 3:20, 21]

5:14 [a][Is. 26:19;
60:1; Rom. 13:11]

5:15 [a]Col. 4:5

thanks always for all things to God the Father [b]in the name of our Lord Jesus Christ, [21a]submitting to one another in the fear of [1]God.

MARRIAGE—CHRIST AND THE CHURCH
(cf. Col. 3:18, 19)

[22]Wives, [a]submit to your own husbands, as to the Lord. [23]For [a]the husband is head of the wife, as also [b]Christ is head of the church; and He is the Savior of the body. [24]Therefore, just as the church is subject to Christ, so *let* the wives *be* to their own husbands [a]in everything.

[25a]Husbands, love your wives, just as Christ also loved the church and [b]gave Himself for her, [26]that He might [1]sanctify and cleanse her [a]with the washing of water [b]by the word, [27a]that He might present her to Himself a glorious church, [b]not having spot or wrinkle or any such thing, but that she should be holy and without blemish. [28]So husbands ought to love their own wives as their own bodies; he who loves his wife loves himself. [29]For no one ever hated his own flesh, but nourishes and cherishes it, just as the Lord *does* the church. [30]For [a]we are members of His body, [1]of His flesh and of His bones. [31a]"For this reason a man shall leave his father and mother and be joined to his wife, and the [b]two shall become one flesh." [32]This is a great mystery, but I speak concerning Christ and the church. [33]Nevertheless [a]let each one of you in particular so love his own wife as himself, and let the wife *see* that she [b]respects *her* husband.

CHILDREN AND PARENTS
(Ex. 20:12; Deut. 5:16)

6 Children, [a]obey your parents in the Lord, for this is right. [2a]"Honor your father and mother," which is the first commandment with promise: [3]"that it may be well with you and you may live long on the earth."

[4]And [a]you, fathers, do not provoke your children to wrath, but [b]bring them up in the training and admonition of the Lord.

BONDSERVANTS AND MASTERS

[5a]Bondservants, be obedient to those who are your masters according to the flesh, [b]with fear and trembling, [c]in sincerity of heart, as to Christ; [6a]not with eyeservice, as menpleasers, but as bondservants of Christ, doing the will of God from the heart, [7]with goodwill doing service, as to the Lord, and not to men, [8a]knowing that whatever good anyone does, he will receive the same from the Lord, whether *he is* a slave or free.

[9]And you, masters, do the same things to them, giving up threatening, knowing that [1]your own [a]Master also is in heaven, and [b]there is no partiality with Him.

THE WHOLE ARMOR OF GOD

[10]Finally, my brethren, be strong in the Lord and in the power of His might. [11a]Put on the whole armor of God, that

5:20 [b][1 Pet. 2:5]
5:21 [a][Phil. 2:3]; 1 Pet. 5:5
5:22 [a]Eph. 5:22—6:9; Col. 3:18—4:1; 1 Pet. 3:1–6
5:23 [a][1 Cor. 11:3]; [b]Col. 1:18
5:24 [a]Titus 2:4, 5
5:25 [a]Eph. 5:28, 33; Col. 3:19; [1 Pet. 3:7]; [b]Acts 20:28
5:26 [a]John 3:5; [b][John 15:3]; 17:17; Rom. 10:8; Eph. 6:17]
5:27 [a][2 Cor. 4:14; 11:2]; Col. 1:22; [b]Song 4:7
5:30 [a]Gen. 2:23
5:31 [a]Gen. 2:24; Matt. 19:5; Mark 10:7; [b][1 Cor. 6:16]
5:33 [a]Col. 3:19; [b]1 Pet. 3:1, 6
6:1 [a]Prov. 6:20; 23:22; Col. 3:20
6:2 [a]Ex. 20:12; Deut. 5:16
6:4 [a]Col. 3:21; [b]Gen. 18:19; Deut. 6:7; 11:19; Ps. 78:4; Prov. 22:6; 2 Tim. 3:15
6:5 [a]Col. 3:22; [1 Tim. 6:1]; Titus 2:9; 1 Pet. 2:18; [b]2 Cor. 7:15; [c]1 Chr. 29:17
6:6 [a]Col. 3:22
6:8 [a]Rom. 2:6
6:9 [a]Job 31:13; John 13:13; Col. 4:1; [b]Deut. 10:17; Acts 10:34; Rom. 2:11; Col. 3:25
6:11 [a][2 Cor. 6:7]

5:21 [1]NU *Christ* 5:26 [1]*set it apart* 5:30 [1]NU omits the rest of v. 30.
6:9 [1]NU *He who is both their Master and yours is*

you may be able to stand against the ¹wiles of the devil. ¹²For we do not wrestle against flesh and blood, but against ªprincipalities, against powers, against ᵇthe rulers of ¹the darkness of this age, against spiritual *hosts* of wickedness in the heavenly *places.* ¹³ªTherefore take up the whole armor of God, that you may be able to withstand ᵇin the evil day, and having done all, to stand.

¹⁴Stand therefore, ªhaving girded your waist with truth, ᵇhaving put on the breastplate of righteousness, ¹⁵ªand having shod your feet with the preparation of the gospel of peace; ¹⁶above all, taking ªthe shield of faith with which you will be able to quench all the fiery darts of the wicked one. ¹⁷And ªtake the helmet of salvation, and ᵇthe sword of the Spirit, which is the word of God; ¹⁸ªpraying always with all prayer and supplication in the Spirit, ᵇbeing watchful to this end with all perseverance and ᶜsupplication for all the saints— ¹⁹and for me, that utterance may be given to me, ªthat I may open my mouth boldly to make known the mystery of the gospel, ²⁰for which ªI am an ambassador in chains; that in it I may speak boldly, as I ought to speak.

A GRACIOUS GREETING

²¹But that you also may know my affairs *and* how I am doing, ªTychicus, a beloved brother and ᵇfaithful minister in the Lord, will make all things known to you; ²²ªwhom I have sent to you for this very purpose, that you may know our affairs, and *that* he may ᵇcomfort your hearts.

²³Peace to the brethren, and love with faith, from God the Father and the Lord Jesus Christ. ²⁴Grace *be* with all those who love our Lord Jesus Christ in sincerity. Amen.

6:12 ªRom. 8:38
ᵇLuke 22:53

6:13
ª[2 Cor. 10:4]
ᵇEph. 5:16

6:14 ªIs. 11:5;
Luke 12:35;
1 Pet. 1:13
ᵇIs. 59:17;
Rom. 13:12;
Eph. 6:13;
1 Thess. 5:8

6:15 ªIs. 52:7;
Rom. 10:15

6:16 ª1 John 5:4

6:17
ª1 Thess. 5:8
ᵇIs. 49:2;
Hos. 6:5;
[Heb. 4:12]

6:18 ªLuke 18:1;
Col. 1:3; 4:2;
1 Thess. 5:17
ᵇ[Matt. 26:41]
ᶜPhil. 1:4

6:19
ªActs 4:29;
Col. 4:3

6:20
ª2 Cor. 5:20;
Philem. 9

6:21 ªActs 20:4;
2 Tim. 4:12;
Titus 3:12
ᵇ1 Cor. 4:1, 2

6:22 ªCol. 4:8
ᵇ2 Cor. 1:6

6:11 ¹*schemings*   6:12 ¹NU *this darkness,*

PHILIPPIANS

GREETING

1 Paul and Timothy, bondservants of Jesus Christ,

To all the saints in Christ Jesus who are in Philippi, with the ¹bishops and ᵃdeacons:

²Grace to you and peace from God our Father and the Lord Jesus Christ.

THANKFULNESS AND PRAYER

³ᵃI thank my God upon every remembrance of you, ⁴always in ᵃevery prayer of mine making request for you all with joy, ⁵ᵃfor your fellowship in the gospel from the first day until now, ⁶being confident of this very thing, that He who has begun ᵃa good work in you will complete *it* until the day of Jesus Christ; ⁷just as it is right for me to think this of you all, because I have you in my heart, inasmuch as both in my chains and in the defense and confirmation of the gospel, you all are partakers with me of grace. ⁸For God is my witness, how greatly I long for you all with the affection of Jesus Christ.

⁹And this I pray, that your love may abound still more and more in knowledge and all discernment, ¹⁰that you may approve the things that are excellent, that you may be sincere and without offense till the day of Christ, ¹¹being filled with the fruits of righteousness ᵃwhich *are* by Jesus Christ, ᵇto the glory and praise of God.

CHRIST IS PREACHED

¹²But I want you to know, brethren, that the things *which happened* to me have actually turned out for the furtherance of the gospel, ¹³so that it has become evident ᵃto the whole ¹palace guard, and to all the rest, that my chains are in Christ; ¹⁴and most of the brethren in the Lord, having become confident by my chains, are much more bold to speak the word without fear.

¹⁵Some indeed preach Christ even from envy and strife, and some also from goodwill: ¹⁶¹The former preach Christ from selfish ambition, not sincerely, supposing to add affliction to my chains; ¹⁷but the latter out of love, knowing that I am appointed for the defense of the gospel. ¹⁸What then? Only *that* in every way, whether in pretense or in truth, Christ is preached; and in this I rejoice, yes, and will rejoice.

TO LIVE IS CHRIST

¹⁹For I know that ᵃthis will turn out for my deliverance through your prayer and the supply of the Spirit of Jesus Christ, ²⁰according to my earnest expectation and hope that

1:1
ᵃ[1 Tim. 3:8–13]

1:3 ᵃ1 Cor. 1:4

1:4 ᵃEph. 1:16;
1 Thess. 1:2

1:5 ᵃ[Rom. 12:13]

1:6 ᵃ[John 6:29]

1:11 ᵃ[Eph. 2:10];
Col. 1:6
ᵇJohn 15:8

1:13 ᵃPhil. 4:22

1:19
ᵃJob 13:16, LXX

1:1 ¹Lit. *overseers*   1:13 ¹Or *Praetorium*   1:16 ¹NU reverses vv. 16 and 17.

in nothing I shall be ashamed, but [a]with all boldness, as always, so now also Christ will be magnified in my body, whether by life [b]or by death. 21For to me, to live *is* Christ, and to die *is* gain. 22But if *I* live on in the flesh, this *will mean* fruit from *my* labor; yet what I shall choose I [1]cannot tell. 23[1]For I am hard-pressed between the two, having a [a]desire to depart and be with Christ, *which is* [b]far better. 24Nevertheless to remain in the flesh *is* more needful for you. 25And being confident of this, I know that I shall remain and continue with you all for your progress and joy of faith, 26that [a]your rejoicing for me may be more abundant in Jesus Christ by my coming to you again.

STRIVING AND SUFFERING FOR CHRIST

27Only [a]let your conduct be worthy of the gospel of Christ, so that whether I come and see you or am absent, I may hear of your affairs, that you stand fast in one spirit, [b]with one mind [c]striving together for the faith of the gospel, 28and not in any way terrified by your adversaries, which is to them a proof of perdition, but [1]to you of salvation, and that from God. 29For to you [a]it has been granted on behalf of Christ, [b]not only to believe in Him, but also to [c]suffer for His sake, 30[a]having the same conflict [b]which you saw in me and now hear *is* in me.

UNITY THROUGH HUMILITY

2 Therefore if *there is* any [1]consolation in Christ, if any comfort of love, if any fellowship of the Spirit, if any [a]affection and mercy, 2[a]fulfill my joy [b]by being like-minded, having the same love, *being* of [c]one accord, of one mind. 3[a]*Let* nothing *be done* through selfish ambition or conceit, but [b]in lowliness of mind let each esteem others better than himself. 4[a]Let each of you look out not only for his own interests, but also for the interests of [b]others.

THE HUMBLED AND EXALTED CHRIST

5[a]Let this mind be in you which was also in Christ Jesus, 6who, [a]being in the form of God, did not consider it [1]robbery to be equal with God, 7[a]but [1]made Himself of no reputation, taking the form [b]of a bondservant, *and* [c]coming in the likeness of men. 8And being found in appearance as a man, He humbled Himself and [a]became [b]obedient to *the point of* death, even the death of the cross. 9[a]Therefore God also [b]has highly exalted Him and [c]given Him the name which is above every name, 10[a]that at the name of Jesus every knee should bow, of those in heaven, and of those on earth, and of those under the earth, 11and [a]*that* every tongue should confess that Jesus Christ *is* Lord, to the glory of God the Father.

LIGHT BEARERS

12Therefore, my beloved, [a]as you have always obeyed, not as in my presence only, but now much more in my absence, [b]work out your own salvation with [c]fear and trembling; 13for

2:12 [a]Phil. 1:5, 6; 4:15 [b]John 6:27, 29; 2 Pet. 1:10 [c]Eph. 6:5

1:22 [1]*do not know* 1:23 [1]NU, M *But* 1:28 [1]NU *of your salvation*
2:1 [1]Or *encouragement* 2:6 [1]Or *something to be held onto to be equal*
2:7 [1]*emptied Himself* of His privileges

1:20
[a]Eph. 6:19, 20
[b][Rom. 14:8]

1:23
[a][2 Cor. 5:2, 8];
2 Tim. 4:6
[b][Ps. 16:11]

1:26 [a]2 Cor. 1:14

1:27
[a]Eph. 4:1;
1 Thess. 2:12
[b]1 Cor. 1:10;
Eph. 4:3 [c]Jude 3

1:29
[a][Matt. 5:11, 12;
Acts 5:41;
Rom. 5:3]
[b]Eph. 2:8
[c][2 Tim. 3:12]

1:30
[a]Col. 1:29; 2:1;
1 Thess. 2:2;
1 Tim. 6:12;
2 Tim. 4:7;
Heb. 10:32; 12:1
[b]Acts 16:19–40;
Phil. 1:13;
1 Thess. 2:2

2:1 [a]Col. 3:12

2:2 [a]John 3:29
[b]Rom. 12:16
[c]Phil. 4:2

2:3 [a]Gal. 5:26;
James 3:14
[b]Rom. 12:10;
Eph. 5:21

2:4 [a]1 Cor. 13:5
[b]Rom. 15:1, 2

2:5
[a][Matt. 11:29];
Rom. 15:3

2:6 [a]2 Cor. 4:4

2:7
[a]Ps. 22:6
[b]Is. 42:1
[c][John 1:14];
Rom. 8:3;
Gal. 4:4;
[Heb. 2:17]

2:8
[a]Ps. 40:6–8;
Matt. 26:39;
John 10:18;
[Rom. 5:19]
[b]Heb. 5:8

2:9
[a][Matt. 28:18];
Heb. 2:9
[b]Ps. 68:18;
110:1; Is. 52:13;
Acts 2:33
[c]Is. 9:6;
Luke 1:32;
Eph. 1:21

2:10 [a]Is. 45:23;
Rom. 14:11;
Rev. 5:13

2:11 [a]John 13:13;
[Rom. 10:9;
14:9]

2:13 ªRom. 12:3;
1 Cor. 12:6; 15:10;
2 Cor. 3:5;
Heb. 13:20, 21
ᵇEph. 1:5

2:14
ª1 Cor. 10:10;
1 Pet. 4:9
ᵇRom. 14:1

2:15
ªMatt. 5:15, 16

2:16 ª2 Cor. 1:14
ᵇGal. 2:2
ᶜIs. 49:4;
Gal. 4:11;
1 Thess. 3:5

2:17
ª2 Cor. 12:15;
2 Tim. 4:6
ᵇNum. 28:6, 7;
Rom. 15:16
ᶜ2 Cor. 7:4

2:19 ªRom. 16:21

2:20
ª1 Cor. 16:10;
2 Tim. 3:10

2:22 ª1 Cor. 4:17

2:25 ªPhil. 4:18
ᵇPhilem. 2
ᶜJohn 13:16;
2 Cor. 8:23
ᵈ2 Cor. 11:9

2:26 ªPhil. 1:8

2:30
ª1 Cor. 16:17;
Phil. 4:10

3:1 ª1 Thess. 5:16

3:2
ªPs. 22:16, 20;
Gal. 5:15;
Rev. 22:15
ᵇPs. 119:115
ᶜRom. 2:28

3:3 ªDeut. 30:6;
Rom. 2:28, 29;
9:6; [Gal. 6:15]
ᵇJohn 4:24;
Rom. 7:6

3:4
ª2 Cor. 5:16; 11:18
ᵇ2 Cor. 11:22, 23

3:5 ªRom. 11:1
ᵇ2 Cor. 11:22
ᶜActs 23:6

3:6 ªActs 8:3;
22:4, 5; 26:9–11

3:7 ªMatt. 13:44

3:8 ªIs. 53:11;
Jer. 9:23;
John 17:3;
1 Cor. 2:2;
[Eph. 4:13]

ªit is God who works in you both to will and to do ᵇfor *His* good pleasure.

¹⁴Do all things ªwithout ¹complaining and ᵇdisputing,² ¹⁵that you may become blameless and ¹harmless, children of God without fault in the midst of a crooked and perverse generation, among whom you shine as ªlights in the world, ¹⁶holding fast the word of life, so that ªI may rejoice in the day of Christ that ᵇI have not run in vain or labored in ᶜvain.

¹⁷Yes, and if ªI am being poured out *as a drink offering* on the sacrifice ᵇand service of your faith, ᶜI am glad and rejoice with you all. ¹⁸For the same reason you also be glad and rejoice with me.

TIMOTHY COMMENDED

¹⁹But I trust in the Lord Jesus to send ªTimothy to you shortly, that I also may be encouraged when I know your ¹state. ²⁰For I have no one ªlike-minded, who will sincerely care for your state. ²¹For all seek their own, not the things which are of Christ Jesus. ²²But you know his proven character, ªthat as a son with *his* father he served with me in the gospel. ²³Therefore I hope to send him at once, as soon as I see how it goes with me. ²⁴But I trust in the Lord that I myself shall also come shortly.

EPAPHRODITUS PRAISED

²⁵Yet I considered it necessary to send to you ªEpaphroditus, my brother, fellow worker, and ᵇfellow soldier, ᶜbut your messenger and ᵈthe one who ministered to my need; ²⁶ªsince he was longing for you all, and was distressed because you had heard that he was sick. ²⁷For indeed he was sick almost unto death; but God had mercy on him, and not only on him but on me also, lest I should have sorrow upon sorrow. ²⁸Therefore I sent him the more eagerly, that when you see him again you may rejoice, and I may be less sorrowful. ²⁹Receive him therefore in the Lord with all gladness, and hold such men in esteem; ³⁰because for the work of Christ he came close to death, ¹not regarding his life, ªto supply what was lacking in your service toward me.

ALL FOR CHRIST

3 Finally, my brethren, ªrejoice in the Lord. For me to write the same things to you *is* not tedious, but for you *it is* safe.

²ªBeware of dogs, beware of ᵇevil workers, ᶜbeware of the mutilation! ³For we are ªthe circumcision, ᵇwho worship ¹God in the Spirit, rejoice in Christ Jesus, and have no confidence in the flesh, ⁴though ªI also might have confidence in the flesh. If anyone else thinks he may have confidence in the flesh, I ᵇmore so: ⁵circumcised the eighth day, of the stock of Israel, ªof the tribe of Benjamin, ᵇa Hebrew of the Hebrews; concerning the law, ᶜa Pharisee; ⁶concerning zeal, ªpersecuting the church; concerning the righteousness which is in the law, blameless.

⁷But ªwhat things were gain to me, these I have counted loss for Christ. ⁸Yet indeed I also count all things loss ªfor

---

2:14 ¹*grumbling* ²*arguing* 2:15 ¹*innocent* 2:19 ¹*condition*
2:30 ¹*risking* 3:3 ¹NU, M *in the Spirit of God*

the excellence of the knowledge of Christ Jesus my Lord, for whom I have suffered the loss of all things, and count them as rubbish, that I may gain Christ [9]and be found in Him, not having [a]my own righteousness, which *is* from the law, but [b]that which *is* through faith in Christ, the righteousness which is from God by faith; [10]that I may know Him and the [a]power of His resurrection, and [b]the fellowship of His sufferings, being conformed to His death, [11]if, by any means, I may [a]attain[1] to the resurrection from the dead.

PRESSING TOWARD THE GOAL

[12]Not that I have already [a]attained,[1] or am already [b]perfected; but I press on, that I may lay hold of that for which Christ Jesus has also laid hold of me. [13]Brethren, I do not count myself to have [1]apprehended; but one thing *I do,* [a]forgetting those things which are behind and [b]reaching forward to those things which are ahead, [14a]I press toward the goal for the prize of [b]the upward call of God in Christ Jesus.

[15]Therefore let us, as many as are [a]mature, [b]have this mind; and if in anything you think otherwise, [c]God will reveal even this to you. [16]Nevertheless, to *the degree* that we have already [1]attained, [a]let us walk [b]by the same [2]rule, let us be of the same mind.

OUR CITIZENSHIP IN HEAVEN

[17]Brethren, [a]join in following my example, and note those who so walk, as [b]you have us for a pattern. [18]For many walk, of whom I have told you often, and now tell you even weeping, *that they are* [a]the enemies of the cross of Christ: [19a]whose end *is* destruction, [b]whose god *is their* belly, and [c]*whose* glory *is* in their shame—[d]who set their mind on earthly things. [20]For [a]our citizenship is in heaven, [b]from which we also [c]eagerly wait for the Savior, the Lord Jesus Christ, [21a]who will transform our lowly body that it may be [b]conformed to His glorious body, [c]according to the working by which He is able even to [d]subdue all things to Himself.

4 Therefore, my beloved and [a]longed-for brethren, [b]my joy and crown, so [c]stand fast in the Lord, beloved.

BE UNITED, JOYFUL, AND IN PRAYER

[2]I implore Euodia and I implore Syntyche [a]to be of the same mind in the Lord. [3][1]And I urge you also, true companion, help these women who [a]labored with me in the gospel, with Clement also, and the rest of my fellow workers, whose names *are* in [b]the Book of Life.

[4a]Rejoice in the Lord always. Again I will say, rejoice!

[5]Let your [1]gentleness be known to all men. [a]The Lord *is* at hand.

[6a]Be anxious for nothing, but in everything by prayer and supplication, with [b]thanksgiving, let your requests be made known to God; [7]and [a]the peace of God, which surpasses all understanding, will guard your hearts and minds through Christ Jesus.

4:7 [a][Is. 26:3; John 14:27]; Phil. 4:9; Col. 3:15

3:11 [1]Lit. *arrive at*   3:12 [1]*obtained it*   3:13 [1]*laid hold of it*   3:16 [1]*arrived*
[2]NU omits *rule* and the rest of v. 16.   4:3 [1]NU, M *Yes*   4:5 [1]*graciousness* or *forbearance*

3:9 [a]Rom. 10:3
[b]Rom. 1:17

3:10
[a]Eph. 1:19, 20
[b][Rom. 6:3–5];
2 Cor. 1:5;
1 Pet. 4:13

3:11
[a]Acts 26:6–8;
[1 Cor. 15:23;
Rev. 20:5]

3:12 [a]1 Cor. 9:24;
[1 Tim. 6:12, 19]
[b]Heb. 12:23

3:13 [a]Luke 9:62
[b]Heb. 6:1

3:14 [a]2 Tim. 4:7
[b]Heb. 3:1

3:15 [a]Matt. 5:48;
1 Cor. 2:6
[b]Gal. 5:10
[c]Hos. 6:3;
James 1:5

3:16 [a]Gal. 6:16
[b]Rom. 12:16; 15:5

3:17
[a][1 Cor. 4:16;
11:1]; Phil. 4:9
[b]Titus 2:7, 8;
1 Pet. 5:3

3:18 [a]Gal. 1:7

3:19 [a]2 Cor. 11:15
[b]1 Tim. 6:5
[c]Hos. 4:7
[d]Rom. 8:5;
Col. 3:2

3:20
[a]Eph. 2:6, 19;
Phil. 1:27;
[Col. 3:1;
Heb. 12:22]
[b]Acts 1:11
[c]1 Cor. 1:7

3:21
[a][1 Cor. 15:43–53]
[b]1 John 3:2
[c]Eph. 1:19
[d][1 Cor. 15:28]

4:1 [a]Phil. 1:8
[b]2 Cor. 1:14
[c]1 Cor. 16:13;
Phil. 1:27

4:2
[a]Phil. 2:2; 3:16

4:3 [a]Rom. 16:3
[b]Ex. 32:32;
Luke 10:20

4:4 [a]Rom. 12:12

4:5 [a]1 Cor. 16:22;
Heb. 10:25, 37;
[James 5:7–9];
Rev. 22:7, 20

4:6 [a]Ps. 55:22;
Matt. 6:25;
1 Pet. 5:7
[b][1 Thess. 5:17,
18]

MEDITATE ON THESE THINGS

[8]Finally, brethren, whatever things are [a]true, whatever things *are* [b]noble, whatever things *are* [c]just, [d]whatever things *are* pure, whatever things *are* [e]lovely, whatever things *are* of good report, if *there is* any virtue and if *there is* anything praiseworthy—meditate on these things. [9]The things which you learned and received and heard and saw in me, these do, and [a]the God of peace will be with you.

PHILIPPIAN GENEROSITY

[10]But I rejoiced in the Lord greatly that now at last [a]your[1] care for me has flourished again; though you surely did care, but you lacked opportunity. [11]Not that I speak in regard to need, for I have learned in whatever state I am, [a]to be content: [12a]I know how to [1]be abased, and I know how to [2]abound. Everywhere and in all things I have learned both to be full and to be hungry, both to abound and to suffer need. [13]I can do all things [a]through [1]Christ who strengthens me.

[14]Nevertheless you have done well that [a]you shared in my distress. [15]Now you Philippians know also that in the beginning of the gospel, when I departed from Macedonia, [a]no church shared with me concerning giving and receiving but you only. [16]For even in Thessalonica you sent *aid* once and again for my necessities. [17]Not that I seek the gift, but I seek [a]the fruit that abounds to your account. [18]Indeed I [1]have all and abound. I am full, having received from [a]Epaphroditus the things *sent* from you, [b]a sweet-smelling aroma, [c]an acceptable sacrifice, well pleasing to God. [19]And my God [a]shall supply all your need according to His riches in glory by Christ Jesus. [20a]Now to our God and Father *be* glory forever and ever. Amen.

GREETING AND BLESSING

[21]Greet every saint in Christ Jesus. The brethren [a]who are with me greet you. [22]All the saints greet you, but especially those who are of Caesar's household.

[23]The grace of our Lord Jesus Christ be with [1]you all. Amen.

4:8 [a]Eph. 4:25
[b]2 Cor. 8:21
[c]Deut. 16:20
[d]1 Thess. 5:22;
James 3:17
[e]1 Cor. 13:4–7
4:9 [a]Rom. 15:33;
Heb. 13:20
4:10 [a]2 Cor. 11:9;
Phil. 2:30
4:11 [a]2 Cor. 9:8;
1 Tim. 6:6, 8;
Heb. 13:5
4:12 [a]1 Cor. 4:11
4:13 [a]John 15:5
4:14 [a]Phil. 1:7
4:15
[a]2 Cor. 11:8, 9
4:17 [a]Titus 3:14
4:18 [a]Phil. 2:25
[b]Heb. 13:16
[c]Rom. 12:1;
2 Cor. 9:12
4:19 [a]Ps. 23:1;
2 Cor. 9:8
4:20
[a]Rom. 16:27
4:21 [a]Gal. 1:2

4:10 [1]*you have revived your care*   4:12 [1]*live humbly*   [2]*live in prosperity*
4:13 [1]NU *Him who*   4:18 [1]*Or have received all*   4:23 [1]NU *your spirit*

THE EPISTLE OF PAUL THE APOSTLE TO THE

COLOSSIANS

GREETING

1 Paul, ᵃan apostle of Jesus Christ by the will of God, and Timothy our brother,

²To the saints ᵃand faithful brethren in Christ *who are* in Colosse:

ᵇGrace to you and peace from God our Father ¹and the Lord Jesus Christ.

THEIR FAITH IN CHRIST

³ᵃWe give thanks to the God and Father of our Lord Jesus Christ, praying always for you, ⁴ᵃsince we heard of your faith in Christ Jesus and of ᵇyour love for all the saints; ⁵because of the hope ᵃwhich is laid up for you in heaven, of which you heard before in the word of the truth of the gospel, ⁶which has come to you, ᵃas *it has* also in all the world, and ᵇis bringing forth ¹fruit, as *it is* also among you since the day you heard and knew ᶜthe grace of God in truth; ⁷as you also learned from ᵃEpaphras, our dear fellow servant, who is ᵇa faithful minister of Christ on your behalf, ⁸who also declared to us your ᵃlove in the Spirit.

PREEMINENCE OF CHRIST

⁹ᵃFor this reason we also, since the day we heard it, do not cease to pray for you, and to ask ᵇthat you may be filled with ᶜthe knowledge of His will ᵈin all wisdom and spiritual understanding; ¹⁰ᵃthat you may walk worthy of the Lord, ᵇfully pleasing *Him,* ᶜbeing fruitful in every good work and increasing in the ᵈknowledge of God; ¹¹strengthened with all might, according to His glorious power, ᵇfor all patience and longsuffering ᶜwith joy; ¹²ᵃgiving thanks to the Father who has qualified us to be partakers of ᵇthe inheritance of the saints in the light. ¹³He has delivered us from ᵃthe power of darkness ᵇand ¹conveyed *us* into the kingdom of the Son of His love, ¹⁴ᵃin whom we have redemption ¹through His blood, the forgiveness of sins.

¹⁵He is ᵃthe image of the invisible God, ᵇthe firstborn over all creation. ¹⁶For ᵃby Him all things were created that are in heaven and that are on earth, visible and invisible, whether thrones or ᵇdominions or ¹principalities or ²powers. All things were created ᶜthrough Him and for Him. ¹⁷ᵃAnd He is before all things, and in Him ᵇall things consist. ¹⁸And ᵃHe is the head of the body, the church, who is the beginning, ᵇthe firstborn from the dead, that in all things He may have the preeminence.

1:1 ᵃEph. 1:1
1:2 ᵃ1 Cor. 4:17
ᵇGal. 1:3
1:3 ᵃ1 Cor. 1:4;
Eph. 1:16;
Phil. 1:3
1:4 ᵃEph. 1:15
ᵇ[Heb. 6:10]
1:5 ᵃ[1 Pet. 1:4]
1:6 ᵃMatt. 24:14
ᵇJohn 15:16
ᶜEph. 3:2
1:7 ᵃCol. 4:12;
Philem. 23
ᵇ1 Cor. 4:1, 2;
2 Cor. 11:23
1:8 ᵃRom. 15:30
1:9 ᵃEph. 1:15–17
ᵇ1 Cor. 1:5
ᶜ[Rom. 12:2];
Eph. 5:17
ᵈEph. 1:8
1:10 ᵃEph. 4:1;
Phil. 1:27;
1 Thess. 2:12
ᵇ1 Thess. 4:1
ᶜHeb. 13:21
ᵈ2 Pet. 3:18
1:11
ᵃ[Eph. 3:16; 6:10]
ᵇEph. 4:2
ᶜ[Acts 5:41];
2 Cor. 8:2;
[Heb. 10:34]
1:12 ᵃ[Eph. 5:20]
ᵇEph. 1:11
1:13 ᵃEph. 6:12
ᵇ2 Pet. 1:11
1:14 ᵃEph. 1:7
1:15 ᵃ2 Cor. 4:4;
Heb. 1:3
ᵇPs. 89:27;
Rev. 3:14
1:16 ᵃJohn 1:3;
Heb. 1:2, 3
ᵇ[Eph. 1:20, 21;
Col. 2:15]
ᶜJohn 1:3;
Rom. 11:36;
1 Cor. 8:6;
Heb. 2:10
1:17 ᵃ[John 17:5]
ᵇHeb. 1:3
1:18 ᵃ1 Cor. 11:3;
Eph. 1:22
ᵇRev. 1:5

1:2 ¹NU omits *and the Lord Jesus Christ*   1:6 ¹NU, M add *and growing*
1:13 ¹*transferred*   1:14 ¹NU, M omit *through His blood*   1:16 ¹*rulers*
²*authorities*

RECONCILED IN CHRIST

[19]For it pleased *the Father that* [a]in Him all the fullness should dwell, [20]and [a]by Him to reconcile [b]all things to Himself, by Him, whether things on earth or things in heaven, [c]having made peace through the blood of His cross.

[21]And you, [a]who once were alienated and enemies in your mind [b]by wicked works, yet now He has [c]reconciled [22a]in the body of His flesh through death, [b]to present you holy, and blameless, and above reproach in His sight— [23]if indeed you continue [a]in the faith, grounded and steadfast, and are [b]not moved away from the hope of the gospel which you heard, [c]which was preached to every creature under heaven, [d]of which I, Paul, became a minister.

SACRIFICIAL SERVICE FOR CHRIST

[24a]I now rejoice in my sufferings [b]for you, and fill up in my flesh [c]what is lacking in the afflictions of Christ, for [d]the sake of His body, which is the church, [25]of which I became a minister according to [a]the [1]stewardship from God which was given to me for you, to fulfill the word of God, [26a]the [1]mystery which has been hidden from ages and from generations, [b]but now has been revealed to His saints. [27a]To them God willed to make known what are [b]the riches of the glory of this mystery among the Gentiles: [1]which is [c]Christ in you, [d]the hope of glory. [28]Him we preach, [a]warning every man and teaching every man in all wisdom, [b]that we may present every man perfect in Christ Jesus. [29]To this *end* I also labor, striving according to His working which works in me [a]mightily.

NOT PHILOSOPHY BUT CHRIST

2 For I want you to know what a great [a]conflict[1] I have for you and those in Laodicea, and *for* as many as have not seen my face in the flesh, [2]that their hearts may be encouraged, being knit together in love, and *attaining* to all riches of the full assurance of understanding, to the knowledge of the mystery of God, [1]both of the Father and of Christ, [3a]in whom are hidden all the treasures of wisdom and knowledge.

[4]Now this I say [a]lest anyone should deceive you with persuasive words. [5]For [a]though I am absent in the flesh, yet I am with you in spirit, rejoicing [1]to see [b]your *good* order and the [c]steadfastness of your faith in Christ.

[6a]As you therefore have received Christ Jesus the Lord, so walk in Him, [7a]rooted and built up in Him and established in the faith, as you have been taught, abounding [1]in it with thanksgiving.

[8]Beware lest anyone [1]cheat you through philosophy and empty deceit, according to [a]the tradition of men, according to the [b]basic principles of the world, and not according to Christ. [9]For [a]in Him dwells all the fullness of the Godhead [1]bodily; [10]and you are complete in Him, who is the [a]head of all [1]principality and power.

Cross references (left column)

1:19 [a]John 1:16
1:20 [a]Rom. 5:1; Eph. 2:14 [b]2 Cor. 5:18 [c]Eph. 1:10
1:21 [a][Eph. 2:1] [b]Titus 1:15 [c]2 Cor. 5:18, 19
1:22 [a]2 Cor. 5:18; [Eph. 2:14–16] [b][Eph. 5:27]; Col. 1:28
1:23 [a]Eph. 3:17; Col. 2:7 [b][John 15:6]; 1 Cor. 15:58 [c]Mark 16:15; Acts 2:5; Rom. 10:18; Col. 1:6 [d]Acts 1:17; Eph. 3:7; Col. 1:25
1:24 [a]2 Cor. 7:4 [b]Eph. 3:1, 13 [c][Rom. 8:17; 2 Cor. 1:5; 12:15]; Phil. 2:17 [d]Eph. 1:23
1:25 [a]Gal. 2:7
1:26 [a][1 Cor. 2:7] [b][2 Tim. 1:10]
1:27 [a]2 Cor. 2:14 [b]Rom. 9:23 [c][Rom. 8:10, 11] [d]1 Tim. 1:1
1:28 [a]Acts 20:20 [b]Eph. 5:27
1:29 [a]Eph. 3:7
2:1 [a]Phil. 1:30; Col. 1:29; 4:12; 1 Thess. 2:2
2:3 [a]1 Cor. 1:24, 30
2:4 [a]Rom. 16:18; 2 Cor. 11:13; Eph. 4:14; 5:6
2:5 [a]1 Thess. 2:17 [b]1 Cor. 14:40 [c]1 Pet. 5:9
2:6 [a]1 Thess. 4:1
2:7 [a]Eph. 2:21
2:8 [a]Gal. 1:14 [b]Gal. 4:3, 9, 10; Col. 2:20
2:9 [a][John 1:14]; Col. 1:19
2:10 [a][Eph. 1:20, 21; 1 Pet. 3:22]

1:25 [1]*dispensation* or *administration*   1:26 [1]*secret* or *hidden truth*
1:27 [1]M *who*   2:1 [1]*struggle*   2:2 [1]NU omits *both of the Father and*   2:5 [1]Lit. *and seeing*   2:7 [1]NU omits *in it*   2:8 [1]Lit. *plunder you* or *take you captive*
2:9 [1]*in bodily form*   2:10 [1]*rule and authority*

NOT LEGALISM BUT CHRIST

[11]In Him you were also [a]circumcised with the circumcision made without hands, by [b]putting off the body [1]of the sins of the flesh, by the circumcision of Christ, [12a]buried with Him in baptism, in which you also were raised with *Him* through [b]faith in the working of God, [c]who raised Him from the dead. [13]And you, being dead in your trespasses and the uncircumcision of your flesh, He has made alive together with Him, having forgiven you all trespasses, [14a]having wiped out the [1]handwriting of requirements that was against us, which was contrary to us. And He has taken it out of the way, having nailed it to the cross. [15a]Having disarmed [b]principalities and powers, He made a public spectacle of them, triumphing over them in it.

[16]So let no one [a]judge you in food or in drink, or regarding a [1]festival or a new moon or sabbaths, [17a]which are a shadow of things to come, but the [1]substance is of Christ. [18]Let no one cheat you of your reward, taking delight in *false* humility and worship of angels, intruding into those things which he has [1]not seen, vainly puffed up by his fleshly mind, [19]and not holding fast to [a]the Head, from whom all the body, nourished and knit together by joints and ligaments, [b]grows with the increase *that is* from God.

[20]Therefore, if you [a]died with Christ from the basic principles of the world, [b]why, as *though* living in the world, do you subject yourselves to regulations— [21a]"Do not touch, do not taste, do not handle," [22]which all concern things which perish with the using—[a]according to the commandments and doctrines of men? [23a]These things indeed have an appearance of wisdom in self-imposed religion, *false* humility, and [1]neglect of the body, *but are* of no value against the indulgence of the flesh.

NOT CARNALITY BUT CHRIST

3 If then you were [a]raised with Christ, seek those things which are above, [b]where Christ is, sitting at the right hand of God. [2]Set your mind on things above, not on things on the [a]earth. [3a]For you died, [b]and your life is hidden with Christ in God. [4a]When Christ *who is* [b]our life appears, then you also will appear with Him in [c]glory.

[5a]Therefore put to death [b]your members which are on the earth: [c]fornication, uncleanness, passion, evil desire, and covetousness, [d]which is idolatry. [6a]Because of these things the wrath of God is coming upon [b]the sons of disobedience, [7a]in which you yourselves once walked when you lived in them.

[8a]But now you yourselves are to put off all these: anger, wrath, malice, blasphemy, filthy language out of your mouth. [9]Do not lie to one another, since you have put off the old man with his deeds, [10]and have put on the new *man* who [a]is renewed in knowledge [b]according to the image of Him who [c]created him, [11]where there is neither [a]Greek nor Jew, circumcised nor uncircumcised, barbarian, Scythian, slave *nor* free, [b]but Christ *is* all and in all.

3:11 [a]Rom. 10:12; [1 Cor. 12:13]; Gal. 3:27, 28 [b]Eph. 1:23

2:11 [a]Deut. 10:16
[b]Rom. 6:6;
7:24; Gal. 5:24;
Col. 3:5

2:12 [a]Rom. 6:4
[b]Eph. 1:19, 20
[c]Acts 2:24

2:14
[a][Eph. 2:15, 16];
Col. 2:20

2:15 [a][Is. 53:12;
Heb. 2:14]
[b]Eph. 6:12

2:16 [a]Rom. 14:3

2:17
[a]Heb. 8:5; 10:1

2:19 [a]Eph. 4:15
[b]Eph. 1:23; 4:16

2:20
[a]Rom. 6:2–5
[b]Gal. 4:3, 9

2:21 [a]1 Tim. 4:3

2:22 [a]Is. 29:13;
Matt. 15:9;
Titus 1:14

2:23
[a]Rom. 13:14;
1 Tim. 4:8

3:1 [a]Rom. 6:5;
Eph. 2:6;
Col. 2:12
[b]Ps. 68:18; 110:1;
[Rom. 8:34];
Eph. 1:20

3:2
[a][Matt. 6:19–21]

3:3 [a][Rom. 6:2];
2 Cor. 5:14;
Gal. 2:20];
Col. 2:20
[b][2 Cor. 5:7]

3:4 [a][1 John 3:2]
[b]John 14:6
[c]1 Cor. 15:43

3:5
[a][Rom. 8:13]
[b][Rom. 6:13]
[c]Eph. 5:3
[d]Mark 7:21;
1 Cor. 6:9, 18;
2 Cor. 12:21;
Gal. 5:19;
Eph. 4:19; 5:3, 5

3:6 [a]Rom. 1:18;
Eph. 5:6;
Rev. 22:15
[b][Eph. 2:2]

3:7 [a]1 Cor. 6:11;
[Eph. 2:2];
Titus 3:3

3:8 [a]Eph. 4:22;
1 Pet. 2:1

3:10 [a]Rom. 12:2;
2 Cor. 4:16
[b][Rom. 8:29]
[c][Eph. 2:10]

2:11 [1]NU omits *of the sins*   2:14 [1]*certificate of debt with its*   2:16 [1]*feast day*
2:17 [1]Lit. *body*   2:18 [1]NU omits *not*   2:20 [1]NU, M omit *Therefore*
2:23 [1]*severe treatment, asceticism*

CHARACTER OF THE NEW MAN

[12]Therefore, [a]as *the* elect of God, holy and beloved, [b]put on tender mercies, kindness, humility, meekness, longsuffering; [13a]bearing with one another, and forgiving one another, if anyone has a complaint against another; even as Christ forgave you, so you also *must do.* [14a]But above all these things [b]put on love, which is the [c]bond of perfection. [15]And let [a]the peace of God rule in your hearts, [b]to which also you were called [c]in one body; and [d]be thankful. [16]Let the word of Christ dwell in you richly in all wisdom, teaching and admonishing one another [a]in psalms and hymns and spiritual songs, singing with grace in your hearts to the Lord. [17]And [a]whatever you do in word or deed, *do* all in the name of the Lord Jesus, giving thanks to God the Father through Him.

THE CHRISTIAN HOME

(cf. Eph. 5:21—6:9)

[18a]Wives, submit to your own husbands, [b]as is fitting in the Lord.

[19a]Husbands, love your wives and do not be [b]bitter toward them.

[20a]Children, obey your parents [b]in all things, for this is well pleasing to the Lord.

[21a]Fathers, do not provoke your children, lest they become discouraged.

[22a]Bondservants, obey in all things your masters according to the flesh, not with eyeservice, as men-pleasers, but in sincerity of heart, fearing God. [23a]And whatever you do, do it heartily, as to the Lord and not to men, [24a]knowing that from the Lord you will receive the reward of the inheritance; [b]for[1] you serve the Lord Christ. [25]But he who does wrong will be repaid for what he has done, and [a]there is no partiality.

4 Masters,[a] give your bondservants what is just and fair, knowing that you also have a Master in heaven.

CHRISTIAN GRACES

[2a]Continue earnestly in prayer, being vigilant in it [b]with thanksgiving; [3a]meanwhile praying also for us, that God would [b]open to us a door for the word, to speak [c]the [1]mystery of Christ, [d]for which I am also in chains, [4]that I may make it manifest, as I ought to speak.

[5a]Walk in [b]wisdom toward those *who are* outside, [c]redeeming the time. [6]*Let* your speech always *be* [a]with grace, [b]seasoned with salt, [c]that you may know how you ought to answer each one.

FINAL GREETINGS

(cf. Eph. 6:21, 22)

[7a]Tychicus, a beloved brother, faithful minister, and fellow servant in the Lord, will tell you all the news about me. [8a]I am sending him to you for this very purpose, that [1]he may know your circumstances and comfort your hearts, [9]with [a]Onesimus, a faithful and beloved brother, who is *one* of you. They will make known to you all things which *are happening* here.

3:12 [a][1 Pet. 1:2]
[b]Luke 1:78;
Phil. 2:1;
1 John 3:17

3:13
[a][Mark 11:25]

3:14 [a]1 Pet. 4:8
[b][1 Cor. 13]
[c]Eph. 4:3

3:15
[a][John 14:27;
Phil. 4:7]
[b]1 Cor. 7:15
[c]Eph. 4:4
[d][1 Thess. 5:18]

3:16 [a]Eph. 5:19

3:17 [a]1 Cor. 10:31

3:18 [a]1 Pet. 3:1
[b][Col. 3:18—4:1;
Eph. 5:22—6:9]

3:19 [a][Eph. 5:25;
1 Pet. 3:7]
[b]Eph. 4:31

3:20 [a]Eph. 6:1
[b]Eph. 5:24

3:21 [a]Eph. 6:4

3:22 [a]Eph. 6:5;
[1 Tim. 6:1];
Titus 2:9;
1 Pet. 2:18

3:23
[a][Eccl. 9:10]

3:24 [a]Eph. 6:8
[b]1 Cor. 7:22

3:25 [a]Rom. 2:11

4:1 [a]Eph. 6:9

4:2 [a]Luke 18:1
[b]Col. 2:7

4:3 [a]Eph. 6:19
[b]1 Cor. 16:9
[c]Eph. 3:3, 4; 6:19
[d]Eph. 6:20

4:5 [a]Eph. 5:15
[b][Matt. 10:16]
[c]Eph. 5:16

4:6 [a]Eccl. 10:12
[b]Mark 9:50
[c]1 Pet. 3:15

4:7 [a]Acts 20:4;
Eph. 6:21;
2 Tim. 4:12;
Titus 3:12

4:8 [a]Eph. 6:22

4:9 [a]Philem. 10

3:24 [1]NU omits *for*   **4:3** [1]*hidden truth*   **4:8** [1]NU *you may know our circumstances and he may comfort*

10a Aristarchus my fellow prisoner greets you, with b Mark the cousin of Barnabas (about whom you received instructions: if he comes to you, welcome him), 11and Jesus who is called Justus. These *are my* only fellow workers for the kingdom of God who are of the circumcision; they have proved to be a comfort to me.

12a Epaphras, who is *one* of you, a bondservant of Christ, greets you, always b laboring fervently for you in prayers, that you may stand c perfect and 1complete in all the will of God. 13For I bear him witness that he has a great 1zeal for you, and those who are in Laodicea, and those in Hierapolis. 14a Luke the beloved physician and b Demas greet you. 15Greet the brethren who are in Laodicea, and 1Nymphas and a the church that *is* in 2his house.

CLOSING EXHORTATIONS AND BLESSING

16Now when a this epistle is read among you, see that it is read also in the church of the Laodiceans, and that you likewise read the *epistle* from Laodicea. 17And say to a Archippus, "Take heed to b the ministry which you have received in the Lord, that you may fulfill it."

18a This salutation by my own hand—Paul. b Remember my chains. Grace *be* with you. Amen.

4:10
a Acts 19:29; 20:4; 27:2; Philem. 24
b Acts 15:37; 2 Tim. 4:11

4:12 a Col. 1:7; Philem. 23
b Rom. 15:30
c Matt. 5:48; 1 Cor. 2:6

4:14 a 2 Tim. 4:11; Philem. 24
b 2 Tim. 4:10

4:15 a Rom. 16:5; 1 Cor. 16:19

4:16
a 1 Thess. 5:27; 2 Thess. 3:14

4:17 a Philem. 2
b 1 Tim. 4:6; 2 Tim. 4:5

4:18 a 1 Cor. 16:21; 2 Thess. 3:17
b Heb. 13:3

4:12 1NU fully assured   4:13 1NU concern   4:15 1NU Nympha   2NU her

THE FIRST EPISTLE OF PAUL
THE APOSTLE TO THE

THESSALONIANS

GREETING

1 Paul, ^aSilvanus, and Timothy,

To the church of the ^bThessalonians in God the Father and the Lord Jesus Christ:

Grace to you and peace ¹from God our Father and the Lord Jesus Christ.

THEIR GOOD EXAMPLE

^{2a}We give thanks to God always for you all, making mention of you in our prayers, ³remembering without ceasing ^ayour work of faith, ^blabor of love, and patience of hope in our Lord Jesus Christ in the sight of our God and Father, ⁴knowing, beloved brethren, ^ayour election by God. ⁵For ^aour gospel did not come to you in word only, but also in power, ^band in the Holy Spirit ^cand in much assurance, as you know what kind of men we were among you for your sake.

⁶And ^ayou became followers of us and of the Lord, having received the word in much affliction, ^bwith joy of the Holy Spirit, ⁷so that you became examples to all in Macedonia and Achaia who believe. ⁸For from you the word of the Lord ^ahas sounded forth, not only in Macedonia and Achaia, but also ^bin every place. Your faith toward God has gone out, so that we do not need to say anything. ⁹For they themselves declare concerning us ^awhat manner of entry we had to you, ^band how you turned to God from idols to serve the living and true God, ¹⁰and ^ato wait for His Son from heaven, whom He raised from the dead, *even* Jesus who delivers us ^bfrom the wrath to come.

PAUL'S CONDUCT
(cf. Acts 17:1–9)

2 For you yourselves know, brethren, that our coming to you was not in vain. ²But ¹even after we had suffered before and were spitefully treated at ^aPhilippi, as you know, we were ^bbold in our God to speak to you the gospel of God in much conflict. ^{3a}For our exhortation *did* not *come* from error or uncleanness, nor *was it* in deceit.

⁴But as ^awe have been approved by God ^bto be entrusted with the gospel, even so we speak, ^cnot as pleasing men, but God ^dwho tests our hearts. ⁵For ^aneither at any time did we use flattering words, as you know, nor a ¹cloak for covetousness—^bGod *is* witness. ^{6a}Nor did we seek glory from men, either from you or from others, when ^bwe might have ^cmade demands ^das apostles of Christ. ⁷But ^awe were gentle among

1:1 ^a1 Pet. 5:12
^bActs 17:1–9

1:2 ^aRom. 1:8;
2 Thess. 1:3

1:3 ^aJohn 6:29
^bRom. 16:6

1:4 ^aCol. 3:12

1:5 ^aMark 16:20
^b2 Cor. 6:6
^cHeb. 2:3

1:6
^a1 Cor. 4:16; 11:1
^bActs 5:41; 13:52;
2 Cor. 6:10;
Gal. 5:22

1:8 ^aRom. 10:18
^bRom. 1:8; 16:19;
2 Cor. 2:14;
2 Thess. 1:4

1:9 ^a1 Thess. 2:1
^b1 Cor. 12:2

1:10 ^a[Rom. 2:7]
^bMatt. 3:7;
Rom. 5:9

2:2 ^aActs 14:5;
16:19–24;
Phil. 1:30
^bActs 17:1–9

2:3 ^a2 Cor. 7:2

2:4 ^a1 Cor. 7:25
^bTitus 1:3
^cGal. 1:10
^dProv. 17:3

2:5 ^a2 Cor. 2:17
^bRom. 1:9;
1 Thess. 2:10

2:6 ^a1 Tim. 5:17
^b1 Cor. 9:4
^c2 Cor. 11:9
^d1 Cor. 9:1

2:7 ^a1 Cor. 2:3

1:1 ¹NU omits *from God our Father and the Lord Jesus Christ*
2:2 ¹NU, M omit *even*   2:5 ¹*pretext for greed*

you, just as a nursing *mother* cherishes her own children. [8]So, affectionately longing for you, we were well pleased [a]to impart to you not only the gospel of God, but also [b]our own lives, because you had become dear to us. [9]For you remember, brethren, our [a]labor and toil; for laboring night and day, [b]that we might not be a burden to any of you, we preached to you the gospel of God.

[10a]You *are* witnesses, and God *also*, [b]how devoutly and justly and blamelessly we behaved ourselves among you who believe; [11]as you know how we exhorted, and comforted, and [1]charged every one of you, as a father *does* his own children, [12a]that you would walk worthy of God [b]who calls you into His own kingdom and glory.

THEIR CONVERSION

[13]For this reason we also thank God [a]without ceasing, because when you [b]received the word of God which you heard from us, you welcomed *it* [c]not *as* the word of men, but as it is in truth, the word of God, which also effectively [d]works in you who believe. [14]For you, brethren, became imitators [a]of the churches of God which are in Judea in Christ Jesus. For [b]you also suffered the same things from your own countrymen, just as they *did* from the Judeans, [15a]who killed both the Lord Jesus and [b]their own prophets, and have persecuted us; and they do not please God [c]and are [1]contrary to all men, [16a]forbidding us to speak to the Gentiles that they may be saved, so as always [b]to fill up *the measure of* their sins; [c]but wrath has come upon them to the uttermost.

LONGING TO SEE THEM

[17]But we, brethren, having been taken away from you for a short time [a]in presence, not in heart, endeavored more eagerly to see your face with great desire. [18]Therefore we wanted to come to you—even I, Paul, time and again—but [a]Satan hindered us. [19]For [a]what *is* our hope, or joy, or [b]crown of rejoicing? *Is it* not even you in the [c]presence of our Lord Jesus Christ [d]at His coming? [20]For you are our glory and joy.

CONCERN FOR THEIR FAITH

3 Therefore, when we could no longer endure it, we thought it good to be left in Athens alone, [2]and sent [a]Timothy, our brother and minister of God, and our fellow laborer in the gospel of Christ, to establish you and encourage you concerning your faith, [3a]that no one should be shaken by these afflictions; for you yourselves know that [b]we are appointed to this. [4a]For, in fact, we told you before when we were with you that we would suffer tribulation, just as it happened, and you know. [5]For this reason, when I could no longer endure it, I sent to know your faith, [a]lest by some means the tempter had tempted you, and [b]our labor might be in vain.

ENCOURAGED BY TIMOTHY

[6a]But now that Timothy has come to us from you, and brought us good news of your faith and love, and that you always have good remembrance of us, greatly desiring to see us, [b]as we also *to see* you— [7]therefore, brethren, in all our

2:8 [a]Rom. 1:11
[b]2 Cor. 12:15;
1 John 3:16

2:9 [a]Acts 18:3;
20:34, 35;
1 Cor. 4:12;
2 Thess. 3:7, 8
[b]2 Cor. 12:13

2:10 [a]2 Cor. 1:12;
1 Thess. 1:5
[b]2 Cor. 7:2

2:12 [a]Eph. 4:1;
Col. 1:10
[b]Rom. 8:28;
1 Cor. 1:9;
1 Thess. 5:24;
2 Thess. 2:14;
[2 Tim. 1:9]

2:13 [a]Rom. 1:8;
1 Thess. 1:2, 3
[b]Mark 4:20
[c][Matt. 10:20;
Gal. 4:14]
[d][1 Pet. 1:23]

2:14 [a]Gal. 1:22
[b]Acts 17:5;
1 Thess. 3:4;
2 Thess. 1:4

2:15
[a]Luke 24:20;
Acts 2:23
[b]Jer. 2:30;
Matt. 5:12;
23:34, 35;
Acts 7:52
[c]Esth. 3:8

2:16 [a]Luke 11:52
[b]Gen. 15:16;
Dan. 8:23;
Matt. 23:32
[c]Matt. 24:6

2:17 [a]1 Cor. 5:3

2:18
[a]Rom. 1:13;
15:22

2:19 [a]2 Cor. 1:14
[b]Prov. 16:31
[c]Jude 24
[d]1 Cor. 15:23

3:2 [a]Rom. 16:21

3:3 [a]Eph. 3:13
[b]John 16:2;
Acts 9:16;
14:22; 1 Cor. 4:9;
2 Tim. 3:12;
1 Pet. 2:21

3:4 [a]Acts 20:24

3:5 [a]1 Cor. 7:5
[b]Gal. 2:2

3:6 [a]Acts 18:5
[b]Phil. 1:8

2:11 [1]NU, M *implored*   2:15 [1]*hostile*

affliction and distress ªwe were comforted concerning you by your faith. 8For now we live, if you ªstand fast in the Lord.

9For what thanks can we render to God for you, for all the joy with which we rejoice for your sake before our God, 10night and day praying exceedingly that we may see your face ªand perfect what is lacking in your faith?

PRAYER FOR THE CHURCH

11Now may our God and Father Himself, and our Lord Jesus Christ, ªdirect our way to you. 12And may the Lord make you increase and ªabound in love to one another and to all, just as we *do* to you, 13so that He may establish ªyour hearts blameless in holiness before our God and Father at the coming of our Lord Jesus Christ with all His saints.

PLEA FOR PURITY

4 Finally then, brethren, we urge and exhort in the Lord Jesus ªthat you should abound more and more, ᵇjust as you received from us how you ought to walk and to please God; 2for you know what commandments we gave you through the Lord Jesus.

3For this is ªthe will of God, ᵇyour sanctification: ᶜthat you should abstain from sexual immorality; 4ªthat each of you should know how to possess his own vessel in sanctification and honor, 5ªnot in passion of lust, ᵇlike the Gentiles ᶜwho do not know God; 6that no one should take advantage of and defraud his brother in this matter, because the Lord ª*is* the avenger of all such, as we also forewarned you and testified. 7For God did not call us to uncleanness, ªbut in holiness. 8ªTherefore he who rejects *this* does not reject man, but God, ᵇwho¹ has also given us His Holy Spirit.

A BROTHERLY AND ORDERLY LIFE

9But concerning brotherly love you have no need that I should write to you, for ªyou yourselves are taught by God ᵇto love one another; 10and indeed you do so toward all the brethren who are in all Macedonia. But we urge you, brethren, ªthat you increase more and more; 11that you also aspire to lead a quiet life, ªto mind your own business, and ᵇto work with your own hands, as we commanded you, 12ªthat you may walk properly toward *those* who are outside, and *that* you may lack nothing.

THE COMFORT OF CHRIST'S COMING

13But I do not want you to be ignorant, brethren, concerning those who have fallen ¹asleep, lest you sorrow ªas others ᵇwho have no hope. 14For ªif we believe that Jesus died and rose again, even so God will bring with Him ᵇthose who ¹sleep in Jesus.

15For this we say to you ªby the word of the Lord, that ᵇwe who are alive *and* remain until the coming of the Lord will by no means precede those who are ¹asleep. 16For ªthe Lord Himself will descend from heaven with a shout, with the voice of an archangel, and with ᵇthe trumpet of God. ᶜAnd the dead in Christ will rise first. 17ªThen we who are alive *and* remain shall be caught up together with them ᵇin the clouds to meet

---

4:8 ¹NU *who also gives*   4:13 ¹Died   4:14 ¹Or *through Jesus sleep*
4:15 ¹Dead

the Lord in the air. And thus [c]we shall always be with the Lord. [18a]Therefore comfort one another with these words.

THE DAY OF THE LORD

5 But concerning [a]the times and the seasons, brethren, you have no need that I should write to you. [2]For you yourselves know perfectly that [a]the day of the Lord so comes as a thief in the night. [3]For when they say, "Peace and safety!" then [a]sudden destruction comes upon them, [b]as labor pains upon a pregnant woman. And they shall not escape. [4a]But you, brethren, are not in darkness, so that this Day should overtake you as a thief. [5]You are all [a]sons of light and sons of the day. We are not of the night nor of darkness. [6a]Therefore let us not sleep, as others *do*, but [b]let us watch and be [1]sober. [7]For [a]those who sleep, sleep at night, and those who get drunk [b]are drunk at night. [8]But let us who are of the day be sober, [a]putting on the breastplate of faith and love, and *as* a helmet the hope of salvation. [9]For [a]God did not appoint us to wrath, [b]but to obtain salvation through our Lord Jesus Christ, [10a]who died for us, that whether we wake or sleep, we should live together with Him.

[11]Therefore [1]comfort each other and [2]edify one another, just as you also are doing.

VARIOUS EXHORTATIONS

[12]And we urge you, brethren, [a]to recognize those who labor among you, and are over you in the Lord and [1]admonish you, [13]and to esteem them very highly in love for their work's sake. [a]Be at peace among yourselves.

[14]Now we [1]exhort you, brethren, [a]warn those who are [2]unruly, [b]comfort the fainthearted, [c]uphold the weak, [d]be patient with all. [15a]See that no one renders evil for evil to anyone, but always [b]pursue what is good both for yourselves and for all.

[16a]Rejoice always, [17a]pray without ceasing, [18]in everything give thanks; for this is the will of God in Christ Jesus for you.

[19a]Do not quench the Spirit. [20a]Do not despise prophecies. [21a]Test all things; [b]hold fast what is good. [22]Abstain from every form of evil.

BLESSING AND ADMONITION

[23]Now may [a]the God of peace Himself [b]sanctify[1] you completely; and may your whole spirit, soul, and body [c]be preserved blameless at the coming of our Lord Jesus Christ. [24]He who calls you *is* [a]faithful, who also will [b]do *it*.

[25]Brethren, pray for us.

[26]Greet all the brethren with a holy kiss.

[27]I charge you by the Lord that this [1]epistle be read to all the [2]holy brethren.

[28]The grace of our Lord Jesus Christ *be* with you. Amen.

4:17
[c]John 14:3; 17:24

4:18
[a]1 Thess. 5:11

5:1 [a]Matt. 24:3

5:2 [a]Luke 21:34;
1 Thess. 5:4;
[2 Pet. 3:10];
Rev. 3:3; 16:15

5:3 [a]Is. 13:6–9
[b]Hos. 13:13

5:4
[a][Acts 26:18];
Rom. 13:12;
Eph. 5:8;
1 John 2:8

5:5 [a]Eph. 5:8

5:6 [a]Matt. 25:5
[b]Matt. 25:13;
Mark 13:35;
[1 Pet. 5:8]

5:7
[a][Luke 21:34]
[b]Acts 2:15;
2 Pet. 2:13

5:8 [a]Is. 59:17;
Eph. 6:14

5:9 [a]Rom. 9:22
[b][2 Thess. 2:13]

5:10 [a]2 Cor. 5:15

5:12
[a]1 Cor. 16:18;
1 Tim. 5:17;
Heb. 13:7, 17

5:13 [a]Mark 9:50

5:14
[a]2 Thess. 3:6,
7, 11 [b]Heb. 12:12
[c]Rom. 14:1; 15:1;
1 Cor. 8:7
[d]Gal. 5:22

5:15 [a]Lev. 19:18
[b]Rom. 12:9;
Gal. 6:10;
1 Thess. 5:21

5:16
[a][2 Cor. 6:10]

5:17 [a]Eph. 6:18

5:19 [a]Eph. 4:30

5:20 [a]Acts 13:1;
1 Cor. 14:1, 31

5:21
[a]1 Cor. 14:29;
1 John 4:1
[b]Phil. 4:8

5:23 [a]Phil. 4:9
[b]1 Thess. 3:13
[c]1 Cor. 1:8, 9

5:24
[a][1 Cor. 10:13];
2 Thess. 3:3
[b]Phil. 1:6

5:6 [1]*self-controlled* 5:11 [1]*Or encourage* [2]*build one another up*
5:12 [1]*instruct* or *warn* 5:14 [1]*encourage* [2]*insubordinate* or *idle*
5:23 [1]*set you apart* 5:27 [1]*letter* [2]NU omits *holy*

THE SECOND EPISTLE OF PAUL
THE APOSTLE TO THE
THESSALONIANS

GREETING

1 Paul, Silvanus, and Timothy,

To the church of the Thessalonians in God our Father and the Lord Jesus Christ:

2ªGrace to you and peace from God our Father and the Lord Jesus Christ.

GOD'S FINAL JUDGMENT AND GLORY

3We are bound to thank God always for you, brethren, as it is fitting, because your faith grows exceedingly, and the love of every one of you all abounds toward each other, 4so that ªwe ourselves boast of you among the churches of God bfor your patience and faith cin all your persecutions and 1tribulations that you endure, 5*which is* ªmanifest1 evidence of the righteous judgment of God, that you may be counted worthy of the kingdom of God, bfor which you also suffer; 6ªsince *it is* a righteous thing with God to repay with 1tribulation those who trouble you, 7and to *give* you who are troubled ªrest with us when bthe Lord Jesus is revealed from heaven with His mighty angels, 8in flaming fire taking vengeance on those who do not know God, and on those who do not obey the gospel of our Lord Jesus Christ. 9ªThese shall be punished with everlasting destruction from the presence of the Lord and bfrom the glory of His power, 10when He comes, in that Day, ªto be bglorified in His saints and to be admired among all those who 1believe, because our testimony among you was believed.

11Therefore we also pray always for you that our God would ªcount you worthy of *this* calling, and fulfill all the good pleasure of *His* goodness and bthe work of faith with power, 12ªthat the name of our Lord Jesus Christ may be glorified in you, and you in Him, according to the grace of our God and the Lord Jesus Christ.

THE GREAT APOSTASY

2 Now, brethren, ªconcerning the coming of our Lord Jesus Christ band our gathering together to Him, we ask you, 2ªnot to be soon shaken in mind or troubled, either by spirit or by word or by letter, as if from us, as though the day of 1Christ had come. 3Let no one deceive you by any means; for *that Day will not come* ªunless the falling away comes first, and bthe man of 1sin is revealed, cthe son of perdition, 4who opposes and ªexalts himself babove all that is called God or

1:4 1*afflictions*   1:5 1*plain*   1:6 1*affliction*   1:10 1NU, M *have believed*
2:2 1NU *the Lord*   2:3 1NU *lawlessness*

that is worshiped, so that he sits [1]as God in the temple of God, showing himself that he is God.

[5]Do you not remember that when I was still with you I told you these things? [6]And now you know what is restraining, that he may be revealed in his own time. [7]For [a]the [1]mystery of lawlessness is already at work; only [2]He who now restrains *will do so* until He is taken out of the way. [8]And then the lawless one will be revealed, [a]whom the Lord will consume [b]with the breath of His mouth and destroy [c]with the brightness of His coming. [9]The coming of the *lawless one* is [a]according to the working of Satan, with all power, [b]signs, and lying wonders, [10]and with all unrighteous deception among [a]those who perish, because they did not receive [b]the love of the truth, that they might be saved. [11]And [a]for this reason God will send them strong delusion, [b]that they should believe the lie, [12]that they all may be condemned who did not believe the truth but [a]had pleasure in unrighteousness.

STAND FAST

[13]But we are [1]bound to give thanks to God always for you, brethren beloved by the Lord, because God [a]from the beginning [b]chose you for salvation [c]through [2]sanctification by the Spirit and belief in the truth, [14]to which He called you by our gospel, for [a]the obtaining of the glory of our Lord Jesus Christ. [15]Therefore, brethren, [a]stand fast and hold [b]the traditions which you were taught, whether by word or our [1]epistle.

[16]Now may our Lord Jesus Christ Himself, and our God and Father, [a]who has loved us and given *us* everlasting consolation and [b]good hope by grace, [17]comfort your hearts [a]and [1]establish you in every good word and work.

PRAY FOR US

3 Finally, brethren, [a]pray for us, that the word of the Lord may run *swiftly* and be glorified, just as *it is* with you, [2]and [a]that we may be delivered from unreasonable and wicked men; [b]for not all have faith.

[3]But [a]the Lord is faithful, who will establish you and [b]guard *you* from the evil one. [4]And [a]we have confidence in the Lord concerning you, both that you do and will do the things we command you.

[5]Now may [a]the Lord direct your hearts into the love of God and into the patience of Christ.

WARNING AGAINST IDLENESS

[6]But we command you, brethren, in the name of our Lord Jesus Christ, [a]that you withdraw [b]from every brother who walks [c]disorderly and not according to the tradition which [1]he received from us. [7]For you yourselves know how you ought to follow us, for we were not disorderly among you; [8]nor did we eat anyone's bread [1]free of charge, but worked with [a]labor and toil night and day, that we might not be a burden to any of you, [9]not because we do not have [a]authority, but to make ourselves an example of how you should follow us.

[10]For even when we were with you, we commanded you

2:7 [a]1 John 2:18
2:8 [a]Dan. 7:10
[b]Is. 11:4;
Rev. 2:16; 19:15
[c]Heb. 10:27
2:9 [a]John 8:41
[b]Deut. 13:1
2:10 [a]2 Cor. 2:15
[b]1 Cor. 16:22
2:11 [a]Rom. 1:28
[b]1 Tim. 4:1
2:12 [a]Rom. 1:32;
1 Cor. 13:6
2:13 [a]Eph. 1:4
[b]1 Thess. 1:4
[c]1 Thess. 4:7;
[1 Pet. 1:2]
2:14 [a]1 Pet. 5:10
2:15 [a]1 Cor. 16:13
[b]Rom. 6:17;
1 Cor. 11:2;
2 Thess. 3:6;
Jude 3
2:16 [a][Rev. 1:5]
[b]Titus 3:7;
1 Pet. 1:3
2:17 [a]1 Cor. 1:8
3:1 [a]Eph. 6:19
3:2 [a]Rom. 15:31
[b]Acts 28:24
3:3 [a]1 Cor. 1:9;
1 Thess. 5:24
[b]John 17:15
3:4 [a]2 Cor. 7:16
3:5 [a]1 Chr. 29:18
3:6 [a]Rom. 16:17
[b]1 Cor. 5:1
[c]1 Thess. 4:11
3:8 [a]1 Thess. 2:9
3:9
[a]1 Cor. 9:4, 6–14

2:4 [1]NU omits *as God*   2:7 [1]*hidden truth*   [2]Or *he*   2:13 [1]*under obligation*
[2]*being set apart by*   2:15 [1]*letter*   2:17 [1]*strengthen*   3:6 [1]NU, M *they*
3:8 [1]Lit. *for nothing*

this: If anyone will not work, neither shall he eat. [11]For we hear that there are some who walk among you in a disorderly manner, not working at all, but are [a]busybodies. [12]Now those who are such we command and [1]exhort through our Lord Jesus Christ [a]that they work in quietness and eat their own bread.

[13]But *as for* you, brethren, [a]do not grow weary *in* doing good. [14]And if anyone does not obey our word in this [1]epistle, note that person and [a]do not keep company with him, that he may be ashamed. [15a]Yet do not count *him* as an enemy, [b]but [1]admonish *him* as a brother.

BENEDICTION

[16]Now may [a]the Lord of peace Himself give you peace always in every way. The Lord *be* with you all.

[17a]The salutation of Paul with my own hand, which is a sign in every [1]epistle; so I write.

[18a]The grace of our Lord Jesus Christ *be* with you all. Amen.

3:11 [a]1 Tim. 5:13;
1 Pet. 4:15

3:12 [a]Eph. 4:28;
1 Thess. 4:11, 12

3:13 [a]2 Cor. 4:1;
Gal. 6:9

3:14 [a]Matt. 18:17

3:15 [a]Lev. 19:17
[b]Titus 3:10

3:16
[a]John 14:27;
Rom. 15:33;
Phil. 4:9

3:17 [a]1 Cor. 16:21

3:18
[a]Rom. 16:20, 24;
1 Thess. 5:28

3:12 [1]*encourage*   **3:14** [1]*letter*   **3:15** [1]*warn*   **3:17** [1]*letter*

THE FIRST EPISTLE OF PAUL THE APOSTLE TO
TIMOTHY

GREETING

1 Paul, an apostle of Jesus Christ, by the commandment of God our Savior and the Lord Jesus Christ, our hope,

²To Timothy, a ᵃtrue son in the faith:

ᵇGrace, mercy, *and* peace from God our Father and Jesus Christ our Lord.

NO OTHER DOCTRINE

³As I urged you ᵃwhen I went into Macedonia—remain in Ephesus that you may ¹charge some ᵇthat they teach no other doctrine, ⁴ᵃnor give heed to fables and endless genealogies, which cause disputes rather than godly edification which is in faith. ⁵Now ᵃthe purpose of the commandment is love ᵇfrom a pure heart, *from* a good conscience, and *from* ¹sincere faith, ⁶from which some, having strayed, have turned aside to ᵃidle talk, ⁷desiring to be teachers of the law, understanding neither what they say nor the things which they affirm.

⁸But we know that the law *is* ᵃgood if one uses it lawfully, ⁹knowing this: that the law is not made for a righteous person, but for *the* lawless and insubordinate, for *the* ungodly and for sinners, for *the* unholy and profane, for murderers of fathers and murderers of mothers, for manslayers, ¹⁰for fornicators, for sodomites, for kidnappers, for liars, for perjurers, and if there is any other thing that is ¹contrary to sound doctrine, ¹¹according to the glorious gospel of the ᵃblessed God which was ᵇcommitted to my trust.

GLORY TO GOD FOR HIS GRACE
(cf. Acts 8:1–3; 9:1–19)

¹²And I thank Christ Jesus our Lord who has ᵃenabled me, ᵇbecause He counted me faithful, ᶜputting *me* into the ministry, ¹³although ᵃI was formerly a blasphemer, a persecutor, and an ¹insolent man; but I obtained mercy because ᵇI did *it* ignorantly in unbelief. ¹⁴ᵃAnd the grace of our Lord was exceedingly abundant, ᵇwith faith and love which are in Christ Jesus. ¹⁵ᵃThis *is* a faithful saying and worthy of all acceptance, that ᵇChrist Jesus came into the world to save sinners, of whom I am chief. ¹⁶However, for this reason I obtained mercy, that in me first Jesus Christ might show all longsuffering, as a pattern to those who are going to believe on Him for everlasting life. ¹⁷Now to ᵃthe King eternal, ᵇimmortal, ᶜinvisible, to ¹God ᵈwho alone is wise, ᵉ*be* honor and glory forever and ever. Amen.

FIGHT THE GOOD FIGHT

¹⁸This ¹charge I commit to you, son Timothy, according to the prophecies previously made concerning you, that by

---

1:2
ᵃActs 16:1, 2;
Rom. 1:7;
2 Tim. 1:2;
Titus 1:4
ᵇGal. 1:3

1:3
ᵃActs 20:1, 3
ᵇRom. 16:17;
2 Cor. 11:4;
Gal. 1:6, 7;
1 Tim. 6:3

1:4
ᵃ1 Tim. 6:3,
4, 20;
Titus 1:14

1:5
ᵃRom. 13:8–10;
Gal. 5:14
ᵇEph. 6:24

1:6
ᵃ1 Tim. 6:4, 20

1:8
ᵃRom. 7:12, 16

1:11 ᵃ1 Tim. 6:15
ᵇ1 Cor. 9:17

1:12 ᵃ1 Cor. 15:10
ᵇ1 Cor. 7:25
ᶜCol. 1:25

1:13 ᵃActs 8:3;
1 Cor. 15:9
ᵇJohn 4:21

1:14 ᵃRom. 5:20;
1 Cor. 3:10;
2 Cor. 4:15;
Gal. 1:13–16
ᵇ1 Thess. 1:3;
1 Tim. 2:15; 4:12;
6:11; 2 Tim. 1:13;
2:22; Titus 2:2

1:15
ᵃ1 Tim. 3:1; 4:9;
2 Tim. 2:11;
Titus 3:8
ᵇIs. 53:5; 61:1;
Hos. 6:1–3;
Matt. 1:21; 9:13

1:17 ᵃPs. 10:16
ᵇRom. 1:23
ᶜHeb. 11:27
ᵈRom. 16:27
ᵉ1 Chr. 29:11

1:3 ¹*command*   1:5 ¹Lit. *unhypocritical*   1:10 ¹*opposed*   1:13 ¹*violently arrogant*   1:17 ¹NU *the only God,*   1:18 ¹*command*

them you may wage the good warfare, [19]having faith and a good conscience, which some having rejected, concerning the faith have suffered shipwreck, [20]of whom are [a]Hymenaeus and [b]Alexander, whom I delivered to Satan that they may learn not to [c]blaspheme.

PRAY FOR ALL MEN

2 Therefore I [1]exhort first of all that supplications, prayers, intercessions, *and* giving of thanks be made for all men, [2a]for kings and [b]all who are in [1]authority, that we may lead a quiet and peaceable life in all godliness and [2]reverence. [3]For this *is* [a]good and acceptable in the sight [b]of God our Savior, [4a]who desires all men to be saved [b]and to come to the knowledge of the truth. [5a]For *there is* one God and [b]one Mediator between God and men, *the* Man Christ Jesus, [6a]who gave Himself a ransom for all, to be testified in due time, [7a]for which I was appointed a preacher and an apostle—I am speaking the truth [1]in Christ *and* not lying—[b]a teacher of the Gentiles in faith and truth.

MEN AND WOMEN IN THE CHURCH

[8]I desire therefore that the men pray [a]everywhere, [b]lifting up holy hands, without wrath and doubting; [9]in like manner also, that the [a]women adorn themselves in modest apparel, with propriety and [1]moderation, not with braided hair or gold or pearls or costly clothing, [10a]but, which is proper for women professing godliness, with good works. [11]Let a woman learn in silence with all submission. [12]And [a]I do not permit a woman to teach or to have authority over a man, but to be in silence. [13]For Adam was formed first, then Eve. [14]And Adam was not deceived, but the woman being deceived, fell into transgression. [15]Nevertheless she will be saved in childbearing if they continue in faith, love, and holiness, with self-control.

QUALIFICATIONS OF OVERSEERS

3 This *is* a faithful saying: If a man desires the position of a [1]bishop, he desires a good work. [2]A bishop then must be blameless, the husband of one wife, temperate, sober-minded, of good behavior, hospitable, able to teach; [3]not [1]given to wine, not violent, [2]not greedy for money, but gentle, not quarrelsome, not [3]covetous; [4]one who rules his own house well, having *his* children in submission with all reverence [5](for if a man does not know how to rule his own house, how will he take care of the church of God?); [6]not a [1]novice, lest being puffed up with pride he fall into the *same* condemnation as the devil. [7]Moreover he must have a good testimony among those who are outside, lest he fall into reproach and the [a]snare of the devil.

QUALIFICATIONS OF DEACONS

[8]Likewise deacons *must be* reverent, not double-tongued, [a]not given to much wine, not greedy for money, [9]holding the [1]mystery of the faith with a pure conscience. [10]But let these

---

1:20
[a]2 Tim. 2:17, 18
[b]2 Tim. 4:14
[c]Acts 13:45

2:2 [a]Ezra 6:10
[b][Rom. 13:1]

2:3 [a]Rom. 12:2
[b]2 Tim. 1:9

2:4
[a]Ezek. 18:23, 32;
John 3:17;
1 Tim. 4:10;
Titus 2:11;
2 Pet. 3:9
[b][John 17:3]

2:5 [a]1 Cor. 8:6;
Gal. 3:20
[b][Heb. 9:15]

2:6 [a]Mark 10:45

2:7
[a]Eph. 3:7, 8;
1 Tim. 1:11;
2 Tim. 1:11
[b][Gal. 1:15, 16]

2:8 [a]Luke 23:34
[b]Ps. 134:2

2:9 [a]1 Pet. 3:3

2:10 [a]1 Pet. 3:4

2:12
[a]1 Cor. 14:34;
Titus 2:5

3:7 [a]1 Tim. 6:9;
2 Tim. 2:26

3:8 [a]Ezek. 44:21

2:1 [1]encourage   2:2 [1]a prominent place   [2]dignity   2:7 [1]NU omits *in Christ*
2:9 [1]discretion   3:1 Lit. *overseer*   3:3 [1]addicted   [2]NU omits *not greedy for money*   [3]loving money   3:6 [1]new convert   3:9 [1]hidden truth

also first be tested; then let them serve as deacons, being *found* blameless. ¹¹Likewise, *their* wives *must be* reverent, not ¹slanderers, temperate, faithful in all things. ¹²Let deacons be the husbands of one wife, ruling *their* children and their own houses well. ¹³For those who have served well as deacons ªobtain for themselves a good standing and great boldness in the faith which is in Christ Jesus.

THE GREAT MYSTERY

¹⁴These things I write to you, though I hope to come to you shortly; ¹⁵but if I am delayed, *I write* so that you may know how you ought to conduct yourself in the house of God, which is the church of the living God, the pillar and ¹ground of the truth. ¹⁶And without controversy great is the ¹mystery of godliness:

ªGod² was manifested in the flesh,
ᵇJustified in the Spirit,
ᶜSeen by angels,
ᵈPreached among the Gentiles,
ᵉBelieved on in the world,
ᶠReceived up in glory.

THE GREAT APOSTASY

4 Now the Spirit ¹expressly says that in latter times some will depart from the faith, giving heed ªto deceiving spirits and doctrines of demons, ²ªspeaking lies in hypocrisy, having their own conscience ᵇseared with a hot iron, ³forbidding to marry, *and commanding* to abstain from foods which God created to be received with thanksgiving by those who believe and know the truth. ⁴For every creature of God *is* good, and nothing is to be refused if it is received with thanksgiving; ⁵for it is ¹sanctified by the word of God and prayer.

A GOOD SERVANT OF JESUS CHRIST

⁶If you instruct the brethren in these things, you will be a good minister of Jesus Christ, ªnourished in the words of faith and of the good doctrine which you have carefully followed. ⁷But ªreject profane and old wives' fables, and ᵇexercise yourself toward godliness. ⁸For ªbodily exercise profits a little, but godliness is profitable for all things, ᵇhaving promise of the life that now is and of that which is to come. ⁹This *is* a faithful saying and worthy of all acceptance. ¹⁰For to this *end* ¹we both labor and suffer reproach, because we trust in the living God, ªwho is *the* Savior of all men, especially of those who believe. ¹¹These things command and teach.

TAKE HEED TO YOUR MINISTRY

¹²Let no one ¹despise your youth, but be an ªexample to the believers in word, in conduct, in love, ²in spirit, in faith, in purity. ¹³Till I come, give attention to reading, to exhortation, to ¹doctrine. ¹⁴ªDo not neglect the gift that is in you, which was given to you by prophecy ᵇwith the laying on of the hands of the eldership. ¹⁵Meditate on these things; give yourself entirely to them, that your progress may be evident

3:13 ªMatt. 25:21
3:16 ª[John 1:14;
1 Pet. 1:20;
1 John 1:2;
3:5, 8]
ᵇ[Matt. 3:16;
Rom. 1:4]
ᶜMatt. 28:2
ᵈActs 10:34;
Rom. 10:18
ᵉRom. 16:26;
2 Cor. 1:19;
Col. 1:6, 23
ᶠLuke 24:51

4:1 ª2 Tim. 3:13;
Rev. 16:14

4:2 ªMatt. 7:15
ᵇEph. 4:19

4:6 ª2 Tim. 3:14

4:7 ª2 Tim. 2:16;
Titus 1:14
ᵇHeb. 5:14

4:8 ª1 Cor. 8:8
ᵇPs. 37:9

4:10 ªPs. 36:6

4:12 ªPhil. 3:17;
Titus 2:7;
1 Pet. 5:3

4:14 ª2 Tim. 1:6
ᵇActs 6:6;
1 Tim. 5:22

3:11 ¹*malicious gossips*   3:15 ¹*foundation, mainstay*   3:16 ¹*hidden truth*
²NU *Who*   4:1 ¹*explicitly*   4:5 ¹*set apart*   4:10 ¹NU *we labor and strive,*
4:12 ¹*look down on your youthfulness*   ²NU omits *in spirit*   4:13 ¹*teaching*

to all. [16]Take heed to yourself and to the doctrine. Continue in them, for in doing this you will save both yourself and those who hear you.

TREATMENT OF CHURCH MEMBERS

5 Do not rebuke an older man, but exhort *him* as a father, younger men as brothers, [2]older women as mothers, younger women as sisters, with all purity.

HONOR TRUE WIDOWS

[3]Honor widows who are really widows. [4]But if any widow has children or grandchildren, let them first learn to show piety at home and [a]to repay their parents; for this is [1]good and acceptable before God. [5]Now she who is really a widow, and left alone, trusts in God and continues in supplications and prayers [a]night and day. [6]But she who lives in [1]pleasure is dead while she lives. [7]And these things command, that they may be blameless. [8]But if anyone does not provide for his own, [a]and especially for those of his household, [b]he has denied the faith [c]and is worse than an unbeliever.

[9]Do not let a widow under sixty years old be taken into the number, *and not unless* she has been the wife of one man, [10]well reported for good works: if she has brought up children, if she has lodged strangers, if she has washed the saints' feet, if she has relieved the afflicted, if she has diligently followed every good work.

[11]But [1]refuse *the* younger widows; for when they have begun to grow wanton against Christ, they desire to marry, [12]having condemnation because they have cast off their first [1]faith. [13]And besides they learn *to be* idle, wandering about from house to house, and not only idle but also gossips and busybodies, saying things which they ought not. [14]Therefore I desire that *the* younger *widows* marry, bear children, manage the house, give no opportunity to the adversary to speak reproachfully. [15]For some have already turned aside after Satan. [16]If any believing [1]man or woman has widows, let them [2]relieve them, and do not let the church be burdened, that it may relieve those who are really widows.

HONOR THE ELDERS

[17]Let the elders who rule well be counted worthy of double honor, especially those who labor in the word and doctrine. [18]For the Scripture says, [a]"You shall not muzzle an ox while it treads out the grain," and, [b]"The laborer *is* worthy of his wages." [19]Do not receive an accusation against an elder except [a]from two or three witnesses. [20]Those who are sinning rebuke in the presence of all, that the rest also may fear.

[21]I charge *you* before God and the Lord Jesus Christ and the [1]elect angels that you observe these things without [a]prejudice, doing nothing with partiality. [22]Do not lay hands on anyone hastily, nor [a]share in other people's sins; keep yourself pure.

[23]No longer drink only water, but use a little wine for your stomach's sake and your frequent [1]infirmities.

5:4 [a]Gen. 45:10
5:5 [a]Acts 26:7
5:8 [a]Is. 58:7; 2 Cor. 12:14 [b]2 Tim. 3:5 [c]Matt. 18:17
5:18 [a]Deut. 25:4; 1 Cor. 9:7–9 [b]Lev. 19:13; Deut. 24:15; Matt. 10:10; Luke 10:7; 1 Cor. 9:14
5:19 [a]Deut. 17:6; 19:15; Matt. 18:16
5:21 [a]Deut. 1:17
5:22 [a]Eph. 5:6, 7; 2 John 11

5:4 [1]NU, M omit *good and*   5:6 [1]*indulgence*   5:11 [1]Refuse to enroll
5:12 [1]Or *solemn promise*   5:16 [1]NU omits *man or*   [2]*give aid to*
5:21 [1]*chosen*   5:23 [1]*illnesses*

²⁴Some men's sins are ᵃclearly evident, preceding *them* to judgment, but those of some *men* follow later. ²⁵Likewise, the good works *of some* are clearly evident, and those that are otherwise cannot be hidden.

HONOR MASTERS

6 Let as many ᵃbondservants as are under the yoke count their own masters worthy of all honor, so that the name of God and *His* doctrine may not be blasphemed. ²And those who have believing masters, let them not despise *them* because they are brethren, but rather serve *them* because those who are benefited are believers and beloved. Teach and exhort these things.

ERROR AND GREED

³If anyone teaches otherwise and does not consent to ᵃwholesome words, *even* the words of our Lord Jesus Christ, ᵇand to the ¹doctrine which accords with godliness, ⁴he is proud, knowing nothing, but is obsessed with disputes and arguments over words, from which come envy, strife, reviling, evil suspicions, ⁵¹useless wranglings of men of corrupt minds and destitute of the truth, who suppose that godliness is a *means of* gain. ²From ᵃsuch withdraw yourself.

⁶Now godliness with ᵃcontentment is great gain. ⁷For we brought nothing into *this* world, *¹and it is* ᵃcertain we can carry nothing out. ⁸And having food and clothing, with these we shall be ᵃcontent. ⁹But those who desire to be rich fall into temptation and a snare, and *into* many foolish and harmful lusts which drown men in destruction and perdition. ¹⁰For the love of money is a root of all *kinds of* evil, for which some have strayed from the faith in their greediness, and pierced themselves through with many sorrows.

THE GOOD CONFESSION

¹¹But you, O man of God, flee these things and pursue righteousness, godliness, faith, love, patience, gentleness. ¹²Fight the good fight of faith, lay hold on eternal life, to which you were also called and have confessed the good confession in the presence of many witnesses. ¹³I urge you in the sight of God who gives life to all things, and *before* Christ Jesus ᵃwho witnessed the good confession before Pontius Pilate, ¹⁴that you keep *this* commandment without spot, blameless until our Lord Jesus Christ's appearing, ¹⁵which He will manifest in His own time, *He who is* the blessed and only ¹Potentate, the King of kings and Lord of lords, ¹⁶who alone has immortality, dwelling in ᵃunapproachable light, ᵇwhom no man has seen or can see, to whom *be* honor and everlasting power. Amen.

INSTRUCTIONS TO THE RICH

¹⁷Command those who are rich in this present age not to be haughty, nor to trust in uncertain ᵃriches but in the living God, who gives us richly all things ᵇto enjoy. ¹⁸*Let them* do good, that they be rich in good works, ready to give, willing to share, ¹⁹ᵃstoring up for themselves a good foundation for the time to come, that they may lay hold on eternal life.

5:24
ᵃGal. 5:19–21

6:1 ᵃEph. 6:5;
Titus 2:9;
1 Pet. 2:18

6:3 ᵃ2 Tim. 1:13
ᵇTitus 1:1

6:5 ᵃ2 Tim. 3:5

6:6 ᵃPhil. 4:11;
Heb. 13:5

6:7 ᵃJob 1:21;
Ps. 49:17;
Eccl. 5:15

6:8
ᵃProv. 30:8, 9

6:13 ᵃMatt. 27:2;
John 18:36, 37

6:16 ᵃDan. 2:22
ᵇJohn 6:46

6:17
ᵃJer. 9:23; 48:7
ᵇEccl. 5:18, 19

6:19
ᵃ[Matt. 6:20, 21;
19:21]

6:3 ¹*teaching*   6:5 ¹NU, M *constant friction*   ²NU omits the rest of v. 5.
6:7 ¹NU omits *and it is certain*   6:15 ¹*Sovereign*

GUARD THE FAITH

²⁰O Timothy! ᵃGuard what was committed to your trust, ᵇavoiding the profane *and* ¹idle babblings and contradictions of what is falsely called knowledge— ²¹by professing it some have strayed concerning the faith.

Grace *be* with you. Amen.

6:20
ᵃ[2 Tim. 1:12, 14]
ᵇTitus 1:14

THE SECOND EPISTLE OF PAUL THE APOSTLE TO

TIMOTHY

GREETING

1 Paul, an apostle of ¹Jesus Christ by the will of God, according to the ᵃpromise of life which is in Christ Jesus,

²To Timothy, a ᵃbeloved son:

Grace, mercy, *and* peace from God the Father and Christ Jesus our Lord.

TIMOTHY'S FAITH AND HERITAGE

³I thank God, whom I serve with a pure conscience, as *my* ᵃforefathers *did,* as without ceasing I remember you in my prayers night and day, ⁴greatly desiring to see you, being mindful of your tears, that I may be filled with joy, ⁵when I call to remembrance ᵃthe ¹genuine faith that is in you, which dwelt first in your grandmother Lois and ᵇyour mother Eunice, and I am persuaded is in you also. ⁶Therefore I remind you ᵃto stir up the gift of God which is in you through the laying on of my hands. ⁷For ᵃGod has not given us a spirit of fear, ᵇbut of power and of love and of a sound mind.

NOT ASHAMED OF THE GOSPEL

⁸ᵃTherefore do not be ashamed of ᵇthe testimony of our Lord, nor of me ᶜHis prisoner, but share with me in the sufferings for the gospel according to the power of God, ⁹who has saved us and called *us* with a holy calling, ᵃnot according to our works, but ᵇaccording to His own purpose and grace which was given to us in Christ Jesus ᶜbefore time began, ¹⁰but ᵃhas now been revealed by the appearing of our Savior Jesus Christ, *who* has abolished death and brought life and immortality to light through the gospel, ¹¹ᵃto which I was appointed a preacher, an apostle, and a teacher ¹of the Gentiles. ¹²For this reason I also suffer these things; nevertheless I am not ashamed, ᵃfor I know whom I have believed and am persuaded that He is able to keep what I have committed to Him until that Day.

BE LOYAL TO THE FAITH

¹³ᵃHold fast ᵇthe pattern of ᶜsound words which you have heard from me, in faith and love which are in Christ Jesus. ¹⁴That good thing which was committed to you, keep by the Holy Spirit who dwells in us.

¹⁵This you know, that all those in Asia have turned away from me, among whom are Phygellus and Hermogenes. ¹⁶The Lord grant mercy to the ᵃhousehold of Onesiphorus, for he often refreshed me, and was not ashamed of my chain; ¹⁷but when he arrived in Rome, he sought me out very zealously

---

1:1 ᵃTitus 1:2

1:2 ᵃ1 Tim. 1:2;
2 Tim. 2:1;
Titus 1:4

1:3 ᵃActs 24:14

1:5 ᵃ1 Tim. 1:5;
4:6 ᵇActs 16:1

1:6 ᵃ1 Tim. 4:14

1:7 ᵃJohn 14:27;
Rom. 8:15;
1 John 4:18
ᵇ[Acts 1:8]

1:8 ᵃ[Mark 8:38;
Luke 9:26;
Rom. 1:16];
2 Tim. 1:12, 16
ᵇ1 Tim. 2:6
ᶜEph. 3:1;
2 Tim. 1:16

1:9
ᵃ[Rom. 3:20];
Eph. 2:8, 9
ᵇRom. 8:28
ᶜRom. 16:25;
Eph. 1:4;
Titus 1:2

1:10 ᵃEph. 1:9

1:11 ᵃActs 9:15

1:12 ᵃ1 Pet. 4:19

1:13 ᵃ2 Tim. 3:14;
Titus 1:9
ᵇRom. 2:20; 6:17
ᶜ1 Tim. 6:3

1:16 ᵃ2 Tim. 4:19

1:1 ¹NU, M *Christ Jesus*   1:5 ¹Lit. *unhypocritical*   1:11 ¹NU omits *of the Gentiles*

and found *me*. [18]The Lord [a]grant to him that he may find mercy from the Lord [b]in that Day—and you know very well how many ways he [c]ministered [1]*to me* at Ephesus.

BE STRONG IN GRACE

2 You therefore, [a]my son, [b]be strong in the grace that is in Christ Jesus. [2]And the things that you have heard from me among many witnesses, commit these to faithful men who will be able to teach others also. [3]You therefore must [a]endure[1] hardship [b]as a good soldier of Jesus Christ. [4a]No one engaged in warfare entangles himself with the affairs of *this* life, that he may please him who enlisted him as a soldier. [5]And also [a]if anyone competes in athletics, he is not crowned unless he competes according to the rules. [6]The hardworking farmer must be first to partake of the crops. [7]Consider what I say, and [1]may the Lord [a]give you understanding in all things.

[8]Remember that Jesus Christ, [a]of the seed of David, [b]was raised from the dead [c]according to my gospel, [9a]for which I suffer trouble as an evildoer, [b]*even* to the point of chains; [c]but the word of God is not chained. [10]Therefore [a]I endure all things for the sake of the [1]elect, [b]that they also may obtain the salvation which is in Christ Jesus with eternal glory.

[11]*This is* a faithful saying:

For [a]if we died with *Him*,
We shall also live with *Him*.
[12] [a]If we endure,
We shall also reign with *Him*.
[b]If we deny *Him*,
He also will deny us.
[13] If we are faithless,
He remains faithful;
He [a]cannot deny Himself.

APPROVED AND DISAPPROVED WORKERS

[14]Remind *them* of these things, [a]charging *them* before the Lord not to [1]strive about words to no profit, to the ruin of the hearers. [15a]Be diligent to present yourself approved to God, a worker who does not need to be ashamed, rightly dividing the word of truth. [16]But shun profane *and* [1]idle babblings, for they will [2]increase to more ungodliness. [17]And their message will spread like cancer. [a]Hymenaeus and Philetus are of this sort, [18]who have strayed concerning the truth, [a]saying that the resurrection is already past; and they overthrow the faith of some. [19]Nevertheless [a]the solid foundation of God stands, having this seal: "The Lord [b]knows those who are His," and, "Let everyone who names the name of [1]Christ depart from iniquity."

[20]But in a great house there are not only [a]vessels of gold and silver, but also of wood and clay, some for honor and some for dishonor. [21]Therefore if anyone cleanses himself from the latter, he will be a vessel for honor, [1]sanctified and useful for the Master, [a]prepared for every good work. [22a]Flee also youthful lusts; but pursue righteousness, faith, love, peace with those who call on the Lord out of a pure heart. [23]But avoid foolish and ignorant disputes, knowing that they generate

---

1:18 [a]Matt. 6:4;
Mark 9:41
[b]2 Thess. 1:10
[c]Heb. 6:10
2:1 [a]1 Tim. 1:2
[b]Eph. 6:10
2:3 [a]2 Tim. 4:5
[b]1 Cor. 9:7;
1 Tim. 1:18
2:4
[a][2 Pet. 2:20]
2:5
[a][1 Cor. 9:25]
2:7 [a]Prov. 2:6
2:8 [a]Rom. 1:3, 4
[b]1 Cor. 15:4
[c]Rom. 2:16
2:9 [a]Acts 9:16
[b]Eph. 3:1
[c]Acts 28:31;
[2 Tim. 4:17]
2:10 [a]Eph. 3:13
[b]2 Cor. 1:6;
1 Thess. 5:9
2:11
[a]Rom. 6:5, 8;
1 Thess. 5:10
2:12
[a][Matt. 19:28];
Luke 22:29;
[Rom. 5:17; 8:17]
[b]Matt. 10:33;
Luke 12:9;
1 Tim. 5:8
2:13
[a]Num. 23:19;
Titus 1:2
2:14
[a]1 Tim. 5:21; 6:4;
2 Tim. 2:23;
Titus 3:9
2:15 [a]1 Tim. 4:13;
2 Pet. 1:10
2:17 [a]1 Tim. 1:20
2:18 [a]1 Cor. 15:12
2:19
[a]Matt. 24:24;
[1 Cor. 3:11]
[b]Num. 16:5;
[Nah. 1:7];
John 10:14, 27
2:20 [a]Rom. 9:21
2:21 [a]2 Cor. 9:8;
[Eph. 2:10];
2 Tim. 3:17
2:22 [a]1 Tim. 6:11

1:18 [1]*to me* from Vg., a few Gr. mss.   2:3 [1]NU *You must share*   2:7 [1]NU *the Lord will give you*   2:10 [1]*chosen ones*   2:14 [1]*battle*   2:16 [1]*empty chatter*
[2]*lead*   2:19 [1]NU, M *the Lord*   2:21 [1]*set apart*

strife. 24And ªa servant of the Lord must not quarrel but be gentle to all, ᵇable to teach, ᶜpatient, 25ªin humility correcting those who are in opposition, ᵇif God perhaps will grant them repentance, ᶜso that they may know the truth, 26and *that* they may come to their senses *and* ªescape the snare of the devil, having been taken captive by him to *do* his will.

PERILOUS TIMES AND PERILOUS MEN

3 But know this, that ªin the last days ¹perilous times will come: 2For men will be lovers of themselves, lovers of money, boasters, proud, blasphemers, disobedient to parents, unthankful, unholy, 3unloving, ¹unforgiving, slanderers, without self-control, brutal, despisers of good, 4ªtraitors, headstrong, haughty, lovers of pleasure rather than lovers of God, 5ªhaving a form of godliness but ᵇdenying its power. And ᶜfrom such people turn away! 6For ªof this sort are those who creep into households and make captives of gullible women loaded down with sins, led away by various lusts, 7always learning and never able ªto come to the knowledge of the truth. 8ªNow as Jannes and Jambres resisted Moses, so do these also resist the truth: ᵇmen of corrupt minds, ᶜdisapproved concerning the faith; 9but they will progress no further, for their folly will be manifest to all, ªas theirs also was.

THE MAN OF GOD AND THE WORD OF GOD

10ªBut you have carefully followed my doctrine, manner of life, purpose, faith, longsuffering, love, perseverance, 11persecutions, afflictions, which happened to me ªat Antioch, ᵇat Iconium, ᶜat Lystra—what persecutions I endured. And ᵈout of *them* all the Lord delivered me. 12Yes, and ªall who desire to live godly in Christ Jesus will suffer persecution. 13ªBut evil men and impostors will grow worse and worse, deceiving and being deceived. 14But you must ªcontinue in the things which you have learned and been assured of, knowing from whom you have learned *them,* 15and that from childhood you have known ªthe Holy Scriptures, which are able to make you wise for salvation through faith which is in Christ Jesus.

16ªAll Scripture *is* given by inspiration of God, ᵇand *is* profitable for doctrine, for reproof, for correction, for ¹instruction in righteousness, 17ªthat the man of God may be complete, ᵇthoroughly equipped for every good work.

PREACH THE WORD

4 I ªcharge *you* ¹therefore before God and the Lord Jesus Christ, ᵇwho will judge the living and the dead 2at His appearing and His kingdom: 2Preach the word! Be ready in season *and* out of season. ªConvince, ᵇrebuke, ᶜexhort, with all longsuffering and teaching. 3ªFor the time will come when they will not endure ᵇsound doctrine, ᶜbut according to their own desires, *because* they have itching ears, they will heap up for themselves teachers; 4and they will turn *their* ears away from the truth, and ªbe turned aside to fables. 5But you be watchful in all things, ªendure afflictions, do the work of ᵇan evangelist, fulfill your ministry.

4:5 ªtim. 1:8 ᵇActs 21:8

3:1 ¹*times of stress* 3:3 ¹*irreconcilable* 3:16 ¹*training, discipline*
4:1 ¹NU omits *therefore* ²NU *and by*

2:24 ªTitus 3:2
ᵇTitus 1:9
ᶜ1 Tim. 3:3;
Titus 1:7

2:25 ªGal. 6:1;
Titus 3:2;
1 Pet. 3:15
ᵇActs 8:22
ᶜ1 Tim. 2:4

2:26 ª1 Tim. 3:7

3:1 ª1 Tim. 4:1;
2 Pet. 3:3;
1 John 2:18;
Jude 17, 18

3:4 ª2 Pet. 2:10

3:5 ªTitus 1:16
ᵇ1 Tim. 5:8
ᶜMatt. 23:3;
2 Thess. 3:6;
1 Tim. 6:5

3:6 ªMatt. 23:14;
Titus 1:11

3:7 ª1 Tim. 2:4

3:8
ªEx. 7:11, 12,
22; 8:7; 9:11
ᵇ1 Tim. 6:5
ᶜRom. 1:28

3:9 ªEx. 7:11, 12;
8:18; 9:11

3:10
ªPhil. 2:20, 22;
1 Tim. 4:6

3:11
ªActs 13:44–52
ᵇActs 14:1–6, 19
ᶜActs 14:8–20
ᵈPs. 34:19

3:12 ª[Ps. 34:19]

3:13
ª2 Thess. 2:11

3:14 ª2 Tim. 1:13;
Titus 1:9

3:15
ªPs. 119:97–104;
John 5:39

3:16
ª[2 Pet. 1:20]
ᵇRom. 4:23; 15:4

3:17 ª1 Tim. 6:11
ᵇ2 Tim. 2:21;
Heb. 13:21

4:1 ª1 Tim. 5:21;
2 Tim. 4:1
ᵇActs 10:42

4:2 ªTitus 2:15
ᵇ1 Tim. 5:20;
Titus 1:13; 2:15
ᶜ1 Tim. 4:13

4:3 ª2 Tim. 3:1
ᵇ1 Tim. 1:10;
2 Tim. 1:13
ᶜIs. 30:9–11;
Jer. 5:30, 31;
2 Tim. 3:6

4:4 ª1 Tim. 1:4

PAUL'S VALEDICTORY

6For [a]I am already being poured out as a drink offering, and the time of [b]my departure is at hand. 7[a]I have fought the good fight, I have finished the race, I have kept the faith. 8Finally, there is laid up for me [a]the crown of righteousness, which the Lord, the righteous [b]Judge, will give to me [c]on that Day, and not to me only but also to all who have loved His appearing.

THE ABANDONED APOSTLE

9Be diligent to come to me quickly; 10for [a]Demas has forsaken me, [b]having loved this present world, and has departed for Thessalonica—Crescens for Galatia, Titus for Dalmatia. 11Only Luke is with me. Get [a]Mark and bring him with you, for he is useful to me for ministry. 12And [a]Tychicus I have sent to Ephesus. 13Bring the cloak that I left with Carpus at Troas when you come—and the books, especially the parchments.

14[a]Alexander the coppersmith did me much harm. May the Lord repay him according to his works. 15You also must beware of him, for he has greatly resisted our words.

16At my first defense no one stood with me, but all forsook me. [a]May it not be charged against them.

THE LORD IS FAITHFUL

17[a]But the Lord stood with me and strengthened me, [b]so that the message might be preached fully through me, and *that* all the Gentiles might hear. Also I was delivered [c]out of the mouth of the lion. 18[a]And the Lord will deliver me from every evil work and preserve *me* for His heavenly kingdom. [b]To Him *be* glory forever and ever. Amen!

COME BEFORE WINTER

19Greet [a]Prisca and Aquila, and the household of [b]Onesiphorus. 20[a]Erastus stayed in Corinth, but [b]Trophimus I have left in Miletus sick.

21Do your utmost to come before winter.

Eubulus greets you, as well as Pudens, Linus, Claudia, and all the brethren.

FAREWELL

22The Lord [1]Jesus Christ be with your spirit. Grace be with you. Amen.

4:6 [a]Phil. 2:17
[b][Phil. 1:23];
2 Pet. 1:14

4:7
[a]1 Cor. 9:24–27;
Phil. 3:13, 14

4:8 [a][1 Cor. 9:25;
2 Tim. 2:5];
James 1:12
[b]John 5:22
[c]2 Tim. 1:12

4:10 [a]Col. 4:14;
Philem. 24
[b]1 John 2:15

4:11
[a]Acts 12:12, 25;
15:37–39;
Col. 4:10

4:12 [a]Acts 20:4;
Eph. 6:21, 22;
Col. 4:7;
Titus 3:12

4:14 [a]Acts 19:33;
1 Tim. 1:20

4:16 [a]Acts 7:60;
[1 Cor. 13:5]

4:17 [a]Deut. 31:6;
Acts 23:11
[b]Acts 9:15;
Phil. 1:12
[c]1 Sam. 17:37;
Ps. 22:21

4:18 [a]Ps. 121:7;
[2 Pet. 2:9]
[b]Rom. 11:36;
Gal. 1:5;
Heb. 13:21;
2 Pet. 3:18

4:19 [a]Acts 18:2;
Rom. 16:3
[b]2 Tim. 1:16

4:20
[a]Acts 19:22;
Rom. 16:23
[b]Acts 20:4;
21:29

4:22 [1]NU omits *Jesus Christ*

THE EPISTLE OF PAUL THE APOSTLE TO
TITUS

GREETING

1 Paul, a bondservant of God and an apostle of Jesus Christ, according to the faith of God's elect and ᵃthe acknowledgment of the truth ᵇwhich accords with godliness, ²in hope of eternal life which God, who ᵃcannot lie, promised before time began, ³but has in due time manifested His word through preaching, which was committed to me according to the commandment of God our Savior;

⁴To ᵃTitus, a true son in *our* common faith:

Grace, mercy, *and* peace from God the Father and ¹the Lord Jesus Christ our Savior.

QUALIFIED ELDERS

⁵For this reason I left you in Crete, that you should ᵃset in order the things that are lacking, and appoint elders in every city as I commanded you— ⁶if a man is blameless, the husband of one wife, ᵃhaving faithful children not accused of ¹dissipation or insubordination. ⁷For a ¹bishop must be blameless, as a steward of God, not self-willed, not quick-tempered, ᵃnot given to wine, not violent, not greedy for money, ⁸but hospitable, a lover of what is good, sober-minded, just, holy, self-controlled, ⁹holding fast the faithful word as he has been taught, that he may be able, by sound doctrine, both to exhort and convict those who contradict.

THE ELDERS' TASK

¹⁰For there are many insubordinate, both idle ᵃtalkers and deceivers, especially those of the circumcision, ¹¹whose mouths must be stopped, who subvert whole households, teaching things which they ought not, ᵃfor the sake of dishonest gain. ¹²ᵃOne of them, a prophet of their own, said, "Cretans *are* always liars, evil beasts, lazy gluttons." ¹³This testimony is true. ᵃTherefore rebuke them sharply, that they may be sound in the faith, ¹⁴not giving heed to Jewish fables and ᵃcommandments of men who turn from the truth. ¹⁵ᵃTo the pure all things are pure, but to those who are defiled and unbelieving nothing is pure; but even their mind and conscience are defiled. ¹⁶They profess to ᵃknow God, but ᵇin works they deny *Him*, being ¹abominable, disobedient, ᶜand disqualified for every good work.

QUALITIES OF A SOUND CHURCH

2 But as for you, speak the things which are proper for sound doctrine: ²that the older men be sober, reverent, temperate, sound in faith, in love, in patience; ³the older women

1:1 ᵃ2 Tim. 2:25
ᵇ[1 Tim. 3:16]

1:2 ᵃNum. 23:19

1:4
ᵃ2 Cor. 2:13; 8:23;
Gal. 2:3;
2 Tim. 4:10

1:5 ᵃ1 Cor. 11:34

1:6
ᵃ1 Tim. 3:2–4;
Titus 1:6–8

1:7 ᵃLev. 10:9

1:10 ᵃJames 1:26

1:11 ᵃ1 Tim. 6:5

1:12 ᵃActs 17:28

1:13
ᵃ2 Cor. 13:10;
2 Tim. 4:2

1:14 ᵃIs. 29:13

1:15 ᵃLuke 11:41;
Rom. 14:14, 20;
1 Cor. 6:12

1:16
ᵃMatt. 7:20–23;
25:12; 1 John 2:4
ᵇ[2 Tim. 3:5, 7]
ᶜRom. 1:28

1:4 ¹NU *Christ Jesus*   1:6 ¹*debauchery,* lit. *incorrigibility*   1:7 ¹Lit. *overseer*
1:16 ¹*detestable*

likewise, that they be reverent in behavior, not slanderers, not given to much wine, teachers of good things— [4]that they admonish the young women to love their husbands, to love their children, [5]*to be* discreet, chaste, [a]homemakers, good, [b]obedient to their own husbands, [c]that the word of God may not be blasphemed.

[6]Likewise, exhort the young men to be sober-minded, [7]in all things showing yourself *to be* [a]a pattern of good works; in doctrine *showing* integrity, reverence, [b]incorruptibility,[1] [8]sound speech that cannot be condemned, that one who is an opponent may be ashamed, having nothing evil to say of [1]you.

[9]*Exhort* [a]bondservants to be obedient to their own masters, to be well pleasing in all *things,* not answering back, [10]not [1]pilfering, but showing all good [2]fidelity, that they may adorn the doctrine of God our Savior in all things.

TRAINED BY SAVING GRACE

[11]For [a]the grace of God that brings salvation has appeared to all men, [12]teaching us that, denying ungodliness and worldly lusts, we should live soberly, righteously, and godly in the present age, [13a]looking for the blessed [b]hope and glorious appearing of our great God and Savior Jesus Christ, [14a]who gave Himself for us, that He might redeem us from every lawless deed [b]and purify for Himself [c]*His* own special people, zealous for good works.

[15]Speak these things, [a]exhort, and rebuke with all authority. Let no one despise you.

GRACES OF THE HEIRS OF GRACE

3 Remind them [a]to be subject to rulers and authorities, to obey, [b]to be ready for every good work, [2]to speak evil of no one, to be peaceable, gentle, showing all humility to all men. [3]For [a]we ourselves were also once foolish, disobedient, deceived, serving various lusts and pleasures, living in malice and envy, hateful and hating one another. [4]But when [a]the kindness and the love of [b]God our Savior toward man appeared, [5a]not by works of righteousness which we have done, but according to His mercy He saved us, through [b]the washing of regeneration and renewing of the Holy Spirit, [6a]whom He poured out on us abundantly through Jesus Christ our Savior, [7]that having been justified by His grace [a]we should become heirs according to the hope of eternal life.

[8a]This is a faithful saying, and these things I want you to affirm constantly, that those who have believed in God should be careful to maintain good works. These things are good and profitable to men.

AVOID DISSENSION

[9]But [a]avoid foolish disputes, genealogies, contentions, and strivings about the law; for they are unprofitable and useless. [10a]Reject a divisive man after the first and second [1]admonition, [11]knowing that such a person is warped and sinning, being self-condemned.

2:5 [a]1 Tim. 5:14
[b]1 Cor. 14:34;
1 Tim. 2:11
[c]Rom. 2:24

2:7 [a]Phil. 3:17;
1 Tim. 4:12
[b]Eph. 6:24

2:9 [a]Eph. 6:5;
1 Tim. 6:1

2:11
[a][Rom. 5:15]

2:13 [a]1 Cor. 1:7
[b][Col. 3:4]

2:14 [a]Is. 53:12;
Gal. 1:4
[b]Ezek. 37:23;
[Heb. 1:3; 9:14;
1 John 1:7]
[c]Ex. 15:16

2:15
[a]1 Tim. 4:13;
5:20;
2 Tim. 4:2

3:1 [a][Rom. 13:1];
1 Pet. 2:13
[b]Col. 1:10

3:3 [a]1 Cor. 6:11;
1 Pet. 4:3

3:4 [a]Titus 2:11
[b]1 Tim. 2:3

3:5
[a][Rom. 3:20];
Eph. 2:4–9
[b]John 3:3

3:6 [a]Ezek. 36:26

3:7
[a][Matt. 25:34];
Mark 10:17;
[Rom. 8:17,
23, 24;
Titus 1:2]

3:8 [a]1 Tim. 1:15

3:9 [a]1 Tim. 1:4;
2 Tim. 2:23

3:10 [a]Matt. 18:17

2:7 [1]NU omits *incorruptibility* **2:8** [1]NU, M *us* **2:10** [1]*thieving* [2]*honesty*
3:10 [1]*warning*

FINAL MESSAGES

12When I send Artemas to you, or ªTychicus, be diligent to come to me at Nicopolis, for I have decided to spend the winter there. 13Send Zenas the lawyer and ªApollos on their journey with haste, that they may lack nothing. 14And let our *people* also learn to maintain good works, to *meet* urgent needs, that they may not be unfruitful.

FAREWELL

15All who *are* with me greet you. Greet those who love us in the faith.

Grace *be* with you all. Amen.

3:12 ªActs 20:4;
Eph. 6:21;
Col. 4:7;
2 Tim. 4:12

3:13 ªActs 18:24;
1 Cor. 16:12

THE EPISTLE OF PAUL THE APOSTLE TO
PHILEMON

GREETING

Paul, a ᵃprisoner of Christ Jesus, and Timothy *our* brother,

To Philemon our beloved *friend* and fellow laborer, ²to ¹the beloved Apphia, ᵃArchippus our fellow soldier, and to the church in your house:

³Grace to you and peace from God our Father and the Lord Jesus Christ.

PHILEMON'S LOVE AND FAITH

⁴ᵃI thank my God, making mention of you always in my prayers, ⁵ᵃhearing of your love and faith which you have toward the Lord Jesus and toward all the saints, ⁶that the sharing of your faith may become effective ᵃby the acknowledgment of ᵇevery good thing which is in ¹you in Christ Jesus. ⁷For we ¹have great ²joy and ³consolation in your love, because the ⁴hearts of the saints have been refreshed by you, brother.

THE PLEA FOR ONESIMUS

⁸Therefore, though I might be very bold in Christ to command you what is fitting, ⁹*yet* for love's sake I rather appeal *to you*—being such a one as Paul, the aged, and now also a prisoner of Jesus Christ— ¹⁰I appeal to you for my son ᵃOnesimus, whom I have begotten *while* in my chains, ¹¹who once was unprofitable to you, but now is profitable to you and to me. ¹²I am sending him ¹back. You therefore receive him, that is, my own ²heart, ¹³whom I wished to keep with me, that on your behalf he might minister to me in my chains for the gospel. ¹⁴But without your consent I wanted to do nothing, ᵃthat your good deed might not be by compulsion, as it were, but voluntary.

¹⁵For perhaps he departed for a while for this *purpose,* that you might receive him forever, ¹⁶no longer as a slave but more than a slave—a beloved brother, especially to me but how much more to you, both in the ᵃflesh and in the Lord.

PHILEMON'S OBEDIENCE ENCOURAGED

¹⁷If then you count me as a partner, receive him as *you would* me. ¹⁸But if he has wronged you or owes anything, put that on my account. ¹⁹I, Paul, am writing with my own ᵃhand. I will repay—not to mention to you that you owe me even your own self besides. ²⁰Yes, brother, let me have joy from you in the Lord; refresh my heart in the Lord.

1 ᵃEph. 3:1
2 ᵃCol. 4:17
4 ᵃEph. 1:16; 1 Thess. 1:2; 2 Thess. 1:3
5 ᵃEph. 1:15; Col. 1:4; 1 Thess. 3:6
6 ᵃPhil. 1:9; [Col. 1:9; 3:10; James 2:14–17] ᵇ[1 Thess. 5:18]
10 ᵃCol. 4:9
14 ᵃ2 Cor. 9:7; 1 Pet. 5:2
16 ᵃEph. 6:5; Col. 3:22
19 ᵃ1 Cor. 16:21; Gal. 6:11; 2 Thess. 3:17

2 ¹NU *our sister Apphia*   6 ¹NU, M *us*   7 ¹NU *had*   ²M *thanksgiving*   ³*comfort*   ⁴Lit. *inward parts,* heart, liver, and lungs   12 ¹NU *back to you in person, that is, my own heart,*   ²See v. 7.

²¹ᵃHaving confidence in your obedience, I write to you, knowing that you will do even more than I say. ²²But, meanwhile, also prepare a guest room for me, for ᵃI trust that ᵇthrough your prayers I shall be granted to you.

FAREWELL

²³ᵃEpaphras, my fellow prisoner in Christ Jesus, greets you, ²⁴*as do* ᵃMark, ᵇAristarchus, ᶜDemas, ᵈLuke, my fellow laborers.

²⁵ᵃThe grace of our Lord Jesus Christ *be* with your spirit. Amen.

21 ᵃ2 Cor. 7:16

22
ᵃPhil. 1:25; 2:24
ᵇ2 Cor. 1:11

23
ᵃCol. 1:7; 4:12

24
ᵃActs 12:12, 25;
15:37–39;
Col. 4:10
ᵇActs 19:29;
27:2; Col. 4:10
ᶜCol. 4:14;
2 Tim. 4:10
ᵈ2 Tim. 4:11

25 ᵃ2 Tim. 4:22

THE EPISTLE TO THE
HEBREWS

GOD'S SUPREME REVELATION
(cf. John 1:1–4)

1 God, who ¹at various times and ᵃin various ways spoke in time past to the fathers by the prophets, ²has in these last days spoken to us by *His* Son, whom He has appointed heir of all things, through whom also He made the ¹worlds; ³ᵃwho being the brightness of *His* glory and the express ᵇimage of His person, and ᶜupholding all things by the word of His power, ᵈwhen He had ¹by Himself ²purged ³our sins, ᵉsat down at the right hand of the Majesty on high, ⁴having become so much better than the angels, as ᵃHe has by inheritance obtained a more excellent name than they.

THE SON EXALTED ABOVE ANGELS

⁵For to which of the angels did He ever say:

ᵃ"You are My Son,
    Today I have begotten You"?

And again:

ᵇ"I will be to Him a Father,
    And He shall be to Me a Son"?

⁶But when He again brings ᵃthe firstborn into the world, He says:

ᵇ"Let all the angels of God worship Him."

⁷And of the angels He says:

ᵃ"Who makes His angels spirits
    And His ministers a flame of fire."

⁸But to the Son *He says:*

ᵃ"Your throne, O God, *is* forever and ever;
    A ¹scepter of righteousness *is* the scepter of
        Your kingdom.
⁹ You have loved righteousness and hated
        lawlessness;
    Therefore God, Your God, ᵃhas anointed You
    With the oil of gladness more than Your
        companions."

¹⁰And:

ᵃ"You, LORD, in the beginning laid the foundation
        of the earth,
    And the heavens are the work of Your hands.
¹¹ ᵃThey will perish, but You remain;
    And ᵇthey will all grow old like a garment;

1:1
ᵃNum. 12:6, 8;
    Joel 2:28

1:3 ᵃJohn 1:14
ᵇ2 Cor. 4:4;
    Col. 1:15
ᶜCol. 1:17
ᵈ[Heb. 7:27]
ᵉPs. 110:1

1:4 ᵃIs. 9:6, 7;
Luke 1:32, 33;
[Phil. 2:9, 10]

1:5 ᵃPs. 2:7;
Acts 13:33;
Heb. 5:5
ᵇ2 Sam. 7:14

1:6 ᵃPs. 89:27;
[Rom. 8:29]
ᵇDeut. 32:43,
LXX, DSS;
Ps. 97:7;
1 Pet. 3:22;
Rev. 5:11–13

1:7 ᵃPs. 104:4

1:8 ᵃPs. 45:6, 7

1:9 ᵃIs. 61:1, 3

1:10
ᵃPs. 102:25–27

1:11 ᵃ[Is. 34:4]
ᵇIs. 50:9; 51:6;
Heb. 8:13

1:1 ¹Or *in many portions*   1:2 ¹Or *ages*, Gr. *aiones*, aeons   1:3 ¹NU omits *by Himself*   ²cleansed   ³NU omits *our*   1:8 ¹A ruler's staff

12 Like a cloak You will fold them up,
And they will be changed.
But You are the ᵃsame,
And Your years will not fail."

13But to which of the angels has He ever said:

ᵃ"Sit at My right hand,
Till I make Your enemies Your footstool"?

14aAre they not all ministering spirits sent forth to minister for those who will ᵇinherit salvation?

DO NOT NEGLECT SALVATION

2 Therefore we must give ¹the more earnest heed to the things we have heard, lest we drift away. 2For if the word ᵃspoken through angels proved steadfast, and ᵇevery transgression and disobedience received a just ¹reward, 3ahow shall we escape if we neglect so great a salvation, ᵇwhich at the first began to be spoken by the Lord, and was ᶜconfirmed to us by those who heard *Him,* 4aGod also bearing witness ᵇboth with signs and wonders, with various miracles, and ᶜgifts¹ of the Holy Spirit, ᵈaccording to His own will?

THE SON MADE LOWER THAN ANGELS
(cf. Ps. 8:1–9)

5For He has not put ᵃthe world to come, of which we speak, in subjection to angels. 6But one testified in a certain place, saying:

ᵃ"What is man that You are mindful of him,
Or the son of man that You take care of him?
7 You have made him ¹a little lower than the angels;
You have crowned him with glory and honor,
²And set him over the works of Your hands.
8 ᵃYou have put all things in subjection under his feet."

For in that He put all in subjection under him, He left nothing *that is* not put under him. But now ᵇwe do not yet see all things put under him. 9But we see Jesus, ᵃwho was made ¹a little lower than the angels, for the suffering of death ᵇcrowned with glory and honor, that He, by the grace of God, might taste death ᶜfor everyone.

BRINGING MANY SONS TO GLORY

10For it was fitting for Him, ᵃfor whom *are* all things and by whom *are* all things, in bringing many sons to glory, to make the captain of their salvation ᵇperfect through sufferings. 11For ᵃboth He who ¹sanctifies and those who are being sanctified ᵇ*are* all of one, for which reason ᶜHe is not ashamed to call them brethren, 12saying:

ᵃ"I will declare Your name to My brethren;
In the midst of the assembly I will sing praise to You."

13And again:

ᵃ"I will put My trust in Him."

1:12 ᵃHeb. 13:8

1:13 ᵃPs. 110:1;
Matt. 22:44;
Heb. 1:3

1:14 ᵃPs. 103:20;
Dan. 7:10
ᵇRom. 8:17

2:2 ᵃDeut. 33:2;
Acts 7:53;
Gal. 3:19
ᵇNum. 15:30

2:3 ᵃHeb. 10:28
ᵇMatt. 4:17
ᶜMark 16:20;
Luke 1:2;
1 John 1:1

2:4 ᵃMark 16:20
ᵇActs 2:22, 43;
2 Cor. 12:2
ᶜ1 Cor. 12:4, 7, 11;
Eph. 4:7
ᵈEph. 1:5, 9

2:5 ᵃ[2 Pet. 3:13]

2:6 ᵃJob 7:17;
Ps. 8:4–6

2:8 ᵃMatt. 28:18
ᵇPs. 8:6;
1 Cor. 15:25, 27

2:9 ᵃPhil. 2:7–9;
Heb. 1:9
ᵇActs 2:33; 3:13;
1 Pet. 1:21
ᶜIs. 53:12;
[John 3:16]

2:10 ᵃCol. 1:16
ᵇHeb. 5:8, 9;
7:28

2:11 ᵃHeb. 10:10
ᵇActs 17:26
ᶜMatt. 28:10

2:12 ᵃPs. 22:22

2:13
ᵃ2 Sam. 22:3;
Is. 8:17

2:1 ¹*all the more careful attention*   2:2 ¹*retribution* or *penalty*
2:4 ¹*distributions*   2:7 ¹Or *for a little while*   ²NU, M omit the rest of v. 7.
2:9 ¹Or *for a little while*   2:11 ¹*sets apart*

And again:

[b]"Here am I and the children whom God has given Me."

[14]Inasmuch then as the children have partaken of flesh and blood, He [a]Himself likewise shared in the same, [b]that through death He might destroy him who had the power of [c]death, that is, the devil, [15]and release those who [a]through fear of death were all their lifetime subject to bondage. [16]For indeed He does not [1]give aid to angels, but He does [2]give aid to the seed of Abraham. [17]Therefore, in all things He had [a]to be made like *His* brethren, that He might be [b]a merciful and faithful High Priest in things *pertaining* to God, to make propitiation for the sins of the people. [18][a]For in that He Himself has suffered, being [1]tempted, He is able to aid those who are tempted.

THE SON WAS FAITHFUL

3 Therefore, holy brethren, partakers of the heavenly calling, consider the Apostle and High Priest of our confession, Christ Jesus, [2]who was faithful to Him who appointed Him, as [a]Moses also *was faithful* in all His house. [3]For this One has been counted worthy of more glory than Moses, inasmuch as [a]He who built the house has more honor than the house. [4]For every house is built by someone, but [a]He who built all things *is* God. [5a]And Moses indeed *was* faithful in all His house as [b]a servant, [c]for a testimony of those things which would be spoken *afterward,* [6]but Christ as [a]a Son over His own house, [b]whose house we are [c]if we hold fast the confidence and the rejoicing of the hope [1]firm to the end.

BE FAITHFUL
(Ps. 95:7–11)

[7]Therefore, as [a]the Holy Spirit says:

[b]"Today, if you will hear His voice,
[8] Do not harden your hearts as in the rebellion,
    In the day of trial in the wilderness,
[9] Where your fathers tested Me, tried Me,
    And saw My works forty years.
[10] Therefore I was angry with that generation,
    And said, 'They always go astray in *their* heart,
    And they have not known My ways.'
[11] So I swore in My wrath,
    'They shall not enter My rest.' "

[12]Beware, brethren, lest there be in any of you an evil heart of unbelief in departing from the living God; [13]but [1]exhort one another daily, while it is called "Today," lest any of you be hardened through the deceitfulness of sin. [14]For we have become partakers of Christ if we hold the beginning of our confidence steadfast to the end, [15]while it is said:

[a]"Today, if you will hear His voice,
    Do not harden your hearts as in the rebellion."

FAILURE OF THE WILDERNESS WANDERERS

[16a]For who, having heard, rebelled? Indeed, *was it* not all who came out of Egypt, *led* by Moses? [17]Now with whom

2:13 [b]Is. 8:18
2:14 [a]John 1:14
[b]Col. 2:15
[c][1 Cor. 15:54–57]; 2 Tim. 1:10
2:15 [a]Ps. 68:18; Is. 42:7; 45:13; 49:9; 61:1; [Luke 1:74]
2:17 [a]Phil. 2:7; Heb. 2:14
[b][Heb. 4:15; 5:1–10]
2:18 [a][Heb. 4:15, 16]
3:2 [a]Ex. 40:16; Num. 12:7; Heb. 3:5
3:3 [a]Zech. 6:12, 13
3:4 [a][Eph. 2:10]
3:5 [a]Ex. 40:16; Num. 12:7; Heb. 3:2
[b]Ex. 14:31; Num. 12:7
[c]Deut. 18:15, 18, 19
3:6 [a]Ps. 2:7; 110:4; Heb. 1:2
[b][1 Cor. 3:16]; 1 Tim. 3:15
[c][Matt. 10:22]
3:7 [a]Acts 1:16
[b]Ps. 95:7–11; Heb. 3:15; 4:7
3:15 [a]Ps. 95:7, 8
3:16 [a]Num. 14:2, 11, 30; Deut. 1:35, 36, 38

was He angry forty years? *Was it* not with those who sinned, [a]whose corpses fell in the wilderness? [18]And [a]to whom did He swear that they would not enter His rest, but to those who did not obey? [19]So we see that they could not enter in because of [a]unbelief.

THE PROMISE OF REST

4 Therefore, since a promise remains of entering His rest, [a]let us fear lest any of you seem to have come short of it. [2]For indeed the gospel was preached to us as well as to them; but the word which they heard did not profit them, [1]not being mixed with faith in those who heard *it.* [3]For we who have believed do enter that rest, as He has said:

[a]"So I swore in My wrath,
'They shall not enter My rest,'"

although the works were finished from the foundation of the world. [4]For He has spoken in a certain place of the seventh *day* in this way: [a]"And God rested on the seventh day from all His works"; [5]and again in this *place:* [a]"They shall not enter My rest."

[6]Since therefore it remains that some *must* enter it, and those to whom it was first preached did not enter because of disobedience, [7]again He designates a certain day, saying in David, "Today," after such a long time, as it has been said:

[a]"Today, if you will hear His voice,
Do not harden your hearts."

[8]For if [1]Joshua had [a]given them rest, then He would not afterward have spoken of another day. [9]There remains therefore a rest for the people of God. [10]For he who has entered His rest has himself also ceased from his works as God *did* from His.

THE WORD DISCOVERS OUR CONDITION

[11a]Let us therefore be diligent to enter that rest, lest anyone fall according to the same example of disobedience. [12]For the word of God *is* [a]living and powerful, and [b]sharper than any [c]two-edged sword, piercing even to the division of soul and spirit, and of joints and marrow, and is [d]a discerner of the thoughts and intents of the heart. [13a]And there is no creature hidden from His sight, but all things *are* [b]naked and open to the eyes of Him to whom we *must give* account.

OUR COMPASSIONATE HIGH PRIEST

[14]Seeing then that we have a great [a]High Priest who has passed through the heavens, Jesus the Son of God, [b]let us hold fast *our* confession. [15]For [a]we do not have a High Priest who cannot sympathize with our weaknesses, but [b]was in all *points* tempted as *we are,* [c]yet without sin. [16a]Let us therefore come boldly to the throne of grace, that we may obtain mercy and find grace to help in time of need.

QUALIFICATIONS FOR HIGH PRIESTHOOD

5 For every high priest taken from among men [a]is appointed for men in things *pertaining* to God, that he may offer both gifts and sacrifices for sins. [2]He can [1]have compassion

3:17
[a]Num. 14:22, 23

3:18
[a]Num. 14:30

3:19
[a]Num. 14:1–39;
1 Cor. 10:11, 12

4:1 [a]2 Cor. 6:1;
[Gal. 5:4];
Heb. 12:15

4:3 [a]Ps. 95:11;
Heb. 3:11

4:4 [a]Gen. 2:2;
Ex. 20:11; 31:17

4:5 [a]Ps. 95:11

4:7 [a]Ps. 95:7, 8

4:8 [a]Josh. 22:4

4:11 [a]2 Pet. 1:10

4:12 [a]Ps. 147:15
[b]Is. 49:2
[c]Eph. 6:17;
Rev. 2:12
[d][John 12:48];
1 Cor. 14:24, 25

4:13 [a]2 Chr. 16:9;
Ps. 33:13–15;
90:8
[b]Job 26:6;
Prov. 15:11

4:14
[a]Heb. 2:17; 7:26
[b]Heb. 10:23

4:15 [a]Is. 53:3–5
[b]Luke 22:28
[c]2 Cor. 5:21;
Heb. 7:26

4:16 [a][Eph. 2:18;
Heb. 10:19, 22]

5:1
[a]Heb. 2:17; 8:3

4:2 [1]NU, M *since they were not united by faith with those who heeded it*
4:8 [1]Gr. *Jesus,* same as Heb. *Joshua*   5:2 [1]*deal gently with*

on those who are ignorant and going astray, since he himself is also subject to [a]weakness. [3]Because of this he is required as for the people, so also for [a]himself, to offer *sacrifices* for sins. [4]And no man takes this honor to himself, but he who is called by God, just as [a]Aaron *was.*

A PRIEST FOREVER

[5a]So also Christ did not glorify Himself to become High Priest, but *it was* He who said to Him:

[b]"You are My Son,
    Today I have begotten You."

[6]As *He* also says in another *place:*

[a]"You *are* a priest forever
    According to the order of Melchizedek";

[7]who, in the days of His flesh, when He had [a]offered up prayers and supplications, [b]with vehement cries and tears to Him [c]who was able to save Him from death, and was heard [d]because of His godly fear, [8]though He was a Son, *yet* He learned [a]obedience by the things which He suffered. [9]And [a]having been perfected, He became the author of eternal salvation to all who obey Him, [10]called by God as High Priest [a]"according to the order of Melchizedek," [11]of whom [a]we have much to say, and hard to explain, since you have become [b]dull of hearing.

SPIRITUAL IMMATURITY

[12]For though by this time you ought to be teachers, you need *someone* to teach you again the first principles of the [1]oracles of God; and you have come to need [a]milk and not solid food. [13]For everyone who partakes *only* of milk *is* unskilled in the word of righteousness, for he is [a]a babe. [14]But solid food belongs to those who are [1]of full age, *that is,* those who by reason of [2]use have their senses exercised [a]to discern both good and evil.

THE PERIL OF NOT PROGRESSING

6 Therefore, [a]leaving the discussion of the elementary *principles* of Christ, let us go on to [1]perfection, not laying again the foundation of repentance from [b]dead works and of faith toward God, [2a]of the doctrine of baptisms, [b]of laying on of hands, [c]of resurrection of the dead, [d]and of eternal judgment. [3]And this [1]we will do if God permits.

[4]For *it is* impossible for those who were once enlightened, and have tasted [a]the heavenly gift, and [b]have become partakers of the Holy Spirit, [5]and have tasted the good word of God and the powers of the age to come, [6]if they fall away, to renew them again to repentance, [a]since they crucify again for themselves the Son of God, and put *Him* to an open shame.

[7]For the earth which drinks in the rain that often comes upon it, and bears herbs useful for those by whom it is cultivated, [a]receives blessing from God; [8a]but if it bears thorns and briers, *it is* rejected and near to being cursed, whose end *is* to be burned.

5:2 [a]Heb. 7:28
5:3 [a]Lev. 9:7; 16:6; [Heb. 7:27; 9:7]
5:4 [a]Ex. 28:1; Num. 16:40; 1 Chr. 23:13
5:5 [a]John 8:54 [b]Ps. 2:7
5:6 [a]Ps. 110:4; Heb. 7:17
5:7 [a]Matt. 26:39, 42, 44; Mark 14:36, 39; Luke 22:41, 44 [b]Ps. 22:1 [c]Matt. 26:53 [d]Matt. 26:39
5:8 [a]Phil. 2:8
5:9 [a]Heb. 2:10
5:10 [a]Ps. 110:4
5:11 [a][John 16:12]; Heb. 7:1–22 [b][Matt. 13:15]
5:12 [a]1 Cor. 3:1–3; 1 Pet. 2:2
5:13 [a]Eph. 4:14
5:14 [a]Is. 7:15; Phil. 1:9
6:1 [a]Heb. 5:12 [b][Heb. 9:14]
6:2 [a]John 3:25; Acts 19:3–5 [b][Acts 8:17] [c]Acts 17:31 [d]Acts 24:25
6:4 [a][John 4:10]; Eph. 2:8 [b][Gal. 3:2, 5]; Heb. 2:4
6:6 [a]Heb. 10:29
6:7 [a]Ps. 65:10
6:8 [a]Is. 5:6

5:12 [1]*sayings,* Scriptures   5:14 [1]*mature*   [2]*practice*   6:1 [1]*maturity*
6:3 [1]M *let us do*   6:6 [1]Or *and have fallen away*

A BETTER ESTIMATE

⁹But, beloved, we are confident of better things concerning you, yes, things that accompany salvation, though we speak in this manner. ¹⁰For ᵃGod *is* not unjust to forget ᵇyour work and ¹labor of love which you have shown toward His name, *in that* you have ᶜministered to the saints, and do minister. ¹¹And we desire that each one of you show the same diligence ᵃto the full assurance of hope until the end, ¹²that you do not become ¹sluggish, but imitate those who through faith and patience ᵃinherit the promises.

GOD'S INFALLIBLE PURPOSE IN CHRIST

¹³For when God made a promise to Abraham, because He could swear by no one greater, ᵃHe swore by Himself, ¹⁴saying, ᵃ"Surely blessing I will bless you, and multiplying I will multiply you." ¹⁵And so, after he had patiently endured, he obtained the ᵃpromise. ¹⁶For men indeed swear by the greater, and ᵃan oath for confirmation *is* for them an end of all dispute. ¹⁷Thus God, determining to show more abundantly to ᵃthe heirs of promise ᵇthe ¹immutability of His counsel, ²confirmed *it* by an oath, ¹⁸that by two ¹immutable things, in which it *is* impossible for God to ᵃlie, we ²might have strong consolation, who have fled for refuge to lay hold of the hope ᵇset before *us.*

¹⁹This *hope* we have as an anchor of the soul, both sure and steadfast, ᵃand which enters the *Presence* behind the veil, ²⁰ᵃwhere the forerunner has entered for us, *even* Jesus, ᵇhaving become High Priest forever according to the order of Melchizedek.

THE KING OF RIGHTEOUSNESS
(Gen. 14:17–20)

7 For this ᵃMelchizedek, king of Salem, priest of the Most High God, who met Abraham returning from the slaughter of the kings and blessed him, ²to whom also Abraham gave a tenth part of all, first being translated "king of righteousness," and then also king of Salem, meaning "king of peace," ³without father, without mother, without genealogy, having neither beginning of days nor end of life, but made like the Son of God, remains a priest continually.

⁴Now consider how great this man *was,* to whom even the patriarch Abraham gave a tenth of the ¹spoils. ⁵And indeed ᵃthose who are of the sons of Levi, who receive the priesthood, have a commandment to receive tithes from the people according to the law, that is, from their brethren, though they have come from the loins of Abraham; ⁶but he whose genealogy is not derived from them received tithes from Abraham ᵃand blessed ᵇhim who had the promises. ⁷Now beyond all contradiction the lesser is blessed by the better. ⁸Here mortal men receive tithes, but there he *receives them,* ᵃof whom it is witnessed that he lives. ⁹Even Levi, who receives tithes, paid tithes through Abraham, so to speak, ¹⁰for he was still in the loins of his father when Melchizedek met him.

6:10 ᵃRom. 3:4
ᵇ1 Thess. 1:3
ᶜRom. 15:25;
Heb. 10:32–34

6:11 ᵃCol. 2:2

6:12 ᵃHeb. 10:36

6:13
ᵃGen. 22:16, 17;
Luke 1:73

6:14
ᵃGen. 22:16, 17

6:15
ᵃGen. 12:4; 21:5

6:16 ᵃEx. 22:11

6:17 ᵃRom. 8:17;
Heb. 11:9
ᵇRom. 11:29

6:18
ᵃNum. 23:19;
1 Sam. 15:29;
Titus 1:2
ᵇ[Col. 1:5];
Heb. 3:6;
7:19; 12:1

6:19
ᵃLev. 16:2, 15;
Heb. 9:3, 7

6:20
ᵃ[John 14:2;
Heb. 4:14]
ᵇGen. 14:17–19;
Ps. 110:4;
Heb. 3:1; 5:10, 11

7:1
ᵃGen. 14:18–20;
Heb. 7:6

7:5
ᵃNum. 18:21–26;
2 Chr. 31:4

7:6
ᵃGen. 14:19, 20
ᵇ[Rom. 4:13]

7:8 ᵃHeb. 5:6;
6:20; [Rev. 1:18]

6:10 ¹NU omits *labor of*   6:12 ¹lazy   6:17 ¹*unchangeableness of His purpose*
²*guaranteed*   6:18 ¹*unchangeable*   ²M omits *might*   7:4 ¹*plunder*

NEED FOR A NEW PRIESTHOOD
(Ps. 110:4)

[11a]Therefore, if perfection were through the Levitical priesthood (for under it the people received the law), what further need *was there* that another priest should rise according to the order of Melchizedek, and not be called according to the order of Aaron? [12]For the priesthood being changed, of necessity there is also a change of the law. [13]For He of whom these things are spoken belongs to another tribe, from which no man has [1]officiated at the altar.

[14]For *it is* evident that [a]our Lord arose from [b]Judah, of which tribe Moses spoke nothing concerning [1]priesthood. [15]And it is yet far more evident if, in the likeness of Melchizedek, there arises another priest [16]who has come, not according to the law of a fleshly commandment, but according to the power of an endless life. [17]For [1]He testifies:

[a]"You *are* a priest forever
According to the order of Melchizedek."

[18]For on the one hand there is an annulling of the former commandment because of [a]its weakness and unprofitableness, [19]for [a]the law made nothing [1]perfect; on the other hand, *there is the* bringing in of [b]a better hope, through which [c]we draw near to God.

GREATNESS OF THE NEW PRIEST

[20]And inasmuch as He *was* not *made priest* without an oath [21](for they have become priests without an oath, but He with an oath by Him who said to Him:

[a]"The LORD has sworn
And will not relent,
'You *are* a priest [1]forever
According to the order of Melchizedek'"),

[22]by so much more Jesus has become a [1]surety of a [a]better covenant.

[23]Also there were many priests, because they were prevented by death from continuing. [24]But He, because He continues forever, has an unchangeable priesthood. [25]Therefore He is also [a]able to save [1]to the uttermost those who come to God through Him, since He always lives [b]to make intercession for them.

[26]For such a High Priest was fitting for us, [a]who is holy, [1]harmless, undefiled, separate from sinners, [b]and has become higher than the heavens; [27]who does not need daily, as those high priests, to offer up sacrifices, first for His [a]own sins and then for the people's, for this He did once for all when He offered up Himself. [28]For the law appoints as high priests men who have weakness, but the word of the oath, which came after the law, *appoints* the Son who has been perfected forever.

THE NEW PRIESTLY SERVICE

8 Now *this is* the main point of the things we are saying: We have such a High Priest, [a]who is seated at the right hand

7:11 [a][Rom. 7:7–14]; Gal. 2:21; Heb. 7:18; 8:7

7:14 [a]Gen. 49:8–10; Num. 24:17; Is. 1:1; Mic. 5:2; Matt. 1:3; 2:6; Rev. 5:5 [b]Matt. 1:2

7:17 [a]Ps. 110:4; Heb. 5:6; 6:20; 7:21

7:18 [a][Rom. 8:3]; Gal. 3:21; Heb. 7:11

7:19 [a][Acts 13:39]; Rom. 3:20; 7:7; Gal. 2:16; 3:21; Heb. 9:9; 10:1 [b]Heb. 6:18, 19 [c]Lam. 3:57; Rom. 5:2; [Eph. 2:18]; Heb. 4:16; James 4:8

7:21 [a]Ps. 110:4; Heb. 5:6; 7:17

7:22 [a]Heb. 8:6

7:25 [a]Jude 24 [b]Rom. 8:34; 1 Tim. 2:5; Heb. 9:24; 1 John 2:1

7:26 [a][2 Cor. 5:21]; Heb. 4:15 [b]Eph. 1:20

7:27 [a]Lev. 9:7; 16:6; Heb. 5:3

8:1 [a]Ps. 68:18; 110:1; Eph. 1:20; Col. 3:1; Heb. 2:17; 3:1; 10:12

7:13 [1]served   7:14 [1]NU priests   7:17 [1]NU it is testified   7:19 [1]complete
7:21 [1]NU ends the quotation after *forever.*   7:22 [1]guarantee
7:25 [1]completely or forever   7:26 [1]innocent

of the throne of the Majesty in the heavens, [2]a Minister of [a]the [1]sanctuary and of [b]the true tabernacle which the Lord erected, and not man.

[3]For [a]every high priest is appointed to offer both gifts and sacrifices. Therefore [b]*it is* necessary that this One also have something to offer. [4]For if He were on earth, He would not be a priest, since there are priests who offer the gifts according to the law; [5]who serve [a]the copy and [b]shadow of the heavenly things, as Moses was divinely instructed when he was about to make the tabernacle. For He said, [c]"See *that* you make all things according to the pattern shown you on the mountain." [6]But now [a]He has obtained a more excellent ministry, inasmuch as He is also Mediator of a [b]better covenant, which was established on better promises.

A NEW COVENANT
(Jer. 31:31–34)

[7]For if that [a]first *covenant* had been faultless, then no place would have been sought for a second. [8]Because finding fault with them, He says: [a]"Behold, the days are coming, says the LORD, when I will make a new covenant with the house of Israel and with the house of Judah— [9]not according to the covenant that I made with their fathers in the day when I took them by the hand to lead them out of the land of Egypt; because they did not continue in My covenant, and I disregarded them, says the LORD. [10]For this *is* the covenant that I will make with the house of Israel after those days, says the [a]LORD: I will put My laws in their mind and write them on their hearts; and [b]I will be their God, and they shall be My people. [11][a]None of them shall teach his neighbor, and none his brother, saying, 'Know the [b]LORD,' for all shall know Me, from the least of them to the greatest of them. [12]For I will be merciful to their unrighteousness, [a]and their sins [1]and their lawless deeds I will remember no more."

[13][a]In that He says, "A new *covenant*," He has made the first obsolete. Now what is becoming obsolete and growing old is ready to vanish away.

THE EARTHLY SANCTUARY
(cf. Ex. 25:10–40)

9 Then indeed, even the first *covenant* had ordinances of divine service and [a]the earthly sanctuary. [2]For a tabernacle was prepared: the first *part,* in which *was* the lampstand, the table, and the showbread, which is called the [1]sanctuary; [3a]and behind the second veil, the part of the tabernacle which is called the Holiest of All, [4]which had the [a]golden censer and [b]the ark of the covenant overlaid on all sides with gold, in which *were* [c]the golden pot that had the manna, [d]Aaron's rod that budded, and [e]the tablets of the covenant; [5]and [a]above it were the cherubim of glory overshadowing the mercy seat. Of these things we cannot now speak in detail.

LIMITATIONS OF THE EARTHLY SERVICE

[6]Now when these things had been thus prepared, [a]the priests always went into the first part of the tabernacle,

8:2 [a]Heb. 9:8, 12
[b]Heb. 9:11, 24

8:3
[a][Rom. 4:25;
5:6, 8;
Gal. 2:20;
Eph. 5:2];
Heb. 5:1; 8:4
[b][Eph. 5:2;
Heb. 9:14]

8:5
[a]Heb. 9:23, 24
[b]Col. 2:17;
Heb. 10:1
[c]Ex. 25:40

8:6
[a][2 Cor. 3:6–8]
[b][Luke 22:20];
Heb. 7:22

8:7 [a]Ex. 3:8; 19:5

8:8
[a]Jer. 31:31–34

8:10 [a]Jer. 31:33;
Rom. 11:27;
Heb. 10:16
[b]Zech. 8:8

8:11 [a]Is. 54:13;
John 6:45;
[1 John 2:27]
[b]Jer. 31:34

8:12 [a]Rom. 11:27

8:13
[a][2 Cor. 5:17];
Heb. 1:11

9:1 [a]Ex. 25:8;
[Heb. 8:2;
9:11, 24]

9:3
[a]Ex. 26:31–35;
40:3

9:4 [a]Lev. 16:12
[b]Ex. 25:10
[c]Ex. 16:33
[d]Num. 17:1–10
[e]Ex. 25:16;
34:29;
Deut. 10:2–5

9:5
[a]Ex. 25:17, 20;
Lev. 16:2;
1 Kin. 8:7

9:6
[a]Num. 18:2–6;
28:3

8:2 [1]Lit. *holies*   8:12 [1]NU omits *and their lawless deeds*   9:2 [1]*holy place,* lit. *holies*

performing the services. ⁷But into the second part the high priest *went* alone ᵃonce a year, not without blood, which he offered for ᵇhimself and *for* the people's sins *committed* in ignorance; ⁸the Holy Spirit indicating this, that ᵃthe way into the Holiest of All was not yet made manifest while the first tabernacle was still standing. ⁹It *was* symbolic for the present time in which both gifts and sacrifices are offered ᵃwhich cannot make him who performed the service perfect in regard to the conscience— ¹⁰*concerned* only with ᵃfoods and drinks, ᵇvarious ¹washings, ᶜand fleshly ordinances imposed until the time of reformation.

THE HEAVENLY SANCTUARY

¹¹But Christ came *as* High Priest of ᵃthe good things ¹to come, with the greater and more perfect tabernacle not made with hands, that is, not of this creation. ¹²Not ᵃwith the blood of goats and calves, but ᵇwith His own blood He entered the Most Holy Place ᶜonce for all, ᵈhaving obtained eternal redemption. ¹³For if ᵃthe blood of bulls and goats and ᵇthe ashes of a heifer, sprinkling the unclean, ¹sanctifies for the ²purifying of the flesh, ¹⁴how much more shall the blood of Christ, who through the eternal Spirit offered Himself without ¹spot to God, ᵃcleanse your conscience from ᵇdead works ᶜto serve the living God? ¹⁵And for this reason ᵃHe is the Mediator of the new covenant, by means of death, for the redemption of the transgressions under the first covenant, that ᵇthose who are called may receive the promise of the eternal inheritance.

THE MEDIATOR'S DEATH NECESSARY

¹⁶For where there *is* a testament, there must also of necessity be the death of the testator. ¹⁷For ᵃa testament *is* in force after men are dead, since it has no power at all while the testator lives. ¹⁸ᵃTherefore not even the first *covenant* was dedicated without blood. ¹⁹For when Moses had spoken every ¹precept to all the people according to the law, ᵃhe took the blood of calves and goats, ᵇwith water, scarlet wool, and hyssop, and sprinkled both the book itself and all the people, ²⁰saying, ᵃ"This *is* the ᵇblood of the covenant which God has commanded you." ²¹Then likewise ᵃhe sprinkled with blood both the tabernacle and all the vessels of the ministry. ²²And according to the law almost all things are ¹purified with blood, and ᵃwithout shedding of blood there is no ²remission.

GREATNESS OF CHRIST'S SACRIFICE

²³Therefore *it was* necessary that ᵃthe copies of the things in the heavens should be ¹purified with these, but the heavenly things themselves with better sacrifices than these. ²⁴For ᵃChrist has not entered the holy places made with hands, *which are* ¹copies of ᵇthe true, but into heaven itself, now ᶜto appear in the presence of God for us; ²⁵not that He should offer Himself often, as ᵃthe high priest enters the Most Holy Place every year with blood of another— ²⁶He then would have had to suffer often since the foundation of the world; but now, once at the end of the ages, He has appeared to put

9:7 ᵃEx. 30:10; Lev. 16:34; Heb. 10:3
ᵇHeb. 5:3

9:8 ᵃ[John 14:6; Heb. 10:20]

9:9 ᵃ[Gal. 3:21]; Heb. 7:19

9:10 ᵃLev. 11:2; Col. 2:16
ᵇNum. 19:7
ᶜEph. 2:15

9:11 ᵃ[Eph. 1:3–11]; Heb. 10:1

9:12 ᵃHeb. 10:4
ᵇIs. 53:12; Eph. 1:7
ᶜZech. 3:9
ᵈ[Dan. 9:24]

9:13 ᵃLev. 16:14, 15; Heb. 9:19; 10:4
ᵇNum. 19:2

9:14 ᵃ1 John 1:7
ᵇHeb. 6:1
ᶜLuke 1:74

9:15 ᵃRom. 3:25
ᵇHeb. 3:1

9:17 ᵃGal. 3:15

9:18 ᵃEx. 24:6

9:19 ᵃEx. 24:5, 6
ᵇLev. 14:4, 7; Num. 19:6, 18

9:20 ᵃ[Matt. 26:28]
ᵇEx. 24:3–8

9:21 ᵃEx. 29:12, 36

9:22 ᵃLev. 17:11

9:23 ᵃHeb. 8:5

9:24 ᵃHeb. 6:20
ᵇHeb. 8:2
ᶜRom. 8:34

9:25 ᵃHeb. 9:7

9:10 ¹Lit. *baptisms*   9:11 ¹NU *that have come*   9:13 ¹*sets apart*   ²*cleansing*
9:14 ¹*blemish*   9:19 ¹*command*   9:22 ¹*cleansed*   ²*forgiveness*
9:23 ¹*cleansed*   9:24 ¹*representations*

away sin by the sacrifice of Himself. 27aAnd as it is appointed for men to die once, bbut after this the judgment, 28so aChrist was boffered once to bear the sins cof many. To those who deagerly wait for Him He will appear a second time, apart from sin, for salvation.

ANIMAL SACRIFICES INSUFFICIENT

10 For the law, having a ashadow of the good things to come, *and* not the very image of the things, bcan never with these same sacrifices, which they offer continually year by year, make those who approach perfect. 2For then would they not have ceased to be offered? For the worshipers, once 1purified, would have had no more consciousness of sins. 3But in those *sacrifices there is* a reminder of sins every year. 4For a*it is* not possible that the blood of bulls and goats could take away sins.

CHRIST'S DEATH FULFILLS GOD'S WILL
(cf. Ps. 40:6–8)

5Therefore, when He came into the world, He said:

a"Sacrifice and offering You did not desire,
But a body You have prepared for Me.
6 In burnt offerings and *sacrifices* for sin
You had no pleasure.
7 Then I said, 'Behold, I have come—
In the volume of the book it is written of Me—
To do Your will, O God.'"

8Previously saying, "Sacrifice and offering, burnt offerings, and *offerings* for sin You did not desire, nor had pleasure *in them*" (which are offered according to the law), 9then He said, "Behold, I have come to do Your will, 1O God." He takes away the first that He may establish the second. 10aBy that will we have been 1sanctified bthrough the offering of the body of Jesus Christ once *for all*.

CHRIST'S DEATH PERFECTS THE SANCTIFIED

11And every priest stands aministering daily and offering repeatedly the same sacrifices, which can never take away sins. 12aBut this Man, after He had offered one sacrifice for sins forever, sat down bat the right hand of God, 13from that time waiting atill His enemies are made His footstool. 14For by one offering He has perfected forever those who are being 1sanctified.

15But the Holy Spirit also witnesses to us; for after He had said before,

16a"This *is* the covenant that I will make with them after those days, says the LORD: I will put My laws into their hearts, and in their minds I will write them," 17then He adds, a"Their sins and their lawless deeds I will remember no more." 18Now where there is 1remission of these, *there is* no longer an offering for sin.

HOLD FAST YOUR CONFESSION

19Therefore, brethren, having aboldness1 to enter bthe Holiest by the blood of Jesus, 20by a new and aliving way

9:27 aGen. 3:19;
Eccl. 3:20
b[2 Cor. 5:10];
1 John 4:17

9:28 aRom. 6:10
bIs. 53:12;
1 Pet. 2:24
cMatt. 26:28
d1 Cor. 1:7;
Titus 2:13

10:1 aHeb. 8:5
bHeb. 7:19; 9:9

10:4 aMic. 6:6, 7

10:5 aPs. 40:6–8

10:10
aJohn 17:19;
[Eph. 5:26;
Heb. 2:11;
10:14, 29; 13:12]
b[Heb. 9:12]

10:11
aNum. 28:3

10:12 aCol. 3:1;
Heb. 1:3
bPs. 110:1

10:13 aPs. 110:1;
Heb. 1:13

10:16
aJer. 31:33, 34;
Heb. 8:10

10:17 aJer. 31:34

10:19
a[Eph. 2:18];
Heb. 4:16
bHeb. 9:8, 12

10:20
aJohn 14:6;
[Heb. 7:24, 25]

10:2 1*cleansed*   10:9 1NU, M omit *O God*   10:10 1*set apart*   10:14 1*set apart*
10:18 1*forgiveness*   10:19 1*confidence*

which He consecrated for us, through the veil, that is, His flesh, 21and *having* a High Priest over the house of God, 22let us ªdraw near with a true heart ᵇin full assurance of faith, having our hearts sprinkled from an evil conscience and our bodies washed with pure water. 23Let us hold fast the confession of *our* hope without wavering, for ªHe who promised *is* faithful. 24And let us consider one another in order to stir up love and good works, 25ªnot forsaking the assembling of ourselves together, as *is* the manner of some, but exhorting *one another,* and ᵇso much the more as you see ᶜthe Day approaching.

THE JUST LIVE BY FAITH

26For ªif we sin willfully ᵇafter we have received the knowledge of the truth, there ᶜno longer remains a sacrifice for sins, 27but a certain fearful expectation of judgment, and ªfiery indignation which will devour the adversaries. 28Anyone who has rejected Moses' law dies without mercy on *the testimony of* two or three ªwitnesses. 29ªOf how much worse punishment, do you suppose, will he be thought worthy who has trampled the Son of God underfoot, ᵇcounted the blood of the covenant by which he was sanctified a common thing, ᶜand insulted the Spirit of grace? 30For we know Him who said, ª"Vengeance is Mine, I will repay," ¹says the Lord. And again, ᵇ"The LORD will judge His people." 31ªIt is a fearful thing to fall into the hands of the living God.

32But ªrecall the former days in which, after you were ¹illuminated, you endured a great struggle with sufferings: 33partly while you were made ªa spectacle both by reproaches and tribulations, and partly while ᵇyou became companions of those who were so treated; 34for you had compassion on ¹me ªin my chains, and ᵇjoyfully accepted the plundering of your ²goods, knowing that ᶜyou have a better and an enduring possession for yourselves ³in heaven. 35Therefore do not cast away your confidence, ªwhich has great reward. 36ªFor you have need of endurance, so that after you have done the will of God, ᵇyou may receive the promise:

37 "For ªyet a little while,
    And ᵇHe¹ who is coming will come and will not ²tarry.
38 Now ªthe¹ just shall live by faith;
    But if *anyone* draws back,
    My soul has no pleasure in him."

39But we are not of those ªwho draw back to ¹perdition, but of those who ᵇbelieve to the saving of the soul.

BY FAITH WE UNDERSTAND

11 Now faith is the ¹substance of things hoped for, the ²evidence ªof things not seen. 2For by it the elders obtained a *good* testimony.

3By faith we understand that ªthe ¹worlds were framed by the word of God, so that the things which are seen were not made of things which are visible.

10:22 ªHeb. 7:19; 10:1 ᵇEph. 3:12
10:23 ª1 Cor. 1:9; 10:13; 1 Thess. 5:24; Heb. 11:11
10:25 ªActs 2:42 ᵇRom. 13:11 ᶜPhil. 4:5
10:26 ªNum. 15:30 ᵇ2 Pet. 2:20 ᶜHeb. 6:6
10:27 ªZeph. 1:18
10:28 ªDeut. 17:2–6; 19:15; Matt. 18:16; Heb. 2:2
10:29 ª[Heb. 2:3] ᵇ1 Cor. 11:29 ᶜ[Matt. 12:31]
10:30 ªDeut. 32:35; Rom. 12:19 ᵇDeut. 32:36
10:31 ª[Luke 12:5]
10:32 ªGal. 3:4; Heb. 6:9, 10
10:33 ª1 Cor. 4:9; Heb. 12:4 ᵇPhil. 1:7
10:34 ª2 Tim. 1:16 ᵇMatt. 5:12 ᶜMatt. 6:20
10:35 ªMatt. 5:12
10:36 ªLuke 21:19; Heb. 12:1 ᵇ[Col. 3:24]
10:37 ªLuke 18:8 ᵇHab. 2:3, 4; Heb. 10:25; Rev. 22:20
10:38 ªHab. 2:3, 4; Rom. 1:17; Gal. 3:11
10:39 ª2 Pet. 2:20 ᵇActs 16:31
11:1 ªRom. 8:24; [2 Cor. 4:18; 5:7]; Heb. 11:7, 27
11:3 ªGen. 1:1; Ps. 33:6; [John 1:3]; 2 Pet. 3:5

10:30 ¹NU omits *says the Lord*   10:32 ¹*enlightened*   10:34 ¹NU *the prisoners* instead of *me in my chains*   ²*possessions*   ³NU omits *in heaven*
10:37 ¹Or *that which*   ²*delay*   10:38 ¹NU *My just one*   10:39 ¹*destruction*
11:1 ¹*realization*   ²Or *confidence*   11:3 ¹Or *ages,* Gr. *aiones,* aeons

FAITH AT THE DAWN OF HISTORY
(Gen. 4:1–16; 5:18–24; 6:5—8:22)

4By faith ªAbel offered to God a more excellent sacrifice than Cain, through which he obtained witness that he was righteous, God testifying of his gifts; and through it he being dead still ᵇspeaks.

5By faith Enoch was taken away so that he did not see death, ª"and was not found, because God had taken him"; for before he was taken he had this testimony, that he pleased God. 6But without faith *it is* impossible to please *Him,* for he who comes to God must believe that He is, and *that* He is a rewarder of those who diligently seek Him.

7By faith ªNoah, being divinely warned of things not yet seen, moved with godly fear, ᵇprepared an ark for the saving of his household, by which he condemned the world and became heir of ᶜthe righteousness which is according to faith.

FAITHFUL ABRAHAM
(Gen. 15:1–6; 21:1–7)

8By faith ªAbraham obeyed when he was called to go out to the place which he would receive as an inheritance. And he went out, not knowing where he was going. 9By faith he dwelt in the land of promise as *in* a foreign country, ªdwelling in tents with Isaac and Jacob, ᵇthe heirs with him of the same promise; 10for he waited for ªthe city which has foundations, ᵇwhose builder and maker *is* God.

11By faith ªSarah herself also received strength to conceive seed, and ᵇshe¹ bore a child when she was past the age, because she judged Him ᶜfaithful who had promised. 12Therefore from one man, and him as good as ªdead, were born *as many* as the ᵇstars of the sky in multitude—innumerable as the sand which is by the seashore.

THE HEAVENLY HOPE

13These all died in faith, ªnot having received the ᵇpromises, but ᶜhaving seen them afar off ¹were assured of them, embraced *them* and ᵈconfessed that they were strangers and pilgrims on the earth. 14For those who say such things ªdeclare plainly that they seek a homeland. 15And truly if they had called to mind ªthat *country* from which they had come out, they would have had opportunity to return. 16But now they desire a better, that is, a heavenly *country.* Therefore God is not ashamed ªto be called their God, for He has ᵇprepared a city for them.

THE FAITH OF THE PATRIARCHS
(Gen. 22:1–14; 48:8–16; 50:22–25)

17By faith Abraham, ªwhen he was tested, offered up Isaac, and he who had received the promises offered up his only begotten *son,* 18¹of whom it was said, ª"In Isaac your seed shall be called," 19concluding that God ªwas able to raise *him* up, even from the dead, from which he also received him in a figurative sense.

20By faith ªIsaac blessed Jacob and Esau concerning things to come.

11:4
ªGen. 4:3–5;
Matt. 23:35;
1 John 3:12
ᵇGen. 4:8–10;
Heb. 12:24

11:5
ªGen. 5:21–24

11:7
ªGen. 6:13–22
ᵇ1 Pet. 3:20
ᶜRom. 3:22

11:8
ªGen. 12:1–4;
Acts 7:2–4

11:9 ªGen. 12:8;
13:3, 18; 18:1, 9
ᵇHeb. 6:17

11:10
ª[Heb. 12:22;
13:14]
ᵇ[Rev. 21:10]

11:11 ªGen. 17:19;
18:11–14; 21:1, 2
ᵇLuke 1:36
ᶜHeb. 10:23

11:12 ªRom. 4:19
ᵇGen. 15:5;
22:17; 32:12

11:13 ªHeb. 11:39
ᵇGen. 12:7
ᶜJohn 8:56;
Heb. 11:27
ᵈGen. 23:4;
47:9;
1 Chr. 29:15;
Ps. 39:12;
Eph. 2:19;
1 Pet. 1:17; 2:11

11:14 ªHeb. 13:14

11:15 ªGen. 11:31

11:16
ªGen. 26:24;
28:13; Ex. 3:6, 15;
4:5 ᵇ[John 14:2];
Heb. 11:10;
[Rev. 21:2]

11:17
ªGen. 22:1–14;
James 2:21

11:18 ªGen. 21:12;
Rom. 9:7

11:19 ªRom. 4:17

11:20
ªGen. 27:26–40

11:11 ¹NU omits *she bore a child*   11:13 ¹NU, M omit *were assured of them*   11:18 ¹*to*

21By faith Jacob, when he was dying, ªblessed each of the sons of Joseph, and worshiped, *leaning* on the top of his staff.

22By faith ªJoseph, when he was dying, made mention of the departure of the children of Israel, and gave instructions concerning his bones.

THE FAITH OF MOSES
(Ex. 2:1–10; 12:31–51)

23By faith ªMoses, when he was born, was hidden three months by his parents, because they saw *he was* a beautiful child; and they were not afraid of the king's ᵇcommand.

24By faith ªMoses, when he became of age, refused to be called the son of Pharaoh's daughter, 25choosing rather to suffer affliction with the people of God than to enjoy the ¹passing pleasures of sin, 26esteeming ªthe ¹reproach of Christ greater riches than the treasures ²in Egypt; for he looked to the ᵇreward.

27By faith ªhe forsook Egypt, not fearing the wrath of the king; for he endured as seeing Him who is invisible. 28By faith ªhe kept the Passover and the sprinkling of blood, lest he who destroyed the firstborn should touch them.

29By faith ªthey passed through the Red Sea as by dry *land, whereas* the Egyptians, attempting to do so, were drowned.

BY FAITH THEY OVERCAME

30By faith ªthe walls of Jericho fell down after they were encircled for seven days. 31By faith ªthe harlot Rahab did not perish with those who ¹did not believe, when ᵇshe had received the spies with peace.

32And what more shall I say? For the time would fail me to tell of ªGideon and ᵇBarak and ᶜSamson and ᵈJephthah, also *of* ᵉDavid and ᶠSamuel and the prophets: 33who through faith subdued kingdoms, worked righteousness, obtained promises, ªstopped the mouths of lions, 34ªquenched the violence of fire, escaped the edge of the sword, out of weakness were made strong, became valiant in battle, turned to flight the armies of the aliens. 35ªWomen received their dead raised to life again.

Others were ᵇtortured, not accepting deliverance, that they might obtain a better resurrection. 36Still others had trial of mockings and scourgings, yes, and ªof chains and imprisonment. 37ªThey were stoned, they were sawn in two, ¹were tempted, were slain with the sword. ᵇThey wandered about ᶜin sheepskins and goatskins, being destitute, afflicted, tormented— 38of whom the world was not worthy. They wandered in deserts and mountains, ªin dens and caves of the earth.

39And all these, ªhaving obtained a good testimony through faith, did not receive the promise, 40God having provided something better for us, that they should not be ªmade perfect apart from us.

THE RACE OF FAITH

12 Therefore we also, since we are surrounded by so great a cloud of witnesses, ªlet us lay aside every weight, and the sin which so easily ensnares *us,* and ᵇlet us run ᶜwith endurance the race that is set before us, 2looking unto Jesus,

---

11:25 ¹*temporary* 11:26 ¹*reviling because of* ²NU, M *of* 11:31 ¹*were disobedient* 11:37 ¹NU omits *were tempted*

the [1]author and [2]finisher of *our* faith, [a]who for the joy that was set before Him [b]endured the cross, despising the shame, and [c]has sat down at the right hand of the throne of God.

THE DISCIPLINE OF GOD
(*Prov. 3:11, 12*)

3 [a]For consider Him who endured such hostility from sinners against Himself, [b]lest you become weary and discouraged in your souls. 4 [a]You have not yet resisted to bloodshed, striving against sin. 5And you have forgotten the exhortation which speaks to you as to sons:

[a]"My son, do not despise the [1]chastening of the LORD,
Nor be discouraged when you are rebuked by Him;
6   For [a]whom the LORD loves He chastens,
And scourges every son whom He receives."

7 [a]If[1] you endure chastening, God deals with you as with sons; for what [b]son is there whom a father does not chasten? 8But if you are without chastening, [a]of which all have become partakers, then you are illegitimate and not sons. 9Furthermore, we have had human fathers who corrected *us,* and we paid *them* respect. Shall we not much more readily be in subjection to [a]the Father of spirits and live? 10For they indeed for a few days chastened *us* as seemed *best* to them, but He for *our* profit, [a]that *we* may be partakers of His holiness. 11Now no [1]chastening seems to be joyful for the present, but painful; nevertheless, afterward it yields [a]the peaceable fruit of righteousness to those who have been trained by it.

RENEW YOUR SPIRITUAL VITALITY
(*Gen. 25:29–34; 27:30–40*)

12Therefore [a]strengthen the hands which hang down, and the feeble knees, 13and make straight paths for your feet, so that what is lame may not be dislocated, but rather be healed.

14 [a]Pursue peace with all *people,* and holiness, [b]without which no one will see the Lord: 15looking carefully lest anyone [a]fall short of the grace of God; lest any [b]root of bitterness springing up cause trouble, and by this many become defiled; 16lest there *be* any [a]fornicator or [1]profane person like Esau, [b]who for one morsel of food sold his birthright. 17For you know that afterward, when he wanted to inherit the blessing, he was [a]rejected, for he found no place for repentance, though he sought it diligently with tears.

THE GLORIOUS COMPANY

18For you have not come [1]to [a]the mountain that may be touched and that burned with fire, and to blackness and [2]darkness and tempest, 19and the sound of a trumpet and the voice of words, so that those who heard *it* [a]begged that the word should not be spoken to them anymore. 20(For they could not endure what was commanded: [a]"And if so much as a beast touches the mountain, it shall be stoned [1]or shot with an arrow." 21And so terrifying was the sight *that* Moses said, [a]"I am exceedingly afraid and trembling.")

12:2
[a]Luke 24:26
[b]Ps. 69:7, 19;
Phil. 2:8;
[Heb. 2:9]
[c]Ps. 110:1

12:3
[a]Matt. 10:24
[b]Gal. 6:9;
Heb. 12:5

12:4
[a][1 Cor. 10:13]

12:5 [a]Job 5:17;
Prov. 3:11, 12

12:6 [a]Ps. 94:12;
Rev. 3:19

12:7 [a]Deut. 8:5;
2 Sam. 7:14
[b]Prov. 13:24;
19:18; 23:13

12:8 [a]1 Pet. 5:9

12:9 [a][Job 12:10]

12:10 [a]Lev. 11:44

12:11 [a]Is. 32:17;
2 Tim. 4:8;
James 3:17, 18

12:12 [a]Is. 35:3

12:14 [a]Ps. 34:14
[b]Matt. 5:8;
[Heb. 9:28]

12:15 [a]2 Cor. 6:1;
Gal. 5:4; Heb. 4:1
[b]Deut. 29:18

12:16
[a][1 Cor. 6:13–18]
[b]Gen. 25:33

12:17
[a]Gen. 27:30–40

12:18
[a]Ex. 19:12, 16;
20:18;
Deut. 4:11; 5:22

12:19
[a]Ex. 20:18–26;
Deut. 5:25;
18:16

12:20
[a]Ex. 19:12, 13

12:21
[a]Deut. 9:19

12:2 [1]originator   [2]perfecter   12:5 [1]discipline   12:7 [1]NU, M *It is for discipline that you endure; God*   12:11 [1]discipline   12:16 [1]godless 12:18 [1]NU *to that which*   [2]NU *gloom*   12:20 [1]NU, M omit the rest of v. 20.

22But you have come to Mount Zion and to the city of the living God, the heavenly Jerusalem, to an innumerable company of angels, 23to the 1general assembly and church of athe firstborn bwho are registered in heaven, to God cthe Judge of all, to the spirits of just men dmade perfect, 24to Jesus athe Mediator of the new covenant, and to bthe blood of sprinkling that speaks better things cthan *that of* Abel.

HEAR THE HEAVENLY VOICE

25See that you do not refuse Him who speaks. For aif they did not escape who refused Him who spoke on earth, much more *shall we not escape* if we turn away from Him who *speaks* from heaven, 26whose voice then shook the earth; but now He has promised, saying, a"Yet once more I 1shake not only the earth, but also heaven." 27Now this, "Yet once more," indicates the aremoval of those things that are being shaken, as of things that are made, that the things which cannot be shaken may remain.

28Therefore, since we are receiving a kingdom which cannot be shaken, let us have grace, by which we 1may aserve God acceptably with reverence and godly fear. 29For aour God *is* a consuming fire.

CONCLUDING MORAL DIRECTIONS

13 Let abrotherly love continue. 2aDo not forget to entertain strangers, for by so *doing* bsome have unwittingly entertained angels. 3aRemember the prisoners as if chained with them—those who are mistreated—since you yourselves are in the body also.

4aMarriage *is* honorable among all, and the bed undefiled; bbut fornicators and adulterers God will judge.

5*Let your* conduct *be* without covetousness; *be* content with such things as you have. For He Himself has said, a"I will never leave you nor forsake you." 6So we may boldly say:

a"The LORD *is* my helper;
I will not fear.
What can man do to me?"

CONCLUDING RELIGIOUS DIRECTIONS

7Remember those who 1rule over you, who have spoken the word of God to you, whose faith follow, considering the outcome of *their* conduct. 8Jesus Christ *is* athe same yesterday, today, and forever. 9Do not be carried 1about with various and strange doctrines. For *it is* good that the heart be established by grace, not with foods which have not profited those who have been occupied with them.

10We have an altar from which those who serve the tabernacle have no right to eat. 11For the bodies of those animals, whose blood is brought into the sanctuary by the high priest for sin, are burned outside the camp. 12Therefore Jesus also, that He might 1sanctify the people with His own blood, suffered outside the gate. 13Therefore let us go forth to Him, outside the camp, bearing aHis reproach. 14For here we have no continuing city, but we seek the one to come. 15aTherefore by

---

12:23 a[James 1:18]
b Luke 10:20
c Gen. 18:25;
Ps. 50:6; 94:2
d[Phil. 3:12]
12:24 a1 Tim. 2:5;
Heb. 8:6; 9:15
b Ex. 24:8
c Gen. 4:10;
Heb. 11:4
12:25 a Heb. 2:2, 3
12:26 a Hag. 2:6
12:27 a[Is. 34:4;
54:10; 65:17;
Rom. 8:19, 21];
1 Cor. 7:31;
Heb. 1:10
12:28 a Heb. 13:15, 21
12:29 a Ex. 24:17
13:1 a Rom. 12:10
13:2 a Matt. 25:35;
Rom. 12:13
b Gen. 18:1–22;
19:1
13:3 a Matt. 25:36;
Heb. 10:34
13:4 a Prov. 5:18, 19
b 1 Cor. 6:9;
Gal. 5:19, 21;
1 Thess. 4:6
13:5 a Gen. 28:15;
Deut. 31:6, 8;
Josh. 1:5
13:6 a Ps. 27:1;
118:6
13:8 a[John 8:58];
2 Cor. 1:19;
Heb. 1:12
13:13 a1 Pet. 4:14
13:15 a Eph. 5:20

12:23 1*festal gathering* **12:26** 1NU *will shake* **12:28** 1M omits *may*
13:7 1*lead* **13:9** 1NU, M *away* **13:12** 1*set apart*

Him let us continually offer [b]the sacrifice of praise to God, that is, [c]the fruit of *our* lips, [1]giving thanks to His name. [16a]But do not forget to do good and to share, for [b]with such sacrifices God is well pleased.

[17a]Obey those who [1]rule over you, and be submissive, for [b]they watch out for your souls, as those who must give account. Let them do so with joy and not with grief, for that would be unprofitable for you.

PRAYER REQUESTED

[18a]Pray for us; for we are confident that we have [b]a good conscience, in all things desiring to live honorably. [19]But I especially urge *you* to do this, that I may be restored to you the sooner.

BENEDICTION, FINAL EXHORTATION, FAREWELL

[20]Now may [a]the God of peace [b]who brought up our Lord Jesus from the dead, [c]that great Shepherd of the sheep, [d]through the blood of the everlasting covenant, [21]make you [1]complete in every good work to do His will, [a]working in [2]you what is well pleasing in His sight, through Jesus Christ, to whom *be* glory forever and ever. Amen.

[22]And I appeal to you, brethren, bear with the word of exhortation, for I have written to you in few words. [23]Know that *our* brother Timothy has been set free, with whom I shall see you if he comes shortly.

[24]Greet all those who [1]rule over you, and all the saints. Those from Italy greet you.

[25]Grace *be* with you all. Amen.

Cross-references

13:15 [b]Lev. 7:12
[c]Is. 57:19;
Hos. 14:2

13:16
[a]Rom. 12:13
[b]2 Cor. 9:12;
Phil. 4:18

13:17 [a]Phil. 2:29
[b]Is. 62:6;
Ezek. 3:17;
Acts 20:28

13:18 [a]Eph. 6:19
[b]Acts 23:1

13:20
[a]Rom. 5:1,
2, 10; 15:33
[b]Ps. 16:10, 11;
Hos. 6:2;
Rom. 4:24
[c]Ps. 23:1;
Is. 40:11; 63:11;
John 10:11;
1 Pet. 2:25; 5:4
[d]Zech. 9:11;
Heb. 10:29

13:21 [a]Phil. 2:13

13:15 [1]Lit. *confessing*   13:17 [1]*lead*   13:21 [1]*perfect*   [2]NU, M *us*   13:24 [1]*lead*

THE EPISTLE OF
JAMES

GREETING TO THE TWELVE TRIBES

1 James, ᵃa bondservant of God and of the Lord Jesus Christ,

To the twelve tribes which are scattered abroad:

Greetings.

PROFITING FROM TRIALS

²My brethren, ᵃcount it all joy ᵇwhen you fall into various trials, ³ᵃknowing that the testing of your faith produces ¹patience. ⁴But let patience have *its* perfect work, that you may be ¹perfect and complete, lacking nothing. ⁵ᵃIf any of you lacks wisdom, ᵇlet him ask of God, who gives to all liberally and without reproach, and ᶜit will be given to him. ⁶ᵃBut let him ask in faith, with no doubting, for he who doubts is like a wave of the sea driven and tossed by the wind. ⁷For let not that man suppose that he will receive anything from the Lord; ⁸*he is* ᵃa double-minded man, unstable in all his ways.

THE PERSPECTIVE OF RICH AND POOR

⁹Let the lowly brother glory in his exaltation, ¹⁰but the rich in his humiliation, because ᵃas a flower of the field he will pass away. ¹¹For no sooner has the sun risen with a burning heat than it withers the grass; its flower falls, and its beautiful appearance perishes. So the rich man also will fade away in his pursuits.

LOVING GOD UNDER TRIALS

¹²ᵃBlessed *is* the man who endures temptation; for when he has been approved, he will receive ᵇthe crown of life ᶜwhich the Lord has promised to those who love Him. ¹³Let no one say when he is tempted, "I am tempted by God"; for God cannot be tempted by evil, nor does He Himself tempt anyone. ¹⁴But each one is tempted when he is drawn away by his own desires and enticed. ¹⁵Then, ᵃwhen desire has conceived, it gives birth to sin; and sin, when it is full-grown, ᵇbrings forth death.

¹⁶Do not be deceived, my beloved brethren. ¹⁷ᵃEvery good gift and every perfect gift is from above, and comes down from the Father of lights, ᵇwith whom there is no variation or shadow of turning. ¹⁸ᵃOf His own will He brought us forth by the ᵇword of truth, ᶜthat we might be a kind of firstfruits of His creatures.

QUALITIES NEEDED IN TRIALS

¹⁹¹So then, my beloved brethren, let every man be swift to hear, ᵃslow to speak, ᵇslow to wrath; ²⁰for the wrath of man does not produce the righteousness of God.

1:1 ᵃActs 12:17

1:2 ᵃActs 5:41
ᵇ1 Pet. 1:6

1:3 ᵃRom. 5:3–5

1:5 ᵃ1 Kin. 3:9;
James 3:17
ᵇProv. 2:3–6;
Matt. 7:7
ᶜJer. 29:12

1:6
ᵃ[Mark 11:23,
24];
Acts 10:20

1:8 ᵃJames 4:8

1:10 ᵃJob 14:2

1:12 ᵃJob 5:17;
Luke 6:22;
Heb. 10:36;
James 5:11;
[1 Pet. 3:14; 4:14]
ᵇ[1 Cor. 9:25]
ᶜMatt. 10:22

1:15 ᵃJob 15:35;
Ps. 7:14; Is. 59:4
ᵇ[Rom. 5:12;
6:23]

1:17 ᵃJohn 3:27
ᵇNum. 23:19

1:18 ᵃJohn 1:13
ᵇ2 Cor. 6:7;
1 Thess. 2:13;
2 Tim. 2:15;
[1 Pet. 1:3, 23]
ᶜ[Eph. 1:12, 13];
Heb. 12:23;
Rev. 14:4

1:19 ᵃProv. 10:19;
17:27
ᵇProv. 14:17;
16:32; Eccl. 7:9

1:3 ¹*endurance* or *perseverance*　　1:4 ¹*mature*　　1:19 ¹NU *Know this* or *This you know*

DOERS—NOT HEARERS ONLY

21Therefore aulay aside all filthiness and 1overflow of wickedness, and receive with meekness the implanted word, bwhich is able to save your souls.

22But abe doers of the word, and not hearers only, deceiving yourselves. 23For aif anyone is a hearer of the word and not a doer, he is like a man observing his natural face in a mirror; 24for he observes himself, goes away, and immediately forgets what kind of man he was. 25But ahe who looks into the perfect law of liberty and continues *in it,* and is not a forgetful hearer but a doer of the work, bthis one will be blessed in what he does.

26If anyone 1among you thinks he is religious, and adoes not bridle his tongue but deceives his own heart, this one's religion *is* useless. 27aPure and undefiled religion before God and the Father is this: bto visit orphans and widows in their trouble, cand to keep oneself unspotted from the world.

BEWARE OF PERSONAL FAVORITISM

2 My brethren, do not hold the faith of our Lord Jesus Christ, a*the Lord* of glory, with bpartiality. 2For if there should come into your assembly a man with gold rings, in 1fine apparel, and there should also come in a poor man in 2filthy clothes, 3and you 1pay attention to the one wearing the fine clothes and say to him, "You sit here in a good place," and say to the poor man, "You stand there," or, "Sit here at my footstool," 4have you not 1shown partiality among yourselves, and become judges with evil thoughts?

5Listen, my beloved brethren: aHas God not chosen the poor of this world *to be* brich in faith and heirs of the kingdom cwhich He promised to those who love Him? 6But ayou have dishonored the poor man. Do not the rich oppress you band drag you into the courts? 7Do they not blaspheme that noble name by which you are acalled?

8If you really fulfill *the* royal law according to the Scripture, a"You shall love your neighbor as yourself," you do well; 9but if you 1show partiality, you commit sin, and are convicted by the law as atransgressors. 10For whoever shall keep the whole law, and yet astumble in one *point,* bhe is guilty of all. 11For He who said, a"Do not commit adultery," also said, b"Do not murder." Now if you do not commit adultery, but you do murder, you have become a transgressor of the law. 12So speak and so do as those who will be judged by athe law of liberty. 13For ajudgment is without mercy to the one who has shown bno cmercy. dMercy triumphs over judgment.

FAITH WITHOUT WORKS IS DEAD
(cf. Gen. 22; Josh. 2)

14aWhat *does it* profit, my brethren, if someone says he has faith but does not have works? Can faith save him? 15aIf a brother or sister is naked and destitute of daily food, 16and aone of you says to them, "Depart in peace, be warmed and filled," but you do not give them the things which are needed for the body, what *does it* profit? 17Thus also faith by itself, if it does not have works, is dead.

1:21 aCol. 3:8
bActs 13:26

1:22
aMatt. 7:21–28;
Luke 6:46–49;
[Rom. 2:13];
James 1:22–25;
2:14–20]

1:23 aLuke 6:47

1:25
a[John 8:32;
Rom. 8:2;
2 Cor. 3:17];
Gal. 2:4; 6:2;
James 2:12;
1 Pet. 2:16
bJohn 13:17

1:26 aPs. 34:13

1:27
aMatt. 25:34–36
bIs. 1:17
c[Rom. 12:2]

2:1 aActs 7:2;
1 Cor. 2:8
bLev. 19:15

2:5 aJob 34:19;
John 7:48;
1 Cor. 1:27
bLuke 12:21;
1 Tim. 6:18;
Rev. 2:9
cEx. 20:6

2:6 a1 Cor. 11:22
bActs 13:50

2:7 aActs 11:26;
1 Pet. 4:16

2:8 aLev. 19:18

2:9 aLev. 19:15;
Deut. 1:17

2:10 aGal. 3:10
bDeut. 27:26

2:11 aEx. 20:14;
Deut. 5:18
bEx. 20:13;
Deut. 5:17

2:12 aJames 1:25

2:13 aJob 22:6
bProv. 21:13;
Matt. 18:32–35;
[Luke 6:37]
cMic. 7:18;
[Matt. 5:7]
dRom. 12:8

2:14
aMatt. 7:21–23,
26; 21:28–32

2:15
aMatt. 25:35;
Luke 3:11

2:16
a[1 John 3:17, 18]

1:21 1*abundance*   1:26 1NU omits *among you*   2:2 1*bright*   2*vile*
2:3 1Lit. *look upon*   2:4 1*differentiated*   2:9 1Lit. *receive the face*

[18]But someone will say, "You have faith, and I have works." [a]Show me your faith without [1]your works, [b]and I will show you my faith by [2]my works. [19]You believe that there is one God. You do well. Even the demons believe—and tremble! [20]But do you want to know, O foolish man, that faith without works is [1]dead? [21]Was not Abraham our father justified by works [a]when he offered Isaac his son on the altar? [22]Do you see [a]that faith was working together with his works, and by [b]works faith was made [1]perfect? [23]And the Scripture was fulfilled which says, [a]"Abraham believed God, and it was [1]accounted to him for righteousness." And he was called [b]the friend of God. [24]You see then that a man is justified by works, and not by faith only.

[25]Likewise, [a]was not Rahab the harlot also justified by works when she received [1]the messengers and sent *them* out another way?

[26]For as the body without the spirit is dead, so faith without works is dead also.

THE UNTAMABLE TONGUE

3 My brethren, [a]let not many of you become teachers, [b]knowing that we shall receive a stricter judgment. [2]For [a]we all stumble in many things. [b]If anyone does not stumble in word, [c]he *is* a [1]perfect man, able also to bridle the whole body. [3][1]Indeed, [a]we put bits in horses' mouths that they may obey us, and we turn their whole body. [4]Look also at ships: although they are so large and are driven by fierce winds, they are turned by a very small rudder wherever the pilot desires. [5]Even so [a]the tongue is a little member and [b]boasts great things.

See how great a forest a little fire kindles! [6]And [a]the tongue *is* a fire, a world of [1]iniquity. The tongue is so set among our members that it [b]defiles the whole body, and sets on fire the course of [2]nature; and it is set on fire by [3]hell. [7]For every kind of beast and bird, of reptile and creature of the sea, is tamed and has been tamed by mankind. [8]But no man can tame the tongue. *It is* an unruly evil, [a]full of deadly poison. [9]With it we bless our God and Father, and with it we curse men, who have been made [a]in the [1]similitude of God. [10]Out of the same mouth proceed blessing and cursing. My brethren, these things ought not to be so. [11]Does a spring send forth fresh *water* and bitter from the same opening? [12]Can a [a]fig tree, my brethren, bear olives, or a grapevine bear figs? [1]Thus no spring yields both salt water and fresh.

HEAVENLY VERSUS DEMONIC WISDOM

[13][a]Who *is* wise and understanding among you? Let him show by good conduct *that* his works *are done* in the meekness of wisdom. [14]But if you have [a]bitter envy and [1]self-seeking in your hearts, [b]do not boast and lie against the truth. [15][a]This wisdom does not descend from above, but *is* earthly, sensual, demonic. [16]For [a]where envy and self-seeking *exist*, confusion and every evil thing *are* there. [17]But [a]the wisdom that is from above is first pure, then peaceable, gentle, willing to yield, full

2:18 [a]Col. 1:6;
1 Thess. 1:3;
Heb. 6:10
[b][Gal. 5:6];
James 3:13

2:21 [a]Gen. 22:9,
10, 12, 16–18

2:22
[a][John 6:29];
Heb. 11:17
[b]John 8:39

2:23 [a]Gen. 15:6;
Rom. 4:3
[b]2 Chr. 20:7;
Is. 41:8

2:25 [a]Heb. 11:31

3:1
[a][Matt. 23:8];
Rom. 2:21;
1 Tim. 1:7
[b]Luke 6:37

3:2 [a]1 Kin. 8:46
[b]Ps. 34:13
[c][Matt. 12:34–37;
James 3:2–12]

3:3 [a]Ps. 32:9

3:5
[a]Prov. 12:18; 15:2;
James 1:26
[b]Ps. 12:3; 73:8

3:6
[a]Ps. 120:2, 3;
Prov. 16:27
[b][Matt. 12:36;
15:11, 18]

3:8 [a]Ps. 140:3;
Eccl. 10:11;
Rom. 3:13

3:9 [a]Gen. 1:26;
5:1; 9:6;
1 Cor. 11:7

3:12
[a]Matt. 7:16–20

3:13 [a]Gal. 6:4

3:14 [a]Rom. 13:13
[b]Rom. 2:17

3:15 [a]Phil. 3:19

3:16 [a]1 Cor. 3:3

3:17
[a]1 Cor. 2:6, 7

2:18 [1]NU omits *your*   [2]NU omits *my*   2:20 [1]NU *useless*   2:22 [1]*complete*
2:23 [1]*credited*   3:2 [1]*mature*   3:3 [1]NU *Now if*   3:6 [1]*unrighteousness*
[2]*existence*   [3]Gr. *Gehenna*   3:9 [1]*likeness*   3:12 [1]NU *Neither can a salty spring produce fresh water.*   3:14 [1]*selfish ambition*

of mercy and good fruits, [b]without partiality [c]and without hypocrisy. [18a]Now the fruit of righteousness is sown in peace by those who make peace.

PRIDE PROMOTES STRIFE

4 Where do [1]wars and fights *come* from among you? Do *they* not *come* from your *desires for* pleasure [a]that war in your members? [2]You lust and do not have. You murder and covet and cannot obtain. You fight and [1]war. [2]Yet you do not have because you do not ask. [3a]You ask and do not receive, [b]because you ask amiss, that you may spend *it* on your pleasures. [4]Adulterers and adulteresses! Do you not know that [a]friendship with the world is enmity with God? [b]Whoever therefore wants to be a friend of the world makes himself an enemy of God. [5]Or do you think that the Scripture says in vain, [a]"The Spirit who dwells in us yearns jealously"?

[6]But He gives more grace. Therefore He says:

[a]"God resists the proud,
But gives grace to the humble."

HUMILITY CURES WORLDLINESS

[7]Therefore submit to God. [a]Resist the devil and he will flee from you. [8a]Draw near to God and He will draw near to you. [b]Cleanse *your* hands, *you* sinners; and [c]purify *your* hearts, *you* double-minded. [9a]Lament and mourn and weep! Let your laughter be turned to mourning and *your* joy to gloom. [10a]Humble yourselves in the sight of the Lord, and He will lift you up.

DO NOT JUDGE A BROTHER

[11a]Do not speak evil of one another, brethren. He who speaks evil of a brother [b]and judges his brother, speaks evil of the law and judges the law. But if you judge the law, you are not a doer of the law but a judge. [12]There is one [1]Lawgiver, [a]who is able to save and to destroy. [b]Who[2] are you to judge [3]another?

DO NOT BOAST ABOUT TOMORROW

[13]Come now, you who say, "Today or tomorrow [1]we will go to such and such a city, spend a year there, buy and sell, and make a profit"; [14]whereas you do not know what *will happen* tomorrow. For what *is* your life? [a]It is even a vapor that appears for a little time and then vanishes away. [15]Instead you *ought* to say, [a]"If the Lord wills, we shall live and do this or that." [16]But now you boast in your arrogance. [a]All such boasting is evil.

[17]Therefore, [a]to him who knows to do good and does not do *it*, to him it is sin.

RICH OPPRESSORS WILL BE JUDGED

5 Come now, *you* [a]rich, weep and howl for your miseries that are coming upon *you!* [2]Your [a]riches [1]are corrupted, and [b]your garments are moth-eaten. [3]Your gold and silver are

5:2 [a]Jer. 17:11; Matt. 6:19 [b]Job 13:28

Cross references:

3:17
[b]James 2:1
[c]Rom. 12:9;
2 Cor. 6:6;
1 Pet. 1:22

3:18
[a]Prov. 11:18;
Is. 32:17;
Hos. 10:12;
Amos 6:12;
[Gal. 6:8;
Phil. 1:11]

4:1 [a]Rom. 7:23;
[Gal. 5:17];
1 Pet. 2:11

4:3 [a]Job 27:8, 9
[b][Ps. 66:18]

4:4 [a]Rom. 8:7;
1 John 2:15
[b]Gal. 1:4

4:5 [a]Gen. 6:5

4:6 [a]Job 22:29;
Ps. 138:6;
Prov. 3:34;
Matt. 23:12;
1 Pet. 5:5

4:7
[a][Eph. 4:27;
6:11];
1 Pet. 5:8

4:8 [a]2 Chr. 15:2;
Zech. 1:3;
Mal. 3:7;
Heb. 7:19
[b]Job 17:9;
Is. 1:16;
1 Tim. 2:8
[c]Jer. 4:14;
James 3:17;
1 Pet. 1:22;
1 John 3:3

4:9 [a]Matt. 5:4

4:10
[a]Job 22:29;
Luke 14:11; 18:14;
1 Pet. 5:6

4:11
[a]2 Cor. 12:20;
Eph. 4:31;
James 5:9;
1 Pet. 2:1–3
[b][Matt. 7:1–5];
Rom. 14:4

4:12
[a][Matt. 10:28]
[b]Rom. 14:4

4:14 [a]Job 7:7;
Ps. 102:3;
1 Pet. 1:24

4:15 [a]Acts 18:21;
1 Cor. 4:19

4:16 [a]1 Cor. 5:6

4:17
[a][Luke 12:47];
John 9:41;
2 Pet. 2:21

5:1 [a]Prov. 11:28;
[Luke 6:24;
1 Tim. 6:9]

corroded, and their corrosion will be a witness against you and will eat your flesh like fire. ªYou have heaped up treasure in the last days. ⁴Indeed ªthe wages of the laborers who mowed your fields, which you kept back by fraud, cry out; and ᵇthe cries of the reapers have reached the ears of the Lord of ¹Sabaoth. ⁵You have lived on the earth in pleasure and ¹luxury; you have ²fattened your hearts ³as in a day of slaughter. ⁶You have condemned, you have murdered the just; he does not resist you.

BE PATIENT AND PERSEVERING

⁷Therefore be patient, brethren, until the coming of the Lord. See *how* the farmer waits for the precious fruit of the earth, waiting patiently for it until it receives the early and latter rain. ⁸You also be patient. Establish your hearts, for the coming of the Lord ¹is at hand.

⁹Do not ¹grumble against one another, brethren, lest you be ²condemned. Behold, the Judge is standing at the door! ¹⁰ªMy brethren, take the prophets, who spoke in the name of the Lord, as an example of suffering and ᵇpatience. ¹¹Indeed ªwe count them blessed who ᵇendure. You have heard of ᶜthe perseverance of Job and seen ᵈthe end *intended by* the Lord— that ᵉthe Lord is very compassionate and merciful.

¹²But above all, my brethren, ªdo not swear, either by heaven or by earth or with any other oath. But let your "Yes" be "Yes," and *your* "No," "No," lest you fall into ¹judgment.

MEETING SPECIFIC NEEDS
(cf. 1 Kin. 18:41–46)

¹³Is anyone among you suffering? Let him ªpray. Is anyone cheerful? ᵇLet him sing psalms. ¹⁴Is anyone among you sick? Let him call for the elders of the church, and let them pray over him, ªanointing him with oil in the name of the Lord. ¹⁵And the prayer of faith will save the sick, and the Lord will raise him up. ªAnd if he has committed sins, he will be forgiven. ¹⁶¹Confess *your* trespasses to one another, and pray for one another, that you may be healed. ªThe effective, ²fervent prayer of a righteous man avails much. ¹⁷Elijah was a man ªwith a nature like ours, and ᵇhe prayed earnestly that it would not rain; and it did not rain on the land for three years and six months. ¹⁸And he prayed ªagain, and the heaven gave rain, and the earth produced its fruit.

BRING BACK THE ERRING ONE

¹⁹Brethren, if anyone among you wanders from the truth, and someone ªturns him back, ²⁰let him know that he who turns a sinner from the error of his way ªwill save ¹a soul from death and ᵇcover a multitude of sins.

5:3 ªRom. 2:5
5:4 ªLev. 19:13; Job 24:10; Jer. 22:13; Mal. 3:5
ᵇEx. 2:23; Deut. 24:15; Job 31:38
5:10 ªMatt. 5:12
ᵇHeb. 10:36
5:11 ª[Ps. 94:12; Matt. 5:10]; James 1:2
ᵇ[James 1:12]
ᶜJob 1:21, 22; 2:10
ᵈJob 42:10
ᵉNum. 14:18
5:12 ªMatt. 5:34–37
5:13 ªPs. 50:14, 15
ᵇEph. 5:19
5:14 ªMark 6:13; 16:18
5:15 ªIs. 33:24
5:16 ªNum. 11:2
5:17 ªActs 14:15
ᵇ1 Kin. 17:1; 18:1
5:18 ª1 Kin. 18:1, 42
5:19 ªMatt. 18:15; Gal. 6:1
5:20 ªRom. 11:14; 1 Cor. 1:21; James 1:21
ᵇProv. 10:12; [1 Pet. 4:8]

5:4 ¹Lit., in Heb., *Hosts* 5:5 ¹*indulgence* ²Lit. *nourished* ³NU omits *as*
5:8 ¹*has drawn near* 5:9 ¹Lit. *groan* ²NU, M *judged* 5:12 ¹M *hypocrisy*
5:16 ¹NU *Therefore confess your sins* ²*supplication* 5:20 ¹NU *his soul*

THE FIRST EPISTLE OF

PETER

GREETING TO THE ELECT PILGRIMS

1 Peter, an apostle of Jesus Christ,

To the ¹pilgrims ᵃof the Dispersion in Pontus, Galatia, Cappadocia, Asia, and Bithynia, ²ᵃelect ᵇaccording to the foreknowledge of God the Father, ᶜin sanctification of the Spirit, for ᵈobedience and ᵉsprinkling of the blood of Jesus Christ:

ᶠGrace to you and peace be multiplied.

A HEAVENLY INHERITANCE

³ᵃBlessed *be* the God and Father of our Lord Jesus Christ, who ᵇaccording to His abundant mercy ᶜhas begotten us again to a living hope ᵈthrough the resurrection of Jesus Christ from the dead, ⁴to an inheritance ¹incorruptible and undefiled and that does not fade away, ᵃreserved in heaven for you, ⁵ᵃwho are kept by the power of God through faith for salvation ready to be revealed in the last time.

⁶ᵃIn this you greatly rejoice, though now ᵇfor a little while, if need be, ᶜyou have been ¹grieved by various trials, ⁷that ᵃthe genuineness of your faith, *being* much more precious than gold that perishes, though ᵇit is tested by fire, ᶜmay be found to praise, honor, and glory at the revelation of Jesus Christ, ⁸ᵃwhom having not ¹seen you love. ᵇThough now you do not see *Him,* yet believing, you rejoice with joy inexpressible and full of glory, ⁹receiving the end of your faith—the salvation of *your* souls.

¹⁰Of this salvation the prophets have inquired and searched carefully, who prophesied of the grace *that would come* to you, ¹¹searching what, or what manner of time, ᵃthe Spirit of Christ who was in them was indicating when He testified beforehand the sufferings of Christ and the glories that would follow. ¹²To them it was revealed that, not to themselves, but to ¹us they were ministering the things which now have been reported to you through those who have preached the gospel to you by the Holy Spirit sent from heaven—things which ᵃangels desire to look into.

LIVING BEFORE GOD OUR FATHER

¹³Therefore gird up the loins of your mind, be sober, and rest *your* hope fully upon the grace that is to be brought to you at the revelation of Jesus Christ; ¹⁴as obedient children, not ᵃconforming yourselves to the former lusts, *as* in your ignorance; ¹⁵ᵃbut as He who called you *is* holy, you also be holy in all *your* conduct, ¹⁶because it is written, ᵃ"Be holy, for I am holy."

1:1 ᵃJohn 7:35; James 1:1

1:2 ᵃEph. 1:4 ᵇ[Rom. 8:29]; 1 Pet. 1:20 ᶜ2 Thess. 2:13 ᵈRom. 1:5 ᵉIs. 52:15; Heb. 10:22; 12:24 ᶠRom. 1:7

1:3 ᵃEph. 1:3 ᵇGal. 6:16; Titus 3:5 ᶜ[John 3:3, 5] ᵈ1 Cor. 15:20; 1 Pet. 3:21

1:4 ᵃCol. 1:5

1:5 ᵃJohn 10:28; [Phil. 4:7]

1:6 ᵃMatt. 5:12 ᵇ2 Cor. 4:17 ᶜJames 1:2; 1 Pet. 4:12

1:7 ᵃJames 1:3 ᵇJob 23:10 ᶜ[Rom. 2:7]

1:8 ᵃ1 John 4:20 ᵇJohn 20:29

1:11 ᵃ2 Pet. 1:21

1:12 ᵃEph. 3:10

1:14 ᵃ[Rom. 12:2]; 1 Pet. 4:2

1:15 ᵃ[2 Cor. 7:1]

1:16 ᵃLev. 11:44, 45; 19:2; 20:7

1:1 ¹*sojourners,* temporary residents   1:4 ¹*imperishable*   1:6 ¹*distressed*
1:8 ¹M *known*   1:12 ¹NU, M *you*

17And if you call on the Father, who awithout partiality judges according to each one's work, conduct yourselves throughout the time of your 1stay *here* in fear; 18knowing that you were not redeemed with 1corruptible things, *like* silver or gold, from your aimless conduct *received* by tradition from your fathers, 19but awith the precious blood of Christ, bas of a lamb without blemish and without spot. 20aHe indeed was foreordained before the foundation of the world, but was 1manifest bin these last times for you 21who through Him believe in God, awho raised Him from the dead and bgave Him glory, so that your faith and hope are in God.

THE ENDURING WORD

22Since you ahave purified your souls in obeying the truth 1through the Spirit in 2sincere blove of the brethren, love one another fervently with a pure heart, 23ahaving been born again, not of 1corruptible seed but 2incorruptible, bthrough the word of God which lives and abides 3forever, 24because

a"All flesh *is* as grass,
    And all 1the glory of man as the flower of the grass.
    The grass withers,
    And its flower falls away,
25 aBut the 1word of the Lord endures forever."

bNow this is the word which by the gospel was preached to you.

2 Therefore, alaying aside all malice, all deceit, hypocrisy, envy, and all evil speaking, 2aas newborn babes, desire the pure bmilk of the word, that you may grow 1thereby, 3if indeed you have atasted that the Lord *is* gracious.

THE CHOSEN STONE AND HIS CHOSEN PEOPLE
(Ps. 118:22; Is. 28:16)

4Coming to Him *as to* a living stone, arejected indeed by men, but chosen by God *and* precious, 5you also, as living stones, are being built up a spiritual house, a holy priesthood, to offer up spiritual sacrifices acceptable to God through Jesus Christ. 6Therefore it is also contained in the Scripture,

a"Behold, I lay in Zion
    A chief cornerstone, elect, precious,
    And he who believes on Him will by no means be put to
        shame."

7Therefore, to you who believe, *He is* precious; but to those who 1are disobedient,

a"The stone which the builders rejected
    Has become the chief cornerstone,"

8and

a"A stone of stumbling
    And a rock of offense."

bThey stumble, being disobedient to the word, cto which they also were appointed.

1:17 aActs 10:34
1:19
aActs 20:28;
1 Pet. 1:2
bEx. 12:5; Is. 53:7
1:20 aRom. 3:25
bGal. 4:4
1:21 aActs 2:24
bActs 2:33
1:22 aActs 15:9
bJohn 13:34;
Rom. 12:10;
Heb. 13:1;
1 Pet. 2:17; 3:8
1:23 aJohn 1:13
b1 Thess. 2:13;
James 1:18
1:24 aIs. 40:6–8;
James 1:10
1:25 aIs. 40:8
b[John 1:1]
2:1 aHeb. 12:1
2:2
a[Matt. 18:3;
19:14;
Mark 10:15;
Luke 18:17];
1 Cor. 14:20
b1 Cor. 3:2
2:3 aPs. 34:8;
Titus 3:4;
Heb. 6:5
2:4 aPs. 118:22
2:6 aIs. 28:16;
Rom. 9:32, 33;
10:11; 1 Pet. 2:8
2:7 aPs. 118:22;
Matt. 21:42;
Luke 2:34
2:8 aIs. 8:14
b1 Cor. 1:23;
Gal. 5:11
cRom. 9:22

1:17 1*sojourning, dwelling* as resident aliens   1:18 1*perishable*
1:20 1*revealed*   1:22 1NU omits *through the Spirit*   2Lit. *unhypocritical*
1:23 1*perishable*   2*imperishable*   3NU omits *forever*   1:24 1NU *its glory as*
1:25 1*spoken word*   2:2 1NU adds *up to salvation*   2:7 1NU *disbelieve*

[9]But you *are* a chosen generation, a royal priesthood, a holy nation, His own special people, that you may proclaim the praises of Him who called you out of [a]darkness into His marvelous light; [10a]who once *were* not a people but *are* now the people of God, who had not obtained mercy but now have obtained mercy.

LIVING BEFORE THE WORLD

[11]Beloved, I beg *you* as sojourners and pilgrims, abstain from fleshly lusts [a]which war against the soul, [12a]having your conduct honorable among the Gentiles, that when they speak against you as evildoers, [b]they may, by *your* good works which they observe, glorify God in the day of visitation.

SUBMISSION TO GOVERNMENT

(cf. Rom. 13:1–5)

[13a]Therefore submit yourselves to every [1]ordinance of man for the Lord's sake, whether to the king as supreme, [14]or to governors, as to those who are sent by him for the punishment of evildoers and *for the* praise of those who do good. [15]For this is the will of God, that by doing good you may put to silence the ignorance of foolish men— [16a]as free, yet not [b]using liberty as a cloak for [1]vice, but as bondservants of God. [17]Honor all *people.* Love the brotherhood. Fear [a]God. Honor the king.

SUBMISSION TO MASTERS

(Is. 53:7–9)

[18a]Servants, *be* submissive to *your* masters with all fear, not only to the good and gentle, but also to the harsh. [19]For this *is* a [a]commendable, if because of conscience toward God one endures grief, suffering wrongfully. [20]For [a]what credit *is it* if, when you are beaten for your faults, you take it patiently? But when you do good and suffer, if you take it patiently, this *is* commendable before God. [21]For [a]to this you were called, because Christ also suffered for [1]us, [b]leaving [2]us an example, that you should follow His steps:

[22] "Who[a] committed no sin,
   Nor was deceit found in His mouth";

[23a]who, when He was reviled, did not revile in return; when He suffered, He did not threaten, but [b]committed *Himself* to Him who judges righteously; [24a]who Himself bore our sins in His own body on the tree, [b]that we, having died to sins, might live for righteousness—[c]by whose [1]stripes you were healed. [25]For [a]you were like sheep going astray, but have now returned [b]to the Shepherd and [1]Overseer of your souls.

SUBMISSION TO HUSBANDS

3 Wives, likewise, *be* [a]submissive to your own husbands, that even if some do not obey the word, [b]they, without a word, may [c]be won by the conduct of their wives, [2a]when they observe your chaste conduct *accompanied* by fear. [3a]Do not let your adornment be *merely* outward—arranging the hair,

2:9 [a]Is. 9:2;
42:16;
[Acts 26:18;
2 Cor. 4:6]

2:10
[a]Hos. 1:9, 10;
2:23; Rom. 9:25;
10:19

2:11
[a][Rom. 8:13];
Gal. 5:17;
James 4:1

2:12 [a]2 Cor. 8:21;
Phil. 2:15;
Titus 2:8;
1 Pet. 2:15; 3:16
[b]Matt. 5:16; 9:8;
John 13:31;
1 Pet. 4:11, 16

2:13 [a]Matt. 22:21

2:16
[a]Rom. 6:14,
20, 22;
1 Cor. 7:22;
[Gal. 5:1]
[b]Gal. 5:13

2:17 [a]Prov. 24:21

2:18
[a]Eph. 6:5–8

2:19 [a]Matt. 5:10

2:20
[a]Luke 6:32–34

2:21
[a]Matt. 16:24;
1 Thess. 3:3, 4
[b][1 John 2:6]

2:22 [a]Is. 53:9;
2 Cor. 5:21

2:23 [a]Is. 53:7;
Heb. 12:3;
1 Pet. 3:9
[b]Luke 23:46

2:24 [a]Is. 53:4, 11;
1 Cor. 15:3;
[Heb. 9:28]
[b]Rom. 7:6
[c]Is. 53:5

2:25 [a]Is. 53:5, 6
[b]Is. 40:11;
[Ezek. 34:23];
Zech. 13:7

3:1 [a]Gen. 3:16;
1 Cor. 14:34;
Eph. 5:22;
Col. 3:18
[b]1 Cor. 7:16
[c]Matt. 18:15

3:2
[a]1 Pet. 2:12; 3:6

3:3 [a]Is. 3:18;
1 Tim. 2:9

2:13 [1]*institution*   2:16 [1]*wickedness*   2:21 [1]NU *you*   [2]NU, M *you*
2:24 [1]*wounds*   2:25 [1]Gr. *Episkopos*

wearing gold, or putting on *fine* apparel— [4]rather *let it be* [a]the hidden person of the heart, with the [1]incorruptible *beauty* of a gentle and quiet spirit, which is very precious in the sight of God. [5]For in this manner, in former times, the holy women who trusted in God also adorned themselves, being submissive to their own husbands, [6]as Sarah obeyed Abraham, [a]calling him lord, whose daughters you are if you do good and are not afraid with any terror.

A WORD TO HUSBANDS

[7a]Husbands, likewise, dwell with *them* with understanding, giving honor to the wife, [b]as to the weaker vessel, and as *being* heirs together of the grace of life, [c]that your prayers may not be hindered.

CALLED TO BLESSING

[8]Finally, all *of you be* of one mind, having compassion for one another; love as brothers, *be* tenderhearted, *be* [1]courteous; [9a]not returning evil for evil or reviling for reviling, but on the contrary [b]blessing, knowing that you were called to this, [c]that you may inherit a blessing. [10]For

[a]"He who would love life
  And see good days,
[b]Let him [1]refrain his tongue from evil,
  And his lips from speaking deceit.
[11] Let him [a]turn away from evil and do good;
[b]Let him seek peace and pursue it.
[12] For the eyes of the LORD *are* on the righteous,
  [a]And His ears *are open* to their prayers;
  But the face of the LORD *is* against those who do evil."

SUFFERING FOR RIGHT AND WRONG

[13a]And who *is* he who will harm you if you become followers of what is good? [14a]But even if you should suffer for righteousness' sake, *you are* blessed. [b]"And do not be afraid of their threats, nor be troubled." [15]But [1]sanctify [2]the Lord God in your hearts, and always [a]*be* ready to *give* a defense to everyone who asks you a reason for the [b]hope that is in you, with meekness and fear; [16a]having a good conscience, that when they defame you as evildoers, those who revile your good conduct in Christ may be ashamed. [17]For *it is* better, if it is the will of God, to suffer for doing good than for doing evil.

CHRIST'S SUFFERING AND OURS

[18]For Christ also suffered once for sins, the just for the unjust, that He might bring [1]us to God, being put to death in the flesh but made alive by the Spirit, [19]by whom also He went and preached to the spirits in prison, [20]who formerly were disobedient, [1]when once the Divine longsuffering waited in the days of Noah, while *the* ark was being prepared, in which a few, that is, eight souls, were saved through water. [21a]There is also an antitype which now saves us—baptism [b](not the removal of the filth of the flesh, [c]but the answer of a good

3:4 [a]Rom. 2:29
3:6 [a]Gen. 18:12
3:7 [a]1 Cor. 7:3; [Eph. 5:25]; Col. 3:19 [b]1 Cor. 12:23 [c]Job 42:8
3:9 [a][Prov. 17:13] [b]Matt. 5:44 [c]Matt. 25:34
3:10 [a]Ps. 34:12–16 [b]James 1:26
3:11 [a]Ps. 37:27 [b]Rom. 12:18
3:12 [a]John 9:31
3:13 [a]Prov. 16:7
3:14 [a]James 1:12 [b]Is. 8:12
3:15 [a]Ps. 119:46 [b][Titus 3:7]
3:16 [a]1 Tim. 1:5; Heb. 13:18; 1 Pet. 3:21
3:21 [a]Acts 16:33; Eph. 5:26 [b][Titus 3:5] [c][Rom. 10:10]

conscience toward God), through the resurrection of Jesus Christ, [22]who has gone into heaven and [a]is at the right hand of God, [b]angels and authorities and powers having been made subject to Him.

4 Therefore, since Christ suffered [1]for us in the flesh, arm yourselves also with the same mind, for he who has suffered in the flesh has ceased from sin, [2]that he no longer should live the rest of *his* time in the flesh for the lusts of men, [a]but for the will of God. [3]For we *have spent* enough of our past [1]lifetime in doing the will of the Gentiles—when we walked in lewdness, lusts, drunkenness, revelries, drinking parties, and abominable idolatries. [4]In regard to these, they think it strange that you do not run with *them* in the same flood of dissipation, speaking evil of *you*. [5]They will give an account to Him who is ready [a]to judge the living and the dead. [6]For this reason [a]the gospel was preached also to those who are dead, that they might be judged according to men in the flesh, but [b]live according to God in the spirit.

SERVING FOR GOD'S GLORY

[7]But [a]the end of all things is at hand; therefore be serious and watchful in your prayers. [8]And above all things have fervent love for one another, for [a]"love will cover a multitude of sins." [9a]*Be* hospitable to one another [b]without grumbling. [10a]As each one has received a gift, minister it to one another, [b]as good stewards of [c]the manifold grace of God. [11a]If anyone speaks, *let him speak* as the [1]oracles of God. If anyone ministers, *let him do it* as with the ability which God supplies, that [b]in all things God may be glorified through Jesus Christ, to whom belong the glory and the [2]dominion forever and ever. Amen.

SUFFERING FOR GOD'S GLORY

[12]Beloved, do not think it strange concerning the fiery trial which is to try you, as though some strange thing happened to you; [13]but rejoice [a]to the extent that you partake of Christ's sufferings, that [b]when His glory is revealed, you may also be glad with exceeding joy. [14]If you are [1]reproached for the name of Christ, [a]blessed *are you,* for the Spirit of glory and of God rests upon you. [2]On their part He is blasphemed, [b]but on your part He is glorified. [15]But let none of you suffer as a murderer, a thief, an evildoer, or as a [1]busybody in other people's matters. [16]Yet if *anyone suffers* as a Christian, let him not be ashamed, but let him glorify God in this [1]matter.

[17]For the time *has come* [a]for judgment to begin at the house of God; and if *it begins* with us first, [b]what will *be* the end of those who do not obey the gospel of God? [18]Now

[a]"If the righteous one is scarcely saved,
    Where will the ungodly and the sinner appear?"

[19]Therefore let those who suffer according to the will of God [a]commit their souls *to Him* in doing good, as to a faithful Creator.

3:22 [a]Ps. 110:1
[b]Rom. 8:38;
Heb. 1:6

4:2 [a]John 1:13

4:5 [a]Acts 10:42;
Rom. 14:9;
2 Tim. 4:1

4:6
[a]1 Pet. 1:12; 3:19
[b][Rom. 8:9, 13];
Gal. 5:25

4:7 [a]Rom. 13:11;
Heb. 9:26;
James 5:8, 9;
1 John 2:18

4:8
[a][Prov. 10:12];
1 Cor. 13:4;
James 5:20

4:9 [a]1 Tim. 3:2;
Heb. 13:2
[b]2 Cor. 9:7

4:10
[a]Rom. 12:6–8
[b]Matt. 24:45;
1 Cor. 4:1, 2
[c][1 Cor. 12:4]

4:11 [a]Eph. 4:29
[b][1 Cor. 10:31];
Eph. 5:20

4:13 [a]James 1:2
[b]2 Tim. 2:12

4:14 [a]Matt. 5:11;
Luke 6:22;
Acts 5:41
[b]Matt. 5:16

4:17 [a]Is. 10:12
[b]Luke 10:12

4:18 [a]Prov. 11:31

4:19
[a]Ps. 37:5–7;
2 Tim. 1:12

4:1 [1]NU omits *for us*   4:3 [1]NU *time*   4:11 [1]*utterances*   [2]*sovereignty*
4:14 [1]*insulted* or *reviled*   [2]NU omits the rest of v. 14.   4:15 [1]*meddler*
4:16 [1]NU *name*

SHEPHERD THE FLOCK

5 The elders who are among you I exhort, I who am a fellow elder and a [a]witness of the sufferings of Christ, and also a partaker of the [b]glory that will be revealed: 2[a]Shepherd the flock of God which is among you, serving as overseers, [b]not by compulsion but [1]willingly, [c]not for dishonest gain but eagerly; 3nor as [a]being [1]lords over [b]those entrusted to you, but [c]being examples to the flock; 4and when [a]the Chief Shepherd appears, you will receive [b]the crown of glory that does not fade away.

SUBMIT TO GOD, RESIST THE DEVIL

5Likewise you younger people, submit yourselves to *your* elders. Yes, [a]all of *you* be submissive to one another, and be clothed with humility, for

[b]"God resists the proud,
    But [c]gives grace to the humble."

6Therefore humble yourselves under the mighty hand of God, that He may exalt you in due time, 7casting all your care upon Him, for He cares for you.
8Be [1]sober, be [2]vigilant; [3]because your adversary the devil walks about like a roaring lion, seeking whom he may devour. 9Resist him, steadfast in the faith, knowing that the same sufferings are experienced by your brotherhood in the world. 10But [1]may the God of all grace, [a]who called [2]us to His eternal glory by Christ Jesus, after you have suffered a while, [3]perfect, establish, strengthen, and settle *you.* 11[a]To Him *be* the glory and the dominion forever and ever. Amen.

FAREWELL AND PEACE

12By [a]Silvanus, our faithful brother as I consider him, I have written to you briefly, exhorting and testifying [b]that this is the true grace of God in which you stand.
13She who is in Babylon, elect together with *you,* greets you; and *so does* [a]Mark my son. 14Greet one another with a kiss of love.

Peace to you all who are in Christ Jesus. Amen.

5:1 [a]Matt. 26:37
[b]Rom. 8:17, 18

5:2 [a]John 21:16;
Acts 20:28
[b]1 Cor. 9:17
[c]1 Tim. 3:3

5:3 [a]Ezek. 34:4;
Matt. 20:25
[b]Ps. 33:12
[c]John 13:15;
Phil. 3:17;
1 Thess. 1:7;
2 Thess. 3:9;
1 Tim. 4:12;
Titus 2:7

5:4 [a]Is. 40:11;
Zech. 13:7;
Heb. 13:20;
1 Pet. 2:25
[b]2 Tim. 4:8

5:5 [a]Rom. 12:10;
Eph. 5:21
[b]Prov. 3:34;
James 4:6
[c]Is. 57:15

5:10 [a]1 Cor. 1:9;
1 Thess. 2:12

5:11 [a]Rev. 1:6

5:12 [a]2 Cor. 1:19;
1 Thess. 1:1;
2 Thess. 1:1
[b]Acts 20:24

5:13
[a]Acts 12:12, 25;
15:37, 39;
Col. 4:10;
Philem. 24

5:2 [1]NU adds *according to God*   5:3 [1]*masters*   5:8 [1]*self-controlled*
[2]*watchful*   [3]NU, M omit *because*   5:10 [1]NU *the God of all grace,*
[2]NU, M *you*   [3]NU *will perfect*

THE SECOND EPISTLE OF
PETER

GREETING THE FAITHFUL

1 Simon Peter, a bondservant and ᵃapostle of Jesus Christ,

To those who have ¹obtained ᵇlike² precious faith with us by the righteousness of our God and Savior Jesus Christ:

²ᵃGrace and peace be multiplied to you in the knowledge of God and of Jesus our Lord, ³as His ᵃdivine power has given to us all things that *pertain* to life and godliness, through the knowledge of Him ᵇwho called us by glory and virtue, ⁴ᵃby which have been given to us exceedingly great and precious promises, that through these you may be ᵇpartakers of the divine nature, having escaped the ¹corruption *that is* in the world through lust.

FRUITFUL GROWTH IN THE FAITH

⁵But also for this very reason, ᵃgiving all diligence, add to your faith virtue, to virtue ᵇknowledge, ⁶to knowledge self-control, to self-control ¹perseverance, to perseverance godliness, ⁷to godliness brotherly kindness, and ᵃto brotherly kindness love. ⁸For if these things are yours and abound, *you* will be neither ¹barren ᵃnor unfruitful in the knowledge of our Lord Jesus Christ. ⁹For he who lacks these things is ᵃshortsighted, even to blindness, and has forgotten that he was cleansed from his old sins.

¹⁰Therefore, brethren, be even more diligent ᵃto make your call and election sure, for if you do these things you will never stumble; ¹¹for so an entrance will be supplied to you abundantly into the everlasting kingdom of our Lord and Savior Jesus Christ.

PETER'S APPROACHING DEATH

¹²For this reason ᵃI will not be negligent to remind you always of these things, ᵇthough you know and are established in the present truth. ¹³Yes, I think it is right, ᵃas long as I am in this ¹tent, ᵇto stir you up by reminding *you*, ¹⁴ᵃknowing that shortly I *must* ¹put off my tent, just as ᵇour Lord Jesus Christ showed me. ¹⁵Moreover I will be careful to ensure that you always have a reminder of these things after my ¹decease.

THE TRUSTWORTHY PROPHETIC WORD
(Matt. 17:5; Mark 9:7; Luke 9:35)

¹⁶For we did not follow ᵃcunningly devised fables when we made known to you the ᵇpower and ᶜcoming of our Lord Jesus Christ, but were ᵈeyewitnesses of His majesty. ¹⁷For He

---

1:1 ᵃGal. 2:8
ᵇEph. 4:5
1:2 ᵃDan. 4:1
1:3 ᵃ1 Pet. 1:5
ᵇ1 Thess. 2:12;
2 Thess. 2:14;
1 Pet. 5:10
1:4
ᵃ2 Cor. 1:20; 7:1
ᵇ[2 Cor. 3:18]
1:5 ᵃ2 Pet. 3:18
ᵇ2 Pet. 1:2
1:7 ᵃGal. 6:10
1:8 ᵃ[John 15:2]
1:9
ᵃ1 John 2:9–11
1:10 ᵃ2 Cor. 13:5;
1 John 3:19
1:12 ᵃPhil. 3:1;
1 John 2:21;
Jude 5
ᵇ1 Pet. 5:12
1:13
ᵃ[2 Cor. 5:1, 4];
2 Pet. 1:14
ᵇ2 Pet. 3:1
1:14 ᵃ[2 Cor. 5:1;
2 Tim. 4:6]
ᵇJohn 13:36;
21:18, 19
1:16 ᵃ1 Cor. 1:17
ᵇ[Matt. 28:18;
Eph. 1:19–22]
ᶜ[1 Pet. 5:4]
ᵈMatt. 17:1–5;
Luke 1:2

1:1 ¹*received* ²*faith of the same value* 1:4 ¹*depravity* 1:6 ¹*patience*
1:8 ¹*useless* 1:13 ¹*Body* 1:14 ¹*Die and leave this body* 1:15 ¹Lit. *exodus, departure*

received from God the Father honor and glory when such a voice came to Him from the Excellent Glory: a"This is My beloved Son, in whom I am well pleased." 18And we heard this voice which came from heaven when we were with Him on athe holy mountain.

19And so we have the prophetic word confirmed, which you do well to heed as a alight that shines in a dark place, buntil cthe day dawns and the morning star rises in your dhearts; 20knowing this first, that ano prophecy of Scripture is of any private 1interpretation, 21for aprophecy never came by the will of man, bbut 1holy men of God spoke *as they were* moved by the Holy Spirit.

DESTRUCTIVE DOCTRINES

2 But there were also false prophets among the people, even as there will be afalse teachers among you, who will secretly bring in destructive heresies, even denying the Lord who bought them, *and* bring on themselves swift destruction. 2And many will follow their destructive ways, because of whom the way of truth will be blasphemed. 3By covetousness they will exploit you with deceptive words; for a long time their judgment has not been idle, and their destruction 1does not slumber.

DOOM OF FALSE TEACHERS

4For if God did not spare the angels who sinned, but cast *them* down to 1hell and delivered *them* into chains of darkness, to be reserved for judgment; 5and did not spare the ancient world, but saved Noah, *one* of eight *people*, a preacher of righteousness, bringing in the flood on the world of the ungodly; 6and turning the cities of aSodom and Gomorrah into ashes, condemned *them* to destruction, making *them* an example to those who afterward would live ungodly; 7and adelivered righteous Lot, *who was* oppressed by the filthy conduct of the wicked 8(for that righteous man, dwelling among them, atormented *his* righteous soul from day to day by seeing and hearing *their* lawless deeds)— 9then athe Lord knows how to deliver the godly out of temptations and to reserve the unjust under punishment for the day of judgment, 10and especially athose who walk according to the flesh in the lust of uncleanness and despise authority. b*They are* presumptuous, self-willed. They are not afraid to speak evil of 1dignitaries, 11whereas aangels, who are greater in power and might, do not bring a reviling accusation against them before the Lord.

DEPRAVITY OF FALSE TEACHERS

12But these, alike natural brute beasts made to be caught and destroyed, speak evil of the things they do not understand, and will utterly perish in their own corruption, 13a*and* will receive the wages of unrighteousness, *as* those who count it pleasure bto 1carouse in the daytime. c*They are* spots and blemishes, 2carousing in their own deceptions while dthey feast with you, 14having eyes full of 1adultery and that cannot

---

1:17 aPs. 2:7;
Is. 42:1;
Matt. 17:5;
Mark 9:7;
Luke 1:35; 9:35
1:18 aMatt. 17:1
1:19
a[John 1:4, 5, 9]
bProv. 4:18
cRev. 2:28; 22:16
d[2 Cor. 4:5–7]
1:20
a[Rom. 12:6]
1:21 aJer. 23:26;
[2 Tim. 3:16]
b2 Sam. 23:2;
Luke 1:70;
Acts 1:16; 3:18;
1 Pet. 1:11
2:1
aMatt. 24:5, 24;
1 Tim. 4:1, 2
2:6
aGen. 19:1–26;
Jude 7
2:7
aGen. 19:16, 29
2:8 aPs. 119:139
2:9
aPs. 34:15–19;
1 Cor. 10:13;
Rev. 3:10
2:10
aJude 4, 7, 8
bEx. 22:28;
Jude 8
2:11 aJude 9
2:12 aJude 10
2:13 aPhil. 3:19
bRom. 13:13
cJude 12
d1 Cor. 11:20, 21

1:19 1Or *We also have the more sure prophetic word*   1:20 1Or *origin*
1:21 1NU *men spoke from God*   2:3 1M *will not*   2:4 1Lit. *Tartarus*
2:10 1*glorious ones,* lit. *glories*   2:13 1*revel*   2*reveling*   2:14 1Lit. *an adulteress*

cease from sin, enticing unstable souls. [a]They have a heart trained in covetous practices, *and are* accursed children. [15]They have forsaken the right way and gone astray, following the way of [a]Balaam the *son* of Beor, who loved the wages of unrighteousness; [16]but he was rebuked for his iniquity: a dumb donkey speaking with a man's voice restrained the madness of the prophet.

[17a]These are wells without water, [1]clouds carried by a tempest, for whom is reserved the blackness of darkness [2]forever.

DECEPTIONS OF FALSE TEACHERS

[18]For when they speak great swelling *words* of emptiness, they allure through the lusts of the flesh, through lewdness, the ones who [1]have actually escaped from those who live in error. [19]While they promise them liberty, they themselves are slaves of [1]corruption; [a]for by whom a person is overcome, by him also he is brought into [2]bondage. [20]For if, after they [a]have escaped the pollutions of the world through the knowledge of the Lord and Savior Jesus Christ, they are [b]again entangled in them and overcome, the latter end is worse for them than the beginning. [21]For [a]it would have been better for them not to have known the way of righteousness, than having known *it,* to turn from the holy commandment delivered to them. [22]But it has happened to them according to the true proverb: [a]"A dog returns to his own vomit," and, "a sow, having washed, to her wallowing in the mire."

GOD'S PROMISE IS NOT SLACK
(Gen. 6:5—8:22)

3 Beloved, I now write to you this second epistle (in *both of* which [a]I stir up your pure minds by way of reminder), [2]that you may be mindful of the words [a]which were spoken before by the holy prophets, [b]and of the commandment of [1]us, the apostles of the Lord and Savior, [3]knowing this first: that scoffers will come in the last days, [a]walking according to their own lusts, [4]and saying, "Where is the promise of His coming? For since the fathers fell asleep, all things continue as *they were* from the beginning of [a]creation." [5]For this they willfully forget: that [a]by the word of God the heavens were of old, and the earth [b]standing out of water and in the water, [6a]by which the world *that* then existed perished, being flooded with water. [7]But [a]the heavens and the earth *which* are now preserved by the same word, are reserved for [b]fire until the day of judgment and [1]perdition of ungodly men.

[8]But, beloved, do not forget this one thing, that with the Lord one day *is* as a thousand years, and [a]a thousand years as one day. [9a]The Lord is not slack concerning *His* promise, as some count slackness, but [b]longsuffering toward [1]us, [c]not willing that any should perish but [d]that all should come to repentance.

THE DAY OF THE LORD

[10]But [a]the day of the Lord will come as a thief in the night, in which [b]the heavens will pass away with a great noise, and

---

2:14 [a]Jude 11
2:15
[a]Num. 22:5, 7;
Deut. 23:4;
Neh. 13:2;
Jude 11; Rev. 2:14
2:17 [a]Jude 12, 13
2:19 [a]John 8:34;
Rom. 6:16
2:20
[a]Matt. 12:45
[b]Luke 11:26;
[Heb. 6:4–6]
2:21 [a]Luke 12:47
2:22 [a]Prov. 26:11
3:1 [a]2 Pet. 1:13
3:2 [a]2 Pet. 1:21
[b]Jude 17
3:3 [a]2 Pet. 2:10
3:4 [a]Gen. 6:1–7
3:5 [a]Gen. 1:6, 9;
Heb. 11:3
[b]Ps. 24:2; 136:6
3:6 [a]Gen. 7:11,
12, 21–23;
Matt. 24:37–39;
Luke 17:26, 27;
2 Pet. 2:5
3:7
[a]2 Pet. 3:10, 12
[b]Matt. 25:41;
[2 Thess. 1:8]
3:8 [a]Ps. 90:4
3:9 [a]Hab. 2:3;
Rom. 13:11;
Heb. 10:37
[b]Ps. 86:15;
Is. 30:18
[c]Ezek. 33:11
[d]Matt. 20:28;
[Rom. 2:4]
3:10
[a]Matt. 24:42, 43;
Luke 12:39;
1 Thess. 5:2;
Rev. 3:3; 16:15
[b]Gen. 1:6–8;
Ps. 102:25,
26; Is. 51:6;
Rev. 20:11

2:17 [1]NU *and mists*   [2]NU omits *forever*   2:18 [1]NU *are barely escaping*
2:19 [1]*depravity*   [2]*slavery*   3:2 [1]NU, M *the apostles of your Lord and Savior*
or *your apostles of the Lord and Savior*   3:7 [1]*destruction*   3:9 [1]NU *you*

the elements will melt with fervent heat; both the earth and the works that are in it will be [1]burned up. [11]Therefore, since all these things will be dissolved, what manner *of persons* ought you to be [a]in holy conduct and godliness, [12a]looking for and hastening the coming of the day of God, because of which the heavens will [b]be dissolved, being on fire, and the elements will [c]melt with fervent heat? [13]Nevertheless we, according to His promise, look for [a]new heavens and a [b]new earth in which righteousness dwells.

BE STEADFAST

[14]Therefore, beloved, looking forward to these things, be diligent [a]to be found by Him in peace, without spot and blameless; [15]and consider *that* [a]the longsuffering of our Lord *is* salvation—as also our beloved brother Paul, according to the wisdom given to him, has written to you, [16]as also in all his [a]epistles, speaking in them of these things, in which are some things hard to understand, which untaught and unstable *people* twist to their own destruction, as *they do* also the [b]rest of the Scriptures.

[17]You therefore, beloved, [a]since you know *this* beforehand, [b]beware lest you also fall from your own steadfastness, being led away with the error of the wicked; [18a]but grow in the grace and knowledge of our Lord and Savior Jesus Christ.

[b]To Him *be* the glory both now and forever. Amen.

3:11 [a]1 Pet. 1:15

3:12
[a]1 Cor. 1:7, 8;
Titus 2:13–15
[b]Ps. 50:3
[c]Is. 24:19; 34:4;
Mic. 1:4

3:13 [a]Is. 65:17;
66:22
[b][Rom. 8:21];
Rev. 21:1

3:14 [a]1 Cor. 1:8;
15:58;
[1 Thess. 3:12, 13;
5:23]

3:15 [a]Ps. 86:15;
Rom. 2:4;
1 Pet. 3:20

3:16 [a]Rom. 8:19;
1 Cor. 15:24;
1 Thess. 4:15;
2 Thess. 1:10
[b]2 Tim. 3:16

3:17 [a]Mark 13:23
[b]Eph. 4:14

3:18 [a]Eph. 4:15
[b]Rom. 11:36;
2 Tim. 4:18;
Rev. 1:6

THE FIRST EPISTLE OF

JOHN

WHAT WAS HEARD, SEEN, AND TOUCHED
(John 1:1–5)

1 That ᵃwhich was from the beginning, which we have heard, which we have ᵇseen with our eyes, ᶜwhich we have looked upon, and ᵈour hands have handled, concerning the ᵉWord of life— ²ᵃthe life ᵇwas manifested, and we have seen, ᶜand bear witness, and declare to you that eternal life which was ᵈwith the Father and was manifested to us— ³that which we have seen and heard we declare to you, that you also may have fellowship with us; and truly our fellowship *is* ᵃwith the Father and with His Son Jesus Christ. ⁴And these things we write to you ᵃthat ¹your joy may be full.

FELLOWSHIP WITH HIM AND ONE ANOTHER

⁵ᵃThis is the message which we have heard from Him and declare to you, that ᵇGod is light and in Him is no darkness at all. ⁶ᵃIf we say that we have fellowship with Him, and walk in darkness, we lie and do not practice the truth. ⁷But if we ᵃwalk in the light as He is in the light, we have fellowship with one another, and ᵇthe blood of Jesus Christ His Son cleanses us from all sin.

⁸If we say that we have no sin, we deceive ourselves, and the truth is not in us. ⁹If we ᵃconfess our sins, He is ᵇfaithful and just to forgive us *our* sins and to ᶜcleanse us from all unrighteousness. ¹⁰If we say that we have not sinned, we ᵃmake Him a liar, and His word is not in us.

2 My little children, these things I write to you, so that you may not sin. And if anyone sins, ᵃwe have an Advocate with the Father, Jesus Christ the righteous. ²And ᵃHe Himself is the propitiation for our sins, and not for ours only but ᵇalso for the whole world.

THE TEST OF KNOWING HIM

³Now by this we know that we know Him, if we keep His commandments. ⁴He who says, "I know Him," and does not keep His commandments, is a ᵃliar, and the truth is not in him. ⁵But ᵃwhoever keeps His word, truly the love of God ¹is perfected ᵇin him. By this we know that we are in Him. ⁶ᵃHe who says he abides in Him ᵇought himself also to walk just as He walked.

⁷ᵃBrethren, I write no new commandment to you, but an old commandment which you have had ᵃfrom the beginning. The old commandment is the word which you heard ²from the beginning. ⁸Again, ᵃa new commandment I write to you,

2:8 ᵃJohn 13:34; 15:12

1:4 ¹NU, M *our*   2:5 ¹*has been completed*   2:7 ¹NU *Beloved*   ²NU omits *from the beginning*

1:1
ᵃ[John 1:1];
1 John 2:13, 14
ᵇLuke 1:2;
John 1:14
ᶜ2 Pet. 1:16
ᵈLuke 24:39;
John 20:27
ᵉ[John 1:1, 4, 14]

1:2 ᵃJohn 1:4;
[1 John 3:5, 8;
5:20]
ᵇRom. 16:26;
1 Tim. 3:16
ᶜJohn 21:24
ᵈ[John 1:1, 18;
16:28]

1:3 ᵃJohn 17:21;
1 Cor. 1:9;
1 John 2:24

1:4 ᵃJohn 15:11;
16:24; 1 Pet. 1:8

1:5 ᵃJohn 1:19;
1 John 3:11
ᵇ[1 Tim. 6:16];
James 1:17

1:6
ᵃ[John 8:12];
2 Cor. 6:14;
[1 John 2:9–11]

1:7 ᵃIs. 2:5
ᵇ[1 Cor. 6:11]

1:9 ᵃPs. 32:5;
Prov. 28:13
ᵇ[Rom. 3:24–26]
ᶜPs. 51:2

1:10 ᵃJohn 3:33;
1 John 5:10

2:1 ᵃRom. 8:34;
1 Tim. 2:5;
Heb. 7:25; 9:24

2:2
ᵃ[Rom. 3:25];
Heb. 2:17;
1 John 4:10
ᵇJohn 1:29

2:4 ᵃRom. 3:4

2:5
ᵃJohn 14:21, 23
ᵇ[1 John 4:12]

2:6 ᵃJohn 15:4
ᵇMatt. 11:29;
John 13:15; 15:10;
1 Pet. 2:21

2:7 ᵃJohn 13:34;
1 John 3:11, 23;
4:21; 2 John 5

which thing is true in Him and in you, [b]because the darkness is passing away, and [c]the true light is already shining.

9[a]He who says he is in the light, and hates his brother, is in darkness until now. 10[a]He who loves his brother abides in the light, and [b]there is no cause for stumbling in him. 11But he who [a]hates his brother is in darkness and [b]walks in darkness, and does not know where he is going, because the darkness has blinded his eyes.

THEIR SPIRITUAL STATE

12 I write to you, little children,
Because [a]your sins are forgiven you for His name's sake.
13 I write to you, fathers,
Because you have known Him *who is* [a]from the beginning.
I write to you, young men,
Because you have overcome the wicked one.
I write to you, little children,
Because you have [b]known the Father.
14 I have written to you, fathers,
Because you have known Him *who is* from the beginning.
I have written to you, young men,
Because [a]you are strong, and the word of God abides in you,
And you have overcome the wicked one.

DO NOT LOVE THE WORLD

15[a]Do not love the world or the things in the world. [b]If anyone loves the world, the love of the Father is not in him. 16For all that *is* in the world—the lust of the flesh, [a]the lust of the eyes, and the pride of life—is not of the Father but is of the world. 17And [a]the world is passing away, and the lust of it; but he who does the will of God abides forever.

DECEPTIONS OF THE LAST HOUR

18[a]Little children, [b]it is the last hour; and as you have heard that [c]the[1] Antichrist is coming, [d]even now many antichrists have come, by which we know [e]that it is the last hour. 19[a]They went out from us, but they were not of us; for [b]if they had been of us, they would have continued with us; but *they went out* [c]that they might be made manifest, that none of them were of us.

20But [a]you have an anointing [b]from the Holy One, and [c]you[1] know all things. 21I have not written to you because you do not know the truth, but because you know it, and that no lie is of the truth.

22[a]Who is a liar but he who denies that [b]Jesus is the Christ? He is antichrist who denies the Father and the Son. 23[a]Whoever denies the Son does not have the [b]Father either; [c]he who acknowledges the Son has the Father also.

LET TRUTH ABIDE IN YOU

24Therefore let that abide in you [a]which you heard from the beginning. If what you heard from the beginning abides

2:8 [b]Rom. 13:12;
Eph. 5:8;
1 Thess. 5:4
[c][John 1:9; 8:12;
12:35]

2:9
[a][1 Cor. 13:2];
1 John 3:14

2:10
[a][1 John 3:14]
[b]2 Pet. 1:10

2:11
[a][1 John 2:9;
3:15; 4:20]
[b]John 12:35;
1 John 1:6

2:12
[a][1 Cor. 6:11]

2:13 [a]John 1:1;
Rev. 22:13
[b][Rom. 8:15–17;
Gal. 4:6]

2:14 [a]Eph. 6:10

2:15
[a][Rom. 12:2];
Gal. 1:4;
James 1:27
[b]Matt. 6:24;
James 4:4

2:16
[a][Eccl. 5:10, 11]

2:17 [a]1 Cor. 7:31;
1 Pet. 1:24

2:18 [a]John 21:5
[b]Rom. 13:11;
1 Tim. 4:1;
Heb. 1:2;
1 Pet. 4:7
[c]2 Thess. 2:3
[d]Matt. 24:5, 24;
1 John 2:22; 4:3;
2 John 7
[e]1 Tim. 4:1

2:19 [a]Deut. 13:13
[b]Matt. 24:24
[c]1 Cor. 11:19

2:20 [a]2 Cor. 1:21;
Heb. 1:9;
1 John 2:27
[b]Acts 3:14
[c]Prov. 28:5;
[John 16:13];
1 Cor. 2:15, 16

2:22 [a]2 John 7
[b]1 John 4:3

2:23
[a]John 15:23
[b]John 5:23
[c]1 John 4:15; 5:1;
2 John 9

2:24
[a]2 John 5, 6

in you, [b]you also will abide in the Son and in the Father. [25a]And this is the promise that He has promised us—eternal life.

[26]These things I have written to you concerning those who *try to* [1]deceive you. [27]But the [a]anointing which you have received from Him abides in you, and [b]you do not need that anyone teach you; but as the same anointing [c]teaches you concerning all things, and is true, and is not a lie, and just as it has taught you, you [1]will abide in Him.

THE CHILDREN OF GOD

[28]And now, little children, abide in Him, that [1]when He appears, we may have [a]confidence and not be ashamed before Him at His coming. [29a]If you know that He is righteous, you know that [b]everyone who practices righteousness is born of Him.

3 Behold [a]what manner of love the Father has bestowed on us, that [b]we should be called children of [1]God! Therefore the world does not know [2]us, [c]because it did not know Him. [2]Beloved, [a]now we are children of God; and [b]it has not yet been revealed what we shall be, but we know that when He is revealed, [c]we shall be like Him, for [d]we shall see Him as He is. [3a]And everyone who has this hope in Him purifies himself, just as He is pure.

SIN AND THE CHILD OF GOD

[4]Whoever commits sin also commits lawlessness, and [a]sin is lawlessness. [5]And you know [a]that He was manifested [b]to take away our sins, and [c]in Him there is no sin. [6]Whoever abides in Him does not sin. Whoever sins has neither seen Him nor known Him.

[7]Little children, let no one deceive you. He who practices righteousness is righteous, just as He is righteous. [8a]He who sins is of the devil, for the devil has sinned from the beginning. For this purpose the Son of God was manifested, [b]that He might destroy the works of the devil. [9]Whoever has been [a]born of God does not sin, for [b]His seed remains in him; and he cannot sin, because he has been born of God.

THE IMPERATIVE OF LOVE
(Matt. 22:39)

[10]In this the children of God and the children of the devil are manifest: Whoever does not practice righteousness is not of God, nor *is* he who does not love his brother. [11]For this is the message that you heard from the beginning, [a]that we should love one another, [12]not as [a]Cain *who* was of the wicked one and murdered his brother. And why did he murder him? Because his works were evil and his brother's righteous.

[13]Do not marvel, my brethren, if [a]the world hates you. [14]We know that we have passed from death to life, because we love the brethren. He who does not love [1]*his* brother abides in death. [15a]Whoever hates his brother is a murderer, and you know that [b]no murderer has eternal life abiding in him.

THE OUTWORKING OF LOVE

[16a]By this we know love, [b]because He laid down His life for us. And we also ought to lay down *our* lives for the brethren.

3:16 [a][John 3:16] [b]John 10:11; 15:13; Gal. 2:20

2:24
[b]John 14:23; 1 John 1:3; 2 John 9

2:25
[a]John 3:14–16; 6:40; 17:2, 3; 1 John 1:2

2:27
[a][John 14:16; 16:13]; 1 John 2:20 [b][Jer. 31:33] [c][John 14:16; 1 Cor. 2:12]; 1 Thess. 4:9

2:28 [a]Eph. 3:12; 1 John 3:21; 4:17; 5:14

2:29 [a]Acts 22:14 [b]John 7:18; 1 John 3:7, 10

3:1 [a][John 3:16; Eph. 2:4–7; 1 John 4:10] [b][John 1:12] [c]John 15:18, 21; 16:3

3:2 [a][Is. 56:5; Rom. 8:15, 16] [b][Rom. 8:18, 19, 23] [c]Rom. 8:29; 2 Pet. 1:4 [d][Ps. 16:11]

3:3 [a]1 John 4:17

3:4 [a]Rom. 4:15; 1 John 5:17

3:5 [a]1 John 1:2; 3:8 [b][Is. 53:5, 6]; John 1:29; [2 Cor. 5:21; Heb. 9:26] [c][2 Cor. 5:21]; 1 John 2:29

3:8 [a]Matt. 13:38; John 8:44; 1 John 3:10 [b]Luke 10:18; [Heb. 2:14]

3:9 [a]John 1:3; 3:3; [1 John 2:29; 4:7; 5:1, 4, 18]; 3 John 11 [b]1 Pet. 1:23

3:11 [a][John 13:34; 15:12]; 1 John 4:7, 11, 21; 2 John 5

3:12 [a]Gen. 4:4, 8

3:13 [a][John 15:18; 17:14]

3:15 [a]Matt. 5:21; John 8:44 [b][Gal. 5:20, 21; Rev. 21:8]

2:26 [1]*lead you astray* 2:27 [1]NU omits *will* 2:28 [1]NU *if* 3:1 [1]NU adds *And we are.* [2]M *you* 3:14 [1]NU omits *his brother*

¹⁷But ^awhoever has this world's goods, and sees his brother in need, and shuts up his heart from him, how does the love of God abide in him?

¹⁸My little children, ^alet us not love in word or in tongue, but in deed and in truth. ¹⁹And by this we ¹know ^athat we are of the truth, and shall ²assure our hearts before Him. ^{20a}For if our heart condemns us, God is greater than our heart, and knows all things. ²¹Beloved, if our heart does not condemn us, ^awe have confidence toward God. ²²And ^awhatever we ask we receive from Him, because we keep His commandments ^band do those things that are pleasing in His sight. ²³And this is His commandment: that we should believe on the name of His Son Jesus Christ ^aand love one another, as He gave ¹us commandment.

THE SPIRIT OF TRUTH AND THE SPIRIT OF ERROR

²⁴Now ^ahe who keeps His commandments ^babides in Him, and He in him. And ^cby this we know that He abides in us, by the Spirit whom He has given us.

4 Beloved, do not believe every spirit, but ^atest the spirits, whether they are of God; because ^bmany false prophets have gone out into the world. ²By this you know the Spirit of God: ^aEvery spirit that confesses that Jesus Christ has come in the flesh is of God, ³and every spirit that does not confess ¹that Jesus ²Christ has come in the flesh is not of God. And this is the *spirit* of the Antichrist, which you have heard was coming, and is now already in the world.

⁴You are of God, little children, and have overcome them, because He who is in you is greater than ^ahe who is in the world. ^{5a}They are of the world. Therefore they speak *as* of the world, and ^bthe world hears them. ⁶We are of God. He who knows God hears us; he who is not of God does not hear us. ^aBy this we know the spirit of truth and the spirit of error.

KNOWING GOD THROUGH LOVE

(cf. John 3:16)

^{7a}Beloved, let us love one another, for love is of God; and everyone who ^bloves is born of God and knows God. ⁸He who does not love does not know God, for God is love. ^{9a}In this the love of God was manifested toward us, that God has sent His only begotten ^bSon into the world, that we might live through Him. ¹⁰In this is love, ^anot that we loved God, but that He loved us and sent His Son ^bto be the propitiation for our sins. ¹¹Beloved, ^aif God so loved us, we also ought to love one another.

SEEING GOD THROUGH LOVE

^{12a}No one has seen God at any time. If we love one another, God abides in us, and His love has been perfected in us. ^{13a}By this we know that we abide in Him, and He in us, because He has given us of His Spirit. ¹⁴And ^awe have seen and testify that ^bthe Father has sent the Son *as* Savior of the world. ^{15a}Whoever confesses that Jesus is the Son of God, God abides in him, and he in God. ¹⁶And we have known and believed the love that God has for us. God is love, and ^ahe who abides in love abides in God, and God ^bin him.

3:17 ^aDeut. 15:7
3:18 ^aEzek. 33:31
3:19 ^aJohn 18:37
3:20
^a[1 Cor. 4:4, 5]
3:21
^a[Heb. 10:22;
1 John 2:28;
5:14]
3:22 ^aPs. 34:15;
[John 15:7];
1 John 5:14, 15
^bJohn 8:29;
Heb. 13:21
3:23
^aMatt. 22:39
3:24
^aJohn 14:23
^bJohn 14:21; 17:21
^cJohn 14:17;
Rom. 8:9, 14, 16;
1 Thess. 4:8;
1 John 4:13
4:1 ^a1 Cor. 14:29
^bMatt. 24:5
4:2
^a[Rom. 10:8–10];
1 Cor. 12:3;
1 John 5:1
4:4
^aJohn 14:30;
16:11
4:5 ^aJohn 3:31
^bJohn 15:19;
17:14
4:6
^a[1 Cor. 2:12–16]
4:7 ^a1 John 3:10,
11, 23
^b1 Thess. 4:9;
[1 John 3:14]
4:9 ^aRom. 5:8
^bIs. 9:6, 7;
John 3:16
4:10 ^aTitus 3:5
^b1 John 2:2
4:11 ^aMatt. 18:33
4:12 ^aJohn 1:18;
1 Tim. 6:16;
1 John 4:20
4:13 ^aJohn 14:20
4:14 ^aJohn 1:14
^bJohn 3:17; 4:42;
1 John 2:2
4:15
^a[Rom. 10:9];
1 John 3:23;
4:2; 5:1, 5
4:16
^a[1 John 3:24]
^b[John 14:23]

3:19 ¹NU *shall know* ²*persuade, set at rest* 3:23 ¹M omits *us*
4:3 ¹NU omits *that* ²NU omits *Christ has come in the flesh*

THE CONSUMMATION OF LOVE

17Love has been perfected among us in this: that ªwe may have boldness in the day of judgment; because as He is, so are we in this world. 18There is no fear in love; but perfect love casts out fear, because fear involves torment. But he who fears has not been made perfect in love. 19ªWe love ¹Him because He first loved us.

OBEDIENCE BY FAITH

20ªIf someone says, "I love God," and hates his brother, he is a liar; for he who does not love his brother whom he has seen, ¹how can he love God bwhom he has not seen? 21And ªthis commandment we have from Him: that he who loves God *must* love his brother also.

5 Whoever believes that ªJesus is the Christ is bborn of God, and everyone who loves Him who begot also loves him who is begotten of Him. 2By this we know that we love the children of God, when we love God and ªkeep His commandments. 3ªFor this is the love of God, that we keep His commandments. And bHis commandments are not burdensome. 4For ªwhatever is born of God overcomes the world. And this is the victory that bhas overcome the world—¹our faith. 5Who is he who overcomes the world, but ªhe who believes that Jesus is the Son of God?

THE CERTAINTY OF GOD'S WITNESS

6This is He who came ªby water and blood—Jesus Christ; not only by water, but by water and blood. bAnd it is the Spirit who bears witness, because the Spirit is truth. 7For there are three that bear witness ¹in heaven: the Father, ªthe Word, and the Holy Spirit; band these three are one. 8And there are three that bear witness on earth: ªthe Spirit, the water, and the blood; and these three agree as one. 9If we receive ªthe witness of men, the witness of God is greater; bfor this is the witness of ¹God which He has testified of His Son. 10He who believes in the Son of God ªhas the witness in himself; he who does not believe God bhas made Him a liar, because he has not believed the testimony that God has given of His Son. 11And this is the testimony: that God has given us eternal life, and this life is in His Son. 12ªHe who has the Son has ¹life; he who does not have the Son of God does not have life. 13These things I have written to you who believe in the name of the Son of God, that you may know that you have eternal life, ¹and that you may *continue to* believe in the name of the Son of God.

CONFIDENCE AND COMPASSION IN PRAYER

14Now this is the confidence that we have in Him, that ªif we ask anything according to His will, He hears us. 15And if we know that He hears us, whatever we ask, we know that we have the petitions that we have asked of Him.

16If anyone sees his brother sinning a sin *which does* not *lead* to death, he will ask, and ªHe will give him life for those

4:17
ª[James 2:13];
1 John 2:28

4:19 ª1 John 4:10

4:20
ª[1 John 2:4]
b1 Pet. 1:8;
1 John 4:12

4:21 ªLev. 19:18;
[Matt. 5:43, 44;
22:39];
John 13:34

5:1
ª1 John 2:22;
4:2, 15
bJohn 1:13

5:2 ªJohn 15:10;
2 John 6

5:3 ªJohn 14:15;
2 John 6
bMic. 6:8;
Matt. 11:30; 23:4

5:4 ªJohn 16:33
b1 John 2:13; 4:4

5:5 ª1 Cor. 15:57

5:6
ªJohn 1:31–34;
[Eph. 5:26, 27]
b[John 14:17]

5:7 ª[John 1:1]
bJohn 10:30

5:8 ªJohn 15:26

5:9
ªJohn 5:34, 37;
8:17, 18
b[Matt. 3:16, 17];
John 5:32, 37

5:10
ª[Rom. 8:16];
Gal. 4:6;
Rev. 12:17
bJohn 3:18, 33;
1 John 1:10

5:12
ª[John 3:15, 36;
6:47; 17:2, 3]

5:14
ª[1 John 2:28;
3:21, 22]

5:16 ªJob 42:8

4:19 ¹NU omits *Him*   **4:20** ¹NU *he cannot*   **5:4** ¹M *your*   **5:7** ¹NU, M omit the words from *in heaven* (v. 7) through *on earth* (v. 8). Only 4 or 5 very late mss. contain these words in Greek.   **5:9** ¹NU *God, that*   **5:12** ¹Or *the life*
5:13 ¹NU omits the rest of v. 13.

who commit sin not *leading* to death. [b]There is sin *leading* to death. [c]I do not say that he should pray about that. [17a]All unrighteousness is sin, and there is sin not *leading* to death.

KNOWING THE TRUE—REJECTING THE FALSE

[18]We know that [a]whoever is born of God does not sin; but he who has been born of God [b]keeps[1] [2]himself, and the wicked one does not touch him.

[19]We know that we are of God, and [a]the whole world lies *under the sway of* the wicked one.

[20]And we know that the [a]Son of God has come and [b]has given us an understanding, [c]that we may know Him who is true; and we are in Him who is true, in His Son Jesus Christ. [d]This is the true God [e]and eternal life.

[21]Little children, keep yourselves from idols. Amen.

5:16
[b][Matt. 12:31]
[c]Jer. 7:16; 14:11

5:17 [a]1 John 3:4

5:18
[a][1 Pet. 1:23];
1 John 3:9
[b]James 1:27

5:19
[a]John 12:31;
17:15;
Gal. 1:4

5:20 [a]1 John 4:2
[b]Luke 24:45
[c]John 17:3; [d]Is. 9:6
[e]1 John 5:11, 12

5:18 [1]guards   [2]NU him

THE SECOND EPISTLE OF
JOHN

GREETING THE ELECT LADY

The Elder,

To the [1]elect lady and her children, whom I love in truth, and not only I, but also all those who have known [a]the truth, [2]because of the truth which abides in us and will be with us forever:

[3a]Grace, mercy, *and* peace will be with [1]you from God the Father and from the Lord Jesus Christ, the Son of the Father, in truth and love.

WALK IN CHRIST'S COMMANDMENTS

[4]I [a]rejoiced greatly that I have found *some* of your children walking in truth, as we received commandment from the Father. [5]And now I plead with you, lady, not as though I wrote a new commandment to you, but that which we have had from the beginning: [a]that we love one another. [6a]This is love, that we walk according to His commandments. This is the commandment, that [b]as you have heard from the beginning, you should walk in it.

BEWARE OF ANTICHRIST DECEIVERS

[7]For [a]many deceivers have gone out into the world [b]who do not confess Jesus Christ *as* coming in the flesh. [c]This is a deceiver and an antichrist. [8a]Look to yourselves, [b]that [1]we do not lose those things we worked for, but *that* we may receive a full reward. [9a]Whoever [1]transgresses and does not abide in the doctrine of Christ does not have God. He who abides in the doctrine of Christ has both the Father and the Son. [10]If anyone comes to you and [a]does not bring this doctrine, do not receive him into your house nor greet him; [11]for he who greets him shares in his evil deeds.

JOHN'S FAREWELL GREETING

[12a]Having many things to write to you, I did not wish *to do so* with paper and ink; but I hope to come to you and speak face to face, [b]that our joy may be full.

[13a]The children of your elect sister greet you. Amen.

1 [a]Col. 1:5

3 [a]Rom. 1:7;
1 Tim. 1:2

4
[a]1 Thess. 2:19, 20;
3 John 3, 4

5
[a][John 13:34, 35;
15:12, 17];
1 John 3:11;
4:7, 11

6 [a]John 14:15;
1 John 2:5; 5:3
[b]1 John 2:24

7
[a]1 John 2:19; 4:1
[b]1 John 4:2
[c]1 John 2:22

8 [a]Mark 13:9
[b]Gal. 3:4

9
[a]John 7:16; 8:31;
1 John 2:19,
23, 24

10 [a]1 Kin. 13:16;
Rom. 16:17;
2 Thess. 3:6, 14;
Titus 3:10

12 [a]3 John 13, 14
[b]John 17:13

13 [a]1 Pet. 5:13

---

1 [1]*chosen* 3 [1]NU, M *us* 8 [1]NU *you* 9 [1]NU *goes ahead*

JOHN

GREETING TO GAIUS

The Elder,

To the beloved Gaius, ᵃwhom I love in truth:

2Beloved, I pray that you may prosper in all things and be in health, just as your soul prospers. 3For I ᵃrejoiced greatly when brethren came and testified of the truth *that is* in you, just as you walk in the truth. 4I have no greater ᵃjoy than to hear that ᵇmy children walk in ¹truth.

GAIUS COMMENDED FOR GENEROSITY

5Beloved, you do faithfully whatever you do for the brethren ¹and for strangers, 6who have borne witness of your love before the church. *If* you send them forward on their journey in a manner worthy of God, you will do well, 7because they went forth for His name's sake, ᵃtaking nothing from the Gentiles. 8We therefore ought to ᵃreceive¹ such, that we may become fellow workers for the truth.

DIOTREPHES AND DEMETRIUS

9I wrote to the church, but Diotrephes, who loves to have the preeminence among them, does not receive us. 10Therefore, if I come, I will call to mind his deeds which he does, ᵃprating¹ against us with malicious words. And not content with that, he himself does not receive the brethren, and forbids those who wish to, putting *them* out of the church.

11Beloved, ᵃdo not imitate what is evil, but what is good. ᵇHe who does good is of God, ¹but he who does evil has not seen ᶜGod.

12Demetrius ᵃhas a *good* testimony from all, and from the truth itself. And we also ¹bear witness, ᵇand you know that our testimony is true.

FAREWELL GREETING

13ᵃI had many things to write, but I do not wish to write to you with pen and ink; 14but I hope to see you shortly, and we shall speak face to face.

Peace to you. Our friends greet you. Greet the friends by name.

1 ᵃ2 John 1
3 ᵃ2 John 4
4
ᵃ1 Thess. 2:19, 20;
2 John 4
ᵇ[1 Cor. 4:15]
7
ᵃ1 Cor. 9:12, 15
8 ᵃMatt. 10:40;
Rom. 12:13;
Heb. 13:2;
1 Pet. 4:9
10
ᵃProv. 10:8, 10
11 ᵃPs. 34:14;
37:27;
Rom. 14:19;
1 Thess. 5:15;
1 Tim. 6:11;
2 Tim. 2:22
ᵇ[1 John 2:29;
3:10]
ᶜ[1 John 3:10]
12 ᵃActs 6:3;
1 Tim. 3:7
ᵇJohn 19:35;
21:24
13 ᵃ2 John 12

THE EPISTLE OF

JUDE

GREETING TO THE CALLED

Jude, a bondservant of Jesus Christ, and ᵃbrother of James,

To those who are ᵇcalled, ¹sanctified by God the Father, and ᶜpreserved in Jesus Christ:

²Mercy, ᵃpeace, and love be multiplied to you.

CONTEND FOR THE FAITH

³Beloved, while I was very diligent to write to you ᵃconcerning our common salvation, I found it necessary to write to you exhorting ᵇyou to contend earnestly for the faith which was once for all delivered to the saints. ⁴For certain men have crept in unnoticed, who long ago were marked out for this condemnation, ungodly men, who turn the grace of our God into lewdness and deny the only Lord ¹God and our Lord Jesus Christ.

OLD AND NEW APOSTATES

⁵But I want to remind you, though you once knew this, that ᵃthe Lord, having saved the people out of the land of Egypt, afterward destroyed those who did not believe. ⁶And the angels who did not keep their ¹proper domain, but left their own abode, He has reserved in everlasting chains under darkness for the judgment of the great day; ⁷as ᵃSodom and Gomorrah, and the cities around them in a similar manner to these, having given themselves over to sexual immorality and gone after strange flesh, are set forth as an example, suffering the ¹vengeance of eternal fire.

⁸ᵃLikewise also these dreamers defile the flesh, reject authority, and ᵇspeak evil of ¹dignitaries. ⁹Yet Michael the archangel, in ¹contending with the devil, when he disputed about the body of Moses, dared not bring against him a reviling accusation, but said, ᵃ"The Lord rebuke you!" ¹⁰ᵃBut these speak evil of whatever they do not know; and whatever they know naturally, like brute beasts, in these things they corrupt themselves. ¹¹Woe to them! For they have gone in the way ᵃof Cain, ᵇhave run greedily in the error of Balaam for profit, and perished ᶜin the rebellion of Korah.

APOSTATES DEPRAVED AND DOOMED

¹²These are ¹spots in your love feasts, while they feast with you without fear, serving *only* themselves. *They are* clouds without water, carried ²about by the winds; late autumn trees without fruit, twice dead, pulled up by the roots; ¹³ᵃraging waves of the sea, ᵇfoaming up their own shame; wandering

1 ᵃActs 1:13
ᵇRom. 1:7
ᶜJohn 17:11, 12

2 ᵃ1 Pet. 1:2;
2 Pet. 1:2

3 ᵃTitus 1:4
ᵇPhil. 1:27

5 ᵃEx. 12:51;
1 Cor. 10:5–10;
Heb. 3:16

7 ᵃGen. 19:24;
2 Pet. 2:6

8 ᵃ2 Pet. 2:10
ᵇEx. 22:28

9 ᵃZech. 3:2

10 ᵃ2 Pet. 2:12

11
ᵃGen. 4:3–8;
Heb. 11:4;
1 John 3:12
ᵇNum. 31:16;
2 Pet. 2:15;
Rev. 2:14
ᶜNum. 16:1–3,
31–35

13 ᵃIs. 57:20
ᵇ[Phil. 3:19]

---

1 ¹NU beloved   4 ¹NU omits God   6 ¹own   7 ¹punishment
8 ¹glorious ones, lit. glories   9 ¹arguing   12 ¹stains, or hidden reefs
²NU, M along

stars ᶜfor whom is reserved the blackness of darkness forever.

¹⁴Now Enoch, the seventh from Adam, prophesied about these men also, saying, "Behold, the Lord comes with ten thousands of His saints, ¹⁵to execute judgment on all, to convict all who are ungodly among them of all their ungodly deeds which they have committed in an ungodly way, and of all the ᵃharsh things which ungodly sinners have spoken against Him."

APOSTATES PREDICTED

¹⁶These are grumblers, complainers, walking according to their own lusts; and they ᵃmouth great swelling *words*, ᵇflattering people to gain advantage. ¹⁷ᵃBut you, beloved, remember the words which were spoken before by the apostles of our Lord Jesus Christ: ¹⁸how they told you that ᵃthere would be mockers in the last time who would walk according to their own ungodly lusts. ¹⁹These are ¹sensual persons, who cause divisions, not having the Spirit.

MAINTAIN YOUR LIFE WITH GOD

²⁰But you, beloved, ᵃbuilding yourselves up on your most holy faith, ᵇpraying in the Holy Spirit, ²¹keep yourselves in the love of God, ᵃlooking for the mercy of our Lord Jesus Christ unto eternal life.

²²And on some have compassion, ¹making a distinction; ²³but ᵃothers save ¹with fear, ᵇpulling *them* out of the ²fire, hating even ᶜthe garment defiled by the flesh.

GLORY TO GOD

²⁴ ᵃNow to Him who is able to keep ¹you from stumbling,
And ᵇto present *you* faultless
Before the presence of His glory with exceeding joy,
²⁵ To ¹God our Savior,
²Who alone is wise,
Be glory and majesty,
Dominion and ³power,
Both now and forever.
Amen.

13 ᶜ2 Pet. 2:17;
Jude 6
15 ᵃ1 Sam. 2:3
16 ᵃ2 Pet. 2:18
ᵇProv. 28:21
17 ᵃ2 Pet. 3:2
18 ᵃActs 20:29;
[1 Tim. 4:1];
2 Tim. 3:1; 4:3;
2 Pet. 3:3
20 ᵃCol. 2:7;
1 Thess. 5:11
ᵇ[Rom. 8:26]
21 ᵃTitus 2:13;
Heb. 9:28;
2 Pet. 3:12
23 ᵃRom. 11:14;
ᵇAmos 4:11;
Zech. 3:2;
1 Cor. 3:15
ᶜ[Zech. 3:4, 5];
Rev. 3:4
24 ᵃ[Eph. 3:20]
ᵇCol. 1:22

19 ¹*soulish* or *worldly*   22 ¹NU *who are doubting* (or *making distinctions*)
23 ¹NU omits *with fear*   ²NU adds *and on some have mercy with fear*
24 ¹M *them*   25 ¹NU *the only God our*   ²NU *Through Jesus Christ our Lord,*
Be glory   ³NU adds *Before all time,*

THE REVELATION
OF JESUS CHRIST

INTRODUCTION AND BENEDICTION

1 The Revelation of Jesus Christ, [a]which God gave Him to show His servants—things which must [1]shortly take place. And [b]He sent and signified *it* by His angel to His servant John, [2a]who bore witness to the word of God, and to the testimony of Jesus Christ, to all things [b]that he saw. [3a]Blessed *is* he who reads and those who hear the words of this prophecy, and keep those things which are written in it; for [b]the time *is* near.

GREETING THE SEVEN CHURCHES

[4]John, to the seven churches which are in Asia:

Grace to you and peace from Him [a]who is and [b]who was and who is to come, [c]and from the seven Spirits who are before His throne, [5]and from Jesus Christ, [a]the faithful [b]witness, the [c]firstborn from the dead, and [d]the ruler over the kings of the earth.

To Him [e]who [1]loved us [f]and washed us from our sins in His own blood, [6]and has [a]made us [1]kings and priests to His God and Father, [b]to Him *be* glory and dominion forever and ever. Amen.

[7]Behold, He is coming with [a]clouds, and every eye will see Him, even [b]they who pierced Him. And all the tribes of the earth will mourn because of Him. Even so, Amen.

[8a]"I am the Alpha and the Omega, [1]*the* Beginning and *the* End," says the [2]Lord, [b]"who is and who was and who is to come, the [c]Almighty."

VISION OF THE SON OF MAN

[9]I, John, [1]both your brother and [a]companion in the tribulation and [b]kingdom and patience of Jesus Christ, was on the island that is called Patmos for the word of God and for the testimony of Jesus Christ. [10a]I was in the Spirit on [b]the Lord's Day, and I heard behind me [c]a loud voice, as of a trumpet, [11]saying, [1]"I am the Alpha and the Omega, the First and the Last," and, "What you see, write in a book and send *it* to the seven churches [2]which are in Asia: to Ephesus, to Smyrna, to Pergamos, to Thyatira, to Sardis, to Philadelphia, and to Laodicea."

[12]Then I turned to see the voice that spoke with me. And having turned [a]I saw seven golden lampstands, [13a]and in the midst of the seven lampstands [b]*One* like the Son of Man, [c]clothed with a garment down to the feet and [d]girded about the chest with a golden band. [14]His head and [a]hair *were* white like wool, as white as snow, and [b]His eyes like a flame of fire;

1:1 [a]John 3:32
[b]Rev. 22:6

1:2 [a]1 Cor. 1:6
[b]1 John 1:1

1:3 [a]Luke 11:28;
Rev. 22:7
[b]James 5:8;
Rev. 22:10

1:4 [a]Ex. 3:14
[b]John 1:1
[c][Is. 11:2];
Zech. 3:9;
Rev. 3:1; 4:5; 5:6

1:5 [a]John 8:14;
Prov. 14:5
[b]Is. 55:4
[c]Ps. 89:27;
1 Cor. 15:20;
[Col. 1:18]
[d]Rev. 17:14
[e]John 13:34
[f]Heb. 9:14

1:6 [a]1 Pet. 2:5, 9
[b]1 Tim. 6:16

1:7 [a]Matt. 24:30
[b]Zech. 12:10–14;
John 19:37

1:8 [a]Is. 41:4;
Rev. 21:6; 22:13
[b]Rev. 4:8; 11:17
[c]Is. 9:6

1:9 [a]Phil. 1:7
[b][Rom. 8:17;
2 Tim. 2:12]

1:10 [a]Acts 10:10
[b]Acts 20:7
[c]Rev. 4:1

1:12 [a]Ex. 25:37;
Zech. 4:2;
Rev. 1:20; 2:1

1:13 [a]Rev. 2:1
[b]Ezek. 1:26;
Dan. 7:13; 10:16;
Rev. 14:14
[c]Dan. 10:5
[d]Rev. 15:6

1:14 [a]Dan. 7:9
[b]Dan. 10:6;
Rev. 2:18; 19:12

1:1 [1]*quickly* or *swiftly*   1:5 [1]NU *loves us and freed;* M *loves us and washed*
1:6 [1]NU, M *a kingdom*   1:8 [1]NU, M omit *the Beginning and the End*
[2]NU, M *Lord God*   1:9 [1]NU, M omit *both*   1:11 [1]NU, M omit *"I am the Alpha and the Omega, the First and the Last," and,*   [2]NU, M omit *which are in Asia*

1:15 ªEzek. 1:7;
Dan. 10:6;
Rev. 2:18
ᵇEzek. 1:24;
43:2;
Rev. 14:2; 19:6

1:16 ªRev. 1:20;
2:1; 3:1
ᵇIs. 49:2;
[Heb. 4:12];
Rev. 2:12, 16;
19:15
ᶜMatt. 17:2;
Acts 26:13;
Rev. 10:1

1:17 ªEzek. 1:28
ᵇDan. 8:18;
10:10, 12
ᶜIs. 41:4; 44:6;
48:12;
Rev. 2:8; 22:13

1:18
ªRom. 6:9;
Rev. 2:8;
10:6; 15:7
ᵇRev. 4:9
ᶜPs. 68:20

1:19
ªRev. 1:9–18
ᵇRev. 2:1
ᶜJohn 16:13;
Rev. 4:1

1:20 ªMal. 2:7;
Rev. 2:1
ᵇEx. 25:37;
37:23;
Zech. 4:2;
Matt. 5:15;
Phil. 2:15

2:1 ªRev. 1:16
ᵇRev. 1:13

2:2 ªPs. 1:6
ᵇJohn 6:6;
1 John 4:1
ᶜ2 Cor. 11:13

2:3 ªGal. 6:9;
Heb. 12:3, 5

2:5 ªMatt. 21:41

2:7 ªMatt. 11:15;
Rev. 2:11, 17;
3:6, 13, 22; 13:9
ᵇ[Rev. 22:2, 14]
ᶜ[Gen. 2:9;
3:22]

2:8
ªRev. 1:8, 17, 18

2:9 ªLuke 12:21
ᵇRom. 2:17
ᶜRev. 3:9

2:10
ªMatt. 10:22
ᵇMatt. 24:13
ᶜJames 1:12

2:11 ªRev. 13:9
ᵇ[Rev. 20:6, 14;
21:8]

2:12 ªIs. 49:2;
Rev. 1:16; 2:16

¹⁵ªHis feet *were* like fine brass, as if refined in a furnace, and ᵇHis voice as the sound of many waters; ¹⁶ªHe had in His right hand seven stars, ᵇout of His mouth went a sharp two-edged sword, ᶜand His countenance *was* like the sun shining in its strength. ¹⁷And ªwhen I saw Him, I fell at His feet as dead. But ᵇHe laid His right hand on me, saying ¹to me, "Do not be afraid; ᶜI am the First and the Last. ¹⁸ªI *am* He who lives, and was dead, and behold, ᵇI am alive forevermore. Amen. And ᶜI have the keys of ¹Hades and of Death. ¹⁹¹Write the things which you have ªseen, ᵇand the things which are, ᶜand the things which will take place after this. ²⁰The ¹mystery of the seven stars which you saw in My right hand, and the seven golden lampstands: The seven stars are ªthe ²angels of the seven churches, and ᵇthe seven lampstands ³which you saw are the seven churches.

THE LOVELESS CHURCH

2 "To the ¹angel of the church of Ephesus write,
'These things says ªHe who holds the seven stars in His right hand, ᵇwho walks in the midst of the seven golden lampstands: ²ª"I know your works, your labor, your ¹patience, and that you cannot ²bear those who are evil. And ᵇyou have tested those ᶜwho say they are apostles and are not, and have found them liars; ³and you have persevered and have patience, and have labored for My name's sake and have ªnot become weary. ⁴Nevertheless I have *this* against you, that you have left your first love. ⁵Remember therefore from where you have fallen; repent and do the first works, ªor else I will come to you quickly and remove your lampstand from its place—unless you repent. ⁶But this you have, that you hate the deeds of the Nicolaitans, which I also hate.

⁷ª"He who has an ear, let him hear what the Spirit says to the churches. To him who overcomes I will give ᵇto eat from ᶜthe tree of life, which is in the midst of the Paradise of God."'

THE PERSECUTED CHURCH

⁸"And to the ¹angel of the church in Smyrna write,
'These things says ªthe First and the Last, who was dead, and came to life: ⁹"I know your works, tribulation, and poverty (but you are ªrich); and I *know* the blasphemy of ᵇthose who say they are Jews and are not, ᶜbut *are* a ¹synagogue of Satan. ¹⁰ªDo not fear any of those things which you are about to suffer. Indeed, the devil is about to throw *some* of you into prison, that you may be tested, and you will have tribulation ten days. ᵇBe faithful until death, and I will give you ᶜthe crown of life.

¹¹ª"He who has an ear, let him hear what the Spirit says to the churches. He who overcomes shall not be hurt by ᵇthe second death."'

THE COMPROMISING CHURCH

¹²"And to the ¹angel of the church in Pergamos write,
'These things says ªHe who has the sharp two-edged

sword: [13]"I know your works, and where you dwell, where Satan's throne *is.* And you hold fast to My name, and did not deny My faith even in the days in which Antipas *was* My faithful martyr, who was killed among you, where Satan dwells. [14]But I have a few things against you, because you have there those who hold the doctrine of [a]Balaam, who taught Balak to put a stumbling block before the children of Israel, [b]to eat things sacrificed to idols, [c]and to commit sexual immorality. [15]Thus you also have those who hold the doctrine of the Nicolaitans, [1]which thing I hate. [16]Repent, or else I will come to you quickly and [a]will fight against them with the sword of My mouth.

[17]"He who has an ear, let him hear what the Spirit says to the churches. To him who overcomes I will give some of the hidden [a]manna to eat. And I will give him a white stone, and on the stone [b]a new name written which no one knows except him who receives *it*.' '

THE CORRUPT CHURCH

[18]"And to the [1]angel of the church in Thyatira write,

'These things says the Son of God, [a]who has eyes like a flame of fire, and His feet like fine brass: [19a]"I know your works, love, [1]service, faith, and your [2]patience; and *as* for your works, the last *are* more than the first. [20]Nevertheless I have [1]a few things against you, because you allow [2]that woman [a]Jezebel, who calls herself a prophetess, [3]to teach and seduce My servants [b]to commit sexual immorality and eat things sacrificed to idols. [21]And I gave her time [a]to [1]repent of her sexual immorality, and she did not repent. [22]Indeed I will cast her into a sickbed, and those who commit adultery with her into great tribulation, unless they repent of [1]their deeds. [23]I will kill her children with death, and all the churches shall know that I am He who [a]searches[1] the minds and hearts. And I will give to each one of you according to your works.

[24]"Now to you I say, [1]and to the rest in Thyatira, as many as do not have this doctrine, who have not known the [a]depths of Satan, as they say, [b]I [2]will put on you no other burden. [25]But hold fast [a]what you have till I come. [26]And he who overcomes, and keeps [a]My works until the end, [b]to him I will give power over the nations—

[27]   'He[a] shall rule them with a rod of iron;
    They shall be dashed to pieces like the potter's vessels'—

as I also have received from My Father; [28]and I will give him [a]the morning star.

[29]"He who has an ear, let him hear what the Spirit says to the churches.' '

THE DEAD CHURCH

3 "And to the [1]angel of the church in Sardis write,
'These things says He who [a]has the seven Spirits of God and the seven stars: "I know your works, that you have a

2:14 [a]Num. 31:16
[b]Num. 25;
Acts 15:29;
[1 Cor. 10:20];
Rev. 2:20
[c]1 Cor. 6:13

2:16 [a]Is. 11:4;
2 Thess. 2:8;
Rev. 19:15

2:17
[a]Ex. 16:33, 34;
[John 6:49, 51]
[b]Is. 56:5; 62:2;
65:15; Rev. 3:12

2:18
[a]Rev. 1:14, 15

2:19 [a]Rev. 2:2

2:20
[a]1 Kin. 16:31;
21:25;
2 Kin. 9:7, 22, 30
[b]Ex. 34:15

2:21 [a]Rom. 2:5;
Rev. 9:20;
16:9, 11

2:23 [a]Ps. 7:9;
26:2; 139:1;
Jer. 11:20; 17:10;
Matt. 16:27;
Luke 16:15;
Acts 1:24;
Rom. 8:27

2:24
[a]2 Tim. 3:1–9
[b]Acts 15:28

2:25 [a]Rev. 3:11

2:26
[a][John 6:29]
[b][Matt. 19:28]

2:27 [a]Ps. 2:8, 9;
Rev. 12:5; 19:15

2:28 [a]2 Pet. 1:19;
Rev. 22:16

3:1 [a]Rev. 1:4, 16

2:15 [1]NU, M *likewise.*   2:18 [1]Or *messenger*   2:19 [1]NU, M *faith, service*
[2]*perseverance*   2:20 [1]NU, M *against you that you tolerate*   [2]M *your wife Jezebel*   [3]NU, M *and teaches and seduces*   2:21 [1]NU, M *repent, and she does not want to repent of her sexual immorality.*   2:22 [1]NU, M *her*
2:23 [1]*examines*   2:24 [1]NU, M omit *and*   [2]NU, M omit *will*   3:1 [1]Or *messenger*

3:3 a 1 Tim. 6:20
b Rev. 3:19
c Matt. 24:42, 43;
Luke 12:39
d 1 Thess. 5:2;
[2 Pet. 3:10;
Rev. 16:15]

3:4 a Acts 1:15
b [Jude 23]
c Rev. 4:4; 6:11

3:5 a [Rev. 19:8]
b Ex. 32:32;
Ps. 69:28;
Luke 10:20;
[Rev. 13:8; 17:8;
20:12, 15; 21:27]
c Phil. 4:3
d Matt. 10:32;
Luke 12:8

3:6 a Rev. 2:7

3:7 a Acts 3:14
b John 14:6;
1 John 5:20;
Rev. 3:14; 19:11
c Is. 9:7; 22:22;
Jer. 23:5
d [Matt. 16:19;
Rev. 1:18]
e Job 12:14

3:8 a Rev. 3:1
b 1 Cor. 16:9

3:9 a Rev. 2:9
b Is. 45:14;
49:23; 60:14

3:10
a 2 Tim. 2:12;
2 Pet. 2:9
b Luke 2:1
c Is. 24:17

3:11 a Phil. 4:5
b Rev. 2:25
c [Rev. 2:10]

3:12 a 1 Kin. 7:21;
Jer. 1:18; Gal. 2:9
b Ps. 23:6
c [Rev. 14:1; 22:4]
d [Heb. 12:22]
e Rev. 21:2
f [Rev. 2:17;
22:4]

3:13 a Rev. 2:7

3:14 a Is. 65:16;
2 Cor. 1:20
b Rev. 1:5; 3:7;
19:11
c [Col. 1:15]

3:15 a Rev. 3:1

3:17 a Hos. 12:8;
Zech. 11:5;
[Matt. 5:3];
1 Cor. 4:8

3:18 a Is. 55:1;
Matt. 13:44
b 2 Cor. 5:3

3:19 a Job 5:17
b Prov. 3:12;
[2 Cor. 11:32];
Heb. 12:6

name that you are alive, but you are dead. ²Be watchful, and strengthen the things which remain, that are ready to die, for I have not found your works perfect before ¹God. ³ᵃRemember therefore how you have received and heard; hold fast and ᵇrepent. ᶜTherefore if you will not watch, I will come upon you ᵈas a thief, and you will not know what hour I will come upon you. ⁴¹You have ᵃa few names ²even in Sardis who have not ᵇdefiled their garments; and they shall walk with Me ᶜin white, for they are worthy. ⁵He who overcomes ᵃshall be clothed in white garments, and I will not ᵇblot out his name from the ᶜBook of Life; but ᵈI will confess his name before My Father and before His angels.

⁶ᵃ"He who has an ear, let him hear what the Spirit says to the churches." '

THE FAITHFUL CHURCH

⁷"And to the ¹angel of the church in Philadelphia write,

'These things says ᵃHe who is holy, ᵇHe who is true, ᶜ"He who has the key of David, ᵈHe who opens and no one shuts, and ᵉshuts and no one opens": ⁸ᵃ"I know your works. See, I have set before you ᵇan open door, ¹and no one can shut it; for you have a little strength, have kept My word, and have not denied My name. ⁹Indeed I will make ᵃ*those* of the synagogue of Satan, who say they are Jews and are not, but lie—indeed ᵇI will make them come and worship before your feet, and to know that I have loved you. ¹⁰Because you have kept ¹My command to persevere, ᵃI also will keep you from the hour of trial which shall come upon ᵇthe whole world, to test those who dwell ᶜon the earth. ¹¹Behold, ᵃI am coming quickly! ᵇHold fast what you have, that no one may take ᶜyour crown. ¹²He who overcomes, I will make him ᵃa pillar in the temple of My God, and he shall ᵇgo out no more. ᶜI will write on him the name of My God and the name of the city of My God, the ᵈNew Jerusalem, which ᵉcomes down out of heaven from My God. ᶠAnd I *will write on him* My new name.

¹³ᵃ"He who has an ear, let him hear what the Spirit says to the churches." '

THE LUKEWARM CHURCH

¹⁴"And to the ¹angel of the church ²of the Laodiceans write,

ᵃ'These things says the Amen, ᵇthe Faithful and True Witness, ᶜthe Beginning of the creation of God: ¹⁵ᵃ"I know your works, that you are neither cold nor hot. I could wish you were cold or hot. ¹⁶So then, because you are lukewarm, and neither ¹cold nor hot, I will vomit you out of My mouth. ¹⁷Because you say, ᵃ'I am rich, have become wealthy, and have need of nothing'—and do not know that you are wretched, miserable, poor, blind, and naked— ¹⁸I counsel you ᵃto buy from Me gold refined in the fire, that you may be rich; and ᵇwhite garments, that you may be clothed, *that* the shame of your nakedness may not be revealed; and anoint your eyes with eye salve, that you may see. ¹⁹ᵃAs many as I love, I rebuke and ᵇchasten.¹ Therefore be ²zealous and repent. ²⁰Behold,

---

3:2 ¹NU, M *My God*   3:4 ¹NU, M *Nevertheless you*   ²NU, M omit *even*
3:7 ¹Or *messenger*   3:8 ¹NU, M *which no one can shut*   3:10 ¹Lit. *the word of My patience*   3:11 ¹NU, M omit *Behold*   3:14 ¹Or *messenger*   ²NU, M *in Laodicea*   3:16 ¹NU, M *hot nor cold*   3:19 ¹*discipline*   ²*eager*

ᵃI stand at the door and knock. ᵇIf anyone hears My voice and opens the door, ᶜI will come in to him and dine with him, and he with Me. ²¹To him who overcomes ᵃI will grant to sit with Me on My throne, as I also overcame and sat down with My Father on His throne.

²²ᵃ"He who has an ear, let him hear what the Spirit says to the churches."'"

THE THRONE ROOM OF HEAVEN

(Is. 6:1–3)

4 After these things I looked, and behold, a door *standing* ᵃopen in heaven. And the first voice which I heard *was* like a ᵇtrumpet speaking with me, saying, "Come up here, and I will show you things which must take place after this."

²Immediately ᵃI was in the Spirit; and behold, ᵇa throne set in heaven, and *One* sat on the throne. ³¹And He who sat there was ᵃlike a jasper and a sardius stone in appearance; ᵇand *there was* a rainbow around the throne, in appearance like an emerald. ⁴ᵃAround the throne *were* twenty-four thrones, and on the thrones I saw twenty-four elders sitting, ᵇclothed in white ¹robes; and they had crowns of gold on their heads. ⁵And from the throne proceeded ᵃlightnings, ¹thunderings, and voices. ᵇSeven lamps of fire *were* burning before the throne, which are ᶜthe² seven Spirits of God.

⁶Before the throne *there* ¹*was* ᵃa sea of glass, like crystal. ᵇAnd in the midst of the throne, and around the throne, *were* four living creatures full of eyes in front and in back. ⁷ᵃThe first living creature *was* like a lion, the second living creature like a calf, the third living creature had a face like a man, and the fourth living creature *was* like a flying eagle. ⁸*The* four living creatures, each having ᵃsix wings, were full of eyes around and within. And they do not rest day or night, saying:

ᵇ"Holy,¹ holy, holy,
  ᶜLord God Almighty,
    ᵈWho was and is and is to come!"

⁹Whenever the living creatures give glory and honor and thanks to Him who sits on the throne, ᵃwho lives forever and ever, ¹⁰ᵃthe twenty-four elders fall down before Him who sits on the throne and worship Him who lives forever and ever, and cast their crowns before the throne, saying:

¹¹ "Youᵃ are worthy, ¹O Lord,
    To receive glory and honor and power;
      ᵇFor You created all things,
      And by ᶜYour will they ²exist and were created."

THE LAMB TAKES THE SCROLL

5 And I saw in the right *hand* of Him who sat on the throne ᵃa scroll written inside and on the back, ᵇsealed with seven seals. ²Then I saw a strong angel proclaiming with a loud voice, ᵃ"Who is worthy to open the scroll and to loose its seals?" ³And no one in heaven or on the earth or under the earth was able to open the scroll, or to look at it.

3:20 ᵃSong 5:2
ᵇLuke 12:36, 37;
John 10:3
ᶜ[John 14:23]

3:21
ᵃMatt. 19:28;
2 Tim. 2:12;
[Rev. 2:26;
20:4]

3:22 ᵃRev. 2:7

4:1 ᵃEzek. 1:1;
Rev. 19:11
ᵇRev. 1:10

4:2 ᵃRev. 1:10
ᵇ1 Kin. 22:19;
Is. 6:1;
Ezek. 1:26;
Dan. 7:9;
Rev. 3:21; 4:9

4:3 ᵃMatt. 5:8;
Rev. 21:11
ᵇGen. 9:13–17;
Ezek. 1:28;
Rev. 10:1

4:4 ᵃRev. 11:16
ᵇRev. 3:4, 5

4:5
ᵃGen. 49:9, 10;
Ex. 19:16;
Rev. 8:5; 11:19;
16:18 ᵇEx. 37:23
ᶜ2 Sam. 7:12;
[Rev. 1:4]

4:6 ᵃEx. 38:8;
Ezek. 1:22;
Rev. 15:2
ᵇEzek. 1:5;
Rev. 4:8; 5:6;
6:1, 6; 7:11; 14:3;
15:7; 19:4

4:7 ᵃEzek. 1:10;
10:14

4:8 ᵃIs. 6:2
ᵇIs. 6:3 ᶜRev. 1:8
ᵈRev. 1:4

4:9 ᵃRev. 1:18

4:10
ᵃRev. 5:8, 14;
7:11; 11:16; 19:4

4:11
ᵃRev. 1:6; 5:12
ᵇGen. 1:1;
John 1:3
ᶜCol. 1:16

5:1
ᵃEzek. 2:9, 10
ᵇIs. 29:11;
Dan. 12:4

5:2
ᵃRev. 4:11; 5:9

4:3 ¹M omits *And He who sat there was,* making the following a description of the throne.   4:4 ¹NU, M *robes, with crowns*   4:5 ¹NU, M *voices, and thunderings.*   ²M omits *the*   4:6 ¹NU, M add *something like*   4:8 ¹M has *holy* nine times.   4:11 ¹NU, M *our Lord and God*   ²NU, M *existed*

[4]So I wept much, because no one was found worthy to open [1]and read the scroll, or to look at it. [5]But one of the elders said to me, "Do not weep. Behold, [a]the Lion of the tribe of [b]Judah, [c]the Root of David, has [d]prevailed to open the scroll [e]and [1]to loose its seven seals."

[6]And I looked, [1]and behold, in the midst of the throne and of the four living creatures, and in the midst of the elders, stood [a]a Lamb as though it had been slain, having seven horns and [b]seven eyes, which are [c]the seven Spirits of God sent out into all the earth. [7]Then He came and took the scroll out of the right hand [a]of Him who sat on the throne.

WORTHY IS THE LAMB

[8]Now when He had taken the scroll, [a]the four living creatures and the twenty-four elders fell down before the Lamb, each having a harp, and golden bowls full of incense, which are the [b]prayers of the saints. [9]And [a]they sang a new song, saying:

[b]"You are worthy to take the scroll,
And to open its seals;
For You were slain,
And [c]have redeemed us to God [d]by Your blood
Out of every tribe and tongue and people and
    nation,
10 And have made [1]us [a]kings[2] and [b]priests to our
        God;
    And [3]we shall reign on the earth."

[11]Then I looked, and I heard the voice of many angels around the throne, the living creatures, and the elders; and the number of them was ten thousand times ten thousand, and thousands of thousands, [12]saying with a loud voice:

"Worthy is the Lamb who was slain
To receive power and riches and wisdom,
And strength and honor and glory and blessing!"

[13]And [a]every creature which is in heaven and on the earth and under the earth and such as are in the sea, and all that are in them, I heard saying:

[b]"Blessing and honor and glory and power
Be to Him [c]who sits on the throne,
And to the Lamb, forever and [1]ever!"

[14]Then the four living creatures said, "Amen!" And the [1]twenty-four elders fell down and worshiped [2]Him who lives forever and ever.

FIRST SEAL: THE CONQUEROR

6 Now [a]I saw when the Lamb opened one of the [1]seals; and I heard [b]one of the four living creatures saying with a voice like thunder, "Come and see." [2]And I looked, and behold, [a]a white horse. [b]He who sat on it had a bow; [c]and a crown was given to him, and he went out [d]conquering and to conquer.

5:5 [a]Gen. 49:9
[b]Heb. 7:14
[c]Is. 11:1, 10;
Rom. 15:12;
Rev. 22:16
[d]Rev. 3:21
[e]Rev. 6:1
5:6 [a]Is. 53:7;
[John 1:29;
1 Pet. 1:19]
[b]Zech. 3:9; 4:10
[c]Rev. 1:4; 3:1; 4:5
5:7 [a]Rev. 4:2
5:8
[a]Rev. 4:8–10;
19:4
[b]Ps. 141:2;
Rev. 8:3
5:9 [a]Rev. 14:3
[b]Rev. 4:11
[c]John 1:29
[d][Heb. 9:12;
1 Pet. 1:18, 19]
5:10 [a]Ex. 19:6
[b]Is. 61:6
5:13 [a]Phil. 2:10;
Rev. 5:3
[b]1 Chr. 29:11;
Rom. 9:5;
1 Tim. 6:16;
1 Pet. 4:11
[c]Rev. 4:2, 3;
6:16; 20:11
6:1 [a]Is. 53:7;
[John 1:29;
Rev. 5:5–7, 12;
13:8] [b]Rev. 4:7
6:2
[a]Zech. 1:8; 6:3
[b]Ps. 45:4, 5,
LXX [c]Zech. 6:11;
Rev. 9:7;
14:14; 19:12
[d]Matt. 24:5;
Rev. 3:21

5:4 [1]NU, M omit *and read*   5:5 [1]NU, M omit *to loose*   5:6 [1]NU, M *I saw in the midst . . . a Lamb standing*   5:10 [1]NU, M *them*   [2]NU *a kingdom*
[3]NU, M *they*   5:13 [1]M adds *Amen*   5:14 [1]NU, M omit *twenty-four*
[2]NU, M omit *Him who lives forever and ever*   6:1 [1]NU, M *seven seals*

SECOND SEAL: CONFLICT ON EARTH

[3]When He opened the second seal, [a]I heard the second living creature saying, "Come [1]and see." [4a]Another horse, fiery red, went out. And it was granted to the one who sat on it to [b]take peace from the earth, and that *people* should kill one another; and there was given to him a great sword.

THIRD SEAL: SCARCITY ON EARTH

[5]When He opened the third seal, [a]I heard the third living creature say, "Come and see." So I looked, and behold, [b]a black horse, and he who sat on it had a pair of [c]scales[1] in his hand. [6]And I heard a voice in the midst of the four living creatures saying, "A [1]quart of wheat for a [2]denarius, and three quarts of barley for a denarius; and [a]do not harm the oil and the wine."

FOURTH SEAL: WIDESPREAD DEATH ON EARTH

[7]When He opened the fourth seal, [a]I heard the voice of the fourth living creature saying, "Come and see." [8a]So I looked, and behold, a pale horse. And the name of him who sat on it was Death, and Hades followed with him. And [1]power was given to them over a fourth of the earth, [b]to kill with sword, with hunger, with death, [c]and by the beasts of the earth.

FIFTH SEAL: THE CRY OF THE MARTYRS

[9]When He opened the fifth seal, I saw under [a]the altar [b]the souls of those who had been slain [c]for the word of God and for [d]the testimony which they held. [10]And they cried with a loud voice, saying, [a]"How long, O Lord, [b]holy and true, [c]until You judge and avenge our blood on those who dwell on the earth?" [11]Then a [a]white robe was given to each of them; and it was said to them [b]that they should rest a little while longer, until both *the number of* their fellow servants and their brethren, who would be killed as they *were,* was completed.

SIXTH SEAL: COSMIC DISTURBANCES

[12]I looked when He opened the sixth seal, [a]and [1]behold, there was a great earthquake; and [b]the sun became black as sackcloth of hair, and the [2]moon became like blood. [13a]And the stars of heaven fell to the earth, as a fig tree drops its late figs when it is shaken by a mighty wind. [14a]Then the sky [1]receded as a scroll when it is rolled up, and [b]every mountain and island was moved out of its place. [15]And the [a]kings of the earth, the great men, [1]the rich men, the commanders, the mighty men, every slave and every free man, [b]hid themselves in the caves and in the rocks of the mountains, [16a]and said to the mountains and rocks, "Fall on us and hide us from the face of Him who [b]sits on the throne and from the wrath of the Lamb! [17]For the great day of His wrath has come, [a]and who is able to stand?"

THE SEALED OF ISRAEL

7 After these things I saw four angels standing at the four corners of the earth, [a]holding the four winds of the earth, [b]that the wind should not blow on the earth, on the sea, or

---

6:3 [a]Rev. 4:7

6:4
[a]Zech. 1:8; 6:2
[b]Matt. 24:6, 7

6:5 [a]Rev. 4:7
[b]Zech. 6:2, 6
[c]Matt. 24:7

6:6
[a]Rev. 7:3; 9:4

6:7 [a]Rev. 4:7

6:8 [a]Zech. 6:3
[b]Jer. 14:12; 15:2;
24:10; 29:17;
Ezek. 5:12, 17;
14:21; 29:5;
Matt. 24:9
[c]Lev. 26:22

6:9 [a]Rev. 8:3
[b][Rev. 20:4]
[c]Rev. 1:2, 9
[d]2 Tim. 1:8

6:10
[a]Ps. 13:1–6;
Zech. 1:12
[b]Rev. 3:7
[c]Rev. 11:18

6:11
[a]Rev. 3:4, 5; 7:9
[b]Heb. 11:40

6:12 [a]Matt. 24:7;
Rev. 8:5; 11:13;
16:18 [b]Is. 13:10;
Joel 2:10,
31; 3:15;
Matt. 24:29;
Mark 13:24

6:13
[a]Matt. 24:29;
Mark 13:25;
Rev. 8:10; 9:1

6:14 [a]Ps. 102:26;
Is. 34:4;
[2 Pet. 3:10];
Rev. 20:11; 21:1
[b]Jer. 3:23;
Rev. 16:20

6:15 [a]Ps. 2:2–4
[b]Is. 2:10, 19, 21;
24:21; Rev. 19:18

6:16 [a]Hos. 10:8;
Luke 23:29, 30;
Rev. 9:6
[b]Rev. 20:11

6:17 [a]Is. 63:4;
Jer. 30:7;
Joel 1:15;
2:1, 11, 31;
Zeph. 1:14;
Rev. 16:14

7:1 [a]Jer. 49:36;
Dan. 7:2;
Zech. 6:5;
Matt. 24:31
[b]Rev. 7:3; 8:7;
9:4

6:3 [1]NU, M omit *and see*   6:5 [1]*balances*   6:6 [1]Gr. *choinix*, about 1 quart   [2]About 1 day's wage for a worker   6:8 [1]*authority*   6:12 [1]NU, M omit *behold*   [2]NU, M *whole moon*   6:14 [1]Or *split apart*   6:15 [1]NU, M *the commanders, the rich men,*

on any tree. [2]Then I saw another angel ascending from the east, having the seal of the living God. And he cried with a loud voice to the four angels to whom it was granted to harm the earth and the sea, [3]saying, [a]"Do not harm the earth, the sea, or the trees till we have sealed the servants of our God [b]on their foreheads." [4a]And I heard the number of those who were sealed. [b]One hundred *and* forty-four thousand [c]of all the tribes of the children of Israel *were* sealed:

[5] of the tribe of Judah twelve thousand *were* sealed;
of the tribe of Reuben twelve thousand *were* [1]sealed;
of the tribe of Gad twelve thousand *were* sealed;
[6] of the tribe of Asher twelve thousand *were* sealed;
of the tribe of Naphtali twelve thousand *were* sealed;
of the tribe of Manasseh twelve thousand *were* sealed;
[7] of the tribe of Simeon twelve thousand *were* sealed;
of the tribe of Levi twelve thousand *were* sealed;
of the tribe of Issachar twelve thousand *were* sealed;
[8] of the tribe of Zebulun twelve thousand *were* sealed;
of the tribe of Joseph twelve thousand *were* sealed;
of the tribe of Benjamin twelve thousand *were* sealed.

A MULTITUDE FROM THE GREAT TRIBULATION

[9]After these things I looked, and behold, [a]a great multitude which no one could number, [b]of all nations, tribes, peoples, and tongues, standing before the throne and before the Lamb, [c]clothed with white robes, with palm branches in their hands, [10]and crying out with a loud voice, saying, [a]"Salvation *belongs* to our God [b]who sits on the throne, and to the Lamb!" [11a]All the angels stood around the throne and the elders and the four living creatures, and fell on their faces before the throne and [b]worshiped God, [12a]saying:

"Amen! Blessing and glory and wisdom,
Thanksgiving and honor and power and might,
Be to our God forever and ever.
Amen."

[13]Then one of the elders answered, saying to me, "Who are these arrayed in [a]white robes, and where did they come from?"

[14]And I said to him, [1]"Sir, you know."

So he said to me, [a]"These are the ones who come out of the great tribulation, and [b]washed their robes and made them white in the blood of the Lamb. [15]Therefore they are before the throne of God, and serve Him day and night in His temple. And He who sits on the throne will [a]dwell among them. [16a]They shall neither hunger anymore nor thirst anymore; [b]the sun shall not strike them, nor any heat; [17]for the Lamb who is in the midst of the throne [a]will shepherd them and lead them to [1]living fountains of waters. [b]And God will wipe away every tear from their eyes."

SEVENTH SEAL: PRELUDE TO THE SEVEN TRUMPETS

8 When[a] He opened the seventh seal, there was silence in heaven for about half an hour. [2a]And I saw the seven angels who stand before God, [b]and to them were given seven trum-

7:3 [a]Rev. 6:6
[b]Ezek. 9:4, 6;
Rev. 22:4

7:4 [a]Rev. 9:16
[b]Rev. 14:1, 3
[c]Gen. 49:1–27

7:9 [a]Is. 60:1–5;
Rom. 11:25
[b]Rev. 5:9
[c]Rev. 3:5, 18;
4:4; 6:11

7:10 [a]Ps. 3:8;
Is. 43:11;
Jer. 3:23;
Hos. 13:4;
Rev. 19:1
[b]Rev. 5:13

7:11 [a]Rev. 4:6
[b]Rev. 4:11; 5:9,
12, 14; 11:16

7:12
[a]Rev. 5:13, 14

7:13 [a]Rev. 7:9

7:14 [a]Rev. 6:9
[b]Is. 1:18;
Zech. 3:3–5;
[Heb. 9:14]

7:15 [a]Is. 4:5, 6;
Rev. 21:3

7:16 [a]Ps. 121:5;
Is. 49:10
[b]Ps. 121:6;
Rev. 21:4

7:17 [a]Ps. 23:1;
Matt. 2:6;
[John 10:11, 14]
[b]Is. 25:8;
Matt. 5:4;
Rev. 21:4

8:1 [a]Rev. 6:1

8:2
[a][Matt. 18:10];
Luke 1:19
[b]2 Chr. 29:25–28

7:5 [1]NU, M omit *sealed* in vv. 5b–8b.   7:14 [1]NU, M *My lord*
7:17 [1]NU, M *fountains of the waters of life*

pets. ³Then another angel, having a golden censer, came and stood at the altar. He was given much incense, that he should offer *it* with ᵃthe prayers of all the saints upon ᵇthe golden altar which was before the throne. ⁴And ᵃthe smoke of the incense, with the prayers of the saints, ascended before God from the angel's hand. ⁵Then the angel took the censer, filled it with fire from the altar, and threw *it* to the earth. And ᵃthere were noises, thunderings, ᵇlightnings, ᶜand an earthquake.

⁶So the seven angels who had the seven trumpets prepared themselves to sound.

FIRST TRUMPET: VEGETATION STRUCK

⁷The first angel sounded: ᵃAnd hail and fire followed, mingled with blood, and they were thrown ᵇto the ¹earth. And a third ᶜof the trees were burned up, and all green grass was burned up.

SECOND TRUMPET: THE SEAS STRUCK

⁸Then the second angel sounded: ᵃAnd *something* like a great mountain burning with fire was thrown into the sea, ᵇand a third of the sea ᶜbecame blood. ⁹ᵃAnd a third of the living creatures in the sea died, and a third of the ships were destroyed.

THIRD TRUMPET: THE WATERS STRUCK

¹⁰Then the third angel sounded: ᵃAnd a great star fell from heaven, burning like a torch, ᵇand it fell on a third of the rivers and on the springs of water. ¹¹ᵃThe name of the star is Wormwood. ᵇA third of the waters became wormwood, and many men died from the water, because it was made bitter.

FOURTH TRUMPET: THE HEAVENS STRUCK

¹²ᵃThen the fourth angel sounded: And a third of the sun was struck, a third of the moon, and a third of the stars, so that a third of them were darkened. A third of the day ¹did not shine, and likewise the night.

¹³And I looked, ᵃand I heard an ¹angel flying through the midst of heaven, saying with a loud voice, ᵇ"Woe, woe, woe to the inhabitants of the earth, because of the remaining blasts of the trumpet of the three angels who are about to sound!"

FIFTH TRUMPET: THE LOCUSTS FROM THE BOTTOMLESS PIT

9 Then the fifth angel sounded: ᵃAnd I saw a star fallen from heaven to the earth. To him was given the key to ᵇthe ¹bottomless pit. ²And he opened the bottomless pit, and smoke arose out of the pit like the smoke of a great furnace. So the ᵃsun and the air were darkened because of the smoke of the pit. ³Then out of the smoke locusts came upon the earth. And to them was given power, ᵃas the scorpions of the earth have power. ⁴They were commanded ᵃnot to harm ᵇthe grass of the earth, or any green thing, or any tree, but only those men who do not have ᶜthe seal of God on their foreheads. ⁵And ¹they were not given *authority* to kill them, ᵃbut to torment them *for* five months. Their torment *was* like the torment of a scorpion when it strikes a man. ⁶In those

8:3 ᵃRev. 5:8
ᵇEx. 30:1;
Rev. 8:3

8:4 ᵃPs. 141:2;
Luke 1:10

8:5 ᵃEx. 19:16;
Rev. 11:19; 16:18
ᵇRev. 4:5
ᶜ2 Sam. 22:8;
1 Kin. 19:11;
Acts 4:31

8:7 ᵃEx. 9:23;
Is. 28:2;
Ezek. 38:22;
Joel 2:30
ᵇRev. 16:2
ᶜIs. 2:13;
Rev. 9:4, 15–18

8:8 ᵃJer. 51:25;
Amos 7:4
ᵇEx. 7:17;
Rev. 11:6; 16:3
ᶜEzek. 14:19

8:9 ᵃRev. 16:3

8:10 ᵃIs. 14:12;
Rev. 6:13; 9:1
ᵇRev. 14:7; 16:4

8:11 ᵃRuth 1:20
ᵇEx. 15:23

8:12 ᵃIs. 13:10;
Joel 2:31;
Amos 8:9;
Matt. 24:29;
Rev. 6:12

8:13
ᵃRev. 14:6; 19:17
ᵇRev. 9:12; 11:14;
12:12

9:1 ᵃLuke 10:18;
Rev. 8:10
ᵇLuke 8:31;
Rev. 9:2, 11; 17:8

9:2 ᵃJoel 2:2, 10

9:3 ᵃEx. 10:4;
Judg. 7:12

9:4 ᵃRev. 6:6
ᵇRev. 8:7
ᶜEx. 12:23;
Ezek. 9:4;
Rev. 7:2, 3

9:5
ᵃ[Rev. 9:10; 11:7]

8:7 ¹NU, M add *and a third of the earth was burned up*   8:12 ¹*had no light*
8:13 ¹NU, M *eagle*   9:1 ¹Lit. *shaft of the abyss*   9:5 ¹The locusts

days [a]men will seek death and will not find it; they will desire to die, and death will flee from them.

[7a]The shape of the locusts was like horses prepared for battle. [b]On their heads were crowns of something like gold, [c]and their faces *were* like the faces of men. [8]They had hair like women's hair, and [a]their teeth were like lions' *teeth.* [9]And they had breastplates like breastplates of iron, and the sound of their wings *was* [a]like the sound of chariots with many horses running into battle. [10]They had tails like scorpions, and there were stings in their tails. Their power *was* to hurt men five months. [11]And they had as king over them [a]the angel of the bottomless pit, whose name in Hebrew *is* [1]Abaddon, but in Greek he has the name [2]Apollyon.

[12a]One woe is past. Behold, still two more woes are coming after these things.

SIXTH TRUMPET: THE ANGELS FROM THE EUPHRATES

[13]Then the sixth angel sounded: And I heard a voice from the four horns of the [a]golden altar which is before God, [14]saying to the sixth angel who had the trumpet, "Release the four angels who are bound [a]at the great river Euphrates." [15]So the four angels, who had been prepared for the hour and day and month and year, were released to kill a [a]third of mankind. [16]Now [a]the number of the army [b]of the horsemen *was* two hundred million; [c]I heard the number of them. [17]And thus I saw the horses in the vision: those who sat on them had breastplates of fiery red, hyacinth blue, and sulfur yellow; [a]and the heads of the horses *were* like the heads of lions; and out of their mouths came fire, smoke, and brimstone. [18]By these three *plagues* a third of mankind was killed—by the fire and the smoke and the brimstone which came out of their mouths. [19]For [1]their power is in their mouth and in their tails; [a]for their tails *are* like serpents, having heads; and with them they do harm.

[20]But the rest of mankind, who were not killed by these plagues, [a]did not repent of the works of their hands, that they should not worship [b]demons, [c]and idols of gold, silver, brass, stone, and wood, which can neither see nor hear nor walk. [21]And they did not repent of their murders [a]or their [1]sorceries or their sexual immorality or their thefts.

THE MIGHTY ANGEL WITH THE LITTLE BOOK

10 I saw still another mighty angel coming down from heaven, clothed with a cloud. [a]And a rainbow *was* on [b]his head, his face *was* like the sun, and [c]his feet like pillars of fire. [2]He had a little book open in his hand. [a]And he set his right foot on the sea and *his* left *foot* on the land, [3]and cried with a loud voice, as *when* a lion roars. When he cried out, [a]seven thunders uttered their voices. [4]Now when the seven thunders [1]uttered their voices, I was about to write; but I heard a voice from heaven saying [2]to me, [a]"Seal up the things which the seven thunders uttered, and do not write them."

[5]The angel whom I saw standing on the sea and on the land [a]raised up his [1]hand to heaven [6]and swore by Him who

9:6
[a]Job 3:21; 7:15;
Is. 2:19; Jer. 8:3;
Rev. 6:16
9:7 [a]Joel 2:4
[b]Nah. 3:17
[c]Dan. 7:8
9:8 [a]Joel 1:6
9:9 [a]Jer. 47:3;
Joel 2:5–7
9:11 [a]Eph. 2:2
9:12
[a]Rev. 8:13; 11:14
9:13 [a]Rev. 8:3
9:14 [a]Gen. 15:18;
Deut. 1:7;
Josh. 1:4;
Rev. 16:12
9:15
[a]Rev. 8:7–9; 9:18
9:16 [a]Ps. 68:17;
Dan. 7:10
[b]Ezek. 38:4
[c]Rev. 7:4
9:17 [a]1 Chr. 12:8;
Is. 5:28, 29
9:19 [a]Is. 9:15
9:20
[a]Deut. 31:29
[b]Lev. 17:7;
Deut. 32:17;
Ps. 106:37;
1 Cor. 10:20
[c]Ps. 115:4–7;
135:15–17;
Dan. 5:23
9:21
[a]Rev. 21:8; 22:15
10:1
[a]Ezek. 1:26–28;
Rev. 4:3
[b]Matt. 17:2;
Rev. 1:16
[c]Rev. 1:15
10:2 [a]Ps. 95:5;
Matt. 28:18
10:3
[a]Ps. 29:3–9;
Rev. 4:5; 8:5
10:4 [a]Dan. 8:26;
12:4, 9;
Rev. 22:10
10:5 [a]Ex. 6:8;
Deut. 32:40;
Dan. 12:7

9:11 [1]Lit. *Destruction*   [2]Lit. *Destroyer*   **9:19** [1]NU, M *the power of the horses*
9:21 [1]NU, M *drugs*   **10:4** [1]NU, M *sounded,*   [2]NU, M omit *to me*
10:5 [1]NU, M *right hand*

lives forever and ever, [a]who created heaven and the things that are in it, the earth and the things that are in it, and the sea and the things that are in it, [b]that there should be delay no longer, [7]but [a]in the days of the sounding of the seventh angel, when he is about to sound, the mystery of God would be finished, as He declared to His servants the prophets.

JOHN EATS THE LITTLE BOOK

[8]Then the voice which I heard from heaven spoke to me again and said, "Go, take the little book which is open in the hand of the angel who stands on the sea and on the earth."

[9]So I went to the angel and said to him, "Give me the little book."

And he said to me, [a]"Take and eat it; and it will make your stomach bitter, but it will be as sweet as honey in your mouth."

[10]Then I took the little book out of the angel's hand and ate it, [a]and it was as sweet as honey in my mouth. But when I had eaten it, [b]my stomach became bitter. [11]And [1]he said to me, "You must prophesy again about many peoples, nations, tongues, and kings."

THE TWO WITNESSES

11 Then I was given [a]a reed like a measuring rod. [1]And the angel stood, saying, [b]"Rise and measure the temple of God, the altar, and those who worship there. [2]But leave out [a]the court which is outside the temple, and do not measure it, [b]for it has been given to the Gentiles. And they will [c]tread the holy city underfoot *for* [d]forty-two months. [3]And I will give *power* to my two [a]witnesses, [b]and they will prophesy [c]one thousand two hundred and sixty days, clothed in sackcloth."

[4]These are the [a]two olive trees and the two lampstands standing before the [1]God of the earth. [5]And if anyone wants to harm them, [a]fire proceeds from their mouth and devours their enemies. [b]And if anyone wants to harm them, he must be killed in this manner. [6]These [a]have power to shut heaven, so that no rain falls in the days of their prophecy; and they have power over waters to turn them to blood, and to strike the earth with all plagues, as often as they desire.

THE WITNESSES KILLED

[7]When they [a]finish their testimony, [b]the beast that ascends [c]out of the bottomless pit [d]will make war against them, overcome them, and kill them. [8]And their dead bodies *will lie* in the street of [a]the great city which spiritually is called Sodom and Egypt, [b]where also [1]our Lord was crucified. [9a]Then *those* from the peoples, tribes, tongues, and nations [1]will see their dead bodies three-and-a-half days, [b]and not allow their dead bodies to be put into graves. [10a]And those who dwell on the earth will rejoice over them, make merry, [b]and send gifts to one another, [c]because these two prophets tormented those who dwell on the earth.

THE WITNESSES RESURRECTED

[11a]Now after the three-and-a-half days [b]the breath of life from God entered them, and they stood on their feet, and

10:6 [a]Gen. 1:1;
Ex. 20:11;
Neh. 9:6;
Rev. 4:11
[b]Dan. 12:7;
Rev. 16:17

10:7 [a]Rev. 11:15

10:9 [a]Jer. 15:16;
Ezek. 2:8; 3:1–3

10:10 [a]Ezek. 3:3
[b]Ezek. 2:10

11:1
[a]Ezek. 40:3—
42:20; Zech. 2:1;
Rev. 21:15
[b]Num. 23:18

11:2
[a]Ezek. 40:17, 20
[b]Ps. 79:1;
Luke 21:24
[c]Dan. 8:10
[d]Dan. 7:25; 12:7;
Rev. 12:6; 13:5

11:3 [a]Deut. 17:6;
Rev. 20:4
[b]Rev. 19:10
[c]Rev. 12:6

11:4 [a]Ps. 52:8;
Jer. 11:16;
Zech. 4:2, 3,
11, 14

11:5
[a]2 Kin. 1:10–12;
Jer. 1:10; 5:14;
Ezek. 43:3;
Hos. 6:5;
Rev. 9:17
[b]Num. 16:29

11:6 [a]1 Kin. 17:1;
Luke 4:25;
[James 5:16, 17]

11:7 [a]Luke 13:32
[b]Rev. 13:1, 11; 17:8
[c]Rev. 9:1, 2
[d]Dan. 7:21;
Rev. 13:7

11:8 [a]Rev. 14:8
[b]Heb. 13:12

11:9 [a]Rev. 17:15
[b]1 Kin. 13:22;
Ps. 79:2, 3

11:10 [a]Rev. 12:12
[b]Neh. 8:10, 12;
Esth. 9:19, 22
[c]Rev. 16:10

11:11 [a]Rev. 11:9
[b]Ezek. 37:5,
9, 10

10:11 [1]NU, M *they*   11:1 [1]NU, M omit *And the angel stood*   11:4 [1]NU, M *Lord*
11:8 [1]NU, M *their*   11:9 [1]NU, M *see ... and will not allow*

great fear fell on those who saw them. [12]And [1]they heard a loud voice from heaven saying to them, "Come up here." [a]And they ascended to heaven [b]in a cloud, [c]and their enemies saw them. [13]In the same hour [a]there was a great earthquake, [b]and a tenth of the city fell. In the earthquake seven thousand people were killed, and the rest were afraid [c]and gave glory to the God of heaven.

[14a]The second woe is past. Behold, the third woe is coming quickly.

SEVENTH TRUMPET: THE KINGDOM PROCLAIMED

[15]Then [a]the seventh angel sounded: [b]And there were loud voices in heaven, saying, [c]"The [1]kingdoms of this world have become *the kingdoms* of our Lord and of His Christ, [d]and He shall reign forever and ever!" [16]And [a]the twenty-four elders who sat before God on their thrones fell on their faces and [b]worshiped God, [17]saying:

"We give You thanks, O Lord God Almighty,
The One [a]who is and who was [1]and who is to come,
Because You have taken Your great power [b]and reigned.
[18] The nations were [a]angry, and Your [1]wrath has come,
And the time of the [b]dead, that they should be judged,
And that You should reward Your servants the prophets
    and the saints,
And those who fear Your name, small and great,
And should destroy those who destroy the earth."

[19]Then [a]the temple of God was opened in heaven, and the ark of [1]His covenant was seen in His temple. And [b]there were lightnings, noises, thunderings, an earthquake, [c]and great hail.

THE WOMAN, THE CHILD, AND THE DRAGON

12 Now a great sign appeared in heaven: a woman clothed with the sun, with the moon under her feet, and on her head a garland of twelve stars. [2]Then being with child, she cried out [a]in labor and in pain to give birth.

[3]And another sign appeared in heaven: behold, [a]a great, fiery red dragon having seven heads and ten horns, and seven diadems on his heads. [4a]His tail drew a third [b]of the stars of heaven [c]and threw them to the earth. And the dragon stood [d]before the woman who was ready to give birth, [e]to devour her Child as soon as it was born. [5]She bore a male Child [a]who was to rule all nations with a rod of iron. And her Child was [b]caught up to God and His throne. [6]Then [a]the woman fled into the wilderness, where she has a place prepared by God, that they should feed her there [b]one thousand two hundred and sixty days.

SATAN THROWN OUT OF HEAVEN

[7]And war broke out in heaven: [a]Michael and his angels fought [b]with the dragon; and the dragon and his angels fought, [8]but they [1]did not prevail, nor was a place found for [2]them in heaven any longer. [9]So [a]the great dragon was cast

---

11:12 [a]Is. 14:13
[b]Is. 60:8;
Acts 1:9
[c]2 Kin. 2:11, 12

11:13 [a]Rev. 6:12;
8:5; 11:19; 16:18
[b]Rev. 16:19
[c]Josh. 7:19;
John 9:24;
Rev. 14:7; 16:9;
19:7

11:14
[a]Rev. 8:13; 9:12

11:15
[a]Rev. 8:2; 10:7
[b]Is. 27:13
[c]Rev. 12:10
[d]Ex. 15:18;
Dan. 2:44;
7:14, 27;
Luke 1:33

11:16
[a]Matt. 19:28;
Rev. 4:4
[b]Rev. 4:11; 5:9,
12, 14; 7:11

11:17 [a]Rev. 16:5
[b]Rev. 19:6

11:18 [a]Ps. 2:1
[b]Dan. 7:10;
[Rev. 20:12, 13]

11:19
[a]Rev. 4:1; 15:5, 8
[b]Rev. 8:5
[c]Rev. 16:21

12:2 [a]Is. 26:17;
66:6–9;
Mic. 4:9;
Gal. 4:19

12:3 [a]Rev. 13:1;
17:3, 7, 9

12:4
[a]Rev. 9:10, 19
[b]Rev. 8:7, 12
[c]Dan. 8:10
[d]Rev. 12:2
[e]Ex. 1:16;
Matt. 2:16

12:5 [a]Ps. 2:9;
Is. 7:14; 9:6;
Rev. 2:27; 19:15
[b]Luke 24:51;
Acts 1:9–11

12:6
[a]Rev. 12:4, 14
[b]Rev. 11:3; 13:5

12:7
[a]Dan. 10:13, 21;
12:1; Jude 9
[b]Rev. 20:2

12:9 [a]Luke 10:18;
John 12:31

11:12 [1]M I   11:15 [1]NU, M kingdom . . . has become the kingdom
11:17 [1]NU, M omit *and who is to come*   11:18 [1]*anger*   11:19 [1]M *the covenant
of the Lord*   12:8 [1]*were not strong enough*   [2]M *him*

out, [b]that serpent of old, called the Devil and Satan, [c]who deceives the whole world; [d]he was cast to the earth, and his angels were cast out with him.

[10]Then I heard a loud voice saying in heaven, [a]"Now salvation, and strength, and the kingdom of our God, and the power of His Christ have come, for the accuser of our brethren, [b]who accused them before our God day and night, has been cast down. [11]And [a]they overcame him by the blood of the Lamb and by the word of their testimony, [b]and they did not love their lives to the death. [12]Therefore [a]rejoice, O heavens, and you who dwell in them! [b]Woe to the inhabitants of the earth and the sea! For the devil has come down to you, having great wrath, [c]because he knows that he has a short time."

THE WOMAN PERSECUTED

[13]Now when the dragon saw that he had been cast to the earth, he persecuted [a]the woman who gave birth to the male *Child*. [14a]But the woman was given two wings of a great eagle, [b]that she might fly [c]into the wilderness to her place, where she is nourished [d]for a time and times and half a time, from the presence of the serpent. [15]So the serpent [a]spewed water out of his mouth like a flood after the woman, that he might cause her to be carried away by the flood. [16]But the earth helped the woman, and the earth opened its mouth and swallowed up the flood which the dragon had spewed out of his mouth. [17]And the dragon was enraged with the woman, and he went to make war with the rest of her offspring, who keep the commandments of God and have the testimony of Jesus [1]Christ.

THE BEAST FROM THE SEA

13 Then [1]I stood on the sand of the sea. And I saw [a]a beast rising up out of the sea, [b]having [2]seven heads and ten horns, and on his horns ten crowns, and on his heads a [c]blasphemous name. [2]Now the beast which I saw was like a leopard, his feet were like *the feet of* a bear, and his mouth like the mouth of a lion. The [a]dragon gave him his power, his throne, and great authority. [3]And I saw one of his heads [a]as if it had been mortally wounded, and his deadly wound was healed. And [b]all the world marveled and followed the beast. [4]So they worshiped the dragon who gave authority to the beast; and they worshiped the beast, saying, [a]"Who *is* like the beast? Who is able to make war with him?"

[5]And he was given [a]a mouth speaking great things and blasphemies, and he was given authority to [1]continue for [b]forty-two months. [6]Then he opened his mouth in blasphemy against God, to blaspheme His name, [a]His tabernacle, and those who dwell in heaven. [7]It was granted to him [a]to make war with the saints and to overcome them. And [b]authority was given him over every [1]tribe, tongue, and nation. [8]All who dwell on the earth will worship him, [a]whose names have not been written in the Book of Life of the Lamb slain [b]from the foundation of the world.

[9a]If anyone has an ear, let him hear. [10a]He who leads into captivity shall go into captivity; [b]he who kills with the sword

---

12:9
[b]Gen. 3:1, 4;
2 Cor. 11:3;
Rev. 12:15; 20:2
[c]Rev. 20:3
[d]Rev. 9:1

12:10 [a]Rev. 11:15
[b]Job 1:9, 11; 2:5;
Zech. 3:1

12:11
[a]Rom. 16:20
[b]Luke 14:26;
[Rev. 2:10]

12:12 [a]Ps. 96:11;
Is. 44:23;
Rev. 18:20
[b]Rev. 8:13
[c]Rev. 10:6

12:13 [a]Rev. 12:5

12:14 [a]Ex. 19:4;
Deut. 32:11;
Is. 40:31
[b]Rev. 12:6
[c]Rev. 17:3
[d]Dan. 7:25; 12:7

12:15 [a]Is. 59:19

13:1 [a]Dan. 7:2, 7
[b]Rev. 12:3
[c]Dan. 7:8; 11:36;
Rev. 17:3

13:2
[a]Rev. 12:3, 9;
13:4, 12

13:3
[a]Rev. 13:12, 14
[b]Rev. 17:8

13:4 [a]Ex. 15:11;
Is. 46:5;
Rev. 18:18

13:5 [a]Dan. 7:8,
11, 20, 25; 11:36;
2 Thess. 2:3
[b]Rev. 11:2

13:6 [a][John 1:14;
Col. 2:9]

13:7 [a]Dan. 7:21;
Rev. 11:7
[b]Rev. 11:18

13:8 [a]Ex. 32:32;
[Rev. 20:12–15]
[b]Matt. 25:34;
Rev. 17:8

13:9 [a]Rev. 2:7

13:10 [a]Is. 33:1;
Jer. 15:2; 43:11
[b]Gen. 9:6;
Matt. 26:52;
Rev. 11:18

12:17 [1]NU, M omit *Christ*   13:1 [1]NU *he*   [2]NU, M *ten horns and seven heads*
13:5 [1]M *make war*   13:7 [1]NU, M add *and people*

must be killed with the sword. [c]Here is the [1]patience and the faith of the saints.

THE BEAST FROM THE EARTH

13:10 [c]Heb. 6:12;
Rev. 14:12

13:11 [a]Rev. 11:7

13:12
[a]Rev. 13:3, 4

13:13 [a]Deut. 13:1;
Matt. 24:24;
2 Thess. 2:9;
Rev. 16:14
[b]1 Kin. 18:38;
2 Kin. 1:10;
Luke 9:54;
Rev. 11:5; 20:9

13:14 [a]Rev. 12:9
[b]2 Thess. 2:9
[c]2 Kin. 20:7

13:15 [a]Rev. 16:2

13:16 [a]Gal. 6:17;
Rev. 7:3;
14:9; 20:4

13:17
[a]Rev. 14:9–11
[b]Rev. 15:2

13:18 [a]Rev. 17:9
[b][1 Cor. 2:14]
[c]Rev. 15:2
[d]Rev. 21:17

14:1 [a]Rev. 5:6
[b]Rev. 7:4; 14:3
[c]Ezek. 9:4;
Rev. 7:3; 22:4

14:2
[a]Rev. 1:15; 19:6
[b]Rev. 5:8

14:3 [a]Rev. 5:9

14:4
[a][Matt. 19:12;
2 Cor. 11:2;
Eph. 5:27]
[b]Rev. 3:4; 7:17
[c]Rev. 5:9
[d]Heb. 12:23;
James 1:18

14:5 [a]Ps. 32:2;
Zeph. 3:13;
Mal. 2:6;
John 1:47;
1 Pet. 2:22
[b]Eph. 5:27

14:6 [a]Rev. 8:13
[b]Eph. 3:9
[c]Rev. 13:7

14:7 [a]Rev. 11:18
[b]Neh. 9:6

14:8 [a]Is. 21:9;
Jer. 51:8;
Rev. 18:2
[b]Jer. 51:7;
Rev. 17:2

[11]Then I saw another beast [a]coming up out of the earth, and he had two horns like a lamb and spoke like a dragon. [12]And he exercises all the authority of the first beast in his presence, and causes the earth and those who dwell in it to worship the first beast, [a]whose deadly wound was healed. [13a]He performs great signs, [b]so that he even makes fire come down from heaven on the earth in the sight of men. [14a]And he deceives [1]those who dwell on the earth [b]by those signs which he was granted to do in the sight of the beast, telling those who dwell on the earth to make an image to the beast who was wounded by the sword [c]and lived. [15]He was granted *power* to give breath to the image of the beast, that the image of the beast should both speak [a]and cause as many as would not worship the image of the beast to be killed. [16]He causes all, both small and great, rich and poor, free and slave, [a]to receive a mark on their right hand or on their foreheads, [17]and that no one may buy or sell except one who has [1]the mark or [a]the name of the beast, [b]or the number of his name.

[18a]Here is wisdom. Let him who has [b]understanding calculate [c]the number of the beast, [d]for it is the number of a man: His number *is* 666.

THE LAMB AND THE 144,000

14 Then I looked, and behold, [1a] [a]Lamb standing on Mount Zion, and with Him [b]one hundred *and* forty-four thousand, [2]having His Father's name [c]written on their foreheads. [2]And I heard a voice from heaven, [a]like the voice of many waters, and like the voice of loud thunder. And I heard the sound of [b]harpists playing their harps. [3]They sang as it were a new song before the throne, before the four living creatures, and the elders; and no one could learn that song [a]except the hundred *and* forty-four thousand who were redeemed from the earth. [4]These are the ones who were not defiled with women, [a]for they are virgins. These are the ones [b]who follow the Lamb wherever He goes. These [c]were [1]redeemed from *among* men, [d]*being* firstfruits to God and to the Lamb. [5]And [a]in their mouth was found no [1]deceit, for [b]they are without fault [2]before the throne of God.

THE PROCLAMATIONS OF THREE ANGELS

[6]Then I saw another angel [a]flying in the midst of heaven, [b]having the everlasting gospel to preach to those who dwell on the earth—[c]to every nation, tribe, tongue, and people—[7]saying with a loud voice, [a]"Fear God and give glory to Him, for the hour of His judgment has come; [b]and worship Him who made heaven and earth, the sea and springs of water."

[8]And another angel followed, saying, [a]"Babylon[1] is fallen, is fallen, that great city, because [b]she has made all nations drink of the wine of the wrath of her fornication."

13:10 [1]*perseverance*   13:14 [1]M *my own people*   13:17 [1]NU, M *the mark, the name*   14:1 [1]NU, M *the*   [2]NU, M add *His name and*   14:4 [1]M adds *by Jesus*   14:5 [1]NU, M *falsehood*   [2]NU, M omit the rest of v. 5.   14:8 [1]NU *Babylon the great is fallen, is fallen, which has made;* M *Babylon the great is fallen. She has made*

9Then a third angel followed them, saying with a loud voice, a"If anyone worships the beast and his image, and receives *his* bmark on his forehead or on his hand, 10he himself ashall also drink of the wine of the wrath of God, which is bpoured out full strength into cthe cup of His indignation. dHe shall be tormented with efire and brimstone in the presence of the holy angels and in the presence of the Lamb. 11And athe smoke of their torment ascends forever and ever; and they have no rest day or night, who worship the beast and his image, and whoever receives the mark of his name."

12aHere is the 1patience of the saints; bhere2 *are* those who keep the commandments of God and the faith of Jesus.

13Then I heard a voice from heaven saying 1to me, "Write: a'Blessed *are* the dead bwho die in the Lord from now on.'"

"Yes," says the Spirit, c"that they may rest from their labors, and their works follow dthem."

REAPING THE EARTH'S HARVEST

14Then I looked, and behold, a white cloud, and on the cloud sat *One* like the Son of Man, having on His head a golden crown, and in His hand a sharp sickle. 15And another angel acame out of the temple, crying with a loud voice to Him who sat on the cloud, b"Thrust in Your sickle and reap, for the time has come 1for You to reap, for the harvest cof the earth is ripe." 16So He who sat on the cloud thrust in His sickle on the earth, and the earth was reaped.

REAPING THE GRAPES OF WRATH

17Then another angel came out of the temple which is in heaven, he also having a sharp sickle.

18And another angel came out from the altar, awho had power over fire, and he cried with a loud cry to him who had the sharp sickle, saying, b"Thrust in your sharp sickle and gather the clusters of the vine of the earth, for her grapes are fully ripe." 19So the angel thrust his sickle into the earth and gathered the vine of the earth, and threw *it* into athe great winepress of the wrath of God. 20And athe winepress was trampled boutside the city, and blood came out of the winepress, cup to the horses' bridles, for one thousand six hundred 1furlongs.

PRELUDE TO THE BOWL JUDGMENTS

15 Then aI saw another sign in heaven, great and marvelous: bseven angels having the seven last plagues, cfor in them the wrath of God is complete.

2And I saw *something* like aa sea of glass bmingled with fire, and those who have the victory over the beast, cover his image and 1over his mark *and* over the dnumber of his name, standing on the sea of glass, ehaving harps of God. 3They sing athe song of Moses, the servant of God, and the song of the bLamb, saying:

c"Great and marvelous *are* Your works,
Lord God Almighty!

14:9
aRev. 13:14, 15;
14:11 bRev. 13:16

14:10 aPs. 75:8
bRev. 18:6
cRev. 16:19
dRev. 20:10
eGen. 19:24;
Ezek. 38:22;
2 Thess. 1:7;
Rev. 19:20

14:11
aIs. 34:8–10;
Rev. 18:9, 18;
19:3

14:12 aRev. 13:10
bRev. 12:17

14:13
aEccl. 4:1, 2
b1 Cor. 15:18;
[1 Thess. 4:16]
c2 Thess. 1:7;
Heb. 4:9, 10;
Rev. 6:11
d[1 Cor. 3:11–15;
15:58]

14:15 aRev. 16:17
bJoel 3:13;
Mark 4:29;
Rev. 14:18
cJer. 51:33;
[Matt. 13:39–41]

14:18 aRev. 16:8
bJoel 3:13;
Mark 4:29;
Rev. 14:15

14:19 aIs. 63:2;
Rev. 19:15

14:20 aIs. 63:3;
Lam. 1:15;
Rev. 19:15
bHeb. 13:12;
Rev. 11:8 cIs. 34:3

15:1 aRev. 12:1, 3
bRev. 21:9
cRev. 14:10

15:2 aRev. 4:6
b[Matt. 3:11]
cRev. 13:14, 15
dRev. 13:17
eRev. 5:8

15:3 aEx. 15:1–21
bRev. 15:3
cDeut. 32:3, 4;
Ps. 92:5;
Rom. 11:33

14:12 1steadfastness, perseverance   2NU, M omit *here are those*
14:13 1NU, M omit *to me*   14:15 1NU, M omit *for You*   14:20 1Lit. *stadia,*
about 184 miles in all   15:2 1NU, M omit *over his mark*

15:3 dPs. 145:17;
Rev. 16:7

15:4 aEx. 15:14
bLev. 11:44;
1 Pet. 1:16;
Rev. 4:8
cPs. 86:9;
Is. 66:23

15:5 aEx. 38:21;
Num. 1:50;
Heb. 8:5;
Rev. 13:6

15:6 aEx. 28:6

15:7 aRev. 4:6
b1 Thess. 1:9

15:8
aEx. 19:18; 40:34;
Lev. 16:2;
1 Kin. 8:10;
2 Chr. 5:13;
Is. 6:4
b2 Thess. 1:9

16:1 aRev. 15:1
bRev. 14:10

16:2 aRev. 8:7
bEx. 9:9–11;
Deut. 28:35;
Rev. 16:11
cRev. 13:15–17;
14:9 dRev. 13:14

16:3
aRev. 8:8; 11:6
bEx. 7:17–21
cRev. 8:9

16:4 aRev. 8:10
bEx. 7:17–20;
Ps. 78:44;
Rev. 11:6

16:5 aRev. 15:3, 4
bRev. 1:4, 8

16:6
aMatt. 23:34
bRev. 11:18
cIs. 49:26;
Luke 11:49–51

16:7 aRev. 15:3
bRev. 13:10; 19:2

16:8 aRev. 8:12
bRev. 9:17, 18

16:9 aRev. 16:11
bDan. 5:22
cRev. 11:13

16:10 aRev. 13:2
bEx. 10:21;
Is. 8:22;
Rev. 8:12; 9:2
cRev. 11:10

dJust and true *are* Your ways,
O King of the [1]saints!
4 aWho shall not fear You, O Lord, and glorify Your name?
For *You* alone *are* bholy.
For call nations shall come and worship before You,
For Your judgments have been manifested."

5After these things I looked, and [1]behold, athe [2]temple of the tabernacle of the testimony in heaven was opened. 6And out of the [1]temple came the seven angels having the seven plagues, aclothed in pure bright linen, and having their chests girded with golden bands. 7aThen one of the four living creatures gave to the seven angels seven golden bowls full of the wrath of God bwho lives forever and ever. 8aThe temple was filled with smoke bfrom the glory of God and from His power, and no one was able to enter the temple till the seven plagues of the seven angels were completed.

16 Then I heard a loud voice from the temple saying ato the seven angels, "Go and pour out the [1]bowls bof the wrath of God on the earth."

FIRST BOWL: LOATHSOME SORES

2So the first went and poured out his bowl aupon the earth, and a [1]foul and bloathsome sore came upon the men cwho had the mark of the beast and those dwho worshiped his image.

SECOND BOWL: THE SEA TURNS TO BLOOD

3Then the second angel poured out his bowl aon the sea, and bit became blood as of a dead *man;* cand every living creature in the sea died.

THIRD BOWL: THE WATERS TURN TO BLOOD

4Then the third angel poured out his bowl aon the rivers and springs of water, band they became blood. 5And I heard the angel of the waters saying:

a"You are righteous, [1]O Lord,
The One bwho is and who [2]was and who is to be,
Because You have judged these things.
6 For athey have shed the blood bof saints and prophets,
cAnd You have given them blood to drink.
[1]For it is their just due."

7And I heard [1]another from the altar saying, "Even so, aLord God Almighty, btrue and righteous *are* Your judgments."

FOURTH BOWL: MEN ARE SCORCHED

8Then the fourth angel poured out his bowl aon the sun, band power was given to him to scorch men with fire. 9And men were scorched with great heat, and they ablasphemed the name of God who has power over these plagues; band they did not repent cand give Him glory.

FIFTH BOWL: DARKNESS AND PAIN

10Then the fifth angel poured out his bowl aon the throne of the beast, band his kingdom became full of darkness; cand

15:3 [1]NU, M *nations*   15:5 [1]NU, M omit *behold*   [2]*sanctuary,* the inner shrine   15:6 [1]*sanctuary,* the inner shrine   16:1 [1]NU, M *seven bowls*
16:2 [1]*severe and malignant,* lit. *bad and evil*   16:5 [1]NU, M omit *O Lord*
[2]NU, M *was, the Holy One*   16:6 [1]NU, M omit *For*   16:7 [1]NU, M omit *another from*

they gnawed their tongues because of the pain. [11]They blasphemed the God of heaven because of their pains and their sores, and did not repent of their deeds.

SIXTH BOWL: EUPHRATES DRIED UP

[12]Then the sixth angel poured out his bowl [a]on the great river Euphrates, [b]and its water was dried up, [c]so that the way of the kings from the east might be prepared. [13]And I saw three unclean [a]spirits like frogs *coming* out of the mouth of [b]the dragon, out of the mouth of the beast, and out of the mouth of [c]the false prophet. [14]For they are spirits of demons, [a]performing signs, *which* go out to the kings [1]of the earth and of [b]the whole world, to gather them to [c]the battle of that great day of God Almighty.

[15a]"Behold, I am coming as a thief. Blessed *is* he who watches, and keeps his garments, [b]lest he walk naked and they see his shame."

[16a]And they gathered them together to the place called in Hebrew, [1]Armageddon.

SEVENTH BOWL: THE EARTH UTTERLY SHAKEN

[17]Then the seventh angel poured out his bowl into the air, and a loud voice came out of the temple of heaven, from the throne, saying, [a]"It is done!" [18]And [a]there were noises and thunderings and lightnings; [b]and there was a great earthquake, such a mighty and great earthquake [c]as had not occurred since men were on the earth. [19]Now [a]the great city was divided into three parts, and the cities of the nations fell. And [b]great Babylon [c]was remembered before God, [d]to give her the cup of the wine of the fierceness of His wrath. [20]Then [a]every island fled away, and the mountains were not found. [21]And great hail from heaven fell upon men, *each hailstone* about the weight of a talent. Men blasphemed God because of the plague of the hail, since that plague was exceedingly great.

THE SCARLET WOMAN AND THE SCARLET BEAST

17 Then [a]one of the seven angels who had the seven bowls came and talked with me, saying [1]to me, "Come, [b]I will show you the judgment of [c]the great harlot [d]who sits on many waters, [2a]with whom the kings of the earth committed fornication, and [b]the inhabitants of the earth were made drunk with the wine of her fornication."

[3]So he carried me away in the Spirit [a]into the wilderness. And I saw a woman sitting [b]on a scarlet beast *which was* full of [c]names of blasphemy, having seven heads and ten horns. [4]The woman [a]was arrayed in purple and scarlet, [b]and adorned with gold and precious stones and pearls, [c]having in her hand a golden cup [d]full of abominations and the filthiness of [1]her fornication. [5]And on her forehead a name *was* written:

[a]MYSTERY, BABYLON THE GREAT,
THE MOTHER OF HARLOTS
AND OF THE ABOMINATIONS
OF THE EARTH.

16:12 [a]Rev. 9:14
[b]Jer. 50:38
[c]Is. 41:2, 25;
46:11

16:13 [a]1 John 4:1
[b]Rev. 12:3, 9
[c]Rev. 13:11, 14;
19:20; 20:10

16:14
[a]2 Thess. 2:9
[b]Luke 2:1
[c]1 Kin. 22:21–23;
Rev. 17:14; 19:19;
20:8

16:15
[a]Matt. 24:43;
Luke 12:39;
Rev. 3:3, 11
[b]2 Cor. 5:3

16:16 [a]Rev. 19:19

16:17
[a]Rev. 10:6; 21:6

16:18 [a]Rev. 4:5
[b]Rev. 11:13
[c]Dan. 12:1;
Matt. 24:21

16:19 [a]Rev. 14:8
[b]Rev. 17:5, 18
[c]Rev. 14:8; 18:5
[d]Is. 51:17;
Rev. 14:10

16:20
[a]Rev. 6:14; 20:11

17:1
[a]Rev. 1:1; 21:9
[b]Rev. 16:19
[c]Is. 1:21;
Jer. 2:20;
Nah. 3:4;
Rev. 17:5, 15; 19:2
[d]Jer. 51:13;
Rev. 17:15

17:2
[a]Rev. 2:22;
18:3, 9
[b]Jer. 51:7;
Rev. 14:8

17:3
[a]Rev. 12:6, 14;
21:10 [b]Rev. 12:3
[c]Rev. 13:1

17:4
[a]Ezek. 28:13;
Rev. 18:12, 16
[b]Dan. 11:38
[c]Jer. 51:7;
Rev. 18:6
[d]Rev. 14:8

17:5
[a]2 Thess. 2:7;
Rev. 1:20; 17:7

16:14 [1]NU, M omit *of the earth and*   16:16 [1]Lit. *Mount Megiddo;* M *Megiddo*
17:1 [1]NU, M omit *to me*   17:4 [1]M *the fornication of the earth*

⁶I saw ᵃthe woman, drunk ᵇwith the blood of the saints and with the blood of ᶜthe martyrs of Jesus. And when I saw her, I marveled with great amazement.

THE MEANING OF THE WOMAN AND THE BEAST

⁷But the angel said to me, "Why did you marvel? I will tell you the ¹mystery of the woman and of the beast that carries her, which has the seven heads and the ten horns. ⁸The beast that you saw was, and is not, and ᵃwill ascend out of the bottomless pit and ᵇgo to ¹perdition. And those who ᶜdwell on the earth ᵈwill marvel, ᵉwhose names are not written in the Book of Life from the foundation of the world, when they see the beast that was, and is not, and ²yet is.

⁹ᵃ"Here *is* the mind which has wisdom: ᵇThe seven heads are seven mountains on which the woman sits. ¹⁰There are also seven kings. Five have fallen, one is, *and* the other has not yet come. And when he comes, he must ᵃcontinue a short time. ¹¹The ᵃbeast that was, and is not, is himself also the eighth, and is of the seven, and is going to ¹perdition.

¹²ᵃ"The ten horns which you saw are ten kings who have received no kingdom as yet, but they receive authority for one hour as kings with the beast. ¹³These are of one mind, and they will give their power and authority to the beast. ¹⁴ᵃThese will make war with the Lamb, and the Lamb will ᵇovercome them, ᶜfor He is Lord of lords and King of kings; ᵈand those *who are* with Him *are* called, chosen, and faithful."

¹⁵Then he said to me, ᵃ"The waters which you saw, where the harlot sits, ᵇare peoples, multitudes, nations, and tongues. ¹⁶And the ten horns which you ¹saw on the beast, ᵃthese will hate the harlot, make her ᵇdesolate ᶜand naked, eat her flesh and ᵈburn her with fire. ¹⁷ᵃFor God has put it into their hearts to fulfill His purpose, to be of one mind, and to give their kingdom to the beast, ᵇuntil the words of God are fulfilled. ¹⁸And the woman whom you saw ᵃis that great city ᵇwhich reigns over the kings of the earth."

THE FALL OF BABYLON THE GREAT

18 Afterᵃ these things I saw another angel coming down from heaven, having great authority, ᵇand the earth was illuminated with his glory. ²And he cried ¹mightily with a loud voice, saying, ᵃ"Babylon the great is fallen, is fallen, and ᵇhas become a dwelling place of demons, a prison for every foul spirit, and ᶜa cage for every unclean and hated bird! ³For all the nations ᵃhave drunk of the wine of the wrath of her fornication, the kings of the earth have committed fornication with her, ᵇand the merchants of the earth have become rich through the ¹abundance of her luxury."

⁴And I heard another voice from heaven saying, ᵃ"Come out of her, my people, lest you share in her sins, and lest you receive of her plagues. ⁵ᵃFor her sins ¹have reached to heaven, and ᵇGod has remembered her iniquities. ⁶ᵃRender to her just as she rendered ¹to you, and repay her double according to her works; ᵇin the cup which she has mixed, ᶜmix double for her.

17:6 ᵃRev. 18:24
ᵇRev. 13:15
ᶜRev. 6:9, 10

17:8 ᵃRev. 11:7
ᵇRev. 13:10; 17:11
ᶜRev. 3:10
ᵈRev. 13:3
ᵉMatt. 25:34;
Rev. 13:8

17:9 ᵃRev. 13:18
ᵇRev. 13:1

17:10 ᵃRev. 13:5

17:11 ᵃRev. 13:3,
12, 14; 17:8

17:12 ᵃDan. 7:20

17:14
ᵃRev. 16:14; 19:19
ᵇRev. 19:20
ᶜDeut. 10:17;
1 Tim. 6:15;
Rev. 19:16
ᵈJer. 50:44

17:15 ᵃIs. 8:7;
Jer. 47:2;
Rev. 17:1
ᵇRev. 13:7

17:16 ᵃJer. 50:41
ᵇRev. 18:17, 19
ᶜEzek. 16:37, 39
ᵈRev. 18:8

17:17
ᵃ2 Thess. 2:11
ᵇRev. 10:7

17:18
ᵃRev. 11:8; 16:19
ᵇRev. 12:4

18:1 ᵃRev. 17:1, 7
ᵇEzek. 43:2

18:2
ᵃIs. 13:19; 21:9;
Jer. 51:8;
Rev. 14:8
ᵇIs. 13:21;
34:11, 13–15;
Jer. 50:39; 51:37;
Zeph. 2:14
ᶜIs. 14:23

18:3 ᵃJer. 51:7;
Rev. 14:8
ᵇIs. 47:15

18:4 ᵃIs. 48:20

18:5 ᵃGen. 18:20
ᵇRev. 16:19

18:6 ᵃPs. 137:8;
Jer. 50:15, 29
ᵇRev. 14:10
ᶜRev. 16:19

17:7 ¹hidden truth　17:8 ¹destruction　²NU, M shall be present
17:11 ¹destruction　17:16 ¹NU, M saw, and the beast　18:2 ¹NU, M omit
mightily　18:3 ¹Lit. *strengths*　18:5 ¹NU, M *have been heaped up*
18:6 ¹NU, M omit *to you*

⁷ᵃIn the measure that she glorified herself and lived ¹luxuriously, in the same measure give her torment and sorrow; for she says in her heart, 'I sit *as* ᵇqueen, and am no widow, and will not see sorrow.' ⁸Therefore her plagues will come ᵃin one day—death and mourning and famine. And ᵇshe will be utterly burned with fire, ᶜfor strong *is* the Lord God who ¹judges her.

THE WORLD MOURNS BABYLON'S FALL

⁹ᵃ"The kings of the earth who committed fornication and lived luxuriously with her ᵇwill weep and lament for her, ᶜwhen they see the smoke of her burning, ¹⁰standing at a distance for fear of her torment, saying, ᵃ'Alas, alas, that great city Babylon, that mighty city! ᵇFor in one hour your judgment has come.'

¹¹"And ᵃthe merchants of the earth will weep and mourn over her, for no one buys their merchandise anymore: ¹²ᵃmerchandise of gold and silver, precious stones and pearls, fine linen and purple, silk and scarlet, every kind of citron wood, every kind of object of ivory, every kind of object of most precious wood, bronze, iron, and marble; ¹³and cinnamon and incense, fragrant oil and frankincense, wine and oil, fine flour and wheat, cattle and sheep, horses and chariots, and bodies and ᵃsouls of men. ¹⁴The fruit that your soul longed for has gone from you, and all the things which are rich and splendid have ¹gone from you, and you shall find them no more at all. ¹⁵The merchants of these things, who became rich by her, will stand at a distance for fear of her torment, weeping and wailing, ¹⁶and saying, 'Alas, alas, ᵃthat great city ᵇthat was clothed in fine linen, purple, and scarlet, and adorned with gold and precious stones and pearls! ¹⁷ᵃFor in one hour such great riches ¹came to nothing.' ᵇEvery shipmaster, all who travel by ship, sailors, and as many as trade on the sea, stood at a distance ¹⁸ᵃand cried out when they saw the smoke of her burning, saying, ᵇ'What *is* like this great city?'

¹⁹ᵃ"They threw dust on their heads and cried out, weeping and wailing, and saying, 'Alas, alas, that great city, in which all who had ships on the sea became rich by her wealth! ᵇFor in one hour she ¹is made desolate.'

²⁰ᵃ"Rejoice over her, O heaven, and *you* ¹holy apostles and prophets, for ᵇGod has avenged you on her!"

FINALITY OF BABYLON'S FALL

²¹Then a mighty angel took up a stone like a great millstone and threw *it* into the sea, saying, ᵃ"Thus with violence the great city Babylon shall be thrown down, and ᵇshall not be found anymore. ²²ᵃThe sound of harpists, musicians, flutists, and trumpeters shall not be heard in you anymore. No craftsman of any craft shall be found in you anymore, and the sound of a millstone shall not be heard in you anymore. ²³ᵃThe light of a lamp shall not shine in you anymore, ᵇand the voice of bridegroom and bride shall not be heard in you anymore. For ᶜyour merchants were the great men of the earth, ᵈfor by your sorcery all the nations were deceived.

18:7
ᵃEzek. 28:2–8
ᵇIs. 47:7, 8;
Zeph. 2:15

18:8 ᵃIs. 47:9;
Jer. 50:31;
Rev. 18:10
ᵇRev. 17:16
ᶜJer. 50:34;
Heb. 10:31;
Rev. 11:17

18:9
ᵃEzek. 26:16;
27:35
ᵇJer. 50:46;
Rev. 17:2; 18:3
ᶜRev. 19:3

18:10 ᵃIs. 21:9
ᵇRev. 18:17, 19

18:11
ᵃEzek. 27:27–34

18:12
ᵃEzek. 27:12–22;
Rev. 17:4

18:13
ᵃ1 Chr. 5:21;
Ezek. 27:13

18:16 ᵃRev. 17:18
ᵇRev. 17:4

18:17 ᵃRev. 18:10
ᵇIs. 23:14

18:18
ᵃEzek. 27:30
ᵇRev. 13:4

18:19 ᵃJosh. 7:6;
Job 2:12;
Lam. 2:10;
Ezek. 27:30
ᵇRev. 18:8

18:20
ᵃIs. 44:23; 49:13;
Jer. 51:48;
Rev. 12:12
ᵇLuke 11:49;
Rev. 19:2

18:21
ᵃJer. 51:63, 64
ᵇRev. 12:8; 16:20

18:22
ᵃEccl. 12:4;
Jer. 7:34;
16:9; 25:10;
Rev. 14:1–3

18:23 ᵃJer. 25:10
ᵇJer. 7:34; 16:9
ᶜIs. 23:8;
Rev. 6:15; 18:3
ᵈ2 Kin. 9:22

18:7 ¹sensually   18:8 ¹NU, M *has judged*   18:14 ¹NU, M *been lost to you*   18:17 ¹*have been laid waste*   18:19 ¹*have been laid waste*
18:20 ¹NU, M *saints and apostles*

18:24
a Rev. 16:6; 17:6
b Jer. 51:49

19:1 a Jer. 51:48;
Rev. 11:15; 19:6
b Rev. 4:11

19:2
a Rev. 15:3; 16:7
b Deut. 32:43;
2 Kin. 9:7;
Luke 18:7, 8;
Rev. 6:10

19:3 a Is. 34:10;
Rev. 14:11

19:4
a Rev. 4:4, 6, 10
b 1 Chr. 16:36

19:5 a Ps. 134:1
b Rev. 11:18

19:6 a Ezek. 1:24;
Rev. 1:15; 14:2
b Rev. 11:15

19:7
a [Matt. 22:2;
25:10];
Luke 12:36;
John 3:29;
[2 Cor. 11:2];
Eph. 5:23, 32;
Rev. 19:9

19:8 a Ps. 45:13;
Ezek. 16:10
b Ps. 132:9

19:9 a Matt. 22:2;
Luke 14:15
b Rev. 22:6

19:10 a Rev. 22:8
b Acts 10:26;
Rev. 22:9
c [Heb. 1:14]
d 1 John 5:10
e Luke 24:27;
John 5:39

19:11 a Rev. 15:5
b Ps. 45:3, 4;
Rev. 6:2;
19:19, 21
c Rev. 3:7, 14
d Ps. 96:13;
Is. 11:4

19:12 a Dan. 10:6;
Rev. 1:14
b Rev. 2:17; 19:16

19:13 a Is. 63:2, 3
b [John 1:1, 14]

19:14 a Rev. 14:20
b Matt. 28:3

19:15 a Is. 11:4;
2 Thess. 2:8;
Rev. 1:16
b Ps. 2:8, 9
c Is. 63:3–6;
Rev. 14:20

19:16
a Rev. 2:17; 19:12
b Dan. 2:47

19:17
a 1 Sam. 17:44;
Jer. 12:9;
Ezek. 39:17

24And ain her was found the blood of prophets and saints, and of all who bwere slain on the earth."

HEAVEN EXULTS OVER BABYLON

19 After these things aI 1heard a loud voice of a great multitude in heaven, saying, "Alleluia! bSalvation and glory and honor and power *belong* to 2the Lord our God! 2For atrue and righteous *are* His judgments, because He has judged the great harlot who corrupted the earth with her fornication; and He bhas avenged on her the blood of His servants *shed* by her." 3Again they said, "Alleluia! aHer smoke rises up forever and ever!" 4And athe twenty-four elders and the four living creatures fell down and worshiped God who sat on the throne, saying, b"Amen! Alleluia!" 5Then a voice came from the throne, saying, a"Praise our God, all you His servants and those who fear Him, bboth1 small and great!"

6aAnd I heard, as it were, the voice of a great multitude, as the sound of many waters and as the sound of mighty thunderings, saying, "Alleluia! For bthe1 Lord God Omnipotent reigns! 7Let us be glad and rejoice and give Him glory, for athe marriage of the Lamb has come, and His wife has made herself ready." 8And ato her it was granted to be arrayed in fine linen, clean and bright, bfor the fine linen is the righteous acts of the saints.

9Then he said to me, "Write: a'Blessed *are* those who are called to the marriage supper of the Lamb!'" And he said to me, b"These are the true sayings of God." 10And aI fell at his feet to worship him. But he said to me, b"See *that you do* not *do that!* I am your cfellow servant, and of your brethren dwho have the testimony of Jesus. Worship God! For the etestimony of Jesus is the spirit of prophecy."

CHRIST ON A WHITE HORSE

11aNow I saw heaven opened, and behold, ba white horse. And He who sat on him *was* called cFaithful and True, and din righteousness He judges and makes war. 12aHis eyes *were* like a flame of fire, and on His head *were* many crowns. bHe 1had a name written that no one knew except Himself. 13aHe *was* clothed with a robe dipped in blood, and His name is called bThe Word of God. 14aAnd the armies in heaven, bclothed in 1fine linen, white and clean, followed Him on white horses. 15Now aout of His mouth goes a 1sharp sword, that with it He should strike the nations. And bHe Himself will rule them with a rod of iron. cHe Himself treads the winepress of the fierceness and wrath of Almighty God. 16And aHe has on *His* robe and on His thigh a name written:

bKING OF KINGS AND
LORD OF LORDS.

THE BEAST AND HIS ARMIES DEFEATED

17Then I saw an angel standing in the sun; and he cried with a loud voice, saying to all the birds that fly in the midst of heaven, a"Come and gather together for the 1supper of the

19:1 1NU, M add *something like* 2NU, M omit *the Lord* **19:5** 1NU, M omit *both* **19:6** 1NU, M *our* **19:12** 1M adds *names written, and* **19:14** 1NU, M *pure white linen* **19:15** 1M *sharp two-edged* **19:17** 1NU, M *great supper of God*

great God, [18a]that you may eat the flesh of kings, the flesh of captains, the flesh of mighty men, the flesh of horses and of those who sit on them, and the flesh of all *people,* [1]free and slave, both small and great."

[19a]And I saw the beast, the kings of the earth, and their armies, gathered together to make war against Him who sat on the horse and against His army. [20a]Then the beast was captured, and with him the false prophet who worked signs in his presence, by which he deceived those who received the mark of the beast and [b]those who worshiped his image. [c]These two were cast alive into the lake of fire [d]burning with brimstone. [21]And the rest [a]were killed with the sword which proceeded from the mouth of Him who sat on the horse. [b]And all the birds [c]were filled with their flesh.

SATAN BOUND 1,000 YEARS

20 Then I saw an angel coming down from heaven, [a]having the key to the bottomless pit and a great chain in his hand. [2]He laid hold of [a]the dragon, that serpent of old, who is *the* Devil and Satan, and bound him for a thousand years; [3]and he cast him into the bottomless pit, and shut him up, and [a]set a seal on him, [b]so that he should deceive the nations no more till the thousand years were finished. But after these things he must be released for a little while.

THE SAINTS REIGN WITH CHRIST 1,000 YEARS

[4]And I saw [a]thrones, and they sat on them, and [b]judgment was committed to them. Then *I saw* [c]the souls of those who had been beheaded for their witness to Jesus and for the word of God, [d]who had not worshiped the beast [e]or his image, and had not received *his* mark on their foreheads or on their hands. And they [f]lived and [g]reigned with Christ for [1]a thousand years. [5]But the rest of the dead did not live again until the thousand years were finished. This *is* the first resurrection. [6]Blessed and holy *is* he who has part in the first resurrection. Over such [a]the second death has no power, but they shall be [b]priests of God and of Christ, [c]and shall reign with Him a thousand years.

SATANIC REBELLION CRUSHED
(cf. Ezek. 38; 39)

[7]Now when the thousand years have expired, Satan will be released from his prison [8]and will go out [a]to deceive the nations which are in the four corners of the earth, [b]Gog and Magog, [c]to gather them together to battle, whose number *is* as the sand of the sea. [9a]They went up on the breadth of the earth and surrounded the camp of the saints and the beloved city. And fire came down from God out of heaven and devoured them. [10]The devil, who deceived them, was cast into the lake of fire and brimstone [a]where[1] the beast and the false prophet *are.* And they [b]will be tormented day and night forever and ever.

THE GREAT WHITE THRONE JUDGMENT

[11]Then I saw a great white throne and Him who sat on it, from whose face [a]the earth and the heaven fled away. [b]And

19:18
[a]Ezek. 39:18–20

19:19
[a]Rev. 16:13–16

19:20 [a]Rev. 16:13
[b]Rev. 13:8, 12, 13
[c]Is. 30:33;
Dan. 7:11
[d]Rev. 14:10

19:21 [a]Rev. 19:15
[b]Rev. 19:17, 18
[c]Rev. 17:16

20:1
[a]Rev. 1:18; 9:1

20:2 [a]Is. 24:22;
2 Pet. 2:4;
Jude 6

20:3 [a]Dan. 6:17;
Matt. 27:66
[b]Rev. 12:9;
20:8, 10

20:4 [a]Dan. 7:9;
Matt. 19:28;
Luke 22:30
[b]Dan. 7:22;
[1 Cor. 6:2, 3]
[c]Rev. 6:9
[d]Rev. 13:12
[e]Rev. 13:15
[f]John 14:19
[g]Rom. 8:17;
2 Tim. 2:12

20:6
[a][Rev. 2:11;
20:14]
[b]Is. 61:6;
1 Pet. 2:9;
Rev. 1:6
[c]Rev. 20:4

20:8 [a]Rev. 12:9;
20:3, 10
[b]Ezek. 38:2;
39:1, 6
[c]Rev. 16:14

20:9 [a]Is. 8:8;
Ezek. 38:9, 16

20:10
[a]Rev. 19:20;
20:14, 15
[b]Rev. 14:10

20:11 [a]2 Pet. 3:7;
Rev. 21:1
[b]Dan. 2:35;
Rev. 12:8

19:18 [1]NU, M *both free*   20:4 [1]M *the*   20:10 [1]NU, M *where also*

20:12 ªRev. 19:5
ᵇDan. 7:10
ᶜPs. 69:28;
Dan. 12:1;
Phil. 4:3;
Rev. 3:5
ᵈJer. 17:10;
Matt. 16:27;
Rom. 2:6;
Rev. 2:23; 20:12

20:13
ª1 Cor. 15:26;
Rev. 1:18;
6:8; 21:4
ᵇMatt. 16:27;
Rev. 2:23; 20:12

20:14
ª1 Cor. 15:26;
Rev. 1:18; 6:8;
21:4 ᵇRev. 21:8

20:15
ªRev. 19:20

21:1 ªIs. 65:17;
66:22;
[2 Pet. 3:13]
ᵇ[2 Pet. 3:10];
Rev. 20:11

21:2 ªIs. 52:1;
[Gal. 4:26];
Heb. 11:10
ᵇIs. 54:5;
2 Cor. 11:2

21:3 ªLev. 26:11;
Ezek. 43:7;
2 Cor. 6:16

21:4 ªIs. 25:8;
Rev. 7:17
ᵇ1 Cor. 15:26;
Rev. 20:14
ᶜIs. 35:10; 51:11;
65:19

21:5
ªRev. 4:2, 9; 20:11
ᵇIs. 43:19;
2 Cor. 5:17
ᶜRev. 19:9; 22:6

21:6
ªRev. 10:6; 16:17
ᵇRev. 1:8; 22:13
ᶜIs. 12:3; 55:1;
John 4:10;
Rev. 7:17; 22:17

21:7 ªZech. 8:8;
Heb. 8:10

21:8 ª1 Cor. 6:9;
Gal. 5:19;
Eph. 5:5;
1 Tim. 1:9;
[Heb. 12:14]
ᵇRev. 20:14

21:9 ªRev. 15:1
ᵇRev. 19:7; 21:2

21:10 ªRev. 1:10
ᵇEzek. 48

21:11 ªIs. 60:1;
Ezek. 43:2;
Rev. 15:8; 21:23;
22:5

21:12
ªEzek. 48:31–34

there was found no place for them. ¹²And I saw the dead, ªsmall and great, standing before ¹God, ᵇand books were opened. And another ᶜbook was opened, which is *the Book of Life*. And the dead were judged ᵈaccording to their works, by the things which were written in the books. ¹³The sea gave up the dead who were in it, ªand Death and Hades delivered up the dead who were in them. ᵇAnd they were judged, each one according to his works. ¹⁴Then ªDeath and Hades were cast into the lake of fire. ᵇThis is the second ¹death. ¹⁵And anyone not found written in the Book of Life ªwas cast into the lake of fire.

ALL THINGS MADE NEW

21 Now ªI saw a new heaven and a new earth, ᵇfor the first heaven and the first earth had passed away. Also there was no more sea. ²Then I, ¹John, saw ªthe holy city, New Jerusalem, coming down out of heaven from God, prepared ᵇas a bride adorned for her husband. ³And I heard a loud voice from heaven saying, "Behold, ªthe tabernacle of God *is* with men, and He will dwell with them, and they shall be His people. God Himself will be with them *and be* their God. ⁴ªAnd God will wipe away every tear from their eyes; ᵇthere shall be no more death, ᶜnor sorrow, nor crying. There shall be no more pain, for the former things have passed away."

⁵Then ªHe who sat on the throne said, ᵇ"Behold, I make all things new." And He said ¹to me, "Write, for ᶜthese words are true and faithful."

⁶And He said to me, ª"It¹ is done! ᵇI am the Alpha and the Omega, the Beginning and the End. ᶜI will give of the fountain of the water of life freely to him who thirsts. ⁷He who overcomes ¹shall inherit all things, and ªI will be his God and he shall be My son. ⁸ªBut the cowardly, ¹unbelieving, abominable, murderers, sexually immoral, sorcerers, idolaters, and all liars shall have their part in ᵇthe lake which burns with fire and brimstone, which is the second death."

THE NEW JERUSALEM
(cf. Ezek. 48:30–35)

⁹Then one of ªthe seven angels who had the seven bowls filled with the seven last plagues came ¹to me and talked with me, saying, "Come, I will show you ᵇthe ²bride, the Lamb's wife." ¹⁰And he carried me away ªin the Spirit to a great and high mountain, and showed me ᵇthe ¹great city, the ²holy Jerusalem, descending out of heaven from God, ¹¹ªhaving the glory of God. Her light *was* like a most precious stone, like a jasper stone, clear as crystal. ¹²Also she had a great and high wall with ªtwelve gates, and twelve angels at the gates, and names written on them, which are *the names* of the twelve tribes of the children of Israel: ¹³ªthree gates on the east, three gates on the north, three gates on the south, and three gates on the west.

21:13 ªEzek. 48:31–34

20:12 ¹NU, M *the throne*   20:14 ¹NU, M *death, the lake of fire.*
21:2 ¹NU, M omit *John*   21:5 ¹NU, M omit *to me*   21:6 ¹M omits *It is done*
21:7 ¹M *I shall give him these things*   21:8 ¹M adds *and sinners,*
21:9 ¹NU, M omit *to me*   ²M *woman, the Lamb's bride*   21:10 ¹NU, M omit *great*   ²NU, M *holy city, Jerusalem*

[14]Now the wall of the city had twelve foundations, and [a]on them were the [1]names of the twelve apostles of the Lamb. [15]And he who talked with me [a]had a gold reed to measure the city, its gates, and its wall. [16]The city is laid out as a square; its length is as great as its breadth. And he measured the city with the reed: twelve thousand [1]furlongs. Its length, breadth, and height are equal. [17]Then he measured its wall: one hundred *and* forty-four cubits, *according* to the measure of a man, that is, of an angel. [18]The construction of its wall was *of* jasper; and the city *was* pure gold, like clear glass. [19a]The foundations of the wall of the city *were* adorned with all kinds of precious stones: the first foundation *was* jasper, the second sapphire, the third chalcedony, the fourth emerald, [20]the fifth sardonyx, the sixth sardius, the seventh chrysolite, the eighth beryl, the ninth topaz, the tenth chrysoprase, the eleventh jacinth, and the twelfth amethyst. [21]The twelve gates *were* twelve [a]pearls: each individual gate was of one pearl. [b]And the street of the city *was* pure gold, like transparent glass.

THE GLORY OF THE NEW JERUSALEM

[22a]But I saw no temple in it, for the Lord God Almighty and the Lamb are its temple. [23a]The city had no need of the sun or of the moon to shine [1]in it, for the [2]glory of God illuminated it. The Lamb *is* its light. [24a]And the nations [1]of those who are saved shall walk in its light, and the kings of the earth bring their glory and honor [2]into it. [25a]Its gates shall not be shut at all by day [b](there shall be no night there). [26a]And they shall bring the glory and the honor of the nations into [1]it. [27]But [a]there shall by no means enter it anything [1]that defiles, or causes an abomination or a lie, but only those who are written in the Lamb's [b]Book of Life.

THE RIVER OF LIFE

22 And he showed me [a]a [1]pure river of water of life, clear as crystal, proceeding from the throne of God and of the Lamb. [2a]In the middle of its street, and on either side of the river, *was* [b]the tree of life, which bore twelve fruits, each *tree* yielding its fruit every month. The leaves of the tree *were* [c]for the healing of the nations. [3]And [a]there shall be no more curse, [b]but the throne of God and of the Lamb shall be in it, and His [c]servants shall serve Him. [4a]They shall see His face, and [b]His name *shall be* on their foreheads. [5a]There shall be no night there: They need no lamp nor [b]light of the sun, for [c]the Lord God gives them light. [d]And they shall reign forever and ever.

THE TIME IS NEAR

[6]Then he said to me, [a]"These words *are* faithful and true." And the Lord God of the [1]holy prophets [b]sent His angel to show His servants the things which must [c]shortly take place.

[7a]"Behold, I am coming quickly! [b]Blessed *is* he who keeps the words of the prophecy of this book."

[8]Now I, John, [1]saw and heard these things. And when I

21:14
[a]Matt. 16:18;
Luke 22:29, 30;
Gal. 2:9;
Eph. 2:20

21:15
[a]Ezek. 40:3;
Zech. 2:1;
Rev. 11:1

21:19
[a]Ex. 28:17–20;
Is. 54:11;
Ezek. 28:13

21:21
[a]Matt. 13:45, 46
[b]Rev. 22:2

21:22
[a]Matt. 24:2;
John 4:21, 23

21:23 [a]Is. 24:23;
60:19, 20;
Rev. 21:25; 22:5

21:24
[a]Is. 60:3, 5;
66:12

21:25 [a]Is. 60:11
[b]Is. 60:20;
Zech. 14:7

21:26
[a]Rev. 21:24

21:27 [a]Is. 35:8;
Joel 3:17
[b]Phil. 4:3

22:1 [a]Ps. 46:4;
Ezek. 47:1;
[Zech. 14:8]

22:2
[a]Ezek. 47:12
[b]Gen. 2:9;
[Rev. 2:7;
22:14, 19]
[c]Rev. 21:24

22:3 [a]Zech. 14:11
[b]Ezek. 48:35
[c]Rev. 7:15

22:4
[a][Ps. 17:15; 42:2;
Matt. 5:8;
1 Cor. 13:12;
1 John 3:2]
[b]Rev. 14:1

22:5 [a]Is. 60:19;
Rev. 21:23
[b]Rev. 7:15
[c]Ps. 36:9
[d]Dan. 7:18, 27;
Matt. 19:28;
[Rom. 5:17];
2 Tim. 2:12;
Rev. 20:4

22:6 [a]Rev. 19:9
[b]Rev. 1:1
[c]Heb. 10:37

22:7 [a][Rev. 3:11]
[b]Rev. 1:3

21:14 [1]NU, M *twelve names*   21:16 [1]Lit. *stadia*, about 1,380 miles in all
21:23 [1]NU, M omit *in it*   [2]M *very glory*   21:24 [1]NU, M omit *of those who are saved*   [2]M *of the nations to Him*   21:26 [1]M adds *that they may enter in.*
21:27 [1]NU, M *profane, nor one who causes*   22:1 [1]NU, M omit *pure*
22:6 [1]NU, M *spirits of the prophets*   22:8 [1]NU, M *am the one who heard and saw*

heard and saw, [a]I fell down to worship before the feet of the angel who showed me these things.

[9]Then he said to me, [a]"See *that you do* not *do that.* [1]For I am your fellow servant, and of your brethren the prophets, and of those who keep the words of this book. Worship God."

[10a]And he said to me, "Do not seal the words of the prophecy of this book, [b]for the time is at hand. [11]He who is unjust, let him be unjust still; he who is filthy, let him be filthy still; he who is righteous, let him [1]be righteous still; he who is holy, let him be holy still."

JESUS TESTIFIES TO THE CHURCHES

[12]"And behold, I am coming quickly, and [a]My reward *is* with Me, [b]to give to every one according to his work. [13a]I am the Alpha and the Omega, the [1]Beginning and *the* End, the First and the Last."

[14a]Blessed *are* those who [1]do His commandments, that they may have the right [b]to the tree of life, [c]and may enter through the gates into the city. [15][1]But [a]outside *are* [b]dogs and sorcerers and sexually immoral and murderers and idolaters, and whoever loves and practices a lie.

[16a]"I, Jesus, have sent My angel to testify to you these things in the churches. [b]I am the Root and the Offspring of David, [c]the Bright and Morning Star."

[17]And the Spirit and [a]the bride say, "Come!" And let him who hears say, "Come!" [b]And let him who thirsts come. Whoever desires, let him take the water of life freely.

A WARNING

[18][1]For I testify to everyone who hears the words of the prophecy of this book: [a]If anyone adds to these things, [2]God will add to him the plagues that are written in this book; [19]and if anyone takes away from the words of the book of this prophecy, [a]God[1] shall take away his part from the [2]Book of Life, from the holy city, and *from* the things which are written in this book.

I AM COMING QUICKLY

[20]He who testifies to these things says, "Surely I am coming quickly."

Amen. Even so, come, Lord Jesus!

[21]The grace of our Lord Jesus Christ *be* [1]with you all. Amen.

22:8 [a]Rev. 19:10
22:9 [a]Rev. 19:10
22:10 [a]Dan. 8:26; Rev. 10:4 [b]Rev. 1:3
22:12 [a]Is. 40:10; 62:11 [b]Rev. 20:12
22:13 [a]Is. 41:4
22:14 [a]Dan. 12:12; [1 John 3:24] [b][Prov. 11:30]; Rev. 2:7 [c]Rev. 21:27
22:15 [a]Matt. 8:12; 1 Cor. 6:9; Gal. 5:19; Col. 3:6; Rev. 21:8 [b]Deut. 23:18; Matt. 7:6; Phil. 3:2
22:16 [a]Rev. 1:1 [b]2 Sam. 7:12; Is. 9:7; Jer. 23:5; Rev. 5:5 [c]Num. 24:17; Luke 1:78; 2 Pet. 1:19
22:17 [a][Rev. 21:2, 9] [b]Is. 55:1; Rev. 21:6
22:18 [a]Deut. 4:2; 12:32; Prov. 30:6
22:19 [a]Ex. 32:33

22:9 [1]NU, M omit *For*   22:11 [1]NU, M *do right*   22:13 [1]NU, M *First and the Last, the Beginning and the End.*   22:14 [1]NU *wash their robes,*
22:15 [1]NU, M omit *But*   22:18 [1]NU, M omit *For*   [2]M *may God add*
22:19 [1]M *may God take away*   [2]NU, M *tree of life*   22:21 [1]NU *with all;* M *with all the saints*

TABLE OF MONIES, WEIGHTS, AND MEASURES

The Hebrews probably first used coins in the Persian period (500–350 B.C.). However, minting began around 700 B.C. in other nations. Prior to this, precious metals were weighed, not counted as money.

Some units appear as both measures of money and measures of weights. This comes from naming the coins after their weight. For example, the shekel was a weight long before it became the name of a coin.

It is helpful to relate biblical monies to current values. But we cannot make exact equivalents. The fluctuating value of money's purchasing power is difficult to determine in our own day. It is even harder to evaluate currencies used two- to three-thousand years ago.

Therefore, it is best to choose a value meaningful over time, such as weighed as a common laborer's daily wage. One day's wage corresponds to the ancient Jewish system (a silver shekel is four days' wages) as well as to the Greek and Roman systems (the drachma and the denarius were each coins representing a day's wage).

The monies chart below takes a current day's wage as thirty-two dollars. Though there are differences of economies and standards of living, this measure will help us apply meaningful values to the monetary units in the chart and in the biblical text.

Monies			
Unit	Monetary Value	Equivalents	Translations
JEWISH WEIGHTS			
Talent	gold—$5,760,000[1] silver—$384,000	3,000 shekels; 6,000 bekas	talent
Shekel	gold—$1,920 silver—$128	4 days' wages; 2 bekas; 20 gerahs	shekel
Beka	gold—$960 silver—$64	$1/2$ shekel; 10 gerahs	bekah
Gerah	gold—$96 silver—$6.40	$1/20$ shekel	gerah
PERSIAN COINS			
Daric	gold—$1,280[2] silver—$64	2 days' wages; $1/2$ Jewish silver shekel	daric, drachma
GREEK COINS			
Tetradrachma (Stater)	$128	4 drachmas	piece of money
Didrachma	$64	2 drachmas	tribute
Drachma	$32	1 day's wage	piece of silver, coin
Lepton	$.25	$1/2$ of a Roman kodrantes	mite
ROMAN COINS			
Aureus	$800	25 denarii	gold
Denarius	$32	1 day's wage	denarius
Assarius	$2	$1/16$ of a denarius	copper coin
Kodrantes	$.50	$1/4$ of an assarius	penny

[1]*Value of gold is fifteen times the value of silver.* [2]*Value of gold is twenty times the value of silver.*

Weights

Unit	Weight	Equivalents	Translations
JEWISH WEIGHTS			
Talent	c. 75 pounds for common talent, c. 150 pounds for royal talent	60 minas; 3,000 shekels	talent
Mina	1.25 pounds	50 shekels	mina
Shekel	c. .4 ounce (11.4 grams) for common shekel, c. .8 ounce for royal shekel	2 bekas; 20 gerahs	shekel
Beka	c. .2 ounce (5.7 grams)	½ shekel; 10 gerahs	half a shekel
Gerah	c. .02 ounce (.57 grams)	⅟₂₀ shekel	gerah
ROMAN WEIGHT			
Litra	12 ounces		pound

Measures of Length

Unit	Length	Equivalents	Translations
Day's journey	c. 20 miles		day's journey
Roman mile	4,854 feet	8 stadia	mile
Sabbath day's journey	3,637 feet	6 stadia	Sabbath day's journey
Stadion	606 feet	⅛ Roman mile	furlong
Rod	9 feet (10.5 feet in Ezekiel)	3 paces; 6 cubits	measuring reed, reed
Fathom	6 feet	4 cubits	fathom
Pace	3 feet	⅓ rod; 2 cubits	pace
Cubit	18 inches	½ pace; 2 spans	cubit
Span	9 inches	½ cubit; 3 handbreadths	span
Handbreadth	3 inches	⅓ span; 4 fingers	handbreadth
Finger	.75 inches	¼ handbreadth	finger

Dry Measures

Unit	Measure	Equivalents	Translations
Homer	6.52 bushels	10 ephahs	homer
Kor	6.52 bushels	1 homer; 10 ephahs	kor, measure
Lethech	3.26 bushels	$\frac{1}{2}$ kor	half homer
Ephah	.65 bushel, 20.8 quarts	$\frac{1}{10}$ homer	ephah
Modius	7.68 quarts		bushel
Seah	7 quarts	$\frac{1}{3}$ ephah	measure
Omer	2.08 quarts	$\frac{1}{10}$ ephah; $1\frac{4}{5}$ kab	omer
Kab	1.16 quarts	4 logs	kab
Choenix	1 quart		measure
Xestes	$1\frac{1}{16}$ pints		pot
Log	.58 pint	$\frac{1}{4}$ kab	log

Liquid Measures

Unit	Measure	Equivalents	Translations
Kor	60 gallons	10 baths	kor
Metretes	10.2 gallons		gallon
Bath	6 gallons	6 hins	measure, bath
Hin	1 gallon	2 kabs	hin
Kab	2 quarts	4 logs	kab
Log	1 pint	$\frac{1}{4}$ kab	log

ABBREVIATIONS FOR THE BOOKS OF THE BIBLE

Acts . . . . Acts

Amos . . . . Amos

1 Chronicles . . . . 1 Chr.

2 Chronicles . . . . 2 Chr.

Colossians . . . . Col.

1 Corinthians . . . . 1 Cor.

2 Corinthians . . . . 2 Cor.

Daniel . . . . Dan.

Deuteronomy . . . . Deut.

Ecclesiastes . . . . Eccl.

Ephesians . . . . Eph.

Esther . . . . Esth.

Exodus . . . . Ex.

Ezekiel . . . . Ezek.

Ezra . . . . Ezra

Galatians . . . . Gal.

Genesis . . . . Gen.

Habakkuk . . . . Hab.

Haggai . . . . Hag.

Hebrews . . . . Heb.

Hosea . . . . Hos.

Isaiah . . . . Is.

James . . . . James

Jeremiah . . . . Jer.

Job . . . . Job

Joel . . . . Joel

John (Gospel) . . . . John

1 John . . . . 1 John

2 John . . . . 2 John

3 John . . . . 3 John

Jonah . . . . Jon.

Joshua . . . . Josh.

Jude . . . . Jude

Judges . . . . Judg.

1 Kings . . . . 1 Kin.

2 Kings . . . . 2 Kin.

Lamentations . . . . Lam.

Leviticus . . . . Lev.

Luke . . . . Luke

Malachi . . . . Mal.

Mark . . . . Mark

Matthew . . . . Matt.

Micah . . . . Mic.

Nahum . . . . Nah.

Nehemiah . . . . Neh.

Numbers . . . . Num.

Obadiah . . . . Obad.

1 Peter . . . . 1 Pet.

2 Peter . . . . 2 Pet.

Philemon . . . . Philem.

Philippians . . . . Phil.

Proverbs . . . . Prov.

Psalms . . . . Ps.

Revelation . . . . Rev.

Romans . . . . Rom.

Ruth . . . . Ruth

1 Samuel . . . . 1 Sam.

2 Samuel . . . . 2 Sam.

Song of Solomon . . . . Song

1 Thessalonians . . . . 1 Thess.

2 Thessalonians . . . . 2 Thess.

1 Timothy . . . . 1 Tim.

2 Timothy . . . . 2 Tim.

Titus . . . . Titus

Zechariah . . . . Zech.

Zephaniah . . . . Zeph.

DICTIONARY-CONCORDANCE

This Dictionary-Concordance will help you to find the meanings of words used in the Bible and in the church and also to locate key passages in which those words occur.

The more difficult words show pronunciation. The meaning follows the word itself (or the pronunciation) and this is followed by the concordance listing. In the concordance listing only the first letter of the word is used — "l." for "love." The references give you the name of the Bible book, then the chapter, and then the verse or verses. Thus, Luke 24:30–51 would be Luke, chapter 24, verses 30 through 51. See the abbreviations for Bible books listed on p. 1713.

A

Aaron The older brother of Moses (Ex. 6:20; 7:7); the spokesman for Moses (Ex. 7:1); brings on plagues with his rod (Ex. 7:10 — 8:17); from him are descended the class of priests in Israel (Ex. 29:9); he makes atonement and stops a plague (Num. 16:41–50); his rod buds (Num. 17:1–11); his death (Num. 20:22–29).

Abba Aramaic for "Father" (Mark 14:36; Rom. 8:15; Gal. 4:6).

Abed-Nego Babylonian name of one of Daniel's companions (Dan. 1:7; 3:16).

Abel Son of Adam; murdered by his brother Cain (Gen. 4:2ff). He is described as righteous (Matt. 23:35; 1 John 3:12). In Hebrews 11:4 he stands at the head of the heroes of faith.

abhor To despise, hate.
I hate and *a.* lying Ps. 119:163
Nations will *a.* him Prov. 24:24
A. what is evil Rom. 12:9

Abiathar A priest in the time of David (1 Sam. 23:6ff).

Abner Commander of the Israelite army under Saul (1 Sam. 14:50; 17:55; 26:5ff; murdered by Joab (2 Sam. 3:27).

abomination Something loathsome.
Wickedness is an *a.* Prov. 8:7
is an *a.* in the sight of God Luke 16:15

Abraham; Abram Israel's first great patriarch or leader. Through faith in God's promise to make of him a great nation, he is led from Ur to Canaan (Gen. 11:31—15:7). God makes a covenant with him (Gen. 15:7– 21); an angel of God promises that Sarah shall give birth to a son (Gen. 18:10); God tests Abraham's faith (Gen. 22:1–19). He stands as the father of all the faithful (Gal. 3:7).

Absalom Son of David and Maacah; turned the people against his father; was defeated and then slain by Joab, to the great sorrow of David (2 Sam. 3:3; 13:20—19:10).

Adam The first man, from whom is descended all mankind. Created on the same day as the animals, he is particularly blessed by God (Gen. 1:27, 28). He and Eve were driven from the Garden of Eden because of their disobedience (Gen. 3:1–24).

adultery Unchastity; unfaithfulness to one's husband or wife.
You shall not commit *a.* Ex. 20:14
You shall not commit *a.* Deut. 5:18
has already committed *a.* with her Matt. 5:28

advise To tell, inform.
I will *a.* you what Num. 24:14

advocate One who speaks in defense of another.
Christ is so called (1 John 2:1).

affliction Distress; pain; adversity.
God has seen my *a.* Gen. 31:42

agape A Greek word meaning "love." It is also used to denote the "love feasts" of the early Christians (Jude 12).

Agrippa King of Judea before whom Paul appeared to plead his defense (Acts 25:13—26:32).

Ahab An evil king of the northern kingdom of Israel in the time of Elijah; married Jezebel, a Sidonian princess, which caused religious turmoil; robbed Naboth of his vineyard and then caused his death (1 Kin. 16:29—22:40).

alien A foreigner.
give it to the *a.* Deut. 14:21

Alleluia Hallelujah; "Praise the Lord" (Rev. 19:1, 3, 4, 6).

Almighty, the God, as being all powerful.
I am A. God Gen. 17:1
as God A. Ex. 6:3
Holy, holy, holy, Lord God A. Rev. 4:8

Alpha and Omega The first and last letters of the Greek alphabet; hence, "the First and the Last." Applied to God (Rev. 1:8, 11; 21:6) and to Christ (Rev. 22:13).

altar Table of sacrifice.
Noah built an a. Gen. 8:20
Moses built an a. Ex. 17:15

Am Exist; be. The reply to Moses' question for the name of the Deity, "I AM WHO I AM" (Ex. 3:14), indicates that the Lord makes Himself present as He wills.

Amen Verily; so be it (Matt. 6:13; Rev. 3:14).

Amos A prophet of Israel; the first to proclaim that God is the ruler of the whole universe; foretold the downfall of the northern kingdom. The OT Book of Amos is the third of the 12 Minor Prophets.

Ananias 1. A Christian of Jerusalem who lost his life for lying and attempting to hold back part of the price of property he had sold (Acts 5:1–10). 2. A Christian of Damascus who received Paul into Christian fellowship (Acts 9:10–17; 22:12–16). 3. A Jewish high priest before whom Paul was tried in Jerusalem (Acts 23:2; 24:1).

Ancient of Days The judge in Daniel's vision; probably intended to be God Himself (Dan. 7:9, 13, 22).

Andrew One of the first of the 12 apostles of Jesus; brother of Simon Peter (Matt. 4:18; 10:2–4; Mark 1:16–20, 29; 3:16–19; 13:3; 6:14–16; John 1:35–42, 44; 6:8; 12:20–22; 21:15–17; Acts 1:13). He was a former disciple of John the Baptist (John 1:35–40). See Simon.

angel A heavenly messenger.
an a. spoke to me 1 Kin. 13:18
a little lower than the a. Ps. 8:5
a. came and ministered Matt. 4:11
the a. Gabriel was sent Luke 1:26
a. of the bottomless pit Rev. 9:11

Angel of the Lord The heavenly messenger whose presence is evidence of God Himself (Gen. 16:7; Ex. 3:2; Num. 22:23; 1 Kin. 19:7; Matt. 28:2; Luke 1:11; 2:9).

anoint To consecrate; to pour oil upon in a ceremony.
a. my head with oil Ps. 23:5
to a. My body Mark 14:8
You did not a. Luke 7:46

answer A reply.
soft a. turns away wrath Prov. 15:1

ant An insect.
Go to the a., you sluggard Prov. 6:6

antichrist Opponent or enemy of Christ.
He is a. who denies 1 John 2:22
deceiver and an a. 2 John 7

Antioch 1. In Syria; the name "Christian" was first used here (Acts 11:26). 2. In Pisidia; visited by Paul and Barnabas (Acts 13:14–52).

anxious Worried; careful.
Be a. for nothing Phil. 4:6

apocalypse A revelation; disclosure; usually a vision. Sometimes used as the title of the NT Book of Revelation.

Apocrypha A number of books included in Roman Catholic versions of the Bible but not in the Hebrew scriptures and not usually appearing in Protestant versions, though sometimes added between the OT and NT.

apostle One of the 12 disciples chosen by Jesus (Matt. 10:2–4) or certain other early Christian leaders (Acts 14:14; Rom. 16:7; Gal. 1:1).

apple A fruit.
a. of His eye Deut. 32:10; Ps. 17:8

appoint 1. To consecrate, or set apart as for the ministry.
a. elders in every church Acts 14:23
a. elders in every city Titus 1:5
2. To establish.
I will a. place 1 Chr. 17:9

Arabia; Arabians The NW part of the large peninsula in SW Asia; scene of many biblical events. The peoples of the area were nomads.

Arameans A Semitic people, traditionally descendants of Shem, the oldest son of Noah (Gen. 10:1, 22, 23). They were nomads, wandering along the W side of the Syrian desert.

Ararat The mountain on which the ark came to rest after the Flood (Gen. 8:4); the land of Ararat is Armenia.

archangel An angel of the highest order.
the voice of an a. 1 Thess. 4:16
Michael the a. Jude 9

ark A floating vessel; ship.
Noah's a. Gen. 6:14—8:19
Noah entered the a. Matt. 24:38

ark of the Testimony The chest which held the two stone tablets on which were

inscribed the Ten Commandments (Ex. 25:10–22). Also called the ark of the covenant (1 Kin. 8:6; 2 Chr. 5:2).

Armageddon The place of the final great struggle between the forces of good and evil (Rev. 16:16).

Artaxerxes The name of two Persian kings: the first, mentioned in Ezra 7 and Nehemiah 2; 13; his grandson, the second, may have been the builder of the palace described in Esth. 1:5, 6.

Ascension The return of the risen Christ to heaven (Luke 24:51; Acts 1:9) on the fortieth day after the Resurrection.

Ascents, Song of A title given to each of Psalms 120—134; probably so called because of their use in a procession ascending to the temple or for pilgrims going up to Jerusalem.

Asher The eighth son of Jacob, the second by Zilpah (Gen. 30:12ff); one of the 12 tribes of Israel.

Ash Wednesday The first day of Lent.

Asia A Roman province in the western part of what we call Asia Minor (Acts 16:6; 20:18; 1 Pet. 1:1; Rev. 1:4).

ask To request.
A., and it will be given Matt. 7:7
a. in prayer, believing Matt. 21:22
do not know what you *a.* Mark 10:38

Assyria One of the two civilizations that flourished in Mesopotamia from the third millennium B.C. till about 600 B.C.

Atonement, Day of An annual fast day of the Jews. Ordained in the Law as a day of humiliation and expiation for sins (Lev. 23:27).

Ave Maria Latin meaning "Hail, Mary!" An anthem in praise of Mary, the Lord's mother; from the salutations of Gabriel (Luke 1:28) and Elizabeth (Luke 1:42) to her.

B

Baal One of the fertility gods of Canaan. There were many local Baals. Elijah met the prophets of Baal in a contest (1 Kin. 18:1–40).

Babel Hebrew form of the name "Babylon," capital of Babylonia; site of the Tower of Babel (Gen. 11:1–9).

babes Infants; small children.
Out of the mouth of *b.* Ps. 8:2; Matt. 21:16

Babylonia One of the two civilizations that flourished in Mesopotamia from the third millennium B.C. till about 600 B.C.

baptism A ceremony in which one enters the church family. It is a way of showing that you have been washed free of sin by the death and rising from the dead of Jesus Christ.
John's *b.* of Jesus Matt. 3:13–17
b. by the disciples John 4:1, 2

Barabbas A robber held in prison by the Roman authorities at the time of Jesus' trial; Pilate freed him and condemned Jesus to death (Matt. 27:20– 26; Mark 15:7–15; Luke 23:18–25; John 18:39, 40).

Barnabas The surname given by the apostles to Joses or Joseph, a Levite of Cyprus, who was sent by them to Antioch to confirm the church there. Accompanied Paul on his first missionary journey (Acts 4:36, 37; 9:27; 11:22, 25, 30; 12:25; 13:1–13, 43–52; 14:12, 14, 20; 15:2ff; 1 Cor. 9:6; Gal. 2:1, 9, 13; Col. 4:10).

Bartholomew One of the 12 apostles of Jesus (Matt. 10:3; Mark 3:18; Luke 6:14; Acts 1:13).

Baruch Jeremiah's scribe, or secretary (Jer. 36:4ff).

basket The container for holding a dry measure.
under a *b.* Matt. 5:15; Mark 4:21; Luke 11:33

bath A liquid measure equal to the dry measure ephah (Ezek. 45:11); about six gallons.
honest ephah, and an honest *b.* Ezek. 45:10

beard The growth of hair on the lower part of a man's face. The Hebrews were forbidden to cut the edges of their beards (Lev. 19:27). The shaving off of beards was an indignity (2 Sam. 10:4, 5).

beast Animal (used for all living things other than man, as a general term); in the Book of Revelation the word is used of both "heavenly" beasts and "beasts from the bottomless pit."

Beatitudes The blessings listed by Jesus in the Sermon on the Mount (Matt. 5:3–12; Luke 6:20–23).

beginning Outset; start.
In the *b.* God created Gen. 1:1
In the *b.* was the Word John 1:1

begotten Having been brought into being.
The only *b.* Son John 1:18

benediction An asking for God's blessing, as by a minister or priest at the conclusion of a church service; a blessing.

Benedictus The song of Zacharias, father of John the Baptist, in celebrating the raising up of a leader from the lineage of David (Luke 1:68–79).

Benjamin The youngest son of Jacob. His mother, Rachel, died at his birth (Gen. 35:18). Especially beloved by his father and by Joseph, his only full brother (Gen. 42:4, 36; 43:14–16, 29, 34; 44:12; 45:12, 14, 22). Ancestor of the tribe of Benjamin, the smallest of the 12 tribes of Israel.

Bethany A small village on the E slope of the Mount of Olives, about one and one-half mi. E of Jerusalem. From here Jesus made His triumphal entry into Jerusalem (Mark 11:1–11); the home of Simon the leper (Matt. 26:6; Mark 14:3); home of Lazarus, Mary, and Martha (John 11:1–44); site of Jesus' final parting from His disciples (Luke 24:50, 51).

Bethel City 14 mi. N of Jerusalem. Near here Abraham built an altar (Gen. 12:8; 13:3, 4); here Jacob's name was changed to Israel (Gen. 35:10–15); the ark of the Testimony rested here (Judg. 20:18–28); Jeroboam made it a place of idolatry (1 Kin. 12:29—13:32), which Josiah destroyed (2 Kin. 23:4–15).

Bethlehem A very old town about six mi. SSW of Jerusalem; the birthplace of Jesus (Matt. 2:1–16; Luke 2:4–15; John 7:42); also associated with David (1 Sam. 16:1–13; 17:12, 15; 20:6, 28), Ruth (Ruth 1:1, 2, 19, 22; 2:4; 4:11), and other persons of the OT.

bird A winged creature.
let b. fly above Gen. 1:20
b. of the air Gen. 6:7; Matt. 6:26

birthright Privilege of the firstborn of a family. Esau despised his b. Gen. 25:34

bishop A high-ranking minister, head of a district or diocese.
A b. then must be blameless 1 Tim. 3:2

blood The life-giving fluid of the body. In the OT it is regarded as the seat of life; but since shed blood signifies death, the word is used of both life and death.
you shall not eat any b. Lev. 7:26; Deut. 12:16
this is My b. Matt. 26:28; Mark 14:24
new covenant in My b. Luke 22:20
eats My flesh and drinks My b. John 6:54
redemption through His b. Eph. 1:7; Col. 1:14
precious b. of Christ 1 Pet. 1:19

Boaz A wealthy Bethlehemite who married Ruth (Ruth 2:1—4:22).

body The physical human being or animal. The church is called "the body of Christ" as the living spiritual community of which Christ is the head and all believers are members. At the Lord's Supper, Jesus broke bread to represent His body given in sacrifice for sinners.
touches the dead b. Num. 19:11
lamp of the b. is the eye Matt. 6:22
this is My b. Matt. 26:26; Mark 14:22; Luke 22:19; 1 Cor. 11:24
many members in one b. Rom. 12:4
you are the b. of Christ 1 Cor. 12:27

Booths, Feast of See Feast of Tabernacles.

bread A food made of a dough of flour or meal and water and baked; sustenance in general. Often used in offerings by OT peoples. In the NT, also used in reference to the coming of the kingdom of God or to Jesus Himself.
not live by b. alone Deut. 8:3
shall eat unleavened b. Deut. 16:8
Cast your b. upon the Eccl. 11:1
not live by b. alone Matt. 4:4
Give us this day our daily b. Matt. 6:11; Luke 11:3
eat b. in the kingdom Luke 14:15
the true b. from heaven John 6:32
I am the b. of life John 6:35

bread, breaking of Since the earliest form of the Lord's Supper involved the "breaking of bread," the term has been used for worship in general (Acts 2:42).

bread from heaven The food miraculously provided by God for the Israelites in their wanderings through the wilderness (Ex. 16:15).

brother A male relative of the same parents; a close associate.
Am I my b.'s keeper Gen. 4:9
b. is born for adversity Prov. 17:17
sticks closer than a b. Prov. 18:24
is My b. and sister and Matt. 12:50

C

Cain Son of Adam; murdered his brother Abel (Gen. 4:2ff); prototype of wicked men (1 John 3:12; Jude 11).

call To summon; specifically in the NT, to summon to discipleship or to accept God's divine invitation for salvation.
to c. those who were invited Matt. 22:3
immediately He c. them Mark 1:20
not come to c. the righteous Luke 5:32
to those who are the c. Rom. 8:28

camel A large animal of desert areas.
a c. to go through Matt. 19:24
and swallow a c. Matt. 23:24

Canaan; Canaanites The land between the Jordan River and the Mediterranean Sea and that part of Syria along the coast (Phoenicia). Peopled by Semites with whom the Hebrews probably merged.

canon The laws of a church; the collection of writings or books of a religion that are considered to be God's Word and that set forth the standards of faith. The OT was, and is, the official collection of holy scriptures of the Jews. These books were recognized as canonical and holy by all orthodox Christians from the beginning. The Roman Catholic Church accepts also certain books which Protestant denominations call Apocrypha. By the end of the fourth century the collection of early Christian writings now known as the NT had been recognized as authoritative.

Capernaum A city on the NW shore of the Sea of Galilee. Jesus lived there (Mark 2:1); home of Peter and Andrew (Matt. 8:5, 14); here Jesus healed the man with an unclean spirit (Mark 1:21–28) and the paralytic (Mark 2:1–12) and held discussions about true greatness (Mark 9:33–37) and paying the half-shekel tax (Matt. 17:24–27).

Carmel, Mount A high headland on the coast of Palestine; scene of contest between prophets of Baal and Elijah (1 Kin. 18:19–40).

catholic Universal; worldwide (as used in the Apostles' Creed); general (as applied to the Catholic Epistles); broad; extensive.

Chanukah See Dedication, Feast of.

cheek The side of the face.
slaps you on your right c. Matt. 5:39; Luke 6:29

cherubim Winged creatures, statues of which were fixed to the mercy seat of the ark of the Testimony. Two cherubim carved from olive wood were placed within the inner room of the temple.
two c. of gold Ex. 25:18
made two c. of olive 1 Kin. 6:23

child A young person of either sex.
a c. is known by his Prov. 20:11
unto us a c. is born Is. 9:6
little c. shall lead Is. 11:6

children Young persons of either sex.
become as little c. Matt. 18:3
Let the little c. come Matt. 19:14

Christians Followers of Christ.
first called c. in Antioch Acts 11:26

Christmas The holiday on December 25 which celebrates the birth of Jesus Christ.

church The people of God; those destined to inherit the kingdom of God. Also, any local group of believers.
I will build My c. Matt. 16:18
Christ is head of the c. Eph. 5:23
head of the body, the c. Col. 1:18
the seven c. Rev. 1:4, 11, 20

clean Free from defilement or dirt. Under the Hebrew law certain animals are declared clean and others unclean (Lev. 11:1–47; Deut. 14:3–21).
c. hands and a pure heart Ps. 24:4
can make me c. Matt. 8:2; Mark 1:40; Luke 5:12
make the outside of the cup and dish c. Luke 11:39
all things are c. Luke 11:41

cloud A visible mass of water particles in the air above the earth.
pillar of c. Ex. 13:21; Num. 12:5
c. covered the mountain Ex. 24:15

Colosse; Colossians A city in Asia Minor. Paul wrote an epistle to the Christians of this city.

commandment Any of the Ten Commandments or laws given to Moses by God at Mount Sinai (Ex. 20:1–17; Deut. 5:6–21); other OT laws.
keep the c. Matt. 19:17
which is the great c. Matt. 22:36
you love Me, keep My c. John 14:15

communicant One who receives or is entitled to receive Holy Communion.

Communion See Holy Communion.

confess To admit to a fault or sin, particularly as a sign of repentance; to acknowledge God's redeeming acts and openly acknowledge that Jesus is the Messiah, Lord, and Son of God (as Peter's great confession in Matt. 16:16; Mark 8:29; Luke 9:20); to offer praise and thanksgiving to God.
c. that he has sinned Lev. 5:5
c. Me before men Matt. 10:32; Luke 12:8
c. their sins Mark 1:5
c. that Jesus Christ is Lord Phil. 2:11
C. your trespasses to one another James 5:16

confirmation A rite in some churches in which a person becomes a full member of a church. Its origins may be found in Acts 8:14–17 and 19:1–7.

congregation An assembly; gathering.
c. of the righteous Ps. 1:5
God stands in the c. Ps. 82:1

converted Changed, as one's religion or belief.
unless you are *c.* Matt. 18:3
Repent . . . and be *c.* Acts 3:19

convinced 1. Persuaded.
not one of you *c.* Job 32:12
2. Convicted.
he is *c.* by all, he 1 Cor. 14:24

Corinth; Corinthians A city of S Greece, capital of the Roman province of Achaia. Paul wrote two epistles to the Christians of Corinth.

counselor An adviser or teacher. Counselors seem to have been court officials of the Israelite kings (1 Chr. 27:33; Job 3:14; Prov. 11:14). The coming Messiah is so called (Is. 9:6).

courier Messenger.
letters were sent by *c.* Esth. 3:13
c. who rode on royal horses Esth. 8:14

covenant A binding agreement. The great covenant between God and Israel was made at Sinai (Ex. 24:3–8); the tablets on which the Ten Commandments were engraved were called "the tablets of the covenant" (Deut. 9:11). The chest in which these tablets were placed was called the "ark of the Testimony" (Ex. 25:22). The new covenant came into being through the blood of Christ.
My blood of the new *c.* Mark 14:24
cup is the new *c.* 1 Cor. 11:25

covet To long for; desire, particularly someone else's property.
shall not *c.* Ex. 20:17; Deut. 5:21
You shall not *c.* Rom. 7:7; 13:9

creation The act of God in making heaven and earth and bringing forth all life; the whole universe.
the story of *c.* Gen. 1:1—2:25
c. which God created Mark 13:19
the whole *c.* groans Rom. 8:22

creator The maker; originator; hence, Creator: God; the Lord.
Remember now your *c.* Eccl. 12:1
C. of the ends of the earth Is. 40:28
creature rather than the *c.* Rom. 1:25

creature Any living thing that God has made.
great sea *c.* Gen. 1:21
called each living *c.* Gen. 2:19
every *c.* of God is good 1 Tim. 4:4

creed A statement of beliefs of a religion; affirmation of faith. In particular, three separate confessions of the early Christian church: the Apostles' Creed, the Nicene Creed, and the Athanasian Creed.

creeping thing Reptile.
every *c.* that creeps Gen. 1:26
C. and flying fowl Ps. 148:10
wild beasts, *c.* Acts 10:12

cross An upright post with cross-beam on which victims of execution were fastened; used by the Romans. A symbol of Christianity.
who does not take his *c.* Matt. 10:38
take up his *c.* Matt. 16:24; Mark 8:34
come down from the *c.* Matt. 27:40
Simon . . . to bear His *c.* Mark 15:21
stood by the *c.* of Jesus John 19:25

crown A headdress of gold, precious stones, etc.; a wreath encircling the head.
A *c.* of glory Prov. 4:9; 16:31
excellent wife is the *c.* Prov. 12:4
c. of thorns Matt. 27:29; Mark 15:17; John 19:2, 5
perishable *c.* 1 Cor. 9:25

Crucifixion, the Jesus' execution on the cross by the Romans at the instigation of the Jewish leaders (Matt. 27; Mark 15; Luke 23; John 19).

crucify To put to death by fastening to a cross.
scourge and to *c.* Matt. 20:19
Let Him be *c.* Matt. 27:22
C. Him Mark 15:13; Luke 23:21; John 19:6

cubit A measure of length of about 18 inches.
add one *c.* to Matt. 6:27; Luke 12:25

cup A vessel from which to drink.
My *c.* runs over Ps. 23:5
c. of cold water Matt. 10:42; Mark 9:41
drink the *c.* Matt. 20:22; Mark 10:39
outside of the *c.* Matt. 23:25
took the *c.* Matt. 26:27; Mark 14:23; Luke 22:17; 1 Cor. 11:25
c. pass from Me Matt. 26:39; Mark 14:36; Luke 22:42
c. which My Father John 18:11

curse To call on God to punish.
c. him who *c.* you Gen. 12:3
Whoever *c.* his God Lev. 24:15
C. God and die Job 2:9
bless those who *c.* you Matt. 5:44; Luke 6:28
began to *c.* Matt. 26:74; Mark 14:71
fig tree which You *c.* Mark 11:21

Cyprus A large island in the Mediterranean 41 mi. from the coast of Asia Minor; home of Barnabas (Acts 4:36); visited by Paul (Acts 13:4–12; 21:3).

D

Damascus A very ancient city, capital of Syria; in OT times the capital of the Aramean kingdom. Site of Saul's conversion (Acts 9:1–22).

Dan The fifth son of Jacob, born of Bilhah (Gen. 30:1–6); one of the 12 tribes of Israel.

dance To move in rhythm, usually to the sound of music.
mourn, And a time to *d.* Eccl. 3:4
you did not *d.* Matt. 11:17; Luke 7:32

Daniel The Jewish prophet at the Babylonian court about whom the OT Book of Daniel is written. Interpreted dreams (Dan. 2:1–45) and the handwriting on the wall (5:17–30); saved by God from the lions (6:16–24).

David The second and greatest king over Israel; youngest son of Jesse (1 Sam. 17:12, 14); slew Goliath (1 Sam. 17:41–50); friend of Jonathan (1 Sam. 19:1—20:42); a fugitive from Saul's wrath (1 Sam. 21–27; 30); king of Judah (2 Sam. 1:1—5:5); king of Israel (2 Sam. 3:6–1 Kin. 2:11); brought the ark of the Testimony to Jerusalem (2 Sam. 6:1–17); his great sin in coveting Bathsheba (2 Sam. 11:1–27); rebellion of his son Absalom (2 Sam. 14–18); his psalm of thanksgiving (2 Sam. 22); names Solomon, his son, to succeed him (1 Kin. 1:11—2:12).

day The time between sunrise and sunset; a period of 24 hours.
God called the light *d.* Gen. 1:5
neither the *d.* nor Matt. 25:13
D. come on you unexpectedly Luke 21:34

day of the Lord In the OT, the day when God punishes evil (Amos 5:18–20); a day of universal disaster (Is. 2; 13; 24; Zeph. 1:7–18; 2:2, 3; 3:8). In the NT, the day of the Last Judgment and the end of the world (1 Cor. 4:5; 5:5; 1 Thess. 5:2; Rev. 16:14).

deacon A servant or minister; an officer of a local church who assists the minister or priest.
with the bishops and *d.* Phil. 1:1
d. must be reverent, not 1 Tim. 3:8

dead Not alive; deceased.
let the *d.* bury their own *d.* Matt. 8:22
the girl is not *d.* Matt. 9:24
raised from the *d.* 1 Cor. 15:12

Dead Sea The salt lake at the mouth of the Jordan River. Biblical names: "Salt Sea" (Gen. 14:3; Num. 34:3, 12; Deut. 3:17; Josh. 3:16; 12:3; 15:2, 5; 18:19); "eastern sea" (Joel 2:20).

death The condition of being without life; the act of dying. Symbol of the final state of the unsaved (John 8:51; Rom. 6:23;

Rev. 20:6), and of the power that rules over man in the age of sin (Rom. 5:14; Rev. 6:8).
valley of the shadow of *d.* Ps. 23:4
swallow up *d.* forever Is. 25:8
not taste *d.* Matt. 16:28; Mark 9:1; Luke 9:27
D., where is your sting 1 Cor. 15:55

Deborah 1. Rebekah's nurse and companion (Gen. 35:8). 2. An early "judge" of Israel; aroused the scattered tribes to opposition to Canaanite oppression; Song of Deborah (Judg. 5:2–31) celebrates her achievement.

debts Obligations; anything owed to another.
forgive us our *d.* Matt. 6:12

Dedication, Feast of An eight-day festival observing the victories of Judas Maccabaeus and the purification and rededication of the temple (John 10:22). Also called Feast of Lights; Hanukkah; Chanukah.

Delilah A woman from the Valley of Sorek; betrayed Samson to the Philistines (Judg. 16:4–22).

deliverer, the In five OT passages (2 Sam. 22:2; Ps. 18:2; 40:17; 70:5; 144:2) God is referred to as "the deliverer"; but even though Christ is the instrument of God's deliverance of mankind from sin, the NT does not use the word except when Paul repeats Isaiah 59:20, using "Deliverer" instead of "Redeemer" (Rom. 11:26).

demon An evil spirit.
sacrifices to *d.* Lev. 17:7; Deut. 32:17
who were *d.*-possessed Matt. 4:24; 9:32; 12:22
He has a *d.* Matt. 11:18; Luke 7:33

den Lair; cave of a wild animal.
into the *d.* of lions Dan. 6:7
a '*d.* of thieves Matt. 21:13; Mark 11:17

detestable Abominable; loathsome.
not eat any *d.* thing Deut. 14:3

devil The chief demon, Satan.
Jesus . . . tempted by the *d.* Matt. 4:1–11
serpent of old, called the *D.* Rev. 12:9; 20:2

die Perish; lose life.
you shall surely *d.* Gen. 2:17
born, And a time to *d.* Eccl. 3:2
for tomorrow we *d.* Is. 22:13
in Me shall never *d.* John 11:26

disciple A learner; a follower, particularly one who follows Jesus Christ.
called His twelve *d.* Matt. 10:1; Luke 6:13
sent two of his *d.* Matt. 11:2
d. rebuked them Matt. 19:13
d. were first called Christians Acts 11:26

Dispersion The widespread settlement of Jews outside of Palestine from the time of the Exile through the following centuries.

doctrine Teaching or instruction, particularly that of Jesus or the apostles concerning God's will.
My *d.* is pure Job 11:4
My *d.* is not Mine John 7:16
the *d.* of baptisms Heb. 6:2

door Entrance way.
will pass over the *d.* Ex. 12:23
and the *d.* was shut Matt. 25:10
I am the *d.* John 10:9
d. standing open in heaven Rev. 4:1

doxology A hymn, usually in a set formula, for expressing praise to God. Luke 2:14 ("Glory to God in the highest") has influenced Christian doxologies.

dreadful Awesome; feared; terrible.
d. day of the LORD Mal. 4:5

drink To swallow a liquid; the liquid so swallowed.
not *d.* wine or intoxicating *d.* Lev. 10:9
Strong *d.* is a brawler Prov. 20:1
d., for tomorrow we die Is. 22:13
D. from it, all of you Matt. 26:27
shall *d.* neither wine Luke 1:15

dust Fine, dry, powdery earth.
God formed man of the *d.* Gen. 2:7
d. you are, And to *d.* Gen. 3:19

E

earring An ornament for the ear.
give me the *e.* from Judg. 8:24

earth The planet on which we live; the soil.
God created the . . . *e.* Gen. 1:1
The *e.* is the LORD's Ps. 24:1
meek shall inherit the *e.* Ps. 37:11
And *e.* is My footstool Is. 66:1
meek, . . . shall inherit the *e.* Matt. 5:5
Your will be done On *e.* Matt. 6:10
on *e.* peace, goodwill Luke 2:14
new heaven and a new *e.* Rev. 21:1

Easter A Christian festival celebrating the resurrection of Jesus; on a Sunday between March 22 and April 25.

eat To consume food.
shall not *e.* of every Gen. 3:1
e. and drink, for tomorrow Is. 22:13
Take, *e.*; this is My body Matt. 26:26

Eden, Garden of A garden of trees planted by the Lord (Gen. 2:8) in which Adam and Eve first lived; actual site unknown; symbolically identified with Paradise.

Edom; Edomites A country to the E and S of Israel; its people had a close relationship to the Israelites, being descendants of Esau.

Egypt A land of NE Africa. Temporary home of Abraham (Gen. 12:10–20); Joseph sold "into Egypt" (Gen. 37:28, 36); Joseph as governor (Gen. 41:37—47:26); Israel in bondage (Ex. 1:1—12:36); the Exodus (Ex. 12:37—14:31); Jesus taken there (Matt. 2:13).

elders Seniors; among the Jews, the old and mature men who were civil and religious leaders; in the Christian church, leaders of the local church.
seventy of the *e.* of Israel Ex. 24:9
tradition of the *e.* Matt. 15:2; Mark 7:3
appointed *e.* in every church Acts 14:23
the *e.* who rule well 1 Tim. 5:17
twenty-four *e.* Rev. 4:4

Eli The priest of Shiloh to whom the boy Samuel was brought (1 Sam. 1–4).

Elijah A prophet from Tishbe to Gilead in the northern kingdom; fed by ravens (1 Kin. 17:6); performs miracles (1 Kin. 17:14–24; 20:30; 2 Kin. 1:10–12; 2:8); taken up by a whirlwind into heaven (2 Kin. 2:11). Malachi prophesies his return before the day of the Lord (Mal. 4:5). In NT times, some thought Jesus to be Elijah (Matt. 16:14; Luke 9:8); others thought John the Baptist to be Elijah (John 1:21). In the early church, John was regarded as the heir to the spirit and power of Elijah (Luke 1:17) or as Elijah reborn (Matt. 11:14; 17:10–13). At the Transfiguration, Elijah appears with Moses (Matt. 17:3, 4; Mark 9:4, 5).

Elisha A prophet; disciple and successor to Elijah; performed many miracles (2 Kin. 2:14–24; 3:16–20; 4:2–7, 32–44; 5:10–14, 27; 6:5–7, 18–20); contact with his bones revives a dead man (2 Kin. 13:20, 21).

Elizabeth Wife of the priest, Zacharias, and mother of John the Baptist (Luke 1:5–66).

Emmanuel *See* Immanuel.

enemies Foes; opponents.
presence of my *e.* Ps. 23:5
love your *e.* Matt. 5:44; Luke 6:27, 35

enter To go or come into.
E. into His gates with thanksgiving Ps. 100:4
E. by the narrow gate Matt. 7:13; Luke 13:24

ephah A dry measure equal to the liquid measure bath; estimated as three-eighths to two-thirds of a bushel.
scales, an honest *e.* Ezek. 45:10

Ephesus; Ephesians A seaport in the Roman province of Asia; visited by Paul on his second and third journeys. Paul's NT Epistle to the Ephesians seems to be a general letter to the churches of Asia Minor.

Ephraim The younger son of Joseph; adopted by Jacob (Gen. 48:1ff); ancestor of one of the most powerful of the 12 tribes of Israel.

Epiphany A Christian festival on January 6, which celebrates the visit of the Magi to worship the infant Jesus.

episcopal Governed by bishops, as applied to Christian churches.

epistle Letter; specifically those letters written by the apostles that are included in the NT. Pastoral Epistles: The NT books of 1 and 2 Timothy and Titus, which are written in the name of Paul as the chief pastor of the churches. General (Catholic) Epistles: The NT books of James, 1 and 2 Peter, 1, 2 and 3 John, and Jude.

Esau Son of Isaac and Rebekah who traded his birthright to his younger twin brother Jacob for a bowl of stew (Gen. 25:22–34; 27; 33:1–16).

Essenes A Jewish community in Palestine at the time of Jesus; strict adherents of Jewish law.

Esther A Jewess of Shushan who became Ahasuerus's queen and thwarted a plot to kill all the Jews, later commemorated by the Jewish festival of Purim. The Book of Esther tells the story.

Eucharist Literally "thanksgiving"; the name sometimes used by Christians to refer to the rite of the Lord's Supper.

Euphrates The largest river in W Asia; marks N boundary of territory promised by the Lord to Israel (Gen. 15:18; Deut. 1:7; 11:24; Josh. 1:4).

Eve The first woman; wife of Adam (Gen. 2:21–25); tempted by the serpent (Gen. 3:1–5).

everlasting Eternal; never ending.
the e. God Gen. 21:33; Is. 40:28
underneath are the e. arms Deut. 33:27
into the e. fire Matt. 18:8; 25:41
inherit e. life Matt. 19:29
have e. life John 3:16, 36; 5:24

evil Wickedness; slanderous or injurious actions.
tree . . . of good and e. Gen. 2:9
I will fear no e. Ps. 23:4
Depart from e. Ps. 37:27
deliver us from the e. one Matt. 6:13

what e. has He done Matt. 27:23; Mark 15:14; Luke 23:22
love of money is a root of all kinds of e. 1 Tim. 6:10

excommunication Exclusion, either permanent or temporary, from the sacraments of or from membership in certain churches. Christian practices are based on ancient Jewish exclusions from the synagogue (Ex. 12:15; Lev. 17:4; Num. 19:20; Ezra 10:8) and NT disciplines (Luke 6:22; John 9:22; 1 Cor. 5:13; 16:22).

Exile, the A period during which most of the people of Judah and Jerusalem were forced to live in Babylonia.

Exodus The going out of Israel from Egypt as recorded in the second book of the OT. It includes the deliverance from slavery, the wandering through the wilderness, the covenant with the Lord at Mount Sinai, and the provision of the tabernacle and ark of the covenant.

eye The organ of sight.
e. of both of them were opened Gen. 3:7
e. for e. Ex. 21:24; Lev. 24:20; Deut. 19:21; Matt. 5:38
lift up my e. to the hills Ps. 121:1
wise in your own e. Prov. 3:7
if your right e. causes you Matt. 5:29; 18:9; Mark 9:47

Ezekiel A major Jewish prophet; author of the OT Book of Ezekiel; one of the captives of the Babylonian exile. Vision of God (Ezek. 1:4–28); parable of the two eagles and the vine (17:1–24); the fall of Jerusalem (24:1–27); various prophecies about other nations (25–32).

Ezra A priest and scribe; supposed author of the OT Book of Ezra, which details the first return of the Israelites from Babylon and the rebuilding of the temple.

F

face The front of the head; the surface or top side; frequently used to indicate the presence of God. Among the Hebrews, "seeking the face of God" referred to attendance at public worship (Ps. 27:8).
on the f. of the deep Gen. 1:2
In the sweat of your f. you shall Gen. 3:19
LORD spoke to Moses f. to f. Ex. 33:11
make His f. shine upon you Num. 6:25
Seek My f. Ps. 27:8
f. of the LORD is against Ps. 34:16
the f. of My Father Matt. 18:10
My messenger before Your f. Mark 1:2
but then f. to f. 1 Cor. 13:12

faith Belief or trust in someone or something. Among Christians, belief in the Holy Trinity.
> your *f.* has made you Matt. 9:22; Mark 5:34; 10:52; Luke 8:48; 17:19
> *f.* as a mustard seed Matt. 17:20; Luke 17:6
> just shall live by *f.* Rom. 1:17
> man is justified by *f.* Rom. 3:28; 5:1; Gal. 2:16; 3:24
> *f.* is accounted for righteousness Rom. 4:5
> saved through *f.* Eph. 2:8
> one Lord, one f., one Eph. 4:5
> *f.* is the substance of Heb. 11:1
> *f.* without works is dead James 2:20

Fall, the A sinking into sin; the disobedience of Adam and Eve whereby sin entered the world (Gen. 3).

falsehood Lying.
> love worthlessness And seek *f.* Ps. 4:2
> destroy those who speak *f.* Ps. 5:6

fast To go without food.
> when you *f.*, do not be Matt. 6:16
> Pharisees *f.* often Matt. 9:14; Mark 2:18

father The male parent or ancestor. In the OT, used of God as the One who made a covenant with the people of Israel.
> be a *f.* of many nations Gen. 17:4
> Honor your *f.* and Ex. 20:12; Lev. 19:3; Deut. 5:16
> who curses his *f.* Ex. 21:17; Lev. 20:9
> David rested with his *f.* 1 Kin. 2:10
> *f.* of the fatherless, . . . Is God Ps. 68:5
> LORD, You are our F. Is. 64:8

Father The First Person of the Holy Trinity.
> glorify your F. in heaven Matt. 5:16, 45
> Our F. in heaven Matt. 6:9; Luke 11:2
> Abba, F. Mark 14:36; Rom. 8:15; Gal. 4:6
> baptizing them in the name of the F. Matt. 28:19
> about My F.'s business Luke 2:49
> who the F. is except the Son Luke 10:22
> the Promise of My F. Luke 24:49
> the only begotten of the F. John 1:14
> one F.—God John 8:41
> I and My F. are one John 10:30
> comes to the F. except through Me John 14:6
> ask the F. in My name John 15:16

fear To dread; to be afraid of; to be anxious.
> I will *f.* no evil Ps. 23:4
> Whom shall I *f.* Ps. 27:1
> F. not, for I am with you Is. 41:10; 43:5

fear of the Lord The term used in the OT for "religion" (Deut. 6:2; 10:20; 28:58; Ps. 111:10; Prov. 1:7; 8:13; Eccl. 12:13). In the NT, "those who fear the Lord" are the faithful (Luke 1:50; 18:4) or converts to Judaism (Acts 10:2; 13:26).

feast A festival; in ancient Israel associated with occasions of religious joy. Those mentioned in the Bible: 1. Passover and Feast of Unleavened Bread (Ex. 12:1–30; Lev. 23:4–14; Deut. 16:1–8). 2. Feast of Weeks or Pentecost (Lev. 23:15–21; Deut. 16:9–12). 3. Feast of Tabernacles (Lev. 23:34–36; Deut. 16:13–15). 4. Purim (Esth. 9:20–28). 5. Feast of Dedication or Feast of Lights (John 10:22).

fellowship Companionship; a group of persons with a common interest. Among Christians, the common bond is their faith in Christ, particularly in partaking of the Lord's Supper.
> into the *f.* of His Son 1 Cor. 1:9
> the right hand of *f.* Gal. 2:9
> any *f.* of the Spirit Phil. 2:1
> our *f.* is with the Father 1 John 1:3

fight Struggle against; do battle.
> F. the good *f.* of faith 1 Tim. 6:12

firmament Sky; heavens.
> Let there be a *f.* in Gen. 1:6
> *f.* shows His handiwork Ps. 19:1

first Before all others.
> *f.* will be last Matt. 19:30; Mark 10:31

First and the Last, the A title used by Isaiah (Is. 41:4; 44:6; 48:12) to convey the idea of God's everlasting sovereignty and eternal majesty and power. The same title is used in Revelation (1:11, 17; 2:8; 22:13) implying God's sovereign lordship manifest in Jesus Christ.

firstborn, firstfruits The eldest; the earliest fruits harvested. The consecration of the first of the male children, of animals, and of fruits was an important part of the religion of Israel.
> LORD struck all the *f.* Ex. 12:29

flesh The soft part of the human body; all mankind.
> All *f.* is grass Is. 40:6; 1 Pet. 1:24
> but the *f.* is weak Matt. 26:41; Mark 14:38
> the Word became *f.* John 1:14

Flood, the The covering of the earth with water because of man's wickedness. Noah's family and the animals of the earth are saved in an ark (Gen. 6:1—8:19).

food Solid food in contrast to that which is drunk.
> You give them their *f.* Ps. 145:15
> trees used for *f.* Ezek. 47:12
> life more than *f.* Matt. 6:25
> have you any *f.* John 21:5

fool A silly or senseless person.
> *f.* despise wisdom Prov. 1:7

f. is right in his own eyes Prov. 12:15
folly of *f.* is deceit Prov. 14:8
f. for Christ's sake 1 Cor. 4:10

foolish Silly; unwise. Parables of Jesus deal with: foolish and wise virgins (Matt. 25:1–13) and a foolish rich man (Luke 12:16–21).

forgive To pardon; show mercy to.
f. us . . . , As we *f.* Matt. 6:12; Luke 11:4
F., and you will be Luke 6:37
Father, *f.* them Luke 23:34

fountain The source, as the spring from which water flows. The Lord is called "the fountain of living waters" (Jer. 2:13; cf. John 4:14) and the "fountain of life" (Ps. 36:9).

frankincense A fragrant incense.
spices . . . and pure *f.* Ex. 30:34
gold, *f.,* and myrrh Matt. 2:11

friend An associate whom one likes.
the rich has many *f.* Prov. 14:20
A *f.* loves at all times Prov. 17:17
a *f.* who sticks closer Prov. 18:24

G

Gabriel An angel of high rank (Dan. 8:16; 9:21; Luke 1:19, 26).

Gad The seventh son of Jacob; born of Leah's maid Zilpah (Gen. 30:10, 11); ancestor of the tribe of Gad.

Galatia; Galatians A region and Roman province in Asia Minor. Paul, in the NT Epistle to the Galatians, tells of his own conversion.

Galilee A region of N Palestine, including the Sea of Galilee on the E side. OT references include: Solomon gives 20 cities of Galilee to Hiram (1 Kin. 9:11); the prophecy of Isaiah (Is. 9:1) concerning "Galilee of the Gentiles" (cf. Matt. 4:13). Called "land of Gennesaret" (Matt. 14:34; Mark 6:53). Jesus' active ministry was almost entirely within its borders.

Galilee, Sea of The larger of the two freshwater lakes on the Jordan River system. Site of miracles: the great catch of fish (Luke 5:1–11); Jesus stills the sea (Matt. 8:23–26; Mark 4:35–39; Luke 8:22–24); Jesus walks on the sea (Matt. 14:25–27; Mark 6:48–51; John 6:19, 20). Also called "Chinnereth" (Num. 34:11; Deut. 3:17; Josh. 13:27); "Chinneroth" (Josh. 12:3); "Gennesaret" (Luke 5:1); and "Tiberias" (John 6:1; 21:1).

gate Doorway.
Enter into His *g.* with thanksgiving Ps. 100:4
Enter by the narrow *g.* Matt. 7:13

Gennesaret A fertile plain on the shore of the Sea of Galilee. *See* Galilee.

Gethsemane A garden on the Mount of Olives where Jesus prayed and where He was betrayed by Judas (Matt. 26:36; Mark 14:32).

Gideon A prophet of Israel especially favored by the Lord with revelations and unusual powers (Judg. 6:11—8:35).

Gilead A rugged, mountainous region E of the Jordan. Possibly also a city (Judg. 10:17; Hos. 6:8) and a tribe (Judg. 5:17).

Gilgal The name of several places in the OT, one of them a city of the tribe of Benjamin, near Jericho; site of the first encampment of the Israelites after crossing the Jordan (Josh. 3; 4); there Saul was made king (1 Sam. 11:14, 15).

give To bestow; hand over to another.
G. us this day our daily Matt. 6:11
it will be *g.* to you Matt. 7:7; Luke 6:38; 11:9
more blessed to *g.* than Acts 20:35

giver One who bestows.
God loves a cheerful *g.* 2 Cor. 9:7

glad tidings Good news; the gospel (used in Luke 1:19; 8:1; Acts 13:32; and Rom. 10:15).

Gloria in Excelsis The proclamation of the heavenly host at the birth of Christ, "Glory to God in the highest" (Luke 2:14).

glory of the Lord The word *glory* is sometimes synonymous with "God" to avoid referring to God in human form (Ex. 33:22). In the OT, used of the fiery presence at Sinai (Ex. 24:16, 17) and of the radiance that filled the tabernacle (Ex. 40:34). In the NT, used of the divine Presence (Mark 8:38; Luke 2:9), of the quality of Jesus' appearance in His transfiguration (Luke 9:29, 31), and of Jesus' Second Coming (Matt. 25:31).

gnat A tiny insect.
strain out a *g.* and swallow Matt. 23:24

God, kingdom of *See* kingdom of God; heaven, kingdom of.

gods Idols.
have no other *g.* before Ex. 20:3

Golden Rule A commandment given by Jesus in the Sermon on the Mount (Matt. 7:12; Luke 6:31).

Golgotha Place where Jesus was crucified (Matt. 27:33, 35; Mark 15:22; John 19:17).

Gomorrah One of the two cities destroyed by the Lord because of their wickedness (Gen. 19:24–28).

good Virtuous; honorable.
  g. name . . . rather than great Prov. 22:1
  No one is *g.* but One Matt. 19:17; Luke 18:19

Good Friday The Friday before Easter; the
  anniversary of the crucifixion of Jesus.

gospel Good news; glad tidings. Hence, the
  teachings of Jesus and of the apostles.
  The NT books of Matthew, Mark, Luke,
  and John are called the Gospels.
  g. of the kingdom Matt. 4:23
  the *g.* of Jesus Christ Mark 1:1
  and believe in the *g.* Mark 1:15
  preach the *g.* Luke 4:18
  hear the word of the *g.* Acts 15:7
  the *g.* of Christ Rom. 1:16

grace OT usage: "favor" in the expression
  "found *g.* in the eyes of" (Gen. 6:8). In
  NT usage: "the unmerited and abundant
  gift of God's love and favor to man,"
  particularly made effective in Jesus
  Christ for the Christian. Used by Paul
  as an opening and farewell greeting
  (Rom. 16:24; 1 Cor. 1:3).
  g. and truth came through Jesus John 1:17
  g. of God and the gift by the *g.* Rom. 5:15
  G. to you and 1 Cor. 1:3; Eph. 1:2
  by the *g.* of God I am 1 Cor. 15:10
  g. of God in vain 2 Cor. 6:1
  g. of our Lord Jesus 2 Cor. 8:9; 13:14
  by *g.* you have been saved Eph. 2:5

guarantee A pledge.
  given us the Spirit as a *g.* 2 Cor. 5:5
  who is the *g.* of our inheritance Eph. 1:14

H

Habakkuk A prophet of Judah; the OT book
  which bears his name is the eighth of the
  12 Minor Prophets.

Haggai A Jewish prophet contemporary with
  Zechariah; the tenth of the 12 Minor
  Prophets of the OT.

Hallelujah "Praise the Lord" (not used in the
  NKJV). *See* Alleluia.

hallowed Made sacred; consecrated.
  H. be Your name Matt. 6:9

hand The end of the arm.
  Into Your *h.* I commit Ps. 31:5
  not let your left *h.* know Matt. 6:3
  if your *h.* or foot Matt. 18:8; Mark 9:43

hands, laying on of A symbolic ritual: 1. Of
  divine blessing (Matt. 19:13–15),
  sometimes accompanied by the gift of
  the Holy Spirit (Acts 19:6). 2. Of divine
  healing (Mark 7:32). 3. Of consecration
  of a man for a specific office (Acts 13:2, 3;

1 Tim. 4:14). 4. Of dedication of an animal
  as for sacrifice (Lev. 16:21).

Hanukkah Hebrew word for "dedication." *See*
  Feast of Dedication.

harp A stringed musical instrument.
  play the *h.* and flute Gen. 4:21
  David would take a *h.* and play it 1 Sam. 16:23

haughty Overbearing; proud.
  h. spirit before a fall Prov. 16:18

heart The physical organ thought of as being
  the seat of the affections.
  A broken and a contrite *h.* Ps. 51:17
  Blessed are the pure in *h.* Matt. 5:8
  Let not your *h.* be troubled John 14:1

heaven A term sometimes used for "God."
  I have sinned against *h.* Luke 15:18
  it has been given to him from *h.* John 3:27

heaven; heavens 1. The sky; the space in which
  the sun, the moon, and the stars move;
  the firmament.
  God called the firmament *h.* Gen. 1:8
  He adorned the *h.* Job 26:13
  h. declare the glory of God Ps. 19:1
  stretch out the *h.* Ps. 104:2; Is. 40:22
  saw *h.* opened and Acts 10:11
  2. The place where God, the risen Christ, the
  angels, and the saints reside; the future home
  of the redeemed.
  new *h.* and Is. 65:17; Rev. 21:1
  till *h.* and earth pass Matt. 5:18
  Father in *h.* Matt. 6:9; Luke 11:2
  looked . . . toward *h.* as Acts 1:10
  eternal in the *h.* 2 Cor. 5:1

heaven, kingdom of Used throughout the
  Gospel of Matthew for "kingdom of God."
  See kingdom of God.
  the kingdom of *h.* is at hand Matt. 3:2; 10:7
  theirs is the kingdom of *h.* Matt. 5:3, 10
  least in the kingdom of *h.* Matt. 5:19; 11:11
  kingdom of *h.* is like Matt. 13:24
  such is the kingdom of *h.* Matt. 19:14

heavenly host *See* host, heavenly.

Hebrews The descendants of Eber (Gen. 10:21);
  sometimes used interchangeably with
  "Israelites."

Hebron An ancient city in the mountains
  of Judah, 19 mi. S of Jerusalem. Here
  Abraham purchased a cave for a family
  burial place (Gen. 23:1–20). David's capital
  city for the first seven and one-half years
  of his reign (2 Sam. 2:1—5:5).

Helper The Holy Spirit; the intercessor promised
  by Christ to help and guide believers
  (John 14:26; 15:26; 16:7).

Herod 1. Ruler of Jewish Palestine under Rome
  (37–4 B.C.); sent the wise men to search

out the infant Jesus (Matt. 2:1–9).
2. Herod Antipas: Tetrarch of Galilee
(4 B.C.–A.D. 39); put John the Baptist
to death (Matt. 14:1–12; Mark 6:14–29;
Luke 3:19, 20; 9:7–9).

Hezekiah The name of four persons in the OT, one
of whom was king of Judah (715–687 B.C.;
2 Kin. 18–20; 2 Chr. 29–32; Is. 36–39).

Holy Communion In Christian churches, the
sacrament of the Lord's Supper. A ritual
during which bread or wafers and wine
or grape juice are blessed and partaken
of by worshipers as the body and blood
of Jesus or as symbolic of them. The
ritual was instituted by Jesus at the Last
Supper (Matt. 26:26–29; Mark 14:22–25;
Luke 22:19, 20; 1 Cor. 11:23–26). Jesus
speaks of the bread as His body and
the cup as the New Testament or New
Covenant in His blood. Paul speaks of the
communion of the body and blood of
Christ (1 Cor. 10:16).

holy of holies The innermost room of the
temple or tabernacle in which the ark of
the Testimony was kept.

Holy Spirit *See* Spirit, Holy.

Holy Trinity *See* Trinity.

Holy Week The week before Easter.

honor To esteem; to give respect.
H. your father and your mother Ex. 20:12;
Matt. 15:4
before *h.* is humility Prov. 15:33
prophet is not without *h.* Matt. 13:57
h. to whom *h.* Rom. 13:7

Horeb, Mount A sacred mountain (Ex. 3:1;
Deut. 1:2, 6, 19; 4:10; 5:2) which may be the
same mountain as Mount Sinai.

Hosea A prophet of Israel; the first of the 12
Minor Prophets of the OT.

Host; host The bread or wafer eaten at Holy
Communion.

host, heavenly 1. The celestial bodies—the sun,
moon, and stars.
all the *h.* of heaven Deut. 4:19; Jer. 8:2
worshiped all the *h.* of heaven 2 Kin. 17:16
2. The mighty army in God's service, including
the angels.
all the *h.* of them Gen. 2:1
heavens, with all their *h.* Neh. 9:6
the *h.* of them Ps. 33:6
brings out their *h.* Is. 40:26
worship the *h.* of heaven Acts 7:42

Hosts, Lord of God, first as Leader of the armies
of Israel (1 Sam. 17:45), then as Leader of
the "heavenly host."

LORD of *h.*, He is the King Ps. 24:10
LORD of *h.* is His name Is. 47:4; 51:15; Jer. 10:16;
31:35
name is the God of *h.* Amos 5:27

house 1. A dwelling place.
not covet your neighbor's *h.* Ex. 20:17
Set your *h.* in order 2 Kin. 20:1
dwell in the *h.* of the LORD Ps. 23:6
Father's *h.* are many mansions John 14:2
2. A family group; a nation.
h. divided against itself Matt. 12:25; Luke 11:17

I

idol A false god; an image or figure regarded as
an object of worship.
Do not turn to *i.* Lev. 19:4
who regard useless *i.* Ps. 31:6
gods of the peoples are *i.* Ps. 96:5
With foreign *i.* Jer. 8:19
the *i.* of the nations Jer. 14:22
keep yourselves from *i.* 1 John 5:21

image A likeness; an idol.
make man in Our *i.* Gen. 1:26
not make . . . a carved *i.* Ex. 20:4

Immanuel A Hebrew name meaning "God-
With-Us," used by Isaiah (Is. 7:14; 8:8) in
foretelling the birth of the Messiah.

immediately Right now.
i. he stumbles Matt. 13:21
end will not come *i.* Luke 21:9

Incarnation The taking by God of human
characteristics in the Person of Jesus;
God's presence on earth.

iniquity Sin; wickedness. *See* sin.
the *i.* of the fathers Ex. 20:5; Deut. 5:9
Pardon my *i.* Ps. 25:11
we bear their *i.* Lam. 5:7

intercession A plea on behalf of another; for
example, Christ's prayer for His followers
(John 17:6–26).
i. for the transgressors Is. 53:12
the Spirit Himself makes *i.* Rom. 8:26
He ever lives to make *i.* Heb. 7:25

Isaac The son of Abraham and Sarah, and half
brother of Ishmael; by his wife Rebekah
he was the father of Jacob and Esau
(Gen. 21:1–12; 22:1–19; 24:62–67; 25:9–11,
19, 20; 26:1—28:5; 35:27–29).

Isaiah A prophet of Israel; the first book of the
OT Major Prophets.

Ishmael The name of six persons in the OT, one
of them Abraham's son by Hagar (Gen. 16;
17:18–26; 21:8–21; 25:12–18).

Israel The name that Jacob received after his mysterious struggle at Jabbok (Gen. 32:22–30); also the name of the whole people descended from him. After the separation into two kingdoms under Jeroboam, the name was confined to the northern kingdom of the ten tribes.

Israelites A name applied to Israel (the people); also called "Hebrews," mostly by foreigners, as was the name "Jews"; the latter arose at the time when Judah, after the fall of the northern kingdom, represented the entire people.

Issachar The ninth son of Jacob, the fifth by Leah (Gen. 30:17, 18); ancestor of the tribe of Issachar.

J

Jacob Son of Isaac and Rebekah; younger twin brother of Esau; father of the people of Israel. Gained by craft the blessing meant for Esau; married Leah and Rachel, the daughters of his uncle Laban; received the name Israel; finally found refuge in Egypt with his favorite son, Joseph (Gen. 25:21–34; 27–35; 37:1–3; 47:28—49:33).

James The name of several persons in the NT. 1. "The Elder," son of Zebedee and brother of John; one of the 12 apostles; martyred under Herod Agrippa (Matt. 4:21; 10:2; 17:1; 20:20; 26:37; Mark 1:19, 20, 29; 3:17; 5:37; 9:2; 10:35, 41; 13:3; 14:33; Luke 5:10; 6:14; 8:51; 9:28, 54; Acts 1:13; 12:1, 2). 2. The son of Alphaeus, also one of the 12 apostles (Matt. 10:3; Mark 3:18; Luke 6:15; Acts 1:13). 3. One of the sons of Mary; known as "the Less" (Matt. 27:56; Mark 15:40; 16:1; Luke 24:10). Tradition regards James (3) to be the same person as James (2). 4. The father of Judas (Luke 6:16; Acts 1:13). 5. "The brother of the Lord"; a pillar of the church at Jerusalem; called "James the Just"; traditionally the author of the Epistle of James (Matt. 13:55; Mark 6:3; Acts 12:17; 15:13; 21:18; 1 Cor. 15:7; Gal. 1:19; 2:9, 12; James 1:1; Jude 1).

jealous Envious; suspicious; full of zeal. When used of God, jealousy describes either His anger against His unfaithful people or His zeal to protect His persecuted people. a j. God Ex. 20:5; Deut. 4:24

Jehovah The LORD; God. Used by some Bible translators for the name of the covenant God of Israel (Ex. 6:3; Ps. 83:18; Is. 12:2; 26:4). See tetragrammaton.

Jephthah A warrior of Gilead; sacrificed his daughter in fulfillment of a vow (Judg. 11:1—12:7).

Jeremiah The name of ten persons in the OT, one of them the prophet Jeremiah (c. 626–580 B.C.). His prophecies, visions, and life story are narrated in the second book of the OT Major Prophets, which bears his name. The almond branch and the boiling pot (1:11–19); the potter's wheel (18:2–10); the good and bad figs (24); Baruch records Jeremiah's prophecies (36:4–32).

Jericho An ancient city at the S end of the Jordan Valley; the fall of the city is told in Joshua 6:1–25.

Jeroboam 1. The first king of Israel (c. 922–901 B.C.); son of Nebat (1 Kin. 11:26—14:20; 2 Kin. 17:21, 22; 2 Chr. 10:2–15; 13:1–20). 2. King of Israel (c. 786–747 B.C.); son and successor of Joash (2 Kin. 14:23–29).

Jerusalem The chief city of Palestine; most sacred city of both Jews and Christians; mentioned under one name or another (Shalem; Salem; City of David; Moriah; Jebus; Zion; Ariel) in about 40 of the 66 books of the Bible. David captured the city (2 Sam. 5:6–9; 1 Chr. 11:4–8) and made it his capital; brought the ark of the Testimony to the city (2 Sam. 6:1–17). Solomon built the temple and other buildings there (1 Kin. 5–7). Captured by Nebuchadnezzar (Jer. 39); rebuilt by Ezra and Nehemiah. Several events in the life of Jesus occurred there: His presentation in the temple (Luke 2:22–38); the cleansing of the temple (John 2:13–25); the conversation with Nicodemus (John 2:23; 3:1–21); and the events of the last week of His life (Matt. 21–28; Mark 11–16; Luke 19:28–24; John 12:12–21).

Jesse Son of Obed; grandson of Boaz and Ruth; father of David (1 Sam. 16:1–13; 17:12ff).

Jesus Christ The personal name of the One whose title gave its name to the Christian religion. Since "Jesus" was a fairly common name in the first century, distinguishing phrases were used when referring to Him (Jesus of Nazareth; Jesus, Son of David; Christ Jesus; the Messiah Jesus; and Jesus Christ). The four Gospels detail His life and ministry: birth (Matt. 1:18–25; Luke 2:1–20); baptism (Matt. 3:13–17; Mark 1:9–11; Luke 3:21, 22); turns water into wine (John 2:1–12); the Sermon on the Mount (Matt. 5:1—7:29; Luke 6:20–49); stilling of the storm (Mark 4:35–41;

Luke 8:22–25); sending the unclean spirits into the swine (Mark 5:1–20); feeding of the 5,000 (Matt. 14:13–21; Mark 6:30–44; Luke 9:10–17; John 6:1–14); walking on the water (Matt. 14:22–33; Mark 6:45–52; John 6:15–21); feeding of the 4,000 (Matt. 15:32–39; Mark 8:1–10); the Transfiguration (Matt. 17:1–8; Mark 9:2–8; Luke 9:28–36); entry into Jerusalem (Matt. 21:1–10; Mark 11:1–11; Luke 19:28–44; John 12:12–19); raises Lazarus from the dead (John 11:1–44); the Lord's Supper (Matt. 26:26–29; Mark 14:22–25; Luke 22:15–20); is arrested (Matt. 26:47–56; Mark 14:43–52; Luke 22:47–50; John 18:2–12); trial before Pilate (Matt. 27:11–14; Mark 15:1–5; Luke 23:1–5; John 18:33–38); the Crucifixion and burial (Matt. 27:32–61; Mark 15:21–47; Luke 23:26–56; John 19:17–42); the Resurrection and Ascension (Matt. 28:1–20; Mark 16:1–20; Luke 24:1–53; John 20; 21).

Jews Hebrews. *See* Israelites. Jesus, King of the Jews (Matt. 27:11, 37; Mark 15:2, 12, 26; Luke 23:3, 38; John 18:33, 39; 19:3, 19).

Jezebel A Phoenician woman, wife of Ahab, king of Israel (1 Kin. 16:30, 31; 21:5–25; 2 Kin. 9:30–37).

Job Chief character in the OT Book of Job; unknown otherwise.

Joel The name of several persons in the OT, including the prophet, son of Pethuel, author of the second book of the 12 Minor Prophets.

John The name of five persons in the NT, among them: 1. John the apostle: A son of Zebedee, brother of James (Matt. 4:21, 22; Mark 1:19, 20; Luke 5:10); sometimes called "the beloved disciple" and "Saint John"; traditional author of the fourth Gospel, the three epistles of John, and the Book of Revelation. 2. John the Baptist: The son of Elizabeth and Zacharias (Luke 1:5–25, 57–66); a prophet, called the forerunner of Jesus (John 1:15–28); baptized Jesus (Matt. 3:13–17; Mark 1:9–11; Luke 3:21, 22; John 1:29–34); imprisoned by Herod and beheaded (Matt. 14:3–12; Mark 6:17–29). 3. John Mark: *See* Mark.

Jonah The name of two persons of the OT, one of whom was the prophet about whom the fifth book of the 12 Minor Prophets is written. Swallowed by a great fish (Jon. 1:17—2:10).

Jonathan The name of 15 persons in the OT, one of whom was the oldest son of Saul; David's friend (1 Sam. 13:2; 14:1–45; 19:1–7; 20).

Joppa The ancient seaport for Jerusalem (Josh. 19:46; 2 Chr. 2:16; Jon. 1:3; Acts 9:36–43).

Jordan The chief river of Palestine, flowing from the slopes of Mount Hermon through Lake Huleh and the Sea of Galilee to the Dead Sea. The waters were miraculously stopped for the Israelites to pass (Josh. 3:14—4:24). Jesus was baptized there (Matt. 3:13; Mark 1:9).

Joseph; Joses The name of 14 persons in the Bible, among them: 1. The son of Jacob and Rachel (Gen. 30:22–24); his coat of many colors (Gen. 37:3); sold into Egypt by his brothers (Gen. 37:18–36); imprisoned on false accusations (Gen. 39:7–23); interpreted Pharaoh's dreams, thus gaining favor (Gen. 41:1–36); as administrator of Egypt (Gen. 41:37—50:26); his brothers come to him for food (Gen. 42–45). 2. The husband of Mary mother of Jesus; resident of Nazareth; descended from David (Matt. 1:16–25; Luke 2:4–7; John 1:45). 3. Joseph of Arimathea: A member of the Sanhedrin; buried the body of Jesus on his own property (Matt. 27:57–60; Mark 15:43–46; Luke 23:50–53; John 19:38–42).

Joshua; Jeshua The name of several persons in the OT, the most important being Joshua, son of Nun, the central figure of the Book of Joshua. This book tells the story of Moses' successor as leader of the Israelites, the conquest of Canaan, and the division of the country among the 12 tribes. His miraculous crossing of the Jordan (Josh. 3:14—4:24); conquest of Jericho (Josh. 6:1–21).

Judah The fourth son of Jacob, by Leah (Gen. 29:31, 35); ancestor of the tribe of Judah.

Judas The name of six persons in the NT, including: 1. A brother of Jesus (Matt. 13:55; Mark 6:3). *See* Jude, The General Epistle of. 2. Judas Iscariot: One of the 12 apostles; the betrayer of Jesus (Matt. 26:20–25, 47–50; Mark 14:18–20, 43–46; Luke 22:47, 48; John 13:21–26). 3. The brother of James; one of the 12 apostles (Luke 6:16; John 14:22[?]; Acts 1:13). *See* Thaddaeus. 4. Judas Barsabas: A Jewish Christian (Acts 15:22, 27, 32).

Jude, The General Epistle of This NT letter designates its author as a "servant of Jesus Christ, and brother of James." *See* Judas (1).

Judea An area of SW Palestine; formerly called Judah.

judge To decide; form an opinion.
J. not, that you be not Matt. 7:1

judge One who forms an opinion. In the OT Book of Judges, one chosen by God to save the people from foreign oppressors; a military leader with both legislative and executive authority.
made you . . . a j. over us Ex. 2:14

Judge God; Christ.
J. of all the earth Gen. 18:25
J. of the living and the dead Acts 10:42
to God the J. of all Heb. 12:23

K

keeper One who guards or takes care of someone or something.
Am I my brother's k. Gen. 4:9

king A chief ruler; among ancient peoples, a religious leader often held to be divine. God and Jesus Christ are called "King."
trees . . . anoint a k. Judg. 9:8
My k. and my God Ps. 5:2; 84:3
the k. of glory shall Ps. 24:7
seen the K., The LORD Is. 6:5
no k. but Caesar John 19:15
K. of kings and Lord 1 Tim. 6:15

kingdom of God The eternal sovereignty or kingly rule of God, manifested in its acceptance by men on earth and the hope for the future; the central theme of Jesus' teaching. The phrase does not occur in the OT, but the idea is present in "Your kingdom," "My kingdom," etc., which are also sometimes used in the NT. "Kingdom of heaven" is used in Matthew's gospel; "kingdom of the Son of His love" (Col. 1:13); "kingdom of our Lord and Savior Jesus Christ" (2 Pet. 1:11).
Yours is the k., O LORD 1 Chr. 29:11
the scepter of Your k. Ps. 45:6
Your k. come Matt. 6:10; Luke 11:2
seek first the k. of God Matt. 6:33; Luke 12:31
with you in My Father's k. Matt. 26:29
k. of God is at hand Mark 1:15
cannot see the k. of God John 3:3
inherit the k. of God 1 Cor. 6:10; Gal. 5:21

L

ladder A framework of uprights and crosspieces on which one may ascend or descend.
Jacob dreams of a ladder (Gen. 28:12).

lamb The young of a sheep, commonly used as the sacrificial animal of the Passover.

God will provide . . . l. Gen. 22:8
a l. to the slaughter Is. 53:7
wolf and the l. shall feed Is. 65:25
Feed My l. John 21:15

Lamb (of God) Christ, whose sacrificial death removed the sins of the world. By extension of "lamb" as the most common victim of OT sacrifices, particularly the "Passover," Christ is our Passover (1 Cor. 5:7).
Behold! The l. of God John 1:29, 36
a L. without blemish 1 Pet. 1:19
stood a l. as though it had Rev. 5:6
L. slain from the foundation Rev. 13:8
L. will overcome them Rev. 17:14

lamp A device producing light.
spirit of a man is the l. Prov. 20:27
light a l. and put it Matt. 5:15
ten virgins who took their l. Matt. 25:1
light of a l. shall not shine Rev. 18:23

lampstand Particularly the seven-branched lampstand of the tabernacle and the temple, and the symbolic one of Revelation.
make a l. of pure gold Ex. 25:31
I saw seven golden l. Rev. 1:12

last The final one.
first will be l. Matt. 19:30; Mark 10:31
I am the First and the L. Rev. 1:17

Last Supper The last meal eaten by Jesus with His apostles, on the night before His crucifixion. See Holy Communion.

law Rules of conduct; particularly rules given by God to Moses by which the Israelites were to live and which were defined in the Pentateuch (the Law of Moses).
l. of the LORD is perfect Ps. 19:7
not . . . to destroy the l. Matt. 5:17
l. was given through Moses John 1:17

Lazarus 1. The beggar in a parable told by Jesus (Luke 16:19–31). 2. A friend of Jesus; brother of Martha and Mary (John 11:1–44; 12:1–11).

Leah Elder daughter of Laban; Jacob's first wife to whom were born six of his sons (Gen. 29:16—30:21).

leaven Yeast or other fermenting agent. It was forbidden to the Israelites in all offerings made with fire (Lev. 2:11; 6:17) and at the Passover (Ex. 12:17–19).
beware of the l. Matt. 16:6
a little l. leavens 1 Cor. 5:6

Lent The 40 weekdays preceding Easter; a period of fasting and repentance in Christian churches.

leopard A wild animal of the cat family.
l. shall lie down with the Is. 11:6

let Allow.
l. me first go Matt. 8:21
L. the little children Matt. 19:14; Mark 10:14;
Luke 18:16

Levi; Levites Third son of Jacob and Leah
(Gen. 29:31, 34); ancestor of the tribe of
Levites, who were charged with the care
of the tabernacle and the temple.

Leviticus The third book of the OT; it deals
mainly with the priests and their duties.

life The union of body and soul. Christ is called
the "Prince of life" (Acts 3:15).
The tree of *l.* was also Gen. 2:9
the resurrection and the *l.* John 11:25

light Brightness; radiance.
Let there be *l.* Gen. 1:3
my *l.* and my salvation Ps. 27:1
the *l.* of the world Matt. 5:14
I am the *l.* of the world John 8:12

Lights, Feast of *See* Dedication, Feast of.

lilies Flowering plants that grow from bulbs.
He feeds his flock among the *l.* Song 6:3
Consider the *l.* of the field Matt. 6:28

locusts Long-winged insects similar to
grasshoppers.
east wind brought the *l.* Ex. 10:13
you may eat: the *l.* Lev. 11:22
his food was *l.* and Matt. 3:4

lord One who has authority over persons or
things; hence, **Lord:** God, as the Supreme
Authority; Jesus, as Leader during His
ministry and as the Son of God. When
large and small capitals are used for
LORD, the original Hebrew reads YHWH
(*See* tetragrammaton).
L. Himself is God Deut. 4:35; 1 Kin. 18:39
the *L.* is one Deut. 6:4
L. of the whole earth Ps. 97:5
says to Me, *L., L.* Matt. 7:21
L. of heaven and earth Matt. 11:25
Son of Man is also *L.* Mark 2:28
My *L.* and my God John 20:28
both *L.* and Christ Acts 2:36
crucified the *L.* of glory 1 Cor. 2:8
is *L.* of *l.* and King Rev. 17:14

Lord of Hosts *See* Hosts, LORD of.

Lord's Day Sunday (Rev. 1:10).

Lord's Prayer The prayer, taught by Jesus to
His disciples, that begins "Our Father"
(Matt. 6:9–13; Luke 11:2–4).

Lord's Supper 1. Holy Communion (1 Cor. 11:20).
2. Last Supper.

lost Mislaid; not to be found.
the *l.* sheep Matt. 18:12–14; Luke 15:4–7
the *l.* coin Luke 15:8–10
the *l.* (prodigal) son Luke 15:11–32

Lot The nephew of Abraham who came with
him to Canaan (Gen. 11:27—13:12). Saved
from Sodom's destruction (Gen. 19:1–38).
His wife was turned into a pillar of salt
(Gen. 19:26).

love 1. A deep affection; devotion.
l. covers all sins Prov. 10:12
Greater *l.* has no one John 15:13
l. of money is a root 1 Tim. 6:10
God is *l.* 1 John 4:8
2. To have deep affection for someone or
something.
l. your neighbor Lev. 19:18; Matt. 22:39;
James 2:8
l. the LORD your God Deut. 6:5; Matt. 22:37
l. your enemies Matt. 5:44; Luke 6:27
God so *l.* the world John 3:16

Luke The evangelist; a companion of Paul;
a physician; traditional author of the
NT books of Luke and Acts (Col. 4:14;
2 Tim. 4:11; Philem. 24).

M

Magi The wise men who came to worship the
infant Jesus (Matt. 2:1–12); because they
offered three gifts, it is often assumed
that there were three Magi.

Magnificat The song of Mary as she rejoices in
the realization of God's redemption of His
people (Luke 1:46–55).

maker One who brings into being; creator;
hence, **Maker:** God.
more pure than his *M.* Job 4:17
man will look to his *M.* Is. 17:7
builder and *m.* is God Heb. 11:10

Malachi An OT prophet, author of the last book
of the OT, one of the 12 Minor Prophets.

man A male human being; the whole human
race.
God is not a *m.* Num. 23:19
m. is born to trouble Job 5:7
M. shall not live by Matt. 4:4
not *m.* for the Sabbath Mark 2:27

mark A sign.
set a *m.* on Cain Gen. 4:15
his *m.* on his forehead Rev. 14:9

Mark; John Mark Son of Mary of Jerusalem;
companion of Paul and other early
Christian missionaries; the traditional
author of the second Gospel (Acts 12:12,
25; 15:37).

marriage The union of one man and one
woman. Explained by Jesus (Mark 10:6–9).
are given in m. Matt. 22:30
M. is honorable among all Heb. 13:4

Mary The name of seven persons in the NT,
among them: 1. The mother of Jesus
(Matt. 1:16, 18–25; Luke 2:5–20). 2. Mary
Magdalene: A Galilean follower of Jesus
(Matt. 27:55, 56, 61; 28:1; Mark 15:40, 47;
16:1; Luke 8:2; 24:10; John 19:25; 20:1,
18). 3. The sister of Martha and Lazarus
(Luke 10:38–42; John 11:1–45; 12:1–8).
4. The mother of James "the Less"
(Matt. 27:55, 56, 61; 28:1–10; Mark 15:40, 41,
47; 16:1–8; Luke 24:1–11). 5. The mother of
John Mark (Acts 12:12).

master A male person in authority; one who
controls someone or something; owner.
is free from his m. Job 3:19
can serve two m. Matt. 6:24; Luke 16:13
nor a servant above his m. Matt. 10:24

Matthew One of the 12 apostles; called "Levi the
son of Alphaeus" in Mark 2:14; traditional
author of the first Gospel.

measure A certain amount; capacity.
have a . . . just m. Deut. 25:15
same m. you use Matt. 7:2; Mark 4:24;
Luke 6:38
good m., pressed down Luke 6:38

mediator One who acts as a go-between in
making an agreement between two
parties. Moses is so designated (Gal. 3:19)
in making the covenant at Sinai. Christ is
called the "one Mediator between God
and men" (1 Tim. 2:5).

meditate To study; contemplate.
he m. day and night Ps. 1:2

meek Humble; gentle.
m. shall inherit the earth Ps. 37:11
Blessed are the m. Matt. 5:5

merciful Forgiving; unwilling to punish.
LORD God, m. and gracious Ex. 34:6
God be m. to us Ps. 67:1
Blessed are the m. Matt. 5:7
m. to me a sinner Luke 18:13

mercy Forgiveness or kindness, particularly to a
wrongdoer.
His m. endures forever Ezra 3:11
they shall obtain m. Matt. 5:7

mercy seat Literally, "covering." The lid of the
ark of the Testimony, from above which
God spoke to His people (Ex. 25:22).

merry Joyous; happy.
m. heart makes a cheerful Prov. 15:13
m. heart does good Prov. 17:22
eat, drink, and be m. Eccl. 8:15; Luke 12:19

Meshach The Babylonian name of one of
Daniel's friends (Dan. 1:7; 3:12).

Messiah Literally, "anointed one"; one sent by
God to save others. In Hebrew belief, the
coming savior of the Jewish people; in
Christianity, Jesus.

Methuselah Noah's grandfather; lived for 969
years, the oldest person mentioned in
the Bible (Gen. 5:27).

Micah A Judean prophet, contemporary of
Isaiah, whose prophecies appear in the
OT Book of Micah, the sixth of the 12
Minor Prophets.

mighty Powerful; very strong.
He was a m. hunter Gen. 10:9
a great and m. nation Gen. 18:18
How the m. have fallen 2 Sam. 1:19
m. in deed and word Luke 24:19

ministry God's service.
to the m. of the word Acts 6:4
m. of reconciliation 2 Cor. 5:18

miracle An event that exceeds the known laws
of nature and science. Usually an act of
God done through human agents.
The OT miracles include:
ten plagues of Egypt Ex. 7:14—12:30
parting of the Red Sea Ex. 14:21–31
feeding with bread from heaven Ex. 16:14–35
walls of Jericho fall Josh. 6:1–21
strength of Samson Judg. 14:1—16:30
Elijah taken by a whirlwind 2 Kin. 2:11
Elisha revives dead child 2 Kin. 4:18–37
three men saved from furnace Dan. 3:19–27
Daniel saved from lions Dan. 6:16–23
Jonah saved Jon. 1:10—2:10
The NT miracles of Jesus include:
the leper cured Matt. 8:2, 3; Mark 1:40–42;
Luke 5:12, 13
centurion's servant healed Matt. 8:5–13;
Luke 7:1–10
the storm stilled Matt. 8:23–26;
Mark 4:35–39; Luke 8:22–24
demons entered into swine Matt. 8:28–32;
Mark 5:1–13; Luke 8:26–33
mute demoniac healed Matt. 9:32, 33
feeding the 5,000 Matt. 14:15–21;
Mark 6:35–44; Luke 9:10–17; John 6:1–14
Jesus walks on the sea Matt. 14:25–27;
Mark 6:48–51; John 6:19–21
feeding the 4,000 Matt. 15:32–38; Mark 8:1–9
ten lepers cleansed Luke 17:11–19
water changed to wine John 2:1–11
Lazarus raised from dead John 11:38–44
Other NT miracles include:
the gift of tongues Acts 2:4–11
Peter restores Tabitha Acts 9:36–41
Peter's release from prison Acts 12:5–10

mite A copper coin of small value.
widow . . . threw in two *m*. Mark 12:42

money Riches; coins.
the tax *m*. Matt. 22:19
no copper in their *m*. belts Mark 6:8
love of *m*. is a root of all . . . evil 1 Tim. 6:10

Mordecai The Jewish hero of the OT Book of Esther.

Moses The great deliverer and lawgiver of Israel; born during the oppression of the Israelites in Egypt (Ex. 1:22—2:2); brought up in Pharaoh's house (Ex. 2:5–10); fled to Midian where he lived 40 years (Ex. 2:15–25); called by God from the burning bush (Ex. 3:2–5) to deliver the Israelites; after performing ten miracles of plagues (Ex. 7:14—12:30) he got Pharaoh's consent to take the Israelites from Egypt; led them 40 years through the wilderness; received the Ten Commandments from God (Ex. 20). The OT books of Exodus, Leviticus, Numbers, and Deuteronomy detail his life and deeds.

Most High, the A name used of God.
When the *M*. divided Deut. 32:8
the *M*. rules in Dan. 4:25
the *M*. does not dwell Acts 7:48

mother Female parent.
Honor . . . your *m*. Ex. 20:12; Matt. 19:19
Like *m*., like daughter Ezek. 16:44
disciple, "Behold your *m*. John 19:27

mourn To grieve for.
Blessed are those who *m*. Matt. 5:4

murder To kill; cause the death of.
You shall not *m*. Ex. 20:13; Deut. 5:17; Matt. 5:21

myrrh An aromatic, resinous substance used in incense and perfumes.
of liquid *m*. Ex. 30:23
frankincense, and *m*. Matt. 2:11
wine mingled with *m*. Mark 15:23

N

Nahum A prophet, the prophecies of whom are given in the OT Book of Nahum, the seventh of the 12 Minor Prophets.

name The word by which a person, place, or thing is called.
n. of the LORD your God in vain Ex. 20:7
How excellent is Your *n*. Ps. 8:1
Hallowed be Your *n*. Matt. 6:9; Luke 11:2
in My *n*. Matt. 24:5; Mark 13:6; Luke 21:8
My *n*. is Legion Mark 5:9
ask the Father in My *n*. John 15:16

Naphtali The sixth son of Jacob, the second born of Bilhah (Gen. 30:7, 8); ancestor of one of the 12 tribes of Israel.

narrow Not wide; small in width.
n. is the gate . . . which Matt. 7:14

Nathan The name of six persons in the OT, one of whom was a prophet contemporary of King David (2 Sam. 7:1–17; 12:1–15, 25; 1 Kin. 1:5–48).

nation A group of people under one government or sharing the same history.
make you a great *n*. Gen. 12:2
n. will rise against *n*. Matt. 24:7; Mark 13:8

Nazareth The town in Lower Galilee where Jesus was brought up (Luke 2:39, 51).

Nebuchadnezzar King of Babylonia (605–562 B.C.).

Nehemiah The name of three persons in the OT, one of whom was the rebuilder of Jerusalem after the Babylonian Exile. The Book of Nehemiah tells his story.

neighbor A person who lives near another.
false witness against your *n*. Ex. 20:16
love your *n*. as yourself Lev. 19:18; Matt. 19:19

new Of recent origin.
nothing *n*. under the sun Eccl. 1:9
n. heavens and a *n*. earth Is. 65:17
A *n*. commandment John 13:34
the *n*. man Eph. 4:24; Col. 3:10

night The period of darkness between sunset and sunrise.
darkness He called *n*. Gen. 1:5
Watchman, what of the *n*. Is. 21:11
the *n*. is coming when no John 9:4

Nineveh One of the oldest and greatest cities of Mesopotamia; capital of Assyria; destroyed 612 B.C. (Gen. 10:11, 12; 2 Kin. 19:36; Is. 37:37; Jon. 1:2; 4:11; Nah. 1:1; 2:8; 3:7).

Noah The ninth descendant of Adam; the survivor, with his family, of the Flood (Gen. 6–9).

Nunc Dimittis The blessing offered by Simeon when Jesus was presented in the temple (Luke 2:29–32).

O

Obadiah The name of 11 persons in the OT, none of whom can be assumed to be the author of the Book of Obadiah, the shortest OT book and fourth of the 12 Minor Prophets.

offering Something given in worship. In the OT we find offerings of: 1. **grain**: Consisting

of unleavened bread, cakes, wafers, or grain mixed with salt and, except when a sin offering, with olive oil (Lev. 2:1–16; 5:11; 6:14–23; Num. 15:4, 6, 9). Sometimes accepted from the poor as a sin offering in place of the burnt offering (Lev. 5:11–13). 2. drink: Consisting of wine and used with the grain and burnt offerings, except in the sin and trespass offerings (Num. 6:17; 15:5, 10). 3. animals, or sacrifice: Cattle, sheep, and goats that were free from blemish (Lev. 1:3). These were used with: a. The burnt offering in which a male lamb, ram, goat, bull, dove, or pigeon was entirely consumed on the altar (Lev. 1; 6:9–13). b. The sin offering in which a bull, a male or female goat, a female lamb, a dove, or a pigeon was given (Lev. 4; 5:7; 6:25–30). c. The trespass offering in which a ram or lamb was used (Lev. 5:6, 15; 6:6; 7:1–8; 14:12, 21). d. The peace offering, including the giving of thanks (Lev. 7:12–15), the payment of a vow (Lev. 7:16–20; Num. 6:13–21), and the voluntary or freewill offering (Lev. 7:16–20); for these any animal without blemish of either sex could be used, except birds (Lev. 3; 7:11–27). In sacrifices, the term "wave offering" is used of those portions consecrated to the Lord by the rite of "waving" (Lev. 7:30–34; Num. 6:17–20); and the term "heave offering" is used of those portions taken away and set apart for the Lord (Lev. 7:14, 32–34; Num. 18:8–32).

oil Any of several greasy liquids that can be burned.
anoint my head with o. Ps. 23:5

Olives, Mount of; Olivet, mount called A mountain E of Jerusalem (2 Sam. 15:30; Zech. 14:4). Closely associated with the last days in the life of Jesus (in the four Gospels and Acts 1:12).

P

Palestine The Greek and Roman names for Canaan; modern usage applies the name to the territory allotted to the 12 tribes of Israel.

Palm Sunday The Sunday before Easter; commemorates the Triumphal Entry of Jesus into Jerusalem (John 12:12, 13).

parable A short story teaching a moral lesson. Among those of the OT are:
Samson's riddle Judg. 14:14
lazy man's vineyard Prov. 24:30–34
two harlots Ezek. 23

healing waters Ezek. 47:1–12
In the NT, parables are only by Jesus, and include:
lamp under a basket Matt. 5:14–16; Mark 4:21–23; Luke 8:16–18
unshrunk cloth on an old garment Matt. 9:16, 17; Mark 2:21, 22; Luke 5:36–39
tares among wheat Matt. 13:24–30
the mustard seed Matt. 13:31, 32; Mark 4:30–32; Luke 13:18, 19
lost sheep Matt. 18:12–14; Luke 15:4–7
laborers in vineyard Matt. 20:1–16
wise and foolish virgins Matt. 25:1–13
the talents Matt. 25:14–30
two debtors Luke 7:41–50
Good Samaritan Luke 10:30–37
Prodigal Son Luke 15:11–32
Pharisee and tax collector Luke 18:9–14
shepherd and the sheep John 10:1–30

Parousia A Greek word adopted as the technical term for the coming of Christ at the end of history; the Second Coming. The English word is coming (Matt. 24:3; 1 Cor. 15:23; 1 Thess. 2:19). Descriptions of the Parousia (Matt. 24:4–44; 25:31–46; Mark 13:5–37; Luke 21:8–36).

paschal Relating to Passover or to Easter.

Passover 1. A seven-day Jewish festival held in March or April, commemorating the slaying of the firstborn just before the Israelites were freed from slavery in Egypt (Ex. 12); combined with the Feast of Unleavened Bread which commemorates the actual Exodus flight (Ex. 13:3–16). 2. The sacrificial lamb of the Passover (Ex. 12:11, 21, 27). Paul refers to Christ as the Paschal Lamb.
Christ, our P., was sacrificed 1 Cor. 5:7

Pastoral Epistles The epistles to Timothy and Titus are so called because they deal chiefly with directions about the work of the pastor of a church.

pasture Grassy land where cattle and sheep graze.
me to lie down in green p. Ps. 23:2

Paul As Saul, the son of Hebrew parents, he persecuted the followers of Jesus (Acts 8:3; Gal. 1:13). Miraculously converted (Acts 9:1ff) and name changed to Paul (Acts 13:9), he became the leading missionary of early Christianity. His life is detailed in the NT Book of Acts. He founded many churches in Asia Minor and Greece and carried on extensive correspondence with them.

peace Freedom from turmoil and war.
of war, And a time of p. Eccl. 3:8

is no *p*. . . . for the wicked Is. 57:21
not come to bring *p*. but a sword Matt. 10:34
on earth *p*., goodwill Luke 2:14
P. to you Luke 24:36; John 20:19

peeled Stripped off the bark.
rods which he had *p*. Gen. 30:38

Pentateuch The first five books of the OT.

Pentecost A Jewish festival on the fiftieth day
after Passover; also called Feast of Weeks
(Lev. 23:15, 16). Observed by the Christian
church as the day on which the gift of
the Holy Spirit was given to the church
(Acts 2:1).

perish To die; to be destroyed.
way of the ungodly shall *p*. Ps. 1:6
believes in Him should not *p*. John 3:15

Peter; Simon Peter A fisherman on the Sea
of Galilee who was called with his
brother Andrew by Jesus (Matt. 4:18–20;
Mark 1:16–18; Luke 5:1–11; John 1:35–41).
He became the "first" of the 12 apostles
(Matt. 10:2), and sometimes spoke for
all the disciples. Jesus changed his
name from Simon to Peter (Matt. 16:18;
Mark 3:16; Luke 6:14; John 1:42).
His mother-in-law healed by Jesus
(Matt. 8:14, 15; Mark 1:30, 31; Luke 4:38,
39); his confession that Jesus is the
Christ (Matt. 16:16; Mark 8:29; Luke 9:20);
his denial of Jesus (Matt. 26:69–75;
Mark 14:66–72; Luke 22:54–62). The
traditional author of two NT epistles.

Pharaoh A title used as a name, or prefixed
to a name, of the king of Egypt. Joseph
interprets Pharaoh's dream (Gen. 41:1–36);
the Pharaoh of the Exodus (Ex. 7–14).

Pharisee A member of a strict Jewish sect,
holding the Mosaic Law and their own
traditions as binding. The parable of the
Pharisee and the publican (Luke 18:9–14).

Philemon A Christian of Colosse to whom the
NT Epistle to Philemon was written by
Paul. In the letter Paul asks Philemon to
pardon Onesimus, a runaway slave whom
Paul has converted.

Philip The name of four persons in the NT,
among them: 1. The apostle (Matt. 10:3;
Mark 3:18; Luke 6:14; John 1:43–48;
6:5, 7; 12:21, 22; 14:8, 9; Acts 1:13). 2. The
evangelist (Acts 6:5; 8:5–40; 21:8).

Philippi; Philippians A city of Macedonia
where Paul founded his first Christian
congregation in Europe. The NT Epistle to
the Philippians was written by Paul to the
church there.

Philistines The people who lived along the S
coast of Palestine; often at war with the
Israelites. Goliath was a champion of the
Philistines (1 Sam. 17:23–51).

Phoenicia A country W of the Lebanon
range and Galilee on the coast of the
Mediterranean Sea (Acts 11:19; 15:3; 21:2);
its chief cities were Tyre and Sidon.

physician A medical doctor.
Is there no *p*. there Jer. 8:22
who are well have no need of a *p*. Matt. 9:12
P., heal yourself Luke 4:23
Luke the beloved *p*. Col. 4:14

Pilate; Pontius Pilate The Roman governor
of Judea (A.D. 26–36); the judge
in the trial and execution of Jesus
(Matt. 27:1–26; Mark 15:1–15; Luke 23:1–25;
John 18:28—19:16).

pillar An upright column.
became a *p*. of salt Gen. 19:26
by day in a *p*. of cloud Ex. 13:21
by night in a *p*. of fire Ex. 13:21

plank A log; a piece of timber.
remove the *p*. Matt. 7:5

plowing will be neither *p*. nor harvesting
Gen. 45:6
in *p*. time and in harvest Ex. 34:21

plowshare The cutting blade of a plow.
their swords into *p*. Is. 2:4
Beat your *p*. into swords Joel 3:10

poor Needy; having little or no goods or money.
the *p*. shall not give less Ex. 30:15
Blessed are the *p*. in spirit Matt. 5:3
have the *p*. with you always Matt. 26:11;
Mark 14:7

prayer Words addressed to God.
house of *p*. Is. 56:7; Matt. 21:13; Mark 11:17;
Luke 19:46
by *p*. and fasting Matt. 17:21; Mark 9:29
you ask in *p*. Matt. 21:22

pride Conceit; vanity.
P. goes before destruction Prov. 16:18

priest A minister. Aaron and his sons, of the
tribe of Levi, were appointed to the
priesthood at Sinai; the office became
hereditary and restricted to that family
(Ex. 28:1; 40:12–15).
p. of God Most High Gen. 14:18

prince One who has authority or influence; a
ruler; hence, Prince: the Messiah; Christ.
made you a *p*. . . . over us Ex. 2:14
Do not put your trust in *p*. Ps. 146:3
P. of Peace Is. 9:6
the *p*. of princes Dan. 8:25
killed the *p*. of life Acts 3:15

prodigal Wasteful. The parable of the Prodigal Son is given in Luke 15:11–32.

prophet A man called by God to be His spokesman.
I will raise up for them a *p.* Deut. 18:18
p. is not without honor Matt. 13:57; Mark 6:4; John 4:44
no *p.* is accepted in his Luke 4:24

propitiation Expiation; removal of guilt by atonement (Rom. 3:25; 1 John 2:2; 4:10).

proselyte A convert.
to win one *p.* Matt. 23:15

Protestant Of or pertaining to any Christian church that grew out of the Reformation or that has developed since then; a member of such church.

psalms (sälms) Songs of praise, particularly those from the OT Book of Psalms.
shout joyfully to Him with *p.* Ps. 95:2
said in the Book of *p.* Luke 20:42
Let him sing *p.* James 5:13

Purim A Jewish festival celebrating the deliverance from massacre (Esth. 9:20–28).

R

Rabbi Master; Teacher.
They said to Him, "*R.* John 1:38

Rachel The younger daughter of Laban; Jacob's second wife; mother of Joseph and Benjamin (Gen. 29:1—31:35; 35:16–19).

Rebekah Wife of Isaac; mother of Esau and Jacob (Gen. 24:10–67; 25:20–26, 28; 26:6–11; 27:5–17).

redeemer One who buys back, rescues (as from sin), or ransoms. Jesus is called "the Redeemer," through His sacrificial death, although the word does not appear in the NT.
I know that my *R.* lives Job 19:25
LORD, my strength and my *R.* Ps. 19:14
R. will come to Zion Is. 59:20

Red Sea; Sea of Reeds The body of water between Arabia and Africa; the miraculous parting of the sea (Ex. 14:21–31) enabled the Israelites to escape the Egyptians.

remember To bring to mind again.
R. the Sabbath day Ex. 20:8
R. Lot's wife Luke 17:32

repent To feel regret; to change one's mind about.
r. in dust and ashes Job 42:6
R., for the kingdom Matt. 3:2

unless you *r.* you will Luke 13:3
R., and . . . be baptized Acts 2:38
R. therefore and be Acts 3:19

rest Repose; quietness.
seventh day you shall *r.* Ex. 23:12
the weary are at *r.* Job 3:17
R. in the LORD Ps. 37:7
labor and have no *r.* Lam. 5:5
I will give you *r.* Matt. 11:28

resurrection A rising from the dead; a return to life; hence, Resurrection: The rising of Christ from the dead (Matt. 28; Mark 16; Luke 24; John 20; 1 Cor. 15).
there is no *r.* Matt. 22:23; Mark 12:18
I am the *r.* and the life John 11:25
This is the first *r.* Rev. 20:5

Reuben; Reubenites The firstborn son of Jacob, by Leah (Gen. 29:32); the ancestor of the tribe of Reuben.

revelation The making known of something previously concealed.
through the *r.* of Jesus Christ Gal. 1:12
The *r.* of Jesus Christ Rev. 1:1

reward To give payment for something done; used particularly of God's blessing upon the obedient and His punishment of the wicked.
r. in heaven Matt. 5:12; Luke 6:23
receive his own *r.* 1 Cor. 3:8

rich Wealthy; having money or property.
Do not overwork to be *r.* Prov. 23:4
for he was very *r.* Luke 18:23

riches Wealth; property; material goods.
r. are not forever Prov. 27:24
deceitfulness of *r.* Matt. 13:22; Mark 4:19

righteous One who does what is right; a virtuous person.
LORD knows the way of the *r.* Ps. 1:6
not come to call the *r.* Matt. 9:13

righteousness Virtue; right action; particularly, conformity to God's will.
in the paths of *r.* Ps. 23:3
hunger and thirst for *r.* Matt. 5:6
grace might reign through *r.* Rom. 5:21

rock A mass of stone; anything hard like a rock.
are my *r.* and my fortress Ps. 31:3
on this *r.* I will build Matt. 16:18

Rock The Lord.
Of the *R.* who begot you Deut. 32:18
The LORD is my *r.* Ps. 18:2

Rome; Romans The capital of the Roman Empire; Christianity probably came to Rome early in the apostolic age. Paul wrote the NT Epistle to the Romans to the Christian community there.

rooster before the r. crows Matt. 26:34, 75

Ruth A Moabite woman who became an ancestress of David through her second marriage, to Boaz. Her story of devotion is told in the OT Book of Ruth.

S

Sabbath The day of rest ordained by God. Among Jews, the seventh day (Saturday); among Christians, the first day of the week (Sunday), the day of divine worship (1 Cor. 16:2).
Remember the S. day Ex. 20:8
a s. of solemn rest for you Lev. 16:31
S. was made for man Mark 2:27

sacrament One of the especially sacred ceremonies in Christian churches, including baptism and Holy Communion or the Lord's Supper; referred to by some Christian churches as ordinances.

sacrifice An offering, usually of the life of a person or an animal, made to God.
s. to the LORD Ex. 5:17
to love Him . . . is more than . . . s. Mark 12:33
put away sin by the s. of Heb. 9:26

Sadducees The aristocratic party of the Jews at the time of Christ. They collaborated with the Romans to maintain their favorable status.

salt A seasoning; a preservative.
became a pillar of s. Gen. 19:26
You are the s. of the earth Matt. 5:13

salvation Deliverance from evil, danger, or trouble; God's gift, through Christ, to save men's souls.
the God of my s. Ps. 25:5
to the Rock of our s. Ps. 95:1
shall see the s. of God Luke 3:6
grace of God that brings s. Titus 2:11
the captain of their s. Heb. 2:10

Samaria; Samaritans The capital city of the northern kingdom, Israel. Also the name of the territory near the city. The term "Samaritan" is usually applied to a member of a religious sect living in that area. The parable of the Good Samaritan told by Jesus (Luke 10:30–37).

Samson A hero of the tribe of Dan, noted for his great strength (Judg. 13–16).

Samuel The last "judge" of Israel; a prophet of the eleventh century B.C. The two OT books of Samuel record his life and deeds and the history of Israel through the reigns of Solomon and David. The Lord calls Samuel (1 Sam. 3); Samuel anoints David (1 Sam. 16:11–13).

sanctify To set apart as holy; to consecrate to religious use; to make holy.
seventh day and s. it Gen. 2:3
s. by the Holy Spirit Rom. 15:16

sanctuary A building or place set apart for religious worship; in the OT, the tabernacle (Ex. 25:8) or the temple (1 Chr. 22:19).

sand Tiny particles of rock, especially as found in deserts and along seashores.
make your descendants as the s. of Gen. 32:12
built his house on the s. Matt. 7:26

sandal strap Thong to fasten a sandal.
whose s. I am not worthy John 1:27

Sarah; Sarai The wife of Abraham; mother of Isaac in accord with divine promise (Gen. 17:15–21; 18:1–15).

Satan The devil; the adversary of God and Christ.
S. casts out S. Matt. 12:26; Mark 3:23
forty days, tempted by S. Mark 1:13
lest S. should take advantage 2 Cor. 2:11
S. will be released from Rev. 20:7

Saul Son of Kish, of the tribe of Benjamin; first king over Israel. The prophet Samuel anoints him to be king (1 Sam. 10:1); he disobeys the Lord (1 Sam. 15); David enters his service (1 Sam. 16:14–23); he tries to kill David (1 Sam. 19:9, 10); David spares his life (1 Sam. 26:6–24).

Saul of Tarsus See Paul.

Savior Literally, "one who saves or delivers"; Christ, as the One who delivers us from the sins of this life and through whom salvation is obtained; God, as the Deliverer of the Israelites from oppression and as the Redeemer of all peoples.
my refuge; My S. 2 Sam. 22:3
A just God and a S. Is. 45:21
rejoiced in God my S. Luke 1:47
Christ, the S. of the world John 4:42
Christ . . . the S. of the body Eph. 5:23
S., the Lord Jesus Christ Phil. 3:20
God our S., Who alone is wise Jude 25

scripture Any writing, particularly that of a sacred nature; hence, Scripture: the Bible. Also "Scriptures"; "Holy Scripture"; "Holy Scriptures."
Have you not read this S. Mark 12:10
search the S. John 5:39
S. is given by inspiration 2 Tim. 3:16

seek To search for; to try to find.
s., and you will find Matt. 7:7; Luke 11:9
none who s. after God Rom. 3:11

Semites The people descended from Shem, the son of Noah (Gen. 5:32), or those speaking one of the Semitic languages.

Sermon on the Mount Name given to a talk by Jesus while teaching His disciples in the hill country of Galilee early in His ministry (Matt. 5:3—7:27). It includes a series of blessings, the Beatitudes (5:3–12); the Lord's Prayer (6:9–13); and the Golden Rule (7:12). A similar discourse in Luke 6:17–49 is called the "Sermon on the Plain."

serpent A snake; in biblical usage, many times synonymous with "Satan."
s. was more cunning than Gen. 3:1
will take up s. Mark 16:18
s. deceived Eve 2 Cor. 11:3
s. of old, who is the Devil Rev. 20:2

Shadrach The Babylonian name of one of Daniel's companions (Dan. 1:7; 3:12).

Sheba, queen of A queen, probably Arabian, who came to test Solomon's wisdom (1 Kin. 10:1–13; 2 Chr. 9:1–12).

Shem The eldest son of Noah who stands as the ancestor of the Semites generally and of the Hebrews specifically (Gen. 5:32; 9:18–27; 10:21–31; Luke 3:36).

shepherd One who herds and takes care of sheep; by extension, the ruler or king of a people. The Lord is the Shepherd of Israel; Christ is the Good Shepherd (John 10:7–18).
The LORD is my s. Ps. 23:1
s. . . . keeping watch over Luke 2:8
one flock and one s. John 10:16
Lord Jesus . . . that great S. Heb. 13:20

Shiloh A city of Ephraim, 10 mi. NE of Bethel; site of the ark of the Testimony and the tabernacle from the time of Joshua to Samuel.

Silas; Silvanus One of the earliest of the apostolic missionaries, associated with both Paul (Acts 16:19ff; 1 Thess. 1:1; 2:1, 2) and Peter (1 Pet. 5:12).

Simeon The name of six persons in the Bible, including: 1. The second son of Jacob, by Leah (Gen. 29:33); ancestor of the tribe of Simeon. 2. A devout man who blessed the infant Jesus when His parents presented Him in the temple (Luke 2:25–35).

Simon The name of nine persons in the NT, including: 1. Simon Peter: See Peter (Matt. 16:17, 18; John 1:42). 2. Simon the Zealot: Also one of the 12 apostles (Luke 6:15). 3. Simon the Pharisee, in whose home Jesus was anointed by the

sinful woman (Luke 7:36–50). 4. Simon the leper, in whose home Jesus was anointed by Mary (Mark 14:3–9; John 12:1–8). 5. Simon of Cyrene, who was forced to carry Jesus' cross (Matt. 27:32; Mark 15:21; Luke 23:26). 6. Simon the sorcerer, who offered money to Peter and John for the power of the Holy Spirit (Acts 8:9–24).

sin 1. An offense or revolt against God (as Adam and Eve in the Garden of Eden); deliberate defiance; wickedness; iniquity; ungodliness.
put to death for his own s. Deut. 24:16
our s. testify against us Is. 59:12
power on earth to forgive s. Matt. 9:6
Who can forgive s. Mark 2:7; Luke 5:21
takes away the s. of John 1:29
He who is without s. John 8:7
gave Himself for our s. Gal. 1:4
2. To commit an offense against God; to be wicked.
is no one who does not s. 1 Kin. 8:46
soul who s. shall die Ezek. 18:4
S. no more, lest John 5:14
cannot s., because he has been born of God 1 John 3:9

Sinai, Mount The sacred mountain where God made the covenant with Israel (Ex. 19–24), near the S end of the Sinai Peninsula. May be the same place as Mount Horeb.

sinful Wicked; full of iniquity.
s. nation, A people laden Is. 1:4
in the likeness of s. flesh Rom. 8:3

sinner One who commits an offense against God.
stands in the path of s. Ps. 1:1
Why does your Teacher eat with . . . s. Matt. 9:11; Mark 2:16; Luke 5:30
come to call . . . s., to repentance Matt. 9:13; Mark 2:17; Luke 5:32
over one s. who repents Luke 15:7
be merciful to me a s. Luke 18:13

Sodom One of the two cities destroyed by the Lord because of their wickedness (Gen. 19:24–28).

Solomon Son of David and Bathsheba; third king of Israel; under his reign the kingdom reached its zenith; noted for his wisdom (1 Kin. 3:16–28) and his gift of expressing himself. The OT books of Proverbs, Ecclesiastes, and Song of Solomon, and Psalms 72 and 127 are attributed to him. He built the temple (1 Kin. 6; 7; 2 Chr. 3); was visited by the queen of Sheba (1 Kin. 10:1–13; 2 Chr. 9:1–12).

son A male child or man as related to his parents; a male descendant.
wise s. makes a glad father Prov. 10:1

Unto us a *s.* is given Is. 9:6

Is this not the carpenter's *s.* Matt. 13:55

Son; Son of God The Second Person of the
Trinity; Christ.

is My beloved *S.* Matt. 3:17; 17:5; Mark 1:11;
Luke 9:35

S. of the living God Matt. 16:16; John 6:69

this is the *S.* of God John 1:34

gave His only begotten *S.* John 3:16

son of man Any human being (Ps. 8:4); the
prophet Ezekiel (used throughout the OT
Book of Ezekiel); in the Gospels, Jesus
uses "Son of Man" as a self-designation,
particularly in the passages relating to
the Parousia.

sons of God Angels (Job 1:6; Dan. 3:25); any
human beings, as created in God's image
(Hos. 1:10); Christians (Rom. 8:14).

soul The life principle of a human being; the
immortal element of man; the spirit; the
living individual.

obey . . . with all your *s.* Deut. 30:2

Hear, and your *s.* shall live Is. 55:3

all *s.* are Mine Ezek. 18:4

destroy both *s.* and body Matt. 10:28

loses his own *s.* Matt. 16:26; Mark 8:36

s. be subject to the governing Rom. 13:1

sow To plant.

s. in tears Shall reap in joy Ps. 126:5

man *s.*, that he will also reap Gal. 6:7

spirit That part of a person's being thought of
as the center of life, the will, thinking,
feeling; that part of man that survives
death.

Into Your hand I commit my *s.* Ps. 31:5

a haughty *s.* before Prov. 16:18

yielded up His *s.* Matt. 27:50; John 19:30

The *s.* indeed is willing Matt. 26:41; Mark 14:38

to the *s.* of just men Heb. 12:23

Spirit, Holy The Third Person of the Trinity; that
divine Spirit, referred to in the OT as
"Spirit of the LORD" or "Spirit of God,"
through which men receive power,
particularly effective through Jesus Christ
in bringing men into fellowship with God.
Some Bible translators use "Holy Ghost"
rather than "Holy Spirit."

in the name of the . . . Holy *S.* Matt. 28:19

baptize you with the Holy *S.* Matt. 3:11;
Mark 1:8; Luke 3:16; John 1:33

be filled with the Holy *S.* Luke 1:15

Holy *S.* was not yet given John 7:39

Helper, the Holy *S.* John 14:26

promise of the Holy *S.* Acts 2:33

witness in the Holy *S.* Rom. 9:1

except by the Holy *S.* 1 Cor. 12:3

communion of the Holy *S.* 2 Cor. 13:14

Spirit of the Lord; Spirit of God; Holy Spirit
The divine source of all life; a special
manifestation of God's divine Presence.

S. of God was hovering Gen. 1:2

S. is poured upon us Is. 32:15

S. of the Lord GOD is Is. 61:1; Luke 4:18

S. descending . . . like a dove Mark 1:10;
John 1:32

God is *S.* John 4:24

not grieve the Holy *S.* of God Eph. 4:30

Stephen The first Christian martyr; one of the
seven men chosen by the apostles for the
special "service of tables"; his death was
the signal for a general persecution of the
Christians (Acts 6:1—8:3).

stew A thick soup.

Esau sells birthright for *s.* Gen. 25:29–34

steward A manager of a household or of
property; used of Christians, particularly
ministers, as guardians of the affairs of
God.

faithful and wise *s.* Luke 12:42

s. of the mysteries of God 1 Cor. 4:1

s. of the manifold grace of God 1 Pet. 4:10

stone A rock; a hard mineral.

dash your foot against a *s.* Ps. 91:12; Matt. 4:6;
Luke 4:11

not one *s.* . . . . upon another Matt. 24:2;
Mark 13:2; Luke 19:44; 21:6

s. to become bread Luke 4:3

sufficient Enough; ample.

S. for the day is its own Matt. 6:34

Supper, Last *See* Holy Communion.

Supper, Lord's *See* Holy Communion.

swear To declare under oath.

not *s.* by My name falsely Lev. 19:12

not *s.* at all Matt. 5:34

sword A sharp-bladed weapon with a hilt or
handle.

beat their *s.* into plowshares Is. 2:4; Mic. 4:3

Beat your plowshares into *s.* Joel 3:10

sharper than any two-edged *s.* Heb. 4:12

synagogue A building where Jewish religious
services and schools and other meetings
are held.

preached the word of God in the *s.* Acts 13:5

T

tabernacle Literally, "tent of meeting"; the
portable shelter used by the Israelites as
a place of worship.

pattern of the *t.* Ex. 25:9

Tabernacles, Feast of One of the three great
joyous festivals of the Jewish year; held

in autumn at the end of the harvest; celebrates a renewal of the covenant and recalls the wilderness pilgrimage (Ex. 23:16; Lev. 23:34–36; Deut. 16:13–15). Also called "Feast of Booths" (Lev. 23:42); "the Feast of Ingathering" (Ex. 23:16; 34:22).

tablets Flat stones bearing inscriptions.
two *t.* of the Testimony Ex. 31:18

talent A unit of money or of weight. Parable of the talents (Matt. 25:14–30).

tax collector Matthew the *t.* Matt. 10:3
a friend of *t.* and sinners Matt. 11:19
saw a *t.* named Levi Luke 5:27

Teacher Title, used of Jesus during His ministry.
your *T.*, the Christ Matt. 23:8, 10
trouble the *T.* Mark 5:35
call Me *T.* and Lord John 13:13

temple A building for the worship of a deity; hence, the temple at Jerusalem.

Temple, Solomon's *See* 1 Kings 5–8 for description of Solomon's temple.
LORD is in His holy *t.* Ps. 11:4
destroy the *t.* of God Matt. 26:61; 27:40; Mark 15:29; John 2:19

temptation An attempt to get someone to do something wrong; a test of character.
not lead us into *t.* Matt. 6:13; Luke 11:4

temptations of Jesus *See* Matthew 4:1–11; Luke 4:1–13.

Ten Commandments The ten laws given by God to Moses on Mount Sinai (Ex. 20:1–17; Deut. 5:6–21).

tent of meeting *See* tabernacle.

testimony In OT: the divine law, especially the Ten Commandments; in NT: witness.
law and to the *t.* Is. 8:20
know that his *t.* is true John 21:24
to the *t.* of Jesus Christ Rev. 1:2

tetragrammaton The four letters YHWH forming the sacred name of the Supreme Deity. Whenever the words LORD and GOD appear in large and small capital letters in the OT, the original Hebrew text uses YHWH.

Thaddaeus One of the 12 apostles of Jesus (Mark 3:18), also called Lebbaeus (Matt. 10:3) and probably Judas. *See* Judas (3).

Thessalonica; Thessalonians An important city of Macedonia where Paul and his associates founded an early Christian church. The two NT epistles to the Thessalonians were among the earliest written by Paul.

Thomas One of the 12 apostles; his incredulity of Jesus' resurrection gained him the name "doubting Thomas" (Matt. 10:3; Mark 3:18; Luke 6:15; John 11:16; 14:5; 20:24–29; Acts 1:13).

Timothy A trusted companion and assistant of Paul, from the early part of the latter's second missionary journey. According to tradition the two epistles to Timothy were written near the close of Paul's life.

tithe The tenth part of one's income paid to support God's work (Lev. 27:30–32).

Titus A gentile Christian associate of Paul (2 Cor. 7:5–7); according to Titus 1:4, 5, Paul wrote the letter bearing his name in order to encourage him in his work in the churches of Crete.

tomb A place of burial.
like whitewashed *t.* Matt. 23:27

Transfiguration Jesus' glorious and radiant change in appearance; witnessed by three disciples (Matt. 17:1–9; Mark 9:2–10; Luke 9:28–36; 2 Pet. 1:16–18).

transgression A sin; rebellion against God's will.
t. of Adam Rom. 5:14

tree A large woody plant with a long trunk.
eat the fruit of the *t.* Gen. 3:2
t. Planted by the rivers Ps. 1:3
good *t.* bears good fruit Matt. 7:17

trespass An offense against God or man. In OT, an animal sacrifice was made for a trespass offering (Lev. 6:6).
if you forgive men their *t.* Matt. 6:14

Trinity The doctrine held by most Christians that there are three divine Persons (Father, Son, and Holy Spirit) united in the one Supreme Divine Being. NT teachings (Matt. 12:32; 28:19; Luke 12:10; Acts 2:33; 1 Cor. 12:4–6; 2 Cor. 13:14) support this doctrine.

trumpet In biblical times, a straight horn of metal, shell, or bone; sometimes the ram's horn; used in ritual.
When the *t.* sounds Ex. 19:13
priests blew the *t.* Josh. 6:20
Gideon's men blew the *t.* Judg. 7:20
with shouting and *t.* 2 Chr. 15:14

trust To have or put confidence in someone or something.
T. in the LORD with all Prov. 3:5
those who *t.* in riches Mark 10:24

truth A proven sincerity, verity, honesty; righteousness.
A God of *t.* and without Deut. 32:4
t. shall make you free John 8:32

I am the way, the *t*. John 14:6
He, the Spirit of *t*., has John 16:13

tunic An outer garment.
made him a *t*. of many colors Gen. 37:3
do not have two *t*. Luke 9:3

U

Ur An ancient city on the Euphrates, called "Ur of the Chaldees"; home of Abraham (Gen. 11:28).

Uzziah The name of three persons in the OT, one of them a king of Judah (c. 783–742 B.C.).

V

vanity Futility; emptiness.
V. of *v*., all is *v*. Eccl. 1:2

viper A poisonous snake.
stings like a *v*. Prov. 23:32

vision Something seen other than by ordinary sight, as in a dream. God's revelations to the prophets were usually by visions.
They err in *v*. Is. 28:7
revealed to Daniel in a night *v*. Dan. 2:19
Tell the *v*. to no one Matt. 17:9

voice A sound uttered through the mouth as in speaking.
a still small *v*. 1 Kin. 19:12
v. of the turtledove Is heard Song 2:12
v. of one crying Is. 40:3; Matt. 3:3; Mark 1:3; Luke 3:4; John 1:23

W

wages The payment for services.
be content with your *w*. Luke 3:14
the *w*. of sin is death Rom. 6:23

walk To move by stepping.
w. through the valley of Ps. 23:4
saw Him *w*. on the sea Matt. 14:26
shall not *w*. in darkness John 8:12

want To lack or need (not in the sense of "to desire").
I shall not *w*. Ps. 23:1

war Fighting with weapons between large groups.
A time of *w*., And a time Eccl. 3:8
w. and rumors of *w*. Matt. 24:6; Mark 13:7; Luke 21:9

wash To clean with water or other liquid.
w. His feet with her tears Luke 7:38
w. the disciples' feet John 13:5

water The colorless fluid that falls as rain.
over the face of the *w*. Gen. 1:2
the flood of *w*. was on Gen. 7:6

Planted by the rivers of *w*. Ps. 1:3
me beside the still *w*. Ps. 23:2
Cast your bread upon the *w*. Eccl. 11:1
baptized you with *w*. Mark 1:8; Luke 3:16; John 1:26

way The direction; path; man's mode of living.
the *w*. of the righteous Ps. 1:6
Train up a child in the *w*. Prov. 22:6
Prepare the *w*. of the LORD Is. 40:3; Matt. 3:3; Mark 1:3; Luke 3:4; John 1:23
I am the *w*., the truth John 14:6

Weeks, Feast of Seven weeks after Passover (Lev. 23:15–21; Deut. 16:9–12). Also called Feast of Harvest (Ex. 23:16). *See* Pentecost.

will Desire; something wished.
Your *w*. be done Matt. 6:10; Luke 11:2
good *w*. toward men Luke 2:14

wine The fermented juice of fruits.
W. is a mocker Prov. 20:1
new *w*. into new wineskins Matt. 9:17; Mark 2:22; Luke 5:38

wise Having good judgment.
tree desirable to make one *w*. Gen. 3:6
man *w*. in his own eyes Prov. 26:12
w. men from the East Matt. 2:1

witness Someone or something that bears testimony to the truthfulness of a statement or to the occurrence of a happening.
be a *w*. between you Gen. 31:44
as a *w*. to all the nations Matt. 24:14
My *w*. is true John 8:14
The people . . . bore *w*. John 12:17
God is my *w*., whom Rom. 1:9
bore *w*. to the word Rev. 1:2

word A spoken sound having meaning.
God spoke all these *w*. Ex. 20:1
w. fitly spoken is like Prov. 25:11

Word; Word of God; word of the Lord God's revealed will; the Holy Scriptures.
the *w*. is very near Deut. 30:14; Rom. 10:8
By the *w*. of the LORD Ps. 33:6
hear the *w*. of the LORD Jer. 29:20
hear the *w*. of God Luke 8:21
for the *w*. of God Rev. 1:9

Word; Word of God A title of Christ.
the *W*. was God John 1:1
concerning the *W*. of life 1 John 1:1
is called The *W*. of God Rev. 19:13

work 1. Labor; effort.
God ended His *w*. Gen. 2:2
the *w*. of Your fingers Ps. 8:3
2. To labor; to toil.
Father has been *w*. John 5:17
all things *w*. together Rom. 8:28
faith *w*. through love Gal. 5:6

works Deeds; efforts.
according to his *w.* Matt. 16:27; 2 Tim. 4:14
w. which the Father John 5:36
its *w.* are evil John 7:7
not of *w.*, lest anyone Eph. 2:9

world The earth; the universe.
the *w.* is Mine, and all Ps. 50:12
You are the light of the *w.* Matt. 5:14
gains the whole *w.* Matt. 16:26
God so loved the *w.* John 3:16
I am the light of the *w.* John 8:12
brought nothing into this *w.* 1 Tim. 6:7

worry Be or become anxious.
by *w.* can add one cubit Matt. 6:27
do not *w.* about tomorrow Matt. 6:34
do not *w.* beforehand Mark 13:11
do not *w.* about your life Luke 12:22

worship To honor; to show reverence for.
you shall *w.* no other god Ex. 34:14
w. at His footstool Ps. 99:5
w. the LORD your God Matt. 4:10; Luke 4:8
where one ought to *w.* John 4:20

wrath Great anger, especially God's punishment
of sin.
soft answer turns away *w.* Prov. 15:1
w. to come Matt. 3:7; Luke 3:7
w. in the day of *w.* Rom. 2:5
delivers us from the *w.* 1 Thess. 1:10

Y

Yahweh The covenant God of Israel, YHWH in
the original Hebrew. According to Jewish
custom, because of reverence the divine
name was not to be spoken, so the
Hebrew words for Lord and God were
substituted. Whenever the words LORD
and GOD appear in large and small capital
letters, the original Hebrew reads YHWH.

Z

Zacchaeus Chief tax collector of Jericho at the
time of one of Jesus' visits (Luke 19:2–8).

Zacharias *See* Zechariah.

Zealot A term used to designate the more
radical Jewish rebels against foreign,
particularly Roman, rule; one motivated
by zeal for the Jewish law.

Zebedee The father of the apostles James and
John (Matt. 4:21; Mark 1:19, 20; Luke 5:10;
John 21:2).

Zebulun The tenth son of Jacob, the sixth by
Leah (Gen. 30:19, 20); ancestor of the
tribe of Zebulun.

Zechariah; Zecher; Zacharias The name of 33
persons in the Bible, including: 1. Son
of the priest Jehoiada (2 Chr. 24:20,
21). 2. One of the OT minor prophets;
contemporary of Haggai; urged the
rebuilding of the temple (Ezra 5:1; 6:14;
Zech. 1:1, 7; 7:1, 8). 3. The father of John the
Baptist (Luke 1:5–67; 3:2).

Zedekiah The name of three persons in the OT,
including the last king of Judah (c. 597–
587 B.C.). Also called Mattaniah (2 Kin.
24:17—25:7).

Zephaniah The name of four persons in the OT,
including a prophet during the time of
Josiah; his prophecies appear in the OT
Book of Zephaniah, the ninth of the 12
Minor Prophets.

Zion; Sion Originally the name of the fortified
hill of pre-Israelite Jerusalem; poetically
extended to refer to the religious capital
of Israel.

A NOTE REGARDING THE TYPE

This Bible was set in the Thomas Nelson NKJV Typeface, commissioned by Thomas Nelson Publishers and designed in Aarhus by Klaus Krogh and Heidi Rand Sørensen of 2K/DENMARK. The letterforms take inspiration from a distinctive typeface found in an early Thomas Nelson *Novum Testamentum*, printed in 1844 in Edinburgh—which in turn reflects the Scotch Roman typefaces created by the celebrated English punchcutter Richard Austin for the type foundry of William Miller, circa 1808–1813.

Just as the NKJV translation inherits the tradition and literary beauty of the King James Bible while updating the language for today's readers, so Thomas Nelson's custom NKJV font family builds on classic letterforms of the past while reflecting cutting-edge typographical design. The result is a type design that is at once beautiful and efficient, traditional and modern—ideal for presenting the sacred words of ancient Scripture to readers today.